Heinrich August Jäschke

# A TIBETAN-ENGLISH DICTIONARY

*Compact Edition*

# A TIBETAN - ENGLISH
# DICTIONARY

*With Special Reference to the Prevailing Dialects*

TO WHICH IS ADDED
AN ENGLISH - TIBETAN VOCABULARY

*By*

HEINRICH AUGUST JÄSCHKE
LATE MORAVIAN MISSIONARY AT KYELANG, BRITISH LAHOUL

MOTILAL BANARSIDASS PUBLISHERS
PRIVATE LIMITED • DELHI

*Reprint :* ***Delhi, 2014***
*First compact Indian Edition: Delhi, 2007*

*First prepared and published at the charge of the Secretary of State for India in Council, London 1881*

*First compact edition published in Japan in 1993*



ISBN: 978-81-208-3093-6

MOTILAL BANARSIDASS
41 U.A. Bungalow Road, Jawahar Nagar, Delhi 110 007
8 Mahalaxmi Chamber, 22 Bhulabhai Desai Road, Mumbai 400 026
203 Royapettah High Road, Mylapore, Chennai 600 004
236, 9th Main III Block, Jayanagar, Bangaluru 560 011
Sanas Plaza, 1302 Baji Rao Road, Pune 411 002
8 Camac Street, Kolkata 700 017
Ashok Rajpath, Patna 800 004
Chowk, Varanasi 221 001

*Printed in India*

by RP Jain at NAB Printing Unit,
A-44, Naraina Industrial Area, Phase I, New Delhi–110028
and published by JP Jain for Motilal Banarsidass Publishers (P) Ltd,
41 U.A. Bungalow Road, Jawahar Nagar, Delhi-110007

# PREFACE.

This work represents a new and thoroughly revised edition of a Tibetan-German Dictionary, which appeared in a lithographed form between the years 1871 and 1876.

During a residence, which commenced in 1857 and extended over a number of years, on the borders of Tibet and among Tibetan tribes, I and my colleagues gathered the materials for this Dictionary.

We had to take primarily into account the needs of missionaries entering upon new regions, and then of those who might hereafter follow into the same field of enterprize. The chief motive of all our exertions lay always in the desire to facilitate and to hasten the spread of the Christian religion and of Christian civilization, among the millions of Buddhists, who inhabit Central Asia, and who speak and read in Tibetan idioms.

A yet more definite object influenced my own personal linguistic researches, in as much as I had undertaken to make preparations for the translation of the Holy Scriptures into the Tibetan speech. I approached and carried forward this task by way of a careful examination of the full sense and exact range of words in their ordinary and common usage. For it seemed to me that, if Buddhist readers were to be brought into contact with Biblical and Christian ideas, the introduction to so foreign and strange a train of thought, and one making the largest demands upon the character and the imagination, had best be made through the medium of a phraseology and diction as simple, as clear, and as popular as possible. My instrument must be, as in the case of every successful translator of the Bible, so to say, not a technical, but the vulgar tongue.

Thus, in contrast to the business of the European philologist, engaged in the same domain, who quite rightly occupies himself with the analysis and commentary of a literary language, the vocabulary and terminology of which he finds mainly deposited in the speculative writings of the Buddhist philosophers, it became my duty to embrace every opportunity, with which my presence on the spot favoured me, to trace the living powers of words and of expressions through their consecutive historical applications, till I reached their last signification in their modern equivalents, as these are embodied in the provincial dialects of the native tribes of our own time.

These circumstances, it is hoped, will excuse and explain the system of my work.

As an inventory of the whole treasure of the language, as a finished key to its literature, this Dictionary, when judged by the high standard of modern lexicography, may seem inadequate; I have, for instance, been unable to consult, much as I could have wished to have done so, all the original and translated treatises in Tibetan which, down to the present, have appeared in Europe, and the reader of a Tibetan work may thus, here and there, look in vain for the assistance he expects. On the other hand, a consistent attempt is here made for the first time, 1. to give a rational account of the development of the values and meanings of words in this language; 2. to distinguish precisely the various transitions in periods of literature and varieties of dialect; 3. to make sure of each step by the help of accurate and copious illustrations and examples. I have done my utmost to arrive at certainty where, heretofore, much was mere guess-work, and I cherish the hope that, from this point of view, my contribution will be welcomed by the comparative philologist, and will be serviceable to the general cause of learning, as well as a useful volume within that narrower circle, whose requirements I was specially bound not to overlook, of persons whose main purpose is to be taught how to write and speak the modern Tibetan tongue.

There are two chief periods of literary activity to be noticed in studying the origin and growth of Tibetan literature and the landmarks in the history of the language. The first is the Period of Translations which, however, might also be entitled the Classical Period, for the sanctity of the religious message conferred a corresponding reputation and tradition of excellence upon the form, in which it was conveyed. This period begins in the first half of the seventh century, when Thonmi Sambhota, the minister of king Srongtsangampo, was sent to India to learn Sanskrit. His invention of the Tibetan alphabet gave a twofold impulse: for several centuries the wisdom of India and the ingenuity of Tibet laboured in unison and with the greatest industry and enthusiasm at the work of translation. The tribute due to real genius must be awarded to these early pioneers of Tibetan grammar. They had to grapple with the infinite wealth and refinement of Sanskrit, they had to save the independence of their own tongue, while they strove to subject it to the rule of scientific principles, and it is most remarkable, how they managed to produce translations at once literal and faithful to the spirit of the original. The first masters had made for their later disciples a comparatively easy road, for the style and contexts of the writings, with which the translators had to deal, present very uniform features. When once typical patterns had been furnished, it was possible for the literary manufacture to be extended by a sort of mechanical process.

A considerable time elapsed before natives of Tibet began to indulge in compositions of their own. When they did so, the subject matter, chosen by them to operate upon, was either of an historical or a legendary kind. In this Second Period the language shows much resemblance to the modern tongue, approaching most closely the present idiom of Central Tibet. We find a greater freedom in construction, a tendency to use abbreviated forms (thus the mere verbal root is often inflected in the place of a complete infinitive), and a certain number of new grammatical combinations.

The present language of the people has as many dialects, as the country has provinces. Indeed, as in most geographically similar districts, well nigh every separate mountain valley has its own singularities as to modes of utterance and favourite collocations of words. Especially is it interesting to note, in respect to pronunciation, how the old consonants, which would seem to have been generally sounded and spoken twelve centuries ago, when the Tibetan written character came into existence, and which, at any rate, are marked by the primitive system of writing, remain still extant; every one of them can still be disinterred, somewhere or other, from some local peculiarity of language, and thus even the very diversity of modern practice can be made to bear testimony to the standards imposed by what was termed above the Classical Period. (Compare my Essay on the Phonetic System of the Tibetan language in the Monthly Reports of the Royal Academy of Science at Berlin 1867, p. 148 etc.)

I have already adverted to the circumstances which, especially in the case of the student, who has for immediate object to learn how to read and write the Tibetan language, render existing dictionaries almost if not quite useless. They give but scanty information concerning modes of construction, variations and limits of actual application, shades of meaning etc. In my own case, I was forced from the beginning to compile my own German-Tibetan dictionary, and found myself for all practical purposes thrown back upon my own resources. But the cause of truth appears to require a further word or two in regard to the Lexicon by Professor I. J. Schmidt of St. Petersburg, the relation of that work to its predecessors having been left by its author in some obscurity.

The first Tibetan dictionary, intended for European students, was published at Serampore, as long ago as 1826. It contains the collections, amassed in view of a dictionary and grammar, by a Roman Catholic missionary, who was stationed in eastern Tibet or close to the frontier in Bhotan. There was nothing to assist him, except the scanty contributions, given by Georgi, in his Alphabetum Tibetanum. He had to cope with an entirely unworked language. He evidently took the one way possible of making acquaintance with it, sufficient to enable him to understand, to speak, to read and write. Each word or sentence was jotted down, as soon as it was heard, or was committed to writing, at the request of the learner, by some native expert. After a while, the attempt could be made to master a book. In the instance of our missionary, Padma Sambhava's book of legends appears to have been selected, a work which represents rather a low level of literature, yet just on that account, perhaps, as a specimen of popular and current literature, not unsuitable to start from. Then, step by step, as best he could, our missionary had to possess himself of some abstract views, which would serve as a preliminary basis for a grammar. And had it been granted to this first occupant of the field to reduce his materials to an ordered system and to prepare them himself for publication, it is possible, that in Europe the knowledge of the Tibetan language might have reached, some fifty years earlier, the stage at which it has now arrived. The very name of that Roman Catholic missionary, however, has been lost. The papers which he left behind him, unsorted and unsifted, came into the hands of Major Latter, an English officer, and were passed on by him to Mr. Schröter, a missionary in Bengal. English was substituted for the Italian of the manuscript, and the East India Company made a grant which defrayed the cost of the Tibetan types and the further expenses of printing. But there was no Tibetan scholar to correct the proofs. The author himself would doubtless, on reconsideration, have detected and dismissed much erroneous or unnecessary matter. As it was, many additional mistakes crept in during the passage through the press. Thus the work, though it has a richer vocabulary than can be found in the later dictionaries, cannot on any questionable point be accepted as an authority, and has only value for those who are already competent, for themselves, to weigh and decide upon the statements and interpretations it advances. I have not been able to extract from it much that was serviceable to me. Nevertheless, any one who knows by experience what time and toil such a work must have cost, though its design remained unfulfilled and its object unaccomplished, will not easily be able to repress his indignation at the tone, in which this book in the preface to his Grammar (p. VI) is recklessly and absolutely condemned by Professor Schmidt.

High praise, however, is awarded by the Professor to a second work, the Tibetan-English Dictionary by Csoma de Körös, which appeared in 1834. This work deserves all eulogy; but the Professor's manner, which imitates that of a master commending a pupil, is, though on other grounds, as unwarranted and as offensive in this as in the former case. The work of Csoma de Körös is that of an original investigator and the fruit of almost unparalleled determination and patience. The compiler, in order to dedicate himself to the study of Tibetan literature, lived like a monk for years among the inmates of a Tibetan monastery. It is to be regretted that, with the knowledge he certainly must have possessed of the later language and literature, he should have restricted the scope of his labours to the earlier periods of literature, and when in his Grammar conversational phrases are quoted as examples, they are almost without exception in the dialect of the Kangyur, and of little practical value.

This Tibetan-English dictionary by Csoma has been adapted for a German public by Professor I. J. Schmidt of St. Petersburg. The translation from English into German is good; in the general alphabetical arrangement improvements have been introduced, and such as are in conformity with the spirit of the language; moreover, three Mongolian dictionaries have been consulted, and from these a certain number of words have been supplemented. But it cannot be said that even on the work of revision Professor Schmidt has bestowed much pains. For example, Csoma's rough grouping of words under the principal headings is left unaltered, though here especially a reduction to alphabetical order was obviously required. Mistakes and superfluities, very pardonable in the case of a first issue of an original publication, are repeated in this translation, and these cannot be so readily overlooked and condoned, when they are made at second hand, and are sanctioned and subscribed to by one, who has assumed so severe a critical and editorial attitude.

The national dictionaries of Tibet itself, so far as I have met with such, are either little handbooks, meant only to furnish a correct orthography, or they are glossaries of antiquated forms. The absence of an alphabetical order in them makes the business of reference very troublesome. It is by great good luck that one sometimes finds an otherwise unknown word after a prolonged search.

My own dictionary, in the main, pursues the object and accepts the plan of the work, which was published by Mr. Schröter. As I said at the beginning, I have not restricted myself to the Classical Period, but I have endeavoured to deal with the Tibetan language as a whole, though I do not pretend to have performed this task exhaustively. My dictionary derives its matter and its principles, so far as possible, equally from the literature and from the speech of the people. Each word has been made the object of observation in its relation to the context as it occurs in books, and in its value and place among others when it is used in common conversation, and then the attempt has been made to define its range and to fix its meaning.

All the words, cited by Csoma and Schmidt, even such as I myself had never seen or heard, I have embodied in this work, stating, in each case, the source from whence I drew them.

The signification in Sanskrit has been added, whenever this seemed likely to be useful or interesting to the student of Tibetan literature. Of proper names only the most important are given.

The great number of diacritical marks will perhaps prove irksome to the English reader; yet, they were not to be dispensed with, if the pronunciation of Tibetan letters and words was to be represented with any degree of exactness, and the method of Prof. Lepsius seemed the most eligible among all the systems available for my purpose. The student, however, need not be disheartened, as he is not obliged to make himself acquainted with all the minutiae of the system, but need only direct his attention to the peculiarities of that dialect, within the limits of which his inquiries, for the time, are confined. And by-the-by it may be observed, that the multitude of little marks, of manifold description, cannot be startling to the Indian reader, who was ever necessitated to make himself familiar with systems quite as complicated, as e.g. the Urdu alphabet.

One word more of apology. Of publications in general it has been said, that "when human care has done its best, there will be found a certain percentage of error". And the probability is but too great, that this dictionary will exhibit a number of deficiencies and faults, in the English text as well as in the Tibetan transcript. Still, I venture to hope that an indulgent Public will be ready to make every reasonable allowance, in consideration of the peculiar difficulties, which attach to the execution of a work like the present, and which, moreover, were not a little increased, in this instance, by the fact that the compositors of the press were altogether unacquainted with English.

I should be guilty of great ingratitude, if I were not to mention my obligations to two friends, without whose kind and efficient aid it would have been impossible for me, in my present infirm state, to complete this work, which was commenced in the days of health and vigour, viz. to the Rev. T. Reichelt, formerly a Missionary of the Moravian Church in South Africa, and to Mr. F. W. Petersen, a relative of mine.

Further, I desire to record my obligations for various acts of kindness, encouragement, assistance and advice, during the prosecution of my researches and the completion of my work, to A. C. Burnell Esq. M. R. A. S., in India; Dr. E. Schlagintweit in Bavaria, Dr. Thomson and Dr. Aitchison of Kew, Dr. Kurz of Calcutta, and R. Laing Esq. M. A., Fellow of Corpus Christi College, Oxford.

Not the least debt of gratitude is that which I owe to Dr. R. Rost in London, Secretary of the Royal Asiatic Society, to whose exertions, indeed, the execution of this work is, properly speaking, entirely due, inas much as he kindly interested the Indian Government on behalf of my undertaking.

Herrnhut, January 1881.

H. A. J.

# INTRODUCTION.

## I. THE TIBETAN ALPHABET.

### CONSONANTS.

The names of all the Consonants sound in a, pronounced like the a in the English word 'far'.

ཀ *ka* pronounced like the French c — car
ཁ *k̔a* like the English c or k — cart
ག *ga* harder than the English (hard) g
ང *ṅa* ng — pang
ཅ *ċa* the soft English g — ginger
ཆ *ča* ch — chart
ཇ *ja* j — jar
ཉ *nya* the French gn — campagne
ཏ *ta* the French t — tard
ཐ *t̔a* the English t — tart
ད *da* dart
ན *na* nard
པ *pa* the French p — pas
ཕ *p̔a* the English p — part
བ *ba* bard
མ *ma* mart
ཙ *tsa* (ts) parts
ཚ *t̔sa* (aspirated)
ཛ *dza* (ds) — guards
ཝ *wa* waft
ཞ *ża* (zh) like the English s in leisure
ཟ *za* like the English z — zeal
འ *a* (basis for vowels)
ཡ *) *ya* yard
ར **) *ra* rasp
ལ *la* last
ཤ *śa* (sh) — sharp
ས *sa* salve
ཧ *ha* half
ཨ *'a* (basis for vowels)

*) ཡ *ya*, when combined, as second consonant, with k- and p-sounds, or with m, is written under the first letter, assuming the shape of ◌ྱ, thus ཀྱ *kya*, པྱ *pya*, མྱ *mya* etc.

**) ར *ra*, when combined as second letter, with k-, t- and p-sounds is written under the first, in the shape of ◌ྲ, thus: ཀྲ, *kra*, ཏྲ *tra*, བྲ *bra* etc. — When combined with another consonant as *first* letter, it is written over the second, thus: རྐ *rka*, རྔ *rṅa*, རྡ *rda* etc., but it is seldom heard in speaking.

The so-called Sanskrit Cerebrals are represented in Tibetan letters by ཊ, ཋ, ཌ, ཎ, ཥ,

and when in this dictionary they are transcribed, they are marked by a dot underneath: *ṭ, ṭ́, ḍ, ṇ, ṣ.*

The figure ཝ (*wa-zur* or small *wa*) attached to the foot of a letter, is often used to distinguish homonyms in writing, e.g. ཚ *tsa* hot and ཚྭ *tsa* (*tswa*) salt.

The dot, which stands at the end of every syllable and of every word, is called Tseg (*ts̀eg*) and is indispensable for a correct writing or reading.

When ག stands as a prefix, it is, when transcribed, represented by *γ*, e.g. གཅིག *γčig*, གཏམ *γtam* etc.

### VOWELS.

The alphabetical order of the vowels is: a, i, u, e, o; they have in Tibetan the same sound as they have in German, Italian, and most other European languages: *a* sounds like the English a in 'far', *i* like ee in 'peer' or i in 'pin', *u* like u in 'rule' or in 'pull', *e* like a in 'fate' or e in 'met', *o* like o in 'note' or in 'not'.

As the vowel a is inherent in every consonant, so that even a single letter may form a word, e.g. བ་ *ba* (cow), ས་ *sa* (earth), there is no special character or letter required for this vowel. The other four vowels are represented by little hooks, ི standing for *i*, ུ for *u*, ེ for *e*, ོ for *o*. The marks for *i, e, o* are placed over the letter, that for *u* under it. Examples: པད་མ་ *pad-ma*, རི་ *ri*, མེ་ *me*, བུ་མོ་ *bu-mo*.

The letter ཨ is used as a basis for initial vowels, thus: ཨ་མ་ *'a-ma;* the letter འ serves as a basis for initial and final vowels: འོ་མ་ *˓o-ma*, དགའ *dga*.

The vowel-sounds of འ, when transcribed, are indicated by the mark ˓: འ *˓a*, འི *˓i*, འུ *˓u*, འེ *˓e*, འོ *˓o*, whilst the ཨ-vowels are denoted by the mark ' placed over the respective letters: ཨ *'a*, ཨི *'i*, ཨུ *'u*, ཨེ *'e*, ཨོ *'o*. — The real nature of the letters འ and ཨ is treated of in the latter part of the Introduction.

Whenever འ is a prefixed letter, the mark ∘, in transcribing, is put under the consonant following the འ e.g. འདུ *˳du*, འགྲོ་བ *˳gro-ba*.

*Note.* For a ready 'finding of words' in the Dictionary, it should be borne in mind, that the articles are arranged in the alphabetical order of the *initial* consonants *and* their *prefixed* and *superscribed* letters. Thus: ག—དག—བག—རྒ—སྒ—སྐ—; ཁ—མཁ—འཁ— etc. etc.

## II. PRONUNCIATION.

With regard to the language, with which I am dealing, it must, on the one hand, be admitted, that distinctions between sounds and, especially, variations in the mode of expressing their values as embodied in a written character, are far more numerous in Tibetan than either in Sanskrit or Hindi, in which two languages there is really little or no opening for mistake or ambiguity in this respect. But on the other hand, Tibetan is scarcely more irregular than French pronunciation, and a few definite rules enjoy universally recognized acceptation.

There is, however, one special difficulty in the case of Tibetan which, at the present stage of that language, renders it practically impossible to set up an equable and authoritative standard of pronunciation, and this is the existence of a great number of independent and well-defined *dialects*. An attempt to deal partially with this difficulty, — to append, let me suppose, to every word from three to five different pronunciations would involve a waste of time and an extension of space quite disproportionate to the value of the result. And yet, if one has to strike a preference in favour of one particular dialect, it is very hard to determine, which is to be selected. At first sight, it might seem the most natural course to fix upon the speech of the best educated classes in the capital city Lhasa. But when this method was followed, or when at least an endeavour was made to act upon it, by Georgi and then by Schröter, only scant approval was bestowed upon it by European critics, and there were and are several reasonable arguments to be urged against its adoption. Of all the dialects this presents to the European ear and tongue the greatest difficulties, and accommodates itself least readily to the written character. Moreover, in my own case, I have to add that I do not consider myself sufficiently master of it to care to risk its application to each individual word. Besides, modern political circumstances make this dialect, for the present, the least available for general use.

Csoma chose a much more manageable and a much more widely circulating mode of pronunciation, though one which presents problems of its own, when it has to be fitted to the written character: the West-Tibetan dialect. Here again, in representing each separate word, one has, in reality, to make choice between two, three or four pronunciations, of which one agrees best with the written character, another conforms closest to the rules of spelling, a third recommends itself as that most frequent in conversational language. In my own smaller Tibetan dictionary I went no farther than to distinguish between two principal groups, which I termed West-Tibetan and Central-Tibetan; but in a more scientific work like the present I may permit myself to call more minute attention to the niceties and refinements of the language before us. I have, accordingly, published a number of specimens from my note-book, in which I kept a collection of typical words, of which I availed myself as often as I had the opportunity of meeting the representatives of remote districts, and of enquiring concerning their manner of speech at home. Whenever in this collection a word had not been entered on sound native authority, or had not been sufficiently discussed, I preferred to mark it with a note of interrogation, and not to allow any conclusion from analogy, or any theory of pronunciation to interfere with the design of my handy-book and its simple and unprejudiced statement of fact. I may therefore, I hope, claim for this list a high degree of trustworthiness, even among collections of the kind, into which words can sometimes have slipped, as they had been heard once, and perhaps were not heard again.

In order to denote the pronunciation, I follow the scheme of Professor Lepsius. Some objections have been urged against this scheme; yet, amongst all systems of the kind, so far as I have become acquainted with them, I have no hesitation in affirming that of Professor Lepsius to be the best, and it is certainly also that most appropriate for my purpose. A thorough study of the 'Standard Alphabet by R. Lepsius, 2nd edition, London, Williams and Norgate. Berlin, Hertz, 1863' may be recommended to all persons, who interest themselves in phonetic investigations. As I can scarcely take it for granted, that the work mentioned will be already in the hands of every one, who may consult my dictionary, I shall endeavour, as briefly as possible, to indicate its essential plan and principles. Its rules may be stated as follows:

In order to mark sound, Lepsius uses the letters of the ordinary Latin alphabet. Where these are insufficient, he calls in the aid of a few Greek letters. Letters are used with the powers they most generally possess in European languages. (Thus z has its usual force, and does not stand for the peculiar sound ts, which belongs to it in the German language alone.) Sounds which lack exact representation are indicated by *diacritical marks*, placed above or below the letters which most nearly correspond. Every simple sound is represented by one and only one simple mark. Explosive and fricative consonants (these terms will be explained below) are denoted by different letters.

The following marks or signs are for *vowels:* the well known sign (˘) for a short, and (¯) for a long vowel; the mark of a modified vowel (¨), German ä, ö, ü, is placed by Lepsius, for practical reasons, below, not above the vowel (*a̤, o̤. ṳ*); a dot under the vowel denotes a close vowel-sound (*ẹ* = a in fate, *ọ* in note); a horizontal line under the vowel denotes a more open vowel-sound (*e̱* in 'there', *o̱* in 'or, cord', which, indeed, supersedes the *a̤* mentioned above); the mark (˜) above the vowel indicates a nasal quality, the breath passing, while uttering the sound, to a considerable extent through the nose (the French *'an, in, on, un'* = *ã, ẽ̱, õ̱, ọ̃*).

In marking *consonants*, there is first the distinction to be noted, that they are partly *explosives*, formed by a rapid process of closing and re-opening the passage of the air at a certain point, partly *fricatives* and *liquids*, formed by a partial process of compressing or narrowing the air-passage; and secondly, they are distinguished in regard to the exact spot, where the process of articulation takes place. The lowest articulation takes place in the *faucal region*, close to the larynx (here, for example, h is formed); next comes the guttural region, at the throat, near the soft palate and uvula (here k is formed); it is marked, when necessary, with a dot above the consonant; then the *palatal region*, the hard palate, (here the German ch is formed in 'ich'); the mark is a stroke like the acute accent in Greek over the consonant; then the *dental region*, at the teeth and gums (d, t, s, sh), and finally the *labial region*, at the lips (b, p, m). There exists a further class of consonants in the Indian languages, and also in modern Tibetan, which are styled *cerebrals;* they are most of them modified dentals, formed by bending or curling the tongue upwards, and bringing the tip of it into contact with the hard palate in the centre or toward the hinder part of its roof; mark, a dot under the consonant.

Many of these letters, in order to become audible, require in pronouncing them a certain *vocalic effort*; others, to say the least, allow or suggest such an effort; the mark of these vocalized consonants is a small *ring* under the letter. When this vocalic effort is made by the medium of the nasal channel alone, the oral passage being simultaneously closed at some one of the points indicated above, we get the nasal consonants as a result. When the stoppage is made at the guttural point, ng is obtained (to be marked *ṅ*); at the dental point, n; at the labial point, m. In order to conform with the two final rules, cited above from Lepsius, the Greek letter χ is used to represent the German ch, when it is guttural and hard, as in the word 'doch'; use is made of the Greek γ, when it is soft or accompanied by a vocalic tone (the Dutch g); χ́ gives the force of a palatal ch (German 'ich' = iχ́, 'milch' = milχ́); ϑ is used to represent the strong English th (as in 'through'); δ renders the softer or vocalized tone (as in 'that'); a hard, sharp and hissing s or ss (as in 'yes', 'press') is marked as s; the soft vocalic s (as in 'his', 'rise') is represented by z; the hard rushing sound sh, German sch, is rendered by š; the sound of the French j by ž. If one attempts to give at the palatal point, where the English y (in 'year'), or the German j (in 'Jahr') is formed, the sound sh, German sch, one obtains the palatal ś̌, or the softened and vocalized ź̌. In the Dictionary ś and ź have been substituted for these marks.

Further, in many languages, what are properly combinations of two consonants come to be regarded as simple forms, this happening, either because they are gradual growths upon an original simpler form, or because they have a natural affinity to each other. Thus properly dental sibilants should be distinguished thus: *tš*, *dž*; but for the sake of simplicity Lepsius, in his second edition, marks them *č* and *ǰ*, or, with their palatal force, *ċ* and *j̇* (instead of *č́* and *ǰ́*).

A further example of the combination of consonants is presented in what is known as *aspiration*, when the letter *h* is brought into more or less intimate connexion with another consonant. This introduces us to a very important distinction, belonging to the Tibetan language, which it is necessary to explain at some length, in accordance with which explosive consonants, as they have the force of tenues, mediae, or aspiratae, are treated. The tenues are produced by a sudden opening of the air-passage at one of the points above mentioned: throat, teeth, lips, such opening being unaccompanied by any sensible operation of the breath whatsoever. Thus, when quite exactly sounded, k, t, p, are produced. The mediae, g, d, b, are produced by the same process, carried out in a milder and less abrupt way, (the peculiar English pronunciation will come under consideration later). The aspiratae require a decided pressure by the breath (they will be found marked by the spiritus asper above the letter: *k̔, t̔, p̔*). In northern Germany, in England, and in Scandinavia, modern educated speech recognizes only mediae and aspiratae, for we give an aspirated sound to every k, t and p. The French and the Magyars distinguish consciously the pure tenues from the mediae; on the other hand they ignore the aspiratae. Tibetan pronunciation makes room and requires a mark for all three gradations. Nay more, it augments the class of explosive consonants or mutae by the addition of the dental sibilants in all three ranks or grades of aspiration: ཅ, ཆ, ཇ and ཙ, ཚ, ཛ, or according to the Standard Alphabet: *ċ, č̔, j̇* and *ts, t̔s, dz*. At a later stage of the language some further modifications were introduced, which we shall subsequently allude to.

Let us now, passing from these general observations, draw attention to a few details of the Phonetic Table, which has been drawn up in deference to a wish that reached me from several quarters.

The first column of the Table, now under review, gives the ancient literal pronunciation, as it was in vogue in the seventh century of our era, and was settled at the time of the invention of the alphabet. Such a pronunciation relies, after all, for its justification on the hypothesis, that the inventors of the alphabet had for their first object to reproduce, as exactly as possible, an artistic reflection of the natural value of sounds as spoken by their contemporaries: that, therefore, a later pronunciation is most in conformity with the original genius of the language, if it gives with the greatest distinctness a special power to each written character. A reference to the Table will amply illustrate the fact, that a pronunciation, adopted on these principles, has actually maintained itself in one or the other provincial dialect, and it is very interesting to notice, that the purest and most striking forms of this survival have their homes in those districts, which are most remote from and least subject to the disintegrating and dissolving influences of the actual centre of Tibetan civilisation, the capital Lhasa. Thus the prefixes and the superscribed consonants, for the most part, are still sounded at each extremity of the whole territory, within which the language is spoken, both on the Western and the Eastern frontier, alike in Khams, which borders on China, and in Balti, which merges into Kashmere. Moreover, in both localities the same minor irregularities occur, transgressions against an exact rendering of the pronunciation according to the letters, the same frequent transformations of the tenues into the aspiratae, g and d (compare lower down) becoming γ or χ, b becoming w. Now, about twenty degrees of longitude separate Balti from Khams, and the former, embracing Islam, long since cut itself adrift from spiritual and religious cohesion with Tibet, and there, too, the dialect in other respects has greatly deteriorated, has admitted many foreign elements and has fallen altogether from the position of a literary language. The resemblances and correspondences noted can, therefore, scarcely be accounted for in any other way, than by assuming that an old and strong instinct of speech lived on in oral tradition for more than ten centuries on the outskirts of the Tibetan domain, which in the intermediate provinces has gradually surrendered and submitted to the spirit of change.

Columns 2—6 contain, on most pages, the provincial dialects in their geographical sequence from West to East. The dialects of Ladak, Lahoul and Spiti correspond to what in my smaller Tibetan dictionary I called the dialect of Western Tibet. The last named, Spiti, represents in some respects the transition to the dialects of Eastern Tibet, under which heading Tsang and Ü are to be classed. At the date of the publication of my former dictionary I was unacquainted with the dialect of Khams. Where a space is left vacant in the columns, the provincial pronunciation agrees with the model provided under column 1. Towards the end of the Table, where the anomalies become much more frequent, I have for the sake of clearness repeated the word.

The sign ◌ྭ (which does not occur in this Table) was pronounced = ཝ, or བ in the substantive terminations *ba* and *bo* (v. Dict. p. 362), viz. = the English w, so that རྭ sounded exactly like the French word *roi*.

The *Accent* has seldom been marked, because, as in our Teutonic dialects, it generally rests on the root of the word. In the case of compounds, it more frequently falls on the last than on the first of the component parts. But accentuation, altogether, is not of great significance in this language.

With regard to *Quantity*, vowels are pronounced shorter, even in open syllables, than is the case for instance in England and Germany. This applies particularly to the Central Provinces. Absolutely long vowels occur only as a peculiarity of dialect. They indicate that a consonant has been dropped, in most provinces, s, in Ü, gs, in Tsang, l. A long vowel may also indicate the blending of vowels. But when in Ü and Tsang the d, (as in *čě'-pa*) and when in Lahoul the g (as in *to', ṕu'-rón*) is partially dropped, the vowel likewise maintains a short abrupt pronunciation. Moreover, the region, to which I have just referred, is that in which the spoken language has been greatly affected by a foreign linguistic principle. A system of Tones has been introduced under manifestly Chinese auspices. I am told by European students of reputation, who have made the Tonic languages of Eastern Asia their special department, that only the first principles of what are known as the *high and low Tones*, have made their way into Tibetan. Here, as in the languages of Farther India, generally, which possess an alphabetic system of writing, the Tone is determined by the initial consonant of the word. This I have generally indicated in column 7, which column applies only to the Spiti, Tsang and Ü dialects. The system of Tones, as in Siam and elsewhere, has become of paramount importance in determining distinctions between words. An inhabitant of Lhasa, for example, finds the distinction between ཤ and ཞ, or between ས and ཟ, not in the consonant, but in the Tone, pronouncing ཤ and ས with a high note (as my Tibetan authorities were wont to describe it 'with a woman's voice', shrill and rapidly), ཞ and ཟ, on the contrary with a low note, and, as it appeared to me, more breathed and floating. This latter distinction is still more apparent with regard to those low-toned aspirates, that in the course of time were introduced in Central Tibet instead of the mediae, in contraposition to which now the original aspirates are used as high-toned; so more particularly in the dialect of Spiti. The low-toned aspirate I have indicated by h, the high-toned by the mark of the spiritus asper ʻ.

Those letters of the alphabet, which as simple initial consonants have a deep tone, become with a superscribed letter or with a prefix high-toned, so also ལ, when subscribed. The tenues remain, it would appear, unaffected by the Tone. With reference to the modifying effect of a final *n, d*, and *ṅ*, in different provinces, the Table may be consulted. The characterisation of the rushing sounds as 'palatals' is no doubt correct and agrees with the generally prevailing pronunciation; but the learner need not consider it as being of much importance.

The two letters, འ and ཨ, introduce us to a very interesting linguistic phenomenon. We meet here with the idea of the *vowel absolute*, the pure vocalic note, freed altogether from any presence of a consonant. This vowel-tone is rendered by the letter of the alphabet འ, in contradistinction to ཨ, which represents the Semitic א, the spiritus lenis of the Greeks, the audible re-opening of the air passage of the larynx. The difference may be observed, for example, in the manner of uttering the words, 'the lily, an endogen' and in the pronunciation of 'Lilian' (a name), in Tibetan ལི་ལི་ཨན and ལི་ལི་འན. Thus, whenever in the middle of a word one vowel succeeds another (hence also in all diphthongs), འ is used. Again, in Tibetan, as in every form of human speech, it cannot but be the commonest of occurrences for a vowel to follow a consonant, and the strict rule might seem to require the vocalic tone to be always indicated, which, according to Csoma, was originally done. However, as the Tibetan language, adopting the principle from Sanskrit, deems the sound of *a* to be naturally inherent in every consonant, while the other four vowels, as mere subspecies of the vowel absolute, are indicated by little hooks above or below the letter, and as the end of a syllable is always marked by a dot (called *tseg*), the function of འ in this capacity was soon seen to be quite superfluous. Its use is necessary only to obviate ambiguities, when for instance one of the five letters, used as prefixes, precedes a consonant with *a*; e.g. the word མད་, would be read *'mad'*; whereas མདའ, written thus, implies that the vowel does not precede but follow the consonant d, and consequently the m is prefix, and the word to be read *'mda'*. If the vowel is not *a*, the sign of such vowel suffices, e.g. མདོ་ *mdo*; མདའོ་ *mdao*, standing now for མདའའོ་. Some practical difficulty attends the pronunciation of the pure vowel as an initial letter. In order that the effect of the consonant ཨ may not be produced, it is necessary, after opening the larynx, to allow the tone gently to set in and then to let it gradually gain fulness and force. I shall indicate this process by the mark ˯. The sound would be still more accurately represented than it is in the Table, thus: ˯*aár-po*, ˯*uúg-pa* etc. Improper are the expedients of some of the dialects, the sound being hardened to *γ* in Khams, to ཨ in Western Tibet; also Csoma's device of indicating it by an h is inadequate. This is a case in which the true pronunciation has been preserved in the Central Provinces, perhaps, because it almost necessarily implies the effort connected with the low Tone, above referred to, so that, when the invading system of Tones had here established its authority, it acted as a conservative element.

Finally, this vocalic tone can be used in connexion with certain consonants. It is unnecessary to indicate it in Tibetan, when it accompanies liquidae (*m, n, ṅ, r, l*) and sibilants; but with the mutae it must be marked, where the effect is that, with which we are familiar in the case of the English mediae, b, d, g, j, for instance in 'be, do, go, jew'. In Tibetan the vocalic effect accompanies aspirates too, and is marked by འ, placed as a prefix, which I transcribe thus ˳, e.g. འདུ་ ˳*du* = the English do. The pause on the tone is of course in the case of mutae a very short one. Here again, though only in the case of the mediae, we find this peculiarity preserved in its purity in Central Tibet. It is not difficult to understand, how, if one is careless about closing the nasal passage, a nasal articulation of this prefix can easily grow common. This has happened throughout Khams, and in the rest of Tibet at least in compound words; at Lhasa it is considered inelegant, as is also the sounding of any prefix. On the other hand, the dialect of Central Tibet neglects the distinction between མ and འ and pronounces the former only as a vocalic initial. In words from the Sanscrit the འ is used in some respect as a 'mora', to denote a long syllable, e. g. ཤྲཱི for श्री; hence the opinion of Lamas of Lhasa, that it expresses prosodical length, when used as above in མདའ.

མྱ་ *mya*, is not found in use in any of the dialects. The sole confirmation of its literal pronunciation depends upon the word *myań-ba* which, perhaps a thousand years ago, found its way into the Bu-nan language (Tibar-skad, Cunningh.) and which the people of Lahoul, when speaking Tibetan, pronounce *nyań-wa*. The process of transition to the cerebral ṭ-sounds in the words *ḱrad-pa* etc. is in many places not yet completed, so that the sound of r is still more or less clearly distinguishable. The *Prefixes* have always constituted the most perplexing phenomena in the Tibetan language, At the time of the invention of the alphabet they must have represented a sort of anticipatory sound in close connexion with the initial consonant of the word. Certain seeming impossibilities of pronunciation, when one has, for instance, to deal with a prefix together with a threefold initial consonant (བསྒྲ་, བསྐྲ་) become less formidable, and not more embarrassing than those which meet us, for example, in the Polish language, when we ascertain that in Balti and Khams the three explosive prefixes are pronounced as fricatives, in which case *v* must be written for *w*. Thus གཅི་ག་ *γči-wa*, བཀྲ་ *wkra*, བསྒྲགས་ *wsgrags* call for no greater exertions, than do the Polish *chciwy, wkrótce, wskroś*. Our strongest ground for assuming this fricative pronunciation to be that of antiquity is, I think, that, had it been explosive, words like གཡུ་, གཡོན་ would have coincided with གྱུ་, གྱོན་. Yet it must be acknowledged that a pronunciation *bču, bka* etc. exists, side by side with *wču, wka* etc. — མ, as a liquid, offers no difficulty. — འ, as a prefix, is no consonant.

A doubt must still cling to ད, and I do not venture to determine its ancient pronunciation. It is by a strange anomaly that, in most dialects, when prefixed to བ, both it and the initial consonant die away into a spiritus lenis; and almost still more singular it is, that where it still asserts an independent force, in Khams and in Balti, it is sounded like ག with the power of *γ*. The investigations of Lepsius go indeed to prove, that ད and ག are complements to each other; but how came, at the beginning, two letters to be chosen as signs for one and the same sound? Most probably the original sound was *ϑ*, which then very soon passed into *γ*. The variations between r and s in Ladak afford no sure hold for drawing inferences.

The purpose, for which the Phonetic Table was drawn up, will have been attained, if I succeed in convincing my readers, 1. that for scientific objects the pronunciation, as it is given in Column 1, is the most suitable, and that with a good conscience it can be recommended in the place of that introduced by Csoma; 2. that its system is regular enough to render it unnecessary to give the pronunciation of every individual word throughout the work; 3. that I present in this Table, in regard to the various dialects, as much in the way of results as, down to the present, it has been possible for European students to acquire and to put into shape for the service of a European public.

# III. PHONETIC TABLE
## FOR COMPARING THE DIFFERENT DIALECTS.

**The columns 2—6 are arranged according to the geographical site of the provinces from West to East.**

### I. Words containing only simple consonants and vowels.

| 1 | 2 | 3 | 4 | 5 | 6 | 7 |
|---|---|---|---|---|---|---|
| | West. Tibet | | Central Prov. | | | |
| | Ladak | Lahoul | Spiti | Tsang, Ü | Khams | |
| *ka-ra* | | | | | | |
| *kug* = cook | | *ku'* | | | | |
| *kun* | | | | *kụn* | *kụn* | |
| *ǩaṅ-pa* | | | | | | in C. high-toned |
| *gaṅ* | | | *ghaṅ* | *ghaṅ* | | |
| *ṅal* | | | | *ṅā* Ts. | | in C. deep-toned |
| *ṅan-pa* | | | | *ṅem-pa* Ü. | | |
| *či* | | | | | *če* | |
| *čad-pa* | | | | *čẹ'-pa* | | |
| *čan-pa* | | | | *čem-pa* | | high-toned |
| *čen-po* | | | | *čem-po* | | |
| *ǰa* | | | *ǰha* | *ǰha* | | deep-toned |
| *nyin* | | | | | *nyen* | |
| *tib-ril* | | | | *tib-rī* Ts. | *teb-rel* | |
| *ťaṅ* | | | | | *ťěṅ* | |
| *ťab* = *ťăp* | | | | | | high-toned |
| *ťog* | | *ťǒ* | | | | |
| *ťod-pa* | | | | *ťọ'-pa* | | |
| *da* | | | *dha* | *dha* | | |
| *dud-pa* | | | *dhud-pa* | *dhụ'-pa* | | deep-toned |
| *nad* = *năt* | | | | *nẹ'* | | |
| *p̌an-pa* | | | | *p̌em-pa* | | high-toned |
| *p̌ug-ron* | | *p̌u'-ron* | | *p̌ug-rọn* | | |
| *ba* | | | *bha* | *bha* | *wa* | |
| *bal* | | | *bhal* | *bhā* Ts. *bhal* Ü. | *wal* | |
| *bu* | | | *bhu* | *bhu* | *wọ* | |
| *bu-mo* | | | *bhu-mo* | *bhu-mo* | *wọ-mo* | deep-toned |
| *bod* | | | *bhod* | *bhọ'* | *wod* | |
| *mig* | | *mi'* | | | | |
| *me* | | | | | | |
| *tsil* | | | | *ťsi* | *tsel* | high-toned |
| *dza-ti* | | | | | | |
| *wa-tse* | | | | | | |
| *ža* | | | *ša* | *ša* | *ža* | |
| *žag* | | *ža'* | *šag* | *šag* | *žag* | |
| *za* | | | *sa* | *sa* | | |
| *zan* | | | *san* | *sen* | | |
| *˯ar-po* | *'ar-po* | *'ar-po* | | | *γar-po* | in C. deep-toned |
| *˯ug-pa* | *'ug-pa* | *'ug-pa* | | | *γug-pa* | |
| *˯o-ma* | *'a-ma* | *'o-ma* | | | *γo-ma* | |
| *˯od* | *'od* | *'od* | | *o͡˯ọ'* | *γod* | |
| *˯ol-mo* | *'ol-mo* | *'ol-mo* | | *o͡˯ǿ-mo* Ts. | *γol-mo* | |
| *yaṅ* | | | | | *yeṅ* | |
| *yan-pa* | | | | *yā-ga* | | |
| *yal-ga* | | | | *yem-pa* | | |
| *yin* | | | | | *yen* | |
| *yul* | | | | *yü, yṻ* Ts. | | |

| 1 | 2 | 3 | 4 | | 5 | 6 | 7 |
|---|---|---|---|---|---|---|---|
| | West. Tibet | | Central Prov. | | | | |
| | Ladak | Lahoul | Spiti | | Tsang, Ü | Khams | |
| *yod* | | | | | *yo̱'* | | deep-toned |
| *ral* | | | | | *rā* | | |
| *rol-mo* | | | | | *rō-mo* Ts. | | |
| *lo-ma* | | | | | | | |
| *ša* | | | | | | | high-toned |
| *šel* | | | | | | | |
| *sa* | | | | | | | |
| *'a-ma* | | | | | | | |

## II. Words terminating in བ or བོ.

| 1 | Ladak | Lahoul | Spiti | Tsang, Ü | Khams | 7 |
|---|---|---|---|---|---|---|
| *za-ba* | | *za-wa* | *sa-wa* | *sa-wa* | | deep-toned |
| *ži-ba* | | *ži-wa* | *ši-wa* | *ši-wa* | *ẓi-wa* | |
| *ši-ba* | | *ši-wa* | *ši-wa* | *ši-wa* | *ši-wa* | high-toned |
| *žu-ba* | | *žu-wa* | *šu-wa* | *šu-wa* | *ẓu-wa* | deep-toned |
| *ǰo-bo* | | *ǰo-wo* | *ǰho-wo* | *ǰho-wo* | | |
| *dar-ba* | | *dar-wa* | *dhar-wa* | *dhar-wa* | | |
| *sol-ba* | | *sol-wa* | | *sō-wa* Ts. | | high-toned |

## III. Words terminating in ས.

| 1 | Ladak | Lahoul | Spiti | Kun. | Tsang, Ü | Khams | 7 |
|---|---|---|---|---|---|---|---|
| *k̔ās* | *k̔as, k̔ē̤* | *k̔ai, k̔ē̤* | *k̔ē̤* | *k̔ā* | *k̔ē̤* | *k̔ē* | high-toned |
| *ris* | *ris, rī* | *rī* | *rī* | *rī* | *rī* | *rī* | deep-toned |
| *gus* | *gus, gṻ* | *gui, gṻ* | *ghṳi* | *gū* | *ghṻ* | *gṻ* | |
| *dus* | *dus, dṻ* | *dui, dṻ* | *dhṳi* | *dū* | *dhṻ* | *dṻ* | |
| *des* | *des, dē* | *dē* | *dhē* | *dē* | *dhē* | *dī* | |
| *k̔os* | *k̔os, k̔ȫ̤* | *k̔oi, k̔ȫ̤* | *k̔ȫ̤* | *k̔o̤* | *k̔ȫ̤* | *kȫ̤* | high-toned |
| *gos* | *gos, gȫ̤* | *goi, gȫ̤* | *ghȫ̤* | *gō* | *ghȫ̤* | *gȫ̤* | deep-toned |
| *'os* | *'os, 'ȫ̤* | *'oi, 'ȫ̤* | *'ȫ̤* | *ō* | *'ȫ̤* | *γȫ̤* | |
| *č̔os* | *č̔os, č̔ȫ̤* | *č̔oi, č̔ȫ̤* | *č̔ȫ̤* | *č̔ō* | *č̔ȫ̤* | *č̔ȫ̤* | high-toned |
| *nags* | *nag*(s) | *nag* | | ? | *nag, nā* | *nāg* | deep-toned |
| *rigs* | *rig*(s) | *rig* | | ? | *rig, rī* | and | |
| *t̔ugs* | *t̔ug*(s) | *t̔ug* | | ? | *t̔ug, t̔ṻ* | so | high-toned |
| *legs* | *leg*(s) | *leg* | | ? | *leg, lē* | forth | deep-toned |
| *p̔ogs* | *p̔og*(s) | *p̔og* | | ? | *p̔og, p̔ō.* | | high-toned |
| *t̔abs* | *t̔ab*(s) | *t̔ab* | *t̔au* | | *t̔ab* | *t̔ab* | |
| *č̔ibs* | *č̔ib*(s) | *č̔ib* | *č̔íu* | | *č̔ib* | *č̔ib* | |
| *šubs* | *šub*(s) | *šub* | *šū* | | *šub* | *šub* | |
| *p̔ebs* | *p̔eb*(s) | *p̔eb* | *p̔ĕü* | | *p̔eb* | *p̔eb* | |
| *'obs* | *'ob*(s) | *'ob* | *'ŏü* | | *'oōb* | *γob* | deep-toned |
| *t̔ams-čád* | *t̔am*(s)*-čád* | *t̔am-čád* | *t̔am-čád* | | *t̔am-čē̤'* | *t̔am-čad* | high-toned |
| *goms-pa* | *gom*(s)*-pa* | *gom-pa* | *ghom-pa* | | *ghom-pa* | *gom-pa* | deep-toned |

## IV. Words with diphthongs.

| 1 | Ladak | Lahoul | Spiti | Tsang, Ü | Khams | 7 |
|---|---|---|---|---|---|---|
| *k̔ai* | *k̔ē̤* | *k̔ai, k̔ē̤* | | *k̔ē̤* | *k̔ē* | high-toned |
| *číi, čī* | *čī* | *čī* | | *čĭ* | *čī* | |
| *bui* | *bui, bṻ* | *bui, bṻ* | *bhui* | *bhṻ* | *bṻ* | deep-toned |
| *dĕĭ* | *dei* | | *dhĕĭ* | *dhĕĭ* | *dī* | |
| *soí* | | | | | *sȫ̤* | high-toned |
| *găŭ* | | | *ghăŭ* | *ghau* | *ga-γo̤* | deep-toned |
| *lĕŭ* | | | | | and so forth | |
| *mĭŭ* | | | | | | |
| *răŏ* | | | | | (*ra-γo*) | |
| *reo* | | | | | | |

| 1 | 2 | | 3 | 4 | 5 | 6 | 7 |
|---|---|---|---|---|---|---|---|
| | West. Tibet | | | Central Prov. | | | |
| | Ladak | | Lahoul | Spiti | Tsang, Ǖ | Khams | |
| *río* | | | | | | | |
| *roo, rō* | | | | | | | deep-toned |
| *ruo* | | | | | | | |

## V. Words with subscribed letters.

| 1 | 2 | | 3 | 4 | 5 | 6 | 7 |
|---|---|---|---|---|---|---|---|
| *kyaṅ* | | | | | | *kyeṅ* | |
| *kyir-kyir* | | | | | | *kyer-kyér* | |
| *kyu* | | | | | | *kyọ̈* | |
| *ḱyi* | | | | | | *ḱye* | |
| *ḱyu* | | | | | | *ḱyọ̈* | high-toned |
| *ḱyed* | | | | | *ḱyĕ'* | | |
| *ḱyod* | | | | | *ḱyọ̈̆'* | | |
| *gyi* | | | | *ghyi* | *ghyi* | | deep-toned |
| *gyon-pa* | Pur: Bal.; | Ld. | | *ghyon-pa* | *ghyọ̈m-pa* | | |
| *ṕyag* | *ṕyag* | *čag* | *čag* | *čag* | *čag* | *čag* | |
| *ṕyi* | *ṕi* | | *ṕi* | *či* | *či* | *či* | |
| *ṕyug-po* | *ṕyug-po* | *čug-po* | *čug-po* | *čug-po* | *čug-po* | *čug-po* | high-toned |
| *ṕye* | *ṕe* | | *ṕe* | *če* | *če* | *če?* | |
| *ṕyogs* | *čog(s)* | | *čog* | *čog* | *čog* Ts. *čō* Ǖ. | *čog* | |
| *bya-mo* | *bya-mo* | *ǰa-mo* | *ǰa-mo* | ? | *ǰha-mo* | ? | |
| *byi-ba, byi-wa* | *bí-wa* | | *bí-wa* | ? | *ǰhi-wa* | ? | deep-toned |
| *bye-ma* | ? | | *be-ma* | ? | *ǰhe-ma* | ? | |
| *byos* | ? | | *ǰos, ǰoí, ǰọ̈* | ? | *ǰhọ̈* | ? | |
| *mya-ṅan* | ? | | *nya-ṅán* | *nya-ṅán* | *nya-ṅẹn* | ? | high-toned |
| *krad-pa* | ? | | *ṭad-pa* | *ṭad-pa* | *ṭẹ̀'-pa* Ts. vlg. *kẹ̀'-pa* Ǖ. | ? | |
| *ḱrag* | *ḱrag* | | *ṭ́ag* | *ṭ́ag* | *ṭ́ag* | *ṭ́ag* | |
| *ḱrims* | | | *ṭ́im(s)* | *ṭ́im* | *ṭ́im* | *ṭ́em* | high-toned |
| *ḱrus* | ? | | *ṭ́us; ṭ́ụ̈* | *ṭ́ui* | *ṭ́ụ̈* | *ṭ́ụ̈* | |
| *ḱron-po* | ? | | *ṭ́on-pa* | *ṭ́on-pa* | *ṭ́ọm-pa* | *ṭ́on-pa* | |
| *gri* | *gri* | | *drí, ḍi* | *ḍhi* | *ḍhi* | *ḍi* | deep-toned |
| *dron-mo* | | | *ḍon-mo* | *ḍhon-mo* | *ḍhon-mo* | *ḍon-mo* | |
| *ṕru-gu* | *ṕru-gu* | | *ṭ́u-gu* | *ṭ́u-ghu* | *ṭ́u-ghu* | *ṭ́ọ̈-gọ̈* | high-toned |
| *bra-bo, bra-wo* | | | *bra-wo, ḍa-wo* | *ḍha-wo* | *ḍha-wo* | *ḍa-wo* | deep-toned |
| *braṅ-sa* | (B. *blaṅ-sa*) | | *ḍaṅ-sa* | *ḍhaṅ-sa* | *ḍhaṅ-sa* | *ḍaṅ-sa* | |
| *sran-ma* | *stran-ma?* | | *ṡran-ma* | *ṡran-ma* | *ṡrém-ma* vulg. *sem-ma* | *stran-ma* | high-toned |
| *sriṅ-mo* | *strin-mo* B. | | *ṡriṅ-mo* | *ṡriṅ-mo* | *ṡríṅ-mo* vulg. *siṅ-mo* | *striṅ-mo* | |
| *hrul-po* | *ṡrul-po* | | *ṡrul-po* | *ṡrul-po* | *šrul-po* | *šrul-po* | deep-toned |
| *klog-pa* | ? | | *log-pa* | *log-pa* | *log-pa* | ? | |
| *glog* | *γlog* B. | | *log* | *log* | *log* | *γlog* | high-toned |
| *bla-ma* | ? | | *la-ma* | *la-ma* | *la-ma* | *wla-ma* | |
| *zla-ba, zla-wa* | *lza* B. | | *(l)da-wa* | *dà-wa* | *dà-wa* | *ldà-wa* | ? |
| *rlaṅs-pa* | | | *(r)laṅ(s)-pa* | *lã-pa* | *laṅ-pa* | *rleṅ-pa* | high-toned |
| *sla-mo* | ? | | *la-mo* | *la-mọ* | *la-mo* | *sla-mo* | |

## VI. Words with superscribed letters.

| 1 | 2 | | 3 | 4 | 5 | 6 | 7 |
|---|---|---|---|---|---|---|---|
| *rkaṅ-pa* | ? | | *(r)kaṅ-pa* | *kaṅ-pa* | *kaṅ-pa* | *rkeṅ-pa* | these and all |
| *rgad-po* | ? | | *(r)gad-po* | *gad-po* | *gẹ̀'-po* | *rgad-po* | the rest are |
| *rṅa* | ? | | *(r)ṅa* | *ṅa* | *ṅa* | *rṅa* | high-toned |
| *rǰes* | ? | | *žes, žē* | *ǰē?* | *ǰē* | *rǰī* | |

| 1 | 2 | 3 | 4 | 5 | 6 | 7 |
|---|---|---|---|---|---|---|
| | West. Tibet | | Central Prov. | | | |
| | Ladak | Lahoul | Spiti | Tsang, Ü | Khams | |
| rnyiṅ-pa | (r)nyiṅ-pa | nyiṅ-pa | nyiṅ-pa | nyiṅ-pa | rnyiṅ-pa | |
| rta | rta, sta, ta | ta | ta | ta | rta | |
| rdo | (r)do | do | do | do | rdo | |
| rnon-po | (r)non-po | non-po | non-po | nọ̈m-po | rnon-po | |
| rba | wa | ba | ba | ba | rwa? | |
| rmig-pa | mig-pa | mig-pa | mig-ba | mig-pa | rṃig-pa | |
| rtsa | sa | sa | ? | tsa | ? | Pur. Bal. |
| rtswa | sa | sa | ? | tsa | ? | rtsoá, stsoá |
| rdza-ma | za-ma | za-ma | ? | dza-ma | ? | |
| lṅa | ṅa, ṡṅa | ṅa | ṅa | ṅa | lṅa | |
| lċaṅ-ma | lċaṅ-ma | ċaṅ-ma | ċaṅ-ma | ċaṅ-ma | lċeṅ-ma | lċaṅ-ma |
| lǰaṅ-k̔u | (l)ǰaṅ-k̔u | ǰaṅ-k̔u | ǰaṅ-k̔u | ǰaṅ-k̔u | lǰeṅ-k̔u | |
| ltad-mo | (l)tad-mo | tad-mo | tad-mo | tẹ̈'-mo | ltad-mo | ltad-mo |
| ldag-pa | (l)dag-pa | dag-pa | dag-pa | dag-pa | ldag-pa | |
| lham | lam | lam | lam | hlam or χlam | lham | lham |
| skom | skom | kom | kom | kom | skom | skom |
| skra | ṡra | ṡra, ṭa | ṭa | ṭa | štra | |
| sgo | γo | go | go | go | sgo | sgo |
| sgra | ḍa, ra | ḍa, ra | ḍa | ḍa | zdra | |
| sṅon-po | ṅon-po | ṅon-po | ṅoṅ-po | nọ̈m-po | sṅon-po | |
| snyiṅ | nyiṅ | nyiṅ | nyin | nyiṅ | snyeṅ | |
| stag | stag | tag | tag | tag | stag | |
| sdoṅ-po | (s)doṅ-po | doṅ-po | doṅ-po | doṅ-po | sdoṅ-po | |
| sna | na | na | na | na | sna | |
| spu | (s)pu | pu | pu | pu | spọ̈ | |
| spyod-pa | (s)ċod-pa | ċod-pa | ċod-pa | ċọ̈'-pa | šwod-pa | |
| sprĕŭ | also ṡrĕŭ | ṭĕŭ | ṭĕŭ | ṭĕŭ | štre-γọ̈ | |
| sbal-ba | (s)bal-wa | bal-wa | bal-wa | bā-wa Ts.<br>bal-wa Ü. | zual-wa | |
| sbyar-ba | żar-wa | żar-wa | żar-wa | ǰar-wa | zuar-wa | |
| sbraṅ-bu | also ḍaṅ-bu | ḍaṅ-bu | ḍaṅ-bu | ḍaṅ-bu | ḍẹṅ-wọ̈ | |
| sman | (s)man | man | man | mẹn | sman | |
| smyon-pa | nyon-pa | nyon-pa | nyon-pa | nyọ̈m-pa | snyon-pa | |
| smra-ba | mra-wa | mra-wa | ? | m(r)a-wa | šna-wa | |
| stsal-ba | (s)tsal-wa | tsal-wa | tsal-wa | tsā-wa Ts.<br>tsal-wa Ü. | stsal-wa | |

## VII. Words with prefixed letters.

| 1 | 2 | 3 | 4 | 5 | 6 | 7 |
|---|---|---|---|---|---|---|
| γċes-pa | ċes-pa | ċē-pa | ċē-pa | ċē-pa | γċī-pa | |
| γtam | tam | tam | tam | tam | γtām | |
| γduṅ-ba | duṅ-wa | duṅ-wa | duṅ-wa | duṅ-wa | γduṅ-wa | |
| γnaṅ-ba | naṅ-wa | naṅ-wa | naṅ-wa | naṅ-wa | γneṅ-wa | |
| γnam | nam | nam | nam | nam | γnam | Bal. γnam |
| γtsaṅ-po | tsaṅ-po | tsaṅ-po | tsaṅ-po | tsaṅ-po | γtseṅ-po | |
| γżu | żu | żu | ṡu | ṡu | γżọ̈ | |
| γzig | zig | zi' | sig | sig | γzig | |
| γyog-po | yog-po | yọ'-po | yog-po | yog-po | (γ)yog-po | |
| γṡer-pa | ṡer-pa | ṡer-pa | ṡer-pa | ṡer-pa | γšer-pa | or gšer-pa |
| γser | ser | ser | ser | ser | γser | Bal. γser |
| dkar-po | kar-po | kar-po | kar-po | kar-po | γkar-po | |
| dkyil | kyil | kyil | kyil | kyil | γkyil | |
| dgu | gu | gu | gu | gu | γgọ̈ | |
| dgra | ḍa | ḍa | ḍa | ḍa | (γ)ḍa | Bal. χṅul |
| dṅul | ṇul (vulgo | mul) ṇul | ṇul | ṇū Ts. ṇul Ü. | γṇul | or χmul |
| dpe-ċa | pe-ċa | pe-ċa | pe-ċa | pe-ċa | γpe-ċa | χpe-ċa |

| 1 | 2 | 3 | 4 | 5 | 6 | 7 |
|---|---|---|---|---|---|---|
| | West. Tibet | | Central Prov. | | | |
| | Ladak | Lahoul | Spiti | Tsaug, Ü | Khams | |
| *ma-dpe* | *mas-pe* | *mar-pe* | *ma-pe* | *ma-pe* | *maγ-pe?* | |
| *dpyid* | *(s)pid* | *pid* | *čid* | *či'* | *χšid* | |
| *dbaṅ* | *uaṅ* | *uaṅ* | *uaṅ* | *uaṅ* (vlg. *aṅ*) | *γweṅ* | |
| *dbu* | *'u** | *'u* | *'u* | *'u* | *wo̤* | * = ཨུ etc. |
| *dbugs* | *'ug(s)* | *'u'* | *'ug* | *'ug* Ts. *'ū* Ü. | *wug* | |
| *dbul-po* | *'ul-po* | *'ul-po* | *'ul-po* | *'ū-po* Ts. *'ul-po, ṳl-po* | *γwo̤l-po* | |
| *dben-pa* | *'en-pa* | *'en-pa* | *'en-pa* | *'em-pa* [Ü. | *γwen-pa* | |
| *dbyar* | *yar* | *yar* | *yar* | *yar* | *wyer* | |
| *dmar-po* | *mar-po* | *mar-po* | *mar-po* | *mar-po* | *(γ)mar-po* | |
| *dmyal-ba* | *nyal-wa* | *nyal-wa* | *nyal-wa* | *nyā-wa* Ts. *nyal-wa* Ü. | *mnyal-wa* | |
| *bka, vka* | *ka* | *ka* | *ka* | *kā* | *vka* | |
| *bkra-šis* | *ṭa-ši(s)* | *ṭa-šī* | *ṭa-šī* | *ṭa-šī* | *bṭa-šī* | |
| *bgo-ba* | *go-wa* | *go-wa* | *go-wa* | *go-wa* | *vgo-wa* | |
| *brgyad* | *gyad* | *gyad* | *gyad* | *gyẹ̀* | *vrgyad* | Bal. *vrgyad* |
| *bču* | *ču* | *ču* | *ču* | *ču* | *vču, bču* | |
| *bčug-sum* | *čug-súm* | *čug-um* | *ču-súm?* | *ču-súm* *ču-sum* | *včug-súm* | |
| *bčub-ži* | *čub-ži* | *čub-ží* | *ču-ži* | *ču-ží* | *včub-ží?* | |
| *brǰed-pa* | *žed-pa* | *žed-pa* | *ǰed-pa* | *ǰĕ'-pa* | *vrǰed-pa* | |
| *btum-pa* | *tum-pa* | *tum-pa* | *tum-pa* | *tūm-pa* | *bto̤m-pa* | |
| *bdun* | *dun* | *dun* | *dun* | *dṳn* | *vdun* | Bal. *vdun* |
| *brtse-ba* | *se-wa* | *se-wa* | *tse-wa* | *tse-wa* | *vrtse-wa* | |
| *brdzun* | *zun* | *zun* | *dzun* | *dzun* | *vrdzun* | Pur. *rdzun* |
| *bži* | *ži* | *ži* | *ši* | *ši* | *vže* | |
| *bžib-ču* | *žib-ču* | *žib-ču* | *ši-ču?* | *ši-ču* | *vžeb-ču?* | |
| *bzaṅ-po* | *zaṅ-po* | *zaṅ-po* | *saṅ-po* | *saṅ-po* | *vzeṅ-po* | |
| *bšal-ba* | *šal-wa* | *šal-wa* | *šal-wa* | *šā-wa* | *všel-wa* | |
| *bsu-ba* | *su-wa* | *su-wa* | *su-wa* | *su-wa* | *vso̤-wa* | |
| *bsreg-pa* | *šreg-pa* | *šreg-pa* | *šreg-pa* | *šreg-pa* *(seg-pa)* | *vstrag-pa* | |
| *bslab-pa* | *lab-pa* | *lab-pa* | *lab-pa* | *lab-pa* | *vslab-pa* | |
| *mṅar* | *k'ar* | *k'ar* | *k'ar* | *k'ar* | *mk'ar* | |
| *mgo* | *go* | *go* | *˳go* | *˳go* | *mgo* | |
| *mgron* | *ḍon* | *ḍon* | *ḍon* | *˳ḍo̤n* | *mḍon* | |
| *mṅar-(b)wa* | *ṅar-wa* | *ṅar-wa* | *ṅar-wa* | *ṅar-wa* | *mṅar-wa* | |
| *mčin-pa* | *čin-pa* | *čin-pa* | *čin-pa* | *čim-ga* | *mčen-pa* | |
| *mǰiṅ-pa* | *ǰiṅ-pa* | *ǰiṅ-pa* | *˳ǰiṅ-pa* | *˳ǰiṅ-pa* | *mǰiṅ-pa* | |
| *mt'iṅ* | *t'iṅ* | *t'iṅ* | *t'iṅ* | *t'iṅ* | *(m)t'eṅ* | |
| *mda* | *da* | *da* | *˳da* | *˳da* | *mda* | |
| *mt'so* | *t'so* | *t'so* | *t'so* | *t'so* | *mt'so* | |
| *mdzo* | *dzo* | *dzo* | *˳dzo* | *˳dzo* | *mdzo* | |
| *˳k'ol-ba* | *k'ol-wa* | *k'ol-wa* | *k'ol-wa* | *k'ō-wa* Ts. | *ṅk'ol-wa* | |
| *˳gul-ba* | *gul-wa* | *gul-wa* | *˳gul-wa* | *˳gū-wa* Ts *˳gul-wa* Ü. | *ṅgul-wa* | |
| *˳čam-pa* | *čam-pa* | *čam-pa* | *čam-pa* | *čam-pa* | *nčam-pa* | |
| *˳ǰam-po* | *ǰam-po* | *ǰam-po* | *˳ǰam-po* | *˳ǰam-po* | *nǰam-po* | |
| *˳t'ag-pa* | *t'ag-pa* | *t'ag-pa* | *t'ag-pa* | *t'ag-pa* | *nt'ag-pa* | |
| *γge-˳dún* | *gen-dún* | *gen-dun* | *ge(n)-dúṇ* | *ge(n)-dṳn* Ts. *ge-˳dṳ́n* Ü. | *γgen-dún?* | |
| *˳dod-pa* | *dod-pa* | *dod-pa* | *˳dod-pa* | *˳dö̤'-pa* | *ndod-pa* | |
| *˳p'ur-ba* | *p'ur-wa* | *p'ur-wa* | *p'ur-wa* | *p'ur-wa* | *mp'ur-wa* | |
| *˳p'yi-ba* | *p'i-wa* | *p'i-wa* | *p'i-wa* | *či-wa* | *nči-wa* | |
| *˳prod-pa* | *ṭ'od-pa* | *ṭ'od-pa* | *ṭ'od-pa* | *ṭ'ö̤'-pa* | *nṭ'od-pa* | |

| 1 | 2 | 3 | 4 | 5 | 6 | 7 |
|---|---|---|---|---|---|---|
| | West. Tibet | | Central Prov. | | | |
| | Ladak | Lahoul | Spiti | Tsang, Ü | Khams | |
| *˳bab-pa* | *bab-pa* | *bab-pa* | *˳bab-pa* | *˳bab-pa* | *mbab-pa* | |
| *vka-˳búm* | *kam-bum* | *kam-bum* | *kam-búm* | *ka(m)-búm* | *vkam-búm* | |
| *˳ťsir-wa* | *ťsir-wa* | *ťsir-wa* | *ťsir-wa* | *ťsir-wa* | *nťsir-wa* | |
| *˳dzin-pa* | *dzin-pa* | *dzin-pa* | *dzin-pa* | *dzim-pa* | *ndzen-pa* | |

# ABBREVIATIONS.

| | |
|---|---|
| abbr. | = abbreviated, abbreviation |
| acc. | according to |
| accus. | accusative case |
| act. | active, -ly |
| adj. | adjective |
| adv. | adverb, -ially |
| A. R. | Asiatic Researches |
| Ar. | Arabic |
| B. | books, book-language |
| Bal. | Balti, the most westerly of the districts, in which the Tibetan language is spoken. |
| Bhar. | Bharata, a dialogue, ed. by Dr. A. Schiefner. |
| Bhot. | Bhotan, province. |
| Burn. I. | Burnouf, Introduction au Buddhism Indien. |
| » II. | Burnouf, Lotus de la bonne loi. |
| C. | Central Tibet, esp. the provinces Ü and Tsang. |
| c. | cum, with |
| c. c. | construitur cum, construed with. |
| c. c. a. | construed with the accusative, etc. |
| ccapir | construitur cum accusativo personae, instrumentativo rei |
| ccirdp | construitur cum instrumentativo rei, dativo personae etc. |
| cf. | confer, compare |
| Chr. P. | Christian writings by Protestant missionaries. |
| Chr. R. | Christian writings by Roman Catholic missionaries. |
| cog. | cognate, related in origin |
| col. | colloquial, -ly |
| collect. | collective, -ly |
| com. | commonly |
| comp. | compound -s |
| conj. | conjunction |
| contr. | contracted |
| corr. | correct, -ly |
| correl. | correlative, -ly |
| Cs. | Csoma de Körös, Tibetan-English Dictionary. |
| Cunn. | Cunningham, General, Ladak and the surrounding country. |
| dat. | dative case |
| deriv. | derivative |
| Desg. | Desgodins, La Mission du Tibet de 1855—1870. |
| Do. or Dom. | Do-mang, a collection of incantations. |
| dub. | dubious |
| Dzl. | Dzanglun, an ancient collection of Legends of Buddha. |

| | |
|---|---|
| e.g. | = exempli gratia, for instance |
| eleg. | elegant, -ly |
| elsewh. | elsewhere |
| emphat. | emphatical, -ly |
| erron. | erroneous, -ly |
| esp. | especially |
| euphemist. | euphemistical, -ly |
| expl. | explain, explanation |
| extr. | extremo, towards the end of a longer article. |
| fem. | feminine gender |
| fig. | figurative, -ly |
| frq. | frequent, -ly |
| fut. | future tense |
| gen. | general, -ly |
| gen. | genitive case |
| Glr. | Gyalrabs, a history of the kings of Tibet. |
| Gram. | native grammarians or grammatical works |
| Gyatch. | Gyatcherrolpa, Biography of Buddha. |
| Hd. | Hindi language. |
| Hook. | Dr. Hooker, Himalayan Journals. |
| ibid. | ibidem, in the same place. |
| id. | idem, the same |
| i. e. | id est, that is |
| imp. | imperative mood |
| impers. | impersonal, -ly |
| incorr. | incorrect, -ly |
| inf. | infinitive mood |
| init. | initio, at the beginning of a longer article. |
| inst. | instead |
| instr. | instrumentative case |
| interj. | interjection |
| interr. | interrogative, -ly |
| intrs. | intransitive |
| i.o. | instead of |
| irr. | irregular, -ly |
| Kh. | Khams, eastern part of Tibet. |
| Köpp. | Köppen, Die Religion des Buddha. |
| Kun. | Kunawur, province under English protection. |
| Lat. | Latin |
| Ld. | Ladak, province. |
| Ld.-Glr. | Ladak-Gyalrabs, a history of Tibet, ed. by Dr. E. Schlagintweit. |
| Lew. | Lewin, Manual of Tibetan. |
| Lex., Lexx. | Lexicons, native dictionaries. |
| Lh. | Lahoul, province. |
| Lis. | Lishigurkhang, glossary. |
| lit. | literally, also literature |
| Ma. | Ma-ong-lung-bstan, a kind of Tibetan Apocalypse. |

masc. = masculine gender
Med. medical works
med. medio, about the middle of a longer article
metaph. metaphorical, -ly
meton. metonymical, -ly
Mil. Milaraspa's hundred thousand Songs.
Mil. nt. Milaraspai nam-tar, Milaraspa's autobiography.
Mng. Man-ngag-rgyud, a medical work.
n. name
neut. neuter gender
nif. ni fallor, if I am not mistaken
n. p. noun proper
N.T. New Testament
num. numeral
obs. obsolete
opp. as opposed to
p. page
partic. participle
pass. passive, -ly
perh. perhaps
Pers. Persian
pers. person, personal
pf. perfect tense
pl. plural number
pleon. pleonastic, -ally
p. n. proper name
po. poetically
pop. popular language
postp. postposition
prep. preposition
prob. probably
pron. pronoun
prop. properly
prov. provincialism, provincial, -ly
Pth. Padma thangyig, a collection of legends of Padma Sambhava.
Pur. Purig, province.
q. v. quod vide, which see
rel. relative
resp. respectful, -ly
Sambh. or Sb. Shambhala, a fabulous country in the north and a book: Guide to Sb.
sbst. substantive
Sch. Prof. Is. J. Schmidt, Tibetisch-Deutsches Wörterbuch.
„ „ Tibetische Grammatik.
Schf. Dr. A. Schiefner.
Schl. = Dr. E. Schlagintweit, Buddhism in Tibet.
Schr. Schröter, editor of the first Tibetan Dictionary.
S.g. Shad-gyud, a medical work.
Sik. Sikkim, province
sim. similar in meaning, similarly
sing. singular number
s. l. c. si lectio certa, if the reading is to be depended upon
S.O. Ser-od, a religious work.
Sp. Spiti, province.
Ssk. Sanskrit
Stg. Stan-gyur, a collection of commentaries.
symb. num. symbolical numeral
syn. or synon. synonymous
Tar. Taranatha, history of the propagation of Buddhism in India.
termin. terminative case
Thgr. Thos-grol, Direction for the departed soul to find the way to eternal happiness.
Thgy. Thargyan, scientific treatises.
Trig. Triglot, a collection of Buddhist terms in Sanskrit, Tibetan and Mongolian.
trop. tropically, figuratively
trs. transitive
Ts. Tsang, province of Central Tibet.
Ü Ü, „ „ „
Urd. Urdu, a dialect of Hindustani.
v. vide, see
vb. verb
vb. a. verb active
vb. n. verb neuter
vulg. vulgar, low expression
vulgo in common life
W. Western Tibet.
Was. Prof. W. Wasiljew, Der Buddhismus.
Wdk. Waidurya Karpo, a mathematical work.
Wdn. Waidurya Nonpo, a medical work.
w. e. without explanation
Will. Williams, Sanskrit-English Dictionary.
Wls. Wilson, Sanskrit Dictionary.
Wts. Wai-tsang-thu-shi, a description of Tibet, originally Chinese, ed. by Klaproth.
Z. Zangskar, a Kashmere-Tibetan province.
Zam. Zamatog, a treatise on Tibetan grammar and orthography.

## EMENDATION.

**Page 122, 1st. column, 4th. line from the top, after dignity, are to be inserted the following words: 2. *Cs.* exaggeration. *sgro-ₒdogs-pa* 1. *Sch.* to bestow the peacock's feather.**

**Other misprints in the English text will be easily recognized as such, and hardly require a specification.**

# TIBETAN-ENGLISH DICTIONARY.

# ཀ

**ཀ་** *ka* 1. the letter **k,** tenuis, = French *c* in *car.* — 2. as numerical figure, used in marking the volumes of a work: **one.** — *ka-ťo* **alphabetical register** *Sch.* — *ká-pa* the first volume of a work. — *ka-dpé* **a-b-c-book.** — *ka-ṕréṅ, ka smad sum-ču, kā-li* the Tibetan **alphabet.**

**ཀ** *ka* 1. an additional syllable, so-called article, affixed to some substantives, numerals and pronouns, v. the grammars. — 2. **pillar,** v. *ka-ba.*

**ཀྭ** *ka (kva)* **oh!**

**ཀ་ཀ་** *ka-ká* **excrement,** (nursery word), **ka-ka taṅ-če** *W.* = French: *faire caca.*

**ཀཱ་ཀ** *kā-ka Ssk.* **crow.**

**ཀྂ་ཀ** *kaṅ-ka, Ssk.* **कङ्क, heron.**

**ཀ་ཀ་ནི་** *ka-ka-ni* a small coin of ancient India *Cs.*

**ཀ་ཀ་རང་** *ka-ka-ráṅ* **cucumber** *Kun.*

**ཀ་ཀོ་ལ་** *ka-ko-la, Ssk.* **कक्कोल,** a plant bearing a berry the inner part of which is a waxlike and aromatic substance. — *ka-ko* prob. means the same.

**ཀ་ཁ** *ka-ḱá* the **a-b-c, alphabet;** *ka-ḱai ťo* **alphabetical register,** *ka-ḱai dpe* **a-b-c-book;** *ka-ḱa-pa* **abecedarian.**

**ཀ་ཁོལ་མ་** *ka-ḱól-ma* v. *ḱol-ma.*

**ཀ་ཅ་** *ká-ča* also *ká-č̔a,* **goods, things;** *ká-čai rjés-su ˳bráṅs-pai rgyálpo* n. of a demon.

**ཀ་ཏ་ཡ་** *ká-ta-ya,* also *ka-tya.* n. of a locality *Mil.*

**ཀ་ཏུ** *ka-tu* v. *ke-tu.*

**ཀ་ཏོ་ར་** *ka-tó-ra,* more correctly *ka-ṭo-ra, Hd.,* **metal cup, dish, basin.**

**ཀ་ཐ་ར** *ka-ťa-ra Kun.* a sort of **peach.**

**ཀ་དག** *ka-dág,* also *ka-nas dag,* pure from the beginning *Lex.*

**ཀ་དར** *ka-dár* (from خبردار *Urd.?*) only in the phrase: **ka-dar čo-če** **to be cautious, take care, take heed,** *-la,* of.

**ཀ་པཱ་ལ་** *ka-pā-la Ssk.* **skull.**

**ཀ་པི་ཏ** *ka-pi-ta* **gum, resin** *Sch.*

**ཀཾ་པོ་རྩེ་** *kam-po-rtse,* absurd spelling instead of *kam-bo-ja Wdk.*

**ཀ་བ་** *ká-ba* **ka-wa** 1. **pillar, post;** *k. ˳dzug-pa* to erect a pillar. — 2. a large vein or artery in the abdomen. — **Comp.** *ka-skéd* shaft of a column. — *ká čan* having columns. — *ka-γčig-sgo-γčig* a small house, poor cottage; also a mode of capital punishment is said to be called so, when the culprit is fastened to a pillar in a dungeon until he dies of hunger. — *ka-γčig-pa* having one pillar, *ka-máṅ-ma* having many pillars. — *ka-čén* the principal p. (cf. στῦλος Gal. 2. 9) *Tar.* 182. 10. — *ka-rtén* base of a p. *Lex.* — *ka-stégs, ka-γdán* pedestal, base of a p. — *ka-spúṅs* many pillars. — *ka-méd* without a pillar; helpless, destitute. — *ka-rtsé, ka-yáṅ-rtse* capital of a pillar. — *ka wá-*

*čaṅ, súl-čan* a channeled pillar. — *ka-γžú* capital of a pillar. — *ka-γžu-γdúṅ* beam of the capital (pillars are mostly made of wood).

ཀ་བེད་ *ka-béd* prob. a sort of **gourd** *Wdṅ.*

ཀ་མ་རུ་ *ka-ma-ru* 1. **alabaster** *Sch.* — 2. n. of a country.

ཀ་མ་ལ་ཤཱི་ལ་ *ka-ma-la-si-la* n. of a famous ancient pandita or Brahmanical scholar.

ཀ་མུལ་རྡོ་རྒྱད་ *ka-mul-rdo-rgyád* is said to denote a sort of **alabaster** or of **steatite** in *C.*

ཀ་ཙ་ལིནྡི་ *ka-tsa-lindi* n. of a fabulous, very smooth, stuff or cloth, *Gyatch.*

ཀ་རྩམ་ *ka-rtsam, Ld.* **ka-sam**, prob. a sort of **oats;** differing from *yug-po,* accounted superior to buckwheat, but inferior to wheat.

ཀ་ཚིགས་ཆེན་པོ་ *ka-tsigs-čén-po* title of a book cited in *Glr.*

ཀྭ་ཡེ་ *ka-yé (kwa-ye)* **oh! holla! hear!** so e. g. at the beginning of a royal proclamation *Pth.*

ཀ་ར་ *ká-ra C. & B.* **sugar;** *šel-ka-ra* crystallized s., sugar-candy, *rgyál-mo-ka-ra* id. *Sch.; byé-ma-ka-ra* ground sugar. — *ka-ra-ǰa* tea with sugar; *Sch.* 'a sweet soup'? — *ka-ra tog-tóg* sugar in lumps. — *kara-šiṅ* sugar-cane. *(W. ka-ra).*

ཀ་ར་བཱི་ར་ *ka-ra-bī-ra*, also *ka-ra-wī-ra(Ssk.)* **oleander flower,** *Nerium odorum.*

ཀ་རཉྫ་ *ka-raṅ-dza Ssk.* a medicinal fruit, *Galedupa arborea.*

ཀ་རནྡ་ *ka-ran-dha Pth.* more correctly *ka-raṇ-ḍa, Ssk.*, a species of **duck.**

ཀ་རུ་ *ká-ru* **wedge.**

ཀ་ལཱ་པ་ *ka-lā-pa* a fabulous place or country in the north of Asia; also n. of a grammar *Cs.*

ཀ་ལ་པིང་ཀ་ *ka-la-piṅ-ka Cs.:* 'Ssk., n. of a bird', *Will.:* '*kalāpin* peacock; the Indian cuckoo'.

ཀ་ལ་ཤ་ *ka-la-śa Ssk.* **pitcher, jar.**

ཀ་ལག་ *ká-lag W.* **mud,** mixture of earth and water used instead of clay *(C. & B.: ǰim-pa)*; the word is also used for other similar compounds.

ཀ་ལནྟ་ཀ་ *ka-lan-taka Ssk.* n. of a bird.

ཀ་ལི་ *ka-li* 1. **skull** *Lex.* — 2. = *ka-lé W.*

ཀཱ་ལི་ *kā-li* the **Tib. alphabet,** v. *ka.*

ཀ་ལིང་ག་ *ka-liṅ-ga Ssk.* n. of different tracts in the eastern part of India; *Sch.:* 'Korea', without giving further explanation; perh. Mongol writers call it so?

ཀ་ལིབ་ *ka-lib, Ar.* قالب **bullet-mould** *W.*

ཀ་ལེ་ *ka-lé.* also *ka-léb,* **saddle-cloth.**

ཀཱ་ཤ་ *kā-śa Ssk.* a sort of grass, Saccharum spontaneum; Tibetans often seem to mistake it for *ku-śa* q. v.

ཀ་ཤི་ཀ་ *ka-śi-ka Ssk.,* adj. of Kāsi (Banāras): inhabitant of Banāras; *ka-śi-kai ras,* a sort of fine **cottoncloth.**

ཀ་ས་ *ká-sa,* also **ká-so, kas** (perh. a mutilated form of *bka-stsal)* resp. **yes, Sir! very well, Sir! at your service!** *(W.* also: **ká-sa-ǰu** v. *žu) W.* frq., also *C.* ni f., never in *B.*

ཀག་གིས་ *kág-gis* **suddenly** *Sch.*

ཀག་མ་ *kág-ma* **mischief, harm, injury** *Cs.*

ཀང་ཀ་ *kaṅ-ka Ssk.* **heron.**

ཀང་དང་ཀིང་ *kaṅ-daṅ-kiṅ* n. of a terrifying deity *Glr.*, prob. = *kiṅ-káṅ,* which is said to signify Rāhula (v. *sgra-γčan & drag-γšed.* in *drag-pa).*

ཀཎྜ་ཀཱ་རི་ *kaṇḍa-kā-ri Ssk.* ('thorny') Wilson: *Solanum Jaquini;* in *Lh.* a sort of wild Rubus.

ཀད་ *kad, Ld.* sometimes instead of the affix *ka,* e. g. *γnyis-kád, tsaṅ-kád;* perh. also in *mnyam-kád, Thgy.?*

ཀན་ *kan Med.* = *bad-kan.*

ཀན་མ་ *kán-ma* **middle finger.**

ཀབ་ཟ་ *kâb-za* (قبضه *Ar.*) *W.* **hilt, handle** of a sword.

ཀབ་ཤ་ *kâb-ša* (كفش *Pers.*) **shoe**; in *W.* esp. the leather shoes of Hindu fashion, which are also bought by wealthier Tibetans.

ཀམ་བོ་ཛ་ *kam-bo-dza Ssk.* n. of a country in the northwest of India, *Wdṅ.*: *kam-po-rtse.*

ཀཽ་ *kau* **watermelon** *Sch.*

ཀར་ *kar*, also *kar-kar*, **great pain, suffering** *Lex.*

ཀརྐ་ཏ་ *karka-ta Ssk.* the constellation of **Cancer.**

ཀར་སྐྱིན་ *kâr-skyin* **loan,** when respectfully requested, cf. *skyin.*

ཀར་ཆག་ *kar-čâg* **register, list.**

ཀརྨ་ *kârma Ssk.* ('deed, action'); *kar-ma-pa* (in Nepal *karmika*) name of a philosophical school of Buddhism.

ཀར་ཡོལ་ *kar-yól* **porcelain, china-ware, -cup** etc.

ཀར་ལང་བ་ *kâr-laṅ-ba*, also *kér-laṅ-ba*, **to stand up, to rise.**

ཀར་ཤ་པ་ཎི་ or ན *kar-ša-pa-ni* or *na*, *Ssk.* कार्षापण, a coin in ancient India, or rather a weight of gold and silver, of different value (not = 'cowries', as *Sch.* seems to think).

ཀལ་ཡ་ *kál-ya*, also *kal-yór*, *W.* col. instead of *kar-yól*, the former seems to be a corruption of قلعي.

ཀི་ *ki* numerical figure: 31, *ki-pa* the 31st (volume).

ཀི་ཀང་ *ki-kán* **wild leek** *Sch.*

ཀི་གུ *ki-gu* n. of the vowel-sign for *i*, ི.

ཀི་མ *ki-ma Dzl.* [illegible] acc. to *Schf.* a corruption of the Chinese *khin*, a lyre with 7 strings. (Pilgrim. of Fa-Hian Calc. 1848 p. 265).

ཀི་ཙི *ki-tsi* **tickling** *W.*, **ki-tsi kúg-če** **to tickle.**

ཀིང་ཀང་ *kiṅ-káṅ* v. *kaṅ-daṅ-kiṅ.*

ཀིམ་པ་ *kim-pa* n. of a fruit, *Lex.*

ཀུ་ *ku* numerical figure: 61; *kú-pa* the 61st (volume).

ཀུ་ *ku, kú-sgra B.*, **kú-čo** *W.* **clamour.**

ཀུ་ན་ལ་ *ku-na-la, ku-nā-la Ssk.*, n. of a bird in the Himalaya.

ཀུ་བ *kú-ba Wdṅ.* **gourd.**

ཀུ་བེ་ར་ *ku-be-ra Ssk.* the god of riches, also *Nag-ku-bera, Rnam-tos-kyi-bú, Rnam-tos-srás, Lag-na-rdó-rje* etc.

ཀུ་མུ་ད་ *ku-mu-da Ssk.* the flower of the red and white **lotus,** *Nymphaea rubra* and *esculenta.*

ཀུ་ཡ་ *kú-ya* **sediment of urine** *Med.*

ཀུ་རུ་ཀུལ་ལེ་ *ku-ru-kul-le* n. of a female deity *Mil.*

ཀུ་རུག *ku-rúg Ld.* **colt of an ass.**

ཀུ་རེ་ *ku-ré*, also *ku-res* **jest, joke,** *ku-re byed-pa* **to jest,** cf. *kyal-ka.*

ཀུ་ལིག *ku-lig* **key,** also **lock;** more accurately: **pé-ku-lig** key, *čug-ku-lig* lock, padlock; **ku-lig-búr-* (or *bor-*) *tse** in *Ld.* a contrivance used instead of a doorlatch. *W.*

ཀུ་ཤ *ku-ša* a sort of grass, Poa cynosuroides, often used in sacred ceremonies.

ཀུ་ཤུ *ku-šu* **apple** *Dzl.*; *W.* (Cf. *sli*).

ཀུ་སུ་མ *ku-su-ma Ssk.* **flower.**

ཀུ་ཧུ *ku-hu* **ring-dove** *Cs.* (*Ssk.*: the cry of the cuckoo).

ཀུག *kug*, also *kug-kúg*, **crooked; a hook;** *gri-kug* a curved knife, short sabre; *lčags-kug* an iron hook; *nya-kug* a fishing-hook; **kug-kug ǰhé-pa** *C.* **taṅ-če** *W.* **to bend, curve; clinch** (a nail); **go kug taṅ-če** *W.* **to nod,** **lag kug taṅ-če** *W.* **of beckon.** (Cf. *kum-pa.*)

ཀུག་རྩེ *kug-rtse*, **kug-se** **cuckoo** *W.*

ཀ

ཀུན་ *kun (C.: *kuṇ*)* **all, every, each; whole;** *spui ḱúṅ-bu kún-nas* from every pore *Dzl.; dé-dag kun* all these; *γžan kun* all the others; also pleon. *kun ṫams-ċád* all of them, they altogether; *kún-gyis mṫóṅ-ba, ṫós-pa* seen, heard by every body, generally known; *kún-tu* 1. into all, in all etc. 2. adv. everywhere, in every direction; *kun-tu-bzáṅ-po* Allgood, n. of the first of the celestial Bodhisattwas, *Samanta-bhadra,* sometimes confounded with Adibuddha, *ṫóg-mai Saṅs-rgyas;* in later works even a *Kun-tu-bzáṅ-mo Yum* is mentioned *Thgr.; kún-tu rgyú-ba* to go everywhere, wander about; *Kun-tu-rgyu* परिव्राजक n. of a class of Brahmans, itinerant monks, *Dzl.; kún-nas* **from everywhere, round about, wholly, thoroughly** e. g. overpowered by passions, cleansed from sin *Dzl.; kún-nas ̥dod-pa* to wish from the bottom of the heart *Thgy.*

**Comp.** *kun-dkris* **general corruptness, misery, sin** *Lex.* — *Kun-kyáb* comprising, pervading all things. — *Kun-mḱyén-(pa)* **omniscient.** — *Kun-dgá-bo, Ssk. ānandā,* n. of the favourite disciple of Buddha; *Kun-dga* is to this time frequently used as a name of (female) persons. — *Kun-dga-rá-ba,* also *kun-dga Thgy.,* or *kun-ra, Ssk.* आराम or संघाराम 'garden of all joys' 1. the **grove** in which a monastery is situated. 2. the **monastery.** 3. in Tibet, which is destitute of groves, more particularly the **auditory** or **library** of a monastery — *Kun-brtágs,* in the Mahayana: a personal, erroneous supposition *Was.* — *Kun-̥dús* **all-gathering, all-uniting.** — *Kun-dbáṅ* **almighty.** — *Kun-rdzób* **altogether vain, delusive;** *kun-rdzób-kyi bdén-pa* subjective truth *Was.* — *Kun-γži* lit.: the primary cause of all things, viz.: 1. the **soul or spirit,** *kun-γžii sems* (opp. to *̥byúṅ-ba bžii lus* the body consisting of the 4 elements), *kun-γžii séms-la ṗo mo ma mċis-te* as no difference of sex exists in souls (we, though being women, would beg etc.) *Mil.* 2. With more precise distinction: *kun-γži* **soul** as the seat of the passions, opp. to *sems-nyid,* the very soul, the spirit as the seat of reason *Mil.* 3. To the followers of the Adibuddha doctrine *kun-γži* is = **God, Adibuddha,** *kun-γžii Saṅs-rgyas.* — *Kun-γzígs* **all-seeing.** — *Kun-slóṅ Lex.* v. *sloṅ-ba.*

ཀུན་ད་ *kun-da Ssk.* **jessamine.**

ཀུན་དུ་རུ་ *kun-du-ru Ssk.* **incense,** Boswellia.

ཀུམ་པ་ *kúm-pa,* also *kum-kúm, kúm-po,* **crooked, shriveled, dried up;** **kum táṅ-ċe* W.* **to bend** together, **to double.** (Cf. *skúm-pa).*

ཀུམ་བྷ་ *kum-bha Ssk.* earthen **jar.**

ཀུམ་བི་ར་ *kum-bi-ra Ssk.* **crocodile.**

ཀེ་ *ke* numeral: 91, *ke-pa* the 91st (volume).

ཀེ་ཀེ་རུ་ *ke-ke-ru,* also *kerketana & ketaka Ssk.* 'n. of a precious white stone' *Cs.;* our Ssk. dictionaries give but the last of these names, and as its only signification the name of the tree Pandanus odoratissima.

ཀེ་ཏ་ར་ *ke-ta-ra Sambh.,* n. of a mountain, prob. Kedāra, part of the Himalaya. *Will.*

ཀེ་ཏུ་ *ke-tu Ssk.* **a fiery meteor, shooting star; the descending node.**

ཀེ་རྩེ་ *ke-rtsé* v. *keu-rtsé.*

ཀེ་རེ་ *ke-ré* v. *kye-ré.*

ཀེ་ལ་ཤ་, ཀཻ་ལ་ཤ་ *ke-la-ša, kai-la-ša Cs.,* कैलास *Will.,* n. of a lofty region of the Himalaya, mythological rather than geographical, seems to be the same as Ti-se q. v., though modern geographers apply the name to different ranges.

ཀེ་ལན་ *ke-lan;* the fraternity or association, which Huc mentions under this name (Voy. II ch. 6), seemed to be totally unknown to our Tashilhunpo Lama, although the expectation of a final war between Buddhist believers and infidels, in which the latter will be destroyed, is widely spread through Tibet.

ཀེ་ཤུ་ཀ *ke-ṡu-ka Wdṅ.* n. of a plant, perhaps *keċuka*, Arum Colocasia, with edible root; or = *keṅ-su-ka?*

ཀེག་མ *kég-ma* = ཀག་མ *kág-ma Cs.*

ཀེང་རུས *keṅ-rús* **skeleton.**

ཀེང་ཤུ་ཀ *keṅ-ṡu-ka Lex., Sambh., Wdṅ.,* n. of a tree.

ཀེའུ་རྩེ *keu-rtse*, also *ke-rtse*, **jacket** *Mil.*

ཀེའུ་རི *keu-ri* n. of a female terrifying deity *Thgr.*

ཀེའུ་ལེ *keu-le Dzl.* [symbol], 1: *keu-lei rgya*, acc. to the Mongol version: **customary seal**, — dubious.

ཀེར་གྱིས *kér-gyis* **suddenly** *Sch.*

ཀེར་བ *kér-ba* **to raise, lift up**, e. g. the finger towards heaven *Glr.*; *ker láṅ-ba* **to rise, stand up.**

ཀོ *ko* 1. num.: 121; *kó-pa* the 121st (volume). — 2. affix, = *ka col. Ld.* — 3. **all, whole** *Schr.*, cf. *kob.*

ཀོ་ཀོ *ko-kó* 1. also *ko-sko*, **throat, chin** *Sch.*, *ko-sko ˏdegs Lex.?* 2. = *ka-ka W.*

ཀོ་ཀོ་ཐང་མ *ko-ko-ťáṅ-ma* n. of a country in or near Ceylon *Pth.*

ཀོ་ཉོན་ཙེ *ko-nyon-tsé*, also *ko-nyol-tsé*, *ko-lon-tsé* the kernel of the pine-apple *Cs.*; more particularly the edible seed of the Neosa-pine in the valley of the Sutledj; also *skan-nyan-tsé Kun.*

ཀོ་ཐ *ko-ťa*, *Ssk.* कोठ, a kind of **leprosy** *Wdṅ.*

ཀོ་པང་ཙེ *ko-paṅ-tsé* a sort of **tea** *Schr.*

ཀོ་ཕོངས *ko-ṗóṅs* **guitar** *Ld.*; it is tuned in 3 fourths.

ཀོ་བ *kó-ba* 1. **hide, skin.** — 2. **leather,** **kó-wa nyé-ḱan** **tanner** *C.*; *gláṅ-ko* **neat's leather.** — *ko-krád* **leather-shoe.** — *kó-mḱan* 1. **tanner.** 2. (acc. to some also:) conductor of a leather-boat, **boatman.** — *ko-btúm* 'leather-wrapping' is said to be a criminal punishment in *C.*, in different degrees of severity, e. g. **lág-pa ko-túm**, when the culprit's hands are cut off, the stumps sewed up in leather, and the wretch thrown as a beggar upon public charity etc. — *ko-ťág* **strap, thong.** — *ko-˳ťágs Cs.*: a small instrument of leather to weave lace with. — *ko-gdán* a piece of leather put under the saddle *Sch.* — *ko-lpágs* **hide, leather.** — *ko-˳búgs Sch.*: three-edged needle for leather. — *ko-ťság* **leather-sieve.** — *ko-rúl* a rotten hide.

ཀོ་བོ *kó-bo* n. of a country *Wdk.*

ཀོ་མ *kó-ma* n. of a bird *Wdṅ.*

ཀོ་ཝག *ko-wág* is meant to express the voice of a raven.

ཀོ་ར *ko-ra*, *Hindi* कोरा, more tibetanized *ko-rás*, unbleached coarse cotton cloth.

ཀོ་རེ *ko-ré*, in compounds *kor W.*, **cup** for drinking; *ṡiṅ-kor* wooden cup, a utensil every Tibetan carries with him in his bosom; *ṡél-kor* (European) **tumbler.** (Cf. *ṗór-pa*).

ཀོ་ལོང *ko-lóṅ*, a dubious word. *Sch.* has *ko-loṅ-ba* to hate, envy, but in a passage in *Mil.*, where the connection admits of no doubt, *ko-loṅ mdzad-pa* must be taken for: to disdain.

ཀོ་ཤམ་བི *ko-ṡam-bi Dzl., Glr., Ssk.:* कौशाम्बी n. of an ancient city on the Ganges, in the Doab.

ཀོ་ས་ལ *ko-sa-la Sambh., Ssk.:* कोसला, = *Ayodhya*, Oude.

ཀོག་པ *kóg-pa* I. subst., also *skóg-pa*, *skógs-pa* **shell, peel, rind;** *ṡún-kog* id.; *ṗyi-kog* exterior shell, **bark;** *kóg-pa ṡu-ba* **to peel, pare.** — II. vb. n. **to splinter off, to chink;** *kog laṅ-ba* 1. id. 2. **to** rise suddenly and run away.

ཀོང *koṅ*, also *koṅ-kóṅ*, 1. **concave, excavated.** — 2. **crooked,** **pí-ṡi tsíg-pa koṅ-kóṅ čo** the cat makes a crooked back *W.* — *kóṅ-po* 1. **cup, bowl.** 2. **crucible.** 3. **breach, gap** *Sch.* 4. n. of a province S. E. of Lhasa. — *kóṅ-bu* small cup, bowl. — *mčód-kóṅ* offering-bowl; *snág-koṅ* **inkstand** for black ink, *mtsál-koṅ* for red ink, vermilion; **lúg-koṅ** **casting-mould** *C.*

ཀ

ཀོད་ *kod* ('a gathering'?) 1. *lag-kód Ld.* an armful of corn, a **sheaf.** 2. affix = *kad, ka, ko: *nyis-kód, ṅa-kód** all the two, all the five *Ld.*

ཀོབ་ *kob* all, *Ld.* col.

ཀོར་ *kor*, root denoting anything round or concave, hence: *kor-kór* 1. adj. **round**, circular *C.* (= **kyir-kyir* W.*); roundish, globular *C.*; concave, deep, as a soup-plate (opp. to flat) *W.* 2. sbst. a thick **loaf** of bread, (opp. to a flat, thin cake) *C.*; **a pan**, saucepan *W.*; a hollow in the ground, a pit not very deep *W.*; *stód-kor* a little circle above a letter, *Ssk.* anuswara; *klád-kor* id., a dot, zero, naught; *ydúb-kor* bracelet *Cs.*; *pád-kor* a certain way of folding the fingers, so as to represent the form of a lotus-flower; *ₒód-kor* a radiant circle *Cs.* Cf. *skór-ba, ₒkór-ba, ko-ré.*

ཀོར་དོ་བ་ *kor-do-ba* **boot** *Ld.?*

ཀོལ་ཏོ་ *kol-to* **dumb, mute** *Sp.?*

ཀོས་ཀོ་ *kós-ko = ko-ko; kos-snyúṅ* with a pointed chin *Sch.*

ཀྱ་སིར་རླུང་ *kya-sir-rlúṅ* v. *kyiṅ.*

ཀྱག་ *kyag*, also *kyag-kyág*, **thick**, run into clots *Cs.*

ཀྱག་ཀྱོག་ *kyag-kyóg* **curved, crooked**; **go kyag-kyóg čo-če* W.* to shake one's head, viz. slowly, in meditating; **ri-mo kyag-(ga-) kyog-(gè)** **a flourish** (in writing) *W.* Cf. *kyog-kyóg.*

ཀྱང་ *kyaṅ* I. adj., also *kyaṅ-kyáṅ, kyaṅ-po*, **straight, slender**, as a stick; **kyaṅ-kyaṅ ríṅ-mo** **tall, slender,** as a man, a tree etc. *W.* — II. adv. = *yaṅ*, **too, also,** always used enclitically, after the letters g, d, b, s.

ཀྱང་ཀྱོང་ *kyaṅ-kyóṅ*, also **kyaṅ-ṅa-kyoṅ-ne**, **indolent, lazy, idle** *W.*; **kyaṅ-kyoṅ čo-če** to lounge, to be idle *W.*

ཀྱར་ཀྱར་ *kyar-kyár*, also *kyar-po* **flat**, not globular *Cs.*

ཀྱར་ཀྱོར་ *kyar-kyór*, also **kyár-ra-kyor-re**, **still feeble,** as convalescents after a disease.

ཀྱལ་ཀ་ *kyal-ka* 1. **joke, jest**, in words *(Liš. ku-rei tsig).* — 2. **jocular trick,** *ku-re daṅ kyál-kai pyir* by way of jest, for fun. — 3. any **worthless, foolish, indecent talk** *Stg.*

ཀྱལ་ཀྱལ་ *kyal-kyál Lex.* w. e.; *Sch.: kyal-kyal-ba* to go round (?).

ཀྱལ་ཀྱོལ་ *kyal-kyól = kyar-kyór, dúd-ₒgro kyal-kyól ₒga* some poor ill-conditioned beast, speaking of cattle, *Mil. nt.*

ཀྱི་ *kyi*, affix I. to sbst.-roots, ending in d, b, s: sign of the genitive case. — II. to verbal roots, after the same final letters, and then without an essential difference from *kyis*, to which we add in this place also examples of the other terminations *gi(s), gyi(s), yi(s), i* (the *s* by itself is not used after verbal roots): a. in the sense of a gerund, meaning **by** (doing something), **because,** *dgós-kyis ₒóṅ-ṅo* we come because it is necessary . . ., or more freq. **though,** *dgai* though she is glad . . . *Dzl.*, in which case it may often be rendered in English by **but**: she is glad, but . . .; *zas bzáṅ-po mi ₒdód-kyis ťa-mál-pa zos* he did not care for dainties, but ate vulgar food *Dzl.*; or it has to be omitted: *bdén-pa yin-gyis rdzún-pa ma yin* it is true, no fiction *Dzl.* — b. as an adjective, forming, like *kyin* (q. v.), with *ₒdug* or *yod* a periphrastical present tense e. g. *ₒgroi ₒdug* he is walking, *ₒoṅ-gi yod* he is coming. — c. at the end of a sentence in the sense of a finite verb and more particularly in the 1. pers. fut.: *ₒgyod mi rmoi* I shall not make you suffer for it *Dzl.*, *ṅas grogs byá-yis* I shall help *Glr.*, *bžag-gi*, and: *bžág-gis* I shall put *Glr.* This use of *kyi(s)* is said to be quite common at the present time in *C.*, whereas in *W.* not only the whole gerundial use, but even the distinction of *kyi, gyi, gi* in the genitive case of a sbst. has disappeared from colloquial language, instead of which the last consonant is repeated and the vowel i added: *śiṅ-ṅi* of the wood, **yid-di** of the mind, **bál-li** of the wool.

Note 1. *kyi(s)* when combined with adjective roots, includes the verb to be, e. g. *máṅ-gi* = *máṅ-po yin-gyi*. — 2. In colloquial language and later literature the genitive of the verbal root often takes the place of the genit. infinitivi, which seldom occurs in the old classical style, e. g. *nam ₒtsoi bár-du* lifelong. — 3. *ʼji nús kyi(s), ʼji túb-kyi(s)* or vulg. **túb-bi**, as much as (I, you etc.) can (could etc.) — 4. *kyi(s)*, when denoting an antithesis, is often followed by a pleonastical *ₒón-kyaṅ*.

ཀྱི་ལྕེ་ *kyi-lče* a medic. plant, Gentiana decumbens *L.*, *k. dkár-po* a variety of it with white flowers.

ཀྱི་ལྡིར་ *kyi-ldír* **iron hoop** *Ld.?*

ཀྱི་བུན་ *kyi-bún* **a feeling cold, a chill** *Sch.*

ཀྱི་ཧུད་ *kyi-húd* the sound of weeping, lamentation.

ཀྱིག་རྩེ་ *kyig-rtse* **unburnt brick** *Sch.*

ཀྱིང་སིར་རླུང་ *kyiṅ-sir-rlúṅ Mil.* also *kya-s. l.*, *C.*, an onomatopoetic word: a **blowing wind.**

ཀྱིན་ *kyin*, used alternatively with *gyin* and *gin*, after a vowel: *yin*, denotes a partic. present, e. g. *smón-lam ₒdébs-kyin soṅ* proceed on your way praying! With *yod* or *ₒdug* it forms a periphrastical present tense: *smón-lam ₒdébs-kyin yod* he is praying (just now): in *Ld.* even as a real subst.: **śug-ra ₒtón-gyin (žig) daṅ** 'with a whistling sound proceeding from it', **ḍó-yin-daṅ** 'together with walking' = in walking.

ཀྱིར་ཀྱིར་ *kyir-kyir W.* (= *kor-kór C.*) **round, circular**; a round thing, **disk**, e. g. the little silver saucer which the women of *Lh.* wear as an ornament on the crown of their head; *kyir-mo* id., esp. **a rupee** *Ld.*; **da kyir-kyir** the disk of the moon.

ཀྱིས་ *kyis*, after d, b, s. 1. sign of the instrumentative case, and therefore generally indicating the personal subject of the action. — 2. combined with verbal roots = *kyi*.

ཀྱེ་ *kye* **oh! holla!** in calling to somebody; in solemnly addressing a person or an auditory; also merely the sign of the vocative case *B.* (in *W.* **wa!**) *kye-kyé* id. emphatically.

ཀྱཻ་ abbrev. for *kye-kyé* v. *kye.*

ཀྱེ་ག་ *kyé-ga* n. of a bird. *Med.*

ཀྱེ་ཕང་(པ་) *kye-p̓áṅ-(pa)* n. of an idol in Lh., consisting like most of the popular idols in those countries of a wooden stick or log decked with rags, but much dreaded and revered; said to be identical with *Pe-dkar* in *C.* Its worship probably dates from a time before Buddhism was introduced.

ཀྱེ་མ་ *kyé-ma* **oh! alas!** mostly expressive of sorrow, often combined with *kyi-hud*; also sign of the vocative case. Seldom it expresses joy. — *kye-mao* id.

ཀྱེ་རེ་ *kye-ré* **upright, erect**; **kye-re laṅ-wa**, resp. **žeṅ-wa C.**, *kyer-kyér-la dad-če*, resp. *žaṅ-če** *W.* to stand; **ₒgo kyer ʼphé-pa** to raise one's head, to look up *C.* Cf. *kyer-ba.*

ཀྱེ་ཧུད་ *kye-húd*, = *kyi-hud.*

ཀྱེ་ཧོ་ *kye-hó* **hollo! heigh! well!** also like the **behold** of the Holy Scriptures.

ཀྱེད་ཀྱེད་ *kyed-kyéd*, also *braṅ-kyéd*, with the upper part of the body stretched forward *Ld.*

ཀྱེར་ *kyer*, v. *kye-re.*

ཀྱོ་བ་ *kyó-ba* **hook** *Sch.*

ཀྱོག་ *kyog*, also *kyog-kyóg*, *kyóg-po*, **crooked, bent, winding,** *rtse kyog* with its point bent, crooked at the top. *Med.*

ཀྱོང་ *kyoṅ*, also *kyoṅ-kyóṅ*, *kyoṅ-po* 1. **hard,** as e. g. stale bread, *ču kyóṅ-po* hard water; **obstinate, unmanageable**; *kyoṅ-ₒbúr* a sort of relievo-work in metal. — 2. **oblong** *Cs.* — *Sch.*: *kyóṅ-ka* **quarrel,** *kyoṅ-mgó* cause of a quarrel (?). Cf. *gyoṅ, k̓a-gyoṅ.*

ཀྱོང་ *kyoṅ*, also *kyóṅ-bu*, **small shovel, scraper** *Sch.*

ཀྱོམ་ *kyom*, also *kyóm-kyom*, 1. **flexible**, but without elasticity, **flabby, loose, lax.** — 2. also *k̔yom-k̔yóm*, **of irregular shape,** not rectilinear.

ཀྱོར་ *kyor*, also *kyor-kyór* **weak, feeble, unfortified** *Cs.*

ཀྱོལ་ *kyol*, also *kyol-kyól* = *kyor Cs.*

ཀྲག་ *krag* v. *bkrag.*

ཀྲང་ངེ་ *kraṅ-ṅé* **standing,** *kraṅ sdod-pa* to **stand** *Zam. Cf. kroṅ.*

ཀྲད་པ་ *krád-pa* **leather half-boot** or **shoe,** as it is worn by the lower class of people, often with a woolen leg; *kradrgyún Cs.* a long narrow piece of leather to fasten the sole to the upper-leather; **tad-kyi** *W.* **ta'-kyi** *C.* (or *gyi*, from *gyina?*) a worn-out leather sole.

ཀྲབ་ཀྲབ་ *krab-kráb* v. *ₒk̔rab-pa.*

ཀྲམ་ *kram W.* **cabbage,** *kram-mṅár* sweet or fresh cabbage; *kram-skyúr* sour or macerated cabbage *Cs.* (?)

ཀྲི་ཀྲི་ *kri-kri* n. of a fabulous king of India *Glr.*, not mentioned in the Ssk. dictionaries.

ཀྲྀཥྞ་སཱ་ར་ *krišṇa-sā-ra Ssk.* **the spotted antelope** *Pth.*

ཀྲུ་ཀྲུ་ *kru-kru W.* **windpipe,** **ṭu-ṭú dam-te ši-ce** to be strangled.

ཀྲེ་ནག་ *kre-nág* **smut** of a kettle *Sch.* (= *sre-nag?*)

ཀྲོང་ཀྲོང་ *kroṅ-króṅ* **standing upright,** e. g. books (opp. to **gyél-k̔an** laid down, lying *W.*); when used of persons it means also: standing on one's knees, kneeling in an upright position.

ཀྲོན་ཀྲོན་ *kron-krón* **hanging,** **ton-ton-la dugce** to hang, to be suspended in the air W.

ཀླ་ཀློ་ *kla-klo* 1. *Ssk.* म्लेच्छ **barbarian.** — 2. in later times: **Moslem, Mahometan; Mahometanism.** *Was.*

ཀླག་ཅོར་ *klag-ćor* **clamour, noise** *Cs.*

ཀླད་ *klad*, acc. to *Liš.* = *goṅ* what is above; hence *klád-pa*, also *glad*, 1. **head.** 2. **brain,** and *klad-ma* **beginning, top** *Sch.*; *gur-klád* chimney of a felt-tent. — *klad-kor* v. *kor.* — *klad-rgyá* the skin covering the brain, **pia mater;** *klad-rgyas*, = *lhá-ba*, 'the bloody marrow in the bones' *Sch.*, or simply **'brain'** *Schf.* — *klad-sgo* the **fontanel** in the infant cranium *Sch.* — *klad-čúṅ* the **cerebellum** *Sch.* — *klad-ɣžúṅ* **spinal marrow.** — *klad-ɣzér* **headache** *Med.* — *klad-šúbs* = *klad-rgyá Sch.*

ཀླན་ཀ་ *klan-ka* 1. **censure, blame** *Cs.*, *klan byéd-pa*, *ₒdebs-pa* to blame, cf. *skur-klán.* — 2. *klan tsol-ba* to seek **brawls** *Pth.*

ཀླན་པ་ *klán-pa* v. *klon-pa.*

ཀླུ་ *klu, Ssk.* नाग, originally: hooded snake, cobra di capello; in this specific sense, however, it is never used in Tibetan, whereas every child knows and believes in the mythological signification: **serpent-demon,** a demigod with a human head and the body of a serpent, living in fountains, rivers etc., commanding over great treasures, causing rain and certain maladies, and becoming dangerous when in anger; *ɣdúg-pa* is therefore a usual epithet of such demons. *klui skad* means the Prakrit language, *klui yi-ge* the Nagari character of *Ssk.* letters, viz. that which is called *varttula*, in contrast to the holy *landza*, *lhai yi-ge.* — *klui ɣnod-pa* or *skyon* diseases of unknown origin. — *klu-mo* a female serpent-demon. —

*klu-sgrúb*, prop. n., Nagarjuna, a famous Buddhist divine. — *klu-mdúd* Codonopsis ovata. — *klu-nad* = *klui-ɣnod-pa.* — *klu-p̔rúg* a young Lu. — *klu-smán* 'n. of a medicine' *Cs.*, but *sman* and *klu-smán* are also synonyms for *klu*, *Glr.*, *Mil.* etc.

ཀླུང་ *kluṅ* **river,** more com. *ču-klúṅ*, *B.*

ཀླུངས་ *kluṅs* 1. **cultivated land, field,** *klúṅs-su skye* it grows on cultivated ground *Wdṅ.* — **2. a complex of fields,** *dkar-*

mdańs-kyi kluń ťsáń-ma all the fields belonging to Kardang (n. of a village).

ཀླུབ་པ་ klúb-pa, pf. klubs, **to cover**, e. g. the body with ornaments Pth.

ཀློག་ klog v. klog-pa.

ཀློག་པ་ klóg-pa I. sbst. **earwax** Sch. — II. vb., pf. (b)klags, ft. (b)klag, imp. klog, lhogs, **to read**, B., C., yid-kyis klóg-pa to read without uttering a sound; klog-pa or klog sbst. reading, klog bzáń-po šés-pa Mil. to be a good reader; klóg-gi slób-dpon a reading-teacher. — klóg-gra a reading-school. — klóg-ťabs, klóg-ťsul art, way of reading.

ཀློང་ kloń acc. to Lex. = Ssk. urmi, **wave;** in the living language it is used for **middle**; in ancient literature for **expanse,** esp. nám-mk̔ai of the heavens, rgyá-mtsoi of the sea; rań-byúń kloń yańs brjod-méd the unspeakably vast uncreated space; hence: the space of heaven, the heavens, klóń-du ldíń-ba to soar, to hover in the sky. This vagueness of meaning makes the word suited to the idle fancies of mysticism, as in: klóń-du ˛gyúr-ba, which seems to denote a soaring into mystic perfection. — dba-klóń Sch.: wave; Tibetans of today, and Schr.: the midst of the waves. — kloń-brdól Glr. was explained by Lamas: emerging from amidst the waves. (The significations 'depth, abyss, plenty, body' added by Sch. seem to be erroneous). Cf. dkyel.

ཀློན་པ་ klón-pa, also klán-pa, **to mend, patch** v. also lhán-pa.

ཀྵ་ཡ་ kša-ya Ssk. prop. **phthisis pulmonalis;** but acc. to Tib. pathology kša-ya nág-po denotes a bilious disease, prob. **icterus niger, black jaundice.**

དཀགས་པོ་ dkágs-po W. for dka-bo.

དཀན་ dkan, also rkan (Ld. *skan*) 1. **the palate,** yá-dkan, the upper, má-dkan the lower part of the palate; *kán-ḍa ˳déb-pa* **to smack** C.; dkan-γnyér the wrinkles of the roof of the mouth Cs. — 2. dkan γzár-po Lex. w. e, Sch. steep declivity, precipice.

དཀའ་བ་ dka-ba 1. adj., also -bo, seld. -mo, **difficult**, slób-pa dká-ba learning is difficult Dzl., gen. with supine: slób-tu or slób-par dka it is difficult to learn, or with the root: go-dká difficult to understand; dkár-ba byuń it has become difficult, it is difficult (to me, to him etc.) — 2. sbst. dká-ba **pains, exertion, hardship, suffering,** dká-ba méd-par without difficulty, easily, dka-ba spyod-pa to undergo hardships = to use exercises of penance (तपस्, कृच्छ्र).

dka-˛grél Cs. 'a difficult commentary', acc. to Tib. dictionaries = पञ्जिका perpetual commentary, lit.: explanation of difficulties. — dka-ťúb, dka-spyód, dka-spyád 1. **penance.** 2. **penitent;** dka-ťúb-pa, dka-spyód-pa, dká-ťub-čan, penitent, ˳ťsó-ba dka-ťúb-ba rtén-pa to live as a penitent. — dka-sdúg **trouble,** dka-sdúg máń-po byéd-pa to take great pains C. — dka-tségs = dká-ba. — dka-lás 1. **a troublesome work.** 2. **trouble, distress.**

དཀར་བ་ dkár-ba I. adj., also -po, seld. -mo 1. **white, whitish, gray.** — 2. **morally good,** standing on the side of virtue — 3. candid, sincere? las dkár-po good action; k̔a-zás dkár-po v. dkar-zás; dkár-la dmar-mdáńs-čan white and red of complexion Pth.

II. sbst. **whiteness.** — dkár-mo sbst. 1. the goddess Durga. — 2. **white rice** Cs.

**Comp.** dkar-skya **light-gray.** — dkar-k̔úń 1. **window-hole** in a wall W. — 2. opening for the smoke in the roof C. — dkar-goń C. a piece of quartz, (acc. to popular belief porcelain is made of quartz,) hence Cs.: 'porcelain-clay.' — dkar-rgyá **rose-coloured.** — dkar-čág **register.** — dkar-ťog = dkar-zas. — dkar-mé a light (?), dkar-mé sbor-ba Sch. 'to light a candle.' — dkar-dmar **light-red** Sch. — dkar-rtsí **white-wash,** consisting of lime or some other earthy colour C., W. — dkar-zás, k̔a-zás dkar-po, dkar-ťog **clean food, lenten**

**diet,** viz. esp. milk, curd, cheese or butter, as *dkar-ysúm Schf. Tar.* (Germ. translat. p. 335); also honey, fruit. — *dkar-yól*, resp. *C.* **žal-kar*, *W. sol-kar** **porcelain, china-ware,** cups or plates of porcelain, *dkar-yol sgrig-pa* to place the china-service on the table, for: to lay the cloth. — *dkar-yyá W.* **tin, pewter,** **kar-yá dan žár-če** **to solder.** — *dkar-sér* **yellowish white.** — *dkar-ysál* 1. **shining white,** *sku-mdog dkar-ysál gáns-ri ₒdra* of a bright white colour like a glacier *Glr.* 2. **window** *Sch.* (?)

དཀུ་ *dku* 1. the **side** of a person's body *Cs.*, *dkur* or *dkú-la rtén-pa* to carry a thing at one's side *Zam.*; *dku brtólba* to open the side (in child-birth, v. *mnal*). — 2. v. *dkú-ba*. *Comp. dku-lči* a heavy feeling in the side, as a symptom of pregnancy. — *dku-mda* (**kúm-da**) *W.* (= *mčan-mda?*) **pocket** in the clothes. — *dku-nád* apparently a disease of the kidneys. — *dku-zlúm*, *Lex.* कचि cavity of the abdomen, womb.

དཀུ་ལྟོ་ *dkú-lto* **craft, cunning, trick, stratagem,** esp. if under specious pretence one person induces another to do a thing that proves hurtful to him.

དཀུ་བ་ *dkú-ba* **'sweet scent'** *Cs.*; *Zam.*: = पति **stench.**

དཀོན་མཆོག་ *dkon-mčog* (*W.*: **kon-čóg, kon-čóg*, *C.*: *kon-čó*) 1. **the most precious thing.** Buddhism has always sought the highest good not in anything material, but in the moral sphere, looking with indifference, and indeed with contempt, on everything merely relating to matter. It is not, however, moral perfection or the happiness attained thereby, which is understood by the 'most precious thing', but the mediator or mediators who procure that happiness for mankind, viz. Buddha, (the originator of the doctrine), the doctrinal scriptures and the corporate body of priests, त्रिरत्न, *dkon-mčóg ysum.* Now, although this triad cannot by any means be placed on a level with the Christian doctrine of a triune God, yet it will be easily understood, how the innate desire of man to adore and worship something supernatural, together with the hierarchical tendency of the teaching class, have afterwards contributed to convert the acknowledgment of human activity for the benefit of others (for such it was undoubtedly on the part of the founder himself and his earlier followers) into a devout, and by degrees idolatrous adoration of these three agents, especially as Buddha's religious doctrine did not at all satisfy the deeper wants of the human mind, and as its author himself did not know anything of a God standing apart and above this world. For whatever in Buddhism is found of beings to whom divine attributes are assigned, has either been transferred from the Indian and other mythologies, and had accordingly been current among the people before the introduction of Buddhism, or is a product of philosophical speculation, that has remained more or less foreign to the people at large. — 2. As then the original and etymological signification of the word is no longer current, and as to every Tibetan *'dkon-mčog'* suggests the idea of some supernatural power, the existence of which he feels in his heart, and the nature and properties of which he attributes more or less to the three agents mentioned above, we are fully entitled to assign to the word *dkon-mčog* also the signification of **God,** though the sublime conception which the Bible connects with this word, viz. that of a personal, absolute, omnipotent being, will only with the spread of the Christian religion be gradually introduced and established.

Note 1. *ran-grub-dkon-mčog* with *Schr.* is evidently the appellation of the Christian God adopted by the Rom. Cath. missionaries of those times. — 2. In the older writings *dkon-mčog* occurs (as far as I know) never without *ysum*, and combinations such as *dkon-mčog-la mčod-pa byed-pa* or *ɣsol-ba ˳debs-pa,* as well as *bla-ma dkon-mčog,* are to be found only in writings of a comparatively recent date. — 3. Instead of the phrase of asseveration: *dkon-mčog šes,* God knows! the mere words *dkon-mčog ɣsum* are frequently used in the same sense.

དཀོན་པ་ *dkón-pa C., B., -mo W.* **rare, scarce,** and therefore **dear, precious, valuable** (in an objective sense, cf. *ɣčes-pa*) *˳ǰig-rtén-na dkón-no* is exceedingly rare in the world *Dzl., ˳ǰig-rtén-na dkón-par bzáṅ-ṅo* it is of a beauty rarely to be met with in the world *Dzl.; k̔yod ˳dra mtóṅ-na dkón-rgyu med* to see a person like you, is nothing particular *Mil.; lče bdé-mo-la lhá čos dkon* with a prattler religion is scarce, there is generally not much religion about him *Mil.* — *dkon-nór* riches, valuables *Mil.*

དཀོར་ *dkór* 1. **wealth, riches.** — 2. *mtil-dkor, yaṅ-dkor, sa-dkor* are expressions current in *C.* which I could not get sufficiently explained. — *dkor-nór* = *nor.* — *dkor-pa Cs., dkor-mi Sch.* **treasurer.** — *dkor-mdzód* frq., **treasury.** — *dkor-rdzogs* (pronounce **kor-zog(s)**) n. of a monastery in southern Ladak, situated 16 000 feet high.

དཀྱར་ *dkyar Z., Ld.,* a sort of **snow-shoes.** *(Sch.:* 'stocking-boots'?)

དཀྱིལ་ *dkyil* **the middle,** *dkyil-du, -na* in the middle, c. genit. in the midst of, amidst; *dkyil-nas* from the middle, from amidst; relative to time: **yar-ri kyil-la* W.,* in the middle of summer. *dkyil-ma* the middle one, e. g. room, = dwelling-room *Ld.*

**Comp.** *dkyil-dkrúṅ* v. *skyil-dkrúṅ.* — *dkyil-˳k̔or* 1. **circle, circumference,** frq. 2. **figure,** e. g. *dkyil-˳k̔or gru-bži-pa* **quadrangle, square**; a certain mystical figure; **diagram, model.** 3. **a circle of objects,** *˳k̔or-gyi dkyil-˳k̔or* the circle of the attendants. 4. **the area of a circle, disk,** e. g. of the sun; *žál-gyi dkyil-k̔or bstan* = he showed his full countenance *Pth.* 5. **sphere,** *rlúṅ-gi dkyil-˳k̔or* the atmosphere, *méi-dkyil-˳k̔or* the sphere of fire, and similarly of the other elements, *lhai dkyil-˳k̔or* may perh. likewise be translated by: the sphere of the power of a certain god. In mysticism and magic, however, several other more or less arbitrary significations are assigned to the word, e. g. it is said to be used for *lús-kyi dkyíl-˳k̔or* the whole extent or bulk of the body, = the body, *dkyíl-˳k̔or-gyi ɣnás-su ˳čáṅ-ba* to wear on one's body (e. g. an amulet); or instead of *čós-kyi dky.: dkyil k̔or mtóṅ-ba* to behold the whole extent of religious doctrine (?).

Note. In Lex. *dkyil* is said to be = मण्ड; perh. merely because *dkyil-˳k̔or* is used for मण्डल? But *mán-dal-gyi dkyil-k̔or* is the Buddhistic map of the world, representing mount Sumeru with the surrounding continents etc.

དཀྱུ་བ་ *dkyú-ba* 1. **to run a race** *Cs.* — 2. **to wring out, to filter** *Sch.* — 3. **to caper about** *Ld.* — *dkyú-byai rta* race-horse *Cs., dkyu-sa* race-course *Cs.*

དཀྱུག་པ་ *dkyúg-pa* **to lose colour** by washing *Ld.,* perh. more correctly *skyúg-pa.*

དཀྱུས་ *dkyus* 1. **length,** *dkyús-su* in length, *dkyus-riṅ* **long** *C., spyan-dkyús* length from one corner of the eye to the other (e. g. in an image) *C. (Sch.:* bold, insolent?) — 2. **untruth, falsehood, lie.** Tar. 108. 7. *dkyus-nyid* seems to be used so, whilst 188, 5 is totally obscure.

དཀྱུས་མ་ *dkyús-ma* **common, every-day,** e. g. *na-bza* every-day clothes, *dbu-ža* work-day hat; hence *mi dkyús-ma* common people (without office or authority) *C.*

དཀྱེལ་ *dkyel* seems to be acc. to *Cs.* a synonym of *kloṅ.* I only met with the word *dkyél-po če* in a medical work; *Sch.* explains it by **universe,** and a native Lex. by *k̔aṅ yáṅs-pa* the wide house, which possibly may signify the same.

དཀྲི་བ་ *dkri-ba pf. dkris, vb. a.* (cf. *˳k̔ri-ba*) **to wind, to wind up,** *grú-gu* a clew or ball of thread, *lús-la gos* (or *gós-*

ཀ

*kyis) dkr.*, **to wrap** a garment round the body; *rtsá-bar ͺkór-lo dkris-pai γčeu Med.* was explained to me: a magic spell in circular writing, wrapped round the lower end of a clyster-pipe, *fig.: sér-snas kún-nas dkris* quite **ensnared** in avarice; *kun-dkris* 'all-ensnaring' = sin. — *dkri-ma (Glr.* 47. where the text has *drima)* means very likely **necker-chief**, which col. is called **kog-ṭi* or *k̔a-ṭi C.* '*og-šri, k̔a-šri, kya-šri* W.* — In the sense of *ͺkríd-pa* to conduct *(Sch.)* it never came to my notice.

དཀྲིགས་པ་ *dkrígs-pa* 1. **darkened, obscured, dim,** = *krigs-pa*. — also *dkrigs-p̔rág*, term for a very large number, *Cs.*: a 100 000 billion, acc. to *Zam.* = *γtáms-pa*, which *Cs.* renders, a 1000 billion. The one may be, after all, as correct as the other, for all these large numbers are, of course, not meant to be used in serious calculations, but are mere imitations of fantastic Indian extravagancies.

དཀྲུག་པ་ *dkrúg-pa pf. dkrugs (W. *šrug-če*)* **to stir, stir up, agitate** (as the storm does the sea); **to trouble, disturb, confound** (as enemies of religion confound the doctrine, or as passions disturb the mind); *dkrugs-šiṅ* 1. **stirring-stick, twirling-stick.** 2. **disturber, enemy** e.g. of the doctrine *Glr.* — *dkrugs Schr.*: turning-lathe (?) — *dkrugs-maSchr.*:quarrel.—*Dzl.* ༢༠༧7. *dkrugs byéd-pa* dubious; a safer reading is *dkú-lto byéd-pa*.

དཀྲུང་ *dkruṅ* v. *skyil.*

དཀྲུམ་པ་ *dkrúm-pa Cs. & Sch.*: **broken.**

དཀྲོག་པ་ *dkróg-pa (= skróg-pa)* 1. **to stir, churn** frq. 2. **to rouse, scare up,** *Glr.* — 3. **to wag** e. g. the tail *W.*

དཀྲོལ་བ་ *dkról-ba* v. *ͺkról-ba.*

བཀག་པ་ *bkag-pa* v. *ͺgégs-pa*; *bkág-ča byéd-pa* **to forbid** *Sch.*

བཀང་བ་ *bkáṅ-ba* v. *géṅs-pa* to fill.

བཀད་ *bkad? Lex.* quote *t̔ágs-kyi bkad*, which was explained to me by: the crossing of threads in weaving; similar: *mgó-spui bkad, mgo-bkád* the crossing or entangling of the hair on the head. — *bkád-pa* seems = *ͺk̔ad-pa.*

བཀད་ས་ *bkád-sa* 1. **a bake-house, kitchen, cook's shop** *Lex.* — 2. **open hall** or **shed,** erected on festive occasions *Tib.-Ssk. Glossary; Tar.* 18, 12.

བཀན་པ་ *bkán-pa* **to put, to press,** *rkáṅ-pa rtsíg-pa-la* one's foot against a wall; **to apply,** *γšó-mo* the plane, *lág-pa* the hand *Zam.*, to put the hand on or to something (or: stretch it out? *Sch.)*

བཀབ་པ་ *bkáb-pa* v. *ͺgébs-pa.*

བཀའ་ *bka (resp.* for *γtam, t̔sig, skad)* **word, speech** of a respected person (wherefore **order, commandment** may often be substituted for it), *rgyál-poi bka* the word of the king, *bká-la γtsógs-pa* to belong to the word, i. e. to be under the commandment or dominion (of somebody) *Glr.*; *rgyál-bai bka* the word of Buddha (this is named as one of the five 'means of grace', so to speak, Glr. fol. 70; the four others are: *mdo-rgyúd* the sacred writings *(sutra* and *tantra), bstan bčós* doctrinal and scientific writings *(šástra), luṅ* oral benedictions and instructions of Lamas, *man-ṅág* admonitions given by them). After quotations *bka* or *bkao (= skad & skad-do)* means: thus says (the holy book or teacher). *bka* as first part of a compound is frequently used to give the word adjoined the character of respectfulness, and is therefore not to be translated separately.

**Phrases and compounds:** *bka bkód-pa* **to publish, proclaim; publication, proclamation** *C.* — *bka-bkyón* (col. **kab-kyon**) 'verbal blows' **reprimand, rebuke** (given by a superior), *bka-bkyón byéd-pa, mdzád-pa B. C.*, **tón-če, p̔ín-če* W.*, *bka bkyón-pa*, all of them construed with dat., **to rebuke** somebody. — *bka-bk̔rims* **law, commandment,** *rgyál-poi bka-k̔rims γnyán-pas* by the cruel order of the king *Dzl.* — *bka bgró-ba* **to consult, to deliberate,** *naṅ-blón bču* *dan bka-žib-tu bgrós-pa-la* deliberating carefully with the ten ministers of the interior *Pth.* (*Schr.* gives also, *bka-grós ₒdri-ba* to ask, — *byéd-pa* to give advice), — *bka-ₑgyur* (**ká-gyur,** com. **kan-gyur, kan-dyúr,** in Mongolia **kan-ǰur**) the word of Buddha, as translated from the original Sanskrit, the holy scriptures of the Buddhists (100 volumes). — *bka ₑgrol-ba* **to dismiss** *Pth.*, *bka-bkrol* **leave of absence,** *ysol-ba* to ask for, *ynan-ba* to grant leave *Schr.* — *bka-rgya, bka-šog,* resp. for *rgya-ma* and *šog-bu,* letter or paper from a superior etc, **diploma, missive, communication** etc. *bka-rgyúd* 1. = *bkai rgyud* 'thread of the word', the oral tradition of the word of Buddha, which is supposed to have been delivered through a continual series of teachers and disciples besides the written scriptures; *bka-rgyud bla-ma* a Lama deriving his religious knowledge in this manner from Buddha himself *Mil.* 2. perh. also = *bka dan rgyud* 'word and tantra', oral and written instruction; *bka-rgyúd-pa* n. of a Lama-sect *Schl.* 73.; *bka-bsgos* **commandment, precept.** — *bka-sgyúr* order, *bka-sgyúr ynan-ba* to issue an order *C.* — *bka sgyúr-ba* 1. to translate the words (of Buddha etc.) 2. to issue an order (viz. in the name of a superior). — *bka sgrog-pa* 1. to publish an order. 2. to proclaim, read, preach the word. — *bka yčog-pa* to act against an order, *yab-kyi bka bčag-tu med* the order of the father must be obeyed *Glr.* — *bka-čéms* resp. for *k̔a-čéms* **testament.** — *bka-mčid* resp. for *mčid,* words or speech of a superior or any person to be honoured. — *bka nyan-pa ccgp.* 1. *vb.* **to obey.** 2. *adj.* **obedient,** *bka mi nyan-pa* 1. to disobey. 2. disobedient. *bka ynyan* 'the cruel commander', acc. to a Lex. = *btsan-pai sa-bdag* 'the mighty lord of the ground', is said to be the first of gods, either Siva or a pre-buddhistic deity. — **ka tan-ce** *W.* **to permit.** — *bka btags-pa* (*Lex.*: = *k̔rims bsgrags-pa*) **a proclaimed order,** cf. *bkar.* — *bka-rtags Cs.*: **mark, seal, precept, maxim** (?) — *bka-stod Sch.*: **'a subaltern, agent'** (?) — *bka-t̔an* **order, edict.** — *bka-drin* resp. for *drin,* **favour, grace, kindness, benefit,** *bka-drinmdzád-pa* to bestow a favour, *mi-la* upon somebody; *blá-mai bka-drin-gyis* through the kindness of his (your) reverence *Mil.*; *bka-drin-čé* the usual phrase of acknowledgment, as our: you are very kind! many thanks! *B.* and *col.* — *bka-drun* **secretary** (of a high person) *C.* — *bka-ydáms,* = *žal-ydáms* **advice, counsel, instruction;** *bka-ydáms-pa* 1. **adviser** *Sch.* 2. n. of a sect of red Lamas, founded by Brom-ston *Schl.* 73. — *bka-ₒdógs-pa* **to proclaim; proclamation.** — *bka-bsdú-ba* collection of the doctrine *Tar.* — **ka-nán** **instruction** *C.* — *bka ynán-ba* 1. *vb.* **to order, command; grant, permit;** 2. *sbst.* **order; permission;** *ned bód-kyi rgyál-poi btsún-mo-la bka ynán-bar žu* I beg you will give her as a consort to my (the Tibetan) king *Glr.* — *bka-p̔ébs Sch.* **a supreme order.** — *bka-p̔rin* **message.** — *bka ₒbáb-pa* the going forth of an order, *bka-ₒbáb* order, edict *Schr.* — *bka-ₒbúm,* vulg. **kam-búm**, the hundred thousand precepts (title of a book). — *bka stsol-ba, pf. stsal* (*stsál-to, stsál-pa*), resp. for *smrá-ba* **to speak, to say** (acc. to circumstances: to command, ask, beg, relate, answer etc.), esp. in ancient literature, in which it is almost invariably used of Buddha and of kings. — *bka-blo-bdé Lex.*: = सुवचस् speaking well, eloquently; *Sch.*: *bka-blo-bdé-ba* to acknowledge to be wrong (?); *bka-blón,* (*bkai blón-po Glr.* f. 94) **prime minister;** any **high official.** — *bka-šóg* any writing of a superior, **decree, diploma, passport, official paper, letter.** — *bka yšágs* 1. **a high official, counsellor.** *C.* 2. **court of justice; judgment-hall.**

བཀར་ *bkar term.* of *bka* in or to the word etc; *bkar ₑdógs-pa Cs.* **to legalize,** *Dzl.* cap. 4: **to proclaim, publish.** *bkár-btags-pa* **published; publication.**

བཀར་བ་ *bkár-ba* v. *dgár-ba.*

བཀལ་བ་ *bkál-ba* v. *ₒkál-ba* and *꜀gél-ba.*

བཀས་ *bkas* instr. of *bka; bkás-pa* v. *꜀gés-pa.*

བཀུ་བ་ *bkú-ba Lex.:* **to extract,** to make an extract of a drug by drawing out the juice *(kú-ba ₒbyin-pa); bkús-te ₒbór-ba id.; smán-bku* medicinal extract.

བཀུག་ *bkug* v. *kug; bkúg-pa* v. *꜀gúgs-pa.*

བཀུམ་ *bkum* v *kum; bkúm-pa* v. *꜀gúms-pa.*

བཀུར་བ་ *bkúr-ba* I. 1. *vb.* **to honour, esteem** (synon. *mčód-pa*), *máṅ-pos bkúr-bai rgyál-po,* महासम्मत, the king honoured by many, frq.; *kún-gyis bkúr-žiṅ mčód-pai ꜀os* worthy of general honour and respect *Mil.; mis bkúr-bar mi ꜀gyur* is not esteemed by men *Dzl.* — 2. *sbst.* **honour;** more frq., *bkúr-sti,* **honour, respect, homage, mark of honour,** *bkúr-stis mčód-pa* to distinguish (a person) by marks of respect *Zam.; ráṅ-la bkúr-sti ₒbyuṅ dus* when honour is shown to yourself *Mil.; bkúr-sti byéd-pa* to do honour frq.; to make a reverence, to salute. — II. *pf.* of *ₒkúr-ba* **to carry;** in the term *máṅ-pos bkúr-bai rgyál-po* the legend combines this signification with the preceding one *Glr.*

བཀོག་པ་ *bkóg-pa* v. *꜀góg-pa.*

བཀོང་བ་ *bkóṅ-ba* v. *꜀góṅ-ba.*

བཀོད་པ་ *bkód-pa* v. *꜀gód-pa.*

བཀོན་པ་ *bkón-pa* v *ₒkón-pa.*

བཀོབ་ལྟ་ *bkób-lta* (**kób-ta**) **the plan** of an undertaking *W.* (vulg. pronunciation for *bkod-blta?*)

བཀོར་འདྲེ་ *bkór-ₒdré Mil.* seems to be a kind of goblins.

བཀོལ་བ་ *bkól-ba* v. *kól-ba.*

བཀྱལ་བ་ *bkál-ba Cs.:* **to talk nonsense,** v. *kyál-ka; bkyál-pai ṅag = kyál-ka Lex.*

བཀྱིག་པ་ *bkyig-pa* v. *ₒkyig-pa.*

བཀྱེ་བ་ *bkyé-ba* v. *꜀gyéd-pa.*

བཀྱེད་པ་ *bkyéd-pa* **to bend back, recline** (vb. nt.), *rgyaṅs byéd-de* bending or turning far aside.

བཀྱོན་པ་ *bkyón-pa* **to beat** (= *rdúṅ-ba) Mil. nt.; bka bkyon-pa resp.* to chastise with words, **to scold,** frq. (v. *bka,* phrases); *Schr.* mentions also *bkyon-bkyál* chiding.

བཀྲ་བ་ *bkra-ba (Lex.:* = चित्र, *cf.* also *krá-bo)* 1. **variegated.** — 2. **beautiful, blooming** (of complexion); **glossy, well-fed** (of animals); *ša-bkrá* n. of a cutaneous disease.

**Comp.** *bkra-bzáṅ* n. of a mountain in Tibet. — *bkra-lam-mé* v. *kra-lam-mé.* — *bkra-šís Ssk.* मङ्गल 1. **happiness, prosperity, blessing,** *ₒbáṅs-rnams-la bkra-šís šog* happiness to my people! may they prosper! *Glr.; *ṅád-med tsád-med ṭa-ši pun-sum-tsóg žu** I wish you good health and immeasurable and perfect happiness! (new year's wish in *W.); bkra-šís-kyi ču* holy water *Glr.; bkra-šis-kyi mál-kri* nuptial bed *Cs.; bkra šis-kyi tsig* or *smon-lam* blessing, benediction; **ṭa-ší šig!** Good bye! May you be happy! **kyód-la ṭa-ši čo!** I wish you joy! (also ironically) *W.; bkra-šis-šiṅ* being happy, enjoying prosperity *Glr.; bkra-šís srúṅ-bai gó-ča* instruments used for insuring happiness (to a new-born infant) *Lt.* — 2. sacrificial ceremony by which blessings are to be drawn down, *bkra-šís byéd-pa* or *mčód-pa* or **yóg-če* (W.,* barley being scattered — *γyog-pa* — on that occasion), to perform this ceremony, — *bkra-šís-pa* **propitious, lucky,** perh. also: **happy;** *bkra-šís-pai ltas* lucky signs; *bkra-šís-pai rtags* lucky configurations or semblances (such as e. g. devout imagination seeks to discover in the outlines of mountains etc. *Glr.* fol. 58.) *bkra-šís-ma* n. of a goddess, *Sch.:* goddess of glory *Dzl.* — *bkra-mi-šís* **misfortune, calamity,** *bkra-mi-šís-pa* **un-**

**happy**; **calamity**, *bkra-mi-śis-pa t́ams-ċád* all manner of calamities. (The expression *bkra-mi-śis* c. dat. for: 'Woe to . . .' in our translation of the New Test. does not rest upon classic authority, but has been adopted as analogous to the above mentioned *bkra-śís śog.) bkra-śis-čos-rdzoṅ (*ta-śi-čo-dzóṅ*)* 'Tassisudon' in Bhot., *bkra-śis-lhun-po (*ta-śi-hlum-po*)* 'Tashilunpo' in Tsaṅ.

བཀྲག་ *bkrag* 1. **brightness, lustre** = *mdaṅs*, also *bkrag-mdáṅs*, e. g. of jewels. 2. **beautiful appearance, colour**, of the face or skin, also *śa-bkrág; śa bkrag-mdaṅs* pure **gloss** of the skin *Mil.; bkrág-čan* **bright**. *bkrag-čór* without gloss, **dim**.

བཀྲབ་པ་ *bkráb-pa* 1. **to select, choose**; *mčóg-tu bkrab* **exquisite, choice** *Lex*. — 2 = *ḱráb-pa, skráb-pa W.*

བཀྲམ་པ་ *bkrám-pa* v. *grém-pa*.

བཀྲལ་བ་ *bkrál-ba* 1. *pf.* of *grél-ba Cs., Tar.* 124, 14. — 2. **to appoint**, *lás-la* to a business.

བཀྲས་པ་ *bkrás-pa* 1. *Sch.: pf.* of a verb *bkrá-ba*, adorned, decorated (?) 2. *Cs.: bkras* abbreviation for *bkra-śís, bkras-btags* for *bkra-śis ḱa-btags* = *ḱa-btags*.

བཀྲི་བ་ *bkrí-ba* 1. for *dkri-ba* to wrap. — 2. for *krid-pa* to conduct. — 3. to try to acquire, **to search for** *Dzl.* ༢༠ **to lay up**, = **śri-ċe* W.*

བཀྲིས་ *bkris* abbrev. for *bkra-śis*.

བཀྲིས་པ་ *bkris-pa* for *dkris-pa* v. *dkri-ba*.

བཀྲུ, བཀྲུས་ *bkru, bkrus*, v. *ḱrúd-pa*.

བཀྲུག་པ་ 1. *Dzl.* ༧༤༦ 1. prob. an incorrect reading. 2. prov. instead of *dkrúg-pa*, v. *ja bkrúg*.

བཀྲེན་པ་ *bkrén-pa* 1. *Cs.* **poor, indigent, hungry**, *sai p̀yogs bkr.* a poor, barren country *Stg*. — 2. **miserly, stingy** *C.*

བཀྲེས་པ་ *bkrés-pa vb.* **to be hungry**; *adj.* **hungry**; *sbst.* **hunger** *B., C.* where it is now used as the respectful term; *bkres-skóm* hunger and thirst; *bkres-skóm-pa-las čóg-par byin-te* leading after hunger and thirst to satiety; *bkrés-rṅab-pa Sch.*: to have a ravenous appetite.

བཀྲོངས་ *bkroṅs* v. *gróṅs-pa*.

བཀྲོལ་བ་ *bkrol-ba* v. *gról-ba*.

བཀླག་པ་ *bklag-pa* v. *klóg-pa*.

རྐ་ *rka* 1. **a small furrow** conveying water from a conduit *(yúr-ba)* to trees or plants; **furrow** between the beds of a garden; hence: 2. **flower-bed**.

རྐང་ *rkaṅ (Ld. *skaṅ, χaṅ*)* 1. **marrow**, *rkaṅ-már* id.; *rkáṅ-bro-ma* tasting of marrow *Sch.; rkáṅ-gi ḱóṅ-nas byáms-pa* love from the innermost heart *Thgy*. — 2. the upper part of the arm or thigh, or the large **marrow-bones** of them, *dpúṅ-rkaṅ, rlá-rkaṅ Med.* — 3. **kernel** of a nut etc. *W.* — 4. = *rkaṅ-pa* no. 5, **stalk**; also **quill** of a feather. — 5. in compounds for *rkáṅ-pa*.

རྐང་པ་ *rkaṅ-pa* (resp. *žabs*) 1. **foot**. — 2. **leg**. — 3 (cf. *lag-pa*) **hind-foot**. — 4. **lower part, lower end**, e. g. of a letter, *rkaṅ-pa-ċan* 'having a foot', so the nine letters are called that extend below the line (ཀ, ཁ etc.) *Glr.* — 5. **stem, stalk**, esp. leaf-stalk, *lo-rkáṅ*. — 6 **verse**, metrical line; *tsig-rkáṅ*, prop.: *ťsigs-su-bċad-pai rkáṅ-pa, id., ťsig-rkáṅ mťar nyis-śád ťob* at the close of a verse a double *shad* is placed; hence: **verse** of the Bible *Chr. Prot.* — 7. **base, foundation**, *rdzu-p̀rúl-gyi rkáṅ-pa bži Dzl.* the four 'pillars' of performing miracles (ऋद्धिपाद) *Trigl. fol.* 17.

**Comp.** **kaṅ-kyóg** **bandy-legged** *C.* — *rkaṅ-kri* a piece of cloth to wrap round the legs *(Lat.: tibiale) Sch.* — *rkaṅ-ḱúm Lex.* w. e., prob. having a foot contracted by disease — *rkaṅ-ḱór* **bandy-legged** *Sch.* *rkaṅ-mgyógs-pa* **nimble-footed**, *rkaṅ-mgyógs-kyi rdzas lham-la byúgs-te* oiling his boots with swiftfootedness, a miraculous ointment imparting this gift *Glr., Tar.* 67. — *rkaṅ-gró* a vassal or subject paying his duty by serving as a messenger or porter *Cs.* — *rkaṅ-ˌgros* or *-brós* 1. **walking on foot.** 2. **domestic cattle; breeding-cattle.** — *rkaṅ-rgyu Cs.*: 'the hollow of the sole'. — *rkaṅ-ɣčig-pa* **one-footed.** — *rkaṅ-rǰén* **bare-footed.** — *rkaṅ-rǰés* **footstep, trace.** — *rkaṅ-ɣnyís-pa* **two-footed, a biped,** po. for **man, mankind.** — *rkaṅ-stégs* **footstool; trestle.** — *rkaṅ-ťáṅ* **on foot,** *rkaṅ-ťáṅ-pa* **pedestrian, foot-soldier,** *rkaṅ-ťáṅ-du grúl-ba (Sch.* also: *rkaṅ-ťáṅ-ba)* to walk, to go on foot. — *rkaṅ-mťil* **sole** of the foot. — *rkaṅ-ˌťúṅ* (erron. also *-ťuṅ) Ssk.* पादप 'drinking with the foot' po. for: **tree** *Mil.* — *rkaṅ-dúṅ* trumpet made of a human thigh-bone (*Hook.* I 173). — *rkaṅ-drúg-pa, rkaṅ-drúg-ldan-pa* **six-footed; insect,** *po.* — *rkaṅ-ɣdúb* **foot-ring** (ornament). — *rkaṅ-ˌdrén* (v. also *žabs-ˌdrén)* **disgrace,** *rkaṅ ˌdrén-pa* c. genit. to get a person into disgrace, to deprive him of his honour and good name, to be a disgrace to another, e. g. a son to his father by criminal actions etc. *rkaṅ-rdúm* **a maimed foot; lame** *Cs.* — *rkáṅ-snam* **trowsers,** *snám-bui rkáṅ-snam ɣčig* one pair of cloth-trowsers. *rkaṅ pags lhuṅ S. g.* fol. 9? — *rkaṅ-ṗyiṅ* felt for covering the legs, v. *rkaṅ-dkri.* — *rkaṅ-ból* upper part of the foot. — *rkaṅˌbám* a disease in the foot, *Sch.*: gout. *rkaṅ-ˌbrós* or *bros* v. *rkaṅ-ˌgrós.* — *rkaṅ-ťségs* v. *ťségs.* — *rkaṅ-mdzub-ˌdzér-pa Sch.*: **corn** (on the toe). — *rkaṅ-mdzér* **iron pricks** fastened to the feet for climbing mountains. — *rkaṅ-bží-pa* **four-footed; quadruped.** — *rkaṅ-lág* hands and feet, *rkaṅ-lag bšál-ba Lt., Schr.*: 'numbness or rheumatic pain in hands and feet'; *rkaṅ-lág sér-kar ˌoṅ* hands and feet chap *Sch.* — *rkaṅ-lám* **foot-path.** *rkaṅ-šiṅ* **treadle,** of a loom. — *rkaṅ-šúbs* **stocking, sock.** — *rkaṅ sór* **toe.**

རྐན་ *rkan* v. *dkan.*

རྐམ་པ་ *rkám-pa* I. *vb.* **to desire, to long,** *nór-la* for money. II. *sbst.* 1. **longing** *(cf. ǩam* extr.) — 2. v. *skam-pa.*

རྐུ་བ་ *rkú-ba, pf. (b)rkus, ft. brku, imp. rkus,* **to steal, to rob,** *brkú-bya* to be stolen, *brkú-byai rdzas* things that may be stolen.

རྐུན་མ་ *rkún-ma* 1. **thief** frq. 2. **theft.** *rk. byéd-pa (W.: *čo-če*)* to steal; **kún-ma zos soṅ* W.* it has been carried away by a thief; **ǩa-kún gyáb-če* W.* 'to steal with the mouth', to promise to pay without ever doing so, or: to deny having known a thing missing, until all inquiry has ceased and it may be safely appropriated (a common practice of servants in India); *dur-rkún* robber of graves. — *rkún-ťabs-su blaṅ-ba* to take away thievishly *Stg.* — *rkún-nor* stolen goods. — *rkún-po, fem. -mo* **thief.** — *rkún-dpon* the head of a gang of thieves or robbers *Cs.* — *rkún-zla* a thief's accomplice.

རྐུབ་ *rkub (Lex.* पायु) 1. **the anus** *B.* — 2. **vulva** *W., C.* — 3. **backside, posteriors** *C.* — *rkub-stégs* **sitting-bench** *C.* — *rkub-ťsós* **buttocks** *Cs.*

རྐེ་བ་ *rké-ba (cf. skémpa)* **lean, meagre** *Cs.*

རྐེད་པ་ *rkéd-pa,* also *skéd-pa, W.: *skéd-pa** 1. **the waist,** *séṅ-ges mčóns-sar was mčoṅs rkéd-pa ˌčag* if the fox takes a lion's leap, he breaks his neck *Mil.*; **skyed kug táṅ-če* W.* **to bow;** **sked-zér** (?) the arms **a-kimbo** *W.*; more particularly that part where the girdle is worn, **loins;** *rked-rgyán* ornament of the girdle; *rkéd-pa-nas gri bton* he took a knife from his girdle *Pth.*; **ke'-pa bhab** 'her waist fell', euphem. expression for: she has got her menses *C.* — 2. **the middle** of a building, of a mountain, **ǩar-skyéd* W.* the middle story of a castle; *rkéd-pa tsam brtsigs ťsár nas* when the building was half finished *Glr.*; *Ti-sei rkéd-pa-na yar bslebs soṅ* he is already half-way up the Ti-se *Mil.*

རྐོ་བ་ *rkó-ba, pf. (b)rkos, ft. brko, imp. rkos* 1. **to dig, dig-out, to hoe,** e. g. *sa* earth; *rko-byéd* digger; po. also a spade, mattock; *brkó-byai sa* soil to be turned up. — 2. **to engrave** *(cf. ˌbúr-ba); brko-spyád* **a gouge** *Sch.*; *brkós ma* **sculpture.**

རྐོ་མ་ *rkó-ma* n. of a bird *Wdṅ.*, prob. = *ko-ma.*

རྐོག་མ་ *rkóg-ma* v. *lkóg-ma.*

རྐོང་པ་ *rkóṅ-pa Cs.*: **itch**, *za-rkóṅ* id.; *Lt.*: *rkóṅ-po.* Others describe it as a scabby eruption of the skin, chiefly affecting animals, but occasionally also men *C.*

རྐོད་པ་ *rkód-pa,* = *rkó-ba Ts.*

རྐོན་པ་ *rkón-pa,* also *skón-pa* 1. **basket**; the word is said to be used in Kun.; perh. also the Ladakian word **kun-dúm**, a large cylindrical or bottle-shaped basket, may be traced to the same form. I never found it in books. — 2. **net**, fowler's net *Lex.*

རྐྱག(པ་) *rkyag(-pa),* also *skyag(-pa),* **dirt, excrement**; **kyág-pa tóṅ-wa* C.*, **kyág táṅ-če* W.* to cack, vulg. — *mig-skyág* the impurity in the eyes *Cs.*; **na-skyág** ear-wax *W.*

རྐྱང་ *rkyaṅ* **the wild ass** or horse of Central Asia, Chigitai, *ṕo-rkyáṅ* male, *mo-rkyaṅ* female of it; *rkyaṅ dár-ma* a young wild ass, *rkyaṅ-rgan* an old one, *Cs.* — *rkyaṅ-ču* n. of a lake in the south of *Ld.*, in the neighbourhood of which these animals are particularly numerous.

རྐྱང་པ་ *rkyaṅ-pa* **simple, single;** *ras rkyaṅ* a single sheet of cotton cloth *Dzl.*, *Mil.*; **mi kyaṅ** a single i. e. free, unemployed man, one that carries no burden *C.*; *yi-ge rkyáṅ-pa* a letter that forms by itself a syllable, or one that is not *brtségs-pa* and without any other consonant or a vowel-sign superscribed; *rkyáṅ-pai graṅs* are called 1, 10, 100 and the further powers of 10; *miṅ rkyáṅ-pa* a word that has no affix-denoting case etc. attached. — **kyaṅ, kyaṅ-kyáṅ, kyáṅ-ka, ḱa-(r)kyáṅ**, col. (in *B. ša-stag*) **only, nothing but**, **pé-ča ṅags ḱár-kyaṅ dug** the book contains nothing but charms. — **kyaṅ-kyáṅ** also: living by one's self, childless *W.* — **kyaṅ-ltab** single folded.

རྐྱང་བ་ *rkyáṅ-ba* v. *rkyóṅ-ba.*

རྐྱང་མ་ *rkyáṅ-ma* n. of a vein, v. rtsa.

རྐྱན་ *rkyan* (*Ld.* **skyan**) 1. a brass-vessel like a tea-pot, with a spout, *rag-rkyan id.*; **ʻo-kyan* W.* milk-pot. — 2. **pot-belly, paunch** *Sch.*

རྐྱལ་ཀ་ *rkyál-ka,* sometimes for *kyál-ka.*

རྐྱལ་པ་ *rkyál-pa,* दृति, **leather bag** *frq.*; *ṕuṅ-po mi-γtsaṅ-rdzás-kyi rkyál-pa* a poetical term for the body *Mil.*; *rkyal-bu* (**kyal-lu**) **small bag, pouch;** *ra-rkyál* bag of goatskin; *ṕye-rkyál* (**če-kyal* C.*, **ṕe-ky.* W.*) bag for flour.

རྐྱལ་བ་ *rkyál-ba* **to swim**, **kyal gyáb-če* W. id.*; *rkyal rtséd-pa* to amuse one's self by swimming.

རྐྱེན་ *rkyen,* प्रत्यय *Will.*: *'with Buddhists: a co-operating cause, the concurrent occasion of an event as distinguished from its proximate* (or rather primary, original) *cause', rgyu* हेतु. (The right meaning was given already by *Schr.*, whereas afterwards, by a mistake of *Cs.*, the totally erroneous sense of 'effect, consequence' has become current among philologists.) 1. **cause, occasion**, *rkyén-gis* c. gen. **by, on account of**, *čii rkyén-gis* whereby? *dei rkyén-gyis* thereby, therefore, *dei rgyu dei rkyén-gyis id.* As a medical term, opp. to *rgyu* (the anthropological or primary cause of a disease) it denotes the pathological or secondary cause of it. — 2. **event, occurrence, accident, case, circumstance**, in a general sense, in as far as the Buddhist conceives every thing that happens in the mutual connexion of cause and effect; *rkyen ṅán-pa* unfortunate accident; *rkyen ṅán-pas ˳das* he has perished by a fatal accident *Glr.*; *ṫse ˳dir byúṅ-bai rkyen ṅán-rnams* the adversities of the present life *Mil.*; *raṅ mi ˳dód-pai rkyen* an event disagreeable to one's own self; *bló-bur rkyen* a sudden accident *Mil.*; *rkyen dé-la brtén-nas* owing to that circumstance *Tar.* 8. 1. *méd-pai rkyén-la bltás-te* or *brtén-te C.* considering the case of not being . . ., not having . . ., thus *nad-kyi rkyen, či-bai rkyen* stands also for: a case of disease, of death; *˳gal-*

rkyén any circumstance or event adverse to the success of an action, **obstacle, hinderance,** any thing opposite or hostile to the existence of another thing, *mťun-rkyén,* **a happy, favorable circumstance, furtherance, assistance, supply,** *mťun-rkyén byéd-pa* c. genit. to assist in, to help to; *mťun-rkyén ₒdzom-po* altogether successful. — 3. **misfortune, ill luck, calamity,** *rkyen zlóg-pa* to avert a misfortune, *ťégs-pa* to endure, *ťúb-pa* to brave it *Mil.* — *cf. rgyu.*

རྐྱོང་བ་ *rkyóṅ-ba pf. & ft. brkyaṅ,* **to stretch, extend, stretch forth** (one's hand to a person), **put out** (the tongue), **spread, distend** (the wings, a curtain), *žabs ɣnyis brkyaṅ-bskúm* one leg stretched out, the other drawn in *Pth.; *kyaṅ-šád-če* W.* to stretch one's limbs. — *brkyaṅ-šiṅ* 1. 'extending-wood', an instrument of torture in Tibet, a wooden frame on which the extended arms and legs of the delinquent are fastened down, whilst burning pitch or sealing-wax is dropped on his naked breast, which procedure is called *brkyaṅ-šiṅ spräd-pa, brkyaṅ-šiṅ-la bčúg-pa* or *brkyáṅ-ba* 2. **cross** *Chr. Prot.* This word has been adopted on account of its etymological signification, although it differs in its form and use from the σταυρός of the N. T., which is unknown in Tibet and India. Additional explanation will be at any rate required on the part of missionaries; but much more so in the case of the *kro-če (Ital. croce)* of the Rom. Cath. missionaries of the last century. In favour of the word *ɣsal-šiṅ,* pointed stake for empaling a delinquent, speaks the circumstance, that this is also the original and classical signification of σταυρός, and that Buddhists from their own legends are well acquainted with the idea of martyrdom inflicted in this manner. Still *ɣsal-šiṅ* leads to a conception of the death of Christ historically untrue and revolting to our feelings and is therefore better not employed; moreover it is to be assumed that in the times of the Evangelists σταυρός was the term generally used for cross, whilst in the case of *ɣsal-šiṅ* no Tibetan thinks of anything else but empaling.

རྐྱོང་ཚེ་ *rkyóṅ-tse W.,* resp. **zim-kyoṅ, zim-tiṅ*, **lamp, candle,** (spelling uncertain).

ལྐུགས་པ་ *lkúgs-pa* 1. **dumb, mute;** *ka lkúgs-par byed-pa* to put to silence *Do.; lkúgs-pa-pa* a dumb man, *-ma* woman *Cs.* — 2. **dull, stupid** *Sch.*

ལྐོག་ *lkog* **secrecy,** *lkóg-gi čuṅ-ma Cs.:* a wife kept secretly, a private concubine, *lkóg-tu* in secrect, secretly frq.: *lkóg-tu gyúr-pa, lkyog-gyúr,* परोक्ष, secret, hidden, out of sight *Mil., Tar.; lkóg-tu gléṅ-ba* to converse secretly; *lk. sdód-pa* to keep in retirement. — *lkog-rṅan* a reward given secretly, a bribe. — *lkog-čós Sch.:* 'a secret doctrine'; but *lkog-čos byéd-pa* is gen. understood: to apply one's self to religious studies or exercises in secret. — *lkog ǰab byéd-pa* to hide one's self in a lurking place: *lkog ǰab byed-nas lta-ba* to watch, to witness from a lurking-place. — *lkog-zán zá-ba Sch.* to take usury-interest in secret. — *lkog-láb* backbiting, slander.

ལྐོག་མ་ *lkóg-ma* (vulg. **og-ma**) 1. **gullet, oesophagus.** — 2. **wind-pipe.** — 3. **throat.** — 4. **neck.** *lkóg-mai lha-góṅ Sch.,* (acc. to others: *lhar-gór)* the larynx, **koi lkóg-ma** or **og-ma šraṅ soṅ* W.* his throat is swollen, he has the croup. — — *lkog-dkár* a small nocturnal carnivorous quadruped with a white throat, marten? — *lkog-gágs* hoarseness of voice *Cs.* — *lkog-šál* **dew-lap** (of oxen). — *lkog-sóg* **craw, maw** (of birds) *Cs.*

ལྐོབ་ *lkob* **fat, heavy, plump** *Sch.*

ལྐོལ་མདུད་ *lkol-mdúd,* also *'ol-mdúd,* **larynx.**

སྐ་ཅིག་ *ska-čig* v. *skad čig, skad* no. 4.

སྐ་ཅོག་ *ska-čóg* n. of a grammarian *Zam.*

སྐ་བ་ *ská-ba* **thick** (of fluids, *cf. slá-ba);* *ska-slád (Ld.: *kas-lád*)* **consistence, density.** — *W.: *skán-te*.*

སྐ་རགས་ *ska-rágs B. & C.*, also *ske-rágs, W.* **kye-rágs**, *resp. sku-rágs* **girdle**, *ska-rags ˳čiṅ-ba* to put on the girdle, *ska-rágs bšur-ba Sch.*: a girdle with a clasp (?).

སྐག་ *skag* 1. *Cs.*: = *kag, keg,* **mischief; unlucky.** — 2. v. *rgyu-skar*.

སྐང་བ་ *skáṅ-ba* = *skoṅ-ba; skaṅ-ɣsó* 1. **satisfaction** *Sch.* — 2. a kind of **expiatory sacrifice,** to make amends for a duty not performed.

སྐང་ཤ་ *skaṅ-ša Sch.*: **sods** cut out.

སྐད་ *skad (C.:* **ka̱***)* 1. **voice, sound, cry** *(cf. sgra), gláṅ-po-čei skad lta-bui sgra* a sound like the voice of an elephant, **ka̱'-la čig-pa dho̱n mi-čig-pa** *C.* (words) equal as to sound, but of different sense (= homophone), *sdug-bsṅál-bai skad ˳byiṅ-pa, snyiṅ-žei skad dón-pa* to utter lamentable cries; *skad stér-ba Sch.*, **kẹ' gyág-pa** *C.*, **skad táṅ-če** *W.* **to sound;** **kẹ' taṅ-wa** *C.* **skad gyab-če** *W. ccdp.* **to call** to a person; *skad mťún-par* with one voice, with one accord. — 2. **speech, words, talk, news,** **ka̱' či naṅ ˳dug** what is your pleasure? what did you say, Sir? *C.*; *zér-ba de či-skad yiṅ* the (words) spoken what speech are they? = what do they mean? *Pth.*; *˳di-skad-(du)* in these words, thus, (before a literally quoted speech), *dé-skad-(čes)* id. (after it); it is also used in a more general sense instead of *dé-ltar: dé-skad ma byed* don't do that *Mil.*; *skad smrá-ba* to give account, to relate *Ld.-Glr. fol.* 12. b. *Schl.*, acc. to another reading instead of *sra smrás-te; skad byéd-pa id., rmi-lám-du byúṅ-ba skad byás-te* reporting it as having been revealed to him by a dream *Pth.* — 3. **language,** *bód-skad* the Tibetan language, *rgya-gár-skad* the Sanskrit language, *bód-skad-du, col. -la,* into or in the Tib. language, *yúl-skad-du* into or in the provincial dialect. — 4. **a snap** with the fingers, always with *čig: skád-čig-(ma)*, gen. as a measure of time: **a moment;** also adv.: for a moment, *skád-čig-la* in a moment, instantly, in one moment, *skád-čig de-nyid-la* in the very same moment. (Some mathematical books compute the *skád-čig* = $^3/_4'''$, others as long as $^1/_3''$).

**Comp. and Deriv.** *skad-˳gágs* **hoarseness of the voice,** *Cs.* — *skad-ṅán* 1. **a bad voice.** 2. **cry, screaming.** — *skád-čan* having a voice, **sounding.** — *skád-ča* 1. *C.*: discourse, conversation, **ka̱'-ča láb-pa** or **ǰhẹ́-pa** to converse, to have a chat. 2. *C.* talk, rumour, **mii ká'-ča re** it is (but) talk of the people. 3. *W.*: news, tidings, intelligence. — *skad-čé, -čén* 1. **a loud voice** *Sch.* 2. n. of an animal *Lt.* — *skad-ɣnyá Sch.*: **a high voice.** — *skad-snyán sgyúr-ba Mil.* to sing or whistle in a quavering, warbling manner, of birds, flute- players etc., *˳gyúr-skad* a singing or playing of this kind. — *skad-dód* **an equivalent word,** *čúṅ-mai sk.* another word for wife *Gramm.* — *skád-pa* v. the separate article below. — *skad-˳dzér Cs.* = *skad-˳gágs*. — *skad-bzáṅ* 1. **a good voice.** 2. *W.*: **good news.** — *skad-lúgs* **dialect.** — *skad-lóg* **clamour, screaming.** — *skad-ɣsáṅs mťo Sch.*: **a loud voice,** *skad-ɣsáṅ nyams-čúṅ ˳gyur* the voice is getting weak *Wdṅ.*

སྐད་ *skad* **ladder,** v. *skás-ka*.

སྐད་པ་ *skád-pa* I. vb. 1. **to say, tell, relate,** *žiṅ-ǩáms šig yód-do skád-par ťos* that a land (of bliss) exists I heard say *Mil.*; more frq. at the end of a sentence *skád-do* or *skad* for: it is said (= dicitur), *grags skad id. Mil.* — 2. **to name, call,** *skád-pa* partic. = *byá-ba* **named, called.** — 3. *Ld.*: **skád-če, χád-če** **to measure, take measure.**— II. sbs. **interpreter; language-master, teacher.**

སྐན་ཏེ་ *skán-te, W.* instead of *ská-ba* **thick, turbid.**

སྐབས་ *skabs* 1. **time, opportunity, case, circumstances;** *mťóṅ-(bai) skabs* opportunity of seeing, *skabs rnyéd-pa* to find an opportunity, *skábs-su* or *skabs-skábs-su* now and then, under certain circumstances,

ཀ

ཀ

*skábs-su* or *skabs* with genit. at the time of, on occasion of, during, while, when; *dé-ka skáb-su* in a moment, instantly, *skabs ˳dir* now, here, in this case, in this place (of a book etc.) frq., *skabs re* once, for a time, **skabs-tóg** *Ld. (col.)* now, *bár-skabs* **interval, interlapse of time** *Tar.*; *dús-skabs, ṫsé-skabs, γnás-skabs*, **time, state, situation,** *skabs daṅ sbyár-ba, dús-skabs daṅ bstún-pa* fit for, adapted, suited to the occasion. — 2. *Cs.* **'mode, method'**, or perh. rather, **way, manner;** so the word seems to be used in *Wdṅ.*: *ldúm-bui skabs la-p̔úg daṅ skyé-lugs ˳drá-bar* the manner (nature) of the plant being similar to that of a radish as to growth. — 3. **section, chapter** *(cf. γtam* no. 3), so esp. in *Tar.*; *skabs bču* the ten sections of Buddhistical theology, also: one that has absolved them.

སྐམ་ *skam* v. *skám-pa* and *-po.*

སྐམ་པ་ *skam-pa* I. *vb.* 1. = *rkám-pa* **to long for.** — 2. = *ském-pa (bskam-pa).* — II. *sbst.* 1. = *rkám-pa* **longing,** 2. **a pair of tongs;** *skam-čúṅ* small tongs, **pincers;** also several other instruments of a similar shape. — III. *adj.*, com. *skám-po* **dry,** *skam-rlón* 1. **dry and wet.** — 2. **dryness** in a relative sense, **skam-ṡi** *Ld.* **very lean** (like a mummy), *skám-sa* **the dry land, the shore,** *skam* id., *skám-sar p̔yin-pa, skam-la sléb-pa* to get ashore, *skam-lam* **journey by land** *Wts.*; **skam-saṅ** *Ld.* **meat perfectly dried.**

སྐར་ *skar;* this and the compounds *skar-ka* and *skar-ṫsad* v. under *ska-ba; skar-k̔úṅ* etc. under *skar-ma.*

སྐར་བ་ *skar-ba Cs.*: 'a penning of cattle, assortment, separation, to pen, to fold, to separate'. But as these significations seem to belong to the spelling *bkar-ba* and *dgar-ba*, it will be safer to confine the verb *skar-ba, pf. bskar, imp. skor*, to the following, 1. **to hang up,** **skar-taṅ-če, ťár-la skár-če** id. *Ld.* (e. g. clothes). — 2. **to weigh,** and **skar** **weight,** **gau ṅul gui skar** a little box weighing 9 rupees (about 4 ounces); **skár-ka* or *-k̔a** **weight;** **skar-ṫsád** **measure, scale.** *W., C.* — 3. **skar-tág táṅ-če** **to inquire rigorously; to restrict, to bind down, to flog;** **skar-lčág** a rigorous inquiring, a flogging *W.*, also *C.*

སྐར་མ་ *skár-ma Ssk.* तारा 1. **star,** fixed star, *nyi zla γza skar* sun, moon, planets and stars; sometimes it is used generally: **skar-čén** a very large, uncommonly bright star, esp. Venus when appearing as evening- or morning-star; *nyín-moi skár-ma* a star seen in the daytime (a thing of very rare occurrence). — 2. **constellation, asterism;** *btsas-skár* constellation of nativity *Med*; *γyaṅ-skár* propitious constellation (such are the nakṡatras no. ༡ to ༢༨, v. *rgyu-skár*).

**Comp,** *skár-k̔uṅ* (the same word as *dkar-k̔uṅ*, but of a different etymology) **window.** — *skar-k̔óṅs Cs.*: 'the angular distance between two stars or planets' (?) — *skar-lṅá* a weight ('5 points' on the steelyard for gold) = 1 *žo* or $^1/_{20}$ ounce; as money = $^1/_3$ rupee. — *skar-čú* 'star-water'; bathing under the constellation *skár-ma rib-čí* (prob. *rewati*, the 28th *nakṡatra*, is meant) in October is considered beneficial for every kind of complaint, because *Saṅs-rgyás smán-pai rgyál-po* (quasi 'Buddha Aesculapius', to whom the origin of the medical science is ascribed by Tibetan Buddhists), bathed in that season, and therefore Tibetans, though not particularly fond of washing and bathing in general, are said to follow this example pretty frequetnly. — *skar-mdá (Cs.: 'ignis fatuus'?)* **a shooting star,** *ltuṅ* or *sa-la dril* is coming down, *˳p̔aṅs Mil. id.* — *skar-dpyád, -rtsís* **astrology.** — *skar-p̔rán* **a small star.** — *skar-ṫsógs* the starry host. — *skar-˳dzín* 'star-catching', making one's self sure of a propitious constellation, e. g. for an intended journey, by a sham departure, conveying luggage or goods to the next village etc., but then interrupting and postponing it to a more convenient time.

སྐལ་བ་ *skál-ba Ssk.* **भाग**, *resp. sku-skál* 1. **portion, share;** *bgo-skál* allotted portion; *zas-skál* portion of food, **ration;** *rań-skál* personal share; *nor-skál* or *syal-nór Glr.* hereditary portion, **inheritance;** *skál-ba ma čád-par* without being shortened of his portion *Mil.; ma mťóń-ba skál-ba ma mčis-pa ₒdra* it does not seem to fall to my lot to see my mother. — *skal-čád* dried up, withered *Sch. (?)* — 2. in a special sense: the portion of good or bad fortune that falls to a man's lot, as a consequence of his former actions, **lot, fate, destiny,** a. relatively: *skál-ba bzáń-po, ńán-pa* good, bad fortune; *ťse ₒdii grogs-s'ál* the matrimonial share of the present life, the connubial fate for which a person is predestinated *Glr.* (The Buddhist priests pretend to be able to calculate the *skál-ba* of any one after his death) b. in a positive and good sense, denoting either prosperity and blessing as a consequence of good actions, or those actions themselves as being pious and meritorious, so that *skal-ldán* means **happy, blessed** as well as **pious, devout,** and *skal-méd* **unhappy, irreligious, impious.** *skal-ldán* are all those who have devoted themselves to virtue and treasured up more or less good works, and who may expect to be promoted in proportion. The term **worthy,** therefore, though not quite correct as to the word itself, is still very appropriate as it regards the subject; even **venerable, holy** may be applied occasionally, cf. **भगवत्** and **भगवान्**. Also some single blessing or spiritual gift may be meant by *skál-ba* and so the Ommanipadmehūm is called the *čos-skál*, 'the religious treasure', of Tibet *Glr.*

སྐས་ཀ་ *skás-ka B., C., skás-ǩa, skás-pa C., skrás-ka* (pronounced **tẹ́-ka C., šrás-ka, šrẹ́-ka W.*), even *skas, skad* **ladder,** generally consisting of the notched trunk of a tree; *rkyáń-skad C.* 'single ladder', the same, compared with two or three of them joined together, to make a sort of staircase with broader steps; **do-tá C., do-šrás, do-šrẹ́* W.* a flight of stone-steps; **gya-šrás, gya-šrẹ W., gya-kẹ́* C. (Schr.)* a regular **staircase** as in European houses; *gru-skás Glr.* prob.: flight of steps at the corner of a building; *gro-skad Glr.* fol. 7 appeared to be unknown to those that were consulted; *skas-kyi rim-pa Cs.* **steps;** **šra-ldań, šral-dáń* W.* **spokes** of a ladder; *skas ˓gram Cs.* the two **side-pieces** of a staircase or ladder; *skas ₒdzug-pa* to apply a ladder *Schr., Cs.*

སྐུ *sku, Ssk.* **काय**, sometimes **मूर्त्ति** 1. also *sku-lus, sku-γzugs, resp.* for *lus:* **body;** by being prefixed to the names of parts of the body and even of everything that has reference to the bodily existence of a person, it imparts to them the character of respectful terms: *sku-stod, -smad* the upper, lower, part of the body; *sku-ša* flesh; *sku-mťsál (for sku-ǩrag)* blood *Cs.; sku-mdóg* colour of the skin, *sku-ná* age; *sku-ťse* lifetime, life; *sku-ǩáms* state of health; *sku-skál* portion, share, *sku-čás* goods, stores *Mil., sku-bsód* virtue, happiness *Tar.; sku-skyés* a present (given to or received from a respected personage); *sku-ₒbág* image, statue *Glr.; sku-mdun-pa (C.: *kun-dụm-pa*)* or *-druń-pa* attendant of a man of rank; **ku-ǰar-wa** ('adherent', v. *ₒbyar-ba) id. C.; sku-nye Sch.* relation, kinsman; *sku-γšegs-pa* dying, death (of a king etc.) *Glr.; sku-bstod* praise *Sch.; sku-šogs* (acc. to *Cs.* instead of *sku γšogs* 'the side' = your presence) a title of honour, when we should say: your or his honour, your or his worship, in *W.* only for clerical dignitaries, in *C.* also for other persons of rank. Even buildings (monasteries etc.) are honoured by these respectful expressions: *sku-dkar γsol-ba* to 'administer' whitewash. — 2. in a special sense: **the person of Buddha,** whom philosophers represent in three forms of existence called *sku-γsum* **त्रिकाय**, viz.: *čós-kyi sku,* **धर्मकाय**, *lońs-spyód-kyi sku* **संभोगकाय** and *sprúl-pai sku* **निर्माणकाय**. These three 'persons', however, have as little as *dkon-mčog-γsum* any thing in common with the Christian Trinity, nor even with the Indian Trimūrtti, for the first state, the 'body of law', the absolute body, is Buddha in the Nirvāna, the so-called first world of abstract existence i. e. non-existence, which is the ultimate aim and end of every existence and the ideal aspired to by every believing Buddhist; the second state, the 'body of happiness or glory' is Buddha in the perfection of a conscious and active life of bliss in the second world (heaven or Elysium), which state however is inferior to the first; the third, the 'body of transformation and incarnation', is Buddha in the third or visible world, as man on earth. Notwithstanding the altogether abstract character of *čós-sku,* as a philosophical conception, Buddhistic fancy is pleased to represent it as a visible image of Buddha, shining in the colours of the rainbow, or at least as a brilliant apparition of light, though impalpable and unapproachable; and this is not only a notion of the vulgar, but is acknowledged also in literature. More recent speculators have even added a *ṅo-bo-nyid-kyi sku* superior to the three, viz. that which is **eternal** in the essence of a Buddha, even *čós-sku,* the absolute body, being described by these philosophers as transient. The unintelligible passage in *Cs.'s* dictionary, p. 305 b. might be corrected thus: 'adding to the former three as a fourth' etc. — To this signification belong the compounds *sku-rím, resp.* for *rim-ₒgro* **reverence, respect,** particularly in the special sense of a solemn **sacrificial ceremony,** performed on public and private occassions, e. g. in cases of disease; *sku-rím byéd-pa* to perform such a ceremony. — *sku-rtén, sku-ṫsáb, sku-γzúgs, sku-ₒdrá (W. *kun-ḍá*)* **image of Buddha** etc. — 3. **image, statue,** of Buddha or other holy persons, *γsér-sku* a gold image, *rdó-sku* a stone image, *ₒǰím-sku* an image of clay, *brís-sku* a painted image, *ₒbúr-sku* a basso-relievo, *rkós-sku* an engraved, *blúgs-* or *ldugs-sku* a molten, *ṫágs-sku* a woven image *Cs.* — *sku-ₒbúm* 'mausoleum' or acc. to another etymology 'the 100 000 images', n. of the famous monastery Kumbúm east of the Kokonor (v. Travels of Huc and Gabet). — *sku γsuṅ ṫugs* 1. (cf. *sku* no. 1) resp. f. *lus ṅag yid* the three spheres of a man's doings or sufferings, works, words and thoughts. — 2. the *rten γsum,* the three representations of Buddha: the image of his person, the books containing his doctrine, the pyramid *(mčod-rtén)* as the symbol of his grace. — *sku-lṅa-rgyál-po* five deities of degenerated Buddhism *Schl.* 157.

སྐུ་རུ་ *skú-ru* a **paddle-wheel,** without a rim; such are the water-wheels of all the mills in the Himalaya *skú-ru-ḱa* **the figure of a cross** + ×. The latter is common in books as an abbreviation like our 'etc.', to save the repeated writing at full length of the same sentence, as refrains etc.

སྐུགས་ *skugs* **the stake** in a game or wager received by the winner. — *skugs-stóṅ Sch. id.?*

སྐུང་བ་ *skuṅ-ba pf. bskuṅs, ft. bskuṅ* 1. **to hide in the ground.** — 2. **to bury, to inter.** — 3. **to tie** in a doubled or twisted position, e. g. a corpse before it is burnt, **to cord** on all sides. — *bskúṅs-sa* **lurking-place, hiding-place** *Mil.*

སྐུད་ *skud sbst.* v. *skúd-pa.*

སྐུད་པ་ *skúd-pa* I. *sbst.* **thread, yarn; wire;** *skúd-pa γčód-pa* to cut off the thread, also *fig. Cs.* to divorce; *ras-skúd* cotton thread, *lčags-skúd* iron wire; *ṫson-skúd* coloured thread; *skud-ró* the thread-ends of a seam; *skúd-bris-mḱan* an embroiderer.

II. *vb. pf. bskus, ft. bsku, imp. skus, col. kú-wa C. *skú-če* W.* **to smear** **tá-gir-la mar skú-če** to butter the bread *W.*, **di-la nág-po ma sku** don't make that dirty *W.;* **to besmear, to daub** *snyiṅ-po(-la) snúm-gyis* a wick with grease *Dzl.; sgó-la rtsi* **to paint** a door; *spós-kyis skúd-pa* **to anoint;** *skud* **ointment,** **šra-skúd** **pomatum** *W.*

སྐུད་པོ་ skúd-po 1. **brother-in-law** *Cs.* — 2. **father-in-law.**

སྐུན་བུ *skún-bu* = *kón-bu Lex.*

སྐུམ་པ་ *skúm-pa pf. bskums, ft. bskum, imp. skum(s)* **to contract, to draw in,** e.g. the leg.

སྐུར་པ་ *skúr-pa,* also *skur-klán, skur-žús* **abuse,** occasionally **blasphemy;** *skur-ₒdebs-pa, byed-pa, smra-ba* **to abuse,** viz.: persons to whom respect is due, esp. holy men or things, e.g. *ₒpʼágs-pa-la* the venerable *Dzl.; dkon-mčóg ɣsum mi bdén-par ltá-žiṅ skúr-pa ₒdébspa* to blaspheme by denying the 'Three Most Precious' *Thgy. sgro-skúr* v. *sgro.*

སྐུར་བ་ *skúr-ba* I. *pf. skur,* at the end of a sentence *skúr-ro,* sometimes for *skúr-pa ₒdebs-pa Mil.* —

II. *pf. ft. & imp. bskur, pf.* at the end of a sentence *bskur-to* 1. **to send, to transmit,** e.g. news, objects, also an army, but not a messenger; *mdún-du skúr-ba* to send on in advance, to have carried before, e.g. a banner; *skur ɣnaṅ mdzád-pa* resp.: to be pleased to send. — 2. **to give, hand over, deliver, consign, give in charge, commit,** e.g. an army to a general; *dbaṅ skúr-ba* to invest with power, **to authorize,** *ɉi dgá-bar gyid-du dbaṅ skúr čig* give me power, permission, to do what I like *Dzl.; rgyál-por dbaṅ skúrba* to authorize somebody to be a ruler, to appoint, create, designate as king. The ceremony observed in such a case is a kind of anointing or baptism, pouring holy water on the crown of the head, *spyi-bo-nas dbaṅ skúr-ba,* and as supernatural powers are supposed to be active during this process, *dbaṅ skúr-ba* means also: **to bless, consecrate, endow** with miraculous power; esp. four mystical powers of meditation are imparted in this way.

སྐུལ་བ་ *skúl-ba pf. bskul,* at the end of a sentence *bskúl-to, Ssk.* **चद्,** **to exhort, admonish, enjoin,** *mi žig las byéd-par* **a** person to do a thing; **to appoint,** *mi žig lás-la,* in the same sense; **to impose,** *mi žig-la las,* work on somebody, — perh. a mere provincialism; *dei ťsig-gis bskúl-nas* **induced** by his words; *rnám-šes las daṅ nyon-móṅs-kyis bskúl-nas* the (departed) soul **urged on, influenced, driven,** by its former works and sins *S. g.; lha-srin mčod skul kyaṅ* though I tried **to determine, to bring round,** the gods and the evil spirits by sacrifices *Pth.; gliṅ sogs drág-tu skúl-šiṅ* flutes and other (instruments) **calling,** resounding, fortissimo and so animating the actors; **yid skúl-če* W.* **to remind, admonish;** **šaṅ** (for *ɣčaṅ*) **skúl-če** **to rouse** by shaking. — *bskúl-ba* and more frq. *bskul-ma* **exhortation, admonition;** *bskúl-ma ₒdébs-pa, C.* also *skúl-rgyag-pa, skul-čág byéd-pa Mil. nt.* **to admonish, exhort.** — **skúl-ǩan W.* **overseer.**

སྐེ་ *ske, vulg. skye,* seld. *skya,* **neck, throat,** *frq.;* neck of a bottle *Cs.; *skye tsir táṅ-če, *kyig-če, sdám-če* W.* **to choke, strangle,** **skyé-la ťág-pa tág-na sád-če* id.; ske ɣčód-pa, ɣtúb-pa, ₒbrég-pa* **to behead, slaughter;** *sker ₒťám-pa* to seize by the throat, to worry *Sch.; sker dógs-pa* to tie round the neck e. g. an amulet; *ske-ₒǩór* necklace *Schr.; ske-čá* ornament for the neck, **necklace** *Mil.; ske-stóṅ Med., Sch.:* cavity of the throat; *ske-rmá Sch.:* a wound of the throat, a **jugular gland that** has opened.

སྐེ་ཚེ་ *ske-ťsé Wdṅ., Ssk.* **राजिका** Sinapis ramosa, **black mustard; mustard seed,** a grain of m. s.

སྐེག་ཚོས་ *skeg-ťsós* **paint, rouge** (for the face) *Sch.*

སྐེད་པ་ *skéd-pa* v. *rkéd-pa.*

སྐེམ་པ་ *ském-pa* I. *vb. pf. bskams, ft. bskam, imp. skom(s)* **to make dry, lean, meagre; to dry up; exsiccate.** — II. *adj.,* also *ském-po,* **dry, dried up; meagre.** — *skem-byéd* a demon that causes drought *Lt.* — *skem-nád Bhar.* consumption.

སྐོ་བ་ *skó-ba, pf. (b)skos, ft. bsko, imp. skos* 1. **to appoint, nominate, commission, charge** a person, *lás-su* with a work *Dzl.,* much more freq.: *rgyál-por,* *dpón-du* to be king, chief; *rgyál-sar skó-ba* to raise to the throne; *ma bskós-šiṅ* without mandate, unbidden *Glr.* — 2. *lás-la bskós-pa* **destined** to the works i. e. destined to a man in consequence of his works; *ṅéd-kyi las-bskós* my **destiny, fate, lot** *Mil.*

*Note.* The signification: to elect, to choose *(Cs., Sch.)* cannot be proved and was expressly denied by Tibetans.

སྐོ་ཙེ *sko-tsé* 1. a kind of wild onion *Cs.* — 2. a mixture of the leaves of several kinds of leek, pounded, formed into balls and dried; when used, a small portion is broken off, fried in butter and then added to the food. This spice forms a lucrative article of commerce and is exported from *Ld.* to Cashmere and from *Lh.* to India.

སྐོག་པ *skóg-pa* v. *kóg-pa.*

སྐོང *skoṅ* v. under *koṅ.*

སྐོང་བ *skóṅ-ba pf. bskaṅs, ft. bskaṅ, imp. skoṅ(s)* 1. **to fulfil,** e. g. a hope, a vow etc., **nyiṅ** the desire *W.*; *k̔a skóṅ-ba* to fill up what is open, to make up a deficiency *Zam.*, also *dgé bai k̔a-skoṅ* to fulfil perfectly the laws of virtue, *k̔a-skóṅ, k̔a-bskáṅs, k̔as-skoṅ* 1. **appendix, supplement,** *γšám-du k̔a-skóṅ-du bšad* will be said, described, below in the appendix *Wdṅ.* 2. By Tibetan copyists of books a short prayer is called so, consisting of a stanza of 4 verses, which they are accustomed to write down or recite after having finished the copy of a work, in order to make amends for the mistakes they may have committed. — *t̔ugs-dám bskaṅ-rdzás* a certain ceremony v. *Schl.* 260. — 2. v. *dpa.*

སྐོན་པ *skón-pa* I. *sbst.* v. *rkón-pa.* — II. *vb. pf. & ft. bskon* **to dress,** to clothe another person (*resp. γsól-ba*).

སྐོབས *skobs* = *skabs Schr., Sch.*

སྐོམ *skom* 1. **thirst,** *skóm-gyis γdúṅs-pa* tormented by thirst *Dzl.* — 2. *resp. žal-skóm,* **drink;** *zas (daṅ) skom* food and drink. — 3. *i.o. skam* the **dry land** *Glr., provinc.* — *skóm-pa* 1. **to thirst, to be thirsty.** 2. **the thirst.** 3. **thirsty,** *skóm-pa-dag ni skóm-pa daṅ brál-bar ₒgyur* the thirsty will get rid of their thirst *S. O.* — *skom-dád (dad-pa = ₒdod-pa)* **thirst** *Med.* — *skom-t̔sád* **burning thirst** *Mil.* — **skóm-ri** **thirst** *W.*

སྐོར *skor (cf. kor)* 1. **circle,** *mig-skor* eyeball *W.*; *sba-skór* hoop of bamboo *Schr.* — 2. **appurtenances,** *yi-ge ₒbri-bai skor* writing utensils, *t̔áb-kyi skor* everything that belongs to the fire-place *C.* (perh. provinc.) — 3. **section, division,** e. g. of a book, similar to *leu,* chapter *Mil., Tar.* — 4. **repetition,** *skor ldáb-pa* to repeat *Schr.* — 5. **theme, subject,** *gaṅ skór-la ₒbri ₒdug* what is the subject of this writing? Answer: *rtai skór-la* a horse *C.*; *de skór-la* on that account, therefore *Ld.* — 6. *skor, skór-zas* **food presented to Lamas;** laymen are deterred from laying their hands on it by the mysteriously menacing verse: *skór-zas zá-la lčag-gi ₒgrám-pa dgos* he that eats Lama's food, wants iron jaws. — 7. v. *skór-ba* no. II.

སྐོར་བ *skór-ba* I. *vb. pf. & ft. bskor* 1. **to surround, encircle, enclose, besiege** *cca & d.*; also of inanimate objects: *dé-la skór-bai ri* the mountains surrounding it *Glr.*; *ri nágs-kyis bskór-ba Sambh.* a mountain surrounded by a forest. — 2. **to go, move, ride round a thing;** esp. the reverential ceremony of प्रदक्षिण transferred from Brahmanism to Buddhism, which consists in going round a holy object with one's right side turned towards it — one of the most meritorious and indispensible religious duties in the eyes of a Buddhist; *č̔ós-skor-la byon* they walked round in the religious direction, i. e. according to the precepts of Buddhism, *bón-skor-du soṅ* in the Bon manner, i. e. the opposite direction *Mil.*; *p̔yag daṅ skór-ba byéd-pa,* as a specification of religious duties: to make salutations and circumambulations.

3. **to wander through, traverse,** *rgyál-ḱams*, the countries, *Mil.* — 4. **to return, go home** *Sch.* — 5. **to turn round, twist,** *mii ltág-pa* a man's neck, i.e. to choke, to strangle him *Glr.*

**Phrases:** *mgo skór-ba, mgo skor byéd-pa (W. *ċo-ċe*)* **to befool, delude, deceive** a person, by intoxication or flattery *Glr.*, also by a flood of words. — **ḱa kór-wa C., kór-ċe* W.* to make one alter his sentiments, to divert one from a plan etc. — **lan** or **dugs skór-ċe** to take vengeance *W.* — **si kór-ċe (v. rtsis) W.* **to count, calculate.** — *ts̀ógs-kyi ḱórlo skór-ba* to arrange the objects of the *maṇḍal* (q.v.) in a circle n.f. — *skor lóg-pa, skor lóg-la ˳gró-ba* to go round the wrong way *Mil.*; **pé-ra kor-re-lóg táṅ-ċe** to talk foolishly, to twaddle *W.* — **lag kór-ċe** the putting a seal under a document which is done by several persons one after another *W.*

**Comp.** *skór-ḱaṅ Glr.*, prob. = *skór-lam.* — *skor-rgyúgs* turning the enemy, getting into his rear *Mil.* — *skór-mḱan, skór-pa* **a turner** *Cs.* — *skor-spyád, skor-šin* a turner's **lathe** *Cs.* — *skor-ṫig* **a pair of compasses.** — *skor-dbyúg* a sling, for throwing *Sch.* — *skor-lám* 1. the pathway round-about a monastery, used for the holy processions. 2. a veranda surrounding a house. 3. col. also: round-about way.

II. 1. **the going, moving round, encircling** etc. — 2. **the way** round a thing, = *skor-lám*, in the compounds: *náṅ-skor* the inner, *bár-skor* the middle, *ṕyi-skor* the outer roundway, *ṕyi-skor čén-po* the outermost. — *sá-skor* round-about way, by-way.

སྐོལ་བ་ *skól-ba* pf. & ft. *bskol* **to boil** (vb. act., cf. *ǰól-ba*).

སྐོས་པ་ *skós-pa* 1. v. *skó-ba.* — 2. *Sch.*: 'to order', but this is *sgó-ba.*

སྐྱ་ *skya* 1. **oar** *C., Thgy.*; *skya-léb* id.; *skya-m̀ǰúg* **rudder;** *skya rgyáb-pa* **to row** *Schr.* — 2. **spatula** *Schr.* — 3. **pot-ladle,** *C.* — 4. **wall** of stone or clay, *bár-skya*, partition-wall, **bhár-kya ċạ'-pa** to make a partition-wall *C.*

སྐྱ་ཀ་ *skyá-ka, skyá-ga Lt.*, n. of a bird, *Cs.*: **magpie.**

སྐྱ་བ་ *skyá-ba* I. vb. 1. pf. *bskyas*, ft. *bskya* 1. *Lex.*: = *˳ṕó-ba* **to change place,** cf. *skyas.* — 2. **to carry, convey** to a place (a quantity of stones, wood, water etc.) *W.*, v. *skyéd-pa.* — 3. *Sch.* **to swim** (?)

II. sbst. 1. **kettle** *Sch.* — 2. prob. = *skya* 1.

སྐྱ་བོ་ *skya-bo, Ssk.* **पाण्डर** and **पाण्डु, whitish gray, yellowish-white;** **skya ċág-ċe* to fry or toast a thing so that its whitish colour turns partially into brown *Ld.*; *mi skya* one clothed in light-gray, (not in red or yellow, as monks are), **a layman;** *sṅo-skya* **light-blue,** *ljaṅ-skyá* **light-green,** and so of the other colours; therefore *ser-skya* ought to denote **light-yellow,** but it is also used as an equivalent of **कपिल,** n. of a saint, (Ser-skyai-˳groṅ = Kapilavastu, an ancient city in Oude, and Buddha's birth-place); originally: 'monkey-coloured', **tawny,** *lto-skyá* 'pale' i. e. poor, insipid, miserable food *Mil.nt.*

**Comp.** **kya-ko-ré, kya-ṫe-ré** **pale, white** *C.* — *skya-skyá* id. *Sch.* — *skya-nár,* **पाटलि** n. of a flower, Bignonia graveolens; *Skya-nár-gyi-bu* n. of a city of Old-India Pāṭaliputra, now Patna. — *skya-snár* acc. to *Stg.* the colour of the skin of the Indians, **brown.** — *skya-rbáb Cs.*: a kind of dropsy, *Sch.*: a grayish oedematic swelling; *skya-rbab-skráṅs Lex.* — **skya-már** **fresh** (i. e. not melted) **butter** *W.* — **skya 'ód* W.*, *skya-réṅs* **morning-twilight, dawn.** — *skya-lám* = *skyá-bo Thgy., C.* — *skya-séṅ* 1. n. of a tree. 2. translation of Pandu, *skya-séṅ-gi bu* a Pandava. — *skya-sér* 1. *Sch.*: **tawny,** cf. *ser-skya.* 2. 'white and yellow' viz.: men, **lay-men and priests** *Mil.nt.*

སྐྱ་རུ་ར་ *skyá-ru-ra* n. of a drug *Med.*

སྐྱག་པ་ *skyág-pa* 1. = *rkyág-pa.* — 2. pf. *bskyags*, ft. *bskyag*, imp. *skyog* **to**

ཀ

**spend, lay out, expend;** *skyag-sgó* **expenditure,** *skyag-ťó* **account of expenses.** — 3. *W.*: **skyag táṅ-ċe** **to slaughter, to murder.**

སྐྱང་ནུལ་ *skyaṅ-núl* **pavement, clay-floor, mud-floor** *Lex., Cs.; skaṅ-núl byéd-pa* **to pave, to plaster** (*Sch.* also; to rub, polish).

སྐྱབས་ *skyabs* (*cf. skyób-pa*) *Ssk.* **शरण protection, defence, help, assistance;** *me-čú-la skyabs* is a protection against water and fire; *skyabs méd-do* I am (or: he is etc.) lost! *skyabs byéd-pa, skyábs-su °gyúr-ba* ccgp. **to protect, help, save** a person, frq. with *srog-gi* added; *skyábs-su °gró-ba* eleg. *mčiba, W.*: **skyab ċól-la yóṅ-ċe** to seek help, *mii* or *mi-la* of some body, *skyabs-°grós* 1. the seeking of help, **शरण गमन** 2. the formula *Saṅs-rgyás-kyi skyabs-su mčio, čós-kyi sky. mčio, dge-°dún-gyi sky. mčio,* the Buddhistic creed or confession of faith.

**Comp.** *skyabs-mgón* **helper, protector, deliverer;** this is applied to certain highly esteemed and respected persons, mythological as well as living, ni f.; *Chr. Pr.* use it for **Saviour, Redeemer, Christ.** — *skyabs-°grós* v. above. — *skyabs-γnás* 1. **place of refuge,** shelter; also of persons, = **helper,** frq ; *mí-la skyabs-γnás byéd-pa Mil.* to take refuge to a person, to seek his assistance. 2. seld. for *skyábs-su γnás-pa* **client,** *ṅá-yi skyábs-γnas ṕó-mo-rnams* all my clients, men and women *Glr.* — *skyabs-sbyin* a gesture of the right hand, like that for giving benediction *Glr.* — *skyabs-yúl* = *skyabs-γnás.* 1.

སྐྱར་གོག་ *skyár-gog* **naked** *Pur.*

སྐྱར་པོ་ *skyár-po Sch.*: **snipe, wood-cock;** *skyar-čúṅ Sch.*: **'a large snipe'** (??); *skyár-mo Sch.* **heron;** *skyar-léb Sch.* **spoon-bill;** *ču-skyar Cs.* **duck,** *Sch.*: **bittern,** but the **कादम्ब** of the *Lex.*, **'a kind of goose'** speaks in favour of *Cs.*

སྐྱར་བ་ *skyár-ba* v. *skyór-ba.*

སྐྱས་ *skyas* a changing of abode; *skyas °débe-pa* to change one's dwelling-place (cf. *skya-ba*), *skyas čén-po °débs-pa* to die

སྐྱས་མ་ *skyás-ma* 1. v. *skyes.* — 2. *Sik.*: **fern.**

སྐྱི་ *skyi Cs.*: the outward side of a skin or hide (opp. to *ŝa*); *skyi γyá-ba* to shiver, tremble with fear *Cs.* **Comp.**: *skyi-dkár Cs.* dressed leather; hide. — *skyi-lpágs Sch.*: chamois, wash-leather. — *skyi-búṅ Mil.?* — *skyi-bún* prob. an itching of the skin *Mil.?* — *skyi-ŝá* 1. outward and inward side of a hide. 2. *Sch.*: the anus.

སྐྱི་བ་ *skyí-ba* I. sbst. 1. a medicinal plant *Med.* — 2. also **kyi-u, ṕi-líṅ kyi-u,** **potato** *C.*

II. vb. pf. *bskyis,* ft. *bskyi,* imp. *skyis* **to borrow,** esp. money or goods (cf. *γyár-ba* and *skyin-pa*).

སྐྱིག་པ་ *skyig-pa* **to hickup;** *skyig-bu* **the hickup** *Med.*

སྐྱིང་སེར་ *skyiṅ-sér Mil.*, eagle, vulture.

སྐྱིད་པ་ *skyid-pa* vb., sbst., adj.: **to be happy, happiness** (*Ssk.* **सौख्य**), **happy;** *skyid-do* (I, thou etc.) am, art etc. happy; *bdé-žiṅ skyid-la* being happy and glad; *skyid-pai nyi-ma* sun of felicity, propitious day *Glr.; skyid-po* = *skyid-pa* adj., frq., *skyid-de-ba* id. *Tar.* 5, 19.

**Comp.** *skyid-glu* **song of joy.** — *skyid-mgo* beginning of **happiness** *Mil.* — *skyid-sdúg* good and ill luck, **happiness** and misery; *skyid sdug ji byuṅ kyaṅ* whatever may happen *Glr.; skyid sdug bsré-ba* to share pleasure and pain. — *skyid-čú* n. of the tributary of the Ya-ru-tsaṅ-po, on which Lhasa is situated.

སྐྱིན་ *skyin* **wild mountain goat,** Capra ibex.

སྐྱིན་གོར་ *skyin-gór* **lizard** *Lex.*, = *da-byid.*

སྐྱིན་ཐང་ *skyin-ťáṅ Sch.*: **hail, sleet.**

སྐྱིན་པ་ *skyin-pa, W. *skyin-po**, resp. *kar-skyin* **a loan,** a thing borrowed; money advanced without interest; *skyin-pa skyi-ba* to ask a loan; *ṅá-la °di skyin-du °tsal* he asked me to lend him this *Dzl.; skyin-pa lén-pa Cs.* to take on credit; *skyin-pa spród-pa, ǰal-ba* to pay back or return a loan *Cs.; nór-skyin* **a loan of** goods or money, *gós-skyin* of clothes. — *skyin-mi Schr.* debtor. — *skyin-ṫsáb C.:* the pledge for a loan; acc. to others, however, it just means the object lent or its equivalent when being returned.

སྐྱིབས་ *skyibs* everything giving **shelter** from above, an overhanging rock, a roof etc.: **čar skyib** shelter from rain; **ḍag-skyib** under a *ṗa-boṅ* q. v. (*gyam* is much larger, *ṗúg-pa* deeper) *W.; bka-sky.* प्रघाण, a covered terrace or small portico before a house.

སྐྱིལ་བ་ *skyil-ba*, pf. & ft. *bskyil* 1. **to bend,** esp. the legs when sitting on the ground after Oriental fashion, also another's leg by a kick from behind; **to** bend the bow. — 2. **to pen up, shut up,** cattle, **to dam up,** a river, also: *ču rdziṅ-du skyil-ba* **to collect** water into a pond *Glr.*, or *rdziṅ-bu sky.*; to dam up a pond (but not 'to dig it' *Schr.*); **to keep back, retain, detain** a person *W.*; **ḱa kyil-če** to keep a person from doing something, to dissuade from *W.* — *skyil-krúṅ*, also *skyil-mo-krúṅ*, the posture of **sitting cross-legged,** *skyil-krúṅ byéd-pa* (resp. *mdzád-pa*), *skyil-mo-krúṅ-gis* (or *du*) *ḍúg-pa* (resp. *bžúgs-pa*) to assume such a posture; *séms-dpai skyil-krúṅ* the usual manner of sitting, in which the feet are not seen, *rdo-rjei sky.* the posture in which the soles of the feet are seen turned upwards, *rdzógs-pai sky.* another posture requiring particular practice. (The spelling *dkyil-krúṅ*, though frequent, is expressly rejected by grammarians.) — **skyil-diṅ** *W.* a small hole filled with water. — **skil-ldir** *W.* **handle, ring** fixed to a thing, for carrying it, hanging it up etc.

སྐྱུ་གང་ *skyu-gáṅ Lex.* w.e., *Sch.:* **a gulp, draught.**

སྐྱུ་རུ་ *skyú-ru* a sour fruit *Med.*; *skyú-ru-ra Med.* (*Lex.:* अम्लल wood-sorrel) the same (?); in later times the word seems to have been used also for the **olive,** and *skyú-ru-šin* **the olive tree,** which in *Sik.* is called *ḱa-skyúr-poi šiṅ.*

སྐྱུ་རུམ་ *skyu-rúm Cs.:* **'condiment, sauce, pickle'**, acc. to others, at least in *W.*, only the resp. word for *spags:* 1. **sauce, gravy.** 2. **dish, mess.**

སྐྱུག་པ་ *skyúg-pa* pf. *skyugs.* 1. **to vomit, eject,** e.g. blood, *skyúg-tu ḥjúg-pa* to cause to vomit, *skyúg-pa drén-pa* to excite vomiting *Tar.*; *skyúgs-pa* (partic. pf.), *ṅan-skyúgs,* **the vomit** (it is the food of certain demons, and being boiled in it, is one of the punishments of hell). — 2 to lose colour, **to stain.**

**Comp.** *skyug-ldád* **rumination,** chewing the cud; *Sch.* also: **eructation.** — *skyúg-bro-ba* nausea, *skyúg-bro-bai nad* disease of nausea; *skyúg-bro-bas* from disgust; *skyug-bro C.* also **impure** with regard to religion, = *W.* **ṫsid-du**. — *skyug-smán* **an emetic.** — *skyúg-log-pa Sch.* to feel disgust.

སྐྱུང་ཀ་ *skyúṅ-ka*, also *lčúṅ-ka*, **jack-daw** (black, with a red bill); *skyúṅ-kas zos Lex.* eaten or stolen by a jack-daw.

སྐྱུང་བ་ *skyúṅ-ba* pf. *bskyuṅs*, ft. *bskyuṅ*, imp. *skyuṅ(s) Cs.* **to leave behind, to lay aside,** e.g. a task *Lex.*, pride *S.g.*

སྐྱུད་པ་ *skyúd-pa* 1. *Cs.:* **to forget, leave off.** 2. *Sch.:* **to comminute; to swallow.** (?)

སྐྱུར་བ་ *skyúr-ba* I. adj. **sour,** sbst. **acidity;** more frq.: *skyúr-po C., -mo W.* adj. **sour,** *Ssk.* अम्ल; *skyur ḥjúg-pa* 1. to turn sour. 2. to suffer a substance to turn sour, v. *ḥjug-pa.* — *ḱa(-ša)-skyúr-po* **olive,** *ḱa (ša)-skyur-pói šiṅ* olive tree *Sik.* — *skyúr-ḱu Cs., raṅ-skyúr Cs., skyúr-ru (Sik.), skúr-mo Lh.* a sour liquid, **vinegar.** (Vinegar seems to be little known as yet in Tibet, and the above mentioned expressions may have been framed by different persons on different occasions, but are not in general use. The same may be said of *Cs.'s skyúr-pa* and *skyur-rtsí* for **acid** in a chemical sense.)

II. vb. pf. & ft. *bskyur* 1. **to throw, to cast,** *ṗyir* out, *lhuṅ-zéd nám-mḱa-la bskyur-nas* having flung his mendicant's-bowl up into the air *Dzl.*, *čur skyúr-ba* to throw into the water, *rgyáb-tu* behind one's self = to turn one's back upon a thing; **to throw away, throw down,** a stone, a corpse etc.; **to eject,** *lúd-pa* phlegm; **to throw off,** a rider; **to give up, abandon,** a work; **to forsake,** a friend; **to abort.** — *skyúr-ma* **abortion** *W.* (?) — *ču skyúr, γyańskyúr* capital punishment in *C.*, when the delinquent, with a weight fastened to his neck, is thrown from a rock into a river.

སྐྱུས *skyus? Sch.: skyus tóg-pa* **altogether;** *skyús-su klóg-pa Gramm.:* to pronounce **jointly,** viz. two consonants without a vowel between them.

སྐེ *ske* 1. v. *ske.* — 2. v. *skyed* and *skyé-ba.*

སྐྱེ་བ *skyé-ba* I. vb. (जन) pf. *skyes* 1. **to be born;** *ńá-la* (seld. *las) bu skyés-pa yin* I have given birth to a son *Glr.; p̓ó-skyes* a man, *mó skyes* a woman, female; *skye-rga-na-ₒči-bai sdug-bsńál* the evil of birth, old age, sickness and death (which constitute what in the opinion of the Buddhist is the greatest evil of all, that of existence); *tóg-ma skyés-nas, má-la skyés-nas B.,* *'á-ma skyé-sa-na* W.* from one's birth; *sk̓ye či-* (or *ši-*) *méd pa* subject neither to birth nor to death, eternal; *skye-ₒgag-méd-Thgy., Lex.,* is said to mean the same. In the special sense of the doctrine of metempsychosis *skyé-ba* has often to be rendered by: **to be re-born,** *mi-ru* as man, *bur* as (somebody's) son. — *mi skyé-bai čós-la bzód-pa* v. *bzód-pa.* — *W.:* **skyé-če** 1. as inf. **to be born, reborn.** 2. as sbst. the being born; **birth.** 3. as adj. being with child, **pregnant; big with young,** also **sk̓yé-če-ma**. — 2. **to become, to begin to exist, arise,** *nad kun mi skye, skyés-paań ži-bai p̓yir* ut ne morbus ullus nascatur, natus quoque sedetur *Med.; skye-ba dań ₒǰig-pa* to arise and pass away; frq. of thoughts, passions etc. (the person as well as the thing in the accus.): *k̓yeu k̓rós-pai sems skyés-te* the youth — thoughts of wrath arising (in him). — 3. **to grow** *(nasci) lúń-pa ₒbru skyé-ba* valleys where corn grows; *ru mgó-la skye* a horn is growing on the head. — 4. **to grow** *(crescere) čer or čen-por skyé-ba* to grow up, to grow tall; *ras kyań lús-k̓yi tsád-du skyés-so* the garment also grew in proportion to the growth of the body, or: with the body *Dzl.; rtúl-pod-par skyés-so* he grew up a valiant man, became a valiant man; **to bud, germinate, sprout,** **sbáns-te skye čúg-ce** to accelerate the germinating of the seed by maceration *W.*; even = *ₒp̓él-ba Dzl.* ༡༧༧ ? — 5. sometimes = *skyá-ba* 2. unless in that case **kyé-če** should be spelled *bskyás-čes W.*

II. sbst. (जाति) 1. the being born, the **birth,** *skyé-ba mťo-ba, skye-mťó or mťón* **high birth;** of high birth, **noble, man,** male; *skyé-ba dmá-ba, skye-dmá, -dmán* **low birth;** of low birth, **ignoble, woman,** *mi-lus ťob kyań skyé-ba dman* born a human being, it is true, but only a female *Mil.; skyes-dmán* col. **kyer mán** in *C.* the usual word for **woman** and **wife,** *ńę k̓yer męn* my wife. — In the special Buddhistic sense: **re-birth** *mir skyé-ba bžén-pa* to take or assume re-birth as a human being; also **period of re-birth = existence, life,** *skyé-ba ₒdi-la* in this, my present, period of life; *skyé-ba bdun* seven periods of life; also **manner of re-birth,** v. *skye-γnás;* in a concrete sense: the **re-born individual,** *yúm-gyi skyé-ba yin* she is the re-birth of the queen dowager, the re-born q. d. — 2. the **arising** etc. — 3. the **growing** etc.

**Comp.** *skye-dgú* v. *skyé-bo.* — *skye-ₒgró* = *ₒgroba* being (q.v.) — *skye-sgó* 1. **entrance to re-birth,** viz. to one of the six regions of birth, v. *ₒgró-ba* II., *skye-sgó γčód-pa* to lock it up. 2. **face,** *légs-pa* a handsome, *žan - pa* an ugly face; also *k̓a-sgó skye-ₒbras légs-pa* is said for: having a handsome exterior *C.* — *skye-mčéd* (आयतन) the five (or six) seats, i. e. **organs, of the senses** (the sixth is मनस् the inner sense); the **senses** themselves; this conception, however, has been greatly altered and varied by the fanciful theories of medical and philosophical authors, cf. *Burn.* I, 500. *Was.* (240). — *skye-γnás* 1. **birthplace; station** or **locality** of a plant.

2. **class** or **region of birth** or re-birth, **class of beings** (v. *gró-ba); byol sóṅ-gi skye-ba* the being born as an animal. 3. **manner of birth** उपपादा, *skyé-ba bži*, also चतुर्योनि. the four kinds or ways of being born: *mṅál-las* (or *nas*) out of a womb (so, acc. to Stg., elephants and some men are born), *sgo-ṅá-las* out of an egg (birds, some *klu*, some men), *drod-γšér-las* out of heat and humidity (insects, some men etc.), *rdzús-te* in a supernatural way (so the *lha*, the Buddhas, when they spring from lotus-flowers; also the inhabitants of infernal regions, souls in the bardo and some men). — *skye-γzúgs* prob. = *byad-γzúgs* **stature, figure.** — *skye-rábs* **series of the births** of a man, **history** of them, and esp. so of the births of Buddha, — so in the title of a work. — *skye-šiṅ* = *skyed-šiṅ Wdn.*

སྐྱེ་བོ་ *skyé-bo* 1. **being,** (animans) *mi-la-sogs-pa skyé-bo* man and the other living beings *Dzl.* — 2. **human being, man,** gen. as a collective noun: **mankind,** *ḱrúl-bčas skyé-bo* infatuated men *Pth.; skyé-bo mḱás-pa γžán-rnams* other sensible people *Tar.; skyé-bo máṅ-poi yid-du óṅ-ba* universally beloved *Dom.; mí nag skyé-bo* **laymen** (on account of the dimness of their religious knowledge); *so-sói skyé-bo* पृथग्जन (cf. *Will.*) the lower clergy, common monks *Tar.*, but also simple laymen, if they are not quite without religious knowledge; *skye-bo-čog*, (*skyeo-čog Cs.* is a less accurate pronunciation), *skyé-dgú*, or (less correctly) *rgu*, **men, mankind**; *skye-dgui-bdág-mo* प्रजापती fem. pr. n., the aunt and first governess of Buddha *Glr., Gyatch.*, also a name of *dpal-lhá-mo's* q.v.

སྐྱེ་ཚེ་ *skye-tsé* = *ske-tsé Lex.*, **mustard.**

སྐྱེ་རགས་ *skyé-rágs W.* for *ska-rags* **girdle.**

སྐྱེག་ *skyeg Cs.:* = *kég, kag* **misfortune.** But *rtsis-kyi skyeg Lex.* w.e.?

སྐྱེགས་ *skyegs* 1. n. of a bird: *ču-sky. Lex.* w.e., *Sch.:* **coot, water-hen;** *ri-skyégs Lex.* w.e., *Cs.:* a large singing-bird, *Sch.;* **grouse, heath-cock.** — 2. *rgya-skyégs* **shell-lac.**

སྐྱེང་བ་ *skyeṅ-ba* and *skyeṅs-pa* **to be ashamed,** also *ḱa-skyeṅ-ba*, B. and col. frq.

སྐྱེང་སེར་རླུང་ *skyeṅ-ser-rluṅ* also *skye-* or *skya-ser-luṅ Mil.*, **cold wind.**

སྐྱེད་ *skyed* and *skye*, 1. **growth, increase,** *skyed če-bar gyur-ba* to grow much; *γžan-gyi zla-skyed-pas dei žag-skyed če* his daily growth was greater than the growth of others in a month etc. *Pth.* — 2. **progress, the getting on, improvement** *skyed yoṅ* progress comes, I am making progress *Mil.;* **profit, gain** *nad-la skyed med* (this) is of no **use** for that disease, of no **benefit** *S.g. fol.* 10. — 3. **interest** *C., dṅul-skyed* of money, *bru-skyed* of corn *C., skyed-du γtoṅ-ba* to give on interest *Cs.; skyed ṗog-pa Cs.:* 'to be the full term of payment', more accurately: *skyed ṗog* I (you, he etc.) am struck or hit by the term of payment; *skyed-čan* yielding interest, profit *Cs.*

སྐྱེད་སྒོ་ *skyed-sgo Mil.nt.* prob. = *rgyal-sgo* principal door.

སྐྱེད་པ་ *skyed-pa* I. vb pf. *bskyed*, act. to *skye-ba*, in *W.* pronounced alike: **skye-če** 1. **to generate, procreate;** seldom in a physical sense: *bskyed-pai yab* ὁ γεννήσας πατήρ *Pth.*, (opp. to *ḃltams-pai yum Pth.*, for which however *skyed-ma Cs.* does not seem to be an appropriate substitute). — 2. **to produce, form, cause** (opp. to *med-par byed-pa* to destroy, annihilate) e. g. diseases, fear, roots of virtue, merit, *bsod-nams-kyi tsogs, sa-bon* (fig.) *Dzl., bras-bu* retribution; **to reproduce,** *zad-pa* what has been consumed *Med.;* to create certain thoughts or affections either in one's self or in others: *spró-ba bskyed-pas dei ṗa-má yaṇ spró-ba čún-zad skyés-nas* by his own rejoicing also to his parents a little joy arising *Dzl.* 22. 5; *ṫams-čad-kyis brtson-grús bskyed-do* they all created zeal, took great pains *Dzl.; čes bsam-pa bskyéd-nas* thus they thought. — 3. **to cause to germinate** or **grow,** *yúr-bai ču-yis žiṅ skyed* ₒ*dra* just as the water of the ditch makes the fields green *Med.; sá-bon Dzl.* (v. before, but it may as well be referred to this signification); *γsos skyéd-pa* **to bring up, to nurse up** *Dzl.; skyed sríṅ-ba* id. *Glr.* — 4. = *skyá-ba,* **to bring on, carry, convey** to a place *Pth.*

**Comp.** *skyed-mos-tsál* **grove, park.** — *skyed-rdzógs,* instead of *skyed-rím* and *rdzogs-rím,* उत्सक्रम and सम्पन्नक्रम, two kinds or degrees of meditation. — *skyed-śiṅ Cs.:* a planted tree (?) prob. a fruit-tree, *Dzl.*

II sbst. 1. **the generating, producing** etc. — 2. = *skyed,* e. g. *skyéd-pa lén-pa* **to gain flesh, to thrive** *C.* — 3. = *rkéd-pa.*

སྐྱེན་པ་ *skyén-pa* adj. 1. **quick, swift** *Lex., k̔ró-* or *sdáṅ-skyen-pa* quick to wrath *Stg.;. byéd-skyen-pa* rash, hasty, precipitate *Glr.* — 2. **nimble, dexterous** *C.W.;* ₒ*p̔óṅ-skyen-pa* dexterous in shooting, **a skilful** archer *Dzl.* (Besides: vb. to make haste, to strive; sbst. zeal, ardour; adj. strong *Cs., Sch.* ??)

སྐྱེམ་པ་ *skyém-pa* resp. **to be thirsty.**

སྐྱེམས་ *skyems* resp. 1. **thirst.** — 2. **drink, beverage,** esp. **beer,** also *žal-skyéms* or *-skyoms, skyems* ₒ*drén-pa* to offer or set before an honoured person something to drink, *bžés-pa* to accept of it, to take it; *skyems-la γsol-rés byéd-pa* to drink beer in company *Glr.; γśegs-skyéms* a carousal on the departure of an honoured person; *γser-skyéms* beer together with grains of corn, as an offering to the gods for the good success of an enterprise, a journey etc., in religious dancing-festivals, *γser-skyéms-pa* sbst. the priest or dancer who offers it. — *skyems-čáṅ* **beer.** — *skyems-čú* **drinkable water.** — **skyéms-ḍaṅ* W.* (?) **brandy.** — *skyéms-tsúgs Sch.:* **cup, dish.** — *skyéms-siṅ* **small-beer.**

སྐྱེར་པ་ *skyér-pa Lex.:* हरित curcuma, **turmeric;** in *W.* **barberry.**

སྐྱེད་དམན་ vulgo for *ske-dmán* **woman** *C.* (v. *skye-ba* II).

སྐྱེལ་བ་ *skyél-ba,* pf. & ft. *bskyel,* imp. *skyol* 1. **to conduct, accompany,** resp. *γdan-skyél-ba; skyól-la śog* conduct him hither! *Pth.; *skyel-la-la** (for **skyél-wa-la**) *soṅ* he has gone to accompany (him) *W.* — *bsu-bskyál* going to meet, and accompanying on departing *Dzl., γśegs-skyél byéd-pa* resp. to accompany an honoured person on departing, to see him off *Mil.* — 2. **to convey, bring, take** e. g. a child to a place, food to somebody, *Dzl., C. W.* id.; **to carry off, to take away** *C.: *śiṅ ma kyal čig** do not bring any more wood! more accurately **kyal śog** bring! **kyal soṅ** take away! — 3. **to send** *B. & C.* e.g. clothes to somebody *Dzl.* — 4. **to risk, to stake,** *raṅ-srog Mil.* — 5. *C.:* **to use, to employ** **bá-laṅ lẹ jhḗ-pa-la** an ox for work; **to spend,** **lẹ jhḗ-pa-la mi-tse** one's whole life in working, **lé-lọ náṅ-na** in idleness. — 6. **k̔a kyél-wa* C.* to kiss; *γnód-pa skyél-ba, B. *kyal-wa* C. W.* col., **to do harm, to hurt, inflict an injury, to play** one **a trick;** *mna skyel-ba B., C.W.,* **to swear,** take an oath; **lo kyél-če* W.* **to rely, depend upon, confide in.** — *skyel-tuṅ byéd-pa* = *γśegs-skyél byéd-pa,* (prop.: to accompany one to a short distance). — *skyel-bdár Lex.,* also col., present of the departing person to those that accompany him. — *skyel-ma* **an escort, convoy;** *skyél-mar yod* he is a guide (to me) *Mil.; skyél-ma žu* we ask for a safe-conduct *Glr.; dmag daṅ bčás-pai skyél-ma* a military escort *Glr.*

སྐྱེས་ *skyes,* also *skyás-ma, skyós-ma, k̔yós-ma,* resp. *γnaṅ-skyés,* **a present,** *skyes skúr-ba* to give or send a present; ₒ*byon-skyés, p̔ebs-skyes* a present given to or received from somebody on his arrival. — *sk̔yas-čáṅ* a present of beer, *skyes-k̔úr* of cakes, *skyes-nór* of merchandise or money; *skyes-lán* a present made in return *Cs.*

སྐྱེས་སྡོང་ *skyes-sdóṅ Sik.* **banana, plantain.**

སྐྱེས་ནག་ *skyes-nág,* also *skye-nág C.* **widower.**

སྐྱེས་པ་ *skyés-pa* 1. pt. pf. of *skyé-ba.* — 2. sbst. **man, male person,** *skyés-pa* *daṅ bud-méd,* men and women *B. & C.*; emphatically: *rgyál-po γčig-po skyés-pa yin* the king alone is a man *Dzl.*; **husband** *Glr.*; = *skyés-bu* **a holy man?**

སྐྱེས་བུ *skyés-bu, Ssk.* **पुरुष man, people;** *skyés-bu gaṅ* **whosoever; man** opp. to the rest of nature *Med.*; **one** (French: *on*), *skyés-bu lág-pa brkyáṅ-ba tsám-gyis* as quick as one stretches out his hand *Dzl.* — Though this word may also be applied to culprits and criminals (*Pth.*), it is chiefly used of **holy men:** *skyés-bu dám-pa* the saint; *dad-ldán sky.* the believing, the faithful *Glr.*; *skyés-bu čén-po,* **महापुरुष** the great saint, in Buddhistic writings nearly identical with Buddha; *skyés-bu mčog* id. (For the 32 chief characteristics and the 80 subordinate marks distinguishing such a person refer to *Köppen.* I. 433. *Burn.* II. 553 ff. *Gyatch.* c. VII.)

སྐྱེས་མ *skyés-ma* 1. fem. of *skyés-pa,* she that has been born *Mil.* — 2. **fern,** = *skyás-ma Sik.*

སྐྱོ་ངོགས *skyo-ṅógs Cs.*: **quarrel,** *Lex.* = *ₒḱrug-lóṅ.*

སྐྱོ་བ *skyóba* 1. vb. **to be weary,** c.c.r: *bdag ḱyim-gyis skyó-ste* I being weary of living in the world *Dzl.*; in a more general sense: **to be ill-humoured, grieved, vexed, to feel an aversion** *Tar.* 12. 13; *skyo mi šés-par* or *skyo mi šés-pa tsám-du* without being tired, **indefatigably;** *nam sḱyo-na* when he was tired of it *Dzl.* — 2. sbst. **weariness** *ₒtsol-ₒtsól-nas skyó-ba yaṅ skyé-bar dug* we are quite tired of that constant seeking *Mil.*; *yid yóṅs-su mi skyó-ba* **indefatigableness, perseverance** *Thgy.* — *skyó-mo* adj., **sems skyó-mo rag** I feel **discontented, disheartened** *Ld.*

**Comp.** *skyo-grógs* **comforter, companion** *Glr., Mil.* — *skyo-glú Cs.*: **a mournful song.** — *skyo-ṅál, skyo-dúb* **weariness,** *skyo-ṅal-méd-pai dád-pa* unwearied faith *Mil.* — *skyo-šás* **disgust, aversion.** — *skyo-sáṅs* **recreation,** *skyo-sáṅs-la ₒgró-ba,* resp. *ₒbyon-pa* **to take a walk or a ride,** to promenade. — *skyo-bsún-pa* **to be grieved** *Sch.*

སྐྱོ་མ *skyó-ma* 1. **pap** of parched meal and beer; any **pap, paste** or **dough;** *skyó-ma ₒbyúg-pa* to spread paste (upon a wound, as a salve) *Med.*; *ša-skyó Med.* ? (it may denote a paste of meat as well as one of mushrooms). — 2. **blame, slander,** *skyó-ma máṅ-la* when he slanders a great deal *Mil.*

སྐྱོགས *skyogs* 1. **scoop, ladle.** — **me-kyóg** **coal-shovel** *C.*; **žu-kyóg** **melting-spoon, crucible** *C. W.* — 3. **drinking-cup, bowl, goblet.** — *γser-skyógs, dṅul-skyógs* gold, silver goblet. *žal-skyógs C. B.,* **don-skyógs** *W.* resp.: drinking-cup. *ḱrag-skyógs* bowl for drinking blood, a skull used for that purpose *Pth.*; **kyog-žáb sal** may I ask your honour for the foot of your cup (viz the remnant of your drink)? *W.* — 3. *srab-skyógs Cs.*: **the rein** of a bridle. —

སྐྱོགས་ལྟོ་འབུ *skyógs-lto-ₒbu* **snail** *W.* *'*ol-skyógs** id.

སྐྱོགས་པ *skyógs-pa* **to turn,** *mgrin-pa* the neck, = to look round, back, *Mil.,* also = to turn away, aside *C.*

སྐྱོང་བ *skyoṅ-ba,* pf. *bskyaṅs,* ft. *bskyaṅ,* imp. *(b)skyoṅ(s)* Ssk. **पा, रक्ष to guard; to keep, to tend,** cattle; **to defend,** the religion; **to save, preserve,** the life, the body; **support, to take care of,** poor people, e.g. *drin bzáṅ-pos* by benefits, favours. *ṫábs-kyis* by various means; **to attend to; to be given to,** *ṫugs-dám* meditation, *lag-léṅ* exercise; *rgyal-srid skyóṅ-ba* to rule, govern a kingdom, *čos bžin-du* in conformity with the law of religion, justly. — *čos-skyóṅ* **'protector, defender of religion', धर्मपाल,** is used for a certain individual deity, or = *ₒjig-rten-skyóṅ,* or for a class of magicians in the monasteries of *C.,* v. *Schl.* 157. *Kö.* II. 259. — *ₒjig-rten-skyóṅ,* **लोकपाल 'guardian of the world';** there are four of them, identical with *rgyal-čen bži* the four great spirit-kings, q.v. — *skyoṅ-dál* **assistance** *C.,* **kyoṅ-dhál jhé-pa** to help. — *skyoṅ-ma* = *brtán-ma* the goddess of the earth.

སྐྱོད་པ *skyód-pa* pf. & ft. *bskyod, Ssk.* **चल, 1. to move, to agitate,** *rlúṅ-gis yál-ga* *skyod-na* when the wind agitates the branches *Dzl.*; **to shake;** hence *Mi-skyód-pa*, Akshobhya, n. of the second Dhyani-Buddha. — 2. *W.*: resp. **to go, to walk,** *(= γšégs-pa, ˛byón-pa B. C.)* **náṅ-du skyod** step in, if you please! — 3. *W.*: **to go down, to set,** of the sun, moon etc., **to expire, to pass, to elapse,** of time.

སྐྱོན *skyon* दोष 1. **fault, defect** (opp. to *yón-tan), skyon gaṅ yaṅ med* I have not to complain of anything, I do not want anything *Dzl.*; **damage, harm, disadvantage, misfortune,** *˛kŕul-pa-la skyon ci yod* what harm is there in erring? *Thgy.*; C.: **mi kyon, kyon me**, no harm, no matter *(W.* more freq.: **mi sto*); γžán-gyi skyon tós-na dgá-ba* rejoicing in the calamities of others, malicious *Glr.*; *skyón-du mtóṅ-bá* to consider it a loss *Glr.* — 2. **bodily defect, fault,** as lameness; **derangement, disorder** in the mixture of the humours *Med.* — 3. **spiritual defect, sin, vicious quality,** *rdzún-du smrá-bai skyon* the sin of lying *Dzl.*; *skyón-gyis ma gos* not defiled by sin; *lar skyon če* but that is very bad (of you) *Glr.*; *skyon byéd-pa Cs.* to commit a fault, *sél-ba Lex.* to remove, amend, correct a fault, *spáṅ-ba* to leave off, to quit it; *mi-la skyon ˛bébs-pa, ˛dógs-pa* (col. **tág-pa, tág-če**) to charge one with a crime, to calumniate *Glr.*; *γžán-gyi skyon gléṅ-ba, rjód-pa*, to name the faults of others, to speak ill of them, to slander *B., C., Schr.* also: to blame, criticise. — *skyón-čan* 1. **faulty, defective, incorrect,** e.g. *dag-yig* the spelling of a word. 2. **sinful,** subject to vice. — 4. symb. num: 18.

སྐྱོན་པ *skyón-pa* pf. *(b)skyon* **to put astride** upon a thing, (causative form to *žón-pa), mi žig rtá-la* (or *rtá-ru)* to cause a man to mount, to go on horseback: to fix something on a stick; *mi žig γsál-šiṅ-la* **to empale** a man.

སྐྱོབ་པ *skyób-pa*, pf. *(b)skyabs*, ft. *bskyab*, imp. *skyób(s) Ssk.* त्रा **to protect, defend, preserve, save** frq., *˛jigs-pa-las* from fear, *˛jig-pa-las* from destruction; *bskyáb-pa* the protecting power, the preserving cause *Mil.* (ni f.).

སྐྱོབས *skyobs* **help, assistance,** seldom for *skyabs; skyóbs-ma Thgy.* id.; **šrog-kyób** col. preservation of life, escape; also: he that saves another's life, helper.

སྐྱོམ་པ *skyóm-pa*, pf. *bskyoms*, ft. *bskyom*, imp. *skyom(s) Cs.*: **to shake, agitate, stir up.** *Lexx.* give: *ču skyóm-pa* and *snód skyom-pa*, to stir the water, to shake a vessel.

སྐྱོར *skyor = kyor*, the hollow of the hand filled with a fluid, e.g. *ču-skyór* a handful of water.

སྐྱོར་བ *skyór-ba* I. vb. pf. & ft. *bskyar* 1. **to hold up, to prop,** — 2. **to paste.** — 2. **to repeat,** *bskyár-te btaṅ* it was repeatedly sent *Dzl.*; to repeat word for word what the teacher says, in order to learn it by heart *Mil.*; to say over again; to **recite by heart** (opp. to *sgróg-pa* to read); *glu de rjes skyór-nas ma bláṅs-na* if one does not sing the hymn afterwards repeatedly *Mil.*; **kyor jaṅ jhé-pa* C.* to practise repeatedly.

II. sbst. **enclosure, fence.**

སྐྱོལ་བ *skyól-ba* sometimes for *skyél-ba.*

སྐྱོས་མ *skyós-ma* v. *skyes.*

སྐྲ *skra*, resp. *dbu-skrá (C.: *ṭa, W.: šra*)* **the hair** of the head, **šra-ló* Ld.* id., used caressingly in speaking to children and women; *skra daṅ ká-spu* the hair of the head and of the beard; *skra bsgril ba Cs.*: plaited or curled hair; *skra nyag γčig* a single hair. — *skrá-čan* having long hair. — *skra-do-kér* the hair plaited together on the crown of the head, as Buddha and Hindu-women wear it. — *skra-mdúd* the bow of ribands at the end of the long plaits of the women in *Ld.* etc. — *skra-tsáb Cs.*: **false hair, a peruke.** — *skra-šeṅ Sch.* thin hair.

སྐྲག་པ *skrág-pa*, with instr., **to be terrified, frightened by, afraid of** something *˛jigs-skrag-pa, dṅáṅs-skr.* id. *B., C.*

སྐྲང་བ་ *skráṅ-ba* pf. *skraṅs*, **to swell**, *ṡraṅs-soṅ* it is swollen, a tumour, a bile, a weal has formed itself *W.*; *skráṅs-po Sch.* a swelling, tumour; *skraṅs-ₒbúr Sch.* an abscess not yet open.

སྐྲན་ *skran* 1. *Ssk.* गुल्म *Cs.*: a fleshy etc. excrescence in the abdomen, a concretion under the skin, in the bowels, womb etc., *Sch.* also: a swelling of the glands. Wise (Commentary on Hindoo Medicine) says, that very different diseases are comprised unter the term *gúlma*, tumours of the pylorus, partial enlargements of the liver, diseases of the large intestines, fixed and moveable swellings; — perhaps also herniae, which I did not find mentioned elsewhere. — In *S.g.* I found *skran-nád* described as a consequence of great fatigue and want of breath, and *skran-γzér* as pain in consequence of suppressed winds. — 2. *rdo-skrán, bad-skrán*, two sorts of **steatite** *C.*

སྐྲབ་པ་ *skráb-pa Cs.*: 'to beat the ground with one's feet,' **to stamp, tread,** cf. *ₒkráb-pa*; *Lex.*: *bró-skrab-pa*, to dance.

སྐྲས་ཀ་ *skrás-ka* v. *skás-ka*.

སྐྲི་བ་ *skrí-ba* 1. *Cs.* **to conduct** (?) 2. *W.* *ṡri-ċe* f. *dkri-ba*.

སྐྲུ་བ་ *skrú-ba* pf. *bskrus* ft. *bskru*, *Sch.*: to wait; the latter would suit well in a passage of *Mil.*, perh. also in *zás-la skru* of the *Lexx.*; but *ṡiṅ-skrus-pa Lexx.* remains unexplained.

སྐྲུན་པ་ *skrún-pa* pf. & ft. *bskrun* **to produce,** fruits *Mil.*, a root of virtue (v. *rtsá-ba*) *Stg.*

སྐྲུམ་ *skrum* **meat,** resp. viz. when spoken of as the food of respected persons.

སྐྲོག་པ་ *skróg-pa* = *dkróg-pa*, perh. also f. *skrág-pa*. *Lexx.* *ḍá-ru skróg-po* **to beat** the drum: *W.* *kopón ṡróg-ċe* **to play** on the guitar.

སྐྲོད་པ་ *skród-pa* pf. & ft. *bskrad* **to expel, drive out, eject,** out of the country *Dzl.*, *Mil.*; to deprive of cast; *ṡrád-de taṅ ċe* to expel a thief publicly out of the village *W.*

བཀ..., བསྐ...; words beginning with these letters will in most cases be found arranged under rk.. and sk..

བསྐང་རྫས་ *bskaṅ-rdzás* a sacrificial ceremony v. *Schl.* 360.

བསྐ་བ་ *bská-ba*, *Ssk.* कषाय, **astringent,** as to taste, *Cs.* erron.: bitter.

བསྐལ་པ་ *bskál-pa*, *Ssk.* कल्प, **a kalpa,** a fabulous period of time; the fantastical reveries of the Buddhists concerning this subject v. *Kö.* I. 266, also *Will.* under *kalpa*. *bskál-pa čén-po* the great kalpa; *bár-(gyi) bskal-pa* the intervening or middle 'kalpa'; *bsk. bzáṅ-po* the happy, blessed period, viz. in which Buddhas appear; *bskál-pa ṅan-pa* the bad 'kalpa'; *bskal-mé* conflagration of the universe.

བསྐུ་བ་ *bskú-ba* v. *skúd-pa* II vb.

# ཁ

ཁ *ka* 1. the letter **k'**, aspirated, like c in *'call'*. — 2. numerical figure: **two,** *ka-pa* the second volume.

ཁ་ *ka* I. additional syllable, = *ka*, but less frequent. —

II. in compounds instead of *ká-ba* **bitter** and *ká-ba* **snow;** for the latter signification it is in *W.* the only form existing.

III. i. o. *kag* **part,** *ka γnyís-su* into two parts (e. g. to cleave) *Stg.*; *ka-gháṅ* one part; in a special sense: the sixth part of a rupee *C.*; *k̔a-čig* part, **some, several,** frq.

IV. (also *Ssk.* ख) resp. *žal*, cf. *k̔á-po* 1. **mouth,** *k̔a k̔a* bitter mouth, bitter taste *Med.*; *k̔a dúl-po* (soft month), manageable, tractable, *k̔a gyóṅ-po* hard-mouthed, refractory; *k̔a sgyúr-ba* (= *k̔a-lo sgy.*) to govern, to rein the mouth (of a horse), to lead, guide, influence other persons *Glr.*, to turn off (a river) *Tar.*; *k̔a ₒt̔én-pa* (to pull the mouth) to stop a beast of draught *Tar.*; *k̔a ₒbyed-pa, W*, **p̔é-če** to open one's mouth, *γdáṅs-pa* to open it wide, *ₒdzúm-pa, W.*, **čug-če** to shut it; *k̔a brdáb-pa* (or *kráb-pa?*) **to smack;** **k̔a dab** (or **ṭab**) **zér-wa** to produce a smacking, snapping sound, col.; *k̔a rég-pa* c. dat. to put one's mouth to a thing, in order to eat or drink it; *k̔a ₒǰúg-pa* c. dat. **to interfere, to meddle with;** *k̔a t̔ál-ba* 1. col. = *k̔a ₒǰug-pa*, 2. *Cs.*: **to promise;** *k̔a γtúgs-pa, k̔a ₒo γtúgs-pa, k̔á-la ₒo byéd-pa, k̔a sbyór-ba B., C.*, **k̔a lán-če* W*, **k̔a kyél-wa* C.* **to kiss;** **k̔a kyé-če* W.*, **to inveigh,** to give ill language; *k̔a bsré-ba* to have intercourse, social connexion with one another, viz. in eating, drinking and smoking together, which is a matter of no little social consequence; *k̔a ₒdzin byéd-pa* c.genit. to receive friendly, to be kind to, assist *Mil.*; *k̔a γtád-pa Glr.* 16. 3. was explained: to bring together personally, to confront, = *k̔a sprád-pa*; *k̔a ₒbúb-tu nyal-ba* to lie in that position; *k̔a bsláṅ-ba* the contrary of the preceding; *k̔a ₒóg-tu bltás-te ši-ba* to be killed by a precipitous fall. Especially: the speaking mouth, *k̔á-nas*, col. also **k̔á-na**, **orally,** by word of mouth, e. g. to state, report, **k̔á-nẹ zér-na** in the colloquial language *C.*; **k̔a dé-mo ṅyiṅ sóg-po* W.* hypocritical; *k̔á-la slá-te dón-la bka* easily spoken after, but difficult to be understood (e. g. a doctrine); **k̔a šór soṅ** 'my (his etc.) mouth has run away', **nor soṅ** 'has erred', the former denoting inconsiderate talk, the latter a lapsus linguae; *k̔as lén-pa, bláṅ-ba* 1. 'to anticipate with the mouth', **to promise** frq., with direct speech or term. inf., sometimes also with the term. of a sbst. e. g. *brán-du k̔as blaṅs* he promised or engaged himself as a servant, — also: **to presume, to arrogate** *Mil.* 2. 'to accept, adopt with the mouth', **to acknowledge, admit** *Tar.*; *k̔as ₒčé-ba B.*, *k̔a t̔ál-ba Cs.*, to promise; *k̔a sṅá-ba, sṅás-pa* to blurt out, speak out inconsiderately; *k̔a ₒčám-pa, mt̔ún-pa, col. *t̔úg-pa** to agree upon; *k̔a sdóm-pa, mnán-pa* to silence, *W.*; **k̔a kág-če, kyíl-če** id.; *k̔a skyór-ba, slú-ba* to speak cunningly, to try to persuade etc.; *k̔a róg-pa*, more freq. **k̔a róg-(te) dúg-pa, dád-pa*, **to be silent;** *k̔a ₒp̔áṅ-ba Tar.*, prob. = *k̔a ₒk̔yam dbyúg-pa C.* to divulge ill rumours; *k̔a lóg-pa* to reply, contradict; *k̔a gáṅ dgar smrá-ba* (**gaṅ tad, gaṅ dran zér-če* W.*) to talk at random; *k̔a- (la) nyán-pa* **to obey,** *k̔a nyán-po* **obedient** (resp. *bka* i.o. *k̔a*); *γsál-k̔a* clear, intelligible language; *k̔a ṅán-du smrá-ba, W.*: **k̔a sóg-po zér-če** to use ill language; also without **ṅán-pa** or **sóg-po, k̔a zér-če** or **k̔a tóṅ-wa** means the same. — 2. **mouth, opening, orifice,** of a vessel, cavern, pit etc., *k̔a γčód-pa, ₒgébs-pa* to cover, shut an opening; *k̔a ₒbyéd-pa* to open, is also used of a book, a letter etc. (for holy books *žal* is employed i.o. *k̔a*); *k̔a ₒbye-ba* to open or unclose itself, to begin to appear, *k̔a ₒbú-ba* id., of flowers; *k̔a búb-tu* the opening turned downward, *k̔a bslán-du* turned upward; *k̔a-t̔úg skóṅ-ba* to fill to the brim; *k̔a skóṅ-ba* to fill up a void, to make up a deficiency, *γžan-nas* or *las* from elsewhere; *k̔a naṅ* the inward brim, *k̔a p̔yi* the outer edge *Glr.* — 3. **the front side, face,** *k̔a lhor stón-pa* or *ltá-ba* to be directed southwards *Glr.* — 4. **surface,** *k̔a ₒbri-ba*, to be diminished, of a fluid the surface of which is sinking; *k̔á ₒp̔ri-ba* to diminish, to make less, by taking away from the surface; **the outside,** *k̔a dkar γtiṅ nag* outside white, inside black, fig. *Mil.*; in a special sense: **colour,** v. *k̔á-dóg*; therefore *k̔á-ru, k̔á-na, k̔á-la, k̔ar* 1. **on, upon, above,** *šiṅ-k̔ar* upon the tree (e. g. he sits), up the tree (he climbs) *Dzl.*; *ču ḱar* on the water; *ṗyogs bži ḱá-ru* all round *Glr.* 2. **on, at,** *ču ḱar* on the river side, *mtso ḱar ṗebs* he came to the lake *Pth.* 3. **above, besides,** = *stéṅ-du Mil.* 4. **towards, in the face of,** *mtson ḱar sra* proof against thrust or blow *Mil.* 5. **at the time of, when,** *sléb-pai ḱar, sleb ḱar, ₒbyon ḱar* when (he) arrived; *ré-bai ḱar* in the hope of; — *ḱá-nas* down from, away from, *rta ḱá-nas ₒbébs-pa* to alight from the horse *Glr.*; **ḱá-na, ḱá-nẹ, ḱá-la** col. for *sgó-nas*, **tábs-si ḱá-na** by way of the opportunity, on occasion, **yun riṅ-gi ḱá-nẹ** by little and little, gradually. — 5. **sharpness, edge,** of a knife etc., **ḱa túg-po soṅ** the edge has become blunt, **log soṅ** has become bad; **ḱa mi ₒdug** the edge is wanting; *meï, čui, rlúṅ-gi ḱa nón-pa* to suppress the sharpness of the fire, water, wind, to stop the flames, floods etc. (viz. by means of incantations) *Glr.*; **ḱa tón-če, ṗiṅ-če** *W.* to grind, to sharpen; *ḱa lén-pa* to become sharp *Sch.*

V. **yesterday,** also: **the day before yesterday,** *ḱai nyin* id., cf. *ḱa-rtsaṅ.*

**Compounds.** *ḱa-dkrí* (*C.* *-*ṭi**, *W.* *-*ṡri**) **neck-cloth,** sometimes worn as a protection against cold. — *ḱá-skóṅ, ḱas-skóṅ* **appendix,** of a book. — *ḱa-skyur-po* **olive, olive-tree** *Sik.* — *ḱa-ḱa-sán* or *siṅ* about two months ago *C.* — *ḱa-ḱébs* **cover, lid** *Sch.* — *ḱa-ḱór, ḱa-ḱyér* **border** *Sch.* — *ḱa-ḱral Cs.*: respect, regard, with respect to. — *ḱa-ₒḱór* the circumference of the mouth *Cs.* — *ḱa-gáṅ* (cf. *ḱa* III) **quadrate, square,** *ḱa-gáṅ-ba* square *adj.*, *ḱa-gáṅ-ma* id., e.g. pieces of cloth so shaped. — *ḱa-gáb Sch.* **cover, lid.** — *ḱa-góṅ* **snow-ball.** — *ḱa-grú* corner of the mouth. — *ḱa-mgál* v. *ḱa-só.* — *ḱa-rgán Mil.* privilege of old age n. f. — *ḱa-rgód Sch.*: ill language; a slanderer. *ḱa-rgyúg Glr.* acc. to the context: idle talk, unfounded assertion. — *ḱa-rgyúd* or *-gyún*, resp. *žal-rgyun*, oral tradition, esp. certain mystical doctrines not allowed to be written down. — *ḱa-bsgós* advice, = *ḱá-ta;* commandment, cf. *bka-bsgós.* — *ḱa-mṅár* bitter and sweet. — *ḱa-čig* (v. *ḱa* III) **some,** — *ḱa-γčáṅ* clever talking, cf. *ḱa sbyáṅ-po* **eloquent.** (*Cs.*: fair words?) — *ḱa-γčód* **cover, lid; cork.** — *ḱa-bčól Sch.* idle talk, prattle. — *ḱa-čág Mil.*, was explained: **abuse,** ill language. — *ḱa-čád*, resp. *žal-čád* **agreement, convention, covenant,** **ḱ. zúm-če** *W.* to conclude a convention. — *ḱa-čár Mil.* snow and rain; *ḱa-ma-čár* both falling promiscuously, sleet. — *ḱa-čiṅs* the appeasing of wild beasts etc. by witchcraft *Mil.* — *ḱa-čú* 1. spittle *Cs.* 2. snow-water. — *ḱa-če* 1. a large mouth. 2. a person that has to command over much (cf. *ḱa-drág, ḱa-žán*). 3. n. of a mask in the religious plays. 4. n. of a country, Cashmere, v. below. — *ḱa-čéms* **last will,** *ḱa-čéms ₒjóg-pa* to make a testament. — *ḱa-čos* **hypocrisy.** — *ḱa-mču* 1. **lip.** 2. *Sch.*: word, voice (?) 3. **quarrel, dispute.** — *ḱa-rjé* 1. great lord, mighty personage *Cs.* (?) 2. good luck, good fortune *Cs.*; but in *C.* it is only used for **fortune = goods, wealth.** — *ḱa-nyúṅ Sch* sparing of words, **laconic.** — *ḱá-ta*, also *ḱá-lta* **good advice, lesson,** *byéd-pa* or *ₒjóg-pa* to give, *C. W.* — *ḱa-tód-la* (or *-na*) *Ld.* = *ḱa-tóg la*, **on, upon.** — *ḱa-tón Cs.*: 'a reading or saying with a loud voice' (*Lex.* वचस), better: **the saying by heart,** *klóg gam ḱa-tón-du dón-nas* reading or saying by heart, *ḱa-tón-du ṡés-pa* to know by heart *Dzl.*; gen. in reference to religious texts. — *ḱa-γtám Cs.* **tradition.** — *ḱa-stóṅ* not yet having eaten anything. — *ḱa-túg C.* to the brim. — *ḱa-tóg-la* or *-na*, = *ḱá-la*, **above, upon,** on the top or surface of, *ḱa-tóg-tu* id.; *ḱa-tóg-nas* down from. — *ḱa-tór Sch.* pustules in the mouth. — *ḱa-dig, ḱa-ldig-mḱan W.* **stammerer.** — *ḱa-dóg*, also *ḱa* (v. *ḱa* IV. 4.) **colour** *skra mton-mtiṅ-gi ḱa-dóg-tu gyúr-to* the hair became blue *Dzl.*; *ḱa sgyur-ba* to change colour, *ḱa ₒgyur* the colour changes, cf. also *mdog.* — *ḱa-drág* 1. **mighty.** 2 **haughty.** — *ḱa-draṅ W.* **over-against, just before, opposite, straight on.** — *ḱa-ṡdáms*, = *ḱá-ta, γdáms-ḱa,* **advice** *W.* — *ḱa-ₒdár*

Cs.: 'one who speaks too fast', Sch.: 'too loud'. — ka-₀díg **cork, bung, stopple.** — ka-nan **yesterday morning** C. — ká-nar-čan **oblong.** — ka-nin **last year.** — ká-po sometimes f. ka 1. **mouth,** e.g. *ká-po dúl-mo* W., *ká dúl-po C., tractable. 2. **speech** Mil. 3. **bitter** C. — ká-lpágs **lip,** góṅ-ma upper, ₒóg-ma lower lip; W.: *kál-pag (s) pág-če, dáb-če* to smack. — ká-spu hair of the beard, skra daṅ ká-spu hair of the head and beard, frq. — ká-pó **boasting,** ka-po-čé id. — ka-pór = pór-pa, **a cup.** — ka-pyis **napkin.** — ká-ba v. below. — ka-bád the humidity of the air or the moisture of the earth caused by snow. — ka-búb mouth or face being turned downwards. — ka-brág v. below. — ka-rbád Cs.: 'a boast, proud speech'; others: idle talk. — ka-sbyáṅ **eloquence** Mil., ka-sbyáṅ-po eloquent, cf. ka-yčáṅ? — ka-ma-čár **sleet,** rain and snow. — ka-múr bit (bridle) Sch — ka-rtsáṅ, ka-sáṅ 1. B. C. **yesterday forenoon,** ka-rtsáṅ-gi byis-pa the boy that was here yesterday forenoon Mil. 2. W. (*kar-sáṅ*) **the day before yesterday;** some days ago; *kar-sáṅ za-nyi-ma* last sunday: *kar-sáṅ (s)tón-ka* last autumn. — ka-tsa 1. **bitter and acrid** Med. 2. **'hot in the mouth'** a. a very acrid sort of radish, e.g. horse-radish. b. aphthae, thrush, a disease of the mouth, incident to horses, cows, sheep. c. ka-tsá riṅ-ṅe-ba Mil. nt. daily warm food. — ka-tsúb **snow-storm.** — ka-tsó **boasting,** ka-tsó šin-tu čé-ba a great swaggerer Glr. — ka-tsón v. below. — ka-mtsúl **muzzle, mouth** (of a dog etc.); the lower part of the human face col. — ka-₀tsóg abuse? *ka-tsóg čém-po* C. a great abuser, reviler. — ka-žán the contrary of ka-drág, low, unimportant, having no authority, ka-žán-pai sdug-bsṅál the misfortune of being of low birth Mil. — ka-žé 1. 'mouth and mind', ka-žé mi mtsúṅs-pa **hypocrisy, hypocrite** C. 2. 'mouth-mind', meaning the same as the phrase just mentioned: **hypocrisy** Mil., ka-že-méd-pa unfeigned, sincere Mil. — ka-žéṅ **breadth, expanse,** e.g. of the heavens Mil. — ka-zás **food, victuals** B. C. — ká-ya lit.: 'being one's partner or match as to speaking', also kai ya, — gen.: **partner; match;** *ká-ya ǰhé-pa* C. to assist, *ko ke ya* (or *ka-ya) ṅe mi tub* I am not his match, not able to compete with him; with regard to things: I am not equal to the task. — ka-ras **neck-cloth,** cf. ka-dkri. — ká-ru-tsa **alum** Méd. — ka-rúd **snow-slip, avalanche,** — ka-ró taste in the mouth. — ka rog v. ka IV. 1. extr. — ka-lán 'mouth-requital' 1. **thanks-giving** Mil. 2. **reply,** esp. angry reply. — 3. **requital** for food received C. — ka-leb **cover, lid.** — ká-lo 1. 'mouth leaves', snoi ká-lo Mil. the young, tender leaves of several wild herbs, used as vegetables. 2. v. below. — ka-šá 1. v. ka-skyúr-po. — ká-sá šá-ba S.g., 'snow-deer', **elk** Sch.; shoe-leather from the skin of this animal is mentioned in Mil., and is known in Tibet. In Sik. however **the deer** of the neighbouring Tarai is called ka-ša, in other parts of the country **the spotted deer,** — ka-šágs **jest, joke,** *ka-šág ṭ'áb-če, táṅ-če* W. to jest. — ka-šúgs-čan, -šéd-čan W. **eloquent.** — ka-šés Cs. **some.** — ka-šób col. **lies, falsehoods; obscene talk; idle talk.** ka-bšád **talk, gossip** Mil. — ka-sáṅ v. ka-rtsáṅ. — ka-síṅ several weeks ago Cs. — ka-só mouth and teeth; similar: ka-mgál mouth and jawbone, *ká-só* or *ka-gál čag yin* I shall break your chops W. — ká-sró? Ld. *ka-šró lám-če* to fry (meat) in butter. — ka-slób, = ka-tón, learnt by heart, (used by children) W. — ka-lhág remnant of a meal Mil.

ཁྭ་ ka (kwa?) v. kwa-ta.

ཁ་ག་པོ་ ká-ga-po Sch.: difficult (?).

ཁ་ཆུལ་ ka-čúl W. col. for ka-če-yul, **Cashmere.**

ཁ་ཆེ་ ka-čé **Cashmere;** amongst other things it produces much saffron, hence ka-če-skyes **saffron;** in Cashmere Buddhism was once flourishing (v. the legend relative to its being introduced there: Introduction du Buddhisme dans le Kashmir par L. Feer Paris 1866), but afterwards it came under Mahometan rulers, and *ka-čé* denotes therefore now in *C.* a mussulman (cf. Huc & Gabet's journey); *ka-čéi dpé-ča* the koran *Schr.; ka-čéi ̥grón-kan* an inn kept by a mussulman *Mil.*

ཁ་ཏ *ká-ta (kva-ta?) Ssk.* 1. **crow.** — 2. **raven,** = *bya-róg, ṗo-róg.* — 3. *ka-ta krá-bo* **magpie.**

ཁ་ཏོ་ཤིང་ *ká-to-šiṅ* is said to be = *ysál-šiṅ,* a pointed stake used for the execution of criminals.

ཁ་ཊྭཱཾ་ག་ *ka-tváṅ-ga, ka-ṭv.,* gen. pronounced *ka-tóm-ga Ssk., Will.:* 'a club or staff with a skull at the top', the weapon of Siva, also carried by ascetics; Tibetans refer it also to the trident.

ཁ་བཏགས་ *ka-btágs* **handkerchief** or **scarf of salutation,** a piece of veil-like and generally worthless silk-fabric, about as large as a small pocket-handkerchief, which in Tibet is given or sent, with or without other presents, to the person one intends to visit; cf. Huc's journey.

ཁ་འདད་ *ka-̥dá,* v. *kan-da.*

ཁ་བ་ *ká-ba* I. col. *C.* **ká-po**, *W.* **kán-te**, *Bal.* **χo** **bitter.** — II. *W.* **ka** **snow,** *ká-ba duṅ ltar ysal* bright as snow and shells *Pth.; ká-ba ̥bab,* col. **ka yoṅ** it snows; **ka páṅ-če** *W.* to remove the snow (with a shovel); *ká-ba-čan* snowy, and as a subst.: the snow-country, Tibet; *ká-ba-čan-pai séms-čan-rnams* the Tibetan beings *Glr.* — III. correspondently to the Arabian word قَهْوَة the missionaries in *Lh.* have given to *ka-ba* the signification of **coffee,** which is otherwise unknown in Tibet.

ཁ་བད་ *ka-bád* 1. the architectural ornament of a Tibetan house formed by the projecting ends of the beams which support the roof (not 'parapet' *Cs.*) — 2. v. *ka.*

ཁ་བྲག་ *ka-brág* **fork** (not generally used in eating); any forked object.

ཁ་མོ་ *ká-mo Cs.* **enchantment, irresistible influence.**

ཁ་ཚར་ *ka-tsár* **fringes, threads,** such as the loose threads at the end of a web.

ཁ་ཚོན་ *ka-tsón Sch.* decision; but in the only passage where I met with this word, viz. *Dzl.* ༢༥༠ 13, this meaning is not applicable, but something like surface or width.

ཁ་ཞུར་ *ka-žúr Sch.* **water-hen.**

ཁ་ཟུར་ *ka-zúr (Ssk.* खर्जूर, *Hindi* खजूर) col. *ka-zúr-pa-ni* **date,** *ka-zur šiṅ* date-tree.

ཁ་གཟེ་ *ka-yzé* 1. *W.:* **rake** (gardening). — 2. *Sp.:* a carrier's **load,** **ka-zé-pa** a cooly.

ཁ་ཡོག་ *ka-yóg* **a false charge,** *C.:* **ma nyé-pe ka-yóg ǰhuṅ** he was innocently accused.

ཁ་ར་ *ká-ra* 1. *W.* f *ká-ra* **sugar.** - 2. *Sch.:* **trough, manger.**

ཁ་རི་ *ka-rí,* or *ka-rú,* v. *kál-ri.*

ཁ་རོག་ *ka-rog,* v. *ka rog-pa, ka* IV. 1. towards the end.

ཁ་ལེ་ *ká-le* v. *kyá-le.*

ཁ་ལོ་ *ká-lo* 1. v. *ka* Comp. — 2. *Schr.* **prow** of a ship, others: **helm;** the word is very often used in the phrase: *ka-lo sgyur-ba,* esp. *gru-yziṅs-kyi,* to turn a ship, to steer, to lead, govern, rule, *ka-lo sgyur-mkas-pa* skilful in driving, *ka-lo-pa* a charioteer. — 3. *Cs.:* the glans penis.

ཁ་ཤྱ་ *ka-šya* n. of a mountainous country in the N.E. of India Tar. 21. 10.

ཁ་སུར་ *ka-súr* v. *ka-zur.*

ཁག་ *kag* 1. **a task; charge, business, duty; responsibility; importance;** *kag ̥kúr-ba* to be charged with, *kág ̥gél-ba* to lay upon; **kag tég-pa** or **kyág-pa** *C.* to warrant, become responsible; *dér ̥tsó-ba yóṅ-ba kag teg* I warrant you will get something to eat there *Mil.;* **kag -tég, kag-kyág** *C.* a bail; *kág-čan* important. — 2. *W.:* **part,** *bču-kág* the tenth part, tithe, **kag-nyi čo-té čád-če** to cut in two; **division, section** (of a book); **place,** **kág nyi-la ṗog soṅ** I have hurt myself in two places; **kag čig-la rúb-če** to press towards one point; in a more general sense: **kag čig-la 'i*

ཁ

*sás-ka čos** finish this work at once! — *yul-ḱág* **province, district;** *rgyal-ḱág* **kingdom.** — 3. *W.: *ḱag** or **ḱág-ga tág-če** **to hang** (by the neck).

ཁག་པོ་ *ḱág po C.* 1. **difficult** (*W. *ḱág(s)-po**); **hard** (to bear), **ḱág-po ǰhuṅ** it proved hard, **ḱág-po ǰhé-pa** to suffer want. — 2. **bad, spoiled, rotten,** **mar ḱág-po soṅ** the butter has become rancid.

ཁག་ལ་ (?) *ḱág-la, Md.: *ḱág-la mar** **fresh** butter, just made.

ཁང་ *ḱaṅ C.:* vulg. f. *ḱoṅ*, sometimes also in books.

ཁང་པ་ *ḱáṅ-pa* **house,** *ḱáṅ-pa-la W.* home, at home; in compounds also for a part of the house: **room, story, floor** etc., *steṅ-, bár-, ˏóg-ḱaṅ* upper story, middle story, ground-floor *Glr.; bár-ma, dkyil-ma* or *ɣzúṅ-ḱaṅ* means also the usual dwelling-room, opp. to *ṗugs* and *sgo* (v. *sgo*): *bzó-ḱáṅ* **workshop;** *báṅ-ḱaṅ* **store-house, store-room;** *sgó-ḱaṅ* **entrance, vestibule;** *skór-ḱaṅ* (*Glr.* 68, 9) seems to be a passage running round a building; **šóg-ḱaṅ* W.* the scooping-form or **mould** used in the manufacture of paper; **ṫsás-ḱaṅ** **bed** (garden).

*ḱaṅ-glá* **house-rent.** — *ḱaṅ-čúṅ* house or room reserved for decrepit parents; *ḱaṅ-čúṅ-pa* inhabitant of such; *yaṅ-ḱaṅ-čúṅ-pa* such a person of the second degree, (if, during his life, his son enters into the same right). — *ḱaṅ-stóṅ* **an empty house,** which is thought a fit place for sorcery and necromancy. — *ḱáṅ-bu* 1. little house, **cottage.** 2. **room,** *mya-ṅán-gyi ḱ.* room of mourning *Dzl.* — *ḱaṅ-mig* **room.** — *ḱaṅ-rtsá* **foundation of a house** *Sch.* — *ḱaṅ-žábs* **flooring** of a room. — *ḱaṅ-bzáṅs* **residence,** chiefly of gods. — *ḱaṅ-rúl Sch.* **a house in ruins.**

ཁང་བུ་ *ḱáṅ-bu Pth.* n. of a (fabulous) country.

ཁད་ *ḱad* 1. **litter, barrow.** — 2. **like, as,** = *ltar Glr.* — 3. = *ḱod*, *ḱad-snyáms* v. *ˏḱod-snyóms.*

ཁད་པ་ *ḱad-pa,* 1. the same as *ˏḱód-pa* **to stick fast, to be seized, stopped, impeded,** v. *ˏḱad-pa;* hence also *ma-ḱád* = *ma-ṫág* **as soon as:** *dbugs čad ma-ḱád-du* as soon as the breathing ceases *Thgr.; *de ma-ḱád** instantly, directly, *bu skyes-ma-ḱád čig Glr.* a child born **just now.** — 2. **to approach, draw near,** with *la*, *núb-la ḱád-pai ṫse* when the evening drew near *Pth.*; frq. with the perfect-root of a verb: *dbugs čád-la ḱád-pai dus* when the ceasing of the breath approaches *Thgr.; zin-la ḱad yód-pa-la* as we were just about to seize him; *ḱád-du* postpos. c.a.: *rtíṅ-pa ḱád-du* **as far as** the heel *Mil.; ḱád-kyis* adv. **by degrees** *Mil.; ḱád-la, ḱád-du* id. *Tar.*

ཁན་པ་ *ḱán-pa*, also *ḱén-pa* 1. sbst. *Schr.:* wormwood, probably a mistake for *ḱám-pa.* — 2. vb. **to add** (arithm.) *Wdk.*

ཁན་ད་ *ḱán-da*, more correctly *ḱáṇ-ḍa*, also spelled *ḱá-ˏdá, Ssk*, treacle or molasses partially dried, **candy;** *dé-la ḱán-da bčos-pa* the candy made of it *Med.; skyér-ḱan-da* candied *skyer-pa.*

ཁན་མན་ *ḱan-máṅ* (corrupted from *ḱa-dmaṅ?*) **modest** *Lh.*

ཁབ་ *ḱab* 1. **court, residence** of a prince, *rgyál-poi ḱáb-kyi mi-rnams* courtiers. — 2. **wife, spouse,** *ḱab čén-ma* the first wife (in rank); *dé-la ḱab ˏós-pa ma rnyéd-nas* as there was not found a wife worthy of him *Glr.; ˏdi ɣnyis ṅai ḱáb-tu byúṅ-ba rmis-so* I dreamt that these two would become my wives *Glr.; ḱáb-tu bžés-pa* to take for a wife, to marry. (*Schr.* has even a verb: *čúṅ-mar ḱáb-pa.*) — 3. **needle,** *ḱab-rtse* point of a needle, *kab-rál(?) Sch.* needle-case, *ḱab-mig* eye of a needle, *ḱáb-mig-tu skúd-pa ˏǰúg-pa* or *rgyúd-pa* to thread a needle; *ṗra-ḱáb* a small needle, *sbom-ḱáb, mo-ḱáb Dzl., ṫa ḱáb W., blo-ḱáb W., ḱab-rúl W.* a large, thick needle, packing-needle; *ḱab-spú* **bristle** *Sik.; ḱab-lén (rdo)* **loadstone, magnet.**

ཁབ་ཏ་ཀ་ *ḱab-tá-ka* col. **knapsack, pouch.**

ཁབ་ལེ་ *ḱáb-le* (or *las?*) *W.* **difficult.**

ཁབས་ *ḱabs* n. of a disease *Med.*

ཁམ་ *k̔am* 1. **a bit**, a small piece of anything, *k̔am-čuṅ* a small bit, *k̔am-gáṅ*, *k̔am γčig* a mouthful, *k̔am-ťsád-du γčód-pa* to cut 'in the size of bits' *Dzl.* (infernal punishment); *k̔am-zán* a mouthful of food *Mil.*; *zas k̔am γčig* id. — 3. *W.*, *C.* **appetite**, **zá-če-la k̔am yoṅ** *W.* I get an appetite for eating; **k̔am dig soṅ** *W.* I have no appetite; *k̔am-lóg* want of appetite, **nausea**, aversion (*Cs.* also: hatred); **k̔am-lóg-pa** inclined to nausea, easily sickened *C.*; **k̔am-lóg-k̔aṅ** *W.* id.; **k̔am-k̔ám čo dug, nyiṅ k̔am-k̔ám čo dug** (with *la*) *W.* he has a desire, a longing for, perh. only provincial pronunciation for *rkám-pa*.

ཁམ་ཁམ་ *k̔am-k̔úm* high and low *Schr.* (?)

ཁམ་དར་ *k̔am-dár* **walnut** *Sch.*

ཁམ་པ་ *k̔ám-pa* 1. **fox-coloured, sorrel, brownish.** — **2. porcelain-clay, china-clay.** — 3. **Tanacetum tomentosum**, a very aromatic plant, frequent on high mountains.

ཁམ་ཕོར་ *k̔am-p̔ór* a cup made of dough, used as a lamp in sacrificing.

ཁམ་བིར་ *k̔am-bír* (perh the *Ar.-Hd.* خمیر leaven) thick bread-cakes leavened with butter-milk *Ld.*

ཁམ་བུ་ *k̔ám-bu* 1. **apricot** *B.*, *C.*, *k̔ám-bui ťsi-gu* the stone of an apricot; *k̔am-bu-már* the oil pressed out of apricot-stones, smelling and tasting of bitter almonds *Med.*; *mṅa-rís kám-bu* dried apricots, v. *p̔á-tiṅ*. — 2. **peach** *Sik.* — 3. v. *k̔am*.

ཁམ་གཡག་ *k̔am-γyág Sch.* cherries, morels; these not being known in Tibet, the word must be either of Khotan or Chinese origin, or else the signification of 'stones of apricots' is to be adopted, as given in *Wts.*

ཁམས་ *k̔ams* (*Ssk.* धातु) 1. physical constitution of the body, **state of health**, *k̔ams bdé ba* healthy constitution, good health; *r̀je-btsún-gyi k̔ams bde lágssam?* is your Reverence well? asks a layman, and the Lama answers: *ṅa šín-tu bde; k̔yed k̔ams bde-am?* I am quite well; are you well? *Mil.*; *W.* more frq.: **k̔am-záṅ-po**, *C.* also *k̔am sáṅ* good health; *k̔ams-rmyá Med.*, acc. to *Cs.* **nausea**, feeling sick; *k̔ams-sós Sch.*: rest, comfort, health, prob. more accurately: recreation, recovery, restoration (of health), so: *k̔ams sós-par gyur Mil.*; sometimes it seems to be a synonym of *lus*, body, *k̔ams dúb-pa bséṅba* to recreate the exhausted body *Mil.nt.* fig.: *γnod-sems-méd-pai k̔ams šas če* the peaceable disposition predominates *Stg.* — 2. (synon. of *yul*) **empire, realm, territory, domain**; *yul-k̔áms* empire, in a geographical and political sense, e.g. Nepaul *Glr.*; *rgyal-k̔áms* 1. for *rgyál-poi k̔ams* kingdom, *k̔a-ba-čan-gyi rgyal-k̔áms* the kingdom of Tibet. 2. for *rgyál-bai k̔ams* the empire of Buddha, the world; *rgyal-k̔áms ₒgrim-pa* to roam over the kingdoms, the countries *Mil.*; **region, dominion**, *bar-snáṅ-gyi k̔ams* the aërial regions, where the *lha* live *Pth.*; in physiology: *mk̔ris-pai k̔ams* the dominion of bile *Med.*; *k̔ams γsum* the three worlds acc. to Buddhistic speculation, viz. the earth with the six heavens of the gods, as the 'region of desire', *ₒdód-pai k̔ams*; above this is the 'region of form', *γzúgs-kyi k̔ams*, and ultimately follows the 'region of formlessness', *γzugs-med-pai k̔ams*. — 3. **element** (syn. *ₒbyúṅ-ba*), *k̔ams drug* the six elements of some philosophical systems, consisting, besides the four elements familiar to us, also of *nám-mk̔a* and *rnam-šés*, the ether and the substance of the mind. In chronology, in naming the single years of the cycle, five elements are assumed, which (according to Chinese theory) are wood, fire, earth, iron, water. — 4. p.n. **Khams**, Great Tibet, the parts between Ü and China; *smad-mdo-k̔ams-sgóṅ γsum* the low-land, the three provinces Do, Kham, and Gong, cf. *mṅa-ris*; *k̔áms-pa* a man from Khams.

ཁར་རྟང་ *k̔ar-rstáṅ* v. *k̔á-rtsáṅ*.

ཁར་གོང་ *k̔ar-góṅ* **steatite, soapstone**, *Sch.*, prob. = *dkar-goṅ*.

ཁར་རྐྱང་ k̔ar-rkyáṅ v. k̔a-rkyáṅ.

ཁར་རྩང་ k̔ar-rtsáṅ v. k̔a-rtsáṅ.

ཁར྄སཱ་པ་ཎི or ཁ་སར་པ་ཎ *k̔arsa-pa-ni* or *k̔a-sar-pa-na* n. of a deity *Glr.*; *Tar.* p. 110 gives a (rather absurd) legend concerning the origin of the name.

ཁལ་ *k̔al* 1. (cf. *sgal*) **burden, load,** *k̔al ₒk̔yér-ba* to carry a burden; *k̔ál-gyi stéṅ-du* on the top of the luggage *Glr.*; *k̔al ₒgél-ba* to load a burden, to put a load upon, *k̔al ₒbógs-pa* to take off the burden, to unload; **load, freight;** as a fixed quantity, *lúg-k̔al* a sheep-load, *bóṅ-k̔al* load of an ass; *ₒbrui k̔al* a load of corn. — 2. **bushel,** a dry measure = 20 bre; therefore = a score or 20 things of the same kind; in *W.* **k̔al-ɣčig* frq. for *nyi-šu*, also with respect to persons; *ɣsór-k̔al* a 'measuring-score', 20 *bre*, actually measured, as is usual with corn; *ₒdégs-k̔al* a 'weighing-score', the weight of 20 points on the steel-yard *(rgya-ma)*, in weighing wood, hay, butter etc.

ཁལ་ཁ་ *k̔ál-k̔a* n. of a Mongol tribe, Khal-ka.

ཁལ་ཁོལ་ *k̔al-k̔ól* **stunned, insensible** *Thgy.*

ཁལ་ཅག་ *k̔al-čág* the best sort of wool for manufacturing shawls, coming from Jang-thang.

ཁལ་པ་ *k̔ál-pa* 1. **wether**, castrated ram. — 2. **sow-thistle,** Sonchus.

ཁལ་མ་ *k̔ál-ma* **beast of burden, sumpter-mule** *B.*, *C. k̔ál-ma-rnams bzán-la skyél-ba* to drive beasts of burden to the pasture, to turn them on grass-land *Glr.*; *Schr.*; **mi k̔al nyis-kyi la* C.* payment for carriers and beasts of burden; though in *W.* it might be understood as: payment for twice twenty men.

ཁལ་རི་, ཁལ་རུ་ *k̔al-ri, k̔al-rú*, also *k̔a-ri, k̔a-rú* twenty bushels.

ཁས་ *k̔as* instr. of *k̔a*; *k̔as-lén-pa* etc. v. *k̔a*, 4; *kas-skón* = *k̔á-skóṅ*, q.v.; *kas-stón* with an empty stomach; *k̔as-dmán*, *kas-žán*, **weak, poor.**

ཁི་ *k̔i* numerical figure: 32.

ཁིའུ་ *k̔iu C.*: **k̔yiu** **a cutting-out knife.**

ཁུ་ *k̔u* 1. numerical figure: 62. — 2. for *k̔ú-lu* (?) *Lil.*

ཁུ་གུ་ *k̔ú-gu Cs.* '1. uncle. 2. an address'(?)

ཁུ་ཏུ་ *k̔ú-tu* **a hut, cottage,** constructed of branches *Lh.*

ཁུ་ནུ་ *k̔ú-nu* p. n. **Kunawar,** also Bissáhar, country on the upper Sutledj, bordering on Tibet, and inhabited in the northern part by Tibetans. Here are situated Kanám, a monastery with a considerable collection of Tibetan books, and Poo, a missionary station of the Church of the United Brethren, founded 1865.

ཁུ་བ་ *k̔ú-ba* 1. **fluid, liquid,** also (but less frq.) *k̔u-čú*; *lhuṅ-bzéd bkrús-pai k̔ú-ba*, the fluid in which a beggar's bowl has been washed *Tar.*; *k̔rús-k̔u* dish-wash, swill *Tar.*; *ₒbrás-k̔u Cs.*: rice-soup, *Schr.*: rice-water; *šiṅ-k̔u, rtsá-k̔u* the sap of trees, of plants *Cs.*; *šá-k̔u* broth, gravy; *már-k̔u* melted butter. — 2. **semen virile,** *k̔u-ba byin-pa* emittere semen; *k̔u-k̔rág* the mixture of the semen with the uterine blood, by which process, acc. to Indian physiology, the fetus is formed, *Med.*, *Ssk.* **संक्लेद.**

ཁུ་བོ་ *k̔ú-bo* **uncle,** on the father's side *B.* and *C.*; *p̔a-k̔ú* father and uncle; *ku-dbón* and *k̔u-tsán* uncle and nephew. But owing to polyandry, the degrees of kindred lose their precision, in as far as all the brothers that have become the husbands of one wife may be called 'father' by the children.

ཁུ་བྱུག་ *k̔u-byúg B.*, also *k̔u-gyúg* and *yug.* **cuckoo,** called *byá-yi ryál-po* and described as a sweetly singing bird, whence prob. *Cs.* has conjectured nightingale, which however is scarcely known in Tibet. — *k̔u-byug-rtsá* n. of a medicinal herb.

ཁུ་མག་ *k̔u-mág Lh.* purse, money-bag, col. for *k̔ug-ma.*

ཁུ་ཚུར་ *k̔u-tsúr Cs.* the clinched hand, **fist,** *k̔u-tsúr snún-pa (Sch.* also *rgyáb-pa)* to strike with the fist. This signification, however, seemed not to be known to the Lamas consulted, who interpreted the word: a religious gesture, the fore-finger being raised, and the others drawn back. Some native dictionaries have मुष्टि fist, others खटक half-closed fist.

ཁུ་ཡུ་ *k̔u-yú*, in *C.* also *'*a-yú**, **hornless,** having no horns, used of cattle *Sch.*

ཁུ་ལུ་ *k̔ú-lu* 1. the short woolly hair of the yak. — 2. *Lh.*: venereal disease, **syphilis.**

ཁུ་ལེ་ *k̔ú-le Sch.*: **steel-yard** and its weight; but *Dzl.* ༢༠, 17 the word refers to an ordinary pair of scales and denotes that **scale** of the two which contains the weights.

ཁུག, ཁུགས་ *k̔ug*, *k̔ugs* **corner,** concave angle, **nook;** of rivers, lakes etc.: **creek, bay, gulf, cove,** also *ču-k̔úg; k̔úg-tu* within a recess, on the farther side of a cavity.

ཁུག་ཏ་ *k̔úg-ta* (or *rta*), *a-li-k̔úg-ta*, a kind of **swallow** *Cs.*; the lights (lungs) of this bird are used as a remedy against pulmonary diseases, *Med.*

ཁུག་རྣ་ *k̔ug-rná* and *k̔ug-sná* **fog, mist, haze,** during a calm, esp. in spring-time.

ཁུག་པ་ *k̔úg-pa* I sbst. 1. *Cs.*: "part of a long period of time" (?) — 2. a certain part of the body *Med.* — II. vb. 1. also *k̔úgs-pa*, **to call** = *gúg-pa Mil.* (cf. also *γyaṅ*). — 2. **to find; get, earn;** *nor k̔úgs-pa-aṅ srid* there is a possibility that we may yet replenish our cash *Mil. nt.*; *γnyid k̔úgs-pa* to get sleep; *sraṅ γsum k̔ugs*, it drew i.e. weighed three ounces.

ཁུག་མ་ *k̔úg-ma* **pouch,** little bag, *me-lčags-k̔ug-ma* tinder-pouch *Mil.*; *dṅúl-k̔ug* money-bag, purse; **rdzóṅ-k̔ug** *Pur.* knap-sack; *rtsám-k̔ug*, resp. *žib-k̔ug*, little bag for flour; *nú-k̔ug* sucking-bag, for babies.

ཁུང་ *k̔uṅ* **hole, pit, hollow, cavity,** originally used only of dark holes and cavities; *sna-k̔úṅ* nostril, *rna-k̔úṅ* the ear-hole, *mčan-k̔úṅ* arm-hole, arm-pit; *brag-k̔úṅ* cleft in a rock, cavern; *byi-k̔úṅ* mouse-hole; *čab-k̔úṅ* a sink; *bso-k̔úṅ* peep-hole; *mda-k̔úṅ* loop-hole; in *C.* *'*i-k̔úṅ*, *mig-k̔úṅ*, *te-k̔úṅ** are used of any hole in walls, clothes etc., caused by decay or daily wear. *γtor-k̔úṅ* a sink, gutter; *k̔úṅ-dregs* soot of an oven or chimney *Sch.*; *k̔úṅ-pa*, *k̔úṅ-po Cs.* a large hole, *k̔ún-bu* a small hole, e.g. *spui k̔ún-bu* pore, passage of perspiration *Dzl.*

ཁུངས་ *k̔uṅs* 1. the original meaning perh. is **mine, pit** *Cs.* — 2. **origin, source** (fig.), *γyoi k̔uṅs snubs*, he stopped the source of the deceit *Ld.-Glr. Schl.* 13, b. *k̔úṅs-čan*, and prob. of similar meaning *k̔uṅs-btsún*, of noble descent, or when applied to statements etc.: well founded; *Cs.* also fine, excellent; *k̔uṅs-méd*, *k̔uṅs ṅán-pa* having no 'origin', mean, pitiful, ill founded; in the last sense it seems to be used of historical accounts, *Tar.* 43, 5, and more esp. of religious records *Pth.*, *Glr.*; *γtam-k̔úṅs Tar.* 66, 18, prob.: historical source, record, document; in *Pth.* facetiously: *γtam-k̔úṅs čaṅ yin* the source of that speech is beer.

ཁུད་ *k̔ud* **coat-lap,** or any cloth serving in an emergency as a vessel; **k̔ụ' ze'** hold forth the lap of your coat, words frequently used to beggars, to whom the alms, chiefly consisting in flour, are poured into that receptacle, *C.*

ཁུད་པ་ *k̔úd-pa* **pocket, pouch** *Sch.*

ཁུད་མ་ *k̔úd-ma* **side, edge** *Cs.*; *k̔úd-du* aside, apart, secretly; *k̔úd-du ̥jog-pa* to put, to lay aside.

ཁུན་ཏི་ *k̔ún-ti*, or **k̔yen-ti**, is stated to be used in *Pur.* for **he, she.**

ཁུན་པ་ *k̔ún-pa* **to grunt** *(Sch.: to groan).*

ཁུན་བུ་ *k̔ún-bu Glr.* 97, 12?

ཁུམ(ས)་ *k̔um(s)* v. *̥gum-pa*; *k̔úms-pa*, **crooked.**

ཁུམས་ *kums Sch.*: so it is said; *Mil.*: *ló-tsťsa-bai snyán-pa rgyáṅ-nas kums* might be rendered: the interpreter's renown was proclaimed from afar; the word, however, is of rare occurrence.

ཁུར་ *k̔ur* 1. **burden, load,** for men, more fully: *mi-k̔ur*; *k̔úr-skyed-pas ̥tsó-ba žig* one that lives by carrying loads *Tar.* — 2. rarely **porter,** carrier of a load; *ḱúr-po* **load, burden;** *ḱúr-bu,* col. **ḱúr-ru** prop. a small load; a load in general; *ḱúr-pá* carrier, cooly; *ḱur-rtsá, ḱur-lám* cooly-station, a day's journey, gen. 10 to 12 English miles; *ḱur-rtsá-pa* a station-cooly.

ཁུར་བ་, འཁུར་བ་ *ḱúr-ba, ˳ḱúr-ba* 1. sbst. *Cs.:* **bread, food,** *Sch.* also forage, fodder. It is, however, not the common word for bread, but only for certain sorts, such as *bra-ḱúr,* bread of buckwheat, *rtsabs-ḱúr* q.v., and more particularly it is applied to cakes and pastry-work baked in fat or oil. — 2. vb. v. *˳ḱúr-ba.*

ཁུར་མ་, ཁུར་མང(ས) *ḱúr-ma, ḱur-máṅ(s)* **dandelion** *C.,* used as a pot-herb and medicinal plant; as the former it is also called *ḱur-ṫsód.*

ཁུར་ཚོས་ *ḱur-ṫsós C.* and *B.* **cheek,** the ruddy part of the face below the eyes (cf. *˳grám-pa); *ḱur-tsóg* W.*

ཁུལ་ *ḱul* 1. *Sch.:* "the soft **down** of furs", abbreviation of *ḱú-lu; ḱul-mal* small basket for wool *Ts.* — 2. **ravine** *Kun.* — 3. **district, province, domain;** *lhá-sa ḱul* all that belongs to Lhasa *Georgi Alph.,* **dei ḱul-la ˳dug** is subject to him *C.*

ཁུལ་མ་ *ḱúl-ma* the bottom, or the side of a thing *Cs.*

ཁེ་ *ḱe* numeral, ninety-two, 92.

ཁེ་, ཁྱེ་ *ḱe, ḱye (Sch.: ḱe-ma)* 1. **profit, gain;** *ḱe-spógs B.* and *C.,* **ḱe-béd** *W.* id.; *ḱe-tsóṅ byéd-pa* **to trade,** to traffic *Pth.; šés-ḱyi ḱe* gain, advantage obtained by knowledge and attainments; *ḱe-pa* **tradesman,** dealer; *ṫsóṅ-˳dus ḱé-pa* trader in a market *Mil.; ḱe-nyén Sch.;* profit and loss, risk; *ḱe-sgrúb-pa Cs.,* **ḱye-béd ṫób-če** *W.,* to make profit, to gain, *ḱe brgyáb-pa,* to make a good bargain *Sch.;* **ḱe-ru ˳do-wa** *C.* to abate, to go down in price; **ḱé-čan, ḱe-me**, profitable, unprofitable; **ḱyé-mo** *W.* **cheap.** — 2. **tetter, herpes, ringworm** (eruption of the skin) *Sch.*

ཁེགས་ *ḱegs* v. *ḱegs.*

ཁེངས་པ་ *ḱéṅs-pa* 1.partic. of *˳ḱéṅs-pa,* filled, replete with. — 2. adj. puffed up, **proud, haughty,** arrogant; sbst. pride etc.; *ḱeṅs-séms, ḱeṅs-drégs* pride. *ḱeṅs-po Med.* with reference to food: producing flatulence.

ཁེན་པ་ *ḱén-pa* 1. *Schr.* worm-wood, prob. erron. for *ḱám-pa.* — 2. *Sch.:* to lean, to repose on, erron. for *bḱán-pa.*

ཁེབས་ *ḱebs,* col., *W.:* **ḱyebs**, *Cs.: ḱébs-ma* **covering,** coverlet: **ḱeb sáṅ-pa**, to take the covering off *C.; čár-ḱebs* a covering against rain, rain-cloak; *stéṅ-ḱebs, lčóg-ḱebs,* table-cloth *Cs.; ṫód-ḱebs Lt.* **cap, hood;** *γdúṅ-ḱebs,* a certain beam or board above the capital of a pillar; *γdóṅ-ḱebs,* **veil,** cloth to cover the head; **dún-ḱyebs** *W.* **apron;** **paṅ-ḱéb** *C.* **napkin, apron.**

ཁེམ་ *ḱem* v. *ḱyem.*

ཁེར་རྒྱག་པ་ *ḱér-rgyag-pa,* **to defraud; to usurp** *Sch.*

ཁེལ་བ་ *ḱél-ba* prob. for *˳ḱél-ba,* **to load** upon; *blo ḱél-ba* is said to be used in *C.* for *blo skyél-ba W.,* v. *skyél-ba* no. 6.

ཁེས་ཉེན་ *ḱes-nyén* the day before yesterday *Sch.*

ཁེས་པ་ *ḱés-pa C.* **to hit,** *˳ṫsáms-la* (or *mtsáms-la?)* to hit the right thing, the exact point or line; *γnád-la* to strike the vital parts, to hit mortally, fatally.

ཁོ་ *ḱo* 1. numeral, 122. — 2. *Bal.* (**χ'o**) for *ḱa-ba,* bitter.

ཁོ་ *ḱo* pers. pron. of the third person, **he, she, it,** but almost exclusively in col. language. In ancient writings it occurs but rarely, being either omitted or supplied by *de,* but in later works that come nearer to the present language, it is to be found the more frequently. *ḱoi* his, her; **ḱó-pa, ḱó-wa** plur. **they,** *W.* and *C.,* v. *Georgi Alph.,* in an edict; **ḱó-čag, ḱó-ṫso** id. *C.;* **ḱó-wa nyi** *W.,* both of them: *ḱo-ráṅ* 1. he himself. 2. he, = **ḱo** col.; with partic.: *ḱo dá-či sṅon la soṅ-ba de, Mil.,* he that just went on in advance, proceded in front.

Note. The word prob. has been originally a sbst., denoting essence, substance (like ṅó-bo); má-ko, γzi-ko, rgyú-ko are said to be used in C. for: the essential, the most important part of a thing, the main point, and the noun substantive may possibly have changed into a substantive pronoun, in a similar manner, as ṅa, I, is connected with ṅó-bo; cf. also kó-na, kó-bo.

ཁོ་ཏི ko-ti C. (Chinese?) **tea-kettle.**

ཁོ་ཐག་གཅོད་པ ko-ťág γčód-pa c. termin. **to despair of** Mil.; **to resign, to acquiesce in, to reconcile one's self to**; also sems ko-ťág γčód pa Pth.

ཁོ་ན kó-na adj. and adv. 1. **just, exactly, the very**, rgyál-pos ˳dod-pa kó-na yin that is just what has been wished for by the king Dsl. ༢༥. 17. sṅá-ma kó-na bžín-du just as before; ˳di kó-na yin-par ṅes he is evidently the very same (man) Mil.; srin-bu kó-na ˳drá-ba just like a worm Thgy.; tsul de kó-nas by the very same process Tar. 13, 12; de kó-na nyid-du gyur čig just so may it happen! (at the conclusion of a prayer) Glr.; but de-ko-na-nyid, as a philosophical term, is also the translation of the Ssk. táttva, essentiality, truth, implying to the Buddhist nothing but **vacuity**, the Nirvâna Trig. 20. — 2. **only, solely, exclusively**, skád-čig kó-na, only for a moment Dzl. ༢༥༢, 12. ˳dod kó-nas brél na, if taken up merely with lust: séms-čan kó-na bdé-bar ˳dód-tsa-na as he intended only the welfare of beings Thgy.; Tar.

ཁོ་བོ kó-bo mas., kó-mo fem. pers. pron. 1st. person, I, pl. kó-bo-čag we, indiscriminately as to the rank of persons, B. and C.; mi kó-boi rnam-šés the soul of me the man, i.e. my human soul Mil.; also pleon. kó-bo ṅa.

ཁོ་བོམ ko-bóm, the Tibetan name for **Khatmandu**, the capital of Nepaul Glr., Mil.; sometimes also called klui p̣o-bráṅ, prob. on account of the mineral treasures supposed to abound in that country.

ཁོ་མ kó-ma, perh. misprinted for kom **knapsack, wallet** Mil., or else a secondary form of that word.

ཁོ་གཡུ ko-γyú, occurs only in *ko-yú skór-če (perh. col. for ˏkor-γyúl) W. **to thrash**, which is done by driving a number of oxen fastened together round a pole that stands in the middle of the thrashing-floor.

ཁོ་ར kó-ra, Cs. also kór-sa, **circumference;** circumjacent space; also **fence**, surrounding **wall**; kó-ra kor-yúg-tu, (kor-) kor-yúg-tu, in a circle, in circumference, frq. in measuring; also round about, all round, e.g. to flow, to encompass; kor-yúg kún-tu in the whole circuit, round about.

ཁོ་ལག ko-lág 1. Cs.: **bigness**, robustness (Lex. पीवरगात्र), ko-lág-yáṅs-pa big, prominent limbs; Sch.: ko-lág čé-ba a large space. — 2. Lh.; **dumpling**, made of rtsám-pa and beer; Ld.: **pap** of rtsám-pa and tea, called spags in C.

ཁོག kog 1. frq. for koṅ(-pa), **the interior, inside**; v. also kóg-pa and kóg-ma. — 2. for kogs, ˏkogs q.v. — 3. for ˳gégs-pa.

ཁོག་པ kóg-pa, sometimes kóg-ma, kog, the trunk of the body, ša-kóg the body of an animal cut up for food; *ša-kóg ḍál-če, šig-ce* to cut up a carcass; *kóg-tu, kog náṅ-du* within the body.

ཁོག་མ kóg-ma C. **pot**, earthen vessel = p̣ru; kog-čén large pot.

ཁོགས kogs **cough** Med., kógs-pa to cough.

ཁོང koṅ, rarely kóṅ-pa, pers. pron. 3d. person, **he, she**; like ko it is of far less frequency in the earlier literature than in the later; at present it is in W. used as the respectful word for he, but in C., acc. to Lewin, as plur., = they; kóṅ-gi his, her; pl. kóṅ-rnams, kóṅ-čag, kóṅ-tso, kóṅ-čag-rnams; koṅ-rán and koṅ-nyid he himself; rgyál-po koṅ-ráṅ yin dgóṅs-nas the king supposing that he himself was meant Glr.

ཁོང་པ kóṅ-pa 1. prov. for kóṅ-pa. — 2. **the inside**, inward parts, prov. kóg-pa (Cs. also: the veins); kóṅ-du, kóṅ-na, kóṅ-nas adv. and postp. **in, within, from**

ཁ

**within, out of;** *ḱóṅ-du* (also *ḱoṅs-su*) *čúd-pa* or *ṫsúd-pa*, with or without *sems* (resp. *ṫugs*) being prefixed 1. **impressed on,** fixed in the mind, thoroughly understood, known. 2. very restless, **uneasy, sorry, anxious** in one's mind; — *ḱóṅ-du sdú-ba* to impress on the memory, to learn (by heart) *Glr.*; *ḱóṅ-nas snyiṅ ṗyúṅ-ba ltar* as if their heart was torn out, *Pth.*; *snyiṅ ḱoṅ rús-pai dkyil-nas γsól-ba btab* he prayed from his inmost heart *Thgy.*; *ḱóṅ-nas šés-pa, smrá-ba* to know by heart, to say, recite by heart *Cs.* **ḱóg-la yid-du med* W.* I have no recollection of it; *ḱóṅ-pai dród-la ṗan* it helps against internal heat *Med.*; *ḱóṅ-par sóṅ-bai dug bžin-no* it is like a poison that has entered into the internal parts (or the veins) *Thgy.*; **ḱóg-paṅḱan-pa**, a bad character *W.*, **ḱóg-pa čén-mo* W.* generosity, magnanimity (?) —

**Comp.** *ḱoṅ-krág*, the blood contained in the veins *Cs.* — *ḱóṅ-ḱro (-ba)* **wrath, anger;** *ḱóṅ-ḱro spóṅ-ba Mil.* to put away, subdue anger, **zá-ba* C.* to 'conceive' anger, take a dislike; *ḱóṅ-mi-ḱro-ba* quiet, calm, mild *Pth.* — **ḱog-ṭ́úg** col. uneasiness, **sorrow, anxiety;** **ḱog-ṭ́úg ǰhé-pa* C.*, **čó-če* W.* to be uneasy, anxious. — *ḱoṅ-gáṅ* full, filled up in the inside, **solid,** *ḱoṅ-stóṅ* **hollow, tubular.** — **ḱog-ṫén, ḱog-ḍén**, *W.* grudge, ill-will, **hatred.** — *ḱoṅ-ṫsil* **suet.** — **ḱoṅ-lóg* W.* **cholera.** — **ḱog-šiṅ* W.* 1. **the core** of a tree, heart-wood. 2. **tenon.** — **ḱog-šúgs** **a groan, sigh** *W.*, **ḱog-šúgs táṅ-če** to sigh, to groan. — **ḱog-šúbs-la sil-če* W.* to read low, softly, whisperingly; **ḱog-sil táṅ-če* W.* to read noiselessly, so as not to be heard. — *ḱoṅ-(γ)seṅ* inner caverns, not opening to the daylight; (those of the Ririab are the habitations of the Lhama-yin or Asura).

ཁོངས་ *ḱoṅs* 1. sbst. *(ḱóṅs-ma Cs.?)* **the middle, the midst;** *gaṅs-ḱóṅs-na* in the midst of alpine snows *Mil.*; respecting time: *žág bdún-gyi ḱóṅs-su* **within, during,** seven days *Pth., Tar.*; respecting money: *de nyid-kyi ḱóṅs-na γnás-so*, (this) is contained, included in that (sum) *Tar.* ༣༢, 15; *ḱóṅs-su γtógs-pa Lex., Cs.:* annexed to, united, incorporated with. — 2. adj. **crooked;** *W.:* **ḱoṅs ča dug** it is **bent, curved,** e.g. paper by heat, the limbs by the gout; **ḱóṅs-kan* W.*, **ḱoṅ-ril* C.* **crippled.**

ཁོད་ *ḱod* I. v. *ḫód-pa* and *ḫgód-pa*. — II. inst. of *ḫod*.

ཁོན་པ་ *ḱon-pa* **anger, grudge, resentment;** *ḱon ḫdzin-pa, ḱón-du ḫdzin-pa* to hate, **ḱón-la ḱúr-če* W.* id.; **ḱon-gúg-ste dád-če* W.* ("to sit waiting with hatred") id.; **ḱon-bér* W.*, the sting, the burning of anger or hatred in the soul.

ཁོབ་ *ḱob* 1. fat, heavy, clumsy *Sch.* — 2. sometimes for *ḫob*. — 3. v. *ḫpebs-pa*.

ཁོམ་ *ḱom* **wallet, leather trunk** *C., Cs.:* felt or skin bag; *γzims-ḱóm Cs.* id. (prob. resp.); *ḱom-ḫbóg Cs.* a cloak-bag; more accurately: the cloth in which the trunk is wrapped and carried by the porter.

ཁོམ་པ་ *ḱóm-pa Schr.*; to be able, esp. **to be enabled** to do a thing by the absence of external impediments; *ḱóm-pa min Cs.*, **ḱóm-če mi rag* W.* I have no time, I cannot do it now; *sdod mi ḱom* I cannot sit and wait now *Pth.*; *mid mi ḱóm-par* without your having time to swallow it down *Dzl.* ༡༧༠, 17. *mi-ḱóm-pa brgyad*, the eight obstacles to happiness, caused by the re-birth in places or situations unfavourable to conversion *Trig.* no. 66. Acc. to *Schr.* the word is also used in that special sense: to be able to carry on a law-suit, to which there are likewise eight obstacles.

ཁོར་མོ་ཡུག་ *ḱor-mo-yúg Sch., ḱor-yúg, ḱór-sa* v. *ḱó-ra*; *ḱor-yúg-tu* **continually, incessantly** *Mil.*

ཁོལ་ *ḱol Cs.* = *ḱól-bu*; *ḱól-du ṗyúṅ-ba*, **abridgment,** epitome *Cs.*

ཁོལ་པ་ *ḱól-pa* 1. *Cs.* **boiled.** — 2. *Sch.* **boiling, bubbling,** *zaṅs ḱól-pa* a bubbling kettle *Dzl.*

ཁོལ་པོ་ *ḱól-po*, also *ḱol-bráṅ*, **servant,** man-servant, *ḱól-por ṙǰés-su bzúṅ-ba* to take, to hire for a servant *Pth.*; frq. fig. *séms-kyi k̔ól-por γda* (the body) is a servant of the mind *Mil.*; *ȷig-rtén srid-pai k̔ól-po* a servant of the world i.e. of mammon *Mil.*

ཁོལ་བུ་ *k̔ól-bu* **a small piece**, *k̔ól-bu nyúṅ-ₒbru tsam žig kyaṅ ma lus Pth.* not so much as a grain of mustard seed is left.

ཁོལ་མ་ *k̔ól-ma* 1. *Cs.* 'anything boiled'; perh. more accurately: anything boiling, *ču k̔ól-ma* **boiling** water; *dúg-mtso k̔ól-ma* a boiling lake of poison. — 2. *Sch.*: an outlet for the smoke in a roof.

ཁོལ་མོ་ *k̔ól-mo* 1. **maid-servant** *B.* — 2. a coarse sort of **blanket** usually given to slaves *Schr.*—3. mowed corn, **a swath** *C.*

ཁོས་ *k̔os* v. *gés-pa.*

ཁོས་པ་ *k̔ós-pa* **wished for,** wanted *Sch.*

ཁྱ་ལེ་ *k̔yá-le Cs.*, **k̔á-le* W.*, as much as fills the hollow of the hand, **a handful,** e.g. of water.

ཁྱག་པ་ *k̔yág-pa* to lift, v. *ₒkyog-pa.*

ཁྱག(ས)་པ་ *k̔yág(s)-pa* 1. **frozen; ice.** — 2. **the frost, cold,** *k̔yág-t̔og-k̔ar* on the ice *Glr.*; *k̔yág-pa ₒk̔yág-pai bód-yul* 'Tibet frozen up with frost' *Pth.*; **k̔yág-la ȷar* (v. *byór-ba*) **soṅ* W.* it has stuck fast by freezing. — **k̔yag-žu-ko-kö* Ts.* mud caused by a thaw, **snow-water.** — **k̔yág-sran-čan* W.* hardened against the cold. — *k̔yag-rúm, k̔yag-róm* ice, pieces of ice, floating blocks of ice (also *čab-róm*); cf. *ₒk̔yag-pa.*

ཁྱད་ *k̔yad* 1. **difference, distinction** *B., C., W.* **gaṅ táṅ-na k̔yad med* W.* it is no matter which you give me; *ṅá-daṅ-p̔rad-pa dáṅ k̔yad-méd-do* it is quite the same as if they came to myself; *séms-la k̔yad byuṅ* a difference of opinion arose. — *k̔yad-ₒčos* mark of distinction. — 2. **something excellent, superior,** *bzoi k̔yad, bzo-k̔yád* an excellent work of art *Glr.*; *bsgrúb-pai k̔yad yoṅ* prob.: it shall be instantly performed in the very best manner *Pth.* — *k̔yad-nór* the principal or chief wealth *Cs.* — *k̔yad-dón* the principal sense *Sch.* — 3. syllable employed to form abstract nouns. A transition to such formations appears in the following sentence: *dkar-nag-čós-kyi če-k̔yád blta Mil.* we wish to examine the difference of greatness or worth of the white and the black religion; so also whenever a certain measure is given, and in general, when such abstract nouns are used in a relative sense, as: *mt̔o-k̔yád* **height,** *zab-k̔yád* **depth,** *p̔yug-k̔yád* **wealth.** — 4. **part, division,** the same as *k̔yád-par* 2; **sa-k̔yád* W.* **place,** corresponding exactly to **sa-ča* C.*

*Derivatives.* **kyeʼ-tsar-čeṅ** = *ṅó-mtsar-čan* wonderful *C.* — *k̔yád-du* adv. especially, particularly, *k̔yád-du ₒp̔ágs-pa* particularly (uncommonly) lofty, sublime *Glr.* *k̔yád-par* adv. = *k̔yád-du Glr.* 50, 7, and more frq. sbst.: 1. **difference, dissimilarity** *B.* and *C.*, *ṅa daṅ k̔yod γnyis k̔yád-par-če* I and you — that is a great difference *Glr.*; *de daṅ kyád-par-ma-mčis-pai rten* an image not differing from this *Glr.*; *míṅ-gi k̔yád-par yin* it is (only) a difference of name *Glr.* — 2. **sort, kind,** *ₒbrás-bui k̔yád-par kun* all sorts of fruit; *ri-dvágs-kyi k̔yád-par žig* a particular kind of game; perh. also: **division, part,** *yúl-gyi k̔yád-par* **province** *Tar.* ༢༠. 14. — 3. = *k̔yad* 2. something of superior qualities, an excellent man *Tar.* ༣༠, 7. *k̔yád-par-čan* **superior, excellent, capital,** *blá-ma k̔yád-par-čan čig Mil.* an excellent spiritual teacher; *k̔yád-par-du* adv. **particularly,** chiefly, especially. Rather obscure as to its literal sense, but of frq. use is the phrase *k̔yád-du γsód-pa, γsád-pa*, c. accus. but also dat., **to despise,** e.g. *dmá-la* an inferior, *rgyu-ₒbrás* the doctrine of retribution, *ṅyon-móṅs-pa* trouble etc.

ཁྱབ་ *k̔yab* v. *k̔yáb-pa.*

ཁྱབ་པ་ *k̔yáb-pa* **to fill, penetrate; to embrace, comprise,** c. accus., also dat., *mi-ȷtsáṅ-bas k̔yáb-pai sa-p̔yógs* a place full of dirt *Thgy.*; *ₒbrúm-pa máṅ-pos* full of, quite covered with pustules, pocks *Med.*; *mk̔rís-*

*pas* filled, impregnated with bile *Med.*; *lus sems dga-bdés ḱyáb-par gyúr-nas* body and soul (filled with) full of joy *Glr.*; *bar ḱyáb-pa* to fill up an intermediate space; **to make** (a country etc.) **full** of light, religion, happiness, frq.; *ťams-čád-la driṅ-gyis* to embrace all creatures with benevolence; *kún-la ḱyab-pa* in grammar: capable of being joined to any word, comprising all of them, *Glr.*; *ḱyab-čé-ba* comprehensive; used also in the way of censure: everywhere and nowhere, to be met with everywhere *Mil.*; *ḱyab-γdál* or *rdól* comprehensive, extensive. — *ḱyab* seems also to be a sbst. in *ḱyab-čé-ba*, and still more so in *rgya bod yoṅs ḱyáb-tu grágs-pa-la* according to what is spoken in the whole compass of India and Tibet *Tar.* 87.

ཁྱབ་འཇུག་ *ḱyab-ǰúg* **Vishnu,** a Brahmanical divinity, appearing, like Brahma and Shiva, also in Buddhist legends, yet principally known in his quality as *γza-sgra-γčan-ₒdzín* (Râhula), conqueror of the demon that threatens to devour sun and moon; hence *ḱyab-ǰug-γzér Med.*, **ḱyab-ǰúg-gi nad* W.*, **ra-hu-lẹ nẹ* C.*, **epilepsy.**

ཁྱམས་ *ḱyams Cs., Sch.* **yard, court-yard,** *Cs.* also gallery. It is, like *ťsoms*, a space that is to be found in many Tibetan houses, and may be compared to the compluvium of the Romans, being open in the middle, and on the sides generally enclosed by verandas. *Ḱyams* may therefore be called court-yard, when it is on the same level with the ground, (so also perh. *Tar.* 89, 4, reading *ḱyams-su* for *ₒḱyams-su)*; but in the upper stories such a construction is unknown in European architecture. *Ḱyams-stód* the upper court-yard, *ḱyams-smád* the lower one; *ḱyams-ťóṅs Cs.*: 'impluvium'.

ཁྱམས་ *ḱyams Cs.*: p. n. = *ḱams*, v. *ḱams* 3.

ཁྱམས་པ་, ཁྱར་པ་, ཁྱལ་པ་ *ḱyáms-pa, ḱyár-pa, ḱyál-pa* v. *ₒḱyáms-pa*, etc.

ཁྱི་ *ḱyi* **dog,** *ḱyi rmug B.* and *C.*; the dog bites, *W.*: barks; **so tab* W.*; bites; **ťam* W.* lays hold of; *ḱyi bós-nas ma brduṅ* proverb: if you call the dog, then you must not beat him *Glr.* — *ḱyi rkaṅ-γnyis Sch.* 'a bastard dog, a cur' (?) — *ḱyi-skád* the barking. — *ḱyi-ḱáṅ* **dog-kennel,** — *ḱyi-gu* **a puppy.** — *ḱyi-rgán* an old dog. — *ḱyi-rṅó* the itch of dogs. — *ḱyi-dám* 'dog's seal', a mark burnt in; **stigma** *C., W.* — *ḱyi-dúg* poison of hydrophobia *Sch.* — *ḱyi-mdúd-pa* the pairing of dogs *Sch.* — *ḱyi-pul* **dog-kennel, dog-house.** — **ḱyi-pal-ǰór* W.* Blitum virgatum. — *ḱyi-spyáṅ W.* **jackal.** — *ḱyi-p̀o* a male dog. — *ḱyi-brú Sch.* a vicious, biting dog. — *ḱyi-sbráṅ* dog's fly. — *ḱyi-mo* a female dog, **bitch.** — *ḱyi-smyón* canine madnes, **hydrophobia** *C., W.*; also mad dog = *ḱyi smyón-pa.* — *ḱyi-rdzi* dog-keeper. — *ḱyi-γžóṅ* trough for dogs and other animals, **manger.** — *ḱyi-šig* **flea.**

ཁྱི་གུ་ *ḱyi-gu* 1. v. *ḱyi.* — 2. *W.* **bud** (of leaves and branches, not of blossoms), **eye** (of a plant).

ཁྱི་ར་ *ḱyi-ra* **chase, hunting,** esp. of single huntsmen, not of a party; stable-stand, cf. *liṅs*; **ḱyi-ra-la čá-če* W.* to go a hunting, **ḱyi-ra čo-če, gyáb-če, gyúg-če** id.; **ḱyi-ra-la čá-ḱan** hunter, sportsman; *ḱyi-ra-ba B.* and *C.*, **ḱyi-ra-pa* W.* huntsman.

ཁྱི་རོང་ *ḱyi-róṅ* p.n., v. *skyid-gróṅ.*

ཁྱི་ལ་ཝ་རི་ *ḱyi-la-wa-ri* a sort of treacle made of *seṅ-ldeṅ Wdṅ.*

ཁྱིག་ *ḱyig* v. *ₒḱyig-pa.*

ཁྱིད་ *ḱyid* breadth of the hand with the thumb extended, a span.

ཁྱིམ་ *ḱyim (Ssk.* गृह) 1. **house,** not as a building, but as a dwelling-place of man, **a home.** Even when in *Sik.* they speak of **šiṅ-ḱyim, nyúg-ḱyim** a house of wood, of bamboo, the idea of habitation, dwelling-place predominates in these expressions. *ḱyim-na* at home, *ḱyim-du* home (to go home); *ḱyim daṅ ḱyim-na* house for house, each in his house *Tar.* 151. 22; *ḱyim spó-ba* to remove to another place; *ḱyim skyóṅ-ba* to have a household, to gain a livelihood; *Kyim-gyi so-tsis* household, housekeeping, farming; *Kyim-gyi rig-pa* knowledge, experience in housekeeping and farming; *Kyim-med-pa* homeless, without a home; therefore esp. as opp. to the life of a homeless and unmarried priest: *Kyim-gyi byá-ba* or *las*, 1. domestic business, 2. lay-life, worldly life; cf. also many of the compounds. *Kyim-la ˎóṅ-ba, γtóṅ-ba* to get married, to be given in marriage, respecting the female part *Glr., Mil.* — 2. **the signs** of the Zodiac, which is called *Kyim-gyi ˳Kór-lo*, viz. *lug* ram, *γlaṅ* bull, *˳Krig-pa* (pairing) twins, *kárkata (Ssk.)* crab, *séṅ-ge* lion, *bú-mo* virgin, *sraṅ* balance, *sdig(-pa)* scorpion, *γžu* (bow) archer, *ču-srin* (sea-monster) capricorn, *búm-pa* water-bearer, *nya* fishes. To these 12 signs however the corresponding Tibetan figures are not ༡ to ༡༢, but o to ༡༡, as seems to be the usage in astronomical science. There is moreover a division into 27 'lunar mansions' much in use; v. *rgyu-skár*. — 3. **double-hour,** the time of two hours; or the twelfth part of the time of the apparent daily rotation of the heavens and consequently also of the zodiac, or, as we should say, the time of the passing of a sign of the zodiac through the meridian. — 4. *Cs.:* **halo,** or circle round the sun or moon. — 5. Symbolic numeral: 12.

**Comp. and deriv.** *Kyim-táb(s)* **husband,** frq.; also wife; *Kyim-táb-la γtóṅ-ba* to give in marriage, to give away a woman for a wife; *Kyim-táb-mo* **wife,** housewife, *Cs.* — *Kyim-bdág* master of the house, **husband;** owner of a house, **citizen;** *Kyim-bdág-ma* fem. — *Kyim-pa* 1. **layman,** 2. *Cs.:* surrounded by a halo *(Kyim* 4); *Kyim-pai p̔yógs-su sbyin-pa* given away to laymen *Dzl.; Kyim-par ˳dug* or *γnas* he lives as a layman; *p̔yis Kyim-pai tsúl-čan-gyi rnál-˳byor-pa* a devout man, who lives outwardly like a layman *Mil.* — *Kyim-pa-pa* **a houseowner, peasant, farmer, husband;** *Kyim-pa-ma* **housewife.** — *Kyim bya* **domestic fowl, cock, hen, poultry** *W., C.* — *Kyim-mi* family of a house, household *Cs.* — *Kyim-tsáṅ* id. — *Kyim-tsér Glr.* 51, 10, usually *Kyim-mtsés, Kyim-mtsés-pa*, fem. *Kyim-mtsés-ma* **neighbour.** — *Kyim-žág, Kyim-zlá, Kyim-ló* 'a zodiacal day, month, year' (?) *Cs.* — *Kyim-sa* earth, **dust,** dirt (in a house), **sweepings** *W.*, **Kyim-sa dú-ce, spúṅ-ce* to sweep (a floor), to sweep together.

ཁྱིམ་ཉ་ *Kyim-nya Sch.:* **whale** (if at all correct, it must be taken as mythological signification, no Tibetan having ever known of the existence of real whales).

ཁྱུ་ *Kyu, Kyú-bo Cs., Kyú-mo Pth.* **flock, herd,** *lúg-Kyu* a flock of sheep, *mdzó-mo-Kyu* a herd of bastard cows, *γnág-Kyu* of horned cattle; *Kyu skóṅ-ba* to keep, tend a flock or herd; **company, band, gang, troop,** *mi-Kyu Cs.* a company of men, *bú-mo-Kyu* a bevy of girls, *dmag-Kyú* a troop of soldiers; *Kyú-nas ˳búd-pa* to exclude from the company *Pth., C.; Kyu-sná ˳drén-pa* to go before, to take the lead of a troop, a flock *Mil.; Kyu-mčóg* **bell-wether;** also the most distinguished amongst a number of men, the first, **chief, head** *Pth., Kyu-mčóg-ma* fem.; *Kyu tságs-pa* vb.n., *Sch.* to collect, to gather in flocks.

ཁྱུ་ *Kyu Sch.* 'ell', prob. incor. for *Kru.*

ཁྱུ་བྱུག་ *Kyu-byúg* acc. to *Lex.* = *ku-hú.*

ཁྱུག་ *Kyug* v. *˳Kyúg-pa.*

ཁྱུང་ *Kyuṅ (Sch.* also *Kyúṅ-mo)* the Garuda bird, a mythical bird, chief of the feathered race. *Kyúṅ-šog-čan* = *p̔yag-rdór.*

ཁྱུང་དཔྱད་ *Kyuṅ-dpyad* a small round **basket** of reed *Cs.; Kyuṅ-ril* is said to be in *C.* a large cylindrical basket, the same as *kun-dúm Ld.*, v. *rkón-pa.*

ཁྱུང་སྡེར་ *Kyuṅ-sdér* ('Garuda claw') *Med., Cs.:* n. of a medicinal root, pseudo-zedoary; *Kyuṅ-rgód Med.* id (?).

ཁྱུད་ *Kyud* v. *˳Kyúd-pa.*

ཁྱུད་མོ་ *Kyúd-mo* **rim** of a vessel *Sch.*

ཁྱུར་མིད་པ་ *kyur-mid-pa* **to swallow** *Med.*; *kyur-mid-du sóṅ-ste* suffering himself to be swallowed (from the story of an Indian idol) *Pth.*

ཁྱུས་ *kyus* wall-side *Ts.* (?)

ཁྱེ་ *kye* 1. for *kyeu Mil.* — 2. for *ke* q.v.; *kyé-mo* v. *ke.*

ཁྱེ་མ་ *kyé-ma* n. of a disease *Med.*

ཁྱེའུ་ *kyeu* (diminutive of *kyó-bo?*) 1. **male child, infant boy.** 2. **youth, adolescent** *B.*

ཁྱེད་ *kyed* pers. pron. 2nd. person, **thou,** and particularly in the plur. **you,** in *B.* eleg., in addressing superiors, but also used by superiors in speaking to inferiors, and even contemptuously: *kyed ltá-bui má-rabs* such vulgar, mean people, as ye are *Dzl.* — *kyéd-kyi* thy, your. — *kyed-ráṅ* (*kyed-nyid* seems to be little used) thou thyself, you yourself; plur. particularly expressed: *kyéd-čag, kyéd-rnams, kyed-tso; dge-tsúl kyéd γnyis* you two Getsuls *Glr.*; *kyed γsúm-po* you three (a mother speaking to her sons) *Glr.*; *kyéd-čág* you, when speaking to one person *Glr.*, = *nyid-čag.*

ཁྱེད་ *kyed* 1. = *kyid W.* 2. v. *ₒkyéd-pa.*

ཁྱེན་ཏི་ *kyén-ti Pur.* **he, she,** v. *kún-ti.*

ཁྱེབས་ *kyebs* v. *kebs.*

ཁྱེམ་ *kyem* (*Sch.* also *kem*) **a shovel,** *W.*: **kyem daṅ páṅ-če** to shovel away, to remove with a shovel; *kyém-gyi ₒdáb-ma* the blade of a shovel, *yú-ba* the handle of it *Cs.* — *gru-kyém, ču-kyém W.* **oar,** *lčags-kyém* **spade;** *me-kyém* fire-shovel; *wa-kyém* a scoop, hollow gutter-shaped shovel *Cs.*; *kyém-bu* spoon *Cs.*

ཁྱེར་ *kyer* v. *ₒkyé-ba; kyér-so* v. *ₒkyer-so.*

ཁྱོ་ *kyo B.* frq., also *kyó-po Pth.* 1. **man** (seldom). 2. **husband,** *kyo byéd-pa* ('to act a husband' cf. *byed-pa* I. 1) to take a wife; *kyod ṅai kyo mi byéd-na* if you do not marry me *Dzl.* — *kyo-méd* **single, unmarried.** — *kyó-mo* wife *Cs.* — *kyo-šúg* husband and wife, married couple; *kyo-šúg γnyis grógs-nas soṅ* these two married people went together; *kyo-šúg mdzá-ba-rnams* a loving couple; *kyim-bdag kyo-šúg γnyis* the citizen with his wife; *γsér-lha kyo-šúg γnyis* about the same as: Mr. and Mrs. Serlha; *kyo-šúg-tu sdú-ba* to join a couple in marriage *Dzl.*

ཁྱོ་ག་ *kyó-ga* 1. **man** emphatically, as: *skyés-bu ṅa hór-pa yaṅ kyó-ga yin* we Turks are men, too; **hero,** *kyó-ga-pa* id. — 3. **heroic deed, exploit.**

ཁྱོག་པོ་ *kyóg-po* **crooked, curved, bent;** *Cs.* also cunning.

ཁྱོག་ཐོང་ *kyog-toṅ* (v. *kyó-ga* and *toṅ*) *W.* **young man, youth.**

ཁྱོགས་ *kyogs* **litter, bier** *Pth.*, **palanquin** *Cs.* also scaffold (?) *Cs.*

ཁྱོང་ *kyoṅ* v. *kyóṅ-ba.*

ཁྱོད་ *kyod* pers. pron. 2nd. person sing. and plur., **thou, you;** *kyod-kyi* thy, thine, your; if plurality is to be especially expressed, it is done by adding *čag: kyód-čag Mil.*; occasionally also *kyód-rnams*, cf. *kyed; kyod-ráṅ* 1. thou thyself, you yourself. 2. thou, you (*W. *kyo-ráṅ**).

ཁྱོན་ *kyon* **size, extension, width, circumference, area, height** e.g. of Dzambuling *Dzl.*, of the Sumeru *Glr.*, of the lunar mansions or the zodiac *Glr.*; *kyon-yáṅs-pa* a wide extent, *kyoṅ-yáṅs sa-γži* all the wide world (earth); *kyon-sdóm Cs.* 1. narrow-extent. 2. sum, contents. — *kyón-nas* **thoroughly,** *kyón-nas mi sdíg-čan* thoroughly a sinner; *kyón-nas med* not at all *C.*

ཁྱོམ་ཁྱོམ་ *kyom-kyóm* 1. **oblique, awry,** irregularly shaped.—2. v. *ₒkyóm-pa.*

ཁྱོར་ *kyor* (*Cs. kyór-pa*) as much as fills the hollow of the hand, **a handful,** cf. *skyor; kyor gaṅ, kyor re* one handful, *kyor do* two handfuls.

ཁྱོལ་བ་ *kyól-ba* v. *ₒkyól-ba; kyós-ma C.* = *skyós-ma, skyás-ma.*

ཁྲ་ *kra* 1. a small bird of prey, **sparrow-hawk, falcon,** used for hunting, also *bya-krá; kra-žúr Sch.*: a species of eagles; *krá-pa* falconer. — 2. v. the following article.

ཁྲ་བོ་ *krá-bo* perh. also *krá-mo* **piebald,** two-coloured, (not many-coloured, which is *bkrá-ba); rgya-stág-krá-bo* the streaked Indian tiger *Mil.; *ta-tá* C.* id.; **ta-wo-pi-wo, ta-si-pi-si* W.* id. (spelling uncertain); *nag-krá* black-spotted, so that black is the predominating colour of the whole; *dmar-krá* red-spotted, red being the predominating colour. — The significations of the various compounds of *kra* have all a reference to the peculiar effect produced on the eye by the blending of two or more colours together, especially when seen from a distance; so: *kra-čam-mé Glr.* is said of a rainbow-tinted meteor, *kra-lam-mé Mil.*, (or *lham-mé,)* of a similar phenomenon, *kra-čem-čém Pth.* of a flight of birds; **ṭa-čám-se, ṭa-čem-mé, ṭa-čém-se* C., *čam-ṭá-ṭiṅ-ṅé* Ld., *ṭa-šig-ge' ṭa-ʼčig-ge, ṭa-róg-ge* C.*, — all these seem to be of nearly the same import. — These compounds have also assumed the character of an adverb, signifying, **together, altogether,** *kra-me-ré Mil.* id.

ཁྲ་མ་ *krá-ma* 1. *Cs.* **register, index.** — 2. *C.* **judicial decree**. — 3. a species of grain, acc. to *Wdṅ.* = *mgyogs-nás* a kind of barley growing and ripening within 60 days; v. *nas.*

ཁྲག་ *krag* (in *Bal.* still pronounced **krag** elsewhere **ṭag**), *Cs.:* resp. *sku-mtsal,* **blood;** **ṅal-ṭág, žaṅ-ṭág* W.* vulg. blood discharged by menstruation, from which, acc. to some authorities, **paṅ-ṭág** blood of the childbed is to be distinguished; *γzuṅ-krág* healthy, nourishing blood *Cs.; nad-krág* bad blood *Cs.: krag ʼdón-pa, W. *tón-če**, to bleed a person; *γtár-ba* id.; *krag γčód-pa* to stop, to stanch the blood; *krag čád-pa* vb. n. to cease to bleed, cessation of bleeding; **nyiṅ-ṭág ʼkól-la rag* W.* I feel my blood boiling, e.g. from ascending a steep hill; *krag ʼdzág-pa* menstruation (the plain undisguised expression): *krag čág-pa* clotted blood, gore *Cs.; krag-šas-čé-ba* plethoric *Med.*

**Comp.** *krag-ʼkrúgs Sch.:* agitation, flutter, orgasm of the blood. — *krág-čan* bloody, e.g. *ral-gri.* — *krag-γčód* n. of a medicinal herb *Med.*, *krag-čags-rtá* a 'blood-bred' horse, i.e. a real horse, opp. to a metaphysical one *Mil.* — *krag-ʼtúṅ* a class of terrifying deities *Thgr.* — **ṭág-tuṅ-bu* W.* **leech.** — *krag-γzér W.* rheumatic pain (?) — *krag-ró* clotted blood (?) *Med.* — *krag-liṅ* a clot of blood. — *krag-šór* hemorrhage, bloody flux (?) *Med.*

ཁྲག་ཁྲིག་ *krag-krig* one hundred thousand million, an indefinitely large number *Cs.;* acc. to *Lex.* = प्रयुत one million, cf. *dkrigs-pa.*

ཁྲག་ཁྲུག་ *krag-krúg Cs.* **complicate, confused;** *Zam.:* like a troop of fighting men, or like the loose leaves of a book, when out of order.

ཁྲག་ཁྲོག་ *krag-króg Lt.?*

ཁྲང་ *kraṅ* v. *mkraṅ.*

ཁྲད་པ་ *krád-pa Cs.* stretched out; *krád-por sdód-pa* to sit (with the legs) stretched out (?). *krád-por skyé-ba Wdṅ.* a botanical term applied to the leaves of plants.

ཁྲབ་ *krab* shield, buckler; coat of mail, scales *Sch.;* acc. to oral communication the word in the first instance denotes **scale** (scale of a fish), and secondly **coat of mail**; consequently *kráb-čan* 1. scaled, scaly. 2. mailed, armed with a coat of mail; *krád-mkan* armourer *Glr.*

ཁྲབ་ཁྲབ་ *krab-kráb* 1. a weeper, one that sheds tears on every occasion *Sch.* — 2. *Mil.* 92, 4?

ཁྲམ་ཁ་ *krám-ka* **a cut, a notch** (in wood), lines cut into wood so as to cross one another, as an ornament; *krám-šiṅ* a club-like implement, carved in the manner just mentioned, representing the attribute of a god. *nyag-krám* a notch.

ཁྲམ་པ་ *krám-pa* I. *C.:* **a liar,** *slu-bar byéd-pai krám-pa Pth.; krám-ma* fem. *Cs.; ka-krám* a lie *Mil.; krám-sems-čan* **lying, mendacious** *Mil.* — II *W.:* 1. **lively, brisk, quick,** like boys, kids etc. (the contrary of *γlén-pa* slow, indolent, apathetic); **ṭám-pa čo* W.* a wish of good speed, addressed to one going on a journey, such as: good success! may all go well! — 2. **modest,** attentive to the wishes of others.

ཁྲལ་ *kral (Lex.* དཎྜ punishment) 1. **punishment, chastisement** for sins, **visitation;** in this sense the word is said to be used still, but much more frq. it signifies 2. **tax, tribute, duty,** service to be performed to a higher master; *kral sdú-ba* to collect taxes, *jál-ba, skór-ba* to pay taxes, *bkál-ba* to impose taxes; *dṅúl-kral* money-tax, tax to be paid in money, *brú-kral* corn-tax, tribute paid in corn, *til-már-kral* tax, tribute to be paid in sesame-oil.

ཁྲི་ *kri (Cs. kri-ma), kri-krág, kri-tsó* **ten thousand,** a myriad, *kri pyed daṅ ɣnyis* 15 000; *nyi-krí* 20 000; *bži-kri* 40 000; *brgyad-kri bži-stóṅ* 84 000, a number frq. occurring in legends.

ཁྲི་ *kri,* also *kriu,* seldom *kri-bo,* resp. *bžúgs-kri,* **seat, chair; throne; couch; frame,** sawing-jack, trestle etc.; **gya-ṭi** an Indian (Anglo-Indian, European) chair; *čós-kri* a professorial chair, pulpit *Pth.,* reading-desk, table for books, school-table; **nyé-ṭi** (v. *snyé-ba*) a contrivance to rest the head on when sleeping on the ground *W. nyál-kri,* resp. *ɣzím-kri,* bed-stead; *sén-ge-kri* throne; *kri-la bskó-ba* to raise on the throne; *kri-la ḱód-pa* to preside, to hold the chair. — As the Tibetans generally sit on the bare ground, or on mats, or carpets, chairs are rather articles of luxury.

**Comp. and deriv.** *kri-ɣdúgs* po. **the sun.** — *kri-pa Cs.* **a chairman;** one sitting on a throne. — *kri-pán* 1. *Cs.:* the height of a chair, a high chair. — 2. *mčod-rtén-gyi kri-pán* the same as *baṅ-rím.* — *kri-mún* or *món Pth., Tar.,* **prison, dungeon.** — **ṭi-šiṅ, ṭiu-šiṅ*,* the common, plain word for chair.

ཁྲི་ལེ་བ་ *kri-le-ba* **fear** *C.* (?)

ཁྲིག་ཁྲིག་ *krig-krig* 1. *so krig-krig byéd-pa* to gnash, grind the teeth *Mil.; ɣzúgs-po* to shiver, shake with cold, terror, rage *Mil.* — 2. col. for *tig-tig.*

ཁྲིགས་ *krigs* **plentiful, abundant** *Sch.; za-ḱóg krigs-se* silk-fabrics, silks, in abundance *Mil.; krigs-se gaṅ* quite full *Sch.; krigs-se byéd-pa* to treat, to entertain plentifully *Sch.*

ཁྲིད་, འཁྲིད་ *krid, krid,* **instruction, teaching;** *krid débs-pa* to give instruction, to instruct, *krid-pas-čog* I am willing to give you instruction, you may have lessons with me *Mil.; krid bšád-pa* to give instruction, to make admonitory speeches, to give parenetical lectures; *krid záb-po* thorough instruction; *slu-krid* instruction to an evil purpose, seduction, v. *slú-ba; sna-krid Lex.* guide, leader. — *krid-mḱan* col. teacher. — *krid-prúg* scholar, pupil. — *krid-pa* v. *krid-pa.*

ཁྲིམས་ *krims* 1. **right,** not in the abstract sense in which the word is generally understood with us, but in more or less concrete applications, such as administration of justice, law, judgment, sometimes also implying **custom, usage, duty.** Accordingly *rgyál-po,* or *btsún-po krims-méd* means an unjust king, an unprincipled priest or ecclesiastic; *krims bžin-du, krims daṅ mtun-par* conscientiously, justly; in conformity with custom, duty, law; *čos-krims* religious right, coming nearest to our abstract right; when, for instance, in *Glr.* king Sroṅ-btsan-sgam-po says: *rgyál-krims čós-krims-su bsgyur* I have changed the right of a king into that of religion, he means to say: I have subjected my own absolute will to the higher principle of universal right. A somewhat different sense conveys *Glr.* 97, 4: *čós-krims jig-pai gros byas* they conspired to extirpate the religious principle of administration. — 2. **law,** *dgé-ba bču daṅ ldán-pai krims* a general law, founded upon the ten virtues *Glr.; des čós-krims daṅ rgyál-krims ɣnyis ɣtán-la pab,* he regulated the spiritual and secular law *Glr.* 97, 1.; *bka-krims* resp. law, as a collection of precepts, **decree, commandment;** *krims čá-ba* to enact a law, to publish a decree, frq.; *krims sgróg-pa* to proclaim an edict; *mťó-ba ḱrims-kyis γnon* he limited the power of the nobility by laws *Glr.*, *ḱrims-yig* code of law *C.*; *ḱrims* also a single **precept, rule, commandment** *Dzl.*; *Burn.* I, 630. — 3. **administration of justice,** *čós-kyi ḱrims* the ecclesiastical, *dpón-gyi ḱrims* the secular civil, exercised by the *ḱrims-dpon*; *lugs γnyis-kyi ḱrims* a twofold jurisdiction, a combination of the ecclesiastical and secular administration of justice (as it existed among the Jews); *ḱrims srúṅ-ba* to observe, to act according to right, custom, duty; also to exercise jurisdiction, to govern, to reign; to bridle, to keep in check *Glr.* 95. 9.; *ḱrims byéd-pa* id. ni f. — *ťsúl-ḱrims* a spiritual precept or duty; also a frequent man's name. — 4. **action, lawsuit,** *W.* also **ṭim-šágs** or only **šags*; *gaṅ žig ṭim-si p̔i-la** *W.* for the sake of some law-suit, **ṭim táṅ-če** to sit in judgment, to try, to hear causes; **ṭim čō'-pa** *C.* = **ṭim táṅ-če** *W.*, means also to pass sentence, to punish, **ṭim ḍág-po tóṅ-wa** to inflict a heavy punishment; *mi-la ḱrims-bčad p̔og* he incurs, suffers punishment *Pth.*; **ṭim žú-če** *W.* to go to law, to commence an action; **ṭim žú-ḱan** *W.* plaintiff; **ṭim táṅ-ḱan** *W.* magistrate, judge; *ḱrims-dpon B.*, *C.*, *W.*, superior judge, chief-justice; **ṭim-kyi dág-po** *C. id.*; *ḱrims-γyóg* apparitor, beadle *Cs.*; *ḱrims-pa* lawyer, advocate *Cs.* (seems to be little used); *ḱrims-ḱan* court, court of justice, tribunal; *ḱrims-ra* id.; place of execution. — 5. **use, custom, usage** — that power to which people in general show the readiest obedience, and which in every sphere of life forms the greatest obstacle to reforms and improvements.

ཁྲིལ་ *ḱril* v. *ˏḱril.*

ཁྲིས་ *ḱris? ḱris-ˏǰágs* **peace,** v. *ˏǰags.*

ཁྲུ་ *ḱru (ḱrú-ma Cs.)* **cubit,** a measure of eighteen inches, from the elbow to the extremity of the middle finger. The average height of a man is assumed to be four cubits, that of a short man three. — *ḱru ˏǰál-ba* to measure with a cubit measure *Cs.*

ཁྲུ་བ་ *ḱrú-ba* sometimes for *ˏḱru-ba.*

ཁྲུ་གཟར་ *ḱru-γzár* a kind of **stew-pan** *Sch.*

ཁྲུ་སློག་ *ḱru-slóg* a pit filled with corn (?) *Sch.*; in *Mil. ḱru-slóg-pa* stands for digging, breaking up the soil, gardening.

ཁྲུང་ཁྲུང་ *ḱruṅ-ḱruṅ* (*Ssk.* क्रौञ्च) **crane,** Grus cinerea.

ཁྲུན་ *ḱrun* **height, length, extension** *Lex.*, *Cs.*

ཁྲུལ་ *ḱrul* 1. *ḱrul γtoṅ-ba* to let fall, **to drop** (several things at intervals), *mči-ma* tears *Mil.* — 2. **da-ṭúl** *W.* **intercalary month.**

ཁྲུལ་པོ་ *ḱrúl-po* *C.* 1. **cheerful, merry.** — 2. **fornicator.**

ཁྲུལ་མ་ *ḱrúl-ma* 1. *W.* **ḱú-wa ṭúl-ma** crooked handle, **crank** (spelling uncertain). — 2. *C.* **a whore.**

ཁྲུམ་ཁྲུམ་ *ḱrum-ḱrúm*, *Sch.*: *ḱrum-ḱrúm byéd-pa*, *Lt.*: *ḱrum-ḱrúm brdúṅ-ba* **to pound** in a mortar.

ཁྲུམས་སྟོད་ *ḱrums-stód*, and *-smád*, two Nakshatras, v. *rgyu-skár* ༢༥.

ཁྲུས་ *ḱrus* 1. pf. of *ˏḱru-ba.* — 2. sbst. **bath, washing, ablution;** *ḱrús-ḱu*, water for bathing, washing or rinsing; dish-water; *ḱrus byéd-pa* to bathe, to use baths *Dzl.*; *ḱrús-la ˏgró-ba* to go to bathe *Dzl.*; *ḱrus γsól-ba* resp. to take a bath *Glr.*, also to administer a bath to another (cf. *γsól-ba*) *Glr.*, *Pth.*; esp. as a religious ceremony, consisting in the sprinkling with water, and performed, when a new-born infant receives a name, when a person enters into a religious order, or in diseases and on various other occasions (cf. *Schl. Buddh.* p. 239, where the word is spelled *bkrus*). Therefore 3. **baptism,** and *ḱrus γsol-ba* **to baptize** *Chr. R.* and *P.*— *ḱrús-kyi rdziṅ*, pond, pool for bathing; *ḱrus-ḱáṅ* bathing-room or house; *ḱrus-sdér* basin, washing-bowl *Sch.*; *ḱrus-búm* sacred watering-pot; *ḱrus-γžóṅ* bathing-tub *Sch.*; *ḱrus-γsér* bathing-water *Sch.*, but in *Lt.* this word relates to a certain medical procedure or method of curing.

ཁ

ཁྲེ ḱre (Ssk. प्रियङ्गु) **millet**, ḱre-čáṅ Murwa-beer *Sik.*, v. *Hook. Himal. Journ.*

ཁྲེ་ཚེ *ḱre-tsé* Chinese **vermicelli** *C.* (*ṭ́e-tse*).

ཁྲེགས་པ *ḱrégs-pa* v. *mḱrégs-pa.*

ཁྲེལ *ḱrel*, resp. *ťugs-ḱrél* 1. **shame, shamefacedness, bashfulness, modesty;** **ṭ́el káb-ce** W. v. *gébs-pa.* — 2. **piety,** esp. *W.* — 3. *C.* **disgust, aversion.**

**Comp. and deriv.** — *ḱrel-gád* a scornful laughter. — *ḱrél-can Cs.* bashful, timid; *W.* **pious, faithful, conscientious.** — *ḱrel-ltás, ḱrel-ltos*, dread of wicked actions; *ḱrel-γdoṅ* (lit. a face capable of shame) id. — **ṭ́él-dad-can, ṭ́él-ₒdod-can** W. fond of making others ashamed. — *ḱrel-ldán* = *ḱrél-can.* — *ḱrél-ba* vb. to make or to be ashamed, **ṭ́el soṅ** he was ashamed, **ṭ́él-ce mi yoṅ** W. he is not put to shame; *C.* also: to get into a passion; sbst. shame, *ḱrél-ba daṅ ṅó-ťsa-ba med* he has no shame nor dread *Dzl.*, **ṭ́él-wa yod** W. it is a shame. — *ḱrel-méd (-pa), W. *ḱrel-méd- (ḱan)* shameless, insolent. — **ṭ́él-ₒo** object of disgust, *C.* — *ḱrél-yod* **chastity, modesty, decency,** *ḱrél-yod-pa* chaste etc., *ḱrél-yod-par byéd-pa* to behave chastely etc. — *ḱrel-šór* = *ḱrel-méd.*

ཁྲེས་པོ *ḱrés-po Thgy.* **load, burden,** = *ḱur.*

ཁྲོ *ḱro* 1. a kind of **bronze,** of about the same quality and worth as *ₒḱár-ba*, but inferior to *li*, q.v.; *ḱró-ču* liquid, melted bronze; *ḱró-čus sdóm-pa* to fill up joints, grooves etc. with melted bronze, to solder *Glr.* — 2. **kettle** *Schr.*

ཁྲོ་པ *ḱró-pa W.* for *ḱrod.*

ཁྲོ་བ *ḱro-ba* 1. **anger, wrath,** (cf. *ₒḱró-ba* vb.) frq; *ḱóṅ-ḱró-ba* inward anger *Thgy.* — 2. **angry, wrathful** *Cs.*; *ḱró-bar byéd-pa, ₒgyúr-ba* to be, to grow angry *Cs.*; *ḱró-bo*, fem. *ḱró-mo* angry, fierce, ferocious, e.g. *γcan-γzán* a ferocious beast; esp. applied to the 54 (or 60) deities of anger and terror (भैरव), e.g. *ḱró-ba-čén-po* = *γšin-rje* the ruler of hades; **ṭ́o-túm-po** furious with rage, raging with anger *C.*: *ḱro-γnyér* distortion of the face by anger; *ḱró-ba-ma, ḱró-ba-can* she whose face is wrinkled with anger, n. of a goddess *Glr.* 17, 12. — **ṭ́o-ṭ́á** W. **dissatisfaction, grumbling.** — *ḱro-món Sch.* prison (perh. *ḱri-món*). — *ḱro-žál* an angry, frowning countenance *Glr.*

ཁྲོག *ḱrog?* — *ḱrog brgyáb-pa* to drink hastily, to gulp down *Glr.*; *ḱrog-ḱrog* plump! the sound caused by something falling heavily on the ground *W.* — *ḱrog-smán* the raw, unprepared substance of a medicine *Sch.*

ཁྲོག་པོ *ḱróg-po* botanical term, used of leaves standing round the stem scattered or alternately.

ཁྲོང་ངེ *ḱroṅ-ṅé* **upright, straight, erect,** (cf. *ḱroṅ*,) *Glr., Mil.*

ཁྲོང་པོ *ḱróṅ-po, *ťóṅ-po* Ts.* **close-fisted, stingy.**

ཁྲོད(པ) *ḱród (-pa), W. *ťó (-pa)** **crowd, assemblage, mass, multitude;** *mi-ḱród* a troop, crowd of men, *ri-ḱród* an assemblage (mass) of mountains; *rtsva-ḱród* a heap, stack, rick of hay; *nags-ḱród* a dense forest, *mun-ḱród* thick darkness; *dur-ḱród* cemetery where the corpses are cut into pieces for the birds of prey; *dei ḱród-du lha-γcig ₒjóg-pas* placing the princess among their (the girls') company *Glr.*; in *W.* **ťó-pai náṅ-na** and **náṅ-du** c. genit. is the usual expression for **among.**

ཁྲོན *ḱron* **claw, fang;** *ḱrón-kyis rkó-bai sde* the class of the gallinaceous birds *S.g.*

ཁྲོན་པ *ḱrón-pa* 1. **well, spring.** — 2. *Lh.*: a wooden **water kennel;** *ḱrón-bu* a little well; also n. of a medicinal herb, a purgative against bilious complaints *Med.* *ḱron-rágs* enclosure of a well *Sch.*

ཁྲོམ *ḱrom* 1. **market-place, market-street, bazar;** *ḱrom skór-ba* to wander, to ride round the market *Glr.*, to ramble through; *γsaṅ-sṅágs króm-du klog* secret spells (magic formulas) are read in the market (a crime and sacrilege in the eyes of a Buddhist). — 2. **crowd of people,** multitude of persons; *ḱrom-čén* a great crowd; *ťsógs-pai ḱróm-rnams* the assembled crowd *Pth.*; *ṗo-ḱróm* a multitude of men; *rgyal-ḱróm* prob. an assembly, a gathering of kings *Mil.*; *ḱrom dmar-nág* ˛*ḱyil-ba* a motley crowd, throng of people *Pth.*

**Comp.** — *ḱróm-čén (po) Thgr.* chief market-place, principal street *Cs.* — *ḱróm-dpon* overseer, police-officer who is charged with the supervision of the market. — *ḱróm-skor-ma* harlot, strumpet *Cs.*

ཁྲོམ་པོ་ *ḱróm-po Glr.*, n. of a province (?), *ḱróm-po-pa* an inhabitant of it.

ཁྲོམ་མེ་ *ḱrom-mé* sparkling, glittering, *zil-pa ḱrom-mé* a sparkling dew-drop *Pth.*

ཁྲོམས་ *ḱroms* v. ˛*grém-pa.*

ཁྲོལ་ *ḱrol* 1. v. ˛*ḱról-ba* and ˛*gról-ba.* — 2. **a sound;** *ḱról-gyis soṅ Glr.* (the ring) slid sounding (across the azure-floor); *ḱrol-dóṅ* is said to denote a large hand-bell, and *ḱrol-lóg* the same as *ḱrog-ḱróg W.* — Cf. ˛*ḱról-ba.* — 3. kettle (?) v. *lčags.*

ཁྲོལ་ཁྲོལ་ *ḱrol-ḱról* adj 1. **bright, shining,** = *ḱról-po.* — 2. *ḱrol-ḱról byéd-pa Glr.*, **mig ṭol-lé ṭol-lé tá-wa** *C.* to stare, *la,* at.

ཁྲོལ་ཆ་ *ḱról-ča* the act of forgiving, pardon *Sch.*

ཁྲོལ་པོ་ *ḱról-po* 1. **sparkling, glistening, dazzling,** e. g. water when the sun shines upon it; **'od ṭól-po** *W.* brightness, splendour. — 2. **distinct, intelligible,** **(s)pé-ra ṭól-po zer mi śe(s)** *W.* he cannot speak distinctly.

ཁྲོལ་མོ་ *ḱról-mo W.* **brittle, fragile,** opp. to *mnyén-po.*

ཁྲོལ་ཚགས་ *ḱrol-tságs Lex., Cs.* **a sieve.**

ཁྲོས་པ་ *ḱrós-pa* v. ˛*ḱró-ba.*

མཁན་ *mḱan,* an affix to substantives and verbal roots, denoting 1. one who knows a thing thoroughly, making a trade or profession of it, *sá-mḱan* one who knows the country, the road, a guide, a pilot (*Dzl.* ༢༧༥, 7); *lám-mḱan* id. *Mil.*; *śiṅ-mḱan,* worker in wood, carpenter, joiner etc. — 2. affixed to a verbal root, it is often (at least in later literature) equivalent to the periphrastic participle, signifying: he who in any special case performs an action; so ˛*dógs-mḱan Glr.*, one who is binding, fastening; also with an objective case: *ṅai bú-mo* ˛*dód-mḱan Glr.* such as are courting my daughter; *bsád-mḱan* the man having killed, the murderer. — 3. In colloquial language, esp. in *W.*, it has on account of its more significant form entirely displaced the proper participle termination in *pa:* **dúṅ-ma ḱyer-ḱan-ni mi** *W.* the men carrying the beam; contrary to its original signification, it is even used in a passive sense: **sád-ḱan-ni lug** *W.* the slaughtered sheep.

མཁན་པོ་ *mḱán-po (Ssk.* उपाध्याय, पण्डित) a clerical teacher, **professor,** doctor of divinity, principal of a great monastery, **abbot,** who, as such, is endowed with the *mḱan-rgyúd*, or spiritual gifts, handed down from Buddha himself by transmission, viz. *dbaṅ, luṅ, ḱrid;* next to him comes the *slób-dpon*, or professor in ordinary. *mḱán-po ťón-mi sámbho-ṭa* Dr. Thon-mi Sambhoṭa; *mḱán-mo* **mistress, instructress** *Cs.*: *mḱán-bu* **pupil, scholar** *Tar.*; *mḱan-čén* a great Doctor, a head-master; *mḱan-slób* for *mḱán-po daṅ slób-dpon*, e.g. *blá-ma mḱan-slób-kyi bka* the words of the Lamas, abbots and masters; also for *mḱán-po daṅ slób-ma Glr.* 100, 4. — *mḱan-rábs* the series or succession of the abbots in the great monasteries *Cs.* — *mḱan-rím* the respective prospects of being elected abbot, as depending on the different ranks of the expectant individuals.

མཁའ་ *mḱa (Ssk.* ख) 1. **heaven, heavens,** gen. *nam-mḱa; mḱa-la* in the heavens, *mḱá-la ṗúr-ba, rgyú-ba, ldiṅ-ba* to fly, wander, soar, in the air. — 2. **ether,** as the fifth element. — 3. symb. num.: **cipher, naught.**

**Comp.** — *mḱa-klóṅ, mḱa-kyáb, mḱa-dbyiṅs* the whole compass or extent of the heavens *Cs.* — *mk̔a-ˌgró-ma*, in *Mil.* gen. *mk̔a-p̔ro-ma*, *Ssk.* **डाकिनी**, fabulous beings of more modern legends, 'wise' women of supernatural powers, sometimes represented like angels, at other times like fairies or witches. — *mk̔a-mnyám Lex.* like the heavens, infinite. — *mk̔a-ldiṅ* the sky-soarer, the bird Garuda, v. *k̔yuṅ*. — *mk̔a-spyód* wanderings through heaven *Tar.* 112, 4, also: enjoyment of heaven, enjoying or inhabiting heaven; *mk̔a-spyód-du γšégs-pa* to go to heaven, to die *Mil.*

མཁར་ *mk̔ar* 1. resp. *sku-mk̔ár*. *Glr.*, **castle**, nobleman's seat or mansion, manor-house, frq.; **citadel, fort** *Pth.*; **house** in general *Mil.* — 2. termin. case of *mk̔a*.

**Comp.** — *mk̔ar-dpón* governor of a castle, commander of a fortress. — *mk̔ar-lás C.* and *B.*, the work of constructing a castle, of raising an edifice; **k̔ar-lén* W.* id. — *mk̔ar-srúṅ* the guard or garrison of a castle, fortress *Cs.* —

མཁར་བ་ *mk̔ár-ba* 1. (also *ˌk̔ár-ba*) *B.* and *C.*, **staff, stick**; *mk̔ar-γsil* staff of the mendicant friars, the upper part of which is hung with jingling rings; *p̔yag-mk̔ár* resp. for *mk̔ár-ba*. — 2. **bronze, bell-metal**, v. *ˌk̔ár-ba*.

མཁལ་མ་ *mk̔ál-ma* **kidney, reins**, *mk̔ál mdog* 'kidney-colour, dark red' *Cs.*

མཁས་པ་ *mk̔ás-pa Ssk.* **पटु**, (originally like σοφός) **skilled; skilful**, in mechanical work, and so it is frq. used in col. language; further in a more general sense: *smán-pa mk̔ás-pa* a skilful, clever physician; **experienced, learned, prudent, shrewd, wise**; c. accus. or dat., in a thing; *so-tsis-la* in farming, *č̔os* in religion; *slób-ma skyóṅ-ba-la mk̔ás-pa* an able tutor, pedagogue *Mil.*; *mk̔as-btsun-bzáṅ* prop. denotes the qualities of a right priest: learned, conscientious, good, but sometimes it indicates only the position in society, the clerical rank, so esp. *mk̔as-btsún* learned clerics, reverends *Glr.*, *mk̔ás-po* or *-pa* a learned man, **a scholar**, *sṅón-gyi mk̔ás-po-rnams* learned men of former times; *mk̔as-grúb* id., *rgya-gár-gyi mk̔as-grúb-rnams* Indian scholars; it is also used like our 'most wise', 'very learned', and similar expressions in a pompous address *Glr.*; *mk̔as-mč̔óg* profound scholar *Zam.* I never found the word applied to inanimate things in the sense of 'wisely contrived', and the correctness of *Cs.*: *t̔abs mk̔ás-pos* 'by wise means' may be questioned.

མཁུན་པ་ *mk̔ún-pa Sch.* v. *k̔ún-pa*.

མཁུར་ཚོས་ *mk̔ur-ts̔ós* v. *k̔ur-ts̔ós*.

མཁོ་བ་ *mk̔ó-ba* **desirable**, to be wished for, *mk̔ó-bai yo-byád*, in *C.* also **k̔o-ǰhe**, desirable things, **requisits**, wants, desiderata; **hindu-t̔én-gyi mi-la k̔ó-wẹ ts̔oṅ-zóg** articles of commerce, goods, commodities, such as they are called for in Hindostan; *nyé-bar mk̔ó-ba* indispensable, most necessary. Cf. *ˌk̔o*.

མཁོས་ཕབ་ *mk̔os-p̔áb Lex.* v. *ˌk̔os*.

མཁྱུད་པ་ *mk̔yúd-pa Cs.*: to keep, to hold, to embrace, = *ˌk̔yúd-pa*; *dpe-mk̔yúd Lex.* w.e.; *Cs.*: unwillingness to lend books, *dpe-mk̔yúd-čan* unwilling to lend books, *dpe-mk̔yúd byed-pa* to be unwilling to lend books; *mk̔yud-spyád* a sort of bag or vessel for carrying something (?); sorcery, witchcraft *Sch.*

མཁྱེན་པ་ *mk̔yen-pa*, resp. for *šés-pa, rig-pa, gó-ba*, **to know**, *yab-yúm-gyis mk̔yén-par mdzód-čig* my esteemed parents may know *Dzl.*; to know, one man from another, *rgyál-po mk̔yén-tam* does the king, does your majesty know the . . . ? (the king himself will answer: *ṅas šés-so*) *Dzl.* It is frq. used of the supernatural perception of Buddha and the saints, *bsám-pa dág-par mk̔yén-pas* as he (the Bodhisattwa) perceived the sentiments (of his scholar) to be sincere *Dzl.*; *mk̔yén-par gyúr-to* perceived, found out, discovered; **to understand**, *mk̔yen sóṅ-ṅam* did you understand it? *mk̔yen-rgyá-čan* possessed of much understanding, very learned *Mil.*; *mk̔yén-ldan-yáṅs-pa* profoundly learned; *mk̔yen-brtsé Glr.* prob.: omniscient-merciful; *t̔ams-čad-mk̔yén* **all-knowing**, a later epithet of Buddha; *ye-mḱyén*, *mṅon-mḱyén* = *ye-šés*, *mṅon-šés*. — *ťugs-mkyén* is known to me only as a sbst. abstr.: the knowing, **knowledge, prophetic sight,** *rje-btsún-gyis ťugs-mḱyén-gyis γzigs-pa lágs-sam* has your reverence seen by your prophetic sight? *Mil.*; acc. to *Cs.*, however, *sku-mḱyén*, *γsuṅ-mḱyén* and *ťugs-mḱyén* are identical in meaning with *mḱyen-mḱyén*, a form of entreaty which, as a Lama told me, properly has the sense: you know yourself best what is good for me! In accordance to this explanation we find in *Mil.* after an entreaty: *blá-ma ḱyed mḱyen-mḱyen*. It is gen. added without any connecting word, like our **pray**, or **please**, but sometimes it is construed with the inf.: *mdzád-pa(r) mḱyen-mḱyén*, please to do.

མཁྲང་(བ་) *mḱraṅ (-ba)*, also *ḱraṅ* **hard, solid, compact**; *srá-mḱráṅ-čan ₒgyur-méd Thgy.* **firm, hearty, sound,** of a strong and robust constitution. — *mḱráṅ-pa* denotes the fourth stage of the development of the foetus *Thgy.*

མཁྲིག་མ་ *mḱrig-ma* **the wrist** of the hand.

མཁྲིགས་པ་ **ṭigs-pa** col. *W.* (also *Bunan*) for:

མཁྲིས་པ་ *mḱris-pa B.* and *C.* (*Ssk.* **पित्त**) **bile, gall.** — 1. the vesicle of the gall, the gall-bladder, as part of the intestines. — 2. generally: the substance of the bile, the bilious fluid, which acc. to Indo-Tibetan philosophy is connected with the element of fire, and which, conformably to its functions, is divided into five species, of which physiology gives the oddest details. — *mḱris-nád* bilious disease: *mḱris-tsád* prob. bilious fever; *gráṅ-mḱris* a feverish shivering, a chill.

མཁྲིས་མ་ *mḱris-ma Lex.* w.e., perh. = *ₒḱris.*

མཁྲེགས་པ་ *mḱrégs-pa*, *W.* **ṭág-mo** (*Ssk.* **सार**) **hard, firm,** e.g. snow; **go-ṭág-čan** *W.* **obstinate, stiffnecked, stubborn.**

འཁང་བ་ *ₒḱáṅ-ba* (not: to put a fault or crime on another *Cs.*, but:) **to hurt or offend, to annoy, to vex,** *tsúr-la ₒḱaṅ* we cause vexation to ourselves (by minding too much the affairs of others): *ₒḱaṅ* **animosity**, *ₒḱaṅ maṅ* there occur many collisions, quarrels *Mil.*, *dpon-slób re ₒḱaṅ ₒbyuṅ* there arise mutual differences, animosities, between masters and scholars *Mil.*

འཁད་པ་ *ₒḱád-pa* esp. *W.* 1. **to sit, to sit firm,** *rtai ḱá-ru* on the back of a horse. — 2. to remain sitting, **to stick fast,** to be stopped, kept back, e.g of a bird, *rnyius*, in a snare: *rḱáṅ-pa ₒḱád-de ₒgyél-ba* to get entangled with the foot so as to fall; *sgo ₒḱad ₒdug* the door sticks. Cf. also *ḱad-pa* and *bkad-pa*.

འཁམ་པ་ *ₒḱám-pa* 1. **to faint away, to swoon.** — 2. *Sch.* also: to take into one's mouth.

འཁར་བ་ *ₒḱár-ba* I. sbst. 1. **staff** v. *mḱár-ba*. — 2. **bronze, bell-metal,** *ₒḱár-(bai) čú* molten, liquid bronze, *ₒḱár-bai mé-loṅ* a metallic mirror; *ₒḱar-ṅá* **gong,** used in India and China instead of bells; *Cs.*: a drum of bronze; yet it is rather a large bronze disk, producing, when struck, a very loud sound like that of a bell. — *ₒḱar-γžóṅ* a dish or basin of metal; *ₒḱar-záṅs* a metallic kettle. — II. vb., in *C.* the same as *ₒḱád-pa*. — 2. in *W.* intrs. to *dgar-ba*.

འཁར་འཁུ་བ་ *ₒḱár-ₒḱu-ba* to resist *Sch.*

འཁལ་བ་ *ₒḱál-ba*, pf. and fut. (imp. *ḱol?*), *W.* **kál-če** 1. *B.*, *C.*, *W.*: **to spin,** *bal*, wool, *skúd-pa* a thread, *srád-bu* yarn. — 2. *W.* **to send, to forward,** things.

འཁུ་བ་ *ₒḱú-ba* **to offend, insult,** *Bhar.* (*Lex.* = **द्रोह** injury); *ₒḱu-ₒḱrig*, acc. to the context, denotes certain passions that disturb the tranquillity of the mind, such as malignity and covetousness; *ₒḱáṅ-ba* is synon. — *Cs.*'s 'to emulate, contemn, hate, long for', and *Sch.*'s 'pride' I am not able to verify.

འཁུན་པ་ *ₒḱún-pa* **to groan,** to fetch **a** deep sigh, not so much as a sign of pain or sorrow, but rather as a mere physical deep and hollow sound *Med.*; ***ₒḱún-sgras ḱáṅ-pa ḱeṅs*** he filled the house with groanings *Pth.*; *sdáṅ-bai dgrá-la γyag ltar ˳ḱun* he groans (grunts, bellows) like a yak against a fierce enemy *Mil.*

**འཁུམ་པ་** *˳ḱúm-pa* pf. *ḱums* (cf. *skúm-pa*) **to shrink**, to be contracted, e.g. of the limbs, by gout; **yúr-ra raṅ-žin ˳ḱúm-ċe yin** *W.* the ditch will get narrower of itself; *ḱúms-pa* shrunk, shrivelled, contracted; fig. reduced, restricted, deprived of power.

**འཁུམས་པ་** *˳ḱúms-pa Lex.* and *Cs.* to comprehend, understand; *Sch.* also: to practise, to impress on the mind.

**འཁུར་བ་** *˳ḱúr-ba* I. sbst. = *ḱúr-ba*, **pastry**. II. vb., pf. and fut. *ḱur*, rarely *bkur* (v. *bkúr-ba*) 1. **to carry, convey**, *ḱur(-ru) ˳ḱúr-ba* to carry a load; *mi ṫég-par ˳ḱúr-ba Med.* to carry too heavy loads, prop to carry what one cannot carry; **ḱur šog** *C.*, **ḱur kyoṅ** *W.* bring! fetch! **ḱur soṅ** *C.*, **ḱur ḱyer** *W.* take away! carry off! *˳ḱúr-du ṫógs-te* taking up in order to carry, taking on one's back *Dzl.*; **lág-par ḱúr-ċe** *W.* to hold in one's hand. — 2. **to carry away** or **off**, *ro ˳ḱúr-ba Pth.*, to carry away a corpse; **to take along with**, in *W.* even: **to pocket**, **sém-la ḱúr-ċe** *W.* to take to heart; **'á-ne ˳ḱúr-ċe** to take a wife, to marry. — *˳ḱúr-ṫag* carrying-girth, rope or strap *Thgy.* Cf. *ḱur*, *ḱúr-ba* etc.

**འཁུར་ཚོས་** *˳ḱur-ṫsós* v. *ḱur-ṫsós*.

**འཁུལ་བ་** *˳ḱúl-ba* **to subdue, to subject** *Cs.*; *Sch.* also: to be uneasy about. *Lex.*: *γyóg-tu ˳ḱúl-ba*; v. also *ḱul* 3. *Zam.*; *ḱral ˳ḱúl-ba* perh. to force a tax, a rate, on a person.

**འཁེགས་པ་** *˳ḱegs-pa* pf. *ḱegs* **to hinder, stop, shut off, debar**, *lam* the way *Mil.*: *ji-ltar bkag ruṅ ma ḱégs-pas Mil.*, although they prohibited, tried to proh. him), he was not prohibited; *rgyál-bai ṗyág-gis kyaṅ mi ḱégs-pa Mil.* not being hindered even by Buddha's power.

**འཁེངས་པ་** *˳ḱéṅs-pa*, pf. *ḱeṅs*, **to be full**, *ċus keṅs yod-pa Glr.*; *blo-grós ma ḱéṅs-te* his mind not being satiated *Tar.* 135, 13.

**འཁེབ་པ་** *˳ḱéb-pa* pf. *ḱebs*, **to cover, to spread over**, *yoṅs-su ḱébs-té* being covered all over *Stg.*; *ḱa ṫams-ċad ḱebs-te* over the whole face *Stg.*; **to overshadow** *Dzl.* ༥༢, 17.

**འཁེལ་བ་** *˳ḱél-ba* pf. *ḱél* 1. **to put on, to load, to pack on**, = *˳gél-ba*; *bċu-ṫóg ḱél-na* when the ten stories or lofts shall have been put on *Mil.nt.* 2. **to spin**, = *˳ḱál-ba C.*, *Glr.*

**འཁོ་བ་** *˳ḱó-ba* (vb. to *mḱó-ba*), **to wish, to want**, to think useful, serviceable, necessary, to have occasion for *Mil.*; *˳ḱó-ste ˳oṅ* he will be able to make use of it *Mil.*; **˳ḱóa mi ˳ḱo** or **˳ḱó-ċe med** *W.* I do not want it, I do not like it; *˳ḱo-bjéd* fit for use, **useful**.

**འཁོགས་པ་** *˳ḱógs-pa* weak from old age, **decrepit, decayed**; *rgan* or *rgas-˳ḱógs* id.; *sṅo-ḱóg, skya-ḱóg* (sic) *Thgy.* with a complexion blue or pale from old age.

**འཁོང་བ་** *˳ḱóṅ-ba* (cf. *sgóṅ-ba*) to contract one's limbs, to sit in a cowering position, **to squat; to hide one's self**; *dpa ˳ḱóṅ-ba* to become discouraged, disheartened *Thgy.*

**འཁོད་, ཁོད་** *˳ḱod, ḱod* 1. **surface, superficies**; *sai ˳ḱod snyóms-pa* to remove inequalities of the surface, to level, to plane, *˳ḱód-snyoms-pa* levelled, made even, plain; also fig.: *bár-gyi ḱod snyoms* gaps were filled up, i.e. distinctions of rank, wealth etc. were done away with, not in consequence of a revolution, but as an act of kindness, forced upon the people by a despotic government. — 2. **a mill-stone**, **yá-ḱo'** the upper stone, **má-ḱo'** the nether stone *C.*

**འཁོད་པ་** *˳ḱód-pa* **to sit down, to sit**; *bar-snáṅ-la*, suspended in the air, floating, soaring, frq. of gods and saints in legends; *rgyal-srid-la* to have been raised to the throne *Tar.*; **to live, to dwell** *Dzl.*; gen. used like a passive to *˳gód-pa* **to be put, placed, established** (in virtue, in a doctrine, = to be converted to); *glegs-bám-du* to be put down in writing, to be recorded *Tar.* Cf. *˳ḱád-pa*.

**འཁོན་པ་** ˳*kʻón-pa* (*Lexx.* have a pf. *bkon*) 1. c.c. *daṅ*, **to bear a grudge** or ill-will against a person, **to be dissatisfied** with a thing; ˳*kʻón-nas* when they (the states) were at war with one another (opp. to *mtʻún-nas* in peaceful relations) *Glr.*; ˳*kʻón-med-par* honestly, without insidious intentions, e.g. in negotiations *Glr.*; *čʻos daṅ* ˳*kʻón-pa* to wish to keep aloof from religion, or to have done with religion; in a special sense: to be tired of the clerical profession *Glr.*; ˳*kʻón-žugs-pa*, ˳*kʻón-du* ˳*dzin-pa* = ˳*kʻón-pa*; ˳*kʻon res byéd-pa Sch.* to quarrel, prob. more accurately, to have a spite against each other. — ˳*kʻón-po* **dissension, discord** *Sch.* Cf. *kʻón-pa*. — 2. *C.* = ˳*kʻar-ba* II.

**འཁོབ་** ˳*kʻób Sch.* **barbarous, rough, rude,** gen. combined with *mtʻa*, *mtʻa*-˳*kʻób*, with or without *yul*, **barbarous border-country.** So the Tibetans always designate their own country, in comparison with India, the holy land of Buddhism, as being *mtʻa*-˳*kʻób kʻá-ba-čan*. The rarely occurring *yaṅ-kʻób* seems to indicate a still more distant and barbarous country.

**འཁོབས་པ་** ˳*kʻóbs-pa* to be startled, agitated, alarmed, in one Lex. however, it is explained by *kʻyáb-pa*.

**འཁོར་** ˳*kʻor* 1. **circle, circumference**; the persons or objects encircling, surrounding (a certain point or place); *lté-ba daṅ dei* ˳*kʻór-rnams* the navel and the circumjacent parts *Med.*; **de-kʻór-la** *W.* thereabout; *nye*-˳*kʻór* v. *nye*; more esp. **retinue, attendants,** ˳*kʻor daṅ bčas-pa* (**सपरिवार**) with attendants, suite: ˳*kʻor rnám-pa bži Tar.* frq., the attendants of Buddha's hearers, divided into four classes (viz. in the earliest times: *dge-slóṅ, dge-slóṅ-ma, dge-snyén*, and *dge-snyén-ma*; at a later period: *nyan-tʻós, raṅ-sans-rgyás, byaṅ-čʻub-séms-dpa*, and *so-sói skyé-bo-rnams* q.v.) ˳*kʻor dgra-bčóm-pas bskór-te* **surrounded by** the retinue of the **Arhants** (v. *dgra-bčóm-pa*); ˳*kʻór-du bsdús-so* **he gathered them** round himself **as his retinue** *Dzl.*; also fig.: the train of **thoughts, reminiscences** etc., which the soul, when passing **into a** new body, cannot take along with it *Thgy.*; it is also used for a single servant or **attendant** (*Cs.* has ˳*kʻór-po* or ˳*kʻór-pa* **male** attendant, and ˳*kʻór-ma* female attendant), ˳*kʻor γčig Mil.*; ˳*kʻor γnyis* two attendants *Glr.*, hence ˳*kʻor-rnams* sometimes for domestics, household servants; but if ˳*kʻor* with a numeral is preceded by *γtsó-bo*, or **a** similar noun, this preceding word is acc. to the Tibetan mode of speaking included in the number given, so that *γtsó-bo* ˳*kʻor lṅa* should be translated: the master and four attendants (not five). — 2. instead of ˳*kʻór-ba*, or *kʻór-lo*, esp. in compound words; *lo*-˳*kʻór* = *lo-skór* a cycle, comprising **a space** of twelve years.

**Comp.** ˳*kʻór-mkʻan* **attendants** *Glr.* — ˳*kʻór*-˳*báṅs* **subjects** *Cs.* — ˳*kʻor-γyóg* = ˳*kʻór* **retinue, servants** etc. — **dhuṅ-kʻór** *C.* **waiting man,** valet de chamber, = *sku-mdún-pa* which is the respectful word for it. — *naṅ*-˳*kʻór* household servants, domestics. — **kʻor-gyág** *W.* **latch.** — ˳*kʻor*-˳*dás* v. sub ˳*kʻór-ba* II.

**འཁོར་བ་** ˳*kʻór-ba* I. vb. (cf. *skór-ba*), **to turn round, to turn about, to go round** in a circle; ˳*kʻór-gin yod* he is walking (running, flying etc.) round the . . . *Glr.*; esp. of the successive transmigrations of metempsychosis, v. II; *mgo* ˳*kʻor* my head turns, I am getting dizzy, confused; also **I am duped,** cheated, imposed on, *kʻyéd-kyi kʻa-sbyáṅ-gyis ṅed mgo mi* ˳*kʻor* we are not to be taken in by the volubility of your tongue *Mil.*; **to pass away, to grow full, to be completed,** *lo-dús* ˳*kʻór-ba-na* when one year was past *Glr.*; *srás-kyis lo* ˳*kʻór-te* when the prince had completed one year, was one year old; **da bú-lon kʻor** *W.* now the debt is entirely paid off, cleared; **kʻor mi tʻub** it cannot be paid off; **mi kʻor**, the sum is not full, not sufficient to cover the debt; **to walk about, roam, ramble** *W.*; **to return** from a journey, to come **home**; **ráṅ-la kʻór-ba** to come or **fall back (on** the head of the author, **originator**); **to** come together, **to contract, to gather, e.g.**

clouds, frq. water, *koi ká-ču kor* W. it makes his mouth water; dgrá-bo ༚kor Mil. enemies are collecting (we create ourselves enemies); also impersonally: *kor soṅ* it has become cloudy; γnam kor the sky is getting overcast, clouded; therefore even **to arise, to be produced, formed,** zíl-pa ༚kor dew is produced, γyá, rust, even: lus-la sras ༚kor a child has been formed, produced, in the womb Pth. —

II. sbst. 1. the turning round or about etc.; more particularly 2. **the orb** or **round** of transmigration within the six classes of physical beings. Though the Buddhist has not a more ardent wish, than to be finally released from the repeated wanderings of the soul, yet he believes so firmly in these migrations, that he will rather follow the doctrines of his philosophers, and doubt the reality of the perception of his senses, than think it possible, that the whole theory of the ༚kór-ba with all its consequences should be nothing but a product of human imagination. — ༚kór-bar ༚kór-ba to turn round, to wander about in the orb of transmigration; ༚kór-bai btsón-ra, ༚dam, mtso the dungeon, the swamp, the sea of the ༚kór-ba; ༚kór-ba-las ༚dás-pa to escape from the ༚kór-ba, = to enter into the Nirwana ༚kór-༚das 1. abbreviation of the foregoing. 2. for ༚kór-ba daṅ ༚das-pa the stay in the ༚kór-ba and the escape from it; ༚kor ༚das γnyis-su ṅas ma mtoṅ I have not seen that there is a difference between these two Mil.

འཁོར་ཡུག ༚kor-yúg **a wall, rampart** Cs., v. kó-ra.

འཁོར་གཡའ་ kór-γyá C. **latch.**

འཁོར་ལོ་ ༚kór-lo (Ssk. चक्र, मण्डल) 1. **circle,** tsógs-kyi ༚kór-lo offerings arranged in a circle, v. tsogs: ༚kór-lo ༚brí-ba to describe a circle Tar. More frq.: 2. a circular body, **a disk, roll, wheel,** any modification of the cylinder, bču-γsum-༚kór-lo the column on the mčod-rtén consisting apparently of thirteen circular disks; ༚kór-lo brtsib-brgyád the wheel with eight spokes, a frq. attribute of deities; rdza-mkán-gyi ༚kór-lo potter's wheel; čós-kyi ༚kór-lo praying-cylinder, cf. below; also a complication of wheels, wheel-work, engine, ༚prúl-(gyi) ༚kór(-lo) 'magic wheel', a phantastic attribute of gods, but also any real machine of a more ingenious construction, e.g. sugar-press Stg., electrical machine etc.; ču-tsod-༚kór-lo a clock; šiṅ-rta-༚kór-lo waggon, carriage, also cart-wheel. — Figuratively: bdé-ba daṅ sdug-bsṅál-gyi ༚kór-lo, vicissitude of fortune; dús-kyi ༚kór-lo (कालचक्र) acc. to Cs.'s Chronological Table (Cs.'s Gram. p. 181) a later philosophical system, contained esp. in the rtsa-rgyúd, Mūlatantra, in which the Adibuddha doctrine, prophecies, chronology etc. are propounded. It was introduced into Tibet about 1000 p. Chr.; cf. also Schl. 45. — ༚kór-lo sgyúr-ba, or skór-ba, with čós-kyi, to turn the wheel of doctrine, = to preach, to teach religion, (vulgo understood only of the turning of the praying-cylinder); *čö-kyi kór-lo léṅ-mor bé-pa* C. to devote one's self to the preaching of religion. On the other hand: ༚kór-los sgyúr-bai rgyál-po (चक्रवर्तिन्) Will.: 'a ruler, the wheels of whose chariot roll everywhere without obstruction, emperor, sovereign of the world, the ruler of a čakra, or country extending from sea to sea'. In this Indian explanation two different etymologies are given, the former of which is undoubtedly the original one. Buddhism and the Tibetan language have added a third signification, 'praying-wheel'; modern scholars a fourth, that of the 'orb' or round of transmigration or metempsychosis: hence the confusion attaching to the import of this word.

འཁོར་ལོག *kor-lóg* is said to be used in col. language instead of ka-ló 3. W.

འཁོར་ས་ ༚kór-sa = skór-lam v. skór-ba I. extr.; ༚kór-sa bár-pa, čén-po Glr.

འཁོར་གསུམ་ ༚kor-γsum, lit. three circles. Ssk. trimaṇḍala; Sch.: **'every thing that belongs to archery'; more correctly: arrow, knife, and spear.**

འཁོལ་བ་ ꜀ḱól-ba I. pf. ḱol, cf. skól-ba, **to boil, to be boiling,** ču ḱol the water is boiling; ꜀ḱol ꜀ǰúg-pa to make boil, to set to the fire for boiling, = skól-ba; **to ferment** (dough), **to effervesce, to sparkle** (beer) *W.* — II. pf. bkol, imp. ḱol 1. to oblige a person to be a servant or bondman, **to use as a servant;** in full: bran-du, also γyóg-tu, ꜀ḱól-ba; therefore bran-ḱól, ḱól-po **servant, man-servant:** bkol-spyód-kyi sdug-bsṅál the calamity of servitude, current expression for designating the lot of animals; γžán-dag-gis dbáṅ-med-par bkól-ba to be enslaved by others, to be compelled to do slave-work *Thgy.*; dgé-bai lás-la bkól-ba to make a person minister to works of virtue. — 2. **to save, to spare,** to enjoy with moderation *Cs.*; zúr-du . . . bkól-ba *Lex.*; *Sch.*: saved, laid up, put by. — 3. *Sch.*: **to become insensible, to be asleep, to get benumbed,** in reference to the limbs; seems to be used in *Med.*

འཁོས་ ꜀ḱos 1. *C.* also ꜀ḱós-ka (cognate to ꜀ḱó-ba), **worth, value, importance** *Cs.*; ꜀ḱós-čan important, mighty, of great influence, ꜀ḱos-méd the opposite of it. — 2. ꜀ḱós-su-ṕab-pa **clyster** *Sch.*; one Lex. has mḱos-páb, w.e.

འཁྱག(ས)་པ་ ꜀ḱyág(s)-pa 1. **to freeze** (of water, earth, provisions); **to coagulate, congeal** (melted fat etc.). — 2. **to feel cold,** ꜀ḱyágs-na gós gyon if you feel cold, put on clothes *Glr.*, *ḱyag ǰhuṅ* *C.*, *ḱyágs-sa rag* *W.* I feel cold; ꜀ḱyágs-gri a feeling cold, a shivering (cf. ltógs-gri) *Mil.*; *ḱyágs-ša* *W.* id., the cold fit of the ague. — ꜀ḱyags-rúm, ꜀ḱyags-róm **ice** *Glr.*; ꜀ḱyags-lhám snow-shoe *Sch.*

འཁྱམ་པ་ ꜀ḱyám-pa **to run about, to wander,** e.g. čá-med yúl-du in an unknown country *Glr.*; ꜀ḱór-bar in the orb or round of transmigration, v. ꜀ḱór-ba; ꜀ḱyám-ste nor mi bdóg-pa žig one who lives as a vagabond *Dzl.*; dé-dag-ni rnám-par ꜀ḱyám-pao they are mistaken, on the wrong track *Wdṅ.*; ꜀ḱyám-du ꜀ǰúg-pa to cause to ramble or rove about, to scatter; ꜀ḱyáms-pa strayed, lost, wandering, vagrant; erroneous, erring *Tar.* 153, 15. — ꜀ḱyám-ḱyi **a vagrant dog.** — ꜀ḱyáms-po 1. a vagabond. — 2. n. of a disease *Med.* — 3. erroneous *Tar.* — ču ꜀ḱyám-pa inundation, flood *Ma.*

འཁྱར་བ་ ꜀ḱyár-ba **to err, to go astray, to deviate from,** *yan ḱyár-la ma čá* *Ld.* do not step out of your rank! do not absent yourself! ꜀ḱyar dogs yod one should be afraid of going astray *Thgy.*; dpe ꜀ḱyár-po a defective simile; tsig ꜀ḱyár-po an inadequate designation. — In *Tar.* 48, 4 dpe ꜀ḱyár-po is translated 'epitome' by *Schf.*, but the whole passage is somewhat obscure.

འཁྱལ་བ་ ꜀ḱyál-ba = kyal-ka q.v.

འཁྱི་བ་ ꜀ḱyi-ba *Sch.*, prob. an incorrect reading for ꜀ḱyil-ba.

འཁྱིག་པ་ ꜀ḱyig-pa, pf. bkyigs, fut. bkyig, **to bind** (a prisoner, a bundle of straw etc.); *kye* (v. ske) *ḱyig-pa* *C.* to strangle, suffocate.

འཁྱིགས་པ་ °ḱyigs-pa **to comprise, encompass** *Pth.*, v. ṕáṅ-pa.

འཁྱིད་པ་ ꜀ḱyid-pa, *Sch.*: mig ꜀ḱyid-pa **to turn** or **roll** one's eyes.

འཁྱིམས་པ་ ꜀ḱyims-pa 1. **to be encircled with** a halo, as the sun and moon sometimes are *Cs.*; ꜀og-꜀ḱyims *Lex.* = परिधि halo; also ꜀ǰa-ód ꜀ḱyims a rainbow-coloured halo appears *Pth.* — 2.: *na-báṅ* or *múg-pa ḱyims, dúd-pa ḱyims*, fog, smoke, **comes floating on.**

འཁྱིར་བ་ °ḱyír-ba **to turn round in a circular course** *Cs.*, *Lex.*: γdugs ꜀ḱyír-ba to turn a parasol round (?).

འཁྱིལ་བ་ ꜀ḱyil-ba vb. n. 1. **to wind, to twist;** duṅ γyás-su ꜀ḱyíl-ba **a triton** or trumpet-shell, wound to **the right, and then** considered particularly **valuable, these shells** generally being wound **to the left; of the** hair: gyén-la ꜀ḱyil-ba **wound or twisted** (on the crown of the **head**) *Glr.*; **ro-smád** °brúl-du ꜀ḱyil-ba **the lower part of the** body being **wound into a serpent** (the usual manner of **representing the 'klu'**); ꜀ód-du ꜀ḱyil-žiṅ, **the body enveloping itself** in light *Mil.*; to roll: **nya γser-mig** ꜀ḱyil-

*ba yod* the fish rolls its golden eye *Mil.*; to whirl, to eddy, to move round rapidly, of the water, so prob. *Dzl.* ༢༢, 13; ༧༨༦, 2; *ḱrom dmar-nág ˳ḱyil-ba* the motley crowd in a whirling motion *Pth.*; to hang or flow down in folds, of a tent or a curtain *Glr.* 33, 12. — 2. **to flow** (whirling) **together**, used of rivulets and brooks overflowing so as to form small lakes *Mil.*; of persons: to meet, to flock or crowd together, *mi múṅ-po dé-ru ˳ḱyil-bar gyúr-te Pth.*; **ḱyil-ču*,* and **ču-ḱyil** col. puddle.

འཁྱུ་བ་ *˳ḱyú-ba*, pf. *˳ḱyus* **to run** *Lex.*

འཁྱུག་པ་ *˳ḱyúg-pa*, pf. *ḱyug* 1. *Cs.*: **to run**; *˳ḱyug-po* a runner; *˳ḱyúg-yig* running hand, current hand-writing, as is used in the writing of letters etc.; *˳ḱyúg-po ˳ḱyú-ba Lex.* is explained by *Sch.*: to run away **hastily**. The signification of running, however, seems to be obsolete, whilst the **usual** meaning is: 2. **to dart** or **sweep rapidly along**, frq. used of a flash of lightning, also of the rapid motion of a fish in the water *Mil.*; of spectral apparitions *Mil.*; of acute rheumatic pains; of the light: to flash, to shoot rays of light, *ḱra-ḱyug-ḱyúg-pa* to gleam, to sparkle with light, to shine in various colours *Pth.*; *ser-˳ḱyúg-ge-ba* glittering in yellow lustre *Mil.*; to glitter, to shine, of the rainbow; to shine through, of the veins through the cuticle etc. — **ḱyúg-šar-čán** *W.* hasty, hurrying, careless.

འཁྱུད་པ་ *˳ḱyúd-pa* 1. **to embrace** frq., *mgúl-nas ˳ḱyúd-pa* to clasp round the neck, **to hug**; to encompass by spanning *Pth.* and elsewhere, cf. *˳ḱyígs-pa*. — 2. **to glide** in or into (as serpents), *mṅál-du ˳ḱyúg-pa* of the soul in the new conception, like the synonym *˳kril-ba*, for *˳ǰúg-pa*. — 3. **to be able**, **nád-pa mál-sa-na láṅ-ṅa** (instead of *laṅ-bar*) **mi ḱyud** the sick man is not able to rise from his bed. — *blos mi ˳ḱyúd-pa byéd-pa Thgy.* (not clear).

འཁྱུར་བ་ *˳ḱyúr-ba Cs.*: to be separated, divorced; *Lex.*: *bskúr-bas ˳kyúr-ba*, therefore prob. the vb. n. to *skyúr-ba*, to be deserted, cast off.

འཁྱེང་བ་ *˳ḱyéṅ-ba* seems to be = *˳géṅs-pa C.* col.

འཁྱེད་པ་ *ḱyéd-pa* (1. cf. *˳gyed-pa*) *Cs.* **to be distributed**, e. g. food, *Dzl.* — 2. *C.* and *W.* **to be sufficient, to suffice, to be enough, to hold out**, **mi ḱyed** there is not enough. — 3. *C.* to gain (a law-suit), **to be acquitted.** — 4. *ṗyir ḱyéd-pa* **to bow** without uncovering one's head, as a less humble way of saluting *Mil.nt.*

འཁྱེར་བ་ *˳ḱyér-ba* pf. *˳ḱyer* (Northern *Ld.* **ḱyers**), at the end of a sentence *ḱyér-ro Tar.* and others, (*Cs. ḱyer-to?*), nearly the same as *˳ḱur-ba*; (the བཤད of the Lexx.: to lead, to guide, does not fully agree with the sense in which it is generally used) — 1. **to carry away, to take away**; *čus* to be carried or swept away by water; fig.: *lé-los* to be overcome, carried away by idleness *Mil.*; *ldé-mig ḱyer* take the key with you! — 2. **to carry, to bring,** in a more general sense, *C.* and *B.*: *ḱyer šog* bring! *ḱyer soṅ* carry off! take away! (in a like manner as *˳ḱúr-ba*); *des ču bláṅ-nas ḱyer ˳óṅ-bai lám-ḱa-na* he having fetched water, being on his way to bring it *Pth.*; *ḱyer-la šog* bring me (word), let me know (the result of your investigation) *Mil.* — *˳ḱyér-so* 1. **appearance,** esp. a neat, handsome appearance of persons or things. 2. **advantage, superiority, pleasantness,** *Mil.*, *C.*

འཁྱེལ་བ་ *˳ḱyel-ba Ld.* **to hit, to strike.**

འཁྱོག་པ་ *˳ḱyóg-pa*, pf. *ḱyag*, imp. *ḱyog*, **to lift, lift up,** = *˳tógs-pa*, *tégs-pa Glr.*; **to carry, bring,** **sól-ǰha ḱyog** bring in the tea *C.*, cf. sub *ḱag.*

(འ)ཁྱོག་པོ་ *˳ḱyóg-po* or *ḱyóg-po* **crooked, bent;** *ḱyóg-poi ri-mo* a crooked figure, a curve, flourish, crescent etc.; *nyas ṗar ˳ḱyog tsur ˳ḱyog byás-šiṅ* the fish winding its body, writhing *Pth.*; *˳ḱyog-čan*, *˳ḱyog-˳ḱyóg* tortuous; *˳ḱyog-bšád* a crooked, out of the way construction or explanation. — *˳ḱyog stón-pa* to fly into a passion (?) *Sch.*

(འ)ཁྱོགས་ ₒkyogs or kyogs **palanquin, sedan-chair, litter** *Pth.*; *ₒkyogs-dpyáṅ* id.; a lath or pole for carrying burdens *Sch.*

འཁྱོང་བ་ *ₒkyóṅ-ba* pf. and imp. *kyoṅ* **to bring** *W.*

འཁྱོམ་པ་ *ₒkyóm-pa* pf. *ₒkyoms* 1. **to rock, to wave,** of a ship *Schr.*, of the water *Sch.* (not quite clear); **kyom-kyom ḍo-ba* C.* **to reel, stagger,** **čáṅ-ghī kyom-pa dug** he is staggering under the influence of beer; to be dizzy *Med.*; *mtso-ₒkyóm* dizziness, vertigo, ni. f.; *lug-glád mgo-ₒkór ₒkyóm-pa ɣso* the brain of a sheep cures the swimming of the head (vertigo) *Med.*

འཁྱོར་བ་ *ₒkyór-ba* 1. **to miss, fail,** not to hit *Cs.* — 2. **to reel, stagger,** from intoxication. — 3. **to warp,** of wood.

འཁྱོལ་བ་ *ₒkyól-ba*, pf. *ₒkyol*, cf. *skyél-ba*, **to be carried, to be brought** (somewhere) *Pth.*; with *ɣnód-pa* to be done, inflicted *Mil.*; **to arrive at, come to, reach,** *sku-tsé mtá-ru* the end of life.

འཁྱོས་པ་, (འཕྱོས་པ་) *ₒkyós-pa* (*ₒpyós-pa*) *Sch.*, *ₒkyós-ma Mil.*, **a present, gift,** = *kyós-ma, skyás-ma.*

འཁྲ་བ་ *ₒkrá-ba* I. vb., pf. prob. *ₒkras* **to lean to, to incline towards** *Cs.*; *ₒkrá-sa* a support to lean against, a prop, back (of a chair) *Lex.* — II. adj. **hard,** = *ₒkráṅ-ba, mkráṅ-ba Sch.*

འཁྲབ་པ་ *ₒkráb-pa*, pf. *bkrab* (?), cf. also *skráb-pa*, 1. **to strike, to beat,** in repeated strokes, as in swimming and rowing; **to thrust, stamp, thump,** tread heavily, *bro ₒkrab-pa* to dance in that manner *Mil.*, *Pth.* — 2. **to winnow, to fan** *Stg.*, col. **ṭáb-pa**. — 3. **mig ṭab ṭab** (or **ṭab-ṭab**) **ǰhé-pa* C.*, **čó-če* W.*, **to blink, twinkle, wink** with the eyes. — 4. **ka-šág ṭab-če* W.* **to jest, to joke,** to crack jokes. — 5. *Sch.*: **to leap, jump,** *Schr.* for joy. — 6. **to scoop out, to bail out** *Sch.* — 7. **to fight, to combat** *C., W.*

འཁྲལ་འཁྲུལ་ *ₒkral-ₒkrúl* **confusion, disorder.**

འཁྲི་བ་ *ₒkri-ba*, pf. *ₒkris*, cf. *dkri-ba*, cognate to *ₒkril-ba*, 1. **to wind, roll; twist** one's self, **to coil** (of snakes) *Dzl.*; *kyim-táb-kyi ₒkri-ba* conjugal embrace *Pth.*; **'óg-ma ṭi-se** (for *ₒkri-ste*) **rag* W.* I have a sore throat, prop. I feel my throat tied up, I am choking; fig.: *kún-la ₒkris-pa*, either as an adj. 'ensnaring', or as a sbst. 'ensnarer' = sin, cf. *kun-dkris* in *dkri-ba*; *ₒkri-šiṅ* = *ₒkril-šiṅ*. — 2. mostly as a sbst.: **the being attached to,** given to, c.c. genit. (synonym of *čágs-pa*): *raṅ-dón-gyi*, to one's own advantage, *bu-smád-kyi* to wife and children *Mil.*; **fondness, attachment;** *žen-ₒkris* id. — 3. *kral ₒkri-ba* **to impose** a tax *C., Lex.*

འཁྲིག་པ་ *ₒkrig-pa* I. sbst. 1. (*Ssk.* **मिथुन**) **coitus** (of the two sexes), **copulation, pairing,** the usual, not exactly obscene, yet not euphemistic term for it; *ₒkrig-pa spyód-pa*, also *ₒkrig-čágs spyód-pa B.* and *C.*, **ṭig-pa čó-če* W.*, to lie with etc.; *ₒkrig-pai čós-la rtén-pa* to indulge in lust, to be given to voluptuousness; *ₒkrig-skád Sch.*, *ₒkrig-tsig Lexx.*, obscene words, unchaste language; *ₒkrig-pa ₒbyin-pa* to talk smut. — 2. a sign of the zodiac, **the twins.** — 3. symb. num.: 2.

II. vb. 1. **to cohere, to stick together** *Cs.* — 2. **to be clouded** (of the sky), *ɣnam ₒkrig* the sky is getting overcast; also **ṭigs soṅ* W.* without a sbst., it has become cloudy, dull; *ₒód-zér daṅ ǰa-ₒód ₒkrig-pa* wrapt in rays of light and the splendours of the rainbow *Pth.*; *taṅ tams-čád mes ₒkrig-pa* the whole plain was enveloped in a flame of fire *Mil.* Cf. *dkrigs-pa.*

འཁྲིད་ *ₒkrid* v. *krid.*

འཁྲིད་པ་ *ₒkrid-pa*, pf. *krid*, fut. *bkri?*, **to lead, to conduct** men or beasts to a place; **to command, to head** (an army); **to bring** along with, *ₒkrid-de ma ₒóṅs-so* he **has not** brought (his wife) with him *Dzl.*; therefore *ₒkrid* equivalent to 'with': *bú-tsa ₒkrid byuṅ-nas* coming out with their children

*Glr.* — *blo ˳ḱrid-pa* perh. a mistake for *brid-pa*.

འཁྲིམས་ *˳ḱrims*, *bréd(-nas)-˳ḱrims Lexx.* w.e.

འཁྲིལ་བ་ *˳ḱril-ba* 1. **to wind** or **coil round** (of serpents), **to embrace** closely, **to clasp round**, e.g. in the act of coition; *ma byams bú-la ˳ḱril* a loving mother clasping her child *Pth.*; *˳ḱril-mḱan* **a plant** furnished with tendrils or claspers *W.*; *˳ḱril-šin Wdṅ.* a climbing plant, creeper. — 2. **to glide, slip into,** of the soul when entering another body, = *˳kyúd-pa*. — 3. *ḱa ˳ḱril-ba W.* to **speak** imperfectly (like children), **to stammer**, — 4. **to heap up,** = *˳dril-ba*, *sgril-ba*.

འཁྲིས་ *˳ḱris* 1. syn. with *˳gram*, **bank, shore, coast,** *rmá-čui ˳ḱris-na yód-pai mḱar*, **a castle** on the banks of the Hoangho *Glr.*; **kyo'-rán-gi ṭ i-na yo'* C.* it lies just before you, under your nose; *blá-mai sku-ḱris-su = blá-mai ṕyógs-la Mil.nt.* — 2. v. *˳ḱri-ba*.

འཁྲུ་བ་ *˳ḱrú-ba* 1. *Cs.* **to wash, to bathe,** = *˳ḱrud-pa*, cf. *ḱrus*. — 2. **diarrhoea, looseness;** dysentery (?); *˳ḱru-nád*, *˳ḱru-sbyóṅs* (**अतिसार**) id.

འཁྲུག་པ་ *˳ḱrúg-pa* 1. vb., pf. *˳ḱrugs*, cf. *dkrug-pa*, *bkrug-pa*, to be in disorder, agitation, commotion, **to be disturbed;** *˳ḱrúg-par ˳gyúr-ba* to get disordered; of the blood: *rtsa ťams-čád ˳ḱrúg-tu bčug*, it made all his blood boil *Glr.*; of the sea frq.; esp. of the mind, disturbed by wrath, fear, anxiety, or some other passion, cf. *ḱog-˳ḱrúgs*; **to quarrel, fight, contend,** *de ɣnyis ˳ḱrúgs-nas*, the two quarrelling; *bod če nan ˳ḱrúg-go*, the nobles of Tibet are contending among one another, have internal feuds; *mči-ma ˳ḱrúg-pa* tears appearing, coming forth, (lit. tears being stirred up, excited *Thgy.*, *Mil.*, *Tar.* — 2. sbst. **disorder, tumult, war,** also **single combat, duel,** *˳ḱrúg-pa šor* disorder arises; *˳ḱrug-dús byas* he appointed the time of the duel *Glr.*; *˳ḱrúg-dpon = dmág-dpon*; *˳ḱrúg-pa byed-pa* to take up arms, to begin war; respecting subjects: to rebel; *˳ḱrúg-pa byéd-pai dús-su* in times of war *Glr.*; *dmag-˳ḱrúg*, *˳ťab-˳ḱrúg* war. — *mi-˳ḱrúgs-pa* n. of a Buddha (not = *mi-skyód-pa*). — *˳ḱrug-lóṅ* is the explanation given by *Lexx.* for *skyo-ṅógs*, hence prob.: **contest, strife.** — **ṭúgs-mḱan* W.* having small cracks, **flaws,** of potter's ware.

འཁྲུང་བ་ *˳ḱrúṅ-ba* or *˳ḱrúṅs-pa* 1. resp. for *skyé-ba* **to be born,** *bčom-ldan-˳dás ˳ḱrúṅs-pa daṅ dus-mnyám-du* at the same time when Buddha was born *Glr.*; *ɣnyis-la sras ma ˳ḱrúṅs-par* as by neither of the two (queens) a son was born *Glr.*; *˳ḱruṅs-dkái skyés-bu* (holy) men, such as are but rarely born (lit. with difficulty) *Mil.*; **to arise, to originate,** *˳ḱruṅs-rábs* legend of the origin . . .; *ḱyed-ráṅ-gi ťúgs-la ˳ḱrúṅs-pai tsig* words as they may just arise in your honour's mind *Mil.*; *snyiṅ-rje ťúgs-la ˳ḱrúṅs-pas* compassion arose in the soul of his reverence *Mil.*; *tiṅ-ṅe-˳dzin ˳ḱrúṅs-pas* meditation arising. — 2. **to come up, shoot, sprout, grow,** of seeds and plants frq.

འཁྲུད་པ་ *˳ḱrúd-pa*, pf. *bkrus*, fut. *bkru* **to wash, to bathe,** *gos* clothes, *ḱa-lág* face and hands *Dzl.*; **to wash off,** *dri-ma* dirt; fig. *sa nán-gyis ˳ḱrud Ma.* is stated to mean: the country is fleeced, thoroughly drained of its resources.

འཁྲུམས་ *˳ḱrums* **carcass, carrion,** game torn by beasts of prey, *Sch.*, (the word seems to be very little known).

འཁྲུལ་བ་ *˳ḱrúl-ba* (*Lex.*: *Ssk.* **भ्रम** to turn out of the way, to wander, to stray, hence perh. originally:) 1. **to be dislocated, sprained, distorted,** **ťsig ṭul* W.* the limb is dislocated; usually: 2. **to be out, to be mistaken,** almost always used in the pf. tense, *˳ḱrúl-pa* mistaken, deceived, *ṅa mig ˳ḱrúl-pa yin-nam* does my eye deceive me? *Mil.*; *rná-ba ˳ḱrul dogs túr-re gyis* take care not to hear wrong *Mil.*; *ɣnyis ɣčig-tu ˳ḱrúl-bar byéd-pa* to make by mistake two to be one, to confound one thing with another *Tar.*; *˳di dge-slóṅ-mar ˳dód-pa ˳ḱrúl-pa yin-la* she being frustrated in her wish to become a nun *Tar.* 85, 1; *˳gró-ba ˳ḱrúl-pa* the deceived creature *Glr.*;

frq. with *snaṅ*: *raṅ-snáṅ ˛ḱrúl-par ˛dug* I have been mistaken, it was a deception of the senses *Mil.*; *snaṅ-˛ḱrúl*, and *˛ḱrul-snáṅ* **illusion, delusion**; *˛ḱrul-snáṅ-ċan* **delusive** *Glr.*; to err, as a syn. of *nór-ba*: *ḱyód-ċag ˛ḱrúl-pai ˛ǰig-rten-pa* ye deluded children of the world! *Mil.*; *žes ˛dón-pa-rnams ˛ḱrul* they who pronounce (read) in this manner, are mistaken; *˛a ˛dogs ˛ḱrul* the adding of *˛a* is a mistake; *nor-˛ḱrúl* mistake, *nor-˛ḱrúl sél-ba Schr.*, **tón-ċe, sál-po gyáb-ċe**, *W.* to remove mistakes, to correct. — 3. **to be insane, deranged,** syn. of *smyós-pa Dzl.* and others. — *˛ḱrúl-pa* 1. adj. **mistaken, deceived.** — 2. sbst. **mistake; frenzy, madness**; *˛ḱrul-γži* **mistake, error**; *˛ḱrúl-so* (*errandi locus*) occasion for committing mistakes, a wrong way, **peril; mistake, error,** cf. *gól-sa*; *˛ḱrul-˛ḱór* artifice *Sch.*, (*Cs.*: machine, contrivance; but this is spelled more correctly *˛ṕrul-˛ḱór*).

འཁྲེན་པ *˛ḱrén-pa* 1. **to wish, to long for,** *zas-skóm Med.*, *ḱyím-la Lex.* — 2. *W.* **to look upon with envy, jealousy.**

འཁྲོ་བ *˛ḱró-ba*, pf. *ḱros*, **to be angry,** *la* at.

འཁྲོག་པ *˛ḱróg-pa* **to roar, rush, buzz, hum,** *rná-ba ḱúr-la ˛ḱrog Med.*, a tingling noise is caused in the ear; *rgyu-lóṅ ˛ḱróg-ċiṅ* a rumbling in the bowels *Med.*; *sbo-˛ḱróg* in the belly; *˛ḱrog-ḱróg* roaring, rushing, buzzing.

འཁྲོལ་བ *˛ḱról-ba* pf. and fut. *dkrol*, imp. *ḱrol* 1. **to cause to sound, to make a noise, to play,** *ról-mo* on an instrument, **to ring** (a bell), **to beat** (a gong, cymbal); *ma dkról-bar* without being played on. — 2. **to sound, resound,** **ḍód-pa ṭ ól-la rag** *W.* my bowels croak; *˛ḱról-po* a player, performer, bell-ringer etc., cf. *ḱról-po*; **ṭrol-lo-lo-tsē** *W.* a tinkling of bells.

# ག

ག *ga* 1. the letter **g**, originally, and in the border countries still at the present time, as initial letter = the English hard g, as final letter = ck; in *C.* as initial deep-toned and aspirated (gh), as final letter more or less indistinct; as a prefix (in *Khams* and *Balti*) fricative = *γ* or *χ*; v. Preface. — 2. as numerical figure: 3, cf. *ka* 2.

ག *ga* affix (article) to some substantives, like *ka*.

ག *ga* (*C.* **gha**) 1. = *˛ga* (*C.* **gā**). — 2. = *gaṅ*.

ག་ཁྲལ *ga-ḱrál C.* (pron. **gha-ṭal**) **tax, duty** (on cattle and butter).

ག་ག *ga-gá W.* a title of honour: **the old gentleman, the old squire** e.g. **ga-gá ta-ra-ċán** the old Squire Tara Chand, opp. to *no-nó* the young Squire; instead of it in *C.*: **'a-ǰho-lág**.

ག་ག་ཚིལ *ga-ga ts̆il*, **tickling** *Cs.*; *ga-ga-ts̆il byéd-pa* **to tickle.**

ག་གེ་མོ *ga-gé-mo* **such a one, such a thing** *Cs.*; **such and such**; v. *če-ge-mo.*

ག་གོན *ga-gón* **a melon** *Cs.* (some Lexx. have: cucumber, others: barley).

ག་ཅེན, ག་ཆེན *ga-ċén, ga-čén* **some** (people), **a good many; a good deal** *W.*, *C.*

ག་ཆད *ga-čád* **without cause, involuntarily,** e.g. to weep *Med.*

ག་ཏ *gá-ta Ssk.*, *ga-tai sde-ts̆an* a particular kind of Indian hand-writing, besides Nagari and Lantsa *Glr.*

ག་ད *gá-da* (गदा), **club, mace.**

ག་དུར་ *ga-dúr* medicinal herb of an astringent taste.

ག་དོར་ *ga-dór Lex.* w.e.: *ṡa-bai ga-dor*; *Sch.* explains: the growth of a new branch on a stag's horn.

ག་འདྲས་ *ga-ₒdrás C.* (pronounced **ghaṅdę**) **how?**

ག་ན་ *gá-na* = *gaṅ-na*, **where**, used interr. and correl., frq.; *gá-na-ba* and *gáṅ-na-ba* the same as a sbst., **the whereabouts** of a person, his place of residence; *rgyál-po gá-na-bar*, (or *gá-na-ba der*, *gá-na ₒdúg-par*, *gá-na bżúgs-par*) *soṅ* he went where the king was *Dzl.*, frq. — **ga-na-méd** *W.* **absolutely, at all events,** **ga-na-méd kal gos** it must be sent by all means; **ga-na-méd lóg-te taṅ yin** I shall give it back at all events (*B. ċis-kyaṅ*).

ག་པུར་ *ga-pur* **camphor** *Med.*

ག་བྲ་ *ga-bra* n. of a medicine *Med.*

ག་ཚམ་ *ga-tsám* **how, how much, how many how long,** interr. and correl.; **as much as,** e.g. as much as you like (you may take) col.

ག་བཙོན་ *ga-btsón* an eruption of the skin *W.*

ག་ཚོད་ *ga-tsód C.* **how much,** **rin gha-tsǫ̈** what is the price?

ག་ཞ་, ག་གཞའ་, ག་ཤ་ *gá-ża, gá-γża, gá-ṡa* **a jest, joke, laughter,** *gá-ża daṅ rtséd-mo rtse Pth.* they jest and play; also adj.: inclined to jesting, **di-riṅ gá-ṡa mi dug** he is not in a good humour, in good spirits, to-day *W.*

ག་ཟུག་ *gá-zug W.* **how,** interr. and correl.

ག་གཟི་ *ga-γzi W.* **squinting.**

ག་རི་, དགའ་རིས་ *ga-ri, dga-ris* = *gá ża W.*; **ga-ri mi rag** I am in low spirits, **dejected.**

ག་རུ་ *gá-ru* = *gan-du* 1. **whither,** which way, to which place, whereto. — 2. **where,** interr. and correl.

ག་རུ་ཌ་ *ga-ru-ḍa* the Garuda-bird. v. *kyuṅ.*

ག་རེ་ *ga-ré* 1. **where is?** *B.* and col. — 2. *Ld.* a species of Lathyrus.

ག་ལ་ *gá-la* for *gáṅ-la*, *ċi-la C.*; **ghá-la tén-ne neʼ ǰhun** owing to what, or from what cause did the disease arise? **ghá-la p̀en** to what does this serve, of what use is this? *Sch.*; **whither,** to what place? **ghá-la ₒdó-ghi yim-pa** *Ü*, where are you going to? — *gá-la-ba* = *gá-na-ba.*

ག་ལེ་ *gá-le C.* **slowly, softly, gently,** gen. in a good sense, opp. to every thing turbulent; therefore in exchanging compliments on meeting or parting: *̨*o-ná ghá-le ku żu naṅ** (perh. to be spelled *sku bżugs snaṅ*) says the person that has paid a visit, *̨*o-ná ghá-le p̀eb** he that received the visit, when taking leave of each other, both phrases implying about the same as our **farewell! good-bye!** Cf. *snaṅ-ba.*

ག་ལོག་ *ga-lóg W.* **squinting.**

ག་ཤ་ *gá-ṡa* 1. v. *ga-ża.* — 2. **girth** or **rope** slung across breast and shoulder in order to draw or carry anything; also **dog-harness;** also the **bandoleer** or **shoulder-belt,** worn as a badge of dignity by constables and the like officers; sobriquet for the rope of meditation, v. *sgom-ťág.*

ག་ཤས་ *ga-ṡás, C.* **gha-ṡę́**, **some, part;** **bhú-mo yaṅ gha-ṡę́ čǫ ǰhę̈-pa yin** even girls, in part, take to religion (become nuns).

ག་ཤེད་ *ga-ṡéd* v. *ṡed.*

ག་ཤེལ་ *ga-ṡél* **glass-beads, glass-pearls** *Sch.*

ག་སིར་ *ga-sír*, instead of تعزير **punishment** *Ld.*

གག་ *gag* 1. **silver** in bars, ingots, small pieces etc., **uncoined** *W.* — 2. **wad, wadding** (for loading muskets) *W.* — 3. *Cs:* = *bya-gág, gag-ťsé* a water-fowl.

གག་པ་ *gág-pa Med.*, a swelling in the throat *Cs.*; *gag-lhóg* id. (?)

གང་ *gaṅ* I. interr. pron. 1. **who? which?** *B., C., W.*; when used adjectively, it generally follows its sbst. (so at least in good language), and if preceding it, it stands in the genit. case: *p̀yogs gaṅ* which region or part of the world? *gáṅ-gi dus* which time? in the latter case it may also mean **whose**: *gáṅ-gi lam* whose way? *ṕyi naṅ γnyis čós lugs gaṅ bzaṅ* which of the two doctrines, the Brahmanic or the Buddhist, is the right one? *ṕyogs gáṅ-nas oṅ, ṅo mi šés-pas* not knowing from what part of the country she comes *Glr.*; *ma ni gaṅ yin bu ni gaṅ yin bye-brág ṕyes* decide which is the mother and which the child *Dzl.*; *gaṅ žé-na* lit. 'if one asks which?' corresponds sometimes to the English 'namely, to wit, viz.'; *gáṅ-na* where? *gaṅ-la* whither? *gáṅ-nas, gáṅ-las* whence? *gáṅ-du* where? whither? *gáṅ-na-ba = ga-na-ba* v. above; *gáṅ-pa, yul gáṅ-pa*, col. **gaṅ-yúl-pa**, from what country? — 2. *C.* for *či* **what?** **ghaṅ zér-ra(m)** what shall I say? **ḱyö̀-kyi miṅ-la ghaṅ zér-ghyi yö̀-dham** what is your name? **gháṅ-la yoṅ** what are you coming for? what do you want? — 2. rel., or rather correl. pron., **who, which, he who, she who, whoever, whichever, whatever,** ὅστις: *gaṅ ṕyir ṭ́óṅ-ba de ni* she who follows *Dzl.*; *gaṅ gos ˳dód-pa-la gos byuṅ* whoever wanted clothes, to him they were given *Dzl.*; *ríg-pa gaṅ rnó-ba čig-la stér-ro* I give it to him who is the sharpest as to sagacity *Glr.*; *ḱyód-kyi ďpá-ba gaṅ yin-pa-la ḱó-bo mgu* the bravery which you have shown pleases me *Tar.* 21, 13; *rgyál-bu gáṅ-du ťse ˳ṕós-pai γnás-su sóṅ-ṅo* they went to the place where the prince had changed life *Dzl.*; *gáṅ-gi lam sṅón-du grub-pa des* . . . he whose way (of sanctification) will be completed first, shall . . . *Stg.* Often *ťams-čád* or a plural-sign accompanies the partic.: *gaṅ mi šés-pa-dag* they who do not understand *Dzl.* Rarely in *B.*, but frq. in the col. language of *W.*, the *pa* after the verb is supplied by a gerundial particle, such as *na, nas*: **gaṅ tán-na ḱyad med** which you intend to give is all the same. Sometimes, however, particularly in more modern literature, no *pa* is added to the verb at all, esp. when *gaṅ* is joined with *yin, yod*, or *dug*, so that such sentences in their form are very similar to the relative sentences of occidental languages; but that this omission of *pa*, although sanctioned by long continued use, is after all an incorrect breviloquence, and that *pa* must always be understood, appears from the frq. occurrence of the plural sign immediately after *yod* etc.: *de γnyís-kyi srid gaṅ yód-rnams* the claims to government which both of these maintained *Glr.*; *gáṅ-ťse — déi-ťse* **when — then;** *gaṅ žig* **whoever, if any body** etc. frq.; vulgo in *W.* often pleon. = any or some, **gaṅ žig ťims-si ṕi-la** on account of some law-suit, instead of *ťims žig-gi ṕyir*; *gaṅ la-lá žig* is of a similar meaning, but less frq. The import of the word is still more generalized by *yaṅ* being added to *gaṅ* or to the verb: *dṅós-po gaṅ mťoṅ yaṅ Mil.* whatever he sets his eyes upon; *gaṅ ltár-na yaṅ, gaṅ yin kyaṅ* whatsoever it may be, however that may be, be that as it may, at all events, esp. *C.*; *gaṅ-yaṅ-rúṅ-ba, gaṅ-rúṅ, gaṅ-či-yaṅ-rúṅ* whosoever he may be, whatsoever it may be, *quicunque*; *γnas gaṅ-yaṅ-rúṅ-ba-na* whereever; *gáṅ-nas gáṅ-du skyes ḱyaṅ* out of which class of beings and into whichsoever I shall be re-born *Dzl.* — 3. indefinite pron., used absolutely, **each, every, any, all,** when followed by a negation = **not any, none, no:** *žo dar ču sogs gaṅ yaṅ ḱa*, curdled milk, buttermilk, water, every thing tastes bitter *Med.*; *saṅs-rgyás gáṅ-gis kyaṅ ma bčágs-pa* not yet trodden by any Buddha *Glr.*; *ṕan gaṅ ťogs gyis* be as useful as ever possible *Mil.*; *gáṅ-dag* all *Glr.* and elsewhere; *dé-dag mi ˳byuṅ gaṅ yaṅ med* these are to be found everywhere; *gáṅ-la gaṅ-˳dul* converting each in the manner best suited to him; *gáṅ-gis kyaṅ = čis-kyaṅ* by all means; *gáṅ-gis kyaṅ dgós-pa méd-pa* altogether useless *Mil.*; *gaṅ daṅ gaṅ Cs., Sch.* (more frq. *gaṅ daṅ či*) every thing whatsoever *Glr.*

**གང་ག་ཆུང་** *gaṅ-ga-čuṅ* an officinal plant *Med.*

**གང་གཱ་** *gaṅ-gā Ssk.* the river **Ganges.**

གང་བ་ gáṅ-ba, sometimes gáṅ-po, also gaṅ 1. **full**, rín-po-čés baṅ-mdzód gáṅ-ba žig a treasury full of jewels Dzl.; ťál-ču ḱól-mas gáṅ-ba-ste being filled with boiling lye Thgy.; ɣser-p̓yé bre gáṅ-po, ɣser ɣžóṅ-pa gaṅ a measure filled with gold-dust, a basin full of gold; ˏóbs-kyi náṅ-na sbrul ɣdúg-pas gáṅ-ṅo lit.: in the ditch it was full of poisonous snakes Dzl.; brgyud gáṅ-bar gyúr-to the progeny increased Glr.; mčód-rten ḱru gáṅ-pa Glr. a pyramid, a full cubit in height. — 2. W. also **heaped** (measure), opp. to *gaṅ-čád* (lit. bčad) **smoothed** (measure).

གང་བུ་ gáṅ-bu **pod, shell, husk** (Sch. also also flower-bud?) ˏod-zér-gyi gáṅ-bur ˳dril-nas enveloping himself in a veil of rays, wrapping himself in a garment of light (another reading: góṅ-por in a lump, in one mass) Glr.; gaṅ-ló an empty pod, freed from the kernels W.

གང་ཟག་ gaṅ-zág 1. **man**, as an intellectual being, **a person**; gaṅ-zág ɣžán-gyis brda sprád-pas another person describing it to you (opp. to what we know by our own perception and observation) Mil.; hence philosophical term for the **I** or **self**, पुद्गल Was.; bstan-bčós-la mḱás-pai gaṅ-žág-rnams learned or lettered men, men of science Glr.; esp. man in relation to religion: čos p̓yi-bšól byéd-pai gaṅ-zág Mil., men who postpone religion, not troubling themselves about it: ˳p̓ágs-pai gaṅ-žág-rnams-kyi rgyál-po the king of reverend persons, i.e. Buddha; lóg-lta-čaṅ-gyi gaṅ-zág heretical people; gaṅ-zág p̓ál-pa, ťa-mál-pá common people Mil. and others; also explicitly: people favourably disposed towards religion, religious people Gyatch. c. 26 & 27. (at present the word is generally understood in the latter sense); dus p̓yis-kyi gaṅ-zág Glr., ma-ˏóṅs-pai gaṅ-zág skál-ba daṅ ldán-pa Mil. a pious posterity. The word, however, so little implies the clerical state, that it is used directly for 2. **layman**, one that has not taken orders Dzl. ༢༦༠, 5 and elsewhere. — 3. (resp. žal-zág) **tobacco-pipe**, not the hukka, but a small sort, similar to ours, gen. made of metal; gaṅ-mgó **bowl** of a tobacco-pipe; gaṅ-mǰúg mouth-piece or **tip** of it C.

གངས་ gaṅs 1. **glacier-ice, glacier**; gáṅs-čan adj. abounding in snow, in glaciers, also as a sbst. a glacier; gáṅs-čan-las ˳byúṅ-bai ču the water issuing from a glacier Med., and even as a p.n.: Tibet; gáṅs-čan-gyi skad the Tibetan language; gáṅs-bšóg-pa to cleave the snow, i.e. to have it trodden down by yaks sent in advance, in order thus to form a path for the travellers (v. Huc Voyage II. 421). — gaṅs-rgyúd a chain of snow-mountains. — gaṅs-čen-mzod-lṅá 'the five receptacles of the vast glacier-ice', or gaṅs-čen-rǰé-lṅá 'the five kings of the same', pronounced *ghaṅ-čen-˳dzo̤'-ṅá*, or *ǰe-ṅá*, n. of a high mountain in Sikkim, commonly spelled Kinjinjunga; gaṅs-čen-mtsó-rgyál name of a deity (?) Glr. — gaṅs-ťigs Med. perh. stalactite. — gaṅs-ri a snow- or ice-mountain, as p.n. = Ti-se. — Seldom 2. col. **ice** in general; *gaṅs-soṅ* it has frozen W. — 3. **snow** in general, *ghaṅ ˳bab* it snows Ts.; *ghaṅ-ma-čár* sleet. — 4. **the sclerotic** of the eye Sch.

གད་པ་ gád-pa 1. **a bluff**; precipitous river-banks, such as frequently inclose the mountain rivers of Tibet. — 2. In W. the word seems to refer more to the species of rock, which is favourable to the formation of such banks: **conglomerate**; gad-p̓ug a cavern in such a bank; gad-rgyál the gigantic walls of conglomerate rock, through which mountain rivers have cut their way.

གད་མོ་ gád-mo **laughing, laughter**, ǰig-rtén-pai gád-mo a laughter, a laughing-stock, to wordly-minded people; ṅai gád-moi ɣnas this is to me an object of laughing, it is ridiculous to me Mil.; gád-mos ˳débs-pa to laugh at a person Tar. 25, 15.

གན་ gan B. and W., gám C., **nearness**, proximity, used only in such connections as gan-du **to, towards, up to**, ṅai gán-du šog come to me; rgyál-poi gán-du he went to the king; ḱáṅ-pai gán-du soṅ he went towards the house; *rgyál-poi gán-nas p̔yin* he came from the king; in col. language also c. accus.: **ḍóg-po gán-du** *W.* close by the brook, and c. termin. case, **čur gán-te** *W.* hard by the water: *rir-gán-pa* one living close to a mountain or hill.

གཉན་ཀྱལ་ *gan-kyál*, and *rkyal*, **supine**, lying on the back, with the face upward, *gan-kyál (du) nyál-ba* to lie in that position; *ₒgyel-ba* to fall backward; *sgyél-ba* to make one fall on his back; **ghan-kyál lóg-pa** to perform a somerset, to tumble over head and heels *C.*

གཉན་རྒྱ་ *gan-rgyá C.*, **gam-rgya** *W.*, **a written contract, an agreement.**

གཉན་དར་ *gan-dár Sch.*: a silk handkerchief offered as a present in exchanging compliments on meeting, = *k̔a-btags*.

གཉན་མཛོད་ *gan-mdzód* **store-room, storehouse** *Sch.*

གནྡྷོ་ལ་ *gándho-la* n. of a famous temple in *rdo-rje-γdán* (Vajrāsana near Gaya in Bengal) *Tar.* 16, 4 and elsewhere frq.; yet the words in *Glr.* 8, 10: *p̔yi gándho-la nán-du lhá-k̔an byás-pas* 'making outwardly a gandhola, inside an idolshrine', seem not to admit of a noun proper; a Lama explained it by *γtsug-lag-k̔an*; more correctly perh. = *dri-γtsan-kan*, i.e. = गन्धकूट. Cf. also ghāṇḍhola.

གཉྫི་ར་ *gánji-ra Glr.* 65, 8 obviously a *Ssk.* word, though not in our dictionaries; Lamas described it as an architectural ornament, consisting in small turrets or spires along the edge of a flat roof.

གཉབ་སྒྲ་ *gáb-sgra W.* **a belch** (vulgar).

གཉབ་པ་ *gáb-pa* **to hide**, to conceal one's self *Dzl.* and elsewhere frq.; *gáb-yig*, writing in secret characters, cryptography *W.*, *C.*; *gáb-sa* a place of concealment, hiding-place.

གཉབ་སྤངས་ *gab-spáns Glr.*, panels or little boards beneath the cornice of a roof, often filled out with paintings.

གཉབ་ཙེ་, གཉབ་ཚེ་ *gáb-tse*, *gáb-tse* **a tableau containing numerous mythological and astrological figures, and used** for fortune-telling.

གཉབ་ཚད་, གཉབ་པའི་ཚ་བ་ *gab-t̔sád*, *gáb-pai t̔sá-ba* a disease *Med.*; acc. to *Schr.* a hectic, consumptive fever.

གཉམ་ *gam* v. *gan*.

གཉམ་བུ་ར་ *gám-bu-ra W.* **citron, lemon.**

གཉའུ་ *gau* 1. **a chest, box** *Pth.*; a little box or case; when containing amulets, it is worn suspended by a string round the neck (v. *Schl.* 174). — 2. a squeaking sound *W.*, **gau zér-če** **to squeak.**

གཉར་ *gar* I. (*Cs. gár-ma*) **a dance**, *gar byed-pa*, *W.* **gár se-če**, to dance; *glu gar rtséd-mo byéd-pa Glr.* to sing, to dance and play; *gár-mk̔an* 1. one dancing, a dancer, a performer, e.g. even Buddha or any saint, when displaying miracles. — 2. n. of a god *Tar.* 11, 17, acc. to *Schr.*, *Siwa*; *gar-stábs* a dancing gesture or motion. — II. = *gá-ru*, *gán-du*, **whither, whereto, where;** *gar yan* anywhere, *gár yan skyé-ba* growing everywhere *Wdn.*; *gar yan mi ₒgró-ba* to go nowhere, to remain where one is *Mil.*; *Pth.* — **gar-méd** *W.* at all events, by all means, = **ga-na-med** — *gar-báb* at random, hit or miss, at hap-hazard *Sch.*

གཉར་ནག་ *gar-nág* n. of a medicine *Lt.*

གཉར་བ་ *gár-ba* **strong**, *gar-čan strong beer.*

གཉར་བུ་ *gár-bu* **solid**, not hollow *Sch.*

གཉར་མོ་ *gár-mo* **thick**, e.g. soup, = *ská-ba*; *gar-slá Sch.*: thick and thin; thickness.

གཉར་ཞ་ *gár-ža*, native name of the district called by the Hindoos Lāhul or Lāhōl (acc. to Cunningham 'Lahul' is a corruption of *lho-yul*, southern country, which latter appellation, however, is not in use in that district itself). Here, in the village of Kyelang, a missionary station was established in 1857, by the Church of the United Brethren (Moravians), together with a school and a lithographic press, for diffusing Christian knowledge by means of books and tracts.

གར་ལོག་ *gar-lóg*, *Tar.* 91, 7. 10. Transl. p. 317: 'acc. to *Was.* a rapacious mountain tribe, north-east of Tibet; in the Tibetan-Sanskrit dictionary mentioned as 'Turushka". They are doubtless the same robbers, that are called 'Kolo' by Huc (II. p. 187), who were known to our Lama from Tashilhunpo as *mgo-lóg*, or *lċaṅ-mo-mgo-lóg*, they having received this name ('queer-heads') in consequence of having their hair closely cropped. Possibly *gar-lóg* is the older and more correct form; cf. *dar-rgyas-gliṅ*.

གར་ཤ་ *gar-šá* the muscles of the thumb (?) *Med.*

གལ་ *gál* 1. **importance,** *gál-du ₒdzin-pa* to consider of importance, to esteem highly *Mil.*; *gál-ċan Cs.*, more frq. *gal-čé-ba* important, *de mi šin-tu gál-čé-bar yód-do Glr.*, *bsláb-bya gal-čé-ba Glr.* important precepts; *gal-čúṅ* unimportant, insignificant; undervalued, slighted *Mil.*; *gál-po* prob. = *gal*, *Schr.*; *gal-po-čé-yi bzá-dpon* the important, indispensable master of the house *Mil.* — 2. **constraint, compulsion,** **ṅa-la ghal ǰhuṅ* C.* I have been compelled. — 3. **trap, snare** *C*, *W.*, also *Mil.*; **gal-ltém* W.* id.; *gal ₒdzúg-pa* to set a trap or snare.

གལ་འགག་ *gál-ₒgág Med.* ?

གལ་ཏ་ *gál-ta W.* **crow-bar, handspike.**

གལ་ཏེ་ *gál-te* I. sbst., *gál-te mčán-kuṅ bċug Pth.* ? — II. conj. **if, in case,** serves to introduce a conditional sentence, ending with *na* (which is the essential word, whereas *gal-te* may be left out as well): *gál-te .. ₒóṅ-na* if .. comes (ἐάν ... ἔλθῃ); also followed by *yaṅ* (*kyaṅ*), although black snow fell *Dzl.* (*nas* instead of *na*, frq. to be met with, is either merely a slip of the pen, or an impropriety of speech). — *gál-te-na* as one word, and with the signification of **perhaps**, or the Greek ἄν (not 'if', *Cs.*) I found only in a few passages of the Kye-lang manuscript of *Dzl.*, where the edition of *Sch.* has *gál-te*, which makes no sense. *gal-srid W.* = *gal-te*. In Lewin's Manual it often occurs in the sense of **but, however.**

གལ་མདོ་ *gál-mdo* n. of a disease *Med.*

གལ་བ་ *gál-ba* **to force, to press** something on a person (cf. *gal* 2), *mi-la btson gal* in-door confinement is forced on men *Mil.*

གལ་རོ་ *gal-ró W.* **refuse, rubbish.**

གས་ *gas* v. *ₒgás-pa*.

གི་ *gi* 1. num. for 33. — 2. affix instead of *kyi*, after *g* and *ṅ*; for the signification v. *kyi*.

གི་གུ་ *gi-gu* the vowel sign ི, **i.**

གི་གུ་ཤེལ་, གི་གུ་ཤ་ *gi-gu-šél*, *gi-gu-šá Sch.*; 'having a white speck in the eye, wall-eyed (of horses)'.

གི་ཝང་ *gi-wáṅ*, *Glr.*, *gi-bám Lt.*, also *giu*, or *giu-wáṅ*, *Cs.*: 'n. of a concretion in the entrails of some animals, used for medicine'. But *Glr.* 35, 9 an elephant has it on its neck, and acc. to oral assertions it is to be found also in the human head; a man, for instance, is said to have *gi-wáṅ* in his brains, if in his sleep he is heard to utter long-drawn humming sounds.

གི་གླིང་ *gi-liṅ* a strong-bodied, durable horse *Sch.*

གི་ལིན་ *gi-lin Wts.* a fabulous animal.

གིང་ *giṅ Pth.* prob. a little drum, or the beating of it, as an accompaniment to dancing.

གིན་ *gin* affix, v. *kyin*.

གིར་མོ་ *gir-mo Ld.* the Indian **rupee,** = 5 *jau*.

གིས་ *gis* instead of *kyis* after *g* and *ṅ*, v. *kyis*.

གུ་ *gu* 1. num. for 63. — 2. sign of diminutives, e.g. *kyi-gu* puppy, little dog. — 3. **extension, extent, room, space** *γnás-sa gu-dóg*, *lúṅ-pa gu-dóg*, *lam gu-dóg* a narrow place, valley, road; *gu-yáṅs* (*-pa*) spacious, roomy, wide, *gu yáṅs-pa ˳dug* there is much room here.

གུ་གུ་ཤ་ *gú-gu-ša Ts.* **plate, flat dish.**

གུ་གུལ་ *gú-gul* (གུགྒུལ) Amyris Agallocha, a costly incense, one kind is white, another black.

གུ་གེ་ *gú-ge* n. of a province in the south-western part of Tibet.

གུ་ཏི་ *gú-ti W.* **deaf** (?).

གུ་རུ་ *gú-ru Ssk.*, spiritual teacher, father-confessor.

གུ་རུག་ *gu-rug Ld.* **colt** or **foal** of an ass.

གུ་ལང་ *gu-láṅ* n. of a deity, resorted to by mothers for being blessed with children; acc. to *Sch.: Siwa.*

གུ་ལེ་ *gú-le W.* for *gá-le* q.v.; *gú-le-la* id., **slowly, softly, gently,** without noise, **go gú-le-la čug** shut the door gently! *gu-yár Sch.* apparently the same.

གུ་སུ་ *gú-su Wdk.* **garment, dress** (?).

གུག་གེ་བ་ *gúg-ge-ba* **bent,** bent downwards (?), of leaves *Wdṅ.*; *gúg-pa* id.

གུག་པ་ *gúg-pa W.* to rub or scratch gently, **to tickle.**

གུང་ *guṅ* I. *Sch.*: 'the broad-headed tiger of Central Asia, Charachula' (*Mongol.*); it is said to differ from *stag*, and is not found in Tibet. — II. also *dguṅ* (*Cs. gúṅ-ma*) 1. **the middle,** *gúṅ-la* in the middle, e.g. the king in the middle (between his two wives); *stód-kyi gúṅ* (*-nas*) *ťon* taken out of the middle of the upper part *Mil.*; *gúṅ-du byéd-pa Thgy.* prob. to divide through the middle, to dissect (anatomically); *gúṅ sgrig-pa Sch.* 'to unite'; with respect to time: *dbyár-gyi gúṅ-la W.* in the middle of summer; *nyin-gúṅ*, and *mťsán-gúṅ* mid-day, mid-night *Cs.*; *guṅ-γnyís*, the two middle times, mid-day and mid-night; *nám-gyi guṅ-ťún-la* at the hour of midnight. — 2. **mid-day,** *guṅ ˳báb-pa* to take a noon-rest on a journey; *guṅ-tsígs* dinner *Schr.*; *guṅ sáṅs-la ˳gró-ba* (*W.* **čá-če**) to take a walk about the middle of the day, at noon; perh. also generally: to take a walk; *guṅ-lón Sch.*: 'at noon', more prob.: afternoon. — 3. **mid-night,** *gúṅ-la* at midnight *Glr.*; *dguṅ-γčig* one night (?) *Sch.* — 4. (Chinese?) title of a magistrate in Lhasa, something like Privy Counsellor; v. *dguṅ.*

གུང་སྟག་ *guṅ-stág* prob. = *stag Ld.-Glr. Schl.* fol. 13, 6.

གུང་ཐང་ *guṅ-ťáṅ* n. of a monastery in *Máṅ-yul Mil.*

གུང་མོ་ *gúṅ-mo* **the middle finger;** **guṅ-dzúg** *C.* id.

གུང་དམར་ལ་ཕུག་ *guṅ-dmár-la-p̔ug C.* **carrot.**

གུང་ལ་ཕུག་ *guṅ-la-p̔ug C.* **radish.**

གུད་ *gud* 1. **slope, declivity** *Cs.* — 2. **separation, solitude, seclusion** *Sch.*; *gúd-du ˳bór-ba* to place obliquely *Cs.*; *gúd-du ɣšégs-pa Dzl.* ༢༢*V*, 18 to separate, to disperse (?) *Sch.* — 3. *C.*: **loss, damage** = *gun, god.* — 4. *Ld.*: **heavy** or **thick of hearing,** **gud-nág** quite deaf, deaf as a post. — 5. *gúd-du ǰúg pa* v. *˳gúd-pa.*

གུད་པ་ *gúd-pa* v. *˳gúd-pa.*

གུན་ *gun* (*Cs. gún-pa*) **loss, damage,** **ṅá-la gun p̔og** *W.* I have suffered a loss (prop. damage has come over me).

གུན་པོ་ *gún-po Lh.* **expensive, dear.**

གུན་དུམ་ *guṅ-dúm* a bottle-shaped or cylindrical **basket** to put fruit in, *Ld.* (perh. akin to *rkóṅ-pa*).

གུམ་པ་ *gúm-pa* v. *˳gúm-pa.*

གུར་ *gur*, resp. *bžugs-gúr*, *γzim-gúr Cs.*, also *dbu-gúr C.*, **tent,** *gos-gúr Cs.* a tent of silk, *p̔yiṅ-gúr* of felt, *sbra* and *re-gúr* of coarse yak's hair felt, *ras-gúr* of cotton cloth; *rgyal-gúr Cs.* 'a king's pavilion', *dmag-gúr* a military tent. — *gur-mčóg* a magnificent tent, or *gur-rgyál*, is used by Chr. Prot. for the tabernacle. — *gur-ťág* the tent-ropes, **gur-bér** *W.*, or *gur-šiṅ Cs.* the tent-poles. — *gur-ťóg Cs.*: 'the upper covering or outer fly of a tent'. — *gur-γžól Cs.*: 'the walls of a tent'. — ***gur-klád* passage for the smoke out of a tent, *gur-***

˳gram lattice in the side of it, and gur-lčám stakes supporting the roof Sch., — peculiar expressions relating to the felt-tents of the Mongol nomads.

gur-kúm, gur-gúm 1. **saffron,** Crocus Glr., Lt. — 2. **marigold,** Calendula, and similar yellow flowers C.

gur-gúr Ld. a small **churn** used for preparing tea.

gur-lpágs a perforated skin, a hide full of holes Sch.

gul-gúl Bal. **slowly,** for gú-le.

gul-nág Lt. n. of a medicine.

gús-pa sbst. **respect, reverence, devotion;** also adj **respectful, devout;** dge-˳dún-la gús-pas p̔yag ˳tsál-lo the priesthood I respect with devotion; ma-gús-pa unbelieving, undevout Thgy.; *gus-žáb čó-če* W. to show a respectful willingness to serve; **humble,** gús-par ˳gyúr-ba Cs.: 'to humble one's self'; in modern letters = p̔ran, your most humble servant.

gús-po C., W., **expensive, costly, dear.**

ge num. for 93.

ge-šá a kerchief for the head hanging down behind.

ge-sár 1. Cs. n. of a flower, Lt. and elsewhere, prob. = केसर; it is said to grow in Nepal, and to be called also pád-ma ge-sár. — 2. Sch.: **pistil,** but, like ze-˳brú, it signifies undoubtedly the organs of fructification in general, as the natural science of Tibet is certainly not acquainted with the sexual difference in the parts of flowers; ge-sár-čan the lotos flower Sch. — 3. n. of a fabulous king in the north of Tibet, with the epithet dmág-gi rgyál-po Glr. and elsewh.; ge-sár-gyi sgruṅ the fabulous history of the same.

gegs **hindrance, impediment, obstacle,** gégs-med-par without hindrance, **unimpeded,** **t̔e-ts̔óm daṅ gegs sél-ba to remove doubts and hindrances Mil.; gegs-byéd bgegs a malignant spirit, causing impediments** or mischief Zam.; čos-mdzád yóṅs-la gegs byéd-pa to throw obstacles in the way of all pious people Pth.; saṅs-rgyás mi t̔ób-pai gegs bži four obstacles to attaining the Buddhaship Thgy.; also without a negation: t̔ób-pai grogs ˳gró-am gégs-su ˳gro will you help me or hinder me in obtaining . . . ? Mil.; ˳grúb-pai gegs impediment to perfection.

gél-pa **branch** of a tree, šiṅ-gel-pa.

go 1. numerical sign for 123. — 2. num. inst. of dgú-bču, in the abbreviated numbers go-γčig etc., 91—99. — 3. for gó-č̔a. — 4. for gó-bo.

gó 1. **place, room, space** (prob. = gu); in this sense it is used in go-mt̔sams-méd-par without intermediate spaces, continuous; ˳bru sna ts̔ogs go-mt̔sams-med-par skyes grain of every kind grew densely, luxuriantly; go-mt̔sams-méd-par gáṅ-ba closely filled Tar. 13; prob. also in go-čod: 'the space is cut off, or filled i e. the matter is done with, settled, satisfaction has been made; col. also: I have got enough, I am full, (the thing lost or missed) has been found, restored; *gho čo̱' soṅ* or *ǰhuṅ* C., *go čód-k̔an yod* W. he has managed the business well, he has executed his commission satisfactorily; des rgyál-bai gó mi čod by this the victory has not yet been fully decided Mil.; t̔os bsam sgom γsúm-gyi go čod (by only once looking at the Ommanipadmehūm) every other hearing, thinking, or looking at is done away with, any thing further is rendered unnecessary Glr.; k̔yéd-la go mi čód-pai čos a doctrine not satisfactory to you Mil.; bu tsab ṅa spyugs či p̔yir go mi čod why should it not be sufficient that I be condemned to exile instead of my son? Pth. — 2. **the proper place** of a person or thing among other persons or things, **position, rank,** condition of life, so in many of the following compounds, the word being seldom used **alone:** p̔ai gór in the place, office, dignity of his **father** Dzl.; gó-nas according to, in pro**portion to Glr.; go rgás-na when rank and** dignity are grown old and gone, when the position in life has been lost *Glr.*; hence *go-rgás* may be applied to an old maid (*Schr.*); *ráṅ-gi go ˳dug* that is my place, my business, like *ča;* also **place, space, spot** in a still more general sense: *'á-mai gó-na* at the place of my mother, with my mother *Glr.*; *raṅ-˳ťág-gi gó-na* near the mill *Glr.; go ldóg-pa* (*zlog-pa, lóg-pa*) to change place, esp. to turn to the contrary *S.g.*; *nád-go* the seat of a disease *Sch.*; *go-byéd* is mentioned as a quality of the air *S.g.*; *sprín-gyi go-bar ǰyé-nas ˳oṅs*, we came parting the space between the clouds *Mil.; sprin dkar ldiṅ-gi go-čóg Mil.?* — 3. **armour,** gen. *gó-čá.* —

**Comp.** *go-skábs* lit. a chance of taking place, of existing, *bdé-bai go-skábs gá-la yod Pth.*, where is there a possibility of being happy? — *go-skál C.* the share or portion due to a person in accordance to his rank. — *go-k̔áṅ* **arsenal** *Schr.* — *go-k̔ráb* coat of mail with helmet, **armour.** — *go-grál* **rank, dignity** *Cs.* — *go-grás* id. *Cs.* — *go-rgás* v. *go* 2. — *gó-ča* 1. **armour;** often fig.: *bzód-pai gó-ča bgó-ba*, or *gón-pa*, to put on the armour of patience; *mi-ǰigs-go-ča* the harness of intrepidity. 2. **gear, implements, tools** in general, *bkra-šis srúṅ-bai gó-ča* (charmed) instruments used for securing future happiness (in behalf of a new-born infant) *Med.* — *go-mnyám C.* of equal rank. — *go-ťém* degree of dignity or rank *Cs.* — *go-˳dún* = *sna-˳dún*, of different sorts, **various** *Lex.* — *go-ldóg* (cf. *go-ldóg-pa*) **the contrary, reverse, opposite; wrong, perverse,** *dé-las go-ldóg* the contrary of it *Med.*: **go ǰug go-lóg-la* W.* head fore-most; **go-lóg čó-če* W.* to go to work in the wrong way, **go-lóg ḍí-če** to write wrong. — *go-p̔áṅ(s)* 1. **degree, rank, dignity,** *blón-poi go-p̔áṅ-la bkód-par ˳gyúr-ba Pth.* to be installed into the dignity of a minister; *go-p̔áṅ spár-ba Lex.* to raise the dignity. **2. model, pattern,** standard of perfection (?) *Cs.* — *go-mťsáms* v. *go* no. 1. — *go-mťsón* harness and weapons. — *go-rím* 1. **order** of rank *Glr.* — 2. **succession,** successive order, turn.

གོ་ཁ་ *gó-k̔a* the place (near the hearth) for firewood *Mil.*

གོ་བ་ *gó-ba* I. vb. 1. **to understand, comprehend,** *W. *há-go-če*; go-dká-ba* difficult, hard to be understood, *go-slá-ba* easy to be understood, intelligible; **gho-dé-wa yoṅ* C.* now it becomes intelligible, thus it will be understood; *go-byed-brdá Lex.* an explaining, illustrating symbol; *gó-žiṅ rtóg-pa* to take in and comprehend; *brdá-ru go* this I understand to be a symbol *Pth.; gó-bai yul, gó-byai yul* a subject intelligible to all *Schr.* — 2. **to mean, to imagine,** *par* that. *Glr.*; *go-nór-ba* to misunderstand, to mistake, to be mistaken. —

II. sbst. **perception, comprehension,** *gó-ba bláṅ-ba Mil.* to come to a right comprehension, a clear perception (of some philosophical or religious truth); *gó-bai mǰál-ba Lex.*: *'mǰál-ba* in the sense of perceiving'.

གོ་བོ་ *gó-bo* a large **eagle** or **vulture,** *C., W.* and *B.*; *go-sér* the common black-bearded vulture of the Himalaya, with a yellow neck; *go-brún* excrements of it *Med.*

གོ་བྱི་ལ་ *go-byi-la Med.* n. of a poisonous medicinal fruit *Cs.*; *go-bye Med.* id.?

གོ་ཡུ་ *go-yú Med.*, n. of a flower *Cs.*

གོ་ར་ *go-rá Cs.*; 'prison, jail'; prop. a court surrounded by a wall.

གོ་རེ་ལོང་ *gó-re-lóṅ* a waiting-servant, **page** *Cs.*

གོ་ལ་ *gó-la Ssk.* **ball, bullet.**

གོ་ལོག་ *go-lóg* v. *go-ldóg* sub *go* Comp.

གོ་ཤེན་ *go-šén* v. *go-čén.*

གོ་ས་ *go-sá* **rank, dignity,** **go-sá čén-po, ťón-po* W.* high in rank.

གོ་ཏ་མ, གཽ་ཏ་མ, གོཽ་ཏ་མ་ *Gó-ta-ma, Gau-ta-ma, Gou-ta-ma,* **the Gotamide,** the descendant of Gotama, which, among others, was the name of the founder of the Nyaya philosophy in India (Banerjea Dialogues on Hindoo Philosophy p. 56f.); but in the Buddhist legends it is mentioned as the name of one of the ancestors of the Sakya-race, on which account Buddha is often called Gautama. The different forms of this name are used promiscuously by Tibetan writers.

གོག *gog W.* for *góṅ-po* **a lump.**

གོག་ཐལ་ *gog-ťál* **ashes,** **gog - ťál yúm - če, yóg-če, tiṅ-če** *W.* to spread ashes (viz. on the snow, in order to increase the effects of the sun, and to accelerate the thawing of the snow).

གོག་པ་ *góg-pa* 1. **to crawl** (of little children). — 2. **to crumble off, to scale off** (of the plaster of a wall, of scurf etc.).

གོག་པོ་ *góg-po* **dilapidated, ruinous,** *ḱáṅ(-pa) góg(-po)* a house in ruins; *mḱar-góg* a dilapidated castle; of clothes: out of repair, ragged; *żiṅ - góg* a field lying waste; *dpe - góg* an antiquated, worthless book; *gog-góg Cs.*: 'the sound of a somewhat broken vessel'.

གོང་ *goṅ* 1. **price, value,** also *goṅ-ťáṅ Glr.*, frq.; *goṅ dpyád-pa* (often also *bčád-pa*, inconsistent with etymology) to apprize, to fix a price; *goṅ brgyáb - pa C.* (*goṅ ˳grig - pa Schr., Sch.*) id. — 2. **the above,** in space as well as in time, (in *Khams* e. g. it is used as a sbst., signifying: elevated, alpine pasture-grounds); **the above said, the former,** referring to a preceding part or passage of a book, *goṅ daṅ mťun, goṅ daṅ ˳drá-bar, goṅ-bżin, goṅ-mťsúṅs* as above (mentioned); *ṕrin goṅ ˳og ˳dzól-ba* to confuse a message, to make a medley of it *Glr.*; *góṅ-du, góṅ-na, góṅ-nas, góṅ-la* 1. adv. over it, on it, thereon, above, from above. 2. postp. c. genit. or accus.: on, above, over, before, *sgo góṅ-du* over the door; *yáb - kyi góṅ - du ˳das*, he died before his father *Glr.*; *déi góṅ-du* before this time *Glr.*; *ma ťsogs góṅ-du* before they are assembled; *góṅ-gi* the former, the above mentioned; *góṅ - gi dé - rnams* those preceding; *góṅ-du bšád-pa ltar* as has been said, explained above; *góṅ - du smós-pa* the above mentioned; *góṅ-gi . . . żes smós-pa* the above statement that . . .; *sṅa goṅ bód-kyi rgyál-po* the former (ancient) Tibetan kings; *goṅ* and *˳og* like our subdivisions of *a* and *b*, the first and second part, division or section of a book, *ba-góṅ* and *ba-˳óg* Volume XV Section 1 and 2; the face and the back of a leaf: *bži-góṅ* folio 4, a. — *goṅ-sku-y̆żógs*, a title, like our: his highness, excellence, eminence *Sch.* v. *sku*.

གོང་པོ་, གོང་བུ་ *góṅ-po, góṅ-bu, W.* **gog**, **lump, mass, heap, clot,** *šá-goṅ-po* a lump of flesh *Dzl.*; *ḱrag-góṅ* a clot of blood *Glr.*; **bol-góṅ** *C.*, **sa-góg** *W.*, clod, glebe; **ḱa-góg** *W.* snow-ball.

གོང་བ་ *góṅ-ba, W.* **góṅ-ṅa**, *gós-kyi góṅ-ba*, **collar,** *goṅ-ba-nas ˳dzín-pa* to seize by the collar.

གོང་མ་ *góṅ - ma* a higher one, **a superior; the former,** the first named, *góṅ-ma bžin-du* like the former; *rgyál-ba góṅ-ma* the most high, the divine Buddha *Mil.*; *góṅ-ma če, góṅ-ma čén-po* the most high, applied to worldly sovereigns, as: *rgya-nág góṅ-ma* the emperor of China *C.*; *góṅ-ma - rnams Mil* the gods (the 'superi' of the ancients), among whom according to the doctrines of Buddhism the Lamas are included.

གོང་མོ་ *góṅ-mo* **ptarmigan, white grouse,** *lhá-bya góṅ-mo B.* and *C.*, **ri-bya góṅ-mo** *W.*, *goṅ-sréǵ* id. (?); *goṅ - yag Sch.*: wood-grouse, cock of the wood, Tetrao urogallus.

གོང་ཞུ་ *goṅ-żú C.* **paper lantern.**

གོད་ *god, W.* **gód-ḱa** *Dzl. gód-pa, Cs. gód-ma* 1. **loss, damage,** *god ˳gyúr-ba Thgy.*, **ghọ'-la ˳dó-wa** *C.*, **god-la čá-če** *W.*, to suffer loss, e.g. *nór - la* or *nor*, a loss of money and property; *gód-pa* vb. id., **nor gód-da** *W.* have you had a loss? 2. *C.* **punishment.**

གོན་ *gon* the common **gourd, pumpkin** *W.*

གོན་པ་ *gón-pa* I. vb. **to put on** (clothes, shoes), *mgó-la ża gón-pa* to put on a cap.

— II. sbst. **coat, clothing** *Sch.*; **gón-če̥* Lh., Ld.*, **gón-ma* Bal.* id.

གོབ་ནོན་ *gob-nón* (spelling uncertain), **gob-nón ċó-ċe, táṅ-ċe, gyáb-ċe* W.* **to tease, vex, irritate.**

གོམ་པ་ *góm-pa* 1. **a pace, step,** *góm-pa ₒbór-ba* to make a step, to pace; *góm-pa bdun ₒbór-ba Glr.* 5, 2 and elsewh.: to make seven steps, as a ceremony, which may also be counted equivalent to a religious pilgrimage, the actual performance of which is not possible: *góm-pa ₒdór-ba* prob. = *ₒbór-ba; góm-pa ₒdébs-pa* and *skyél-ba Lt.* ?? — *góm-pai stabs* the (peculiar) manner of stepping *Zam.*; **ṗrú-gu-la gom-ṫáṅ láb-ċe* W.* to teach a little child to walk; **gom čág-ċe** to stride solemnly along; **gom-ǰór** col a veranda (?). — 2. **the 'pas'** in dancing.

གོམས་པ་ *góms-pa* **accustomed, wonted, wont** c. dat.; *klóg-pa-la góms-šiṅ* practising (the art of) reading *Dzl.*; *góms-par byéd-pa*, and *ₒgyúr-ba* c. dat. and accus., to accustom one's self to a thing, to practise; *mi góm-pa* unaccustomed; **mí daṅ góm-te* W.* accustomed to man, tame, domesticated: **ghom-ky̆e̥* C.* a habit, custom.

གོར་མ་ *gór-ma Cs.*: a general name for stone; *Sch.*: stones, rubble, bowlder-stones.

གོར་མ་ཆག་ *gor-ma-čág*, eleg. *gor-ma-bkúm*, **certain, sure, indubitable,** *de ₒbyúṅ-ba gor-ma-čág-go* his coming is quite sure *Wdṅ.*; *dé yin gor-ma-čág-go* that it is this, is quite certain *Stg.* frq; *gor-ma-čág-par* adv. certainly.

གོར་མོ་ *gór-mo* 1. **round, circular** *Sch.*; *gor-gór Med.* id. — 2. *W.* **a rupee.**

གོར་ཤི་ཤ་ *gór-ši-ša* v. *tsán-da-na.*

གོལ་བ་ *gól-ba* v. *ₒgól-ba.*

གོས་ *gos* 1. resp. *ná-bza*, **garment, dress.** — 2. in some compounds **silk.** — *rgyán-gós* fine clothes *Glr.*; *rgyún-gos C., W.*, an every day coat; *čos-gos* clerical garb or garments *Schl.* 170, *Burn.* I. 306, *Köpp.* I. 339, II. 266; *mṫáṅ-gos* a sort of petticoat worn by the monks, having many plaits and folds, like the kilt of the Highlanders, but longer and of one colour; *ṗó-gos* man's dress; *blá-gos* an upper garment, a kind of toga; *mó-gos* a woman's gown; *γzáb-gos* holiday clothes, opp. to *rgyun-gos C., W.* — *gos gón-pa, gyón-pa* to put on, *ₒbúd-pa* to take off, *brǰe-ba* to change clothes; *brtségs-pa Sch.*: to put one garment over the other; *gos btég-pa* to tuck up, by drawing the front skirts under the girdle; *gos ldáb-pa* to lay or fold a coat together; *gos spú-ma* a coat of napped cloth.

**Comp.** *gos-skúd* **silk-thread.** — *gos-sgáb* **skirt** or **flap** of a coat. — *gos-sgám* box, chest, or press for clothes, **wardrobe.** — *gos-čén*, col. *go-šén*, silk fabrics, **silks.** — *gos-rnyiṅ* an old coat or dress. — *gos-ṫúṅ* **trowsers** *Glr., C.* — *gos-mṫá* = *gos-sgab.* — *gos-nág* a black garment, a female dress. — *gos-bzáṅ* a beautiful dress, fine clothes (as an object of show), festival raiment. *gos-lág* (in *W.* also pronounced **goi-lág, go-lág** in *C.* **gho-lág**) **dress, clothes,** body-linen; **gos-lág ṭú-ċe* W.* to wash linen.

གོས་པ་ *gós-pa* pf. of *bgó-ba.*

གྱ་ *gya* num. instead of *brgyád-ċu*, in the abbreviated numbers *gya-γċig* etc. 81—89.

གྱ་ *gya*, a root, the meaning of which is not quite settled yet; it occurs in the following combinations: *gya-gyú* (*Cs.*: crookedness?) **intrigues,** secret machinations *C., W.*; *γnód-séms daṅ bslú-bai gya-gyú sogs* malice, deceitful tricks and the like; *gya-gyu-ċan* crafty, deceitful, fraudulent, e.g. *sems*; *gya-gyú byéd-pa* **to** intrigue, to plot. — *gya-ma-gyú* 1. of rivers etc.: **quiet, calm,** gently flowing along *Mil.* 2. of a man: **cautious, close, reserved,** so that one does not know what to think of him, ni f. — *gya-nyés Mil.* was explained: **marvelous, inexplicable,** of men, occurrences etc. — *gya-nóm-pa Cs.*: 'contentment, joy'; yet the context in several passages of *Mil.* suggests the signification: abundance, sufficiency. — *gya-rtsóm, gya-tsóm* haste, hurry, rashness *Cs.*

གྱ་བ་ *gyá-ba* **deformed, disfigured,** having lost his or her former beauty *Cs.*

གྱག་པ་ *gyág-pa* diminished *Cs.*; v. *°gyág-pa.*

གྱང་, གྱེང་ *gyaṅ, gyéṅ* **pisé,** earth or clay stamped into moulds, and frequently used as building-material in *Sp., Ld.,* and other parts of Tibet; *gyaṅ-sgróm* pisé-mould; *gyaṅ-skór* pisé-wall round an estate or village *Glr.*; *gyaṅ-ra* cattle-yard constructed of pisé; *gyaṅ-tse* terrace wall of pisé *Ld.*; *gyaṅ-rím* one layer of pisé, i.e. as much as is stamped in at a time, about one ell in height; this frequently serves for a measure of the depth of the snow *Mil.*; *gyaṅ-ris* fresco or wall-painting.

གྱད་ *gyad,* also *gyád-pa, Ssk.* मल्ल 1. **a champion,** a man of great physical strength, **an athlete,** frq.; *da-dúṅ gyád-gyi tsal °gran* let us try once more our strength in fighting *Mil.*; *gyád-rdo* giant-stone, i.e. a stone which only a giant is able to lift *Mil.* — 2. n. of a people *Tar.* 11, 10.

གྱན་རྒྱུ་ *gyan-rgyu Med., gyan-rgyui bu-ga, gyan-rgyui mṫu?*

གྱམ་ *gyam* **a shelter, a grotto** large and wide, **but** not deep (cf. *skyibs*), *brág-gyam* a shelter under a rock; *gád-gyam* a grotto beneath a conglomerate rock; *ṗoṅ-gyám* (for *ṗa-boṅ-gyam*) a shelter under a beetling rock: *gyám-bu* a little cover or shelter *Cs.*

གྱར་གྱོད་ *gyar-gyód* prob. = *gyod-ḱa, god-pa* loss, damage.

གྱི་ *gyi* for *gyi,* after *n, m, r, l*; v. *kyi.*

གྱི་ན་(བ་) *gyi-na (-ba)* 1. **bad, coarse, mean, poor, miserable,** of food, clothes etc.; *gyi-na °ťsó-ba* a miserable, starving life *Pth.* — 2. **unsteady, fickle** *Schr.*

གྱི་ལིང་ *gyi-liṅ Glr.* n. of an excellent breed of horses.

གྱིག་ *gyig* **caoutchouc, India rubber,** *gyig-šiṅ, gyig-sdóṅ* caoutchouc-tree *Sik.*

གྱིང་ *gyiṅ* n. of a deity *Pth.,* perh. = *kiṅ-káṅ.*

གྱིང་མོ་ *gyiṅ-mo W.* gently **sloping,** gradually descending or subsiding.

གྱིན་ *gyin* v. *kyin.*

གྱིམ་བག་ *gyim-bág* **amalgam;** *gyim-bág-gis °byúg-pa* to gild in the fire *Schr.*

གྱིས་ *gyis* 1. inst. of *kyis,* after liquid letters. — 2. v. *bgyid-pa.*

གྱུ་ *gyu Cs.* = *gya-gyú*; cf. also *sgyu.* — *gyú-ba* v *°gyú-ba.*

གྱུང་རོ་ *gyúṅ-ro* v. *gyóṅ-ro; gyur* v. *°gyúr-ba.*

གྱེ་གུ་ *gyé-gu* **crookedness, curve; hunch, hump,** crookback, crooked; *gyé-gu-čan* of a camel, *gyé-gur °dúg-pa* being crooked, of trees, opp. to *draṅ-po, Stg.*

གྱེ་གོང་ *gye-góṅ* n. of a Bonpo idol (?) *Mil.*

གྱེང་ *gyéṅ* v. *gyaṅ.*

གྱེད་པ་ *gyéd-pa* v. *°gyéd-pa.*

གྱེན་ *gyen* (opp. to *ṫur*) **up, upward, up-hill,** mostly followed by *du* or *la, gyén-du °dzég-pa* to mount up, to ascend; *gyén-du rdzé-ba* to turn up, to cock (a hat or cap); above, on the surface, *gyén-du lús-pa* to keep above (water) *Glr.* **gyen-la ḍáṅ-po** *W.* **perpendicular, vertical;** *gyen-čád* (opp. to *man-čád*) the upper part of a country, *pú-rig gyen-čád* Upper Purig, *Ld.-Glr. Schl.* 26, b. also sbst.: *gyen γzár-po* a steep ascent *C.*

གྱེར་ *gyer* v. *dgyér-ba.*

གྱེས་ *gyes* v. *°gyé-ba.*

གྱོ་མོ་ *gyó-mo* 1. **gravel, grit** *Dzl., Stg.* — 2. **potsherd** *Cs.*; *gyo-dúm* id. — 3. **tile, brick** *Sch.*; *gyo-mgó* id.; clay-vessel. In an allegorical comparison of the body with a house, the hair of the head is said to be like a *ṗó-gyo mo-gyói rdza Med.? gyo-rtsí Wdṅ.?*

གྱོག་པ་ *gyóg-pa* **curved, crooked** *Cs.*; *gyóg-po* **left-handed, awkward** *Sch.*

གྱོགས་ *gyogs C.* pronounced **ghyog, ghyo**, for *sgyogs* **cannon,** large gun.

གྱོང་ *gyóṅ* **want, need, indigence,** *lto-gós-kyi gyóṅ ťeg-pa* to be able to endure want of food and clothes *Mil.*; *°ḱur-ba* to be reduced to want. — *gyóṅ-po* (cf. *kyoṅ-po*) **hard, harsh, rough, rude, impolite,** (*srab-*) *ḱa-gyóṅ-po* hard-mouthed; *gyoṅ-ró* a dried up body, a mummy *Sch.*; metaph. *dgra-gyóṅ* a hard, cruel, dangerous enemy; *ḱa-gyoṅ-čé* very rude, impudent *Mil.*

གྱོད *gyod* v. *ˬgyód-pa.*

གྱོད་ཁ *gyód-ḱa* **loss; quarrel, law-suit** *Sch.*

གྱོན་པ *gyón-pa* **to put on, to wear** = *gón-pa*; *lús-la gyón-pai gos* the garment that one wears *Dzl.*; *gyón-rgyu* materials for clothing *Mil.*

གྱོས་པོ *gyós-po* **father-in-law**, *gyós-mo* mother-in-law, *gyos-sgyúg* parents-in-law *Dzl.*, *Stg.* (In *Ld.* this word is rather avoided, sounding, as it is pronounced there, much like the obscene *rgyó-ba.*)

གྲྭ *grva* 1. **angle, corner** *Dzl.* ༢༢༥, 13; **lap, lappet, extremity,** *gós-kyi grva* coat-tail *Tar.* 98, 10 (seldom used). — 2. **school,** *klóg-grva* a reading-school *Cs.*; *sgóm-grva Glr.* and elsewhere: a meditating-school; *sṅágs-grva* a school for mystical theology *Cs.*; *ˬdúl-grva Glr.* a training-school, seminary; *smán-grvá* a medical school; *rtsís-grva* a school where mathematics are taught; *yíg-grva* a writing-school *Cs.* — 3. **a cell** *Cs.* (?) — 4. sometimes for *grvá-pa.*

**Comp.** *grvá-ḱaṅ* **school-house, school-room;** **láb-ḍa-ḱaṅ** *W.* id. — *grvá-pa* **scholar, disciple,** generally; **monk,** the lowest ecclesiastical grade; *grvá-pa byéd-pa* to become or to be a monk. — *grvá-dpon* **school-master** *Cs.*. — *grva-ṗrúg* **school-boy.** — *grvá-ṫsáṅ* the apartments in great monasteries, where the monks belonging to the same theological confession live together. — *grva-tsógs* convention of monks. — **ḍa-šág** **cell** *C.*, *W.* — *grva-sa* **monastery,** *grva-sa čén-po* a great monastery; a school attached to such a one; *mṫsan-nyid-kyi grvá-sa žig* a school of the Tsannyidpa sect; *dei stón-pa-rnams* the teachers of such a school *Mil.*

གྲ་ཏི *grá-ti* **plate, dish** *Ld.*

གྲ་བ *grá-ba* 1. sbst., also *gra-ṗád* **'a muzzle'** *Sch.*; a net before the window, to prevent passers-by from looking into the room *Schr.* — 2. vb. to carve in wood.

གྲ་མ *grá-ma* 1. **a beard** of corn, **awn,** *ˬbru grá-ma-ċan* bearded, awned plants, such as corn etc. (opp. to *ˬbru gáṅ-bu-ċan* leguminous plants) *S.g.*; **the bones** of fish v. *nya.* — *Zam.*: a tree or shrub, prob. the Tibetan **furze,** Caragana versicolor. — 3. a disease of the genitals, perh. venereal boils (condyloma) *Med.*

གྲག་པ *grág-pa* I. sbst. 1. **noise, rumour, talk,** *Cs.* — 2. the principal or most distinguished amongst several persons *Mil.* — II. vb. = *ˬgrág-pa, miṅ yaṅ mi grág-par* so that not even the name is mentioned any more *Pth.*

གྲགས་པ *grágs-pa* I. vb. 1. **to bind** *Thgy.*, *C.*, *W.*, e.g. *grés-po* a load, a burden, also *grás-pa Thgy.*; perh. also *ˬgrágs-pa*, *ˬgrógs-pa* q.v. — 2. pf. of *ˬgrág-pa.* — II. sbst. 1. **fame, reputation,** character by report, *grágs-pa ṅán-pa* ill name, bad repute *Pth.*; **rumour, report,** *deï grágs-pa čén-po byuṅ* the report of it spread, was circulated; in most cases it signifies **good name, renown,** *snyán-pa daṅ grágs-pas sai steṅ ṫams-ċád ḱyáb-pa Glr.* the whole earth was filled with (his) fame and renown; *snyan-grágs* id. (*Cs.*: good tidings); *grágs-pa-ċan*, *snyán-grags-ċan* illustrious, renowned; *rgyáṅ-nas grágs-pa če-ba* of great renown, of celebrity at a distance, (of less significance when more closely examined); **fame, glory,** *rnyéd-pa daṅ grágs-pa-la čágs-pas Dzl.*, greedy of gain and fame; *grágs-pa-čén-po* is also the name of a goddess = *dpal-lhá-mo.* — *grags* = *grágs-pa*: *grágs-ˬdod-ċan* desirous of glory *Mil.*; *grágs-ċan W.* (pronounced **rág-čán**) **famous, renowned; beautiful, splendid, glorious; proud, haughty** (in this case perh. for *drégs-pa-ċan*). — *grágs-ˬdzín-ma*, *Ssk.* **यशोधर, यशोवति,** the second wife of Buddha, acc. to others the second name of his first wife. — 2. **cry, outcry, clamour** (perh. better written *grág-pa*), *dga-grágs ˛úr-ba* to raise shouts of joy.

གྲང་བ་ *grán-ba*, *W.* **ḍán-mo**, I. adj. **cold, cool**, *grán-bai ɣnas* a cool place; **dán-mo rag** *W.*, **ḍhán-ghi ˳dúg** *C.* I am cold.

II. sbst. **coldness, cold**, *grán-ba ni dró-bar gyur* the cold changed into warmth *Dzl.*: **mén-ťog ḍán-mo ṗog** *W.* the cold has struck, killed, the flowers. — *graṅ-ṅád* the cold fit of the ague, **ḍhaṅ-ṭ̣i** (lit. *mk̔ris*) *C.* id. — **daṅ-ṅád** *W.* synon. with *grúm-bu*, **gout, rheumatism, arthritic pain**; *graṅ-dro* **cold and warmth**, *graṅ-dro-méd-pai ras-kyáṅ ˳di* this thin cloth which constitutes my clothing, in warm and in cold weather *Mil.*, v. *méd-pa*; also warmth in a relative sense, **temperature.** — *graṅ-šúm Lt.*, *graṅ-šúm byéd-pa* to shiver with cold *Schr.*

III. vb., also *graṅs-pa* 1. **to get** or **grow cold**, *gráṅs-su bčúg-pa Lex.* to let grow cold; *graṅs ˳gró-bar ˳dug* it will grow cold *Mil.*; *graṅ mi bya* one must not suffer (the child) to catch cold *Lt.* — 2. **to count, judge, consider**, v. *bgráṅ-ba*; also *Zam.*: *čes gráṅ-naaṅ* though such may be supposed; *Cs.* and *Schr.* have also *graṅ* **perhaps**, *yin graṅ* perhaps it may be so.

གྲངས་ *graṅs*, col. also **ḍaṅ-ka**, *Ssk.* संख्य **number**, frq., *lan graṅs-dú-mar* a number of times *Mil.*; *graṅs-méd-pa*, eleg. *graṅs-ma-mčís-pa* innumerable; *gráṅs-čan* numerous (?) *Cs.*; *gráṅs-čan-pa* the atheistic Sankhya sect of the Brahmans (Ban. p. 66); **dá-ḍaṅ žág-ḍaṅ gyáb-če** *W.* to date (lit. to write down the number of month and day); *graṅs ˳débs-pa* or *rtsi-ba* to count *Cs.* — *graṅs-brdá* (*Cs.* Gram. § 235) symbolical numerals, certain nouns, which in some books are used instead of the usual numerals, e.g. *mig*, eye, for 'two'.

གྲངས་པ་ *gráṅs-pa* to grow cold, v. *grán-ba* III.

གྲབ་རྒྱག་ *gráb-rgyág* pride, boasting *Sch.*

གྲབས་ *grabs* 1. **preparation, arrangements, measures; a contrivance**, *grabs byéd-pa* to make preparations for, to be on the point of, frq., *˳gró-bai grabs byéd-pa*, to make preparations for departing, *ɣsód-grábs yód-pai tsé-na* just as preparations were made for slaughtering them *Mil.*; **k̔o kyug ḍhab ǰhe'** *C.* he is getting sick, is going to vomit; *k̔áb-grabs*, *˳dziṅ-grabs* the making one's self ready for combat. — 2. col. also for *gros*, **deliberation,** **nẹ čir dhab ǰhe' dug** *C.* they are deliberating about me; **naṅ-náṅ-ṅi ḍabs ťún-nẹ** *W.* on mutual agreement.

གྲམ་པ་ *grám-pa* 1. **swamp, marsh, fen** *Lex.* — 2. *˳grém-pa Mṅg.*

གྲལ་ *gral*, *Ssk.* पङ्क्ति 1. **row, series, class,** esp. a row of persons, *gral(-du) sgrig-pa* to order, to dispose in rows, in rank and file; *grál-gyi ťóg-ma, ltag, goṅ*, more frq. *gral-mgó* the upper end of a row, the uppermost place, the seat at the head of the table; *ťá-ma*, *˛og* or *gral-mǰúg(-ɣžug)* the lower end; *gral mgó-ma* the first, the head person *Mil.*; *ɣyas-grál* the right-hand end, *ɣyon-grál* the left-hand end; *gral-rim C.* **claim, title**, *rgan-ɣžon-gral-rim* the right of seniority; *grál-pa* a beer-house customer; *gral-ɣtám* tap-house talk *Mil.*; *dbaṅ-grál* the row of supplicants for a benediction; *mčed-grógs daṅ dbaṅ-grál mťun dús-su Mil.* if you sit with your fellow-believers in one row, on one mat; **če-ḍál-la čud soṅ** *W.* he has entered into the row, the class, of adults. — 2. **bench.** — 3. **proportionality** (?), **žeṅ-riṅ ḍal-méd daṅ** *W.* with his disproportioned length and breadth, his unwieldiness. — 4. **mi žig-la ḍal žig ḍig-če** *W.* (lit. *sgrig-pa*) *W.* to play **a trick** to a person.

གྲལ་མ་ *grál-ma* a small beam, **rafter**, *Cs.*; *grál-bu*, *gral-ṗyám S.g.* roof-laths, sticks which are laid close together and covered with earth.

གྲས་ *gras* **class, order, series; rank, dignity; tribe** *Cs.*

གྲས་པ་ *grás-pa* 1. for *drás-pa.* — 2. **to bind,** v. *grágs-pa.*

གྲི་ *gri* (so pronounced in *Pur.*) 1. **knife,** *gris ɣčód-pa*, **ḍi daṅ čád-če** *W.*, to cut with a knife, but also *grir ṙṅám-pa*, *ɣsód-pa*, *˳gúm-pa Ma:* to kill with a knife;

gri-só, gri-dṅó, gri-ḱá the edge of a knife; gri-lám lit. 'the path of the knife', the cut, incision; gri-gúg Pth. a short, crooked sabre or sword, **falchion, cimeter;** gri-śá flesh of a man that has been killed with a sword, (used in sorcery). — 2. Lt.: dar-mai gri?

གྲི་མག་ gri-mág v. grib-ma.

གྲིན་པ་ grin-pa Mil., prob. = sgrin-po **skilful, clever.**

གྲིབ་ grib 1. **shade**, grib-kyi ṕu Glr. the shady part of a valley on the north side of a mountain range, cf. sribs; grib-ṕyogs the side not exposed to the sun, north side, col., grib-lhágs the coolness of the shade, the cool shade Sch.; grib-ma *ḍi-mág* W. **shadow** (cast by an object); dei grib-ma gáṅ-la ṕóg-pa on whom his shadow falls; grib-ṫsód a dial Cs. — 2. **spot, filth, defilement, contamination,** mostly in a religious sense: grib yoṅ pollution arises; ro-grib defilement by a corpse; grib-sél name of a Buddha; grib-(kyis) nón-gyi ɣdon a demon that defiles and poisons the food, a harpy; *ḱó-la ḍib ṕog soṅ* W. C. he is crack-brained, not in his right mind; *ḍib-čan* stubborn, refractory, whether from stupidity, or from ill-will.

གྲིམ་པ་ grim-pa **to hasten, to hurry** Sch.

གྲིམ་ཙེ་ grim-tse Sik. a pair of **scissors.**

གྲིམས་ grims Med.? (Lex. चतुरस्र quadrangular, regular, harmonious) Schr.: intelligent, clever.

གྲིལ་ gril (cf. ˛gril-ba) **a roll**, śog-gril rolled paper, a paper-roll; gos-gril a garment folded up Cs.; gril-ḱa byéd-pa to make up a parcel Sch.

གྲུ་ gru 1. **boat, ferry, ship, vessel,** also a hide blown up with air, used for crossing rivers = *ko-ḍhú* C.; gru-śán id.; gru-śán-pa ferry-man; grú-la žón-pa to go on a ferry. **Comp,** grú-ḱa, gru-śán-ḱa, grú-btaṅ-sa C. starting- or landing-place of a ferry. — gru-glá, gru-btsás fare, passage-money, a boat-man's fee. — grú-pa ferry-man. — gru-dpón ship-master, master of a vessel. — grú-bo, gen. gru-ɣzíns, ship. — gru-˳dzin (पोतल) ancient name of Tatta, at the mouth of the Indus, ancestral seat of the Shākya race, whence the name is transferred to the residence of the Dalai Lama in Lhasa, v. Köpp. II, 342. — 2. (Cs. grú-ma) **angle, corner,** convex or concave, also **edge, border, brim;** gru-ɣsum, gru-bži etc. triangle, quadrangle; gru-ɣsúm-pa triangular; dkyil-˳ḱor gru-bži-pa žig ˳brí-ba to draw a quadrangular figure, a square; ˳dom-gáṅ gru-bži, a surface six feet square; dbyibs gru-bžir yod S.g.; *ḍu-nar-čan* W. rhomboidal; gru-yon, Cs. gru-gyél, oblique angled; gru-dráṅ right-angled Cs.; gru-ḱún v. mṫo-gon. — yúl-gru **place, village, town, country.** — 3. **lustre,** of precious stones, gru-dmár a reddish lustre Mil.nt.

གྲུ་གུ་ grú-gu 1. **clew, hank.** — 2. n. of a country.

གྲུ་ཆར་ gru-čár 'a fine, fertile rain' Sch.

གྲུ་མོ་, གྲེ་མོ་ grú-mo, gré-mo **elbow,** grú-mor ḱa-tvám-ka bzúṅ-ba holding a trident in his arm Pth.; dé-la grú-moi ṕul-rdég čig byás-nas pushing him with his elbow Mil.; gru-súg byéd-pa id.; grú-moi ḱug, the hollow of the elbow-joint Glr.

གྲུ་ཤ་ gru-śá, or gru-śá, n. of a country Pth.

གྲུག་པ་ grúg-pa to break into small pieces, **to crumble, to bruise** Dzl.; grúg-pai ˳bras bruised rice Schr.; rúś-pa čag-grúgs fracture of a bone Med.; grúgs-bu something broken.

གྲུང་བ་, གྲུང་པོ་ grúṅ-ba, grúṅ-po, fem. grúṅ-mo 1. **wise, prudent** Mil.; also: grúṅs-pa lags very learned Sir! Thgr. — 2. **meek, mild, gentle** Cs.

གྲུབ་ grub Ld. **all,** *ḍub śi soṅ* all are dead; *ḍub zas soṅ* it has all been eaten up, (v. the next word).

གྲུབ་པ་ grúb-pa, pf. of ˳grúb-pa 1. **made ready, complete; perfect;** (ma grúb-pa also: not existing); grúb-pai raṅ-byón spyan-ras-ɣzigs Glr. the perfect, by himself originated, Awalokiteswara = lhún-gyis grúb-pa; don ṫams-čád grub-pa, don-grub, सर्वार्थसिद्ध, सिद्धार्थ 'the fulfilment of every wish' n. of Buddha, also of a spell or magic formula. — *grúb-pa lus Med.* either: the frame, the structure of the body, or more prob. an abbreviation of *ṗúṅ-po lṅá-las grúb-pai lus Med.*, v. *ṗúṅ-po*. — 2. **the state of perfection,** *grub-pa ťob-pa* to attain to this state, *grub-ťób* सिद्ध one that has attained to it, **a saint;** *grub-brnyés, grub-mčóg* id.; *grub mťá* (*C.*col. **ḍhum-tá**) *Ssk.* सिद्धान्त **opinion, theory** *Zam.; ṗyi-náṅ-gi grub-mťa ma ₒčáms-par Glr.* there being no conformity of opinion between Brahmanists and Buddhists; also n. of a philosophical work, *Was.* 262. — *ma-grúb-pa, grub-pa-méd-pa?*

གྲུམ་པ་ *grúm-pa* 1. *S.g.* n. of a burrowing animal, *Sch.*: **badger.** — 2. pf. of *ₒgrúm-pa* **lamed, crippled,** *grúm-po* a maimed person, a cripple; *grúm-bu, grum-nád* **gout, rheumatism,** = *ťsig-nád; drag-grúm* gout, podagra; **ša-ḍúm* W.*, a feeling of lameness in the limbs.

གྲུམ་ཙེ་ *grúm-tse* a thick woolen **blanket** *Mil.nt.*

གྲུལ་བུམ་ *grul-búm* a class of demons, *grul-búm-mo* female demons; there are also horned demons of this kind.

གྲུས་པོ་ *grús-po C.* a yak two or three years old.

གྲེ་ *gre* a Naksatra, v. *rgyu-skár.*

གྲེ་ག་ *gré-ga C.* **a sheet of paper** (*W. *šog-gáṅ**)

གྲེ་བ་ *gré-ba* the fore-part of the neck, the **throat,** both the wind-pipe and the gullet; **ḍé-wa dé-mo**, or **nyán-pa dug* W.* he has a good voice, sings well; *gre (-ba) gágs(-pa) Med.* hoarseness; **ḍé-wa táṅ-če* Ld.* to join in singing or shouting; *gré-ba dár-ba* a snoring or rattling in the throat; **ḍe-bsál táṅ-če* W.* to hawk, to hem, to clear the throat.

གྲེ་བོ་ *gré-bo* a species of demons; *gré-mo* 1. female demons of this kind. — 2. v. *grú-mo.*

གྲེ་མག་ *ḍe-mág*, vulg. for *grá-ma* **awn.**

གྲེ་མོག་འབུ་ *gré-mog-ₒbu W.* **ant, emmet.**

གྲེའུ་ *greu* **pea, pease,** *món-sran-greu* acc. to *Wdṅ.* = माष.

གྲེས་མ་ *grés-ma* **the flashing, lightening, shining** *Schr.*

གྲོ་ *gro* 1. **wheat,** *gro-yós* parched grains of wheat, parched corn; *gro-sóg* stalk of wheat, wheat-straw. — 2. **breakfast,** taken late in the forenoon or about noon, *gro ₒdégs-pa Glr.*, also **ḍho ₒbóg-pa* C.* to take breakfast, = *ťsál-ma zá-ba.* — **ḍo žig* W.* a morning's march, short day's march, reaching quarters already at 10 or 11 o'cl. a.m.

གྲོ་ག་ *gró-ga, W.* also **ḍó-wa**, the thin **bark of the birch-tree,** frq. used to write on (esp letters), or for ornamenting bows etc. *Mil.*

གྲོ་བོ་, གྲོ་མོ་ *gró-bo, gró-mo* **reddish gray.**

གྲོ་མ་ *gró-ma* 1. = *gro* 2. — 2. n. of a medicinal herb *Wdṅ.* — 3. **ḍhó-ma, gya-ḍhó* C.* **potato.**

གྲོག་པོ་ *gróg-po* (*Lex.* दवभ्र) 1. a deep **dell, ravine,** lateral valley *C.*; *gróg-ču* brook, rivulet; *grog-yzár* a torrent pouring down in a ravine. — 2. *W.* = *gróg-ča.*

གྲོག་མ་, གྲོག་མོ་ *gróg-ma, gróg-mo* **ant, emmet;** *grog-tsáṅ, grog-mk'ár* ant-hill; *grog-spúr* acc. to some = *gróg-ma*, acc. to others some other insect.

གྲོག་ཞིང་ *grog-žiṅ* n. of a medicine *Wdṅ.*

གྲོགས་ *grogs*, col. **rog** 1. **friend;** the more definite form is *grógs-po*, fem. *grógs-mo; k'a-grógs* a seeming friend, a false friend; *ytiṅ-grogs* a true friend; *sdig-pai grógs-po-la rten-na* if he attaches himself to bad friends *Dzl.*; *snyiṅ-gi grógs-po* intimate friend, bosom-friend *Pth.*; *grógs-po(r) byéd-pa* to make friendship, to enter into connexion with, to make a league, *ma-mťoṅ-ma-ṗrád-pai grógs-po byas*, they joined in friendship without knowing each other *Glr.* — *kye grógs-po* ho, friend! *Pth.* — 2. **associate, companion, comrade,** *grógs-po-dag* company, society *Dzl.* also used as address: comrades! friends! or more respectfully: honoured friends! honoured gentlemen! *Stg.;* **fellow,** *grógs-k̔yeu* play-fellow, play-mate *Dzl.; dpúṅ-grógs* fellow-combatant, brother in arms; *ₒdúg-grogs,* resp. *bžúgs-grogs* inmate, fellow-lodger *Mil.,* **ḍáṅ-rog* W.,* (v. *braṅ-sa*) id.; also neighbour *W., C.; dgá-grogs, γtán-grogs, grogs,* companion in life, **spouse, husband, wife,** *grogs mi rnyed* she cannot get a husband *Mil.; ts̔e ₒdii grogs-skál* a man's destination as to marriage, the matrimonial lot assigned by fate *Glr.; ₒdód-grogs, mdzá-grogs, bzáṅ-grogs C.* one beloved, **lover, sweet-heart,** *mál-grogs* resp. *γzim-grogs* bed-fellow (not only 'concubine' *Cs.*); *dmág-grogs* ally, confederate (in war), hence also: — 3. **assistant, fellow-labourer,** *lás-grogs* journeyman, under-workman; *grogs byéd-pa* to help; *rgán-mo mčód-rt̔en skúd-pai grogs byas* they helped the old woman in anointing the pyramid *Dzl.; rtsig-grogs byéd-pa* to help in building a house; at present in *C.* a word of courteousness in making requests: **ṭen rog naṅ (γnaṅ)* be so kind as to show me; **naṅ rog dzé'** would you kindly give me; **dha ṅa t̔oṅ rog dzọ'** now please let me go! cf. *rogs.*

གྲོང་ *groṅ* an inhabited place, a human habitation, **house, village, town,** *brgyá-groṅ, stóṅ-groṅ* a place of a hundred, of a thousand houses or house-holds (*mi-k̔yim*). —

**Comp.** *groṅ-k̔yér* 1. a large town, **city,** *B.* and *C., groṅ-k̔yer (gyi) mčog* chief city, capital *Tar.* 2. fig. **place, scene, sphere,** (e.g. this world is a scene of illusions *Mil.*) — *groṅ-graṅs* the number of houses in a village or town. — *groṅ-mčóg Mil., groṅ-mčóg ₒdrím-pa, ₒgró-ba, rgyúg-pa* one that wanders about among the peasantry as a fortune-teller; clerical charlatan, hedge-priest. — *groṅ-γtám* prob. = *groṅ-tsig* — *groṅ-rdál* (*Lex.* जनपद 'an extension of houses') a large town, also a suburb. — *groṅ-pa* 1. *W.* **a villager, peasant.** 2. *C.* = *groṅ.* — *gróṅ-po* = *groṅ Mil.* — *gróṅ-dpon* **village-chief,** *Sch.* — *gróṅ-mi* **peasant.** — *groṅ-tsig Lex.* **provincialism.** — *gróṅ-tso* **village, borough.** — *groṅ-bžis* **farm** *Sch.* — *gróṅ-yul* **village** *Mil.*

གྲོང་བ་ *groṅ-ba C.* col. for *graṅ-ba* **cold,** in *Glr.* occasionally.

གྲོད་པ་ *gród-pa* 1. **belly,** *grod-tsíl* **suet.** — 2. col. **stomach;** of ruminating animals the first stomach or paunch. — 3. a dried paunch, or bullock's stomach, for keeping oil etc. *Glr.*

གྲོན་ཅན་ *grón-čan* disadvantageous, injurious, *gron-čé* very noxious, *gron-méd* harmless, innoxious *Lex.*

གྲོལ་བ་ *gról-ba* pf. of *ₒgról-ba,* as sbst. = मुक्ति the having been delivered, **deliverance** (from the pain of existence).

གྲོས་ *gros* 1. **advice, counsel,** *gros ₒdebs-pa B.* to give advice; *gros byéd-pa B.,* **dós gyáb-če* W.,* to consider, to deliberate; to resolve, decide; *gros ₒdri-ba* to ask (a person's) advice, to consult (with one); *grós-ₒdri-sa* the place where advice may be asked, **an oracle** *Glr.; grós-pa* adviser, counsellor, senator; *grós-mi* id., head-man of a village; *gros mt̔ún-par* by unanimous decree, unanimously *Dzl.* — 2. **speech, talk,** = *γtam Mil. nt.* — 3. **council** (?). — 4. *Cs.:* **care, heed, caution,** *grós-čan* careful, cautious, *grós-med* careless, heedless.

གླ་ *gla* **pay, wages, fee,** *gla zá-ba* to live on wages, to work for daily wages *Dzl.; gla-ltó* food and wages; *glá-pa, glá-bo* (col.), *gla-mí* a day-labourer, hired workman, *glá-mo* (*Cs. glá-pa-mo*) fem.

གླ་བ་ *glá-ba* 1. **the musk-deer,** Moschus moschiferus, *glá-mo* the female of it, *gla-p̔rúg* the young of it; *glá-bai lté-ba* musk-bag (lit. navel); *glá-rtsi* (*W.*lar-si**), *Ssk.* कस्तूरी **musk,** *glá-rtsi-me-tog* Pedicularis megalantha, **gla-dá-ra* W.* Delphinium moschatum, two alpine plants smelling strongly of musk; *gla-sgáṅ* n. of a medicinal root *Cs.; gla-glád* v. *glaṅ-glad.* — 2. n. of a pretty large tree, similar to, or the same as *stár-bu Glr.*

གླག, བྱ་གླག *glag, bya-glág* **eagle, vulture;** *glag k̔rá-mo Sch., *lag-kyi* W.* (an eagle which is said to bark like a dog), rgyab-glág perh. different species of eagles.

གླག་པ་ glág-pa often used erroneously instead of rlag-pa.

གླགས་ glags **opportunity, occasion, possibility**, glags ˳tsól-bá to seek an occasion, to look for an opportunity; da glags rnyéd-par dug now the favourable point of time seems to have come Glr.; esp. opportunity of doing harm to another, of getting a hold on him; glags rnyéd-par mi gyur, he will not be able to get at you, to do you harm; γsó-glags med there is no possibility of helping him, he is incurable Med.; bzód-glags med intolerable, insupportable, frq.

གླང་ glaṅ (Bal. *χlaṅ*) 1. **ox, bullock.** — 2. **elephant.** — 3 **Taurus,** the Bull, in the zodiac.

**Comp.** glaṅ-glád 'bullock- or elephant-brains'; soap being made of such, acc. to popular belief: C. **soap** (Schr. gla-glad). — gláṅ-to the Indian **bison**, Bos taurus indicus, Lh. — glaṅ-ťúg, glaṅ ˬóg-čan **a bull.** — glaṅ-dár-ma n. of a king of Tibet, living about 1000 after Christ, notorious for his hostility against the hierarchy of the Lamas. — glaṅ-dór **a team** of bullocks. — glaṅ-sná **the trunk** or proboscis of an elephant; a plant so called on account of the long spiral spur of its corolla, Pedicularis Hookeriana. — glaṅ-po = glaṅ. — glaṅ-po-čé, glaṅ-čén, **elephant**, gláṅ-mo a female elephant, glaṅ-ṗrúg the young of an elephant. — glaṅ-bu a young bullock, glaṅ-rú a bullock's horn; also a large fork used by the Tibetan soldiers to rest the musket on, when firing (Hook. II., 235). — ṗa-gláṅ = glaṅ-ťúg.

གླང་, གླང་ཐབས་ glaṅ, glaṅ-ťabs Med., γzer-gláṅ W., **colic, gripes, spasms** in the stomach, and similar affections; glaṅ-šú Med.?

གླང་མ་ gláṅ-ma a large kind of alpine **willow.**

གླད་ glad 1. **the head**, glád-la round the head, e.g. to brandish a sword, Glr.; as postposition used in a general sense: **close over,** čui glád-la close over the water. — 2. **brain** Med., cf. klád-pa.

གླད་པ་ glád-pa **to thin** Sch. Cf. lhad, slád-pa.

གླན་པ་ glán-pa 1. = glón-pa, **to patch, botch, mend;** glan brgyáb-pa Sch., glán-par byéd-pa Lt. id.; lhán-pa glán-pa to sew on a patch Lex. — 2. **to return,** lan an answer, to reply, rejoin Lex. — 3. C. col for glén-pa; so also occasionally in books.

གླལ་བ་ glál-ba **to yawn.**

གླིང་ gliṅ, द्वीप, prop. **island,** but usually: **continent,** part of the globe, viz. one of the four imaginary parts of the earth, as taught by the geographers of Tibet, or rather of ancient India: lus-ṗágs the part east of the Sumeru, of a semicircular shape; ˳dzam-bu-gliṅ in the south, triangular; ba-glaṅ-spyód in the west, circular; sgra-mi-snyán in the north, square. The general character of the first of these parts is described as being ži-ba tranquil; that of the second as being rgyás-pa rich; that of the third as being dbaṅ-ldán strong, and that of the fourth as being drág-po wild. In a more general sense: **region, country,** so Nepal is frq. denominated rín-po-čei gliṅ the country of jewels and treasures, Urgyan mǩa-groi gliṅ the country of the Dakini, as is also Lahoul, in local chronicles; byai gliṅ region or country of birds Glr.; the word is also not unfrequently a component part of the names of towns and villages. — gliṅ-ṗrán prop. a little island, generally one of the small continents, of which there are eight, acc. to the above mentioned geographical system; also island in general. — gliṅ-ka a small uncultivated river-island, or low-land C.

གླིང་བུ་ gliṅ-bu (Ssk. वंश) **fife, flageolet,** made of one piece of wood and much like those used in Europe as play-things for children; it is the common musical instrument of herdsmen, and often consists of two pipes; ṗred-gliṅ **flute, piccolo-flute,** mostly of metal; dge-gliṅ a larger musical instrument like **a hautboy,** used in sacred ceremonies; *rkaṅ-gliṅ* lit. a fife made of the human femural bone, but sometimes also of metal.

གླུ་ *glu* (*Ssk.* गीति) **song, tune**, mostly, though not always, of a profane nature, opp. to religious hymns; *glu-dbyáṅs, glu-sgrá*, id.; the word is also used of the singing of birds; *glu-čúṅ* a little song, ditty, hummed by a person *Glr.; glu-rés* alternate song; *glu-gar-rtséd-po* rejoicings of every kind *Glr.; glu lén-pa B.*, **lu gyáb-pa** *C.*, **táṅ-čé** *W.*, to sing.

གླུད་, བླུད་, གླུད་ཚབ་ *glud, blud, glud-tsab* **a ransom,** a thing given as a ransom, *sróg-gi glud* a ransom for one's life *Lex.; ḱoi glúd-du lug brgya γsód-pa*, to slaughter a hundred sheep as a ransom *Mil.;* **lü-la taṅ** *C.* he is made an expiator, a scape-goat; **mi-lü** *C.* in a special sense: a man's image which in his stead is cast away in the *γtór-ma:* therefore **ḱo mi-lü yin** *C.* he is a curse, an anathema, one deserving to be cursed (ni.f.).

གླུམ་ *glum* **boiled barley, wheat,** or **rice,** used instead of malt in brewing beer (not for food).

གླེ་ *gle* 1. *Glr.* 60. a small uncultivated island, = *gliṅ-ka* (*Ld.* **zal**). — 2. n. of the capital of Ladak, usually *sle.*

གླེ་འདམས་ *gle-ₒdams* n. of a distemper *Cs.;* involuntary discharge from the bowels, or of urine *Sch.*

གླེགས་ *glegs* (*Cs. glégs-ma*) **table, board, plate;** *záṅs-kyi glégs-bu* copper-plate *Tár.* 26, 10; *glegs-bám* (पुस्तक) **book,** also *dpé-ča glegs-bám Glr.; glegs-bám máṅ-po bžéṅs-so* he made a present of, dedicated, many books (for the use of a temple); *glegs-šíṅ* the wooden boards which in a Tibetan book supply the binding; *glegs-ṫág* a thong etc. fastened round a book; *glegs-čáb* a buckle, clasp, or ring attached to this thong. — *sgó-glegs* the pannel of a door; **núm-lag** writing-tablet, a small board, blackened, greased, and strewed over with scraped chalk, on which the school-children write with wood-pencils.

གླེང་བ་ *gléṅ-ba*, pf. *gleṅs* **to say, talk, converse,** *γtam (-du) gléṅ-ba* id., resp. *γsuṅ gléṅ-ba; 'lám-la ma ṫar' žes gléṅs-nas* as word was sent: 'the road is not passable!' *Glr.; γtam gléṅ-ba ni bdág-gis byas* I have made this speech *S.O.; γčig gléṅ γnyis gleṅ rim-pas mčéd-de btsún-moi bár-du gléṅ-žiṅ* the rumour spreading from one to the other, until it came before the queen *Pth.; čós-kyi sgrog-gléṅ byéd-pa*, (resp. *mdzád-pa*), **to preach** *Glr.; gros-gléṅ* **council, consultation,** perh. also disputation.

**Comp.** and **deriv.** *gléṅ-brjód, gléṅ-mo* sbst. **conversation, discourse, lecture,** *gléṅ-brjód ma maṅ dar-γčig γson* listen a little to a short discourse *Mil.; čós-γtam gléṅ-mo byed* let us converse on religious subjects *Mil.; gléṅ-mo* the act of speaking, opp. to *yi-ge*, the act of writing, the written letter etc. *Lex.* — *gleṅ-γži* 1. **the subject** of a discourse *Cs.* 2. table of contents, **index** *S.O.* and elsewh. 3. **place, scene,** of a conversation or discourse *Stg.* frq. — *gléṅ-ba-po, gléṅ-mo-mḱan* a story-teller *Cs.; glen-ₒbúm* 'a hundred thousand stories', title of a book, *Sch.*

གླེན་པ་ *glén-pa* 1. *B.* and *C.* **stupid, foolish,** *glen lkugs bkol-spyód-kyi sdug-bsṅál* the misery of stupidity, of dumbness and of servitude (the state of animals) *Thgr.; byol-sóṅ-las kyaṅ glén-po* more stupid than a brute *Mil.;* **fool,** *ḱyód-rnams re glen* fools that you are all of you *Dzl.;* often in the sense of 'fool' in the Bible, = the wicked, the ungodly: *glén-pa γti-mug-čan* infatuated fools *Dzl.* ༢༠, 9 = profaners of holy things; **len-nág** *W.* id.; **len-nág-gi pé-ra** foolish talk. — 2. *W.:* **idle, lazy, dull, imbecile,** e.g. a sickly child, an animal affected with a disease (opp. to **ṭám-pa, šáṅ-po** being in good health, active, lively).

གླེབ་པ་ *gléb-pa*, pf. *glebs*, **to make flat, plain** *Cs.*, *léb-mor gleb Lex.*

གླེམ་པ་ *glém-pa* **to press, squeeze; to crush, squash** *Stg., C.*

གློ་ *glo* (*Ld.* ལྡོ་ **ldo**), resp. *gžogs*, 1. **the side,** esp. of the body, *glos ṗáb-pa* to lie down on one's side (lit. by means of the side); *gló-ča* (*Ld.* **ldó-ča**) ornaments, suspended on the side of the body, strings of pearls, shells etc., worn by women in the girdle; also in a general sense: *sráṅ-gi glo γyas γyón-na* on both sides of the street *Stg.*; perh. also side of a house, wall, in the expression: **kún-mẹ lo tol** the thieves broke through the wall *W.*; *glo-skár* window *Pth.* — 2. **saddle-girth** *W.* — 3. **cough**, **lo gyág-pa** *C.* to cough; (*Sch.* has: to err, to act foolishly, to lose, to neglect); **lo láṅ-wa** *C.* to cough; *gló-k'a sra* a bad cough *Sch.*; **lo-k'óg** *C., W.*, cough; *glo-rgyál Lt.* a chronic cough; *glo-bstúd Lt.* a permanent short cough. — 4. Not quite clear is the etymology in *glo rdég-pa Sch.:* to be frightened, timid, and *glo rdég* (*-tu*) suddenly, = *gló-bur* q.v.

གློ་བ་ *gló-ba* **the lungs**, *gló-ba ma lṅa* prob. the five posterior lobes of the lungs, *gló-ba bu lṅa* the five anterior ones *Med.*; *gló-k'a* of a colour like the blood of the lungs, **pale-red** *Sch.*; *glo-dóṅ* **windpipe** *Cs.* — *glo-rdól* a disease of the lungs; *glo-rkó* perh. the same. — *glo-sbúbs* (*Sch. spub*) wind-pipe. — **gló-ro** *W.* prob. pulmonary consumption. — *glo lú-ba Lt.* 'convulsion of the lungs' *Cs.*, or simply: cough, v. *lú-ba*.

གློ་བུར་ *gló-bur* 1. **suddenly, instantaneously,** also *gló-bur-du, gló-bur-bar*; *glo-bur-du mi máṅ-po* ˳*či-bai sdug-bsṅál* the calamity of many men dying suddenly; *glo-bur-nád* diseases that arise on a sudden (opp. to *lhan-skyés* inherited diseases) *Med.* — *gló-bur-ba* adj., *gló-bur-bai don* the signification of suddenness *Lex.* — 2. *Cs.:* 'recently, *gló-bur-du* ˳*óṅs-pa* a new comer'.

གློ་འབུར་ *glo-*˳*bur* **a rise**, an elevation above a surface *Sch.*

གློག་ *glog* (*Bal.* and *Kh.* **χlog**), col. also *glóg ka*, **lightning**, flash of lightning; *glog* ˳*bar* it lightens; *glog k'yug* id.; *glog k'yúg-pai yun tsám-las ma lón-par* with the rapidity of lightning *Mil.*; *glog rgyú-ba* the flashing of light, *Dzl.*; *glog-spriṅ* thunder-cloud, also as a symbol of the transitoriness of things.

གློག་པ་ *glóg-pa* a disease, = *lhóg-pa.*

གློད་པ་ *glod-pa* 1. **to loosen, relax, slacken** vb.a. *Cs.* — 2. **to comfort, console; to cheer up** *Sch.*; *glód-la rgyún-du bžugs* your honour may be easy about staying here always *Mil.*, cf. *lhód-pa*. — 3. *Ü:* **to give**, *ma bzuṅ ma glód*(*-par*) without any regard to taking or giving *Glr.*

གློན་པ་, གླན་པ་ *glón-pa, glán-pa* 1. **to return an answer, to reply.** — 2. **to patch, to mend**, cf. *klón-pa* etc.

གྷན་དྷོ་ལ་ *ghán-dho-la* n. of a mountain in *Lh.*, perh. incor. instead of *gan-dho-la* q.v.; it may also be derived from घण्टा bell, and thus the word would signify the same as *dril-bu-ri*, which is the name of another holy mountain, at the foot of which the nobleman's seat **Gondla** is situated.

དགག་པ་ *dgág-pa* v. ˳*gégs-pa.*

དགང་བ་ *dgáṅ-ba* v. ˳*géṅs-pa.*

དགང་གཟར་ *dgaṅ-γzár* v. *γzar.*

དགད་མོ་ *dgád-mo* v· *gád-mo.*

དགབ་པ་ *dgáb-pa* v. ˳*gébs-pa.*

དགའ་བ་ *dgá-ba* (*Ld.* col. **γá-ċe**) I. vb. **to rejoice**, to be rejoiced or glad, *la* at, in, or of; *dé-la dgá-ste*, rejoiced at it, glad of it, — *mi dgá-ste* grieved, vexed, indignant at it; *k'rims yód-pa-la dgá-nas* if you wish to have the law introduced *Glr.*; *γsód-pa-la dgá-žiṅ* sanguinary, delighting in blood-shed *Dzl.*; *bu-mo de-nyid-la dgá-bas*, as I wish to have none other but this girl *Dzl.*; *bód-la dgá-ba γċig kyaṅ ma byuṅ* nobody took an interest in Tibet *Glr.*; *k'yed ċii p'yir mi dga* why are you so dejected, low-spirited? *dga bžin-du* with pleasure (e.g. I shall accept it); rarely with the gerund: *bram-ze da-ruṅ* ˳*dug-ste rab-tu dga-nas* much rejoicing, very glad, when (that) the Brahmin was still there *Dzl.*; with the termin. of the inf.: to do a thing readily, willingly, *nyán-par dgá-ba* **to like** to hear, to listen eagerly; **to be willing,** *su žig* *ₒdúg-par dgá-na* if anybody will stay here voluntarily *Dzl.;* **to have a mind, to intend, to wish,** *k̔yod ráb-tu byúṅ-bar dgá-am* do you intend to take orders? *Dzl.; bdág-gis ras ₒdi ... sbyin-par dgao* I should like to present this cloth to ... *Dzl.: méd-par byá-bar dgá-na* as I wish to annihilate ... *Dzl.; gar dgá-bar* (or *gar dgá-ba der*) *soṅ* go whereever you like *Dzl.;* seldom with the accus.: *ₒdzóm-pa de dga-ste* as you now enjoy an abundance *Mil.;* with the instr. case: *des dgá-bar šóg-čig,* may you be cheered, comforted by it *Dzl.*; frq. absolutely: *dgá-bar byéd-pa* to make glad, to rejoice, *C.* also: to caress, to fondle.

II. sbst. **joy,** *dgá-bai γtam byéd-pa* to express one's joy *Dzl.*; *dgá-bai sems* id.; *dé-la ráb-t̔u dgá-bai sems skyés-so* he found great delight in it *Dzl.*; compounds v. below.

III. adj. 1. **glad, pleased, enjoying,** *ṅa dgá-ba ma yin-pas* as I was not pleased with it *Dzl.; de-la mi dgá-ba, W.* **mi gá-k̔an**, not favourably disposed towards, unfriendly, inimical to; *dgá-bar byéd-pa* to make glad, to delight, *bu čuṅ dgá-ba byéd-pai yo-byád* things which delight little children, play-things *Glr.* — Less frq. 2. **charming, sweet, pleasing, agreeable, beautiful,** *lhág-par dgá-ru ₒgro* she is getting more and more beautiful; *C.* in a general sense: **good,** cf. below: *dga-bdé.* — 3. as a proper name = नन्द *Tar.*

**Comp. and deriv.** *dga-grágs ˛úr-ba* to give cheers, to raise shouts of joy *Mil.* — *dga-grógs* a participator of joy, gen. with reference to husband or wife (col. **ga-róg**). — *dga-mgú* great joy, *dga-mgú-ba, dga-mgu-ráṅ-ba* to have great pleasure, to be very glad, to be delighted, frq., *dgá-žiṅ mgú-la yi-ráṅs-pár ₒgyúr-ba* id. *Glr.* frq.; yet *dga-mgúr spyód-pa* to indulge in sensual pleasure *Pth., Stg., bú-mo daṅ* with a girl. — *dga-stón* **feast,** public festivity; *dga-st̔ón-gyi γdán-sa* the place of a feast *Glr.*; *bsú-ba dgá-ba* festivities of welcome *Glr.*; *dga-stón byéd-pa* to celebrate a festival; *ₒgyéd-pa* to spread a feast, to distribute festival dishes; fig. *rná-bai dga-stón* a feast or treat to the ears *Glr.* — *dga-bdé* 1. **joy,** *lus sems dga-bdés k̔yáb-par ₒgyur Glr.* 2. (*Ts.* col. **gan-dē**) **good,** = *yág-po,* (of servants, dogs etc.) *C.*; **mí-la ga-dé ǰhē-pa** to treat a person kindly, with affection *C.* — *dga-ₒdún* wedding, nuptial festivities *Sch.* (seems to be a word not generally known). — *dga-ₒdód* n. of the plain of Lhasa, or at least of the northern part of it. — *dga-ldán* joyful 1. n. of a residence of gods, or of one of the heavens, *Ssk.* तुषित v. *Köpp.* I. 265. 2. n. of one of the great monasteries near Lhasa, founded by Tsongkhapa, about the year 1407, v. *Köpp.* II, 345. 3. *γžúṅ-sa dga-ldan* n. of the royal castle of residence at Lhasa; *dga-ldán-pa* n. of a sect = *dge-lúgs-pa.* — *dgá-bo* = *dga-bdé* 2. **good** *C.* — *dga-sdug-drag-žan* good and bad, strong and weak, of articles of merchandise and the like *C.* — *dga-spró* **joy,** *dga-spró dpag-tu-méd-pa t̔ób-pa yin* he entered into a state of indescribable joy *Mil.* — *dgá-ma* n. of the goddess of joy *Cs.* — *dga-ma-ₒdár C., W.* (col. **gá-man-dár**) the trembling with joy, the state of being enraptured, in ecstasy. — *dgá-mo* 1. **delightful, pleasing, charming,** of news, of a speech *W.*, of a landscape *Mil.* 2. **delighted, joyous, cheerful** *W.*, **sem gá-mó rag** I am cheerful; **gá-mo-čan** *W.* id.; **gá-mo ǰhē-pa** *C.* to caress, to fondle. 3. **pure,holy** *Sch., Dzl.*, prob. also *Mil.*; *čós-pa dgá-mo* a godly priest. — *dga-t̔sór* **joy,** **k̔o ga-t̔sór máṅ-po ǰhē** *C.* he is very joyful; *dga-t̔sór čé-ba* gratifying, delightful *Mil.* — *dga-ráṅs* being glad, **rejoicing,** **dhé-la ga-ráṅ ḍhág-te** *C.* being greatly delighted with it, — *dga-rís* v. *ga-ri,* = *gá-ža.*

དགར་ *dgar* = *dgá-bar, raṅ-dgár* **at pleasure,** ad libitum, frq.: *či dgar Pth.* seems to mean: **why.**

དགར་བ་ *dgár-ba* I. **to separate, confine, fold up** (men, cattle, goods), *dgar-byai p̔yugs* cattle to be penned in a fold *Cs.*; *γnás-nas dgár-ba* **to banish,** to exile; *dgár-bai dón-du* **in a** special sense, in particular *Sch.* — **gár-te bór-ċe* W.* to set apart, exclude, shut out; to lock up, shut up, to lay up or by, to preserve; **gár-gya ċó-ċe* W.* to store up; **tób-ċi gár-ċe** to button up. — 2. **to hang up, to fasten, to attach,** **dhar-ċóg ṫúg-pa-la* C.* a flag to a rope. Cf. *skár-ba.*

དགལ་བ *dgál-ba* v. *˳gél-ba.*

དགས་པ *dgás-pa* v. *˳gás-pa.*

དགུ *dgu* 1. **nine,** *dgú-bċu (ṫám-pa)* ninety; *dgú-bċu rtsa γċig,* or *go-ċig, W. *gu-bċu-go-ċig** ninety one etc.; *dgú-pa* 1. the ninth. 2. having, comprising, measuring, nine, e.g. *ḱru-dgú-pa* measuring nine cubits (in length, height etc.); *dgú-po* the nine, those nine; *lan-dgú* nine times; *dgu-níṅ* three years ago col. — 2. **many,** *dgú-ċig* id. *Mil.*; *ṫabs dgus bsags,* gathered by many efforts, with great difficulty; used as sign of the plural: *skyé-dgu* men, *skye-dgui bdág-po (Ssk.* प्रजापति) the lord of creatures, the lord of men; *skye-dgui-bdág-mo* n. of the aunt and wet-nurse of Buddha; *yód-dgu Lex.* those that are, the existing beings; *nor yód-dgu-ċog Mil.* the goods that one has, property; *bzáṅ-dgu Lex.* the good and the brave (among men); *lus ˳dod dgur sgyúr-ba* to be changed, transformed, ad libitum *Mil.*; *ṅan-dgu ṫúb-pa Lt.* to overcome every evil; *mi šes dgu šés-po Thgy.* he that knows every thing; **mí ǰhe' gu ǰhe' mi yoṅ gu yoṅ* C.* if you do many things which ought not to be done, many things will take place which ought not to take place; *ši-ba yid-kyi dgú-la mi byéd-de Thgy.* not counting death among things to be thought of. — 3. inst. of *dgun, dgu-zlá* winter-month *Mil.* frq — *zer-dgu, smra-dgu??*

དགུ་ཁྲི *dgu-ḱri* **litter, bier** *C.*

དགུ་གཏོར *dgu-γtór,* for *ṫses nyer-dgúi γtor-ma,* a sacrifice on the 29th day of the month *W.*

དགུ་ཐུབ *dgu-ṫub* 'all-conquering', n. of a plant.

དགུ་ཕྲུགས *dgu-ṕrúgs Mil., Thg.,* **a particular kind of meditation.**

དགུ་བ *dgú-ba* 1. vb. **to bend,** to make crooked; **go gú-ċe* Ld.* to bend, bow, stop; to submit. — 2. sbst. the act of bending, bowing, **inflection.** — 3. adj. **bent, stooping;** *dgú-po, dgú-mo Cs.* id.

དགུ་རྩེགས *dgu-rtségs* n. of a yellow flower *Cs.*

དགུ་ཚིགས, དགུ་ཚིགས་སྐྱ་མོ *dgu-tsigs, dgu-tsigs skya-mo* **the galaxy, the milky way** *Mil.*

དགུ་མཚན *dgu-mtsán* **prize** (of combat) *C.*

དགུག་པ *dgúg-pa* v. *˳gúg-pa.*

དགུང *dguṅ,* another form for *guṅ* (the former of the two appears to be prevalent) 1. **the middle.** — 2. **noon, mid-day.** — 3. **mid-night.** — 4. **heaven.** *dgúṅ-la reg* it reached up to heaven *Mil.*; *dguṅ sṅón-po* the blue heaven, *yá-gi dguṅ-sṅón* the blue heaven above *Mil.*; *dgúṅ-du* (or *-la*) *γšégs-pa* (lit. to repair, to withdraw, to heaven) to die *Mil.* and elsewh. — 5. before dates, esp. before the word *lo,* it serves as a respectful word, and is e.g. frq. used in stating the age of a Buddha or a king; yet it occurs also in compounds, where no such bearing is discernible: *dguṅ-žág, dguṅ-zla Cs.*; *dguṅ-do-núb Mil.* this evening, to-night; *dguṅ-snyiṅ* a year, a year of one's life; *dguṅ-ḱág* division of time (?); *dguṅ-bdún* a week. (*Cs.* has also *dguṅ-ṫig,* and *dguṅ-ṫig-gi dkyil-˳ḱor,* which terms were prob. framed by him, and meant to denote the meridian line and meridian circle.)

དགུང་མོ *dgúṅ-mo* **evening** *Sch,* perh. a corruption of *dgóṅ-mo.*

དགུན, དགུན་ཀ *dgún, dgún-ka, W. *gún-ka** **winter;** *dgún* is also used adverbially: in winter(-time), during winter; *dgún-dus* winter-time; *dgun-ṫóg, dgun-ṫog-ṫág, W. *gun-ṫag-ṫóg*,* all the winter through; **gun ṫse re* W.* every winter; *dgun grán-bai dús-na* during the cold of winter *Dzl.*; *dgun-nyi-ldog* the winter solstice; *dgun-nyi-ldog-gi ťig*, or *ǩor-ťig* the tropic of Capricorn *Cs.* (cf. the remark at the end of *dguṅ*); *dgun-stód*, *dgun-smád* the first and the last half of winter, (v. *dus*).

དགུམ་པ་ *dgúm-pa* v. *˳gúm-pa*.

དགུར་, རྒུར་, སྒུར་ *dgur*, *rgur*, *sgur*, three different spellings of the same root, all of them pronounced **gur**, **crooked,** *dbyibs-dgur* of crooked stature *S.g.*; *rgur źig* stoop down! bend your back! *Dzl.*; *sgúr-te* writhing (with pain) *Dzl.*; *sgúr-po* crooked, hump-backed, by birth *Lt.*; with age *Thgy.*; *C.* col. **gur-gúr** id.; *mgo dgúr-ba* to duck, to bend vb.n.; to submit, to humble one's self (cf. *dgú-ba*). *Cs.: dgúr-po*, *dgúr-mo* a crooked man, a crooked woman; *ťsigs-dgúr* a crooked back, crook-backed; *lag-dgúr* having crooked hands etc.; *dgur-˳gro* of a stooping gait.

དགུས་ *dgus* 1. instr. of *dgu.* — 2. *C.*, *W.*, **this day five days** (the present day included).

དགེ་བ་ *dgé-ba* (*Ssk.* शुभ, कुशल, श्रेयस; also स्वस्ति, कल्याण, seldom शुद्ध) 1. **happiness, welfare; happy, propitious,** *dgé-źiṅ śis-pa Wdṅ.* More frq.: 2. **virtue** (opp. to *mi-dgé-ba*, and *sdíg-pa*), also adj. **virtuous,** *sems dgé-ba* a virtuous mind *Glr.*, *las dgé-ba*, *mi-dgé-ba* good and bad actions *Stg.*; *dgé-bai rtsá-ba* roots of virtue, meritorious actions, from which afterwards the fruits of reward come forth; *dgé-rtsa skyéd-pa* frq., *spyód-pa Thgy.*, *byéd-pa Mil.* to produce such a root, to achieve a meritorious action; *dgé-ba séms-par ˳gyúr-ba* to become inclined to virtue, i.e. converted *Dzl.*; *dge-ťsógs* (v. *ťsogs*) a virtuous work, a good deed; *dgé-ba bču* the ten virtues, viz. 1. *srog mi γčód-pa*, not to kill anything living (by which Buddhism has replaced our scriptural interdiction of murder); 2. *ma byín-par mi lén-pa* not to take what has not been given (those who closely stick to the word go even so far, that they will not touch or accept an alms, unless it be put into their hands); 3. *lóg-par mi γyém-pa* not to fornicate; 4. *rdzun mi smrá-ba* not to tell a lie; 5. *ťsig-rtsúb mi smrá-ba* not to abuse or revile; 6. *ṅag-kyál* (or *˳ǩyal*) *mi smrá-ba* not to talk foolishness (cf. *kyál-ka*); 7. *ṕrá-ma mi byéd-pa* not to calumniate; 8. *brnáb-sems mi byéd pa* not to be avaricious or covetous; 9. *γnód-sems mi byéd-pa* not to think upon doing harm or mischief; 10. *lóg-lta mi byéd-pa* not to entertain heretic notions, or positively, *yáṅ-dag-par ltá-ba Stg.* to be orthodox. — 3. **fasting, abstinence,** in the phrase: *dgé-ba srúṅ-ba* to fast, to abstain from food, frq. — 4. **alms, charity; banquet, treat,** as a religious work, *śí-dge γsón-dge* largesses, treats, taking place at funerals, or given in one's life time *Mil.* (*W.* **yá-tra**, and **ku-rim**).

**Comp. and deriv.** *dge-bskos* **censor,** and at the same time **provost** and **beadle** in a monastery, who has to watch over strict order, and to punish the transgressors Köpp. II. 259, 276; in *Ld.* he is also called *čos-ǩrims-pa* (vulg. **čosrimpa**). — *dge-rgán* **surety, moral bail,** a monk that is made answerable for the moral conduct of an other, who is placed under his care and called *dge-γžón*; also in a gen. sense: **teacher, schoolmaster.** — *dge-bsnyén*, fem. *dge-bsnyén-ma* (*Ssk.* उपासक and उपासिका) 1. the pious of the laymen who retaining their secular occupations have renounced the five cardinal sins (murder, theft, fornication, lying, and drunkenness) and provide for the maintenance of the priests (so in *Dzl.* and gen. in the earlier writings). 2. in in later times as much as **a novice, probationer, catechumen,** i.e. either a kind of clerical apprentice (the Shabi of the Mongols, *śrāmanera Ssk.*, v. *Köpp.* II., 252), or one of a next higher degree, a candidate (v. *Schl.* 162). — *dge-ltás S.g.* **a propitious omen,** a favourable prognostic. — *dge-˳dún* (col. **gen-dún**), prop. *dge-slóṅ-gi ˳dun* (*Burn.* II., 435) *Ssk.* संघ, the whole body of the clergy, **priesthood;** *dge-˳dun-dkon-mčóg* the priesthood as one of the three great jewels, or as part of the godhead (in which latter sense the word now is usually understood) cf. *dkon-mčóg*; *dge-ₒdun-dpal-čén Mahāsāṅghika*, n. of a Hinayāna school *Tar.*, *Was.*; *dge-ₒdun-grúb-pa* n.p., the first Dalai Lama about the year 1400; *dge-ₒdun-rgyá-mtso* n. of the second Dalai Lama, v. *Köpp.* II., 131. — *dge-ldán* **virtuous**; *dge-ldan-pa* n. of the most numerous sect of Lamas, founded by Tsonk'apa; it is also called *dge-lúgs-pa*, or *dga-ldán-pa* from Galdan, a monastery near Lhasa which, as well as Sera and Ḍa-puṅ, belongs to his sect. The Lamas of this community wear for the most part yellow garments; they are said to approach nearer to perfection in mysticism (the highest aim of Buddhist priests) than any other sect, since they apply themselves more systematically to the preparatory studies of morality etc. — *dge-sdig* for *dge-ba daṅ sdig-pa*. — *dge-sbyóṅ Ssk.* श्रमण a Buddhist ascetic, or mendicant friar, *Burn.* I. 275. *Köpp.* I., 330. — *dge-sbyór* seems to have corresponded in its original acceptation to our conception of piety, sanctification and practical religion, but in later times the sense of expertness in the art of meditation was attached also to this word, as: *dge-sbyór p̔el* (this man's) expertness increases, is making progress *Mil.* — *dgé-rtsa* instead of *dgé-bai rtsá-ba* v. above. — *dge-rtsis* the amount of virtue, the sum of merit, *dge-rtsis rgyás-pa* a considerable amount of merit. — *dge-ts̔úl* 1. a young monk; in the older writings it may be understood as novice; 2. in later literature it denotes the degree next to the *dge-bsnyén*, being that of a subordinate or under-priest, *Köpp.* II. 252, 335. *Schl.* 162.; *dge-ts̔ul-ma* a young nun, a novice. — *dge-mtsán* a lucky omen *Glr.* — *dge-γžón* v. *dge-rgán.* — *dge-γyóg* (seems to be pronounced **ger-yóg** in col. language) **constable, beadle,** a servant of the *ts̔ógs-čén zal-ṅó*, or chief-justice of Sera and other monasteries. — *dgé-las* a good deed or action, but by later writers also applied to magic ceremonies and the like. — *dge-lúgs-pa* v. *dge-ldán-pa.* — *dge-légs* good fortune, prosperity *Glr.* — *dge-slóṅ* Gelong, 1. originally 'beggar of virtue', mendicant friar, भिक्षु one that has entirely renounced the world and become a Buddhist priest, 2. in later writings the highest clerical degree, a priest that has received the highest ordination, v. *Köpp.* I., 335. The Gelong is bound to observe all the 233 commandments of the *so-sór t̔ar-pai mdo.* — *dge-slób-ma* a young nun *Cs.* — *dge-bšés* 1. v. *bšes-γnyén.* 2. n. of priests or monks. — *dge-sloṅ-šiṅ* is said to be a provincial name of the cedar, Cedrus Deodara.

དགེང་ལ་ *dgéṅ-la*, also *dgáṅ-la*, **on, upon, in, at** *Ts.*

དགེར་བ་ *dger-ba* = *γyo-ba*, **to prepare,** (food), *ₒk̔úr-ba dgér-ba* to bake pastry; **t̔ṳ́-ma gér-wa** *C.* = *ₒt̔úd-pa.*

དགེས་པ་ *dgés-pa* = *dgyés-pa* frq.

དགོ་ *dgo*, in *Lexx.* explained by *dúm-bur*, to divide (?).

དགོ་བ་ *dgo-ba*, a species of **antelope**, living on high mountains, Procapra picticaudata *Hodgson*, v. *Hook.* II. 157 and 139; *dgó-ba-mo* the female of this antelope *Cs.*

དགོག་ *dgog Lexx.* w.e.; *dgog-tiṅ* **pestle** *C.*

དགོང(ས)་ *dgoṅ(s)*, also *dgóṅ(s)-mo*, *Sch.* *dgóṅ(s)-ka* 1. **evening,** *dgoṅs-γčig* one evening, once on an evening *Glr.*; *naṅ re dgoṅs re* every morning and evening; **goṅs-zán** *W.*, **góṅs-zé** *C.*, resp. *dgoṅs-γsál* evening-meal, supper; *dgoṅs-ₒǰám* resp. evening-soup; *dgóṅs-su Dzl.*, *dgóṅs-mo* and *dgoṅs Glr.* in the evening; *dgoṅs daṅ t̔o-ráṅs* in the evening and in the morning *Med.* frq.; *dgoṅs ₒbáb-pa* to hold an evening's rest, to take up night-quarters. — 2. **supper** *C.* — 3. **a day's journey,** *dgoṅs-žág* col. id.; *rta-dgóṅs* a day's journey for one travelling on horseback, *lug-dgóṅs* a day's journey for a drove of sheep.

དགོངས་པ་ *dgóṅs-pa*, resp. for *sém-pa*, *snyám-pa* etc., and *sems*, *blo* etc. I. vb.

1. **to think, to meditate,** *dgoṅs-pa-la ḥjug-pa* to enter into meditation *Glr.*; *ₒdi snyám-du dgóṅs-par gyur-to* he thought so in his mind *Dzl.*; *rgyál-po ḱoṅ-ráṅ yin dgóṅs-nas* the king thinking that he himself was meant, referring the allusion to himself *Glr.*; **to regard as,** *bu daṅ ₒdrá-bar dgóṅs-pa* to treat one like a son *Dzl.*; **to remember, to think of, to devise,** *mṅa-ris-kyi ḥdúl-bya-la* remembering those of Nari that were to be converted, thinking of the conversion of Nari *Glr.*; also with *p̔yir Pth.*; *ṅá-la t̔ugs-brtsé-bar dgoṅs-šig* remember me graciously, frq.; so in a similar manner: to hear graciously, to take a kind interest, share, or concern in, to interest one's self for, to try to promote; so our Lama explained the passage *Glr.* 101, 9: *saṅs-rgyás-kyi bstáṅ-pa-la dgóṅs-nas* = *bstáṅ-pa ₒp̔él-bai p̔yir bsám-blo btáṅ-nas*; **to intend, to purpose,** with the termin. of the inf., frq., *t̔ugs-kyis ma dgoṅs-so* he did not intend, he had no mind *Pth.* — 2. **to die,** *més-kyi dgóṅs-dus-kyi mčód-pa btsug Glr.* is stated to mean: he instituted sacrifices for the remembrance of his grandfather's death; and so similarly in other passages.

II. sbst., also *t̔ugs-dgóṅs*, 1. the act of **thinking, meditating, pondering,** *t̔ugs-dgóṅs ḥtóṅ-ba Mil.* to meditate; **thought,** *rgyál-poi t̔úgs-kyi dgóṅs-pa-la 'gáṅ-du p̔yin' snyám-pa* lit. in the king's 'mind-thoughts' was thought: where shall I go? *Glr.*; **meaning, sense,** esp. the sense of sacred words or writings, therefore *dgóṅs-pa ₒgrél-ba* to explain that sense, *dgoṅs-ₒgrél*, *dgoṅs-bgról* commentary; **a will, a wish,** *rgyál-poi* (or *-pos*) *dgoṅs-pa bžin-du bsgrub nús-so* I am able to fulfil your majesty's wish *Dzl.*; *skyóṅ-bai dgons-pa-čan Glr.* 104, poetically, one having the desire of protecting, one wishing to protect. — 2. **soul,** *dgóṅs-pa mya-ṅán-las ₒdás-so* his soul quitted (the abode of) misery. — 3. **permission** *C.*, *W.*, **góṅ-pa žú-wa** to beg leave, to ask permission, **góṅ-pa táṅ-wa**, resp. **náṅ-wa** to give permission, in *Sik.* also: to grant admission; but gen. it is used for **leave of absence**, and **ḱó-la góṅ-p̔og ḥjhuṅ soṅ** *C.* signifies: he has been dismissed, turned out.

དགོད་པ་ *dgód-pa* 1. **to laugh,** *Glr.*; gen. in such expressions as the following **gọ'-dhó** (lit. *bro*) *yim-pa** *C.* to make one's self ridiculous, a laughing-stock, also *Glr.*; **hab-gód čo-če** *W.* to set up a loud laugh, to burst out into laughter; *dgod-bág* a jest, joke *Sch.*; cf. *bgád-pa.* — 2. v. *ₒgód-pa.*

དགོན་པ་ *dgón-pa* 1. **a solitary place; desert, wilderness,** *dgón-pai ḥnas* a desolate place or region *Stg.*; *dgon-dúṅ* a sandy desert, sands *Sch.* (*Zam.* जङ्गल and *dgón-pa:* अरण्य forest). — 2. **hermitage.** — 3. **monastery,** frq.; *dgón-pa-pa* 1. a man dwelling in a desert, a hermit. 2. a man dwelling in a monastery, a monk; *dgon-pa-ma* fem.

དགོས་པ་ *dgós-pa* I. vb. implying necessity, as well as want: **to be necessary, to be obliged** or **compelled; to want,** to stand in need of; also where we use 'ought'; it is gen. used with the verbal root or with the termin. of the inf. present, *byed dgos*, but sometimes also of the inf. future or perfect, e.g. *rin-po-čes brtsigs dgós-na rin-po-če méd-pas sá-las bya dgos* though it ought to have been built of precious stones, yet for want of such, it will have to be constructed of earth *Dzl.* — *la* gen. denotes the person standing in need of a thing, e.g. *ṅá-la dgos* I want, I stand in need of, but it also refers to the object for which a thing is wanted: *rgya-gár-du ₒgró-ba-la ḥser dgos-pa yin* for a journey to India gold is wanted (required); in such a case the termin. may also be used: *či žig-tu dgos*, for what purpose is it wanted? *zas za ma dgos* I did not want to eat *Mil.*; *dgós-pai dús-su blaṅs* they took them when they wanted them *Glr.*; *bžéṅs ma dgos* he was not obliged to erect . . . *Glr.* — In commanding, the word is used to paraphrase the imperative of a verb: *ₒóṅ-bar dgos* come! in entreating, the respectful term is chosen: *ₒbyon dgos Mil.*, or in *W.*: **skyod dgos žu** 'you must come, pray!' =

please, do come! *˳krid ḋgós-pai γsól-ba*, or *żú-ba*, a request to be taken along with (by another person) *Mil. C.*: **to wish,** *ḱyo̤' śe-pa ˳di ṅa go̤-pa yin* I wish you to know this *Lew.*

ག

II. sbst. **necessity, want, use, purpose** (*W. dgós-če*, pronounced **gó-śe(s)**), *mán-po ˳tsol dgós-pa byuṅ* we have been under the necessity of looking for you a long time *Mil.*; *ṅá-la γyui dgós-pa med* I have no use for that turkois, I do not want it *Mil.*; **tiṅ-la gó-śe ṗi-la* W.* for future use; *dgós-pai čún-bas* as it is rather useless; *dgós-pa ċii ṗyir* for what purpose? frq.

III. adj. (*C.* also **go̤-gyu**, and **go̤**, *W. *gó-śe**, as in II.), **necessary, due, needful, useful,** *med kyaṅ dgos-pai ḱral-bsdud* a tax necessarily to be paid, unrelentingly exacted *Mil.*; *ráṅ-la dgós-pai skál-ba* the portion due to you *Mil.*; *dgós-pai bsláb-bya* useful doctrines *Glr.*; *dgós-pa yin* or *yod B.* and *C.*, **gó-śes yod* W.* it is requisite; *dgas(-pa) med B.*, **go̤-gyu me̤n* C.*, **gó-śe man** or **med* W.*, it is unnecessary, unfit, not wanted; *mi-dgós-pa* **useless, noxious,** *mi-dgós-pai ṗra-mén* pernicious witchcraft *Pth.*; *dgos-byéd* **useful,** *don dgos-byéd ċi ˳dug* what there is in it of useful contents *Mil.*; *dgos-˳dód* **wishes and wants,** *dgos-dód ˳byúṅ-bai dpal* a treasure out of which all wishes and wants come, i. e. are satisfied *Glr.*; *dgos-˳dód nags-ťsál* a forest for wishes, i.e. a forest which grants every wish; *dgos-˳dód* necessary expenses *Cs.*

དགྱེ་བ་ *dgyé-ba* **to bend, to be curving** or **crooked**; *dbyibs dgyé-ba* stooping, cringing, ducking *S.g.*

དགྱེར་བ་ *dgyér-ba*, *glu dgyér-ba* for *glu lén-pa* **to sing, chant,** expression of the Bonpas; the word is also pronounced **ghyér-wa**.

དགྱེལ་བ་ *dgyél-ba Sch.* = *sgyél-ba.*

དགྱེས་པ་ *dgyés-pa*, resp. for *dgá-ba*, **to rejoice, to be glad**; often with *ťugs*: *rgyál-poi* (or *-po*) *ťugs dgyes* the king rejoiced; with *la* (to rejoice) at or in, (to be glad) of; **to please, to be pleased, to choose,** *ió-bo ˳byón-pa-la ťugs-dgyés-par ˳dug* it seems the lord is pleased to walk *Glr.*; *mi dgyés-te* sorrowful, sad, discouraged, dejected; angry, indignant; cf. *dgá-ba.*

དགྱེས་སུ་འཛུག་པ་ *dgyés-su ˳ǰúg-pa* **to bend,** to double down *Sch.*, v. *dgyé-ba.*

དགྲ་ *dgra*, also *dgrá-bo*, *Ssk.* शत्रु 1. **enemy, foe,** *sdáṅ-bai dgra* the hating enemy, (opp. to *byáms-pai γnyén*), frq. used of imaginary hostile powers, that are to be attacked and withstood only by witchcraft; *dgra γnyen med* there is no difference between friend and enemy = no such thing exists (viz in the golden age); *dgrar ˳gyúr-ba* to become an enemy (to one) *Tar.*; *dgra byéd-pa*, *dgrá-ru ldáṅ-ba*, *láṅ-ba* to act in a hostile manner, *la*, against; *dgra slóṅ-ba*, causative form, to make a person one's enemy *S.g.*; *dgrar sém-pa*, *˳dzín-pa* to look upon one as an enemy, to take him for an enemy; *dgrar śés-pa* id.; *dgrá-bċóm-pa* Arhant, Arhat, the most perfect Buddhist saint (*Ssk.* अर्हन्त venerable; the Buddhists, however, explain it as a compound of *ari* enemy and *han* to extirpate, he who has extirpated the enemies i.e. the passions *Burn.* I. 295, II. 287. *Köpp.* I. 400). Also *dgra bgegs ˳dúl-ba Glr.* is interpreted as referring to the subduing of spiritual enemies. — *sṅá-dgrá* a former foe, *dá-dgra* a present foe, *ṗyi-dgra* a future foe *Cs.*; *ṗyi-dgra* prob. also a foreign enemy. — *˳čí-dgra* a mortal, deadly enemy *Cs.* — *dgrá-ča* weapon, arms *Wdṅ.*, *dgrá-sta* battle-axe; *dgrá-lha* v. *lha.* — 2. In *W.* also **punishment,** **ḱó-la ḍa ṗog soṅ** he was punished; also for any self-incurred misfortune: **ḱyód-la ḍa ṗog yin** you will draw upon yourself trouble, fatal consequences.

དགྲམ་པ་ *dgrám-pa* v. *˳grém-pa.*

དགྲོང་བ་ *dgróṅ-ba* v. *˳gróṅ-ba.*

དགྲོལ་བ་ *dgról-ba* v. *˳gról-ba.*

བགག་པ་ *bgág-pa Cs.* another form for *˳gégs-pa.*

བགད་པ་ *bgád-pa* to laugh *Dzl.*, cf. *dgód-pa.*

བགམ་པ་ *bgám-pa* v. *ₒgám-pa.*

བགེགས་ *bgegs* 1. = *gegs*, **hindrance, obstruction**, seldom. — 2. an evil spirit, **demon, devil**, like *ɣdoṅ*; *bgégs-kyi rgyál-po bi-nā-ya-ka Mil.* frq. (*Ssk.* **विनायक** a remover, of obstacles; the god Ganesha etc.).

བགོ་བ་ *bgó-ba* I. vb. 1. **to put on clothes** etc., pf., imp. *bgos; lham rtág-tu bgos* always wear shoes *S.g.*; esp. to put on armour. — 2. v. under *bgód-pa.*

II. sbst. **clothes, clothing**, *bgó-ba daṅ bzá-ba* food and clothes *Dzl.*

བགོད་པ་ *bgód-pa* (*bgog-pa Sch.* is perh. a provincialism) pf., imp. *bgos*, fut. *bgo*; *W.* inf. **gó-ċe**; imp. **gos ťóṅ** **to divide**, *nor* an inheritance; **to divide** in ciphering, *graṅs* a number; **to distribute**, *ṡas-ṡás-su* into shares, *mi-rnams-la* to or amongst people *Dzl.*

**Comp.** *bgod-byéd* **divisor** *Wdk.*, and accordingly also *bgo-byá* **dividend.** — *bgo-skál* 1. **share, lot**, *B.* and *col.* 2. **the doctrine of strict retribution** *Thgr.* frq. — **gó-ǩan* W.* **sharer, partaker, heir, joint-heir,** — *bgo-bṡá* = *bgo-skál, bgo-bṡá byéd-pa* to distribute, allot, apportion, *nor* the property *Thgy.*, *la* among *Stg.*

བགོམ་པ་ *bgóm-pa*, pf. *bgams Sch.*, **to walk, to step, to stride**, *góm-pa bgóm-pa Lex.* to make steps; *ₒťém pa-la bgóm-pa* to step over the threshold; *bgom ₒgró-ba* to pace, to walk slowly; *bgoms ťúb-pa* to begin to walk (?) *Sch.*

བགོར་ *bgor*, supine of *bgó-ba.*

བགོར་བ་ *bgór-ba*, *Cs.* = *ₒgór-ba.*

བགྱང་བ་ *bgyáṅ-ba*, acc. to *Zam.* = *brgyáṅ-ba*, v. *rgyóṅ-ba.*

བགྱི་བ་ *bgyí-ba*, eleg. for *byá-ba*, 1. fut. of *bgyid-pa.* — 2. sbst. **action, deed.**

བགྱིད་པ་ *bgyid-pa*, pf. *bgyis*, fut. *bgyi*, imp. *gyis*, eleg. for *byéd-pa* 1. **to make, to manufacture**; *gyis zér-bai ɣzugs* the images regarding to which there had been said: 'make them!' i.e. the bespoken, ordered images *Glr.*; **to do, to act, to perform**, *las bgyíd-pa* to do a work, *bká bżín-du bgyio* according to the word will be acted *Dzl.*; *nye-ɣnás bgyíd-pa* to act the disciple = to be a disciple *Dzl.*; *mi-la ɣnód-pa bgyis* I have hurt the man, I have done him harm *Dzl.*; *bu yód-par gyis ṡig* make, bring it about, that a child be (born)! *Dzl.*; *rgyál-bu ma ṡór-ba gyis ṡig* see that yo do not let the prince escape *Pth.* (*ba* for *bar* in the more careless popular style). — 2. **to say**, *żes bgyis* so he said *Dzl.*; *żes bgyi-ba* the so called *Dzl.*

བགྲང་བ་ *bgráṅ-ba*, pf. *bgraṅs*, **to number, count, calculate** *bsód-nams-kyi ťsad* the amount of merits *Glr.*; *bgráṅ-bya* what may be numbered, numerable; *bgráṅ-bar mi byá-ba, bgráṅ-du méd-pa, bgraṅ-yás* innumerable; *bgraṅ-ṗréṅ* rosary, beads *Glr.*, also the garland of human skulls, often seen as an attribute of terrible deities.

བགྲད་པ་ *bgrád-pa* 1. **to open wide**, *mig bgrád-pa* to stare, goggle, *ǩa bgrád-pa* to gape *Glr.*, *Cs.*; *rkáṅ-pa* to part the legs wide, to straddle, cf. *bsgrád-pa.* — 2. **to scratch** *Sch.* (spelled more corr. *ₒbrád-pa*).

བགྲུང་བ་ *bgrúṅ-ba*, pf. *bgruṅs* to cause to deposit, **to strain, to depurate** *Cs.*, e.g. *rnyóg-ma* impure water *Lex.*.

བགྲུད་པ་ *bgrúd-pa*, pf. *bgrus*, fut. *bgru*, to clear from the husks, **to husk, to shell**, *bgrús-pai ₒbras Lex.* husked rice.

བགྲེ་བ་ *bgré-ba*, pf. *bgrés*, resp. **to grow old**, often with an additional *sku-nas* in years (v. *na*) *Dzl.*; *bgres-rgyúd* weakness of old age, infirmity *Pth.*: *bgrés-po*, in *W.* pronounced **ré(s)-po**, an old man, a man gray with age, hoary; **ré(s)-mó** fem.

བགྲེང་བ་ *bgréṅ-ba*, occasionally for 1. *sgréṅ-ba.* 2. *bgráṅ-ba.*

བགྲེན་པ་ *bgrén-pa*, *Sch.* = *bkrén-pa.*

བགྲོ་བ་ *bgró-ba*, pf. *bgros* (resp. *bka-bgrós mdzád-pa Pth.*) **to argue, discuss, deliberate, consider**; the subject discussed is gen. a direct quotation: *ċii ṗyir ₒdi-ltar gyur ċel bgrós-nas* to converse on the cause of the present state of things *Dzl.*; *żes ṗan-*

ṫsún-du bgrós-nas thus declaring their opinions to one another *Tar.*; **to ask advice,** *ċi-ltar bya žes bgrós-nas* asking what they should do *Dzl.*; **to resolve, decide,** *byá-bar* to do *Dzl.*; *bgro-gléṅ byéd-pa* to dispute, to debate *Lex.*

བགྲོང་བ *bgróṅ-ba Tar.* = *bgráṅ-ba* **to count.**

བགྲོད *bgrod* 1. **the walk, gait,** mode of walking. — 2. symbol. num.: 2.

བགྲོད་པ *bgród-pa* **to walk,** *bgród-la ṗan* this assists in learning to walk *Lt.*; **to go, wander,** *lam bgród-pa* to travel over *Glr.*; **to get through,** *ḱyód-kyis bgród-pai skabs med ruṅ* although until now you have not been able to get to this place *Mil.*; *ču bgród-par dká-ba* a river difficult to cross; *nyi-ma-lho-bgród* the sun's going to the south, in the winter half-year, the sun's south **declination,** *byaṅ-bgrod,* north declination, *bgród-dus γnyis S.g.* both declinations; *bud-méd-la bgród-pa* to lie with a woman *Schr., Cs.*

བགྲོས་པ *bgrós-pa* v. *bgró-ba.*

མགར *mgar* n. of a noted crafty vizier of the king Srontsangampo *Glr.*

མགར་བ *mgár-ba* (col. **gár-ra**) **smith,** *mgár-bai bzo* smith's work; **gár-zo ċó-ċe* W.* to forge; *mgár-ḱaṅ, mgár-sa* smithy; *γser-mgár* gold-smith *Cs.*

མགལ *mgal* **jaw, jaw-bone,** *ya-mgál* the upper, *ma-mgál* the lower jaw-bone; *mgal-čág* a broken jaw-bone, *mgal-búd* a dislocated jaw-bone *Cs.*

མགལ་པ *mgál-pa,* also *ₒgál-pa* **a billet of wood;** *mgal-dúm* 1. a large piece of wood split or cut, 2. a piece of wood half-burnt *W., C.*; **gal-dó, gal ṫsig* W.*, **gal-rő* C.* id.; **gal-mé** a burning piece of wood, **a fire-brand; torch,** consisting of long chips or thin billets of wood; *mgal-méi ₒḱór-lo* a circle of light produced by whirling round a fire-brand.

མགུ་བ *mgú-ba* **to rejoice, to be glad, joyful, content;** *mgú-nas* delighted *Mil., Tar.*; *mgú-bai lan ma byuṅ* he did not receive a gratifying, satisfactory answer *Tar.* 17, 27; *ṫams-ċád byin yaṅ mgú-dus med* he is never content though every thing be given him *Mil.*; *mgú-bar byéd-pa, W.*: **gu ċúg-ċe**, to exhilarate, to gladden, to make content; *dga-mgú-ba, dga-mgu-ráṅ-ba* are intensive verbs; *mgur* = *mgú-bar.*

མགུར *mgur* (*Ssk.* कण्ठ) resp. 1. **throat, neck,** *gyu mgur-du ṗul-nas* presenting (the great teacher) with a turkois for his neck *Ma.* — 2. **voice,** *mgur snyán-pa* a sweet, harmonious, voice *Cs.* — 3. (col. **gúr-ma**) **song, air, melody,** hence a religious song is always designated by the respectful word *mgur* (not by *glu*), although the term in itself has no immediate reference to it. *mgur (-du) γsúṅ-ba, bžés-pa* resp. for *glu léṅ-pa* to sing a song; *Sch.*: *mgur ṫen-pa* id. — *mgur-ₒbúm* a hundred thousand Songs, title of the Legends of Milaraspa, which are richly interwoven with songs. — *Sch.*: *mgur bsál-ba* to clear the throat, to hawk, to hem; *čú-boi mgur* 'by-water', a tributary, a subsidiary stream (?).

མགུར་ལྷ *mgúr-lha* the god of hunting with the Shamans *Sch.*

མགུལ་(པ) *mgúl (-pa) Ssk.* कन्धर 1. **neck, throat,** *mgul-du ₒdógs-pa* to tie, fasten to one's neck e.g. magic objects; *ráṅ-gi mgúl-pa γċód-pa* to cut one's own throat *Dzl.*; *mgúl-pa sub* his throat is stopped, choked *Mṅg.*; *mgúl(-pa)-nas ₒdzín-pa, ₒǰú-ba,* to seize by the throat, sometimes also used for *mgúl-pa-nas ₒḱyúd-pa* to fall on a person's neck, to embrace. — *mgúl-nad* disease of the throat, **sore throat.** — *mgul-ċiṅs dkár-po* a white **neck-cloth** *Pth.* — *mgul-dár* or *dpa-dár* a silk cloth tied round the neck as a badge of honour. — 2. **the shoulder** of a mountain *Mil.*, *γyón-mgul-na* on the left slope.

མགེའུ *mgeu* = མགོའུ *mgou Cs.* v. *mgo.*

མགོ *mgo* (*Ssk.* शिर) resp. *dbu* 1. **head,** **gó-la zug rag** I have a headache, a pain in my head *W.*; **mgo ₒḱor** my head turns, I feel dizzy, I am getting confused, perplexed; *mgo skór-ba* to cheat, swindle, deceive; *mi-mgo ma skor* do not cheat people! *Mil.; mgo dgú-ba, dgúr-ba* v. *dgú-ba, mgo ₒtóm-pa* v. *ₒtóm-pa; mgor ǰóg-pa* to carry on the head *Sch.*; **go yúg-ce** *W.* to shake one's head, **kug táṅ-ce** *W.* to nod with the head, either as a sign of affirmation, or of beckoning to a person; **kyog-kyóg cò-ce** to wave the head from one side to the other, expressive of reflection. — 2. **summit, height, top,** *ri-mgo ká-bas γyogs Mil.* the hill-tops were covered with snow. — 3. **first place, principal part,** *mgo byéd-pa* to lead, to command, to be at the head *Glr.*; to educate cf. *dbu mdzád-pa*; to inspect, look after, superintend, control, *bú-mo žig-gis mgo byéd-pai mi máṅ-po* a number of (labouring) people looked after by a girl (the farmer's daughter) *Mil.;* **ḍos gó cò-ce** *W.* to preside in a consultation. — 4. **beginning,** *W.*, **go-ma**; *grós-mgo* the beginning of a consultation; *mgo ₒdzúg-pa* to begin; *bod sdúg-pai mgo ₒdzugs* that was the beginning of the misfortunes of Tibet *Ma*; *brtán-gyi skyid-mgo dé-nas tsugs* with this my constant good-fortune commenced *Mil.; ló-mgo-la* at the beginning of the year *Mil.*; *mgó-nas* from the beginning *Dzl.* — 5. *Gram.:* a superscribed *r, l, s* e.g. *rá-mgoi ka,* རྐ, *k* with *r* superscribed; *dé-rnams bas pul sá-mgoi kao* these are the words beginning with *bsk*.

**Comp. and deriv.** *mgo-klád* **brain** *Cs.* — *mgo-dkyil* col. crown of the head, **vertex.** — **go-kár**, or **gar** *Ld.* a tight under-garment, drawn over the head when put on, (*Ssk.* परिधान, *Hd.* प्रहिरवन) something like a shirt, but not in general use. — *mgo-skór* **imposture, deceit,** *bdud-kyi mgo-skór de ṅa mi ₒdod* I detest these diabolical tricks *Mil.* — *mgo-skyá* a gray head, *mgo-skyá-can* a gray-headed person *Cs.* — **go-kyóṅ** *C., W.*, **protector, patron,** = *mgo-ₒdren.* — *mgo-kra* scald, scald-head *Sch.* — *mgo-mkrégs-can* **obstinate, pertinacious, stubborn,** esp. in buying and bartering, selfish, bargaining, haggling: **go ṭag cò-ce** *W.* to have these qualities. — *mgo-rgyán* head-ornament. — *mgo-can* having a head, **mi-go-can** having a man's head, such as English rupees and other coins (bearing the image of a head) *W.* — **go-ciṅ** *C., W.* = *go-ₒdrén.* — **go-(l)cág** a blow or knock on the head *Ld.* — *mgo-lcógs* little **shoots, sprouts, branches** *Sch.* — *mgo-čá* = *mgo-rgyán.* — *mgo-mǰug* beginning and end (head and tail), *šiṅ ₒdii mgo mǰug gaṅ yin-pa bye-brág pyes šig* find out which is the upper and which the lower end of this piece of wood *Dzl.* — *mgo-ǰóṅ Cs.:* 'an oblong head.' — *mgo-rǰén* bare headed. — *mgo-nyág Cs.:* 'a compressed, contracted head'. **go-nyī-pa** *C.* two-headed, double-tongued; a double-dealer, backbiter. — *mgo-snyóms* indifferent, unconcerned. — **gor-tiṅ tsáṅ-ma** from head to heel, the whole from top to toe, = **go-lus-ča-tsaṅ**. — *mgo-ₒdón* = *mgo-ₒdrén,* with *byed-pa* = *mgo ₒdon-pa* to bring or draw forth, to raise, to lift up a person's head, gen. with *raṅ*, one's own head, used in the sense of: **to be self-dependent,** one's own master, to come off well, **to be uppermost** *Mil.*; *mgo ₒton-pa* id. — *mgo-ₒdrén* **protector, patron,** used frq. in letters as a complimentary title. — *mgo-nág* po. for **man** *Glr.* — *mgo-nád* **headache.** — **gó-bu** *W.* **first-born.** — *mgó-ma* 1. adj. **first,** *gral-mgo-ma* first in order, the first in a row or line of persons *Mil.* 2. sbst. **the beginning** *W.*, **go-ma tsug-ce** to begin. 3. adv. **in the beginning, at first** *W.* — *mgo-tsém* 'stitched at the head' denoting a book which is so stitched, that the lines run parallel to the back, whilst one stitched in our way is called *rta-mgó-ma.* — *mgo-γžún,* col. **gog-žún** **crown** of the head. — *mgou, mgeu* a small head *Cs.* — *mgo-yór* = *tsá-bai nad Ts.* — *mgo-γyógs* **a covering for the head** (hat, cap etc.). — *mgo-ril* 1. **a round head.** 2. **cattle without horns** *W.* — *mgo-rég* for *mgo brégs-pa* one that has his head shaved, **a monk;** *mgo-rég btsún-ma Lt.* monks and nuns, or: nuns that have their heads shaved. — **go-lus-ča-tsáṅ** a complete **suit of clothes,** **gor-tiṅ-tsáṅ-ma** id.; **go lus sum kón-ce** *W.* to furnish a person with new clothes; **go lus spó-ce** *W.* to give one's own clothes to a person (e.g. when a king honours any body by arraying him in splendid garments). — *mgo-lèb* a flat head *Cs.* — *go-šóg*, resp. *u-šog* **cover,** of a copy-book etc. *Cs.* — *mgo-srín* n. of a disease *Lt.*

མགོན་པོ་ *mgón-po*, *Ssk.* नाथ **protector, patron; principal, master, lord; tutelar god;** *˳gro-mgón* protector of beings; *skyabs-mgón* v. *skyabs; čii ɉyir ṅai mgon mi byed* why do you not assist me? *Dzl.*; *lhai, bdúd-kyi, γšin-rɉei mgón-po* the principal of the gods, of the devils, the lord of death *Cs.*; *mgón-po mčód-pa, stód-pa; rbúd-pa* to honour, to praise, the tutelar god, to stir up or urge him to aid one's cause. The special tutelar god of Tibet, called *mgón-po* by preference, is Awalokiteśwara, Spyan-ras-γzigs; *˳ɉig-rten-mgón-po*, or *mi-mɉed-žiṅ-gi mgón-po* lord of the world, *˳ɉig-rten γsúm-gyi mgón-po* (Hindi: *triloknāth*), lord or ruler of the three worlds, an epithet 1. of Buddha, 2. of Awalokiteśwara, 3. of the Dharma-Rājā of Bhotān.

**Comp.** *mgon máṅs* many patrons or defenders of religion; many small pyramidical sacred buildings *Cs.* — *mgon-méd* unprotected, *mgon-med zas-sbyin*, अनाथपिण्डद, n. of a certain house-owner in Buddha's time, often mentioned in legends.

མགྱོགས་པ་ *mgyógs-pa*, *C.* **gyóg-po** **quick, speedy, swift;** *mgyógs-par* (seldom *mgyógs-la Mil.*) adv. **quickly, speedily, soon;** **gyog-riṅ** *W.* speedy, hasty, rash, **gyog-lám** *W., C.*, a straight, short way, a short cut; *rkaṅ-mgyógs* v. *rkaṅ*. — *su-mgyógs*, pronounced **sun-gyóg(s)** *W.*, (lit. 'who is quick?') a race, a racing or running-match.

མགྲིན་པ་ *mgrin-pa*, (*Ssk.* ग्रीवा) 1. **neck,** *mgrin riṅ-ba*, a long neck, *mgrin túṅ-ba* a short neck *Lt.*; *mgrin-sṅón* blue-necked, an epithet of gods. — 2. **throat,** as passage or organ of the voice, *mgrin γčig-tu* (to call as) with one voice, frq.; *mgrin-bzáṅ* a loud voice *Cs.*

མགྲོན་ *mgron* **feast, treat, banquet, entertainment,** *mgron γtóṅ-ba*, resp. *sku-mgrón ˳búl-ba* to entertain; **ḍón-taṅ-k̔an** *W.* host, entertainer; *mgrón-la ˳bod-pa*, resp. *mgrón-du spyan-˳drén-pa*, to invite to an entertainment; *mgrón-du ɉnyér-ba* to treat, to regale *Dzl.*; *mgrón-du ˳gró-ba* to go to an entertainment, a party *Dzl.* (cf. *˳grón-du ˳gró-ba* to go abroad); *zas-mgrón* an entertainment consisting in eating; *ja-mgrón* a tea-party; *čaṅ-mgrón* a treatment with beer or wine *Cs.*

འགག་ *˳gag* 1. **obstruction, stoppage,** esp. in comp.: *yi-ga-˳gág* want of appetite; *γčin-˳gág*, also *-dgag*, strangury. — 2. a place or spot that has to be passed by all that proceed to a certain point, **zám-pe gág-tu gúg-na kụ́m-ma ˳dzin tub** *C.* the thief may be stopped, if you are on the watch in the thoroughfare of the bridge; *ri-bo dpal-˳bár-gyi ˳gag* the place on the Palbár mountain, where there is the only passage *Mil.*; *sgo-˳gág* the door of the house, because through it all that enter or leave have to pass; *k̔a-˳gág* the mouth, through which every thing must pass that is eaten; fig.: *tar-lám-gyi γnad-˳gág*, the main point for obtaining salvation; *˳gag γčig-tu dril-ba* to unite, to be concentrated in one point *Mil.*

འགག་པ་ *˳gág-pa* 1. vb, (cf. *˳gegs-pa*) **to stop, to cease,** to be at a stand-still; mostly in the perfect form *˳gags; dáṅ-k̔a ˳gags* the appetite is gone *Mil.*; it is also used of the passions having been suppressed, having ceased *Mil.* — 2. sbst. **door-keeper,** v. *sgo-˳gág* sub *˳gag*.

འགང་ *˳gaṅ* v. *rgaṅ*.

འགངས་པ་ *˳gáṅspa* **difficult, troublesome** *Sch.*

འགང་(པོ་) *˳gáṅ(-po)* the **burden** of an office, business, commission, *˳gan ˳k̔úr-ba* to bear such a burden, *bskúr-ba* to impose it on a person.

འགབ་ *˳gáb* = *mtá-ma, mɉúg-ma,* **the end,** of a bench, a garment etc. *Mil.nt.*; as postpos. c.genit. **after, behind** *C.*

འགབ་པ་ *˳gáb-pa* 1. *Sch.*: **to take care, to be cautious; orderly, decent.** — 2.

*W.* **to suffice,** **mi gáb-če med** the workmen will not suffice.

འགམ་པ་ ˳*gám-pa*, pf. *gams Sch.*, *bgams Cs.*, fut. *bgam*, imp. *goms* 1. **to put,** or rather **throw, into the mouth,** e.g. grains of wheat, a mouthful of meal, as Tibetans use to do; *ṗye ťúr-mgo re tsam* ˳*gams* I took a small spoonful of meal *Mil.* — 2. **to try,** *bgám-mo* I will try him, I shall put him to the proof *Dzl.*; *ťsód* ˳*gám-pa* id. *Lex.* — 3. *W.* **to threaten, to menace.**

འགའ་ ˳*ga* (˳*ga-bo Cs.?*) **some, a few, several,** *ḱyi-ra-ba* ˳*ga* some huntsmen *Mil.*; *γžón-pa* ˳*ga žig* some young men *Mil.*; *ḱo-ráṅ* ˳*ga* some of them *Mil.*; ˳*ga-ré* = ˳*ga žig Pth.*; *gál-te nón-gyis* ˳*ga žig bžág-na* if I appoint some by a peremptory decree *Dzl.*; *skabs* ˳*gar* in some cases; *lan* ˳*ga* (*žig*) sometimes, now and then (opp. to frequently, as well as to once, one time); *res* ˳*ga* 1. sometimes. 2. col. for some, several; *bar* ˳*ga* sometimes; *lan* ˳*ga* — *lan* ˳*ga*, *res* ˳*ga* — *res* ˳*ga*, *bar* ˳*ga* — *bar-*˳*ga* at one time — at another time, some — others; ˳*ga tsam* a few, few *Thgy.*: ˳*ga šás* some, part (of them) *Mil.*; ˳*ga yaṅ* followed by a negation: no, no one, not any, none.

འགའ་ ˳*ga Glr.*, also ˳*ga - ti* n. of a place in the east of Tibet.

འགར་ ˳*gar*, termin. of ˳*ga*.

འགར་བ་ ˳*gár-ba* 1. sbst. (*W.* also **gár-ru**, *Ts.* ***˳*gar, gir**) masc. ˳*gár-po*, fem. ˳*gár - mo*, a mixed breed of cattle, of a *mdzo* (q.v.) and a common cow, or a bull and a *mdzó-mo*. — 2. vb. v. sub *dgár-ba*.

འགལ་དུམ་ ˳*gál-dúm* v. *mgal*.

འགལ་བ་ ˳*gál-ba*, c. *las* or *daṅ*, **to be in opposition** or **contradiction to,** as: *rtág-pa daṅ dṅós-po γnyis* ˳*gál-ba yin* the ideas of 'perpetuity' and of 'thing' are contradictory; commonly of persons: **to counteract,** to act in opposition to, **to transgress, violate, infringe, break,** a promise, law, duty; *yid daṅ mi* ˳*gál-bar Dzl.*, resp. *tugs daṅ mi* ˳*gal-bar*, (he gives them) to their wish, to their heart's content; *bka bžin - du mi* ˳*gal-bar bgyio* I shall act faithfully according to the order *Dzl.*; **gal mi dug** *W.* he has not committed anything, he is innocent; *lha* or *klu daṅ* ˳*gal - ba* not to honour a Lha or Lu according to duty.

**Comp.** ˳*gal - rkyén* **mishap, untoward accident, impediment** (opp. to *mťun-rkyen*); ˳*gal-rkyen sél-ba*, or *méd - par byéd-pa*, or *zlóg-pa* to avert, to remove such accidents or impediments. — ˳*gal-*˳*ḱrúl* **transgression,** ˳*gal -* ˳*ḱrúl spaṅs - te*, conscientiously; **gal-ṭúl só-wa** to make amends, to atone for a transgression. — ˳*gal-mťún-šes-pa Chr. Prot.*, the knowledge of what is conformable or contrary to the divine law, meant to express our **'conscience'**; the term was formed after the Tibetan phrase: *dge mi-dgé šés-pa*, or *rig-pa*, knowledge of what is virtue and what is vice; cf. however *šés-bžin*, *γnóṅ-ba*, and *byas-čós*. — ˳*gál-ba-po Cs.*, ˳*gál-po Sch.*, a transgressor. — ˳*gal-ťsábs Cs.* a great fault, a crime; ˳*gal-ťsábs-čan* faulty, criminal, a criminal (?).

འགས་པ་ ˳*gás-pa*, pf. *gas* (cf ˳*ges-pa*) **to be cleft** or **split,** of rocks etc.; **to chap,** of the skin, the lips; to break open, **to burst,** of a bag etc., *ḱa lṅá-ru* into five rents, in five places; **to crack, to break** or **burst asunder,** of a vessel, the heart, a fruit, *bdún-du* into seven pieces; *šiṅ-gi rigs - la byás-na ni* ˳*gas* if it be made of wood, it will split, crack *Glr.*

འགིའུ་ ˳*giu* v. *gi-wáṅ*.

འགུ་མདའ་ ˳*gu-mdá* **gun-stock,** (spelling not certain) v. *sgum-mdá*.

འགུ་བ་ ˳*gú-ba*, incorr. for *mgú-ba*.

འགུག(ས)་ ˳*gug(s)* **a mesh** *W.*

འགུག(ས)་པ་ ˳*gúg(s)-pa*, pf. *bgug*, fut. *dgug*, imp. *ḱug* 1. (cf. *kug*) **to bend,** to make crooked, *γnya* ˳*gugs-pa C.* to bend, bow, stoop; *mgo* ˳*gugs-*˳*gúgs-par sóṅ-ṅo* he went off bowed down, crestfallen. — 2. **to gather,** to cause a gathering, *rnág-tu* of matter, pus, to suppurate. — 3. **to call, to summon, to send for,** e.g. the gardener *Dzl.*,

ཀ

one's daughters *Dzl.*; **to conjure up,** ghosts, *des bdag ˳gúg-par ˳gyúr-ro* by this (charm) I may be conjured up; *blo náṅ-du k̔úg-la* calling the spirit back into its inner domain, abstracting the mind from the external world. — 4. **to draw back, to cause to return, to convey back** *Mil.*, *C.*

འགུད་པ་ *˳gúd-pa*, pf. *gud*, = *rgud-pa*? *gúd-du bċúg-pa* **to ruin,** to reduce to an extremity *Schr.*; *rtsa byiṅ-gúd dal Med.* a pulse slow and sinking.

འགུམ་པ་ *˳gúm-pa* 1. pf. *gum*, *˳gums* eleg. **to die.** — 2. pf. *bkum*, *fut. dkum*, imp. *k̔um(s)*, **to kill,** to put to death *Dzl.* frq.; **to slaughter** (butcher), *ɣsár-du bkúm-pai ša*, meat of an animal just killed, fresh meat *Dzl.* — 3. **to bend, curve,** make crooked, to contract, v. *kum* and *skúm-pa*.

འགུལ་ *˳gul* **neck,** v. *mgul*.

འགུལ་བ་ *˳gúl-ba* (cf. *sgul-ba*) to change place or posture, **to move, shake, to be agitated,** **ri-gu ḍód-pa-la gul dug** the kid moves in the womb (of the goat); *˳gul-dká* (the limb) moves with difficulty *Med.* frq.; *˳gul yaṅ ma nús-so* (they) would not even stir (from terror) *Dzl.*; **to waver, tremble, shiver,** *˳dár-žiṅ ˳gúl-ba*; *'sa-˳gúl* (pronounced **saṅ-gúl**) earthquake *W.*

འགེག(ས)་པ་ *˳gégs-pa* pf. *bkag*, fut. *dgag*, imp. *k̔og* **to hinder, prohibit, stop,** *bdág-gis bkág-na yaṅ ma ťúb-kyis* though I was preventing it, I could not (carry my point) *Dzl.*; *ma bkág-ste náṅ-du btaṅ* he admitted him without impediment *Dzl.*; **kág-ċe med zér-k̔an-gyi ka-šóg** a warrant, a permit to traffic without hinderance, a pass-bill, and the like *W.*; **to shut, to lock** (up), **to close,** *sgo* the door *Glr.*, *lam* the road frq., to close one's nose with the hand *Pth.*; **to retain, keep back** excretions *Med.*, *bšaṅ-dgág* obstruction (cf. *˳gag*); **zá-ċe kág-te ši** *W.* his food sticking fast he died; **to lock up, shut up** (things for keeping), **to pen up** (sheep, cattle), **kág-te bór-ċe** *W.* id; *dgag-dbyé* the ending of the seclusion, viz. of the monks who have to stay in their houses during the rainy season *Schf.*, *Tar.* 10, 10, cf. *Köpp.* I, 369; **to forbid,** *dgag-sgrúb Sch.*: 'to forbid and to allow' (?); *gág-pai sgra*, *˳gag-ťsig* a prohibitive particle *Gram.*; *bkág-ča byéd-pa* to forbid, prohibit *Sch.*; **k̔a kág-ċe** *W.* to silence, to hush; *dgág-pa* a negative, a negation; *bkág-ča* the negative side *Was.* (282).

འགེངས་པ་ *˳géṅs-pa*, pf. *bkaṅ*, fut. *dgaṅ*, imp. *k̔oṅ* 1. **to fill,** *ťib-ril čus* or (seld.) *čú-las*, or *ťib-ril-du čus*, or *ču*, (to fill) a tea-pot with water; **to soil, smear, stain,** the bed with blood *Glr.*; *dgáṅ-dka* difficult to be filled, not to be satisfied, insatiable *Stg.* — 2. **to fulfil** (more frq. *skóṅ-ba*) *ťugs-dám Lex.* — 3. *gžu ˳géṅs-pa*, *mda ˳géṅs-pa* to prepare bow and arrows for shooting, frq.; **ťú-pag káṅ-ċe** *W.* to load a gun.

འགེད་པ་ *˳géd-pa*, *Cs.* = *˳gyéd-pa*.

འགེབས་པ་ *˳gébs-pa*, pf. *bkab*, fut. *dgab*, imp. *k̔ob* (*W.* **bkob**), **to cover,** e.g. one's breast with the hand; to cover up, *k̔a* an opening, aperture; **to spread** over or on, **to set up, to put on,** a cover, lid, cork, plug etc.; **to protect,** *btsún-mo mi-ma-yin-gyis ˳gébs-su ˳júg-pa* to have the queen protected by ghosts; **to disguise,** metaph: **bkáb-ste** in disguised language, euphemistically *W.*, **káb-ċe p̔í-la** in order to express it euphemistically.

འགེམས་པ་ *˳gém-pa*, acc. to *Cs.* another form for *˳gúm-pa*, **to kill, to destroy;** *Schr.*: *klád-pa ˳géms-pa* to surprise; to overthrow an argument by reason; cf. *mgo-˳géms Lex.* w.e.; as a partic.: stupid *Schr.*; the few passages, where I met with the word, leave its meaning doubtful.

འགེལ་བ་ *˳gél-ba*, pf. *bkal*, fut. *dgal*, imp. *k̔ol*, 1. **to load, to lay on** a burden, *brui k̔al ċig bkál-te* loaded with a load of grain *Dzl.*; fig. to put a yoke upon a person's neck, *byur* to bring down misery on a person; *W.* to bring accusations against a person, **mi 'ós-pe lás-ka žig mi žig-la kal táṅ-na** *Ld.* if one is accused of an unlawful action; *k̔ral ˳gél-ba* to impose tribute *Lex.*; **to commission, to charge with, to make, appoint, constitute**, **mi žig gád-po-la kál če* Ld.* to appoint some one to be an elder or senior, cf *ₒčól-ba.* — 2. **to put, to place** on or over, *ydúṅ-ma bkál-ba* a beam placed over it *S.g.*; **to set** or **put on**, e.g. a pot on a trevet; **to hang up**, *gos-ₒgel-ydáṅ* a stand to hang clothes on; fig. *ₒči-bar nús-pai tog ₒgel dgos* one must set on it the roof of being able to die, i.e. one must crown the whole edifice by being free from fear of death *Mil.*

**འགེས་པ་** *ₒgés-pa*, pf. *bkas*, fut. *dgas*, imp. *k̔os*, trs. to *ₒgás-pa*, **to split, cleave, divide**, *bkas-šiṅ Lex.* cleft or chopped wood; *dúm-bur* (to divide) into pieces *Lex.*, **to cut up** or **open**, e.g. a fish, gourd, pumpkin, *Dzl.*

**འགོ་** *ₒgo*, = *mgo* in some figurative applications of the word: *dmág-ₒgo* **commander** of an army *Cs.*; *mk̔ár-ₒgo, rdzóṅ-ₒgo* commander of a fort *Cs.*; *ₒgo snám* a sort of fine cloth made of shawl-wool, or also: Europe-cloth, i.e. broad cloth = *sag-lád*; *ₒgó-pa* **officer, captain, head-man** of a village or district, esp. in *W.*; in a general sense: **kon-čóg ɉig-ten-gyi gó-pa yin** God is the ruler of the world; **koṅ-čóg-gi saṅ gó-pa med** God is the only and highest ruler; **ₒgo-pọ́n* C.* **rector, director, head-master, principal** e.g. of a school; *ₒgó-ma Zam.* **beginning, origin, source;** *ₒgó-mi Lex.* = *ₒgó-pa*; **go-yód** = *ₒgó-pa Ld.*; *ₒgor* in the beginning, at first, originally *Sch.*, *sér-bai ₒgor* when it began to hail *Mil.nt.*

**འགོ་བ་** *ₒgó-ba*, pf *gos* (or *ₒgos*), cf. *bsgo-ba*, 1. **to stain,** to lose colour; **to dirty, sully** one's self, *dé-la* with it, *naṅ-skyúgs lús-la* to soil one's self with vomit. — 2. **to infect**, with a disease, *ₒgó-bai nad, ₒgo-nád, ₒgó-bai rims*, a contagious or epidemic disease, **a plague**, frq.

**འགོག་པ་** *ₒgóg-pa*, pf. *bkog*, fut. *dgog?* imp. *k̔og* 1. **to take away** forcibly, **to snatch, tear away, pull out,** *rtsá-ba* a root *Lex.*, **so** a tooth *Schr.*; **to tear up**, e.g. a floor *W.*; **to peel** *Sch.*; **kóg-te k̔yér če* W.* **to rob, plunder** frq.; **kóg-te k̔yers* Ld.* it has been robbed. — 2. **to take off**, a cover, a lid, a pot from the fire *W.*

**འགོགས་ཀ་** *ₒgógs-pa* another form for *ₒgégs-pa*, **to prevent, to avert** unfortunate events, fatal consequences; **to suppress,** the symptoms of a disease by medicine; **to drive back** or **away, to expel** e.g. spirits, ghosts; **to repel** people that are trying to land.

**འགོང་བ་** *ₒgóṅ-ba* 1 *Cs.*: to bewitch, enchant (?), *góṅ-ba-po, ₒgóṅ-po* **an enchanter, sorcerer,** *góṅ-ba-mo* enchantress, sorceress *Cs.*; more frq. *ₒgóṅ-po* **an evil spirit, demon,** also fig. demon of concupiscence, of fear, of terror *Mil.*; *ₒgóṅ-mo* fem. — 2. pf. *bkoṅ*, perh. more corr. *sgóṅ-ba, spú-sgoṅ-ba Lex.* **to despond.**

**འགོད་པ་** *ₒgód-pa*, pf. *bgod*, fut. *dgod*, imp. *k̔od* (cf. *k̔ód-pa*), the Latin *condere*, 1. **to design, to project, to plan** *Schr.* — 2. **to found, to etablish, to lay out** (a town), **to build** (a house); hence *bkód-pai rig-byéd* books on architecture *Glr.*; **to manufacture, to form, to frame.** — 3. **to put, to fix, to transfer,** into a certain state or condition, *bdé(-ba)-la Dzl.*, *bder Lex.*, into a happy state, *dge-ba-la Dzl.* into virtue, *čós-la Pth* into the true doctrine, *rnám-par ₒgról-ba-la Dzl.* into salvation, *mya-ṅán-las ₒdás-pa-la* into delivery from existence *Dzl.*; *žag-gráns* **to fix** a certain time or term *Schr.*; *ts̔ad* (to determine) the measure or size of a thing *Schr.* — 4. **to set, put,** or **place in order,** *gral-p̔yám bgód-pa ₒdra* as the rafters of a roof are placed side by side *S.g.*; *mt̔ar dgód-pa* **to add** or **affix** e.g. ciphers to a certain number *Wdk.*; *bkód-par mdzés-pá* beautiful as to arrangement, nicely ordered, *(b)rgyan dgód-pa Lex.* to arrange ornaments (tastefully), **to decorate, adorn, to construct** or **adjust** grammatical forms, sentences *Zam.* — 5. to put down in writing, **to record,** *miṅ ká-ba-la* to write names on a column *Pth.*; **to compose, draw up, write,** a narrative etc., frq.; **to mention, to insert,** in a writing; **ka kọ́-pa* C.* **to publish**, to make known. — 6. **to rule, to govern** *Schr.*; *byol-sóṅ bkód-pai rgyál-*

po yin he is king over all subjugated animals *Mil.*

The partic. pf. *bkód-pa* is also sbst.: 1. **plan, ground-plan, draught** of a building *Schr.* — 2. **delineation, sketch,** *žiṅ-bkód* **map.** — 3. **form, shape, figure** *Schr.* — 4. **sample, copy,** even of one's own body, e.g. when a person multiplies himself by magic virtue, = *sprúl-ba.* — 5. **building, edifice, structure,** *bkód-pa mdzes* the structure (is) beautiful *Glr.* — 6. **frame, body,** *bkód-pa lus* id. *Mil.*; *ṅai bkód-pa nám-mk̔ai raṅ-žin* my body of an ethereal nature *Pth.*

*Note.* The Lexx. have for *bkód-pa* always **न्यास** putting down, depositing; but often it has the signification of **व्यूह** orderly arrangement; as vb. it comes nearest to **उपरच्**. As the meaning of the word is almost quite the same as that of *κτίζειν* and *condere*, it recommends itself as the most suitable term for **'to create'**, to call into existence, *˳gód-pa-po* for **creator,** and *bkód-pa* for **creature,** notions which are otherwise foreign to Buddhism.

འགོམ་པ་ *˳góm-pa*, *Cs.* = *góms-pa*, *Sch.* also = *˳gém-pa*, *˳gúm-pa.*

འགོར་ *˳gor* 1. v. the following article. — 2. termin. of *˳go*, in the beginning, at first *Sch.* — 3. supine of *˳gó-ba.*

འགོར་བ་ *˳gór-ba* **to tarry, linger, loiter,** *W.* frq. **máṅ-po gor soṅ** you stayed away very long; **lám-la gor** he lingers on the way; **máṅ-po ma gór-te** without long delay, = *riṅ-por ma lón-par*, and *riṅ-por mi t̔ogs-par B.*; *de ˳gor-γží yin* that impedes, delays; *zlá-bu γnyis ˳kor* (the work) lasted two months *Glr.*

འགོལ་བ་ *˳gól-ba*, pf. *gol* 1. **to part, to separate** vb.n.; *˳gól-bai γnas* a hermitage *Pth.*, *˳gól-po* hermit, recluse. — 2. **to deviate, err,** go wrong or astray; *˳gól-sa* 1. the place where two roads separate. 2. **error, mistake.**

འགོས་ *˳gos* n. of a monastery *Tar.*

འགོས་པ་ *˳gós-pa* v. *˳gó-ba.*

འཁྱག་པ་ *˳kyág-pa* cf. *skyág-pa*, **to be sold, spent, expended** *Cs.*

འགྱང་བ་ *˳kyáṅ-ba*, pf. *˳gyaṅs*, **to be delayed, deferred, postponed,** *p̔yir ˳gyaṅ-na* if one defers it; **nyin ˳gyaṅ žag ˳gyaṅ ǰhē-pa* C.* to delay again and again; *lo maṅ-po mi ˳gyaṅ-bar* before many years shall have passed; *dus ˳gyaṅs Lex.* w.e.

འགྱིང་བ་ *˳gyiṅ-ba* 1. to look about haughtily, **to look down upon, to slight,** *mi-la* a person; also of things: **to despise, contemn, neglect** them *B.* and col.: **˳gyiṅ-bhág ǰhē-pa* C.*, **gyiṅ čo-če* W.* id.; **gyiṅ-čan** supercilious, contemptuous. — 2. = *sgyiṅ-ba Glr.*; *Mil.* — *šél-kyi ˳gyiṅ-˳k̔ar* a sceptre of crystal, an attribute of gods, in pictures represented as a plain, unadorned staff.

འགྱུ་བ་ *˳gyú-ba*, pf. *˳gyus*, **to move quickly** to and fro, e.g. as lightning, the quivering air in a mirage, the motion and versatility of the mind etc.

འགྱུར་བ་ *˳gyúr-ba* I. vb., pf. *gyur(-to, -pa)* imp. *gyur (-čig)*, cf. *sgyúr-ba*, 1. **to change,** to be altered *B.* and col.; *mi-rnams-kyi spyód-pa ˳gyur* the behaviour of men changes *Ma.*; *˳gyúr-bai čos* a changeable (and therefore perishable) thing *Cs.*; and *˳gyúr-du yód-pa* changeable, variable, *˳gyúr-du méd-pa*, *˳gyur-med* unchangeable, invariable; sometimes **to decrease, abate, vanish, die away,** *mt̔u-stóbs, nád-med-pa, γzi-rǰid yóṅs-su ˳gyur-ba* the total decay of strength, health, and esteem (in old age) *Thgy.*; *bdág-gi sems ma gyur, ma nyáms-so* my mind has not been altered, nor my resolution weakened *Dzl.*; also with *las: dád-pa ˳di-las ma gyur čig* do not **depart** from that belief *Mil.* (I have therefore availed myself of this word, combined with the active (transitive) form *sems sgyúr-ba* 'to change the mind' for expressing the *μετανοεῖν* and *μετάνοια* of the N. T., though the Buddhist is wont to regard the *mi-gyúr-ba* as the thing most to be praised and desired.) With the termin. it signifies **to be changed, transformed into,** *B.* and col.; hence — 2. **to become, to grow,** *dge-slóṅ-du ˳gyúr-ba, rgyál-por ˳gyúr-ba* to become a monk, a king *Dzl.*; *skra mťon-mťiń-gi ḱa-dóg-tu gyúr-to* his hair turned azure (sky-blue) *Dsl.*; *sbrúm-par ˳gyúr-ba* to get with child; *bdún-du ˳gyur-ba* to reach the number of seven *Dzl.* (In all these cases the more recent writings and the col. language in *C.* usually have *˳dó-wa*, *in W.* *čá-c̀e*.) *˳gyúr-ba* is also frq. used in conjunction with verbs: *yód-par ˳gyúr-ba* 'to become being', i.e. to begin to exist, 'to become having,' i.e. to gain possession; *sróg-la mi ltá-bar ˳gyúr-pai dṅós-po ˳di-dag* these acts of having become indifferent to life, i.e. acts of contempt of death *Dzl.*; *ná-bar gyúr-na ˳di mťóń-ba tsám-gyis nad sós-par ˳gyúr-ro* when taken ill, they get well again, as soon as they obtain a sight of this *Glr.*; *c̀an mi smrá-bar gyúr-to* he became speechless *Dzl.*; *˳gyúr-ba* denoting both the pass. voice, and the fut. tense, the context must decide in every instance, how it is to be understood: *su žig rgyal-srid byéd-par ˳gyur* who shall have the government, who shall rule? *Tar.* 21.; *de rgyál-por ˳gyúr-bar šés-so* they knew that this man is made king (for: would be made king); *ḱó-mos ḱyód-kyi bu bsád-par gyúr-na* if your son has been killed by me *Dzl.*; *ḱyod mí-ša zá-bar gyúr-c̀ig* may you be obliged to eat human flesh! *Dzl.*; *c̀ii ṗyir ḱyod ˳di-ltar gyur* by what means have you come into this state? *Dzl.*; *ya-mtsán-du* (or *-par*) *˳gyúr-ba* to be surprised, astonished; with *γnás-su:* **to come** to a place, **to arrive** at *Mil.*; *˳dód-pai dṅos-grúb-tu ˳gyúr-ba* to be endowed with the perfect gift of wishing, viz. of having every wish fulfilled; **to happen, to take place, to occur**, *ya-mtsán-du ˳gyúr-ba c̀i yod* lit. what is there that has wonderfully happened, what wonderful things have happened? *γyós-par ˳gyúr-ba* to become moving, to begin to move. — 3. **to be translated,** *bod-du* into Tibetan *Tar.*; *bka-˳gyúr* the translated word, v. *bka*; cf. *sgyúr-ba.* — 4. joined to numbers it signifies **time** or **times,** *γžán-pas brgya-˳gyúr stoṅ-˳gyúr-du ˳ṗágs-pa* a hundred times, nay a thousand times more sublime than others *Dzl.*; *ḱyód-pas brgya-˳gyúr-bas lhág-par bzáṅ-ba yod* there are (girls) a hundred times prettier than you *Dzl.*; *γsum-˳gyúr ltá-bur* three times as much *Dzl.*; *de γnyis-˳gyúr tsam žig* one twice as large as that *Mil.*

II. sbst. **change, alteration, vicissitude,** *dus bžii ˳gyúr-bas* through the change of seasons *Thgy.* — *˳gyur-skád*, or also *˳gyur-ḱúgs* singing or humming a tune in a trilling manner *Mil.*; *˳gyur-lc̀am nya Mil.* perh. a fish swiftly moving to and fro; *˳gyur-rtén bžág-pa* to pay money in hand, as an earnest that the bargain is not to be retracted. — Instead of the imp. *gyur*, *šóg* is frq. used.

འགྱེ་བ་ *˳gyé-ba*, pf. (and imp.?) *gyes,* **to be divided**, e.g. a river that is divided into several branches; *rnám-pa γnyis-su* (a ray of light divided) into two parts *Dzl.;* **to separate, to part,** *bem rig ˳gyes dus* when body and soul part from each other *Mil.;* **to disperse,** of a crowd, with or without *so-sór Dzl.* and elsewh.; of a single person: **to part, withdraw, go away,** *mi-tsóg dan ghyč-ne* *C.* withdrawing from the crowd; **to issue, proceed, spread,** *dé-dag-las gyés-so* they have proceeded from those (their ancestors); of a disease: *gyén-du gyes* (opp. to *ťúr-du zug*) *Med.?*

འགྱེད་པ་ *˳gyéd-pa* (*W.* *kyé-c̀e*) pf. *bgyes,* fut. *bkye,* 1. **to divide** (trs.), **to scatter, disperse, diffuse,** e.g. rays of light; it is also used when the neutral form *˳gyé-ba* would seem to be more correct; **to let proceed,** *sprúl-pa,* an emanation; hence **to send,** a messenger *Lex.* and *Schr.*; **to dismiss,** *ťsogs*, an assembly *Sch.* — 2. *˳ťáb-mo ˳gyéd-pa, γyul ˳gyéd-pa,* also *˳gyéd-pa* alone, to fight a battle, **to fight, to combat,** *˳gyéd-pai ťse* in the dispute; similarly *˳dzíṅ-ga bkyé-ba* **to quarrel** *Med.*; hence prob. *W.:* *ḱa kyé-c̀e* to abuse, to menace. — 3. *stón-mo ˳gyéd-pa* frq. **to give** an entertainment, banquet, prop. to dispense a feast; *nor ˳gyéd-pa* **to distribute** a property *Lex.*

འགྱེར་བ་ *˳gyér-ba* **to drop** or let fall, to throw down *Schr.;* **to quit, abandon,** throw away *Sch.*

འགྱེལ་བ་ ˌgyél-ba, pf. gyel (-to), imp. gyel, **to fall, to tumble,** *gyel ma gyel* W. don't tumble, take care not to fall; *gyél-kan* W. lying, (not standing), e.g. a bottle.

འགྱེས་པ་ ˌgyés-pa, another form for ˌgyé-ba, p̓yi-gros-su ˌgyés-par ˌgyur back foremost they retreat Glr.

འགྱོད་པ་ ˌgyód-pa (Ssk. कौकृत्य) vb. (W. *gyód-če*) **to repent, to grieve for,** and sbst. **repentance,** sorrow for, not only for bad, but also for good actions, when the latter are attended with disadvantage or loss; p̓yis ˌgyón-par ˌgyur you will have to repent it hereafter Dzl.; with la, to repent of a thing; ˌgyód-pa skye repentance arises, I feel repentance, I repent frq.; sems ˌgyód-par ˌgyur id.; *da gyód-pa yoṅ dug* W. id.; ˌgyód-pa med I do not regret it; ˌgyód-pa-čan repenting Pth.; ˌgyód-pai sems méd-par k̓yód-la sbyín-no I give it you readily and with all my heart Pth.; ˌgyód-med without repentance, without grudging, also: in good earnest; ˌgyod-ts̓áṅs byéd-pa, ˌt̓ól-žiṅ ˌgyód-pa, ˌgyód-čiṅ bšág-pa Dzl. to acknowledge repentingly, to confess with compunction; ˌgyod-ts̓áṅs byéd-par γnáṅ-ba to accept a repentant confession = to forgive, to pardon Dzl. (p. ༤༧, ༥༢, ༦༠, ༢༢༩); ˌgyód-rmo-ba, c. la, to make repent, to make one suffer, feel, or pay (for a thing) Dzl.; γnoṅ-ˌgyód repentance proceeding from consciousness of guilt Pth.

འགྲག(ས)་པ་ ˌgrág(s)-pa, pf. grags, **to sound,** to utter a sound, of men, animals, thunder etc. Dzl.; **to cry, to shout,** dei rná-lam-du ˌgrágs-par ˌgyúr-na if it is shouted into his ear; čes grags so it is called, so he was called, by this name he goes, under that name he is known, celebrated; bód-la yi-ge med čes grags Tibet, so it is said, was without letters, without a written language; Zam.

འགྲགས་པ་ ˌgrágs-pa **to bind,** v. grágs-pa.

འགྲང་བ་ ˌgráṅ-ba 1. Cs. **to number, to count,** v. bgráṅ-ba. — 2. **to satisfy** with food, **to satiate,** *ḍáṅ-če med* W. he is insatiable; gen. only the pf. is in use: ˌgraṅs rǰes after having eaten one's fill Med.; šá-ba bšád-pas mi ˌgráṅ-te not yet having enough of deer-killing Mil.

འགྲད་པ་ ˌgrád-pa Cs. = bgrád-pa, **to spread, to extend** (vb. a).

འགྲན་པ་ ˌgrán-pa (Ssk. स्पर्ध) 1. **to vie** with, **contend** with, **to strive** (for victory), wa séṅ-ge-la a fox (contending) with the lion Dzl.; čo-ˌp̓rúl in magic tricks Dzl.; rig-pa in shrewdness, cunning Glr.; p̓yug-k̓yád rnam-t̓ós-kyi bu daṅ ˌgrán-te to cope even with Plutus as to riches Dzl.; bstód-par ˌgran let us vie with one another in songs of praise Glr.; ˌgrán-pas čog let us now draw a parallel between (these two) Glr.; ˌgrán-du ˌǰúg-pa to cause (two persons) to strive (for the victory) Dzl. — 2. in a general sense, **to fight,** to defend one's self, to make resistance.

**Comp.** ˌgran-ts̓ig words of contention, **a quarrelling speech** Glr. — ˌgran-sems 1. **contention, emulation.** 2. **jealousy.** 3. **quarrelsome temper, spirit of controversy;** ˌgran-sems γčóg-pa to stop, put an end to contention. — ˌgrán-zla (pronounced *ḍál-za* in the north of Ld.), **rival, competitor,** equal match; ˌgrán-zla-med-pa, ˌgran-zla daṅ brál-ba, also ˌgrán-gyi do-méd, ˌgrán-ya-med, without a rival, **matchless, unequalled,** applied also to things.

འགྲམ་ ˌgram 1. **shore, bank,** ču-ˌgrám id.; ču čén-poi ˌgrám-du soṅ they went to the bank of a large river Dzl. — 2. **side,** sgo-ˌgrám γyás-na on the right side of the door Glr.; sgoi p̓yi-ˌgram-na before the door, outside, out of doors Pth. — 3. **wall,** k̓áṅ-pai ˌóg-ˌgram the lower wall of a house (opp. to the roof) Mil.; ˌgram-γži C., S.g. **foundation, basis,** ˌgram-γži ˌdíṅ-ba to lay a foundation. — In a more general sense: ˌgrám-du **near, close to, just by,** rgyáṅ-nas sgra čé-la ˌgrám-du don čuṅ he has a great voice, is making much noise, at a distance, but looking nearer, you do not find much in him Mil.; šiṅ-gi ˌgrám-du close to the tree.

འགྲམ་པ་ ₒgrám-pa **cheek** (cf. *k̔ur-ṫsós*), **ḍám-pa hom soṅ* W.* his cheeks are fallen; *lág-pa ₒgrám-pa-la rtén-pa* to lay one's hand on the cheek (in a pensive or sorrowful mood) *Dzl.*

**Comp.** *ₒgram-lčág* a slap on the face, box on the ear; **ḍam-čág gyáb-če* W.* to box a person's ears. — *ₒgram-ču ldaṅ* that makes one's mouth water *Sch.* — *ₒgram-p̔ug Lt.?* — **ḍam-dzóg* C.* a blow or cuff with the fist upon the cheek, **gyág-pa** to deal such blows. — *ₒgram-rús* **cheek-bone, jaw-bone.** — *ₒgrám-ša* the flesh of the cheek. — *ₒgram-γšóg* the hinder part of the jaw-bone *Sch.* — *ₒgrám-so* **cheek-tooth**, molar-tooth, grinder.

འགྲམ་ཡིག་ *ₒgram-yig* **edict, proclamation, publication** *Sch.*

འགྲམས་པ་ *ₒgráms-pa* **to hurt** *Lt.*; of wounds: to get inflamed, ni f. *Mil. nt.*

འགྲམས་ཚད་ *ₒgrams-ṫsád*, a disease, fever in consequence of great exertions *Med.*

འགྲས་པ་ *ₒgrás-pa* **to hate,** to bear ill-will, to have a spite against, **ṅa k̔ó-la že ḍé ₒdug* C.* I hate him in my heart.

འགྲིག་འགྲིག་ *ₒgrig-ₒgrig* 1. **gelatine, jelly** of meat *C.* 2. v. the following article.

འགྲིག་པ་ *ₒgrig-pa* (cf. *sgrig-pa*) **to suit, agree, correspond, to be right, adequate, sufficient,** in *B.* seldom, col. very frq., **ḍig-pa yin* C.* that will do, I am satisfied; **da ḍig* W.* now that will do! just enough now! **ḍig-ḍig* W.* to be sure! quite so! of course! **ₒo ḍig gog* W.* yes, to be sure! **tsó-če mi ḍig* W.* it is not yet time for cooking; **ṫó-re tság-na ḍig-ga* W.* will it be early enough, if I sift it to-morrow? **de yaṅ mi ḍig-pa dug* W.* also that is not practicable; *ṅa ǰọ'-yaṅ di ma ḍig-na* if my pronunciation is not correct *C.* (Lewin).

འགྲིབ་པ་ *ₒgrib-pa*, pf. *grib,* 1. **to grow less, to decrease, to be diminished,** syn. to *ₒbri-ba; mi ₒgrib mi lúd-pa* neither to grow less nor to flow over *Dzl.*; but gen. *ₒp̔él-ba* is opposed to *ₒgrib-pa*, and both words refer not only to bulk, size, and quantity, but also to strength, well-being etc., so that *ₒgrib-pa* also means to sink, decay, be reduced; *bskál-pa mar ₒgrib*, acc. to *Schr.* = Treta yuga v. *dus* 6; *mar ₒgrib-pa* also opp. to *yar skyé-ba* to be re-born in lower regions. — 2. **to grow dim, to get dark,** cf. *sgrib-pa Cs.*

འགྲིམ་ *ₒgrim*, in *lag-ₒgrim Glr.* 45: *lag-ₒgrim-gyis brgyus-pas* passing from hand to hand, v. *ₒgrim-pa* II, 1.

འགྲིམ་པ་ *ₒgrim-pa* I. sometimes for *ₒbrim-pa Pth.* II. pf. *ₒgrims* 1. **to go, walk, march about, perambulate, to rove** or **stroll** idling about, *rgyal-k̔ams* over the countries *Mil.*; *γčig-pur ri-k̔ród-la Mil.*; *bár-dor* in the bardo (q.v.) *Thgr.*; *mi-sér ǰág-pai ₒgrim-sa yin* it is a resort of robbers *Mil.*; it is also used of the course of the veins in the body *Med.* — 2. *W.* **to go off, to sell,** to meet with a ready sale. — 3. *rig-pa ₒgrim-pa* v. *rig-pa.*

འགྲིལ་བ་ *ₒgril-ba*, pf. *gril* (cf. *sgril-ba*) 1. **to be twisted** or **wrapped round,** *Dzl.* ༢༥, 17. acc. to one manuscript, for *ₒkri-ba Sch.*; to be collected, concentrated, to flock or crowd together, *kun ₒgril-nas* all in a heap, all together *Mil.* — 2. **to be turned, rounded, made circular** or **cylindric,** e.g. a stick *Mil.* — 3. **to fall,** e.g. leaves from a tree; in *B.* seldom, in *W.* frq. (*ₒdril-ba* is the same word).

འགྲིས་ *ₒgris* v. *ₒdris.*

འགྲུ་བ་ *ₒgrú-ba*, pf. *grus*, **to bestow pains** upon a thing, *slob-pa-la* upon study *Dzl.*

འགྲུབ་པ་ *ₒgrúb-pa*, pf. *grub* 1. **to be made ready, to be finished, accomplished;** *ₒgrúb-pa mi srid* it is not possible that this be accomplished *Glr.*; *ma ₒgrúb-par* before its having been finished *Glr.*; *ma-ₒgrúb-pa-rnams ₒgrúb-par ₒgyur-ro* (frq. of charms, regarding their desired effect) prob. means: all that has not yet been effected, will be accomplished by it; *grúb-pa-rnams* is applied in a special sense to the ordained Gelongs (v. *dge-slóṅ*); *šúgs-la ₒgrub* the thing is brought about quite of itself *Mil.*; so esp. in the phrase: *lhún-gyis grúb-pa* being produced spontaneously (opp. to making, procuring) e. g. clothes, food etc. were always at his disposal, viz. in a supernatural way *Dzl.*; *dpál-las grub* it devolved on me in consequence of my perfection, my superior qualities *Mil.*; *dón-la grúb-pa med kyaṅ* though it did not actually happen so (still, being meant to frighten by appearances etc.) *Glr.*; *byéd-na don čen ₒgrub* if you do so, you will have many advantages (lit. great welfare) by it *Mil.*; *gru ₒgrúb-pa Tar.* 25,6; 34,20 *Schf.*: to take in a full cargo, though from the wide meaning of the word, it may also signify: to accomplish a journey happily, so esp. in the passage *Tar.* 35,3 — 2. **to be made, fabricated,** *rdó-las* out of stone. — 3. **to be fulfilled, granted,** of wishes etc., also with *bžin-du.* — 4. **to be performed according to rule,** of charms; cf. *sgrúb-pa* and *grúb-pa.* — *ₒgrúb-sbyór* is an expression occurring in almanacs, relative to the proving true of certain astrological prognostics of good luck, similar to, but not identic with *rten-ₒbrél.*

འགྲུམ་པ་ *ₒgrúm-pa*, pf. *grum*(?), **to pinch** or **nip off** (the point of a thing), **to cut off, to prune, lop, clip,** the wings, *W.*, cf. *grúm-pa.*

འགྲུལ་བ་ *ₒgrúl-ba* I. 1. **to walk, to pass, to travel,** *ₒgrúl-bar byéd-pa* to cause to go, to send off, despatch, a messenger *Dzl.*; **ṅún-la ḍul* W.* walk first! take the lead! *ₒgrúl-ba-po*, *ₒgrúl-po Sch.*, **ḍúl-ḱan, ḍúl-mi* W.* a walker, foot-traveller, pedestrian; *ₒgrúl-pa Sch.* id.; *ₒgrúl* sbst. passage, the possibility of passing, *γnya-náṅ-gi ₒgrul čád-pas* the passing from Nyanaṅ being made impracticable (viz. by snow) *Mil.* — 2. fig. **to walk, to live, act,** or **behave,** **ṭim-si** (or **tim-mi*) *naṅ-tar* W.* (to live) in conformity with one's duty, in accordance to the law. — 3. **to pass, to be good, current,** of coins.

II. i. o. *brúl-ba Mil.*

འགྲུས་པ་ *ₒgrús-pa* 1. pf. of *ₒgrú-ba.* — 2. sbst. **zeal, diligence, endeavour;** more frq. *brtson-ₒgrús.*

འགྲེ་བ་ *ₒgré-ba* 1. **to roll** one's self, *sá-la* on the ground; *ₒgre-ldóg Glr.* (or *ₒgre lóg Pth.*) *byéd-pa* id., e.g. from pain, despair etc.; also of horses etc. — 2. **to repeat** *Cs.*

འགྲེང་བ་ *ₒgréṅ-ba* (cf. *ₒsgreṅ-ba*) **to stand** (not in use in *W.*) *dóṅ-gi ḱar ₒgréṅ-nas* standing at the top of the pit *Dzl.*; *dṅáṅs-pa ltar ₒgréṅ-bar ₒgyur* they start up as if frightened *Dzl.*; of the *ṗo-mtsán*: to be erected *Med.*; *mi ₒgreṅ γsum* three lengths of a man *Tar.* — *ₒgréṅ-bu*, also *ₒgréṅ-po* (*Glr.*) the sign of the vowel e.

འགྲེམ(ས)་པ་ *ₒgrém(s)-pa*, pf. *bkram*, fut. *dgram*, imp. *ḱroms* (*W.* **ṭam-če**, imp. **ṭom**) 1. **to put** or **lay down** in order, e.g. beams, spars etc. *B.* and col.; **to spread out, to display,** goods, books, on the table or ground; **to scatter,** blossoms by the wind *Stg.*; **to draw,** a curtain. — 2. **to sprinkle,** water, *B.* and col. — 3. **to distribute,** for *ₒbrim-pa C.*

འགྲེལ་བ་ *ₒgrél-ba*, pf. *bkral*, another form for *ₒgrol-ba*, **to explain, comment, illustrate,** *dgóṅs-pa* the import (of the words or writings of the saints); *ₒgrél-ba Cs.*, *ₒgrel-pa Zam.*, *Tar.* explanation, explication, commentary; *don-ₒgrél*, resp. *dgoṅs-ₒgrél* explanation of the meaning; *tsig-ₒgrél* explanation of a word, of the words; *γžuṅ-grél* 1. explication of the text 2. text and commentary; *raṅ-ₒgrél* prob. self-explanation, an explanation contained in the book itself *Wdṅ.*; *ₒgrél-ba-po Cs.*, *ₒgrél-po Sch.*, *ₒgrel-byéd Cs.* an explainer, commentator. (*ṗan-tsún ₒgrél-ba*, and *ḱral ₒgrél-ba Lexx.*?)

འགྲོ་སྒོ་ *ₒgró-sgo C.* **expense, expenditure,** of money, **ḍo-gor táṅ-ba** to lay out (money), to spend.

འགྲོ་ལྡིང་ *ₒgro-ldiṅ* Dramila, country in the south of India *Schf.*; another reading gives Draviḍa (coast of Coromandel).

འགྲོ་བ་ *ₒgró-ba* I. vb., pf. and imp. *soṅ*, the imp. *ₒgro(s)* seldom used, 1. **to**

**walk,** *k̔yeu ₒgro mi nús-pa góg-pa tsam* an infant, a child, that creeps only, and is not yet able to walk *Dzl.*; *ₒgró-ba daṅ nyál-ba daṅ ₒdúg-pa* the walking, lying and sitting *Dzl.*; com. in a more gen. sense: **to go, to move,** *ₒgró-am mi ₒgro* will you go or not? *rgyál-poi mdún-la ₒgró-bai lág-ča* the things going, i.e. carried, before the king *Glr.*; **to go away,** *da ṅa ₒgró-bar žu* now I beg to be permitted to go *Pth.*; *γnás-nas ₒgró-ba* to go away from a place, to leave, *k̔yim-nas ₒgro mi p̔ód-na* if one cannot leave his house, part from home *Pth.*; **to go out,** *k̔yod nyin-par rtág-tu ₒgró-na* if during the day you always go out, are from home *Dzl.*; **to travel,** *p̔an-tsún-du ₒgró-ba Dzl.*, *p̔ar ₒgro t̔sur ₒgró-ba Pth.* travelling there and back; *yar ₒgro mar ₒgró-ba* to travel up and down, up hill and down hill *Glr.*; *ₒgró-čos-su* as a spiritual vademecum *Mil.*; *ₒgró-t̔se* on the way, on the road; opp. to *ₒóṅ-ba* (more fully: *p̔ar ₒgro t̔sur ₒoṅ-ba*, col. *yoṅ-ba*) to go and to come back; hence *ₒgro-t̔se* may also mean: on the way thither; *ₒgro-ₒoṅ-méd-pa* a thing that is neither going nor coming, but always remaining in its place *Mil.*; **to go, move on,** to continue one's way, esp. in the phrase *soṅ(-soṅ)-ba-lus.* Connected with adverbs and postpositions: *p̔yir ₒgró-ba* to return, go home, to come back, also: to go out, *mdún-du, sṅón-du, sṅún-la ₒgró-ba* to go before, pass before, precede (*mdún-du* referring to space only, *sṅón-du* and *sṅún-du* both to space and time); *rǰés-su ₒgró-ba* to follow, come after or later, to succeed, also to give one's self over to, to addict one's self to (e.g. ill courses) *Ld.-Glr. Schl.* p. 7, b; *ₒgro čug, C.* let it be, let it take its course! — *rkyál-ₒgro* a swimming fish *Cs.* — *dgúr* (or *rgur*)-*ₒgro* = *dud-ₒgro.* — *ₒgrúl-ₒgro* pacing, walking *Cs.* — *rgyúg-ₒgro* running, galloping *Cs.* — *ṅán-ₒgro* going to damnation, *ṅán-soṅ* having gone to damnation, *ṅán-soṅ γsum* the three damned, or not saved, classes of beings (v. sub II); *ṅán-soṅ γsum* **is opposed to** *bdé-ₒgro,* **and often used in** a general sense = 'hell'. — *sṅón-ₒgro* 1. **preceding, foregoing, previous, former.** 2. **preface, introduction,** opp. to *dṅos-γži*, the thing itself, the text etc. *Thgr.* and elsewh. — *čos t̔ams-čád-kyi sṅón-ₒgroi sláb-bya* Petersb. Verzeichniss no. 409) does not mean: 'advice given by the former (teachers)' *Sch.*, but: introductory and preparatory doctrines. — *mčóṅ-ₒgro* (going in leaps) **a frog** *Cs.* — *nyál-ₒgro* (creeping, crawling) **a worm.** — *ltó-ₒgro* (crawling, sliding on the belly) **worm, snake,** frq. — *dúd-ₒgro* (*Ssk.*, **तिर्यञ्च**) walking in an inclined posture, **an animal,** v. sub. II — *bdé-ₒgro* going to happiness: **the happy, the blessed,** also *bdér-ₒgro Was.*, opp. to *ṅán-ₒgro*, v. above; usually in a gen. sense, like our 'heaven'; *bdé-ₒgro mto-ris-kyi lus t̔ób-pa* to receive a heavenly, glorified body, v. *lus.* — *ₒdúr-ₒgro* **trotting** *Cs.* — *ₒp̔ur-gro* **a bird** *Cs.* — *ₒp̔yé-ₒgro* = *ltó-ₒgro.* — *láṅs-ₒgro* walking erect, **man.** — 2. **to get, to get into, to enter** *čí-bdag-gí dbáṅ-du sóṅ-ba* having got into the power of death *S.g.*; *grál-gyi t̔á-mar soṅ* they got (in a miraculous manner) to the end *Dzl.* ༢༦, 4. b.; *de nyid mig-tu sóṅ-na* if the same (a little hair) gets into the eye *Thgy.* — 3. **to find room in, to be contained in,** like *šóṅ-ba*: *til-rǰáṅ k̔al brgyád-ču ₒgró-ba žig* a sesame store-room that will hold 80 bushels; *k̔al γčig ₒgró-bai žiṅ* as much land as can be sown with a bushel of corn (prop. a field holding a bushel) *Pth.* — 4. **to turn to, to be transformed into,** syn. to *ₒgyúr-ba* and often used instead of it, but only in more recent writings, and in the col. language of *C.* (in *W.* **čá-če** is much more in use): *dúg-tu ₒgro* it turns to poison, it is changed into poison *Mil.*; *k̔yi-mo žig-tu soṅ* she was changed into a bitch *Mil.*; *mt̔ar gyúr-nas sdug-bsṅál-du ₒgró-bas-na* because they finally change and are turned into misery *Thgy.*; *lóg-par ₒgró-ba* to take an unfavourable turn, to have a fatal issue (of a cure) *Lt.*; *da sgrúb-γnas-su soṅ yod* it has now become a place of meditation, it has been transformed into sacred ground

Mil.; *stobs čúṅ-du ˳gró-ba* the state of declining, the decay of strength *Med.*; *ćól-bar ˳gro* they get intermixed, confused *Ma.*; similarly *Tar.* 210,10; *las zin ˳gró-na* when there is no more work, when work ceases. In a somewhat different sense: *mé-tog smán-la ˳gro* the blossom is used for medicines. — 5. In *W.* *˳gró-ba* is gen. joined to a supine in *te,* and used to express uncertainty or probability: **dí-riṅ der léb-te do** he has probably arrived there to-day; **zér-te yod do** very likely he has said so; **šro ži-te do** his anger will have abated, I think. The origin of this particular use of the word may perh. be traced to such sentences as the one following: *p̔úṅ-ste ˳gro* we are going to be ruined, we are likely to be ruined. — 6. **to be spent, expended,** v. *˳gró-sgo*; **sóṅ-to** col., account of expenses.

II. sbst. **a being, a living creature,** *˳gró-ba mi* the being 'man', *Mil.*; *˳gró-ba rin-čén Cs.*, *˳gro-mčóg,* **the** highest being, or creature, man; *˳gró-bai rigs drúg*, *˳gro-drúg* the six classes of beings, viz. *lha, lha-ma-yin, mi, dúd-˳gro, yi-dvags, dmyál-ba-pa.* The *lha-ma-yin* are sometimes omitted, or placed after man. — *˳gro(-bai) don byéd-pa*, or *mdzád-pa* to care for the welfare of beings, which expression is frq. applied to the benevolent activity of the Bodhisatvas etc., at present as much as: to perform divine service, to officiate, = *sku-rim byéd-pa.* — *˳gro-p̔án* = *˳gro-dón Tar.* 13,16. — *˳gró-sa* 1. **way, road** *W.*, **dó-sa med** one cannot go there. 2. **aim, scope,** *˳gró-sar p̔yin* he reaches his aim, attains his end *Glr.* 3. **access, approach,** *˳gró-sa mi ˳dug* one cannot gain access, admission.

འགྲོགས་པ་ *˳grógs-pa* 1. (cf. *grogs*) **to be associated,** *k̔yo-šúg γnyis ˳grógs-na* husband and wife together *Dzl.*; *de daṅ ˳grógs-te ˳oṅs* he came with him, had joined him *Dzl.*; *˳grógs-te dóṅ-ṅo* let us go together *Dzl.*; *ṅa daṅ k̔yéd-rnams ˳bral-méd rtág-tu ˳grogs* I and you, we shall always remain inseparably united *Glr.*; *˳grógs-dgos-rnams* those with whom we are to keep close fellowship, our nearest relations and associates *S.g.* — 2. cf. *˳grágs-pa, sgróg-pa*) **to cry, to shout** *Dzl.*, esp. joined with *˳bod.* — 3. (cf. *grás-pa, grágs-pa* I.) **to bind, to tie,** *t̔ág-pa-la dar-lčog*, a flag to a rope; **to hang, fix, fasten,** *nyí-mai zér-la* hanging on a sun-beam *Glr.*

འགྲོང(ས)་པོ་ *˳gróṅ(s)-po*, or *˳gróṅs-pa*, **straight,** = *bsráṅs-pa, Ts.*

འགྲོང་བ་ *˳groṅ-ba* 1. pf. *groṅs* 1. resp. **to die;** *˳gróṅs-ka* the very time of one's death *Cs.*, cf. *˳čí-ka*; sometimes it stands 2. for *˳drén-pa, Mil.* and *C.* — 2. pf. *bkroṅs*, fut. *dgroṅs*, resp. **to be killed, murdered, put to death,** of Lamas and kings.

འགྲོད་པ་ *˳gród-pa*, = *bgród-pa*, **to go, to travel** *Glr.*

འགྲོན་ *˳gron* **alienism,** the state of being a foreigner; *˳grón-du ˳gró-ba* to go on travels, to go abroad *Dzl.*; *˳grón-po*, fem. *˳grón-mo*, guest, foreigner, stranger, traveller frq.; *˳grón-po ˳bód-mk̔an* one inviting guests, an inviter col.; *γžis-˳gron* a native guest, *byés-˳gron* a foreign guest *Cs.*; *˳gron-k̔áṅ* inn, public house *Mil.*; *˳gron-γnyér* 1. that servant in a household who has to announce visitors, to receive and hand over requests etc.; in *W.* an official in the monasteries attending on strangers and travellers. 2. a mediator, one supporting a petition, one taking care of sacrifices etc. — *˳gron-lám* road *Cs.*

འགྲོན་པ་ *˳grón-pa, Cs.* = *˳gród-pa.*

འགྲོན་བུ་ *˳grón-bu* (*W.* col. **rúm-bu**) **a small shell, cowry,** at present chiefly used as ornament, or as a medicine, after having been burnt and pulverized; *˳grón-bui t̔al* the ashes of this shell *Med.*; *˳gron-t̔ód* an ornament for the head, consisting of cowries *Mil.*

འགྲོར་ *˳gror*, supine of *˳gró-ba.*

འགྲོལ་བ་ *˳gról-ba* I. vb. neut., pf. *grol*, **to become free, to be liberated, released from,** *bčiṅs-pa gaṅ yin-pa dé-dag ni gról-bar gyúr-to* all that were bound were released: *lus dé las* from this body *Glr.*; *nád-las* from disease, *ṅas* by me *Mil.* In a specific Buddhistic sense: *yid*, or *sems rnám-par grol* the soul or spirit is released, made free, viz. from every impediment arising from imperfect knowledge or perception, the latter being no longer subject to dimness and uncertainty, but perfectly clear; *raṅ(-sar) gról-ba* what has become clear of itself (without any study or exertion) *Glr.*; yet *raṅ gról-ba* seems also to denote: to be set free, to get released (from the *ₒk̔or-ba*) through one's self; *č̔os-nyid-kyi gliṅ-du ₒgról-ba* to be released and elevated into the region of the highest perception *Glr.*; *ₒgról-ba*, used absolutely, always signifies, like *t̔ár-ba*, to be released from the evil of existence.

II. vb. act., pf. *bkrol*, fut. *dgrol*, imp. *k̔rol* (*W. bkrol*, pronouneed *ṭol*) 1. **to loose, untie, unbutton, unfasten**, a knot, a bag, a garment; **to put down, take off**, arms, ornaments etc. — 2. **to release, redeem, liberate**, *bčiṅs-pa-las* from fetters *Tar.* — 3. **to remove**, do away with, put an end to, *sdug-bsṅál* misery, *t̔e-ts̔óm* doubts. — 4. **to remove obscurities**, to free from uncertainties, **to explain, interpret, comment**, = *ₒgrél-ba*, e.g. *dgóṅs-pa* the sense, import *Lex.*; *ₒgrol-byéd*, *ₒgról(-ba)-po* commentator *Cs.*

**འགྲོས་** *ₒgros* the act of **going, walking**, *p̔yi ₒgrós-su* v. sub *ₒgyés-pa*; *skyabs-ₒgrós* v. *skyabs*; *spyod-ₒgrós* manner of walking, gait, carriage; *séṅ-gei spyod-grós Mil.* the manner of a lion; also manner or mode of living, of transacting business, *dé-tso ṅá-yi spyod-ₒgrós yin* these are my occupations *Mil.*; *mig-gi spyod-ₒgrós* the language of the eyes, of looks; *rkaṅ-grós* 1. a going or travelling on foot, a march. 2. breeding cattle, *rkaṅ-ₒgrós spél-ba* to breed cattle, to be a grazier. — *č̔u-ₒgrós* a current of water; *šiṅ č̔u-ₒgrós-la kyál-če* to float timber *W.* — *ₒgros-č̔én* amble (of a horse) *Sch.*

**རྒ་བ་** *rga-ba*, pf. *rgas* 1. **to be old, aged**, *rga-šis yzír-ba* to suffer under (the infirmities of) old age *Zam.* (cf. *skyé-ba* init.); *rgás-pai stéṅ-du* beside my being already old *Dzl.*; *rgas-k̔ógs* v. *ₒk̔ógs-pa*. — 2. fig. **to go down, to set**, of the sun etc.; *go-rgás* v. *go* 2.

**རྒ་ཝང་ཀྲད་ཀྱི་** *rga-waṅ-k̔rád-kyi*(?) **bat, flitter-mouse** *Ts.*

**རྒག་ཅིག་** *rgag-čig* a large gray species of **lizard** *Ld.*

**རྒང་** *rgaṅ*, also *ₒgaṅ-yzér-ma* **hedgehog** *Sch.*, or perh. rather **porcupine.**

**རྒད་པ་** *rgád-pa*, or *rgán-pa*, **old, aged;** more frq. *rgád-po* 1. an **old man**, a man gray with old age. 2. an **elder, senior, headman** of a village; *rgád-mo* an old woman; *rgan-bgrés* old people *Sch.*; *rgan-rgón ɟnyis Sch.*: 'both the old man and the old woman' (?); *rgan-rgón-rnams-kyi skyo-grógs* the comforter of old people (so *Mil.* calls himself). — *rgan-byis* old people and children, old and young *Mil.* — *rgan-mi-máṅ* = *rgan-ɣsum*. — *gan-tsir-žón-tsir W.*, *gẹn-žọn-ḍhal-rim C.* the privileges of seniority. — *rgan-žúgs* those that are grown old *Cs.*, 'an old monk' (?) *Sch.* — *rgan-rábs* the aged, *rgan-rábs-la rim-gro byéd-pa Stg.*, *rgan-rigs p̔u-dúd-du k̔úr-ba S.g.* to respect old age. — *rgan-ɣsúm*, *rgan-mi-máṅ* the elders of a village.

**རྒལ་** *rgal W.* **a ford.**

**རྒལ་ཅིག་པ་** *rgal-čig-pa* = *rgag-čig Ld.*

**རྒལ་བ་** *rgál-ba*, pf. and fut. *brgal*, imp. *rgol*, c. *las*, or accus., or *la*, **to step** over (a threshold) *Glr.*; **to pass** or **climb** over (a mountain); *la brgál-bai byáṅ-ṅos* the north-side of a pass crossed *Glr.*; **to leap** over (a wall) *Dzl.*; **to ford** (a river); **to travel** through, **to sail over, to pass** (a river or lake), *rgyá-mtso-la gru-ɣziṅs-kyi lám-nas brgál-te* after having crossed the sea in a ship.

**རྒལ་ཚིགས་** *rgal-tsigs Sch.* = *sgal-tsigs.*

**རྒས་** *rgas*, v. *rgá-ba.*

**རྒས་ཀ་** *rgás-ka* **old age;** *rgás-ka sṛa* a vigorous old age.

**རྒུ་** *rgu* sometimes for *dgu*; *rgu-t̔ub* = *dgu-t̔ub Med.*; *-gu-drús?*

**རྒུད་པ་** *rgúd-pa* **to decline, to sink, to get weak, frail,** esp. with old age *Mil.*, *Pth.*; in *W.* used in a more general sense: **gud soṅ** 1. he has grown thin. 2. he is impoverished, much reduced, in declining circumstances; *dar-rgúd* the rise and fall in the world.

**རྒུན་** *rgun* **the vine; grape;** *rgun-dkár* white grapes, *rgun-nág* black, or purple grapes *W.*; *rgun-rgód W.* **raisins;** *rgun-ₒbrúm* grapes; raisins; *rgun* (-*ₒbrum*)-*śiṅ* vine; *rgun*(-*ₒbrum*)-*tsás* **vineyard;** *rgun-čáṅ Mil.* **wine,** resp. *rgun-skyéms Cs.*

**རྒུར་** *rgur* v. *dgur.*

**རྒོ་** *rgo*, sometimes for *sgo.*

**རྒོ་བ་** *rgó-ba* = *dgó-ba.*

**རྒོངས་** *rgoṅs S.g.?*

**རྒོངས་མོ་** *rgóṅs-mo Mil.* for *dgóṅs-mo* (?).

**རྒོད་** *rgod* 1. **laughing, laughter** *S.g.* — 2. **bird of prey.** — 3. **wild.** — 4. **prudent** (v. the following word).

**རྒོད་པ་** *rgód-pa* I vb. 1. **to laugh,** aloud *Mil.*; (*Bal.* **rgód-ča**) cf. *gád-mo, dgód-pa, bgád-pa.* — 2. **to grow weak, languid,** or **indolent,** syn. to *γyéṅ-ba*, often joined with *byiṅ*, for emphasis; *rgód-bag-čan* weak, languid, indolent *Stg.*

II. adj. 1: **wild,** *ra-rgód* wild goat, *p̔ag-rgód* wild boar, *γyag-rgód* wild yak or ox; *rgod-γyag-rwá* horn of the wild yak *S.g.*; *bya-rgód* vulture, bird of prey = *bya-rgyál*; *rgód-po*, and *rgod* id.; *rgód-kyi rtse-rgyál* an eagle's feather, stuck as ornament on the hat *Pth.*; *mi-rgód* a wild or savage man; a robber, ruffian; *mi-rgód byéd-pa* to rob (usually named together with murdering and lying) *Dzl.*, but as the Tibetan always attaches to this word *mi-rgód* the notion of some gigantic hairy fiend, it cannot in every instance be applied to beings really existing. — Fig. furious, angry (seldom); *dbugs-rgód Med.?* — 2. **prudent, able** *C.*, *Zam.*

**རྒོད་མ་** *rgód-ma*, *rta rgód-ma* (*Bal.* **gún-ma** **a mare;** *rgod-skám-ma* a barren mare *Sch.*; *rgod-brúṅ* dung of a mare *Med.*

**རྒོལ་** *rgol* 1. v. *rgál-ba.* 2. v. *rgól-ba.*

**རྒོལ་བ་** *rgól-ba*, pf. and fut. *brgol*, **to dispute, combat, fight,** *mi-la* with or against a man; *p̔á-rol-poi dmág-la rgól-du ₒgró-ba* they are about to fight against the hostile army *Dzl.*; *γžán-gyis rgol ma nús-so* nobody could fight them, could make head against them *Glr.*; **to offer resistance,** to make opposition, *sus kyaṅ rgól-ba ₒdzúgs-pai mi ma byuṅ* nobody arose to offer resistance *Pth.* (evidently incorrect; it should be either; *sus kyaṅ rgól-ba ₒdzúgs-pa* [inf.] *ma byuṅ*, or: *rgól-ba ₒdzúgs-pai* [partic.] *mi su yaṅ ma byuṅ*); sometimes as much as **to accuse, to charge,** *k̔yód-kyis ṅai bu bsád-do žes brgál-te* 'you have killed my son', thus accusing me *Dzl.*; *t̔sur γnyis rgol* he quarrels at a double rate *Mil.*; *mi-la rgól-ba zú-ba* to find fault with another (higher in rank), to pick a quarrel with him *Mil.*; *rgól-bai žu-dón* a speech provoking a quarrel with a superior *Mil.*; *p̔as-rgól* a quarrel or contest begun by the counter-party *Sch.*; *p̔as-rgol-mi*, *p̔as rgól-pa mi* adversary, opponent *Dzl.* ༢༦༠, ༢. — *sṅá-rgol*, and *p̔yi-rgol* (*Ssk.* **पूर्ववादिन्** & **परवादिन्**) 1. acc. to *Cs.* **plaintiff** and **defendant,** but these terms are not quite adequate, as *sṅá-rgol* prop. denotes him who begins a quarrel, **the aggressor, assailant,** both in war and in common life, e.g. in court, and *p̔yi-rgol* designates him, who is intent on defending himself against the attacks and accusations of the opponent, by surpassing him in abusive language and esp. by having recourse to witchcraft. Hence *p̔yir-rgól-bai γnód-pa* is a kind of danger against which every one tries to protect himself, and chiefly again by charms and witchcraft. — 2. *sṅa-rgol* and *p̔yi-rgol* are also said to signify those students that are contending with one another in academical disputations.

**རྒྱ་** *rgya* 1. resp. *p̔yag-rgyá*, **seal, stamp, mark, sign, token;** (*p̔yag-*) *rgyás ₒdébs-*

pa, Cs. rgya brgyáb-pa, to seal, to stamp; to seal up, búm-pa-la a bottle Glr.; nám-mḱai dbyáṅs-su (to seal up) into the heavenly regions, i. e. to cause to disappear, to hide for ever Glr.; to confirm or pledge solemnly by a sealed document; ri-rgya lúṅ-rgya ₒdzúg-pa 'to seal up hills and valleys', i. e. to protect the living beings inhabiting them from being harmed by huntsmen or fishermen, an annual performance of the Dalai Lama, consisting in a variety of spells and incantations; rgya yčóg-pa to break open a seal Cs. — Further expressions v. compounds. — 2. (Cs. rgyá-bo?) **extent, width, size,** rgyar dpag-tu-méd-pa immeasurable in extent Glr.; séms-čan-gyi rgyai ťsad ni či tsam how vast must be the extent (of love) with respect to beings! Thgy.; rgyá-čan having extent, mḱyén-rgya-čan of extensive learning Mil.; rgya-čén(-po) of very large size, very extensive, of a building, a pond etc.; grand, enormous, prodigious, of banquets feasts, sacrifices, assemblies; c. accus. very rich in. Schr.; in a general sense: great, stón-pa rgya-čé-ba a great master or teacher Thgy.; rgya-čén spyód-pai blá-ma may be rendered: a very virtuous Lama, po.; rgya-čúṅ denotes the contrary of all this; rgya-če-čúṅ v. rgya-ḱyón in Compounds; rgya-čér adv. = rgyás-par in detail, at large, at full length, e.g. to explain; rgya-čér byéd-pa to extend Feer Introd. etc. p. 72; rgya-čer-ról-pa Lalitavistara or Lalitavistāra, title of a biography of Buddha, translated and edited by Foucaux (a conjecture concerning the signification of the Sanskrit word v. Fouc. Rgyatcherr. II. p. XXII.; some statements relative to the Chinese translations of this work, v. ibid. p. XVI., and Was. 176; on the historical value of it v. Was. 3, 4); rgya bskyéd-pa Zam., Cs. to widen, augment, enlarge, extend, rgya bskúm-pa to contract, to diminish the extent. Lastly, it also denotes, like dkyíl-ₒḱor, a plain surface, a disk: nyi zlai rgya dkar šar Mil. the bright disks of the sun and moon appear, cf. rgyas in zla-rgyás; v. also the compounds. — 3. (Cs. rgyá-mo, perh. also rgyá-ma) **net;** byá-rgya fowling-net, nyá-rgya fishing-net, ri-dags-rgya hunting-net, — 4. for rgyá-ma, v. compounds. — 5. for rgyá-mo **beard,** rgyá-čan having a beard, bearded C. — 6. for rgya-gár, rgya-gár-pa, and rgya-gár-skad. — 7. for rgya-nág, rgya-nág-pa, and rgya-nág-skad. — 8. for rgya-ru. — 9. for rgya-skyégs. — 10. erron. for brgya.

**Comp. and deriv.** rgya-dkár 1. nyi-zlái rgya-dkár v. above no. 2. extr. 2. Cs. = rgya-gár India, 3. Cs. a dog with white spots on the nose. — rgya-skád 1. Sanskrit language, 2. Chinese language. — rgya-skás (W. *gya-šrẹ*) **a** (European) **staircase,** cf. skás-ka. — rgya-skégs, rgya-skyégs, Ssk. लाचा, Williams: 'a kind of red dye, lac, obtained from an insect as well as from the resin of a particular tree'; in medical works it is mentioned as an astringent medicine; the adjectives dkar-rgyá light-red, and rgya-smúg violaceous C. are derived from this word. — rgya-ḱúr Med.? — rgya-ḱyi a Chinese dog. — rgya-ḱyón **width, extent, area** Pth., col. *gya-če-čúṅ*. — rgya-ḱrí C. **chair.** — rgya-gár (the 'white extent or plain') **India,** rgya-gár-pa an Indian, rgya-gar-skad Sanskrit language. — rgya-grám a figure like a cross; rdo-rje-rgya-grám shaped like a quadrifid flower; rluṅ rgya-grám žés-pa Glr. seems to be = rlúṅ-gi dkyil-ₒḱor atmosphere (connected with some phantastic association); lám-po rgya-grám a cross-road Sch. — rgya-čáṅ a kind of girdle Lex. — rgya-čan v. rgya 2 and 5. — rgya-ču-ḱúg-pa n. of a river in China near the Tibetan frontier (also rgya-ču-rabs-med) Glr. — rgya-če etc. v. rgya 2. — rgya-ṭám Bhot. = ṭám-ka, the third part of a rupee. — rgya-rtags **mark, signature, stamp** Sch. — rgya-tél a kind of seal or stamp Cs. — rgya-mťóṅs 1. a platform, an open pavilion on the house-top, 2. a vent-hole for smoke. — rgya-ₒdré **a quarrel** Mil.nt. — rgya-nág (the 'black extent') **China,** rgya-nág-pa, and -ma a China-man and woman; rgyá-rnams the Chinese Glr.

ག

— *rgya-nón W.* the great royal seal, of a square form; surpassing (*nón-pa*) all others in influence and power. — *rgya-dpé* a Sanskrit book *Tar.* 33, 2. — *rgya-ṗi-liṅ* n. of the country, *rgya-ṗi-liṅ-pa*, n. of the people, through which the Tibetans heard first (prob. at the beginning of the eighteenth century) of the civilized nations of the occident, hence n. for **British India**, for Englishman, or European resident of British India, and also (sometimes without *rgya*) for Europe and European in general. The word is of course not to be found in literature. Some derive it from 'Feringhi', which term, in the slightly altered form of *ṗa-ráṅ*, *ṗe-ráṅ*, is current in *C.*, along with the above mentioned *rgya-ṗi-liṅ*; it is therefore not improbable, that *ṗi-liṅ* represents only the more vulgar pronunciation of the genuine Tibetan word *ṗyi-gliṅ*, an outcountry, a distant foreign country and esp. **Europe**, *Chr. Prot.* — *rgya-ṗib(s)*, *rgya-ṗúb(s)* a Chinese roof *Glr.* — *rgyá-ba* 1. vb. to be wide, extensive, pf. *rgyas* (q.v.), 2. sbst. width, extent, 3. adj. wide; *rgyá-bar* ˳*gyúr-ba* to extend, to increase, to become copious *Cs.*, perh. no longer in use. — *rgyá-bo* 1. *Cs.* and *Lex.* **beard.** 2. a **Chinese** *Glr.*, but not without an allusion to the former signification. — *rgya-dbáṅ rin-po-čé* title of the Dalai Lama, v. *Huc* II., 275, where '*kian ngan*' stands erroneously. — *rgyá-ma* 1. **a large steel-yard** *C.*, *rgyá-ma-la* ˳*dégs-pa* to weigh *Glr.*, **gyá-ma-la tég-ne** *C.* being weighed out by retail, e.g. meat; **gyá-ma-la ma tég-ne** *C.* wholesale. 2. a sealed paper, document. — *rgya-mí* a **Chinese.** — *rgyá-mo* 1. **net** *Cs.* 2. **a Chinese woman** *Glr.*; *rgyá-mo-bza* id. — *rgya-rmá* **the venereal disease** *Sch.* — *rgya-smúg* **violet colour** *C.* — *rgya-tsá* **sal ammoniac** *Med.* — *rgya-tsós Med.*, perh. = *rgya-skyégs.* — *rgyá-mtso* 1. **sea, ocean;** *rgyá-mtsor* ˳*júg-pa* to go to sea *Dzl.*, *γtóṅ-ba* to let one go to sea *Dzl.*; *ṗyii rgyá-mtso* the outer sea, ocean; *náṅ-gi rgyá-mtso* an inner sea, inland sea, lake. 2. *Bal.* (**rgyám-tso**) **river.** 3. **dropsy** *Mṅg.* 4. symb. num.: *four.* — *rgya-γżi W.* is stated to be a kind of *γtór-ma.* — *rgya-zór Mil.* = *zor* **reaping-hook, sickle.** — *rgya-γzéb Sch.* 'a large net', *C.* a large **rake,** used in reaping. — *rgya-yúl* 1. a large country 2. China *Glr.* — *rgyá-ra*, *rgyá-ru*, occasionally *rgya* alone, **the Saiga-antelope** *Sch.* — *rgya-ri* **a portion of meat,** (= *sder-gáṅ* a plateful) small or large, *Pth.*, *W. C.*; it also denotes a measure = ½ *dum*, or ¼ *lhu.* — *rgya-róg* **beard** *C.* — *rgya-láb* **talk, gossip.** — *rgya-lám*, **high-road, high-way.** — *rgya-śóg* **Chinese paper.** — *rgya-sér* 1. **gap, cleft, fissure, chasm,** in rocks, glaciers etc., 2. a dog with yellow spots about the nose *Cs.* 3. **Russia,** *rgya-sér-pa* a Russian; cf. *rgya-gár.* — *rgya-sóg* 1. *W.* **a saw** 2. *Sch.*: 'a Chuichui, or Chuichur, an infidel, a Mahometan; also Turkestan'. — *rgya-sráṅ* the open **street** (opp. to house) *Glr.*

རྒྱག་པ *rgyág-pa* another form for *rgyáb-pa*, used esp. in *C.*, **to throw, cast, fling,** *mda rgyág-pa* to shoot arrows *Glr.*; *brág-la ču rgyág-pai* ˳*ṗraṅ* a path along a precipice, where the water rushes against the rock, i.e. where there is a cataract *Glr.*; *dgón-pa żig rgyág-pa* **to found** a monastery (= ˳*débs-pa*) *Georgi Alph. Tib.*; **gó-la zug gyag** *C.* = *mgó-nad* ˳*debs.*

རྒྱགས *rgyags*, or *brgyags*, **provisions, victuals, food,** in full: ˳*tsó-bai rgyags*, ˳*tso-rgyágs*; *lam-rgyágs* provisions for a journey; *dgun-rgyágs* prov. for the winter; *rgyágs-ṗye*, provisions of meal or flour; *rgyags-zóṅ* merchandize to buy or barter victuals with.

རྒྱགས་པ *rgyágs-pa* **fat, stout,** *Schr.* also **mighty, powerful, proud;** *rgyags-ṗrúg Pth.*, *Schr.*: bastard-child.

རྒྱང *rgyaṅ* (so pronounced in *Bal.*) instead of *gyaṅ*, **wall.**

རྒྱང་བ *rgyáṅ-ba*, for (*b*)*rkyáṅ-ba*, *Pth.*: *rgyáṅ-nas bżag* they laid him down with his hands and feet stretched out.

རྒྱང་མ *rgyáṅ-ma* **distance** 1. absolutely: *rgyáṅ(-ma)-nas* at a distance, from afar, e.g. to see, to call to; *rgyáṅ (-ma)*

-*nas grágs-pa čé-ba* famous, celebrated, from afar *Mil.; rgyáṅ-du lás-pa* lingering far behind *Sch.; rgyaṅ mig mi mṫóṅ-mk̇an W.* short-sighted; *rgyaṅ mčoṅ btáṅ-gin* moving forward by long leaps; *rgyáṅ-so* ₒ*dzúgs-pa* to look over *Sch.*, (ought perhaps to be spelled *rgyaṅ-zo* one looking, spying into a distance); *rgyaṅ-šèl* spy-glass, *rgyaṅ-bsriṅs-pa* lengthened to a great distance *Lex.*; *rgyaṅ-ṗán, rgyaṅ-ṗén* n. of a philosophical (atheistical *Cs.*) sect in ancient India, *Tar.* 22, 8: ₒ*jig-rten-rgyaṅ-ṗán.* — 2. used relatively: *rgyaṅ-riṅ-po* **far**, *rgyaṅ-riṅ-por soṅ* he went far away *Mil.; rgyaṅ-ṫúṅ-ba* **near**; *rgyaṅ-grágs* the reach of hearing, **ear-shot**, (gen. the distance at which the sound of a trumpet may be heard, i.e. about 500 fathoms; however, as this number is much in favour with the Tibetans, such estimates are not to be depended upon). — *mig-rgyáṅ Glr.* distance of sight, i.e. the distance at which a man may be well distinguished from a woman, or a horse from an ass; — *rgyáṅs* adv. far, *rgyaṅs bkyéd-de Mil.nt.* moving far away, e.g. in order to increase one's distance from an unpleasant neighbour at table).

ཀྱང་རྩེ་ *rgyáṅ-tse* n. of a village and monastery in Tibet, not far from the frontier of Bhotan, *Köpp.* II., 358.

ཀྱན་ *rgyan* I. 1. **ornament, decoration,** *rgyán-gyis brgyán-pa* decked with ornaments *Dzl.; rgyan-*ₒ*dógs-pa* to adorn one's self *Mil.; k̇a-rgyán* an ornament at the mouth, edge, or brim of a vessel, e.g. peacock's feathers about the mouth of a *búm-pa* (sacred bottle), flowers in a glass etc.; *k̇a-rgyán-čan* decorated in the front-part, e.g. a coat trimmed with fur of different colours, an arrow gaily painted at its notched end; *rgyán-rnams Dzl.* ornaments, *rgyán-ča* id.; *rgyan-gós Glr.* festival garment, beautiful vesture; *dbu-rgyán* an ornament of the head, a diadem. — 2. in relation to spiritual things: *séms-kyi rgyan* something good, **a blessing,** for the heart *Mil.; rgyán-du* ₒ*čar* it proves a blessing, a moral advantage or benefit *Mil.*

II. 1. **a stake** or **pledge** at play, = *skugs*, **gyan tsúg-če* W.* to bet, to wager, e.g. a rupee: (also *rgyal? Schr.*). — 2. **lot,** *rgyan rgyáb-pa* to cast lots, without religious ceremonies, whereas *rtags-ril* and *mo* are connected with such.

ཀྱབ་ *rgyab,* resp. *sku-rgyáb, Ssk.* पृष्ठ 1. **the back** of the body, the back part of any thing; *rgyáb-kyis ṗyógs-pa,* in later literature also *rgyab-ṗyógs-pa Thgy.* to turn one's back to a person or thing, c. *la,* also fig. *Dzl.; rgyáb-kyis ṗyógs-par byéd-pa* to put to flight; *rgyab stón-pa* to turn one's back, to turn round *Glr.*; *rgyáb-tu skyúr-ba* to throw to the back, to leave behind, to give up, to quit, frq.; *rgyáb-tu* ₒ*bór-ba* id.; *rgyab brtén-pa* to lean one's back against or upon, to lean or rest on, to rely upon, confide in *Mil.; rgyab byéd-pa* to protect *Sch.; rgyáb-tu, rgyáb-na, rgyáb-la* **behind,** behind hand; **after, back**; *rgyab-nas* from behind; *rgyab mdún γnyis-la Glr.*, **gyab daṅ dún-la** col. behind and before; *ṫi-seï byaṅ-rgyáb-tu sleb ṫse* as we came behind to the north-side of the Tise *Mil.; rgyáb-kyi skyed-mos-ṫsal-du γšégs-so* let us go into the garden behind us *Dzl.*; *rgyab-rdzi* one standing behind working people, in order to watch and superintend them. — 2. as much as one is able to carry on his back, **a load,** *drel-rgyáb γsum* three mules' loads *Glr.*

**Comp.** *bal-rgyáb,* or **rgyab-bál* W.* **a fleece** of wool. — *rgyab-k̇ál* 'a back's load', a burden carried on the back *Sch., Schr.* — *rgyab-sṅás* a cushion or pad for the back *C.* — *rgyab-rtén* something to lean against, a safe retreat, **prop, support** *Mil.*, *rgyáb-rtén byéd-pa* to be a support *Mil.* — *rgyab-riṅ* **serpent, snake** *Sch.* — **gyab-lóg ǰhe'-pa* C.* 1. **to turn one's back** 2. **to rebel, revolt;** **gyab-lóg dád-če* W.* to sit backward, with the back in advance. — *rgyab-lógs* **the back, back-part, reverse** of a thing.

ཀྱབ་པ་ *rgyáb-pa,* pf. and fut. *brgyab,* imp. *rgyob,* **to throw, to fling,** aiming at a certain point, hence **to hit,** also **to beat** with a stick, = *rdúṅ-ba*; **to strike,** *mó-la mčus brgyáb-nas bsad* he (the male bird) killed his mate by a stroke of his bill *Bhar.*; **tsá-ge-la gyob** *W.* throw into the centre! hit the mark! *sdóṅ-po-la brgyab ṗog* (the ray of light) fell upon the stem *Glr.; dé-la ču rgyob* sprinkle this with water! *Pth.*; *ṗyugs nágs-seb-tu rgyáb-pa* to let the cattle run into the wood; **žag-ḍáṅ gyab-če** *W.* to put down the date, to date; **la gyab-če** to cross a mountain pass. — *rgyáb-pa* is particularly used in *W.* in many phrases, whilst in *C. rgyág-pa*, and in *B.* ₒ*débs-pa* are more in use, as may be seen by referring to the several substantives, e.g. **lud gyáb-če**. *W.* to throw dung upon the fields, to manure; **par gyáb-pa** *C.*, and **gyáb-če** *W.*, to print; *gyáb-pa* stands also alone, elliptically: **ka gyab dug** here (is printed) the letter *ka*.

རྒྱམ་ཚྭ་ *rgyam-ṫsva Med.*, *Cs.*: 'a kind of salt, like crystal'.

རྒྱར་ *rgyar* v. *rgya* 2.

རྒྱལ་ *rgyal* 1. **victory**, in certain phrases: **gyal ṫób-če** *W.* to gain the victory, to conquer, overcome; to win a law-suit, opp. to **ṗam ṗóg-če**. — 2. *Schr.* and *Sch.*: *rgyal-rgyán* **a pledge, a stake,** *rgyal btsúg-pa* to bet, wager gamble *Sch.; rgyàl bžag-pa* to contend with another person about the first place, to try to get the precedence (?) *Sch.*; perh. also ornament, v. sub *rgód-pa* 2. — 3. **fine, penalty,** for theft *C.* — 4. n. of two lunar mansions, v. sub *rgyu-skár*; *rgyál-gyi zlá-ba, skár-ma rgyál-la báb-pai nyin-par, skár-ma rgyal daṅ* ₒ*dzom-par, dpyid-zla rá-bai skár-ma rgyál-gyi nyin-par*, are dates relating to them. — 5. for *rgyál-po* and *rgyál-ba*.

རྒྱལ་བ་ *rgyál-ba* I. vb. neut. **to be victorious,** to obtain the victory, always with the sbst. in the nom. (not instr.) case, and gen. with *las*, **over** or **against**, *nág-poi ṗyógs-las* over the powers of darkness, ₒ*jigs-pa-las* over fright, fear; also *ɣyúl-lás* in battle; prob. also *ṫsod ltá-ba-las* to pass **an** examination successfully; but also without *las, rtsód-pa* (to win) in a contest *Glr.*; very frq. *rgyál-bar* ₒ*gyúr-ba* id.; *ṅa ṗám soṅ ḱyod gyal soṅ* I have lost, thou hast won (also in business); **to be acquitted,** to gain a law-suit; *dmag-*ₒ*ḱrúgs-kyi rgyal-ṗám-gyi ɣnas-ṫsúl ḱol* send (us) news concerning the progress of the war; in a similar sense: *rgyal ṗam či-ltar byuṅ B.; rgyál-bar gyúr-čig, rgyál-ba daṅ ṫse-riṅ-bar šog čig* victory and long life! *Dzl.*

II. sbst. 1. (*Ssk.* जय) the act of conquering, **the victory**, **ḍi gyál-wa ṫob** *C.* this bears away the palm or prize, this is the most excellent of all. — 2. the conquering party or person, he that prevails, **the conqueror** (opp. to *ṗám-pa* the conquered, vanquished). Much more frq.: 3. **the most high, Buddha** (*Ssk.* जिन), *rgyál-bai sku* his person, *rgyál-bai bka*, his word; *rgyal daṅ de sras* (po. instead of *rgyál-ba daṅ dei sras*) Buddha and his children, his disciples *Pth.* 1, 1; *rgyál-ba góṅ-ma* the highest Buddha, **God,** *Mil.* — 4. *rgyál-ba rin-po-čé* His Highness, His supreme Majesty, title of the Dalai Lama.

III. adj. 1. **conquering, superior, eminent, excellent,** *rnám-par rgyál-bai ḱaṅ-bzáṅs* the most magnificent palace (of Indra) *Glr.* — 2. *W.* (gen. pronounced **gyálla**, in *Pur.* **rgyál-wa**) **good,** instead of *bzáṅ-po*; **gyál-la dád-če** or **lús-če** to continue in good condition, entire, uninjured; *mā gyalla* excellent! capital!

**Comp. and deriv.,** belonging partly to *rgyál-ba*, partly to *rgyál-po*: **gyal-kár** **window** *C.* — **gyál-ḱa, ḱa-gyál** **victory, gain, advantage** *W.* — *rgyal-ḱág* **country, empire.** — *rgyal-ḱáms* 1. **kingdom.** 2. **realm, dominion of Buddha, the world.** — *rgyal-ḱrid Ld.* for *rgyal-srid*. — *rgyal-ḱrims* v. *ḱrims*. — *rgyal-*ₒ*góṅ* n. of a demon *Mil.* — *rgyal-brgyúd*, and *rgyal-rábs* 1. succession of kings of the same line or family, **dynasty** *Glr.* 2. a single **generation** of a dynasty, *rgyal-brgyúd lṅá-bču-na* in the fiftieth degree (in the line of descent). — *rgyál-sgo* **principal door,** entrance-door, **gate** *C.* — *rgyal-sgrúṅs*, legend of the kings, esp. that of Gesar. — *rgyal-čén bži* the four kings of the spirits or guardians of the universe

(ˌjig-rten-skyóṅ v. skyoṅ-ba), residing just below the summit of Meru, the protectors of the gods against the Asuras, v. *Köpp.* I, 250; II, 261. — *rgyal-stód* lunar mansion v. *rgyu-skár*. — *rgyál-po* 1. **king,** *rgyál-po čén-po* **great king, emperor**; *rgyál-por ˌjúg-pa, bskó-ba,* to inaugurate a king, to raise to the royal throne; *mi-la rgyál-po ˌčól-ba* id. *Pth.*; *rgyál-po byéd-pa* to act the king, to be(a) king; *ṅa rgyál-po mi ˌdod* I do not wish to be king *Dzl.*; *rgyál-po mi ťób-na* if I do not obtain royalty *Dzl.*; *ṅas ni rgyál-po mi nús-so* I cannot be king *Dzl.* The word is also used for: government-authorities, police etc.; *rgyál-poi čád-pa* public punishment, *rgyál-pos γsód-pa* to be publicly executed. (As a characteristic sign of Asiatic views it seems worth mentioning, that the *rgyal-po* is usually spoken of much in the same manner, as robbers, conflagrations etc. are, i.e. as a kind of calamity against which protection is to be sought, esp. by charms and spells, cf. *ˌjigs-pa*). 2. a local god, *ˌgro-ťáṅ rgyál-po* the Dewa of Dotaṅ *Mil.* 3. fig. something excellent, superior in its kind; not only as with us the word is applied to the lion, as the king of animals, but also to distinguished flowers: the Udumbara (Ficus glomerata), to mountains, Meru and others; and col. *gaṅs-rgyál* a large glacier, *brag-rgyál* a huge rock, *smón-lam-gyi rgyál-po* a very comprehensive prayer, the *bzaṅ-spyód Glr.* 4. symb. num.: 16. — *rgyal-ṗrán* vassal or feudatory prince. — *rgyál-bu* prince. — *rgyal-blón* king and ministers, council of state. — *rgyál-mo* 1. queen. 2. pupil of the eye, together with the iris; *rgyál-moi mdaṅs nyams* the brightness of the eyeball disappears *Med.* 3. like *rgyál-po* 3, e.g. a charm of particular power. — *rgyal-smád* lunar mansion, v. *rgyu-skár*. — *rgyal-ťsáb* (for *rgyal-poi ťsab*) 1. vice-roy, regent. Such a vice-roy under Chinese supremacy is now the king of Tibet, who about a century ago was still an independent ruler. 2. **successor** of a king. 3. (for *rgyál-bai ťsab*) **Maitreya,** the future Buddha. — *rgyal-mťsán* sign of victory, **trophy,** a kind of decoration of cloth, of a cylindrical shape, erected upon a flag-staff, or carried on a pole. — *rgyal-rábs* 1. = *rgyal-brgyúd.* 2. **history, annals,** of the kings, title of several books. — *rgyal-rigs* 1. **the royal family, house, lineage,** 2. **warrior-caste** क्षत्र. — *rgyál-sa* 1. **a king's** or prince's **residence,** city where a court is held, and hence often **capital, metropolis.** 2. col., esp. in *W.*: **town.** 3. **throne** fig.; *rgyál-sar γšégs-pa* to ascend the throne, *rgyal-sa bzúṅ-ba* to occupy the throne, *rgyál-sar bskó-ba* to raise to the throne, *rgyal-sa ˌṗrog-pa* to usurp the throne; *ˌdi-nas rgyál-sa rgyai miṅ rgyál-po-la šor* from him the dominion passed over to the Chinese Ming-dynasty *Glr.* — *rgyal-srás* 1. **prince.** 2. **son of Buddha, a saint;** *sṅón-gyi rgyal-srás* saints of the olden time, of past ages. — *rgyal-srid* 1. **government, reign,** *rgyal-srid bzúṅ-ba* to enter upon the reign, to take possession of the throne. 2. *rgyal-srid sna-bdún* the seven jewels of royal government, v. *rin-čén.*

རྒྱས་པ *rgyás-pa* (prop. pf. to *rgyá-ba*) 1. vb. **to increase** in bulk or quantity, **to augment, to spread,** *bá-yi nu ltar rgyas* (the swollen uvula) gets as big as a cow's dug (these are in Tibet particularly small) *Lt.*; *ˌja-ťsón rgyás-pa ˌdra* like an expanded rainbow *Glr.*; *bstán-pa rgyás-šin* the doctrine gaining ground, spreading *Glr.*; **to grow, develop** itself, of blossoms frq., of the body etc. — 2. adj. **extensive, large, ample, wide; copious, plentiful, manifold, numerous; rich in, abounding in; great in, strong in** cca.; **detailed, complete, full;** esp. adv. *rgyás-par* (col. **gyás-pa, gyę-pa**), *rgyás-par šes ˌdód-na,* often also *rgyás-par ˌdód-na* if you wish to know it fully, to hear it in detail; **ťsáṅ-ma gyás-pa zér-na** *W.* if all the particulars are to be told; *rgyás-par byéd-pa* 1. to make bigger, to augment, to increase, to bestow or confer plentifully, *mi-la* on a person *Glr.* 2. to describe, narrate, state at large, in detail frq.; *don rgyás-par byed-pa* to be very useful, to exert a beneficial influence, *la* on, *Glr.* — *zla-ba rgyás-pa* full moon *Pth.*; *nya-rgyás zla-ba* id. — *rgyás-pai ťsá-ba, rgyas-ťsád* n. of a disease *Med.* — *ži-rgyás* etc. v. *glin*, and *ži-ba.*

རྒྱུ *rgyu Ssk.* हेतु I. 1. **matter, substance, material**, *rgyu šél-las* crystal being the material; *čán-rgyu* ingredients for making beer, i.e. barley, barm etc.; *rgyu dgé-ba bságs-pas ťób-pa yin* (the human body) is a substance obtained by accumulating virtue *Thgy.*; *ná-la dgós-rgyu čun* I have few wants *Mil.*; also for substance in an emphatical sense, = nervus rerum, money *Mil.*; *bzó-rgyu* matter or substance of which any thing is made or manufactured, material *Glr.*; *zá-rgyu med* we have nothing to eat *Glr.*; hence **opportunity, chance, possibility**, *dá-ltar rgyu žig snán-no* an opportunity offers now *Dzl.*; **arrangements, preparation**, **dó-gyu ǰhé-pa* C.* to make preparations for a journey. In a special sense: material, stuff for weaving, **warp, chain.** — 2. **cause, reason, motive**, main condition, *mya-nán-las dás-pai rgyur gyur* it becomes the cause of Nirwana, i.e. it leads to Nirwana *Dzl.*; in elliptical speech: *lha dan mii rgyur gyúr-pai dgé-ba* the virtue that leads to (the re-birth amongst) gods or men *Dzl.* ༢༧, 17 (*Sch.* incorr.); in the same manner *nán-son rgyú-ru gro*; *rgyus* c. genit. by reason of, on account of, in consequence of *Tar.*; *čii rgyus* why *Stg.*; *rgyu méd-du, méd-par* without the impulse of a foreign cause, spontaneously; without sufficient reason, without good cause, the Latin *temere*; *rgyu dan rkyen Cs.* and *Sch.* 'cause and effect', more correctly (cf. *rkyen*): primary and secondary cause, which, certainly, sometimes coincides with 'origin and further development', and so, too, with 'cause and effect'; *rgyu dan rkyen deï pyir, deï rgyu deï rkyén-gyis, deï rgyu-rkyén*, therefore, on that account; in *Med.*: *nyé-bai rgyu* the three anthropological causes or conditions of diseases, the three 'humours', air, bile, and phlegm; *rin-bai rgyu* the ultimate cause of diseases, and of every evil, viz. ignorance (*ma-rig-pa*, v. *rig-pa*); *skyéd-byed rgyu* the creative cause *Zam.*; *pél-bai rgyu ni lté-ba* the main condition, the efficient cause, of growth is the navel-string *Med.*; *rgyu byéd-pa* to be the principal cause of, to lie at the bottom of a matter *Mil.*; *rgyu skyéd-pa* to lay the foundation of *Dzl.* — 3. after verbal roots *rgyu* implies necessity, like our **I am to, I have to, I am obliged to, I ought to**; in later literature, as well as in the present col. language of *C.*, it indicates the fut. tense: *čós-skor γyás-nas byéd-rgyu-la* whereas the holy circumambulation (v. *skor-ba* I, 2) ought to be performed from the right (to the left) *Mil.*; *sdán-dgra yál-rgyu-la* as the enemy must vanish, or: is sure to come to an end *Mil.*; **sol-čóg ṭal-ḍig ǰhá-gyu yin-nam* C.* am I to lay the cloth? **dhá-ta tó-ča zá-la dó-gyu yin* C.* now I will go and dine; *nai drún-du ón-rgyu yin-pa* those that intended to come to me (the Latin 'venturi') *Glr.*; *dé-la rgyal-srid γtád-rgyu-la* when the government was to be conferred upon him, when he was to enter upon his reign *Glr.*; *rta žón-rgyu med* (riding-) horses were not to be had *Glr.* — When appended to adjectives, it is a mere pleonastical addition: *dkón-rgyu med* that is not a very precious thing, there is nothing particular in that *Mil.*; *čún-rgyui lha-kán* a very small temple *Mil.*; *γžán-pas légs-rgyu med* he is not more beautiful than others *Glr.*; *ya-mťsán-rgyu-med* that is not to be wondered at; **gó-gyu man* C.* that is useless.

**Comp.** *rgyu-rkyén* (v. above sub no. 2) **connection**, meaning, signification, *rgyu-rkyen bšad-du γsol* please explain to me the connection, which is often used in a general sense = what does that mean? what is that? *Glr.*, but also in a special sense relative to law-suits: **kyö-kyi gyu-kyén žú-la do* C.* I am going to tell what it is with you, i.e. I shall inform against you, bring an action against you. — *rgyu-čá* col. that which belongs to a thing, **an appurtenance**, necessary implement etc. —

*rgyu-ₒbrás* cause and effect or consequence, gen. in a moral sense: actions and their fruits (*lás-kyi rgyu-ₒbrás*); also the doctrine treating on this subject, the doctrine of retribution, the principal dogma of Buddhism, prop.: *las-rgyu-ₒbrás-kyi čos*; *las-rgyu-ₒbrás-la yid-čes-pa* to believe in the doctrine of retribution *Glr.* — *rgyu-mtsán* (*Ssk.* निमित्त) 1. **cause,** *rgyu-mtsán ₒdri-ba* to ask after the cause *Glr.*; *rgyu-mtsán lo-rgyús ₒdri-ba* to question closely, to examine rigorously *Mil.*; **the connection of events,** the manner in which a thing has come to pass, *ṅai náṅ-nas ṗye k̔yér-bai rgyu-mtsán šod* tell me how it was that you could fetch the flour from my house, how you were able to accomplish it *Mil. nt.* 2. **token, sign, characteristic, proof, evidence,** *ₒdúg-pai rgyu-mtsán* as an evidence of being . . . *Glr.*

II. instead of *rgyú-ma.*

རྒྱུ་བ་ *rgyú-ba* **to go, walk, move, wander, range,** of men, animals, and fig. of lifeless things, *čú-la rgyú-bai ₒdab-čágs* birds frequenting the water; *kún-tu rgyú-ba* to wander from one place to another, hence: *kun-tu-rgyú* itinerant monk, n. of a sect of the Brahmans *Dzl.*; *rluṅ rgyú-bai rtsa* those veins in which air is circulating, cf. *rtsa* and *rluṅ*; also c. accus.: *yul*, or *groṅ rgyú-ba* to rove through countries, through villages; *rgyu-sráṅ*, *btsán-gyi rgyu-sráṅ* the road that is frequented by the *btsan* (a kind of demons). — *rgyu-skár* v. below.

རྒྱུ་མ་ *rgyú-ma* 1. **entrails, intestines, bowels,** esp. the small intestines, opp. to *loṅ-ka* the large intestines; *rgyu ₒk̔ril-ba convolvulus intestinorum Sch.*(?); *rgyu ₒk̔róg-pa* the croaking of the bowels *Sch.*; *rgyu-sgróg* the **caul,** covering the lower intestines; *rgyu-stód* the upper bowels, *rgyu-smád* the lower bowels *Cs.*; *rgyu-nád* disease of the bowels; *rgyu-γžér* **colic.** — 2. **sausage,** **gyú-ma gyáṅ-wa* C.* (v. *sgyóṅ-ba*), **k̔áṅ-če* W.* to stuff sausages; **gyú-ma kar-gyáṅ** meat-sausage, meat-pudding, **gyú-ma nag-gyáṅ** black-pudding *C.*

རྒྱུ་སྐར་ *rgyu-skár* **the lunar mansions,** *Ssk.* नक्षत्र, or those 'constellations' through which the moon 'passes' in her revolution round the heavens; acc. to *Wdk.* and others they are the following: ༠ *t̔a-skar* (also *dbyug-gu*) three stars in the Ram's head; ༡ *bra-nye* (conceived by the Brahmans to be the image of the *yoni*); ༢ *smin-drug*, the Pleiades; ༣ *be-rdzi, snar-ma*; ༤ *mgo, smal-po*; ༥ *lag*; ༦ *nabs-so, rgyal-stod, nam-so*; ༧ *rgyal-smad*; ༨ *skag, wa*; ༩ *mču, rta-pa, rta-čen* (with Regulus its brightest star); ༡༠ *gre, rtau, rta-čuṅ*; ༡༡ *dbo, k̔ra*; ༡༢ *me-bži, bya-ma*; ༡༣ *nag-pa, byau* (with Spica); ༡༤ *sa-ri*; ༡༥ *sa-ga*; ༡༦ *lha-mtsams, lag-sor*; ༡༧ *snron, ldeu* (with Antares); ༡༨ *snrubs, sog-pa*: ༡༩ *ču-stod*; ༢༠ *ču-smad, ṗul*; ༢༡ *gro-bžin* and *byi-bžin* (considered as one constellation); ༢༢ *mon-gre, mon-dre*; ༢༣ *mon-gru, sgrog*; ༢༤ *k̔rums-stod*; ༢༥ *k̔rums-smad*; ༢༦ *nam-gru, še-sa.*

རྒྱུག་པ་ *rgyúg-pa*, pf. *brgyugs*, fut. *brgyug* 1. **to run,** frq.; **to make haste, to hurry, to rush,** *sgor* to the door (out of the room) *Dzl.* . . . *kyi t̔óg-tu* upon . . . *Dzl.*; **há-la gyug** be off! get you gone! *C.* 1. **to start** (of a rail-way train) *W.*; *rta-rgyúg-pa* to ride full speed, **to gallop**; also sbst. **race** *Glr.* — 2. **to go, to pass, to circulate, to be current; to be valid, to have force.**

རྒྱུགས་ *rgyugs Lex.*; *Sch.*: **limit, term, aim, end**; *W.*: **task, lesson.**

རྒྱུགས་པ་ *rgyúgs-pa* **pride, ambition** *Sch.*; **grief, sorrow** *Schr.*(?).

རྒྱུང་བ་ *rgyúṅ-ba* **the nerves, sinews** *Sch.*; cf. *brgyúṅs-pa.*

རྒྱུད་ *rgyud* 1. *Ssk.* तन्तु, तन्त्री **string, cord,** but only in certain relations: the string of a bow; *rgya-rgyúd* Chinese string *Mil.*; string, chord, of a musical instrument, *rgyud-máṅs* harp; chain, v. *lu-gu*; mostly fig.: *ri-rgyúd, gaṅs-rgyúd* chain of mountains, ridge of snowy hills; also thread of tradition, i.e. continuous, uninterrupted tradition, so in: *k̔a-rgyúd, dgoṅs-rgyúd, čos-rgyúd, bka-rgyúd* (v. *bka*, compounds); *snyan-rgyúd=bka-rgyúd*, frq. in *Mil.*; *γtam-rgyúd Zam.* legendary tradition. — If used for expressing a succession of generations or families, the word is gen. written *brgyud*, rarely *rgyud*, e.g. *rje-btsún slob-rgyúd daṅ bċas-te* his reverence (the venerable divine) with his race of scholars, in as much as the disciples of a saint are frequently called his spiritual children *Mil.* — 2. **treatise, dissertation**, *Ssk.* तन्त्र, also *rgud-sdé*, esp. the necromantic books of the mysticism of later times *Was.* (184), in four classes, the so-called four classes of Tantras (*rgyud-sdé bži*): *byá-bai rgyud, spyód-pai rgyud, rnal-ₒbyór rgyud, rnal-ₒbyór bla-na-méd-pai rgyud;* yet *rgyud bži* is also the short title of a medical work consisting of four parts: *rtsá-bai rgyud, bšád-pai rgyud, man-ṅág rgyud, pyi-mai rgyud.* — 3. **connection, relation, reference**, e.g. of a word. (?). — 4. **character, disposition** of mind, natural quality; **heart, soul**; *rgyud bzáṅ-po* a good disposition, *rgyud ṅán-pa* a bad disposition; *rgyud ži-ba* a mild disposition, good nature, *rgyud ₒjám-pa* a soft temperament *Cs.*; *rgyud ma-rúṅs-pa* a wicked character *Thgy.*; *sem-gyü C.*, *šē-gyü C.*, *Mil.*, prob. also *rig-rgyúd Mil.*, character; *raṅ-rgyúd ṅán-pai ₒgóṅ-po tul* restrain the demon of your own wicked heart *Mil.*; of thoughts, feelings, passions, also of a *tiṅ-ṅe-ḍžin* is said: *rgyúd-la skye* they arise in the soul; *rgyud smin* the mind ripens *Mil.*; in some phrases and passages it designates a man's whole personality: *ráṅ-gi rgud tóg-tu lén-pa* to take (other people's) sufferings altogether upon one's own person (not merely to heart) *Glr.*; *raṅ-rgyúd-la brtág-pa, γžan-rgyúd-la sbyár-ba* to think a matter through in one's own mind, to draw conclusions from an attentive observation of others, *Thgy.* — Concerning *raṅ-rgyúd*, and *γžan-rgyúd* (स्वतन्त्र & परतन्त्र) in the more recent philosophical writings, and in medical works, v. *Was.* — *rgyud-čágs Tar.* 15, 14, acc. to *Schf.* sentence, thesis, point. — *don-rgyúd, sgrub-rgyúd Mil.?*

བརྒྱུད་པ་ *rgyúd-pa* I. vb., pf. *brgyus* and *brgyud*, fut. *brgyu*, imp. *rgyud*, 1. **to fasten** or **file** on a string, to string, *tá-gu-la brgyús-pa* strung, filed on a string *Stg.*; *γsér-nyag-tag γyu brgyús-pa* a gold chain with turquoises inserted *Mil.* — 2. **to pass** through or over, **to traverse** (later literature and col.) *mú-ge rgyúd-nas ₒoṅ* famine passes over, prevails in the country *Ma.*; **náṅ-na naṅ gyúd-de dul* W.* he passes from one room to the other, he visits room after room; **nyúṅ-ti-ne gyúd-na gár-la ton* W.* he is passing through Kullu to Gar; *lag-ₒgrim-gyis brgyús-pas* v. *ₒgrim; yig-nór brgyúd-pa* an error in writing has crept in *Tar.*; *stón-pa γsum ras-čúṅ-pa brgyúd-nas zer* the three teachers, using *Ras-čuṅ-pa* as a go-between, said ..., = they sent word by *Ras-čuṅ-pa* to this effect *Mil.*

II. sbst. and adj. 1. prop. a participle used a. actively; *rgyúd-pa* (or *brgyud-pa*) one that is transmitting knowledge, **a teacher**; *rgyúd-pa bzáṅ-poi byin-rlabs-čan* one that enjoys the blessing of having an excellent spiritual teacher *Mil.*; *ṅai rgyúd-pa rdo-rje-ₒčaṅ-čén yin Mil.* (in this instance it would be justifiable to write *brgyúd-pa*, and, regarding this as a derivative of *brgyúd*, to translate it with 'ancestor'). — b. used passively: *rdo-rje-ₒčáṅ-nas nyams-rtógs rgyúd-pa de ná-ro lags* he to whom knowledge was communicated by *Dor-je-čáṅ* is *Nāro Mil.*; *nā-ro čen-poi rgyud-pa* **a scholar** of great *Nāro Mil.* — 2. a derivative of *rgyud* 2., a Tantrika, **a mystic.**

རྒྱུད་རིས་ *rgyud-ris* a term used in architecture, **wall, panel** (?).

རྒྱུད་ལོང་ *rgyud-lóṅ* **bolt, door-bar** *Sch.*

རྒྱུན་ *rgyun*, *Ssk.* स्रोतस a continual flowing, **the flow, current** or **stream** (seldom river; perh. *smig-rgyui rgyun Lex.* a river seen by a mirage or fata morgana(?); *gáṅ-gai rgyun* the river Ganges); *ču-rgyún-gyis ₒkyér-ba* to be carried away by the current; *rgyún-du žúgs-pa* v. *ₒbrás-bu bži*; frq. fig. *túgs-rjei rgyun* stream of grace *Glr.*, and sim. in some compounds; often in reference to time, hence *rgyún-du* **continually, perpetually, always**, *dus-rgyún-du* id.; **dhū-gyün ta-bhu jhē šig* C.* make it as usual!

sṅár-gyi rgyun all the time before, opp. to *da-ltar* now; also for **ordinarily, predominantly,** e.g. ordinarily it is white, only by way of exception it is of another colour; *k'a-rgyún* = *ka-rgyúd* tradition; *rgyún-gos* an every day coat, opp. to *γzúb-gos; rgyun-ˌgág,* and more frq. *rgyun-čád* an interruption of flowing, of progress, hence *rgyun-čad-méd-par,* or *rgyun-mi-čád-par* uninterruptedly; *rgyun-zás* daily food; *rgyun-riṅ-ba* lasting, of long continuance; *rgyun-lám* an endless, interminable way, to be pursued again and again, e.g. *ˌk'ór-bai* of transmigration, *byaṅ-čúb-kyi* of virtue, holiness *Mil.*

རྒྱུས་ *rgyus* 1. v. *rgyu.* — 2. (*Cs. rgyús-ma*) **notice, intelligence, knowledge,** *ṅá-la dé-ī gyus yod* I am acquainted with it, I know the thing, I am up to it, frq; *W.:* **gyus yód-k'an** one that knows about it; **gyus yód-pai lam** a well-known road; *č'a-méd yúl-du rgyus-méd ˌk'yam* as a stranger I am rambling through a foreign country *Glr.*; *lo-rgyús* 1. **annals, chronicle,** 2. in a general sense **history, story, tale, narrative,** *lo-rgyús bšád-pa* to relate a story *Glr.*, **ṅá-la lo-gyús šád-če máṅ-po yod** *W.* I have much to relate, to tell; *lo-rgyús žib-tu ˌdri-ba* to ask closely, to inquire minutely into a story *Mil.*; *góṅ-gi lo-rgyús bšád-do* he reported what was related above *Pth.*; also used of any short notice or intelligence, without reference to things past: *der ˌbyóṅ-pai lo-rgyús γsuṅs* he mentioned that he was going there *Mil.*

རྒྱུས་པ་ *rgyus-pa* the fine threads or **fibres** of which animal muscle, plants etc. are composed; *rgyús-pa-čan* fibrous; *rgyus-skúd* **catgut.**

རྒྱོ་བ་ *rgyo-ba,* pf. *brgyos,* fut. *brgyo,* imp. *rgyos,* to unite in sexual embrace. This word is an undisguised, and therefore somewhat obscene expression, which in books and in col. language is avoided, though referring to an act not criminal in itself, as *Cs.* seems to have understood it, when he translates *rgyo-ba* by: to abuse, constuprate, ravish; hence it is allowable, yet vulgar, to say: **'á-pa daṅ 'á-ma gyó-wa ǰhe'** *C.*

རྒྱོང་བ་ *rgyóṅ-ba,* pf. *brgyaṅs,* fut. *brgyan,* seems to be a secondary form of *rkyóṅ-ba,* **to extend, stretch, spread** (vb. a.); the word is to be found in *Lexx.*, but seems to be little used; *brgyáṅs-pai má-ts'a Pth.* a disease consisting in some parts of the body being morbidly distended (?).

རྒྱོབ་པ་ *rgyób-pa Cs.*, a secondary form of *rgyáb-pa,* prob. but a provincialism.

སླ་ *lga,* also *sga,* ཤྲྀང་ཝེར་ **ginger** (fresh or dried); *lga-rlon* fresh ginger.

སླང་ངེ་ *lgaṅ-ṅé Pth.: skya-lgaṅ-ṅé,* is stated to mean: **perfectly white.**

སླང་པ་ *lgáṅ-pa, lgaṅ-p'úg* **urinary bladder** *Med.*

སླང་བུ་ *lgáṅ-bu,* = *gáṅ-bu,* **husk, pod, shell.**

སླའུ་གསེར་ *lgau-γsér Cs.* = *lga-rlon.*

སློ་ *lgo Cs.* = *p'a-ba-dgo-dgó* **puff-ball.**

སྒྱམ་ཚྭ་ *lgyám-ts'wa* = *rgyám-ts'a Zam.*, a kind of **rock-salt.**

སྒ་ *sga* 1. gen. *lčá-sga, bča-sga,* **ginger,** = *lga*; *sga-skyá Lt.* id. (?); *sgá-pi-p'o Lt.* prob. for *sga daṅ pi-pi-liṅ daṅ p'ó-ba-ri* ginger and two kinds of black pepper; *sga-spyód Sch.* = *sga-skyá.* — 2. **saddle,** *rta-sga* (*Ld.* **stásga**) horse-saddle; *sga bstád-pa,* resp. *čibs-sga bstád-pa Glr.*, to lay the saddle on, to saddle; *sga-k'ébs* saddle-cloth, *Sch.:* the leather cover or coating of a saddle; *sga-gló* saddle-girth *W., C.*; *sga-lág Cs.:* frame of the saddle; saddle-bow, saddle-tree; *sga-šá* straps for fastening the travelling-baggage to the saddle, cf. *ša-stág* 2.

སྒ་ཕོང་ *sga-p'óṅ* **bat, flitter-mouse** *Sch.*

སྒང་ *sgaṅ* 1. a projecting **hill** or **spur,** on the side of a larger mountain; *sgaṅ-γšóṅ* elevations and depressions on a hill-side, in *Kun. sgaṅ-k'úl*; *sgáṅ-k'a-la yod* (the village) is situated on a mountain-spur; **sgaṅ gyáb-na** *W.* when you have passed round the extremity of the hill. — 2. *ču-*

*sgáṅ* **a blister,** caused by vesicatories, by long marches etc., *C.*, *W.*; cf. *bsgaṅ.*

སྒང་བ་ *sgaṅ-ba*, pf. *bsgaṅs*, fut. *bsgaṅ*, **to grow** or **become full** *Cs.*; *bud-méd ná-so sgaṅ* a marriageable girl.

སྒབ་པ་ *sgab-pa*, secondary form of *ˌgébs-pa*, *byá-mas bú-la sgab-pa* the covering of a young bird by its mother *Glr.*; *gos-sgáb Lex.*, skirt or lap of a coat, *sgab-ťúṅ* a short skirt.

སྒམ་ *sgam* **chest, box, trunk;** *sgam-čúṅ* a little chest or box; *sgam-bu* id.; *sgam-sgo-máṅs* a chest of drawers, cabinet *C.*; *śiṅ-sgam* a wooden chest, *lčágs-sgam* an iron chest; *kó-sgam* a leather trunk; *ró-sgam*, resp. *spúr-sgam* coffin *Cs.* — syn. *sgrom.*

སྒམ་པ་ *sgám-pa*, or *sgám-po Cs.* **deep, profound,** *Sch.* also **prudent, quiet;** *Lex. blo-sgam* w.e. Only the following phrase came under my notice: *ťugs śin-tu sgám-mo* he (the prince) is very clever (as a legendary explanation and confirmation of the name *sroṅ-btsan-sgám-po*). Prob. obsolete.

སྒར་ *sgar* **camp, encampment,** *dmag-sgár* a military camp, *sgar ˌdébs-pa* to pitch a camp; *sgar-míṅ C.* watch-word, parole, = *bso-sgrá.*

སྒལ་ *sgal* **load** of a beast of burden, *rta-sgal* a horse-load, *śiṅ-rtai sgal* a cart-load, waggon-load *Cs.*; *sgal ˌgél-ba* to put on a load, *ˌṗán-ba* to throw it off, *ˌbógs-pa* to take it off, *sgal bsráṅ-ba* to adjust or balance it; *sgál-rta* pack-horse, *sgál-ṗyugs* beast of burden.

སྒལ་པ་ *sgál-pa* 1. **the small of the back,** *sgál-ˌdabs* the lumbar region *Med.* — 2. **the croup, crupper,** back of a horse *Glr.*; **gál pa ťon dug** *W.* the back comes out, i.e. has become sore or galled; *sgal-ťsigs-Med.*, *sgal-rus* col. backbone, spine; *sgal-rmá* a sore on a animal's back caused by the load.

སྒུ་སྟེགས་ *sgu-stégs Lex.* w.e.; *Sch.* **elbow, angle.**

སྒུ་རྡོ་ *sgu-rdó* **a sling** *Sch.*

སྒུག་པ་ *sgúg-pa*, pf. *bsgugs*, fut. *bsgug*, imp. *sgug(s)*, **to wait,** *zlá-ba γčig sgúg-pa* to wait for a month *Glr.*; **to await, to expect,** *ˌči-ba* death *Mil.*; *lám-na sgúg-pa* to wait on the road *Mil.*; *sgúg-čiṅ sdód-pa*, *W.*: **gúg-te dád-če** to sit waiting; **'i-ru gúg-te dód** *W.* wait here! *sgug-tu ˌjug-pa* to keep one waiting *Glr.*; **to lie in wait** (for a person), **to waylay;** *ǰág-pas sgúg-pai sa* a place where robbers are lying in ambush *Mil.*; **kon gúg-te dád-če** *W.* to bear a grudge, to have a spite against a person.

སྒུང་ *sguṅ Ld.* **clap, crack, crash, report** (of a gun).

སྒུད་པོ་ *sgud-po* **father-in-law,** *sgud-mo* mother-in-law *Sch.* prov.

སྒུམ་མདའ་ *sgum-mda Schr.* butt-end of a gun, **gun-stock** *C.*, *W.*; spelling dubious.

སྒུར་ *sgur* v. *dgur.*

སྒུལ་བ་ *sgúl-ba* vb. a. (cf. *ˌgul-ba*), pf. and fut. *bsgul*, **to move, agitate,** put in motion, *rgyud kyaṅ ma sgúl-to* he could not even move the bow-string *Dzl.*; to pull (e.g. the bell-string).

སྒེའུ་ *sgeu* 1. diminutive of *sga*, **ginger,** *sgeu-γsér Med.*, *Ssk.* आर्द्रक (*Hind. adrak*), fresh ginger. — 2. **a small door.**

སྒེག་པ་ *sgég-pa Cs.*: **to boast, brag;** yet not so much with respect to words as to looks and demeanour, so that it may be applied to the airs of coquettish girls (*sgég-čiṅ mdzés-pa* coquettish *Mil.*, *Stg.*) as well as to the bearing of insolent youngsters and bullies. *sgég-ma* n. of a goddess; *sgég-mo Lex.* लास्या, a dancing girl.

སྒེང་ལ་ *sgéṅ-la*, or *dgeṅ-la* (?) **on, upon** *Ts.*

སྒེར་ *sger Sch.*: 'different, dissimilar, foreign'. This word I repeatedly met with in books of physical science, without finding the signification given above applicable.

སྒོ་ *sgo* 1. **door,** the aperture itself, as well as the wood-work of the door: *sgo ˌbyéd-pa*, *W.* **ṗé-če**, to open the door; **ǰúg-pa** 1. *C.* to put in a door, to hang a door on hinges 2. *W.* to close, to shut the door;

*yčód-pa* 1. to shut, 2. to lock (a door); **gyág-pa, gyáb-pa** C., to shut (the door); *ytán-pa Sch.*: 'to lock up', prop. to bolt, to bar, v. *sgo-ytán; bkúm-pa, bskúm-pa Cs.*: resp. to shut (a door); *sgo bdúṅ-ba* to knock, to rap at the door; **go šrúg-ga rag** *W.* I hear a rattling or rapping at the door. The ground floor of a house into which the door leads, is generally occupied by the cattle, hence: *sgoi p̓yugs* the cattle near the door, opp. to: *p̓úgs kyi nor* the money in the inner chamber farthest from the door, cattle and money being thus the two poles or terminating points of household property. — *rgyál-sgo* the principal door or entrance of a house or chamber (in *Ld.* also: **gyáz-go**). — *sgrig-sgo* folding-door *Cs.* — *čáb-sgo* resp. for *sgo Cs.*, cf. *ysáṅ-sgo*. — *rtá-sgo* a door which may be passed through on horseback, viz. the door or gate of a court-yard or garden, open at the top, or a high castle-gate; in the latter case syn. to *rgyál-sgo*. — *náṅ-sgo* the innermost door, *bár-sgo* the middle door, *p̓yi-sgo* the outer door *Pth.* — *tsé-sgo* v. 2, *lás-sgo* v. 3. — *šél-sgo* glass-door; wing of a window, casement; *ysáṅ-sgo* secret door; *Cs.* resp. for *sgo* (?). — 2. **the boards** that form the pane or square of a door, hence **board, plank,** v. *sgo-ṙñám*; *tsé-sgo* a Chinese punishment, consisting of a thick board with an opening for the neck of the culprit, and resting on his shoulders; *sgo yyóg-pa* to put on the board of punishment. — *bsé-sgo daṅ lčágs-sgo bdun sbrags* a door constructed of sevenfold layers of leather and iron, used as a butt for shooting at. — 3. the aperture of a door, and hence **aperture** in general: *sgo kún-nas* from all the apertures (of the body); *žál-gyi sgo* resp. mouth *Dzl.*; *mṅál-sgo* the opening of the womb (v. *mṅal*) frq.; *skyé-bai sgo* id. less frq. *Thgy.*; *dkyíl-ˏkor sgo-bži-pa* a square figure with four openings, about thus: ⌜⌟; the opening of a semicircle; **entrance, passage, outlet,** connecting passage, communication; also fig.: way of mediation, of bringing an agreement about, *ṅan-sóṅ-gi sgo* the entrance, the road, to misery viz.: to hell; *dbáṅ-poi sgo* the organs of sense, also *sgo lṅa* alone; *sgo-ysúm* the three media or spheres of moral activity, *lus, ṅag, yid*, action, word and thought frq.; *bzá-ba daṅ btúṅ-bai sgo ˏp̓rog-pa* to cut off the supply (of provisions) *Pth.*; *bdag čos sgor ˏjug-pa žu* I beg to allow us to enter religion, to receive us as students or disciples *Mil.*; *ˏgró-sgo Schr.* 1. also *búd-go, kyág-go W.*, expense, expenditure 2. *dó-go-tar šė́-pa C.* to relate accurately how a thing came to pass; *lás-sgo* 'door of intercourse, of trade', a commercial place or town, emporium *Glr.* Hence *sgó-nas* with the genit. **by means of, by,** in the way of, according to, but never as connected with a person or joined to an infinitive: *tabs dú-mai sgó-nas* in different ways, variously (often coinciding with: by various means); *lus ṅag yid-kyi sgó-nas* in or by actions, words, and thoughts (e.g. to strive for virtue, cf. above *sgo-ysúm*) *Dzl.*; *rnám-pa sna-tsógs-kyi sgó-nas* in every possible way *Dzl.*; *dpei sgó-nas* (to explain) by way of comparison *Thgy.*; *mtsan-nyid-kyi sgó-nas* (to describe a thing) according to its characteristics *Thgy.*; *rigs-kyi sgó-nas* (to divide) according to the species *Lt.*; *ˏdrá-bai sgó-nas btags-miṅ ste* it being a name given to it from its resemblance to ... *Wdṅ.*; ... *la p̓rag-dóg-gi sgó-nas* from envy of ... *Mil.*; *mi-snáṅ-bai sgó-nas* by way of invisibility, by being invisible *Wdṅ.*

**Comp. and deriv.** *sgo-káṅ* the entrance into a house, **vestibule, porch, portal.** — *sgo-kúṅ* opening of the door *Mil.* — *sgo-kyi* a door-guarding dog, **watch-dog.** — *sgo-ˏkór* **hinge** of a door or gate. — *sgo-glágs Zam.* = *sgo-ytán* (?). — *sgo-glégs* **the board** or **plank** of a door *Cs.* — *sgo-ˏgrám* the space near the door. — *sgo-ˏdrig* (*Ld.* **sgon-dig**) **door-frame**, window-frame. — *sgo-rgyáb* the space behind the door, within the door *Glr.* — **go-čág** (*lčags*) *C.* **lock** of a door. — **go(g)-tán** a bar or bolt (a small beam) to secure the door with. —

ག

*sgo-ťém* **threshold,** also **the head-piece** of a door. — *sgo-bdág* = *sgo-dpón*. — *sgo-rnám* a single **board**, e. g. of the floor. — *sgó-pa*, resp. *čábs-sgo-pa* **door-keeper, porter;** *sgo-dpón* the first, principal door-keeper. — **go-ṗiṅ** *W.* **door-hinge.** — *sgo-ₒṗár* **board** or **plank** of a door *Cs.* — *sgo-bár Ld.* **chinks** between the separate laths of a door (for of such the doors in Tibet frequently consist, owing to the scarcity of wood). — *sgó-ma* 1. **pane** or **square** of a door, **fold** of a folding-door; 2. a masked dancer in religious dramatic entertainments, representing one of the four guardians of the world (v. *rgyal-čén*). — *sgó-mo* 1. **a large door, a gate, castle-gate, town-gate;** 2. **beginning,** *rtsis-kyi sgó-mo Pth.* = *rtsis-ₒgo Cs.* (Chronol. Table) beginning of a new epoch. — *sgo-mtsáms* the small opening left between door-post and door, when the latter does not perfectly fit. — *sgo-yig Cs.* 1. **inscription,** 2. **lampoon, libel,** 3. a magisterial **advertisement** fastened to a door. — *sgo-lá* n. of a high and difficult mountain-pass between Lhasa and Pan, v. Huc. I. p. 244. — *sgo-sruṅ* **door-keeper, porter** *Dzl.*

སྒོ *sgo*, in *skyé-sgo* v. sub *sgó-po*.

སྒོ་ང་ *sgo-ṅá* or *sgoṅ-ṅá* and *sgoṅ*, **egg, eggs, spawn,** also egg as a measure *Lt.*; *sgoṅ-dkrís* the pellicle, membrane of an egg *Sch.*; *sgóṅ-čú* the white of an egg *Sch.*; *sgoṅ-šún*, or *kog*, the shell of an egg; *sgoṅ-sér* yolk of an egg *Sch.* — *sgo-ṅa ṗyed* a scholastic term, v. *Was.* (274).

སྒོ་པུར་ *sgo-púr* **foreskin, prepuce** *C.* vulg.

སྒོ་པོ་ *sgó-po*, also *sgó-bo*, (*Ld.* **gó-po**) *W.* 1. **the body,** with respect to its physical nature and appearance, **gó-po čén-mo, riṅ-mo, go-riṅ, go-záṅ** tall, **gó-po čuṅ-se** of small stature, short; **róm-po** stout, lusty; **ťá-mo** slender, thin; **dé-mo** healthy, well; **go-yál** a man that has lost his own body by gaming and become the slave of another. — 2. = *skyé-sgo* **face, countenance,** *skye-sgo legs* a beautiful face, *žán-sgo* an ugly face *Mil.* — *sgó-lo* 1. **body,** 2. **face,** as a flattering word; also directly for a nice or pretty face, **gó-lo min dug bag ťsogs yod** she has not a pretty face, but looks like a fright *W.*

སྒོ་བ་ *sgó-ba*, pf. *bsgo* (*bsgos* in *Lexx.*, prob. obsolete) **to say,** when used of superiors, hence mostly **to bid, to order** (cf. the article *bka* init.), frq. in early literature, in later times more and more disappearing, being unknown to the common people.

སྒོ་ཙམ་ *sgo-tsám* **a little** *Sch.*

སྒོ་ལོ་ *sgó-lo* 1. v. *sgó-po*. — 2. *Ld.* also = *sgo-ṅá*.

སྒོག་པ་ *sgóg-pa*, (*Ssk.* लशुन) **garlic, leek,** (Allium); *ri-sgóg Med.* Allium sphaeroceph. *L.*, or a species allied to it; *sgog-skyá Med.* Allium nivale Jacqm. (?); *sgog-snón Med.* perh. A. rubellum, a blue species, very common in the Himalaya. — *sgog-tiṅ* mortar, *sgog-ɣtún* pestle, for bruising leek.

སྒོག་པ་ *sgóg-pa* 1. *Cs.*: 'pf. *bsgags*, fut. *bsgag*, to make one swear, *sgóg-po* one that makes a person swear.' I only met with *mna-sgóg Lex.* w. e. — 2. *ɣya sgóg-pa* v. *ɣya*.

སྒོང་ *sgoṅ* 1. v. *sgo-ṅá*. — 2. n. of a country, prob. = *koṅ Glr.* — 3. *sgoṅ-ťóg-pa* n. of a plant *Med.*

སྒོང་བ་ *sgóṅ-ba*, pf. *bsgoṅs*, fut. *bsgoṅ*, imp. *sgoṅ (s)*, 1. **to make round, globular** *Cs.*; so it is prob. to be understood in: *bu-rám bsgár-žiṅ bsgráṅs-nas bsgoṅs Lex.*, he having boiled down the sugar and allowed it to grow cold, formed it into balls (in this form the sugar is usually kept in Tibet). — 2. **to hide** or **conceal** a thing *Sch.*, thus in **góṅ-te bór-če** *W.*; cf. also *dpá-sgoṅ-ba*.

སྒོབ་སྒོབ་ *sgob-sgób* **unable, deficient,** wanting in strength *Sch.*; **lág-pa gob-soṅ** *Kun.* the hands are unable (to move), stiff (from cold).

སྒོམ་ *sgom* **reflection, meditation, contemplation,** *sgom šór-gyi dógs-pa* the fear lest contemplation should be prejudiced or rendered impossible *Mil.*; *sgom srúṅ-ba* to sustain, to preserve meditation (undisturbed) *Mil.*; *sgom-méd* without meditation *Thgr.*

**སྒོམ་པ་** *sgóm-pa* I. vb., pf. *bsgoms*, fut. *bsgom*, imp. *sgom(s)*, resp. *ṫugs sgóm-pa* (*Ssk.* भू, *causative* भावय) 1. originally: **to fancy, imagine; meditate, contemplate, consider,** c. accus. and dat.; **to have, to entertain, to produce** in one's mind, = *skyéd-pa*, e. g. *bzód-pa, snyíṅ-rje, byáms-pa* etc.; *rgyún-du nam ₒči čá-med sgom* always consider that it is uncertain at what time you shall die *Mil.*; with the accus. and termin., or with a double accus.; **to look upon,** to represent to one's self as ..., *ₒgró-drug-séms-čan ṗá-mar sgom* look upon the beings of the six classes as being your parents *Mil.*, viz. with the same respect and affection, or even so, that you imagine your father's or your mother's soul inhabiting just now the animal body of one of those beings; *rmi-lam sgyú-ma sgom* look upon it as being the illusion of a dream *Mil.* — 2. In later times *sgóm-pa* became the usual term for the systematic **meditation** of the Buddhist saint, so that this word, and the expressions *tiṅ-ṅe-ₒdzin-du ₒjúg-pa*, and *bsam-ytán sgrúb-pa*, which in classical writings denote the concentration of the mind upon one point or subject, e. g. upon a certain deity, *lha*, prob. imply one and the same thing. Three degrees of this systematic meditation are to be distinguished, viz. *ltá-ba* contemplation, *sgóm-pa* meditation, properly so called, (which requires *ysal daṅ mi-rtog má-yyeṅs ysum*, i.e. that it be performed in a clear and decided manner, without suffering one's self to be disturbed or distracted by any thing), and the third degree *spyód-pa*, exercise and practice, which three distinctions will be somewhat elucidated by the following: *bzá(-bai)-ytad(-so) yód-na bltá-ba min, byiṅ-rgod yód-na sgóm-pa min, bláṅ-dor yód-na spyód-pa min*, if one lives plenteously, there is no contemplation (possible); where there is inattention and a distracted mind, meditation cannot take place; where there is desire or disgust, exercise and practice are not (to be thought of) *Mil.* 14, 11. Hence contemplation would seem to be more immediately opposed to the rule of sense, meditation to the rule of imagination, practice to the rule of passion; v. also *Was.* (137), *Köpp.* I, 585. Sometimes contemplation and meditation are also opposed to *ṫós-pa*, and *bsám-pa*, hearing and knowing, as to mere acts of memory and intellect. — *sgóm(-pa)-po Cs.*, *sgom-byéd*, *sgóm-mḱan Mil.* one that meditates, **an ascetic;** *sgóm-ma* fem. *Mil.* — *sgom-čén* 1. **a great meditator** (so *Mil.* often calls himself). 2. a kind of **field-mouse,** Lagomys badius *Hook.* II, 156. — *sgom-ṫág* 'meditating-cord', a cord or rope slung by the laxer sects round their bodies, in order to facilitate the effort of maintaining an erect and immoveable posture during meditation, which expedient of course is scorned by the more rigid devotees.

II. sbst. 1. **meditation.** — 2. *Cs.*: 'the state of being accustomed to' (prob. erron. for *goms-pa*).

**སྒོམ་འབྲོག་** *sgom-ₒbróg* (?) **holly,** Ilex. *Sik.*

**སྒོར་** *sgor* a spindle in turning-lathes? v. the next word.

**སྒོར་བ་** *sgór-ba* 1. pf. and fut. *bsgar*, **to boil down,** to condense by boiling, e. g. *bu-rám* sugar. — 2. **to turn** on a lathe, *W.* **gór-la ṫen-če**.

**སྒོར་མོ་** *sgór-mo* (perh. also *skór-mo*) 1. **round,** e. g. of leaves, *Wdṅ.* and elsewh. — 2. **a circle.** — 3. **a disk, a globe;** hence a rupee *W.*; a semi-globular bowl or vessel *W.*, *sgor-ṫig* circular line, circumference, circle; *sgor-ṫig ṗyé-ba Cs.*, *ṗyéd-ka Schr.* semicircle.

**སྒོས་** *sgos*, in compounds and as adverb: **private, separate, distinct; privately** etc., opp. to *spyi*, e. g. *spyi-ydugs* a parasol for several persons, awning, shelter, *sgos-ydugs* a parasol for one person *Glr.*; *sgós-skal* share of a single person, individual lot

*Mil.*; *sgós-su,* or *sgos* adv., (opp. to *spyir*) particularly, especially; *sgos-(kyi), dpon* a subaltern officer *Cs.*; *sgós-pa Sch.*: 'to choose, to find the right thing'.

སྒྱིཝ་, སྒྱིག་གུ *sgyiu, sgyig-gu* **bag, purse;** *sgyig-gu čád-poi dbáṅ-du sóṅ-nas* our purse being at low ebb; *dṅul-sgyig* money-bag, purse.

སྒྱིང་བ་ *sgyiṅ-ba*, pf. *bsgyiṅs*, fut *bsgyiṅ*, 1. acc. to *Lexx.* = *Ssk.* जम्भ syn. to *glál-ba,* **to yawn, gape,** and perh. to stretch one's self after having slept; it is almost exclusively used in describing the attitude of a dying lion, and so also the dying attitude of Buddha. — 2. perh. also = *ˬgyiṅ-ba.*

སྒྱིད་(པ་) *sgyid(-pa)* 1. the hollow of the knee, bend of the knee; **knee-joint;** *sgyid-pa γcód-pa* to lame the knee-joint, to hamstring (a horse) *Glr.* — 2. **the calf** (of the leg) *Mil.*; *sgyid skyúr-ba* acute pain in the knee and leg e.g. of a woman with child *Med.; Cs.*: 'to despair'? — *sgyid-k̔úṅ* the hollow of the knee *Med.* — *sgyid-k̔yól* one lame in his legs *Cs.* — *sgyid-lug-pa Lex.* w. e., *Cs.*: slothful, idle, lazy; *sgyid-lhód Sch.* id.

སྒྱིད་བུ་ *sgyid-bu*, also *sgyéd-bu*, **a hearth, fire-place,** consisting of (three) stones on which the kettle is placed; *lčags-sgyid* iron trevet, tripod, cf. *sgyéd-po.*

སྒྱུ་ *sgyu* **artifice, imposture** *Dzl.* and elsewh., *γyo-sgyú* id.; *γyo-sgyu-med-na* if he is without guile *Dzl.; sgyu-čan* artful, crafty, cunning, *Cs.* — *sgyu-ˬp̔rúl-ma,* माया, the name of Buddha's mother. — *sgyú-ma,* माया, **illusion,** false show, deception of sight, opp. to *dṅos* reality; *sgyu-ma sprul-ba* to exhibit a false show *Cs.*; *ṅas snáṅ-ba tams-čád sgyú-mar šes* I know that every thing visible, the whole external world, is only an illusion *Mil.; sgyú-mai nor* apparent riches, hence riches in general *Mil.* (cf. *sgyu-lús*); *sgyú-ma-mk̔an* **a juggler** *Mil.*; *sgyú-ma-mk̔an-gyi mčán-bu, sgyu-mai mčán-bu* a juggler's apprentice *Lexx.* — *sgyu-rtsál* **art, skill, dexterity,** frq., the Indians, and so also the Tibetans counting 64 arts (or 60 in a round number) *Tar.* 21, 2. — *sgyu-zóg* **deception, hypocrisy** *Pth.* — *sgyu-lús* 1. the immaterial, subtile and pure body of the soul in the Bardo, hell etc., hence = *yid-kyi lus Thgr.* 2. the animal and human body in general, in as much as it is only an apparent body, a phantom, when considered from a higher philosophical point of view *Mil.*

སྒྱུག་མོ་ *sgyúg-mo* **mother-in-law** *Stg.*; *mna-sgyúg* both daughter-in-law and mother-in-law.

སྒྱུར་བ་ *sgyúr-ba*, pf. and fut. *bsgyur*, (vb. a. to *ˬgyúr-ba*) 1. **to transform,** *lus ˬdod-dgúr* to transform one's body (i. e. one's self) at pleasure, (*Dzl.* ༢༦ *lus* is to be supplied, or *gyúr-te* to be read); to transform the royal prerogative into a religious one, v. *k̔rims.* — 2. **to change** (colour, one's mind), **to alter** (something written), hence **to correct, to revise.** — 3. **to give up, leave off** (customs, scruples, doubts, timidity) *Glr., p̔yi-rol-pai čós-lugs* the non-Buddhist religion. — 4. **to turn** off or aside (the course of a river); **to dissuade, divert,** *las,* from *Dzl.* — 5. **to turn,** **ǰiṅ pa gyúr-če** *W.* to turn round on one's heel; **ǰiṅ-pa gyúr-te ltá-če** *W.* to look back; *k̔ór-lo sgyúr-ba* to turn a wheel = *skór-ba*; *skad sgyúr-ba* to vary, to modulate the voice, also to hum a tune, to sing or whistle, as birds do. — 6. **to govern,** *rtai k̔a sráb-kyis,* a horse's mouth by the bridle; also fig. **gyál-pọ k̔a lọ́n-gyi gyur, k̔yọ̄ k̔a čúṅ-mẹ̄ gyur** *C.* the king is governed by his minister, the husband by his wife; *ˬdod-čágs ṅán-pas k̔a-sgyur* he is governed by evil passions *Mil.*; *k̔á-lo sgyúr-ba* to govern, prop. and fig., v. *k̔á-lo*; *šiṅ-rta sgyúr-ba* to drive a carriage; in a similar sense *dbaṅ sgyúr-ba* c. *la,* to have command or control of, to command, dominate, frq.; prob. also to possess *Mil.* — 7. **to translate,** *sgra sgyúr-ba* id. — 8. **to multiply** *Wdk.* (cf. *ˬgyúr-ba* 4, and *lóg-pa*); *bsgyúr-bya* the multiplicand *Wdk.* — 9. *Lad., Pur.* **to kill, to slaughter.** — 10. **to publish, proclaim, announce** **ka-sál gyúr-če** *W.* to publish an order; *lon gyur* W. announce me! send in my name!

སྒྱེ་སྒུར་ sgye-sgúr **crooked** Sch., better dgye.

སྒྱེ་བོ་ sgyé-bo is said to denote in C. one of the lower classes of officials or noblemen.

སྒྱེ་མོ་ sgyé-mo 1. sbst. **a bag** (not of leather); ras-sgyé a bag of cotton stuff Pth.; sgyeu diminutive. — 2. adj. **quiet, gentle** (of horses) Sp.

སྒྱེད་པོ་ sgyéd-po a stone for a fire-place, **hearth-stone,** three of which are so placed together, that a fire may be kindled between them and a kettle put on; sgyéd-bu a fire-place constructed in this manner.

སྒྱེལ་བ་ sgyél-ba, pf. and fut. bsgyel, vb. a. to ˳gyél-ba, **to throw down, to overthrow, overturn,** gan-kyáb on the back Lex.; **to lay** or **put down** (a bottle, a book); **to thwart** (the charm of an enemy); **to kill** (horses); *mi se', ta gyel* manslaughter and the killing of horses, C.

སྒྱོགས་ sgyogs 1. a warlike engine to shoot darts or fling stones with, **catapult, ballista,** sgyógs-kyi ˳p̔rul-˳k̔ór Thgr. id; sgyogs-rdo a stone flung from such a machine Sch.; in later times: 2. **mortar, cannon, gun,** in Tibet even at the present day without wheels, col. *ghyog*. — 3. a surgeon's instrument for setting broken limbs Cs.

སྒྱོང་བ་ sgyóṅ-ba, pf. bsgyaṅs, fut. bsgyaṅ, perh. originally = sgóṅ-ba to hide, but actually used 1. in C.: *gyú-ma gyáṅ-wa* **to fill, to stuff** (a sausage) 2. col. in W.: *gyáṅ-če* **to put** into (the pocket, a box, a coffin); *gyáṅ-du bór-če* **to keep, lock,** or **shut up** (things); *úgs gyáṅ-če* to hold one's breath; gla p̔yir sgyóṅ-ba **to retain** the wages due to another person Sch. The form rgyaṅs often occurs in Mil., in passages where 'to retain, lock up, put into' or a similar term would suit very well. Other passages cannot yet be sufficiently accounted for, and upon the whole the roots gyaṅ and kyaṅ (rgyaṅ etc.) require to be more closely investigated.

སྒྲ་ sgra, W. also *ra*, 1. **a sound, noise; voice;** há-sgra the sound h Glr.; sgrá-bčas ˳bru noisy evacuations take place Lt.; ˳ón-pa-dag sgrá-rnams t̔os the deaf hear sounds; sgra sgróg-pa to produce sounds, noises Mil.; sgra dag γsal γsum (read) loud, correctly, and distinctly, those three (a precept for reading or reciting); *nyid-ra táṅ-če* W. to snore; *šóg-ra* the noise made by a flight of birds passing; miṅ-sgra a mere word, name, or sound Was., as a philosophical term. — 2. **word, syllable,** bdág-sgra Cs., bdág-poi sgra Gram., the name given in grammar to the so-called article pa, e.g. in rtá-pa horseman, rider; dgág-sgra prohibitive or negative particle. — 3. **language,** science of languages, **philology.**

**Comp.** sgra-skád (= sgra 1.) **sound, voice,** sgra-skád snyán-pa frq. — sgrá-čan **sounding, sonorous.** — sgra-čé **far-famed, renowned** Mil.. sgra čer gragspa Stg. id. — sgra-snyán 1. **a well-sounding, agreeable voice,** 2. C. **a guitar.** — sgra-brnyán **echo** Mil. — sgrá-ldar **sounding, sonorous.** — sgra-dbyáṅs 1. **pleasing tone, harmony, euphony,** e.g. glu daṅ ról-moi Tar. 2. n. of a goddess Cs. — sgra-sbyór Zam., Tar., Schf., a coalition or connection of letters. — sgra-mi-snyán (a disagreeable voice) n. of a larger and two smaller northern continents of the fabulous geography of ancient India. — sgra-t̔ád (sgra daṅ t̔sad-ma) Tar., Schf.: grammar and logic; yet yi-gei sgra-t̔ád, sgra-t̔sad-yi-ge Glr. seem to denote philology.

སྒྲ་གཅན་ sgra-γčán, Ssk. राहु Rāhu, 1. a demon or monster of Indian mythology, esp. known by his being at enmity with the Sun and Moon, on whom he is continually wreaking his vengeance, occasionally swallowing them for a time and thereby causing their eclipses. The Buddhist representation of the Rahu-legend is given by Schl. p. 114. — 2. Cs.: **the ascending node** of the moon, determining the time of the obscurations. — sgra-γčán-

*dzin*, राहुल *Rāhula* 1. 'seized by Rāhu' (*Fouc. Gyatch.* II, LVII), obscured, eclipse of the sun or moon, 2. 'catcher of Rāhu,' acc. to the Tibetan legend an epithet given to the deity *p̓yag-rdór*, acc. to Indian mythology, to Vishnu, who in Tibetan is called *k̓yab-ʼjúg* (also *k̓yab-ʼjug-ɣsód Cs.*); sometimes, however, he is identified with Rāhu himself, for the names *ɣza-sgra-ɣċan*, *ɣza-sgra-ɣċan-dzin*, *ɣza-k̓yab-ʼjúg*, *ɣza-rā-hu-la*, and even *ɣza-du-ba-ʼjug-riṅ* (comet!) are used promiscuously. — 3. a son and disciple of Shakyamuni, who received this name on account of an eclipse of the moon taking place at his birth, v. *Fouc. Gyatch.* II, 389.

སྒྲང་བ *sgráṅ-ba*, *Cs.*: pf. *bsgraṅs*, fut. *bsgraṅ*, imp. *sgroṅ*, 1. **to enumerate**, to reckon up separately. — 2. **to upbraid, to reproach.**

སྒྲལ་བ *sgrál-ba* **to cut** into small pieces, viz. the picture of an enemy whom one wishes to destroy.

སྒྲིག་པ *sgrig-pa*, pf. *bsgrigs*, fut. *bsgrig*, imp. *sgrig(s)*, *W.* **rig-ċe**, **to lay** or **put in order, to arrange, adjust,** *paṅ-léb* boards or planks, *so-p̓ág* bricks or tiles *Glr.*, *kar-yól* plates and dishes, = to lay the cloth; *ɣdan* stuffed seats or chairs *Dzl.*; **to put** or **fit together, to join** the separate parts of an animal body *Glr.*; to put close together, side by side, hence *W.*: **žiṅ de nyis rig-te yod** these two fields are adjacent, **t̓a daṅ rig-te yin** it is situated close to the border; **to compile, to write** books *Glr.* — **rig-mo* W.* **tight, close,** e.g. a joint, commissure, seam.

སྒྲིན་པོ *sgrín-po*, *Zam.*: = *mk̓ás-pa*, **prudent, skilful, clever,** *blo sgrín-pa* a penetrating mind *Sch.*

སྒྲིབ་པ *sgrib-pa* 1. vb. pf. *bsgribs*, fut. *bsgrib*, imp. *sgrib(s)*, *W.* **rib-ċe**, to deprive of light, **to darken, to obscure,** *W.* **rib ma rib** get out of my light! *nyi-mai ʼod-zér bsgribs-nas* the light of the sun being obscured, by clouds *Glr.*, by a curtain *Zam.* — 2. sbst. the state of being darkened, **obscuration,** gen. fig., mental darkness, **sin,** also *sgrib*; *séms-ċan t̓ams-ċád-kyi sgrib-pa sél-ba* frq., hence *sgrib-pa-rnam-sél* n. of a Boddhisatva; *sgrib-pa lṅa Dzl.*, the five obscurations caused by sin, prob. = पञ्चकषाय *Burn.* II, 360. — 3. adj **darkened, obscured, dark; sinner,** *bdag-ráṅ sgrib-pa ċé-am* am I so great a sinner? *Pth.* — **ḍib-ma* C.*, **rib-ma* W.* **shelter, fence,** e.g. at the side of a field against the wind.

སྒྲིམ་པ *sgrim-pa*, pf. *bsgrims*, fut. *bsgrim*, imp. *sgrim(s)*, *Cs.*: **'to hold fast, to force** or **twist together; to endeavour'**; *Sch.* also: **'to squeeze in, cram in; to be over-hasty, confused'.** Only the following phrases came to my notice: **kụ̓-pa ḍim-pa* C.* to twist or twine a thread; **rig-pa ḍim* C.* take care! (collect your thoughts!); **ḍim-tog-ċan* Sp.* inquisitive, curious. Some passages in *B.*, e.g. *blo-bsgrims* (explained by *blo-ʼdás Zam.*) are as yet dubious as to their sense.

སྒྲིལ་བ *sgril-ba*, pf. and fut. *bsgril*, *W.* **(s)ril-ċé**, (cf. *ʼgril-ba* 1. and *ʼk̓ril-ba*), 1. **to wind** or **wrap round** e.g. a bit of cloth round one's finger; **to roll, wrap,** or **wind up;** *ril-bur* to roll or form into a pill *Med.*; **to make fast** or **tight,** *lhód-pa* what is loose; *p̓yogs ɣċig-tu sgril-ba* to gather into a heap, **to heap** or **pile up, to sweep together;** hence *sgril-bas* (also *dril-bas Glr.*) **to sum up all,** taking all together, in short *Lt.*; *mjúg-ma sgril-ba* **to wag** the tail, *mi-la* at a person (of dogs) *Mil.*; **to roll,** e.g. a large stone to some place. — 2. **to multiply** *Wdk.*, frq.; *bsgril-ma* a doubled and twisted thread or cord *Sch.*; *sgril-šiṅ* a wooden roll, round which paper etc. is wound; the rolling-pin of bakers. — *sgril-šóg*, *W.* **šog-ril**, rolled paper *Cs.*

སྒྲུག་པ *sgrug-pa*, pf. *bsgrugs*, fut. *bsgrug*, imp. *sgrug(s)*, *W.* **rúg-ċe(s)**, **to collect, gather, pluck, pick up** e.g. wood, flowers, vermin etc.

སྒྲུང(ས)་ *sgruṅ(s)*, *Ld.* **šruṅs**, *C.* **ḍum**, **fable, legend, tale** (to the uncultivated mind of the Tibetan, destitute of any physical and historical knowledge of the countries and people beyond the boundaries of his native soil, the difference between truth and fable is but vague and unsettled); *sgruṅ ₒčád-pa* to relate fables, stories etc.; *sṅon-rábs sgruṅ Zam.*, *sṅón-gyi sgruṅ-rgyúd Glr.*, *sgruṅ-γtám* tales of ancient times, of the days of yore; *sgrúṅ-mḱan Cs.*, *sgrúṅ-pa Sch.* the inventor or writer of fables and tales, also a narrator of tales.

སྒྲུང་བ་ *sgrúṅ-ba*, pf. *bsgruṅs*, fut. *bsgruṅ*, 1. **to mix.** 2. **to invent, to feign** *Cs.*

སྒྲུན་པ་ *sgrún-pa*, pf. and fut. *bsgrun* 1. **to compare** c. *la* and *daṅ Dzl.* — 2. **to emulate, vie, contend with** *Cs.*

སྒྲུབ་པ་ *sgrúb-pa* I. vb. pf. *bsgrubs*, fut. *bsgrub*, imp. *sgrub(s)* (cf. *ₒgrúb-pa Ssk.* साध) 1. **to complete, finish, perform, carry out,** an order, a wish, hence usually with *bžin-du Dzl.*; **to make, achieve, manufacture, obtain, attain,** *dṅúl-rdo-la dṅul bsgrúb-tu btúb-pa ltar séms-čan-la Saṅs-rgyás bsgrúl-tu btúb-pa yin-no* in like manner as silver is obtained from silver-ore, Buddha may proceed from beings *Thgy.*; *don sgrúb-pa* to attain to one's aim, to obtain a blessing, a boon; *ṫse ₒdii don sgrúb-pa* to care for the wants of this life; **to procure,** *rgyágs-ṗye* flour, as provision for a journey *Mil.*; *nor sgrúb-pa* **to gain** riches; **to furnish with, to supply,** one's self or others *Mil.* — 2. *lha-sgrúb-pa* implies, in accordance to Brahmanic-Buddhistic theology, not so much the making a deity propitious to man (*Cs.*), as rendering a god subject to human power, forcing him to perform the will of man. This coercion of a god seems to be effected in a twofold manner. The practise of the common people is to perform a vast amount of prayers and conjurations, specially intended for the god that is to be made subject. Another method is adopted by saints, who are advanced in every kind of religious knowledge. They continue their *sgóm-pa,* or profound meditation, for months and years, until the deity, finally overcome, stands before them visible and tangible, nay, until they have been personally united with and, as it were, incorporated into the invoked and subjected god. Whilst the conatus, the labouring in this arduous undertaking, is often called *sgrúb-pa*, the arriving at the proposed end is designated by *ₒgrúb-pa*, e.g. *rgyál-pos rta-mgrin sgrúb-pa mdzád-pas ₒgrúb-nas rta-skád btón-pas* etc., the king began to coerce *Taḍin* (*Hayagriwa*), and when the latter was made obsequious, so as to appear, a neighing was heard etc. *Glr.*; *sgom-sgrúb byéd-pa* for *sgóm-pa daṅ sgrúb-pa byéd-pa Mil.* — *bsgrub-ḱáṅ*, *sgrub-γnás*, *sgrub-ṗúg* the house, the place, the cavern, where a saint applies himself to *sgrúb-pa*; *sgrúb-pa-po* one effectuating the coercion described above, *Sambh.* frq. — *sgrub-rtágs* tokens, proofs of perfection, of an accomplished saint. — *sgrub-ṫábs* the method of effecting the coercion, of obliging a god to make his appearance; *sgrub-byéd* 1. he that accomplishes the coercion (cf. *Schl.* p. 247). 2. a kind of bile *Med.* — *sgrub-γšén* the Bon-doctrine *Mil.*

II. sbst. 1. one that contemplates and meditates, like *sgom-čén Mil.* 2. n. of a sect of Lamas, with whom marriage is permitted.

སྒྲེ་བ་ *sgré-ba* I. *Cs.* adj. **naked,** gen. *sgren-mo.*

II. vb. pf. *bsgres,* fut. *bsgre* (cf. *ₒgre-ba*) 1. **to roll** *Glr.*, *Pth.* — 2. **to multiply** *Wdk.* — 3. **to repeat** *Cs.* — 4. **to put** or **place in order, to put together, to compare,** e.g. records *Tar.* 174, 14 *Schf.*

སྒྲེ་གློག་ *sgre-zlóg* a sea-washed beach *Sch.*

སྒྲེག་པ་ *sgrég-pa* 1. vb. pf. *sgregs,* **to belch.** — 2. sbst. **belch, eructation,** *sgrég-pa ₒdón-pa, ₒbyin-pa Med.* *rul-ḍág* *C.* a belch of a fetid smell.

སྒྲེང་བ་ *sgréṅ-ba*, pf. *bsgreṅs*, fut. *bsgreṅ*, imp. *sgreṅ(s)*, cf. *ₒgréṅ-ba*, 1. **to raise, erect,** lift up, hold up, plant up, e.g. a finger, a beam etc. — 2. **to stretch out** a limb and hold it stiff *C.*

སྒྲེན་མོ་ *sgrén-mo* **naked,** *sgrén-mor ₒbyúṅ-ba* to appear in a naked state, to show one's self naked *Dzl.*; *Bhar.* 59. *Schf.* 'orbus', orphaned (coġ. to *bkren?*).

སྒྲོ་ *sgro* 1. a large **feather,** esp. quill-feather, used for an ornament of arrows, as a charm etc.; *sgro-mdóṅs* peacock's feather, as a badge of dignity. 2. **to elevate, exalt, increase;** *Cs.*: **to exaggerate.** *Was.* however has p. (305): 'Vorurtheil (Anerkennung des Nichtwahren), Gegensatz: *skur-ₒdébs* Lästerung (Leugnung des Wahren)', and p. (297): '*sgro-skúr* Verneinen und Lästerung'. *Cs.* renders *sgro-skúr* by 'exaggerated praise and blame'; *sgro-skúr ₒdébs-ba* occurs also in *Mil.* The phrase *sgro-ₒdógs γčód-pa* might therefore be rendered: to put an end to overrating and to prejudice; this meaning, however, does not suit in every instance, and acc. to expressions heard from people in *C.*, *sgro-ₒdógs γčód-pa* would signify: to turn to account, to work one's way up, to contest for a prize. Finally ought to be mentioned that acc. to *Schr.* *sgro-ₒdógs spyód-pa* (sic) denotes 'logic'. A connection between these heterogeneous significations is not discernible, but a clew may perhaps be found hereafter. — 3. **sack, bag** (?), *ťál-sgro Glr.* was explained by: a sack full of ashes.

སྒྲོ་ག་ *sgro-ga C.* the little bubbles in sparkling beverages, **čáṅ-la ḍó-ga ḍug** the beer sparkles.

སྒྲོ་གུ་ *sgró-gu*, v. *sgróg-gu* sub *sgrog.*

སྒྲོ་བ་ *sgró-ba* I. sbst. 1. *Wdṅ.*, acc. to *Sch.* **the bark** of a species of willow, but prob. the same as *gró-ga.* — 2. *C.* **the penis.**

II. **vb.**, pf. *bsgros,* fut. *bsgro,* imp. *sgro-Lexx.* w.e., *Cs.*: **to debate, discuss,** so that it would be only another form of *bgro-ba*; but in *C.* **ḍo-šę' ǰhé'-pa** is said to mean: **to talk at random,** to chatter away thoughtlessly.

སྒྲོག(ས)་ *sgrog(s)* **cord, rope,** for tying, fettering: **fetters** *Mil.* and *C.*; *lčags-sgróg* iron fetters, chain; *lčags-sgróg lág-pa sbrél-nas* the hands tied or chained together; *lčags-sgróg-pa* a convict put in irons; *šiṅ-sgróg* fetters made of twisted twigs *Cs.*; *lham-sgróg* **shoe-strap,** lace, latchet. — *sgróg-gu, sgró-gu, W.* **róg-bu**, **string, strap,** for binding, fastening, strapping; *Sch.* also button; *sgrog-ril Sch.* **button,** *sgrog-ril sgróg-pa* to button up.

སྒྲོག་པ་ *sgróg-pa*, pf. *bsgrags*, fut. *bsgrag*, imp. *sgrags(s)*, **to call, call out,** call to *Dzl.* and elsewh.: **to publish, proclaim, promulgate,** *γtam-snyán* good news *Mil.*; *ši-bai γtam bsgrágs-na* if his death becomes known, *Tar.*: *čos sgróg-pa*, resp. *čós-kyi sgrog-gléṅ mdzád-pa Glr.* **to preach;** *dril-sgrog-pa* to publish by ringing a bell, to publish, proclaim; *sgróg-pa-po* a proclaimer, a preacher *Cs.* — 2. **to shout, to scream,** *ṅú-skad drág-por sgrog* (the infant) weeps and screams *Lt.* — 3. *C.* (in *W.* only resp.) **to read,** *γsuṅ sgróg-pa* to read words of Buddha *Ma.*; even: *séms-kyis sgróg-pa* to read silently. — 4. **to bind,** like *ₒgrógs-pa*; v. also *sgrog* extr.

སྒྲོད་པ་ *sgród-pa*, another form of *ₒgród-pa* to go; not much used.

སྒྲོན་མ་ *sgrón-ma* **a lamp, lantern, torch,** *sgron-mé* a burning lamp, (prop. a lamp-fire); often fig. — *sgroṅ-pa* vb. **to light, to kindle,** *dpé-ča-la me sgrón-nas* lighting (burning) the book *Pth.* — *sgron-bskál* the enlightened age *Cs.*, opp. to *mun-bskál* the dark age. — *sgron-drégs* **lamp-black.** — *sgron-(me-) šiṅ Sch.* the yew-leaved fir, Pinus picea, which tree, however, is scarcely known in Tibet; in *Sik.* it denotes Pinus longifolia, and prob. also in every other province, the most resinous species of coniferous trees prevailing there.

སྒྲོན་པ་ *sgrón-pa*, pf. and fut. *bsgron* 1. **to cover, to lay over, adorn, decorate** *Glr.* — 2. **to light, to kindle,** v. *sgrón-ma.*

སྒྲོབ་ *sgrob* **haughtiness, arrogance, pride,** *Lexx.*

སྒྲོམ་ *sgrom* **box, chest, trunk, coffer** = *sgam*; *sgróm-bu* a small box or chest: *smyug-sgróm Cs.* = *γzéb-ma* a chest or trunk made of bamboo; *ro-sgróm, rús-pai sgrom Zam.* **coffin.**

སྒྲོལ་བ་ *sgról-ba*, pf. and fut. *bsgral* 1. **to rescue, deliver, save,** *las* from, out of, *sgról-bai ded-dpón-du ₒgyur* he becomes a guide to salvation *Glr.* — 2. **to lead,**

**transport, carry, to cross** (a river) by boat or ferry, *ču-bsgrál Lex.:* तीर्ण passed over; *čú-boi ṕá-rol-tu bsgrál-bar mdzód-čig* have the goodness to take me over to the other bank *Sambh.*; *ₒḱór-ba bsgrál-bai gru-γziṅs yin Glr.* it is a boat that carries over the river of transmigration. — 3. **to remove,** do away with, drive away, *ₒdré-rnams ṕyii rgyá-mtso čén-po-la bsgrál Glr.* the demons were driven to the uttermost parts of the sea; *bdud sgról-ba* to expel the devil; *sdig-čan rgyál-po sgról-bar ₒgyur* the guilty king will be removed out of the way! *Glr.*; *dgra-bgegs bsgral-bai ša ḱrag rus-pa daṅ naṅ-rol glo snyiṅ bčás-pa mčod-par ₒbul* the flesh, blood, bones, heart, lungs and entrails of slaughtered enemies of the faith are offered by us as a sacrifice. This saying, the tendency of which is often justified by the sophism, that it is an act of mercy to kill an enemy of the faith and thus prevent him from accumulating more sin, shows that even 'mild Buddhism' is not incapable of bloody fanaticism, and instances like that of king Laṅ-dar-ma of old, and of the recent martyrdom of Roman Catholic christians at Bonga confirm this fact from experience.

སྒྲོལ་མ་ *sgról-ma*, sometimes also *sgrol-yúm Cs., W.* **ról-ma**, 1. n. of two goddesses, *Ssk.* तारा, known in the history of Tibet as the white and green Tara, incarnated in the two wives of Srongtsangámpo, *Schl.* 66 and 84; *Köpp.* II., 65. — 2. a name of females, of frequent occurrence.

སྒྲོས་ *sgros* 1. *Cs.* **manner, method, way,** *bšád-sgros* way of explaining, instructing, informing: *sgrogs bšád-sgros Sch.:* 'the method of instruction which is to be proclaimed' (?); *γtám-sgros Cs.:* 'way or manner of speaking' (?). — 2. *Cs.* **edge, brim, lip;** *Sch.* also mark from a wound, **scar;** *žál-gyi mču-sgrós* seems to signify only 'lip'.

བརྒད་པ་ *brgád-pa* = *bgád-pa* to smile, to smile on *Stg.*

བརྒལ་ *brgal* 1. v. *rgál-ba*, 2. v. *rgól-ba.*

བརྒོལ་བ་ *brgól-ba Sch.* 'das Gegenseitige', mutual relation, contrast, contrary?

བརྒྱ་(ཐམ་པ་) *brgya* (*ťám-pa*) **a hundred,** one hundred; *brgya-ṕrág* the hundred, a century; *brgya-ṕrág bču* 1000; *brgyá-pa* the hundredth; *brgyá-po* consisting of one hundred (cf. under *dgu*); *brgya daṅ bču-bži* 114; *brgya-nyi-šu* 120; *bži-brgya* (*daṅ*) *go-brgyád* 498; *brgyá-rtsa* v. *rtsa; brgyá-la* (*Cs.: brgya-ma-lan-γčig*, or *brgyá-lam-na?*) once among a hundred (cases or times) i.e. very rarely, e.g. (*dus*) *brgyá-la brnyed kyaṅ* though it be found for once at last *Mil.* frq., cf. *Schf.* Erläut. zu *Dzangl.* p. 45; also = finally, in short, the Latin *denique, Mil. nt.*; *brgyá-čan* erron. for *rgyá-čan.* — *brgya-mčód* a hecatomb of 100 lamps, offered on certain festival occasions *Sik.* — *brgyá-ₒdaṅs* about or nearly a hundred *Sch.* — *brgyá-dpon* a captain of a hundred men, the Latin centurio. — *brgya-byin* (शतक्रतु) '(honoured by) a hundred sacrifices', epithet of Indra, cf. ἑκατόμβαιος) 1. Indra. 2. n. of a medicine *Wdṅ.*

བརྒྱ་ *brgya?* 1. in *smrá-bai brgya Sch.:* noisy conversation; *Lexx.* simply आलाप speech, conversation (with the remark that the word is obs. and prov.). — 2. often erron for *rgya.*

བརྒྱང་བ་ *brgyáṅ-ba* 1. v. *rgyoṅ-ba* 2. **to call** to a person from a distance, *C.*

བརྒྱད་ *brgyad* **eight**; *brgyád-pa* the eighth, *brgyad-po* consisting of eight, *brgyád-ču* eighty, *brgyad-ču-rtsa-γčig* (*W.* **gyad-ču-gya-čig**), *gya-γčig* 81; *brgyad-brgyá* 800; *brgyad-stóṅ* 8000; *brgyad-ḱri* 80 000.

བརྒྱད་(བ)ཀག་ *brgyad-(b)kág* **a reproach, rebuke,** *brgyad-kág byéd-pa* to rebuke, to chide *Dzl.*

བརྒྱན་པ་ *brgyán-pa*, vb. **to adorn, decorate; to provide with** (c. instrum.), cf. *rgyan* sbst.; *nya mgo sá-yis brgyán-pa* the letter *nya* (ཉ) being provided with an *s* above it, = *sny..*, *Zam.*

བརྒྱལ་བ་ *brgyal-ba* 1. **to sink down** senseless, **to faint;** **brgyál-te dád-če**

*W.* to lie in winter-sleep; *˳o-brgyál-te* very much exhausted, v. *˳o.* — 2. **to howl**, of the fox. *Sch.*

བརྒྱུངས་པ་ *brgyúṅs-pa Lex.*; *Cs.*: **'the marrow in the back-bone'.**

ག

བརྒྱུད་ *brgyud*, cf. *rgyud*, *Ssk.* परम्पर **family** (*gens*), **lineage; relations, ancestors, descendants, offspring**, *mi-brgyúd* 1. = *brgyud, dei mi-brgyúd yin-pa* being of his family *Glr.* 2. people, nation, *bód-kyi mi-brgyúd* the Tibetan nation. 3. the human race, mankind *Cs.*; *rigs-brgyúd*, resp. *γduṅ-brgyúd* family; issue, progeny, *rigs-brgyúd ˳pél-bar ˳gyur* there will be a numerous offspring; *bla-rgyúd* succession or descent of Lamas *Cs.* — **mig ná-če gyúd-la yod** *W.* diseases of the eye frequently occur in that family; **dé-ne̤ gyud mi čad yin** *W.* then the race will not die out; **spél-gyud-la bór-če** *W.* to set apart cattle for breeding; *brgyúd-nas brgyúd-du* from generation to generation *Cs.*; *bu ťsa brgyúd-du bdeo* he is blessed even to his children and children's children *Dzl.*

**Comp.** *brgyud-brgyúgs* a continuous succession *Sch.* — *brgyúd-čan* like his progenitors *Cs.* — *brgyúd-pa* 1. belonging to a race or family. 2. v. *rgyud* and *rgyúd-pa.* — *brgyud-méd* degenerate *Cs.*, cf. *brgyúd-čan.* — *brgyúd-ma* 1. *Cs.* = *brgyúd-čan.* 2. *W.* fruitful, fertile. 3. *brgyud-ma-brgyab Lex.* w.e. — *brgyud-˳dzín* a first-born male, heir and successor.

བརྒྲད་ *brgrad* is acknowledged by *Lexx.*, but evidently an incorrect form for *bgrad.*

བསྒ... *bsg*... words beginning thus will for the greater part be found under *sg*...

བསྒག་པ་ *bsgág-pa* v. *˳gégs-pa* and *sgóg-pa.*

བསྒང་ *bsgaṅ* (*Lexx.* = *dṅos-γži*, मूल?) **point of time, moment, instant, conjuncture,** *lo-γsar-bsgáṅ-gi lhágs-ma* a chilling gale on newyear's day *Mil.*; esp. **the proper time** or season for doing a thing, *byá-bai bsgaṅ; ˳bri-bai, zá-bai bsgaṅ* the time for writing, eating. (A different word from *sgaṅ*).

བསྒོ་བ་ *bsgó-ba* 1. v. *sgó-ba.* — 2. pf. *bsgos*, vb. a. to *˳gó-ba*, **to soil, stain, defile,** lit. and fig., **kyo̤n-ghyī ma gō** *C.* he was not tainted with any spot or blemish, nothing could be laid to his charge; **to infect** with disease; rarely in a good sense: *dri sna-ťsogs-ǩyis legs-par bsgos-pa Stg.* well **anointed** with salves and perfumes.

བསྒྲང་བ་ *bsgráṅ-ba* 1. **to enumerate, count up** (?) *Cs.* — 2. **to cause to grow cold** *Lexx.*

བསྒྲད་པ་ *bsgrád-pa Lexx.* = *bgrád-pa.*

# ང

ང་ *ṅa* 1. the letter *ṅ*, sounded as a nasal guttural, the English ng in singing, in the Tibetan language often the initial letter of a word. — 2. as numerical figure: 4. — 3. as numeral adjective = *lṅá-bču*, in the numbers 51—59.

ང་ *ṅa*, pers. pron., first person sing. and pl. **I, we,** the usual word in familiar speech; *ṅai* my, our; mine, ours; *ṅa mi rgan* old man that I am *Mil.*; *ṅa rgyál-po sroṅ-btsan-sgám-po daṅ* with me, king Srongtsangampo *Glr.*; *blá-ma ṅa* I, the Lama *Mil.*; *de mi rgan ṅai ǩá-la nyon* listen to my word as that of an old man *Mil.*; *ṅai ˳di* this my (doing) *Glr.*; *ṅai rje-btsún* my honoured masters! *Mil.*; *ṅai* *yid-ₒóṅ* my dearest! *Pth.; ṅa-ráṅ* I my self, esp. col. very frq.; **ṅa ráṅ-ka** *Ts.*, **ṅa tsog** *Ü, ṅa nyid, ṅa ḱó-na, ṅa bdag* (?), *ṅa-bo* (??) *Cs.* id.; *ṅa ráṅ-gi yaṅ* moreover, what concerns my own affairs *Mil.* Distinct expressions for the pl. **we** are: *ṅá-ĉag B.* and *C.*; **ṅá-ža** *W.*, **ṅá-ya** *Bal.*; in *W.* **ṅá-ža** seems to be used in an exclusive sense: I and my people, i.e. excluding you or the person or persons addressed, so that when Europeans use it in *Ld.* or *Lh.*, in addressing their hearers, meaning to include themselves (all of us, we and you), they are generally misunderstood; **ṅa daṅ** 'he or those with me', is said to be used in a similar manner; **ṅa daṅ nyis** both of us; *ṅa-rnams* we *Cs.* Synonyms are: *ṅed, ṅos, bdag,* **ḱo-bo**; and *ṅaṅ, ṅo, dṅo, dṅos, ṅogs* may prob. bederived from the same root.

ང་རྒྱལ་ *ṅa-rgyál* ('I the first') **pride, arrogance,** frq.; *ṅa-rgyál skyéd-pa* to be proud *Dzl.*; *γĉog-pa* to break (another's pride), to humble, humiliate *Mil.*; *ṅa-rgyál-ĉan* proud; *W.* also naughty, of children.

ང་ངུར་ *ṅa-ṅúr* a species of **duck,** v. *ṅúr-ba*; perh. Anas casarca.

ང་བ་ *ṅá-ba*, rarely for *ṅán-pa*; *dri ṅá-ba* stench *Stg.*; cf. *nyám-ṅa-ba, yá-ṅa-ba.*

ང་ར་ *ṅá-ra* (cf. *ṅad*) **air,** *ṅa gáṅs-kyi ṅá-ras mi ǰigs* I am not afraid of the air of glaciers *Mil.*; **ṅá-ra ḍáṅ-mo rag, ǰám-po rag** *W.* I perceive the air to be cold, to be mild; esp. cold air, *ṅá-ra-ĉan* fresh, cold.

ང་རོ་ *ṅá-ro* **a loud voice, a cry,** *kye-húd-kyi ṅá-ro ₒbód-pa* to raise woeful cries *Pth.*; *skád-kyi ṅá-ro ĉĕn-pos bsgrágs-so* they proclaimed, shouting at the top of their voices *Pth.*; *séṅ-gei ṅá-ro* the loud voice, the roaring, of a lion *Mil.*; *γdúg-pai ṅá-ro* prob. voices foreboding mischief *Mil.*; **the roar, roaring, rushing,** of waves etc.; *ṅá-ro sgróg-pa* to roar, to rage; in a relative sense: *skád-kyi ṅá-ro drag-žán* a loud and a low sound, the different force or effort required in producing it *Gram.*; *ṅá-ro-ĉan* loud, noisy, roaring; a crier, bawler, noisy fellow.

ངག་ *ṅag*, sometimes *dṅags*, resp. *γsuṅ*, **speech, talk, word,** *ṅág-gi nyés-pa* sins committed with the tongue, in words, (*rdzun, ṕrá-ma, ťsig-rtsúb,* prob. also *kyál-ka*); *ṅag-gi lhá-mo* the goddess of speech, of eloquence, Sarasvati; *ṅág-gi dbaṅ-ṕyúg* = *ₒǰam-dbyáṅs* Manjusri; *ṅag ₒǰám-po* kind, polite speech or words; *ṅag-ₒǰám smra-mḱás* of a soft tone in speaking and prudent in words *Glr.*; *smán-pai ṅag bžin-du byed-pa* to obey the words of the physician; *ṅag sdóm-pa, ṅag bĉád-pa* silence, as a monastic duty or religious exercise, resp. *γsuṅ-bĉád Mil.*; *γžan-gyi ṅag γĉóg-pas* not doing according to another's word, not obeying him *Tar.*, frq.; *ṅag mnyán-pa* to be obedient *Dzl.*

**Comp.** *ṅag-kyál*, or *-ₒḱyal* = *kyál-ka.* — *ṅag-ₒgrós, smrá-bai ṅag-grós* 'a manner of speaking or uttering words' *Cs.* — *ṅag-rgyún* tradition, not recorded history, *Cs.* — *ṅag-snyán, snyan-ṅág, snyan-dṅágs* 1. **poetical expression, figure, metaphor.** 2. **poem,** piece of poetry *Glr.* — *ṅag-dbáṅ* 1. **eloquent.** 2. p. n., e. g. *ṅag-dbáṅ blo-bzáṅ rgyá-mťso* Dalai Lama, born 1615. — *ṅag-sbyór* arrangement of speech *Cs.* — *ṅag-ťsig* = *ṅag.* — *ṅag-lám žú-ba* to apply to a person by word of mouth, resp.

ངང་ *ṅaṅ* (not in the earlier literature) 1. **the nature, essentiality, idiocrasy** of a person, the peculiarity of a thing, *saṅs-rgyás-kyi ṅaṅ yin* he is (partaking) of the nature of Buddha, Buddha-like (corresponding to our 'divine', which consequently might be expressed by *dkon-mĉóg-gi ṅaṅ*) *Mil.*; *stóṅ-pai ṅaṅ-nyid* the essentiality of the vacuum itself *Glr.*; frq. used only paraphrastically or pleonastically: *tiṅ-ṅe-dzin-gyi ṅáṅ-la žúgs-pa* to enter into meditation *Mil.*; *ťugs-mnyés bžin-pai ṅáṅ-la* in a cheerful mood *Mil.*; *ĉágs-med-kyi ṅáṅ-la γnás-par gyis* continue in that passionless state of mind *Thgr.*; *ₒǰigs-skrág-gi ṅáṅ-nas ₒĉi-ba* to die of fear or anxiety; *ṅáṅ-nas* in general is used nearly like *sgó-nas Mil.* frq.; **character, disposition,** *ṅáṅ-bzáṅ, ṅaṅ-ṅán Sch.*; *ṅaṅ-ťsúl,* and esp.

*ṅaṅ-rgyúd* id., *ṅaṅ-rgyúd bzáṅ-po Wdṅ., dgé-ba Glr.*, a naturally good, virtuous character; very frq.: *ṅaṅ-rgyúd riṅ-ba* forbearing, longsuffering, not easily put into a passion *Glr.*; not easily excited to action, **phlegmatic,** cool, also **ṅaṅ riṅ-wa* C.*; even *ṅaṅ* alone may have this meaning: *ṅaṅ ma tuṅ* don't lose your patience *Mil. nt.*; *ṅáṅ-gis adv.* not only signifies spontaneously, of one's own accord, but also **slowly, gradually, gently** *Mil.* (so already *Schr.*) — 2. **dominion, sphere, province,** parallel to *kloṅ* and *dbyiṅs Mil.; *ṅa ma-ši-kai ṅáṅ-la dug** I belong to the kingdom of Christ, said one of our Christians, in order to show the meaning of **ṅaṅ**. Hence it might be used for expressing the ἐν of the N. T. (I John 5, 6 and many other passages) denoting a pertaining to, belonging to, being connected with. *ṅáṅ-la ₒjóg-pa (bžág-pa) Mil.* and *C.* is an expression not explained as yet.

ངང་པ་ *ṅáṅ-pa* 1. **goose,** more accurately *ṅáṅ-pa* a gander, *ṅáṅ-ma* a goose *Cs.* The domestic goose and the breeding of it is not yet known in Tibet, at least not in *W.* — 2. **a light-bay horse,** an isabel-coloured horse *Ld.-Glr.*

ངད་ *ṅad* 1. cog. to *ṅá-ra*, **air,** **ṅád-la skám-če* W.* to dry in the air; in a general sense the air in its chemical qualities, in its influence on the senses: **scent, fragrance,** *spós-kyi ṅad ldáṅ-ba* the rising of an aromatic breeze; *ṅad yal* the fragrancy, the aroma evaporates; **vapour,** *ḱá-ṅad, čú-ṅad* snowy vapour, aqueous vapour; **aromati csubstance,** *sṅó-ṅad* aromatic vegetables, such as onions *Med.;* **cold air, the cold, coldness,** v. *ṅad-čan.* — 2. *W.* (cf. *ṅár-ba, ṅár-ma*) **severity, roughness,** **ṅe ṅad ǰigs dug** he fears I might address him harshly; *ṅád-čan* 1. fragrant, fresh, cool, *W.* cold. 2. *W.* rough, impetuous.

ངན་ *ṅan* 1. **evil, mischief, misfortune,** *ṅan čén-po byas* it has done great mischief *Glr.;* esp. harm done by sorcery and witchcraft *Mil.*; *ṅan-dgú* every possible evil *Lt.* — 2. **curse, imprecation,** *ṅan ₒdébs-pa, W. *táb-če**, to curse, to execrate; *mťu ṅan ₒdébs-pa* to curse by means of witchcraft. Cf. *mṅan.*

ངན་པ་ *ṅán-pa*, col. also **ṅán-po**, **bad,** of food etc.; **mean, miserable** *Dzl.;* **poor, humble, low,** (prop. *rigs-ṅán*), *ṅan-lóṅ* poor and blind (people) *Glr.*; *lo ṅán-pa* a year yielding no crops, an unfruitful or bad year; of men, actions etc.: **wicked,** *ṅán-pa ḱyod γnyis* ye two villains! *Glr.*; **noisome, pernicious,** *γsol-ṅán* pernicious food, i.e. poison, resp., *Glr.; . . . la ṅán-du rǰód-pa* to revile, blaspheme; *mi-la mig ṅán ltá-ba* to look with an evil or envious eye upon a person *Glr.; ráṅ-rnams spyod ṅan byás-nas dus ṅan zer* acting badly themselves they speak of bad times *Ma.* — *ṅan-ₒgro, ṅan-soṅ* v. *ₒgro-ba* I. extr. — *ṅan-ṅón Cs.* mean, pitiful, very bad. — *ṅan-ṅón tsám-gyis čog šés-pa* prob.: to be satisfied with any thing, and be it ever so poor. — *ṅan-ne-ba* bad. — **ṅan-ṗe* W.* meal of parched barley, roasted meal. — *ṅán-so* 'bad place', hell; cf. *ṅán-ₒgro* under *ₒgró-ba* I. extr.

ངན་བུ་ *ṅán-bu C.*, **we,** eleg., = *bdag,* when speaking humbly of one's self.

ངམ་གྲོག་ *ṅam-gróg, Cs.* 'torrent', *Sch.* 'ditch filled with water, water-ditch; the bank of a river grown high and steep by having been gradually washed out by the current'; (only this latter sense of the word was authenticated to me). In *Glr.* Tibet is poetically called '*ṅam-grog-čė*', which is a very appropriate name when rendered: having large and deep erosions.

ངམ་དུར་ཅན་ *ṅám dur-čan* given to gluttony and drinking *Stg.*

ངམ་རུ་ *ṅam-ru* n. of a disease *Med.*

ངམ་ཤུགས་ *ṅam-šúgs* **reluctantly.**

ངར་ *ṅar* 1. **fore-** or **front-side, forepart,** *ṅar-γdóṅ* id.; esp. of the leg, the shin-bone, also knuckle ni f.; *lag-ṅár, rkaṅ-ṅár* fore-arm, lower part of the leg; *rǰe-ṅar* seems to be an appellation for both, (in *W.* **nyar** instead of it). — 2 v. *ṅár-ba* 1. —

3. termin. of *ṅa*, 'to one's self', *ṅar-*ₒ*dzin* = *bdag-*ₒ*dzin*, selfishness, self-interest. *Mil.* — 4. *ṅar* ₒ*dón-pa* to set on or against, **to instigate**, *nyams-kyi ṅar* ₒ*dón-pa* irritations of the mind, excitements *Mil.*; *nyam-ṅár Lex.* id. (?) — 5. v. *ṅar-ṅár-po.*

ངར་སྐད་ *ṅar-skád* **the roaring,** of lions etc., ₒ*dón-pa*, *sgróg-pa Mil.*; *W.* **táṅ-ce** also to call to, to shout at.

ངར་ངར་པོ་ *ṅar-ṅár-po* **hoarse, husky, wheezing,** e.g. in old age *Thgy.*; *ṅar-ṅár* ₒ*k'ún-sgra* a hoarse groaning *Pth.*; *ṅar-glúd* hoarseness and phlegm *Med.*; *gré-ba ṅar-ba* a hoarse throat *Med.*

ངར་ཅན་ *ṅár-can* v. *ṅár-ba.*

ངར་སྣབས་ *ṅar-snábs* **mucus, snivel,** (affords food to certain demons).

ངར་པ་ *ṅár-pa* **stalk** of plants *Med.*

ངར་པོ་ *ṅár-po W.* **strong, ferocious,** of the tiger etc.

ངར་བ་ *ṅár-ba* 1. **strength, force; hardness,** of steel; cold, frost, cold wind *Mil.* (cf. *ṅá-ra*, *ṅad*); *ṅar γtoṅ-ba*, *W.* **táṅ-ce*, *ċúg-ce**, *Sch.* also *ldúd-pa*, to steel, to temper. — *ṅár-ċan* 1. strong, vigorous 2. tempered; *ṅár-ldan* id.; *sems ṅár-ldan* a strong mind *Mil.*; *ṅar-méd* weak, soft. — 2. (v. *ṅar* 1.) a sort of flap (of breeches).

ངར་མ་ *ṅárma* 1. **irritable, passionate, impetuous** *Sch.* — 2. **strong, powerful,** e.g. a powerful protection, *Mil.*

ངལ་བ་ *ṅál-ba* **to be fatigued, tired, wearied; fatigue, weariness,** resp. *sku ṅál-ba*, or *t'ugs ṅál-ba*, also *mnyél-ba*; *ṅal soṅ* I am tired; *spóbs-pa ṅal* the strength decreases *Med.*; *ṅál-čad-pa*, *ṅál-dub-pa* intensive forms of *ṅal*; *ṅal* ₒ*ǰúg-pa* vb. a. **to tire, fatigue, weary;** *ṅal γsó-ba* 'to cure weariness', **to rest,** frq.; *ṅal-stégs* a rest, a sort of crutch or fork, which coolies sometimes carry with them, to support their load, whilst taking a momentary rest in standing: also any bench or seat inviting to repose. To provide such conveniences for wayfaring men is considered a meritorious act.

ངས་ *ṅas* 1. instr. of *ṅa*. — 2. *mi-ṅas Tar.* 37, 16. is undoubtedly a typographical error, instead of *mi-nad*. *Schf.* has left it without an annotation.

ངི་ *ṅi* num. fig.: 34.

ངུ་ *ṅu* num. fig.: 64.

ངུ་བ་ *ṅu-ba*, pf. *ṅus*, resp. *šúm-pa*, 1. **to weep,** 2. *W.* also **to roar,** used of swelling rivers, not of the wind; *Schr.*: 'to groan like a turtle-dove'; **ṅu ma ṅu** *W.* do not weep! *ṅús-pai mči-ma* tears that have been shed *Dzl.*; *ga-čád ṅús-pa* weeping without a cause, hysterical weeping *Med.*; *ṅú-ru* ₒ*ǰúg-pa* to cause to weep *Lt.*; **ṅú-ma-god** *W.* weeping and laughing at the same time; *šes ṅús-so* thus he said weeping *Glr.*; **ṇu ḍhó-wa** (lit. *gro-ba*) *C.* to be sorrowful, sad. — *ṅú(-ba)-po Cs.*, *ṅú-mk'an* col. one weeping, a weeper. — *ṅú-šur-ċan Sch.*, *ṅú-mk'an* col. a child that is continually crying. — *ṅu-*ₒ*bód*, *ṅu-rdzi*, *W.* **ṅu-zi**, sbst. a crying, howling, lamenting.

ངུ་རུ་ *ṅú-ru W.* for *ṅúr-ba* 1.

ངུག་པ་ *ṅúg-pa Ts.* = *ṅúr-ba* 2, **to grunt; to snore; to pur** (of cats).

ངུད་མོ་ *ṅúd-mo* **a sob** *Cs.*, *Schr.*

ངུར་བ་ *ṅúr-ba* 1. sbst. **duck,** esp. the red wild duck, चक्रवाक Anas casarca; *ṅúr-ka* as red as fire, fiery red; *ṅur-smrig* yellowish red, **saffron colour,** the original colour of the monks' habit, though not the common high-red of the Brug-pa monks in *Sik.* and in *W.* — 2. vb. **to grunt,** of pigs and yaks.

ངུས་ *ṅus* v. *ṅu-ba.*

ངེ་ *ṅe* num. fig.: 94.

ངེད་ *ṅed* pers. person. first person, eleg. for *ṅa*, **I, we;** *ṅéd-kyi* my, our; *ṅed γnyis(-ka)* we two; *ṅed γsum(-po)* we three; *ṅed spun γsum* we three brothers *Glr.*; *ṅéd-kyi bu-dód mdzod* have the goodness to become our foster-son *Mil.*; sometimes *ṅa* and *ṅed* are used promiscuously in the same sentence, so: *ṅas* I, and directly after: *ṅéd-kyi* our *Mil.* The plural number is specially indicated in: *ṅéd-cag*, *ṅéd-tso*, *ṅéd-rnams*, *ṅéd-dag Mil.*; *ṅéd-čag-rnams Cs.* — *ṅed-rán* 1. I myself, we ourselves. 2. I, we *Glr.*; *ṅed-nyid*, *ṅed-ḱó-na Cs.* id. (*Ld.* **ṅad**).

ངེའུ་ཅག *ṅeu-čag Dzl.* ༢༥༢, 11.15. is prob. an incor. reading in *Sch.'s* edition, instead of *ˬu-bu-čag.*

ངེས་པ *ṅés-pa* 1. adj. **certain, true, sure, firm,** *bdág-la ṅés-pa žig stsál-du ɣsol* I ask you to communicate to me something certain, i.e. authentic news; *ṅés-par byéd-pa* to fix, settle, establish, ascertain, e.g. facts of chronology, v. *Wdk.* chronological table in *Cs.'s* Grammar; to ratify *Schr.*; *ˬči-bar ṅés-pa yin* or *ṅés-so* death is certain; *de bdén-par ṅés-sam* is it certain that this is true? *Glr.*; *mi btúb-tu ṅés-na* as it is certain that I am not able (to do it) *Dzl.*; *nam ˬḱyer ṅés-pa med* it is not certain at what time they will be carried off *Glr.*; *bdag ḱyód-kyi bu yin ṅés-na* if I am actually, for certain, your son *Pth.*; *p̔an ṅés-pai čos* that religion which is sure to lead to salvation *Mil.*; *ṅés-pai dón-las gol* he is missing the true sense *Pth.*; *ma-ṅés-pa* untrue *Tar.* 109, 17; *ɣnás-la ṅés-pa méd-pa yin* as to abode I am changeable, I have no fixed abode *Mil.*; also *ṅes-méd* alone: **homeless** *Mil.*; **undefined**, *ṅes-méd-kyi rí-la* somewhere on the mountains *Mil.*; sometimes it is but a rhetorical turn, like the English **evidently, obviously,** *bú-la bkra-mi-šis ṅés-kyis*, as our son has evidently met with an accident *Dzl.*; *bud-méd yin-du ṅés-so* they are evidently women, they do not deserve to be called men *Dzl.*; also sbst. **certainty, surety, truth**; *ṫsé-la, ṅág-la, lús-la ṅés-pa med* (man's) life-time, word, body have no certainty, are transient *Glr.* Hence *ṅés-pa-čan* **real, actual,** *ṅés-pa-čan-du* really, truly, in fact, in reality, opp. to deceitful appearances, false opinions, wrong calculations etc. *Glr.*; *ṅes-pa-nyid-du* adv. 1. in reality *Glr.* 2. truly, in truth, verily *Glr.*; *ṅés-par* adv. 1. really, certainly, to be sure, frq.; *sdig-pa byás-na rnam-par-smín-pa ṅés-par myóṅ-ste* as retribution for a sin committed is sure to take place, will certainly follow *Dzl.*; *dé-ɖra-ba žig ṅés-par yód-na* if such a one is really present *Dzl.*; *ṅés-par čí-ba* the certain dying, the certainty of death *Thgy.*; *bdag ṅés-par byao* I will surely do it *Dzl.* 2. **by all means,** to add force to the imperative mood *Tar.* 16, 11. — 2. often it is used subjectively, esp. in *C.*, when *séms-la* is to be supplied, so that it may be rendered by **to know:** *bdén-par ṅes*, *rdzún-par ṅes* I know (I am certain) that it is true, untrue; *ṅés-pa čer med* I am not quite sure, I do not know for certain, I do not fully understand, I do not clearly see through it *Mil.*; *séms-čan ˬdi bdág-gi p̔a-má yin ṅés-na*, if we take it for granted, if we try to realize the fact, that this being is our father or mother *Thgy.*; to remember, to bear in mind **sém-la ṅē ṫúb-bam** *C.* shall you be able to remember that? *ṅés-dón*, also *yáṅ-dag-doṅ*, is said to mean immediate knowledge of the truth, which may be obtained mystically by continued contemplation, and is opp. to *dráṅ-don*, knowledge obtainable through the medium of the sacred writings *Mil.*, also *Lexx.*; *ṅes (-par) ˬbyuṅ-(ba) Mil.* frq., *Schr.*: 'deliverance from the round of transmigration', *Sch.*: 'to appear, to prove true'; another explanation still: 'knowledge of one's self' is not borne out by etymology. — *ṅes-bzúṅ* acc. to *Lexx.* a synonym of *bráṅ-pa*, q. v. — *ṅes-(par) légs(-pa) Thgy.*, 'that which evidently is the best', is said to denote deliverance from the round of transmigration.

ངོ *ṅo* num. fig: 124.

ངོ་ *ṅo* 1. resp. *žal-ṅó* (cf. *ṅó-bo*, *ṅor*, *ṅos*) **face, countenance, air, look,** as the expression of a man's personality and mind (*ṅo mdzés-pa Cs.*, and *ṅán-pa Schr.* are dubious), *bdág-gi ṅó-la ɣzigs-nas* when she (my mother) shall see my face, *ṅod kár-po* a cheerful face; *ṅo nág-par ˬdug-pa* to sit with a sad and gloomy face *Glr.*; *ṅo nág-par ˳gyúr-ba* to grow sorrowful, to turn pale with fright, pain etc.; *ṅo bab* courage fails(me); *ṅo srúṅ-ba* frq. 'to watch the countenance', to pay much or even too much regard to other people's opinions; *ṅo ḍzín-pa Mil.* seems to signify the same, and *ṅo čógs-pa* the contrary: not to comply with a person's wishes *Mil.*; *ṅo spród-pa* to lay open the features, to show the nature of a thing, to explain; *ṅo ˳ṗród-pa* to understand, to learn, in later literature frq.; *ṅo šés-pa* to know *ccap: ṅa ṅo kyód-kyis ma šés-na* if thou dost not know me *Mil.*; with termin. inf.: to know (that something happens); to find out, e.g. by calculation; to perceive; *ṅo mi šés-pa* 1. not to know 2. unacquaintance, ignorance 3. unknown: *ṅó-mi-šes-pa-la ldáṅ-ba* to rise before a stranger; *ṅó-mi-šes-pai yul* an unknown country *Thgy.; ṅo ltá-ba Glr.* is said to signify: to submit (vb. n.); **ṅo lén-če* W.* to beg pardon, cf. *ṅos bláṅ-ba*; *ṅo ldóg-pa* or *lóg-pa* to turn away, always fig. = to desert, *˳ḱór-bai yul ṅo lóg-na* if you will desert, get rid of, the land of transmigration; more frq.: *ṅo-lóg byéd-pa* to revolt, rebel, *rtsóm-pa* to bring about a revolt, *ṅo-lóg-mḱan* mutineer, agitator, *ṅo-lóg-čan* seditious, faithless, *ṅo zlóg-pa ccg.* to oppose, resist, not comply with a person's wish *Dzl.* — 2. **side,** like *ṅos*, esp. *W.*: **'a ṅó-la soṅ** he has gone to that side, in that direction; **sám-pa 'a ṅo 'i ṅó-a soṅ** he is absent, inattentive. — 3. **self, the thing itself**, cf. *ṅó-bo* and *ṅos;* v. *˳jál-ba*; also sbst. **the self, the I,** *ṅo-tsáb* the representative of the I; cf. also *ṅo-čén.* — 4. **likelihood, prospect of,** c. genit. inf. or root, *˳kyér-bai ṅo* a probability of its being taken away; *bu čig ˳byuṅ ṅo če* a great chance of (getting) a son. — 5. (also *ṅos*) a. **the waxing** and **waning moon,** with regard to shape; one half of the lunar month with regard to time, *yar-ṅo* the former, *mar-ṅo* the latter half; *yár-ṅo zla ltar* like the crescent moon. b. in a special sense the **increasing moon,** or the first half of the month; thus vulgo; so also in *B.: zlá-ba dgu ṅo bču lón-pa-na Glr., ṅo bčú-nas, zlá-ba ṅo bčú-na Pth.* in the first half of the tenth month (to denote the duration of pregnancy).

**Comp. and deriv.** *ṅo dkar* v. above 1. — *ṅo-lkog* prop. adj.: **public** and **private, open** and **secret,** but it is generally used as a synonym of *zol* or *rdzun*, **fraud, imposture, deceit, eye-service.** It may be explained by its contrary: *ṅó-med lkóg-med* acting in the same manner in public as in private life, the open and the secret conduct being alike *Mil.* (cf. *ṅos*). — *ṅó-čan* natural (?) *Cs.* — *ṅo-čén* ('the greater self'), a man of influence interceding for another person, **an intercessor;** *ṅo-čén byéd-pa* to intercede *Glr.*; *mi-la ṅo-čén ˳čól-ba* to use a person as negotiator, to make inquiries through him *Glr.* (*Sch.* incorr.) — *ṅo-rtóg W.* 1. (like *ṅés-pa* of *B.*) **certain,** e.g. **ṅo-tóg šé-če** to know for certain. 2. (like *dṅos, yaṅ-dag-pa*) **real, actual; true, genuine,** **˳ṫul yin-na ṅo-tóg yin** is it counterfeit or genuine? illusion or reality? **ṅo-tóg sád-ḱan** the actual murderer, he who really occasioned the death. — **ṅó-stod-ḱan W.* he who praises another to his face, **a flatterer.** — *ṅo-nág* v. above 1. — *ṅó-bo-nyid*, **entity,** *ṅo-bo-nyid-méd-pa* non-entity *Tar.* 90,2.; **essence, nature, substance,** e.g. *séms-kyi Mil.;* **character** *Was.* (278. 294); **marrow, main substance, quintessence** (= *snyiṅ-po*) *Glr.* and elsewh.; *ráṅ-gi ṅó-bos* in itself, according to its intrinsic nature *Mil.;* also col. **ṅó-bo ḱo-ráṅ* C.* the thing itself, opp. to a surrogate; *ṅó-bo ɣčig rtógs-pa ɣnyis Was.:* 'one quality, two (different) ideas' (*Schl.* has *ldóg-pa* instead of *rtóg-pa*). — *ṅo-˳báb-pa* adj. **discouraged, timorous, bashful** *W.* — *ṅó-ma* acc. to *Cs.* = *ṅo.* — *ṅó-ma-ɣyog C.:* master and servant. — *ṅó-mig W.* **boldness;** **ṅó-mig-čan**, or **čén-po** bold, daring, courageous; **ṅó-mig čuṅ-se** shy, timid, faint-hearted *W.* — *ṅó-tsa* ('heat of the face') 1. the act of **blushing, shame,** *ṅó-tsai ɣnas* shameful things *Sch., Schr.; ṅó-tsa-čan,*

ང

*ṅó-tsa-śes-pa* shamefaced, chaste, ashamed: *ṅó-tsa-med-pa, mi-śes-pa* shameless, barefaced, impudent; **ṅa ṅó-tsa rag** I am ashamed, **ko ṅó-tsa dug, ṅó-tsa-čan dug** *W.* he is ashamed; *ṅó-tsa byéd-pa* to be ashamed. 2. a shameful thing, *kyod ṅó-mi-tsa-la ṅó-tsar byed* you are ashamed where there is no occasion for it *Mil.*; *ṅó-tsa-ba* to be indecent, indecorous, unbecoming, *yúl-du lóg-na ṅó-tsa-la* as it would be a shame if we returned *Glr.*; *γčér-bur ̥gró-ba ṅó-tsa žin* as it would be indecorous to go naked *Pth.* — *ṅo-mtsár-ba* v. *mtsár-ba.* — *ṅó-ru, ṅor* 1. into the face *Sch.*, e.g. *skúd-pa* to smear; *rtsúb-pa* to say rude things to another's face *Thgy.*; *ṅo-rán-du* id. 2. in the face of, before the eyes, *γžán-gyi* of others. 3. by reason of, in consequence of, *des bskúl-bai ṅor* in consequence of a summons, of a request of him *Glr.* and elsewh. — *ṅo-śés* **an acquaintance, a friend** (the usual word in *W.*). — *ṅo-só* **joy,** *ṅo-só čé-bar ̥oṅ* you will have great joy, you will be delighted, highly satisfied; *sbyin-pa ṅo-só byéd-pa* to make presents to another to his full satisfaction *Mil.*, also *Tar.* 211, 2. — *ṅo-srúṅs* regard to the opinion of others, an aiming at applause *Mil.*

ངོགས་ *ṅogs* 1. **mountain-side, slope** (cf. *ṅos*); river-side, **bank, shore,** *rgyá-mtsoi Dzl.* — 2. **ford,** *ču-ṅógs* id. *C.*

ངོམ་པ་ *ṅóm-pa*, pf. *ṅoms*, 1. **to satisfy one's desire** by drinking, *krág-gis*, also *krág-las Dzl.*; *ma ṅoms* I am still thirsty; *ṅóm-par*, also *ṅoms-tsád, ̥túṅ-ba* to drink one's fill; also of sleeping, *nyid ma ṅom* I have not yet had my full share of sleep; fig.: *čós-kyi bdud-rtsis*, to fill one's self with the nectar of doctrine *Dzl.*; *bltá-bas mi ṅoms mdzés-pa* so beautiful, that one cannot gaze at it long enough, frq.; also *bltá-bas mi ṅoms bžin-du* not being able to look at it sufficiently *Pth.*; *ṅoms(-pa)-méd(-pa)* insatiable. — 2. **to show** with design (boastingly, or indecently, e.g. one's nakedness) *Glr.*, *Pth.* — 3. col. for *snóm-pa* to snuffle, to pry into, to spy.

ངོར་ *ṅor* 1. v. under *ṅo, Comp.* — 2. n. of a monastery of the Saskya, *Wdk.* chronological table in *Cs.*'s Gram.

ངོས་ *ṅos* 1. **side,** *mdún-ṅos* front-side, front of the body *Lt.*; of a pyramid, a mountain, *lhó-ṅos* southern side or slope of a mountain, **side, margin, edge,** of a pond etc.; *rgyáb ṅos γyás-na* on the right hand behind, *γyás ṅos mdún-na* on the right hand before *Glr.*; **surface, plain,** of the table; *sai ṅos* surface of the earth *Cs.*; hence *ṅós-su* (opp. to *lkog-tu*) *Mil.*, **ṅú-la** (opp. to *sbás-te* (**bé-te**) *W.* manifestly, notoriously, publicly, openly (cf. *ṅo*); **side, direction,** like *pyogs, W.* — 2. a thing itself (cf. *ṅo* 3), examples v. under *̥ǰál-ba.* — 3. pers. pron. first person **I, we;** esp. in *Ld.* in epistolary correspondence, eleg. — 4. instrum. of *ṅo,* = *ṅó-yis*; *ṅos dzín-pa Mil.* (*dṅos dzín-pa Thgy.*) vb. 1. to be selfish, self-interested, also adj. selfish, cf. *ṅos* 3. 2. more frq. to perceive, to know, to discern, also *ṅó-yis dzín-pa*; *ṅos zin-par gyis śig*, know it! be sensible of it! *Thgr.*; with the termin.: to acknowledge as, to take for, to look upon as *Tar.* 189, 1. In a special sense: diagnosis, discriminating a disease *Med.* **nóṅ-ṅo láṅ-wa** *C.* (lit. *γnoṅ ṅos blaṅ-ba*) = **ṅo lén-če** v. **ṅo** 1.

དངགས་སྙན་ *dṅags-snyán* v. *ṅag* (*Lex.* = काव्य).

དངང་བ་ *dṅáṅ-ba*, pf. *dṅaṅs* 1. **to be out of breath, to pant,** to feel oppressed e.g. when plunging into cold water *C.*, but esp. when frightened and terrified, hence 2. to be frightened, **to fear, to be afraid,** *sbrúl-gyis* of a snake; *čes dṅáṅs-nas* thus he spoke in dismay *Dzl.*; *dṅáṅ-par ̥gyúr-ro* you will (or would) be terrified *Dzl.*; *dṅaṅ-skrág, skrag-dṅáṅ* great fear, fright, terror; *dṅaṅ-skrág-pa* intensive form of *dṅáṅ-ba*, frq.

དངན་འཐེན་པ་ *dṅan-̥tén-pa Lex.* not to return things taken away from another.

དངར་ *dṅar* 1. for *mṅar*, **sweet** *Mil.* and elsewh. — 2. also *zil-dṅár Lex.* w.e.;

*Sch.*: order, succession(?); *ťsár-du dṅar Lex., Sch.* put in order, placed in array.

དངུད་མོ་ *dṅúd-mo* = *ṅúd-mo Sch.*

དངུལ་ *dṅul* (col. often **mul**) 1. **silver.** — 2. **money.** — 3. **a rupee.** — 4. **a tola** or Indian half ounce; *dṅúl-gyi ťóg-nas dṅul γsúm-ču ťob* he gets 30 rupees out of the ready money; *dṅúl-ka* a silver mine, a vein of silver; *dṅul-kúg, dṅul-sgyig* money-bag, purse; *dṅúl-ču* quicksilver, mercury; *dṅul-dúl-ma* refined silver *Sch.*; *dṅul-rmig*, lump, bar, ingot, of silver *Sch.*; **ṅul-záṅ(s)* W., C.*, silvered or plated copper.

དངོ་ *dṅo* 1. **shore, bank** *Lex.* — 2. **edge** of a knife *Cs.*; fig. *rta-lčág-gi dṅo* whip-cord, lash of a whip *C.* — 3. handle of a knife(??) *Cs.*

དངོམ་པ་ *dṅóm-pa, dṅom-brǰid*, **brightness, splendour;** *dṅóm-po, dṅóm-čan* shining, bright *Cs.*; *Lex. dṅom-čé* very bright. Cf. *rṅám-pa.*

དངོས་ *dṅos* 1. **reality, real,** *dṅos daṅ sgyú-ma* reality and illusion; *rgyál-bu dṅos* the real prince (opp. to a spurious one); **proper, true, genuine; positive** (opp. to negative) *Gram.*; **personal,** *dṅós-la yód-pa* to be personally present; *dṅós-su*, resp. *žal-dṅós-su* **bodily** e.g. to appear bodily; *ˏá-yig dṅós-su med kyaṅ*, even though the *ˏa* is not actually written there, *Gram.*; *dṅós-su grúb-pa méd-pa* to have no real existence *Thgy.* — 2. *Cs.*: pers. pron. **I,** cf. *ṅos*; *dṅos-ḍzin-pa* to be selfish *Thgy.*; *dṅos-ḍzín* **selfishness, selfinterest,** *dṅos-ḍzín γdón-gyis zin-pa* to be possessed by the demon of selfishness *Thgy.*; *dṅos-ḍzín-čan* selfish, self-interested. Thus it was explained by Lamas, though it cannot be denied that sometimes the version: belief in existence, a clinging to reality, a signification equally justifiable by etymology (v. below), would be more adequate to the context. — 3. *Tar.* 150, 14: thou, you; except in this passage I did not meet with the word in this sense, yet it may be used so, in the same manner as *nyid* q.v.

**Comp. and deriv.** *dṅos-grúb, Ssk. siddhi*, 1. **perfection, excellence,** any thing of superior value, e.g. honour, riches, talents, and esp. wisdom, higher knowledge, and spiritual power, as far as they are not acquired by ordinary study and exercise, but have sprung from within spontaneously, or in consequence of long continued contemplation. This *dṅos-grúb* is, as it were, the Buddhist caricature of the χαρίσματα of the N.T. (v. I. Cor. 12,4). — 2. name of male persons, col. **ṅo-rúb* W.* — *dṅos-ṅán* having little flesh, **ill-fed,** emaciated *Mil.* — *dṅós-čan* **material, real** *Cs.* — *dṅós-dad* true faith, opp. to *blún-dad* 'a fool's faith', superstition *Mil.* — *dṅos-sdig* prob.: real, or still effective sin, unatoned, unexpiated sin *Dzl.* ༧༡, 14; or less emphatically: sinful actions in general ༦༠, 15. — *dṅós-po, Ssk.* **भव, वस्तु, thing, natural body,** *ser dṅúl-la sógs-pai dṅós-po Glr.*; **matter, subject,** *dgá-bai dṅós-po* matter of rejoicing *Wdṅ.*; **goods, utensils,** *dge-slóṅ-gi* wearing-apparel of a Gelong; **occurrence, event, action,** *dṅós-po sgrúb-pa* to bring a thing about, to set it on foot or a going *Dzl.*; as a philosophical term: **substance, matter,** *Was.* (270. 294); *dṅós-por ḍzin-pa* the belief in the reality of existence *Mil.* — *dṅós-ma Cs.* **natural** (opp. to artificial), natural productions. — *dṅós-miṅ* 1. **the proper** or **real name** for a thing; so *Zam.* uses the paraphrase: *p̀o-mtsán-gyi dṅós-miṅ*, in order to avoid the plain expression *mǰe*, which is considered obscene. 2. **noun substantive,** *Chr. Prot.* a newly coined grammatical term. — *dṅos-med Lex.* = *Ssk. abhava, Cs.* **immaterial,** not existing, *Was.* (281): **not real.** — *dṅos-slób* a real, **a personal pupil** *Tar.* often. — *dṅos-γži* (*Lex.* = *Ssk. mūla*) the main part of a thing, **the thing itself,** e.g. the subject-matter of a treatise, the ceremony itself, opp. to *snóṅ-ˏgro* introduction, *sbyór-ba* preparation, and eventually also *rǰes* that which follows.

མངག་པ་ *mṅág-pa*, pf. *mṅags*, **to commission, charge, delegate, send** (a messenger, commissary etc.) *Dzl.*; also used of Buddha's sending a Bodhisatva on the earth to convert all mortals. — *mṅag-γžúg* **a servant, slave,** but esp. a messenger of the gods.

མངན་པ་ *mṅán-pa* **to curse, to execrate;** *mṅan bsgraṅ-ba Cs.* 'enumeration of curses'; but *mṅan mi bgraṅ? Lex.* w.e.

མངའ་ *mṅa*, resp. for *dbaṅ*, **might, dominion, sway,** *mṅa mdzád-pa* to govern, to rule, *la* over; *mṅa brnyés-pa* to have obtained power *Glr.; mṅa sgyúr-ba Tar.* id.; to possess (books, knowledge etc); to have mastered, to understand thoroughly; *mṅa γsól-ba* 1. to name, nominate, appoint, *rgyál-por* a king *Pth.; btsún-mor* to declare a woman one's wife *Glr.* 2. to praise *C.*; *bkra-šis mṅa γsól-ba C.* to congratulate. — *mṅa-ṫáṅ* **power, might.** — *mṅa-bdág* **ruler, master, owner,** frq. — *mṅá-ba* 1. vb. resp. for *yod-pa*, **to be** (to have), *rgyál-po-la sras γsum mṅá-ste* the king having three sons *Dzl.; btsún-poi skú-la bsnyuṅ mi mṅa lágs-sam* (I trust) your majesty is not unwell? *Glr.* 2. adj. (partic.) being owned by, **belonging to,** *Dzl.* ༧༥, 3: **having, owning,** = *daṅ ldán-pa*, frq. — *mṅa-mdzád* = *mṅa-bdág.* — *mṅa-žábs Glr., mṅa-˛óg Glr., mṅa-ris Lexx.* **subject to; a subject.**

མངའ་རིས་ *mṅa-ris* p.n., in a wider sense the whole country round the sources and the upper course of the Indus and Sutledge, together with some more western parts; the Cashmere, English, and most western Chinese provinces, where Tibetans live; in a more limited sense *mṅa-ris skor γsum* denotes Rutok, Guge, and Purang. — *mṅa-ris-ḱám-bu C.* (*ṗá-tiṅ* W.), **dried apricots** from Balti; *mṅa-ris ču, mṅa-ris γtsáṅ-po*, also *γyas-ru-γtsáṅ-po*, and *rta-mčóg-ḱa-bab*, the principal river of Tibet.

མངར་བ་ *mṅár-ba, W.* *ṅár-mo*, *C.* *ṅár-po*, **sweet,** frq.; *mṅar γsum* the three sweets, sugar, molasses, and honey; cf. *dkar γsum.*

མངལ་ *mṅal*, resp. *lhums* (གརྦ) **womb;** *mṅál-gyi dri-mas ma gós-par* not contaminated by the impurity of the womb (so all the Buddhas are not born like other mortals, but come forth out of the side of the breast); *mṅal daṅ ldán-par ˛gyúr-ba* to be with child; *mṅal mi bdé-bar ˛gyúr-ba* to be taken by the labours of childbirth; *mai mṅál-nas byúṅ-nas rtág-par* constantly from one's birth; *mṅál-du čágs-pa* 1. the originating in the womb, conception, 2. the foetus or embryo *Med.; mṅál-du ṫógs-pa* a disease; *mṅál(-du) γnás (-pa)* foetus, embryo *Thgy.; mṅál-du ˛júg-pa* to enter the womb, relative to a Buddha: his incarnating himself, his assuming flesh; *mṅál-du ˛dzín-pa Wdṅ.* to conceive, to be with child. — *mṅál-ḱa* mouth of the womb, orifice of the uterus *Med.* — *mṅal-grib* contamination of the womb; *Cs.* adds: original sin, yet prob. it signifies nothing more than *mṅál-gyi dri-ma* v. above; (the said contamination is considered to extend to the least contact with a woman in childbed). — *mṅál-sgo* the canal of the uterus, vagina; also in a more special sense the extreme orifice of the vagina *Med.;* frq. without any immediate physiological reference, the same as *mṅal*, e.g, when the subject of re-birth is spoken of. — *mṅal-ṫúr* a spoon used in midwifery for extracting a dead fruit (in the artificial delivering of a live child the obstetric art in Tibet is rather helpless). — *mṅal rlúgs-pa* **abortion,** *mṅal rlúgs-par byéd-pa* to cause abortion *Cs.*

མངོན་པ་ *mṅón-pa* **conspicuous, visible,** e.g. continents, because they stand out of the water; more frq. fig.: **evident, manifest, clear,** *mṅón-par ˛gyúr-ba* to become manifest; to be verified, proved, e.g. gold by refining *Dzl.* — Tibetan writers regularly translate the *Ssk. abhi* by *mṅón-pa*, hence *čos mṅón-pa Dzl.*, and *mṅón-pai bka Pth.*, the *Abhidharma* (v. *Köpp.* I., 595; *Was.*), *mṅon-pai sde-snod Abhidharma-piṭaka, mṅon-pa-mdzod Abhidharma koša* (v. *Burn.* I. and *Was.*); as a vb.: to be evident, to appear clearly, *bdén-par čis mṅon*, from what is it evident that it is true? *Dzl.; γnód-par bgyid-du mṅóṅ-no* they are evidently bent on doing mischief *Dzl.; mṅón-du byéd-pa* to manifest, to make public; to show something to others; *Tar.* 24, 1 should be understood: to make clear or manifest to one's self, to perceive, know, understand; *mṅón-du ₒbyin-pa* to disclose, reveal (secrets, the future) *Glr.*; to make known (one's wishes) *Glr.*; *mṅón-du ₒgyúr-ba* to be revealed or disclosed, to make one's appearance, *raṅ-byúṅ ye-šés mṅón-du gyúr-pas* as the self-originated wisdom has revealed itself to us *Mil.* — *mṅón-par* adv. manifestly, openly, evidently; often = entirely, highly, greatly, very, *mṅón-par rdzogs Was.* (246) complete fulfilment; in the sense of 'very' it may also be taken in *mṅón-par dgao*, in the legends of Buddha, 'they rejoiced very much', though also one of the other significations of *abhinanda* might help to explain these words.

**Comp.** *mṅón-(par) brjód(-pa)* = *abhidāna*, a collection of synonyms, of which some are mentioned in *Burn.* I. and II. — *mṅon-rtágs* **proof, argument**; sign or token of the truth of a thing *Dzl.* ༢༣, 2. — *mṅon-(par) rtógs(-pa)* 1. a clear comprehension *Was.* (287). 2. a hymnlike description of a Lha from top to toe, v. also *Schl.* 260. — *mṅon-mtó* re-birth as Lha or as man *Thgy.* (*Schr.*); also n. of a region in Paradise. — *mṅón-pa-pa* an Abhidharma scholar. — *mṅon-spyód Sch.* cruelty, severity; *Schf.* more corr.: **witchcraft,** *Ssk. abhičāra*, *Pth.*, *drág-po mṅon-spyód-kyi las Tar.* frq. — *mṅon-mtsán Lex.* w.e., *Sch.*; an evident sign. — *mṅón-(par) šés(-pa)*, resp. *mḱyén(-pa)*, *Ssk. abhijñā*, a kind of **clairvoyance**, gift of supernatural perception, of which five species are enumerated, viz. assuming any form at will, seeing and hearing to any distance, knowing a man's thoughts, knowing a man's condition and antecedents; originally used as a vb.: to be clear-seeing *Pth.* — *mṅon-súm-du* 1. **openly, publicly** *Dzl.*; more frq. 2. **bodily, personally**; like *dṅós-su*, e.g. to appear, to instruct, in person (*Tar.*); to know by one's own personal experience (*W.*).

རྔ་ *rṅa* I. **kettle-drum, drum,** *ₒḱár-rṅa* v. *ₒḱar*; *rdzá-rṅa Glr.*, *Cs.*: 'a drum of earthen ware'; *rgyál-rṅa* the beating of drums after a victory, *bág-rṅa* at nuptial festivities, **lhá-ṅa** *Ld.* for the king; **žéṅ-ṅa**, and **zím-ṅa** *Ld.* a morning and evening serenade with an accompaniment of drums; *ḱrims-kyi rṅá-bo če brdúṅs-te* the beat or sound of the large proclamation drum (prop. law-drum) *Glr.* —

**Comp.** *rṅa-sgrá* 1. sound of the drum, or kettle-drum 2. n. of a Buddha, = *dón-yod-grub-pa* or Amoghasiddha. — **ṅa-lčág** *W.*, *rṅa-rdég Sch.*, *rṅa-dbyúg Cs.*, *rṅa-yáb Sch.* **drum-stick.** — *rṅá-pa* **a drummer** *Cs.*, *rṅa-dpón* a chief drummer. — *rṅa-lpágs* **drum-skin.** — *rṅa-yu* handle of a kettle-drum (the larger kettle-drums being held up during the play by means of a handle or stick). — *rṅa-šiṅ* the wooden body of a drum *Cs.* — *rṅa-šón* kettle-drum music *Sch.* — *rṅa-ɤsáṅs* (also *rṅa-bsaṅs*) a loud beat or roll of the kettle-drum *Sch.*

II. for *rṅa-bóṅ*, and *rṅá-ma.*

རྔ་བ་ *rṅá-ba*, pf. *brṅas*, fut. *brṅa*, imp. *rṅos*, **to mow, to cut, to reap,** *ₒbru*, or *lo-tóg zór-bas* to cut the harvest with a sickle; *brtsás-ma brṅás-pa* the reaped corn; *rṅá-mḱan* the mower, reaper.

རྔ་བོང་ *rṅa-bóṅ W.*, **ṅa-móṅ** *C.*, **camel,** *rṅa-ɤséb* male camel, *rṅá-mo* female camel; a camel in general; *rṅa-ṗrúg* the young of a camel; *rṅa-rgód* a wild camel; *rṅa-bál* camel's hair.

རྔ་མ་ *rṅá-ma* 1. **tail.** 2. in a special sense: **yak's tail** *Mil.* — *rṅá-ma ɤyúg-pa Sch.*, **ṅá-ma ṭóg-če** (lit. *skrog-pa*) *W.*, to wag the tail. — *rṅa-yáb* 1. a yak's tail, used for fanning and dusting. 2. *rṅa-yáb*, and *rṅa-yab-ɤžán*, n. of two fabulous islands in the south of Asia *Cs.*

རྔན་ཆེན་ *rṅan-čén Lex.*, *C.* and *W.*, **contempt, disdain;** **ṅan-čén ǰhé-pa** *C.*, **čó-če** *W.* to despise, contemn.

རྔན་པ་ *rṅán-pa* I. sbst. 1. **reward, fee, hire, wages;** *rṅán-pa máṅ-po* the wages are high; *rṅán-pa sbyin-pa* or *ɤtóṅ-ba* to pay wages; to bribe, to corrupt. — 2. in *C.* at present a kind of **sacrifice.**

II. vb. **to reward, to recompense**, perh. better *brṅán-pa.*

ངབ་པ་ *rṅáb-pa* 1. (cf. *rṅam-pa*) **to desire** earnestly, **to crave**, *bkrés-rṅab-pa* to be greedy, to have a craving appetite *Lex.* — 2. *W.* col. for *rṅá-ba* **to mow;** **ṅáb-sa** (lit. *ṅáb-rtsva*) *W.* grass or corn that is to be mown or cut.

ངབས་ར་ *rṅábs-rva Med.*, a hollow horn, used for sucking *Sch.*

ངམ་པ་ *rṅám-pa* 1. sbst. (cf. *dṅom*), also *rṅam-brǰid, rṅom-brǰid*, **splendour, magnificence, majesty**, an appearance, commanding awe or inspiring terror (but not = awe *Cs.*); *rṅám-pai ṅá-ro* a voice of that kind; *rṅám-po, rṅám-čan* adj. bright, shining, grand, majestic. — 2. vb., also *rṅáms-pa*, pf. *brṅams*, **to breathe**, *rṅám-pa bde* the breathing is regular *Mṅg.*, frq ; *rṅám-pa tuṅ* short breath *Sch.*; esp. to breathe heavily, **to pant**, *rṅám-pa rgod* wild puffing *Med.*; c. dat. **to pant for, to desire ardently**, *srog γčód-pa-la* to be blood-thirsty *Ma.*; *rṅám-pai ṫsúl-gyis* greedily (devouring) *Thgr.*; *rṅám-čan* adj. greedy, avaricious, covetous; **za-ṅam-pa** voracious, gluttonous, ravenous *W.*; to rush upon, fly at, throw one's self on, *γžán-la* on others *Mil.*; **to rage**, to be in a fury; **to destroy** or murder in a state of fury; *mi ṗal-čér grir rṅom* (like *grir γsod*) the people are in numbers murdered by the sword *Ma.*; to call out in a rage, *čes ḱrós-rṅam-nas* thus she called furious with rage *Dzl.*; *rṅáms-pai* (*ḱro*)-*žal* an angry face, wrathful look *Glr.*

ངམས་ *rṅams* **height;** in height *Glr.*, *rṅáms-su* id.

ངས་ *rṅas*, v. *sṅas.*

ངུ་ *rṅu* **pain,** v. *zug-rṅu.*

ངུབ་པ་ *rṅúb-pa*, pf. (*b*)*rṅubs*, fut. *brṅub*, imp. *rṅubs*, **to draw in**, *dbugs* air, *snar* into the nose *Med.*; to breathe *Med.*; *dbugs rṅub mi ˳ton* (?) is mentioned as a sign of great sadness and affliction *Pth.*

ངུལ་ *rṅul* **perspiration, sweat**, *rṅúl-ču* id., esp. col.; *rṅul ˳du Med.*, *˳byuṅ Dzl.*, *rṅúl-ču ˳ton*, **yoṅ**, col. perspiration is breaking forth; *rṅul ˳dón-pa* to cause to sweat or perspire *Cs.*; *rṅúl-ba*, pf. *brṅul*, to sweat, to perspire *Cs.*

ངེའུ་ *rṅeu* 1. also *rṅeu-čúṅ, rṅa-čúṅ*, a little drum, diminutive of *rṅa.* — 2. the young of a camel, v. *rṅa-móṅ.*

ངོ་ *rṅo*, is stated to be a kind of **leprosy,** covering the whole body, of a whitish colour, itching very much, and contagious; **ṅo ṗog, gyab** he is affected with leprosy; *rṅó-čan* leprous (cf. *mdze*).

ངོ་བ་ *rṅó-ba* **to be able** *Cs.*, *rṅo-ṫóg-pa* id., so *Fouc. Gyatch.* ༢༣༠, 9, **ṅób-če** *Ld.*; *Sch.* has: *rṅo mi ṫóg-pa* to look at one with uncertainty, not being able to recognize; the passage of *Mil.*: *rṅo ma ṫogs kyaṅ* is not to be explained by either of these significations; *Lex.*: *rṅo mi ṫogs* w.e.

ངོ་བག་ཅན་ *rṅó-bag-čan Cs.* v. *rṅom-bag-čan.*

ངོ་ལེན་པ་ *rṅó-len-pa* **to roast, fry,** (?) *Sch.* v. *rṅód-pa.*

ངོག་ *rṅog* 1. also *ze-rṅóg*, **the hunch** or **hump** of an animal *Lex.*, more esp. a hump consisting of fat (like that of the camel); *ṫsil-rṅóg* the fat around the kidneys, suet *Mil.*; *rús-kyi rṅog Lex.* w.e. — 2. *rṅog*(*-ma*) **the mane** of horses etc. (not of the lion, v. *ral-pa*), *rta-rṅóg* a horse's mane, *dre-rṅóg* a mule's mane; *dreu-rṅóg* a kind of stuffed seat or mattress *Cs.*, a thick-haired carpet *Sch.*; *rṅóg-čan, rṅóg-ldan* having a mane; *rṅogs-čágs* a beast that has a mane *Cs.*

ངོད་པ་ *rṅód-pa* I. pf. *brṅos*, fut. *brṅod Cs.* (perh. erron. for *brṅo*) imp. *rṅod, rṅos, W.* **ṅo-če** 1. **to parch** (barley), *ser tsam* (to parch a thing) so that it turns yellowish *Glr.* — 2. **to roast, to fry** e.g. meat in a pan.

II. **to deceive** (acc. to *Cs.* = *rṅón-pa* to deceive wild beasts, to hunt); **to seduce,** esp. to sensual indulgence, *bud-méd Lex.*; similarly *Tar.* 39, 2.

རྔོན་པ་ *rṅón-pa* 1. vb., pf. and fut. *brṅon*, **to hunt, pursue**, wild animals *Cs.*, *Sch.*; **to fish** *C.* — 2. sbst. a hunter, huntsman *Dzl.* and *Ler.*; *rṅón-pa-mo* a hunting woman, a huntress *Cs.*

རྔོབ་པ་ *rṅób-pa Ld.* **to be able**, v. *rṅó-ba*.

རྔོམ་བརྗིད་ *rṅom-brjid* (cf. *rṅám-pa* 1) **splendour, stateliness, majesty**; *rṅóm-bag-čan*, also col. **ṅóm-jig-čan**, grand, majestic; terrible, of a judge, of terrifying deities. (A sbst. *rṅóm-bag* = *rṅom-brjid Cs.* prob. does not exist.)

ལྔ་ *lṅa* (*Bal.* **ya**), **five**, *lṅá-bču(-tam-pa)* fifty; *lṅa-brgya* five hundred; *lṅa-bču-rtsa-γčig* (*W.* **ṅa-bču-ṅa-čig**) or *ṅa-γčig*, fifty one etc.; *lṅá-pa* the fifth, *lṅa-po* consisting of five, cf. *dgu*; *lṅá-ga Cs.*, *lṅá-ka Pth.* all the five, each of the five. The number five very often occurs in legends, as well as in sacred science, v. the Index to *Burn.* II., and to *Fouc. Gyatch.* II. under '*Cinq*'. *lṅa-lén*, *Ssk.* पञ्चाल, n. of a country in the north of ancient India.

སྔ་ *sṅa* (पूर्व) a root signifying **before, soon, early**, rarely referring to space, and seldom used alone as adj. or adv., e.g. *Dzl.* ༢༣༥, 8: *ₒdá-ba ni há-čaṅ yaṅ sṅa čés-so* deliverance (sc. from existence) takes place much too soon; *ṅa ni ťém-pa sṅa brgal yin* I was the foremost, the first, to cross the threshold *Glr.*; *bstán-pa sṅa dar bar dar p̔yi dar γsum* the first, intermediate, and last propagation of the doctrine *Glr.*; gen. it is used with an adjective termination, with postpositions, or in compounds.

**Deriv.** *sṅá-ba* 1. adj. **ancient**, belonging or referring to former ages, *rgya-nág-gi rgyál-po sṅá-ba* an ancient king of China *Glr.*; of an early date, long ago, . . . *las dá-lta sṅá-ba ₒdúg-gam* is it already a long time, since . . . ? *Mil.*; 2. sbst. **antiquity**, the olden time; **the morning**; = *sṅá-dro*, *Mil.*; 3. vb. pf. *sṅas*, **to be the first, to come first, to be beforehand**, (φϑάνειν): *rjé-yi sku mťoṅ ṅa sṅá-bas* **as I was the first** to see the king's face *Glr.*; *ₒgran-ťsig sṅás-pa yin* you were **beforehand** with me in disputing *Glr.*; **ka ṅe soṅ** *Sp.* you promised it. — *sṅá-bar* in former times, **formerly, in the morning**; *saṅ sṅá-bar* to-morrow morning *Glr.* — *sṅá-ma* adj. 1. **earlier, former, preceding, afore-said**, frq.; *sṅá-ma sṅá-ma* always the anterior in time and place; *sṅá-ma ltar*, or *bžin-du*, as before, frq. 2. **the first**, the foremost in a series or succession *Dzl.*; *ldáṅ-bai sṅá-ma* she who takes the first turn in getting up *Mil.* — *sṅá-mo* 1. **earlier, by-gone**; *sṅá-mo-nas* **long ago** *Mil.*; 2. *W.*: **the morning**, in the morning, **mā ṅá-mo** early in the morning, **ťó-re ṅá-mo** to-morrow morning; also: **early enough**, in due time (opp. to **p̔i-mo**). — *sṅá-ru* v. *sṅar*, as a separate article. — *sṅá-na* **before, previously**, (gen. *sṅar* is used inst. of it). — *sṅá-nas* id., prop. of former times.

**Comp.** *sṅá-góṅ(-nas)* adv. **before, previously, at first**, a little while ago, **just now** *Mil.*; **formerly**, = late, deceased, *sṅa-góṅ yab* your late father *Glr.*; *sṅa góṅ bód-kyi rgyál-po* the earlier Tibetan kings *Glr.* — *sṅa-dgóṅs* morning and evening *Sch.* — *sṅa-sṅá* very early *Sch.* — *sṅa-čád* **formerly, hitherto**, till now, up to this time *Dzl.*, = *sṅan-čád*, *sṅon-čád*. — *sṅa-rtiṅ-du* **earlier** or **later**, not at the same time, e.g. *brós-so* they escaped *Glr.* — *sṅa-ltás* **omen, presage, prognostic**; also the fate or destiny portended. — *sṅa-ťóg* 1. **forenoon.** 2. the **first-fruits** of harvest *Cs.* — *sṅa-dús* **antiquity, time of old.** — *sṅa-dro* **the morning**, the earlier part of the forenoon, 'the time before the heat of the sun'; *sṅá-dro γčig-la* in half a forenoon *Glr.*; *sṅá-dro dgóṅs-mo* morning and evening *Sch.* v. **above**; *saṅ sṅá-dro* to-morrow morning *Mil.* — *sṅa-p̔yí(r)* **sooner** or **later**, like *sṅa-rtiṅ-du* v. above *Dzl.* frq. — *sṅá-rol* **time of old, past ages** *Cs.*; *sṅá-rol-tu* before *Tar.* (cf. *sṅón-rol*). — **ṅá-lo** *W.* **last year.** — *sṅa sugs ₒdrén-pa Cs.*: 'the accenting of the first syllable'. — *sṅa-sár* **early**, *sṅa-sar-sár* very early *Cs.* — *sṅa-sór* 1. in the first place, first of all, **at first** (cf. *rtiṅ-sor*) *Glr.* 2. **anciently**, in old times *Cs.*

སྔ་སྔོ་ *sna-snó* **vegetables, greens** *Thgy.* (v. *sno*).

སྔག་པ་ *snág-pa*, also *snágs-pa*, pf. *bsnags*, fut. *bsnag*, imp. *snog*, **to praise, commend, extol; to recommend;** *ₒgró-bar snags* it is recommended to go *Wdn.*; *bstod-snág-pa* to praise, to sing praises, frq.; *snág-(pa-)po* a praiser, commender, *Cs.*; *snag-(par) ₒos(-pa)*, *snág-ldan* praiseworthy; praised; also n. of the horse of Buddha *Cs.* — *snag-γsól* **praise, thanks.**

སྔགས་ *snags* (मन्त्र, also धारणी & तन्त्र) 1. **incantation**, magical formula, a set of words, consisting mostly of a number of unmeaning Sanskrit syllables, in the recital of which however perfect accuracy is requisite; hence detailed rules and instructions for a correct pronunciation of the Sanskrit sounds have been drawn up for Tibetan devotees. (On magical formulas v. *Burn.* II., 21, and note; on Buddhist magic in general v. *Was.* 142. 177, *Köpp.* II., 29.) — *γzuns-snágs*, *rig-snágs*, and *γsan-snágs* prob. = *snags*. — *snags sgrúb-pa*, *spél-ba*, *zlá-ba*, *C.* also **gyág-pa**, to recite, to pronounce charms, incantations; *ₒčán-ba*, *ₒdzin-pa*, to carry (charms) about one's self. — *snágs-kyi tég-pa* Tantrayāna, Mantrayāna, v. *tég-pa*. — *snágs-pa*, *snágs-mkan*, one versed in charms and their use, i.e. in orthodox and legitimate magic, as contained in the sacred books of religion. Opposed to this are *nan-snágs*, *nan-snags-mkan*, diabolical sorcerers and necromancers, and also common swindlers, jugglers, conjurers, fortune-tellers etc. — 2. *praise, encomium Cs.*

སྔངས་ *snans* = *dnans*, v. *dnán-ba Glr.*, *Pth.*

སྔན་ *snan*, for *sna*, *snon*, e.g. *snan-čád*, **formerly, before, previously, beforehand,** opp. to now *Mil.*; *snan-čád tó-ₒtsams-pa bzód-par γsol* pardon our former scoffing *Mil.*; esp. *W.*: **nán-la** for *snón-la*, *snar*, before, previously; **nán-ma** for *sná-ma*, **nán-me gyál-po** the former or last king, **nán-ma nán-tar** just as before.

སྔན་བུ་ *snán-bu* a medicinal herb, *Wdn.*

སྔར་ *snar*, prop. *sná-ru*, **before, beforehand, previously, formerly, at first;** *snar de byás-pai ₒóg-tu* not until that has been previously done *Dzl.*; *snar méd-pa*, *snar ma byás-pa*, *snar ma skyés-pa* what has not existed, or has not been done before, where we only say **new**, frq.; *snar lons* get up first! *Dzl.*; *snár-bas kyan(lhag-pár)* still more so than formerly, frq.; *snár-gyi* what has been hitherto in use, frq.; *snár-gyi yi-ge rnyín-pa-rnams* the old writings of antiquity *Glr.*; *snar yin-na* adv. = *snar Mil.*; *snar ltar*, *snar bžin* as before; *snár-nas* from before, from former times *Mil.*; also with reference to space: foremost, ahead, in advance, on, onward, joined to verbs of motion *Dzl.*; *snár-ba* the former, first-mentioned (?). In the sense of a postposition (c. accus.) *snar* is used but seldom, as far as I know only in *spyan-snár*.

སྔར་མ་ *snár-ma* **intelligent,** quick of apprehension *Sch.*

སྔས་ *snas* **a bolster, pillow, cushion;** *yo-byád snás-su ₒjúg-pa Glr.*, *C.* col. **yo-jhe-la ne čúg-pa** using the luggage as a pillow; *snas-stán*, *snas-ₒból*, resp. *dbu-snás* pillow; *rgyab-snás* a cushion for the back; *snas-mál* a couch constructed of pillows or cushions; *snas-ₒpáns* (?) pillow, cushion *Cs.*; *W.* **nye** for *snas*.

སྔས་པ་ *snás-pa* v. *sna-ba*.

སྔུན་ *snun*, col. for *snon*; *snún-la* c. genit. **before, ago,** like *gón-du*; **dá-wa nyis-si nún-la** two months ago; **nún-la son** he walked in advance, or ahead; **nún-ma** former, last; **nún-ma-žag** *W.* two days before yesterday, **yan nún-žag** three days before yesterday.

སྔུར་བ་ *snúr-ba* **to snore** *Lex.* (cf. *nur-ba*).

སྔེའུ་ *sneu Lex.*, *Cs.*: a kind of pulse or pease; *Sch.* = *món-sran*, v. *greu*.

སྔོ་ *sno*, a root signifying **blue** or **green;** as sbst. **plant, herb, vegetable, greens** *Mil.*; *sno skyé-na* when it is getting green or verdant.

**Comp.** *sno-skyá* **blue bice, pale blue,** e.g.

the skin of emaciated persons *Med.*; *ṅo gyaṅ-gyáṅ* *W.* greenish-yellow (spelling dubious). — *sṅo-sgá* officinal herb, *Wdṅ.* (green ginger?) — *sṅo-ṅád* v. *ṅad.* — *sṅo-ljáṅ* **bluish green.** — *sṅo-tóg Schr.* 'unripe, sour, of fruits'(?); more corr.: green, unripe fruits. — *sṅo-drégs* green mud or mire *Sch.* — *sṅo-nág* **deep blue.** — *sṅó-ba* 1. vb. **to get green, verdant;** 2. adj., also *sṅó-bo,* more frq. *sṅón-po, sṅón-mo* **blue, green,** also used of the livid colour of diseased or famished people *Glr.* — *sṅo-smán* a medicinal herb. — *sṅo-ṫsód* **vegetables; herbs.** — *sṅo-ló* the leaf of a plant; *Cs.:* '*sṅo-ló ₒčár-ba* to become notorious'. — *sṅo-sáṅs* **pale blue** e.g. of the sky; *sṅo-sáṅs-ma* night *Sch.*

སྔོ་བ་ *sṅó-ba, Cs.* also *sṅód-pa,* pf. *bsṅos,* fut. *bsṅo,* imp. *sṅos,* 1. **to become green** *Cs.* — 2. (*Lex.* परिणाम?) **to bless,** *ṅó-wa gyáb-ce* *W.*, though in most cases as a requital for a present given; *Dzl.* ༢༥༣, 16: to bless, to pronounce a benediction, hence also in litanies the words of the priest seem to be indiscriminately called *sṅó-ba,* whereas the responses of the congregation of monks are termed *mtun-ₒgyúr*; generally: **to dedicate, devote,** e.g. one's property to the *dkon-mčóg γsum,* i.e. in reality to the priesthood; *dgé-ba ₒgro-drug dón-du sṅos,* to devote alms, charitable gifts, to the (temporal and eternal) welfare of beings. *Mil.*; also **to design, to intend,** *ṅá-la bsṅós-pai γyu* the turkois intended for me (by you) *Mil.*; *Dzl.* ༧༥༥, 3: *sá-la ḱáṅ-bu daṅ rin-po-čér bsṅós-nas rtse-ba,* fancying the earth to consist of cottages and jewels, and thus playing with it.

སྔོག་པ་ *sṅóg-pa Lexx.*, prob. pf. *bsṅogs,* fut. *bsṅog,* imp. *sṅogs,* **to vex, to annoy**; cf. *skyo-ṅógs, skyo-sṅógs.*

སྔོན་ *sṅon = sṅa* and *sṅan,* **formerly, before, previously;** *sṅon tós-na* having formerly heard *Dzl.*; *sṅon máṅ-du ḱyer yaṅ* although you have taken a good deal with you before; *sṅon ₒdás-pai* or *byúṅ-bai dús-na* in by-gone times, frq.; *sṅon bčom-ldan-ₒdás* a former Buddha *Glr.*; *sṅon mi dbúl-po de* this man formerly poor *Dzl.*; *bdág-las sṅon bdág-gi ṗa* my father before me (has . . .); *sṅón-gyi* adj. former, last; *sṅón-ma* the former (when two persons or things are spoken of), *sṅón-ma-rnams* the former (persons or things) *Glr.*; **beginning,** *lha-ḱáṅ ȷ̀ig-pai sṅón-ma lhá-sa-la byás-te* making a beginning with the destruction of the temples in Lhasa *Glr.*; *sṅón-du* adv. and postp., **before,** at the head, in advance, in the front of, *sṅón-du ₒgró-ba* to go before or in advance, to precede, also of words and letters; *sṅón-du ₒȷ̀úg-pa* to put or place before, *Gram.*; *sṅón-la = sṅón-du: sṅón-la soṅ* walk first! *Mil.*; *stón-pai sṅón-du* (he died) before the Teacher (Buddha) *Tar.*; sooner, earlier, before the time supposed, *sṅón-la ṫsár-ro* they were first in finishing (their task) *Glr.*; *ₔo-ná sṅón-la ₒdi ṗul čig* oh yes, but first give me that *Mil.*; *sṅón-nas* from a former time, from the beginning *Mil.*; *sṅón-bžin* as formerly *Mil.*

**Comp.** *sṅon-skyés* **the first-born,** eldest son. — *sṅon-gró* v. *ₒgró-ba* **compounds.** — *sṅon-čád, sṅon-čád Dzl.*, v. *sṅan-čád.* — *sṅon-ₒȷ̀úg* **a prefixed letter** *Gram.* — *sṅon-dús, sṅon-ṫsé* **antiquity;** adv. **anciently,** in times of old. — *sṅon-byúṅ Cs.* = *sṅon-rábs.* — *sṅón-rábs* ancient race, ancient history, **antiquity,** पुराण. — *sṅón-rol* (cf. *sṅá-rol*) **former time** or **period,** *ma γtád-pai sṅón-rol žig-tu* formerly, in former times, when (the chair) was not yet transferred (to . . .) *Tar.* — *dus ná-niṅ sṅón-bai sṅón-rol-na* a year ago (an expression with an unnecessary redundancy of words!) *Mil.* — *sṅon-lás* **former actions.**

སྔོན་ *sṅon = sṅo, sṅón-po,* v. *sṅo.*

སྔོན་བུ་ *sṅón-bu* n. of a medicinal plant, acc. to *Cs.* poisonous; in *Lh.* Delphinium Cashmirianum, officinal. — *sṅon-bum* n. of a botanical work: 'the hundred thousand vegetables' *Cs.*

བརྔ་བ་ *brṅá-ba,* v. *rṅá-ba.*

བརྔད་པ་ *brṅád-pa Sch.:* 'ausziehen, ausreissen'.

བརྙན་པ་ brñán-pa, = rñán-pa sbst. Glr., vb. Lex.

བརྙབ་པ་ brñáb-pa 1. Sch. = brñád-pa. — 2. Lex. = rñáb-pa, rñams-pa.

བསྙལ་བ་ bsñál-ba **to be faint** or exhausted Cs.; v. sdug-bsñál.

བསྙས་པ་ bsñás-pa to place upon a cushion Sch.

བསྔོ་བ་ bsñó-ba 1. v. sñó-ba. — 2. **a blessing**, cf. sñó-ba. — 3. Cs. also: **mouldy, rotten** (prob. only livid, discoloured, v. sño).

# ཙ

ཙ་ ċa 1. the letter ċ, tenuis, palatal, like the Italian ci in *ciascuno*, or c in *cicerone*. — 2. as numerical figure: 5. — 3. = lċa **excrement**, alvine discharges, ċa dór-ba to discharge excrements *Mil.*

ཙ་ཅིར་ ċa-ċir lark *Ld.*

ཙ་ཙུས་ ċa-ċús **warped, distorted, awry** *Sch.*

ཙ་ཙོ་ ċa-ċó **clamour, cries,** *snyiṅ tsim-gyi ċa-ċo* shout, exclamation of joy *Pth.*; **noise**, of many people *Thgy.*; *da ċa-ċó ma zer* now do not make such a noise! (so *Mil.* rebukes the aërial spirits); **chirping, twitter** *Glr.*; *ċá-ċo-ċan* **shouting, bawling; talkative, loquacious** *Stg.*

ཙ་དར་ ċá-dar, also *ṫsá-dar, tsá-sar*, **a sheet, blanket, toga.**

ཙ་ར་ར་ ċa-ra-rá, or *ċi-ri-rí*, *W.* **ċár-pa ċa-ra-rá yoṅ dug**, it rains heavily, **it is pouring.**

ཙ་རི་ ċa-rí *W.* **bug.**

ཙ་རེ་ ċa-ré **continually, always** = *ċar.*

ཙག་ ċag termination of the plur. of pers. pronouns.

ཙག་ཀྲུམ་ ċag-krúm **cartilage, gristle;** *snai ċag-krúm* bridge of the nose.

ཙག་དཀར་ ċag-dkár *W.* **quartz.**

ཙག་ག་ ċág-ga, *C.* **ċág-ga ȷhé-pa**, = *nyá-ra byéd-pa*, c. *la*, **to take care of;** **ċág-ga dág-po ȷhé-pa** to look after, to keep, preserve carefully; **ċág-ga dág-po** careful, orderly, regular, tidy, of persons.

ཙག་ཙག་, ཙག་པ་ ċag-ċág, ċág-pa **smacking** in eating *Cs.*

ཙག་ཅེར་རེ་ ċag-ċer-ré closely pressed or crowded, in standing or sitting *Ld.*

ཙག་རྡོ་ ċag-rdó = ċag-dkár *W.*

ཙང་ ċaṅ, (v. ċiaṅ, ċi-yaṅ), **every thing, any thing whatever,** *ċaṅ-ṡés* knowing every thing, epithet of deities or saints; more frq. followed by a negative particle and then signifying: **nothing;** **ċaṅ mi sto** it does not matter, it is indifferent (to me), frq.; **ċaṅ med** there is nothing here, or at hand; also = **ċaṅ mi sto; ċaṅ mi ṡés-k̇an** ignorant, stupid; blockhead, simpleton.

ཙང་ཏེའུ་ ċaṅ-téu *Glr.*, also *ċaṅ-ċaṅ-téu* (ཙམས) a sort of **small drum** *Pth.*

ཙན་ ċan, affix, adjective termination, prop. signifying: **having, being provided with,** = *daṅ ldán-pa*, corresponding to the English adj. terminations -ous, -y, -ly, -ful, e.g. *tsér-ma-ċan* thorny; sometimes also = -like or -ish: *bón-ċan* Bon-like, heretical *Mil.*, *hin-du-ċan* Hindoo-like, Hindooish; seldom affixed to verbs: *byéd-pa-ċan* a doer, maker; in *C.* also for the possessive pron.: *ṅá-ċan, k̇ó-ċan*, my, his (her), **nag-góṅ sá-hib-ċeṇ** the Sahib's inkstand. It may also be **affixed to a set of words that form one expression:** *tsér-ma nón-po-ċan* **having sharp thorns,** *séṅ-gei mgó-ċan* **having a lion's head.**

**ཙན** c̀an, po., prop. c̀án-du, postp. c. accus., **to, with,** k̔oṅ c̀án-du mi ˳gro I do not go to him *Mil.*, *Pth.*; ṅa c̀án-du with me, in my presence *Mil.* The word seems to be rather obsolete; more recent editions having gán-du and drúṅ-du instead of it.

**ཙན་ཙིལ** c̀an-c̀il (?) *W.* the green shell of a walnut.

**ཙན་ཙེ, ཙན་ཙེར, ཙན་ཉེ** c̀an-c̀é, c̀an-c̀ér, c̀an-ñé, *Sch.*; a small bowl or dish; *Cs.*: continually.

**ཙན་དྭང** c̀an-dvaṅ **green, unripe** *W.* (?).

**ཙན་ས** c̀án-sa (?) **kitchen, fire-place** *W.*

**ཙབ་ཙོབ** c̀ab-c̀ob *Cs.* **nonsense** e.g. smrá-ba.

**ཙམ** c̀am 1. *Cs.* **slow**; *Lex.* c̀ám-gyis ǰog, and several other passages, the sense of which is not quite clear, cf. čam-mé. — 2. **glistening, glittering** (?) cf. lčam-mé. — 3. *W.* **whole, unimpaired,** *sa* (*lit.* rtsva) *c̀am-mé yod* the whole store of hay is still left (entire).

**ཙམ་པ་ཏ་ལོ** c̀ám-pa-tá-lo *Ts.* **mallow.**

**ཙམ་པོད** c̀am-pód *Ld.* **a bunch** of flowers, sprigs etc., a handful of ears of corn.

**ཙར** c̀ar 1. *Lex.* c̀ar-ré, *Cs.* c̀a-ré, *Sch.* also c̀ar-már, **always, continually** *Cs.* — 2. also čar, čár-du, with numerals, esp. γc̀ig-c̀ar **at the same time, simultaneously,** opp. to one after the other, successively (viz. doing or suffering a thing, sleeping, dying etc.) *Dzl.*; **at once, on a sudden,** opp. to gradually *Mil.*; lṅá-čar all the five together *Thgy.*, γnyis-čar, drúg-čar etc.

**ཙར་རས** c̀ar-ras v. ˳doms-ras.

**ཙལ** c̀al *Cs.*: '**noise,** c̀al-c̀al id.; c̀al-rgyúg rumour, (false) report'; c̀al-c̀ól idle talk, nonsense, c̀al-c̀ól γtam id. *Mil.*

**ཙས** c̀as *Pur.*, v. c̀es 2.

**ཙས་ཙུས** c̀as-c̀ús *Sch.* = c̀a-c̀ús.

**ཙི** c̀i **num. figure: 35.**

**ཙི** c̀i I. interr. pron. in direct questions:

1. **what?** (*C.* gen. gaṅ instead of c̀i) c̀i šes (like the *Hind.* **क्या जाने**) who knows? col. *W.*; also pleon. at the end of a question after the... am: ṅa ṅó-šes-sam c̀i? do you know me? do you? *Dzl.*; c̀ii of whom? whose? followed by ṗyir, don, čed, slad (-du): why? wherefore? inst. of c̀ii pyir also c̀i-pyir etc.; de c̀ii ṗyir žé-na 'this wherefore? (= why this?) if so it is asked'. (This phrase, besides the gerundial particles — esp. pas — is the only way in which in *B.* the causal conjunction 'for' (*Lat. nam, enim*) can be expressed, and in translating into Tibetan, the English conjunction must therefore often be altogether omitted.) c̀ii ˳brás-bu what sort of fruit? c̀ii ri what kind of a mountain? i.e. of what consisting? *Pth.*; c̀i also, like an adj., is placed after the word to which it belongs: rgyu c̀i-las for what reason? on what account? *Thgy.* — 2. **why? wherefore?** but only in negative questions: bdág-la des c̀i ma čog why should not that suffice me? *Thgy.*; c̀i mi sgrub why do you not procure...? inst. of the imp. procure! *Mil.*; bsám-na c̀i ma legs if you considered..., why would not that be a good thing? = you had better consider, you ought to consider *Mil.*; frq.: de ˳byúṅ-na c̀i ma ruṅ if that happened, why should it not be desirable? = would that it happened! oh, may it happen! — 3. **how?** in conjunction with other words, v. below. — 4. inst. of a note of interrogation, e.g. in: c̀i γnaṅ, for γnáṅ-ṅam, γšégs-par c̀i γnaṅ do you allow (me) to come? *Dzl.* [illegible], 13; [illegible], 5.

II. correlatively: **which, what; whatsoever; every thing,** much like gaṅ, q.v., esp. the syntactical explanations given there. c̀i, as a correlative, ought prop. always to be written ǰi, yet not even in decidedly correlative sentences is this strictly observed: c̀i byed(-na-˳aṅ) whatever I may do *Glr.*; c̀i bgyi bka nyan(-te) ṅéd-kyis bsgrub whatever we may be bidden to do, we shall obediently perform *Pth.*; **c̀i myur,** also c̀i myur žig-la *Pth.* **as quick as possible;**

also *ci* alone: by all means, at all events, *spyan ci draṅs* he must be conducted here at all events *Glr.*

**Comp. and deriv.** *ci-ga* **what?** col. — *ci-dgar, ci dgá-bar* whatever one may wish, **at pleasure, ad libitum.** — *ci snyed* v. *snyed.* — **ci toṅ** (lit. *γtoṅ*) **zig** **some, something** col. — *ci lta-bu* **of what sort,** manner, **fashion,** quality or nature? *Lat. qualis.* — *ci ltar* **how?** in what manner? **what?** *da ci ltar bya, W.* **da ci có-ce**, what is now to be done? — *ci ltar gyúr-pai γtam byás-so* he related what had happened, frq. — *ci-ste,* followed by *na* or (rarely) *te,* in most cases = the *Lat. sin,* **but if,** if however; even supposed that; sometimes for *gál-te,* **if,** in case. — *ci sto* what does it matter? *śi yaṅ ci sto* if he dies, what does it matter? *Thgy.* (cf. *caṅ*). — *ci-ₒdra-ba* similar to what? of what kind? also: of whatever description it may be *Glr.* — *ci-nas* from which or what? out of which or what? by which? etc. (*Bal.*: **ci-nę** how?), *ci-nas kyaṅ* = *cis kyaṅ* q. v. — *ci tsam* **how much?** *B., W.*; *ci tsam yod kyaṅ* though he have ever so much *Mil.*; *ci tsám-du* how far? to what distance? — *ci-tsug Cs.,* col. **ci-zug, gá-zug** how? in what manner? — *ci zig* 1. **what? what a?** 2. **some one, any one, something, anything;** *ci zig-tu dgos* for what (purpose) is it wanted? *Dzl.*; *ci zig-na* once, one time, at any time *Pth.*; *ci zig-nas* after that, afterwards *Pth.* — *ci yaṅ, ci-aṅ, caṅ* **whatever,** any thing, all kinds of things, **ṅul yǫ-na tsóṅ-gyu ci yaṅ yǫ** *C.* if there is money, you may sell any thing; followed by a negative: **nothing.** — *ci rigs-pa* adj., *ci rigs-par* adv. 1. **in some measure,** to a certain degree; in part, partly *Tar.*; 2. **of every sort** *Dzl.* and elsewh. — *ci-la* **why? wherefore?** *Glr., W.* col.; also for the *de cii ṗyir zé-na* of *B.*; further it is used inst. of an affirmative; e. g. question: shall we get rice there? answer: **tob yin; ci-la mi tob** of course, why not? **ci-la zu** **why! well!**

ཅི་ལིམ་ *ci-lim* (*Hind.* چلم) 1. the **bowl** of a **hukka** (water-pipe). — 2. a **hukka.**

ཅི་ཙེ་ *ci-tse Kun.,* also *tsé-tse,* **millet.**

ཅིག་ *cig,* enclitic, a modification of *γcig,* after *s* usually changed into *śig,* after vowels, and the liquids *ṅ, n, m, r, l* into *zig* (exceptions, however, in provincialisms and in literature are not unfrequent) 1. after nouns, the indefinite article **a,** or **a few,** when following after a plural; sometimes also untranslatable: *bud-méd-dag cig* some women; *máṅ-po zig* many (sometimes expressly opp. to *máṅ-po, the* many, *Tar.* 7, 15); *gaṅ zig* v. *gaṅ*; **a little, some,** *śiṅ zig ₒtú-ru ₒgro dgos* I must go and pick up some fire-wood *Mil.*; after infinitives: *k̔rims daṅ ₒgál-ba zig byéd-pa* to commit a trespass, to make one's self guilty of a transgression *Dzl.*; *tse ṗós-pa gráṅs-med-pa zig myaṅ* he suffered innumerable deaths *Dzl.*; it is even added to numerals, and not only when 'nearly', 'about' or similar words leave a given number undefined (*mi lṅa tsam zig* some five people), but also in sentences like the following: *cu-mig bzi zig yod* there are four springs or fountains. In all these cases, however, it may also be omitted. The numeral for 'one' ought always to be written *γcig* and never *cig,* but prefixing the *γ* is so often neglected (e. g. in *tabs. cig-tu, lhan cig* etc.) that even grammarians let it pass. — 2. when affixed to verbs (to the root of the imp. mood, or, in negative sentences, to the root of the present tense) it is a sign of the imperative. In ancient literature it is used without reference to rank, whether it be in making prayers to Buddha, or in giving orders to a servant; at present in *C.* only in the latter way; in *W.* it is of rare occurrence.

ཅིང་, ཤིང་, ཞིང་ *ciṅ, śiṅ, ziṅ,* a gerundial particle, the initial letter of which is changed acc. to the rules obtaining for *cig*; it corresponds to the English participle in **ing,** is used in sentences beginning with **when, after, as,** and is affixed to verbal roots and adjectives, in the latter case including the auxiliary verb to be: *γsón-por dúr-du bcug-ciṅ bui śa zá-bar* *gyúr-čig* (= *bčúg-nas*, or *bčúg-ste*) may I, after having been buried alive, be obliged to eat my own son's flesh! *Dzl.*; usually however employed in the minor clauses of accessory sentences: *brós-šiṅ gáb-pas* having hid themselves after running away *Dzl.*; frq. also where coordinate ideas are in English connected by **and** or **but:** *šá-la zá-žiṅ ḱrág-la ₒťúṅ-ba* eating flesh and drinking blood; *čé-žiṅ légs-pa* tall and well-shaped; *drod ɣnód-čiṅ bsíl-ba p̓an* heat is hurtful (but), cold is beneficial *Lt.* It is also used like the ablative of the gerund in Latin: *nya bšór-žiṅ ₒtsó-o* we live by fishing (piscando) *Dzl.*; and = *kyin* (q.v.): *ri-la draṅ-sroṅ byéd-čiṅ ₒdúg-go* he sits on the mountain acting the part of an anchorite *Dzl.*; *smre-sṅágs ₒdón-čiṅ ₒdug* he sits wailing *Dzl.*; *raṅ-dgár ₒgró-žiṅ ɣda* he is wandering at pleasure *Mil.*; *čes smrá-žiṅ yód-pa-la* as they were thus speaking *Glr.*; *čos stón-čiṅ yód-pai ťse* as he was just giving religious instruction *Tar.* 11, 12.

ཅིའུ་རི་ *čiu-ri* n. of a female demon *Thgr.*

ཅིར་, ཅི་རུ་ *čir*, *či-ru*, termin. of *či*, 1. **whereto** etc., little used. — 2. with *yaṅ:* **everywhere**, in every direction, for any purpose, by all means, with a negative: **nowhere** (so at least it is to be explained in several passages of *Pth.* and *Thgy.*).

ཅིས་ *čis*, instr. of *či*, *čis yid-čes-par ₒgyur* **by what** am I to believe it? what shall make me believe it? **whereby** can I know it to be true? *Dzl.*; *čis kyaṅ mi skrág-pa yin* he is not to be frightened by any thing *Dzl.*; *čis kyaṅ*, and *či-nas kyaṅ* frq. used as adv.; **by all means**, at all events, at any rate, *čis kyaṅ ₒgró-na* if you wish to go by all means, at all hazards; *da čis kyaṅ gegs byao* now I will at any rate play him a trick *Dzl.*; *čis kyaṅ bžes-pa žu* I beg of you most earnestly to accept it *Mil.*; *čis kyaṅ slobs* **never mind**! teach it me at any rate! *Pth.*

ཅུ་ *ču* 1. num. figure: 65. — 2. inst. of *bču*, used in compound numerals for the tens, when the preceding numeral ends with a consonant: *sum-ču*, *drug-ču*, *bdun-ču*, *brgyad-ču.*

ཅུ་གང་ *ču-gaṅ Med.*, *Cs.*: 'a sort of lime used for medicine'.

ཅུ་ཏི་ *ču-ti* (?*ɣču-ti*) **pig-tail, cue**, worn by boys and men in Tibet proper, *Ld.* and *Sp.* Cf. *čo-to.*

ཅུ་ལི་, ཅོ་ལི་ *ču-li*, *čo-li* 1. *W.* **a fresh apricot.** — 2. *C.* **dried apricots** without stones. — 3. a sort of wild-growing vegetable *Sik.*, *C.* — *ču-li ta-gir* the pulp of apricots boiled down to a conserve and formed into cakes *W.* — *bun-ču-li* a kind **of peach** *Kun.*

ཅུག་ཅུག་ *čug-čúg* = *čag-čág Sch.*

ཅུང་ *čuṅ* 1. *C.* **gourd, pumpkin.** — 2. n. of a place. — 3. for *čuṅ žig: da ḱyod čuṅ ₒp̓yis-pa yin* you are **a little** too late now *Pth.*; *čuṅ yó-ba* a little slanting *Glr.*

ཅུང་ཞིག་, ཅུང་ཟད་, ཆུང་ཟད་ *čúṅ-žig*, *čúṅ-zad*, *čúṅ-zad*, **a little,** *B.* and *C.*, *mú-ge čúṅ-zad čig* a partial famine *Mil.*; *čúṅ-zad-kyi p̓yir* for the sake of a trifle, through an insignificant circumstance *Dzl.* ༢༢༥, 15; **some,** *Lat. nonnulla*, of rare occurrence, *Was.* (242); *čuṅ žig skyéṅ-bar gyúr-nas* rather ashamed, somewhat confounded *Glr.*; *čúṅ-žig p̓áṅ-nam blta* I shall see, whether it will help, or has helped, a little *Mil.*; a little while, a short space of time, *čúṅ-zad čig sdod čig* wait a little (while) *Dzl.* When followed by a negative, it may either be translated as in: *čúṅ-zad ma bdé-ba* a little unwell, uneasy etc. *Mil.*, or as in: *dbaṅ čúṅ-zad med*, there is not even a slight possibility = there is no possibility **at all** *Pth.* and elsewh.

ཅུང་ཞོ་ *čúṅ-žo*, also *čúṅ-žu*, *čuṅ-ži*, *ɣčoṅ-ži*, a kind of white stone.

ཅུབ་ *čub W.*, from the *Hind.* चुप, **čub čád-de dug** he keeps silence, **holds** his peace.

ཅུར་ *čur*, in *čur mid-pa* **to devour** food **entire** *Sch.*

ཙུར་ནི་ *ċúr-ni* **meal, flour,** only in medical writings.

ཙེ་ *ċe* numer. figure: 95.

ཙེན, ཤེན, ཞེན *ċé-na, šé-na, žé-na* (cf. *ċig*), inst. of *ċes smrá-na,* **'if one says so, asks so'** etc., after words literally quoted, frq. (*W.* **zér-na**).

ཙེ་སྤྱང་ *ċe-spyáṅ* **jackal.**

ཙེ་རེ་, ཙེར་རེ་ *ċe-ré, ċer-ré* **envious, jealous,** *mig ċe-ré* (*ċér-gyis Thgr., ċér-te Glr.*) *ltá-ba* to look with an evil or envious eye upon; *ċe-ré lóṅ-ba* dim-sighted, purblind *Cs.*

ཙེམ་མེ་བ་ *ċém-me-ba* **bright, shining,** of polished metal *Glr.*, cf. *kŕá-bo.*

ཙེམ་ཙེ་ *ċém-tse* **scissors** *C.*

ཙེའུ་ *ċeu* 1. a small **sucking-pipe** for drinking the Murva-beer, in which millet grains are swimming *Sik.* (v. *Hook.* I., 175). — 2. **a clyster-pipe.**

ཙེར་ *ċer,* v. *ċe-ré.*

ཙེས་ *ċes* 1. (*Lex.* इति), also *šes* and *žes* (cf. *ċig*) **so, thus,** in ancient literature regularly placed after words or thoughts that are literally quoted, and so continuing the sentence; the quotation itself is gen. preceded by *ₒdi skád-du,* or *ₒdi snyám-du.* In later literature *ċes* and the introductory words are often omitted, in col. language always. Inst. of *ċes smrás-so, ċes γsúṅs-so,* so he said, thus he spoke, so has been said or spoken, so it is said, often only *ċés-so* is used, and in like manner *ċés-pa* for *ċes smrás-pa,* this word, this speech; *ċés-pa-la sogs-pa* these and similar words; *ċés-pa ₒdi yaṅ* also the preceding poem (is written by him); *snyun žés-pa nád-kyi miṅ yin* the word *snyun* is a term for 'disease' *Zam.*; *žés(-pa) daṅ* 'such, and', if a quotation is followed by another, where we say 'further', 'moreover'; *ċés-pa-la* after words have been quoted, which form the subject of further discussion; *ċes byá-ba,* or *ċés-pa* the so called, frq. after names; ***ċés-su*** rarely for *ċes.* — 2. acc. to the usual spelling and pronunciation (*ċes, ċe*) of the Lamas of *Ld.* it is the ordinary termination of the infinitive in *W.* (in *Pur.* and *Bal.* *ċas,* in *Kun.* *ċä*), though etymologically as yet not accounted for; sometimes used also as a sbst. or adj. i.e. partic.: *bsád-ċes* killing, *bsád-ċes yin* it is to be killed; *skyé-ċes* pregnant, v. *skyé-ba.*

ཚོ་ *ċo* 1. num. fig.: 125. — 2. *ċo-ₒdri-ba Lex., C.,* **to blame, reproach, slight; to vie with.**

ཚོག, ལྕོག *ċó-ga, lċó-ga Mil.* **lark** (not common in Tibet).

ཚོ་གེར་ *ċó-ger*(?), *ċó-ger bžugs Glr., W.* vulgo: **ċó-gan dug** he sits **motionless.**

ཚོ་ཏོ་ *ċó-to,* also *ċó-ti, Cs.*: **a tuft of hair** on the head, thus *Lex.*: *ċó-toi tor-ċóg* (= *ċú-ti?*); cf. *lċaṅ-lo.*

ཚོ་རི་ *ċó-ri = ċor, čáṅ ċo-ri Lex.*(?).

ཚོ་ལི་ *ċó-li = ċu-li.*

ཚོ་ལྫ་ *ċó-lc* **the prattling** or **chattering** of little children *Mil.*; cf. *ċá-ċo.*

ཚོག་ *ċog Cs.*: a plural-sign; *Schr.* all (people). This, or a similar original meaning of the word is also to be traced in an expression usual in *Ld.*: *ċóg-mdo* a place where three roads meet, v. *mdo*; cf. also *ċag.* When affixed to a word, it must be preceded by the vowel *o,* the final consonant of the root being at the same time repeated. Affixed to verbs, it seems to convert them into participles: *ₓóns-so-ċog-la Dzl.* ༢༥, 6, to those arrived, to the (persons) arrived, *yin-no-ċog, yód-do-ċog* those being, existing (things or persons); *Cs.*: *γċés-so-ċog* things that are valuable, precious, to a man.

ཚོག་ཚོག་པ་ *ċóg-ċog-pa W.* **grasshopper, cricket.**

ཚོག་པ་ *ċóg-pa C.* **to have leisure** *ċóg-na yoṅ go* if you have leisure, come! **ċóg-ka** **leisure,** **dhe-riṅ ċóg-ka me'** to-day I have no leisure; **ċóg-ka ǰhé** is an affirmative answer, when having been asked for some little service, something like: well, I'll do it.

ཚོག་བུ་ *čóg-bu* a sort of **small tent** *Cs.*

ཚོག་ཙེ་ *čóg-tse*, v. *lčog-tse.*

ཚོག་ལ་མ་ *čóg-la-ma* a mineral(?) *Med.*

ཚོང་ *čoṅ* 1. *Lex.* a musical instrument, *Schr.*: a bell. — 2. *Mil: čoṅ-la skyur-ba* to push one down a precipice in order to kill him (the only meaning the context here will admit); cf. *tson-dóṅ.* — 3. v. *γčoṅ.*

ཚོང་ཅི་ *čóṅ-či* a small **bowl** or **dish** *Sch.*; v. *čan-če.*

ཚོང་ཚོང་ *čoṅ-čóṅ* **jagged, indented, serrated.**

ཚོང་མོ་ *čóṅ-mo*, col. for *lčúṅ-mo.*

ཚོང་བ་ *čóṅ-ba*, *Pth.*: *ṅu-ₒbód čóṅ-ba* acc. to the context: to raise loud lamentations, wailings (at funerals); perh. etymologically connected with *čo-ṅés.* Cf. *γčóṅ-skad.*

ཚོང་ཞི་ *čóṅ-ži* = *čúṅ-žo.*

ཚོང་རོང་ *čoṅ-róṅ*, perh. = *čoṅ-čóṅ*, *Mil. čoṅ-róṅ tsér-ma.*

ཚོད་པན་ *čod-pán*, मुकुट, ornament for the head, worn by kings, **tiara, diadem, crown; the crest** of gallinaccous birds.

ཚོབ་དར་ *čób-dár Ld.-Glr.*, *Schl.* p. 29, a (?).

ཚོར་གང་, ཚོར་ཅིག་ *čor-gáṅ, čór-čig* **a mouthful, a gulp, a little** *Sch.*; cf. *čo-ré.*

ཚོལ་ཚུང་ *čol-čúṅ Thgy.* childish **prattle** or **babbling.**

གཅགས་པ་ *γčágs-pa* 1. **to apprehend, to grasp** (with the understanding), **to impress,** gen. with *yid-la*, on the mind, e.g. the doctrine *Dzl.*; also *bka nan-γčágs čén-po γnáṅ-ba* to give a thoroughly solid, impressive instruction; *γčágs-po byéd-pa* = *γčágs-pa;* with additional force: **do čág-po ǰhé-pa* C.* to impress (to one's mind) as firm as a rock. — 2. relative to persons it is synon. to *čágs-pa* **to love.**

གཅང་པོ་ *γčáṅ-po*, *W.* **šáṅ-po** **clever; lively, sprightly;** *W.* also **attentive to, regardful of;** *γčáṅ-po drúṅ-po* clever and sagacious *Mil.*, *γčaṅ-drúṅ ldán-pa* id. *Pth.*; hence also *γčaṅ* sbst. sagacity, cleverness; *k̔a-γčáṅ* clever words, clever speech *Cs.*; cf. also *k̔a-sbyáṅ*; *W.*: **šaṅ čó-če** to watch for; to keep guard, to watch; **šaṅ-rig čó-če** to be very attentive, to listen with fixed attention, **šáṅ-rig-čan**, *C.* **čáṅ-rig-čen** very attentive; *W.*: **šaṅ skúl-če** 1. to exhort, admonish 2. to wake, to rouse from sleep; **čós-si šaṅ-skúl táṅ-če** to give religious exhortations, to hold parenetic lectures.

གཅུད་པ་ *γčúl-pa*, v. *γčód-pa.*

གཅན་(གཟ) ཟན་ *γčan-(γ)zán* frq. **beast of prey,** *Lat. fera*, but more in a systematic sense, so that the cat, and even the dog may be included; *Glr.* po. *γčan-(γ)zán t̔á-ma* 'the last of the beasts of prey', the cat.

གཅམ་བུ་ *γčám-bu Cs.* **humbleness, servility, flattery,** *Sch.* also **untruth, lie;** *γčám-bui ṅag*, or *tsig* a servile speech; *γčám-bu smrá-ba* to speak submissively *Stg.* (not much used).

གཅར་བ་ *γčár-ba* 1. *Sch.*: **cut out, put out, knocked out,** e.g. *mig* an eye (cf. *bčar-ba.* — 2. *Mil.?*

གཅལ་བ་ *γčál-ba, γčál-du bkrám-pa* **to spread, display, lay out** e.g. precious stones, jewels, on a table, on the ground, *Glr.*, also *Lex.*

གཅི་བ་ *γči-ba* 1. vb. v. *γčid-pa.* — 2. sbst. = *γčin*; *bšaṅ γči* both kinds of alvine discharges. *Dzl.*

གཅིག་ *γčig*, num. **one**; *γčig kyaṅ* even but one; **one and the same,** *dus γčig-tu* at the same time (whereas *dus čig-na* once, one day, which however is also written *dus γčig-na*); *γčig byéd-pa* to unite (vb. n.), to join (in an act), to act in concert; sole, alone; **dear,** beloved, *yab γčig* dear father! *Glr.*: *šin-tu γdúṅ-bai ma γčig* my own (only) beloved mother! somebody, some one *Dzl.*, *γčig . . . γčig* the one — the other, somebody or other, very frq.; *γčig-gis γčig*, *γčig-la γčig* etc. one another, each other frq.; *mi-γčig C.* **differing, different.**

**Comp. and deriv.** *γčig-ka* **single, only,** opp. to several, *Mil.* — *γčig-čar, γčig-čar* v. *čar.* — *γčig-čig*, pronounced **čig-čig**, **a certain, some one,** εἷς τις, *slób-ma-las γčig-čig Dzl.; bud-méd γčig-čig Dzl.* ༢༥༦, 5 (where *Sch.* has *čig-γčig* erron.); *γčig-γčig*, pronounced **čig-čig**, 1. **one at a time; separately, alone,** esp. *W.*; 2. **of the same kind, not different** *W.* (v. *Fouc. Gram.* p. 21. 42), 3. adv. **by one's self, only, solely** *W.* — *γčig-čog* **all-sufficient** *Glr.* — *γčig-nyid Cs.* 'unity'(?) — *γčig-tu* 1. **into one,** into one body, **together,** *γčig-tu sdú-ba* to unite e.g. six countries, *Dzl.*; to contract, to simplify *C.* 2. at once, wholly, altogether *Dzl.* ༢༢, 3; 3. firstly, in the first place, *γčig-tu-ni*; then follows *γnyis-su-ni* etc. *Dzl.* 4. only, solely *Thgy.* — *γčig-dú* unity and plurality, *γčig-du-brál* not having these two qualities *Was.* (308). *γčig-pa* 1. **the first** *Wdṅ.* (little used). 2. **naving** etc. **one,** cf. *dgu.* 3. **of one kind,** not different or manifold, *mi-γčig-pa* different *B.* and *C.* — *γčig-pu* (also *γčig-bu?*) **alone, single,** *γčig-pus mi stoṅ túb-pa* to be able to cope alone with a thousand men *Dzl.; γčig-pur lus-pa* to remain alone behind *Glr.*; **only, sole,** *bu γčig-pu* the only son, frq. — *γčig-po* 1. **alone,** *rgyál-po γčig-po skyés-pa yin* the king alone is a man, *Dzl.* 2. **being one,** or the one, *ma γnyis-la skyés-pai bu γčig-po* thou (being the) one son of two mothers, viz. claimed by two, *Glr.* 3. *Pur.* **the one — the other.** — *γčig-šós* **the other**, when speaking of two.

གཅིད་པ་ *γčid-pa*, also *γči-ba*, pf. *γčis*, fut. *γči*, imp. *γčis*, to make water, to piss.

གཅིན་ *γčin* **urine,** *γčin γčid-pa*, or *γči-ba*, *W. táṅ-če*, to make water; *γčin šor* urine is discharged involuntarily; *γčin-rkyág*, both discharges, vulg.; *γčin-ˌgág* the retention of urine *Med.*; *γčin-snyi* gonorrhoea, clap(?) *Med.*

གཅིའུ་ *γčiu* 1. clyster-pipe = *čeu*; *γči-ui sman* clyster *Lex.* — 2. *clyster*(?) *Cs.*

གཅིལ་བ་ *γčil-ba* **to spoil, to destroy** *Sch.*

གཅུ་བ་, ལྕུ་བ་ *γčú-ba, lčú-ba*, v. *γčúd-pa*; *γču* or *lču-ˌkór Cs.*, *γču-skór W.*, *γčús-bu Ts.*, **screw.** — *γčú-ti* v. *ču-ti.* — *γču-dóṅ* screw-box *Cs.*

གཅུ་གལ་ *γču-gál* **importance,** *Cs.*

གཅུགས་པ་ *γčúgs-pa*, prob. not different from *γčágs-pa*. The word occurs in: *yid(-la) γčugs(-pa)* beloved, a friend *Dzl.*; *mdza-γčúgs byéd-pa* to treat amicably *Wdn.*; *ḱon-γčúgs* having conceived a hatred *Lex.*

གཅུང་པོ་ *γčúṅ-po*, resp. **a younger brother.**

གཅུད་ *γčud? γčud-(la) ˌbór(-ba) Lexx.* w.e.; *Sch.*: **to forsake, to cast out, to reject;** (cog. to *čul-zán?*)

གཅུད་, ལྕུད་པ་ *γčúd-pa, lčúd-pa*, pf. *γčus, lčus*, fut. *γču, lču*, imp. *γčus* (?) **to turn,** turn round, **twist, twine, plait, braid;** **čud log táṅ-če* W.* to untwist, untwine a rope; **čus zum táṅ-te nol dug* W.* they wrestle and scuffle (prop. they fight scuffling); **sen čus gyáb-če* W.* to press and bore with the knuckle; **čús-spu** a low expression for the hair; *lág-pa γčus Zam.?*

གཅུན་པ་ *γčún-pa*, secondary form of *ˌǰún-pa*, *Lexx.*: *rtsád-nas γčún-pa*, prob. **to subdue** completely; *γčúr-žiṅ γčún-pa* prob. to beat or press a thing until it is soft.

གཅུར་བ་ *γčúr-ba*, secondary form of *ˌǰur-ba*; *γčúr-ṗe Ld.* a coarse sort of **vermicelli.**

གཅེ་བ་ *γčé-ba* **to esteem, to hold dear, to love** *Sch.*

གཅེན་ *γčen* (*Cs. γčén-po*) resp. *Cs.*: one's **elder brother** *Dzl.* ༣༦, 11; acc. to *Zam.*: first-born son.

གཅེར་བ་ *γčér-ba* v. *bčér-ba.*

གཅེར་བུ་ *γčer-bu* **naked,** col., also *Mil.*; *γčer-nyál* id.; *Kun.*: **čer-góg**; resp. *sku γčér-bu*; *γčér-bu-rnams ˌgábs-par byéd-pa yin-pa* being one that covers the naked *Stg.*; *γčér-bur ˌbyin-pa* to make naked, to strip *Pth.*; *γčér-bu byúṅ-ba*, *W. *čer-nyál tóṅ-če** to show one's self naked; *γčer-*

bu-pa, γčér-nyal-mḱan Mil. (Ssk. nirgrantha a naked man, gymnosophist; čós-sku γčer mtóṅ-du gról-bas having been delivered so far as to see the čós-sku (v. sku) unveiled Glr.

གཅེས་པ་ γčés-pa (Lh. *šé-pa-*) **dear, beloved,** ... ltar γčés-na yaṅ although he is to me as dear as ... Glr.; ṅéd-kyi mi γčés-pa a man dear to us, our beloved, our darling Mil.; γčés-ma a favourite, sweetheart Cs.; γčes-ṕrúg dear child Mil.; **excellent, precious, valuable,** šín-tu γčes-pai lḃa the five important letters (viz. the prefixed letters) Glr.; šés-pa γčes it is of importance to know Med.; often as superlative: ˳jig rtén ˳di-na γčés-pa raṅ-srog yin the dearest thing in the world is one's own life Pth.; γčés-par byéd-pa Stg., ˳dzin-pa Glr. c. accus., W.: *šé-pa čó-če* gen. with the dat., to hold dear, to love, to esteem, persons or things, but not applicable to the deeper affections of the heart. — γčes-bsdús Lex. w.e.; γčes-btús Cs. choice pieces (out of books).

གཅོག་པ་ γčóg-pa, pf. bčag, imp. čog(s), W. *čág-če*, imp. *čog* trs. to ˳čág-pa, **to break,** dúm-bur to pieces; **to break off,** or **asunder; to smash,** a glass; **to crack,** nuts; **to burst; split, blast,** a gun, a rock; fig.: **to break, to violate,** a promise, a vow, a law etc. frq., yáb-kyi bka bčág-tu med the word of my father may not be violated (by me) Glr.

གཅོང་, གཅོང་ནད་ γčoṅ, γčoṅ-nád, **consumption, phthisis,** γčoṅ-čén dmú-ču prob. dropsy in the chest or in the pericardium Med.; gen. any **chronic disease** *čoṅ-la ťsu' ma soṅ-ṅam* C. it has not taken a chronic turn, has it? also fig.: *sem čóṅ-po duŋ* C. the heart is sick, afflicted.

གཅོང་སྐད་ γčóṅ-skad Lex., Sch.: **lamentations, wailings, plaintive voices,** cf. γčóṅ-ba.

གཅོང་བ་ γčóṅ-ba 1. pf. bšoṅs, **to excavate, wash out, undermine** through the action of water, túr-du γčoṅ-bar mi γyúr-ro they are not undermined (by the water) Stg.; γčoṅ-roṅ a narrow passage, a defilé Cs. — 2. from γčoṅ, **to get faint, languid, wearied** in mind, C.

གཅོང་ཞི་ γčoṅ-ži, v. čoṅ-ži.

གཅོད་པ་ γčód-pa, pf. bčad, fut. γčad, imp. čod, W. *čád-če*, imp. *čod* 1. **to cut,** ; čád-bya γčód-pa secanda secare Gram.; **to cut asunder,** ḱam-tsad-du into small bits; **to cut off, chop off,** the hands; **to cut down, to fell,** trees; **to cut out,** the tongue Dzl.; **to rend asunder, to break,** a thread, a rope, chains, fetters. — 2. **to cut off** fig.: ču, the water, by damming it out, frq.; **to reduce,** the wages; **to cure,** a disease; **to suppress,** a passion; **to discontinue, to give up,** zan, zas, eating i.e. to abstain from food, to fast; srog, to kill, to murder, frq.; **to stop** a thing in its origin, **to obviate, prevent, avert; to avoid; to lock,** the door, frq.; ... kyi, or la, bár-du γčód-pa to throw obstacles in a person's way, to hinder, impede, frq.; sróg-la bár-du γčód-pa dé-dag all these life-endangering beings Glr.; (for more examples refer to bar); **to stop,** to make a pause, in reading, šad yoṅ-na drág-por bčád-pa making a marked stop, when there is a shad, Gram.; rnam(-par) γčód(-pa), or bčad(-pa), section, paragraph; stop, pause; yoṅs-γčód id. Gram.; **to decide,** čes bčád-do thus he decided Dzl.; ḱrims, or (Dzl.) žal-čé, to pass sentence or judgment; to judge, condemn, cf. also ťág-γčod-pa. — 3. **to cross** (little used), čú-bo grú-yis a river in a boat Glr. — 4. rjes γčód-pa **to follow** the track, used both of men and dogs; *már-dzi* (to follow) the smell of butter (viz. of roast-meat), *kyúr-dzi čo'-pa* C. to follow the sourish smell (viz. the smell of beer); (γ)sár- (also ťsar Pth.) γčod-pa to search into, to investigate, to examine or study thoroughly Ld.-Glr. Schl. p. 20, b. — čád-pas γčód-pa and other phrases v. under the respective noun. — *čo'-táṅ* C. **the Tibetan rupee,** having lines (radii) of division marked, by which they may be cut into smaller pieces. — Note: In some phrases the spelling of γčód-pa and the assonant verbs *spyód-pa* and *dpyód-pa* is variable.

གཙོམ་, བཅོམ་ *γčom*, *bčom*, **pride, haughtiness, arrogance**, *bskyúṅ-ba* to put it off, give it up *Lexx.*; *bčom čuṅ-ṅus Tar.* 20, 6 despondingly, low-spirited; *gros-γčóm Lex.* obs. or prov. for *gros-bčám*, v. *˳čám-pa*.

ཙ

གཙེར་བ་ *γčór-ba* **to spread, scatter, disperse** *Cs.*

བཅག་པ་ *bčág-pa* v. *γčóg-pa* and *˳čág-pa*.

བཅང་ *bčaṅ? Sch.*: *'bčaṅ-rgya-čén-po* comprising much, comprehensive, very extensive; *bčaṅ-rgyár mdzad-pa* resp. to apply one's self, to bestow pains upon'.

བཅད་ཀ་ *bčád-ka W.* a whole that has been cut into, or a piece cut off.

བཅད་པོ་ *bčád-po W.* something **old, torn, worn out.**

བཅབ་པ་ *bčáb-pa* v. *˳čab-pa*.

བཅམ་བཅོམ་ *bčam-bčóm Sch.*: trivial things, medley, hodge-podge.

བཅའ་སྒ་ *bčá-sga* v. *sga*.

བཅའ་བ་ *bčá-ba* 1. v. *čá-ba*. — 2. sbst. drinking; gen. used connected with *bza-ba; bčá-ba daṅ bzá-ba,* or *bza-bča* food and drink.

བཅའ་འཕྲང་ *bča-˳pŕáṅ Mil.*, declivity, precipice *Sch.*

བཅའ་མག་ *bča-mág*, the usual pronunciation of *lčags-mag*.

བཅར་བ་ *bčár-ba* 1. = *bčir-ba* **to squeeze, to press** in a press *Thgy.*; **to crowd, to throng**, **yár-la bčar** *C.*, stand (or sit) more closely together! — 2. **to pull** or **force from, to wrest** *Cs.* — 3. *Lexx.*: *mig bčár-ba* the same as in *γčar-mig* (?). — 4. *Sch.*: *logs bčár-ba* to prop sideways. — 5. *Sch.*: *bčar bžúgs-pa* to have a permanent residence (this would however be more correctly expressed by *čar*). — 6. *bčár-bai rta- bčibs*, and *lan-bčár? Lexx.* w.e.

བཅལ་བ་ *bčál-ba* v. *˳ǰál-ba*.

བཅས་པ་ *bčás-pa* 1. originally pf. of *˳čá-ba*, little used. — 2. adj. **together with, connected with, having, possessing, containing** a thing, with *daṅ* or termin. (the latter in prose only when a second *daṅ*, signifying 'and', occurs in the sentence); gerundially: *bčás-te*, sometimes also *bčás-pas* or *bčás-šiṅ*; adverbially: *bčás-su* frq.; *˳ḱor daṅ bčás-pa(-te, -su)* with attendance, with a retinue or suite, frq.; *bu-mo bču bod-blón daṅ bčás-pas skór-te* surrounded by ten virgins together with the Tibetan ambassadors *Glr.*; *btsún-mo daṅ srás-su bčás-te* with (his) wife and son *Glr.*; *gos daṅ bčás-su* (to go into the water) having one's clothes on *Dzl.*; *žal ˳dzúm-pa daṅ bčás-te* with a smiling face *Glr.*; *šér-sna daṅ bčás-pa* infected with, subject to, avarice; without *daṅ* or termin. (esp. po.); *˳ḱrúl-bčas* infatuated, fascinated *Pth.*; *˳bru-ťáṅ ťun bčas* together with a small parcel of Dutan tea; it is also, like *rnams*, a collective sign, used in enumerations, referring to several nouns, *Wdṅ.*, or like *la-sógs-pa* and other (things), and more (such things), and the like: *rgyags daṅ bčas bskyál-lo* provisions and other necessaries we shall supply *Mil.*

བཅིང་བ་ *bčiṅ-ba*, fut. of *˳čiṅ-ba* **to bind.**

བཅིངས་པ་ *bčiṅs-pa*, pf. of *˳čiṅ-ba* **to bind.** Both verbs (*bčiṅ-ba* and *bčiṅs-pa*) are also used as substantives: **bonds, fetters,** whether of a material, spiritual, or magical nature.

བཅིབ(ས)་པ་ *bčib(s)-pa* v. *˳čib-pa; Sch.* also: **carriage, conveyance.**

བཅིར་བ་ *bčir-ba* v. *˳čir-ba*.

བཅིལ་བ་ *bčil-ba* v. *˳ǰil-ba*.

བཅུ་ *bču* (*Bal.* **wču**) **ten**, *bču ťam-pa* id.; *bču-pŕag* a decade; *bču-γčig, bču-γnyis* (*Bal.* **wču - ṅas**) eleven, twelve etc., (v. also *bčo*); *bčú-pa, bčú-po* as in *dgú-pa, dgú-po*. — *bču-skór ˳ton, bču-gyúr ˳ton* (the field) yields a tenfold crop. — **čú-ḱa, čú-ḱai ṭal** *C.*, **ču-ḱág** *W.*, tithe, tithes; *bču-ḱág-pa* a collector of tithes, *bču-ḱag ˳dón-pa* to tithe, to decimate *Cs.* — *bču-dpón* corporal, Lat. *decurio*, *bču-˳óg* (**ču-*

*wáġ* Ts.*) a band of ten soldiers. — *bču-γčig-žál* the eleven-faced (Awalokiteswara) *Glr.*

བཙུ་བ་ *bčú-ba* v. *˳ču-ba.*

བཙུག་པ་ *bčúg-pa* v. *˳ǰug-pa.*

བཙུགས་ *bčugs*, from the phrases: *sems ḱón-med-pa dan̓ bčúgs med-pa dan̓ γnód-pa med-pa Stg.*, and *Pratihārya Avadāna* (v. *Feer*) p. 3: *lha-byin-gyis bčugs byás-te* = देवदत्तविगृहीतेन, it appears, that *bčugs* signifies hatred, hostility, damage, loss, which when compared with *γčugs* seems rather strange, yet is in accordance with कौशल्य (for this must probably be read inst. of कोशल).

བཅུད་ *bčud* (रस) **moisture, juice, sap**, but gen. combined with the notion of a certain inherent virtue or power; *zlá-bai bčud* a fructifying moisture, to be compared in its effects to the warmth of the sun, and prob. means night-dew (if after all it is any thing real); hence **essence, nutriment**, *rkán̓-gis bčud ˳gyur* nourishment comes from the marrow *Med.*; *bčúd-la son̓*, *Mil.* also *bčúd-la bor*, (this food) has proved a nutritious fluid, it agrees with him; *bčúd-čan* nutritious, succulent, of grass, food etc.; *bčud-méd* not nutritious, *Med.*; invigorating **cordial, quintessence**, *bčud-lén* an elixir of life; frq. fig.: *čos ṫams-čád bsdús-pai bčud Glr.*

བཅུམ་པ་ *bčúm-pa* 1. v. *˳ǰúm-pa.* — 2. **to use artifices, to chicane** *Sch.*

བཅུར་བ་ *bčúr-ba* 1. **to be flattened down** *Sch.* — 2. *Kun.* **lún̓-po čúr-te yon̓** there is a draught (here). — 3. *C.* like *bkág-pa* **to bar, obstruct, block up**, e.g. of snow obstructing a road. Cf. *˳ǰúr-ba.*

བཅེ་, བཅེས་ *bče, bčes* v. *˳čé-ba.*

བཅེར་བ་ *bčér-ba* 1. **to heap** or **pile up** *Cs.*; *Lex.: šin̓ pún̓-por bčér-ba* to pile up wood. — 2. = *bčir-ba* 1. **to squeeze, to press** *C., W.*; **to squeeze in**, *ri-brág γnyis-kyi bár du* something between two rocks *Pth.*; **čer tán̓-če** *W.* to squeeze, press, screw in; **čer-čér tán̓-če** *W.* to throng, to crowd.

བཅོ་ *γčo*, for *bču* in *bčo-ln̓á* 15, and *bčo-brgyád* 18; *lo ln̓a γsum bčo-ln̓á* 3 times 5, 15 years (*ln̓a γsum* standing pleon.) *Mil.*

བཅོ་བ་ *bčó-ba*, pf. and imp. *bčos*, prop. root of the fut. tense of *˳čós-pa*, but in *W.* the usual word for *byéd-pa* **to make, perform; to prepare, manufacture, construct;** employed in all kinds of phrases; **ḱo-la zún-čan čo** *W.* (he) makes him a liar.

བཅོག་ *bčog? Glr.* 99.

བཅོམ་ *bčom* for *γčom*, **pride.**

བཅོམ་པ་ *bčóm-pa*, pf. of *˳ǰóms-pa*, **conquered, subdued; having conquered** or **subdued**, e.g. *dgrá-bčoms-pa*, v. *dgra*; **victory** *Cs.*; *˳ṗrog-bčóm*, and **čom-ṫóg** *W.* **robbery** and **acts of violence.** — *bčom-brlág* p.n., Mathura, town of ancient India, in the neighbourhood of Agra, *Zam.*, *Tar.* — *bčom-ldán* victorious *Cs.*; *bčom-ldan-˳dás* (*Kh.* **wčom-ldan-dę̈**, *Ld.* **čom-dan-dás**, *C.* **čom-dän-dę̈**) भगवत् *Cs.*: victorious, *Sch.*: 'the victoriously consummated', *Burn.* le bien-heureux, the usual epithet of Buddha, *Burn.* I., 71.

བཅོལ་བ་ *bčól-ba*, v. *˳čól-ba*; *bčól-ma* a thing committed to a person's charge, **a trust.**

བཅོས་པ་ *bčós-pa*, a verb of its own, though as to form resembling a participle, 1. **to treat medically,** hence **to cure, to heal**, *mḱas kyan̓ bčós-su med* he cannot be cured even by the best physicians *Med.*; *bčós-(pai) ṫabs* the way of treating, the method of curing *Med.*; *sman-bčós* medical treatment *Med.* — 2. to do (a thing) for the sake of appearance, for form's sake, **to affect,** *bčós-su byéd-pa* **to perform a sham work,** e.g. blowing into a blazing fire *C.*; hence as sbst.: **a false conception,** wrong idea, *bčós pa dan̓ ˳ḱrúl-bar gyúr-ba* to give way to odd fancies, to have crotchets in the brain, e.g. in consequence of old age *Thgy.* — 3. partic.: made or contrived by art,

ཙ

**artificial, feigned, fictitious,** *ma-bčós* artless, unaffected, genuine; it also seems to denote an absence of mental activity, or a forbearance of exercising such activity, in short that indifference to the world, which is so highly valued by the Buddhist, *Mil.* — *bčós-pai ras,* or *ras bčós-bu,* washed or prepared cotton-cloth *Cs.*; calico, chintz *Cs.;* in *S. O.* it seems to denote a costly, valuable fabric; *bčós - ma* sbst. and adj., a production of art, any thing made or contrived by art, esp. every thing imitated, counterfeit, mock, sham, not genuine, frq.; *bčós-ma ma yin-pa* natural, unfeigned, genuine, e.g. respect, reverence *Glr.* — *ṫsúl-bčos-mḱan,* one that is shamming, a hypocrite. Cf. *ₒčós-pa.*

ལྕ *lča*, *Ld.* for *lči - ba*, **excrement, dung, manure.**

ལྕ་སྒ *lčá-sga* = *bča-sga*, **white ginger,** v. *sgá.*

ལྕ་བ *lčá-ba* 1. *Cs.:* a sort of **carrot,** *Med.* frq., but not known to the common people, at least not in *W.* — 2. **कम्बल** acc. to *Was.* a garment made of wool or felt *Tar.*

ལྕག *lčag* 1. **rod, switch, stick, whip;** *glaṅ-lčág* ox-whip; *rṅa - lčág* kettle - drum stick; *lčaṅ - lčóg Lex.* willow - twig, osier-switch; *rta - lčág* horse-whip, whip in general, also a scourge, consisting of several straps with sharp knots; *spa-lčág* a cane, bamboo *Mil.*; *ber(-ma)-lčág* stick *Mil.* — 2. (*lčág - ma*) **stroke, blow, cut, hit,** *lčag rgyáb-pa* to give a blow or cut, *rtá-la* to the horse *Glr.*; *mgo-lčág* (*Ld.* **go-lčág**) a blow or stroke upon the head; *ₒgram-lčág* a smack on the cheek, slap on the face, box on the ear *Cs.; ṫal-lčág* id. — 3. forepart of a coat of mail *Sch.* — 4. a kind of Daphne, v. *re-lčag-pa.*

**Comp.** *lčág-rdo W.* **flint,** flint-stone. — *lčag-ₒbrás Mil.* **whip-cord,** lash of a whip; *lčag-ₒbréṅ*, and *lčag-dṅó* id. — *lčag-ṫsán* = *rta-lčág C.* — *lčag-yú* **whip-stick,** handle of a **whip.**

ལྕག་ལྕིག *lčag-lčig Lex.* w.e.

ལྕག་པོད *lčag-pód* **a girdle,** made of plaited and interlaced strips and resembling a chain; one *Lex.* adds: *dáṅ-mai ₒdríl-du lhás-pa* (?).

ལྕགས *lčags* 1. **iron,** *lčágs-kyi* of iron; *lčágs-bton-mḱan* a miner digging for iron; *rgya-lčágs* Chinese iron; *ṗo - lčágs* an inferior sort of iron, *mo - lčágs* a finer and better sort of it, *Cs.* steel (?) — 2. an iron instrument, tool, esp. **lock** (of doors), **fetter, shackle,** *sgo ṫams - čad lčags btab - čiṅ* locking every door *Pth.; *káṅ-čag lág-čag* C.* fettered on hands and feet; *γnam-lčágs* 1. thunderbolt, 2. a flash of lightning just striking an object; *me - lčágs* a steel to strike fire with, fire-steel.

**Comp. and deriv.** *lčags-kyú B.* an iron hook, esp. fishing-hook, angle; often fig.: *ṫúgs-rǰei*, or *čós-kyi lčags-kyús ₒdzín-pa* to seize with the hook of grace or of religion *Dzl., Glr.* and elsewh. — *lčags-dkár* tinplate, white iron plate. — *lčags-skúd* **thin wire.** — *lčags - ḱém* or *ḱyém* **a spade.** — *lčags - ḱról Sch.* a big iron kettle (= *W.* **čag-dol** **stew-pan,** large iron pan or pot?) — *lčags - mgár* iron smith, **black-smith.** — *lčags-sgór* iron pan. — *lčags - sgyíd* **trevet, tripod.** — *lčags - sgróg* **fetter, shackle.** — *lčags - čás* **implements of iron, hardware.** — *lčags - tíg* a kind of **gentian,** cf. *tig - ta.* — *lčags-ṫág* **chain** or **chains.** — *lčags - ṫál Cs.* an iron **dish** or **plate,** prob. from *ṫá-li.* — *lčags - drégs* (*W.* **čag - rág**) 1. **iron dross,** scoria or slag of iron; 2. **dirt** of the intestines. — *lčags - rdó* 1. perh. more correctly *lčag - rdó* **flint - stone.** 2. iron - stone, **iron ore** (?). — *lčags - ṗrá Ü,* a kind of musket, imported from Rum (Turkey). — **čag-bér** *W.* an iron bar, **crowbar, handspike.** — *lčágs-mag, bčá-mag,* the Turkish چقمق **flint-stone, tinder-box** *W.* — *lčags-tságs* an iron **cribble** or **sieve, colander.** — *lčags-zám* iron bridge. — *lčags - záṅs* iron kettle. — **čag-záṅ** *C.* good iron, **steel.** — *lčags-γyá* **rust** *Med.* — *lčags-ri* **a wall encircling an estate, a town etc.** — *lčags-sláṅ* **a large iron pan for roasting or kiln-**

drying corn. — *lčags-šán* iron hoop, hasp, cramp-iron. — *lčags-sá* iron ore *Cs.* — *lčags-bsró* **smoothing-iron** *Sch.*

ལྕང་མ་ *lčáń-ma* **willow**, Salix viminalis, almost the only leaved tree in Tibet, frq. planted in the vicinity of villages; *rgyál-lčań* the specific name of this tree in *Kun.; róń-lčań, sér-lčań* different species of it; *lčań-dkár Kun.* a white kind with birch-like bark, cf. *šo*; *lčań-ló* willow-leaves, 2. (जटा) **matted hair**, *lčáń-lo-čan*, or *-pa*, one with matted hair, a penitent; also n. of a place in ancient India, of another in Lhasa, and of a third on the top of the fabulous Rirab. 3. **queue, pigtail** *C.* — *lčań-rlóm* a flat willow basket *Ts.* — *lčań-šiń* willow-tree, willow-wood. — *lčań-šól Sch.*: 'the red willow'. — **čań-sil* W.* coolness, shade under a willow-tree.

ལྕང་ལྕོང་ *lčań-lčóń Cs.* = *sań-šóń* **a craggy place, a broken country.**

ལྕམ་ *lčam*, also *p̓yam*, 1. **lath, pole, rafter, spar** of a roof. In Tibet the rafters are placed horizontally, and support a layer of earth; in Mongol tents they are slanting, supporting the felt-covering. — 2. also *brag-lčám*, n. of an officinal herb used for healing wounds *Med.* — 3. *gyur-lčám* prob. denotes a glittering fish, or a fish rapidly darting along — 4. v. *lčám-mo.*

ལྕམ་མེ་བ་ *lčám-me-ba*, perh. **variegated, shining, dazzling** *Glr.*

ལྕམ་མོ་ *lčám-mo*, resp. for *spun*, and esp. for *sriń-mo*, acc. to *Cs.* also for *čúń-ma*, **a royal consort**, a great man's **sister** or **wife**; *lha-lčám* a princess *Pth.*; *lčam-čúń* a young princess or lady, a young unmarried lady of noble rank; *lčam-drál, mčéd-lčam-dral, lčam-sriń* brother and sister.

ལྕམ་པ་ *lčám-pa* 1. n. of a flower *Wdń.*; 2. n. of a kind of vegetables *S.g.*

ལྕི་བ་ *lči-ba* 1. sbst. (*Ld.* **lča**, *Lh.* **či-a, čé-a**), **dung**, esp. of cattle; *bai lči-ba, bá-lči* cow-dung; *lči-skám* dry dung (used as fuel), *lči-rlón* fresh dung. — 2. adj. **heavy,** *W.* **čin-te**, *yań-lči* 1. light and heavy; 2. weight, **yań-či dán-da čó-če** *W.* to balance equally, to counterpoise; with regard to food, perh. heavy, oppressing the stomach; but also in a favourable sense: **substantial, nutritious;** fig.: **weighty, important,** *k̓yéd-kyi skyes dań bka-stsál lči-ba des* in consequence of your weighty presents and requests *Glr.*; **nám-čog čin-te** *W.* hard of hearing; *k̓a-na-ma-t̓ó-ba lči-ba* a heavy, deadly sin, frq.

ལྕིད་ *lčid* v. *ljid.*

ལྕིན་ཏེ་ *lčin-te* v. *lči-ba.*

ལྕིབས་ *lčibs* denotes a. things, which serve to protect the hands, when having to deal with hot or otherwise disagreeable objects; so gloves may be called *lčibs Sch.*, but esp. *tsa-lčibs* (*W.* **tsalčib**) **pot-cloth** (to take pots from the fire), **rę-čib** *C.*, also **lag-čib** id.; hence prob. *mig-lčibs*, resp. *spyan-lčibs* **eyelid**; *mig-gi lčibs-t̓ór* sty, wisp in the eye, and perh. from some remote similarity *sgo-lčibs, sgoi ya-lčibs* the lintel or head-piece of a door; *nya-lčibs* fishgills, *Lex.* and *Cs.*; b. contrivances to facilitate the handling of different objects, as: **the handles** of pots and vessels, the handles, **hilts, bows, ears, loops** etc. of knives, scissors, pincers and other working-tools.

ལྕུ་བ་ *lčú-ba* v. *γčú-ba.*

ལྕུག་པ་ *lčúg-pa Cs.*, *mnyen-lčug Lex.*, **flexible, pliant; a supple branch;** *lčug-lčúg byéd-pa* to bend repeatedly *Cs.*; *lčúg-ma* **a root-shoot** of a willow or a poplar-tree, **a rod, switch;** **čúg-gu** *C.* the bud of a twig; *lčug-p̓rán* a thin branch or twig.

ལྕུགས་ *lčugs, gri-yi lčugs Lex.* w.e.

ལྕུང་ཀ་ *lčúń-ka* = *skyúń-ka*, **jack-daw.**

ལྕུང་མོ་ *lčúń-mo* **thimble** *Glr.*

ལྕུད་པ་ *lčud-pa* v. *γčud-pa.*

ལྕུམ་ *lčum Med.*, *lčum-tsa Cs.*: **'a plant, the stalks of, which are used as a purga-**

tive'; *lċum-dkár* prob. another species of that plant *Med.*

ལྕེ *lċe* 1. resp. *ljags* (जिह्व) **tongue,** *lċe rkyaṅ-ba* to put forth, to show the tongue *Mil.*; *lċe brgyá-yis yon-tan ċuṅ-zad brjód-par nus ma mċis* even with a hundred tongues we should not be able sufficiently to praise the merit... *Pth.* — 2. **blade,** *Cs. gri-lċe.* — 3. (अशनि) **thunderbolt,** *lċe ˳bébs-pai glog* a flash of lightning accompanying a thunderbolt. — 4. **flame,** *me-lċe.*

ཆ

**Comp.** *lċe-kyigs* **the frenum** of the tongue *Cs.* — *lċe-čúṅ* **uvula,** *lċe-čuṅ ˳babs* inflammation of the uvula *Med.* — *lċe-ɣnyis-pa* **double-tongued, deceitful,** *lċe-ɣnyís byéd-pa* to be double-tongued. — *lċe-ṫéb, lċe-˳drá* a fleshy excrescence below the tongue *Cs.* — *lċe-bdé* a nimble tongue a babbler *Mil.* — *lċe-spyáṅ* = *ċe-spyáṅ Thgy., Stg.* — *lċe-˳búr* a swelling on the tongue *Cs.* — *lċe-myaṅ-ṫsá* **alum** *Med.* — *lċe-rtsá* the root of the tongue, *lċe-rtsá-ċan* a letter pronounced from the root of the tongue, a guttural. — *lċe-rtsé* the tip of the tongue *Cs.*, *lċe-rtsé-ċan* a letter sounded with the tip of the tongue, a lingual. — *lċe-ṫsá-(-ba)* a sharp-tasted, pungent medicinal herb *Med.* — *lċe-ɣžór* a tongue-scraper *Cs.*

ལྕེག *lċeg* a coat of mail for a horse *Sch.*

ལྕེབ་པ *lċéb-pa* to go to kill one's self, **to seek death,** esp. by a leap into the water or down a precipice, but not every kind of suicide; also used of insects that fly into a flame etc.

ལྕོ་ག *lċó-ga*, also *lċóg-ma* or *mo* **lark.**

ལྕོག *lċog* 1. *B., C.* **a turret** on a house-top, pinnacle (*W. *speu**). — 2. v. *lċóg-tse.*

ལྕོག་པོ *lċóg-po* prob. **low,** *lċóg-por skye* (a certain plant) is low-growing, it does not grow high.

ལྕོག་ཙེ, ལྕོག་རྩེ *lċóg-tse, lċóg-rtse,* resp. *ɣsol-lċóg,* **table,** in Tibet, esp. in *W.*, a very rare piece of furniture, and always small and low; *lċog-ḱébs* table-cloth, *lċog-ḱébs btiṅ-ba* to lay the cloth; *rgya-lċóg* a large table, a European table; *mdun-lċóg* 'fore-table', a sort of table before an idol, for spreading offerings on it, v. e.g. *Hook.* I, 172; but it is not the same as altar.

ལྕོགས *lċogs, zer-lċógs* **pronunciation** *C.*(?)

ལྕོག(ས)་པ *lċóg(s)-pa* I. **to be agitated, to shake, to tremble,** *mé-tog mgo-lċóg Zam.* a flower shaking, waving its head (little used).

II. 1. vb. **to be able,** *de ma lċóg-na* if (he) is not able (to do that); *ji lċóg-kyi Mil.* as much as possible, to the utmost; **ṅa-ráṅ-ghi gaṅ ċóg-pa* C.* as far as I am able. More used: 2. adj. **able,** *ṡéd-kyis mi lċóg-pa* unable, feeble, weak, *rig-pas mi lċóg-pa* ignorant; **ṅẹ ṫsar ċig-la ċóg-pa me'** I am not able to carry the whole at once *C.*; **ċóg-ċan** clever, skilful, handy, **ċog-méd** awkward *W.*; **ḱẹ ċog mi dug** he does not get on with his mouth, he lisps; also **ḱa ċóg-pa** irreverent, disrespectful in speaking *W.*(?)

ལྕོང *lċoṅ, sbol-lċóṅ* a frog in its first stage of development, **tadpole** *Pth.*

# ཆ

ཆ *ča* 1. the letter *č*, the aspirated *ċ*, pronounced hard and forcibly, like **ch** in *chap* or *church.* — 2. numerical figure: 6, *ča-pa* the sixth volume.

ཆ *ča* I. **part, portion, share** 1. opp. to the whole, *ča ɣsúm-du bgos* divide it in three parts! *brgyai ča* $\frac{1}{100}$ *Glr.*; *stóṅ-gi ča* $\frac{1}{1000}$; *baṅ-mdzód ɣsum-ča ɣċig* one third of the provisions *Dzl.; dbui ča tsam čig γsér-gyis ma lón-bar* there being still wanting about as much gold as (the weight of) his head *Glr.; nán-par sná-bai ča* the following day's first part, i.e. the following morning *Mil.*; *sá-ča* a piece of land *Glr.*, *C.*, also land, territory, country in general, *ghai sa-ča* the country of Gha *Glr.; zúr-ča* frontier parts, frontier province; *ča-snyoms* at equal parts, equally, e.g. *ču sbyar* mixed with the same quantity of water *Lt.; ča-mnyám* id., *ča-mnyám žib btey* accurately weighed in equal parts *Lt.; ča tsam, ča ₒdra tsam* in part, in some measure; *ča ma ₒdra* or *ma mťún-pa* partly not equal, differing a little; *ča tsam šes kyaṅ* even if one knows but a little *Mil.*; *yid smon ₒos ča tsam mi γdá-bas* it being not in the least desirable; *ča-rdzógs* being complete in every part, entire, integral *Sch.* — Esp. 2. **the half,** *nám-gyi ča stod*, the first half of the night, *nám-gyi ča smad* the second, the last half of it. Hence 3. **the one part** of a pair, similar to *ya*, *lham ča γčig* the one boot; *ča sgrig-pa* to pair, to match, to couple *Sch.*; an equal, a match, *ča-mťún-pa, ča-ₒdrá-ba*, *C.* also **ča-lóṅ-wa**, similar, resembling *Wdṅ.* and elsewh.; *la-lá ťár-pa ča-mťún dgé-ba med* some have no virtue befitting (i.e. leading to) final salvation *Thgy.; ča-méd* without an equal, matchless; *čá-ma-yin-pa* unfit, improper, unbecoming *Sch., ṅag γčóg-pa ni ča ma yin* not obeying will not do, is out of place *Tar.* 110, 11. — 4. **a pair,** = *zuṅ Sch.*; *Zam.*: युग. — 5. **share, portion, lot,** *mťsar-sdúg bltá-bai čá-nas mnyam* being equal as to their (respective) share of beauty *Glr.*; *dmán-ča ₒdzin-pa* to choose the humbler (inferior) share, i.e. to be humble, = *dmán-sa ₒdzin-pa Mil.*; in general: ***ča ₒdzin-pa*** c. genit. to adhere, to be attached to a person or thing *Pth.*; *žiṅ rmó-ba ṅai ča yin* ploughing is my business, my lot, my department *Dzl.*; *čá-la* equally, in equal parts, equally divided, *ká-ba nyin dgu mťsan dgu babs, čá-la nyin mťsan bčo-brgyád babs Mil.* there was a fall of snow during nine days and nine nights; it fell equally portioned out to days and nights, (together) eighteen (the peculiar mode of reckoning is here to be noticed).

II. **news, intelligence, notice,** construed like *rgyus* and *γtam; γtám-ča ₒdri-ba* = *γtam ₒdri-ba; ča yod, ča med* like *rgyus yod* and *rgyus med; nam ₒči ča méd-kyi čos* the doctrine of the uncertainty of the day of death *Mil.; ... par ča mčis-te* there coming news or intelligence that ...; *skád-ča* v. *skad*; physically: **voice, sound,** *brág-ča* echo; intellectually: **prospect, auspices,** *Mil.*: *sróg-ča* prospects of life (as to its length and preservation), *kyím-ča* prospects regarding the household, *dgra-ča* prospects, expectations as to one's enemies; **lám-ča** *C.* prospects of a safe journey (cf. *ṅo* 4).

III. **thing, things,** relating to clothes, ornaments, materials etc., cf. *čas;* **go-lus-ča-tsáṅ** *W.* a complete suit of clothes; but mostly used in compounds: *ské-ča* neck-ornaments, *glo-ča* ornaments suspended to the belt or girdle, e.g. strings of shells; *dgós-ča* necessary things *Cs.*; *mčód-ča* things necessary for sacrifices, requisites for offerings *Glr.*; *mťsón-ča* weapons; *yig-ča* prob. writings, deeds, documents *Glr.*; **rẹ-ča** cottons, cotton fabrics *C.*; *lag-ča* implements, utensils, goods, baggage etc. *Glr.* — There is still to be noticed the expression: *ča-bžág-pa*, lit. to add one's own share to a thing, 1. to adhere, stick, or cling to, to follow, obey (laws); *saṅs-rgyás-kyi bká-la ča bžag* they adhere to the words of Buddha; *rgyál-poi bká-la* to obey the king's commandment. 2. to refer to (?) *C.*

ཆ་རྐྱེན་ *ča-rkyén Lex., Sch.*: 'share of destiny, of fate; consequence of one's actions' (?).

ཆ་མཁན་ *čá-mkan* **soothsayer, fortune-teller** *Sch.*

ཆ་ག་ *čá-ga Mil.*, **hem, edge, border;** *čá-ga ₒdebs-pa* to hem, to turn in (the edge of cloth).

ཆ་ག་འབུ. *čá-ga-ₒbu C.*, *Lex.* also *čá-ga-pa*, **grasshopper.**

ཆ་ཆོ *čá-čo Lex.*, *Sch.*: 'things homogeneous, matched'.

ཆ་བ *čá-ba*, pf. and imp. *soṅ* (the regular form *čas* being nearly obs. at present), in *W.* the usual word for *ₒgro-ba* to go, in *B.* little used and only in later writings, 1. **to go,** **šór-te čá-če** to retire, to retreat slowly; **da ča yin**, or **da čen** adieu, good bye, farewell! **da čen žu** resp., your servant! (in taking leave); **'á-ru-soṅ** go thither, or that way! **'á-ru ma ča** do not go to this place, do not step this way! **to travel,** **gyál-la** (or *dé-mo, yág-po*) *ča žig** I wish you a safe journey, a pleasant trip to you! **lóg-te čá-če** to return, to go or come back; **tiṅ-la čá-če** to follow, to come after or later; **ča čug** let (him) go! give (it) up! let (it) alone! **to be gone, consumed, spent, used, wasted,** **šiṅ mán-po ča yin** a great deal of wood will go, will be consumed. — 2. **to become, grow, get, turn,** **tsan ča dug** it grows night, it is getting dark; **gas čá če** to grow old; **nág-po soṅ** that has turned black; **šés-kan čá-če** to get information; also with *la*: **bág-ma-la čá-ba** (= *bág-mar ₒgró-ba, ₒgyúr-ba*) to become a bride *Ma.*; **mán-lami ča** this is not used for medicine. — 3. with a supine (*B.*) or a verbal root (col.): **to be about, to be on the point, to be going,** *sléb-tu čá-bai tse* when they were on the point of arriving *Mil.*; *nyi-ma ₒčár-du čá-ba daṅ* when the sun was just going to rise *Mil.*; **me ši ča dug** the fire is on the point of going out; **nad ži ča dug**, the disease is decreasing. — 4. with the gerund it expresses a continuous progress, a gradual operation, an effect by little and little, **ču pél-te ča dug** the water increases from day to day. — 5. with the inf. it is used in the sense of the future tense, or like the Greek μέλλειν: **to intend, to purpose,** **či šrid-de dir šriṅ-če ča dug** how long does he (do you etc.) intend to stay? **nam lug sád-če ča dug** when are you going to kill the sheep?

ཆ་བུ *čá-bu*, a kind of little ornament worn in the ears *Ld.*

ཆ་བྱད *ča byád* 1. **thing, implement, instrument,** e.g. a musical instrument *Dzl.*, a surgical instr. *Med.* — 2. **clothing, dress,** *mi-sdúg-pai ča-byad-čan* poorly clothed, ragged *Mil.*; **external appearance,** also of animals.

ཆ་ཚམ *ča-tsám* v. *ča* I, 1.

ཆ་ཚད *ča-tsád* = *čag-tsad.*

ཆ་ཚན *ča-tsán* **species, division, class** *Sch.*

ཆ་འཛིན *ča-ₒdzin* v. *ča* I., 5.

ཆ་རྫོགས *ča-rdzógs* v. *ča* I, 1.

ཆ་ར *čá-ra* **1. oak,** also *mon-čá-ra* (on account of its growing only on the southern ranges of the Himalaya mountains, inhabited mostly by Non-Tibetans) in several species, with pointed, evergreen leaves, a tree much inferior in beauty to the English oak. *čá-ra ṗreu Sch.*: 'the stunted or dwarf-oak'. — 2. also *ča-ri, ča-lí, ča-lú*, a coarse sort of **blanket** made of yak's hair.

ཆ་ལ *čá-la* v. *ča* I., 5.

ཆ་ལག *čá-lag* 1. *C.* **implements, instruments,** required for the carrying on of a business. — 2. *W.* **things, effects,** luggage. — 3. *Tar.* 43, 18: *čá-lag daṅ bčás-pa rdzógs-par šés-pa Schf.*: 'the systematic and complete understanding'.

ཆ་ལང *ča-láṅ* joined with *rdéb-pa Lex.* and *Mil.*, meaning not known; *Wts.* gives: petite lance des bonzes.

ཆ་ལམ *čá-lam* = *há-lam*, **some; for the most part, rather** *C.*

ཆ་ལི, ཆ་ལུ *ča-li, ča-lú* v. sub *čá-ra.*

ཆ་ལུགས *ča-lúgs* **clothing, costume, appearance.**

ཆ་ཤས *ča-šás* **part, portion, share,** *lús-kyi ča-šás* a part of the body, a limb etc.

ཆ་ཧར *ča-hár* Chakhar, a Mongol tribe *Sch.*

ཆག་ *čag* 1. **dry fodder** for horses and other animals, as hay, barley etc.; *čag-γžoṅ* trough, manger, crib. — 2. **the fourth finger** *Med.* — 3. resp. for **shoe** *Glr.*, also *p̒yag(-lhám).* — 4. *čag-p̒éb-pa Glr.* = *p̒yag p̒éb-pa.* — 5. **the breadth of a fist,** *čag gaṅ* id, *Mṅg.* frq. — 6. v. *čág-pa.*

ཆག་(ད)ཀྲུམ(ས)་ *čag-(d)krúm(s)* **piece, fragment** *Lex.*, *Thgy.*; **čag-ṭúm-la soṅ* C.* it has gone to pieces.

ཆག་སྐྱ་བ་ *čag-skya-ba Sch.*: 'having only one purpose, pursuing but one aim; unremitting, indefatigable'.

ཆག་ག་ཆོག་གེ་ *čag-ga-čog-gé* (or *p̒yag-ga-p̒yog-gé?*) various things mixed up or thrown together, medley.

ཆག་གྲུམ་ *čag-grúm Lex.* = *čag-dkrúm(?).*

ཆག་རྒྱག་པ་ *čag-rgyág-pa* **to doubt** *Sch.*

ཆག་ཆག་ *čag-čág* I. 1. with *byed-pa*, *ₒdebs-pa*, **to sprinkle, besprinkle,** *čus* with water, *k̒áṅ-pa, lám-rnams* the house, the streets *B., C.* (*W.* **čab-čáb**). — 2. *Sch.*: *čag-čág γdab-pa* **to starch, to stiffen.**

II. *W. čag-čág* **cò-ce** **to tread, to trample,** e.g. the narrow paths or furrows between garden-beds; **to clap the hands.**

ཆག་ཆད་ *čag-čád* **rent, break, rupture** *Sch.*

ཆག་དུམ་ *čag-dúm* **fragment, piece, crumb, scrap, bit.**

ཆག་འདིང་ *čag-ₒdiṅ* **doubtful, incredible** *Sch.*

ཆག་པ་ *čág-pa* 1. a large **tuft** or **bunch** of flowers, ears of corn etc. — 2. pf. of *ₒčág-pa*, **broken;** *ma-čág(s)-pa*, and esp. adv. *ma-čág(s)-par* also *čág-med-par* uninterrupted, unintermitting; uninterruptedly; *gas-čag-méd* without a crack, flaw, or chink. — 3. *lam čág-pa* v. *ₒčag-pa.*

ཆག་པོ་ *čág-po* **broken; a broken vessel, pot** etc., **a pot-sherd;** *tsel-(po) čág(-po)* a broken dosser or pannier.

ཆག་བུ་ *čág-bu*, diminutive of *čag-pa*, **a little bunch.**

ཆག་མོ་ *čág-mo* **bunch,** *ₒbrás-bu čág-mo* a fruit growing in the form of bunches or clusters, like the grapes of the vine, the berries of the elder etc. *W.*

ཆག་ཙེ་ *čág-tse* a small **grain,** e.g. of ground grits, **čág-tse-ċan** **granulous;** **bág-p̒e čág-tse-ċan** ground grits, *W.*; *Hind. soojee.*

ཆག་ཚད་ *čag-tsád Sch.*: **the right measure,** *dug ster čag-tsád* if a sufficient quantity of poison has been administered to a person, *Med.*

ཆག་ཤིང་ *čag-šiṅ* a wooden **splint** for a broken limb, **ċug-ċe** to put it on *W.*

ཆགས་པ་ *čágs-pa* I. frq. for *čág-pa* 2.

II. vb. **to be begotten, produced;** *ma-čágs-pa* not begotten or produced in the usual way of propagation, but = *rdzús-te skyés-pa*, or *lhún-gyis grúb-pa Pth.* frq.; *mṅál-du čágs-pa* to be produced in the womb, as the foetus is; hence *čags* in compounds: animal, *ₒdab-čágs*, *γšog-čágs* winged animal, bird; *srog-čágs* in general: a living being, an animal, = *séms-ċan*; *ₒp̒rúl-gyi ṭsul-čágs Glr.* prob. as much as a wonderful child, a prodigy; *šiṅ-la čágs-pa* to grow on a tree, of fruits; and in general: **to rise, arise, spring up, originate,** of the world, of new works, buildings, empires, customs, of eruptions on the skin; **zíl-pa čags soṅ** *W.* dew has fallen; **to come forth, to appear,** = *ₒbyúṅ-ba*, e.g. *ₒód-du čágs-pa* to come to light, to appear *Mil.*; * *ṅul čags* * *W.* sweat comes forth, breaks out, I perspire; even: *ráb-tu čágs-pa* = *ráb-tu ₒbyúṅ-ba* to become a cleric (little used); *čags-rábs* genesis, history of the beginning, esp. of the world; *čags-ṭsúl* 1. manner of beginning, origin, procreation *Med.* 2. *W.* form, figure, demeanour, **čags-ṭsúl sóg-po** coarse, rude, rough.

III. 1. vb. **to love,** (ἐρᾶν), *bú-mo-la* a girl; *skyés-pa daṅ na-čúṅ γčig čágs-pa* the mutual affection between a man and a maiden; tender attachment in general, connubial, parental and filial love, *yid-la čágs-pai bú-mo-rnàms* my dearly beloved daughters *Pth.*; ardent desire or longing for something, *grágs-pa-la* for glory; **to be attached to, to cling to,** e.g. *lus daṅ srógla čágs-pa* to life, *yúl-la* to one's home, to one's native country; often: to suffer one's self to be enticed by a thing, **to indulge in;** *čágs-par mi bya ʼjigs-par mi byá-ste* allowing neither desire nor fear to have any influence upon himself *Samb.* — 2. sbst. **love** (ἔρως), **lust, passion** for, **affection, attachment,** *čágs-pa skyés-so* he fell in love *Dzl.*; *čágs-pa spyód-pa* = *ʼkrig-pa spyód-pa.* According to Buddhistic theory all *čágs-pa* is a great evil, as it betrays a troubled state of mind, and a reprehensible attachment to external things; yet even a saint, so far advanced in dispassion and apathy as Milaraspa, may sometimes be caught in very tender affections and sensations of *čágs-pa,* very like those of other human creatures.

**Comp.** *čags-sdáṅ* 1. *Schr.* **love and hatred,** 2. *Glr.*, *Pth.* **jealousy** (love showing itself in hatred), also *čags-sdáṅ-gi ṗrag-dog.* — *čags-spyód* **coition, copulation,** cf. *čágs-pa* III., 2. — *čags-žén,* also *žen-čágs* = *čágs-pa* sbst. *Mil.*; **čags-žén ċó-ċe* W.*, to love, c. *la*; *čags-žén méd-pa* dispassionate, indifferent to all terrestrial things. — *čags-séms* = *čags-žén.* — *čágs-sred-ċan Pth.* **lustful, libidinous, wanton.**

ཆང་ *čaṅ* (मद्य) resp. *skyems, ysól-čaṅ, mčód-čaṅ C.*, a fermented liquor, **beer, wine,** (not 'brandy' *Sch.*); *bu skyés-pa-la miṅ, čaṅ dráṅs-pa-la yťam* proverb: to the new-born child a name (is due), to the beer to be drunk a talk; *nás-čaṅ* beer made of barley (the usual kind); *brás-čaṅ* of rice *Glr.*; *gró-čaṅ* of wheat *Cs.*; *bú-ram-čaṅ,* or *búr-čaṅ* of sugar *Med.*; *rgún-čaṅ* wine; *sbráṅ-čaṅ Med.* honey-wine, mulse, mead? *rús-čaṅ Med.?* — *zás-čaṅ, zán-čaṅ* eating and drinking, meat and drink. — *sloṅ-, tig-,* and *bsu-čaṅ* v. sub *bág-ma.* — Fig.: *btúṅ-ba dran-šes bdúd-rtsii čaṅ* my drink is the wine of wisdom's **nectar** *Mil.* —

Here the process of brewing may be mentioned. When the boiled barley (*Ld. *sbo-bód*, Ts. *ťab**) has grown cold, some **ṗabs** (q. v.) is added, after which it is left standing for two or three days, until fermentation commences, when it is called *glum.* Having sufficiently fermented, some water is poured to it, and the beer is considered to be ready for use. If proper care is taken (and the people of Ü and Ladak generally do so), the pale beer, thus obtained, is not amiss, and sparkles a good deal, but not being hopped it does not keep long. The people of Lahoul are accustomed to press out the *glum* with their hands, instead of filtering it, and mismanage the business also in other respects, so that their *čaṅ* is a gray muddy liquor, that has hardly any resemblance to beer. The residue of malt, called *sbáṅ-ma,* may be mixed with water or milk, pressed through a strainer, and used instead of barm in baking bread, cakes etc.

**Comp.** *čáṅ-ḱaṅ* **beer-house, pot-house, tavern.** — *čáṅ-ċan* **drinking-cup** or **bowl** *Sch, Wts.* — *čáṅ-čem-ċan* **an intoxicated person.** — *čáṅ-čem-sa Lex.* prob. = *čáṅ-sa.* — *čáṅ-ʼtuṅ-mḱan* **a beer-drinker;** **čáṅ-ʼtun-ḱan máṅ-po dzom** a great beer-drinking bout takes place *W.* — **čáṅ-dad-ċan** **a drunkard, tippler** *W.* — *čáṅ-ťsúgs* = *čaṅ-ċan Sch.* — *čáṅ-ʼťsoṅ-gi ḱyim* **beer-house** *Dzl.* — *čáṅ-sa* 1. **beer-house** 2. **beer-carousal,** *čáṅ-sa čén-po byéd-pa* to give or arrange a great beer-drinking bout *Mil.*

ཆང་ཆུང་ *čaṅ-čúṅ* **a little** *Sch.*

ཆད་ *čad* 1. also *čad-dón, čad-mdó, W.* **čád-ka*,* **promise, engagement, agreement** *ḱa-čád* oral, verbal engagement, *lag-čád* pledge of faith by hand; *čad-dón byéd-pa, *čád-ką ċó-ċe, zúm-ċe* W.*, to give a promise, make a contract; *ytóṅ-(bai) čad(-don) byéd-pa* to agree about giving; *čad-dón ltar byéd-pa* to keep, fulfil a promise; *čad-rdó* 1. the stone which is broken in the ceremony of *rdo yċóg-pa* q. v. 2. monument, memorial of a covenant. — 2. in compounds also for *čád-pa* punishment, *lus-čád* corporeal punishment.

ཆད་པ་ *čád-pa* I. sbst., resp. *bka-čád*, **punishment**; the preceding genit., contrary to our usage, is the genit. of the punishing person, thus: *rgyál-poi čád-pa* a punishment of the magistrates, i. e. a punishment decreed or inflicted by the magistrates, frq.; seldom, if ever, genit. of the punished action, and never that of the punished person. In classical language the usual construction of the words is the following: *čád-pas γčód-pa* to punish, *mi žig-la* somebody, ...*pas* or ... *pai ṗyir* for having...; in more recent literature: *čád-pa γčód-pa Thgr., Glr.*; *čád-pa ťób-pa* 1. to receive the fine incurred by another 2. to suffer punishment, to pay a fine; *ṅá-la čád-pa ṗog* punishment is inflicted on me, I am punished.

II. 1. **to promise,** e.g. *bká-las mi ˳gál-bar* to obey. — 2. v. sub *˳čád-pa*.

III. adj. **begotten, born, descended** from; the Tibetans are *sbreu daṅ srin-mo-nas* (or *las*) *čád-pa* the offspring of a monkey and a Rakshasi *Glr.*; *šá-nas čád-pai bu* a full child *Glr.*

ཆད་པོ་ *čád-po* 1. **rent, torn, worn-out, ragged, tattered,** *sgyi-gu čád-po* a leaky purse. — 2. a limited time, **a term** *Sch.*

ཆད་ཡིག *čad-yig* **a written contract**; *čad-mál-gyi yi-ge Glr.* id.

ཆད་ལུས་པ་ *čád-lus-pa* not to obtain the things hoped for, to be disappointed *Sch.*

ཆད་སོ་ *čád-so* 1. a limited time, **a term.** — 2. **a time-purchase** *Sch.* — 3. **an agreement** *Tar.*

ཆན་ *čan*, also *čan-ťúg Sch.*, **boiled corn** or **barley** etc.; *˳bras-čán* rice-pap, *nas-čán* barley-pap.

ཆན་པ་ *čán-pa* a pair of **scissors**, but the common people know only **shears**, which are for various purposes; the scissors mentioned in surgical books are prob. of a nicer construction.

ཆབ་ *čab*, resp. and eleg. for *ču* 1. **water,** *dri-čáb* scented water; *sṅa-čáb, ṗyi-čáb*, water which at the beginning and close of the meetings in the large monasteries is handed round, and of which every one present takes a few drops on his tongue, as a symbol of purification, in place of the original ablutions. — 2. for other fluids, as *spyan-čáb* **tears**, *žal-čáb* **spittle**, *γsaṅ-čáb*, or *čab-γsáṅ* **urine**, *ba-čab* cow's urine (so with the Hindoos in *Lh.*, the cow being to them a sacred animal). — 3. in some compounds: **power, dominion, authority.** — *čab-rkyán* **brass can, brass-(tea) pot** with a long spout for pouring out tea, *W.*; also n. for Tibet, perh. on account of the large consumption of tea there. — *čab-ǩúṅ* **privy** *Cs.* — *čab-sgó* **door,** *čab-sgo-pa* **door-keeper, porter.** — **čab-ḍá** (spelling dubious) a wooden **pail,** of a similar shape as *čab-rkyán W.* — *čab-bróm, čab-róm* **ice.** — *čab-blúg C.* a vessel for rinsing one's mouth with water. *čab-mig* eleg. for *ču-mig* **fountain, spring.** — *čab-ťsód* eleg. **a watch, a clock.** — *čab-˂óg* what is subjected to a person's sway, territory, dominion etc., *čab-˂óg-tu sdú-ba* to subject; *čab-˂óg-gi rgyál-po* a vassal, feudal tenant *Trig.*; *čab-˂óg-pa*, also *čab-˳báṅs* one owing allegiance to a sovereign, a subject. — *čab-šóg Cs.* eleg. for **letter, diploma** etc. — *čab-sér* eleg. for *ču-sér* **matter, pus.**

ཆབ་མ་ *čáb-ma W., C.*, also *Mil.*, **lid, valve; buckle, clasp,** *čáb-tse*, or *čáb-rtse C.* id.

ཆབས་ *čabs Lex. čabs-γčig Sch.* = *ťabs-γčig* **together.**

ཆམ་ *čam*, in *čám-la ˳bébs-pa Lex.* w.e.; *Sch.*: to throw down, to cause to lie down; to subdue, subject; to spend, consume, **to have done with**; by this last signification it would be a syn. to *zin-pa*, and the circumstance that *čams* is used in Balti as an auxiliary vb. of the pf. tense agrees with that supposition, e. g. **zan zós-se čams** I have done eating, = *zos zin B.*

ཆམ་པ་ *čám-pa* 1. **cold** (in the head), **catarrh**; *sne-čám* id.; *gre-čam* catarrh in the throat, bronchial catarrh; *glo-čám* catarrh in the lungs; *rims-čám* an infecting or epidemic catarrh. — 2. *Cs.* = ̥*čám-pa* **accord, accordance.**

ཆམ་མེ་ *čam-mé* **slowly, by degrees, gradually** *Schr.* (cf. *čem-mé*).

ཆར་ *čar*, termin. of *ča*, 1. **into parts**, e.g. *bgó-ba* to divide into parts. — 2. **as an equal, as a match,** ... *la čar mi ṗod* he is not an equal to, cannot come up to... *Thgy.*; ... *dan stón-ṗrag-čar mi nye* prob.: he does not come up to... at all (lit. not for the thousandth part) *Pth.*; so in a similar manner: *brgyai čar yaṅ mi sleb Tar.* — 3. affixed to numerals, and sometimes, though less correctly, written *čar*, q.v. The terminations of the cases mag be affixed to it: *lṅa* **čár-gyis** every fifth day *Thgy.*

ཆར་ *čar*, also *čár-pa*, 1. **rain**, *čar čén-po* a plentiful rain, *čar drág-po*, or *drag-čár* a heavy rain; *čar čén-pas* or *čé-bas* as it rained heavily *Pth.*; *čar ̥bébs-pa* to cause to rain; *čar ̥bab* it rains, *W.* **čár-pa yoṅ**; *čár-gyi rgyun* a sudden or violent shower of rain *Tar.* — 2. at Kyelang for **watering-pot**; this utensil having never been seen there before, the word was at first applied to it jestingly, but is now generally adopted; *ču-ṫság* 'water-sieve' would be more correct.

**Comp.** *čar-skyibs* **a shelter, pent-roof,** protecting from rain. — *čar-kébs* dress against rain, **rain-cloak.** — *čár-čan*, *čár-ldan* rainy *Cs.* — *čár-ču* **rain-water.** — *čár-dus* **rainy season.** — *čar-̥dód (-byeu)* n. of a bird, water-ousel. — *čar-sprin* a rain-threatening cloud. — **čar-bhi** (?) *C.* rain-cloak. — *čar-rlúṅ* rain and wind *Cs.* — **čar-šiṅ** = *čar-skyibs W.* — *čar-lén* the coping or water-tile of a wall *Cs.*

ཆལ་ *čal*, *sku-čál* resp. **belly, abdomen,** *Cs.*

ཆལ་ཆིལ་ *čal-čil Lex.*, wavering, fluctuating *Sch.*

ཆལ་ཆོལ་ *čal-čól Tar.* 184, 20 = ̥*čal-la-̥col-le.*

ཆལ་མར་བརྡལ་བ་ *čál-mar brdál-ba* to spread equally, uniformly (vb. a.)

ཆས་ *čás* (*Sch. čás-ka*) cf. *ča* III., 1. **thing, tool, requisite** etc., *sé-mo-do-la sógs-pai čás-kyis brgyán-te* adorned with ornaments of pearls and other things *Mil.*; *dga-stón-gyi čas rgya čén-po* grand festival arrangements; *čas dé-rnams bšig* overturn the whole affair! *Glr.*; *bág-mar rdzóṅ-bai čas* things to be given to her as a dowry *Tar.* 121, 5; *lčágs-čas* iron tools or utensils; *ltó-čas* food; *dmag-čas* military stores, requisites for war *Pth.*; ̥*ṫsó-čas* provisions *Mil.*; *lág-čas* tool, instrument *Cs.* — 2. **dress, garment,** *ṗó-čas* man's dress; *čas-gós*, *W.* **gón-čē**, coat, dress; in a more general sense: **appearance, form, shape,** *búd-med-kyi čás-su byáste* appearing in the shape of a woman *Glr.*; *hór-čas byed* he puts on a Mongol dress *Ma.*; *bú-moi čás-su žugs* he puts on a girl's dress, disguises himself as a girl *Glr.*, *Pth.*; *čas sgyúr-ba* to put on, to assume another dress.

ཆས་པ་ *čás-pa*, originally the pf. of *čá-ba*, but always used as a separate vb. 1. **to set out, set forth, depart,** *čas dgós-par* as I must depart from here *Thgy.*; *bód-du čás-so* they set out for Tibet *Glr.*; *dus-γčig-tu čás-so* they departed at the same time *Dzl.*; *čás-su ̥júg-pa* to send away, dispatch; *mgyógs-čas γtóṅ-ba* to rush, run towards. — 2. **to set about, to begin,** *γsód-par* to kill; ̥*gró-bar čás-pa-las* when he made arrangements to depart *Dzl.*; also in the following manner; *da ṗyir ̥dóṅ-ṅo žes čás-pa* 'now we will return' they said, making preparations, or: saying thus, they made preparations *Dzl.*; *ṫugs čás-so* he had set his mind on departing *Mil.*

ཆི་ *či* num. fig.: 36.

ཆི་ཀ་ *čí-ka* **wallet, knapsack** *W.*

ཆི་ཏྲ་ *čí-tra W.* **variegated, figured,** of fabrics.

ཆི་ལི་ལི་ *či-li-li* onomatopoetic word for snuffing up scents by the nose; **žim-žim ḍi-ma či-li-li kyer** *C.* sweet odours of cakes are meeting us; *mé-tog dri-ma či-li-li* the perfumes of flowers are perceptible *Mil.*

ཅིག *čig* = *γčig* **one**, as the first part of compound numbers: *čig-bču* 10, *čig-brgya* 100, *čig-ston* 1000, *čig-ḱri* a myriad etc.; also: *čig-rkyáṅ Lex.*, *Schr.*: 'separate, single, one alone'; *čig-skyés Med.*, *čig-táṅ Med.?* — *čig-ťúb* n. of a plant *Med.*; *Sch.* also: *čig-ťúb-pa* to be able to do a thing alone; *čig-dril Sch.*: rolled, wrapped, packed up (in one parcel or bundle); *čig-láb byéd-pa* to talk to one's self, to hold a soliloquy *Schr.*

ཅིང(ས)་ *čiṅ(s)* v. *˳čiṅ-ba.*

ཅིད་པ་ *čid-pa* v. *ṗyid-ba.*

ཅིབ་པ་ *čib-pa* equal, uniform, suitable *Sch.*

ཅིབས་(པ) *čibs (-pa)* resp. **horse**, riding-horse, saddle-horse, *čibs-la ˳čib-pa* (for *rtá-la žón-pa*) to get on horseback, to mount; to go on horseback, to ride; *čibs-las γžól-ba* to dismount, **čibs žól-la naṅ** *C.* may your honour please to dismount; *ḱyéd-kyi čibs-su ˳bul* I give it you for a riding-horse *Mil.*

**Comp.** *čibs-ka ˳ḱrid-pa* to lead a horse by the bridle *Schr.*; *čibs-ḱa ťúb-pa* to have the command of the bridle, fig.: to be expert in ruling *Ld.-Glr.* p. 14, a, *Schl.* where *ṗyibs* is incorr.). — *čibs-čás* a horse's furniture, **harness** *Cs.* — *čibs-ťur* **the head-piece** of a bridle. — *čibs-dpón* a master groom, **equerry.** — *čibs-rá* **a stable** for horses.

ཆུ *ču* I. num. fig.: 66.

II. sbst. (resp. *čab*) 1. **water;** *ču daṅ sai bu* is said to be a poetical name for wood; *˳báb-ču* lit. descending water, viz. brook, river, also rain. — 2. **brook, river,** *ču ˳ḱyám-po* overflowing rivers, floods *Ma.*; *ťáṅ-ču* a river or rivulet of the plain; *ri-γzár-ču* cataract, mountain torrent *Glr.* — 3. **water in the body:** *snyiṅ-ču* dropsy in the pericardium, *págs-ču* anasarca *Med.*; *págs-ču-zugs* one suffering from anasarca; v. also *ču-sér;* esp. euphem. for **urine;** *mi-ču* urine of men, *bá-ču* of cows *Med.*; *ču ni ču ˳dra* the urine is like water *Med.* — 4. v. *ču-žéṅ.*

**Comp.** *ču-klúṅ* **river,** e.g. *ču-kluṅ gaṅ-gā* the river Ganges *Dzl.* — *ču-klóṅ Cs.*: 'the body of a river', yet v. *kloṅ.* — *ču-dkyil* the middle of a river. — *ču-rkyál* a leather bag for water *Cs.* — *ču-skád* the voice of the waters, the sound of rushing water. — *ču-skór*, *raṅ-ťág-ču-skór* **water-mill** *Glr.* — *ču-skyúr* n. of a bird *Thgy.*, *Sch.*: **'bittern, snipe'**; also n. of a plant. — *ču-skyúr* 1. *Lt.*: acidulous mineral waters 2. *C.*: **vinegar.** — *ču-skyés* 'water-born', the lotus *Glr.* — *ču-skyór* a handful of water. *ču-ḱa* the bank or brink of a river. — *ču-ḱúg* **bay, gulf.** — *ču-˳ḱúr* containing water, po. for **cloud;** a native proposed to use this word also for **sponge,** which is a commodity hitherto unknown in Tibet. — *ču-˳ḱyil* **puddle, pool.** — *ču-gáṅ* 1. full of water. 2. = *ču-sgáṅ* (v. *sgaṅ*) which latter is prob. the more correct spelling. 3. *Dzl.* ༡༡༦, 2; ༢༤༡, 18 = **सत्त्व** virtue, honesty, v. *Schf.* on this passage. — *ču-grí* a sort of knife; *Tar.* 43, 1 *Schf.* razor; also the attribute of a god, a weapon with a curved blade *Stg.* — *ču-gróg Sch.*: rivulet, brook; dish-water, rinsings; boiled water (?). — *ču-mgó C.* **source** or **head** of a river. — *ču-gágs* stoppage or retention of urine, **ischury,** *ču-gágs ˳bigs* the ischury is removed (lit. bored through) *Med.* — *ču-˳grám* **bank** of a river; *ču-grám-gyi šiṅ* a tree on the edge of a river, a metaphor for frail and perishable things. — *ču-rgyún* the streaming, continual flowing, **current,** often fig. — *ču-sgóṅ* the water-egg, po. for moon *Sch.* — *ču-ṅógs* v. *ṅógs.* — **čú-ta-gir** *W.* flour-dumplings, boiled in water. — **ču-stáṅ** *W.* **swaddling-cloth.** — **ču-ťág** *W.* calamus, sweet-scented flag, or some similar plant. — *ču-ťúms Sch.*: 'a swelling in the flesh, or a tumour filled with water'. — *ču-mťá* the side or **bank** of a river, **ču-ťá tsúg-pa** (the avalanche came down) even to the river side. — *ču-dár Wdk.* a small prayer-flag stuck up close to the river, in order to avert inundations. — *ču-dúg Sch.*: 'a poisonous plant, hemlock', but Tibetans usually understand by it the stupefying power ascribed to certain rivers. — *ču-dóṅ* **a deep well.** —

ཆ

— ču-mdá **a jet,** a spouting forth of water *Med.* — *ču-mdó* 'mouth (of a river), spout (of a tea-pot)' *Sch.;* but v. *mču.* — *ču-mdóg* the colour of urine *Med.* — *ču-rdó C.* small rounded pebbles, as in brooks. — *ču-nág* inundation, flood (?) *Ma.* — *ču-rnág* matter, pus *Sch.* — *ču-snód* 1. **pitcher, jug.** 2. *Schr.:* **chamber-pot** (yet in *W.* at least this article of luxury is not known). — *čú-pa* **water-carrier.** — *ču-pyág-pa* is enumerated among other synonyms to *grú-pa,* signifying **a ferry-man,** water-man. — *ču-prán* a little river, **brook.** — *ču-bár* 1. ('between the waters') **isthmus,** neck of land. 2. p. n. of a place in Tibet. — *ču-bál* n. of an aquatic plant *Wdṅ.* — *ču-bún* white paint for the face *Sch.* — *ču-bór* 1. **bubble,** also *čui ču-búr* 2. **blister, bladder, vesicle,** e.g. occasioned by a burn or a vesicatory *Lt.* 3. **boil, ulcer, abscess** *Thgy.,* 4. *šai ču-búr* a word describing the foetus five days after conception *Thgy.* — *čú-bur-čan* 1. n. of a hell *Thgy.* 2. the eye *Schr.* — *čú-bo* **river,** frq., *čú-bo-ri* n. of a mountain with a monastery two days' journey from Lhasa *Glr.* — *ču-byá* **a water-bird;** *Sch.:* *ču-byá dkár-po* swan, *ču-byá mgo-dmár* stork (not known in *W.*). — *ču-byí* **water-rat** *Sch.* — *ču-lbág* v. *lbag.* — *ču-sbúr* 1. *Sch.:* 'driftwood and the like', prob. more correctly: thin pieces of wood, chips, chaff etc. floating on the water. 2. **water-beetle** *Med.* — *ču-sbrúl* **water-snake,** not a mythological conception, like *klu,* but a really existing animal, though for Tibetans a somewhat faboulous one, as they have never seen the creature itself. The eel (*Sch.*) can hardly be meant by it. — *ču-mig* 1. **spring, fountain** frq. 2. n. of a vein *Med.* — *ču-rtsá* v. *ču-ču,* as a separate article. — *ču-tságs* 1. **a strainer, sieve,** 2. **watering-pot.** — *ču-tsán* 1. hot water, 2. warm water, not too hot for drinking *Med.* 3. a hot spring *Sch.* — *ču-tsód* 1. the clepsydra or **water-clock** of ancient India. 2. **clock** in general, *ču-tsod-ₒkór-lo* a wheel-clock. 3. **the Indian hour** = ⅕ *kyim* or 24 minutes. 4. **the European hour;** *W.:* **ču-tsód nyis ma leb** it is not yet two o'clock. — *ču-ₒdzin* po. **cloud** *Mil.* — *ču-rdzá* earthen vessel for water, **water-jar.** — *ču-žén* (*Lex.* तरिणाह) **long and broad, area, superficial extent,** *ču-žén kru-brgyád-pa* eight cubits long and broad *Dzl.;* also *ču-žeṅ-gáb-pa,* e.g. *ču-žeṅ-gáb-pa-la dpag-tsád brgyád-ču Glr.;* *ču-žeṅ-srab-túg* in length, breadth and height; also separately: *čur dpag-tsád* ༢༥༠༠, *žén-du yaṅ* ༢༥༠༠, *mta-skór-du dpag-tsád* ༡༠༠༠༠ *yód-pa* 2500 miles in length, 2500 miles in breadth, 10000 in circumference; yet except in this connexion *ču* alone is never used for length. As another signification of *ču-žeṅ-gáb-pa Schr.* mentions moreover: proportioned, symmetrical; others have: beautiful, great, considerable, which e.g. is its proper meaning in: *ču-žeṅ-gáb-pa nya-grodha Stg.* the stately fig-tree. — *ču-zém* **water-tub.** — *ču-zlá* 1. the image, the reflexion of the moon in the water; a sort of deception of the senses by witchcraft. 2. the water-month, the first month. — *ču-yzár* a large **ladle** *Cs.* — *ču-bzóm* **a covered bucket** for carrying water. — *ču-ₒóbs* **water-ditch** *Sch.* — *ču-yar* col. water-rat (?) — *ču-rágs* **dam, dike.** — *ču-rí* 'hill of water', **billow.** — *ču-rúd* water rushing in, **inundation, deluge.** — *ču-rlábs* **wave, billow** *Dzl.* — *ču-lág* the arm of a river *Glr.* — *ču-lúd Sch.* dung, manure (?) — *ču-ló* n. of an edible plant *S.g.* — *ču-lóg* **floods.** — *ču-lón,* **dam, dike** *Tar.* 56, 15. *Liš.* — *ču-šiṅ* wood drifted away by the water = *ču-ₒgrám-gyi šiṅ* v. above; or the translation of कदली plantain or banana-tree with its spongy wood, in the place of which the Tibetan thinks of the *ₒóm-bu,* a shrub of similar qualities, at any rate a symbol of perishableness, of the frailty of life. — *ču-šúṅ Sch.* surface of the water (?) — *ču-šél* v. *šel.* — *ču-ysóṅ Dzl.* ༡༥༦, 17. a ravine containing water. — *ču-sá* **river-mud,** as manure. — *ču-sér* 1. animal water, **serum,** whether normal, or of a morbid character *Med.* — 2. **matter, pus.** — *ču-sráṅ,* = $\frac{1}{60}$ *ču-tsod,* i.e. **a minute;** the Indian or Tibetan minute is equal to 24 of our seconds, = 6 *dbugs Wdk.*, cf. *ču-tsód.* — *ču-srin* a water- or **sea-monster,** also Capricorn in the Zodiac. — *ču-lhá* **water-god** (*Varuṇa*); also = *klui rgyál-po.*

ཆུ་ཆུ་ *ču-čú,* = *la-čú,* **rhubarb,** *ču-rtsá* its root, used as dye and as a laxative *C.*

ཆུ་ཉིང་ *ču-niṅ* **four years ago** *C., W.*

ཆུ་པ་ *čú-pa* 1. *C.* a man's dress, **coat,** — 2. **water-carrier.**

ཆུ་བ་ *čú-ba* a large **sinew,** of which there are 16 acc. to Tibetan anatomy; *čú-ba ldóg-pa* a contraction of the sinews *Cs.*, *žá-ba* lameness, paralysis of the sinews *Sch.* — *ču-rgyús* (स्नायु) sinews, ligaments and nerves (there are 900 *rgyús-pa*); with respect to these, as well as to the veins, Tibetan science seems to be rather in the dark. — *ču-rtsá* 'sinew-veins', a term coming nearest to what we call the nerves. — *ču-ba-lṅa-ldán,* and *lṅa-lén Cs.* names of countries in India.

ཆུ་མ་རྩི་ *ču-ma-rtsí* a medicinal herb *Med.*

ཆུ་མ་ལོང་ *ču-ma-lóṅ,* **ṭu-gu ču-ma-loṅ** *Ld.* **an infant, baby.**

ཆུ་སོ་ *ču-só* the external and internal **urinary organs.**

ཆུག *čug* v. *ȷúg-pa.*

ཆུང་བ་ *čúṅ-ba* 1. adj. col. *čúṅ-nu, W.* also **čúṅ-se**, **little, small,** *čuṅ-čés-pas Dzl.* when he was very little; **young,** *bu čúṅ-ba* or *-ṅu* the younger or the youngest son; *lo-čúṅ* young in years; *ma-čúṅ* the younger sister of the mother; *'*á-pa čúṅ-ṅu** the younger brother of the father; the younger or the youngest of the fathers (in polyandry); *čúṅ-ṅu-nas* up from infancy; *čuṅ-grógs* an early friend, friend of one's youth; *čuṅ-zád* a little, cf. *čuṅ-zad*; *čuṅ-(gyi) sri* a devil devouring infants, infants-devil; **nyiṅ-ḱám-*, *ṅo-mig-*, *ṗod-**, or **nyom-čúṅ-se** *W.* shy, timid. — 2. vb. **to be little, small** etc., *snyiṅ ma čuṅ čig Glr.*, be not timorous, do not fear! *dún-ma rgya ma čuṅ čig* let the consultation not be trifling, let at once something of moment be consulted; *dún-ma rgya mi čúṅ-bar byed-do* let us now decide on important things *Glr.*; *čúṅs-pa* pf., *čúṅs-pa yin-nam* is it too unimportant? *Mil.* (*čuṅ-ȷúg* v. *ȷa*).

ཆུང་མ་ *čúṅ-ma, C.* also **čuṅ-grógs, čuṅ-dris**, resp. *btsún-mo,* **wife, consort, partner** *B., C.*; *lén-pa* to marry; *mi žig-gi čúṅ-mar byéd-pa* to be made a man's wife, to be married.

ཆུད་ *čud* occurs only in *čúd-ɣzon-pa, -ɣson-pa, -ɣsan-pa, -za-ba,* seldom *-dza-ba* (*Lex.*) **to consume, spend, waste;** *čud mi zá-ba* inexhaustible.

ཆུད་པ་ *čúd-pa* = *tsúd-pa, ȷúg-pa,* **to go, get in** or **into, to enter, to put in** or **into** etc., to go into a town *Dzl.*; of food entering the body *Dzl.*; *gaṅ yaṅ rúṅ-ba mi čúd-pa med* all without distinction may enter (my religion), says Buddha, in opposition to the aristocratic exclusiveness of Brahmanism *Dzl.*; *ťugs-su čúd-pa,* resp., to impress on one's mind; *ḱoṅ-du* v. *ḱoṅ-pa*; *ǒg-tu* to subject *Tar.*; *gräbs-su* c. accus. to procure, to provide or furnish one's self with a thing *Mil.*

ཆུན་ *čun,* occurs in *žiṅ-čun* one that is watering or taking care of fields, *ťsás-čun* gardens *ól-čun* meadows *Ld.*

ཆུན་པོ་ *čún-po* (दामा) 1. **bunch, bundle.** 2. **tuft, tassel, ornament,** of silk, pearls etc.

ཆུན་མ་ *čún-ma* **the second wife** in rank.

ཆུན་ཙེ་ *čún-tse Bal.* **little, small.**

ཆུབ་པ་ *čúb-pa,* a corruption of *čúd-pa, kun čúb-par byao* all this is to be well impressed on the mind; *dbaṅ-po ťams-čád-du čúb-pa* to pass through, to penetrate, every organ *Stg.*

ཆུམ་པ་ *čúm-pa, ȷigs-čum-pa Mil.*, **to shrink, to crouch** with fear.

ཆུར་ *čur,* termin. of *ču*; *čur ci-ba* to be drowned.

ཆུར་བ་ *čúr-ba* a kind of vermicelli, prepared from butter-milk boiled *Med., Ld.* **čurṗe**.

ཆུས་ čus 1. instrum. of ču; Sch. also čús-γtoṅ-ba 'to melt'; more correctly: **to gild, to plate** (in the warm or in the cold way), to overspread with a gold or silver liquid. — **after five days** C., W., or, the present day included, on the sixth day, cog. to bču.

ཆེ་ če 1. num. fig.: 96. — 2. v. če-ba.

ཆེ་གེ་མོ་ čé-ge-mo **such a one,** lo čé-ge-mo žig-la in such and such a year Dzl.; čé-ge-mo k̔yod you so and so Thgr.

ཆེ་འགྲན་ če-ˌgrán W. being jealous of one's own honour, ni f.

ཆེ་ཐབས་ če-t̔ábs **arrogance, haughtiness,** sde-pai če-t̔abs the arrogance of the great Ma.; *če-t̔ábs-med-k̔an* W. affable, condescending, kind; če-t̔ábs-čan proud, arrogant, haughty; če-t̔ábs byéd-pa B., *čo-če* W., *zuṅ-wa* C., to be arrogant, haughty.

ཆེ་དོན་ če-dón **a missive** to an inferior, **an edict.**

ཆེ་བ་ čé-ba 1. adj. **great,** (for čén-po); bu čé-ba the eldest son, the elder; čé-bar ˌgyúr-ba to become great or greater, to grow, increase e.g. of passions; čé-bar ˌgró-ba, čer ˌgró-ba id., cf. čer, čé-bar byéd-pa to make great; frq. in conjunction with nouns: že-sdáṅ čé-ba great with respect to anger, i.e. very prone to anger; rigs čé-žiṅ being of high extraction; also in compounds, v. below. — 2. sbst. **greatness, high degree** Mil.; **superiority, excellence,** ... kyi čé-ba stón-pa to show the superiority of a thing Mil.; *čé-wa śrúṅ-wa* Ld. to behave decently, respectably. — 3. vb., pf. čes **to be great,** not only in čé-žiṅ, če-o, but also in: ṅa-rgyál ma čé-žig do not be great in pride, i.e. do not allow pride to become great Mil., and so in similar cases; cf. čes.

**Comp.** čé-ka Sch.: 'chiefly; the plurality'. — če-kyád **greatness, size** Dzl. — *če-ḍál* W., *če-dál-la čud soṅ* he has entered the class of adults, he has come to full age. — čé-rgyu = čé-ba, cf. rgyu 3. — če-brgyúd perh. lineage by the eldest sons Glr. — če-čúṅ **great and small; size;** če-čúṅ ni in size. — če-ˌdón the coming to full age Mil. nt. — *če-mi* W. **an adult.** — *če-lóṅs* C. grown up, **adult** (Sch. 'chiefly'?)

ཆེ་ཞེ་ če-žé one's **elder sister** Cs., **the elder wife** Sch.

ཆེ་བཞི་ če-bži Liš. = bden-dpáṅ, **witness, eye-witness; witness, testimony,** če-bžir dris-te being questioned as a witness, or asked for a testimony Stg.

ཆེད་ čed, as sbst. of rare occurrence, Schr.: reason, signification = don; Sch.: čed čén-po a great thing, an important business or affair. Mostly čéd-du postp. c. genit. **on account of, because of, for;** ltá-bai čéd-du yin it is in order to see Pth.; riṅ-gyi čéd-du as an equivalent Pth.; lhai čéd-du ˌdzin-pa or γnyér-ba, also ṙjés-su ˌdzin-pa or γnyér-ba to admit to the discipleship or communion of a god Mil. — As an adv. čed-du seems to signify 1. for a certain purpose, **designedly, purposely, expressly,** e.g. with byéd-pa to do, to make a thing; mṅágs-pa to send off, dispatch. — 2. **again, once more, once again,** = p̔yir Mil. — dgos-čéd the construction of any noun with p̔yir-du, čéd-du etc., regarded by Tib. grammarians as a case of declension.

ཆེད་དོན་ čed-dón v. če-dón.

ཆེན་པོ་ čén-po B. and C., *čén-mo* W., **great** (čén-mo in B. only as fem. Dzl. ༡༠, b), čén-por ˌgyúr-ba, W. *čen čá-če*, to become great, to increase, col. also for to grow up; skyes-bu čén-po a great man, a man of great worth (by his talents and actions), a saint; *mi čén-mo* W. a man of quality, of rank, a nobleman, a rich man; čén-ma the first wife in rank; čen čun γnyis the first and second wife Glr.; *čén-mo* W. also: **old,** *ṭ̔ú-gu lo ču čen-mo* a child ten years old.

ཆེམ་མེ་བ་ čém-me-ba Lex., Cs. **stillness, silence,** čém-mer ˌdúg-pa Schr., čém-mer ˌk̔ód-pa C., to sit still without speaking.

ཆེམ(ས)་ čem(s) in compounds: 1. čaṅ-čém(s) v. čaṅ. — 2. k̔a-čém(s), resp. žal-čéms(s), bka-čém(s) **farewell exhortation; last will, testament,** srás-la k̔a-čém(s) ₒjóg-pa to deposit a testamentary disposal or devise for a son Glr.

ཚེམ(ས)་ཚེམ(ས)་ čem(s)-čém(s) 1. **the noise** made by thunder, by the shock of an earthquake etc., ₒbrúg-sgra čem-čém sgrógs-pa the rolling, roaring, clapping of thunder; bžad-gád ₔur čém-pa a roaring laughter. — 2. k̔ra čem-čém v. k̔rá-bo.

ཚེར་ čer termin. of če, čer ₒgró-ba to grow, increase; čer skyé-ba to become great; to grow up, čer skyés-pa partic. grown up, adult; da-dúṅ čer t̔oṅ go on! go on! Mil.; rgyal-srid byá-ba čer ma byuṅ Glr. his government was not (yet) of much consequence (as he was too young); ṅés-pa čer med this is not quite evident to me Mil.; perh. Tar. 36, 16; 101, 22; 120, 21; 169, 14 will allow a similar interpretation of čer. — čér-na S.O. yea; still more (?).

ཚེས་ čes 1. instrum. of če. — 2. pf. of čé-ba, as adv. **very,** k̔a-zás ṅan čés-kyi as the food is very bad Dzl.; čes sgrin-pa very prudent or clever Sch.; čes dár-bar gyúr-to it spread very much Tar.

ཚེས་པ་ čes-pa 1. pf. of čé-ba to be great, ha-čaṅ yaṅ čes-so he is much too great Dzl.; dmag-dguṅ čes-pa a great army; dbaṅ čes-pas being very mighty Glr.; čar čes-pas as it rained heavily Pth.; dga čes-nas greatly rejoicing Mil. — 2. **to believe,** but only when preceded by yid (resp. t̔ugs), or bden (col.), c. la, also c. accus., or par, that, Dzl. ༧༥, 18.

ཚོ་ čo 1. num. fig.: 126. — 2. as a word for itself seldom to be met with, e.g. Ld.-Glr. Schl. fol. 13, 6, Tar. 129, 20; signification not clearly to be made out. *čó-med-pa* C. = dón-med-pa to no purpose, vain; fickle.

ཚོ་ག་ čó-ga (विधि) the way or **method** of doing a thing, e.g. of solving an arithmetical problem Wdk., of curing maladies S.g., esp. used of magic performances, čó-ga-pa Cs., čó-ga-mk̔an Mil., a performer of such ceremonies. Whether it may safely be used for religious rites or ceremonies in general, is doubtful.

ཚོ་གོ་ čo-gó Bal. **great.**

ཚོ་ངེ་, ཚོ་ངེས་ čo-ṅé, čo-ṅés, **lamentation, wailing,** esp. lamentations for the dead, dirge, ₒdébs-pa Dzl., ₒbód-pa, ₒdón-pa in more recent literature, byéd-pa Sch., to lament, wail, cry, clamour; with la to cry to a person; the crying of a new-born child Thgy.

ཚོ་འཕྲུལ་ čo-ₒp̔rúl **magical trick, jugglery,** often put to rdzu-ₒp̔rúl, also used of the apparitions and doings of goblins Mil. Cf. rdzu-ₒp̔rúl.

ཚོ་བ་ čó-ba **to set on** (a dog), čó-čo-ba to set on repeatedly Cs.

ཚོ་འབྲང(ས)་ čo-ₒbráṅ(s) Mil.; Cs.: the mother's family or lineage; čo-rígs Dzl. frq. Cs.: 1. the father's lineage, descent by the father's side; 2. an honourable extraction. — čo-rís Mil., frq. = čo-rigs, also applied to things, e.g. a cane: čo-rís yé-nas btsún-pa a cane of an excellent kind, not coming from any mean or noxious plant.

ཚོ་ལོ་ čó-lo 1. **die, dice,** game at dice. — 2. **seal**(?) — čó-lo-mk̔an a dice-player Cs., čó-lo rtsé-ba to play at dice Cs.; čó-lo-ris Glr. the figure of a die, a square figure, in Glr. 47, 9 the Mongol translation substitutes a wheel, v. ₒk̔ór-lo; a checkered colouring or pattern, e.g. of cotton cloth C.

ཚོག་ čog 1. for čó-ga; bón-čog Mil. the ceremony of the Bonpos. — 2. v. γčóg-pa. — 3. v. čóg-pa.

ཚོག་པ་ čóg-pa vb., sbst., adj. 1. **to be sufficient, sufficiency, sufficient,** ccdpir: ṅéd-la dé-kas čog it is sufficient for us, we are satisfied Mil.; dris-pas (instr. of pai) čog-go Dzl. ༢༠༧, 10 (there has been) enough of asking, = don't ask any more! gáṅ-du bžugs kyaṅ čóg-par ₒdug it is sufficient (for him) wherever he may live, i.e. he is satisfied with any place of living Mil.; ṅéd-la nor loṅs-spyód-kyis čóg-pa yod we have money and goods enough Mil.; ₒdi γsúm-gyis čóg-na if these three are sufficient for you Mil.; rin-po-čes čóg-par *gyúr-nas* when they had precious stones enough *Dzl.*; *˳di-tsam-gyis čóg-pa ma yin-no* that is not enough, that will not do *Dzl.*; *sgál-pa mi brgya żon čóg-pa* his back (is) large enough for a hundred men to ride on it *Glr.*; adv.: *čóg-par* sufficiently, e.g. *sbyin-pa* to give *Dzl.*; **ma čóg-pa** or **-ga* W.* (col. for *čóg-par*), **dúń-če ma čóg-ga sad soń** he not only struck but killed him; *ṕyin-pas čóg-gi* it being sufficient (for the present) that I have come *Mil.*; *ťams-čád-la čóg-par gyúr-te* as all were satisfied *Dzl.*; *čóg-par ˳dzin-pa* to deem a thing sufficient, to be contented or satisfied with it; *čog šés-pa* vb., sbst., adj. to be contented, contentment, content; *ltá-bas čog mi šés-pai rdzas* a thing at which one cannot look enough *Glr.*, *Pth.*; *yo-byád-kyi* (better *kyis*) *čog šés-pa* easily satisfied as to the necessaries of life. — 2. **to be allowed, permitted, at liberty,** construed in the same manner: *ḱrid-pas čog* you may have lessons with me, I will instruct you *Mil.*; *˳grán-pas čog* I am quite at liberty to compete with you, we may safely compete with each other *Glr.*; *˳tsó-ba dráńs-pas čog* you can have meat set before you *Mil.*; with a root: *bu byin čog* then you may render up your son; hence it is in *W.* the usual word for *rúń-ba*, **náń-du ča čóg-če yin-na man** is it allowed to enter or not? **šrád-ma za čog** eating pease is allowed, also: pease are edible; **lé-na ḱyoń čog ka tań** he issued an edict, that it should be permitted to fetch wool, i.e. he (the Maharajah of Kashmir) permitted the export of wool; **léb-na ṕul čog* when it arrives, I shall take the liberty of sending it to you.

ཆོགས་པ་ *čógs-pa* seldom for *˳čág-pa* **to be broken** *Mil.*

ཆོང་, མཆོང་ *čoń*, *mčoń* a transparent, variegated, half-precious stone brought from India to *Ld.* and considered less valuable than *γzi*; perh. cornelian or sardonyx?

ཆོད་ *čod* 1. *C.* **the cutting off; deciding;** **ṭ al-čǫ́ gya čém-po ǰhé-pa** to bring about a great remission of taxes, **bhu-lǫn-čǫ́** remission of debts; **sa-čǫ́ gya čem-po ǰhé-pa** to make a great way; cf. however *ṕyod*. — 2. **partition-wall** *Sch.*, *čod rgyág-pa* prob. to construct a partition-wall. — 3. v. *γčód-pa*.

ཆོད་པ་ *čód-pa* 1. **to be cut off,** *lám-sgo γnyis ḱá-bas čód-de* both approaches being cut off or obstructed by snow *Mil.*; *bčad kyań mi čód-do* impossible to be severed, *caedendo non caeduntur*, *Glr.*; *mi-čód-rdó-rje* a diamond that cannot be cut to pieces, an epithet of a firm unbending king *Pth.* — 2. **to be decided, settled, fixed,** *goń-ťáń dpyád-kyis* (or *pas*) *mi čod Glr.* the value (of the stone) cannot be fixed, though one should attempt to apprize it i.e. it is invaluable, priceless; *go čód-pa* v. *go*.

ཆོད་པོ་ *čód-po W.* 1. **split, cut through;** 2. **distinct,** of words or writings.

ཆོན་ *čon* 1. *W.* (cog. to *čud?*) **useless,** to no purpose, *rin čon soń* the payment has been useless, thrown away; gen. adv. **čón-la** gratuitously, in vain, for nothing, **čón-la ḱón-če** to hate without cause or reason; **čón-la dád-če** to sit idle, to spend one's time unprofitably. — 2. **tent** (?), *čon-tág* tent-rope *Mil.*, *čon-ṕúr* tent-pin.

ཆོམ(ས)་ *čom(s)* 1. **robbery,** *čóms-kyis zas ˳tsól-ba* to live on robbery *Ma.*; *čóm-po* robber *Dzl.*, *čóm-po rkún-ma* robber and thief, gen. *čom-rkún*, *čom-rkún-gyi ˳ǰigs-pa* fear of robbers and thieves; *čom-rkún-pa* id. *Stg.* — 2. imp. of *˳ǰóms-pa*.

ཆོམ་པ་ *čóm-pa* **to be finished, accomplished,** *W.*, **tó-re čom yin** to-morrow it will be finished, **da čom soń** now it is done, completed; cf. *čam*.

ཆོལ་ *čol* 1. **inconstant** *Cs.*; *dpyid-čol* fickle spring-weather. — 2. *Cs.*: for *čó-lo* in compounds, *rus-čol* **a die** made of bone; *šiń-čól* a wooden die; *duń-čól* shells used inst. of dice (?).

ཆོལ་ཁ་ *čol-ka Sch.*: 'a hole made by a blow; a nest'.

ཆོལ་ཟངས་ *čol-zańs* a shallow shore *Sch.*

ཆོས་ čos (धर्म) 1. **doctrine**, a particular doctrine, **tenet**, or **precept**; *ɣsáṅ-bai čos šig* an esoteric doctrine, a mystery *Dzl.*; *ḱyád-čos* for *ḱyad-par-čan-gyi čos* a peculiar, distinguished, sublime, and therefore difficult doctrine; *ʼjig-rtén-gyi čos brgyad* the eight doctrines or principles of the world (though frq. mentioned, I found them nowhere specified) cf. Foucaux Gyatcherr., Translation p. 264; *čos-brgyád-mḱan*, a man of the world, worldling *Mil.* — More esp. 2. **moral doctrine,** whether any separate dogma, or the sum of various doctrines, **religion** in general, both theoretically (system of morality, ethics) and practically (faith, exercise of religion); *lha-čós* the religion of the gods or (Buddhist) deities, i.e. the Buddhist religion, as the only true one, in opposition to all other heresies and false religions (*log-čós*), as well as to irreligiousness (*čos ma yin-pa*); *ḱa-čós* profession with the lips, hypocrisy *Glr.*; *ʼḱrig-pai čós-la brtén-pa* those practising the religion of voluptuousness (an expression designedly forcible, like St. Paul's: 'whose god is their belly'); *mí-čos* v. below; *čos ʼčád-pa*, or *bšád-pa*, *stón-pa*, *smrá-ba*, *sgróg-pa*, resp. *čós-kyi sgrog-gléṅ mdzád-pa Glr.* to expound, to teach, to preach religion; *čos smrá-bai žál-la ltá-ba* to watch the mouth of the preacher *Pth.*; **čo dóg-pa** *C.* to read a religious book; **čos šád-ḱan** *W.* a preacher; *čos ʼčád-pai ʼdun-ḱáṅ* place where sermons are delivered, church *Dzl.*; *čos nyán-pa* to hear religious discourses *Dzl.*; *čos žú-ba* to ask for religious discourses; partic.: one eagerly desiring or asking for religious instruction, an inquirer *Pth.*, *Mil.*; *čos byéd-pa* to act or live religiously, righteously, = *čos bžin-du byéd-pa;* also merely to wish to become pious, to strive after piety; *ḱyed snyiṅ-nas čos byéd-na* if you are in good earnest about religion, if piety is the aim of your heart *Mil.*; lastly in a special sense: to become or to be a monk *Pth.*; *čós-la sems sgyúr-ba Mil.* to show an inclination for religion, to turn religious; *čós-su*, or *čós-la ʼjúg-pa* 1. vb. nt. to enter into religion, to be converted, also: to go over to a religion, to turn (Buddhist), 2. vb. act. to convert, to turn a person from a bad life to a good one, to make him a believer, to make another a convert, a proselyte; *čós-la ʼgód-pa* = *ʼjúg-pa 1*; *čos spyód-pa* to practise religion; the exercise of religion, worship *S.g.*; *bka-čós* the word of Buddha, the doctrine as taught by Buddha himself; *rtógs-pai čós Thgy.* the knowledge acquired by meditation, independently of books, scarcely different from *ṅes-dón*, or *ṅon-šés; bstán-pai čos Thgy.* any knowledge derived from other sources. — 3. in a special sense the **religion of Buddha**, Buddhism, *dám-pai čos*, and frq. *dám-pa čos* id. (cf. ἡ πίστις Acts 6, 7); *čos daṅ bon* Buddhism and Bon-religion *Mil.*; *čós-la lóṅ-spyod-par ʼgyúr-ba* to live in the enjoyment of true faith. — 4. **religious writings**, and **writings, books, literature** in general, in as much as the Tibetans derivate every science from religion; *bón-gyi čos ťams-čád* all the Bon-writings *Mil.* — 5. **custom, manner, common usage, fashion,** *mí-čos* manners of the world *Mil.; mi-čos-kyi dús-su* as long as he lived according to the ways of the world *Mil.*; *yúl-čos-kyis* according to the custom of the country *Dzl.*; *kyád-čos* the way of distinguishing, of pointing out the characteristics *Glr.* (cf. under 1); **nature, quality,** *Dzl.* ༢༤༢, 18 cf. *čos-nyid.* — 6. **substance, being, thing,** *čos ťams-čád mi-rtág-pa yin-gyi* as every thing existing is perishable *Dzl.* — Other philosophical expressions containing the word *čos* v. *Was.* (296).

**Comp.** **čós-skad** *W.* **book-language,** as opp. to *pál-skad.* — *čós-sku* v. *sku.* — *čos-skyóṅ* v. *skyoṅ-ba.* — *čos-ḱri* **reading-desk, lecturer's chair, pulpit** *Pth.*; **reading-table, school-desk.** — *čos-ḱrims* v. *ḱrims.* — *čos-ḱrims-pa* v. *dge-bskós.* — *čos-ʼḱór* vulgo **prayer-mill**; the column of disks on the *mčod-rtén Pth.* v. *ʼḱór-lo* 2, also *ʼḱór-lo* extr. — *čos-grá* **school.** — *čos-(kyi) rgyál (-po)* 1. honorary title of kings deserving well of religion. 2. = *γšín-rje Schl. Buddh.* 93, 3. also as a p. n. — *čos-rgyúd* **religious tradition,** also = **confession, creed,** *rje-btsún-gyi čos-rgyúd ₒdzin-pa-rnams* those embracing the religious tradition of his reverence, his fellow-believers *Mil.*; *čos-rgyúd γčig-pa* one confessing the same faith or religion *Thgr.* — *čós-čan* 1. **pious, devout.** 2. v. *čos* 5, *ₒjig-pai čós-čan yin* **having the properties** of perishableness, being subject to the law of mutability *Thgy.* — *čos-rjé* 'lord of the faith', viz. 1. Buddha *Lex.*, 2. devout or righteous lord, title of honour given to distinguished scholars *Tar. transl.* 331, and elsewh.; perh. also = *čos-rgyál.* — *čos-nyid* 1. = *čos* 5, **quality, nature,** *rgyá-mtsoi čos-nyid-kyis* in a manner peculiar to the sea, *Dzl.* ༥༨, 9 (112, 9?). 2. philosophical term: **existence, entity,** = *de-bžin-nyid* (acc. to *Thgy.*) by which the Buddhist however means a negation of being, non-existence, non-entity. — *čos-stégs W.* = *čos-kri.* — *čos-stón* religious festive entertainment given to saints *Glr.* — *čos-dráṅ-po* **righteous** with regard to the laws of religion (adopted by Prot. Miss. for the scriptural term 'righteous' or 'just'), *čos-dráṅ-ba* justice, righteousness. — *čos-ldán* = *čós-čan.* — *čos-sdé* **convent, monastery,** *Wdk., Glr.* — *čós-pa* a religious man, **a divine, a monk.** — *čos-spún* **a religious brother;** such brotherhoods e.g. are formed by two devotees, before going on a pilgrimage. After having been consecrated by a priest, who consults the lot on such an occasion, they owe hospitality and mutual assistance to each other for life. — *čos-spyód* **exercise of religion;** *čos-spyód-bču* = *dgé-ba-bču.* — *čos-sbyin* is said to be frq. used in book-titles: *bkra-šis-lhún-po-nas čos-sbyin ₒdzad-méd spel ṗyir bris* written from Tashilhunpo as a religious gift for infinite increase and blessing. — *čos-blón* **a pious functionary** or official (*bdud-blon* an impious or wicked one) *Glr.* *čós-ma* a religious woman, **a nun** *Cs.* — *čos-méd* without religion, **irreligous, wicked.** — *čos-myón* **religious frenzy,** *W.*: **čos-nyón žugs** he has become deranged, his brains are turned (in consequence of meditating). — *čos-zóg* **priestcraft** *Mil.* — *čos-lúgs* religious party, **denomination, sect.** **čós-sem-čan* W.* inclined to religion, **pious.**

མཆད་པ་ *čád-pa Lex.*: = 'tomb, sepulchre; = *pramārita Ssk.* killed, slain; *mčád-pa-med-pa* entire, perfect; *mčád-par byá-ba* = *mahimān Ssk.* greatness; also the magical power of increasing size at will'.

མཆན་ *mčan* 1. **the side of the breast,** *mčán-gyi bu* bosom-child, darling, *mčán-gyi mčis-bráṅ* bosom-wife (cf. our 'bosom-friend'); *mčán-du ₒjúg-pa* to put into one's bosom *Glr.*; *mčán-kuṅ* **arm-hole, arm-pit,** often = *mčan*; *mčán-kuṅ γyás-pai rtsíb-mai bár nas* (the Buddhas are born) from between the ribs of the right side (cf. *mnal*); **čán-da* W.* **pocket,** in clothes, cf. *dkú-mda.* — 2. v. the following article.

མཆན་བུ་ *mčán-bu* 1. **apprentice,** *bzoi* in a handicraft, trade or art, *rig-pai* in a science, disciple *Cs.*, *sgyú-ma-mkan-gyi* appr. of a juggler, conjurer *Zam.* — 2. *yi-geï mčán-bu* words or lines, printed or written in a smaller character than the rest, and inserted in the text (called *má-yig Cs.*) like our parenthesis, but without brackets; hence 3. **note, annotation** (*Sch.* also: testimony?).

མཆི་བ་ *mčí-ba*, eleg. for 1. **to come, to go,** *slád-bžin-par mčio* I shall come later *Dzl.*; **to appear,** used of a god; *skyábs-su* (to put one's self) under the protection of another person, ccd.; *ₒbáṅs-su mčio* I will obey *Mil.* — 2. **to say,** *žes mčio* thus he said.

མཆི་མ་ *mčí-ma*, resp. *spyan-čáb* **a tear,** *ₒbyin-pa*; *ₒdón-pa Glr.*, *blúg-pa Dzl.*, *γtón-ba Mil.* to shed (tears); *ském-pa* to dry up tears *Cs.*; *ₒṗyi-ba* to wipe off tears *Cs.*; *mčí-mas brnáṅ-ba* to be choked with tears, to sob violently *Sch.*

མཆིག་ *mčig* 1. *Cs.* a stone for grinding spice etc., **a mortar;** *mčig-gu* a small mortar *Sch.*, **a pestle** *Cs.* — 2. **the nether mill-stone,** *mčig-ma* the runner or upper mill-stone, *Sch.*, *mčig skór-ba* to grind *Sch.*

མཆིང་ *mčiṅ Cs.* = *kloṅ*; one *Lex.* = *dkyil*; v. *kloṅ*.

མཆིང་བུ *mčiṅ-bu Cs.* = *˳čiṅ-bu*.

མཆིད་ *mčid, bka-mčid, γsuṅ-mčid, W.* **mol-čid** resp the talk, discourse, speech (of an honoured person) *Cs.*; *mčid-lán* answer to such speech *Mil.*

མཆིན་པ་ *mčin-pa*, resp. *sku-mčin* **the liver;** *mčin-dri, mčin-rí* **the midriff** or **diaphragm;** *mčin-ḱa* liver-coloured; *mčin-nán* 'liver-pressing', first breakfast, because according to popular belief water rises from the human liver in the morning, which is depressed and appeased by taking some food; *mčin-nán byed-pa* to breakfast.

མཆིལ་པ་ *mčil-pa* 1. **fishing-hook** *Dzl.*, *mčil-pas nya ˳čór-ba* to fish with a hook, to angle *Cs.* — 2. **a little bird,** *W.* **či-pa**, *Ts.* **čil-pig*; *či-pa skyá-wo** *W.* sparrow; *mčil-ḱra* sparrow-hawk; *mčil-mgó* a fabulous stone, like a bird's head, supposed to possess a variety of marvelous qualities.

མཆིལ་མ་ *mčil-ma* 1. *W.* **mčil-mág**, resp. *ǰags-mčil, ǰags-čáb* **spittle,** prob. also other similar fluids *Lt.*; *˳dór-ba* (*W.* **ṗáṅ-ce*) to spit; *mčil-lúd* (*W.* **mčil-ldúd**) morbid saliva, e.g. of people affected with a cough or with hectic fevers; *mčil-snábs* prob. id.; *mčil-snód*, resp. *žal-bzéd*, spitting-box; *mčil-zúm, mčil-bkáb W.* slavering-bib or cloth. — 2. = *mčil-lhám Tar.* 72, 9?

མཆིལ་ལྷམ་ *mčil-lhám* **shoe, boot,** *mčil-lhám γnyis ˳dor-ba* to lose both shoes *Wdṅ.*; *mčil-lhám-mḱan* shoemaker, cobbler, seller of boots; *mčil-lhám-gyi yú-ba* the leg of a boot *Cs.*

མཆིས་པ་ *mčis-pa* 1. also *mčis-lágs-pa*, eleg. for *yod-pa*, **to be, to be there, to exist,** *du mčis* how much is there, how many are there? *Cs.*; *sú-la dám-pai čos mčis-pa* whoever has the holy doctrine *Dzl.*; *yul dbús-nas mčis-so* (he) is (comes) from the country Ü *Dzl.* — 2. pf. of *mči-ba* 1. *lam riṅ-po-nas mčis-te* having come from afar. 2. *žes mčis-pa* so-called.

མཆིས་བྲང་ *mčis-bráṅ* 1. eleg. **dwelling, abode, domicile;** also when speaking modestly of one's own dwelling: *bdág-gi mčis-bráṅ* my humble roof *Dzl.* — 2. *Lex.* **wife, partner.**

མཆིས་མལ་ *mčis-mál* **bed, bed-stead** *Cs.*

མཆུ་ *mču* 1. **lip,** *ya-mču* upper lip, *ma-mču* lower lip; *mču btud mḱas Wil.* prob.: one must be wise in lowering the lips, i.e. one must yield, giving up pouting; *ḱa-mčú*, resp. *žal-mčú* 1. **lip** 2. word, voice (?) *Sch.* 3. quarrel, strife, *ḱa-mčú rgyal-ṗám ǰi-ltar byuṅ žé-na* if one asks, which are the details of the quarrel; **ḱam-čú ǰhé-pa** *C.* **gyág-pa** *Cs.* to quarrel. — 2. **beak** or **bill** of birds, *mčú-la ťógs-te ˳gró-ba* to fly, carrying something in the bill *S. O.*; *mču-lto* (or *ču-mdo?*) *W.* id. — 3. n. of one of the lunar mansions, v. *rgyu-skar*.

**Comp.** *mču-skyé* muzzle *Sch.* — *mču-sgrós* v. *sgros*. — *mču-ťár Sch.* (prob. a mis-print for *mču-ťór*) pustules, tubercular elevations on the lips. — *mču-riṅs* long-beaked, n. of a bird, and also of an insect (a large musquito).

མཆེ་བ་ *mčé-ba, Cs.* also *mče-só*, **corner-tooth, canine tooth, eye-tooth, fang, tusk** of an animal, *mčé-la γtsigs-pa, W.* **žé-ce**, to show one's teeth, to grin; *mče-ba-čan-gyi sde* the class of the tusked animals, viz. the carnivora (lion, tiger, leopard), and the tusked pachydermata (elephant, boar etc.).

མཆེད་ *mčed, sku-mčéd, mčed-lčám*, resp. for spun, **brother, sister;** *mčed γnyis* my two brothers *Dzl.*; *srás-mo lha-lčám mčed bži* four princesses, sisters; *deï mčed* his illustrious brother, in reference to a king, prince etc. *Glr.*; esp. of gods: *mčed bži* four divine brothers *Glr.*; *mčed-grógs, grogs-mčéd* clerical brother, *mčed-grógs máṅ-po ťsógs-par* where many clerical brothers assemble; *mčed-grógs dam-ťsig γčig-pa Thgr.* betrothed brothers, religious brothers, = *čos-spún*; also *mčed-lčám* has this signification.

མཆེད་པ་ *mčéd-pa* 1. **to spread**, to gain ground, esp. of a fire. frq.; also fig.: *bdág-gi* ₒ*dod-čágs-kyi me mčéd-pas* as the fire of voluptuousness spread or increased within me *Dzl.*; also in the following sense: *már-me γčig-la γčig mčed ltar* as one kindles one light by another *Mil.*; *γčig gleṅ γnyis gleṅ rím-pas mčéd-de* as (the news) spread more and more by gossiping people *Pth.* — *skye-mčéd* v. *skye.* — 2. = *γyó-ba, mi-mčed-pai dád-pa* = *dád-pa brtán-po.*

མཆེར་པ་ *mčér-pa* **the milt, spleen.**

མཆོག་ *mčog* **the best**, the most excellent in its kind, *skyés-bu mčog, mii mčog, rkaṅ-γnyis-rnams-kyi mčog* Buddha; *nyes-ltúṅ-gis ma ṕóg-pa* (or *na*) *mčog yin-te ṕog-rtíṅ bšágs-pa byéd-pa rab yin Mil.* the best thing is, not to have been surprised by sin, but after having been surprised, it is the best to confess it (and thus to atone for it); *γsuṅ-mčóg* chief or fundamental doctrine, main dogma, principal commandment etc. *Glr.*; *ṅa ni* ₒ*jig-rtén* ₒ*di-na mčog* I am the highest in the world (says Buddha immediately after his birth) *Glr.*; *γnas-mčóg* the most glorious or splendid country *Glr.*; *ro-mčóg* excellent taste or flavour *Mil.*; *mḱas-mčóg-rnams* most learned gentlemen *Zam.*; also as a complimentary word; *mi mčog ḱyod* most honoured Sir! *Pth.*; *mčog-dmán, mčog daṅ ťun-móṅ, mčog daṅ ṕál-pa*, good and bad, first-rate and common, fine and ordinary, of goods etc.; eminent and ordinary, of mental gifts, talents etc.; *mčóg-tu gyúr-pa* = *mčog*, e.g. *mi-rnams-kyi náṅ-na mčóg-tu gyúr-pa γčig* one that has risen among men, so as to become their chief *Glr.*; *yúl-rnams-kyi mčóg-tu gyúr-pa* the most splendid of countries. — Adv.: *mčóg-tu* very, most, with verbs: *bón-po-la mčóg-tu mós-pa žig* a great admirer of the Bonpos *Mil.*; gen. with adjectives: *ro mčóg-tu mṅár-ba* extremely sweet; with the comparative: much, far, by far, greatly, *dé-bas mčóg-tu čeo* . . . is far or much greater than that *Dzl.*

**Comp.** *mčog-sbyin ṕyag-rgyá* a gesture made in practising magic, in conjuring up or exorcising ghosts. — *mčog-zúṅ* the model pair, the two most excellent amongst Buddha's disciples, Shariibú and Maudgalgyibú, v. *Köpp.* — *mčog-riṅ* longest *Thgy.*

མཆོང་ *mčoṅ* v. *čoṅ.*

མཆོང་བ, མཆོངས་པ་ *mčóṅ-ba, mčóṅs-pa* to leap, to jump, frq., e.g. *čur* into the water; *mí-seb-la* among the people, e.g. of a mad dog).

མཆོད་པ་ *mčód-pa* (पूज) I. vb. 1. **to honour,** revere, respect, receive with honour, *kún-gyis bkúr žiṅ mčód-pai* ₒ*os* worthy of being honoured and praised by all; usually ccapir. (rarely dp.) in the special sense: to honour saints or deities by offering articles of food, flowers, music, the sound, odour and flavour of which they are supposed to relish, hence to treat, entertain, regale (the gods), and in a more general sense applied also to lifeless objects, e.g. to honour a sepulchre in such a manner; *Glr. mčód-pa* may therefore in English be sometimes translated by: to offer, to sacrifice, but it should always be borne in mind, that no idea of self-denial or yielding up a precious good (as is implied by the English word), or of slaughtering, as in the Greek *θύειν*, can be connected with the Tibetan word itself, though in practice bloody sacrifices, abhorred as they are by pure Buddhism in theory, are not quite unheard of, not only animals being immolated to certain deities, but also men notoriously noxious to religion slaughtered as *dmar-mčod*, red offering, to the *dgrá-lha* q.v. — 2. *C.* resp. **to eat, drink, take, taste,** (in *W.* expressed by **dón-če**).

II. sbst. **offering, oblation, libation,** *mčód-pa* ₒ*búl-ba, W.* **ṕúl-če** frq., also *byéd-pa*; *ról-mo mčód-par* ₒ*búl-ba* to bring an offering of music *Mil.*: *mčód-pa sna-ṫsógs ṫógs-te* carrying along with them all sorts of offerings *Glr.*; *mčód-pai ḱyád-par bču* the ten kinds of offerings *Tar.*; *lha-mčód* offering or libation brought to a *lha*; *ₒbru-mčód* an offering consisting of grain; *dus-mčód* offerings presented at certain times *Pth.*; *rgyun-mčód* daily offering; fig. *dád-pai mčód-pa Mil.*; *ɣtaṅ-rág-tu sgrúb-pai mčód-pa ṕul* as a thanksgiving bring the offering of meditation! *Mil.* —

**Comp.** *mčód-ḱaṅ* **house** or **place of offerings,** of worship, *Pth.*; adopted as an appellation for the temple of the Jews, as *lhá-ḱaṅ* could not be used *Chr. Prot.* — *mčód-ḱri* **offering-table,** Jewish **altar,** *Chr. Prot.* — *mčod-lčóg* prob. the same, *C.* — *mčod-čá Glr.* = *mčod-rdzás.* — *mčod-brǰód* words of adoration, doxology. — *mčod-rtén Ssk.* **चैत्य** (religious building) and **स्तूप** (elevated place, elevation, tumulus) 1. etymologically; receptacle of offerings; 2. usually: a sacred pyramidal building, of a form varying in different countries and centuries, esp. near temples and convents, where often great numbers of these structures are to be seen. They were originally sepulchres, containing the relics of departed saints, and therefore called *ɣduṅ-rtén*; afterwards they were erected as cenotaphs, i. e. in honour of deceased saints buried elsewhere, but in more recent times they are looked upon as holy symbols of the Buddhist doctrine, v. *Köpp.* I, 533. — *mčod-stégs* offering-table, **altar.** — *mčod-stód Sch.*: an offering with a hymn of praise. — *mčod-stón* **an entertainment,** as sort of libation, given to the priests *Dzl.*; perh. also **a sacrificial feast.** — *mčod-sdóṅ* 1. *Sch.* = *mčod-rten* (?), 2. **offering-lamp** *Sch.*, 3. **the wick** of such a lamp (in this sense it is used in a little botanical book). — *mčod-ɣnás* 1. prop. place where there is offered, **place of sacrifice.** 2. the object to which veneration is shown, image of a god *Glr.*, **sanctuary.** 3. the offering priest, **the sacrificator.** — *mčód-pa-po* a sacrificer *Cs.* — *mčod-ₒbúl* the offering of a sacrifice *Cs.* — *mčod-sbyin* id. (though elsewhere *mčod-pa* sbst., as a gift to deities, is distinct from *sbyin-pa* a gift to men), also: sacrificer; *mčod-sbyin-gyi ₒdun-ḱáṅ* house where people assemble in order to perform sacrifices; *sróg-gi mčod-sbyin* bloody offerings or sacrifices *Tar.* — ***mčod-mé* offering-lamp,** lighted in honour of a deity, and very common in the houses of Buddhists; **čod-mé ṕúl-če** *W.* to light such a lamp, (prop. to offer it). — *mčod-rdzás*, *mčod-čá*, *mčód-pai yo-byád* instruments, utensils, requisite for festival processions in honour of a deity. — *mčod-šóms* or *-bšáms* the upper shelves in the holy repositories, containing the little statues of Buddha etc.

མཆོར་པོ་ *mčór-po*, sometimes *ₒṕyór-po* 1. **pretty, handsome,** neat, elegant, *ṕo mčór-po* a handsome man, *bud-méd mčór-mo* a pretty woman, esp. a smart gaily dressed female. — 2. *W.* also **vain, conceited.**

འཆག་ཅན་ *ₒčág-čan* col. **trodden, stamped; solid, firm, compact,** like the Hindustani *pakka.*

འཆག་པ་ *ₒčag-pa* I. pf. *čag* (s) 1. **to break** vb. n., *snod čag-pa* a broken vessel *Dzl.*; fig. *ṅa-rgyál čag* my pride is broken, frq.; *der-ₒbyón-stabs čag* the opportunity of going there has been cut off *Mil.*; **lam čág-pa* (also *šog-pa*)* *C.* a. a beaten, practicable road (a road broken through, v. *ₒčég-pa*) b. *W.* an impracticable, broken-up road. — 2. **to be broken off,** abated, beaten down from the price, *žu-čág-med-par* there being no room for either asking or abating *Mil. nt.* —

II. also *čágs-pa*, pf. *bčags*, fut. *bčag* (imp. *ₒčog?*) 1. **to tread, to walk, to move,** esp. when speaking respectfully or formally, *yab-més-kyi žábs-kyis bčágs-pai sá-ča* the place where my ancestors did walk *Glr.*; *žabs čágs-pai ṕyag ṕyir ₒgro* follow me on my walk *Mil. nt.* — *ₒčág-tu* or *ₒčágs-su ₒgró-ba* to take a walk *Dzl.*; **góm-čag-če** *W.* to step along solemnly; *čág-ṕeb-pa* v. *ṕyág-ṕeb-pa.* — 2.

like ˳gró-ba in a more general sense: *bžón-pa-la*, *čibs-la* to ride in a carriage, on horseback *Cs.*

འཚགས་པ་ ˳*čágs-pa* 1 v. ˳*čág-pa.* — 2. sometimes for ˳*čég-pa.*

འཚག(ས)་ས་ ˳*čág(s)-sa* a place for walking, *Lexx.*, *Cs.*

འཚང་བ་ ˳*čáṅ-ba*, pf. *bčaṅs*, fut. *bčaṅ*, imp. *čoṅ(s)*, 1. **to hold, to keep,** to take hold of, *skrá-la* by the hair *Mil.* — ˳*čaṅ-zúṅs* handle, crook of a stick, *Mil.* — 2. **to carry, to wear,** to carry about one, e.g. amulets etc. — 3. (*yid-la*) **to keep** in memory, in one's mind. — 4. **to have, to assume,** e.g. the body of a goddess, of a Rakshasi *Pth.*

འཚངས་པ་ ˳*čáṅs-pa W.* a (closed) handful e.g. of dough; **čáṅs-bu** a clod (of clay), a snow-ball etc. formed in the hand.

འཚད་པ་ ˳*čád-pa* I. pf. *čad*, vb. n. to *γčód-pa*, like *čód-pa*, **to be cut** into pieces, **to be cut off, to decay,** *dúm-bur* (to fall) to pieces *Med.*; **to cease, end, stop,** of diseases *Glr.*, of life *Lex.*; **to cease to flow** or **to blow,** of water or wind; **to die away, to become extinct,** of a family, a generation; **to be consumed,** of provisions *Pth.* of bodily strength *Thgy.*; **to be decided,** *k̔yód-kyis bsád-par* ˳*čád-na* you being determined to kill me *Dzl.* —

II. pf. and fut. *bšad*, imp. *šod* 1. **to explain,** ˳*óg-tu* ˳*čad* it will be explained below *Lt.*; *yid-la byos šig daṅ bšád-do* give heed, and I will explain it to you *Stg.*; ˳*čad nyán-pa* to listen to an explanation *Sch.*; ˳*ǰig čos γtam* ˳*čád-pa* to teach the transitoriness of existence *Sch.* (?) — 2. **to tell, to relate.**

འཚབ་པ་ ˳*čáb-pa*, pf. *bčabs*, fut. *bčab*, imp. *čob* **to conceal,** to keep secret, ˳*čáb-pa-med-pai sems* a candid mind, open-heartedness *Stg.* (cog. to ˳*ǰáb-pa*).

འཚམ་པ་ ˳*čám-pa* I. vb. (pf. *bčam Lex.*), also adj. and sbst. **to accord, to agree, agreeing, agreement,** *srid-la mi* ˳*čám-pas* as they did not agree about the government *Glr.*; ˳*čam byéd-pa* to make agree, to reconcile *Mil.*, **čam mi čam** col. they do not agree; *k̔a* ˳*čám-pa* to agree upon, to concert, e.g. an escape; *k̔a* ˳*čám-par* by concert, unanimously.

II. 1. **to dance,** ˳*čám-par byéd-pa Sch.* 2. a dancer, *k̔ro* ˳*čám-pa* a dancer with a frightful mask; *gar-*˳*čám(s)* a dance; ˳*čám-po* a dancer *Glr.*; ˳*čam-dpón* leader of a dance; ˳*čám-yig* book or programme of a dance.

འཚའ་ ˳*ča Ld.*, *Sp.* **cupboard.**

འཚའ་བ་ ˳*čá-ba* I. pf. *bčas*, rarely ˳*čas*, fut. *bča*, imp. *čos*, **to make, prepare, construct,** but used only in reference to certain things; 1. *γnas*, vulg. *ṫsaṅ*, ˳*čá-ba Pth.* to prepare a place, house or abode, to settle; *mal* ˳*čá-ba* to make a bed or couch *Cs.*; *dmag-sgár* ˳*čá-ba* to pitch a camp; *k̔rims-ra* ˳*čá-ba* to establish a court of justice *Glr.* — 2. *rgyal-k̔rims* ˳*čá-ba* to draw up a law, to give laws, frq. — 3. *dam* ˳*čá-ba* to make a vow, **to promise, assert, protest,** frq.; *yi-dam* ˳*čá-ba* id.; also to utter a prayer; *dám-bča* v. sub *dam.* — 4. *skyil-krúṅ čá-ba* = *skyil-krúṅ byéd-pa*, v. *skyil-ba.* — 5. *blo-γtád* ˳*čá-ba*, c. c. *la*, **to place confidence in.**

II. **to bite,** *γčig-la γčig*·˳*čá-žiṅ zá-la* to bite and devour one another *Dzl.*; *so* ˳*čá-ba* to bite with the teeth (?) *Mṅg.*, or to gnash or grind the teeth (?); *šiṅ* ˳*čá-ba* **to gnaw** at a piece of wood *Stg.*

འཚར་རྒྱན་ ˳*čar-rgyán*, or ˳*čar-čán* a present given reluctantly *Sch.* (?)·

འཚར་བ་ ˳*čár-ba*, pf. *šar*, **to rise, appear,** become visible, of the sun etc., also of the sun's appearing above a mountain, from behind a cloud etc., frq.; **to shine,** *gaṅs-ri-la nyi-ma šar-ba* the shining of the sun upon a mountain covered with snow, a snowy mountain lit up by the rays of the sun *Glr.*; *γzugs-brnyán mi* ˳*čar-ba* the not appearing of the image which is formed by the reflection of a mirror (as something strange and surprising) *Wdṅ*; *γzugs* ˳*čár-ba byéd-pa* to cause an image to be reflected (in the water);

dpyid-ka ŝar spring has appeared; frq. of thoughts: nyáms-su, or yid-la ̥čár-ba (thoughts) rising in one's mind; yid-la ŝar kyaṅ Mil. though I can figure it in my mind; grógs-su ̥čar (they) appear as friends Mil.; rgyán-du ̥čar Mil. it turned into a blessing. — ̥čár-sgo **thought, idea, conception,** ̥čár-sgo ̥byuṅ an idea comes, a (happy) thought, a (new) light, bursts upon me Mil.; ̥čar-ga Mil. **the rising, the rise.**

འཆལ་བ་ ̥čál-ba, secondary form to ̥čól-ba II., 1. Cs.: **to fluctuate** mentally; in this sense prob. Zam. γtad-méd ̥čál-ba to fluctuate, to waver, without aim or object. — 2. **to be confused,** in disorder, smra-̥čál, also ̥čal-γtám smra Lt., as a morbid symptom, prob. he raves, he talks nonsense. — 3. morally: tsul-k̒rims ̥čál-ba S.g. **to break** one's vow, bsláb-pa to act contrary to the doctrine, **to violate** it Tar.; in a more restricted sense: — 4. **to fornicate,** to commit adultery, bud-méd smad-̥čál byéd-pa a whore, harlot Mil.; ̥čál-pa, -po lecher, fornicator Stg.; ̥čál-pa-rnams-kyi tsig obscene language, mentioned as sub-species of kyál-ka; ̥čál-mo whore. — *čal-la-čol-lé* W., čal-čól Tar. 184, 20 confusedly, pellmell.

འཆི་བ་ ̥či-ba, pf. ŝi, 1. vb. **to die,** of a flame: to go out; raṅ ̥čio I will seek death Dzl.; ̥či-ba yin he dies, will die S.g.; ̥či or ŝi-ba-las sós-par ̥gyúr-ba Dzl. to be saved from imminent danger of death (but not: to rise from the dead); ̥či-bar byéd-pai ču water causing death Sambh.; ŝi-bar gyúr-to they perished Pth. — 2. sbst., the state of dying, **death,** ̥či-ba tsám-du ̥gyúr-ba to die almost (of grief etc.) Mil.; dus-min ̥či-ba nyúṅ-ba yin premature death rarely occurs Sambh.; ̥či-ba nam yoṅ ča med Mil. when death will come one does not know, (W. *ŝi-če* to die; death; *ŝi soṅ* he has died, *ŝi yin* he will die).

**Comp.** ̥či-k̒a Cs.: 'the very act of dying,' but I doubt whether such a sbst. exists; I only know the adv. ̥či-kar at his very dying, at the point of death Mil., when being exstinguished Glr. (v. k̒ar sub k̒a IV. 4, 5), and ̥či-ka-ma 1. adj. dying, dúd-̥gro ̥či-k̒a-ma a dying animal Glr.; 2. sbst. the dying, ̥čí-ka-ma-ru = čí-k̒ar (doubtful); ̥či-kar and ̥či-gar may be incorrect spellings. — ̥či-ltas, more rarely ̥čí (-bai) rtágs **forebodings, foretokens of death** Med. — ̥či-bdág the lord of death, perh. = γŝín-rje, but it seems to be more a poetical expression than a mythological personage; ̥či-bdág bdud id. — ̥či-nád a disease causing death, **a fatal disease** Tar. — ̥či-ba-po Cs.; a person dying (?) — ̥či-(ba)-méd(-pa) immortal; cf. ŝi-ba. — Note. ̥či ̥p̒ó-ba is prob. only a rather incorrect, yet common expression for tse ̥p̒ó-ba to change one's place of existence, to transmigrate.

འཆིག(ས)་པ་ ̥čig(s)-pa **to bind** Sch., prob. an incorr. spelling for ̥kyig-pa.

འཆིང་བ་, འཆིངས་པ་ ̥čiṅ-ba, ̥čiṅs-pa I. vb., pf. bčiṅs, fut. bčiṅ, imp. ̥čiṅ(s), W. *čin-če*, **to bind** (in general); **to fetter** (a prisoner) Dzl.; **to bind** or **tie up, to cord,** a bundle or package; **to tie round,** to put on, a girdle Glr.; **to bind up, to dress,** wounds; fig. **to render harmless, to neutralize, paralyze,** esp. by witchcraft, **to exorcise,** frq.; bčiṅs ̥gról-ba to untie, to loosen, to take off the dressings Lt. —

II. sbst. any binding-material 1. **ribbon,** mgul-čiṅs necklace, neckcloth, neckerchief. — 2. **fetter, shackle,** also fig. for magic curse, anathema. — 3. **string, tie.** — 4. **cramp, spasm** C.

འཆིང་བུ་ ̥čiṅ-bu a spurious, glass jewel (Schf. Tar. 142, 9); bsam-yas-̥čiṅ-bu p. n. Ma.

འཆིབ(ས)་པ་ ̥čib(s)-pa, pf. bčibs, fut. bčib, imp. čibs resp. **to ascend, to mount,** a horse or carriage, rtá-la, or more correctly čibs-la, **to ride,** to proceed on horseback.

འཆིམས་པ་ ̥čims-pa **to be full, to get full** Sch.

འཆིར་བ ˳čir-ba, evidently a present-form of the pf. *čír-ba*, **to press, to squeeze.**

འཆུ་བ ˳*čú-ba* I. acc. to grammatical analogy 1. vb. n. to *γčúd-pa*, **to be twisted, distorted**, pf. ˳*čus.* — 2. sbst. **curvature, crookedness, distortion.** — 3. adj., more frq. ˳*čús-pa* **crooked, wry,** *ka-˳čús Wdṅ.* the mouth being wry, distorted *Lt.*; also obstinately perverse; fig. *yig-˳čús Med.* frq., prob. = *kam-lóg.*

II. pf. *bčus*, fut. *bču*, imp. *čus*, *W.* **ču-če**, 1. **to lade** or **scoop** (water), *ču-mig-la ču* to draw water from a well *Dzl.*; *ču-tóm* water-conduit *Sch.* — 2. **to irrigate, to water,** *žiṅ* a field *Cs.* (?)

III. *nán-gyis* ˳*čú-ba-la Tar.* 127, 6, when he was pressed hard, was urged with importunity; (this signification, however, seems to rest only on this passage).

འཆུག་པ ˳*čúg-pa* **to be mistaken** *Pth.*, v. ˳*pyúg-pa.*

འཆུན་པ ˳*čún-pa*, evidently vb. n. to ˳*júṅ-pa*, hence 1. **to be tamed, subdued, made to yield,** *stóbs-kyis* by force, *lás-kyis* by hard work. — 2. **to confess** *Cs.* — 3. **to wrap** or **twist** *Sch.* — 4. **to fix** *Sch.* — 5. **to fix one's self** *Sch.*; ˳*čál-sar* ˳*čun* entangled in vicious indulgences *Sch.*

འཆུམ(ས)་པ ˳*čúm(s)-pa* 1. **to wish, to long for** *Lex.* — 2. **to shrink** *Cs.*

འཆེ་བ ˳*če-ba*, pf. *bčes*, ˳*čes* (*Sch.*), fut. *bče*, imp. *čes*, 1. **to assure, to promise,** *kas* ˳*čé-ba Lex.*, resp. *žál-gyis* ˳*čé-ba* id. — 2. resp. for *smrá-ba*, like *γsún-ba* (?)

འཆེག་པ ˳*čég-pa*, also ˳*čág(s)-pa*, pf. *bšags*, fut. *bšag*, imp. *šog*, *W.* **šág-če**, 1. **to cleave, to split,** *šiṅ* wood; *sóg-les* ˳*čég-pa* to saw *Sch.*; ˳*čeg-byéd* (a thing) that cleaves, a hatchet *Cs.* — 2. **to confess, to acknowledge;** v. also *bšág-pa* and *šóg-pa.*

འཆེད་པ ˳*čéd-pa* an incorr. form of *čád-pa* or *mčéd-pa.*

འཆེམས་པ ˳*čéms-pa*, pf. *bčems*, fut. *bčem*, **to chew** *Med.*

འཆེལ་བ ˳*čél-ba Cs.* 1. **to believe, give credit to;** *blo-˳čél-ba* (?) col. id. — 2. *Lexx.* = *žén-pa* **to wish** (?).

འཆོག ˳*čog* **wall** *Sch.*

འཆོང་བ, འཆོངས་པ ˳*čóṅ-ba*, ˳*čóṅs-pa Sch.* = ˳*čáṅ-ba.*

འཆོམས་པ ˳*čóms-pa* 1. = ˳*čám-pa Glr.* and *Lexx.* — 2. vb. n. to ˳*jóms-pa* 4 *W.*, **da čoms soṅ** now it is done.

འཆོར་པོ ˳*čór-po* = *mčor-po.*

འཆོར་བ ˳*čór-ba* I. vb. n., pf. *šor*, 1. **to escape, slip, steal away; to drop from,** *stón-mo šór-gyis* as the meal escaped him, as he was deprived of the meal *Dzl.*; *rtsa-krág* ˳*čór-ba* hemorrhage, bloody flux *Med.*; *bkrag-˳čór* without splendour, lustreless; *nor* ˳*čor* the money is gone, spent, lost *Thgy.*; *sdóm-pa* ˳*čor* the duty is violated *Glr.*; *mé-la, čú-la* ˳*čór-ba* to be consumed by fire, carried off by water; **čaṅ mi tuṅ dé-ne ka mi šor* W.* I will not drink any beer, then the mouth cannot run away, i. e. then no indiscreet words will escape my mouth; **to flow out, to run,** of a leaking vessel, **to run over,** of a full one. — 2. **to come out, to break out,** frq. of fire; ˳*krúg-pa šor* a quarrel, a war broke out, also of water breaking through an embankment etc. — 3. **to go over, to pass,** from one person or thing to another, *rgyál-sa Bód-nas Me-nyág-la šor* the supreme power passed from Tibet to Tanggút *Glr.*; *γžán-gyi dbáṅ-du šor* then I shall get into the power of another *Mil.*; *rkún-ma-la šor* it became the prey of a thief. — 4. *W.* **to run away, flee, escape, elope,** inst. of ˳*brós-pa*, **šór-te ča-dug** he retires, falls back.

II. vb. a., pf. (*b*)*šor*, fut. *γšor* (?) 1. **to pursue, chase, hunt** after, *ri-boṅ rgyas* hares by means of nets; *nya* ˳*čór-ba* to fish *Dzl.*; *Cs.* also to strain (?); ˳*čor-sgég* a seducer; a swaggerer *Sch.* (cf. *sgég-pa*). — 2. **to light, kindle, set on fire** (?)

འཆོལ་པ ˳*čól-pa* 1. **disorderly, dissolute, immoral.** — 2. disorderly action or conduct, **dissoluteness,** ˳*čól-pa sna-tsógs spyád-pa* committing several acts of immorality *Wdṅ.* — *kro-bo-˳ól-pa* n. of a demon. (Cf. ˳*čól-ba* II).

**འཆོལ་བ** ˳*čól-ba* I. pf. *bčol*, fut. *γžol* (?) 1. **to entrust** a person with a thing, to commit a thing to another's charge; **to make, appoint**, *dé-la rgyál-po ˳čól-lo* they made him king *Pth.*; *btsún-mo-la rtá-rdzi bčól-lo* they made the queen tend the horses *Glr.*; *ṫab-;yóg ˳čól žig* he may be employed as a kitchenboy, scullion *Pth.*; *dbaṅ-méd-du ˳čól-ba* to make one powerless, to compel by authority *Glr.*; *bčól-bai γnyer Lex.* manager; *˳čól-bai ṅo Ler.* intercessor; *pi-wáṅ-la ram-˳dégs bčól-nas glu blaṅs* she sang with accompaniment of the guitar (lit. committing the accompaniment to the guitar) *Glr.*; **kyab čól-la** (for *˳čol-du*) **yoṅ-če** *W.* to place one's self under another man's protection. — 2. **to commit, commend, recommend,** *lás ˳čól-ba* to commission one with an affair or transaction; resp. *p̔rin (-las) ˳čól-ba*, though *p̔rin (-las)* seems to be sometimes a mere pleonasm: *bán-so yul deï lha-srúṅ-rnams-la p̔rin-bčól mdzád-do* (the king) recommended the sepulchre to the tutelar gods of the country *Glr.*; **čól-te bór-če** *W.* to deposit a thing for temporary keeping.

II. = *˳čál-ba* 1. *Cs.* **to change, to turn aside** (?) — 2. **to be thrown together** confusedly, e.g. of the loose leaves of a (Tibetan) book; *˳čól-bar byéd-pa* to put in disorder, to confuse, to confound *Ma.*; *dge-sdíg ˳čól-bar ˳gro* virtue and vice are confounded *Ma.*; **'i lé-ka čól dug** *W.* this affair goes wrong, turns out badly; in a special sense: **to rave, to be delirious** *C.*; **čol-láb gyáb-pa** *C.* id.; **nyid-čol láb-pa, gyag-pa** *C.*, to talk confusedly whilst being heavy with sleep; **čól-k̔a** *C.* senseless talk; **čól-k̔an-ni ṭ̔ú-gu, čol-ṭ̔úg** *W.* being of a mixed race; illegitimate or bastard child, bastard. — 3. morally: **to break a vow;** **a-ne čol son** he has broken his vow on account of a woman, i.e. by having married.

**འཆོལ་མ** ˳*čól-ma Cs.*: 1. a thing committed to another's care. — 2. **a sly, crafty woman,** *Sch.* **a dissolute woman.**

**འཆོས་པ** ˳*čós-pa* I. pf. *bčos* or *˳čos*, fut. *bčo*, imp. *čos*, supine *bčós-su Dzl.* ༢, 4, *W.* **čó-če**, pf. and imp. **čos**, **to make, make ready, prepare, to construct, build,** a bow, a road etc. *Glr.*; *˳čós-sam* am I to build? *Glr.*; *drés-ma ṫág-par ˳čós-pa* to make ropes out of *drésma* (a kind of grass) prop. to work *drésma* into ropes, *Glr.*; *γzab ˳čós-pa* to adjust one's ornaments *Sch.*; *lus ˳čós-pa* to dress, to trim one's self up *Sch.*; *γsár-du ˳čós-pa* to renew, renovate, repair *Sch.*; *ltúṅ-ba p̔yir ˳čós-pa Tar.* 95, 20 perh. to retouch, amend, correct, improve. — *ṫsúl-˳čos* hypocrisy, a mere outward performance of religious rites and observances *Mil.*, *ṫsul-˳čos ma byas spyód-pa* to live without hypocrisy *Mil.*; *ṫsúl-˳čos-mk̔an* hypocrite. — *ṫsúl-˳čos-pa* or *bčós-pa* acc. to *Cs.* also an established rule or canon.

II. *Sch.*: **to gnaw off** (secondary form to *˳čá-ba*).

# ཇ

**ཇ་** *ǰa* 1. the letter *ǰ*, media, palatal, like the Italian *gi* in Giovanni, *g* in giro; in *C.* as initial deep-sounding and aspirated, *ǰh.* — 2. numerical figure: 7. — 3. **tea,** resp. *γsol-ǰa.* For the trade in Central Asia it is pressed into brick-shaped lumps, a portion of which, when to be used, is pulverized and boiled, having been well compounded with butter and salt or soda (*bul*) by means of a kind of churn of bamboo (*gur-gúr*), after which it is drunk as hot as possible. Of late years tea grown on the southern slopes of the Himalaya Mountains finds its way into

Central Asia. The tea called ₒbru-ťáṅ is considered the best, and of other teas Čs. mentions rtsé-ǰa, zi-liṅ-spú-ǰa hairy (?) tea from Siling, (a province in the neighbourhood of the Kokonor); Schr.: γnám-ǰa, míṅ-ǰa, ₒbó-ǰa, ǰa-γzúṅs, zau, hu-čág, ₒu-si; bzaṅ-ǰa, or ko-tse is, acc. to Cs., good ordinary tea, čuṅ-ₒǰug, or čuṅ-čuṅ are sorts of inferior quality. The shepherds in W. make use of a surrogate, viz. the Potentilla Inglisii (spáṅ-ǰa), growing on the mountains at a height of 15 000 feet; poor people in Sik. use the leaves of the maple (γya-lí).

Other **comp.** ǰa-bkrúg (pronounced *ǰhab-ṭúg*), prob. for ǰa-dkrúg, **twirling-stick** Ts. — ǰa-mčód, libation of tea. — ǰa-ₒťág, or btág **grinding-stone,** in India and Tibet used for kitchen purposes inst. of our little mortars. — ǰa-dám Sch. **tea-pot** (?) — ǰa-blúg W. a little pitcher-shaped **brass vessel.** — ǰa-ₒbíṅ (pronounced *ǰham-bíṅ*) C. **tea-kettle, tea-pot.** — ǰá-ma the man that prepares the tea in a monastery, **tea-cook;** ǰai dpon head-tea-cook. — ǰa-ril 1. W. **grinding-stone;** 2. Lex. **skull.** — ǰa-sun-čan 'a cup of tea, or: as much as a cup of tea' Sch. — ǰa-seg tea-dust Sch.

ཇ་ཧོད་ ǰa-hód Lex. **yellowish red.**

ཇག་ ǰag **robbing, robbery,** ǰag rgyág-pa to rob, to be a robber; rku-ǰag-gyu-zól byéd-pa Glr.; ǰág-pa frq. robber (not robbery Sch.); ǰag-dpón captain of a gang of robbers Mil.

ཇི་ ǰi 1. num. fig.: 37. — 2. the correlative form of the pron. či, **what.** For the construction of a sentence containing či or ǰi, v. gaṅ II. The explanation there given shows, that in correct language ǰi is always followed by a participle: ǰi yód-pa de ṗul žig offer what you have, make a libation of what you have. Owing, however, to the slight difference in the pronunciation of či and ǰi, the former is frq. written in the place of the latter; ǰi, of course, is used in conjunction with the same words as či; a few more instances may follow here: ǰi-skad whatever, relative to words spoken: ṅas ǰi-skad smras kyaṅ whatever I may say Glr. — ǰi-snyéd 1. as much as, as great as; 2. C. very much, every thing possible. — ǰi-lta-ba 1. adj. of what kind, of what nature, ...ǰi-lta-ba bžin-du... la yaṅ de-bžin-no as it is with... so it is with... Stg. 2. sbst. quality, nature, condition Cs. — ǰi-lta-bu such as, like as, Lat. qualis. — ǰi-ltar adv. as, in what manner; 'á-mas ǰi-ltar zér-pa bžin-du according to what the mother has said Glr. — ǰi-ste = či-ste. — ǰi nús-kyis to the utmost, to the best of one's ability Dzl. — ǰi ma ǰi-bžin-du (?) according to custom or common usage Sch. — ǰi-mi-snyám-pai bzód-pa a patience prepared for every event Sch. (?) — ǰi-tsam = ǰi-snyéd; lo lṅa lón-pa ǰi-tsam-pa de-bžin-no they are (as tall) as (children) five years old Stg.; ǰi tsam byas kyaṅ whatever they had done Tar.; ǰi-tsam-na or nas as soon as, when. — ǰi-bžin as, like, how, ǰi-bžin ₒtso mi ruṅ (he) can in no wise, by no means, continue to live Lt.; ǰi-bžin-du γsuṅs elliptically: he said how (it was), he answered according to the state of the case (Schf.) Tar. 89, 9. — ǰi-srid as long as.

ཇུ་ ǰu num. fig.: 67.

ཇུ་ཐིག་ ǰu-ṭig denotes a way of drawing lots by threads of different colours, whence a class of Bonpos is called ṗya-bon ǰu-ṭig-čan Glr.

ཇུ་པོ་ ǰú-po Liś., *ǰu-lúm* W., a globular stone used for grinding spices, = ǰa-ril.

ཇུས་ ǰus C. **strategy.**

ཇུས་མ་ ǰús-ma a sort of silk stuff Cs.

ཇུས་ལེགས་ ǰus-légs 1. Sch.: 'possessed of good manners, of propriety of conduct, **decent, agreeable;** ǰus-bdé sincere' (?) — 2. Cs. **clever, skilled, able, experienced.** *žiṅ-gi lẹ* in agriculture, *mag* in military matters C.

ཇེ. ǰe 1. num. fig.: 97. — 2. a particle, used for expressing the comparative degree of an adj. or adv., and esp. a gradual growing or increase, often with termin. or *la: ǰe man ˳gro* (they) go on increasing or multiplying in number *Mil.*; *ǰe ɣsál-du soṅ* it has become more and more clear or evident *Thgr.*; gen. repeated: *ǰe nye ǰe nye són-ste* going nearer and nearer *Mil.*; *ǰe čuṅ ǰe čúṅ-la soṅ*, also *ǰe čúṅ ǰe nyúṅ Mil.* less and less; sometimes also for the superlative degree, *Cs.*: *ǰe dáṅ-po* the very first, also *Lex.* — 3. *ǰé-žig* a little while, = *ré-žig Lex.* — 4. *Bhar.* 14, *Schf.*: 'an adhortative particle, often connected with a vocative'; *Sch.* has: *ǰe kyod* 'now you, you first!' — 5. = *dbyaṅs Lex.*

ཇོ་ *ǰo* 1. num. fig.: 127. — 2. v. the following word.

ཇོ་བོ་ *ǰó-bo* (आर्य) 1. *C.* **the elder brother,** also **ǰo-ǰó** and **'á-ǰo** (the latter also in *W.*), resp. *ǰo-légs.* — 2. **lord, master,** esp. **nobleman, grandee,** *W. *ǰo*, yar-lúṅ ǰó-bo Glr.* the lord of the manor of Yarlung; **ti-nán ǰo* W.* the nobleman of Tinan; *ǰo-ǰo miṅ-po* my noble brothers (says a princess) *Glr.*; in *C.* used as honorary title for noblemen and priests, in *W.* also for noble Mussulmans; in ancient times for certain divine persons, and idols, particularly for two, famous in history: *ǰó-bo mi-skyod-rdó-rǰe*, and *tsan-dán-gyi ǰó-bo*, also *ǰó-bo šá-kya, ǰó-bo rin-po-čé* v. *Glr.*

ཇོ་མོ་ *ǰó-mo* 1. **mistress**, the female head of a household, a woman that governs as mistress of her servants *Dzl.* — 2. **lady,** esp. **a cloistress, nun** *Mil.*; in *W.* frq. – 3. **goddess** (cf. sub *ǰo-bo* 2), *ǰo-mo sgrol-ma* the goddess *Dolma Glr.* — 4. p. n. *ǰo-mo-lha-ri* one of the highest mountain summits in West-Bhotan, usually called 'Chumulhari'; *ǰo-mo-ka-nag* another summit in southern Tibet.

མཇལ་བ་ *mǰál-ba*, imp. *mǰol*, 1. **to meet** c. *daṅ*, = *˳prad-pa*, without any respect to rank, *Mil.* often. More frq. 2. resp.: **to obtain access** to an honoured person; *žal-dṅós-su mǰál-bar yod* he (the incarnated Buddha) may personally be seen and spoken to *Glr.*; **to wait on, to pay one's respects** to a person, *yab daṅ mǰal ˳tsál-lo* I will pay a visit to my father *Dzl.*; *pyis myúr-du mǰál-du yoṅ* I shall take the liberty of soon coming back *Mil.*; *rgyál-bai sku daṅ ta-mal mǰal* to thee, Buddha, my own humble self approaches (says a prince to his father who appears to be an incarnated Buddha) *Glr.*; *mǰál-bar žú-ba* to ask for an audience *Glr.*; *mǰál-du mi btub* (they) cannot get in, cannot obtain admittance *Pth.*; **ǰal-čág čó-če** (or **čag-ǰál* Cs.*) *W.* to salute, to exchange compliments on meeting; *mǰal-prád-byéd-pa* = *˳prad-pa*; used also of a king and his ministers: *mǰal-prád daṅ dgá-bai ɣtam máṅ-po mdzad* (they) exchanged many compliments and expressions of joy *Pth.*; to visit or pay one's respects to holy places, as pilgrims do, **to go on a pilgrimage,** also *žal mǰál-ba Mil.*; *ɣnas mǰál-ba* id., *ɣnas-mǰál-pa* partic., a pilgrim, palmer; *˳di mǰól žig* do make your pilgrimage to this place. — 3. **to understand, comprehend,** *Zam.*: *'gó-bai mǰál-ba* ज्ञा'; *don mǰál-ba* to understand the sense *Mil.*, yet cf. *˳ǰál-ba* 3. — 4. often erron. for *ǰál-ba.*

**Comp.** *mǰál-ka* **audience, access, admittance,** *mǰál-ka ɣtóṅ-ba*, or *ɣnáṅ-ba* to give audience, *˳gégs-pa* to refuse it *Mil.* — *mǰal-dár* = *ka-btágs.* — *mǰál-sna-pa* **an usher,** master of ceremonies *Cs.* — *mǰal-pyág* **salutation.** — *mǰal-máṅs* a visit paid by many together, a grand reception *Cs.*

མཇིང་པ་ *mǰiṅ-pa* 1. = *˳ǰiṅ-pa.* — 2. *rtswa-mǰiṅ* **meadow** *Bhar.* 82, *Schf.*

མཇུག *mǰúg* what is behind, **hind part,** e.g. of the body, resp. *sku-mǰúg,* **posteriors, back-side, tail,** often also *mǰúg-ma*; *mǰug skór-ba* col. to turn one's back (on another); *mǰúg-ma sgríl-ba* to wag the tail; fig.: the further progress and final issue of an affair, **the consequences** = *rǰes*, opp. to *dṅos-ɣži* the thing itself, and to *sṅón-˳gro* the preparations *Thgy.*; **the lower end** or extremity, e.g. of a bench, a stick, a river (= mouth), of a procession, train etc.; with regard to time: **the end,** *zlá-ba brgyád-pai mǰúg-la,* at the end of the eighth month;

in general mǰúg-la, mǰúg-tu adv. and postp., = mťar, at the end of, at last, behind, after, with the genit. inf., or the verbal root, gen. opp. to *mgo.* — *mǰúg-sgro* (*W.* *ǰúg-ro*) lower or inferior part, underpart, buttocks (cf. *γžug*); *mǰúg-to* id. — *mǰug-btág* (for *btég*), and *mǰug-ldéb W.* wagtail. — *mgo-mǰúg* above and below *Dzl.*

མཇེ་ *mǰe*, resp. *γsáṅ-mǰe*, लिङ्ग, शेफ **the penis;** *Zam.* avoids the term by making use of circumlocutions, others employ it, esp. *Med.*; also in vulgar use; *mǰe láṅ-ba* erection of the penis; *mǰe sbúbs-su nub* the penis recedes; *mǰe-mgo* glans penis. — *mǰe-rlíg* the penis and testicles. — *mǰe-śúbs* the membraneous covering or sheath of the penis.

མཇེད་པ་ *mǰéd-pa*, *Zam.* सह suffering, enduring, bearing patiently; *Cs.*: obnoxious; *mi-mǰéd* prop.: free; gen. **the world, the universe,** acc. to Buddhistic ideas; except in the last mentioned sense the word seems to be little used.

འཇག་པ་ *˳ǰág-pa*, pf. *ǰags*, *Cs.*; *Sch.*: to establish, settle, fix, found; hence prob. *bde-˳ǰágs* and *ḱris-˳ǰágs*, *˳ǰags-ḱris* (*Lexx.* and elsewh., but not frq.) **time of prosperity,** of peace, of rest, a time without disturbances, war, epidemies etc. (*ḱris* by itself is not known).

འཇག་པོ་ *˳ǰág-po* 1. *Lex.* = *klu*, or n. of a Lu, also *˳ǰóg-po.* — 2. vulgo = *yág-po.*

འཇག་མ་ *˳ǰág-ma* 1. *Sch.*: a sort of **coarse** and **thick grass** of inferior quality; so *Pth.* of a hut: *˳ǰág-mas ṕúb-pa* covered with such grass. — 2. *Lex.* वीरण **a fragrant grass,** Andropogon muricatus. — 3. *Glr.*: **a blade** (of grass), **stalk** (of corn), *˳ǰág-ma reï stéṅ-na* on every blade, *kú-śai ˳ǰág-ma ṕon ċig* a bundle of blades of Kusha grass; *˳ǰag-rgód Sch.* horse-tail, pewter-grass, Equisetum. — 4. *Sik.* **squirrel,** perh. = *bya-ma-byí Sch.* (?).

འཇགས་ *˳ǰags*, v. sub *˳ǰág-pa.*

འཇགས་པ་ *˳ǰágs-pa C.* **to give,** to make a present *Georgi Alph. Tib.*

འཇང་བ་ *˳ǰáṅ-ba* **to devour, swallow,** *Sch.*

འཇན་པོ་, འཇན་མོ་ *˳ǰán-po*, *˳ǰán-mo* **consort, husband, wife** *Cs.*

འཇན་ས་ *˳ǰán-sa*, v. *ċán-sa.*

འཇབ་པ་ *˳ǰáb-pa*, pf. prob. *bžabs*, fut. *bžab*, **to sneak, slink,** creep privily; **to lie in wait,** in ambush, *tsé-la ˳ǰáb-pa* to attempt a person's life *Pth.*; *ṕág-ne ǰáb-te sad táṅ-ċe* *W.* to assassinate; *lkog ˳ǰab byéd-pa* v. *lkog*; *˳ǰáb-bus ma byin-par lén-pa Thgy.* to steal clandestinely. Cog. to *˳ċáb-pa.*

འཇབ་ཙེ་ *˳ǰáb-tse* nippers, tweezers.

འཇམ་མགོན་ *˳ǰam-mgón* = *˳ǰam-dpál.*

འཇམ་པ་ *˳ǰám-pa B.*, *ǰám-po* *W.*, *˳ǰam-˳ǰám* *C.* col. (opp. to *rtsúb-pa*, *rtsíṅ-ge*) **soft, smooth, tender, mild,** e.g. of cloth, hair, a meadow, a plain without stones or rocks, of fruit, the air, the character of a person, a person's way of speaking (*ṅag C.*, *pé-ra* *W.*, *pé-ra ǰám-po daṅ* with mild expressions, fair words, in a friendly manner), of a law; of beverages: **weak** *W.*; of a (hay-)rake: **close** *W.*; *ǰám-po ṅáb-ċe* *W.* to mow off close; *˳ǰam-˳búd* blowing or playing (the flute) softly, piano; *˳ǰam-rtsi Med.*, seems to be a kind of medicine; *ǰam-sáṅ* *W.*, *C.*, plain, without ornaments.

འཇམ་དཔལ་ *˳ǰam-dpál* (मञ्जुश्री) *˳ǰam-mgón* (०नाथ), *˳ǰam(-pai)-dbyáṅs* (०घोष) one of the two great Bodhisattvas of the northern Buddhists, the Apollo of the Tibetans, the god of wisdom, demiurge, and more particularly the tutelar god and civilizer of Nepal (v. Köpp. II, 21), incarnated in *Thonmi Sambhota*, and afterwards in king *Kri-sroṅ-sde-btsán* and others. Cf. *spyan-ras-γzigs.*

འཇམ་མ་, རྗེ་འཇམ་ *˳ǰám-ma*, *rǰe-˳ǰám*, resp. for *ťug-pa*, **soup.**

འཇམ་མོ་ *˳ǰam-mo* **post-stage** *Sch.*

འཇའ་, འཇའ་ཚོན་ *˳ǰa*, *˳ǰa-tson* **rainbow** frq., *˳ǰa-˳od* light, splendour of the rainbow *Pth.*; *༵ja-tson yal-ba* the vanishing of the rainbow frq.; *༵ja-lus* v. *lus.*

འཇའ་བ་ *༵ja-ba* 1. also *༵ja-mo Sch.* **lame,** gen. *ža-ba*; *༵ja-bar byed-pa* to make lame, to lame *S.g.* — 2. **to bespeak, to concert, to confederate** *Sch.*

འཇའ་ས་ *༵ja-sa*, *༵ja-mo*, **edict, diploma**, a permit *Cs.*, who declares this word to be Chinese.

འཇར་བ་ *༵jar-ba Lex.* w.e., acc. to *Cs.* = *༵byar-ba* **to stick together, to cohere.**

འཇལ་བ་ *༵jal-ba*, pf. *bčal*, fut. *γžal*, imp. *༵jol*, *W.* **čal-če**, 1. **to weigh,** *༵jal-byed srań* (a pair of) scales for weighing *Lex.*, *sráń-la γžal-ba Glr.* — 2 **to measure,** *riń-tuń-tsád ༵jál-ba C.* to measure the length. — 3. **to appraise, to tax**; to weigh in one's mind, **to ponder**; more fully expressed by *blos-༵jal-ba* to understand *Sch.*, although native grammarians refer this signification with less probability to *m༵jal-ba.* — 4. **to pay, pay back, repay,** *bú-lon* a debt, *skyin-pa* a loan, *kral* a tax; **to retaliate, return, repay,** esp. with *lan: pan-lán γnód-pas* or *légs-pai lan nyés-pas* to return evil for good. The following is a Buddhist principle of law, but prob. existing only in theory: *dkon-mčóg-gi rdzás-la kri ༵jal, dge-༵dún-gyi rdzás-la brgyád-ču ༵jal, pál-pai rdzás-la bdún-༵gyur ńo brgyad ༵jal* divine or sacred objects are to be repaid or made good tenthousandfold, things or property of the clergy eightyfold, of ordinary men sevenfold, and besides the object itself, hence eightfold *C.*; in *Glr.* there is the following passage: *brkús-pa la brgyad ༵jal ńos dań dgu.* — 5. often erron. for *m༵jál-ba*; thus prob. also in: *༵jal ༵búl-ba* to bring a present *Sch.* (more correctly: a present of salutation). — *༵jál-ka* the act, or business of measuring *C.*

འཇི་བ་ *༵ji-ba* 1. *Cs.*, also *l༵ji-ba*, **a flea.** — 2. *Lex.* and *Cs.*: = *༵jim-pa.* — 3. *Cs.* = *༵jám-pa* **soft, smooth.** — 4. *Sch.*: **disgusting, nasty,** e.g. of a fishy smell.

འཇིག་རྟེན་ *༵jig-rtén* (receptacle of all that is perishable) 1. **the external world:** a. acc. to the common (popular) notion: the whole earth, the universe, *༵jig-rtén-na dkón-pa*, what is rare, the only thing of its kind in the world *Dzl.*; *༵jig-rtén-gyi lha* the god of the world, a deity of the Bonpos *Mil.*; *༵jig-rtén-las ༵dás-pa* one that has escaped from this world, one emancipated, blessed *Cs.* — b. the external world acc. to Brahmanic and Buddhist theories, as set forth: *Köpp.* I, 231; *༵jig-rtén-gyi kams* id. *Glr.*; *༵jig-rtén čágs-pa* origin, beginning, *γnás-pa* duration, *༵jig-pa* destruction, *bžág-pa* arrangement of the world, cosmography (title of a volume of *Stg.*) *༵jig-rtén γsum* the three worlds, earth, heaven, and hades; *༵jig-rtén* (*γsúm-gyi*) *mgón-po* (*Triloknāth Hind.*) lord or patron of the three worlds, which is also the title of the third of the three highest Lamas, viz. of the Dharma Raja, residing in Bhotan, v. *Cunningh. Ladak* 371; Buddha *Sakya-túb-pa* seems to have the same title, *Pth.* — c. fig.: *bdé-ba-čan-gyi ༵jig-rtén,* or *bdé-༵gro mto-ris-kyi ༵jig-rtén* the world of the blessed, like our 'heaven', but of rare occurrence. — 2. **world,** in a spiritual sense, *༵jig-rtén-gyi byá-ba* worldly things or affairs; *༵jig-rtén-la dgós-pa* (or *pán-pai*) *bsláb-bya* useful maxims of life, moral rules *Glr.*; *༵jig-rtén-gyi čos brgyad*, v. *čos*; *༵jig-rtén byéd-pa* short expression for *༵jig-rtén-gyi las byéd-pa Mil.* — 3. symb. num.: **three.** — *༵jig-rtén-pa* 1. an inhabitant of the world, or the inhabitants of the world, the world as the totality of men, and more particularly of the worldly-minded; *༵jig-rtén-pa ni ma-dúl-ba yin-pas* as the world is unconverted, in which sense also *༵jig-rtén* (by itself) seems to be used. 2. a layman.

འཇིག་པ་ *༵jig-pa* I. vb. 1. act. pf. *bžig*, fut. *γžig*, imp. (*b*)*šig*, *W.* **šig-če*, *šig táń-če**, **to destroy,** buildings etc., frq.: **to cut to pieces, to divide,** e.g. a killed animal *W.*; **to ruin, to annihilate,** existing institutions or things, also other people; **to abolish, annul,** a law *W.*: **to dissolve,** an enchantment; **to lay aside** an assumed appearance or manner (= to unmask one's self) *Mil.*; **to break, violate,** one's duty, a vow, *Dzl.*;

rma-̥jig *Med.* was explained: **healing wounds.** ̥*jig-par byed-pa* = ̥*jig-pa*, frq. — 2. vb. n. pf. *bžig*, and more frq. *žig*, *W.* **žig-če, žig ča-če**, **to be ruined, undone,** e.g. by mischief-making people *Dzl.*; **to fall to pieces, to decay, to rot,** of the human body etc.; **to be lost, to perish,** ̥*jig-par śin-tu sla* (earthly goods) may be easily lost again *Thgy.*; **to vanish, disappear,** ̥*jig* (or *žig*)-*par* ̥*gyur-ba* id.; *sem žig soṅ W.* he was quite dejected or cast down; *žig ysós byed-pa B., C.*, **žig-só* (or -*sób*) *čó-če* or *táṅ-če** *W.* to 'restore from destruction', to rebuild c. dat. frq., also c. genit. *Pth.*; prob. also c. accus. — 3. **to suck,** draw out moisture *Sch.*, v. ̥*jib-pa*.

II. sbst. **decay, destruction, ruin,** entire overthrow, *skyé-ba daṅ* ̥*jig-pa kún-la srid-na* as it is the lot of all men to rise and to decay *Dzl.*; *lús-kyi mťar* ̥*jig-pai ltas* symptoms of the final decay of the body *Wdṅ.*; **čáṅ-la k'oi žig-pa yod** beer proves his ruin, beer is his destruction *W.*; ̥*jig-pe čó-čen** *C.*, ̥*jig-pa-čan Cs.* frail, perishable.

III. adj., but only in conjunction with a negative: *mi-*̥*jig-pa* **imperishable;** *mi-*̥*jig rtág-pa* as explanation of a synonym *Lex.*

འཇིགས་པ་ ̥*jigs-pa* I. vb. (भी) resp. *tsábs-pa*, to be afraid of a thing, is gen. connected with the instr. (lit. 'by'), in later literature and col. with *la*, *srin-pos* ̥*jigs-śiṅ* from fear of the Rakshasa *Dzl.*; *dé-la ṅa mi* ̥*jigs* I am not afraid of that *Mil.*; in *W.* frq. in conjunction with **rag**: **k'ó-la* ̥*jig rag** I am afraid of him; also relative to the future, like *dógs-pa*: *yi-ge máṅs-pas* ̥*jigs-nas* = *máṅ-gi dógs-nas*, fearing lest there should be too much writing, i. e. from want of room *Pth.*; ̥*jigs-su-ruṅ-ba* dreadful, frightful, frq.; *̥*jig-te dár-ri spé-ra zér-če** *W.* to speak trembling and shaking with fear; **máṅ-po* ̥*jig soṅ** *W.* I am very much afraid; ̥*jigs-par* ̥*gyur-ba* to be frightened, ̥*jigs-par byéd-pa* to put in fear, to frighten.

II. sbst. (भीरु) **fear, dread,** *srin-poi* ̥*jigs-pas* from fear of the Rakshasa *Dzl.* ཀུ, 14 (unless *srin-pos* ought to be read, as above); ̥*jigs-pa brgyad* the eight fears of life (so among the rest: *rgyál-poi* ̥*jigs-pa* the standing in fear of the king, who in the East is always supposed to be an arbitrary despot); *mi-*̥*jigs-pa* 1. fearlessness, intrepidity; *mi-*̥*jigs-pa sbyin-pa* to impart intrepidity; *mi-*̥*jigs-pai lág-pa* a fearless hand, heroic vigour. 2. pardon, quarter, safety *Cs.* — ̥*jigs (-pa)-čan Cs.* 1. fearful, timorous. 2. dreadful, frightful (I never found it used in this sense).

III. adj. 1. (fearing) **fearful, timorous,** ̥*jigs-pai* ̥*gró-ba-rnams* timorous beings *Pth.* — 2. (feared) **dreadful, frightful,** ̥*jigs-pai mťsón-ča* dreadful weapons; *kyod-pas lhag-par* ̥*jigs-pa yod* there is something even more formidable than you are *Dzl.*

**Comp.** *bár-do-la* ̥*jigs skyób-mai smón-lam* a prayer efficacious in the Bardo-horrors *Thgr.* — ̥*jigs-skrág* **fear;** also a terrible object, ̥*jigs-skrág-tu soṅ* he has been changed into **a fright,** a monster *Mil.*; *̥*jig-tág tóm-pa** *C.* (lit. *btón-pa*) to frighten, deter; intimidate, threaten; ̥*jigs-skrág-pa* to fear, to be afraid *Dzl.* — ̥*jigs-mk'an* col. **timid, timorous.** — ̥*jigs-čan* v. ̥*jigs-pa-čan* above. — ̥*jigs-čúm-pa* v. *čum-pa*. — ̥*jigs(-pa)-po* one afraid *Cs.* (?) — ̥*jigs-byéd* one that is terrifying *Sch.*, appellation of Yamāntaka, who is invoked, e.g. in drawing lots. — ̥*jigs-brál*, ̥*jigs-méd* **fearless, intrepid, bold;** also noun pers. — *̥*jigs-ri** *W.* **fear, terror,** *̥*jig-ri tsór-če** to be afraid, *̥*jig-ri kúl-če** to frighten, to menace, to intimidate. — ̥*jigs-sa Mil.*, ̥*jigs-sa čé* it is a very dangerous quarter or region, in that place there is much occasion for being afraid.

འཇིང་ ̥*jiṅ* 1. acc. to *Cs.* = *mčiṅ*, *kloṅ*, e.g. *rgyá-mťsoi*; *Sch.*: *mtso-*̥*jún* the whole circumference of a lake; prob. more corr.: **the middle,** *Lex.*: *lus-*̥*jám* ̥*jág-po mťsó-*̥*jiṅ* ̥*jug* the smooth-bodied Lu alights in the middle of the lake. — 2. *srod-*̥*jiṅ Lex.*; or *srod-byiṅ* **twilight.**

འཇིང་པ་ ̥*jiṅ-pa*, also *mjiṅ-pa*, **neck,** resp. *sku-*̥*jiṅ*; **jiṅ-pa gyúr-če** *W.* to turn or move round (as vb. n.), *ǰiṅ-pa gyúr-te ltá-če* W. to look round, or back; *ǰiṅ-pa čág-če* W. to break one's neck; *ǰiṅ-pa zúm-če* W. to hug, to embrace; ʼǰiṅ-kyóg a wry neck Cs.; ʼǰiṅ-kúṅ the nape of the neck Glr.; ʼǰiṅ-ltág the back part of the neck Cs.

འཇིབ(ས)་པ ʼǰib(s)-pa (Sch. also ʼǰigs-pa) pf. bžibs (γžibs), fut. bzib (γžib), **to suck**, e.g. of a suckling baby; mčus with the lips Lex.; ḱrag ʼǰibs-pa to suck blood Lex.; **to suck out, in,** or **up, to imbibe, absorb,** also **to blister,** ǰib-mán W. vesicatory.

འཇིབ་རྩི ʼǰib-rtsi 1. Cs. a kind of sirup. — 2. Wdṅ. a medicinal herb.

འཇིམ་པ ʼǰim-pa B., C., a compound of earth and water, **mud, clay, loam** etc. (W. *ká-lag*); ʼǰim-skoṅ a small cup of clay, a crucible Cs.; ʼǰim-γzugs a figure formed of clay Glr.; rdó-rǰei ʼǰim-pa v. rdó-rǰe.

འཇིལ་བ ʼǰil-ba, pf. bčil, fut. γžil, **to expel, eject, remove, turn off,** ṕyir ʼǰil-ba Lex. id., e.g. noxious animals, vices etc.

འཇུ་བ ʼǰú-ba I. vb. 1. pf. ʼǰus, **to seize, grasp, take hold of,** c. dat., dpràl-bai mdá-la ʼǰú-ba grasping the arrow sticking in his forehead Glr.; γčig-la γčig ʼǰú-ba taking firmly hold of each other (in a storm at sea) Glr.; to seize a person (in taking him prisoner) Pth.; lág-pa-nas to grasp by the hand, to shake hands (in greeting) Dzl. — 2. pf. bžus, fut. bžu, W. *žú-če (or ǰu-če?)* **to melt, to digest,** zas ʼǰú-ba to digest the food; ʼǰu slá-ba digestible, ʼǰu dká-ba difficult of digestion; *ra ǰú-če* W. to digest intoxication, to sleep the fumes of wine away; ʼǰu-byéd a sort of bile, the bile as the promoter of digestion Med. Cf. žú-ba II.

II. sbst. 1. **digestion,** ʼǰú-ba slao the digestion is in order, is easy Med.; ʼǰu-stóbs čuṅ the digestive power is weak Med. — 2. **a flea** Sch. = ʼǰi-ba.

འཇུག ʼǰug, sometimes for mǰug.

འཇུག་ངོགས ʼǰug-ṅógs Cs. **entrance,** way of access, to a tank or river, Ghāt (Hind.).

འཇུག་པ ʼǰúg-pa, I. pf. and imp. žugs, W. *žúg-če*, vb. n., 1. **to go** or **walk in, to enter,** ḱáṅ-pai, or čui náṅ-du ʼǰúg-pa to go into the house, or into the water; rgyá-mtsor ʼǰúg-pa to put to sea, to set sail Dzl.; lám-du ʼǰúg-pa to set out, to start, to prosecute a journey; *mál-sa-la žúg-če* W. to go to bed. In a special sense: a. of a demon, entering into a man to take possession of him, hence *ḍé-žug-ḱan* W. possessed (by a demon); ʼǰúg-sgo Med. the place where the demon entered the body. b. dgé-ba-la ʼǰúg-pa to walk in the path of virtue; acc. to Schr. ʼǰúg-pa by itself, without dgé-ba-la, implies the same, and in conformity with this a Lama gave the following explanation of the expression ʼǰúg-pai las in Thgy.: works that are a consequence of having really entered upon the practice of virtue, positive good works, opp. to the negative good works of the ten virtues. čós-la ʼǰúg-pa to turn to religion, to be converted; čos or bstán-pa žig-la ʼǰúg-pa to adopt a certain religion, a certain doctrine. c. bud-méd-la ʼǰúg-pa to lie with, sleep with a woman Med.; *bár-la žúg-če* W. euph. expression for: to commit adultery. d. *dún-du žúg-če* W. to appear, in reference to gods. e. rǰés-su ʼǰúg-pa v. rǰés-su. — 2. **to set** or **fall to, to begin,** rig-pa sbyáṅ-bas rtsóm-pa kún-la ʼǰug a skilled, an experienced man is prepared for anything, knows how to set about it, how to manage it Med.; gen. with the inf.: to begin to do, to commence doing a thing, rtóg-pa-la, resp. dgóṅs-pa-la ʼǰúg-pa to begin to think upon Dzl., Glr.; stón-pa-la ʼǰúg-pa to begin to show Dzl.; γčig-la γčig rnám-par brlág-pa-la žúgs-pas being in the best way of entirely exterminating one another Stg. — 3. pass. of ʼǰúg-pa II, 3, of letters: **to be combined, to be preceded, to be followed,** zla yig sṅón-du ba žúgs-čan (words) having zl preceded by b, i.e. beginning with bzl Zam. — 4.

**to take place, to exist,** če-čuṅ-k̔yád žúgs-par mṅón-pas as evidently a difference in size is existing (?) *Dzl.* ༧༠, 3.

II. pf. *bčug* (perh. also *ˏǰugs Lex.*), fut. *γžug*, imp. *čug*, *W.* **čúg-če**, vb. a., with *náṅ-du* or termin.: 1. **to put into,** e.g. meat into a pan, a key into the key-hole, a culprit into prison; **to infuse, inject,** *γžúg-par bya* this must be infused *Med.*; also fig. **nyíṅ-rus čúg-če* W.* to inspire with courage. In a special sense: a. *dé-la blo ˏǰúg-pa* to set one's mind on, to apply one's self to *Glr.* b. *mi žig č̔ós-la ˏǰúg-pa* to convert a man, to induce him to adopt a certain religion; *ˏǰúg-pa* also without an object, to missionate successfully *Feer Introd. du B. au Cachem.* 68. — 2. **to make, render, appoint, constitute,** with the accus. and termin., or col. with two accus.: *mi zig rgyal-por ˏǰug-pa* to make one king *Dzl.*; *mṅon-du ˏǰug-pa* to make public or manifest, to disclose, to show *Samb.*; **siṅ čug-če* W.* to clear, clarify; frq. with the supine or root of a verb: a. **to cause, compel, prevail on,** *zar ˏǰug-pa* to prevail on another to eat something *Dzl.*; *skrod-du γžug-go* I shall induce (them) to expel (you) *Dzl.*; *bžugs ˏǰug rgyu yin* he will induce (the god) to take his abode *Glr.*; *ˏgroṅ-su ˏǰug-pa* to be the cause of somebody's death *Mil.*; *yid-la ˏǰug-tu ˏǰug-pa* to cause a thing to enter a person's mind, to put in mind, to remonstrate; *ˏp̔el-bar ˏǰug-pa* (resp. *mdzad-pa*) = *spel-ba* to increase, as vb. a.; **ǰuṅ čug-če* W.* to cause to exist, create, procure; **k̔ol ǰug-če* W.* = **skol-če** to cause to boil; *dar-du čug čig* cause it to spread *Glr.* b. **to command, order, bid,** *dmag ˏdzin-du bčug* he ordered the soldiers to take (the man) prisoner (but he escaped) *Dzl.* ༢༢༢, 3; *byed-du ˏǰug-pa* to bid one do a thing, frq.; *btsun-mo blon-pos ˏgebs-su bčug* he gave orders for the queen being protected by the minister. c. **to let, suffer, permit,** *smon-lam ˏdebs-su čug* allow me to say a prayer; *rtsig-tu mi ˏǰug* I shall not give permission to build *Glr.* d. **to give an opportunity** *Thgy.* e. in a general sense: *dal-du ˏǰug-pa* to do things slowly, to be slow *Mil.* — 3. **to put** grammatically: *sṅon-du ˏǰug-pa* to put or place before, *sṅon-ˏǰug* a prefixed letter, a prefix; *rǰes-ˏǰug* final letter, *yaṅ-ˏǰug* the last but one; also to put, to use a word in a certain signification, *rgyu-mtsan-la ˏǰug* is used with reference to cause *Gram.* — 4. **to banish, to exile** (prob. erron. for *spˏúg-pa*), *byáṅ-la* to northern regions *Glr.* — 5. *sgo ˏǰúg-pa* v. *sgo.* — 6. inst. of *ˏbyúg-pa.*

འཇུག་པ་ *ˏǰúg-pa* sbst. 1. **the going into, the entering;** in a special sense 2. the beginning, **the first stage** of a disease *Mṅg.* — 3. (अवतार) the incarnation of a deity.

འཇུངས་པ་ *ˏǰúṅs-pa* **avarice,** *Dzl., Lex.*; *ˏǰúṅs-pa-čan* avaricious; *ˏǰuṅs-ˏǰúr* a miser, niggard.

འཇུད་མཐུན་མ་ *ˏǰud-mt̔ún-ma*, or *ˏǰud-ˏt̔ún-ma Lex.* ('accessible to all') **a prostitute;** *ˏǰud-mt̔ún byéd-pa* to be a harlot.

འཇུད་པ་ *ˏǰúd-pa*, and more frq. *ˏdzúd-pa*, secondary forms of *ˏǰúg-pa.* Cf. *čúd-pa, ˏtsúd-pa.*

འཇུན་པ་ *ˏǰún-pa*, pf. *bčun*, fut. *γžun* (cf. *bžun, žun*) *W.* **čún-če**, *Cs.*: **to subdue,** make tame; to make confess; *W.*; **to make soft, to soften,** e.g. iron; **to punish,** by words or blows; **to convert.**

འཇུམ་པ་ *ˏǰúm-pa*, pf. *bčum*, fut. *γžum*, imp. *čum*, **to shudder, to shrink.** (Acc. to grammatical analogy *ˏǰum-pa* ought to be vb. a., to cause to shudder, and *ˏčúm-pa* vb. n.) *ša ˏǰúms-pa Lex.*, contraction of the muscles, shrinking, shuddering *Sch.*

འཇུར་ *ˏǰur*, supine of *ˏǰú-ba*; *ˏǰur mi ˏdod* indigestible *Sch.* (?).

འཇུར་བ་ *ˏǰúr-ba* 1. (pf. *bčur*, q. v.) *Cs.*: complication; *Sch.* also: to struggle against, to resist. *Pth.*: *ˏǰúr-bar ˏgyúr-ba* **to be entangled;** *ˏǰúr-bu Sch.*, **ˏǰúr-pa* C.* tangled yarn; *srád-bui ˏǰúr (-pa) Lexx.* w. e., *Sch.*: 'the tightness of the yarn'; *ˏǰur-mt̔úg* wrinkled, as the skin is in old age *Thgy.*; *ˏǰur-míg* a wire-drawing plate, *ˏǰur-mig-nas ˏdrén-pa* to draw through this plate *Thgy.* — 2. = *ˏdzúr-ba*

**to evade, to shun,** to go out of the way, *˛jur-méd* unavoidable *Mil.*

འཇུས་ *˛jus*, v. *˛ju-ba* I, 1.

འཇེབས་པ་ *˛jébs-pa, ˛jébs-po,* **well-sounding** *Stg.*; *snyan - ˛jébs* harmony, euphony.

འཇེམ(ས)་པ་ *˛jém(s)-pa* 1. **dexterity, cleverness** *Lex.* 2. **skilled, clever;** *Sch.* **decent;** *˛jéms-po* id.

འཇོ་སྒེག *˛jo - sgég* a coquettish, alluring, seducing attitude or posture; *Lex.*: *˛jud-mťún ˛jo-sgég ˛jog* the harlot assumes such an attitude.

འཇོ་བ་ *˛jó-ba*, pf. *bžos*, ft. *bžo*, imp. *˛jos,* **to milk,** *rá - ma ˛jó - ba* to milk a goat, *˛o-ma ˛jo-ba* 'to milk the milk'; *ǩyód-kyis ˛ó-ma bžos dug, ṅas ni bžós-pa med,* it is you, not I, that have 'milked out the milk' *Glr.*; *˛jó (-ba) -po, ˛jó - mǩan,* milker, milk-man, *˛jó(-ba)-mo* milkmaid; *˛dód - ˛joi ba* a cow that is able to fulfil every wish.

འཇོག་པ་ *˛jóg-pa* I. pf. *bžag*, ft. *γžag*, imp *žog*, *C.* col. **žág - pa**, 1. **to put, to place,** e.g. the foot on the ground; also to place persons, to assign them a place *Dzl., Glr.*; fig. = *˛gód-pa* (e.g. *dgé-ba-la, byaṅ-čúb-la, byaṅ-čúb-kyi lám-la*) v. *˛gód-pa* 3; **to put in order, to arrange,** *˛jig-rtén-bžag-pa* the arrangement (system) of the world; *lus dráṅ - por bžág - ste* sitting straight, bolt-upright *Dzl., Mil.*; *bžág - nu mi sdod* if one places her any where, she will not remain there *Mil.*; *stéṅ - du yar bžag* (the anchors) were placed above, were weighed *Pth.*; *lás-su ˛jóg-pa* to set one a task, to employ one in a certain service *Dzl.*, *rgyal-srid-la ˛jóg - pa* to appoint one to the government i.e. to make one king; *šéms* (resp. *ťugs*)*-la ˛jóg-pa* to take to heart *Glr., Mil.*; *lús-la grui ˛du-šés bžág - la* if we fancy the human body to be a ship *Thgy.*; *nám-mǩa ráṅ-gi ṅáṅ-du žog* transfer it to the nature of the ethereal space, i.e. figure it to yourself as ether *Mil.*; *p̒yir ˛jóg-pa* 1. to leave behind, at home *Dzl.;* 2. to put by, to lay aside *Dzl.*; (another reading omits *p̒yir*). — 2. **to lay** or **put down,** a burden etc., **žóg-la šog** put (it) down and come! *C.*; *nor* (*γ*)*sog ˛jog med* heaping up treasures and depositing them was not, i.e. was never heard of; *γsóg-˛jog-mǩan* a hoarder up, a miser *Cs.*; **to leave, to leave behind,** *lag - rjés* a trace or mark of activity, monumentum *Glr.*; **to leave, quit, abandon,** *ráṅ - gi yul* one's own country *Glr.*; *p̒óṅs-par ma bžág-par* so that it is not abandoned, given up, to poverty *Thgy.*; **yúg-le žog* C.* (= **p̒áṅ - té bor* W.*) throw it away! **to depose,** *yí - ger bris ˛jóg - pa* to depose in writing, *literis mandare Glr.*; *sá-bon, γduṅ-brgyúd ˛jóg-pa* to leave an offspring behind, to propagate the species; **to lay up, to keep,** as holy relics; **to lay aside,** *ré-žig žóg-la* setting aside, apart, for a while *Dzl.*; *mnyám-par ˛žóg-pa* v. *mnyám-pa*; *sgról-lam ˛jog* shall we turn them out or leave them? *Mil. nt.*

II. pf. (*b*)*žogs*, fut. *γžog*, imp. *žog*, *W.* **žog-če,** **to cut, to hew, to square,** a pen, timber etc.; **to carve, to chip,** a thin piece of wood etc.

འཇོག་པོ་ *˛jog-po* n. of a Lu *Mil.*, = *˛jag-po.*

འཇོང་ *˛joṅ* = *lčoṅ*, **tadpole.**

འཇོང་འཇོང་ *˛joṅ - ˛jóṅ* col., *Sch.* *˛jóṅ - po,* **oblong, longish, oval, elliptical, cylindric, bottle-shaped** etc.; col. also applied to stature: **tall;** *˛joṅ - nyáms - čan Wdṅ.* oblong shaped, in relation to leaves, cones of fir etc.; *ló-ma ˛joṅ-stábs nyág-ga-čan* split into narrow slips, wing-cleft (leaves of caraway) *Wdṅ.*; *dbyibs - ˛jóṅ* an oval form.

འཇོང་ཙེ་ *˛jóṅ-tse Cs.* = *lčóg-tse.*

འཇོམས་པ་ *˛jóms - pa*, pf. *bčom*, also *žom*, fut. *γžom*, imp. *čom*, *W.* **čóm-če** 1. **to conquer, subdue, oppress, suppress,** an enemy; *˛dód-čágs-kyis kún-nas ˛jóms-pa* to be quite overpowered by lust; *nad ˛jóms - pai sman* a medicine for a disease (to overcome it); *ráb-tu γžóm-pa ˛di* the following overpowering (charm);

*bċóm-mo* an exclamation like: I am done for! *perii*! — 2. **to destroy**, towns etc. *Glr.*; *bċóm-la γžág-go* id. *Glr.* — 3. **to plunder, spoil, rob,** *˳ǰóms-pai grabs byás-pa-la* as they were about to rob him *Mil.* — 4. **to finish, accomplish** *W.*, cf. *čóm-pa.*

འཇོར་ *˳ǰor* 1. *C.*, also *γžor*, **hoe, grubbing-hoe, mattock, pick-axe** (*W.* **tóg-tse**), *˳ǰór-gyis rkó-ba* to turn up with the hoe; *˳ǰór-po* a large mattock, pick-axe, spade, *˳ǰór-bu* a small one, a hoe; *˳ǰor-yú* the handle of a hoe, *˳ǰor-lċágs* the iron of a mattock *Cs.* — 2. supine of *˳ǰó-ba.*

འཇོལ་བ་ *˳ǰól-ba* I. vb. 1. **to hang down,** of a cow's udder, of the long hair on a yak's belly, of tails etc.; *˳ǰol-˳ǰól* hanging-belly, paunch. — 2. gen. *˳byól-ba* **to turn aside, to make way.**

II. sbst., also (*Cs.*) *˳ǰol-˳ǰól* and *γžól-ba*, **train, trail; retinue** *Cs.*; *˳ǰól-gos Cs.*, *˳ǰól-ber Wdk.*, *Pth.*, a robe or garment with a train; *˳ǰól-ċan* having a train; *˳ǰol-méd* without a train *Cs.*

འཇོལ་ལེ་ *˳ǰol-lé* **hanging,** cf. *p̀yaṅ-ṅé*, *gród-pa ˳ǰol-lé* hanging-belly, paunch, cf. *p̀yal Lex.*

འཇོལ་མོ་ *˳ǰól-mo*, acc. to the descriptions given by natives, a bird of the size of a blackbird, of lively motions and an agreeable whistling, in the neighbourhood of Lhasa, building in willow-trees and thorn-bushes; *Cs.* has: a turkey-hen.

རྗང་མ་ *rǰáṅ-ma*, or *rdzaṅ-ma*, **store-room** *Thgy.*

རྗིད་པ་ *rǰid-pa* **lean** *Cs.*, gen. *rid-pa.*

རྗིབ་ལས་ **žib-las** (?) *W.*, **service** done in socage, compulsory service, in the fields, on roads etc.

རྗུད་པ་ *rǰúd-pa*, *rdzúd-pa*, = *rgúd-pa Lex.*

རྗུན་ *rǰun*, *nad-rǰún Mil.* a disease.

རྗེ་(བོ་) *rǰé(-bo)*, also *rǰe-u*, **lord, master,** 1. **ruler, king,** *yúl-gyi rǰe mdzád-nas* ruling over a country, acting the part of a sovereign *Glr.*; *bod-k̀áms-kyi rǰé-bor gyur* he became sovereign of Tibet *Wdk.*; *sá-yi bdág-po mi-yi rǰe Mil.* lord of the ground, ruler of the people; *rǰé-bo daṅ bran*, *rǰe-k̀ól Stg.*, master and servant; *rǰe-blón* king and minister; *rǰe ċi lags* sir, what does that mean? *Glr.*; also a title before names, esp. names of kings, *ǰó-bo rǰe Dipangkāra Glr.*; *rǰe-bdúd rǰe-btsáṇ* the gentlemen devils and the gentlemen goblins (messieurs les diables et messieurs les farfadets); *rǰe dkon-mċóg-la γsól-ba ˳débs-pa Mil.* is in fact an empty phrase in the mouth of a Buddhist philosopher, but may nevertheless be used in Christian language for addressing God as 'our Lord'. — 2. **a nobleman,** a person of rank, *rǰeu(i) rigs*, *rǰe-rigs* = *rgyal-rigs* the caste of nobility. — *rǰe-dpón* (*Lex.* आर्य) = *rǰe*, master, lord, prince *Cs.*; *rǰé-ma*, also *γċés-ma Cs.*, col. **šé-ma**, a lady of rank, *rǰe-ċúṅ* a young lady, a miss; *rǰé-srás* a young gentleman; also a term of address *Cs.* — *rǰe-btsún* **reverend sir,** a title of the higher priesthood, *rǰe-btsún-ma* fem. — *rǰé-sa* (or *žé-sa*) *byéd-pa* to show deference, to pay one's respects; *žé-sai γtam*, or *žé-sai skad* courteous words, esp. ceremonial and complimentary terms, e.g. *dbu* for *mgo* etc. *W.*: **yá-ša ċó-ċe, yá-šẹ pé-ra**.

རྗེ་ངར་ *rǰe-ṅár* the lower part of the leg, **the shank** (*W.* **sug**); *rkaṅ-lág rǰe-ṅár* the lower part of the arms and the legs *Med.*

རྗེ་བ་ *rǰé-ba*, pf. *brǰes*, fut. *brǰe*, imp. *brǰes*, *W.* **žé-ċe**, **to barter,** to give or take in exchange; *˳di-dag-gis brǰeo* it may be exchanged for these *Dzl.*; **zan daṅ srog žé-ċe** *W.* to risk one's life for the necessary food (as thieves do); *brǰé-byai nor* articles of barter; in a more general sense: **to change, to shift,** *miṅ* the name, *gos* the clothes *Dzl.*, *γnas* the place, *tse* the life, i.e. to die *Cs.* — *brǰé(-ba)-po* a barterer *Cs.*

རྗེད་པ་ *rǰéd-pa*, pf. and fut. *brǰed* 1. **to honour, reverence** c. dat., *mċód-ċiṅ brǰéd-pa* id. *Dzl.*; *brǰéd-pai ˬos* venerable *Lex.* — 2. **to forget,** frq. (cf. *lus-pa*); *brǰéd-du ˳ǰúg-pa* to make forget, to cause to forget.

**Comp.** *rjéd-ṅas-čan Lexx.* (**मुषितस्मृति**) **forgetful, oblivious;** *Cs.* gives inst. of it: *rjéd-ṅes-čan*, but also thus no clear etymological explanation is obtained. — *rjéd-ču* draught of oblivion, of Lethe *Cs.* — *rjed-bsnyén* (etymology?) *sgúg-pa* technical term for the common practice of Indian servants to hide an object belonging to their master in some obscure corner, and after waiting (*sgúg-pa*) for some months, until it may be assumed that the thing is altogether forgotten (*brjéd-pa*), to appropriate it to themselves. — *rjéd-to* list of notes, memorandum-book, journal, diary, cash-book etc. *Glr.*, *C.*, *W.* — *rjed-rdó* prob. monumental or **memorial stone.** — *rjed-byáṅ* specifications or **lists of goods,** pieces of luggage etc. which the Tibetans number and mark with the letters of the alphabet. — *rjed-byéd* 1. a demon that takes away the power of memory, also *rjed-byéd-kyi γdon.* 2. epilepsy (**अपस्मार**) *Med.* — *rjed-zás Cs.:* 'the meat of forgetfulness'.

རྗེན་ནེ་བ་ *rjén-ne-ba* v. the following word.

རྗེན་པ་ *rjén-pa* 1. not covered, **bare, naked,** *B., C.* (*W.:* **čer-nyál**), *rkaṅ-rjén* (*-pa*) barefooted, unshod; *žabs-rjén-par γdá-ba* or *γšégs-pa*, resp., to be barefooted, to go barefoot; *γdoṅ rjén-du sdód-pa* to sit with unveiled face, *mgo-rjén-pa* with uncovered head, *rgyab-rjén* with a naked back *Cs.*; *rjén-par ₒdón-pa C.* to strip perfectly; *dmar-rjén* stark naked *Sch.*; *rál-gri rjén-pa* a naked sword; **žén-pa toṅ** *W.* give it (me) not wrapped up! *sa-rjen* the bare ground, not covered with a carpet *Cs.*; *rjén-ne-ba* undisguised, obvious to the understanding, manifest *Mil.* — 2. **raw,** not roasted or cooked, *ša-rjen* raw meat, *dmar-rjén* red raw meat; *mar-rjén* not melted butter; *nas-rjén* raw barley, not prepared or roasted; also the meal of it: *W.* **nar-jén** barley-flour, cf. *Sch.: bra-rjén* buckwheat-meal. — *rjen-zás Med.* (*Cs.* also *rjen-rigs*) victuals that may be eaten raw. — 3. not ripe, **unripe** *W.*

རྗེས་ *rjes* 1. **trace, track, mark left,** impression made (on the ground), *pyi-rjés Med.* prob. id.; *mi-rjés* a man's track, *rta-rjés* a horse's track *Glr.; šiṅ-rtai rjes* the track of a waggon or cart, a rut; *rkaṅ-rjés*, resp. *žabs-rjés*, the trace of one's foot, footprint, *rkaṅ-rjés byuṅ* a footprint is made; *rkaṅ-rjés ₒjóg-pa* to leave a footprint behind *Mil.; byas-rjés* proof of an accomplished deed, whether it be the work itself or some indubitable result of it; *lag-rjés*, resp. *pyag-rjés* impression or mark left of one's hand, hence fig.: action, deed, charitable institution, pious legacy, whereby a person wishes to immortalize his name. — 2. **the hind part** of a thing *Sch.* (?) — 3. inrelation to time: that which follows, **the consequence, the course** or **progress** of a thing, **the last,** = *mjug.* — 4. adv. and postp. inst. of *rjés-su*, v. below. — *rjes γčód-pa* 1. *Sch.* to destroy, blot out, efface a track or trace, in *Med.* to eradicate the trace of a disease, to cure it thoroughly, 2. *Sch.*: to separate, disjoin the hind part(?) 3. *W.* **žes čád-če** to follow a trace or track, to find out or to come upon the track. — *rjes dzin-pa* to 'seize' the track, to overtake *Glr.*, also to be able to follow the track, *rá-ma kyui rjes mi zin-pa* a goat that cannot follow the flock *Mil.* — *rjés-la, rjés-su, rjes*, adv. and postp., afterwards, hereafter, for the future, later; after, behind, *deï rjés-la, de-rjés* after that, afterwards, later *Mil.*; *dé-dag ₒdás-pai rjés-su* after these were gone *Glr.*; *bžag-rjés po.* = *bžág-pai ₒóg-tu Lt.*; *ṅai rjés-su* after my death. *rjés-su* in conjunction with verbs corresponds to the *Ssk.* **अनु** and is often not to be translated, or serves only to give additional force to some other word or expression: *rjés-su ₒgró-ba, ₒbráṅ-ba* to go after, to follow, to come after; also fig.: *spyód-pa tams-čád ya-rábs-kyi rjés-su ₒbróṅ-ba* to imitate the nobility, the free-born, in their whole demeanour *Glr.*; *lé-lo daṅ spyód-pa ṅán-pai rjés-su ₒgró-ba* to imitate idleness and wickedness, or idle and wicked people *Ld.-Glr.*; *slób-dpon-gyi rjés-su brjód-de* saying after the teacher *Thgy.* — *rjés-su ḥdzín-pa* **to receive** *Pth.*: *ḱól-por rjés-su bzúṅ-nas lto-gós-kyis bskyáṅ-du γsol* pray take me (the orphan) into your service, and provide me with food and clothes; to receive as a disciple or follower = *čéd-du ḥdzín-pa* frq.; **to draw after** (after death) *Mil.*; **to assist**, *ḥdi rjés-su zuṅ žig* do take care of, or provide for this man (as a future co-disciple) *Mil.*; finally with respect to charms and spells: to commit to memory or keep in memory ni f. — *rjés-su ḥjúg-pa* 1. vb. a. **to add, affix,** 2. vb. n. **to follow,** *bdag daṅ bdág-gi rjés-su ḥjúg-pai slób-ma-rnams* I and the disciples that follow me *Mil.*; in a similar sense: *mi-la rjés-su slób-pa* to follow another as a disciple *Dzl.* ༢༦༠,3 (༡༦༢,7 seems to be a corrupt reading). Also in the following phrases *rjés-su* may be understood in the sense of: afterwards, subsequently: *rjés-su drán-pa* **to remember, recollect,** keep in mind, *rjés-su drán-par byéd-pa* to bring to one's remembrance, to remind *Pth.*; *rjés-su ḥgyód-pa* **to repent** *Cs.*; pleon. or without any obvious meaning in: *rjés-su mtún-pa Thgy.* **to agree,** to accord, *rjés-su rnyéd-pa Stg.* **to find,** *rjés-su dpág-pa* **to weigh, to ponder** *Cs.*, *rjés-su snyiṅ-brtsé-ba Thgy.* **to pity,** *rjés-su bstán-pa Tar.* **to instruct,** and thus in similar expressions, esp. in one of frq. occurrence in legends: *rjés-su yi-ráṅ-ba*, resp. *rjés-su ťugs-ráṅ-ba* (*Sch.* erron. *ťúgs-pa!*) **to rejoice, to enjoy,** for which sometimes also *rjés-su ṗyógs-pa* is used, e.g. *dbyé-ba-rnams-la rjés-su yi-ráṅ-ba* to rejoice at people disagreeing, to enjoy dissensions and jarrings *Stg.*

**Comp.** *rjes-skyés* (अनुज) born later; younger brother. — *rjes-grúb-kyi miṅ* **by-name, surname** *Cs.* — *rjes-ḥjúg* 1. **following,** coming after, *ṗyi-rábs rjes-ḥjúg ťams-čád* all the following generations *Pth.* 2. **final consonant.** — *rjes-ťóg* prob. the same as *rjés-la Wdṅ.* — *rjes-ťób Mil.* is said to denote short interruptions of meditation by taking food, but no more than is absolutely necessary for the preservation of life. — *rjes-dpág* 1. consideration, deliberation. 2. *Was.* (297) a syllogism consisting of three propositions. — *rjés-ma* = *rjes* 2 hinder part *Cs.* — *rjes-méd* without leaving any traces, **trackless,** *ḥjig-pa* to destroy thoroughly *Glr.*

རྗེས་པ་ *rjés-pa* v. *rjé-ba.*

རྗོད་པ་ *rjód-pa* pf. and fut. *brjod*, **to say, pronounce, utter,** e.g. a charm or magic formula; *ṅe miṅ žód-da rag* W.* I hear my name mentioned; *saṅs-rgyás-kyi mtsán-nas* to pronounce or invoke the name of Buddha *Dzl.*; **to propound, promulgate,** *čos* a religious doctrine; **to enumerate, set forth,** *légs-pa* or *nyés-pa* the good or bad qualities, actions etc., *yón-tan* the excellence or superiority of a person *Dzl.* and elsewh.; **to treat** of a subject in writing: *lhág-pa-rnams ni ḥdir brjód-bya* we have now to treat of the rest *Zam.*; an author even says *žes bržód-de* with regard to his own words (after a bombastic poetical exordium, like the 'dixi', of Roman orators) *Glr.*; *rjód-du méd-pa* unspeakable, inexpressible, ineffable, *rjód-du méd-čiṅ dpág-tu méd-pa* id. *Dzl.*; *brjod(-kyis) mi láṅ-ba* (or *lón-ba*) id.; also vb.: to be inexpressible or inexhaustible, frq.; *re-reï miṅ-nas rjod mi laṅ* one cannot mention or enumerate them all *Mil.*; *don mdzád-pa rjod mi láṅ-ṅo* his utility is beyond description *Dzl.*; *rjód-kyis mi láṅ-bai ṗyir mi bkod* I do not write it down, because it is impossible to relate every thing *Pth.* (v. *brjod*).

ལྗགས་ *ljags*, resp. for *lče*, **tongue,** *ljágs-kyis čab ḥdór-ba* to spit, to spit out; *ljags-čáb* spittle, saliva; *ljags-dbúgs* breath.

ལྗང་མོ་ *ljáṅ-mo* p. n. of a district 1. in Ü, 2. in Kams.

ལྗང་ཁུ་ *ljáṅ-ku*, or *ljáṅ-gu Lt.*, *W.*, **green** (gen. expressed by *ṅón-po*, notwithstanding the ambiguity), *ljaṅ-skyá* greenish white, *ljaṅ-nág* greenish black, dark green. — *ljáṅ-pa* green corn, in the first stage of its growth (in the second stage it is called sóg-ma, in the third snyé-ma). — lo-ljáṅ-ba having a green blade. — ljáṅ-bu greenness, verdure (grass, foliage, shrubs), Lex.: श्याम — ljaṅ-dmár greenish red; ljaṅ-sér greenish yellow.

ལྗང་དུང་ ljaṅ-dúṅ (spelling?), **solid**, not hollow, W.

ལྗན་ལྗིན་ ljan-ljin **filth, dirt, dust, sweepings;** lúd-pa ljan-ljin maṅ a great deal of foul mucous expectoration Lt.

ལྗབ་ ljab W. **flat, plain, even;** *ljab-ljáb-ba bor* lay or put it down flat; *ljab čó-te dug* sit down flat (on the ground)!

ལྗི་བ་ lji-ba, 1. a flea (ˌji-ba). — 2. **heavy, weighty.**

ལྗིད་པ་ ljid-pa, **heaviness, weight,** γser daṅ ljid-pa mnyám-pa dgos it must be weighed up with gold Glr.; de daṅ ljid mnyám-pa of equal weight, equal in weight Med.; ljid-čan, ljid-ldán heavy; ljid-čé-ba very heavy; ljid-méd light, not heavy; lus ťams-čád-kyi ljid ṗab he sat down with the whole weight of his body Cs.; ljid-kyis nón-pa pressing down by his(its) weight.

ལྗེན་པ་ ljén-pa Cs. **to enter, to penetrate,** bló-la one's mind, = to be perceived, understood; ťson-ljén a die or colour penetrating and remaining fixed in cloth etc. Cf. žén-pa.

ལྗོངས་ ljoṅs **a large valley, principal** or **main valley; region, district, province** Dzl.; ljoṅs daṅ yul-ˌḱór countries and provinces; ljoṅs čén-po a large country; ḱá-ba-čan-gyi ljoṅs ˌdi, gáṅs-čan(-gyi) ljoṅs Tibet, frq.; nágs-ljoṅs woody country; smán-ljoṅs a country of medicinal herbs Zam.; mú-geï ljoṅs a very poor country, starving country Mil.; ljóṅs-la in the valley, in the plain; ljóṅs-mi-rnams country-people Cs. — ljoṅs (-su) rgyú-ba to rove about, ljoṅs sgyúr-ba the end of the estival fast of the monks (about the end of August), when they are permitted to rove about the whole district of their monastery.

ལྗོན་པ་ ljón-pa a country of gods, **paradise;** ljon-šíṅ a tree from paradise, or any large and beautiful tree; ljón-pai nágs a beautiful forest.

བརྗིད་ brjid, Tar. 11, 14, but more frq. γzi-brjid, **brightness, splendour, lustre,** gen. of gods and saints, v. γzi; also dpal-brjid Lex.; brjid-pa to shine, glisten, glitter Cs., brjid-kyis brjid shining with brightness Lex.

བརྗེ་བོ་ brjé-bo a making up, a compensation by **barter,** brjé-bo byéd-pa Glr., *brjé-bo gyáb-če* W., to give an equal measure in bartering, e.g. of salt for barley.

བརྗོད་ brjod (cf. rjód-pa) **sound; talking; speech,** brjod bdé-ba euphony; also well-sounding, agreeable speech; **brjod mi** bdé-ba the contrary; also: *dha jọ mi de* C. it is not meet now to speak **about it;** brjód-pa speech, utterance; mṅon-**brjód** synonymy, explanation of words; Cs. **also:** 'a poetical term'; mčod-brjód **praise, eulogy,** Sch.: invocation of a deity; če-brjód Schr.(?), and čéd-du brjód-pa, Tar. 140, 2 acc. to Schf.: preface, introduction, in C.: to approve, sanction, commend, Was. (270) in the title of a book: = उदान वर्ग w.e.

**Comp.** brjód-bya sbst., Zam. also brjód-pa, = वाच्य an attribute, predicate Lex. — brjod-méd 1. a speech not earnestly meant, empty words, mere talk. 2. Mil.: the unspeakable, the transcendental, identified by some with the Nirvana, by others not. — brjod-ˌdód Tar. 210, 7: brjod-ˌdód-tsam acc. to Schf.: 'a mere supposition'; but in a passage in Mil. it seems to denote the (conceited) habit of constantly proposing one's own opinion, and so it might also be understood in Tar.

# ཉ

ཉ་ *nya*, I. the letter *ny*, double-consonant, distinctly pronounced like *n* + *y* (*Ssk.* ञ्य), and used only as initial letter; therefore differing in its nature and sound from the *Ssk.* ञ, though representing it in Sanskrit words.

II. symb. num. for eight.

III. **fish** (मत्स्य), *nya ₒdzin-pa*, *W.* **nya zúm-če**, *nya ₒčór-ba* (or *bsor-ba*) *Dzl.*, *nya lén-pa* (*bláṅ-ba*) *Pth.* to catch fish; *ₒdám-nya Ld.*, an eel *Cs*; *rgyál-poï γsól-nya* the king's table fish *Pth.*

IV. also *nyá-ču* (cf. *čú-ba*). 1. **tendon, sinew**; *W.*: **ḱáṅ-pẹ nya ḍid soṅ** my foot is asleep. — 2. col. **mark**, left by a blow, **a weal**, **nya laṅs** the blow has left a weal *W.*

V. 1. the fifteenth day of a lunar month, the day of the full moon. — 2. = *ts̀es* ni f.: *zlá-bai nya drúg-la* on the **sixth day** of the month *Mil.*

VI. *nya Sch.* 1. lock (?) — 2. **muscle** *Med.*, *nya-bží* the four principal muscles, viz. those of the arms and the calves of the leg, v. also the compounds.

VII. **ṇya čád-če** *W.* to arrive sooner by a short cut; cf. also **ťad-nya**.

**Comp.** *nya-rkyál* **the bladder** of a fish *Cs.* — *nya-skyogs* **gills.** — *nya-ḱrá* **sea-eagle,** white-tailed eagle *Sch.* — *nya-ḱráb-čan* **carp** *Sch.* — *nya-ḱrab-čén* **sturgeon** *Sch.* — *nya-ḱróm* **fish-market.** — *nya-gáṅ* 1. full of fish *Sch.* 2. full moon *Cs.* — *nya-grá*, *nyai grá-ma* small **fish-bones.** — *nya-ₒgyúr* = *nya-lóg* 2 *S.g.*, *C.* — *nya-rgyá* **fishing-net.** — *nya-rgyáb C.*, earth heaped up (like the back of a fish) on the top of outer walls to prevent the entering of the wet. — *nya-rgyás* (*zlá-ba*) full moon *Pth.* — *nya-sgóṅ* **fish-spawn, roe** of fish. — *nya-lčibs* **fish-gills** *Cs.*; mother of pearl *Schr.* — *nya-čú* **tendon, sinew**; perh. also a large nerve in the nape of the neck. — *nya-dól* fishing-net; **nya-dól-pa** fisherman *W.* — *nyá-dós* a load of fish *Sch.* — *nya-ldir* 'a muscle' *Sch.* — *nyá-pa* **fisherman** *Cs.* — *nya-p̀yís* (*Cs.*: fish-gills) **mother of pearl** *S.g.* and col — *nya-mid Sch.*: a sea-monster (this word seems not to be generally known). — *nyá-mo* **a** (female?) **fish** *Mil.* — **nya-tsél** bow-net, kiddle *W.* **nya-tság** *C.* id. — *nya-ťsil* the fat of a fish. — *nya-ťser* **fish-bones** *Sch.* — *nya-ťsóṅ-pa* **fish-monger.** — *nya-ₒdzin Cs.*, **nya-kúg** *W.*, angle, fishing-hook. — *nya-zán* a fish-eater, one feeding on fish *Cs.* — *nya-rús* fish-bone *Cs.* — *nya-lóg* 1. *Cs.*: 'a contraction or sinking of the sinews'. 2. *Sik.*: **cholera** (*Urd.* هيضه) — 3. *Med.*, also *nya-lhóg*, a name for a disease. — *nyá-ša* 1. flesh of fish 2. *W.*: meat cut into long narrow strips and dried in the sun, in *C.* **ša-bčúg**. — *nya-γšóg* the fin of a fish *Cs.* — *nya-ság* fish-scale. — *nya-sóg* prob. the backbone with the bones attached to it, resembling a saw.

ཉ་ག་, ཉག་ *nyá-ga, nyag,* a steel-yard.

ཉ་བོ་ *nyá-bo* body, figure *Sch.*

ཉ་མ་ *nyá-ma* (*Sch.*: 'mistress of the house, housewife'?) **hearer** of a Lama, without being a regular disciple *Mil.* frq.; *nyá-ma p̀ó-mo-rnams Mil.* (cog. to *nyán-pa?*)

ཉ་ར་ *nyá-ra* **care**, *nyá-ra byéd-pa Sch.*, **nyá-ra čó-če** *W.*, to take care of, to provide for a person, to keep a thing well; **nyar gọ** *C.* for *nyá-ra byed dgos*; cf. *γnyér-ḱa*.

ཉ་ར་ཉོ་རེ་ *nya-ra-nyo-ré* **weak, feeble, frail,** e.g. of a worm *Thgy.*

ཉག་ *nyag* 1. v. *nyá-ga*. — 2. v. *nyág-ma*. — 3. also *nyág-ga*, *nyag-ḱrám*, **notch, indenture,** *ló-ma p̀rá-la nyág-ga-čan* having multifid leaves, like those of caraway *Wdn.*; *nyág-ga méd-pa* not cleft, not indented. — 4. of wool, *nyág-tu ₒdrén-pa* to draw out into threads, to spin *Mil.*

ཉག་ཉིག *nyag-nyig Cs., Sch.* also *nyag-nyóg* **filth, dirt.**

ཉག་ཉུག *nyag-nyúg Mil.* = *sna-ťsogs* (?), of rare occurrence.

ཉག་ཐག *nyag-ťág* **thread; chain,** of gold *Mil.*, of iron *Mil.*; cord for stringing turkoises *Mil.*; a cable *Schr.*

ཉག་མཐིལ་ *nyag-mťil* **scale of a steel-yard,** *nyag-rdó* weight of a steel-yard.

ཉག་ཕྲན *nyag-ṗrán* a small beam, **a pole** *Cs.*; **an arrow**; *nyag-ṗran-mdá* arrow *Mil.*

ཉག་མ་ *nyág-ma*, also *nyag-ré*, **single;** *nyag γčig* 1. id., *skra*, or *spu nyag(-ma) γčig* a single hair, frq.; *skrá-yi nyág-ma* id. (a man has 21 000 of them *Med.*) — 2. **a minimum** *Mil.* — 3. *Sch.* also: **bachelor,** old voluntary bachelor. — *saṅs-rgyas-nyag-γčig Thgy., Pth.*, only Buddha, or nothing less than Buddha.

ཉག་མོ་ *nyág-mo Lex.* w.e.; **woman** *Sch.*

ཉག་ཤིང་ *nyág-šiṅ* **beam of a steel-yard.**

ཉང་ཀ, ཉང་གེ་ *nyáṅ-ka, nyáṅ-ge Sp.* **currant,** Ribes.

ཉན་ཏི་ *nyán-ti Pur.* **thy, your** (?).

ཉན་པ་ *nyán-pa* (*nyán-to, nyán-tam*), imp. *nyon* 1. (also, though seldom, *mnyán-pa*) c. dat. or accus. **to hear,** to give ear to, **to listen** (cf. *ťos-pa*); *slób-dpon-gyi ťád-du čos nyán-pa* to attend to the religious instruction of the teacher; *ṅag* or *ťsig nyán-pa Dzl.*, *ǩá-la*, or resp. *žál-la*, or *bka-nyán-pa* to obey, to yield; *ṅas ǰi-ltar zér-pai ǩá-la nyán-na Glr.*, *ṅá zer nyán-na Mil.* if you listen to my word; *Tar.* 14, 14; 17, 16 c.c. *las.* — 2. **to listen secretly,** to be an eaves-dropper, **ṗag-nyẹn ǰhé-pa* C.*, **ṗag-nyán čò-če, táṅ-če* W.*, id.; *nyán-mǩan* col. *nyán(-pa) -po*, fem. *nyan (-pa) -mo*, *B.*, a hearer, auditor; *nyan-ťós* id.; but esp. of the personal disciples of Buddha, the Sravakas, *Köpp.* I., 419; *Burn.* I., 296; *nyan-ťós bču-drúg* the sixteen *γnas-brtán* q.v.; *nyan-ťós-ma* a female hearer; *ǩa-la nyán-po, nyán-mkan* obedient, *ǩá-la mi nyán-po* disobedient. — 3. **to be able,** later *B.*, and col., gen. with a negative: *ₒgró ma nyán-pas* not being able to walk (on account of illness) *Mil.*; also like *ma btúb-pa* not being willing; without a negative: **nyán yin* W.* yes, I shall be able; inst. of *rúṅ-ba*: **za-nyán yód-na kyoṅ* W.*, bring it me, if it is still eatable.

ཉམ་ *nyam*, also *nyam-tiy, nyam-yós* **cricket, locust** *Sik.*

ཉམ(ས)་ *nyam(s)*, resp. *ťugs, ťugs-nyám(s)* 1. **soul, mind,** *nyáms-kyi grogs* companions of the soul, viz. the murmuring springs and rivulets in the solitude of alpine regions *Mil.*; *nyáms-kyi čaṅ* the soul's wine, i.e. religious knowledge *Mil.*; *nyams dgá-ba* 1. well being, comfort, cheerfulness, *nyams mi-dgá-ba* an unhappy state, discomfort, *nyams-dgá glú-ru bloṅs* sing a song of joy! *Mil.* 2. gen. adj.: agreeable, delightful, charming, *nyáms-dga-bai sa-γnás* a charming country *Glr.*. — 2. **thought,** *nyams skye* or *šar* a thought rises. — 3. **strength, magnitude, height, state, manner,** *nyams-(kyi) ťsád byéd-pa Pth.* (also with *bčád-pa* or *lén-pa C.*) to try, to put to the test, e.g. one's strength; *ťugs-dám-gyi nyams sád-pa* to try the degree of a person's devotion or spiritual progress *Mil.*; *smra-nyáms, byed-nyáms* manner, — and particularly a pleasing, agreeable manner, — of speaking or dealing.

Other phrases are: *nyáms-su lén-pa* to take to heart, to interest one's self in or for a thing *Dzl.*, to commit to memory, to learn (v. below); *nyáms-su myóṅ-ba* to suffer, undergo, experience *Dzl.*; *nyams ṅá-ba* v. the compounds; *nyams bčád-pa C.* to try, to examine; *nyams ₒbrú-ba C.* to irritate, provoke, vex; *nyams myóṅ-ba* = *nyáms-su myóṅ-ba*; *nyams bžág-pa* is said to be = *drán-pa nyé-bar bžág-pa*, v. *nyé-ba*; *nyams lén-pa* 1. = *nyáms-su lén-pa*, v. above, 2. col. to measure out, to

ཉ

take the measure, the dimensions of, to survey, *sa* land, *nor* the property, to take an inventory, to ascertain or compute the state of one's property, 3. *C.* = the following; *nyams sád-pa* ccg. 1. to try, to test, *byéd-dam mi byed* whether he will do it or not *Mil.*, to tempt, *ťugs-dám-gyi nyams sád-pa* v. above. 2. to mock, scoff, trouble maliciously, provoke, irritate *C.*

**Comp.** *nyams-dgú* v. *nyams-ťábs.* — *nyams-rgyúd Mil.* = *nyams*, *nyams-rgyúd-la sbyáṅs-pa*, intellectually skilled, well versed. — *nyams-ṅá* **anxiety, fear, dread,** of a thing, with the dat. or instr. *Mil.*; *nyams-ṅá-las ťár-ba* to be delivered from anxiety *S.g.*; *nyams-ṅá-ba* vb. to be alarmed, to be in great anxiety *Sch.*; adj. dreadful, horrible, *nags-ťsál nyams-ṅa-ba* a horrible forest *Dzl.* — *nyams-bčág* is said to be used resp. or euphem. for *skyon*, e.g. for damage done to an image of a god by water *C.*; *nyams-čágs* sin *Schr.*; in *Thgr.* it seems to be used in this sense. — *nyáms-čúṅ* 1. **faint, weak, languid, exhausted,** by hunger, illness etc. *Dzl.*; **poor** in learning, destitute of knowledge, ignorant *W.*; destitute of money, destitute of virtue *C.* 2. *W* col. for *snyems-čúṅ.* — *nyams-rtógs* resp. **knowledge, cognition, perception,** *nyams-rtógs šig yod*, *nyams-rtógs bzáṅ-po skye* or *ʼkruṅs*, a perception, a good thought arises (in my mind); in a general sense: *nyams-rtógs-kyi mťar pyin-pa* to obtain perfect knowledge *Mil.*, frq. — *nyams-stóbs* **strength,** *zin* is gone *Med.* — *nyams-stoṅ-ysál* v. *ysál-po.* — *nyams-brtás byed-pa* **strengthening, restorative, nourishing** *Med.*, (but *nyams-brtas* he recovered, grew well, got up again *Dzl.*) — *nyams-ťág-pa* **suffering, tormented, exhausted** *Dzl.*; *nyams-ťág-pai skad* or *sgra* lamentation, doleful cries. — *nyams-ťábs*, *nyams-dgú Sch.*: 'appearance, colour, figure, state' (?). — *nyams-myóṅ Tar.* **enjoyment, delight,** *nyams-myóṅ ma skyes ruṅ*, although I had no real enjoyment of it *Mil.nt.*; *ťsór-bai nyams-myóṅ* prob. perception by the senses, knowledge acquired through the medium of the senses *Mil.* — *nyams-rtsál Dzl.* ༢༥༤, 7 **skill.** — *nyams-mťsár-ba C.* **wonderful,** most beautiful. — *nyams-lén* a memorial verse, a rhyme or verse serving to retain things in memory *Mil.*

ཉམས་པ་ *nyáms-pa* **injured, hurt,** e.g., by a fall *Dzl.*; of lifeless things: **spoiled, damaged** *C.*; **impaired, imperfect,** *stobs-nyams*, *dbáṅ-po nyáms-pa*, *yán-lag nyams Lex.* (as explanation of *ža-bo*); *smra-nyáms* (the sick person) speaks little *Med.*; **sem-nyám sóṅ-k̔an** *W.* discouraged, disheartened; esp. relative to a violation of duty, failing in, *tsúl-ǩrims* (or *ťsúl-las*) *nyáms-pas* because he has failed in, acted against the moral law *Dzl.*; *bzód-pa nyáms-par ʼgyúr-bas* because their patience failed *Dzl.*; also **stained** *Glr.*, e.g. *ǩrág-gis* with blood; *nyáms-par byéd-pa Wdṅ.*; *nyáms-su ʼjúg-pa Glr.* to spoil, deteriorate, destroy; *ma nyáms-pa* entire, complete, untouched, uncorrupted.

ཉར་ *nyar* 1. v. *nya-ra.* — 2. *Cs.*, also *nyar-nyár*, **oblong.**

ཉར་གདོང་ *nyár-ydóṅ W.* inst. of *ṅar-ydóṅ*, **shin, shin-bone.**

ཉལ་ཉིལ་ *nyal-nyil*, or *nyal-nyól* **filth, dirt,** foul matter, loose and dry dirt that may be removed by sweeping *Pth.*, *Dzl.*

ཉལ་བ་ *nyál-ba*, imp. *nyol*, 1. **to lie down,** e.g. before a tigress *Dzl.*; to lie down, **to sleep,** *nyal(-du) soṅ* (he) went to bed *Glr.*; *rgya-sráṅ-la nyal ʼdúg-go* (he) slept in the street *Glr.*; *mi nyal tsám-la* when people go to bed, at curfew *Mil.*; *rta nyal byéd-pa* to make a horse lie down *Glr.*; rarely of things: *rtsva nyal* the grass is laid-down (by the wind or rain) *Dzl.*; *ra ʼog nyál-bai nya* so *Zam.* calls the letter *rnya*; fig. to rest, *bdé-bar nyál-du méd-do* (he) had no rest, viz. from envy *Dzl.* ༢༣༠, 12. — 2. with *daṅ* or *la*, **to lie with** (a woman) *Dzl.* and elsewh. — 3. fig. **to dwell, to live** *Mil.*

**Comp.** *ṅyal-ǩri* **couch, bed, sofa** *C.* — *nyal-gós* **counterpane, quilt, blanket** *Sch.* — *nyál-po* **coition,** *nyál-po byéd-pa* to practise cohabitation, *máṅ-du* immoderately *Med.* —

*nyál-bu* bastard, whoreson *Ma.* — *nyál-sa* sleeping-place.

ཉི *nyi* 1. num. fig.: 38. — 2. num. inst. of *γnyis* in compounds, *nyi-brgyá*, *-stóṅ*, *-ḱri* etc., *nyi-ḱri* also title of a book, the Prajna Paramitā, containing 28 000 Sloka. — 3. for *nyi-ma*.

ཉི་ཁུད *nyi-ḱud* a lake in Nepal *Pth.*

ཉི་མ *nyi-ma* (*Bal.* **nyó-ma**, 1. **the sun,** *˳čar* becomes visible, rises; *šar* id., also: has risen, shines; *nub*, *rgas*, *W.* also **skyod*, *bud**, sets, is setting; *nyí-ma nub ťse bar* (for *ťseï bár-du*) until sun-set *Sch.*; *nyi-mai γnyen* akin to the sun, the Sâkya race *Cs.*; **da nyi-ma ríṅ-mo** *W.* now the sun stands already high in the heavens; **nyi-ma-gaṅ-šár** sun-flower, Helianthus. — 2. **day,** = *nyin-mo*, opp. to night, frq.; **nyi-ma-ťsé** *W.* the whole day, all day long; **nyi-ma-ṕéd** *W.* noon, mid-day; *nyi-ma γčig* one day, once *Dzl.*: *nyí-ma-re-ŕér* daily.

**Comp.** *nyi-dkyil* **disk of the sun** *Sch.* — *nyi-gúṅ*, *nyí-mai guṅ* **noon, mid-day;** meridian(?) *Cs.* — *nyi-dgá* seems to be the n. of a medicinal herb *Med.* — *nyi-rgás* **sun-set.** — *nyi-ldóg* **the solstice,** *dgún-nyi-ldog* winter solstice, *dbyár-nyi-ldog* summer solstice *Wdk.* — *nyi-núb* = *nyi-rgás.* — *nyí-ťsé* 1. *Sch.*: the time or duration of one day. 2. *Lex.*: = प्रदेश direction, place, country(?); *nyi-ťsé spyód-pa Lex.*: a kind of ascetic; *nyi-ťsé-ba Sch.*: ephemeral; single, simple; *Thgy.*: n. of a class of infernal beings. — *nyi-tsód* **sun-dial,** *nyi-tsód-kyi ḱór-lo* the circle of a sun-dial *Cs.* — *nyi-˳dzin* **eclipse** of the sun (cf. *sgra-γčán*). — *nyi-zér* **sun-beam,** *nyi-zér rtá-la žón-nas* riding on a sun-beam *Mil.* and elsewh.; *nyi-zér-gyi rdul* a mote floating in a sun-beam. — *nyi-zlá* sun and moon; also the figures of sun and moon connected, crowning the top of the *mčod-rtén*; *nyi-zlá bsdad mi oṅ* sun and moon will not stand still *Mil.* — *nyi-˯óg* below the sun; the earth *Was.* (49); *nyi-˯óg-gi rgyal-ḱams Glr.* id.; it seems, however, to denote a certain country, acc. to Mahāvyutpatti the same as Aparāntaka, *Williams*: the western country; cf. *Schf.* on *Tar.* 72. — *nyi-˳od* **sun-shine.** — *nyi-yól* any **screen** or **shelter** from the sun's rays: awning, curtain, parasol, pent-house *Sch.*; **nyi-ríb** (prop. *sgrib*) *W.* id., umbrella. — *nyi-šár* **sun-rise** *Cs.* — *nyi-lhag Sch.* a cold day (?) — Cf. *nyín-mo*.

ཉི་ཤུ *nyí-šu* (inst. of *nyis-ču*), often in conjunction with *ťám-pa*, **twenty,** *nyi-šu-rtsa-γčig B.*, *C.*, **nyi-šu-nyer-γčig** *W.*, *nyer-γčig*, twentyone.

ཉིག་ཉིག *nyig-nyig W.* **loose, slack, lax,** not tight or tense.

ཉིང་ཁུ *nyiṅ-ḱu*, *Ssk.* मण्ड *Cs.*: 'heart, spirit, essence', cf. *snyiṅ-po*.

ཉིང་ཏོ *nyiṅ-to Sch.*: **sure, trustworthy,** *Lex.*: *nyiṅ-tor* = *ṅes-par*.

ཉིང་ལག *nyiṅ-lag*, a category not familiar to us; gen. mentioned together with *yán-lag*; it might be translated by: members of a second order, parts of the *yán-lag*; the exact meaning must however remain undetermined, as the Tibetans themselves are not able to give a clear definition of it. In *C.*: inner parts of the body, opp. to outer. In books, phrases like the following are to be found: *yán-lag daṅ nyiṅ-lag ťams-čád daṅ ldán-pa*; *yán-lag daṅ nyiṅ-lag ná-ba*; *yán-lag daṅ nyiṅ-lag γčód-pa*; evidently the *nyiṅ-lag* are smaller, but more numerous than the *yán-lag*. In *Pth.* also *nyiṅ-sprúl* is found besides *yaṅ-sprúl*, emanation of the third order; v. *sprúl-pa*.

ཉིང་མཚམས་སྦྱོར་བ *nyiṅ-mťsáms sbyór-ba* **to be re-born** *Stg.*

ཉིད *nyid* 1. **self, same,** opp. to other persons, *ma nyid* the mother herself *Dzl.*; *mi de ni rgyál-po nyid yín-no* this man are you yourself, o king! *Dzl.*; the very, just he, just it etc., *las byéd-pai γnas nyid-la* just where I am working *Dzl.*; *deï druṅ-nyid-na* (or *du*) close by, to, or before, **hard** by, *Thgy.*; *dus de-nyid-du* at the **very** moment, frq.; *mčód-bya nyid* that which is venerable par excellence *Tar.* 15, 13; *yón-*

*tan nyid Tar.* 15, 14 id.; *dé-nas mi riṅ-ba-nyid-na* a very short time after *Tar.*; when added to adjectives it denotes abstract nouns, as in English the terminations: -ness, -ship, -ty, -cy, -y etc., but it is chiefly limited to the language of philosophical writings, from which a few expressions only (such as *stoṅ-pa-nyid* the emptiness, the Buddhist vacuum) have found their way into col. language. — 2. In the more recent literature it is used resp. for *ḱyod*, **thou, you**; *nyid-kyi* **thy, your** *Pth., Ma.*; *nyid-ráṅ* **you** (col. **nyi-ráṅ, nyo-ráṅ**) *W., C.*, resp., like the German *'Sie'*; *nyid-ċag(-raṅ)* **you**, addressed to one person or to several, *C.* (in *Glr. ḱyed-ċag* seems to be used in the same way). — **3. only,** *graṅs-kyi lṅa nyid Zam.* only the numeral *lṅa*; *za nyid-do* the letter *za* alone (without a prefix).

ཉིན(མོ) *nyin(-mo)* 1. **day,** =*nyi-ma* 2; *nyin-gyi riṅ-la* during the day-time *Pth.*; *nyin-mor ˳gyur* it dawns *Cs.*; *nyin-mor byed* 'making day', an epithet of the sun *Cs.*; *nyin* adv. in the day-time *Glr.*; *nyin-ċig* one day, once *Dzl.*; *nyin ċig bžin-du* daily *Dzl.*; *nyin-par* during the day-time *Dzl.*; by day-light *Dzl.*; *deï nyin-par* on that day, frq. *Dzl.*; *ṗyir nyin, ṗyi de nyin, deï ṗyi nyin* the following day, on the f.d. *Dzl.*; *ṫses bċo-lṅái nyin* the 15th., on the 15th. *Glr.*; fig.: *bstán-pa nyin-par mdzád-pai skyés-bu* a saint that restores the doctrine, a reformer of faith; hence *Schr.*: *dád-pai nyin-byed* evangelist, apostle. — 2. **propitious day;** **ṅa ča nyin-mo mi ˳dug** *W.* this day is not propitious for me to go.

**Comp.** *nyin-dkár* a white, a **lucky day** *Sch.* — *nyin-gáṅ, nyin-ṫog-ṫág* (*W.* **ṫag-ṫog**) all the day long. — *nyin-gúṅ* **noon.** — *nyin-gla* daily pay, a day's hire *Cs.* — **nyin-ṫse-ré** *W.* all the day long, the live-long day. — *nyin-mṫsán* 1. **a day and a night,** *nyin-mṫsán bċo-brgyád Mil.* for nine days and nine nights. 2. **day and night** *Dzl., nyin-mṫsan-méd-par* id., frq.; *nyin-med-ṫsán-med W.* id.; *nyin-mṫsán-du* id. *Mil.*; *nyin-mṫsán mnyám-pa* equinox. — *nyin-žág(-γċig)* 1. a day with the night, 24 hours, divided into 12 portions of time, called *ḱyim* (q. v.): *nam-ṗyéd* midnight, *nam-ṗyed-yól* 2 o'clock a. m., *ṫo-ráns* 4 o'cl. a. m. (in popular language also: **ǰá-po dáṅ-po** about 2 o'cl., **nyís-pa** 3 o'cl., **súm-pa** 4 o'cl., *nam-láṅs* 6 o'cl. a. m. (i. e. the time when the sun first illumines the mountain tops; it is from this moment, and not from midnight, that in daily life the date is counted); *nyi-šár* 8 o'cl. a. m. (when the sun rises upon the valley); *dros-ǰám* (col. **nyi-ḍúl**) 10 o'cl. a. m.; *nyin-gúṅ, nyi-ṗyéd* 12 o'cl., noon; *ṗyed-ċól* (*W.* **zá-ra ṗí-mo**) 2 o'cl. p. m., *myur-smád* 4 o'cl. p. m., *nyi-rgás* 6 o'cl. p. m., *srod-˳ḱór* 8 o'cl. p. m. (col. **sa-rúb, srod-rúb**), *srod-ċól* 10 o'cl. p. m. (col. **tiṅ-nyí**) — thus acc. to *Wdk.* By adding the names of the 12 years' cycle (*nam-ṗyéd byi-ba, ṗyed-ċól glaṅ* etc., v. the word *lo*), these terms have been rendered still more convenient for astrological calculations. Of course, all the terms given are strictly correct only at the time of the equinoxes, and deviate at the summer and winter solstices for more than an hour from the time indicated by our clocks. 2. *nyin-žág* as symb. num.: 15. — *nyiṅ-bžin-gyis Pth., nyin-ré bžin Glr.*, daily adv., with-*gyi* adj. — *nyin-lám* a day's journey *Glr.*, *rkaṅ-ṫáṅ-gi, rtá-pai, lúg-pai nyin-lam* a pedestrian's, a horseman's, a sheep-driver's daily march. — *nyin-ráṅs Tar.* (= *ṫo-ráṅs*) day-break, morning twilight *Schf.*

ཉིབ་ཕྱོགས་ *nyib-ṗyógs, W.* **nyib-ċóg(s)** the sunny side of mountains.

ཉིལ་བ་ *nyil-ba* **to decay,** to crumble to pieces, of rocks, mountains etc.; rarely to run down, of tears, to flow down, of locks of hair.

ཉིས་ *nyis* 1. instrum. of *nyi*. — 2. in compounds for *γnis*.

ཉུ་ *nyu* num. fig.: 68.

ཉུ་ཏི་ *nyú-ti* **pear** *Ld.*

ཉུག་པ་ *nyúg-pa* 1. **to besmear,** *spos* to perfume; **to rub gently, to stroke, to caress** *Sch.*, in this sense perh. *Gyatch* ꝏ, 14. — 2. **to touch,** = *rég-pa* ccd. *W.*; *C.*? — 3. **to search after** (feeling, groping) *Cs.* — 4. **to put out, stretch out,** *ču-nas mgo* one's head out of the water, to look or **peep out**, resp. *dbu nyug mdzád-pa Glr.*; *nyug-nyúg-pa Tar.* 80, 21 **to stand out, to project** (*Sch.*: to run to and fro?).

ཉུག་རྩ་མེ་ཏོག་ *nyúg-rtsa mé-tog* **Carthusian pink** *C.*

ཉུག་རུམ་, ཉུང་རུམ་ *nyug-rúm, nyuṅ-rúm* **a eunuch** *Dzl.*

ཉུང་བ་ *nyúṅ-ba* 1. adj. col. **nyúṅ-ṅu**, **little;** **nyuṅ-ṅu žig**, *Ld.* col. **nyúṅ-ṅa-rig**, *nyúṅ-zad čig* id. *Dzl.*; *nyuṅ-šás Wdṅ.*, **a little, a few, some;** *nyúṅ-bar byéd-pa* to make less *Cs.* — 2. vb. **to be little.**

ཉུང་མ་ *nyúṅ-ma* **turnip,** *la(-p̔ug daṅ) nyuṅ (-ma)* radishes and turnips *Glr.* — *nyúṅ-k̔u, nyúṅ-loi ǰa* turnip-soup, turnip-tea, an infusion of dried turnip leaves, much used, e.g. in Bhotan, and considered very nourishing(?). **nyuṅ-dő** *C.*, mentioned by *Wts.* p. 137. as 'navets ronds', large sweet, red turnips (perh. turnip-rooted cabbage?). — *nyuṅ-γži* seed-turnips (*Cs.* turnip-seed). — *nyúṅ-lo* a turnip leaf.

Note. In writing and speaking this word is often confounded with *yuṅ(s)* mustard, so that e.g. *yúṅ-ma* is said for turnip inst. of *nyúṅ-ma*, *nyuṅs-dkár* for white mustard, inst. of *yuṅs-dkár*.

ཉུང་རུམ་ *nyuṅ-rúm* v. *nyug-rúm.*

ཉུལ་བ་ *nyúl-ba* **to wander** or **rove about, to pass privily** or **steal** through, e.g. towns, countries, mountains *Mil.*, burying-places, tombs (as jackals) *Mil.*; (*lta*) *nyúl-pa, nyúl-mi Pth.*, *sa-nyúl* a spy *Cs.* (Also *γnyúl-ba, myúl-ba.*)

ཉེ་ *nye* num. fig.: 98.

ཉེ་ཏི་ *nyé-ṭi* a pear *Schr.* (cf. *nyú-ti, nyó-ti*).

ཉེ་བ་ *nyé-ba* I. vb., **to be near, to approach,** always with the supine of a verb, *dus byéd-du nyé-bas* when he was near dying *Dzl.*; *zlá-ba ťsáṅ-du nyé-bas* (when she was) near the completion of the months, i. e. the time of giving birth to a child *Dzl.*, frq.; *slób-dpon p̔yir ˏóṅ-du nyé-bas* when the time of the teacher's return drew near *Dzl.*; *zín-du mi nyé-ste* being not near having done *Dzl.*; even used as follows: *γnas der sléb-tu nyé-bai ťse* when he came near the place *Mil.*

II. adj., col. **nyé-mo** **near,** both as to space and time, *lam-riṅ-gi γnyén-pas k̔yim-mťses nye* the neighbour is nearer than a kinsman living far off; *ká-ba daṅ nyé-bai sar* at a place near the pillar *Glr.*; *ťag-nyé-ba* id.: *ri ťag-nyé-ba žig* a near or neighbouring hill *Ma.*; standing near, fig. being closely connected with by consanguinity: *nyé-ba-rnams C.* relations, kindred (*Dzl.* ꝏ, 13 *γnyén-pas* prob. is preferable to *mo nyé-bas*); allied by similarity: *mťsáms-med-pa lṅa daṅ de daṅ nyé-bai sdig-pa* the five worst sins, and those coming nearest to them; near by friendship and affection: **nyé-mo yin** *W.* he is closely connected with us, he is desirous to enter into an intimate connection with us; *blo*, or *snyiṅ*, or *sems nyé-ba* (or **nyé-mo**), friendly, kind, amicable, *blo nyé-ba ltar byéd-pa* to affect a friendly manner *Glr.*; **nyé-mo ǰhé'-pa** *C.* to love, **e. g.** parents loving their children or vice versâ; *nyé-bai sras brgyad Glr.* the eight intimate disciples (of Buddha, not historical, but mythical persons, Mandshusri etc.).

III. adv. *nyé-bar* or *nyer* 1. **near,** *daṅ* to, *dé-dag daṅ nyé-bar lhá-k̔aṅ bžens* near to them he built a temple *Tar.*; *nyé-bar ˏóṅ-ba, sléb-pa*, to come near, to approach; *nyé-bar ˏgyúr-ba* id, *stóṅs-su nyé-bar ˏgyúr-ba daṅ* when it was nearly empty *Pth.*; *dár-la nyé-bar gyúr-to* it began to spread, to extend itself *Pth.*; *nyé-bar γnás-pa* **to** be near, to stand near, e.g. of a star *Wdṅ.* — 2. *nyé-bar byéd-pa*, with la, **to adhere to, to keep** (one's promise) *Pth.* — 3. *nyé-bar bžág-pa* **to make use of, to employ,** *drán-pa nyé-bar bžág-pa* (स्मृत्युपस्थान, *Burn.* I.,

626. ཉཔ near, though Tibetan dictionaries write ཉབ) to make use of one's intellectual powers. To do this rightly forms part of Buddhist wisdom (v. *Köpp.* I, 436) and instruction (*Dzl.* ༡༥༥, 7, where *Sch.*'s version is incorr.), being divided into four divisions or degrees (*Burn.*); *saṅs-rgyás-la dkón-pai ₒdu-šés nyé-bar bžág-pa* to apply to Buddha the notion of rareness *Tar.* 5, 13. — 4. **intensely, urgently, speedily,** *ₒjigs-pa nyé-bar ži* fear is speedily allayed *Glr.*; *nadnyé-bar ₒtso* the disease is speedily cured *Thgy.*; *nyé-bar lén-pa Mil.*, *Thgy.* to seize eagerly, to strive for earnestly, to aspire to, esp. to the re-birth as a human being; cf. also *nyer-lén*; *nyé-bar mk̔ó-ba* of urgent necessity, frq. *Tar. nyer ₒp̔el* it increases rapidly *Med.*

IV. sbst. v. *nyé-šiṅ.*

**Comp.** *nye-sk̔ór Sch. nye-ₒk̔ór* **those about us,** the company around us, *k̔yed-ráṅ-gi nye-k̔ór-gyi ldóm-bu-ba* a beggar belonging to the people around you *Mil.*; esp. relations, kindred, *des nye-k̔ór yaṅ šúgs-kyis yoṅ* in this way family-connections are formed of themselves *Mil.* — *nye-mk̔ón = nye-riṅ Cs.* (?) — *nye-gróġs* **neighbour, fellow-creature** *Cs.* — *nye-čár* **now** *Sch.* — *nyé-dag Cs.*, *nyé-du*, and most frq. *nye-ₒbrél* (*ɣnyen-ₒbrél*) **kindred, relations** (these being considered a main obstacle to moral perfection, they are to be shunned accordingly). — *nye-ɣnás* **disciple,** *kyéd-kyi nye-ɣnás bgyio, nye-ɣnás-su mčio* I wish to become your disciple *Dzl.* — *nye-ṫsán, nye-rigs* **relative, kinsman.** — *nye-riṅ* 1. **near and far,** near and distant relations. 2. **distance,** *sgor nye-riṅ ċi-tsam yod* how far is it from here to the gate? 3. **partial,** *rgyál-po nye-riṅ čes* the king is very partial *Glr.*, *nye-riṅ-méd-pa* impartial *Glr.* — *nye-lám* **near; now** *Sch.*

ཉེ་ཞོ *nye-žo* **damage, mishap, accident** (syn. to *bar-čad*), *nye-žo-méd-par* without an accident, safely *Dzl.*

ཉེ་རེག་པ *nye-rég-pa Lexx.* **to wash.**

ཉེ་ཤིང་ *nyé-šiṅ*, or *nyé-bai šiṅ Med.*, a tree the fruits of which are used as a sweet medicine.

ཉེག་མ, ཉེག་ཐག *nyég-ma, nyeg-ṫág*, v. *nyág-ma.*

ཉེད་པ *nyéd-pa = mnyéd-pa.*

ཉེན་ *nyen* 1. = *nye*, *nyen-kór*, or *nyen-skór* = *nye-ₒk̔or* **a relative,** *Pth.*: *nyen-kór žig yin* he is a kinsman; also alone, like *ɣnyen.* — 2. with a vb.: **danger, risk,** *myúr-du ₒjig-nyen yod* there is a danger of its being soon destroyed *Glr.*; *dmyál-bar ₒgro-nyén ɣda* there is a danger of going to hell; *sróg-gi bar-čád-du ₒgró-bai nyen yod Mil.* of risking one's life; **dúṅ-nyen** *C.* he has the chance of receiving a good beating; occasionally also: to be near, to impend, in reference to happy events; in col. language it is simply used for danger, *nyén-ċan* dangerous, e.g. *lam, las, sbrul* etc.

ཉེན་པ *nyén-pa*, pf. *nyén-to*, **to be pained, pinched, pressed** hard, e.g. by hunger, cold, enemies; **to toil and moil, to labour hard, to drudge;** v. *baṅ.*

ཉེར་ *nyer* 1. = *nyé-bar.* — 2. v. *nyi-šu.*

ཉེར་སྣོགས *nyer-snógs Thgy.*, **theme, task** *Sch.*

ཉེར་ཉེར་ *nyer-nyér, nyer-že*; *W.* **dregs, sediment.**

ཉེར་བ *nyér-ba* 1. *Sch.* **to tan, curry, dress,** make soft. — 2. *W.*, also **nyer-kád ṫáṅ-ċe**, **to snarl, growl.** — 3. *W.* **to tarry, stay, linger** (*snyér-ba* for *bsnár-ba?*).

ཉེར་མ *nyér-ma W.* for *ɣyér-ma*, **red pepper.**

ཉེར་ལེན་ *nyer-lén*, or *nyé-bar lén-pa*, is said to be = *rgyui rgyu*, original cause.

ཉེལ་བ *nyél-ba* taken **ill, sick** *Sch.*

ཉེས་པ *nyés-pa* I. sbst. any thing **wrong** or **noxious,** or liable to become so, and the consequences of it; hence 1. **evil, calamity, damage,** *nyés-pa ṫams-ċád deï lús-la ₒduo* all sorts of plagues are collecting upon his body *Dzl.*; *lo-nyés* a bad harvest, failure of crops, *lo-nyés byúṅ-bai ṫse* when the harvest had been bad; in a special sense in medicine: the three **humours** of the body, air (v. *rluṅ*), bile, and phlegm, gen. called त्रिदोष ) *nod-byéd nyés-pa γsum* the three noxious matters (most diseases being ascribed to a derangement of one of them). — 2. **moral fault, offence, sin, crime,** *nyés-pai skyon*, being contaminated by a crime *Dzl.; lus daṅ ṅág-gi* (or *ḱai*) *nyés-pa* sin in word and deed *Dzl.*; *nyés-pa byéd-pa* to commit a fault, a crime; to sin, frq.; also: *mi žig-la nyés-pa byuṅ* a slip has occurred to a person *Dzl.*; *bdág-la nyés-pa či žig yód-de ma γnaṅ* what crime have I committed, that you will not give me permission? *Dzl.* — 3. **punishment** *C.* **nyē-mig** id., resp. **ka nyē*; *nye-pa ṕog-ḱan** he that has got a punishment.

II. vb. **to commit an offence,** *ₒdis či nyés-te bzuṅ* what offence has he committed that he is taken prisoner? *Dzl.* (cf. above); *sṅón-čad bdág-gis nyés-pa bden* it is true that formerly I committed a fault *Dzl.; sṅár ma sbrán-pa nyés-so* the not reporting sooner was a fault *Dzl.*; *γyógs-pa nyés-so* you have committed a fault by covering ... *Dzl.*; *bdag nyés-na* if harm is done to me; hence *či nyés* in a general sense: *ḱyod či nyés-pa smros šig* tell me what has happened to you *Dzl.*; *btsóṅ-na či nyés* quid mali, si vendideris? *Dzl.*; *mi drán-nam či nyes* is she out of her senses, or, what is the matter with her? *Dzl.*; *či nyés-na* why, *či nyés-na ḱáṅ-pai náṅ-na rdziṅ-bu bskyil* why is there a pond within the house? *Dzl.*; *ma nyés-pai ₒgró-ba* innocent beings *Mil.*; *ma nyés-pa ṕyir byuṅ* he came out again unhurt *Dzl.*; *nyés-byas* a wicked action, a sin *Cs.*; *nyés-ltuṅ* sin, sinful deed, trespass, *nyés-ltuṅ-gis ṕog* he has been overtaken by a sin *Mil.*

ཉོ་ *nyo* 1. num. fig.: 128. — 2. **carrot** *Cs.*

ཉོ་ཏི་ *nyo-ti* **a pear** *Ld.*

ཉོ་བ་ *nyó-ba*, pf. and imp. *nyos*, 1. **to buy,** *dṅul brgyas* for a hundred rupees; *nyó-(ba-)po* a buyer, purchaser, *nyo-(ba-)mo* fem.; *nyó-mḱan* a buyer, customer; *nyó-ťo* account, bill; *nyo-ₒtsóṅ* commerce, traffic; *nyo-ₒtsóṅ byéd-pa* to trade. — 2. **to take at rent, to take the lease** (of a field, by buying the crop).

ཉོག་པ་ *nyóg-pa* **soiled, dirtied,** made unclean, e.g. of victuals *Mil.*; *nyóg-ma Sch.*, *ču-nyóg Lex.* muddy, foul water; *nyog-nyóg-po* confused (story) *Tar.*

ཉོགས་བྱིང་ *nyogs-byiṅ Sch.*: **too soft;** *nyog-nyóṅ Sch.* **soft, tender, weak,** inclined to weep; **šés-nyog-čan** (for *γčés-nyog-čan*) dandling, fondling *W.*

ཉོད་པ་ *nyód-pa* **food** *Lex.*

ཉོན་མོངས་པ་ *nyon-móṅs-pa* (seldom without -*pa*), *Ssk.* क्लेश 1. **misery, trouble, pain,** frq.; also used as a verb: *nyon-móṅs-šiṅ*; *tsá-bas nyon-móṅs-te* molested by the heat *Dzl.*; *nyon-móṅs-par ₒgyúr-ba* to get into trouble *Dzl.*; *nyon ma móṅs-sam* had you to experience any hardship? *Dzl.* — 2. in a restricted sense: **the misery of sin,** *nyon-móṅs-pa-las ṕan-pai don med* this does not avail for being delivered from such misery *Dzl.*; **sin,** *nyon-móṅs-pai nad, dri-ma Dzl.*; *sér-sna-la sógs-pai nyon-móṅs-pa* avarice and other sins *S.O.*; *nyon-móṅs-pa-méd-pa* free from sin, sinless *S.O.*; *nyon-móṅs-čan-gyis nyá-ša nyos Zam.* the offender buys the flesh of a fish.

ཉོབ་ཉོབ་ *nyob-nyób* weak, feeble-minded *Sch.*

ཉོར་ *nyor* 1. v. *nyó-ba*. 2. **a rectangle** *Cs.*

ཉོལ་ *nyol*, imp. of *nyál-ba*; *nyól-ba* prov. for *nyál-ba*.

ཉོས་ *nyos*, imp. of *nyó-ba*; *nyos-mi* a slave *Cs.*

གཉང་བ་ *γnyáṅ-ba Sch.*, prob. = *rnyáṅ-ba*.

གཉན་ *γnyan* 1. a pestilential disease, epidemic, or contagious disorder, **plague,** *mdze daṅ ₒbrum-bu γnyan Ma.*; *γnyan-nád* id.; *γnyan-dúg* a poison against, or a remedy for the plague *Med.*; *dka-γnyán* a destructive plague *Sch.* — 2. **a species of wild sheep, argali** (Ovis ammon).

ཉ

**གཉན་པ་** γnyán-pa **cruel, fierce, severe,** *lha γnyán-rnams Glr.* gods of vengeance, deities of terror; *klu-γnyán* id.; *k̔rims γnyán-pa* a cruel commandment, frq.; *dam-ts̔ig γnyán-pa* prob. a rigid vow, a solemn oath *Mil.*; of mountains: **wild, rugged, precipitous**; *γnyán-sa* a rugged country *Mil.*; in *γnyán-pai γnad* (v. *γnad*) prob.: dangerous. — *γnyán-po* sbst. *Mil.?*

**གཉའ་(བ)** *γnya(-ba)* 1. **neck, nape,** *γnyá-ba brtuṅs* the neck is contracted or shortened *Med.* — *γnyá-ko* hide, or leather of a beast's neck *Cs.* — *γnya-k̔óbs* screen of the neck (attached to a helmet) *Sch.* — *γnya-rgyáb* (?) *C.* breast-work, parapet. — *γnya-rtsé* vertebra prominens, the cervical vertebra with its projecting process *Mil.* — *γnya-ts̔igs* cervical joint. — *γnya-réṅs* stiff neck, *γnya-réṅs-čan* 1. having a stiff neck; 2. stiffnecked, obstinate. — *γnya-šiṅ* a yoke (for oxen) *Glr.*, *Lex.* — 2. *skad-γnyá* v. *skad.*

**གཉའ་ནང་** *γnya-náṅ*, or *snya-náṅ*, a village on the frontier of Nepal

**གཉའ་བོ་** *γnyá-bo* **a witness,** one that gives evidence *Cs.*, *Lex.* = *dpáṅ-po*; *γnyá-bo byéd-pa* to pledge for, to be surety for; *Dzl.* ༡༡༥: *bskyi-γnyá byas*, *Sch.*: 'he made an attested loan'.

**གཉི་ག་** *γnyi-ga* for *γnyis-ka Stg.*; *γnyi-zér* for *nyi-zér Lex.*

**གཉིག་ཏུ** *γnyig-tu Lex.* = *γčig-tu.*

**གཉིད་** *γnyid*, resp. *mnal*, **sleep**, *γnyid-du ˳gró-ba* to fall asleep *Glr.*, *Mil.*; *W.* **nyid ma yoṅ** sleep has not come, I am sleepless; **nyid ma k̔ug, nyid k̔ug ma nyan**, also **nyid saṅ soṅ** id.; *γnyid mi t̔ub* he cannot find sleep *Med.*; *γnyid-t̔úm-pa* one uninterrupted portion of sleep *Glr.*; *γnyid mt̔úg-pa* a sound sleep, *γnyid-sráb* a light sleep, a slumber *Med.* — *γnyid-log-pa* (prop. *γnyid-kyis lóg-pa*) *Dzl.* to fall asleep, *Dzl.* ༡༥༣, 16; ༢༡༤, 9 (thus correctly translated already by *Schr.*), prob. also to sleep; *γnyid-la ˳gro-ba*, *W.* **ča-če**, to fall asleep; *γnyid t̔úg-por soṅ* he fell into a deep sleep *Mil.*; **da-rúṅ γnyid ma lóg-mk̔an-˳dug* W.* I am still awake; *γnyid sád-pa* to awaken, to awake vb. n.; *γnyid-yúr-ba* to be overcome by sleep *Sch.*, *Tar.* 31, 22, *Pth.*, — *γnyid-rdól C.* somnambulism; **nyid-ma-mún-la dúl-če** id., *Ld.*; **nyi'-čól gyáb-pa** id. *C.* — *γnyid-čan* sleepy *Cs.*; *γnyid-méd* having no sleep, sleepless; *γnyid-yér* morbid sleeplessness; *γnyid-yár Med.*, *Pth.*, id.? *γnyid-lam C.* = *rmi-lam* dream.

**གཉིས་** *γnyis* 1. also *γnyis šig* (v. *čig*), **two,** *de γnyis, γnyís-po, γnyís-ka* the two, both; *γnyis(-su)-méd(-pa)*; *mi-γnyis-pa Tar.*, not being two, i.e. not differing, identical, the same, *ṅa daṅ rgyál-ba γnyis-su med* I and Buddha, we are one, i.e. I am an incarnation of Buddha *Glr.*; *Cs.* also: indubitable, thus perh. used by *Mil.*; *γnyis-su ˳byúṅ-ba* to be divided into two, to become two *Glr.* — 2. **a** (married) **couple,** *brám-ze γnyis* Brahmin man and wife. — 3. **both** (v. above), in Tibetan often added, where two nouns have the same predicate, either disjunctively, and then usually followed by *re: jó-bo daṅ byams-mgón γnyis mdzó-mo reï stéṅ-du bžugs* both the lord and the Maitreya were mounted on bastard-cows *Glr.*; *ṅa-ráṅ re γnyis* either of us *Mil.*; *p̔yi naṅ γnyis čós-lugs gaṅ bzaṅ* which is the better of the two religions, the esoteric, or the exoteric? *Glr.*; — or copulatively: *k̔yo-šúg γnyís-la rás-čug γčig-las mi bdóg-ste* as they both, husband and wife, had only one cloth together *Dzl.*; — and reciprocally: *čos daṅ bon γnyis rtsód-pa* the contest between the religion of Buddha, and the religion of the Bons *Glr.*; *k̔yod daṅ ṅa γnyis bza-mi byao* we two shall marry each other *Glr.* In most cases mentioned sub 3, *γnyís-po* (the two), *γnyís-ka*, *(γ)nyi-ga*, *W.* col. also **nyi-ko, nyi-kad, nyi-kod**, *Sp.* **nyi-mo**, may be used inst. of *γnyis*; *γnyis* may also refer to several nouns on one or on both sides: *k̔yed daṅ ṅa γnyis* both you (referring to several persons) and I; but it may also be quite omitted, as in other languages: *ga daṅ bai ˳jug-tsúl* the way of employing the (two) letters g and b *Gram.*

**Comp. and deriv.** *γnyis-skyes* one that is **born twice** i.e. a bird *Cs.;* also one that has entered into a religious order *Cs.* — *γnyis-čár* v. *čar.* — *γnyis-γnyis* **two a piece.** — *γnyis-ldáb* **twofold, double,** v. *ldab.* — *γnyis-ₒťúṅ* (द्विप) 'drinking twice', the elephant. — *γnyis-pa* 1. **the second.** 2. **having two,** possessed of two, e.g. *mgo-γnyis-pa* having two heads. two-headed; also double-tongued, deceitful *W.* 3. **having doubts, doubting**(?) *Wdn.* — *γnyis-po* the two, both (v. above). — *γnyis-méd* v. beginning of this article. — *γnyis-ₒdzin* prob. the state of being affected or influenced by contrary things: doubt, unsteadiness, wavering *Glr.; γnyis-ₒdzin ltá-ba* prob. to look upon two things as differing, to think them different *Mil.*

གཉུག་མ་ *γnyúg-ma Cs.* **natural,** opp. to *bčós-ma* artificial, hence (*Sch.*) = *dṅos-ma; Lexx.* = निज innate, peculiar. It occurs in the expressions: *sems γnyúg-ma,* and *γnyúg-mai sems Mil*; *γnyúg-mai ye-šés Mil.*; *;nyúg-mai don Mil.* and *Lex.*; *ma-bčós γnyúg-mai ṅáṅ-du ₒdres,* perh.: is dissolved into the uncreated primordial existence *Mil.* Our Lama explained it differently in different passages, and was not certain of the true meaning of the word.

གཉུང་དཀར་ *γnyuṅ-dkár* **rape-seed** for pressing oil; but cf. *nyúṅ-ma.*

གཉུལ་བ་ *γnyúl-ba* = *nyúl-ba.*

གཉེ་བ་ *γnyé-ba, Glr.* also *γnyeo, smyé-bo,* **a wooer, courter.**

གཉེ་མ་ *γnyé-ma* the twisted part of the **colon** or **great gut,** *Med.* and col. (*Sch.* erron.: rectum).

གཉེན་ *γnyen,* resp. *sku-γnyén* 1. **kinsman, relative,** *byáms-pai γnyen* loving relations, frq.; *γnyén-la byáms-pa byéd-pa* to love one's relatives; *γnyén-gyi sgyúg-mo, sgyúg-mo* as a degree of relationship *Lex.*; *γnyen byéd-pa* to become related, or allied, by marriage *Dzl.* — 2. gen. *γnyén-po* **helper, friend, assistant,** esp. spiritually: *rgyud γnyén-po bzáṅ-bar byin-gyis rlobs* bless my soul, that it may become a good spiritual helper (to these people) *Mil.*; *γnyén-po-la ma ltós-par* without looking up to a spiritual adviser *Mil.*; frq. used of supernatural helpers: *bod ₒdúl-bai γnyén-po* the promoter of the conversion of Tibet (the special Saviour of Tibet, as it were), Awalokiteswara, frq.; applied to things: **remedy, means, expedient, antidote,** *nád-la γsó-bar byéd-pai γnyén-po* assistants in curing maladies (e.g. medicine, diet etc.) *Med.*; *dei γnyén-por* as a remedy for *Thgy.*, frq.; *sgrúb-pai ťabs mi šés-pai γnyén-por* as a remedy for helplessness in acquiring a certain object, i.e. direction or instruction how to obtain it *Thgy.; γnyén-po γsáṅ-ba* mysterious helpers, or sources of good (relative to fetish-like objects frq.) — 3. *Cs.*: '*γnyén-po* adversary, antagonist, enemy; contrary, opposite, adverse'; *Sch.*: '*γnyén-por rtén-pa* to adhere to the counter party'; *Lexx.* have '*spáṅ-byai γnyén-po*' a *γnyén-po* to be shunned, explaining *γnyén-po* by प्रतिभव (prob. to be corrected into पक्ष) opponent, adversary. Sure proofs of this signification of *γnyén-po* I seldom met with in literature, but Lewin mentions some instances scarcely to be doubted. — 4. i. o. *mnyen* and *bsnyen.*

**Comp.** *dpuṅ-γnyén* **helper, assistant,** frq. — *ṗá-γnyén, má-γnyen* a relation on the father's side, on the mother's side *Cs.* — *bšes-γnyén* friend, esp. spiritual friend, v. *bšes.* — *γnyen-grás* (*Sch.?*), *γnyen-ₒbrél,* **nyen-ḍúṅ-po** *W.* relations, esp. of the same blood; *γnyen-sdé, γnyen-ťsán, γnyen-srid Mil.* id., col. — *γnyen-ₒdún* 1. *Sch.*: '**concord, harmony,** amongst kinsmen', in which sense it seems to be used in *Stg.*: *γnyen-ₒdún zád-pa yin* this harmony ceases. 2. **relations,** *ṗa yaṅ ma yin, γnyen-ₒdún min* neither father nor relations *Thgy.* — *γnyen-zlá* prob.: qualified, fit for matrimonial alliance (as to birth etc.), *kyéd-rnams kyaṅ ṅed rgya-nág-pai γnyen-zlá yin-pas* as ye Tibetans may enter into connubial connexion with us Chinese *Glr.*; in a concrete sense: a good match, *γnyen-zlá ma rnyéd-*

*kyis Dzl.* ༣༤, 14; *k̔yod daṅ ɣnyen-zlá min* I am not allied with you by marriage, with you I am not on terms of affinity. — *ɣnyen-šál* (?) reconciliation *C.* — *ɣnyen-bšés* relatives and friends, also separately: *k̔yód-la ɣnyen med bšes kyaṅ med Mil.*

གཉེར་བ་ *ɣnyér-ba* c. accus. **to take pains with, to take care of, to provide for,** to try to get; **to procure, to acquire,** *ɣnyer byéd-pa* id.; as a sbst. *Tar.* 165, 22: the procurer, provider *Schf.*; gen. in conjunction with *don* in various ways, as: *bdag don žig ɣnyér-te* as I have to look after a business *Dzl.* ༢༠, 7; *don ɣnyér-ba* to earn money; *dón-du ɣnyér-ba* c. accus., rarely c. dat.: to provide for, to strive to procure, *nor dón-du ɣnyér-ba* to endeavour to make money, frq.; *yo-byád dón-du ɣnyér-ba-rnams* people who desired to have goods *Tar.* 169, hence *don-ɣnyér* **exertion, effort, zeal,** *don-ɣnyér čén-po dgos* great exertions are necessary *Mil.*; in this sense prob. also *Tar.* 4, 8: earnest exertion (in investigating); *don-ɣnyér byéd-pa* c. *la* to study, investigate (a thing) *Glr.*; *don-ɣnyér-čan* 1. zealous, painstaking. 2. *Sch.* also: liked, welcome, *mgron* a welcome guest. — *dkon-ɣnyér Tar.* 183, 21, *Schf.*: administrator of valuable property; acc. to others: the first secular functionary of a *ɣtsúg-lag-k̔aṅ*, about the same as **bailiff** (steward) of a convent, = *lha-ɣnyér* Georgi Alph. Tib. (in an edict); also the manager of the daily sacrifices (*dgon-ɣnyér?*); *slob-ɣnyér* **a student,** *čos-slob-ɣnyér* a religious scholar (a student of theology) *Mil*, *slob-ɣnyér gáṅ-du bgyis* where did you study? *Mil.* — *ɣtad-ɣnyér byéd-pa* to trust (a person with), to intrust (a thing to) *Glr.*; *čéd-du ɣnyér-ba*, and *rǰés-su ɣnyér-ba* v. *čed.* — *ɣnyér-k̔a* **attention, care,** *ɣnyér-k̔a byéd-pa ccg.* to pay attention to, attend to, take care of *Pth.*; *ɣnyér-k̔a ɣtád-pa* to commit (a thing) to a person's charge, to put a person in trust of *Glr.* — *ɣnyér-pa* **farm-steward,** in convents etc. — *ɣnyér-byáṅ* prob. = *ɣnyér-k̔a.* — *ɣnyer-tsáṅ* **store-room, store-house,** (if under the charge of a special *ɣnyér-pa*).

གཉེར་མ་ *ɣnyér-ma* a fold of the skin, **wrinkle** *Med.*; *ɣnyer-ma réṅs-pa* *ˬgyur* the wrinkles are made straight, are smoothed *Stg.*; *ɣnyér-ma-čan* wrinkled; *k̔ro-ɣnyér* (भृकुटि) a frown, a severe or angry look v. *k̔ró-ba*; *ɣnyér-ba* to wrinkle, *sna-góṅ ɣnyér-ba* to knit the brows, to frown *Pth.*

གཉེལ་བ་ *ɣnyél-ba* = *mnyél-ba Sch.*

གཉོག་པ་ *ɣnyóg-pa* **to desire,** to wish earnestly *Cs.* v. *snyóg-pa.*

གཉོད་ *ɣnyód* **strength, durability, stoutness** of cloth etc., *C.* and *W.*, *ɣnyód-čan* strong; *ɣnyod-čúṅ*, *ɣnyod-méd* weak; *Lex.* *lus ɣnyod-čúṅ* a weakly body or constitution.

གཉོད་པ་ *ɣnyód-pa* **to draw, stretch, strain** *C.*, *W.*

མཉན་ *mnyan C.* **boat, skiff, wherry;** *mnyán-pa* boat-man, ferry-man.

མཉན་པ་ *mnyán-pa* 1. = *nyán-pa Dzl.* etc. — 2. v. *mnyan.*

མཉན་ཡོད་ *mnyan-yód*, श्रावस्ती, a town in the northern part of Oudh.

མཉམ་ *mnyam* v. the following word.

མཉམ་པ་ *mnyám-pa* (सम) col. **nyám-po*, 1. **like, alike, equal, same,** *mnyám-po yód* they are alike, equal, not differing, col.; with *daṅ*, seldom with the termin., *lha daṅ mnyám-pa yod* they are like unto the gods *Pth.*, *Glr.*; *zlúm-por mnyám-pa* roundish *Sambh.*; *rigs mnyám-pa* of equal birth, rank *Dzl.*; *dus mnyám-pa* contemporary, simultaneous, frq. *mnyám-par gyúr-ba* to become equal, to be equal *Dzl.* — 2. **even, level, flat,** *lag-mt̔il ltar mnyám-pa* flat like the palm of the hand *Glr.* and elsewh.; *mnyám-pa* (or *-par*) *byéd-pa* to make even or level, to even, to equalize *Dzl.*; to divide equally; *sems mnyám-pa* imperturbation, evenness of mind, not to be affected by kindness or the reverse; *sems mnyám-par ˬǰóg-pa* to compose the mind to perfect rest, for meditation, frq.; *mnyám-pa sbyór-ba* id. (?) — *mnyám-du* adv. (col. **nyám-po**) c. *daṅ:* together with, in company of, *blá-ma daṅ nyám-du ˳grogs dús-su Mil.*; *ma daṅ mnyám-du ˳čí-ba Thgy.*; col. **ṅa daṅ nyám-po ṡog** or merely **nyám-po ṡog** come along with me! **nyam sóṅ-te** going along with; *nyí-ma ṡár-ba daṅ mnyám-du* with the rising sun *Mil.*; col. **ḍul daṅ nyám-po** in walking, *ambulando*; **ťen daṅ nyám-po** in taking it away (it was broken); **ǩúr-pa nyám** (to send something) by (with) a cooly. — *mnyam-méd*, *mnyam-brál* unequalled, matchless; *mi mnyám-pa* 1. unequal, 2. uneven. — *ṕyag* (or *lag*) *γnyis mnyám-bżag-tu yód-pa* both hands laid together on the stomach, *mnyám-bżag ṕyág-rgya-čan* id. — *mnyam-pa-nyid*, **समता**, equality, parity; impartiality, justice.

མཉེད་པ་ *mnyéd-pa*, pf. and imp. *mnyes*, fut. *mnye*, *W.* col. **mnyo-če**, 1. **to rub**, between the hands or feet, e.g. ears of corn; one's body *Tar.*; esp. hides, hence **to tan, curry, dress;** *kó-ba mnyés-pa* a tanned hide, dressed leather; **ṡed daṅ nyé-če** *W.* to rub in or into with force. — 2. *Cs.* also: **to coax.**

མཉེན་པ་ *mnyén-pa*, *W.* **nyén-mo**, **flexible, pliable, supple; soft, smooth,** of the voice frq.; of the mind *Dzl.*; *mnyén-par byéd-pa* to make soft, smooth, flexible, *˳gyúr-ba* to become soft, of the skin etc. *Med.*; *mnyen-mnyél-ba* to make soft by tanning *Sch.* — *mnyen-mnyés γṡin-pa* to caress, to fondle *Sch.*

མཉེལ་བ་ *mnyél-ba* 1. also *γnyél-ba*, **to tan, to dress** (hides) *Sch.* — 2. resp. for *ṅál-ba* **to get tired** *Pth.*

མཉེས་པ་ *mnyés-pa*, resp. for *dgá-ba*, in more recent writings and col. for the *dgyés-pa* of ancient literature, **to be glad, to take delight in,** c c d.; **to be willing, to wish,** often with *ťugs*; *mnyés-par byéd-pa* to make glad, to give pleasure; e.g. to the king by presents *Glr.*, to Buddha by worshipping him *Glr.* — *mnyes-bṡín-pa Lexx.*, *Sch.*: to love much; to be rejoiced at.

མཉོ་མཉོ་ཅན་ *mnyó-mnyo-čan W.* fondling, petting, *ṕrú-gu-la* a child.

རྙ་ལོ་, སྙ་ལོ་ *rnyá-lo*, *snyá-lo*, several wild-growing species of Polygonum *Med.*

རྙང་བ་ *rnyáṅ-ba Cs.* = *bṡál-ba*, **to rinse;** *W.* to suffer diarrhoea, *rnyaṅ-nád* diarrhoea; *rnyáṅ-pa* diarrhetic stool; *rnyáṅ-ma*, *γnyáṅ-ma* id., ni f.

རྙང་རྙིང་ *rnyaṅ-rnyiṅ*, **worn-out clothes, rags** *Cs.*

རྙན་ *rnyan* = *γnyan* wild sheep, **argali.**

རྙབ་རྙབ་པ་ *rnyab-rnyáb-pa* **to seize or snatch together** *Sch.*

རྙས་ *rnyas*, sometimes used for *brnyas.*

རྙི་, སྙི་ *rnyi*, *snyi*, *W.* **nyiu*, *nyíṅ-ṅu** (cf. *rnyoṅ*) 1. **snare,** for catching wild animals, *rnyi ˳dzúg-pa* to lay snares, also fig. — 2. **trap,** *ṕúr-rnyi* mouse-trap (consisting of a flat stone supported by a little stick (*ṕúr-pa*). — 3. **net** *Sch.* (?).

རྙིང་པ་ *rnyíṅ-pa* **old, ancient,** of things, e.g. clothes, *γsar-rnyiṅ* new and old; *sṅár-gyi yi-ge rnyíṅ-pa-rnams* ancient records *Glr.*; *brda-rnyíṅ* the ancient orthography *Zam.*; *lo-rnyin* = *na-niṅ* last year *Wts.*; *draṅ-srón rnyíṅ-pa* the old rishi, i.e. the well-known, of long standing, opp. to a new-comer *Dzl.* — *rnyíṅ-ba* vb., pf. *brnyiṅs*, to grow old, *gos brnyiṅs* old clothes, *lham brnyiṅs* old shoes *Lex.*; *rnyiṅ-bar ˳gyúr-ba* id.; *rnyiṅ-bar byéd-pa* to wear out or away in a short time *Dzl.*

རྙིང་མ་ *rnyíṅ-ma*, n. of the most ancient sect of Lamas, clothed in red, v. *Köpp.*; *Schl.* 72; *rnyín-ma-pa* one belonging to this sect.

རྙིད་པ་ *rnyid-pa*, pf. *brnyid*, (*b*)*rnyis*, fut. *gnyid*, 1. **to wither, to fade,** also fig. — 2. **to grieve,** (vb. n.) *Sch.*

རྙིལ་, སྙིལ་ *rnyil*, *snyil*, *so-rnyil*, **the gums.**

རྙིལ་བ་ *rnyil-ba* v. *snyil-ba.*

རྙེད་པ་ *rnyéd-pa* I. vb., pf. *brnyed*, *brnyes*, fut. *brnyed*, (**लाभ**) **to get, obtain, acquire; to meet with, find,** *B.*, *C.*, frq.; *gáṅ-*

ཉ

*nas rnyed* where did you get that? *Dzl.*, also: whence shall I get it? *Dzl.*; *mi rnyéd-du mi rúṅ-ṅo* it must be got or procured by all means *Dzl.*; *ṅas rnyed* I obtain; *rnyéd-par dká-ba* दुर्लभ difficult to be obtained, found, or met with, frq.; *sdug-bsṅal daṅ bsdós-te čos rnyéd-pa* to purchase the acquisition of religion by suffering tortures *Dzl.*; *zas daṅ skom ma rnyéd-de* having nothing to eat or to drink, frq.; *don rnyéd-pa* v. *don*; *da ni ré-ba rnyéd-do* now my hopes are realized *Dzl.*; *gri rnyéd-pas* as he found a knife *Dzl.*; *skabs rnyéd-pa* to find an opportunity *Dzl.*; *btsál-na yaṅ ma rnyéd-de* not finding it in spite of every search *Dzl.*, (*W.* *ťob-če*).

II. sbst. लाभ **profit, gain, acquisition, property, goods**, *rnyéd-pa máṅ-po rnyed-pa* (or *ťób-če*) to gain much profit; *bdag rnyéd-pa daṅ ldán-na mi dga* if I have got some earnings, he envies me for them; often in conjunction with *grágs-pa* and similar expressions: riches and honour. — *rnyed sdú-ba, rnyéd-pa ṕróg-pa Sch.*: to make booty, to plunder. — *rnyed-bkúr Lex.*, prob. riches and honour. — *rnyed-nor* v. *ťob-nór*.

རྙོག་པ་ *rnyóg-pa* (cf. *nyóg-pa*) vb., pf. *brnyogs*, fut. *brnyog*, 1. **to trouble, to stir up** *Cs.*; also adj.: **thick, turbid.** **ču nyóg-pa** *W.* — 2. **to rub** one's self, *ká-ba-la* against a pillar *Dzl.* (*snyóg-pa*). — **nyóg(-pa)-čan, nyóg-po** *C.*, troubled, turbid, dirty; *rnyóg-pa méd-pa* clear, limpid, *mťso Wdṅ.* — *rnyóg-ma* dirty, muddy water; mud, mire, *rnyóg-ma-čan* muddy, miry.

རྙོགས་ *rnyogs Lt.?* *rnyogs-ťsád* a disease *Med.*

རྙོང་ *rnyoṅ* seems to be the same as *rnyi Lexx.*; *rnyóṅ-ba*, pf. *brnyoṅs*, fut. *brnyoṅ* 1. *Cs.*: 'to ensnare, entrap'. — 2. *Sch.*: 'to stretch out'. I met with *rnyoṅ* in the following expressions, not satisfactorily to be explained either by *Cs.* or by *Sch.*: *rkáṅ-pa rnyoṅ Lex.*; *dku ma rnyoṅs Lex.*; *lus rnyóṅ-ba S.g.*; frq.; *γyal-rnyóṅs S.g.*; *mgul-rgyáb zug daṅ rnyoṅ S.g.*; *rnyoṅs-ťsád Mṅg.*

སྙ་ནང་ *snya-náṅ* v. *γnya-náṅ*.

སྙ་ལོ་ *snyá-lo* v. *rnyá-lo.*

སྙག་པ་ *snyág-pa*, col. for *snyég-pa;* also in *Mil.*

སྙགས་ *snyags Lex.* w.e.; *C.* = *dbyaṅs* music, harmony.

སྙད་ *snyad* **malicious** or **false accusation** or **imputation**, *snyad ˳dzúg-pa* (*W.* **tsug-če**) to bring in an action against, to prosecute; **nyad ḍú-če** *W.*, **nyẹ' kó-wa** *C.* id., esp. to irritate, to provoke another, by accusations; *snyad ˳dágs-pa* id. *Glr.; snyad ˳dág-pa, W.* **dág-če** to clear one's self of an accusation, to refute it; *snyad byéd-pa* c.dat. to use as a pretence or pretext *Glr.*; **nyẹ' čọ'* (or *čẹ'*) *táṅ-wa** *C.*, **nyad-sé tág-če** *Ld.* to weary another by too great punctiliousness, ni f.; **nor-nyád čó-če** *W.* to extort money by false accusations, *la* from; *snyad méd-par* without cause, pretence, or provocation *Thgy.*; **nyád-zer-čan** *W.* one that makes false accusations.

སྙད་པ་ *snyád-pa*, pf. and fut. *bsnyad*, imp. *snyod*, **to relate, to report**, e.g. *lo-rgyús* a story *Pth.*, *rmí-lam* a dream *Dzl.*; *γtam snyád-pa* 1. to speak, state, inform, give notice (*W.* **hun táṅ-če**). 2. *Cs.*: 'to rehearse' (?).

སྙན་ *snyan* 1. resp. **the ear,** *rgyál-poi snyán-du ťos* it came to the king's hearing *Glr.; snyán-du žus* or *brjod* they told or informed him *Pth.; snyán-du zuṅ* listen, pay attention, give ear to! *Pth.; snyán-du ṕul* they sang to him or before him (lit. they made him hear) *Mil.* (cf. sub *snyán-pa*); *snyán-(gyis) γsán-pa* to hear *Mil.*; *snyan-γsán bébs-pa* to give ear to one, to hear one *Cs.*; **nyẹ̄n-žu ˳bul-wa** *C.* to address a superior, to apply to him; *snyan-kúṅ* the ear-hole; *snyan-dbáṅ* the organ of hearing *Cs.*; *snyan-šál* the lap or tip of the ear *Cs.*; *snyan-ṕrá žú-ba* to slander, *mi mi-la* to calumniate one person to another. — 2. = *γnyan* **argali.**

སྙན་པ་ *snyán-pa* (यशस्) 1. sbst. **renown, glory, fame, praise, rumour,** *ḱyód-kyi* *snyán-pa pʻyogs bčur grags* every part of the world rings with thy praise; *deï snyán-pa rgyáṅ-nas tʻos Mil.* his praises are heard far and wide; *čes deï snyán-pa brjód-čiṅ* thus speaking praisingly of him *Mil.*; *čés-pai snyán-pa-la rtén-nas* owing to a rumour of this purport *Mil.*; *čes snyán-pa daṅ grágs-pa čén-po byuṅ* so was said far and near *Mil.*; *deï snyán-du* to his praise *Mil.* (cf. *snyan*). — 2. adj., *W.* **nyán-po**, **well-sounding,** sweet to hear, of voice, words etc.; **tʻsor-náṅ-la nyán-po* W.* pleasant to the ear; also: *dge-slóṅ dbyaṅs ráb-tu snyán-pa* a monk having a well-sounding voice *Dzl.*; *tʻsig snyán-par* with pleasant words *Dzl.*; *snyán-pai tʻsig-gis* id.; **low,** not loud; *snyan-skád* also *C.*: elegant, well-sounding, poetical language; *mi snyán-pa* 1. unharmonious; 2. offensive, insulting, *gaṅ žig bdág-la rtsód-čiṅ mi-snyán-brjod* he who in a dispute says to me insulting words; *mi-snyán-par zér-ba dáṅ-du lén-pa* to put up with, to pocket offensive remarks. 3. lamentable, *skad mi snyán-pa zér-ba* to utter lamentable cries, plaintive tones, also of animals, *Dzl.*; *γtam-snyán(-pa)* 1. good, joyful news, glad tidings, *byéd-pa* to bring them *Dzl.*, *Mil.* 2. a pleasing talk, conversation *Cs.* (?) — *snyan-grágs* v. *grágs-pa.* — *snyan-rgyúd* oral instruction of the Lamas, = *bka-rgyúd.* — *snyan-(d)ṅág(s)* v. *ṅag.* — 3. vb. **to praise, extol, glorify,** *stód-čiṅ snyán-par grágs-te* he extolled him in songs of praise *Dzl.* (?)

སྙབ་པ *snyáb-pa* **to smack** with the lips *Sch.*

སྙམ་པ *snyám-pa* 1. vb. **to think, suppose, fancy, imagine,** *bdág-čag riṅ-po-če btaṅ* (better: *γtaṅ*) *snyám-mo* we think we shall give jewels *Dzl.* ༢༥, 16.; *ṅa lčeb dgos snyám-nas* thinking, I must seek death (v. *lčéb-pa*) *Pth.*; *yón-tan daṅ ldán-par snyám-ste* fancying to be possessed of excellent qualities *Dzl.* — 2. sbst. **thought, sense, mind, feeling,** *čos byás-na snyám-pa yóṅ-gin γda* (cf. *na* III., 2) we have a mind to renounce the world *Mil.*; similarly: *ʼjigs-so snyám-pa yod re-skán* I am far from any thought of fear *Mil.*; most frq. *snyám-du bsams* he thought in his mind; *snyam-byéd*: *pʻan snyam-byéd kyaṅ* though one may imagine that it will help *Med.*; *skyúg-pa, brduṅs, dkris snyam-byéd* there arises a feeling like that of nausea, like that of being beaten, of being (tightly) wrapt up, *Med.*

སྙི *snyi* v. *rnyi.*

སྙི་བ *snyí-ba* 1. adj., also *snyi-bo, snyí-mo, snyin-po Cs.*, **nyin-te* W.*, **soft, smooth,** to the touch; **tender, delicate,** of the skin; **easily broken** or **injured; loose, crazy,** not durable, not strong or stout, of cloth, ropes etc.; not hard or tough, **tender,** of meat, rendered so by beating or boiling. — 2. sbst. **softness.** — 3. n. of a plant.

སྙི་ཕུལ *snyi-pʻúl* corn of luxuriant growth *Sch.* (?)

སྙི་མ *snyi-ma* prov. for *snyé-ma*; also *Glr.*

སྙི་ཤང་ཀ་ཏྱ *snyi-śaṅ-ka-tya*, and *snyi-śaṅ-gur-rta*, names of mountains in Nepal.

སྙིགས་པ *snyigs-pa* **degenerated, grown worse** *Cs. snyigs-ma* (कषाय) 1. **impure sediment,** *már-gyi* in butter; *daṅs snyigs ˳byéd-pa* to separate the clear (fluid) from the sediment *Med.* — 2. the degenerated age (iron age), prop. *snyigs-(mai) dus.*

སྙིང་ *snyiṅ* (हृद) **the heart** 1. physically, also *snyíṅ-ka, snyiṅ-ga*, resp. *tʻugs (-ka)*; also **the breast;** **nyiṅ-ka pʻár-ra rag* W.* I feel my heart palpitate; *snyiṅ ˳dár-žiṅ ˳gul* the heart trembles (with fear) *Domaṅ*; *bdág-gi lús-kyi snyiṅ ltar γčes* as dear to me as my own heart *Glr.* — 2. **intellectually: the mind,** *snyiṅ dgá-ba,* ***snyiṅ bdé-ba*** gladness, cheerfulness; *snyiṅ* ***daṅ mig*** *˳pʻróg-pa* to transport, to ravish ***Sch.***; **courage,** *snyiṅ ma čuṅ čig* be not afraid! sentiment, feeling, will, **nyiṅ sóg-po čó-te ma čag* W.* I have not broken it wilfully; **kʻa daṅ nyiṅ ma ḍé-te* W.* **hypocritical;** **nyiṅ-sém dáṅ-po* W.* sincere, **candid; in a more general sense:** ***snyiṅ γdón-gyis bslus*** the heart is infatuated by a demon *Glr.*; even madness may be attributed to the heart *Do.* — *snyiṅ-nas* 1. heartily, zealously, earnestly, e.g. looking for or to a thing *Dzl.*; *snyiṅ ťág-pa-nas* with all one's heart, most earnestly, devoutly, e.g. to say one's prayers *Thgy.* 2. actually, really, *ḱoṅ snyiṅ-nas mi ₒbyiṅ-ba yin* really he does not sink! (the water actually bears him) *Mil.* 3. v. *snyiṅ-po.*

**Comp. and deriv.** *snyiṅ-ku* v. *nyiṅ-ḱu.* — *snyiṅ-ḱáms* **courage** *Sch.* — **nyiṅ-ṭ́ág ḱol** *W.* my heart's blood is boiling (with anger etc.) — *snyiṅ-dgá* v. above. — *snyiṅ-čan* **courageous, spirited** *Ld.* — **nyiṅ-č́u žug** *W.* **afflicted with dropsy in the pericardium,** hydrocardia. — *snyiṅ-rje,* resp. *ťúgs-rje* (करुणा) **kindness, mercy, compassion,** *mi-la snyiṅ-rje sgóm-pa* to commiserate, to pity a person *Mil.*; *snyiṅ-rjes ḱyáb-pa* id. with respect to a great number of beings, to embrace with affection *Dzl.*; *snyiṅ-rjes nón-te* overpowered by compassion; **nyiṅ-že ťsór-če** *W.* to have compassion; *snyiṅ-rje-čan, snyiṅ-rje daṅ ldán-pa* compassionate, merciful *Dzl.*: *snyiṅ-rje-skad* lamentation, a cry of compassion *Dzl.*; *snyiṅ-rje-mo:* 1. *ḱyod snyiṅ-rje-mo raṅ žig ₒdug* you are much to be pitied *Mil.* 2. col.: **dearest, most beloved, amiable, charming;** also *snyiṅ-rje* for *snyiṅ-rje-mo, snyiṅ-rje mdzá-bo* my poor little friend. — *snyiṅ-nyé-ba,* col. **nyiṅ nyé-mo**, **friendly, amicable, loving, affectionate; friend; friendship,** *snyiṅ-nye bú-mo* a woman connected by friendship with, a woman, the friend of (a sick person mentioned) *Lt.* — *snyiṅ-γtam* **a confidential speaking,** for exhortation, consolation, or encouragement; *brtsé-bai snyiṅ-γtam* affectionate exhortation *Glr.*; *p̔án-pai snyiṅ-γtam* useful admonition etc. *Mil.* — *snyiṅ-stobs* **courage.** — *snyiṅ-ₒdód-pa* **to wish, to desire, to long for,** *za-snyiṅ-ₒdód-pa* to wish to eat, to be craving for food *Thgy.*; *ₒgro-snyiṅ-ₒdód-pa* to wish to go. — *snyiṅ-rdúṅ-ba* palpitation of heart *Sch.* — **nyiṅ daṅ* (etymol. dubious) *čó-če** *W.* c.d. to **interest one's self for, to take an interest in.** — *snyiṅ-sdúg W.* **liked, beloved; darling, favourite,** e.g. a child; *nyiṅ-dúg šig dug** *W.* he is a general favourite; **ṅa di nyiṅ-dúg čo dug** *W.* I am very fond of this, it is my favourite (pursuit etc.); but *snyiṅ-ma-sdúg* bad people *Mil.* — *snyiṅ ná-ba* 1. = *snyiṅ-nád.* 2. **'heart-sickness', grief,** on account of injury suffered from others, curable only by indemnity paid or revenge taken. — *snyiṅ-nád* **disease of the heart.** — *sniṅ-po* (सार, गर्भ) **the chief part, main substance, quintessence,** e.g. the cream of the milk *Med.*; the soft part of a loaf, the wick of a lamp *Dzl.*; frq. fig.: the main substance of a doctrine, a book etc., *don-snyiṅ ₒbyin-pa* to give a summary, the sum and substance (of a writing); *séms-čan tams-čád saṅs-rgyás-kyi snyiṅ-po-čan yin-na* if all beings have the pith and essence of the nature of Buddha in themselves *Thgy.* 5, 8; the Ommanipadmehūm is called the *snyiṅ-po* of religion *Glr.*; *snyiṅ-po-méd-pa* worthless, null, void, *snyiṅ-pos dbén-pa* id. *Tar.* 185, 2; *de-bžiṅ-γšégs-pai snyiṅ-po* the spirit of Tathāgata *Was.*; *snyiṅ-po-byaṅ-čúb-* (or *byaṅ-čub-snyiṅ-po*) *-la mčís-pa* to become Buddha *Thgy.*; *srog(-gi) snyiṅ(-po) ₒbúl-ba Mil.* frq. to offer one's heart's blood, to pledge one's own life. — *snyiṅ-rtsa* (col.) the great veins connected with the heart, perh. = *snyiṅ-luṅ.* — *snyiṅ-rtse* the tip or apex of the heart, mentioned by *Mil.* as a particular dainty (perh. only by way of a jest). — *snyiṅ-brtse-ba,* resp. *ťúgs-brtsé-ba,* vb., also sbst. and adj., not much differing from *snyiṅ-rje*: **love, pity** etc. frq.; *Dzl.: bú-la snyiṅ-brtse-nas*; *ťams-čád-la snyiṅ-brtse-ba yín-na*; *de-dag-la snyiṅ-brtse-bai p̔yir*; *snyiṅ-brtse-bai sems skyés-te* etc. — *snyiṅ-ťsim* **contentment, satisfaction,** sometimes also pleasure felt at the misfortune of others *Pth.*, *snyiṅ-ťsim ₒdébs-pa* to manifest such an enjoyment. — *snyiṅ-ťsil* the fat about the heart *Cs.* — *snyiṅ-žo-ša* v. *žó-ša.* — *snyiṅ-rús,* resp. *ťugs-rús* (acc. to *Mil.: snyiṅ-gi rús-pa ťón-par gyis* let energy and diligence arise in you); **firmness of mind** (heart) i.e. 1. **diligence, zeal, perseverance**

*Mil.* and *C.* 2. **courage** *W.* — *snyiṅ-re-rjé* (*snyiṅ-rje*, with *re* placed between, v. *re*) **o the poor man!** the poor people! either standing absolute or as predicate to a preceding noun: *ₒdi-rnams snyiṅ-re-rjé* these (people) are indeed much to be pitied *Mil.*; *kyod-raṅ . . . ₒdzín-pa snyiṅ-re-rjé* you (would) comprehend that? poor wretches that you are! *Mil.*; even as an adjective: *séms-ċan snyiṅ-re-rjé* the poor creatures! frq.; *snyiṅ-re-rjé-bai sdig-ċan* the lamentable sinner! — *snyiṅ-rluṅ Sch.*: 'low spirits, melancholy, mental derangement'; I met with it only in *Mil.*, as signifying **heart-grief, deep sorrow,** e.g. *snyiṅ-rlúṅ drág-po ldaṅ* great affliction is caused. — *snyiṅ-lam-na Sch.*: 'in one's mind'. — **snyiṅ-lúṅ** *W.* the heart, liver, and lights of a slaughtered animal, the **pluck.** — *snyiṅ-śúbs* **pericardium.**

སྙིང་བ་ *snyiṅ-ba W.* **to swell** (in water), **lum nyiṅ soṅ** the soaked barley has swollen.

སྙིད་པ་ *snyid-pa* prob. = *rnyid-pa Pth.*

སྙིད་མོ་ *snyid-mo Lex.* the sister of a woman's husband.

སྙིན་པ་ *snyin-pa*, *snyin-po*, *snyin-te*, v. *snyi-ba.*

སྙིམ་པ་(གང་) *snyim-pa(-gaṅ)* a measure for liquids, as well as for flour, grain and the like, as much as may be taken up by both hands placed together.

སྙིལ་ *snyil* = *rnyil.*

སྙིལ་བ་ *snyil-ba*, or *rnyil-ba*, pf. and fut. *bsnyil* (cf. *nyil-ba*) 1. **to pull** or **throw down, to break down, to destroy,** houses, rocks etc.; *pyé-mar snyil-ba* to reduce to powder *Lex.*, *Sch.* — 2. *pyir* (*bskrad*) *snyil-ba Lex.*; *Sch.*: **to expel, banish, exile.**

སྙུག་པ་ *snyúg-pa*, also *smyúg-pa*, pf. *bsnyugs*, fut. *bsnyug*, **to dip in, to immerge.**

སྙུག་མ་ *snyúg-ma*, more frq. *smyúg-ma*, **reed, rush, bulrush**; *snyúg-gu* reed-pen; *snyúg-bzo* basket-work of reeds *Pth.*; *snyúg-śiṅ* bamboo.

སྙུགས་ *snyugs C.* **duration, continuity, time** *Cs.*; **nyúg-ċen** *C.* continual; *snyugs-sriṅs Lex.* protracted, lengthened out.

སྙུགས་སྦྲུལ་ *snyugs-sbrúl* **lizard** *Sch.*

སྙུང་ *snyuṅ*, resp. for *nad*, *W.* **nyuṅ-zúg**, **disease, illness, sickness,** *btsún-pai skú-la snyuṅ mi mṅá-am* is your Majesty well? *Glr.*; *snyúṅ-du mdze byuṅ Glr.* leprosy arose to him as a disease, he was attacked with the disease of leprosy; *snyuṅ mdzes btab* id. *Tar.*; *snyúṅ-γži* = *nád-γži.*

སྙུང་བ་ *snyúṅ-ba* I. vb., pf. *bsnyuṅs*, fut. *bsnyuṅ*, 1. **to make less, to reduce, to diminish**; *Sch.*: **to disparage.** — 2. resp. **to be ill, sick, indisposed;** *tugs snyúṅ-bai mi* people that are disagreeable, annoying to others *Mil.*

II. sbst. 1. the state of being ill, **illness, indisposition.** — 2. *W.* **awl, pricker, punch;** also *snyúṅ-bu.*

སྙུན་ *snyun* = *snyuṅ*, *skú-la snyún-gyis bzuṅ* he was taken ill *Dzl.*; *snyun ₒdri-ba Mil.*, *rmé-ba Sch.*, *γsól-ba Dzl.*, *snyún-dri žú-ba Mil.*, to inquire after a person's health; to wait on, to pay one's respects *Dzl.* ༢༤༥, 16.

སྙུན་པ་ *snyún-pa*, pf. and fut. *bsnyun*, **to be ill,** to labour under a disease.

སྙེ་ཐང་ *snye-taṅ* a village and convent near Lhasa.

སྙེ་བ་ *snyé-ba*, pf. *bsnyes*, fut. *bsnye*, imp. *snye* **to lean against, to rest on,** *rtsig-pa-la* against a wall; **to lie down, recline, repose on,** *mál-stan-la* on a bed, *sṅás-la* on a cushion or pillow; **gyáb-nye** col. a support or cushion for leaning against with one's back. — *snye-kri* v. *kri.* — *snye-stán*, *snye-ₒból* **pillow** or **cushion** to rest on.

སྙེ་མ་ *snyé-ma*, also *snyi-ma*, 1. **ear** of corn. 2. **corn forming ears** (v. *ljáṅ-pa*), *snyé-ma mig-ċan* fruitbearing ears, **nye-lóṅ** *W.* empty ears; **nye-ma ton** *W.* the corn blows, is in flower; **nye ċág-pa** *C.* to thrash, **nye-ċág-gi dhu'-ḍo** an animal used for treading out the grain. — *snye-dkár* diseased ears. — *snye-mgó* = *snyé-ma* 1.

སྙེག(ས)་པ་ *snyeg(s)-pa*, pf. *bsnyegs*, fut. *bsnyeg*, imp. *snyog(s)*, *W.* **nyág-če**, 1. c. accus. **to hasten** or **run** after, **to pursue,** frq.; also with *ṙjés-nas*, *ṙjés-su*, *ṙjés-bžin-du*, *ṗyi-bžin-du*; *raṅ-ₒgró-sa snyogs* hasten towards your aim! *Mil*; *snyég-sar snyogs Lex.* id.; *bsnyég-tu*, or *snyégs-su ₒdoṅ-ba* to walk hastily, to make haste or speed *Dzl.* — 2. **to overtake,** *snyégs ma nús-pas* not being able to reach *Dzl.* — 3. c. dat. **to hasten** to some place, *ltád-mo-la* to the play *Mil.*; **to rise,** *γnám-la* rising up to heaven, as a flame, *Glr.*, a cedar *Wdṅ.*, frq.; **to strive** or **struggle for, to aspire to,** *nór-la* riches, *sde-čén-la* increase of territory, *żiṅ-ḱams-bzáṅ-la* the region of eternal bliss. — *snyég-ma* pursuer *Dzl.*

སྙེགས་ *snyegs* **straight, stretched out** *Sch.*

སྙེང་བ་ *snyéṅ-ba* 1. inst. of *rmyéṅ-ba*, to stretch *Mil.* — 2. also *snyéṅs-pa*, resp. for *ₒjigs-pa*, vb. (pf. *bsnyeṅs*, fut. *bsnyeṅ*) and sbst., *rgyál-pos ma snyeṅs šig* do not be afraid of the king! *Dzl.*

སྙེད་ *snyed* I. the **crupper** attached to a saddle *Sch.* II. = *tsam*: 1. *ₒdi-snyéd (-čig)*, *de-snyéd(-čig)* **so much, so many,** frq.; also for: **how many!** e.g. . . . *yón-tan ₒdi-snyéd mṅao* how many excellent qualities has . . .! *Dzl.*; *či-snyéd*, *ji-snyéd* how much? how many? also *snyed* alone (examples v. sub *byé-ma*). — 2. after round sums: **about, near,** *stoṅ snyed*, also *stoṅ ji-snyéd Mil.* about a thousand.

སྙེན་པ་ *snyén-pa Cs.*: 1. **to come** or **go near, to approach,** gen. *bsnyén-pa*. — 2. **to gain, to procure,** inst. of *rnyéd-pa*(?).

སྙེམ(ས)་པ་ *snyém(s)-pa* 1. vb., pf. *bsnyems*, **to be proud** or **arrogant, to boast,** *ṅa-rgyál snyéms-pas* to be swollen with pride *Dzl.*; *mťu-rtsál* (to be proud) of one's strength *Dzl.* — 2. sbst. **pride, haughtiness,** *snyém-pa-čan* prideful, proud, *snyems-čúṅ* 1. prideless, humble, affable, kind, col. **nyom-čúṅ**, and **nyam-šúṅ**. 2. poor, indigent *C.*

སྙེས་ *snyes* v. *snyé-ba*.

སྙོ་བ་ *snyó-ba* sometimes for *smyó-ba*.

སྙོག་པ་ *snyóg-pa*, or *bsnyóg-pa*, secondary form of *snyég-pa*, esp. when signifying **to wish earnestly, to crave** for or **lust** after, also *ḱa-snyóg-pa Cs.*

སྙོད་ *snyod*, = *go-snyód*, **caraway.**

སྙོད་པ་ *snyód-pa* I. pf. *bsnyad*, 1. **to draw out** and **twist,** as in spinning *Stg.*, *C.* — 2. *Cs.*: **to tell, to relate,** = *snyád-pa*.

II. pf. *bsnyod*, *bsnyos*, fut. *bsnyod*, **to feed,** to give to eat and to drink, *ccapir.*

སྙོན་པ་ *snyón-pa* I. 1. pf. and fut. *bsnyon*, **to deny, to disavow dishonestly,** *Dzl.* ༢༩, 2; ༢༠, 8 **to assert falsely,** *snyon byéd-pa Glr.* — 2. **nyon dú-če** *W.* is said to signify the same as **nyad du-če** v. *snyad*.

II. inst. of *smyón-pa*.

སྙོབ་པ་ *snyób-pa*, pf. *bsnyabs*, fut. *bsnyab* 1. **to stretch out,** e.g. the hand, *Lex.* — 2. *W.* **to reach,** by stretching one's self out, **to arrive at,** **nyob mi ťub**.

སྙོབས་ *snyobs* = *snyoms Lex.*

སྙོམ(ས)་ *snyom(s)*, *Lex.* = तन्द्रि I. 1. **weariness, lassitude; laziness, idleness,** *lus snyoms-lčí-ba yin* one is exhausted and dull *Med.*; *snyóms-la ṅúl-ba* to be tired and exhausted. — *snyóms-las* 1. **indolence, unconcern,** esp. religious indifference, *Glr.*; *snyóms-las byéd-pa*, or *drán-pa Glr.* to be lazy, indolent, indifferent; *snyóms-las-čan* adj. lazy etc. *Glr.* — 2. *Sch.*: an idle person(?).

II. col., also *Mil.*, inst. of *snyems*.

སྙོམ(ས)་པ་ *snyóm(s)-pa* I. vb., pf. *bsnyoms*, fut. *bsnyom*, to make even 1. **to level,** *γnas* a place, *Dzl.*; *sá-la snyóms-pa* to level with the ground, **to demolish** *Dzl.* — 2. *ṗan-tsun* **to equalize** different things, **to arrange uniformly,** *zas* one's meals, i.e. not cold and warm promiscuously *Thgy.*; **to level, to reduce** to an equality of condition, *ltogs-ṗyúg* rich and poor (according to the principles of the communists) *Glr.*; similarly *bú-lon Tar.* 74; *ťams-čád-la snyóms-na bdag kyaṅ snyóms-par mdzad* ₒtsal I wish to be treated fairly like any other people *Dzl.* ༧༥; *k̔á-lo snyóms-pa* to regulate (a matter), **to manage** or **direct** (a business) **justly**, uniformly *Glr.* — *snyóm-du med*, he has not his like *Dzl.*; **tag nyóm-la** *C.* always uniformly, without variation.

II. sbst., also *btaṅ-snyóms*, evenness, or **calmness of mind, equanimity**, *snyóms-par ₒjúg-pa* to assume it, = *sems mnyám-par bžág-pa*, v. *mnyám-pa*. — *snyoms-ₒjúg byéd-pa* 1. id., 2. euphem. for *ₒk̔rig-pa spyód-pa*. — *mgo-snyóms* impartial *Mil.* — *snyóms-po* equal, even, uniform, e.g. in every part equally thick.

སྙོལ་བ་ *snyól-ba*, pf. and fut. *bsnyal* (cf. *nyál-ba*) 1. **to lay down; to bed** a person, to assign him his couch or bed *Pth.*; **ṭú-gu mál-du** *C.* (to lay) a child on its bed, to put to bed; **nyál-te žág-pa** *C.*, *bór-ce W.*, to lay or put down, opp. to *laṅ-te* etc., to set or place upright, to set on end, e.g. a book. — 2. fig.: **me nyál-wa** *C.* to put the fire to bed, i.e. to scrape it together and cover it with ashes; *spu snyól-ba* to smooth down the bristling hair, i.e, to abate one's anger; *čaṅ, žo, snyól-ba* to allow the beer to ferment, the milk to curdle, in a state of rest (undisturbed).

བརྙ་བ་ *brnyá-ba*, pf. *brnyas*, 1. **to borrow** *Dzl.* ༢༥༠, 12. 14; ༢༥༢, 6. 2. **to seize** by force, **to usurp** *Sch.*

བརྙང་ *brnyaṅ Lex.* prob. = *rnyáṅ-pa*.

བརྙད་པ་ *brnyád-pa* for *bsnyád-pa*.

བརྙན་པ་ *brnyán-pa Cs.* **to borrow**; *brnyán-po* borrowed; also fig.: borrowed, reflected, *γzugs-brnyán* (*Lex. snaṅ-brnyán*) a reflected image **प्रतिबिम्ब** frq.; also image, picture in general; even a little statue *Pth.*; *rmi-lam-gyi γzugs-brnyán* vision, visionary image; *sgra-brnyán*, **प्रतिश्रुत** reflected sound, echo; *mgo-brnyán* a mask, a fearful apparition *Thgr.*, *mgo-brnyán sér-po Schl.* 234. — *p̔yag-brnyán* servant *Cs.* — *brnyán-poi gos Cs.*: 'a garment marked with the figures (sic) of the rainbow' — *brnyán-poi brnyas Lex.* interest for a loan, rent for things borrowed *Sch.*

བརྙབས་པ་ *brnyábs-pa* **diligence, painstaking; to take pains** *Sch.*

བརྙས་པ་ *brnyás-pa* I. borrowed, v. *brnyá-ba*.

II. 1. **to despise, contemn** c. dat., frq.; *ma brnyás šig* do not despise! *Dzl.*; *brnyas smád-pa* id. *Dzl.* — **contempt**, *brnyás-pa byéd-pa*, *W.* **nya-šé tág-ce**, ccd. to despise, to treat contemptuously, frq.; *brnyas-bčos* (*Thgy. brnyas-čos*) contempt, scorn.

བརྙོངས་ *brnyoṅs* **convenient, suitable** *Sch.*

བསྙིགས་པ་ *bsnyigs-pa* 1. **to return, restore, deliver up** *Cs.* 2. **sediment.**

བསྙུག *bsnyug* full *Sch.*; *skyu-gaṅ bsnyug Lex.* a full draught (?).

བསྙུལ་བ་ *bsnyúl-ba* to wash *Lex.*

བསྙེན་པ་ *bsnyén-pa* 1. **to approach, to come near,** c. dat., also *drúṅ-du*, *k̔ó-boi drúṅ-du bsnyen čig* come to me *Dzl.*; *góm-pa re-ré bór-žiṅ ₒči-ba-la bsnyén-pa ltar* as with every step we come nearer to our death *Thgy.*; **to join, to stick to** a person *Dzl.* — 2. **to propitiate, soothe, satisfy,** a deity *Cs.* — 3. **to accept, receive, admit** *W.*; *bsnyén-par rdzógs-pa* to be ordained, consecrated, frq.; c. *las* by *Tar.* — *dge-bsnyén* v. *dgé-ba*. — *bsnyen-bkúr* **reverence, veneration, respect,** *byéd-pa* to pay one's duty or respect, esp. to the priesthood by various services, *ṅá-la bsnyén-pa byás-te Dzl.* and elsewh., frq., also *bsnyén-žiṅ bkúr-ba Glr.*, and **nyen kúr-ce** *W.*; *bsnyén-bkur žú-ba* to ask permission for performing such services *Mil.* — *bsnyen-bsgrúb* priestly function, religious office, esp. *snags* q. v. — *bsnyen-γnás* fasting, abstinence; *bsnyen-γnás srúṅ-ba*, *W.* **zúm-ce**, to abstain from food, to fast.

བསྙེར་བ་ *bsnyér-ba* to make grimaces or gesticulations *Cs.*



ཉ

བསྙེལ་བ *bsnyél-ba, Lexx.:* resp., **to forget;** *bsnyel-méd* not forgetting or forgetful, mindful; *bsnyel-γsó-ba* to remind, to put one in mind of a thing *Mil. nt.*

བསྙོན *bsnyon* v. *snyon.*

བསྙོར་བ *bsnyór-ba*, *Lex. nas bsnyór-ba*, acc. to *Sch.:* to sift barley.

## ཊ

ཊ *ṭa*, the letter *ṭ*, cerebral *t*, *Ssk.* ट.

ཊཱ་ཀཱ *ṭá-kā*, *Hind.* टका in *W.* imaginary coin, money of account, = 2 paisa or 1 d. — Different from it is

ཊྃ་ཀ, ཊང་ཀ, ཊང་ཁ, ཏང་ཀ *ṭáṅ-ka, ṭaṅ-ka, ṭaṅ-ka, taṅ-ka, Hind.* तङ्का 1. in *C.* ½ rupee = 9 d., v. also *γčod-taṅ* (v. *γčod-pa* comp.). — 2. a gold and silver coin *Tar.* 112, 6. — 3. *W.* **money** in general.

ཏི་ཀེཊ, ཏྲི་ཀེཊ *ti-ked, tri-ked* **card, ticket; postage-stamp.**

## ཌ

ཌ *ḍa*, the letter *ḍ*, cerebral *d*, *Ssk.* ड.

ཌཱ་ཀི *ḍá-ki* (डाकी *Hind.:* 'husband of a Dākini,' *Shaksp.*) in *Mil.* prob. = *Dākini, mkʼá-ₒgro-ma.*

ཌ་མ་རུ, ཌ་རུ *ḍá-ma-ru, ḍá-ru,* (डमरु) a small **tympan** or **drum,** with a handle and two balls fastened to it by a strap.

ཌཱཀ *ḍāk*, gen. **drag**, *Hind.:* डाक, **the post, letter-post.**

ཌཎ་ཌི *dan-ḍi*, *Hind.* डण्डी, **the beam** of a pair of scales; a kind of litter.

## ཏ

ཏ *ta*, 1. the letter t, tenuis, French t. — 2. num. fig.: 9. — 3. inst. of *btags*, v. *ya-btags.*

ཏ་ཀ་རི *tá-ka-ri* (*Hind.* तराकड़ी) common **scales,** *Ld.*

ཏ་ཀུ *tá-ku W.* stick with a hook, hooked cane, **crutch;** **ta-ku-rú-ku* Ld.* **crooked, contracted, crippled.**

ཏ་གིར *tá-gir W.* **bread,** esp. the flat breadcakes of India, commonly called '*chapátee*'; **ču-ta-gir* Ld.* boiled flour-dumplings; **túl-ta-gir** pancakes.

ཏ་བ *tá-ba* (Pers. تابا) gen. **tao* W.* a flat **iron pan** without a handle.

ཏ་བག *tá-bag W.*, *tár-ₒbag C.*, **a plate,** **tá-bag dal-dál* W.*, **ter-tér* C.*, a flat plate, *kor-kór* a deep plate, soup-plate.

དབེར་ ta-bér (spelling?) W. **fence** of boards or laths.

ཏ་ཟིག *ta-zig*, or *ta-zig-yúl*, **Persia**, *ta-zig* (*-pa*) a Persian.

ཏ་ར་ཙེ་ *ta-ra-tsé* (*Pers.* ترازو) W. a small pair of scales, **goldweights.**

ཏ་རེ་ *ta-ré* v. *re.*

ཏ་ལ་ *tá-la* 1. ताल **the palmyra tree,** *Borassus flabelliformis* (not the date-tree *Cs.*) *B.* — 2. In more recent times, and already in *Mil.*, *tá-la* seems to denote **the plantain** or banana tree, *Musa paradisiaca.*

ཏ་ལ་ལ་ *ta-la-la Lex.* **lamp, lantern.**

ཏ་ལའི་བླ་མ་ *ta-lai-blá-ma* (*ta-lai Mong.* ocean, sea), the Dalai Lama, v. *Huc.* II., 155. *Köpp.* II., 120.

ཏག་ཏག *tag-tág W.* the imitative sound of knocking, **tag-tág zer* there is a knock, **tag-tág čó-če* to knock at the door.

ཏང་ *taṅ* **through,** v. *toṅ* and *lteṅ.*

ཏང་ཀུན་ *taṅ-kun* n. of a medicinal herb *Med.*

ཏང་ག *taṅ-ga* v. ཊཾ་ཀ *ṭaṅ-ka.*

ཏཏྐཱ་ལ་ *tatkā-la Ssk.* **the present moment** *Wdk.*

ཏན་དུར་ *tan-dúr Ld.* a sort of hard **cake** or bread, resembling biscuit or rusk.

ཏབ་ཏབ་ *tab-táb* v. *tob-tób.*

ཏར་ཏར་ *tar-tár*, **tar-tár-čó-če* Ld.* to smooth (wrinkles or folds in cloth, paper etc.)

ཏལ་པ་ *tál-pa*, or *tál-ma*, *Cs.*: 'a moment', *Sch.*: 'quick, decisive, penetrating'; *tál-par*, *Cs.* also *tál-mar*, 1. **instantly, immediately, quickly** *C.*, e.g. *soṅ* go without delay! *Lex.* — 2. *Sch.*: **completely, quite through**, *γčód-pa* to hew, to cut (quite through), *ˬbigs-pa* to bore through, to perforate; also *tal ˬbigs-pa.*

ཏལ་བ་ *tál-ba* a tool with holes in it, used by nailers *Sch.*

ཏི་ *ti* 1. num. fig.: 39. — 2. Not originally Tibetan, designating 'water'; this word has found its way into *Ld.*, where it however occurs only in **ká-ti** saliva (water of the mouth), and in **ná-ti** mucus (running from the nose). — 3. v. *spyi.*

ཏཱི་ཀ *ti-ka* (**टीका**) **explanation, commentary.**

ཏི་ཐུག *ti-túg*, (*Sch. γti-tug*) **bad, mean, silly** *Cs.*; **obstinate, stubborn** *Schr.*

ཏི་ནག *ti-nág* **heath-cock** *Sch.*

ཏི་པི་ *ti-pi*(?) *W.* **cap, hat** (from the *Hind.* **तोपी**?).

ཏི་ཕུ་ *ti-p̔u*, *Sch.*: *ti-p̔u mǰug-riṅ* **pheasant.**

ཏི་ཙ་ *ti-tsa Stg.*, *tú-tsa Sch.*, **anvil.**

ཏི་ཚ་ *ti-ts̔a* 1. *tig-ts̔a* **zinc** *Med.*; *ti-ts̔a sér-po* cadmia, calamine (?) *Med.* — 2. a musical instrument, constructed of metal *Sch.*

ཏི་སེ, ཏེ་སེ *ti-se*, *té-se*, the snow-peaks around the lake Manasarowar in *Mṅaris*, which are considered to be the highest and holiest of mountains.

ཏིག *tig* 1. also *tig-tig*, *Lex.* w.e.; *Sch.*: 'certainty, surety; **certain**'. In col. language **tig, ḍig, tiγ, ṭig**, is frq. used for: **to be sure! well, well! very right!** also as an adj.: *nór-dag tig-tig* the right, the lawful heir. Cf. **ˬgrig; tig ltá-če, tig tsam**, *tig-ts̔ád* v. sub *tig.* — 2. *Sik.* the great **hornet.**

ཏིག་ཏ *tig-ta* (from **तिक्तक** the n. of several bitter herbs, e.g. of Gentiana Chirayta) several species of **gentian.**

ཏིག་མེན *tig-mén Cs.*, *tig-tsé Ld.*, the ribands which are wound round the felt-gaiters that cover the lower part of the legs.

ཏིག་ཚ་ *tig-ts̔a* = *ti-tsa.*

ཏིག་རིག *tig-rig Sp.* inst. of *ta-gir.*

ཏིང་ *tiṅ* 1. a small **cup** of brass used esp. in sacrificing. — 2. the sound of metal, **tiṅ zér-ra rag** W. I hear a tinkling.

ཏ

**ཏིང་ངེ་འཛིན་** *tiṅ-ṅe-˳dzin* (**समाधि** *Trigl., Was.* also **समापत्ति**) **contemplation**, profound meditation, perfect absorption of mind, cf. *bsam-γtán*, and *sgóm-pa*; *tiṅ-ṅe-˳dzin byéd-pa Sch.*, gen. *tiṅ-ṅe-˳dzin-du ˳júg-pa* to be absorbed in deep meditation; *tiṅ-ṅe-˳dzin ˳k̔ruṅ* devout meditation takes place; also meton.: the faculty, the power of meditating e.g. *p̔el Mil.*

**ཏིང་རྗིང་** *tiṅ-rjiṅ Sik.* **shrew**(-mouse).

**ཏིང་ཏིང་** *tiṅ-tiṅ* **clean, well-swept** *Ld., Ts.*

**ཏིང་ཏི་ལིང་** *tiṅ-ti-liṅ* **snipe** *Ld.*

**ཏང་(ཏིང་)ཤགས་** *tiṅ (-tiṅ) - šags* little bells moved by the wind *Sch.*

**ཏིབ་རིལ་** *tib-ríl*, resp. *γsol-tib*, **tea-pot**, *zaṅs-tib* a copper tea-pot, *rdza-tib* an earthen tea-pot.

**ཏིམ་པི་** *tim-pi Mil.* goat's leather, kid-leather, from India, dyed green or blue.

**ཏིམ་བུ་** *tim-bu Ts.* **funnel.**

**ཏིལ་** *til* (**तिल**) **sesame,** *til-már* sesame-oil, seed-oil.

**ཏུ་** *tu* 1. num. fig.: 69. — 2. an affix, denoting the terminative case, or the direction to a place, joined to the final consonants g and b; cf. *du, ru, su.*

**ཏུ་པག་** *tú-pag* (*Turk.* توپک) *W.* **gun, musket, fire-lock, fowling-piece,** **gyáb-če** to discharge, fire off; **tú-pag-man** gunpowder.

**ཏུ་རུ་ཀ་** *tu-ru-ka Ma.* **the Turks, Turkomans,** **तुरुष्क**, ترک.

**ཏུ་ཙ་** *tú-tsa* v. *ti-tsa.*

**ཏུ་ལཱ་** *tú-lā* (*Ssk., Hind.*) **a balance, pair of scales,** *C. *tú-la tég-pa** to weigh.

**ཏུག་གིན་འདུག་** *túg-gin ˳dug* 'cannot' *Sch.* (?)

**ཏུག་རིང་** *tug-riṅ*, or *tug-čúm*, prob. also *tug-čém, Cs.:* a wooden rattle's sound or noise; *Sch.* also: the trotting of horses heard in the distance; *tug-riṅ-čan Stg.* noisy (?).

**ཏུབ་** *tub, tub γčig-tu rgyúd-do?*

**ཏུབ་ཏུག་** *tub-túg Lex.* w.e.; *Sch.:* 'either — or, whether I be able (to do it) or not' (?).

**ཏུར་བ་** *túr-ba* (?) *W.* **to darn** (stockings).

**ཏུར་རེ་** *túr-re* **clear, distinct.** syn. to *wál-le*; *yid túr-re ˳dug* it is clear to my mind; *túr-re bzuṅ Mil.* prob. watch it! have a sharp eye upon it! *že-sdáṅ laṅs dogs túr-re gyis Mil.* take care lest an emotion of anger arise in your mind! *túr-gyis sad Mil* prob.: he awakes, stirs, is evidently roused; *túr-re-ba Glr.*; adj. (or abstract noun), *ṙjed-yeṅ-méd-par túr-re-ba* clear, firm with regard to perceptions, opinions etc., without omission or digression.

**ཏེ་** *te* 1. num. fig.: 99. — 2. an affix denoting the gerund, and used after the final letters *n, r, l, s* (v. Grammar), to be translated by the participle in ing, or sentences beginning with when, after, as etc.; also used as a finite tense (though seldom in *B.*), and in that case followed by *˳dug* or *yod*, or also without these words: **dád-de ˳dug** I sit *W.*; *˳gró-ba yin-te Mil.* I go.

**ཏེ་པོར་** *té-por Lex.* = *légs-par*; *Sch.:* very, really, actually.

**ཏེ་བོར་** *té-bor Sch.* constantly, continually.

**ཏེ་སེ་** *té-se* v. *ti-se.*

**ཏེག་པ་** *tég-pa*, imp. *tog, C., W.,* = *˳tégs-pa*, **to pack up, put up; to put in** or **into,** **am-bág-la** into one's bosom; **tag-ṭul** or **ṭug** preparations for a journey, **taṅ-če* W.* to make.

**ཏེའུ་** *teu? Ld.-Gir.* (*Schl.* f. 25, b); *teu sér-po; Mil.* 59, 4 of my edition; *Lex.: teu šiṅ-k̔ri*, where *Sch.* translates: a square table.

**ཏེལ་པ་** *tél-pa Cs.:* an instrument for burning *Med.*; *lčágs-tel* such an instrument of iron *Cs.*; *sprá-tel Lt.?*

**ཏོ་** *to* 1. num. for 129 — 2. affix added to certain verbs, when they terminate a sentence.

**ཏོ་ཏོ་ལིང་ལིང་** *to-to-liṅ-liṅ W.*, an adv. denoting a swinging motion;

hence **to-to-liṅ-liṅ sed sé-ce** to play at swinging, to swing.

ཏོ་ལ་ *tó-la* for *tú-lä C.*

ཏོག་ *tog* 1. (केतु *Cs.*: **'the top** of any thing, **a top ornament'**; esp. the button on the cap of Chinese dignitaries, as a mark of distinction; *tog-dkár*, श्वेतकेतु n. of Buddha in paradise (*dga-ldán*) before his incarnation *Ld.-Glr.* 8, a.; *mdúṅ-tog* point, thorn, nail. — 2. for *tog*, and thus prob. also used in *skabs-tog* now, at present *Ld.*

ཏོག་སྒྲ་ *tóg-sgra*, *tóg-tog-sgra Lex.*, a rolling sound *Sch.*, acc. to *Wdṅ.* also a cracking sound.

ཏོག་ཏིལ་ *tog-til* **a bump, a swelling,** by a knock against the head.

ཏོག་ཙེ་ *tóg-tse W.*, *tóg-rtse Lex.*, **hoe, mattock, pickaxe** *W.* (in *C.* *jor*); *tog-lcags* the iron of the hoe, *tog-yu* the handle of it; *tog-leb* a spade (?) *Cs.*

ཏོང་ཏོང་བྱེད་པ་ *toṅ-tóṅ byéd-pa Lex., Sch.*: to perforate; to produce a whirling noise.

ཏོབ་ཅི་ *tob-ci W.* **button,** **tób-ci brgyáb-ce** to button up; cf. *tób-cu*; (buttons are not in general use in Tibet).

ཏོབ་ཏོབ་སྨྲ་བ་ *tob-tób smrá-ba* to talk confusedly *Sch.*; *W.*: **tab-táb**, or **tab-tób ma co** keep your temper! do not talk with such agitation!

ཏའུ་ལོ་ *tou-lo* **polecat** *Sch.*

ཏོལ་ *tol? Mṅg. bem-tól? Sch. tol-ycód-pa* = *tal-ycód-pa* q.v.

ཏྲམ་པ་ *trám-pa* hard (of rare occurrence); *sa-trám*, *rus-tram*, *rtsa-tram*, *tram-dkár*, *tram-nág*, are different species of gout *Med.*

ཏྲི་ཀེད་ *tri-ked* v. *ṭi-ked.*

ཏྲི་ཤུ་(ལ་) *tri-šu(-la)*, from त्रिशूल trident *Wdk.*

ཏྲེ་ཏྲེ་ཧོ་ *tre-tre-ho* (by the context) a dangerous disease of the stomach or a serious symptom of it *Pth.*

ཏྲེ་བ་ཅན་ *tré-ba-can* coloured *Sch.*

ཏྲེ་སམ་ *tré-sam* a medicine in the shape of a powder *Med.*

ཏྲོན་ *tron* **diligence, industry** *Cs.*; *tron byéd-pa* to be diligent, to exert one's self.

གཏག་གཏོང་ *ytag-ytoṅ Lex.* w.e.; *ytag-ytoṅ-ba* to disperse *Sch.*

གཏང་རག་ *ytaṅ-rág* **thanks, thanksgiving,** and prob. also thank-offering, esp. rendering thanks to a deity; *ytaṅ-rág byéd-pa*, *búl-ba Mil., Lt., W.* **có-ce, púl-ce** to render thanks.

གཏད་ *ytad* (v. *ytód-pa*), in the direction of, **towards,** *yyón-gral-du ytad pyín-nas* going towards the left end of the row *Glr.*; **doṅ-tád* W.* directly opposite, just over against.

གཏད་པ་ *ytád-pa* 1. vb, v. *ytód-pa,* also *brtád-pa.* — 2. sbst. **hold, steadiness, firmness,** *ytád-pa-med* it has no hold, no firmness *Mil.*; *ytad-méd cál-ba Zam.* prob. to vacillate, to waver, to be unsteady.

གཏད་སོ་ *ytád-so* a refuge, resource, esp. store of provisions; **tẽ-so žág-pa* C.* to procure such a store.

གཏན་(པ་) *ytán(-pa) Cs.*: 'series, order, system; a bar for a door'; *Sch.* also 'anvil', and 'to lock up'. People from *C.* knew only one signification of *ytán-pa*, viz. **mortar,** = *ytun*; **bar, door-bar** occurs in *sgo-ytán C.* and *W.* But a different word seems to be *ytan*: 1. **order, system,** in the current phrase *ytán-la bébs-pa* to put in order, to arrange, to reduce to a system, *bre-sráṅ* measure and weight *Glr.*, the Tibetan alphabet *Glr.*, the civil law and the canon law *Glr.*, laws, books, = to compose, draw up, write *Glr.*; *raṅ-séms ytán-pa* in a mystic sense: to regulate, compose, and purify the mind *Glr.*; also to fashion, to train *C.*, to set right *Mil.* (Cf. *bsam-ytán.*) — 2. **duration,** perh. also entireness, completeness, hence *ytán-gyi* constant, continual, *ytan-grogs* consort, partner for life *Mil.*; *ytan-méd Sch.*: 'perishable, without duration or continuity'; *ytán-du* 1. **always, continually, for ever,** *ytán-du bzúgs-pa* living there continually *Tar.* 2. **entirely, completely** (which is the usual signification of *ɣtan-du*) e.g. to cut off, to deliver completely; *ɣtán-nas* id.; *ɣtan-k̒rigs* agreement, stipulation, convention, *ɣtan-krigs byéd-pa Mil.*

Note. Owing to its second signification *ɣtan* is often confounded with *brtan(-po)*, or even with *bstan(-pa)*. Not only illiterate people, but well-educated Lamas from *C.* were occasionally doubtful as to the correct spelling of this word.

གཏན་ཚིགས་ *ɣtan-ts̒igs* (*Ssk.* हेतु, *Stg., Do,* ཐེ f. 344 *ɣtan-ts̒igs-kyi de-k̒o-na-nyid bstán-pa* = हेतुतत्त्वउपदेश) 1. **argument,** syllogism *Cs.*; evidence before a court of justice *Dzl.* ༢༢༥, 6. — 2. *Sch.*: **a standing proposition,** indisputable point *Thgy.* (where in my *Ms. brtan-ts̒igs* is erron. written; v. the note to the preceding word). — 3. **logic, dialectics** *Cs.*; *ɣtan-ts̒igs-méd-par smrá-ba* is in *Stg.* the term applied to a kind of *kyál-ka*, evidently: illogical, irrational talk; *ɣtan-ts̒igs-su bžéd-nas Glr.* 96. wishing to clear up, to render evident (?); *ɣtan-ts̒igs-mk̒an* dialectician, logician.

གཏམ་ *ɣtam* (कथा) **talk, discourse, speech,** 1. in a general sense: **tam ċig-pa* C., *tam ċig-ċig* W.*, that is one and the same talk, that means the same; *ɣtam bsdúr-ba* to compare depositions, to examine, to try judicially, **tam-dúr* W.* trial, judicial examination. — 2. **news, tidings, intelligence,** *ɣtám bzáṅ-po* good news; *p̒yis ɣtam mi ˳dug* after which there are no further accounts *Mil.*; **tam šád-ċe** to tell a tale, a story *W.*; **report, rumour, fame,** *de p̒ul zér-bai ɣtam rgyál-pos t̒ós-nas* when the king heard the report that ... had been delivered up *Pth.*; *t̒ag-riṅ-gi ɣtam* fame of remote matters or events; *bdág-gis ɣtám-du t̒ós-na* as I have learned, have been told *Dzl.* — 3. **section, chapter** *Tar.*, frq.

**Phrases.** *ɣtam gléṅ-ba S.O., Dzl., ɣtám-du gléṅ-ba Dzl.* to speak, to converse, to discourse; *ɣtam byéd-pa, smrá-ba, zér-ba* id.; *ɣtam byar ˳groo* I shall go and speak to him *Dzl.*; the genit. preceding *ɣtam* always denotes the person or thing spoken of, not the person speaking; *ċi-ltar gyúr-pai ɣtam byas* he gave an account of the manner how it had happened *Dzl.*; *mt̒ún-pai ɣtam byéd-pa* to negotiate about peace *Glr.*; *c̒os (-kyi) ɣtam byéd-pa* to begin a religious conversation *Mil.*; *na dé-ltar byéd-pai ɣtam mi-la ma lab* do not tell any body that I am doing this *Mil.*; in a similar manner: *mi rúṅ-bai ɣtam bsgrág-go* he shall declare it to be unbecoming *Thgr.*; *p̒a-mái ɣtam dris* he inquired about his parents *Dzl.*; *bú-moi ɣtam t̒os* he heard of the girl *Dzl.*

**Comp.** *ɣtam-rgyúd* **tradition, oral account;** *deï ɣtam-rgyúd* the legend of him. — *ɣtam-ṅán* **ill report,** slander. — *ɣtam-snyán* **joyful news, glad tidings,** *sgróg-pa* to announce *Mil.* — *ɣtam-bsdúr* v. above. — *ɣtám-dpe* a proverb, a saying *Cs.* — *ɣtam-rtsúb* rough speech, **abusive language.** Note. In *W.* **(s)pé-ra** is more in use than **tam**.

གཏམ(ས)་པ་ *ɣtám(s)-pa* 1. adj. **full,** *spú-gri ɣtám(s)-pa* quite full of razors *Thgy.*; also *Lexx.*; more frq. it is spelled *(b)ltám(s)-pa.* — 2. vb. to appoint, to commission, of rare occurrence. — 3. sbst. *Cs.*: a term for a thousand billion, yet v. the remark to *dkrigs-pa.*

གཏའ(མ་) *ɣtá(-ma) Lexx.* (cf. *ɣté-pa*) **pawn, pledge,** *ɣtá-mar ˳júg-pa* to pawn, to give as a pledge, *ɣtá-ma blú-ba* to redeem a pledge *Cs.*; **nór-ta* W.* jewels, precious stones, given as a pledge (*Cs.*: 'pecuniary security, bail'); *mi-ɣta* a hostage *Cs.*

གཏར་བ་ *ɣtár-ba*, with *k̒rag*, **to bleed,** to let blood *Med.*; *ɣtár(-bar) byéd-pa, rtsá-ba-la* from a vein, or also *ɣtár-ga ˳débs-pa* id.

གཏི་ཁེ་ *ɣti-k̒é* a kind of louse *Sch.*

གཏི་ཐུག་ *ɣti-t̒ug* insane, mad *Sch.*, = *ti-t̒ug.*

གཏི་མུག་ *ɣti-mug* (तमस्) **gloom, mental darkness, ignorance, stupidity,** *glén-pa ɣti-mug-ċan* infatuated fools *Dzl.*; *mtsán-mo ɣti-mug-ɣnyid-du soṅ* at night I fell into a profound sleep *Mil.*; in a special sense: the lowest of the three *guṅa* or psychological qualities of animated beings, **सत्त्व, रज, तमस्**, virtue, passion, stupidity, acc. to the Brahminical theory, for which however Buddhism has substituted the three moral categories: *₀dod-čágs, že-sdáṅ, γti-mug*, voluptuousness, anger, inconsiderateness (*Köpp.* I, 33); *γti-mug*, as for example, is the source of falsehoods told with a pretended good intention, *Stg.*; the symbol for it is the pig *Wdṅ.* Note. The philosophical term *ma-rig-pa* is altogether different from *γti-mug.*

**གཏིག(ས)་པ་** *γtig(s)-pa Lex.* **to fall in drops, to drop, to drip.**

**གཏིང་** *γtiṅ, Ld.* **ltiṅ**, **bottom,** *rgyá-mtsoï γtiṅ-dkrugs* he turned up the bottom of the sea; *γtiṅ-du núb-pa* to sink to the bottom *Cs.*; **depth,** hence *γtiṅ záb-po Dzl., γtiṅ riṅ-ba* deep, *γtiṅ nyé-ba* not deep, shallow; *rgyá-mtso-bas γtiṅ-záb-bo* it is deeper than the sea *Dzl.*; *γyáṅ-sa γtiṅ-riṅ-ba* a deep abyss *Thgr.*; *ču-bo γtiṅ-záb-po žig* a deep river *Dzl.* ༢༠༢, 1. (in the third line however *záb-bo* would be the correct reading for *zab-po*); *γtiṅ-zab-ḱyád ḱru-brgyád-pa* eight cubits deep (lit. with regard to depth holding eight cubits) *Dzl.* ༡༢༦, 5; fig. *γtiṅ-nas* from the bottom of the heart, *ṅá-la dád-pa γtiṅ-nas gyis* believe in me with all your heart *Mil.*; *ḱa-grógs* and *γtiṅ-grógs* v. *grogs*; *ḱa-dkar-γtiṅ-nág* white without, and black within (fig.) *Mil.*; the following passage of *Mil.*: *rgyá-mtso čé-la dpe lóṅ-la ḱa-γtiṅ-méd-pai sgom čig gyis*, is not perfectly clear, yet the real sense seems to be: resembling the ocean, be so lost in contemplation, that you do not know any longer a difference between surface and bottom; *γtiṅ-rdó* a stone or piece of lead (*žá-nyei γtiṅ-rdó Pth.*) fastened to a rope, and used as plummet, as anchor, as a clock-weight, as a means for drowning delinquents etc.; **ču nyóg-po-če-la tiṅ med* W.* a very muddy water has no depth; *γtiṅ-čan* deep, *γtiṅ-méd* shallow *Cs.*; also fig. deep, reserved, covert, difficult to fathom, to form an opinion of, and the contrary: shallow, superficial; *γtiṅ-mi-lón C.* of unknown depth; *γtiṅ-dróṅs-pa* fathomed, penetrated, ascertained *C.*

**གཏིབ(ས)་པ་** *γtib(s)-pa* 1. **to be gathering;** of clouds, *sprin-ṕuṅ γtib-pa* thick clouds gathering *Wdṅ.*; *bdug-spós sprin-bžin γtib* incense wafts along like clouds *Glr.*; *mún-pa γtib Lex.*, col. also **nam-ḱa tib-tib yod** cf. *₀tib-pa.* — 2. sometimes for *rdib-pa.*

**གཏིམ་པ་** *γtim-pa* v. *tim-pa.*

**གཏུག་པ་** *γtúg-pa*, pf. *γtugs*, also *btúg-pa*, cognate to *túg-pa*, 1. **to reach, to touch,** *yi-dam-gyi túgs-kar γtúgs-nas* putting or pressing (his forehead) against the breast of the image *Glr.*; *mi žig-gi žábs-la mgó-bos γtúg-pa*, or only *žábs-γtug-pa* to touch as a supplicant a person's feet (or skirt) with the brow, to cast one's self at another's feet, frq.; *btug túg-pa daṅ* was explained: when it (the danger) draws quite near *Ma.*; **to overtake, to reach,** ni f., e.g. *mta* the end *Lex.*; **to meet with, to join** *Tar.* 172, 14. — 2. to bring an action against a person, **to sue** *Sch.*, thus prob. *Dzl.* ༢༢༩, 3, and *Pth.* — 3. = *zád-pa* to be exhausted, to be consumed(?) *Zam. zád-pai γtúgs-pa.*—

Note. Not only *γtúg-pa*, but also many of the following words have b as well as g for their initial letter, and moreover a corresponding form beginning with *t*, of the same or nearly the same signification.

**གཏུན་** *γtun, Sch.* also *rtun*, col. **gog-tún** (spelling dubious) 1. **pestle;** there are small ones, like ours and large ones, in shape of poles, as thick as a man's arm, and about 6 feet long, by means of which the pounding is effected in an excavation made in a rock, called *γtun-ḱúṅ*; *γtun(-gyis) rdúṅ-ba* to pound with a pestle *Dzl.*; *γtún-po* mortar *Cs.*; *γtun-bu, γtun-šiṅ* pestle *Cs.* — 2. **mallet, knocker** *Dzl.*.

**གཏུབ་པ་** *γtúb-pa*, more frq. *btúb-pa*, = *túb-pa*, **to be able,** *ṕyir ₑóṅ-du btúb-pa-am* shall you really be able to come back? *Dzl.*; *mi btúb-pa* very frq. not to be able to prevail upon one's self, **to be unable,** also: **to be unwilling, to have no mind** (to do a thing).

གཏུབ(ས)་པ་ *γtúb(s)-pa, btúb(s)-pa, Ld.* **stúb-če**, = *ₒtúb-pa*, **to cut to pieces, to cut up,** meat, wood etc.; in *W.* also **to mince;** (in *C. btsáb-pa*); *γtubs-spyád* chopper *Sch.*

གཏུམ་པ་ *γtúm-pa* 1. **ferocity, rage;** also adj. **furious;** *ḱró-žiṅ γtúm-la snyiṅ-rje-med* in furious wrath, merciless *Dzl.*; *γdúg-čiṅ γtún-pai ḱlu* a Lu in a deadly rage *Sambh.*; *γtúm-pai sgra sgróg-pa* to roar furiously *Pth.*; *ḱró-γtum-pa* furious with rage *Glr.*; *γtúm-žiṅ rgód-pa* obstinate and unmanageable, of a boy; *γtúm-po Mil., γtúm-čan, γtum-ldán* cruel, fierce, furious *Cs.*; *blá-ma ťugs-γtúm-po ₒoṅ* the Lama grows angry *Mil. nt.*; *γtúm-mo* fem. a fury of a woman *Dzl.* ༢༠༠, 10; *Sch.* also: hangman (?); *rluṅ γtúm-mo Cs.* a furious wind, a hurricane — 2. = *btúm-pa, ₒtúm-pa*, **to veil, to cover; to wrap up,** e.g. the head; with the instr. to wrap up or cover with a thing.

གཏུམ་པོ་ *γtúm-po* 1. v. *γtúm-pa* 1. — 2. चण्ड (hot) in the more developed mysticism the power which meditating saints by dint of long continued practice may acquire of holding back their breath for a great length of time, by which means the air is supposed to be drawn from the *ró-ma* and *rkyáṅ-ma* (two veins, v. *rtsá-ba*) into the *dbú-ma* (*sróg-rtsa, dhú-ti,* aorta?) thus causing a feeling of uncommon warmth, comfort, and lightness inside, and finally even emancipating the body from the laws of gravity, so as to lift it up and hold it freely suspended in the air, *Mil.* frq.; v. also *Tar.* 186, 20; *γtúm-poi bde-dród* the feeling of warmth just mentioned *Mil.*; *γtúm-po ₒbar* the warmth of meditation commences *Mil.* The three above-named veins are symbolically represented by *a-shád*, i.e. the second half of an ཨ, viz. ་, hence *a-šad-γtúm-po* the three veins'-meditation-warmth, *Mil.* — 3. n. of the goddess Durga or Uma.

གཏུར་བུ་ *γtúr-bu Lex.* w.e.; *Cs.* **bag, sack, wallet.**

གཏུལ་བ་ *γtúl-ba* **to grind, to pulverize,** colours, medicinal substances etc.; cf. *ₒťág-pa.*

གཏེ་པ་ *γté-pa W.* (*Ld.* **sté-pa**) *γté-ba, γté-ma C., γtèn-pa Lexx.*, **pawn, pledge, bail** (*Sch.* also: a present); cf. *γtá-ma*; *γteu* id.? hostage? *Tar.*

གཏེར་ *γter* (निधि, कोष) 1. **treasure,** frq. — 2. symb. num. for 9. — *γter-mdzód* **a treasury.** — *γtér-ḱa* **a mineral vein, mine,** *nór-gyi γtér-ḱa rnyéd-pa* to find a mine of precious metals.

གཏོ་ *γto Lt., Thgy.* a magic ceremony for the purpose of averting misfortune; *γto-bčos* id.

གཏོག་པ་ *γtóg-pa* 1. also *btóg-pa, ₒtóg-pa,* **to pluck off, gather, crop, tear out** (one's hair) *Lex.* — 2. v. *se-gol.*

གཏོགས་པ་ *γtógs-pa* **to belong, appertain to; belonging,** *rgyál-poï γdúṅ-la γtógs-pa yin* you belong to the royal blood or family *Dzl.*; *deï náṅ-du mi γtógs-sam* am I not included in them? *Dzl.*; *ₒdzam-bui-gliṅ-la γtógs-pa* belonging to Dzambuling *Glr.*; **di lé-ka daṅ ma tog** *W.* do not meddle with that! *ma-γtógs-pa*, gen. adv. *ma γtógs-par* **except, besides.** — *γtogs-ₒdód Sch.*: 'to love, to like, to wish; a good-for-nothing fellow' (?).

གཏོང་བ་ *γtóṅ-ba*, pf. *btaṅ*, fut. *γtaṅ*, imp. *toṅ* (*W.* **taṅ-če**, imp. **toṅ**) त्यज 1. **to let** a. **to let go,** to permit to go, **to dismiss,** *čii pyir bdág-čag-rnams-kyis γtoṅ* why should we let you go, suffer you (our teacher) to go? **to let escape** (a prisoner) *Dzl.*; **to let loose** (a dog against a person) *Mil.*; **to let go,** to quit one's hold *ma γtoṅ*, col. **ma taṅ** don't let him go, stop him! **to leave, abandon, renounce,** *čos* one's religion; more definitely: *blos γtóṅ-ba*, v. *blo*; *yóṅs-su γtóṅ-ba* to abandon altogether *Dzl.*; to leave off, to abstain from, *γsód-par byá-ba γtóṅ-ba* to leave off killing *Dzl.* b. **to let in, to admit,** *sgó-nas* through the door *Dzl.*, *náṅ-du γtóṅ-ba* to permit to enter. — 2. **to let go,** i.e. to make go, **to send,** *mi* a man, a messenger, very frq.; *°dzam-bui-gliṅ kún-tu btáṅ-nas* he made him go all over the country of Dzambuling *Dzl.*; *skyél-du γtóṅ-ba* to dispatch for conveying (a message); *lén-du γtóṅ-ba* to send (a person) for (a thing); *°tsól-ba btáṅ-ba-las* he sent out searchers (people in search) *Dzl.* ༢༠, 18., unless this passage should be read *°tsól-bar.* — 3. **to let have, to give,** so in *W.* almost exclusively; *sman γtóṅ-ba* to give medicine, *γtóṅ-tsul* the way of giving medicine, for 'a dose' *Med.*; *γtóṅ-p̓od-čan* liberal, bounteous *Mil.*; *γtóṅ-sems-ldan* id. *S.g.*; *γtóṅ-sems* liberality, bounty; **tóṅ zer** he says, give me! he wants to have, he tries to get *W.*; *čós-la γtóṅ-ba* to give a person up to religion, i.e. to destine him for the priesthood, to make him take orders. — 4. **to make, to cause,** e.g. a smoke by lighting a fire *Glr.*; with the termin. **to turn into,** *byé-tan néu-taṅ-du* sandy plains into meadows *Glr.*; *rims(-nad) γtóṅ-ba* to cause, **to send down,** epidemies, plagues (of gods); **to construct, fix, place,** chains before a building *Glr.*; in *W.* **(s)kad táṅ-će** to utter sounds, **kú-čo, bọ-ra táṅ-će** to raise, to set up a cry; **kug** or **kum táṅ-će** to make crooked, to bend; in forming intensive verbs: **go čád táṅ-će** to decapitate; **tón toṅ, p̓iṅs toṅ** take out! throw out! **tsa toṅ** put salt into it! **ču táṅ-će** to water (the garden); **lud táṅ-će** to manure (the fields). The participle **taṅs-pa** is used adverbially in *Ld.*; **ī-ne táṅs-pa ǎ tsúg-pa** from here to there, from this place to that place (= *bzuṅs-te*).

གཏོད *γtod?* *γtód-la mnán-pa*, of the sun *Pth.*, of the galaxy *Mil.*, evidently denotes the disappearing of these celestial bodies by enchantment or only as a poetical figure; perh. = *γdos*, or to be explained by *γtód-pa* II.

གཏོད་པ *γtód-pa* I. also *γtád-pa*, pf. *btad, γtad*, fut. *γtad*, imp. *btod* (*Mil.*; *Cs. tod?*) 1. **to deliver up,** *lág-tu* into the hand, to hand over *Glr.*, to hand to a person the subject for a theme or problem *Glr.*, to commit the management of the household to another *Dzl.*, to commit a child to a teacher *Dzl.*, *dge-°dún-la dbaṅ* to confer important offices on the priesthood *Glr.*, *rig-pa* to teach; *γčig snyiṅ γčig-la γtád-pa* to communicate one's feelings to one another *Glr.* — 2. **to lean against** or **upon** c. dat., e.g. to rest one's head on one's arm; to lay or put against, to, or on, one's mouth to a person's ear *Thgr.*, the tip of the tongue against the palate *Gram.* — 3. **to direct, to turn,** *mí-la mgó-bo*, one's face towards a person *Lt.*, *mí la mdzúb-mo*, or *sdig-mdzúb* to point at a person (with the finger) *Glr.*; *sgo nub-p̓yógs bál-poi yúl-du γtod Glr.*, the door points south, towards Nepal; *°bém-la* to take aim, to aim at *Lex.*; *rná-bai dbáṅ-po γtód-pa* to listen to, to give a person a hearing *Mil.*; *sems*, resp. *tugs, γtód-pa Mil.* id.; *˂od-zér-la γtád-nas γzigs-pas* turning after a ray of light, following it with the eye (= *brtén-nas*) *Glr.*; also used absolutely: *dkar-kúṅ γtód-pa* the projecting windows *S.g.* (?) — *ka γtód-pa Glr.?*

II. inst. of *rtód-pa*, **to fasten** (cows etc.) to a stake (driven into the ground), **to tedder.**

གཏོམ་པ *γtóm-pa* **to talk, to speak** *Sch.*, cf. *γtam* (?).

གཏོམས་པ *γtóms-pa* **filled up, full,** for *bltáms-pa, γtáms-pa, Sch.*

གཏོར་བ *γtór ba* (*Lexx.* अवक्ष) cf. *°tór-ba*, 1. **to strew, to scatter** ccirdp., *mé-tog-gis γtór-ro Dzl.* they strewed flowers, also *γtór-to Dzl.*; *ṅá-la sas γtór-ba* they that threw earth upon me *Dzl.*; *sá-la γtór-ba* to scatter over the ground *Glr.* — 2. **to cast, to throw,** ccar., books into the water *Glr.*, a ring into the air *Glr.*; to throw out, e.g. spittle into a person's ear, for healing purposes (= *°dór-ba*); **to cause to circulate** the chyle through every part of the body *Med.*; **to waste, to dissipate** *Dzl.*, occasionally with the accus. of the vessel containing the substance thrown out: *nú-*



ཏ

*ma γtór-ba Glr.* (a cow) emptying its udder by discharging the milk. — 3. *Sch.*: '*srub γtór-ba* **to rend,** to tear to pieces'.

གཏོར་མ་ *γtór-ma* **strewing-oblation,** an offering brought to malignant demons, either as a kind of exorcism or as an appeasing gift, in order to prevent their evil influences upon man; *mčód-pa daṅ γtór-ma sbyin-pa* to offer such an oblation, *γtór-mar sṅó-ba* to devote something for it. The ceremonies are similar to those used in *sbyin-srég Schl. Buddh.* 249; the offerings consisting of things eatable and not eatable, of blood, and even of animal and vegetable feces, scattered into the air (the benefit being shared by the *dri-za* q.v.). There are various sorts of Torma-offerings, according to the nature of the substances offered (*ču-* or *čab-γtor, ṕye-γtor; lhag-γtor,* an oblation of the fragments of a meal *Mil.*), or according to the time at which (*dgu-γtór* v. *dgu*), and the purpose for which they are offered (*mtsun-γtor* v. *mtsun*). Other names of Torma-offerings are: *blud-rgyá, mar-me-rgyá, tiṅ-lo(?)-rgyá, ča-γsúm* etc. Tormas in general belong to the ceremonies most frequently performed; *γtor-čá* are the vessels and other implements used for that purpose; *γtor-sdéb Sch.*: 'a bowl for these offerings'(?). — *γtor-zán Lex.* बलि oblation of the remnants of the daily meal to creatures of every description.

གཏོལ་ *γtol*, only in *γtol-méd*, = *ča-méd*, **not known, dubious,** *ṕó-ₒam mó-ₒam γtol-méd-do* one does not know yet, whether it will be a boy or a girl *Dzl.*; *ċi byá-bai γtol méd* not knowing what to do *Dzl.*; *gar tál-bai γtol med* not knowing where she had gone to; *bdág-la γtol méd* I do not know any thing about it *Dzl.* — (*Sch.* has a verb *γtól-ba* to perforate, pierce; to discover, disclose; v. *rtól-ba*).

གཏོས་ *γtos* **size, width, quantity,** *ri-boi γtos tsam* as high as a mountain *Lex.*; *rim-gro γtos-čé-ba*, like *rgya-čé-ba*, great marks of honour, extraordinary homage.

བཏག་པ་ *btág-pa* v. *ₒtág-pa*.

བཏགས་པ་ *btágs-pa* v. *ₒdógs-pa*, and *ḱa-btágs*.

བཏང་བ་ *btáṅ-ba* v. *γtóṅ-ba*.

བཏད་པ་ *btád-pa* v. *γtód-pa*.

བཏབ་པ་ *btáb-pa* v. *ₒdébs-pa*.

བཏང་སྙོམས་ *btaṅ-snyóms* (cf. *snyoms*) उपेक्ष complete **indifference,** perfect **apathy** (acc. to *Schr.* prop 'a liberality perfectly impartial'?).

བཏང་བཟུང་ *btaṅ-bzúṅ Lex.* मुचिलिन्द n. of a hill where Buddha was teaching.

བཏིག་པ་ *btig-pa*, pf. *btigs*, *Cs.* **to drop,** to let fall in drops, *rná-bar sman*, medicine into the ear, v. *ₒtig-pa*.

བཏིང་བ་ *btiṅ-ba* v. *ₒdiṅ-ba*.

བཏུ་བ་ *btú-ba* v. *ₒtú-ba*.

བཏུང་བ་ *btúṅ-ba* v. *ₒtúṅ-ba*.

བཏུག་པ་ *btúg-pa* v. *γtúg-pa*.

བཏུད་པ་ *btúd-pa* v. *ₒdúd-pa*.

བཏུད་མར་ *btúd-mar Glr.* in rapid or close succession, **tụ́-tụ́-pa-la** *C.* id.

བཏུབ་ *btub*, *Lex.* = *ruṅ*, **fit, convenient, practicable, becoming,** *btúb-bo* it is convenient etc.; *btúb-pa* v. *γtúb-pa*.

བཏུམ་པ་ *btúm-pa, γtúm-pa*, 1. **to wrap round, to envelop;** hence 2. in *W.* **to shut,** a book, valuable books being wrapped up in a cloth before being laid by; *btum-ṕóg* **bunch** or **knot**, produced by money and the like being tied up in the girdle.

བཏུལ་བ་ *btúl-ba* v. *ₒdúl-ba, γtúl-ba*.

བཏེག་པ་ *btég-pa* v. *ₒdégs-pa*.

བཏོད་པ་ *btód-pa* 1. = *rtód-pa*, **to fasten** (grazing horses or cattle) by a rope to a stake, **to tedder;** *Mil.* declares relations to be the *btod-tág* (the tedder) in the hands of the devil. — 2. **to erect, raise up, produce, cause, occasion;** *srol-btód-*

pa (*Lex.* w.e.) may accordingly imply: to introduce a custom.

བཏོན་པ་ *btón-pa* v. *ₒdón-pa.*

བཏོལ་བ་ *btól-ba Sch.* = *γtól-ba.*

རྟ་ *rta* (*rtá-po C., Mil.*), resp. *čibs*, 1. **horse,** *ṕo-rta* a gelding, *mó-rta*, or *rta-rgód-ma*, a mare; *rta ₒdúl-ba* to break in, train, a horse; *rta rgyúg-pa* to gallop; to run horses for a wager, to race *Glr.*; **sta śrul-če* Ld.* id.? — 2. the lower front part of a pair of breeches, *dór-rta, ăṅ-rta.*

**Comp.** *rta-rkyá(-pa)*, or *-skyá(-pa)* one skilled in horsemanship. — *rta-bskrágs* (**stab-rágs* Ld.*) a clattering train of horsemen. — *rta-gál Ts.* pouch or bag of a horseman, saddle-bag. — *rta-grás* = *rta-rá.* — *rta-bgád* a horse-laugh, *rta-bgád-kyis ₒdébs-pa* to set up a horse-laugh *Sch.* — *rta-mgó* a horse's head; *rta-mgó-ma* v. *go-ťsém.* — *rta-mgrin* (**हयग्रीव**) n. of a demon (*Schl.* 110), a terrifying deity. — *rtá-sga, W. *té-ga**, **saddle.** — *rta-sgám* a large box or chest. — *rtá-sgo* v. *sgo.* — *rta-sgyél*, gen. connected with *mi-bsád*, the slaughtering of men and killing of horses. — *rta-ṅán* Tibetan horses, small, strong, unshod, v. *Hook.* II, 131, and so already in *Marco Polo*'s travels. — *rta-rṅa* **horse-tail,** **te ṅá-ma yod* W.* it is (made) of horse-hair. — *rta-lčág* horse-whip; whip in general. — *rta-čág* dry fodder or provender given to horses, corn, oats. — *rta-mčóg* the best horse, a splendid horse, state-horse; gen. a fabulous horse, a sort of Pegasus, thus e.g. *Glr.* chp. 6, where it partakes of divine properties (*rtai rgyál-po čan-šés bá-la-ha*; acc. to *Schl.* p. 253 *rlúṅ-rta* is the same). — *rta-mčóg-ka-ₒbab* = *γyas-ru-γtsán-po* = *mṅá-ris-ču* n. of the principal river of Tibet. — *rta-ljáṅ* he with the green horses, the sun, po. *Glr.* — *rta-rná* horse-ear, n. of one of the seven gold-mountains, surrounding the Rirab. — *rtá-pa* horseman, rider, **tá-pa ta-žón* Ld.* a balancing-board, **see-saw;** *rtá-pai dpúṅ* horse, **cavalry** *Cs.* — *rta-lpágs* a horse's skin; n. of a medicinal herb *Med.* — *rta-bábs* 1. a large stone or raised place for alighting from a horse(?) *Cs.* 2. the superstructure of a large door or gate, the arch of a gate-way, *Lex. twa-ra-ṇa*, **द्वारणा**? — *rta-dbyáṅs* **अश्वघोष** n. of a great scholar *Thgy.* — *rta-bél* a horse's front-hair *Cs.* — *rta-sbáṅs* **horse-dung.** — *rta-rmig* a horse's hoof; n. of a plant *Med.* — *rta-rmig-ma* a lump of silver bullion like a horse's hoof *Cs.* — *rta-rdzí* one that tends horses; **a groom** *Glr.* — *rta-žún* a good horse. — *rta-zám* 1. **post-station,** *rta-zám-gyi ťsúgs-pa* a post-house; *rta-zám gyi spyi-dpon* postmaster-general *Cs.* 2. in *Ld.* also for *rta-zám-pa.* — *rta-zám-pa* **postillion, courier, express, estafet.** An estafet rides day and night, mounting fresh horses at certain stations, and making the way from Lé to Lhasa (for ordinary travellers a journey of 4 months) in 18 days. — *rta(i)-ₒú-lag* a compulsory service consisting in the supply of horses. — *rta-rá*, *rta-grás* **inclosure, stable,** for horses. — *rta-šá* 1. horse-flesh. 2. the oblique abdominal muscles of the hips. — *rta-šád* **curry-comb** *Sch.* — *rta-γsár* a horse not yet broken in or dressed *Schr.* — *rta-bséb* **stallion.** — With regard to the colour of horses (*spú-ka*), the following distinctions are made: *rta-dkár* a gray or white horse; *rta-rkyaṅ-nág*, or *kam-nág Sch.* a dark-brown horse; *rta kám-pa Ld.* a yellowish-brown horse (*Sch.* a dark-brown horse); *rta-kam-dmár Sch.* a light-bay horse, a sorrel horse; *rta krá-bo* a piebald or a dappled horse *Ld.-Glr.*, *Schl.* fol. 26, a; *rta-gró Sch.* a gray horse, *rta gro-dkár* a light-gray horse, *rta gro-sṅón Sch.* a dapple-gray horse, *rta gro-dmár* a roan horse, a roan; *rta rgya-bo Sch.* a chestnut-bay horse (a bayard, a brown horse) with white breast and muzzle; *rta ṅáṅ-pa* an isabel *Ld.-Glr.*; *rta rṅog-dkár* a bright bay horse; *rta-sṅo-kra, rta-sṅo-ťig-čan Sch.* a dapple-gray horse; *rta-sṅo-nag Sch.* a dark-gray horse; *rta-ťig-kra Sch.* a spotted horse; *rta nag* a black horse; *rta-brau* = *rgya-*

bo *Sch.*; *rta-mog-ro Glr.* a yellowish-brown horse; *rta zag-pa Sch.* a horse having gray and white spots; *rta ˛ól-ba Mil., Ld.-Glr.*, a black horse; *rta ra-rá Sch.* a yellow-dun horse; *rta rág-pa Ld.* a tawny horse (*Sch.*: 'a white and red spotted horse'); *rta rag-rág* an ash-gray horse; *rta rag-sér*, or *rta ser-sér Sch.* a yellowish-red horse; *rta sram-srám Sch.* a gray horse with a black mane and tail.

ཏ

རྟག་པ་ *rtág-pa* (नित्य) 1. **perpetual, constant, lasting, eternal.** 2. **perpetuity, duration** to all futurity, a quality which, acc. to Buddhist views, can be ascribed only to the vacuum, to absolute emptiness, the *stoṅ-pa-nyid*; *mi rtág-pa* not durable, perishable; *de yaṅ mi-rtag ṫsul-du yda* this, too, is subject to the law of perishableness *Mil.*; *mi rtág-pai čos* the principle of transitoriness; *rtág-par ˳dzin-pa* to look upon (transitory things, i.e. the world) as lasting, and hence: to be worldly-minded *Glr.*; as partic. one that is earthly-minded, a worldling; *nyál-ba-la rtág-pa* steady in lying, i.e. disposed to lie down, to be continually at rest, *Stg.*; *rtag-čad* lasting and transitory, frq.; *rtag-par*, or more frq. *rtag-tu*, **always,** i.e. 1. continually, 2. at each time (*Dzl.* ༢༥, 5); *rtág-tu-ba* perpetuity, eternity *Cs.* — *rtág-po, Ld.* **stágs-po**, **lasting,** durable, reliable, *rtag-brtan* id. *C.*; *rtag-snyóm-la C.* adv. uniformly, equally. — *rtag-rés ˳kór-ba Sch.*: a constant change(?).

རྟགས་ *rtags* (cf. *rtógs-pa*) 1. resp. *ṗyag-rtágs*, **sign, token, mark, characteristic,** **tag-żi** *W.*, **tags-pa** *Ld.*, id.; *rtags byéd-pa*, vulg. **tag rgyáb-pa** to make a mark; *ráb-tu byúṅ-bai rtags yód-pa* (partic.) one having the outward marks of an ecclesiastic *Glr.*; *bkra-ṡis rtags* v. *bkra-ṡis*; **omen, prognostic,** = *ltas*, *bú-mo skyé-bai rtags* a prognostic of a girl being born *Med.*; **proof** of a thing, c. genit., frq.; *mṅon-rtágs Dzl.* id.; **proof, argument, evidence,** **či tágs-pa-nẹ zum** *Ld.* upon what evidence have they seized him? **tágs-pa żig gos** you must prove it, **ṫágs-pa-aṅ mi dug** there is no trace, no evidence, left. — 2. **inference, deduction** *Was.* (320). — 3. **the black, the centre** of a target, *W.* **túg-la čúg-če** to take for a mark. — 4. **sexual organ,** organ of generation, *rtágs-sam bhá-ga* as two synonyms for the same thing *Wdṅ.*, *ṗó-rtags*, *mó-rtags* frq. — 5. **gift, present,** resp. *ṗyag-rtágs*. — 6. any mark for denoting grammatical distinctions, such as terminations etc., ni f.; *rtags ˳jug-pa* using such marks, making grammatical distinctions, seems to imply about the same thing as our etymology, the etymological part of grammar. — *rtags-yig* 1. **stamp, type**(?) *Cs.* 2. letter of recommendation, **credentials** *W.* — **tag-ril** *W.*, **lot,** **tag-ril táṅ-če** to cast or draw lots (a half-religious proceeding) cf. *rgyan*.

རྟབ་པ་ *rtáb-pa*, also *rtab-rtáb-pa*, and *stáb-pa*, **to be in a hurry, to be confused, frightened,** in a state of alarm, e.g. of fowl frightened by some cause (*Zam.* = *bréd-pa*); *rtáb-po* adj.; *stab-stáb-por sóṅ-nas* having become quite startled and confounded *Pth.*; *rtab-rtób* sbst., *rtab-rtób-tu náṅ-du ṗyin-te* she ran into the house in haste (full of joy) *Mil.*; *rtab-rtáb-la ra mi ˳dren* I cannot help you with such speed *Mil. nt.* It is also spelled *brtabs-pa*.

རྟས་པ་ *rtás-pa* v. *brtá-ba*.

རྟིག་གི་ *rtig-gi Ts.* for *rtéu*, **foal, colt.**

རྟིང་ *rtiṅ* (in more recent literature and col.) what is **behind** or **after,** with regard to space, and more particularly to time, *rtiṅ-du, rtiṅ-la, rtiṅ-na* adv. **afterwards,** *rtiṅ-du bčós-so* they were made afterwards, were added later *Glr.*; postp. c. genit., or less corr. c. accus., after; *byon rtiṅ-la* after their appearance *Pth.*, *byuṅ-rtiṅ* after he has come *Mil.*; *de-rtiṅ-la* after that *Glr.*; **tiṅ-nẹ ḍáṅ-če** *W.* to follow, to come after or later; *rtiṅ-ma* adj. and sbst. the last *Tar.*; *ytám-gyi rtiṅ-ma yin* this is my last, my farewell-speech *Glr.*; without *ma*: **dus tiṅ żig-na** *W.* some day hereafter, some future day; **tiṅ-ma żag, tiṅ-ma nyi-*

*ma** W. the following day; **tiṅ-ǰúg** remaining part, the last remainder, **di-riṅ ǰa tiṅ-ǰúg len soṅ** W. to-day I have used the last of my tea. — *rtíṅ-pa* 1. the end, extremity, lowest part, e.g. of a stick *Glr.*; gen.: 2. the heel of the foot, *rtíṅ-lčags* a spur, *rtiṅ-lčags rgyáb-pa* to prick with the spurs, to spur; *rtíṅ-ču* the Achilles-tendon.

རྟིབ་པ་ *rtib-pa*, pf. *brtibs*, fut. *brtib*, imp. *rtib(s)* **to break** or **pull down** (cf. *rdib-pa*).

རྟིའུ་ *rtiu*, sometimes for *rteu*, **a foal.**

རྟུག་པ་ *rtúg-pa* 1. **excrement, dirt** *rtug-skám* or *-ském* dry excrements *Med.*; *rgyal-srid rtúg-pa bžin-du dór-ba* to throw off royalty like dirt *Pth.*; *rtúg-pa p̔yis-pai rdo* a stone for wiping one's self *Mil.* — 2. *C.* **wind, flatulence.** — 3. *(b)rtug* v. sub *ťógs-pa.*

རྟུང་བ་ *rtúṅ-ba*, pf. *brtuṅs*, fut. *brtuṅ*, also *stúṅ-ba*, **to make shorter, to shorten, to contract,** e.g. a rope, a dress; *ɣnyá-ba brtuṅs* his neck is contracted *Mṅg.*

རྟུན་ *rtun* v. *ɣtun*; *rtun-ril* **a trituration-bowl** *Sch.*

རྟུན་པ་ *rtún-pa*, *brtún-pa*, **diligence,** *rtún-pa skyed-pa* to be diligent *Zam.* Cf. *dún-pa.*

རྟུལ་པོ་ *rtúl-po*, or *rtúl-ba*, **blunt, dull,** *mtson-rtúl* a blunt weapon *Cs.*; gen. fig.: *dbáṅ-po rtúl-po* (opp. to *rnón-po* or *rnó-ba* sharp, and *ˌbriṅ-po* middling) dullness, stupidity, imbecility of mind; dull, stupid; *blo-rtúl* weak intellect. — *(b)rtul-p̔ód-pa* (वीर) boldness, courage; bold, brave *Dzl.*

རྟེའུ་ *rteu* **foal, colt,** *rteu ˌbraṅ-ba* to bring forth a colt, to foal *Cs.*

རྟེན་ *rten* (cf. the next article) that which contains, keeps, or supports a thing, 1. **a hold, support,** esp. in compounds: *ka-rtén* the plinth or base of a pillar *Cs.*; *rkaṅ-rtén* (resp. *žabs-rten*) a foot-stool *Cs.*; *žu-rtén* a present given to support a supplication, and never omitted by Orientals when making a petition; **sem-tén** W. token, keep-sake; — esp. **a visible representation, a statue** or **figure** of Buddha or of other divine beings, which the pious may take hold of, and to which their devotions are more immediately directed (v. the explanation in *Glr.* chp. II, init.) — 2. **receptacle,** resp. *ɣduṅ-rtén*, for the bones or relics of a saint, *mčód-rten* for oblations, v. *mčód-pa*, compounds; *rig-pai rten* receptacle of the soul, i.e. the body *Schr.*; *rig-pa rtén-med-pa*, *rten daṅ brál-ba* the houseless, bodiless soul *Thgr.*; *ˌǰig-rtén* v. *ˌǰig*; *snyiṅ ni ťse srog séms-kyi rten* the heart is the seat of life and of the soul *Mṅg.*; **seat, abode, residence,** of a deity, **sanctuary, temple** (*Dzl.*), **shrine,** *rtén-gyi ɣtsó-bo* the deity residing in a shrine. *Glr.*; **visible representation, symbol,** of divine objects or beings, esp. the *rten ɣsum: skú-rten* an image of Buddha, *ɣsúṅ-rten* symbol of the doctrine, gen. consisting in a volume of the holy writings, *ťúgs-rten* symbol of grace, a pyramid, *Köpp.* II, 294. Hence *rten* might very suitably be used for denoting the material element in the Christian sacraments, viz. the water, and the bread and wine. — 3. **present, gift,** prop. for *žú-rten* (v. sub no. 1), and then in a more general sense, resp. *p̔yag-rtén*, *W.*, for *p̔yag-rtágs*; also **offering, oblation.** — 4: **sex,** specified as male, female, or hermaphrodite, independently of age *S.g.*; sometimes comprising age *S.g.*; or denoting age alone, as child, man, old man *Lt.*; **calling, situation** in life *Tar.* 163, 15 (where *gyi* ought to be changed into *ni*) 176, 15; 178, 18; some compounds follow still at the end of the next article.

རྟེན་པ་ *rtén-pa* 1. vb., pf. and fut. *brten*, imp. *rton* (*brten?*), **to keep, to hold, to adhere to, to lean on,** *ˌk̔ár-ba-la* on a staff *Pth.*; *ká-ba-la* against a pillar; *lág-pa ˌgrám-pa-la* to lean one's head on one's hand, in meditating *Dzl.*; fig. **to depend** or **rely on,** *brtén-pai blá-ma* the priest to whom one holds; *snúm-la rtén-pa* to keep to the fat, i.e. to eat much fat *Med.*; *ˌk̔rig-pai čós-la* **to be given, addicted,** to sensuality; **ču táṅ-wa máṅ-po-la tén-ne** *C.* if

ཏ

one is intent on watering; ₒtsó-ba dka-śúb-la v. dká-ba compounds; k̓yéd-kyis ɣsúṅ-ba-la brtén-nas following, obeying (your) orders *Glr.*; ṅai nús-pa-la rtén-nas relying on my strength, i.e. by the help of my strength (you will be able to get to that place) *Mil.*; hence (b)rtén-nas is frq. used for: in consequence of, with respect to, concerning etc.: rkyen dé-la rtén-nas in consequence of this event (the doctrine spread) *Tar.* 8, 1; *gha-la tén-nas* why? wherefore? *C.*; yul k̓yád-par-čan-la rtén-nas (to sin) with regard to a noble object *Thgy.*; **to hang on, to depend on, to arise** or **issue from**; rtén-par ₒbrél-ba v. rten-ₒbrél; **to be near, to border on,** *tén-te yod* *W.* (the two villages) are contiguous to each other; = ɣtád-pa, stón-pa to be directed, to be situated, to lie towards, lhó-p̓yogs-la to be situated towards the south *Sambh.*; ₒod-zér-la rtén-nas ɣzígs-pa to look after or pursue with one's eye a ray of light, like ɣtód-pa I. 3. Cf. stén-pa. — 2. sbst. **that which holds, keeps up,** rgyál-poi rtén-pao (these) are **the supports** of kings *Dzl.*; brtén-pa rús-pai ɣnás-lugs bstán-pa 'the doctrine of the hold-giving bones', osteology *Mṅg.* 3. adj. attached to, faithful *C.*

**Comp.** rtén-grogs, ṫse hril-por ₒgrógs-pai rtén-grogs perh. erron. for ɣtán-grogs. — rtén-ɣnas *Gram.*: the case which denotes the place of a thing or person, **the locative.** — rten-ₒbrél, or in full: rtén-par ₒbrél-bar ₒgyúr-ba or ₒbyúṅ-ba 'the coming to pass in continuous connection' (the explanation of *Burn.* I, 623 is grammatically not quite correct) i.e.: 1. in a general sense: **the connection between cause and effect;** in a special sense, the Buddhist doctrine of the rten-ₒbrel bču-ɣnyis, निदान, the twelve causes of existence *Wdk.* 551 (with illustrations); *Schl.* 23, *Burn.* I. 485, *Köpp.* I., 609. 2. **the auspices** of an undertaking, in as much as the complete knowledge of the causal connection of things implies also a certain prescience of future events; rten-ₒbrél rtóg-pa to investigate the auspices, śés-pa to know them, (a physician e.g., when treating a patient, must try to find out the auspices) *Med.*; rten-ₒbrél bzaṅ or legs good auspices, ṅan bad auspices, frq.; so also frq. col. — rtén-ma **prop, support, pillar** *S.g.*, *tén-śiṅ* *W.* a pole used as a prop; rtén-sa *Mil.?*

རྟོག་གེ་བ་ rtóg-ge-ba (तर्क) the act of **arguing, reasoning; dialectics** *Cs.*; *Sch.* distrust, suspicion (?); k̓a-bšád rtóg-geï slób-dpon seems to describe a teacher who talks in a hypocritical manner with a mere appearance of wisdom. — rtóg-ge-pa an arguer, disputer, reasoner, dialectician *Cs.*

རྟོག་པ་ rtóg-pa I. vb., pf. brtags (rtogs q.v.), brtag, imp. rtog(s), 1. **to consider, examine, search into, look through,** cca. (also dat.), brtágs-na mi śes though one meditates (upon the soul), one cannot understand or fathom it *Mil.*; frq. with a single or double indirect question: to examine whether (or whether not); brtag-dpyód (or rtóg-ɣžig) ɣtóṅ-ba *Pth*, *Mil.* id.; brtags-dpyód examination, trial *Zam.*; c. termin. **to discern, to recognize** as, e.g. mk̓rís-par brtag it is ascertained to be bile, to be caused by bile *Med.*; so-sór rtóg-pa *Stg.* prob. to recognize as being different. — 2. **to muse, to ruminate,** to trouble one's head about a thing, which is considered a fault much to be guarded against, and the more so, as religious faith as well as meditation require the mind to be strictly directed and entirely devoted to the one subject in question; hence ma-rtóg tiṅ-ₒdzín *Mil.* contemplation without any disturbing reflections and by-thoughts; cf. no. II. — 3. v. dog-pa.

II. sbst. 1. **consideration, deliberation, reflection,** cf. I., 2; rtóg-pa skyé-ba, rtóg-pa-la ₒjúg-pa to reflect on a thing, to indulge in musings *Dzl.* — 2. **scruple, hesitation,** rtóg-pa skyés-te to grow doubtful, hesitating *Mil.*; rtog(-pa)-med(-pa) simple, unsophisticated; simplicity; singleness of heart. — dé-la rtog-ₒjúg mi byed *Glr.* he does not meddle with that.

རྟོགས་པ་ rtógs-pa (prop. the pf. of rtóg-pa, like novi of nosco) 1. vb. **to per-**

**ceive, to know, to understand,** *dpyád-na ma rtógs-so* they did not understand, though they inquired into it *Dzl.*; *rtógs-par ₒgyúr-ba* to obtain information, to convince one's self of a thing *Dzl.*; *rtógs-par byéd-pa* to teach, to demonstrate, to convince a person of *Dzl.*; *má-rtógs-pa* stupid, ignorant; ignorance *Mil.* — 2. sbst. (but in Tibetan always construed as an infinitive with the accus. inst. of the genit., and with an adv. inst. of an adj.) **knowledge, perception, cognition,** frq.; *sems rtógs-pa* the knowledge of (one's own) soul *Mil.*; *mṅón-par rtógs-pa* (**अभिसमय**) clear understanding or perception, in modern Buddhism the same as *stoṅ-pa-nyid Trig.* 21. — *rtógs-pa-čan, rtogs-ldán* rich in knowledge *Mil.* — *rtógs-(pa) brjód(-pa)*, for **अवदान** cf. *Burn.* I. 64, a moral legend. — *rtogs-spyód* theory and practise, *rtogs-spyód byéd-pa* to know and to do, *rtogs-spyód la mḱás-pa* theoretically and practically religious. — *rtógs-ₒdod-čan* desirous of knowing or learning, inquisitive *Mil.* — Sometimes for *ťogs-pa*.

ཏོད་པ་, གཏོད་པ་, བཏོད་པ་ *rtód-pa, γtód-pa, btód-pa* 1. sbst. also *rtod-ṕúr*, **a stake,** in the ground, for teddering a horse, for securing a boat etc.; **a peg,** in a wall, for hanging up things; *rtod-ťág* a tedder (v. *btod-pa*); *rtód-pa brgyáb-pa* to drive in a stake or peg 2. vb. **to tedder, fasten, secure** *Dzl.*

རྟོན་པ་, བརྟོན་པ་, བརྟན་པ་ *rtón-pa, brtón-pa, brtán-pa*, with or without *yid*, ccd., **to place confidence in** a person, **to rely on.**

རྟོལ་ *rtol? čos-rtól Tar.* 164, 20, *Schf.* the pith or marrow of a doctrine; *rtól-skyes-kyi šés-pa Mil.?* — *brtól-šes-pa Tar.* 197, 8, *Schf.* to know thoroughly.

རྟོལ་ *rtol Cs., rtol-góg Lex.* w.e.; *Sch.*: **a bastard,** an animal of a mixed breed, *rtól-po* a male, *rtól-mo* a female bastard *Cs.*; acc. to Desgodins the cross-breed of a yak-bull and a *ₒgar-mo*. Cf. *ltor*.

རྟོལ་བ་ *rtól-ba*, pf. *brtol* (*Ld.* **stól-če**) 1. **to bore, to pierce,** to bore into, cci. & t., *Stg.*; to bore through, **to perforate** cca., a board etc., *sgo-ṅa* the shell of an egg (of chickens creeping out) *Sch.*, **to open** (an abscess) by a puncture; **to make an incision;** **bi-gaṅ* W.* to bore a hole. — 2. **to come to, to get to, to arrive at,** *γnás-su* to (at) a place *Lex.* (cog. to *ťál-ba, ťél-ba*); *yoṅs-ₒdus-brtol Lex.* w.e.; *Tar.* 30, 22, *Schf.*: **पारिजातक**, the coral-tree, Erythrina indica; also a tree of paradise. (In *Dzl.* ༢༤༢, 13 the manuscript of Kyelang has: *dé-dag-las rtól-ba* it outpassed them).

ལྟ་ *lta* 1. more correctly *blta*, v. sub *ltá-ba*, I. 1., **we will see,** *Mil.*, frq. — 2. in various phrases and expressions, in which its special signification is no longer clearly discernible: a. *lta či smos Dzl.* and elsewh., the most frq. form, *lta smos či dgos Thgy*, *lta smos či ₒtsal* (eleg.) *Stg.*, *W.* more distinctly: **lta dgos či yod**, also **zer dgos či yod**, **far from, not to mention, to say nothing of, how much less, how much more;** with a preceding infinitive or noun: *ₒdi-dag ₒdul-ba lta či smos* to say nothing of the conversion of these! how much easier is it to convert these! *Dzl.*; *ₔó-skol lta či smos* how much more we! *Thgy.*; *lta žog* is much the same: *lo zlá-ba lta žog* to say nothing of years and months; **tar žog, tá-la žog* C.* id. — b. the word is frq. used after participles or adjectives ending with *pa*, when, judging in each case from the connection in which it happens to stand, it may be deemed equivalent to: **evidently, indeed, thus then** etc., spoken either with emphasis, or ironically, or in a sorrowful tone. As it is next to impossible to learn from the Tibetans the exact import of those little words, which slightly modify the grammatical and logical relations of a sentence, European translators have generally passed them over. Cf. *Dzl.* ༢༠༠, 18, ༢༥༦, 2 (where a shad ought to be added), ༤༢, 7 (where *ste* means though), ༢༦༩, 18; *Tar.* 7, 17, 19. In *Dzl.* ༢༠༢, 7 *lta*, in accordance with the manuscript of Kyelang, is to be omitted. — c. **like, as,** (*ltá-ba* sbst. abstr., *ltá-bu* adj., *ltá-bur* or *ltar* adv.), *dú-ba ltá-bur yód-*

*pa żig* one having the nature or the colour of smoke *Glr.*; *rta bčus rgyúg-pa ltá-bui sgra* a noise as if ten horses were galloping *Glr.*; ... *ltá-bu mk̔ás-pa żig* a man as wise as ... *Dzl.*; *p̔a-má ltá-bur gyúr-to* he was (to him) like a father *Dzl.*; *bai dzí-ma ltá-bu daṅ ldán-te* having eyelashes like those of a cow *Stg.*; *rán-la mi-mk̔ó-ba bú-la byiṅ-pa ltá-bu ma yin* not as if she (the mother) would give her child only what she does not want herself *Thgy.*; *żés-pa ltá-buo* is the usual expression for quoting a passage from an author, and always follows the quotation; *k̔yod ṅá-lta-bu min* you are not my equal, and also: you are not in my situation *Mil.*; *ₒdí-lta-bu, dé-lta-bu*, one like him, such a one as he; *či-lta-bu* what sort of? *saṅs-rgyas šes byá-ba či-lta-bu yin* the so-called Buddha, what sort of being is he? what is meant by 'Buddha'? *Dzl. či-lta-bu-la bskal-pa żes bgyi* what sort of a thing is called 'Kalpa'? *ǰí-lta-ba* v. *ǰi*; *ǰi-lta-bu* of what kind, as a rel. pron. Sometimes *lta* alone is used for *lta-bu*: *k̔yód-lta* your equal *Mil.*; so prob. also in the passage *Dzl.* ༧༢༥, 8, where *yód-pa lta či mt̔oṅ* would be = *yód-pa ltá-bu gaṅ mt̔oṅ* (better than taking *lta či mt̔oṅ* for *lta či smos Schf.*). In *Dzl.* ༢༤༢, 13, and ༢༤༤, 3 *ltá-żig* is prob. to be altered into *ltá-żog*, v. sub a, 2, above. — d. *lta* is sometimes a mere expletive, e.g. in *dá-lta* (v. *da*), and after the conditional *na* (*Dzl.* ༧༢༦, 1; ༤༦, b; ༥༣, 16, ༢༥༤, b.).

ལྟ་བ་ *ltá-ba* I. vb., pf. *bltas*, fut. *blta*, imp. *ltos*, *blta*, resp. *γzígs-pa* (cf. *ltos-pa*) 1. **to look** (as an act of the will, cf. *mt̔óṅ-ba*), **to view**, often with *mig*, or *míg-gis* (v. below); *bltás-na mi mt̔oṅ* though you look (for it) you do not see it *Mil.*; **nán-tan żíb-ča ltos* Ld.* look at it accurately! **to̱ šig* C.* look (before you)! have your eyes open! **to̱ šig nyo̱n čig* C.* attention! mind! be careful! *ltá-bas čog mi šés* I never can look enough at it; with *nas*: to look from or through, *sgo-séṅ-nas* (to peep) through the narrow opening of a door *Tar.*; *bltá-na sdúg-pa* pleasing when looked upon, charming to look at; also n. of the city of gods on the Rirāb *Stg.*, and of one of the seven golden mountains around the Rirāb *Glr.*; *ltá-ru soṅ* go there and look (at it)! **lta-la toṅ* W.* let me look (at it)! show it me! *p̔an-ts̔un-du ltá-ba* to look around *Dzl.*; **čog-čóg-la**, or **ye-yóṅ-la** col. id.; *p̔yi mig*, or *p̔yir* (to look) back *Dzl.*; **p̔i mig log lta-če**, or **ǰiṅ-pa gyúr-te ltá-če* W.* id.; **to inspect**, ccd., rarely c.a., frq. *Glr.*, *Dzl.*; *k̔yed mi-nús-pa-la bltás-na* if one views, considers, your inability *Dzl.*; *ṅas ma bltas-na* if I do not inspect it *Glr.*; **gháṅ-la te̱ ruṅ* C.* whatever one may fix his eyes upon = whatever it may be; **to look after** or **into, to revise, to examine, to try,** *rtsa ltá-ba* to feel a person's pulse *Med.*; *p̔án-nam blta* I will see, if I can help *Mil.*; also: I will see, whether it has done good; *su če blta* let us see who is taller *Mil.*; *e' ts̔ud ltos šig* see, if you can put it through *Glr.*; *rtíṅ-sor blta* we shall see that afterwards *Mil.*; *yáṅ-dag-par ltá-ba* to examine or search into minutely *Mil.*; **tsod ltá-ba** in col. language is the expression most in use for **to examine,** to put to the proof, **to test, to try, to sound** etc. Lastly, as a mere act of the mind: **to meditate, reflect, muse, ponder, investigate,** *du ₒdug blta* let us see how many there are *Mil.*; *lta rtog byéd-pa*, or *γtóṅ-ba Mil.* to investigate closely. Also in a mystic sense, v. *sgóm-pa* I, 2. — 2. ccd. (or accus.) and termin., to look upon a thing as, *šés-pa-la zóg-tu* to look upon knowledge as deceitful; *dkon-mčóg γsum mi bdén-par ltá-ba* to think the three treasures to be untrue, not real, = not to believe in them. — 3. c. dat. (rarely termin.): **to have regard to, to pay attention to, to take notice of,** and with a negative: **to be indifferent to, not to care about,** *sróg-la mi ltá-ba* not to care about one's life (from heroism or desperation). — 4. **to be situated** or **directed towards,** *mdo ni núb-tu lta* the lower part of the valley is situated towards the west. — 5. *ṅas bltás-pa* in my opinion;

ná-la bltás-na(s), or rtén-nas, with regard to me, as for me, for my sake *Glr.*; *γžán-ma-rnams-la bltás-pas* as far as the others are concerned, with regard to the others *Glr.* —

II. sbst. 1. the act of **looking, beholding,** v. I, 1. 2.; *ltá-ba yáṅs-šiṅ* circumspect *Glr.* — 2. **contemplation** (mystical) v. *sgóm-pa* I, 2. — 3. (दर्शन) **opinion, doctrine, theory, philosophical system, school** (in Tibetan a verb, cf. *rtógs-pa* II), *rtág-par ltá-ba* the theory of perpetual duration (of earthly things); *ṅán-par ltá-ba* a false opinion, = *lta-lóg*.

**Comp.** *lta-nyúl-pa* **a spy, scout,** *lta-nyúl byéd-pa* to spy, to explore, v. *nyúl-ba*. — *lta-stáṅs*, resp. *γzig-stáṅs Pth.* **the look,** or manner of looking, air, mien, *ži-bai lta-stáṅs* a mild look, or countenance, *Cs.*; *kró-bai lta-stáṅs* an angry or fierce look *Cs.*; esp. the magical and powerful look of a saint, *lta-stáṅs šig mdzád-pa* to cast such a magical look *Mil.*; *lta-stáṅs-la bžúgs-pa*, *lta-stáṅs-kyi ṅáṅ-nas čá-ba Mil.* to sit, or stride along, with such a look, i.e. with great solemnity of deportment, as of one in a trance; *lta-stáṅs-bži* the four magical looks, viz.: *ₒgúgs-pai lta-stáṅs* the attracting look, *skród-pai lta-stáṅs* the repulsive look, *lhúṅ-bai lta-staṅs* the precipitating look, *réṅs-pai lta-stáṅs* the paralyzing look *Cs.*; also *séṅ-geï, gláṅ-po-čeï lta-stáṅs-kyis γzigs-pa* to look at a person with a lion's look, with an elephant's look. — *lta-lóg*, in later lit. and col. *lóg-lta*, **false sentiment,** not only false doctrine, heresy, but any irreligious impulses of the mind, perverse and sinful thoughts, e.g. *lóg-lta skyés-te* is used for conspiring against a person's life *Glr.*, giving way to doubt or weakness of faith *Glr.*, falling in love with a woman *Pth.*; *mí-la lóg-lta byéd-pa* to slander, to abuse a person *Glr.*

ལྟག་ལྕིན་ *ltag-lčin* **puff-ball** *Sch.*

ལྟག་པ་ *ltág-pa* 1. the back part of the neck, **nape** *Med.* and elsewh., frq. — 2. **the upper part** or **place,** *grál-gyi* of the divan, the seat of honour *Dzl.* — 3. **the back,** *gri-ltag* the back of a knife. — 4. *ltag ₒog sgyúr-ba* to turn upside down *Dzl.*; *ltág-na(s), ltag,* **above,** *sgó-ltag* above the door, *gróṅ-ltag dgón-pa Mil.* the convent above and behind the village, the front-side of the houses being gen. turned towards the valley and the river; thus 'behind' is equivalent to 'higher up'; *ltág-na-med-pa* (of rare occurrence) for *blá-na-med-pa* the highest, अनुत्तम; *ltag skór-ba* to strangle, to suffocate *Glr.*; *ltag γčód-pa* 1. *Cs.* to cut off a man's neck, to behead. 2. *W.* to make a person change his mind, to alter his sentiments; **ṅe kó-la gyóg-pa tag čad yin** I hope I shall talk him out of it, shall dissuade him from doing it; *ltag nyal-ba* to lie backward *Sch.*

**Comp.** *ltág-sgo* the back-door of a house, v. above. — *ltag-γčód* or *-čód* 1. **decapitation,** 2. *Sch.*: **changeable, fickle, inconstant.** *ltag-čú Med.*; *Sch.*: 'sinew of the neck, the covering of the neck'. — *ltag-mdúd Sch.*, *ltag-sdúd Lt.*, the hole in the occiput, the connexion of the brain with the spinal marrow. — *ltág-spu* neck-hair, **mane,** of the horse, of the lion *Ld.-Glr.* — *ltág-ma* what is uppermost, e.g. words written over other words.

ལྟང་ *ltaṅ* 1. **a bale** of goods, carried on one side of a beast of burden, half a load, *ltaṅ γnyis* two bales, or a whole load. — 2. also *lteṅ*, *W.*: **through, quite through,** **ṗi-sta-ṅe náṅ-la ltaṅ ṫoṅ dug** one sees from the outside into the interior; **ltaṅ bug toṅ** bore through! **ltaṅ ṫón-te ča dug** he is passing through, he does not make a stay here. — Cf. *toṅ*.

ལྟད་མོ་ *ltád-mo*, col. also **ltán-mo**, resp. *γzigs-mo*, the looking on, **a sight, scene, spectacle,** *ltád-mo-la ₒtsogs* they came together in order to look on *Glr.*; *ltád-mo ltá-ba* to look at a scene, to be an eye-witness; *ltád-mo ltá-bai sa* a place where there is something to be seen; **a theatre.** — *ltád-mo-ḱaṅ* a playhouse, exhibition, puppet-show etc. — *ltád-mo-pa Pth.*, **ltád-mo-lta-mi**, **ltád-mo-la yóṅ-ḱan**

**W.**, a spectator, a visitor; *ltád-mo-mḱan*, ***ltád**-mo stón-pa* a showman, actor, mimic etc. — *gróṅ-yul-gyi ltád-mo ma dran žig Mil.* forget the scenes of village life!

ལྟབ་པ་ *ltáb-pa*, pf. *bltabs*, fut. *bltab*, imp. *ltob* (*W.* **ltabs toṅ**), **to fold** or **gather up**, **to lay** or **put together**, **kyaṅ-tab, nyi-tab tab-če** *W.* to fold single, to fold double; *γsúm-ltab byéd-pa* to fold or bend together threefold, e.g. a corpse previous to cremation; *ltáb-ma Cs.* **a fold, crease, plait;** *ltab-gri* a clasp knife.

ཏ ལྟམ(ས)་པ་ *ltám(s)-pa*, pf. *bltams*, fut. *bltam*, 1. **to be full**, also *γtáms-pa*. — 2. resp. **to be born**, *skyéd-pai yab daṅ bltáms-pai yum* the father by whom one is begotten, and the mother by whom one is born *Pth.*

ལྟར་ *ltar* 1. also *bltar*, supine of *ltá-ba*, **in order to see;** *bltár-ruṅ-ba* visible; *Sch.:* 'pleasing to the eye'; *gaṅ ltár-na yaṅ, či ltár-na yaṅ*, be that as it may *Glr.* — 2. postp. c. a., **like, as,** after the manner of, *ri-ltar* like a mountain; *ṕyag byéd-pa ltar byéd-pa* to make a saluting gesture *Glr.; ṅo-šes ruṅ mi šés-pa ltar byas* although they knew . . ., they affected not to know . . . *Mil.; ̥bral mi ṕód-pa ltar yód-na yaṅ* being like one that cannot part with, = being scarcely able to part with, *Glr.*; *ltar snáṅ-ba* to appear like, hence prob. *ltar-snáṅ* appearance, similarity *Sch.*, (*Lex.* w.e.); *lúṅ-bstan-pa ltar* (to do a thing) in conformity with a prediction *Tar.*; also *ltár-na*, and *ltár-du*, *mi-lo ltár-na . . . yod* computed by human or terrestrial years it amounts to . . . *Thgy.*; *bód-rnams ltár-na* according to Tibetan (sources) *Tar.; či-ltar(-na)* how? in what manner or way? *či-ltar* also serves to paraphrase the English 'so that', e.g. 'he played so that all were enraptured' is thus expressed: he played — how did he play? — all were enraptured; *ji-ltar(-na)* as *ji-ĺta ji-ltar . . . dé-lta dé-ltar Sambh.* even as . . . so; *̥di-ltar, dé-ltar(-na)* so, thus, in that manner; *̥di-ltar mi rgan ḱyod* such an old fellow as you are; frq. also in referring to the words of others, where we use 'that': *dé-ltar bdén-na* if that is true.

ལྟར་ལྟར་པོ་ *ltár-ltar-po Lex., Cs.*: of a liquid nature, as an embryo first in the womb.

ལྟས་ *ltas* **prognostic, omen,** more distinctive *sná-ltas;* **miraculous sign, miracle, prodigy,** more accurately: *ṅo-mtsár-bai ltas; bkra-šis-pai ltas* a propitious omen; *rmi-ltas bzáṅ-po* a good sign in a dream *Pth.*; *dgé-ltas* a favourable sign; *ṅán-ltás*, or *ltas-ṅán* a bad sign *Dzl.; ltás-mḱan* a soothsayer, fortune-teller; *ltas stón-pa* to soothsay *Cs.*

ལྟི་རི་ *lti-ri* **pitcher** *Sch.*

ལྟིག་ཐུང་ *ltig-ťúṅ C.* a person of small stature, perh. a corruption of *lte-ťúṅ*.

ལྟིབ་པ་ *ltíb-pa* to fall through *Sch.*

ལྟིར་བ་ *ltír-ba* v. *ldír-ba*.

ལྟུང་བ་ *ltúṅ-ba* 1. vb., pf. *lhuṅ*, **to fall, to fall off, down, into;** fig.: *mtó-ba de yaṅ mtar lhúṅ-ṅo* what is high will finally fall down *Dzl.*; more esp. to fall into sin, to commit sin, hence *nyes-ltuṅ* an actual sin, a sinful deed, *ltúṅ-byed* a transgression, crime; also *ṅán-soṅ-du* (v. *̥gró-ba* I, 5), or *dmyál-bar* to fall into damnation. — 2. sbst. **the fall,** esp. the moral fall, *ltúṅ-bas gós-pa* polluted by sin; *ltúṅ-ba bšágs-pa* confession of sin.

ལྟེ་བ་ *lté-ba* 1. **navel-string, umbilical cord,** *γčód-pa* to cut it *Med.* — 2. **navel,** *lté-bai ḱúṅ(bu) Lt.* id.; *glá-bai lté-ba* musk-bag. — 3. the middle of a thing, **centre,** *dkyíl-̥ḱor-gyi* of a circle; *mu-ḱyúd γsúm-gyi lté-bar* in the middle of three (concentric) circles *Lt.*; *raṅ-ťág-gi lté-ba* the axle-tree of a water-wheel *Glr.*; *sai lté-ba* the centre of the earth, in the opinion of the natives: *Tibet*; also cognomen of several fabulous kings of Tibet *Köpp.* II., 52. — *lté-ba γžuṅ-ráṅ* Lhasa, or, in a more special sense, the palace of the Dalai Lama — *lte-ťúg W.* = **tig-ťúṅ** *C.*

ལྟེང་ *lteṅ* 1. v. *ltaṅ*. — 2. *lteṅ-rgyás* n. of a Buddha.

ལྟེང་ཀ ltéṅ-ka **pool, pond** *Dzl.*

ལྟེབ་པ ltéb-pa (cog. to *ltáb-pa*), **to double down, to turn in,** *mťa,* or *snḗ-mo* to hem, by turning in the edge, cf. *snḗ-mo.*

ལྟེམ་རྒྱང ltem-rgyáṅ **humour, whim, caprice,** *ltem-rgyáṅ byéd-pa* to be whimsical or capricious *Cs.*

ལྟེམ་པ ltém-pa the state of being full, e.g. a vessel full of water; **full, overflowing,** *ltém-po* full; *ltem-ltém* so full that it runs over.

ལྟོ lto, seldom *ltó-ba* (*C., Mil.*) 1. **food, victuals,** *lto(b)za-ba* 1. to eat, *lto yaṅ ma zos* he did not eat anything *Glr.*; 2. to gain or get one's living *C.*; *ltó-la byin* give him to eat! *Lt.*; *lúg-la lto ster* feed the sheep; *lto γyó-ba* to prepare food *Mil.*; **to nyo ṡroŋ ťsoṅ** *C.* he risks his life in order to procure food; *gla-ltó* wages and food; *lto-gós, lto-rgyáb,* food and clothes *Mil.*; *lto-rgyab-skyid Lex.* prob. food, clothes, and good health (comfort); **dha tó-če za gyu yin** *C.* now I will go and eat (something). — *lto-čúṅ, lto-rán Sch.*: a person temperate in eating. — *ltó-ₒdun-čan* **an epicure, parasite, sponger.** — *lto-žiṅ* provision ground which a person receives for his subsistence. — *žím-lto-čan* dainty-mouthed, lickerish. — 2. **goat's beard,** Tragopogon, used as a kitchen-vegetable.

ལྟོ་བ ltó-ba **belly, stomach**; also the belly of a bottle; *ltó-ba sá-la ₒbébs-pa* to prostrate one's self.

**Comp.** *lto-gáṅ* a full belly, also: with a full belly or stomach. — *ltó-ₒgro, ltós-ₒgró* 1. moving or creeping on the belly, **a worm, a snake.** 2. symb. num.: 8. — *lto(-ba)-ₒgróg(-pa) Cs.*: 'belly-fretting, a nervous excitement of the belly'. — *lto-stóṅ* with an empty stomach, **jejune, empty.** — *lto-ldir* belly of a vessel, *ltó-ldir-čan* swelling out, bellied, like vessels. — *ltó-na-ba, ltó-zug* stomach-ache. — *lto-ₒp̓yé* crawling or creeping on the belly, a snake; *lto-ₒp̓ye čén-po,* **महोरग**, a fabulous monster of the serpent kind, similar to the klu.

ལྟོག་འདྲེ ltog-ₒdré a demon *Sch.*; *ₒdre-ltágs* prob. the same

ལྟོགས་པ ltógs-pa I. vb. 1. **to be hungry,** *ltógs-so* I am hungry *Cs., ltógs-su ₒbór-ba* to suffer a person to hunger, to starve *Dzl.* — 2. *Sch.*: **to regret,** *ltogs nyal ma byeb* do not always lie in grief and regret! *Sch.* (?); *ltógs-par bžúgs-pa* resp. to be full of regret.

II. sbst. **hunger.**

III. adj. **hungry,** *séms-čan ltógs-pa-rnams Dzl.*; *ltógs-par ₒgyúr-ba* to grow hungry; *ltógs-gri Mil*, col. **ltóg-ri** *W.* hunger, **ṅa(-la) ltóg-ri rag** I am hungry, **k̓yod (-la) ltóg-ri rag** you are hungry, **k̓o ltóg-pa yod** he is hungry. — *ltogs-p̓yúg* hunger (i.e. poverty) and wealth *Glr.* — *ltog-tsór* the feeling of hunger, *ltogs-ťsor če* I am very hungry *Mil.*

ལྟོང་ག ltóṅ-ga **notch, incision, indentation,** *mdá-ltoṅ* the notch in an arrow; **a depression,** *ri-tóṅ* in a ridge of mountains, *la-tóṅ* the indentation of a mountain-pass.

ལྟོངས ltoṅs **summit** *Mil.*, frq

ལྟོབ ltob v. *ltáb-pa.*

ལྟོར ltor, *sras-ltór* a bastard prince *Glr.*

ལྟོས ltos 1. v. *lta-ba.* 2. *Sch.* = *γtos.*

ལྟོས་པ ltós-pa 1. vb., = *ltá-ba,* **to look at,** on, or to, ccd., *γnyén-po-la ma ltós-par* without looking to a spiritual guide *Thgy.*; *k̓yod dé-la ltos mi dgos-pa žig yin* you need not care for that *Mil.*; *ré-žiṅ ltós-pa Glr.* to look at (a thing) hopefully; *dé-la ltós-na* if I look at, consider, this *Mil.*, if one compares this with… *Thgy.*; *(s)*ṅá-ltos či-čug* (?) *tsáṅ-ma čó-k̓an** *W.* a person acting with great circumspection — 2. sbst. **the looking** at or on, *ltós-pa méd-par* without looking at it (e.g. in playing at dice); **relation, respect, regard** *Cs.*

སྟ་མགོན sta-gón **preparation, arrangement,** *sta-gón byéd-pa* to make preparations, to prepare, arrange, fit out; *ₒtsó-*

ཏ

***bai sta-gón-la bžeṅs*** he rose to make preparations for dinner *Mil.*

སྟ་ཟུར *sta-zúr* **hip, hip-bone,** e.g. as the seat of strength *Mil.*; *stá-zúr yan-čád* from the hip upward *Dzl.*

སྟ་རི *sta-ri W.*, originally *sta-gri Mil.* and *C.*, *sta-ré B.*, **axe, hatchet**; *dgrá-sta* battle-axe *Lex.*; *star-ltág Cs.* the back of an axe or hatchet, *star-mig* the hole for putting the handle in, *star-yú* the handle, *star-só* the edge of an axe.

སྟག *stag* 1. **tiger,** *rgya-stág* the Bengal tiger *Mil.*; *stag-ṕrúg* a young tiger, *stág-mo* a tigress; *stag-ťsán* a tiger's den; *stag-ris* the stripes of a tiger's skin. — 2. *Tar.* 166, 2?

སྟག་ཆས *stag-čás Mil.* utensils carried by men about them, such as a knife, smoking-implements, weapons etc.

སྟག་པ *stág-pa* **birch-tree;** *stág-ma* n. of another tree.

སྟག་གཟིག *stag-yzig* a not unfrequent form (which prob. has been adapted to Tibetan etymology) for *ta-zig*, **Persia, Persian.**

སྟག་ཤ *stag-ša* a medicinal herb, *Glr., Med.*; *stag-ša-dé-ba Glr.*

སྟག་ཤར *stag-šár* **a youth, young man** *C., Mil.*

སྟང་ཟིལ *stan-zil Cs.*: n. of a black stone, acc. to *Zam.* a silver-ore.

སྟངས *staṅs*, *Sch.* also *stáṅ-ka*, **manner, style, posture,** *góm-pai staṅs* manner of walking, gait; *brdég-staṅs byéd-pa* to assume a fighting posture *Mil.*; *ltá-staṅs* v. *ltá-ba* comp.; *stón-pai bžugs-staṅs* the sitting posture of Buddha; *C.*: **ko ghó-ghon-tan dé-mo** his style of dressing is fine, he is well dressed; **tám-zer-taṅ ké-pa** eloquent; even like a mere termination for forming verbal substantives: **zá-taṅ**, or **tún-taṅ lég-mo** good eating, drinking.

སྟད་པ *stád-pa*, pf. and fut. *bstad*, imp. *stod*, **to put on, to lay on,** *rtá-la sga* to put the saddle on a horse, to saddle; *rtá-la* ˳*gró-čas* to load the baggage on a horse.

སྟན *stan* **mat, carpet,** esp. a carpet for sitting on, also **a cushion,** resp. *bžugs-ydan*; **saddle-cloth;** *stan* ˳*diṅ-ba* to spread a mat (on the ground), ˳*gébs-pa* to lay (a mat) on; **ču-stán** swaddling-cloth *W.*; **bol-tén** mattress, **ṭul-tén** (lit. *ṕrul-stán*) a light travelling-mattress *C.*; sometimes substratum of any kind, also of hard materials, e.g. *ytsub-stán, btsab-stán.*

སྟབ *stab* 1. v. *rtab.* — 2. *Sch.*: *stab stáṅs-pa* to suffer, to tolerate, to yield.

སྟབས *stabs* (cog. to *ťabs*, also syn. of *staṅs*), **mode, manner, way, measure,** *séṅ-gei stábs-kyis* (or *su*) ˳*gró-ba* to walk in the manner of a lion; *gar-stábs* v. *gar*; **opportunity,** ˳*byón-stabs* an opportunity for going; **tábs-si ká-na** (also **ká-ne*, or *ká-la**) *W.* when an opportunity offers; *riṅs-stabs-su* hastily, speedily *Mil.*; **kón-stabs** dearth, famine, want *Ld.*; **riṅ-stabs** a describing at full length, copiousness (*stabs*, in this instance, corresponds to the English termination 'ness', changing the adj. into an abstract noun).

སྟར *star*, for *sta-ri* q.v.

སྟར་ཀ *stár-ka Sch.*, *stár-ga Lex.*, *stár-ka Glr.*, **walnut,** *star-(gai) šiṅ*, *ljón-šiṅ stár-ka* walnut-tree *Glr.*; *star-skógs* nutshell; *star-sdóṅ* trunk of a walnut-tree. *stár-ka byéd-pa Ld.-Glr. Schl.* f. 15, b (?).

སྟར་བ *stár-ba*, pf. and fut. *bstar*, imp. *stor*, 1. **to file** on a string, e.g. pearls; **to tie fast, to fasten to,** e.g. sheep to a rope, in a bivouac, *stár-la rgyúd-pa* id. — 2. **to clean, to polish** *Lex.* — 3. *Sch.*: **to ornament, decorate** (?).

སྟར་བུ *stár-bu*, or *star-žun Med.*, frq., the berries of Hippophaë rhamnoides, a shrub or tree very frequent in Tibet; acc. to a *Lex.* also a kind of Rumex in India.

སྟི་བ *sti-ba*, pf. *bstis*, fut. *bsti*, imp. *stis*, 1. **to rest, to repose, to refresh** one's self, *sti-(bai) ynas* resting-place. — 2. **to honour** (?); *(b)sti-stáṅ* **honour, respect, reverence,** *byéd-pa* ccd., to show a person honour, frq.; **kó-la ti-tán čaṅ med** *W.* he is not esteemed at all, he enjoys no credit whatever: *bkúr-sti* id., v. *bkúr-ba*.

སྟིང་བ་ *stiṅ-ba*, pf. *bstiṅs*, fut. *bstiṅ*, imp. *stiṅs*, **to rebuke, scold, abuse** *Lexx.*

སྟིབ(ས)་པ་ *stib(s)-pa* to offer (sacrifice), rarely used.

སྟིམ་པ་ *stim-pa*, pf. *bstims*, fut. *bstim*, imp. *stims*, prop. vb. causative to *ₒtim-pa*, gen. = *ₒtim-pa*, **to enter, penetrate, pervade, to be absorbed in**, *tugs čos-nyid-kyi klóṅ-du stim Pth.* the soul is absorbed in the expanse of the *čos-nyid*.

སྟུ་ *stu* **cunnus**, orifice of the vagina, the vulg. and obscene expression for the pudendum muliebre.

སྟུག(ས)་པ་ *stúg(s)-pa* 1. abstract noun and adj., **thickness, density, thick;** *stugs-po* adj., = *ₒtúg-pa*, *ₒtúg-po*, **thick, dense**, e.g. a forest, *Dzl.*; **sound, heavy** (sleep, clouds etc.); *dpal-stúgs* right noble, most noble *Cs.*; *stugs-po-bkód-pa Pth.* one of the heavens of Buddha. — 2. **a wind,** flatulence *C.*

སྟུང་བ་ *stúṅ-ba*, pf. *bstuṅs*, fut *bstuṅ*, imp. *stuṅs* = *rtúṅ-ba*.

སྟུད་པ་ *stúd-pa*, pf. and fut. *bstud*, **to repeat, to reiterate**, to give or offer repeatedly (medicine, food, beer etc.), *bstúd-na* if it is repeated *Mṅg.*; *sbrid-pa máṅ-po stúd-ciṅ ₒoṅ* repeated sneezing ensues *Lt.*; *bstúd-nas ná-ba* to be always ill *Sch.*; cf. *btúd-mar*.

སྟུན་པ་ *stún-pa*, pf. and fut. *bstun*, prop. causative to *ₒtún-pa*, gen. = *ₒtún-pa*, **to agree**, *dgé-ba bčú-la bstún-pai rgyal-ḱrims* a law agreeing with the ten virtues *Glr.*; *ₒdod-yón lṅa daṅ stún-pai loṅs-spyód* a life of pleasure in accordance with the five enjoyments *Glr.*; *dus-skábs daṅ stún-te* agreeably to the (proper) time, in due time *Glr.*; *ṅai žiṅ rmó-ba ₒdi daṅ stún-pai mgúr-ma* a song having reference to this my labour in the fields *Mil.*; *γžuṅ daṅ stún-pa Lex., Cs.*: 'to confer, to make agree with the original text'.

སྟུབ་པ་ *stúb-pa*, or *sté-pa*, *Ld.*, for *btúb-pa*, *γté-pa*.

སྟེ་ *ste* an affix for the gerund, inst. of *te*, after *g*, *ṅ*, and vowels, v. *te*. — As *ste* contains the copula, it may be added also to other words than verbs, e.g. *kyod rigs čé-žiṅ mtó-ba-ste* as you are of high and noble extraction *Dzl.*; like *ₒdi-lta-ste* it is also used for **namely, to wit, videlicet** (viz.), that is to say, esp. before translations of foreign words and names: *ṡi-ra-ste mgó-bo žes-byá-ba Tar.* 11, 11; 4, 11; 189, 2 and elsewh. In the latter case it may also be rendered by **or** (Lat. *sive*). After an enumeration of several things, it serves to point back, or to comprise: *ža, za, a, ya, ṡa, sá-ste drug-ni* the six letters *ž*, *z* etc.; *γsum ná-ro kyi-gu gréṅ-bu-ste* three signs, o, i, and e *Glr.*, *Tar.* 188, 16; *dá-ste žag bdún-na* as to the being now, in seven days, i.e. in seven days from to-day *Dzl.*; sometimes *ste* seems to stand in the place of a preceding verb, *Feer Introd.* 73, s.l.c.; at other times it is used, where its exact meaning is not obvious.

སྟེའོ་ *sté-po*, or *steu*, carpenter's **axe, adz,** an axe with its blade athwart the handle (*Cs.*: 'paring axe'), used by Indian and Tibetan carpenters, *Hind. basūla*, *ste-ltág* its back, *ste-yú* its handle, *ste-ḱá Cs.* its edge, though in *S.g.* 32 *sté-ḱa so-γnyis-pa* it must be the name of the tool itself. — *ste bžog γtóṅ-ba* to pare, to smooth, to hew with the axe. — **ṗág-ste** *W.* a plane.

སྟེགས་ *stegs*, also *stégs-bu*, any contrivance for putting things on, **a stand, board, table, stool** etc.; *ká-stegs* the pedestal or base of a pillar *Cs.*; *rkáṅ-stegs* foot-stool, jack, horse (wooden frame with legs); **kyóṅ-stag** *W.* candlestick; **čós-stag; čó-tag** *W.*, book-stand; *ₒdug-stegs* a board, stool, bench, to sit on *Cs.*; **do-tég** *C.* a stone-seat, whether artificial or natural; *snód-stegs Cs.* 'a board to put vessels on'; *ṗór-stegs* a cupboard *Cs.*; **ṗó-stag** *W.* a bench; *žábs-stegs* resp. for *rkaṅ-stegs*; **žǔn-teg** *C.* candlestick; *γžag-stegs* a board to place things on *Cs.*; *zá-stegs* dining-table *Schr.*; *γsól-stegs* id resp., and table in general, col. **sol-tág**; *lám-stegs* seat, resting-place by the road-side *Glr.*; **ǒṅ-teg** *C.* candlestick.

ཏ

སྟེང་ steṅ **that which is above, the upper part, top, surface,** *sai steṅ ťams-ċád* the whole face of the earth *Glr.; sén-moi stéṅ-gi sa* the earth here upon my finger nail *Dzl*; *stéṅ-gi nám-mk̒a* the heavens above *Dzl.*; *stéṅ-gi p̒yogs* the zenith; *steṅ-ˏóg* above and below, *steṅ-ˏóg-gi γdon* demons of the upper and lower regions; *stéṅ-na* adv. and postp.: above, overhead, on high, up-stairs, on the surface, answering to the question where or in what place; *stéṅ-du* adv. and postp. 1. id., answering to the question whither, to **what** place, but also where or in **what place,** e.g. to sit on a lotos, to throw down to the ground, to send **a thing** or a messenger to a person *Dzl.*, frq. 2. above, over, moreover, besides, **in addition** to, *rgás-pai stéṅ-du* in addition to my old age *Dzl.*; *byás-pai stéṅ-du* he made it and besides... *Dzl.*; *bdug čós-la mi mós-pa méd-pai stéṅ-du bón ráṅ-la mos* I am not only no despiser of religion, but a regular Bon-worshipper *Mil.*; *stéṅ-nas* down from. — *stéṅ-ka* (*W.* **táṅ-ka**), also *stéṅ-tse* a terrace. — *stéṅ-k̒aṅ* upper story of a house, garret. — **steṅ-dúṅ**(?) *W.* pestle, pounder.

སྟེན་པ་ *stén-pa*, pf. and fut *bsten*, imp. *sten*, **to keep, to hold; to adhere to, to stick to, to rely** or **depend on,** almost like *rtén-pa*, but c. accus., *blá-ma mk̒ás-pa stén-pa* to adhere to a learned Lama; to stick or keep to certain victuals, medicines etc., using them regularly, frq.; even *sdug-bsṅál* to have to taste misfortunes *Thgy.*; **to addict one's self** (to virtues or vices), *sér-sna* to avarice *Stg.*; *mi stén-pa* = *spáṅ-ba* to avoid, shun, abstain from *Glr.*; *Cs.* also: *γyog stén-pa* to keep a servant in pay.

སྟེམ་པ་ *stém-pa*, pf. and fut. *stems* (= *stén-pa*?), **to hold, to support** *Mil. nt.*; **to shut** or **fasten** a door, **to secure** it by a beam or bar. *C.*

སྟེམས་ *stems* **curse** (?) *Tar.* 181, 20. Cf. *byad.*

སྟེའུ་ *steu* v. *sté-po.*

སྟེར་བ་ *stér-ba*, pf. and fut. *bster*, ccdp. 1. **to give** *B.*, *C.*, frq.; **to bestow, present, grant, concede, allow;** with the supine or root of a verb: **to let, permit,** *náṅ-du ˳gro(r)*, *náṅ-du ˏóṅ-du* to let enter to grant admission *Dzl.* — 2. *W.* in a special sense: to give to eat or to drink, **to feed** (infants, animals). — 3. **to add** (in arithmetic) *Wdk.* — **tér-go** **aid, contribution** *C.*

སྟེས་དབང་ *stes-dbaṅ Lex.*, where *staṅs-legs* is added for explanation; in *Tar.* 134, 7 *stes-dbaṅ-gis* is translated by *Schf.*: power of fate.

སྟོ་ཐག་ *sto-ťag* **rope** *Sch.*

སྟོ་བ་ *stó-ba*, most frq. in the col. phrase *ċaṅ mi sto* it does not matter, it makes no difference, it is all the same (also *ċaṅ mi rtog*); *Mil.*: *ṡi ruṅ mi stó-ba ˳dug* it does not matter if they die; *ṡi yaṅ ċi stó-ste* what does it matter if they die?

སྟོ་ར་ (?) *stó-ra W.*, a circle of dancers.

སྟོང་ *stoṅ* 1. **thousand,** *stoṅ-p̒rág* id., *stoṅ-p̒rag-brgyá-pa* (the work) containing ten thousand (viz. Sloka) *Köpp.* II, 272; *Burn.* I, 462. — *stóṅ-dpon* a commander over a thousand; *stoṅ-˳k̒ór-lo* a wheel with a thousand spokes; *las stoṅ byed Med.* that is a remedy producing a thousand good effects. — 2. **a fine for manslaughter,** to be paid in money or goods to the relatives of the person killed; *če-čúṅ-gi stoṅ byéd-pa Glr.*, to proportion this fine to the rank of the man killed. — 3. v. *stóṅ-pa.*

སྟོང་གྲོགས་ *stoṅ-grógs* v. *stóṅs-pa.*

སྟོང་པ་ *stóṅ-pa* (शून्य) **empty, clear,** *k̒áb-kyi rtsé-mo tsam γzúgs-pai sa stóṅ-pa* about so much clear space, as to allow the point of a needle to be stuck in *Dzl.*; **hollow,** not charged or loaded (of a gun); not written upon, **blank; indifferent,** having no distinct or definite quality, e.g. as to taste or smell; *rlúṅ-gi raṅ-bžín ni stoṅ mód-kyi* though wind (or air) in itself is without smell *Dzl.*; **waste, deserted,** *brag-stóṅ* a rocky desert, *luṅ-stóṅ* a desolate valley *Mil.*; **žaṅ - stóṅ** *Ld.*, **dom - stóṅ** *Pur.*, bare-bottomed, having the bottom bare, vulg.; **mi tóṅ-pa** *W.*, = **mi kyaṅ**, v. *rkyaṅ-pa; k̔aṅ - stóṅ* a desolate house, as a place suitable for enchantments; fig. **sem tóṅ - pa rag** *W.* I feel lonely. — *stoṅ-pa-nyid.* शून्यता, **emptiness, vacuity, the void**, the chief product of the philosophical speculations of the Buddhists, and the aim and end of all their aspirations, v. *Köpp.* I, 214; *Burn.* I, 442; 462. (Five synonyms v. *Trig.* f. 20). *stóṅ - zád - la skyél - ba* to squander, to waste, *ts̔e* one's life *Mil.*; *stoṅ-saṅ-ṅé* absolute vacuity, *stóṅ-saṅ-ṅé byás-nas* making tabula rasa, keeping, retaining nothing whatever *Thgy.* — *stoṅ-ɣsál* v. *ɣsal-po.* — Adv. *stóṅ-par* in vain(?) *Mil.*

སྟོང་ཟིལ་ *stoṅ-zil*(?) *W.* Corydalis meïfolia.

སྟོངས་པ་ *stóṅs-pa* 1. pf. *bstaṅs* (*Dzl.*), fut. *bstaṅ*(?), **to accompany**, **tóṅ - te ḍó-wa** *C.* to go along with a person; *čis kyaṅ mi stóṅs-par* ₒ*či* I die without any thing following me *Thgy.*; more frq. *stoṅ-gróġs byéd-pa* cc gp. (also dat.?) **to help, to assist** a person *Mil.* — 2. **to make empty; to be empty**, **to become waste** or **desolate**, *ráṅ-gi ɣnas stóṅs-šiṅ S.g.*, *raṅ-šúl stóṅs-nas Mil.*, your own place becoming desolate; *stóṅs-su nyé-bar gyur* it had become nearly empty, was almost spent or exhausted *Pth.*; *mis stóṅs-pai k̔áṅ-ro* ruins forsaken by men; *saṅs-rgyás-kyis stóṅs-pa Thgy.* the period during which no Buddha appears, a *mi-k̔óm-pa* v. *k̔óm-pa*; *sa-ɣžír stóṅs-pa* to level with the ground, to raze, to demolish entirely.

སྟོད་ *stod*, *Ssk.* उत्तर, **I. the upper, higher, former part** of a thing, **the upper half** opp. to *smad*; 1. esp. the upper part **of the body**, resp. *sku-stód Pth.*; *stod-k̔óg* the upper part of a carcase *Sch.*, also *stód-po Mil.*; *stod-k̔yébs* a sort of frill or ruffle of the Lamas; *stod-ₒgág* doublet of the Lamas, without sleeves; *stod - túṅ* a short coat, jacket. — 2. the upper or higher part **of a country**, *stód-pa* an inhabitant of it, highlander. — 3. with respect to time: **the first part**, of the night *Dzl.*, of life *Glr.*, of winter and the like; *stód-la* at the upper part of, above.

II. v. *stád-pa*, and *stód-pa.*

སྟོད་པ་ *stód - pa* 1. vb., pf. and fut. *bstod* ('to raise, to exalt', opp. to *smád-pa*) **to praise, commend, laud**, *bdág-stod-pa*, *W.* **ráṅ-tod-če**, **to praise one's self**, **raṅ-tod - čan** **a self-admirer, self-flatterer; to extol, to glorify**, men, **gods etc., frq.**; *stod-(čiṅ) bsṅags-pa* id.; *stod-ts̔ig* an epithet of praise, a commendable quality. — 2. sbst. **praise, eulogy**, also **tód - ra** *W.*; **compliments**, complimentary phrases e.g. in letters; hymn of praise, also *stod - bsṅágs*, *stod-dbyáṅs*, *stod-glú*; *stód-pa(r) byéd-pa*, *W.* **p̔ul - če**, ccd. (the former also c. accus.) to praise, to extol; *stod-ₒós* laudable, commendable, worthy of praise.

སྟོན་ *ston* 1. **autumn** (more about it v. *dus*), *ston brgya mt̔óṅ - bar gyúr čig* may he live to see a hundred autumns! *Lt.* — 2. **in autumn**, during autumn *B.*, frq. — 3. = *ston-tóg.*

**Comp.** *stón-ka*, *stón-k̔a*, **autumn**, **stón-ka - na*, *stón - ka - la** in autumn, during autumn. — *ston-tóg* autumnal fruit, **harvest**, *ston-tóg sdú-ba* (*W.* also **dóg-če**) to gather in the produce of the fields, to harvest. — *ston-dús* **harvest-time, autumn**, — *ston-zlá* autumnal month.

སྟོན་པ་ *stón-pa* I. vb., pf. and fut. *bstan*, at the end of a sentence *bstán-no* (so prob. also in *Dzl.* ༧༠, 10 the correct reading), *W.* *(*s*)*tán-če**, **1. to show**, *lam stón-čig B.*, *(*s*) *tán toṅ** *W.*, **ṭen rog ǰhe šig** *C.* show me the way! *stón-mk̔an žig yod* somebody has shown *Glr.*; *bú-mo sgo stón - mk̔an* the girl that has shown the door *Mil.*, *mts̔án-mk̔an-la bu stón-pa* to show the soothsayer a child *Dzl.*; *lus stón-pa*, applied to deities etc.: to show one's self, to appear *Dzl.*; *rdzu-ₒp̔rúl stón-pa* to show, to exhibit magic tricks, v. *rdzu*; *dmág-pa yin-no žes bstán-te* 'this is the bridegroom!' with these words showing, i. e. introducing him as the bridegroom

ད

*Dzl.* ༢༥, 3. — 2. = *ɣtód-pa*, **to face, to front, to look towards,** *sgo lhó-ṗyogs-su ston* the door faces the south *Glr.* — 3. **to point out, to indicate, describe, explain,** *čé-ba* the greatness or superiority of a thing *Mil.*; *bú-mo skyé bar ̥gyúr-bar stón-pa yin* it indicates that a girl will be born *Wdṅ.*; *ci-̥dra ži̇g (yod) ston dgos* give me a description of her person *Glr.*; *bstán-par byao* now I will explain that, frq.; *ǰi-ltar byón-pa bstán-pai leu* the chapter describing the arrival; hence **to teach,** *čos* religion; *luṅ* v. *luṅ*. — 4. *W.* **to make** one **undergo** or **suffer, to inflict** (just as **ťóṅ-ċe** to suffer), **mi-la nag stón-pa** to torture a person, **dug-ṅálstón-pa** to plague, torment, grieve. — 5. *W.* as a vb. nt., **to show one's self, to appear,** *'*i-ru tán-te yod** this appears here, this turns up or occurs here.

II. sbst. **a teacher,** frq., *lúṅ-ston-pa* **a prophet,** v. *luṅ;* the *stón-pa* par excellence is Buddha, frq.; — *ston-min,* and *tse-min* two false doctrines *Glr.* 92, 3. (the translation given by *Sch.* is but an arbitrary one).

སྟོན་མོ་ *stón-mo* **feast, banquet** (v. also *yá-tra*), *stón-mo bzáṅ-po, čén-po,* a grand, splendid feast *Dzl.*; *šóm-pa* to prepare, arrange (a feast), *byéd-pa* to give, hold, celebrate it, also c. dat. in honour of; *stón-mo ̥drén-pa* to serve it up *Mil.*, *̥gyéd-pa* to distribute the dishes, *dmáṅs-kyi stón-mo ̥gyéd-pa* to distribute of the **viands** of the table to **the common people** ***Mil.***, *zá-ba* to eat, or **partake, of such a festive** entertainment *Dzl.; stón-mo-ɣnaṅ-sbyin* a present of meat, of provisions *Glr.*; *dgá-ston* festive entertainment, frq.; *rná-bai dgá-ston* a feast or treat to one's ears *Glr.*; *čós-ston* a religious feast *Glr.* (might be used for agapē, love-feast, feast of charity); *dús-ston* a periodical festival, one connected with certain times or periods *Tar.; bág-ston* wedding-feast, frq.; *miṅ-ston* feast given at the solemnity, when a name is given to a child; *ráb-ston* a feast after settling some important business *Cs.; btsás-ston* a feast given after the birth of a child; *tsógs-ston* sacrificatory feast; *ɣšid-ston* funeral feast.

སྟོབ་པ་ *stób-pa*, pf. *bstab* (*Cs. bstob*), fut. *bstob Cs.*, imp. *stob*, (causative to *ťob-pa?*), to put into another's mouth, esp. food, **to feed;** also applied to a mare that shoves the grass to her foal *Dzl.*; *nán-tan-gyis stób-pa* to press a person to accept of a dish etc. *Dzl.*; in a more general sense: *láṅ-ste stan stób-par byéd-pa* rising to offer one's own seat *Stg.*; to make a donation *Dzl.*; also capir.: *yo-byád ťams-ċád-kyis stób-pa* to provide a person with every thing within one's power *Tar.*

སྟོབས་(པོ་) *stóbs(-po)* **strength, vigour, force,** frq.; *lús-stobs* bodily, *snyiṅ-stobs* mental strength; *̥ǰú-stobs* digestive power *Med.; stóbs-po če* of great physical strength *Dzl.; stóbs-kyis* by virtue, by means of; *stobs-̥ṗel-nyams-brtás byéd-pa* strengthening, nourishing, of food *Med.*; *stóbs-ċan, stobs-ldán*, strong, robust; *stobs-čúṅ, stobs-méd*, powerless, weak; the five powers of a Buddha v. *Burn.* II, 430; *Köpp.* I, 436; the ten powers v. *dbaṅ bċu*. — *stobs-čén* 1. n. of a Lu-king, *S.O.* — 2. **rammer, pile-driver,** (or *rdob-čén?*) *C.*

སྟོར་བ་ *stór-ba* **to be lost, to perish, to go astray,** *bu stór-ro* a child has been lost *Dzl.*; *lus daṅ srog* (to lose) one's life *Dzl.*, *sems* one's senses, *lam* one's way (**also** fig. to err from true religion *Pth.*); **tor ma ċug** *W.* do not lose it, do not drop it, carry it carefully; *stór-sa med* it cannot be lost or antiquated *Mil.* — *stór-ǩuṅ* for *ɣtór-ǩuṅ* drain, gutter *Lex.*

བརྟ... *brt...* v. chiefly sub *rt.*

བརྟ་བ་ *brtá-ba*, pf. *brtas*, *Lex.*: *lus sems brtas*, explained by *rgyás-pa*, **to grow wide, to extend;** gen. **to grow stout,** esp. with *nyams* ~~*Dzl.*;~~ cf. also the expression for strengthening sub *stóbs(-po)*; also *rtas byéd-pa Med.*; fig. strong or great: *̥gyód-pa rtas* the greatest, the sincerest repentance *Pth.*; *bág-čags rtás-pa* high passion *Thgy.*

བརྟག(ས)་པ་ *brtág(s)-pa*, v. *rtóg-pa;* as sbst., preceded by a genit., **inquiry, examination,** *Stg.*, frq.; gen. c. accus. *rmí-lam brtág(s)-pa* examination of dreams *Stg.*; *rin-po-če brtág(s)-pa-la mkʻás-pa* connoisseur of precious stones *Dzl.*; *brtágs-pa brgyad Tar.* 21, 2.?

བརྟད་ *brtad* a kind of imprecation, which consists in hiding the image and name of an enemy in the ground underneath an idol, and imploring the deity to kill him; *brtad ˳ǰúg-pa* to perform that ceremony *Mil.*

བརྟད་པ་ *brtád-pa* 1. *Lex.* = *bló-bur* **new, recent.** — 2. *Sch.* **haste, speed,** for *rtáb-pa(?)* (*Tar.* 180, 2 it should prob. be *ɣtád-na.*)

བརྟན་པ་ *brtán-pa* adj. and abstract noun; *brtán-po* adj., **firm, steadfast, safe; firmness** etc.; *brtán-par ɣnás-pa*, **tán-po dád-če* W.*, to last, hold out, abide, continue, frq.; *brtán-pa tʻób-pa* to become firm or durable (lit. to acquire firmness or durability) *Mil.*; *brtáṅ-par ˳gyúr-ba*, **tán-po čá-če* W.* id.; *brtán-gyi skyid* a continued or abiding happiness *Mil.*; *dbaṅ brtan* their strength is holding out *Med.*; *brtán-du ˳ǰúg-pa Glr.*, **tán-po čó-če* W.*, to watch, keep, preserve carefully; **tán-po kur* W.* carry it carefully or safely! *dám-bčas-pa brtán-par šes* he knew his word to be inviolable *Dzl.*; *yi-dam-la brtán-pas* because he firmly kept his word *Dzl.*; *dus brtán-gyi bdé-ba* eternal welfare, everlasting happiness *Mil.* (perh. this ought to be *ɣtan*).

བརྟན་མ་ *brtán-ma*, or *bstán-ma*, and *bstán-pa-mo*, n. of the goddess of the earth, (also *skʻóṅ-ma*, *yá-ma*), used in practising magic.

བརྟུལ་བ་ *brtúl-ba* 1. **deportment, behaviour** *Cs.* — 2. *Sch.* also diligence, painstaking(?). — *brtul-žúgs*, व्रत 1. *Cs.* manner, way of acting. 2. *Sch.* and gen.: exercise of penance, *brtul-žugs byéd-pa* or *spyód-pa*, to perform such exercises, to do penance. 3. penitent. — *brtul-žugs-čan* penitent (adj. and sbst.) — *brtul-pʻód-pa* v. *rtul-pʻód-pa.*

བསྟང་བ་ *bstáṅ-ba* v. *stóṅs-pa.*

བསྟན་པ་ *bstán-pa* 1. v. *stón-pa.* — 2. sbst. **doctrine,** a single doctrine, or a whole system of doctrines; *saṅs-rgyás-kyi bstán-pa* the doctrine or religion of Buddha, *tʻub-bstán*, for *tʻúb-pai bstán-pa*, id.; *ɣnás-lugs bstán-pa* the doctrine of the position of... *Med.*; *bstán-pa ɣnyis* with Urgyan Padma etc., the same as *mdoi* and *sṅágs-kyi lam*, v. *mdo* extr. — *bstán-˳gyur* the second great literary production of Buddhism, containing comments on *Kan-˳gyur*, and scientific treatises (v. *bka-gyur* in *bka*) *Köpp.* II, 280. — *bstan-bčos* (शास्त्र) a scientific work. — *bstan-rtsís* a chronological work relative to the year of Buddha's death. — *bstan-˳dzín* follower, adherent of a doctrine, *saṅs-rgyás-kyi bstan-˳dzin Mil.*, Buddhist; also frq. used as a noun personal. — *bstan-(b)šig* col. a destroyer of the doctrine, in general a good-for-nothing fellow, a mischief-maker, an obnoxious person or thing. — *bstan-srúṅ* 1. **a keeper, guardian of the doctrine;** perh. also = *bstan-˳dzín.* 2. **keeper, warden, guardian** in general, *lha-kʻáṅ-gi bstan-srúṅ*; *lhá-sai bstan-srúṅ* the tutelar goddess of Lhasa, acc. to *Glr.* = *dpal-lhá-mo.* 3. in general the contrary to *bstan-bšig.*

བསྟིར་ *bstir* supine of *sti-ba; bstir-méd* 'restlessness', one of the infernal regions.

བསྟུགས་པ་ *bstúgs-pa* **to make lower, to lower** *Sch.* (?).

བསྟེན་པ་ *bstén-pa* 1. vb. v. *stén-pa.* 2. sbst. **confidence,** = *brtón-pa Bhar.*

བསྟོད་པ་ *bstód-pa* v. *stód-pa.*

# ཐ

ཐ་ ťa, the letter t aspirated, like the English t in 'tea'.

ཐ་ ťa 1. num. fig.: ten. — 2. **every thing, all, total** *Sch.* (?).

ཐ་སྐར་ *ťa-skár* a certain star, *ťa-skár-zla-ba* a month, prob. = **वैशाख** (April-May); *ťa-skár-gyi bu* **अश्विनी** twin half-gods.

ཐ་ཁབ་ *ťa-ḱáb Lh.* a large **needle**.

ཐ་ག་པ་ *ťá-ga-pa* **a weaver** *Dzl.*

ཐ་གུ་ *ťá-gu*, vulg. *ťi-gu*, 1. a short **cord** or **rope**. — 2. **string, twine**, for making garlands *Stg.*; a bell-rope *Dzl.*

ཐ་གྲུ་ *ťa-grú*, originally *ťag-grú Pth.*, **extension, width, breadth**, *ₒdzam-bu-gliṅ-gi ta-grú kún-la Glr.* in the whole extent of Dzambuling; *ťa-grú čé-ba Pth.* extensive.

ཐ་རྒོད་ *ťa-rgód* 1. **obtuse, rounded off** *Sch.* — 2. *Mil.?*

ཐ་ཆད་ *ťa-čád* **very bad, mean** *Cs.*

ཐ་ཆུང་ *ťa-čúṅ* **the last month** of a season (v. *dus*), e.g. *dpyid-zla ťa-čúṅ* the last month of spring, opp. to *rá-ba*, (and *ₒbriṅ-po*); **the youngest** of three or more sons, opp. to *rab* (and *ₒbriṅ-po* the middle one).

ཐ་སྙད་ *ťa-snyád* 1. **appellation**, *žes ťa-snyád-du grags* so it is called *Wdṅ.*; *Tar.* 96, 13; 178, 3; *Was.* (296): **supposition; condition**, *ťa-snyád-pai bdén-pa* conditional truth. — 3. *Schr.*: **etymology**, *Cs.* only: part of grammar; so frq. used by grammarians, e.g. *tsig daṅ ťa-snyád slób-pa* to learn spelling and etymology. — 4. In col. language I heard it used only for talking or disputing in a conceited, foolish manner, so also in *Mil.* — *Lex.* in conformity with each of these significations = **व्यवहार**, from **व्यवह** to distinguish, to name; to dispute. — *ťa-snyad-γčig-pa* n. of a school, of a system or doctrine *Tar.*; *ťa-snyad-grúb-pa* n. of a literary work.

ཐ་དད་པ་ *ťa-dád-pa* **different, various, sundry**, gen. opp. to *γčig* or *γčig-pa*; *dgós-pa ťa-dád-pa* the various wants of a man *Dzl.*; *ťa-mi-dád-pa* alike, equal.

ཐ་ན་ *ťá-na* **even, so much as, up to**, *ťá-na-srog-čágs gróg-sbur yan-čád* even the smallest insect *Stg.*; *ťá-na yig-ₒbru re-ré yan-čád* even every single letter *Thgy.*; at the close of an enumeration: **finally also** *Ld.-Glr. Schl.* 20, 6.

ཐ་པི་ཐུ་པི་ *ťa-pi-ťú-pi* **confusion, disorder** *Sch.*

ཐ་པག་ *ťá-pag* v. *ťár-dpag.*

ཐ་བ་ *ťá-ba* (= *ťú-ba*) **bad** *Mil.*

ཐ་མ་ *ťá-ma* **the last** of several things, with respect to number, time, rank, the lowest, meanest, most inferior, often opp. to *rab* and *ₒbriṅ*, and also to *ḱyád-par-čan*; it appears somewhat singular, that *γčan-zán-gyi ťá-ma* signifies a cat, and *ₒdab čágs-kyi ťá-ma* a hen *Glr.*; *dús-kyi ťá-ma-la* in the last times *Glr.*, prob. also alluding to the general decline taking place towards the end of the Kalpa; sometimes it is to be translated: **in the last place, finally, at last** *Glr.*, like *ťá-mar Dzl.* ༢༠, 11; last = parting (parting-cup, parting-kiss); for the last time: *γnyén-gyi ťá-mas bskor* he sees his relations for the last time around him, *zás-kyi ťá-ma za* he eats for the last time *Thgy.*; *ťá-ma-la* c. genit. at the end of, after. — *ₒṕrád-pai ťá-ma ni ₒbral, γsón-pai ťá-ma ni či-ba yin* the end of every meeting is parting, the end of every living is dying.

ཐ་མ་ཁ་ *ťa-ma-ḱa Cs.*, vulg. *W.* *ťá-mag*, **tobacco**, *ₒťuṅ-ba*, *W.* resp. *dón-če* to smoke (tobacco).

ཐམལ་པ་ *ta-mál-pa* (*ta-mál* abbreviated from *tá-ma-la*) 1. **mean, vulgar, plebeian**, *ta-mál-par ₒdúg-pa* to live like the vulgar *Dzl.* — 2. **ordinary, usual**, *ta-mál-pa ma yin* that is no usual thing *Dzl.*; *ta-mál* adv. = *p̓al-čér.*

ཐ་ཚིག *ta-tsig Sch.* 'oath'; but in two passages of *Dzl.* *ċii ta-tsig* can only mean: **'what signifies?'**

ཐ་ར་ཐོ་རེ་ *ta-ra-to-ré W.* **wide asunder, wide,** **ta-ra-to-ré žág-pa** *C.* to scatter, to throw loosely about.

ཐ་རམ་ *ta-rám* 1. *Sch.*: 'the breadth of a plain'. — 2. a medicinal herb *Med.*, in *Lh.* Plantago major.

ཐ་རུ་ *ta-rú Tar.* 20, 17, *Schf.*: 'the utmost limits', or it may be a p. n.

ཐ་ལི་ *ta-lí W.*, **te-li** *C.*, *Hind.* **थलिया, a tin plate.**

ཐ་ལོང་ *ta-lón W.* a sort of red cloth.

ཐ་ཤལ་ *ta-šál Sch.*: 'the end, the consequence; bad'; *Bhar.*: *skyés-bu ta-šál nyid Schf.*: homo nequam, a good-for-naught.

ཐག *tag* 1. sometimes for *ₒtag*, *Glr.* — 2. **distance** a. relatively (prob. from *tág-pa* measuring-cord, surveyor's chain) only in: *tag-rin-ba* adj. and abstract noun, *tag-rin(-po)* adj., *W.* **tag-rin-(mo)** **distant, a great distance,** *sa tag-rin(s)* a far country *Glr.*; with *dan* or *las* far from; *tag-mi-rin-ba* not far *Pth.*; *tag-rin(-po)-nas* from afar, from a distance *Thgy.*; *tag-nyé-ba* **near; proximity;** *W.* adj. **tag-nyé-mo**; *tag ċi-tsam* how far? *Cs.*; *tag-grú* v. *ta-gru*. b. absolutely, only with respect to time, in: *ma-tág* **but just, just now**, gen. with a verbal root, *sleb ma-tág yin-pa* he that has arrived just now *Glr.*; *snar bšad ma-tág-pa* (the passages) that have been explained just now *Gram.*; as an adv. gen. *ma-tág-tu*, or only *ma-tág*, frq., e.g. *tos ma-tág-tu* as soon as he had heard; *de ma-tág-tu* directly, immediately, in *W.* **ma-tóg-tse**. — 3. *tag-tóg* v. *tog-tág.* — 4. *tag-γċód-pa* v. *tág-pa* I.

ཐག་ཐག *tag-tág*, with **ǰhé-pa** *C.*, **ċó-ċe** **to knock,** *sgo* at the door.

ཐག་པ་ *tág-pa* I. **rope, cord** (in *Lh.* hempen ropes, as a foreign manufacture, are often distinguished from other ropes, by being called रस्सी, *bal-tág* rope made of wool, *ral-tág* rope of goat's hair, *rtsid-tág* rope of the long hair of the yak, *rtsa-tág*, or *p̓on-tág Glr.* rope of grass; *lċágs-(kyi) tág-pa* chain, wire-rope, used as fetters or otherwise; **ras-tág** *W.* **bandage;** *tag-mig* **mesh** of a net *Sch.*; *tag-zó* **rope-maker's work** *Pth.* — *tág γċód-pa* vb. a. (*tag čód-pa*, or *čád-pa* vb. n. or pass.) 1. to cut a cord, *bdag nyé-du dan ₒbrél-tag bċád-pas bde* I am glad of having cut the cord (tie) which united me with my family *Mil.*; gen. with *re*, the cord of hope, e.g. *ₒgró-bai ré-tag čad* the cord of the hope of going on a journey is cut off, i.e. the journey has been given up *Glr.; Schr.*: *ₒó-tag γċód-pa* to wean (a child); *bló-tag-ċod* deliberation is cut off, the matter is decided or resolved upon; hence frq. without *blo*: 2. **to decide, resolve, determine,** *rgyal-po bkrón-bar tag-bċád* it was determined to murder the king *Glr.*; *k̓yod γnyis ná-la čún-ma mi len tág-čód-pa-na* if you positively refuse to give me a wife *Pth.*; **tag-ċád mi k̓yud** *W.* I have no right to decide on that point; *tag-čód-pa byéd-pa* to decide, pass sentence, give judgment *Mil.*; **to be sure, decided, certain,** ... *gróns-par tag-bċád-de* (cf. above) as it is quite certain that he has died *Mil.*; ... *yod tag-čód* there are certainly ... *Glr.*; *čos dar ₒón tag-čód* it is quite certain that religion will spread *Mil.*; *ltá-bas tag-bċád-nas* being immovable in contemplation; with termin.: to know for a certainty, to understand or see clearly, *rán-sems čós-skur tag-čód-ċin* knowing one's own mind to be vain and frail (v. *čós-sku* sub *sku* 2) *Mil.*; *snán-ba séms-su* the visible world as a thought, as imaginary, i.e. as nothing *Mil.*; *tag-čód* **certainty, surety, evidence,** *ₒón-kyan tag-čód byed dgos* but one should know it for certain, one must be sure of it *Mil.*; *ltá-ba tag-čód-kyi rnál-ₒbyor-pa* you, the ascetic, firm in meditation! *Mil.* — **tag-čǫ'-rbę'-čǫ'** *C.* resolute.

II. prob. = *dág-pa*, in *snyiṅ* (or *že*, or *bsám-pa*) *ťág-pa-nas* with a faithful heart, with all my heart, **heartily**, *že ťág-pai žú-ba Mil.* a sincere prayer or entreaty.

Note. In *ťag-pa* and other words beginning with *ť*, (e.g. *ťaṅ*, *ťo*), *d* sometimes takes the place of *ť*, and this **uncertainty** in the use of the initial letter **dates perh.** from a time, when the **aspirated pronunciation** of the media first **began to be adopted** in *C.*, and was not **yet generally** introduced.

**ཐགས་** *ťags* **texture, web,** ***ťags*** *˳ťúg-pa* to weave *Dzl.*, *ťágs-˳ťag-mkan* col. for *ťá-ga-pa*, also *ťágs-mkan* ***Pth.*** **a** weaver; **ťser-ťág** *W.* thorn-hedge, **fence** consisting of thorn; *ťags-ǩri* (weaver's) loom *Ld.-Glr.*; *ťágs-gra-˳bu Cs.*, ***ťágs-ǩan-bu*** *W.*, **spider**; *ťágs-ča* weaver's implements; *ťágs-ɣnas*, *ťágs-ra*, a weaver's place or shop *Cs.*; *ťags-brán byéd-pa Mil.*, **ťag rán-če** *W.*, to begin the warp.

**ཐགས་ཐོགས་** *ťags-ťógs* **impediment** *Cs.*

**ཐང་** *ťaṅ* 1. also *ťáṅ-ma Mil.*, *ťáṅ-bu Dzl.* Ms., **ťáṅ-ka** *W.*, flat country, **a plain, steppe**; also fig. like *žiṅ*, *bde-čén-gyi ťaṅ* land of bliss *Mil.*; *ťáṅ-la* (from the house) into the plain or steppe, = into the open air *Dzl.*; *ťáṅ-la ltúṅ-ba* to fall to the ground; **ma-ťáṅ** *W.* the unfloored bottom of a room; *gram-ťáṅ* a fenny or swampy plain *Cs.*; *spaṅ-ťáṅ* a green grassy plain or steppe, meadow, prairie; *byaṅ-ťáṅ* the northern steppes or plains of Tibet (used as a noun proper); *bye-ťáṅ* a sandy desert or plain; *˳ol-ťáṅ* ground covered with (snail-) clover, **pasture ground**, grassy plain; *śag-ťáṅ* a gravelly plain; *ťáṅ-du byéd-pa Cs.* to lay waste, to make a desert of, *ťáṅ-du ˳gyúr-ba* to become a desert. — 2. *Cs.* **price, value,** perh. also amount; *rin-ťáṅ* id. *Dzl.*; *rín-ťaṅ-čan* **dear, precious,** *Mil.*; *yoṅ-ťáṅ* 1. *W.* **income, profit,** 2. *C.* = *yón-tan* **talent,** natural gift, faculty; *lo-ťáṅ* yearly tribute, *ɣčód-pa* to fix, to order it *Tar.*; *za-ťáṅ* (a person's) capability of eating *Thgy.* — 3. *W.* for *dwaṅs* **clear, serene,** **nam ťaṅ** a cloudless sky, fine weather; **daṅ ṗi-ro ťáṅ-te yod** (the sky) was cloudless last night. — 4. **potion** *Med.* — 5. = *bka-ťáṅ*, **order, command,** (*bka*) *ťaṅ-yig* **decree;** *pad-ma-ťaṅ-yig* is the abridged title of a collection of legends about Padma Sambhava. — 6. (**resin?**) *ťaṅ-čú* **resin, gum,** e.g. of fruit-trees. — 7. a very short space of time (the statements as to its length vary from five seconds to one minute and a half), **a moment, a little while,** gen. *ťaṅ ɣčig*, not seldom joined with *skad čig* and *yud tsam*; *ťaṅ tsam* id. *Pth.*; *čig-ťaṅ*, *bži-ťaṅ* one moment, four moments; *Lt.*, *ťaṅ-ré S.g.*, one after the other *Sch.* — 8. v. *ťaṅ-ka*. — In a few instances the meaning of *ťaṅ* is not quite evident.

**Comp.** *ťaṅ-ǩrúṅ* bastard *Sch.* — *ťaṅ-čú* v. *ťaṅ* C. — *ťaṅ-stóṅ* uninhabited, desolate; wilderness. — *ťaṅ-˳brú Sch.* 'cedar-nuts', perh. = *ko-nyon-tsé* q.v. — *ťaṅ-múr* tar *Cs.* — **ťaṅ-ma-la-la-tsé** a small lizard *Ld.* — *ťaṅ-ɣží* market-price, **ťaṅ-ži čag** *C.* the market-price abates. — **ťaṅ-zi** *W.* fata morgana — *ťaṅ-rág* cedar (?) *Sch.* — *ťaṅ-śiṅ* fir, pine.

**ཐང་ཀ, ཐང་ག** *ťáṅ-ka*, *ťáṅ-ga*, resp. *žal-ťáṅ*, *W.* **sku-ťáṅ**, *Tar.* *ťáṅ-sku*, **image,** prop. of human beings, at present = picture, **painting,** in a gen. sense, also of landscapes etc.

**ཐང་དཀར་** *ťaṅ-dkár* the white-tailed eagle *Sch.*

**ཐང་ཐང་** *ťaṅ-ťáṅ* v. the following word.

**ཐང་པོ་** *ťáṅ-po*, **tense, tight, firm** (= *˳ťáṅ-po?*); *ťaṅ-lhód* tight and loose; also tenseness fig. *Mil.*; *ťáṅ-śa ɣčód-pa* to strain, to stretch, *čód-pa* vb. n. or pass. *Stg.*, *Mil.*, *C.*; **zúg-po ťaṅ-ṅam** *C.* are you well? — *rkaṅ-ťáṅ-du* or *la* **on foot,** v. *rkáṅ-pa* comp.; *ťaṅ ɣčod-pa* **to tire, to fatigue** *Mil.*, *ťaṅ čod-pa* or *čad-pa* to be tired, wearied *Pth.*; **gom-ťáṅ láb-če (ťú-gu-la)** *W.* to lead a child in walking, to teach a child to walk; *śa-ťáṅ-ťáṅ* to the utmost of one's power *Sch.*

**ཐང་ཕྲོམ་** *ťaṅ-ṗróm* a medicinal herb *Med.*, *Wdṅ.* = *dha-tu-ra* thorn-apple (?).

ཐང་ཤ་ *ṫáń-ṡa* v. sub *ṫań-po; ṫań-ṡiń* v. *ṫań* comp.

ཐད(ཀ) *ṫád(-ka)* 1. **the direction straight forward,** *steṅ daṅ ˏog daṅ ṫád-ka ṫams-ċád-du* upward and downward, and in every other direction *Stg.; steṅ-ˏog-ṫád-kar* straight upward and downward *S.g.; ṗo-bráṅ-gi ṫád-kar ṗyin* they came straight towards the castle; *ṫád-ka-na* directly before *Thgy.; deï nub-ṫád-kyi* that which is situated to the west of it *Tar.;* most frq. *ṫád-du* c.genit. **towards,** in straight direction; **over against; in presence of** e.g. to assemble, to propound, to lay before one, to study under a professor *Dzl.*; **exactly in the place** of a thing *Tar.* 17, 1; *ṡai ṫád-nas čod Tar.* 159, 4 prob.: cut off only from the flesh; **ṫę'-kya, ṫę'-kaṅ-la** *Ts.* **straight on;** *ṫad-draṅ-na* **directly before** *Wdṅ.;* **ṫad-nyá** *W.* **over against, opposite, facing;** *ṫád-so-na* = *ṫád-ka-na Mil.* — 2. *ṫad-kar* **each for himself** *Glr.* — 3. **entire, whole, untouched, safe** (integer) *C.* and perh. *Thgy.*

ཐོད་ frq. abbreviation for ཐམས་ཅད་ *ṫams-ċád,* **whole, all.**

ཐན་ *ṫan, Hind.* थान, = *yug,* **a piece of cloth.**

ཐན་ཀོར་ *ṫan-kór, ṫan-skór Lex.,* surrounding country *Sch.*

ཐན་ཐུན་ *ṫan-ṫún* (*Schr. ṫad-ṫún*) **a little** *Sch.*

ཐན་པ་ *ṫán-pa* **dry weather, heat, drought** *Glr.*

ཐབ་ *ṫab* 1. resp. *ɣsol-ṫáb,* **fire-place, hearth,** *me-ṫáb,* id.; also for **stove,** *lċags-ṫáb* iron stove; *ṫab ṡor* 'the hearth is running over', i.e. the food placed on it runs over in boiling, a mis-hap the more serious, as the household god is offended by the evil smell caused thereby. — 2. v. sub *čaṅ.*

**Comp.:** **ṫáb-ka** *W.* fire-place, **ṫáb-ka tsam yod** how many fire-places, i.e. households, are there? — *ṫab-ḱúṅ* opening or mouth of a stove, furnace, or fire-place; v. also *Schl.* 249. — *ṫab-ɣnás* fire-place, furnace, oven *Cs.* — **ṫab-tsáṅ** *W.* kitchen. — *ṫab-ṗyis, W.* **ṫab-ṗis** clout, dish-clout, wiper. — *ṫab-ɣžób* burnt smell. — **ṫab-lás ċó-ḱan** *W.* cook. — *ṫab-ɣyóg* kitchen-boy, scullion *Pth.* — *ṫab-ṡiṅ* fire-wood, fuel. — *ṫab-lhá* deity of the hearth.

ཐབ་ཐོབ་ *ṫab-ṫób W.* = *ṫom-ṫóm.*

ཐབས་ *ṫabs* (cog. to *stabs*), **opportunity, chance, possibility,** **ṫóṅ*-or *ḍúl-ṫáb ma ǰuṅ** *W.* I had no opportunity of seeing or going; **ṫab ṡig nyi-ráṅ-ne mi ǰúṅ-na** *W.* if you offer no chance, if on your part it is not made possible; *ṫabs mi ṫub Dzl.* and col. I am not able, I cannot; *ɣdan-dráṅs-pai ṫabs med* I then shall lose the opportunity of meeting (the princess) *Glr.; ˳brós-pai ṫabs med* there is not any chance of escape *Glr.; lám-la ɣžól-ṫabs med* there is no occasion for stopping or tarrying on the road *Mil.;* **way, manner, mode,** *klog-ṫabs* way of reading, e.g. Sanskrit; *rḱún-ṫabs-su* in a thievish manner, by theft *Stg.; rgyál-poi ṫabs ɣtóṅ-ba* to give up the way (of life) of a king, to resign the crown *Dzl., ṫabs ɣċig-tu* together, in company, jointly, e.g. to sit down with one another, to go together to a place, frq.; **means, measures,** *ṫabs byéd-pa, W.* **ċó-ċe, ḱyóṅ-ċe** to use means, to take measures; *blo ṫabs ˳tsól-ba* to contrive means *Ma.; ṫabs stón-pa* to show means or ways, to give directions, to instruct *Glr.; ˳tsó-ṫabs* **livelihood, subsistence;** *ṫabs zad* there is nothing else to be done *Glr.; ži-bai ṫábs-kyis* in a fair way, amicably, not by constraint or compulsion *Glr.*; *ṫábs-kyis* by various means, by artifice, cunningly, craftily; *ṫábs(-la)-mḱás-pa, ṫábs-ṡes-pa, W.* also **ṫáb-ċan**, **skilful, dexterous, clever, full of devices;** *da bód-du ˳gró-ṫabs gyis ṡig* now take steps, make preparations, for a journey to Tibet *Glr.*; *de ɣsón-poi ṫabs yód-dam* is there a means of recalling those men to life? *ṫabs-čág Mil.,* **ṫab-ṡág** or **ṫeb-ṡág** vulgo, a shift, make-shift, surrogate; *ṫabs (daṅ) ṡes (-rab)* the mystical union of art and science, or (*Sch.* less correctly) of matter and spirit, cf. *Was.* (144).

ཐམ་ག, ཐམ་ཀ *ṫám-ga, ṫám-ka* **a seal, sign** *Cs.,* v. *dám-ḱa.*

ཐམ་ཐམ་ *tam-tám Sch.* 1. also *tám-me-ba*, **unconnected, scattered, dispersed.** — 2. *tam-tám (byed) -pa* = *ₒtám-pa.*

ཐམ་པ་ *tám-pa* (sometimes *tém-pa*) **complete, full,** almost exclusively used as a pleon. addition to the tens up to hundred.

ཐམས་ཅད་ *tams-čád* **whole, all;** added to the singular number: *rgyal-ḱáms tams-čád* the whole empire *Glr.*; *lus tams-čád na* the whole body aches (opp. to one part of it); *bód-kyi zaṅs tams-čád* all the copper of Tibet *Glr.*; more frq. added to a plural (though usually in the form of the singular number): all (the persons or things), *de tams-čád*, rarely *dé-dag tams-čád*, all those; *tams-čád-kyis so-só-nas* all of them one by one, each.

ཐམས་པ་ *táms-pa (= ₒtám-pa?), sa,* or *bye-táms-su ₒjug-pa* to suffer (a person or beast) to stick fast in the mud, in the sand (?) *Glr.* 84.

ཐའུ་ *tau Wdṅ.* **capsule** (?), *Wts.* **peach** (?).

ཐར་ *tar* v. *tar-tór.*

ཐར་ཐོར་(ལ་) *tar-tór(-la)* = *ta-ra-to-ré* (cf. *ₒtór-ba*); **tar čós-se dug** *Ld.* sit wide asunder, not too close together! *tar byed-pa Mil.* **to break to pieces, to smash, to crush.**

ཐར་ནུ་ *tár-nu* a purgative *Med.*

ཐར་དཔག་ *tar-dpág, C.* **tar-ₒbág**, *W.* **tá-bag** a large **plate, dish, platter.**

ཐར་བ་ *tár-ba* **to become free, to be saved,** **tar gos*, or *goi** *W.* he must become free, *las* from; to be not hindered or prevented, **to get through, to get on, to be able to pass,** *čú-la* through the water *Mil.; zas mi tar* the food cannot pass through *Med.*; to be released, acquitted, discharged, **ṭ ím-na** *C.* by a court of justice; *tár-du ₒjúg-pa* to set at liberty, to acquit, with *tse* (col. **tse-tár-la táṅ-wa**) to pardon (a malefactor), to grant him his life, frq., to let live (animals) *Mil.;* often in a religious sense (with or without *rnám-par*) **to be saved, freed, released,** viz. from the transmigration of souls; more frq. the pf. *tár-pa* 1. to be free etc., *lam tar* the road is free, passable. 2. sbst. **freedom, liberty, happiness, eternal bliss,** मोक्ष, *tár-pai rgyur ₒgyur* it will be serviceable for (my) liberty; *tár- (pai) lam* the road to happiness (a common expression); *tar-méd-kyi dmyál-ba* hell without release. 3. adj. **free,** *tár-par ₒgyúr-ba* to become free, *byéd-pa* to make free, to liberate, to save; *tár-sa* place of refuge, asylum *Thgy.*

ཐལ་ *tal*, sometimes for *ta-li*; *tál-gyis* v. *tál-ba* II. 3.

ཐལ་བ་ *tál-ba* I. sbst. 1. **dust** (cf. *rdul*), **ashes,** and similar substances; *gog-tál* ashes; **tug-tál** ('soup-dust') roasted barley-flour *C.* — *tal-kár* a kind of elephant, *Cs.*, perh. the ash-coloured. — *tál-ču* lye. — *tal-čén* ashes of the dead; also a sort of light gray earth, representing the former, and used for bedaubing the face in masquerades *Mil.* — *tal-tág Ld.* unleavened bread. — *tal-mdóg* ash-coloured, cinereous. — *tal-pyágs* broom *Sch.* — *tal-byi* the gray or cat-squirrel. — *tal-tsá* a sort of salt *Med.* — 2. *bya-tal* **dung of birds** *Glr.*

II. vb. (*Cs.* also *ₒtál-ba*) 1. **to pass, to pass by,** **tal ča dug** *W.* he goes past, he does not come in; **zám-pa tal ča dug**, he goes past the bridge, does not pass over it; to **miss** the mark, of an arrow or ball; *rba tal-tál ₒoṅ* the waves flow past *Mil.* — 2. **to go, step, pass beyond,** *lo lná-bču tál-nas* when the age of fifty has been passed *Wdṇ.*; **ču-tsód γčig tsá-big tal** *W.* a little past one o'clock; *sṅo-ba-las tal-nas dmar-žiṅ* Thgy., prob. inclining from blue to red; **to be in the advance** *C.*; **to project, to be prominent,** hence *tal-túṅ* different lengths, one object projecting beyond another; **to play a prominent part, to take the lead** *W.*; *tál-čes-pa* **to exceed the due measure** *Sch.*; **ḱa tal-wa** to be forward in speaking, bold. — 3. **to go or pass through,** *brág-la yar tal mar tal,* and *ṕar tal tsur tál-du ₒgró-ba* to soar up and down before a rock, and to pass actually through it (the saints not being subject to the physical laws of matter) *Mil.*, *Thgr.*; **to shine, to light through**; *tal-ᵒbyúṅ-du ₒgró-ba* to go straightforward, to act without ceremony or disguise *Dzl.* ༡༥༢, 3; *tál-ma Sch.*, *tál-le C.*, **through and through**; *tál-gyis* **directly, straightway, unhesitatingly** *Mil.* — 4. **to come or get to, to arrive at** (*W.* **tél-ce**), *tál-nas lo γsum lon* three years have elapsed since they arrived; *p̀a-má gar tál-bai )tol-méd*; *bzaṅ-tál* safe arrival *Thgr.*; *yár-gyi bzáṅ-tal čén-por ₒgró-ba* to arrive at, attain to (a blessed state) in a pleasant and speedy manner *Thgr.* — 5. **to be over, past, finished, done,** *tál-lo* of a song: it is over, finished *Mil.*; *drúg-ču tál-lo* the number of sixty is full; *yál-nas tál-ba Mil.* having disappeared, vanished; *stór-te* (or *stór-nas*) *tal* he is undone, it is all over with him *Mil.* frq.; *rim-gyis ȷe nyúṅ ȷe nyúṅ tal* by degrees it vanishes, dies away *Mil.*; *sṅar čad-tsig tal* the former agreement is no longer valid; *tal soṅ* col. = *tsar soṅ.* — *Tar.* 46, 5. 12? 172, 5: *tál-gyur-pa Schf.* **follower, adherent,** or the name of a certain sect.

ཐལ་མོ་ *tál-mo* **the palm of the hand,** *tál-mo sbyár-ba* to hold together the palms of the hands, as a gesture of devotion; *tál-mo snún-pa Dzl.*, more frq. *tal-lčág rgyáb-pa* to give a slap on the face, a box on the ear; *tal-brdáb-pa* to clap with the hands *Sch.*

ཐི་ *ti* num. fig.: 40.

ཐི་གུ་ *ti-gu* v. *tá-gu*; *ti-gu-kró-bo* (?) *C.* = **ar-gón* W.*

ཐི་བ་ *ti-ba* 1. **wood-pigeon, stock-dove** *Sch.*; *ti-bo* **plover, peewit, lapwing** *Sch.* — 2. *C.* = *té-ba.*

ཐིག་ *tig*, prob. from *ti-gu*, 1. **carpenter's cord** or string to mark lines with, **marking-string,** *tig(-gis) ₒdebs-pa* to use such a string, to draw lines. — 2. any instrument used in drawing lines; *skor-tig* a pair of compasses, *γya-tig* slate-pencil, lead-pencil; also a line drawn with a lead-pencil; **tig-ta taṅ-ce* W.* c. genit. to examine, try, test. — 3. **a line,** *tig-ₒdebs-pa*, *rgyag-pa*, *rgyab-pa*, to draw lines; *guṅ-tig* the meridian line *Cs.*; *nag-tig* or *snag-tig* a black line, *tsal-tig* a red line; *tsaṅs-tig* diameter; equator *Cs.* — 4. symb. numeral for **zero.** — 5. v. *tig.*

**Comp.** *tig-skód* string to mark lines with. — **tig-nyá* W.* **over against.** — *tig-nág Stg.*, *Sch.*: that part of hell, where the damned are sawn to pieces, lines being drawn upon them. — *tig-tsám* **a little.** — *tig-tsád Cs.* **proportion, symmetry,** *Ld.-Glr.* f. 27, 6, *tig-tsad byéd-pa* to proportion; **tig-tsád zúm-ce* W.*, to determine the relation or proportion of things. — *tig-šiṅ* **a ruler,** to rule lines with.

ཐིག་ལེ་ *tig-le* 1. **a spot** like that of a leopard's skin, *tig-le-čan* **spotted, speckled;** *tig-ma* W.* id., of variegated woolen fabrics; *čos tig-le nyag čig Mil.*, the centre of all religion, in which finally all the different sects must unite. — 2. **zero, naught** *Wdk.* — 3. **semen virile.** — 4. **contemplation.** The two latter significations are mystically connected with each other, as will be seen from a passage of *Mil.*, which is also a fair specimen of the physiological and mystical reveries of the more recent Buddhism: *yoṅs lús-la γtúm-mo ₒbár-bas bde; rluṅ ro rkyaṅ dhú-tir čúd-pas bde; stod byaṅ-čub-séms-kyi rgyún-ₒbab bde; smad dáṅs-mai tig-le kyáb-pas bde; bar dkar dmar tug p̀rad brtsé-bas bde; lus zag-med-bdé-bas tsim-pas bde; de rnál-ₒbyor nyáms-kyi bde drug lags*, he (the Yogi) feels well in general, when the warmth of meditation is kindled (cf. *γtúm-mo*) in his body; he feels well, when the air enters through *ró-ma* and *kyáṅ-ma* into the *dhúti*; he feels well in the upper part of his body by the flowing down of the *bődhi*; he feels well in the lower parts by the spreading of the chyle (chylous fluid, semen); he feels well in the middle, by being affected with tender compassion, when the red (the blood in the *kyáṅ-ma*) and the white (the semen in the *ró-ma*) unite; the whole body is well, being pervaded by the grateful feeling of sinlessness; this is the sixfold mental happiness of the Yogi.

ཐིགས་པ *tigs-pa* **a drop,** *tigs-pa re-ré-nas* in drops, by drops *Glr.*; *čar-tigs* a drop of rain; *γsér-tig-po* (sic) *Mil.* seems to denote a drop or globule of molten gold, which in this form is offered for sale by gold-washers.

ཐིང *tiṅ* v. *ˌdiṅ-ba.*

ཐིབ་པ *tib-pa* v. *ˌtib-pa* and *γtib-pa*; *tib-tib* **very dark** *Sch.*; *byin-rlábs tibs-tibs Pth.* seems to imply the descending of a blessing upon a person; *tib(s)-po, mo* **dense,** *Cs.* or perh. nothing but **obscure, dark,** *nags Stg.*

ཐིམ་པ *tim-pa*, also *ˌtim-pa, γtim-pa* and *stim-pa*, gen. with *la* or *náṅ-du*, **to disappear** by being **imbibed, absorbed; to evaporate,** of fluids; of a snake: **to creep away,** to disappear in a hole; frq. of the vanishing of rays of lights, of gods etc.; **to be melted, dissolved** (salt or sugar in water); **to sink,** *dran-méd-du* into unconsciousness *Mil.*

ཐུ *tu* 1. num. fig.: 70. — 2. **tu gyáb-če* W.* **to spit,** with *la*, to spit at or on. — 3. often erron. for *mtu.*

ཐུ་བ *tu-ba* 1. also *tú-pa*, **skirt, coat-flap** *Glr.* — 2. rarely *ˌtú-ba*, **bad,** e.g. wood *Mil.*; **gyal-tú* W.* good and bad promiscuously; *sdug-bsṅál tú-ba* a bad accident *Thgy.*; **malicious, wicked, vicious** *Glr.* — 3. vb., v. *ˌtú-ba.*

ཐུ་བོ *tú-bo* **ཛྱེཥྛ a chief; an elder brother,** *Dzl.*, *Tar.*; *tú-mo Cs.*: mistress, lady (?).

ཐུ་མི *tu-mi* p. n., v. *ton-mi.*

ཐུ་རེ *tu-ré* **uninterrupted** *Sch.*

ཐུ་ལུམ *tu-lúm* **a lump of metal** *B.*; *W.* **cannon-ball:**

ཐུག *tug*, *C.* also **túg-pa**, c. accus. **until, to,** in reference to time and space; **žag zib-ču tug** for forty days; only col.

ཐུག་ཚོམ *tug-čóm Sch.*: **'dreadful noise'**; *Thgr. tug-tsóm*; *Mil. tug-sgrá* id.

ཐུག་པ *túg-pa* I. sbst. **soup, broth,** *ˌbras-túg* rice-soup, *bag-túg* meal-soup, gruel, *rgya-túg* Chinese soup, a sort of vermicelli-soup *C.*; *tug-tál* v. *tál-ba.*

II. vb. 1. **to reach, arrive at, come to,** c. dat. or termin., *tseï mtar túg-pa* to reach the natural term of life *Dzl.*; to come or go as far as *Dzl.*; *rús-pa-la túg-pa* to pierce to the quick *Dzl.*; *ši-la tug tse Mil.*, *ˌči-bar túg-pa-la Lt.* when one is near death; ... *la túg-gi bár-du* till, until *Dzl.*, *Tar.*, *Pth.*; *bzúṅ-la tug* he was just on the point of seizing her *Dzl.*; **sád-da tug* W.* going to kill; *ši-la* (or *bsád-pa-la*) *túg-pa* often means deserving death (of culprits) *Dzl.*; *tse ˌpó-ba-la tug kyaṅ* though life is at stake *Dzl.*; in like manner *W.*: **lus šrog daṅ túg-te ča dug** he goes at the peril of his life; *tug-yas* not to be reached, endless *Cs.* — 2. **to meet, to light upon,** c. *la* or *daṅ*, = *ˌṕrád-pa*, esp. col. **nyi-ráṅ-la túg-ga-la yoṅs* W.* he has come to see you; **tug yin* W.* we shall meet again, = till we meet again! à revoir! *ǰág-pa daṅ túg-pa Mil.* to fall in with robbers; *γdoṅ túg-pa* = *túg-pa*; *či-la tug ruṅ Mil.*, **ghá-la tug kyaṅ* C.* whatever may happen to me; *tug-čád* agreement to meet *Sch.* — 3. col. **to touch, to hit or strike against,** *W.*: **ï-ru túg-kan** here it touches, or strikes against; here is the rub; **lag-pa mi tug yin** I shall not touch it, I shall not come near with my hand; **dé-la tug kyaṅ ma tug* W.* do not even touch it!

ཐུགས *tugs*, resp. for *snyiṅ, yid, sems, bsám-pa, blo* etc., and whenever mental qualities or actions are spoken of in respectful language, v. below. 1. **heart, breast,** in a physical sense, gen. *túgs-ka*; *túgs-kyi sprúl-pa* the incarnation of a deity, originating in a ray of light which proceeds from the breast of that deity *Glr.* — 2. **heart,** in a spiritual sense, **mind, soul, spirit, will,** v. below; **design, purpose, intention,** *sbyin-pai tug zlóg-tu γsol* we beg to desist from the intention of giving *Dzl.*; **understanding, intellect** *Glr.* (v. *sgám-pa*); *túgs-*

*su čúd-pa* = *ḱoṅ-du čúd-pa*; *ťúgs-su* *₀byóṅ-pa* to be kept in mind, in memory *Mil.*; also = *yid-du ₒóṅ-ba* ni f.; cf. *₀gró-ba*. — 3. *ťúgs-la btúgs-so* v. *₀dógs-pa*. — 4. for *ťúgs-rǰe* or *bka-drin*, *ťugs mdzád-pa* **to grant or show a favour** *Dzl.* — 5 in the phrase *ťugs mi ťúb-pa*, with the genit. of the inf., it is used without ceremonial distinctions for **to venture, to risk, to dare** *Dzl.*

**Comp.** *ťúgs-ka* v. above — *ťugs-mḱyén* resp. for *mṅon-šés Mil.* — *ťugs-₀ḱrúgs* resp. for *ḱoṅ-₀ḱrúgs Ma.* — *ťugs-dgóṅs* = *dgóṅs-pa* II.; *ťugs-dgóṅs γtóṅ-ba* = *bsam-bló γtóṅ-ba* **to muse, meditate, reflect** *Mil.* — *ťúgs(-su) ₀gró-ba* resp. for *yid-du ₒóṅ-ba* **to be agreeable; agreeable, pleasant, delightful; pleasure, delight,** ... *la* in (a thing) *Mil.* — *ťugs-ṙgyál* resp. **anger, wrath, indignation** *Mil.*, *ťugs-rgyál bžeṅs* anger arises, is roused. — *ťugs-ṅán* **grief, sorrow, affliction** *Dzl.* — *ťúgs-čes-pa* resp. for *yid-čes-pa* to believe. — *ťúgs-rǰe* prop. respectful word for *snyiṅ-rǰe* **pity, commiseration, compassion;** gen. **grace, mercy, generosity,** *ṅa-la ťúgs-rǰe(s) γzigs* pray, look graciously upon me! *Mil.*; even thus: *sá-bon žig ťúgs-rǰe γzigs dgos*, pray, be so kind as to send me some seeds! *W.* — *ťúgs-rǰes ₀dzin-pa*, *ťúgs-rǰe mdzád-pa* id. — *ťúgs-rǰe-čan* **gracious, merciful, generous.** — (*lha*) *ťúgs-rǰe čén-po* the All-merciful, Awalokiteswara. — *ťugs-dám*, prop. resp. for *yi-dam*, 1. **oath, vow, solemn promise,** e.g. *bčá-ba* to take (an oath), to make (a vow). 2. **a prayer,** a wish in the form of a prayer, = *smón-lam*. 3. **contemplation,** the act of contemplating a deity (cf. *sgóm-pa* and *sgrúb-pa*); **meditation** in general, *Mil.* frq., *ťugs-dám ₀pel* meditation increases, proceeds successfully; **devotion.** 4. **a deity, a tutelar god** or **saint, a patron** *Glr.* — *ťugs-nyid* v. *sems-nyid*, sub *sems.* — *ťugs-múg* resp. for *yi(d)-múg* despair. — *ťugs bdé-ba*, *mi bdé-ba*, v. *bdé-ba*. — *ťugs-γtsigs-pa* to be cautious *Sch.*; v. however *γtsigs-pa*. — *ťugs-brtsé-ba* **love, affection of the heart, compassion,** resp. for *snyiṅ-brtsé-ba*, frq., *ťugs-brtse-bar dgóṅs-pa*, *γzigs-pa*, with *la*, to look upon compassionately, to remember in mercy. — *ťugs-ráb Sch.* = *šes-ráb*. — *ťugs-rús Mil.* = *snyiṅ-rús*. — *ťugs-(kyi) srás Mil.*, *Tar.*, **spiritual son,** an appellation given to the most distinguished scholars of saints.

ཐུང་ང་ *ťuṅ-ṅa* **three years old,** of animals *Sch.*

ཐུང་བ་ *ťúṅ-ba*, col. *ťúṅ-ṅu*, *Ld.* **ťúṅ-se**, **short,** relative to space, time, quantity of vowels etc.; *ťuṅ-ṅu ₀gro-ba* to become shorter; but the word is not so much used as 'short' is in English; *yid ťúṅ-ba Dzl.*, *spro ťúṅ-ba Wdṅ.* **passionate, hot-tempered, hasty.**

ཐུད་ *ťud* **cheese** made of buttermilk, or of *čur-pe*, butter and milk *Ld.*, *Glr.*, *Pth.*; *ₒo-ťúd* milk-cheese, made of curd, or of milk coagulated with runnet.

ཐུན་ *ťun* I. a regular amount, a fixed quantity 1. of time, a certain length of time, as long as a man is able to work without resting, **a shift,** six, four, or three hours; *Schf.* translates *Tar.* 67, 17 even by one hour; **a night-watch,** *mel-tse ťun ₀ḱor* the night-watch is over *Dzl.*; *ťun bžii rnal-₀byor* the meditation of a whole day *Mil.*; **ťun čád-če** *W.* (the cock) announces the watch (by crowing); *ťun bzuṅ-ba Pth.* prob. to have the watch; *nam-gyi guṅ-ťun-la* at or about midnight; *sród-kyi gúṅ-ťun-la Mil.* prob. id. — 2. **a dose of medicine** *Med.* frq. — *ťun-log?*

II. **in sorcery:** bodies or substances which are supposed to be possessed of magic virtues, such as sand, barley, certain seeds etc., *ťun-dóṅ* a hole in which such substances are concealed; *ťun-rá* a horn to carry them; *ťun γsó-ba* to revive a charm *Mil. nt.*

III. one who collects, **a gatherer** (from *₀ťú-ba*), *šiṅ-ťún* one who picks up or gathers sticks *Mil.*; *rtsa-ťun* a gatherer of grass, *snye-ťún* a gatherer of ears of corn *Cs.*; *ťun-zór* reaping-hook, sickle *Sch.*

IV. *ťun*, or more frq. *ťun-móṅ(s)*, **usual,**

**daily,** what is done or is happening every day; **common, general,** *dṅos-grub ṫun-moṅs* earthly goods, as well as intellectual endowments, considered as common property, but not spiritual gifts; *ṫun-min, ṫun-moṅs ma yin-pa* **unusual, uncommon,** not for every body; **ċig-la ċig ṫun-móṅ ċo** take good care to live together in harmony *W.*; *ṫun-móṅ-du* or *su* **in common, in company, jointly;** *ṫun-moṅ* by itself is also used as adv., = *ṫun-spyir,* **in general.**

ཐུབ་པ *ṫúb-pa* (**शक्**) I. vb., c. accus., sometimes c. dat., 1. **to get the better of, to be able to cope with, to be a match for** (an enemy), **to be able to stand or bear** (the cold etc.), **to be able to do one harm, to get at one,** *dug-gis ma ṫub-ċiṅ* as the poison could not do him any harm *Dzl.*; **to be able to quench, extinguish, keep off** e.g. fire, hail *Glr.*; *γžán-gyis mi ṫúb-pa* **invincible,** not to be overcome; *ṅan dgu ṫúb-pa* to be able to subdue every thing that is bad *Lt.*; **to have under one's command** or **control, to keep under,** e.g. one's own body; **to be able to bear,** e.g. *mis ṫúb-par dka* (water from a glacier) is not easily borne by man, i.e. does not agree with him *Med.*; *ras rkyaṅ ṫub-pa* to be able to bear a simple cotton dress *Mil.*; *lo brgya ṫúb-pa* to live to (the age of) a hundred years, frq. — 2. with a supine or verbal root, **to be able,** col. the usual word, in B. gen. *nús-pa*; cf. *γṫúb-pa.*

II. sbst. 1. **शाक्य a mighty one, one having power and authority,** *śā-kya-ṫub-pa* Buddha; a wise man, a sage, a saint in general, **मुनि**. — 2. symb. num. for 7.

ཐུམ(ས)་ *ṫum(s),* also *ṫúm-pa Cs., ṫúm-po Sch.,* 1. **cover, covering, wrapper,** of a book or a parcel; *rgyáb-pa Sch.* to put (a cover round a thing), to wrap up; **śig-pa* C., W., *śáṅ-pa* C.* to take off (a covering); *ṫúm-ċan* having a cover. — 2. **a parcel wrapped up** (in paper etc.); *ₒbru-taṅ-ṫúm bċas* together with a small parcel of tea.

ཐུམ་པ *ṫúm-pa* 1. v. *ṫum.* 2. v. *γnyid.*

ཐུམ་བུ, ཐོམ་བུ *ṫúm-bu, ṫóm-bu* **a large spoon, a ladle;** *rag-ṫúm* a brass ladle, *zaṅs-ṫúm* a copper ladle.

ཐུར་ *ṫur* 1. *Cs.* **a declivity** (?), prob. only adverbially: **down;** *ṫur-lám* a downhill road; *ṫúr-la, ṫúr-du* down, downward, *ₒgró-ba* to go down, *núb-pa* to sink down; *mgo ṫúr-du bstán-te* head down, head over heels *Stg.*; **ṫi-pi ṫúr-la súb-ċe* W.* to uncock one's cap. — 2. v. *ṫúr-mgo,* and *ṫúr-ma.*

ཐུར་མགོ *ṫúr-mgo* 1. **the tip of a spoon,** *ṫúr-mgo tsam* as a measure *Mil.* — 2. also *ṫór-mgo* halter, **ṫúr-go ċúg-ċe* W.* to bridle, to bit (a horse); **ṫúr-la ṫén-ċe* W.* to strive, to struggle against; to rear. — *ṫur-ṫág* the rein, *ṫur-mṫa* the end of the rein.

ཐུར་བུ, ཐུར་རུ་ *ṫúr-bu, ṫúr-ru* **foal, colt, filly.**

ཐུར་མ *ṫúr-ma, W. *ṫur-maṅ*,* 1. **spoon.** — 2. Chinese **chopsticks.** — 3. **a pole** *Dzl.* ༢༧༢, 4. — 4. a whole class of surgical instruments *S.g.*

ཐུལ་ *ṫul* 1. **egg** (acc. to Cunningham a Cashmiri word), *ṫúl-ta-gir* pancake. — 2. v. *ₒdúl-ba,* also substantively: *ṫul de min* besides this **way of converting** (people) *Pth.*; *ṫul ₒóg-tu ₒjúg-pa Tar.* 25, 16 to keep a tight hand over a person, to discipline one; *žiṅ-gi ṫul ₒdébs-pa Ld.-Glr.* to clear land for tillage, ni f.

ཐུལ་པ་ *ṫúl-pa, Cs.* also *ṫúl-po,* dress made of the skins of animals, **a furred coat** or **cloak** *Mil.*; *lúg-ṫul* dress of sheep-skin, *rá-ṫul* dress of goat-skin, *ṫúl-lu* the common sheep-skin dress; **ṫúl-ċan* W.* wide, not fitting close or tight.

ཐུལ་བ *ṫúl-ba* 1. pf. to *ₒdúl-ba,* **to tame, curb, check, restrain,** *Mil.*: *ṅás ₒdré-rnams ṫúl-nas* the goblins having been subdued by me; *las nyon-moṅs ṫúl-ba dka* it is difficult to check a sinful deed *Mil.*; participle: tamed, civilized; converted. — 2. **to roll** or **wind up** *Lh.*

ཐུལ་ལེ་ *ṫúl-le Ld.* **impressive,** nearly the same as *ṫúr-re.*

ཐུས་པ *ṫús-pa* 1. **bad** = *ṫú-ba,* prov.; 2. v. *ₒṫú-ba.*

ཐེ་ *te* 1. for *té-mo*; 2. num.: 100.

ཐེ་རྟོག་ *te-rtóg* **scruple, doubt, uncertainty, hesitation,** occasionally used for *te-tsóm.*

ཐེ་བ་ *té-ba, C.* also **ti-ba**, pf. *tes Sch.*, the col. syn. of *γtógs-pa*, seldom in *B.*, 1. **to belong, appertain to,** c. *la.* — 2. **to occupy one's self** with a thing, **to meddle with, to interfere,** c. *dan* (= *ₒdri-ba*); *té-mk'an* belonging together, c. *la*, belonging to a thing; **ma-té-a* W.* for *ma-té-bar*, = *ma-γtógs-par*; *te-rég* the connexion or relation of ownership, *di-la yáb-kyi te-rég med* to this my father has no claims *Mil. nt.*

ཐེ་བོ་, ཐེ་བོང་ *té-bo, te-bón W.* **thumb,** v. *téb-mo.*

ཐེ་མོ་ *té-mo*, col. *té-tse*, diminutive *teu*, resp. *p'yag-té* **seal, signet, stamp,** **té-tse gyáb-če*, or *nán-če** to seal, to stamp; *sa-té Tar.* 79, 12(?); **té-tse lag-kór tán-wa** to engage, to bind one's self by a seal in some common concern.

ཐེ་ཚོམ་ *te-tsóm* **doubt, scruple, uncertainty, perplexity,** *te-tsóm skyes, byed* (*W.* **čo**), *za, te-tsóm-du gyur* I am doubtful; *te-tsom za-ba-rnams* scrupulous, irresolute persons *Pth.*; **te-tsom man-po rag* W.* I am in great perplexity, I am quite at a loss; *te-tsom žig ₒdri-ba* to utter a doubt *Dzl.*

ཐེ་རང་ *te-ran* v. *teu-ran.*

ཐེ་རེ་ *te-ré* col. **straight, upright, firm; smooth,** without folds or wrinkles; *te-ré tin C.* draw (the carpet) smooth.

ཐེ་རེལ་ *te-rél W.* **incomplete, defective, unfinished,** *te-rél-la lus son* (the loaf) is not whole, there has already been cut from it.

ཐེ་ལི་ *te-li* v. *ta-li.*

ཐེག་པ་ *tég-pa* I. sbst. **यान**, 1. **vehicle, carriage, riding-beast,** *rtai tég-pa-la žon* he mounted on horseback *Dzl.*; *tég-pa lna-brgyá bsams* he procured five hundred conveyances (horses, elephants, carriages) *Dzl.* 2. for attaining to salvation, *tég-pa γsum* **three conveyances** are generally mentioned, but in most cases only two are specified, viz. *tég-(pa) dman(-pa)*, **हीनयान**, and *teg(-pa) čen-po*, **महायान**, gen. called 'the little and the great conveyance or vehicle', by means of which the distant shore of salvation may be reached. Yet mention is also made of a *snágs-kyi tég-pa*, **मन्त्रयान** *mantrayāna*, e.g. *Tar.* 180, 13. For more particulars about these vehicles, and other more or less confused and contradictory notions, the works of *Köppen* and esp. *Wasiljew* may be consulted.

II. vb. 1. **to lift, raise, hold up, support** *Mil., Glr.*; hence *k'ri-tégs* leg of a table *Sch.*; *teg-k'úg C.* knapsack, travelling-bag. — 2. **to raise, set up fig.** *bšad-gád* to raise a loud laugh *Mil.* — 3. most. frq. **to be able to carry,** *ji tég-pa* as much as you are able to carry *Dzl.*; *mis teg-tsád γčig* as much as one man is able to carry *Tar.*; esp. with a negative: *ma teg* he was not able to hold him up *Dzl.*; *mi-teg k'ur* to carry what is too heavy to be carried (by ordinary muscular strength), to strain one's self by lifting, *Med.*; to endure, tolerate, stand, *k'ón-rnams-kyi nan ma teg-par* not being able to stand their urgent demands *Mil.*; **to bear, to undergo without detriment,** *skyid teg sdug teg* to be able to bear good fortune and ill fortune. Cf. *ₒtégs-pa, ₒdégs-pa.* —

ཐེང་ *ten* 1 *ten-ró Mil.*, **ša-tén* Ld.*, the dead body of an animal killed by beasts of prey. — 2. **tén-la* C.* **down, downward,** e.g. **kyúr-wa, yúg-pa, bór-wa**, to fling down.

ཐེང་པོ་ *tén-po Pth.*, *tén-bu Sch.*, **tén-k'an* W.*, **lame, hobbling, limping.**

ཐེངས་ *tens* **time, times,** *tens lna* five times *Pth.*; *dbugs-tens čig-la* in one breathing, at a stretch; without intermission *Pth.*

ཐེན་ *ten* 1. **a little while, a moment.** — 2. v. *ₒten-pa.*

ཐེན་པ་ *tén-pa* **tax, duty, impost** *Sch.*

ཐེབ་ *ťeb* 1. for *ťem*, **full** *Glr.* — 2. for *ťabs* *Glr.*, *C.* — 3. *ťéb-mo*, *ťeb-čén* the thumb, *ťeb-čúṅ* the little finger; v. *mťe-boṅ*.

ཐེབས་ *ťebs* **series, order, succession** *Sch.*, *ťebs-re byed-pa* to do successively; *ťébs-pa* v. *ₒťebs-pa*.

ཐེམ་པ་ *ťém-pa* I. 1. **threshold**, *rgál-ba* to cross it *Glr.*; *sgo-ťém* door-sill, threshold; *yá-ťém* head-piece of a door-frame, lintel, *ma-ťém* sill, threshold *Glr.* — 2. **staircase, stairs, flight of steps,** *ťem-skás* id.; **ťem-só** *W.* **step, stair;** *ťem-rim* *Cs.* 1. the several steps of a staircase. 2. **rank, dignity.** — *rdo-ťém* stone staircase; *ǩor-ťém* winding stairs *Cs.* — II. 1. **to be full, complete,** *zla-dus ťem-pa daṅ* when the time of the months was fulfilled *Glr.* frq.; *žag γčig ma ťém-pa-la* one day being still wanting *Glr.*; *brgya ťém-pa* v. *ťam-pa Glr.* — 2. *W.*: **to be sufficient, enough.** — 3. **to receive** (?) *Sch.*

III. *Sch.* = *ťén-pa*, **tax, impost, tribute.**

ཐེམ་བུ་ *ťém-bu*, *ťem-tsaṅs* **stopping, closing, shutting up; a stoppage** *Sch.*

ཐེམས་ཡིག་ *ťems-yig Sch.* **memorial.**

ཐེའུ་རང་ *ťeu-ráṅ Glr.*, *ťe-bráṅ Lt.*, *ťe-ráṅ Ma.*, a sort of **demons.**

ཐེར་ *ťer* 1. **bald, bare,** *spyi-ťér Thgy.* a bald head; a bald-headed person; *ťer-ťér C.* flat. — 2. = *ťe-ré* (?) *ṗyi ťer naṅ gog* strong and hale outside, decayed within *Mil.*; *ťer-zúg-pa* = *rtág-pa Thgr.*

ཐེར་འབུམ་ *ťer-ₒbúm Sch.* 1 000 000 000; *ťer-ₒbum-čén-po* 10 000 000 000.

ཐེར་མ་ *ťér-ma* a kind of thin woollen cloth, a flannel-like fabric, *le-ťer* made of shawl-wool, *bal-ťer* of common wool.

ཐེལ་ *ťel* for *ťe-li*, *rag-ťél C.* a plate made of latten brass.

ཐེལ་བ་ *ťél-ba W.* frq. = *sléb-pa* **to arrive,** cf. *ťál-ba* II., 4.

ཐེལ་སེ་ *ťél-se Sch.* and *Wts.* **a seal, stamp,** = *ťe-tse.*

ཐེས་པ་ *ťés-pa Sch.* pf. to *ťé-ba*; = *ťes-bsún Lt.?*

ཐོ་ *ťo* 1. num. for 130. — 2. **register, list, catalogue, index;** *ťo ₒbrí-ba* to register, to make out a list or catalogue *Schr.*; *sléb-ťo*, *ₒbyúṅ-ťo* account of receipts, *sóṅ-ťo*, *búd-ťo*, *skyág-ťo* account of expenditures; *btáṅ-ťo* account of money or goods lent out; *nyó-ťo* account of goods bought, bill; *lo-ťo* **calendar, almanac;** *dei lág-tu ṗrin-bor-ťo* list of orders or directions given to him (lit. laid down in his hands); *dei rgyúd-la ťób-ťo* a list of things which his relations shall receive.

ཐོ་གར་ *ťo-gár Pth.*; acc. to *Sch.* **the Turkomans;** *Tar.* 18, *Schf.*: **Tukhara,** name of a people in the northwest of India; prob. the **Togarmah** of the Bible.

ཐོ་ཅོ་ *ťo-čo Mil.*, **a foolish joke,** unbefitting a sensible man.

ཐོ་ཕྱི་ *ťo-ṗyi Schr.* **love** (?), in *Pth.* it seems to signify the **sky.**

ཐོ་བ་, མཐོ་བ་ *ťó-ba*, *mťó-ba*, **a large hammer,** *ťó-bas rdúṅ-ba* to hammer, to forge; *rdó-ťo* a stone hammer, *śiṅ-ťo* a wooden hammer, mallet; **ťo-čúṅ** 1. an ordinary hammer. — 2. **the cock of a gun.** — 3. **a soldering-stick.** *Lh.*

ཐོ་འཚམ་པ་ *ťo-ₒtsám-pa* **to scorn, scoff, jeer, sneer at, vex, insult, mock,** c. *la*, by words *Dzl.*, also by actions *Dzl.*; *snan-čud ťo-ₒtsám-pa bzód-par γsol* pardon our having sneered at you before! *Mil.*; also *mťo-mťsám-pa*, *-btsám-pa*, *-brtsám-pa*.

ཐོ་ཡོར་ *ťo-yór* **stone pyramid, heap of stones** (cairn).

ཐོ་རངས་ *ťo-ráṅs* 1. **dawn, break of day, early morning,** *ťo-ráṅs(-kyi) dús-su* early in the morning; 2. **the following, the next morning,** c. genit.; both also adverbially: *de daṅ mǰal-bai ťo-ráṅs* on the morning after having met him.

ཐོ་རེ་ *ťó-re W.* **to-morrow** (*B.*, *C.* *saṅ*).

ཐོ་རེ་བ་ *ťó-re-ba*, *ťor-tsál Cs.*: **a few;** *Mil.*, *ťog-re-tsal* **a little while.**

ཐོ་ལུམ་ *ťo-lúm* v. *ťu-lúm*.

ཐོ་ལེ་ *ťo-lé* 1. *ťo-lé ₒdébs-pa* **to spit,** c. *la*, at or on *Pth.* (cf. *ťu*). — 2. **button** *C.* — 3. *ťo-lé dkár-po C.* **chalk.** — 4. *ťo-le-rgyal Mil.?*

ཐོ་ལོག་ *ťo-lóg C.* **mule, hinny.**

ཐོག་ *ťog* I. **what is uppermost** 1. **roof,** *ťog ˳búbs-pa* to cover with a roof, to roof (a house) frq.; *ťog ˳gél-ba* id.; also fig. **to complete, to crown a thing** *Mil.*; **ťóg-sa nán-ċe* W.* **to roof, to finish a roof** by beating and stamping down the earth or sods, of which the covering consists; *ťog-rdzis γtón-ba Mil.* id.; also fig. **to impress,** c. genit., *Mil.* — **ťog-kár* W.*, the opening for the smoke in a roof. — *ťog-ċan* having a roof, **ťóg-yog* W.* under cover. — 2. **ceiling;** *yá-ťog* ceiling, *má-ťog* floor of a room. — 3. **story,** *dgu-ťóg* having nine stories or floors, frq. — 4. in a general sense: *ťog ˳drén-pa Mil.* **to be at the head, to lead, direct, govern;** *ťog-ḱar, W. *ḱa-ťóg-la**, **on, upon,** *ḱyág-ťog-ḱar* on the ice *Glr.*; *ťóg-tu*, and *ťog-ťóg* adv. **up, up to; above;** *yáṅ-ťog-tu* in the uppermost place, quite at the top, *Glr.*; postp. c. genit. (or accus.) 1. **on, upon,** e.g. to lay on, to place upon *Pth.; sems ťóg-tu ľǰi-bar byúṅ-nas* lying heavy, weighing heavily, upon one's mind *Glr.; ṅai ťóg-tu byuṅ* my heart was smitten (by that); that has touched, has grieved my heart *Mil.*; *ťog-tu ḱel-ba Mil.*, vb. act. to it. 2. **above** *Glr.* 3. **towards,** in the direction of, e.g. running towards, *mai ťog-tu Dzl.*; *yá-ťog, má-ťog* ad. **above, below,** or **up to, up stairs,** and **down, down stairs** *Mil.* 4. **to,** e.g. to send to *Dzl.* 5. *dmag-ťog* **at the head of** the army, or only **with** the army. 6. **during, as long as, throughout; whilst** (*ťog* gen. without *-tu*), *dgun-ťog* throughout the whole winter; **dir ḁ-ḱu sem ťser ťog** whilst her husband is here in great anxiety *Ld.; bgros-ťog* during the walk. Cf. also *ṅa-og, p̀i-ťog* as sbst.: **morning, evening, forenoon, afternoon** *W.* 7. **directly after,** *bżos-ťog ˳ó-ma* fresh milk, *S.g.* (s.l.c.). — *ťog-nas* 1. **above, more than,** **lo ṅab-ču̧ ťog-nȩ ma lus* Ld.* they remained, i.e. lived not more than fifty years. 2. **on the part of,** *Thgy.*, analogous to *p̀yógs-nas.*

II. **thunderbolt, lightning;** *ťog daṅ sér-ba* lightning and hail, *ťog-sér-gyi γnód-pa* damage done by the elements; *ťog ˳báb-pa* lightning descending, *rgyab-pa* striking, *ťog-bábs-su ˳byón-pa* to arrive, to approach quick or suddenly like lightning *Tar.*, resp.; *ťóg-gis γsód-pa S.g.*, *ťog báb-ste ˳či-ba Do.* to be killed by lightning.

III. 1. **fruit, produce,** *dkár-ťog* v. *dkár-po; żiṅ-ťog* produce of the fields *Dzl.*; *lo-ťóg* a year's produce; *śiṅ-ťóg* produce of a tree or other plant, fruit; *γsar-ťóg* this year's crop *S.g.*; *ťog-p̀úd* **first-fruits, as an** offering; *ťog-śás* id.(?). — 2. *W.* **fortune, wealth, property,** **ṅúl-li ťog** property in money, cash in hand; *(s)pi-ťog* common property, property belonging to a community.

IV. in *ma-ťog(-ťse)* for *ma ťag*, col. and *Thgy.*, s.l.c., v. *ťag*. Cf. also *ťog-ťág, ťóg-ma, ťógs-pa.*

ཐོག་ཐག་ *ťog-ťág*, prob. augmentative of *ťog*, v. *ťóg-tu* 6, also *ťag-ťóg*, **during, as long as, throughout; quite,** *mťsan ťog-ťág-tu* all night long; *nyi-ma-γčig-gi bár-du ťog-ťág* during a whole day; *lam ťog-ťág gáṅ-ṅo* the roads were quite full (of snow) *Dzl.*

ཐོག་མ་ *ťóg-ma* **what is uppermost,** 1. **the upper end, the uppermost place,** *grál-gyi ťóg-ma-la ˳dúg-go* they sat down in the first, or uppermost, place *Dzl.*; gen. 2. **origin, beginning;** *ťóg-mai saṅs-rgyás kun-tu-bzáṅ-po* Adibuddha Samantabhadra, so a deity is called, by which a prayer has been appointed that is supposed to be particularly efficacious; *ťóg-ma ťo-rigs mťó-ba* of noble birth, as regards his origin *Dzl.*; *ťóg-ma btsás-pai ťsé-na, ťóg-ma btsás-nas, ťóg-ma skyés-nas* already at his birth, from his very birth *Dzl.*; *ťog-ma méd-pa-nas, dus ťog-méd-nas* time out of mind, from eternity; *ťóg-ma-nas* from the very beginning; of itself; as a matter of course *Dzl.; bsúbs-pai ťog-ťág-la* as soon as they began to fill up *Glr.; ťog-mťa-bar-du* at first, later, in conclusion (lit. in the beginning, end, and middle) *Lt.*; most frq. *ťóg-mar* 1. **at first, first,** the Lat. primum,

ཐ

primo, and primus. — 2. postp. c. genit. **before**, with respect to time *Mil.* — *tog-drans-pa Pth., Glr., Sch.*: 'at first, begun'; our Lama explained it by **'to lead, to guide'**, v. *tog* I, 4.

ཐོག་ཚད་ *tog-tsád W.* **story** (of a house); *tóg-so Mil. nt.* id.

ཐོགས་ *togs* v. *ₒdógs-pa*, and *ₒtógs-pa*.

ཐོགས་པ་ *tógs-pa*, c. *la*, **to strike, stumble, run against** (like *túg-pa* v. 3); **to be hindered, impeded, delayed,** frq.; *mi kyi gáṅ-laaṅ tógs-pa méd-du* without being hindered by men, dogs, or anything else *Mil.*; *togs-pa-méd-pa, togs-méd, togs-brdúgs-*(or(b)*rtug-*)*méd-pa*, असङ्ग **not hindered, unimpeded, unchecked; all-searching, all-penetrating.**

ཐོང་ *toṅ*, *toṅ-ṡól* **a plough.**

ཐོང་ཁ་ *tóṅ-ka Mil., toṅ-ga Mṅg.?*

ཐོང་པ་ *tóṅ-pa* 1. *Cs.* **a ploughman.** — 2. *Cs.*: **'a ram** that is castrated, **wether;** *ra-toṅ* a castrated he-goat'; according to my authorities, however, *tóṅ-pa*, and *ra-tóṅ* signify a ram and he-goat **one year old,** *toṅ-tsér* and *ra-tsér* being the feminine forms (?) — 3. *tóṅ-pai lo Mil.* the years between childhood and manhood, **juvenile years,** *Sch. tóṅ-po*, cf. *kyóg-toṅ*.

ཐོང་སྤུ་ *tóṅ-spu* **mane of the camel** *Sch.*

ཐོངས་པ་ *tóṅs-pa Mil.?*

ཐོད་ *tod* 1. *Cs.* **a head-ornament, crown;** gen. the usual covering for the head in the East, **turban,** *la-tód Glr.* id.; *dbu-tód* resp.; *sá-yig tód-du bċiṅs-pai ka* the letter k having for a crown the letter s: སྐ *Zam.* — 2. = *tog* I.: **go-tọ̈** *C.* **over** or **above** the door; *ka-tód-la, ka-tóg-la, ka-tód-la,* **up, upon** *Ld.* — 3. **threshold,** *yá-tod, má-tod* = *yá-re, má-re.* — 4. v. *tód-pa.* — 5. *tod-rgál čé-ba* (*toṅ?*) *Mil.*, acc. to the context: **angry, wrathful.** — 6. *tod-tód* v. *su.*

ཐོད་པ་ *tód-pa* 1. **skull, cranium;** skull of a dead person, **death's head;** *tod-skám* **a** dry skull, *tod-rlón* a fresh skull *Thgr.*; *tod-krág* a skull filled with blood *Thgr.*; *tod-pór* a drinking-cup made of a skull. — 2. col. **forehead, brow;** *tod-rtsá* vena frontalis *Lt.*; *tod-čiṅs, tod-kébs, tod-brgyán*, turban.

ཐོད་ལེ་ཀོར་ *tod-le-kór Lex.* **alabaster;** *Tar.* 67, 18 *Schf.* = खटिका, chalk.

ཐོན་ *ton* v. *ₒtón-pa* and *ₒdón-pa; tón-pa C.* also: **good, fair, beautiful;** *smrá-bar tón-pa* eloquent.

ཐོན་མི་ *tón-mi*, or *tú-mi sam-bhó-ṭa* n. of the minister that was sent to India by king Sroṅbtsansgampo, in order to procure an alphabet for writing.

ཐོབ་ *tob* 1. v. *tób-pa.* — 2. v. *ₒdebs-pa.*

ཐོབ་ཆུ་ *tob-ču Schr.*, **tob-če, tob-čí, teb-ču** *C.*, **button** (v. *tob-ċi*).

ཐོབ་པ་ *tob-pa* I. vb. (synon. to *rnyed-pa*, and exclusively in use in *W.*) 1. **to find,** frq. — 2. **to get, obtain,** *ṅas tob B., ṅá-la tob* col., I find, I get; *tob-par ₒgyúr-ba* id.; **to partake of, to come to,** *dád-pa* faith (to come to the faith) *Mil.*; **to obtain, to get possession of, to subject to one's power** *Dzl.*; *da-drág tob-mtár Gram.*: after (words) that have got a *da-drág*; *saṅs-rgyás, rgyál-po, bdág-po, tób-pa* (lit. to get the Buddha etc.) **to become** a Buddha, a king, a lord; **čag-dzód tob-ċe** *W.* to become frq. (cf. *rgyál-po*). —

II. sbst. that which has been got or obtained: **the sum, result,** of a calculation etc. *Wdṅ.*

III. **tób-ċe(s)** *W.* adj. that which is **to be got** or **received,** e.g. **búlon tób-ċes-si bún-yig** a list of demands to be called in, of money owing.

**Comp.** *tob-rgyál byéd-pa* **to rob, pillage, plunder** (?) *Sch.*; *tob-čá* the share which one gets *C.* — *tob-táṅ Cs.* 'income, revenue'; more accurately: that which falls to one's share, as a reward or pay, for work, services etc., e.g. bits of cloth or silk, which a tailor may keep for himself. — *tob-nór* 1. **share, quota.** 2. **quotient.** — *tob-bló C.* **desire,** *bkúr-sti tób-pa* **ambition** *Schr.* — *tob-tsír* (lit. the turn of getting, receiving) **claim, right; duty, due,** *tob-tsir ná-la yod* I have a claim, a right to it *W.*; **tob-tsir tán-ce* W.* to give each his share in his turn (prop. acc. to the due turn). — *tob-rim Glr.* id. — *tob-yig* **repertory, index.** — *tob-sról* prob. = *tob-tsir,* **right of succession** *C.* — *tob-šá C.* **contest, quarrel, strife; scramble,** e. g. for money thrown among the people.

ཐོམ་བུ་ *tóm-bu* = *túm-bu.*

ཐོམས་པ་ *tóms-pa* v. *ₒtóms-pa.*

ཐོར་ཁོད་ *tor-kód*, or *tor-gód*, **a Mongol tribe.**

ཐོར་མགོ་ *tor-mgó* v. *tur-mgó.*

ཐོར་ཅོག, ཐོར་ཙུགས་ *tor-còg, tor-tsúgs,* (also *do-kèr*) **a plaited tuft of hair, toupet,** *Lex.*: *cò-toi tor-cóg*; *tor-cóg dar sna lna bcins Pth.* he bound his tuft of hair with a silk string of five colours; prob. = *ytsug-tór* q.v.; *tór-to(r) Lex.* id.

ཐོར་པ་ *tór-pa,* also *ₒtór-pa Med.,* **the small-pox** *Sch.*; in *Sik. tór-ba* signifies **pimple, pustule,** but the usual word for this is *srin-tór*, and in *W.* **pul-tór** has a similar meaning, whereas *tór-bu Med.* denotes a whole class of diseases, comprising dyspepsy and cutaneous disorders. — *dmar-tór* **measles** *Sch.*

ཐོར་བ་ *tór-ba* 1. v. *ₒtór-ba.* — 2. v. *tór-pa.*

ཐོར་བུ་ *tór-bu* **single, separate**; *Tar.* 120, 19: *prá-mo tór-bu-pa* separate little works, books *Schf.*

ཐོར་མོ་ *tór-mo* the growing fat of cows, goats etc. in consequence of sterility *Sch.*

ཐོལ་བ་ *tól-ba* 1. v. *ₒtól-ba,* pf. to *rtól-ba,* what has come forth, what has been raised, elevated (?) *Sch.* cf. *tol-tól Mng.*; *tol-byún* to arise, to begin, suddenly *Sch.*

ཐོས་པ་ *tos-pa* 1. vb. **to hear** *B., C.* (*W.* **tsór-ce**), *rgyál-po žig-gi ytam tós-sam,* or only *rgyál-po žig tós-sam Dzl.* have you heard of a king? *ₒbrós-so zér-bai ytam rgyál-poi snyán-du tós-so* it came to the king's hearing that he had escaped. *Glr.* — 2. adj. *mán-du tós-pa* **far-famed, renowned,** frq.; *ma tós-pa* **unheard of**; *tos-gról* the title of a book which is read to the soul of a deceased person (**tō-dhól* C.*, **to-dól* W.*), and the full title of which is: *tós-pa tsám-gyis gról-ba tób-pai cos* a doctrine by the hearing of which a man is instantly saved *Thgr.*; *tos-cún Mil.* **hearing little.**

ཐྲིག་ཐྲིག་ *trig-trig* **the creaking of shoes.**

ཐྭག་ *twag Ld.* the sharp sound, **the cracking,** which is heard, when a branch of a tree is breaking off; cf. *tsa-rág* and *ldim.*

མཐང་ *mtan Cs.*: **the lower part of the body,** *mtan-gós* a vestment for it, a sort of petticoat (acc. to others: toga) worn by Lamas.

མཐའ་ *mta* (cf. *tá-ma*) 1. **end, ending,** 1. relative to space: **edge, margin, brink, brim,** of a well *Glr.*, skirt of a forest, gen. *mtá-ma*; **limit, bound, border, confines, frontiers,** *mta skór-ba* to go round the confines (of a place); *mtá-las ₒdás-pa* exceeding all bounds, very great, e.g. *sdug-bsnál Thgr.*; used even thus: *rgyál-po bžúgs-pai mtá-la bskor* to walk round him that sits on a throne *Glr.*, po.; adverbially: *dé-mta* round this (mountain) *Mil.*; *mta dbus kún-tu* in the whole country (in the frontier districts and in the central parts); *mtai rgyal-kams* neighbouring or border-country; *mta* id., e.g. *mta bži* the four border-countries, i.e. all the surrounding territory, frq.; *mtai nor* the treasures of the border-country *Glr.*; *mtai dmag* border-war.; in the Tibetan part of the Himalaya mountains *mta* denotes in a special sense **Hindoostan**; — in grammar: **termination,** *na ma ra la žés-rnams mtá-can* words ending in n, m, r, l; *ga-mtá* a final g. 2. relative to time: *bskál-pai mta Dzl.* the **termination** of a Kalpa; *dus-mtái me* the conflagration at the end of the world, the ecpyrosis; in a more general sense: *mta nán-pas* as this will end badly; *mta ycig-tu Wdn.* and *Tar.* 4, 7 *Sch.*: **on the one hand, in part, in a certain degree, in some respect**; *Schf.*: 'schlechthin' (?) —

*mta-ɣčód-pa* final or definitive sentence or judgment *Sch.; dei mta ɣčod-pai ṗyir* in order to settle it definitely, viz. by counterproof, *Gram.*; *yáṅ-dag-mta* the true end, i.e. objective truth *Was.* (297); **the rest, remainder,** *re-dógs-kyi mta spaṅ* having given up also the last remnant of fear and hope *Glr.*, cf. *mtá-dag; mtá-ru, mtar* 1. **towards the end,** towards the boundary or the neighbouring country; **at the end** etc.; *mtar túg-pa* to reach, to attain to the end, frq.; *tsei mtar túg-pai graṅs* the number of those that reach the (natural) end of life *Dzl.; mtar-tug-pa-méd-pa* inexhaustible *Dzl.*; *mtár-ṗyin-pa* (rarely *mtar-ₒkyil-ba*) id.; also absolutely as sbst. *mtár-ṗyin-pa* **a perfect, a holy person, a saint;** *mtár-ton-pa* id. (?) *Mil.; mtár-byed-pa* to give a work its finish *C.*, (*Sch.*: 'to destroy, demolish'?) 2. adv. **lastly, finally, in conclusion** *Dzl., Thgy.*; perh. also **to the very last, wholly, altogether.** 3. postp. with genit. **after, behind,** *rgyal-rábs sum-brgyái mtar* after 300 royal generations *Glr.*; *sá-mtar šiṅ, šiṅ* is to be written after a final s, *Gram.* — 2. **aim, purpose** *Cs.* — 3. **system,** opinion *Tar.* 107, 4 *Schf.*, perh. for *grub-mta.*

**Comp. and deriv.** *mtá-klas-pa Cs.* = *mtá-med-pa*, yet v. *mtas.* — *mta-skór* **circumference, perimeter,** v. *dpag-tsád.* — *mta-ₒkób* v. *ₒkob.* — *mta-grú Glr.* 42? — *mta-rgyás* **very wide** *Schr.* — *mta-lčags* frame, of a mirror etc. *Schr.* — *mta-čag Med.?* — *mta-rtén* final consonant *Gram.; mta-rten-med-pa* ending with a vowel *Gram.* — *mta-tig* boundary line *Sch.* — *mta-tog-tág* **unceasing** (?) *Sch.* — *mtá-dag* **several, sundry; all,** frq.; *maṅ-tsig mtá-dag* the plural sign *mta-dag Gram.* — *mta-draṅs Gram.?* — *mtá ma* **the end,** *grál-gyi mtá-mai bú-mo* the girl at the end of the row (opp. to the middle or the other end, not necessarily to the beginning, like *mǰúg-ma*); **border, hem, seam,** of dresses *Dzl.; deṅ mtoṅ-ba mta-ma* to-day we see (him) for the last time *Glr.* (*tá-ma* would be more correct, like *Dzl.* ༡༧, 16). — *mta-mal-pa* sometimes for *ta-mal-pa.* — *mtá-mi* **borderer; neighbouring people.** — *mtá med-pa, mtá-yas-pa* **infinite, endless.** — *mta-ɣséb Wdṅ.?*

མཐར་ *mtar* 1. v. *mta.* 2. for *tar.*

མཐར་སྐྱོལ་ *mtar-skyól* the bringing to an end, **carrying through, persistence, perseverance** *Mil.*

མཐར་གྱིས་ *mtár-gyis* **by turns, successively,** *Dzl.*; **by degrees, gradually.**

མཐས་ཀླས་ *mtas-klas, Zam.* = पर्यन्त, **border, limit?** cf. *mta* compounds.

མཐིང་ *mtiṅ* acc. to *Cs.*: 'indigo', and '*mtiṅ-šiṅ* indigo-plant'; acc. to a Lama from Lhasa however: 1. **mountain-blue** (which is found, together with malachite, in the hills near Lhasa). — 2. from the resemblance: **indigo-colour** (whereas indigo as a substance is *rams*), and esp. a light **sky-blue, azure;** cf. *mton-mtiṅ.*

མཐིང་རིལ་ *mtiṅ-ril, Lex.* a certain bird; *Sch.*: a sort of wild duck; acc. to *Pth.* a smaller bird.

མཐིའུ་ *mtiu* v. *mteu.*

མཐིལ་ *mtil* 1. **bottom,** of a vessel, of the sea; **floor,** of a room *Glr.*; **foundation,** of a house. — 2. the lower side of a thing; **inner or lower part of a thing,** *lág-mtil* (resp. *ṗyág-mtil*) **the palm of the hand;** *lag-mtil-na* in the closed hand; *lag-mtil gaṅ* a closed handful; *rkaṅ-mtil* (resp. *žabs-mtil*) the sole of the foot; *lham-mtil*, the sole of a shoe; *mtil bži* the palms of the hands, and the soles of the feet. — 3. **the background, the far end,** of a cave, a tunnel etc. — 4. *C.*: **the centre, the principal or chief part,** of a town; **the principal place, chief city, capital,** of a country.

མཐུ་ *mtu* 1. **power, force, strength,** of the body, of the mind, of Buddha, of a prayer, of witchcraft etc.; **ability, power** or **authority** to do a thing; *mtu daṅ ldán-pa* **strong, powerful, efficacious, able** etc., *mtu-méd* **powerless, feeble, unable;** **mi za tu mé** *C.* I must eat it; *bsgrub-mi-nus-mtu-méd-la soṅ* we must be able to fulfil it *Mil.*; *mtu-*

*žig-gis* by an extraordinary manifestation of power or strength *Dzl.*; *klui mtu yin* that is an effect of the Lus, is produced, comes from the Lus *Stg.*; *mtus* **by virtue of,** frq.; *mtu-stóbs* = *mtu.* — 2. **magic, witchcraft,** *mtu γtóṅ-ba Mil.*, *mtu ˳débs-pa*, *tāb-ce* *W.*, to practise witchcraft, to injure a person by magic spells, to bewitch *Mil.* and col. frq.; *mtu ser brtad γsúm-po rdzógs-par bslabs* conjuring, raising tempests, exorcising ghosts, all these things I have learned thoroughly *Mil.*; *mtu-bo-čé* **high-potent, high and mighty** *Tar.*

མཐུག་ *mtug* v. *˳tug.*

མཐུད་པ་ *mtud-pa* v. *˳tud-pa.*

མཐུན་པ་ *mtún-pa*, also *˳tún-pa*, **to agree, to harmonize; agreement, harmony; agreeing** etc., 1. in a general sense, c. c. *daṅ*, . . . *yin-par don mtún-no* they agree in the opinion of her being . . . *Glr.*; *mtún-par byéd-pa* to make agree, to bring to an agreement, to make consistent, *mtún-par ˳gyúr-ba* to be made agreeing or consistent *Glr.*; *dgóṅs-pa γčig-tu mtún-pa* unanimous; *lhai lugs daṅ mtun* god-like (in deeds) *Glr.*; *rigs mtún-pa* of equal birth; *lo mtún-pa* of the same age, contemporary; *blo mtún-te* being of the same mind, similarly disposed, *čos byá-bar* with respect to religion *Glr.*; *ka mtún-par* with one mouth, *gros mtún-par* with one accord, unanimously, as one man; *grabs mtún-pa* to live in harmony; — **to be adequate, corresponding to,** e.g. *yid (daṅ) mtún-par*, resp. *túgs daṅ mtún-par*, to one's wish, as one could desire = *yid bžin-du*; *nad daṅ mtún-par* corresponding to the disease, fit or proper for the disease. — 2. in a special sense 1. viz. *yid daṅ*, **to be wished for, desirable,** particularly in *mtun-rkyén*, v. *rkyén*; also: **to wish, to like, to delight in,** *kyed-rnams-kyis mtún-pai rdzas* things wished for by you, desirable to you *Mil.*; 2. with or without *γčig-la γčig*: *mtún-nas* whenever they (the two nations) lived in peace with each other (opp. to *˳kón-nas*) *Glr.*; *mtún-pai γtam byéd-pa* to converse amicably *Glr.*, to enter into negotiations of peace *Glr.*; *mtún-par byéd-pa* 1. v. above, 2. **to caress, to fondle, to dandle** *Glr.*; *šin-tu mtún-par yod* they are on the best terms with each other, are making love to each other *Glr.*; *mtún-po bsdad ˳dug* col. id.; *mtún-po byéd-pa* to be kind, affable, condescending *Mil.* (opp. to being proud, cold, reserved); *rgya bod γnyis mtun ˳oṅ* there will be a good understanding between China and Tibet *Glr.*; *mi mtún-pai pyogs tams-čád-las rgyál-ba* to gain the victory over all the hostile parties; *mtún-˳gyur-gyi yi-ge C.* **letter of recommendation;** *mtún-čan W.* **gentle, peaceful.**

མཐུར་ *mtur*, also *mtúr-mgo*, v. *túr-mgo*, **halter,** *rta-mtur Lex.* id.; *mtur-tág* **rein, reins** *Sch.*; *mtur-mtá* the end of the reins, e.g. to place them into the hands of another.

མཐུས་ *mtus* v. *mtu* 1.

མཐེ་བོ་ *mté-bo*, col. *mté-bóṅ*, *mte-čén*, *mtéb-mo* (v. also *te bo*), **thumb,** *rkáṅ-pai mté-bo* **the big toe;** *mteb-čúṅ* the little finger, the little toe *Glr.*

མཐེའུ་ *mteu* 1. **a little hammer;** 2. *mteu-čúṅ* **the little toe.**

མཐོ་ *mto* 1. **a span,** from the end of the thumb to the end of the middle finger when extended; *mto ˳jál-ba* or *γžál-ba*, *W.* *tāb-ce*, to span, to measure by the hand with the fingers extended; *mto gáṅ*, *mto ré tsam* a span (in length), *mto do* two spans. — 2. v. *mtó-ba.*

མཐོ་གོང་ *mto-góṅ* a little triangular receptacle into which the likeness of an enemy is placed, to whom one wishes to do harm by witchcraft *W.*

མཐོ་རྒྱབ་ *mto-rgyáb* **earnest-money** *W.*

མཐོ་བ་ *mtó-ba* 1. **to be high; highness, height; high, lofty, elevated,** *B.* (cf. *mtón-po*), frq. fig.; *rigs če-žiṅ mtó-ba-ste* being of high and noble birth *Dzl.*; *dé-las mtó-ba* more elevated than that, surpassing, surmounting that; c. accus. or instrum., high as to (stature, rank etc.) *mťó-na* when I am high, when I rise; *mťó-ba γnón-pa* to lower what is high, to bring down, to humble, frq.; *ṅas mťo-mťó byás-pas dma-dmá byuṅ* **the** more I was aspiring, the more I was brought low *Pth.*; *sbyin-pa mťó-ba Stg.* was explained: gifts or alms bestowed from a sincere heart. — 2. **hammer,** v. *ťo-ba*; *mťo-po-tog* a stone used as a hammer *Cs.*

**Comp.:** *mťo-ḱyad* **height, highness** *Dzl.* — *mťo-dógs Pth.* (together with *γyo-sgyú*, and *ṗrag-dóg*) perh. mistrust, suspicion; **ťón-dod-čan** *W.* **ambitious,** aspiring, aiming at things too high. — *mťo-spyód W.* a haughty manner. — *mťo-dmán* 1. *Cs.* high and low, uneven; also *Schr.* 2. **height,** *mťo-dmán mnyám-pa* of equal height *Glr.* — *mťo-ₒtsám(s)-pa* v. *ťo-ₒtsám-pa.* — *mťo-rís* **heaven,** abode of the gods, **paradise,** Elysium.

མཐོང་ག་ *mťóṅ-ga Sch.*, *mťoṅs-ḱa Pth.*, **chest, breast,** *mťóṅ-ga-nas ₒdzin-pa* to seize by the breast *Pth.*

མཐོང་བ་ *mťóṅ-ba* **to see,** 1. vb. n. to have the power of vision, often with *mig(-gis)*; *mťóṅ-bar ₒgyúr-ba* to obtain the faculty of seeing, to recover one's sight; *mťóṅ-bar byéd-pa* to make (the blind) see *Dzl.*; *mig-gis nye mťoṅ riṅ mi mťoṅ* he sees only when the object is near, not when it is far, he is short-sighted *Med.*; *nye-mťóṅ* short-sighted *Sch.* — 2. vb. a. 1. **to perceive,** by the eye, **to see, to behold,** *bód-kyi ri mťóṅ-bai ri* an eminence from whence one can see the mountains of Tibet *Glr.*; *mi γžán-gyis mťóṅ-sar* (a place) where one can be seen by others; *de bú-mos mťóṅ-bar mdzád-do* he made it visible to the girl, he made her see it *Dzl.*; *mťóṅ-ba žig yód-na* if there is one that has seen it, if there exists a witness *Dzl.*; *de mťóṅ-ste šes* seeing this, I came to know, i.e. from this I saw, I perceived; *mťoṅ ťos dran reg*, frq., the seeing, hearing, touching, thinking of (e.g. a form of prayer, or magic formula); *ma ₔóṅ-bar*, (or *ₔóṅ-ba*) *mťóṅ-nas* as he saw his mother coming. 2. with accus. and termin.: **to regard, consider, take for,** *Thgy.*; *rdzas dkar sér-por mťoṅ Lt.* taking white things for yellow ones. 3. **to meet, find, catch.** 4. **to know, understand, perceive** (mentally) *Mil.* 5. col. **to undergo, suffer, endure,** misfortunes, pain etc. (cf. *stonpa* 4), *mi mťoṅ mťóṅ-ba* to suffer what is not to be suffered, not bearable n i f., cf. *ltá-ba.*

**Comp.** *mťóṅ-ḱuṅ Cs.* **'a window',** prob. for *mťoṅs-ḱuṅ.* — *mťóṅ-sgom-čan Thgy.* was explained: one who instantly knows and understands every thing he sees(?) — *mťóṅ-ₒḱor, mťóṅ-mťa,* **the reach of sight, range of vision** *Cs.*, **ťóṅ-ₒḱor-la bor** *W.* do not take them (the horses) farther than you can see them; **the horizon** *Cs.*; *mťoṅ-dúg* ('eye-poison') **evil-eye** *Sch.*; **envy, grudge, jealousy.** — *mťoṅ-snáṅ* v. *snaṅ-ba.* — *mťoṅ-byéd* that which sees, the eye *Cs.*; the substance which is the source of vision, a species of gall, **आलोचक.** *Med.* — *mťoṅ-lám* the path of obtaining the power of sight, a mystical state *Was.* (139) — *mťoṅ-lugs* the way of beholding, of viewing a thing; **notion, idea, opinion** = *snáṅ-ba, mťóṅ-lugs γsúm-du byuṅ* three different opinions were forming *Glr.*

མཐོངས་, རྒྱ་མཐོངས་ *mťoṅs, rgya-mťoṅs* 1. **an opening for the smoke** in a ceiling or roof, also *mťóṅs-ḱuṅ.* — 2. also *mťóṅs-ḱa*, **pavilion, platform, open gallery,** on a flat roof *Glr.* (*Cs.:* 'impluvium, or the opening in the middle of a square building', for which, however, the Tibetan word seems to be *ḱyams* or *ḱyams-mťóṅs*).

མཐོངས་ཀ་ *mťóṅs-ka* **silk ornaments** on the borders of a painting *Cs.*

མཐོངས་པ་ *mťóṅs-pa Cs.:* **to lose one's senses;** perh. *ₒťóms-pa.*

མཐོན་ཀ་ *mťón-ka,* or *mťón-ga Lex.*; *Cs.* 1. **azure, sky-blue** (?). — 2. n. of a flower. — 3. *Glr.* one of the five celestial gems; *mťón-ka čén-po* another of these gems. —

མཐོན་པོ་ *mťón-po* **high, elevated,** *B.* and col. (cf. *mťó-ba*), of water **deep,** of the voice **loud,** of weight and measure **full,** of rank **high;** **čós-skad ťón-po** *W.* high-sounding words, pompous style; *lág-len tón-po* W. highly skilled, well practised. — mton-mtiṅ 'the high blue (thing)' viz. the hair of the head of Buddha, always represented as of a light sky-blue.

མཐོལ་བ་, འཐོལ་བ་ mtól-ba, ₒtól-ba, **to confess, to avow**, nyés-pa Dzl.; mtol tsáṅs (cf. ₒgyod-tsáṅs) **confession, acknowledgment**, mtol-tsáṅs byéd-pa Dzl., mtol bšags-pa to make confession, to confess, which acc. to Buddhist doctrine involves atonement and remission of sins.

མཐོས་ mtos 1. Ld. **high, elevated**, *ṭim-si saṅ tos ma len* do not take more than is right! — 2. Mil.?

འཐག་པ་ ₒtag-pa, pf. btags, fut. btag, imp. tog, 1. **to grind**, raṅ-tág-gis in a mill Dzl., gro wheat, pyé-mar to flour; to reduce to powder, **to pulverize**, by means of two stones (cf. ɣtun); **to mash**. — 2. **to weave**, snám-bu cloth; ₒtág(-pa)-po, ₒtág-mkan **a weaver**; dar-tag-bú-mo the daughter of a silk-weaver Glr. — ₒtag-stán loom Sch. — ₒtag-rdó **mill-stone, grinding-stone**(?) Sch.

འཐང་པོ་ ₒtáṅ-po Wdṅ. a bodily defect or deformity, prob. téṅ-po.

འཐད་ ₒtad **liking, pleasure; will; joy**, v. the following article.

འཐད་པ་ ₒtád-pa I. 1. **to be pleasant, agreeable, well-pleasing** ccdp., ɣsuṅ de kun šin-tu séms-la ₒtád-pa žig byuṅ all these sayings have pleased me very much Mil. — 2. (not governing a case) **to please, to be acceptable, to be considered as good**, to be (generally) **admitted**, mi ₒtád-par mtoṅ I see that (this reading) is not generally accepted Zam.; žes-paaṅ ₒtád-do it occurs also in this form Zam.; mi-ₒtád-de **wrong!** Was. (294): **to be fit, proper, suitable** (syn. to ₒos-pa), sems zér-ba mi ₒtád-la as it is not proper to call it soul, as it cannot fitly be called soul Mil. — 3. a familiar word, very frq. used, in W. almost the only word for dgá-ba and ₒdód-pa, *sem tád-de* cheerfully, joyfully W., ₒtád-rgyu méd-pa tsam žig-la prob.: as he became angry Mil.; *sém-mi náṅ-ne̤ tad soṅ*, also *tiṅ (q. v.) *tág-pa-ne̤ tad-soṅ* W. I have been heartily glad; ₒtad-ₒtád-ₒdra yaṅ Mil. though apparently rejoicing; *mā tad-tád* W. I am very glad of that; *sem tád čúg-če* W. to make glad, to exhilarate; *sá-heb-bi žó-la mi tád-da* W. does your honour not like curdled milk? *tád-kan* W. willing, ready; *gá-ru tád-na soṅ* W. go wherever you like; lóg-pa-ₒtad let us turn back Glr.; ráṅ-ñi ₒtád-la voluntarily, spontaneously.

II. Sch. = ₒtán-pa, ₒtad-ldán = ₒtán-po.

འཐན་ ₒtan **bad**, ₒtan-ₒdré a demon Sch.

འཐན་པ་ ₒtán-pa (cog. to brtán-po and táṅ-po?) Cs. also ₒtád-pa, **firmness, constancy**, in Lex. explained by nán-tan; mi ₒtán-po a steady, resolute man Cs.

འཐབ་པ་ ₒtáb-pa **to combat, to fight**, in a battle; **to quarrel, to dispute, to brawl**; ka-tsúb daṅ ₒtáb-pa to struggle with a snow-storm Mil.; ₒtáb-pa méd-čiṅ ši-ba to die peaceably, without a struggle; ₒtáb-pa ₒdúm-na when quarreling (persons) are reconciled; ka-ₒtáb Cs. a fighting with the mouth, altercation; lag-ₒtáb Cs. a fighting with one's hands, a close fighting, a scuffle (Sch. gesticulation?); ₒtab-król Lex. dispute, contest; ₒtab-ₒkrúg prob. id.; (Lex. **आयुध** weapon?); *tab-ḍháb* C. weapons, arms; ₒtab-čás ammunition, requisites for war Schr.; ₒtab-brdúṅs, á-kui ₒtab-brdúṅs the quarreling and thrashing of my uncle Mil.; ₒtáb-mo quarrel, fight, row, fray, battle, B. and col. frq., ₒtáb-mo byéd-pa B., *čó-če* W., to quarrel, fight etc.; ₒtáb-mó spród-pa to fight a battle, to join battle Glr.; ₒtab-žób a dry cough Sch. — ₒtáb-rtsód altercation, quarrel, brawl, frq. — ₒtab-ya antagonist, kyód-kyis ṅai ₒtáb-ya byed dgos thou must contend with me Glr. — bdúd-moi ₒtáb-ya a termagant, a she-devil to struggle with Mil.; ɣnás-skabs-kyi ₒtáb-ya the antagonists of life, i. e. the family and relations a secular man has to struggle with Mil. — ₒtab-rágs intrenchment, breast-work, fortification C.

འཐབ་འབུ་ ₒtáb-ₒbu **a cricket** *Sch.*

འཐམ་པ་ ₒtám-pa, pf. ₒtams, 1. **to seize,** to lay hold of, **to grasp**, to take a firm hold of, esp. with the teeth (dogs), or the jaws (serpents *W.*); to sting (of bees *W.*); **to embrace,** **rkaṅ-pa ₒtám-ċe** *W.* to put one's arms around a person's feet, as a supplicant; to grasp intellectually, to comprehend (?) *Glr.* — 2. **to gnash,** *so* one's teeth; **to shut closely,** *ka* one's mouth, frq. — 3. **to join, unite** (vb. n.), *grógs-su, grógs-por Stg.*, in friendship, *byá-bar* in an act, an undertaking *Dzl.*

ཐ

འཐལ་བ་ ₒtál-ba v. *tal-ba.*

འཐས་པ་ ₒtás-pa, *Lex.* = *mkrégs-pa*, **hard, solid;** *bag-čágs rgyúd-la ₒtas* prob.: inordinate desire has taken a firm hold of your minds; *sra-ₒtás Sch.* **strong, robust, sinewy;** *á-ₒtas-te*, and *á-ₒtas-kyi bag-čags Pth.?*

འཐིག་པ་ ₒtig-pa 1. vb. n., pf. ₒtigs **to drop, to fall in drops, to drop from,** *krag ma ₒtigs-par Lt.* without any blood dropping out. — 2. vb. a., pf. *btigs*, fut. *btig* **to cause to fall in drops, to instil** etc.

འཐིང་སླད་ ₒtiṅ - slad *Cs.* a term of blame or abuse; *Lexx.*

འཐིབས་ ₒtibs **a cover, covering;** *ₒtibs - ₒog tsud? S.g.*

འཐིབས་པ་ ₒtibs-pa, pf. *tibs* and *ytibs* (cf. *ytibs - pa*), **to gather,** of clouds, storms; *ná-bun bžiṅ-du ₒtibs-par gyúr-to* (all the Buddhas) came drawing nearer like clouds of mist *Glr.;* **to condensate,** vb. n. *ljón-šiṅ tams-cád dgá-bai tsál-du ₒtibs* all the trees afford a delightful shade *Glr.; byiṅ ₒtibs* drowsiness overcomes me; po. and fig. **to grow dark or dim,** *šés-pa* consciousness *Med.* — *ₒtibs - po* **dark, close, dense.**

འཐིམ་པ་ ₒtim-pa v. *tim-pa.*

འཐུ་བ་ ₒtú-ba 1. adj. v. *tu-ba.* — 2. vb., also *ₒtún-pa*, pf. *ₒtus, btus*, fut. *btu*, imp. *tus, btu* (*Cs.*), **to gather, collect, pick up,** *šiṅ, me-tog*, frq.; *tus-mi* an assemblage of men, council, *Cs.*

འཐུང་བ་ ₒtúṅ-ba, pf. *ₒtuṅs* (*Cs.* also *btuṅs* I have drunk out), (fut. *btuṅ Cs.*), imp. *ₒtuṅ*, (*Cs.* also *btuṅ* drink out!), *W.* **túṅ-ċe**, **to drink,** frq.; **to suck, to smoke** (tobacco), **to eat** (soup); **to be soaked, drenched** (cloth) *Dzl.*; *ṅóms - pa ₒtúṅ - ba* to drink one's fill *Dzl.; žo-ₒtuṅs, ₒo-ₒtuṅs* suckling baby; *žo-ₒtuṅ dus-na* during the time of giving suck *Med.*; *ₒtúṅs-pa tsám-gyis* immediately after drinking *Thgy.*; *ₒtúṅs - so* they were engaged in drinking *Glr.*; *ₒtúṅ-du rúṅ-ba, W. *tuṅ-čóg**, **drinkable;** *btúṅ-ba* sbst. **drink, beverage,** *bzá-ba daṅ btúṅ-ba, bza-btúṅ* (*W. *zabtúṅ**) meat and drink, frq.; *btúṅ-ču* water for drinking *Mil.* —

འཐུག་པ་, མཐུག་པ་ ₒtúg-pa, *mtúg-pa*, adj. and abstr. sbst., *ₒtúg-po* adj , **thick,** *mta-ₒtúg* thicker toward the margin or edge *Mṅg.*; gen. of woven stuffs, opp. to *sráb-pa*; *srab-ₒtúg* 1. **thin and thick,** 2. **thickness** relatively; also **consistency,** of liquids, opp to *slá-ba Med.;* **dense,** *nags*, frq.; **sound, heavy,** *ɣnyid ₒtúg-po* a sound sleep; **strong,** *bag - čágs ₒtúg - po* a strong inclination *Mil.*

འཐུད་པ་, མཐུད་པ་ ₒtúd - pa, *mtúd - pa* **to make longer** by adding a piece, to piece out, to prolong, *pu-dúṅ W.* a sleeve; *skyé-ba ₒtud mi dgos* he has no need of adding a re-birth, a new period of life *Pth.*; *ₒtud - ma* 1. **addition, prolongation,** **sróg-gi túd-ma táṅ-ċe* W.* prolonging life (by medicine, careful nursing). — 2. **aid, assistance, subsidy,** e.g. to a needy betrothed couple; also **a gift of honour**, a present, offered to a departing benefactor or respected Lama *W.*; *dmag - ₒtúd* **subsidies; auxiliary troops.** — 3. **help, assistance** in general.

འཐུན་ ₒtun **gatherer,** *šiṅ-ₒtún* a gatherer of wood, *rtsa-ₒtún* of grass.

འཐུབ་པ་ ₒtúb-pa, pf. *ₒtubs*, fut. *ɣtub*, imp. *ₒtub, btub, W. *túb-ċe**, **to cut into pieces,** v. *ɣtúb-pa.*

འཐུམ་པ་ ₒtúm - pa, pf. *ₒtums, btums*, fut. *btum*, imp. *ₒtum, btum, W. *túm-ċe**, **to cover** or **lay over, to put over,** to

**coat,** *záṅs-kyis Glr.*; **to wrap up, to envelop,** v. *ɣtúm-pa.*

འཐུམས་ ˳*tums* **barren, sterile; addled** (eggs); *blo-˳túms* **stupid** *Lexx.*

འཐུར་ ˳*tur* supine of ˳*tu-ba.*

འཐུལ་བ་ ˳*túl-ba* **to rise, to spread,** of smoke, vapours, perfumes, *ga-pur ˳tul* it smells of camphor *Lex.*; *rdul mi ˳túl-bar byás-pai ˳óg-tu* after having laid the dust *Dzl.*; *la-lás bdug-spós ˳tul* some persons were spreading perfumes *Pth.*

འཐེགས་པ་ ˳*tégs-pa Cs.* **to set out on a journey.** (To me only **tág-ce* W.* is known.) 1. **to pack up.** 2. **to depart.** It prob. signifies the same as *tég-pa*, ˳*dégs-pa* **to lift, raise, take up,** cf. *ɣżi btág-ces,* or ˳*degs-pa* **to shift, to change,** lodgings, to remove; *teg-k'úg* carpet-bag, knapsack.

འཐེང་ ˳*teṅ*, perh. only another spelling for *teṅ*; *Sch.* has ˳*téṅ-la* ˳*bór-ba* **to throw away as unfit,** and if that be correct, it may serve to explain both significations mentioned under *teṅ.*

འཐེང་བ་ ˳*téṅ-ba Cs.* **to be lame, to go lame,** cf. *téṅ-po*; also adj.: *bsu-mk'an byiu ˳teṅ-ma cig kyaṅ med* not even a lame chicken came to meet me *Mil. nt.*

འཐེན་པ་ ˳*tén-pa* 1. **to draw, to pull,** *gyén-la* up, upward, *mdún-du* forth, out; *p'ar ˳ten tsur ˳ten* they pulled to and fro, this way and that way *Pth.*; *nur-gyis* by jerks, by little and little *Glr.*; *yól-ba ˳tén-pa* a curtain drawn before *Glr.*; **u' tén-ce* W.* to draw breath, to breathe; in *W.* esp. used for **to draw out** (a cork) **to take off** (a pot-lid), **to draw** or **take away** (a pot from the fire). — 2. **to stop, to stop short, to wait,** ˳*tén-pa bzaṅ* it will be advisable to stop, to wait. — In *W.* also = *rtén-pa* to lean, recline, repose on. — **gór-la tén-ce* W.* to form on a lathe, to turn. — *Sch.*: ˳*ten-˳k'yér* forgetting and remembering (?).

འཐེབ་ ˳*teb* **overplus, extra, supernumerary,** *gos-˳téb* a supernumerary dress *Lex.*; *mal-gos ˳teb-kyis ˳túm-pa* to wrap up in an extra blanket *Lex.*; *żag ɣcig ˳teb* one day over, or too much; ˳*téb-pa* to have too much (?) *Sch.*

འཐེབས་པ་ ˳*tébs-pa*, pf. *tebs*, (prop. the passive or neuter vb. to ˳*débs-pa*, but often not differing from it, v. ˳*débs-pa*) 1. **to be thrown, strewed, scattered,** *sá-bon Mil.*; **to be afflicted with, befallen by,** *nád-kyis* a disease, frq., also with *lús-la Glr.*; *lan ˳tébs-pa* to answer; *ɣsal ˳tébs-pa* to be explained minutely; to be understood perfectly *Thgr.* — 2. *W.* **to be hit** or **struck** (= *k'és-pa*; **'i-ru teb soṅ** I have been hit here (stung, bitten etc.); **teb cúg-te toṅ** put it down, hitting (the right place), i.e. put it just in its proper place; **mi téb-ce** not to hit the mark, to miss the aim; **ma teb** the blow did not strike home; even of a prayer is said: **teb**, it has hit, it has been heard. — 3. *Cs.* in a general sense: **to take, seize, hold fast;** ˳*tebs-lcib Cs.*: 'a tailor's instrument for holding fast cloth etc. in sewing; a thimble'; but the latter is undoubtedly to be spelled *mteb* (or *teb*)*-lcibs*; v. *lcibs.*

འཐེམས་པ་ ˳*téms-pa Cs.*: '**to shut, comprise, cover, include;** v. ˳*tams-pa*'; the *Lexx.* have only: *nan-čags-˳téms*, and ˳*tems-nán* w.e. In *W.* it is 1. vb.n. to ˳*tams-pa*: **lág-pa tem** my hand has been squeezed in, **tém-cei čá-lag** a thing (e.g. a machine) giving chances of being squeezed. — 2. **to suffice,** = ˳*k'yéd-pa, ldáṅ-ba.*

འཐོ་འཚམས་པ་ ˳*to-˳tsáms-pa* v. *to* etc.

འཐོག་པ་ ˳*tóg-pa Cs.* = *ɣtóg-pa*, *Sch.* also = ˳*tág-pa.*

འཐོགས་པ་ ˳*tógs-pa* pf. and imp. ˳*togs*, 1. **to take, to seize, to take up,** a knife, a sword *Dzl.*, provisions in order to distribute them *Dzl.*, esp. **to carry** *Dzl.* and elsewh.; *ról-mo ˳tógs-pa Glr., Tar.* 21, 16, prob. to carry musical instruments (or to make music?); = *tób-pa* to receive, **mii lus togs re-ré*, or *togs tsád** all that have received human bodies by the metempsychosis *C., W.* — 2. = ˳*dógs-pa* with *p'an*, frq., v. ˳*dógs-pa*; *Tar.* 159,16 = **to name, to call.**

**འཐོན་པ་** ˳*tón-pa*, pf. and imp. *ton*, vb.n. to ˳*dón-pa*, in *W.* very frq., in *B.* less so, = *byúṅ-ba*, 1. **to come out, to go out,** **dág-sa k̔áṅ-pa-ne̱ ton** he is just coming out of the house; *kun p̔yir* ˳*tón-te* all coming out *Mil.*; **to remove** (from a house or place), **to leave,** **ton-čág** *W.* the last farewell; **to depart, to emigrate;** *ču p̔á-gar tón-nas* when I shall be beyond the river *Mil.*; more carelessly: **yul tón-na, lúṅ-pa tón-na** *W.* when one has passed through, the village, the valley; **dún-du tón-ce** to step or come forth (from the crowd etc.); **to rise, arise, originate,** v. *snyiṅ-rús.* — 2. for ˬ*óṅ-ba*, **to come,** esp. *Bal.* — 3. **to come from, to proceed from, to have origin,** *bod k̔o-ráṅ-nas* ˳*tón-pa yin* these are products of Tibet itself; hence: **to occur,** like ˬ*oṅ-ba*, *ts̔óṅ-pas k̔úr-nas* ˳*ton* ˳*dug* (these goods) occur as imported, are imported; *rig-pa-ˬcan miṅ* ˳*ton yin-te* known as being acute, sagacious.

**འཐོབ་པ་** ˳*tób-pa*, v. *tób-pa.*

**འཐོམ(ས)་པ་, ཐོམས་པ་** ˳*tóm(s)-pa, tóm(s)-pa*, **to be dim, dull, clouded,** of the senses and the understanding, **nyid tóm-ce** *W.* **to slumber, to doze.** **nyid yúr-ce** id.; *mgo-(bo)* ˳*tom* consciousness is clouded or darkened, by intoxication, disease *Med.*; also of religious darkness *Pth.*; **mig tom-tóm ča dug** *W.* he is dazzled (by the brightness of the sun): *ldoṅs-šiṅ* ˳*tóms-par gyur* having become blind *Dzl.*

**འཐོར་** ˳*tor* **fragment,** of a book *Tar.*, cf. *tór-bu.*

**འཐོར་བ་** ˳*tór-ba*, pf. *btor*, fut. *ytor*, imp. ˳*tor*, 1. prop. vb.n. **to be scattered,** of leaves by the wind *Dzl.*, **to fly asunder, to be dispersed; to fall to pieces, to decay,** of the body after death *Mil.*; **to burst,** of a gun; but also vb.a.: *mé-tog* ˳*tór-ba* to strew flowers *Glr.*, *Dzl.*; ˳*tor-*˳*tuṅ* **libation** *Cs.*, *ču-*˳*tór* libation of water *Sch.*; cf. *ytór-ba.* — 2. *W.*: **to have notches, flaws,** of edge-tools.

**འཐོལ་བ་** ˳*tól-ba* v. *mtól-ba.*

# ད

**ད་** *da* 1. the letter **d**, originally, and in the frontier districts also at present, pronounced like the German d, i.e. not quite so soft as the English d; in *C.* as initial aspirated and low-toned, **dh**; as final letter half dropped, and changing a preceding a, o, u into *a̤, o̤, ṳ*; as prefix in *Kh.* and *Bal.* = *γ*, not differing from the prefixed **g.** — *da-drág* is a term used by **grammarians,** for the now obsolete *d* as second final, after n, r, l, e.g. in *kund*, changing the termination *du* into *tu*; *no, ro, lo* into *to*; *nam, ram, lam* into *tam.* — 2. num. **figure for 11.**

**ད་** *da* 1. gen. at the head of a sentence: **now, at present, just,** esp. before the imp. mood: *da kar-dáṅ-la soṅ* just go to Kardang! **directly, immediately, forthwith, instantly;** in narration sometimes (though rarely) for **then, at that time.** — 2. in col. language after the emphatical word of the sentence: **it is true, to be sure, indeed,** **loṅ da yod ṅul med** time I have, it is true, but no money.

**Comp.** *da-ko Sch.* = *da.* — *dá-ci* **a little while ago, lately.** *Mil.* and col. — *dá-ča* **in future, henceforward.** — *da-nyid* **the present time; but just now.** — *dá-lta(r)*

1. **now, at present,** *dá-ċi-nas dá-lta ṕán-la* from lately till now *Thgy.*; *dá-ltai* (or *dá-ltar-gyi*) *bár-du* until now; *dá-ltai spyód-lam* our course of acting during this life *Glr.*; *dá-ltar-gyi byá-ba*, or *dṅós-po* a person's experience or actions during the present period of his life *Dzl.*; *da-lta-nyid-du Glr.*, *da-lta-ráṅ Mil*, *Pth.*, instantly; *dá-lta-ba Cs.*, *dá-ltar-ba Gram.*, *dus dá-lta-ba* the present time, presence; the present tense 2. *W.* **hereafter, afterwards,** **dág-sa mi gos, dál-ta toṅ** I do not want it now; give it me afterwards. — *dá-ste* **henceforth, from this time forward** *Dzl.* — *da-dúṅ* (frq. pronounced and spelled *da-rúṅ*) v. below. — *da-dé Glr.* and *C.* **now.** — *da-náṅ* **this morning.** — *dá-ni* 1. **now,** 2. **henceforth** *Glr.* *da-ṕyi(n)-ċad Dzl.*, *da-ṕyis Glr.* **henceforth.** — *dá-byuṅ* a man of yesterday, **an upstart.** — *dá-tsam* about this time. — *da-ťsún* henceforth *Pth.* — *da-γzód* **but now, but just, not until now.** — **da-ráṅs* C.* = *da-naṅ.* — *da-rúṅ*, *da-dúṅ* **still, still more,** *da-rúṅ ťoṅ* give still more! *da-rúṅ légs-par γsúṅ-bar žu* please, explain it more in detail *Ma.*; **still longer, once more,** *da-rúṅ yaṅ* again and again, over and over again; **da-rúṅ ťsá-big ma ťsar* W.* it is not quite finished yet. — *da-rés* (*Sch.* also *da-ré-ba?*) 1. **now, now at least, but for this time** (opp. to *sṅán-čad, sṅar, ṕyis*) *Mil.* 2. *W.* **formerly, heretofore** (opp. to *da* **now**). — *dá-lo* **this year, in this year.**

ད་ཁ་ *dá-ka* **horse-shoe,** **dhá-ka gyáb-pa** to shoe a horse *C.*

ད་ཅི་ *dá-ċi* (*stá-ċi?*) **sickle hook,** for cutting off briers *Lh.*

ད་ཆུ་ *dá-ču* **mercury** *Med.*

ད་ཏྲིག་ *da-trig* a medicine *Med.*

ད་དྲག་ *da-drág* v. the letter d.

ད་ཕྲུག་, དྭ་ཕྲུག་, ད་ཚེ་ *da-ṕrúg*, *dwa-ṕrúg*, *da-tsé*, **orphan.**

དྭ་བ་ *dwá-ba* a plant *Med.*, yielding an acrid drug; *da-ťsód* id.(?); *da-rgód*, and *da-γyúṅ* are two species of this plant, the former of which is considered to be of greater virtue *Wdṅ.*

ད་བག་ *dá-bag* v. *tá-bag*, *ťar-ₒbág.*

ད་བེར་ *da-bér* v. *ta-bér*, *mda-bér.*

ད་བྱིད་ *da-byid* **lizard,** *Med.*; *Lex.* = *skyin-gór.*

ད་ར་ *dá-ra* col. and sometimes *B.* = *dár-ba* **buttermilk.**

ད་ལི་ *da-lí* several low-growing kinds of Rhododendron.

དག་ *dag* 1. sign of the plural, eleg. for *rnams*; often added to the pronouns *de* and *ₒdi*, and sometimes to numerals; also in the combination *dag-rnams.* In translations of Sanskrit works it denotes the dual number. — 2. *ṅá-dag*, *ǩyéd-dag*, seems in *Mil.* often to be used for *ṅá-lta-bu-dag* **my equal,** or **equals** (another reading is *ṅá-lta*, v. *lta* 2). — 3. *W.* col. = *da*, esp. in the compounds **dág-sam, dóg-sa** now; also **certainly, it is true** (v. *da* 2) *Mil.* — 4. v. *dág-pa.*

དག་ཁ་ *dág-ka* is said to be used in *Ts.* for *dé-ka.*

དག་ཅི་ *dág-ċi Lh.* **mint,** aromatic plant, Mentha Royliana.

དག་ག་དོག་གེ་ *dag-ga-dog-gé Ld.* for *dog-dóg.*

དག་པ་ *dág-pa* (prop. pf. of *ₒdág-pa*), **clean, pure; cleanness, purity;** as adj. also *dág-po*, *W.* **dág-mo**; *dág-par ₒgyúr-ba* to become clean, *dág-par byéd-pa* to make clean, to cleanse, to purify, *dág-par ₒǩrú-ba* (*W.* **dág-mo ṫú-ċe**) to wash clean; more frq. fig.: **ǩa ma dhag* C.* impure, incorrect, vulgar pronunciation, cf. *sgra* 1; *rigs ma dag* impure blood or kindred; com. **pure** with regard to religion and morals, (also = **holy, sacred,** relative to lifeless objects), *lus daṅ ṅag daṅ yíd-kyi las yóṅs-su dág-pa* quite pure in word and action *Dzl.*; *lus dag sems dag dbáṅ-po dag*, also *lus-γtsaṅ* etc. id.; *dág-par ₒťsó-ba* to lead **a** pure, a virtuous life; *smón-lam dág-pa* is stated to mean a **sincere** prayer *Glr.*; *rnám-(par) dag(-pa)* quite pure, most holy, frq.;

hence *rnam-(par) dag(-par) rtsi-ba*, or *mdzád-pa* is used for: to justify, in a scriptural sense, by *Chr. Prot.*; *mi or ma-dág-pa* **impure; impurity,** *bkrús-na mi-dág-pa méd-do* when they have bathed they are quite clean *Dzl.* — Adv. *dág-par*, e.g. *ˌkrú-ba* v. above; *dág-tu* **assuredly, certainly** *Lt.*(?); *dág-gis* purely = quite, entirely *S.g.*(?); **dág-mo** *W.* id., **dág-mo šrág-če** to burn completely, **dág-mo za-če** to eat all, to consume entirely. — *yáṅ-dag-pa Skr.* **सम्यक्** *Trigl.*, **actual, real,** *yáṅ-dag-par ču yin* in reality it is water *Dzl.*; more frq. construed thus: *de yin yáṅ-dag-na* if it is really that, *btsoṅ yáṅ-dag-na* if you are really willing to sell it, *ˌdod yáṅ-dag-na* if you really wish it, *ḱyód-la yod yáṅ-dag-na* if you really have *Dzl.*; *yáṅ-dag-pa daṅ bdén-pai tsul bžiṅ-du* in truth and in reality *S.O.*; *yaṅ-dag-pa ni bden-pa-ste* since that which is real is true *S.O.*; *yaṅ-dag-pa-nyid* reality *S.O.*; *dgé-bai čós-rnams yáṅ-dag-par bláṅ-ba* to assume, to adopt, virtuous habits earnestly *Stg.*; *yáṅ-dag-par rdzógs-pa* really accomplished *S.O.*; *yaṅ-dag-par ltá-ba* to be orthodox, v. *dgé-ba bču*; *yaṅ-dag lam* the right way, = *ťár-lam Mil.*; *yaṅ-dag-dón* seems to be = *ṅes-don Mil.*, but *yáṅ-dag dón-du ynyér-ba* to aim at, to aspire to, truth *Mil.*; *yáṅ-dag-pai dón-la ˌjúg-pa* to be pious *Thgy.* —

**Comp.** *dag-brjod* orthoepy *Cs.* — *dag-ťér-ba, dag-ťér byéd-pa Sch.* to clean, to cleanse; *Tar.* 189,22; *dag-ster(-čer)mdzád-pa.* — *dag-(pai) snaṅ(-ba) Schr.* 'good opinion'(?), prob.: **a pure, sound view** or **knowledge** *Glr.*; in *Mil.* it has a similar meaning; **dhag-náṅ jón-wa** *C.* to lead a holy life. — *dag-žiṅ* holy country *Sch.* — *dag-yig* orthography; *sṅón-gyi-dag-yig* the older orthography; *brda-dág* = *dag-yig.*

**དགག་པ་** *dág-pa, W.* **dag-če**, v. *tég-pa.*

**དང་** *daṅ*, postp. c. accus, **with** (Lat. cum), *ṅa daṅ* with me (often with the addition of *bčás-pa, lhan-yčig, mnyám*, q. v.), e.g. to go, speak, play, quarrel with; *bud-méd daṅ nyál-ba* to lie with a woman; in some cases it must be omitted in English, or rendered by other words, as: *groṅ-kyér daṅ nyé-ba, riṅ-ba* near the town, far from the town; *de daṅ ˌdrá-ba* equal to that. Some particular ways of using *daṅ* are the following: 1. for **and,** *yser daṅ dṅúl daṅ lčags-la-sógs-pa* gold, and silver, and iron, and the other (metals). The shad is here always put after *daṅ*, which shows that in the mind of the Tibetan *daṅ* never ceases to be a postposition; it can therefore be used only for connecting nouns and pronouns. In enumerations it is employed in different ways, and often quite arbitrarily, e.g. after every single noun or pronoun except the last one, or also after the last; it is used or omitted just as the metre may require it; or when a sum is mentioned, in the following manner: *byúṅ-ba bži ni: sa (daṅ) ču (daṅ) me (daṅ) rluṅ daṅ bžio* the four elements: earth, and water, and fire, and air, four they are; or, esp. in col. language, thus: *sa daṅ yčig, ču daṅ ynyis* etc. — 2. **distributively:** *žag daṅ žag, lo daṅ lo*, day by day, every year; *ḱyim daṅ ḱyim-na Tar.* every one in his house. — 3. after a personal pronoun col. almost like a sign of the plural: *ṅa daṅ ynyís-ka* we two, both of us. *ṅa daṅ tsán-ma* all of us. — 4. after the inf., and in *W.* after the gerund in *gin*, *nyi-ma šár-ba daṅ* at sun-rise, as soon as the sun rises, when the sun rose; *lo brgya lón-pa daṅ* when a hundred years had (or shall have) passed away, after a hundred years; *smrás-pa daṅ ḱyim-du soṅ* with saying so, he went home, is gen. translated: he said so and went home, and so frq. in narration; *W.*: **šúg-ḍa ton daṅ** with a whistling, **ťóṅ-gin žig daṅ** at beholding. — 5. after an imperative for **and,** *sgo rduṅs šig daṅ de-dag ˌoṅ-ṅo* knock at the door, and they will come *Dzl.*; *yíd-la byos šig daṅ bšád-do* give heed, and I will explain it to you *Stg.*; or it is used in the following manner: *légs-par sems šig daṅ ma nór-ram* consider it well; have you not made a mistake there? *nyon čig daṅ sṅón-dus-na* listen to me!

Now, there was in olden times etc. *Dzl.* and elsewh., frq.; *loṅ žig daṅ ṅá-la dbáṅ yod* do take it! I have the power, you know, i.e. I shall answer for it *Dzl.*; in more recent times it is used (also when not followed by any other words) as an imperative particle = *čig*: '*da zo daṅ*' *byas-pas* saying 'eat!' *Glr.*; '*da ltos daṅ*' *ysuṅs* 'now just see', he said *Mil.*; even after *žu*, which in its application is like a verb in the imperative: '*ysúṅ-ba žu daṅ*' *žes zér-bas* saying 'pray, teach (us)!' *Mil.* — 6. In *W. daṅ* is used improperly for the instrum.: **bér-ka daṅ duṅ** strike with the stick! and for by or through with respect to persons: **yóg-po daṅ šab-šób zer** he cheats me, tells me a lie, through his servant.

དང་ *daṅ* 1. **meadow** *Lh.* — 2. *daṅ*, or perh. better *taṅ*, (cf. *tiṅ*), **taṅ táṅ-ce*, or *taṅ čó-ce, taṅ šan čó-ce**, **to read in a singing or drawling manner** *Ld.* — 3. *dáṅ-du lén-pa*, c. *la*, **to submit, yield to, comply with,** *Glr.*, *Tar.*; c. accus. **submissively to put up with** (*Sch.* and *Wts.* are hardly right).

དང་ག, དང་ཁ་ *dáṅ-ga, dáṅ-ka*, 1. **appetite,** *daṅ-ga ₒgag* my appetite is gone, *mi bde* is bad, *Med.* and *Mil.* (*Sch.* 'the **will**'?). — 2. *C.* for *dám-ka*.

དང་པོ་ *dáṅ-po* 1. **the first,** with respect to number, time, rank, *dáṅ-poï ytam de sus zer Pth.* who spoke (raised) the first rumour? who was it that first got up the rumour? *dáṅ-poi nyin-par* on the very first day; *na-tsód dáṅ-po-la ynás-pa* being still in the prime of life *Wdṅ.*; the former, he that is mentioned before another, *dáṅ-po ynyis* the two first named *Thgy.*; **the former, the earlier,** he that precedes another in point of time, = *sṅá-ma*, opp. to *pýi-ma, ₒóg-ma,* **the latter.** — 2. **the first thing, part** etc., *nyin-moï dáṅ-po-la* at the beginning of day, at day-break *Tar.*; *daṅ-po-nyid-du* **in the first place, before the rest, above all, before every other thing** *Thgy.*; *dáṅ-po-nas* from the very beginning *Thgy.*, *Tar.*; *dáṅ-por,* and very frq. *dáṅ-po* adv., **firstly, in the first place; at first, in the beginning.** — *las-dáṅ-po-pa* **a beginner,** *las-dáṅ-po-pai dús-su* as long as he is only a beginner *Thgy.*; *las-dáṅ-po-pai byis-pa* like νήπιος (child) in the N.T., *Mil.*

དང་བ་ *dáṅ-ba* 1. **to be pure,** *nám-mka dáṅ-nas Mil.*; gen. adj. **pure, clear,** *ₒbras dáṅ-ba* picked rice *Lt.*; of inclinations, dispositions, feelings: *séms-čan kún-la rab dáṅ-ba* full of love towards all creatures; *dge-séms dáṅ-ba* a pure, sincere disposition to virtue *S.O.*; most frq. **devout, pious; devotion, faith;** *dáṅ-bai sems* id. (in *W.* often confounded with *ydeṅ-ba*). — 2. *lag dáṅ-ba* = *dár-ba*, v. *darba* II. 2.

དང་ཙེ་ *dáṅ-tse W.* **a field-terrace.**

དང་ར་ *dáṅ-ra* (spelling dubious) **stable,** for cattle, *C.*, *W.*

དང་ལ་ *dáṅ-la* 1. *Sch.* **'a tract of land abounding in springs'.** — 2. n. of a high mountain pass, north of Lhasa, called *Tantla* by Huc II., 231.

དྭངས་པ་ *dwáṅs-pa*, *C.* also **dháṅ-po**, **pure, clean, clear,** = *daṅ-ba* I., of air, water; *ynam-dwáṅs* a clear sky, fine weather (*W.* **taṅ**); *daṅs-smug* reddish gray *Sch.* — *dwaṅs-ma* 1. **the chyle,** *Ssk.* रस, concerning which Brahmanical and Buddhist physiology has led to a great many phantastical ideas, *Med.* frq.; also fig., mostly in an obscure and unintelligible manner. — 2. *Sch.*: **'the spirit; the soul',** a signification not found hitherto in any book, but acc. to a Lama's statement the word denotes the soul, when purified from every sin, and to be compared to a clear and limpid fluid, in which every heterogeneous matter has been precipitated. — *daṅs* is also not seldom met with erron. used for *dṅaṅs* and *mdaṅs*.

དད་པ་ *dád-pa* 1. secondary form of *ₒdód-pa* **to wish** *Dzl.* and elsewh.; hence in compounds: *skom-dád* **thirst,** **tágs-dad-čan** **fond of dress or finery** (cf. *ₒdogs-pa*) *W.*, **and in similar expressions.** — **2. to believe** (cf. श्रद्) **in a religious sense, more significant than** ***yid-čes-pas*** **and including a devotedness full of confidence, like** πιστεύειν in the N.T.; **also sbst. faith, more fully** ***dád-***

*pai sems*, and adj. **faithful, believing**, *yón-bdag dád-pa* the faithful giver of alms *Mil.*; more fully *dád(-pa)-čan, dad-ldán*; *ma-dád-pa*, and *dad-méd* **unbelieving**; often with *mos* or *gus*: *kun dad-dad-mos-mós-su ₒdúg-pa-la Mil.*; *dad-čiṅ-gus-par ₒgyur-ba Glr.*; *dad-par ₒgyúr-ba, dád-pa byéd-pa* **to become faithful or believing, to believe**, frq.: *dád-bžin-du* full of faith; *dad-brtsón* for *dád-pa daṅ brtson-ₒgrús Tar.* — Note. **mi žig-la dád-pa ťob* W.* col. a man becomes a believer, v. *ťób-pa*; but *Tar.* 35, 1 *p̓ágs-pa Dhi-ti-ka-la dád-pa ťob* means: he was brought to believe by hearing the Reverend Dhitika.

ད

དནད་ *dán-da*, and *dan-róg*, medicinal herbs *Med.*

དནདལི་ *dán-da-li*, or *dan-dál*, *Ld.* **a sieve**, gen. consisting of perforated leather and a wooden frame; *rás-dan-dal* a sieve made of cloth (inst. of leather).

དནམོ་ *dán-mo* (spelling?) the female of the ibex, and of the musk-deer.

དམ་ *dam* (a root signifying bound, fast, fixed, from which the following compounds, as well as *sdóm-pa*, are to be derived), sbst., also *dam-ťsig* and *yi(d)-dam*, resp. *ťugs-dam*, **a solemn promise; vow, oath, confirmation by oath,** like *bden-ťsig*: *dam bčá-ba* 1. **to promise,** 2. **the act of promising, the promise**; also *dám-bča Mil.* and col.; *dám-bča ₒbúl-ba* resp. to make a promise, e.g. *mi ₒbáb-pai* not to descend *Mil.*; to promise solemnly *Mil.*; hence *yi-dam*, and (more popularly) *dám-bča* **the sacrament** *Chr. Prot.*; *dam bčás-pa* a promise made; *dam srúṅ-ba, dám-la ɣnás-pa*, or *nyé-bar byéd-pa, dám-bčas-pa spyód-pa, dám-bčas-pa bžin-du byéd-pa, dám-bčas-pa daṅ mi ₒgál-ba*, to keep one's promise; *nyáms-pa* to break (a promise, a vow); *dam-nyáms-kyi lás-rnams* **violations of duty**; *dám-la ₒdógs-pa* **to exorcise** demons etc. *Glr., Pth.*, but only by gentle persuasion, which induces them to promise to do no harm anymore, not by magic power (so it was expressly stated by a Lama); *dám-la ₒjóg-pa Tar.* 125 id. (ni f.); *dám-čan, dam-ťsig-čan Mil.* bound by an oath etc.; *dám-ču* prob. water which is drunk in taking an oath *Pth.*

དམཁ་ *dám-k̔a Glr.*, *dám-ga Wts.*, *ťám-ga Cs.*, **a seal, stamp,** resp. *p̓yag-dám*, esp. for the seals of Lamas; *dám-k̔a rgyáb-pa* **to seal, to stamp**; *k̔yi-dam* v. *k̔yi*; *dam-rgyá* = *dám-k̔a Tar.*: **dam-čug* W.* seal of a Lama, used as an amulet.

དམཔ་ *dám-pa*, acc to the explanation of a Lama: **bound by an oath** or **vow, consecrated**; but *Lexx.* render it by परम, श्रेय i e. = *mčog*, thus *Dzl.* ༢༢༣, 4; ༢༡, 9, and *Cs.*: **noble, brave, excellent,** which is prob. also the sense of the word when compounded with *čos, skyés-bu*, and other words. Its usual rendering, however, is 2. **holy, sacred**, *blá-ma dám-pa, skyés-bu dám-pa*, a holy Lama, a holy man, and most frq. *dám-pai čos, dám-pa čos, dám-čos*, the holy doctrine, the holy religion of Buddha. Yet, in the interpretation of passages the original meaning (noble, excellent) ought to be resorted to much oftener. So also *ɣyóg-mo dám-pa čig Glr.* signifies an excellent, a favourite female slave, but not exactly a holy or a faithful one.

དམཔོ་ *dám-po* 1. **strong, firm; tight, narrow**, of fetters etc.; gen. adverbially *dam-du*, e.g. to bind, to lock up, to seize firmly, securely. — 2. of laws, commandments, **severe, strict, exact.**

དམདུམ་ *dam-dúm* **various** *Sch.*; yet cf. *dum.*

དར་ *dar* I. 1. **silk**, *dár-gyi* **of silk, silken**; *mṅal-dár* resp. for *k̔a-btágs C.*; *rgyaï naṅ dar* fine Chinese silks *Thgy.* — *dar-dkár* white silk *Glr.* — *dar-skúd* silk-thread; *gos-méd dar-skúd ₒdra* stark naked *Ma.* — *dar-gós* silk dress, *Cs.* also silk-stuff. — *dar-čún* a bunch or fringe of silk *Cs.* — *dar-čén Ld-Glr.*, acc. to *Schl.* = *k̔a-btágs*, yet cf. the significations given sub I. 2. — *dar-ₒťág-mk̔an* a silk-weaver; *dar-ₒťag-bu-mo Glr.* the daughter of a silk-weaver. — *dar-p̓ón* = *dar-čún.* — *dár-bu* a coarse kind of silk *Cs.* — *dar-búbs* a whole piece of silk-stuff rolled together. — **dhar-ma-rẹ* C.* 'neither silk nor cotton', half silk half cotton; acc. to others velvet. — *dar-dmán-pa* raw silk *Schr.* — *dar-tsóṅ-pa* a dealer in silks, a silk-mercer. — *dar-záb* the finest silk, frq.; a piece of such silk. — *dar-yáb* a silk fan. — *dar-yúg* a narrow ribbon-like piece of silk-stuff *Glr., Mil.* — *dar-liṅ* = **dhar-ma-rè**. — *dar-šám* the lower border of a silk dress *Glr.* — *dar-(gyi) srín(-bu)* silk-worm. — 2. **a cloth**, made of whatever material; **flag** *Wts.*, **sail** (v. *γyór-mo*); *ₒp̀yar-dár* a hoisted flag; *mduṅ-dar* a little flag fixed to a lance; **ru-dhár** *C.* military banner. — *dar-lčóg* little flags fixed on houses, piles of stones, and the like (v. *Schl. Buddh.* 198). — *dar-po-čé* 1. **a large flag** fastened to a flag-staff; 2. **flag-staff, mast.** — *dar-tsó* a military division, squadron *Sch.* — *dar-šiṅ, dar-bér*, prob. flag-staff.

II. **ice, icy plain;** *dar čágs* ice is forming; also substantively = *dar, mtsó-la dar-čágs btab Mil.* — *dar-zám* ice-bridge. — **dar-ǰár** ('clinging to the ice'?) *W.* a dark-gray aquatic bird.

III. v. *dar-γčig, dár-ba, dár-ma.*

དར་རྒྱས་གླིང་ *dar-rgyas-gliṅ* v. *rdo-rǰe-gliṅ.*

དར་སྒ་ *dár-sga* **walnut.**

དར་གཅིག་ *dar-γčig* (col. also *dal-γčig*), **a little while, a moment;** *dar-γčig lón-pa-na* after a little while *Glr.*; adverbially: **for a little while, for a moment** *Mil.*: **directly, instantly, in a moment** *Mil.*; *dár-tsam Sch.* id.

དར་དིར་ *dar-dir* **humming, buzzing** *Mil.*; **wailing, lamenting** *Pth.*

དར་རྡོ་ *dar-rdó* **grinding-stone** for Indian ink *Sch.*; *bdár-rdo* would perhaps be more correct.

དར་པོ་, དར་མོ་ *dár-po, dár-mo*, col. for *dál-po, dál-mo*, v. *dál-ba.*

དར་བ་ *dár-ba* I. sbst., also *dá-ra, dar*, **buttermilk,** *dar-γsár* fresh buttermilk.

II. vb. 1. **to be diffused, to spread**, of influence, power, opinions, diseases, *čes dár-ba* to gain much ground, to increase exceedingly *Lt.*; *dár-du ₒǰúg-pa* (act.) to extend, enlarge, e.g. academies *Glr.*; *dar-gúd* spreading and decaying, increase and decrease; **dhár-po** *C.* **grand, magnificent,** of a feast, drinking-bout. — 2. with *lag*, **to take in hand, to put hand to a work,** c. *la Dzl.*; also *dáṅ-ba.*

དར་མ་ *dár-ma* 1 **the age of manhood, manly age, prime of life.** gen. reckoned from 30 to 50, but acc. to *S.g.* from 16—70; *dár-la báb-pa*, or *dar-báb*, a person in the prime of life, frq.; *dar-γáṅ* col. id.; *dar-yól* a person beyond that age. — 2. **a man,** and *dár-mo* **a woman in the prime of life.**

དར་མོ་ *dár-mo* v. *dár-po, dár-ma.*

དར་སྨན་ *dar-smán* v. *dar-tsúr.*

དར་ཙམ་ *dár-tsam* v. *dar-γčig.*

དར་ཚིལ་ *dar-tsil Sch.* 'groin' (?).

དར་(མ)ཚུར་ *dar-(m)tsur Wdṅ.* = *dar-sman*, **alum** *Sch.*

དར་ཡ་ཀན་ *dar-ya-kan* a medicinal herb *Med.*

དལ་ཡམས་ *dal-yáms Mil., rims-dál Mil.*, **epidemic disease, plague,** or perh. n. of a particular disease.

དལ་ཅིག་ *dál-čig*, col. for *dar-γčig.*

དལ་ཐོག་འཇུག་པ་ *dal-tóg ₒǰug-pa* **to attack and disperse an enemy** *Sch.*

དལ་བ་ *dál-ba, dál-bu*, **slowness, ease, quietness, leisure** (opp. to haste, hurry, vehemence), **dhál-wa* (or *dhál-bu*) *yŏ'-dham** *C.*, have you time? *dál-ba žig-gi skábs-su* when he happened to have nothing to do *Dzl.*; *dál-bar ₒdúg-pa* to be disengaged, unemployed; *dál-ba brgyad* **the eight conditions of rest**, the state of being free from the eight *mi-k̀óm-pa*; to these belong the *ₒbyor-pa bču*, i.e. ten goods or blessings which, in part, are but more particular definitions of the eight rests, yet include also other blessings; hence both together are called *dal-ₒbyór bčo-brgyád* (another instance of this peculiar way of reckoning v. sub *nyin-mtsán*). As these various conditions are partly characteristics of 'humanity', and attainable only by human beings, they might be denominated 'the (eighteen) specific blessings of humanity'. Often they are also used directly for 'condition of humanity, or of human nature', this kind of existence being, from a religious point of view, the best and most desirable. *rnyed-dkái dál-ba mi lus*, and similar expressions frq. occur (*Cs.* has calmness, tranquillity of mind, evidently mistaking it for *rnal-ₒbyor*). *dál-ba, dál-bu, dál-po, dál-mo, W.* also **dál-čan*, **quiet, calm,** of the mind, the water; **gentle,** of the wind; **slow, lazy;** **šé-gyú dhál-wa*, or *šé-pa dhál-wa* C.* phlegmatic disposition. — Adv. *dál-bar* (v. above), *dál-gyis, dál-bus*, **slowly, softly, gradually,** e.g. to draw, opp to *drág-tu*; *dál-ₒgroi rgyun bžin* like a stream flowing gently and softly; *mi-dál-bar Dzl.* incessantly.

ད

དལ་མོ་ *dál-mo* **chine, loin.**

དལ་བཙོང་ *dal-btsóṅ* (spelling dubious), **dal-tsóṅ táṅ-če* W.* **to carry on compulsory trade.** This is frequently done by Eastern rulers, who in time of personal need make a sale of goods, compelling people to buy at fixed prices.

དི་ *di*, num. fig.: 41.

དི་གར་ཙེ་ *di-gar-či* is said to be a provincialism, and secondary form of *γži-ka-rtsé*, n. of a town near Tashilunpo.

དི་མར་ *di-mar Sch.*: 'a certain worm or insect'.

དི་རི་རི་ *di-ri-rí* **buzz, murmur, hum, low confused noise,** as of crowds, of a number of praying people, of wailing prisoners, of birds on the wing *Glr.*

དིག་ *dig*, the Persian دیگ, **a large kettle, washing-copper, brewer's copper.**

དིག་པ་ *dig-pa* 1. *Cs.* **a stammerer,** also *ka-dig*, cf. *ₒdig-pa*. — 2. *C.* **reeling, staggering, intoxicated.**

དིང་དིང་ *diṅ-diṅ, gád-mo diṅ-diṅ Tar.* 158, 4 prob. an onomatopoetic word, *Schf.* **'laughing aloud'.**

དིང་སང་ *diṅ-sáṅ* = *deṅ-saṅ*.

དུ་ *du* 1. num. fig.: 71. — 2. for *tu* (q.v.) after final *ṅ, d, n, m, r, l.* — 3. **how many?** *bslébs-nas zlá-ba du lon* how many months is it ago that he came? — *du-dú* **how much, how many each time?** *dú-žig* how much about? *dú-ma* many, *žag dú-ma* many days; *dú-mar ₚ́ye* it is divided into **several** (parts) *Wdṅ.*; *lan dú-mar* **many a time, often** *Cs.*; **dú-ma ráksa* C.* col. a great many, very much (perh. 'devilishly much', from *rākšas*).

དུ་བ་ *dú-ba* (cf. *dúd-pa*) **smoke,** *ₒtul*, or *gyén-du ₒₚ́yur* smoke rises *Zam.*; *dú-ba-pa Sp.* very poor people that pay but a trifling tax, **proletarians** (prop. 'smoke-people' that have nothing but the smoke of their fire). — *du-ba-mjug-riṅ* **a comet.** — *du-žág C.* the smoke or vapour hanging over towns and large villages in the morning.

དུག་ *dug* **poison,** *dug blúd-pa* to administer a poisoned potion to a person, to give him poison to drink; *dug-mi-γnód-par ₒgyur* he becomes proof against poison *Dom.*; *čú-la dug ₒdébs-pa* to poison the water *Pth.*; *dug γsum* in a moral sense, *ₒdod-čágs, γti-mug, že-sdáṅ*; sometimes *dug lṅa*, five moral poisons, are mentioned.

**Comp.** *dúg-čan* poisonous. — *dug-γnyén* an antidote *Cs.* — *dug-mdá* a poisoned arrow. — *dug-sbrúl* venomous serpent. — *dug-méd* not poisonous. — *dug-šóg* poisonous paper *Mil., Pth., Glr.* — *dug-sél* that which neutralizes a poison *Cs.* — *dug-srúṅ* a preservative against poison *Cs.*

དུག་ཏི་ *dúg-ti* (or *dúg-ste?*) *Ts.*, **so, thus, in this manner,** also *núg-ti*.

དུག་པོ་ *dug-po*, esp. *Ü* (= **ču-pa* Ts.*, **gon-čę* W.* **coat, garment, dress** *Mil.*

དུགས་ *dugs*, esp. in medical writings; it seems to denote 1. **heat:** *Tar.* 31, 21 *tsád-pai dugs-kyis* by the glowing heat of the day *Schf.*; *S.g.*: *čui dri dugs rláṅs-pa če* the water (i. e. urine) has a strong smell and emits much heat (?) and vapour; *Lt.* ༧༡, 4. 5; ༧༢, 4; ༥༦, 5; ༦༥, 4; ༧༥༠, 10. *čui rigs šin-tu dúgs-pa Mṅg.* adj.? — 2. **revenge, grudge, rancour,** **dug kór-če, dugs-*

*lán ldón-če** to take vengeance, to revenge one's self.

དུགས་པ་ *dúgs-pa W.* 1. **to make warm, to warm**, *mé-la* at the fire, e. g. one's hands, a plate. — 2. **to light, to kindle,** **me dúg-če** to light a fire; **kán-pa mes dug soṅ** the house has begun to burn, has caught fire; **zá-če dug ťsár-ǩan** burnt food, a burnt meal; **dúg-ḍi** a burnt smell.

དུང་ *duṅ* 1. **a tortoise shell,** *duṅ-rdó* a petrified tortoise shell *Cs.* — 2. **a shell,** both small shells, worn as an ornament (*skye-duṅ-p̔réṅ* necklace of shells), and more particularly **the great trumpet-shell,** which is sounded on certain occasions; it is usually of a pure white, hence *duṅ-dkár* 1. **trumpet-shell,** 2. **white rose** *C.*, *dúṅ-so* snow-white teeth *Pth.*, *dúṅ-ru* snow-white horns *Mil.*; a trumpet-shell wound to the right (*γyás-su ˳ǩyíl-ba*) is regarded as valuable as it is rare *Glr.* — 3. **trumpet, tuba,** *duṅ ˳búd-pa* to sound, to blow a trumpet; *ǩrims-duṅ* judgment-trumpet, trumpet used in courts of justice, *čos-duṅ* church-trumpet, trumpet used in religious ceremonies, *dmag-duṅ* war-trumpet, *liṅs-duṅ* hunting-bugle; *rkaṅ-duṅ* a trumpet or cornet made of a hollow thigh-bone; *zaṅs-duṅ* a copper trumpet, a bass tuba eight feet long; *dbaṅ-duṅ* a similar instrument, but of less dimensions; *rwa-duṅ* a trumpet of horn, *rag-duṅ* a brass trumpet. — 4. **skull** (?) *Sch.* has: *duṅ-čen* 1. skull, 2. = *rkaṅ-duṅ*; in *Glr.* Brahma is called *duṅ-gi tor-ťsogs-čan.*

དུང་ངེ་ *duṅ-ṅe* **constant, continual** *Dom.*; *duṅ-ṅe-ba Thgr.* id.

དུང་དུང་ *duṅ-dúṅ* **staggering, reeling, tottering, wavering** *Sch.*

དུང་པན་ *duṅ-pán*, *C.* **dhuṅ-pẹ́n**, **basin.**

དུང་འཕྱར་ *duṅ-˳p̔yár Pth.*, **100 million** *Sch.*

དུངས་པ་ *dúṅs-pa*, secondary form of *γdúṅs-pa*, **love,** *dád-pa daṅ dúṅs-pa žig skyés-te Mil.*, frq.; *yid-dúṅs* = *snyiṅ-brtse-ba*, frq.; **dhúṅ-bhu** *C.* love, **ṭ́u-gu-la dhúṅ-bu ǰhé̄-pa** cf. *γčés-pa.*

དུད་པ་ *dúd-pa* I. sbst. (cf. *dú-ba*, and the Pers. دود) **smoke,** *W.*: **ǩáṅ-mig dúd-pa mā méd-ǩan dug** there comes very little smoke into the room. — *dúd-ǩa Sch.* 1. having the colour of smoke, **dark-gray.** 2. **family, household.** 3. **chimney** (?). — *dúd-ǩu Sch.* 'liquid soot'; prob. soot mixed with water, smut; *Lt.* compares morbid evacuations or matter ejected from the stomach with *dud-ǩu.* — *dud-bál* soot *Sch.*, prob. **flocky soot.** — *dud-bún* a cloud of smoke *Cs.* — *dud-rtsi* soot, smut *Cs.* — *dud-lám* chimney.

II. vb. 1. **to tie, to knit, to knot,** v. *mdúd-pa.* — 2. pf. of *˳dúd-pa*, **stooping, bent,** hence *dúd-˳gro* **quadruped, beast, animal,** opp. to man that walks erect *Stg.*

དུན་པ་ *dún-pa* **great diligence, assiduity,** *dún-pa drág-po*; **dún-čan** very diligent *W.* (cf. *˳dún-pa*, and *rtun*).

དུབ་པ་ *dub-pa*, vb. **to be** or **get tired; adj. tired;** sbst. **fatigue;** *mi dúb-bo* they do not get tired *Dzl.*; *ṅál-žiṅ dúb-nas Glr.*; *lus daṅ ṅag yid dub Pth.* he is tired in body, mouth, and soul, i.e. he has no strength for doing, saying, or thinking anything good. — *dúb-čan* **tiresome** *Cs.* — *dúb-rgyu* **anxious, sorrowful** *Sch.*

དུབས་ *dubs*, *Stg.* **frq.:** *nyé-žiṅ dubs nyé-bar* acc. to the context it might mean: **very probably;** but the word seems to be little known.

དུམ་ *dum* **a piece,** frq.; as a measure or certain quantity of meat, v. *γzugs*; *dúm-po* **a large piece** *Cs.*; *dúm-bu* **a small piece,** frq.; *dúm-bur γčóg-pa, γčód-pa, byéd-pa* to break, to cut to pieces. — *dam-dúm* several small pieces or things *Cs.*; perh. = *dum-dúm Ld.*, e.g. *yul dum-dúm*, or *groṅ dum dúm* several scattered farms, hamlets or villages, which have together one common name.

དུར་ *dur* **tomb, grave,** *dúr-du ˳ǰúg-pa*, *˳dzúd-pa* (*Cs.* *˳débs-pa*) **(s)kúṅ-če** *W.*, **to bury;** *dur rkó-ba* to dig a grave. — *dúr-rkun* grave-robber, plunderer of tombs. — *dúr-ǩuṅ* **grave, tomb.** — *dúr-ǩrod* acc. to etymology denotes **a cemetery, burial-**

**ground**, but in Tibet it signifies a place to which corpses are brought to be cut into pieces for hungry dogs and vultures, this being considered a very honourable mode of burying (or rather disposing of) dead bodies, *Köpp.* II, 322. These places of course are haunted by demons and foul spirits; *dúr-ḱrod-pa* an ascetic living at such a place, *Burn* I, 309. — *dúr-rgyas* the last food which a dying man eats. — *dúr-sgam, dúr-sgrom* **coffin.** — *dúr-rdo* **tomb-stone** *Cs.* — *dúr-spyaṅ* **jackal.** — *dúr-ṗuṅ* **barrow, tumulus, mound, cairn.** — *dúr-byaṅ* **epitaph** *Cs.* — *dúr-ṫsun, dúr-ṫsod,* food offered to the dead *Cs.* — *dur-mṫséd* a place for burning dead bodies *Sch.* — *dúr-sri* a grave-devil, a sort of sepulchral vampire.

དུར་བ *dúr-ba.* 1. sbst. **weed, weeds,** *Sch.* — 2. vb. **to run** *Mil., dúr-te rgyúg-pa* to run towards a place or object, to hasten to, *zás-la dúr-ba* to hasten to dinner, *lás-la* to work *C.*; cf. *ṅám-dur-ċan.*

དུར་བིན *dur-bin W.*, the Persian دوربين **spy-glass.**

དུར་བྱ *dúr-bya* **a paring-axe; a hoe** *Sch.*

དུར་བྱིད *dur-byid* **a purgative root,** prob. = *ṫár-nu S.g.*, acc. to *Wdṅ.* = *tri-byi-ta* (sic), prop. त्रिवृता, Ipomoea Turpethum.

དུལ་བ *dúl-ba*, prop. pf. of *ₒdúl-ba*, **soft,** of the skin etc.; **tame; gentle** (temper), **easy** (disposition), **mild;** also sbst. **softness** etc.; *dul-po, W. *dúl-mo** id., but only adj.; *ma dul-ba* **untamed, rude,** *Dzl.*; **sráb-ḱa* (or *ḱá-po*) *dúl-mo* W.* **soft-** or **tender-mouthed; tame, manageable, tractable.** *Tar.* 11, 14 a better reading prob. would be: *dbaṅ-po ₒdul-bai brȷ̇id* a splendour that dazzles the senses.

དུལ་མ *dúl-ma* a kind of **water-colour** made of pulverized gold and silver, for painting and writing.

དུས *dus* 1. **time,** in general, *dús-kyi ḱór-lo* v. *ḱór-lo*; *dús-kyi* means also: **happening sometimes** *Mil.*; *dus* adv., for a while, for some time *Lt.*; *deï dús-su, dus de tsa-na, dé-dus, dus der,* at the time, at this time; *dus de-nyid-du* then immediately, directly afterwards; *dáṅ-poi dus nyid-du* in the very first time; *dús-su*, or *dus-dús-su, dus ₒga-ré,* sometimes, now and then: *de daṅ dus mnyám-du* simultaneously with that *Glr.*; *dus γċig-tu* or *la* at one and the same time, together; *dús-ċig-na* (erron. *γċig*), also *dus re* (or *nam*)-*żig-gi ṫse, dus-re* (-*żig*), once, one day, some day; *dus lan-ċig* id. *Glr.*; *dus ṗyi żig-na* some future day; *dus γżan żig-na* another time; *dus ċi tsam-na* at what time? when? *Glr.*; *dus*(-*na*) after a genit., inf., or verbal root = when, after, *żag γnyis soṅ dus* when two days had, or will have passed *Mil.*; *ṅa bú-moi dús-na yin-te* when I was still a girl *Glr.*; *mgú-dus med* the time of being satisfied never arrives *Mil.*; *btsá-dus-te* as the time of giving birth has come *Lt.*; frq. with *ₒbáb-pa: bdag ₒdúl-bai dús-la bab* the time of my conversion has come: sometimes *dús-la sleb Lt.*; col.: *dus sleb* the time is come; *ₒgro-bai dus ₒdébs-pa Dzl., byéd-pa* frq., to fix a time for going, also thus: *nam ₒgró-bai dus byéd-pa Dzl.*; *dus kún-tu, dus rgyún-du* always; almost pleon. in: *dus dá-nas* henceforth, from this time forward *Mil.*; *de daṅ dus ₒdzom* as to time it coincides with that *Glr.* — 2. **the right time, proper season; for** is expressed by the genit. of the inf. (cf. above: the time of my conversion); *dús-su* at the right or proper time, e.g. for paying off *Glr.*; *dus ma yin-pa* the wrong time; *dus ma yin-par, dus-min* unseasonably, not in due time; esp. too soon, prematurely, e.g. to die; *dus-ma-yin-pa spóṅ-ba* to abstain from doing unseasonable things. — 3 *dus γsum* **the three times,** viz. *dá-ltai*, or *dá-ltar-gyi, ₒdás-pai,* and *ma-ₒóṅs-pai*, frq., thus in *dus γsúm-gyi saṅs-rgyás* the Buddhas of the three times; often also with special reference to metempsychosis, **the present, the former,** and **the future period of life;** with respect to the times of the day: **morning, noon, evening;** besides *nyin-dus γsum*, also *mṫsán-dus γsum* occurs. —

4. **season.** Here Tibetans, of course, distinguish the four seasons of the temperate zone, *dpyid* spring, *dbyar* summer, *ston* autumn, *dgun* winter; but in books, originally written in India, either three are counted, *ťsá - dus* hot season, *grán - dus* cold season, *čár-dus* rainy season, or more accurately six: *dpyid* (वसन्त) spring, i. e. March and April, *sos-ka* (ग्रीष्म) hot season, May, June, *dbyar* (वर्ष) rainy season, July, August, *ston* (शरत्) damp season, September, October, *dgun - stód* (हेमन्त) first part of winter, November, December, *dgun-smád* (शिशिर) last part of winter, January, February. — 5. **conjunctures, times, circumstances,** *dus dé - mo* *W.*, *dhu̥ - dé (sa - ͺjám)* *C.*, *dús-kyi ͺḱrúg-pa méd-pa Ld.-Glr.*, *dus bzán-po Dom.*, peace. — 6. **a particular period of time, as distinguished from others, an age,** युग (= $\frac{1}{1000}$ कल्प), *yar-ldán*, or *rdzogs-ldán* (कृत or सत्य) *yar-rábs*, or *γsum-ldán* (त्रेत) *rtsod - ldán*, or *γnyis - ldán* (द्वापर) *snyigs - ma* (कलि), to be compared to the four ages of Greek mythology. — 7. **year** *Lt.* — 8. symb. num.: 6. — Note. *dus byéd-pa* also signifies (cf. 1 above) **to fulfil the time,** *ťsei dus byéd-pa* to die, to perish, also to commit suicide *Dzl.* frq.; *ͺči-bai dus byed-pa* id. *Wdn.* — *dus dzin-pa* to take the day-service upon one's self (?) *Dzl.* ༢༥༢, 3.

**Comp.** *dus-skabs* v. *skabs.* — *dus-čén, -bzán, -stón,* **festival,** *byéd-pa* to keep one. — *dus-mčód* v. *mčod-pa.* — *dus-sbyor Cs.*: **'judicial astrology',** *dus-sbyor-pa* an astrologer. — *dus-me* **comet** *Cs.* — *dus-rtsi-ba Cs.* **'the counting of time'.** — *dus - ťsig Sch.*: '*dus - ťsig γsár - ba* new, fresh provisions, **'produce of the year'** (?). — *dus-ťsigs, dus-mťsams* 1. **period, epoch;** 2. **season** *Cs.* — *dus - tsód* 1. **space** or **measure of time.** 2. often for *dus*, *deï dus - ťsód-kyi mi-rnams* the men of that time or period, *deï dus-ťsod - la* at that time; also for hour. — *dus-zin Sch.*: 'time of depravity'. — *dus-bzán* v. above *dus-čén.* — *dus-rlábs* **'wave of time'** i. e. **ebb** and **flood, the tides,** *Stg.* — *dus - lóg* a year yielding no crops, **a sterile, bad year** *Pth.*

དེ་ *de* 1. num. figure: 101. — 2. affix of the gerund, for *te*, after a final *d.*

དེ་ *de* demonstrative pron. (in *B.* gen. placed after the word to which it belongs, in col. language before it, even without the termination of the genitive) **that, that one,** opp. to *ͺdi* this, this one, yet with occasional exceptions. 1. when words or passages are literally quoted, the Tibetan begins with *ͺdi-skad* or some similar expression, and places a *čes* or *dé-skad* after it. *ͺdi*, in such a case, corresponds about to **'the following',** *de* to **'such',** or **'thus',** (cf. τοῦτο and τόδε). But elsewhere *ͺdi* may also refer to what has been said before, e.g. in a reply: *ťsig ͺdi ni bdén - pa yin-nam* is this word (that has just been said) true? *Dzl.* In the context of a narrative, however, *de* is usually employed. — 2. It frq. stands in the place of the definite article **the:** *p̓a de lóg-ste són-no* the father went back *Mil.*; esp. after adjectives and participles, where it adds to perspicuity: *γžón - nu de na - ré* the younger one said *Mil.*; *snón-la són-ba de* he that has gone on before *Mil.*; *deï dón-du, deï p̓yir(-du), čéd-du, slád-du,* **therefore, on this account, for this reason;** *deï ͺóg-tu* **under that, after that, afterwards;** *deï dús-su, ťse(-na)* **there, then, at that time.** — 3. **he, she, it,** for *ḱo*, which in classical style is not in use. — 4. for *deï*, in *de-p̓yir, de-dus,* (abbreviations of *deï p̓yir-du, deï dús-su,* v. above). **Plural:** *dé-dag, dé-rnams, dé-ťso.*

**Comp. and deriv.** *dé-ka, dé-ḱa,* **the very same,** *γsa dé - ka na yin* the very same snow-leopard (you saw) was I myself *Mil.*; *dé - ka ltar* **just so** *Thgy.*; *dé - ka yod* (in answer to a question) **indeed! yes, yes! to be sure!** *Mil.*, *C.*, frq.; *dé - ka lags Mil.*, id.; *de ḱyed lags Pth.*, oh, this ... is you?! — *de-ḱó-na, de-nyid,* col. *de-rán,* **the very same,** cf. *ḱó-na; de - nyid,* and *de-ḱo-na-nyid* are also sbst.: **essence, nature** *Thgy.*; *séms-kyi de-nyid* the essence of the soul

*Mil.* — *de-snyéd* **so many.** — *dé-ltu, dé-ltar* (*-du*, or *-na*) **so,** *p̔a ni dé-lta ma yin-te* as it is not so with the father *Stg.;* *dé-lta-bu* of that kind, quality, or manner, **such,** esp. in *B.* — *de-dé* = *de*, but more emphatic, **exactly that;** *de-de-bžin-no* **yes, so it is!** **dhén-ḍa, ḍe** *C.* = *dé-lta* etc. — *dé-na* **therein, in that place, there, here.** — *dé-nas* **from, thence, from that place; afterwards, then, at that time,** very frq. — *dé-pa, dé-ma Cs.* one of that place, sect, religion etc. — *dé-bas* 1. after a comparative, **than that;** 2. also *dé-bas-na, dés-na, des,* **therefore, consequently, now then** (δή) *B.* frq. — *dé-bo* = *de Cs.* — *dé-tsam* **so much;** *dé-tsam-na, dé-tsa-na,* **then, at that time.** — *dé-tsug, W.* gen. **dé-zug**, **so, thus.** — *dé-bžin(-du)* **according to that, thus, so;** frq. for **it,** *dé-bžin-du γnáṅ-ṅo* he allowed it *Dzl.;* *dé-bžin ṅó-šes-nas* perceiving it *Glr.* — *de-bžin-nyid* (तत्त्व) **essence,** *Was.* (272), **identity** (297), like *č̔os-nyid* and some other similar expressions, = *stoṅ-pa-nyid, Trigl.* fol. 20. — *dé-zug* = *dé-tsug.* — *dé-yaṅ, dé-aṅ,* 1. **this,** or **that, too; he also.** 2. **namely, to wit, viz.,** preceding specifications and detailed statements, sometimes also after a gerund, in which case it cannot be rendered in English. — *de-rag* **directly, immediately** *Sch.* — *de-ráṅ* = *de-k̔ó-na, de-ráṅ yin* that is just the thing! exactly! to be sure! col. — *de-riṅ B.* and *C.* **to-day,** *de-riṅ-gi* **of this day.** — *dé-ru, der,* 1. **into that, thereinto, into that place, thither, that way.** 2. **in that, therein, in that place, there,** frq. — *dé-la* **to this, to that; in, on,** or **at this; thereat, therewith, thereto, thereon; about that, concerning that; thereof, therefore.** — *dé-las* **from, out of, from that;** after a comparative and *γžan,* **than that.** — *de-srid* to such a length of time.

དེ་བ་ *dé-ba* a medicinal herb, *Med.*

དེང་ *deṅ*, also *diṅ*, **to-day,** *déṅ-nas* from this day forward *Mil.*; *deṅ p̔yin-čad* or *čad Dzl.* id.; *déṅ-gi dus* the present time or age; *deṅ-sáṅ* to-day and to-morrow; **now-a-days;** *deṅ-sáṅ lhá-rje* the physicians of the present day *Wdṅ.;* *déṅ-dus smán-pa Lt.* id.

དེང་བ་ *déṅ-ba*, pf. and imp. of *ₒdéṅ-ba,* **to go, to go away;** *déṅs-pa* seems to be the same form: *so-sói γnás-su deṅs Mil., ráṅ-sar déṅs-so Pth.* they went each to his own place; *nám-mk̔ar deṅ Mil.* prob. it melted away, dissolved into air; *sór-mo-rnams deṅs mdzád-pa* to turn the fingers upwards (?). *Schr. déṅs-pa* to ascend.

དེད་པ་ *déd-pa*, pf. of *ₒdéd-pa.*

དེབ་(མ་) *déb(-ma)* **poultice, cataplasm,** applied to sores and inflamed parts of the body *Sch.*

དེབ་ཐེར, གཏེར, སྟེར་ *deb-t̔ér, -γtér, -stér,* tibetanized form of the Persian دفتر **documents, records, catalogues, registers, lists, books;** *deb-t̔ér-pa, deb-t̔er-mk̔an Cs.* keeper of the archives or records, **recorder, archivist, librarian;** *déb-k̔aṅ* **chancery, government office** *Schr.; déb-yig* **cover, envelope, stitched book** *Sch.*

དེམ་ཙི་ *dém-tsi* (perh. *Bu-nan*); **a small, narrow bridge, foot-bridge** *Lh.*

དེའང་ *déaṅ*, v. sub *de.*

དེའུ་(རེ་) *déu(-re)* **one day, some future time,** *Dzl.* frq.; *deu ... deu ...* now ... now, at one time ... at another time *Mil.* (*Tar.* 165, 18 is prob. an incorr. reading).

དེར་ *der*, for *dé-ru*, esp. as adv., **then, at that time;** *der zad, der bas Cs.* that is all, there is nothing more, finis.

དེས་ *des* 1. instrum. of *de; des čog* with that it is enough, **that will do** *Sch.* — 2. for *dé-bas*, v. *de* comp.

དེས་པ་ *dés-pa Cs.:* **'fine, brave, noble, chaste;** a title'; occurs frq. in *Dzl.* as a commendable quality of women.

དོ་ *do* 1. num. figure: 131. — 2. **two, a pair, a couple,** used only in counting, measuring etc.: *žo do re* two drams of each *Med.;* **tá-bag do** *W.* two platefuls. — 3. **this,** *Schr.: dó-yi dón-du;* gen. only in *do-núb* this evening, to-night *Mil.; bdag do-núb sáṅ-gi mi* I, a man only for to-day and to-morrow *Mil.; Cs.* also *do-žág, do-*

*mód* to-day. — 4. **an equal, a match; a companion, associate,** *W.* **yá-do** **fellow, yoke-fellow, mate, comrade, consort;** *do-zla* 1. id. *Mil.*; 2. **party** in a lawsuit(?); **dó-da ǰan-tsún žib čé-pa** *Cs.* seems to mean: carefully to investigate (the right of) both parties; *do-med* unequalled, matchless; **dho-med zaṅ-po**, *C.*, *W.*

དོ་ཀེ(ར)་ *do-ké(r)* = *tor-tsúgs Lex.*

དོ་གར་ཁ་ *do-gar-ḱá W.* **light-blue.**

དོ་གལ་ *do-gál* **importance, weight; important, weighty** *C.*, *W.*; **dho-ghál mi ǰhé-pa** *C.*, **do-gál mi čó-če** *W*, to treat lightly, to make light of, to slight; **di tsig-po dho-ghál mi dug** *C.*, this word is unimportant, of no consequence; *do-gál-čan* important, of consequence *Cs.*

དོ་དམ་ *do-dám* **commission, charge, superintendence;** **dho-dhám ǰhé-pa** *C.*, **do-dám ḱúr-če** *W.*, to have the superintendence, direction, or charge of a business, to have the keeping of a thing; *do-dám-pa* 1. a commissioned, authorized person, **overseer** etc. 2. **bishop** *Chr. Prot.*

དོ་པོ་ *dó-po* **a load,** for a beast of burden, cf. *dos*; **do-góm** *W.* saddle-cloth, housing; *do-lógs* the load on one side of a sumpter-horse, half a load, *do ya-γčig*; *do-nón-pa* the equalizing of the load, by increasing or lessening it on one of the sides.

དོ་བ་ *dó-ba* 1. Jerusalem artichoke *Sik.* — 2. secondary form of *sdó-ba* c. accus., to be a match for, to be equal in strength etc., to cope with *Mil.*; **šrog dhaṅ dhón-da re** *C.* his life is at stake (*da?*).

དོ་བོ་ *dó-bo Med.*, prob. = *dó-ba* I.

དོ་མོད་ *do-mód* **to-day,** this day, v. *do.*

དོ་ར་ *do-rá Mil.?*

དོ་རེ་ *do-ré* v. *do* 2.

དོ་ཤཱ་ལཱ་ *do-šā-lā Hind.* a thick **shawl** or **wrapper** *W.*

དོ་ཤལ་ *do-šál Cs.* n. of an ornament hanging down from the shoulders; *Schr. mu-tig-gi do-šál* pearl-necklace; *Mil.* id.

དོ་སེ་ *do-sé* (from *tse?*) **now, at present** *Bal.*

དོག་ *dog* col. an auxiliary vb., acc. to Lamas of *W.* and *C.* = *rtóg-pa*, but of different pronunciation (*W.* **dog**, *C.* **dhog**). It seems to correspond to the expressions: as far as I know, as much as you know, to your knowledge etc. So a person may be asked: **yóg-mo me bar dóg-ga(m)** has your maid-servant, for what you know, lighted a fire? whilst, if the servant herself were asked, the question could only be: **me bar-ra(m)*, or *bar tsar-ra(m)**.

དོག་ *dog* sbst., in *B.* mostly *dóg-pa*, 1. **bundle, clew, skein,** e.g. of wool, weighing about two pounds, as much as one can hold conveniently with the hand or twist round it (*lag-dóg*). — 2. **capsule,** *ǎr-dza-kai* of the cotton plant. — 3. **ear of corn** *Lex.*; *Col.* more in use: *dog-dóg* a larger piece, *ḱá-ra dog-dóg*, lump-sugar (opp. to ground sugar); **clod, clump, lump, loaf,** **dog-dóg čó-če** *W.* to form loaves; or in general: to press, to press together, to crush, to crumple; **a piece of wood, a log** *W.* (differing from *rdog*); **dág-ga-dog-gé** *Ld.* broken in pieces, e.g. *ḱa-ra.*

དོག་པ་ *dóg-pa* 1. v. *dog* sbst. — 2. adj. and sbst., **narrow, narrowness;** *dóg-po*, *dóg-mo* adj.; *dóg-pai γnas-las ṫar-ba Wdṅ.*; fig. *šin-tu dóg-par gyúr-to* they were kept within narrow bounds *Glr.*; **ṭim dhóg-po** *C.* strict administration of justice.

དོག་ལེ་ *dóg-le* an iron pan with a handle *C.*, *W.*

དོགས་པ་ *dógs-pa* 1. vb., **to fear, to be afraid of, to apprehend,** gen. with the root of the pf tense, which in earlier writings is placed in the instrum. case: *nyés-pa byúṅ-gis mi dogs Dzl.*; whereas *Glr.*: *ser byuṅ dógs-pai dús-su* (fearing) when a hail-storm is threatening; *Tar.* 188. 9: *rgyal-srid ma zin-gyi(s) dógs-te* being afraid (the prince) might not be able to govern; *ma zin dógs-pas Glr.* fearing lest he should not finish the matter; *γsó-mk̔an ma byuṅ dógs-nas Glr.* fearing that no deliverer would make his appearance; hence for **that not, lest** and similar expressions, *bu mis mt̔óṅ-gis dógs nas* that his son might not be seen by the people *Pth.*; *že-sdáṅ laṅs dogs túr-re gyis* be on your guard lest anger should arise, take care not to grow angry! *Mil.*; *ˌgos dógs-pai lčibs* dusters to prevent (things) from getting dirty *Lex.*; *γžán-gyis γsál-bar šés-kyis dogs(-na)* using distant allusions, so that the drift of a speech is not at once clear and intelligible *Gram.*; rarely with the supine: *dé-dag bág-tu*, or *ˌbrós-su dogs* fearing lest they should become faint-hearted or take to flight *Dzl.* — 2. sbst. **apprehension, fear, scruple,** *dógs-pa skyes-te Dzl.*; also *dogs skyés-te Glr.*; *dogs bsál-ba, dogs γčód-pa* to remove doubts or apprehensions *Tar.*; *dogs dpyod ni dogs γčód-do* examining a scruple is as much as removing it *Sch.*; *re-dógs* hope and fear (things which a saint ought to be no longer subject to) frq.

དོང་ *doṅ* 1. **a deep hole, pit, ditch,** an excavation deep in proportion to its breadth, e.g. a trench in fortifications, *Glr.*; *sa-dóṅ* id.; *ču-dóṅ* **a well, a deep cistern;** *me-dóṅ* a fiery abyss, pool of fire *Dzl.*; *Sch.* proposes to use it also for **crater.** — 2. **depth, deepness, profundity;** *dóṅ-čan Cs.*, **dóṅ-po** *W.*, **deep;** *doṅ-méd* not deep, shallow *Cs.* — 3. v. *ˌdóṅ-ba.*

དོང་ག་ *dóṅ-ga* n. of a tropical climbing plant, and of a sweet-tasted lenient purgative *Med.*

དོང་པ་ *dóṅ-pa* **padlock,** *dóṅ-pa ˌjúg-pa* to put a padlock on.

དོང་པོ་, ལྡོང་པོ་ *dóṅ-po, ldóṅ-po* 1. **tube,** any hollow cylindrical vessel, = *pu-ri*; *dóṅ-bu* a small ditto; *spa-dóṅ* a tube etc. of bamboo, *šiṅ-doṅ* a tube etc. of wood; *lčags-doṅ* of iron; *mda-doṅ* **a quiver,** *dóṅ-ba Glr.* id.; *dóṅ-mo, ldóṅ-mo* **a small churn,** = *gur-gúr.* — 2. **a shuttle,** made of a piece of bamboo.

དོང་ཙེ་ *dóṅ-tse, Sch.* also *dóṅ-ťse, dóṅ-rtse,* piece of money, **coin,** *γsér-gyi* gold coin *Dzl.*; esp. a small coin, used (like penny) proverbially for a small sum, *Dzl.* ༢༩༡, 9; ༼༼, 6.

དོང་ཟིལ་ *doṅ-zil* (?) *W.* Corydalis meïfolia.

དོང་ཟེ་ *dóṅ-ze* **wasp** *Cs.*

དོད་ *dod* **an equivalent,** **ṅul méd-na dod ʼiṅ tob gos** *W.* if you have no money, I must receive an equivalent; *dei dod či-ˌdra yod* what is the equivalent, what shall we get for it? *Mil.*; *bu-dód* adoptive son, *ṅéd-kyi bu-dód mdzod* pray, suffer yourself to be adopted by us *Mil.*; *skad-dód* verbal equivalent, **synonym, translation** *Lex.*; *dód-du* **as an equivalent, as payment, for, instead of, at,** e.g. at a moderate price; *k̔yód-kyis ṅai stóbs-kyi dod mi p̔er Glr.*, gen. **mi nun** *C.*, you cannot cope with me in strength, you are no match for me.

དོད་པ་ *dód-pa* **to project, to be prominent,** gen. with *ˌbur-du*; also **elongated** (Botany) *Wdṅ.*

དོན་ *don* (Ssk. अर्थ), resp. (at least in some of its applications) *žabs-don Pth.* 1. **sense, meaning, signification,** *gó-ba* to understand, *ˌgrél-ba* to explain; *don rnyéd-par dká-bai yig-ˌbrú* letters the meaning of which is not easily understood *Glr.*; *don mi ˌdug* that makes no sense; *ˌdii don či yin* what does that mean? *žal ni k̔ai don yin: 'žal'* signifies the same as *k̔a*; *dpe bži don daṅ lṅai mgur* a psalm, containing four parables, together with their explanation, as being the fifth (part) *Mil.*; *ráṅ-gi-séms-la don gyis* refer the signification, make the application, to your own soul *Mil.*; ... *kyi dón-du bšad,* it is explained in the sense of ..., as having the same meaning as ... *Gram.*; *don mt̔ún-no* they agree in this sense, on that point, they say so unanimously *Glr.*; *don dé-la soms* think over this sense, i.e. over the meaning of this significant example *Mil.*; *žu-dón* application, petition, request; contents, *Tar.* 45, 19.; also opp. to *ťsig* (word, form); *čos-byuṅ-na spri-ti-ma zer-ba ˌdug-ste don mtun* in the *čos-byuṅ*, it is true, he is called Spritima, but the contents (i.e.

the things related about him) agree, are the same *Glr.*; *ńés-don*, and *dráṅ-don* v. *ńés-pa* extr.; **idea, notion, conception** *Was.* (283); as the heading of a chapter or paragraph, e.g. *sdíg-pa dág-pai don* of the expiation of sin. Rarely in a subjective sense: *don-méd byís-pa* thoughtless children *Mil.* — 2. **the true sense, the real state of the case, the truth,** (cf. *don-dám*), esp. *dón-la*, sometimes also *dón-gyis Tar.* 102, 12, in truth, in fact, really *Glr.* and elsewh.; to speak the truth *Thgy.*; *dón-la bltá-na* col. id.; also for: true! surely! indeed, forsooth. — 3. **intent, purpose, design; profit, advantage,** *₀dii don ċi yin* what is your meaning and intent (of doing that)? *soṅ-sóṅ-bai don med Dzl.* going on is to no purpose; *don med bžin-du* without seeing the use of it, without understanding the purpose *Wdn.*; with the genit. of the noun: **the profit, advantage, the good,** of a person, *mii don byéd-pa* to promote a person's welfare; esp. with reference to holy men, *₀gro(-bai) don byéd-pa* to work for the welfare of (all) beings, very frq.; of priests col.: to act officially, to sacrifice; **gain, profit,** v. *γnyér-ba*; in a concrete sense: **some particular advantage, prerogative, good** or **blessing** obtained, frq.; *p̀án-pai don* a useful thing, *bdé-bai don* a gift of fortune, *rnyéd-pa* to obtain it; *dṅos-grúb mčóg-gi don* the excellency of the highest perfection; hence *dón-du* postp. c. genit. 1. **for,** for the good or the benefit of; 2. **for the sake of, on account of**; c. genit. of inf. **in order to, that**; 3. rarely: **in the place of, instead of, against, for,** *zas nór-gyi dón-du ₀ts̀óṅ-ba* to sell food for money *Mil.* — 4. in a general sense: **affair, concern, business,** *raṅ-(gi) don* one's own affairs, one's own interest (cf. n. 3); *γžan-(gyi) don* the interest of others; also meton. for **disinterestedness** *Mil.* (*Ssk.* परार्थ); *don máṅ-bas* on account of much business (syn. *brel-bas*) *Dzl.*; **chief or main point** (ni f.), *γsó-ba-rig-pai dón-rnams mdor sdú-ba* to sum up the principal points of medical science; *čos don γsúm-la ₀dús-te* religion being reduced to three main points (*lus, ṅag, yid*) *Glr.*; *don sgrúb-pa*, or *₀grúb-pa* to settle an affair, to obtain one's end, to attain to happiness. — 5. in anatomy *don lṅa* are: **the heart, lungs, liver, spleen,** and **kidneys** *Med.*; cf. *snod.* — 6. **document,** *čád-don* a written contract, agreement; *ċe(d)-don* a letter (to an inferior person).

**Comp.** *dón-ċan*, *don daṅ ldán-pa* 1. **useful, profitable, expedient,** e.g. *tsig Thgy.* 2. **enjoying an advantage.** 3. having a certain sense. — *don-mt̀un* **a merchant** *Cs.*; *dpal daṅ ldán-pai don-mt̀ún-dag* most honourable merchants! — *don-dág* 1. *Sch.* business, affairs (?). 2. col. = *don* 1. *don-dám* (परमार्थ), **the true sense,** subjectively: **good earnest,** col. *W. yáṅs-pa man don-dám yin* it is not (said in) jest, but in good earnest; objectively: *don-dám-par dbyer-méd* in truth, (after all, upon the whole, in the end), it is all the same *Gram.*; *don-dám rnám-par ńés-pai čos Glr.* prob. = *don-dám-pai bdén-pa* absolute truth *Was.* (293); in later times = *stoṅ-pa-nyid Trigl.* 20; *Mil.* — **don-ḍás* W.* (lit. *-₀bras*) = *če-dón?*

དོན་ *don* num. for *bdún-ċu*, *don-γċig* etc. 71, 72 etc. to 79.

དོན་པ་ *dón-pa* for *₀tón-pa Glr.* in one passage, prov. in *C.*

དོབ་དོབ་ *dob-dób*, *dob-dób smrá-ba* **to talk stuff, nonsense** *Sch.*

དོམ་ *dom* **the brown bear**; *dóm-bu* 1. *Sch.* the cub of a bear, 2. *Cs.*: a species of black dogs, resembling a bear.

དོམ་དོམ་ *dom-dóm Cs.*: ornamental fringes hanging down from the neck of a horse; *Wdṅ.*: *mé-tog rtá-yi dom-dóm ₀dra.*

དོམ་ར་ *dóm-ra* **screen, shade** for the eyes and the like *Sch.*

དོར་ *dor* **a pair** of draught cattle; *glaṅ-dór* a yoke of oxen

དོར་བ་ *dór-ba* v. *₀dór-ba.*

དོར་མ་ *dór-ma* **breeches, trowsers,** *dor-t̀ún* short breeches, *dor-ríṅ* long drawers, trowsers *Cs.*; *snam-dor* from *snam-bu*; *dór-rta* 1. that part of the breeches which covers the privy parts, v. *rta*; *yúgs-sa-moi dór-rta des γza sruṅ, rmá-la p̀an Wdṅ.*, the

ད

middle part of a widow's drawers prevents epilepsy and heals wounds. — 2. *W.* = *dór-ma?*

དོལ་ *dol* 1. **net**, esp. fishing-net, **ṭám-pa** to spread, to fix it *C.*, *W.*; *(nya-)dól-pa* **a fisherman**, cf. *ɣdól-pa*. — 2. *W.* **stew-pan.** — 3. *dol ɣċód-pa* **to split, to cleave** *Sch.*

དོས་ *dos* **a load** (of a beast of burden) that has to be carried by compulsory service, without being paid for; *k̔al-dós* id.; *ǰa-dós* a load of tea carried in this manner; *dos ₒgél-ba* to load (on), **to pack,** *dos ₒbógs-pa* (not *ₒp̔óg-pa Cs.*) **to unload;** *dós-pa* a conductor of such loads *Cs.*, *dos-dpon* the leader of a caravan of such loads; *dos drág-pa* 1. *Mil.* prob.: **hard compulsory service;** 2. perh. also: **severe in exacting it,** e.g. a feudal lord.

ད྄ྲ་ཅི་, དྲང་ཅི་ *drá-ċi, dráṅ-ċi Pur.* a flat basket.

དྲ་པ་ *drá-pa* a small copper coin, used in the western part of the Himalaya, **a thick paisa,** of the value of half a penny.

དྲ་བ་ *drá-ba* I. sbst. जाल, 1. **grate, lattice; net, net-work,** *lús-la drá-bar ₒbrel* (the veins) are spread throughout the body like net-work *S.g.*; *rús-pai drá-ba* the frame-work of bones, the skeleton *Thgy.*; *ₒod-zér-gyi drá-la* a pencil or aggregate of rays of light (lit. lattice-work of rays) *Glr.*; *dra mig* id., esp. col.; *lċágs-(kyi) dra(-mig)* **iron railings; grate; gridiron;** *rgyá-dra* **wooden rails, fence** *C.*, *W.*; *dra-(ba) p̔yed(-pa) Lex.*, *Glr.* 'half-lattice', technical term for a kind of silk ornament; *drá-ba-ċan* latticed, grated; *dra-lag-drá-lag-ċan* having many forked ends or branches, of the horns of a stag. — 2. a bag made of net-work *Cs*, *dra-p̔ád*, *dra-čúṅ* id. — 3. the web of water-fowls.

II. vb., pf. *dras*, *W.* **ḍé-ċe**, **to cut, clip, lop, dress, prune, pare** (leather, cloth, paper, wings etc. with knife or scissors); also fig.: *p̔ai miṅ-nas drás-te* borrowing (a syllable) from the father's name *Glr.* (twice); cf. also *Tar.* 107, 13; **ṭéb-ḍhe-pa** *C.* one that cuts the strings (of a purse) on his thumb, i.e. **a cut-purse, pick-pocket;** *gos-drás* cloth cut out for a garment *Cs.*; *dras-spyád* **scissors** *Sch.*; *dra-grí Cs.*: 'a tailor's knife used for shears'; *drai* (sic) *ro Sch.*, **ḍe-rúg, ṭa-ḍe** *W.* **clippings, cuttings, remnants.**

དྲ་མ་ *drá-ma* **experienced, practised, learned** *Sch.*; so perh. *Pth.*, where however *bra-ma* and *tra-ma* is the usual form.

དྲ་ཟུ་ *dra-zu*, or **dra-su** *W.* a small pan with a handle; **a ladle.**

དྲག་ *drag* 1. *W.* **the post; any parcels** or **goods conveyed by post,** the *Hind.* डाक. — 2. **expedient, profitable, of use,** *p̔úl-ba drág-gam* will it be of any use, well-applied, if I give? *Mil.*; *ǰi byas kyaṅ ma drag* whatever I did, it was of no use *Pth.*; *na ċi-ltar byás-na drag* what course will it be expedient to take?, what shall I do best? *Pth.*; **ċi ḍhag, ghaṅ ḍhag** *C.* what is right? what is expedient? *nád-pa drág-pas čog* it is sufficient, if the patient is getting better *Mil.*

དྲག་པ་ *drág-pa* 1. **noble, of noble birth** *C.*, **drág-po** *W.*; *mi drág-pa*, or merely *drág-pa*, **a nobleman;** *drag-rigs* **nobility, gentry;** *drág-par byéd-pa* to raise to nobility, *drág-par ₒgyúr-ba* to become a nobleman *Cs.*; *drag-šos* an inferior officer or magistrate *Cs.* — 2. gen. *drágs-po*, *W.* also *drag-ċan*, (*Ssk.* तीव्र, उग्र) **strong, vehement, violent** *ču drag-pa* a rapid river, violent current; *brtson-ₒgrus drag-pa ₒbád-pa* or *ₒdún-pa drag-pa* unbending, unwearied application; *skad drag-pa* a powerful voice; *k̔rims drag-pa* a severe punishment; *snyiṅ-rǰe drag* yearning compassion; **strong, forcible,** of expressions or language; moreover an epithet of terrifying deities, particularly of Siwa (*Ssk.* रुद्र), *drag-mo* fem.; *ži rgyas dbaṅ drag* v. sub *ži-ba*. — Adv. *drag-tu* **vehemently, violently,** e.g. to pull, to lament, to implore; **hastily, speedily,** e.g. to come *Wdṅ.*; *drág-por*, e.g. *drág-por bċad-de bklág-par byao* in reading a marked stop should be made *Gram.*; *ha-ċaṅ mi-drág-par* very gently, softly; *drág-gis, dád-pa* to believe firmly *Mil.* — 3. *drág-pa* possessing a quality in a high degree, *dug-drag-pa Stg.* very poisonous. — 4. symb. num. 11.

**Comp.** *drag-nád*, v. *dreg-nád*, **gout.** — *drág-rtsal-čan* = *drág-po*, of deities. — *drag-žán* **strong and weak,** e.g. the relative force of sound *Gram.*; also **high and low,** with respect to rank. — *drag-šúl* **frightfulness,** *drag-šul-čan* **frightful, terrible, powerful; cruel,** frq., yet chiefly with respect to the power manifested by gods and sorcerers. — *drag-γšed* lit. 'cruel hangman', a terrifying deity v. *Schl.* 111, 214.

དྲགས་ *drags* adv. **very, much, greatly,** *mań-drags Mil.* **very much**; adj. **much, strong, intense,** *bza-btuń-drags* eating and drinking a great deal *S.g.*; *dran-drágs* an intense, most vivid, remembrance of a person *Mil.*, an ardent longing or desire; *dga-drágs-nas* being very happy, highly rejoiced *Pth*, *C.*; *ˌgyod-drágs-nas* feeling deep repentance *Mil.*; *bsten drágs-na* if one continues it too long *S.g.*

དྲང་ *drań* a kind of bear *Sch.*

དྲང་པོ་ *dráń-po* (ऋजु) **straight** 1. not deviating from the direct course, not crooked or oblique, *tig*, *lam* etc. frq.; *lus dráń-po ˌǰóg-pa* to sit straight; **k'a búb-ne dáń-po čó-če** *W.* to place a thing straight or upright again; **ṭ'éd-la dáń-po** *W.*, horizontal. — 2. **right,** e.g. *lam*, opp. to *lóg-pa.* — 3. **sincere, honest, upright, truthful,** *dráń-poi rań-bžin-čan-gyi p'yir* because they have an upright character *Dzl.*; *las dráń-po* good actions, righteous deeds, opp. to *rtsúb-po* violent, unjust *Stg.*; *k'rims dráń-po* 1. **a just sentence, righteous judgment,** opp. to *log-pa.* — 2. applied to men, with regard to their acting according to justice and the law (v. *k'rims*); *čós-drań-po* **honest, upright,** with respect to religion and the divine law; also *dráń-po* alone, whenever it is not to be misunderstood, may be used for our **just.** — *drań-por, tsig dráń-por smrá-ba* **to be candid, to speak the truth,** frq. *drań-don* v. *ńés-pa* extr.

དྲང་བ་ *dráń-ba* 1. abstract noun to *dráń-po.* 2. pf. to *ˌdrén-pa.*

དྲང་སྲོང་ *drań-sróń*, ऋषि, 1. **a holy hermit,** an order of men, introduced from Brahmanism into Buddhism. These saints are looked upon partly as human beings, partly as Dewas, and at any rate as being endowed with miraculous powers *Dzl.* frq. — 2. At present the Lama that offers *sbyin-sreg* is stated to bear that name, and whilst he is attending to the sacred rites, he is not allowed to eat anything but *dkar-zas* (v. *dkar-po*). — 3. symb. num.: 7.

དྲན་དྲི་ *drán-dri Lh.* **the beam of a pair of scales,** *Hind.* डण्डी.

དྲན་པ་ *drán-pa* I. vb. स्मृ, 1. **to think of,** c. accus., with or without *yid-la*, gen. to think of past events, **to remember, recollect, call to mind,** *drin* benefits, v. *drin*; *byúń-ba-rnams* that which has happened *Glr.*; more emphatically: *rǰés-su drán-pa* frq.; but also *dkon-mčóg drán-pa* to think of, to remember, God; *sdúg-po yóń-ba de ma drán-pa yin* do not think of, do not trouble yourself about, future evils *Mil.*; *bskyis-par mi drán-no* I do not recollect having taken anything on credit *Dzl.*; *drán-pa tsám-gyis* as soon as one thinks of it, quick as thought *Thgr.*; *so-só-nas . . . drán-par gyis šig* every body should think of . . . *Dzl.* (the simple imp. seems not to be used); *(rǰés-su) drán-par byéd-pa* also: **to remind of, to put in mind of, to revive the memory of,** = *drán-du ˌǰúg-pa*, *dran-skúl byéd-pa Lex.* — 2. **to become conscious of, to recollect,** *rmi-lam* a dream *Pth.*; *drán-par ˌgyúr-ba* to recover one's senses, to be one's self again *Dzl.*; *čiań mi drán-pa* insensible *Dzl.*; *mi drán-pai ˎóg-tu* after they had become insensible *Dzl.* — 3. **to think of with love** or **affection, to be attached to, to long for,** *ǎ-ma* for the mother col.; **dran-sém** *W.* **love, affection, attachment;** *dran-mčog-rǰe* dearest Sir! *Mil.*

II. sbst. स्मृति, स्मर, 1. **remembrance, recollection, reminiscence; memory** frq.; *drán-pa γsál-po* a retentive memory. — 2. **consciousness,** *stor* is lost; *t'ugs dran-méd-du tim-pa* to lose one's senses, resp. *Mil.*; *dran-méd-du brgyál-pa* id.; *drán-pa rnyéd-*

*pa* to recover one's senses *Pth.*; *γsó-ba* id.; *dran-ₒdzin-méd-pa* being out of one's senses (with joy) *Glr.*; **self-possession, consideration,** *dran-méd* without consideration, inconsiderate; *séms-čan smyón-pa-dag drán-pa so-sór rnyed* insane persons regained the respective faculties of their minds *S.O.*, *drán-pa γžúṅs-pa* prob. quickness of apprehension, good capacity; *drán-pa nyáms-pa* weak-minded; *dran-yód, dran-ldán*, remembering, being in one's senses *Cs.*; *dran-šés* for *drán-pa daṅ šes-ráb Mil.*; **ḍhẹm-pa maṅ-po ko-la šar* C.* he is uneasy, troubled, full of scruples and apprehensions.

ད

དྲལ་ *dral* 1. v. *lčam-mo.* 2. v. *ₒdral-ba.* 3. for *gral.*

དྲལ་ཙེ་ *dral-tse* a kind of courier or messenger *Cs.*

དྲས་ *dras* v. *dra-ba* II.

དྲི་ *dri*, col. also *dri-ma*, **odour, smell, scent,** *dri-žim(-po), dri-bsúṅ Dzl.* an agreeable smell, sweet scent; *dri-bzáṅ(-po)* 1. id., 2. *Cs.* also **saffron;** *dri-ṅán*, prob. also *dri-lóg, W. *dri sóg-po*, Cs. dri-mi-žim* an unpleasant smell, a stench; *dri bró-ba* to exhale an odour *Glr.*; **ḍi núm-pa* or *nóm-pa** to inhale an odour; *W.: *kyúr-ḍi, nyiṅ-ḍi, dúg-ḍi, mé-ḍi, rúl-ḍi, hám-ḍi rag** I perceive a sour, stale, burnt, smoky, putrid, mouldy smell; **tsig-ḍi, žob-ḍi** a smell of burnt food, burnt wool; *dri lṅa* five odours or perfumes used in offering; *dri-ka Sch.*: urinous smell (?); *dri-ṅád* vapour, exhalation, fragrance; *dri-čan lté-ba* bag of the musk-deer; musk *Wdṅ.*; *dri-ču* scented water, perfume *Cs.* (yet cf. *dri-ma*), *dri-čén* a medicinal herb *Lt.* — *dri-γtsaṅ-káṅ*, **गन्धकूट, a sacred place, a chapel,** conjectures about the etymology of the word v. *Burn.* I, 262. — *dri-ₒdzin* po., the nose. — *dri-za*, also *dri-za-mo* fem., **गन्धर्व an eater of fragrance,** in Brahmanism **the heavenly musicians,** and so also in Buddhism painted as playing on guitars, but usually (in accordance with the etymology) thought to be **aërial spirits,** that feed on odours of every description. They are supposed not only to be fond of flowers and other fragrant objects, but also to visit dunghills, flaying-places, shambles etc., the various substances of which are accordingly dedicated to them (cf. *γtór-ma*). The insects, swarming about such places, the Tibetan believes to be incarnated *dri-za.* — *dri-zai groṅ(-kyer)* **mirage, fata morgana.**

དྲི་བ་ *dri-ba* **question,** *dri-ba ₒdri-ba* to ask a question, *mi-la* a person; *dri-bai lan, dris-lán*, answer; *dri-rtóg ma maṅ Mil., C., *ḍhi gya ma ǰhé* or *če* Cs.*, don't ask long! do not ask many questions!

དྲི་བོ་ *dri-bo* **an enchanter, sorcerer, magician,** *dri-mo* **enchantress, witch** *Mil.*

དྲི་མ་ *dri-ma*, **मल, 1. dirt, filth, impurity; excrement, ordure;** *lag-(pai) dri(-ma)* marks left by dirty fingers on books etc.; *sná-dri* mucus, snot, snivel *S.g.*; *dri-ma γzum* the three impurities, excrement, urine, sweat; but sometimes more are enumerated; frq. fig.: *nyés-pai, nyon-móṅs-pai, ka-na-ma-tó-bai dri-ma*; *dri-ma kun zád-nas* after all impurities have been put off *Dzl.*; *dri-ču* 1. **urine,** *ₒdór-ba* to urinate *Glr.*; *rés-ₒga raṅ-byuṅ-gi dri-ču sten* sometimes (in my extremity) I had recourse to my own water *Mil.* — 2. v. sub *dri.* — *dri-čén* feces of the intestinal canal. — *dri-ma-čan* **dirty, sluttish,** as to dress; *dri-ma-méd-pa* clean, cleanly. — 2. for *dkri-ma*, v. *dkri-ba.*

དྲིང་ *driṅ Cs.* = '*drin* **kindness, favour;**' yet, *γžan driṅ mi ₒǰog Lex.*, *γžán-gyis driṅ-la mi ₒǰog-čiṅ raṅ-gi čos žugs-so Dom.?* One dictionary renders it by **प्रत्यय,** knowledge; certainty, faith, confidence

དྲིན་ *drin*, resp. *bka-drin*, rarely *sku-drin Glr.*, **kindness, favour, grace,** *blá-mai drin-gyis* by the grace of my Lama, of my spiritual father, of my patron saint *Mil.*; in addressing a person, *kyed* (or *kyod*)-*kyi bka-drin-gyis* is gen. used; *mai drin* benefits conferred by a mother *Thgy.*; *drin-čan, drin-čé* **kind, gracious, benevolent; benefactor,** *drin-čan pa-má* the parents, these benefactors; *drin-čan már-pa*, Marpa full of grace (Milaraspa's Lama); *tse ͺdí-la drin če-šós ráṅ-gi ma yin* the greatest benefactress for this life is one's own mother; *bód-la bka-drín čé-ba lags-so* this turned out the greatest benefit for Tibet *Glr.*; *ǎ-ma drin-čén* kindest mother! (says a king to a wonder-working female saint) *Pth.*; *drin drán-pa* as a vb., **to acknowledge a kindness, to feel obliged**; as a sbst. **thankfulness, gratitude** *Thgy.*; *k̔yód-kyi drin rtág-tu drán-pas* as I shall always feel greatly obliged to you *Dzl.*; *dei bka-drín drán-čiṅ* full of thankfulness towards him *Dzl.*; *drin rǰéd-pa* unmindful of obligations; *drin γzó-ba, drín-du γzo-ba, drín-lán glán-pa, drin-lán bsáb-pa, W.* **ḍin-zó taṅ-če** to return benefits, to show one's self grateful; *drin γzó-žiṅ lan byao* you shall not have done it for nothing *Dzl.*; *drin-lán-du* as a gift made in return, a return-present.

**དྲིབ་ཤིལ་** (*drib-šil*) **ḍib-šil**, a corrupt form for *dril-bu γsil, Ld.*, = *γyér-k̔a.*

**དྲིམ་** *drim* (spelling?) **stump, trunk**, of a tree or plant, deprived of top and branches *Ld.* —

**དྲིའུ་** *driu* v. *dre.*

**དྲིལ་** *dril*, gen. *dríl-bu*, **bell**; *dril sróg-pa* to ring the bell; to publish by ringing a bell; *dríl-lče* the tongue of a bell, the clapper; *dril-γzúgs* the body of a bell *Cs.*, *Glr.*; *dril-sgrá* the voice or sound of a bell, peal of bells; *dril-k̔aṅ* bell-tower, belfry; *dril-stégs* the frame of timber, on which bells are suspended.

**དྲིལ་བ་** *dríl-ba* v. *ͺdril-ba.*

**དྲིས་པ་** *drís-pa* v. *ͺdri-ba.*

**དྲུ་བུ་** *drú-bu* = *grú-bu, grú-gu*, **a clue** or **ball**, of wool etc.

**དྲུག་** *drug* num. **six**, *drúg-pa, drúg-po* cf. *dgu*; *yi-ge drúg-pa* or *-ma* the prayer of the six letters, the Ommanipadmehūm, *Glr.*; *drúg-ču* sixty; *drúg-ču-rtsa-γčig* (*W.* **ḍug-ču-re-čig**), or *re-γčig*, sixty one; *drug-brgyá* six hundred; *drug-stóṅ* six thousand; *drug-ču-skór* a cycle of sixty years. — *drúg-sgra* the so-called article, presenting itself in the following six forms: *pa, ba, ma, po, bo, mo.*

**དྲུག་དཀར་, དྲུག་དམར་** *drug-dkár, drug-dmár*, **two sorts of turkoise** *Cs.*

**དྲུང་** *druṅ* the space **near**, and esp. **before** a person or thing, *p̔o-bráṅ-gi druṅ gáṅ-na-ba der ͺdúg-nas* alighting on the place before the palace *Dzl.* ༢༧, 3; gen. with *na, du, nas.* 1. adv. **near to, near by, to** or **at the side of, before, to, off from;** *drúṅ-du rtóg-pa* to examine personally, face to face, orally *Dzl.*; *drúṅ-du ͺgró-ba* to go near or up to. 2. postp. c. genit. (less corr. c. accus.), *šiṅ-gi drúṅ-na* near, or under the tree, *drúṅ-du* id.; to or towards the tree; *drúṅ-nas* away from (the tree); *rgyál-poi drúṅ-du* to the king, before, in presence of (coram) the king; *drúṅ-pa*, resp. *sku-drúṅ-pa*, one standing near, **a waiting man, a page in ordinary** *Cs.* — *drúṅ-ͺk̔or* **train, retinue.** — *drúṅ-γnas-pa* **companion, associate.** — *drúṅ-yig(-pa)* **secretary.** — *drúṅ-ͺtso-ba* **private physician,** physician in ordinary *Cs.* When preceded by *žabs* it becomes a respectful term, e.g. in the direction of a letter, where it stands for our **'to'** (lit. 'to the feet of *N.N.*').

**དྲུང་པོ་** *drúṅ-po* 1. **prudent, sensible, judicious, wise** *Mil.*, in conjunction with *γčáṅ-po*; so also *Pth. γčaṅ-drúṅ-ldaṅ-pa.* — 2. **sincere, candid** *C.* — 3. **diligent?**

**དྲུངས་** *druṅs* **root,** of rare occurrence; *druṅs* (*-nas*) *p̔yuṅ* exterminated, destroyed root and branch, *Lex.*

**དྲུངས་པ་** *drúṅs-pa* **clarified, clear** *Cs.*; *bžes-druṅs* resp. for *čaṅ*, **beer,** *Ts.*

**དྲུད་** *drud* 1. v. *ͺdrud-pa.* — 2. *drud-drúd* **pelican** *Sch.*

**དྲུབ་པ་** *drúb-pa* v. *ͺdrúb-pa.*

**དྲུམ་པ་** *drúm-pa* **to have a strong desire, to long, languish, pine,** for, *Sch.*

**དྲུས་མ་** *drús-ma* **millet** *Sch.*

**དྲེ་** *dre Ts.*, *dreu Lex.*, *ḍiu Lh.*, *drel Glr.*, **mule,** *dré-p̔o, p̔ó-dre* he-mule, *dré-mo, mó-dre* she-mule.

དྲེ་བོ་ *dré-bo Lt., dré-mo Mṅg.*, **de-món** *W.*, **elbow.**

དྲེག་པ་ *drég-pa, drégs-pa* 1. any **dirt** that is removed by scraping, whereas *dri-ma* is washed off; more particularly: — 2. **soot,** which is also used as a medicine *Wdṅ.*; *k'un-dreg* id.; *sgrón-dreg* lamp-black; *sláṅ-dreg* soot on a kettle; *lčágs-dreg* v. *lčags*; *t'ál-dreg, rdó-dreg Med.?* — *só-dreg* **tartar** incrusting the teeth *Med.* — *dreg-bál* flakes of soot. — *dreg-nád* **gout;** *dreg-grúm* id.

དྲེགས་པ་ *drégs-pa* 1. **pride, haughtiness, arrogance,** *k'eṅ-drégs* id.; *drégs-pa nyams* pride is put down, humbled; *drégs-pa skyáṅ-ba* to lay aside, to put off pride; *nór-gyis dregs* purse-proud *Lex.* — 2. **proud, haughty, arrogant,** = *drégs-pa-čan*; *drégs-pa (-čan t'ams-čád* the great, the proud, the people of high rank, the great ones of this world *Pth.*; in the world of spirits, with or without *bgegs*: the powerful demons. — 3. as a vb.: *ró-tsas dregs t'se* when the sexual impulse **is strong** *Med.*

དྲེད་ *dred* (*Zam.* तरक्षु) **hyena,** which name has prob. been transferred by the inhabitants of the mountainous districts to the *dred*, an animal better known to them) **the yellow bear;** *mi-dred* a bear that devours men *Mil.*; *p'yúgs-dred* a bear destructive to cattle; *dréd-p'o* he-bear, *dréd-mo* she-bear. — *dred-tsáṅ* a bear's den. — *dred-siu-šiṅ* hazel-nut tree *Sch.*

དྲེད་པོ་ *dréd-po* 1. *Sch.*: **'evasive, lazy'**, yet *čos-méd dréd-po zol-zóg γyo-rgyú-čan?* — 2. **load, burden,** esp. a heavy load *C.*, *dréd-po dréd-pa* = *k'rés-po grág-pa*, to cord a load.

དྲེད་མ་ *dréd-ma, rtsa-dréd-ma Glr.* = *drés-ma*; *dám-dréd-ma Mil.?*

དྲེའུ་, དྲེལ་ *dreu, drel*, v. *dre*; *dreu-rṅóg* 1. **the mane of a mule.** — 2. **a couch,** or **stuffed-seat** *Cs.* — 3. a kind of **long-haired cloth.**

དྲེས་མ་ *drés-ma* 1. *C.* a kind of grass, of which ropes and shoes (of great durability) are made; *Glr. dréd-ma*; *drés-mai ge-sár S.g.* the filaments of *drés-ma*; *dres-ₒbru Cs., dres-ₒbrum S.g.* the seeds of *drés-ma.* — 2. *W.* Iris kamaonensis.

དྲོ་ *dro* (cf. *dró-ba*), 1. **the hot time of the day,** from about 9 o'cl. a. m. till 3 o'cl. p. m.; *dró-la báb-nas* when this time arrived *Dzl.*; *sṅá-dro* the morning, *p'yi-dro* 1. the later part of the afternoon, 2. *W.* **p'i-ro** evening, night. — 2. a meal taken about noon, **lunch;** *dro btáb-pa* to lunch; *dro-lúg* a sheep intended to be eaten for a luncheon; *dro-šá* meat intended for such a purpose.

དྲོ་བ་ *dró-ba* 1. **to be warm,** v. *drós-pa*; gen. adj. **warm,** *dró-bai γnas* a warm place; *dró-bar ₒgyúr-ba* to grow warm. — 2. **warmth** (*bág-dro* v. sub *ur*).

དྲོགས་ *drogs Sch.*: 'packed up, made up into pack or parcel'.

དྲོང་(ས་) *droṅ(s)* v. *ₒdren-pa.*

དྲོང་མ་ *dróṅ-ma* **a large basket** or **dosser,** provided with a lid, and carried on the back, *Hind.* पतारा.

དྲོད་ *drod* 1. **warmth, heat,** e.g. of the sun; *drod-γšér* warmth and moisture; *dród-kyi šiṅ* a tropical tree *Wdṅ.*; *me-drod* 1. **the heat of the fire** *Lt.* 2. prob. **animal heat,** perh. because it is supposed to arise from a union of the fiery element with a germ originated by conception. — 2. *k'a-dród zuṅ γčig* a small piece of food, = *k'a-zás*, and prob. incorrect for *k'a-bród* enjoyment of the mouth. — *lám-la drod t'ób-pa Mil.* was explained: to have a cheerful mind, free from doubts and apprehensions on the way (to heaven), *drod*, therefore, seems to stand here for *brod.* — *drod-rtags, Mil.*, was explained as being new knowledge, new perceptions, as a fruit of long meditation; one *Lex.* has *dród-rig-pa* = मात्रज्ञ experienced or well-versed in measure.

དྲོན་མོ་ *drón-mo* col. **warm,** *zan-drón* warm food.

དྲོལ་ *drol* v. *ₒdrol-ba.*

དྲོས་ *dros, Sch.* = *dro*; *dros-čén* **noon, mid-day,** *dros-čúṅ* forenoon(?).

དྲོས་པ་ *drós-pa*, pf. of *dró-ba*, **heated, grown warm,** esp. of the ground by the heat of the sun, of men, by warm clothing; *dros soṅ* the ground has grown warm, the snow is beginning to melt; *drós-na* when it is getting warm; *di gón-na dros lags* if you put that on, you will be warm *Mil.*; *tse γċig drós-pai gos* warm clothing for one period of existence *Mil.* — *ma-drós-pa* n. of the Manasarowara or lake of Mapam in Nari. The Hindoos describe it as something like a northern ocean, inhabited by Nagas (v. *klu*), and the Tibetans in good faith repeat such fables, at least in their literature, although they know better.

ད་མན་ *dha-mán Ld.-Glr. Schl.* fol. 17, b., v. *lda-mán.*

དྷུ་ཏི *dhú-ti*, (धुति a shaker, agitator?) a word of more recent mystical physiology, 'the middle vein', = *dbú-ma* (cf. *γtúm-po* and *t́ig-le*) *Thgr.*, *Mil.*, *Wdṅ.* The Lamas consulted by me asserted, not quite in accordance with books, *dhu-ti* to denote a kind of *rluṅ* in the body (which would agree with धू to blow, and with πνεῦμα), a vital power closely connected with the soul, supporting it during lifetime, and leaving it only when separated by death. This would be a new or second signification of *dhu-ti*, although I cannot vouch for the correctness of the above statement, nor am I able to decide, whether *dhu-ti* and *ȧ-ba-dhuti* are quite the same. — *ȧ-ba-dhuti-pa Tar.* 187, 8 is a proper name, *Schf.*

དྷེ་ལ་ *dhe-la*, *Hind.* धेला, **half a paisa,** the smallest coin, equal to the tenth part of a penny, *W.*

གདག(ས)་ *γdag(s)* 1. fut. of *˳dogs-pa.* — 2. *γdags* **the light, day** *Cs.*, opp. to *sribs.* — 3. in *Stg.* *γdágs-pa* occurs frq. as a translation of प्रज्ञा **wisdom.**

གདང་, རྡང་ *γdaṅ*, *rdaṅ* (*ldaṅ*?) 1. **clothes-stand, rack** or **rail** for hanging up clothes, *γdáṅ-la gos ˳dzár-ba*, *˳gél-ba*; *γdáṅ-bu* 1. **peg** or **nail,** for the same purpose. 2. *skás-kyi γdaṅ(-bu) Lex.*, **s̀ral-dáṅ* W.*, **step of a ladder.** — 2. col. for *γdeṅ.*

གདང་བ་ *γdáṅ-ba*, *γdáṅs-pa*, to open wide, mouth and nostrils, **to gape** *B.* and col.; *γdáṅ-pai k̔ro-žál* an angry face with the mouth wide opened *Glr.*

གདངས་ *γdaṅs* 1. **music, harmony, melody,** = *dbyaṅs*, *snyags*, also *γdaṅs-snyan*; *γdaṅs byéd-pa* to make music *C.* — 2. resp. for *dprál-ba* **forehead** *Cs.*

གདངས་པ་ *γdáṅs-pa* 1. v. *γdáṅ-ba.* 2. resp. one recovering from illness, **convalescent,** with *snyun*, *bsnyuṅ-ba Lex.*; **ra daṅ* W.* he has recovered from his drunken fit, has become sober again.

གདན་ *γdan*, आसन, resp. *bžugs-γdan W.*, **a bolster,** or seat composed of several quilts or cushions, put one upon the other (five for common people, nine for people of quality), cf. *˳bol*; *γdan-k̔ri* **a throne** *Glr.*; *γdan-rábs* **a succession of teachers** *Tar.* 199, 4. The word is much used in polite expressions: *γdan ˳dégs-pa* **to take leave, to withdraw, to depart;** *γdán-sa* 1. **place of residence,** *bla-mai Mil.*; *dga-ston-gyi* place of a festival *Glr.* 2. **situation, position, rank,** ni f., *Mil.*; *γdán-˳dren-pa* **to invite,** = *spyán-˳dren-pa*, **to appoint, to nominate,** *dpon-du* a chief, a leader *Glr.*; **to go to meet** *Glr.*; **dan-su-ċe* W.* id.; **dan-kyal-ċe* W.* **to accompany,** as a mark of attention; *dan-p̔eb-pa* **to arrive** *Sch.*

གདབ་པ་ *γdáb-pa*, fut. of *˳debs-pa.*

གདམ་ཀ་ *γdám-ka W.*, *γdam-ṅa Lex.*, **choice, election,** **dám-ka ċó-ċe* W.* **to choose, to elect;** *γdám-ṅa byéd-pa Lex.* id.

གདམས་པ་ *γdám-pa*, fut. of *˳dóms-pa*, *γdáms-pa*, pf. of *˳dóms-pa*, **to advise,** *rgyál-po-la γdám-pai mdo* adviser of kings, a mirror for sovereigns *Thgy.*; *γdáms-pa* sbst. **advice, counsel, doctrine, precept,** *γdáms-ṅág*, *W.* **γdáms-ka*, *γdáms-k̔a** (cf. *k̔á-ta*, *k̔á-lta*), resp. *žal-γdáms*, *bka-γdáms* id.; *γdáms-pa ċig žu* we ask for some advice *Glr.*; *p̔án-pa γdáms-pa* a good advice; *γdams-ṅág stón-pa Lex.*, **dám-ka*, or *k̔á-ta táṅ-ċe* W.* to give an advice, to advise; *γdams-ṅág ˳dóms-pai tsig* **the imperative mood,** expressing command or exhortation *Gram.*

གདའ་བ་ *γdá-ba*, eleg. for *˳dúg-pa B.* and *Khams*, 1. **to be, to be there,** *du* γda how many are there here? *Zam.*; *sgyúr-gin γda Glr.*; *rtóg-tu γdao* he or it may be discerned, distinguished *Dzl.*; *ṕyin-nas γda* he had arrived *Mil.*; no other negative than *mi* can precede it: *žábs-mtil-la ču rég-pa tsám-las mi γda* the water did not reach above the soles of the shoes *Mil.* — 2. with *par* it expresses uncertainty, vagueness, *γšégs-par γda* he may possibly go, *Pth.*; *ₒdi yin-pa* (col. for *par*) *γda* he seems to be this (man) *Pth.*; cf. *ₒdug-pa.* — 3. to say, cf. *mči-ba.*

གདལ་བ་ *γdál-ba* another form for *rdal-ba.*

གདིང་བ་ *γdiṅ-ba* another form for *ₒdiṅ-ba*; also sbst.: *γdiṅ-ba daṅ bgo-ba* **carpets and clothes,** i.e. all sorts of textures, *Stg.*

ད

གདུ་བ་ *γdú-ba* 1. another form for *sdú-ba* **to gather, to collect.** 2. another form for *γdúṅ-ba* (?) *Sch.:* **to love**; cf. *rnyed-la γdu Zam.*

གདུ་བུ་ *γdú-bu Glr.*, *γdú-gu Glr.*, *γdúb-bu* the usual form, **ring for the wrist, bracelet,** or for the ankle, an ornament of Hindoo women; *lag* (resp. *ṕyag*)-*γdub* bracelet; *rkaṅ* (resp. *žabs*)-*γdub* foot-ring; *sór* (col. *ser*)-*γdub* finger-ring *Glr.*; *γser-γdub* gold-ring, *dṅul-γdub* silver-ring; *γsér-ser-γdub* a golden finger-ring; **tág-če** *W.* to put on (a ring).

གདུག་པ་ *γdúg-pa* 1. **poison** = *dug*, *γdúg-pa γsum Dzl.* = *dug γsum*; *zás-su γdúg-pa zá-ba Dom.* — 2. in general: any thing hurtful, or any injury, mischief, harm done; as adj. **noxious, mischievous, dangerous,** *γdúg-pa-čan*, of animals, demons, wicked men; *dug-sbrúl γdúg-pa-čan* dangerous venemous serpents *Glr.*; *dre-srin γdúg-pa maṅ* many mischievous demons *Glr.*; *γdúg-pai bsám-pa* propensity to destroy, destructiveness, ferocity, of beasts of prey *Glr.*; *γdúg-pai ṅá-ro* wild screams *Mil.*; *γdug-rtsúb* **ferocity, malice, spite** *Mil.*; *stár-bu γdúg-pa tsér-ma-čan* **buckthorn** with horrible spines *Wdṅ.*; also for **mischief done by evil spirits** *Mil.*

གདུགས་ *γdugs* I. resp. *dbu-γdúgs* 1. **parasol, umbrella,** *B., C.* — 2. **canopy, baldachin**; *spyi-γdugs* a covering, shelter, awning, for several persons *Glr.*; *γdugs ₒbúbs-pa* to raise a canopy, to put up a shade or screen; of peacocks: to spread the tail.

II. eleg. **mid-day, noon,** *sáṅ-gi γdúgs-la* for to-morrow noon *Dzl.*; noon-tide heat (cf. *dugs*), *γdugs-méd γdóṅ-pa γdúgs-kyis γdúṅs* an unprotected face is molested by the heat *Lex.*; *γdugs-ťsód* 1. **noon-tide, dinner-time,** 2. **dinner.**

གདུང་ *γduṅ*, resp. for *rus* (-*pa*), 1. **bone, bones, remains,** esp. as *riṅ-srél*, also *γduṅ-rús*, *sku-γdúṅ*; *γser-γdúṅ*, *dṅul-γdúṅ* the gold and silver palls covering the remains of the highest Lamas. — 2. **family, lineage, progeny, descendants,** *rigs ni rgyal-rigs-so, γduṅ-ni gau-ta mao* as to caste, he belongs to that of the ruler, as to family, he is a descendant of Gotama; also fig.: *saṅs-rgyás-kyi γduṅ Dzl.* the spiritual children of Buddha, the saints; *γduṅ-brgyúd yod* the house, the family, is still existing *Glr.*; *γduṅ* (*brgyud*) *ₒdzin-pai sras* a first-born male, by whom the lineage may be continued, frq.; also for any single descendant *Glr.* — *γduṅ-sgróm Sch.* **coffin,** *Schr.* **funeral urn.** — *γduṅ-rtén* funeral pyramid containing relics, cf. *mčod-rten.* — *γduṅ-rabs* **generation,** *ṅá-nas γduṅ-rábs lṅá-pa-la* in the fifth degree after me *Glr.*

གདུང་བ་ *γdúṅ-ba*, *γdúṅs-pa* I. vb. 1. **to desire, to long for,** *zás-la, ltó-la, Glr.* and elsewh.; **duṅ duṅ čó-če** *W.* id. — 2. **to love,** *šin-tu γdúṅ-bai ma γčig* my own dearly beloved mother! cf. *brtse-γdúṅ.* — 3. **to feel pain, to be pained, tormented, afflicted,** by heat or cold, thirst, lust, distress; **nyiṅ dúṅ-te** *W.* sad, sorrowful; *γdúṅ-bar byéd-pa* to make sad, to distress, *γžán-gyi séms-la*, the mind of others. — 4. **to be dried,** *nyi-mas* by the sun, of a dead body *Dzl.*

II. sbst. 1. **desire, longing, lust,** *γdúṅ-ba ži* (sensual) desire ceases *Stg.* — 2. love, *mos-gus-γdúṅ-ba dpag-méd skye* immense veneration and love arises *Glr.* — 3. **affliction, misery, distress, torment, pang,** *γdúṅ-bai skad* a plaintive voice, doleful cry *Glr.*

III. adj. 1. **longed for, earnestly desired.** — 2. **beloved,** v. above. — 3. **grieved, tormented** frq.; *yduṅ-dbyáṅs* a song expressive of longing or of grief, an elegy *Mil.*; *yduṅ-séms* love-longing *B.*, and col.; **ǎ-ma-la dúṅ-sem-čan ₒdug** *W.* he tenderly loves his mother.

གདུང་མ་ *ydúṅ-ma* **beam, piece of timber,** *má-yduṅ* principal beam, *bú-yduṅ* cross-beam; *yduṅ-ḱébs* beams projecting over the capital of a column *Glr.* — *yduṅ-sgrig* a raft *Ld.* — *yduṅ-ₒdébs S.g.* pedestal, base(?) — *yduṅ-zám* a bridge of timber or of poles. — *ydúṅ-šiṅ Sik.* fir-tree (Pinus abies).

གདུད་པ་ *ydúd-pa* **love, longing** *Sch.*, cf. *ydú-ba.*

གདུབ་བུ་ *ydúb-bu* v. *ydú-bu.*

གདུབ་པ་ *ydúb-pa Stg.*: *zás-la*, adj., **frugal, temperate?**

གདུམ་(པོ) *ydúm(-po)* **a piece** *Sch.* = *dum.*

གདུལ་ *ydul* v. *ₒdul-ba.*

གདུས་ *ydus* v. *ydú-ba.*

གདེག་ *ydeg* v. *ₒdégs-pa.*

གདེང་ *ydeṅ* **confidence, assurance, cheerfulness** *Mil.* very frq.; *ydeṅ ṫób-pa* to become confident, to take courage, to be reassured; *ₒči-tse ydeṅ čiaṅ med* when dying, he has no confident hope *Mil.*; *mi-ₒǰigs-pai ydeṅ* a strong confidence *Mil.*, *Thgr.*; *ydeṅ-tsád* id., *de-riṅ tsam yaṅ sdód-pai ydeṅ-ṫsád ma mčis-pas* not being sure whether his life will be spared for one day more; *ₒči-bród ydeṅ-tsád med* without confidence, without any readiness to die *Mil.*; *blo-ydeṅ Mil.* and col. = *ydeṅ.*

གདེང་བ་ *ydeṅ-ba*, pf. *ydeṅs*, *Cs.* **to threaten, to menace;** *Sch.* **to brandish** in a menacing way, *mtson-ydeṅ* brandishing a weapon *Lex.*; I also met with: *lag ydeṅ-ba Glr.* to raise and move one's hand (in a suppliant manner), cf. *dáṅ-ba* II., and: *bya yšog ydéṅ-pa* a bird with its wings raised and spread *Ma.*

གདེངས་ཀ་ *ydéṅs-ka* **head and neck of a serpent,** *sbrúl-gyi Glr.*

གདེངས་པ་ *ydéṅs-pa* 1. v. *ydéṅ-ba*, 2. = *ydeṅ*(?) **dáṅ-pa-čan** *W.*, **ló-deṅ-pa** *C.*, **deserving** or **enjoying confidence; faithful, trusty,** of servants, husbands, wives etc.

གདོང་(པ) *ydoṅ(-pa)*, resp. *žal-ydoṅ*, 1. **face, countenance,** *ydoṅ skya* a pale face *Lt.*; *ydoṅ-dmar bod-yul* the country of the red-faced (more accurately: brown-faced) Tibetans *Pth.*; *ydoṅ-nág(-po)* 1. **a** black face; 2. **a frowning countenance;** *ydoṅ-čúṅ* dejected, disheartened, *ḱrel-méd ydoṅ-čúṅ mi byed-par* impudent and saucy *Glr.*; **doṅ-šrán táṅ-če** *W.*, **doṅ-šran-te čá-wa** *Kun.*, to be forward, bold, brazen-faced; *ṗág-gi ydóṅ-pa* pig's face, pig's head *Sambh.*; *ydoṅ-bži-pa* Brahma ('the four-faced'). — 2. **surface, superficies,** *sa-yži*; **fore-part, front-part,** *dóṅ-la* adv. **in front, in advance** e.g. to go *C.*; *ydoṅ-ytád*, *Ld.*: *doṅ-stád* **just opposite;** *ydoṅ(-la)-ₒdéd-pa* **to push** or **press forward,. to urge on** (a donkey, a coward to the fight), **to haul** (a culprit before the judge); *snáṅ-ba ydóṅ-ded-pa* to pursue one's course regardless of others (both in a good and in a bad sense) *Mil.*; *ydoṅ-ṗyis* handkerchief *Sch.*; **doṅ-si** *W.* complexion, *gyur soṅ* he has changed colour; to *ṫúg-pa* and *bsú-ba* it is joined pleon.; *ydoṅ-lhógs* is stated to imply the same as *grúm-bu Lt.*

གདོད་མ་ *ydód-ma* = *yzód-ma*, **the beginning,** *ydód-mai dus*; *ydód-mar* **in the beginning, at first** *Mil.*; *ydód-kyi(s)* **first, at first, previously, before** *Mil.*; *ydód(-ma)-nas* from the beginning; *ydód-nas dág-pa* of primitive purity *Mil.* and elsewh.; *da-ydód Lex.* prob. = *da-yzód.*

གདོན་ *ydon* (ग्रह) **evil spirit, demon,** causing diseases etc, *steṅ ₒog-gi* superior and inferior (spirits), Rahu e.g. is *stéṅ-gi ydon*, an evil spirit of the aërial or heavenly regions; *stéṅ-ydon-gyis ₒči-ba Glr.* = *yzas ṗóg-pa* to die of epilepsy (*W.*?), or of apoplexy (*Sch.*); *ydon-čén bčo-lṅá*, or *bčo-brgyád*, frq.; *ydón-gyis brláms-pa Lt.*, *brlábs-pa Sch.*, infatuated or possessed by some evil spirit; *ɣdon ₒǰúg-pa* the entering of a demon into a person; *ɣdón-mi-za-ba* **certainty, surety**; *de byuṅ-ba-la* or *de byuṅ-bar ɣdon mi za* there is no doubt of such a thing having happened; gen. adv.: *ɣdón-mi-za-bar* undoubtedly, indubitably, *ɣdon-mi-ₒtsal-bar Dzl.* id.

གདོན་པ་ *ɣdon-pa Cs.* fut. of *ₒdon-pa.*

གདོལ་པ་ *ɣdól-pa*, *Lexx.* = *rigs-ṅán*, चण्डाल, **an outcast**, a man of the lowest and most despised caste, still below the *dmáṅ-rigs.* The Tibetan word for this caste was perh. originally *dól-pa* fisherman, and has afterwards been transferred to all persons that gain their livelihood by the killing of animals, and consequently are despised as professional sinners.

གདོས་ *ɣdos* 1. **fetter, chain**; *ɣdos-ťág* fetter in a fig. sense, bondage, *Thgy.* — 2. **material existence** (?), **matter** (?). *ɣdos-bčás*, (*b*)*rdos-bčás*, **material, corporeal**, *ɣdos-bčás-kyi lus Thgr.*, frq.; *ɣdos-bčas-su grúb-pa med* (these things) are nothing material, they have no substance *Thgr.*; *ɣdos-méd* **immaterial, unsubstantial**; *ɣdós-su čé-ba* seems to be the same as *ɣdos-bčas*, and perh. also *ɣdós-pa ₒdzin Lex.* — 3. *ɣdos brgyáb-pa C.* for *W.* **ka kun gyáb-če**, v. *rkún-ma.*

གདོས་པ་ *ɣdós-pa* 1. = *ɣdos* (?) — 2. *Cs.* **mast, sail-yard**; acc. to Lexx. something pertaining to a ship; *ɣdós-bu* oar *Sch.*

བདག་ *bdag* 1. **self**, *ṅa bdag* for *ṅa nyid Dzl.* ༧༦, 14; gen. in the objective case: **myself, thyself, one's self**; *bdag ston ɣžan smad* to praise one's self, to blame others; *bdag sruṅ-ba* to devote one's self to solitary contemplation; or as a genit.: *bdág-gi* one's own, my, mine; *bdág-gi séms-la smad* he reproved himself *Dzl.*; *bdág-tu ₒdzín-pa*; *bdag-ₒdzin* the clinging to the I, the attachment to one's own self, **egotism**, frq.; *bdag daṅ bdág-gir ₒdzin-pa* attachment to the I and mine *S.O.*; *bdág-tu ltá-ba* prob. id., *Tar.* 35, 18, *Schf.*: Atmaka-theory, *bdag-méd-pai čos Tar.* 36, 1 the Anātmaka, the contrary; *bdag-méd rnám-pa ɣnyis* are mentioned in *Thgy.*, prob. = *gáṅ-zág-gi bdag-méd*, and *čós-kyi bdag-méd Mil.* c. XII.; *bdág-gir med S.O.*; *bdag-méd* ultimately coincides with *stoṅ-pa-nyid*, *Burn.* I., 462 med. In common life, *bdag-med* is also used for **another**, **dag-méd-kyi mi** id.; **dag-méd-la ma taṅ** do not give it to another; *bdag-ɣžan* I and others, one's self and others; *bdag-nyíd* 1. = *bdag* **I myself, thou thyself, he himself**, *bdag-nyíd-la ɣsón-čig* listen to me! *Pth.*; *rgyál-po bdag-nyid* the king himself *Dzl.*; *ka-čig ni bdag-nyid ráb-tu ₒbyúṅ-bar ɣsol* some ask for the permission of becoming priests themselves *Dzl.*; *bdag-nyid ₒba-žig* only for their own persons *Thgy.* 2. sbst. **the thing itself, the substance, the essence**, *byaṅ-čub-séms-kyi bdag-nyid yin* I am the essence of bōdhi, the personified bōdhi, says *Mil.*; *ťúgs-rǰei bdag-nyid dkon-mčog-ɣsum* o grace personified, Triratna! *Glr.*; the Ommanipadmehūm is *saṅs-rgyás ťams-čád-kyi dgóṅs-pa ťams-čád ɣčig-tu bsdús-pai bdag-nyid Glr.*, i.e. the sum and substance of all the sentences of all the Buddhas concentrated in one word; *bdag-nyid-čén-po*, *čé-bai bdag-nyid* = *rdzógs-pai saṅs-rgyás* chief Buddha, Sākyathubpa, *S.O.* — 2. sbst. pronoun, first person, **I**, eleg., expressing modesty and respect to the hearer or reader, without amounting to our 'my own humble self', v. *prán-bu*; plur. *bdág-čag*, *bdág-rnams*, *bdág-čag-rnams*, also in a general sense: we mortals *Thgy.*; *bdág-čag tsóṅ-pa-rnams* we, these merchants here *Dzl.* — 3. **the I**, the ego = *gáṅ-zag Was.* (269). — 4. **master, lord**, for *bdág-po*, v. below. — 5. in natural philosophy **the element of solid matter**; also for **air** *Stg.* — *bdág-po* 1. **proprietor, master, lord**; *bdág-poi sgra* the syllable *pa*, as denoting the active agent, i.e. him that has to do with a thing, e.g. *rtá-pa* (not to be taken as 'definite article' *Cs.*); thus in many compound words: *káṅ-bdag*, *kyim-bdag* etc.; *ťúgs-rǰei bdág-po* lord of grace, Awalokiteswara, *Glr.* init.; supreme lord, liege-lord, *klui bdág-po* = *dbáṅ-po*, *rgyál-po*; patron. 2. **husband, lord, spouse**; hence **a-ma dág-po*, or *sriṅ-mo dág-po**, a vulgar and obscene word of abuse. — *bdag(-po) byéd-pa* to reign over, to possess, prop. with *la*, but also with accus. *gha-sá-ča bód-kyis bdag byas* Tibet reigned over the province of Gha; *W.* also: to treat rudely, to handle roughly; *bdág-tu byás-pai bud-méd* a married woman *Thgy.*; *bdag-po-med-pa* (col. *mk̔an*) **unowned**, e.g. of a dog, *Pth*; **forlorn, friendless,** without a patron, **a vagabond;** also for an unmarried woman; also as an abusive word.

**Comp.** *bdag-rkyén* (as yet not found in books) seems to denote **kindness, attention, help,** received from a superior, (yet, it would seem, not without some obligation or other existing on the part of the latter, and thus the word differs from *bka-drín*). — *bdag-nyid, bdag-méd* v. above. — *bdag-bzúṅ Glr.* prob. = *bdag-po*. — *bdag-bsrúṅ* **hermit.**

བདའ་བ་ *bdá-ba* I. adj. resp. **savoury, well-tasted,** for *žim-pa*; *C.* col. **dán-te**.

II. vb., pf. *bdas* = *˳déd-pa*, 1. **to drive, to drive out,** *p̔yugs* cattle; **to chase, to put to flight** *Dzl.*; *lás-kyis, lás-kyi rlúṅ-gis bdás-nas* in consequence of works, of certain actions, frq. — 2. **to carry away, along,** or **off, to hurry off,** *čú-bos bdás-pai gliṅ* land carried away by water *Cs.* — 3. **to call in, collect, recover,** *bú-lon* debts *Dzl.* — 4. **to reprove, rebuke, accuse** *Sch.*; *bda-˳déd byéd-pa Lex.*, *Cs.*: 1. **to drive, to carry.** 2. **to examine, to investigate.**

བདར་ *bdar* for *bda-bar*.

བདར་བ་, རྡར་བ་ *bdár-ba, rdár-ba*, **to rub,** i.e. 1. **to file, to polish** *Glr.*, **to grind, to whet;** *bdár-rdo* whet stone, hone. 2. **to rasp,** e.g. sandal-wood *Glr.*; **to grind, to pulverize,** *p̔yé-mar bdár-ba* to grind to powder, *Lexx.*; *lčágs-bdar* **a file,** *sá-bdar* **a rasp.** — 3. *so bdár-ba C.* **to gnash** or **grind the teeth;** *p̔yag bdár-ba* to sweep *B.*; *byi* and *p̔yi bdár-ba* **to clean, to polish** *Dzl.* — *Ma.* in two passages: **to pray earnestly,** which is the meaning required by the context, confirmed also by several Lamas. — *mdún-du bdár-ba Lex.*: पुरस्कृ, to place in front: to lead; to appoint; show; inspect; prefer; honour. — *skyel-bdár* fee or reward given to an escort *Sch.* — *brdár-ša Sch.*: '*séms-kyi brdár-ša* the nerves, sinews'(?); *bdár-ša γčód-pa*, and *rtsa-brdár γčód-pa* to examine closely *Mil.*; *raṅ-gi séms brdar-ša čod C.* take it seriously to heart.

བདལ་བ་ *bdál-ba* v. *rdál-ba*.

བདུག་པ་ *bdúg-pa* 1. vb. pf. *bdugs*, **to fumigate, to burn incense, to swing the censer** *Dzl.* — 2. sbst. **the burning of incense; perfume, frankincense,** more frq. *bdug-spós*, *bdug-spós-kyis bdúg-pa, Dzl.*; *bdug-spós ˳t̔ul* odours of incense arise *Pth.*

བདུང་བ་ *bdúṅ-ba* v. *rdúṅ-ba*.

བདུད་ *bdud*, *Ssk.* मार, Mong. *šimnus*, the personified evil principle, **the Evil One, the Devil,** the adversary of Buddha, and he that tempts men to sin, but not like Satan of the Bible, a fallen spirit, nor like Ahriman of the Persians, an antagonist of Buddha of equal power and influence, but merely an evil genius of the highest rank, by whose defeat Buddha will finally be the more glorified. He is also identified with the god of love (Cupid), काम; v. *Köpp.* I. 88. 111. 253. In later times he has been split into four, and subsequently into numerous devils; also female devils, *bdúd-mo*, are mentioned. — *bdúd-rtsi* (अमृत. सुधा) 1. **the drink of gods, nectar,** frq.; fig.: *čos-kyi bdúd-rtsi* the nectar of the doctrine, and similar expressions; even common beer, when drunk by a Lama, may resp. be called so. — 2. a praising epithet of medicines; *bdud-rtsi-lṅa-lúm* a bath prepared of a decoction of five holy plants, viz. *šúg-pa, bá-lu, ṫse-pád, k̔ám-pa*, and *˳óm-bu*. — 3. **myrobalan,** Terminalia citrina, *Wdṅ.* — 4. a kind of brandy(?) — 5. *bdud-rtsi-dmár-po* a demon.

བདུན་ *bdun* 1. **seven,** *bdún-pa, bdún-po*, cf. *dgu*; *bdún-ču* seventy; *bdun-ču-rtsa-γčig*, (*W.* **bdun-ču-don-γčig**), *don-γčig*, seventy one etc.; *bdun-brgyá* seven hundred, *bdun-stóṅ* seven thousand etc. — *lús-kyi bdún-po* the seven (principal) parts of the body, viz. hands, feet, shoulders, and neck, (those of holy men are of a goodly size, long and stately) *Stg.* — *bdun-phrág* (ἑβδομάς) seven days, a week, *S.g.* — **dún-na-tse** *W.* a child born before the natural time, a seven months' child.

བདུར་བ་ *bdur-ba Sch.* **to belong to a class** (?).

བདེ་བ་ *bde-ba* (शुभ, सुख) vb., adj., sbst., *bdé-po* adj. *Mil.*, *C.* (of rare occurrence), *bdé-mo* adj., col., esp. *W.*, 1. **to be happy** or **well**; **happy**; **happiness**; *mi bdé-ba* the contrary of *bdé-ba*; *ṅa bdé-ste* as I am quite happy *Dzl.*; *bdeo* he is happy, prospers, flourishes; *bdé-bar byéd-pa* to make happy; *bdé-bar phyin-pa* to come to a state of happiness, of rest, to a place of safety; *bdé-bar gnás-pa* to be happy, to live in prosperity; *bdé-bar gtóṅ-ba* to let alone, to let another be happy; *khyod bdé-bar btaṅ mi yoṅ* we shall not allow you to be quiet *Mil.*; in *C.* col.: **żo' dé-mo-la mi żag** id.; *bdé-bar gyúr-čig*, resp. *bżúgs-šig*, **be happy! farewell!** *W.* **dé-mo ča żig**; *bdé-bar btsá-ba B.*, **dé-mo-la kyé-če** *W.*, to be safely delivered of a child; *bde-bar gšégs-pa* he that has entered into eternal bliss, the blessed, *Sch.* (*Köpp.* I, 91?) an epithet of former Buddhas, *Ssk.* सुगत; *lus daṅ sems mi-bdé-bar ḥgyúr-ba* to be bodily and spiritually afflicted *Dzl.*; *mi-bdé-bai bág-med-na* fearless of adversity *Dzl.*; *mi-bdé-bar ḥgyúr-ba* **to ache,** of parts of the body; *mṅal mi-bdé-bar ḥgyúr-ba* to be in travail, to suffer the pangs of childbirth; *sems-bdé, blo-bdé, snyiṅ-bdé* **cheerful, merry, glad;** *šin-tu thugs-ma-bdé-bar dám-bčas-te* promising with a heavy heart, very reluctantly *Glr.*; *dga-bdé* v. *dgá-ba* comp.; *dus-bdé* (**-mo** *W.*) **peace, a state of peace,** in *C.* frq. in conjunction with *żod-ḥjágs* or *sa-ḥjám*; *żi(-bai)-bdé(-ba)* **the happiness of rest, a happy tranquillity** *Glr.*; **peace** *Thgy.*; esp. the happiness of Nirwana *Thgy.*, *Mil.*; *ḥjig-rtén-gyi bdé-ba-la čágs-te* fond of a worldly life of pleasure *Dzl.*; *bdé-ba daṅ ldán-pa* happy, *bdé-ba-čan* v. below; *gnas-skábs-kyi bde-ba* a happy situation *Glr.*; *mya-ṅán-las ḥdás-pai bdé-ba thób-pa* to attain to the happiness of Nirwana *Dzl.*; *dus-brtán-gyi bdé-ba-la bkod dgos* I must help him to attain to eternal bliss *Mil.*; *phan-bde* v. *phan.* — 2. **good, favourable, suited to its purpose** ... *na bdeo* (*W.* **dé-mo-yin**) the best thing will be, if I ... *Dzl.*; **gho dé-wa yoṅ** *C.* so it becomes intelligible; **good, well-qualified, well-adapted,** *kha lče bdé-ba* with good organs of speech *Pth.*; *smra-bdé-žiṅ* knowing to speak well, well-spoken *Pth.*; *nyáms-rtogs-kyi smra lče bde* a tongue skilled in speaking wisdom *Pth.*; in *W.* it is opp. to *rtsóg-po*: **lam de-mo** the road is good, may be passed without risk. — 3. in *W.* *bde* is also the usual word for **beautiful,** more accurately: **(l)tá-na de-mo*; *mā de-mo** splendid indeed! **dé-mo man-na-méd** it is only for show.

**Comp.** *bde-skyid* **happiness, felicity,** frq.; *bdé-ḥgro* going to happiness, joining the happy (spirits in heaven), also *bdér-ḥgro*, opp. to *ṅán-ḥgro*; usually in a genêral sense, like our 'heaven'; *bdé-ḥgro mtho-ris-kyi lus thób-pa* to receive a heavenly (glorified) body. — *bde-čén* felicity, consummate bliss, frq. — *bde-mčóg*, शम्बर. सम्वर, a deity of more recent Buddhism, *Schl.* 108; *Tar.* — *bde-ḥjágs* **prosperity, welfare.** — *bde-stóṅ* (acc. to a Lama's statement for *thabs bdé-ba, šes-rab stoṅ-pa-nyid*), an expression for contemplation, v. *Was.* (144 and 141). — *bde-spyód* *W.*, **de-čód** *C.* **de-čö**, col. euphemism for **privy.** — *bdé-ba-čan* सुखवति, *bdé-ba-čan-gyi žiṅ-khams* **the land of bliss,** a sort of heaven or paradise, in the far west, the abode of Dhyani Buddha Amitabha, v. *Glr.* chapt. IV., *Köpp.* II., 27. — *bde-byéd* he who or that which makes happy *Cs.*, शंकर. — *bde-byúṅ* शम्भु, शम्भल, source of happiness, n. of *Siwa*; as symb. num.: 11. — *bde-blág* **ease, content** *Cs.*, acc. to our Lama: **quickness, speed,** *nád-pa bde-blág-tu gsós-par ḥgyúr-bai mtshan-nyid Wdṅ.* a sign that the patient will soon recover. — *bde-légs* **well-being;** ... *las bde-légs-su gyúr čig* they shall recover from ..., they shall prosper again after ... *Dom.*

བདེན་པ་ *bdén-pa*, सत्य, I. vb. 1. **to be true,** and adj. **true,** *khyod zér-ba bdén-no* what you say is true, you are right *Dzl.*; *bdág-gis nyés-pa bdén-gyis* it being true that I committed a fault *Dzl.*; *dé-bžin-du bden srid* it might be true after all *Glr.*; *šin-tu yaṅ bden* to be sure, that is true! *Glr*; *de bdén-par ṅés-sam* is it quite certain that this is true? *Glr.*; *ċ'bden ltós-la bdén-par* ₒ*dúg-na* ... see whether it is true, and if it is, then ... *Pth.*; *bdén-par* ₒ*dzín-pa* to believe to be true, to take for granted *bdén-*ₒ*dzin žig-na* the illusion being destroyed *Thgr.*; **dèn-če-ċe* W.* (for *yid-čes-pa*) to believe, to be persuaded of the truth, frq.; *bden bden* very true indeed! certainly; *bden-bdén-ma* prob. something in which there is much truth *Tar.* — 2. to be in the right, to be right, *kyed bod-blon-rnams bden* ye Tibetan ambassadors are in your full right *Glr.*; **ṅa á-sál-la dén-pa soṅ* W.* I have evidently been right.

II. sbst. 1. **truth**, in the abstract; but usually: **something true**, true words etc., *bdén-pa smra-ba* to tell or speak the truth; as adj.: **true, veracious** *Stg.*, (*W. *dén-pa zér-k'an**); *mi-bden-rdzún* this is not truth but falsehood *Glr.*; *bden-pa mt'óṅ-ba* to discern, to know, the truth, a degree of Buddhist perfection *Tar.*; *bdén-pa bži* the four truths, the four realities, viz. pain, the origin of pain, the annihilation of pain, and the way of annihilating it, v. *Köpp.* I., 220. Whether, when *bdén-pa gnyis* are mentioned, they refer to two of the just named realities, or whether they always denote absolute (objective) truth (*don-dám-pai bdén-pa*) and subjective truth (*kun-rdzób-kyi bdén-pa*) as mentioned by *Was.* (293), I am not prepared to decide, nor am I able to explain the meaning of *lám-gyi bdén-pa* and ₒ*góg-pai bdén-pa* (*Thgy.* frq.). *bden-pa-nyid* seems to be a technical term for truth, though the Buddhist understands by it nothing but *stoṅ-pa-nyid.* Nevertheless, the possibility of its being misapprehended from this reason ought to be no obstacle to the word being used in its original sense, and re-established in its proper right, the more so, as Buddhist philosophy makes but a mockery of truth, by identifying it with a negation of reality. — 2. = *bden-tsig*, v. below, *Mil.*

**Comp.** **dén-daṅ, dén-du* W.* **in truth, certainly.** — *bden-po* **a true, a just man** *Cs.* — *bden-brál Cs.*: 1. **'void of truth, unjust.** 2. **southwest part** or **direction'.** — *bden-tsig* 1. a true word *Mil.*, but usually 2. a solemn asseveration, often combined with a prayer, to which the power of securing infallible fulfilment is ascribed *Dzl.* and elsewh., frq. — *bden-*ₒ*dzin* v. above.

བདེར་ *bder* = *bdé-bar*; *gaṅ-bdér* **whichever you like, at your pleasure;** *ċi-bdér* has a similar meaning. v. *Tar.* 69, 14, and prob. also 192, 4; *bder-bkod* v. ₒ*gód-pa bdér-*ₒ*gro* v. *bdé-ba.*

བདོ་བ་ *bdó-ba* 1. *Cs.* **'abundance, exuberance'**; more corr., acc. to *Zam.*, where it is explained by *dár-ba* and तीव्र (unbounded), **to extend** (intr.) **without bounds.** — 2. with *la*, **to hurt, to injure** a person *Dom.* and elsewh.; *dgra bdó-ba* v. *sdáṅ-ba.*

བདོག་པ་ *bdóg-pa* I. vb. 1. *W.* **to get** or **take possession of, to stow away, to house,** **ston-tóg** the harvest; **to put into,** **gám-mi náṅ-du** something into a box; **to lay up or by, to keep,** esp. **dóg-te bór-ċe** in store, on hand; **ug náṅ-du dóg-ċe** to hold one's breath — 2. *B.* **to be in possession, to be possessed of,** gen. with *la*, like *yód-pa*, *dé-la rás-yúg gċig bdog* he is in possession of only one piece of cloth *Dzl.*; *k'yód-la* ₒ*di-*ₒ*dra-bai slób-ma bdóg-gam* have you such scholars? *Dzl.*; *nor mi bdóg-pa Dzl.* poor; *dgón-pa ni gáṅ-na bdog Mil.* where have you (where is) your monastery? *bdág-la p'úg-pa bdog* I have a cavern *Mil.*; in an absolute sense: *t'abs bdóg-gam mi bdog* are there any means or not? *Ma.*; *W. *yin-dog-ċan** is stated to mean **proud, arrogant;** **yóg-dog-ċan** one that saves money, a scraper.

II. sbst. **wealth, riches,** *B.*; cog to *bdág-po.*

བདྲལ་བ་ *bdrál-ba*, pf. of ₒ*drál ba*, *Dzl.* frq. (s. l. c.)

མདག་པ་ *mdág-pa* a sort of large **unburnt bricks** of mud or clay *Cs.*

མདག་མ, མེ་མདག *mdág-ma, me-mdág,* **glowing embers, live** or **burning coals,** *mdág-mai doṅ* a pit for keeping them, e.g. for the purpose of melting metals *Stg.*

མདང་ *mdaṅ,* also *mdaṅs,* 1. *C., B.* **yesterday evening, last night,** frq.; *mdáṅ-gi rmi-lam,* also *mdaṅ-súm-gyi rmí-lam Glr., Pth.,* last night's dream. — 2. *W.* **yesterday** (cf *ḱa-rtsáṅ*); *mdaṅ-sáṅ Lex., Cs.:* 'yesterday and to-morrow, now-a-days'; perh. erron. for *deṅ-sáṅ.*

མདང་བ་ *mdáṅ-ba Sch.: mdáṅ-bai γnas* **place of cremation,** the spot where the burning of the dead takes place.

ད མདངས་ *mdaṅs* I. *Ssk.* ओजस्. तेजस्, 1. resp. *sku mdaṅs* **brightness of face, fresh and healthy complexion,** also with *bžin-gyi Cs.; míg-gi mdaṅs* bright eyes *Lt.; γzi-mdáṅs* = *mdaṅs*; *dmár-bai mdaṅs* fresh, ruddy complexion *Glr.: dmár-bai mdáṅs-kyis* with a face beaming with joy *Dzl.* and elsewh.; the brightness is destroyed by disease, *ₒṕrog,* frq., or is fading away, *ₒčor Lt.;* in a relative sense: **appearance, exterior, look,** *mdaṅs-ṅán* bad, ugly appearance *S.g.* — 2. *Med.:* a hypothetical fluid, the most subtile part of the semen, a substance that pervades the whole body, esp. the skin, and is the primary source of vitality; cf. *Wise,* Hindu Syst. of Med., Calcutta 1845, p. 42. 54. 201. — *mdaṅs-bsgyúr* n. of a species of bile. — 3. **brightness, lustre, splendour,** in general, *nyi-mai, ₒȷ̀ai B.* and col.; fig.: *dbáṅ-poi mdáṅs-ma mig ni ṅá-la med Pth.* I am destitute of the eye, that brightest of the senses, as much as: the most excellent of possessions is denied to me.

II. resp. *dprál-ba* **forehead.**

མདའ་ *mda* 1. **arrow,** *rgyáb-pa, ₒṕén-pa* to shoot (an arrow); *smyúg-mda* an arrow of reed, *lčágs-mda* an iron arrow; *dúg-mda* a poisoned arrow *Mil.; dprál-bai mda* an arrow lodged in the forehead *Glr.; mé-mda* 1. **a fiery dart.** 2. **gun, firelock** *C.* — 2. any straight and thin pole or piece of wood, e.g. the stem or tube of a tobacco-pipe; *šiṅ-rtai mda* pole or beam of a carriage; *lčágs-mda* an iron bar or rod, a ramrod etc.; *čú-mda* a jet or shoot of water, frq.; **(s)kár-da* W.* a shooting star. — 3. = *mdo* 1. — 4. symb. num.: 5.

**Comp.** *mda-ḱúṅ* **loop-hole, embrasure.** — *mdá-mḱan* 1. **an archer.** 2. **an arrow-maker** *Glr.* — *mda-rgyáṅ* the range of an arrow-shot *Glr.* — *mda-sgró* the feathers of an arrow *Cs.* — *mdá-ču* the waters discharged from the lower parts of a valley, opp. to *ṕú-ču,* those of the upper part *Glr.* — *mda-ltóṅ* the notch at that end of an arrow which is placed on the bow-string *Pth.* — *mda-dár* a little flag fastened to an arrow; esp. an arrow with silk ribbons of five different colours. By hooking such an arrow into the collar of a bride, the match-maker draws her forth from among her maiden companions *Glr.* — *mda-dóṅ* **quiver.** — *mdá-pa* **an archer;** *mda-dpón* **the commander of the archers,** a high military rank *C.* — *mda-sprád* v. *spród-pa.* — *mda-bér* perh. the more correct form of *ta-bér.* — *mdá-bo* a large arrow. — *mda-mó* **arrow-lot,** a kind of fortune-telling by means of arrows. — *mda-rtséd byéd-pa* to amuse one's self with the shooting of arrows *Cs.* — *mda-ts̒o* a troop of archers *Cs.* — *mda-γyu* bow and arrows *Dzl.* — *mdá-bzo-pa* arrow-maker. — *mda-yáb Glr.* 1. *Lex.* = *ṕú-šu,* **fence;** hence **parapet, railing;** yet a Lama from Tashilhunpo declared it to be the projecting part of the (flat) roofs of large temples, on which the parapet is erected. — 2. **a covered gallery** on the top of a house *C.*

མདུང་ *mduṅ* 1. **lance, spear, pike,** *mduṅ-skór-ba* to brandish, to whirl a spear *Cs.; mduṅ-kyim Dzl.* 96, 9 a frame for leaning spears against; *mdúṅ-mḱan* a maker of spears; *mduṅ-ťúṅ,* or *ₒťáb-mduṅ* a short lance or pike, a javelin. — *mdúṅ-ťogs Mil., mdúṅ-pa* a spearsman, a lancer. — *mduṅ-dár* a lance with a little flag at the top. — *mdúṅ-rtse* top of a spear, spear-head; *mdúṅ-šiṅ* shaft of a lance. — *mdúṅ-bzo-pa* =

*mdúṅ-mḱan.* — *mduṅ rtse-ɣsúm-pa* trident. — 2. **sting,** of insects *C.*, *W.*, *mduṅ brgyáb-pa* to sting. — 3. *ɣser-mdúṅ, dṅul-mdúṅ* prob. the **two frontal muscles** *Med.*

**མདུད་** *mdúd Lt.* a medicine (?).

**མདུད་པ་** *mdúd-pa* **a knot,** *mdúd-pa bór-ba* frq., *dúd-pa Lt.*, *byéd-pa Cs.*, **gyáb-ce** *W.*, to tie or make a knot, *sgrol-ba, ˳grol-ba,* to untie (a knot); **ḍól-dud** *W.* sliding-knot, slip-knot, **šin-dud** *W.* a regular knot; *skra-mdúd* knot or bow of ribbons holding together the long plaits of the women; frq. fig. *sér-snai mdúd-pa* bonds of avarice *Mil.*; **nyiṅ-dud ḍól-ce** *W.* (to untie) to open one's heart to a person; *mdúd-pa-ćan.* 1. **full of knots, knotty.** 2. **cloddy** (?) *S.g.* — *mdúd-˳dra* a disease of the membrum virile, prob. paraphimosis *Mṅg.*

**མདུན་** *mdun* **the fore-part, the front-side of a thing; the vis-à-vis,** *mdún-gyi nám-mka-la* in the heavens before him, over against him, *Glr.* and elsewh.; *mdún-gyis* adv. coram, **face to face,** *mdún-gyis ltá-ba* to behold face to face; gen. c. *la, na, du, nas:* 1. adv. **before it, at it, to it, from it;** 2. postp. **before, at, to** etc.; *mdún-la ˳óṅ-ba,* or *sleb-pa* to come up or near, *ráṅ-gi mdún-la sleb ma bćug* he did not allow (the pursuer) to come near; *mdún-du skúr-ba* to send in advance; *mdun-du ṗyin-pa* to come near, to approach; to hasten to *Pth.*; *mi máṅ-po tsógs-pai mdún-du* in the presence of a great number of people *Dzl.* — *sku-mdún-pa* **a waiting-man, valet de chambre,** v. *sku.* — *mdun-lćog* v. *lćóg-tse.* — *mdun-na-˳don* (*C.* **dụn-nán-dọn**) 1. *Lex.* **पुरोहित, court-chaplain, domestic chaplain** or **priest**; so prob. also *Tar.* 58, 17. — 2. at present: **a high civil officer** or **functionary,** = *bka-blón,* vizier, *Stg.* and elsewh.

**མདུན་མ་** *mdún-ma,* frq. in later lit.; one Lama explained it by *mós-pa,* another by: 1. **wife,** 2. **things, concerns;** *˳jig-rtén-gyi mdún-ma* = *˳jig-rtén-gyi bya-ba.*

**མདེའུ་** *mdeu, Sch.* also *mde-ka,* **arrow-head** *B.*; *mde-súl Cs.*: 'the furrows or grooves of an arrow-head'.

**མདོ་** *mdo* 1. **the lower part of a valley,** where it merges into the plain (opp. to *ṗu*), = *mda;* more frq. the place where one valley opens into another, hence in general: the point where two valleys, roads (*lám-mdo*), rivers (*ćú-mdo*) meet; *lám-sraṅ-mdor* at the street-corners *Dzl.*; *ɣsúm-mdo, bži-mdo, ćóg-mdo* the point where three, four, several (roads etc.) meet, esp. *bží-mdo* **a crossing, cross-road,** as a place of incantations; *mdo* prop. n. (in full: *dar-rtse-mdo*) province of the eastern part of Tibet, v. *ḱams*; **˳dó-ru** in *C.* used as postp. = near, with, by, **ṅe ˳do-ru** with me, **yul-gyi ˳do-ru** near the village. — 2. *Ssk.* **सूत्र, aphorism, short sentence** or **rule, axiom;** hence *mdó-ru, mdor, mdó-tsam sdu-ba* to contract, abridge, epitomize, to give only the main points, frq.; *mdor(-sdu)-na* **in short, in general, altogether, on an average,** denique, frq. — 3. **Sūtra,** in the more recent Buddhist sense, religious treatise or dissertation, a sacred writing, *mdo-sdé* a collection of Sūtras, a part of the Kangyur; *mdo-sdé-pa, mdo-sde-˳dzin* Sautrāntika, a school of philosophers, v. *Tar.*; *mdo-máṅ* title of several collections of Sūtras; in quoting passages: *mdó-la, mdó-las,* in the *mdo,* according to the *mdo* (viz. is said, is written etc.) *Stg.*; *mdo-sṅob* giving a benediction to the host for his entertainment *Mil.*, cf. *Köpp.* I, 143. At present a distinction is to be made between *mdoi* or *dbú-mai lam,* and *sṅágs-kyi lam,* i. e. between the doctrine of the sacred writings and a faithful and systematic study of them, — and of the more modern mysticism, which is mixed up with Siwaism, and seeks to obtain spiritual gifts by means of witchcraft, thus saving trouble and time; v. *Was.* (142. 177), *Köpp.* II, 29. — 4. *Cs.* *mdó-ćan* **prudent,** *mdo-med* **imprudent,** cf. *˳do.* —

**མདོ་ལེ་** *mdo-lé,* the tibetanized **डोली** *Hind.* **sedan-chair** *Pth.*

ད

ད

**མདོག་** *mdog*, resp. *sku-mdóg*, **colour** (cf. *ḱa-dóg*) *B.*, *C.*; *mdog-légs* of a beautiful colour; *mdog-mdzés* 1. id., 2. **a rose.** *Cs.*; *mdog-dkar-ḱá* perh. the more corr. spelling for **do-gar-ḱá** *W.*, light-blue; *mdog-ysál* a species of gall, lit. **'purifier of the skin'**, *Med.*

**མདོངས་** *mdoṅs* 1. the white spot, **blaze, star** on the forehead of a horse *Glr.* and elsewh.; 2. **the eye in a peacock's feather;** *rmá-byai mdoṅs*, *sgro-mdóṅs*, *mdóṅs-sgro* **peacock's feather;** *mdóṅs-mťa-čan* **turkey-hen** *Cs.*

**མདོངས་པ་** *mdóṅs-pa* = *ldóṅ-ba*, **blind,** physically and morally, *B.*, *mig-mdoṅs-pa*, *mdóṅs-par ˳gyúr-ba*, to get blind, to be made blind *Dzl.*

**མདོངས་གསོལ་བ་** *mdóṅs-ysol-ba Mil.*, *mdoṅs-sól žu-ba* or *byéd-pa Cs.*, **to congratulate, to wish joy** to another *Cs.*; *Zam.* explains it by *˳dún-pa* to wish, another *Lex.* by *ṅó-dga* joy; in the passage of *Mil.* it seems to signify thank-offering.

**མདོམས་** *mdoms*, sometimes written for *˳doms.*

**མདོས་** *mdos* a cross formed of two small sticks, the ends of which are connected by coloured strings ⊕, and used in various magic ceremonies.

**འདག་པ་** *˳dág-pa* 1. *Sch.*: **'clay; cleaving, adhesive, sticky.'** In *C.* = *˳jim-pa* (*W.* **ká-lag**) a mixture of clay and water; *˳dag-žál S.g.* prob. id.; *˳dág-pa sbyáṅ-ba* to make such a mixture, *Cs.*; *˳dag-sbyár* covering, or stopping up with clay, e.g. the chinks of a wall or door, **˳dag-ǰár ˳búl-ba** to render such service to a meditating Lama as an act of piety. In *Pth.* *˳dág-pa* is mentioned as a kind of plastic art, and evidently signifies to mould, to model, to shape. — 2. = *ldág-pa Cs.*; *˳dág-gu Lex.* = *skyó-ma*, pap, pulp, prob. = *ldé-gu.* — 3. pf. *dag*, 1. **to clear, to wash away, to wipe off,** *dri-ma*, frq.; *rtá-la sol-byúg* (to clean) a horse marked or blackened with charcoal *Glr.*; *sdig-sgrib* (to wash off) the filth of sin *Glr.* 2. **to disappear,** of sinful thoughts *Glr.*, sometimes *ynás-su* to their own place, is added pleon. *Mil.* — Participle *dág-pa* clean, v. *dág-pa.*

**འདང་** *˳daṅ* v. *˳dad.*

**འདུང་བ་** *˳dúṅ-ba Sch.* **to come to, to arrive at**; cf. also *brgya-˳daṅs*, sub *brgya.*

**འདད་, འདང་** *˳dad*, *˳daṅ*, resp. *sku-˳dad* or *daṅ Lex.* **funeral-repast.**

**འདབ་** *˳dab* **a train** of persons, *˳ḱor-˳dab* **retinue** *Cs.*

**འདབ་མ་** *˳dáb-ma* 1. **wing,** *sprúg-pa* to shake (the wings) *Cs.*, *yyób-pa* to clap them *Cs.* — 2. **ladle, float-board** of a water-wheel. — 3. **petal,** flower-leaf, frq.; *˳dab-brgyad* eight-petaled *Glr.*; v. *Schl. Buddh.* 248. — 4. **any leaf, a broad leaf,** also *lo-˳dab.* — 5. **fan** *Cs.* — 6. **flag** *Cs.* — *˳dab-čags* a winged animal, **bird,** frq. — *˳dab-ráṅs-pa* **full of leaves;** with leaves fully developed *Sch.* — *˳dab-ysóg* **flag-feather, quill-feather.**

**འདབས་** *˳dabs*, rarely *˳dab*, **the side, lateral surface,** of a hill, of the body etc.; **surface,** *mčin-˳dabs* of the liver *Med.*; in a more general sense: *sgál-˳dabs* **the lumbar region** *Med.*; pleon.: *nágs-˳dabs-na* = *nágs-na* in the woods *Mil.*

**འདམ་** *˳dam* **mud, mire, swamp,** earth and water, = *˳dág-pa*, but as a product of nature; *˳dam rdzáb B.*, **dam-tsóg** *W.* id.; *˳dám-du*, *˳dam-rdzáb-la ˳byiṅ-ba* to sink into a swamp; **dam-pág(s)** *W.* muddy plash, slough. — *˳dám-bu* **reed** for thatching, writing etc.; *Cs.* also **sugar-cane;** *˳dam-bu ka-ra?* prob. a species of reed in wells or ponds *Wdn.*; **dam-búr** *W.* sugar-cane.

**འདམ་ཀ་** *˳dám-ka Zam.*, *˳dám-ga*, *˳dám-ṅa*, *˳dám-pa Cs.* **choice, option,** *deṅ saṅ ˳dám-ka byéd-pa* to choose whether to-day or to-morrow *Zam.*; cf. *ydám-ka.*

**འདམ་པ་** *˳dám-pa* (or *˳dóm(s)-pa Glr.* prov.) pf. *˳dams*, imp. *˳dom(s)*, **to choose, to select,** a bride *Glr.*; *mi-ytsáṅ-ba ˳dám-pa* such as choose impure things, cynical, lascivious characters *Stg.*; *˳dam-riṅ* choosing, turning over in one's mind a long while; *dgrá-bo yáṅ-pa mi ytaṅ ˳dam-riṅ ťábs-kyis ydul* prob.: not losing sight of your enemy, constantly watching, put him down, as soon as an opportunity offers, *S.g.*, and hence *že-sdáṅ ₒdam-riṅ* a long lingering, lurking grudge *S.g.*

འདའ་བ་ *ₒdá-ba*, pf. *ₒdas* (prob. vb. n. to *bdá-ba, ₒdéd-pa*) **to pass over, 1. to travel over, to clear a certain space,** *t̔aṅ de* this plain *Sambh.*; *žag dú-mai lam* (to perform) many day's journeys *Dzl.* — 2. c. *las:* **to go beyond, to surpass** *Dzl.; lhá-las dás-pai spos* incense surpassing that of the gods, i.e. that which is burnt to them *S.O.*; **to exceed,** *t̔sád-las* the measure *Lt.*; *gráṅs-las dás-pa Tar.* surpassing number, innumerable; *bsám-byai yúl-las* (surpassing) the understanding or imagination, inconceivable *Glr.;* **to transgress, to trespass against,** *bká-las, k̔ríms-las*, a commandment, a law = *ₒgál-ba*; **to get over a thing, to get the better of, to overcome,** = *rgyál-ba*; **to go away from,** *mya-ṅán-las* q.v.; **to let go, leave off, abandon,** *č̔ós-las* one's religion *Thgy.*; *bló-las dás-pa?* — 3. with or without *dús-las, t̔se*, resp. *sku*, **to depart this life, to die;** *das-po* **the deceased, defunct, late,** *Lex.*; **dẹ-lóg* W.* the soul of a deceased person, **ghost, apparition;** the re-appearing is possible only for about forty days after death, as long as the Bardo lasts, v. *bar-do*. — 4. **to pass by,** = to disappear, *nyi-zlá ₒdás-nas* when the sun and the moon have disappeared (for a time); very frq. relative to time: **to pass away, to elapse,** *ₒdás-pai dus* the time that has passed, is gone, past time, v. *dus* 5.; *zla dgu ₒdás-nas* after nine months *Lt.*; *ₒdas-ló* the year past, *ₒdas-zlá* the month past, *ₒdas-žág* the day past; **dẹ-zág-la* W.* **the other day, lately;** *nyin-mt̔sán č̔ós-kyis ₒdá-bar bya* day and night are spent in religious exercises; *dgé-bai byá-ba k̔ó-nas dus ₒda Tar.* (time) spent in none but works of virtue. — *ₒdá-ga (-ma) Cs.* **hour of death,** *ₒda-ga-ye-šés* मृति ज्ञान, knowledge of the hour of death (title of a book).

འདར་བ་ *ₒdár-ba* **to tremble, shudder, shiver, quake,** *gráṅ-bas ₒdar-ba* to shiver with cold; *ₒjigs-pas* (to tremble) with fear; *ₒdár-žiṅ ₒgúl-ba* id.; *ₒdár-bar ₒgyúr-ba* to begin to tremble; *ₒdar-yám Sch.* doubting, wavering, undetermined, *ₒdar-yám byéd-pa* to doubt, to waver.

འདལ་ *ₒdal*(?) *ru-ₒdál, ru-ₒdrél* **a single horn** *Sch.* — *bad-ₒdál* prov., being left exhausted on the road, sinking under fatigue.

འདལ་འདལ་ *ₒdal-ₒdál* v. *tá-bag.*

འདལ་བ་ *ₒdál-ba* = *dál-ba, č̔u-ₒdál* **still water** *Lex.*

འདི་ *ₒdi* demonstr. pron. **this,** *ṅai bu ₒdi* this my son; *ṅai ₒdi* this of me, i.e. that which I am doing just now *Glr.*, what I am experiencing just now *Mil.*; **the present, the respective,** *ₒgrúb-pa-po ₒdi* the respective performer (of an incantation) *Dom.*; such a one, *bdag miṅ ₒdi žes-byá-ba* I, such and such a one *Thgr.*, also *ₒdi daṅ ₒdi (-lta-bu)* and similar expressions, *ṅas k̔yód-la ₒdi daṅ ₒdí-lta-bu žig sbyin-no* I give you such and such a thing. On the difference between *ₒdi* and *de* v. *de*; the plural forms and derivatives of both of them are in conformity; only the following may be particularly mentioned: *ₒdi-ka-ráṅ* is used also for **just here, just now** *Mil.; ₒdí-lta-ste* **for instance, to wit, such as, viz.;** also pleon. with *žé-na: γnyis gaṅ žé-na ₒdi-lta-ste Wdṅ.; ċi p̔yir žé-na ₒdi-lta-ste Pth.; ₒdi-ltar* **so, in this manner,** *ċii p̔yir k̔yod ₒdi-ltar gyur* in what manner have you become so, how did you get into this condition? *Dzl.* frq.; *ₒdi-ltar-ro* it ran thus, it was to this effect, of this purport *Glr.* frq.; *ṅa ₒdi-ltar yin* such I am, I am, live, go, just as you see me here *Mil.;* in the verse: *ₒdus-byas č̔os-rnams ₒdi-ltar blta* 'compounded things must be regarded thus' — the word *ₒdi-ltar* is meant to be accompanied by a snap of the fingers (*se-gól*, or *skád-ċig-ma*); *ₒdi-nas* **from this place, from this time present, as yet, still.** *ₒdi (daṅ) p̔yi (-ma)* the present and the future life, frq.; *ₒdi p̔yid sdéb-pa, rjé-ba* to exchange this life for the future one, i.e. *t̔se p̔yi-ma blós-btaṅ-ste ₒdii don sgrúb-pa* to be earthly minded *C.*; **dí-zug, ʼi-zug* W.*, so, thus; **dí-riṅ* W.* to-day; *ₒdi-ru* (come) **in here, into this place; here, at this place,** frq.; **now,** seldom.

འདིག་ ˳dig **stopper, stopple,** also *k̔a-˳dig; *dig-če* Ld.* to put in a stopper; **to stop up,** to close with a stopper; **dig-ril* C.* **musket-ball.** Cf. *dig.*

འདིང་བ་ ˳*diṅ-ba,* pf. *btiṅ, fut. ydiṅ, imp. t̔iṅ(s),* **to spread on the ground,** a mat, carpet etc.; **to scatter, sprinkle, strew,** grass or hay to lie upon, ashes on the snow etc.; **btin-ba** sbst. *W.* **a small carpet,** on which the Lamas use to sit; **mal-btin* C.* **bedding, pillow,** or **blanket.** — ˳*diṅ rgyáb-pa Sch.* **to weigh in one's mind,** to consider; to suspect, to entertain a suspicion.

འདུ(ན)་ཁང་ ˳*dú(n)-k̔aṅ* **meeting-house, house of assembly;** *čos˳čád-pai*(quasi) **church, chapel** *Dzl.*

ད

འདུ་འཁྲུག་ ˳*du-˳k̔rúg* **tumult, riot, uproar** *Cs.*

འདུ་བ་ ˳*dú-ba,* pf. ˳*dus,* (vb. n. to *sdúd-pa*) 1. **to come together, to assemble,** of men and animals; ˳*dun-k̔áṅ-du Dzl.;* ˳*dús-sam ma* ˳*dus* are they already assembled? *daṅ* with (a person) *Tar.*; in order to fight *Stg.*; of things: *nyés-pa t̔ams-čád dei lús-la* ˳*duo,* v. *nyes-pa;* ˳*du-ba* and ˳*dus-pa* sbst. **a coming together, an assembling, a gathering,** esp. in *Med.* a (somewhat indefinite) **disease, or cause of disease;** ˳*dus-sa* **meeting-place** *Glr.*; *las-mi maṅ-po* ˳*dus-sa* an establishment comprizing many workmen, **manufactory, workshop, workhouse,** **dzóm-˳du yóṅ-gin ˳dug* C.* they flock or crowd together; *tsoṅ-˳dus* the assembled traders or dealers, **the market** frq.; *skyabs-kun-˳dus* 'a collection of all the refuges' is a name given to Milaraspa. — 2. **to unite, to join one another,** *k̔yo-šúg-tu* as husband and wife, **to get married;** in a special sense in philosophical language: 1. **to unite** (opp. to ˳*brál-ba*), e.g. the soul uniting with an organ of sense, like *sdéb-pa, Mil.* 2. ˳*dus-byás* composed of two or more ingredients, ˳*dus-ma-byas* consisting of one thing, simple, elementary; only this is eternal, every thing compounded is perishable, frq. — 3. **to be pressed** or **crowded together,** **šril dús-te dug* Ld.* they stand crowded, in serried files or ranks; intellectually: *dam-čos* ˳*dus-pa* a compressed system of religion. — 4. ˳*dús-pa* **to consist of** or **in,** *ynyís-su* ˳*dus-so* (religion) consists of two things *Thgy.*; *snaṅ-srid séms-su* ˳*dús-te yda* the external world consists of spirit, is spirit, i.e. is nothing *Mil.* — 5. col.: **to be drawn together, to contract, to shrink,** **dus ča dug* Ld.* it shrinks, e.g. wood or paper from heat; **tsa-˳du* C.* prob. **cramp, spasm, convulsion;** **dús-k̔an* Ld.* **elastic, springy.**

འདུ་བྱེད་ ˳*du-byéd, Ssk.* संस्कार, (the Tibetan word is nothing but a literal translation of the *Ssk. saṅskāra;* cf. also ˳*du-šés* and *p̔úṅ-po*) 'one of the obscurest and most difficult terms of Buddhist philosophy' *Köpp.* I, 603, where the various translations are enumerated that have been attempted, such as: idea, notion, imagination (cf. *Burn.* I, 503), action (*Was.*) etc. It should, however, at once be acknowledged, that the word cannot be translated into a European language, as the meaning given to it is not the result of honest research and observation, but a product of arbitrary and wild speculation.

འདུ་འཛི་ ˳*du-˳dzi* **noise, bustle, din, clamour,** ˳*du-˳dzi méd-pai dbén-pa* ˳*di* this solitude without any noise *Mil.*; ˳*du-˳dzi-la ynás-pa* to live in the midst of the bustle of worldly affairs; ˳*du-žiṅ,* ˳*du-lóṅ Cs.* id.

འདུ་ཤེས་ ˳*du-šes, Ssk.* संज्ञा ('con-scientia') corresponds in most cases to our **idea, notion, conception, image,** although sometimes **perception, feeling, sense, thought, consciousness** may be employed for it: *nór-la rtág-tu yód-pai* ˳*du-šés skyéd-pa* to combine with earthly goods the idea of constant possession *S.O.* and thus frq.; *lús-la grui* ˳*du-šés* ˳*jug-pa* to unite with the human body the idea of a ship, to represent the body as a ship, *Thgy.*; *skyó-bai* ˳*du-šes byuṅ* the perception, the feeling of discomfort arises *S.g.*; *k̔ró-bai* ˳*du-šés-spáṅ-ba* to detest the idea, the thought of anger *Dzl.*; *dgé-bai p̔yógs-la* ˳*du-šés čuṅ-zad kyaṅ ma yyos* no thoughts, no inclinations, tending to virtue, arose (in him), virtuous emotions never stirred in his mind; *čágs-pai* *ₒdu-ŝés-ĉan* entertaining thoughts of sensual pleasure *Glr.; ₒdu-ŝés slar rnyéd-pa* to recover from a state of insensibility; as vb.: *ₒdu-ŝés-pa, mya-ṅan-ₒdás ťob du-ŝés-te* imagining that I shall obtain Nirwāna *Thgy.* As one of the five *p̓úṅ-po* it is translated by **idea** (*Burn.* I, 511), by **perception** (*Köpp.* I, 603). The three terms *ₒdu-ŝes-ĉan, ₒdu-ŝes-méd-pa, ₒdu-ŝes-med-mín* may be rendered: having the faculty of thinking, having no faculty of thinking, neither thinking nor not thinking (*Dzl.* ༢༢༦, 7), *ₒdu-ŝes-ĉan* refers to human beings, the two other terms relate to celestial beings (v. *Köpp.* I, 261, 17 and 26), that are evidently so much the more excellent and exalted, as they are far above all reasoning and thinking. According to another, and (it would seem) more natural interpretation, the first of these three terms implies **rational** beings (man), the second **irrational** beings (higher animals), and the third **quite irrational** creatures (lower animals, worms, reptiles, that are not even possessed of the sensitive powers of the higher animals), whilst the 'long-lived Lhas' of the 17th. heaven are classed together with the common Lhas (who however taken strictly, belong to the 'first world') and on account of their stupidity are believed to be incapable of ever being converted, *Thgy.*

འདུག་པ་ *ₒdúg-pa* (eleg. *γdá-ba*, resp. *bžúgs-pa*) 1. **to sit**, syn. with *sdód-pa*; with *na, la* etc.; **to sit down** with termin. or *la*; **to sit up** (in bed); *ₒdúg-par ₒgyúr* **to get seated** *Dzl.* ༥༦, 6; **to remain sitting,** to keep one's seat, *Dzl.* ༥༦, 7; **to remain, to stay,** *ₒdír ma ₒdúg-par soṅ žig Dzl.*; **to remain behind, to stay at home,** with or without *p̓yir, ḱyim-na* etc. *Dzl.* — 2. **to be, to exist, to live** *Glr.*: ... *skabs-med ₒ'dug-go!'* there is no chance of ... Yes, there is! ... *ₒdug ŝés-nas* knowing that ... is still alive *Dzl.; dráṅ-sroṅ byéd-ĉiṅ ₒdug* he lives as a hermit *Dzl.;* **to be, to live at a certain place,** *γnás-na ₒdúg-pa* the being somewhere *Gram.*; *p̓a-má gáṅ-na ₒdug* where are my parents now? **to be at home** *Dzl.* and elsewh.; **to be extant, to be found,** *ĉaṅ mi ₒdug* nothing is, or was to be found, nothing was there *Mil.*; as partic. joined with, or put inst. of the possess. pron.: *ḱo-ráṅ daṅ* (*ḱoi*) *bu brgyad ₒdúg-pa* he and his eight children being with him *Mil.* (*yód-pa* is construed in the same manner); in quotations: to be found, to be written, to be met with, ... *yod zér-ba ... na ₒdug* the account of being ... is to be found in ..., *Glr.* — 3. **to be**, as copula, in *B.* often with termin.: *ḱyim-par ₒdúg-pa* to be a layman *Stg.*; *rkáṅ-pa ḱrá-bor ₒdug* the foot was variously coloured *Dzl.*; *ₒdí-rnams mi-ma-yin-du ₒdúg-pas* as these are spirits *Mil.* Generally speaking, this termin. case is not to be pressed, nor always to be explained by: **to have become,** or to be translated by: **in,** as in the following: *rgya-gár-gyi yi-ger ₒdúg-pas* to be (written) in the Indian language *Glr.* — 4. **to be,** as auxiliar vb., 1. with the termin. of the inf., often merely paraphrastically, e.g. *yód-par ₒdúg-pa* = *yód-pa Glr.*; frq., however, indicating doubtfulness and uncertainty: *ṅa ni ŝaṅ ĉi-bar ₒdug* may be I shall die to-morrow *Glr.*; *ḱyed ... yin-par-ₒdug* you seem to be, you are, I dare say *Mil.*; *ₒgro dgós-par ₒdug* I suppose you must go *Glr.*; *stér-bar ₒdug* it will probably be given *Glr.*; *ma mťóṅ-na mi rtógs-par ₒdug* if we had not seen it, we should probably not have known it *Mil.*; in the same manner it is used with *yód-pa*, q. v. — 2. with a verbal root, in ancient lit. hardly ever occurring, in more recent writings used paraphrastically like *ₒdúg-pa,* with the termin. of the inf. (v. above 1), but not indicating a certain tense, e.g. *rdol ₒdug* it makes its appearance, comes to light, *Glr.*, *bŝig ₒdug* they were destroyed *Glr.*; in col. language (in *W.* at least) it is gen. a sign of the pres. tense: *zer ₒdug* I say, thou sayest etc.; only in *Bal.* it indicates the fut. tense. — 3. with the gerund in *te* or *nas* vulgo for the pres. or preterite tense, frq.; in *B.* of so rare occurrence, that it is prob. to be regarded as a vulgarism to be charged on the copyists, and to be corrected accordingly. — 4. with *gin* (*B.* and col.) and *ċiṅ* (*B.*), denoting **a continued action, state,** or **condition,** as in English: I am looking. — *ₒdúg-ɣnas*, *ₒdúg-sa*, **place of residence, abode.**

འདུད་པ་ *ₒdúd-pa*, pf. *btud*, fut. *ɣdud* (*Cs.*), imp. *dud*, *tud* (*Cs.*), **to bend** or **bow down, to incline,** *rná-ba*, to incline one's ears to hear, (also used of animals), cf. our 'to prick the ears', *Dzl.*; **to bow, to make a bow,** *la*, to a person; *żábs-la* at a person's feet, to kneel down before a person.

འདུན་ *ₒdun*, *go-ₒdún*, = *sna-ts̓ogs* **of several kinds, divers, sundry, various,** *Lex.*

འདུན་པ་ *ₒdún-pa* 1. vb. **to desire, to wish earnestly,** with *la*, *nyán-pa-la mi ₒdún-par* they not having any desire to hear *Pth.*; *dgé-ba-la* to strive after virtue, frq.; also *ₒdún-pa* alone (without *dgé-ba-la*) id. *Thg.*; **lo č̓ó-la ₒdụ́m-pa** *C.* religious interest, concern for religion; to be zealous, to take a warm interest *Mil.* — 2. sbst. **a desire** *Thgy.*; **a supplication** *Dzl.*, *Glr.* Cf. *dún-pa*.

འདུན་མ་ *ₒdún-ma* 1. **advice, counsel,** *ṅán-pa* a bad advice *Ma.*; *ₒdébs-pa* to give advice; *byéd-pa* to take a resolution *Mil.* — 2 **consultation** (v. examples sub *č̓úṅ-ba*), *ₒdun-grós* id.; *da lán-gyi ₒdun-grós ₒdí-la* at this present consultation *Glr.*; **ₒdụ́m-ma ǰhé-pa** *C.* to consult, to confer with (a person about a matter). — 3. **council,** *ₒdún-mar bsdus* they called a council together *Mil.*; esp. in compounds: *ₒdún-ḱaṅ* = *ₒdú-ḱaṅ* q.v.; *ₒdún-sa* **meeting-place, assembly,** frq.; **union, association, society,** *dge-ₒdun* an association of clerical persons. — 4. v. *ₒdum?* *ɣnyen-ₒdun* harmony amongst relations, *Stg.* — 5. **the state of being a bride; bride,** *C.*, and perh. *Glr.*; cf. also *dga-ₒdún* sub *dgá-ba*. — 6. = *mdún-ma?*

འདུབ་སྙོམས་ *ₒdub-snyóms Sch.* **a state of comfort, ease;** *ₒdub-ₒḱrúgs*, an interruption of that state, discomfort.

འདུམ་པ་ *ₒdúm-pa* 1. vb. **to reconcile one's self to, to be reconciled with,** *t̓áb-pa ₒdúm-na* if contending parties are reconciled with one another; *rtág-tu mi ₒdúm-mo* they are constantly at variance *Dzl.*; **dúm-ṭa** (lit. *ḱra*) *C.* contract, agreement, = *č̓ad-don*. — 2. sbst. **concord, unison, peace** *Cs.*

འདུར་ *ₒdur* **thick and clammy** *Sch.*

འདུར་བ་ *ₒdúr-ba* **to trot;** *ₒdur-grós* **the trot.**

འདུལ་བ་ *ₒdúl-ba* I. vb., pf. *btul*, *tul*, fut. *ɣdul*, imp. *tul*, *W.* **túl-ċe** 1. **to tame, to break in,** *rta*; **to subdue, conquer, vanquish,** *dgra*; sometimes even **to kill, to annihilate** *Pth.* — 2. **to till, cultivate,** waste land; **to civilize,** a nation, which with the Buddhist is the same as **to convert,** frq.; **to educate, to discipline, to punish;** *ɣdúl-bai rigs-pa* those fit for and predestinated to conversion *Dzl.*; *ɣdúl-bya* id. frq.; also used substantively: *ₒgró-ba ṅá-yi ɣdúl-bya yin* the beings are to be converted by me *Glr.*; *bdag ḱyéd-kyi ɣdúl-byar šog ċig* may we become your converts!

II. sbst. **विनय** 1. **the taming** etc. — 2. also *ₒdúl-bai sde*, the disciplinary part of the Kangyur, *ₒdul-ba-las* from, or according to the Dulwa; *ₒdúl-bai brda* an expression (taken) from the Dulwa.

འདུས་པ་ *ₒdús-pa*, v. *ₒdú-ba*.

འདེ་གུ་ *ₒdé-gu*, v. *ldé-gu*.

འདེ་བ་ *ₒdé-ba*, v. *ldé-ba*.

འདེག(ས)་པ་ *ₒdég(s)-pa*, pf. *bteg(s)*, fut. *ɣdeg*, imp. *t̓eg*, *W.* **tág-ċe**. imp. **tog**, **to lift, to raise, to elevate,** the head, the tail, also fig.; *sgrón-me Glr.*, *'*od-ṭo** *W.*, to hold up a lamp, a light; also fig.: to let one's light shine to others; *grágs-pai gó-sar ₒdégs-pa* to raise to a high rank; **to support, sustain, maintain, keep up,** *Pth.*; *rám-bu ₒdégs-pa* to join in singing, to fall in with, *Dzl.* and elsewh. (*Sch.* erron. 'to bawl, to blare'); *rá-mda ₒdégs-pa* to help; for **żi tág-ċe** and similar phrases cf. the secondary forms *tég-pa*, *tégs-pa*, *ₒt̓égs-pa;* with or without *srán-la*, *rgyá-ma-la* etc.: to put on the balance, **to weigh,** *B.*; *żib-btégs* weighed accurately

*Lt.*; ₒ*dégs-ḱal* 'a bushel by weight' *Cs.*, or rather: twenty points on the large steelyard. — **ǰug-tág* W.* **water-wagtail.** — **dég-ḱa* C., W.*, **weight.** — ₒ*dégs-dpon* is said to denote a military dignity, but is not generally known; as 'servant waiting at table', it ought to be spelled *stégs-dpon.* — ₒ*dégs-śiṅ Sch.* **yoke,** fitted to a person's shoulders, for carrying water-buckets etc.

**འདེང་བ་** ₒ*déṅ-ba*, pf. *deṅ*, imp. *deṅ(s)*, **to go,** esp. *ṗyir déṅ-ba* **to go back, to return,** *Dzl., Lex.* Cf. ₒ*doṅ-ba.*

**འདེད་པ་** ₒ*déd-pa*, pf. and imp. *ded*, sometimes preceded by *rǰés-su*, **to go** or **walk behind,** hence 1. **to drive,** cattle, the herdsman walking behind the animals, whereas of the shepherd ₒ*ḱrid-pa* is used; *rlúṅ-gis gru* ₒ*ded* the wind drives the ship, frq.; also to drive through (a tube) by blowing, to blow through *Glr.*; to drive (animals, birds) from a place of rest, **to rouse, start.** — 2. **to pursue, chase, run after,** *rgód-ma* ₒ*déd-pa* to be in the rut (of a stallion); **ded táṅ-ċe* W.* to chase, to hunt; **déd-de bó-ċe* W.* to call after a person. — 3. vb. n. **to follow in succession, to succeed,** *rim-pa bžin* successively, of generations, *Glr.* — 4. **to call in, to recover,** money, debts; *bú-lon-*ₒ*ded drág-po* a severe dun *Mil.*; ₒ*déd-mi* a driver, e.g. the person walking behind the horse of a rider, driving it on *Lt.*; **the pursuer** of a fugitive *Glr.* — Cf. *bdá-ba.*

**འདེབས་** ₒ*debs* 1. **puncheon** (tool). — 2. **time, times,** = **lan* W.*(?).

**འདེབས་པ་** ₒ*débs-pa*, pf. *btab*, fut. *γtab*, imp. *ṫob*, supine ₒ*débs-su*, and *γdáb-tu*, *W. *táb-ċe**, imp. **tob**; **to cast, throw, strike, hit,** variously applied, cf. *rgyáb-pa*, in *B.* gen. with instr., even if there is a dative in the same sentence, v. the examples; **ċog-tse-la táb-ċe* W.* to strike upon the table; *rlúṅ-gis, γdón-gyis, nád-kyis* ₒ*débs-pa*, to be beaten by the wind, to be possessed by a demon, to be seized with an illness, frq.; *sṅágs-kyis* ₒ*débs-pa B., mtu btáb-pa* col., **to pronounce a charm** against a person or thing, with *la*; *lan, ṅo-spród, gros* ₒ*débs-pa*, **to answer, to explain, to advise;** *γsól-ba* ₒ*débs-pa* **to make a request,** *smón-lam* ₒ*débs-pa* to offer up a prayer; *γsal-*ₒ*débs byéd-pa* **to remember well** *Mil.*: *γsal-*ₒ*débs-su śés-pa* prob. **to have a distinct recollection of a thing** *Glr.*; *rtsis* ₒ*débs-pa* prob. **to cast up an account, to reckon, to compute,** *dei rtsis-γdáb bdág-la med* I do not take that into account *Mil.*; *lús-la γzér(-gyis)* ₒ*débs-pa Dzl.*, **zér tab-ċe,* or *gyab-ċe* W.*, knocking nails into the body; *rgyas* ₒ*débs-pa* **to seal;** **lúd tab-ċe,* or *gyáb-ċe* W.* to spread dung (on the ground), to manure; *ċus* ₒ*debs-pa* to sprinkle with water *Dzl.*; *ṫsa, śa ṫúg-pa-la* ₒ*débs-pa* to put salt, meat, into the soup; *sá-bon* ₒ*débs-pa* to sow; *gur* ₒ*débs-pa, sga-*ₒ*débs-pa*, to pitch a tent, a camp (driving in the tent-pins); also without a sbst.: *sṅar btab-pai ċu-γśoṅ-du* (pitching) in the same dell where they had encamped before *Dzl.* ༢༥༢, 1. (*Sch.* incorr.): hence in general: **to found, to establish,** e.g. a monastery, frq.; *dus* ₒ*débs-pa* to fix a time.

**འདེམ་པ་** ₒ*dém-pa* **to prove, to examine** *Sch.*

**འདེར་** ₒ*der Glr.* prob. for *lder.*

**འདོ་** ₒ*do*, for *mdo* 3., *Cs.* ₒ*do-yód* **prudent, clever,** ₒ*do-méd Lex., Cs.* **imprudent, silly.**

**འདོ་བ་** ₒ*dó-ba* 1. sbst. *Sch.*: **'a breed of fine horses';** one *Lex.* has ₒ*do-rta* w. e. — 2. vb. *Cs.*: = *zló-ba*, **to say, to repeat;** *ma-*ₒ*dos-par* **unspeakable** (?) *Dzl.* ༢༥༥, 4 (the reading of *Sch.* dubious, v. *Schf.*'s remarks on this passage).

**འདོག་པ་** ₒ*dóg-pa*, prob. an incorr. reading for *dógs-pa.*

**འདོགས་པ་** ₒ*dógs-pa*, pf. *btags* (also *γdags?*), fut. *γdag(s)*, imp. *ṫogs*, *W. *tag-ċe**, imp **tog* or *tag toṅ**, 1. **to bind, fasten, tie to,** (opp. to ₒ*gról-ba*), *W. *ḱyi túg-te bor**, tie up, fasten, the dog well; (v. ₒ*bór-ba*); *la* to a thing, frq.; also in a more general sense: **to fix, to attach,** e.g. a balcony to a house *S.g.*; **to tie round, to buckle on,** *go-mtsón lús-la* the armour *Pth.*; **to**

**put on,** *rgyan* gay clothes, finery, *rgyan bzáṅ-po btágs-pa* beautifully attired *Mil.*; col. also without *rgyan*, e.g. **tág-dad-čan* W.* fond of dress and finery. — 2. in particular phrases: *bkar-ₒdógs-pa* v. *bkar*; *mi-la skyon ₒdógs-pa* **to charge a person with a fault, to upbraid;** *sgro ₒdógs-pa* v. *sgro*; *ťúgs-la ₒdógs-pa* **to interest one's self in** or **for, to take care of;** *ḱyod ťúgs-la mi ₒdógs-pa ₒdi či yin mi šes* why he does not interest himself in your behalf, I know not *Mil.nt.* 37, 6.; with reference to things: **to have near at heart;** *ťúgs-la btágs-so* you have taken great care of me, a phrase frq. used, where we should say: I am much obliged to you! though Tibetans deny its implying acknowledgment and expression of thanks. — *dám-la ₒdógs-pa* v. *dam*; *p̓an ₒdógs-pa* v. *p̓án-pa*; *miṅ ₒdógs-pa* **to give a name;** *drá-bai sgó-nas* according to likeness or analogy *Mṅg.*; *ḱyeui miṅ či-skad γdags* how is the boy to be called? *Dzl. miṅ mi-ŷdúṅ-ba žes* (or *mi-γdúṅ-bar*) *btágs-so* they named him... *Mil.*, *Dzl.*; *miṅ* may also be wanting. — 3. *Gram.* **to join, subjoin, affix,** *rar btags ga* a *g* joined with *r*, i.e. *rg*; *ra-la ǰa* a *ǰ* joined with *r*, i.e. *rǰ*; *sa-la btags-pai ta-yig, st*; *ya-btags*, or shorter, *yá-ta*, the *ya* which is written underneath, the subscribed *ya*, = ◌ྱ; *yá-ta btágs-pa yi-ge bdun*, seven letters are joined with *yá-ta(gs) Glr.*; *smád-ₒdogs γsum* the three subscribed letters, *ya*, *ra*, and *la Zam.*; *ₒdogs-čan* 1. having a letter subscribed; 2. an open syllable with a vowel-sign, as *go* གོ, *de* དེ, *mdo* མདོ, etc. (not *da* ད or *mda* མདའ) *Zam.*; *a-ₒdogs* consonants with *a* (འ) subscribed, syllables with a long vowel. — 4. in philosophical writings: *btágs-pa* **conditional,** not absolute, *Was.* (228. 270), *btags-méd* **nominal** *Was.* (281).

འདོང་བ་ *ₒdóṅ-ba*, pf. and imp. *doṅ* or *ₒdoṅ*, **to go, to proceed,** *so-sór Dzl.* **to separate, to disperse;** *rgyál-poi tád-du* (to go) to the king; *p̓yi-rol-tu ₒčág-čiṅ* to take a walk *Dzl.*; *dóṅ-ṅo* let us go *Dzl.*; *lóg-la ₒdoṅ-ṅo* let us turn back *Glr.*

འདོད་པ་ *ₒdód-pa* I. vb. (*W.* more frq. *ťád-pa*), **to have a mind, to like, to be willing,** *zas bzáṅ-po mi ₒdod Dzl.*; *mi za ₒdod ťsul byed* he pretends not to like this food *Lt.*; *sbyin (-par) ₒdód-pa ₒgyur* he gets inclined to give; *mi ₒdód-par ₒgyúr-ba* to feel no longer inclined; **to wish,** *nyán (-par)* to listen; *či daṅ či ₒdód-pa* whatever you may wish *Dzl.*; *rgyál-po ₒdód-pa* to wish to be a king *Dzl.*; as adj.: **wished for, desirable,** esp. with negatives, v. below; *ₒdód-par byá-ba* adj. **agreeable, pleasing, obliging, flattering,** *Stg.*, *Cs.*; **to desire, to long for,** *ḱyim ₒdod* I wish I were at home *Dzl.*; *me daṅ nyi-ma* (I am longing) for fire and for sunshine *Med.*; *bú-mo ṅa mi ₒdod* I do not wish for a girl; *raṅ-ₒdód-žen-pa* **self-love** *Glr.*; (*raṅ-*) *bzáṅ-ₒdod* **self-complacency, vanity,** *Glr.*; **to ask for, to demand,** *koṅ-ǰo ₒdód-pa-la slebs* they came in order to ask for *Koṅǰo* (in marriage) *Glr.*; **to strive for, to aspire after,** *saṅs-rgya-bar* for holiness, for being like Buddha, for Buddhaship, *Dzl.*; **to be willing, to intend;** also ironically: *ná-ₒdod-pa* one that wants to grow ill, that does not take any care of himself; **to be ready, willing,** *bsnyen-bkúr byéd-par* to take charge of the waiting on (Buddha); *ₒdód-par byéd-pa* to make willing, disposed, to persuade to it *Dzl.*; **to maintain, to assert; to suppose; to pronounce to be** (cf. *ₒťád-pa?*) *Mṅg.*, *Tar.* and elsewh. frq. — *mi ₒdód-pa* to be not willing, not liking; **to detest,** *btsógs-pas kún-gyis mi ₒdód-na* as she was detested by all on account of her sluttishness *Dzl.*; **to be angry, indignant,** *žes mi ₒdód nas* thus exclaiming indignantly *Dzl.*; *mi-ₒdód-pa*, and *ma-ₒdód-pa* adj. **not wished for, disagreeable, adverse,** *mi-ₒdód-pai las* hard drudgery; *mi-ₒdod(-lóg)-pai rluṅ* adverse wind, frq.; **ťsig mi-dód-pa zer-ḱan* W.* one that slanders.

II. sbst. *Ssk.* काम 1. **lust, desire** in general; *ₒdód-pa kun zád-de* after all desires have ceased *Dzl.*; *ₒdód-pa-rnams-la čágs-pa* to indulge one's desires or passions; in a special sense, **carnal desire, lust, vo-**

**luptuousness**, = ₒdod-čágs, frq.; meton., coitus, ₒdód-pa spyód-pa to practise it; ₒdód-pai dus ₒdébs-pa to agree upon the time for cohabiting *Tar.* — 2. *Ssk.* इच्छ, **a wish**, ₒdód-pa γsum γnáṅ-na if three wishes are granted *Dzl.*; meton. the object of desire, ₒdód-pa ťób-pa; ₒdód-pa daṅ ₒbrál-ba to be separated from the object of one's desire. — 3. **supposition** *Tar.* 45, 21. — 4. *W.* semen virile. — 5. **Kama, Cupid,** the god of love and of lust. — 6. symb. num.: 13.

**Comp.** ₒdod-ḱáms the world of sensual pleasure, the world of Brahma; ₒDod-ḱams-bdág-ma, prop. n. = Skye-dgui-bdág-mo, = Dpal-lhá-mo. — ₒdód-mḱan he that wishes, seeks, sues, **a lover, suitor**, cca., nai bú-mo ₒdód-mḱan máṅ-po ₒdug there are here many suitors of my daughter *Glr.* — ₒdod-dgu all wishes, lus ₒdod-dgúr sgyúr-ba to transform one's self at pleasure *Mil.*, *Stg.* — ₒdód-čan, ₒdod-ldán, ₒdód-pa-čan eager, desirous *Cs.* — ₒdod-čágs (राग) **passion, carnal desire, lust,** frq., ₒdod-čágs skyés-te, ₒdod-čágs-kyis γdúṅs-te; as the highest of the three **guna** (cf. γti-mug) it corresponds to सत्त्व, **virtue,** and is symbolized as cock or hen, though Tibetan readers probably never understand anything else by it than sensual indulgence. — ₒdod-ₒǰó v. ₒǰó-ba. — ₒdod-dún strong desire *Cs.* — ₒdod-dpál prop. n. **Dodpál,** a large hardware-manufactory and mint at the foot of the Potala in Lhasa. — ₒdod-brál, ₒdod-méd, free from passions. — ₒdod-(pai) yón-(tan) 'wished for goods', earthly goods and pleasures, whatever is grateful to the senses, such as ₒdód-pa lṅa, a delight to the ears, the eyes, the palate etc. — ₒdod-lóg **unchastity, lewdness, prostitution,** spyód-pa to have illicit, esp. incestuous intercourse, daṅ with. — ₒdód-sred-čan **avaricious, greedy** *Pth.*, yet cf. čags-sred-čan; both words prob. signify the same. — ₒdod-lha = ₒdod-pa 5.

འདོན་ ₒdon *Lt.*, n. of a medicine (?) dkar, dmar, skyur-ₒdon.

འདོན་པ་ ₒdón-pa, pf. bton, fut. (*Cs.*) γdon, imp. ton, *W.* *tón-če*, the vulg. word for ₒbyin-pa, vb.a. to ťón-pa, ₒbyúṅ-ba, **to cause to go out** or **to come forth,** i.e. 1. **to expel, throw out, eject,** from the house, village etc.; to take out, from a box; **to draw forth; to dig out,** metals: *záṅ-ton-sa* *W.* a copper-mine; *tón-te bór-če* *W.* **to put, set, lay, place out; to let out,** of prison *Pth.*; **to drive** or **turn away, to dismiss,** a servant, a wife etc., frq.; *ṅa ḱoi ḱa-nẹ čaṅ ma ton* *W.* I could not get or force any thing out of him; mčí-ma ₒdón-pa to shed tears *Glr.*; with skad and similar words: **to utter, to set up** (a cry), **to make one's self heard;** hence 2. **to pronounce,** yi-ge γnyis-γnyis-su ₒdón-pa to pronounce two consonants as two distinct sounds *Gram.*; to pronounce a magic formula; klóg-pa daṅ ₒdón-pa-la góms-šiṅ practising reading and pronouncing *Dzl.*; **to say, to repeat; to recite** (sacred texts) with a singing, drawling tone, like that of mendicant friars; hence in general, to perform one's devotions; žal-ₒdón-du mdzád-pa, *Tar.* 95, 11, prob. resp. = ḱa-tón byéd-pa to repeat by heart; ťúgs-la ₒdón-pa prob. to read silently. — 3. fig. **to elevate, to raise,** ḱri ťóg-tu *Pth.*, or rgyál-sar *Glr.*, to raise to the throne; mgo v. mgo-ₒdon, sub mgo compounds; γžán-gyi srog to prolong a person's life, by affording him a (scanty) subsistence *Thgy.*; *sróg-ton-ḱan(-po)* *W.* the giver of life, ζωοποιός. — 4. *ḱa tón-če* *W.* **to sharpen** a scythe **by means of a hammer.** — 5. **to edit, to publish,** books, *Tar.* 47, 17. — 6. čos mťá-ru ₒdón-pa to arrive at the end and scope of religious knowledge *Mil.* — 7. *W.* resp. **to take, to taste,** to eat or to drink, don yin-na would you like a taste of that? dón-ḱaṅ dining-room; dón-gir resp. for ta-gir; dón-rag for ǎ-rag.

འདོམ་པ་ ₒdóm-pa 1. **to come together** *Lex.*, *Lt.* — 2. for ₒdám-pa **to choose, to make a choice** *Glr.* — 3. also ₒdóms-pa, pf. γdams, ft. γdam, imp. ₒdoms, 1. **to advise,** cf. γdám-pa. 2. **to exhort,** bág-med-pa-rnams-la wicked persons, brtsón-par to give diligence *Tar.* 3. **to recommend** *Glr.*, **to bid, to command,** v. γdám-pa. — 4. *Cs.*: **importance; business, occupation** (?).

འདོམ(ས)་(པ) ˳*dóm*(*s*) (*-pa Cs.*) 1. a long-measure, **a fathom,** = 6 feet, ˳*dom-gáṅ* one fathom, *S.g.*, as the usual length of a man, = *k̔ru bži; šiṅ* ˳*dom dó* a piece of wood two fathoms long *Dzl.;* ˳*dom bčui doṅ* a well ten fathoms deep; ˳*dóm-gyis*, or ˳*dóms-su* ˳*ǰál-ba* to measure by fathoms *Cs.*; ˳*dom-gaṅ-gru-bži* 1. adj. measuring a square fathom, also a cubic fathom; 2. sbst. **a strong jail** or **dungeon.** — 2. imp. of ˳*dam-pa* **to choose.**

འདོམས ˳*doms* the pudenda, **privities,** regio pubis, ˳*doms*(*-kyi*)*-spu* the hair of that region, ˳*doms-spu* ˳*t̔óg-pa* to pluck out such hair *Cs.*; *rṅa-ma* ˳*doms óg-tu* ˳*ǰúg-pa* col. to take to one's heels; ˳*doms-stóṅ* vulg. without breeches; *sdoms-lpágs* foreskin, prepuce (?); ˳*doms - γtsáṅ* (*-ma*) *C.* a pure virgin; a nun; ˳*doms - γtsáṅ - pa* a chaste monk (if not rather *sdom* is meant); ˳*doms-rás* (also *čar - rás Cs.*) a small apron to cover the privy parts *Cs.*

འདོར་བ ˳*dór-ba*, pf. and imp. *dor* (cog. to *γtór - ba, stór-ba, byi-dór, p̔yag-dár*). 1. **to throw** or **cast away,** like *γtór-ba* and ˳*bór-ba Stg.;* esp. **to throw out, to eject,** spittle, frq.; *drí-ču* ˳*dór-ba* to make water *Glr.*; fig. *srog* ˳*dór-ba* to fling away one's life *Dzl.;* **to sweep out** or **away** *Dzl., Stg.* — 2. (opp. to *léṅ - pa, bžéd - pa*) **to decline, refuse, reject, despise,** things offered *Dzl.;* to reject, a reading, a passage *Gram.*; **to disapprove,** of an action as immoral; *blaṅ-dór,* ˳*dor-léṅ*, accepting and rejecting, deciding for or against, e.g. *dge-sdig-gi Glr.* — 3. **to subtract,** *dór-bai lhág-ma Wdk.* the remainder left after subtracting; perh. also **to divide.** — 4. *srog* ˳*dór-ba* also signifies: **to endanger life,** or **to deprive of life,** used e.g. of diseases *S.g.*; *góm-pa* ˳*dór-ba* (= ˳*bór-ba*), to pace, to step, to stride, frq.; *dmód-pa* ˳*dor-ba* v. *dmód-pa.*

འདོལ་ས ˳*dól-sa Lex.,* **fertile ground** or **soil** *Sch.*

འདྲ་བ ˳*drá-ba* 1. adj., *C.:* **ḍá-té**, **similar, equal** (which two notions gen. are not strictly distinguished from each other); ˳*drá-ba* ˳*di-dag* these equal things, for: these comparisons, *Pth.*; *kyed γnyis* ˳*drá-bar* ˳*dug*, ˳*dra - ba yin*, ˳*drao*, you two resemble each other very much; with a pleon. *mnyam*: *riṅ-t̔úṅ mnyám-la* ˳*drá-ba* equally long *Dzl.*; gen. with *daṅ* or accus., seldom with termin., in various applications: *k̔yed*(*daṅ*) ˳*drá-ba ni* your equals *Dzl.; bud-méd-du* ˳*drá-bai náṅ-na* amongst womanlike, effeminate (men), *Dzl.;* ˳*dii byin t̔sáṅs-pa daṅ* ˳*drao* his brightness is equal to (that of) Brahma *Dzl.*; *γžán-gyi dón-laaṅ ráṅ-gi* ˳*drar séms-pa* esteeming our neighbour's advantage as high as our own *S.g.; t̔ams-čád-la bu γčig-pa daṅ drao* he behaved to all as (to) an only son *Dzl.;* with a negative: *γžan yaṅ de daṅ* ˳*drá-ste γnáṅ-ba med* others shall allow it just as little as he himself *Dzl.; Saṅs-rgyás daṅ* ˳*drá-bar byá-bai p̔yir* in order to be equal to Buddha, to come up with Buddha *Dzl.*; *brtsigs-pa mi* ˳*dra skyés-pa* ˳*dra* not as if (it had been) built, but as if it had grown up spontaneously *Glr.*; *bdag* ˳*dra bud-méd blo-dmán kyaṅ* even a stupid woman like myself; *skra* ˳*drá-ba yód-dam* whether any thing like hair is still left? *Mil.; t̔én-ro* ˳*dra rnyed* he found the remnants of a carcass or something like it *Mil.*; *ro daṅ* ˳*drá-ba* as much as dead *Wdṅ.*; *mnyán-pa daṅ* ˳*drá-bai bšes-γnyén* a teacher like as a ferryman (conveying to the shores of happiness) *Thgy.*; *rtag - rtág* ˳*dra yaṅ* seemingly eternal *Mil ; skyid-skyid* ˳*dra yaṅ* even if it appears a blessing *Mil.; rúṅ-ba daṅ* ˳*drá - na* if it appears feasible *Dzl.*; *ster dgós-pa* ˳*dra* it seems I shall be obliged to give it *Glr.; da-lán k̔yod nús-pa če-čé* ˳*dra bžin byúṅ - ste* as your strength this time at least seems to be rather great *Mil.; k̔yed slu-slú* ˳*dra* you might easily be ensnared *Mil.; mi-*˳*drá-ba* **unequal, unlike, different,** *sṅon-čád daṅ mi* ˳*drá-bar* quite otherwise than formerly *Dzl.*; *čós-pa mi* ˳*drá-bar* not like, not befitting, a priest *Mil.*; **various, several,** **k̔a-zé mi-ḍá-wa** *C.* several dishes; ˳*di-*˳*dra-ba, dé-*˳*dra-ba* **such**; *dé-dras*, (**dhéṅ-dẹ** *C.* vulg.) **so, thus**; *či-*˳*dra-ba, ǰi-*˳*dra-ba* **of what kind** (qualis), *či-*˳*dra čig légs-*

*par ston dgos* you must tell me minutely how she looks, what kind of appearance she has *Glr.*; *p̒ug ci ˳dra cig ˳oṅ* what will be the upshot? where is this to end? *Glr.*; *ṅa ji-˳dra-bar de bžin ˳gyur* he becomes just what I am *Stg.*; **ghán-de** *C.* col. **how?** *˳dra-˳dra* (*W.* **d̤án-d̤a**) very frq. for *˳drá-ba*, e.g. *ša-dkár-gyi ɣyu ˳drá-˳dra-la tig-rtse-zer* something similar to the substance of tin is called zinc; *˳dra mi ˳dra* like and unlike; **equality, likeness, similarity,** *˳dra mi ˳dra ltá-ba* to examine the likeness *Glr.* — 2. sbst. 1. **resemblance, likeness,** v. *˳dógs-pa* 2. — 2. **form, shape, appearance, phase.** *Thg.*

འདྲངས་ *˳draṅs* v. *˳graṅs.*

འདྲད་ *˳drad* v. *˳brad.*

འདྲན་ *˳dran* v. *˳gran.*

འདྲལ་བ་ *˳drál-ba*, pf. *dral* (cf. *rál-ba* and *hrál-ba*), **to tear to pieces, to rend asunder;** also **to pull down,** a house; **to rip up, to cut open,** an animal.

འདྲི་བ་ *˳drí-ba*, pf. and imp. *˳dris*, 1. **to ask,** ... *la*, *W. nas*, a person; with accus. **to enquire after** or **about** a thing; *grós-˳dri-sa* a place for asking advice, **oracle** *Glr.*; *blá-ma ˳drí-ba* to inquire after one's Lama *Mil.*; *p̒a-mái ɣtam* after one's parents *Dzl.*; *˳drí-bai ts̒ig* **interrogative pronoun,** e.g. *ci Gram.*; v. also *dri-ba*. — 2. inst. of *˳bri-ba*.

འདྲིང་བ་ *˳driṅ-ba Glr.* fol. 57, 12? another reading: *ldiṅ-ba.*

འདྲིད་པ་ *˳drid-pa* for *˳brid-pa.*

འདྲིམ་པ་ *˳drim-pa* for *˳brim-pa.*

འདྲིལ་བ་ *˳dril-ba*, pf. *dril*, I. vb. n., cf. *˳gril-ba* and *hril-ba*, 1. **to be turned, rolled round** or **twisted into** a thing, *od-zér-gyi gáṅ-bur* to be wrapped into a covering of light *Glr.*; **to gather, to flow together,** as *p̒ó-bai bád-kan*, the gastric phlegm *Med.*; fig.: *blo-séms ɣcig-tu ˳dril-te* whilst our minds were flowing together *Glr.*; *yúl-pa-rnams k̒á-˳dril-te ṅó-log-pa* **a conspiracy** *Schr.* — 2. **to roll down,** *ri-bo ṅos-la* the slope of a hill *Thgy.* — 3. **to fall, to fall down** *W.*

II. vb. a., cf. *sgril-ba*, **to wrap up,** *rás-kyis* in a kandkerchief *Glr.*, *dar sna lṅas* in five sorts of silk *Glr.*; *zaṅs-kyis* (covered or sheathed) with copper *Mil.*; **to heap together, to pile up,** *mé-tog p̒úṅ-por dril* the blossoms are aggregated, heaped together in a panicle *Wdṅ.*; *dril-bas* **in short, to sum up all, in summa** *Glr.* — *l̤ags ˳dril-ba Sch.*: to play with the tongue, moving it to and fro.

འདྲིས་པ་ *˳dris-pa* **to be accustomed to, to be acquainted with,** gen. with *daṅ*, *Glr.* and col.; rarely with accus.: *ɣnyen ji tsam ˳dris bžin* the more friends you get familiar with; *mig ˳dris c̒és-na* if persons constantly see one another, get perfectly used to one another, *Mil.*; mostly adj. (= *góms-pa*) **accustomed, used,** *mi* or *k̒áṅ-pa daṅ*, to men, to one's house; also *dris-pa* used absol. = **tame** *W.*; *dris-pa mi* an acquaintance, a sympathizing friend, an assistant *Thgy.*; *sṅar-dris-kyi mi* an old acquaintance, an old crony *Thgr.* A derivation of *dris-pa* from *˳drid-pa*, *˳brid-pa*, to deceive, to bait, to decoy, and hence to tame, was suggested by some Tibetans, but is after all scarcely to be authenticated.

འདྲུ་བ་ *˳drú-ba* v. *˳brú-ba.*

འདྲུགས་པ་ *˳drúgs-pa* **to fall into small pieces, to crumble** (away) *Sch.*

འདྲུད་པ་ *˳drúd-pa*, pf. and imp. *drud* (*˳drus?*), rarely *˳brúd-pa*, 1. **to rub,** *lus* the body; **to file, to rasp,** *šiṅ* wood, *Lex.*; **to rub off, to scour,** **bé-ma daṅ W.*; **to polish, to smooth, to plane,** *p̒ag-ste* with a plane *W.*; **to grind, to powder, to pulverize** (?). — 2. **to drag, to draw** or **pull along** on the ground, by a rope, *ro sá-la* a dead body on the ground (*ma-˳drús-par* without slipping (?) *Med.*) — 3. **d̤úd-de gyur toṅ** *W.* move, or push it a little aside; *d̤ud cád-ce W.* to cut off obliquely (?).

འདྲུབ་པ་ *˳drúb-pa*, pf. and imp. *drub* (*s*) 1. **to sew** *Sch.*, so perh. *Dzl.* ༢༢༠, 11.

— 2. **to embroider** *C.* — 3. **to heal**, *rma* wounds *S.g.* — *ťsem-drúb* needle-work *Sch.*

འདྲུལ་བ་ *ₒdrúl-ba*, pf. *drul*, gen. *rul* (q.v), **to become putrid, to rot, to putrefy**, *drúl-bar gyúr-ba* id.; *ₒdrúl-bar byéd-pa* to cause to be decomposed *Med.*; *rten-ₒdrúl* prob.: putrefied substances, *bšaṅ-γčis ₒbyin-par-byed* are removed with the faeces *Med.*

འདྲེ་ *ₒdre*, also *lhá-ₒdre*, *W.* **lán-ḍe**, **goblin, gnome, imp, demon, evil spirit, devil,** col. the most frq. word for such beings; quite in a general sense: *klu-γnyán-la sógs-pai lha-ₒdre-rnams; byá-ₒdre, ₒdre-rgód Lt.* prob. two particular species of demons; *zá-ₒdre* is said to be a word for 'owl'; *ₒdres ₒk̔yér-ba* to be carried off by goblins *Ma.*; *ₒdres-γnód, ₒdrei γnód-pa* mischief done by evil spirits; *ₒdre ₒjúg-pa* the entering of evil spirits, the state of possession; *ₒdré-žugs-pa* (*W.* *-*k̔an**) one possessed by a devil, a demoniac; *skród-pa* to cast out, *ₒdúl-ba* to subdue (devils).

**Comp.** *ₒdre-ₒjigs-šiṅ = gu-gul-šiṅ*, 'devil's fear', a resinous wood, by the burning of which goblins are smoked out. — *ₒdre-paṅ-k̔a* n. of the fruit of *sgóṅ-ťog Wdṅ.* — **ḍe-p̔u* (or *bu?*)-*ťsúb** *W.* **whirlwind, water-spout.** — *ₒdré-p̔o* a male devil, *ₒdré-mo* a female d., *ₒdré-bu* a young d., an imp *Cs.* — *ₒdre-me-bud* ignis fatuus, will-o'the wisp, Jack with the lantern *Schr.* — *ₒdre-dmág* a goblin host. — *ₒdre-lág* the left hand, the left side of the body being supposed to belong to the evil spirits *C.* — *ₒdré-šig* **'devil's louse', bed-bug** *C.* — *ₒdre-srin* goblins and Rakshasas, demons in general, frq.

འདྲེ་བ་ *ₒdré-ba* I. pf. and imp. *ₒdres*, prop. vb. n. to *bsré-ba*, 1. **to be mixed with,** *de γnyis ₒdrés-(-na) Lt.* if the two are mixed with each other; *p̔yogs-γčig-tu ₒdres* mixed together, miscellaneous *Lex.*; *ₒdres-mťsáms* (*ₒťsams Tar.*) the 'limit of mixing', *rgyá-mťso daṅ gáṅ-gā ₒdrés-mťsáms* the influx of the Ganga into the sea *Tar.* 178, 9; *ťsig γžaṅ ma ₒdrés-par* without mingling other talk with (the conversation); *k̔a daṅ snyiṅ ma ₒdres* a man with whom word and sentiment differ, **a hypocrite;** *čos daṅ čos ma yín-pa ₒdres* right and wrong were mixed together; in an absol. sense: *spyód-pa ₒdrés-te mú-stegs-par gyúr-to* his course of life degenerated, and he became a Brahmanist *Pth.*; *dúd-ₒgro ₒdrés-pa* an animal of a mixed race, **half-breed, mongrel;** *ma ₒdrés-par* without any confounding or mixing together, sharply discriminating *Mil.*; *ma-ₒdrés-pa* prob. **pure, unadulterated.** — 2. **to interfere, to meddle with,** **de lé-ka daṅ ma ḍe** *W.* do not meddle with that; **to have intercourse with, to engage in,** *B.* and col.; *ráṅ-sems blá-ma ₒdrés-pas bde* through your, the Lama's, intercourse with my soul, in your society, I am happy *Mil*; *γtam ₒdré-ba* id.

II. erron. for *ₒgré-ba Pth.*

འདྲེག་པ་ *ₒdrég-pa* v. *ₒbrég-pa.*

འདྲེགས་ *ₒdreγs* v. *drég-pa.*

འདྲེད་པ་ *ₒdréd-pa* **to slide, glide, slip,** **ḍéd-de gyel** *W.*, **ḍéd-tag(?) šór-ne gyel** *C.* he slipped and fell.

འདྲེན་པ་ *ₒdrén-pa*, pf. *draṅ(s)*, fut. *draṅ*, imp. *droṅ(s)*, 1. **to draw, drag, pull,** a carriage *Glr.*; a person by his arm *Dzl.*; *drág-tu* violently *Dzl.*; **to draw tight,** a rope *Dzl.*; **to draw from, to pull out,** an arrow out of a wound *Glr.*; **to press** or **squeeze out,** matter, pus, *Med.*; **to tear out,** *γsóṅ-poi rgyú-ma* the intestines of a living person; fig. *k̔a-čig ťser-sṅón-gyi rigs-suaṅ ₒdren* some reckon it (lit. **draw** it) to the species of Meconopsis *Wdṅ.*; **to cause, to effect,** *bde-čén* felicity *Thgy.*, *skyúg-pa* vomiting *Tar.* — 2. **to conduct,** water (*W.* **rán-če**); **to lead, to guide;** with or without *sna*, *lam ₒdrén-pa* to direct a person in his way; also sbst. **guide,** *ₒdren-méd* without a guide, without a king *Dzl.*; esp. to lead to happiness, felicity, frq.; opp. to *lóg-ₒdren-pa* q.v.; *yúl-du-dmag* to lead an army into a country, to wage war against it, frq. — 3. **to cite, to quote,** *luṅ* a religious authority *Cs.* — 4. **to invite,** a guest; **to call, to go to meet; to cause to appear, to conjure up,** a ghost, a deity; resp. *spyán-ₒdren-pa, γdán-ₒdren-*

pa; also for **to fetch, to go for,** if the object is of a sacred character, e.g. relics; *spyan ma dráṅs-par ༎gró-ba* to go uninvited *Cs.* — 5. **to place before one, to serve up,** dishes, meals; **to pour out,** beer, wine etc., ccdpar., frq.; resp. with *žál-du Pth.*; **to taste,** to eat or drink what has been offered, resp. *W.* (cf. *mčód-pa, γsól-ba*). — 6. **to count, to number,** esp. with *re*, or *re-ré-nas*, separately, one by one, *Glr.*, *Mil.*; **to enumerate,** *ma draṅs* ... are here not enumerated *Wdṅ.*; c. termin. **to count for, to consider, to look upon as,** *dpé-ru* as a parable, as not existing *Mil.* — 7. *W.* in a general sense: **to convey, to remove,** **zá-če túr-maṅ daṅ den** food is conveyed by a spoon, **ka kyem daṅ den** snow is removed by a shovel. — 8. further: *rkaṅ* (resp. *žabs*) *༎drén-pa* **to insult, to scoff, to deride** *Thgy.*, *C.* — *me ༎drén-pa* the blazing, flaring of a flame *Sch.* — *mgo-༎dren* v. *mgo*, comp.

**འདྲེན་མ, འདྲེས་མ** *༎drén-ma, ༎drés-ma,* **mixture, medley,** e.g. in border-districts a mixed dialect, a mixed religion; a mixed colour, e.g. gray.

**འདྲོངས་པ** *༎dróṅs-pa* = *༎drén-pa*, esp. in conjunction with *spyan*: *spyán-༎droṅs-sam ltos šig*; *mi ༎droṅs-na* try whether you can invite him (whether he will come); if not, then ... *Mil.*, also *Mil. nt.*

**འདྲོག་པ** *༎dróg-pa* 1. **to wince, shrink, quiver, start,** from fear; **to shy,** of horses; *༎dróg-čan* **shy, skittish, easily frightened** *W.* 2. — *༎drog-slóṅ-ba Sch.*: **to take by surprise, to deceive by cunning, to outwit;** *blo-༎dróg Lex.* w.e.

**འདྲོབ་སྐྱོང** *༎drob-skyóṅ Sch.*: 'the keeper of light' (?).

**རྡང** *rdaṅ* v. *γdaṅ.*

**རྡབ་པ** *rdáb-pa* v. *rdéb-pa.*

**རྡར་བ** *rdár-ba* v. *bdár-ba.*

**རྡལ་བ** *rdál-ba*, pf. and fut. *brdal*, imp. *rdol*, also *γdál-ba, bdál-ba*, 1. **to spread,** sand, stones, manure, esp. if done by means of a stick, rake, shovel etc.; **to extend,** a canopy *Pth.*; **to cover,** *rdziṅ-gi žabs byé-mas*, the bottom of a pond with sand *Dzl.*; fig. *dam-čos taṅ-mar bdál-ba-la* now when holy religion lies before you as if it were spread out in a plain, i.e. when it is accessible to all, *Mil.*; *kyab-γdál* or *rdál* spreading far and wide, all-embracing, *sems nám-mka ltá-bu, čós-kyi kloṅ, čos-dbyiṅs*, and the like; *groṅ-rdál* v. sub *groṅ.* — 2. *sos-γdál Lex.* w.e.; *Sch.*: **slowly, not in a hurry.**

**རྡིག** *rdig* = *yo-byád*? *náṅ-gi rdig kun Mil.* seems to mean: all the utensils and furniture of a house.

**རྡིགས་པ** *rdígs-pa* **to beat** *Sch.*, prob. = *rdég-pa.*

**རྡིབ་པ** *rdíb-pa*, pf. *rdibs*, vb. n. to *rtíb-pa*, **to fall to pieces, to give way, to break down,** of a roof, rock, tree, the heavens. — 2. **to get dinted,** battered, like tin-vessels by a blow or knock, *C.*, *W.*

**རྡུ་བ** *rdú-ba Cs.* **thistle,** not generally known, but perh. the same as *ma-rdu.*

**རྡུག་པ** *rdúg-pa*, pf. *brdugs*, fut. *brdug*, 1. **to conquer, to vanquish** (?), *klú-rnams-kyis lha-ma-yin túb-čiṅ rdúg-par byás-te* the Nagas having overcome and vanquished the Asuras *Stg.*; hence prob. **to annihilate, destroy, undo,** *der tabs brdugs-pas* as all resources were destroyed *Pth.* — 2. **to strike against, to stumble at,** *C.* (cf. *túg-pa* II, 3); *togs-rdug* (or *brtug*)-*méd-pa*, v. *tógs-pa*, without impediment.

**རྡུང** *rduṅ*, **a small mound, hillock,** *Ld.*

**རྡུང་བ** *rdúṅ-ba*, pf. *brduṅs*, fut. *brduṅ*, imp. (*b*)*rduṅ*(*s*), also *bdúṅ-ba*, **to beat, to strike,** a person, a drum etc.; **to cudgel, to drub,** also *rdúṅ-༎tsog-pa* (*Sch.* -*༎tsob-pa*?); **to beat with a hammer, to hammer,** *lčags*; *rdúṅ-du rúṅ-ba* malleable, ductile; **to knock,** *sgo* at a door; **to break to pieces, to smash,** *rdo-yis* with a stone (the sacrificial vessels) *Glr.*; **to beat out,** *brá-bo* buckwheat, with a stick; hence to beat out with a flail, **to thrash; to pound, to bray;** *stéṅ-rduṅ* a pestle *Ld.* — *bro rdúṅ-ba* **to dance.** — *γžu rdúṅ-ba* **to bend the bow,** v. *Schf.* on *Dzl.* ༢༥༢, 11. — *rdúṅ-mkan* **a fighter, bully;** of horses:

**a kicker**; of oxen, **butting.** — *rduṅ-γtág Lex.* w.e., prob. a drubbing, a sound thrashing; *rduṅ-γtag byuṅ* I have got a drubbing.

རྡུམ་པོ *rdúm-po Cs.* **maimed, mutilated,** *rdúm-po byéd-pa* **to mutilate**, *lag-rdum* a maimed hand, *rkaṅ-rdúm* a maimed foot, *rwa-rdúm* a mutilated horn; having a maimed hand, foot etc. *Mil.*

རྡུལ་ *rdul* **dust,** not so much as a deposited mass, but rather as particles floating in the air, **motes, atoms**; thus esp. *rdul-ṗrán, rdul-ṗrá-mo, rdul-ṗra-ráb, nyi-zér-gyi rdul*, yet less to express minuteness than infinite number; **atom**, in a philosophical sense, *ḱu-ḱrág-gi rdul ťams-čád* all the atoms of the procreative fluid *Wdṅ.*; **monad,** *rdul-ṗra-rab-ča-med*, acc. to *Was.* (279); *rdul ˳tul, ldaṅ*, dust arises *Dzl.*; *rdul mi túl-bar* (or *ma ldáṅ-bar*) *byéd-pa* to lay the dust *Dzl.*; *sprúg-pa, W.* **śrúg-če**, to shake off, to beat out; *rdúl-du rlóg-pa* (in this case also *ťál-bar rlóg-pa*) to crush or pound a thing, until it is reduced to powder *Lex.*; *glaṅ-rdúl Cs.*: 'a mote in the dung of an ox'(?), *Sch.*: 'a small particle of cow-dung.' — *rdo-rǰei rdul* diamond-powder(?) *Lex.*; *sól-bai rdul* coal-dust.

**Comp.** *rdúl-čan* **dusty.** — *rdul-ṗyágs* **dusting-whisk, dusting-brush** *Sch.* — *rdul-ťsub* **a** whirling cloud of dust. — *rdul-ťsón* coloured stone-dust, employed in certain ceremonies, for making figures drawn in the sand more visible *Mil. nt.* — *rdul-γzán* a blouse(?), travelling-cloak against the dust, *Wdk. fol.* 144 a Lha wears such a garment.

རྡུལ་པོ་ *rdúl-po*, prob. erron. for *rtúl-po Dzl.* ༢༣༥, 2.

རྡེ་ *rde* in compounds for *rdeu.*

རྡེ་བ་ད་རུ་ *rde-ba-da-ru Wdṅ.*, tibetanized from देवदारु, **cedar.**

རྡེག(ས)་པ་ *rdég(s)-pa*, pf. *(b)rdegs*, fut. *brdeg*, imp. *(b)rdeg(s)*, **to beat, strike, smite,** c. accus., or (less corr.) c. dat., chiefly in *B.*, *rdég-čiṅ spyód-pa*, verberando concumbere, to compel a wife by blows to fulfil the conjugal duty *Thgy.*; *mé-loṅ-la brdég-čiṅ* beating the looking-glass in anger *Glr.*; *rdeg-˳ťsóg-gi sdug-bsṅál* the ill-fortune of getting a beating *Thgy.*; **to push, thrust, knock, kick,** *ṗul-rdég* a blow with the fist, *byéd-pa* to give one *Mil.*; *rdeg-čós Lex.* w.e., *Sch.* a dance; *rdeg-čós-pa* to dance, so perh. *Thgy.*, if *brdog-čós-pa* is not a better reading, *glo-rdég(-tu)* = *glo-búr-du*, **suddenly.**

རྡེབ་པ་ *rdéb-pa*, sometimes for *sdéb-pa.*

རྡེབ(ས)་པ་ *rdéb(s)-pa*, prob. the original form, but of rare occurrence, for *rdáb-pa*, pf. *brdabs*, fut. *brdab*, 1. **to throw down with a clap,** to clap the coat-tail on the ground *Glr.*; with a clashing sound, a potsherd *Tar.*; **to fling or knock down,** a person *Mil.*; *lus sá-la* **to prostrate one's self,** very frq.; *rtas* (to be thrown) by the horse *Sch.*; **ḱa dáb-pa** 1. *C.* **to fall upon one's face.** 2. *W.* **to smack with the tongue,** also of the snapping of a spring, of the clapping down of a lid or the cover of a book; **ká-lpags déb-pa* W.* to smack with the lips (in eating). — 2. **to throw to and fro, to toss about,** *mgó-bo rdébs-śiṅ ˳dré-ldog-pa* to turn one's head this way and that way *Pth.* — 3. **to stumble** *Sch.*, so perh. *Lt.* fol. 196, 6; *čal rdáb-pa Lex.*, *rdáb-čal-ba Sch.* to slip and stumble. — 4. **to kill, to slaughter** *Bal.* — 5. **deb-śóg śé-pa, táṅ-wa* C.*, **ur deb táṅ-če* W.*, **to talk big, to exaggerate.**

རྡེའུ་, རྡེ་, རྡེལ་པོ་ *rdeu, rde, rdél-po*, dimin. of *rdo*, 1. **a little stone, pebble,** *rdeu bskúr-ba bžin* like a little stone thrown on the ground *Glr.* — 2. **the stone,** calculus, in the bladder or the kidneys, *ṗo-rdé* calculus in males, *mo-rdé* in females; *rdeu čágs-pa* the concrescence of a calculus, *rdeu ˳dón-pa* the removing it *Cs.* — *rdel-dkár* a white pebble, *rdel-ḱrá* a coloured pebble *Cs.* — *rde-˳grám* ('the spreading of little-stones') the counting with pebbles *Cs.* — *rde-γžál* a pavement of pebbles. — 3. **a musket-ball** *C.*, *rdeu-pár* a bullet-mould; a bullet-founder *C.*

རྡོ་ *rdo B., C., rdó-ba* in *W.* the usual form, in more recent lit. frq., 1. **stone.** — 2. **weight,** for weighing things by a balance, col.; *rdoi* of stone, *rdoi ťúb-pa* a stone Buddha *Glr.*; *rdo skyéd-pa, skyá-ba,* to carry or drag stones to a place; **do-čág čóg-pa** *C.* a ceremony observed in making a contract, by breaking a stone and using the fractured side as a seal, cf. *mdzúg-gu ₒtúd-pa*; *rdo-bčál btín-ba Sch.*: 'stones arranged according to their species'; **do-rúb-la táṅ-če, do-rúb táṅ-te sád-če** *W.* to pelt, beat, or kill with stones, **to stone;** *rdo rus ťug* to the last extremity *Sch.*; *dṅúl-rdo* a stone containing silver, silver-ore *Lex.*; *sprin-rdo* a sort of marble *Cs.*; *sbrá-rdo Sch.*, (perh. *spra-rdo?*) asbestus; *mé-rdo* fire-stone, flint; *rmaṅ-rdo* foundation-stone; *zúr-rdo* corner-stone; *ɣsér-rdo* a stone containing gold, gold-ore *Cs.*

**Comp.** *rdo-klád* a stone resembling a sheep's brain, and used as a remedy for diseases of the brain *S.g.* — *rdo dkár Cs.* a white stone; *Sch.* **alabaster.** — *rdo-skrán* a kind of steatite or soap-stone. — *rdo-ǩá* a vein in a stone. — *rdo-ǩóg* a stone pot. — *rdo-mǩris* gall-stone (?) *S.g.* — *rdo-rgyúd* various kinds of soft stone, as serpentine, soap-stone, chalk. — *rdo-rgyús S.g.? *do-čág* C.* oath taken in the above mentioned ceremony. — *rdo-čál Sik.* = *rdo-ɣžál.* — *rdo-čár* a shower of stones; **hail** *Schr.* — *rdo-ₒčáṅ, W. *dom-čáṅ**, a stone of such a size as may be grasped by the hand. — *rdo-mnyen Cs.* = *ka-ma-ru* a soft kind of stone, alabaster. — *rdo-snyiṅ* jasper *Sch.* — *rdo-ťál Cs.* stone-ashes, **calcined stone;** *Sch.* **quicklime,** *Schf. Tar.* 103, 14: **chalk;** *rdo-ťál byúgs-pa* to rough-cast, to plaster. — *rdo-drég S.g.? Sch.* dirt on stones. — *rdo-snúm* **rock-oil, petroleum** *Schr.* — **do-pé** *W.* stone-dust, small particles or grains of stone. — *rdo búṅ-ba* a shining black stone *Cs.* — *rdó-bos* (perh. *do-bos*) **a large hammer, mallet** *Ld.* — *do-dbyúg* **a sling-stone** *S.g.* — *rdo-ₒbum* a sacred heap of stones, **a mani.** — *rdo-sbóm* large, heavy stones *Sch.* — *rdo-rtsig* stone-wall — *rdo-tsád* (= *yám-bu, rta-rmig-ma Cs.*) **a bar of silver-bullion,** of about 156½ tolas (4 pounds) in weight, the common medium of barter in Central Asia. — *rdo-žun Lt.* = *brag-žun* **bitumen, mineral pitch** (?) — *rdo-žó* **lime,** both quick lime and slaked lime *C.* — *rdo-ɣžál* **a stone-pavement.** — *rdo-ɣžógs* a cut or wrought stone *Cs.* — *rdo-zám* a stone-bridge; a rock-bridge, natural bridge formed by overhanging rocks. — *rdo-riṅ(s)* a stone pillar, obelisk, as a land-mark, monument, or an ornament of buildings *Glr.* — *rdo-ríl* a globular stone *Pth.* — *rdo-léb* a stone slab to sit upon; or to write on etc. — *rdo-sraṅ* a stone weight *Cs.* — *rdo-srín Glr.* 50, 10, evidently a corruption of *dar-srín.*

རྡོ་རྗེ *rdó-rje*, gen. **dór-je** *W.* **dór-že**, वज्र, (*Zam.* also उपल) 1. **precious, stone, jewel,** esp. **diamond,** more precisely: *rdó-rje pa-lám*; *rdo-rjei ɣtun* a knocker made of precious stones *Dzl.*; *rdó-rjei sku* an adamantine body *Pth.*; *rdó-rjei ťse* an adamantine life *Glr.*; *zag-med-rdó-rje-lta-bui ťsé-la mňa brnyéd-pas Pth.* as much as immortality; *rdó-rjei ₒjim-pa*, or *rin-po-čei ₒjim-pa Glr.* mortar composed of pulverized precious stones and water, and considered a cement of marvelous properties. — 2. **thunderbolt,** originally the weapon of Indra, with the northern Buddhists the ritual sceptre of the priests (v. *Köpp.* II, 271; *Was.* 193), held by them during their prayers in their hands and moved about in various directions; symbol of hardness and durability, also of power; source of many phantastic ideas and practices; frq. forming part of names. — 3. euphem. for *po-rtágs C.*

**Comp.** *rdo-rje-gliṅ* seems to be the popular spelling of the Sanitarium in British Sikkim, which by the English generally is written Darjeeling. (Here Csoma died, and Dr. Hooker staid here for some time.) Acc. to several titles of books in the Petersb. list of manuscripts, it ought properly to be spelled *dar-rgyas-gliṅ.* — *rdo-rje-rgya-grám* v. *rgya* comp. — *rdo-rje-ɣčód-pa*, वज्रच्छेदिका, title of a religious book most extensively used among Buddhists; *Was.* (145), *Burn.* I, 465. — *rdo-rje-ₒčáṅ*, वज्रपाणि, less frq. *ₒdzin*,

ད

॰धर, also *lág-na*, or *ṕyág-na-rdo-rje*, and abbreviated *lag-*, or *ṕyag-rdór*, **holder of the sceptre**, originally the Indra of the Brahmans; in Buddhism, in the first place, the Dhyani Bodhisatva of the Dhyani Buddha Aksobhya, and secondly a terrifying deity, the guardian of the mystical doctrine (*Was.* frq.), hence confounded with the *čos-skyoṅ-bži*, as well as with *ku-be-ra*, prince of the *γnod-sbyin*, and special deity of Milaraspa; v. *Köpp.* and *Schl.* — *rdo-rje-γdán*, वज्रासन, prop. the diamond seat or throne of Buddha at Gaya, *Köpp.* I, 93, and hence also proper name applied to that town, frq. — *rdo-rje-ṕa-lám* diamond v. above. — *rdo-rje-ṕág-mo*, वज्रवाराहि or भद्रोाहि (*Wts.* 136) 'diamond-sow', a goddess of later Buddhism, frq. worshipped (also in *Lh.*, where she has a sanctuary at Markula near Triloknath), and incarnated as abbess in a nunnery, situated on an island of the lake Pal-te, v. Georgi *Alph. Tib.*, *Wts.* 135. — *rdo-rje-ṕúr-pa Glr.* an instrument the upper part of which is a dorje and the lower a purpa. — *rdo-rje-légs-pa*, abbrev. **dor-lág**, a local deity in *Lh.*, originally an honest village black-smith. — *rdo-rje-sems-dpa*, वज्रसत्त्व. gen. = *rdo-rje-ₒčáṅ* (*Was.* 188), sometimes differing from it, v. *Schl.* p. 50; also = *mi-skyód-pa*, Aksobhya; also *mi-skyoṅ-rdó-rje Glr.* Respecting the word *rdo-rje* cf. *Burn.* I, 526.

རྡོ་ར་ *rdo-ra*, or *rto-ra* **circle of dancers** *W.*

རྡོག་ *rdog C.* **root**, **dog dhaṅ ló-ma** root and leaves; **lab-dog** radish-root; yet cf. *rdóg-po.*

རྡོག་པ་ *rdóg-pa* **step, footstep; kick,** *rdóg-pa ₒbór-ba* **to step, to pace, to walk** *Cs.*; *rdóg-sgra* the sound of steps, the clattering of hoofs; *rdog-stán* a straw-mat for cleaning one's shoes *C.*; *rdóg-pai ₒóg-tu ₒjúg-pa Dzl.* ༢༥༡, 13 (*Ms.*; *Sch.*: *rdóg-pai žábs-su?*) to prostrate, to throw under one's feet; *rdóg-pas rdúṅ-ba Sch.*, *ₒṕúl-ba Sch.*, *snón-pa*, *mnán-pa Sch.*, *rdog-ṕúl rgyáb-pa Pth.*, **dog-tó ṕúl-wa* C.*, **dog-čóṅ gyab-če* W.* to strike with the foot, to apply a good kick, to stamp the ground; *rdog-bstád byéd-pa* prob. id.; prop. to load, to pack on(?).

རྡོག་པོ་ *rdóg-po* (*Cs.* also *rdóg-ma*), **a grain of corn, sand, sugar; a drop of rain** *Glr.*; *sran rdog bdun* seven peas; *ₒṕreṅ-rdog* the bead of a rosary, which often consists of grains of seed; **a piece,** *rdog-γčig* (how many turnips do you want?) one *C.*

རྡོངས་པ་ *rdóṅs-pa* v. *sdóṅs-pa.*

རྡོམ་ཆང་ *rdom-čáṅ* v. *rdo-mčáṅ.*

རྡོར་ *rdor* 1. in compound words for *rdó-rje.* — 2. n. of a monastery in Tibet *Cs.* Chronolog. Table 1223 p. C. — 3. = *sdor Cs.*

རྡོལ་པ་ *rdól-pa* **a cobbler** *Cs.*, prob. = *γdól-pa.*

རྡོལ་བ་ *rdól-ba*, pf. and fut. *brdol*, vb. n. to *rtól-ba*, 1. **to come out, to break forth from, to gush forth, to issue from,** of a well of water (issuing from) *Pth.*; **to come up, to sprout, to shoot,** of seed; **so ma dol* W.* the teeth are not yet cutting; *kóṅ-nas rdól-bai glu* a song streaming forth from within *Mil.*; *mi-nad rdól-žiṅ* diseases breaking out among men *Mil.*; **to flow** or **run off,** of the water of a lake; *kloṅ rdól-ba* to come forth, to proceed from the middle or the midst of *Glr.* (the meaning of this passage is not quite clear); *rdol-γzér* an instrument for boring metals *Sch.* — 2. of vessels: **to leak, to be not tight, to have holes,** *snod žabs-brdól* a vessel with a leaky bottom *Thgy.*; also of shoes, covers, tent-cloth etc. not being watertight; **to break, to burst,** of ulcers, wounds; *glo-rdol Med.* v. *gló-ba*; *rdol-γnyán Sch.*: 'fistula; gonorrhea'. — 3. **to rave, to delirate; to be sleep-walking, lunatic,** also *bla rdól(smrá)-ba Lex.*, where it is explained by *bab-čól*; *γnyid-rdól*, *mig-rdól C.* id.

རྡོས་པ་ *rdós-pa* 1. sbst., *Cs.* = *γdos*; *lus rdos-čé Lex.* w.e. — 2. vb. n. *Sch.*: **'to break, burst, flow out,** *dbú-ba*, or *lbú-ba* the bursting of a bubble'.

ལྡ་་ *lda . . . Ld.* frq. for *kla . . .*, *gla . . .*, *zla . . .*

ལྡ་གུ་ *ldá-gu* **discourse, speech, conversation;** *W.*: **ldá-gu táṅ-če** **to speak;** **ldá-gu šé-če med** one cannot understand what is spoken or said; *ldá-gu-čan* **talkative** *Cs.*

ལྡ་མན་ *lda-mán*, *Ld.-Glr. dha-mán*, **a couple of small kettle-drums,** one hanging in front, the other behind, the latter being beaten by a second person that follows the bearer.

ལྡ་ལྡི་ *lda-ldi* a kind of ornament of silk or cotton, **a fringe** or **tassel,** *dár-gyi, rin-po-čei,* esp. worn in sacrificing, *Lex.*

ལྡག་པ་ *ldág-pa,* pf. *bldags,* fut. *bldag,* imp. *ldog,* **to lick,** *k'rag* blood; *klad ldág-pa* the brain being licked up, a punishment of hell *Thgy.*; *ná-bza-la,* or *-nas* to lick a person's coat *Mil.*; **ldag-ldog** *W.* = *p'e-srul,* lit. **'a lick',** i.e. a pap prepared of *rtsám-pa* and *čaṅ,* licked from the fingers, or eaten with a spoon.

ལྡང་ *ldaṅ* 1. v. *ldáṅ-ba.* — 2. for *γdaṅ* **stand, frame, trestle.** — 3. *W.* **ldaṅ-ldáṅ-la kur** carry it lengthways! opp. to *p'red*; **ldaṅ-ldáṅ-la dád-če** to rock with one's chair.

ལྡང་མགོ་ *ldáṅ-mgo* **the yarn-beam** of a loom *Sch.*

ལྡང་སྒོ་སྐ་ *ldáṅ-sgo-ska. Ssk.* शरभ, *Fouc. Gyatch.* २८८; if the text is correct, it would seem preferable to connect *ri-dags* with *ldáṅ-sgo-ska,* and to render it: 'the animal Sarabha', a fabulous eight-footed creature of the snowy mountains.

ལྡང་བ་ *ldáṅ-ba,* pf. *ldaṅs* or *laṅs,* imp. *ldoṅ,* 1. vb. n. to *sláṅ-ba,* **to rise, to get up** (cf. the more frq. secondary form *láṅ-ba*), *ˌgyél-ba-las* from a fall *Wdṅ.*; *nyál-las* from a lying position *Lex.*; *stán-las* from a seat; *t'o-ráṅs* in the morning *Lt.*; *ṅó-mi-šes-pa-la* before, or in presence of a stranger; also used of the bristling of the hair, *Lt.*, of the rising of vapours, perfumes, dust, of a wind springing up; **to extend, to spread,** *dri ṅán-pa p'yogs bčur ldaṅ* an offensive smell is spreading in every quarter *Tar.*; *ˌk'rúgs-pa dbús-nas* the rebellion (spread) from the province of Ü, *Ma.*; **to break out,** *mé-ro ldaṅ* the smothered flame breaks out again; in a special sense of morbid matter that has accumulated (*γsóg-pa*) *Med.* frq., e.g. *k'a-zás žú-nas ldaṅ* during digestion the symptoms break out anew; *dgrá-ru ldáṅ-ba* to show one's self an enemy, to break out into hostilities frq.; **to arise, originate, break out,** of disease, despair, *Mil.*; also for: **to have risen, to stand,** but only in certain combinations, *ldaṅ dub byéd-pa* tired from having been standing (so long) *Lt.* — 2. *W.* **to suffice, to be sufficient, enough** (cf. *loṅ-ba*) = *ˌk'yéd-pa,* of food, clothes, money; hence *ldaṅ*: **complete, perfect, entire, whole,** **ras náṅ-ša rág-ma gos ldaṅ čig** cotton cloth with lining (sufficient) for a whole dress; **ḍú-gu gos ldaṅ nyis** woolen yarn for two complete dresses. — *ldaṅ* prob. signifies also quite through, cf. *ltaṅ* II.; *ldaṅ-tsád* occurs in medical works, and in many cases seems to imply **quantity;** *neu-ldáṅ Lex.* = *na-mnyám* of the same age (*Sch.* not corr.).

ལྡད་པ་ *ldád-pa* 1. vb. pf. and fut. *bldad,* imp. *ldod,* **to chew** *Zam., W.*; *skyug-ldád Cs.*, v. *skyug bldeg-čiṅ ldad-pa* (?) *Sch.* to chew the cud, to ruminate; *log Cs.* 1. id., 2. rumination, deliberate reflection; *Pur.*: **spá ldad-čas** to taste, to try; *Ld.*: **ḍi ldad-če** to smell at. — 2. *Ld.* for *glád-pa*

ལྡན་པ་ *ldán-pa* I. sbst., also *mdán-pa Lex.*, **cheek,** *ldán(-pai) so* cheek-tooth, molar tooth; *ldan-lčág Cs.* a blow on the cheek, a box on the ear; **dẹn-tsóg** *C.* id.; **mi dhé-la dẹ́n-tsog gyag* (or *gyab*) *soṅ, mi dhe dẹ́n-tsog-ghī máṅ-po duṅ soṅ** his ears have been soundly boxed; metaph. *grog-ldán* the cheek or side of a ravine *Mil. nt.*

II. vb. and adj. 1. originally: **to be near to, hard by,** a thing, (juxta), hence *W.* **ldán-la, ldán-du**, adv. and postp., **near to, by,** **ṅẹ-ldán-la dug** sit down by my side; **šiṅ-gi ldán-du** close by the tree; **ṅai ldán-du šog** come near to me! **gám-mi ldán-du** near the box; **tser-máṅ-ṅi ldán-la ḍúl-če** to go along the side of a hedge. — 2. in *B.* and *C.* only used with reference to possession (penes), mostly as partic. or adj., and construed like *bčás-pa*, **having, being possessed of, provided with**, = *čan* (which in *W.* is almost exclusively used in this sense). The objects may be things of any description, also physical and mental properties, so that *ldán-pa* differs in this respect from *bčás-pa* (*Tar.* 136, 14. 15); *nor daṅ ldán-pa* rich, wealthy; *sems-čan daṅ ldán-pa* with child; *bu daṅ bu-mor-ldán-pa* having children; *rig-pa daṅ ldán-pa* wise; with a negative: *nor daṅ mi ldán-pa*; *daṅ ldan-par ˳gyúr-ba* **to get, to obtain**, frq.; *ldán-du lén-pa Glr.* 101, 1 is stated to mean the same. Poetically, and forming part of certain expressions and names, without *daṅ* and *pa*, like *čan*: *nor-ldán, dga-ldán, ˳byor-ldán.* — 3. *ldán-pa* and *ldan daṅ ˳dús-pa* seem to imply: **mixed, compound** (opp. to *rkyáṅ-pa*) with regard to temper and disposition of mind *S.g.* — 4. **to add up, sum up**, *Wdk.* — 5. *W.* **gún-ka ṫsúg-pa ldan yin** it will be **enough**, it will hold out, till winter-time, prob. only a corruption of *ldáṅ-ba.* — 6. *Pur.* = *˳grig*, **regularly, properly, duly, rightly.**

ལྡན(པ)པོ *ldán(-pa)-po* one that has, that is able, a man of ability *Cs.*

ལྡནམ་ *ldán-ma* n. of a country *Ma.*

ལྡན་ཚད་ *ldan-ṫsád* equivalent to *˳dus-ṫsád Mṅg.* 35 (?).

ལྡབ་ལྡིབ་ *ldab-ldib* (*skad*) *Lex.* **silly talk, tittle-tattle.**

ལྡབ་ལྡོབ་ *ldab-ldób Lex.* w.e., *Cs.* **indolence, dullness, drowsiness**; acc. to others, **a hasty, volatile manner.**

ལྡབ་པ་ *ldáb-pa*, pf. *bldabs*, fut. *bldab*, imp. *ldob*, 1. *Cs.* **to do again, to repeat**; *skyár-ldáb Lex., Sch.*: **repeatedly, anew, afresh, again**; *nyis-ldáb Lex., Sch.*: for the second time, doubly, twice; **čú-(l)dab de saṅ čén-mo yod* W.* it is ten times as large as that, yet cf. *ltáb-pa*; **ldáb-ste zér-na* W.* saying it once more, again, in short. — 2. ? *Ld.*: **ldab zúm-te k̔yer** take a firm hold of him (or it) with your hand, and carry him (or it) away!

ལྡམ་ལྡམ་ *ldam-ldám Cs.*, *ldam-pa*, **very idle, slothful.**

ལྡམ་ལྡུམ་ *ldam-ldúm Cs.*: **'mean, pitiful, sorry, idle'.**

ལྡམ་ལྡེམ་ *ldam-ldém Ld.* **dubious, uncertain,** used of things.

ལྡར་བ་ *ldár-ba Cs.* **to be weary, tired, faint, languid**, *ldar-ldár-du ˳gyúr-ba.*

ལྡི་རི་རི་ *ldi-ri-rí* (v. *ldír-ba*) **the rolling of thunder** *Thgr.*

ལྡིག་པ་ *ldig-pa* **to fall** or **sink through** *Sch.*

ལྡིང་བ་ *ldiṅ-ba* **to be swimming, floating,** cf. *rkyál-ba*, *W.*: **čáṅ-ṅi k̔a-ṫóg-la p̔abs ldiṅ dug**, opp. to **ṫil-la ner* or *nub*;* **to be suspended, floating, soaring** (in the air), *γnám-la, nám-mk̔a-la*; *mk̔á-ldiṅ* v. *mk̔a.*

ལྡིང་ཁ་ *ldiṅ-k̔a* v. *ltiṅ-k̔a.*

ལྡིང་ཁང་ *ldiṅ-k̔aṅ* **a bower** formed by the branches of a tree, **the leafy canopy** of a dense wood *Mil.*; *šiṅ γyú-lo rgyás-pai ldiṅ-k̔aṅ* the wide shady porches of turkois-leaved trees.

ལྡིང་དཔོན་ *ldiṅ-dpon* an officer over fifty, acc. to others, over a hundred men, = *brgyá-dpon*, a sergeant, captain, distinguished by a copper button on his cap, *Hook.* II, 160. 200.; *ldiṅ-˳og Sch.*, *ldiṅ-ṫso*, the troop under this officer's command.

ལྡིང་སེ་ *ldiṅ-se*, or *ldiṅ-si Ld.*, adv. **quite, very, very much**, **ṅa ldiṅ-se k̔ams záṅ-po yod** I am quite well; **ṅa ldiṅ-se ma ˳ṫád soṅ** I was very much displeased, very vexed; perh. also **ldiṅs ṫág-pa-nas** for *γtiṅ*, cf. *líṅs-pa*, or perh. in *Ld. ldiṅ* is the form for *γtiṅ.*

ལྡིབ་པ་ *ldib-pa* 1. vb., pf. *bldib*, *Sch.* = *ldig-pa.* — 2. adj. *Cs.*: **not clear, not intelligible**, **k̔a-dib* W.* **stammering, stuttering**; *ldib-ldib* = *ldab-ldib.*

ལྡིམ་ *ldim W.* **the crash** of a falling tree, **the report** of a gun, **ldim zér-ra rag** I hear a crack.

ལྡིར་ལྡིར་ *ldir-ldír* is said to be = **di-ri-ri* C.*

ལྡིར་བ་ ldír-ba 1. also ltír-ba, **to be distended, inflated, to belly;** lto-ldír a big belly; ltó-ldir-čan big-bellied. — 2. **to rush, to roar,** of the wind W.; **to roll,** of the thunder, ˳brag ldir it thunders; ldír bžin like thunder; ldír-sgra a thundering, roaring noise; ldir-čé-ba thundering Thgr.

ལྡུ་གུ་ ldú-gu = γdú-ba, γdú-gu.

ལྡུག(ས)་པ་ ldúg(s)-pa, pf. ldugs (Lex.), blugs (usual form), fut. blug, imp. blug(s), col. blug-pa, **to pour,** snód-du; lág-ču blugs pour some water on my hands, give me water for washing; **to sprinkle,** to strew, sand Glr.; **to cast, to found,** metals. Cf. blugs and lugs.

ལྡུད་པ་ ldúd-pa, pf., fut. and imp. blud, col. blúd-pa, **to give to drink, to water,** cattle etc., with accus of the drink given, dug blúd-čiṅ mi ˳či he does not die by a poisoned draught, btúṅ-ba blud he gives (him) to drink Thgr.; túg-pa légs-par blúd-čiṅ making (another) eat plenty of soup Lt., as one also says: túg-pa ˳túṅ-ba to eat soup.

ལྡུམ་ ldum 1. **vegetables, greens,** in general. — 2. W. **lettuce, salad;** ldum-nág, a kind of lettuce Cs.; ldúm-bu 1. Cs. **plant, stalked plant.** 2. prob. for ldóm-bu Mil.; 3. C. vulgar pronunciation for sdóṅ-po. — — ldúm-ra 1. W. **kitchen-garden;** 2. **fruit-garden, orchard,** and 3. esp. **flower-garden** (better sdúm-ra); ldúm-ra-pa **gardener** Pth.

ལྡུམ་པོ་, ལྡུམ་ལྡུམ་ ldúm-po, ldum-ldúm, 1. for dúm-po Glr.; 2. Ld. for zlúm-po, **round;** Mil. also ldúm-la ˳gril-ba made round, rounded off.

ལྡུར་ལྡུར་ ldur-ldúr Lex.; Sch.: **roaring, rushing.**

ལྡེ་ lde? Lexx. miṅ(-gi)-lde w. e.; lde-ka Sch.: **'belonging together, of the same species'.**

ལྡེ་གུ་, ལྡེའུ་ lde-gu, ldeu Med. 1. Cs. **mixture, syrup** (?); 2. **ointment** Wdṅ.

ལྡེ་བ་ ldé-ba (Sch. also ˳dé-ba), pf. (b)ldes, fut. blde, imp. ldes, **to warm one's self,** c. accus., me, at the fire; nyi-ma, in the sun (not me-la).

ལྡེ་མིག་ lde-mig B. and C. (Ts. col. *de-mág* Bal. *le-mig, otherwise not in use in W.) 1. **key,** lde-čáb Glr. prob. id. — 2. **introduction, preface** Cs.

ལྡེའུ་ ldeu 1. Cs. also sdeu, a kind of **pease,** Hind. मुङ्गा — 2. v. lde-gu.

ལྡེག་པ་ ldég-pa (pf. bldeg?) **to quake, shake, tremble,** e. g. of the palace of the gods Dzl.

ལྡེང་ཀ་ ldéṅ-ka, ldiṅ-ka, v. ltéṅ-ka, **a pond.**

ལྡེབ་ ldeb 1. Sch. **leaf, sheet,** of paper; 2. = ldebs 1.

ལྡེབ་པ་ ldéb-pa 1. Cs. = ldég-pa; 2. Sch. **to bend round** or **back, to turn round, to double down.**

ལྡེབས་ ldebs 1. **side,** Lex. = ˳dabs, e.g. of a mountain Sch., the flat side of a sword or knife Cs.; rús-pai ˳búr-poi ldebs by the side of, near, the protuberance of a bone. — 2. **compass, enclosure, fence** Sch. — 3. C., W. **a large cloth,** in which a person is carried by several others, either by means of a pole, or by taking hold of the four corners. This mode of conveyance is called **Dandi** (डण्डी Hindi). — 4. in the Wdṅ. it seems to have still another signification.

ལྡེམ་ ldem 1. v. ldém-pa I. — 2. **statue, idolatrous image, idol,** standing upright, cf. ldém-pa II., C. — 3. **suspension-bridge** (?) Ld.-Glr. Schl. 17, a; v. ldém-pa III.

ལྡེམ་པ་ ldém-pa I. sbst. 1. Cs.: **'contrariety, opposition, irony',** which seems not to be quite inconsistent with the explanation given by Zam., draṅ-min, as being an intentional concealing of the true sentiment. — ldém(-po) **riddle, enigma** (cf. tsód-bya); mi-ldem, byá-ldem, bém-ldem an enigma or allegory applied to men, to birds, to inanimate beings; ldém-poi ṅag, ldém-γtam **parable, allegory;** ldem-dgóṅs Lex. = Ssk. अभिसंधि, prob.: a concealed deceitful intention, Sch.: 'a mysterious opinion'; ldem-rjód-pa Cs. to say a riddle or parable, *ldem ṭad-če* W. to propose a riddle, ldem tsód-pa Cs., čód-pa Sch., to solve a riddle. — 2. W. **a trap** (C. *púr-nyí*), *bi-ldém* mouse-trap, **wa-ldém** fox-trap, **tsúg-če** to put a trap.

II. adj. 1. (*Schr. ldém-po*) **straight, upright; tall, well-made,** *Mil.*, prob. also *Wdṅ.* — 2. partic. of III., **inconstant; unstable, variable, perishable** *Cs.*

III. vb., also *ldem-ldém-pa Sch.* **to move up and down,** striking, trembling, vibrating; *γšog-sgró ldém-pa* the clapping of wings *Mil.; ldem-ldém* **flexible, supple, elastic, pliant.**

ལྡེར *lder, Ts.* = *ldebs* I., *skyai ldér-la* **on the side** of a wall, **on a wall,** e.g. to paint, to scrawl; *rii lder.*

ལྡེར་བ *ldér-ba Cs.:* '1. **toughness, clamminess,** 2. **potter's clay**'. *lder-tso Cs.* 1. **clay,** 2. **an idol made of clay** *Mṅg.* — *ldér-sku Glr.* prob. = *ldér-tso* 2.; acc. to others: a picture on a wall. — *ldér-bzo* figures modelled of clay, **plastic work,** *ldér-bzoi lha Zam.* = *ldér-tso* 2.; *lder-bzoi-ldebs Lex.* a clay-enclosure (?) — *ldér-so Glr.* 88, 1. 2., by the context also **figure, image.**

ལྡོ *ldo* side, *Ld.* for *glo.*

ལྡོག་པ *ldóg-pa*, pf. and imp. *log*, vb. n. to *zlog-pa*, 1. **to come back, to return, to go home, to depart.** — 2. **to come again,** often with *p̔yir*, of diseases, = to relapse; in a specific religious sense v. *ₒbrás-bu bži*, frq.; *dgrar* to come forward again as an enemy, to renew the war (ni f.) *Mil.* — 3. **to change, to undergo a change**), as to colour, smell etc. *Med.*; *ₒgyúr-ldog*, and *ldog-ₒgyúr Mṅg.* **changeableness, inconstancy, fickleness.** — 4. **to turn away** (vb. n.) *las* from; *blo ldóg-pa* id *Thgy.*; *ṅo ldóg-pa* v. *lóg-pa*. The partic. as adj.: *dé-las ldóg-pai* (the thing) **opposed** to that, **contrary** to it, *Wdṅ*; *go-ldóg* id. *Lt.*; *mgoldóg Lex.?* — *Sch.* has also *ldog-p̔yé-ba* **distinguished, different,** from each other, and *ldóg-pa* **reciprocal, mutual, each separately.** Cf. *lóg-pa.*

ལྡོང་བ *ldóṅ-ba* 1. vb., pf. *ldoṅs, loṅ,* **to become blind, to be blind; to be infatuated.** — 2. adj., also *ldóṅs-pa, mdóṅs-pa,* **blind; infatuated.** Cf. *lóṅ-ba.*

ལྡོང་མོ *ldóṅ-mo*, resp. *γsol-ldóṅ*, **a small churn,** used for preparing tea, = *gur-gúr*, v. sub *ǰa.* Cf **doṅ-dús** *Ld.* **a stave;** *ldoṅ-rus?*

ལྡོང་རོས *ldoṅ-ros Cs.:* n. of a yellow earth, **bole, ochre,** used for staining the walls of houses; *ldoṅ-ros-sa Lt.*

ལྡོན་པ *ldón-pa* **to give** or **pay back, to return,** = *klón-pa, glón-pa*, esp. with *lan,* **to answer** *Dzl.*

ལྡོབ་པ *ldób-pa* **to apprehend quickly; to be witty, to be quick in repartee** *Cs.*; *ldobs-skyén Lex.*, explained by *šés-sla-ba* understanding readily?

ལྡོམ་པ *ldóm-pa? rag-ldóm-pa* is stated to be = *rag-lús-pa Ld.*

ལྡོམ་བུ *ldóm-bu*, less frq. *ldúm-bu*, often preceded by *ro-snyóms* **alms,** consisting of food; *ldóm-bu byéd-pa* to ask such alms; *ldóm-sa* alms-house, house where beggars receive food; *ldóm-bu-ba* a person living on alms, a beggar, *Mil., Pth.*

སྡང་བ *zdáṅ-ba*, pf. *sdaṅs*, I. **to be angry, wrathful,** *mi dgá-žiṅ sdáṅ-ste* growing angry, flying into a passion *Dzl.*; gen. c. *la:* **to hate, to be inimically disposed,** frq.; *sdáṅ-bai dgra* opp. to *byáms-pai γnyen*; *sdáṅ-bar séms-pai dgrá-bo* id. *Wdṅ.*; *k̔yim-mtses-kyi dgrá-sdaṅ-ba*, or *dgrá-bdo-ba* the neighbour's grudge; *sdáṅ(-bai) sems, sdáṅ-blo*, most frq. *že-sdáṅ*, **hatred, enmity, hostility, ill-will;** (cf. dug) *sdáṅ-ba t̔ams-čád ₒǰig-pa* to subdue all hostile powers; *sṅar sdáṅ-ba* the former, the old hatred *Mil.*; *sdaṅ-mig Lex.* an angry look, a scowl.

II. for *γdáṅ-ba.*

སྡང་བུ *sdáṅ-bu* v. *γdáṅ-bu.*

སྡད་པ *sdád-pa* v. *sdód-pa.*

སྡམ་པ *sdám-pa* v. *sdóm-pa.*

སྡར་མ *sdár-ma* **trembling, timorous, timid** *Dzl., Zam.*

སྡི་བ *sdi-ba*, pf. *bsdis*, v. *sdig-pa.*

སྡིག *sdig* 1. **thick** (?) *γsús-pa sdig Mṅg.* — 2. **foundation** *C.*, *rgyág-pa* to lay a foundation.

སྡིག་པ་ *sdig-pa* I. also *sdig-pa rwá-čan*, col. **rá-tse**, **scorpion,** also as sign of the zodiac; *sdig-pa dkár-po, nág-po*; *sdig-rwá*, the sting of a scorpion; *sdig-dúg* the poison of a scorpion; *sdig-ťsáṅ* a scorpion's nest; *sdig-srin* **crab, crawfish**, used both as food and medicine *Med.*, but not as designation for the respective sign of the zodiac, v. sub *kyim*; *sdig-srin-ₒbu Lt.* id.?

II. (पाप) **sin**, moral evil as a power, *sdig-pa-la yid-čes-pa Dzl.* ༢༥༣, 11 to believe in sin as such; *ₒjóms-pa* to conquer sin, as something hostile to man *Dom.*, and so meton. = sinners, adversaries; sometimes perh. for **sinfulness**, sinful state, but gen. in a concrete sense: **offence, trespass,** in thought, word, or deed, *ka-na-ma-ťó-bai sdig-pa*, or *nyés-pa* prob. a grievous sin *Dzl.*; also with a genit., *rgyál-poi sdig-pa sbyóṅ-ba* to wash away, to expiate, the king's sin; also *ₒdág-pa, sél-ba, W.* **čád-ce**; *ₒbyáṅ-ba* id., but more in an intransitive or passive sense; so also *ₒčégs-pa* (*γšág-pa, bšags-pa*) to confess, as acc. to Buddhist views, confession is almost tantamount to expiation of sin, cf. also *ₒgyód-pa* and *bzód-pa;* there seems to be, however, no word strictly corresponding to our 'forgiving' of sin; *sdig-(pai)-las* a sinful deed; *sdig-pa-la dgá-ba* **to love sin, to be wicked;** *sdig-(pai) grogs* a companion in vice, an associate in crime *Dzl.*; *sdig-pa byéd-pa, spyód-pa,* **to commit sin, to sin;** *sdig-pa mi byéd-pai yul* a country where no sins are committed, a pious country; *sdig-byéd, sdig-spyód* **impious, wicked; a wicked person,** *sdig-pa-rnams byás-pa* id. (more accurately: πολλὰ ἡμαρτηκώς) *Stg.*; *sdig-čan* id. (*sdig-pa-čan* seems not to be in use); *sdig-sgrib* the filth, the contamination of sin, *sdig-sgrib ťams-čád sél-ba* to cleanse from every defilement of sin *Glr.* (which the Ommanipadmehūm is sufficient to do); *sdig-po* **a sinner, a bad character,** *sdig-po če* a vile sinner *Glr., Mil.*; *rdig-to-čan*, पापीय, = *sdig-čan*, but only as epithet of Dud; *sdig-blón* a wicked officer *Glr.*

སྡིག(ས)་པ་ *sdig(s)-pa*, pf. *bsdigs*, fut. *bsdig*, imp. *sdigs*, and *sdí-ba*, pf. *bsdis*, ft. *bsdi*, 1. **to show, to point out,** *sdigs-mdzúb* a pointing finger, ... *la sdigs-mdzúb γtád-pa* to point at ... (with scorn or derision); *sdigs-mdzúb nám-mka-la γtad* pointing with the fingers toward heaven, yet not in a 'menacing' (*Cs.*) way. — 2. **to aim** *C.*, *bsdí(g)s-sa* the place that is aimed at, **aim, butt; goal** *Thgy.*; *bsdís-pai p̔yógs-su* in the direction of the aim *Thgy.* — 3. **to menace, to threaten,** *čád-pas* with punishment *Mil.* (ni f.); **dig-če p̔i-la** *Ld.* as an alarm-shot; *ₒdi-la bdág-gis ₒjigs-pa žig-gis ma bsdigs-na* if I do not threaten him with something frightful, if I do not strike him with fear, *Dzl.*; *sdigs-mo byéd-pa* to assume a menacing attitude *Mil.*, to threaten tauntingly *Thgy.*

སྡིངས་ *sdiṅs* **a cavity** or **depression,** *spáṅ-sdiṅs* a depression on a grassy plain, *ri-sdiṅs* on a mountain-ridge; the significations given by *Cs.*, 'middle part, heart, core', were not known to our men of Tashilunpo.

སྡིབ་པ་ *sdib-pa* 1. *Sch.* = *ldib-pa.* — 2. *Tar.* 8, 18 = *rtib-pa.*

སྡུག་པ་ *sdúg-pa* I. adj. **pretty, nice,** *ltá-na* to look at *Dzl.*; **tsa-ḍhi-dúg-pa** *C.* **mint,** Mentha, ἡδύοσμον; gen. with reference to a person: what is **agreeable, pleasing, dear,** to a person *Ssk.*: प्रिय, *bdág-gi bu náṅ-gi sdúg-pa-la* the most beloved of my sons *Dzl.*; *ṅai bu sdug* my dear son *Pth.*; *sdúg-par ₒdzin-pa Dzl.*, *sém-pa Dzl.* frq., *rtsí-ba Mil.*, to love, c. dat., gen. with regard to parental love; *sdúg-par ₒgyúr-ba* to become dear to a person, to be endeared to, *Dzl.; mi-sdúg-pa* **not fair, ugly, disagreeable,** of the body, of a country etc.; *mi-sdúg-pai tiṅ-ṅe-ₒdzin Tar.* 10, 11 contemplating one's self and the world as a foul, putrid carcass (v. *Tar.* Transl. 285, foot of the page); *mi-sdúg-par byéd-pa* to disfigure, pollute, profane, a temple *Dzl.; sdúg-gu* beautiful, pretty, handsome, *bud-méd sdúg-gu ťams-čad* all pretty women *Dzl.*; there is also a form for the fem. gender: *sdúg-*

*gu-ma Dzl.*; *sdú-ge-ba Cs.*: 'the state of being somewhat pleasing'(?); in a prayer occurs: *bod-báṅs sdúg-ge snyiṅ-re-rǰé* the good, poor Tibetans, just as in W. **sdug-pa-ṫsé** is used; often (but not necessarily) rather pityingly: *k̔o sdug-pa-ṫsé* the good man (will do his utmost); **ri-pa sdug-pa-ṫsé** the good fieldmouse (speedily made off); but also: **sab dug-pa-ṫsé ӑ-lu żig toṅ* W.* good sir, give me a few potatoes!

II. vb. **to be oppressed, afflicted, grieved,** like *γdúṅ-ba*, *sems lás-kyis sdúg-nas* by sorrow *Mil.*; **sem máṅ-po máṅ-po dug soṅ* C.* I was very, very sorry for it; . . . *pas sdúg-go* we are miserable, because . . . *Dzl.*; *sdúg-par ˳gyúr-ba* to become unhappy, to get into distress *Dzl.*

III. sbst., *Ssk.* दुःख, **affliction, misery, distress,** *bod sdúg-pai mgo ˳dzugs* that is the beginning of the misfortunes of Tibet *Ma.*; *ṅéd-la sdúg-pai ré-mos bab* (then) came our turn of being visited by affliction *Mil.*; more frq. *sdug*, and *sdug-bsṅál* (v. below) *sdúg-tu mi yoṅ ˳dug-gam* are you not in distress? *Mil.*; *sdug k̔ur byéd-pa* to undergo hardships (voluntarily), to bear affliction (patiently), to suffer, in an emphatical sense, *Mil.*; *sdug mi ṫeg* you cannot endure the hardships *Mil.*; **ka-dúg máṅ-po ǰhē-pa* C.* to work hard, to drudge; *skyid-sdúg* good and adverse fortune, good luck and ill luck, very frq.; *bde-sdúg* id.; *sdug-sógs byéd-pa* (the contrary to *ṫsogs-sógs byéd-pa*) to accumulate misery upon one's self *Mil.*; **dug máṅ-po táṅ-wa* C.* to plague or vex a good deal, to inflict injury, c. *la*; *γżan-sdúg-gi sdig-pa* the sin of having done evil to others *Mil.*; **dug zṓ-la táṅ-wa* C.* **to torture, to put to the rack;** *sdug ˳báb-pa* **to be in mourning** *Cs.*; *sdug srúṅ-ba* **to mourn** *Cs.*; *sdúg-čan* col. **fatiguing, worrying.** — *sdug* as adj., **unhappy, miserable,** *Pth.*, is of rare occurrence.

**Comp. and deriv.** *sdug-k̔áṅ* **a chamber of mourning,** a darkened room *Cs.* — *sdug-gós* **a mourning dress** *Cs.* — *sdug-bsṅál* the most frq. word for **misfortune, misery, suffering; also pain,** *sdug-bsṅál-gyis γdúṅs-pa Dzl.*, *sdug-bsṅál myóṅ-ba* (*W.* **ṫóṅ-če**) to be in calamity, to suffer pain; **dug-ṅál tóṅ-wa, tér-wa* C.* (**táṅ-če* W.*), to inflict pain, to grieve, to torment; *sdug-bsṅal daṅ ldán-pa*, *sdug-bsṅál-čan* **unhappy, miserable; misery, distress, affliction;** **dug-ṅál ǰhē-pa* C.* to lament, wail, moan; *sdug-bsṅál-du ˳gyúr-ba* to become sorrowful or melancholy; **ṅá-la ná-ga-ri ma šés-pę dug-ṅál yod* Ld.* I regret my not knowing Sanskrit; *sdug-bsṅál-ba* (vb.) **to be unhappy,** (sbst.) **the state of unhappiness,** *Thgy.*; *sdug-bsṅál-bai skad* lamentable, doleful cries. — *sdug-mṫúg C.* accumulating calamity. — *sdug-˳dré* a demon *Sch.* — **dúg-pò* C.* **wretched** (road), **savage** (dog), **ill-bred, naughty, unamiable; evil** (sbst.), *dúg-po byéd-pa* to do evil *Mil.*; **mi-la dúg-po táṅ-wa* C.* to do evil to a person, to molest, trouble, annoy, injure, a person. — *sdug-p̔óṅs-pa Stg.*, *C.*, **poor.** — *sdug-żwa* a mourning-hood *Cs.* — *sdug-srán* inured to hardships; the being hardened *Mil.*

སྡུད་ *sdud* 1. *Sch.*: the **folds** of a garment; *sdúd-k̔a* string for drawing together the opening of a bag, **drawing-hem.** — 2. *Cs.* **synthesis,** *˳byed-sdúd* analysis and synthesis.

སྡུད་པ་ *sdúd-pa*, pf. *bsdus*, fut. and likewise for the pres. tense) *bsdu*, imp. *sdus*, *bsdu*, vb.a. to *˳dú-ba*, 1. **to collect, gather, lay up, amass, assemble,** riches, flowers, broken victuals, taxes, crops, earnings, men, cattle etc., frq.; **to put together, to compile,** *miṅ-rnams . . . nas bsdus* the names have been put together out of . . . *Glr.*; **to brush** or **sweep together,** *W.*: **k̔yim-sa ŏl-mo-nę* (or *daṅ*)* the dust with a broom; *dbáṅ-du* **to subject, subdue,** frq. — 2. **to unite, join, combine,** *šiṅ γsum mgo* three pieces of wood at their upper ends *Dzl.*; six kingdoms into one *Dzl.* (to join) actions, words, and thoughts in the path of virtue *Dzl.*; *dmág-rnams k̔ór-du* (joining) the troops with his retinue *Dzl.*; *k̔yo-šúg-tu* to unite in matrimony, to give in marriage. — 3. **to condense, to comprise,** all moral precepts in three main points, the letters of the alphabet in five classes *Gram.*; esp. with *nyúṅ-ṅur*, zúr-tsam, **to contract, compress, abridge,** frq., *de yaṅ bsdú-na* if one shortens it still more, if it is abridged a second time *Gram.*; **dús-ḱan* W.* **brief, concise, compendious;** **dú-yig* C.* **abbreviation, abridgment;** *bsdus-ˏgrel* an abridged commentary *Tar.* 177,7; **to close, conclude, finish, terminate,** *mǰug sdúd-pa* to close a train, opp. to *sna ˏdrén-pa Mṅg.*; *slár-bsdu-ba* concluding a sentence or period with the finite verb in *o*, *Gram.* — 4. *bsdús-pa* **to consist of** or **in**, c. instrum., e.g. *yi-ge drug-gis* of six letters *Thgy.* — 5. **to boil down, to inspissate** *Lt.*, *bsdús-ḱu, γdús-ḱu,* a preparation thus obtained *Med.*; *bsdus-ťáṅ* prob. id. *Med.* — 6. scil. *bsód-nams: bsdú-ba rnam bži* the four ways of collecting merit *Glr.* — 7. *dbugs sdúd-pa Med.?* *bsdú-ba* sbst. **collection, gathering** *Tar.* 33, 16. — *bsdus-γžom* or *ˏǰom Schr.*: a machine for executing criminals constructed in such a manner, that the head is crushed by two stones striking together; *Stg.*: n. of one of the hells

སྡུམ་པ་ *sdúm-pa* 1. vb., pf. *bsdums*, fut. *bsdum*, imp. *sdum(s)*, vb.a. to *ˏdúm-pa*, **to make agree, to bring to an agreement,** *mi-mťún-pa-rnams* things not agreeing *Sch.*, **to reconcile, to conciliate,** *mi-mdzá-ba-rnams* enemies *Thgy.*; *sdúm-par byéd-pa* id.; *sdum-byéd* (resp. *mdzad*), *sdúm(-pa)-po, sdúm-mḱan,* **conciliator, pacifier, peacemaker;** *res ˏḱrúgs-pa res bsdúm-pa máṅ-du byúṅ-ṅo* at one time they were at odds, at another they were at peace with one another *Tar.* — 2. sbst. **house, mansion** *C.*; *γzim-sdum* (resp.) **bed-room;** *sdúm-ra* garden near the house, cf. *ldúm-ra*.

སྡུར་བ་ *sdúr-ba*, pf. and fut. *bsdur*, **to compare,** *go-sdúr byéd-pa* id., v. *go* 2; *nyams sdur byéd-pa C.* to compare different texts; **tam-dúr* W.* **judicial examination, trial.**

སྡུར་ལེན, སྡུར་བླང *sdur-lén, sdur-blaṅ,* **amber** *Ts.*, for *sbur-lén*.

སྡེ་ *sde* (*Ssk.* in compound words सेना) **part, portion,** of a whole, e.g. of a country, also *yúl-sde*, **province, district, territory,** even **village** *C.*, *bón-sde* the places or villages of the Bonpas *Glr.*; *sde-čeṅ-la snyég-pa* to aim at an extension of territory *Dom.*; part of the human race: **nation, people, tribe, clan, community,** *ṕá-rol-gyi sde ˏǰóms-pa* to conquer hostile nations; **class,** e.g. of letters: phonetical class; *sde sder bgó-ba* to divide into classes *Cs.*; classes of books: *mdó-sde* the Sūtras, v. sub *mdo; rgyúd-sde* the Tantras, v. sub *ryyud; sbyór-sde bži* the four volumes treating of pharmacy *Glr.*; of monks: community of monks, body of conventuals (consisting of not less than four persons); hence **convent, monastery,** *sde btsugs* he founded convents *Glr.*; *čos-sde* id.; class of religious followers, philosophical school, *sde bži* the four (principal) schools *Tar.*; *lha srin-gyi sde brgyad, lha klú-la sógs-pai sde brgyad* the eight classes of spirits, frq.; it is also used for **a great quantity, great many, lots of;** and by improper use, or by way of abbreviation for *sdé-pa, sde-dpon,* commander, ruler.

**Comp. and deriv.** *sde-skór Glr.* **district.** — *sde-ḱrugs* **insurrection,** general revolt of a people, *byéd-pa* to excite one *Ma.* — *sde-snód γsum,* त्रिपिटक, **'the three baskets',** viz. the three classes of the sacred Buddhist writings, *ˏdúl-bai* (discipline), *mdo-sdéi* (Sūtras), *sṅágs-kyi sde-snód* (Mantras, i.e. metaphysics and mysticism), hence *sde-snód-la sbyáṅ-ba* to study the sacred writings *Mil.* — *sdé-pa* 1. **the chief** or **governor** of a district *C.*, = *ˏgó-pa W.*, **majordomo** of the Dalai Lama, *Köpp.* II., 134; in a general sense: **a man of quality, a nobleman** *Ma.* 2. **a. letter** of a certain phonetic class, or the phonetic class itself, *sdé-pa bži-pa* the fourth phonetic class, the labials *Gram.* So the word is also used for denoting a certain class or **school** of Buddhist philosophers. *Tar.*, frq. — *sde-dpón* = *sdé-pa* 1, signifies also a class of **demons** *Dom.* — *sde-ťsán* **class,** e.g. phonetic class, = *sde*; a particular kind of writing, *nā-ga-ri sde-ťsán Glr.*; — *sde-γzár Sch.* **lawlessness, anarchy,** *sde-γzár čén-po* general anarchy (?) — *sde-yaṅs* (spelling?) **court, court-yard,** = *ḱyams*. — *sde-rigs* **dominion, territory,**

*Glr.* — *sde-srid* 1. **province, kingdom** *Cs.* 2. **regent, administrator,** in more recent times title of the *sdé-pa* of the Dalai Lama, and the rulers of Bhotan. *Köpp.* II., 154.

སྡེ་བ་ *sde-ba*(?) *W.* **ʼi-ru dé-če med** there is here no room any more.

སྡེབ་ *sdeb* (? *ˎdebs*) **time, times,** = *lan W.*, e.g. four times.

སྡེབ་པ་ *sdéb-pa*, pf. *bsdebs*, fut. *bsdeb*, imp. *sdebs*, 1. **to mingle, mix, blend** (*ṗyogs*) *γčig-tu* together, *Lex.*, cf. *sbyir-ba*. — 2. **to join, unite, combine,** *drás-su sdéb-pa Mil.*, by the context: sewed well together, — but *drás-su?* — Gen. vb.n.: **to join, to unite,** *dan* with, also *la*, *sems mig dan bsdébs-nas lta, rná-ba dan bsdébs-nas nyan Mil.* the soul sees by joining the eye, it hears by joining the ear; **to join company, to associate, to hold intercourse with,** *Mil.*; also to have sexual intercourse *Pth.*, cf. *ˎdré-ba, ˎgrógs-pa, dzóm-pa.* — 3. **to prepare, dress, get ready** (victuals) *Sch.*, cf. *sbyór-ba.* — 4. **to exchange, barter, truck for,** **bág-ṗe ḍás-la** *W.* flour for rice; in this sense prob. also used by *Mil.*; **to change,** money, **nul deb sal** please change me a rupee (not so in *C.*). — 5. **to make poetry, to compose verses,** at the end of poems: *żés-pa . . . kyis sdéb-pao* the above verses have been composed by . . .; = *sbyór-ba*.

སྡེབ་སྦྱོར་ *sdeb-sbyór* 1. **composition,** esp. poetical, **poetry,** — 2. *yi-gei sdeb-sbyór* **orthography** *Schr.*, *Cs.*, *Sch.*

སྡེར་མ་ *sdér-ma*, resp. *γsol-sdér*, **dish, platter, plate, saucer;** *sder-gáṅ* a plateful, a dish (of meat etc.), esp. *C.*

སྡེར་(མོ) *sdér(-mo)* **claw, talon,** *sdér-kyu Sch.* id.; *sdér-mo rno* a sharp claw; *sdér-čan* furnished with claws, *sder-méd* without claws; *sder-ˎdzin byéd-pa* to seize with the claws *Cs.*; *stag(-gi)-sdér* a tiger's claw *Lt.*; *sder-čágs* animals provided with claws *Mil.*

སྡོ་ཁམ་ *sdo-ḱám Sch.* **belonging together, a pair**(?).

སྡོ་བ་ *sdó-ba*, pf. (*b*)*sdos*, fut. *bsdo*, imp. *sdos* (also *dó-ba* q. v.) 1. **to risk, hazard, venture,** gen. c. *dan*, also c. dat. or accus., *bdág-gi lus* one's own body *Dom.*; *lus srog dan* frq., *lus dan sróg-la Dzl.* — 2. **to bear up against,** *sdug-bsṅal, nyon-móṅs-pa dan*, against heavy trials, against toil and drudgery *Dzl.*; **to bid defiance,** to an enemy *Dzl.*, also **to behave with insolence, contemptuously** *Dzl.* — 3. *lág-pas Dzl.* ༧༧༩, 6(?).

སྡོང་པོ་ *sdóṅ-po* (*C.* vulg. **dúm-po** 1. **trunk, stem, body** of a tree *Glr.* — 2. **stalk,** of a plant, *pádmai* of a lotus; *sdóṅ-po ḱoṅ-stoṅ* a hollow stalk *Wdṅ.*; *sdóṅ-poi sde* the class of stalked plants *Cs.* — 3. **tree,** also *śiṅ-sdóṅ(-po)* frq.; *śiṅ-sdóṅ rkaṅ-γčig* a tree of a single stem *Glr.*; *śiṅ-sdóṅ ḱoṅ-rúl* a tree rotten at the core; col. fig. barren, of females, prob. jestingly. — 4. **block, log.**

**Comp.** *Cs.*: *sdar-sdóṅ* trunk of a walnut-tree, *śug-sdóṅ* stem of a juniper-tree; *ṫsil-sdóṅ* **a tallow-candle;** *ḱyags-sdóṅ* **an icicle.** — *mčod-sdóṅ* (*Sch.* = *mčod-rtén*), in a botanical work it was explained by 'wick', = *sdoṅ-rás*, which seems to be more to the purpose, as a blossom is compared with it. — *sdoṅ-rkáṅ* v. *sdoṅ-rás*. — *sdoṅ-dúm* **stump of a tree,** *sdóṅ-dúm ṫsig-pa* the burnt stump of a tree *Cs.* — *sdóṅ-bu Cs.* 1. **a small trunk.** 2. **stalk.** 3. **wick.** — *sdoṅ-rás, sdoṅ-śiṅ, sdoṅ-rkáṅ C.* a wick of cotton, of wood, of pith; cotton wicks are used esp. for sacred lamps.

སྡོང་བ་, སྡོངས་པ་ *sdóṅ-ba, sdóṅs-pa* (*Sch.* also *rdóṅs-pa*) pf. *bsdoṅs*, fut. *bsdoṅ*, **to unite, to join** (in undertakings), **to enter into a confederacy, to associate one's self with,** c. *dan* (also accus.?); *ḱyod dan ṅa sdóṅ-ste ˎgro* you and I, we will go together; *sdóṅs-zla* prob. = *zla-grógs*.

སྡོད་པ་ *sdód-pa*, pf. and fut. *bsdad*, resp. *bżés-pa*, *W.* **dád-če**, 1. **to sit,** frq., **sil-la dod** *W.* sit down in the shade! *dál-bar sdód-pa* to sit still *Lt.* — 2. **to stay, to tarry, to abide,** *ṫóg-mar der bsdad* for the present I will stay here yet a little longer *Mil.*; *nyál-nas bsdad-ˎdug-pa* to lie down and to continue lying *Mil.*; **ḍọ̈-du ˎǰúg-pa** to receive hospitably, **mi ˎǰúg-pa** to deny reception, to send away *C.*; **to stop, to halt,** in running, walking *Dzl.*;

**to wait**, *re žig ma bsád-par sdód-čig* wait a little yet before beginning to kill *Dzl.*; *skád-čig kyaṅ sdód-pai loṅ méd-par* without waiting even for a moment *Glr.*; *Ld.*: **ltós-te dád-če** to wait and see whether etc.; **sám-te dád-če** to wait for, hope for, to look forward to, **gúg-te dád-če** id.; *mdó-sde ₒdi ₒtsó-žiṅ sdód-na* as long as the authority of this book is acknowledged *Dom.*; **zag daṅ kyir-kyír dad dug** *W.* (this thing) always remains round (crooked), it will not get straight. — 3. **to be at home,** **dẹ' yọ'** he is at home, **dẹ' me'** he is not at home *C.*; **to live, reside, settle at** *B.* and col.; *bka-sdód Lex., C.*: 1. **attendant, waiting servant,** 2. **aid-de camp.**

སྡོམ་ *sdom* 1. *Lex.* and *C.* **spider.** — 2. **summary, contents,** *spii sdom* 1. **table of contents, index** *S.g.* 2. **general introductory remarks, introduction,** also *sdom-tsig; sdóm-la* **summarily, to be brief, in short.**

སྡོམ་པ་ *sdóm-pa* I. vb., pf. *bsdams, bsdoms,* fut. *bsdam, bsdom,* imp. *sdom(s), W. *dám-če** 1. **to bind,** *lčags-sgróg-gis* **to fetter** *Cs.*; **to bind** or **tie fast, to pinion; to bind up, to dress,** wounds. — 2. **to fasten, to fix firmly,** e.g. by a screw-vice; *kro-čús* by melted metal, i.e. to solder; *so,* to press, grind, or strike the teeth together, **to gnash,** as in anger *Pth.*; **to fasten securely,** the door *Dzl., Pth.*; *rtsá-ka* **to close** an opened vein *Med.*; hence in general, 3. **to stanch, stop, to cause to cease,** *rtsa-krág šór-ba* the bloody flux *Med.*; **to bind, constrain, render harmless, to neutralize,** *nyés-pa* an evil *Lex., Sch.* — 4 *W. *káb-ša dam dug** the shoe **pinches.** — 5. to make morally firm, **to confirm,** *spyód-pa,* one's conduct, to conform it strictly to the moral law. — 6. with or without *bdag-nyid,* **to bind one's self, to engage** *Cs.* — 7. **to add together, to cast** or **sum up,** *rgyud bži bsdóms-pas leu* ༡༥༤ all the four Gyud together have 154 chapters; *yóṅs-su bsdús-pa-la* taking all together *Tar.*

II. sbst. **सम्बर obligation, engagement, duty,** *sdóm-pa lén-pa Glr., ₒdzín-pa Cs.,* to enter into an engagement, to bind one's self to perform a certain duty, *mi-la ₒbógs-pa* **to bind a person by duty,** by oath, **to swear in** *Glr.* (e.g. in convents, in the relations of priests and laymen); *srúṅ-ba* **to be true to** one's duty, to keep one's engagements; *ₒčor* a duty is violated *Glr.*; *ṅá-la sdóm-pa med* I have renounced my vow *Glr.* — *sdóm-pa ɣsum,* acc. to *Glr.* and other more recent authors, are: *so-tár* (v. *so-só*), *byaṅ-séms,* and *ɣsaṅ-sṅágs-kyi sdom-pa.*

**Comp.** *sdom-ltóṅ*(?) **neck-bell,** bell attached to the neck of cattle. — *sdom-byéd* 1 **one that binds,** by duty etc. 2. **an astringent medicine** *Cs.* — *sdom-ɣzér* **rivet of a pair of scissors or tongs** *Sch.*

སྡོམ་བུ་ *sdóm-bu Sch.*: **a ball; a round tassel.**

སྡོར་, རྡོར་ *sdor, rdor* 1. (like ὄψον) that which gives relish to food, **seasoning, condiment,** esp. *túg-sdor* that which gives substance to soup, viz. **meat;** *tsa-sdór* salt and meat. — 2. **spice,** *sdór-gyi rkyál-pa* spice-bag *S.g.*; *sdor-tál* spice-powder *Sch.* —

བརྡ་ *brda* (**संकेत**) **sign,** i.e. 1. **gesture,** *čágs-pa ₒdód-pai brda máṅ-du bstán-nas* making many wanton gestures (or giving hints, intimations v. 2), *lág-brda* signs with the hand, *saṅs-rgyás la ɣsól-čig čes lág-brda byas* they beckoned to him to ask Buddha *Dzl.*; **mig-da táṅ-če** *W.* to give a hint with the eye, to wink. — 2. **indication, intimation, symptom, token,** *mi-rtág ₒgyúr-bai brdao* it is an indication of their frail condition *Thgy.*; **symbol** *Pth.*, *brdar* as a symbol, symbolically; *de gaṅ yin ₒdri-bai brda stón-pa* to ask for a thing by symbolic signs, in symbolic language *Glr.*; *brda spród-pa, ₒpród-pa, sbyór-ba, ₒgrol-ba* **to explain, describe, represent,** with accus., and prob. also with genit.: *yin-lugs-kyi brda ₒgról-ba Mil.* to explain the essence or nature of things (ni f.); meton. *dei brda či lags* what may be the symbolical meaning of it *Mil.* — 3. **word,** *ₒbód-pai brda* interjection *Liš.*; *ₒdúl-bai brda* word out of the Dulwa *Zam.*; *dris-pai brda-rnyiṅ* an obsolete word for 'being asked', *Lex.*; *brdá-sgyur-pa Sch.* **interpreter, dragoman** *Sch.*; *brdai blá-ma* is stated to be a Lama who instructs by word of mouth *Mil.;* esp. with regard to the spelling of words: *brda yaṅ mi ˳dra sna-ṫsogs gyur* there came also into use various spellings *Zam.*; *brda - rnyiṅ* old orthography, *brda-ɣsár* new orthography *Zam.*; *bód-kyi brdai bstan-bčós* title of the Zamatog; *ṫsig-brda = ṫsig, ṫsig-brda-yis ˳grol-ba* to explain by words *Mil.*

**Comp.** *brdá-skad* **language by symbolical signs** *Mil.*; prob. also nothing but the usual language by words *Glr.* — *brda-čád* (prob. for *˳čad*, from *˳čád-pa* II.), *me-loṅ-gi brda-čád* the language or evidence of the mirror; so prob. also *Tar.* 210, 22. — *brda-spród, brda-sbyór* 1. **explanation**, *miṅ - dón brda-spród* explanation of the import of names, title of a small Materia Medica by a certain Wairocana. 2. **orthography** *Gram.*, *Pth.* — *brda - lon Mil.* is said to be *= ṫsig-lan*, verbal answer. — *brda-lags* 'insignis', acc. to *Cs.* in *Journ. As. Soc. Beng.* V, 384.

བརྡུལ་བ་ *brdúl-ba* 1. *Lex.* w.e.; *Sch.* **to deceive, to cheat.** 2. *Sch.* **to swing, brandish, flourish,** *ɣyáb-mo* a fly-flap.

བརྡོག་འཆོས་པ་ *brdog-˳čos-pa* **to slip, to slide, to lose one's footing.**

བསྡར་བ་ *bsdár-ba, Sch.*: *mdún-du bsdár-ba* **to hope, to expect** or **wait for a** favour. In *Dzl.* ༧༢༨, 18 the better reading (accordant with the manuscript of Kyelang) is *sdur* (*= sdú-bar*).

བསྡོགས་པ་ *bsdógs-pa*; the *Lexx.* add: *grabs, Cs.* **to compose, prepare, make ready,** *nyer bsdógs-pa* id.; *sna-ṫág bsdógs-pa* to wind the rope, which is fastened in the nose of an ox or a camel, round the horns or the neck of the animal.

# ན

ན *na* 1. the letter **n.** — 2. num. figure: 12.

ན་ *na* **meadow,** *C.* also *ná-ma*; *nar skye* it grows on meadows, *Wdṅ.* and elsewh. (cf. *neu*).

ན་ *na* I. sbst. 1. **year** (?) v. *ná-niṅ.* — 2. **stage of life, age,** also *na-ṫsód*, and *ná-so*, resp. *sku-ná* (also *sku-nás?*); *na-ṫsód rgás - pas Wdṅ.* old, of an advanced age; *ná-so ɣžón-te Glr.* young; *sku-nás ṗrá - mo Mil.* of a tender age; *na-ṫsód-kyi dbyé - ba* the different ages or stages of life; (*sku-*) *nár-son-pa* (*Sch.* grown old?) *Glr.*: of full age, adult, grown up; **ná-so-tsir-la** *W.* according to age; *na - čúṅ* girl, maiden, virgin, *na - čúṅ bzáṅ - mo bču* ten beautiful girls *Dzl.*; *na-mnyám, -˳drá, -zlá, neu-ldáṅ Lex.* of the same age, coetaneous; **ná-da-toṃ-mo** *C.* a festivity given by wealthy parents on their son's birthday to him and his playmates, also **ló-da-toṃ-mo**; *na-ṗrá young*, tender; *na-ɣžón = ɣžón - nu.* II. postp. c. accus., signifying the place where a thing is, 1. added to substantives, **in,** (more accurately *náṅ-na* c. genit.), sometimes also to be rendered by **on, at, with, to** etc. *mdó-na* in scripture, *lo-rgyús-na* in a book of history *Glr.*; *dé - na* there, in that place; of time: *dus-ɣčig-na* at the same time, *dei ṫsé-na* at that time, then etc. — 2. added to verbs, either to the inf., or more frq. (col. always) to the verbal root: **in, at, during** (the doing or happening of a thing), hence a. **when, at the time of,** *bós-na* when I called *Dzl.*, *zér-ba-na* when he said *Tar.*; *bdág-gi ṗa ṫse ṗós-na* when my father shall have died *Dzl.*; with *nam*: *nam dús-la báb-na* (*W.* **dus léb-na**) when the time comes, frq.; *nam ₒgró-na* when I (you etc.) go, was going, shall go. — b. **if, in case, supposing that** (ἐάν), the different degrees of possibility, however, cannot be so precisely expressed by the mood in Tibetan, as in other languages; with or without a preceding *gál-te*, *ċi-ste* etc. (cf. the remarks sub *gaṅ* II.); ... *ma mtóṅ na* ... *mi rtógs-par dug* if we had not seen ..., we should not have known ... *Mil.*; but in most cases also the vb., to which it is subordinate, is put in the gerund: *ₒdi byás-na brám-ze ma yin-pas* as I should be no longer a Brahmin, if I were to do that *Dzl.*; further: **if even** ..., how much the more ...! in asseverations: **if** ..., then indeed may ...! then I would that ...! it is well, that ..., it will be well, if ..., *na légs-so* frq.; if *légs-so* is elliptically omitted, *na* answers to: **o that! would that!** also: **I will**; in an interrogative sentence, viz. '*légs-sam*' being omitted, to: **must I? shall I?** *Mil.*: *čos byás-na snyam* (when we are with you) we think, we will be pious! *ₒjig-rtén byás-na snyam* (when we have come home) we think, let us take care of temporal things! *ċi drág-na* (better *ċi byás-na drag*) what shall we consider the most advantageous? — c. of a more general signification: **as, since, whilst, by** (with the partic. pres.), = *te* or *pas Dzl.* frq., *dug zós-na yaṅ* even by eating poisonous things (he was not hurt) ༢༤, 3; *na* is used thus, however, only in conjunction with *yaṅ*, and *dug zós-na yaṅ* is the more popular phrase for *dug zos kyaṅ* In careless speaking or writing *na* is also used for *ċé-na Thgy.* frq. — 3. pleon. added to the termination of the instr. of substantives and verbs: *rgyu dés-na* **for that reason, therefore,** *ċii rgyús-na* **for what reason, why, wherefore** *Stg.*; *dé-bas-na* **hence, thus, so then, accordingly,** very frq.; *kúr-bas-na* because they carried *Glr.*; also added to the termination of the termin.: *ʒi-ltar-na* frq.; *γċig-tu-na*, *γnyis-su-na*, **in the first place, firstly** etc. *Dzl.*; *slád-du-na Dzl.*; *rgya-gár skád-du-na Thgy.* — 4. incorr. for *nas*, col. frq.; its being used for the termin. is very questionable, and the rare instances of this use in books may be regarded as errors in writing (e.g. *Dzl.* ༢༥༦, 17 *náṅ-na soṅ* inst. of *naṅ-du*), whereas the contrary, *du* for *na*, occurs frq., and is to be considered as sanctioned.

III. conj. **and**, *Bal* (?) – IV. v. *ná-ka*, *ná-ba*.

ན་ཁ་ *ná-ka*, = *spaṅ*, **greensward, turf.**

ནཱ་ག་ *nā-ga*, *Ssk.* for *klu*.

ནཱ་ག་རི་ *nā-ga-ri* **Sanskrit, Sanskrit-letters.**

ན་གི་ *na-gi Sch.* 1. **being ill**(?). 2. **the claws of a sea-monster**(?).

ནཱ་གེ་སར་ *nā-ge-sar Lt.* = Hindi, for **नागकेसर**, Mesua ferrea.

ན་འཛའ་ *na-ₒʒa W.* **mock-suns** and similar phenomena, v. *na-bún*.

ན་ནིང་ *ná-niṅ* (*Cs.*: 'for *na-rnyiṅ*') **the last year**; gen. adv. **last year**; *ná-niṅ-gi* adj. **of last year** or **last year's** (crop).

ན་བ་ *ná-ba* 1. **to be ill, sick**; inf. also the state of being ill, **illness, sickness,** *ná-ba γsó-ba* to cure it *Lt.*, though *nad* is more in use; partic.: a sick person, **patient,** *ná-ba daṅ ₒċi-ba* disease and death; *skye rga na ₒċi* v. *skyé-ba* I., *rgás-pa daṅ ná-ba* old and sick people; *mi-ná-ba γnás-pa* to remain in health *S.g.*; *ná-ba-pa*, *ná-ba-ma Cs.* a sick person, an invalid (male and female); *ná-mo* a female patient *Mil.*; *ná-ba-mkan* a sickly person, an invalid *Cs.*; *ná-ba-ċan* sickly, *na-ba-méd* healthy *Cs.*; *na-tóg* after falling ill *Sch.* — 2. of the separate parts of the body: **to ache,** *rná-ba* (not *-bai*) *ná-ba* pain in the ear, earache; *lus tams-ċád na* (my) whole body aches *Dom.*; *so ná-na* having the toothache; *nán-na na* it aches, when pressed (with the fingers) *S.g.*; *klád-pa ná-ba-la* (good) for the headache, for diseases of the brain; *na-ₒʒrén* complication of diseases or fits *Sch.*; *na-(ba daṅ)zúg(-rṅu)*, *na-tsá* disease and pain.

ན་བུན་ *na-bún* **fog, thick mist,** *tibs*, *ₒkyims* comes on; *byin-rlabs-kyi* prob. **a cloud, a flood, of blessing** *Mil.*

ནམ་ *ná-ma* 1. v. *na* I. 2. also *ná-mo*(**नमस्**), **praise, glory, adoration,** *na-mo gu-ru* **praise** to the teacher!

ནྣམ་ *ná-ma Ssk.* = *žes byá-ba* **so called,** frq. in titles of books.

ནབཟའ་ *ná-bza* (**ná-za**, vulg. **náb-za, nám-za**) resp. for *gos*, **garment, dress,** frq.; *γsól-ba* to put it on.

ནཙུན་ *na-ún* obs. or vulg. for *na-bún*, old edition of *Mil.*

ནརག་ *na-rag, Ssk.* **नरक, hell.**

ནརམ་ *na-rám* medicinal herb, *Med.*; in *Lh.* Polygon. viviparum.

ནྣ་རི་ཀེ་ལ་ *na-ri-ke-la Ssk.* **cocoa-nut.**

ནརེ་ *ná-re*, by form and position an adv., like *ₒdi-skad-du*; before words or sentences that are quoted literally, mostly followed by *smrás-nas, zér-ba-la*, but not always, in which latter case it stands for **'he says, he said'** etc., the noun being always put in the nom. case, never in the instr.: *ₒṕags-pa na-re* the Reverend said; rarely in accessory sentences: *gál-te γžán-dag ná-re* (not *ná-re-na*) si forte alii dixerint *Wdṅ.*; even without *gál-te* in the same sense *Thgy.* It hardly occurs in old classical literature, nor in the col. language of *W.*, but pretty frq. in later literature. In *Kun.*, however, there exists a vb. *ná-čas* (**ná-čā**), pf. *nas* (**nā**), *imp. nos* (**nö**) which is used for *zér-ba* (not in use there), and is construed with the instr.: *ǎ-pa-su nā soṅ* the father has said.

ནརོ་ *ná-ro* the sign for the vowel **o,** ◌ོ.

ནྣརོ་ *nā-ro* n. of a holy Lama *Mil.*; *nā-ro-pa Tar.* 181, 10 id.? *ná-roi sems-ₒdzin-gyi lčags-ťág* a sort of puzzle.

ནལནྡ་ *na-landa Pth. nā-len-dra Wdk.*, n. of a monastery in Magadha.

ནལི་ *ná-li* **bowl, basin,** an iron or china dish *W.*

ནལེ་ཤག་ *na-le-šag Lt., šal S.g.,* = *ši-kru Wdṅ.* (**शिग्रु**?) n. of an acrid medicine.

ནག་ *nag* (blackness?) **crime, offence, transgression,** v. *nág-pa* comp.; *nag-ku-be-ra* v. *ku-be-ra.*

ནག་པ་, ནག་པོ་ *nág-pa*, gen. *nág-po*, **black,** *ber ṕyi nág-pa naṅ dkár-ba* a garment outside black, inside white *Glr.*; **nág-po ma ḱu** do not blacken it, do not soil it! of the countenance **dark, frowning, gloomy, mournful** *Glr.*; *mi nag* (-*po or-pa*) a black one, a layman, (on account of his not being clad in a red or yellow clerical garb); *nág-po* n. p. **Krishna** *Tar.*, *nág-po čén-po* = **महाकाल Siwa;** *nág-mo* 1. **a black woman,** 2. **Kali, Uma;** *nág-moi-ₒbaṅs* or *ḱol* Kālidāsa. — 3. **woman,** in general *Sch.* — *nag-ₒgrós, năg-po ₒgro-šés* 'easy to be understood' *Sch.*; acc. to our Lama from Tashilunpo *nág-po ₒgro-bšér* implies: illustrating a sentence by comparing it with similar passages; *nág-čan* 1. **a person guilty of a crime** *Sch.*; *mi nág-čan dóṅ-nas ťar-pa* a criminal released from prison *Mil.* 2. **a married man** *Sch.* — *nag-ǩágs* **black-cattle, horned cattle** *Sch.*; v. also *γnág-pa.* — *nág-ču* n. of a river north of Lhasa, *Huc* II, 238; *nág-ču-ḱa-pa* people living on its banks, notorious for their thievish propensities. — *nag-čén, nag-nyés C.* **a heinous crime.** — *nag-ťúm, nag-ťóm, Sch., nag-siṅ-ba Thgy., nag-hur-ré Sch.,* **coal-black, jet-black.** — *nag-nóg* (-*čan*) **dirty, dingy; not clear,** as bad print; fig. **stained, polluted,** with sin, guilt, *sems.* — *nag-ṕyógs* v. *ṕyogs.* — *nag*(-*ma*)-*ťsúr* **a black mineral colour,** *Sch*: **green vitriol**(?). — *nag-ťsig* **a point, dot,** *W.* — *nag-zúg* (?) **darkness,** *nag-zúg-la snóm-bžin soṅ* he groped about in the dark.

ནག་ཤ་ *nág-ša Sch.*: **linden-tree, lime-tree** (hardly to be found in Tibet; the word perhaps introduced from Mongol dictionaries).

ནགས་(མ་) *nágs* (-*ma Glr.*) *B, C., W.,* **forest,** *rtsi-šiṅ-nags-kyis mdzes* beautified by forests, richly wooded *Glr.*; *ₒťúg-po* dense forest; *nags-ḱród* a thicket *Glr.*; *nágs-čan* woody, covered with forests; *nags-ljóṅs* woodland country, a well-wooded province; *nags-sbál Lt.* tree-frog (?); *nags-ťsál* = *nags*, *nyám-ṅa-ba* a dreadful forest *Dzl.*; *yid-du-ₒoṅ-ba* a lovely wood *Sambh.*; *nags-*(*γ*)*séb* an intersected forest, v. (*γ*)*seb.*

ནང་ *nan* I. the space within a thing, 1. **the interior, the inside,** *ṗúg-pai nan kun* the whole interior of the cavern *Mil.*; *γžóṅ-pai, dóṅ-gi nan* the interior of a basin, of a pit (e.g. being filled up) *Dzl.*; *k̔áṅ-pai nan pyag-dár byéd-pa* to sweep the inside of a house *Dzl.* — 2. **space, room, apartment, chamber** col. — 3. **dwelling, domicile, house,** esp. *C.* — 4. meton **inmates, family, household,** **nan ṫsaṅ** *W.* the whole family. — 5. **the interior** (spiritually), **heart, mind, soul,** *ye-šés náṅ-na šar* wisdom begins to shine in the mind; *žen-ₒdzin naṅ-nas ₒgrol* affection, interest, disappears from the heart *Glr.* — 6. sometimes adv. for *náṅ-na.*

II. *náṅ-gi*, genit., used 1. as an adj.: **inner, inward, esoteric** (opp. *to ṗyi*), *náṅ-gi k̔rims, náṅ-k̔rims,* a private law, an esoteric precept or doctrine not intended for the public; **ge-dụn-gyī náṅ-ṫim dhaṅ ₒgal ṫse** *C.* if priests violate their special moral duties, (very different from *náṅ-pai k̔rims* the Buddhist law, merely opp. to Brahmanism); *náṅ-gi sbyin-pa* inward offerings, i.e. spiritual sacrifices, opp. to outward and material offerings; but *Dzl.* ༢༣༠, 4 it denotes personal sacrifices, the surrendering of parts of our own self, e.g. a member of the body, opp. to outward property; the meaning also reminds of Rom. 12, 1, and I Pet. 2, 5. — *náṅ-gi byá-ba* internal affairs *Glr.*; v. also the compounds. — 2. for *náṅ-na* **among, amidst,** frq. c. accus.: *bu náṅ-gi ṫa čuṅ, ṗúg-ron náṅ-gi čúṅ-ṅu Dzl.* the smallest among etc.; for *dé-dag-gi náṅ-na* **of it, of them, among them** etc.: *náṅ-gi čúṅ-ṅu* the least of them *Dzl.*; *náṅ-gi lhá-mo sṅá-ma* the foremost among the goddesses; sometimes more pleon., without distinct reference to a preceding noun, *Dzl.* ༡༠༦, 18; ༡༣༠, 16 (where *Sch.* prob. translates incorr.).

III. with *la, na, du, nas;* 1. as sbst., acc. to the significations given above, e.g. *nád-pai náṅ-du ₒjúg-pa* to go **into** the room of a sick person *Wdṅ.*; *dei náṅ-du γdan-dráṅs-te* inviting **into** their house *Mil.* — 2. as adv. *náṅ-na* **in it, therein, within, among it** or **them;** *náṅ-du* and *náṅ-la* **thereinto, into it;** *náṅ-nas* out, thereout, from among; among it or them = *náṅ-na.* — 3. postp.: **in, into, among** etc., e.g. *rdziṅ-gi náṅ-na k̔rus byéd-pa Dzl.* to bathe in a pond, *čui náṅ-du žúgs-pa* to go into the water; *groṅ-k̔yér dei naṅ daṅ ṗyi-rol-na* in the town and out of it *Dzl.*; **sém-mi náṅ-na zér-pa** *W.* he said to himself; *snai náṅ-nas byuṅ* it came out of his nose (again) *Dzl.*; *mii náṅ-na(s) bzáṅ-po žig* one very beautiful among men *Dzl.*; *gliṅ dé-rnams-kyi náṅ-na(s) mčóg-tu gyúr-pa* the most important among or of these countries *Glr.* (here at least the sing. is as frq. als the plur.); in col. language the word is much used, though often inaccurately; so it is frq. employed, where the later literature has *ṅáṅ-la, ṅáṅ-nas;* **wáṅ-gi náṅ-na** by force; **só-mẹ náṅ-na zer gos** *W.* that should have been mentioned, when it was fresh (in remembrance); **lo tóṅ-ni náṅ-na ṫsá-pig ma ṫsar** not yet quite in a thousand years, i.e. it is not full a thousand years *W.* — There is still to be noticed: *naṅ* = *naṅ-mo.* — *naṅ-méd-la* col. frq. suddenly; in *B.* of rare occurrence; *naṅ-méd nor rnyéd-pa* to become rich unexpectedly *S.g.*

**Comp. and deriv.** *naṅ-kyóg Sch.*: having legs bending inward, **bandy-legged.** — *naṅ-skór* v. *skór-ba* extr. — *naṅ-k̔rims* v. above. — *naṅ-k̔ról*, vulgo *-rol*, **bowels, entrails, intestines;** also any separate part of them; *naṅ-k̔ról dróṅ-ba* spasmodic contractions of the bowels *Sch.*; *naṅ-k̔rol-bžág* seems in *Lexx.* to be taken synon. with *mnyam-bžag.* — *naṅ-góg* v. *ṫer.* — **naṅ-gyóg** *W.* **a large bolt, door-bar.** — *náṅ-ča* = *naṅ-k̔rol.* — *naṅ-čags-su* in one's self, in one's own mind *Sch.* — *náṅ-rje* **minister of the interior, home-minister** *Sch.* — *náṅ-lta Glr* 89, 11? — *naṅ-ṫáb byéd-pa* to be involved in intestine war *Pth.*, = *naṅ-ₒk̔rúgs.* — *naṅ-dág* 1. *Sch.* 'the interior being cleansed'. 2. col. (or *naṅ-brtags?*) v. *snaṅ.* — *náṅ-don* **the intrinsic meaning, the true sense,** *náṅ-don rtóg-pa* to investigate, to study, the real meaning; **náṅ-don tóg-k̔ẹn,**

or *ghó - k̔ẹn** *C.*, **nán - don - čan* (or *-yod-k̔an)** *W.* most learned, very erudite; acc. to *Cs.* more particularly the mystical sense of religious writings, a higher degree of theology, as it were; *nán - don - gyi rab-ˌbyáms - pa* a Doctor of Divinity *Cs.* — *nan-nán-gi, nan-nán-nas = nan-gi, nan-nas* among. — *nán - pa* **Buddhist**, opp. to *p̔yi-pa*, Non-Buddhist, Brahmanist; *nán-pai lta-ba, bstán-pa, čos, stón-pa, čá-lugs*, the theory etc. of the Buddhists. — *nán-po* an intimate, a bosom - friend *Sch.* — *nán-mi* members of a household, inmates (ni f.) *Dom.* — *nán-mig* room, apartment, *C.*, *W.* — **nan-yáns** *W.* wide, spacious, roomy. — *nan-ról = nan-k̔rol* — *nán-ša* lining, **nán-ša tán-wa** to cover on the inside, to line, **nán-ša-čẹn** *C.* lined. — *nan-sél* **dissension, discrepancy.** — *nan-ɣsés* **reciprocal, mutual** *Wdn.* frq.

ནང་མཆོད་ *nan-mčód* **a sort of potion** (thin pap?) consisting of the 'ten impurities', viz. five kinds of flesh (also human flesh), excrements, urine, blood, marrow, and '*byan-séms dkár-po*' (?), all mixed together, transsubstantiated by charms, and changed into *bdúd-rtsi* or **nectar**, a small quantity of which is tasted by the devotees, with the Lama at their head. This delicious drink is considered of great importance by the mystics, who seek to obtain spiritual gifts by witchcraft (cf. *mdo* extr.); hence every offering is sprinkled with this potion.

ནང་ལྟར་ (*nán-ltar*) **nán-tar** *W.*, *C.*, **nán-žin** *C.* col. for *bžin-du, ltar*, **according to, in conformity with, like, as,** c. genit. or accus., *bka nán-tar, bkai nan-tar.*

ནང་མེ་ *nán-me*, resp. for *me* **fire** *W.* (*snán-me?*).

ནང་མོ་ *nán-mo* (*ma Pth.?*) **the morning;** in the morning; *nán-mo ɣčig bžin-du* every morning *Pth.*; *nan re* id.; *nan re dgons re* every morning and evening; *da-nán* this morning; *da-nán ni gán-nas byon* where do you come from to-day? *Mil.*; *da-nán-gi tsó-ba* this day's breakfast *Mil.*; *nan-núb* in the morning and in the evening; *nan - núb nyi - p̔yéd ɣsúm - la* in the morning, in the evening, and at noon. — *nan-par* 1. in the morning, *nan-par snar* early in the morning *Dzl.* 2. **the morning,** esp **the following morning,** *nán - par - kyi skál-ba* the allowance, the ration for the following morning *Glr.*

ནངས་ *nans W.* (?) *nan - čun yod* that is a mere **trifle,** not worth while, cf. *mnog.*

ནངས་པར་ *náns-par Cs.*, **nán - la** *W.*, **the day after to-morrow,** *B. ɣnan.*

ནད་ *nad* **disease, distemper, malady, sickness,** cf. *ná-ba*; (the Tibetan science of medicine distinguishes 404 kinds of diseases); *mi - nad p̔yúgs - nad* diseases among men and animals *Glr.*; *nad ɣsó - ba* to cure a disease, *nad ˌtsó-ba, nad sós - par*, or *ži-bar*, or *dan brál-bar ˌgyúr-ba* to be cured of a disease, to get well, to recover; *nád-kyis ˌdébs-pa, ˌt̔ébs-pa*, to be attacked by a disease, to be taken ill *B.*; *C.* more frq.: **nẹ̈-kyi gyáb-pa, zir-wa**, *W.*: **ṅá-la nad yon(s)**; *nád-kyi rgyu*, and *rkyen*, v. *rkyen* 1 and 2.

**Comp.** *nad - rkyál Wdk.* emblem of a deity (meaning not clear). — *nád - k̔an* **hospital** *Cs.* — *nád - go* **seat of a disease** *Sch.* — *nád-čan* **ill, sick** (little used). — *nád-pa* 1. **a sick person,** male or female. 2. adj. **ill, sick,** *séms-čan nád-pa-dag S.O.* = *nád-po* and *nád-bu = nad Cs.*, **nád-bu-čan** *W.*, weak in health, **sickly, poorly.** — *nad - méd* **healthy, hale, in health,** (the usual word); *nad-méd-par gyúr-čig* may you recover your health, may you remain in good health, all hail to you! *Cs.* — *nád-med-pa* **health,** *nád-med-pa t̔ób-pa, rnyéd-pa* to get well, to recover one's health; *nád-med-pa ˌgyúr-ba* declining health *Thgy.* — *nad tsúl* **the character of a disease** *S.g.* — *nad-ɣži* **seat, primary cause** of a disease(?) *Lt.* — *nad - ɣyóg* one attending to sick persons, **a nurse**; *nad-ɣyóg byéd-pa W.* **čó-če**, **to nurse.**

ནན་ *nan* **the act of pressing, urging; pressure, urgency, importunity,** *k̔ón-rnams-kyi nan ma t̔égs-par* not being able to resist their importunity *Mil.*; *nán-gyis* with urgency, pressingly, e.g. *žú-ba* to request, to solicit *Glr.*; *nán-gyis zar ̥ǰúg-pa* to urge, to compel (a person) to eat *Dzl.*; *nán-gyis skór-ba* to press, to crowd, round *Dzl.*; *nán-gyis ̥gúg-pa* to make a person come near by calling to him *Mil.*; *nan-čágs* 1. sbst. **certainty, surety,** **da nan-čág t̔ob soṅ** *W.* now I have certainty, now I know for sure; *nan-čags ̥t̔ems? Zam.* 2. adv. **certainly, surely** *W., C.*; adj. **lon nan-čág** *W.* certain news. — *nán-tan* 1. sbst. **earnest desire, application, exertion** *Cs.*; *byaṅ-čúb-la nán-tan byéd-pa* to strive earnestly for perfection *Dzl.*; *nán-tan-du byéd-pa Thgy.*; in *čós-kyi nán-tan γsuṅs Pth.* '*kyi*' is perh. to be cancelled. 2. adv. *C*: **certainly, positively,** **ṅe nén-ten láb-pa, neṅ-čág zér-pa**, I have told him so definitively, as my unalterable decision; *W.*: **earnestly, ardently, accurately,** **nán-tan žib-ča ltos** look at it, examine it, accurately! **nán-tan čos** do it well, most carefully! **nán-tan šrág-če** to burn entirely. — *nán-tar* very, *nán-tar bzaṅ Lex.*; **very much, all the more, altogether** *Mil.*; *nan-túr*, of rare occurrence, = *nán-tan*. — *nón-pa, γnán-pa* are cog. to *nan.*

ནན་ཏེ་ *nán-te* 1. *Ts.* for *ná-ba* **sick, ill.** — 2. *W.* **ču nán-te kyoṅ**, for *ran-te, ̥dren-te*, conduct the water this way!

ནན་ཞག་ *nán-žag W.* **late, recent,** what has happened a few weeks or months ago.

ནབས་ *nabs* **put on** (your clothes)! *Sch.*, v. *mnáb-pa.*

ནབས་སོ་ *nábs-so* **one of the lunar mansions,** v. *rgyu-skár* ༥.

ནམ་ *nam* I. sbst. 1. **night,** *nam láṅs-te*, or *-nas*, when night departs, **at day-break,** frq.; *nam-gáṅ Sch.*: the last day of the lunar month on which there is no moonshine at all; *nam-gúṅ* **midnight,** *nám-gyi gúṅ-t̔un-la* in the hour of midnight *Dom.*; *nam-stód* the first half of the night, *nam-smád* the second half of the night; *nám-gyi č̔a stod, smad*, id. — *nam-p̔yéd* **midnight** *Dzl., Glr.*; *nam-žóṅ* (?) *Sch.* in the morning; *nam-riṅ Sch.* a long day (??) — *nam-láṅs* **day-break,** *nam-laṅs-kyi-bar-du Dzl.* — *nam-sród* **darkness of night,** *nam-sród byiṅ soṅ-bai t̔se* as it was almost quite dark *Mil.*, **nam-šród yol sóṅ-nas** *C.*, *nam-srós-nas Sch.* id. — 2. for *nam-mk̔a* q. v.

II. adv. of time, also *dus-nám-žig*, 1. **when?** frq., **how long a time?** seldom; *rgyún-du nam ̥č̔i č̔a med sgom* always keep in mind that you do not know when you will die *Mil.*; *dus-nám-žig-gi tsé-nas* **since when? since what time? how long ago?** *Mil.*; relatively: *nam ̥gró-bai dus byéd-pa* to appoint the time, when one is going to start *Dzl.*; *nam žig sgyú-lus ̥ǰóg-pai t̔se*, when he shall lay aside his phantom-body *Mil.*; **nam t̔súg-pa k̔o ma léb-na, de t̔uy**..., as long as he has not come, so long . . . *W.* — 2. *nám(-du) yaṅ* (col. **nám-aṅ, náms-aṅ**) with a negative, **never,** in sentences relating to the past, or the future, or containing a prohibition, cf. *mi* and *ma*, *nam-yaṅ mi ziṅ-to* it will never be finished *Dzl.* ༢༣༦, 9; *sṅon nam yaṅ ma t̔os* (that) has never been heard of formerly; without a negative in *B.* rarely, col. frq.: **always;** *nam žag brtan Mil.*; **nám-žag gyún-du** *C.* id.

ནམ་མཁའ་ *nám-mk̔a* (cf. *mk̔a* and *γnam*) the space or region above us, **heaven, sky,** where the birds are flying, and the saints are soaring, where it lightens and thunders etc.; **the ether,** as the fifth element *S. g.*; **the principle of expansion and enlargement** *Wdṅ.*; *nám-mk̔a daṅ mnyám-pa* like unto the heavens, as to wide expanse, frq.; inaccurately also for an **innumerable multitude,** *nám-mk̔a daṅ mnyám-pai séms-čan-rnams Mil.*; *nám-mk̔ai dbyiṅs, nám-mk̔a-ldiṅ(-mo)* v. sub *mk̔a*; *nám-mk̔ai mt̔oṅs* **celestial vault, firmament** *Glr., S. O.*; *nám-mk̔a-mdog* the blue colour of the sky, **azure;** it is supposed to be produced by the southern side of mount Rirab, which consists entirely of azur-stone, *Mil.*; *k̔yim-gyi nám-mk̔a-la* in the air above the house, like *bar-snáṅ-la*, *Tar.* ༢༦, 2; *nam-̥p̔áṅs γčód-pa*, also *nam-*

*dpáṅs spyód-pa Mil.*, to cross the height of the heavens, to fly across the sky. — *nam-gru* v. *rgyu-skar.*

ནམ་ཟླ་ (*nám-zla*) pronounced **nám-da*, and *nám-la**, *Mil.*, *Pth.*, col., **season**, *nám-zla dus bži* the four seasons; *da nam-da ston šar* now autumn has set in; **da nam-da ḍaṅ-mo soṅ**; fig. *nám-da das* the (favourable) season has passed *Mil.*

ནམ་སོ་ *nám-so* = *nábs-so.*

ནར་ *nar* v. *na* I. and II., 2; also *ná-ḱa.*

ནར་མ་ *nár-ma* adj., and *nár-mar* adv., continuous, without interruption *Sch.*; **či-ma nár-te ṫon* or *šor* C.* torrents of tears gushed from his eyes, cf. *ḱrul*; *nár-re Mil.*, more vulg. **nár-ra-ra** in a long row or file, *grúl-ba* to walk.

ནར་མོ་, ནར་ནར་པོ་ *nár-mo*, *nár-nar-po* **oblong** *Mil.*, *Med.*; *ḱa-nar-čan* having the shape of a rectangle; *gru-nar-čan* **rhombic, lozenge-shaped.** Cf. *(b)snár-ba.*

ནལ་ *nal* n. of a precious stone *Sch.*

ནལ་(མ་) *nál(-ma) Cs.* **incest, fornication;** *nal-grib* pollution by it. *nal-ṗrúg* frq., **nal-ḷé* Ts.*, bastard-child; *nál-bu Sch.* a libidinous woman (??).

ནལ་བྱི་ *nál-byi Pth.* n. of a poison-tree.

ནས་ *nas* I. sbst. 1. **barley,** in three varieties: *mgyógs-nas* (*Ld. yáṅ-ma*, or *drug-ču-nas*, *Wdṅ. ḱrá-ma*) early barley, ripening in about 60 days; *sér-mo* late barley, the best sort; *če-nas* a middling sort. — 2. **barley-corn,** *nas-tsam* as much as a barley-corn *Glr.* — *nás-čaṅ* beer brewed of barley. *nas-ṙjén* v. *ṙjén-pa.* — *nas-ṗyé* barley-flour. — **nas-zír** (spelling not certain) aim or sight on a gun *W.*

II. postp., sign of the ablative case (almost like *las*) 1. added to sbst.: **from,** *byáṅ-ṗyogs-nas* from the north, often joined with *bzúṅ-ste* (*Ld. *táṅs-te**), commencing **from,** extending **from,** with a following **to, as far as; till, until,** with respect so space and time; **by,** *lág-pa-nas dzin-pa* or *jú-ba* to take a person by the hand, *míṅ-nas ṙjód-pa*, *smó-ba* to call by name, *ṫígs-pa re-ré-nas* (to count) by single drops, *so-só-nas* **one by one, each by himself; through,** *dúṅ-nas bšád-pas* speaking through a trumpet *Glr.*, *sgo-sáṅ-nas ltá-ba* looking through the chink of a door *Tar.*; *sgó-nas γtóṅ-ba* to admit through the door *Dzl.*; **bi-yaṅ-nẹ ṗaṅ* W.* he flung it through the hole (cf. also *rgyúd-pa* I., 2); made, manufactured, built etc. **of,** *ṗá-gu-nas* of bricks; (made, worked, struck etc.) **with,** **lág-pa-nẹ duṅ* W.* struck with the hand; denoting **distance:** *rgyaṅ-grágs γčig-nas pó-ta-la yod C.*, Potala lies within reach of the ear; *di-nas gáṅs-ri-la* far from here on the snowy mountain *Glr.*; with respect **to time: after,** *šag bdún-nas* after seven days: *dé-nas* **after that, afterwards, then.** — 2. added to verbs, as gerundial particle, rarely to the inf., gen. (col. always) to the verbal root, prop. **after, since;** also equivalent to *te*, when added to a pres. or pf. root (instances of which are to be met with almost on every page of Tibetan books); together with *dug* or *yod* added to a pres. or pf. tense, col. frq., in *B.* rarely: *ṅa lčeb dgos snyám-nas yod* I think I must seek death *Pth.*; *ṫsós-nas yod* it is boiled *Pth.*; *só-nam-gyi byá-ba-la žúgs-nas yód-pa-la* as they began to till the ground *Glr.* — Col. also for *na.*

ནི་ *ni* I. 1. particle, col. also **niṅ**; *Cs.* justly remarks: 'an emphatical particle', serving to give force to that word or part of a sentence, which rhetorically is most important, esp. also (though not exclusively, *Sch.*) to separate the subject of a sentence from its predicate, thus adding to perspicuity: *ḱyod dir óṅs-pa ni ṅai mṫus óṅs-so* thy coming hither has been effected by my (magic) power *Dzl.*; *bdag ni brám-ze yin* myself am a Brahmin *Dzl.*; *de ni ṅa yin* that one am I; *di ni mi ṗód-do* this I am not able to do *Dzl.*; ***ṫa-mál-pa ni ma yin*** a vulgar person she is not *Dzl.*; *des ni* it is by this (**that**...); ***stobs ni*** as to strength (I...); ***gál-te nús-na ni*** if he can (— well!); *da ni, snar ni, ₒdi-las ni, snon-čad ni* etc.; *šin-mḱan ni* now, as to the carpenter, he ... *Dzl.; dár-ba ni* now, with respect to the propagation (of the doctrine). In a similar manner it is frq. used, where we begin a new paragraph, heading it with its principal contents. In col. language the word before *ni* is rendered still more emphatic by repeating it once more after *ni*: **zer ni zer dug* W.* (it is true) they say so; **ḍi ni ḍi-te yod** it has been written, (to be sure); **ǰhe ni ǰhe* C.*, **čo ni čo dug* W.* (certainly) they are working at it, (but ...). In metrical compositions, esp. in mnemonic verses, it is often added as a mere metrical expletive, without any meaning, esp. after *dan*. — 2. *Ts.*: demonstrative pron., **ri ni-lẹ ní to-wa dug** this mountain is higher than that.

II. num. figure: 42.

ནི་ལ་ *ni-la* (*Hindi* नील blue) 1. *Cs.* **indigo.** — 2. *W.* **the blue pheasant** of the South Himalaya, manāl.

ནི་ལམ་, ལི་ལམ་ *ni-lam, li-lam* (*Hindi*; Shaksp.: 'from the Portuguese *leilam*') **auction, public sale.**

ནིང་ *nin* 1. col. for *ni*. 2. for *rnyin?* v. *na-nin, že-nin*.

ནིམ་བ་ *nim-ba*, निम्ब, n. of a plant, Melia Azedarachta.

ནིའི་ལི་ *nii-li Sch.*: **the great buzzard** or **mouse-hawk** (?).

ནུ་ *nu* num. fig.: 72.

ནུ་བ་ *nú-ba* pf. and imp. *nus*, **to suck** *Cs.*, *nu(-ba)-po, mo*, **a suckling** *Cs.*, *nu-ḱug* sucking-bag.

ནུ་བོ་ *nú-bo*, resp. *γčún-po, W.* **no**, **a man's younger brother** *B.* and *C.*

ནུ་མ་ *nú-ma, Cs.* also *čáb-nu* (resp.?), **breast,** as two correspondent parts of the body, 1. **mammary gland, female breast, bosom** *S.g.* — 2. **nipple, teat,** also of males. — 3. **dug, nipple** of a cow's udder; *nu-ḱyim, -γdan, -ₒbur, -ₒbor, Cs.* id. — *nú-ša* **the thoracic muscle.** — *nu-rtsé, nu-sór Cs.* the tip of the breasts, nipple. — *nú-žo* mother's milk, *mai nú-žo Dzl.*; *nú-žo snún-par byéd-pa* to suckle, to give suck, *Lt.*; *nú-žo skám-na* if she has no milk *Lt.*

ནུ་མོ་ *nú-mo* 1. *W.* **nó-mo**, **the younger sister of a female,** *B.* and col. — 2. v. *nú-ba*.

ནུག་སྟེ་ *núg-ste* (pronounced **núg-te**) *Ts.*, **so, thus.**

ནུད་པ་ *núd-pa* **to suckle,** *W.*: **pi-pi nud ton** give to suck! (= *snún-pa*).

ནུབ་ *nub* 1. **the west,** *nub-(kyi) ṕyogs(-rol)* id.; *núb-ṕyogs-su* towards the west; *nub-byán* north-west; *núb-kyi* of the west, western; v. also *bdé-ba-čan*. — 2. **evening,** *do-núb* this evening, to-night.

ནུབ་པ་ *núb-pa* 1. vb., **to fall gradually, to sink,** *mťil-la* to the bottom; **to sink in,** *pús-mo núb-pa tsam* knee-deep *Dzl.* frq.; **to go down, to set,** of the sun, moon, frq.; fig. **to decay, decline,** of religion; *núb-par ₒgyúr-ba* id.; *núb-par byéd-pa Sch.* = vb. a. *snúb-pa*. — 2. sbst. **an inhabitant of the West.**

ནུབ་མོ་ *núb-mo* **evening; in the evening,** frq.; *nub grán-gi* happening every evening *Sch.*

ནུམ་ *num, W.* col. for *mun*.

ནུར་ནུར་པོ་ *núr-nur-po* denotes the form of the embryo in the second week: **oval, oblong;** *mér-mer-po* id.

ནུར་བ་ *núr-ba* (cf. *brnúr-ba, snúr-ba*), 1. **to change place** or **posture, to move a little,** **rig-te nur** (v. *sgrig-pa*) *W.* move a little nearer together, stand or sit a little closer! *núr-gyis ₒťén-pa* to pull gradually, to give short pulls *Glr.*; *ṕa-bón ₒdam rdzis-pa bžin-du nur* the rock yielded, i.e. received impressions, like foot-prints on soft clay, *Mil.*; **to step aside, to draw** or **fall back; to get out of its place, to be dislocated;** **ṕi núr-la ḍúl-čé, ṕi-log-la núr-če* W.* to move slowly back. — 2. **to crumble to pieces,** *Mil.* of mountains during an unearthly storm, according to some Lamas, cf. *snúr-ba*. — 3. *Cs.*: **to approach, to come near to**(?), yet cf. *snúr-ba*.

ནུས་པ་ *nús-pa* I. 1. vb. **to be able, to have** sufficient moral or physical power, also = ṗód-pa; ǯi (or frq. ċi) *nús-kyis* **to one's best ability; to be able to do** or **to perform,** *dká-las gaṅ yaṅ mi nus* he cannot perform any difficult task *Thgy.*; *rgyál-po mi nus* he cannot be a king; **to venture, to dare,** *ɣgro nús-pa* one that dared to go. (In *W.* **ťúb-pa** is used almost exclusively instead of it.) — 2. adj. **able,** *nús-pa su čé-ba lta* let us see who is more able, more efficient, who can do more, *Mil.*; *C.* also **active, diligent, assiduous.** — 3. sbst. **power, ability, faculty, capability,** c. genit.: *ṅai nús-pa-la brtén-nas* by my power, through my agency (you shall obtain it) *Mil.*; *rtsig-pai nús-pa yód-dam med* whether there will be a capability of building . . . *Glr.*; **de čós-la nús-pa med* W.* this religion has no power; *nús-pa bšig-pa ťams-ċad* all the destructive powers; *byéd-nus-pa, sťón-nus-pa* the capability of doing, of showing *Thgy.*; *rnam-smin-nus-pa* the power of retributive justice (Nemesis, as it were) *Mil.*; **efficiency, efficacy, virtue** (of a remedy), *smán-nus ǯoms* they hinder the efficacy of the medicines *Med.*; *nús-pa smin* the efficacy becomes complete *Mil.*; in a more particular sense: **the effect of a medicine** in the stomach (opp. to its taste etc.); there are eight different effects: *lċi, snum, bsil, rtul, yaṅ, rtsub, ťsa, rno S.g.*; *nús-pa ɣnyis daṅ ldan* they have both qualities *S.g.*; *nus-stóbs* = *nús-pa Sch.*

II. pf. of *nú-ba*.

ནེ *ne* num. figure: 102.

ནེ་ཐང་, ནེའུ་ཐང་ *ne-ťáṅ, neu-ťáṅ,* **meadow, grass-plot, green-sward,** *B., C., W.*

ནེ་ནེ་མོ *né-ne-mo* **aunt,** the father's sister, or wife of the mother's brother.

ནེ་མ་ *né-ma* **meadow, green-sward,** *C., W.*

ནེ་ཙོ་ *né-tso* **parrot.**

ནེ་རེ་, ནེར་ནེར་ *ne-ré, ner nér* (v. *ner-ba*), *W.* **sediment, settlings, dregs.**

ནེ་ལེ་ *ne-lé Sch.*: **'mouse-hawk',** a species of large hawk or vulture, differing from *gó-bo,* frequently to be met with in Kullu, but not in Ladak.

ནེ་ཝེ་ *ne-we Sch.* mason's **trowel,** *ne-we rgyag-pa* to plaster, to roughcast.

ནེ་གསིང་, ནེ་བསིང་ *ne-ɣsiṅ, ne-bsiṅ* = *neu-(ɣ)siṅ.*

ནེན་པ་ *nén-pa W.* col. for *lén-pa,* **to take, lay hold of, seize; to take out, off, away; to hold.**

ནེམ་ནེམ་ *nem-ném* denotes **a nodding, waving,** or **rocking motion,** *Mil.*; cf. *nems* and *snem.*

ནེམ་བུ་ *ném-bu* **doubt, error** *Sch.*

ནེམས་ *nems*; *Stg.* describes an elastic floor in the following manner: *rkáṅ-pa bžág-na ni nems šes byéd-de, rkáṅ-pa btégs-na ni spar žes byed*: hence *nems,* **it sinks a little, gives way.**

ནེའུ་ལྡང་ *neu-ldáṅ Lex.* = *na-mnyám* one of the same age, **coetaneous, contemporary**; *Sch.*: *neu-ldáṅ* **friend,** and *neu-ldáṅs* **protector, defender.**

ནེའུ་ལེ་ *neu-lé, Hindi* नेवला, *Ssk.* नकुल, **ichneumon,** Herpestes Pharaonis, *Liš.*; represented in *B.* as a fabulous animal, cat-like and vomiting jewels.

ནེའུ་(ག)སིང་ *neu-(ɣ)siṅ* 1. *C.* = *ne-ťaṅ.* — 2. **grass-plots** on high mountains, **alpine pastures** (*C. spaṅ*).

ནེར་བ་ *nér-ba* **to sink, to fall gradually,** *mťil-la* to the bottom, = *núb-pa.*

ནེར་ནེར་ *ner-nér* = **ne-re* W.*

ནོ *no* 1. *W.* for *nú-bo.* — 2. num. fig.: 132.

ནོ་ནོ་ *no-nó Ld.* title of young noblemen, *no-nó čén-mo* the eldest of a nobleman's sons, *bár-pa* the second, *čúṅ-se* the youngest; *Sp.* title of the highest magistrate of the country.

ནོ་མོ་ *nó-mo* (*Bal. nó-ño*) *W.* for *nu-mo.*

ནོག *nog Sch.*: **cervical vertebra; hump of a camel.**

ནོག་པ་, ནོག་པོ་ *nóg-pa, nóg-po,* prob. prov. for *nág-po*; *nog-nóg* **very dark, deep-black.**

ནོང་བ་ *nóṅ-ba*, pf. *noṅs*, **to commit a fault, to make a mistake, to commit one's self**, *ċi noṅs* what have I done amiss? *bdág ma nóṅs-par ͦdí-ltar γnód-pa bgyis* I have thus been injured without my fault *Dzl.*; *nóṅs-pa* **fault, crime,** *nóṅs(-pa) mi byéd-pa* not to commit a fault or crime *Dzl.; bzód-pa* to pardon, to forgive, v. *bzód-pa*; *nóṅs-pa bzód-par γsól-ba* to ask pardon for a fault committed (in *C.* even: **nóṅ-pa sol-wa**); *nóṅs-pa-ċan* **culpable, liable to punishment;** **noṅ-ċan-ni (s)pe-ra* W.* a reprehensible speech.

ནོངས་པ་ *nóṅs-pa* resp. **no more alive, dead** *Dzl.*, *rje-btsún sku ma nóṅs-par ṕébs-pa* that your Reverence has arrived safe and sound *Mil.*

ནོད་པ་, མནོད་པ་ *nód-pa, mnód-pa*, pf. and imp. *mnos*, **to receive** instruction, directions, favours, from a superior, esp. priest, *Dzl.*, *Glr.*; but also to receive punishment.

ནོན་པ་ *nón-pa* I. also *γnón-pa*, pf. *γnan, mnan*, 1. **to press,** **máṅ-po ma non** do not press too hard! **nán-te ṕé-ċe* W.* to open a thing by pressing; with or without *rkáṅ-pas* to tread under foot, to crush; **to pour over, to cover with,** *sas, byé-mas*, with earth, with sand; **to be drenched,** *čár-pas* by a shower of rain *Dzl.*; to lay over, to overlay with *Tar.* 9, 11, 21; more frq. fig. **to oppress, suppress, overcome, conquer, humble, keep under,** *mťó-ba ḱrims-kyis* the great people by laws *Glr.;* enemies frq.; evil spirits by magic, e.g. *sri γnán-pa* by burying heads of animals in the ground, in order that the evil spirits may remain shut up there; *bgegs nón-pa* to keep the spirits away from the fields during harvest by hatchets etc. stuck in the ground; po. *ḱá-bai γdoṅ sri mnan* I have crushed, subdued, the face of the snow (i.e. its surface) that was adverse to me *Mil.; sa γnón-du* the sitting posture of a saint, when his left hand rests in his lap, and his right hand hangs down, keeping down, as it were, the earth and her powers; cf. *mnyam-bžág*. — Frq. also: *mya-ṅán-gyis, snyiṅ-rjes* etc. to be overcome by misery, by compassion. — 2. **to overtake, to catch, to reach,** *bdás-pas* in the pursuit *Mil.* and *W.* — 3. *sgo-ṅa* **to brood, to hatch, eggs,** *Sch.*

II. *W. lo tsam-non*, for *lon*, how old is he?

ནོམ་པ་ *nóm-pa*, pf. *noms*, 1. *Cs.* **to be satisfied, contented** (*ṅom-pa?*) — 2. **to seize, to lay hold of** (*snóm-pa*); *Sch.*: *noms-nyúg byéd-pa.*

ནོར་ *nor* I. (*Ssk.* धन, also वसु) 1. **wealth, property, possessions,** *nor(-la) gód-pa Mil.* to suffer a loss of property; **nor gód-da** or **ṕóg-ga* W.* have you suffered damage or loss? **nor nyams ċǫ́-pa* C.*, **lén-ċe* W.*, to examine the inventory, the amount of property; *ṕágs-pai nor bdun Mil.* the seven (spiritual) possessions of a saint, v. *Trig.* 17; proverb: **ráṅ-nor-la man mí-nor-la dhug* (sc. *tar tọ*)* *C.* look upon your own property as a medicine, upon that of others as a poison; **thing, substance,** much the same as *rdzas*, *Zam.* (nif.). — 2. more or less exclusively: **money,** *nór-la ltá-ba* to care for money, to be avaricious, easily bribed etc.; *nor skyí-ba* to borrow money, *nor bsri-ba* to save money, to scrape together; *nor sog-ͦjóg-pa* to accumulate riches. — 3. *Sch.*: **cattle,** even in such phrases as: *nọr ͦḱrig-pa* the pairing of cattle. *Sch.*, *nor-dpon Desg.* chief neatherd (provincialism of *C.?*). — 4. **heritage, inheritance,** *bkó-ba* to divide (it among the heirs); *ṕá-nor* heritage from the father, *má-nor* heritage from the mother. — 5 symb. num.: 8 (cf. *nór-lha*).

**Comp.** *nór-skal* **inheritance, hereditary portion;** *nór-skal-rnams* **funds, capital** *Mil.* — *nor-rgyún* imperishable riches *Cs.*; *nor-rgyún-ma* a goddess, *nor-ċan* **wealthy, opulent, rich** *Cs.* — *nór-bdag* 1. **a man of wealth.** 2. **an heir.** 3. **a money-changer, usurer,** *Hind.* महाजन, *nór-bdag-mo* fem. of it; also n. of a goddess; *nór-bdag-bu* heir. — *nór-ͦdus Pur.* **the gathering of taxes.** — *nór-brnab-ċan* covetous, greedy of money. — *nor-ṕyúgs* **amount, or stock of cattle,** *nor-ͦbrú* **store of corn.** — *nór-bu* v. that article.

— nor-ₒdzín po. **the earth.** — nor-rdzás = nor I., 1. B. and col. — nór-lha = ku-be-ra, god of riches; there are eight such gods.
II. v. sub nór-ba.

ནོར་བ་ nór-ba **to err, to make a mistake, to commit a fault**, gas ₒṗul nór-ro it is wrong (to write it) with the prefix γ Gram.; nor soṅ it is a mistake, I (thou, he etc.) am wrong; ka, lág-pa, lam nor soṅ, it was a slip of the tongue, I got hold of the wrong thing, I lost my way; to stray, dé-las ₒdi-ru from one thing to another Thgy.; mi-nór-ba, ma-nór-ba, nor-ba-méd-pa **infallible,** not liable to fail, e.g. of a charm; where one cannot miss or go wrong, lam; mi-nór-bar, strictly according to prescription or direction. — nór-ba, nór-pa Cs. 1. **a wanderer,** from the right way. 2. **an error, a mistake.** — nor-ₒkrúl id., frq.; nór-ra-re Sch.: he might possibly be mistaken.

ནོར་བུ་ nór-bu (मणि) 1. **jewel, gem, precious stone**, nór-bu-čan adorned with jewels, set with precious stones; nór-bu-pa, nór-bu-mkan Cs. **a jeweler**, a connoisseur of gems; nór-bu-ₒṗreṅ-ba a rosary or chaplet composed of precious stones; also as title of a book; nór-bu rín-po-čé, चिन्तामणि, a very costly jewel; also jewel, par excellence, a fabulous precious stone, the possession of which procures inexhaustible riches; acc. to Wdk. 488, it has the shape of an oval fruit of the size of a large lemon. — 2. **a noun personal**, or family name, much in use. — 3. gen. pronounced *nór-ru, nór-ro*, **good, excellent, noble,** e.g. mi, Bal., Pur.

ནོར་སོ་ nór-so, nór-so-čan, Wdṅ. 173, 11; 182, 4?

ནོལ་བ་ nól-ba to agree, to come to terms Cs.

ནོས་པ་ nós-pa v. nód-pa.

ནྱ་གྲོ་དྷ་ nya-gro-dha Ssk., Ficus indica, = byaṅ-čub-šiṅ.

གནག་པ་ γnág-pa, a secondary form of nág-pa, of rare occurrence, 1. **black;** γnag-sbágs **sooty** Sch.; γnag-ṗyúgs **black cattle**, esp. the yak; γnag rta lug γsum cattle, horses, and sheep, these three; γnag-kyú a herd of cattle; γnag-rdzi a keeper of cattle, cow-herd; γnag-lhás an enclosure for cattle. — 2. fig. black-hearted, **wicked, impious.** — 3. (looking black upon) **frowning;** Glr. fol. 96: sems šin-tu γnág-par byuṅ (notwithstanding their friendly appearance) they had a spite against each other in their hearts. — 4. sbst. **misfortune, grief, affliction, pain,** γnág-pa daṅ ldán-pa unfortunate, unhappy Stg.; *nag-čan* W. **cruel, tormenting;** *nag stán-pa* Ld. to torture, to torment. — 5. Sch.: (well) **considered,** (carefully) **weighed** in the mind; v. however brnág-pa.

གནང་བ་ γnáṅ-ba I. vb., pf. γnaṅ(s), imp. γnoṅ, B., C. (in W. stsál-ba is gen. used for γnáṅ-ba) 1. **to give,** resp., i.e. only used when a person of higher rank gives or is asked to give; cf. ₒbúl-ba; *dág-la dá-wa čig-gi ṗog kyáb-rog náṅ-wa žu* C. please, have the kindness to give me my month's pay; sometimes it is preceded by a pleon. rjés-su, Cs., **to bestow, to confer, upon,** frq.; **to commit to,** to place under a person's care, e.g. a pupil (resp. for γtód-pa) Mil.; **to grant, to concede,** what has been asked, γnáṅ-du γsol (ancient lit.), γnáṅ-ba žu (later lit.) I request you to grant; skur-γnáṅ mdzád-pa mkyen-mkyén I beg you for the favour of sending me... (in modern letters); **to allow, permit, approve of, assent to,** γšégs-par γnáṅ-no he accepted the invitation, he promised to come Dzl.; bdag ráb-tu ₒbyúṅ-ba(r) γnoṅ žig allow me to take (holy) orders, to become a priest Dzl.; bdag ni sbyín-pa žig byéd-kyis γnoṅ žig allow of my making a donation Dzl.; de bžin-du γnáṅ-ṅo yes, I permit it Dzl.; yid bžín-du γnáṅ-ṅo we allow it; do according to your pleasure! — či γnaṅ v. či I., 4. — In a looser sense: blón-por γnáṅ-ṅo he appointed him his minister; mi γnáṅ-ba **to forbid, prohibit,** čos byar mi γnáṅ-bai krims bčas he published a prohibitory law concerning the exercise of religion Glr.; (bkas) ma γnaṅ Pth. he refused it, declined to grant it, byon-du ma γnaṅ he refused to come *Glr.* — 2. sometimes **to command, to order,** complete form: *bka γnáṅ-ba; γnáṅ-ťsig skúl-ba* to order a person to do a thing *Pth.* — 3. in complimentary phrases used in *C.* the precise meaning of *γnáṅ-ba* is not always quite obvious: *γnaṅ-rógs mdzad-pa* (v. above) to give, to help to, to assist in(?); **góṅ-pa ťsóm-pa ma naṅ**, do not be put out, do not give way to any misgivings (towards me)! sometimes *snaṅ* (q.v.) would make a better sense.

II. sbst. **concession, permission, grant,** *ˏgró-bai γnáṅ-ba žú-ba Mil.; mí-las γnáṅ-ba ťób-pa* to obtain permission from a person; *bka-γnáṅ-ba* (magisterial) permission, order (of government); *γnaṅ-sbyin* very frq., **gift, donation, present,** *stón-mo γnaṅ-sbyin* a present of provisions *Glr.*; **gift of honour, reward, favour, privilege, price of victory** held out etc.

གནང(ས)་ *γnaṅs* adv. 1. **on the third day,** e.g. he came *Glr.*; gen. of the future: **the day after to-morrow,** *saṅ γnaṅs Glr.*; **ťó-re náṅ-la* W.* to-morrow and the day after to-morrow; *saṅ ˏgro γnaṅs ˏgro yód-pa yin* to-morrow or the day after to-morrow I must be off *Pth.*; *γnaṅs-γžés* on the third and fourth day *Lex.* — 2. *γnaṅs-čé* **rather** (too) **large,** *γnaṅs-čún* **rather** (too) **small** *Mil.nt.*

གནད་ *γnad*, *Ssk.* मर्मन्. 1. **the main point, object** or **substance, the pith, essence,** *γnad ˏgról-ba* to explain the main point *Mil.; γnad-dón* the proper meaning, the pith of the matter *Tar.*, *Schf.*; **γnád-šes-mk'an* W.* one that knows a thing thoroughly, that is up to it, knows how to do it; **nẹ' šẹ'-pa, nẹ'-kyi žú-wa búl-wa* C.* to excuse one's self, to defend or justify one's self (prop. to account for the circumstances that led to an action); **ṗog da ṗog; nad-du* (or *nad-čan*) *ma ťeb* W.* I have hit (him), but not mortally; so *B.*: *γnád-du snún-pa* to pierce mortally. — 2. in anatomy: by *γnad bdun*, or 'the seven important parts of the body', acc. to *S.g.* are meant: flesh, fat, bones and veins, and *ču-rgyus, don,* and *snod* (*Wise*, Hindoo Medicine p. 69, gives a somewhat different explanation). — 3. in mysticism: the seven physical conditions requisite for successful meditation, *lág-pa mnyam-bžág-tu bžág-pa* (the hands joined over the stomach in such a manner, that the fore-joints of the fingers cover each other, whilst the thumbs are stretched out without touching), *lus rdo-rje-skyil-krúṅ sdód-pa, gal-ťsig mda ltar srúṅ-ba, dpúṅ-pa rgód-šog-pa ltar srúṅ-ba, mig sna-rtsér ˏbébs-pa, mču raṅ-ˏbab-tu bžág-pa, lčé-rtse ya-dkán-la sbyár-ba;* there are also *séms-kyi γnad Mil.* certain conditions of the mind required, such as abstaining from *rtóg-pa*, speculative thinking.

གནན་པ་ *γnán-pa* v. *nón-pa.*

གནབ་པ་ *γnáb-pa* v. *mnáb-pa.*

གནམ་ *γnam* 1. **heaven, sky,** = *nám-mk'a; γnám-ga* id. *Cs.*; *γnám-gyi gó-la* **the sphere** or **globe of heaven** *Cs.*(?); *γnam ˏgyúr-ba Mil.*, mentioned in connexion with an earthquake, and prob. corr. translated by *Schr.* with thunderstorm, tempest; **nam kar-kór* W.* now the sky is cloudless, now overcast (inst. of **dkar-ˏkor*?*); *γnám-sgo* 1. *Sch.* **the gate of heaven**(?). 2. *C.* **trap-door.** — *γnam-lčags, γnam-lče Cs.* **thunderbolt, lightning** that has struck; *γnam-stóṅ* the thirtieth day of the lunar month, the day of new moon *Pth.*; **nam-ťáṅ* W.* serene sky, fine weather. — *γnam-ťel-dkár-po Glr.* 99 is said to be a deity of the Horpa or Mongols, as likewise *sa-ťel-nág-po*, and *bar-ťel-k'rá-bo.* — *γnám-mda Pth.* shooting an arrow straight up into the air. — *γnám-rdo Cs.* = *γnam-lčágs, Schr.* **hail.** — *γnam-zlúm* vault of heaven *Sch.* — *γnam-yás Glr.* 95 is said to be a n. p., the name of a building. — *γnam-rú*, resp. for *γžu*, **bow** (for shooting), *Cs.* **rainbow.** — *γnám-sa* heaven and earth, *γnám-sa brdéb-pa tsam* so that heaven and earth were mixed *Glr.* — 2. v. *nam*, **faulty, incorrect.**

གནའ་བ་ *γná-ba Glr.*, *Lt.*, *rnab Sg.*, *Ld.* **ná-po*, fem. *ná-mo**, an **antelope,** found in *Ld.*, *Sp.*, *Kun.*, *Nepal* and other countries;

its flesh is well-tasted, and its hair is supposed to cure cases of poisoning(!) *Med. Hook.*, (Him. Journ. II, 132) seems to mean this animal by his 'gnow', prob. confounding *γna* with *γnyan* (q.v.) which latter, acc. to Cunningham's Ladak p. 198, and by the statements of the natives, is the argali.

གནའ་བོ་ *γná-bo* **ancient** *Cs.; γna-sṅón* **formerly, in old times** *Cs.*; *γná-dus Lex.* **former times, time of yore**; *γná-nas ma mtoṅ* never seen or heard of before *Dzl.*; *γná-rabs Cs.* men who lived in old times, the ancients.

གནའ་མི་ *γná-mi Lex.* w.e.; *Sch.* **witness.**

གནས་ *γnas* 1. **place, spot,** *B.*, *C*, (in *W. sa(-k'yád), sa-čá) dbén-pai γnas ṡig* a lonely place; *mtó-bai γnas* a raised place, an elevation *Dzl.*; *γnás-na ˳dúg-pa, γnás-su sdód-pa* the being somewhere, *γnás-su ˳gró-ba* the going somewhere, *γnás-nas skrod-pa* the expelling from a place *Gram.* — 2 **place of residence, abode, dwelling-place,** (in *W.* not in use) *γnas ˳bébspa Sch.*, *˳čá-ba Ma.*, *˳débs-pa*, to establish one's self at a place, **to settle,** *γnas γtóṅ-ba, ṡóm-pa,* **to quarter, lodge, take in,** a person *Stg.*, *γnas méd-par ˳gyúr-ba* to become homeless; a house, family, or race no longer existing, extinct, *Dzl.; γnás-su sóṅ-ṅo* they returned to their place, their home *Dzl.; γnas daṅ skyabs méd-par ˳gyúr-ba* to be at one's wit's end, not knowing what to do *Schr.* — 3. **a holy place, place of pilgrimage; hermitage, monastery;** **nás ǰal-pa, nás-kor-pa* W.* **a pilgrim;** **dor-ǰe-liṅ-gi nɛ** the hermitage, or Buddhist parsonage in Darjeeling; acc. to *Sch.* also Lama, cf. *mčód-γnas.* — 4. **a clerical dignity** or **degree,** *γnas sbyin-pa* to confer such *Sch.* — 5. (cf. the Latin *locus*) **object,** like *yul*, but not so frq., *gád-moi γnas* an object of laughter; *ṅó-tsai γnas* words, actions, which ought to be an object of shame *Schr.*; **point, head, item** *Was.* (225); **sphere, province,** fig. *S.g.*; *ríg-pai γnas lṅa* the five classes of science. — *γnas ˳gyúr-ba Sch.:* to appear embodied (?); *γnás-su ˳gyúr-ba* and *byéd-pa S.O.* and elsewh.?

གནས་པ་ *γnás-pa*, (imp. prob. only in the periphrastical form *γnás-par byos*) 1. **to be, live, lodge, dwell, stay,** of persons, animals and things, *mṅál-na γnás-pai k'yeu* the babes in their mother's womb *Dom.* — 2. **to remain, hold to** or **on, adhere to,** e.g. a doctrine, opinion, way of acting etc., *dgé-ba bčú-la γnás-pa* to persevere in the ten virtues; *byáms-pai sems-la γnás-pa* to remain, to continue in love; in a general sense: *čós-la γnás-pa* 'one abiding in religion', a clerical person *Dzl.* ༢༩, 13; **to exist permanently,** opp. to the moment of first taking existence *Was.* (278). — 3. **to hesitate** (?). — *ráb-tu γnás-pa* v. *ráb-tu.*

**Comp. and deriv.** (also of *γnas*)*: γnás-skabs* 1. **state, condition,** or perh. more accurately **period,** *mṅál-gyi γnás-skabs ltár-ltar-po Lex.* 2. **temporal life,** *γnas-skabs-kyi bdé-ba* temporal happiness (opp. *to mtár-tug-gi snyiṅ-po,* or *don, ˳brás-bu, Schr.*, the essence or result of perfection, here, therefore, = eternal felicity); *γnás-skabs-tse-yi bar-γčód mi ˳byúṅ-ẑiṅ* if my temporal life be not endangered. — *γnás-k'aṅ* **dwelling, dwelling-house** or **room** *Dzl.*; *γnás-k'aṅ-la sógs-pa* a furnished house or room *Dzl.* — *γnas-čén* a great resort of pilgrimage, a great sanctuary *Tar.* — *γnas brtán* (loco firmus, stabilis, lit. translation of **स्थविर** 1. firm, 2. old) **an elder, senior,** n. of the (16) highest disciples of Buddha; afterwards, when various schools had been formed, n. of the orthodox Buddhists, *Burn.* I, 288; *Köpp.* I, 383; *Was.* (38). (*Cs.* seems to have confounded *brtan* with *brten*, when he translates: subaltern, vicar). — *γnás-po* **host, landlord, master of a house, head of a family** *C.*, *γnás-mo* fem. *Glr.* — *γnas-mál Lex.*, **शयासन**, sleeping-place, night-quarters, couch *Schr.*; *Cs.* dwelling-place (?) — *γnas-med* v. *γnas* 2. — *γnas γtsáṅ-mai ris* n. p., name of an abode of the gods. — *γnas-tsáṅ* **dwelling, quarters, lodgings,** *mí-la γnas-tsáṅ γyár-ba* to ask for a lodging; to be lodged, to be received into another's house *Tar.*; **nẹ-ṫsaṅ ̥juṅ** *C.* you will be lodged here, you may stay here (over night), *W.* **ḍáṅ-sa.** — *γnas-ṫsúl* 1. **the state** in which one is, good or bad, **condition of life,** *séms-kyi* the state of one's soul or heart. 2. **an account**, of one's state of mind. 3. **story, tale, narration; event,** col. 4. in philosophy: **the reality of being** (opp. to non-existence) *Was.* (297). — *γnas-γží* 1. = *γnas* 3, *Tar.* frq. 2. **the locative,** that case which relates to being **in** or **at** a place *Gram.* — *γnás-lugs* 1. **position, disposition, arrangement,** *lús-kyi* arrangement of the parts of the body, the science of anatomy *Med.* 2. in mystical works: *γnás-lugs rtógs-pa* **the knowledge of the essence of things,** the knowledge of all things, or in a Buddhist sense, of the non-existence of all things, *Tar.* and elsewh. — *γnas-bšád* 1. **topography and geography** col. 2. narration of legendary tales connected with some holy place. — *γnás-sa* (v. *γnás-pa*) the permanent residence of a person, or the constant place of a thing, opp. to **bór-sa** *W.* temporary place or residence; **place, room,** in general, **nẹ́-sa yáṅ-pa dug** *W.* there is much room here. — *γnas-bsrúṅ* 1. *W.* ('locum tenens') **earnest, earnest-money, pledge, security;** it might also be used for **ticket,** ticket of admission etc. 2. *Sch.:* **guardian,** or **warden** of a monastery.

གནོང་ *γnoṅ* 1. v. *γnaṅ-ba.* — 2. **consciousness of guilt,** *γnoṅ laṅ* (his) conscience smites (him) *Mil.*; *̥gyod-čiṅ γnoṅ bkúr-bai sems* repentance and a sense of guilt *Dzl.*

གནོང་བ་ *γnóṅ-ba* 1. **to be conscious of one's guilt, to feel remorse,** to be stung in one's conscience, *γnóṅ-žiṅ ̥gyód-pai sgó-nas* from a consciousness of guilt *Pth.*, *γnoṅ-̥gyód drág-pos* id. *Pth.*; **nóṅ-ṅo láṅ-na ṭím-čọ' de** *C.* where there is repentance, it is easy to pass judgment. — 2. **to be seized with anguish,** as the effect of poisoning. —

གནོད་པ་ *γnód-pa* 1. vb. (cf. *snád-pa*) **to hurt, harm, injure, damage,** *rkáṅ-pa-la γnód-par ̥gyúr-gyi dógs-pas* in order not to hurt one's foot *Dzl.*; *γnód-par ̥gyúr-bai dgra* a dangerous enemy *Dzl.*; **ṅá-la nod yin** *W.* (he or it) will hurt me. — More frq.: 2. sbst. **damage, harm, injury,** *byéd-pa, skyél-ba, Glr., Mil.,* **kyál-če** *W.* **to do harm, to inflict injury, to hurt,** with *la; γnód-pa med-par, ma ̥gyur-nas* without any harm, without injury *Sch.*; *γnod-byed-nyés-pa* v. *nyés-pa* I. — *klui γnód-pa* damage done by Nagas. — *γnod-sbyin,* यक्ष, a class of demons.

གནོན་པ་ *γnón-pa* v. *nón-pa.*

གནོབ་ *γnob* v. *mnáb-pa.*

མནག་པ་ *mnág-pa Sch.* = *γnág-pa* 5.

མནད་མནད་ *mnad-mnád Sch.:* **falsehood, calumny;** *W.* **nad-nád čó-ḱan** one doing damage maliciously.

མནན་པ་ *mnán-pa* v. *nón-pa.*

མནབ་པ་, (ག)ནབ་པ་ *mnáb-pa,* (*γ*)*náb-pa,* resp. for *gyón-pa,* **to put on,** *ná-bza Lex.* the garment; v. also *nabs.*

མནབ་རྩལ་ *mnab-rtsál Cs.* **mean, worthless;** *Lex.* and *Sch.:* **nourishment, food,** *mnab-rtsál-gyi bu(-ṫsa) Cs.:* the child of an indigent person, *Sch.:* **foster-child;** the word is not much known.

མནམ་པ་ *mnám-pa* **to smell of,** cca., *drí-ma glá-bai ríl-ma mnam* as to its smell, it smells of the dung of a musk-deer; **to smell agreeably, to exhale fragrance,** e.g. the scent of lotus *Glr.*; more frq. **to smell badly,** to spread an offensive smell, to stink, *rṅul maṅ dri mnam* profuse and badly smelling perspiration *Lt.*; *lus btsóg-pa mnám-pa* (or *-po*) *̥di Dzl.* this foul stinking body. Note: The transitive signification (to smell = to perceive by the nose) belongs only to the form *snám-pa*, and *Dzl.* ༢༥, 14 should be translated: the medicine stank.

མནའ་ *mna* **oath,** *mna ̥bór-ba, ̥dór-ba, byéd-pa, skyél-ba B.,* **kyál-če** *W.,* **to take an oath, to swear;** *lha dpáṅ-du btsúgs-nas mna byéd-pa* to swear by the Lha *Glr.*; *̥di-skad čes mna bór-ro Dzl.*; *bar daṅ mná-*

dpaṅ byéd-pa to act as a mediator and witness of the confirmation of the peace by oath *Glr.*; **mna zá-ba* C.* **to swear falsely, to commit perjury.**

མནའ་མ་ *mná-ma Dzl.* and elsewh., *Cs.*: a son's or grand-son's wife, **a daughter-in-law;** but the word is also used for the daughter-in-law 'in spe', i.e. for the bride of the son, who is usually selected by the parents and lives with these for one or two years before being married; so also bridegroom and son-in-law are nearly synonymous; v. *bág-ma* and *mág-pa*; cf. also the Hebrew חָתָן and כַּלָּה.

མནར་བ་ *mnár-ba* **to suffer, to be tormented,** *B., C., sdug-bsṅál p̔úṅ-pos* under a mountain of misery *Glr.*; *nyes-méd γtsó-bo rgyál-poi ˳ǰigs-pas mnar* the innocent lords had to suffer in consequence of the king's fears *Pth.*; *lás-kyis mnár-ba* to suffer in consequence of former actions, to be damned; *lás-kyis mnár-˳bai brág-srin-mo žig* a Srinmo in the state of damnation; *raṅ-nyid mnar-sdaṅ (?) byed* you make yourselves suffer the torments of damnation *Mil.*

མནལ་ *mnal*, resp. for *γnyid*, **sleep,** *mnál-du p̔éb-pa* or *˳gró-ba* to fall asleep, *mnál-ba* to sleep, *mnál-γzim-pa* id.; *mnal sád-pa* to awake *Mil.*; *mnal-láb* the talking in one's sleep; *mnál-lam* **dream** *Glr.*

མནོ་བ་ *mnó-ba* 1. **to think, fancy, imagine,** *de ṅá-la zér-ba yin mnós-nas* thinking it had been said **to him.** — 2. **to think upon, to consider,** *sṅa bsam p̔yi mno méd-par* neither considering before hand, nor thinking of the consequences; *bsam-mnó γtóṅ-ba* id., *Mil.* (cf. *bsam-bló*).

མནོག་པ་ *mnóg-pa* **contentment** *Cs.*; *zas-mnóg Lex.* w.e.; *Sch.*: moderate fare, frugal diet; *mnog-čúṅ* insignificant, trifling, v. *naṅs.*

མནོང་བ་ *mnóṅ-ba* v. *γnóṅ-ba.*

མནོད་པ་ *mnód-pa* v. *nód-pa.*

མནོལ་གྲིབ་ *mnol-grib Cs.* = *mnal-grib*; *mnol-ríg* **weak intellect,** want of quick perception *Sch.*

མནོས་ *mnos* 1. v. *nód-pa.* — 2. v. *mnó-ba.*

རྣ་བ་ *rná-ba* 1. resp. *snyan*, col. **nám-čog*, or *ǎm-čog**, (*Pur., Bal. *rna, sna**). **the ear,** *séms-čan ˬón-pa-dag rná-bas sgrá-rnams t̔os* the deaf hear; *rná-bai ṅé-loṅ* the drum or tympanum of the ear *Cs.*; *rná-bai dgá-ston* a treat for the ears *Glr.*; *rná-bai dbáṅ-po γtod* lend me your ear, listen to me *Mil.*; *ṅed rná-ba mi sun* I am not tired of hearing *Mil.*; *rnar snyán-pa* pleasant to the ear, tickling the ear *Stg.*; *rná-ba ˳dúd-pa* v. *˳dúd-pa*; *rná-ba byá-ba, byó-ba, blág-pa Sch.*, **to listen,** *rná-ba ná-ba* disease of the ear, **ear-ache;** *rná-ba ˬúr-ba Med.* a tingling, humming, or buzzing in the ears; *rná-ba sra* hard or dull of hearing *Sch.* — 2. v. *γná-ba.*

**Comp.** *rna-kór* ear-ring *Sch.*—**na-kyág* W.* ear-wax, cerumen. — *rna-k̔úṅ* ear-hole, *˳či-bai rná-k̔uṅ-du* (or *rná-bar*, or *rnar*) *brǰód-pa* to cry into a dying man's ear. — *rna-k̔ébs* that part of a helmet which protects the ear *Sch.* — *rna-gyán* ornament worn in the ears, e.g. *mé-tog-gi Stg.*; *rna-čá* id., *γsér-gyi Mil.* — *rná-mčog* col. 1. = *rná-ba.* 2. the pan of a fire-lock. — *rna-ltág* the back-part of the ear *Cs.* — *rná-t̔eg-čan, bzód-pa sgóm-pai rná-t̔eg-čan* one that is able to listen to all that (stuff) with patience *Mil.* — *rna-γdúb* ear-ring *Cs.* — *rna-mdá γzér-ba C.* the piercing of the ear with an arrow, a chinese punishment. — *rna-spág* (sic), or *-spábs* ear-wax *Sch.* — *rna-rál* an ear torn by pendants. — *rna-lúṅ Cs.* **the ear or handle of a vessel.** — *rna-šál Med.* ear-lap, tip of the ear. — *rna(-pa)-γšóg Lex.* and *Lt.*, perh. = *sna-γšog.* — *rna-slán* (**nas-lán**) a fur-cover for the ears, worn by Tibetan ladies.

རྣག་ *rnag* **matter, pus, suppuration,** *rnag smin-pa* pus grown ripe *Cs.*; *˳drén-pa Sch.*: 'to draw out the pus'; (I only met with *rnag sná-˳dren-pa S.g.*, which can hardly have this signification); *rnag-rdól-ba* discharge of matter; *rnag-rtól-ba* prob. causing such a discharge by a puncture; *rnag ˳dzág-pa* the dropping or running of pus

*Cs.*; *rnág-par rnág-pa* to form pus, to ulcerate *Cs.* — *skráṅs-pa rnág-tu k̔ug* v. *gug-pa.* — *rnag-k̔rág* matter and blood. — *rnág-čan* containing pus, purulent. — *rnag-ₒbrúm* abscess *Sch.* — *rnag-šubs* prob. the core of an ulcer.

རྣགས་ *rnags W., C.,* **ready money, cash,** **nag kyaṅ** id.; **nag-zog** money and goods; **gir-mo gyad nag** *Ld.* eight rupees in cash.

རྣང་བ་ *rnáṅ-ba* pf. *brnaṅs* **to be checked, stopped, shut off**; with or without *grébar*, to stick fast in one's throat; **to be choked** (complete form *brnáṅs-te ₒči-ba*); *dbúgs-kyis rnáṅ-šiṅ* (his) breath stopping short (from fright) *Pth.*; *skád-kyis rnáṅ-te* not being able to utter a word *Dzl.* ༢༧, 1; *zás-kyis rnáṅ-te* the food sticking fast in his throat, *mya-ṅán-gyis* from sorrow *Dzl.*

རྣམ་ *rnam*, in compounds for *rnám-par*, v. *rnám-par* extr.

རྣམ་པ་ *rnam-pa* 1. **piece, part,** e. g. the parts of a panel of a door, **riṅ-gi nám-pa** a longitudinal piece, **žéṅ-gi nám-pa** a cross piece *W.*; *rnám-pa γnyis-su gyes* (a ray of light) is divided into two parts or rays; **section, distinct part of a treatise; part, ingredient,** *lús-kyi rnám-pa p̔rá-rags-rnams* the subtile and the coarse ingredients of the body *Wdṅ.*; *rnám-pa kún-tu, t̔ams-čád-du* in every respect, to all intents and purposes, through and through, entirely, perfectly; this phrase is used, whenever people of rank are addressed: *rnam-kún t̔úgs-rje mgo-ₒdrén bkadrín mt̔suṅs-brál* most honoured patron, altogether incomparable as to grace and goodness! or, *rnam-kún t̔úgs-rje daṅ bkadrín mt̔suns-brál*; European gentlemen are thus addressed in letters: *rnam-kún t̔úgs-rje ₒgyur-méd sá-heb* most honoured Sahib, invariably kind in every respect! — 2. things or persons taken **individually,** often pleon., *ₒod-zér rnám-pa bži* four (separate) rays of light; *jó-bo rnam(-pa) γnyis* the two lords (sc. gods) *Glr.*; *bdag ₒdir t̔sogs bú-mo rnám-pa lṅa* we five girls here assembled *Mil.*; **sá-heb nám-pa nyi** *W.* the two European gentlemen; *čo-ₒp̔rúl* *rnám-pa bčo-brgyád* the eighteen wonderful feats; *ₒbyúṅ-ba rnám-pa lṅa Wdṅ.* the five elements; *žal-zás rnám-pa Dzl.* ༧༦, 17 the separate dishes of a meal (another reading: *žal-zás-rnams*); when used in quite a general sense, the exact meaning is to be understood only by the context: *lhá-sa rnam-pa γnyis t̔sár-nas* after finishing the two Lhasa affairs, viz. the erecting of two buildings previously mentioned; *rnám-pa t̔ams-čád mkyén-pai ye-šés S.O.*, or *spyan Dzl.*, as much as omniscience; *γzugs ní k̔a-dóg daṅ dbyíbs-kyi rnám-pao* '*γzugs*' is that in which both colour and form are included *Wdṅ.* — 3. **division, class, species,** *dpuṅ rnam bži* the four species of troops (cavalry, elephants, chariots, infantry); *rnám-pa bži* of four different kinds. — 4. **manner, way,** *rnám-pa sna-t̔sógs-kyis, rnám-pa sna-t̔sógs-kyi sgó-nas* in manifold manner, variously, frq.; *rnám-pa drúg-tu* (the earth shakes) in six ways, i.e. directions (whenever extraordinary works of charity are performed by holy men) v. *Burn.* I., 262 (not 'six times' *Sch.*); *rnám-pas* = *sgó-nas*, or *p̔yir*, *bslú-bai rnám-pas* by arts of seduction *Dzl.*; *dé-la mi dgá-bai rnám-pas* from vexation at it *Mil.*; *bsér-mai rnám-pas* in consequence of the cold wind *Mil.* — 5. **outward appearance, exterior, आकार**, as to form, figure, shape: *lčágs-kyui rnám-pa* in the shape of a hook, hooked *Wdṅ.*; *stón-pai rnám-par sprul* he assumed the appearance of the Teacher *Tar.*; *č̔ós-skui rnám-par ₒgyúr-ba* to appear in a misty form *Glr.*; *lus ₒdi ni roi rnám-par ₒgyur* this body turns into a corpse *Thgy.*, and so in most cases with regard to the whole appearance; of colour alone it is used only, when *dbyibs* (the shape) has already been stated, as in a passage from *Pth.*: as to its *rnám-pa* (colour), it is spotted like a leopard; **deportment, demeanour, gesture,** *yid-du ₒóṅ-bai rnám-pas* of graceful manners *Mil.*; further: **state, manner of existence,** of certain inhabitants of hell *Thgy.*; in philosophical writings: 'Form der Erkenntniss' *Was.* (274); men-

ན

tally: **disposition, temper, state of mind** *Thgy.*; **ko nám-pa-la** = *sám-pa-la C.* in his mind.

རྣམ་པར་ *rnám-par* 1. termin. of *rnám-pa:* **into the form** etc., v. above. — 2. as postp. **like,** = the Lat. instar, *Wdn.* — 3. adv. (possibly an abbreviation of *rnám-pa kún-tu*), **entirely, perfectly, thoroughly;** in negative sentences: **by no means, on no account;** often only adding force to another word, *Ssk.* वि; frq. in the shorter form *rnam.*

The following expressions most in use, containing the adv. *rnám-par* or *rnam,* are alphabetically arranged with reference to the second word: *rnám-par klúb-pa* **to adorn, embellish** *Cs.* — *rnam-gráṅs* 1. **enumeration,** *rgyál-poi* of kings *Glr.* 2. **the whole amount, sum total,** *S.g.*; **full number** or **quantity,** where nothing is wanting *Glr.*90, 3.; *mtsán-gyi rnam-gráṅs* the component parts of his name according to their etymological value *Tar.* 69, 3. 3. **treatise, dissertation, a paper,** *čós-kyi* frq. 4. by grammarians the signification of *de* is thus defined: *rnam-graṅs-yžan-brjód-pa* demonstrative pronoun(?). — *rnam-ₒgyúr* (cf. above *rnám-pa* 5) 1. **form, figure, shape,** *yi-gei rnam-ₒgyúr* the form of the letters (written or printed) *Glr.*, or in this passage also = the graceful form of letters, caligraphy, penmanship, v. below. 2. **behaviour, demeanour,** *lus-ṅág-gi Wdn.*; of a sick person *S.g.;* **gesture,** e.g. devout gestures *Mil.*; *rnam-ₒgyúr rdzés-pa Pth.* mimic gestures, mimical performance, ballet. More esp.: 3. **beautiful form, graceful carriage** of the body, **graceful attitudes** (of dancers etc.) *Pth.*; *bzoi rnam-ₒgyúr* the beauty of a work *Glr.* 4. **pride** *C., W., Mil.*; *rnám-ₒgyur-čan* **fine, smart, gayly dressed; proud, vain, foppish** col. — *rnám-par rgyál-ba* conquering completely, gaining a full victory *Pth.*; *rnam-rgyál* a surname much in use; *rnam-rgyal-púṅ-pa,* acc. to *Schl.* 247 *búm-pa,* water-bottle for sacred uses. — *rnam(-par)-bčád(-pa)* section, paragraph, *rnám-par bčad-pa daṅ-po-o* first paragraph; also mark of punctuation at the end of a paragraph, i.e. double-shad. — *rnam-bču-dbaṅ-ldan* a certain way of writing the Ommanipadmehūm, v. *Schl.* p. 121; but I should rather explain it in accordance to *rnám-pa* 2, as the 'ten powerful things', scil. letters or written characters, else the words would have been: *rnám-par dbaṅ-ldán bču.* — *rnám-par ₒjóg-pa* v. *rnam-bžág.* — *rnám-par rtóg-pa* (cf. *rtóg-pa* I. 2, and II., 2), gen. sbst. *rnam-rtóg* (विकल्प distinction; doubt, error) 1. **discrimination, perception;** so perh. *S.g.*: *rnam-rtóg ṅan bčom* the perception of what is disagreeable is weakened; **reasoning, mental investigation,** opp. to *ye-šes,* the sublime wisdom of the saint. 2. **scruple, hesitation,** *rnam-rtóg ma mdzád-par čaṅ ₒdi ysol* please drink this beer without any scruple! *Pth.;* so also in col. language. 3. in philosophy: **obscuration,** viz. of the clear and direct (nihilistic) knowledge of truth by reasonings in the mind of the individual, **error,** *Was.* (305). 4. in pop. language **disgust, distaste,** *rnám-rtog skyéd-pa* to feel disgust *Glr., zá-ba Pth.* prob. id. — *rnám-(par) tár(-ba).* 1. **to be entirely released** or **delivered,** and sbst. **complete deliverance,** *rnam-tár ysum Trigl.* fol. 12, three ascetic notions (in themselves of little consequence), *stoṅ-pa-nyid, mtsán-pa-med-pa,* and *smón-pa-med-pa.* 2. sbst. *rnam-tár* **biography, legendary tales** about a saint; **tale, story, description,** in general. — *rnam-tós-(kyi) bu, sras, rnam-sras* = Kuvera, *Ssk.* वैश्रवण. — *rnam-(par) dág (-pa)* thoroughly cleansed, frq.; by *rnam-(par) dág(-par) rtsi-ba,* or *mdzád-pa* I have attempted to express the Scriptural doctrine of δικαιοῦν or **justification.** — *rnam-ₒdúd* n. of one of the seven golden hills round Mount Meru. *Glr.* — *rnam-ₒdrén* (cf. *ₒdrén-pa* 2) the saviour, Buddha; *rnam-log-ₒdrén* the reverse. — *rnam-par-snaṅ-mdzád,* वैरोचन, n. of the first of the Dhyani Buddhas. — *rnam-(par) ₒprul(-ba)* **sorcery, magic tricks,** *byéd-pa Dom.* — *rnam-pyé, rnam-pyéd,* prob. = *rnam-(par) dbye(-ba)* 1. **distinction, division, section.** 2. *rnam-dbyé* **case** or **cases,** of which the Tibetan grammarians, from an excessive regard of the Ssk. language and in fond imitation of its peculiarities, have also adopted seven in number. — *rnam-(par) smin(-pa)* **retaliation, requital,** of good or evil deeds, committed in former lives, of good actions by prosperity (*las-˳ṗró*), of bad ones by misery and sufferings (*lan-čágs*), very frq.; *sdig-pai rnam-par smin-pa myóṅ-ba Dzl.* — *rnam-(par) bžág(-pa)* 1. **to distinguish, to put in order, arrange, classify** *Wdṅ., Thgy.,* . . . . . *sgó-nas* according to . . . (**certain** points or facts). 2. to consider a person or thing as fully equal or equivalent to another, to substitute one for the other, *C.*; *rnam-bžag* sbst., *Lex.* **व्यवस्था** 1. **placing apart, separating; distinction.** 2. **arrangement, position,** = *γnás-lugs* 1. — *rnam-(par) rig(-pa)* and *šés(-pa)*, as a vb., 1. **to know fully, to understand thoroughly.** 2. *rnám-par šés-pai lús-čan-rnams Dom.* **rational,** or at least **animated,** beings, opp. to inanimate nature; as a sbst., gen. *rnam-šes*, **विज्ञान**: 1. etymologically: **perfect knowledge, consciousness,** *Köpp.* I, 604. 2. in philosophy: one of the five *ṗúṅ-po*, **perceptions, cognitions,** *Was.* (of which there are six, if the knowledge acquired by the inner sense is included) also in *Mil.* frq., e. g. *sgó lṅai rnam-šes* (cf. *sgo γsum*). 3. in pop. language: **soul,** e.g. of the departed, (later literature and col.) (The significations 2 and 3, I presume, should be distinguished, as is done here, according to the different spheres in which they are used and not be explained one out of the other, as is attempted *Burn.* I, 503. *Schr.* gives here, as in most cases, the signification used in col. language.) 4. *rnam-rig Was.* (307) **idea, notion;** *Tar.* often = **न्याय**, also **विज्ञ**, *rnam-rig-tu bkrál-pa* 'explained in the sense of the idealists', *Schf.*; *rnam-rig daṅ rtóg-gei bstan-bčos* logical and dialectical Shastras. — *rnam-bšád* **explanation** *Tar.*

རྣམས་ *rnams*, in *B.* the usual sign of the plural, in col. language little used, esp. in *W.*, meaning, acc. to its etymology, **piece by piece;** hence its use is not a strict grammatical rule, but more or less arbitrary; it is mostly omitted, when the plural is otherwise indicated, e. g. after definite and indefinite numerals; it may be used, however, not only in these instances (*˳k̔or máṅ-po-rnams* many servants), but also after collective nouns (*dge-˳dún-rnams*), at the end of enumerations (= *de t̔ams-čád*), after general expressions, such as: *gaṅ yód(-pa)-rnams* whatever they were, after other plural-signs (. . . *dag-rnams* etc.). Cf. *rnám-pa* 2.

རྣར་ *rnar*, for *rná-bar*, q. v.

རྣལ་(མ་) *rnál(-ma)* I. 1. **rest** *Cs.*, *lus rnál-du γnás-par gyúr-to* his body obtained rest *Tar.*; esp. **tranquillity of mind, composedness, absence of passion,** *sems rnál-du mi γnás-par* his soul having no rest *Tar.*: *rnál-du ˳dúg-pa*, or *˳k̔ód-pa*, *Mil.*: *rnál-mar sdód-pa* id.; *rig-pa rnál-du ˳bébs-pa* to give one's mind up to perfect rest *Thgr.*; *rnal-˳byór* 1. **योग**, **meditation,** nearly the same as *tiṅ-ṅe-˳dzin* and *bsam-γtán Mil.*, but chiefly when it is considered as the business of life; *rnal-˳byor-rgyúd*, **योगतन्त्र**, *Tar.* frq. 2. often for *rnal-˳byór-pa.* — *rnal-˳byór-pa* **योगिन्**, **योगाचार्य**, **devotee, saint, sage, miracle-worker** frq. — 2. *Sch.* also: **personal, visible, essential** (?) — *Tar.* 201, 6. 22: *bstán-pa rnál-ma*? — II. often for *mnal.*

རྣུར་བ་ *rnúr-ba* v. *snúr-ba.*

རྣོ་བ་ *rnó-ba B.*, རྣོན་པོ་ *rnón-po* usual form, 1. **sharp, acute, edged, pointed;** *rno-méd C.* **dull, blunt;** *rno ṗyúṅ-ba* to sharpen, grind, whet *Sch.* (like *k̔a ˳dón-pa*); *rno lén-pa* to get sharp, to be sharpened; *rno-ṗyuṅ* name of males. — 2. this word is applied by the Tibetans to the chemical qualities of things, though not quite in the same way as we do, as they ascribe a 'sharp' taste to the flesh of beasts of prey, to the bile etc. *Med.* — 3. *rig-pa rnó-ba* **sharp, clever, shrewd,** *Glr.*, *blo rnó-ba* **talented, gifted,** *dbáṅ-po rnó-ba* **acute, sagacious.**

རྣོང་ rnoṅ Mil.? rnóṅ-la ₒṗog.

སྣ sna 1. (resp. śaṅs) **the nose,** B.; in col. language *sna-mtsúl*, v. below; *snai rús-pa* bridge of the nose, *snai čag-krúm* cartilage of the nose; *skad sná-nas ₒdón-pa* to utter (nasal) whining tones *Mil.*; *sná-nas ₒḱríd-pa* to lead or turn by the nose; *sna ₒṗyi-ba* to blow one's nose. — 2. **trunk, proboscis,** *ṗág-pai Glr.*; *gláṅ-sna* v. *glaṅ*. — 3. a mountain projecting from some other mountain in a lateral direction, **a spur** *Glr.*; it might also be used for **cape, promontory.** — 4. **end,** *ťig-śna* the end of a string *Glr.*, *rál-pai sna* the end of a lock of hair *Glr.*; **hem, edge, border,** *gós-kyi sna* the border of a garment *Cs.*; esp. **the nearer end, fore-part,** *ₒod čén-po żig-gi sná-la* foremost of a bright ray of light (that was approaching) *Mil.*; *sna ₒdrén-pa* **to lead, to head** (a body of men) cf. *mỳug-ma*; *dmág-sna ₒdrén-pa* to take the command of an army *Pth.*; more indefinitely, like *ₒdrén-pa*: **to draw along, to lead, to guide,** esp. with *lam*, to direct the way or course of a person, (having the person always in the genit. case); *ₒgrǫ drúg-gi lam-sna ₒdren* as a guide he leads all beings *Mil.*; **čú-na ḍem-pa** *C.* **to conduct water** (by a water-course); **to bring upon, to cause,** v. below, compounds; *rnág-sna ₒdrén-pa* to cause suppuration *Med.*; *lám-sna ₒdzín-pa* to have taken a certain road *Mil.* — In some cases it is difficult to account for the signification, so: *sna-čén-po* *Cs.* **a deputy; commissioner;** *sna-lén byéd-pa* c. genit. **to shelter, harbour, lodge, take in,** *Pth.*, *C.*; *sna (b)stád-pa Lex.*, *bdág-gi sna-stád ḱyód-la re Cs.* I place my full confidence in you; **ná-do ťóg-nẹ** *C.*, (**nár-do gyáb-te** *W.*) **ₒgyél-ba** either: to fall by striking with the fore-part of one's foot against a stone, or by striking one's foot against a stone lying before one. — 5. **sort, kind, species,** mostly with *ťsógs (-pa)*, *W.* with **so - sǫ́**, **diverse, various, all sorts of,** *spos sna-ťsógs-kyis ₒdébs-pa Dzl.* to strew all sorts of spices over . . . .; *rnám-pa sna-ťsógs* frq.; less frq. *sna-maṅ Lex.*, *sna dpag-tu-méd-pa Glr.*, *sna-ťsád Glr.* **of every sort;** *rín-po-če sna-bdun* seven kinds of jewels; *dár-sna lṅa* five sorts of silk; also *sna* alone is added to substantives, inst. of *sna-ťsógs*, or = *rnams*: *śíṅ-snai dúd-pa* smoke from different sorts of wood *Glr.*; *ₒbrú-sna smíṅ-pa* the ripening of corn *Glr.*; *sna-γčig* a single one *Mil.*; *čós-sna Tar.* 166, 4 prob. is not so much a kind, as a part of doctrine, *Schf.* — 6. *mi-sna*, *bló-sna* v. *mi* and *blo*.

**Comp.** *sná-skad*, **ná-kád ton** *W.*, he speaks through his nose. — *sna-ḱúṅ* nostril. — *sna-ḱrág*, *sna-ḱrág ₒdzág-pa* a bleeding from the nose, *sna-ḱrág γčód-pa* to stop it, *čad*, it ceases, it is stanched. — *sna-ḱríd* guide, leader; the leader of a choir. — *sná-ga* col. = *sna* 3. — *sna-góṅ* trunk, proboscis *Sch.* — *sna-sgáṅ* bridge of the nose *Cs.* — *sna-sgrá* the noise made through the nostrils *Cs.*, snuffling. — *sna-čú* a running nose, *sna-čú ₒdzag* mucus is dropping from the nose *Lt.* — *sna-čén Thgr.* a demon (?). — *sna-mčú* an elephant's trunk *Pth.* — *sna-ťág* 1. a rope passed through the nose of a beast to lead it by. 2. proboscis, *sna-ťág* or *sna-mčú sríṅ-ba* to stretch it forward *Pth.* — *sna-dri* prob. = *snabs Med.* — *sna-γdóṅ* bridge of the nose *Sch.* — *sna-ₒdág* (spelling?) *W.* **snuff.** — *sna-ₒdrén* **leader, commander;** *sdug-bsṅál-gyi sna-ₒdrén* **one that causes misfortune, author of it.** — *sna-nád* disease of the nose. — **na-či** *C.*, **na-ṗi** *W.*, pocket-handkerchief. — *sna-bábs* the glanders *Sch.* — *sná-bo* 1. **leader, commander, chief.** 2. **a guide,** *gom γsum tsam-laaṅ sná-bo dgos* about every third step one wants a guide *Mil.* — *sna-búg S.g.*, *sna-sbúgs Cs.*, nostril. — *sna-sbyóṅ*, *sna-smán* snuff *Med.* — *sná-ma Lex.* w.e., *Cs.* = *sna* 4. — *sna-rtsá* root of the nose *Cs.* — *sna-rtsé* tip of the nose. — *sna-ťsógs* v. *sna* 5. — **nam-ťsúl** *W.*, **nam-súl** *Bal.* = *sna* 1 and 2. — *sna-ₒdzúr* an aquiline or crooked nose *Cs.* — *sna-léb* a flat nose *Cs.* — *sna-śá* the flesh of the nose; the nose *Cs.*; *sna-śá sbyín-pa* to suffer one's self to be led by the nose *Cs.* — *sna-γšóg* 'the hair in the nostrils'; *sna-γšógs* 'the wings of the nose (alae nasi), together with the nostrils' *Sch.*; *sna-γšór* id. *Sch.* — *sna-bšál Lt.*, prob. an injection into the nose.

སྣ་ནམ་ *sna-nám* **Samarkand** *Glr.*

སྣ་སྙེམ་ *sna-sném, sna-sném ma ˳dúg-čig* do not sit here so idly, without any particular object! *Sch.*

སྣ་སྦྲང་ *sna-sbráṅ* **arrow-head** *Sch.*

སྣ་མ་ *sná-ma* 1. *Cs.*: 'the blossom of the nutmeg-tree'(?). — 2. v. *sna*, compounds.

སྣ་རུ, རྣ་རོ་ *sná-ru, rná-ro,* = *ná-ro Sch.*

སྣག་ *snag* 1. = *rnag Cs.* — 2. also *snág-ŧsa* **ink, Indian ink,** *rgya-snág* China ink, *bod-snag* Tibetan ink, *če-snág* Cashmere ink; **nág(-ŧsa) lug soṅ** *W.* the ink has run, i. e. a blot has been made. — **nag-koṅ** *W.*, **nag-bhum** *C.*, inkstand. — *snag-ŧig* an ink-spot, a dash, a stroke, made with the pen. — *snag-ṗyé* ink-powder. — *snag-ris rgyág-pa* to paint over with ink. — 3. *mig-gi snág-lpags Pth.?*

སྣག(ས)་ *snag(s)* = *ma-γnyén*, **relationship by the mother's side;** *snág-gi γnyen-mŧsáms* id. *Pth.*; *snag-dbón Lex.* w.e.

སྣང་བ་ *snáṅ-ba* I. vb. 1. **to emit light, to shine, to be bright;** *snáṅ-bar byéd-pa* **to fill with light, to enlighten, to illuminate,** *˳gyúr-ba* **to be filled with light, to be enlightened,** e.g. by the light of wisdom *Dzl.*; *šin-tu mi-snáṅ-bai mún-pa* darkness entirely devoid of light *Dzl.* — 2. **to be seen** or **perceived,** to show one's self, to appear, e.g. blood appears on the floor *Dzl.*; (*ṗyi*) *snáṅ-ba ŧams-čád Mil.*, *ṗyi snáṅ-ba gaṅ ˳byuṅ Mil.*, *ṗyi snáṅ-bai yul Mil.*, *snaṅ-ŧsád Glr.*, every thing visible, all that is an object of sense, the external world; *dá-lta rgyu žig snáṅ-ṅo* now an opportunity shows itself *Dzl.*; *lus mi snaṅ yaṅ γsuṅ snáṅ-ba ma-čád-pa byuṅ* although the body had become invisible, yet the voice continued to appear, to be heard *Tar.* 127, 11; it seems even to be capable of being extended to mental perceptions, the partic. being equivalent to imaginable; **to have a certain appearance, to look** (like), *čád-pa ltar* as if it had been suddenly cut off *Wdṅ.*; *snúm-bčas* (to look) greasy *S.g.*; *˳ṗrúl-du snáṅ-ṅo* it looks like sorcery *Glr.* (cf. *˳ṗrul*); *mi-snáṅ-ba* **invisible,** *mi-snaṅ-bar ˳gyúr-ba* to disappear frq.; *btsún-mo-rnams mi snáṅ-ba daṅ* as their wives were not to be seen, were not present *Dzl.* ༡༠, 17; *mi-snáṅ bar byéd-pa* to make invisible, to efface the traces of a thing. — 3. = *yód-pa Lex.*, sometimes in *B.*, and in the col. language of certain districts; *žes ṗrál-skad-la snaṅ* so it occurs in vulgar language *Gram.*; *zér-ba snaṅ* it is said, *dicitur*, *Tar.* 34, 4, and in a similar manner 33, 22; 34, 14; prob. also: **to be in a certain state** (of health), **in a certain condition, situation** etc., *C.*: **dhá-ta ghaṅ náṅ-ghin yọ̈-dham** how are you now? **čag peb žu naṅ** is the usual salutation in *C.*, like our: good morning! or: how do you do? however, the literal sense of it seems to have been forgotten, as even educated Lamas seldom know how to write it correctly. The proper way of spelling it seems to be: *ṗyag ṗeb bžud snaṅ*, and the words hardly imply much more than those addressed to inferior people, viz. *da leb soṅ* well, so you are come! well, there you are! Cf. *gá-le.*

II. sbst. (**दर्शन, आलोक** etc.) 1. **brightness, light,** *snáṅ-ba yód-pai dús-su* when there is light, broad day-light *Thgy.*; fig. *čós-kyi snáṅ-ba* the light of doctrine *Dzl.* — 2. **an apparation, phantom,** *mi máṅ-pos déd-pai snáṅ-ba ˳byúṅ-ṅo* there is an appearance as of being pursued by many people, i.e. a phantom of many pursuing people *Thgr.*; *rmi-lam-gyi snáṅ-ba-rnams Mṅg.* — 3. physically: **seeing, sight,** *bdag-ráṅ-gi snáṅ-ba ma dág-pa yin* my faculty of vision, my sight, is dimmed *Tar.*; more frq. intellectually: **view, opinion,** *saṅs-rgyás-kyi snáṅ-ba-la . . . γzigs-so, mi-nág-gi snáṅ-ba-la . . . mŧóṅ-ṅo* by the Buddhas he was looked upon as . . ., by laymen as . . . *Glr.*; **thought,**

**idea, notion, conception,** c. genit., *ₒdi ťams-čád ráṅ-gi séms-kyi snáṅ-ba yin* all these things are only conceptions of your mind, your fancies *Thgr.*; *skyid-sdúg-gi snaṅ-ba ŝar Thgr.*; *ₒḱyágs-pai snáṅ-ba ₒbyuṅ Mil.*; *bkres-snáṅ ye-méd-par gyúr-to* he was even without a thought of hunger *Mil.*; absolutely: **ḱyód-di náṅ-wa gá-ru taṅ soṅ** *W.* where are your thoughts wandering? *čós-la snáṅ-ba sgyur* turn your mind to religion! *Mil.*; *snáṅ - ba ₒgyúr - ba* (τὸ μετανοεῖν) change of heart, conversion (not to be confounded with *snáṅ-bar ₒgyúr-ba* v. above). *snáṅ-ba bdé-ba* **pleased, cheerful, happy** *Pth.*; in some expressions it is equivalent to **soul.** Most of the significations mentioned sub 3 seem not to have been in use in the older language. — *ₒḱrul-snáṅ, ₒṕrul snáṅ* **illusion, deception of the senses, deceit, error** *Mil.*, *Glṙ.*, col. — *ɣnyis-snáṅ* the arising of two ideas in the mind, *ɣnyis-snáṅ-gi rtóg - pa* **hesitation, irresolution, wavering** *Mil.* — *mťoṅ-snáṅ* 1. **the act of seeing, the sight,** *mťoṅ-snáṅ-gi sprúl-pa* phantom, apparition, **ťoṅ-náṅ dé-mo** *W.* a sight beautiful to look at, **ťoṅ-náṅ sóg-po** of ugly appearance. 2. *Cs.*: **manner** or **mode of viewing, point of view;** *ɣzigs-snáṅ* id. resp.; *Pth.*: *ɣzigs - snáṅ - la* according to his (supernatural) **intuition** (with reference to a holy person). — *tsor-snáṅ* **the hearing,** **tsor-náṅ-la nyán-po** *W.* delightful to hear, pleasing to the ear. — *bar-snáṅ* v. *bar.* — *raṅ - snáṅ* one's own thoughts, ideas *Mil.*; **the own mind** *Glr.*; *raṅ-snáṅ ₒḱrúl-pa* an illusion of fancy *Thgr.*; *snaṅ - ġrágs* **things seen and heard** *Mil.* — *snaṅ-stoṅ Mil.* frq., prob. not 'empty show, delusive appearance' *Sch.*, but: **things (really) appearing and (yet) void,** one of those frq. instances, where two words of opposite meaning are placed together, *dbyer - méd* often being added, as a tertium quid (cf. *Köpp.* I, 598). — *snaṅ - dág* (*naṅ - rtágs, brtág?? Ld. naṅ-stag*) col. **the inward man, the heart, the soul,** **naṅ-dág-la sám-pa ŝar soṅ** *W.* a thought has risen in my soul; **naṅ - dág čad soṅ** now he has felt it in his inmost soul, this will have struck home to his heart *W.*; **ṅá-la naṅ-dhág ma ǰhuṅ** *C.* I have not heard it, perceived it, minded it; **naṅ-dhág ma ǰhḗ** *C.*, **ma čo** *W.*, I was not heedful, I made a mistake! — *snáṅ-ba-mťa-yás* = *ₒod-dpag-méd* Amitabha, the fourth Dhyāni Buddha. — *snáṅ-me* v. *naṅ - me.* — *snaṅ - ťsád* v. above I., 2. — *snaṅ-ťsúl* 1. the outward appearance, of a landscape = **scenery** *Mil.*; 2. **appearance** opp. to essence, *ɣnas-ťsul Was.* (297). — *snaṅ - mdzád* v. *rnám - par.* — *snaṅ - ŝás* **thoughts, fancies** (?) — *snaṅ-srid* (*Ssk.* **संसार**) **the visible, external world** frq. — *snaṅ-ɣsál* **shining brightlo, brilliant;** *čós-kyi snaṅ-ɣsál sgrón-me* the bright light of doctrine *Pth.* — *snaṅ-ṅor ral ₒdrum Tar.* 16 (?).

སྣད་པ་ *snád-pa*, pf. *bsnad*, imp. *snod*, **to hurt, to harm, to injure,** c. accus., *lus snád-nas* being hurt in the body *Dzl.*; *ṅai rta snad ₒgro* or *ₒoṅ* my horse might be hurt *Mil.*; *snád - kyis dógs - te* afraid of hurting him *Dzl.*; of horned cattle: **to butt** *Sch.*

སྣབས་ *snabs*, resp. *ŝaṅs*, **mucus, snivel, snot,** *snabs ṕyi - ba* to blow one's nose, *snabs-ṕyis* pocket-handkerchief; *snabs-lúg* snotty nose, snotty fellow *Sch.*; *snabs-lúd*, prob. also *dar-snábs Dom.* = *snabs*; *bé-snabs* thick phlegm *Cs.*; *snám-pa* v. *snom.*

སྣམ་བུ་ *snám-bu* **woolen cloth;** the common sort is not dyed, very coarse, and loosely woven; *snám-bu spú-čan* hairy cloth, napped cloth; *snam-ṕrúg, dbus-snám Mil.*, fine cloth; *ₒgo-snám C.* id.; *snam-sbyár Lex.* a sort of loose mantle for priests *Cs.* — **nám-ya** *W.* **trowsers.** — *snam-yúg, yúg-snam* a whole piece or roll of woolen cloth. *snam rás* woolen cloth and cotton cloth *Mil.*

སྣམ་བྲག་ *snam-brág* (*Ü:* **ám-bág**) **bosom,** *snam-lógs, snam-ɣžógs* resp. **side.**

སྣར་ *snar*, termin. of *sna*; *snar-bkáb Wdk.* fol. 464 **nose-band** (?) **pocket-handkerchief** (?); *snár - kyu* **guide-rope** for camels, passing through their nose.

སྣར་ཐང་ *nar-ťáṅ* n. of a monastery, *Köpp.* II. 256; n. of a philologist *Gram.*

སྣར་པོ་, སྣར་མོ་ *snár-po, snár-mo Cs.* 1. of **a white** or **light red colour** (cf. *skya-nár*). — 2. **long, oblong,** cf. *nár-mo.*

སྣར་བ་ *snár-ba* prob. the original form of *bsnár-ba*.

སྣར་མ་ *snár-ma* n. of one of the **lunar mansions,** v. *rgyu-skar* 3.

སྣལ་བ་ *snál-ba* v. *bsnál-ba*.

སྣལ་མ་ *snál-ma* **thread, silk-thread, woolen thread** etc.; **knitting-yarn**, or yarn used for other purposes; also for **warp, abb-yarn.**

སྣུན་པ་ *snún-pa*, pf. and fut. *bsnun*, 1. **to prick** *Lt.*; **to stick** or **prick into**, e.g. a stick into the ground *Mil.*, *mtson* a weapon *Lex.* — 2. **to suckle** (cf. *nú-ba*, *núd-pa*), *nú-ma* or *nú-žo snún-pa Pth.*, *Lt.*, id. — 3. **to multiply** *Wdk.* — *ɣnad snún-pa Lex.* w.e, *Sch.*: 'to excavate the interior, to get or penetrate into the inside'(?).

སྣུབ་པ་ *snúb-pa*, pf. *bsnubs*, fut. *bsnub*, imp. *snub(s)* vb.a. to *núb-pa*, **to cause to perish**; gen. fig. **to suppress, abolish, abrogate, annul, destroy, annihilate**, a religion, a custom etc.

སྣུམ་པ་ *snúm(-pa S.g., -po Cs.)*, 1. **fat, grease, any greasy substance,** *snúm-gyis skúd-pa* **to grease, to smear**; in *C.* esp. **oil** (*W.* **már-nag**), *snum-zád-kyi már-me* a lamp, the oil of which is consumed; also fig., *snum* being added pleon., e.g. *Mṅg.*: *lus-zúṅs snum-zád*, and parallel to it: *lus-zúṅs zad Lt.*; *rlan-snúm* raw fat, *žun-snúm* melted fat *Cs.*; *sol-snúm* cart-grease, composed of pulverized charcoal and fat *Glr.* — 2. fig. of luxuriant grass or pasture, *ri snúm-pa* a hill clothed with luxuriant pastures *C.* (cf. *rug-gé*); *snúm-la ǰám-pa* luxurious and soft *Mil.* — *snum-kóṅ* a little bowl for oil etc. — *snum-ₒkúr* a kind of pastry baked in suet. — *snum-glégs*, *W.* **num-lág**, a wooden tablet, blackened, greased, and strewed with ashes, used for writing upon with a wood-pencil, thus serving for a slate. — *snúm-čan*, *snúm-bčas*, *snum-ldán* **fat, oily, greasy.** — *snúm-dri* a smell of fat. — *snúm-nag* **oil** *Kun.* — *snúm-rtsi* a greasy liquid, **oil** etc.; **greasy, oily** *C. snúm-pa* vb. = *snóm-pa* I.

སྣུར་བ་ *snúr-ba*, pf. and fut. *bsnur*, vb.a. to *núr-ba*, 1. **to put** or **move out of its place, to remove, to shift** *W.*; **to move** or **draw towards one's self** *Cs.*, so *mdún-du snúr-ba Zam.* is explained by *ₒtén-pa*. — 2. *Sch.*: **to cut into pieces, to fracture, to crush,** *žib-mor* into small pieces (to reduce), to powder; so it seems to be frq. used in *Lt.*, though one *Lex.* explains it by *ₒdás-pa* (scarcely corr.). — 3. *Cs.* **to bring near = to shorten,** *dus* a term, a space of time. Cf. *brnú(r)-ba Lexx.*

སྣེ་(མོ་) *sné(-mo)* 1. **extremity, end,** *snál-mai Lex.*, of a thread, *ťág-sne* the end of a rope *Sch.*; **hem, seam,** *né-mo* **ltáb-če** *W.* to fold down and sew the edge of a piece of cloth, **to hem;** **né-mo gyáb-če** *W.* to trim with cord or lace. *sne-ₒkór* **to warp, to get twisted** *Sch.* — 2. *sne-rgód*, *sne-dmár*, *sne-ťsód*, *món-sne*, *sneu*, names of plants.

སྣེམ་པ་ *snémpa* **to shake, to cause to move slightly,** *bsném-byai sa-ɣži* a quagmire, shaking or yielding under one's feet *Sch.*; *nem-ném bsném-pa Lex.*, pf. *bsnems.*

སྣོ་བ་ *snó-ba Cs.* = *snúr-ba*, **to reduce to small pieces, to crumble.**

སྣོད་ *snod* I. sbst. (**भाजन**) 1. **vessel,** *snod-spyád* id., *Lex.* and col. frq.; *ɣser-snód* a gold vessel; *p̀ye-snód* a vessel for meal or flour; *ču-snód* water-pot, pitcher; *bu-snód* **uterus, womb,** *Lt.* and col.; *snód-kyi ka* mouth of a vessel, *snód-kyi žabs* bottom or foot of a vessel, stem of a glass. — 2. in anatomy: *snod drug* (the six vessels) are: gall-bladder, stomach, the small and the large intestine, urinary bladder and spermatic vessels (in the female: uterus); *don-snód*, the six vessels and the five *don* together, v. *don* 5. — 3. with reference to religion v. *sde*, compounds. — 4. fig. 1. in ascetic language denoting **man**, as far as he is susceptible of higher and divine things; so already in *Dzl.* a man is called *snod yóṅs-su dág-pa* a very pure and holy vessel; *snod-ldán slób-ma* a disciple eager to be instructed *Mil.*; *snód-du rúṅ-ba* one fit for, worthy of (instruction); *snód-du méd-pa* unfit, insusceptible, rude, vulgar.; *ṅés-par légs-pai snod mčog*, *ṅes-legs bsgrúb-pai snod* *mčog* a most perfect vessel of religion (most susceptible of etc.) *Thgy.*; *snod ma yin* insusceptible of religion *Thgy.*, *Tar.* — 2. in metaphysics: *p̔yi-snód* **the external world,** or rather **inanimate nature,** *p̔yi-snód-kyi ˳jig-rtén Glr.* and elsewh. frq., opp. to *naṅ-bčúd*, viz. the sentient beings composing it; so *Mil.*; *Sch.*: matter and spirit. — II. v. *snád-pa.*

སྣོན་ *snon* **rest, remainder**(?) *Dzl.* ༢༥༢, 4, *Sch.*

སྣོན་པ་ *snón-pa*, pf. and fut. *bsnan*, 1. **to add, superadd, increase, augment,** **la nán-če* W.* to add to the wages, to raise the wages; **ǰa tsá-big nan sal* W.* please give me some more tea! *γnyis bsnán-te* two being added to them, (their number) increasing by two *Mil.*; *máṅ-du snón-pa* to augment by a great number frq. — *nón-ka*, or *nón-k̔a W.*, **increase, growth, augmentation,** and in a special sense: **agio, premium**; *snón-ma*, *bsnán-ma*, id.; **puṅ-nón* W.*, **gyab-nón* C.*, *dmag-tsógs snón-ma* **reinforcements, auxiliary troops.** — 2. **to add up, sum up** *Wdk.*

སྣོབ་ཟོག་ཅན་ *snób-zog-čan* (spelling?) **curious, inquisitive,** **nob-zóg čò-če* W.* to pry into, to ferret.

སྣོམ་པ་ *snóm-pa* I. also *snúm-pa*, pf. *bsnums*, fut. *bsnum*, imp *snum(s)*; and *snám-pa*, pf. *bsnams*, fut. *bsnam*, imp. *snom(s)*, 1. **to smell**, to perceive by the nose (cf. *mnám-pa*), *snas dri-rnams bsnáms-pa* to perceive scents by the nose *Stg.*; **da num* W.* there, smell at that! **zi núm-te ḍúl-če* W.* to go about smelling and prying; **ṅa čiaṅ mi num* W.* I do not smell any thing. — 2. **to grope,** **mụn-nag-la nom-nẹ čin* = *nag-zúg-la nóm-žin soṅ* C.*, v. *nag-zúg.*

II. pf. *bsnams*, fut. *bsnam*, *W.* **nám-če**, resp. for *lén-pa*, *˳dzín-pa*, *tógs-pa*, *˳čáṅ-ba*, **to take,** relics from a sepulchre *Glr.*; **to seize, to take up,** the alms-bowl *Dzl.*; **to hold,** a stick *Mil.*; **to put on,** a sacred garment; **nam yin-na* W.* would you please (to take), would you like (to have a cup of tea etc.)?

སྣོར་བ་ *snór-ba*, pf. and fut. *bsnor*, **to confound, mingle, mix, disturb** *Cs.*

སྣོལ་བ་ *snól-ba*, pf. and fut. *bsnol*, 1. **to unite, join, put together, fit together,** e.g. bricks or stones in building *W.*; *Cs.* **to adjust**; *Sch.*: to mend holes in stockings, **to darn**; **to cross** one's hands, *bráṅ-k̔ar*, resp. *t̔úgs-kar*, on the breast *Thgr.* and elsewh. frq.; *˳t̔am snól-ba* **to put together, to embrace** *Cs.*; *ltá-snol-ba* to look at each other, *˳ó-snol-ba* to kiss each other, 'and thus frq. denoting reciprocity' *Cs.* (though not to my knowledge). — 2. **to wrestle, scuffle, fight,** of boys, dogs frq., also *Mil.*; *stag snól-ba* a fighting tiger that rushes upon the enemy *Ma.*; **to contend with, fight against, subdue,** *me*, a fire *Tar.*

སྣྲུབས་, སྣྲོན་ *snrubs, snron*, the names of two of the lunar mansions, v. *rgyu-skár.*

སྣྲེལ་(ག)ཞི་ *snrel-(γ)ži Lexx.* = *p̔red*; *Cs.* **sloping, oblique**; *Sch.*: **confusedly, pellmell**; *Cs.* also **mediocrity.**

བརྣག་པ་ *brnág-pa* 1. **to devise, contrive, to take care, to be concerned about, to strive for** or **after,** . . . *žes γčig-tu brnágs-pas* striving only after (that one thing) *Tar.*; as sbst. *brnág-pa čoṅs* keep (it) well in your mind, pay all attention (to it)! c. genit., cf. *brnán-pa.* — 2. *Lex.* = *bzód-pa*, **to suffer, to endure**; *brnag-dka* **intolerable, insupportable** *Lex.* — 3. *Cs.*: **to be full of corrupt matter.**

བརྣང་བ་ *brnáṅ-ba* v. *rnáṅ-ba.*

བརྣན་པ་ *brnán-pa* 1. *Cs.* **to attend, to look on attentively,** *˳bri-klóg brnán-pa* to attend while a person is reading or writing. — 2. *Sch.*: **'to be desirous of, to long for,** *čós-la* for religious instruction, *ltó-la* for food'. With the first signification agrees a quotation in *Zam.*: *nán-tan-brnan*, with the second the word **zá-nan-čan* W.*, = *zá-brnab-čan.*

བརྣབ་སེམས་ *brnáb-sems Cs.*: **covetousness, selfishness**; *Thgy.*: *bdág-gi-la brnáb-sems* predilection for one's own things, *γžán-gyi-la brnáb-sems* desire for things belonging to others; *W.*: **zá-nab-ċan** **greedy, ravenous;** **nór-nab-ċan** **greedy of gain** or **money, covetous.**

བརྣུ་བ་, བརྣུར་བ་ *brnú-ba, brnúr-ba Lexx.; Cs.* **to draw to, to attract,** (*Sch.* also: 'to remove a thing from its place?'), prob. another form for *snúr-ba.*

བརྣོགས་པ་ *brnógs-pa* **to hide, conceal,** *Lexx.*

བསྣང་བ་ *bsnáṅ-ba* v. *rnáṅ-ba.*

བསྣད་པ་ *bsnád-pa* v. *snád-pa.*

བསྣན་པ་ *bsnán-pa* v. *snón-pa.*

བསྣམ་པ་ *bsnám-pa* v. *snóm-pa.*

བསྣར་བ་ *bsnár-ba* 1. **to extend in length, to lengthen, to pull out,** e.g. a piece of India rubber *W.* — 2. **to draw** or **drag after, to trail,** *mǰúg-ma Lex.* the train of a robe, the tail etc.; fig. **to have in its train, to be attended with,** *nyon-moṅs-bsnár* the consequences of sin *Sch.*

བསྣལ་བ་ *bsnál-ba* **to spin out, to protract** *Cs.*

བསྣུན་པ་ *bsnún-pa* v. *snun-pa.*

# པ

པ *pa* 1. the letter *p*, (tenuis), the French p. — 2. num. figure: 13.

པ་ *pa*, an affix, or so-called article, the same as *ba* (q. v.) which, when attached to the roots of verbs, gives them the signification of nouns, or, in other words is the sign of the infinitive and the participle; in the language of common life, however, it is frq. used for the finite tense, and for *par;* affixed to the names of things, it denotes the person that deals with the thing (*rtá-pa* horseman, *ċú-pa* water-carrier); combined with names of places, it designates the inhabitant (*bód-pa* inhabitant of Tibet); with numerals, it either forms the ordinal number (*γnyis-pa* the second), or it implies a counting, measuring, containing (*bú-mo lo-γnyís-pa* a girl counting two years, i. e. a girl of two years; *k̔ru-gáṅ-pa* measuring one cubit; *súm-ċu-pa* containing thirty viz. letters, like the Tibetan alphabet); frq. it has no particular signification (*rkéd-pa* etc. etc.), or it serves to distinguish different meanings (*rkaṅ* marrow, *rkáṅ-pa* foot) or dialects (*k̔á-ba B.*, **k̔a* W.* snow); *pa daṅ* with a verb, v. *daṅ* 4; in certain expressions it stands, it would seem, incorr. inst. of *pai*: *γsó-ba rig-pa* science of medicine, *grúb-pa lus* structure of the body, *dám-pa čos* holy doctrine (of Buddha).

པ་ཏ་ *pá-ta W.* **cross,** St. Andrew's cross (thus ×).

པ་ཏིལ་ *pa-til* v. *ṗa-til.*

པ་ཏོ་ *pá-to* **a medicinal herb** *Wdṅ.*

པ་ཏ, more corr. པཏྲ, *pā-tra* (also *pa-ṭa Pth.*) *Ssk.*, **cup, basin, bowl** (esp. for sacrifices); beggar's bowl = *lhuṅ-bzed.*

པ་ཎ་ *pa-ṇa Ssk.* = *ṭaṅ-ka Tar.* 112, 6; in Bhotan 1 rupee *Schr.*; in *W.* (also **pé-ṇa**) a copper-coin = Paisa, esp. of foreign coinage.

པ་ཎི་ *pa-ṇi Hind.* **पानी, water** *Lt.*

པ་བེན་ *pa-ben* **a strip of wood, ledge, border** (?) *W.*

པ་(ཝ་)སངས་ *pa(-wa)-sáṅs* 1. **the planet Venus.** — 2. **Friday.**

པ་ཡག་པ་ pa-yag-pa a medicinal herb = *smug-čuṅ Med.*

པ་ཡུ *pa-yu* salt *Bal.*

པ་ཡོ་དོ་ཡོ་ *pa-yo-tó-yo*, **srog daṅ pa-yo-tó-yo taṅ-te soṅ** *Ld.* for *srog daṅ bsdos*, v. *sdo-ba.*

པ་ར་ཁ *pá-ra-ḱa W.* **cross** (a straight one +).

པ་རང་ *pa-ráṅ* (spelling doubtful, at any rate not *p̓a-raṅ*) n. of a mountain pass, 19 000 feet high, between Ladak and Spiti.

པ་རི་ *pá-ri W.*, *pá-ru C.*, *B.* 1. **box**, cylindrical or oval, high or flat, of wood or metal. — 2. *pá-ru*, also *pá-tra Sch.* — 3. v. *bá-ru.*

པ་ཤི *pa-ši Sch.* **'a teacher'**; *Lex.*: n. of a Tibetan priest that went to China.

པ་སངས་ *pa-saṅs* v. *pa-wa-saṅs.*

པག, པག་བུ *pag*, *pág-bu Bal.*, *pág-gu Dzl.*, *pau W.*, *p̓ag Glr.*, *p̓au Wdṅ.*: **brick**; *pág-gu byéd-pa Dzl.*; *p̓ibs-pag* roof-tile *Cs.*; *wá-pag* gutter-tile *Cs.*; *rdzá-pag*, *só-pag Glr.* burnt-brick *Cs.*; *sá-pag Glr.* unburnt-brick *Cs.*; *pag(-bu)-mk̓an* mason *Cs.*; *pag-rtsig* brick-wall *Cs.*; **pag-tsír W.* a row or layer of bricks; frq. used as a measure = a small span, **ḱa pag-tsír nyis yod** the snow is as deep as two layers of bricks. — Not quite plain is the etymology of *˳og-pag*, *Lex.*: *ska-rágs-kyi rgyan*, *Sch.*: 'a girdle ornamented with glass-beads'; and of *pag-p̓ór Sch.* cup or vessel with a lid.

པགས་པ་ *págs-pa*, *Mil.* also *-po* (cf. *lpags*) 1. **skin, hide**; *šu-ba* to skin, acc. to *Schr.* also merely to fret the skin; *págs-pai gos* skin or fur-clothing *S.g.* — 2. **foreskin**, when the connection of words does not admit of a misconception, *Mng.* — 3. **skin** or **peel** of fruit, **the bark** of trees, also *pags-šún*, and *šún-pags*; **pag-t̓ág** *C.* bark-cord, match-cord; *págs-ču* anasarca, skin-dropsy; *págs-ču-žugs* affected with this disease.

པང་ *paṅ*, ཕང་ *p̓aṅ*, resp. *sku-páṅ*, 1. the bend or hollow formed by the belly and the thighs in sitting, **lap**, *B.*, *C.*, *W.*; *paṅ-du soṅ* he sat down on the lap of ... *Glr.*; *paṅ-ḱebs* apron; *paṅ-ḱrag* the blood flowing off during child-birth; **paṅ-big** *W.* urinary bladder; **paṅ-ri* (for *dri?*) *suṅ** *C.* she has the bloody flux; *páṅ-γyog-ma Cs.* midwife (a kinswoman generally has to officiate as such; a hired one receives a new dress for her services). — 2. the bend or hollow formed by the arm and the chest in carrying something; **bosom**, usually *páṅ-pa*; *šiṅ-paṅ-pa gaṅ* an armful of wood; *páṅ-par ˳kyér-ba* to carry (a child) on the arm *Dzl.* and elsewh.; *sdóṅ-po páṅ-pas ma ˳kyigs-pa tsam žig* a tree not to be encompassed by a man's arms *Pth.*; **paṅ-gód*, *paṅ-kód** *W.* an armful.

པང་ཀ་ *páṅ-ka*, *páṅ-ḱa* 1. *W.* an implement for stirring the fire; for scraping = *rbad.* — 2. *Ts.* = *paṅ.*

པནྩ, པན་ཙ་ *pańtsa*, *pan-tsa*, seems to be the n. of a tree *B.*, *C.*; *Ssk.* only: five.

པད་པ་ *pád-pa C.* = *srin-bu pád-ma*, v. *pád-ma.*

པདྨ, པད་མ་ *padma*, *pad-ma Ssk.* in *C.* pronounced **pé-ma** 1. **water-lily, lotos, Nymphaea**, if not nearer defined, the blue species, whilst the less frq. form *pád-mo* (acc. to *Glr.* fol. 62) seems to denote the white kind of this flower. — 2. (not in *Ssk.*, at least acc. to *Wls.* and *Williams*, though *Köpp.* II, 61 seems to dissent): **genitals**, of either sex, *Med.* — 3. *srin-bu pád-ma* **leech**. — *pad-kór*, *pad-skór* 1. a particular way of folding the fingers during prayer *Cs.* and *Sch.*; a certain gesture with the hand. 2. a kind of **toupet** of the women, also *pad-ló C.*, *W.* — *pád(-ma) dkár(-do)* 1. white lotos. 2. **title** of a celebrated **Sutra**, translated by Burnouf, *Was.* (151). — *pad-dkár žal-laṅ* an astronomical work by Púgpapa, v. *Cs.* time-table. — *pad-ma-čan* full of lotos; more particularly lotos-lake, with and without *mtso Glr.* — *pad-(ma daṅ nyi-ma daṅ) zlái γdun Glr.* and elsewh., carpet with representations of lotos, sun and moon. — *pad-ma-pa-ni* lotos-bearer, name of Awalokiteswara, *Köpp.* II, 23. — *Pad-ma-ₒbyuṅ γnás, Sskr.* P. Sambhava, also: *U-rgyan-pád-ma*, one of the most famous divines and holy magicians, in the 8th century, from Urgyén (*Ssk.* Udayana) i.e. Kabul, who acc. to his own declaration (v. the fantastic legend concerning him, entitled: *pad-ma t̔aṅ-yig*) was greater than Buddha himself, v. *Köpp.* II, 68. – *pad-ma-ra-ga Ssk.* ruby. — *pád-rtsa* a medicinal herb *Wdṅ* (= *pe-tsé?*).

པཎྜི་ཏ་ *paṇḍi-ta Ssk.*, **Pandit**, Indian scholar or linguist; *paṇ-čén* great Pandit; *paṇ-čén rin-po-čʻé, bog-do* (Mongolian) *rin-čen*, title of the second Buddhist pope, residing at Tashilunpo, *Köpp.* II, 121. — *pan-ža* Pandit-cap.

པན་པོན་ *pan-pón* (also *pan-pún?*) not considered perfect in dignity, as for instance the Lamas in *Lh.*, that are married; yet cf. *ban-bón*.

པར་ *par* I. **form, mould,** *blugs-par* casting-mould; *rdéu-par* bullet-mould; *blúgs-par*, as well as *śiṅ-par*, printing form, a stereotype plate cut in wood; *par rkó-ba* to cut types; *rgyáb-pa, par-du ₒdébs-pa*, to print, to stamp; *par (-yig) ₒbri-ba* to write the exemplar or manuscript for printing. — *pár-rko-pa, pár-rko-mk̔an*, cutter of types. — *pár-k̔aṅ* printing-office. — *par-rgyáb* print, **par-rgyáb tsógs-se** *W.* like a print or impression. — *par-snág* printing-ink. — *pár-pa* printer *Cs.* — *pár-dpon* fore-man of a printing-office. — *pár-ma* a printed work, book; **di pár-ma yaṅ yod** this is also to be had printed. — *par-γyóg* a printer's man, assistant. — *par-śog* printing-paper. — *par-γži* = *par*.

II. v. *pár-ma*. — III. termin. of *pa*, also sign of the adverb; combined with verbs, it represents the supine, or adverbial sentences, commencing with **whilst, so that;** *mi byéd-par* without doing.

པར་ཏང་ *par-taṅ Lex.*, **a hairy carpet** *Sch.*

པར་པ་ཏ་ *par-pa-ta* n. of an officinal plant *Med.*

པར་བུ་ *par-bu Lexx., Sch.* = *pa-tra.*

པར་ཙ་སོ་ཏི་ *par-tsa-só-ti W.* **a kind of cotton cloth.**

པལ་ལ་ཏུ་ལ་ *pal-la-tú-la Hind.* **scales of a balance** *Sik.*

པས་ *pas* 1. the instr. of *pa*; combined with verbs, it signifies **by, in consequence of, because;** also **as, since, when.** — 2. = *las*, as sign of the comparative; after vowels, however and the final consonants d, r, l, *bas* stands in its place; *rtá-bas k̔yi čʻúṅ-ba yin* the dog is smaller than the horse; *k̔yód-pas, stág-pas, rtá-pa-bas, śnár-bas*, or *śná-ma-bas čʻe*, bigger than you, than a tiger, than a rider, than formerly; it rarely stands for the partitive: *bu lṅa-brgyá-bas γčig*, or for *las* with the signification: except, *Mil.*

པི་ *pi* num. fig.: 43.

པི་ཅག་ *pi-čág* (*Turk.* چاكو) **large butcher's knife.**

པི་པི་ *pi-pi* 1. *Schr., Sch.* **fife, flute.** — 2. *W.* **nipple, teat;** **pi-pi nud táṅ-če** to suckle. — 3. **icicle** *W.*

པི་(པི་)ལིང་ *pi(-pi)-liṅ, Ssk.* **पिप्पली**, Piper longum, a spice, similar to black pepper, yet more oblong.

པི་ཕོ་ *pi-p̔o* v. *pi-śi.*

པི་ཙེ་ *pi-tse* **skin,** or **leather bag** for water etc. *Lh.*

པི་ཚི་ *pi-t̔si*, and *ma-t̔si*, interjections of anger, *Foucaux Gyatch.* ༢༥༤, *transl.* 292.

པི་ཝང་ *pi-wáṅ* or *pi-báṅ, Zam.* = **वीणा**, **guitar,** also *da-nyén-pi-waṅ C., pi-waṅ ról-mo Glr.* = *k̔ó-poṅ W.*; *pí-waṅ rgyud γsum* a three-stringed guitar *Stg.*; *rgyud-máṅ* a guitar with many strings *Cs.*; *sgróg-pa* to play (the guitar); *pi-waṅ-mk̔an*, or *pi-waṅ-pa* a player on the guitar.

པི་ཤི་ *pi-śi* (perh. from the Persian) **cat,** *W.*; *pi-p̔o* male cat, *pí-mo* female cat.

པིག་མོ་ *pig-mo* v. *pús-mo.*

པིར་ *pir* **brush, pencil;** *byúg-pir* large brush, for house-painting; *bšád-pir* small brush or pencil for artistic painting, Chinese writing; *pir-ťogs(-pa)* painter *Cs.* — *pir-doṅ* receptacle or case for brushes. — *pir-spu* pencil-hair. — **pir-nyúg** *W.* = *bčad-pir*; also for lead-pencil. — *pir-šiṅ* pencil-stick.

པིར་བ་ *pir-ba* (spelling?) **to crush, to grind** (to powder) = *mnyéd-pa Ld.*

པིལ་ཙེ་ *pil-tse Ld.* **sieve.**

པིས་མོ་ *pis-mo* v. *pús-mo.*

པིཔྤལ་ *pispal*, acc. to *Cs. Ssk.*, yet not to be found in *Lexx.*, **the wild fig-tree,** *Hindi: pipal.*

པུ་ *pu* num. figure for 73.

པུ་ཏི་ *pú-ti* **milfoil,** (millefolium), yarrow; *Lh.*

པུ་ཏྲི་ *pú-tri* (*Ssk.* पुत्री, daughter), a common female name (perh. *bu-ǩrid.*)

པུ་སྟི་ *pú-sti, Glr.* = *pó-ti*, **book** (perh. formed out of *pústak*).

པུ་ན་ཁ་ *Pu-na-ǩa* town in Bhotan.

པུ་བྱི་ *pú-byi* v. *spú-byi.*

པུ་ཙེ་ *pú-tse, pú-se*, a little rat-like animal, v. *bra* and *zlum*; *pu-tse-šel* prob. = *pu-šel-tse.*

པུ་ཚེ་ *pu-ťsé* **husks of barley** *W.*; *Cs.* **bran.**

པུ་རངས་ *Pu-ráṅs Mil.*, a district in *Mṅa-ris.*

པུ་རི་ *pu-rí* **tube,** any thing tubular and hollow, box of tin or wood, pencase etc.; also = *dóṅ-po* the Tibetan shuttle; **pu-ri méd-ǩan** *W.* full, solid, not hollow, cf. *pá-ri.*

པུ་རུ་ཥ་ *pu-ru-ša Ssk.* **man; soul;** = *skyés-bu.*

པུ་ལིང་ག་ *pu-liṅ-ga Cs.: Ssk.* **masculine gender.**

པུ་ལུ་ *pú-lu* **hut,** built of stones, like those of the alpine herdsmen *W.*, (*Ts. rdzi-skyor*); *k̇yi-pul* dog-kennel.

པུ་ཤུ་ *pú-šu* **fence,** *Lex.* = *mda-yáb* and *lúṅ-kan.*

པུ་ཤེལ་ཙེ་ *pu-šel-tse* a medicinal herb *Med.*

པུག་ཏ་ *púg-ta* (?) **shelf, partition** in a box.

པུག་མ་ *púg-ma Pur.* **collar-bone.**

པུང་པ་ *púṅ-pa, ṗúṅ-pa C., W.* **an urn-shaped vessel** of clay or wood, for water, beer etc. (seems not to be the same with *búm-pa*).

པུན་པ་ *pún-pa W.*, **pún-če** = *lúd-če* to run over.

པུཎྜ་རཱི་ཀ་ *puṇḍarika Ssk.*, **white lotos.**

པུར་ *pur Cs.* 1. **steel-yard.** — 2. *púr-gyis* v. *ₒṗur-ba.* — 3. v. *spur.*

པུལ་ *pul* v. *pú-lu.*

པུཥྐར་ *puškara Ssk.* **blue lotos.**

པུསྟ་ཀ་ *pustaka Ssk.* **book.**

པུས་མོ་ *pús-mo, W.* **pis-mo, pig-mo**, **knee;** *pis-mo sa-la ₒdzug-pa* to kneel; **pig-mo tsúg-če, pi-tsúg gyáb-če** *W.* id.; **pig-mo tsúg-te dad-če** to sit in kneeling (which is considered indecorous); cf. *tsog.*

པེ་ *pe* num. figure: 103.

པེ་(ད)ཀར་ *pe-(d)kár*, also *be-kár, pe-há-ra. bi-hár Lt., Glr., Mil.*, a much worshipped deity, v. *kye-ṗáṅ*, and *Schl.* 157.

པེ་ཏེ་ཧོར་ *pe-te-hor* n. of a people *Sch.*

པེ་ནེ་ *pe-ne, pé-na* v. *pa-ṇa.*

པེ་བན་ *pe-bán* (*Pers.* پیوند), **graft, scion;** **pe-bán tsúg-če** *W.* to graft.

པེ་ཙམ་ *pe-tsám* **little, small, a little** *Sch.*

པེ་ཙེ་ *pe-tsé, pi-tsi, Chin. pai-tsái,* **Chinese white cabbage** in *C.*; of late also known in Europe.

པེ་ར་ *pé-ra* **a flat basket.**

པེ་ས་ *pé-sa, paisa, Hind.*, copper coin, not quite a half-penny.

པེན་ཙེ་ *pén-tse* a kind of wood of which vessels are made *Cs.* (= *pán-tsa?*)

པོ་ *po* 1. sign of nouns, in like manner as *-pa*; it particularly designates concrete nouns and the masculine gender, frq., in contradistinction to abstract nouns with *-pa* or *-ba*, and to feminines with *-mo;* connected with a numeral, it supplies the definite article: *lṅá-po* the five (just mentioned); *γnyis-po* the two, both, = *γnyis-ka.* — 2. num. figure: 133.

པོ་ཏ་ལ་ *pó-ta-la* (*Ssk.* पोत ship, ल to receive, hence: harbour, port; *Tib. gru-dzin*) 1. ancient n. of Tatta, a town not far from the mouth of the Indus. — 2. n. of a three-peaked hill near Lhasa, with the palace of the old kings of Tibet, now the seat of the Dalai Lama. (The spelling '*Buddha-la*' arises from an erroneous etymological hypothesis, and the fact of its being found even in Huc's writings may be attributed merely to a thoughtless adherence to what had become a custom; v. *Köpp.* II, 340.)

པོ་ཏི་ *pó-ti* (acc. to one *Lex.* a corruption of *pu-sta-ka*, for which also the form *pu-sti* seems to speak) = *glegs-bam*, **book** (of loose leaves).

པོ་ཏུམ་ *po-túm Sik.* **large wasp.**

པོ་ཏོ་ *po-tó C.* **bullock.**

པོ་ཏོག་ *po-tóg* v. *mto-po-tog.*

པོ་ལ་ *po-lá* the well-known Turkish mess of **pilaw**, *Hind.* **pulao**, rice boiled with fowl; in *Ld.* however sweet rice, prepared with butter, sugar, and 'pating'; fig. *bsámbloi pó-la byéd-pa* to concoct and deal in plans and plots.

པོ་ལོ་(ན)་ཤན་ *po-lo(n)-šán* n. of the mountains bordering on China *Ld.-Glr. Schl.* 21, a (where in the translation the word has not been recognized as being a proper name).

པོག་ཕོར་ *pog-pór* **censer, perfuming-pan.**

པོགས་ཏ་ *pógs-ta* v. *púgs-ta.*

པོད་ *pod, pon, pón-to* v. *pod, pon, pón-to.*

པོབ་ *pob C.* **castrated ram.**

པོལ་ *pol Ts.* = *tsá-bai nad.*

པྲ་ *pra* small **turkoises**, 1 or 2''' in size, strung together for finger-rings, v. *tsom.*

པྲ་(མོ་) *pra(-mo) Cs.* 1. **lot**; *pra ˳débs-pa* to cast lot. — 2. **sign, token, prognostic**; *Sch.*: *pra ˳bebs-pa* 'ein Zeichen geben, ein Bild darstellen'.

པྲ་ཅལ་ *pra-čál, spra-čál Lex.* w.e. *Sch.* **jest, joke, fun,** nonsensical talk; *byédpa* to make sport, to play the buffoon; *slóṅ-ba* to cause merriment; *pra-čál-pa*, or *-mkan* wag, buffoon.

པྲ་ལི་ *pra-li Sch.*: hill-mouse (marmot?), hare (?); cf. *brá-ba.*

པྲང་འགོས་ *praṅ-˳gós* an alpine herb, said to be very wholesome to sheep (so for instance in Purig); acc. to recent investigations, of little value. Acc. to *Cs.* = *á-króṅ*, but this is denied by the people of Lahoul.

པྲི་ཡང་གུ་ *pri-yaṅ-gu Ssk.*, n. of several kinds of Indian aromatic plants *Med.*

པྲོག་, ཟེ་པྲོག་ *prog, ze-próg Lex.*, **the crest of a cock** *Cs.*; *próg-žu, bróg-žu, spróg-zu* = *čod-pán.*

དཔའ་(བ་) *dpá(-ba)* (शूर, वीर), also *spá-ba* 1. **bravery, strength, courage; brave, strong, courageous;** *dpa bsgóṅ-ba Lex., kóṅ-ba Thgy.*; *góṅ-ba, bkóṅ-ba Lex.*, to despond; to dishearten (?); *šin-tu dpá-žiṅ* he becoming very brave *Dzl.*; *dpá-la stobs kyaṅ gyad daṅ bnyám-ste* being brave, and in strength equal to an athlete *Dzl.* — 2. **beauty; beautiful.** — 3. *W.* **taste, agreeable taste, flavour.**

**Comp.** *dpá-čan* 1. brave. 2. beautiful. 3. *W.* savoury. — *dpa-méd-kan W.* tasteless, v. also *ldád-pa.* — *dpa-čén* very brave; a great hero. — *dpa-dár* = *mguldár*, a piece of silk, tied round the neck, as an honourable distinction for some brave deed. — *dpa-ldán* = *dpá-čan* 1 and 2. — *dpá-bo*, विर, 1. strong man, hero. 2. demigod. — *dpa-bo-dkár* a medicinal herb *Med.* — *dpá-mo* 1. heroine (more frq. than the masc. *dpá-bo*). 2. = *mka-gro-ma*, Dākini *Mil., Thgr., Glr.* — *dpa-tsúl Mil.* = *dpá-ba* 1. sbst., ni f.

དཔག་ཚད་ *dpag-tsád* **mile,** acc. to *Cs.* = 4000 fathoms, hence a geographical mile; yet there are mentioned *dpag-čén* and *dpag-čúṅ*, the latter = 500 fathoms. The word seems altogether to belong more to the phantastic mythical literature, than to common life; so at least in *W.*

དཔག་པ་ *dpág-pa* v. *dpóg-pa.*

དཔག་གཡེངས་ *dpag-γyéṅs* the bustle or tumult of a festival *Ld.*

དཔག་བསམ་ཤིང་ *dpag-bsam-šiṅ* n. of a fabulous tree, that grants every wish; acc. to *Pth.* = *tsán-dan-sbrúl-gyi snyiṅ-po.*

དཔང་(པོ་) *dpáṅ(-po)* **witness,** both the deponent, and the evidence deposed. Fully authenticated are as yet only: *lha dpáṅ-du* ˳*dzúg-pa* to call a deity for a witness in taking an oath, to appeal to *Glr.*; also: *dpaṅ byéd-pa* to bear witness, to attest, v. *mna.* More conjectural are the meanings of: *blo-séms dpáṅ-du ɔ̓óg-pa Glr.*, or *raṅ-séms dpáṅ-du* ˳*dzúg-pa Mil.*, to be sincere, to be conscious of speaking the truth; *dpáṅ-du* ˳*gyúr-ba* to be witness of, to see, to know (cf. *spyán-du* ˳*gyúr-ba*); *bden-dpáṅ Liš.* as explanation of *če-bži*, witness or proof for the truth of a thing; **páṅ-po lóg-pa zér-ces** *W.* to give false evidence (*Schr. rdzun-dpáṅ*). — *mi-dpáṅ* (*Ld.* **mir-paṅ**) *W.*, *C.*, is used as syn. to *dpáṅ-po* (also *Schr*), 1. witness. 2. defender, advocate; *mi-dpaṅ* (or *dpaṅ-po*) *byéd-pa* c. genit. or dat., to defend in a court of justice; (*dpáṅ-pos dpóṅ-ba Sch.* seems to be unknown and doubtful).

དཔངས་ *dpaṅs* **height;** *dpáṅs-su* in height *Samb.*; *dpaṅs-mtó Lex.* high, cf. ˳*pʻaṅs.* — *dpaṅs-tsád* great heat *Schr.* (?).

དཔར་བ་ *dpár-ba* v. *dpór-ba.*

དཔལ་ *dpal Ssk.* श्री 1. **glory, splendour, magnificence, abundance;** *dpal reg-pa-méd-pa* unattainable glory *Glr.*; *yón-tan dú-mai dpal* splendour of numerous accomplishments; *skyéd-pai dpál-la loṅs-spyód-pa* enjoying the utmost happiness *Glr.*; frq. as an epithet, or part of the names of deities, e.g. *dpal-čén hé-ru-ka*, and esp. *dpal(-ldan)lhá-mo*, *dpal-čén-mo*, Durga Uma, Kāli, the much adored spouse of Siva; ˳*dod-dgúi dpal* the fulness of all that can be desired *Glr.*; *dpál-gyi dúm-bu*, श्रीखण्ड, 1. sandal-wood. 2. *Cs.* a kind of syrup, prepared of *bsé-šiṅ*, used as a purgative. — 2. **wealth, abundance,** *Glr.* and elsewh. — 3. **welfare, happiness, blessing,** ˳*gró-bai* of creatures *Mil.* and elsewh.; *kún-gyi dpál-du* ˳*gyúr-ba* or *šár-ba* to be (become) the salvation, the saviour of all beings *Glr.* and elsewh.; *dpal skyéd-pa*, *γžán-gyi*, *ráṅ-gi dpal* to work for the elevation of others or for one's own. — 4. nobility, *dpál-gyi γnáṅ-ba* privilege of nobility; *dpál-gyi γnaṅ-šóg* diploma of nobility, *dpál-gyi γnaṅ-šóg-pa* one having a diploma of nobility *Cs.* — *dpal-kʻyád Dzl.* = *dpal* 1. — *dpal-rtúg* majesty, full glory *Sch.* — *dpal-ldán* a man's name (very common). — *dpal-pʻó* an illustrious man, *dpál-mo* an illustrious woman *Cs.* — *dpal* (-*gyi*) -*béu* is said to denote the figure ࿕ *Glr.* — *dpal-byéu* glow-worm *Sch.* — *dpal-byór* 1. glory, wealth, magnificence, as a man's possession. 2. *W.* strawberry; 3. a man's name (very common).

དཔུང་ *dpuṅ* 1. **host, great number,** ˳*baṅs tams-čád-kyi Dzl.*; esp. of soldiers. — 2. **troops, army,** *dpuṅ bži* the four species of troops: *rtai*, *gláṅ-po-čei*, *šiṅ-rtai*, and *rkaṅ-tʻáṅ-gi dpuṅ* (or *dpuṅ(-bu)-čuṅ*); *dpuṅ-(gi) tsógs*, *dmag-dpúṅ*, army frq.; *dgra-dpúṅ* hostile army. — 3. (auxiliaries?), **help, assistance,** **púṅ-la táṅ-ce** *W.* to send assistance. — *dpuṅ-grógs*, *-rogs*, helper. — *dpuṅ-(gi) γnyen* friend, protector, defender, assistant, frq. — **puṅ-nón** *W.* reinforcement.

དཔུང་པ་ *dpúṅ-pa* 1. **shoulder,** *dpúṅ-pa kʻar* on the shoulder *Glr.*; *dpuṅ-pa daṅ dpyi γnyis* both the shoulders and hips *S.g.*; upper arm, *dpuṅ-pa-rkáṅ* upper arm-bone; *dpuṅ* ˳*júm-pa Sch.* to contract the arm (?); *dpuṅ-pa-lág* upper and lower arm *Cs.*; *dpuṅ-pa-rgyán* an ornament for the arm *Cs.* — 2. **sleeve,** *gos dpúṅ-pa-čan* a garment with sleeves *Cs.*; *dpuṅ-pa-bċád* the part of a woman's dress covering the chest *Zam.*; *Sch.: dpuṅ-bċad-rás.*

དཔེ་ *dpe*, *Ld.* **spe**, 1. **pattern, model,** *dé-la dpe Glr.*, or *de dper byás-nas Zam.*, taking this for a pattern; *rgyá-yul-nas rtsis-kyi dpe blaṅs* it was from China that mathematics were learned *Glr.*; . . . *pai dpe mi ₒdug* there are no patterns for . . . *Glr.*; *dpe ċi ltar* with what to be compared? according to what analogy? *Thgy.*; similitude, parable, example, *mṫún-pai dpe* an example that may be followed, a good example; *bzlóg-pai dpe* an example to the contrary, a warning example *Thgy.*; **pe záṅ-po*, and *ṅém-pe pe*,* as well as **yár-la* and *már-la żág-pe-pe*, or *mar-pe** *C.* id.; *dpe stón-pa* to teach or to prove by examples; hence the participle, used substantively, serves as an epithet of the Sautrantikas, *Was.* (112); *dpe bṡád-pa*, *dpe bżág-pa* = *dpe stón-pa; dper rjód-pa* to set up for a parable or comparison; *dpér-na*, in later times also *dpé-ni*, *dpe byéd-na Mil.*, **pe gyáb-na** *W.*, 1. (in order) to quote an example, by way of a comparison, just as if, followed by *bżin-du* or *ltar*, very frq.; 2. like our 'for instance', e.g., before enumerations, where in the older writings gen. *ₒdi-lta-ste* is used; *dper ₒós-pa Cs.* what may be compared, *dper mi ₒós-pa* not to be compared; occasionally also: worthy or not worthy of imitation; *ḱá-dpe*, *γtám-dpe* proverb, adage *Cs.*; *ₒdrá-dpe* allegory, parable *S.g.*; *má-dpe W.*, *Ld.* **má-spe**, *Lh.* **már-pe**, pattern, (writing-) copy (cf. also *má-dpe* and *bú-dpe* below). — 2. **symmetry, harmony,** beauty, (in certain phrases). — 3. **book,** *ḱrims brgyad-kyi dpe* the book of the eight commandments *Dzl.*; *ká-dpe*, *ka-ḱái dpe* abc-book, primer; *ṗyág-dpe* resp. for *dpe*, if used by a Lama (cf. *ṗyag-mḱár*); *má-dpe*, *bú-dpe* original and copy of a book *Cs.*; *yig-nág dpe* a real book, not of a fig. meaning, as the book of nature, *Mil.*; *dpe rtsóm-pa* to write, to compose, *bṡú-ba* to copy a book; *ₒdógs-pa*, *ₒṫsém-pa* to bind, to stitch a book.

**Comp.** *dpé-ka* little book, vulgo. — *dpe-ḱáṅ* library; bookseller's shop. — *dpe-ḱri* a table to put books on, book-stand. — *dpe-mkyúd*, *ₒḱyud Cs.* v. *mḱyud-pa.* — *dpe-mgó*, *dpe-mjúg* beginning, end, of a book. — *dpe-sgám* chest for books, book-case. — *dpé-ča* not frq. in *B.*, but vulgo the common word for book. — **dpé-ča ṗé-ċe, túm-ċe** *W.* to open, to close a book; v. *btúm-pa.* — *dpe-rjód* v. *dper.* — *dpe-ṫó* list of books. — *dpe-byád* proportion, symmetry, beauty, *dpe-byád bzáṅ-po brgyád-ċu* the eighty physical perfections of Buddha. — *dpe-byád-ċan* well-proportioned. — *dpé-ṫsoṅ-pa* bookseller. — *dpe-ṡúbs* case or covering for a book. — *dpe-bṡús* copy of a book. — *dper* v. 1. — *dpe-brjód* 1. example, comparison, *dpe-brjód byéd-pa* to compare, to cite an example *Cs.*; *dpe-brjód rtógs-pa Gram.* id. (?). 2. paradigm, example *Gram.* —

དཔེ་སྒྲ་ *dpé-sgra* (?), *(*s*)*pé-ra** *W.*, **speech,** for *γtam*; *(*s*)*pé-ra zér-ċe*(*s*), *táṅ-ċe*(*s*)*, to speak, to talk; *ī-zug* (*s*)*pé-ra ma taṅ* do not say so! *(*s*)*pé-ra zér-ċe*(*s*) *med-ḱan soṅ** he became speechless (with terror etc.).

དཔེར་ན་ *dpér-na* v. sub *dpe.*

དཔོག་པ་ *dpóg-pa*, pf. *dpags*, fut. *dpag*, 1. **to measure, to proportion, to fix,** *γtóṅ-tsul če-čúṅ-la* (to proportion) the dose to the size *Lt.*; . . . *kyi ṫsád-las* after the measure of . . ., *Lt.*; *nad-stóbs-la* according to the violence of the disease *Lt.*; *dpag* (*tu*) *méd* (*-pa*), less frq. *dpag-brál*, *dpag-yás*, immensely large, very much; *ṫugs dpag-méd* infinite grace, *mdzád-pa* to show *Dzl.* — 2. **to outweigh, to counterbalance,** *loṅs-spyód ṫams-ċád-kyis mi dpóg-pa* not to be counterbalanced by all the wealth . . . *Tar.* — 3. **to weigh, to judge, to prove,** *rjés-su dpóg-pa* to examine *Tar.*; *rjes-dpág Zam.* **अनुमान,** inference, conclusion.

དཔོན་པོ་ *dpón-po* **master, lord,** over men (generally); (cf. *bdág-po* owner) master, over working-men, overseer, foreman, leader, *grá-pai dpon-po*, **director,** =

*ₒgó-dpon*; **dpón-po-la čag p̓ul dug žu zer, ťug-šró ma kyod, ṅa yóṅ-loṅ med** W. make your master my compliment, and he should not take it amiss that I had no time to come; *ḱríms-dpon* 1. prop.: superior judge, lord chief-justice. 2. now: high officer of state, prefect, = *mi-dpón*; *mḱar-dpón* commander of a fortress; *ₒḱrúg-dpon* general *Ma.*; *ₒgó-dpon* v. *go*; *brgyá-dpon* centurion, captain; *bčú-dpon* corporal; *číbs-dpon* master of the horse, equerry; *rje-dpon* = *rje*; *rtá-pa-dpon* (sic) (cf. *pa* extr.) general of cavalry *Glr.*; *stégs-dpon*(?) v. *stegs*; *stoṅ-dpon* leader of a thousand (seems to be no longer in use); *déd-dpon* sea-captain; *mdá-dpon* is said to be in *C.* the modern word for general, and *ₒdégs-dpon* the same as *stóṅ-dpon*; however v. *stegs*; *ldiṅ-dpon* v. *ldiṅ*; *spyi-dpon* governor general *Cs.*; *mi-dpon* prefect; *rtsig-dpon* master-mason; *rdzóṅ-dpon* = *mḱár-dpon*; *yúl-dpon* prefect of a district *Wts.*; *rú-dpon* something like colonel; *šiṅ-dpon* master-carpenter; *slób-dpon* teacher, frq., also title of the higher and more learned Lamas, corresponding, as it were, to *M.A.*, master of arts; *γsól-dpon* head-cook, butler. — *dpón-mo* fem., *ṅai dpón-mo yin* she is my mistress *Glr.* — *dpón-yod* standing under a master or mistress. — *dpon-méd* free *Cs.* — *dpon-γyóg* master and servants, frq. — *ḱoṅ-jo dpon-γyóg* (princess) *koṅ-jo* and her suite *Glr.* — *dpon-tsáṅ* physician *Schr.* and *Sch.* — *dpon-yig* secretary *Schr.* — *dpon-slób* 1. inst. of *dpón-po daṅ slób-ma Ma.* and elsewh. 2. title of the four independent rulers in Bhotan, the 'Penlow' of English news-papers, acc. to the pronunciation of **pọn-lob, pọn-lo**.

དཔོར་བ་ *dpór-ba*, pf. and fut. *dpar*, **to dictate**, *Cs.*; **por-tsóm (je')-pa** *C.* id.

དཔྱ་ *dpya* **tax, duty, tribute,** *ₒbúl-ba* to pay, *Dzl.*, *ₒbébs-pa* to impose *Tar.* 21, 11; *dpya-ḱrál* id., *rgyál-poi dpya-ḱrál Lex.*; likewise *dpya-ťáṅ Cs.*

དཔྱང་བ་ *dpyáṅ-ba*, *spyáṅ-ba*, **to suspend, to make hang down,** prop. vb. a. to *p̓yáṅ-ba*, with pf. *dpyaṅs* and *spyaṅs*, imp. *dpyaṅs*, *Sch. dpyoṅs*, but also vb. n., **to rock, to pitch** (of a ship) *Pth.*; *dpyáṅ-la γtóṅ-ba* trs. *Thgy.*; **gyóg-čaṅ**, perh. more corr. **ḱyog-čáṅ**, also **p̓eb-čáṅ** *C.* sedan-chair, palanquin; *dpyaṅ-ťág*, *ₒp̓yaṅ-ťág*, cord or rope, by which a thing is suspended, e.g. a plummet, a bucket, a miner; hence fig. *ťugs-rjei dpyaṅ-ťág γčód-pa Thgr.*; *ču-snod daṅ dpyaṅ-ťag sbá-ba* to hide the bucket together with the rope *Schr.*; a rope-swing, *dpyaṅ-ťág rtséd-pa* to swing (one's self); *dpyaṅs*, *spyáṅs-pai p̓an*, hanging ornaments, *dar-dpyáṅs* silk ornaments *S.g.*

དཔྱད་ *dpyad* 1. v. *dpyód-pa*. — 2. *Stg.*: an instrument to open the mouth by force; perh. also in a more general sense: crow-bar(?); *dpyád-pa* v. *dpyód-pa*.

དཔྱས་པོ་ *dpyás-po* **offence, fault, blame** *Cs.*; *dpyás-čan* faulty, blamable; *dpyas-méd* faultless, blameless *Cs.*; *dpyas ₒdógs-pa* to blame *Tar.*; cf. *ₒpyá-ba.*

དཔྱི་ *dpyi* (*Cs.* also *spyi*) *W.* **(s)pi**, **hip** *Lt.*; *dpyi-mgó Cs.*, *dpyi-zúr*, *dpyi-rús*, hip-bone; *dpyi-míg* socket of the hip-bone, perh. also vulg. = hip.

དཔྱིད་ *dpyid* (cf. Phonetic Table), **spring,** also adv. in spring *Dzl.*; cf. also *dus* 4; *dpyid-ka*, **pid-ḱa** *W.*, id., also *Glr.*; *dpyid-zla* month of spring.

དཔྱིས་ *dpyis*, *dpyis p̓yin-pa Sch.*: to come to the last, to arrive at the end; *dei rig-pa ₒdi dpyis p̓yin-pa sus kyaṅ mi šes dgóṅs-nas Schf.*: as he reflected, that no body would thoroughly understand his arguments.

དཔྱོང་བ་ *dpyóṅ-ba*, perh. primitive form of *dpyáṅ-ba*.

དཔྱོ་བ་ *dpyó-ba* **to change** *Sch.*

དཔྱོད་པ་ *dpyód-pa*, pf. and fut. *dpyad*, **to try, to examine,** *nyés-pa daṅ ma-nyés-pa* innocence and guilt, right and wrong *Dzl.*; *dpyád-na ... ma rtógs-so* after ever so much investigating ... they found out nothing *Dzl.*; *bye-brág-tu dpyád-pa ste* having now been separately examined *Zam.*; *sa-dpyád*, or *ri-dpyád γzigs-pa* to examine the country, or the mountains, i.e. their general features, with regard to omens and auspices *Glr.*; *sai dpyad bzáṅ-bar šés-pa* to know that this examination will turn out favourably *Glr.*; **rin čád-če** (gen. written **bčad-če**, cf. *bčód-pa* extr.) *W.* to tax, to estimate; *goṅ-ťáṅ dpyád-kyis* (or *-pas*) *mi čod Glr.* v. *čod-pa* 2; esp. in medicine: *smán-pas ... dpyad byás-te ... žes dpyad byás-so* the physician having tried, tried thus, (pronounced the following as the result of his examination) *Dzl.* ༢༥༢, 12; *sman-dpyád byéd-pa* to treat medically, *dpyad má-la bya* then the mother (not the child) must be placed under medical treatment *Lt.*; *ₒbrás-kyis btsún-moi sman-dpyád byed-pa* to cure (the illness of) the queen with rice *Dzl.*; *sman-dpyád-la mkás-pa* to be skilled in medical science *Dzl.*; *ča-byád dpyád-kyi γnas* instrumental therapeutics i.e. surgery *S.g.*; *rtog-dpyód, brtag-dpyád*, examination; *rtog-dpyód ráb-tu γtóṅ-ba* to examine very closely *Pth.*; *rtog-dpyód ťoṅ* examine! *Mil.*; *bzaṅ-dpyód* examining the worth of a thing. — *dpyód-pa-pa*, and *spyód-pa-pa*, *Ssk.* **मीमांसक**, an Indian sect of philosophers (the former of the two spellings seems to be more correct).

དཔྲལ་བ་ *dprál-ba* (resp. *γdaṅs Cs.*), **ṭál-wa**, *Ld.* **šrál-wa**, **forehead,** *dprál-bai mda* an arrow sticking in the forehead *Glr.*; *dprál-bai mig bžin-du* 'like the eye of the countenance', to designate something highly valued (as the scriptural 'apple of the eye'); *dprál-bai p̒yógs-kyi ťad dráṅ-na* just before one in front *Wdṅ.*; fig. **ṭal-wa ṅán-pa** *W.* unlucky; a luckless person.

དཔྲུལ་དཔྲུལ་ *dprul-dprúl* (or *p̒rul-p̒rúl?*), **ṭul-ṭúl-la tóṅ wa** *C.* to hang one's self.

ལྤགས་ *lpags*, as second part of compounds inst. of *págs-pa*, e.g. *wá-lpags* fox-skin, *stág-lpags* tiger-skin; *šún-lpags* skin, bark, peel, shell.

སྤ་ *spa* 1. v. *dpa.* — 2. also *sba*, **cane** (seems to be distinguished from *smyúg-ma* more in a popular and practical way, than scientifically); *spa-skór* hoop of a cask *Schr.*; *spa-ǩár Mil.*, *spa-lčág Mil.*, *spa-bér Pth.*, *spa-dbyúg Lex.*, walking-cane; *spa-gliṅ* cane-flute *Sch.*; *spa-til* lunt, match, v. *p̒a-til*; *spa-dóṅ* or *-ldoṅ* little cask, made of bamboo, prob. = *gur-gúr dóṅ-mo*; **pa-ₒbár** *C.*, *W.* torch; *spa-dmyúg* or *-smyug*, cane *Cs.*; *pa-šíṅ Sik.* strong bamboo sticks.

སྤ་མ་ *spá-ma* 1. **juniper,** Juniperus squamosa, and some other small species; cf. *šúg-pa.* — 2. **cypress** *Sik.*

སྤག་པ་ *spág-pa* 1. v. *spóg-pa.* — 2. **ǩál-pag pág-če** *W.* **to smack** (in eating). — 3. *C.*, *W.* **to dip,** e.g. meat into the gravy; cf. the following.

སྤགས་ *spags*, resp. *skyu-rum*, 1. *C.* = *zan* (= **ǩó-lag, pág-ǩu** *Ld.*), **pap,** esp. made of tea and 'tsampa'. — 2. *W.* = **ša-rúg** *C.*), **sauce, gravy,** for dipping in (sops); **dam-pág** *W.* mire, sludge. — 3. **food, dish, mess**; *W.*, *C.* **pag na so-só**.

སྤང་ *spaṅ*, I. also *spáṅ-po*, 1. **turf, greensward, meadow,** *mdún-na spáṅ-po mé-tog bkra* in front a flowery meadow-ground *Mil.* — 2. **moss,** also *ču-spaṅ Cs.* — 3. **bog,** *spaṅ-skóṅ* 1. p.n. ('turf-ditch'), a large valley, with a lake in it, on the frontier of Ladak and Rudog. 2. *spaṅ-skóṅ p̒yag-rgyá-pa* n. of an ancient work on religion *Glr.*; *spaṅ-rgyan* a medicinal herb *Med.*; *spáṅ-čan* covered with turf; *spáṅ-ču* green mud *Sch.*; *spaṅ-ljóṅs* grassy country; *spaṅ-ťáṅ* a plain covered with verdure; *spaṅ-spós* Waldheimia tridactylites, a pretty, very aromatic composite, growing on the higher alps; *spaṅ-bóg* piece of turf, sod; *spaṅ-ma Med.*, **तुत्थ**, blue vitriol; *spaṅ-rtsi S.g.* (?); *spaṅ-žún* verdigris *Sch.*; *spaṅ-ri* a grassy hill *Mil.*; *spaṅ-γšóṅ* a mountain-meadow *Mil.*

II. **board, plank,** gen. *spaṅ-léb Glr.* and vulg.; also **a slab, slate, flag** *Lh.*; *spaṅ-sgó* board or panel of a door *Cs.*; *spaṅ-ǩri Schr.*, **ṭi-páṅ** *Ld*, **paṅ-dáṅ** *Ld.*, bookstand.

སྤང་བ་ *spaṅ-ba* v. *spoṅ-ba.*

སྤངས་ *spaṅs*, sometimes inst. of *dpaṅs.*

སྤད་ *spad*, only in *p̒a-spád* **father and children;** cf. the more frq. *ma-smád*, *Lex.*

སྤན་སྤུན་ *span-spún* **brothers, relatives** *Cs.*

སྤབས་ *spabs, rna-spábs C.* **ear-wax;** *Lexx.* also *ṙṅul-* (or *rdul-?*) *gyi spabs* w.e.

སྤར་ *spar* for *par* 1. *Sch.*

སྤར་ཁ་ *spar-ḱa, spar-ḱa brgyad* the **pah kwah,** or eight diagrams of Chinese science, ═══ etc.

སྤར་བ་ *spar-ba* I. sbst., also *spar-mo* (*Ld.* **wár-mo**, acc. to the spelling *sbar-mo*) 1. **the grasping hand, paw, claw,** *spráṅ-poi spár-mor spa-dbyúg sprad* he puts the staff into the beggar's grasp (hand) *Lexx.; *wár-mo gyáb-ċe* W., spár-mos ₒbrád-pa* to clutch, to scratch; *spár-mos ₒdébs-pa Cs., spar byéd-pa Sch.,* to seize with the hand, the paw, or the claws; *γdoṅ ťams-ċád spar-ṡád rgyáb-pa Pth.* to scratch the whole face ('combing it with the claws'); **sbar-ₒju* C.* rail, for taking hold of; *spár-mo ₒbyéd-pa, bsdám-pa* to open, to close the hand *Cs.* — 2. as a measure: as much as may be grasped with the hand, **a handful** (of wood, grass, earth etc.), **(s)pár-ra γaṅ** one handful, *(s)pár-ra gaṅ do* two handfuls etc.; *spar-ťsád lṅa-brgyá* 500 handfuls *S.g.; sa spar-gáṅ Mil.* a handful of earth.

II. vb. v. *spór-ba.*

སྤར་མ་ *spár-ma* a low-growing shrub of very hard wood *Mil.nt.*

སྤི་ཏི་ *(s)pí-ti* **Spiti,** the valley, situated to the west of Lahul, watered by the Spiti river, belonging to the British Punjāb, and inhabited by a race of pure Tibetans.

སྤིའུ་ *spiu* col. for *spéu.*

སྤུ་ *spu, Ssk.* रोमन्, 1. **hair** (*'pilus'*, cf. *skra*), *lús-kyi* of the body in general, *Lex.; mgó-spu, ḱá-* or *γdóṅ-spu, mčán-spu, ₒdoms-spu* (or *spu-ṅán Cs.*), *bráṅ-spu,* hair of the head, the beard, arm-pits, lower-parts, chest; *bá-spu* the little hairs of the skin, frq.; *rtá-spu* horse-hair; *spu ₒṕyi* or *γtog* the hair is plucked out *Lex., byi* falls off *Dzl., γżob byed* is singed off *Sch., ldaṅ, laṅ Dzl., lóṅ-γyo Mil.,* the hair bristles, stands on end; *spu ziṅ byed B., brtse Sch., *se-ziṅ* W.,* a shuddering of fear comes over (me, him etc.); *ťams-ċád spu-ziṅ byéd-ċiṅ Pth.; byad spus ḱeṅs-pa* with a face all hairy *Glr.; spui ḱúṅ-bu* passage of perspiration, pore *Dzl.; spu nyág-ma tsám-gyi ₒgyód-ṕai sems* repentance as much as one single little hair *Dzl.* — 2. **feather,** *byá-spu rluṅ-gis ḱyer-ba* a down (feather) blown off; **feathers, plumage.**

**Comp.** *spú-ḱa* **colour** of horses and other hairy animals. — *spú-gri* 1. **razor;** also allegorically, as a title of books. 2. knife *C.* — *spú-ċan* hairy. — *spu-ċim(?)* false hair *Sch.* — *spú-ja* v. *ja.* — *spú-byi nág-po, spu-nág* also *pú-byi,* **sable** (furred animal) *Sch.* — *spú-ma* hairy, carded (cloth). — *spu-méd* hairless. — *spu-γtsaṅ-ma* v. *spus.* — *spu-hrúg* short-haired *Sch.*

སྤུ་རངས་ *spu-ráṅs Glr.* v. *pu-ráṅs.*

སྤུག་ *spug Lexx.* n. of a precious stone *Cs.*

སྤུང་ *spuṅ* **heap,** col. also for *ṕúṅ-po; spúṅ-ba* pf. and imp. *-spuṅs,* to heap, accumulate, pile up (coals etc.); *rin-čén spúṅs-pa* a heap of precious stones *Glr.*

སྤུད་པ་ *spúd-pa* **to decorate;** *rgyáṅ-gyis Lex.* (cf. *spus*).

སྤུན་ *spun* 1. children of the same parents, **brothers, sisters,** *ḱó-mo-ċag spun γnyis* we (his) two sisters *Dzl.* ༧༨༠, 17; *ṅed spun γsum* we three brothers *Glr.; ḱyed bú-mo spun lṅa-po* you five sisters *Mil.*; pleon. *bu spun γsum Tar.; spun γżán-rnams* his other (six elder) brothers *Tar.; spun-γċés* dear brother! *Chr. P.* — *ṕá-spun,* brothers and sisters of the same father; *má-spun* of the same mother; *spún-zla, (s)pun-da,* or *-la* 1. = *spun;* 2. in *C.* it is said to be used also for attorney, advocate; *spún-ma* sister, as a more particular designation of the sex. — 2. in a wider sense: **cousins, brothers-** or **sisters-in-law;** *grógs-spun* mate, comrade; *čós-spun* a brother of a religious order; *ṕá-spun, ṕás-spun,* several neighbours or inhabitants of a village, that have a common Lha, and thus have become **'rus-pa ċig-ċig'**, members of the same family; this common tie entails on them the duty, whenever a death takes place, ofcaring for the cremation of the dead body (cf. *čos-spún*) *Mil.* and elsewh.; *mdza-spún* friend *Cs.* — 3. **weft, woof** in weaving.

སྤུན་པ་ *spún-pa* 1. sbst., also *sbún-pa B., C., sbur(-ma) Dzl., Ld.*, **chaff, husks** etc. — 2. adj. a botanical term, description of the stalk of a plant *Wdṅ.*

སྤུབ་པ་ *spúb-pa*, pf. *spubs*, vb. a. to *˳búb-pa* **to turn upside down.**

སྤུར་ *spur*, *pur*, also *sku-spúr*, resp. for *ro*, **dead body, corpse,** *spur sbyáṅs-pa C.* to burn a dead body; *spur-k̔aṅ* house for keeping dead bodies, or rather, in most cases, the place of cremation; *spur-sgam* or *sgrom* coffin; *spur-t̔al* ashes of a dead body; *spur-t̔sa* the salt for preparing a dead body; *spur-šiṅ* wood for burning a corpse.

སྤུར་བ་ *spúr-ba*, vb. a. to *˳p̔úr-ba*, **to make fly, to scare up, to let fly;** *dus spúr-ba* to pass time quickly *Cs.*; *stoṅ-spúr* exaggeration, bombast *Cs.*

སྤུས་ *spus* 1. **goods, merchandize, ware,** *spus ltá-ba* to examine goods before purchase *Cs.*; **spus gyúr-če* W.*, **pu ˳gyúr-wa* Cs.* = **dal tsoṅ táṅ-če**. — 2. **goodness, beauty,** *spús-čan, spus-γtsáṅ, spus-bzáṅ*, of fine appearance; *spus-méd* ill-looking, unsightly. — 3. *Sch.*: for *spos.*

སྤེའུ་, སྤིའུ་ *speu*, *spiu*, **turret,** on a castle or gate *W.*, (*C. lčog*). High towers or steeples are seldom met with in Tibetan architecture; **peu gyá-čan riṅ-mo**, *mk̔ar* or *k̔áṅ-pa dgu-t̔óg* are the terms denoting such.

སྤེག་ཤིང་ *speg-šiṅ Cs.*: n. of part of a cart.

སྤེན་ཏོག་ *spen-tog*, **ornament, finery.**

སྤེན་པ་ *spén-pa*, *γza-spén-pa* 1. the planet **Saturn;** the proper meaning is said to be a broom, hence the sign for it is somewhat resembling that implement *Wdk.* — 2. **Saturday.**

སྤེན་མ་ *spén-ma*, *spén-šiṅ*, n. of a tree, prob. tamarisk; *spen-bád* a parapet, formed of the stems of tamarisk and raised on the roofs of monasteries.

སྤེལ་བ་ *spél-ba*, vb. a. to *˳p̔el-ba*, 1. **to augment, to increase,** *nor* the wealth *Lex.*, *bkra-šis* the welfare; *rkaṅ-˳gròs spél-ba* to breed cattle *Dzl.* and elsewh.; **spel-gyúd-la bor-če* W.* to keep cattle for breeding. — 2. **to multiply** (arithm.) *Wdk.* — 3. **to spread, to propagate** (news, secrets) *Dzl.* and elsewh.; more emphatically: *spel rgyás-par*, or *sgróg-par byéd-pa* to blaze about *Sch.* — 4. **to join, to put together,** e.g. letters (almost = to spell); to mingle, to mix; *spél-ma* mixture, e.g. of prose and verse *Cs.*; acc. to *Was.* however, couplets, similar both as to metre and contents; composition, combination, *γser γyu spél-mai k̔ri* a chair of gold and turkoises *Pth.*; *spél-mai nor* mixed goods *Cs.*; *spél-gos* clothes of various colours *Cs.*; *spel-t̔sig Sch.*: a combination of verses, poetry(?); *spél-mar byéd-pa* to mix *Lex.*

སྤེས་ *spes* **edge, brim, border,** *Sch.*

སྤོ་ *spo* **summit of a mountain,** *brag-dmar spo-mt̔ó-nas* from the height of Bragmar *Mil.*; *rdo-rje-γdán-gyi spó-la* on the top of Gayā *Pth.*; *spó-bo* 1. (top, point =) bud *Ts.* 2. district to the east of Lhasa *Glr.*

སྤོ་ཏོ་ *spo-to* 1. **bullock** *C.* — 2. n. of a village in Panyul.

སྤོ་རེ་ *spo-re* v. *spor.*

སྤོ་བ་ *spo-ba*, pf. and imp. *spos*, vb. a. to *˳p̔ó-ba*, **to alter, to change;** with and without *γnas* (*W. *sa**): to change the place (of residence), to remove, to shift; also to transpose, transplant; *miṅ spó-ba* to change the name *Mil.*; *gos spó-ba* to change one's dress; *mgo-lús* v. *mgo* extr.; to remove (an officer) to another station; to dismiss (a servant), *W.*, also *B.* frq.; *γžan mk̔ás-pa yód-na spós-pa bzaṅ* if another skilful (physician) is to be had, it will be better to dismiss (the present one); to alter, to mend, to correct *W.*; *spó-sa* a place newly occupied by nomads *Sch.*

སྤོག་པ་ *spóg-pa*, pf. *spags*, fut. *spag*, **to remove and to bring near by turns** *Cs.*; *Lexx.* w.e. —

སྤོགས་ *spogs* **gain, profit,** *k̔e-spógs* id.; *spogs byed-pa* to make profit, to gain money; *tsoṅ-spógs byéd-pa* to gain money by traffic *Dzl.*; *t̔soṅ-spógs-la ˳gró-ba Dzl.*; *skyed-spogs* interest (of money); *spógs-su γtóṅ-ba* to give money on interest *Cs.*; **mi-póg lém-pa* C.* to demand a tax from emigrants or travellers.

སྤོང་བ་ *spóṅ-ba, spáṅ-ba*, pf. *spaṅs*, fut. *spaṅ*, imp. *spoṅ(s)*, (*Ssk.* वृच्) 1. **to give up, to declare off,** *bdag daṅ bdag-gir Sambh.* to give one's self up and all that one has; *sman-dpyád mi byéd-par spóṅ-na* if he gives (the patient) over without even attempting a cure *Dzl.* ༦༠, 1; **to renounce** (all pleasures) frq.; **kód-gu-ru spaṅ mi p̔od** he cannot give up Kotgur (his former residence) or forget it; without an object: *yóṅs-su spóṅ-ba* (partic.) they (the Bodhisattvas) who entirely renounce *Thgy.*; **to shun, avoid, abstain from** (faults, sins, certain food) frq.; **to reject** = *˳dór-ba: bde-sdúg-la spaṅ-blaṅ med* between happiness and unhappiness there was no need to choose (sc. because only bliss prevailed) *Glr.; spoṅ-bláṅ ˳dzín-pa žig-pa* the cessation of every inclination and disinclination, or also, of every interest in choosing or rejecting. — 2. **to throw off, to drop,** a letter, *p̔yi-tség* (to omit) the dot after a syllable *Gram.*

སྤོང་བྱེད་ *spoṅ-byéd* **Vaisali,** ancient town near Allahabad, *Tar.* 7, 5 and elsewh.; also Vriji, acc. to *Schf.*

སྤོད་ *spod* **spice** *Med.*; *spod ˳débs-pa* to season; *spód-čan* seasoned.

སྤོད་པ་ *spód-pa* 1. **hermit,** *spód-k̔aṅ* hermitage *Sch.* — 2. **vow,** *spód-pa nyáms-pa* one that has broken his vow *Sch.*

སྤོབས་པ་ *spóbs-pa* (*W.* also **spós-pa**), 1. vb. **to dare, to venture,** *˳ǰú-bar mi spóbs-pas* not daring to take hold of *Pth.*, also *Dzl.* ༧༤༧, 4; ༢༦༢, 16; *spóbs-par byéd-pa* 1. id. 2. to enable, empower, authorize *Cs.* — 2. sbst. **courage, confidence.**

སྤོམ་ཡོར་ *spom-yór* diffuse (in words), **prolix, long-winded,** *byéd-pa, smrá-ba, čád-pa Cs.* 'to say circumstantially'.

སྤོར་ *spor, spo-ré,* **steel-yard;** *W.* particularly a little one.

སྤོར་བ་ *spór-ba, spár-ba*, pf. and fut. *spar*, 1. **to lift up,** *rdó-rje* the praying-sceptre *Dom.*; (a hatchet) to fetch a blow; *W. *šed spár-la* (or *spár-te*) *rgyob** swing (the hatchet) well and strike! **spár-la čoṅ** run and leap! cf. also *nems;* to raise, promote, advance, *go-p̔án* in rank *Lex.* — 2. v. *dpór-ba.*

སྤོལ་ *spol Ts.* for **me-mé* W.* (v. *mes-po*).

སྤོས་ *spos* 1. sbst. **incense;** *bdug-spós* id.; less frq. **perfume** in general; *byug-spós* sweet-scented water or ointment; *spos sbyór-ba, sgrúb-pa,* also *rgyáb-pa* and *rgyág-pa Cs.*, to prepare incense, perfumes, *bdúg-pa* to burn (incense); *˳byúg-pa* to cover (with perfume); *rgya-spós, brag-spós, spaṅ-spós,* different kinds of perfume; *spos-(kyi) réṅ (-bu)* pastil, long and thin straws being covered with an odoriferous substance, which generally consists of pulverized *šugpa*, and sandal-wood, combined with some *gugul*, musk and the like; they are made by the Lamas, and frequently presented to travellers as an offering of welcome. *spos-dkár* frankincense, = *gugúl dkár-po.* — *spós-mk̔an* perfumer. — *spos-čúg* incense in pieces or cakes. — *spos-čú*, resp. *čab*, sweet-scented water, diluted ointment, *lús-la ˳byúg-pa Pth.*; *spós-čus čag-čág ˳débs-pa Pth.* to sprinkle with such water. — *spos-snod Cs.*, *spos-p̔ór* (also *pog-p̔ór*), censer, perfuming-pan. — *spós-t̔soṅ-pa* = *spós-mk̔an.* — *spos-γžóṅ* basin for incense *Cs.* — *spos-šél* (col. **po-šél**) amber. — 2. vb. v. *spó-ba* and *spóbs-pa.*

སྤྱ་དངོས་ *spya-dṅós Cs.* = *yo-byád; Lex.* *spyad-dṅós* and *dṅos-spyád,* as explanations to *ka-ča.*

སྤྱང་ཀི་ *spyáṅ-ki Mil., Sg., -gi Dzl., -ku, -gu, k̔u Cs., Lh. *šáṅ-ku**, **wolf.** (Wolves, where more frequent, as e. g. in Spiti, commit ravages among the sheep; but are other wise not much dreaded by man). *spyáṅ-mo* female wolf; *spyaṅ-p̔rúg* young wolf; *spyaṅ-t̔sáṅ* wolf's den; *spyaṅ-dóṅ* wolf's trap (used in *Sp.*); *spyáṅ-ku ṅú-ba* the howling of a wolf *Cs.; če-spyáṅ Lex.*, lċe-spyáṅ Stg., dur-spyáṅ Cs., *k̔yi-ċáṅ* W., jackal. — spyaṅ-dug-pa Cs., spyaṅ-t̔sér Med., thistle, or kind of thistle, mentioned as an emetic.

སྤྱང་བ་ spyáṅ-ba 1. sbst. and adj.; spyáṅ-po adj., **skill; skilful, clever,** Lexx., Glr. and elsewh.; prob. = γċáṅ(-po), q. v.; sometimes confounded with sbyáṅ-ba, sbyáṅs-pa, practiced, expert; rig-pa spyáṅ-bas rtsóm-pa kún-la ₒjug Lt. the clever man finds his way in every thing; spyaṅ-γlén Cs. the clever man and the dunce; Glr.: spyaṅ γlen ma nór-ba ċig byed dgos, prob. to be read ₒbyed, and to be translated: then it must evidently appear, who is clever and who is stupid. — 2. vb. = dpyáṅ-ba.

སྤྱད་ spyad v. spya.

སྤྱད་པ་ spyád-pa v. spyód-pa.

སྤྱན་ spyan, resp. for mig, **eye**; spyan bgrád-pa, γdáṅ-ba, to stare Cs.; spyan ₒgyúr-ba v. spyán-pa; spyan ₒdrén-pa, rarely dróns-pa, resp. for ₒdrén-pa, to invite, v. ₒdrén-pa; spyan ₒp̔yi-ba to wipe the eyes; spyan btsúm-pa to shut the eyes Cs.

**Comp. and deriv.** spyan-kyúg or k̔yug eye-brow Cs. — spyan-dkyús v. dkyus. — spyan-bskyúṅs mdzád-pa to protect, to preserve the eyes Sch. — spyán-sṅa before, with, in presence of a dignitary, spyán-sṅai grá-pa-rnams the scholars standing in presence of his Reverence Cs.; mostly in the termin. case: spyán-sṅar, as adv. and postp., rgyál-poi spyán-sṅar k̔rid-pa to lead (another) before the king, frq.; rarely in reference to the first pers.: ṅai spyán-sṅar ₒoṅ they came to me, before my face (sc. Buddha's) Dzl.; less corr. spyán-sṅar mdzés-pai skúd-ris Mil. in front (on the fore-part of the shoes) beautifully embroidered figures. — spyán-ċan having eyes. — spyan-lċibs eye-lid. — spyan-čáb tears, ₒbyín-pa to shed; čór-ba to flow from; also to shed, rgyál-bu spyan-čáb šór-ro Pth. the prince shed tears. — spyan-ₒdrén one who invites, one that calls to dinner. — spyán-pa Cs. 1. eye-witness; 2. commissary; 3. Sch. overseer; spyán-du ₒgyúr-ba = dpáṅ-du ₒgyúr-ba, to see, to know; spyán-pa byéd-pa to watch, guard, keep, protect, inspect Sch.; bá-glaṅ-gi spyán-pa cow-herd(?) Sch. — spyan-ₒbrás apple of the eye. — spyan-mig-bzáṅ the western 'king of ghosts', v. rgyal-čén sub rgyál-ba. — spyan-dmígs Sch.: 'the object of vision; the inclination of the mind'. — spyan-smán medicine for the eyes. — spyan-rtség the wrinkles of the eye-lids Cs. — spyan-zúr Sch., corner of the eye. — spyan-γzígs, costly offerings dedicated to the gods, Mil.; also applied to presents of food, offered to men, Mil.; ₒbúl-ba to offer such; also ₒdrén-pa. — spyan-yás, Sch., without eyes, blind. — spyan-rás, Sch. the brightness of the eye, a glance of the eye. — spyan-ras-γzigs W.; *ċan-re-zig* Cs.: *čen-re-sig or -si*, Ssk. अवलोकितेश्वर, the other (cf. ₒjam-dpal) of the two great half-divine Bodhisattvas of the northern Buddhists, who more particularly is revered as begetter (not creator), redeemer, and ruler of men, and in the first place of the Tibetans, incarnate as king Sroṅ-tsan-gám-po, Köpp. II, 22. — spyán-lam-du seems to be = drúṅ-du, spyán-sṅar, Mil. and elsewh.

སྤྱི་ spyi, I. adj. (synon. t̔un, also dbyiṅs, opp. to sgos) 1. **general, relating to all, standing higher than all:** *ṭim-pọn ċi*, chief prefect, governor general C.; adv. spyi, spyir(-du), less frq. spyi-la, spyi-na, spyir-gyis, **generally, in general,** frq. followed by sgos(-kyis), k̔yád-par, **in particular, singly;** also like cum tum in Latin; spyi daṅ ₒdir, generally, and here, in this work, Wdṅ.; spyii sdom, v. sdom; — spyii k̔og ji daṅ ji bžin-du (?) Sch.: 'according to general custom'. — 2. **all,** C.; lhá-k̔aṅ spyii bstan-srúṅ Glr. — 3. for spyi-bo, v. below. — spyi-sgra Cs., **general meaning,** more corr. sgra-spyi, Was. (294), **general expression.** — spyi-γċér, spyi-t̔er Cs., bald-headed. — spyi-t̔ór = gtsug-tór Lex. spyi-t̔óg, property of the community, common property; W.: *pi-t̔og-ne toṅ* bestow it out of the common funds! — spyi-gdugs, v. sgos. — spyi-pa, **head, chief, leader, superintendent,** Sch.;

པ

*spyi-dpon*, much the same, v. *sgos*; *spyi-bo*, 1. (rarely *spyi*), **crown of the head**, top, *spyi-bor ᵒḱúr-ba* to carry on the head; — *spyi-bos ṕyág-ᵒtsal-ba* to bow down bending the head; *žabs spyi-bor lén-pa*, frq., to place the foot of a superior on one's own head; *dei spyi-bo-nas byúg-nas*, pouring over his head, anointing him, *Domaṅ*; more frq: *spyi-bo-nas dbaṅ skúr-ba*, v. *skur-ba*; *spyi-bo-nas dbaṅ bskúr-bai rgyál-po*, the anointed king; *spyi-glugs*, the vessel used for anointing (resembling a tea-pot). — 2. the end of a piece of cloth, *dar-yúg-gi*, *Glr.* — 3. name of a king of China *Glr.*; *spyi-miṅ* common appellation: *dḱor ni nór-gyi spyi-miṅ*, '*dḱor*' is a general word for property, *Lex.* — II. often incorr. for *ċi*, also *dpyi*.

སྤྱི་ཏི་ *spyi-ti*, a fantastic, mystical doctrine of **Urgyen-Padma**, *ṫég-pa č́én-po spyi-ti*, *spyi-ti yóg-brdai dkyil-ḱor Pth.*; *yáṅ-ti*, another of his doctrines.

སྤྱི་བརྟོལ་ *spyi-brtól*, *Cs.*: **impudence, impertinence**, *Sch.*: **lewd**; *spyi-brtól-ċan*, impudent; *spyi-brtól byéd-pa*, to be impudent *Cs.*

སྤྱིང་བ་ *spyiṅ-ba*, pf. *spyiṅs*, imp. *spyiṅ(s)*, the vb. a. to *ᵒbyiṅ-ba*, **to sink, to lower, let down, dip under**; *čur*, *Lexx.*

སྤྱིན་ *spyin* (*W.* *(s)pin*), **glue, paste**: *spyin skól-ba*, to manufacture glue; *skúd-pa* (*Sch.* also *bdár-ba?*) to spread glue on; *pin daṅ ǰár-ċe* *W.* to glue; *ko-spyin*, glue made of skins, *nya-spyin*, fish-glue, isinglass; *bág-spyin* paste or rather a kind of putty, compounded of flour and glue; *rá-spyin* glue made of horn; *ša-spyin*, meat-jelly; *spyin-ṗor* glue-pot.

སྤྱིམས་ *spyims* (? *ċims*), *Ld.* = *spyi*; *ċimsi miṅ* = *spyi-miṅ*.

སྤྱིར་ *spyir* v. *spyi*.

སྤྱིལ་པོ་ *spyil-po*, 1. **hut** *Mil.*, *Pth.*; *rtsai*, **thatched hut** *Lex.*; *spyil-bu*, id; *lo-mai spyil-bu*, hut constructed of twigs, fastened together on the top, **arbour**; **a cot**, a mean house. — 2. **inmate of such a one**, *Cs.*; also *spyil-pa*, fem. *-ma*.

སྤྱུག་པ་ *spyúg-pa*, pf. *spyugs*, imp. *spyug(s)*; **to expel, to turn out, to banish**; *yúl-nas* out of the country; *yul gžán-du Glr.*; *mṫá-la*, *mṫar* into the neighbouring country, over the frontier (v. *mṫa*); when the place of banishment is named, the otherwise faulty spelling *bċúg-pa* is allowable; v. *ᵒǰúg-pa*.

སྤྱོ་བ་ *spyó-ba*, pf. and imp. *spyos*, **to blame, to scold** *Dzl.*; *č́úṅ-ma rtág-tu spyó-žiṅ*, as my wife is always scolding; *ċes spyós-so* thus they spoke in a blaming way, *Dzl.*; *Cs.* also: **to mock, to ridicule**(?). synon. *gšé-ba*.

སྤྱོང་བ་ *spyóṅ ba* = *dpyáṅ-ba*.

སྤྱོད་པ་ *spyód-pa*, I. vb., also *spyád pa*, pf. *spyad*, *Ssk.* चर 1. — *byéd-pa*, **to do, to act**, v. *tsáṅs-par*, yet gen. with an object in the accus. **to accomplish, perform, commit**; *sdig-pa*, *sdig-pai las*, *dgé-ba*, *dká-ba* (v. *dká-ba*), *č́os spyod-pa*; *mi-dge-ba dé-dag spyód-na* if one commits these sins *Thgy.*; *bdag ċi spyád-pas ᵒdir skyes*, what having done, or because of which doing of mine am I re-born here? *Dzl.*; even like *byéd-pa* = to be, *mṅa-ᵒóg spyód-pai ᵒbáṅs Glr.*, simply = subjects; rarely c. dat.: *sdig-pa ᵒbá-žig-la spyód-pa*, *Thgy.*, *dgé-ba bċú-la*, *Dzl.*, denoting a habitual doing; cf. *zá-ba*. — 2. **to treat, to deal with**, *zas-skóm légs-par spyód-pa*. (to deal with) food and drink in the right manner *S.g.*; gen. with the dat.: *žiṅ-la lhú-ru spyad*, the fields were disposed of in lots, divided *Glr.*; hence gen. **to use**, to make use of, to employ, to enjoy: *bá-glaṅ nyin-par* to use an ox during the day (for ploughing) *Dzl.*; *yun-riṅ-dus-su bdé-bar spyad kyaṅ*, even if one has long and in tranquillity used, enjoyed (this world's goods), *Thgy.*; so frq. with *loṅs*: *lóṅs-spyod-pa*; to have for a sphere of activity, v. *mḱá-spyod*, *sá-spyod*, *sa-ᵒóg-spyod*; also a euphemism for sensual indulgence: *bud-méd-la spyód-pa* to use, to cohabit with, a woman, *Dzl.*; *mi-rigs-par* or *lóg-par*, to violate (a woman) *Thgy.* & others; *dga mgúr spyód-pa*, of a like meaning; the other synonymous phrases: *ₒdod-lóg spyód-pa, mi ₔós-pai spyód-pa byéd-pa, Glr., nyál-po, čágs-pa, ₒḱrig-pa spyód-pa*, belong by their construction properly to 1; so also: *bud-méd brgya spyod nus* he can get done with a hundred wives, *Lt.*

II. sbst. 1. **action, practice, execution,** opp. to *ltá-ba*, theory. esp. in mysticism, v. *sgóm-pa*. — 2. **activity:** *spyód-pa śin-tu dóg-par gyúr-to* they were much restrained, narrowly watched *Glr.*; *séms-kyi spyód-pa* seems to be: faculty of mind, *Wdṅ.* — 3. **way of acting, conduct, course of life,** = *spyód-lam*; *byaṅ-čub-séms-dpai* frq : *ṅán-* or *nyés-spyod* bad actions, *bzáṅ-* or *légs-spyod* good actions *Cs.*; *spyód-pa žib-pa*, 'the strict', a monastic order *Pth.*; **behaviour, deportment,** frq.: *spyód-pa rtsiṅ-ba*, rude, rough, in manners *Glr.*; *spyód-pas skád-čig kyaṅ mi ťsugs*, of an extremely variable conduct (lit. not for one moment the same) *Glr.*

**Comp.** *spyod-ₒgrós* **gait and deportment** *Mil.* — *spyod-ṅán* = *ṅán-spyod, spyod-ṅán byéd pa.* — *spyód-ťsul, Sch.* = *spyód-pa* II. *spyód-yul*, **sphere of activity;** *kún-gyi spyód-yul ₒdi ma lags*, that is not a thing to be attempted by every body *Mil.*; *mťóṅ-bai spyód-pa* range of vision *Tar.*; cf. गोचर. — *spyód-lam*, 1. **demeanour, deportment, mode of life** frq.; 2. **good behaviour,** graceful demeanour, noble deportment; otherwise *spyód-pa mdzés-pa*; hence *spyód-pa daṅ ldán-pa, spyod-ldán* of genteel manners *Dzl.*; *spyód-pa daṅ mi ldán-pa Dzl.*, **čod-ṅán-čan** *W.*, **čọ̈-lóg ǰhé-ḱẹn**, *C.* **rude, unmannerly, ill-bred, disobedient.** 3. *Med.*: **diet,** and more particularly **bodily exercise;** *zas-spyód*, food and exercise. 4. **attitude:** *spyód-lam rnam-bži* the four attitudes of sitting, lying, standing and walking.

སྤྱོད་པ་པ་ *spyód-pa-pa* v. *dpyód-pa*, extr.

སྤྱོད་པད་ *spyod-pad* or *dpyod-pád* (spelling not quite certain), pronunc.: **čọ̈-pẹ̈**, **lemon, citron** *C.*

སྤྱོན་པ་ *spyón-pa*, rarely for *ₒbyon-pa.*

སྤྱོམ་པ་ *spyóm-pa*, pf. *spyoms*, **to boast, to exhibit with ostentation,** e.g. virtues, (the Greek *καυχᾶσθαι*). Notwithstanding the detailed explanations of the *Lexx.*, the word is after all so little known, that I never met with it in books, nor heard it used by the people. — *spyoms*, sbst., **self-praise, boasting** *Zam.*

སྤྲ་ *spra*, monkey. *Mil.*, prob. the large dark-gray, long-tailed **monkey** of the southern Himalaya; *sprá-mo*; *spra-ṕrúg.*

སྤྲ་(ཏ)ཅལ་ *spra-čál* v. *pra-čál*; *spra-tél* v. *tél-pa.*

སྤྲ་བ་ *sprá-ba*, I. sbst. *W.* **śrá-wa**, **spunk, German tinder,** prepared of the fibres of a thistle (Cousinia); *spra-mé*, glowing tinder, *Pth.*; *ṕyi ni sprá-ba dkár-por γyogs*, white-nappy, as a botanical term, *Wdṅ.*, the colour of the tinder, referred to, being a light gray; *sprá-bai ťóg-gu* a medicinal herb *Wdṅ.*

II. vb. pf. *spras*, imp. *spros*, 1. **to adorn, to decorate:** *rgyán-gyis* frq., *mtsán-dpes Mil.* and elsewh. — 2. *γčes spras, Lex.? sprá-ba byéd-pa* **to love, to caress.** — 3. perh. identical with **śrá-če(s)**, **to empty** (a dish). — 4. *spra ₒḱrid-pa* **to lead, to direct right.** — Cf. also *γtsaṅ sprá-wa.*

སྤྲ་ཚིལ་ *spra-ťsil, Med., C.* **wax** (*W.* **mum**).

སྤྲག་པ་ *sprág-pa* v. *sbrág-pa.*

སྤྲང་བ་ *spráṅ-ba, Cs.*, **to beg;** (the verb I never met with, and *Zam.* explains the sbst. only by *nor-méd*); *spráṅ-po*, **beggar,** *Dzl., Glr.*, frq. (*Wts.* 'filou', rather bold, though not far from the truth); **ṭaṅ-lóṅ** *C.*, id.; *spraṅ-rgán Mil.*, an old beggar; *rdzús-mai spráṅ-po* a sham-beggar *Glr.*; *spraṅ-ṕrúg* beggar boy; *spraṅ-bán* mendicant friar *Glr.*; *spraṅ-zás* beggar's livelihood *Mil*; *dkar-spraṅ* begging for lenten food, also such food obtained by begging, v. *dkar-zás*; *skyur-spráṅ* begging for beer *Mil.*

སྤྲད་པ་ *spród-pa* v. *spród-pa.*

སྤྲི་སྟི་མ་རྫ་ཡ་, སི་ཆེན་ *spri-sti-ma-rdza-ya, si-čén*, n. of the emperor of China, during whose reign Buddhism was introduced into that country,

པ

*Glr.*; acc. to Chinese accounts: *Miṅg-ti*, 58—76 after Christ.

སྤྲི་མ་ *spri-ma, spris-ma, sris-ma, W.* *śri*, **cream,** and other fatty substances, gathering on the surfaces of fluids; *ₒó-mai spris, Lt., žo(i)-spris, Wdṅ.*; gen. *ₒo-sri*, cream (of milk); *ťúg-spri*, the greasy surface of soup; ditto of urine *Med.*

སྤྲིང་བ་ *spriṅ-ba*, pf. *spriṅs*, **to send a message, to give information, to send word;** *p̔rin*, tidings *Dzl.*; *žes spriṅ-ṅo* so I send him word *Dzl.*

སྤྲིན་ *sprin*, *ṭin*, *Ld.* *śrin*, *Bal.* *spin*, **cloud,** also as an emblem of transitoriness frq.; *śrin ṭigs, k̔or*, *W.*, clouds are spreading; *sprin-gyi ysėb-nas* from between the clouds *Glr.*; *ylóg-sprin* thunder-cloud *Glr.*; *čár-sprin* rain-cloud; *ₒjá-sprin* cloud tinged with rainbow colours *Pth.*; *mig-sprin* v. this; *lhó-sprin* a southern cloud, picturesque expression, the clouds in Tibet generally coming from the south *Mil.*; *sprin-skyés* lightning; *sprin-dmár* clouds reddened by the sun, morning or evening red; *sprin-p̔úṅ, sprin-ťsógs*, an accumulation of clouds; *sprin-yyi p̔ó-nya* the messenger of the clouds, Meghadūta, a poëm by Kalidāsa *Tar.*

སྤྲིབས་པ་ *spribs-pa* **to be hungry** *Sch.*

སྤྲིས་མ་ *spris-ma* v. *spri-ma.*

སྤྲུ་མ་ *sprú-ma, Cs.*, **hellebore;** *sprú-dkár, -nág Med.*

སྤྲུག་པ་ *sprúg-pa*, pf. and imp. *sprugs*, *ṭúg-pa*, *W.* *śrug-če* **to shake, to shake off, to beat out,** *rdul* dust; **to stir up,** *rdul-ťsúb*, **to raise,** whirl up dust; *lus sprúg-sil-ba, lus sprug-sil byéd-pa Glr.*, to shake one's self (used of horses); fig. *nus mťu rtsal sprúg-pa*, to strain every nerve, to work with might and main *Pth.*; **to shake about, to stir up** (synon. *śrul-če, rum-če* *W.*); *Cs.* also: to rub, to scratch, to brush??

སྤྲུལ་བ་ *sprúl-ba* (cf. *ₒp̔rúl-ba*), **to juggle, to make phantoms** (*sprúl-pa*) **appear, to change, to transform** (one's self), which according to the doctrines of Buddhism is the highest acquisition of any man, that by his own holiness has assumed divine nature, viz. as long as he is capable of acting, not having yet been absorbed into the blessed state of nothingness. This power of transformation on the part of the Buddhist is the evidence of what he understands by divine omnipotence; but as this conception is a mere product of fancy, it varies in its import. On the one hand it is opposed to reality, *dṅos*; thus e. g. beings, whom no Buddha could convert through his personal agency, *sku-dṅós-kyi sgó-nas*, are converted (acc. to *Pth.*) *sprúl-pai ťábs-kyis*. Frequently Buddha avails himself of jugglery, *rdzu-p̔rúl ston*, converting thousands of beings in a trice, *Dzl.* & elsewh.; further: *drág-poi sprúl-pa byás-pa yin Glr.*, I caused terrifying phantoms to appear, viz. the spectral bodies of executed culprits, in order to scare the rude Tibetans into the way of virtue. From the foregoing it is evident that the term in question by no means conveys the scriptural idea of **a creative and miraculous power**; the Tibetan, however, when he becomes acquainted with christianity, is always apt to substitute his *sprúl-pa* or *rdzu-ₒp̔rúl*, and *sprúl-ba* for it. On the other hand, a real and material existence is as often attributed to a *sprul-pa*, when it designates the incarnate and embodied person, the Avatāra of a deity, (Mongol. Chubilgan), who like any human being is capable of acting, and exerting an influence on the material world around him, or of suffering by it, without any docetic admixture. Occasionally it is also to be translated by **emanation:** *yáṅ-sprul*, emanation of the second degree, i.e. one emanation going forth from another; *nyiṅ-sprul* or *ysúm-sprul*, an em. of the third degree *Pth.*; *sprúl-pa ₒgyéd-pa*, to let emanations go forth, *Lexx.* — Further: *sprúl-pa mkyén-pa*, to be an adept in the art of *sprúl-pa*, i. e. witchcraft, *Glr.*; *ri ynyis sprúl-te* producing two mountains by magic, *Dzl.*; ... *mťó-ba* ... *bžúgs-pa sprúl-nas*, changing himself into a high enthroned person, *Dzl.*; *dge-*

*slóṅ žig-tu*, transforming himself into a friar, *Dzl.* frq.; *dúd-ₒgro ťsim-par sprúl-ba*, to satiate animals by fictitious food *Dzl.*; *ťams-čád sprúl-par ₒdúg-pa*, these were all metamorphoses, mocking phantoms, *Glr.*; *sku-lús-kyi sprúl-pa brgya-rtsa-brgyád mdzád-de* or *sprúl-te*, to centuple one's self, *Glr.*; *sprul-pai rgyál-po*, the phantom-king, viz. Buddha, Avalokitesvara, or some other divine person, incarnate as a king; *gaṅ-la-gaṅ-ₒdúl-gyi sprúl-pa*, all-converting Avatara, frq.

སྤྲེ་ *spre*, gen. *spreu*, rarely *sprel* (*Ld.* **ṡreu*; *spriu**) **monkey**, of a grayish yellow brown, common in the forests of the southern Himalaya, (cf. *spra*); sometimes a distinction is made between *spre* and *spra*, in which case the former is the long-tailed monkey. — *spré-mo*, female monkey, *Cs.*; yet also *spreu žár-ma*, a blind female monkey, *Dzl*; *spre-ṕrúg*, young monkey. — *spre-rtséd*, apish tricks; foolery.

སྤྲོ་བ་ *spró-ba* I. vb. pf. *spros*, prop. the transitive of *ₒṕró-ba* **to make go out, to disperse, to spread**; gen. however intransitive: 1. **to go out, to proceed, to spread,** of rays of light, of the wind, *Wdṅ.* — 2. fig. **to enlarge upon**, by way of explaining, representing, *Zam.*, *Pth.*; *γčig-las sprós-pa*, *Was.* (115), enlarging (proceeding) from the number one in an ascending progression of numbers; *rnám-par sprós-pa*, to have come to a full development and restoration from the consequences of sins, *Stg.*

II. 1. vb. (pf. unaltered), **to feel an inclination for, to delight in:** *dgé-ba-la*, in virtue, *Dzl.*; *byá-ba gáṅ-la yaṅ spró-ba čuṅ*, feeling little inclination for doing any thing, *Thgy.*; *bsád-par spró-ba su yaṅ ma byuṅ*, none was found that had a mind to kill, *Stg.*; so also *Tar.*; **to be willing, to wish,** *Tar.*; in an absolute sense: *sems*, or resp. *ťugs*, *spró-bar ₒgyúr-ba*, **to get cheerful, merry,** *Mil.* — 2. sbst. **joy, cheerfulness:** *spró-ba skyéd-pa*, to feel joy, pleasure, *Dzl.* and elsewh.; *spró-ba skyé-bai ṕyir-du*, for an encouragement, for a comfort, *Glr.*; *spro-siṅ-ba Sch.*, great joy (cf. *siṅ*); *spro-siṅ-gé-ba*, *Sch.*, to one's wish (?); *spro ši-ba*, *Sch.*, 'not to be joyful', lit. the cessation of joy; *spro ťúṅ-ba*, 'short cheerfulness', i.e. a passionate disposition; or as adj. **passionate, irascible,** *Wdṅ.*; *dga-spró*, **joy,** *dga-spró dpag-tu-méd-pa ťob*, he got into a most cheerful humour, *Mil.*—**ṭo-ḱáṅ**, *C.*, pleasure-house, summer-house, pavilion; *spro-séms* and (*Ld.*) **spro-ṡés, ṡro-ṡés**, joy; *spro-séms*, *Thgy.* also youthful joy, alacrity, cheerfulness in working, readiness to act.

སྤྲོག་མ་ *spróg-ma*; *Sch. spós-kyi spróg-ma*, **little box for frankincense.**

སྤྲོག་ཞུ་ *spróg-žu* v. *ṕrog*.

སྤྲོད་པ་ *spród-pa*, secondary form *sprad*, the vb. a. of *ṕrod-pa* (by the illiterate it is often used for *γtod-pa*, not very current in common life) 1. **to bring together, to put together, to make to meet:** *ṅai blá-ma-la spród-do*, we will bring you together with our Lama, *Mil.*; so also resp. . . . *γnyis žal spród mdzád-pa*; in another passage *de daṅ žal-spród-du bžúgs-šin* prob. means sitting exactly opposite to one another, (a whimsical idea, relative to two idols many miles distant from each other; possibly it should be read *γtod-du*); *bdág-čag spród-čig*, bring about a meeting between our two parties! *Dzl.*; *γyul* or *ťáb-mo*, to commit a battle; *rál-ḱa*, *Ma.*, to put the edges of the swords together, prob. meaning the same; *mťeb spród-pa*, to put the finger to the bow-string, *Glr.*; **lág-tọ̀ ťéb-tọ̀ kál-wa**, to suspend by the thumb and big toe, a kind of torture in *C.* (The special meaning: to cohabit, *Cs.*, never came to my notice). — 2. **to deliver** (a letter, message) *Pth.*; *spár-mor*, *lág-tu*, *Lex.*, to put into one's hand; **to set, to put, to propose,** **gyugs, ldem**, a task, a riddle, *W.*; **to pay** (cf. *ₒṕrod-pa*), *ṕyir sprod-pa*, to repay. — Moreover: *ṅó-sprod-pa*, **to explain,** *don daṅ spród-pa* seems to signify the same in *Mil.*, *Pth.*; *brdá-sprod-pa*, **to explain, to describe** v. *brda*; *brda-spród*, ibid. seems to denote grammar.

སྤྲོས་པ་ *sprós-pa*. 1. pf. v. *spró-ba* I. — 2. **business, employment, activity;** *Cs.:*

'spros-pa-čan, busy, **employed, occupied;** sprós-bčas, id.; čós-kyi and ₒjig-rtén-gyi sprós-pa, spiritual and secular business'; *Sch.*: 'spros kun, all affairs'; I met only with sprós-pa méd-pa or čód-pa, or spros-brál, denoting the state of an absolute inactivity, such as belongs to Buddha in the state of čos-sku, (v. sku 2) *Pth.*, *Mil.*

# ཕ

ཕ ṕa 1. the letter ṕ, aspirate, the English p in pass. — 2. num. figure: 14.

ཕ་ ṕa I. vulgo ཨ་ཕ་, ཨ་པ་, ǎ-ṕa, ǎ-pa, (*Cs.* also ཨ་ཏ་ ǎ-ta) 1. **father**, resp. *yab* (yet also ṕa is used, e.g. when Milaraspa is addressed by his female disciples, as well as in prayers to defunct saints *Mil.*) — 2. a male, not castrated, animal (vulg. likewise ǎ-ṕa). **Comp.** ṕa-gláṅ bull. — ṕa-rǰes-bú, *Sch.*, a child born after its father's death. — ṕa-rtá, stallion. — *ṕa-nór*, patrimony *C.*, *W.* — ṕa-spád (*Sch.* also ṕad) v. *spad;* ṕa-spún v. *spun.* — ṕa-ṕág, boar. — ṕa-má, parents, ṕa-má-la gús-pa, *Stg.*; *ṕa-ma-méd-ḱan*, *W.*, orphan; also father or mother, parent; ṕa-má-γčig-pa, brothers and sisters born of the same parents. — ṕa-miṅ, relations on the father's side; btsún-moi ṕa-miṅ bós-so, *Glr.*, he invited the relations of his wife's father; ṕa (daṅ) més (-po), ancestors; ṕa-més ši-bai dón-du, for the (defunct) ancestors, *Wdṅ.*; — ṕa-tsáb 1. foster-father, guardian, *Sch.* 2. father to a country (?). — ṕa-tsán, *Mil.* 1. cousin by the father's side (patruelis) *C.* 2. also = ṕa-spún (?). — ṕa-γži = *ṕa-nór*, *C.* — ṕa-yáṅ, *Sch.*, step-father; — ṕa-yúl, fatherland, native country, frq.; ṕa-yúl-la čágs-pa or srég-pa, love of country. — ṕa-γyág, yak-bull. — ṕa-γyár, step-father, foster-father, *Cs.* — ṕa-rá, he-goat, buck.

II. root for the terms: **beyond, onward, farther on**; ṕá-ga, the opposite side; ču ṕá-gar ṫón-nas, to get to the opposite bank or shore, *Mil.* (not frq.). — ṕá-gi, 1. that which is on the other side, *Sch.* 2. *C.*, also *Pth.*, *Mil.*: **yonder;** ṕá-gii ri de, that mountain yonder, *Pth.* 3. col.: **he.** — ṕá-gir, **there, thither.** — ṕá-ṅos = ṕá-rol, ṕá-rol-tu *Lh.* — ṕá-mṫa, the other end, the other boundary, *Cs.*; ṕa-mṫa-méd, without boundary, endless, *Cs.* — ṕa-ṕyogs *C.* = ṕá-ga. — ṕa-tsád, ṕa-zád, **distance;** ṕa-ṫsád čig-na, at a small distance (from the town), *Pth.*; dé-nas ṕa-zád čig-na, a bit farther on, *Dzl.*; ṕa-ṫsad čig-tu ₒtón-nas, stepping a little aside, *Pth.*; ṕa-zád ₒgró-ba, to go on, *Dzl.* frq. — ṕa-ri the mountain on the other side. — ṕá-rol, in *B.* very frq. **1. the other side; opposite side, counterparty.** 2. for ṕá-rol-pa, -na, -tu v. below; ṕá-rol-tu, over to the other side, skyél-ba, to carry, ṕyin-pa, to get to the other side, esp. in reference to the Mahāyāna doctrine of crossing the stream of time to the shore of rest, of Nirwāṇa; gen. as sbst. = **पारमिता**, means of crossing (*Was.* **perfections**, *Köpp.* **cardinal-virtues**); gen. six of them are reckoned: sbyin-pa, ṫsúl-ḱrims, bzód-pa, brtson-ₒgrús, bsam-γtán, šes-ráb; sometimes only five, at other times even ten, by adding ṫabs, smón-lam, stobs, ye-šés; sbyin-pai, šes-ráb-kyi ṕá-rol-tu ṕyin-pa, to have stepped over or crossed by means of beneficence, wisdom etc. (or more naturally: to have got to the end of beneficence etc., to have fully achieved, accomplished it; sbst. the full accomplishment of etc.). — ṕá-rol-na, adv., **on the other side;** postp. e. gen. **beyond, behind,** with regard to space, *Sambh.*; **extending**

**beyond**, both as to the future and the past, e.g. *bskál-pa gráṅs-med-pai ṕá-rol-na*, innumerable Kalpas ago, frq.; *ṕá-rol-pa*, 1. **one living on the other side.** 2. also *po*, **enemy, adversary**, *ṕá-rol-pai rgyál-po, ṕá-rol-pai dmag, ṕá-rol-gyi dmag-ts̀ógs*, the hostile king, hostile army; *ṕá-rol ɣnón-pa*, to vanquish the enemy; *ṕá-rol-gyis mi ts̀úgs-par ͦgyúr-ba*, not to be molested by the enemy. 3. also *po*, **the other; the neighbour;** *ṕá-rol-gyi lén-pa*, to take away the neighbour's property; *ṕá-rol-gyi rdzas, yo-byád, nor, Stg.*; *ṕá-rol ɣnón-pa, Tar.* 12,20: excelling others, *Schf.* **exceedingly.** — Cf. also *ṕar* and *ṕan* II.

ཕ་གུ་ *ṕá-gu*, *Sch.* **wall; edge, border;** in two passages of *Glr.* the latter meaning does not suit at all, and the former not well; rather: **tile**; v. *pag*.

ཕ་ཏིང་ *ṕá-tiṅ*, *W.*, **sweet dried apricots,** in *C.* **ṅa-ri-k̀ám-bu**, in Hind. خوباني, in Russia *bokhari*, *bokharki*, also called Persian fruit, much exported from Balti, Kabul, and other countries f western Asia.

ཕ་ཏིལ་ *ṕa-til*, *pa-til* (*Ar.* فتيلة) *W.*, **lunt, match**; **dug-c̀e**, to light (a match).

ཕ་བ་དགོ་དགོ་ *ṕa-ba-dgo-dgó*, **puff-ball, bull-fist** (a kind of fungus) *Wdṅ.*

ཕ་བོང་ *ṕa-bóṅ*, *Glr.* and elsewh., *C.*, *ṕa-ͦóṅ Pth.*, *Bal.*, *ṕa-lóṅ Ld.*, **a large rock** or **block**, above ground.

ཕ་ཝང་ *ṕa-wáṅ*, 1. **bat** (animal) *Lt.*, *Thgr.*, *C.*; **ṕo-loṅ-hel-kyí*, *ṕa-waṅ-áṅ-kyé*, *-ár-k̀yi**, *W.*, **ṕa-waṅ-t̀ár**, *Sik.*, id. (= *bya-waṅ*). 2. *rdo ṕa-waṅ*, *Ssk.* sālagrāma, **ammonite.**

ཕ་ར་ *ṕá-ra*, 1. **breeding-buck.** — 2. v. *ṕár-ba*.

ཕ་རང་ *ṕa-ráṅ*, 1. also *ṕe-ráṅ*, = **ṕi-líṅ**, *C.*, **Feringhi, European.** — 2. vulg. **venereal disease.**

ཕ་རི་ *ṕa-rí* 1. *Lh.*, **a coarse covering** or **carpet.** — 2. a mountain on the other side.

ཕ་ལ་ *ṕá-la Ssk.*, **fruit**, *Lt.*

ཕ་ལམ་ *ṕa-lám*, *rdo-rje-ṕa-lám*, **diamond**, *Lt.*

ཕ་ལི་ *ṕa-li*, **shield, buckler.**

ཕ་སོད་ཤེད་འདུག་ *ṕa-s̀od s̀edͦdug*, **he changes colour, turns pale,** with consternation, *Ld.*

ཕག་ *ṕag*, I. v. *pag*. — II. in *B.* gen. *ṕág-pa*, **swine, hog, pig** (introduced into *C.* from China, and largely consumed; in *W.* somewhat known from India, **ri-ṕag* and *lúṅ-ṕag** being distinguished as the wild boar and the tame hog); *ṕág-pai sna*, *Glr.*; *rús-pa*, *Med.*; *b̀cud*(?) *Lt.*; *ṕág-gi ɣdoṅ*, a pig's face, *Sambh.*; *ṕá-ṕag*, not castrated, *ṕó-ṕag*, castrated boar; *mó-ṕag*, sow. — *ṕág-k̀yu*, herd of swine. — *ṕág-mgo*, 1. **boar's head** (a valued protective against demons, it being hid in the ground under the threshold of the door). 2. *S.g.* fol. 26, it seems to be **a mineral** used in medicine. — *ṕag-rgód*, wild boar. — *ṕag-mc̀e*, tusks of a boar. — *ṕag-t̀úṅ*, *Sch.*: a large boar(?). — *ṕag-ṕrúg*, young pig. — *ṕág-ma*, *Sch.*, gelded hog. — *ṕág-mo*, 1. sow. 2. a goddess v. *rdo-rje*. — *ṕag-ts̀áṅ*, pig-sty. — *ṕag-ts̀íl*, hog's lard; bacon. — *ṕag-ts̀ógs* = *ṕag-k̀yu*. — *ṕag-rdzí*, swine-herd. — *ṕag-zé*, hog's bristle, *Wdṅ.* — *ṕag-yar-ma*, *Sch.*, the fattening of pigs(?) — *ṕag-ril*, pig's muck(?) *Lt.* — *ṕag-s̀a*, pork.

III. (*Cs. ṕág-ma*), **something hidden; concealment:** *ṕág-na mi yód-pa*, a man concealed behind, *Dzl.*, *ṕág-gam gru z̀ig-tu*, in a corner, in obscurity, *Dzl.*; **ts̀á-big ṕág-la yod**, it is somewhat hidden, cannot be seen well (from this place), *Ld.*; **ṕág-la zá-c̀e**, to eat (dainties) by stealth, *W.*; *nyí-ma rii ṕág-tu ͦgró*, *Thgy.*, the sun hides himself behind the mountain; *sgo-ṕág-nas bltás-pas*, to watch, spy, lurk behind the door, *Glr.*, v. also *ͦjáb, pa*; *ṕag nyan táṅ-c̀e W.*, **to listen.** — **ṕag-sté**, *W.* ('a hidden paring-axe' v. *sté-po*) plane; **ṕag-sté gyáb-c̀e, dúd-c̀e, s̀rúb-c̀e**, to plane. — *ṕag-ts̀óṅ*, smuggling, *c̀ó-c̀e*, to smuggle, *W.* **táṅ-k̀an**, smuggler, *W.* — *ṕág-ra*, parapet. — *ṕag-rágs*, rampart, intrenchment. — *ṕag-lám*, secret path (of smugglers). — **ṕag-súg**, bribery, *C.*, *W.*; **ṕag-súg táṅ-c̀e**, to bribe; *zá-c̀e*, **to accept a bribe,** *W.*

ཕག་ཕག་ *p̒ag-p̒ág*, the name given in *Pur.* to **Codonopsis ovata**, the thick roots of which plant are cooked like turnips or ground and baked; v. *klu-mdúd.*

ཕང་ *p̒aṅ* I. *ₒp̒aṅ* (*p̒áṅ-ma*, *p̒áṅ-bu Cs*) **spindle;** *p̒aṅ-ló*, 1. the **whirl** of the spindle. 2. *šiṅ-rtai p̒aṅ-ló*, **waggon wheel,** *Dzl.*

II. v. *paṅ*.

ཕང་འགྲོ་ *p̒aṅ-ₒgró, Sch.*, the belly or body of a stringed instrument.

ཕང་བ་ *p̒áṅ-ba, p̒áṅs-pa* (*Glr.* also *p̒óṅs-pa*, prov.) **to save, to spare, to use economy:** *srog* to spare one's life; *mi-p̒áṅs-te* or *-par* e.g. *ₒbúl-ba*, to give largely, not sparingly; *p̒áṅ-sems*, **thriftiness;** *p̒áṅ-sems-čan*, **thrifty, frugal;** **p̒aṅ-sem čo-če**, *W.*, **to be thrifty, frugal.**

ཕང་མ་ *p̒áṅ-ma*, **a medicinal plant,** *Med.*

ཕ ཕང་མེད་ *p̒aṅ-méd*, stated to be = *rin-méd*, *Ts.*

ཕང་ལོ་ *p̒aṅ-lo* v. *p̒aṅ* I.

ཕང་ལོང་ *p̒aṅ-lóṅ*, **vertebra**(?) *S.g.*

ཕཊ་ *p̒aṭ Ssk.*, an unmeaning sound, frequently used in magic spells, on which subject Milaraspa speaks rather obstrusely.

ཕད་ *p̒ad*, **a large bag** or **sack**, *rás-p̒ad, rál-p̒ad, rtsid-p̒ad*, sack of cotton cloth, goat's hair, yak's hair; *p̒ad-ḱá, -skéd, -mtil*, **the mouth, middle,** and **bottom** of a sack; *p̒ad-gáṅ*, a full sack, a sackful; *p̒ad-stóṅ*, an empty sack; *p̒ád-snam*, sack-twine, sack-cloth; *p̒ád-tsa*, very coarse sack-cloth.

ཕན་ *p̒an* I. sbst., **hanging ornaments,** lappets of silk, similar to the decorations of our tent-cloths, awnings etc., *ka-, sgo-, γduṅ-p̒an*, on pillars, doors, beams; *p̒an-γdugs*, a parasol so decorated, *S.g.*

II. = *p̒a* II., gen. in the combination of *p̒an-čád* (*Glr.* also *p̒an-čód*), also *p̒án-la* or *p̒an*, **towards, until:** *dá-či-nas dá-lta p̒án-la dar čig soṅ*, from 'but just' till 'just now' a moment has passed, *Thgy.*; *ná-niṅ-nas da p̒an-čád lo γčig son*, *Thgy.*; **da p̒an**, **until now,** *C.*; ... *nas diṅ-saṅ p̒an* (*-la*) *Glr.* from ... till now; *p̒yi-ma p̒an-čád-du ₒgró-ba yin*, I am proceeding towards the future, *Thgy.*; *p̒an-čád* also **beyond:** **de p̒ẹn-čẹ' ma ḍo* C.* do not go any farther than that place; combined with its contrary *ťsun*: *p̒an-ťsún(-du) gró-ba*, to walk to and fro, there and back; to walk past, frq.; *p̒an-ťsún-du p̒úl-ba*, to push hither and thither, *Glr.*; *p̒an-ťsún mťún-pai γtam*, assurances of mutual friendship, *Glr.*; *p̒an-ťsun γčig-gis γčig-la γi-ge γtóṅ-ba, p̒yag byéd-pa, γnód-pa byéd-pa*, mutual correspondence, m. greetings, m. encroachment; *p̒an-ťsún sdúr-ba sdébs-pa*, to compare with one another, to mix one with the other, *Zam.*; *γnyis-γnyis-dag p̒an-ťsun-gyi ₒdra-bai yi-ge*, two equal letters (ă, ā etc.) at a time *Gram.*: *ma-p̒áṅ-gi ₒgram p̒an-ťsún-du* on each of the two shores of lake *Ma-p̒aṅ*, *Mil.*; *don p̒an-ťsún bsdú-rgyu ẙód-pa*, **correlative terms,** having reciprocal relation, *Gram.*: *p̒an-ťsún ťor-ba*, **to scatter, to disperse;** *p̒an-ťsún-dag, Cs.*, both parties.

III. v. the following articles.

ཕན་དིལ་ *p̒án-dil W.* **kettle, pot** (of tinned copper, the common cooking-vessel in Tibet and India, having the shape of a broad urn); in *C.* **zaṅs(-bu)**, *Pers.* and *Hd.* دیگچی (*dēgčí*); *p̒an-čuṅ*, a small vessel of that kind.

ཕན་པ་ *p̒án-pa* I. vb. **to be useful:** *de ni bdag-la mi p̒an*, that is no more of use to me; *p̒án-par mi ₒgyur*, it will be of no use; *bu ₒdis ṅá-la p̒án-par dka*, this son will hardly be useful to me, *Glr.*; *p̒án-par dgá-ba-rnams*, such as wish to make themselves useful, they who are ready to serve, *Thgy.*; *bgród-la p̒an*, useful for learning to walk, *Lt.*; *nad kún-la p̒án-pa yin*, that is good for all diseases, *Lt.*; *ṅai nád-la p̒án-pa yin-pas*, because I have recovered, *Glr.*; **p̒an soṅ**, it has helped, it has got better; ... *na pan*, if ..., then I shall get well, *Glr.*; *p̒án-pa žig srid*, recovery might be possible, *Pth.*; *mi p̒an*, it is useless, = **hurtful;** also: **it is not enough,** *Mil.*; *mi p̒án-par ₒdód-pa ťams-čád*, all the malevolent, *Domaṅ*: *ḱá-la p̒an*, lit. 'it is a mere enjoyment of the mouth', i. e. an outward, temporary enjoyment or advantage; hence *ṕán-pa* and *ṕan-pa yin-pa*, adj., **useful**: *ṕán-pai don*, a useful thing, valuable possession, frq.; *bdag nyon-móṅs-pa-las ṕan-pai don med*, after all it is of no use to me in my misery, *Dzl.*; *bslab-bya ṕan-pai ṫsig*, a wholesome instructive word, *Glr.*; *ṕan-pai grós*, useful advice, *Dzl.*

II. sbst. **use, benefit, profit**: *bstán-pa-la ṕán-pa žig byed-pa*, *Stg.*; *ṕan-γnod-méd-pa*, bringing neither profit nor harm, *Mil.*; *ṕán-pa daṅ bdé-ba*, *ṕan-bdé* **happiness and blessing**, very frq.; *ṕan-ₒdóγs-pa*, *ṕan-ₒdógs byéd-pa*, **to be of use**, and adj. **profitable**, frq.; *ṕan-ṫógs*, **profit**; *ṕan-ṫógs če*, *Thgy.*, **čén-mo**, *W.*, **very profitable**; ... *la ṕan gaṅ ṫogs gyis*, render services to ... in every way possible! *Mil.*; *ṕan-grogs* a helping (useful) friend, *Pth.*; *ṕan-γnód*, profit and loss, *ṕan-bdé* v. above; *ṕan-zás*, wholesome diet, *Med.*; *ṕan-yón*, **benefit, blessing,** as a reward for a meritorious action, frq.; *ṕan-(pai) sems*, **benevolence, readiness to help.**

ཕབ་པ་ *ṕáb-pa*, I. v. *bébs-pa*. — II. *Sch.*: **to fall down** (?).

ཕབས་ *ṕabs*, 1. **dry barm** (prepared for inst. in Balti, is said to consist of flour, mixed with some ginger and aconite). — 2. **lees, yeast** (of beer).

ཕམ་པ་ *ṕám-pa* v. *ₒṕám-pa*.

ཕའུ་ *ṕau* v. *pag*.

ཕར་ *ṕar* I. sbst. **interest** (of money), *W.*: **ṅúl-la ṕar kál-če**, to impose, demand interest, **čál-če**, to pay interest; **exchange, agio.**

II. in later writings and col. for *ṕa* II.; also for *ṕan-čád*, *ṕa-zád*: **farther**; *ṕar ₒgró-ba*, to go on; *ṕar ₒkyám-pa*, to roam farther and farther, *Thgy.*; **ṕár-tsam**, *C.*, = *ṕar*; *ṕar ₒgro ṫsur ₒgró-ba-rnams*, people going, travelling, hither and thither; **away, off**: *di-nas ṕar*, away from here; *ṕar mi mčio*, I do not go away, *Dzl.* ༢༢༠, 6 (*Sch.* erron. 'to the father'); *ṕar bžud*, go away!; ... *la ṕar lta-ba*, **to look** (in a certain direction) *Mil.*, **away from one's self**, as opp. to: *raṅ-rig-séms-la ṫsur ltá-ba*, to look into one's own heart *Mil.*; *glu ṕár-čig ṫsúr-čig lén-pa*, **alternative song**, *Mil.*; *ṕár-slob ṫsúr-slob yin*, they are mutually scholars one of the other, *Tar.*; *ṕar γčig láb-na ṫsur γnyis rgol*, if you say one word 'towards her', she gives you smartly a double charge back, *Mil.*; *ṕar-ṫsúr-la*, *W.* also = **so-sór**, **in opposite directions**; **ṕar-ṫsúr-la čo-če** to separate vb. a.; **ḍo-če**, to separate vb. n.

**Comp.** *ṕár-ka*, *Thgy.* *ṕár-ka* = *ṕá-rol*, **the opposite side** (of a valley &.) vulgo frq. — *ṕár-ṅos*, id., *čui ṕar-tsúr-gyi-lam.* — *ṕar-ṕyin* abbreviation for *ṕá-rol-tu ṕyin-pa* v. *ṕá-rol*, *ṕa* II. *Mil.* — **ṕár-tsam**, *C.*, = *ṕa-zád*. — *ṕar-ₒdzúg* and *tsur-rgól* prob. = *sṅá-rgol* and *ṕyi-rgol*. — *ṕar-zád* = *ṕa-zád*. — *ṕár-la*, 1. = *ṕar*, **away, onward**, *Schr.* 2. = *ṕá-rol-tu*, *na*, esp. with regard to time: vulgo *lo γčig ṕár-la*, after one year; *W.* esp. after the gerund in *nas*: **zan zós-nẹ ṕár-la**, after dinner. — *ṕár-lam*, **way** or **journey thither**, *Sp.* ni f.

ཕར་བ་ *ṕár-ba*, I. 1. **wild dog** (barks, and commits its ravages like the wolf, yet being afraid of man) in *Ld.* — 2. wolf *C.*, also *ṕar-spyáṅ*. II. v. *ₒṕár-ba*.

ཕར་རྫས་ *ṕar-rdzás*, *Sch.*, **an old heir-loom.**

ཕལ་ *ṕal*, I.? *Ld.* 1. **ṕal čós-se (or te) dug**, **step aside! make way!** — 2. **ṕal-ṕál čá-če**, **to feel flattered.** II. v. the following.

ཕལ་པ་ *ṕál-pa*, **usual, common**; *ṕal-pai miṅ*, his usual (common) **name**, *Thgr.*; *ṕál-pa-las ṕags-par* **bzáṅ-ba**, **a more than** ordinary beauty *Dzl.*; **mi** or *gaṅ-zág ṕál-pa*, common people, *Mil.*; *ṫsoṅ-ṕál-rnams bór-ro*, they left the common tradespeople behind, *Dzl.*; *ṕál-pai rdzas* v. *ₒjál-ba*; *šiṅ ṕál-rnams*, common trees, *Mil.*; *snod ṕál-pa*, common vessels, *Mil.*; *ṕal*, the common people; *ṕál-gyi náṅ-na γnás-pa*, to live among the people *Dzl.*; *ṕál-gyis rgyáb-nas ded ṕál-gyis bskór-te*, the people running after and crowding round him, *Pth.*; **ṕál-(pai) skad**, 1. *W.* the language of common life, opp. to **čós-skad**, book-language (*C.* **ṭ́ál-kẹ'**). 2. *Sch.*: **rough-copy, waste-book; *ṕál-po-* (*Cs.* also *-mo*) *če*, a host, a troop**; *mi-rgód ṕal-po-če žig*, a troop or set of monsters (v. *rgód-pa* II.); gen. like *οἱ πολλοί*, the mass of the people, majority, great part or number; *ṕal-čé-ba* id. — *ṕal-čén*, **a philosophers' school**, called Mahasanghika. — *ṕal-čér*, **manifold, for the most part, ordinarily**, also = **universally**; *ṕal-čér čo-ṅés ̥dégs-so*, they raised a general lamentation *Dzl.*

ཕལ་ཅན་ *ṕál-čan W.*, **broad, wide**, e.g. a broad valley; *ṕal-méd*, narrow.

ཕས་ *ṕas*, instrum. of *ṕa*, I. **by the father**; v. also *ṕas-spún*, sub *spun*. II. **of the opposite side, of the counter-party**, e.g. *ṕas rgól-ba.*

ཕི་ *ṕi*, 1. num. figure 44. — 2. *W.* for *ṕyi*, *ṕí-pa* for *ṕyí-pa.*

ཕི་ཀེར་ *ṕi-ker* (Urdu فكر, *Ar.* reflexion) *W.* **čaṅ ṕi-ker med** = *čaṅ mi sto* it is no matter, it makes no difference.

ཕི་ལིང་ *ṕi-liṅ* v. under *rgya.*

ཕིག་ཕིག་ *ṕig-ṕig*, a kind of jelly *C.*

ཕིང་ *ṕiṅ*, *Sch.*: 1. **earthen-ware pitcher.** — 2. **cup, cupping-glass.** — 3. *W.*: **sgó-ṕiṅ**, **door-hinge.**

ཕིང་པ་ *ṕiṅ-pa* v. ཕྱིང་པ་; ཕིང་བ་, ཕིང་ཅེས་ v. འཕྱིན་པ་

ཕིར་བ་ *ṕir-ba*, **ṕir-če** *W.* **to fall down.**

ཕུ་ *ṕu* numerical figure: 74.

ཕུ་ *ṕu*, I. sbst. 1. **the upper part** of an ascending valley or ravine; *ṕu bar mdo* (or *mda*), the upper, middle, and lower part of such a valley; *ṕu-ču*, **mountain-torrent**, frq.; *ṕur ma ̥gro, ṕu yá-gir ma ̥gro. Glr.*, do not go to the upper part of the valley; *ṕu-lhágs*, higher situated and colder places or districts, opp. to *rgya-šód*, lower and milder parts. The not unfrequent phrase: *ṕu-ťág γčód-pa* or *čód-pa* was **traced** by our Lama to its original meaning: the upper part of the valley is shut up (with snow etc.), which is now used in a general sense; *ḱrúl-bai ṕu-ťág čod, Mil.*, prob. shut out all error, prevent every mistake! *ṕu-ťag-čód-lugs-kyi čos šig, Mil.* seems to be an instruction for making a decision; *ṅa rgás-pa daṅ séms kyi ṕu-ťág čód-pas ̥gró-ba mi yóṅ-bar ̥dug*, prob.: I being old and my spiritual affairs settled (not calling for further improvement), shall probably not travel any more (to India; but you may do so) *Mil.* cf. *ṕugs.* — *ṕú-pa*, the inhabitant of an elevated valley. Fig.: *ṕu γyo mda dkrug*, there is agitation above and below, the higher and the lower faculties of the mind are troubled, excited, *Mil.* — 2. prop. n. **Pu**, e. g. **a village in Upper Kunawar**, missionary station of the Church of the United Brethren. — 3. vulgo **the spirit** or **gaseous element of liquors**, causing them to foam, effervesce or explode, cf. *dbugs;* perh. to be referred to no. II.

II. interjection and imitative sound: *ṕu ̥débs-pa Glr.*, **ṕu gyáb-če** *W.*, **to make pooh, to blow, to puff, to inflate**; *ṕu skoṅ*, puff it up (the skin etc.), lit.: fill it with pooh! *ṕus*, with the breath; *ṕus ̥débs-pa Sch.* **to blow, howl, cry** (?); *sna-rtsa-ṕu*, **n. of a disease**, *Lt.*

ཕུ་དུང་ *ṕu-dúṅ*, also *ṕu-ťúṅ Glr.*, *ṕu-rúṅ Cs.*, **sleeve**; **ṕu-rdzús** *C.* (false sleeves), *ṕu-dúṅ-* (or *-ťuṅ-*) *rtse* (sleeve-edges) **hand-ruffles;** mittens, cuffs (to keep the wrist warm).

ཕུ་དུད་ *ṕu-dúd*, **honour, respect, esteem**; *ṕu-dúd-du byéd-pa, Glr.*, *ṕúd-du ḱúr-ba, S.g.*, to show honour, respect.

ཕུ་བ་ *ṕú-ba*, pf. of *̥búd-pa*, **to blow**, col. used for the latter.

ཕུ་བོ་, ཕོ་བོ་ *ṕú-bo, ṕó-bo*, (*Sch.* also *ṕun*), a man's **elder brother**: *ṕu-nú*, the elder and the younger, i. e. the two brothers; also the elder and the younger sons (for examples refer to *tsan-dán*); in the passage of *Dzl* ༢༠༦, 14, *nu* ought to be canceled, and *ṕu-nú-mo*, ༡༦, 6. 9. should be translated by sister-in-law. *ṕu-grás, Sch.*, **the elder brothers, dub.**

ཕུ་རོན་ ṕu-rón Pth., ṕug-rón, (*ṕur-gón* vulg.) **pigeon**; ṕu-rón-gyi kyu Pth.; ṕug-skyá Sch. of a light blue colour, like pigeons.

ཕུ་ལ་, ཕོ་ལ་ ṕú-la, ṕó-la Ld. (from the Turkish), **pilaw**, a dish of boiled rice, with butter and dried apricots.

ཕུ་ཤུད་ ṕu-šúd **hoopoe.**

ཕུ་སེ་ ṕú-se, **mouse, souslik** and similar rodent quadrupeds (cf. bra).

ཕུག་ ṕug, 1. = ṕugs. — 2. = sbugs, ṕúg-pa; lgáṅ-ṕug-gaṅ, **the bladder,** in reference to its capaciousness, S.g.; mje ṕúg-tu nub, the penis recedes into its cavity, Wdn.; **the eye of a needle,** Lt. — 3. pf. and imp. of ˳bug-pa. — 4 = ṕub Schr. — 5. for ṕug-ron, q.v.

ཕུག་པ་ ṕúg-pa, **cavern**; brag-ṕúg, rock-cavern, grotto; gad-ṕúg, cavern in a steep river-bank, or in conglomerate; dbén-ṕug, the solitary cavern of an anchorite, Ma.; ṕúg-pa-pa, n. of an astronomer of the 15th. century, v. pád-ma; ṕug-rtsis, and likewise ṕug-lúgs Wdn., his calculations.

ཕུག་རོན་ ṕug-rón v. ṕu-rón.

ཕུག་ཤུབ་ཤེ་ལེ་ ṕug-šub-še-le (?) W., **hoopoe;** perh. = ṕu-šúd, which occasionally is also spelled ṕu-ɣšud

ཕུག(ས)་ ṕug(s), (cognate to ṕu; also ˳búg-pa and sbugs), **end, termination;** ṕug-mda-ťúg-pai lóṅ-ka, the entrails, the beginning and end of which lie close together, Mil. (mda, v. under ṕu); **innermost part, an innermost apartment,** = sbúgs; ṕúgs-kyi nor v. sgo init.; perh. also ṕúg-gi spa-rim ltá-bu Glr. 45, 4 may be referable to this meaning. séms-kyi ṕugs-ťag čod-pas bde, happy (am I), because the final aim of my mind is decided and settled, Mil., evidently = ṕu-ťag čod-pa, the former being perh. etymologically more correct. Similarly: bu ťse ˳dii bló-ṕugs čós-la ɣtód-čig Mil., may the boy direct the aim of his mind for this life unto religion! — **Time to come, futurity,** (opp. to ˳ṕral, the present moment); ṕúgs-su, ṕugs-na, **hereafter, at last, ultimately** (Sch. always?); ṕugs-či ˳dra čig ˳oṅ, how will it end? what will be the final issue? Glr.

ཕུགས་ཏ་ ṕugs-ta, ṕógs-ta, pogs-ta, W. (Pers. پخته), **firm, strong, durable;** ṕúgs-ta btsems, sew it well (so that it will hold)!

ཕུང་པ་ ṕúṅ-pa v. ṕúṅ-pa.

ཕུང་པོ་ ṕúṅ-po, 1. **heap;** ṕúṅ-por spúṅ-ba, Lex. also bčér-ba, to gather into a heap; nás-ṕuṅ, rtsá-ṕuṅ, lúd-ṕuṅ, sá-ṕuṅ, a heap of barley, hay, dung, earth; **mass,** me-múr-gyi ṕúṅ-po, a glowing mass, a mass of fire; sprin-ṕuṅ, clouds, a gathering of clouds Glr.; ɣnyér-mai ṕúṅ-po (the skin becomes) a heap of wrinkles, Thgy.; the body is called mi-ɣtsáṅ-ba rnám-pa sna-ťsógs-kyi ṕúṅ-po, dug ɣsúm-gyi ṕúṅ-po, ˎjig-pai ṕúṅ-po, zin-pai ṕúṅ-po, Thgy.; **accumulation, mass,** bsod-nams-kyi, čós-kyi, e.g. čós-kyi ṕúṅ-po ༨༤༠༠༠, the whole mass of the 84 000 religious lectures of Buddha(!) Mil. — 2. In metaphysics: स्कन्ध, **the so-called five aggregates** (Cs.) or **elements of being,** viz. ɣzugs, ťsór-ba, ˳du-šes, ˳du-byéd, rnam-šés, (v. Köpp. I. 602, and esp. Burn. I. 475 and 511), which in the physical process of conception unite, so as to form a human individual or **the body** of a man, (ṕuṅ-po lṅa-las grub-pai lus Wdn.) which by some of the later and more popular writers is itself called ṕúṅ-po. So this word, as being synonymous to lus, has found its way into the language of the people, and not in a low sense, in as much as one of our Christian converts used the expression: ye-šui ṕúṅ-po dur-kuṅ-ne žens. — 3. Symb. num. for 5.

ཕུང་བ་ ṕúṅ-ba v. འཕུང་བ་ ˳ṕúṅ-ba.

ཕུད་ ṕud, sbst. I. (v. ˳ṕud-pa, pf. ṕud), **a thing set apart,** used particularly of the first-fruits of the field, as a meat- or drink-offering, in various applications: zas-čáṅ-gi ṕud meat- and drink-offering Glr.; ťóg-pud, ló-pud, an offering of the first-fruits of harvest; srús-ṕud id., consisting of ears of corn, wound round a pillar of the house; *bán-ṗud*, first-fruit offering of the barn; *rdó-ṗud, sá-ṗud*, an offering of stones or earth, when a house is built, these materials then being used for manufacturing images of gods, *Glr.*; **initiatory present**, e.g. the first produce of a work, that has been committed to one *Glr.* (so, according to circumstances, it may be as much as **a specimen**); in a general sense, **a thing done for the first time**; *bág-mai ṗud*, prob the first cohabitation. — II. for *ṗu-dúṅ* and *ṗu-dúd*, q.v.

ཕུད་པ་ *ṗúd-pa*, I. pf. of *˳búd-pa*.

II. *Cs.* sbst. 1. **spindle covered with yarn.** — 2. **hair-knot, tuft of hair;** *ṗúd-čan*, being provided with such a one.

ཕུན(སུམ)་ཚོགས་(པ) *ṗun(-sum)-ṫsógs(-pa)* 1. adj. **perfect, complete,** possessing every requisite quality, e.g. *dgón-pa*, a hermit's dwelling; **excellent, exquisite, distinguished,** e.g. *ro*, taste, *bsnyén-bkur*, distinctions, marks of honour *Mil.*, *nor daṅ loṅs-spyod Domaṅ*; adv. *dgé-ba bču ṗun-sum-ṫsógs-par spyód-pa*, *Dzl.*, to practise the ten virtues to perfection. — 2. sbst. **perfection, excellence, superior good,** frq.; *ṗa-ról-poi ṗun-sum-ṫsógs-pa-la čágs-pa* to covet the excellent things which another possesses, *Thgy.* — 3. *ṗun-ṫsógs*, frequent **name** for **males** and **females.**

ཕུབ་ *ṗub* 1. **shield, buckler,** *Glr.*, of a convex shape, with the rim bent round; *ko-ṗúb*, a leather buckler; *ṗub-šúbs*, the cover of a buckler, *Cs.*; *ṗúb-kyi mé-loṅ*, the centre of the shield, *Cs.* — 2. v. the following.

ཕུབ་པ་ *ṗúb-pa*, pf. of *˳búb-pa*.

ཕུབ་མ་ *ṗúb-ma*, **short straw**; *ṗúb-ma žig*, a small stalk, a bit of chaff; **ṗúb-ma ṭáb-če* or *ṭab táṅ-če**, to fan, to winnow; *ṗub-ldir Cs.*, chaff; *gró-ṗub*, wheat-straw.

ཕུམ་ཕུམ་ *ṗum-ṗúm*, **posterior, anus** *Pth.*

ཕུར་ *ṗur* 1. v. *ṗu.* — 2. v. *˳ṗúr-ba.* — 3. v. *ṗúr-pa.*

ཕུར་པ་ *ṗúr-pa*, **peg, pin, nail**; *rtsig-pur Schr.*, **ṗur-ča* or *ša** (?) *Ld.*, a peg on a wall, to hang up things; *lčágs-ṗur*, **iron nail**; *šiṅ-ṗur*, **wooden peg**; *ṗur-rnyi* v. *rnyi*, *ṗur-bži brkyáṅ-ba* to fasten the hands and feet of a culprit to four pegs driven into the ground, when he is to undergo the punishment of the *rkyaṅ-šiṅ*, v. *rkyoṅ-ba.* 2. **iron instrument** in the form of a short dagger, used for expelling evil spirits, and fancied to possess great power, *Schl.* 257; *sá-ṗur ˳débs-pa*, to stick such a dagger into the ground, whereby the subterranean demons are kept off; fig. *mig ṗúr-ṫsugs-su ltá-ba Glr.*, to look at one with a piercing glance of the eye; **lha-la sól-wa ṗúr-tsug-tu ˳déb-pa* C.*, to implore a god very earnestly. *ṗúr-bu* 1. = *ṗúr-pa*; the usual form of incantation is: *ṗúr-bus γdáb-bo, ṫó-bas brdúṅ-ṅo, ṗyág-rgyas mnán-no!* 2. (*γza*) *ṗúr-bu*, **the planet Jupiter**; its day: **Thursday.**

ཕུར་བ་ *ṗúr-ba*, *Sch.*: **to emboss;** *ṗúr-ma* or *˳búr-ma*, **relief work, embossment.** — 2. **to scratch,** v. *˳ṗúr-ba*; *mgo-ṗúr*, n. of a disease *Lt.*

ཕུར་བུ་ *ṗúr-bu*, v. under *ṗúr-pa.*

ཕུར་མ་ *ṗúr-ma*, v. *ṗúr-ba.* — 2. *ṗyé-mai ṗúr-ma*, **a decoration** resembling **a flag.**

ཕུར་མོ་ *ṗúr-mo*, a medicament *Wdn.*; *ṗur-tál? S.g.*

ཕུལ་ *ṗul* 1. **a handful,** also *ṗul-gáṅ*, e.g. of corn, *Dzl.*, beer *Lt.* (in which case = *skyor*). — 2. **end?** only in the phrase: *ṗúl-tu ṗyin-pa*, **to reach the highest degree, to be victorious**, to have the better of an argument; *yi-gei sgrá-la ṗúl-tu ṗyin*, he has finished his studies in grammar, *Glr.*; *mḱás-pai ṗúl-tu ṗyin-par gyúr-to*, he became a great scholar, *Pth.*; also *ṗul-(tu) byúṅ(-ba)*, **accomplished, perfect, eminent** *S.g.*; p. n. = *ȧ-ti-ša.* — 3. *ṗúl-čan*, **thick** = **róm-po* Ld.*

ཕུལ་བ་ *ṗúl-ba* v. *˳ṗúl-ba* and *˳búl-ba.*

ཕེ་ *ṗe* 1. *W.* for *ṗye*; *ṗé-ku-lig*, **key.** — 2. num. figure: 104.

ཕེ་རང་, ཕ་རང་ *ṗe-ráṅ, ṗa-ráṅ*, **Feringhi, Europeans,** *C.*

ཕེག་རྡོབ་ *ṗeg-rdób* v. under *ṗeb-pa.*

ཕེད་, ཕེན་ *ṕed, ṕen W.* for *ṕyed, ṕyen*; *ṕed-ṕed* v. *ṕyad-ṕyad.*

ཕེབ་པ་ *ṕéb-pa*, 1. pf. *ṕebs*, resp. **to go** *C.*; **to come** *C.* and *W.*; also *čág* (or *ṕyág*)-*ṕeb-pa;* scarcely in ancient lit., but *Glr.*, *Pth.*, *Mil.*; **nyi-ráṅ-la ṕéb-loṅ yód-na** W., if you have time to come; **o-ná ghá-le ṕeb** *C.*, well, good bye! **dha sá-hib ṕeb**, id. in speaking to a European; *čag ṕeb žu naṅ* v. *snáṅ-ba* I. extr.; *ṕéb-par smrá-ba Schr.*, to salute; *Sch.* also: to speak politely (??); *ṕéb-par ṕág-pa*, *Sch.*, to rise gracefully, to walk decently (?); *ṕéb-sgo ltar Sch.*: 'according to the given order', but cf. *ₒgro-sgo ltar* under *sgo* 3; *ṕéb-rdog-pa* 'to tramp arrival', to go to welcome a high Lama or other honoured person on his arrival with dance and music *C.*, *Lexx.*; *Cs.* however mentions *ṕeg-rdób* as a musical instrument, 'a small brazen plate for music', and in *Stg.* the same word occurs along with *sil-bsnyán.* — 2. for *ₒbab;* so it seems to be used, *Lt.*: *ťúr-du mi ṕebs*; *ṕó-bar mi ṕebs*, it won't go down his throat.

ཕེར་བ་ *ṕér-ba* **to be able** *Mil. nt.*, cf. also *dod*; *Cs.*: 'to become, to be fit' etc.

ཕོ་ *ṕo* I. num. figure: 134.

II. **man**, opp. to woman, **male**, *ṕo lo lṅá-bču-pa*, men of the age of fifty (opp. to *bú-mo lo-gnyis-ma*) *Ma.*; *ṕo mčór-po*, a handsome man (opp. to *bud-méd mčór-mo*) *Pth.*; as a pleonastic apposition to the pers. pron., like *mi*, *Mil.*; common in *C.*: **ṕo-ṅá**, I (masc.) = *ḱó-bo*; esp. in reference to animals: **male, he** (ass), **cock** (bird), *Dzl.* and elsewh.; as apposition to the names of domestic animals when castrated: *ṕo-rtá*, **gelding**; *rá-ṕo*, **a castrated he-goat.** — *ṕo-skyés*, **man, male person**, *Pth.* — *ṕo-gós*, man's dress, man's coat; *ṕo-čás*, *Mil.* id. (?) — *ṕo-čén Wts.*, *Sch.*, gelding. — *ṕo-tó Bal.*, stallion. — *ṕo-rtágs* 1. *Physiol.* = *ṕo-mťsán.* 2. *Gram.*: sign for the masculine gender, *Cs.* — *ṕo-nád*, 1. *W.* andromany, inordinate desire after men. 2. v. *ṕó-ba.* — *ṕo-mó*, man and woman, men and women, male and female; *ṕo-mó med*, no difference of sex exists. **ṕo-ťsé** *Bal.*, male sex. — *ṕo-mťsan*, membrum virile, man's yard, esp. the penis; the rather vague expression *ṕo-mťsán* (or *ṕo-rtágs*) *bčád-pa* is asserted to apply not to castration (*Schr.*), but only to circumcision (which, however, is not generally known in Tibet, Mussulmans being found only in some of the larger cities of the country). — *ṕo-yan Sch.* and *ṕo-raṅ Cs.*, *ṕo-hraṅ C.*, an unmarried man. — **ṕo-ri** *W.*, **ṕo-ré** *C.* a male kid. — *ṕo-lhá*, 1. tutelary deity of a man's right side (ni f.) *Glr.* 2. *Cs.*: **Sir**, as polite address. — (Observation: The circumstance of the consonants of the alphabet and the prefix-letters being divided by Tibetan grammarians into masculine, feminine and neuter, is of no practical moment: careful investigations on that head have been made by Schiefner and Lepsius).

III. v. *ṕó-so.*

ཕོ་གྱོག་ *ṕo-gyóg Sch.* (perh. *ṕo-gyó* v. *gyo-mo*), **hollow tile.**

ཕོ་ཉ་ *ṕó-nya*, less frq. *ṕó-nya-ba* (*Ssk.* दूत), 1. **messenger**, e.g. sent for a physician; *ṕó-nya γtóṅ-ba*, *ṕó-nya-mṅág-pa*, to send, dispatch a messenger; *brtsi-ba*, *Cs.* to receive one (?) — 2. **ambassador, envoy.** — 3. Passages like *γšin-rjei ṕó-nya* messenger of death, angel of death, and *bdé-ba-čan-gyi ṕó-nya*, honourable epithet of a king, that is looked upon as a demi-god (similarly to ἄγγελος τοῦ παραδείσου) **sufficiently** justify the application of the word to the scriptural notion of **angel**, which may be rendered still more intelligible by adding *nám-mḱai*, *Chr. P.* (P. Georgi retains the Italian *angelo*, spelling it *án-ₒbye-lo*). Buddhist mythology has no available type for it, and *lha* (*Cs.*) could only be made use of, if already whole generations of the Tibetan nation had become Christians.

ཕོ་ནོ་ *ṕo-nó Bal.* for *ṕu-nú.*

ཕོ་བ་ *ṕó-ba* (resp. *sku-ťog Cs.*) 1. **stomach** — 2. the second cavity of the stomach or **reticulum** of ruminating animals (cf. *gród-pa*). *ṕo-ba ljid-pa*, *Cs.* to overcharge the stomach, to clog; *šól-ba Cs.* to purge, to cleanse; *ṕo-bai ḱa Cs.*, the upper orifice of the stomach, joining the oesophagus; *ṕo-ñan*, a weak st., *bzaṅ*, a good, sound st. *Cs.* — *ṕo-tér*, swag-belly *Sch.*; *ṕo-nád*, disorder of the st. — 2. v. *ṕo*, above.

II. pf. of *ₒbó-ba* for *ṕos Glr.*

ཕོ་བ་རི་ *ṕó-ba-ri*, also *-ris* or *ṕo-ris Lt.*, **black pepper**; the col. form: *ṕo-ba-ríl-bu* **'stomachic pills'** prob. is merely a popular etymology (similar to the English 'sparrow grass', corrupted from asparagus).

ཕོ་བྲང་ *ṕo-bráṅ* resp. for *káṅ-pa*, **house, dwelling**; often also implying **hall, castle, palace,** *B.* and col.; *slei ṕo-braṅ*, the castle (palace) of Lé.

ཕོ་ཚོས་ *ṕo-ťsós Schr.* **red paint**; *dúṅ-la ṕo-ťsós bskús-pa*, red paint put on a shell *Pth.*; *ṕo-ťsos-ťsal Pth.*

ཕོ་རིས་ *ṕo-ris* v. *ṕo-ba-ri.*

ཕོ་རོག *ṕo-róg*, **raven,** perh. also **crow**; cf. *ḱwá-ta*; *ṕo-rog-mig*, **medicinal herb,** *Wdṅ.*

ཕོ་ལ་, ཕུ་ལ་ *ṕó-la*, *ṕú-la W.*, v. *pó-la.*

ཕོ་ལད་ *ṕo-lád W.* **steel,** *Pers.* پولاد ,فولاد.

ཕོ་ལོ་ལིང་ *ṕo-lo-liṅ W.* **peppermint.**

ཕོ་ལོང་མདུད་ *ṕo-loṅ-mdúd Mil.* a kind of knot, complicated, and of magic virtue.

ཕོ་ལོང་ཧེལ་ཀྱི་ *ṕo-loṅ-hél-kyi* etc. v. *ṕa-wáṅ.*

ཕོ་སོ་ *ṕó-so*, *W.* **haughtiness, pride;** **ṕo-so čo-če**, to demean one's self haughtily, *W.*; **ṕó-so-čan**, proud, haughty, puffed up; *ká-ṕo Mil.* bragging about things, which in reality one is not able to do; *ṕo-tsod*, prob. the same as *ṕo-so*, *Mil.*: *ṕo-tsód mṅón-šes ma ₒčad čig*, do not boast of prophetic sight.

ཕོག *ṕog*, 1. *Wts.* **beam, rafter;** *Sch.*: 'the principal beam of the roof'. — 2. v. *ₒṕóg-pa* and *ₒbóg-pa.*

ཕོགས་ *ṕogs*, **wages, pay, salary;** *lo-, zla-, nyin-ṕogs* annual, monthly salary, daily wages; *d ́il-ṕogs*, *smár-ṕogs*, *Cs.*, payment in money; *zóṅ-ṕogs Cs.* payment in goods. 2. **providing for another person in natural produce,** even without any service being done in return, e.g. the maintenance of Lamas; *ṕogs-dód*, maintenance by an allowance of money (in exceptional cases).

ཕོང་ *ṕoṅ*, v. *ₒṕáṅ-ba*; *ṕóṅ-ba Glr.* for *paṅ-ba.*

ཕོངས་པ་ *ṕóṅs-pa* (cf. *ₒṕóṅs-pa*) 1. **poor, needy;** *séms-čan nyam-ťág-póṅs-dgu*, the poor and miserable creatures, *Glr.*; *sdúg-ṕoṅs-pa*, id. *Stg.*, *C.* — 2. **poverty.**

ཕོད་ *ṕod*, *skár-ma ṕod*, *Cs.*, *Sch.*, **comet.**

ཕོད་ཁ་ *ṕód-ḱa*, **masquerade garment** with long sleeves.

ཕོད་པ་ *ṕód-pa*, 1. **to be able,** esp. in a moral sense, **to prevail on one's self,** *ₒbral-mi ṕód-pa ltar yód-na yaṅ*, although he was scarcely able to part with . . . *Glr.*; *ₒdi ni mi ṕód-do*, that I cannot do (moral impossibility) *Dzl.*; *lta mi ṕod*, I cannot bear to see that, *Dzl.*; to be able to resist: *zas žim gos bzaṅ su-yis ṕod* who can resist good food and fine clothes? hence *ṕod-pa-čan*, *Cs.*, **bold, daring;** **ṕod-čúṅ-se**, *W.* **timid, cowardly.** — 2. **to come up to, to be nearly equal in worth,** with *ťsam(-la)*: *deï bsód-nams ťsam-la ṕód* it is nearly of equal merit as . . . *Dzl.*

ཕོན་(པོ་?) *ṕón(-po) Glr.* and elsewh., *ṕób-ṕon Cs.*, *ṕón-po(n)*, *ṕón-to*, *pod-ṕód*, *W.*, 1. **bundle, truss,** of hay, straw, reeds; **sheaf.** *C.* — 2. **bunch, wisp, cluster, umbel,** *W.*; **tuft, tassel;** *dár-ṕon*, *skúd-ṕon*, *Cs.*

ཕོབ་ *ṕob* v. *ₒbébs-pa.*

ཕོར་པ་ *ṕór-pa C., B.* (*W.* **kó-re**, resp. **don-kyóg**), **bowl, dish, drinking-cup,** generally made of wood and carried in the bosom, to have it always ready for use; cups made of other materials are called *lčágs-ṕor*, *dṅúl-ṕor*, *γsér-ṕor*, and a glass tumbler *šél-ṕor*. The word is also applied to vessels used for other purposes: *spyin-ṕor*, glue-pot, *póg-ṕor*, perfuming-pan. — *ṕór-ṕyis*, cloth for wiping the cup; *ṕor-kúg*, id. (?); *ṕor-šúg* (*šubs*?), the pocket or fold in the coat for receiving the cup, *C.*

ཕོལ་ *ṕol*, *W*. 1. **blister** caused by burning, *ṕol-mig*, **a bad sore, ulcer, abscess,** *C.*, *W*. — 2. *Thgy.*, **a kind of fungus** (mould).

ཕོས་ *ṕos*, 1. v. *ₒbó-ba*. — 2. v. *ša*.

ཕྱ་, ཕྱ༹་ *ṕya*, **lot**, *ṕya débs-pa* to cast lots *Cs.*; **lot, fortune** *Cs.*, *ṕya brtág-pa* to judge of lots or fortune *Cs.*; **prognostic** *Sch.*, *ṕya-bzáṅ*, *-ṅán* good, bad fortune or prognostics *Cs.*; *nór-ṕya*, *k̔yim-ṕya* prognostics relative to property, family etc., in drawing lots or playing at dice; *ṕya (daṅ) γyaṅ* lot (good luck) and blessing, *ṕya daṅ γyaṅ ₒgúg-pa* to call forth good luck and blessing, to secure it by enchantment *Glr.*, *rgya-nág-gi ṕya-γyáṅ nyáms-pas* as China's fortune and welfare were prejudiced *Glr.*; *ṕyá-mk̔an* fortune-teller *Cs.*, but v. also the next article.

ཕྱ་མཁན་ *ṕyá-mk̔an*, 1. = *rdzá-mk̔an*, **potter.** — 2. v. the foregoing.

ཕྱ་ཅན་ *ṕya-čan Lt.?*

ཕྱ་ལ་ལེ་བ་ *ṕya-la-lé-ba*, *Sch.*, **coarse, rude, negligent, disorderly** (?).

ཕྱ་ར་ *ṕyá-ra*, **curtain before a door,** *Schr. Sch.*

ཕྱག་ *ṕyag*, 1. resp. for *lag*, **hand**; *bčom-ldan-ₒdás-kyis ṕyag sá-la brdebs*, Buddha struck with his hand on the earth, *Dzl.*; *ṕyag brgyáṅ-ba*, to stretch forth one's hand, *Sch.*; with *la* it denotes also the imposition of hands as a holy ceremony, *W.*: **čag gyaṅ sál-če**. — 2. **bow, compliment, reverence**: *ṕyag dáṅ-po-la*, whilst making the first bow, *Glr.*; also **compliment** in letters: . . . *la ṕyag graṅs-med bčans*, with a thousand compliments to . . . (a Lama even of a higher order concluded his letter to a nobleman with 10000 compliments to him as the head of the family, and then to the rest according to rank and age in a descending line with 1000, 100 etc.); therefore *ṕyag byéd-pa* (eleg. *gyid-pa*; resp. *mdzád-pa*, when e.g. a king is addressed by a Lama, *Pth.*), in *Balti* **ṕyag byá-ča*,* *W.* gen. **čag ṕul-če* or *čo-če*, resp. *ǰal-čag čo-če**, to salute, to pay one's respects, with *la*, e.g. ministers waiting on the king, *Glr.*; **čág-ga yoṅ**, he comes to pay his respects, *W.*; *ṕyag daṅ skór-ba byéd-pa*, to make bows and circumitions, *S.g.*; with or without a preceding *ṕyi* (vulg. *ₒt̔on*), **to take leave, to bid adieu,** *B.* and vulgo (cf. *ṕyi* below), **dé-ne čag ṕul yin**, *W.*, so then I shall take my leave now. — *ṕyag ₒt̔sál-ba*, pf. *btsal*, imp. *t̔sol*, to make a very low reverence, the head almost touching the ground; more at large: *γžán-gyi žábs-la mgó-bos ṕyag ₒt̔sál-ba*, esp. in use before Lamas and kings; in the introductions of books, also, the authors generally address both deities and readers with the phrase: *ṕyag ₒt̔sál-lo.* — 3. **impurity, dirt**(?); v. some of the following compounds and also *ₒṕyág-pa.* — 4. sometimes for *čag*.

**Comp.** *ṕyag-mk̔ár* resp. for *mk̔ar-ba* **staff.** — *ṕyag-ₒk̔ur W.* = *ṕyag-rtén.* — *ṕyag-goṅ* the back of the hand *Cs.* — *ṕyag-rgyá* (मुद्रा) 1. resp. for *rgya* (I.) **seal**; *ṕyag-rgyás ₒdébs-pa* to seal, to confirm by a seal, v. *rgya* I. This meaning is at present hardly any longer known, but only: 2. gesture, the manner in which the hand and fingers are held by Buddha, by stage-players, Lamas or saints etc, when performing religious ceremonies or sorceries; *ṕyag-rgyás mnán-pa* to overcome evil spirits by such gesticulations *Dom.*, *ₒgról-ba* to set them free, by dissolving the charm *Pth.* There is a great number of these gesticulations. *ṕyag-rgya-čen-po* is said to be a figurative designation of the Uma-doctrine. (The other meanings given by *Cs.* and *Sch.* are rather uncertain.) — *ṕyag-ṅár* wrist *Cs.*, yet v. *ṅar* I. — *ṕyag-ča Sch.* 'wrought by the hand; an implement', resp. for *lag-ča*, v. *ča* III. extr.; *ṕyag-čás* attributes, carried in the hand, in performing religious dances, cf. *ṕyag-mt̔sán.* — *ṕyag-čáb* water for washing the hands and the face. — *ṕyag-mčód Mil.* for *ṕyag daṅ mčod-pa byéd-pa.* — *ṕyag-snyigs Lexx.* = *ṕyag-dár.* — *ṕyag-rtágs* 1. resp. for *lag-rtágs* sign of the hand, impression of a blackened finger in the place of a seal. 2. = *ṕyag-rtén* (?). — *ṕyag-*

*rtén B.* and col. **a present of welcome,** frq., **a present** in general, also **a fee** *Glr.*; *ṕyag-rtén rgya-čén* immense presents *Glr.* — *ṕyag-mtíl* resp. **palm of the hand.** — *ṕyag-mtéb* resp. **thumb.** — *ṕyag-dár* **sweepings, dust, rubbish**; *ṕyag-dár byed-pa Dzl.* and elsewh., *ṕyág-pa Lex.*, **gyáb-če** *W.* to sweep, to clean; *ṕyag-dar-pa* a sweeper *Dzl.*; *ṕyag-dár-gyi ṕúṅ-po, ṕyag-dar-ḱród* dust-heap; *ṕyag-dar-ḱród-kyi čós-gos* or *ná-bza* vestment or cowl of a mendicant friar, which according to the rules of his order is to be patched up of rags gathered from heaps of rubbish *Burn.* I, 305. (The explanation given by *Sch.* seems to rest on mere hypothesis.) — *ṕyag-na-rdó-rje, ṕyag-rdór* v. *rdo-rje-ₒčaṅ.* — *ṕyag-dpé* resp. for *dpé-ča* v. *dpe* 3. — *ṕyag-dpúṅ* resp. for arm. — *ṕyág-ṕyi* **attendant, man-servant** = *žabs-ṕyi*; *ṕyág-ṕyi byéd-pa* to be a servant; *ṕyág-ṕyi-la* or *ṕyag-ṕyir ₒbréṅ-ba* to be a follower (of a Lama); collect. train of servants, retinue. — *ṕyag-ṕyis* resp. **towel.** — *ṕyag-brís* resp. 1. **hand-writing, manuscript.** 2. **drawing** *Glr.* 3. **letter** *W.*, *brtsé-bai ṕyag-brís* your kind letter, your friendly correspondence. — *ṕyag-ₒbúl* resp. **gift, present.** — *ṕyag-sbál Cs.* resp. = *ṕyag-goṅ*; *Sch.* *ṕyag-sbál-du bčúg-pa* to hold one's hand ready for taking or receiving, v. *sbal.* — *ṕyag-smán* 1. resp. for *sman C.* 2. = *ṕyag-rtén W.* — *ṕyag-ma* **broom, duster, mop** *C.*, *Lexx.* — *ṕyag-tsaṅ Sch.*: 'the all-filling One, the all-universalizing One' (?) — *ṕyag-mtsán* the attributes or emblems of Buddha and of different deities, carried in the hands (it is indeed nothing else than what, when carried in the hands of men, is called *lag-* or *ṕyag-čás Glr.* and elsewh.). — *ṕyag-mdzúb* resp. for **finger.** — *ṕyag-mdzód* **treasurer,** of kings or in large monasteries. — *ṕyag-rdzás* resp. for *nor-rdzás Mil.* — *ṕyag-žabs* resp. for *rkaṅ-lág Schr.* — *ṕyag-ra* (prob. for *ṕyag-gra*) **privy. water-closet.** — *ṕyag-rás* resp. for **towel** *Sch.* — *ṕyag-lán* the return of a salutation, **reciprocal greeting** *Mil.* — *ṕyag-lás W.* resp. for *las* = *ṕrin-las B.* — *ṕyag-lén* resp. for *lag-lén* **practice, exercise,** also **ceremony** (?) **religious rite** (?); . . . *la-ṕyag-lén ₒdebs-pa Pth?* . . . *la-ṕyag-lén-du ₒgro-ba Mil.* (?) — *ṕyag-šiṅ* an attribute of idols, resembling a rod (birch) or besom *Wdk.* — *ṕyág-sa* = *ṕyag-ra*; *ṕyag-sén* resp. for *sén-mo*; *ṕyag-sór* resp. for *sór-mo.* — *ṕyag-sról* **law, regulation; practice, use; tradition.**

ཕྱང་ངེ་བ་ *ṕyáṅ-ṅe-ba, Cs.*: = *ǰól-le-ba,* **hanging down** (belly, v. *ṕyal*); *Lexx.* give **ཡཱམ**, slender, slight-made; *Sch.*: **straight, stretched** (?); *ṕyaṅ-ṕrúl* or *-ₒṕrul Lexx.* pendent ornaments.

ཕྱད་ཕྱད་ *ṕyad-ṕyád,* vulg. *ṕed-ṕed,* **awkward gambols,** clumsy attempts at dancing.

ཕྱད་པ་ *ṕyád-pa,* also *ₒṕyád-pa,* **constant, firm, persevering;** *ṕyád-par,* **always, continually, perpetually;** *Lexx.* = *rgyún-du* (of rare occurrence); *ṕyad ma ṕyod Mil.?*

ཕྱམ་ *ṕyam* = *lčam* (*Sbh.* also *ḱyam*), *ṕyam-ṙnas, -rten, -stegs,* **support** (of rafters); *Sch.*: the resting-point of a beam.

ཕྱམ་ཕྱམ་པ་ *ṕyam-ṕyám-pa, Thgr.* **glittering;** cf. *lčám-me-ba.*

ཕྱམ་མེ་བ་ *ṕyám-me-ba, Glr.* **slow, not hasty, not greedy, indifferent to.**

ཕྱར་ཁ་ *ṕyár-ḱa Sch.* **blame, affront, insult** (v. *ₒṕyá-ba?*) *ṕyar-γyáṅ Sch.* id.; *Lexx. ṕyar-γyéṅ?*

ཕྱལ་ *ṕyal,* resp. **belly, stomach,** *Cs.*; *ṕyal-ṕyaṅ-ṅe, Lexx.* = *gród-pa ǰól-le-ba,* **paunch, swag-belly;** *ṕyál-mo* id.?

ཕྱི་ *ṕyi* (*W.* **ṕi**) I. **behind** adv.: *ṕyi-bkan-du nyál-ba Sch.*, to lie on one's back; *ṕyi-gros-su gyé-ba, Glr.*; **či-ḍọ gyáb-pa** *C.*, to retreat, to recede, with the back in advance; *ṕyi lús-pa,* to lag behind; *ṕyi-rtiṅ Sch.*, **heel;** *ṕyi-sdér, Sch.* **the spur of birds;** *ṕyi-na, Cs.;* **behind;** *ṕyi-nas, Cs.*, **from behind;** **ṕi-nur-la** or **ṕi-log-la ḍúl-če**, to walk backward, *W.*; *ṕyi-γnón yoṅ,* pursuing he comes rapidly near, *Mil.*; *ṕyi mig ltá-ba,* to look round (back), *Glr.*, *ṕyi mig ma ltá-bar,* without looking round; *ṕyi mig čig γzigs-pas,* resp. just looking round (back), *Mil.*; **ṕi* (*mig*) *lóg-te ltá-če** *W.* id. — *ṕyi-ṕyir,* behind, following, e.g. *ṕyi*

*˳gró-ba*, to walk behind or after another person, *Pth.* — *p̓yi ˳brán Lex.* (also *mčis-brán*), spouse, wife. — *p̓yi-ma*, the posterior *Schr.*(?) — *p̓yi-bžin* adv. and postp., **after**; *˳gró-ba*, *˳brán-ba*, frq.; *ri-dags-kyi p̓yi-bžin rgyúg-pa*, to pursue game, deer; *p̓yir-bžin*, id.; *p̓yi-la*, later lit. and *C.*, id.; . . . *kyi p̓yi-bžin p̓yin-pa*, *˰óṅ-ba*, *˳gró-ba*, to go after; v. also *p̓yir* and *p̓yis*.

II. **after**; adv.: *sṅa-p̓yi*, sooner and later; also adj.: the former, the latter; the earlier, the later; *˳di-p̓yi* sc. *ṫse*, the present and the future life; frq.; *dus p̓yi žig-na*, at a later period, some time afterwards *Dzl.*; *deï p̓yi nyin* on the following day *Dzl.*; *nyi-ma deï p̓yi de nyin k̔ó-na*, id., *Tar.* — *p̓yi-dgra* v. *dgra.* — *p̓yi-čad* = *p̓yin-čad* q.v. — *p̓yi-ṫog W.*, the later part of the afternoon. — *p̓yi-dro*, *p̓yi-ro* (also *Mil.*) *W.*, gen. **p̓i-ṫog, p̓i-ro** id., also evening. — *p̓yi-nas*, **in future**, in time to come, *Mil.* — *p̓yi-p̓réd Tar.*: *nyi-ma p̓yi-p̓red-kyi bar-du Schf.*, until sunset; *Schr.*: evening. — *p̓yi-p̓yág byéd-pa*, to greet for the last time, to bid farewell, to take leave. — *p̓yi-ma* adj.: **later, subsequent,** following, *sṅá-ma ma šu p̓yi-ma zá-ba*, not having digested the first (meal), to eat (consecutive) additional quantities *Lt.*; *p̓yi-ma p̓yi-ma*, each following one, every one consecutive in a series, *S.g.* and elsewh.; *nyál-bai p̓yi-ma*, the last going to bed, *Mil.*; *p̓yi-ma-rnams*, the later ones, the moderns, frq. — *p̓yi-mo* adj. **late**, *da (nyi-ma) p̓yi-mór soṅ dúg-pas*, it having grown late (in the day) *Mil.*; **'i go p̓i-mo p̓e dug**, this door is not opened until later (in the day), *W.* **p̓i-mo čó(s)-k̔an-ni tá-gir**, the last baked, newest bread, *W.* — *p̓yi-rabs*, the later generation, posterity. Cf. *p̓yin*, *p̓yis*.

III. **outside,** *p̓yii žiṅ*, the field outside, as a third part of the property, exclusive of cattle and money (cf. *sgo* init.); *p̓yii só-nam*, husbandry, farming *Glr.*; *p̓yii-rgya-mṫso*, the outer sea, the ocean, *Glr.*; *p̓yii mi Dzl.* (Ms.), people from abroad, other, strange people, not belonging to the family, *mgrón-nam p̓yi-mi-dag ˰óṅs-na*, if (when) guests or strangers come, *Dzl.*; *p̓yi-na*, **out of doors, abroad**; *p̓yi-nas*, from without, from abroad; *p̓yi-ru*, *p̓yir*, **out** (proceeding from the interior of a place to the exterior), less frq., v. *p̓yi-rol*; *p̓yi-la*, id., *B.* and *C.* frq. - *p̓yi-k̔yóg Sch.*: with knees bent outward. — *p̓yi-gliṅ* v. *rgya-p̓i-liṅ* under *rgya* comp.; *p̓yi-dgrá* v. *dgra.* — **p̓i-(s)ta-la* and *-ru**. *W.* for *p̓yi-ról-na* etc.; **p̓i-sta-la čá-če**, euphemist. for 'going to the water-closet'. — *p̓yi-náṅ*, **the outside** and **inside,** **p̓i naṅ lóg-če**, *W.*, *bsgyúr-ba*, *Schr.* to turn inside out, e.g. a bag; *lčágs-kyi sgróm-la-sógs-pa sgrom p̓yi naṅ rim-pa bdun tsam*, an iron box (coffin) and moreover a series of 7 boxes one within the other *Tar.* 28; *p̓yi naṅ γnyis-ka smin-pa*, ripe both as to the outside and inside, *Dzl.*; *p̓yi naṅ γtsaṅ*, pure as to thought and action. With respect to religion, this expression generally denotes the difference between Non-Buddhism — or in a more limited sense Brahmanism — and Buddhism; frequently *γsaṅ* is added as a third item, being explained by: *p̓yi lus naṅ ṅag γsáṅ-ba yid*, which explanation however is insufficient, e.g. in the passage: *čos p̓yi naṅ γsaṅ Pth.*, in which moreover merely a classification within the Buddhist religion seems to be spoken of. Political distinctions are made in *Glr.*: *p̓yi naṅ bar γsúm-gyi byá-ba byéd-pai blón-po*, yet without sufficiently elucidating the subject. The terms *p̓yi lta* and *naṅ lta*, *Glr.* fol. 89, as well as *p̓yi ltár-du* and *naṅ ltár-du*, *Pth.* p. 10 I am at a loss to explain. — *p̓yi-pa* 1. *B.* and col. **a Non-Buddhist,** more particularly **a Brahmanist,** also for *p̓yi-pai čos*, the doctrine of Brahma *p̓yi-pa-la dga Glr.* 2. *Chr. Prot.*: **heathen,** one that is neither a jew nor a Christian. — *p̓yi-yul* 1. *Sch.* **foreign country.** 2. *p̓yi snáṅ-bai yul*, **the external world,** opp. to: *náṅ-gi sems*, *Mil.* — *p̓yi-rol*, 1. **the outside,** *mál-gyi p̓yi-rol*, the outside of the bed, *Glr.*; *p̓yi-rol-na*, *-tu*, *-nas*, in *B.* **gen.** for *p̓yi-na*, *-ru*, *-nas*; adv. outside, out of doors, out, from without; postp. on the outside before (the door), (he was turned) out

of (the house), (he comes) from without (the village), frq.; **ṕi-log* W.* id.; **čág-ri ṕi-log la**, outside before the (garden) wall. 2. mystic: *ɣdon bgegs ṕyi-rol-tu ˳dzin-pa*, to believe goblins and demons to be really **existing in the outer world** *Mil.* — *ṕyi-sa*, **excrements** *S.g.*; the supposed food of certain demons *Thgy.* — *ṕyi-lha?*
IV. *ṕyi-la*, **on account of**, v. *ṕyir*.

ཕྱི་ལྕག *ṕyi-lčág*, *Cs.*; **a blow** with the side of the hand.

ཕྱི་ཐན *ṕyi-ťán*, **threat, menace**, *Mil. nt.*

ཕྱི་བདར (or བརྡར) བྱེད་པ *ṕyi-bdár* (or *brdar*) *byéd-pa*, **to clean, to cleanse** *Dzl.* and elsewh.; *byád-kyi ṕyi-bdár bšól-nas kyaṅ* though you do not wash your face *Mil.*

ཕྱི་ཕུར *ṕyi-ṕúr*, a kind of **ornament**, similar to *ṕan*.

ཕྱི་བ *ṕyi-ba S.g.*, *˳pyi-ba Lt.*, 1. the large **marmot** of the highlands of Asia, Arctomys Boibak. — 2. v. *˳byi-ba*.

ཕྱི་མོ *ṕyi-mo*, I. col. **ǎ-ṕyi, ǎ-pi**, **grandmother**, *Cs.* II. v. *ṕyi* II.

ཕྱིང་པ *Pur.* **ṕyiṅ-pa**; *Ld., Lh.* **ṕiṅ-pa**, elsewh. *čiṅ-pa*, **felt**, *˳déd-pa*, to make felt, to mill, to full *Sch.*; *ṕyiṅ-gúr*, felt-tent, a Tartar hut; *ṕyiṅ-stán*, felt-carpet, felt-covering; *ṕyiṅ-déb Sch.*: a wrapper or cover made of felt.

ཕྱིད *ṕyid* = *ṕyi*, **after, following**; *ṕyid-nyin*, the day after to-morrow, *Cs.*

ཕྱིད་པ *ṕyid-pa* I. (v. *ṕyi* ni f.) **to retard, prolong, maintain,** with *ťse:* to maintain one's life, to earn a livelihood, *W.* e.g. **gár-ra čó-te** or **čós-si náṅ-ne ťse ṕid-če**, to maintain one's self as a smith, or by religion, (being a Lama). — II. **to freeze,** **káṅ-pa ṕid-soṅ**, the foot is frozen, suffering from chilblains; **mig ṕid soṅ**, the eyes are inflamed, snow-blind, *W.* (*C.* **či**). — III. v. *˳ṕyid*; *byid*.

ཕྱིན *ṕyin* for *ṕyi*, in certain phrases: 1. *ṕyin-čád, -čád*, **later, afterwards**, *ṕyin-čád sdom*, bound over for the time to come, e.g. not to do a thing again; *da ṕyin-čád*, from the present moment, from henceforth, frq.; *˳di ṕyin*, id.; *de ṕyin-čád*, rarely *de ṕyin-nas*, *Tar.* 57, 2 since, since that time, ever since. — 2. **outside**, *ṕyin rtsig-pa méd-de* as there was no wall outside *Glr.*; *ṕyin-dgrá* a foreign enemy *Glr.*; *ṕyin-las* outward business, foreign affairs *Dzl.*

ཕྱིན་ཅི་ལོག *ṕyin-či-lóg*, anything **wrong, incorrect, deceptive, fallacious; perversity**; *ṕyin-či-lóg-gis bslád-de* corrupt, depraved by perversity *Dzl.*; *ṕyin-či ma lóg-pao* it is infallible (of a spell), synon. to *bdén-pa*; *ltá-ba ṕyin-či ma lóg-pa* correct view, opinion *Pth.*; *ṕyin-či-lóg-tu stón-pa* to teach a false doctrine; *blo ṕyin-či ma lóg-par*, with a never erring mind *Mil.*

ཕྱིན་པ *ṕyin-pa* I. *B., C.* **čin-pa**, *Sp.* **ṕin-pa**, little used in *W.*: 1. **to come, to get to, advance, arrive**; *lam ṕyed tsám-du*, having got about midway, *Dzl.*; *der ṕyin-pa daṅ*, frq.; *ču ṕrág-pa tsám-du ṕyin-to*, the water reached up to his shoulders, *Dzl.*; **ṕin-na** *Sp.*, is he arrived? *sbyin-pai ṕá-rol ṕyin*, that goes farther than alms-giving, surpasses it, *Glr.*: *dpag-tsád lṅar ṕyin-pa*, to be five miles in length, *Dzl.* — 2. **to go, to proceed**, *sṅón-la ṕyin-pa*, *Pth.*; *ma ṕyin-par sleb*, without going, without moving from the place, he arrives at . . . *Mil.*; *bud-méd deï rtsar ma ṕyin*, he did not go to the woman (euphemist.) *Glr.*; *stab-stob-du naṅ-du ṕyin-te*, he went in, ran in, in a great hurry. (Probably the word is cog. to *ṕyi*, and therefore = *˳byúṅ-ba, ˳ťón-pa*.) — II. v. *˳byin-pa*.

ཕྱིར *ṕyir*; prop. the termin. of *ṕyi*: I. 1. adv. **back, towards the back, behind;** *ṕyir ˳óṅ-ba*, to come back, to return *Dzl.* and elsewh., frq.; also used in a special sense rel. to re-birth *lan-ɣčig ṕyir ˳óṅ-ba, ṕyir mi ˳óṅ-ba* v. *˳brás-bu* (*bži*); *ṕyir ˳gró-ba, ṕyir ˳dóṅ-ba* etc., id.; *ṕyir ˳dúg-pa*, to remain behind, at home, *Dzl.*; *ṕyir ˳jóg-pa*, to leave behind, at home, to lay aside, to lay up, *Dzl.*; **again** (*rursus*), *ṕyir láṅ-ba*, to get up again, after having fallen; *ṕyir ldóg-pa, lóg-pa*, to come back again, to return; *ṕyir ldóg-pai lam*, the way back, the return, *Dzl.*; *ṕyir mi ldóg-pa*, the not taking place of relapses, the prevention of them, *Lt.*; *p̓yir zlóg-pa*, to bring back, to draw off, to divert from; *p̓yir sós-par ˳gyúr-ba*, to return to life; *p̓yir sáns-nas*, having come to himself again, having recovered, *Dzl.*; *p̓yir má-la smrás-pa*, he replied to his mother, *Dzl.*; *p̓yir-lóg skyón-pa*, to make one ride backward, with the face to the horse's tail. — 2. postp. e.g. **behind, after,** *ńai p̓yir e' ˳gro Pth.*, will you follow me? come with me? instead of this more carelessly: *ńa p̓yir Mil.*; *p̓yir-bžin* = *p̓yi-bžin* frq. —

II. **afterwards, hereafter**, at a later time *Thgy.*; *p̓yir ˳óń-ba*, to come too late *Dzl.*

III. **out**, *p̓yir-la* out (motion from an interior to an exterior place), *p̓yir ťón-pa, ˳gró-ba, ˳dén-ba, γšégs-pa* to go out, *skyúr-ba*, to cast out, *p̓yir bstán-nas*, turned inside out (the lining of a coat) *Glr.*; *p̓yir ˳búd-pa Sch.*: 'to put out, to remove; to come to an end, to be completely exhausted'; *sgo p̓yir mi γtóń-ba*, not to let out at the door, to keep locked in or shut up *Pth.* In *C.* also *p̓yi-la* is used in this sense. — *p̓yir-žiń* acc. to *Lexx.* = भूयंस more (exceeding in number or degree).

IV. postp. c.g., also *p̓yir-du*, more rarely *p̓yir-na*(*W.* **p̓í-la**) **on account of**, 1. (propter) = **by** or **through**, *či p̓ir k̓yod di-ltar gyur*, whereby or through what have you got into this plight? *Dzl.*; without *k̓yod*: where does that come from? *Dzl.*; **i nad či p̓í-la yoṅs**, by what has this disease been caused? *W.*; *γnód-pai p̓yir-du*, because I have done you harm *Mil.* 2. **for, for the sake of** (*causa*), for the good or benefit of, from love to *Dzl.*; **for the purpose of**, *brtág-pai p̓yir-du*, in order to try or to prove *Glr.* Whether *p̓yir* with the infinitive, esp. of one-rooted verbs, is to be resolved by **because** or **in order that**, can be determined only by the context.

ཕྱིས་ *p̓yis* I. adv. **behind**, *p̓yis ni sgra ˳byuń*, behind, i.e. behind your back, voices are heard; gen. with respect to time: **afterwards, later,** *p̓yis ˳byúń-ba*, to arise, to follow, to come later *Wdń.*; also in reference to things past, of a later date than others that had happened before them *Glr.*; *p̓yis-nas kyań*, **also in future, in after times** *Mil.*; *p̓yis-nyin*, on the following day (= *sań*) *Dzl.*; at some future time, some (future) day, *Dzl.*; *da p̓yis* = *da p̓yin-čád Glr.*; *dus p̓yis* = *dus p̓yi žig-na*, subsequently, hereafter *Pth.*; *p̓yis skye-ba-méd-pa*, one that in future will not be re-born *Mil.*; on the other hand: *p̓yis skyes bu Sch.*, a son born after the death of his father; *sú-bas kyań p̓yis* last of all *Dzl.*; *p̓yis-pa* v. *˳p̓yi-ba* (I.); it is also construed like a sbst.: ... *ťob-pai p̓yis šig-na*, at a time subsequent to his having obtained, = after he had obtained *Tar.* — II. sbst. in compounds: **clout, rag, duster, cloth**, *sná-p̓yis, lág-p̓yis, p̓yág-p̓yis*; *p̓yis-pa*, v. *˳p̓yi-ba* II.

ཕྱུག་པ་ *p̓yúg-pa* adj. **rich**, also fig.: *yón-tan du-mai dpál-gyis p̓yúg-par šog*, may I grow rich in the splendour of numerous accomplishments! *p̓yúg-po*, adj. **rich**, sbst. **a rich man**, *p̓yúg-po čén-po žig* a rich nobleman *Mil.*; *p̓yúg-mo* a rich lady; *p̓yug-k̓yád* riches, wealth, opulence *Dzl.*; *p̓yúg-par ˳gyúr-ba* to grow rich, *byéd-pa* to make rich; *p̓yug-dbúl* rich and poor; *p̓yug dbul med* no difference between rich and poor *Dzl.*

ཕྱུགས་ *p̓yugs*, **cattle**, *sgoi p̓yugs* v. *sgo*; *p̓yugs ˳ťsó-ba* to tend cattle *Glr.*; *p̓yúgs-kyi siń-rta Cs.*, a bullock cart; *p̓yúgs-nad* disease of cattle, murrain; *nor-p̓yúgs*, chattels, all kinds of property *Dzl.*

ཕྱུར་བུ་ *p̓yúr-bu Sch.* **hay-rick, shock of sheaves, heap of sticks** (*Schr. ˳p̓yúr-ba*, to heap up).

ཕྱེ་ *p̓ye W.* **p̓e**, resp. *γsáń-p̓ye, žib*, 1. **flour, meal**, esp. 2. **flour of parched barley,** = *rtsám-pa*. — 3. for *p̓yé-ma*, **dust, powder** etc.; *p̓ye ˳ťág-pa, ťság-pa*, to grind corn to flour; to sieve; *p̓yer ˳ťág-pa*, to reduce to flour. — 4. v. *˳byéd-pa*. — *rgyágs-p̓ye* flour as provision for a journey *Glr.*; **ńán-p̓e** *W.* = *rtsám-pa*; also parched meal. *lčágs-p̓ye* iron filings; *rdó-p̓ye*, stone reduced to powder, small particles of stone; *spós-p̓ye, tsándan-gyi p̓yé-ma*, sandlewood powder, fumigating powder; *bág-ṗyé* wheat flour; *brág-ṗye* small fragments of stone, produced by stone-cutting *Glr.*; *śiṅ-ṗye* saw-dust; *γsér-ṗye* gold-dust; *ṗye-ḱug* flour-bag; *ṗye-sgye* flour sack; *Cs.*: 'a double pouch for meal'; *ṗye-snód*, flour-tub; *ṗye-ṗór Cs.* a box for meal; *ṗye-ṗád*, flour-bag; *ṗye-baṅ*, flour-store; *ṗyé-ma*, dust, powder; saw-dust, filings etc.; *ṗyé-mar* termin. of *ṗyé-ma*; *ṗye-már* (*Hindi* घीसत्तू) flour roasted with melted butter, sweetened with sugar, considered a dainty.

ཕྱེ་མ་ལེབ་ *ṗye-ma-léb Lex*, **ṗe-ma-leb-tsē** *W.*, **butterfly.**

ཕྱེད་ *ṗyed* I. **half**; *ṗyed-daṅ-γnyis* ('which with an additional ½ would be = 2') **one and a half** etc.; *brgya-ṗrág ṗyed-daṅ-γsúm*, two hundred and fifty; **yáṅ-čē' C.*, **yáṅ-ṗed, ṗéd-di(saṅ) ṗed, ṗéd-yaṅ-ṗed** *W.* one fourth, a quarter; *yúṅ-ṗyed* one eighth (little used); *mi-ṗyéd* half a man, also used for woman *Pth.* (n.f.); *zla-ṗyéd* v. *zlá-ba*; *zla-ba-ṗyéd-pa*, lasting half a month, e.g. a disease. — *ṗyéd-ka, -pa, -ma, Cs.*, *ṗyéd-po Cs.* and vulg. one half; *ṗyéd-ma* also: partner to one half; *˳dii náṅ-na ṅai ṗyéd-ma žig kyaṅ yód-de*, as I have still a partner in this business; *ṗyed-krúṅ*, half a *skyil-krúṅ* (q. v.), drawing in one leg, and stretching out the other *Glr.*; *ṗyed-gliṅ*, peninsula; *ṗyed-brgyád* = *ṗyed-daṅ-brgyad* hence sbst.: half a rupee, = 7½ points on the gold-steel-yard *C.*

II. v. *˳byed-pa.*

ཕྱེན་ *ṗyen* (vulg. *ṗen*), **wind, flatulence** *Med.*; *γtóṅ-ba*, to let go a wind; *ṗyen śor soṅ*, a wind has escaped (me etc.); *ṗyen-dbúgs Cs.*, id.; *ṗyén-dri*, a low, soft wind.

ཕྱོ་ཕྱོ་ *ṗyo-ṗyó*, **čo-čó zér-wa**, **to set on** or **at** (to set a dog at a person) *C.*

ཕྱོགས་ *ṗyogs* 1. **side, direction**; *ṗyogs gaṅ-nas* from whence? *ṗyogs der*, **there, thither,** in that direction; *yul dei ṗyógs-su* or *-la*) *soṅ*, proceed in the direction of yonder village; *ltág-pa* (for *-pai*) *ṗyógs-su Wdṅ.* towards the nape of the neck; *ṗyogs γčig-tu* or *-la* towards one side, in one direction; also for **together**, e.g. to sweep together, to heap together; vulgo also for **at the same time, at once**; *ḱyim-pai ṗyógs-su byin-pas*, bestowing on lay-men *Dzl.*; *čos ṗyógs-su γtóṅ-ba* to spend for pious purposes *Mil.*; in the same manner: *dge-bai ṗyógs-su*, to devote to benevolent designs *Mil.*; **for, in behalf of, for the benefit of:** *γtán-grogs ṗyógs-su śi-lčébs byéd-pa*, to die, to undergo death for the sake of husband or wife *Mil.*; in letters usually: *dé-ṗyogs-su*, there with you, *˳di-ṗyogs-su*, here with us. — 2. **quarter** of the heavens, **the cardinal points** of the horizon; *ṗyogs bži*, the four points of the compass; *ṗyogs bžir*, round about, in all directions; c.g. **round** (a person or place); *ṗyogs bži-nas*, from all sides; frequently also *ṗyogs bču*, the ten points of the compass are spoken of, which are the following: *śar, śar-lhó, lho, lho-núb, nub, nub-byáṅ, byaṅ, byaṅ-śár, steṅ-* and *˳óg-ṗyogs* (Zenith and Nadir); *ṗyogs-skyóṅ, ṗyogs-skyoṅ-rgyál-po, lha čén-po ṗyogs-skyoṅ-ba bču* similar to *ḃig-rtén-skyoṅ* (v. *skyóṅ-ba*), yet ten in number; *rgya-gár-gyi śar-ṗyogs-na*, to the east of India; *rgya-gár śár-ṗyogs-pa-rnams*, the eastern Indians. — 3. *sa-ṗyogs*, **country, region, neighbourhood, part,** *dben-pai sa-ṗyógs*, lonely region, solitary part; *ḃigs pai sa-ṗyógs*, an unsafe country; *yul-ṗyógs* id., *ṅai sa-ṗyógs-na* in my country *Mil.*, *C.* — 4. **part, party,** also *ṗyogs-ris*; *γžán-la ṗyogs ˳gyúr-ba*, to take another man's part, to side with a certain person *Thgy.*; *ṗyogs-(ris) byéd-pa* c. genit. *W.*, **čog-(ri) čó-če**, *ṗyogs ˳dzín-pa Tar.*, *ṗyogs tsam rig-pa Tar.* 119, 4 id.; *ṗyogs-méd* impartial, *sine ira et studio*, gen. in a Buddhist ascetic sense: indifferent to every thing; *ṗyógs-ča Mil.*, *ṗyógs-lhuṅ Lex.*, prob. also *ṗyógs-žen Tar.* 184, 22, partial, interested; *ṗyogs-čai rtóg-pa*, hesitation, scruples, arising from still feeling an interest in a thing *Mil.*; in a general sense it is used in: *ṗyogs-mtsúṅs-pa* **similar** *Wdṅ.*, *Tar.*; *ṗyogs-mtun-du Tar.* 190, 16 ought to be rendered: **appropriate, suitable, adequate;** *ráṅ-ṗyogs* one's own party, *γžán-ṗyogs* the other or opposite party; *γnyén-ṗyogs* friends, *dgrá-ṗyogs* enemies; *dkár-ṗyogs* **the good,**

**the well-disposed,** esp. the good spirits, *nág-ṕyogs, sdig-čan-gyi ṕyogs* **the bad, malicious,** esp. the evil spirits, devils. — 5. in popular language the word is used also with respect to time: **k̔a-saṅ-stón-čogs* Ld.*, **last autumn.**

ཕྱོགས་པ་ *ṕyógs-pa* I. vb. **to turn** vb. n., *čós-la* to turn to religion *Schr.*; *ṕyir ṕyógs-pa* to turn one's self back, to turn aside (*Schr. ṕyir ṕyógs-par byéd-pa*, to divert from, to dissuade from) *Tar.* 12, 14 28, 9. *ₒči-k̔ar ṕyógs-pa* turned to dying = near dying? *k̔ór-ba-la rgyáb-kyis ṕyógs-pa*, to turn one's back to the orb of transmigration; *mṅón-du ṕyógs-pa*, 1. **to be visible, to be evident, to be exposed to view** (?), *lho-ṅos-su mṅón-du ṕyógs-pai brág-las ₒbyúṅ-ba* growing on a surface rock on the south-side *Sambh.*; *don de mṅón-du ṕyógs-par byá-bai ṕyir*, in order to bring this meaning to the light, to express it clearly *Gram.* (?). 2. **to be openly** or **evidently attached to, to adhere to** (?) *rgyúd-la* to a Tantra or treatise *Sambh.*

II. adj., sbst., **attached to, following; a partizan, an adherent.**

ཕྱོད་པ་ *ṕyod-pa Cs.* **progress**, *ṕyod čé-ba*, great progress; *Lex.*: *sa-ṕyod-če* v. *čod.*

ཕྱོར་ *ṕyor Mil.*, prob. for *mčor.*

ཕྲ་ *ṕra*, *ₒṕra*, **ornament** (?), **jewel** (?) *ṕra rgyág-pa, rgyáb-pa, ₒgód-pa, ₒdébs-pa*, *Sch.* also *ṕras sprá-ba*, to insert an ornament of jewels, to stud with jewels; *rmog-la pad-ma-rā-gai ṕra btáb-pa de*, this set of rubies on the helmet, this helmet studded with rubies *Glr.*; *rin-čén sna-ts̔ógs-kyis ṕra bkód-pa Mil.*; *ṕra-ts̔óm* border, trimming, *Lex.*

ཕྲ་རྒྱས་ *ṕra-rgyás Was.* (241) = *bág-la nyál-ba*, **vanities**, i.e. passions, errors, erroneous notions.

ཕྲ་དོག་ *ṕra-dóg* v. *ṕrag-dóg.*

ཕྲ་བ་ *ṕrá-ba* 1. v. *ₒṕra-ba.* — 2. *Lt.* a disease of children. — 3. adj., gen. *ṕrá-mo* (*Cs.* also *bo*) **thin, fine, minute,** opp. to *sbóm-po* q.v., *sbrul ṕrá-mo žig Tar.*; in a general sense, **little, small,** *séms-čan ṕrá-mo-rnáms; ná-ṕra-mo*, little as to age, young, *Mil.*; **trifling, little, slight,** *rnám-rtog ṕrá-mo* slight scruples, *Mil.*; *rdzun ṕrá-mo*, a little lie, a fib, *Thgy.*; **ṭ́á-mo-nẹ ťóṅ-wa, láb-pa**, to see, to inspect most accurately, to learn the minutest details, *C.*; **thin, high,** rel. to voice *W.*; *ṕra-žib Lex.*, fine and exact; *šin-tu ṕrá-ba*, in reference to the doctrine of Buddha, implying prob. its subtilties. Cf. *ṕran.*

ཕྲ་མ་ *ṕrá-ma*, **calumny, slander,** esp. through tell-tales and intermeddling persons *B.* and col.; *ṕrá-ma byéd-pa Dzl.*, *smrá-ba Cs.*, *ȷ́úg-pa B.* and *C.*, **čó-če* W.*, resp. (when referring to a person of higher rank) *γsól-ba, žú-ba*, to calumniate, slander, vilify, blacken; *ṕrá-ma-mk̔an Cs.* **calumniator, slanderer.**

ཕྲ་མེན་ *ṕra-mén*, **sorcery, witchcraft** *Schr.*; so prob. *Pth.*: *mi-dgos-pai ṕra-mén-gyi ṅan-sṅágs*, an evil magic spell of pernicious necromancy; *ṕra-men-po* and *-pa* masc., *-mo* and *-ma* fem., necromancer, wizard, witch; *ṕra-mén rdzá-ki* (for *dzo-gi*, **योगिन्**) id.

ཕྲ་མོ་ *ṕrá-mo*, v. *ṕrá-ba*; ཕྲ་ཤགས་ *ṕra-šags*, v. *ₒṕrá-ba.*

ཕྲག་ *ṕrag* provinc. also *dbrag, srag*, 1. **intermediate space, interstice, interval,** hence *ṕrág-tu* = *bár-du Thgy.*; **a hollow, ravine, defile;** *smin-ṕrág* v. *smin-ma.* — 2. after cardinal numbers it seems to correspond about to the Greek subst. termination ας: *bču-ṕrág* a decade, *brgya-ṕrág* a hundred (century), *stoṅ-ṕrág* a thousand (chiliad), *brgya-ṕrág γčig, brgya-ṕrag bčú*; *stoṅ-ṕrág bži-bču-žig*, a number of forty thousand *Dzl.*; *bdun-ṕrág*, ἑβδομάς, week (recognized as a measure of time, but in common life not much in use).

ཕྲག་པ་ *ṕrág-pa*, 1. sbst., resp. *sku-ṕrág* **shoulder,** *ṕrág-pa-la ₒgél-ba Glr.*, *ťógs-pa Sambh.* to load on one's shoulder; *grógs-poi ṕrág-pa-la ₒdzég-pa*, to mount the shoulder of one's companion *Dzl.*; **upper arm,** *ṕrág-pa γnyis-kyi ša Dzl.*, *ṕrag-góṅ*

23

*Lt.* id. — 2. vb., also *ₒp̔rág-pa*, **to envy, to grudge**, *Cs.*; *p̔rag-dóg*, *p̔ra-dóg*, the envy, *p̔rag-dog skye* envy is stirring within me, I envy, frq.; *p̔rag-dóg-čan*, envious, grudging, jealous *Pth.*

ཕྲང་ *p̔raṅ*, v. *ₒp̔raṅ.*

ཕྲད་ *p̔rad*, *ṫsig-p̔rád*, *p̔rád-kyi yi-ge*, **particle**, e.g. *rnám-dbye-p̔rad* the signs of the cases, *kyi, la* etc.

ཕྲད་པ་ *p̔rád-pa* v. *ₒp̔rád-pa*; *p̔rád-po* for *k̔rád-po Wdṅ.*

ཕྲན, ཕྲན་བུ་ *p̔ran*, *p̔rán-bu*, (*Ts.* also *p̔rán-te*) = *p̔rá-mo*, **little, small, trifling**, yet more in particular phrases, and less used in books, than in common life, esp. in *C.*: **rin ṭém-bhu ṭè-dhe** (lit.: *sprad-de*) having paid, spent a trifle; **žú-ba ṭém-bhu žig** a small request; **ṭem-bhu čig** a little bit *C.*; as sbst.: 1. **part of the body** (whether in a general or a more particular sense, I have not been able to ascertain); in medical writings the *p̔ran-bui nad* form a class of their own; *yan-lág-gi p̔ran γčód-pa Glr.*, to maim, to mutilate parts of the body (not necessarily to castrate *Sch.*). — 2. **knives** and other small instruments used in surgery *Med.* — 3. *p̔ran-ráṅ* in the polite epistolary style the person of the writer, 'my own little self', 'your humble servant'; *p̔rán-la ráṅ-gi* = to me my..., inst. of: *ṅá-la ṅa-ráṅ-gi.* — *p̔ran-ṫségs*, **trifles, minor matters**; *ₒdúl-ba p̔ran-ṫségs-kyi γži* the minutiae of religious discipline, Dulva.

ཕྲན་རྩག་ *p̔ran-rtság*, *p̔ran-ne-rtsag-tsi* stated to be = *p̔yin-či-lóg Ld.*

ཕྲན་ཚེགས་ *p̔ran-ṫségs* v. *p̔rán-bu* extr.

ཕྲལ་ *p̔ral* v. *p̔rál-ba*; ཕྲི་བ་ *p̔ri-ba* v. *ₒp̔ri-ba*; ཕྲིད་ *p̔rid* v. *sbrid-pa.*

ཕྲིན་ *p̔rin*, *ₒp̔rin*, **news, tidings, intelligence, message**, *p̔rin bzáṅ-po*, good tidings, favourable accounts; *p̔rin-bkur-mk̔an*, messenger, vulgo; *p̔rin skúr-ba*, *spriṅ-ba* to send word, information, *k̔yér-ba*, to bring tidings, intelligence; *spród-pa*, *ₒp̔ród-pa* to deliver; *smrá-ba*, *rjód-pa*, *byéd-pa* to report, to deliver messages orally; to superiors: *γsól-ba*, *žú-ba*; to inferiors: *sgó-ba*, *γsúṅ-ba*; *k̔ó-boi p̔rin yaṅ dé-la byós šig* deliver a message to him also from me *Dzl.*; *p̔rin-γtam* message, report *Cs.*; *p̔rin-pa* messenger; newsmonger *Cs.*; *p̔rin-bzáṅ* gospel *Chr. Prot.*; *p̔rin-yig* letter, epistle; *p̔rin-lán* answer to a message. — *p̔rin-lás* (*W.* **čag-lás**) 1. resp. for *las* **labour, business; deed, work**, frq.; *ráb-tu-γnás-pai p̔rin-lus mdzad* (the Buddhas) performed the work of consecrating *Glr.*; *p̔rin-lás rnam bži* the same as *ži-rgyas-dbaṅ-drág-gi p̔rin-lás Glr.*, v. explanation under *ži-ba*; *p̔rin-lás čól-ba*, *p̔rin-bčól byéd-pa* ccdpar. to commit a thing to another person's care or trust, e.g. before going on a journey; in reference to gods: to recommend to their protection or blessing *Glr.* and elsewh. — 2. po. for *p̔rin-lás-pa* **commissary** *Glr.*, where Avalokitesvara is called *p̔rin-lás* of all Buddhas. — 3. **efficiency, power** *Mil.*

ཕྲུ་གུ་ *p̔rú-gu* v. *p̔rug.*

ཕྲུ་བ་ *p̔rú-ba*, *ₒp̔rú-ba* = *k̔óg-ma* **earthen pot, pan, stew-pan.**

ཕྲུ་མ་ *p̔rú-ma*, *ₒp̔rú-ma* 1. **uterus, matrix of animals**, or acc. to *Cs.* merely the integuments of the eggs; acc. to some, also **the urinary bladder.** — 2. **encampment**, = *dmag-sgár Lex.*

ཕྲུག་ *p̔rug* 1. in compounds for *p̔rúg-gu*, *p̔rú-gu* **child, a young one** (of animals); *p̔rúg-gu-mo* a little girl *Cs.*; *p̔rúg-gu skyéd-pa* to beget children, *γsó-ba* to rear, to bring up (children); *p̔rúg-gu skye* a child is born; *šor* a miscarriage, abortion, takes place; *p̔rúg-gui dus* childhood; *dá-p̔rug* orphan; *nal-p̔rug* bastard; *gláṅ-p̔rug* the young one of an elephant; *séṅ-p̔rug* a lion's cub etc.; metaph. of disciples and subalterns: *ṫsoṅ-p̔rúg* the merchants of a caravan in their relationship to their leader *ṫsoṅ-dpón.* — 2. **fine cloth** or **woollen stuffs** *Wts.*, *snam-p̔rúg* id., *dbus-p̔rug* woollen goods from Ü *Mil.*

ཕྲུགས་ *p̔rugs* one day with the night, a period of 24 hours, — but this signification does not hold good in every case.

ཕྲུད་གཞོང་ *ṕrud-γžoṅ* v. *γžoṅ-pa.*

ཕྲུམ་ *ṕrum Lt.* and *S.g.?* *prum-rús* **cartilage, gristle.**

ཕྲུམ་ཕྲུམ་ *ṕrum-ṕrúm Sik.* = *ṕum-ṕum.*

ཕྲེའུ་ *ṕreu Cs.* = *ṕrá-mo.*

ཕྲེང་བ་ *ṕréṅ-ba* v. *˳ṕréṅ-ba.*

ཕྲེད་ *ṕred*, *˳ṕred*, **cross, transverse; across, athwart, obliquely;** *ṕréd-du*, col. **ṭ éd-ṭ éd-la**, crossways, in a cross direction; *ṕréd-lam*, a path (horizontal or inclined) leading along the side of a mountain, (cf. on the other hand *˳ṕraṅ*); *ṕred-γtán* bolt or bar of a gate; **ṭ éd-la ḍáṅ-po**, horizontal *W.*

ཕྲོ་བོ་ *ṕró-bo* something like: **a child's frock** or **chemise** *Ld.* (?)

ཕྲོག་ *ṕrog* etc. v. *˳ṕrog*; ཕྲོབ་, ཕྲོལ་ *ṕrob, ṕrol* v. *˳ṕrob*, *˳ṕrol.*

ཕྲོས་ *ṕros* v. *˳ṕró-ba.*

འཕག་པ་ *˳ṕág-pa*, pf. *˳ṕags*, .. **to rise, to be raised**, e.g. a post or stake raised by the frost; **to soar up**, to fly up to heaven, a miraculous feat often performed by the saints of legends, *Dzl.* and elsewh.; of rays of light, *Dzl.* and elsewh.; fig.: to be higher, more elevated, *deï stéṅ-du* (or *dé-las*) *dpag-ts̀ád brgyad-k̀ri* (or more accurately *k̀ris*) *˳ṕágs-so Glr.*, *Pth.*, (this region) lies by 80000 miles higher than that *Stg.*; **to grow larger, longer**, of the apparent lengthening of the teeth when aching *W.*; of horses: **to rear, to rise up** on the hind-legs; more particularly of the deifying of saints; thus the demi-god-like king Srontsansgampo in his farewell speech says: *k̀yed kun ˳ṕágs-pai byin-rlabs yin* I am the divine instrument of your elevation (your elevation-blessing), he who will effect your ascent to heaven or deification; part. pf. *˳ṕágs-pa* (*Ssk.* आर्य), **sublime, exalted, raised above,** *ṕál-las ˳ṕágs-par bzáṅ-ba* a more than ordinary beauty *Dzl.*; *γžan-pas ˳ṕágs-par gyúr-to* he far excelled others *Dzl.*; *k̀yád-(par) ˳ṕags-(pa)*, **distinguished, excellent, glorious,** *yúl-las k̀yad-˳ṕags rgya-gar-yul* India, the most glorious country; *nór-sna k̀yád-par ˳ṕágs-pa brgyai ˳búl-ba* an offering of a hundred of the most costly kinds of jewels *Pth.*; esp. in reference to holy persons, things, places etc.; title of saints, and teachers of religion, with the fem. *˳ṕágs-ma*; *˳ṕágs-pa* 'par excellence' is Avalokitesvara, in *W.* esp. the one, that has his throne at Triloknath in Chamba, v. *re-˳ṕágs*; the word is also frq. used as an epithet, placed at the head of the title-pages of religious writings; lastly it is a name of common persons. — *˳ṕágs-pai nor bdun* the seven treasures of the saints: *sbyin-pa, ts̀úl-k̀rims, dád-pa* and the like *Mil.* — *˳ṕágs(-pai) yul* 1. elevated country, highland. 2. the holy land of the Buddhists, the tracts of the middle Ganges; *˳ṕags-pai skad*, the Sanskrit language *Lex.* — *˳ṕags-rgyal Tar.* and elsewh. = उज्जयिनी *Schf.*, town and district of Ujain. — 2. the word is stated to imply also **to play, to joke, to make sport** *C.*

འཕང་ *˳ṕaṅ* 1. v. *ṕaṅ* I. — 2. also *˳ṕaṅs*, *dpaṅs*, *spaṅs*, **height,** *˳ṕáṅ-du*, *˳ṕáṅs-su* in height; *k̀ri-˳ṕaṅ* v. *k̀ri*, *go-˳ṕaṅ* v. *go*; *γnam-˳ṕaṅ*, the height of the heavens *Lex.*, *Mil.*; *dbu-˳ṕaṅ* fig. highness, sublimity, *dkon-mč̀óg-gi dbu-˳ṕáṅ smád-pa* to lower, to detract from the sublimity of God (v. *dkon-mč̀og*), to blaspheme God *Domaṅ*; *˳ṕaṅs-mt̀ó* high *Dzl.*; *˳ṕáṅs-mt̀o-ba*, *˳ṕaṅs-mt̀on-dmán* relative height *Dzl.*

འཕང་བ་ *˳ṕáṅ-ba* fut., *˳ṕaṅs-pa* pf. of. *˳ṕéṅ-pa.*

འཕངས་པ་ *˳ṕáṅs-pa* 1. frq. for *ṕáṅs-pa* **to spare, to save** *Dzl.*; kindly and carefully to protect from harm, e.g. a drunken Lama *Thgy.*; hence prob. the version प्रियंस; *˳ṕaṅs-méd γtóṅ-sems-ldan* liberal, bounteous, without restriction *S.g.* — 2. *Glr.* also for *˳ṕóṅs-pa* provinc.

འཕན་ *˳ṕan* I. v. *ṕan* (I). — II. *˳ṕáṅ-yul Glr.*, *˳ṕáṅ-po Huc* II, 242; name of the nearest alpine valley north of Lhasa, the inhabitants of which are said to speak an indistinct dialect.

འཕམ་པ་ ₒp̓ám-pa, pf. p̓am, opp. to *rgyál-ba* **to be beaten, conquered, to come off a loser, to get the worst of,** *γyúl(-las)* in battle *Dzl.*; *lha-ma-yin-las* by the Asuras *Dom.*; in law-suits, in traffic etc.; *ₒp̓ám-par ₒgyúr-ba B.*, **p̓am ḍó-wa* C.* id; also with *p̓am*, as if it were a sbst.: **p̓am kúr-wa* C.* to put up with, to bear a loss, damage, defeat; *ₒp̓am bláṅ-ba Glr., Pth.* prob. id.; *ₒp̓ám-par byéd-pa* to beat, to defeat, to conquer, *rgyá-rnams ₒp̓ám-par byas* he conquered the Chinese *Glr.*; *rás-pas bón-po čós-kyis p̓ám-byas-te* Raspa overcoming the Bonpo by the doctrine of Buddha (v. *čos* 3.) *Mil.*; **p̓am čúg-če* or *kál-če*, W.* id.; *p̓am p̓og soṅ* I have met with a loss, I suffered damage, opp. to *gyal t̓ob soṅ*; *p̓am-rgyál ma bsrés-na* if one is not inclined now for a serious struggle, will not stand the chance of ... *Mil.*; *yid-ₒp̓ám-pa Mil.*, **sems p̓ám-po* C.* dejection; *yid-ₒp̓ám-ma* a low-spirited, dejected woman *Mil.*; *p̓ám-pa Glr.*, *pám-po* the vanquished etc.; **p̓am-pe ṅo-lén čó-če* W.* to give in, to ask pardon; *mi-ₒp̓ám* 1. **invincible.** 2. **a man's name.** 3. *mi-ₒp̓am mgón-po Zam.*, also *mi-ₒp̓ám čós-kyi rje* is stated to be = *ₒjam-dbyáṅs*.

འཕར་ ₒp̓ar *Cs.* in compounds: **board,** *sgo-ₒp̓ar* board or leaf of a door.

འཕར་བ་ ₒp̓ár-ba I. sbst. v. *p̓ár-ba*.

II. vb. (vb. n. to *spór-ba*) 1. **to rebound,** of stones, **bar-náṅ-la* W.* **to splash up,** of water, **to fly up,** of sparks; **to leap, to bound, to throb,** of the veins, *rtsa ₒp̓ar*, the pulse is beating; **p̓ar tá-če* W.*, to feel one's pulse; **nyiṅ-ka p̓ar dug** his heart is throbbing, palpitating; **p̓ár-ra rag** I have heart-throbbing (v. *rag*); *ₒp̓ár-ₒp̓ro čad* v. *ₒp̓ró-ba* 2; *sá-la ₒp̓ár-ba*, **to fidget, to be restless, to jump,** from fear *Pth.*; *pár-gyis ₒp̓ár-ba Lex.* prob. the same as *ₒp̓ár-ba*. — 2. *Cs.* **to be raised, elevated, promoted, advanced.**

འཕར་མ་ ₒp̓ár-ma, *Sch.* **'double, manifold'**; *brgya-ₒp̓ar-ma*, *Sch.* 'more than hundred'.

འཕལ་ག་ ₒp̓ál-ga *Cs.*, **incision, indentation, notch.**

འཕིག་པ་ ₒp̓ig-pa, p̓ig-pa, pf. ₒp̓igs *Sch.* = *ₒbig(s)-pa*.

འཕིར་བ་ ₒp̓ir-ba *Ts.* = *ₒp̓úr-ba*, **to fly.**

འཕུག་པ་ ₒp̓úg-pa *Sch.* = *ₒbúg(s)-pa* (?).

འཕུང་བ་ ₒp̓úṅ-ba, pf. p̓uṅ, **to sink, to begin to decay, to be in declining circumstances, to get into misery,** either by one's own fault, or that of others (opp. to *t̓séṅ-ba*) *Glr.* and elsewh.; *bód-yul ₒp̓úṅ-bai las* a deed to the detriment of Tibet *Glr.*; in a similar manner *bód-yul ₒp̓úṅ-bai p̓uṅ-góṅ*, mischievous conjurers in order to inflict an injury on Tibet *Ld.-Glr. Schl.* 21, b; *mgár-gyis rgyá-yul p̓úṅ-bar byás-pa-rnams dráṅ-nas*, remembering the calamities brought on China by Mgar *Glr.*; *ₒp̓uṅ-bar ₒgyúr-ba B.*, **p̓úṅ-du ḍó-wa* C.*, **p̓uṅ čá-če* W.*, to be ruined, to perish, *ₒp̓uṅ-bar byed-pa B.*, *ₒp̓úṅ-la sbyór-ba Mil.*, prob. also *γtóṅ-ba*, *ₒjúg-pa* to ruin, to undo *Pth.*; *raṅ-ₒp̓úṅ* having been reduced by one's own fault; *ₒp̓uṅ-dkrol* or *k̓rol* **the decay of fortune, ruin, destruction** *Mil.* and elsewh.; *ₒp̓uṅ-γži* cause, occasion of decay *Mil.*

འཕུད་པ་ ₒp̓úd-pa **to lay aside, to put away, to separate,** = *ₒbúd-pa Cs.* (?), *šúg-pa ₒp̓úd-pa*, to clear, to part the flour from the bran, to sieve *Sch.* (?)

འཕུབ་པ་ ₒp̓úb-pa = *ₒbúb-pa* **to cover with a roof** *Sch.* (?)

འཕུར་བ་ ₒp̓úr-ba, pf. p̓ur, 1. **to fly;** *p̓úr-gyis ₒp̓úr-ba Lex.*, prob. id.; cf. *p̓ar-ba*. — 2. **to wrap up, envelop, muffle up;** *Dzl.* ༢༧༦, 10: *rin-po-če gós-kyi mt̓á-mar* the gem into the skirt of the coat, and likewise *Dzl.* ༢༥༧, 13 read: *gós-mt̓ar p̓úr-te*, inst. of *byúṅ-ste*; *mgo gós-kyis Mil.* (col. not used). — 3. = *mnyéd-pa* **to rub with the hand,** e.g. linen in washing, leather in tanning *Glr.*; to scratch (softly) *C.*

འཕུལ་(ཡིག) ₒp̓ul(-yig) **prefix,** *de sogs da-yig gás-ₒp̓ul-čan*, these and others have *d* with the prefix *g*: *bás-ₒp̓ul-kao* words beginning with *k* with the prefix *b*; *bá-yis ₒp̓úl-bai sla*, viz. *bsla* ...; *das-ₒp̓ul-méd* these receive no *d* as prefix; *sa-*

*ra-lá-rnams ᵒṕúl-tsul ni* the manner in which prefixes are joined with words beginning with *s, r* or *l*; *rkyaṅ-ᵒṕul* words beginning with a simple consonant (to which also *ya-, ra-,* and *la-tags* are reckoned), preceded by a prefix; *brtsegs-ᵒṕul,* words beginning with two consonants and a prefix *e.g. bsku Gram.*

འཕུལ་བ་ *ᵒṕúl-ba* I. v. the preceding article. — II. vb. 1. = *ᵒbúl-ba,* **to give.** — 2. **to push, to jostle;** **ṕul-ṫúg gyáb-ĉe**, to push with the fist, with the trunk, (of elephants) etc., *W.; grú-moı ᵒṕul-rdeg ĉig byéd-pa,* to jostle with the elbow *Mil.*; vulgo **ṕul-dag* or *ṫag* W., *ᵒṕul-tsúg* C.*

འཕེག *ᵒṕeg* v. *ṕeg.*

འཕེན་པ་ *ᵒṕen-pa* pf. *ᵒṕaṅs,* fut. (and frq. for the pres.) *ᵒṕaṅ,* imp. *ṕoṅ, ṕaṅs,* 1. **to throw, to cast, to fling;** *nám-mḱa-la* into the air *Dzl.*; *ḱór-bar,* to throw into the orb of transmigration *Mil.*; *dmyál-bar,* to cast into hell *Thgy.*; **ḱa pán-ĉe**, to shovel snow (out of the road, from the roof); **ṕáṅ-te bór-ra tsig-te bor** am I to throw down the wood, or pile it up? *W.*; **pu ṕáṅ-ĉe** to cast the hair *W.*; hence *ᵒṕaṅ,* spindle, and *ᵒṕén-śiṅ,* acc. to *Sch.*, a weaver's shuttle (it being flung). — 2. **to fire off, to discharge, to let fly,** *mda,* an arrow, *γžan-la,* at another *Dzl*; *ᵒṕen-duṅ* dart, javelin *Stg.*; **to shoot,** *ᵒṕen-mi śés-pa, W. *ṕaṅ-mi-śes-ḱan**, one that does not know how to shoot. — 3. *Sch. ᵒṕen-pa btaṅ-ba* **'to intend, to have a mind, to think upon, to consider',** (yet in the only passage, in which I met with the word, in *Thgr.*, the above meaning does not seem applicable).

འཕེལ་བ་ *ᵒṕél-ba* I. vb. pf. *ṕel* (བྲྷ) vb. n. to *spél-ba,* opp. to *ᵒgríb-pa,* 1. **to increase, augment, multiply, enlarge,** frq.; **sum lan nyí-la tsam ṕel** how many are two times three? *W.*; *ᵒṕel-ᵒgrib-kyi dbáṅ-gis* in consequence of the increase and decrease *Gram.*; *ᵒṕel-ᵒgrib-nád,* prob. diseases arising from an excess or deficiency of humours *Wdṅ.* — 2. **to improve, to grow better,** *bsam-γtán* or *tugs-dám ᵒṕél-ba yin* meditation has improved, has proceeded better *Mil.* — II. sbst., *Sch.* also *ᵒṕél-ka,* 1. **increase.** 2. **development** *S.g.*

འཕོ་བ་ *ᵒṕó-ba* pf. and imp. *ᵒpos,* prop. intrans. to *spó-ba,* = *γnas-spó-ba*; 1. **to change place, shift, migrate** frq.; *myur-du ᵒpos-śig,* go speedily elsewhere! *Dzl.*; in a more general sense **to change,** *ᵒṕo-méd bdé-ba* changeless happiness; in a similar sense *ᵒṕo-ᵒgyur-méd-pai rnal-ᵒbyór Mil.*; yet frq. also vb. a.: *ḱú-ba yaṅ ᵒṕo yaṅ ᵒṕo byás śiṅ* pouring off the gravy again and again *Pth.*; very frq. *ṫse ᵒṕó-ba, ᵒĉi-ᵒṕó-ba, śi-ᵒṕó-ba,* to exchange life, **to die,** (in the earlier literature the most common expression for it); the last of the above terms prob. may be explained by *ĉi-žiṅ ᵒṕó-ba*; *ĉi-ᵒṕo-ba ᵒdébs-pa, Thgr.* frq. seems to mean: to help the soul to a happy departure. — 2. *C.* **to fall out, to shed,** of wheat and corn in general.

འཕོག་པ་ *ᵒṕóg-pa,* pf. and secondary form *ṕog,* **to hit, strike, touch, befal, meet,** *mṅár-bai dris ᵒṕóg-pa ṫams-ĉád* all whom the sweet odour met, to whom it became perceptible *Dzl.*; gen. with *la*: *ₒod-zér, grib-ma mi-la ᵒṕog,* a ray of light, a shadow falls upon that man *Glr.* frq.; *ḱó-la nad, ṫsád-pa, ĉád-pa ᵒṕog,* disease, heat, punishment etc. has befallen him; *γza-ᵒṕog-mḱan* **an epileptic person** *W., C.*; the signification: **to hurt,** seems to be less inherent to the word than dependent on contingent circumstances.

འཕོང་ *ᵒṕoṅ Cs.* **archery,** *ᵒṕoṅ-sa* archery ground, *ᵒṕóṅ-mḱan* archer, *ᵒṕoṅ-skyén* good, skilful archer *Dzl.*

འཕོང་ཚོས་ *ᵒṕoṅ-tsos Cs.* **buttocks;** *ᵒṕoṅs* sitting-part, posteriors *Lt., Wdṅ.*; *ᵒṕóṅ-la skyón-pa Sch.* 'the riding of two persons on one horse'.

འཕོངས་པ་ *ᵒṕóṅs-pa* 1. vb., pf. *ᵒṕoṅs* or *ṕoṅs,* **to be poor, indigent;** *ᵒṕóṅs-par bžúg-pa* to let (another) pine in poverty *Thgy.*; with instrum. **to be deprived of, to lose,** *rgyál-po srás-kyis ᵒṕóṅs-nas* the king having lost his son *Pth.* — 2. also *ṕóṅs-pa,* sbst. **poverty,** and adj. **poor**, v. *ṕóns-pa*; perh. also **dejected, disheartened.**

འཕོད་པ་ *ₒṕód-pa = ṕód-pa*, *Cs.*; འཕོན་པོ་ *ₒṕón-po = ṕón-po*; འཕོབ་པ་ *ₒṕób-pa = ₒbébs-pa Sch.*

འཕྱ་བ་ *ₒṕyá-ba*, pf. *ₒṕyas*, acc. to *Lex.* = *smód-pa* **to blame, censure, chide**; the context however, in which the word occurs, seems to suggest the meaning: **to scoff, to deride,** (*Sch.*) e.g. *Dzl.* ༡༢༢, 13. ༡༥༨, 7. ༢༨༠, 15; also *Pth. mis ₒṕyá-ru ₒoṅ*, people will laugh at you.

འཕྱག་པ་ *ₒṕyág-pa*, pf. *ₒṕyags* or *ṕyag?* **to sweep, to clean** *Lex.*, *Pth.*; cf. *ṕyag-dár.*

འཕྱང་བ་ *ₒṕyaṅ-ba*, pf. *ₒṕyaṅs*, vb. n. to *dpyáṅ-ba*, **to hang down,** *dar sṅon-poi ge-ša ₒṕyaṅ-ba* a handkerchief of blue silk hanging down from the head *Sambh.*; *má-mču ťúr-du ₒṕyáṅ-ba* the lower lip hanging down, as a sign of death *S.g.*; **to cling to a person,** from love etc.; *rǰe-btsún-gyi skú-la Mil.*, to the Reverend's person (or body?); *ǰú-žiṅ ₒṕyáṅ-ba* to cling to, to take a firm hold of *Thgy.* — *ₒṕyaṅ-ťág* **plumb-line, sounding-line** *C.* also *dpyáṅ-ťag.* — **čáṅ-ḱe̤m-pa** **rope-dancer,** esp. at the festivities of new-year *C.*

འཕྱང་མོ་ཉུག་ or ཡུག་ *ₒṕyaṅ-mo-nyug* or *-yug Sch.*, **singular, strange.**

འཕྱད་ *ₒṕyad Sch.* = *ṕyad.*

འཕྱན་པ་ *ₒṕyán-pa Lexx.* = *yán-pa* **to ramble, to range, roam about, wander, stray from;** *ₒṕyán-te ₒgró-ba Dzl.* ༢༦༩, 4.

འཕྱར་ཁ་ *ₒṕyár-ḱa Sch.*, **blame, affront, disgrace.**

འཕྱར་བ་ *ₒṕyár-ba*, imp. *ₒṕyor* and *ṕyor* 1. **to raise, to lift up**; *ṕrú-gu nám-mḱa-la Glr.* to lift the infant up to heaven; **to hold aloft,** e.g. the *dor-ǰe* in practising magic, pointing it towards heaven; so also *sdig-mdzúb* to raise the finger *Mil.*; *rál-gri*, to lift up the sword to fetch a blow; to lift up the grain in a shovel, hence: **to fan, to sift, to winnow.** — 2. **to hoist,** a flag, frq.; *ₒṕyar-dár* or *dar-ₒṕyár*, a flag; in a general sense: **to hang up,** so esp. *W.* **čár-la** (*Lad.* **čás-la** for *čárs-la*), **bór-če** id.; **čár-la tún-če** to hang a man; *čár-šiṅ* gallows; occasionally too: to cling or stick to an object. — 3. *Cs.* **to show, to represent, to excite, to waken;** *ₒṕyar-γyeṅ*, engaging, winning behaviour (= *ₒǰog-sgégs*), *ṕyár-ba byéd-pa* to assume an alluring attitude; *ₒṕyár-ka-čan*, tempting, graceful, charming.

འཕྱི་བ་ *ₒṕyi-ba* I. sbst. **marmot,** *ṕyi-ba.* — II. vb. pf. *ṕyis*, *ₒṕyis* 1. **to be late, to be belated, to come too late;** *gál-te ₒṕyis-na*, if I come too late *Dzl.*; *da ḱyod čuṅ ₒṕyis-pa yin* you come just a little too late *Pth.*; *ₒṕyi-mo* v. *ṕyi* II. — 2. also *ₒṕyid-pa* **to wipe, to blot out,** *mig* to wipe the eyes *Pth.*; *mčí-ma* the tears *Glr.*; **to pull out,** *spu* the hair *W.*; **to tear out,** *rlig-pa* the testicles *Sch.*; *ₒṕyi-rás Cs.*, **wiper, wiping-clout, duster;** *lág-ₒṕyi Cs.*, **towel,** v. *ṕyis* II.

འཕྱིག་པ་ *ₒṕyig-pa, Sch.* **to bind,** better *ₒḱyig-pa.*

འཕྱིད་པ་ *ₒṕyid-pa* v. *ₒṕyi-ba.*

འཕྱིལ་བ་ *ₒṕyil-ba* for *ₒḱyil-ba* **to wind, to twist,** (the hair) *Wdṅ.*

འཕྱུག(ས)་པ་ *ₒṕyúg(s)-pa*, rarely *čúg-pa* **to be mistaken,** also *W.*; **to miss,** *lam*, the road *Lex.*; *ču-tsód*, to mistake the hour *Pth.*

འཕྱུར་བ་ *ₒṕyúr-ba* 1. **to mount, to rise up,** of smoke; **to overflow; inundate,** of rivers and lakes *Lex.* — 2. *Sch.* **to heap up, to accumulate?** v. *ṕyúr-bu.*

འཕྱེ་བ་ *ₒṕyé-ba*, pf. *ₒṕyes*, **to crawl, to creep,** like snakes; esp. *lto-ₒṕye*, 'belly-creeper', **snake, serpent;** *ₒṕyé-ba čén-po*, **महोरग**, name of a demon; *ₒṕyé-bo*, fem. *mo* **cripple** *Lex.* = *rkaṅ-med.*

འཕྱེན་ *ₒṕyen Mil.* = *pyen*, **wind,** *γtóṅ-ba*, to let go a wind.

འཕྱོ་བ་ *ₒpyó-ba* pf. *ₒṕyos?* 1. **to swim,** of fishes, *Mil.* — 2. **to soar, to float,** in the air *Thgy.* — 3. **to flow, heave, swell,** of fluids *Mṅg.*; *ₒṕyo-dár-ba Sch.*, to undulate. — 4. **to range, roam about, gambol,** *rtse-žiṅ ₒpyó-ba*, of deer *Mil.*; *rí-la ₒṕyo* *dgu*, po. the wild animals of the field *Sch.* — 5. *snyiṅ ˳p̒yo Sch.*, 'the heart is swelling, courage is rising'; however *šés-pa ˳p̒yo Med.*, seems rather to imply: consciousness gives way, is wavering, flitting; *sems ˳p̒yo Lt.?*

འཕྱོང་བ་ *˳p̒yóṅ-ba Lt.* perh. = *˳p̒yáṅ-ba*; occasionally, like *˳p̒yoṅs-pa* used incorr. for *mč̒óṅs-pa*.

འཕྱོངས་རྒྱས་ *˳p̒yoṅs-rgyás Sch.*, **pride, haughtiness, insolence.**

འཕྱོན་མ་ *˳p̒yón-ma*, **harlot, prostitute,** *byéd-pa*, to whore, to fornicate *Lex.*

འཕྱོར་བ་ *˳pyór-ba*, v. *p̒yár-ba*, also for *č̒ór-ba*; *˳p̒yór-po* for *mč̒ór-po*, hence *˳pyór-dga Sch.* **dandy, fop.**

འཕྱོས་མ་ *˳p̒yós-ma Sch.*, purchase-price of a bride.

འཕྲ་བ་ *˳p̒rá-ba* I. vb., also *prá-ba*, pf. *˳p̒ras*, **to kick, to jerk, to strike with the foot,** *˳p̒ra-šágs* a stroke or kick with the foot, *byéd-pa* to kick about with the feet, in a paroxysm of pain or anguish, *Pth.*; **ṭ̒a-šag gyáb-pa**, to give one a kick. — II. = *p̒rá-ba, prá-mo.*

འཕྲག, འཕྲག་པ་ *˳p̒rag, ˳p̒rág-pa*, **to envy, grudge,** v. *p̒rag.*

འཕྲང, ཕྲང་ *˳p̒raṅ, p̒raṅ, lam-˳p̒ráṅ*, **a foot-path** along a narrow ledge on the side of a precipitous wall of rock (not 'a defile or narrow pass' *Sch.*), frq.; *bar-doi ˳p̒raṅ* the road of the abyss of the *bar-do*, (as with us: the valley of death) frq. *Thgr.*; *bár-doi ˳p̒raṅ-sgról*, prob. a prayer for deliverance from that abyss *Thgr.*

འཕྲང་འཕྲུལ་ *˳p̒raṅ-˳p̒rul Sch.* **something hanging down.**

འཕྲད་པ་ *˳prád-pa* pf. and fut. *p̒rad* **to meet together**; *daṅ* **to meet with, to fall in with, to find;** *de daṅ p̒rád-do*, you shall see him *Dzl.*; *de ni ṅa dan prad mi t̒ub*, him I cannot admit *Dzl.*; *bdag daṅ ˳p̒rád-par šog čig*, come to see me *Dzl.*; *sṅar ṅa daṅ ˳p̒rád-pai ˳óg-tu* not until they have met me (sensu obscoeno) *Dzl.*; *byis-pai ro žig daṅ p̒rád-do* he found the dead body of an infant *Dzl.*; *˳p̒rad-t̒sams Sch.*, intersecting line of two plains, **corner, angle.**

འཕྲབ་པ་ *˳p̒ráb-pa* = *˳p̒rá-ba* and *˳k̒ráb-pa*; *˳p̒ráb-byéd-pa* **to flutter,** of a bird wounded by a shot.

འཕྲལ, ཕྲལ་ *˳p̒ral, p̒ral*, prob. to be regarded as a sbst., like *druṅ, mdun, sṅa* etc., expressing **immediate nearness;** 1. in reference **to space,** but seldom, as for instance *˳p̒rál-du k̒yi k̒ríd-de*, having a dog near at hand *Glr.*; gen. 2. with respect **to time:** *p̒ral daṅ p̒ugs*, what is going to happen immediately and at a later period, presence and futurity; *˳p̒ral-p̒úgs-kyi ˳gal-rkyén t̒ams-čád sél-bar byed Glr.* to avert immediate and subsequent disasters; *˳p̒ral p̒ugs gáṅ-la bzaṅ* that is good both for the nearest and the more distant future; *˳p̒ral daṅ yún-du* now and for a long time to come; *˳p̒ral-sog-˳jog-méd-par* without having gathered or laid up any thing for daily use *Mil.*; *˳p̒rál-gyi ˳dug-t̒sugs ṅán-pa* a poor temporary dwelling, or also: a common, ordinary dwelling, v. no. 3; *˳p̒ral-du ša yžan ma rnyed-de* as at the moment he was not able to procure any other meat *Dzl.*; *˳p̒rál-du sleb yoṅ Mil.* I shall come immediately; *˳p̒rál-du dgós-pai yo-byád* the things necessary for daily use *Dzl.*; *˳p̒rál-du ˳byór-ba ma yin* that is not to be had at a moment's bidding *Dzl.*; also postp. c.g.: *deï ˳p̒rál-la p̒an* that will help the moment directly after it; more frq. after verbal roots = *ma-t̒ág-tu*: *p̒ebs-p̒rál* as soon as he had arrived *Mil.*; *smras-p̒rál* as soon as it has been spoken *S.g.*; *skyes-p̒rál* immediately after birth *Lt.*; in compounds: *p̒ral-rkyén, p̒ral-dgós, p̒ral-p̒úgs* cf. above; *p̒ral-grig* finished, ready, prepared, in proper case, (vulgo, esp. in *W.*, a word much used) **ṭ̒al-ḍig čó-če** to prepare, to get ready. — 3. fig., **common, ordinary, of daily occurrence, common-place,** *p̒rál-skad B., C.*, (*W. *p̒ál-kad**) common dialect; *žes p̒ral-skad-la snaṅ* so you may hear it in the language of the common people, *Gram., Wdṅ.*

འཕྲལ་བ་ *˳p̒rál-ba*, pf. *p̒ral*, fut. *dbral*, imp. *p̒rol*, vb.a. to *˳brál-ba*, **to separate, to part,** **k̒a ṭ̒ál-wa**, id., *C.*; *daṅ* from;

པ

*rtags daṅ ṕral* he deprived them of their insignia *Glr.; srog daṅ ₒṕrál-ba* to put to death, to inflict capital punishment *Glr.; zúg-tu ₒṕrál-ba* to cut into quarters (cattle) *Mil.*; *ltó-ba ṕrál-ba* to cut open, to rip up the belly *Tar.*; *dbrál-bar dka* difficult to part, hard to be kept asunder *Lex.*

འཕྲས་པ་ *ₒṕrás-pa* 1. pf. of *ṕrá-ba;* as sbst. **stroke, blow, kick** with the foot, *Cs.*; *rkaṅ-ₒṕrás*, id.; *rtas-ₒṕras rgyag-pa*, the kicking of a horse; *lag-ₒṕrás*, a blow with the hand, *Cs.*; *ₒči-ₒṕrás Lexx.*, *ši-ₒṕrás* vulg. (*W.* **šin-ṭás* or *ṭe**), the kicking, struggling, moving in convulsions, of a dying man or animal, **agony.** (*Sch. ₒṕras*, to lie on one's side?). — 2. instrum. of *ₒṕra*, *Sch.*: *ṕras spras-pa.*

འཕྲི་བ་ *ₒṕri-ba* pf. and imp. *ṕri(s)*, fut. *dbri*, vb.a. to *ₒbri-ba*, **to lessen, diminish; to take away from,** **ḱa ṭi-če** to take off at the top, e.g. from too full a measure *W.*; more in the special sense of subtracting, with different construction: *de* (or *dé-yis* or *dé-la*) *ťig-ro ṕri-ba-yis* 60 diminished by this, or: this being subtracted from 60; (*ťig-ró* = cipher six) *Wdk.*

འཕྲིག་པ་ *ₒṕrig-pa* 1. **to struggle, flutter,** *Cs.*; **to throb, pulsate,** *Lt.* — 2. *Sch.* **to desire, covet, demand.** — 3. *Sch.* **to be suspected.** — 4. **error?** *Sch.*: *ₒṕrig-ldán*, **erroneous, mistaken, faulty, incorrect.**

འཕྲིན་ *ₒṕrin* v. *ṕrin*; *ₒṕrin-pa* **to inform** *Cs.*

འཕྲུ་བ་ *ₒṕrú-ba*, འཕྲུ་མ་ *ₒṕrú-ma* v. *ṕrú-ba* etc.

འཕྲུག་པ་ *ₒṕrúg-pa*, pf. *ṕrugs*, **to scratch one's self,** *ṕrúgs-na Lt.* if one scratches; *za-ₒṕrúg byed* he scratches himself on account of an itching *Med.*

འཕྲུགས་ *ₒṕrugs S.O.*, perh. = *ṕrug* II.

འཕྲུལ་ *ₒṕrul*, **jugglery, magical deception,** the abstract noun to *sprúl-ba*, q.v.; *ₒṕrul-če-ba* great in magic power *Glr.*; *ₒṕrul-gyi rgyal-po* the magic king, enchanted king, phantom-king *Glr.*; *ₒṕrúl-ghi koṅ-jo* the enchantress *Koṅ-jo Glr.*; *ₒṕrul-gyi spyan-gyis* with a magic eye, by means of magical vision *Dzl.*; *ṕá-rol ɣnón-pai ₒṕrul daṅ ldán-pa* possessing magic power for subduing an enemy *Sambh.*; *rnám-(par) ₒṕrúl (-ba)*, *čo-ₒṕrúl*, *rdzu-ₒṕrúl*, frq.; *sgyu-ₒṕrúl* less frq., id.; *mig-ₒṕrul*, optical deception *Cs.* — *ₒṕrul-gyi ₒḱor-lo*, *ₒṕrul-ₒḱor*, **magic wheel,** in ancient literature merely a phantastic attribute of gods etc.; in modern life applicable to every more complicated machine with a rotating motion, e.g. a sugar-mill *Stg.*, an electrifying machine and the like. *ₒṕrul-dgai lha*, *dga-bži-ₒṕrul-gyi lha*, *ɣžan-dga-ₒṕrul-dbaṅ-byed-kyi lha*, the names of various regions that are residences of gods. *ₒṕrul-snáṅ* 1. **delusion, mockery.** 2. n. of a monastery in Lhasa founded by the Nepal wife of *Sroṅ-btsan-sgam-po's.*

འཕྲུལ་ཕུར་ *ₒṕrul-ṕur S.g.* seems to be **catheter.**

འཕྲུལ་བ་ *ₒṕrúl-ba*, 1. by its form intrs. to *sprúl-ba*; acc. to *Cs.* both are identical in meaning; I met with it only as an abstract noun = *ₒṕrul* in *rnám-par ₒṕrúl-ba* (v. under *ₒṕrul*), e.g. *rnám-par ₒṕrúl-ba dú-ma*, many transformations, magic tricks, for which *rnam-ₒṕrúl* gen. is used. — 2. **to be mistaken, to err, to make blunders** *Mil.*, better *ₒḱrúl-ba.* — 3. **to separate, part, discriminate,** the good from the bad, truth from falsehood *Ld.* (= *ṕrál-ba?* like *drúṅ-po* and *dráṅ-po*).

འཕྲེ་བ་ *ₒṕre-ba* pf. *ₒṕres Cs.*, *ₒṕre byéd-pa Sch.*, **to incline, to lean against; to put down, to lay down;** *Dzl.* ༡༥, 12, where however the context is not perfectly clear.

འཕྲེང་(བ་), ཕྲེང་(བ་) *ₒṕreṅ(-ba)*, *ṕreṅ(-ba)* sbst. col. *W.* **ṭáṅ-ṅa**, *Ü*: **ṕaṅ**) *Ssk.* माल, **a string, a thread** or **cord,** on which things are filed, strung, or ranged, e.g. *mé-tog-gi ₒṕréṅ-ba Glr.* a wreath, garland of flowers; *ₒṕreṅ-ba dmar-po* a wreath of red flowers *Wdṅ.*; *gaṅs-rii* a circle of snow-mountains *Schr.*; *nags-kyi*, of woods *Sambh.*; *šiṅ-rtai ₒṕreṅ-ba rim-pa bdun* 7 circles of chariots *Pth.*; *yig-ₒṕreṅ* a line of letters; *ₒṕréṅ-ba ₒdógs-pa* to bind a wreath; *ₒṕreṅ-skúd*, *ₒṕreṅ-ťág* the string or cord of the wreath; *ₒṕreṅ-rdóg* bead, hence ₒp̔réṅ-ba esp.: a string of beads, **rosary**; *bgraṅ-ₒp̔reṅ*, rosary for counting the repetitions of prayers and magic spells, being used also in arithmetic, as an aid to memory; *mú-tig-ₒp̔reṅ* string of pearls, rosary composed of pearls; *nor-bu-ₒp̔reṅ-ba* of precious stones; also title of a book; fig. *don ma go tsig-gi ₒp̔réṅ-ba bzuṅ*, they only keep to the string of words, without understanding their import *Mil.*

འཕྲིང་བ་ *ₒp̔réṅ-ba* vb.n. **to love, to be fond of, greatly attached to,** with accus. of the person, *séms-la* and similar supplementary words being generally added; *blá-ma yid-la ₒp̔réṅ-bai rtags*, *bú-mo séms-la ₒp̔réṅ-bas Glr.*; *yáb-kyi t̔úgs-la p̔réṅ-bar gyúr-te*, or *ₒp̔réṅ-bžin-du* as she was very dear to her father *Glr.*; *šín-tu ₒp̔róṅ-ba žig byuṅ* an ardent longing for home came over me *Mil.nt.*

(འ)ཕྲིང་ *ₒp̔reṅ*, sometimes incorr. for *p̔raṅ*.

འཕྲིད་ *ₒp̔red*, v. *p̔red*. — འཕྲེས་ *ₒp̔res*, v. *ₒp̔ré-ba*.

འཕྲོ་བ་ *ₒp̔ró-ba*, pf. *ₒp̔ros*, prop. vb.n. to *spró-ba*, 1. gen. with *las*, from, **to proceed, issue, emanate from, to spread,** in most cases rel. to rays of light; *sku ₒod-zér ₒp̔ró-ba* a body from which rays of light proceed, a body sending forth light *Glr.*; *Cs.* also relative to odours, fame etc.; occasionally in reference to descent or parentage *Thgy.* — 2. **to proceed, to go on, continue,** and *ₒp̔ro* **continuation,** opp. to being finished, at an end (*Sch.* incorr.: 'the end'); **láb-'ṭo žen-ghyi čẹ̈-pa* C., Schr.*: the interruption of a conversation by another person; *ₒjig-pro bčad* the process of destruction came to an end *Glr.*; *sbyin-pai ₒp̔ro čád kyaṅ slóṅ-mo-pai ₒp̔ro ma čad Pth.* the gifts had come to an end, but not the begging; *ₒp̔ar-ₒp̔ro čad* the pulse no longer beats *Thgr.*; *čos-bsgyúr-ₒp̔ro-rnams bskyur* the continuations of translating were thrown aside *Glr.*; of the soul: *yód-ₒp̔ro-la mi yoṅ* whilst it is still existing, it does not come forth, i.e. it vanishes imperceptibly, as soon as an attempt is made to find out its seat and to demonstrate its essence *Mil.*; *ₒp̔ro t̔úd-pa* to annex the remainder, to append the continuation; **'ṭo žág-pa* C.* to lay the continuation aside; **šól-wa** to put it off, both expressions implying an interruption of work; *ₒp̔ro lus soṅ* or *las soṅ* a remainder is still left of what has not been used or consumed; **ₒdi ghaṅ 'ṭó-te** after this has been filled up (by pouring in the wanting quantity) *C.*

འཕྲོག་པ་ *ₒp̔róg-pa*, pf. and imp. *p̔rogs*, fut. *dbrog* 1. **to rob, take away; to deprive of,** c. gpar. *nor, gos, rgyál-poi lág-nas rgyál-sa* to deprive the king of his throne *Glr.*; hence *rgyál-sa p̔rógs-pai mi* usurper *Glr.*; *tsád-pas mii mt̔u-stóbs ₒp̔rog* the heat deprives a man of his strength *Med.*; yet also: *sems-yid ₒp̔róg-pa* to take another man's heart, to run away with his affections, to captivate him *Glr.*; *ₒp̔rog-byéd*, and also *ₒp̔róg-ma = dbaṅ-p̔yúg* 1. ईश्वर i.e. Shiwa, or also Indra. 2. symb. num.: 11. — *rku-ₒp̔róg*, robbery *Ma.*, **čom-* or *čom-ṭóg**, id., *W.*; **čóm-'ṭóg táṅ-kan** robber, **waṅ daṅ čom-'ṭóg čó-te** by violence, *W.* — 2. **to make one lose a thing,** *bdág-gi glaṅ p̔rogs* (by his negligence) he has made me lose my ox *Dzl.*; *sdóm-pa ₒp̔róg-tu byuṅ* my vow is lost to me, i.e. the meditation I had vowed has been disturbed, thwarted *Glr.*, to deprive a person of his power or place, **to overthrow,** kings, dignitaries etc. *Stg.*, analogous to *γyo-ba, ₒgul-ba, ₒk̔rugs-pa.* — 3. **to remove, do away with, expel,** demons *Glr.*

འཕྲོང་ *ₒp̔roṅ Glr.*, provinc. for *ₒp̔raṅ* and *ₒp̔reṅ*, v. *ₒp̔reṅ-ba*.

འཕྲོད་པ་ *ₒp̔rod-pa* 1. vb.: pf. *p̔rod*, vb. n. to *spród-pa*, **to have been delivered, transmitted,** *lág-tu* into the hands of a person, hence *ₒp̔rod-ₒdzin*, **ṭod-zin** *W.* **receipt, quittance;** *ṅo* or *ṅos-ₒp̔rod-pa* **to know, perceive, understand;** so prob. also *snyiṅ-la γsál-bar ma p̔rod Schr.* — 2. adj. **fit, proper, suitable, agreeing with, congenial to,** *p̔ó-bar* agreeing with the stomach *Med.*; *mi-ₒp̔rod zas* unwholesome food *Med.*; *mi-ₒp̔rod-pa* also signifies adverse fortune, adversity *C.*;

*k̔aṅ-pa e' ₒṕrod c̀e-na* if the question is, whether the house is likely to prosper.

འཕྲོབ་པ་ *ₒṕrób-pa Sch.* = *ₒṕráb-pa*, འཕྲོལ་བ་ *ₒṕrol-ba Sch.* = *ₒṕrál-ba.*

འཕྲོས་པ་ *ₒṕrós-pa* v. *ₒṕro-ba*; *ₒṕros γtóṅ-ba Schr.*, *ₒṕros-par byed-pa Sch.* **to spread, to pour forth,** e.g. light, *ₒṕros Tar.* 48,3, acc. to *Schf.*: a detailed work; but *Tar.* 143, 13?

# བ

བ *ba* 1. the letter **b**, originally, and in the frontier districts still at the present day, corresponding to the English b; the pronunciation of it, however, varies a good deal in the different dialects of the country: in *C.* this letter, as an initial, is at present deep-toned and aspirated = *bh;* in *Sp.* as a final letter, it is softened down to w; and this softening of its sound prevails throughout Tibet in the substantive terminations *ba* and *bo*, when preceded by a vowel or by *ṅ, r, l*; as a prefix it is sounded in *Bal.* and *Kh.* = *b* or *w*. Regarding the irregularities in the pronunciation of initial *db* v. the Phonetic Table. — 2. num. figure: 15.

བ་ *ba* I. (also *bá-mo Cs.* ?) **cow,** *ₒdod-ₒ̀joi ba* v. *-ₒ̀jo-ba*; *ba-k̔ó* cow-leather; *ba-kyú* herd of cows; *ba-gláṅ* v. below; *ba-γc̀ín* urine of a cow; *ba-lc̀í* cow's dung; *ba-č̀u*, resp. *-čab* = *ba-γc̀ín* (used by hindooizing Tibetans, the cow being sacred to the Hindoos); *ba-nú* 1. a cow's dug. 2. a stone resembling it in appearance *Med.*; *ba-ṕrúg* calf; *ba-rmig* a cow's hoofs; *ba-rmig-gi č̀u* the water collected in the impression of a cow's foot on the ground, to denote a very small quantity of water *Dzl.*; *ba-o* for *bai ₒó-ma*; *ba-rdzí* cow-herd; *ba-rá* pen or stable for cows; *ba-rú* 1. a cow's horn. 2. vulg. cup for scarifying, the hollow tip of a cow's horn being used as such; *ba-ṡá* cow-beef.

II. affix or so-called **article,** for *pa*, to substantives the roots of which end with a vowel or with *ṅ, r, l*, except when *pa* has its particular signification, as in *č̀u-pa* etc. (v. *pa*); in adjectives it is either syn. with *po* (as: *dmár-bai mdaṅs*, a ruddy complexion), or it denotes **'having'** (= . . . *po-c̀an*, as: *sna-dmár-ba* or *sna-dmár-po-c̀an* having a reddish trunk), or it is the sign of the verb formed from it (*dmár-ba*, to be red), or of the abstract substantive (*dmár-ba*, redness).

བ་དཀར་ *ba-dkár* **lime, lime-stone** *Schr.*

བ་གམ་ *ba-gám*, *S.g.* and elsewh.; *Cs.*: 'low wall, parapet'; acc. to my authorities a certain part of the timber work of a roof, something like pinnacle, battlement; so also *Tar.* 80, 21: the king with his retinue beheld the pinnacles of the Naga palace rising above the surface; v. *nyúg-pa* 4.

བ་གླང་ *bá-γlaṅ* **ox, bull;** **ba-laṅ ťsogs** *W.*, like an ox, stubborn, stupid; also dirty, filthy, nasty, for which our vulgar expression is swinish; *ba-glaṅ-spyod* appellation for the western part of the globe, v. *γliṅ*. — 2. for *bál-γlaṅ Dzl.*

བ་ཊི་ *bá-ṭi*, *Hind.* **बाटी, a large brass dish.**

བ་ཏི་ཀ་ *bá-ti-ka Stg.*, a small long-measure, ¼ of a barley-corn.

བ་ཐག་ *bá-ťag W.*, also *Sambh.*, 1. **root.** — 2. **stalk of fruit.**

བ་དན་ *ba-dán* 1. **पताका,** of which the word is a corruption acc. to *Liš.*, an **ensign** with pendent silk strips *Dzl.*, *Gyatch.*, *Glr.* — 2. also *šes-rab-ral-gri*, stated to be a kind of **dagger**, set upright, a semblance of which often attends apparitions of the gods; thus the signification of 'sword', given by *Sch.*, seems to be justified, and also *Schr.* refers to it under *spa-dám*; I never met with it in *B.* in that sense.

བ་དམ་ *ba-dám*, *Pers.*, *Urd.* بادام, from the *Ssk.* वाताम्र, 'windmango' *Shksp.*, **almond.**

བ་སྤུ་ *bá-spu* **a little hair,** the little hairs of the body, *bá-spu lan* or *ldan*, the little hairs stand up, I shudder, *B.*, *C.*; similarly: *bá-spu gyo Glr.*, *Mil.*; *ba-spu tsam yan med* (I feel no repentance) even as great as a hair *Dzl.*; *bá-spu-čan* **hairy, covered with hair,** *ba-spu-méd* bald; *bá-spui bú-ga* or *kun (-bu)* **pores.**

བ་བུ་ *bá-bu* (*Pers.* پاپوش, *pāpōš*) **a soft shoe,** *skúd-pai* knitted shoe, *pin-pai* felt-shoe, but in general they are made of wool or goat's hair.

བ་བླ་ *ba-bla* (*Ts.* **bhá-bla**) *Med.* **arsenic.**

བ་འབོག་ *ba-ₒbog W.* **clod, lump of earth.**

བ་མེན་ *ba-mén Mil.*, *Wdn.*, *Cs.* and *Sch.*: 'a species of wild cattle with large horns'; *Sch.* also: **buffalo-calf;** though in *Sambh.* *gans-ri-ba-mén* are spoken of.

བ་མོ་ *bá-mo* **hoar-frost,** *B.* and col.; *ba-tsa* (Campbell in Summer's Phenix p. 142, 5: *pen-cha*), inferior, **impure soda,** incrusting the ground near salt-lakes; it is mixed with the food of cattle (from which circumstance the word may be translated 'cow-salt'), occasionally also for the want of something better put into the tea; *bá-tsai skyúr-rtsi Cs.* muriatic (hydro-chloric) acid.

བ་ར་ཎ་སི་ *bā-ra-ṇa-si*, v. *wā-ra-ṇa-si.*

བ་རུ་ར་ *ba-ru-ra* an astringent medicament *Med.*

བ་ལ་ཧ་ *bá-la-ha*, *čan-šés bá-la-ha*, n. of a demon, v. *rta-mčóg.*

བ་ལུ་ *ba-lu* = *da-li*, various low alpine species of **Rhododendron.**

བ་ལེ་ཀ་ *bá-le-ka* medicinal plant, belonging to the climbers *Med.*

བ་ཤ་ *bá-ša* 1. v. *ba* I. — 2. prob. = *bá-ša-ha* a bitter-tasted officinal plant, acc. to *Wdn.* an Indian tree; in *Lh.* a rather insignificant radiated flower.

བ་ཤུ་ *bá-šu*, *W.* **a virulent boil, ulcer.**

བ་ཤོ་ *bá-šo Ld.*, *ba-šo-ka C.*, **currants, small raisins.**

བ་སོ་ *bá-so* **elephant's tooth, ivory;** *bá-so-mkan* worker in ivory.

བག་ *bag* I. a primary signification of this word seems to be: **a narrow space;** thus with *Sch.* fig. *bág-dog-pa* to be straitened, in necessitous circumstances, poor; in another application more frq.: *bág-tsam* a little, *nor bág-tsam re* a little money *Mil.*; *bag-ré Thgr.*, perh. the same; *dán-ga bág-tsam bde* the appetite is growing a little better *Lt.*; *tsér-ma bág-tsam yód-pa* having a few prickles *Wdn.*; *bág-tsam-pa* **slight, insignificant, trifling,** *sdug-bsnál*, a slight misfortune *Thgy.*; *ma-bdé-ba bág-tsam-la bzód-pa mi byéd-pa Mil.* to be fretting on account of a trifling mischance; most frq., however, the word has a moral bearing: **attention, care, caution,** relative to physical and moral evils or contaminations; *bag-méd*, in a gen. sense: *rá-ro dán-po bág-med-pa* the beginning of intoxication is the disappearing of attention; in a special sense (*Ssk.* प्रमाद): **careless, heedless, fearless;** *mi-bdé-bai* fearless of misfortune *Dzl.*; *ₒdi-lta-bui bag méd-par ₒgyur* I shall be freed from the fear of such things *Dzl.*; **fearless,** without fear or consideration, without regard to consequences or to the judgment of others etc., *čán-la bag-méd ₒdi-tsam ₒtún-ba Pth.* without shame drinking such great quantities of beer; *mi-dgé-bai las bág-med-par byéd-pa* to sin without fear or restraint *Dzl.*; *ₒdod-čágs-la bág-med-pas* to indulge in sensuality without restraint *Dzl.*; **heedlessness** with regard to good and evil *Tar.* 4, 22; **moral carelessness, indifference, want of principle,** *bág-med-la nyál-ba C.*, stated to be = *bág-la nyal-ba*. v. *bag* II; of an opposite meaning: *bag-yód(-pa)* **reverence, fear, shame,** often parallel to *ṅó-ťsa*, *ₒdzém-pa*; **conscientiousness,** almost **religious awe;** adj. **conscientious;** *spyód-pa bág-yod-pa* conscientious dealings (pious course of life) *Dom.*; *bág-yod-par mdzód-čig* act conscientiously, take care not to commit sin (here = do not kill) *Tar.* 32, 7; *de bág-yod-pai ṗyir* as he was conscientious (here = chaste) *Tar.* 39, 2; *bag daṅ ldán-pa* id.; *bag daṅ ldán-par mdzod Glr.*; *bág-ťsa-ba* **to be afraid;** *bag mi ťsa* I am not afraid *Mil.*; sbst. **fear, timidity, anxiousness** *Mil., Stg.*; *bág-ťsa méd-pa* fearlessness *Mil.*; *bag byéd-pa* c. *la*, to fear, to dread, a person *Dzl.*, to take care of, one's clothes *Dzl.*; *bag-yaṅs-su* (or *-kyis*) *Sch.* (*'cura relaxata'*) without fear, fearlessly, coolly; *bag ₒḱúms-pa Sch.* to be afraid; *bag ₒbébs-pa* to drop, abandon, cast away all fear, *γžan-la* the dread of a person *Mil.* frq.; *bág-pa Dzl.* ༤༥, 15 *Ms.* as a vb. to be afraid, to be fearful, *dé-dag bág-tu dógs-nas* afraid lest they should take fright (another reading: *brós-su*) *bágs-kyis* with fear, with awe *Mil.*; *bágs-kyis byéd-pa* to act carefully, with caution *Dzl.* ༢༦༧, 15; *ma bags-kyis* without fear, unrestrained *Dzl.* ༢༥༥, 1 (*Ms.*; with *Sch. ma* is wanting, and both passages are rendered incorr.); *bág-po* adj. = *bág-yod-pa Cs.*; *bag-zón* dread, fear, anxiety *Sch.* —

II. **inclination? passion?** *bág-la nyál-ba Was.* (241) **'vanities** (in Chinese: lullings into security'), the usual sinful temptations, lust, anger etc.; the etymological derivation of the term is, however, not perfectly clear; *bag-méd-la nyál-ba*, which acc. to its primary signification ought to be placed sub I, is said to imply the same. More frq. *bag-čágs* denotes **passion, inclination, propensity,** gen. in a bad sense, *las-ṅan bag-čágs*, *ṅán-pai bag-čágs*, also occasionally without any addition, id.; *bag-čágs yid-kyi lus* the 'intellectual' body of passions *Thgr.*, v. *lus*; less frq. in a good sense: *Tar.* 32, 7 = love, affection; *bag-čágs bzaṅ*, *Mil.* —

III. in compounds also for *bag-ṗyé* and *bág-ma*.

བག་པ་ *bág-pa* 1. vb. **to be afraid,** v. *bag* I. — 2. **purity?** *Cs.*

བག་པོ་ *bág-po* 1. = *bag-yód Cs.* — 2. **bridegroom.**

བག་ཕྱེ་ *bag-ṗye* (*W.* **bág-ṗe**) **wheat-flour;** *bag-skyó* thin pap or porridge of meal; *bag-zán* thick pap, dough; *bag-drón*, warm porridge; *bag-sbyár* paste; *bags-sbyin* **lute, putty,** a compound of meal and glue; *bag-léb*, resp. *bžes-bág C.* a cake of bread (*Hind. chapāti*).

བག་མ་ *bág-ma* **bride,** *lén-pa* to choose, to take frq.; *bág-ma-la* (or *bág-mar*) *lén-pa* to choose for a bride, *γtóṅ-ba* to give for a bride (wife), *ₒgró-ba*, *čú-ba Ma.*, **čá-če* W.*, to become a bride, to get married; **bág-ma ṭi-te* (or *láṅ-te*) *bór-če**, *W.* to leave the chosen bride with her parents, sometimes for years, which frequently is the case, as betrothals, from reasons of expediency, are often brought about by the parents at a very early age. The common custom is that the young man desirous of marrying proceeds to the parents of his chosen one with the 'wooing-beer', *slóṅ-čaṅ*, which step however may remain yet a private affair; after some time he brings *tig-čaṅ*, the 'settling-beer', and finally *bsú-čaṅ*, the 'taking-home-beer', whereupon follows the wedding, *bág-ston*, and the consummation of marriage, *bza-mí byéd-pa*. — *bag-gós* **wedding-garment;** *bag-grógs-mo* **bride's maid** *Cs.*; *bag-zoṅ Cs.* (prob. more correctly: *rdzoṅs*) **dowry.**

བག་ཙམ་ *bág-tsam* v. *bag* I.

བག་ཙེ་ *bág-tse* a little **basket for wool** or **clews of wool,** *W.*

བག་ཤིས་ *bág-šis* (also *báxis*, *bóxis* etc.) *Ar.* بخشيش 1. **fee,** drink-money. — 2. *Sp.* **a present, alms.**

བགས་ *bags* v. *bag* I.

བང་ *baṅ* 1. **foot-race,** *baṅ ni γžán-las mgyógs-pa* to be quicker in running than another; *de daṅ baṅ mnyám-par rgyúg-pa* to run with equal swiftness as . . . *Pth.*; *baṅ rgyúg-pa Cs.*, **bhaṅ táṅ-wa* C.*; **baṅ táṅ-*

če* W.; ban ˳grán-pa to run a race; ban-rtsál sbyón-ba Mil. to exercise one's self in racing; ban dan ˳gró-las-dag-gis nyén-pa or ban-˳grós nyén-pa to overexert one's self in running Med.; *bhan-gyóg, bhan-čón* C. **running-match, race**; ban-čén(-pa, also -po) Pth., Glr. **swift messenger, courier**; *bhan-mi* C., *ban-mi* W., id. — 2. v. bán-ba.

བང་བ་ bán-ba, bán-kan, bán-mdzod **store-room, store-house, corn magazine,** also **treasury** Dzl.; šin-ban Kun. a large box for grain, half underground; bán-p̔ud first-fruit offering from the barn; *bhan-gha* Ts. **repository**; (dbus-ban, pronounced:) *ü-bhán* Ts. **cupboard, press, case.**

བང་རིམ་ ban-rim = k̔ri-˳p̔án, the part of the mčód-rten which has the form of a staircase. — 2. Sch. 'a separate part of a house connected by a staircase' (?).

བང་སོ་ bán-so **grave, tomb,** γsón-por bán-sor ˳dzúg-pa to bury alive Glr.; **sepulchre, monument,** bán-so ˳débs-pa, or rtsig-pa to build a sepulchre Glr.; bán-so mčód-pa to perform funeral sacrifices, to honour a grave Glr.

བངས་པ་ báns-pa Sch. 1. = sbáns-pa. — 2. = bán-ba. — 3. = bán-so.

བཏ་ཏི་ bát-ti (Hindi) 1. a weight = 2 ser, about 4 pounds. — 2. **balance, pair of scales**; *bát-ti tág-če* to weigh W.

བད་ bad 1. **moisture, humidity,** *šin bad k̔ór-na* W. when wood attracts humidity; *bád-čan* moist, humid, damp, from rain or dew W. — 2. **hoar-frost** = bá-mo Sch., Wts. — 3. in compounds for bád-kan. — 4. **edge, border,** bad ni γser the edge is of gold Sch.; mk̔ar-bád S.g. = k̔a-bad? bad-˳búr Mil.?

བད་ཀ་ bád-ka C. a plant, similar to mustard, yielding oil.

བད་ཀན་ bád-kan mucus **phlegm,** a. as normal substance of the body comprizing 5 kinds: rten-byéd mucus in the joints of the neck and shoulders, myag-byéd in the stomach, myon-byéd in the tongue and palate, tsim-byéd in the brain, eyes etc., ˳byor-byéd in the rest of the joints; b. in a morbid state, as a cause of disease: bád-kan-las gyúr-pai nad mucous diseases; bad-kan-lhén mucus in the cardiac regions, prob. = gastric catarrh; bad-kan-lčags-drégs intestinal catarrh; bad-kan-mgul-˳gágs mucous consumption; bád-kan grúm-bu dkár-po etc. Med.; bad-kan-rlún phlegm and air, bad-kan-mk̔ris phlegm and bile; bad-kan-k̔rag phlegm and blood Med.

བན་ ban 1. C. **beer-jug, pitcher.** — 2. v. the following articles.

བན་ཆུང་, བན་བུན་ ban-čún, ban-bún **a little, a bit**; kyod-rán nyams-ban-bún-gyi snán-ba-la you, with your little bit of spiritual light Mil.; rtsi-šin sna-ts̔ógs ban-ma-bún forest-trees of every kind not a few (or also variously mixed?) Mil.; ban-če in moderate quantity, 'tolerably many'.

བན་དྷ་ bán-dha Sch. **skull, cranium**; frq. spelled bhán-dha, hence perh. = **भाण्ड** vessel, in which sense it is gen. to be understood in books; accordingly it may be a skull used as a drinking-vessel.

བན་དྷེ་, བན་དེ་ bán-dhe, bán-de, acc. to Hodgson's learned Nepalese authority (Illustr. 75) = **वन्द्य**, *reverendus, salutandus*, for which also in the Tibetan language btsún-pa is always used as an equivalent: **a Buddhist priest;** hence originally = Buddhist in general, the term being also applied to women Mil.; ban-rgán an old priest Glr.; ban-sprán and sprań-bán a mendicant friar; ban-čún ('pen-kiong' Desg. 370) pupil, disciple in a monastery; ban-lóg col., a priest that has turned apostate; ban-bón Mil. and elsewh. 1. (acc. to our Lama:) Buddhist and Bonpo. 2. (acc. to Sch.): **a Bon-priest,** in which case, however, the word prob would be bon-bán.

བན་ཟོན་ ban-zón Sch.: for bag-zón **dread, fear.**

བབ་ bab v. ˳báb-pa.

བབ་ཅོལ་ bab-čól **hastiness, rashness,** want of consideration in speaking and acting = γzu-lúm; sdig-pa bab-čól-du byéd-pa to sin recklessly, without heed or regard Mil.

བབ་མོ་, བས་མོ་ báb-mo, bás-mo (?) *Ld.* **soft, mild;** also **chaste, modest** (corrupted from *bág-mo*?).

བབས་ *babs* 1. **sunk, settled,** v. *ˌbáb-pa*; *nú-ma-la raṅ-bábs-kyi rdzas byúg-ste* rubbing the breasts with a medicine, so that they sank down of themselves, as if they were full *Glr.*; *bábs-sa* **settlement, colony** *Sch.* — 2. **shape, form, appearance** *Sch.* — 3. *rta-babs* v. *rta*, comp.

བམ་(པ་) *bám(-pa)* 1. **rotten, decayed, putrid,** *ro bám-pa* putrid corpse *Tar.*, *bam-ró*, id.; prob. also corpse in general, esp. in connection with sorcery; *bam-čén*, id.? *Thgr.* — 2. **mould,** white film on liquids; **mouldy, fusty, musty** *W.*

བམ་པོ་ *bám-po* 1. **bundle** of wood or grass *Schr.*, *Sch.* — 2. **division, section,** of books, (of greater length than a chapter); in metrical compositions it is said to comprize a number of 300 verses; *glegs-bám* v. *glegs*; *bam-šiṅ Sch.* **board,** prob. = *glegs-šiṅ*.

བམ་རིལ་ *bam-ril* 1. *Sch.* **dull, weak,** from old age or long labour, **worn out,** by much usage. — 2. *W.* **mould.**

བར་ *bar* sbst. (*Cs.* also *bár-ma*) 1. **intermediate space, interstice, interval,** *mḱar ɣnyis-kyi bar zám-gyis sbrél-ba Glr.* overbridging the space between the two castles; *sa-bár* **straits, narrow sea;** *ču-bár* **isthmus, neck of land;** **páṅ-gi bar, láṅ-ḱe bar, ˌče bar** **shelf** of a repository, cup-board etc. *W.*; **intermediate, middle, mean,** *stod smad bar ɣsum* upper, lower and middle country *Ma.*; *bar ˌdir* here in the middle countries *Glr.*; *bár-gyi*, id., as adj. *Tar.* and elsewh.; *bár-gyi sder-čágs*, in *Wdṅ.* a lizard, as an amphibium partaking of two natures; *bár-na, bár-du, bár-la* adv. and postp. c. genit. (and accus.), *lám-gyi bár-na* in the middle of the road (there is a well); on the road, in or on the way, on the journey *Dzl.*; *brág-bar btsir-ba* to be squeezed between two rocks *Thgy.*; *ló-ma daṅ yál-gai bár-du* between leaves and branches *Dzl.*; *rgya bod bár-la ˌgró-bai mi* people travelling between China and Tibet *Glr.*; *deï bár-la, de-bár* between *Glr.*; **in the mean time, at the same time,** *Glr.*; *zla-ba ɣsum-gyi bár-du* (to provide for a person) for the space of 3 months *Dzl.*; *žag bdún-gyi bár-du* for seven days (he had not eaten any thing) *Dzl.*; *ťúṅ-čin byá-bai sá-ča bár-du byon* he went as far as the country called *tuṅ-čin Glr.*; *dá-ltai bár-du Glr.*, *da-tsam-gyi bár-du Dzl.*; *da-bár*, *Mil.* **until now, hitherto;** *de(i) bár(du)* id., when referring to what is past = **until then;** *ˌbrás-bui bár-du ťób-pa* to obtain all, even to the fruit (inclusive of the fruit) *Dzl.*; *lan ɣsum-gyi bár-du* at three (different) times *Dzl*; frq. with verbs: *rtsé-mo-la ťúg-gi bár-du* till even touching the top *Dzl.* and so frq.; rel. to time gen. with a negative, being then equivalent to **as long as,** *ma ťób-pai bár-du* as long as it has not been obtained = until its having been obtained *Dzl.*; *ṅa ma ši bár-du* till or up to my death *Mil.*; *ma bsleb bár-du* as long as we have not reached, attained *Glr.*; seldom without a negation: *mya-ṅán-las ˌdás-pai bár-du Dzl.* ꝖV, 4 (s. l. c.); *bár-nas* **from between,** *rtsíb-mai bár-nas* from between the ribs *Glr.* — 2. fig. *bar byéd-pa* to interpose, intercede, mediate *Glr.*, cf. *bár-mi*. — 3. Termin. of *ba*, and cf. *par* III.

**Comp. and deriv.** **bhár-kya** partition-wall *C.* — *bar-skábs* space of time, period *Tar.* — *bar-skór* veranda, exterior gallery of the middle story of a house. — *bar-ḱaṅ Sch.* a building between two other houses; *Schr.* a room between two others. — *bar-gós Schr.* waist-coat. — *bár-ˌga* some, several; several times, now . . . now . . . *Dzl.* — *bar-čód, -čad*, perh. also *-ɣčod*, sbst. to *bar-du ɣčod-pa*, (v. *ɣčod-pa*) **hinderance, impediment; danger; damage, failure, fatal accident;** *ťsé-la bar-čád ˌoṅ*, or *byuṅ* (my) life is in danger; *lús-kyi, sróg-gi bar-čád-du ˌgyur* id.; also: to meet with an accident, to perish, to be lost *Dzl.* and elsewh.; **bar-čad-la ši* W.*, he met with a violent death; *bar-čád sél-ba* to protect against fatal accidents, of magic spells frq.; *ṅá-la bar-čád méd-par* without meeting with an accident *Mil.*; *bar-čád rtsóm-pa* to meditate evil, to brood mischief *Mil.*; *bar-čád ma ťsúgs-par* without having played me a roguish trick *Mil.*; also in a moral sense: temptation; sin, trespass, *bár-du γčód-pa* to commit sin, to trespass *Mil.* — **bár-ta* W.* cloth round the loins. — *bar-stóṅ Sch.* empty space. — *bár-do* 1. also *bar-ma-do* the intermediate state between death and re-birth, of a shorter or longer duration (yet not of more than 40 days, ni f.); although on the one hand it is firmly believed, that the place of re-birth (whether a man, an animal, or a god etc. go forth from it), unalterably depends on the former course of life, yet in *Thgr.* the soul is urged and instructed to proceed at once into Nirwana to Buddha (inconsistently with the general dogma). *bár-do γčód-pa Mil.* is explained as putting off and preventing the intermediate state after death, as well as re-birth, by penitentiary exercises. 2. *W.:* **hard, difficult; difficulty,** — perh. Bunan. — *bar-snáṅ* (seldom *bar-snáṅ-ba*) **atmospherical space**; *stéṅ-gi bar-snáṅ-la* in the heavens, in the air, frq.; *bar-snáṅ-la ₒṕar* (a fragment of a blasted rock) flies up into the air; *bar-snáṅ-du* or *-la* c. genit., the common word for **over**, *goi bar-náṅ-la*, over (his) head. — **bár-pa* W.* the middle one, e.g. of three brothers. — *bar-bár-du Ma.* **at intervals, from time to time, now and then**; *bar-bár-la* id.; **mā bar-bár-la**, at long intervals, seldom *W.* — *bár-ma* the middle one of three things *Glr.* — *bar-mi* **mediator, intercessor, umpire.** — **bar-ťsód* W.* middling, **lúṅ-po bar-ťsód** a moderate wind. — *bar-mťsáms*, *bar-ₒťsáms* **interval** (*Sch.:* room; leisure, convenience, comfort?). — *bar-lág-pa* = *bar-mi Sch.* — **bar-lhag** gap, vacancy, deficiency *W.*, **bar-lág káṅ-če** to fill up a gap or vacancy, to supply a want, or deficiency.

བར་ལིག *bar-lig W.* **a field** or **estate** let to a person for the term of his life, for usufruct.

བལ་ *bal* **wool**, *bál-gyi* woolen, *bal daṅ ldán-pa* woolly *Wdṅ.*; *bal séd-pa* the first coarse plucking of wool, *rmél-ba* the second, of the finer wool, *śiṅ-ba* the third, of the finest *W.*; **bal táb-če** to beat wool *W.*; *lug-*, *ra-*, *rṅá-bal* sheep-wool, goat's and camel's hair; *rás-bal*, *śiṅ-bal* cotton *Cs.*; *śiṅ-bal* prob. also the down on willow-blossoms *Sch.*; *srín-bal Wdṅ.*, *Schr.*: raw silk, yet perh. also cotton; *čú-bal* a kind of moss on stones in brooks *Cs.* — *bal-skúd* a woolen thread or yarn, worsted. – *bal-skyé Sch.:* mould on fermented liquors. — *bal-gláṅ*, *Cs.* also *bál-gyi glaṅ-po-čé*, a kind of elephant, for which sometimes incorr. and ambiguously *bá-laṅ* is used, *Dzl.* and elsewh. — *bal-ťér* thin woolen cloth *Cs.*; **bal-ₒdáb* W.* tuft of wool, as is used for spinning. — *bal-ṕrúg* thick woolen cloth. — *bal-yás Sch.* wool-card (?)

བལ་པོ་ *bál-po*, *bal(-po)-yúl* **Nepal**, frq. designated as *rín-po-čei gliṅ*, and as the favourite country of the *Klu*, or serpent-demons; *bál-po-pa*, fem. *bál-po-ma*, *bál-mo Glr.*, a Nepal man or woman; *bal-nyiṅ C.*, (*-snyiṅs*) a Nepal rupee; *bal-srán Tar.*, Nepal pease.

བས་ *bas* I. v. *bás-pa*. — II. instrum. of *ba*; *bas-bldágs*, 'licked by a cow', n. of a disease combined with the sensation, as if the skin had been licked off by a cow, cow-itch, cow-pox *Cs.* (?) — III. v. *pas*, where there is to be added: **to say nothing of, much less,** e.g. *kron ₒdom dgu-brgyá-bas brgya yaṅ ₒbru mi ťub*, a well a hundred fathoms deep cannot be dug, to say nothing of 900 fathoms (much less one of 900 f.) *Glr.*

བས་པ་ *bás-pa* (cf. Pers., Hind. بس) *Cs.:* pf. of *byéd-pa* inst. of, *byás-pa* in the signification of **'done (with), settled'**; *bás-par byéd-pa*, id. *Sch.*; in *Bal.* frq.: **bas, byas, bas-se*, or also *byás-te yód** it is finished, completed, ready, all right; *der bas* that is all of it, nothing more is left *Sch.*; in *bgyis-su bás-kyis* after having been made, caused, occasioned *Mil.*, it stands as a sign of the preterite, similar to *zin*; or like *zad*: *mi γčig-gi smán-du ma bás-kyis* not only for one man it serves as a medicine *Dzl.*; *bas-mta* **border-country** *Sch.*

བས་མོ་ *bás-mo* v. *báb-mo*.

བི་ *bi* 1. num. figure: 45. — 2. in *W.* gen. for *byi.* — 3. *bi* and *biu Pur.* for *bya* **bird, fowl, hen.**

བི་གང་, བི་ཡང་ *bi-gáṅ, bi-yáṅ* in compounds *big,* **hole** *W.* for *bú-ga*, cf. *ₒbig-pa*; *bi-gáṅ-čan* having holes.

བི་ཏང་ *bi-taṅ, Lh.* **door,** prop. Bunan.

བི་ནཱ་ཡ་ཀ *bi-nā-ya-ka Ssk.*, v. *bgegs.*

བི་ཤྭ་ཀར་མ *bi-šwa-kar-ma Ssk., lhai bzó-bo* the smith of the gods, the Brahman-Buddhist Vulcan *Dzl., Glr.*

བི་ཥ་ *bi-ṣa* (*Ssk.* word for poison) n. of certain medicinal plants, e.g. *bi-ṣa-dkar* Polygonatum, in *Lh.*

བིག་པན་ *big pan Cs.* **vitriol;** *Sch.* **potash, garlic-ashes;** mentioned in *S.g.* as a caustic.

བིག་བི་ལིག *big-bi-lig Kun.* **quail.**

བིད་བིད་ *bid-bid*(?) *Ld.* **mouth-piece of a hautboy, hautboy reed.**

བིམ་པ་ *bim-pa* **बिम्ब, विम्ब.** Momordica monadelpha, a cucurbitaceous plant with a red fruit *Wdṅ.*, along with *ka-bed*; the fashion of Indian poets to compare red lips with the bimpa fruit, has been adopted also by the Tibetans, *Gyatch.* p. ༦༢; transl. p. 108; so also *Pth.: mču-sgrós bim-pa ltá-bur mdzes* (where *Sch.* gives the signification of **peach,** on which the name possibly may have been transferred, although 'lips of the shape of a peach-tree leaf' seem to be rather a strange fancy).

བིར་བིར་ *bir-bir W.* **crumbs, bits, scraps.**

བིལ་བ་ *bil-ba Ssk.* **बिल्व**, *Hind. bilb, bél,* Aegle marmelos, tree with a nourishing and wholesome fruit; the word seems to have been transferred also to the cocoa-nut.

བུ་ *bu* I. sbst., resp. *sras*, 1. **son,** common in *B.* and *C.*; **čé-bu** *W.*, the eldest son. — 2. child, *bu btsá-ba* the bringing forth of children, children being born *Dzl.*; *bu máṅ-bar ₒgyúr-ba* to get many children; *bu mi γsós-pa* not being able to keep a child alive *Dom.*; esp. in reference to the mother: *ma-bu*, mother and children; also transferred on animals: *rta ma brgya bu brgya* a hundred mares with as many foals *Dzl.;* the word is moreover used in many other instances, e.g. with regard to letters which in writing are placed under other letters, in reference to principal beams and smaller cross-beams, to capital and interest; also as a friendly address of a teacher to his hearers *Mil.* — The fem. *bú-mo* v. below.

**Comp.** *bu-ₒkrid* (or *pu-tri*?) a fem. noun proper. — *bu-grógs Cs.* **step-brother, foster-brother.** — *bu-rgyúd* **offspring, issue, progeny, generation** *Tar.* 168. 11. — *bu-dód* foster-child, adopted son, *ṅéd-kyi bu-dód mdzod* deign to be adopted by us *Mil.* — *bu-γdúṅ* a small cross-beam *Mil.* — *bu-nád* child-bed, *bu-nád log* the child-bed terminates unfavourably *Pth.* — *bu-snód* **uterus, womb** *Med.* — *bú-po* male child, son *Dzl.* — *bu-prug* children. — *bú-mo*, vulg. also *bó-mo* 1. **daughter,** frq. 2. **girl,** *ṅa bú-moi dús-na yin-te* when I was still a girl *Glr.* — *kyeu daṅ bú-mo* lads and lasses *Dzl.*; **maiden, virgin;** *bú-mo γtsáṅ-ma, γsár-ma, γsár-pa* a girl that is still in a virgin state. 3. young woman *Dzl.*; *W.* gen. for *bud-méd*, frq. — *bu-smád, Cs.* also *bu-mád* family, children, nearest relations *Mil.* and elsewh. — *bu-tsá* (*Dzl.* ed. *Sch.* also *bu-tsá*) 1. **children's children** *Thgy.*; family = *bu-smád* 2. *W.*, **son,** gen. for *bu*; **boy,** **bú-tsa daṅ bó-mo**. — *bu-tsáb Cs.* = *bu-dod.* — *bu-tsás ₒbrél-ba Glr.* (acc. to the context) to cohabit. — *bu-sriṅ* brother and sister. — *bu-slób* scholar, disciple, follower of a clerical teacher, opp. to *nyá-ma* hearer, who still continues in his secular calling. — II. num. figure: 75.

བུ་ག *bu-ga* 1. **छिद्र**, in compounds *bug,* **hole, opening, orifice; aperture,** *bá-spui bú-ga* pore, passage of perspiration *Dzl.;* *sna-búg* nostril; *bú-ga dgu(-po)* the nine orifices of the body (eyes, ears, nostrils, mouth, urethra, anus); *tsáṅs-pai bú-ga* and perh. also *yid-ₒjug bú-ga Med.*, appears to be = *mtsog-ma* **the fontanel** or vacancy in the infant cranium, with which various fables are connected; **cavity, vessel,** (anatom.), also **veins** *Med.* — 2. symbol. num.: 9.

བུ་གུ་ *bú-gu* **hole,** *sgoi* key-hole *Dzl.*

བུ་སྟོན་ *bu-stón* name of a learned Lama and author of *čos-byúṅ*, about the year 1300 *Glr.*, an adherent of the Adi-buddha doctrine, v. *Cs. Gram.*

བུ་རྡོ་ *bú-rdo Sch.*, **idle talk, tittle-tattle.**

བུ་ཡུག་ *bu-yúg* **snow-storm** *Mil.*

བུ་རམ་ *bu-ram Hindi* गुड़, *gur*, hence *W.* **gu-rám**, **raw sugar, muscovado; treacle**, *Mil.*, *Lt.*; *bu-rám sgór-ba* to boil down raw sugar *Lex.*; *bu-ram-šiṅ, bur-šiṅ*, vulg. **gur-šiṅ** **sugar-cane;** *bu-ram-šiṅ-pa*, इक्ष्वाकु, name of the first king of the solar dynasty in India, *Glr.*; *bu-ram-čaṅ, bur-čaṅ* sugar-beer *Lt.*; *bur-dkár? Lt. bur-stáṅ γčig* (more correctly *ltaṅ*) *Sch.*, a bale of raw sugar packed up in leather.

བུ་ལོན་ *bú-lon* (cf. *bun*) **advanced money, debt,** **ṅul gyg bú-lon mi-la táṅ-če* W.* to lend a person a hundred florins; (*bú-lon byéd-pa* to contract debts *Schr.*, *Sch.*??) *bú-lon ˳ǰál-ba* (*W.* **čál-če**), *spród-pa Sch.* to pay a debt, *sél-ba* to put out, to cancel a debt, *déd-pa, bdá-ba* to call in, to recover a debt, *čágs-pa* prob. the beginning and running up of debts *Dzl.*; *bú-lon-pa* **debtor,** *dṅul brgyai* of a hundred rupees.

བུ་ཧག་ *bu-hág* v. *sbugs-hág.*

བུག་པ་ *búg-pa* 1. sbst. **hole,** *búg-pa ˳búg-pa* to bore holes *Glr.*, cog. to *bú-ga.* — 2. *Sch.*, to get holes (?).

བུག་ཞོལ་ *bug-žól* v. *sbugs.*

བུག་སུག་ *bug-súg Ld.* **birdsfoot-trefoil,** Melilotus.

བུང་བ་ *búṅ-ba* 1. a humming and stinging insect, **bee** etc.; *buṅ-lčág* sting, and also the wound caused by it; **buṅ-ba čág taṅ soṅ* W.* the bee has stung. 2 *Cs.* a bright black stone.

བུངས་ *buṅs* **mass, heap, bulk,** *buṅs-čén* a large heap *Lt.*; *dri-čui buṅs-če* a great quantity of urine *Mṅg.*; *buṅs byéd-pa* to heap one upon another, pile up. — *buṅ* **many** (?).

བུད་ *bud*, every darkening of the air through dry matter, **a cloud of dust,** more exactly *ṫal-búd*; *bud-ṫsub* dust from threshing; *búd-kyis btab* wrapt in vapour *Mil.*; perh. also **snow-storm** (*Sch.*), yet not exclusively.

བུད་དྷ་ *búd-dha Ssk.*, **Buddha,** n. of the founder of the religion which is called after him, occurring but rarely in Tibetan writings, and among the people (at least in *W.*) almost unknown, v. *saṅs-rgyas*; *bud-dhai ṗreṅ-ba*, **búd-dé ṫáṅ-na** **rosary** *Ts.*

བུད་པ་ *búd-pa* 1. *Sch.* = *sbúd-pa.* — 2. pf. cf. *˳búd-pa.*

བུད་མེད་ *bud-méd B.* and *C.*, 1. **woman,** *bud-méd sdúg-gu* a fair woman *Dzl.*; *bud-méd daṅ sbágs-pa* to defile, corrupt one's self with women *Dzl.* — 2. **wife, spouse,** not frq. *Dzl.* (*W. bú-mo* and *ă-ne*).

བུད་ཤིང་ *búd-šiṅ* **fire-wood, fuel,** also dung used as such; *búd-šiṅ bšág-pa* to cleave or chop wood.

བུན་ *bun* 1. = *bú-lon Mil.*, *bun ṫoṅ* **lend us!** *Mil.*; *bun btáṅ-du ma nyán-pas* not willing to lend any thing *Mil.*; *k̔yéd-rnams-la bun dgós-na* if you want an advance (of money) *Mil.* — *bún-ṫo, bún-yig* 1. **debtor's account-book.** 2. **bond** or obligation, **bill of debt.** — *bun-bdág* 1. **creditor.** 2. **money-changer, banker.** — *bún-yig* v. *bún-ṫo.* — 2. **interest,** **bhu̱n kyé-pa** to bear interest *C.*; *bun ˳ǰál-ba* to pay interest *Cs.* — 3. (house) **rent** *Sch.* (?) — 4. *bun-ré Sch.* **a small matter,** cf. *ban-bún*; *bun-bún Sch.* piece-meal, scattered, dispersed. — 5. v. *˳bún-pa.*

བུན་ལོང་ *bun-lóṅ* — *ču bun-loṅ-lóṅ byed* it is whirling up and down, an expression used of boiling water which contains impurities or extraneous matter; hence *bun-lóṅ-gi snaṅ-sás* troubled, impure, sinful thoughts.

བུབ་པ་ *bub-pa* v. *˳bub-pa.*

བུབས་ *bubs* = *yug*, also *ṫan* (थान *Hind.*) 1. an entire **piece of cloth** rolled up; *gos-bubs* cotton-cloth *Cs.* — 2. in a general sense one whole, something entire *Sch.*; *bubs-ril* prob. whole, entire, *bubs-ril lus S.g.* the whole body, opp. to separate parts.

བུམ་པ་ *búm-pa*, **bottle, flask**; the water-flask of the hukka; bottle-shaped ornaments in architecture, e. g. on the cenotaphs or Chodtén; *rdzá-mai* earthen-bottle, pitcher; *šél-bum* glass-bottle; *čàṅ-bum* beer-bottle; *mčód-bum Cs.* vessel used in sacrificing; *mé-bum* cupping-glass *Lt.* (cf. *puṅ-pa*).

བུར་ *bur* 1. **bolt, bar**, vertically fastened to a door etc., *ťóg-bur* upper, *yóg-bur* lower bolt. — 2. for *bu-rám*. — 3. for *ₒbur*.

བུར་རྟིང་ *bur-rtiṅ* (or perh. *tiṅ*) *Sch.*, a kind of **bell** or **gong** in temples.

བུར་ཙེ་ *búr-tse* n. of certain plants in *Ld. & Kun.*

བུལ་ *bul W.*, **bhul, bhu̥l, bhu̥* and *bhu̥-tog* C., Med.*, (the spellings of Campbell, *peu* — v. *bá-mo* — and of *Schl.*, *phuli*, have prob. resulted from a mistake in hearing), **soda**, not unfrequently found in Tibet as a white powder on the ground, and used as a medicine, as a ferment, as a means for giving additional flavour to tea, and for various technical purposes.

བུལ་པོ་ *búl-po* **slow, heavy, tardy,** *ₒgro búl-te* slow in walking, making but tardy progress *Dzl.*; *W.*: **d̥úl-ce búl-po**.

བུལ་ཧ་རི་ *bul-ha-ri*, **bul-gar* W.*, **Russia leather, jufts.**

བུས་པ་ *bús-pa* 1. for *byís-pa Lt.* — 2. v. *ₒbúd-pa*.

བེ་ *be*, 1. num. figure: 105. — 2. *W.* for *bye*. — 3. for words here not noted refer to *pe*.

བེ་ཁུར་ *be-ǩur S.g.?*

བེ་གེ་ *be-gé* v. *beg-gé*.

བེ་ཅོན་ *be-čon*, also *-tson*, *Ssk.* गदा, 1. **club,** with an ornamental knob, prob. merely an attribute of gods. — 2. n. of a goddess *Thgr.*

བེ་ཏ་ *be-ta* a geographical prop. name, prob. = Himalaya, *Pth.*

བེ་ཏོ་, བེ་དོ་ *bé-to, bé-do*, vulg. **calf.**

བེ་དྷ་ *bé-dha* v. *ₒbé-dha*.

བེ་སྣབས་ *be-snábs Cs.*, **thick slime** or **mucus,** e.g. the mucus flowing at child-birth from the vagina *Lt.*

བེ་བུམ་ *be-búm*, also *beu-búm*, **writing, scripture, book** *Glr.*, perh. the same word as the following.

བེ་འབུམ་ *be-ₒbum*, are stated to be the sacred writings of the Bonpos, which — as our Lama candidly owned — 'are also perused by Buddhists for their edification'.

བེ་མོ་ *bé-mo* **cow-calf,** female calf *C.*

བེ་རྫི་ *be-rdzi* Nakshatra, v. *rgyu-skár* 3.

བེ་ཟ་ *bé-za W.*, from the *Hind.* ब्याज, **interest,** *ṭá-ka bé-za* a double paisa interest, of 1 rupee, = 4—6 pCt. pro month.

བེ་རག་ *be-rag* (spelling?), **fillet** of the women in *Ld.*, ornamented with coloured stones.

བེ་ལེ་ཀ་ *be-le-ka S.g.*, a kind of **surgical instrument.**

བེ་ལོག་ *be-log Sch.* **great-grandfather.**

བེ་ཤིང་ *be-šiṅ* **oak-tree,** = *ča-ra*; *be-ǩród* oak-forest *Wdṅ.*

བེག་གེ་ *beg-gé Lt.*, a disease; *Sch.*: measles.

བེག་ཙེ་ *bég-tse* a hidden **shirt of mail.**

བེང་ *beṅ Sch.*, **stick, cudgel, club.**

བེད་ *bed*, 1. = *ǩe, ǩe-béd*, **advantage, profit, gain, high price,** *ťsá-la drúg-ču bed yód-pai skábs-su* at a time when salt was a sixty times dearer (than barley) *Glr.*; **bed ťób-ce* W.* to gain, to make profit; *bed-čód Mil.* is stated to be the same as *loṅs-spyód*; *bed-čód ťsod bčád-de* to be temperate, to keep moderation in the indulgence of the appetites. — 2. **interest,** *C., W.*

བེན་ *ben* **a large pitcher; jug, beer-pot,** *Glr.*; **ču-bhén**, water-pot, *C.*

བེམ་པོ་ *bém-po* 1. **dead matter,** mostly applied to the body, as opp. to the soul, *rig-pa*, e.g. *bem rig ₒgye-dus* when body and soul are parting, *Mil., Thgr.*; *lus bem-rig γnyis-kyi so-mtsáms-su* on the boundary between the physical matter of the body and the soul *Mil.*; *Was.* (272) *bem-reg* is perh. a mistake in writing, although it also makes sense. — 2. *Sch.* **a pestilential disease**; in the *Mṅg. bem tol rgyáb-pa* seems to denote a surgical operation. — 3. some receptacle, **box, bag** etc., *bém-poi náṅ-nas γser bton* she took gold out of the . . .?

བེའུ་ *beu Cs.* **calf.**

བེའུ་བུམ་ *beu-búm* v. *be-búm*, *Mil.*

བེའུ་རས་ *beu-rás*, in *Stg.* mentioned as a material for clothing; *Schr.*: **'fine linen'**, which however is as yet unknown in Tibet.

བེར་ *ber* 1. **cloak**, *bér-gyi ťú-ba* tail of the cloak *Glr.*; *ber nág-po* a black cloak *Glr.* and elsewh.; *ˌjol-bér* dress with a train *Wdk.*, *Pth.*; *ťsem-bér* a cloak patched up of many pieces *Pth.*; *ber-čen* gown of a priest, sacerdotal cloak, without sleeves, with *gos-čén* for a collar; *ber-ťúl* fur-cloak. — 2. **strength, sharpness, keenness, pungency,** of spices, spirits, snuff etc.; *ber-čan* sharp, pungent, piquant; **ǎ-rág-la ber màṅ-po yod** the gin is very strong *W.*; **bér-ra rag, lčeï bér-če máṅ-po rag** it bites, burns my tongue; *za-bér Cs.* the burning sensation caused by the stinging of nettles; cf. *gár-ba*.

བེར་ཀ་ *bér-ka W.*, *bér-ma*, *ber-lcág Mil.*, **stick, staff** (cf. *dbyúg-pa*); *spai bér-ma* cane, bamboo *Mil.*; *ber-ma lčag γčig* a simple staff *Mil.*; *lčags-bér* iron-bar, crow-bar; *smyug-bér* cane, walking-stick.

བེལ་ *bel Cs.* **leather bag.**

བཻ་ཌཱུར་ཡ་ *wai-dūr-ya*, *Ssk.*, **azure stone, lapis lazuli** *Dzl.* *wai-dūr-ya dkar-po* and *sṅon-po*, v. table of abbreviations.

བཻ་རོ་ཙ་ན་ *wai-ro-tsa-na Ssk.*, *Tib.*: *rnam-par-snaṅ-mdzad*, 1. n. of the first Dhyani-Buddha. — 2. a Lotsawa v. *Köpp.* II., 69.

བོ་ *bo*, 1. num. figure: 135. — 2. **affix**, to designate some words as nouns.

བོ་ཏོག་པ་, བོ་ལོང་བ་ *bo-tóg-pa*, *bo-lóṅ-ba* *Ts.*, **ankle, ankle-bone.**

བོ་དེ་ *bo-de Cs.*: 'n. of a tree, the fruits of which are used as beads for rosaries'.

བོ་དྷི་ *bo-dhi Ssk.*, **wisdom**; also n. of the **Indian fig-tree**, ficus religiosa, *byaṅ-čub-šiṅ*; n. of the **white narcissus** (*Lh.*).

བོ་བ་ *bó-ba*, prob. pf. of *ˌbó-ba*.

བོ་མོ་ *bó-mo W.* for *bú-mo*.

བོ་ལོ་ *bó-lo*, **ball**, for playing *Ld.*

བོག་པ་ *bog-pa* v. *ˌbógs-pa*.

བོག་ར་ *bóg-ra Sch.* **roof.**

བོགས་ *bogs*, *Cs.*, **gain, profit, advantage;** *bogs ˌdón-pa Sch.* to yield profit; whereever I met with the word, it was used only in a religious sense: **gain for the mind,** benefit for the heart, furtherance of devotion. of meditation, *Mil.*

བོང་ *boṅ* 1. also *boṅs*, **size, dimensions, volume, bulk,** *boṅ-čé*, *-čén* large, *boṅ če don čuṅ*, large of size, and small of significance are e. g. the lungs (in as far as roasted or boiled they yield little substantial food) *Mil.*; *lus-boṅ-čé*, *-čúṅ*, *ˌbriṅ* big, little, middling, as to size of body, *S.g.*; *boṅ-ťúṅ* little in stature; *boṅ-ťsád*, *boṅ-ťsód* = *rdzógs-pa* full size, a full-grown body *Thgy.* — 2. v. *boṅ-na*. — 3. also *bóṅ-ba*, *Cs.*: 'general name for small stones, pebbles etc.'; in medical works *zíṅ-gi bóṅ-ba* are mentioned as remedies; in *Pth.* the word occurs in an enumeration of temporal goods, precluding the above signification. — 4. v. *boṅ-bu*. — 5. provinc. for *baṅ Glr.*

བོང་ཁྲ་ *boṅ-krá Sch.* a species of **falcon.**

བོང་གུ་ *bóṅ-gu* v. *bóṅ-bu*.

བོང་ང་ *boṅ-ṅá*, various species of **wolf's bane,** aconite, *boṅ-dkár*, *-nág*, *-dmár*, *-sér*, used as medicines, or even as poisons.

བོང་ནག་ *boṅ-nág* v. the preceeding and the following article.

བོང་བུ་ *bóṅ-bu*, *Sch.* also *bóṅ-bo*, 1. **ass,** *bóṅ-p̓o* or *p̓o-bóṅ* he-ass, *bóṅ-mo* or *mo-bóṅ* she-ass, *boṅ-p̓rúg* colt or foal of an ass; *boṅ-sgál* an ass's load; *boṅ-sbáṅ* dung of an ass; *boṅ-rdzí* keeper or driver of an ass; *dre-bóṅ Cs.* 'an ass generating a mule'. — 2. n. of insects, *rgyás-poi bóṅ-bu* sugar-mite, lepisma, *Ld.; boṅ-nág* (perh. *buṅ-nág*) dung-beetle *Lh.* — 3. *Cs.*: **blockhead, fool.**

བོད་ *bod* 1. *Ssk.* **भोट, Tibet**, *bód-(kyi) yul* id. 2. for *bód-pa, bod ḱa-čig* some **Tibetans** *Tar., ḱyed bód-rnams* ye Tibetans. — 3. for *bód-skad* the **Tibetan language**, *bód-du bsgyur ̥jug* I will have it translated into Tibetan *Pth.*; *bód-skad,* in a more limited sense, also implies the common language of conversation, opp. to book-language *W.*; *bód-pa, bód-(kyi) mi* Tibetans, *bód-mo* fem.; *bód-kyi mi-rigs* or *mi-brgyúd* the people of Tibet. in contradistinction to other nations, *bod-̥báṅs* the Tibetan people, opp. to its ruler.

བོད་པ་ *bód-pa* 1. v. *bod.* — 2. = *̥bód-pa.*

བོན་ *bon* (acc. to *Schf.* = **बीज**) 1. n. of the early religion of Tibet, concerning which but very imperfect accounts are existing (v. Report of the Royal Bavarian Acad. of Sc., 13. Jan. 1866); so much is certain, that sorcery was the principal feature of it. When Buddhism became the religion of state, the former was considered heretical and condemnable, and *lha-čos* and *bon-čos*, or shorter *čos* and *bon*, were placed in opposition, as with us christianity and paganism; v. *Glr.* and *Mil.*; at the present time, both of them seem to exist peaceably side by side, and the primitive religion has not only numerous adherents and convents in *C.*, but manifold traces of it may be found still in the creed of the Tibetans of to-day. — 2. = *bón-po*, follower of this religion.

བོར་ *bor*, v. *̥bór-ba.*

བོར་ར་ *bór-ra*, **a sack of corn,** holding about 30 *ḱal W.*

བོལ་ *bol, bol-góṅ* 1. **the upper part of the foot** *Stg.* — 2. **the leg of a boot** *W.* — 3. **clod of earth** *C.* — 4. v. *̥bol.*

བོལ་གར་ *bol-gár* = *búl-ha-ri.*

བོལ་པོ་ *ból-po* v. *̥ból-po.*

བོས་ *bos*, v. *̥bód-pa.*

བྱ་ *bya* 1. sbst. **bird, fowl, hen,** cf. the following articles. (*Pur. biu* [v. *byiu*], *bi*). — 2. vb. fut. root of *byéd-pa*, v. this and the sbst. *byá-ba.* — 3. **ja čó-če* W.*, **to castrate, to geld.**

བྱཱ་ཀ་ར་ཎ་ *byā-ká-ra-ṇa*, **व्याकरण**, prop.: **explanation**, 1. = *luṅ-du-ston-pa* **prophecy**, cf. *Burn.* I, 54 sequ. — 2. in later times: **grammar.**

བྱ་ཀྲི་ *bya-kri Mṅg., bya-tri Lt.*, n. of a medicine.

བྱ་རྐང་ *bya-rkáṅ*, 1. **a bird's foot.** — 2. n. of **a vein** *Med.* — 3. officinal plant, in *Lh.* a blue kind of orobanche.

བྱ་སྐད་ *bya-skád*, also *bya-sgrúṅs, bya-čos* title of a book of satirical fables, in which birds are introduced speaking.

བྱ་སྐོན་ *bya-skón* **fowler's net** *Lex.*

བྱ་སྐྱི་ *bya-skyi Stg.*; *Sch.*: **roof, shelter.**

བྱ་ཁང་ *bya-ḱáṅ Cs.* **bird-cage.**

བྱ་ཁྱུང་, ཁྲ་, ཁྲུང་ *bya-ḱyúṅ, -ḱrá, -ḱrúṅ* = *ḱyuṅ, ḱra* and *ḱruṅ-ḱrúṅ.*

བྱ་གག་ *bya-gág Dzl.* and elsewh., a species of ducks, *Sch.*: **the gray duck.**

བྱ་དགའ་ *bya-dgá* **gift, present,** esp. as a reward; *sbyin-pa* to bestow a gift, frq.; *bya-dgár* as a present, for a reward, *stér-ba* to give.

བྱ་རྒོད་ and རྒྱལ་ *bya-rgód* and *-rgyál* **bird of prey** *B.* and col.; *bya-rgod-spos Med.*, vulgo *la-da-ra* (v. *gla*) *bya-rgod-ṕúṅ-poi ri*, **गृध्रकूट**, vulture-hill, in Magadha, a preaching-place of Buddha.

བྱ་རྒྱ་ *bya-rgyá* **fowler's net.**

བྱ་སྒབ་ *bya-sgáb* n. of one of the smaller lobes of the lungs.

བྱ་སྙེན་ *bya-snyéṅ* v. *bya-rmyéṅ.*

བྱ་ཏྲི་ *bya-trí* v. *bya-krí.*

བྱ་ཐལ་ *bya-t́ál Glr.* light-gray **bird's dung.**

བྱ་འདབ་ *bya-ₒdáb* 1. lit. **a bird's wing.** — 2. a part of the roof or vertical projection of the same, a kind of façade, admitting of pictorial decoration *Glr.*

བྱ་འདྲེ་ *bya-ₒdré Sch.*, a winged diabolical creature, **harpy.**

བྱ་ན་ *bya-na* (acc. to *Liś.* corrupted from व्यञ्जन) **seasoning, condiment, sauce,** in a legend; prob. also in a gen. sense: **meat, food,** *byá-nai yo-byád Lex.*, *byá-na-ma*, prob. id.; *ťsá-ba byá-na-ma žig ǩyér-nas* bringing some warm food *Mil.*

བྱ་ནག་ *bya-nág* **raven,** or some similar bird *S.g.*; *bya-nag-rdó-rje Mil.* id., because the raven is said to reach an age of a thousand years.

བྱ་ནན་ *bya-nán Sch.* (sub. *byá-ra*) **earnest endeavour.**

བྱ་པ་ *byá-pa Cs.* **fowler, bird-catcher.**

བྱ་པོ་ *byá-po* 1. **cock,** the male of the domestic fowl, more definitely: *byá(-po) mtsa-lu B.* and col.; *byá-po dáṅ-po, ɣnyís-pa* etc., the first, the second cock-crow *C.* — 2.**byá-po skyá-po** *W.* **sparrow.** — 3. *bya-po-tsi-tsi Med.*, a medicinal plant, stopping the monthly courses; in *Lh.* the great balsamine, Impatiens Roylei.

བྱ་སྤུ་ *byá-spu*, **down** (feather), *byai spu B.* and col.

བྱ་ཕོ་ *bya-p̔o*, **cock,** the male of any bird.

བྱ་ཕྲུག་ *bya-p̔rug* 1. **a young bird.** — 2. **a young fowl, chicken.**

བྱ་བ་ *byá-ba* 1. inf. and part. fut. of *byéd-pa*, q.v. — 2. sbst. **deed, action, work,** without any reference to time, *ₒjig-rtén-gyi byá-ba* and *čós-kyi byá-ba* secular and religious works, frq.; *mai byá-ba byéd-pa* to act as a mother, to perform a mother's part *Tar.*; *byá-ba zin-pa* an action completely past *Gram.*; *byá-ba maṅ yaṅ ₒbrás-bu čúṅ-ba* much labour and little fruit, much work and little profit *Tar.*; *der rgyál-po daṅ blón-po-rnams-kyi byá-ba byúṅ-ba yin* then the affairs of the kings and their officers, the concerns of the state and its functionaries, gained ground; also in an absolute sense *byá-ba* = **secularity, worldliness,** *byá-ba btáṅ-ba ǰig rgyán-du če* a resigning of worldly things is fraught with great blessing *Mil.*; *bya-byéd* the doing, doings: *bya-byed nyúṅ-ba ǰig rgyán-du če* the doing little brings great blessing, and so in a similar manner: *byá-rgyu byéd-rgyu ma maṅ ǰig* do not give way to a bustling disposition *Mil.*, i.e. do not permit your contemplative state to be interrupted by a distracting activity of your mind; *bstán-pa-la* (or *bstán-pai*) *byá-ba byás-pai lo-rgyús* an account of what has been done for the spread of the doctrine *Tar.*; *byá-ba daṅ ₒbrél-ba* seems to be a grammatical term relating to the verb.

བྱ་བང་ *bya-báṅ* v. *bya-wáṅ*.

བྱ་བལ་ *bya-bál Sch.* **down** (feathers); *Lt.* 121?

བྱ་བྲལ་བ་ *bya-brál-pa* one free from business, one that has renounced all worldly employment, **an ascetic,** *Ld.-Glr.*

བྱ་མ་ *byá-ma* **a female bird, hen, brood-hen.**

བྱ་མ་རྟ་ *byá-ma-rta* **courier, estafet.**

བྱ་མ་བུམ་ *bya-ma-búm* a tea-pot shaped vessel used in sacrificing.

བྱ་མ་བྱར་སྐྱག་ *bya-ma-byar-skyág*(?) **dandelion,** Taraxacum *Ld.*

བྱ་མ་བྱི་ *bya-ma-byí S.g.*; *Sch.* **flying squirrel.**

བྱ་མ་ལེབ་ *bya-ma-léb Sch.* **butterfly,** = *p̔ye-ma-léb.*

བྱ་མོ་ *byá-mo* 1. **the female** of any kind of birds. — 2. **hen, female fowl,** also in conjunction with *mťsá-lu*, cf. *byá-po*(?).

བྱ་རྨྱང་བ་ *bya-rmyáṅ-ba Sch.*, *bya-rmyéṅ* (another reading *snyeṅ*) *byéd-pa*, **to yawn** *Mil.*

བྱ་དམར་ *bya-dmár* **flamingo** *Sch.*

བྱ་ཚང་ *bya-ťsáṅ* **bird's nest.**

བྱ་ཚེ་རིང་ *bya-ťse-riṅ Sch.* **the white crane.**

བྱ་ཚོགས་ *bya-ťsógs* **a flight of birds.**

བྱ་རྫི་ *bya-rdzi* **one attending to poultry.**

བྱ་ཝང་ *bya-wáṅ S.g.; Sch.:* **night-hawk, goat-sucker,** caprimulgus; **bat.**

བྱ་བཞོན་ **bya-bžón* Bal.* **egg.**

བྱ་ཞེ་ *bya-žé* **crest, tuft** (of feathers) of birds *Sch.*

བྱ་འུག་ *bya-ˌúg* prob. **owl**; *Sch.* quail(?).

བྱ་ར་ *byá-ra Cs.*: 'heed, care, caution'. This word belonging to the language of the people and to later literature, is not so much an abstract, as a concrete noun, signifying **a watchman,** superintendent (chiefly by day, cf. *mél-ťse* night-watch); it denotes more particularly that individual of a community, who has to see to it, that the compulsory post-office duties be punctually performed, and that messages from the lord or magistrate of the place be duly dispatched and forwarded to their place of destination; in a more gen. sense *byá-ra b̓yéd-pa Glr.*, **čó-če* W.*, *ɣtoṅ-ba Mil.* c. *la*, **to give heed, to pay attention, to look sharp, not to lose sight of;** also, **to be on one's guard against, to take a thing seriously,** e.g. *nád-la* a disease *Lt.*; **ǰá-ra ˌi-mig** (prop. *yid-mig*) **čo**, pay strict attention! *W.*

བྱ་རོག་ *bya-róg* **crow, raven,** mentioned in S. O. as an inveterate enemy of the *ˌug-pa* (owl).

བྱ་ལས་ *bya-lás,* **labour, work,** *zin-pa-méd-pai bya-lás* endless labours *Mil.*

བྱ་ལོ་པ་ *byá-lo-pa* 1. v. *lo.* — 2. *Sch.* 'keeping poultry'(?).

བྱ་སོ་མ་ *bya-so-ma Ts, Ld.* **bat.**

བྱག(-པ) *byág(-pa)* 1. *Cs.* **pliancy, nimbleness, agility of body;** *byag-mk̓an* rope-dancer *Lex.* — 2. sometimes erron. for *ǰag* and *ǰág-pa.*

བྱང་ *byaṅ* 1. **north;** *byaṅ-p̓yógs* and prob. also *byáṅ-k̓a Mil.* id.; *byáṅ-gi, byaṅ-p̓yógs-kyi* northern; *byaṅ-ṅós* north side, northern brow or slope of a hill; also n. pr., *Glr.; byaṅ-ťáṅ* n. pr. the heaths or steppes in northern Tibet, more esp. those bordering in the west on *Ld.* — 2. **northern country,** coinciding with *byaṅ-ťáṅ: byáṅ-la bčúg-go* he was banished to the north country *Glr.; byáṅ-pa* a man from *Jaṅ-ťáṅ* — 3. the significations of *byaṅ-snyom-pa Sch.* **to tailor, to cut to a proper shape,** and of several other compounds, require a different etymology yet unknown. — 4. for *byáṅ-bu.*

བྱང་རྐྱང་ *byaṅ-rkyáṅ* **trowsers, small-clothes, breeches** *Mil.*

བྱང་ཁོག་ *byaṅ-k̓óg* 1. **the inside of the body,** *byaṅ-k̓og-stód* the upper part of the body, cavity of the chest, *byaṅ-k̓og-smád* lower part of the belly, abdomen, bowels *S.g.*; **ǰaṅ-k̓óg-la zug rag** I feel a pain in my bowels *W.* — 2. **rump;** opp. to *yan-lág* limbs *Lt.*

བྱང་ག་ *byáṅ-ga Lt.?*

བྱང་སྒྲ་མི་སྙན་ *byaṅ-sgra-mi-snyán* the northern continent of the ancient geography of India, v. *gliṅ.*

བྱང་ཆུབ་ *byaṅ-čúb,* **बोधि**, prop. wisdom; with the Buddhists **the highest perfection and holiness,** such as every Buddhist desires to obtain, which however to its full extent only the real Buddha himself possesses, v. *Köpp.* I, 425, 435; *byaṅ-čub-mčóg* id., frq.; *byaṅ-čub-mčóg-tu sems* (or resp. *ťugs*) *skyéd-pa* to create the thought of such holiness, to direct the mind to it *Dzl., Glr.*; *byaṅ-čub ˳dód-pa* to aim at it, to be anxious to obtain it *Dzl.*; *lén-pa* to attain it; *byaṅ-čub-séms* the mind intent on and suited for it, universal charity; *snyiṅ-rǰe-byaṅ-čub-séms-kyis kun blaṅ-nas* submitting to every thing with a loving and charitable mind; *byaṅ-čub-séms-dpa,* **बोधिसत्त्व**, frq. with the addition of *sems-dpa-čen-po* the saint that has attained the highest station next to Buddha, merely for the welfare of men still tarrying in this world, designated Buddha, as it were; *Köp.* I, 422; *byaṅ-čub-séms-ma* fem. of it *Thgr.*; *byaṅ-čub-šiṅ,* **पिप्पल**, the bodhi-tree, holy fig-tree, ficus religiosa (not indica), emblem of mercy; *byaṅ-čub-snyiṅ-po* **बोधिमण्ड**, n. pr. = *rdo-rǰe-ydan.*

བྱང་རྡོ་ *byaṅ-rdo Cs.* **monument,** prop. inscription-stone.

བྱང་པ་ *byáṅ-pa* 1. v. *byaṅ.* — 2. *S.g.? byaṅ-pa-srin Sch.*: an insect.

བྱང་བ་ *byáṅ-ba*, pf. of *ₒbyáṅ-ba* q.v.; *byaṅ-séms* **a pure, holy mind** *Mil.*, prob. = *byaṅ-čub-séms.*

བྱང་བུ་ *byáṅ-bu*, བྱང་མ་ *byáṅ-ma* 1. **inscription, direction, label.** — 2. the **tablet** on which an inscription is written, *záṅs-kyi byáṅ-bu-la* (to write) on a copper plate or tablet *Glr.*; *yig-byáṅ, ḱa-byáṅ*, resp. *žal-byaṅ*, = *byáṅ-bu* 1; *sgo-byáṅ* inscription over a door, *dur-byáṅ* on a sepulchre; *rtags-byáṅ* a mark on a thing *Cs.*; *bJed-byáṅ* list of marked luggage; *miṅ-byáṅ*, resp. *mtsan-byáṅ* list of names *Pth.*; *šog-byáṅ* cards *Sch.*; *byaṅ-rdó* a stone monument.

བྱད་ *byad* I. 1. *Cs.* **proportion, symmetry, beauty,** *dpe-byad Dzl.*, id.; *byád-čan* well-proportioned, fair, beautiful; *byad-méd* the contrary *Cs.* — 2. **face, countenance** *Lex.*; *byad spus ḱéṅs-pa* a hairy face *Glr.*; *byád-kyi bkrags Thgy.*, *mdaṅs Lt.*, brightness, radiancy, beautiful complexion; *byad-bžin* face *Dzl.*, मुख *Lex.*; *byad-γzúgs, Sch.*: stature, prob. more correctly: countenance and body *Dzl.* and elsewh. —

II. (*Cs.* also *byád-ma*) 1. **enemy.** — 2. **a wicked demon,** *byád-ma rmé-ša-čan Wdṅ.* — 3. also *byad-stem(s), S.O.* and elsewh., **imprecation, malediction,** combined with sorcery, the name of an enemy being written on a slip of paper and hid in the ground, under various conjurations; *γžán-gyi byad, ṕá-rol-poi byad-stéms* a malediction practised by another; *byád-du* or *stéms-su Júg-pa*, prob. to curse a person with conjurations.

III. in compounds, *yo-byád, ča-byád* q.v. — IV. frq. for *byed.*

བྱན་ *byan* 1. *Ld.* frq. for *byá-na*, **Jan čo-ḱan, Ján-ma** **cook.** — 2. v. the following.

བྱན་པོ་ *byán-po Cs.* **married man**; *Sch.*: a free man, one divorced from his wife; *byan-mo Cs.* **wife, spouse**; *Sch.*: 1. **a divorced woman.** — 2. **a whore.** Only this latter signification seems to be known among the common people, e.g. **ǎ-pe̥ Ján-mo**, as a vulgar abusive term; *byan-ťsud-pa Sch.* 'to allure, entice, seduce'; these significations are, however, not sufficient to explain: *byán-moi byi-bor* (or *-por*) *raṅ byan ťsud Lex.*, and: *séms-la raṅ byan ťsud Mil.*

བྱབ་པ་ *byáb-pa* 1. **to clean, cleanse, wash, wipe,** *naṅ ťams-čád-la* to clean the whole house *Domaṅ.* — 2. **to take up, to gather with both hands,** e.g. barley *C.*; *byab-zed Sch.* instrument for cleaning, brush; *byabs-ḱrus Sch.* shower-bath.

བྱམས་པ་ *byáms-pa* 1. **kindness, love, affection,** *byáms-sems* id. — 2. **kind, loving, affectionate,** used of the love of parents to their children, of the beneficent to the needy, but not in the contrary order, nor of love to inanimate objects; *byáms-pai tiṅ-ṅe-ₒdzin* the meditation of love, compassion, frq.; *mi kún-la byáms-šiṅ* being kind towards every body; *byáms-pai γnyen* kind, affectionate relations, frq.; *byáms-pa máṅ-na* when I have many well-wishers, patrons *Dom.*; *byáms-pa* as a n. pr., also *byáms-pa mgón-po* **Maitreya,** the Buddha of the future period of the world, who at present is enthroned in the Galdan heaven, and who is frequently represented in pictures, v. *Köpp.*; *byams-bžúgs* sitting like Maitreya, i.e. after European fashion on a chair, with his legs hanging down, opp. to *ťub-bžúgs*, like Sākyathubpa; yet he is by no means uniformly represented in that posture.

བྱར་ *byar*, supine of *byéd-pa*; *byar-méd* 1. prop.: *non faciendum*, **not to be done.** — 2. sbst. **inactivity,** inaction in the specifically Buddhist sense, **apathy, indifference,** *byar-méd-kyi ṅáṅ-la γnás-par gyis Thgr.*

བྱས་པ་ *byás-pa*, pf. of *byéd-pa*; *byás-na 'si feceris', 'sin feceris'*, after a preceding prohibitive *ma byed* also to be rendered by **else;** as sbst. 1. *'factor'*. 2. *'factus'*: *byéd-pa byás-pa* a doer of deeds, as the first grade of holiness; *byás-pa šés-pa, γzó-ba Sch.* to keep in mind a thing done, to requite, to reward; *byas-čos Mil.*, also known in *C.*, seems to be a notion akin to our **conscience,** **Jhe̥-čǒ záṅ-po, ṅém-pa* C.*, **Jhe̥-le̥** id.

བྱི་ byi 1. *Glr.*, *Pth.*, *byi byéd-pa* **to commit adultery** or **rape of females**, *byi-čád* punishment for it. — 2. v. *byi-ba*. — 3. *Pur.* *bi* **bird**, cf. *byiu*.

བྱི་ཏང་(ག) *byi-táṅ(-ga)* **a medicine** *Med.*

བྱི་ཐུར་ *byi-ṫur* or *dur*, 1. n. of an animal, inhabiting caves *S.g.*; *byi-dur-ma Sik.* **porcupine.** — 2. **spine** of a porcupine or a hedgehog *Sch.*

བྱི་དར་ *byi-dár* a kind of silk stuff? *Wdk.*

བྱི་དུར་ *byi-dúr* v. *byi-ṫúr*.

བྱི་དོར་ *byi-dór* **the wiping, cleaning;** *ṗyag-bdár žés-pa byi-dór-gyi las dei miṅ* the word *ṗyag-bdár* denotes the act of cleaning *Lex.*; commonly *byi-dór byéd-pa* e.g. *ɣnás-su* to clean, to sweep a place *Dzl.*; spiritually; to cleanse one's thoughts *Mil.*; *byi-bdár byéd-pa Dzl.* **to dress, trim, decorate one's self, to make one's self smart.**

བྱི་པོ་ *byi-po Sch.* **bosom.** — 2. *W.* **male-cat, tom-cat.**

བྱི་བ་ *byí-ba* I. sbst. *B.* and *C.*; col. *C.* *ǯhi-tsi* *Ld.*, *Pur.* *bi-tse*, *Ld.*, *Lh.* *sa-bi-li(g)*, **rat, mouse,** and various other animals: *byi-ba-rkaṅ-riṅ Sch.* rabbit (?); *dṅúl-byi Sch.* white rabbit. — *byi-dkár Sch.* white hare. — *byi-ḱúṅ* mouse-hole. — *byi-rdo Sch.* rat's-bane, arsenic. — *byi-ldém* mouse-trap. — *byi-nág Sch.* fitchet, polecat. — *byi-ṗrúg* young mouse. — *byi-brún Dzl.* mouse-dung. — *byi-blá* v. sub *byi-la*. — *byi-ṫsáṅ* mouse-nest, mouse-hole. — *byi-ṫsér* medicinal herb *Med.* — *byi-₀dzin Cs.* mouse-trap; *byi-bzúṅ Lt.*, *bi-zúm* *W.*, etymol. id.; but applied to that troublesome plant, **the bur** (burdock), which is stuck into mouse-holes, to fasten in the skin of the mice. — *byi-loṅ* etym. blind-mouse *Sch.* mole. — II. vb.: *byi-ba byéd-pa Cs.*, = *byi byéd-pa* 1. **to mouse; to steal, to pilfer.** 2. **to commit adultery.** — III. pf. of *₀byi-ba* q. v.; *byi-ba spu*, *Sch.*, hair that has fallen off.

བྱི་བོ་ *byi-bo Lex.*; *Sch.* **little child, infant,** = *byis-pa*.

བྱི་བཞིན་ *byi-bžin* n. of one of the lunar mansions, v. *rgyu-skár*.

བྱི་ཟེ་ *byi-zé Cs.* = *tabs*, **manner, way, method.**

བྱི་རུ་ *byi-ru* **coral,** frq., also *byú-ru*; *byi-ru mdog* light red *Glr.*

བྱི་རུག་ *byi-rúg* medicinal plant *Med.*

བྱི་ལ་ *byi-la*, *B.*, *W.* *bi-la, bi-li* (*Hind.* *billā*), **cat;** *byi-lai brun*, cat's dung *Lt.*; *byi-bla Wdk.* id.? In the latter work it is mentioned as the name of a certain monster, whilst *byi-blai rgyal-mṫsán* is an attribute of the gods, resembling a flag with a cat's head at the top.

བྱི་ལམ་ *byi-lám Wdk.*?

བྱི་ཤང་ *byi-šáṅ Wdṅ.*?

བྱིང་བ་ *byíṅ-ba* v. *₀byíṅ-ba*.

བྱིང་བྱིང་ཐུ་ལུ་ *byiṅ-byiṅ-ṫu-lu S.g.* n. of an animal (?).

བྱིངས་པ་ *byíṅs-pa* 1. *Cs.* **general, common.** — 2. *Sch.* **hidden, concealed.** — 3. *Cs.* **root.** The word seems to be a secondary form of *spyi* ano *dbyiṅs*, yet in various passages of medical works none of the above meanings is applicable.

བྱིན་ *byin* 1. **pomp, splendour, magnificence**, e.g. of kings; *byin-čé-bar bžúgs-pa* to be enthroned in great splendour *Dzl.*; *ɣzi-brǰid daṅ byin če Dzl.* *mṫu daṅ byin Dzl.*: *byin-čan* magnificent, splendid, brilliant, *byin-méd* the contrary. — 2. **blessing,** a bestowing of blessings, a power working for good, *byin-báb Lex.*, *-ṗáb Sch.*: conferring blessings (?), *bčom-ldan-₀dás-kyi byin-gyis* by the blessing, the miraculous power of Buddha; yet also applied to devils, v. below: most frq. *byín-gyis rlób-pa*, pf. *brlabs*, fi. *brlab*, imp. *rlobs*, **to bless,** *mi* a person, *sa-ɣzi* a place *Mil.*, also followed by the termin.: *séms-čan-gyi sdug-bsṅál ži-bar byiṅ-gyis rlobs* grant thy blessing, that the misery of beings may be assuaged *Mil.*; *bu mṫun-rkyén ₀dzóm-bar byin-gyis rlobs* bless the son, that all happiness may be accumulated on him *Mil.*; *rgyud ɣnyén-po bzáṅ-bar* **bless my soul, that it may be an efficient help (to these people)** *Mil.*; relative to devils: *log-*

*ˌdrén bdúd-kyis byin-gyis brlabs* heretical teachers sent and fitted out by the devil; so also *Tar.* 46, 13; **to create, to change into** *Mil., Tar.*; hence *byiṅ-rlabs* blessing, *byin-rlabs byéd-pa*, resp. *mdzád-pa* frq., *γtóṅ-ba*, resp. *stsól-ba Cs.*, = *byiṅ-gyis rlób-pa*; *byin-rlabs-čan, byin-rlabs daṅ ldán-pa* blessed, sanctified, highly favoured, men or things *Pth.*; so also *byin-rlabs žúgs-pa Mil.*; *ˌdre-ˌdúl byin-rlabs* blessing pronounced against demons, exorcism of devils *Mil.*; meton.: I am the *ˌṕágs-pai byin-rlabs* of all of you, he who will help you to go to heaven *Glr.*

བྱིན་རྟེན་ *byin-rtén Cs.*, the **relics** of a saint, or the place where they are kept ('depository of blessings'); also in the shape of pills, which liberal donors receive from their Lamas, and which they swallow, particularly in the hour of death.

བྱིན་པ་ *byin-pa* 1. sbst. **calf of the leg**, *byin-pa ná-ba* pain in the calf; *byin-súl Cs.* 'hollow on the inward side of the thigh' (?). — II. pf. of *sbyin-pa*.

བྱིན་པོ་ *byín-po Sch.* **all, the whole; general**; *byin-gyis ṕrá-ba* by degrees, more and more fine etc.?

བྱིན་རླབས་ *byin-rlabs* v. *byin* 2.

བྱིབ་པ་ *byib-pa*, pf. *byibs* 1. **to cover, to wrap up**, *gós-kyis Lt.* — 2. *Cs.* **to hide, conceal, keep secret, hush up.**

བྱིའུ་ *byiu* 1. *Pur.* **biu**, **little bird, bird** *S.g.* — 2. *Sch.* **alpine hare.**

བྱིལ་བ་ *byil-ba* **to stroke**, *mgó-bo-la byil-byil byéd-pa* to stroke a person's head *Pth.*

བྱིལ་མོ་ *byil-mo* **naked** *Sch.*

བྱིས་པ་ *byis-pa* 1. **child**, esp. **little child**; *byis-(pai) nad* disease of children *Med.*; *byis-pa btsá-tabs* obstetric science *Med.*; *byis-stón* v. *ná-zla* sub *na* I, 2; *byis-pai blo Cs.* childishness, want of judgment; *byis-pai skyé-bo* **a plain, ignorant person**, a person not initiated *Thgy.*, *S.O.*; *mo-byis* girl, lass *Mil.*; *byis-pa-zúṅ-žig Cs.*, twins. — 2. **boy, lad,** till about the age of 16 years, frq. (*W.* not in use).

བྱུ་རུ་ *byú-ru* = *byi-ru*.

བྱུག་པ་ *byúg-pa* 1. **unguent, ointment, salve,** whether as colouring-matter, medicine or sweet scent *Dzl.*, *Med.*; *byúg-pa ska* thick ointment, thick plaster; *byúg-pa sla* thin unguent *Cs.* — 2. **foot-bath** *W.*, perh. better: *bčúg-pa*.

བྱུག་རིས་ *byug-ris*, *Lex.* = *gral*, **place**, in a certain succession or row; *byug-ris žog* make room, leave a place empty *Sch.*

བྱུགས་ *byugs* v. *ˌbyúg-pa*; *byugs-spos* **anointing-oil** *Sch.*

བྱུང་ *byuṅ* v. *ˌbyuṅ-ba*; *byúṅ-tsul* **history, story, particulars** of any event, *ṅai byúṅ-tsul dé-ltar γda* that is my story *Mil.*; *byuṅ-rábs Sch.* id.

བྱུར་ *byur B.*, esp. of later times and col., *Ld.* also *byus*, **misfortune, mishap, accident**, *byur čé-žiṅ bu mi γsós-na* if one has the great misfortune not to be able to keep a child alive *Dom.*; *mi-la byur ˌgél-ba* to draw down misfortune on a person *Dom.*; **ṅá-la ǰur čug soṅ* W.*, **ǰhur* C.*, I have had misfortune, I have been unfortunate; *byúr-gyi*, also *byúr-čan* unlucky, disastrous, perilous. — **ǰhur-nág** great calamity *C.* — *byur-sél* preservative against misfortune. — *raṅ-byur-rdó* was explained: a sling-stone with which one hits one's self.

བྱུར་པོ་ *byúr-po*, *Cs.* also *-bu*, vulg. *byur-byúr* **heaped**, a heaped measure of corn or meal; *byúr-por bkaṅ Thgy.*

བྱེ་ *bye* 1. = *byeu* **little bird**, *bye-gliṅ* bird's nest *Ma.*; *bye-ṕrúg* a young little bird *Dzl.*, also *bya-ṕrúg*; *bye-brún* bird-dung *Wdṅ.*; *byeu ˌúr-pa Sch.* **partridge.** — 2. v. *byé-ma*.

བྱེ་མགོ་ *bye-mgó* 1. **bird's head.** — 2. **an officinal mineral** *S.g.*

བྱེ་བ་ *bye-ba* **ten million**, *byé-ba-ṕrag γsum daṅ sá-ya-ṕrag drug* thirty-six million; *byé-ba sa-ya*, eleven million; it seems to be among the larger numbers one of the most popular, as the word million is in English.

བྱེ་བྲག་ *bye-brág*, **विशेष**, 1. **difference, diversity**, *ḱó-bo daṅ saṅs-rgyás ˌye-brág či yod* what difference is there between me and Buddha? *Dzl.*; *bye-brág ˌbyéd-pa* to find, to show a difference, c. genit. in, of, between things; to analyze, to explain; variety, diversity *Was.* (266); *bye-brág bšád-pa* = *vibhāshā Was.* (147), also *bye-brag-bšad-mtšó* or *-ču-γtér*, title of books; *byé-brag-čan Cs.* different, *bye-brag-méd-pa Cs.*, *mi-p̔yéd-pa Dzl.* equal; *bye-brág-tu smrá-ba Thgy.*, *bye-brág-pa*, वैशेषिक, name of a school of philosophers, Atomists *Köpp.* I, 69. — 2. **division, section, class, species,** *dúd-ˌgroi, ról-moi bye-brag* a species of animals, a kind of musical instrument etc. *Lex.*; *yúl-gyi bye-brág* a part of the country, province, *Tar.* 33, 6; *bye-brág-tu* (to go through) according to the separate classes *Zam.*

བྱེ་མ་ *byé-ma* (*C.* **jhé-ma**, *W.* **bé-ma**) 1. **sand,** frq. — 2. **sandy plain, sands,** *γsér-gyi byé-mai dkyíl-na* in the middle of a plain of gold sand *Glr.* — 3. **gravel** (disease) *Schr.* — *byé-ma ˌbru γčig* a grain of sand *Cs.*; *gáṅ-pai klúṅ-gi byé-ma tsam* as much sand as there is on the Ganges; *bye-ma-ká-ra* brown sugar, ground sugar, *Hind.* चीनी, *C.* — *bye-dkár* white sand, *bye-nág* black sand. — *bye-čáb Lt.* sandy water, water standing on sandy ground. — *bye-ljóṅs* a sandy tract *Cs.* — *bye-t̔áṅ* a plain of sand, a sandy desert *Glr.* — *bye-p̔úṅ* heap of sand. — *bye-tsúb* sand raised by a whirlwind. — *bye-ríl* (*Schr. hril*), small sugar-balls, Indian sweet-meat, imported into Tibet, *C.*

བྱེད་པ་ *byéd-pa* I. vb., pf. *byas*, fut. *bya*, imp. *byos*, vulgo *byas* (*Sp., Bal.* **béd-pa**; in *Ld.* and *Lh.* instead of it gen. **čó-če**), resp. *mdzád-pa*, eleg. *bgyíd-pa*, 1. **to make, to fabricate,** with the acc., e.g. a house, an armour etc.; with *las* or *la*, to make out of or of: *γsér-las* out of gold, *šín-la Tar.* 160, 11 of wood; with the acc. and termin. to form to, to work into, *págs-pa šog-šog-tu* to work or manufacture skin into parchment *Dzl.*; with the instrum.: to do with, to make of: *ˌdis či žig bya* what are you going to do with it, to make of it? *Dzl.* **to cause, to effect:** *lhúṅ-ba de ṅas byás-pa yin Mil.* it was I that caused this falling; with the supine, **to take care that:** *byéd-par ˌdod-par byéd-pa* to make him inclined to do it *Dzl.*, *ma šór-bar byos šig Pth.* take care, that he do not escape; *yód-par byéd-pa* **to produce, procure, provide,** *dei γnás-k̔aṅ-la sógs-pa byás-nas* he provided for him a dwelling with appurtenances *Dzl.*; to fit out, equip (a ship) *Glr.*; **to act:** *rgyál-po, draṅ-sróṅ* etc. *byéd-pa* to act a king, a saint, as much as: to rule as a king, to live as a saint *Dzl.*, *blá-ma byéd-pa* to be a priest *C.*; in a gen. sense: **to do:** *byá-ba daṅ bya-ba-ma-yin-pa stón-pa* to teach what men ought to do and what they ought not to do *Thgy.*; **to commit, perform, execute:** *nyés-pa byed-byéd-pa* one that has repeatedly committed himself, *las* or *byá-ba byéd-pa* to perform an action, *las či žig byed* what are you doing, what is your business? *t̔abs yód-de byéd-mk̔an med* there is an expedient, but no one that carries it into effect *Ma*; *mi byar mi rúṅ-bas* as it must be performed, lit. as it cannot remain undone *Dzl.*; *bsám-pa ltar myúr-du byás-na* if an intention is speedily executed, performed; *las byéd-pa* **to work, to be efficient** (of a medicine); **to act, proceed, pretend, affect:** *či ltar byás-na legs* how proceeding is good? i.e. which is the best way to proceed, how shall I manage best? *Glr.*; *bsám-γtan-la yód-pai lugs byas* he pretended, affected to meditate *Glr.*; *dei lúgs-su byao* I will act as he does, I will do like that man *Glr.*; *gá-le byéd-pa Mil.* to proceed slowly, to be slow; **to take, to assume, to count:** *žag bži-pa dáṅ-por byás-na* if the fourth day be taken for (counted as) the first *Wdn.*; *byéd-pa* with the termin. of the inf. is frequently used periphrastically or to give force to other verbs; such forms are: *γsód-par byéd-pa* to kill, *p̔a-más šés-par byos* (or *gyis*) *šig*, resp. *yab-yum-gyis mk̔yen-par mdzod čig* dear parents, you must know! *Dzl.*; on the other hand: *p̔á-la rig-par gyis šig* let your father know about it *Tar.* 37, 7; in such cases the proper sense is merely to be gathered from the context. Besides the simple fut.: *ˌdúg-par byao* I shall remain *Tar.*, *k̔ó-mo grogs byá-*

*yis* as I shall be with you *Glr.*; — the form *byao* frq. serves to express necessity: *btsál-bar bya* I must seek *Dzl.*; esp. with a negation: *brjód-par mi byao* they are by no means to be pronounced; the participles in the short forms of *γtoṅ-byéd* and *γtoṅ-byá* differ, in as much as the former is used in an active sense, e.g. one giving, a giver, the latter in a passive sense, one to be given; they may be formed of any verb. For specific combinations, in which *byéd-pa* is differently to be translated, as *dpe byéd-pa*, *yid-la byéd-pa* etc., refer to these words. — 2. **to say, to call**, yet chiefly only in the pf. tense: *žes byás-pa Dzl.* thus said, so called; *sṅar byás-pa bžin* according to what has been said before *Dzl.*; *byas-kyaṅ* though saying *Pth.* — and in the fut., which in that case, however, frq. stands for the present: *(žes) byá-bai sgra byúṅ-no* a voice thus speaking was heard *Glr.*; *dé-la dbyaṅs šes byao* these are called vowels *Gram.*; *(žes-) byás-pa*, or more frq. *byá-ba*, the so called, being often joined to a name, that is mentioned for the first time, e.g. Anu, the so called, whilst we should say, a man, called Anu, or of the name of A.; *byá-ba* also implies: of the purport, to the effect, just as *čés-pa* is also used: *'tsol-žig' byá-bai luṅ byúṅ-nas* an order being given to make a search *Glr.* — 3. **to go away, to disappear**: *byas soṅ* he disappeared *Glr.* —

II. sbst. 1. *byéd-pa* and *byéd-mk̔an*, the person that does or has done a thing, **the doer, performer** etc.; **author**, *bstan-bčós byéd-mk̔an* the author of the work *Tar.* — 2. *byéd-pa* **the instrumentative case** *Gram.* — 3. *byéd-pa* **the doing, dealings**, with noun in the instrum. case: *dé-ₒdra-ba mi-rigs-pa rgyál-pos byéd-pa* such wrong being done by the king, such unjust dealings of the king *Dzl.*; in the genit. case: *bló-yi byéd-pa dbyíṅs-su sbos* hide the working of your understanding in the heavens, i.e. let it disappear in nothingness; **effect**, also with the noun in the genit. case, *Wdṅ.* — 4. *byéd (-pa)-po*, **doer, accomplisher** etc., *mčód-sbyin byéd-pa-por bos* he invited him as sacrificing priest *Tar.*; *ₒdúl-bar byéd-pa-po* converter *Tar.*; *bkra-šís spél-bai byéd-po* augmenter of eternal happiness (from a hymn); *byéd-pa-po* **instrumentative case** *Gram.*; as the twelve *byéd-pa-poi skye-mčéd* I here cite the following from *Wdk.*, without being able to offer an explanation: *bdag, séms-čan, srog, ₒgró-ba, γsó-ba, skyés-bu, gaṅ-zág, šéd-čan, šed-bdág, byéd-pa-po, ts̔ór-ba-po, šés-pa-po, mt̔óṅ-ba-po*, where, by the by, it is to be observed, that thirteen are here enumerated, *byed-pa-po* being mentioned again with the rest (a want of accuracy, which is not unfrequently to be met with in the scientific works of the Tibetans). — 5. *byá-ba* q. v.

བྱེའུ་ *byeu* (also *byiu* q.v.) **little bird**; *byeu-zúl byéd-pa* v. *zul*; *byeu-la-p̔ug S.g.*, a medicinal herb *Cs.*

བྱེར་བ་ *byér-ba* v. *ₒbyér-ba.*

བྱེས་ *byes*, *Lexx.* and col.; **foreign country; abroad**, *byes t̔ag-riṅ-ba* a far distant country *Cs.*; *byés-su ₒgró-ba* to go abroad, to travel; *byés-su ₒdég-pa* to remove, to emigrate *Lex.*; *byés-nas sléb-pa* to come from abroad *Lex.*; *byés-pa* traveller, foreigner, stranger; **lam-róg bés-pa yód-pa yin-te** *W.* proceeding together as fellow-travellers.

བྱོ་བ་ *byó-ba Cs. rná-ba byó-ba* **to hear, hearken, listen.**

བྱོན་པ་ *byón-pa* v. *ₒbyón-pa.*

བྱོལ་བ་ *byól-ba* v. *ₒbyól-ba.*

བྱོལ་སོང་ *byol-sóṅ* **animal**, esp. **quadruped**; *byol-sóṅ-bas glén-pa* more stupid than a brute *Mil.*; *byol-sóṅ rgyál-po* the lion *Mil.*

བྲ་ཀ་ *brá-ka* v. *t̔á-ka.*

བྲ་ཉེ་ *bra-nyé*, n. of a lunar mansion, v. *rgyu-skár* ?.

བྲ་བ་ *brá-ba*, 1. sbst., n. of a small **rodent**, living under ground (not mole *Cs.*, but rather **suslik, earless marmot** *Sch.*); *brá-p̔u-se Ld.* a similar animal (= *pra-li?*); *bra-mk̔ár, bra-tsáṅ Cs.*, burrow of it; *bra-brúṅ*

*Lex.*, *bra-ril Cs.*, dung of it; *bra-lpágs* skin of it. — 2. vb. **to have** or **to be in great plenty, to abound** (?), *rán-gis za ma bra, btuṅ ma bra, gon ma bra* she allowed herself no abundance of food, drink, or clothing; **za-, tuṅ-, čin-, lab-, zér-ḍha-te** eating, drinking plentifully, walking, speaking, talking a great deal *C.*; **ťsa-, ḍho-, ḍháṅ-ḍha-te** being very hot, warm, cold *C.*

བྲ་བོ *brá-bo* (prov. **brau**, *Pur.* **bro**) **buckwheat**; *bra-pýé Lex.*, *rjen Sch.* buckwheat flour; *bra-sóg* buck-wheat straw, serving as a poor sort of fodder during winter.

བྲག *brag* **rock**, *brag rtse-γsúm-pa* a three-pointed rock; *brag-skéd* the middle height of a rock, opp. to *brag-mjug* and *rtse* its foot and top *Cs.* — *brag-spós* prob. an aromatic herb, used for incense *Lt.* — *brag-skíbs* beetling rock. — *brag-rgyál* a prominent, high and precipitous rock, towering rock. — *brág-ča, -ča* echo; also fig. for something unsubstantial, shadowy, not existing *Mil.* — *brag-mjúg* foot of a rock *Cs.* — *brag-pug* rock-cavern. — *brag-pye* dust produced by hewing stones *Glr.* — **ḍhag-bhóṅ** = *pa-bóṅ C.* — *brag-dmár* name of a rock in or near Lhasa, alledged not to be identic with *dmar-po-rí* (*Sch.*). — **ḍag-tsél-wa, ḍag-šig-pa** mite, tick *W.* — *brag-rtsáṅ* rock-lizard. — *brag-rtsé* top of a rock. — *brag-žún* mineral pitch, bitumen, is said to cure fevers and even fractures. — *brag-rí* rocky hill. — *brag-rúd* fall of a rock. — *brag-róṅ* chasm in a rock, ravine. — *brag-šig* v. *brag-rtsél-ba.*

བྲང *braṅ* 1. resp. *sku-bráṅ* **chest, breast,** (cf. *nú-ma*); *braṅ rdúṅ-ba* to beat one's breast *Glr.*; **ṭú-gu ḍáṅ-la čir-te ǩyér-če* W.* to carry a child pressed against one's breast. — *braṅ-kyéd* (?) *Cs.* a high, prominent chest. — *braṅ-dkyil* middle of the breast, cardiac region. — *braṅ-lkóg Mil.* prob. = *lkóg-ma.* — *braṅ-skás Sch.* the dorsal vertebrae opposite to the chest. — **ḍaṅ-kúd** **string** of the *braṅ-ǩún* (*-guṅ, -ǩoṅ, -goṅ*), **pellet-bow,** a bow furnished with two strings, to shoot pellets or small stones, *braṅ-rdi* or *-rdeu*, with it *W.* — **ḍhan-ǩóg* C.* cardiac-region, pit of the stomach. — *braṅ-sgró* snake, serpent (like *lto-ₒgró*). — *braṅ-búr* the middle convex part of the *rdó-rje Ma.* — *braṅ-ťsig Lh.*, prob. heart-burning. — *braṅ-(γ)žól Cs.* dew-lap. — *braṅ-ze Mil.* prob. breast-bone, sternum. — *braṅ-γyúṅ Sch.* tame, gentle. — *braṅ-rus Med.* breast-bone. — **ḍaṅ-lág* W.* the hands crossed on the breast. — *braṅ-so Glr.* breast, brisket of a butchered animal. — 2. also *ₒbraṅ*, gen. *ₒbráṅ-sa*, eleg. *mčis-bráṅ* (q.v.), resp. *γzim-bráṅ*, *bžugs-bráṅ* **night-quarters, halting-place,** whether under a roof or in the open air; also as much as **stage** (of a journey); *bráṅ-sa ₒdébs-pa Tar.*, prob. also **bór-če* W.*, to take up night-quarters; **dwelling,** particularly a temporary one, **lodgings**; but also a permanent **abode,** esp. in *W.*; **ḍáṅ-sa táṅ-če, yár-ce** to take in, to lodge a person over night *W.* (cf. *γnas* 2). — *bráṅ-ǩaṅ*, dwelling-house, dwelling-room *Pth.* — *braṅ-grógs* house-mate, bed-fellow. — *braṅ-dpón* master of the house, landlord. — *po-bráṅ* v. *po*; *bla-bráṅ* v. *bla.*

བྲང་ངེ *braṅ-ṅé Lex.* = *kraṅ-ṅé.*

བྲང་པ *bráṅ-pa* v. *ₒbráṅ-pa.*

བྲན *bran* 1. **slave, servant,** *mi-bráṅ* 'vir servus' *S.g.*; *bran byéd-pa* to be a servant, to serve *Cs.*; *brán-du ₒgyúr-ba* to become a servant *Cs.*; *brán-du ₒǩól-ba* to make another be a servant, to use him as a servant *B.*; *brán-du skúl-ba* to engage a person as a servant, to get him to work for one's self *Glr.*; *brán-du ǩas-bláṅs-so Pth.* they promised to serve him; *lus ṅag yid γsum brán-du púl-te* devoting heart, mouth, and body to his service *Pth.*; *naṅ nub lto-gós-kyis brán-du ǩol* morning and night I am a slave to food and clothing *Mil.*; **subject,** one owing allegiance, **la-dágs-si gyál-po-la ḍán-yul-ťso** a village subject to, belonging to, the king of Ladak *W.*; *brán-po* servant, slave *Tar.*; *brán-mo* maid-servant, female slave; *bran-ǩól, bran-γyóg* = *bran*; also collectively, servants, domestics, household. — 2. **texture,** in the compound *ťags-brán byéd-pa* to weave *Mil.*; *nye-brán Mil.* seems to be some decoration of the shoes; *sṅo-brán Mil.* something similar. — *ču-brán Glr.*, and *mťso-brán*??

བྲན་པ་ *bran-pa* **to pour out** *Tar.*

བྲན་མོ་ *brán-mo* 1. v. *bran* 1. extr. — 2. also = **ḍan-tsós** *W.* **finger, toe.**

བྲབ་པ་ *bráb-pa* v. *ₒbráb-pa.*

བྲམ་ཟེ་ *brám-ze*, from ब्रह्मन् 1. **Brahmin,** Hindoo priest; *brám-ze-mo* female Brahmin; *brám-ze rig-byéd ₒdón-pai sgra* the voice of a Brahmin reciting the Vedas, being taken as a sign of good luck; *brám-ze-pa* an adherent of Brahma. — 2. **a priest** in general *S.O.* (Acc. to *Fouc.* transl. of *Gyatch.* 13 and 52 also = *brāhmaṇa*, the theological part of the Vedas; this is however against the tenor of the Tibetan text, which requires the word to be taken in the former sense.)

བྲལ་ *bral* v. *ₒbrál-ba.*

བྲི་ *bri* v. *ₒbri-ba.*

བྲིད་པ་ *brid-pa* 1. *Sch.* '**to continue, to reiterate, to repeat continually;** *brid-la γtón-ba* to give again and again'. — 2. v. *ₒbrid-pa.*

བྲིད་བྲིད་པ་ *brid-brid-pa Sch.* **to float,** to move confusedly, before one's eyes.

བྲིད་རྩ་ *brid-rtsa Lt.*?

བྲིམ(ས)་ *brim(s)* v. *ₒbrim-pa.*

བྲིས་ *bris* v. *ₒbri-ba*; *bris-sku, sku-bris* **picture of a saint,** drawn or painted *Cs.* — *bris-ₒbúr* the art of painting and carving images. — *bris-ma* written book. — *nag-bris* a drawing *Cs.*; *ťson-bris* a coloured picture.

བྲུ་བ་ *brú-ba* v. *ₒbrú-ba.*

བྲུ་བ་ཚ་ *bru-ba-tsá Lex.* **hunger.**

བྲུ་ཞ་ or བྲུ་ཤ་ *bru-žá* or *bru-šá Wdk.*, prob. = *gru-žá* and *gru-šá Pth.*, *ₒbru-šál* or *ₒbru-šál Ld.-Glr. Schl.* 19, b. 21, **a.** name of a country to the west of Tibet, bordering on Persia.

བྲུག་པ་ *brúg-pa* **to flow, to stream, to gush** *Cs.*; sbst. **current, flow, flux** *Cs.*; *ču brúg-pa* flowing-water *Lex.*

བྲུན་ *brun* **dirt, dung, excrements,** *mi-brúṅ, bya-brún, sbraṅ-brún* etc. feces of men, birds, flies etc. *Med.* and elsewh.

བྲུབ་པ་, བྲུབས་པ་ *brúb-pa, brúbs-pa* v. *ₒbrub-pa.*

བྲུལ་ *brul* **small particles, fritters, bits, crumbs,** *bag-brul C.* crumbs of bread; *brúl-ba Mil., C.* **to fall,** into an abyss *Thg.*; to fall off, fall out, fall down, of leaves, seeds etc.; *brúl-bu, brúl-lu* = *brul W.*

བྲུས་ *brus* v. *ₒbrú-ba.*

བྲེ་ *bre*, **ḍe**, *Sskr.* द्रोण, 1. **a measure for** dry things as well fluids, about 4 pints; acc. to *Cs.* $\frac{1}{20}$ of a *ₒbo*; *bré-bo če, breu čúṅ* large and small *bre, Cs.*; *γsér-p̔ye bre gaṅ Glr.* one (small) measure of gold-dust; *bre-do* two measures; *bré-la γšoṅ* that will just fill a *bre Zam.*; *bres bšar-ba* to measure with a *bre Lex.*; *lha-ḱaṅ bre-ťsad tsam žig* a miniature temple, not larger than a *bre Glr.*; vulgo also that part of the *Chod-rten*, which has the shape of a corn-measure; in a general sense, **measure,** *bre-sráṅ γtáṅ-la ₒbébs-pa Glr.* to regulate measures and weights. — 2. **bre* Ld. Lh.* **bre-sé* Kun.* Eremurus spectabilis, a plant of about a man's height, belonging to the asphodels. — 3. v. *bré-ba..*

བྲེ་ཀོ་ *bré-ko* **basin for washing** *C.*

བྲེ་ག་ *bré-ga* **medicinal herb**; *bré-gu*, id.(perh. the same plant) *Med.*

བྲེ་བ་ *bré-ba* v. *ₒbre-ba*; *bla-bré, ka-bré Sch.* **capital, chapiter, upper part of a column** or pillar.

བྲེ་མོ་ *bré-mo Sch.* **unfit, useless, worthless;** *bré-moi γtam Thgy.*

བྲེགས་པ་ *brégs-pa* v. *ₒbrég-pa.*

བྲེང་བ་ *bréṅ-ba* v. *ₒbréṅ-ba.*

བྲེད་པ་ *bréd-pa* **to be frightened, afraid, in fear** = *rtáb-pa*, *B.* and *C.*; *sbrúl-gyis dṅaṅs-šiṅ bréd-pa* to be frightened by a snake *Wdṅ.*, or *bréd-čin dṅáṅs-pa Pth.*;

*bdúd-kyis bréd-na* if you are afraid of the devil *Glr.*; *bred-ₒtoms Lex.*; **ḍhé-po** fearful, frightful, terrible *C.*

བྲེལ་བ་ *brél-ba* I. vb. (not the same as *ₒbrél-ba*) 1. **to be employed, busy, engaged, to have business** or **work on hand,** *ṅed mḱar-las-kyis brel-nas loṅ mi ₒdug* being engaged in building, we have no time to spare *Mil.*; *ₒdod ḱó-nas brél-na* if one is entirely taken up with lust and pleasure; **dhe-riṅ ṅá-la ḍhél-wa yọ', saṅ-nyin śog** to-day I have a great deal to do, come to-morrow *C.*; *brél-bas* on account of much business *Dzl.* — 2. synon. with *ṕóṅs-pa* **to be poor, to be without, wanting, destitute of,** c. instrum.: *loṅs-spyod-kyis brél-ba Dzl.* ༡༢༩, 7; more frq. with a negative: *ċis kyaṅ mi brél-bar byás-so* they did not let him want anything *Dzl.* ༡༢༠, 17, *Sch.*; *ₒtsó-bai yo-byád-kyis mi brél-bar* abounding in every necessary of life *Dzl.* ༡༥༥, 3 (acc. to a better reading); combined with another word: *ṕóṅs-brel-te*; *brel-ṕoṅ-méd-ċiṅ Dzl.*, *mi brel-bar* not sparingly, scantily, niggardly, e.g. to bestow *Dzl.* frq. — II. sbst. 1. *C.* and *B.*, a being engaged in **a multiplicity of business** v. I, 1. — 2. *W.*: **business, affair, concern,** **ṅá-la ḍél-wa żig yod** I have some particular business, concern, suit; **ḍél-wa ċi yod** what do you want, what are you about, what are you doing there?

བྲེས་ *bres* 1., *W.* also *brés-kyu* **manger;** *rta-brés* manger for horses. — 2. v. *bre.* — 3. v. *ₒbré-ba.*

བྲོ་ *bro* 1. **oath,** *bro-tsál-ba* to take an oath (?) *Pth.*, *bro ₒbór-ba* id., *dbu-bsnyuṅ daṅ bro bór-ro Glr.* they swore by their heads, nif. — 2. **dance,** *bro skráb-pa Lex.*, *ḱráb-pa Mil.*, *brdúṅ-ba Glr.*, resp. *żabs-bró mdzád-pa Mil.* to dance, leap, gambol, as a manifestation of gladness and mirth, whilst *gar byéd-pa* is a regular kind of dancing, with gentle and waving motions of the body; *rṅa-bró* drums and dancing *Glr.*; *bró-mḱan Cs.* dancer. — 3. *Pur. bro* v. *brá-bo.* — 4. v. *bró-ba.* — 5. *bro-nád Lex.*, *Mil.* and elsewh.; *Sch.* 'an epidemic disease'; *bro-ₒtsál Sch.* '**cold** (in the head), **cough, catarrh;**' *Tar.*: *ṕágs-pa lo maṅ-por sku-bro ₒtsal-te*; *Mil.*: *śin-tu bro-ₒtsál-bar gyúr-nas.*

བྲོ་བ་ *bró-ba*, I. vb. 1. **to taste, to smell,** vb. a. & n.; *γnyid kyaṅ mi bró-bas*, not even enjoying (tasting) sleep *Dzl.*; *ḱá-ro skyá-ba bro* one has an astringent taste in the mouth *Med.*; *spos bro-o* it smells of incense *Dzl.*; *dri-γsúṅ żím-pa bro-o* it has a pleasant smell *Dzl.* — 2. *C.* **to desire, to wish,** = *ₒdód-pa*, *bló-bro-ba* id.; *ṅu bró-ste* being about to weep *Mil.* — II. sbst. **taste, savour, flavour,** col. *bro-blág* (**ḍob-lág**), *lán-tsa ḱa-zás kún-gyi bró-ba skyed* salt imparts flavour to any kind of food *S.g.*; *bro ltá-ba* or *myoṅ-ba*, col. **ḍob-lag nyaṅ-ċe** *W.* to taste, to savour; to try the taste; *bró-ba-ċan Cs.*, **ḍób-lag-ċan** *W.* savoury, pleasing to the organs of taste, exciting the appetite; *bro-(ba-)med* tasteless, insipid *Cs.*

བྲོ་མ་ *bró-ma* v. *gró-ma.*

བྲོག་ཞུ་ *bróg-żu* v. *próg-żu.*

བྲོད་ *brod*, = *bró-ba*, **taste** (*żím-po*) **ḍhọ'-ċẹn** *C.*, **ḍód-ċan** *W.*, well-tasted, savoury; **ḍhọ' ċém-po** *C.* of a strong, powerful taste.

བྲོད་པ་ *bród-pa* **joy, joyfulness,** *bród-pa skyéd-pa Mil.*; *dga-bród* id. *C.*; *ċi-bród* readiness to die *Mil.* — Here may be quoted also *drod* 2 and 3.

བྲོབ་, བྲོལ་ *brob, brol* v. *ₒbráb-pa, ₒbrál-ba.*

བྲོས་ *bros* 1. v. *bro* 5; *bros-tebs Sch.* — 2. v. *ₒbros-pa.*

བླ་ *bla* I. the space **over, above** a thing, chiefly occurring in compounds; *blá-na* above *Lex.*; *bla-na-méd-pa*, अनुत्तर, having nothing higher over it, the upper-most, the very highest, e.g. *byaṅ-ċúb*, *śes-ráb* and the like frq; *bla-na-méd-pai lam*, *bla-med-rdo-rjei tég-pa*, = *sṅágs-kyi lam*, the mystical method, v. *mdo* 3; *sá-bla*, above the earth, above ground, opp. to *sa-stéṅ*, *sa-ₒóg* upon and under the earth. Generally fig.: **superior, better, preferable,** *baṅ-mdzód stoṅ yaṅ blao* then even an empty treasury is preferable *Dzl.*; commonly with the pf. root of a vb.:

*ťse ₒṕos kyaṅ blao Dzl.* then I will rather die; less frq. with *na*: *ši-na yaṅ blai* since even death is to be preferred *Dzl.*; frq. it may be rendered by 'may', *rgyál-bar gyur kyaṅ blao* then may rather . . . gain the victory (than that I should . . .) *Dzl.*; also pleon.: *kyod mig-gis mi mťoṅ yaṅ blai* be it that you do not see it (it is of no consequence whether you see or not) *Dzl.* ༢༡༠, 7. In the passage *Tar.* 123, 8 *bla* seems to stand as an adv. for 'very', *Schf.* —

**Comp.** *bla-gáb, bla-gós* (*W.* vulgo **tsá-dar, tsá-sar**) = *γzán-gos*, upper garment, cloth, serving Indians, and occasionally also Tibetans as a covering, = toga, ἱμάτιον; *bla-gáb ṕrág-pa γčig-tu γzár-ba* to throw the toga over one shoulder, frq.; *bla-gab-méd-pa*, 1. without upper garment *Dzl.* 2. having no wish, no desire, free from passion(?) — *bla-bré*, also *bla-re*, canopy, dais *Dzl.* and elsewh. — *blá-ma* उत्तर 1. **the higher, upper, superior**; *blá-mar byéd-pa* to esteem highly, to honour, syn. to *bkúr-sti byéd-pa Domaṅ, Tar.*; the exact grammatical explanation of *mii blá-mai čós-kyi čo-ₒṕrúl Dzl.* ༤༨, or of the similar passage *mii čos blá-mai rdzu-ₒṕrúl Burn.* I, 164, offers some difficulties, although it is evident, that *Burn.* has hit the sense better than *Sch.* Of later date is the signification: 2. **the superior**, i.e. spiritual teacher, father confessor, गुरु, with the genit. of the person *Pth.*; in a more gen. sense: **ecclesiastic, priest, 'Lama'** *Thgr., Pth.*; in East. Tib. a title designing a high eccles. degree, something like 'D.D.' v. Desg. 247, 371; *bla-mčód* for *blá-ma daṅ mčod-γnás* ecclesiastic and sacrificing priest, whether it be one and the same person, or two different individuals *Pth., Mil.*; *bla-(ma-) čén (-po)* **chief Lama, Grand-Lama.** — *bla-bráṅ* resp. for dwelling-room or house of a Lama or Lamas, whilst *γzim-ḱáṅ, ṕo-bráṅ* are the resp. expressions for secular dignitaries. — *bla-slób, blá-ma daṅ slób-ma*, the Lama and his disciple *Sch.* — *smán-gyi-bla* v. *sman.* —

II. *Sch.* **'soul, life'**; acc. to oral explanations: 1. **strength, power, vitality,** e.g. in food, scents etc., just like *bčud.* — 2. **blessing, power of blessings,** like *γyaṅ*, e.g. **ṭim-mé mi-la la čém-po mi dug = yaṅ mi čag* C.*, no blessing attends a contemner of the law. — 3. an object with which a person's life is ominously connected; thus very commonly *bla-šiṅ* a tree of fate (gen. a juniper or in *W.* a willow-tree, *ral-lcáṅ*), planted at a child's birth; *rgyál-poi bla-gyú* the king's turkois of life *Glr.*; *bla-dár* a little flag on the house-top, on which benedictions are written; *bla γnás* the omen is lasting, propitious, *nyams* it is vanishing, foreboding danger; so prob. also *Dzl.* ༢༠, 17, where it is not at once equivalent to 'soul' (*Sch.*). —

III. frq. incorr. for *sla.* — IV. in some combinations it has a signification not yet accounted for, e.g. *bla rdól-ba Sch.* to find fault with, to blame, abuse, without a reason; *bla-ťse*(?) *Lex.*

བླ་གབ་, བླ་གོས་ *bla-gáb, gos* v. *bla* I.

བླ་ཆེན་, མཆོད་ *bla-čén, -mčód* v. *blá-ma* sub *bla* I.

བླ་གཉན་ *bla-γnyán Med.*?

བླ་ཐབས་ *bla-ťabs Lex.*

བླ་དགས་ *bla-dágs Gram.*; *Sch.*: 'a primitive word, an abstract noun'.(?)

བླ་ན་ *blá-na* v. *bla* I.

བླ་བོར་ *blá-bor Sch.*: 'well! that may be! so much the better!'

བླ་བྲང་ *bla-bráṅ* v. *blá-ma* sub *bla* I.

བླ་འཚོ་, གླ་འཚོ་ *bla-ťsó, gla-ťso Sch.*: **hereditary portion, inheritance.**

བླ་གཡུ་ *bla-γyú*, བླ་ཤིང་ *bla-šiṅ* v. *bla* II.

བླ་རེ་ *bla-ré* v. *bla-bré* sub *bla* I.

བླག་ *blag* 1. sub *bde-bláγ* q. v. — 2. sub *btso-blag* q. v.

བླག་པ་ *blág-pa* 1. pf. *blags*, *rná-ba blág-pa = rná-ba γtád-pa Lex.*: **to incline one's ear to, to lend one's ear, to listen to** (*blág-pa* not by itself 'to hear' *Cs.*). —

2. *mči-ma blág-pa* **to shed tears.** — 3. in *blág-pa méd-pa*, the free translation of आभ्यवकाशिक, *Burn.* 1, 309 takes it in the signification given by *Sch.* to *bdé-blág*, and explains it by 'bare of every convenience or comfort'.

བླང་བ་ *bláṅ-ba* v. *lén-pa.*

བླད་པ་ *blád-pa* **to chew,** secondary form to *ldád-pa Lex.*

བླན་པ་ *blán-pa* = *glán-pa Cs.*

བླར་ *blar,* frq. incorr. for *slar.*

བླུ་བ་ *blú-ba,* pf. *blus,* **to buy off, to ransom, to redeem,** *mi de blú-ru γtóṅ-ba* to pay in order to redeem a man, to pay as a ransom for him *Glr.; ṗug-ron-gyi srog blus* he redeemed the life of the dove *Dzl.*; *˳dí-dag-gis rgyal-poi mgo blu-o* therewith I will redeem the king's head *Dzl.*; to recover, to redeem, *γté-ba,* a pawn, pledge, security *C.*; *blu-rin* the money or price paid for the redeeming of persons or goods, ransom.

བླུག་པ་ *blúg-pa* v. *ldúg-pa.*

བླུགས་སྐུ་ *blúgs-sku* **molten image;** *blúgs-pár* casting-mould; *blúgs-ma* **cast metal, statues, relievos** (cf. *˳búr-ba*); *blugs-γzár, dgáṅ-blugs* v. *γzar*; *ǰá-blugs* urn-shaped vessel for pouring out tea etc.; *spyi-blugs* v. *spyi-bo* sub *spyi*; *már-blugs* oil-pitcher.

བླུད་པ་ *blúd-pa* 1. vb. *ldud-pa.* — 2. sbst. to *blú-ba,* **release, ransom, redemption** *Sch.* — *blúd-bu* v. *rlúd-bu.*

བླུན་པ་ *blún-pa* **dull, stupid; stupidity, foolishness;** *blún-po* **stupid, foolish; fool, idiot;** *blún-po la-lá . . . ˳dzin* some fools consider it . . .; *blúṅ-poi lugs* foolery, fool's opinion, fool's wisdom, expressions frq. used in scientific works to defeat antagonistic views; *dgé-ba mi byéd-pai mi ni blún-po yin* the man without virtue is a fool; *˳dod-yón-la čags šin-tu blun* to be given to lust is folly *Pth.*; *byol-soṅ-ṗyúgs-pas blun* more stupid than a beast *Mil.; blún-γtam, blún-tsig* foolish talk, foolery; *blún-dad* superstition *Mil.* (cf. *dṅos-dad*).

བླུས་ *blus* v. *blú-ba; blús-ma* **ransom** *Cs.*

བློ་ *blo* I. rarely *bló-ba* **mind** (*Was.* 314 बोधि) 1. the intellectual power in man, **understanding,** *mḱás-pai blo daṅ ldán-pa Dzl.*, *blo rno-ba Glr.* talented, gifted; *blo čén-po* (*čúṅ-ṅu*) of great (small) mental abilities *C.*; *blo γsál-te* of a clear understanding, sharp-witted *Dzl.*; *šes-pai blo* sagacity, intelligence, judgment *Dzl.*; *blo-rgyá Sch.* comprehensive intellectual power; *blo myur-žiṅ* being of quick comprehension, sharp *Dzl.*; *blo-ráb, -˳briṅ, -dmán-pa* of sound, moderate, weak intellects or mental faculties *Mṅg.*, the last expression is frq. used in modestly speaking of one's self *Glr.* and elsewh.; *bló-yi mún-pa* intellectual darkness, a darkened mind *Glr.*; *blo-bág* narrow-minded, weak in intellect *Sch.; ḱyod ni blo nór-ro* you are mistaken; *blos-lčógs-pa* 'to be competent in mind or judgment' *Sch.*; *bló-na-˳bab* 'I understand' *Sch.* (?) — 2. **mind, thought, memory,** *čos daṅ yi-ge-la blo ǰúg-pa* to direct one's thoughts to religion and to learning to read *Glr.*; *bló-la sbyór-ba* to impresss on the mind, to inculcate *Glr.*; *bló-la bžúgs-pa* what is retained by, treasured up in the memory *Tar.*; *bló-la bzúṅ-ba* to learn by heart *Glr.*, *W.*: **loa* or *ló-na zúm-če**; *blo-ťag-čód* v. sub *ťág-pa* I. — 3. **mind, sentiment, disposition** (here in part = *yid*), *bló-la ˳dód-pa* to desire; *blo ˳dún-pa* interest, concern, v. *˳dún-pa; mčód-pa byéd-pai bló-čan de* he that has a mind, is disposed, to sacrifice *Dzl.*; *raṅ bdé-bar ˳dód-pai blo méd-par* without any regard to his own welfare *Thgy.*; *blo nyé-ba* friendly sentiment; also: kindly disposed *Glr.*; *sdáṅ-bai blo* a hating mind, malevolent disposition *Lt.*; *blo gró-ba Sch.*: 'to get soft, moved, touched, sad', acc. to a native authority: to be agreeably affected by; *blo mťún-pa* to be of the same mind, like-minded, with supine also: to agree *Glr.*; perh. also: to be unanimous, peaceable, on friendly terms *Sch.*; *ḱyéd-kyi blo daṅ mťún-pa* agreeably to your wish *Mil.*; *blor ma šoṅ Sch.* 'the mind could not take it in' *Tar.* 51, 7, *Schf.*: 'it did not please me, I could not reconcile myself to it'; **blo skyél-ba** W., **k̔el-ba** C., *čel-ba* Cs. (?), to rely, to depend upon, *blo gél-ba* to hope Sch. (the correct spelling as yet doubtful); *blos γtóṅ-ba* to give up, resign entirely, to risk, venture, e.g. *ráṅ-gi srog* Glr., Mil., *blo spáṅ-ba*, id. Mil.; **t̔se-ₒdi lō-táṅ** monk C.; *ₒó-čag blos ma t̔óṅs-par* as she was so much attached to us Mil.; *raṅ-blos ma t̔oṅs-pa* a man attached to himself, in love with himself; *blo γtód-pa* Schr. to trust, confide (cf. compounds); *dé-las blo zlóg-pa* Thgy., to subtract, to draw off, divert, dissuade from; *blo brid-pa* to deceive, impose upon, cheat Glr. (*bló-yi bdag* 'conscience' Sch., acc. to Schr. not an authenticated expression).

**Comp.** *blo-k̔og-čé* confident, courageous, intrepid, undaunted. — *blo-grós* **sense, intellect, understanding;** *blo-grós-kyi šés-bya* what is to be discerned by the understanding; *blo-grós daṅ ldán-pa, blo-grós-čan* sensible, judicious (of persons), *blo-grós čén-po* C. of much sense, of an excellent understanding, *čúṅ-nu* C., *žán-pa* Mil. of little understanding; *blo-gros-méd* unintelligent, injudicious; *blo-gros-rgyal-po* n. of a medicinal plant, = *smug-čúṅ* Wdṅ. — *bló-čan* having mind, sense; *byis-pai blo-čan* having the mind or sense of a child, thinking like a child Cs.; having a mind, v. above *mčód-pa byéd-pai bló-čan de*. — *blo-nyés* **ill-meaning, malicious** Glr. — *blo-γtád, blo-γdeṅ* **hope, confidence, assurance,** *bdág-gi blo-γdéṅ sú-la ₒča* in whom am I to place my confidence. — *blo-γdeṅ čós-la byéd-pa* Glr.; W.: **lor-tád* or *lo-dáṅ čó-če, kyél-če (s)**, c. *la*. — *blo-rtóg* prob. = *blo-grós, blo-rtóg t̔a-dád-pa* Pth. people of different mental abilities. — *blo-stóbs* 1. C., W. **courage.** 2. W., **generosity, magnanimity,** or perh. also **equanimity, self-command,** e.g. if a person remains kind and forbearing towards disobedient servants. — *blo-t̔ábs* counsel, expedient, *blo-t̔ábs tsól-ba* Ma. — *blo-bde* **cheerful, happy.** — *blo-ₒdód* **covetous, greedy.** — *bló-sna* 1. *bló-sna maṅ-ba* Glr. was explained by our Lama: having manifold thoughts, being restless, flighty, giddy. 2. W. disposition, turn of mind, **ló-na riṅ-mo** slowness, irresolution, also longsuffering, **lo-na t̔úṅ-se** resoluteness, determination, promptness, both also adj.: slow, irresolute, and: resolute, determined etc. — *blo-méd* injudicious, foolish Cs. (Dzl. ༧༤༤, 18 makes no sense, there being prob. an error in the text. The translation of Sch. seems to be a mere conjecture). — *blo-bzáṅ* 'sound sense', col. **'lob-zaṅ'**, a very common name of persons. — *blo-šéd* Sch. 'memory, intellectual power'. — *blo-séms* **mind, soul, heart,** *blo-sems-bdé* = *blo-bdé* Mil. — *blo-bsám* intellect; W.: **lo-sám méd-k̔an** foolish, one not knowing what he is about.

II. frq. incorr. for *glo*.

བློ་བ་ *bló-ba* I. vb. **to be able** = *p̔ód-pa*; *k̔yod mi ló-na* if you cannot; **di mi lo** that you cannot (dare not) do, prob. only W. vulg. — II. sbst. = *blo*, frq. used by Mil. for the sake of the rhythm.

བློ་བུར་ *bló-bur* = *gló-bur* **sudden, suddenly;** *k̔yed dá-ltar-gyi dád-pa bló-bur yin* thy present faith is new, but just sprung up in thee Mil.; *mi-spyod bló-bur-du ₒgyur* the conduct of men suddenly changes Ma.

བློང་མོ་ *blóṅ-mo*, for *lóṅ-mo*, **bones** or **knuckles** used as dice Mil.

བློན་ *blon* 1. Lex. = *gros, blón ₒdébs-pa* **to give advice, to counsel;** Cs.: to make arrangements. — 2. v. the following.

བློན་པོ་ *blón-po* **officer** (prop. counsellor), any magisterial officer of higher rank; *blón-po daṅ ₒbaṅs* commanding and obeying, higher officers and subalterns Glr.; more particularly **minister** (of state); *blon(-po) čen(-po)* Glr., *blón-po bká-la γtógs-pa* Glr., more commonly *bka-blón(-po)*, **high officer of state, minister, governor;** *k̔rims-blón* minister of justice, officer of justice; *rgyal-blón* king and minister, also = council, privy-council, Glr.; *čós-blon* 1. (opp. to *bdúd-blon*) an orthodox, faithful minister etc. 2. *čos-blon čén-po* minister of public worship Glr.; *rje-blón* the same as *rgyal-blón* Glr. — *spyi-blon* chief officer Cs. — *p̔yi naṅ bar γsúm-gyi blón-po* Glr., lit. outer, inner, middle

བ

minister, a distinction not quite intelligible. — *dmág-blon* military, *yúl-blon* civil officer *Cs.* — *naṅ-blon* 1. v. above *p̔yi-naṅ* etc. 2. *Lh.* country-judge.

བྷ་ *bha*, sometimes written for བ, either from ignorance, or in order to appear learned, as is also དྷ for ད, and so forth.

བྷ་ག་ *bhá-ga Ssk.* **the female genitals**, *Pth.*

བྷ་ར་ཏ་ *bhá-ra-ta, bhá-ra-tai dúm-bu, bhár-ta, bár-dha, Ssk.* भरतखण्ड country between Lanka and the Sumeru, viz. Hindustan; also North-India, *Mil.* and elsewh.

བྷ་ལད་ *bha-lad, Urd.* وِلايت, *Beng.* belati, 'a far distant country', = *p̔i-liṅ*, for **Europe.**

བྷང་གེ་ *bhaṅ-ge W., Ssk.* भङ्गा, **hemp.**

བྷེ་ད་ *bhe-da* v. *ₒbe-dha.*

དབའ་ *dba* 1. *Lex.* = *že-sa* **reverence, respect,** obs. 2. (or *rba*) = the following.

དབའ་ཀློང་ *dba-klóṅ Glr., rba-kloṅ Mil., Dzl., dba-rlábs* **wave, billow**; *rba-skya* whitish waves *Mil.*; *dba-tsúb* surge, roar, turmoil of waves *Cs.*; *dba-byi* water-rat?

དབག་པ་ *dbág-pa*, pf. *dbags Sch.*, v. *dbog-pa* and *bag-pa.*

དབང་ *dbaṅ* (**waṅ*, vulg. *'aṅ**) 1. **might, power, potency,** *blón-po dbaṅ čés-pas* because the minister was very potent *Glr.*; *dbaṅ dge-ₒdún-la γtad Glr.*, not only: 'he granted great privileges to the priesthood' *Sch.*, but: he invested it with magisterial power and jurisdiction; rarely used of physical power or strength *S.g.*; *bsdad-dbaṅ-med* it is not in my power to stay *Thgy.*; *búm-pa ǰó-moi yin-te dbaṅ ma mčis-so* as the pitcher belongs to my mistress, I have no power over it, I have not to dispose of it *Dzl.*; *sdod-dbaṅ-méd-par* having no strength, not being able to wait (from eagerness, avidity etc.) *Glr.*; *dbaṅ-méd*, prob. *sdod* to be supplied (if the text be correct), this won't do so any longer *Glr.*; *(raṅ-)dbaṅ-méd-du* or *par* involuntarily, not being able to help it, e.g. to weep, rejoice, believe, *Mil.*: *dbaṅ-méd-du mči-ma ₒčór-du ₒǰúg-pa* to make one weep; *dbaṅ-méd-du ₒčól-ba* to make a person powerless, to force by absolute power *Glr.*; *dbáṅ-du ₒgyúr-ba* to get into another's power, to be overpowered *Tar.*; *ₒdód-pai* to get into the power of the passions, to be led away by them *Dzl.*; *dbáṅ-du gyúr-pa* seems also sometimes to mean: he who has brought every thing into his power (?), along with *nyon-moṅs-pa-méd-pa* and *sems-rnam-par-gról-ba*; *dbáṅ-du sdúd-pa* to reduce under one's power *Pth.*; *snyiṅ-rǰe* to make the principle of mercy one's own, to practise it freely *Glr.*, (where *ₒdú-ba* stands); *ₒgró-ba* to comprise all beings, *Glr.*; *dbáṅ-du byéd-pa* id.; *dbaṅ byéd-pa* c. la, 1. to rule over, to govern, frq. 2. to possess, *bdág-gis dbaṅ byar méd-pa* what one does not possess *Thgy.* — *dbaṅ-sgyúr-ba c. la,* to govern, to rule, frq.; *dbaṅ ₒgrúb-pa* id. seldom. — *dbaṅ skúr-ba* v. *skur-ba* and *dbaṅ,* 2. **waṅ táṅ-če* W.* to make efforts, to exert one's self, also = the next. — *dbaṅ zá-ba* to offer violence *Dzl.* ༡༤༥, 3. — *dbáṅ-gis* like a postposition, by, by means of, in virtue of, in consequence of, e.g. *lás-kyi* of former actions *Glr.*; *ṅa-rgyál-gyi dbáṅ-gis* from or in consequence of pride *Tar.* — 2. more especially in mythology, *dbaṅ bču Dzl.* ༢༥༢, 14, also *stobs-bču Trigl.* 8, 6; *Gyatch.* II, 46, *Burn.* II, 781 seqq. 1. the ten powers of knowledge of Buddha, v. *Köpp.* I, 437 seqq. 2. in later times *γžan rǰés-su ₒdzin-pai dbaṅ bču* ten powers tending to the benefit of others are ascribed to the Bodhisattva, *Thgy.*: *ts̔é-la dbáṅ-ba* (respecting this form v. below) power over the length of one's own life; *séms-la dbáṅ-ba* power according to one's own pleasure to enter into any meditation; *yo-byád-la* to shower down provisions for the support of creatures; *lás-la* to mitigate the punishments for their sins; *skyé-ba-la* to effect one's own re-birth in the external world, without danger of being infected by its sin; *mós-pa-la* at pleasure to change one object into another; *smón-lam-la* to see every prayer for the welfare of others fulfilled; *rdzu-ₒp̔rúl-la* to exhibit wonderful feats for bringing about the conversion of others; *ye-śés-la* to understand all writings on religion (ni f.); *č̔ós-la* to convey the publication of religion to all creatures at the same time and in every language. 3. in practical mysticism: various supernatural powers (v. *skúr-ba*), e.g. *p̔yi naṅ γsáṅ-gi dbaṅ skúr-ba Pth.* is alledged to signify: to convey externally, i.e. into the mouth, the power of *snaṅ-ba-mt̔a-yás* (this and the two following are names of Buddhas and demons), internally, into the body, the power of *spyan-ras-γzigs* and lastly into the mind perfect purity, i.e. the *rta-mgrin*, and together with it power over the demons. — 3. **regard, consideration**(?). In later writings the composition of *dbáṅ-du byás-na* (*mdzád-na* etc.) c. genit. (instead of which in *C.* also *dbáṅ-du śór-na, sóṅ-na* are said to be in use), is frq. to be met with, signifying as much as: when... is concerned, when... is in question, for the purpose of, or merely: respecting, as regards: *légs-pai, ǰígs-pai, btsán-pai* when beauty, firmness, formidable appearance (of a royal castle) are concerned, are the points in question *Glr.*; *sṅágs-kyi dbáṅ-du rtsís-pai śló-ka* prob. the Slokas being numbered with a regard to the Mantras, i.e. including the latter *Tar.* 127, 16. — 4. symb. num.: 5 (*dbaṅ* being taken for *dbáṅ-po*).

**Comp. and deriv.** *dbaṅ-bskúr* consecration, inauguration, initiation *Was.* (189), = *dbaṅ-bskyúr* might, power, e.g. *saṅs-rgyás-kyi Glr.* — *dbaṅ-grál* the row of those that are to be ordained or consecrated. — *dbáṅ-čan* mighty, powerful *Cs.* — *dbaṅ-t̔áṅ* 1. **might,** = *mṅa-t̔aṅ, dbaṅ-t̔aṅ-méd-pa* low, mean, of inferior rank *Dzl.* 2. **time, chronology** *Lexx.* 3. **destiny, fate, predestined fate,** or rather the destiny of any creature consequent to its former actions, *t̔se daṅ dbaṅ-t̔áṅ*, frq.; *dbaṅ-t̔aṅ-méd-pa* may therefore imply: having no destiny, i.e. no particular destiny. — *dbaṅ-ₒdus-p̔o-bráṅ* 'Angdophorung' of the Indian papers, n. of a fort in Tibet. — *dbaṅ-ldán* mighty, powerful; *dbaṅ-ldán-gyi p̔yogs Domaṅ, dbáṅ-poi p̔yogs Sbh.*, is said to be north-east. — *dbáṅ-po* v. the next article. — *dbaṅ-p̔yúg* 1. adj. mighty, also sbst.: *dbaṅ-p̔yúg γžán-las č̔é-ba Glr.* 2. symb. num.: 11. 3. **noun proper** a. Iswara, Siva *Glr.*, hence also the Lingam as his emblem *Glr.* b. Avalokitesvara *Glr.* — *dbáṅ-ba* 1. vb. c. *la* = *dbaṅ byéd-pa*, e.g. *rgyal-srid-la mi dbaṅ* he does not succeed to the throne; gen. with accus. *γčig ₒdi dbáṅ-ba yin* one ... belongs to this one *Mil.*; *bdag dbáṅ-bai rgyal-p̔rán* the vassals under my sway *Dzl.* 2. sbst. = *dbaṅ*, e.g. *t̔sé-la dbáṅ-ba* (v. above). — *dbaṅ-rís* prob. domain, dominion. — *dbaṅ(-po)-lág(-pa)* a medicine, said to be prepared from a viscid, aromatic root, shaped like a hand. — *dbaṅ-śés* perception, by means of the organs of sense *Was.* (278).

དབང་པོ་ *dbáṅ-po* 1. **possessed of power, dominion,** *nór-gyi dbáṅ-por gyur Dzl.* (*Ms.*); **lord, ruler, sovereign,** esp. divine rulers: Indra, also *lhai dbáṅ-po*; further *rgyál-bai dbáṅ-po, t̔úb-pai dbáṅ-po* the highest of the Buddhas *Glr.* — 2. **organ of sense,** *dbáṅ-po lṅa(-po)* a. the five organs of sense, eyes etc., also *dbáṅ-poi sgo lṅa Med.* b. *Trigl.* 17, 6, five immaterial, transcendent senses of Buddha, which are in unison with his five powers, *stobs lṅa*, as stated by *Burn.* II, 430, v. *Köpp.* I, 436. In natural philosophy six organs of sense frq. are mentioned, मनस् being added as the sixth; medical writings also treat of *dbáṅ-po dgu* or *dbáṅ-poi sgo dgu*, v. *bú-ga*. — 3. **sense, intellectual power,** *dbáṅ-po rnón-po* of acute intellect, *dbáṅ-po rdúl-po* of obtuse intellect, also as common expressions for sagacious or dull *Dzl.*; *dbáṅ-po nyams* the senses are weakened, become dull *Med.*; *lus sems dbáṅ-po* body, soul, and senses (are glad, are pure etc.) *Dom.*; *dbáṅ-po γsó-ba* to gladden, strengthen, revive, the senses *Mil.*; *ráṅ-gi séms-las dbáṅ-poi rnam-śés ₒbyuṅ* out of the spirit (of the personality which during the time between two periods of existence is in a disembodied state) the sense-endowed soul (of the new individual) is generated (in the process of conception)

S.g. — 4. **genitals,** Wdn. and elsewh.; *dbáṅ-po lág-pa* v. *dbaṅ-lág* sub *dbaṅ.*

དབར་མི་ *dbár-mi Sch.* **a faint-hearted, timorous man.**

དབལ་ *dbal Lex.* = *tog* and *rtsé-mo* **top, summit, point** e.g. of a *mčod-rten Glr.*; the point, or acc. to some the grooves of the *p̔úr-pa* or exorcising dagger; *rtai dbal bzaṅ-ṅan Lex.?* — *dbál-ba* v. *˳bal-ba.*

དབུ་ *dbu* resp. for *mgo*, **head,** frq.; **beginning, commencement,** e.g. of holy doctrine *Glr.*; *'u lán-če* W., the mode of greeting between Lamas, by touching each other with their fore-heads; to bless (a layman by imposition of hands); *dbu mdzád-pa* to be the head, the principal person, e.g. in an assembly of believers *Mil.*; more definitely: *dbu mdzád-do* he was my instructor *Mil.* — *dbu-skrá* the hair of the head. — *dbu-rgyán* ornament of the head, diadem *Mil.* — *dbu-rṅás Sch.* pillow. — *dbu-čan* furnished with a head, i.e. with a thick stroke at the top (of a letter), hence the name of the Tibetan printing characters. — *dbu-čen* 1. **higher officer.** 2. *dbu-čuṅ* **subaltern officer** *Cs.* — *dbu-rje* **Reverence, Reverend,** title of Lamas. — *dbu-snyúṅ bžés-pa Sch.*, *dbu-snyúṅ daṅ bro ˳bór-ba Glr.* resp. to swear by one's head. — *dbu-t̔ód* royal cap, crown. — *dbu-mt̔úṅ drúṅ-du* resp. the same as *žabs drúṅ-du* in directing letters: To ... — *dbu-˳p̔áṅ* **elevation, high rank, dignity,** *stód-pa* to praise, *smád-pa* to despise, to revile (dignities). — *dbú-ma* 1. n. of the goddess **Durga,** the wife of Siva. 2. **principal vein,** v. *rtsá-ba.* 3. **the middle** (-doctrine), **middle-road,** मध्यम, which endeavours to avoid the two extremes *Was.*, also *dbú-mai lam* or *ltá-ba*; *dbú-ma-pa* an adherent of this doctrine *Sch.*, cf. however *mdo* extr. — *dbu-méd* **the Tibetan current hand-writing,** cf. *dbú-čan.* — *dbu-rmóg Zam.* w.e.; in W. *gyál-po u'-móg čo žig* is said to signify: Long live the king! — *dbu-rtsé* the top, pinnacle, of a temple, monastery *Glr.* — *dbu-mdzád* (cf. *dbu mdzád-pa* above) **chairman, principal, warden,** in convents an official that takes the lead in performing the prayers. — *dbu-žwá* cap. — *dbu-šóg* title-page *Sch.*

དབུ་བ་ *dbú-ba* v. *lbú-ba.*

དབུགས་ *dbugs* 1. **breath, respiration,** *dbugs rṅúb-pa daṅ ˳byín-pa* or *˳byúṅ-ba* to respire, to inhale and exhale air *Med.*, W. *tón-če* for *˳byúṅ-ba*; *dbugs ˳byin-pa* to stop for rest, to recover one's breath *Sch.* (and perh. *Pth.*); *dbugs-dbyúṅ t̔ób-pa* to be eased in one's mind, after despondency *Tar.*; *'ug gyaṅ bór-če* W. to stop, to keep back one's breath; *'ug sub* or *kor táṅ-če* W. to choke, suffocate, strangle, throttle; *skyé-˳gro t̔ams-čád-kyi dbugs lén-pa* to take away the breath of beings (which is ascribed to the demon *pe-dkár*) *Glr.*; *p̔yi-dbugs* seems to be the last breath of a dying man, but *náṅ-dbugs* is some fantastic physiological notion *Thgr.*; *dbugs mdé-ba* and *mi-bdé-ba* an easy and a hard breathing *Med.* frq.; *dbugs-t̔úṅ* short breath; *dbugs rdzáṅ-ba* or *brdzáṅs-pa* shortness of breath, asthma, as a complaint of old age *Thgy.*; *dbugs lheb-lhéb byéd-pa* to pant, to be pursy *Med.* — *dbugs-rgód Lt.?* — *dbugs-ṅán Sch.* flatulence. — *dbugs t̔ebs-rél Sch.* 'in one breath'? — 2. **a breath, one respiration,** as smallest measure of time = $\frac{1}{1800}$ *kyim* = 4 seconds.

དབུང་ *dbuṅ Lex.* = *dbus.*

དབུབ་པ་ *dbúb-pa* v. *˳búbs-pa.*

དབུར་ *dbur* termin. of *dbu, Sch.* **first, at first.**

དབུར་བ་ *dbúr-ba*, also *˱úr-ba*, *'úr-ba* **to smooth,** *šóg-bu* paper, *ras* woollen stuff, *γžál* a pavement *Cs.*; *'ur gyág-pa* C., *gyáb-če* W. to iron, to smooth linen etc., *'ur-čag* smoothing-iron.

དབུལ་བ་ *dbúl-ba* I. vb. v. *˳búl-ba.* — II. adj. **poor, indigent** *Dzl.*; sbst. **poverty, want, penury,** *dbúl-ba sel-ba* to relieve want *Glr.*; *dbul-žiṅ ˳p̔óṅs-pai rigs* **a** poor and indigent generation *Dzl.*; **hence frq.** *dbúl-p̔oṅs* poor, **a poor man, pauper** *Mil.*; poverty *Glr.*; usually *dbúl-po*, fem. *dbúl-mo*, poor.

དབུས་ *dbus* (*Ld.* *'us*, *C.* *'ü*) 1. **middle, midst, centre,** *t̔ág-pai dbus tsám-du* *ṗyin-nas* having proceeded about to the middle of the rope *Dzl.*; *skyé-boi dbús-su* in the midst of the people *Tar.*; *ṫaṅ γnyis-kyi dbus-ri* the hill (mountain) in the middle between the two plains *Glr.*; *dbús-kyi ri-rgyál* Sumeru standing in the centre (of the world) *Mil.*; seldom relative to time: *bžúgs-pai dbús-su* whilst he was sitting *Glr.*; in metaphysics: *dbus daṅ mṫa* 'the medium and the extremes' *Cs.* Asiat. Researches XX, 577 — *dbús-ma* the middle one (of three or more persons) *Mil.*, (of inanimate things) *Glr.* — 2. in a specific sense: **the central province** of a country, a. of India, hence = Magadha, the holy land, land of Buddha *Thgy.* b. of Tibet, the province Ü; *dbús-pa* an inhabitant of it; *dbus-γtsán Ü* and *Tsaṅ*.

དབེན་པ་ *dbén-pa* **solitary, lonely,** e.g. a road *Dzl.*; **solitude, loneliness,** *dbén-pa ₒdí-na* in this solitude *Dzl.*; *dbén-par ₒgró-ba* or *γnás-pa* frq.; *dben*, id.: *dbén-la dga Ma.*; *dben-(pai) γnas, sa* solitary place, esp. hermitage; *dbén-γnas čén-po ḃrgyád-kyi sa* earth from the eight great hermitages, sacred places of pilgrimage in India *Glr.*; like *bstoṅs-pa* the word is construed with the instrum. case: *mas dbén-pa*, solitary as to a mother, i.e. motherless; *snyiṅ-pos dbén-pa* = *snyiṅ-po méd-pa Tar.*

དབོ་ *dbo* 1. n. of a lunar mansion, v. *rgyu-skár*, no. 22. — 2. the belly-side of fur.

དབོ་བ་ *dbó-ba* v. *ₒbó-ba*.

དབོན་པོ་ *dbón-po* (*W.* *'ón-po*, *C.* *'o̤m-po*) 1. *B.* resp. for *ṫsá-bo* **grandson; nephew**; *dbon-srás* id. *Glr.*; *dbón-mo* fem.; *mes-dbón* ancestor and grandchild *Glr.*; *dbon-žáṅ Glr.* 95 seems to denote son-in-law and brother-in-law, with which also *Sch.*'s Mongol transl. agrees, Geschichte d. Ost-Mong. p. 359 med. — 2. **Lama-servant** *C.* — 3. a certain sect of Lamas, clad in red, shorn, and married, = **sor-kyim-pa**, *C.*, *W.* — 4. a Lamā skilled in astrology, who for instance, when a person has died, performs those ceremonies, that serve to **avert harm from the survivors** *W.*

དབོལ་བ་ *dból-ba Cs.* = *rtól-ba*, *Lex. rdziṅ dból-ba*.

དབྱངས་ *dbyaṅs*, **yaṅ(s)** 1. **singing, song, tune, melody,** *glu-dbyáṅs* id.; *luṅ-bstán-gyi dbyaṅs* prophetic song, psalm *Mil.*; *dbyaṅs(-su) lén-pa, dbyaṅs byéd-pa* to sing *Dzl.*; *stód (-pai) dbyaṅs* song of praise, hymn of thanksgiving, **ǰhé-pa** *C.*, **ṗúl-če** *W.*; *γduṅ-dbyáṅs* a song of aspiration *Mil.* — *dbyáṅs-čan Glr.* a deity, prob. = *ₒjam-dbyáṅs-čan-ma* Saraswati, goddess of euphony. — *dbyaṅs-snyán* sweet singing. — *dbyáṅs-pa* singer *Cs.* — **yaṅ-žú** bow for a violin, fiddle-stick *W.* — 2. **vowel,** hence *dbyaṅs-yig* 1. the (four) **signs of the vowels,** *Gram.* 2. *Cs.*: **notes** (of music) or **any contrivance for marking the modulation of sounds**; so perh. also *Glr.*

དབྱར་ *dbyar* **summer,** in India: **rainy season** (cf. *dus*); also *dbyár-ka, dbyár-ḱa Mil.*, *W.*, *dbyár-dus*, *Cs. dbyár-mo*; *dbyar-dgun-méd-par* summer and winter *Mil.*; *dbyar B.*, *dbyár-ka-la* col. in summer; *dbyar-γnás* 1. summer-abode, *Sch.* 2. the solitary summer-fasting of the monks; *dbyar-skyés* 'summer-born'; *dbyar-ṙṅá* summer-drum, po. expression for thunder *Cs.* — *dbyar-čár* summer-rain *Cs.* — *dbyar-žwa* summer-hat.

དབྱར་པ་ *dbyár-pa* (*Pur.* **sbyár-pa**, elsewh. **yár-pa**) **poplar,** various kinds of which tree are found in the vicinity of villages, cultivated or growing wild. (*Wdṅ.* also *sbyár-pa.*)

དབྱི་ *dbyi* (**yi*, com. *'i**) 1. **lynx,** *dbyí-mo* the female of this animal, *dbyi-ṗrúg* a young one; *dbyi-ṫsáṅ* lair of it. — 2. in Ü: **beer,** = *čaṅ*.

དབྱི་གུ་ *dbyí-gu* = *dbyig-gu* **little stick,** cf. *dbyig-pa*.

དབྱི་བ་ *dbyí-ba*, prob. only fut. to *ₒṗyí-ba*, **to wipe off, to blot out, to efface,** *Lex.*: *ri-mo*, a drawing. *Sch.* however notices also a perf. *dbyis*.

དབྱི་མོ་ *dbyí-mo* **flax** (?).

དབྱི་མོང་ *dbyi-moṅ* **medicinal herb, used against delirium** *Med.*; *Cs.*: **'a plant** of an acrid taste, used as tea'; in *Lh.* Potentilla Salesovii, of which neither the one nor the other fact is known to me.

དབྱིག(ས)· *dbyig(s)* 1. = *nor* **wealth, riches, treasures**, *nor-dbyig* id. *Dzl.*; *dbyig-čan* rich, *dbyig-med* poor *Cs.*; *dbyig-máṅ Lex.* — 2. prob. = *dbyig-γnyén*, **precious stone** or a kind of such *Glr.* and elsewh.

དབྱིག་པ· *dbyig-pa* **stick**, = *dbyúg-pa*.

དབྱིག་པུ· *dbyig-pu Sch.*: 'implement for cleaning, scouring, polishing'.

དབྱིང་ཞ· *dbyiṅ-ža Sch.*: **summer-hat** (?).

དབྱིངས· *dbyiṅs* 1. syn. with *kloṅ*, com. *nám-mkʻai dbyiṅs* or *dbyiṅs* alone: **the heavens, celestial region**, *rgyáb-la brag dmar nám-mkʻai dbyiṅs* red rocks behind and the expanse of heaven *Mil.*; *kʻyeu dbyiṅ-su yal* the youth disappearing was carried up to heaven *Pth.*; *dbyiṅs-na bžúgs-pai ḍá-ki-ma Mil.* — 2. **height** *Schr.*; the above passage was also rendered: red rocks behind, as high as heaven. — 3. in metaphysics an undefined idea of **extent, region, space**, **धातु**, (cf. *kloṅ*), *čós-kyi dbyiṅs*, **धर्मधातु**, not 'the wide diffusion of religion' *Sch.*, but a mere fanciful notion, or as it is expressed *Wts.* 143: le monde intellectuel de Bouddha; of highly learned Lamas the words are used: *tʻugs-dgóṅs čos-dbyiṅs-su tʻim C.*; and also *dbyiṅs* alone: *bló-yi byéd-pa dbyiṅs-su sbos Glr.* hide your mental activity in the heavens, i.e. let it be reduced to nothing; so prob. also *Tar.* 38, 10, *pʻúṅ-po lhág-mo méd-pai dbyiṅs-su*, where nothing of the skandha is left remaining. *Sch.*: *dbyiṅs-su* in a body, in one mass, whole, entire (?).

དབྱིན· *dbyin* or *γyin byéd-pa Sch.*, **to incite, instigate, set on.**

དབྱིབས· *dbyibs* **shape, figure, form**, *byá-dbyibs-čan* having the shape of a bird *Lt.*; *šiṅ-rtai dbyibs daṅ ˳dra* shaped like a waggon or carriage *Glr.*; *skyés-pai dbyibs-la ṅós-bzuṅ-ba* to learn the nature (of plants) from the shape in which they grow; **ă-mẹ yib dug** he quite resembles his mother in shape *W.*; *dbyibs légs-pa B.* a fine figure, **sóg-po** an ugly figure *W.*, or also: of a handsome (or ugly) form; *dbyibs zlúm-por yod* it has a round shape *Glr.*

དབྱུག་གུ, དབྱུ་གུ *dbyúg-gu, dbyú-gu* 1. **small staff, wand, rod,** e.g. used as a magic wand, sun-dial etc. *Cs.* — 2. *Lex.*: = *ču-tʻsod* q.v.; *Sch.*: *dbyúg-gu re-bži*, '64 equal parts of weight or measure; 64 quarters of an hour, or 16 hours'; but 64 *ču-tʻsod* would make as much as 25 $\frac{3}{5}$ hours.

དབྱུག་རྡོ· *dbyúg-rdo W.* **sling-stone**; *B.*: *rdo-γyúg*.

དབྱུག་པ· *dbyúg-pa* I. vb. pf. *dbyugs* 1. **to swing, brandish, flourish,** a stick, a sword; **to wag**, *ṙná-ma* the tail *Cs*; **yug yug ǰhe'-pa** *W.*, to swing to and fro, to dangle; **yug toṅ** *W.*, swing! dangle! — 2. **to throw, cast, fling,** **gyál-kar-nẹ do** *C.*, to fling a stone through a window; to throw away, to throw down, **yúg-lẹ žog** *C.* (= **pʻáṅ-te bor** *W.*), throw it away! — II. sbst, **stick**, *C.*; **yúg-pa gyáb-pa** *C.* to strike, to beat with a stick. *dbyúg-to Glr.*, *dbyúg-tʻo*, id. (*Sch.* club?) *Lex.*: = *bér-ka*, **दण्ड**; *dbyug-to-čan* wielding a stick; n.p.

དབྱུང་བ· *dbyúṅ-ba*, fut., and in *C.* secondary form to the pres. *˳byin-pa*.

དབྱེ་བ· *dbyé-ba*, (regular pronunciation **yé-wa*, com. *'é-wa**). I. vb. fut., and in *C.* secondary form of *˳byéd-pa*. — II. sbst. 1. **parting, partition, division, distinction, classification** *Thgy.* — 2. **section, part, class, species**, *dbyé-ba nyí-šu γsuṅs* twenty different species are named *Lt.*; *yi-ge ˳di dbyé-ba γnyis* these letters are divided into two classes; hence like *sna-tʻsogs*: *sgyu-rtsál dbyé-ba* manifold arts, artifices *Smbh.* — *dbyé-brál Lex.*: **discord, dissension.**

དབྱེན་པ· *dbyén-pa* (**yén-pa*, com. *'én-pa**, = *dbén-pa*), **difference, dissension, discord, schism**, *dge-˳dún-gyi dbyén-pa byéd-pa* to create discord, to cause a schism among the priesthood *Dzl.*; *dbyen ˳byéd pa* **to make** a difference, to discriminate *Sch.*

དབྱེར་མེད, དབྱེ་རུ་མེད་པ, དབྱེར་ཕྱེད་པ, *dbyer-méd, dbye-ru-méd-pa, dbyer-mi-pʻyéd-pa* **in-**

**separable, not to be distinguished, quite the same, identical** *Glr.* and elsewh.; *blá-mar dbyér-med* prob.: identical with a Lama; esp. in the higher philosophy in reference to the impossibility of distinguishing between good and evil (!).

དབྱེས་ *dbyes Schr.:* **magnitude, size, dimensions,** so perh. where *dprál-bai dbyes če* is mentioned as a characteristic of beauty.

དབྲག་ *dbrag*, v. *ṗrag*, **intermediate space, interstice;** ravine, glen, defile, *C.; Sch.* also: vise, handvise.

དབྲད་པ་ *dbrád-pa* v. *ₒbrád-pa.*

དབྲབ་པ་ *dbráb-pa* v. *ₒbráb-pa.*

དབྲལ་བ་ *dbrál-ba* v. *ₒbrál-ba.*

དབྲི་བ་ *dbrí-ba* v. *ₒbri-ba.*

དབྲེ་བཙོང་ *dbre - btsóṅ* (?) *Sch.*; *Lex. dbre-btsog* dirt, filth.

དབྲོག་པ་ *dbróg-pa* v. *ₒṗróg-pa.*

འབའ་ *ₒba Sch.:* 'seizure, distraint'; or rather the liability of paying higher interest, payment not having been made at the appointed time; *ₒba-gan, ₒba-gan-yig* warrant for thus proceeding against a debtor *C.*

འབའ་ཆ་ *ₒba-ča Wdṅ.*; *Sch.:* **lees** from distilling brandy.

འབའ་པོ་ *ₒbá-po* **magician, sorcerer, conjurer;** *ₒbá-mo* sorceress, witch *Cs., W.*

འབའ་བ་ *ₒbá-ba* 1. **to bleat,** *W.* *ba tán-če*. — 2. **to bring, to carry,** *ₒbā - šog* bring it hither! *Sik., ₒba-soṅ* take it there! — 3. **to commit adultery** *C.*

འབའ་བོ་ *ₒbá-bo, Cs.* = *ṗug-pa*, **hole, cave, cavern,** *brág - gi* cleft in a rock, grotto; *ₒbá-bo-čan* **hollow, excavated.**

འབའ་བྱི་ *ₒbá-byi* a kind of cake, baked of parched rice or maize meal, frequently eaten with the tea *C.*

འབའ་ཞིག་ *ₒbá-žig B.* **only, solely, alone,** *bdag ₒbá-žig tár - ro* I alone escaped *Dzl.*; *rkáṅ-pa ₒbá-žig* the foot alone (appeared party-coloured) *Dzl.*: *blón-po de ₒbá-žig-gi čúṅ-ma* only this officer's wife *Dzl.*; mere, nothing but, *γser daṅ dṅul ₒba-žig-gis gaṅ Sbh.*

འབག་ *ₒbag* 1. **mask, guise, disguise;** cf. also sub *sgo-lo.* — 2. **imitation, effigy, likeness, figure,** *ₒdra-ₒbág* resp. *sku-ₒbag, žal-ₒbág* id.; *ₒdra-ₒbag-gyon-mi* masked persons *Pth.* — *ₒbag-ₒčam*, prop. **masquerade,** masked ball; *Cs.:* buffoonery, grimaces.

འབག་པ་ *ₒbág-pa* I. vb. pf. *ₒbags*, fut. *dbag?* cf. *sbág - pa*, **to defile, to pollute one's self,** *bud-méd daṅ* with women *Dzl.*; *ₒdod-čágs-la* through lust *Dzl.*; **to defile, to soil, to dirty,** *snód-la* a vessel *Dzl.* ༢༢༡, 7? — 2. *C.* **to take away, to steal, to rob; to covet, to wish to take,** c. *la Mil.* (acc. to oral information).

འབག་འབོག་ *ₒbag-ₒbóg* a slight elevation, **hillock** *W.*

འབག་རག་ *ₒbag-rág* **spider,** *ₒbag-rág-gi tsaṅ* cob-web *Sik.*

འབགས་ལྷག་ *ₒbags-lhag* **rest, remainder, remnant** (of food) *Mil.*

འབང་བ་ *ₒbáṅ-ba* **to be soaked, macerated,** softened by soaking *Cs.*, cf. *sbáṅ-ba.*

འབངས་ *ₒbaṅs* **subject,** *rgyál-po ₒbáṅs-su ₒoṅ* the king turns into a subject *Ma.*; *ₒbaṅs byéd-pa* to obey, *bkai ₒbaṅs bgyíd-par* (or *bka-ₒbaṅs-su*) *ḱas-blaṅs-so* they promised to obey, to perform the commandment *Mil.* frq.; *báṅs-su byéd-pa Cs.* to reduce under one's dominion; gen. collectively: **the people, the subjects,** opp. to *blón-po* officers, magistrates, or *rje, rgyál-po* etc. — *lha-báṅs Tar.* 165, 22 *Schf.:* slaves belonging to a temple.

འབད་པ་ *ₒbád-pa* I. vb., imp. *ₒbod*, **to endeavour, to exert one's self, apply one's self,** c. *la* or the termin.; *dus-rgyún-du čós-la ₒbád-pa de* this (habit of) constantly applying one's self to religion *Mil.*; also c. acc.: *dká-ba brgya-ṗrág* to perform a hundred exercises of penance; col. **to cultivate, raise, rear, take care of,** *žiṅ* or *sa-γzí* to cultivate the ground, *rgun-ₒbrúm* to grow vines, *dúd-ₒgro* to breed cattle; *slób-par* to apply one's self to learning, *gléṅ-mo ḱó-nar* to devote one's self exclusively to public speaking, preaching *C.* — II. sbst.

**application, study, exertion,** ₒ*bád-pa drág-pos* with most persevering application; ₒ*bád-pa daṅ rtsól-ba méd-par* without any exertion *Glr.*; hence ₒ*bad-rtsól* id.; *skyés-bus srúb-pai* ₒ*bad-rtsól* an assiduous rubbing with a human hand *Wdṅ.*; *dei* ₒ*bad-rtsól-gyis* through his endeavours *Thgy.*; prob. also: **volition, energy of will** *S.g.*; the passage in *Thgy.*: *byaṅ-čúb č̓i ťób-la* ₒ*bad* ₒ*tsál-lo,* is perh. not quite correct.

འབབ་ ₒ*bab* 1. **a fall of snow** *Mil.* — 2. **tax, duty** *Sp.*

འབབ་པ་ ₒ*báb-pa*, pf. *bab(s)*, imp. ₒ*bob Cs.*, *bobs Glr.*, **to move downward** 1. **to descend**, *lá-nas* col., a defile, in *B.* gen. with *las*, e.g. *rtá-las Dzl.*, also *rtá-ḱa-nas Glr.* to alight from a horse, mostly with *la*, although *rí-la* ₒ*báb-pa* may also mean: to alight (flying) on a mountain *Dzl.* ༢༥༣, 2. — 2. **to fall down,** *γnám-la ḱá-ba* ₒ*bab* snow falls from heaven *Dzl.* — **to flow,** the usual word; to flow off; *mi-γtsáṅ* ₒ*báb-pai γtór-ḱuṅ* sink-hole, for dirty water to run through *Lex.* — 4. **to alight on, to enter into**, of demons *Lt.* — 5. in a general sense, like **to get:** *nya skám-la* ₒ*báb-pa* a fish that has got on dry ground; *ṅá-la ré-mos* ₒ*bab Pth.*, or *res* ₒ*bab Tar.* it is my turn; *sróg-la* ₒ*báb-bo Dzl.* life is at stake; frq. in reference to time: *či-bai dús-la báb-bo* it has come to the time of dying, the hour of death has arrived; without a genit.: it is time; *skábs-la báb-bo* there is now an opportunity *Dzl.* — ₒ*bab-ču* **river, rivulet, brook;** also **rain.** — ₒ*bab-stégs* access or descent to the water, steps leading to a bathing-place *Hind.* **ghāṭ.* — ₒ*báb-mo** *W.* **condescending, affable.**

འབམ་ ₒ*bam* 1. *rkaṅ-*ₒ*bám* a disease of the foot *Sch.*: **gout.** — 2. ₒ*bám-yig* v. *yi-ge.*

འབམ་པ་ ₒ*bám-pa Cs.* **putrefaction, rottenness; to be putrid, rotten,** cf. *bám-pa.*

འབར་བ་ ₒ*bár-ba* (vb.n. to *sbár-ba*) 1. **to burn,** *me* ₒ*bár-bai ḱáṅ-pa* a burning house *Thgy.*; **to catch fire, to be ignited; to blaze** *Dzl.*; also in reference to the passions frq.; **to beam, radiate,** ₔ*ód-du* in light *Tar.*; ₒ*bár-du rúṅ-ba Cs.* combustible. — 2. **to open, to begin to bloom, to blossom,** frq. — 3. **to talk, tattle, to be garrulous, babbling,** *ₒ*bar* ₔ*ó-pa me'** it is not worth while to talk about it *C.*; *ḱo ṅá-la máṅ-po* ₒ*bar* ₒ*dug* he treats me to a long gossip *C*; esp. **to brawl, quarrel, chide,** *ḱa-*ₒ*bár* **quarrelsome, brawling** *Mil.*; *máṅ-du* ₒ*bár-du byúṅ-ba-las* as she was going to brawl still longer *Mil.*; **bar-kád táṅ-če** to rail at a person *W.* — 4. *dpal* ₒ*bar-ba Cs.* **to be celebrated,** famous.

འབར་འབར་ ₒ*bar-*ₒ*bár* 1. sbst. **a high, pointed hill,** cf. ₒ*bag-*ₒ*bóg.* — 2. adj. **uneven, rough; pock-marked.**

འབལ་བ་ ₒ*bal-ba,* used only with *skra,* 1. **to part, dress, arrange,** the hair, as it is customary with the monks and nuns of certain sects; in Kham also national costume; *skra γyas* ₒ*bal γyon* ₒ*bal byéd-pa* (of a nun) *Pth.*; **bál-*ₒ*go-čen** a person wearing the hair thus dressed *C.*; *skrá-*ₒ*bal-čan,* prob. id.; *C.*: name of an old Indian sect. — 2. as a sign of mourning, **to have the hair disheveled,** hanging down in disorder *Pth.*; so also *Dzl.* ༡༣༥, 17, acc. to correct reading; ₒ*bal-*ₒ*bál* **shaggy** *Sch.*

འབི་འབི་ ₒ*bi-*ₒ*bi* **small lumps of clay** *Cs.*

འབིག(ས)་པ་ ₒ*big(s)-pa*, pf. *ṗigs*, fut. *dbig*, imp. *ṗig(s)* and ₒ*búg(s)-pa*, *ṗug, dbug, ṗug,* also *ṗig-pa, ṗúg-pa,* 1. **to sting,** of insects *Stg.*; **to pierce,** *rdó-rje-yis ni rin-čén ṗug* the diamond pierces the precious stone *Pth.*; **to bore,** *šiṅ-la búg-pa* ₒ*búg-pa* to bore holes into wood *Glr.*; in a gen. sense, **to make a hole,** *rkáṅ-pa ḱyis ṗug* the dog bit my foot *Mil.*; *ḱáṅ-pa* ₒ*big-pa Thgy.* and elsewh., **to break into, to break open;** *ₒ*big gyáb-pa**, id. *C.*; *ču-*ₒ*gágs* ₒ*bigs* it removes strangury *Med.* — 2. *C.* **to deflower, to lie with,** obscene. — **búg-če** *W.* to make remarks on an absent person, **to criticize.** — *bigs-byéd*, n. p., n. of the Vindhya mountains (v. विन्द).

འབིང་ ₒ*biṅ*, **jham-biṅ** *C.*, resp. **sol-*ₒ*biṅ** **tea-pot.**

འབིབ(ས)་པ་ ₒ*bib(s)-pa* = ₒ*búb(s)-pa Sch.*

འབུ་ ₒbu **worm, insect**, any small vermin, esp. euphem. for louse; ₒbu-srin, srin-ₒbu, id.; ₒbu-skyógs **snail** *Med.*; ₒbu-tags *Cs.*, **cob-web**; *bu-yáṅ* (prob. a mere corruption of búṅ-ba) **humble-bee** *W.*; *ₒbu-riṅ* **snake** *W.*

འབུ་བ་ ₒbú-ba, pf. ₒbus 1. **to open, to unfold,** of flowers, esp. with *ḱa Pth.* — 2. *Cs.*: **to be lighted, kindled, set on fire**.

འབུ་མ་ ₒbú-ma *Sch.*: tool used in forging nails.

འབུ་རས་ ₒbu-rás a coarse silky material, stated to be imported into Tibet from Nepal, and to come from some other insect than the silk-worm.

འབུ་ལ་ ₒbú-la 1. *C., W.* shoe of plaited straw. — 2. *C.*: *kó-wa bú-la*, a kind of leather, resembling chagreen.

འབུ་སུ་ཧང་ ₒbu-su-háṅ medicinal herb *Med.*

འབུག ₒbug *Sch.* **awl, puncher; chisel.**

འབུགས་པ་ ₒbúgs-pa v. ₒbígs-pa.

འབུངས་པ་ ₒbúṅs-pa, prop.: **to fall upon in a body, to rush in upon,** = rúb-pa; čós-la ₒbuṅs apply yourselves with might and main to religion! it is also used of one person: ₒbad ₒbuṅs he summons all his strength, strains every nerve *Dzl.*

འབུད་པ་ ₒbúd-pa I. pf. bus, ṕu(s) (the latter form prob. transit., the former intransit.) fut. dbu, imp. ṕu(s) 1. vb.n **to blow,** lás-kyi rluṅ ₒbúd-čiṅ whilst the wind of works is blowing; čós-kyi duṅ bus the trumpet of religion blew (was blown). — 2. vb.a. **to blow,** duṅ the trumpet; **to blow away,** rluṅ-gis sbúr-ma bús-pa ltar like chaff blown off by the wind *Dzl.*; to blow up, to fan, me the fire, frq.; **to blow into, to inject,** e.g. to apply a clyster *C.*; **to blow** or **breathe upon,** bsér-bus to be encountered by a cold wind *Med.*; **to inflate, to distend** by injecting air, lus kun bús-pa ltar skraṅs *Mṅg.*; ₒbud-ₒduṅ *Wdk.* = duṅ trumpet. Cf. sbúd-pa and ṕu. — *W.* *ṕú-če*. — II. pf. imp. ṕud, fut. dbud *W.* *ṕud-če*, trs.: 1. **to put off, pull off, take off** *C., W.*, the turban, hat, coat, ring etc. *Glr.* and elsewh.; **to throw down,** ṕud bžág-go *Glr.*, = *ₒpaṅ-ste* bor *W.*, v. sub ₒṕén-pa. — 2. **to drive out, expel, cast out, chase away,** with the accus. of the person and place, yul out of the country *Tar.*; yul-ṕud an exile *Schr.*; drag-pos by force *Mil.*; **to let out** (out of a cage); **to set free, to set at liberty, to allow to pass** *W.*; **to lay out, to spend,** *ṅul tsam ṕud soṅ* how many rupees have been laid out, spent? — 3. **to pull out, tear out, extract, uproot,** so a tooth, *C., W.* — 4. **to take away, to subtract,** *gú-ne (or gu tóg-ne) ži ṕúd-pa (or ṕúd-na) ṅa lus* 4 taken from 9 leaves 5 *W.* — III. pf. ₒbud, vb.n. (limited perh. to *W.*) 1. **to fall from, escape from, drop, fall down,** *lág-pa-ne bud soṅ* it escaped, dropped out of my hand; **to fall off,** of leaves; **to fall through,** *sól-wa ḍa-míg-ne bud soṅ* the coals are fallen through the grate. — 2. **to go away, to leave,** e.g. to leave the service. — 3. **to go out of sight, to disappear,** *nyi-ma bud soṅ* the sun is gone down; *búd-ḱan* a departed (deceased) person; **the ancients, those of old,** *pristini*; **to pass away,** *dus-ṫsód bud* time passes away (make haste!); *pid-ka šar-na gun bud soṅ* when spring begins, winter has passed away; *bud čug-če* **to cause to be lost,** or **to suffer to be lost, to lose.**

འབུན་པ་, བུན་པ་ ₒbún-pa, bún-pa **to itch;** *buṅ, zá-bun* **the itch, itching** *W.*; *bun rag* I feel an itching (*B.* ɣyá-ba).

འབུབ་པ་ ₒbúb-pa, pf. bub, imp. bub(s), 1. **to be turned over, upside down,** frq. with *ḱa*, ḱa-ₒbúb-tu nyal he lies with his face undermost; ḱa-ₒbub-tu bžag or bor it is placed with its top lowermost, inverted, tilted, turned over; lag-ₒbúb (or -bubs) byéd-pa *Sch.*: stumbling to fall on the hands. — 2. fig., **to be overthrown, destroyed, spoiled,** with regard to meditation *Mil.*

འབུབས་པ་ ₒbúbs-pa, pf. imp. ṕub(s), fut. dbub, *W.* *ṕub-če*, **to put on a roof,** or something for a roof; ṫog **to make, construct a roof;** gur to pitch a tent; gru-ṕúbs corner-pavilion *S.g.*

འབུམ་ ₒbum **one hundred thousand,** ₒbúm-ṫso id.; rgyai dmag ₒbúm-ṫso lṅa

500 000 Chinese *Glr.*; *˳bum-ṕrág γčig* a hundred thousand; *˳búm-tso drug* 600 000; *mgur-˳búm* the 100 000 songs, v. *mgúr-ma.*

འབུམ་པ་ *˳búm-pa* **tomb, sepulchre** *Cs.*, *sku-˳búm*, *γduṅ-˳búm Cs.*, id.; *sku-˳búm* (**kum-búm**) n. p., a large monastery on the Chinese frontier, v. Huc, also *Köpp.*, who traces the name back to the preceding word.

འབུར་བ་ *˳búr-ba*, I. vb. 1. **to rise, to be prominent,** *sbáṅ-la brág-ri ˳búr-ba čig* a rocky hill rising from the green-sward *Mil.*; *˳búr-du dód-pa* v. *dód-pa*; *˳búr-du rkó-ba* to emboss, to work out relievos *Glr.*; **˳bur-kó gyáb-pa** *C.*, **búr-la tón-če** *W.* id. — 2. **to spring up, come forth, bud, unfold,** **ṅo bur dug** it is getting green *W.* — 3. **to increase, augment,** **ṅo kyé-na ŏ-ma bur dug** when the fields are getting green, milk becomes more plentiful *W.* — *kyoṅ-˳bur* gold and silver ornaments in relievo on some other metal. — *glo-˳búr*, *blo-˳bur* seems to be a technical term for some part of a building *Glr.* — *bris-˳búr* paintings and sculptures. — *˳búr-rko-mkʼan*, *˳búr-bzo-pa* engraver. — *˳búr-sku* relief-picture — *˳bur-rgód* (s.l.c.) *Ld.-Glr.*, *Schl.* 17, b., mentioned among various musical instruments (?). — *˳bur-ǰóms* with *byéd-pa* to reduce elevations, to smooth uneven ground; fig. *Mil.*, to prostrate an opponent in disputation. — *˳búr-po* 1. *Sch.*: **projecting, prominent; a protuberance, tumor,** *rús-pai ˳búr-poi ldebs* near the protuberance of the bone *Med.* 2. **having protuberances, uneven, rough,** opp. to *˳ǰám-po*, of the skin *Med.* — *˳búr-ma* embossment, relievo. — II. sbst. **protuberance,** e.g. a boil, pustule etc.

འབུལ་བ་ *˳búl-ba* I. vb., pf. imp. *ṕul*, fut. *dbul* (**ul*, *ụl**), *W.* **ṕúl-če** 1. **to give,** when the person receiving is considered to be of higher rank (cf. *γnáṅ-ba*), *či tsam žig dbúl-bar bgyi* how much shall we give you? *Feer Introd.* p. 70, 18; **to bring in,** e.g to place a criminal before the king *Dzl.*; *gar daṅ rtséd-mo rgyál-po-la ˳búl-ba* to perform dances etc. before the king *Dzl.*; *γtsúg-lag-kʼaṅ rgyál-po-la γzigs-par ˳búl-ba* to show the king the convent-temple *Glr.*; **to lay before, represent, report,** like *γsól-ba*, *ťsul rgyas ṕúl-bas* as they had given him a minute report of the manner in which . . . *Mil.*; *ṕul žig* communicate it to me *Mil.*; *˳bul-bar ṕul-nas Mil.*, prob. proposing to give, offering; *lam* to put a person in the way of, to put in a condition, to enable *Mil.*; specifically in dating letters: *dkar-mdáṅs-nas ṕul* given at Kardang. — 2. **to add** (arith.) *Wdk.* II. sbst. **offering, gift, present,** *˳búl-ba maṅ-po ṕul Mil.*, also *byéd-pa Pth.*

འབུས་པ་ *˳bús-pa* 1. v. *˳bú-ba.* — 2. = *˳búr-bar*, **prominent.**

འབུས་ཤིང་ *˳bus-šiṅ Sch.* **a coppice of young trees.**

འབེ་དྷ་ *˳be-dha* (**bé-da**), a class of **itinerant musicians,** cf. *mon W.* (This seems not to be a Tibetan word, but to belong to one of the mountain dialects; its spelling also — acc. to *Ld.-Glr.*, *Schl.* 25, b. p. 15 — may be wrong).

འབེན་ *˳ben Pth.*, **˳bem** *W.*, *C.*, 1. **aim, goal, target,** *˳ben ˳dzúgs-pa* to set up a target; *˳bén-la γtod-pa* to aim, to take aim; *˳bén-sa* the place where the target is to be set up; specifically: the central part of the target, the mark. — 2. **scope** *Cs.* — 3. **putrefaction** *Sch.*, = *˳bam.*

འབེན་དུག་ *˳ben-dúg Cs.* **rags, tatters.**

འབེབས་པ་ *˳bébs-pa*, pf. *ṕab*, fut. *dbab*, imp. *ṕob W.* **ṕáb-če**, causative to *˳báb-pa* 1. **to cast down, throw down,** *ltó-ba sa-la* to cast one's self on the ground *Dzl.*; *sa-rdúl ˳bebs bčug* he made (the pigeon) throw down dust *Glr.*; **to cause to rain** (e.g. jewels) frq.; *kʼyeu ču ˳bébs-kyi ri-mo* a picture representing two youths who, driven by piety, conveyed by means of an elephant skins filled with water to the fishes in a dried-up pool *Glr.*; *mig sna-rtsér* to keep one's eyes directed towards the tip of the nose. — 2. **to subject** *Dzl.* ༢༦༠, 12. — 3. **to put off, to lay aside,** e.g. *bag* I. — 4. **used in** a variety of phrases: *γnas ˳bébs-pa W.* **ži ṕáb-če** to take up one's residence in a place; *dpya ˳bébs-pa*, with *la*, to impose taxes *Tar.*, cf. ˳*bab; skyon* ˳*bébs-pa* to impute a crime to a person, to calumniate *Glr.*; *(s)*kad p̓ab-če** *W.* to translate; *blo*, resp. *t̓ugs*, e.g. *yul-p̓yogs* ˳*di-ru* ˳*bébs-pa* to direct one's thoughts to a certain place, to have a mind to settle there; *ytán-la* ˳*bébs-pa* v. *ytan*; **nā ṅúl-la p̓áb-ča** to turn the barley into money *Kun.*

འབེམ་ ˳*bem* v. *ben.*

འབེར་ ˳*ber Cs.*: 'a sort of plastic mass used by smiths'.

འབེལ་(མ་) ˳*bel(-ma)* the hair on the forehead of a horse *Cs.*

འབེལ་པོ་ ˳*bél-po Sch.*: **'temperate, saving, economical**; ˳*bél-po* ˳*dug* a good deal has been saved (by economy), ample provision has been made; ˳*bél-du* ˳*júg-pa* to enjoin temperance, frugality' (?).

འབོ་ ˳*bo* **a dry measure,** which seems to be very variable as to quantity, and little used; *k̓al-bó Cs.* **bushel.**

འབོ་བ་ ˳*bó-ba*, pf. ˳*bos, bo, p̓o*, fut. *dbo W.* **bo-če, p̓o-če**, **to pour out,** *k̓rag* ˳*bó-ba* to shed blood *Ma.*; *ma bó-ba byúṅ-nas* there being no spilling *Glr.*; *bdúd-rtsi p̓ó-bas* pouring out nectar *Glr.*; **p̓os toṅ** *Ld.* pour out! — 2. **to swell (up), to rise,** **bós-te rag** I see it has swelled *W.*; ˳*bós-pai nas Sch.* swelled barley; *srán-ma p̓ós-pa tsam* as big as a swelled pea *Lt.*; *srád-ma p̓os-p̓ós* grain swelled, and afterwards parched. — 3. **to sprout, shoot forth,** of wild-growing plants, *sa* ˳*bo* ˳*dug* the ground is verdant *C.*

འབོག་ ˳*bog*, a kind of **upper-garment,** *p̓o-*˳*bóg*, for men, *mo-*˳*bóg* for females *Cs.* — 2. *W.*: **a square cloth,** for wrapping up and carrying provisions, also **bog-ča**, hence **bog-ṭes** a burden thus formed. — 3. *W.*, **a small hillock;** **sa-bóg, be-bóg** a sand-hill; **ri-bóg** a projecting hill, also a clod; **paṅ-bóg** a piece of turf.

འབོག་ཆོལ་ ˳*bog-čol* v. *sbug-čol.*

འབོག་ཐོ་ ˳*bog-t̓ó, žwá-mo* ˳*bog-t̓o Cs.*, **hat with a broad crown of yellow cloth, and trimmed with long-haired fur.**

འབོག(ས)་པ་ ˳*bog(s)-pa*, pf. *bog, p̓og*, fut. *dbog? W.* **bog-če**, **to be rooted out, uprooted, pulled out,** of teeth *W.*; **to be put out of joint,** *tsigs W.* — 2. **to be taken down** (opp. to ˳*gél-ba*), *k̓ál-rnams p̓og Glr.* the loads were taken off; **zaṅ mé-ne** the kettle from the fire *W.* — 3. **to grow loose, to come off, to drop off,** leaves from a tree *C.* — 4. **to sink down, to fall to the ground,** esp. in a fainting-fit, ˳*bog-čiṅ brgyál-ba Thgy.*, *brgyál(-žiṅ)* ˳*bóg-pa Pth.*, id.; ˳*bog yun-riṅ-na Lt.* prob.: when the fainting-fit has lasted a long time; *smyo-*˳*bóg* **madness, insanity,** ˳*byuṅ* sets in, takes place *Glr.*; ˳*bog-ši* being quickly carried off, by cholera etc. *W.* — 5. **to wade, to dip into, to submerge,** *č̓ú-la Dzl.* also *ču Lex.* to wade through the water.

འབོགས་པ་ ˳*bógs-pa*, pf. *p̓og*, fut. *dbog, dbag*, imp. *p̓og*, 1. **to give, to impart,** *ydams-ṅág, luṅ* counsel, advice, directions *Tar.*; *k̓rid, bsláb-pa Mil.* instruction; *sdóm-pa* to impose religious duties, i.e. to receive into holy orders *Glr.*; to bequeath, to give (?), *nor Lex.* — 2. *yži-ma* **to fit up a dwelling,** = ˳*bébs-pa Glr.*; *gro* ˳*bógs-pa* to take breakfast. — 3. **to blot, stain, pollute,** v. ˳*bág-pa.*

འབོང་བ་ ˳*bóṅ-ba Cs.*, **roundness, rotundity,** ˳*boṅ-*˳*bóṅ*, **round;** acc. to my informants **boṅ-bóṅ** **loose, slack, incoherent** *W.*

འབོད་ ˳*bod* 1. v. ˳*bód-pa.* — 2. v. ˳*bád-pa.*

འབོད་པ་ ˳*bód-pa, bód-pa*, pf. imp. *bos, W.* **bo-če, bos (boi, bo)**, 1. **to call, to exclaim,** *sdod čig čes bós-so* he exclaimed: wait! *Dzl.*; *mi žig B.*, *mi žig-la* col., to call a person; *rtsar Glr.*, *mdún-du Pth.* to call near; *náṅ-du* to call in; ˳*bód-pai brda* or *t̓sig* **interjection** *Gram.*; *č̓áṅ-la* ˳*bod-pa* to call, to invite, to a cup of beer *Dzl.*; *ma bós-par* ˳*óṅ-ba* to come uninvited *Dzl.*; *kú-čos* ˳*bód-pa Wdṅ.*, ˳*bod-grógs-pa Dzl.* to cry repeatedly; **bós-ra** *Ld.*, **boi-ra, bo-ra** *Lh.*, **táṅ-če** or *gyáb-če** id. *W.*; *ṅu-*˳*bód* howling, v. *ṅú-ba.* — 2. **to call, to name, to denominate,** *yúl-skad*... ˳*bód-pa* commonly called, styled ... *Wdṅ.*

འབོབས་ ₒbobs, not exactly 'stocking' (*Sch.*), but a soft, warm stuffing of the stockings; **bob-zὀn** a shoe provided with such stuffing *C.*

འབོར་བ་ ₒbór-ba, pf. imp. *bor*, 1. **to throw, cast, fling,** e.g. the mendicant's bowl up in the air, the sword to the ground *Dzl.*; *zám-pai ₒóg-tu* to precipitate a person from a bridge *Dzl.*; *p̔yir* to cast out *Thgy.*; **ma bhor-wa ɉhe** *C.* don't throw it away! **bhor soṅ** I've lost it *C. bor-ɣtór, bor-stór, bor-dór, dór-ₒbor-ba Mil.* and elsewh. id.; to throw away, pour away, *ču* water *C.*; to waste, to squander *Dzl.* — 2. **to leave, forsake,** *k̔yim-t̔ab* husband or wife *Dzl.*; to leave behind, *mi žig bód-du* to leave a person behind in Tibet; *yáb-kyis bór-bai tse* when I was left by my father, when my father died *Pth.*; *de bór-la t̔oṅ* let that alone, give it up, keep away from it *Mil.*; **ṅa lé-ka bor taṅ yin** *W.* I shall now leave off working, I shall put aside my work. — 3. = *ₒɉóg-pa*, **to place, put, lay,** in *W.* the word commonly used, in *C.* and *B.* only in certain phrases: **'i-ru bor** put it here! **tán-ni k̔ar bór-če** to seat a person on the carpet, to invite to a seat on the carpet; **mii lág-tu ṭin bór-če** to place a charge into somebody's hands; **nyér-pa só-ma bór-če** to appoint a new manager; frq. with gerund: **k̔yi tág-te bór-če** to fasten a dog (to a chain). — 4. in particular combinations, e.g. *góm-pa*.

འབོལ་ ₒbol (v. *bol*) **cushion, bolster, mattress;** *snye-ₒból* pillow, v. *snye-ba*.

འབོལ་པོ་ ₒból-po *B., C.*, **ₒból-mo** *W.* 1. **soft,** of the ground, beds, leather, fruit etc.; **soft, gentle, pliable,** also as to disposition of mind; *ₒból-le šig-ge sdód-pa* to sit still, to remain quiet, tranquil *Mil.* — 2. *C.* = *mód-po*.

འབོས་ ₒbos 1. v. *ₒbo.* — 2. v. *ₒbo-ba.* — 3. sbst. **boil, bump, tumour** *C.*

འབྱང་བ་ ₒbyaṅ-ba **to clean, cleanse, purify** *Cs.*, *ₒbyaṅ-k̔yád* custom *C., W.*

འབྱམས་པ་ ₒbyám-pa, pf. *byams Cs.*, **to flow over, to be diffused.** *ₒbyam-klás-pa Lex., Cs.*: unlimited, infinite; *rab-ₒbyáms Lex., Cs.*: widely diffused, far spread; *rab-ₒbyáms-pa Cs.*: a man of profound learning, a doctor of theology or philosophy; also *Schr.*; *Köpp.* II, 253.

འབྱར་བ་ ₒbyár-ba v. *ₒbyór-ba.*

འབྱི་བ་ ₒbyí-ba, pf. *byi*, also *p̔yi* and *p̔yis*, vb. n. of *p̔yí-ba* **to be wiped off, blotted out, effaced** *Cs.*; **to fall off,** of the hair *Dzl.* and elsewh.

འབྱིང་བ་ ₒbyíṅ-ba, pf. *byiṅ* 1. **to sink in, to sink down, to be swallowed up,** *šiṅ-rṭa byé-ma-la ₒbyiṅ Glr.* the carriage sticks fast in the sand; *gru čú-la* the ship sinks in the water *Dzl.* and elsewh. — 2. **to grow faint, languid, remiss,** *rig-pa byíṅ-ba bsér-ba* to lift up again one's fainting soul *Mil.*; *byiṅ-rgod* seems to signify **languor, distraction,** *byiṅ-rmúgs Mil.*, id., *byiṅ-rmugs-méd-pai sgom*; so also *byiṅ-t̔ibs Lt.*; *sems-byiṅ-ba* **drowsiness, indolence, depression of spirits.** — 3. *C.* **ɉhiṅ soṅ, ɉhiṅ log soṅ**, they have dispersed, separated, are all gone home. — 4. v. *ₒɉiṅ*, 2.

འབྱིད་པ་ ₒbyíd-pa, pf. *byid*, *p̔yid* 1. **to glide, to slip** *Lex.* = *ₒdréd-pa.* — 2. **to disappear, to pass away,** e.g. *mi-t̔se ₒbyid* human life passes away *Lex.*; in *W.* **tse p̔íd-če** vb. a., to earn a livelihood, **gár-ra čó-te** by smith's work (*C. lto zá-ba*).

འབྱིན་པ་ ₒbyin-pa, pf. imp. *p̔yuṅ*, fut. (in *C.* also pres.) *dbyuṅ Ld.* **p̔íṅ-če**, trs. of *ₒbyuṅ-ba*, **to cause to come forth: 1. to take out, to remove,** a pillar from its place *Dzl.*; **p̔iṅs(toṅ)** take it out (out of your pocket, out of the box etc.) *Ld.*; **to draw out, pull out,** a sword, a thorn etc., frq.; **to tear out, to put out,** one's eyes etc., *mig dbyúṅ-ba dé-dag* the men whose eyes are to be put out *Dzl.* p. ༢༩, 10, acc. to an emended reading; **to draw forth, produce, bring to light,** something that was hid *Dzl.* — 2. in a more gen. sense: **to let proceed from, to send out, to emit,** rays of light, frq.; *lus-la k̔rag* to draw blood by scratching one's self *Dzl.*; *mči-ma Glr.* to shed tears; *skad* to make the voice to be heard, of a bird *Dzl.*; *sdug-bsṅál-gyi skad* to utter complaints, lamentations *Dzl.*; *skad čén-po* to cry aloud *Dzl.*; **to exhibit, to extol,** *bstán-paí čé-ba* the grandeur of the doctrine *Tar.* 48, 9, *Schf.*; **to drive out, turn out, expel,** *γnas ˳byin-pa Tar.*, **yúṅ-wa** *Ts.*, to banish, so also *Ld.* **piṅ-ce**; **to cast out, throw away** *Ts.*; **to save, rescue, liberate, release,** *nas* from, *Dom.*; absol. *Tar.* 121, 19. — 3. particular phrases, such as *ḱól-du ṗyúṅ-ba*, *yid ˳byin-pa* etc. v. in their own places.

**འབྱུག་པ་** *˳byúg-pa*, pf. and imp *byugs* 1. **to wet, moisten, smear, spread over, anoint,** with *la*: *ša skám-la ṫsá-ču byúgs-pa* salt-meat *Glr.*; *γdóṅ-la sol-snúm ˳byúg-pa* to daub one's face with coal-salve *Glr.*; also with accus. and instrum.: *lha-rtén spos daṅ byúg-pas* covering the little temple with spices and ointments *Dzl.*; *γser ˳byúg-pa* prob. to gild *Pth.* — 2. **to stroke, to pat,** *mgó la* a person's head *Dzl.*

**འབྱུང་བ་** *˳byúṅ-ba* 1. vb., pf. imp. *byuṅ* (intrs. of *˳byin-pa*) **to come out, to emerge,** often with a pleon. *ṗyir* etc., from the water, from an egg, a vessel etc. *Dzl.*; *˳ḱór-ba-las* = to be set free, to be liberated *Dom.*; to go out, *ḱyim-nas Dzl.*; *ṗyi-rol-tu ˳byúṅ-ba* to go out into the open air *Dzl.*; **to make one's appearance, to become visible** *Dzl.*; **to show one's self, to appear** *rgyál-poi rmi-lam-du byúṅ-bai lha-γčig* the princess that appeared to the king in a dream *Glr.*; also: *ṅá-la rmi-lam bzáṅ-po byuṅ* I have had an auspicious dream *Mil.*; *sgrén-mor ˳byúṅ-ba* to go abroad naked *Dzl.*; **to be heard, to resound,** *skad* frq.; **to be said, to be told** *Tar.*; **to turn out, to prove, to be found,** *ma bzi-ba su byúṅ-ba* he who is found not intoxicated *Glr.*; *ṅán-pa byuṅ* it proved to be ill founded *Mil.*; ... *pa su yaṅ ma byuṅ* none was to be found that ... *Pth.*; to step forward, from the crowd; to step forth, to appear *Glr.*; **to step up to,** with *rtsar* to *Glr.*; *brgyúgs-nas byuṅ* they came running up or near *Pth.*; **to go to, to proceed to, to come,** *rii rtsé-mor Dzl.*; **ka-náṅ-wa ma júṅ-na** *W.* if no order (permission etc.) comes; *dbugs ṗyir byuṅ-nas* when breathing returned, when they recovered from fainting *Dzl.*; *mun-pai bskal-pa lṅa-brgya byuṅ-ṅo* then came, followed, 500 dark Kalpas *Pth.* — 2 **to rise,** as kings, frq.; **to arise, to originate, to become,** with *nas*, *las*, from, in consequence of, by, *dé-nas byuṅ* it derives its origin from that *Glr.*; *˳brás-bu ˳byúṅ-bai šiṅ* trees on which fruit is growing *Stg.*; *mi ˳byúṅ-bar ˳gyúr ba* not to come to a fair beginning, to be suppressed in its first beginnings *Glr.*; *ḱyeu žig byuṅ ˳dug* by that time a boy had become of it *Glr.*; *γnyis-su byuṅ* they became two, they split in two (systems of doctrine); *ráb-tu ˳byúṅ-ba* to become a priest, v. *rab*; to come in (money); **to happen, to take place,** very frq., *ltas či byuṅ* what signs have taken place? *Dzl.*; *mi žig-la nyés-pa čén-po byuṅ* = a man has committed etc. *Dzl.* frq.; *ro ˳di-rnams-la či byuṅ-ba yin* what has happened to these corpses, what is their history? *Glr.*; *sṅar byuṅ ba* and *ma byuṅ-ba* things heard of and unheard of *Tar.*; *ḱá-ṗye-nas yód-pa dé-aṅ de dús-su byúṅ-ṅo* 'at that time also the opened position (of the hands of the image) took place' *Glr.*; *blá-ma-la yaṅ byuṅ lágs-sam* did the same thing happen to your Reverence? *Mil.*; *ṅéd-kyis ˳di-bžin byuṅ* it is I that brought this thing about *Glr.*; *ṗyis-byuṅ* or *˳byuṅ* the later time, time to come, also adv. afterwards, latterly, *Tar.* — 3. The word more and more assumes the character of an auxiliary in such phrases as the following: *˳gro-ṫub-pa byuṅ* they were able to proceed (the possibility of proceeding was brought about) *Glr.*; *da bla-ma der bžúgs-pa byúṅ-na* in case your Reverence should stay there *Mil.*; with the supine: *˳búl-du, žér-du, stón-du byúṅ-ba-la(s)* as they gave, said, showed *Mil.*; *ṫugs-dám ˳ṗél-bar byuṅ* meditation increased; lastly, with the root only: *bod daṅ ˳brel byuṅ* came into communication with Tibet *Glr.*; *sleb byúṅ-ba-la* when he appeared *Mil.*; *rdo dbyug byuṅ* he threw a stone; and so it is commonly used now, esp. in *C.*; it supplies the place of a copula in: *γsuṅ de kun séms-la šin-tu ˳ṫád-pa žig byuṅ* this song was truly heart-affecting *Mil.*

**Comp.** ₒbyúṅ-ḱuṅs 1. = ču-mig **a well, spring** *Sambh.* 2. **origin** *Pth.* 3. **ablative case** *Gram.* — ₒbyúṅ-ḱuṅs-kyi ḱams *Cs.*, 'a mineral, *byuṅ-ḱuṅs-kyi ḱáms-kyi bċud* a mineral elixir'(?) — ₒbyuṅ-γnás (सम्भव), **place of origin** (cf. *padma* ₒbyuṅ-γnás); **primitive source,** *yón-tan ťams-ċád-kyi* ₒbyuṅ-γnás source of all accomplishments; *byuṅ-bai γži* id.; *p̒an-bdé ťams-čád* ₒbyúṅ-bai γži primordial source of all happiness. — II. sbst. 1. **a coming forth, an originating, the state of being,** ₒbyuṅ-ba-nyid *Tar.* 4, 4 *Schf.* the true state of a case. — 2. **element**, usually 4: ₒbyúṅ-ba bžii γnód-pa damage done by fire, water, wind and sand *Glr.*; ₒbyuṅ-ba bžii *lus* the physical body, very frq.; ₒbyúṅ-ba *γyo* the elements are in motion, are raging *Ma.*; higher philosophy numbers 5 elements, adding the ether, *mḱa*, as the fifth; accordingly physiology teaches, that in the composition of the human body earth constitutes the mucus of the nose, water the saliva, fire produces the pictures formed in the eyes, air the sensations of the skin, ether the sensations of the ear; even 6 elements are spoken of, v. *Köpp.* I, 602. — 3. symb. num. for 5.

འབྱུང་པོ་ ₒbyúṅ-po (भूत) 1. **being, creature,** ₒbyúṅ-po kun all beings *Cs.*; ₒbyúṅ-po čén-po the great being, Buddha *Cs.* — 2. **demon, evil spirit, foul sprite,** frq., ₒbyuṅ-po-srúṅ a preservative, talisman, against such; ₒbyúṅ-mo fem. *Cs.*

འབྱེ་བ་ ₒbyé-ba, pf. and imp. *bye*, *W.* *be-če(s)*, intrs. of ₒbyéd-pa 1. **to open,** *padma ḱá-bye-ba* a lotos-flower that has opened *Glr.*; *mṅal ḱá-bye-nas* when the mouth of the womb has opened itself *S.g.* — 2. **to divide, separate, resolve,** *ska sla γnyis-su bye* it resolves into thick and thin matter *Med.*; *dúm-bu stóṅ-du dbyé-bar* ₒgyur it separates into a thousand pieces *Glr.*; *bye-brág ma byé-bai bár-du* as long as the separation has not evidenced itself *Dzl.*

འབྱེད་པ་ ₒbyéd-pa, pf. and imp. *p̒ye*, *p̒yed*, *p̒yes*, fut. *dbye*, *W.* *p̒é-če(s)*, pf. and imp. *p̒e(s)*, vb. a., 1. **to open,** *ḱa p̒e(s) toṅ* *W.* open your mouth; *sgo p̒yés-nas* ₒǰóg-pa *Pth*, *p̒é-te bór-če* *W.* to open the door without shutting it again; fig. *čós-kyi sgo rnám-par* ₒbyéd-pa; *mig* to open one's eyes, opp. to ₒdzúm-pa; *lóṅ-bai mig* ₒbyéd-pa to open a blind man's eyes *Dzl.*; to open again what had been shut or stopped, to restore, *dáṅ-ga, yi-ga B.*, *ḱam W.* the appetite; *ba-p̒yéd* the open b, b pronounced like w, *Gram.*; to get out, work out, fetch out, stone-shivers by means of a chisel *Glr.* — 2. **to separate, to keep asunder, to disentangle,** threads *W.*; to disunite, to set at variance, *dé-dag dbyé-bai p̒yir* in order to set them at variance, to create enmity between them *Stg.*; to part, separate, *byaṅ-ḱóg-stod-smad mčin-dris dbyé-ba ste* the cavity of the chest and the abdomen being separated by the diaphragm *S.g.*; **to divide, classify,** *rígs-kyi sgó-nas dbyé-na* if they are classified according to the different species *Lt.*; **to pick, to sort,** pease; hence, **to pick out, choose, select,** *p̒é-te kyoṅ* make your choice, and bring it here! *W.*; *séms-ċan-rnams lás-kyis rnám-par p̒ye* the beings are severed by their deeds *Thgy.*; *ḱá-p̒ye-ba* to open, to separate, e.g. when hands, that were laid in each other, are separated again *Glr.*; *ḱá-p̒ye-ba* also **to open, to begin to bloom**; ₒbyéd-pa **to dissect, to anatomize** *Thgy.*; esp. with *rnám-par*, **to analyze,** to explain grammatically and logically, *don*, the sense, import, *Stg.* frq.; as *sdúd-pa* is the opposite of it: ₒbyed-sdúd **analysis and synthesis** *Cs.*; ₒbyed-sdúd-kyi sgra term for the affix *am*, the disjunctive particle (ni f.) *Glr.*; *mi-p̒yéd-pa* **inseparable, indivisible, imperishable,** *sku Sch.*; **unshaken, immovable,** *dád-pa Mil.* frq.

འབྱེད་དཔྱད་ ₒbyed-dpyád *Sch.* **tongs, pincers.**

འབྱེམ་པ་ ₒbyém-pa, with *byéd-pa*, 'to act with promptness, determination and good success' *Sch.*

འབྱེར་བ་ ₒbyér-ba pf. and imp. *byer*, **to disperse in flight,** to flee in different directions *Dzl.* *ťsóṅ-*ₒ*dus byér-nas mi* ₒdúg-ste the market-people having fled, and no body remaining *Pth.*; **to give way, to be**

**removed,** of diseases *Lt.*, opp. to *γyas* and *bsags.*

འབྱོ་བ་ *₀byó-ba*, pf. *p̓yo, p̓yos*, imp. *p̓yo, byo, byos,* **to pour out, to pour into another vessel, to transfuse** *Lex.* and *Cs.*

འབྱོག་པ་ *₀byóg-pa*, pf. *byogs* **to lick** *Lex.* and *Cs.*

འབྱོང་བ་ *₀byóṅ-ba* I. pf. *byáṅ-ba* 1. **to be cleansed,** purified, v. *byáṅ-ba.* — 2. **to be skilled, well versed,** *rig-byéd-la* in the Vedas *Tar.* — II. pf. *₀byoṅs-pa* **to be finished, perfect, complete,** frq. with *snyiṅ-rǰe Mil* and elsewh., to exercise full compassion(?) cf. *sbyóṅ-ba.* (The above arrangement is nothing more than an attempt; in order to arrive at any certainty as to these roots, a far greater number of observations would be required.)

འབྱོན་པ་ *₀byón-pa*, pf. and imp. *byon*, resp. **to go, proceed, travel,** *dé-nas byón-pa-na* then in proceeding on the way *Glr.*; **to arrive, appear, become visible;** also for *₀byúṅ-ba*, e.g. *raṅ-byón*; with root of the verb: *p̓úr-byon-pas* preparing to fly *Mil.*; *ma-byón-pa* = *ma-₀óṅs-pa* future (Buddhas) *S.O.*; to rise, to appear; with dat. inf. = *₀ǰúg-pa* **to begin, to set about** a certain work *Tar.* 125, 16.

འབྱོར་པ་ *₀byór-pa* **wealth, riches, goods, treasures,** *₀byor-pa zád-mi-šes-pa daṅ ldán-pa* one possessing inexhaustible wealth, *bdé-ba daṅ ₀byór-pa* joy and treasures *S.O.*; *₀byór-pa drug Pth.*, prob. six kinds of temporal goods; *ráṅ-gi ₀byór-pa lṅa* and *γžan-gyi ₀byor-pa-lṅa* five subjective and five objective goods, of a similar nature as those mentioned sub *dal-₀byor*, yet without any evident reason for being thus divided *Thgy.*; *₀byor-ldán* rich, mostly used as a noun personal.

འབྱོར་བ་, འབྱར་བ་ *₀byór-ba, ₀byár-ba* I. intrs. of *sbyór-ba* 1. **to stick to, adhere to** *Med.*; **k̓yág-la ǰar soṅ**, it is frozen fast *W.*; *₀byár-byed spyin* glue *Lex.*; *₀byor-sman* sticking-plaster *W.*; **to infect,** of diseases, *₀byor-nad* an infectious disease *Cs.* also mentally: **lo* or *sém-la ǰar** it sticks fast, is remembered, borne in mind. — 2. **to be prepared,** ready, at hand, extant, *ša ma byór-nas* there being no meat prepared *Dzl.*; *₀p̓rál-du ₀byór-ba ma yin* that is not at once in readiness *Dzl.*; *či ₀byór-ba des mčód-pa byéd-pa* to offer sacrifice of such things as are at hand *Dzl.*; *či-ste ₀byór-bar mi ₀gyúr-na* but if he has not such a thing at his disposal *Sambh.* — 3. **to agree,** *mi-₀byór-ba k̓á-čig* some disagreements, contradictions *Tar.* — II. resp. **to come, arrive,** *W.*, *C.*; **k̓yö́-kyi ku dǘn-du ǰár-gyu yin** I shall appear before your Honour *C.*; **nyúr-du ǰar yoṅ** I shall immediately attend *C.*

འབྱོལ་བ་ *₀byól-ba*, pf. and imp. *byol*, fut. (and pres. in *C.*) *dbyol* **to give or make way, to turn out of the way, to step aside,** *γčig-gis γčig-la Dzl.*; *₀byól-te ₀gro* in walking I make way (to people) *Dzl.*; *W.* with accus.: **rul, las, dig-pa ǰól-če** to step out of the way of, to shun, a serpent, toil, sin. Sometimes *₀ǰól-ba.*

འབྲ་གོ་ *₀brá-go* n. of a medicine *Med.*

འབྲང་ *₀braṅ* v. *braṅ* II.

འབྲང་རྒྱས་ *₀braṅ-rgyás Mil.* **sacrifice,** offering of eatables.

འབྲང་བ་ *₀bráṅ-ba* 1. pf. *₀braṅs*, imp. *₀broṅ*, **to bear, bring forth, give birth; to litter,** *bráṅ-mo* an animal going with young, bearing *Cs.* — 2. also *₀bréṅ-ba*, pf. *₀braṅs*, imp. *₀breṅs Mil.* (*₀broṅ Sch.?*) **to follow, to walk at another's heels,** with *p̓yir*, *p̓yi-bžin* (*-du*), *rǰés-su*, *W.* **tiṅ-la** with genit., **to follow, pursue, hunt after,** *dbyúg-pas* with a stick *Pth.*; **to pursue,** in one's thoughts.

འབྲད་པ་, འདྲད་པ་ *₀brád-pa, ₀drád-pa*, pf. *brad*, imp. *brod* **to scratch, to scrape,** with the nails, claws etc.; **to lacerate by scratching,** *γdoṅ Dzl.*; also **to gnaw, nibble at.**

འབྲབ་པ་ *₀bráb-pa*, pf. *brab*, imp. *brob* 1. **to catch suddenly, to snap away, snatch away,** a fly with one's hand, the prey with a bound. — 2. **to beat, to scourge,** *ts̓er-lčág-gis* with thorns *Thgy.* — 3. **to throw out, to scatter,** magical objects, such as grains of barley etc.

**འབྲལ་བ་** *ₒbrál-ba*, pf. *bral*, imp. *brol*, intrs. of *ₒṕrál-ba*, **to be separated, parted from, deprived of,** c. *dań*, e.g. from one's retinue, of the light of doctrine *Dzl.*; *ₒbrál-bar mi ṕod bú-mo ḱyod* thou, my daughter, from whom I am not able to part *Glr.*; *čúń-ṅu-nas ṕa-má γnyis dań brál-te* from a child bereft of parents, an orphan from infancy *Pth.*; **to lose, to be bereft,** frq. used in reference to the death of near relations; *mdo-sdé dań lág-pa mi brál-žiń* as the sacred writings never came out of his hands; *skóm-pa dań brál-bar gyúr-to* he got rid of his thirst; *nad dań brál-bar gyúr-to* he recovered from his illness, frq. (in such cases often confounded by the illiterate with *nád-las bsgral* etc.); more particularly: *srog dań* etc. **to die, perish,** frq.; *ₒjig-čiń ₒbrál-bar ₒgyúr-ba* to be dissolved, of the human body *Dzl.*; *ₒdú-ba yód-na ₒbral-bar oń* what was solid, is dissolved in dust *Dzl.*; *ₒbral(-bar) med (-pa)* **inseparable, indissoluble,** frq.

**འབྲས་** *ₒbras*, *C.* also *ₒbrás-mo*, resp. *bsań-ₒbrás* (*Pur.* **bras**, *Ld.* **ḍas**, *Lh.* **ḍai**, *C.* **ḍę**) 1. **rice;** *ₒbras-dkár(-mo)* white rice, *ₒbras-dmár* red rice (the inferior and cheaper sort); of the former there seem to be distinguished: *ₒbo-tsa-li* (*Hd.* **basmati**), *rgyal-mo-γsán, ham-dzém, ₒdzin-ₒdzin* the second sort, acc. to *Cs.*; *ₒbrás-kyi srus* peeled rice *Sch.*; *ₒbras-sá-lu* 'wild rice' *Sch.*; *ₒbras-so-ba Sch.* and *Schr.*, rice not husked *ₒbrás-mo spos-šel* or *dkar-ₒdzóm Ts.* maize.

**Comp.** *ₒbras-čáṅ* rice-wine, rice-beer. — *ₒbras-čán* boiled rice. — *ša-ₒbrás* rice mixed with small pieces of meat. — *ₒbras-túg* rice-soup. — *ₒbras-žiń* rice-field. — *ₒbras-zán* dish of rice. — *ₒbras-yós* parched rice *Med.* — *ₒbras-sil C.* boiled rice, got up with butter, sugar, apricots etc., *W.* **ṕu-lá, ṕo lá**, پلاو. — 2. **tumour,** esp. larger swellings in the groin etc.

**འབྲས་ལྗོངས་** *ₒbras-ljóń* (**ḍe-jóń**) n. p., **Sikim.**

**འབྲས་སྤུངས་** *ₒbras-spúńs* n. p., monastery near Lhasa.

**འབྲས་བུ་** *ₒbrás-bu* 1. **fruit,** e.g. *šiń-gi Mil.*; *ₒbrás bu ye-méd-kyi sa* a country producing no fruit *Thgy.*; **corn, grain,** *ₒbrás-bu zín-bas brńá-ba Mil.*; *ₒbras-ńan* a failure of fruit. — 2. **testicle** *Wdń.* cf. *rlig-pa*; *mig-ₒbrás* apple of the eye. — 3. fig. **effect, consequence,** esp. as opp. to *rgyu*, hence *rgyu-ₒbrás* cause and effect, more esp. in moral philosophy = **retribution, requital, recompense, reward,** three grades being distinguished: 1. *rnám-par smin-pai ₒbrás-bu* full recompense, in the worst case by the punishments of hell; 2. *rgyu bťún-pai ₒbrás-bu* by adversity during life; 3. *dbáń-gi ₒbrás-bu* by unpleasant local circumstances, — so *Thgy.*; *rgyu-ₒbrás* and *ₒbrás-bu* also directly denote **the doctrine of final retribution,** *ₒbrás-bu mi bden* the doctrine of requital is not true *Thgy.*; further: *ₒbrás-bu* reward of ascetic exercises, the various grades of perfection, of which four are distinguished: a. *rgyún-du-žugs-pa* स्रोतापत्ति or as partic. ०पन्न, he who enters the stream (that takes from the external world to Nirwana); b. *lan-γčig-ṕyir-ₒoń-ba* सकृदागामिन्, he who returns once more (for the period of a human birth); c. *ṕyir-mi-ₒoń-ba* अनागामिन् he who returns no more, being a candidate of Nirwana; d. *dgra-bčom-pa* अर्हन्त, the Arhat, the finished saint; v. *Köpp.* I, 398.

**འབྲི་ཁུང་** or **གུང་** *ₒbri-ḱúń* or *-guń* sect of Lamas and monastery in Tibet, *ₒbri-ḱúń-pa* member of that sect.

**འབྲི་ཏ་** *ₒbri-ta* a form of medicine, prob. a kind of extract *Med.*; *ₒbri-ta-sa-ₒdzin* medicinal herb, an emetic, *Med.*; in *Lh.* Cuscuta, which however does not agree with the descriptions.

**འབྲི་བ་** *ₒbri-ba*, I. pf. and imp. *bri*, intrs. of *ₒṕri-ba* **to lessen, decrease, diminish,** of water, frq. in conjunction with *ḱa*, at the surface, used with regard to size, number and intensity (synon. *ₒgrib-pa*). — II. pf. and imp. *bris* (*Glr.* also *bri*) 1. **to draw, design, describe,** *dkyil-ₒḱor žig* to describe a circle or other figure; also to paint *Glr.* 2. **to write,** *yi-ge* letters, a letter (epistle); *yi-ger 'literis mandare'*, to record, to write down, something from hearing *Dzl.*: *ₒbri-smyúg* writing-reed, pen, pencil etc.

**འབྲི་མོ་** *˳bri-mo*, **चमरी, tame female yak;** *rgod-˳bri Pth.*, or *˳broṅ-˳bri Cs.*, wild female yak; *˳bri-zal* young female yak *Ld.-Glr.*, *˳bri-o* yak-milk; *˳bri-mar* yak-butter; *˳bri-mdzo* (*W.* **brim-dzo**) bastard of bull and yak.

**འབྲི་མོག་** *˳bri-móg* medicinal herb *Med.*

**འབྲིང་** *˳briṅ* **middle, midst, mean, middling, moderate,** *˳briṅ žig* something moderate, of middling quality, = *ṫsád-ma* or *ṫig-ṫsád W.*; *briṅ-po* the middle one, of three sons *Dzl.* and elsewh.; between *stobs čé* and *čúṅ-nu Lt.*; *bzaṅ ṅan ˳briṅ γsum*; *rnal-˳byór ˳briṅ-po* one that is moderately advanced in contemplation *Thgr.*; *zlá-ba ˳bríṅ-po* v. *zla-ba*; *˳bríṅ-gis* **middling, moderately,** adv.

**འབྲིང་བ་** *˳briṅ-ba*, in *žabs-˳briṅ byéd-pa* for *bráṅ-ba Mil.*

**འབྲིད་པ་** *˳brid-pa* 1. also *˳dríd-pa*, pf. *brid*, **to deceive, cheat, impose upon,** *blo ˳brid-pa* id. *Glr.*; *˳brid-de rṅód-pa-las Tar.*, as she wanted to seduce him deceitfully; *ḱa-mṅar-brid* deceitfully, insidiously sweet, being followed by a nauseous, acrid or burning taste *Med.* — 2. *Cs.* = *˳ṗri-ba.*

**འབྲིམ་པ་** *˳brím-pa*, I. vb., pf. *brim(s)* 1. **to distribute, deal out, hand round,** sweet-meats, flowers, poems *Dzl.*, *Tar.*; *... la*, to ... — 2. *Ld.* **to throw away,** what is worthless, = **ṗáṅ-čes**. — II. sbst. **distributer, dispenser, waiter at table** *Dzl.*; *˳brím (-pa) -po*, id. *Cs.*

**འབྲུ་** *˳bru* **grain, corn, seed,** frq.; grain of sand, *byé-ma ˳bru rei stéṅ-na* on every grain of sand *Glr.*; *˳bru ˳ṫag-pa* to pound grains *Lex.* — 2. a single **grain, piece, letter,** *yi-ge ˳bru γčig* a single letter; also without *yi-ge*: *˳bru drúg* the six letters = *yi-ge-drúg-pa*, v. *drug.* — 3. collectively, **grain, corn,** in gen. *˳brui ḱal* a load of grain *Dzl.*; *˳brú-sna mi ˳ḱruṅs* no kind of grain is growing *Glr.*; *˳bru gáṅ-bu-čan* pulse, legume *S.g.*; *nor dan ˳bru-rnams ˳ṗel* money and corn multiply. — *˳bru-rdóg* grain of seed. — *˳brú-sna* v. above. — *˳bru-báṅ* granary. — *˳bru-˳bú* corn-worm, weevil *Cs.*

*˳bru-már* oil extracted from seeds; lamp-oil *Dzl.* — *˳brú-ṫsoṅ-pa* oil-merchant.

**འབྲུ་ཐང་** *˳bru-ṫáṅ*, n. of a superior sort of tea.

**འབྲུ་བ་, བྲུ་བ་** *˳brú-ba, bru-ba*, pf. and imp *brus*, *˳drú-ba, drus* 1. **to dig,** *ḱúṅ-bu, dur, doṅ* (cf. *rkó-ba*). — 2. **to chisel, carve, cut.** — 3. *Sch.* **to look through,** *yig* a writing; **to examine,** *˳bru* grain; hence *mṫsaṅ ˳bru-ba* to spy out, smell out, faults, stirring up brawls and quarrels by it, *Stg.* **to irritate, vex, provoke,** *mṫsaṅ ˳brú-bai ṫsig* provoking words *Lex.*; *snyad, snyon ˳brú-ba* **to accuse** *W.*

**འབྲུ་མ་** *˳brú-ma* **tumour, swelling, weal** *Sch.*

**འབྲུ་ཚ་** *˳bru-ṫsa* an angular kind of Tibetan current handwriting, v. *Csoma Gram.*

**འབྲུ་ཤལ་, འབྲུ་ཤ་** *˳bru-šál, ˳bru-šá* v. *bru-šá.*

**འབྲུག་** *˳brug* (*Bal.* **blug**) 1. **thunder,** *˳brug-skád, ˳brug-sgrá* id.; *skad-čen ˳brug* loud thunder; *˳brug ˳bód-pa Cs.*, *grág-pa Dzl.*, *ldír-ba Lex.* and elsewh., thundering. — 2. **dragon** (to which thunder is ascribed *Sch.*); *γyu-˳brúg sṅón-po* blue dragon *Glr*

**འབྲུག་པ་** *˳brúg-pa* I. sbst. 1. **sect of Lamas,** clothed in red, *Schl.*73., established in the province of Bhotan, acc. to *Sch.* = *ža-dmár*, = *sá-skya.* — 2. **Bhotan.** —

II. vb. for *˳brúb-pa Mil.* frq.

**འབྲུད་པ་** *˳brúd-pa*, = *˳brú-ba*, also *˳drúd-pa.*

**འབྲུབ་པ་** *˳brúb-pa* 1. gen. with *ču*, **to cause to overflow, to gush, to spout forth to flow over,** *Mil.*, *Tar.* and elsewh.; *ču-˳brub Lex.*, *˳brubs Sch.* water that has flown over (?). *˳brub-po* **fluid, liquid; fluidity, a fluid,** *Cs.* (?). — 2. *Cs.* **to deal out.** — 3. *Sch.* **to shut up, wrap up.**

**འབྲུམ་པ་** *˳brúm-pa* 1. *Cs.* **grain, minute particle,** *˳brum-rdog*, *˳bru-rdóg* a single grain, = *˳bru*; **fruit,** *rgun-˳brúm* grape; *se-˳brúm* hip (fruit of wild brier) *Sik.* — 2. **pustule, pock,** gen. *˳brúm-bu*; *˳brum-nad* small-pox; *˳brum-nág* black or deadly small-pox; *˳brum-dkár* white small-pox; *˳brum-ḱrá* coloured small-pox *Med.*, *˳brum-*

*pa* and *ₒbrúm-pa nág-po* as name of a disease of the groin, prob. bubo *Med.* — *ₒbrum-rjes* pock-mark. — *ₒbrúm-po* a large grain *Cs.; ₒbrúm-bu* a small grain; pock, pustule, v. above.

འབྲུམ་ལྷ་མོ་ *ₒbrum-lha-mo Sch.* a tutelar goddess of little children, worshipped by the Shamans.

འབྲེ་བ་ *ₒbré-ba*, pf. and imp. *bres* **to draw over** or **before, to spread, to stretch,** a net *Glr.*, a curtain *Glr.*, a canopy, awning *Lex.*; **to wrap a thing up in a cloth,** in order to carry it, as books, a corpse *Thgy.*

འབྲེག་པ་ *ₒbrég-pa*, pf. *breg(s)*, imp. *brog(s)*, also *ₒdrég-pa* **to cut off,** *šiṅ-ta-lai lo-ma bregs-pa* a plantain branch cut off, as representing a being irremediably cut off from its former state of existence *Mil.;* **to mow** *Sch.;* of parts of the body: *ske* to cut off a person's neck *Thgr.*, *ṕo-mṫsán* the membrum virile *Schr.*, *rtai súg-pa* the foot of a horse, prob. only the tendon of it, as much as to lame, to disable *Glr.*; also to sever with a saw; most frq. in reference to the hair, to cut off, **to shave,** with the scissors or a razor, *skra daṅ ḱá-spu* frq.; *ₒbrég-mḱan* **barber, hair-cutter** *Dzl.; ₒbreg-spyád* a sharp small knife *Sch.*

འབྲེང་པ་ *ₒbréṅ-pa Cs., bréṅ-ba* **strap, rope,** *ko-ₒbréṅ* leather strap; *ša-ₒbreṅ Mil.*; *ₒbreṅ-ṫag Cs.* cane-ribbon, made of buck-leather; leading-rope, guide-line. — *ₒbréṅ-bu Cs.* cobbler's strap.

འབྲེང་བ་ *ₒbréṅ-ba* frq. for *ₒbráṅ-ba.*

འབྲེལ་ *ₒbrel* sbst. v. *ₒbrél-ba* II.

འབྲེལ་པ་ *ₒbrél-pa* **connection, conjunction,** yet only in certain applications: 1. **connection between cause and effect,** used also at once for **effect, consequence, efficacy,** *smón-lam-gyi ₒbrél-pa* the efficacy of prayer *Mil.* frq.; *ₒjog-pa* to apply, make use of it *Mil.* — 2. **the vascular and nervous system conjunctively,** the two systems in their totality, ni f., *Med.* — 3. **genitive case,** the sixth case of Tibetan Grammarians, *ₒbrél-pai sgra*, the termination of it, *kyi.* — 4. **a small quantity, a little, a bit,** *zás-kyi ₒbrél-pa žig dgos* I ask for a little bit to eat *Mil.* frq.; *čos(-kyi) ₒbrél(-pa) ṫób-pa* to snatch up a little bit of religion *Mil.*

འབྲེལ་བ་ *ₒbrél-ba* I. vb., intrs. of *sbrél-ba,* 1. **to hang together, to cohere, to be connected,** *rtsa daṅ rus-pa tsam ₒbrél-ba* connected only by veins and bones, nothing but skin and bone *Dzl.; ₒod-zér-gyi drá-bas ₒbrél-te* covered with a continuous net of rays *Glr.;* gen. with *daṅ, bod daṅ rgyai ₒbrél-ṫsul* the connection with, or the intercourse between Tibet and China *Glr.; de dan ₒbrél-bai las* the functions connected with, and peculiar to (a certain organ) *Lt.; ₒbrel-mṫsams* 1. **joint,** or **rivet** of pincers etc. *S.g.* 2. **boundary,** *W.* — 2. **to come together, to meet, to join,** *ₒbrél-γtam* gossipings in meeting on the road *Mil.* — 3. **to meet sexually, to cohabit,** *de daṅ lus ₒbrél-ba* to cohabit with (him or her) *Glr.; (lháṅ-du) ₒbrél-ba-la(s) bu skyes* they having cohabited, a child was born *Glr.* — II. sbst. *ₒbrél-ba* or *ₒbrel* **union, communication, connection,** *bod daṅ ₒbrel byuṅ* the union with Tibet took place *Glr.*; *rgya bod γnyis ₒbrel čád* the union ceases *Glr.; *nor-ḍél čó-če, nor-ḍél-la čá-če* W.*, to form a mercantile connection, to enter into commercial intercourse. — *las-ₒbrel* = *las-ₒṕro* q.v. — *γnyis-ₒbrél, γsum-ₒbrél* a double, triple consonant, e.g. *sk, skr.*

འབྲོག་ *ₒbrog* **solitude, wilderness, uncultivated land,** esp. **summer-pasture** for cattle in the mountains; thus *ₒbrog-skyoṅ-ba Ld.-Glr., Schl.* 15, 6 might imply: to attend to a mountain dairy; *gám-ₒbrog* a near, *rgyáṅ-ₒbrog* a remote summer-pasture; *ₒbrog-ḱyi Cs.* a large shaggy shepherd's dog; *ₒbróg-dgon, ₒbróg-stoṅ, ₒbróg-sa* = *ₒbrog. ₒbróg-γnas* 1. **pasture-land** 2. **people occupying it.** — *ₒbróg-pa, ₒbróg-mi* id.; more particularly, **inhabitants of the steppe,** nomadic Tibetans *Sch.*, *ₒbróg-mo* wife, *ₒbrog-ṕrúg* child of such a nomad. — *ₒbrog-žád Sch.* rude, rough, boorish, *ₒbrog-žad stón-pa* to be rude etc.

འབྲོང་ *ₒbroṅ* 1. (**चमर**) = *γyag-rgod,* **wild yak** *Glr.*; *byáṅ-ḱai ₒbroṅ,* the yak of

Jang-thang; ˳broṅ-˳brí cow, ˳broṅ-p̔rúg calf, ˳broṅ-ko skin, leather, ˳broṅ-ša flesh, ˳broṅ-ru or -ra Glr. horns of the wild yak. — 2. v. ˳bráṅ-ba.

འབྲོམ་ ˳brom noun personal; ˳brom-stón a celebrated Lama and scholar in the 11th. century.

འབྲོས་པ་ ˳brós-pa, pf. and imp. bros, **to flee, to run away** (W. *šor-če*), ˳brós-šiṅ gáb-pa to flee and hide one's self Dzl.; p̔yir ˳brós-so (the army) took to flight Glr.; ˳brós-pai γnas Dzl., ˳brós-sa Glr. place of refuge; fig. mig k̔uṅ-du bros his eyes are sunk, hollow S.g. — ˳bros-ša a large dorsal muscle Med. — γnyid-˳brós-pa = γnyid-lóg-pa (?) Dzl. ༢༧༨, 9.

རྦ་ rba v. dba.

རྦད་ rbad 1. Sch. a large species of **eagles.** — 2. W. **crutch,** = paṅ-ka. — 3. = rbab. — 4. **great** (?) v. k̔a-rbad; rbad-sgra a strong voice Sch.; cf. rbod-rbód. — 5. **quite, wholly, entirely** (?) rbád-γčod-pa, rbad-tsér γčód-pa Mil. to cut off entirely, to extirpate; *t̔ag-čǒ be'-čǒ* **resolute** C.

རྦད་སྐྱོགས་ rbad-skyógs Sch. **residue, residuum, dregs, husks** etc.

རྦད་པ་ rbád-pa 1. vb., imp. rbod, **to set on, incite,** Tar., C., e.g. kyi; **to excite, instigate, animate,** Cs.; rbad-k̔a S.g. an inciting talk (?). — 2. adj. **undulating, undulatory** Sch.

རྦད་རྦོད་ rbad-rbód, **thick, dense, close, strong, great** Cs., skra rbad-rbód Lex.

རྦབ་ rbab, 1. Med., Sch.: a kind of **dropsy,** skya-rbáb Sch., also ša-rbab Lt. id. (?) — 2. **the rolling down,** also rbad, e.g. rdo-rbáb loose stones rolling down, a frequent annoyance in high mountains Pth., rbab ži-bas after the rolling of detritus had ceased Mil.; *bad p̔og soṅ* a piece of rock rolling down hit him W.; rbab sgríl-ba Lex. to roll down, trs.; rbáb-pa id. intrs.; már-la rbáb-tu šor it rolled down and away Mil.

རྦེ་ rbe Sch. **'the fur of the stone-fox'.**

རྦོ་ rbo Sch. **milt of fish.**

རྦོད་ rbod v. rbád-pa.

ལྦ་བ་ lbá-ba 1. **wen, goitre.** — 2. **knots, excrescenses** on trees, on account of their speckled appearance often worked into drinking-bowls; lbá-tsa Med., prob. a kind of salt, used as a curative of goitre.

ལྦག་ lbag **bubbles** (?), *ču bag gyáb-če* to strike the water, so as to make it splash and foam W.

ལྦུ་བ་, དབུ་བ་ lbú-ba, dbú-ba **bubble, foam, froth, slaver;** čú-lbu Lex.; lbú-bčas nyuṅ producing little froth Lt.; lbú-ba bsál-ba to scum or skim off Cs.; grogs čú-yi lbú-ba daṅ ˳dra a friend is like water-bubbles.

སྦ་ sba v. spa.

སྦ་ནག་ sba-nág Sch. **a mean house, hovel, hut.**

སྦ་བ་ sbá-ba 1. vb. fut. of sbed-pa q.v. — 2. sbst. **privy parts, pudenda** Stg.

སྦག་པ་ sbág-pa, pf. sbags, imp. sbogs (cf. ˳bág-pa), **to soil, stain, defile, pollute,** dri-mas Lex. — 2. **to mingle, intermix,** Lex.

སྦང་བ་ sbáṅ-ba v. sbóṅ-ba.

སྦང་མ་ sbáṅ-ma malt from which beer has been brewed, v. čaṅ; sbaṅ-skóm id. dried, sbaṅ-p̔yé id. reduced to flour (of an inferior quality) Cs.; glum-sbáṅ Ts. = sbáṅ-ma; sbaṅ-ču barm prepared from it W.

སྦངས་ sbaṅs dung of larger animals, rtai sbaṅs Glr. (*stal-báṅ(s)* Ld.), boṅ-sbaṅs, glaṅ-po-čei sbaṅs Cs.; sbaṅs-lúd id., used for manure; sbaṅs-skám id. dried for fuel.

སྦབ་ཅ་ sbáb-ča C., *sbáb-ǰa* W. a certain number or quantity of trading-articles, e.g. of paper, a quire of 10—100 sheets, a bundle of matches etc.

སྦམ་པ་ sbám-pa, pf. sbams, imp. sboms, **to put** or **place together, to collect, to gather,** p̔yogs γčig-tu Lex.; smyúg-ma sbáms-pa ˳dra like reeds laid together Wdṅ.

སྦར་བ་ sbár-ba, v. sbór-ba.

སྦར་མོ་ sbár-mo v. spár-mo.

**སྦལ་** *sbal* (perh. the same as the following *sbal-pa*), *lág-pai* the soft muscles of the inner hand, cf. also *p̓yag-sbál;* the soft part of the paw of animals.

**སྦལ་པ་** and བ *sbál-pa* and *-ba* **frog** (rather scarce in Tibet), one *Lex.* **कर्कट, crab, crawfish**(?); *sbál-pa dkár-po Stg.* stated to be a large species of frog; *nágs-sbal Lt.* prob. tree-frog; *rús-sbal* **tortoise;** *sbal-čúṅ* or *-lčoṅ Pth.* 1. a young frog, **tadpole** *Cs.* 2. vulg. (from ignorance) **lizard;** *sbal-rgyáb S.g.* tortoise-shell.

**སྦལ་མིག** *sbal-mig* **bud, eye, gem, sprout, shoot,** *˳ton* comes forth, *˳bye* opens *Stg.*

**སྦིད་པ་** *sbíd-pa Ts.* for *sbúd-pa* **bellows,** instrument for blowing.

**སྦུ་གུ་** *sbú-gu* **hollow, cavity,** in the stem of a plant or a grass-blade *Mil.*

**སྦུ་བ་** *sbú-ba* v. *lbú-ba.*

**སྦུ་ལ་ཁ་** *sbú-la-k̓a Ts.* = *bka-blon-sram* **sable,** *mustela zibellina.*

**སྦུ་ལྷན་** *sbu-lhán Ts.* (*bu-hlẹn*) **plane,** tool used in joinery.

**སྦུག་ཆོལ་, སྦུབ་ཅལ་,** *sbug-čól, sbub-čál Cs.,* *˳bog-˳čol* (?) *Ld.-Glr.;* *sbug-žál, sbum-žól* *W.* **large brass cymbal;** *dúṅ-če, p̓áb-če* *W.* to play the cymbals.

**སྦུག་པ་** *sbúg-pa* = *˳búgs-pa,* **to perforate, to pierce.**

**སྦུག་(སྦུག་)པོ་** *sbug-(sbug-)po Cs.* **hollow.**

**སྦུག་(ས་)** *sbug(s)*, more frq. *sbubs,* **hollow, cavity, excavation, interior space,** *k̓úṅ-bui Lex.* tubular cavity, in bones etc. *S.g.;* **subterraneous passage, conduit, sewer** *C.;* *sbúbs-su ˳júg-pa, sbúbs-nas ˳tón-pa* to put into an underground hole or recess, to come forth from it *Glr., Mil.;* *sbúg-tu nor sbá-ba* to hide money in such a place *Lex.;* **hiding-place, hidden recess,** = *saṅ-señ;* **hole** for inserting the handle of some instrument *Sch.;* *šáṅs kyi sbubs γnyis* hollow, expanded nostrils *Cs.;* *sbubs-˳byár Med.* disease of the penis, prob. stoppage of its orifice by gonorrhoea, cf. *mje.*

**སྦུགས་དགག་** *sbugs-hág* (*bu-hág*) 1. the **panting** of a dog *Sik.* — 2. **bassoon** with a large and nearly globular bell-mouth *W.* —

**སྦུད་པ་** *sbúd-pa* 1. vb. **to light, kindle, set on fire,** seldom, *Lex.:* *mé-čas sbúd-pa* q. v. — sbst. **bellows,** usually consisting of two skin-bags, the orifices of which are opened and shut by the hands, and which are then squeezed together, so that the compressed air passing through a tube is driven into the fire; *sbúd-pa ˳búd-pa Cs.* or *rgyáṅ-ba Sch.* to blow or work the bellows; *sbud-rgyál* = *sbúd-pa.*

**སྦུན་པ་** *sbún-pa* v. *spún-pa.*

**སྦུན་གཏེར་** *sbun-γtér Pth.* a small building in the style of a monument, in which sacred writings are deposited.

**སྦུར་** *sbur* **ant** *Cs.,* prob. identical with the following (cf. *gróg-sbur*).

**སྦུར་པ་** *sbúr-pa* **beetle,** *čú-sbur S.g.;* *sbur-čén, -čúṅ, -dmár, -mgyógs Cs.,* denoting various kinds of beetles.

**སྦུར་མ་** *sbúr-ma,* = *sbún-pa,* **chaff, husks** etc.; *rlúṅ-gis sbúr-ma bús-pa ltar Dzl., sóg-sbur čus γyéṅ-ba ltar Pth.* like chaff scattered by the wind, carried along by the water; *sbu-lén* or *-lóṅ* **amber** *Wts.*

**སྦེ་ག་** *sbé-ga Lex.* w. e.

**སྦེ་བ་** *sbé-ba Sch.* **to scuffle, wrestle.**

**སྦེག་པ་** *sbég-pa* **lean, lank, thin** *S.g.*

**སྦེད་པ་** *sbéd-pa,* pf. *sbas,* fut. and common secondary form *sba,* imp. *sbos, W.* *sbá-če*, pf *sbas,* **to hide, conceal,** *γter* a treasure, *mdzód-du* in a store-house; *má-mo sbéd-pai p̓ug* cavern in which a Mamo is concealed *Mil.;* *dpúṅ-gi ts̓ogs ts̓ál-du* to conceal troops in a wood *Dzl.;* *γtér-du* to deposit as a treasure *Glr.;* *sai ˳óg-tu* in the ground *Dzl.;* also as much as to inter, to bury *Dzl.;* *sbás-te* or *bẹ́-te bor-če* *W.* = *sbéd-pa;* *sbás-te* **secretly, clandestinely, by stealth** *W.;* *mi sdig-čan-la lus sba p̓yir* in order to hide our form before sinful men, in order not to be recognized by them *Mil.;*

**to hide from, to guard, secure, protect from,** *srúṅ-žiṅ sbá-ba* id.; **to keep, preserve,** *sba-sri-med-par* (to bestow) freely, amply, without restriction.

སྦེད་མ་ *sbéd-ma* **a veiled woman;** name of a wife of Buddha *Cs.*

སྦོ་ *sbo Sch.* **the upper part of the belly;** *sbo-ṫsil* **bacon** *C.; sbo-rkún-pa* **pickpocket** *C.*

སྦོ་བ་ *sbó-ba* pf. *sbos* = *ₒbó-ba* 2, **to swell(up), to distend,** *ltó-ba sbos Lt.* the belly is swollen, turgid; *sbó-ₒk̔rog-pa Sch.* 'to wheeze from inflation' (?).

སྦོག(ས)་པ་ *sbóg(s)-pa* v. *sbág-pa; rán-gi bú-ṫsai ṫsig-sbóg Mil.*, seems to imply a man that is receiving abusive language from his own sons (?).

སྦོང་བ་ *sbóṅ-ba*, pf. *sbaṅs*, fut. *sbaṅ* **to steep** in water, **to soak, to drench;** **báṅ-te bor* W.* soak it in water!

སྦོད་པ་ *sbód-pa* **tassel, tuft.**

སྦོམ་པ་ *sbóm-pa*, more frq. *sbóm-po* **thick,** *p̔ra-ba-las zlog sbóm-po Zam.* the contrary to *p̔rá-ba* is *sbom-po*; *sbom-p̔rá daṅ riṅ-ṫúṅ mnyam* of equal length and thickness *Dzl.*; **stout; coarse, clumsy, heavy,** also applied to sins; *sbóm-ma* a stout woman *Cs.*; sbst. **thickness, stoutness, heaviness.**

སྦོར་བ་ *sbór-ba*, pf., fut. and secondary form *sbar*, trs. of *ₒbár-ba*, **to light, kindle, inflame.**

སྦོར་ལོ་ *sbór-lo* Anemone polyantha *Lh.*

སྦྱང་བ་ *sbyáṅ-ba* v. *sbyóṅ-ba.*

སྦྱར་བ་ *sbyár-ba* v. *sbyór-ba.*

སྦྱར་པ་ *sbyár-pa Wdṅ.*, n. of a tree, prob. = *dbyár-pa.*

སྦྱིག་པ་ *sbyig-pa, sbyig-mo Lex.* w.e.

སྦྱིན་པ་ *sbyin-pa*, I. vb., pf. and imp. *byin*, 1. **to give, to bestow** (in *B.* a common word, in *W.* almost unknown; yet v. *smín-pa* II.), without any ceremonial difference between high and low; **to hand, deliver; to give up, deliver over; to give back, give for a present; to offer, proffer, hold out,** *rín-la byin-no* he offered as an equivalent *Pth.*; *ma byin-par mi lén-pa* v. *dgé-ba.* — 2. **to add, to sum up** *Wdk.* —

II. sbst. **gift, present, alms;** the expression *sbyin-pa γsum* comprises: *zaṅ-ziṅ-gi* the bestowing of goods, *mi-ₒǰigs-pai* the affording of protection, and *č̔ós-kyi sbyin-pa*, the giving of moral instruction *Cs.*, *sbyin-γtóṅ* distribution of gifts, *sbyin-γtoṅ čen-po byed-pa Dzl.* — *sbyin-bdag* dispenser of gifts, more especially in the first beginnings of Buddhism a layman manifesting his piety by making presents to the priesthood, v. *Köpp.* I, 487, and in almost all legends; also the reverse, *len-pa* **the receiver of gifts,** Dulva v. Feer Introd. p. 71. — *sbyin-sreg*, होम, **burnt-offering,** v. *Was.* (194), *Schl.* 251 sqq.

སྦྱུ་ *sbyu*, sometimes for *sgyu Sch.*

སྦྱོང་བ་ *sbyóṅ-ba*, pf. *sbyaṅs*, fut. *sbyaṅ* ཀྱོང 1. **to clean, remove by cleaning,** clear away, as *ₒdág-pa*, esp. *sdig-pa Tar.*, *sgrib(-pa) Thgy.*; less frq. in a physical sense, e.g. removing phlegm by vomiting *Med.*, *ₒk̔ru-sbyóṅs* diarrhoea *Lex.*; **to cleanse,** *sbyóṅ-byed* 1. **cleansing, purifying,** *raṅ sbyoṅ-byed-kyi šes-rab Mil.* the knowledge how a man may be purified by his own doings. 2. *Med.*: **purging medicine.** — 2. **to remove, take away,** in a general sense *Cs.*; **to subtract,** *de-rnams ṫig-mtsams sbyaṅ-ste Wdk.*, 60 being subtracted, cf. *ₒp̔ri-ba*; **to cease,** of diseases *Med.* — 3. **to exercise, to train,** *blo* one's mind *Cs.*, *k̔a* one's mouth, hence *k̔a-sbyáṅ* eloquence *Mil.* (having reference also to *k̔a-γčáṅ* q. v.); *sṅon yón-tan sbyáṅs-pa sóṅ-bai mṫus* by dint of formerly cultivated abilities *Glr.*; *ṫugs yóṅs-su sbyáṅs-pai skyés-bu Mil.* a saint of a thoroughly cultivated (or purified) mind; **to exercise, to practise,** *da-rúṅ sbyaṅ dgos* that must be practised still better; **to study,** *sde-snód-la* the holy scriptures *Mil.*, and with accus. *γžúṅ-lugs Tar.* 14, 9 (where *byaṅ* stands); *rtsis-la sbyáṅ-ba* to learn mathematics *Pth.*; **to practise, to perform; to recite, to repeat,** formulas, *bšar-sbyáṅ byéd-pa Mil.*, **kor ǰaṅ č̔ó-če* W.*; **to accustom, familiarize,** **mi daṅ*

བ

*ǰaṅ-k̔an** accustomed to man, tame, also without **mi daṅ** *W.*; **ǰaṅ-k̔yád** **custom, use, habit** *W.* — 4. **to accumulate** (?) *Cs.* — 5. **to conjure to the spot, to call by magic** (?) *Tar.* 76,15 *Schf.*

སྦྱོར་བ *sbyór-ba* I. vb., pf. and fut. *sbyar*, *W.* **žár-će**, trs. of *ₒbyór-ba*, 1. **to affix, attach, fasten, stick**, a writing, a plaster *W.*: **žar gyab-će**; **to apply** *lćé-rtse dkán-la Gram.*; fig. *bló-la, séms-la* **to impress;** **kár-ya daṅ** **to solder** *W.*; **zer gyáb-la žor** nail it fast! *W.*; **me-skám žar tsar** the trigger is drawn *W.*; **to put on,** a plaster, v. above, an arrow on the bow-string; **to subjoin, take up, resume,** a subject in a treatise *Thgy.*, *Tar.* 127,14; **to put together, to join, unite,** *rús-pa čág-pa Med.*, *dbáṅ-po γnyis* v. sub II.; **to compile, compose,** a book; *k̔a* 1. **to close, shut,** one's mouth, = *ₒt̔áms-pa Pth.* 2. **to kiss** *C.*; **to insert, to dispose** in proper classes or divisions *Gram.*, *byá-bai sgra ma sbyar yaṅ* also without the word *bya* being added; *bdé-ba-la, byaṅ-čúb-la Mil.*, like *ₒgód-pa* 3; **to join, connect, combine,** words, letters; *ts̔ig de don daṅ sbyár-tsa-na* if these sentences are joined with their significations, i.e. if their explanation is given *Mil.*; *rtsís-su* **to count together, to sum up** *Dzl.*; *sbyór-la*, gen. written *žor-la*, **joined, connected, combined,** **ts̔ig nyi sum žór-la yoṅ** two or three words are found joined to one another; this word is frq. used to express simultaneousness of action, where in English expressions as 'along with', 'together with', 'at the same time' etc. are used: *žór-la ₒgró-ba* to go along with (another person) *Mil.*; *žór-la k̔ur-k̔yer* take this also along with it! **k̔o čá-te žor daṅ kal soṅ** *W.* as he was going, we sent it along with him; *žor-la gyel soṅ* it fell at the same time (by coming in contact with some other falling body); **žór-la k̔yér-wa** to take hold of and take away at the same time; *k̔ó-la žor p̔óg-pa* he was also (simultaneously) affected by (the loss); **žór-la zér-k̔an žig** or even **ts̔ig-gi žor** a mere expletive, without any appreciable meaning *C.*; *bdag sdig-sgrib čés-pai žór-la* (the calamity has befallen the others too), owing to their connection with such a great sinner as I am *Mil.nt.* — 2. **to prepare, procure, to get ready,** *yo-byád* the appurtenances *Dzl.*, *ₒts̔ó-ba* victuals *Dzl.*; *rta daṅ sbyár-bai šiṅ-rta* a carriage ready to start *Stg.* (or acc. to no. 1, a carriage attached to the horses); **to mix,** *ču daṅ* with water *Dzl.* and elsewh.; *γžán-du* **to prepare, to turn one thing into another, to change, transform** *Thgy.*; frq. **to prepare one's own mind, to compose one's self,** *dád-pa-la sbyór-bar gyis* make up your mind to believe *Mil.* — **to join, fit together, adjust, make agree,** esp. one's course of action; **to conform one's self to,** with *daṅ*, *k̔ó-moi yid daṅ sbyor čig* accommodate yourself to my wishes *Dzl.*; *k̔rims daṅ sbyár-ro Dzl.* then we must conform to the law; most frq: ... *daṅ sbyár-nas* or *-te* **corresponding, agreeable to, according to,** *k̔rims* according to the law, to usage etc. *Dzl.*; *bú-moi yid* according to the wish of the daughter *Dzl.*; also **to compare** *Tar.* 89, 16, *Thgy.*; *γžan-rgyúd-la sbyór-ba* seems to imply: to gain knowledge by observing others, opp. to *raṅ-rgyúd-la brtág-pa*, to ascertain by one's own immediate judgment. — 4. **to compose poetry,** ... *kyis sbyár-bao* = *sdeb-pa* 5 — II. sbst. 1. **adjunction, conjunction, union,** *dbáṅ-po γnyís-kyi sbyór-ba byéd-pa*, '*membrorum amborum conjunctionem efficere*' *Wdṅ.*; hence **coition, cohabitation,** *bud-méd-la sbyór-ba byéd-pa* to effectuate it with a woman *Pth.*; *sgra-sbyor-ba* a joining or combination of sounds (letters), **orthography** (?) *Zam.* — 2. **a mingling, a mixture,** e.g. of medicines, also *sbyar-t̔ábs Med.*; *sbyor-sde-bži* the four departments of pharmacy *Glr.* (apparently the title of a book); **preparation** = *sṅón-ₒgro Schl.* 240, also mental preparation, esp. the preparation of the mind for prayer, and the arrangement of it, meditation preparatory to it (ni f.) cf. *mts̔ams sbyár-ba.* — 3. **syllogism** *Was.* (278). — 4. **comparison, agreement, harmony,** *γtám-gyi* the harmony of history *Schf.*

སྦྲ *sbra* 1. *W.* **(s)bra**, *C.* **ḍa** **felt-tent,** *sbra-gúr* id.; *sbra-t̔ág* ropes, *sbra-šiṅ* frame-work, *sbrá-pa* inmate, of such a tent. 2. v. sub *ɣtsaṅ*.

སྦྲག་པ་ *sbrág-pa*, pf. *sbrags*, *C.* **ḍág-pa**, *W.* **rág-če** **to lay, to put**, a thing over or by the side of an other, *p̓yogs-ɣčig-tu Lex.*; gen. used only in the gerund: **ťsa dor rág-nẹ** together with salt and spices *W.*; **ṅá-ža daṅ rág-te mi dug** he does not belong to us *W.*, or in compounds: *nyi-rág* **double-barreled gun** (one barrel beside the other), *W.*raṅ-bár ḍug-rág** six-barreled pistol, **revolver** *W.*, *bse-sgo bdun-sbrag Pth.*, sevenfold skin-door, used as a target for shooting at.

སྦྲག་མ་ *sbrág-ma* **hay-fork,** *Cs.*

སྦྲང་བུ་ *sbráṅ-bu C.* **ḍáṅ-bu**, *W.* **ráṅ-ṅu, ra-uṅ** **fly,** and similar insects without a sting; *sbráṅ-ma* 1. id. 2. *C.* **bee,** *sbráṅ-mai ťsogs* swarm of bees. — *sbráṅ-rtsi W.* **ráṅ-si** **honey;** **ráṅ-si ráṅ-ṅu** *W.* bee. — *sbráṅ-čaṅ* **mead** or something similar. — *sbraṅ-ťsáṅ* and *sbraṅ-dóṅ Cs.* cells in a honey-comb, the honey-comb itself. — *sbraṅ-búg* bee-hive *Sch.* — *sbraṅ-byí* marten *Sch.* — *sbraṅ-yáb* flap, fly-brush *Cs.*

སྦྲད་པ་ *sbrád-pa* = *˳brád-pa* **to scratch** *Sch.*

སྦྲན་པ་ *sbrán-pa* = *sbrón-pa.*

སྦྲམ་བུ་ *sbrám-bu* **unwrought gold** *Cs.*

སྦྲིད་པ་ *sbríd-pa* 1. **to sneeze** *Med.*; *sbríd-pa ˳byuṅ* I am seized with a sneezing *Med.* — 2. **to become numb, torpid,** **kʿáṅ-pẹ nya ḍid soṅ** my foot is asleep *W.* — 3. *Dzl.* ༢༥༩, 5 *Sch.* **to flutter** before one's eyes (?).

སྦྲུད་པ་ *sbrúd-pa*, pf. and imp. *sbrus*, fut. and sec. form *sbru*, *W.* **rú-če** **to stir** with one's hand, *zan Lex.*; **to knead** (*Cs.*) is *rdzí-ba* which is not identical with *sbrúd-pa*, at least not in *W.*

སྦྲུམ་པ་ *sbrúm-pa* **pregnant, big with young;** *mi daṅ srog-čags sbrum-ma-rnams Dzl.* women with child and beasts with young; *sbrúm-par ˳gyúr-ba* to conceive, to become pregnant, frq.; *sbrúm-par ťsór-nas* feeling pregnant *Pth.*: *p̓rú-gu sbrum byúṅ-bas* having conceived, being with child *Pth.*

སྦྲུལ་ *sbrul*, *Pur.* *sbrul*, *Lh.* **rúl**, *C.* **ḍul** 1. **serpent, snake;** *sbrul* and *sbrúl-mo* also mythical demoniac beings; *sbrul ɣdúg-pa* or *dug-sbrul* venomous serpent; *sbrul kʿas sdigs-po Sch.* serpent-tamer; *sbrúl-gyi snyiṅ-po* v. *tsán-dan.* — *sbrúl-mgo* 1. a serpent's head. 2. v. *˳aṅ-ke.* — *sbrul-sgóṅ* a serpent's egg. — **ḍul-nyá** **eel** or some other esculent snake-like fish *C.* — *sbrul-dúg* venom of serpents. — *sbrul-mig* 1. a snake's eye. 2. n. of **a certain vein** *Med.* — *sbrul-ťsil* snake's grease *Med.* — *sbrul-žágs* v. *žags.* — *sbrul-ló* serpent-year, *sbrúl-lo-pa* one born in such a year v. *lo.* — *sbrul-śún* slough, skin of a snake. — 2. symb. num.: 8, = *klu.*

སྦྲེ(ད)་ *sbre(d) Lex.* n. of an animal; *Sch.*: **stone-fox.**

སྦྲེ་བོ་, རེ་བོ་, རེ་བ་ *sbré-bo, ré-bo, ré-ba* a coarse material manufactured of yak's hair for tent-coverings.

སྦྲེང་བ་ *sbréṅ-ba*, pf. *sbreṅs*, *Cs.*: **to play** an instrument; acc. to *Dzl.* ༦༡, 16, **to jerk,** a chord, a bow-string.

སྦྲེབས་པ་ *sbrébs-pa Cs.*: resp. for *ltógs-pa* **hungry.**

སྦྲེལ་བ་ *sbrél-ba*, *W.* **rél-če(s)** **to stitch together,** paper; **to stitch to, to sew on; to fasten on,** a package on a horse; *lčags-sgróg lág-pa sbrél-nas* having one's hands shackled together; *bar zám-gyis sbrel* the chasm is overarched by a bridge *Glr.*; (iron chains) *séṅ-ge daṅ* fastened to (stone) lions; in a gen. sense: **to connect, to join,** *ɣnyis-sbrél, ɣsum-sbrél* two or three consonants joined together, cf. *miṅ-ɣži.*

སྦྲེས་པ་ *sbrés-pa Cs.* **frozen, stiff, hard.**

སྦྲོན་པ་ *sbrón-pa*, pf. and fut. *sbran* 1. **to call to the spot,** *rá-mda, grogs* for assistance *Lex.*; **to send for,** the minister *Glr.* — 2. **to call to** *Thgy.*; **to give information, notice, intelligence,** *rgyál-po-la rmi-lam-du* to warn the king by a dream *Dzl.*; *mi žig sbrán-du btáṅ-nas Dzl.* to dispatch a man in order to convey intelligence. — 3. **to sprinkle, to stain, to pollute,** *ťig-les Sch.*

# མ

**མ** *ma* 1. the letter **m.** — 2. numerical figure: 16.

**མ** *ma* I. sbst. 1. **mother,** col. *ǎ-ma*, resp. *yum; mai rum* womb, matrix; *ráṅ-gi ma γčig-pai sriṅ-mo* full sister by the same mother, whilst *mas dbén-pai sriṅ-mo* denotes half-sister, step-sister, by another mother. — 2. frq. used metonymically, e.g. **capital,** v. below; **ma tsam yod* W.*, what is the amount of the sum advanced? **original text, copy to write after, pattern** v. below; **a letter** written **above** another. — **Comp.:** *ma-k̔ál* amount in bushels of grain lent out. — *ma-k̔ú* mother and uncle, v. *k̔á-bo.* — *ma-rgyúd Sch.* 1. **original, primary cause.** 2. **line of descent** by the mother's side, when however it should be spelt *brgyud.* — *má-ču* the first infusion of malt or stronger beer, v. *č̔aṅ.* — *ma-čúṅ Cs.:* 'a mother's younger sister', perh. more correctly: a father's second wife, as to rank; *ma-čen* 1. *Cs.:* 'a mother's elder sister', or a father's principal wife. 2. v. the respective article. — *ma-p̔ár* capital and interest *W.* — *ma-bu* mother and son; capital and interest; original and copy; *ma-bú mt̔ún-pa ₒbri-ba* to copy accurately *Schr.;* a letter written above and below another letter; principal and cross beam etc. — *má-mo* v. that article. — *ma-tsáb* foster-mother *Sch.* — *ma-γži* v. sub II. — *ma-γyár* step-mother *Cs.* — *ma-ró* a mother's corpse *Pth.*

II. a root signifying **below,** opp. to *ya: má-gi* the lower one, e.g. *čú-bo Mil.; ma-gi-na* below, at the bottom, *má-gi-nas* from below, out of the valley, in *Sik.:* from, out of, the Indian plain (v. *mt̔a*); *má-mču* lower lip. — *má-t̔em* sill, threshold. — *má-t̔og* v. *t̔og* I, 2. — *má-rdo* = *rmáṅ-rdo.* — *ma-rábs* mean descent, people of low extraction *Dzl.* — *ma-ri Sch.* downward (?) — *ma-ré* = *ma-t̔ém,* v. *re.*

III. negative adv. **not,** however only in some cases: a. in the simplest form of prohibition, where in the Tibetan language inst. of the imperative the root of the present with *ma* is used: *ma ₒgro* do not go, *ma byed* do not do (it). With the form of the future *mi* is placed: *rjód-par mi byao* it shall not, should not be pronounced *Dom.*; *mi de dgrar mi bslaṅ* they should not make the man their enemy *S.g.* — b. with the preterite: *ma soṅ* he did not go, *ma byas* he did not do (it). — c. with the present tense also in conjunction with the words *yin, lags, mčis, red.* — d. without any evident reason, and perh. not always correctly, with many substantives and adjectives that are formed of infinitives or participles, and are conveying a negative sense: *ma-rig-pa* a not knowing, ignorance; *ma-rúṅ-ba* v. *ruṅ-ba* (v. *mi*).

IV. In the col. language of *Lh. ma* is used as an **interrogative,** when a question is returned by a question: **k̔yód-di miṅ či zer** what is your name? **miṅ ma?** my name?

V. Affix, so-called article, frq. denoting the fem. of the masc. in *pa*, if *mo* is not used inst. of it; gen. put to the names of inanimate things, utensils etc., as also to compound adjectives: *zaṅs ru-bži-ma* a four-handled kettle (cf. *bu lo-γnyis-pa* a boy two years old, sub *pa*).

VI. *mai nyin* **two days before yesterday** *C.*, = *sṅón-ma žag W.*

**མཱ** *mā W.* always with a marked accent and long vowel, prob. abbrev. of *maṅs* **very,** before adjectives and adverbs, **mā máṅ-po** very much, **mā gyál-la** very good.

**མ་ཀར** *ma-kár* (Hind. مکر impostor) *W.* **deceit, imposition, intrigue,** **ma-kár čó-te zer** he speaks hypocritically, with some secret design; *ma-kar-čan,* **hypocritical, fawning.**

མ་ཀ་ར་ *ma-ka-ra Ssk.* **sea-monster.**

མ་ཁ་ *ma-ḱá* 1. *Lt.* = *mtsan-dbye.* — 2. **Mecca** *Stg.*

མ་ཁལ་ *ma-ḱál* v. *ma* I.

མ་མཁན་ *ma-mḱán* v. *ma-rgán.*

མ་གལ་ *ma-gál Wdṅ., W.* **poplar-tree.**

མ་གི་ *má-gi* v. *ma* II.

མ་རྒད་ *ma-rgád,*mar-gád* Glr.,* from मरकत, **emerald.**

མ་རྒན་ *ma-rgán W. *mar-gán** 1. **matron, grandam.** 2. *C.* also **ma-ḱe̱n** **cook; quarter-master.**

མ་ཆེན་ *ma-čén* 1. v. *ma* I. — 2. **head-cook.**

མ་ཏྲི་མུ་ཏྲི་སལ་ལེ་འཛུ་ *ma-tri-mu-tri-sa-la-ₒdzu* is said to be a form of prayer of the Bonpos, as the Ommanipadmehūm is of the Buddhists; *Desg.* p. 242 has: *ma tchri mou me sa le gou.*

མ་དང་ (?) *ma-dáṅ Ld.* a place on the roof of a house cleared for spreading grain there.

མ་གདན་ *ma-ɣdán, W. *mag-dán*, C. *ma-de̱n** **ground, basis, foundation;** also for *ma-ɣdán-gyi ri-mo* **ground-plan.**

མ་རྡུ་, མ་དུ་ (?) *ma-rdú, *ma-dú W.* **thorn, prickle,** *má-rdu-čan* **thorny, prickly.**

མ་རྡོ་ *má-rdo, *mar-do* W.* prob. a careless pronunciation of *rmáṅ-rdo.*

མ་ནིང་ *ma-niṅ* 1. **without sexual distinction** *Med.* and *Gram.* — 2. **impotent, unable to beget** *S.g.* — 3. **barren, childless** *Wdṅ.* (explained by *bu-ťsa-méd-pa*). — 4. *Cs.*: also **hermaphrodite,** *Wdṅ.* however denotes this explicitly by *mťsan-ɣnyis-pa.*

མ་ནུ་ *ma-nu Med.? Cs* : = मनु, मनस्, *yid*; as symb. num.: 14.

མ་ནུ་པ་ཏྲ་ *ma-nu-pa-tra* a medicine *Wdṅ.*; in *Lh.* Bryonia dioeca.

མ་ཎི་ *má-ṇi* (*Ssk.* precious stone) 1. abbrev. of Ommanipadmehūm; **má-ni táṅ-če* W.* 1. **to mutter prayers.** 2. **to purr like a cat.** Hence 2. **praying-cylinder,** prop. *ma-ni-ĉos-ₒḱór Schl.* 230. — 3. **consecrated stone-heaps** or **stone-walls** (Mongul *Obo*) *Schl.* 196; *ma-ni bka-ₒbúm* title of a book; as to its contents v. *Schl.* 84.

མ་ཕང་ *ma-p̓áṅ Mil., ma-p̓ám Cs.* = *ma-drós-pa,* v. *drós-pa.*

མ་མ་ *má-ma* **children's nurse** *Dzl., Glr., Cs.*: *nú-ma snún-pai* wet-nurse, *dri-ma ₒp̓yi-bai* nurse for cleaning, *páṅ-du ₒḱúr-bai* for carrying, *rtséd-grogs-kyi* for playing.

མ་མུན་ *ma-mún Ld.* col. for *na-bún,* **fog.**

མ་མོ་ *má-mo* 1. *Sch.* **grandmother.** — 2. *Sch.* **ewe,** sheep that has lambed. — 3. *Mil.* and elsewh. frq., a kind of wicked demons.

མ་ཞི་ *ma-ži Lt.* medicinal plant (?).

མ་ཞུ་ *má-žú* v. *žú-ba.*

མ་གཞི་ *má-ɣži, W. *máb-ži** 1. **ground-work, basis, elementary principle, component part; prime colour; principal thing, main point.** — 2. *Sch.* **originally** (?).

མཱ་ཡཱ་ *mā-yā Ssk.* = *Tib. sgyu-ₒp̓rul-ma* **'delusion',** n. of the mother of Buddha Sākyamuni.

མ་གཡོག་ *ma-ɣyóg* = *ťab-ɣyóg* **kitchen-boy, scullion** *W.*

མ་རི་, མ་རེ་ *ma-ri, ma-ré* v. *ma* II.

མ་རུ་ *má-ru* n. of a castle, perh. = *rmé-ru.*

མ་རུ་རྩེ་ *ma-ru-rtsé* 1. n. of a medicine *Med.* — 2. n. of a country *Pth.*

མ་ལ་ *ma-la Sch.* **excellent! capital!** — In *Feer Introd.* p. 69 it was explained by our Lama as = *'é-ma* **ah, well!** Also Feer has: *Eh bien!*

མ་ལ་ཁན་ *má-la-ḱan Ld.* **snake-charmer, conjurer.**

མ་ལ་ཡ་ *má-la-ya* **the western Ghauts** famous for sandal-wood; the tracts along their foot, **Malayalim, Malabar.**

མ་ལ་ལ་ཙེ་ *ma-la-la-tsé Ld.* **small lizard.**

མ་ལག་ *má-lag Ld.* **somerset;** **má-lag lóg-če** to perform a somerset, to play the tricks of a mountebank; to roll on the ground with legs turned up, of horses etc.

མ་ལམ་ *má-lam* **high-road, broad passage** *W.*

མ་ཤ་ *má-ša* 1. *Ssk.* **माष**, **pea**, Phaseolus radiatus, = *mon-srán* or *greu Wdṅ.* — 2. *W.* the contrary of *ya-ša*, **contempt, scorn, disregard.** — 3. *W.* **trigger of a musket.**

མ་ཤ་ཀ་ *ma-ša-ka Ssk.* **माषक**, *Cs.*: a small gold weight and coin in ancient India.

མ་ཤི་ཀ་ *ma-ši-ka* name formed from the Hebrew מָשִׁיחַ, for **Christ**, the Greek word not being adapted to the Tib. language *Chr. Prot.*

མ་ཧཱ་ *ma-hā Ssk.* **great**, used in names and titles: *ma-hā-kā-la* and *de-ba* = Siva *Glr.*; *ma-hā-tsī-na*, *ma-hā-tsin* the modern name of China, formerly *rgya-nág*; *ma-hā-tsi-nai skad* the Chinese language *Wdk.*; *ma-hā-rā-dzā* the great king, title of some princes, particularly that of Kashmere.

མ་ཧེ་ *ma-he*, *Ssk.* **महिष**, **buffalo** *Glr.*, *ma-he-mo* female of it.

མག་པ་ *mag-pa* 1. **son-in-law** *Dzl.*, *mag-skud* son-in-law and father-in-law *Dom.* 2. **bridegroom** col.

མག་མལ་ *mag-mal*, *Ar.* مخمل, **velvet** *W.*

མང་ *maṅ* 1. *C.* col. for *mi oṅ*, *mi ₒdug* (?); so also in some passages of the *Ma.* — 2. v. *máṅ-po.*

མང་ག་ལཾ་ *maṅ-ga-lam Ssk.* = *bkra-šis.*

མང་པོ་ *máṅ-po* 1. **much, many**, *mi maṅ-po* (*rnams*) **many people**, also (like *οἱ πολλοί*) **most people, the gross** or **bulk of the people**, for which *W.* **máṅ-če**, e.g. **máṅ-če zer dug** most people say, or, mostly it is said etc.; *ₒk̔or máṅ-po* (*rnams*) the numerous retinue *Dzl.*; *máṅ-por* adverb **mostly** (not frq.) *Zam.*; *ču maṅ-nyúṅ ltos* look after the height of the water, whether there is much or little of it; *γčig bsgyúr-ba-la maṅ-nyuṅ med* if you multiply by 1, you will get neither more nor less *Wdk.* — 2. **very, very much,** with verbs, chiefly col., *maṅ-po ₒjigs* I am very much afraid.

**Comp. and deriv.** *maṅ-bkúr* = *máṅ-pos bkúr-ba* v. *bkúr-ba* I. and II. — *maṅ-γé-mo* long ago, long since (?) *Cs.* — **maṅ-ṅa* W.* col. for *máṅ-por*, *máṅ-ba(r)*; **žag daṅ žag máṅ-ṅa máṅ-ṅa táṅ-če** to give a little more every day. — *máṅ-če* v. above. — *máṅ-ja* a liberal distribution of tea *Ld.-Glr. Schl.* fol. 27, a, and p. 72. *máṅ-du* is not only the termin. case, but also a compound of *maṅ* and the synon. *du*, being used exactly like *máṅ-po*, both in the nomin. and accus case, *γdams-ṅág máṅ-du bstán-pas ₒbrás-bu bži t̔ób-pa máṅ-du byuṅ* as he gave manifold instructions, many became obtainers of the four fruits *Tar.* 14, 3.

མང་བ་ *máṅ-ba* I. vb. pf. *maṅs*, **to be much,** *ₒdi máṅ-ṅam de maṅ* is this much or that? i.e. which is more, this or that? *Dzl.*; *dgra máṅs-pas* as the enemies had become very numerous *Dzl.*; *sman-dpyád máṅs-pas p̔án-rgyu med* by making much of medical treatment he will not grow well *Mil*; *ma máṅ čig* be it not much, let it not grow too much *Mil.* and elsewh.; *máṅs-kyis dógs-pa* fearing lest it should grow too much *Wdṅ.* — II. adj. 1. *máṅ-po.* — 2. **having much,** *bu maṅ-bar ₒgyúr-ba* to get many children, *bu-máṅs* rich in children *Pth.* — *máṅs-t̔sig* a sign of the plural number, e.g. *dag Gram.* — III. also sbst. **plenty.**

མང་ཡུལ་ *máṅ-yul*, a province of Tibet bordering on Nepal, in which *skyid-gróṅ* is situated, v. *skyid.*

མན་ཛི་ར་ *man-dzi-ra S.g.* a mineral medicine; perh. *man-dza-ri Ssk.* **pearl.**

མཎྜལ་ *maṇḍal Ssk*, prop. *Tib. dkyil-ₒk̔or* jewels, viands etc. presented as offerings, and arranged in **a cirle** *Glr.* and elsewhere, cf. *t̔sogs.*

མད་ *mad* 1. = *nad* (?) *lus mad-méd-čiṅ Sambh.* — 2. sometimes for *smad.*

མད་པ་ *mád-pa* **true,** *kyed mad γsúṅ-žiṅ* as you speak what is true *Mil.*; *ma nyés-pai bden-t̔sig mád-po smras kyaṅ* although he solemnly declared not to have committed it *Pth.*

མན་ *man* I. sbst., also *mán-na*, *má-na Hind.* a **'man'** or Indian hundredweight, equal to about 80 pounds, anglicized **maund.** — II *W.* for *ma yin* (*B. min*) 1. it is not;

*'i man* this it is not; *mán-na* is it not so? isn't it? is it? In conjunction with a negative it is col. almost the only word for **only, but** etc.: *de mán-na mi yoṅ, de mán-na med* only this one is to be met with, besides this there are none; *la-dág-gi lug čún-se mán-na mi yon* there are only small sheep in Ladak; *dún-la mán-na mi ťoṅ-k'an* he who sees only what is close before him, a short-sighted person; *ḍé-bu lo gyad tiṅ-la mán-na mi yoṅ* fruit will appear only after a space of eight years; *di-riṅ mán-na ma ťoṅ* I have seen (him, it) only to-day, i.e. to-day for the first time cf. *min.* — 2. **no.** — III. = *ma* II., *man-yán* **below** and **above** *Cs.*; *man-čád, -čád, -čód* 1. adv.and postp.c.accus., **below, downward, on the lower side of, as far as,** *lté-ba man-čád ču náṅ-du nub Glr*, he was immerged in the water below his navel, i.e. up to his navel; inst. of *man-čád* also merely *man: pús-mo goṅ man Mil.*, lit below the parts over the knee i.e. higher than the knee; *de man-čód*, below that *Glr.*; in reference to time, **from,** *do-núb man čad* from this evening *Mil.*; *de man-čád* **since, from that time forward** *Mil.*; *rmaṅ btiṅ-ba man rab-ɣnás mdzád-pa yán-la* from the foundation up to the consecration *Glr.*; **even to** (the last man), (all) **except** or **save** (one), also *mán-pa, mán-pe, mán-k'an, man-ra* *W.* (*B. min-pa*). — 2. sbst. **lower part** of a country, **lowland,** thus in *Lh.* as a proper name.

མན་ངག *man-ṅág*, *Ssk.* उपदेश, **advice, direction, information,** *stón-pa* to give, *man-ṅag (-gi) -rgyúd* v. *rgyud* 2; in later writings and in the mind of the common people, it coincides with *sṅags*, in as much as the esoteric doctrines of mysticism, i.e. magic art, are concerned, which are communicated in no other way than by word of mouth; cf. *k'a-rgyan.*

མན་ཅད, ཆད, ཆོད, པ, ལྷག *man-čad, čad, čod, pa, lhag*, v. *man* II. and III.

མན་དཱ་ར་བ *man-da-ra-ba*, मन्दारव, a tree in paradise *Stg.*

མན(ན)མུན(ནེ) *man(-na)-mún(-ne) Ld.*, **turbid, muddy, dingy, dim, dull, dusky,** as to water, flames of light etc.

མན་ཙི *mán-tsi Sch.* a kind of silk-cloth.

མན་ཛི *man-dzi* 1. *Sch.* 'a small **square table**', acc. to others **a tripod** with long curved feet, for sacrificial purposes. — 2. *W.* **bed** *Hindi* मञ्च.

མན་ཤེལ *man-šel* **crystal, glass** *Pth.*

མར *mar* I. sbst., resp. *ɣsol-már* 1. **butter** *Thgy*, *C.*, *W.* — 2. col. also **oil.** — **Comp.** *skya-már*, *Ld. k'ág-la mar* fresh, not melted butter; *ba-már* cow-butter; *ₒbri-már* yak-butter; *ₒbru-már* oil from oleaginous seeds, rape-seed oil etc. *Dzl.* and elsewhere; *rtsi-már* oil from the stones of apricots etc.; *mdzo-már* butter from the bastard-cow; *žun-már* melted butter, *ghi (Hind.)*, the usual form of butter in India and frq. also in Tibet, highly esteemed both as food and as medicine; *žum-már-pa* *C.* **lamp;** *mar-dkár Med.* = *skya-már.* — *már-k'u* melted, liquid butter. — *mar-rnyiṅ* old, rancid butter, recommended by physicians for diseases of the mind, fainting-fits, wounds. — *mar-nág* *W.* oil, *nyuṅ-dkar-mar-nág* rape-seed oil. — *mar-blúg* *W.* a small urn-shaped vessel for butter or oil. — *mar-mé* **lamp,** at present only for holy uses, thus: *mar-mé ghyen-tsẹn* holy, heavenward burning lamp *C.* (formerly any lamp *Dzl.* ꣽ, 11; *Glr.*); *mar me mdzád* Buddha Dipankara, v. *Dzl.* XXXVII.; — *mar-žógs Mil.* a part cut off, one half of a *mar-ril*, i.e. a globular lump of fresh butter, about one pound in weight, not unfrequently offered to travellers as a gift of courtesy. — *mar-ɣsár* fresh butter *Lt.* — II. termin. of *ma* I., to or 'into' the mother; *mar-gyur ₒgró-ba* regarded as a mother, a creature loved like a mother, *Mil.*; v. *ma* II. down, downward, *már-la* id., *B.* and *C.*; v. *rbab* and *ₒgrib-pa*; *mar-ṅo* v. *ṅo* 5.

མར་ཀ་ལ་ག *mar-ka-la-ga* (?) a fine ochreous earth, found e. g. on the Baralasa pass between *Lh.* and *Ld.*, used as ground-colour in staining houses with *dkár-rtsi Ld.*

མར་རྒན་ *mar-rgán* v. *ma-rgán.*

མར་ངོ་ *mar-ṅó* v. *ṅo* 5.

མར་དོན་ *mar-dón* perh. *dmar-ₒdón.*

མར་པ་ *már-pa,* n. of a holy Lama, teacher of Milaraspa, by whom he was highly respected.

མར་བ་ *mar-ba* provinc. for *dmár-ba Sch.*

མར་ཡུལ་ *már-yul Ma.,* n. p. = *la-dwags* Ladak.

མལ་ *mal,* the place where a thing is, its **site, situation,** **mál-du žág-pa** *C.* **bór-ċe** *W.,* to put a thing in its own place; also where a thing has been, its **trace, vestige,** *šiṅ-rtai* rut, wheel-mark, track; *mal γċig-tu mi ₒdúg-pa* prob. to be unstable, changeable, fickle, restless; more esp. place of rest, **couch, bed,** *mál-gyi ₒog-tu* under the bed *Glr.; dgoṅs-mal* resp. for night-quarters *Dzl.* ༢༩༠, 3 (so acc. to the xylographic copy; *Sch.* having the less appropriate *dgons-lam*); **mal dúg-ċe** *W.* to live in a strange place, ἐπιδημεῖν; *mal bdé-ba Sch.* a quiet sleep, *ṅai lus sems mál-du bde* I now may safely lie down, fig. for: the danger is now over *Glr.* — *mal-k̔ri* bed-frame, bed-stead. — *mal-gós Cs., mal-ċá Lex.,* **mal-čẹ́** *C.,* **-stán** *C., W.. Dzl.* bedding, bed-clothes. — *mal-ldaṅ Sch.* 'cradle', rather improb., perh. hammock. — *mal-yól* bed-curtain. — *mál-sa,* resp. *γzims-mál* couch, bed.

མལ་ལ་མུལ་ལེ་ *mal-la-múl-le Ld.* **lukewarm,** tepid.

མལ་ལི་ཀ་ *mal-li-ka Ssk.,* properly name of a flower, Jasminum Champaca, used as an epithet in pompous titles of books.

མས་ *mas* 1. instrum. case of *ma* mother. — 2. v. *ma* II, **the lower part,** gen. however with terminative meaning, **downward, towards the lower parts,** *mas btáṅ-ba Med.* to move downward, to purge; **backward, last** *Sch.;* used also as a sbst.: *más-kyi* the last, e.g. *yi-ge* final letter *Cs.; más-la* downward, below *Sch., más-nas* from below *Sch.;* cf. the contrary *yás.*

མི་ *mi,* I. num. figure: 46. — II. sbst. **man,** *mi γsod-pa* to kill men, to murder, *mi-méd ri-k̔ród* uninhabited, desolate mountains *Mil.; mi-rnams ná-re* people said *Mil.; mi-la ma lab* tell no body else of it *Mil; ráṅ-gis bságs-pa mi-yis spyod* what we gathered ourselves, is enjoyed by others *Mil.; mi-nor raṅ slóṅ-ba* to gather by begging what belongs to others *Mil.; mii bú-mo* 1. daughters of men, opp. to *lhai bú-mo* e.g. witches appear in the shape of daughters of men *Mil.* 2. daughters of others, opp. to *ráṅ-gi bú-mo Mil.,* cf. also *mi-bu* further on; pleon. before a pers. pron. of the first person: *mi-ṅá, mi-bdág* I, *Mil.* (cf. *p̔o*), and with certain sbst.: *γtsó-bo mi drug* (we) six lords *Glr.;* plur. also *mi-ts̔ó Sch.*

**Comp.** *mi-k̔a,* (idle) talk of the people, common talk, *yúl-sdei náṅ-nas mi-k̔a sdud* in the whole neighbourhood one is an object of gossip, nif.; defaming talk; imprecating speech, with or without *ṅán-pa, mi-k̔á zug* or *p̔og* (damnation) lights on (me, him) *Dom.* — *mi-kyim* 1. **human dwelling, house,** (the Chinese capital contained) *mi-kyim ₒbúm-ts̔o* 100 000 houses *Glr.* 2. *Ld.-Glr. Schl.* 20. b. and *Glr.* 94, 7 it seems to imply **the people of a household, domestics,** the same as *k̔yim-ghi mi.* — *mi-ₒgréṅ* v. *ₒgréṅ-ba.* — *mi-rgód* v. *rgód-pa* II. — *mi-brgyúd* v. *brgyud.* — *mi-rǰé* sovereign, king, *mi-rǰé mdzád-pa* to be king, to reign *Glr.* — *mi-nyid Cs.* 'humanity, honesty'; *mi-nyid-ċan* 'humane, honest'(?) — *mi-brdág.* 1. = *mi-rǰé.* 2. symb. num.: 16. — *mi-mda* (vulgo *min-da*) *Mil.* and *C., W.:* men, persons preceded by a numeral, e.g. six men, six women (prop. a line or row of people). — *mi-sdé* v. *sde. Sch.* has also: *lha-sdé mi-sdé* princes and nations. — *mi-sná* 1. **race of men, class of people** (seldom). 2. **messenger, delegate,** not frq met with in books, yet not unknown in *C.* and *W.,* and used esp. of messengers with an errand or charge given them in words; in our translations introduced for **apostle**, *p̓ó-nya* having been adopted for 'angel'. — *mi-dpón* prefect *Glr.*, *C.* — *mi(i)-bu* 1. **a child of man, a mortal,** po., *Mil.*, cf. *mii bú-mo* above. 2. **son of man,** when Christ speaks of himself as such, otherwise *mii sras Chr. Prot.* — *mi-bo Cs.*, rarely for *mi.* — *mi-dbaṅ*, prince, potentate. — *mi-ma-yin(-pa)* अमनुष. one that is not a human being, *mi daṅ mi-ma-yin-pa t̓ams-ċád* all human and not human (adversaries) *Dom.*, esp. ghosts, demons, *dur-k̓ród-kyi mi-ma-yin-pa-rnams* the ghosts of a grave-yard (not the souls of the dead); *mk̓á-la rgyú-bai mi-ma-yin* the ghosts that walk in the air *Mil.*; *dkár-p̓yogs-kyi mi-ma yin-rnams* good genii *Mil.*; *mi-ma-yin-gyi čo-ₒp̓rúl* apparitions of ghosts *Mil.* — *mi-mo* **woman,** yet only in contraposition to *lhá-mo* and other not human female beings *Mil.* and elsewh. — *mi(i)-yul* human world, lower world, earth, opp. to regions of the gods or of infernal beings *Glr.*, *Pth.* — *mi-rabs* mankind. — *mi-rigs* v. *rigs.* — *Mi-la-rás-pa*, often only *Mi-la*, name of a Buddhist ascetic, of the 11 century (*Wdk.*), who between the periods of his meditations itinerating in the southern part of Middle Tibet as a mendicant friar, instructed the people by his improvisations delivered in poetry and song, brought the indifferent to his faith, refuted and converted the heretics, wrought manifold miracles (*rdzu-ₒp̓rúl*), and whose legends, written not without wit and poetical merit, are still at the present day the most popular and widely circulated book in Tibet. — *mi-lág* servant, **mi-lág-tu ₒḍó-wa** to do servant's work, to perform drudgery *W.* — *mi-lús* 1. the human body. 2. v. *lús-pa.* — *mi-ser* 1. **subject, servant, menial, drudge.** 2. **robber, thief, sharper.** — 3. v. below.

III. negative adv.: **not,** in all such cases where *ma* (q.v.) is not used. With simple verbs the place of the negation is always immediately before them, in compound forms gen. before the last of the component parts, e.g. *ₒbyúṅ-bar mi ₒgyúr-ro*, unless logically it belongs to the first, in which case often *ma* inst. of *mi* is employed. This rule, however, is not always strictly observed, so *Glr.* 70: *de daṅ nám-du yaṅ mi ₒbrál-bar gyis šig*, and immediately after: *skad ɣċig kyaṅ ma brál-bar gyis šig* do never part with it

མི་ཉག་, མེ་ཉག་ *mi-nyág*, *me-nyág*, and ཏང་གུད་ Tanggud, names of two provinces closely connected with each other, situated in the north-eastern part of Tibet and forming in ancient times a separate kingdom *Glr.*

མི་མ་ *mi-ma Sch.* **tears.**

མི་སེར་ *mi-sér* 1. n.p., formed after مصر, *mi-sér yul* Egypt, *mi-sér-pa* Egyptian, *Chr. Prot.* — 2. v. *mi.*

མིའམ་ཅི་ *miam-ċi*, *Ssk.* किंनर, fabulous beings of Indian origin, nearly related to the *ₒdri-za*, and belonging to the retinue of Kuvera; fem *miam-ċi-mo.*

མིའུ་ *miu* 1. **a little man, dwarf,** also *miu-t̓úṅ Wdn.*; *mig-gi miu* v. *mig.* — 2. perh. applicable also **to puppet, doll.**

མིག་ *mig*, resp. 1. **eye.** — 2. **eye of a needle; hole** in a hatchet or hammer, to insert the handle — 3. symb. num.: 2. — *mig-gi gaṅs Sch.*, the white of the eye; *mig-gi rgyál-mo* or *miu*, 'the queen or the little man in the eye': 1. **pupil.** 2. **iris** *Stg.*; *mig-gi snág-ṫsa* or *-mṫso Cs.*, vulgo *mig-gi nág-po* id.; *mig-gi mé-tog Sch.* the luminous point of the eye: *mig nyáms-pa Cs.* weak eyes; *mig ltá-ba* to see with the eyes, to look up, to look round *Glr.*; *mig ₒdzúm-pa* to shut the eyes, *ₒbyéd-pa* to open the eyes, v. *ₒbyéd-pa* 1; *ₒdón-pa*, *ₒbyin-pa* to cut or tear out the eyes, to squeeze them out by a particular instrument, as a torture or punishment *C.*; *mig bċár-ba Lex.*, acc. to *Sch.* id.; *mdóṅs-pa*, *mdóṅs-par ₒgyúr-ba* to get blind or blinded, to be deprived of sight *Dzl.*; *mig ₒk̓yid-pa Sch.*, to distort or roll the eyes; *mig skú-ba Dom.* (*bskú-ba?*) n. of a certain magic trick; *mig čid-pa* inflammation of the eyes through cold, snow-blindness *C.* (perh. *p̓yid-pa*); **mig zug soṅ** it has struck my eyes, I should like to have it *C.*, *W.*; **mig log ltá-ce** to eye one obliquely, with envy or jealousy *W.* —

**Comp.** *mig-kyóg* squinting *Sch.* — *mig-rkyén Mil.*, is said to be the same as *mig-ltós.* — **mig-skyór** *W.* eye-ball. — *mig-skyág* the impurities in the eyes *Cs.* — *mig-k'úṅ* eye-hole, socket *Sch.* — *mig-ₒk'rul Mil.* v. *mig-ₒp'rul.* — *mig-grogs* one's sweetheart *Cs.* — *mig-ₒgram* edge of the eye *Sch.* — *mig-rgyaṅ* 1. v. *rgyaṅ-ma.* 2. far-sightedness, *mig-rgyáṅ-čan* one that is far-sighted, *mig rgyaṅ-t'úṅ* short-sighted *Bhar.* *mig-sgyu* mirage, looming, Fata Morgana, *sós-kai t'áṅ-la mig-sgyu ₒgyú-ba bžin Thgr.* like the mirage on a plain in the hot season. — *mig-sgyur-ma* = *mk'á-ₒgro-ma Mil.* — *mig-čaṅ* 1. having eyes. 2. having seeds or grains, fructified, of ears of corn *W.* — *mig-čér* v. *če-re.* — *mig-lčibs* eye-lid *Med.* — *mig-ču* 1. tears *W.* 2. hydrophthalmia *Med.* 3. *mig-ču dzág-pa* blear-eyes *Schr.* — *mig-brnyás ₒk'yér-ba Mil.* c. dat., to slight, to treat contemptuously. — *mig-rtúl* dim, dull eyes *Sch.* — *mig-lta* (resp. *žál-lta, žál-ta*) *byéd-pa* to inspect, superintend (**mig-ta-k'an** overseer of workmen); to keep, to guard; to care for, to minister, to serve. — *mig-ltág Sch.* = *mig-skyóg* (?) — *mig-ltós* 1. eye-sight, look, mien *Cs.* 2. *C. W.* learning by observation and close ocular attention, **gár-ža-pe̱ hin-dui mig-tós k'ur,** or *k'yon,* or *lob dug** *W.* the people of Lahoul copy the Hindoos; **mig-tós ṅán-pa k'ur,** or *lob soṅ** *W.* he has imitated what is not good. — **mig-tọ-la p'ẹm-pa,** or *nọ'-pa** *C.* to derive profit or harm from observing and imitating others (?) **mig-tọ-la p'ém-pe̱ 'ṭim** deterring punishment. — **mig-t'ág tón-wa** a kind of torture in *C.*, little hooks, connected by strings, being fastened in the lower eye-lids as well as in the chest, by which means the former are constantly drawn down and prevented from closing. — *mig-t'úṅ* short-sightedness *Cs.*, *mig-t'úṅ-čan* short-sighted. — **mig-ḍa** snow-spectacles, shades formed of a texture of horse-hair. — **mig-dól** *C.* = *γnyid-rdól.* — *mig-ldán* = *mig-čan* po. needle. — *mig-nád*, disease of the eye. — *mig-po* = *mig Cs.*, *mig-po-čé* a large eye *Cs.* — **mig-pág** *C.*, *W.* eye-lid. — *mig-sprin* 'a white spot in the eye' *Sch.*; acc. to *Lt.* it seems to be the white of the eye, sclerotica, in *C.* the cataract is called so. — *mig-p'ór Cs.* = *mig-k'úṅ.* — *mig-ₒk'rúl Mil.* optical deception, *mig-ₒk'rul-mk'an* a showman *Cs.* — *mig-bu* 'Augenklappe' *Sch.* (?) — *mig-ₒbúr* goggle-eyes. — *mig-ₒbras* apple of the eye, eye-ball, **mig-ḍás lóg-če,** or *mig-kór lóg-če** *W.* to roll the eyes; *bdág-gi mig-gi ₒbras ltar γčés-na yaṅ* although she is as dear to me as the apple of my eye. — *mig-máṅ(s)* chess-board, game at tables, *mig-máṅ rtsé-ba Dzl.* to play at chess, *mig-maṅ-rís-su bris-pa Glr.* chequered, painted or in-laid work after the pattern of a chess-board. — *mig-méd* eyeless, blind. — *mig-dmár* 1. red eye, as a symptom of disease *Lt.* 2. the planet Mars. — *mig-smán* eye-medicine. — *mig-rtsa* 1. prob. Vena facialis externa *Med.* 2. the blood-vessels of the sclerotica, *mig-rtsa ₒk'rúgs-pa* the blood-vessels irritated, reddened *Med.* — **mig-sál** *W.* sharp-sightedness, **mig-sál-k'an** sharp-sighted, **mig-sal-nyám** the contrary. — *mig-rtség* the wrinkles of the eye-lid *Cs.* — *mig-ts'il*, 1. fat in the eye *Mil.* 2. the white in the eye *Cs.* — **mig-ts'ig(-če)** *W.* inflammation of the eye, **k'á-mig-ts'ig** caused by snow, **dúd-mig-ts'ig** caused by smoke. — *mig-zi* mist before the eyes *Sch.* — *mig-zúr* corner of the eye *Sch.* — *mig-γzúgs S.g.* optical perception, a picture of objects being formed on the retina by reflected rays of light (merely guessed by Tibetan science, not ascertained by observation and research). **mig-yáṅ(s)** *C.*, *W.* liberal, bountiful. — *mig-yór*, 1. *Sch.* = *mig-rtúl.* 2. = *mig-sgyú Thgr.* — *mig-rig-rig Mil.* timidly, anxiously looking to and fro, hither and thither. — *mig-riṅ-čan* = *mig-rgyáṅ-čan Cs.* — *mig-ris* artificial eye-brows *Cs.* — *mig-rús* eye-bone *Cs.* — *mig-slobs* the act of accustoming the eyes to . . ., *mig-slóbs ṅán-pa skye Mil.* you habituate yourself to a faulty look, i. e.

downward, to what is earthly. — **mig-ṡóg** *W.* eye-lash. — *mig-sér* 1. jaundice, also **gya-nág mig-sér* W.* 2. envy, jealousy, *mig-sér-čan* envious, jealous. — *mig-hu-ré* v. *hu-re.*

མིང་ *miṅ*, resp. *mtsan*, **name,** *k̓yód-kyi miṅ či yin Mil.* or **či zer* W.* what is your name? *dei miṅ yaṅ med Glr.* such a thing is or was not known at all, such a thing does not exist; *miṅ-tsam-gyi dge-slóṅ Dzl.* priest only by name; *W.*: **miṅ-gi náṅ-na** id.; *C.* also: **ṭál-gyi miṅ tsám-lẹ me** this tax exists only nominally; **appellation, designation, word,** *t̓én-pai miṅ* a word for drawing (pulling) *Gram.*; *miṅ-gi mdzod* **dictionary;** **k̓yod-sụ miṅ daṅ** or **sụ miṅ-ṅi náṅ-na** or **sụ miṅ nén-te** or **sụ miṅ-la t̓én-te ča dug* W.* in whose name or business, upon whose order are you going? **čii miṅ daṅ* W.* for what cause, in behalf of what affair? *miṅ-nas rǰód-pa*, or *smó-ba Dzl.* and elsewh., to call by name, also to call upon the name of, hence . . . *kyi miṅ-nas brǰód-de* in the name of; *miṅ ₒdógs-pa* to name v. *miṅ* 2; *dṅós-miṅ* v. *dṅos*; *btágs-miṅ* a name given (e.g. a Christian name) *Cs.*, *rǰes-grúb-kyi miṅ* a surname *Cs.*, *rus-miṅ* a family name *Cs.*

**Comp.** *miṅ-rkyáṅ* a single syllable or name *Cs.*; cf. *miṅ-sbyár.* — *miṅ-grógs* one's name-sake *Cs.* — *miṅ-sgrá* a mere name, word, or sound (philosophical term.) *Was.* — *miṅ-ṅán* a bad name, infamy *Cs.* — *miṅ-čan* having a name, *dpal-ₒbyór miṅ-čan* one of the name of Paljor. — *miṅ-t̓on* v. *ₒt̓ón-pa.* — *miṅ-mt̓á* final letter *Cs.* — *miṅ-sbyár* compound name. — *miṅ-méd* 1. nameless. 2. the fourth finger. — *miṅ-tsig* word, appellation. — *miṅ-γži* the first letter of the root of a word, in contradistinction to the second, the third, and the prefix-letters, *miṅ-γži rkyáṅ-pa* a single initial, e. g. ཀ, including ཀྱ, ཀྲ, ཀླ, *Zam.*; *γnyis-sbrél, γsum-sbrél* a double, triple, letter, like རྐ, རྐྱ, *Cs.*(?) — *miṅ-bzáṅ* good reputation *Cs*

མིང་པོ་ *miṅ-po* **brother** in relation to his sister, *miṅ-sriṅ* brother and sister; *de ṅa daṅ miṅ-sriṅ-du byao Dzl.* her and myself I shall make to be sister and brother, i.e. I shall raise her to be my sister.

མིད་ *mid* **a large fish** *Cs.*; *mid-mid* id.

མིད་པ་ *mid-pa* 1. sbst. **gullet, oesophagus** *Mil.* and elsewh.; *mid-skráṅ* a tumour of it, incident to horses *Sch.* — 2. vb. **to swallow, to gulp down,** frq.

མིན་ *min*, *W.* **man**, 1. for *ma yin* (he, she, it) **is not,** *ṡa-mịn-tsil-min Mil.* they are neither 'flesh nor fat'. — 2. abbrev. for *min-pa* and *min-par* v. below; *btaṅ-min* for **btaṅ yin-nam ma yin* W.* will it be given or not? *min-pa* and *ma yin-pa* **to be not;** often as a participle supplying the place of a prep. or adv. (for *min-par*), **excepted, except, besides,** *de ma yin-pai ṡiṅ Stg.* the other trees except this one; *klu ma yin-pa γžan mi t̓ub Dzl.* except he that is a Lu cannot . . .; *saṅs-rgyás min-pa sus kyaṅ mi ṡes Mil.* besides Buddha no one knows of it, no one knows it except Buddha; *ṅas yug γčig min-pa mi bsdad Mil.* I have been sitting down only this moment; *ro zér-ba min-pa skyab-pai miṅ mi yoṅ-ba ₒdug Mil.* one can only say 'corpse', and the appellation '*skyab-pa*' is not admissible; *de min* **besides, otherwise, else, apart from, setting aside** *Mil.*; even: *de-min-rnams Glr.* those that are not doing so. Cf. *man.*

མིན་ད་ *min-da* v. *mi-mda*, sub *mi* compounds.

མིམ་ *mim*, the Hind. *mĕm*, **Madam,** *mim sá-heb* the mistress or lady of the house.

མིར་ *mir* termin., མིས་ *mis* instrum. case of *mi.*

མུ་ *mu* 1. num. fig.: 76. — 2. sbst. **border, boundary, limit, edge, end,** *žiṅ-mu-la γnás-pai lha* deity residing on the landmark; *mú-la skye* (the plant) grows on the edges of fields *Wdṅ.*; *mt̓a méd-čiṅ mu med Stg.* there is neither limit nor end; *mu bži* = *mt̓a bži Mil*, *S.g.* seems to be used in a philosophical sense for 'perfect limitedness'; *mu-k̓yúd* **circumference, compass, the hoops** of a cask *Sch.*, the **rim** of a wheel *Stg.*; *mu-k̓yud-ₒdzin* n.p., the least of the seven mountains surrounding the Sumeru. *mú-stegs-pa*, also *mú-stegs-čan Ssk.* तीर्थिक (overlooking the word *stegs*) it is gen. explained in an intellectual sense, so by Cunningham: adherents of the doctrine of finite existence (Bhilsa Topes), *Cs.*: the doctrine of perpetual duration or of perpetual annihilation(?); but should not rather *mú-stegs* be the same as *˳báb-stegs* (v. *˳báb-pa*), being a literal translation of तीर्थ, and therefore prop. a Brahmanic ascetic (v. *Ssk.* dict.), in Buddhist literature always equivalent to Brahmanist, Non-Buddhist, heretic (infidel)? — 3. *Sch* has besides: *mú-la* in a circle, continuously; *mu-ltar* or *mú-nas* = *bžin-du C.*; in *W* they say: **mu čig-la bor** throw it together on a heap!

མུ་གེ་ *mú-ge* 1. *W.* **desire, appetite,** **zaṅ za-če** or **čaṅ ťún-čeï mú-ge rag** I have a longing for food, for beer; *mú-ge-čan* fond of dainties, lickerish, of men and animals. — 2. *B.* and col., **famine,** *mú-ge ˳byuṅ Dzl., Mil.* a famine is caused, breaks out.

མུ་ཅོར་ *mu-čór* **nonsense,** *smrá-ba Stg.* to talk nonsense.

མུ་ཏིག *mú-tig* **pearl** frq., *mú-tig-rgyan* a pearl ornament *Cs*; *mu-tig-čún-po, mu-tig-drá-ba Glr.* garland formed of pearls; *mu-tig-ṗreṅ* string of pearls.

མུ་ཏི་ལ་ *mu-ti-la* **mother of pearl** *Sch.*(?).

མུ་ནི་ *mu-ni Ssk.* **saint, ascetic, anchorite,** chiefly in names: *Sā-kya-mu-ni* the saint of the Sākyas, Buddha.

མུ་ནི་ཏིད་ *mu-ni-ti Sch.* = *mu-tig*(?).

མུ་མེན་ *mu-mén Glr., Mil.* a precious stone, of a dark blue, yet inferior to the azure-stone, occasionally used for rosaries; mention is also made of *mu-mén dmár-po Wdṅ.*

མུ་རྩོད་ *mu-rtsód*(?) **colt's foot,** Tussilago farfara *Lh.*

མུ་ཟི་ *mú-zi* **brimstone, sulphur** *Med.*, *mú-zi-čan* containing sulphur, sulphurous; *mú-zii skyúr-rtsi* (*snum Schr.*) sulphuric acid *Cs.*(?).

མུ་རན་ *mu-rán* **hoop,** of casks etc. *Sch.*

མུ་ལ་ *mū-la Ssk.*, **root;** particular roots, such as those of Arum campanulatum, so perh. *Lt.*

མུག་གེ་ *múg-ge* sometimes for *mú-ge.*

མུག་པ་ *múg-pa*, 1. sbst. **moth, worm,** *múg-ma* id. *Glr.*, also *múṅ-ma*; *gós-mug* clothes-moth, *bál-mug* id., *lčágs-mug* a worm that eats iron away(?) *Cs.*; *múg-zan* moth-eaten, destroyed by worms *Cs.* — 2. vb. with *yid-*, *yi-*, resp. *ťugs-*, **to despair** *Pth.*; *blo múg-po* a gloomy, doleful way of thinking *Sch.*

མུན་པ་ *mun-pa* 1. sbst. **obscurity, darkness,** frq. — *mún-pai smag-rúm* id., frq.; *mún-pa-nas mún-par ˳gro Dzl.* they wander in eternal darkness; *mún-pa sél-ba* to lighten the darkness; frq. fig. with and without *bloi.* — 2. adj. **obscure, dark.** — 3. vb. in *W.*, *mun soṅ* he has become insensible. — **Comp.** *mún-ḱaṅ* dark room, e.g. the sanctuary containing the images of the gods *Glr.*; prison *Cs.* — *mún-ḱuṅ Dzl.* prison, dungeon. — **mun-ṭig* Lh.*, *mun-ḱród Dzl.*, **mun-nág* W., C.*, *mun-brág Sch.* and *Lh.*(?) close darkness. — **mun-ḍúl*, or *mun-nyúg táṅ-če* W.* to grope in the dark. — **mún-ču, núm-ču* W.* the dusk of evening, **mún (-ču) rub** sets in. — **mún-(s)pe-ra táṅ-če* W.* to talk confusedly, wildly. — *mun-sprúl Tar.* 56,17, to judge by the context: ignorance, stupidity; so *Schf.* — *mun-sribs Lex.* the darkness of night. — *mun-sró* furious passion, **mún-sro yoṅ dug* W.* he rages in his passion. — **mun-srós* = *mún-ču* W.*

མུམ་ *mum* (*Hind.*) *W.* **wax.**

མུར་ *mur* 1. termin. of *mu*, hence *mur-ťug* **to the extremity, till the end of** *Cs.*; perh. also *mur-dúm* (or *-zlum*?) *Ld.* **dull,** of knives, hatchets; *múr-˳dug* = *mú-stegs-pa Sch.* — 2. **gills** of fish.

མུར་གོང་ *mur-goṅ* **the temples** *Sch.*; *mur-˳grám* id. *Cs*; **jaw, jaw-bone** *Sch.* — *mur-ťór* ulcers in the mouth *Sch.*

མུར་བ་ *múr-ba* 1. **to gnaw,** to destroy by gnawing, to bite asunder, e.g. bones *Thgr.* — 2. **to masticate, to chew**(?).

རྨུལ་ཐུག mul-ťug W. **fist**, *mul-ťúg čó-če, gám-če* to threaten with the fist, *gyáb-če* to strike with the fist.

མེ་ me I. num. fig.: 106. — II. sbst. 1. resp. žugs C.; *nán-me* W., **fire**, me ₒbar the fire burns, šor breaks out, mčed spreads, ši is extinguished; *me són-na* W. is the fire burning (again)? ḱán-pa mes (vulgo *méla*) bsregs, šor, ḱyer the house is burnt down, *dugs soṅ* W. ignited, burnt (partially); me sbór-ba, ₒbúd-pa, γtóṅ-ba B., *(s)bár-če, ṕú-če, dúg-če* W. to light a fire, γsó-ba, *són-te čó-če* W. to stir, poke, trim the fire, *nyál-če* W. to cover the glowing embers with ashes, in order to preserve the heat; rgyáb-pa 1. **to set on fire,** ḱyim-la a house Glr. 2. **to strike fire** W., me ldé-ba B. and col., to warm one's self at the fire. — 2. symb. num.: 3. —

**Comp.** me-skám cock (of a gun), *mekám ǰar ťsar* W. the gun is cocked. — meskyógs C. a shovel for live coals. — mesgyógs, gyogs = sgyogs 2. — me-mgál **firebrand,** me-mgál-gyi ḱór-lo the circle made by a firebrand, when quickly swung round Cs. — *me-ḍọ́n* **torch** C. — mé-čan fiery, containing fire. — me-lčágs fire-steel, pocketfire. — mé-lče flame of fire. — me-čá firesteel(?) Sch., *me-čẹ́* C. every thing requisite for kindling a fire, as it is got in readiness for the following morning. — me-mnyam-rlúṅ v. rluṅ. — *me-tág* C. 1. (rtags) a mark of burning. 2. (ltag or stag) **spark, sparklet,** a bit of live coal in the ashes. — me-ťáb fire-place, hearth; stove. — me-dóṅ Dzl. fire-pit, pool of fire. — me-dród v. drod. — *me-dá* C., musket, pistol; *meda pag-čén* canon Schr.; *me-dá gyáb-pa* to discharge a gun; *me-da-šiṅ* resinous wood, the coal of which is particularly used for making gun-powder. — *me-dág* (mdag) C. coals glowing underneath the ashes. — me-rdél bullet, musket-ball Sch. — me-rdó flint Cs. — me-núr Sch. = me-mdág. — me-snód, or -ṕór coal-pan, chafing-dish, perfuming-pan. — me-púṅ, me-búm cupping-glass, cup Lt. — mé-ba Dzl. = me. — mébo = me a large fire; mé-bo če Dzl. — me-dbál a disease Med.; it is said to be a cutaneous eruption, hot and smarting, perh. erysipelas? — me-múr = me-mdág Dzl.; me-ma-múr Thgy. id.? — me-btsá v. btsa. — *me-ťság* spark W. — *me-dzẹ́* **gunpowder** C. — me-γži anvil Sch. — me-γžób mark of singeing, of having caught fire. — *me-zí* W. = me-ltág. — me-ₒóbs = me-dóṅ Sch. — mé-rí fire-mountain, introduced by us for **volcano.** — me-ris a figure resembling a flame Sch. — me-ró an extinguished fire, fig. bstán-pai me-ró laṅ Glr. the extinct doctrine revives again. — *meliṅ* W. flame. — me-lén fire-tongs. — me-šél burning-glass. — me-lhá the god of fire, v. Schl. 251 sqq. — III. v. also mé-tog.

མེ་ཉག me-nyág v. mi-nyág.

མེ་ཏོག mé-tog, W. *mén-tog*, 1. **flower,** métog ₒbar, ḱa ₒbus the flower opens, begins to bloom, mé-tog-gi ṕréṅ-ba chaplet, wreath of flowers. — 2. W. **tuft** or **crest** on the head of some birds. — 3. W. **snow-flake.**

མེ་ལོང་ mé-loṅ 1. **mirror, looking-glass,** frq.; lás-kyi mé-loṅ a magic mirror, revealing the future Glr.; also fig., esp. in titles of books, e.g. rgyal-rábs-kyi γsál-bai mé-loṅ A bright Mirror of the History of Kings. 2. **plain surface,** flat body extending in length and breadth, e.g. the flatness of the shoulder-blade, table-top, door-pannels etc., hence sgo mé-loṅ-čan Glr. an opening provided with a frame of boards to close it, not merely an 'ostium', of which description most of the inner doors in Tibetan houses are.

མེའའུ་ meaₒo **the mewing of a cat.**

མེད་པ་ méd-pa for mi yód-pa **to be not, to exist not** (v. yód-pa), med he is not here, he is gone etc.; *ḱa-čúl-du soṅ-te med* W. he is off, having gone to Kashmere; *čagmag ǎ-pẹ ḱyér-te med* W. the tinder-box is not here, father has taken it with him; *ši-te med* W. he is dead and gone; skabs med Dzl. there is, or there was, no opportunity; čos-kyi miṅ tsam yaṅ med Glr. religious law does not, or did not, exist at all; med kyaṅ even if nothing is extant, though the thing does not exist in reality; **ni méd-na yaṅ yoṅ dug** the '*ni*' may be dispensed with, though '*ni*' be omitted, it will be all right; *rgyá-la méd-pai yí-ge drug Glr.* six letters not existing in Sanskrit; *méd-kyaṅ-ruṅ-bai yig-ₒbru γčig* a letter that may also be wanting, a dispensable letter, e.g. ཀྵ *Glr.*; *méd-kyaṅ dgós-pai k̒ral-bsdúd Mil.* a taxation necessary, and even if one possesses nothing, yet as it were inexorable; *méd-pa* (*W. *méd-k̒an**) not being, not existing, not having; *blá-ma-la bžúgs-grogs méd-pa lágs-sam Mil.* has your Reverence no fellow-resident in your house? fem. *méd-ma Mil.*; *W. *mā dud-pa-méd-k̒an** very or quite smokeless; *mi brnáṅs-pa skyúg-tu méd-pa mid-du méd-pa Dzl.* a man about to be choked, being neither able to spit out, nor to swallow down; *bdag* (or *bdag-la*) *čaṅ dbul-du med Dzl.* we are not able to give any thing; *med-mi-rúṅ-gi bu-ts̒á Mil.* the sons and grandsons that are to get something (as a heritage); *k̒yim der méd-du mi γtúb-pa*, or *mi rúṅ-ba* indispensable in the house *Thgy.*; so also *med-t̒abs-méd-pai blón-po Glr.*; *méd-par ₒgyúr-ba* to be annihilated, to disappear, *stág-mo méd-par gyúr-to Pth.* the tigress disappeared; *γnam daṅ sa yaṅ med-gyur-na Dzl.* when heaven and earth shall pass away; **da ṅa čiaṅ méd-k̒an soṅ* W.* now I am quite undone; *blón-po-rnams ₒgran-sems-méd-par gyur-to Glr.* the ministers lost their litigiousness, gave up quarreling; *zas brim-du méd-par gyúr-to Dzl.* the distribution of the dishes became impossible; **p̒é-ra zér-če méd-k̒an soṅ* W.* he became speechless; *med-par byéd-pa* to annihilate, an enemy *Dzl.*, to put an end to, a quarrel *Glr.*; frq. *méd-pa(r)* may be rendered by 'without': *rgyál-po žig méd-na mi ruṅ*, or *t̒abs méd Pth.* we cannot do without a king; *m̒ta-rten-méd-pai m̒ta* a termination without a final consonant *Gram.*; *rgyu méd-par S.g.* without cause; or by 'instead of': *rgyál-po méd-par Glr.* instead of the king, *sṅár-gyi lus méd-par Glr.* instead of the former shape; *nyin-mts̒an-méd-par* making no difference between day and night, *p̒o-mo-méd-par* between male and female, *rgan-byis-méd-par* old and young; vulgo also *nyin-med-mts̒án-med* etc. — *méd-po*, *W. *méd-k̒an**, fem. *méd-mo*, a poor man, pauper.

མེན་ *men Mil.* **an ornament, piece of finery.**

མེནྡི་ *mendi*, *Ssk.* मेन्धी, Lawsonia alba, a plant used for staining the finger-nails red *Mil.*

མེན་ཙེ་ *mén-tsi* **a coloured silk handkerchief** *W.*

མེན་ཧྲི་ *mén-hri* a kind of **fur**? *mén-hri dmár-poi slóg-pa* a fur-coat of red *men-hri* is mentioned as the vesture of a Lha.

མེར་ *mer* termin. of *me*.

མེར་བ་ *mér-ba Cs.*: 'a quaking; thinness; *mér-po*, *mer-mér* thin, as liquids'; *Sch.*: '*mér-gyis gaṅ* full to the brim'. I met with 1. *mer* in *žig-mér* q.v. — 2. *mér-ba* as adj. for *mts̒o* the lake *Mil.* — 3. **mer-mér* W.* adj. **like a thin pap**, and sbst. **a muddy substance**, e.g. street-mire; **mer-mér čó-če** to make a mire. — 4. *mér-mer-ba* adj in connection with such sbst. as light, ray, beam, brightness *Thgr.*, *Mil.* — 5. *mér-mer-po* used in medical writings in a similar manner as *núr-nur-po*, to define the shape of an embryo, **oblong, oval**; these descriptions, however, though partly founded on observation, are frequently very arbitrary, vague, and even contradictory. In *W.* the word has only the signification 3; a Lama from *C.* rendered it with **'full'**, which would agree with *Sch.* and no. 1, as well as with 'glittering, quivering', having some relation to no. 2 and no. 4.

མེལ་ཚེ་ or ཙེ་ *mél-ts̒e* or *-tse* 1. **watch, watchman, sentinel; watcher, spy,** *mél-ts̒e byéd-pa* to watch, to keep watch *Dzl.*; *ǰá-ra-mel-ts̒e* = **mel-ts̒e* W.* — 2. **steatite** or **soap-stone**, of a greenish colour.

མེས་པོ་ *més-po*, vulgo **me-mé**, **grandfather**; also **forefather, ancestor, progenitor,** *saṅs-rgyás t̒ams-čád-kyi spyi-mes kun-tu-bzáṅ-po Thgr. Kuntuzaṅpo*, the common progenitor of all the Buddhas; *mes rgyál-po Glr.* merely equivalent to 'the old king';

*ṗa-més* the grandfather by the father's, *ma-més* by the mother's side *Cs*; *yaṅ-més* great-grandfather *Glr.*; *že-* or *γži-més Sch.* great-great-grandfather; *mes-dbón* grandfather and grandchildren, resp., e.g. *rgyál-po mes-dbón* the kings from one generation to another, the royal ancestors *Glr.*; *mes-rábs* id. *Sch.*; **me-mé**, reverential name given to men of a more advanced age *W.* also *C.*

མེ་ཏྲི་ *me-tri*, मैत्र, v. *byáms-pa Mil.*

མོ་ *mo*, I. num. figure: 136.

II. **woman, female**, opp. to *ṗo*, = *bud-méd*: *mo na-re* the woman said *Glr.*, *Mil.*; of animals: **female**. — **mo-kyáṅ** *W.* virgin. — *mo-gós* woman's gown, petticoat. — *mo-brgyúd* female line of descent. — *mo-bi* female calf. — *mo-byís Mil.*, *mo-dbyis* (**mo-yi**) *C.* girl, female child. — *mo-btsún* nun *Glr.* — *mo-mtsán*, *moi dbáṅ-po* female genitals. — *mo-ráṅ-(mo)* 1. **single, unmarried woman**, so perh. in the passage, *γdoṅ ṅán-gyi ḱyó-bas mo-ráṅ skyid* happier is a single woman than one with a husband of a bad face; more frq., the word implies 2. **a poor, destitute female**, one who did not get a husband *W.* 3. **she, herself** *C.*, *Lew.* — *mo-rí*, *mo-ré* a female kid. — *mo-rigs* female sex. *Cs.* — *mo-lús* the female body *Sch.* — *mo-γšám* a barren female, hence *mo-γšám-gyi bu* a nonsense, an incongruity.

III. **lot**, *mo ˳débs-pa* to cast the lot, always a religious ceremony performed by Lamas (cf. *rgyan* and *rtags-ril*), which however does not preclude the possibility of an imposture; *mó-pa* one dealing with these practices, a soothsayer, *mó-pa ˳dre mtóṅ-ba* a soothsayer that pretends to have seen a ghost; *mó-mḱan Cs.*, *mó-rtsis-pa Glr.* id. (the latter expression in the respective passage = court-astrologer); *mo-ma* the feminine of it *Cs.*, which however is at variance with *Mil.*, who in several places has *bla-ma mḱas-pai mo-ma*.

IV. affix, so-called article, corresponding to the masc. terminations *po* and *pa*, and denoting the fem. gender of persons, *bú-mo* daughter, *bód-mo* a Tibetan woman.

མོ་ཁབ་ *mo-ḱab* v. *ḱab.*

མོག་པ་ *móg-pa* **dark** (coloured) *Cs.*; *móg-ro* of horses, yellowish-brown *Glr.*

མོག་མོག་ *mog-móg* 1. *Cs.* = *móg-pa.* — 2. **meat-pie**, meat-balls in a cover of paste.

མོག་ཤ་ *móg-ša* **mushroom** *W.*

མོགས་ཙ་ར་ *mógs-tsa-ra Lt.* n. of a plant; in *Lh. mog-ša-ras* is a large species of Ferula or Dorema, of a yellow flower and a fetid smell.

མོང་གོལ་ *móṅ-gol* **a Mongul** *Tib. sóg-po.*

མོང་རྟུལ་ *moṅ-rtúl Lex.* = *blúṅ-po* **dull, stupid.**

མོང་ལོ་ *móṅ-lo*, *W.* for *lóṅ-mo* **knuckle, anklebone.**

མོད་ *mod* **moment**, occurring only in the following combinations: *láṅ-bai mod (de-nyid)-la* at the very moment of rising *Pth.*, *Mil.*, *dei mód-la* the moment after *Glr.*; gen. *mód-la* **instantly, immediately**, *mód-la dráṅs-so Glr.* he immediately pulled it out; *ḱra yaṅ mód-la ṗyin-te Dzl.* immediately after there came also the hawk; *dé-nas mód-la* id. *Dzl.*

མོད་པ་ *mód-pa* (cognate to *mád-pa*?) an emphatic word for **to be**, 1. as an augmentative of *yin*, sometimes superadded to this word; occasionally untranslatable, sometimes = **indeed, to be sure**, *žes smras mód-kyi Dzl.* though indeed you may say so; *dpag-tu-méd mód-kyi* though indeed it is immeasurable *Dzl.*; *γsa dé-ka ṅa yin mod Mil.* the snow-leopard indeed was I myself; *di ma yin mod ˳on-kyaṅ* ... to be sure, it is not this one, yet... *Tar.*; *˳gró-ba yin mod* (although not invited) yet after all you must go. — 2. as augmentative of *yod*, signifying abundance, plenty *B.*, *C.*, *W.*; *de mi byéd-na dgra mod* if you omit to do this, you will have plenty of enemies, *nad mod* plenty of diseases; *sti-bstáṅ-gi ḱrims šin-tu mód-kyi* although they abounded in compliments; *mód-pa* having an abundance, *loṅs-spyód mód-par ˳gyur* he becomes the owner of great wealth *Dzl.*; *šiṅ-tog mód-*

pa Glr. abounding in tree-fruit; *mód-po* adj. plentiful, abounding, *kúl-lu-ru śiṅ mód-po* in Kullu wood is plentiful, or *śiṅ mód-poi yul* (Kullu is) a country abounding in wood, opp. to *dkón-po*, hence 'cheap' may occasionally stand for it.

མོན་ *mon* 1. n. p., general name for the different nations living between Tibet and the Indian plain *Mil : món-yul-gyi bán-dhe* a monk from Nepal; *Glr.: dpal-gro món-la* Paldo in Bhotan; *mon-ta-waṅ* is stated to be a commercial place in Assam, from whence much rice is brought to Tibet; the people of Lahoul are looked upon by the real Tibetans as Mon, though for the most part they speak the Tibetan language, and they in their turn consider the Hindoos in Kullu as Mon; that this appellation is often extended to the Hindoos in general, appears from such names as, *món-gre, món-sran* Indian pea, *Phaseolus radiatus*, माष; *món-ča-ra* the ever-green oak and its fruit, of the southern Himalaya ridges *Wdṅ.*; in *Ld.* the musicians (*Ld.-Glr. Schl.* 25, b), carpenters, and wood-cutters coming from the south, are likewise denominated Mon. — The form *mon-pa Cs.* is not known to me; *mon-mo* fem. *Pth.* — 2. sometimes for *mun.*

མོན་ཞ་ *mon-ža* (or perh. *γža*) *W.*, **popularity, respect, reputation**, *món-ža tob* he makes himself generally beloved, is highly respected; *món-ža-čan* **beloved, popular**.

མོར་ *mor* termin. of *mo.*

མོལ་བ་ *mól-ba* the usual resp. term, esp. in *W.*, for **to say, to speak,** as *bsgó-ba* and *bká-rtsal-ba* are used in earlier, and *γsúṅ-ba* in later literature and in *C.*, hence it is often to be rendered by 'to order'; **śá-heb-la sa-lám mol žu** have the goodness to present (say) my compliments to that gentleman; **mól-lče táṅ-če** to flatter, to caress; **mól-la táṅ-wa* C.* to make known(?).

མོས་པ་ *mós-pa* vb. and sbst. **to be pleased,** *la* **with, to wish, to have a mind,** *ˌgró-bar mós-so Glr.* I took a fancy to go there; *ču-la sógs-par mós-na Thgy.* if you wish for water or something of the kind; *mós-pa daṅ ˌdód-pa S.O.* desiring and coveting (are the origin of all the misery of sin); **to take pleasure in, to rejoice at,** *mós-pai glu Glr.* song of rejoicing; as sbst.: **pleasure, satisfaction, esteem**. — 2. **to respect, to esteem,** with *la,* to respect with devotion, **to revere, to adore** *čós-la* frq.; *kyod gáṅ-la mos* to whom do you direct your devotions? *Mil.; mós-nas ˌbúl-ba yin* I give it merely from devout veneration, i.e. I shall take nothing for it *Pth.*; frq. joined with *gús-pa*: *yid-mos-gús drág-pos* with fervent veneration; *dad-mós* devotion; *mos spyód-pa* as participle, a pious man, a devotee *Tar.* 109, 7.

མྱ་ངན་ *mya-ṅán*, **trouble, misery, affliction,** *mya-ṅán-gyis γdúṅ-ste Dzl.*; *mya-ṅán či yaṅ med Dzl.* I have no trouble, no uneasiness, whatever; *mya-ṅán bsal Tar.* the time of mourning is at an end; *mya-ṅán byéd-pa* to lament, to wail; *mya-ṅan-méd*, अशोक, n. of a famous king of ancient India *Glr., Tar.* ch. VI; *mya-ṅán-las ˌdás-pa*, abbr. *myaṅ-ˌdas* (and so also pronounced, as for instance in a verse of *Mil.*, where it occurs as a trochee) 'having been delivered from pain', the usual, illiteral, Tibetan version of निर्वाण, the absolute cessation of all motion and excitement both of body and mind, which is necessarily connected with personal existence; absolute rest, which by orientals is thought to be the highest degree of happiness, imagined by some as a perfect annihilation of existence, by others, more or less, only as a cessation of all that is unpleasant in human existence, — well set forth by *Köpp.* I. 304 sqq.

མྱ་ངམ་ *mya-ṅam* **a fearful desert** *Lex., Thgy.*

མྱག་པ་ *myág-pa Sch.* **'to chew'**; acc. to medical writings, **the chemical decomposition** of the chyme in the stomach; **to cause putrefaction**; pf. *myags; myágs-par byéd-pa* = *myag-pa S.g.*; *rul-čiṅ myágs-pa Dzl.* decomposed, putrefied; *ro-myágs* the watery product of putrefaction, '*tabes*' *Thgy.*

མྱང་བ་ *myáṅ-ba* v. *myóṅ-ba.*

མྱད་པ་ *myád-pa Sch.* = *mid-pa* sbst.

ཨྨྱིང་ *myiṅ Sch.* = *miṅ.*

སྨྱུ་གུ་ *myú-gu,* སྨྱུག་ *myug,* 1. *Sch.* **reed, rush, flag,** also = *smyú-gu.* — 2. *Cs.* **sprout,** the first shoot of corn etc., *myú-gu̓ sṅón-po Thgy.* the young green corn.

སྨྱུག་པ་ *myúg-pa, myúg-myug-pa* 1. **to run, roam, stroll idle about** *Sch.* — 2. **to show, exhibit ostentatiously, to boast with** *Cs.* v. *dmyúg-pa.*

སྨྱུར་བ་ *myúr-ba* **quick, swift, speedy,** *myúr-po* id. *Mil.*; mostly as adv., *myúr-du* **quickly, speedily; soon;** *ċi-myúr* as speedily as possible; *myur-du-btsá-rtags* symptoms of immediate parturition *Med.*

སྨྱུལ་བ་ *myúl-ba* **to examine closely, to search into, to scrutinize,** c. accus. or termin. of place *Stg.*, *Mil.*, prob. but a different spelling for *nyúl-ba.* — *lċe-myúl Mṅg.*, *Lt.* a symptom of disease, acc. to *Wise* p. 282: a quivering motion of the tongue.

སྨྱོ་བ་ *myó-ba* v. *smyó-ba.*

སྨྱོང་བ་ *myóṅ-ba,* pf. *myaṅs,* also *myoṅ,* fut. *myaṅ W.* **nyáṅ-ċe**, 1. **to taste** *Dzl.*; **to try by tasting,** *myaṅ-bas žim-po ṫsor-nas* perceiving the relish by tasting; *ro myóṅ-ba* **dob-lág nyáṅ-ċe** *W.*, id.; **to enjoy,** *mṫo-rís-kyi loṅs-spyód* the bliss of paradise *Dzl.*; *myóṅ-bar byéd-pa* to make, or to permit to, enjoy, *k̓yod ċ̓ós-kyi zas myóṅ-bar byao* I shall make thee enjoy the food of religious doctrine *Sch.*, yet it may be rendered also more simply: thou wilt enjoy . . . *Dzl.* ༧༥༢, b. — 2. in philosophy: **to perceive,** in relation to the perceptions of sense, *Ssk.* वेदन. — 3. **to experience, to suffer,** both good and evil, *sdug-bsṅal,* distress etc. frq.; **to get,** *mi-sdúg-pai lus* an ugly body; seldom with termin., *γnás-skabs γžán-du myóṅ-bar ₒgyúr-bai lás-rnams* works which would bring upon their author another state of existence (after his death) *Thgy.*; *myóṅ-bar mi ₒgyúr-ba* to be preserved from *Dom.*; *raṅ-gi byás-pa ráṅ-gi myóṅ-ba yin Pth.* your own doings are your own sufferings; as you have brewed, so you must drink. — 4. auxil. of the pf. like ***byuṅ,*** but chiefly in negative sentences: *btsal ma myoṅ Dzl.* I have never yet sought, *mṫoṅ ma myoṅ Mil.* I have never yet seen, *ṫos ma myoṅ Mil.* I have never yet heard, — a construction, that has originated from the earlier one c. inf.: *rdzun smrá-ba ma myoṅ, dgé-bai sems skyéd-pa ma myoṅ* dealing with falsehood, producing virtuous thoughts, has never happened to me yet *Dzl.*

དམའ་བ་ *dmá-ba* **to be low,** *dbus dma mṫa γnyis mṫó-na* if (in pregnancy) the middle parts of the body are low, and the sides high *Med.*; sbst. **lowness;** adj., also *dmá-mo,* **low,** low water, low voice, low rank, short measure or weight, frq.; *dmá-la k̓yád-du γsód-pa* to despise the low and humble *Lt.*; *dmá-na* if I live in humble circumstances *Dom.*; *ṅá-yis mṫo mṫo byás-pa dma dma byuṅ* aspiring higher and higher, I fell deep *Pth.*; of religion: *ċ̓úṅ-zad dmá-bai dús-su* as it had somewhat fallen into decay *Pth.*; *dma ₒbébs-pa* (frq. written *sma*) *W.* **ma bab kál-ċe**, and intrs. *dma ₒbáb-pa* to lower, to degrade, by words: **to abuse, to vilify** *Do.* by deeds: **to deface, to deform, to mar** *Pth.*; **to disgrace, dishonour, profane** *Pth.*; **to humiliate** *Tar.*; **to oppress, to ruin** *Schr.*; **ma-bab-ċan** *W.* humiliated, brought low. — *dmá-sa* 1. *Sch.* low land (?) 2. = *dmán-sa.* — Cf. *dmán-pa.*

དམག་ *dmag Lexx.* सेना 1. **army, host,** *dmag-tsógs, dmag-dpúṅ,* less frq. *dmag-γséb* id.; *dmag daṅ bċás-pa* with an army *Tar.*; *mí-la dmag skyúr-ba* to commit the command of an army to a person *Glr.*; *yúl-la dmag ₒdren-pa* to lead an army against, to invade a country, frq.; *dmag rgyág-pa Glr.*, **mag ṫáb-pa** *C.* to war, to make or wage war, *dmag-rgyág* (or *dmag-ₒdrén*) *res máṅ-du byéd-pa* to make war upon each other *Glr.*; *mú-stegs-pai dmág-gis bzuṅ* he was made a prisoner by an army of Brahmanists *Glr.*; *dmag stoṅ* 1000 men *Pth.*; *dmág-gi ṫsogs stoṅ-p̓rág súm-ċu* an army of 30 000 men *Dzl.* — 2. in a gen. sense, **multitude, number, host,** **mag-líṅ(s)** *W.* a beating up of game, a battue; **mag-nór** property of the community, = *(s)pi-nor* *W.* — 3. *Cs.* and *Sch.* **war.** —

ཨ

**Comp.** *dmag-ḱrims* 'martial law' *Cs.* — **mag-ṭúg* W.* **war, contention, contest.** — *dmag-mgó Ma.* vanguard, front or first line of the army. — *dmag-sgár* encampment, *ₒdégs-pa* to pitch a camp. — *dmag-bsgrig* troops drawn up, battle-array *Sch* — *dmag-č̔ás* requisites for war, military stores, ammunition *Pth.* — **mag-ťáb* C., W.* war. — *dmag-nór* v. above sub no. 2 *mag-nór.* — *dmag-sná* = *dmag-mgó Ma.* — *dmag-dpúṅ* army. — *dmag-dpón* commander, general. — *dmag-bráṅ* = *dmag-sgár.* — *dmag-mí* warrior, soldier. — *dmág-mo* = *dmag*, *dmág-mo če bskúr-ba Pth.* to send out a great army. — *dmag-ťsógs* = *dmag-dpúṅ.* — *dmag-líṅs* v. above.

**དམག་པ་** *dmág-pa* v. མག་པ་ *mág-pa.*

**དམངས་** *dmaṅs* **the common people, populace, multitude, vulgar;** *dmáṅs-kyi stón-mo* a banquet for all *Mil.*; *dmaṅs ṕál-pa* the vulgar, the common people; one of the common people; *dmáṅs-rigs* id.; used also as an abusive word: **mean fellow;** when referred to Indian matters = शूद्र the caste of craftsmen, not so low as *γdól-ba.*

**དམད་པ་** *dmád-pa Sch.* invective, abuse, (does not suit to *S.g.* 21).

**དམན་པ་** *dmán-pa* (cf. *dmá-ba*) 1. **low,** v. *mtó-ba*; gen. fig., in reference to quantity, **little,** *dman lhag log* either too little, or too much, or badly constituted, e.g. gall, and other humours of the human body *Med.*; *bsód-nams dmán-pa* having little merit, *blo dmán-pa* having little sense *Glr.*; with *skye-ba* v. *skye-ba* II.; in reference to quality: **indifferent, inferior** *Ssk.* हीन, *rim-pas dáṅ-po mč̔og yin ṕyi-ma dman* in the order (of enumeration) the first is always better, the next following inferior *S.g.*; **mẹn-šár** maiden, girl, virgin *C.* (cf. *skye-dmán*); **depressed in spirits** *Wdṅ.*; **poor, pitiable,** *ri-dwágs dmán-ma* the poor deer *Mil.*; *dmán-sa* or *dman-č̔a, ₒdzín-pa* to choose the low, humble part, to be humble, to humble one's self, frq.; *dmán-sa zuṅ daṅ mtó-sar sleb Mil.* choose what is low, and you will obtain what is high. — 2. *dman* for *skye-dmán* **woman,** opp. to *ṕo Mil.* — 3. in *Mil.* sometimes also for *má-mo, srín-mo.*

**དམར་** *dmar* **profit, gain, good success,** *dmar čuṅ* a small profit *Mil*; *dmár-po* adj., *ťugs-dám dmár-po byúṅ-ṅam* did it go on well with your meditation? *Mil.*, *dmar-ḱrid Cs.* 'practical instruction', e.g. in the healing art; acc. to my authorities it signifies the last 'finishing' instruction, in religion *Mil.*, in medical science *Med.*

**དམར་པོ་** *dmár-po*, fem: *dmár-mo* (seldom), *dmár-ba*, adj. 1. **red,** frq., *mdog-dmár-po* one red-coloured (lit. red as to colour) *Dom.*; *dmár-bai spyan* red eyes *Glr.*; *sna dmár-ba* having a red trunk or proboscis *Glr.*; *dmár-ba*, also **redness and to be red.** — 2. v. *dmar.* — **Comp.** *dmar-skyá* pale red. — *dmar-ḱrá Lt.*, red-spotted. — *dmar-ḱrid* v. *dmar.* — **mar-žén* W.* raw meat *W.* — *dmar-ljáṅ* greenish red *Mil.* — **már-ťag čọd* W.* the red of evening has vanished from the mountains. — *dmar-ťáb?* — *dmar-ťór* v. *ťór-pa.* — *dmar-mdáṅs Sch.* 1. **bright red**(?) 2. **ruddy complexion.** — *dmar-ₒdon Lt.* medicinal herb; in *Lh.* = *bya-po-tsi-tsi.* — *dmar-nág, skud-pa dmar-nág γnyis* two threads, one black, the other red, used in magic. — *dmar-smyúg* blackish red. — *mar-zaṅ-záṅ* scarlet-red. — *dmar-yól* red chinaware (? opp. to *dkar-yól*) *Med.* — *dmar-bšál Sch.* dysentery, bloody flux. — *dmar-sér* (*-po*) reddish yellow, honey-coloured *Glr.*

**དམས་པ་** *dmás-pa Cs.* **wounded.**

**དམིག་པ་, དམིག་བུ་** *dmig-pa, dmig-bu Lex.* and *Cs.* **hole.**

**དམིགས་** *dmigs* sbst. v. the following.

**དམིགས་པ་** *dmigs-pa* 1. vb. (analogous to *sgom-pa*), **to fancy, to imagine** *Tar.* 73, 5. prob.; **to think, to construe in one's mind,** *dmigs-te Glr.* or vulgo *dmigs-la* in imagination, e.g. to do a thing in one's mind, which at the time one is not able to perform in reality; this according to a Buddhist's belief is permitted in various cases (e.g. **sém-mi míg-la ṕúl-če* W.*, to bring an offering in mind, in imagination); it is attended with the same beneficial effects, as if actually done, and in legends, especially, it is generally followed by a happy realisation of what had been desired. — *dmigs-so S.O.* prob.: it is imaginable, it may be done in mind; *don dmigs-pa* to intend a benefit or profit for another person *Mil.* — Generally 2. sbst., **thought, idea, fancy** **आलम्बन**, vulgo**mig(s)**; *dmigs-pai rten* prob.: a thing only supposed, an object imagined *Thgr.*; *dmigs-pa ži̇g ston-pa, ˳bógs-pa* to give (to another person) an idea of, to make a suggestion *Mil.*; **mig-la čo go** *W.* means also: do it, execute it, according to your own mind, I cannot supply you an exact pattern of it; *dmigs-čan* **ingenious, skilful** in contriving *W.*; *dmigs-pa-las ˳dás-pa = bsám-byai yúl-las ˳dás-pa?* — *yéṅs-med(-par) dmigs-pa (daṅ) brál-bas-na* indisturbable by fancies of the mind, free from every working of the imagination *Mil.*; *dmigs-pa-méd-pai snyiṅ-rje Mil.* seems to be, acc. to *Thgy.* the pity which the accomplished saint, who has found every thing, even religion, to be vain and empty, feels towards all other beings, in as far as they are still subject to error and mistake, opp. to *séms-čan-la dmigs-pai snyiṅ-rje,* and *čós-la dmigs-pai snyiṅ-rje* the tender sympathies called forth by the sight of beings that are really suffering and of those defective in morality — a play upon empty phrases, in as much as in the very narrative, from which the passage above is quoted, the natural softness of Milaraspa is evidently excited by a very positive case, and not by any reflexions of an abstract nature. — **mig-pa-ne zu-pa** (v. *bzó-ba*) *C.* done only in thought, supposed, fictitious; *dmigs tams-čád brjéd-nas* forgetful of all the beautiful fancies, schemes, and airy notions; *dmigs-pa ytód-pa* prob.: to direct one's thoughts, fancies, *la* to *Tar.* 189, 2. (where, no doubt, *ytád-na* is to be read); *dmigs-ytád* **mental object,** *dmigs-ytád brál-bai rnál-˳byor-pa* a saint that is free from such objects; acc. to our Lama also = *ytád-so* q.v.; *dmigs-ysál Lex.*; (*Sch.*: 'a clear notion'), perh. misspelt for *dmigs-bsál* exception from a rule *Gram.*; a particular mention, marking out, exemption of a person, in magisterial orders or enactments *W.* — *dmigs-bu* a blind man's leader *Dzl.*, *Lex* = *lóṅ-ḱrid-pa.* — *nyes-dmigs Mil.* and elsewh., punishment. In the last three examples the etymological relationship is not quite evident.

དམུ་, རྨུ་ *dmu, rmu* a kind of **evil demon,** rarely mentioned *Lex.*; *rmu-rgód* **wild, angry, passionate;** a violent fellow, not safe to deal with *Mil.*; *dmu-bló* a wild, irascible mind *Sch.*; hence *dmus-byúṅ* terrifying, frightful *Sch.*; perh. also *dmus-lóṅ* blind, bodily blind, whilst *loṅ-ba* may be applied also to spiritual blindness *Dzl.*, *Glr.* and elsewh., and *dmu-ču* **dropsy,** esp. in the chest and in the belly *Med.*; *dmu-skrán Sch.* an oedema, tumour filled with water.

དམུན་པ་ *dmún-pa* **darkened, obscured,** *blo*; *mún-pa.*

དམུལ་བ་ *dmúl-ba* v. *˳dzúm-pa.*

དམུར་བ་ *dmúr-ba* v. *múr-ba.*

དམུས་ལོང་ *dmús-loṅ* v. *dmu.*

དམེ་བ་ *dmé-ba* v. *rmé-ba.*

དམོད་པ་ *dmód-pa* I. vb. *Cs.* **to curse, accurse, execrate,** *dmód-pa byéd-pa* id. *Tar.* 14. 17. — II. sbst. *dmod-pa Dzl.*, *dmod, Glr.* and elsewh., **imprecation, execration, malediction;** *dmód-mo* id.; joined with *˳bór-ba, ˳dór-ba, ˳dzúg-pa, smó-ba:* 1. **to curse, to execrate,** *draṅ-sroṅ-gis dmod-pa bor-bai lo bču-ynyis* the twelve years on which a curse had been pronounced by the saint *Dzl.* 2. **to swear,** to confirm a treaty by an oath *Glr.* 3. **to pronounce a prayer** or **conjuration,** *lha-la* to the deity *Glr.* 4. **to affirm,** e.g. to say '*"*kon-čóg še** or the like. The word seems to be nearly related both to *smód-pa,* and to *smón-pa,* but, as expressly stated by the *Lexx.*, is not synon. with these verbs.

དམྱལ་བ་ *dmyál-ba* I. vb. **to cut up,** to cut into little pieces, meat at dinner *Dzl.*, a punishment of hell *Dzl.* — II. sbst. **hell,** also *sems-čan-dmyál-ba; dmyál-bar ˳gró-ba* to go to hell, *dmyál-ba bčo-brgyád* the 18 regions of hell; *ťsa-dmyál* the hot hell, *grań-dmyál* the cold hell. — *dmyál-ba-pa, -po*, occupant of hell. — **nyál-wa-čan** *W.* **poor, miserable, wretched**; also like غريب *Urd.*, = my own little self, for 'I', in humble speech.

དམྱུག་པ་ *dmyúg-pa Cs.* **to show**, *dmyúg-dmyug-pa, dmyúg-pa byéd-pa* to show repeatedly, **to boast.** Yet cf. *myúg-pa.*

རྨ་ *rma* **wound** *B., C.*; *ńá-la rma byuń* I was wounded; *rma ˳byin-pa* to wound, *rma γsó-ba* to heal a wound; *rmai lhá-ba Sch.* 'a wound growing worse'; yet cf. *lhá-ba.* — *rmá-ǩa* 1. **the orifice** or **edges** of a wound. 2. *W.* inst. of *rma* **wound,** **rúl-li ťám-te má-ǩa ťon** he has been wounded by the bite of a serpent. — *rma-čás Sch.* **plaster, cataplasm, dressing, bandage.** — *rma-r̀yes Sch.* **scar**, cicatrix. — *rma-rnyiń* an old wound. — *rma-smán, rma-rtsis* medicine or salve for a wound. — *rma-mťsan* scar *Bhar.* — *rma-ró Sch.* scurf, scab. — *rma-ŝú* a festering, suppurating wound. — *rma-ŝúl* scar. — *rma-srol Sch.* the act of wounding, the wound received(?) — *rma-γsál* a fresh wound.

རྨ་ཆུ་ *rmá-ču* n.p., the river **Hoangho** *Glr.*

རྨ་ཆེན་ *rma-čén* v. *rmá-bya.*

རྨ་བ་ *rmá-ba*, pf. *rmas* 1. **to ask**, obs., *Lex.* 2. **to wound** *Dzl.*

རྨ་བྱ་ *rma-bya* (vulgo often **máb-ja**), मयूर, **peacock,** living wild in India, an object of superstition with Buddhists and Brahmanists. — *rma-bya-čén-po* n. of a deity *Dom.*; *rma-čén Wdk.*, महामायूरी *Will.*: 'one of the 5 tutelar deities of the Buddhists'; *Sch.*: *rma-čen ˳bom-ra* 'lord of the yellow stream' (?).

རྨང་ *rmań*, provinc. *rmiń Glr.* **ground, foundation,** *rmań ˳diń-ba* to lay a foundation *Glr.*; *rtsig-rmáń* id.; *rmáń-rdo* foundation-stone.

རྨང་འཚེར་ *rmań-˳ťsér, smań-˳ťsér* or *-ťsar Sch.* 1. **pincers** to pluck out hairs; *Cs.* instrument for cleaning the nostrils. — 2. *Sch.* **rake** (instrument).

རྨང་ལམ་ *rmáń-lam Sch.* = *rmi-lam*, of rare occurrence.

རྨད་པ་ *rmád-pa* or rather usually: *rmád-du byúń-ba, rmad-byúń* **wonderful, marvelous,** and *ńo-mťsar-rmád-du ˳gyúr-ba* to wonder, to be surprised at, fq.

རྨན་པ་ *rmán-pa Sch.* **wounded;** *rmás-pa* v. *rmá-ba.*

རྨི་བ་ *rmi-ba*, pf. *rmis*, **to dream**; *rmi-lam* resp. *mnál-lam* **a dream,** *rmi-lam za-zi* a troubled dream *Lt.*; *mi-bzań-ba* a portentous, ill-boding dream *S.g.*; *rmi-lam mťóń-ba, rmi-ba* to dream, *rmi-lam-du rál-bar rmis-so* he dreamt that he had been torn to pieces *Dzl.*; *rmi-lam-du ˳byúń-ba* to appear in a dream *Dzl.*; *rmi-lam brtág-pa Cs.* to judge of dreams, *bśád-pa Cs.* to interpret dreams.

རྨིག་སྒ་ *rmig-sga Sch.* **a saddle** that may be folded together.

རྨིག་པ་ *rmig-pa* 1. **hoof,** *rmig-pa ǩa-brág, rmig-brág Cs.* a cloven hoof, *mig-pa-ǩa-brág-čan* cloven-footed; *rmig-zlúm* an undivided hoof; *rta-rmig* a horse's hoof, also name of a plant *Wdń.*; *γyág-rmig* a yak's hoof; *rmig-lčágs* **horse-shoe** *Cs.*; *rmig-(γ)zer* horse-shoe nail, hob-nail *Cs.* — 2. *W.* **horse-shoe,** *gyab-če* to put on a horse-shoe, to shoe.

རྨིག(སྨ)་པ་ *rmig(s)-pa* **lizard,** of a small kind *S.g.*

རྨིང་ *rmiń* v. *rmań.*

རྨུ་ *rmu* v. *dmu.*

རྨུ་བ་ *rmú-ba Cs.* 1. **dullness, heaviness.** — 2. **fog.** — *rmus-pa* 1. *Cs.* **dull, heavy;** *Lex.* **peevish, loath, listless.** 2. **foggy, gloomy, dark,** *nam rmús-pa* a dark night *Dzl.*, cf. *rmúgs-pa*; covered with fog, *yul, Dzl.* — *rmu-ťag* 1. **a cord to which little flags are attached,** on convents etc. 2. *Glr.* fol. 24, sqq., here the word seems to denote some supernatural means of communication between certain ancient kings and their ancestors dwelling among the gods.

རྨུག་པ་ *rmúg-pa*, pf. *rmugs*, 1. **to bite,** *B., C.,* — 2. **to hurt, to sting,** of bees etc. *W.*;

**to gall,** the feet by friction of the shoes *W.* — 3. **to bark** *W.*

རྨུགས་པ་ *rmúgs-pa* 1. **a dense fog,** *ḱyim* fog is coming on, *ₒtib Cs.* id.; *saṅs* has cleared away *Cs.*; *rmúgs-pa-čan* **foggy;** *nam rmúgs-pa Dzl.* ༢༢༠, 12, a dark, foggy night (another reading: *rmús-pa*); *Dzl.* ༧༤༠, 15, *nyin-mtsán-du yul rmúgs-pa* (*rmús-pa*), covered with fog, wrapt in darkness. — 2. *Sch.* **eyes heavy with sleep.** — 3. **inertness, languor, laziness** *Mil.*; **inert, languid, sluggish,** *rmúgs-par byéd-pa Dom.*

རྨུན་པོ་ *rmún-po Cs.* **dull, heavy, stupid;** *żo rmún-po S.g.* sour milk (?).

རྨུར་བ་ *rmúr-ba* to gnarl and bite each other, of dogs *Lex.*

རྨུས་པ་ *rmús-pa* v. *rmú-ba.*

རྨེ་བ་ *rmé-ba* I. **to be economizing, parsimonious** *Lex.*; *bsris-* (*Sch. srid?*) and *sér-rme-ba Lex.* id. —

II. also *dmé-ba* and *smé-ba* 1. sbst. **spot, speck, mark,** a natural mark, on a cane *Mil.*; **mole, mother-spot;** **mé-żól* W.* mark of burning; **a detestable sin,** esp. murder; **uncleanness of food,** *rme-γtsaṅ-méd* or *γtsaṅ-rme-méd* making no difference as to clean or unclean food *Mil.*; *rme-grib* **moral defilement;** *rme-ša-čan Wdṅ.*, **me-ša za-kan* W.*, eating unclean flesh, as an animal that devours its own young. — 2. adj., also *rmé-ba-čan, rmé-čan Wdṅ.*, *rmé-po Lex.* **unclean, defiled, contaminated.**

རྨེ་རུ་ *rmé-ru,* n.p. 1. mountain on the Chinese frontier *Glr.* — 2. a castle in Lhasa *Glr.*

རྨེག་པ་ *rmeg-pa* = *γtan* **order, series, row** *Lex.*, *rmég-med-pa* disordered, not regulated.

རྨེད་ *rmed* **crupper,** attached to a saddle, *sgá-yi rméd Lexx.*; *góṅ-rmed Pth.*

རྨེད་པ་ *rméd-pa* I. also *sméd-pa,* pf. *rmes,* **to ask,** *dri-żiṅ sméd-par mdzád-pa* id. resp. *Mil.*; *snyún-dri sméd-pa Mil.* = *snyún-dri żú-ba.* — II. **to plough and sow;** *rméd-du ǰúg-pa* to cause to be ploughed and sown, e.g. rice *Dzl.*

རྨེན་པ་ *rmen-pa Lex. rmén-bu Lt.*, *ša-rmén Mil.* and vulgo, **gland,** swelling of the glands, **wen.**

རྨེལ་བ་, སྨེལ་བ་ *rmél-ba, smél-ba* 1. **to pluck out,** *C.*, *W.*, *Lex.*, v. *bal.* — 2. **to become threadbare** *W.* — 3. *Sch.* **to appoint, to call, to invite.**

རྨོ་སྔགས་ *rmo-sṅags Sch.* = *smre-sṅágs.*

རྨོ་མོ་ *rmó-mo* 1. *Cs.* = *ma-čúṅ.* — 2. *Sch.* **grandmother.**

རྨོ་བ་ *rmó-ba,* pf. and imp. *rmos* 1. **to plough** (**up**), *żiṅ* frq.; **to sow and plough in** *ₒbras Dzl.*; *ma rmós-pai lo-tóg* 1. **a fabulous kind of grain** in the mythical age. 2. **maize,** *C.*, *W.* — *rmó-po, rmó-mḱan* ploughman. — 2. *ₒgyód-rmo-ba* v. *ₒgyód-pa.*

རྨོག་ *rmog* **helmet** *Glr.*; *rmog-tsáṅs Cs.* 'the padding in a helmet'; *ḱrab-rmog* coat of mail and helmet.

རྨོང་བ་ *rmóṅ-ba* vb. and sbst., pf. *rmoṅs* **to be obscured; obscurity,** chiefly in a spiritual sense; also adj. **obscured, stultified** *Stg.*; more frq. *rmoṅs-pa,* e.g. *blo,* the mind darkened, by false doctrine *Thgy.*; by sorrow, despondency, = despairing, despondent, unnerved *Dzl.*, with *la* or termin., as to, with regard to . . .; *blo ma rmóṅs-pa,* or *rmoṅs-méd Mil.* a mind lively, unimpaired, susceptible, *la* of; *kun-tu-rmóṅ šas-čé-ba* an ample share of irrationality, the principal obstacle to the happiness (*ma-ḱóm-pa*) of those beings which are born as beasts; *rmóṅ-par ₒgyúr-ba* to be obscured, darkened, *byéd-pa* to obscure, to darken *Glr.*, also: to confound, perplex, deceive, = *mgo skór-ba Tar.*; *rmóṅ-bu Lex.* without expl., *Cs.*: 'a kind of distemper'; *rmóṅ-spu* hair of the abdomen and the pudenda, *ra-túg rmoṅ-spus lhog-pa ₒǰom S.g.* the belly-hair of a he-goat tends to heal cancer.

རྨོད་པ་ *rmód-pa Cs.* **to plough,** *rmod-gláṅ* a plough-ox; *rmod-lám Sch.* **furrow.**

རྨོན་པ་ *rmón-pa* 1. **the act of ploughing;** *rmón-pa rgyáb-pa* to plough *Cs.* — 2. **a plough-ox,** *rmon-dór* a yoke of plough-oxen.

རྨྱ་བ་ *rmyá-ba S.g.* **sickness, nausea,** *ḱams-rmyá Lex.* id.

རྨྱང་བ, རྨྱེང་བ rmyáṅ-ba, rmyéṅ-ba = snyéṅ-ba **to stretch one's self**, to stretch forward the neck; *bya-rmyáṅ byéd-pa* id. *Cs.* also: to yawn.

སྨ *sma* v. *dma.*

སྨ་ར *smá-ra* **beard** *Mil.*, *smá-ra-čan* **bearded.**

སྨག *smag* 1. a sort of **medicine** of an astringent taste *Med.*; *smág-rgyu* **black pepper.** — 2. **dark; darkness;** *mún-pai smag-rúm* id. *Glr.*

སྨང་ཚེར *smaṅ-ťsér* v. *rmaṅ-ₒťser.*

སྨད *smad*, अधर, 1. **the lower part,** opp. to *sťod*; *smád-la* downward *Sch.*; *lús-kyi smad* the lower half of the human body, frq.; *smad ₒṗyés-pa Sch.*: 'to move the posterior to and fro' (?). — *lus-smad-lṅa sá-la γtúg-pa* to bring the five lower parts of the body, the belly, the knees, and the points of the feet in close contact with the ground, i. e. to prostrate one's self; hence *čos-gos smad lṅa Dzl.* ༧༢༠, 16, the five lower pieces of the priestly apparel, perh. breeches, stockings and boots; the meaning, however, of *sems-smád bčo-brgyád Pťh.* I am not prepared to settle. — 2. **lowland** = *man-čád.* — 3. **low rank,** v. *smad-rigs* below. — 4. with regard to time, **the latter part, the second half,** उत्तर, of the night, *Dzl.*, of winter, of life etc. — 5. **children,** in relation to their mother, gen. preceded by *ma* or *bu*, thus: *ṅed ma-smád* I and my mother *Mil.*; *rgán-mo ma-smád γsum* the old woman with her (two) sons, those three *Dzl.*; also of animals: *rgód-ma ma-smád γnyis* the mare and her foal, the two *Dzl.*; *bu-smád* (*Cs.* also *mad*) wife and children, family; *nád-pa dei bu-smád Mil.* the sick man's family; *bu-smád-rnams* (my) wife and children *Mil.*

**Comp.** *smad-ₒčal* **lewdness, dissoluteness, prostitution,** *byéd-pa* to indulge in, to practise *Mil.* — *smad-ₒdógs* a subscribed letter *Gram.* — *smád-ťsoṅ-ma 'meretrix'*, prostitute, harlot, frq. — *smad-γyógs* nether integuments, breeches, trowsers *Wdṅ.* — *smad-rigs* common people, lower caste *Dzl.*

སྨད་པ *smád-pa* I. vb. 1. **to bend down; to hand, to reach down,** the alms bowl to a little boy *Dzl.*; (*Sch.* 'to stoop'?); *γdoṅ smád-pa* to cast down one's eyes, to be abashed, dejected *Tar.*; *sems* to humble one's self, *la* before *Dzl.*, *ťugs* id. resp.: **to be condescending, lowly, meek** *Dzl.* — 2. **to vilify,** c. *la* or accus.: **to blame, to chide,** *bú-mo* one's own daughter *Dzl.*, *bdág-gi séms-la* to blame one's self *Dzl*; **to abuse, defame, degrade, traduce,** *ťsig ṅár-pas ₒṗágs-pa-la* (to abuse) the venerable man with base words *Dzl.*, *dkon-mčóg-gi dbu-ₒṗáṅ* (to degrade) the highness of the excellent, = to blaspheme; **to despise,** the doctrine *Glr.*; **to dishonour, violate, ravish,** *bu-moi lus* a girl *Pth.*; *má-ga-dha nyáms-smad-pai ťse Tar.* 192 when (the country of) Magadha had been brought low, had decayed in its prosperity; *smád-pai ťsig* or *ṅag* **abusive word, invective, libel;** *smád-ra* (prop. *sgra*) id., more in the language of the common people, but also *Mil.*; *smád-ra γtóṅ-ba Mil.*, **taṅ-če* W.* to abuse, to revile; *smad-rigs* common people.

II. sbst. **blame, reproof, reproach, disgrace, contempt.**

སྨན *sman* 1. **medicine, physic, remedy,** both artificially prepared and crude: **medicinal herb, drug;** *rii sman ₒťú-ba* to gather officinal plants on the mountains *Dzl.*; *mén-la ₒdo* C.*, **man-la ča* W.*, (the plant) is used as a medicine; *sman sbyór-ba* to prepare a medicine, *γtóṅ-ba* to administer, *zá-ba* or *ₒťúṅ-ba* to take (physic); different forms of medicine are: *ťáṅ-gi sman* liquid medicine, infusion, decocture; *ṗyé-mai sman* powder; *ríl-bu* pill; *ldé-gu* electuary, sirup; *sman-már* oily medicine (*Tar.* 39, 8); *sman-čáṅ* prob. alcoholic tincture; *ₒbrí-ta* extract(?). — Further: *k̔óṅ-sman* medicine taken internally, *byúg-sman* used externally, unguent; *ₒbyár-sman* plaster; *bzi-sman* soporiferous potion; *skyúg-sman* emetic; *bšál-sman* purgative. — *smán-gyi bla*, or *smán-bla Glr.* nnd *Med.*; *Sch.*: 'physician general', yet to my knowledge it is never used in that sense, but only as a god or Buddha of therapeutics; there are eight such gods, revered by students of medicine, and frequently invoked in medicinal writings, as well as in medical practice, v. *Schl.* p. 266 sqq. (*sman-gyi lha Glr.*, is prob. but a misprint). — Other compounds: *sman-rkyál* medicine-bag, smaller or larger leather-bags being the usual receptacles for the commodities of grocers and the drugs of physicians. — *smán-k'an* apothecary's shop. — *sman-k'úg* medicine-bag. — *sman-sgá* a kind of officinal ginger (?) *S.g.* — *sman-sgám* medicine-box. — *sman-mčód* the best, or a very superior medicine *Pth.* — *sman-ljóṅs* a country rich in medicinal plants. — *sman-rtá* the vehicle or substance in which medicine is taken *Med.* — *sman-snod* medicine glass or vessel. — *smán-pa* physician *Dzl.*, *Glr.*, *Med.* — *smán-dpe* medical book. — *sman-dpyád* v. *dpyád-pa.* — *sman-blá* v. above.

II. the same as, or something like *klu Glr.*, *Mil.*

III. *Lex.* = *p'an*; *Sch.* also has: *sman-séms* 'a beneficent mind, a mind intent on working good'.

IV. incorr. for *dman.*

སྨར་བ་ *smár-ba* 1. sbst., **ready money,** gen. *smar-rkyáṅ*; *zoṅ min smar* money, and not goods *Lex.* — 2. vb. careless and incorr. pronunciation of *smrá-ba.*

སྨལ་པོ་ *smál-po* n. of a lunar mansion v. *rgyu-skár.*

སྨས་པ་ *smás-pa Sch.*, v. *rmás-pa.*

སྨིག་རྒྱུ་ *smig-rgyú* **mirage** *Lex.* = **मरिचि**; prob. also a reflection in water, *čur-ₒkrul-smig-rgyú.*

སྨིག་བུ་ *smig-bu* **lizard** *Sch.*, v. *rmig(s)-pa.*

སྨིག་མ་ *smig-ma*, provinc. for *smyúg-ma* **cane, reed** *Do.*

སྨིན་དྲུག་ *smin-drúg* 1. also *skár-ma-smin-drúg* **कार्त्तिक. the Pleiades;** *smin-drug-zlá-ba* the month in which the moon standing near the Pleiades is full, Oct. or Nov., *Glr.*; *smin-drug-bú*, **कार्त्तिकेय,** the son of Siva, god of war *Lex.* — 2. *Pur.* Eremurus spectabilis, v. *bre.*

སྨིན་བདུན, སྨེ་བདུན་ *smin-bdún*, *sme-bdún* **the Great Bear,** *Ursa major.*

སྨིན་པ་ *smin-pa*, I. (**विपाक**) **to ripen, ripeness, maturity;** most frq. **ripe,** *ₒbrás-bu smin-no B.*, *smin soṅ* vulgo, the fruit is ripe; *smin-par ₒgyúr-ba Glr.* *smin ₒóṅ-ba* to ripen; the growing on to maturity of an animal germ; also the 'stadium maturationis', or the full development of a disease *Med.*; applied to conversion *Pth.* and elsewh.; *rgyud smin-čiṅ gról-bar byin-gyis rlobs* give them the benediction for being saved (absorbed into Nirvana) after having attained to maturity of mind *Mil.*; *smin-gról-la* or *smin-gról-gyi lám-la ₒgód-pa* to lead to conversion and salvation *Glr.*; *rnám-par smin-pa* v. *rnám-pa.* — *smin-grol-gliṅ* n. of a monastery *Cs.*

II. *Bal.* to give (*sbyin-pa*).

སྨིན་མ་ *smin-ma* **eye-brow,** *smin(-mai) dbrag Med.*, *smin-p'rag Mil.*, *smin-mts'ams Glr.* the space between the eye-brows.

སྨུག་ཆུང་ *smug-čuṅ Med.* a plant = *smug-rtsi* (?).

སྨུག་པ་ *smúg-pa Sch.* for *rmugs-pa* **fog.**

སྨུག་པོ་ *smúg-po* 1. sbst. a disease, acc. to *Cs.* = *ₒdus-nád*, v. *ₒdú-ba*, 1. — 2. adj. **dark bay, cherry-brown, purple-brown;** **gya-múg** *C.* violet coloured; *dmar-smug* brownish white *Wdṅ.*; *smug-smúg Sch.* dark red. — *smug-rtsi* 1. **red colour,** with which sacrificial utensils are painted *Lex.* — 2. Macrotomia, a plant with dark-red root, used for dyeing, *smug-tsós* paint or colour yielded by this plant *Cs.*

སྨེ་བདུན་ *sme-bdún* v. *smin-bdún.*

སྨེ་བ་ *smé-ba* 1. v. *rme-ba.* — 2. *rtsis-kyi smé-ba Lex.* a kind of arithmetical figure in geomancy, which is used together with the Chinese diagrams, *spar-k'a Mil.*

སྨོ་བ་ *smó-ba*, pf. and imp. *smos*, not frq., yet in some cases of constant use, for *smrá-ba* **to say,** *miṅ-nas smó-ba* to call by name, to name *Do.*; . . . *žes smós-pa* the assertion that . . . *Wdṅ.*; *goṅ-du smós-pa* above-mentioned *Do.*; *lta či smos* v. *lta.*

**སྨོད་པ་** *smód-pa*, pf. *smad, Lex.* **निन्द** v. *smád-pa*, **to blame,** *bdag stod γžan smod* to praise one's self, disparaging others; *γžogs-smód byéd-pa* to slander, calumniate *Thgy.*; **to depreciate, to make contemptible,** *smód-par ˳gyúr-bas Stg.* because it would be disreputable, would detract from his honour. For *smod-˳dzúg-pa* it would prob. be better to write *dmod-˳dzug-pa*.

**སྨོན་པ་** *smón-pa* **to wish, to desire,** with *la*, *skyid-pa γžán-la ṅa mi smon* for another happiness I do not wish *Mil.*; more frq. with termin. of the infinitive, and then = to pray for, *rgyál-po skyé-bar* (to pray for) being re-born as a king *Dzl.*; *smón-pa bžin-du byéd-pa* to fulfil a prayer *Dzl.*; *smón-pai γnas* the object of a wish or prayer *Cs.*; *yid-smón* **wish, desire,** *de ťsúr-šog-gi yid-smon ṅá-la med* I do not wish that he should come *Mil.*; *riṅ-po-nas ˳di-lta-bur yid-smon byéd-par gyúr-te* having long ago entertained this wish *Stg.*; *yid-smon ˛os* worth wishing, desirable; *smon-˳ǰúg* a wish and its accomplishment, *smon-˳ǰúg γnyis*; *smón-lam*, **प्रणिधि**, prayer, whether it be in the general way of expressing a good wish or offering a petition to the deity, or in the specific Brahmanic-Buddhistic form, which is always united with some condition or asseveration, as: if such or such a thing be true, then may . . ., **wishing-prayer.** — *smon-(lam) lóg(-par) ˳débs-pa* to curse, to execrate.

**སྨོན་མགྲིན་** or **འདྲིན་** *smon-mgrin* or *˳drin* **comrade, companion, associate,** = *grógs-po Lex.*

**སྨྱན་** *smyan? Sch.: smyan byéd-pa* to travel on business; *smyan-byed blo-žan* a traveling clerk not very shrewd *Bhar.* 108; this would seem preferable to the Ssk. equivalent, mentioned in *Schf.'s* edition.

**སྨྱར་བ་** *smyár-ba Sch.* **to stretch one's self,** after sleep.

**སྨྱི(ག)་གུ་, སྨྱུ(ག)་གུ་** *smyí(g)-gu, smyú(g)-gu* **thin cane, writing-cane, reed-pen;** **ḍoi nyí-gu* C.* goose-quill, **čág-gi nyí-gu* C.* steel-pen.

**སྨྱིག་མ་**, com. **སྨྱུག་མ་** *smyig-ma, smyúg-ma* 1. **cane, bamboo,** *smyúg-mai sbubs* tube of bamboo *Cs.* — 2. **a pen of reed,** *˳ǰóg-pa, W. *žóg-če** to make a reed-pen; **ḍi-nyúg** id, improp. also lead-pencil.

**Comp.** *smyug-ǩróg Cs.*, acc. to others, *smyug-sbróg* tube of bamboo; pen-case; small churn, = *gur-gúr Cs.* — **nyug-ǩyim* C.* house constructed of bamboo. — *smyúg-mǩan* a worker in cane *Cs.* — *smyug-sgám* a chest made of reed *Cs.* — *smyug-gri* penknife. — *smyug-lčág* flag, flag-stick; long bamboo *Cs.* — **nyug-váľ* C.* a flat basket. — *smyug-ťógs* writer *Cs.* — *smyug-dóṅ Cs.* = *gur-gur.* — *smyug-γdán* mat of reed, cane-mat. — *smyug-γdúgs* an umbrella made of split reeds *Cs.* — *smyug-sdér* plate, dish or flat basket, constructed of reed *C.* — **nyug-tsá-me-tog* C.*, Carthusian pink. — *smyug-ťsigs* knot, node, joint, of reeds. — **nyug-lóm* C.* flat basket. — *smyug-bšád* comb made of bamboo.

**སྨྱུང་བ་** *smyúṅ-ba* **to fast, to observe a strict diet** *Med.*; often in a religious sense, *smyúṅ-bar byás-pa* and *ma byas-pa* he who has strictly observed fasting, and he who has not *Do.*; *smyuṅ-γnás* **the fast, the act of fasting;** **nyén-nẹ nyúṅ-nẹ zúm-če* W.* to fast, to practise abstinence. V. *Schl.* 240.

**སྨྱུར་བ་** *smyúr-ba* **to be quick, expeditious, in a hurry, to hasten** *Cs.* Cf. *myúr-ba.*

**སྨྱོ་བ་, མྱོ་བ་** *smyó-ba, myó-ba*, pf. *smyos, myos* **to be insane, mad,** *či-˛aṅ mi drán-par myós-so* they lost their senses and ran mad (with grief) *Dzl.*; *smyos-sam* is she mad? *Dzl.*; *snyiṅ myós-pas Do.*, being deranged; **nyo dug* W.* he is crazy; **to be mad,** as dogs *Schr.*; **to be intoxicated,** *smyó-bai ǩú-ba* intoxicating liquor *Dzl.*; *rťág-tu myós-pai γnas* pot-houses, fuddling-places *Stg.*; fig. *˳dod-čágs-kyis myos Dzl.* he is mad with lust; *smyó-bar byéd-pa* to make one mad or drunk. — *smyo-byéd* 1. **narcotic,** *smyo-byéd-kyi rdzas* narcotic medicine, soporiferous potion, maddening drink. 2. *smyo-byed(-kyi) γdon* a demon that causes a state of stupefaction or insanity. 3. **frenzy, madness.** 4. symb. num.: 13.

སྨྱོན་པ་ *smyón-pa* **insane, frantic, mad,** *la-dág-pa nyón-pa* a madman from Ladak; *gláṅ-po-če Dzl.* a mad elephant, *k̔yi* a mad dog; **nyón-pa čo dug* W.* he raves, he is stark mad; **čo-nyón žug* W.* he has been seized with religious insanity, is deranged, which is stated to be occasionally the effect of severe and long continued meditation. Cf. *lhoṅ*.

སྨྲ་བ་ *smrá-ba*, sometimes སྨོ་བ *smó-ba*, also སྨར་བ *smár-ba*, pf. *smras*, imp. *smros* 1. **to speak, to talk,** *smra ma nús-te Dzl.* growing dumb, speechless, not being able to speak (physically); *čaṅ mi smrá-bar gyúr-to* they grew speechless, did not know what to say *Dzl.*; *smra šés-nas mir gyúr-to* they received the faculty of speech and became men *Glr.*; *bslú-bai rnám-pas k̔yeu daṅ smrás-te Dzl.* speaking to the youth in a seductive manner; *tsig snyán-par smrá-ba Dzl.* to speak in a friendly way; *čos smrá-ba* **to preach,** *čos smrá-bai žál-la ltá-ba* to hang on the preacher's lips, to listen very attentively *Pth.*; *da ma smra žig Dzl.* do not lose another word; *smra-mk̔as(-pa)* speaking shrewdly, well-spoken, eloquent *Dzl.*, *Glr.*; *smra-ₒdód* **talkative, loquacious** *Cs.*; *smra-nyúṅ* sparing of words, **taciturn,** *Lt.*; *smra-bčád* forbearing to speak; not being bound to speak *Mil.*; *smra-mčóg*, *smrá-bai dbaṅ-p̔yúg*, *smrá-bai rgyál-po* = *ₒjam-dpál*; also **to treat of,** with reference to books *Was.* — 2. **to say,** *mi-la* to a person; when it precedes the words that are quoted as they were spoken, (the so-called 'oratio obliqua' being very seldom made use of, one instance v. further on): (*di-skad-čes*) *smrás-pa* or *smrás-so;* when placed after the words spoken, (*čes*) *smrás-so*, *smrás-te* etc.; *smrás-pa* also is equivalent to **he continued** *Dzl.*; sometimes it is used impersonally, **it is said,** e.g. it is said in that letter, where we should say, 'that letter says', *Stg.*; *smrá-rgyu ma byúṅ-ṅo* there remained nothing more for him to say (v. above); rarely with termin. inf.: *γtúg-par ni ṅa mi smrao* that they will reach it, I do not pretend to say *Thgy.*; *šés-par smrá-ba* to profess to know, to understand, like '*artem profiteri*' *Dzl.*; *dṅós-por smrá-ba* to acknowledge a thing in substance *Was.*, *med-par smrá-ba* to deny it in sum and substance.

Note. The word which forms the subject of this article, though constantly to be met with in books, seems to be hardly ever used in conversational language.

སྨྲང་, སྨྲེང་ *smraṅ*, *smreṅ Cs.* **word, speech;** *smraṅ γsól-ba* to beg the word, to beg leave to speak

སྨྲེ་བ་ *smré-ba* 1. = *smrá-ba*(?) — 2. **to wail, to lament** *Pth.*; more com *smre-sṅágs ₒdón-pa* to utter lamentations; *smre-sṅágs-kyi sgó-nas* whining (with joy) *Mil.* — *smre-γtsáṅ*?

# ཙ

ཙ *tsa*, 1. the letter sounding **ts**; tenuis, as in the words 'it got so cold', cf. however ཚ *tsa;* ཙ, ཚ and ཛ represent in *Ssk.* and Hindi-words the palatals च, छ and ज (ཛྷ = झ). — 2. num fig.: 17.

ཙྭ་ *tswa Ld.* **spunk,** German tinder.

ཙ་ཀོར་ *tsa-kór*, *Ssk.* चकोर **partridge,** = *sróg-pa.*

ཙཀྲ་བཱ་ཀ་ *tsa-kra-bā-ka* **red goose,** *Anas casarca.*

ཙ་དར, ཙ་སར *tsa-dar, tsa-sar, Pers., Hind.* چادر **shawl, plaid, cloak, toga** *W.* —

ཙ་ན, ཙ་ནས, ཙ་ལ *tsá-na, tsá-nas, tsá-la* v. *tsam.*

ཙ་ན་ཀ *tsa-na-ka*, more corr. ཙ་ཎ་ཀ *Ssk.*, **chick-pea**, *Cicer arietinum.*

ཙ་བིག *tsá-big*, v. *ťsa-big.*

ཙ་རག *tsa-rág,*tsa-rág zér-če* Ld.* **to crackle,** of fire, breaking twigs etc.

ཙ་རུ *tsá-ru* 1. *W.* **curled, frizzled,** as hair and similar things. — 2. *Lex.*: *Ssk.* **meat-offering** to the manes.

ཙ་ཤ(ཀ) *tsa-ša(-ka)*, चाष, *Coracias Indica*, **jay, roller.**

ཙག་གེ *tság-ge W.* **the black mark in a target,** *tság-ge-la gyob* hit the mark!

ཙན་དན, ཙནྡན *tsán-dan, tsándan*, चन्दन, **sandal-tree,** *Sirium myrtifolium*, sandal-wood, used for elegant buildings, images of the gods, perfumes, medicines *Glr.*, *Med.*; in different varieties: *dkár-po, dmár-po* etc., also of fabulous kinds: *tsán-dan sbrúl-gyi snyiṅ-po, gór-ši-ša, gláṅ-mgo Glr.*, *Dzl.*; fig. **something superior in its kind,** *p̔a tsán-dan p̔ú-nu mi-lag-tu soṅ* the elder and younger sons of a distinguished father perform menial services.

ཙན་དོང *tsan-dóṅ* v. *btson-dóṅ.*

ཙབ་ཙུབ, ཙབ་ཙོབ, རྩབ་རྩུབ *tsab-tsúb, tsab-tsób, rtsab-rtsúb* **hurry, haste** *Cs.*, *tsab-tsúb-čan* hasty *Cs.*; *tsab-tsúb mi bya Lex.* take your time, don't be in a hurry! *rtsab-rtsub-méd-par* not flitting, like a butterfly, from one object to another *Mil.*; *tsub-liṅ Sch.* hastily, in a hurry(?) — *rtsab-hrál Lex.*; *Sch.* a loose, dissolute course of life(?) — *rtsáb-pa Sch.* to hurry, to hasten(?).

ཙབས་རུ *tsabs-rú* 1. a kind of **salt,** *tsabs-ru-ťsá S.g.* — 2. **a tube of horn** *Sch.*

ཙམ *tsam* mostly affixed as an enclitic, = *snyed* (sometimes carelessly for *tsám-pa* or *tsám-du*) I. in a relative sense, 1. **as much as** *ₒdí-tsam* as much as this, = so much, so many; *mi ₒdi tsam γsód-pa* to kill so many men *Glr.*; *dé-tsam* id.; also emphat.: *čos de tsam žig bšád-nas* after having given you so much religious instruction *Mil.*; by way of exclamation: *či-tsam* **how much!** *W.* and *B.*, *či-tsam byas* how much have you not done! *Glr.*; *ji-tsam ... dé-tsam* how much... so much (as much as) *Cs.* — 2. denoting comparison, as to size, degree, intensity, **like, as-as, so-as, so that:** *ri-ráb tsam* like Sumeru (in height) *Cs*; *yúṅs-ₒbru tsam* as big as a grain of mustard-seed; **de ri ťón-po tsam dug dé-tsogs di yaṅ yod* W.* as high as yon mountain is also this one; *pús-mo núb-pa tsam* even to sinking in up to the knees (knee-deep); *nyi-ma ₒgrib-pa tsam* so much that the sun was darkened *Glr.*; *mťai rgyál-po yaṅ dbáṅ-du ₒdús-pa tsam byuṅ* he became so (powerful), that he could also subdue — or could have subdued — the neighbouring kings *Glr.* — 3. denoting contingency and restriction: **perhaps, if need be, almost, only, but, all but:** *ťsab ruṅ tsám-mo Wdṅ.* this may perhaps be used instead, this may, if need be, supply its place; *btaṅ-na nam-mk̔ai bya yaṅ zín-(pa) tsam γda* if I let him loose, he might almost catch a bird in the air, = *zín-pa daṅ ₒdrao Mil.*; with a partic.: *rtags yód-pa tsám-la* = *rtags daṅ yód-pa-la* to every one that has the mark *Glr.*; *rtsa daṅ rús-pa tsam Dzl.* nothing but skin and bones; *ₒgro mi nús-pa ₒgóg-pa tsam Dzl.* one only creeping, not being able to walk; *ča tsam šes kyaṅ* if one knows but a particle, but a little bit; *sems tsám-mo* they exist only in our fancy *Was.*; *ťsigs-ma tsam yód-dam Dzl.* is not the sediment at least still left? *lhág-ma tsam žig Dzl.* but a remnant; *brgya tsam* may mean: about one hundred, or: only one hundred; in some cases *tsam* is untranslatable: *lṅa-brgyá tsam ťams-čád ťsei dus byas-so* the 500 merchants died all *Dzl.* (15, 9 s. l. c.); *bdén-pa tsam yod Mil.* some grain of truth is in the matter; *ťsig daṅ rnám-par ₒdrá-ba tsam ₒdúg-na-ₒaṅ Mil.* though it is all but equal to the words, i.e. very much like the real tenor or wording; it may also be combined with the signs of the cases: *ṅa miṅ tsám-gyi dgé-sloṅ ma yin Dzl.* I am Bhikshu not only by name, I am not merely called so; *da tsám-gyi bár-du Dzl.* till about the present time (standing here rather pleon., as frq. is the case); *brám-ze γčig tsám-gyi sláddu Dzl.* for the sake of a single Brahmin; *spu nyóg-ma tsám-gyi ₒgyód-pai sems Dzl.* but a whit (lit. a little hair) of repentance. — 4. *tsám-na* referring to time: **about a certain time, at the time when, when:** *nam-ṗyéd tsám-na* about midnight; *de tsám-na* then, at that time; esp. with verbs: *k̔yim-du ṗyin tsám-na Dzl.* when he came home; inst. of *tsám-na* it is very common to say *tsá-na; byéd-gin yod tsá-na* as he was just doing it *Glr.*; *γnyid sad tsá-na* when he awoke *Glr.; zlá-ba brgyad soṅ tsá-na* when eight months had passed *Glr.*; esp. col.: **yoṅ tsá-na* W.* as we came, on our journey hither, when incorr. **tsa-nẹ* (or *sá-nẹ*)* is said, which is justifiable only in such cases, as: **ἅ-ma kyé-sa-nẹ** from one's birth; *ɔ̓i-tsam-na* or *-nas* **when**, yet mostly pleon., in as far as the sentence beginning with *ɔ̓i-tsam-na* after all concludes with *nas, pa daṅ, dus-kyi t̔se* etc., v. *Feer Introd.* frq., also *Tar.* — 5. *tsám-du* denoting extent, degree, intensity: **as far as, about so far, nearly up to, even to, till, so that,** and *tsam* in various other applications: *lam ṗyed tsám-du* about half way; frq. with verbs: *bá-spu láṅs-pa tsám-du skrags Dzl.* he was so frightened, that his hair stood on end; *dúm-bur bčád-pa tsám-du sdug-bsṅál-gyis γdúṅs-te Dzl.* tormented by a pain, as if he were cut to pieces; *bus ma mtóṅ-ba tsám-du dgá-ste Dzl.* 'being glad even to a mother's being seen by her child', i.e. so glad as a child is, when beholding its mother again; sometimes *tsám-la* for *tsám-na* and *tsám-du Mil.* yet not frq. and more col.: *ḍib tsám-la* in the shade; **šiṅ-ni tsám-la* W.* under, before, near a tree; *tsám-gyis* instrum.: *ṅan-ṅon tsám-gyis čóg-šes-pa* content with every thing, as poor as it may be; com. added to the inf.: *smrás-pa tsám-du* as soon as it had been said *Dzl.* frq., or also: 'in the mere saying so' *Stg.*; inst. of it, col.: **zer tsam ẑig-la*; W.*: **zér-ra tsám-ẑig-ga**. — *tsam yaṅ* with a following negative: **not the least,** *mós-pa tsam yaṅ mi byéd-pa Mil.* to pay not the least respect; **not in the least, not at all:** *nyi-ma daṅ zlá-ba tsam yaṅ ltar med Dzl.* neither sun nor moon is to be seen at all. — *tsám-pa* adj., *mi-t̔sad-tsám-pa* man-sized, **having the size of a man** *Tar.* — *tsám-po Mil. mi tsám-po yóṅs-kyi sems-la ₒjug* prob: I shall enter into the soul of the very first man I meet with; also = *gaṅ* (cf. *rtags gaṅ yód-pa-la* above). — *Cs.* has besides: *tsám-po-ba* a comparing, estimating; *tsam-poi t̔sig* a comparative expression; *tsám-poi don* a comparative sense (?). II. used interrogatively: **how much? how many?** **rin tsam?* W.* how dear?

ཙམ་པ་ *tsám-pa* 1. v. *tsam* towards end of preced. article. — 2. sbst. **flour** from parched barley, v. *rtsám-pa*. — 3. n. of a country *Tar.* 10,14; 20,16; acc. to *Ssk. Lexx.* = Bhagalpore, v. *Köpp.* I, 96; in modern geography: the small Hindu mountain-province **Chamba** on the river Ravi, under British protection.

ཙམ་པ་ཀ་ *tsám-pa-ka Ssk.* **magnolia,** *Michelia Champaca.*

ཙམ་ཙོམ་ *tsam-tsóm* **tripping to and fro, fidgeting about** *W.* (cf. *tsab-tsób*).

ཙར་མ་ *tsár-ma* n. of a place, freq. resorted to by *Mil.*

ཙི་ *tsi* num. fig.: 47.

ཙི་ཏྲ་ཀ་ *tsi-tra-ka Ssk.* 1. a painted mark on the forehead, being the badge of various sects *Sch.* — 2. name of several plants, esp. *Ricinus communis*, so perh. *Lt.*; in *Lh.*: *Anemone rivularis*, common there.

ཙི་སྟག་ *tsi-stág* n. of a purgative *Med.*

ཙི་ན་ *tsi-na* चीन, *China Cs.*; now com. *ma-ha-tsin.*

ཙི་ཙི་ *tsi-tsi* **mouse** *C.*, *tsi-ghi* id. *Ts.*; *tsi-čuṅ* **shrew** (mouse) *Sch.*; *táṅ-gi tsi-tsi* **field-mouse** *Schr.*; *sai tsi-tsi* **mole** *Schr.*; *tsi-tsis-ₒdzin* n. of a plant *Wdṅ.*

ཙི་ཙི་ཛོ་ལ་ *tsi-tsi-dzó-la Cs.*, *tsi-tsi-dzó-ba Sch.* **cancer** (disease), said to be a Nepalese word.

ཙི་ཙེ *tsi-tsé* v. *tse-tsé.*

ཙིག་ཙིག *tsíg-tsig byéd-pa* **to quarrel, to be at variance** *Sch.*

ཙིཏྟ་ *tsitta Ssk.* **the heart** as seat of the intellect, v. *Burn.* I, 637.

ཙིད་ *tsid* **anvil** *Sch.*

ཙུ *tsu* num. fig.: 77.

ཙུ་ད་ *tsú-da, tsú-dai śiṅ* n. of a tree *Sch.*

ཙུག *tsug* for *ċi-ltar* adv. interrog. and correlat., **how, as,** rarely occurring in books; *Pth.*: *de gar ˳gro, tsug byed* where she is going, and what she is doing. In *W.* com. in the form *zug*, in such combinations as: *gá-zug* for *ċi-tsug, ċi-ltar*; **ĭ-zug* or *˳di-zug*, and *ă-zug** or **dé-zug**: **so;** **daṅ de-zug de-zug** and more of that kind; *de-tsug lags* in *Lexx.*

ཙ

ཙུག་ཙུག *tsug-tsúg* the noise of **smacking** in eating, *tsug-tsúg mi bya* do not smack *Zam.*

ཙེ *tse* num. fig.: 107.

ཙེ་གུར་ *tse-gúr Sch.*: 1. a small **tube.** — 2. **a little.**

ཙེ་པོ, ཙེལ་པོ *tsé-po, tsél-po* **a basket** carried on the back, dosser, esp. *W.*; **ċáṅ-tse* or *ċág-tse** a wicker basket, **nyúṅ-tse* or *nyúg-tse** a cane basket *Ts.*; **tsel-ċúg** the wands used for such a basket; **tsel-ċág** a broken dosser *W.*; **tsel-rá** the frame-work of a basket *Cs.*; **tsel-lúṅ** string or strap for carrying it.

ཙེ་ཙེ, ཙི་ཙེ *tse-tsé, tsi-tsé* **millet** *Cs.*

ཙེ་རེ་ *tse-ré* 1. **song, tune** *Lex.* — 2. = *ťse-ré.*

ཙེག་ཙེག་ *tseg-tség, tseg-tség zér-ba* **to rustle,** 'to make a noise like dry hay' *Cs.*

ཙེབ་ཙེབ *tseb-tséb* **sharp-pointed,** of needles, thorns.

ཙེམ་ཙེ *tsém-tse* = *ċém-tse* **small scissors.**

ཙེའུ་རི་ *tseu-ri* a species of female demons *Thgr.*

ཙེར་ཙེར་ *tser-tsér, tser-tsér byéd-pa* **to tremble, shake, quake** *Sch.*

ཙེལ་པོ་ *tsél-po* v. *tsé-po.*

ཙོ *tso* num. fig.: 137.

ཙོ་ར་ *tsó-ra Wdṅ., Ssk.* n. for the medicinal herb *srúb-ka;* in *Ssk. Lexx.* no botanical explication is given, but only the notice, that it is a perfume; in Kullu a sweet-scented white lily is called so.

ཙོག་པུ་ *tsóg-pu* (acc. to one *Lex.* = उङ्कटुक, which is not to be found; on the other hand *Burn.* I, 310 gives *tsóg-pu-pa* = नैषद्िक one sitting down) **the posture of cowering, squatting, crouching,** *tsog(-tsog)-pur sdód-pa, ˳dúg-pa* resp. *bźúgs-pa Pth.*, col. **tsoṅ-tsóṅ, tsom-tsóm**, **to cower, squat, crouch;** *tsóg-pu mi nus* he cannot even cower, of one sick unto death *Thgy.*; *tsog mi γzúg-pa* of a similar sense *Sch.* — (The version 'to sit on one leg drawn in' *Sch.*, which has also been adopted by *Burn.*, may possibly be founded on a mistake of *Sch.*, who in *Cs.*'s explanation: 'sitting in a crouching posture upon one's legs', prob. read 'upon one leg').

ཙོང་ཁ་ *tsóṅ-ka* n. of a place in Eastern Tibet *Ma.*; *tsóṅ-ka-pa* 1. inhabitant of that place. 2. n. of a celebrated teacher of religion and reformer, about the year 1400.

ཙོང་ཙོང་ *tsoṅ-tsóṅ* 1. = *tsog-tsóg* v. *tsóg-pu.* — 2. *tsoṅ-tsóṅ-la kur* carry it straight *W.*

ཙོན་དོང་ *tson-dóṅ* v. *btson-dóṅ.*

ཙོབ་ཙོབ *tsob-tsób, *tsob-tsób-la dúg-ċe* Ld.* to stand or sit in different groups, not in rows.

ཙོར་མོ་ *tsór-mo* **a five-finger pinch** *Cs.*

གཙག་པ་ *γtság-pa* v. *˳tság-pa*; *γtság-bu* also *btságs-bu* **lancet** for bleeding.

གཙང་ *γtsaṅ* 1. **clean, pure** v. *γtsáṅ-ba.* — 2. n. of a province in *C.*, where Tasilhunpo is situated; *γtsáṅ-pa* inhabitant of it.

གཙང་བ་ *γtsaṅ-ba* 1. vb. **to be clean, pure** *Dom.* — 2. sbst. **cleanness, purity.** — 3. adj. **clean, pure.** Most frq. as sbst. with negation: *mi-γtsáṅ-ba* impurity, foulness, filth *Dzl.* and elsewh.; excrement *S.g.*; *mi-γtsáṅ-ba 'rnám-pa sna-ts'ógs-kyi p'úṅ-po* heap of all kinds of filth, mass of corruption, sometimes applied to the human body *Dzl.*; *γtsáṅ-ma* adj., clean, as to the body, clothes etc.; *de ni rab-bkrús γtsáṅ-ma yin* that man is well washed and clean *S O.*; *γtsaṅ-btsog-méd(-pa)* one that knows no difference between clean and unclean (cf. *med*); **dirty, slovenly; rude, uncouth** *Glr.*; *γtsáṅ-mar byéd-pa* 1. **to clean.** 2. **to make one's self clean, smart, tidy;** **tsáṅ-ma ǰhé'-pa* C.*, **čó-če* W.* is said to be a euphemism for circumcision. — **šul-tsáṅ-po* C.* one that clears his plate, empties his cup; one that does a thing thoroughly. — *γtsáṅ-k'aṅ Cs.*, com. *dri-γtsaṅ-k'aṅ* v. *dri.* — *γtsaṅ-sbrá* religious purity, शुचि; *γtsaṅ-sbrá-čan* (or *daṅ ldán-pa*) morally pure, *γtsaṅ-sbra-méd-pa* impure *Do.*— *γtsaṅ-ris Sch.*: the pure country and its inhabitants, the pure, the saints.

གཙང་པོ་ *γtsáṅ-po*, *Ld.* **tsáṅs-po** **river, stream**; esp. the large stream flowing through Tibet from west to east, gen. called **Yarutsaṅpo**; *γtsaṅ-čú*, resp. *γtsaṅ-čáb*, id.

གཙང་བུ་ *γtsaṅ-bu* **screen, parasol** *Sch.*

གཙང་གཙོང་ *γtsaṅ-γtsoṅ* (or **ₒdzaṅ-ₒdzoṅ*?*) *Ld.*, **steep, rugged, mountainous.**

གཙབ་པ་ *γtsáb-pa* **to detach with a crow-bar.**

གཙི་བ་ *γtsi-ba*, pf. *γtsis*, **to invite, summon, call, appoint** *Sch.*

གཙིགས་ *γtsigs* 1. **importance** *Cs.*, *γtsigs(su)* *-če* very important *Lex.*; *γtsigs čé-bar byéd-pa* to make much of *Cs.*; *Sch.* also *mi-γtsigs* **insignificant; unapt,** and *ma-γtsigs* **unimportant; without difficulty,** whereas in one *Lex.* *mi-γtsigs spyód-pa* is explained by *mi-rigs-pa.* — 2. *Pth.* 85: (but as a girl was born, the king and his ministers were quite in despair, and) *btsún-mo-la yaṅ t'ugs γtsigs-čuṅ-bar gyur-to* also the queen's mind was much dejected(?). — 3. *Mil.*: *γtsigs-la ₒbébs-pa* frq.; by the context: **to subdue, to force, compel,** also with supine, *ₒbaṅs bgyid-par* to compel to obey. — 4. *Sch.*: *γtsigs-pai blo* quick comprehension, retentive memory.

གཙིགས་པ་ *γtsigs-pa*, with or without *mčé-ba*, **to show one's teeth, to grin** *Glr.*; *rnam-par γtsigs-pa* id. *Glr.*

གཙིར་བ་ *γtsir-ba* v. *ₒtsir-ba.*

གཙུག་ *γtsug* 1. **crown of the head, vertex** *Lt.*, *spyi-γtsug* id. *Glr.* frq.; *γtsúg-tu ₒčiṅ-ba* to fasten on the head; fig. *sá-yig γtsúg-tu bčiṅs-pai ga*, cf. *tod.* — 2. **tuft, crest,** of birds *Sch.* — 3. **whirlpool, eddy, vortex,** in the water *Sch.*; *γtsug-ₒk'yil Wdṅ.*, also *rtsub-ₒkyil*, perh. id.(?); *γtsug-rgyán* head-ornament, *γtsug-(gi) nór(-bu)* jewel of the head; frq. fig.: most high, most glorious among . . ., c.genit.; also *γtsúg-gi nór-bur gyúr-pa Glr.*, = *mčóg-tu gyúr-pa.* — *γtsug-tor* = *tor-čog*, उष्णीष, conical or flame-shaped hair-tuft on the crown of a Buddha, in later times represented as an excrescence of the skull itself, v. *Burn.* II., 558. *Schl.* 209.

གཙུག་ལག་ *γtsug-lág* 1. **sciences, 'literae'**; *γtsug-lág rnám-pa bčo-brgyád* the eighteen sciences; *k'yod γtsúg-lag čé-ziṅ ₒdzúṅs-pa* thou, who art rich in knowledge and wisdom. — 2. **scientific work** or **works,** frq.; *γtsug-lag-k'aṅ* विहार, academy, convent-temple and school, cf. also *gándho-la*; *γtsúg-lag-mk'an* or *-pa Cs.* a learned man.

གཙུགས་པ་ *γtsúgs-pa* **to bore out, scoop out, excavate** *Sch.*(?).

གཙུབ་པ་ *γtsúb-pa*, pf. *γtsubs*, **to rub,** *γtsub-šiṅ*, a piece of dry wood that is rubbed against another (*γtsub-stán* or *-γtán*) in order to make fire *Cs.*

གཙེ་བ་ *γtsé-ba*, pf. *γtses* v. *ₒtsé-ba.*

གཙེགས་པ་ *γtségs-pa* = *ₒdzigs-pa Sch.*

གཙེང་བ་ *γtsén-ba* = *γtsi-ba Sch.*

གཙེར་བ་ *γtsér-ba* = *ₒtsé-ba Lex.*

གཙོ་ *γtso* 1. v. *γtsó-bo.* — 2. v. *γtsod.*

གཙོ་བོ་ *γtsó-bo* (*Ssk.* **प्रधानं**, consequently = *mčog*) 1. **the highest** in perfection, **the most excellent** in its kind, *γtsó-bor* or *γtsor byéd-pa, lén-pa* to place foremost, to consider the first or most excellent; *γtso byás-pai bú-mo lṅa* the five noblest of the girls *Mil.*; *γtso byéd-pa-rnams* the most respectable, the leaders, the heads *Mil.*; *des γtsó-byas dpon-γyóg-rnams* the higher and lower people subject to him *Pth.* (*γtsó-byed-pa* to be the first, belongs however rather under the head of no. 2); *sṅágs-kyi γtsó-bo, smón-lam-gyi γtsó-bo* (the same as *rgyál-po*) chief spell, principal prayer; *yi-ge γtsó-bo súm-ču* the 30 principal letters, (the letters of the alphabet) *Glr.*; *nad-rnams kún-gyi γtsó-bo* the principal disease, viz. fever *Lt.* (more correct from an Indian than from a Tibetan point of view); *γtso-čé-ba* **very important** *Thgr.*; **eminent** *Tar.*; *γtsó-bor* and *γtso-čér*, adv., **especially, chiefly, principally.** Hence: 2. **a chief, a principal, master, lord,** *rkaṅ-γnyís-kyi* (lord) of men, i.e. Buddha *Dzl.*; *rten-gyi γtso-bo* the 'lord' of the shrine, the deity to whom a shrine is consecrated, which in the lord's absence is guarded by some servant deity, e.g. *Dzl.* chap. VI.; *čós-kyi γtsó-bo čén-po* grand-master of the doctrine, a title of Sariibu *Dzl.*; **gentleman,** but chiefly as a title = Sir, Mr., *blón-po γtsó-bo drúg-po, γtsó-bo mi drug* the six (gentlemen) ministers *Glr.*; *γtsó-mo* the most distinguished lady, the noblest, first in rank, *bú-mo γtsó-mo* the most excellent among the girls; *γtsó-mor ˳ós-pa žig* the one most deserving of preference, the one of the noblest appearance *Mil.*; *γtsó-mo mdzád-pa* to be mistress, resp.

གཙོ་མ་, བཙོ་མ་ *γtsó-ma, btsó-ma* **hemp** *Sch.*

གཙོད་, བཙོད་, གཙོ་ *γtsod, btsod, γtso* (*Ld.* vulgo **stsod**), **the so-called Tibetan antelope,** with straight horns standing close together and in the direction of the longitudinal axis of the head *S.g.*, *γtsód-mo* fem., *γtsod-pʼrúg* the young one, *γtsod-rús* the bones, *γtsod-kʼul* the wool of it (used for shawls).

བཙའ་ *btsa* (*btsa-ba Sch.?*) 1. **rust,** *lčágs-kyi btsa* rust of iron; *btsas-zas Sch.*, *kʼyer Lex.* destroyed by rust. — 2. **rust, blight, smut,** of corn *Sch.* — 3. = *btsag, Sch.* — *me-btsá* **moxa** *Lt.*; *mi-rus-btsa?*

བཙའ་བ་ *btsá-ba* 1. pf. *btsas*, **to bear, to bring forth,** *čuṅ-ma-la bu btsas* his wife bore, gave birth to, a son *Dzl.*; *bu btsá-bai tʼabs mi tʼub* they could not bring forth *Dzl.*; *btsás-pa* what is begotten, new-born children or animals *Do.*; *btsá-zug laṅs* pains of labour ensued *Sch.* — 2. resp. **to watch, look on, spy,** *spyán-gyis Cs.*

བཙའ་མ་ *btsá-ma* **fruit** *Sch.* 2. = *btsa Sch.*

བཙག་ *btsag*, **गैरिक**, **red ochre** *Med.* and *Lex.*; used also of earths of a different colour; *btsag-tʼáṅ, btsag-ri, btsag-lúṅ* plain, hill, valley, of red earth; *btsag-yug* some other officinal mineral *Med.*

བཙག་པ་ *btság-pa* v *˳tság-pa.*

བཙག་མོ་ *btság-mo* a certain beverage, = *rtsáb-mo.*

བཙང་བ་ *btsáṅ-ba* prob. = *˳tsáṅ-ba.*

བཙང་པོ་ *btsáṅ-po* title of sovereigns *Glr.*, alledged to be but Khams-dialect for *btsán-po.*

བཙན་ *btsan* 1. a species of demons, residing in the air, on high rocks etc., mischievous, *Glr., Dom.* — 2. v. the following article.

བཙན(པོ་) *btsán(-po)* **strong, mighty, powerful,** of kings, ministers etc., esp. as title of honour: **high-potent,** *Dzl., Glr.*; hence of family, race, descent: **illustrious, noble,** *lhá-mo btsán-rnams* the queens of high descent, in opp. to a third of low extraction *Glr.*; *btsan-(žiṅ) pʼyug(-po)* noble and rich *Dzl., Mil.*; **strong, violent,** *btsan-dúg* a virulent poison *Dzl.*; **forcible, violent,** *btsan-˳pʼrógs byéd-pa* to commit a robbery connected with violence *Pth.*; *btsan-tʼabs-su* by violent means *Pth.*; **coercive, strict, severe** *bka, kʼrims Glr.*, *btsán-par mdzád-pa* rigorously to enforce (a law); **firm, staunch, immovable, not wavering,** *ṅag-btsán* steadfastly abiding by one's word *Sch.*; **firm, safe,**

**sure,** *dben-γnás Mil.* a safe, inaccessible retreat; *rdzoṅ btsan* a firm stronghold *Lex.*; = concealed, hidden, hence *btsan-k̔aṅ* the innermost dark room in a temple, in which the gods reside, or an apartment for the same purpose on the top of a house; **definite, decided, without uncertainty,** *saṅs-rgyás-kyi bstán-pa mi núb-čiṅ mt̔a btsán-par byéd-pai p̔yir* in order that the doctrine of Buddha by being accurately defined may be secured against subversion *Pth.*

བཙབ་པ་ *btsáb-pa* imp. *btsob,* **to cut small, to chop,** wood; **to hash, to mince,** meat *C.*; *bstab-stán* chopping-block *C.*

བཙམ(ས)་པ་ *btsám(s)-pa* for *˳tsám-pa,* v. *t̔o.*

བཙལ་བ་ *btsál-ba* v. *˳t̔sól-ba.*

བཙས་པ་ *btsás-pa* v. *btsá-ba.*

བཙས་མ་ *btsás-ma* 1. also *rtsás-ma* **harvest,** *btsás-ma rṅa-ba* **to reap, to mow** *C.* and *Lex.*, *btsás-ma ran tsa-na* in harvest time *Mil.*— 2. **wages, pay,** *gru-btsás Lex.*, fare, passage-money; *la-btsás Lex.*, *la-čan-gyi btsas?*

བཙིར་བ་ *btsir-ba* v. *˳t̔sir-ba.*

བཙུག(ས)་པ་ *btsúg(s)-pa* v. *˳dzúgs-pa.*

བཙུད་པ་ *btsúd-pa* v. *˳dzúd-pa*, *˳t̔súd-pa.*

བཙུན་པ་ *btsún-pa* 1. **respectable, noble,** of race, family, *rigs čé-žiṅ btsún-pa* id. *Dzl.*; *btsún-pai bud-méd Dzl.* a lady of rank. — 2. **reverend,** as title of ecclesiastics, *btsún-pa-rnams* the ecclesiastics, priests *Glr.*, = *ban-dhe* and *Ssk.* भदन्त (*Tar.* Transl. p. 4, note 7); even *btsún-pa k̔rims-méd* wicked Reverends *Ma.* — 3. **creditable, honourable, faithful** in observing religious duties, so frq.: *mk̔as btsun bzaṅ γsum* v. *mk̔as-pa*; *t̔sig-btsún-pa* grave and virtuous discourse *Schr.*, *Sch.*: polite words (?), *t̔sig mi btsun-pa Thgy.* was explained to me: one whom nobody believes; applied to things: **good;** thus *Mil.* says of his cane: *spa čo-ris yé-nas btsún-pa de* this cane of quite an excellent quality. — *btsún-po* = *btsún-pa* 1., *rgya-rǰé btsún-po* the noble emperor of China *Glr.*; as a title v. *snyuṅ; btsún-por byéd-pa Cs.* to reverence. — *btsún-ma* priestess *Cs.* — *btsún-mo* 1. woman of rank, **a lady;** also as a term of address: your ladyship, e.g. in a legend, when a merchant speaks to the wife of a judge *Dzl.*; **spouse, consort,** esp. **queen consort,** with and without *rgyál-poi,* frq.; *btsún-mo čé-ba* = *čen-ma* the principal wife; *btsun-mo-čan* having a wife, *btsun-mo-méd* not having a wife *Cs.* — 2. **nun,** *mo-btsún,* id. *Glr.*, *C.*

བཙུམ་པ་ *btsúm-pa* v. *˳dzúm-pa.*

བཙེ་བ་ *btsé-ba* v. *˳t̔sé-ba.*

བཙེམ་པ་ *btsém-pa* v. *t̔sem-pa.*

བཙོ་ *btso,* **purification, refining** (?) **ser-la tso taṅ-wa* C.* to refine gold (which term eventually is the same as 'to boil') v. *˳tsod-pa; btsó-ma, btsós-ma* a purified substance, *γser btsó-ma,* purified gold, very frq. with regard to a bright yellow colour *Glr.*

བཙོ་བ་ *btsó-ba* v. *˳t̔sód-pa*; *btso-blag-pa* **to dye, to colour,** *btso-blág-mk̔an* **a dyer,** *Lex.*

བཙོ་མ་ *btsó-ma* 1. = *γtsó-ma.* — 2. v. *btso.*

བཙོག་པ་ *btsóg-pa* I. vb. v. *˳t̔sog-pa.*

II. adj., also *(b)rtsóg(s)-pa, W. *sóg-po** 1. **unclean, dirty, nasty, vile,** *˳di-ni šin-tu rtsóg-pai sa yin* this is a very vile place, says the prince of hades to a saint visiting there; so also every Tibetan will say to a stranger entering his house; *ṅa btsog-čiṅ* when I am getting unclean, i.e. when I am confined *Dzl.*; *lus btsog-pa mnyam-pa ˳di* this vile stinking body *Dzl.* — 2. in *W.* the common word for **bad** in every respect, **useless, spoiled, troublesome, perilous** (e.g. of a road); **injurious;** also in a more relative sense, **inferior, poor,** of goods; *btsog-nág* tobacco-juice, oil from the tobacco-pipe.

བཙོང་ *btsoṅ* **onion** *Med.* and vulgo, eschewed by pious Buddhists and ascetics, but a favourite food of the bulk of the people; *btsoṅ srég-pa* to roast onions.

བཙོང་བ་ *btsóṅ-ba* v. *ₒtsóṅ-ba.*

བཙོད་ *btsod* n. of an animal, = *γtsod*, q v. — 2. n. of a plant, **madder** **मञ्जिष्ठा**, (*Rubia Manjit*); *btsod-ₒbru* seeds of this plant, *btsod-žiṅ* field on which it is grown.

བཙོན་ *btson*, also *btsón-pa*, **a captive, prisoner,** *nyés-pa byás-pai btson žig* an imprisoned criminal *Dzl.*; *btsón-du ₒdzín-pa* to take prisoner *Dzl.*; *ₒjúg-pa* to put to prison; *btsón-nas ₒdón-pa* to set free, *tár-ba* to be released; *bzáṅ-btson* undeserved imprisonment or detention (ni f.), e.g. of hostages, fig. of people that are snowed up *Mil* — *btsón-kaṅ*, *btson-ra* prison. — *btsón-doṅ* 1. **dungeon,** keep; *Mil.*: *γnás-skabs-kyi btsón-doṅ* the dungeon of life. — 2. *W.* **deep abyss, gulf,** **tsón-doṅ tóṅ-na mi máṅ-poi go kor** many are getting dizzy, when looking into a deep abyss. — *btsón-rdzi*, *btsón-sruṅ* jailer, turnkey. — *btsón-rdzas* prison-fare.

བཙོལ་བ་ *btsól-ba* v. *ₒtsól-ba.*

ཙ ཙ་ *rtsa* I. sbst., more col. *rtsá-ba* (*W.* **sá-wa**) or *rtsá-bo S.g.* 5, 1. **vein,** *rtsa γčód-pa* to open a vein *Dzl.*, **sá-wa gyáb-če** *W.* id. Owing to the imperfect state of Indian and Tibetan anatomy, resulting from inveterate prejudices both of a religious and intellectual nature, great confusion prevails also in the department of angiology, many different vessels of the human body, and even part of the nerves being classed among the veins, so that it is impossible to find adequate terms for the Tibetan nomenclature. This applies e.g. to the division of the *rtsa* in *čágs-pai*, *srid-pai*, *ₒbrél-pai*, and *tséi* or *sróg-gi rtsa*, which last term does not correspond to what we understand by artery (*Cs.*); so it is also with respect to the three principal veins, which by a mystic theory are stated to proceed from the heart, *dbú-ma* the middle one, white, *rkyáṅ-ma* the left one, red, and *ró-ma* the right one, white, concerning which cf. the articles *γtúm-mo* and *tig-le*; *rtsa-dkár*, also *rlúṅ-rtsa Med.*, are perh. in most cases the same as **artery,** acc. to the well-known supposition of the ancients, that the veins of dead men, appearing empty, contain air; *par-rtsa* id., as in the living body it pulsates; *rtsa-nág* or *krág-rtsa*, vein, blood-vessel; *rtsa-sbúbs* is mentioned *Lt.* 147, 10, as a surgical instrument. Some names are more or less clear: *mig-rtsa* seems to be the Vena fac. ext., *rtsa-čúṅ* Vena jugul. ext., *rtsa-čén* or *rtsa-bo-čé* V. saphena magna, *pó-mtsan-ghi dbus-rtsa* V. dorsalis penis. *rgyú-grog-rtsa*, on the other hand, are the ureters, ni f., which are represented as proceeding from the small intestine. — *rtsa-rgyus Med.* 1. *Sch.*: 'veins and sinews' (?); *rtsa-rgyus-ₒgag* an obstruction of the veins *S.g.* 2. title of a book: Directions how to feel the pulse. — *rtsa-čús*, *C. rtsa-ₒdus* cramp. — *rtsa-mdúd* an inturgescence of the veins. — *rtsa-γnás Mil.* seems to be a net of veins, vascular plexus, any connection of things that may be compared to it, as e.g. the causal connection of the 12 Nidanas (v. *rten-ₒbrel* sub *rtén-pa* comp.) — *rtsa-spún* tissue of veins *Sch.* — 2. **pulse,** so in *rtsa ltá-ba*, or *rtog-pa Med.* to feel one's pulse, and *mtson-*, *kan-*, or *čag-rtsa* the feeling one's pulse with the second, third or fourth finger.

II. sbst, for *rtsá-ba.*

III. particle in conjunction with numerals: 1. gen. connecting the tens with the units, equivalent to **and:** *nyi-šu-rtsa-γčig* twenty and one; less frq. after *brgya* and *stoṅ*, where also *daṅ-rtsa* is not unusual, yet examples as the following: *S g.*, fol. 5, where the sum of 62, 33, 95 and 112 is stated to be = *sum-brgya-rtsa-γnyis*, and *Pth.* p. 34, twice *lṅa-brgyá-rtsa γčig* = *stoṅ-daṅ-rtsa-γnyis*, — exclude any doubt as to the proper use of the word. — 2. inst. of *nyi-šu-rtsa-γčig* to *nyi-šu-rtsa-dgu*, *rtsa-γčig* etc. is also used by itself, as an abbreviation, e.g. *S.g.* p. 3, in describing the growth of an embryo from week to week; this use of the word may account for the assumption, quite general in *W.* and *C.*, that *rtsa* in itself is equivalent to 20, for even Lamas of both districts could be convinced only by an arithmetical proof, that the numbers mentioned in the above passages were 302 and 1002, and not 322 and 1022. — 3. In *bčú-rtsa nyí-šu-rtsa, brgyá-rtsa*, without any units following, e.g *Tar.* 120, 10, the word evidently stands but pleonastically, like *ťam-pa.*

རྩྭ་ *rtswa (Bal., Pur. rtswa, stswa) C.* **tsa**, *Lh., Ld.,* **sa**, **तृणं**, **grass, herb, plant**, *rtsa-ǩai* (or *rtsa-rťsei*) *zil-pa* the dew on the grass *Glr.*; *rtsa nyag γčig* a single blade of grass *Cs.*; *sṅó-yi rtsa, rtsa-sṅón* green grass; *rtsa-skám*, and often *rtsa* alone, **hay**, *rtsa rná-ba* to mow grass, *ₒťú-ba*, to gather (grass); *rtsá-ǩa C., W.* pasture, pasturage, **sá-ǩa gyál-la** *W.* good pasturage. — *rtsá-čan* covered with grass, grassy. — *rtsa-mčóg* Kusha-grass *Lex.*, v. *ku-ša*; *rtsa-mčog* (*-groṅ*) town in West Assam, where Buddha died *Glr.*; Kamarūpa. — *rtsa-ťág* grass-rope *Dzl.* — *rtsa-ťún* grass-gatherer *Sch.* — *rtsa-γdán* grass-mat *Sch.* — *rtsa-γyáb* manger *Sch.* — *rtsa-ras Sch.* 'linen', prop. the same as *la-ta* q. v. — 2. euphemism for *rkyag*; **tsa táṅ-wa** *C.* to go to stool; *rtsa ču bsdams Mil.* he suffers from obstruction and strangury.

རྩ་བ་ *rtsá-ba*, I. cf. *rtsaṅ* and *rtsad, Ssk.* **मूल**. 1. **root** (*W.* com. **bá-ťag** for it), **stalk of fruits**; *rtsá-ba lṅa* five (medicinal) roots, viz. *rá-mnye, lčá-ba, nyé-šiṅ, ǎ-šo* (better *ǎ-ša*)*-gandha, γzé-ma*; *rtsá-ba-nas ₒbyin-pa* etc. to pull out with the root, to eradicate, extirpate, mostly fig., v. below. — 2. **the lower end** of a stick, trunk of a tree, pillar; *má-ťog rtsá-ba* id. *Mil.*; the **foot** of a hill, mountain-pass, the latter also *lá-rtsa W.* **lár-sa**; *rtsá-bai žal, lag* the lower faces or hands of those images, that represent deities with many faces and hands *Glr.*; *rtsá-bai ṅos* base of a triangle *Tar.* 204, 1; **fundament, foundation-pillar,** and the like; in later literature and vulgo *rtsá-bar* and *rtsar*, rarely (*Glr.*) *rtsá-ru* postp. with genit., **to, at,** e.g. to go to, to come to, to be at, both of persons and things, *bud-méd-kyi rtsar nyál-ba* or more euphem., *ṕyin-pa* to go to a woman *Glr., šiṅ-gi rtsar*, even *čui rtsar Glr.*; **at, near, to,** a tree, river etc.; so also *rtsá-la* **to, at;** *rtsá(-ba)-na Glr.* and vulgo (incorr.) **tsá-nę** *C.* **at, near**; without a case following: *rtsar byúṅ-nas* coming near, stepping up to *Glr.* — 3. **root** fig. **origin, primary cause,** also *γži-rtsa*, e.g. *ₒǩor-bai γži-rtsa γčod-pa Mil.* to cut off the root of transmigration, to deliver a soul from tr.; *rtsá-ba-nas ₒbyin-pa, ₒdón-pa, ₒgóg-pa* etc., also *tsáṅ-nas, tsád-nas γčód-pa* etc., to exterminate (root and branch), to annihilate; on the other hand: *rtsa-brdár-γčod-pa Mil.*, *rtsád-γčod-pa* to examine closely, to investigate thoroughly. — *nyon-móṅs-kyi rtsá-ba γsum* are the three primary moral evils, viz. *ₒdod-čágs, že-sdaṅ, γti-mug; rtsa-brál* therefore might signify: he who has freed himself from them; but it seems to mean also: without beginning or end, **unlimited,** e.g. *snyiṅ-rje Glr., sems nyid Mil.; dgé-bai rtsá-ba, dgé-rtsa* a virtuous deed, as a cause of future reward, *skyéd-pa, spyód-pa, byéd-pa* to perform such a deed; *rtsá-bai* . . . **the original, primary, principal** . . ., e.g. *don*, primitive or first meaning *Cs.*; *rtsá-bai nyon-móṅs-pa Cs.*: 'original sin', *Sch.*: 'sin inherited from former births'; at all events not identical with the original sin of Christian dogmatics, although the word grammatically might denote it; *rtsa (-bai) rgyud* an introductory treatise, giving a summary of the contents of a larger work, e.g. of the *rgyud-bži*, mentioned sub *brgyud;* also title of other works, *Ssk.* **मूलतन्त्र**, v. *Cs. Gram.*, chronol. table; whether *Sch.'s* translation 'cause and effect' is altogether correct, may admit of some doubt, yet v. below; *rtsá-ba daṅ ˛grél-ba Cs.* 'text and commentary'; in *rtsá-bai ma Thgy.* the genitive case stands prob. for the apposition: the mother that is the root of me, in a similar manner as *rtsá-bai raṅ-bžin* nature *Cs.; rtsá-bai blá-ma* seems to denote the teaching priest, the one by whom in any particular case the instruction is given, opp. to *brgyúd-pa*, he to whom it is imparted. A good deal of confusion however prevails here, owing to the ambiguity of the verbal form in *brgyúd-pa* and the variable spelling;

v. *rgyúd-pa* extr. — *rtsa-ťór Sch.*: 'lower end and top' (?) (should perh. be *rtsa-ťog*); *rtsa-mi Tar.* 191, 3 is rendered by *Schf.* with 'Haupt-Mann', principal man. — *rtsa-lág* (*Schr.*: root and branches) *Lex.* बन्धु relations, kindred; *rtsa-lag-čan* having relations, *rtsa-lag-med* without relations *Cs.* — *rtsa-šés Sch.*: primitive wisdom. — 4. symb. num.: 9. — II. v. *rtsa* **vein.**

Note. *rtsa*, vein, is traced by Tibetan scholars back to *rtsá-ba*, the veins being the 'roots of life'; in a dictionary the words are better treated separately.

ཙ་ལ་ *rtsá-la* v. *rtsá-ba* I, 2.

ཙང་ *rtsaṅ* = *rtsá-ba* seldom, v. *rtsá-ba* I, 3.

ཙངས་པ་ *rtsáṅs-pa* lizard, *brag-gi Lt.* (*W.* **gag-čig**).

ཙད་ *rtsad* = *rtsá-ba* **root**, *rtsád-nas γčód-pa Mil.* to root out, to eradicate; *rtsad γčód-pa*, = *rtsa-brdár γčód-pa*, = *ťsar* and *γsar γčód-pa*, to search, investigate *Mil.*; *gar bžugs rtsad bčád-nas* to inquire, search for a person's place of abode *Pth.*

ཙབ་པ་, ཙབ་ཙབ་ *rtsab, rtsab-rtsab* v. *tsab-tsub.*

ཙབས་ *rtsabs* **ferment, barm, yeast,** prepared of barley-flour; *rtsabs-ǩur* a sweetish sort of bread, made up with it *Ld.*; *rtsábs-mo* a beverage brewed from roasted meal (*rtsám-pa*) and water, and made to ferment by adding butter-milk, esp. liked in winter; also called *btság-mo; žó-rtsabs Sch.* milk-brandy, not known to us.

ཙབས་རུ་ཚ་ *rtsabs-ru-ťsa Lt.* n. of a medicine.

ཙམ་པ་ *rtsám-pa*, I. sbst. 1. **roast-flour,** flour from roasted grain, *ₒbras-rtsam* of rice, *gro-rtsam* of wheat, *nas-rtsam* of barley, this last the most common; stirred with water, beer, or tea into a pap, it is the usual food in *C.* — *rtsám-ₒbru* roast-flour and grain = victuals in gen. *Kun.* — *rtsám-rín* the price of flour *Sch.* — 2. **urine** *Lt. rtsam-mdóg* colour of urine.

II. vb. v. *rtsóm-pa.*

ཙར་ *rtsar* v. *rtsá-ba* I, 2.

ཙལ་ *rtsal* 1. **skill, dexterity, adroitness, accomplishment;** in the first place **physical skill,** *lag-rtsal-čan* of a skilful, practised hand *W.*; *sgyu-rtsál* id., *stobs daṅ sgyu-rtsál* strength and dexterity *Glr.*, skilfulness; *rtsal(daṅ) ldán(-pa)* skilful, expert, adroit, *rtsal-méd* the contrary; *rtsal ₒgran-pa* to vie in skill, *rtsal sbyóṅ-ba* to practise, or improve one's self in skill *Mil.*; *rtsal šor* all skill is gone, *rgud id. Sch.*; *stobs-(kyi) rtsal, Lex.* पराक्रम, strength, energy, *mťu-rtsál* and *rtsal-mťu* prob. id. *Dzl.*, *S.g.*; *rtsal-čé-ba* or *rtsal-po-čé* adroit as a gymnastic, wrestler etc.; also sbst. athlete, juggler etc. *Dzl.*; *rtsál-gyi mčoṅs* a gymnastic feat *Lex.*; *rtsal-sbyoṅ* bodily exercise, nimbleness, agility, *báṅ-rtsal-sbyoṅ* nimbleness in running, *γšóg-rtsal-sbyoṅ* agility in flying *Mil.*; *ču-rtsál* feats performed in the water; the art of swimming *Pth.*; vulgo *W.* also for natural, innate abilities: *míg-rtsal-mǩan* keen-sighted, *mig-rtsal nyams* of a weak sight; *rtsal-ťôn Sch.* 'skilful, masterly' (?) — 2. in later times used in a special sense of **skill, expertness in contemplation,** cf. *sgóm-pa;* so frq. with *Mil.*; *byaṅ-čub-séms-kyi rtsal γsum*; *lam-ₒgag-méd-kyi rtsál-ǩa* such accomplishments 'as will clear the road', — ascetical terms familiar only to the initiated.

ཙས་མ་ *rtsás-ma* v. *btsás-ma.*

ཙི་ *rtsi* 1. all fluids of a somewhat greater consistency, such as the **juice** of some fruits, **paints, varnish** etc., *rtsi-čan* **viscid, sticky, clammy;** **tsi gyág-pa** *C.*, **si gyáb-če, kú-če, táṅ-če** *W.* to colour, to paint, **tsi táṅ-wa** *C.* also to solder; *ldab-pa*(?) *Sch.* to lacker, to varnish; *sbráṅ-rtsi* **honey;** *nád-kyi rkyen rtsi* a medical draught, potion *Dzl.* ༢༧, 7, (another reading: *sman*); *bdúd-rtsi* nectar; *tsón-rtsi* painter's colour, *dkár-rtsi* white-wash, *nág-rtsi* black paint, *dmár-rtsi* red paint; **sér-tsi** *C.* gilding, **ṅúl-tsi** silvering *C.* — 2. applied to external appearance: **dóṅ-si** *W.* **complexion;** even *spa rtsi ₒjam ǩa-dóg légs-pa de* this cane, as to its outside smooth, as to colour beautiful *Mil.* (unless *rtsi* be = shell, bark, rind?)

— *rtsi-ťóg* juicy fruit; *rtsi-śiṅ* 1. **fruit-tree** *Pth.* 2. **tree,** in gen. *Glr.* and elsewh., frq. — *rtsi-gu* fruit-kernel, the kernel in a fruit-stone (not the latter itself *Sch.*); *W.* for **ťsi-gu**, q.v.; *rtsi-gu-mar-nag* oil extracted from the stones of apricots; *rtsi-már Lt.* id.

རྩི་བ་ *rtsi-ba*, pf. *(b)rtsis*, fut. *brtsi*, imp. *(b)rtsi(s)* 1. **to count,** **si-te bór-če* W.* to pay down, money; cf. also *rtsis.* — 2. **to count, reckon, calculate,** *mi ré-la ṗul re-réi ťád-du* reckoning a handful to each *Dzl.*; *żag súm-ču-la zlá-ba γčig, zlá-ba bču-γnyis-la lor rtsí-ba* to reckon a month at 30 days, a year at 12 months *Thgy.*; *mi-lo-ltar rtsí-ba* to count by the years of a man *Thgy.*; *gaṅ bzaṅ rtsí-ba* to calculate which (day) be a propitious one *Glr.*; *dus rtsí-ba* to reckon up, to compute the time *Mil.*; **če-miṅ ḍál-la si-če* W.* to reckon among the adults; *yón-tan-la skyón-du rtsí-ba* to consider good qualities as faults, = *ltá-ba* I, 2; *brduṅ rtsi* he may be reckoned to strike, i.e. he is very likely to strike, threatens to strike *C.*; *brtsís zin* 1. **the account is closed,** the bill is ready. 2. **product, sum total.**

རྩིའུ་ *rtsiu* n. of a plant, = *pri-yáṅ-ku Wdṅ.*

རྩིག་པ་ *rtsig-pa* I. vb., pf. *(b)rtsigs*, fut. *brtsig*, imp. *(b)rtsig(s)*, 1. **to build,** whether of stone or of wood, *ǩáṅ-pa.* — 2. **to wall up,** *sgo* a door *Glr.* — II. sbst. **wall, masonry.**

**Comp.** *rtsig-skyábs Stg.* is said to be = *rtsig-rmáṅ.* — *rtsig-ṅós* side of a wall. — *rtsig-rdó* stone for building. — *rtsig-dpón* master-mason, architect. — *rtsig-ṗúr* a peg in a wall, wall-hook, to hang up things. — *rtsig-rmáṅ* fundament of a wall. — *rtsig-zúr* edge or ledge of a wall *Thgy.* — *rtsig-bzó-pa* brick-layer, mason. — *rtsig-γyóg* journeyman mason.

རྩིགས་ *rtsigs*, *Sch.*: '*rtsigs-čé* **very gracious and well-affected**' (?), prob. should be *rtsis-če* q. v. no. 3.

རྩིགས་མ་ *rtsigs-ma* **turbid matter, sediment, impurity,** = *tsigs-ma S.g.*

རྩིང་བ་ *rtsiṅ-ba* adj. and sbst., **coarse, clumsy, rough, rude; coarseness** etc., *B.*; *rtsiṅ-po B.* and *C.*, *rtsiṅ-ge C.*, *W.* id., but only adj; *ṗye* coarse meal, grits (opp. to *żib-po, ˳ǰám-po*); *spyód-pa rtsiṅ-ba* of rude manners *Glr.*

རྩིད་པ་ *rtsid-pa* **the long hair of the yak,** *rtsid-ťágs* = *re-ťágs* coarse cloth manufactured of it; *rtsid-stán* saddle-cloth *Mil.*; *rtsid-gúr* tent-covering made of it.

རྩིབ(ས)་མ་ *rtsib(s)-ma* 1. **rib,** *rtsib-mai bár-nas* from between the ribs *Glr.*; *rtsib-lógs γyas γyon* all the ribs of the right and left side *Dzl*; *rtsib-logs ná-ba* pain about the ribs *Do.*; *rtsib-riṅ* the upper ribs (?) — 2. **spoke** of a wheel, frq.; *rtsib-kyi mu-ǩyúd* fellies composing the rim of a wheel *Cs.*; in ornamental designs the *rtsib-ma* are often fanciful figures, supplying the radii of the circle; further: **the sticks** or **ribs** of a parasol, canopy etc. *Glr.*; **the spars** of a felt-tent, **the ribs** or **futtocks** of a boat *Schr.* — *rtsib-ri* n. of a mountain, = *śri-ri.*

རྩིས་ *rtsis* 1. **counting, numbering, numeration,** *rtsis-las ˳das-pa* innumerable *Mil.*; **bód si-la, món-si-la* W.* according to Tibetan, according to Indian counting or computation of time (is to-day the twentieth); **mi-si, ḍóṅ-si* W.* numbering of the people, of the domiciliated; **mág-si táṅ-če* W.* to hold a numbering of military forces. — 2. **account,** *rtsis byéd-pa Glr.*, *˳débs-pa Mil.*, *γyáb-pa C.*, *W.* **kor-če, (l)ta-če** **to calculate, to compute,** *rtsis-su sbyár-ba* to count together, to sum up *Dzl.*; **calculation, computation** (beforehand), **scheme;** **żag nyi-śu-la ˳gro- (or ča-rtsis yod)* W.* in about 20 days we calculate, i.e. we intend, to go; **śiṅ-ta gyúg-si yód-pe dus-ťsód-la* Ld.* at the hour, when according to their calculation the carriage was to start; *rtsís-kyis* (or *rtsis byás-nas*) *ṅó-śes-pa* to find by computation *Glr.* — *skár-rtsis* **astrology, astronomy;** *dkár-rtsis, nág-rtsis*, acc. to *Cs.*: Indian and Chinese astronomy and chronology. — 3. **estimation, esteem,** *rtsis-po čén-po byéd-pa* to value, to make much of, *lús-kyi rtsis-po-če* one that makes much of his own body, by indulging and adorning it *Thgy.*; *rtsis-rtsis byéd-pa Sch.* id.; *dé-la bla-*

*lhág-tu rtsis-su byed* he respected her beyond measure *Tar.*, *Schf.* — **si-rúg** vulgo *W.* for *rtsis* in most of its significations.

**རྩིས་པ** *rtsis-pa* 1. also *rtsis-mk̔an* **mathematician, astronomer, soothsayer; accountant** *Cs.* — 2. n. pr. *rtsis-pa ȧ-mgrón* secular, *rtsis-pa mgron-γnyér* spiritual name of the late Resident of the Sikim government at Darjeeling, called by the English Cheboo Lama, † 1866, v. Hooker Journ. — *rtsis-dpon* a chief mathematician, chief accountant, receiver general *Cs.*

**རྩུབ་པ** *rtsúb-pa* I. vb. **to revile, abuse,** v. *ṅor rtsub-pa* sub *ṅo.*

II. adj., com. *rtsúb-po*, *rtsúb-mo Ssk.* **परुष, uneven, rough, rugged,** of the skin, cloth etc.; **coarse-grained**, powder; **rough, wild, dreary,** countries, *roṅ-rtsub* with wild ravines *Glr.*; **bristly**, hair; **harsh, tart, astringent,** of taste *Med.*; also applied to any thing of a highly **aromatic, pricking, pungent** or **acerb** taste, such as onions and similar vegetables, liable to cause both dietetic and religious scruples; *rtsub-zás* food of this description; in music: **strong, forte;** of sentiment and behaviour: **rude, unfeeling, regardless, callous** *S.g.*, *Glr.*

**རྩེ(མོ)** *rtse(-mo)* 1. **point, top, peak, summit,** *k̔aṅ-, gri-, ri-, śiṅ-rtse*, or *k̔aṅ-pai* etc., *rtsé-mo* **gable** of a house, point of a knife, top of a hill, head of a tree; of convents, royal palaces, resp.: *dbú-rtse Glr.*; *lá-rtse*, *W.* **lár-se** (cf. *rtsá-ba* I, 2.) **lá-se** **summit** of a mountain-pass; *rtse daṅ logs-su* terminal and lateral *Wdṅ.*; *rtsé-sgro Glr.* flag-feather, pinion; *ża rtse-riṅ* hat with a high crown *Tar.*; *rtse γčil-ba Sch.*: to break off the point, to blunt; *rtse-reg-čé Mil.* very sensitive, touchy, not to be touched with the tip of the finger. — 2. **point, particular spot,** *rtse γčig-tu ltá-ba* to look at one point; also adv., to look **steadily, unremittingly,** as: *rdṅ-gi grib-ma-la rtse-γčig-tu ltá-ba Wdṅ.*, also *Tar.* frq.; *sems rtse γčig-tu byed-pa* to direct the mind to one point, frq.; *sems rtse-γčig-tu byás-pai tiṅ-ṅe-ˌdzin-la żúgs-te Dzl.*; aim, *tse ˌdii rtse γčig* as this life's only aim *Mil.*

**རྩེ་བ** *rtsé-ba*, pf. *rtses*, imp. *rtse(s)*, **क्रीड,** (different from *brtsé-ba*) 1. **to play,** *mig-máṅ* at chess *Dzl.*; **to sport, to frolic,** used also of animals *Dzl.*; *rtse bro γtóṅ-ba* to run to and fro, playing and skipping, of deer *Mil.*; **to joke, to jest,** *rtsé-żiṅ dgá-ba, rtse-dgá spyád-pa* id.; **yáṅ(s)-pa sé-če** *W.* id.; **to enjoy, amuse, divert one's self, to take recreation,** *ṫsal-gyi naṅ-du rtser soṅ* they went on a pleasure party into the woods *Dzl.*; euphem. of cohabitation, *ˌdi daṅ rtsé-bar byao Pth.* I mean to enjoy her.

**Comp.** *rtsé-mk̔an* player, gambler, gamester. — *rtse-grógs, rtsed-grógs* play-mate. — *rtse-dgá* v. above. — *rtse-rgód* sport and laughter. — *rtsé-sa* play-ground, place of amusement. — *rtse-sems* a mind fond of play; *k̔yód-kyis rtsé-sems yin mod k̔yaṅ* though you may still relish pleasures *Pth.*

2. **to touch,** *W.* **lág-pa ma se** do not touch it with your hand. — 3. **to shudder** (cf. *spu*).

**རྩེ་ཅུང** *rtse-čúṅ* = *rtsa-čúṅ*, Vena jugularis externa.

**རྩེག་པ** *rtség-pa*, pf. *(b)rtsegs*, fut. *brtseg*, imp *rtsog*, *W.* **sóg-če(s)** 1. **to lay one thing on or over another, to pile up, stack up, build up,** wood, boards; to put slices of meat on bread; fig.: *ná-ro γnyis brtseg* two 'naro' one above the other, ◌ྐྐ, *Gram.*; gen. **double;** *k̔aṅ-pa rtsegs-pa* 1. **'a house of two stories'** = a stately building, palace; by this word *Wdṅ.* explains *k̔aṅ-bzáṅ*, v. *bzáṅ-po.* 2. acc. to other *Lexx.*, **an apartment built on another,** an upper chamber; balcony on the roof of a house, **कूटागार;** *rgya-grám brtségs-pai mčód-rten* a chod-ten with a cross (v. *rgya-grám*) on the top *Pth.* — 2. **to tuck up,** clothes *Cs.* — 3. *dbugs rtségs-pa, gyén-du dbugs(-kyis) rtség-pa Med.*, **short-breathed, asthmatic, panting, gasping,** from fright etc., or as a sign of approaching death. — *dkon(-mčóg) brtségs(-pa)*; **रत्नकूट** title of a book.

**རྩེང་བ** *rtseṅ-ba*, pf. *brtseṅs*, fut. *brtseṅ*, imp. *(b)rtsoṅ(s)* **to tuck up, truss up.**

**རྩེད་པ** *rtséd-pa* I. also *rtsén-pa*, = *rtsé-ba* **to play;** ***rtsed rtsé-ba*** id.; *rtséd-mo*

**play, game,** *dgá-bai rtséd-mo byed-pa Dzl.*; *glu gar rtséd-mo byéd-pa* to sing, dance and play *Glr.*; *rtséd-mo* **toy,** *byis-pai* children's toy *Mil.*; *rtséd-mo-čan* **playful, sportive, merry** *Cs.*; *rkyál-, gár-, grí-, čól-, mčón-, rtá-rtsed* the sport of swimming, dancing, fencing, dicing, leaping, riding *Cs.*; *γyeṅ-rtséd* **play, amusement, diversion**; *rtsed-dgá* id. *Sch.*; *to-to-liṅ-líṅ rtsed* q. v.; *rtséd-ˌǰo, rtsén-ˌǰo*, *W.* **sén-ǰo** **sport, public amusement, popular pleasure;** *γžón-nu rtséd-ˌǰoi ťsógs-kyis bskór-nas* surrounded by a number of youthful playmates; **sén-ǰo táṅ-če* W.* to arrange a sport.

II. **to varnish** (?).

རྩེད་མ་ *rtséd-ma* the disagreeable feeling in the teeth produced by acids *Sch.*; *rsed-ǎm* a shivering, cold shudder *Sch.* v. *rtsé-ba* 3.

རྩེད་མོ་, རྩེན་པ་ *rtséd-mo, rtsén-pa* v. *rtséd-pa.*

རྩེན་གོག་ *rtsen-góg Mil*, acc. to *Sch.*: **calf of the leg.**

རྩེས་ *rtses* v. *rtsé-ba.*

རྩོག(ས)པ་ *rtsóg(s)-pa* v. *brtsóg-pa.*

རྩོད་ལྡན་ *rtsod-ldán* n. of a certain era or period of the world v. *dus* 6.

རྩོད་པ་ *rtsód-pa*, I. vb., pf. *brtsad* **to contend, to fight with arms** *Dzl.*; with words: **to dispute, debate, wrangle,** frq., *daṅ* with, *la* about; *rtsód-čiṅ mi-snyán rǰód-pa* to speak evil words, to use bad language, in quarreling.

II. sbst. **dispute, contention, quarrel; disputation** *Glr.*; *rtsód-pa ˌgrán-pa* to compete in disputation *Glr.* — *ťsád-mai rtsód-pa* a learned debate about words; *rtsód-pa-rnams* points of controversy *Tar.* 132,18, *Schf.* — *rtsod-γží* the subject of a disputation.

རྩོན(མ) *rtsón(-ma) Pur.* **nausea, vomiting,** **rtson ṗog** he grows sick; **rtsón-čas** **to be sick, to vomit.**

རྩོམ་པ་ *rtsóm-pa* I. vb., pf. *(b)rtsams, rtsoms,* fut. *brtsam*, imp. *rtsom(s)* 1. **to begin, commence** a work, **to be about, to set about** an undertaking; *ˌbrós-par brtsáms-te* being about to run away *Dzl.*; *čós-las brtsáms-te rtsód-do* it was about religion that our dispute began *Tar.*; *ṅo-lóg brtsáms-pa-las* beginning, stirring up an insurrection *Glr.*; *dé-nas brtsáms-te* beginning at this place, **from here, from that time** (cf. *bzúṅs-te* sub *bzúṅ-ba*). — 2. **to make, to accomplish,** *γsó-bai las mi brtsáṃ-mo* so he will not accomplish the business of healing; com. **to compose, to draw up,** in writing, *bstán-bčos rtsom-mi* author, writer, composer *Pth.*; *brtson-ˌgrús rtsóm-pa Dzl.* frq., to work diligently, carefully; **to take pains, to exert one's self,** *rtsóm-par*, or *rtsóm-pa-la mǩás-pa* a clever writer, an elegant composer, which title in Tibet is applied to any one, that exhibits in his style high-sounding bombast with a flourish of religious phrases; *čad rtsod rtsom γsum-gyi bšad-gra Glr.* prob. a school, in which religion is taught and explained, combined with disputations and written compositions. —

II. sbt. **beginning, commencement** (**आरंभ**), *rtsóm-pa daṅ-po* the first beginning *Ld.-Glr.*; **a doing, proceeding, undertaking, deed** *Tar.*

རྩོལ་བ་ *rtsól-ba* 1. vb. **to endeavour, to take pains, to give diligence;** *rtsól-bar* adv. **diligently, zealously;** *ǩyód-kyis rtsól-bai dús-la bab* now you must use dispatch *Pth.*; *rtsol-méd* **unsought,** *rtsol-méd ˌgró-bai don byéd-pa* to seek the welfare of beings without their caring for it *Glr.*; *srog rtsól-ba Lex.* and *Mil.*, acc. to *Sch.*: **to draw breath, to take fresh courage,** which seems to be implied by *dbugs rtsól-ba Ma.*; *nyal-po rtsol drag(-na)* if cohabitation is immoderately indulged in *Med.* — 2. sbst. **zeal, endeavour, exertion.** *rtsól-ba skyéd-pa* to use diligence *Zam.*

སྩོལ་བ་ *stsól-ba*, pf. and fut. *stsol* (**sól-wa, sál-wa**), 1. **to give, bestow, grant,** when the person that gives is respectfully spoken to, much the same as *γnaṅ-ba* q.v.; *stsál-du γsol* please to give, to grant etc. *Dzl.*; *bdág-gi lám-rgyags stsol čig* pray, give me provisions (provender) for the journey *Dzl.*; **to give back, to return** what had been lent *Dzl.*; **to grant, bestow, afford, give** (as a present); also for γtóṅ-ba **to send, to send out,** so at least in *W.*; further: *W.* *ǰa sal, śu-gu sal, deb-sal** please to give me some tea, to lend me some paper, pray, give me change; or more pressingly: *ǰa sal gos** I earnestly request you for some tea etc., I entreat you to . . .; *sal mi gos** I thank you, I do not want it; *bká-stsal-ba* v. sub *bka; dṅos-grúb stsól-ba* to bestow spiritual gifts(?). — 3. sometimes incorr. for *bsál-ba* (*sél-ba*) **to clean, to clear, to remove** *Dzl.*

བརྩད་པ་, བརྩམ་པ་ *brtsád-pa, brtsám-pa* v. *rtsód-pa, rtsóm-pa,* sometimes incorr. for *btsád-pa, btsám-pa.*

བརྩེ་བ་ *brtsé-ba* vb. **to love,** sbst. **love, affection, kindness,** nearly the same as *byáms-pa,* frq. preceded by *snyiṅ,* resp. *tugs,* q. v.; *brtsé-bas* out of love, kindness, e. g. *γnáṅ-ba* to give something out of love; **with love, lovingly, kindly,** e. g. *skyóṅ-ba* to protect; *brtsé-bai tsig* words of love, kind exhortations *Glr.*; *brtsé-bai p̔yag-bris* your very kind letter; *snyiṅ-brtse-ba,* resp. *túgs-brtse-ba = brtsé-ba; brtsé-ba-čan, brtse-ldán* **loving, affectionate, kind;** *brtse(-ba)-méd(-pa)* **unkind, unmerciful, ungracious;** *brse-γdúṅ* **love, affection,** *p̔a-má brtse-γdúṅ če yaṅ či žig bya* what could even parental love do? *Glr.; lha-p̔rúg γžón-nui brtse-γdúṅ de* this proof of love on the part of young goddesses towards me *Mil.*

བརྩོན་པ་ *brtsón-pa* 1. vb. with *la,* **to strive, to aim at, to exert one's self for,** *tsógs-pa-la* an accumulation of merits, frq.; *brtsón-par byéd-pa,* or *˳gyúr-ba,* also with *mṅón-par* preceding it; **to apply one's self,** *lás-la* to business, *tugs-dám-la* to meditation *Dzl., Mil.* — 2. sbst. (*Ssk.* वीर्य, *virtus*) **endeavour, effort, care, exertion,** *byá-ba-la brtsón-pa* alacrity, readiness to act *Wdṅ.*; more frq. *brtson-˳grús* v. below. — 3. adj. = *brtsón-pa-čan, brtson-ldán Mil.,* **diligent, assiduos, studious,** *sgrúb(-pa)-la* eager to obtain power over demons *Mil.*; *brtsón-par* **on purpose, with intention, wilfully;** as sbst. mostly *brtson-˳grús,* with *skyéd-pa, byéd-pa, rtsóm-pa* to use diligence, to show energy, zeal etc.; *brtson-˳grús drág-po* intense application; *brtson-˳grus-čan* **assiduous, studious,** *brtson-˳grus nyáms-te Stg.* having lost one's energy.

# ཚ

ཚ 1. the letter *tsa,* the aspirate of ཙ (cf. ཛ), sounded *ts.* — 2. num. fig.: 18.

ཚ་ *tsa,* 1. **hot,** v. *tsa-ba.* — 2. **grandchild,** v. *tsá-bo.* — 3. v. *tsa-tsa.* — 4. resp. **illness, complaint** *C.*

ཚྭ་ *tswa* **salt,** *tswa ˳débs-pa* **to salt,** with *la*; **tsa nyén-če* W.* to taste, to try, food prepared with salt; *k̔a-ru-tswa* **alum** *Med.*; *rgya-tswa* **sal-ammoniac** *Med.*; *lče-myaṅ-tswa* **alum** *Lt.*; *rdo-tswa* **rock-salt** *Cs.*; *ba-tswa* **impure soda,** v. *bá-mo.* — *bód-tswa Lt.?* — *lán-tswa = tswa.* — *tswa-k̔a* salt mine *Cs.* — **tsa-(k̔u-)čan* W.* **saline, salinous.** — *tswa-sgo* place where salt is found. — **tsa-tsé** **sal-ammoniac** *C.* — **tsa-ču** **salt-water, brine;** acc. to some, **vinegar** (?).

ཚ་སྐོར་ *tsa-skór* v. *tsá-bo.*

ཚ་ཁང་ *tsa-k̔áṅ* v. *tsa-tsá.*

ཚ་འཁྲུ་ *tsa-˳k̔rú* v. *tsa-ba.*

ཚ་ག་འབུ་ *tsá-ga-˳bu,* also *čá-ga-˳bu, tsag-tság* **grasshopper, locust** *C.*

ཚ་གཅིག་མ་ *tsa-γčig-ma* **thick blanket, quilt** *C.*

ཚ་ཆུ་ *tsa-ču* v. *tsa-ba.*

ཚྭ་ཚུ་ *tswa-ču* v. *tswa.*

ཚ་དྲག་ *ťsa-drág* **haste, hurry,** **ťsa-ḍág ǰhe šig* C.,* **ťsa-rág toṅ* W.* make haste! — adv. *tsa-drág-tu Sch.* but also **mā ťsa-rág šog* W.* come quickly, without delay!

ཚ་སྣ་ *ťsá-sna* **anxiety** about, **tender care** for a thing, ni. f; **ťsa-na-čan* W.* **solicitous, careful, attached,** **ťsa-na-méd-ǩan* W.* **indifferent, unfeeling, callous;** *ǩán-pe *ťsá-na ǩúr-ǩan* W.* one that has to care for the welfare of a household or community, superintendent etc.

ཚ་སྣག་ *tsa-snág Sch.* = *snág-tsa* **ink.**

ཚ་པན་ཚེ་ *tsa-pan-tséC.* **dresser, kitchen-table.**

ཚ་བིག་ *tsá-big Ld.* **a little.**

ཚ་བ་ *ťsá-ba* I. vb. **to be hot,** *só-ga-(la) nyi-mai ˛od-zér ráb-(tu-) ťsá-bas* as at the time of the Soga the rays of the sun are very hot.

II. sbst. 1. **heat,** *ťsá-bas ɣdúṅ-ba* to be tormented by the heat *S.g.*; *ťsá-bai dus-su* during the heat of the day, at noon, cf. *dro Mil.*; *ťsá-ba ni bsíl-bar gyúr-to* the heat changed into coolness *Dzl.*; *tsa ɣzér-ba* the burning of the heat, or of the sun *Sch.*; *ťsá-bai nad Lt.* the fever-stage in diseases; *tsa sél-ba* to cure an acute disease *Sch.*; *ťsá-bas rmyá-ba* to lose one's appetite in consequence of great heat *Sch.* — 2. **warm food,** *stér-ba, ˛drén-pa Mil.*; *tsa-ɣčig-ma* one that in twenty-four hours takes but one regular meal. — 3. **spice, condiment,** *ťsá-ba ɣsum* त्रिकुटक, black pepper, long pepper, ginger.

III. adj. (vulgo **tsém-mo* C.*, **tsán-te* W.*) 1. **hot, warm.** — 2. **sharp, biting, pungent,** of spices etc. — 3. **stinging, prickly, thorny** *Pth.* —

**Comp.** *ťsa-˛ǩru* colic, gripes *Lt.* — *ťsa-gón* forenoon *Sch.* — *ťsa-graṅ* 1. hot and cold. 2. (relative) warmth. — **tsan-gyal* W.* inflammatory fever. — *tsa-lčib* v. *lčib.* — **tsa-čú** 1. a hot spring *C.* 2. a warm bath *C.* — *tsa-bra* dinner *Sch.(?)* — *ťsa-mig* red pepper *Ld.* — **tsém-mo C.* hot, warm. — *ťsa-dmyál* hot hell. — *ťsa-zér* 'glowing ray', po. for sun. — **tsan-láṅ* W.* hot, passionate, ardent; in the rut — *tsa-lam Sch.*: half a day's journey, a march before breakfast, = *ťsal-mai lam.* — *tsa-bsubs Lt.?*

ཚ་བོ་ *ťsá-bo*, resp. *dbón-po B.*, *sku-tsa C.* 1. **grandchild, grandson,** *Ld.* **mē-mé-tsa-wo**. — 2. **nephew, brother's son** *Dzl.*; *Ld.*: **ȧ-žáṅ-ťsa-wo**. — *bú-tsa* v. *bu*; *yáṅ-tsa* **great-grandchild,** *yúṅ-tsa* **great-great-grandchild,** *ɣži-tsa* id. *Sch.* — *ťsa-skór* grandchildren *Sch.* — *ťsá-mo* 1. **granddaughter.** 2. **niece.** 3. **wife** *Lh.* — *ťsa-žáṅ* nephew and uncle *Mil.* — *ťsa-ɣzúg* nephews and nieces *Sch.* — *tsa-yúg* grandchildren, *tsa-yúg máṅ-poi čó-lo* the many grandchildren's tattling *Mil.*; offspring, in gen., *bu-tsa-yúg* id. *W., C.*; **ťsá-wo ťsa-yúg yáṅ-ťsa yúṅ-tsa* W.* children and children's children.

ཚ་མིག་ *tsa-mig* v. *ťsá-ba* comp.

ཚ་མོ་ *ťsá-mo* 1. v. *ťsá-ba.* — 2. v. *ťsá-bo.*

ཚ་ཚ་ *ťsá-ťsa* 1. little images of Buddha, and conical figures, moulded of clay and used at sacrifices *Schl.* 194, 206; *tsá-ǩaṅ* place for keeping them *Cs.*; fig. *ǩá-nas mé-yi ťsá-ťsa ˛pro* from his mouth proceeded cones of fire *Pth.* — 2. *Bal.* for *tsa-drág* **hastily, quickly;** *ťsa-ťsa-méd* **slow, slowly.**

ཚ་གཟུག་ *tsa-ɣzúg* v. *ťsá-bo.*

ཚ་ཟར་ *tsá-zar* v. *tsá-dar.*

ཚ་རག་ *tsa-rág* v. *ťsa-drág.*

ཚ་རུ་ *tsa-rú* **lamb-skin,** **ťsar-lág* W.* coat made of lamb-skins.

ཚ་ལ་ *tsá-la* a kind of medicine *Med.*, acc. to *Wdṅ.* = *dar-ťsúr.*

ཚ་ལུ་ *tsa-lú* 1. also *mtsa-lú*(?) **cock,** *bya (-po)-ťsá-lu Wdṅ., C.*; in *W.* applied only to red-breasted cocks, from *mtsal* vermilion (*Sch.* hen?). — 2. v. *ťsál-ba.*

ཚ་ལུམ་པ་ *tsa-lúm-pa C.* **sweet orange,** frq. in *Sik.*

ཚ་ལེ་ *tsá-le* 1. *Ssk.* सुभग, *Hd.* सुहागा, *Pers.* تنكار, *Ar.* بورق, **borax,** *ťsá-lei skyúr-*

**rtsi** boracic acid *Cs.*; *ťsa-le byéd-pa* to solder *Sch.*(?). — 2. *ťsá-le žáṅ-po Lh.*, n. of a flower, *Hemerocallis fulva.*

ཚག *ťsag*, 1. v. *ťsags*. — 2. *ťság-sgra* **an appalling tone** *Sch.*(?); **ťsag gyab** *W.* a stinging pain is felt. — 3. **ťsag-ṭ̔úg, ťsag-yá** *W.* **twins**; **ťsag-lúg** twin-sheep.

ཚག་པ་ *ťság-pa* (cf. *˳ťság-pa*), *mar ťság-pa* **oil-miller** *Sch.* — *ťság-ma* **sieve, filter,** also *ťsags*, q. v. — **ťsag-rẹ́** bolting-cloth, bolter *C.*, *W.* — *ťsag-ró* residuum after sifting, as bran etc.

ཚག་ཚིག *ťsag-ťsig* **dark spots** or **speckles,** on wood etc. *Mil.*; **freckles** *C.*

ཚག་ཚེ *ťsag-ťse* **bruised barley** or **wheat** *Sch.*

ཚག་ཤ་ *ťság-ša* **flesh of larger animals,** of cattle etc.

ཚགས *ťsags* 1. **cap,** *gos-ťságs* coat and cap *Dzl.* — 2. = *ťság-ma, ťsags-kyis, btsags Lex.*; *ko-ťságs* a sieve made of leather, the one most in use; *k̔rol-ťságs* = *ťság-ma Lex.*; *nya-ťságs* **weel,** for catching fish *C.* — 3. **thin-split bamboo,** for making baskets *Sik.* — 4. *Sch.*: **'the right sort, a choice article,** *ťsags-bzáṅ byás-nas* making a good choice'. — 5. **density**(?) **ťság-čan, ťsag-ťúg-mo** *W.* standing close together, e.g. trees, books; *ťsags-dám* dense and strong, as stuffs *Sch.*; *so ťsags-dam-žiṅ* the teeth standing close and firm *Glr.*; **ťsag čó-te dug** sit close together! *Ld.*; *ťsags-lhód* not dense or compact *Sch.*; relative density. — 6. *ťsags byéd-pa* (*W.* **čó-če**), *ťságs-su ˳ǰúg-pa* and *čúd-pa Mil.* **to save, spare, lay up** as provision for the future, *ťse p̔yi-mai grabs či yaṅ ťságs-su ma čud* I have not made any provision yet for the future life *Mil.*; **to economize, to be sparing,** *mé-la* of the fire; to be niggardly; *ťsags-˳dod-čan* **stingy, griping, avaricious.**

ཚང་ *ťsaṅ* 1. **nest,** *byá-ťsaṅ S.g.*; *ťsaṅ bzó-ba* to build a nest *Sch.*; **den, hole, lair, kennel, burrow,** *stág-ťsaṅ, wá-ťsaṅ, p̔yi-ťsaṅ* (cf. *p̔yi-ba*); **cell, honey-comb, hive,** *sbráṅ-ťsaṅ Cs.* — 2. variously applied to human places of abode: *γnas-ťsaṅ* **habitation, house;** *ťsáṅ ˳čá-ba* to build a nest, to establish a household *Schr.*; *grwa-ťsaṅ* v. *grwa*; **ťab-ťsáṅ** in *W.* the common word for **kitchen,** *γsól-k̔aṅ* being the resp. term for it; *ťsáṅ-zla* perh. brothers and sisters, beside *p̔a-má Mil.* — 3. v. *˳ťsáṅ-ba.*

ཚང་ཉུ་ *ťsáṅ-ṅu* **cradle** *Sch.*

ཚང་བ་ *ťsáṅ-ba* I. vb., pf. *ťsaṅs*, **to be complete, full, entire,** *zlá-ba dgu ťsáṅ-ba-na, ťsáṅ-ba daṅ, ťsáṅ(s)-nas* when the nine months were full, completed *Dzl.*, *zlá-ba ťsáṅ-du nyé-bas* towards the end of the months of pregnancy *Dzl.*; **dá-wa ťsaṅ soṅ = bud soṅ** *W.* the month is completed, is expired; *rgyál-po γčig* (also *γčig-gis*) *ma ťsáṅ-ba-la* as one king was still wanting, the number not being yet complete *Dzl.*; *ťsaṅ-nas yod* they are complete (in number) *Pth.* —

II. sbst. (seldom) **completeness, entireness,** *yin-min-gyi(s) ma-ťsáṅ-ba byuṅ-na* when there is no completeness, no absolute certainty as to right and wrong. —

III. adj. 1. **complete, entire;** more frq.: 2. **having things complete,** *yón-tan dé-ťso ťsáṅ-bai bú-mo* a girl in full possession of all these qualities *Pth.*; *k̔a-dóg lṅa ťsaṅ-ba* having all the five colours complete *Glr.*; *dbáṅ-po ma-ťsáṅ-ba* one not in full possession of his five senses *Glr.* — *ťsáṅ-ma* 1. **whole, entire, perfect** (the usual adjective form), *bya-p̔rúg ťsáṅ-ma žig* a perfect young bird, i.e. perfectly developed *Dzl.* — 2. esp. *W.* **all,** for *tams-čád.* — **ťsáṅ-ka** *W.* **all together, in all,** with regard to smaller numbers. — *ťsáṅ-po* forming a whole. — *ťsaṅ-skám* **perfectly** dry, *ťsaṅ-rlón* **perfectly** wet; *ťsaṅ-˳grig* **all right,** frq., **ťsaṅ-ḍig ǰhẹ́-pa* or *čó-če** *W.*

ཚང་ཚིང་ *ťsaṅ-ťsiṅ*, *Cs.*: **wood, grove, copse, thicket;** *Sch.*: a wild, dismal place; *ťsaṅ-ťsiṅ ˳k̔rigs-pa Sch.*: 'dense thicket; horrible and awful'; *'ťsaṅ-ťsiṅ srid-pai γnas* the horrible existence in the external world *Mil.*

ཚང་ཡ་ *ťsaṅ-yá* **double-barreled gun** *C.* and *W.*

ཚང་ར་ *ťsaṅ-ra* v. *˳ťsaṅ-ra.*

ཚངས *tsaṅs*, *W.* **kú-lig-gi tsaṅs**, key-hole, col. for *mtsams* (?).

ཚངས་པ *tsáṅs-pa* (evid. preterite of *₀tsáṅ-ba*) 1. **purified, clean, pure, holy,** *tsáṅs-par gyur čig* prob. be clean! be forgiven! *Dzl.* ༧༠༢, 13; *₀gyod-tsáṅs, mtol-tsáṅs,* v. the two; *tsáṅs-par spyód-pa, tsáṅs-pai spyód-pa spyód-pa, tsáṅs-par mtsúṅs-par spyód-pa* 1. to be clean, chaste, holy, to do what is right, to lead an honest, upright life. 2. to be a priest, to belong to a holy order, and as sbst. priest, cleric; *mi-tsaṅs-par spyód-pa,* not to be clean, chaste etc., esp. with *bud-méd-la* to commit one's self with a woman *Mil.* — *tsaṅs-skúd*, *Sch.:* 'holy cord, the bond of spirits' (?) — *tsaṅs-tig* **equator,** prob. of *Cs.*'s construction, cf. *dguṅ* extr. — 2. **ब्रह्म, Brahma,** an Indian deity transplanted into Buddhism; he is occasionally called *lha čén-po* (*Glr.*) and proverbial for his melodious voice, yet otherwise not of any consequence. — *tsáṅs-pai bú-ga* = *mtsóg-ma Med., Pth.*

ཚད *tsad* (cf. *tsod*) 1. **measure,** a. **in a general** sense, **size:** *če-čúṅ-gi tsád-la* according to the size, in size *Glr.*; *mi-tsad* size of a (full-grown) man *Tar.*; *sku-tsád* stature, size of body, resp. *Glr.*; *zlá-bai dkyil-₀kór-gyi tsad* the size of the moon's disk *Stg.*; *stobs gyad stóbs-po-čei tsád-du pyin-te* his strength was equal to that of a powerful athlete *Dzl.*; **ṭu súm-čui tsad čo gos* W.* make it thirty cubits in size; *kam-tsád-du γčód-pa* to cut into bits piecemeal *Dzl.*; *ču-rgyún kyab-tsád-du* as far as the waters covered it *Tar.*; *ṅóm-tsad(-du) ₀túṅ-ba* to drink one's fill; *γnás-tsad* seems to express chronology *Wdk.*; *mnan-tsad* direction how the pulse is to be felt (or pressed) *Med.*; *kyéd-rnams-kyi čós-bslab-tsad* according to your view of religious studies *Mil.*; *dró-tsad* thermometer, *graṅ-droi tsad* id.; *yaṅ-lčii tsad* barometer; *mto-dman-gyi tsad* scale for the rising and falling (of the barometer); all these appear to be proposals of *Cs.* for the respective physical terms; *pa-tsád* distance (v. sub *pa* II); *tsad-méd(-pa)* **unmeasured, immeasurable, innumerable,** e.g. *yón-tan Dzl.*; *tsad-med(-pa) bži* the four immeasurables (viz. merits): *byáms-pa, snyiṅ-rje, dká-ba* and *btaṅ-snyóm Dom.*, *spyod-pa* to practise them, *tob-pa* to attain to them *Dzl.*; *ṅa-bas mi tsad γžan yaṅ* an infinity of others besides me *Mil.*

b. **the full** measure, which is **not short** of the proper quantity, **standard,** *tsád-du pyin-pa, skyé-ba* (*Sch.* also *₀kyól-ba*) to grow, so as to reach the proper measure; *tsád-du skyés-pa* grown up, full-sized, adj. *Dzl.*; **tsẹ' žág-pa** to set up a pattern, or as a pattern *C.* *tsad-ldán* right (as weight), about the same as 'gaged', just, fair, with regard to persons (ni f.) *C.*

c. **the right** measure, which does **not exceed** the proper quantity: *tsád-γčod-pa* to limit, *bed-čód* the enjoyment *Mil.*; *bza-btúṅ-la* to observe the proper measure in eating and drinking, **tsẹ' dzim-pa,* or *žág-pa* C.* id.; *tsád-las ₀dá-ba, tál-ba* to exceed the proper measure frq.; *yid-pám-pa-la tsád-las ₀dás-pa yoṅ* the dejection increases to an excess *Mil.* — To 1, a. may be referred d. those instances in which the word assuming the character of an affix serves to form abstract nouns, such as *γdeṅs-tsád*, or *rtogs-tsád*, *Mil.* in several passages (cf. also *tsod*) further to 1, b may be reckoned e. the signification **all,** *dgé-ba byed tsad* all the pious *Pth.*, to which also *Tar.* 54, 15 may be referred; *sna-tsád* **of every kind, of all sorts** *Glr.*; **žẹ tsẹ' čụ'-du soṅ C.* all his eating agreed with him extremely well; *₀dir ldóm-bu-ba byuṅ tsad* all the beggars that show themselves here *Mil.*; *mi yoṅs tsad* all the people that come; *snaṅ tsad čós-skur šar* all that happens appears as *čós-sku Glr.*; *γsuṅ tsad* all that is ordered, proclaimed *Sch.*; *tsogs tsád* all the people assembled *Sch.*; and f. **enough,** esp with a negation: *₀dra-ba mi tsad* not having enough of the comparisons, not resting satisfied with them; **ma tsád-de* W.* = *ma zád-de B.* not only. — 2. a certain **definite measure,** in compounds: *dpag-tsád* **a** mile, *sor-tsád* an inch: also pleon. *kru-tsad* an ell *Cs.* = *kru.* — 3. **goal, mark,** the point to which racers run *C.*

— 4. *tsad rgyág-pa* **to guess, conjecture, suppose** *Sch.*, cf. *tsod.* — 5. sometimes for *tsád-pa* **heat**; for *tsad-ma* **logic**, *dbu-tsád* Madhyamika logic *Tar.* 179, 17, *Schf.*

ཚད་པ *tsád-pa* I. sbst. 1. **heat**, in gen.; *tsád-pa byuṅ-tse* when it grows hot *Glr.*; *tsád-pas γdúṅ-ba* to be tormented by the heat *Glr.*; *tsád-pas*, or vulg. *tsád-pa-nas*, *p̒óg-pa* to be struck by the heat, to receive a sun-stroke; also to be taken ill with dysentery, to which the Tibetans, used to the dry atmosphere of the northern Himalaya, are very liable, when during summer they venture into the southern subtropical regions; *tsád-čan* hot, e.g. *yul*; *tsad-ldán* prob. id.; *me-búm tsád-čan, Lt.* a hot cupping-glass (?). 2. morbid heat of the body, **fever** (*W.* **tsan-zug**); *tsad-pai nad* id., but also **dysentery**, v. above *Glr.*, *C.*; *tsad-pa žag-γnyis-ma* tertian fever *Schr.*; *gya-tsẹ' Sik.* Indian or jungle-fever; **roṅ-tsẹ'** *Sik* common intermittent fever. — II. vb. *Cs.*: **to measure,** = *tsád-du byéd-pa, tsad ˳ǰál-ba.*

ཚད་འབུ *tsád-˳bu* **grasshopper, locust** *Sch.*

ཚད་མ *tsád-ma*, प्रमाण *Cs.*: **'measure, rule, model, proof, argument; logic'**; *tsád-ma-pa*, or *-mk̒an*, *Cs.* logician, dialectitian; *tsád-mai bstan-bčós* a dialectical work *Pth.*; *tsad-ma γžuṅ* an original work on dialectics *Cs.*; *tsád-ma ˳grél-ba* commentary to it *Cs.*; *saṅs-rgyás-kyi bka tsád-mar bžág-pa* the words of Buddha reduced to a dogmatical system (?) *Pth.* — *tsád-ma kun-˳dús, tsád-ma sde bdun* titles of books mentioned by *Was.*

ཚན *tsan*, 1. a root = *tsa* in *tsá-ba* **hot, warm** *C.* and *B.*; *tsán-mo* (**tsẹ́m-mo**), *in W.* **tsán-te**, e.g. with *ču*, **ču tsẹ́m-mo** *C.*, **ču-tsán** *W.*, hot water *Dzl.*, warm water *Lt.*; *zan-drón tsán-mo* warm food *Lt.*; *ču-skól tsán-mo* boiling water *Mṅg.*; **ša tsọ́-pa tsẹ́m-mo** boiled meat, in Lhasa brought warm to the market; **tsẹn-˳ḍi táṅ-wa** *C.* to proceed capitally against, ni. f.; *tsán-te* **sharp, biting, pungent,** *W.* also sbst.: **spice,** esp. **red pepper.** — *tsan-žug W.* **fever.** — *tsan-ró Sch.*: **'hot,** the sensation of heat'. — 2. = *tsá-bo*: **p̒a-tsẹ́n** cousin by the father's, **ma-tsẹ́n** by the mother's side *C.*; *p̒a-tsán* also = *p̒a-spún*; *k̒u-tsán* v. *k̒ú-bo.* — 3. **series, order, class,** *sde-tsán* id.; *bži-tsán* a class or collection of four things, tetrad *Gram.*; *drug-tsán-du sdébs-pa* to put together in classes of six *Mil.*; *don-tsán Tar.* 96, 14, a certain class of ideas, range of thoughts *Schf.* — 4. as termination of some collective nouns: *γnyen-tsán, nye-tsan* **kindred, relations,** *nye-tsán bdúd-kyi bsol-˳débs yin Mil.*; *blón-po-tsan lṅá-po* the five embassies, ni f. *Glr.* — 5. *náṅ-tsan* **part,** of a country, **district,** *Tar.* 90, 20. — 6. *čos-tsan* any treatise under **a distinct head** or **title** in a volume *Cs.* — 7. **difference** *Sch.*; *le-tsan* different divisions, sections, chapters. — 8. **much, large, copious, great,** **k̒a tsan čin-te** *W.* much deep snow; *tsan-čé-ba, tsan-čen* **very much, a great deal,** *las ṅán ni tsan-čé* a great many bad actions *Thgr.*; *lo tsan-če-ba* a plentiful harvest, rich crop *Glr.*; hence *tsán-po* **a dignitary, grandee** *Pth.*; *k̒ams-tsán*, 1. **prefect of a provincial association,** in large convents, such as Sera and others. 2. **association, club.**

ཚབ *tsab* (cf. *˳tsáb-pa*), **representative,** com. *tsáb-po C., W.*, **kó-la tsáb-po yod** he has got a representative, proxy; in reference to a thing: **equivalent, substitute,** *des tsab ruṅ* it may be replaced by this, *tsab ruṅ tsam-mo* this may perhaps be used as a substitute *Wdṅ.*; **táb-p̒ii tsab čó-če** *W.* to use as a mop; *ṅas tsab byao* I shall supply his place *Tar.*; *tsáb-tu* **instead of, in the place of,** *már-mei* instead of a lamp, for a lamp *Glr.*; in *W.* **tsáb-la** very common. Chiefly in compounds: *sku-tsáb* resp. = *tsáb-po* **representative of a superior,** hence, as may be the case, **vice-roy, delegate, commissioner, agent.** — *rgyal-tsáb* v. *rgyál-ba.* — *do-tsab Schr.* prob. = *tsáb-po* = *sku-tsáb.* — *rta-tsáb* a thing given as an equivalent for a horse *Cs.* — *nor-tsáb* goods serving as a compensation for something else. — *p̒a-tsáb* **guardian, trustee.** — *bla-tsáb* representative of a Lama, **Vice-Lama.** — *bu-tsáb* **adopted child, foster-child.** — *mi-tsáb Schr.* **negociator, mediator; hostage** (?).

ཚབ་ཚབ་ *ṫsab-ṫsáb, mig ṫsab-ṫsáb byéd-pa* **to blink** or **twinkle** with the eyes *C.*, also *W.*

ཚབས་ *ṫsabs* 1. mostly with *če, čén-po*, **very great, very much**, *sdig-pa ṫsabs-čé-bar ˳dug* it proves a very great sin, *mgó-bo ˳ḱor ṫsabs-čé-na* when much dizziness intervenes *Lt.*; **ṭim-dhaṅ-gal ṫsab čém-po* C.*, great, serious transgression; *˳gál-ṫsabs-čan* sinning heinously. — 2. *ṫsábs-pa* and *-po Cs.*, who also designates it as resp., **peril, fear, sin** (rather questionable); **difficulty, trouble** (might perh. be more adequate); *búd-med ˳ó-ṫsabs-la ṗan Wdṅ.* it is of use in milk-diseases of the women.

ཚམ་དམ་ *ṫsam-dám* **noisy, blustering, alarming** *Sch.*

ཚམ་ཚུམ་, ཚམ་ཚོམ་ *ṫsam-ṫsúm, ṫsam-ṫsóm* (cf. *ṫsóm-pa, ṫé-ṫsom*) **doubt, hesitation, wavering,** *ṫsam-ṫsúm byéd-pa* **to doubt, hesitate, waver;** *ṫsam-ṫsúm-čan, ṫsam-me-ṫsom-mé* **doubtful, wavering, undecided,** *ṗan-ṫsúṅ ṗyág-la ṫsam-me-ṫsom-mér lús-pai ṫse* whilst both of them were uncertain as to saluting (who should salute first) *Pth.*

ཚའི་ཏའུ་ *ṫsai-tau* (Chinese) **chopping-knife** *C.*

ཚའི་སྐྱོགས་ *ṫsai-skyógs* **scoop, basting-ladle** *C.*

ཚར་ *ṫsar* 1. also *ṫser* **time** *Pth.* vulgo; *ṫsar-γčig* one time, once; *ṫsar γčig-la* also = *srib-γčig-la* in one moment; *ṫsar γsum* threefold, in three specimens, copies *Tar.*; *ṫsar bži Dzl.* ༧༢, 8, in four divisions, sorts, qualities (?) — 2. also *ṫsar-ṫsar* **ends of threads, fringes,** in webs, *ḱa-ṫsár Ld.* also *ru-ṫsár* fringes at the beginning, *ṗon-ṫsar* at the end of a web *Cs.* — 3. **thin strips of cane,** for wicker-work, *ṫsar-zám* cane-bridge *C.* — 4. *ṫsar-slág* v. *ṫsa-ru.* — 5. v. *˳ṫsar-ba.*

ཚར་བོང་ *ṫsar-boṅ* officinal plant in *Lh.*, *Carduus nutans*, but not agreeing with the description in *Wdṅ.*

ཚར་མ་ *ṫsár-ma*, fem. *ṫsár-mo Bal.* **old.**

ཚར་ཚར་ *ṫsar-ṫsar* v *ṫsar* 2.

ཚལ་ *ṫsal* 1. provinc. also *ṫsol*, **wood, grove,** as a place for hunting and recreation, *ṫsal stúg-po Dzl.*; *nags-ṫsál* id.; **garden,** *mé-tog-gi* flower-garden *Ph.*; *ṫsal yaṅ-ṫse* (*Chin.*) *C.* kitchen-garden. — 2. *smyu-gui-ṫsal* one kind of the fabulous food of man in the primitive world *Glr.*; also the 'unploughed rice' is called *˳bras sa-lu-ṫsal.* — 3. v. *mṫsal.*

ཚལ་པ་ *ṫsál-pa* (*Sch. ṫsal-ba?*) 1. also *šiṅ-ṫsal* **chip** (of wood), **splinter,** *nón-po* a sharp, piercing splinter *Dzl.*; **billet** *Glr.*; **thin board, veneer** etc.; **shiver, fragment,** *ṫsál-pa bdún-du gas Dzl.*; *ṫsál-bu* dimin., small chip or shiver *W.*: **ṫsál-bu ṫon soṅ** a small piece is broken out. — 2. **bunch,** of flowers, of ears of corn etc., a lock of hair cut off *W.*

ཚལ་མ་ *ṫsál-ma* vulgo for *dro*, **breakfast,** *ṫsal-ma *za-ba* **to breakfast,** *ṫsál-ma zá-ba-rnams* 'companions at a great man's table' (?) *Cs.*; *ṫsál-mai lam* = *ṫsa-lám* v. *ṫsá-ba* extr.; *ṫsal bóg-pa* = *dro btáb-pa* to make a morning-halt on a journey; *ṫsal-rtiṅ* the time from breakfast till dinner, opp. to *sṅá-dro*, q. v.

ཚས་ *ṫsas* (*ṫsás-po Cs.*) 1. *W.* for *ṫsal* **garden,** *ṫsas-skór, ṫsás-ḱaṅ* garden-bed, *ṫsás-mḱan* gardener. — 2. of a woman in child-birth: *ṫsas-kyis γso* (?) *Med.*

ཚི་ *ṫsi* num. fig.: 48.

ཚིཀ་ *ṫsi-ka* (or *ṫsi-rka?*) *C.* **furrow** in a ploughed field.

ཚིགུ་, ཚིག་གུ་ *ṫsi-gu, ṫsig-gu* 1. **kernel** or **nut** contained in the stone of a stone-fruit, *ḱám-bui* of an apricot *Lt.*, *C.* (*W.*: **rtsi-gu**). — 2. *Ld.* a large **muller** or **grinding-stone** = *ju-lúm*; **musket-ball, bullet.**

ཚི་བ་ *ṫsi-ba C.*, *W.* **ṫsi** **tough, viscous, sticky matter,** esp. **clammy dirt,** e.g. in the wool of sheep; *ṫsi dám-po* solid dirt, *bád-kan-gyi ṫsi-ba Med.* **tenacious slime;** *ṫsi(-ba)-čan* **sticky, clammy, dirty;** **ṫsi-du* W.* **dirty, unclean, filthy,** esp. in a religious sense, = **kyug-ḍho* C.*; **ṅe zúg-po ṫsi-du soṅ** **says** a girl euphemistically for: I have the menses.

ཚིག་ *ṫsig* 1. **word,** in its strict sense, '*bdé-bar γšégs-pa ni' bde-ba daṅ γšegs-pai ṫsig γnyis-las med, bde-bar γšegs-pa* **are only** two words, viz. *bde-ba* and *γšegs-pa Lex.*; *ₒdri-bai tsig* interrogative (word), such as *či; tsig sgrig-pa* to connect or arrange words; as a sbst.: **construction**, the order in which words are to be placed; **grammatical form**, *dá-ltar-gyi tsig* form of the present tense; *tsig-gróg-s, tsig-grógs-kyi dbáṅ-gis Tar.; Schf.*: 'by the force of construction' (?) *tsig-ₒgrél Tar.* **explanation of words**; *tsig-ₒgrós Sch.*: '**course of speech**, connexion of words'; *tsig-p̓rad, tsig-rgyán* **particle**, a small word not inflected; *tsig-ₒbrú Schr.*: **a separate word** or **syllable**, *tsig-ₒbrú-γnyer-pa Sch.* 'linguist, philologist, purist'; *tsig-ₒbru-lčibs Lex.?* — 2. **word, saying, speech,** subject of a discourse, *tsig-snyán(-pa)* kind word, friendly speech, *tsig-ǰám* id., *brtse-bai tsig* an affectionate word *Glr.*; **tsig-súb** *W.* hard, angry, bad words; **tsig-ṅán, tsig-zúr** *W.* id.; *rtág-par ma mtóṅ-bai tsig tos-nas* always receiving the answer, that (she who was sought) had not been seen; *tsig-med-par ₒgyúr-ba* not being able to utter a word (from pain) *Dzl.; but k̓a-tsig-méd-par γsól-ba ₒdébs-pa Mil.* prob. to pray without hypocrisy; *tsig nyúṅ-la don čé-ba Mil.* saying much in few words; *tsig-k̓yál-pa = kyal-ka Dzl.*; *γžán-gyi tsig γčod-pa* to interrupt one in his speech; *tsig-γsal* **a clear word, perspicuous style** *Cs.*; *tsig-ₒból* **easy** or **fluent style** *Cs.*; *tsig-la mk̓as-pa* skilful in selecting words *Cs.*; *bdén-tsig* v. *bdén-pa* extr.; *brdzún-tsig* **falsehood, lie** *Cs.*

ཚིག་གུ *tsig-gu* v. *tsi-gu.*

ཚིག་པ *tsig-pa* 1. v. *ₒtsig-pa.* — 2. sbst., *W.* also *tsig-po* **anger, indignation, vexation, provocation,** *tsig-pa zá-ba* **to be angry** *Pth.*, frq.; **tsig(-po) k̓ol** *W.* his anger kindles.

ཚིག་པོ *tsig-po* 1. = *tsig Cs.* — 2. v. *tsig-pa* 2.

ཚིགས *tsigs*, less frq. *tsigs-pa, tsigs-ma* 1. **member** between two joints, hence *tsigs-mtsáms* joint *S.g.*; **joint**, *sor-tsigs* the joints of the fingers, **knuckles** *Cs.*; *tsigs ₒbúd-pa Cs.*, **ṭúl-če, bóg-če** *W.* to put out of joint, **to dislocate, to sprain;** *tsigs ǰúg-pa* to reduce a dislocated joint *Cs.*; *tsigs-nád, tsigs-zúg* articular disease, pain in the joints, gout; joint of the back-bone, **vertebra; spine,** also *sgal-tsigs*, vulgo *tsigs-rús*, hence **tsig-gúr** *W.* hump, hunch; **joint, knee, knot,** *sog-tsigs* knot of a stalk of corn or straw, *smyug-tsigs* knot of cane *Cs.*; member of a generation *Glr.*; **metrical division, verse,** *tsigs-su bčád-de smrá-ba* to speak in verse, *tsigs (-su) bčad(-pa)* **strophe, stanza,** *tsigs-bčád byéd-pa* to compose verses, to speak in verse *Dzl.*; *dus-tsigs* **division of time,** e.g. season *Pth.* — 2. *tsigs-ma* **sediment, residuum, residue,** *smán-gyi* of a medicine *Dzl.*; *már-gyi Dzl.* olive-husks, oil-cake; *tsigs-ró = tsigs-ma.*

ཚིབ(ས) *tsib(s), tsib-nad* **measles** *Sch.*

ཚིམ་པ *tsim-pa* vb. **to be content;** gen. adj. **content, satisfied, satiated, consoled,** frq.: *yid tsim-par gyur* he was satisfied, appeased, consoled; *ǰi ₒdód-pai yid tsim-ste* all her (their) wishes being satisfied *Glr.*; *dga-bdés tsim-par gyúr-čiṅ* being indeed over-happy *Pth.*; *tsim-par byéd-pa* to satisfy, with the dat. or accus. of the person.

ཚིམ་ཚིམ *tsim-tsim, mig tsim-tsim ₒdug C.* the eye is **dazzled.**

ཚིར *tsir* **order, course, succession, turn,** prob. only col., **ṅá-la tsir yoṅ* or *bab** it is my turn; **ná-so tsir-la** succession by seniority; **gán-tsir žón-tsir** id.; **tsir-la, tsir-du, tsir daṅ** by turns, every one in his turn or course, one thing after the other.

ཚིར་བ *tsir-ba* v. *ₒtsir-ba.*

ཚིལ *tsil* **fat,** not melted, *tsil-bu* id. *S.g.*; *lúg-tsil* **mutton fat,** *p̓ág-tsil* pork-fat, **bacon;** *k̓ál-tsil, k̓óg-tsil, gród-tsil* **suet, lard;** *sbó-tsil* **bacon;** *lóṅ-tsil* **intestinal fat.** — *spra-tsil* **wax** *B., C.* (*W.* **mum**); *tsil-ku* liquid fat, in the living body, or melted fat *Pth.* — *tsil-čan, tsil-ldán* **fat,** *tsil-méd* **lean.** — *tsil-ró* remains of lard after melting. — *tsil-šúbs* 1. **straight-gut, rectum** *Med.* 2. **sausage** *Cs.* —

ཚིལ་དིང *tsil-diṅ Ld.* **mortar and pestle.**

ཚིས *tsis Mil., Thgy.* prob. secondary form of *rtsis.*

ཚུ་ *tsu* 1. num. fig.: 78. — 2. the contrary of *p̓a* II., root of the words signifying **hitherward, on this side**; *tsú-k̓a Cs.* (*tsúr-k̓a* q v.), more frq. *tsú-rol* **this side** (opp. to *p̓á-rol*), *tsú-rol-na* adv. **on this side**, postp. with genit. adj. **on this side**; *tsú-rol-tu*, this way, to this place; *tsú-rol-nas* from this side; *tsú-rol-pa* one on this side, one belonging to this (our) party *Stg.*; *tsu-bi* one of this side, *p̓a-bi* one of the other side *Cs.*, provinc. (?). Cf. *tsun, tsur.*

ཚུའུ་ *tsu-u*(?) *C.*, prob. Chinese, for the Tibetan *skyúr-ru*, acc. to some: **vinegar,** acc. to others: **a pulpy product,** prepared of various kinds of fruit, mixed with vinegar, sugar, and spices, and having been left to ferment, used, like mustard, as a condiment, which in India is called 'chutney'.

ཚུག་ *tsug* 1. *Sch.:* **'group, object'** (?); *tsúg-so W.* all the households or villages placed under one Gopa. — 2. rarely for *tsug*; thus *ǰi-tsug Glr.* 49, inst. of *či-tsug*.

ཚུག་པ་(ལ་) *tsúg-pa*(*-la*) *W.* **to, up to, till,** *gaṅ tsúg-pa* **how far, how long?** **ṅa Nyúṅ-ti-ru čá-če tsúg-pa-la** until I go to Sultanpur; *gaṅ tsúg-pa ... de tsúg-pa* **so far as.**

ཚུགས་པ་ *tsugs-pa* 1. v. *ₒtsugs-pa.* — 2. **to do one harm, to hurt, to inflict,** mostly with a negative, *bar-čád ma tsúgs-par* without having hurt me *Mil.*; *ṅá-la mes, nad-kyis* etc. *mi tsugs* fire, disease etc. can do me no harm, *Glr., Mil.*, frq. — 3. sbst., also *tsúgs-k̓aṅ*, *W.* **tsug-sa**, **caravansary,** or merely a level, open place near a village, where traveller's may encamp, or where public business is transacted; also for **धर्मशाला, hall of judgment; hospital.**

ཚུད་པ་ *tsud-pa* v. *ₒtsud-pa.*

ཚུན་ *tsun* = *tsu* 2., gen. with *čad* or *čad* or *la*, signifying **within, by, not later than,** as postp. c. accus., *rabs bdun tsun-čád* within seven generations, (they will be happy) even to the seventh generation, *Dzl.*; *sáṅ-gi nyi-ma-p̓yéd tsún-la* by to-morrow noon (it must be finished) *Glr.*; **dá-wa če' tsun 'é leb** *C.* shall he come in less than half a month? *bu daṅ bú-mo tsun-čád* even to the children, not even the children being excluded *Tar.* 119, 3. —

Note. In the terms *p̓an* **and** *tsun*, like *yan* and *man*(*-čad*), the significations given by *Cs.:* **from, from a certain place or time forward, till, until,** are not properly inherent to the word, but are to be inferred in each separate instance from the figurative application of the original sense of the root.

ཚུབ་མ་ *tsúb-ma, ₒtsúb-ma* **storm,** *tsub-čéb, rluṅ-tsúb* **gale, hurricane,** *k̓a-tsub* snow-storm; *bu-tsub* (*p̓u-tsub?*) gust of wind, (*lha*) *ₒdrei bu-tsub* whirlwind; fig. *p̓rag-dóg-gi tsúb-ma Mil.* **a violent fit of envy;** *sems-tsúb* **trouble of mind** *Cs.*

ཚུར་ *tsur* **hither, to this place, hitherward** (cf. *p̓ar*), *tsur šog* (resp. *γšegs*, in later lit. *byon*) come hither, come here! also in an objective sense: *tsur ˛óṅ-ba* **to return home** *Pth., Tar.*; *ₒdi-nas tsur bšád-nas* speaking to me through this (tube) *Glr.*; almost pleon. in *tsúr-la nyon* listen to me! *Mil.* frq.; *tsúr-ka* **this side,** the this side river-bank, declivity, party etc., similarly: *tsúr-logs, tsúr-p̓yogs.*

ཚུར་(མོ་), མཚུར་(མོ་) *tsúr*(*-mo*), *mtsúr*(*-mo*) **colouring matter, pigment,** prob. = *sa-tsúr Stg.*, acc. to *Cs.* **mineral paint,** *nag-* black, *ser-* yellow, *dmar-tsúr* red-paint; for *nag tsúr Sch.* has: green vitriol; in *Zam.* also *rús-kyi tsur* is named.

ཚུལ་ *tsul* शील 1. **manner, way, form, character, nature,** *tsul ǰi-ltar ... de bžin-du* as — so *Wdṅ.*, *zér-tsul, ₒgrúl-tsul, bsám-tsul* the way in which a person speaks, walks, thinks; *γnás-tsul* v. *γnás-pa*; *γnás-tsul* and *snáṅ-tsul* **being** and **appearing,** philosoph. terms for **reality** and **appearance** *Was.* (297); *γtóṅ-tsul* the way of giving, i.e. a certain quantity given, dose *Stg.*; *mi sdug-pai sna-tsógs-kyis* (to damage) in various vicious ways *Mil.*; *tsul de k̓ó-nas* **by that same** way of proceeding *Tar.*; hence *tsúl-gyis* in consequence of, by means of *Pth.* and elsewhere; *snan smrás-pai tsul* the character of his last speech *Dzl.*; *rgya-bód-kyi ₒbrél-tsul* the mode or kind of intercourse, the

ཚ

relations between Tibet and China *Glr.; p̓yág-gi tsúl-du* in a way as if he were saluting *Mil.*; *gus-gús-kyi tsúl(-du) byéd-pa* to make a semblance of veneration, to make gestures of reverence *Mil.; mi mk̓yén-pai tsúl-du byás-te* pretending not to know *Mil.;* (cf. *tsúl-₀čos-pa* v. *čos-pa*); *dge-slóṅ-gi tsúl-du* in the guise of a monk *Tar.; mai tsul ₀dzin-pa* to assume the mother's form, figure *Tar.; glaṅ-čén-gyi tsúl-du*, (Buddha came down) in the shape of, or as, an elephant *Glr.*; *dád-pai tsúl-gyis* in the way of faith, with a believing mind *Pth.; mi-rtág tsúl-du γda* it exists in the way of transientness, it is of a transitory nature *Mil.; mdzád-pa bču-γnyis-kyi tsúl-gyis* in the manner, in the order, of the twelve deeds *Glr.*; *šas čé-bai tsúl-gyis* for the most part, *Tar.* 50, 15; **way of acting, conduct, deportment, course of life,** *sṅá-mai tsul* your former conduct *Mil.*; *dé-lta-bui dgé-bai tsul de t̓ós-nas* hearing such an example of virtue related. — 2. emphat.: **the right way**, good manners, order, rule; *tsul (daṅ) mt̓ún(-pa)* **orderly, regular, sensible, reasonable,** *brgyá-la tsul-mt̓ún re tsam ₀byúṅ-na Mil.* if but once in a hundred cases something sensible is uttered; *tsul-ldán, tsúl-čan* regular, methodical *Cs.*; also **just**, conformable to duty, *tsúl-bžin-pa* adv. *tsul-bžin-du* id.; *tsul-méd, tsul-bžin-min* **irregular, unjust** *Cs.; srid-žui tsul spyód-čiṅ* fulfilling a child's duty; *tsúl-las nyams* **growing remiss in one's duty,** neglecting, breaking one's duty; esp. *tsúl-k̓rims* **religious or moral duty, moral law; monastic vows,** *tsúl-k̓rims-čan* 1. being bound by such *Sch.*; 2. observing such *Cs.; tsúl-k̓rims srúṅ-ba* to keep them, *₀jig-pa, nyáms-pa* to break them; *tsúl-k̓rims,* as a personal name, is much in favour. — 3. **species, kind,** *nád-tsul* species or kind of disease, *zás-tsul* species of food *S.g.* (not frq.). — 4. joined to the root of a verb: *yóṅ tsul,* **when,** or **as,** he came, *W.*

ཚེ་ *tse* I. num. figure: 108.

II. sbst. 1. **time,** in a gen. sense, = *dus B.; yód(-pai) tse(-na),* **when** it is, **when** it was; *gáṅ(-gi) tse(-na), de(i) tse(-na)* **at which time, at that time, then,** frq. *tse-ré* all the time(?), *nyin-tse-ré* the whole day, *tsan-tse-ré* the whole night *W.* — 2. **time of life,** **tse-ghaṅ-tsǫn-čug** imprisonment for life *C.*; *tse γčig-gi drós-pai gos* v. *drós-pa;* **life,** *tse ₀di* this, the present, life, *tse-p̓yi(-ma)* a future period of life (also merely: *₀di p̓yi,* without *tse*); *tse sṅá-ma* an earlier period of existence, relative to the transmigration of souls, yet *tse ₀di* and *p̓yi* may also be used in a Christian sense; *tse riṅ-ba* long life, *tsę t̓úṅ-ba* short life; *tse-riṅ* is also a very common name both of men and women; *rgyál-ba daṅ tse-riṅ-bar šóg-čig* happiness and long life (to the king)! *Dzl.; tse(-daṅ) -ldán(-pa),* आयुष्मान्, title or epithet of Bodhisattwas; *tse-dpag-méd* name of Buddha; **tse p̓id-če** *W.* to earn a livelihood; *tse ₀k̓yér-žiṅ šór-ba* to come off with one's life, to have a narrow escape; *tse t̓ár-du ₀júg-pa* v. *t̓ár-ba*; *tse(-las) ₀dás(-pa)* having died *Dzl.* — 3. *Bal.* **sex,** **p̓ó-tse, mó-tse**, male, female sex.

**Comp.** *tse-skábs* v. *skabs.* — *tse-čú* water of life *Glr.* — *tse-γnyis-pa* of an amphibious nature *Cs.* — *tse-ltógs* a poor, starving vagrant, beggar *W.* — *tse-mdáṅs Lt.* = *byad-mdaṅs* healthy appearance, a fine, fresh complexion. — *tse-tsád* duration of life. — *tse-mdzad, Wdk.* 457, an attribute of the gods, resembling a small plate with fruit. — *tse-rábs* period of existence, duration of a re-birth, a great many of which acc. to Buddhist doctrine every man has to pass through *Dzl.; tse-rábs-kyi blá-ma Mil.* a man that is always re-born as a Lama.

ཚེ་པད་ *tse-pád Ephedra saxatilis*, a little alpine shrub with red berries, which are said to be roasted and pulverized, to give greater pungency to snuff.

ཚེ་རེ་ *tse-ré* 1. v. *tse.* — 2. v. *tsér-ka.*

ཚེག་ *tseg W.* **tsag** 1. **point, dot,** also *nag-tség.* — 2. more particularly **the point separating syllables,** *bar-tség,* id.; *p̓yi-tség* likewise, in as far as it follows a letter *Gram.*; *tseg-bar* that which stands between **two** points or tsegs, **a syllable.**

ཚེགས *tsegs* **troublesome, difficult, hard,** *tsegs-če* very troublesome, *rkaṅ tsegs-čé* ***Mil.*** much (fruitless) running to and fro; ***tsegs-méd*** it is not difficult; *tsegs-méd(-par)* easily adv.; *tségs-pa* trouble, toil, difficulty *Sch.; ṕran-tsegs* little troubles or difficulties *Cs.*

ཚེམ(པོ) *tsém(-po)*, **seam,** cf. *ₒtsém-pa; tsém-bzo-pa, tsém-pa* **tailor** *W.*; *tsém-po ₒgrol* the seam opens, comes loose; *tsem-méd* without a seam; *tsém-bu Lex., Sch.*: what has been stitched, darned, quilted.

ཚེམས *tsems*, resp. **tooth,** *tséms-šiṅ* tooth-pick *Dzl.*

ཚེམས་པ *tsems-pa* to have the disadvantage, to come off a loser, not receiving a full share *Sch.*

ཚེར *tser* 1. = *tsar* **time** vulgo; *tser-tsér, Mil.*, prob. **many times, repeatedly.** — 2. v. the following.

ཚེར་ཀ *tsér-ka W.* also *tse-ré, tse-ri* **sorrow, grief, pain, affliction,** **tse-ré čo mi go** do not grieve! **tser čúg-če** to afflict, to grieve (not in *B.*).

ཚེར་མ *tsér-ma, W.***tser-máṅ** 1. **thorn, prick, brier,** *Dzl. tser zug soṅ* I have run a thorn into (my hand, foot); *tser-mai mgo* a deer's head po. spoken of *Mil.; tsér-ma ₒdón-pa* to pull out a thorn; *nya-tsér* fish-bone *Sch.*; *tsér-ma-čan* 1. thorny, prickly, briery. 2. like thorns, *Thgy.*— 2. **thorn-bush, bramble, brake** *tser-dkár, tser-stár*, buck-thorn, *Hippophaë rhamnoïdes*, **tser-tar-lú-lu** *Ld.*, the berries of it (extremely sour). — *tser-tágs* thorn-hedge (in Tibet gen. dead hedges). — *tser-lúm* yellow raspberry *Sik. tser-lhág* n. of a disease *Lt.*

ཚེས *tses* अहन्, 1. **day of the month,** *tses-gráṅs* **date,** always expressed by the cardinal number, *tses-γčig* etc., *tses-bčú* the tenth, in certain months a festival day, *tses-bču-mčód-pa* sacrifice and beer-drinking on that day; *tses-bčúi ₒčám-yig* programme of the religious dances performed on that occasion; *zlá-ba tsés-pa* and *tses-γsum-zlá-ba.* — 2. symb. num.: 15.

ཚོ *tso* 1. num. figure: 138. — 2. sbst. **troop, number, host,** yet hardly ever standing alone, or governing a genit. case, but like a termination affixed: *gróṅ-mi-tso* the peasants (of the village), *kyéd rnál-ₒbyor-pa-tso* ye saints! In some instances its substantive character is more apparent, thus in *tsóṅ-pa-tso, mkás-pa-tso, bá-tso* it may be rendered by: **a troop of merchants, a society of learned men (or the learned), a herd of cows** (*Cs.*); but most frq. it stands (at least in later lit.) as plural termination of pronouns, so: *ṅéd-tso* **we,** *koṅ-tso* **they,** *ₒdi-tso* **these,** or it is affixed to numerals: *ₒbum-tso* 100 000. — *yul-tso* v. *yul.* — 3. adj. **hot** *Bal.*

ཚོ་བ *tsó-ba* **fat, greasy,** *tso-kú* fat gravy, *tso-ldír* unwieldy with fatness (*tso ₒdug mi ₒdug*, or *bud ma bud*, is it fat or not? being with young or not? *Sch.?*)

ཚོ་ལོ *tsó-lo W.* vulg. = *ₒṕoṅs*, cf. *ₒṕoṅ-tsos.*

ཚོགས *tsogs Ssk.* गण, (cf. *ₒtsógs-pa*) 1. **an assemblage** of men (implying, however, compared with *tso*, a larger number of individuals, not at once to be surveyed), *Cs.*: *tsogs sdú-ba* to call an assembly, *ₒgyéd-pa* to dismiss it; *tsogs ₒdu* an assembly meets, *ₒgye* it dissolves; *W.*:**šol soṅ** it is adjourned, **tol soṅ** it is broken up; *dpuṅ(-gi), dmag (-gi)-tsogs* army frq.; *yul-tsogs* village community, country-parish, **yul-tsog nyi laṅ-te yod** *W.* two parishes have set out; **human society,** *tsógs-kyi náṅ-nas ₒbyúṅ-ba Stg.*, **tsog dhaṅ gyé-wa** *C.* to retire from society; *tsógs-naṅ mi ₒgró-ba* not mixing with society *Dó.; čós-tsogs* has been introduced by us, with the concurrence of our native Christians, as the word for **'congregation, church,** ἐκκλησία'. — 2. **accumulation, multitude,** of things, **šiṅ-tsog** *W.* wood, thicket, copse, bush, shrub; *mé-tsogs* mass of fire, *Thgy.*; in a more special sense = *dgé-bai tsogs*, or *bsód-nams-kyi tsogs*, accumulation of merit acquired by virtue, *tsogs γsóg-pa* to accumulate such frq.; *tsogs ma bság-pai mi* almost the same as a wicked, godless person; *tsogs(-kyi) ₒkor(-lo)*, गणचक्र, sacrificial offering, a quantity of victuals, trinkets, and other articles being disposed in

ཚ

a circle as an oblation, *Mil.* and elsewh.; *tsogs-ₒkór skor-ba* prob., like *śóm-pa* to prepare such an offering; *tsogs γnyis Glr.* was explained by *bsod-nams-kyi tsogs daṅ ye-śes-kyi tsogs*; *sna-tsógs* of all kinds, merely signifies 'many'. — 3. *tsogs drug Mil.* and elsewh., *Was.* 290, **'kinds' of perception** by the senses, which are supposed to be more or less in number, yet the etymology of the word rather suggests the groups of objects perceptible by means of the (6) senses. —

**Comp.** *tsogs-kàṅ* meeting-house *Cs.* — *tsogs-ₒkór* v. above. — *tsogs-grál Mil.* 1. row of people in an assembly 2. row of offerings, ni f. — *tsógs-čan-ma Sch.* 'song-stress, prostitute'. — *tsogs-mčóg* a most splendid assemblage, *tsogs-mčog-dge-ₒdún Thgy.* — *tsogs-γtám* speech addressed to a meeting *Cs.* — *tsogs-stón* a high sacrificial festival *Pth.* — *tsogs(-kyi)-bdág(-po)* गणेश, son of Siwa, the god of wisdom, furnished with a thick belly and the head of an elephant; appears also in the Buddhism of later times. — *tsogs-dpón* president or chairman of a meeting *Cs.* — *tsogs-záṅs Sch.*: 'the meeting-kettle, the point of union or its symbol'. — *tsogs-sa* place of meeting *Cs.* — *tsogs-γsóg* accumulated merit, tantamount to offerings and gifts bestowed on priests, also any service or work done to or for a priest *Mil.*

ཚོང་ *tson* (*Cs.* = *zon* merchandize, but more corr.:) **trade, traffic, commerce,** **pag-tsón** *W.* smuggling-trade, **čó-če, táṅ-če**; *tsóṅ-gi ke* profit, gain, *gun* loss in trading; *tsoṅ byéd-pa Glr.*, **gyag-pa** *C.*, **gyab-če** *W.* (cf. above), to carry on trade; *tsoṅ brgúd-pa* id. *Sch.*

**Comp.** *tsoṅ-skad* commercial language, business-like style, terms of trade. — *tsóṅ-kaṅ* store-house, magazine. — *tsoṅ-gru* trading-vessel, merchantman. — *tsóṅ-grogs* commercial friend, correspondent. — *tsoṅ-čaṅ* pledging in beer, after a bargain has been struck. — *tsóṅ-čad* bill of purchase, deed of sale. — *tsoṅ-mtun* commercial intercourse. — *tsóṅ-ₒdus* market people *Pth.* — *tsóṅ-ₒdus-sa* market-place. — *tsóṅ-rdal* that quarter of a city which is chiefly inhabited by merchants. — *tsoṅ-pa* **merchant, trader, seller;** *ₒbru-tsoṅ-pa* corn-merchant, *čaṅ-tson-pa* dealer in wine and other liquors. — *γser-daṅ-dnul-(gyi) tsóṅ-pa* exchanger of gold and silver coins. — *tsóṅ-dpon, Hind. čaudhari*, head of a commercial establishment, the principal merchant in a city, under whose control all the rest, and the market in general, are standing; the chief leader of a caravan, to whom all that have joined in it are subordinate *Glr.* — *tsoṅ-spógs* proceeds of trade; *tsoṅ-spógs byéd-pa, tsoṅ-spógs-la ₒgró-ba* to engage in commercial speculations *Dzl.* — *tsoṅ-ₒprúl* commerce, *tsoṅ-ₒprúl-gyi γnas* market. — *tsoṅ-zán* (cf. *tsoṅ-čáṅ*) meal after settling a business. — *tsoṅ-zóṅ* goods, merchandize. — *tsóṅ-sa* commercial place, market.

ཚོང་ཚོང་ *tsoṅ-tsóṅ* 1. a kind of **ornament** *Cs.* 2. = *tsoṅ-tsóṅ*.

ཚོད་ *tsod* (prop. the same as *tsad*) 1. **measure, proportion,** in a general sense = **the right and just measure;** *tsod ₒdzin-pa*, (*bzúṅ-ba*) *W.* **zúm-če** 1. to take measure, to measure, to measure out, to survey, *yul* land, **yul-tsód-zum-kan** land-surveyor *W.* 2. to estimate, to rate, to appraise, to tax, *raṅ-gi tsod mi ₒdzin* he overrates himself (his own powers) *Dzl.* 3. to observe the right measure, to be temperate, *zas-čáṅ-la* in eating and drinking *Glr.*; *zás-tsod ma zin čuṅs gyúr-na* when below the proper measure, i.e. when too little is eaten *S g.* 4. to try, to tempt, to lead into temptation *W.*; *tsod-ltá-ba, lén-pa B.* and vulg., *Cs.* also *tsod bgám-pa* **to try, prove,** **tsod ma ltos** I have not tried it yet *W.*, **tig-tsód ma ltos** id., *tsod ltá-ba, len-pa* also **to sound, to sift, examine, spy out,** *tsód-len-pa* sbst., **spy;** *séms-kyi* or *nyáms-(kyi) tsod lén-pa* to examine, find out or sift another's thoughts or sentiments, also **kog-tsǫ' lém-pa** *C.*; *tsod ₒjal-ba* to measure; *tsod-śes-pa* **to keep measure,** and adj.: **observing due measure, temperate,** *tsod-mi-śés-pa* not keeping measure, intemperate. — *tsod-čan, tsod-ldan* 1. **moderate.** 2. **punctilious, strict, grave** *W.* — *tsod-méd* intemperate, immoderate, impudent. — 2 **measure, instrument for measuring,** *ču-ṫsód* water-clock. — 3. **division, portion, quantity,** *ṫsod-čig* part, **nor ṫsod čig** part of the money, of the estate *W.*; esp. of time, **point of time,** certain hour, cf. *ču-ṫsod* and *dus-ṫsod; *duṅ ṗú-če ṫsód-la* W.* at the time when the signal with the trumpet is given; **ṫsam ṫsod* W.*, at which hour? — 4. **estimation, supposition, conjecture, guess;** *ṅai ṫsod-la* according to my estimation, *ṫsod* *ₒdzin-pa* v. above; **dha léb-pe̱ ṫso̱' yo̱'** by this time he will have arrived, I guess *C.*; hence **ṫsod-če* W.* to guess; *ṫsód-šes, ṫsód-bya* **riddle** *Cs.*, *ṫsód-šes smrá-ba* to propose a riddle, *mi-ṫsod* about men, *bem-ṫsód* about inanimate objects *Cs.*(?); **ṫsod-ṫsód* W.* at random *Sch.* — 5. *ṫsod* affixed to an adj. serves to form abstract nouns, thus: *rnyéd-par dká-ṫsód* the difficulty of obtaining, *ₒǰig-par slá-ṫsod* the facility of destroying, *ṗan-ₒdógs čé-ṫsod* the greatness of the advantage *Thgy.*

ཚོད་མ་ *ṫsód-ma* 1. **vegetables, greens,** *ṫsód-ma rgod-skyés Cs.*: wild-growing greens, frequently gathered by the Tibetans in spring-time, such as dandelion, nettles, Eremurus etc.; *ṫsód-ma γyuṅ-skyés Cs.* cultivated vegetables. — 2. **boiled greens, vegetable-soup** *Mil.* and vulgo. — *sṅo-ṫsód* = *ṫsód-ma*; *nyuṅ-ṫsód* a dish of roots, turnips etc. *Cs.*; *ldum-ṫsód* a variety of roots *Cs.*(?) — *lo-ṫsód* all sorts of cabbage; *ša-ṫsód Cs.*, 'meat',(?) or more probably: prepared mushrooms. — *ṫsod-sdér* **plate, dish** *Sch.*

ཚོན་ *ṫson*, I. (cf. *ṫso-ba* and *ṫsos*) **colour,** 1. colouring matter, **paint,** = *ṫsón-rtsi*, or *rtsi-ṫsón*; *ṫsón-rtsi dkár-pos ₒbri-ba* to mark with white paint; *ₒbyúg-pa* **to paint;** *ṫson lén-pa* to take, imbibe colour *Cs.; ṫson sbyór-ba* to mix, to prepare colours *Cs.*; *ṫsón-gyis btso-ba* **to colour, to dye;** *ṫson-skúd* dyed thread *Do.*; *ṫson-spél* a coloured strip *W.* — 2. **colour** = *mdog W.* — II. v. *mṫson.*

ཚོན་པོ་ *ṫson-po* 1. **fat, plump, well-fed** *W., C.* 2. **resinous.**

ཚོན་མོ་སྟེང་ *ṫson-mo-steṅ* a metal (not known) *Stg.*

ཚོབ་ *ṫsob* for *ṫsab Sch.*

ཚོམ་པ་ *ṫsóm-pa* I. also *ṫsóm-po Cs.* **bundle, bunch,** *ṫsóm-bu* id., *mé-tog-gi ṫsóm-bu* bunch of flowers *Pth.*; *rṅá-ma nág-poi ṫsóm-pa btágs-pa Mil.*, a kind of collar, made of black yak's tail; *pra-ṫsóm* a border or trimming set with jewels or pearls. Acc. to our authorities, however, the word properly signifies a mixture or variety of colours, something **variegated, gay-coloured,** e.g. **dii náṅ-du ṫsom máṅ-po** there is much colouring in this, it is manycoloured, **ṫsom-ṫsóm** id. — II. vb. **to doubt, hesitate;** to be timid, bashful, shy; to be ashamed *C.;* sbst. **doubt, timidity** etc.; *ṫsom-ṫsóm, ṫsam-ṫsóm, ṫe-ṫsóm* id.

ཚོམས་ *ṫsoms C., W.* 1. = *ḱyams*, also *ṫsoms-skór* **court-yard,** *ḱan-pai ṫsoms Lex.* — 2. **set, division, part, chapter** *Sch.*, so perh. in the title of a book, *čéd-du brǰód-pai ṫsoms Thgy.*; **kye-ča yu daṅ zii ṫsóm-čan* W.* a neck-lace or string of pearls in sets, divided by turkois-drops and *γzi.*

ཚོམས་རྔམས་ *ṫsoms-rṅams* **noise, din, clatter** *Sch.*

ཚོར་བ་ *ṫsór-ba* 1. **to perceive,** sbst. **perception;** as one of the five skandhas = वेदना, a sensation, a feeling; **to perceive,** *γžán gyis ma ṫsór-bar* without any one perceiving it *Dzl.;* also without *γžán-gyis*: *ma ṫsór-bar rkú-ba* to steal unobserved, the contrary to robbing forcibly *Thgy.*; **žim-po ṫsor** he found it well-tasted; *sbrúm-pa ṫsór-nas* feeling herself to be with child *Pth.;* **yáṅ-mo ṫsor soṅ* W.* it felt light to the touch. — 2. **to hear,** for *ṫós-pa*, common in *W.* —

ཚོར་ལོ་ *ṫsór-lo* a (flying) **report, rumour.**

ཚོལ་བ་ *ṫsól-ba* v. *ₒṫsól-ba.*

ཚོས་ *ṫsos* 1. **paint, dye, colouring matter;** *ṫsos rgyág-pa, rgyáb-pa* **to dye, to colour** *Sch.*; *ṫsos gyur* (or *log*) *soṅ* it has lost colour, it is faded; *ṫsós(-kyi) ḱu(-ba)* liquid paint, = *ṫsón-rtsi Glr.*; *ṫsós-mḱan* dyer, *ṫsos-lu Sch.*: a cosmetic, wash(?); *rgyá-ṫsos* a red pigment from India, perh. kermes *Med.* — 2. **a medicament** *Med.* — 3. v. *ḱur-ṫsos, ₒṗoṅ-ṫsos.*

ཚ

མཚའ་ལུ་ *mtsá-lu* 1. also *rtá-mtsa-lu Lex., Sch.*: a horse with white feet. — 2. v. *tsa-lu*.

མཚགས་ *mtsags Sch.* = *tsags* 4, *tsags-bzáṅ byéd-pa*.

མཚང་ *mtsaṅ* v. *ₒtsaṅ-ba*.

མཚན་ *mtsan* 1. resp. for *miṅ*, **name**, esp. the new name which every one receives that takes orders; *mtsan γsól-ba* 1. to give a name *Glr.* 2. to take, to assume, a name *Glr.*, title *W.* — 2. **mark, sign,** v. *mtsan-ma*. — 3. **night**, *mtsán-mo*.

མཚན་(མ་) *mtsán(-ma)* लक्षण, 1. **sign** (*rtags* and *ltas*), **mark, token, badge, symptom,** *dón-med-pai mtsán-ma yin* it is a sign that it would be fruitless *Wdṅ.*; *mtsán-ma ₒdébs-pa* to make a mark, to mark (e.g. with paint) *Glr.*; *btsún-mo-la ma ₒjigs-šig byás-pai mtsán-ma byin-nas* making a sign to the queen, signifying: do not fear! (that she had nothing to fear); *mtsán-mas mtsón-pa* to represent a thing by a sign or mark *Lex.*; *rgyal-poi mtsán-ma* (or *rtags*) *lṅá-po* (acc. to Indian notions) the five royal insignia, turban, parasol, sword, fly-flap and coloured sandals; **shape** and **peculiar characteristics of separate parts of the body,** *lus-kyi mtsan Dzl.* ༧༥, 5, esp. as marks of beauty, *skyés-bu čén-poi mtsan sum-ču-rtsa-γnyis* cf. *skyés-bu*; *mtsan daṅ dbyibs* as to limbs and stature *Dzl.*; *mtsan(-ma) bzáṅ(-po)* and *ṅán(-pa)* good and evil signs, tokens, symptoms, prognostics, frq.; *bkra-šís-pai dge-mtsan* propitious signs *Glr.*, emphat., good, favourable sign, some special (good) quality, *mtsan daṅ ldan-pa* possessing such quality, **superior, excellent,** frq.; *mtsán-ma rtóg-pa* to prove, to examine, signs; *mtsán-mar sgóm-pa* to take as an omen *Sch.*, *mtsán-mar ma bzuṅ* do not regard it as an (evil) omen, be not surprised or alarmed *Sch.* — *mtsan(daṅ) bčás(-pa)*, and *mtsan-méd* having characteristics and having none, (v. also *Was.* 297), terms with which Buddhist speculation loves to play, cf. *Köpp.* I, 597. — 2. **genitals** *Med., Pth.*, gen. preceded by *p̓o* or *mo*; *mtsan-dbye* prob. the genitals open themselves *Med.*; hence in Lhasa the word *tsan-zúg* (q.v.) might be misunderstood for painful affection of the genitals. — 3. *šín-tu mtsan čé-bar gyúr-te* is at one time applied to Buddha, at another to men, thus leaving the true meaning doubtful.

**Comp. and deriv.** *mtsán-mkan* soothsayer, astrologer, frq. — *mtsan-gráṅ* and *dgu-mtsan* prize, crown of victory *C.* — ***mtsan*-*brjód*** calling upon the name of a deity, enumerating its characteristics and attributes *Cs.*; *mtsan-dón* something similar(?). — ***mtsan-nyid*** prop.: **'the sign'**, the essential characteristic, sometimes even implying the true, innermost essence of a thing, whilst, on the other hand, it is also used merely for 'mark' in general; *čós-kyi mtsan-nyid stón-pa, kóṅ-du čúd-pa* prob. to show the true essence of doctrine, to receive it into one's own mind *Dzl.*; *mtsan-nyid-pa Mil.* n. of a philosophical school of the present day, stated to be the same as *bye-brág-pa*; it is much in favour with the Gelugpa-sect, and the principal object of their studies is, to ascertain the literal sense and original spirit of their doctrine; they love disputations on these subjects, and may be considered the representatives of speculative science among the Tibetan clergy. — *ₒdus-byás-kyi mtsan-nyid mi-rtág-pa yin* the essential property of all that is compounded is liability to decay *Glr.*; **property, quality** *Domaṅ*; **symptom, indication,** *nád-pa sós-pai mtsan-nyid* an indication that the patient will recover *S.g.*; *mtsan-nyid γsum* the three marks or characteristics in the doctrine of 'perception' of the Mahayanists, *kun-btágs, γžán-dbáṅ, yoṅs-grúb Was.* 291; *mtsan-nyid bšád-pa Schr.*: **definition**; so it seems to be used in *Thgy.* — *mtsan-rtágs* = *mtsán-ma Wdk.* — *mtsán-pa* **marked,** *ₒkór-los* being marked with the figure of a wheel *Glr.* — *mtsán-dpe* for *mtsan daṅ dpe-byad Glr.* — *mtsan-γži Lex., Sch.*: 'the cause of a sign or symptom, an object' (?).

མཚན་མོ་ *mtsán-mo W.*, **tsan**, **night** **tsan ča dug**, *W.* **night sets in; adv. at**

**night, by night, in the night time** *Dzl.*, *W.*: **tsan-la**; *dei mtsán-mo Dzl.* in that night; *tsan gáṅ, tsan tog-tág, W.* also **tsan-tse-ri**, the whole night; also adv., all night; *mtsan-dkyil, mtsan-gúṅ, mtsan-pyéd* **midnight;** *mtsan-stód, mtsan-smád* the first, the second half of the night; *mtsan-stód-kyi rmi-lam* a dream before midnight *Med.* — *mtsan-dús* **night time.** — *mtsan-byí* (*W. *tsan-bi**) **bat.** — *tsan-śiṅ W.* 1. **chip of pine-wood,** 2. **pine-wood.** 3. **pine-tree.** — *mtsan-só byéd-pa* to keep watch during the night *Sch.*

མཚམས་ *mtsams* 1. **intermediate space, interstice, border, boundary-line,** *rgya-gár daṅ bál-poi mtsáms-na, rgya-bál-gyi mtsáms-su* on the border between India and Nepal *Glr.*; *mtsáms-kyi nags-króod* boundary-forest *Glr.*; *sa-mtsáms* (vulgo *san-tsám*) frontier of the country *Glr.*; *dé-nas ˳doms lṅa-brgyái mtsáms-nas* at a distance of 500 fathoms from that place; *bar-mtsams-na yod* it lies in the middle between; *ri taṅ mtsáms-su* where the mountains are contiguous to the plain; *byaṅ śar mtsáms-su* in the north-east (cf. no. 2 below); *ču ˳gram mtsáms-su* (between the water and the river's bank) close to the edge *Wdṅ.*; *dei mtsáms-su* (with regard to a royal dynasty) **intervening, a usurper,** interrupting the regular succession *Glr.*; *čés-pai tsig mtsáms-nas* when these words were uttered, at these words *Tar.* 127, 11; *sgo(i)-mtsáms* a narrow opening of the door, *sgo-mtsáms-nas sleb* (he or it) enters through the cleft of a door, equivalent to our 'through the key-hole'; **tsám-la čúg-če* W.* to preserve, to put (plants) between (paper), to pack up (glass in straw). — *mtsams sbyor-ba* 1. **to close interstices, to stitch up, to sew together** (the separate parts of a shoe) *Mil.* 2. *Sch.*: **to occupy a certain space, to enter a womb',** to embody one's self in human flesh, so it seems to be used in *Thgr.* and *Mil.* 3. **to take a resolution, to form a plan, to conceive an idea, to settle in one's mind,** like *˳gód-pa*, cf. *sbyór-ba* I, 2; II, 2 *C.*, *W.* — *mtsams ˳byé-ba* to split(?), *skra smin γsár-du mtsams-bye rtsub ˳kyil S.g.* the hair of the head and the eye-brows splits, divides again, is growing thin, crisp, and interspersed with bald places, which is alledged to be a symptom of approaching death, yet hardly founded on correct observation, nor by any means clearly defined; *Schr.* has: *skra mtsams ˳byéd-pa* to part the hair on the top of the head. — *mtsams-med-pa* 1. adj., *Ssk. ānantarya*, without interstices, continuous, = *go-mtsams-med-pa* v. *go* 1, *Dzl.* 2. sbst., *Ssk. ānantarya*, *Was.* (240), 'where nothing is to be interposed between a deed and its consequences, where the consequences are not to be averted', **a deadly, capital sin** *Dzl.* and elsewh.; *mtsáms-med-pa lṅa*, i. e. inexpiable sins, are: parricide and matricide, murder of an Arhat (*dgrá-bčom-pa*), or of a Tathāgata, likewise causing divisions among the priesthood. — *dus-mtsáms* **intermediate time** *Cs.* — *mtsams-sbyór* the Sanskrit diphthongs ē, ō, ai, au; *mtsams-sbyór-pa* and *-ma*, **a** bawd, *Cs.* — *mtsams(-kyi)-žu(-ba)*, also *˳tsams-žu*, an expression gen. occurring in modern Tibetan letters, winding up the complimentary phrases of the introduction, and passing over to the proper business of the letter; for the immediate sense of the phrase I found no explanation. — 2. **the points of the compass,** *mtsams bži* the four cardinal points of the horizon; *mtsams brgyad* includes the intermediate points, south-east etc., *mtsams drug* denotes the four cardinal points together with the zenith and nadir. — 3. **demarcation, partition, break, pause, stop,** *mtsams γčod-pa* to make a stop or pause with the voice in reading *Gram.*; esp. to draw a line of demarcation about one's own person, whether it be by a magic circle (*Dom.*), or by retiring to a solitary house, either for the sake of private study (*Zam.*), or which is most frq. the case, for religious meditation, (**tsám-la dád-če* W.*) in the cell of a cloister, or in a hermitage or cave in the mountains, the seclusion lasting sometimes for several months, during which time the scanty food is silently received from without through a small aperture. Such seclusions are undergone by some in the sincere belief, that they will acquire thereby higher gifts and abilities, by others merely to increase their odour of sanctity. *mtsams sdóm-pa Mil.* has a similar signification. — *spyad-mtsáms* **rules, instructions,** defining the extent and limits of a person's duties. — 4. symb. num.: 6, v. *mtsams drug* above.

མཚར་བ *mtsár-ba* 1. **fair, fine, beautiful,** = *mdzés-pa Zam., Glr.* frq., *mtsar sdug dan ldán-pa* id., e.g. *bú-mo Glr.*; also of flowers; **bright, shining,** of metals *Stg.*; **nyám-tsar-wa, ló-tsar-wa** admirably fair, wonderfully fine. — 2. **wondrous, wonderful, marvelous,** gen. with *no, nó-mtsar-čan žig* a wonderful, distinguished, eminent man *Mil.*; *rten no-mtsar-čan* a wonderful image (of some deity) *Glr.*, in both instances equivalent to **wonder-working, miraculous;** *no-mtsar-mčód-pa* a marvelous, extremely rich offering *Mil.*; more frq. *no-mtsar-čé-ba* e.g. **marvelous things, events, miracles** *Dzl.*; *mi srid no-mtsar-če* impossible! most wonderful! *Glr.*; *no-mtsar-čé-ba ma yin* that is not so very wonderful *Dzl.*; **strange, ridiculous,** *γtam šin-tu no-mtsar-čé Glr.* — 3. *no-mtsár* **wonder, surprise, astonishment,** *no-mtsár skyé-ba, no-mtsár-du* ₒ*gyur-ba* or ₒ*dzin-pa, no-mtsar-rmád-du* ₒ*gyúr-ba* to wonder, to be surprised. — 4. *no-mtar-čé* an expression of thanks, = *bka-drin-če, dé-ltar yin-na kyed γnyis-ka no-mtsar-čé* if that is so, then both of you receive my best thanks! *Mil.*; *yóns-pa no-mtsar-čé* thanks to you for your coming! *Mil.*

ཚ

མཚལ *mtsal Cs.* also *tsal* **vermilion,** used (among the rest) inst. of red ink for writing; *mtsal-pár* a printing with red ink *Cs.*; *mtsal-lčógs-pa*(?) *Sch.*: 'clear vermilion'(?); *sku-mtsál* resp. for *krag* blood *Cs.*

མཚུངས་པ *mtsuns-pa* (*W.* **tsogs**) **similar, like, equal,** *ka-dog* as to colour *S.O.*, *sna-ma dan* like the former, *bdud-rtsir* like nectar *S.g.*; *bdud dan mtsuns* you are to me like a satan, you are a satan to me *Pth.*; *lhai sdug-bsnál dan ča-mtsúns-pai stén-du* besides their sharing all the imperfections of the gods *Thgy.*; *dús-mtsuns-pa* **a contemporary** *Mil.*; *mtsuns-méd, mtsuns-brál,* **without an equal, matchless, incomparable;** *sems dan mtsuns ldán-pa* explained by *Was.* (241) as: manifestations of mind, those outward signs by which the mind manifests itself as existing.

མཚུན *mtsun* (*Zam.* = *Ssk.* क्रव्य, raw flesh) 1. *Cs.*: **meat for the manes of the dead,** *γtón-ba* to bring an offering to the dead, *skyel-ba* to send one; *mtsun-γtór* explained in *Wdn.* by *ši-bai dón-du γtór-ma γtón-ba*; *mtsun-γtór stér-ba Wdn.* — 2. *Sch.*: **tutelar deities, household-gods,** or rather **the souls of ancestors;** so *Dzl.* ༢༠, 16 (another reading is *btsun*); also in *mtsun-γtor*, if *mtsun* be taken as a dat., it may have this signification; *mes-mtsún* household-gods of the Shamans *Sch.*

མཚུར *mtsur* v. *tsúr-mo.*

མཚུལ་པ *mtsúl-pa* **the lower part of the face,** nose and mouth, **the muzzle** of animals *Mil.*; **bill, beak** *Sch.*; *W.* **nám-tsul** **nose;** *mtsúl-pa* ₒ*gag* the effect of the gall entering the nose(?) *Mng.*; *ka-mtsúl* (*W.* **kam-tsúl**) **face,** seldom in *B.*

མཚེ་སྐྱོང *mtse-skyón Wdn.?*

མཚེ་ལྡུམ *mtse-ldúm* n. of a medicinal herb *S.g.*

མཚེ་མ *mtsé-ma* (*W.* **tsag-túg**) **twins,** *bu mtse-ma γnyis dus γčig-na* ₒ*kruns-so Pth.* two twin-sons were born simultaneously; *mtsé-ma γsúm-po* three-twin-child, trigemini *Wdn.*

མཚེད *mtsed, Sch.*: *dur-mtséd,* **place for burning the dead.**

མཚེའུ *mtseu* **a small lake,** *mtso dan mtseu* lakes and lakelets *Pth.*

མཚེར་བ *mtser-ba* = ₒ*tser-ba.*

མཚོ *mtso* 1. **lake,** frq. — 2. for *rgya-mtso* sea, rarely. — 3. symb. num.: 4. — **Comp.** *mtso-dkyil, mtso-dbús* the middle of a lake. — *mtso-*ₒ*kór* an assemblage of many lakes *Cs.* — *mtso-*ₒ*kyóms* v. ₒ*kyoms.* — *mtso-*ₒ*grám, mtso-mtá* border of a lake. — *mtso-snón Glr.*, **sóg-po tso-nón** *C.* the blue lake, Kokonor, in Mongolia. — *mtso-čú* water, *mťso-rláṅs* vapours, *mťso-rlóbs* waves of a lake. — **ťso-lág* C.* **inlet, creek, cove.** — **ťo-lag-ḍél* C.* **strait, channel.**

མཚོག་པ་ *mtsóg-pa* v. *˳tsóg-pa.*

མཚོག་མ་ *mtsóg-ma Lt.*, also *mtsog-ɣsén Cs.*, 'spot or tender part of the head', vacancy in the infant cranium, = *tsáṅs-pai bú-ga.*

མཚོགས་ *mťsogs* adv., **ťsógs-se** adj., *W.* for *mtsuṅs* or *˳dra*, **similar, like, equal;** **aṅ-ré-zi ťsogs rgyál-la mi dug** they are not so good as the English; **ǩo daṅ ṅá-la dug-ṅál ťsóg-se yod** with him and with me there is the like disaster, misfortune visits us equally.

མཚོན་ *mtson*, 1. also *mtsón-ča*, any **pointed or cutting instrument,** *mtsón-čas ɣtúb-pa* to cut to pieces with such an instrument *Dzl.*; **weapon, arms;** *mťson ťogs-pa* to seize a sword, to take up arms *Dzl.*; *mťsón-gyis ˳ǰig-pa* to destroy, to conquer, with the sword *Ma.*; *mťsón-ča rnám-pa bži Stg.*: sword, spear, dart, arrow; *go-mťsón* armory and arms; *ru-mtsón* v. *ru*; *mťson-ǩrág* blood drawn by cuts or stabs (used for sorceries) *Lt.* — *mtsoṅ-gyi dru-bu* an attribute of the gods, resembling a coil or ball of thread *Wdṅ.*; *mtson-skúd sgríl-ma Thgr.* id. (?). — 2. also *ťson* **fore-finger,** *mtsón-rtsa* the pulse to be felt with the fore-finger; *mťson gaṅ* a finger's breadth; *mťson gaṅ mar* a finger's breadth lower *Med.*; *mťsón-pa* a four-fingers' pinch(?); *šiṅ mťsón-pa žig* a handful of sticks *Mil.*

མཚོན་པ་ *mtson-pa* 1. v. *mtson.* — 2. vb. **to set forth, bring forward, adduce, state, quote, exhibit,** examples of grammatical forms etc. *Gram.*; *˳dis mťsón-nas* illustrating it by this, setting this up as an example *Gram.*; *des kyaṅ sgyú-mai dpe čig mťson* also in this may be seen an instance of deception *Mil.*; *dpes mťsón-pa* to illustrate by parables *Mil.*; *mtsán-mas* by a sign *Gram.*; so prob. also: *ǎm-ban ɣnyis dei mtsón-pai dmág-mi* the soldiers brought forward by the two Chinese officials; it is also alledged to stand for **to make, to prepare** *C.* — *rnám-mǩa mťsón-pai rnál-˳byor-pa* prob.: the saint that represents the heavens, that resembles the heavenly space *Mil.*

འཚའ་ལུ་ *˳ťsa-lu* v. *mťsa-lu.*

འཚག་པ་ *˳ťsag-pa* 1. vb., pf. *ťsags, btsags,* fut. *btsag*, imp. *ťsog* (trans. to *˳dzag-pa*), **to cause to trickle, to strain, filter, sift, squeeze, press out,** *˳bru-már ťság-pa* (partic.) oil-miller *Dzl.*; **to draw off,** *dmú-ču* to tap (a dropsical person) *S.g.* Cf. *ťság-ma, tsags.* — 2. adj. **thick, fat, obese** *Lex.*

འཚང་, མཚང་ *˳ťsaṅ, mťsaṅ* **fault, error, offence, sin,** *de ˳ťsáṅ-du če* that is very wicked, a great offence; *mii* or *mí-la ˳ťsaṅ brú-ba* or *drú-ba* 1. **to spy out another's faults,** to upbraid him with them, to accuse him *Do., C., W.*; **ťsaṅ ˳og ḍhú-wa* C.* id. — 2. **to irritate, provoke, make angry** *C.*

འཚང་བ་ *˳ťsáṅ-ba*, vb. I. pf. *ťsaṅs*, fut. *btsaṅ*(?) 1. **to press into, to stuff** *Sch.*, *˳ťsáṅ-ǩa byéd-pa* id. *Sch.*; *náṅ-du ˳ťsáṅs-pa Lexx.* prob. pressed into, stuffed inside, so *Sch.*: *ǩri naṅ ťsáṅs-čan* a stuffed seat; *dbugs ǩar ˳ťsáṅs-pa* out of breath, panting (in the heat of pursuit) *Mil.*; *dbugs stod-du ˳ťsaṅs-nas skad mi ťon Mil.* I am pressed for breath, my breath stops, I cannot utter a word (for ardent longing); *stod-˳ťsáṅs, rluṅ-˳ťsáṅs, ˳ťsáṅs-la ṗan*, all these expressions imply a want of breath, not sufficiently to be reconciled to the original meaning of the word. — 2. **sú-la ťsáṅs-se yóṅ-če* Ld.* **to attack a person with open violence,** opp. to a stealthy attack. — II. pf. *saṅs*, which verb, however, occurs only in *˳ťsaṅ-rgyá-bar ˳gyúr-ba* to become Buddha *Dzl.* frq., *˳ťsaṅ rgyá-bar ˳dód-pa* to aim at Buddhaship, and *saṅs-rgyás* (having become) Buddha. Besides this form, there exists also a verb *sáṅ-ba*, pf. (*b*)*saṅs*, to clean, as may easily be proved by examples. The whole will perh. become clear, if we presume, that the form *˳ťsaṅ-ba* for the present tense is now obsolete, occurring only in reference to Buddha, as quoted above, and that the root *saṅ* is now used as present tense in the following significations: 1. **to remove** (impurities) — like *˳dág-pa* — **to make clean,** *daṅ sáṅ-te med* W. (the soot) having yesterday been removed, there is none just now; *saṅ dug, saṅ ċos* W. it is cleansed, swept clean, *ₒbag saṅ, nyé-pa saṅ* the contamination, the sin, has been removed, done away with C.; snyun saṅs the disease is removed Pth.; skyo-sáṅs byéd-pa to remove melancholy, to recreate or amuse one's self; to comfort others; skyo-sáṅs-la ₒgró-ba, skyo-sáṅs byéd-pa to take a walk, to take a ride Pth., C.; mya-ṅáṅ sáṅ-ba **to comfort** Pth., **to console one's self**; esp. 2. **to recover, to come again to one's senses,** ra-ro-ba-las from intoxication Dzl.; γzím-pa-las from a deep sleep Dzl.; also construed as before: bzi Glr., *ra* W. from a drunken fit, and this agrees with a sufficiently authenticated signification of the Ssk. root budh, so that saṅs-rgyás would after all be the literal translation of बुद्ध (contrary to Burn. I, 71 med.), taking the signification of the name, accord. to Tibetan notions, to be: 'the man that has entirely recovered from error and come to the knowledge of absolute truth'. That saṅs-rgyás be the same as **perfect, holy,** seems to be a mere etymological conjecture of Cs. — 3. **to take away, to take off,** *ḱeb sáṅ-wa* C. to uncover. — 4. **to be spoiled, to become unfit, useless,** *wó-ma saṅ soṅ* C. the milk is spoiled, zom saṅ ₒdug = ṡaṅ ₒdug the casks are leaky, are running out.

ཚ

འཚང་ར་ ₒtsaṅ-ra Sch.: the neck of the thigh-bone; tsáṅ-rai tsil the fat attached to it C.

འཚབ་པ་ ₒtsáb-pa, pf. tsabs, bsabs, fut. bsab, imp. tsob, **to pay back, repay, refund,** skyín-pa a loan Lex.; cf. tsab.

འཚབ་འཚུབ་ ₒtsab-ₒtsub **hurry, confusion, perplexity, fear** Sch.; also: ₒtsab-ₒtsáb-mor γnás-pa to tarry in fear, to hesitate in apprehensions Tar.

འཚབས་པ་ ₒtsábs-pa, pf. tsabs, imp. tsobs Sch.: resp. **to be afraid;** Lex. blo-ₒtsábs id. (?).

འཚམ(ས)་པ་ ₒtsám(s)-pa 1. = ₒčam-pa(?) **fit, suitable, in accordance to, in conformity with,** de daṅ ₒtsám-par S.g.; so-sói ₒbyór-pa daṅ ₒtsám-par Tar. according to their ability, in proportion to their property. — 2. frq. and mostly erron. for mtsáms-pa.

འཚར་བ་ ₒtsár-ba, pf. tsar 1. **to be finished, completed, terminated,** sṅón-la tsár-ro Glr. it was the first that was finished; **to be at an end, consumed, spent,** *nor tsár-te soṅ* W. the money is all spent; esp. as an auxiliary, to denote an action that is perfectly past or completed (where in the earlier literature zin stands), in later books with the termin. inf., yóṅs-su rdzógs-par tsár-te when ... was completely finished Glr.; vulgo the mere root is used, esp. in W., *tsog tsar-ra ma tsar* are they assembled, has the meeting begun already? *lam-la żug tsar, soṅ tsar, kal tsar* he is on the way, he is gone, it is dispatched; tsár-ba byéd-pa, tsár-du ₒǰúg-pa Cs., *tsar ċug-ċe* W. **to bring to a close, to finish, to terminate.** — tsár-γċod-pa 1. **to destroy, annihilate,** e.g. diabolic influences, infernal powers Pth.; **to defeat, overcome,** in disputation Mil.; **to excel, surpass,** sgyu-rtsál-gyis Glr.; **to punish** Tar. 2. for γsár-γċod-pa Pth. — 2. **to grow, grow up, thrive,** of little children W.; ₒtsar-skyéd growth Mil.

འཚལ་ ₒtsal, sgro-bai-ₒtsal-gyi ḱa-brgyan Mil.?

འཚལ་བ་ ₒtsál-ba, imp. ₒtsol eleg. 1. **to want, wish, desire, ask;** when followed by a verb, the latter stands in the termin. inf., or the mere root of it, and more esp. that of the perf. form, yab daṅ mǰal ₒtsál-lo I have a mind to go to see my father Dzl.; bltás-par ₒtsál-te wishing to see Dzl.; túgs-la bżag ₒtsal I wish it may be borne in mind Glr.; γsuṅ ₒtsal I beg you to speak Mil., bzuṅ ₒtsal please take Pth.; pleon. ₒḱrid-par żu ₒtsal Glr.; esp. as an intimation of willingness, dé-ltar ₒtsál-lo yes, we will do that Mil., or like our: very well! Further: ṗá-la nor ma ₒtsál-tam has he not asked the money from his father? Dzl.; gum yaṅ ċi ₒtsal why does (the king) want to kill me? Dzl.; deï don mi ₒtsal the profit of it I do not desire Glr. — 2. **to eat,** btsan-dúg poison *Dzl.*; *byi-bas ₒtsál-te* eaten by mice *Dzl.*; *ɣdon mi ₒtsál-bar* eleg. for *ɣdon mi zá-bar* without doubt *Dzl.* — 3. **to know** *Cs.*; so *ṅo-ₒtsál-ba* appears to be used for *ṅo-šes-pa*, and in a passage of *S.O.* it seems to imply **to understand.** — 4. in certain phrases: *ₒbad ₒtsál-ba* **to use diligence** *Thgy.*; *bro ₒtsál-ba* 1. **to swear** *Pth.*(?), 2. **to have a cold** *Mil.*; *p̔yag ₒtsál-ba* **to greet, salute,** v. *p̔yag.*

འཚལ་མ་ *ₒtsál-ma Cs.* = *tsál-ma.*

འཚིག་པ་ *ₒtsig-pa*, pf. *tsig*, **to burn, to destroy by fire,** *groṅ-k̔yer mi daṅ bčas-pa* (he burned) the town with its inhabitants *Pth.*; *mes*, *mer*, vulgo **mé-la** with fire; *rnám-par* entirely, completely *Dzl.*; more loosely: *tsig soṅ* he burnt himself, scalded himself etc.; also of food, burnt, injured by the heat; *ₒtsig-gam* am I burning? (thinks one suffering of fever) *Med.*; of inflammation, v. *mig-ₒtsig*; of any violent pain *Dom.*; **to be glowing**, of the evening-sky *W.*; **tsig ₒǰug ₒdug** *C.* **to be in the rut**, the copulating of larger animals.

འཚིང་ and འཚིངས་པ་ *ₒtsiṅ* and *ₒtsiṅs-pa Mṅg.?*

འཚིར་བ་ *ₒtsir-ba*, pf. *tsir*, *btsir*, fut. *ɣtsir*, *btsir*, imp. *tsir W.* **btsir-če** **to press,** *mig* with the finger on the eye *Med.*; *nán-gyis* to press hard *Stg.*; **to press out**, an ulcer; **to wring**, a wet cloth; **to crush out,** *til-már* sesame-oil *Lex.*; *ₒo-ma ₒtsir-ba* **to milk;** **tsir tag ǰhé-pa*, or *táṅ-wa** *C.* **to press hard, to examine closely, to hold a rigorous inquest;** *btsún-mo-la yaṅ tugs ɣtsir čúṅ-bar gyúr-to Pth.* also the queen's mind was much depressed.

འཚུགས་པ་ *ₒtsúgs-pa*, pf. *tsugs* (intrs. of *ₒdzúg-pa*), 1. **to go into** (more frq. *ₒtsúd-pa*), **to enter upon, begin, commence,** *stód-pa ₒbúl-ba-la tsugs* he began to praise, to flatter. — 2. **to penetrate by boring,** v. *p̔ur-pa*; **to take root, to establish one's self, to settle,** *rtsá-ba ma tsugs* it has not struck root; *ₒbrog ₒtsúgs-su ye ma-ₒdod Mil.*, prob.: they had no longer any mind to establish themselves in this alpine solitude; *brtán-gyi skyid-mgo dé-nas tsugs* this was the beginning of my lasting happiness *Mil.*; most frq. *tsúgs-pa* as partic. or adj.: **firm, steady,** *rk̔aṅ-lúg ma tsúgs-te sá-la ₒgyél-to* his limbs not remaining firm (in consequence of a paralytic stroke), he fell to the ground *Dzl.*; **káṅ-pa tsúg-kyin dug** sit quiet with your feet! *Ld.*; *ₒdug mi tsúgs-pa Med.*, *sa ɣčig-tu mi tsugs-pa Pth.*, **dö̆-tsug mé-pa** *C.*, **dád-du mi tsúg-k̔un** *W.* not being able to sit still; not stationary, **unsettled, roving, restless, volatile, flighty, inattentive,** *spyód-pas skád-čig kyaṅ mi tsúgs-pa Glr.* id.; **tsúg-la dod** *W.*, be attentive! **to be able** *C.*

འཚུད་པ་ *ₒtsúd-pa*, pf. *tsud* (intrs. to *ₒdzúd-pa*) **to be put into** (a hole), to prison *Glr.*; **to go into, to enter, to get into** (a good and wholesome way), **to go to** (hell); *k̔oṅ-du* v. *k̔oṅ ₒtsud-pa.*

འཚུབ་པ་ *ₒtsub-pa*, pf. *tsubs*, 1. **to whirl**, of whirlwinds, snow-storms, smoke etc. *Mil.* and elsewh. — 2. **to be choked,** esp. **to be drowned,** *ṅya čab-la ₒp̔yo-ba ₒtsub mi srid* the fish swimming in the water cannot be drowned *Mil.*; *čus ₒtsúb-pa Mil.*; **tsub-te ši** *W.* he has been drowned. — 3. *spyód-pa ₒtsúb-pa* **pugnacity,** of fowl *Glr.*

འཚེ་བ་ *ₒtse-ba* 1. vb. pf. *btses*, fut. *btse*, *ɣtse* (*Dzl.*) **to hurt, damage, injure, persecute, torment,** *mi-la ₒtsé-žiṅ ɣnód-pa byéd-pa*, or *ɣnód-čiṅ ₒtsé-bar byéd-pa* id.; also sbst., **enemy**, **persecutor** *Mil.*; *ɣčan-zán-la sógs-pai ₒtsé-ba daṅ bčás-pa* (a place) haunted by beasts of prey or any other noxious creatures *Thgy.*; the term is also applied to horses that bite each other. — 2. sbst. (spelling uncertain) **psalterium,** the third stomach of ruminating animals *W.*

འཚེག་པ་ *ₒtség-pa*, pf. *tsegs*, imp. *tseg(s)*, **to repay** *Cs.*

འཚེང་བ་ *ₒtséṅ-ba*, pf. prob. *ₒtseṅs*, 1. **to increase, improve, thrive,** opp. to *ₒp̔úṅ ba W.* — 2. **to be content, happy** *Mil.*

འཚེད་པ་ *ₒtséd-pa* 1. v. *ₒtsód-pa.* — 2. v. *bséd-pa.*

འཚེམ་པ་ *ₒtsém-pa* pf. *tsems*, *btsems*, fut. *btsem*, imp. *tsems*, *W.* **tsém-če** **to sew,** **gos tsém-čeï ras** materials for a gar-

ཚ

ment; ₒtsem-skúd **thread** for sewing; ₒtsem-kʻáb **needle.** — ₒtsem-drúb **needle-work** *Cs.* — ₒtsem-srúb *W.* **seam.** — ₒtsem-méd without a seam; *Sch.* also: without interruption.

འཚེར་བ་ ₒtsér-ba, I. vb. **to neigh** *Pth.* and vulgo. — II. also *mtsér-ba* 1. vb. **to grieve, to sorrow,** and sbst. **grief, sorrow,** resp. *tugs-ₒtsér*, cf. *tsér-ka*; ₒtsér-čan **sorrowful, anxious,** ₒtser-méd **free from sorrow, easy.** — 2. **to be afraid, to fear** *C., Mil.* — 3. **to shine, to glitter,** and sbst. **lustre, brightness, splendour, brilliancy,** of light *Lex.*, of jewels *Dzl.*; *dkár-žiṅ* (or *dkár-la*) ₒtsér-ba to be of a shining white *Mil.*

འཚེར་ས་, མཚེར་ས་ ₒtsér-sa, mtsér-sa 1. *Sch.*: **cause of uneasiness, source of care.** — 2. an old deserted settlement or dwelling; ₒtser-rnyiṅ id. *Sch.*

འཚོ་བ་ ₒtsó-ba, I. vb. a. intrs, pf. and imp. *sos*, 1. **to live,** *riṅ-du* a long time, *lo brgya* a hundred years *Med.*; *nam* (or *ji-srid*) ₒtsoī bár-du **for life, life-long,** *čós-kyis, rig-pas, rṅón-pas* to gain a livelihood by religion, science, hunting *Cs.*, or: to lead the life of a cleric, scholar, hunter; *srid* ₒtsó-ba to pass life, **to continue** in a state, **to exist,** frq.; ₒdú-ₒdzii náṅ-du ₒtso mi pʻód-do in the throng of the world I cannot exist *Dzl.* (*W.* *són-če and *tse pʻid-če**). — 2. **to remain alive,** to be maintained in life, ₒdi ma byás-na mi ₒtsoo else we shall not remain alive, we shall not be able to live *Dzl.*; **to revive, to recover,** from sickness etc. *Dzl.*; *sós-par ₒgyúr-ba* id, frq.; *ši-ba-las* to be rescued from peril of death *Dzl.* — 3. **to last, to be durable,** of clothes etc., *W.*: *máṅ-po tsó-če* to last long, to be very durable; ₒtsó-žiṅ *sdód-pa* to remain valid, binding, to retain its virtue, efficacy, of laws, doctrine etc. — 4. **to feed, to graze.** — b. trs., pf. (*b*)*sos*, fut. *γso*, 1. **to nourish,** *lus* the body; to sustain, *srog* life; **to pasture, to feed,** *pʻyugs* ₒtsó-ba-la kyér-ba to lead the cattle to pasture *Pth.*, *pʻyugs* ₒtsor pʻyin-pa id. — 2. **to heal, to cure,** *nad Lt.*; in this sense the fut. form is used as a vb. for itself, q.v.; ₒtso-byéd, *tso-mdzád* **'life-giver',** i.e. physician, **medicine.**

II. sbst., also ₒtso, 1. **life,** *mi žig-gi* ₒtsó-ba bšól-ba to prolong life *Dzl.*; ₒó-čag ₒtsoī rje the lord of our lives, viz. the king *Glr.*; ₒtso skyóṅ-ba to spare, preserve, protect another's life; **to rear, bring up, educate.** — 2. **livelihood, sustenance, nourishment, entertainment,** *zlá-ba γsúm-gyi bár-du* ₒtsó-ba sbyór-ba to board a person for three months *Dzl.*; ₒtsó-ba-la ma bltá-ste not caring for the entertainment *Dzl.*; ₒtsó-bab záṅ-po good eating and drinking *Mil.*

འཚོག་ཆས་ ₒtsog-čas **goods, effects, chattels, tools, necessaries,** =*yo-byad Lex.*; also **provisions, provender.**

འཚོག་པ་ ₒtsóg-pa, pf. *btsags*, fut. *btsog*, imp. *tsog*, *W.* *tsóg-če* 1. **to hew, chop, cut, pierce; to inoculate, vaccinate,** *brúm-pa* the small-pox. — 2. **to cudgel,** ₒtsóg-čiṅ rdúṅ-ba *Pth.*, *brdóg-ₒtsog-pa* id. *Dzl.* — 3. also *mtsóg-pa* **to find fault with, to blame, censure, carp at, teaze** *Sch.*

འཚོག་མ་, འཚོགས་མ་ ₒtsóg-ma, ₒtsógs-ma = *mtsóg-ma.*

འཚོགས་པ་ ₒtsogs-pa, pf. and imp. *tsogs*, **to assemble, to gather, to meet,** frq.; *kʻyed ₒdir tsogs*, ye, that are here assembled *Mil.*; *mi máṅ-po tsógs-pai mdún-du* before many assembled people *Dzl.*; ₒbyúṅ-ba lṅa tsógs-pa the five elements meeting *S.g.*; ₒtsogs rtén-gyi zas-čáṅ food and drink to entertain the people assembled *Glr.*; **to unite, to join** in doing something, **to associate,** to make common cause; examples v. *lugs.*

འཚོང་བ་ ₒ**tsóṅ-ba,** pf. *btsoṅs*, fut. *btsoṅ*, imp. *tsoṅ*, *W.* *tsóṅ-če*, **to sell,** *dri* ₒtsóṅ-bai γnas place where perfumes are sold *Stg.*; *daṅ gón-če tsóṅ-kʻan-ni mi* *W.* the man that yesterday had a coat to sell.

འཚོད་པ་, འཚེད་པ་ ₒtsód-pa, ₒtséd-pa, (*Cs.* ₒtsó-ba?) pf. *btsos*, fut. *btso*, imp. *tsos*, *tsod*, *W.* *tsó-če*, 1. **to cook, to dress,** in boiling water, meat, vegetables; *ču-tsós* *W.* 'water-boiled', dumplings, = *čú-ta-gir*. — 2. **to bake** provinc. — 3. **to dye,** *gos* a garment. — 4. *tsós-pa*, *tsós-mkʻan* *W.** **ripe,** *tsos soṅ* is ripe; *ldád-pa ma tsos* *Ld.*, he is a green-horn.

འཚོབ(ས)་པ་ ₒťsób(s)-pa **to be a deputy, representative, substitute** *Cs.*; *rigs ₒťsób-pa* to be the first-born male in a family, the support of a family *Dzl.*; *ₒťsób-par byéd-pa* **to substitute**, to put in the place of another *Dzl.*; *γduṅ-ₒťsób-po* resp. for **first-born** *Dzl.*

འཚོལ་བ་ *ₒťsól-ba*, pf. and fut. *btsol*, imp. *ťsol*, *W.* **tsál-če**, 1. **to seek, to search, to make research**; *ťabs* **to think upon means.** — 2. **to try to obtain**, *zas*; **to procure, acquire** *Mil.*; **to fetch** *Thg.*

# ཛ

ཛ *dza* 1. the letter sounding **dz**; cf. the observations to ཙ *tsa.* — 2. numerical figure: 19.

ཛ་ *dza* 1. v. *dza-ti.* — 2. *dzá-brduṅ-ba* **to break through** *Sch.*

ཛ་ཏི་ *dzá-ti*, prop. ཛཱ་ཏཱི་, *Ssk.* जाती, **nutmeg** *Lt.* and vulgo; sometimes *dza* for it, po. *Lt.*

ཛ་བོ་ཤིང་ *dza-bo-śiṅ Lex.* **a hollow tree** *Sch.*

ཛ་ཡ་ *dzá-ya* 1. *Sch.*: '**muddy deposit**, green slime in the water'. — 2. *C.* **the markings of wood**, speckled and variegated, in consequence of a disease of the tree, cf. *lbá-ba.* — 3. n. of an ancient king of China *Glr.*

ཛ་ལནྟྲ་ *dza-lantra*, more accur. ཛ་ལནྡྷ་ར་ *dza-lán-dha-ra*, n. of a province in the Punjâb, now 'Jellundur'.

ཛ་ལུ་ཀ་ *dzá-lu-ka*, *čui dza-lu-ka Sch.* '**water-spider**'; in *Ssk.* however: **leech.**

ཛབ་ར་ *dzáb-ra*, prob. to be spelt *rdza-bra* q.v.

ཛམ་བུ་ *dzám-bu*, gen. *ₒdzám-bu*, जम्बु, **the rose apple-tree**, *Eugenia*, which figures also in mythology; *dzám-bui gliṅ*, *dzam-bu-gliṅ*, *dzam-gliṅ*, जम्बुद्वीप, acc. to the ancient geography of India and Tibet, that part of the world which comprizes these countries, the triangular peninsula of Hindostan, occasionally including the immediate border-lands; but as in Brahman and Buddhist literature all that does not belong to these two religions is considered as not existing, or at least as hardly human, *ₒdzam-bu-gliṅ* is simply used for **earth, world**, and *ₒdzam-bu-gliṅ-pa*, for inhabitant of the world, **man.**

ཛམ་བྷ་ལ་ *dzám-bha-la*, also *dzám-bha*, *Glr.* the Tibetan **Plutos, god of riches,** = *rnam-ťos-srás*, also *rmugs-ₒdzin Lex.*, *γnod-ₒdzin*, and acc. to *Schf.'s* conjecture (*Tar.* 6, 1) also *γnód-pa-čan*; *dzam-sér* this god painted yellow, *dzam-nág* painted black *Cs.*

ཛི་ *dzi*, num. figure: 49.

ཛི་ན་མི་ཏྲ་ *dzi-na-mi-tra Ssk.* n. of a Buddhist scholar.

ཛུ་ *dzu*, num. figure: 79.

ཛུ་ཏ་ *dzu-ta Hindi*: **shoe** *C.*, *W.*

ཛུབ་ཛུབ་ *dzub-dzúb C.* **dhsub-dhsúb ǰhé-pa** **to wag, to whisk** the tail, of horses and cattle.

ཛེ་ *dze*, num. figure: 109.

ཛེ་ཙེ་ *dze-tse C.* **dhse-tse**, vent-hole for the smoke, **chimney.**

ཛོ་ *dzo* num. figure: 139.

ཛོ་ཀི་, ཛྭོ་ཀི་ *dzó-ki*, *dzwo-ki Mil.*, *Wdṅ.*, vulg. for *yó-gi*, v. *rnál-ₒbyor-pa.*

མཛའ་བ་ *mdzá-ba* (*Lex.* = *mťún-pa*) **to love,** as friends or kinsmen do, *ǩyo-šúg* *mdzá-ba-rnams* a loving married couple *Dzl.*; *mdza-žiṅ sdúg-par ˳gyúr-ba* loving each other, e.g. like brothers or sisters, *Dzl.*; *mi-mdzá-ba ťams-čád* any hostile, malignant (creatures or powers) *Dom.*; *mi-mdzá-ba-rnams sdúm-pa* to reconcile those that are at variance *Thgy.*; *brám-ze mdzá-žiṅ šés-pa žig yód-de* he had a Brahmin for his intimate friend *Dzl.*; *mdza-bšés* **friend,** frq. in conjunction with *nyé-du* or *ǩyim-mťses Glr.*; *mdzá-bo* id. *Dzl.* etc. and vulgo, rarely *mdzao Thgy.*; still more vulg. *Ts.*: **dzán-te, dzá-mo** fem.; **dzá-wo ǰhé-pa**, *C.*, = *mdzá-ba*; *mdza-grógs* intimate friend *Sch.*; *C.*: **husband**, wife.

**མཛངས་པ** *mdzaṅs-pa* (*Ssk.* पण्डित) 1. **wise, learned,** frq.; *mǩás-šiṅ mdzáṅs-pa, γtsug-lag-če-žiṅ mdzáṅs-pa*; *mdzaṅs-bluṅ* the wise man and the fool, a relig. composition, publ. by Schmidt, together with a German translation, containing an endless variety of examples relative to the Buddhist doctrine of future rewards and punishments; *mdzáṅs-ma* a wise woman *Glr.* — 2. **gentle, noble,** distinguished as to rank, *ya-rábs mdzáṅs-kyi bu Glr.* po. — (The spelling *˳dzáṅs-pa* is not of unfrequent occurrence, but seems to be objectionable.)

**མཛད་པ** *mdzád-pa*, imp. *mdzod* (*W.* also **dzad**), **to do, to act,** resp. for *byéd-pa* in all its significations, whenever the person acting is the object of respect, hence almost without exception with regard to Buddha; but also in common life: **či dzad dug* W.* what is your honour doing? also together with *byed-pa*, *grogs byéd-par mdzód čig* pray, help me! further as a sbst.: **the act of doing, the thing done, the deed,** *mdzád-pa bču-gnyis* the twelve deeds (or prop. incidents) of an incarnated Buddha, viz. the descending from the gods, conception, birth, exhibition of skill (i.e. going through certain chivalrous exercises), conjugal diversion, relinquishing family-ties, engaging in penitential exercises, conquering the devil, becoming Buddha, preaching, dying, being deposited in the shape of relics; sometimes even hundred (or rather 125) such deeds are enumerated *Cs.* —

**Comp. and deriv.** *mdzád(-pa)-po* a maker, composer etc.; also to be used for creator. — *mdzad-spyód* resp. deed, action *Mil.*; deportment, conduct, like *spyód-lam Mil.*; course of life, way of acting, e.g. of a heretical king *Pth.*

**མཛར་ར་མཛེར་རེ** *mdzár-ra-mdzer-ré Ld.* pitted with the small-pox, **pock-marked; warty, blotchy,** v. *mdzér-pa.*

**མཛུབ་མོ**, vulgo **མཛུག་གུ** *mdzúb-mo, mdzúg-gu*, 1. **finger,** esp. **fore-finger**; *ťams-čád ǩar mdzúb-mo čúg-la sdod Glr.* now sit down and put your finger into your mouth (for our: put your finger upon your mouth), i.e. be silent, as becomes the vanquished; **dzúg-gu ṭ̌ü'-pa* C.* a kind of covenanting, the two parties wetting their fingers with saliva and then striking them against one another, which ceremony is considered more stringent than that of **do čóg-pa**, v. *rdo.* The different fingers are: *(m)ťé-bo, (m)ťéb-mo* **thumb**; *mdzúb-mo B.*, **dzúg-gu** vulgo, *ston-byéd Cs.*, *mťsod Med.* **fore-finger**; *srin-lád, bar-mdzúb Cs.*, **gúṅ-dzug* C.*, *kán-ma Med.* **middle-finger**; *srin-mdzub Cs.*, **srín-dzug** vulgo, *miṅ-méd* (*Cs.*, acc. to *Ssk.*) *čad Med.* **the fourth finger**; *(m)ťe(-ba)* or *ťeu-čúṅ*, **dzug-čúṅ* C.* **the little finger.** — 2. **toe.** — 3. **claw.**

**Comp.** *mdzub-kér, -kyér* or *-kyáṅ Cs.* a stiff finger. — *mdzub-brkyáṅs Cs.* an extended finger. — *mdzub-skyis* finger-ring (= *ser-γdub*) *Lew.* — *mdzub-ǩrid* a pointing with the finger, hint, intimation, direction, *blo-ťé-ťsom sél-bai mdzub-ǩrid byas* he made an intimation that removed every scruple of the mind *Glr.* — **dzug-gáṅ* W.* a span, measured with thumb and fore-finger. — *mdzub-gúg* a crooked finger *Cs.* — **mdzub-rtén** vulgo, thimble — *mdzub-mťó* 'a span measured with the thumb and middle-finger' *Sch.* prob. = *mdzug-gaṅ.* — *mdzub-rdúb* a mutilated finger *Cs.* — *mdzub-brdá* a hint or sign given with a finger *Cs.* — *mdzub-rtsé* tip of a finger *Cs.* — *mdzub-ťsigs* joint of a finger *Cs.* — *mdzub-žú* thimble *Cs.* — **dzug-ri* W.* = *mdzub-brdá*, **dzug-ri-táṅ-će** to beckon. — *mdzub-šúbs* a fingered glove *Sch*

**མཛེ་** *mdze, Ssk.* **कुष्ठ**, **leprosy** (not cancer, yet infectious, the skin growing white and chapped) *Glr.*, *Med.*; *mdzé-ćan* **leprous.**

**མཛེར་པ་, འཛེར་པ་** *mdzer-pa*, *˳dzér-pa* **knot, excrescence** of the skin, **wart** etc. *Med.*; *rus-mdzér S.g.* bony excrescence, exostosis (?); **knag, knot,** in wood *Dzl.*; *mdzer-mál* knot-hole, in boards.

**མཛེས་པ་** *mdzés-pa* **fair, handsome, beautiful,** *mdzés-pai* or *-mai bú-mo Glr.*; *bú-mo mdzés-pa* as a tender address to a daughter *Glr.*; *ri-bo nags-ťsál dú-mas mdzés-pa* a mountain beautified by numerous woods; *mdzés-par byá-bai p̔yir* for show, serving as finery, ornament *Stg.*; fig.: *spyód-lam mdzés-pa* a deportment outwardly unblamable *Dzl.*; *lus-mdzés* a well-made body, *γdoṅ-mdzés* a handsome face, *mig-mdzes* a beautiful eye *Cs.*; *mdzes-mdzés* **pomp, extravagance, profusion, debauchery** *Sch.* — *γnod-mdzés* name of the *rig-sṅágs-kyi rgyál-po* (?) *Dom.*, *Lex.*

**མཛོ་** *mdzo* mongrel-breed of the yak-bull and common cow *Lt.*, whilst *˳bri-mdzo* (*W. *brim-dzo**) is the hybrid of a common bull and a yak-cow, *mdzó-p̔o* a male, *mdzó-mo* a female animal of the kind, both valued as domestic cattle; *mdzó-mo-k̔yu* a herd of such animals; *mdzo-rgód* wild cattle; *mdzo-p̔rúg* calf of such cattle; *mdzo-kó* leather, *mdzo-már* butter from a bastard cow, *mdzo-sgál* load for the same *Cs.*; *mdzo-ťsá Wdṅ.* n. of a medicine (cf. *ba-ťsá?*).

**མཛོ་མོ་** *mdzó-mo*, 1. v. *mdzo.* — 2. **oats** *Sch.*

**མཛོད་** *mdzod, Ssk.* **कोष**, 1. sbst. **store-house, magazine, depository, strong-box,** *mdzód-du ˳júg-pa*, *sbéd-pa* to secure, to hide a thing in a depository, *mdzód-nas ˳dón-pa* to fetch forth from it; *dkor-mdzód*, *γter-mdzód Glr.* treasury; *baṅ-mdzód* corn-magazine, granary; *dbyig-mdzód* a safe for valuables, *γser-mdzód* for gold; *p̔yag-mdzód* (*Cs.* also *mdzód-pa*) **treasurer,** with kings, in large monasteries; *míṅ-gi mdzod* a treasury of words, **dictionary.** — *mdzod-k̔aṅ* store-room, larder. — *mdzod-srúṅ* treasurer *Dzl.* — 2. vb. v. *mdzád-pa.*

**མཛོད་སྤུ་** *mdzód-spu, Ssk.* **ऊर्णा**, *smin-mťsams-kyi mdzód-spu Glr.*, acc. to *Cs.* **a single hair,** acc. to the majority, **a circle of hair,** between the eye-brows, in the middle of the forehead, one of the particular marks of a Buddha, from which, e.g., he is able to send forth magic or divine rays of light.

**མཛོལ་བུ་** *mdzól-bu Lex.*; *Sch.*: **'grief, dejection; a snare, a trap'** (?).

**འཛའ་** *˳dza* 1. **exchange, agio** *C.* — 2. **interest** or **premium** paid for the use of money borrowed *Lh.*

**འཛའ་བ་** *˳dzá-ba*, prob. only in the word *ćúd-˳dza-ba* **to be expended in vain** *Cs.* (?).

**འཛག་པ་** *˳dzág-pa*, pf. (*γ*) *zags*, fut. *γzag*, (intrs. to *˳ťsag-pa*), **to drop, drip, trickle,** *sna-k̔rág*, *sna-ću dzag* blood, water, dripping from the nose *Med.*; **ṅal-ṭ̔ag zág-će** the menstrual flow of females (plain expression for it) *W.*; *mći-ma Dzl.*; *˳ó-ma ˳dzág-pa dé-las ˳byuṅ* milk is trickling from it *Wdṅ.*; *˳dzag-˳dzág-pa* to trickle constantly *Sch.*; in a more gen. sense: **to flow out** spouting; *k̔rag γzágs-pa* the blood that has been shed *Dzl.*; *mťso žábs-nas zágs-te méd-par soṅ* flowing off at the bottom, the lake dwindled away *Mil.*; **k̔á-ću zag dug* W.* he foams (with rage); *bžin zags-te* the face dripping (with perspiration); **šú-gu zags soṅ* W.* the paper runs, blots; sometimes used transitively: *kún-la snyiṅ-btse mći-ma γzag* he is shedding tears of universal pity *Dzl.* ୨୨, 16; *sor bar-nas ˳dzág-nas* letting (the ashes) fall through between his fingers *Mil.*

**འཛག་འཛོག་** *˳dzag-˳dzóg* **mixed, mingled, promiscuously, pell-mell** *Lexx.* = *˳k̔rúgs-pa.*

**འཛང་འཛོང་** *˳dzaṅ-˳dzóṅ* = *γtsaṅ-γtsóṅ.*

**འཛངས་པ་** *˳dzaṅs-pa*, *Lex.* = *zád-pa* **spent, consumed, exhausted,** construed with *nor*, of rare occurrence.

འཛད་པ་ ₒ*dzád-pa*, pf. *zad* 1. **to be on the decline,** pf. **to be consumed, spent,** frq., *bságs-pai nor ₒdzad* the gathered wealth goes to an end *Pth.*; *snúm-zad-kyi már-me* a lamp the oil of which is exhausted *Glr.*; *k̔yód-kyi bsód-nams zád-pai ťsóṅ-p̔rug-rnams* ye (poor) partners in trade, whose stored-up merits are now at an end (whilst the speaker by the strength of his virtue is saved from the danger in which the others perish) *Glr.*; *rgyágs-la zad* that has been spent for provisions *Mil.*; *brlai ša zad kyaṅ yaṅ-ṅo* the flesh of the upper part of the thigh, even after it had been used (after all had been laid on the scales), was nevertheless lighter than .... *Dzl.*; *ťabs-zád* helpless *Glr.*; *ťse-yóṅs-su zád-pa-las* whilst life is consuming itself *Do.*; *ťse-zád-kar Do.*, prob. the same as ₒ*či-k̔ar*, at the hour of death; frq. referred to sin: ₒ*dod-čágs-kyi sems, dri-ma kun, nyés-pai skyon ťams-čád, ₒdód-pa kun yóṅs-su zád-de* sensuality and all sin, desire and defilement being done away with, having ceased *Dzl.*; *dug lṅai lás-la zád-pa med* the effects of the five poisons (q.v.) never cease; ₒ*dré-la zad-pa med* of devils there is an infinite number *Mil.*; *zad (-pa) méd(-pa), zad-mi-šes-pa* incessant, endless, everlasting — 2. ₒ*dis zad* **with this it is done,** i.e. a. this is **the only thing,** besides which no second is existing; ₒ*dis don-γnyer-žiṅ ₒťsó-bar zád-na* as this is our **only means** of making a living *Dzl.*; *bu ni k̔yod γčig-pur zád-de* as thou art **our only son** *Dzl.*; *mťóṅ-ba k̔ó-mo k̔ó-nar zád-de* as I am **the only person** that has seen .... *Tar.*; *mťsóṅ-bar zád-de* this is limited to seeing, this refers **only** to sight *Dzl.* ༤༥, 12; *γnyis ni miṅ γčig-pa tsám-du zád-pas* as the two have **only one name** *Tar.*; hence the frequent *ma zád-de* with the termin. case, **not only,** *srog ₒdór-ba ₒdi ₒbá-žig-tu ma zád-de* having lost his life not only this time (but often so before) *Dzl.* ༧༣, 13; *der ma zad(-kyi)* not enough with that, still more, further, yea even *Thgy.* — b. **it is decided, settled, unquestionable,** *nor rgyál-pos bžés-par zád-na* as the fortune unquestionably falls to the king.

འཛབ་ ₒ*dzab* **magic sentence,** *bzlá-ba* to pronounce one *Lex.*

འཛབ(ས)་པ་ ₒ*dzáb(s)-pa* **to strive, endeavour; to be studious, to give diligence** *Sch.*

འཛམ་བུ་ ₒ*dzám-bu* v. *dzám-bu.*

འཛམ་བུར་ ₒ*dzam-búr*, **gun, cannon,** **gyáb-pa** *C.* to discharge.

འཛར་ ₒ*dzar* **bob, tassel, tuft** *Lex.*

འཛར་བ་ ₒ*dzár-ba Cs.*: **'to hang down'**; yet it is evidently the prop. present-form to the pf. *bzar* and the fut. *γzar,* which frq. are used without regard to tense: **to hang up,** clothes on a line *Dzl.;* **to hang** or **throw over,** the toga over one's shoulder *Dzl.* and elsewh.

འཛི་བ་ ₒ*dzi-ba* **to abstain from, to be abstinent, temperate** *Sch.*

འཛིང་བ་ ₒ*dziṅ-ba* **to quarrel, contend, fight,** *mče-, sder-, rwa-ₒdziṅ byéd-pa* to fight with tusks, claws, horns *Cs.*; ₒ*dziṅ-mo* **quarrel, contention, dispute.**

འཛིངས་པ, གཟིང་བ་ ₒ*dziṅs-pa, γziṅ-ba*, gen. with *skra*, rarely with *mgo Glr.*, **bristly, rugged, shaggy,** of beggars *Dzl*, infernal monsters *Dzl.* — *sprin-sna ₒdziṅs-mťiṅ-nág Mil.?*

འཛིན་ ₒ*dzin* 1. **the act of seizing, seizure, grasp, gripe,** v. ₒ*dzin-pa*, e.g. *nyi-ₒdzin* eclipse of the sun, *zla-ₒdzin* lunar eclipse, (the heavenly bodies being seized by the dragon Rahula, v. *sgra-γčan*), *ril-ₒdzin* total, *ča-ₒdzin* partial eclipse *Wdk.* — 2. **he that seizes, holds fast, a holder, keeper; receptacle;** *rdo-rje-ₒdzin* v. *rdó-rje*; *ču-ₒdzin* po. cloud, *ro-ₒdzin* po. tongue *Lex.*; **adherent,** e.g. in *srol-ₒdzin.* — 3. **bond, obligation, certificate,** e.g. *p̔rod-ₒdzin* **receipt, acquittance.** — 4. **contract, agreement, treaty,** **žág-pa** *C.*, **táṅ-če** *W.*, to conclude, make, a bargain, a treaty; *yig-ₒdzin* **a written agreement.**

འཛིན་ཅན་ ₒ*dzin-čan W.* **sticky, glutinous** (?).

འཛིན་པ་ ₒ*dzin-pa* I. vb. pf. *(b)zuṅ*, fut. *γzuṅ*, imp. *zuṅ(s)*, also *γzúṅ-ba, bzúṅ-ba* and *zin-pa* in all tenses, *W.* **zúm-če**, *Bal.* **zún-čas**, 1. **to take hold of, to seize, grasp,** *lág-pa-nas* to grasp a person's hand *Mil.*; *mgó-nas* taking hold of a skull *Dzl.* ༢༧, 6; *gós-kyi mťá-ma* to seize the coat-tail *Dzl.*; *mi* a man, = to catch, frq.; *čuṅ-mar ₒdzin-pa* to take wives *Glr.*; **to hold,** *lág-na rál-gri* to hold a sword in one's hand *Glr.*; **k̔yi zum toṅ* W.*, **k̔yi dzin* (or *zin*) *rog ǰhẹ* C.*, hold the dog fast! **to catch,** a ball, rain-water etc.; *bzuṅ-bas mi zin capiendo non capitur*, it (the soul) cannot be taken hold of *Mil.*; *bdág-gi γduṅ-brgyúd ₒdzin-pai rgyál-bụ* a prince upholding my race *Glr.*; **to hold, support,** a certain doctrine; **to embrace,** another religion *Glr.*, v. below; to take upon one's self, some religious duty. — 2. **to get, receive, obtain.** — 3. **to occupy, to take possession of,** hold in possession, a country *Ma.*, *rgyál-sa* the throne; **to be seized,** *nád-kyis zin-pa* seized with a malady *Mil.*, — 4. intellectually: **to take in, comprehend, grasp, conceive,** by the faculty of perception or imagination: *dbáṅ-po-rnams-kyi nús-pa zad-pas yul mi ₒdzin-pa-amγžán-du ₒdzin-pa* to perceive things not as they are, or not at all, in consequence of weakened senses *Thgy.*; with reference to mind or memory: *séms-la, yid-la, bló-la B.* and *col.*; **to be taken in, affected, seized, captivated,** *sdig-pas zin-pa* to be affected, taken, by sin *Mil.*; *ťúgs-rǰes zin-pa* to be kindly, graciously, affected towards a person; *ťugs-ma zin-pa* to be not graciously inclined *Mil. nt.*; *bú-mos zin-pa* taken in love with a girl *Pth.*; *ₒdzin-pa ťams-čád* all that captivates me; **to choose, to follow,** *ri-k̔ród* to choose the solitude of mountains *Mil.*, *dmán-sa* to follow humility, to choose lowliness *Mil.* and elsewh.; **to embrace,** another religion, v. above; **to take for, to consider, esteem,** *ṅa-la dgrar* taking me for an enemy *Dzl.*; *mi* or *mí-la γčés-par* or *sdúg-par* to value, esteem, love, a person, v. *γčẹ́s-pa*; *p̔ar, mar* to esteem, respect one, as a father, as a mother *Stg.*; *méd-pa-la yód-par* to consider the not existing as existing *Thgr.*; *γnyis-su* to consider as different, to find a difference between two things, which according to Buddhist philosophy are one and the same, cf. *γnyis-ₒdzin*; also absolutely, without an object being mentioned: *dṅós-por ₒdzin-pa* to believe in the reality (of a thing) *Mil.* — 5. *rǰés-su ₒdzin-pa* v. *rǰes*.

II. sbst. 1. **he that seizes, holds, occupies,** *rigs-sṅags ₒdzin-pa* the holder of a magic sentence; **adherent, keeper** etc. — 2. **that which affects, captivates,** in an intellectual sense, v. above *ₒdzin-pa ťams-čád*; the being seized or affected with, or as we should say, **taking an interest in,** v. sub *spóṅ-ba*; also cf. *γzuṅ-ₒdzin*. — *ₒdzin-skyóṅ*, *p̔o-bráṅ ₒdii ₒdzin-skyóṅ gyis* occupy this palace and take care of it *Glr.* — *ₒdzin-pa* **the earth,** as a receptacle of beings *Sch.*

འཛིམ་པ་ *ₒdzim-pa Lt.?* acc. to one *Lex.* = *ₒdzin-pa*.

འཛིར་བ་ *ₒdzir-ba*, = འཛག་པ *dzág-pa* **to drop, to drip** *Lex.*

འཛུ་བ་ *ₒdzu-ba*, pf. *ₒdzus*, **to enter** *Sch.*

འཛུགས་པ་ and ཟུག་པ་ *ₒdzugs-pa* and *zug-pa*, pf. *btsugs*, *zugs*, fut. *γzugs*, imp. *zug(s)*, (trs. to *ₒťsugs-pa*) 1. **to prick** or **stick into, to set,** to prick a stick, to set a plant, into the ground, **to plant,** frq.; **to run, thrust, pierce,** to run one's self a splinter into the flesh etc. *W.*; **to erect,** a pillar, **to raise,** a standard. — 2. **to put down, to place,** a kettle *Dzl.*; to place before, *mi-la p̔ór-pa* to place a drinking-bowl before a person (more genteel than *bžag-pa*) *Glr.*; **to put or place on, to touch with,** *mdzúb-mo* the finger; esp. *pús-mo(-i lha-ṅá) sá-la* to place the knee on the ground, to kneel down, v. *pús-mo*; *žábs-ₒdzugs-kyi dga-ston* feast given, when a little child begins to walk *Glr.* — 3. **to lay out,** a garden, **to found,** a town, a convent; **to institute,** a sacrificial festival *Glr.*; **to introduce,** *srol* a custom *Lex.*, hence in a general sense, **to begin, commence,** any business, with or without *mgo*; **ku-rim tsúg-sa ma tsugs* W.* has the ceremony already begun? is it a going? *rgól-ba ₒdzúgs-pa* to offer resistance *Pth.* — 4. **to prick, sting, pierce,** *mdas* with arrows *Dzl.*, fig. *mi-k̔a zúg-pa* hurting by malicious words *Do.*;

*tsig kún-tu zúg-pa* a sarcastic, offensive speech *Stg.* — 5. intrs., **to bore or force itself into, to penetrate, to take hold, to stick to,** mostly fig., e.g. *sman ma zug* the medicine has not taken hold yet, does not work *Thgy.*; *zlá-la ḱyéd-kyis mi zug* you do not çling or stick to a companion *Mil.*; **dé-la sem zúg-pa* C.* to be attached to, to be pleased with a thing; **zúg-pa* C.*, attached. — 6. **to sting,** like nettles, **to prick,** *tser ltar* like a thorn *Mil.*; *ló-ma zúg-par byed* the leaves sting *Wdṅ.*; *zug-rgyu-méd-pa* not smarting *Wdṅ.*

**འཛུད་པ་** *˳dzúd-pa*, pf. *btsud*, *Sch.* also *zud*, imp. *tsud* (trs. to *˳tsúd-pa*, synon. to *˳ǰúg-pa*), **to put, to lay,** into a box, into the grave; **to lead, to guide,** into the right way, to virtue, to religion = to convert; to reduce, to despair, *sdig-pa-la* to seduce to sin *Pth.*; **to prompt** one to do a thing *Gyatch.*; *˳dzúd-˳dzud-pa* to put into *Sch.*

**འཛུབ་མོ་** *˳dzub-mo*, sometimes erron. for *mdzúb-mo*.

**འཛུམ་** *˳dzum* **smile,** *byáms-pai ˳dzúm-γyis* with a friendly smile; *˳dzum byéd-pa* **to smile;** *˳dzum daṅ ldan* **smiling** *Pth.*; *˳dzum skyóṅ-ba* to preserve a friendly countenance, to be always mild and gentle; *˳dzum-skyoṅ* in a special sense, the exhortation given to every daughter on her marriage, to treat visitors with a friendly smile; also fig., **an engaging appearance,** *rí-mo ˳dzúm-gyis ma bslús-par* not to be deceived by an enticing appearance of colour *Mil.*; *ṅo-˳dzúm*, **smile,** in a relative sense, *ǎ-nei ṅo-˳dzúm dkar nag bltas* I watched whether the smile, the mien, of my aunt was friendly or unfriendly *Mil.*; *ṅo-˳dzúm nág-ste* looking sad *Dzl.*

**འཛུམ་པ་** *˳dzum-pa*, pf. *btsum*, *zum*, fut. *γzum*, imp. *tsum* 1. **to close, to shut,** yet only in certain applications, more esp. **to close one's eyes, to shut one's mouth,** *mig mi-˳dzúm-par ltá-žiṅ* to have one's eyes immovably fixed upon *Dzl.*; also *pád-mai ḱa zum bžin S.g.* just as the lotus-flower closes; *má-ḱa mi zúm-žiṅ Wdṅ.* if the wound will not close; *ḱa zum* the orifice (of the urethra) is closed *Mṅg.* — 2. **to wink,** prob. only **dzum-dzúm ǰhḗ-pa* and *čó-če**. — 3. **to smile,** *ráb-tu* to look very friendly *Glr.*; sbst. **the smile,** *bčom-ldan-˳dás-kyi žal ˳dzúm-pa daṅ bčás-pai sgó-nas* from the portals of Buddha's countenance graced with a smile *Glr.*; *žal-˳dzúm mdzád-pa* resp. to smile *Glr.*; *bžín-gyi ˳dzum* the smile of the countenance; adj. **smiling; sweet, beautiful** *Mil.*

**Comp.** *˳dzúm-ḱa* a smiling mouth; *lha-mo ˳dzúm-ḱa-mo* a smiling goddess *Mil.* — *˳dzúm-bag-čan* (of a child) sweetly smiling *Mil.* — *˳dzum-ltag-dgyé Cs.*: 'a smile between the teeth, a sardonic smile, a grin'; *˳dzum-mdáṅs* a smiling air *Cs.* — *˳dzum-múl* or *-dmúl* a smile; *dzum-múl-gyis šor* a smile escaped him *Glr.*; *˳dzum-(d)múl-ba* to smile. — *˳dzum-méd* frowning, austere *Cs.* — *˳dzum-˳dzúm* 1. the winking. 2. the smiling; *˳dzum-waṅ-wáṅ Cs.*: smiling look.

**འཛུར་** *˳dzur*, 1. sup. of *˳dzu-ba*. 2. v. the following.

**འཛུར་བ་** *˳dzur-ba*, pf. *bzur*, fut. *γzur*, imp. *zur*, *Cs.* **zúr-wa** **to give** or **make way,** *lam(-nas)* to step aside; **to keep aloof** *Mil.*; *lás-la ˳dzúr-ba* to shun work, to evade labour *Lex.*

**འཛུལ་བ་** *˳dzúl-ba* 1. vb. **to slip in,** *rtsa-γséb-tu* between the grass *Thgy.*, *sgor* through the door *Lex.*; *čú-la*, *čur* into the water, i.e. to dive. — 2. sbst. *Sch.*: **'a tippler'.**

**འཛུས་** *˳dzus* v. *˳dzú-ba*.

**འཛེག་པ་** *˳dzég-pa*, pf. *˳dzegs*, imp. *˳dzog*, **to ascend,** *rí-la* frq.; *šiṅ-sdoṅ-po-la Glr.*

**འཛེང་** *˳dzeṅ*, *˳dzeṅ-rdo* **whsettone, hone** *Lex.*

**འཛེང་བ་** *˳dzéṅ-ba* **to stick** or **jut out, to project, to be prominent** *Sch.*

**འཛེད་པ་** *˳dzéd-pa*, pf. *bzed*, fut. *γzed*, vulgo *bzéd-pa*, **zḗ-pa* C.*, **zéd-če* W.*, **to hold out** or **forth,** *ḱud* the coat-tail, *snod* a vessel *Dzl.* (The significations given by *Cs.*: **to receive,** and by *Sch.*: **to meet with,** seem not to be sufficiently warranted.)

**འཛེམ་པ་** *˳dzém-pa* **to shrink,** *la*, from, **to shun, avoid,** *mi-dgé-ba-la Glr.*, *sdig-*

pa-la frq.; ṅó-ťsa-la mi ˳dzém-pa Cs. **insensible to shame, shameless**; *nád-rigs-la-mi ˳dzém-na* unless one is on his guard against the several diseases; also **to feel ashamed**, **ṅe'-nam-la mi ˳dzem-mam* C.* do you not feel abashed in our presence? *˳dzém-pa-čan ˳dzém-bag-čan* **bashful, modest, temperate** *Cs.*; *˳dzém(-pa)-med(-pa)* the contrary; *ǩrel-˳dzém* **modesty** *Cs.*

འཛེར་པ་ *˳dzér-pa* v. *mdzér-pa.*

འཛེར་བ་ *˳dzér-ba* 1. **to say**, to speak, *Stg.* ཁུ་ 57, 6, obs., v. *zér-ba.* — 2. **to be hoarse**, *˳dzér-pò* hoarse, *skad Dzl., Med.; skad ˳dzer-˳dzér-du ṅú-ba* to weep with a very hoarse voice *Pth.* — 3. **to solder** *Sch.*

འཛོ་སྒྲེལ་ *˳dzo-sgrél Mil.?*

འཛོག་པ་ *˳dzóg-pa*, pf. *btsogs*, fut. *btsog* **to heap together, to jumble, to throw disorderly together** *Cs.*

འཛོང་འཛོང་ *˳dzoṅ-˳dzóṅ Ts.* **˳dzog-˳dzóg** 1. **jagged, pointed, conical.** — 2. **oblong, cylindrical** *C.*

འཛོམ(ས)་པ་ *˳dzóm(s)-pa* **to come together, to meet**, **dzom ťsár-ra ma ťsar** are they already assembled? *dág-pa mṅón-dgai žiṅ-ǩams der ˳ó-skol ˳dzóm-par γdon mi za* that we shall meet again in the realms of pure bliss, that is certain *Mil.*; *ťses bčo-lṅá daṅ ˳dzóms-pas* as it just fell upon the 15th. *Glr.*; **dzom mi dzom* W.* they do not agree with each other; *dé-rnams rnyéd-par dká-ste mi ˳dzom* as it is difficult to obtain these things, we shall not be able to get all of them together *Glr.*; **dzóm-pa mé'-pa čig kyaṅ me'* C.* there is nothing that does not find its way there, that is not to be had there; **to be plentiful** *Mil.*; as partic. with termin. case: **rich in, abounding** *Mil.* — *dál-˳byor ˳dzóm-pai lus Mil.* v. *dál-ba.* — *ǩun-˳dzóm* 'where all meet', name of mountain-passes, e.g. between *Lh.* and *Sp.*, and of females; in a similar manner *gaṅ-˳dzóm* and *˳byor-˳dzóm* ('conflux of goods'). — *˳dzóm-po* rich in *C.*, *rtsa-ču ˳dzóm-po* abounding in grass and water, fertile *C.*; *mťun-rkyén ˳dzóm-po* fortunate, successful, through a favourable concurrence of circumstances; *ťsos-sna-˳dzóm-po* variegated, many-coloured.

འཛོལ་པ་ *˳dzól-pa* **fault, error, mistake,** *dé-la ˳dzól-pa γsum byuṅ* he fell into three mistakes, committed three errors *Glr.*

འཛོལ་བ་ *˳dzól-ba* **to shake about, to stir** or **shake up**, e.g. a feather-bed; **to confound, to confuse,** *p̔rin goṅ-˳og ˳dzol-ba* to deliver a message confusedly, making a mess of it *Glr.*; *W.: *zol-zól čo-če*.* — **˳dzól-ťso* C., *zol-zól* W.* **difference.**

རྫ་ *rdza, W. *za**, 1. **clay**, gen. *rdzá-sa.* — 2. in comp. for *rdzá-ma*, e.g. *čáṅ-rdza* **beer-jug**, *čú-rdza* **water-pitcher** *Cs.* —

**Comp. and deriv.** *rdza-kór* earthen bowl, little dish. — *rdza-ǩáṅ* pottery *Schr.* — *rdza-ǩúṅ* clay-pit. — *rdza-mǩán* potter, *rdza-mǩán-gyi ˳kór-lo skór-ba* to turn the potter's wheel *Dom.* — *rdza-rṅá* kettle-drum of burnt clay. — *rdza-čág* potsherd. — *rdza-čú*, or more refined *rdza-čáb*, water issuing from clay-slate rocks *Mil.* and elsewh. — *rdza-čén* a large, *rdza-čúṅ* a little pot, v. *rdzá-ma.* — *rdza-snód, rdza-spyád* earthen vessel. — *rdza-pág* tile, (Dutch) tile for stoves. — *rdza-p̔ór C.* = *rdza-kór.* — *rdza-búm* 1. **pitcher, jar, bottle**, formed of clay. 2. **jar**, in gen., *lčágs-kyi rdza-búm* iron jar *Stg.* — *rdzá-bo* an earthen vessel *Cs.* — *rdzá-ma* **pot** (unglazed, urn-shaped, bellied vessels of various size, not for cooking, but only for holding water, butter and the like). — *rdza-γžóṅ* earthen basin. — *rdza-ri* mountain consisting of clay-slate. — *rdza-sá* argillaceous earth, clay. — *dza-brá, C. *dzab-ra*, W. *zab-ra** a mole-like animal.

རྫ་ཀི་ *rdzá-ki Mil.*, for *dzó-gi, yó-gi.*

རྫང་ *rdzaṅ* **chest, box**, for various store = *báṅ-ba Thgy.*

རྫང་བ་ *rdzáṅ-ba* v. *rdzóṅ-ba.*

རྫབ་ *rdzab*, *˳dam-rdzáb*, **mud, mire** (*Cs.* **clay**); *rdzab-dóṅ* **sink, slough.**

རྫབ་རྫུབ་ *rdzab-rdzúb* **sham, emptiness, falsehood**, *rmi-lam rdzab-rdzúb-čan* an empty dream *Cs.*

རྫས rdzas 1. **thing, matter, object** (= *dṅós-po Lex.*), *rdzas dkar sér-por mtoṅ* white objects appear yellow *Lt.*; *rdzas ka-sáṅ yód-pa dé-riṅ med* the thing of yesterday is to-day no more *Mil.*; *mi-ɣtsáṅ-bai rdzas* something impure *Pth.;* natural bodies, **substances**, from which e.g. medicines are prepared *S.g.*; **materials, requisites,** *dei rdzas* requisites for this purpose; especially for sacrifices, sorceries etc., hence also used as identical with **magic agency** *Wdṅ.*; **remedy,** *smyo-byéd-kyi* narcotic, soporific *Glr.*; **ointment,** v. *rkáṅ-pa* and *bábs*; *rdzás-las* ₒ*byúṅ-bai bsód-nams Tar.* 20, 9, not: merits arising 'from works or any material causes', but: the good, the blessing accruing from a right application of *rdzas*, wonder-working medicines, and consisting in long life etc., with which also *Trigl.* fol. 20, b is in unison, if the Sanskrit word is read *dzaiwatrikam*; *srog-rdzás* **provisions, victuals** *Pth.;* in the context *rdzas* is also found standing alone in the same sense, where it perh. would be more correct to read *zas*; *mé-mdai rdzas, me-rdzás*, also *rdzas* alone, **gun-powder,** **dzẹ-kúg** *C.* cartridge-box, **dzẹ-mé** (a gun) not loaded *C.*; **goods, property,** *rdzas gaṅ yód-pa-rnams* all his property *Mil.*; *nor (daṅ) rdzas* money and money's worth *Mil.* and elsewh.; **treasures, jewels, valuable productions,** *rgya-gár-gyi Glr.* — 2. in philosophy: **matter** *Was.;* **real substance, realities** *Was.*

རྫི rdzi, *W.* **zi**, 1. **wind,** *rdzi-rlúṅ* id., also *bsér-bui, rlúṅ-gi rdzi Do.*; *pu-rdzí*, or *stod-rdzí* a wind blowing down the valley, *luṅ-* or *mdo-rdzí* blowing up the valley; *dri-rdzi ldaṅ* a fragrant breeze, a wind fraught with the odours of flowers is blowing *Stg.*; **šár-zi yóṅ-ṅa rag** *W.* I perceive an east-wind is setting in; *rdzi-čár* heavy rain with wind, *rdzi-čár drág-po* rain-storm *Tar.* and elsewh.; **zi núm-če* or *tsór-če** *W.* **to smell, sniff, snuffle,** of dogs. — 2. in comp. for *rdzi-bo, rdzi-ma.* — 3. v. *zi.*

རྫི་བ rdzí-ba, pf. *(b)rdzis*, fut. *brdzi*, imp. *(b)rdzi(s)*, *W.*, **zi-če**, *Pur.* **dzi-čas** **to press, to knead,** dough; **to tread, to beat** (clay, *gyaṅ* q. v.); *gál-te tsér-ma brdzís-na* **if I should tread into a thorn** *Dzl.*; **to crush, a worm; to oppress, to distress;** *rdzi-méd Lex., Sch.:* 'powerless', but *stóbs-rnams-la rdzi-ba-med-pa Stg.* evidently signifies: of invincible strength.

རྫི་བོ rdzí-bo **herdsman, shepherd, keeper,** frq.; also *rdziu Dzl.*; *rdzi-po* a male, *rdzí-mo* a female keeper; *pyúgs-rdzi* herdsman, *ɣnág-rdzi* neat-herd, *gláṅ-rdzi* cow-keeper; *rá-rdzi* (**rár-ži** *W.*) goat-herd; *kyi-rdzi* dog-feeder, *byá-rdzi* person attending to the poultry; *mí-rdzi* 'guarder of man, a god' *Cs.* yet a king might also be thus designated; *rdzi-skór* shepherd's hut = *pu-lu. Sch.* has besides: *dpe-rdzi* **index, register.**

རྫི་མ rdzí-ma (vulgo **zi-ma**) **eye-lashes** (the eye-lashes of Buddha are sometimes compared to those of a cow).

རྫིག་རྫིག rdzig-rdzig, with **taṅ-wa** *C.*, **to address harshly, to fly at.**

རྫིང rdziṅ **pond,** gen. *rdziṅ-bu* e. g. for bathing *Dzl.*; v. also *skyil-ba*; *rdziṅ-po* or *-čén* a large pond *Cs.*

རྫིངས rdziṅs, *gru-rdziṅs Lt.*, gen. *ɣziṅs* **ship, ferry.**

རྫིའུ rdziu 1. for *rdzi-bo.* — 2. **fin of a fish** *Sch.*

རྫུ་བ rdzú-ba, pf. *(b)rdzus*, fut. *brdzu*, imp. *(b)rdzu(s)* **to give a deceptive representation,** to make a thing appear different from what it is (cf. *sprúl-ba*), with termin. case **to change into,** also **to change** (one's self), **to be changed,** *srin-por* to change into a Rakshasa *Zam.*; **to disguise** one's self, *rnál-byor-par* as a mendicant friar; *rdzús-te skyé-ba* v. *skyé-ba*; *yig-rdzu* a letter filled with falsehoods, a lying epistle *Mil. nt.*; *šá-ru rdzú-bai rgyú-ma* entrails feigning to be flesh, looking like flesh *Mil.*; *rdzu-*ₒ*prúl* (*Ssk.* ऋद्धि) **delusion, miraculous appearances, transformations,** *stón-pa* to produce such, ₒ*jig-pa* to destroy the illusion, e.g. by seeing through it *Mil.*; *rdzu-*ₒ*prúl-gyi mtu*, or *stobs* **witchcraft, magic;** *rdzu-*ₒ*prul-čan* gifted with magic power *Thgy. rdzu-*ₒ*prul* is the highest manifestation of the acquired moral perfection, that is known to Buddhism; there is, however, an essential difference between it and the miracles of holy writ, the former bearing the stamp of non-reality and mere appearance, as is not only implied by the name, but also universally acknowledged; and it differs again from *čo-ₒṗrul,* in as much as the latter requires the help of natural magic (jugglery), or of demoniacal influences, and never can be produced, like *rdzu-ₒṗrúl,* at the pleasure of the saint by his own immanent power. Yet there is no doubt that the term *čo-ₒṗrul* is also often used in connection with *rdzu-ₒṗrúl,* and as identical with it; v. *Dzl.* ༢༦ and ༥༩.

ཪྫུན་ *rdzun, C.*dzun*, W.*zun*, Pur.*rdzun*,* also *brdzun* **untruthful speech, falsehood, lie, fiction, fable**; *rdzun-tsig,* id.; *mi-bden rdzún* that is falsehood and not truth *Glr.*; *rdzun-smrá-ba,* resp. *ɣsúṅ-ba B., byéd-pa B., C., *zér-če* W.* **to lie**, *rgyál-ba-rnams-kyis rdzun ɣsúṅ-ba mi srid* it is impossible that Buddhas should lie; **to tell tales, to make believe, to impose upon**; **zun yin* W.* you are not in earnest, you only want to quiz me; **zun gyáb-če* W.* to lie, to act the hypocrite; **mi še zun gyab* W.* to feign, to pretend ignorance, to disown a person or thing, **mi ṫsor zun gyab* W.* he pretends not to hear it. — *rdzun-ₒḱrab Sch.*: 'an adroit liar and deceiver'. — *rdzún-ma* 1. = *rdzun Dzl.* 2. **liar** *Mil.* — **zún-yag-čan* W.* **clown, buffoon, merry Andrew.**

ཪྫུབ་ *rdzub* **deceit, imposture** *Lex.*, *byéd-pa* **to make a false assertion** *Tar.*; cf. *rdzab-rdzub.*

ཪྫུས་མ་ *rdzús-ma* something **counterfeit, feigned, dissembled,** *rdzús-mai spráṅ-po* a disguised beggar *Glr.*

ཪྫེ་བ་ *rdzé-ba* pf. *(b)rdzes,* fut. *brdze,* imp. *(b)rdze(s) W. *zé-če*,* 1. **to tuck up, truss up,** clothes; **to cock,** a hat; **to turn up,** the upper-lip *Wdṅ.*; *skra gyén-du brdzés-pa* the hair bristling *Do.*; **so* or *čé-wa zé-če* W.* to show one's teeth, to grin. — 2. **to threaten** *Cs.*

ཪྫེའུ་ *rdzéu* dimin. of *rdzá-ma,* **a small pot, pipkin.**

ཪྫོག(ས)་ *rdzog(s)?* **fist,** also **dzog-ril* C.*

ཪྫོགས་པ་ *rdzogs-pa* 1. vb. **to be finished, to be at an end, to terminate** (*Lex.* = *zin-pa*), *lam rdzógs-pai mṫsáms-su* just where the road terminates *Mil.*; **dá-wa zóg-nẹ* W.* as the month has expired; **ʼi-ru pi-ti yúl-ṫso zog soṅ* W.* here the villages of Spiti have an end; *mdzád-pa yóṅs-su rdzógs-nas* having accomplished all his deeds *Glr.*; *ɔ̀i-ltar smón-pa bžin-du yoṅs rdzógs-pas* all prayers and wishes being fully realized *Dzl.*; *yóṅs-su rdzógs-par ṫsár-te* when the whole (of the building) was completed *Glr.* — 2. adj. **perfect, complete, blameless,** **gó-lo zog dug* W.* the body (of this horse) is without fault; *stón-pa dág-par rdzógs-pai saṅs-rgyás* the most perfect teacher, Buddha *Glr.*; so in a similar manner *rdzogs (-pa)-čén(-po)*; also *yé-šes yóṅs-su rdzógs-pa* is an appellation of Buddha. — *rdzógs-par* adv. **perfectly, completely, fully** (cf. *lhúg-par*), *bsnyád-pa* to report circumstantially *Dzl.*, *ɣdams-ṅág ɣnáṅ-ba* to counsel well *Mil.*; *rdzógs-par šés-pa žig* one thoroughly conversant *Mil.*; *rdzógs-par bsláb-pa* to learn thoroughly *Mil.* — *bsnyén-par rdzógs-pa* or *bsnyen-rdzógs mdzád-pa* to ordain, v. *bsnyén-pa.* —

**Comp.** *rdzogs-ldán* v. *dus* 6. — *rdzogs-ṫsig* v. *slár-sdu-ba.* — **dzog-yél* C.* obeisance to Chinese officers, in a kneeling posture. — *rdzogsrim* v. sub *skyéd-pa.*

ཪྫོང(ས)་ *rdzoṅ(s),* 1. (*C.* vulgo **dzum**) **castle, fortress**; *rdzóṅ-dpon* lord or governor of a castle, commander of a fortress; **dzoṅ-kyél* C.*, **zoṅ-lén* W.* letter-post from one nobleman's seat to another. — 2. **the act of accompanying, escorting,** *ₒdebs-pa* **to accompany, to escort** *Dzl.*, **fee for safe-conduct,** travelling-present; **dowry,** *byéd-pa* to bestow.

ཪྫོང་བ་ *rdzóṅ-ba* pf. *(b)rdzaṅ(s),* fut. *(b)rdzaṅ* **to send, to dispatch,** presents, ambassadors; **to expedite, send off, dismiss; to give to take along with.** — *dbugs rdzóṅ-ba* **shortness of breath, asthma** *Thgy.* and elsewh.

ཪྫོབ་པོ་, མོ་ *rdzób-po, -mo,* 1. **vain, empty, spurious, void**; *kun-rdzób* v. *kun.* — 2. **vain, fond of dress** *W.*

# ཝ

ཝ *wa* 1. the letter **w**, which occurs but rarely, and only as an initial, yet it is a true Tibetan letter, the *Ssk.* व being gen. represented by བ, and as second constituent of a double consonant denoted by ྭ (called *wa-zúr* angular or small *wa*); the pronunciation in general is the same as that of the English w. — 2. num. fig.: 20.

ཝ *wa* 1. **water-channel, gutter,** gen. of wood (*Cs.* also: trough); *wa-k̔a Lex.* id., *Cs.*; *wa-mču* **spout, lip,** or **beak** of vessels. — 2. **fox** (the name corresponding to the sound of barking) *Dzl.*, vulgo *wa-tsé; wa brgyal* the fox yelps *Sch.* The fox is the riding-beast of the goblins; whenever his barking is heard, it is in consequence of his receiving lashes from his rider. — *wa-skyés* fox-born *Cs.* — *wa-gró* a bluish fox, *gro-gró* a gray fox *Sch.* — *wa-rgán* **an old fox, a knave** *Cs.* — *wa-ldéb* fox-trap *W.* — *wa-nág* a blackish fox *Sch.* — *wa-lpágs* fox's skin. — *wa-spyaṅ Mil*, *wá-ma-spyaṅ Cs.* **jackall.** — *wa-p̔rúg* young fox, cub. — *wá-mo* she-fox. — *wa-ťsaṅ* fox-hole. — *wa-róg* black fox *Sch.* — *wa-ťswá* a kind of salt *S.g.* — 3. n. of **a lunar mansion**, v. *rgyu-skár*. — 4. *wa-lóg-pa* **to perform somersets** *Sch.* — 5. *W.* **ho**! calling for one.

ཝ་ར་ཎ་སཱི་, or སེ་, བ་ར་ཎ་སི་ *wa-ra-ṇa-sí* or *sé, ba-ra-na-si* **Banaras,** a city in the valley of the Ganges, frq. mentioned in legends, as a residence of Buddha, at the present time a principal seat of Brahmanism.

ཝ་ལེ་, ཝལ་ལེ་, ཝལ་ལེ་བ་ *wa-lé, wal-lé, wal-lé-ba* **clear, distinct, plain,** *wa-lér drán-pa* to recollect distinctly *Cs.*; *yid-la* floating distinctly before one's mind *Lex.; don wa-lé gyis* try to gain a clear understanding of the sense of it *Mil.*; also *skad-wál* = आशब्द(?).

ཝ་སི་ *wa-si* a kind of apples *Sch.*

ཝི་ *wi* num fig.: 50.

ཝུ་ *wu* num fig.: 80.

ཝུ་རྡོ་ *wu-rdo* **pumice stone** *Sch.*

ཝེ་ *we* num. fig.: 110.

ཝོ་ *wo* num. fig.: 140.

# ཞ

ཞ *ža*, 1. a letter of the alphabet, represented by *ž*, originally, and in the frontier-provinces to the present day, the soft sibilant, which is pronounced like *j* in French, or like the English s in leisure, (*zh*), (still more accurately like the Polish *ż* in *zima*); in *C.* it differs now from ཤ only by the following vowel being deep-toned. — 2. numerical figure: 21.

ཞྭ་, ཞྭ་མོ་ *žwa, žwa-mo,* resp. *dbu-žwa,* a covering of the head, **hat, cap;** fig. *ṅa yig sá-yi žwá-čan* the letter ང having ས for a cap: སྔ *Zam.*; *žwa gón-pa, gyón-pa* to put the cap on, *ˌbúd-pa* to take it off (in *Ts.* by way of salutation); *rgya-, bod-, sog-žwa* Chinese, Tibetan, Mongolian cap; *dgun-žwa* winter-cap, *dbyar-žwa* summer-hat (light felt-hats adapted to the warmer season); *p̔yiṅ-žwa* hat or cap made of felt; *wa-žwa* cap made of the fur of a fox. — *žwa-dkár, -nág, -dmár, -sér* white, black, red, yellow cap, denoting occasionally also **the wearers** of such caps, esp. **red-caps** and **yellow-caps**, as belonging to different Lama-sects — *žwa-k̔ébs* the covering of a hat *Cs.* — *žwa-t̔og* top ornament of a hat *Cs.*, prob. a button, v. *t̔og.* — *žwa-ɣzól* brim, *žwa-ri* crown of a hat *Cs.*, in *Ld.* however *ri* denotes the brim or flap. — *Schl.* p. 171 calls a low conical cap of the Chief Lama *ná-t̔on-ža.*

ཞ་ཉེ་ or ཞ་ནེ་ *žá-nye* or *žá-ne*, also *rá-nye Cs.*, **lead**, *žá-nyei ɣtíṅ-rdo* **sounding-lead, plummet** *Pth.*; *ža-nye-rdó* **lead-ore** *Cs.*; *žá-nyei čus sbyár-ba* to fill up (a groove or juncture) with molten lead *Glr.*; *žá-nye dkár-po C.*, **tin**, also *ža-dkár, ɣša-* or *bša-dkár*; *žá-nye nág-po* lead, (*Cs.*'s 'white lead and black lead' seem to be a mere conjecture); *ža-šóg* (**tin-foil** *Sch.* (?)), thin plates of lead.

ཞ་བ་ *žá-ba* **lame; lameness**; gen. *žá-bo* **lame, halting;** a lame person, **cripple,** *B.* and col.; *žá-mo* fem.; **žá-wo čo dug* W.* he is lame, he limps; *rkáṅ-* or *lág-ža-čan* having a lame foot or hand.

ཞ་འབྲིང་ *ža-ˌbriṅ* v. *žabs* extr.

ཞ་ལ་ *žá-la Glr.* and vulgo, v. *žál-ba.*

ཞ་ལུ་ *žá-lu* **cup, bowl,** = *p̔or-pa, ko-re Cs.*

ཞ་ལུ་པ་ *žá-lu-pa, žá-lu lóts-tsa-ba* or *lo-čén* n. of the author of a little glossary, called **Zamatog.**

ཞག་ *žag* 1. *žág-pa* (only *Schr., Cs.*), **žág-po* W*, **žág-ma* Lt., W.*, resp. *dguṅ-žág* **a day,** the time from one sun-rise to another (cf. on the other hand *nyí-ma* 2); *žag čig* **a day,** and adv : **once day, once;** **žag čig-gi žág-la* W.* is also used of a future day: **žag čig de dus leb yin* W.* once the time will come; *žag ˌga-nas* after a few days *Mil.*; *žag dú-ma lón-par* after many days *Dzl.*; *ṅa dí-riṅ ná-niṅ léb-žag* W.* this is the day of our arrival a year ago; **dę́-žag* W.* **lately,** the other day, a short time ago; **dáṅ-žag* W.* **yesterday; recently,** **dáṅ-zag za-nyi-ma* W.* last sunday; **nán-žag* W.* some time ago, **nán-žag stón-ka* W.* last autumn; **k̔ár-saṅ-žag* W.* **the day before yesterday;** *žág-nas žág-tu* **from day to day;** **žág-daṅ(-žag)* W.* **every day, always;** *žag bdun* seven days, *žag-bdun-p̔rág* **a week,** *žag-bdun-p̔rág že-brgyád* forty-eight weeks *Thgy.* — *žag-gráṅs* **the date,** **žag-ḍáṅ gyáb-če* W.* **to date.** — *žag-mál* **a station, day's journey, quarters** *Cs.*, *žág-sa* id. *Cs.* — **žag-záṅ* W.* **holiday.** — 2. **fat, grease,** in a liquid state, = *tsil-k̔u S.g.*; also melted and congealed again *W.*; fig. **the fat of the country, fertility,** *yúl-la žag med* the country is barren *Ma.*; *žág-čan* greasy, oily, *žag-méd* lean; *žag-p̔ór* a cup, vessel, for grease *Cs.* — 3. **fog, smoke, dry vapour,** filling the atmosphere in autumn.

ཞགས་པ་ *žágs-pa* **leash,** rope with a noose, e.g. for catching wild horses, *žags-t̔ág Cs*, *žags-dbyúg Sch.* id., *rgyáb-pa Cs.*, *p̔en pa Sch.* to throw the noose; *žags-pas, žags-t̔ag-gis ˌdzín-pa* frq. fig., as *Schl.* 213; *sbrul-žágs* noose consisting of a serpent, for catching any hurtful creature *Glr.*; frq. as an attribute of the gods.

ཞང་(པོ་) *žáṅ(-po)*, vulgo *á-žaṅ*, **uncle** by the mother's side, **mother's brother;** *žaṅ-brgyúd* his offspring *Cs.*; *žaṅ - nyén* in a gen. sense, relations by the mother's side *Dom.*; *žaṅ-tsá* sister's son. — *tsa-žáṅ*, resp. *dboṅ-žáṅ* 1. nephew and uncle, by the mother's side, also applied to spiritual brotherhood *Mil.* — 2. **son-in-law** and **brother-in-law** *Glr.*

ཞང་བློན་ *žaṅ-blón Glr.* seems to be a kind of **title** given to a minister (or magistrate).

ཞང་ཞུང་ *žaṅ-žúṅ* ancient n. of the province of **Guge** *Glr.*

ཞན་པ་ *žán-pa* **weak, feeble,** frq., the opp. to *drág-po*; *ṅa ji-ltar žan yaṅ* as weak, as miserable as I am (says a cripple) *Pth.*;

*kams žáṅ-pa Mil.* of a weak body, of delicate health; also applied **to sounds, accent** and the like; cf. *ṅá-ro*; **ugly** opp. to *légs-pa*, v. *skye-sgo*.

ཞབས་ *žabs* 1. **bottom** of a lake, of a vessel *Dzl.*, *Mil.*; lower end of a staff *Mil.*; for **under** in compounds, as *mṅa-žábs* q.v. — 2. resp. for *rkáṅ-pa* **foot**, *mi žíg-gi žábs-la ₒdúd-pa Cs.*, *mgó-bos btúg-pa S b.*, *ˏo byéd-pa Cs.* to bow down at another person's feet, to touch them with one's head, to kiss them; *žabs drúṅ-du* c. genit **to the feet of ...**, for **to ...**, in directions of letters; *žabs rjén-par* **barefooted**, e. g. *γšégs-pa Mil.*; *žabs ₒdegs-pa Sch.* to help, prob. = *žabs-tóg byéd-pa* v. below; *žabs ₒčág-pa* = *ₒčág-pa* II. —

**Comp.** For the most part they are the same as those of *rkáṅ-pa*; there are to be mentioned more especially: *žábs-kyu* 1. **spur** *Cs.* (?). 2. n. of the vowel-sign ུ for u *Gram.* — *žábs-mgo Tar.* point of the foot *Schf.* — *žabs-sgróg* garter *Cs.* — *žabs-bčágs Sch.*, 1. partic. of *žabs-ₒčag-pa*. 2. = *žábs-čágs*. 3. **grounds, territory.** — *žabs-čág(s)*, *-ṕyágs*, resp. shoe, boot. — *žabs-tóg* 1. **service** rendered to superiors, esp. to priests, convents etc., by the erection of buildings, or keeping them in repair, or by any aid or work done in their behalf; *ₒtsó-bai žabs-tóg* or *žabs-tog* alone: distribution of victuals, *žabs-tóg bzáṅ-po ṕul* he placed dainty food before him *Mil.*; *žabs-tóg ˏo mi brgyál-ba ₒbul* we shall provide you with every thing, so that you shall not suffer want *Mil.*; *žabs-tóg byéd-pa* a. **to render such services** b. **to feed, treat, provide,** offer, *Glr.* and elsewh. 2. = *žabs-tóg-pa* 1. **servant,** regularly employed in monasteries, by Lamas etc., **an official,** *rgyál-poi sku-γsuṅ-túgs-kyi žabs-tóg* royal page, *Glr.* 2. **dispenser, benefactor** *žabs-tóg-ma* fem. — *žabs-rtiṅ* **heel.** — *žabs-rtén* 1. **footstool** *Cs.* 2. **boot** *Sch.* — *žabs-ₒdrén* **shame, disgrace,** from *mii žabs ₒdrén-pa* to bring shame upon another, to be a disgrace to him, e.g. a child proving a disgrace to his parents, by a dissolute life, disrespectful deportment etc. *Thgy.* *žabs-rdul* dust on one's feet *Cs.* — *žabs-pád* lit.: 'a padma below the foot', seems to be an attribute of divine persons, but sometimes nothing more than a high-sounding complimental expression for 'foot'; *byin-pa 'e-na-ya ₒdra žabs-pad ₒbur* his leg displays a calf like that of Enaya *Pth.*; *žabs-pad-la*, *Zam.* init., seems to stand like *žabs druṅ-du*, so also *žabs-pád kri drúṅ-du*, in letters; *mii žabs-pad stén-pa Tar.*, fig. for *žabs-tóg byéd-pa* **to serve; to be a scholar, pupil** *Schf.* — *žábs-ṕyi* **servant** (male or female), in the widest sense of the word, servant to an individual, as well as a minister of the state or the church, only that the latter service is always referred by an Asiatic to the 'person' of the king or priest; collectively: **retinue**; occasionally also to be understood as **an attending, a waiting on,** thus: *rjé-yi žábs-ṕyi ₒgran*, we will vie with one another in our attending the lord *Glr.*; *žábs-ṕyir ₒbráṅ-ba*, *žábs-ₒbraṅ-ba* or *ₒbriṅ-ba* to follow as a servant, *žam-ₒbriṅ(-pa) Do.*, *žam-riṅ Cs.*, *ža-ₒbriṅ Sch.* servant. — *žabs-bró*, *žabs-bró mdzád-pa* **to dance** *Sch.* — *žabs-ma* drawers, under-petticoat. — *žabs-sén* nail of the toe *Sch.* — *žabs-bsil* water for washing an honoured person's feet. — *žabs-lhám* = *žabs-čág*.

ཞམ་ཆུ་ *žám-ču Sch.*: 'the scum left by the evaporation of water' (?); **žám-če** *W.* to take off, *lbú-ba* the froth, scum; yet cf. *γžám-pa*.

ཞམ་མེ་བ་ *žám-me-ba* **being plentiful, abounding in** *Mil.*

ཞར་བ་ *žár-ba*, fem. *ma*, 1. = *yan lag ma tsaṅ* being not in full possession of one's members, *mig-žár* **one-eyed, half or totally blind**; *lag-žár* having only one hand, being lame in one or both hands; so in a similar manner *rkaṅ-žár*. — 2. (= *mig-žár*) *C.*, *W.* **blind,** rarely in *B.* — **žar-tẹ** (*žar-ltas*) the winking with one eye *C.*

ཞར་ལ་ *žar-la*, *Schr.* **'following, succeeding',** prob. = *žór-la*, q.v.

ཞལ་ *žal* resp. for *ka* 1. **mouth** 2. **face, countenance** *žál-du γsól-ba*, *W.* **žál-la rág-če**, to eat, to drink; **tsá-big žál-la rag** or **žal-rág dzod** please to take some ...!

rgyal-poi žál-nas ysuṅs the king spoke Glr. frq.; žál-gyi sgo the door of the face, the mouth (cf. also ₒdzúm-pa); žál-la mi nyán-pa Glr. to be disobedient; žál-gyis bžés-pa Glr. or ₒčé-ba Sch. to promise, and other significations of k'as lén-pa, e.g. to accept Tar. 126, 10; žal bgrád-pa and ydáṅ-ba **to gape** Sch., ₒbyéd-pa to open the mouth, žal ₒdzúm-pa to smile; with ltá-ba 1. žál-la ltá-ba, e.g. čos smrá-bai to watch the mouth of the preacher, to hang on his lips Pth.; in a similar manner: gús-pai séms-kyis ṅá-yi žál-la lta Pth. 2. žal ltá-ba, žál-lta byéd-pa **to serve** (v. žál-ta), žal yaṅ k'yéd-la lta mčód-pa yaṅ k'yéd-la ₒbul they serve you and honour you Glr.; žál-lta-ru byuṅ he came to serve him Mil.; žal ydáms-pa **to bid, order, exhort** Glr.; žal dón-pa **to pronounce, to deliver, state, report**; žal mjál-ba Mil. **to visit, to come to see**; žal mt'óṅ-ba to see a person's face Tar.; 'in order to attain the highest dṅos-grúb, one must séms-kyi raṅ-žál mt'óṅ-ba, and in order to be able to do this, one must penetrate into the Buddhist doctrine' — thus Mil. teaches a Bonpa; p'yis žal mt'óṅ-bao afterwards his face was seen, he made his appearance Tar.; žal-yzigs-pa v. sbst. žal-yzig.

**Comp.** For the most part expressions of civility: žal-k'ár, resp. for k'ar-yól plates and drinking-vessels. — žal-dkyil face Cs. — žal-bkód order, ordinance Sch.(?). — žal-skóm, žal-skyéms drink. — žal-skyín Glr. countenance. — žal-skyógs cup, goblet Mil. — žal-k'ébs cover of an image of Buddha Sch. — žal-k'rid oral or personal instruction Mil. — žal-ₒk'aṅ biting words of a superior (Sch. prob. not quite correct). — *žal-gyá' (rgya? brgya) *jhé'-pa or žē-pa* to promise C. — žal-rgyán mustaches C. — žal-ṅó 1. = ṅo, žal-ṅó nág-par bžugs he was sitting there with a mournful face Glr. 2. ts'ogs-čen-žal-ṅó title of the chief-justices of the great monasteries of Sera, Gadan and Depung. 3. Sch.: 'žal-ṅo or ṅor (?), noble sons, princes' (?) — žal-dṅós **bodily**, in one's own body or person, saṅs-rgyás žal-dṅós-kyi ₒk'rúṅs-yul Pth., the place where Buddha was born bodily; žal-dṅós-su mjál-bar yod Glr. he is bodily to be seen. — žal-sṅa Cs. = spyan-sṅa. — žal-čol resp. for 'ar-čól handkerchief, napkin C. — žal-čád v. k'a-čád. — žal-ču, žal-čáb Schr., Cs. spittle, saliva. — žal-mčú lip, v. k'a-mčú. — žal-čé **judgment, decision**; des ₒú-bu-čag-yi žal-čé ycád-do he shall pass sentence on us Dzl. ༢༦༢, 15, and elsewh. (the text of Sch. is not quite correct); žal-čé bču-drúg-pa and bču-ysúm-pa '(the code) with the 16 and that with the 13 judgments'; these are two distinct bodies of law, both of them in C. of standard authority; žal-čé-pa judge Dzl. — žal-čéms v. čems 2. — žal-nyód favourite dish Sch. — žál-ta 1. also žál-lta a. **service, turn.** b. **inspection, visitation, revision**; žál-ta byéd-pa a. **to serve**, b. **to inspect, review, superintend; to visit**, the poor, the sick and to take care of them; **to guard**, žiṅ-la the field. 2. resp. for k'á-ta, k'a-ydáms **direction, instruction, counsel, advice**, žál-ta žib-rgyás žú-ba to ask for accurate and detailed instructions Mil.; žál-ta-pa = sku-mdún-pa, žábs-p'yi waiting-man, valet-de-chambre C., Tar. 56,2: servant in a convent; more frq. fem., žál-ta-ma waiting-woman, lady's maid, chamber-maid. — žal-ydáms **instruction, advice**, jig-rtén-la dgós-pai žal-ydáms ysúṅs-so he imparted to her useful maxims Glr.; **order, command** Glr. (v. above); also, žal-ydáms bris-mk'an **author**, in as much as all printed books are considered to be sacred, and the authors generally are Lamas, whose words are looked upon as divine. — žal-ydóṅ **countenance.** — žal-bdág in large religious meetings a Lama, who walks about with a wand in order to preserve good order, a verger. — žal-ₒdébs **a free-will offering** or **present** Cs. — žal-lpágs **lip.** — žal-p'yis resp. **napkin.** — žal-bád (or pad?) C. **chief overseer, superintendent.** — žal-byáṅ **title, superscription, inscription.** — žal-ts'óm (for ág-ts'óm) Pth. **beard.** — žal-ts'ós Sch. (Cs. žal-ts'us) = žal-zás Dzl. **food.** — žal-zág **tobacco-pipe**, v. gaṅ-zag. — žal-yzigs 1. **looking with the face**, lhor, southward Glr. 2. **apparition**, žal-yzigs t'ób-pa to see an ap-



ཞ

parition, *bžúgs-par žal-γzigs-šiṅ* appearing in a sitting posture *Mil. nt.* (cf. *spyan-rás*). — *žal-bsró Tar.* 76, 12, *Schf.*: **the act of consecrating,** e.g. a temple.

ཞལ་བ *žál-ba* I. sbst., also *žal, žá-la, žál-rtsa* or *-rdza Sch.* **clay, lime-floor,** *Lex.*: *žál-ba = skyáṅ-núl*; *mtíl-gyi žá-la Glr.* **clay, cement of a floor,** cf. *ǎr-ga*; **plastering, rough-cast,** *sgó-la žal bgyis-te* plastering the door with clay *Glr.*, also applied to the anointing of sacrificial objects with butter *Mil.* — II. vb. **to serve up food, to spread a repast** *Sch.*

ཞི་ *ži* num. fig.: 51.

ཞི་གིལ་ *ži-gil* **chaff** and other impurities removed from the grain by washing.

ཞི་བ་ *ží-ba*, *Ssk.* शम्, **to become quiet, calm, to abate, to subside; to settle,** of a swelling *W.*; **to be allayed,** of passion, malice etc. *Glr.*; **to be appeased, relieved, to cease,** of pain, quarrels, intoxication, maladies etc. *Glr.* and elsewh.; **to be atoned, blotted out,** of sins *Tar.*; *ží-bar ˳gyúr-ba B.*, **ži čá-če* W.*, id.; **ra, šro ži soṅ* W.* the drunken fit, the paroxysm of passion has passed over; *ži-la soṅ* (the hobgoblins) became quiet, held their peace *Mil.*; *ži-bar byéd-pa* **to still, sooth, appease, mitigate,** **ži čúg-če* W.*; *ži-byed* a composing draught, संशमन *Wise* 130; more particularly with reference to the affections: **to be dispassionate**, not subject to any mental emotion, *ži-ba čén-por ˳gyur* he is getting very free from passion *Do.*, v. below *ži-γnás;* also sbst. **tranquillity, calmness,** and adj. **tranquil, calm,** *ži-ba daṅ bde-légs-su ˳gyúr-bar mdzád-du γsol* permit us to attain to peace and happiness *Dom.*; *ži-bai tábs-kyis* **amicably, in a fair way** *Glr.*; so also *ži-bai γtam smrá-ba Glr.; ži-bas mi tul drág-pos ˳dul dgos ˳dug Pth.* if he will not submit by fair means, he must be converted or subdued by force; *ži-bai žal Pth.* the expression of calmness about his mouth, his peaceful countenance; *ži-bar γšégs-pa* to go to rest, to die *Cs.*; *ži-bai* or *lóṅs-skui lha-tsogs že-γnyis Thgr.* the good, the peaceable deities, opp. to those called *kró-bo;* differently again the word is used in: *ži-ba daṅ kró-ba daṅ ží-ma-kro Pth.*, which has been explained by *Sch.* as: the medium between calmness and passion, 'calm indignation'. *Cs.* moreover mentions *ži-ba* or *rtag-ži-ba*, as 'a name or epithet of Iswara and certain Buddhas', so that *ži-ba* would be equal in sound as well as in meaning to शिव, *ži-ba-pa* and *-ma* being his male and female disciples. A good deal of obscurity attaches, further, to the frequent mention of the *ži-rgyas-dbaṅ-drag*, as the characteristic properties of the four parts of the world (v. *gliṅ*), and likewise as qualities and functions of the Buddhas, gods and saints, viz. allaying diseases, conferring happiness and wealth, ruling over all creatures and subduing all that is unruly and hostile; to which are to be added four kinds of burnt-offerings, in the same fourfold sense, v. *Schl.* 250. Finally, in mysticism the term *ži-ba* acts a prominent part: *ži(-bar) γnás(-pa)* and *lhag(-par) mtoṅ(-ba)*, शमथ and विपश्यन, shortened *ži-lhág*, implies an absolute inexcitability of mind, and a deadening of it against any impressions from without, combined with an absorption in the idea of Buddha, or which in the end amounts to the same thing, in the idea of emptiness and nothingness. This is the aim to which the contemplating Buddhist aspires, when, placing an image of Buddha, as *rten*, (v. *rten* 1) before him, he looks at it immovably, until every other thought is lost, and no sensual impressions from the outer world any longer reach or affect his mind. By continued practice he acquires the ability of putting himself, also without *rten*, merely by his own effort, into this state of perfect apathy, and of attaining afterwards even to *dṅos-grub*, the supernatural powers of a saint. The stories that are related of such achievements, and with which the work of Taranātha abounds, are, notwithstanding their absurdity, readily believed by every faithful Buddhist. That there are also cases of failures, cf. *smyón-pa*.

ཞི་མ་ *ží-ma* **sieve,** of cane or wood *Ts.*

ཞི་མི་ *ži-mi Schr.* and *Wts.* (where *ši-mi* stands), gen. *žím-bu Glr.*, or *žúm-bu* **cat**, *C.*

ཞིག་ *žig* 1. = *čig.* — 2. v. *ₒjig-pa* I., 2, *žig-rál-ba* **demolished, ruined** *Mil.*

ཞིག་མེར་ *žig-mér* (sbst. or adj.?) **dense throng,** or **crowded together** in a mass *W.*

ཞིང་ *žiṅ*, I. sbst. ཞེཅ (*Cs.*: *žiṅ-ma, žiṅ-po, žiṅ-bu*, perh. provincialisms), 1. **field, ground, soil, arable land;** *táṅ-žiṅ* fields in a plain, level land, *ri-žiṅ* fields on a mountain, hill-land; *túl-žiṅ W.* (ni f.) cultivated land; *žiṅ-ḱa* = *žiṅ*, *žiṅ-ḱai bú-mo* the girls in the field *Mil.*; *žiṅ rmó-ba* frq., to plough a field; to carry on agriculture; *ₒdébs-pa* to till, to sow a field, *mi γčig-gis btáb-pai* a field that has been sowed by one man *Glr.*; *žiṅ ₒčú-ba* to irrigate a field (?) *Cs.*; *rná-ba* to mow, to reap, a field, *žiṅ-mḱan* **reaper;** **žiṅ bád-če* W.* to pursue husbandry; *žiṅ bgód-pa* to divide or distribute land *Cs.* — 2. fig., cf. *žiṅ-ḱams, bsód-nams-kyi žiṅ daṅ ₒṗrád-pa* to enter the field of merit, to turn into the path of virtue *Dzl.*; *γdúl-byai žiṅ-du γzígs-te Pth.* seeing him in the land of conversion (yet v. also 3, a.); **region,** *žiṅ bču* (*Sch.*: 'the ten regions') is said to signify something like: the reign of Evil. — 3. equivalent to *saṅs-rgyás-kyi žiṅ* the kingdom of Buddha, a. in an earthly sense: **a holy land, a land of salvation,** where Buddha resides, or at least where Buddhism prevails; so also *ₒdúl-bai žiṅ* land of conversion *Glr.*; acc. to *Wts.* it is a name of the earthly seat of Buddha, the residence of the Dalai Lama at Lhasa; b. supernaturally: **heaven, paradise, Elysium** i.e. one of the heavens inhabited by the Buddhist gods, or also the state of non-existence, Nirwāna; *žiṅ-la ṗéb-pa* = *bdé-bar γšégs-pa* **to die.** — 4. **body,** v. *žiṅ-čén, žiṅ-lpágs.* —

**Comp. and deriv.** *žiṅ-bkód* map *C., W.*, *žiṅ-gi bkód-pa* v. *Asiat. Res.* XX., 425. — *žiṅ-ḱaṅ* 1. summer-house, pleasure-house, pavilion *W.* 2. field and house, the whole estate or property *W.* (= *yul-γžis*) — *žiṅ-ḱáms* = *žiṅ* 2 and 3, frq. — *žiṅ-ₒḱrúṅs, žiṅ-gi ḱrúṅs-pa* or *-ma* the produce of the field *Cs.* — *žiṅ-ḱród* many fields together *Cs.* — *žiṅ-rgód* rough, uncultivated ground *Sch.* — *žiṅ-čén* and *-čúṅ* a large and a small field; also: a large and a small body or corpse *Thgr.* — *žiṅ-mčóg* paradise, a most delightful country, an Eden, an Eldorado *Pth.* — *žiṅ-bdág* proprietor of a field, land-owner. — *žiṅ-pa* husbandman, farmer *Dzl.* — *žiṅ-lpags* a skin (pulled off), hide. — *žiṅ-mu* boundary of a field, landmark. — *žiṅ-bzáṅ* good land, productive soil *Cs.* — *žiṅ-γšin* dead, arid, burnt soil *Cs.* — *žiṅ-sa* 1. ground, soil, arable land *Cs.* 2. province *Sch.*

II. gerundial termin. = *čiṅ*, q.v,

ཞིབ་ *žib*, resp. **fine flour,** also **flour in general,** *žib-ḱúg* bag, *žib-ṗór* box, for flour *Cs.*

ཞིབ་པ་ *žib-pa, B., žib-po Cs., žib-mo C., W.* 1. **fine,** of powder and similar things, *žib-rtsiṅ* fine and coarse *Zam.*; *žib-par byéd-pa, B.* **žib-mo čó-če* W.*, to make fine, to pound, to reduce to powder. — 2. **accurate, exact, strict, precise,** *ltá-ba yáṅs-šiṅ spyód-lam žib-par mdzod* be wide in your views, but strict in your actions *Glr.*; so *Sch.* understands also *žib-žib yod*; *žib-po med, žib-rgyu med*, which ought however to be translated: 'I have accurate information, I have no precise information, I have no particulars to communicate'; *žib-mo šés-pa* to know accurately; more frq. adv. *žib-par, žib-tu B.*, **žib-ča* *vulg., **exactly, precisely, thoroughly** *žib-tu γsól-ba, γtam žib-tu byéd-pa* to report accurately *Dzl.* (the former resp.); *žib-par bšád-pa Glr.* id.; *žib-par (šes-) ₒdód-na* if you wish to know it accurately *Glr.*; *bka žib-tu bgros-pa* resp., to consult carefully *Pth.*; *bka-mčíd γsuṅ-glén žib-tu bgyid* gentlemen, discourse as freely as you please! *Mil.*; *las-rgyu-ₒbras žib-tu mi rtsi-na* if one does not strictly regard the doctrine of retaliation *Mil.*; **žib-ča ltos* (or *tọ**) *W.* look at it well, carefully; **žib-ča zer* W.* pronounce it accurately; **žib-ča čọ'-pa* C.* to examine closely; **žib-sál* W.* accurately and distinctly.

ཞིམ་ཐོག་ལེ་ *žim-ṫog-le* n. of a medicinal herb *Med.*

ཞིམ་པ་ *žim-pa*, gen. *žim-po*, **well-tasted, sweet-scented,** **žim-po rag* W.* I find the

ཞ

taste or smell of it agreeable; *ša ̥di lhág-par žim-na* this meat being of a better taste *Dzl.*; *žim-rgyui zas* food prepared of savoury things *Zam.*; *dri-žim, dri-ɣsúṅ žim-po* pleasant odour *Dzl.*; *dri mi žim-pa* disagreeable smell *Glr.*; **žim-zẹ** also **žim-žim** *C.*, **žim-zag** *W.* sweet-meats, confectionery; **žim-zag-tsóṅ-k'aṅ** *W.* confectioner; **žim-lto-čan** *W.* dainty-mouthed, a sweet-tooth.

ཞིམ་བུ་ *žim-bu* v. *ži-mi.*

ཞུ་ *žu*, 1. num. figure: 81. — 2. v. *žú-ba.*

ཞུ་དག་ *žu-dág*, ཞུས་དག་ *žus-dág* **amendment, improvement, correction**; the word is also added at the end of written books, e.g. of Taranātha, as an attestation of a careful revision; *žu-dág byéd-pa* **to mend, improve, correct**; *raṅ-rgyúd žu-dág byéd-pa* to examine and reform one's self *Cs. žu-dag-mk'an* **reviser, corrector, censor** *Cs.*, *žu-čén-gyi lóts-ṫsa-ba* a great corrector or commentator (of *Ssk.* writings), seems to have become a current title.

ཞུ་བ་ *žú-ba* I. vb., pf. *žus* (esp. in later writings and vulgo, in ancient literature gen. *ɣsól-bar* for it) signifies 1. every kind of speaking to a person of higher rank, therefore **to request, to prefer a suit or petition, to make a report, to put a question** etc., *žú-žiṅ ɣsól-ba-la ̥gró-bai ṫse* when I have to bring in a petition *Dzl.*; *'mnál-lam de ɣžán-la mi ɣsúṅ-bar žu' žús-so* 'pray, do not relate the dream to others', he begged *Glr.*; *ɣnáṅ-bar žu byás-pas* saying, 'I beg you will permit', *Glr.*; *snar mt'óṅ-bai dṅós-po dé-dag žuo* I will ask him about the things lately seen, I shall request an explanation of him *Dzl.*; *ṅá-la gáṅ-dag žú-ba de légs-so* it is very right of you, thus to ask me about every thing *Do.*; *rgyál-poi drúṅ-du rmi-lam žús-pa* he related the dream before the king *Pth.*; *ston-pa žu* (*pa* col. for *par*) I request (you) to explain *Mil.*; *der ̥byón-pa žu* 'thither to come I request' *Mil.*; *dé-la mk'án-po žus* they besought him to be their abbot *Glr.*; *ɣnáṅ-ba žú-ba* to ask permission *Cs.* — 2. In *W.* this *žu* has become a word of civility to the widest extent, as it is not only added to almost every sentence of a speech or a letter, something like our 'with your permission' or 'if you please', e.g. **žan či méd-na ṅa ḍo yin žu** if you have nothing further (to say), I shall go, with your permission; **k'o leb soṅ žu** he is arrived, if you please; but it also supplies every kind of salutation in coming or going, hence **žu zér-če**, resp. **žu žú-če**, to make or give one's compliments, **ă-pa-nẹ žu máṅ-po žu dug** my father's best respects (cf. *p̓yag*). Inst. of *žu*, *ǰu* is also frq. heard (vulgo), e.g. **ǰu sab ǰu!** good day, Sir, good day! which prob. is only an intensation of sound, and not to be referred to the Indian जी. — **či-la žu** *W.* **why, well then, mind!** **či-la žu, nyi-ráṅ ṅẹ tsar ma kyód-pa yun-riṅ kyod** well, I have not seen you this age! — The word is also used as a sbst., for **request, wish, question,** **žú-wa ̥búl-ba** *C.*, **p̓úl-če** *W.*, *ɣtóṅ-ba Glr.* to make a request, to put a question; *ɣdan-̥drén-pai žú-ba náṅ-čan p̓úl-bas Mil.* assailing him with pressing invitations.

II. (prop. fut. of *̥ǰú-ba*) pf. (*b*)*žu*(*s*), fut. (*b*)*žu*, (imp.?) 1. **to melt**, trs. and intrs., *bžu-btúl* v. sub *lugs*; *bžu-byai ɣser* gold to be melted *Cs.*; *žú-bai k'ams* whatever is melting or fusible, **metals** *Sch.*; *žuo* it melted (from the heat) *Dzl.*; *̥ód-du žu-nas* dissolving in light *Glr.* frq. — 2. **to digest**, *žú-byed-kyi sman* digestive medicine *Cs.* (cf. *̥ǰu-byéd*); *ma-žú*(*-ba*) undigested, *zas ma žú-ba* undigested food, also **indigestion,** sufferings arising from it; *ma-žúi nad* id.; *ma-žú ̥ǰú-ba* to decompose what is undigested *Med.*; opp. to *žu-rǰés* it seems to denote more particularly **the chyme** before it is mixed with bile, and perh. also **the duodenum** where this takes place; so the region of *žu daṅ ma-žúi bár-na* is stated to be the place, where the bile is principally operating *S.g.* Cf. *̥ǰú-ba.*

**Comp.** *žu-skyogs W.* crucible, melting-spoon. — *žú-mk'an* 1. **petitioner.** 2. **digester;** n. of an officinal plant, = *spaṅ-žún Wdṅ.*

— *žu-gléṅ, žu-gléṅ byéd-pa* to address, accost, resp. *C.* — *žu-rgyá* (v. *rgya-ma*) 1. petitionary letter, petition, suit. 2. any writing addressed to superiors. — *žu-rgyú* the subject of a petition or suit. — **žu-ṅó-pa**, *C.*, intercessor, advocate, mediator, **žu-ṅó ǰhé-pa** to intercede, to advocate. — *žu-rǰés* 1. **the chyme mixed with bile** (cf. *ma-žu* above). 2. **the place of it,** *žu-rǰés na* I feel a pain there *Med.* 3. **eructation, rising,** *ḱá-la zu-rǰés skyur S.g.* caused by beer; *ro daṅ žu-rǰés mṅár-mo Med.* a sweetish taste and rising (from the stomach). — *žu-rtén* **the present** which, according to oriental notions, has necessarily to attend or introduce a petition. — *žu-dón* prop. drift, subject of a petition; in a general sense = *žú-ba* request, suit, address, communication etc. — *žu-sná* (pronounced **žu-ná**) *W.* = *žu-ṅó.* — *žú-po, žú-ba-po* = *žú-mḱan* 1. — *žu-byéd* v. above — *žu-ₒbúl*, pronounced **žum-búl**, petitioning, making a suit in an humble posture with folded hands *Cs.* — *žú-yig, žú-šog, žú-bai ṗrin-yig* a petition, *žú-yig-gi rten* = *žu-rten.* — *žu-lán* answer to a petition. — *žu-lóg* a feigned, false, designing suit, **gyáb-pa** to address such a one *C.*

ཞུགས་ *žugs*, resp. **fire,** e.g. the fire lighted for cremation *Tar.* 7, 4.

ཞུགས་པ་ *žúgs-pa* v. *ₒjúg-pa.*

ཞུང་ཞུང་ *žuṅ-žúṅ* with *byéd-pa* **to nod or bow repeatedly,** of a pigeon *Mil.*

ཞུད་པ་ *žúd-pa* 1. **to twine, to twist** *W. *žúd-če, žú-če**. — 2. **to spin** *Cs.*, *žu-ḱór* spindle, distaff. — 3. **to rub** *Cs.* — 4. **to hang up, to suspend** *Ts.* — *žud-ťág* = *dpyaṅ-ťág.*

ཞུན་པ་ *žún-pa* **melted** *Cs.*; **žun ťáṅ-če* W.* **to melt,** trs; *žun-ťár byéd-pa* to melt and beat to pieces *Mil.*; *žun-ťigs* spark flying from red-hot iron *W.*; *žún-ma* that which is melted, *γser sogs žún-mai ṗúṅ-po* heaps of melted gold and other metals *Glr.* — *žun-mar* v. *mar.* — *žún-mo* melted, whatever melts easily *Cs.* (who spells it *bžun-mo*).

ཞུམ་པ་ *žúm-pa* 1. sbst. **fear, dismay, despondency, faint-heartedness,** *sems žúm-na* if I continue undismayed *Dzl.*; *dkon-mčóg γsúm-la žúm-pa-med-par bkúr-bsti byéd-pa* to honour the three most Precious undauntedly, with a cheerful heart; *sems ráb-tu žúm-par gyúr-ťo* they became greatly dejected in mind, their spirits were much cast down *Pth.* — 2. vb. **lbú-wa žúm-če* W.* **to scum, to skim** (off).

ཞུམ་བུ་ *žúm-bu* = *ži-mi.*

ཞུར་ *žur*, 1. **snout, muzzle, trunk.** — 2. sup. of *žú ba.*

ཞུལ་ཞུལ་ *žul-žúl, Ts.*: **žū-žū ǰhé-pa** **to stroke, to caress.**

ཞུས་དག་ *žus-dág* v. *žu-dág*, ཞུས་པ་ *žús-pa* v. *zú-ba.*

ཞེ་ *že* (cf. *žen*) 1. **inclination, affection, heart, mind; volition;** there is a proverb in *C.*: **mi ḱá-ṗo-čé-la že me', ču nyóg-po-čé-la tiṅ me'** a braggart has no mind, as muddy water has no bottom, i.e. as in muddy water you cannot see the bottom, so you cannot rely on the solid principles of a braggart; *ḱa-žé* v. *ḱa*, comp.; *že bkon-pa* or *ₒḱon-pa* a hating mind, *rkám-pa Sch.* a covetous, *ťág pa Mil.* a sincere, *nág-po C.* a wicked, *γtsáṅ-ba Sch.* a pure heart or mind, or also hating, covetous etc. as to mind (several other combinations of this kind, given by *Sch.*, are too doubtful to be copied); *že-γčód-pa Sch.*: 'to lose courage, to have no longer any inclination for', perh. better, **to resign,** and *že-bčád* **resignation,** as a Buddhist virtue *Mil.*; on the other hand, *že γčod-pai ťsig Sch.*: 'slanderous words' which, e.g. *Dzl.* ༢༩, 11, well agrees with the context, but is not clear in point of etymology. — *že-dúg* damage, destruction *Sch.*, *byéd-pa* to cause, to inflict. — *že-lóg* v. *žen-lóg* sub *žén-pa.* — *že-sún* angry, cross, ill-humoured, vexed. — 2. numerical word for *bži-bču* in the abridged numbers *že-γčig* etc., 41 to 49. — 3. numerical figure: 111.

ཞེ་ན་ *žé-na*, rarely *žés-na*, v. *čé-na.*

ཞེ་ས་ *žé-sa* **reverence, respect, civility, politeness,** *žé-sa daṅ bčás-pa* **reverential, respectful** *Pth.*; *dei dús-su mis ṗyag daṅ* žé-sa mi šés-pas because at that time people knew little of compliments and politeness *Pth.*; žé-sa byéd-pa to show honour, respect, rnám-gyur mdzés-pai žé-sa ₒbul-ba to arrange mimic performances in honour of some persons, (which also at the present time is frequently done in these countries); complimentary word (for žé-sai tsig), rná-bai žé-sa snyan the complimentary word for rna-ba is snyan *Zam.*

ཞེང་, གཞེང་ žeṅ, γžeṅ *Cs.* (*W.* *žaṅ*) 1. **breadth, width,** žéṅ-čan **broad** (road, valley), **wide, spacious,** *žéṅ ka-čém-po* *C.* id.; žeṅ-méd, žeṅ-ṗrá-mo, *žeṅ-čúṅ-se* *W.* **narrow;** žéṅ-du in breadth *Sambh.*; žeṅ-šiṅ writing-tablet = snum-glegs. — 2. **plain, surface, side,** žeṅ-čé-ba γnyis the two broad sides (of a pillar) *Glr.*

ཞེད་པ་ žéd-pa **to fear, to be afraid,** synon. to ₒjigs-pa *Thgr.* frq.; žéd-nas full of apprehensions *Pth.*

ཞེན་པ་ žén-pa (cf. že), vb. c. la, 1. **to desire, to long for, to be attached to, to be partial to, to be taken with,** ḱyéd-la žén-čiṅ čags I love you ardently (ἐρῶ) *Glr.*; bod-ₒbáṅs ṅá-la žen-čé-žiṅ dgá-ba-rnams the people of Tibet, that are affectionately attached to me *Glr.*; sbst.: **desire, longing,** e.g. to hear more of a thing *Mil.*; also **greediness, covetousness;** ráṅ-ₒdod-žen-pa **self-love, selfishness, egotism** *Glr.*; ṗyógs-žen *Tar.* 184, 22, **party-spirit, party-agitation;** čágs-med žén-med free from passion or interest *Mil.*; žén-pa zlog suppress your passion *Mil.*; tse ₒdí-la žen ldóg-pa to be disgusted with this life *Thgy.*; *žém-pa ma lóg-na dhe'-pa mi yoṅ* *C.* before one has renounced every desire, one cannot believe. —

**Comp.** žén-ḱa, žé-ḱa = žén-pa sbst., *Sch.* — žen-ḱris *Mil.*, žen-čágs frq., also vulgo, žen-ₒdzín *Glr.* inclination, desire, passion, attachment, *žen-dzín čó-če* *W.* to love, to be attached. — žen-dón, resp. bžed-dón, object of desire *Cs.* — žen-lóg(-pa, cf. above), disinclination, antipathy, disgust; in an ascetic sense: resignation *Mil.*; ₒjig-rtén žen-lóg-gi gaṅ-zág a man tired of this world *Mil.*; žen-lóg-pa, or -mḱan fastidious, squeamish, easily disgusted; *že-mi-lóg-ḱen* *C.* one that is not easily disgusted, not squeamish. — 2. = ljén-pa **to penetrate, to be fixed,** of colours etc., ras dkar-po tson žen-pa ltar as a colour is fixed in white cloth, is **lasting** *Dzl.*

ཞེམ་ཞེམ་ žem-žém *Ld.* an inferior kind of silk, of which the handkerchiefs consist, that are presented to foreign visitors etc. as a welcome or mark of respect, cf. ḱa-btágs.

ཞེར་ žer, žer ₒdébs-par byéd-pa *Cs.*: **to chide, rebuke,** which, however, in the only passage, where I met with the word, does not suit the sense very well.

ཞེར་པོ་ žer-po **'mean, pitiful, coarse'** *Cs.*

ཞེས་ žes v. čes.

ཞོ་ žo, 1. **dram,** a small weight = $\frac{1}{10}$ ounce, of skar-lṅa, v. skár-ma; γser-žo-gaṅ *Pth.* a dram of gold; γser žo γsum-brgyá between 1 and 2 pounds of gold; as a coin it is stated to be = $^2/_3$ rupee. — 2. resp. γsol-žo **thick milk, curds,** žo bsnyál-ba to place milk to curdle; **milk** in gen., esp. mai nú-žo *Dzl.*, má-žo col., mother's milk; žo-ₒtúṅ dús-na during the time of suckling, žo-spáṅs zas zai dús-na after the child has been weaned *Med.*; žo dkróg-pa, skróg-pa, bsrúb-pa **to churn, to butter** *Lex.* — 3. **a small white spot,** sen-žo on a finger nail, so-žo on a tooth *Glr.* — 4. num. figure: 141.

**Comp.** žó-ka prob. = žo, *Thgy* — žo-skyá *Med.?* — žo-čágs *Med.?* — žo-ṗrúm *Sch.*: 'a vessel for thick milk' (?), perh. ṗru. — žo-rás *Med.*, *Sch.*: spoiled milk. — *žo-ri* *W.*, (like rú-ma *C.*) **sour milk,** used to acidify new milk; in a gen. sense: **ferment, leaven.** *žo-dzi* *Ts.* — žo-ši *Sch.* = žo-rás. — žo-srí, žoi spris-ma *Wdṅ.* **cream.**

ཞོ་ཤ་ žo-šá 1. **force, efficiency** *Cs.* — 2. n. of a medicinal fruit, žo-šá γsum, viz. mḱál-žo-ša kidney-shaped, healing diseases of the kidneys (in *W.* the chesnut bears this name), snyiṅ-žo-ša heart-shaped, healing diseases of the heart; gla-gor-žo-ša is said to be given to horses; besides mčin-pa-

and *mčér-pa-žo-ša* are mentioned. — 3. **toll** (?), **pay** (?), *žo-šás ₒtsó-ba Tar., Stg.* a publican *Cs.*, a soldier *Schr.*, prob. any officer that receives salary or pay.

ཞོག་ *žog*, imp. of *ₒjóg-pa*.

ཞོགས་ *žogs* v. *mar-žógs*.

ཞོགས་པ་ *žógs-pa Med., žóg-ka Sch.*, = *sná-dro* **morning, fore-noon**; *žógs-ja* **tea at breakfast** *Cs.*

ཞོང་ *žoṅ* **lower, nether**, *žóṅ-kaṅ-pa* the lower part of the house, *žoṅ-rtsé* the lower and the upper part; *žoṅ-žóṅ* **deepened, excavated, hollow, uneven** *C.*

ཞོད་ *žod* 1. the original meaning of the word is yet uncertain; at present used in *C.*: **žo' dé-wa, žo-jág**, **peace, quietness, tranquillity**, **ko žo'-dé-la mi žag** he gives him no rest, causes him much trouble; **sém-kyi zo' dé-mo** peace of mind, evenness of temper; **žo'* or *zo' dé-mo* or *ₒjám-pa* gentleness, meekness. — 2. *Sch.*: **high-water, floods, inundations** *Wts., C.; sna tan pyi žod* first drought, then inundation *Wdk.* — 3. **udder** *W., C.*

ཞོན་པ་ *žón-pa*, resp. *ₒčíb-pa* **to mount**, c. *la*; *rtá-la žón-pa* to ride, on horseback, *šiṅ-rta-la* to ride, in a carriage, frq.; *rtá-la žón-nas lhó-pyogs-su ₒgró-ba* to ride southward, to travel on horseback towards the south *S.g.*; also c. accus.: *bžón-pa žón-pa* to mount a horse or a carriage *Lex.*; *žón-du ₒjúg-pa* (= *skyón-pa*) to let mount.

ཞོམ་པ་ *žóm-pa*, = *ₒjóms-pa*? *rgas žóm-ste* **weighed down by old age** *Sch.*; cf. *γžóm-pa*.

ཞོར་ *žór*, ཞོར་ལ་ *žór-la* etc. v. *sbyór-la*.

ཞོལ་ *žol* 1. *žol-γyág*, **yak-bull**, *Bos grunniens Sch.*; *rá-ma žól-mo* a long-haired goat *Mil. nt.* — 2. **village belonging to a convent** *Mil.*, so Shikatse is the *sde-žól* of Tashilhunpo. — 3. postp., **under**, *Sch.* (cf *γžol-ba* II).

གཞའ་བ་ *γža-ba Sch.*: 1. **to sport, joke, play, sing**, (cf. *ga-γža*). — 2. **to believe, trust, confide.**

གཞའ་ཚོན་ *γža-tson* earlier form for *ₒja-tsón* **rain-bow.**

གཞའ་གསང་ *γža-γsaṅ* = *γyuṅ-druṅ Lex.*

གཞག་པ་ *γžag-pa* v. *ₒjóg-pa*.

གཞང་ *γžaṅ* 1. **anus** *Med., γžáṅ-ka* id.; *γžaṅ-nád, γžaṅ-ₒbrúm* **piles, hemorrhoids** *Med.*; *γžaṅ-srín* a kind of intestinal worms *Lt.* — 2. **privy parts**, **žaṅ-ₒtʼág* W.* catamenial blood; **žáṅ-tsoṅ-ma* W.* = *smád-tsoṅ-ma*; **žaṅ-stoṅ* W.*, without breeches, with a bare posterior.

གཞད་གད་, གཞད་མོ་ *γžad-gád, γžád-mo* v. *bžád-pa*.

གཞན་ *γžan, γžán-pa, γžán-ma* (the last esp. in *W.*), 1. adj. and sbst., **other, the other, another**, *žan mi* the other men *Dzl.*, *γžán-pas lhág-par* more than others *Dzl.*; *slób-ma γžán-dag* the other scholars *Dzl.*; *mtsan γžán-pa* the other signs *Dzl.*; *blón-po γžán-ma-rnams* the other ministers *Glr.*; *bú-mo γžán-pas čé-rgyu med* she is not taller than the other girls (*pas* = *las*, not from *pa*) *Glr.*; *γžan rgol ma nus* others were not able to resist them (= nobody could do them any harm) *Glr.*; *γžán-du* to some other place, *ₒgró-ba* to go (to some other place) = **to go away, to start; elsewhere; in another way**, v. example *ₒdzin-pa* 1, 4; also: *γžán-du ma sems šig Dzl.*, suppose or believe nothing else, do not think that the matter can be otherwise, frq. used like our 'of course'; *γžán-na* **elsewhere**; *γžán-nas* **from some other place**; *γžán-nas ₒgrúb-tu med* it cannot be accomplished from any other quarter, by any body else *Mil.* — 2. adv. **otherwise, else, on the other hand** *W.*; *γžán-yaṅ* **further, furthermore, or else**, (just) to mention some other circumstance, frq. — *γžan-bsgrúb Lex.* seems to be some logical term *Gram.* — *γžan-ₒprúl* n. of a heaven inhabited by certain gods *Glr., Mil.* — *γžan-dbáṅ* **dependent on others** *Was*, cf. *raṅ-dbáṅ*.

གཞབ་པ་ *γžáb-pa* **to lick** *Sch.*

གཞམས་པ་ *γžáms-pa* v. *bžáms-pa*.

ཞ

གཞར་ཡང་ γžár-yaṅ *Lex.* = *nám-yaṅ*; *Pth.*: *γžar-yaṅ mi* **never** (*Sch.* and *Schr.* prob. incorr.).

གཞལ་བ་ *γžál-ba*, fut. of *ˏǰál-ba*, **to weigh**, *sráṅ-la γžál-bar nús-kyi* if one could weigh with a pair of scales *Glr.*; *γžál-dgos-kyi rdzas Sch.*; 'goods for which duties are to be paid', liable to duty, to custom; *γžal-du-méd-pa* **imponderable** *Stg.*; **immensely much** *Pth.*; **immeasurable, incomparable, infinite, vast**; *γžal méd*, *γžal-yás* id.; *γžal-med-k̔áṅ*, more frq. *γžal-yas-k̔aṅ*, also *γžal-med-kaṅ-bžaṅ* palace, rarely used of human palaces (so *Glr.* in one passage, when speaking of the house of a Brahmin), mostly of the abode of gods *Pth.* and elsewh.; also Tibet, in po. language, is called a *lha-γnás γžal-yas-k̔áṅ*, the heavens with the sun a *ṅo-mtsár lhai γžal-yas-k̔áṅ*. — *γžal-ťsád* **measure, scale, standard** *Sch.*

གཞས་ *γžas* **play, sport, jest, joke** *Sch*, *Lex.*: *glu-gžas.*

གཞི་(མ་) *γži(-ma)* 1. that from which and on which a thing arises, exists, depends; **ground, foundation, original cause, exciting cause** (मूल *Was.* 234); *dge-légs tams-čád ˏbyúṅ-bai γži(-ma)* the primitive source of all happiness (is the doctrine of Buddha) *Glr.*; *γži-skye-méd* without origin and birth *Mil.*; *γžir bžág-pa* prob.: to use as a foundation *Mil.*, *Tar.*; **gór-ži** *W.* cause of delay; *má-γži* v. as an article of its own sub *ma*; *rtsig-γži* foundation of a wall *Cs.*; *nyúṅ-γži*, *lá-γži* turnips, radishes, left for seed (being the foundations, as it were, of new plants); in *γži-sems-nyid*, *γži-čos-nyid* it prob. stands as an apposition, in the sense of *kun-γži*: the spirit, the primeval cause; in a special sense: the innermost essence, inherent nature; *γži-nas* **actually**, opp. to 'apparently' *Mil.*; **fundamental law, statute**, *γži čén-po* title of a book *Was.* 264; in certain cases it may be translated by **action**, v. *ruṅ-ba* 2, c. — 2. **ground, floor**, *γži-ma gru-bži* a square floor *Glr.*; *stéṅ-gi γži* the upper base, top-surface *Stg.* — 3. **residence, abode, home**, *γži ˏdzin-pa* to take up one's residence in a place *Mil.* and elsewh.; *γži ˏbébs-pa W.* **p̔ab-če** id.; *γži-ma rab čig p̔óg-nas bžág-go* he assigned to him a nice dwelling-place and established him there *Glr.*; **seat, place**, *čos-γži* seat of religion, monastery *Tar.* and elsewh.; school of religion *Tar.* 44, 17; *γži γčig-tu skád-čig kyaṅ mi sdód-de* in no place resting for a moment (the arrow flies towards its goal) *Thgy.*; **ži čig-tu** *C.* the same as *rtse γčig-tu*. — 4. in philosophy: **axiom, proposition** *Was.* (58); **contents, tenor** (299); **basis, support** (273). — 5. *Sch.*: **enmity**?? — 6. also *že* (cf. *γžes*) a definition of time or of relationship: *γži-niṅ*, *že-niṅ* two years ago, *γži-més* great-great-grandfather, *γži-més-mo* great-great-grandmother, *γži-ťsá* great-great-grandchild *Sch.* —

**Comp.** *γži-dgón* monastery of the place, in or near a village, usually very small and harbouring but a few monks. — *γži-ǰi-bžin-pa* a recluse, 'who stays where he is' *Burn.* I, 310. — *γži-bdág* lord of the manor, lord of the soil, may denote a king or nobleman, but gen. it is **a local deity**, presiding over a certain district, to whom travellers are bound to offer sacrifice, and whom to offend they must carefully avoid.

གཞིག་པ་ *γžig-pa* 1 **to examine, search, try**, *rtog-* (or *brtag-*) *γžig légs-par γtóṅ-ba* to select and arrange carefully, e.g. books *Pth.*; *lo daṅ zlá-bar rtog-γžig žib-tu γtóṅ-ba* to search minutely as to the day and year *Pth.*; *bsam-γžig γtóṅ-ba* = *bsam-bló γtóṅ-ba* to weigh, consider *Pth.* — 2. fut. of *ˏǰig-pa.*

གཞིབ་པ་ *γžib-pa* fut. of *ˏǰib-pa.*

གཞིབས་པ་ *γžibs-pa* **to put** or **lay in order** *Lex.*, **žib-žib čó-če(s)** *W.*, **toṅ-wa** *C.* id.

གཞིལ་བ་ *γžil-ba* fut. of *ˏǰil-ba*, = *ˏǰóms-pa.*

གཞིས་ཀ་ *γžis-ka* **native place, native country** *Lex.*; *yul-γžis* house, estate, property *Mil.* = *žiṅ-k̔áṅ* paternal estate; *p̔a-γžis* the father's domicile as inheritance; *γžis sgril-ba* to change one's abode, to remove to another place *Sch.*; *γžis-pa* **a native** *Sch.*; *γžis-mad* **family, household, wife, children** and

**domestics**; *γži-byés Sch.*: native and foreign, at home and abroad.

གཞུ་ *γžu*, also *γžu-mo Mil.*, resp. *γnam-rú B.* and col., 1. **bow**, for shooting, *γžu bčos* he constructed a bow *Glr.*; *γžu ₒgén-ba*, *W.* **kán-če**, to bend the bow and have it ready, frq.; *ₒtén-pa Pth.*, and *ₒgúgs-pa Cs.*, id.; *ₒbúd-pa* to unbend (the bow) *Cs.*; *rdúṅ-ba* (*Dzl.* ༦༤, 15, ༡༦༦, 11. *Gyatch.* ༡༢༤, 10), acc. to explanations given by Lamas: to make the bow-string sound by a sudden pull or jerk, = *γžú-rgyúd sbréṅ-ba Dzl.*, which both as to matter and language seems preferable to other explanations that have been given. — 2. **arch**, in architecture *Cs.*, *γžú-lugs-su ₒbúb-pa* 'to arch in the form of a bow' *Cs.*; **capital**, **chapiter**, v. *ka-ba*. — 3. resp. for **žum-már-pa** **lamp**, **zim-žu** id., **góṅ-žu** lantern *C.* (spelling uncertain).

**Comp.** *γžú-mk'an* bow-maker. — *γžu-rgyúd* bow-string *Dzl.* — *γžú-čan*, *γžu-ldán* furnished with a bow. — *γžu-mčog Lex.*, *Sch.*: 'the two ends of a bow'; *γžu-mčóg ₒdzúgs-pa* to rest one end of the bow on some object(?) *Mil.* — *γžu-t'óg* an arched roof *Cs.* — *γžu-t'ógs* holding a bow, archer *Ld.-Glr.* — *γžu-brtán* n. of an ancient Indian king *Gl.* — *γžu-dóms* a cord, fathom, as a standard measure, opp. to any abitrary measure (so explained by a Lama). — *γžú-pa* bow-man, archer. — *γžur-šúbs*, bow-case *Wdṅ.*

གཞུ་བ་ *γžú-ba* **to strike, to lash**, *lčág-gis* with a whip.

གཞུག་ *γžug* 1. = *mǰug*, q. v., **end, extremity**; *γžug-gu*, *γžug-čuṅ Med.* **coccyx**; **rump** or **ventlet** of birds *Sch.*; *γžug-rmén* the glands of it *Sch.*; *gral-γžúg* the end of a row *Glr.*; *mgo-γžúg* upper and lower end, e.g. of a stick *Glr.*; *lo-γžúg-la* at the end of the year *Mil.*; *mṅag-γžúg* household-servants, suite *Sch.* — 2. v. *ₒǰúg-pa*.

གཞུང་ *γžuṅ* 1. **the middle, midst.** — 2. **spinal marrow** *S.g.*, also *klad-γžuṅ Sch.*, *γžuṅ-ríṅs Mil.* — **gyab-žúṅ-la zug rag** *W.* I feel a pain in the middle of my back; *lče-γžuṅ* the middle of the tongue; *γžuṅ-nas* in a direct way, opp. to *zúr-nas*.

**Comp.** **žúṅ-go** *C.* middle door, principal door or gate. **žuṅ-čág** *W.* partition-wall, **čád-če** to construct one. — *γžúṅ-pa* a man from the middle part of the country, neither *stód-pa* nor *šám-pa W.* — *γžúṅ-ma* 1. **the middle of a thing** *Cs.*; as a proper name: the middle part of Lhasa, containing the royal palace, also *γžuṅ-sa-dga-ldán*. 2. the back-part of fur *Sch.* 3. **kernel**, **pith**, **main substance** *Sch.* 4. **the original**, **the source**, **text**; *γžuṅ-lúgs* id. *Tar.*

གཞུང་བ་ *γžúṅ-ba* pf. *γžuṅs Cs.*: '**to attend, to be heedful**; **attention**, *γžúṅs-pa* heedful'; *Sch.* has: 'sincere, orderly', and for the current phrase *yid γžúṅs-pa* he gives: 'a quiet and prudent mind or behaviour'. But the way in which the word is used in books, where it frequently occurs in conjunction with *mk'ás-pa*, as well as in the popular expressions *žúṅ-k'an* and *žuṅ-méd-k'an* = *blo-rnó* and *blo-dmán*, would rather suggest the version: **acuteness of perception**, a good and quick comprehension.

གཞུད་པ་ *γžud-pa Sch.*: '**to go, to walk, to put into**'.

གཞུན་པོ་ *γžún-po* **excellent in its kind**, *γser γžún-po* the purest gold, *ston-tóg γžún-po* a capital crop *C.*

གཞུར་བ་ *γžúr-ba* **to shear, shave, cut off**, **ṭa** the hair *C.*, leaves, branches *Cs.* (cf. *bžár-ba*?).

གཞེ་ར་ *γžé-ra* **parsley** *C.*

གཞེང་ *γžeṅ* v. *žeṅ*.

གཞེན་ *γžen* the act of **remembering** or **reminding**, **nyiṅ-la žen yóṅ-če p̔i-la di** *W.* in order not to forget it, I have written it down; *γžen skúl-ba Lex.* to remind a person; *γžen btád-pa* or acc. to another reading *btáb-pa*, i.e. *ₒdébs-pa* to admonish, exhort *Dzl.* ༢༥༡, 9.

གཞེན་པ་ *γžén-pa* **to light, kindle, inflame** *Sch.*; *ráṅ byuṅ-gi mes žúgs-la*, prob. to be set in flames by spontaneous fire (?) *Tar.* 7, 4.

གཞེས་ *γžes* **the second day after to-morrow** *Lex.*; **to-re naṅ-la že-la** *W.* to-morrow, the day after to-morrow, on the fourth day; *γžes-rnyin Cs.* = *γži-nin*.

གཞེས་པ་ *γžés-pa* (= *bžugs-pa* yet less used), resp. for **to sit, stay, wait**, *čuṅ tsam γžes šig* wait a little! *Dzl.* ༢༢༡, 12 (another reading: *bžugs šig*).

གཞོ་བ་ *γžó-ba* for *bžó-ba*, v. *ˌjó-ba*.

གཞོག་པ་ *γžóg-pa* v. *ˌjóg-pa*.

གཞོགས་ *γžogs* **the side of the body**, = *glo*; *γžogs γyas γyon* the right and left side *Sch.*; *γžógs-su* sideways *Sch.*; *γžogs slóṅ-ba Lex.*, *γžogs-sloṅ byéd-pa Cs.* to speak allusively; *γžogs-smód byéd-pa* to prejudice a person against another insidiously, to create enmity *Thgy.*; it is also used like a verb: *γžógs-te rtsáb-pa* to be insolent with a fair appearance, opp. to *ṅor* downright *Thgy.* — *γžogs-p̔yéd ná-ba Do.* prob. an inaccurate expression for pain in one side.

གཞོང་པ་ *γžóṅ-pa* **wooden basin, trough, tub, washing-tub**; *k̔yi-γžóṅ* (col. **k̔yib-žóṅ**) trough for feeding dogs and other animals, also manger *W.*; **t̔ud-žoṅ* W.* prob. id.; **čag-žóṅ* W.* trough for dry horse-meat; **tab-žóṅ** winnowing-tray, inst. of a shovel; in books the word is used in a wider sense, in such expressions as *γser-, dṅul-, ˌk̔ar-, rdo-γžoṅ*.

གཞོངས་ *γžoṅs Lex.* = *ljoṅs*.

གཞོན་པ་ *γžón-pa* 1. sbst. v. *bžón-pa*. — 2. adj. **young**, *γžón-pa de na-ré* the younger one said *Mil.*; *rgyál-po sku-ná γžón-pa* the young king; *bdag γžón-pas* as I am still young, I as the younger one, the youngest *Dzl.*; *γžón-pa ˌgá-žig* some young people *Mil.*; *γžón-dus bu-méd* who in their younger years had no children; *γžón-nu* **a youth**, frq., *γžón-nu-t̔so* plur. *Mil.*; *γžón-nu-ma* or *bú-mo γžón-nu Dzl.* **virgin, maiden, girl**; *sé-ba γžón-nu* a young rose *Wdṅ.*; *γžón-nu daṅ brál-bar byéd-pa* to deprive a girl of her virginity *Cs.*, *γžon-nu-brál* a girl that has lost her virginity *Cs.*; *γžón-nu-nas* from a child, from infancy *Mil.*; *γžon-grógs* youthful companion *Mil.*; *γžón-ša-čan* with youthfnl flesh, *γžón-ša-čan-du ˌgyúr-ba Glr.* to grow young again.

གཞོབ་ *γžob* 1. *me-γžób* **singeing**, or what has been **singed**, wool, hair, feathers etc.; **a mark** from burning; *γžób-drí Sch.* also *γžob-ró* smell of singeing; *γžób-tu ˌgyúr-ba* to be singed, seared *Pth.*; **žob gyáb-pa* C.* to singe off; fig. *ṅai lus-séms γžób-tu t̔al Glr.* my body and soul were seared, deeply afflicted. — 2. *W.* **a crash**, e.g. of a tree breaking down.

གཞོམ་པ་ *γžóm-pa* 1. v. *ˌjoms-pa*. — 2. **to break in two, to tear** *Sch.*; in *W.* used of metal vessels **bent** or **bruised**.

གཞོར་ *γžor* v. *ˌjor*.

གཞོལ་བ་ *γžól-ba* 1. **to apply one's self diligently** *Cs.*, *čós-la t̔ugs γžól-ba Pth.* id. resp. — 2. **to comprehend, to fathom**(?) *Sch.* — 3. resp. for *ˌbáb-pa* **to alight, light from, dismount**, v. *čibs*; cf. also *žol*.

གཞོས་ *γžos* for *bžos*, v. *ˌjó-ba*.

བཞར་ *bža*, in *Lexx.* mentioned as the same with *brlán-pa*.

བཞག་ *bžag* 1. **large intestine**, = *γnyé-ma*; *bžag-sgór-mo* the windings of the intestines *Glr.*, *Mil.* — 2. certain muscles under the arms *Mṅg.* — 3. *Sch.*: 'flesh of animals that died of disease'.

བཞག་པ་ *bžág-pa* 1. v. *ˌjóg-pa*. — 2. **to tear, wear**, intrs., of cloth etc.; **to burst, crack, split** *C.*, *W.*

བཞད་ *bžad*, also *bžád-pa Pth.* **swan**; *bžad-dkár Lex.*; *bžad-ldán Schr.*: 'a pond with swans on it'.

བཞད་པ་, གཞད་པ་ *bžád-pa*, *γžád-pa* **to laugh, smile** *Glr.*; *bžád-k̔a-ma* a girl with a smiling face *Mil.*; *bžad-gád* **laughter**, *t̔ég-pa* to raise (a laughter) *Mil.*, *bžad-gád-mk̔an Tar.* buffoon, jester; *bžád-mo* **smile, laughing, laughter**, *bžád-mo bžád-pa* to laugh; *bžád-pa-mo*, *bžad-ldán-ma* n. of a goddess, *Ssk.* Hāsawati *Cs.*

བཞབ་པ་ *bžáb-pa* v. *ˌjáb-pa*.

བཞམས་པ་ *bžáms-pa* 1. also *γžáms-pa Schr.*? **to stroke**, *p̔yág-gis* resp. with the hand, **to coax, caress**; hence *bžáms-te Dzl.*

२२,5, might perh. be rendered: **to appease, to pacify.** — 2. *bžams-bsgó byéd-pa Lex.* **to remind of, to call to mind.**

བཞར་བ་ *bžár-ba* **to scrape,** with a knife, **to shave** or **shear,** with a razor *Med.*; *skra bžár-ba* the hair.

བཞི་ *bži* 1. **four;** *bži-pa, bží-po* cf. *dgu*; *bži-bču* (col. *žib-ču*) 40, *bži-bču-rtsa-γčig* (*W.*žib-ču-že-čig*), *že-γčig* etc. the numbers 41—49; *bži-brgyá* 400, *bži-stoṅ* 4000 etc.; *bži-ča* one fourth, a quarter; *bži-ṫsan-gyi-sdé-pa pyed-daṅ-brgyád* the 7½ tetrads (of letters) *Gram.* — 2. often incorr. for *ži* or *γži*.

བཞིན་ *bžin* 1. sbst. **face, countenance,** *ráb-tu mi-sdúg-pa* (of) a very ugly face *Dzl.*, *légs-pa, mdzés-pa Glr.* (of) a handsome, a pretty face; *bžin-mdžés-ma* a woman or girl with a pretty face; *bžin zágs-te* the face dripping (from perspiration); *bžin ˳dzúm-pa daṅ bčas-pa* with a friendly smiling countenance *Mil.*; *bžin-pags sér-po* the skin of the face being yellow (as in bilious complaints) *Mṅg.*; *bžin-rás* the appearance, *ṅán-pa Med.*; *bžin-bzáṅ*, fem. *bzin-bzaṅ-ma*, a polite address: my dear Sir; *kye bžin-bzaṅ-dag* much respected gentlemen! also in other instances as a word of politeness: *bžin-bzáṅ-ma dé-dag laṅs-te* the ladies rose and ...; it seems to be particularly in favour, when apparitions are addressed *Mil.* — 2. particle, the meaning of which corresponds in part to that of the Greek prep. κατά c. acc., gen. used as an adv. *bžin-du* or *bžin*, but also as an adj. with *pa:* a. joined to verbal roots, *bžin* serves to form with them a partic. pres., and *bžín-du* a gerund, *ṫugs-mnyés-bžin-pai ṅáṅ-la* in a rejoicing frame of mind, in a joyful mood *Mil.*; *ḱri-la bžúgs-bžin-du* sitting on the chair *Dzl.*; *skrág-bžin-du* from fear *Dzl.* (cf. καθ' ὕπνον); *mdaṅs ˳gyur bžin-du* whilst his colour changes *Dzl.*; *mi šes bžin-du šes-so žes zer* not knowing it he pretends to know it *Stg.*; *dád-bžin-du log soṅ* 'credentes discesserunt', believing they went away *Mil.* b. *bžin(-du)* as postp. c. acc., **agreeably, in conformity, according to,** very frq.; *čos bžin-du* according to the precepts of religion *Dzl.* (cf. κατὰ νόμον), *rgyál-pos bsgó-ba bžin-du sgrúb-pa* to execute a thing according to the king's command, to perform his order frq.; *ḱyod ǰi-skad smrás-pa bžin-du γžán-dag-la bsnyád-de* relating to the others according to what has been said by you, = relating what you have said *Dzl.*; *yid-bžin-du* to heart's content frq.; **like, as,** *ri ˳gyél-ba* like the breaking down of a mountain *Dzl.*; also with a pleonastic *ltar: mḱán-po ǰi-ltar γsúṅ-ba bžin Glr.*, or, which would be the same, *ǰi-bžin γsúṅ-ba ltar*, as the very learned gentleman has said, foretold; *de bžin-du* **so** = *dé-ltar; de-de-bžin-no* yes, that is so; *de-bžin-nyid* (**तत्त्वता**), **truth, reality, substance, essentiality** *Was.* (272), **identity** (297), in mysticism = *čos-nyid Thgy.*, v. *čos*, comp.

c. *ṗyi-bžin(-du)*, *ṗyir-bžin(-du)* **afterwards, subsequently** (cf. κατόπισθε). — d. distrib. *nyin-ré-bžin(-du)*, **daily, per day** (καθ' ἡμέραν), *nyin-γčig-bžin-du* id.; *re-re-bžin-gyi mdzad-pa Glr.* his daily doings.

བཞུ་བ་ *bžú-ba*, v. *žú-ba* II. and *˳ju-ba*, **to melt.**

བཞུགས་པ་ *bžúgs-pa*, resp. for *sdód-pa* and *˳dúg-pa*, 1. **to sit,** *bžúgs-su γsol B*, *bžugs(-žu)* col., please sit down! — *bžúgs-ḱri* chair; throne. — 2. **to dwell, reside,** *bžúgs-pai ṗo-bráṅ* castle of residence *Dzl.*; *bžúgs-pai rten* a small temple in which a deity resides *Dzl.*; *bžugs-grógs* fellow-lodger: — 3. **to remain, stay, exist, live,** *˳jig-rtén-du bžúgs-pa* to be in the world, to live on earth, of Buddha and saints; also, still to remain in the world; *stón-pa bžúgs-pai dús-su* during the life-time of the Teacher (Buddha) *Tar.*; *ḱyed ˳dir bžugs čos-mdzád ye* devout here present = my devout friends! *Mil.*; **žug yǫ-dham* C.* are you at home? **ku žug naṅ yǫ-dham* C.* are you coming? = welcome! well-met!; transferred to writings, texts etc., **to be contained,** so in titles of books: *mdzaṅs-blúṅ žes-byá-ba bžúgs-so* the so-styled 'Sage and Fool' is contained (in the present volume); *bló-la bžúgs-pa daṅ glegs-bám-du bžúgs-pa tams-čád yi-ger spel* all that was found in the memories (of individual persons) and in books, was recorded *Tar.*

བཞུད་པ་ *bžúd-pa*, resp. **to go away, to depart**, *B.* frq.; *ṕar bžud* pray, go away! (opp. to *ťsur-byon*).

བཞུན་ *bžun* v. *žun*.

བཞུར་བ་ *bžúr-ba* 1. = *γzúr-ba*, *bžár-ba Cs.* — 2. **to strain, filter**, *Sch.*

བཞུས་པ་ *bžús-pa* v. *žú-ba*.

བཞེང་བ་ *bžéṅ-ba*, pf. and imp. *bžeṅs Glr.*, resp. for *slóṅ-ba*, **to raise, erect, set up**, an image, temple; **to manufacture, compose**, sacred things, e.g. pictures, books; **to draw up, frame, write, print**, or cause it to be done; **to found, endow, give**, books to monasteries etc.

བཞེངས་པ་ *bžéṅs-pa* 1. pf. of *bžéṅ-ba*. — 2. resp. for *láṅ-ba* **to rise, get up**, intrs. to *bžéṅ-ba*; also with *yár(-la) Glr.*; **nyi - ráṅ žáṅs(-sa**) *W.* are you risen? **žaṅ(s)** please to get up!

བཞེད་པ་ *bžéd-pa* I. vb., resp. for *˳dód-pa*, **to wish, desire**, *rgyál-po γzigs bžéd-dam* does your Reverence wish to see the king? *Dzl.*; *rgyál-po náṅ-du ˳byón-par bžéd-pa-la* as the king wished to enter *Glr.*; *rta mi bžéd-na* if your Reverence does not wish to have the horse *Mil.*; in science: **to accept**, *mḱán-pa ṕyí-ma-dag mi bžéd--pa legs* it is well that learned men of later times do not accept it, approve of it *Gram.*; **to assert, maintain**, *so-sói bžéd-ťsul máṅ-na yaṅ* although many different propositions are to be met with *Wdk.*; *sṅá - mas bžed* earlier writers are of opinion, insist on *Gram.*; of letters: *ga-˳ṕul bžed* certain letters require ག for a prefix *Zam.* — II. **supposition, view, opinion** *Tar.* 113, 21. — *bžed-don* resp. **wish, desire** *Cs.*, *bžed - don ˳grub* it happens according to one's wish, as one could wish *Cs.*

བཞེས་པ་ *bžés-pa* I. vb., resp. for *lén-pa* **to take, receive, accept; to seize, confiscate**, *B.*, *C.* (*W.* **nám-če** synon.); *ḱáb-tu bžés-pa* and *žál-gyis bžés-pa* v. *ḱab* and *žal*; esp. at meals, **to take, to eat**, *ɉi bžéd-pa bžes šig Dzl.* please take whatever you like, *bžés-na* if he would take it, if it should be to his liking *Mil.*; instead of *lón-pa* in: *dgúṅ-lo bču-γnyis bžés-pa* he got twelve years old. — II. sbst. **food, meat**, *bžés-pa ˳drén-pa* to offer, to serve up meat *Mil.*, *Pth.* — **Comp.** **žē-ḍho** *C.* food, sweet-meats (cf. *gro*) *bžes-ťáṅ* food (?) *Sch.* — **žē-ḍhúṅ** (?) *Ts.* beer. —**žē-bhág** *C.* bread —**žē-rág** *W.* brandy. —**žē-hór** *C.*, hookah, oriental tobacco-pipe, the smoke of which passes through water.

བཞོ་བ་, བཞོས་པ་ *bžó-ba*, *bžós-pa* **to milk.**

བཞོག་པ་ *bžog-pa* v. *˳ɉog-pa*.

བཞོགས་ *bžogs* = *γžogs*.

བཞོང་ *bžoṅ* = *γžon*.

བཞོན་པ་ *bžón-pa* (sometimes incorr. *γžón-pa*) vehiculum, **riding - beast, carriage, vehicle**; *bžón-pa šóm-pa* to order the horses to be put to *Dzl.*; *bžon-pas ˳brós-pa* to take to flight in a vehicle or on horseback *Dzl.*; *mi-srun bžón-pa* a not gentle riding-beast *S.g.*

བཞོན་མ་ *bžón-ma* **milking cow** *Cs*, *bžon-ṕyugs* milking cattle *Glr.*

# ཟ

ཟ་ *za* 1. the letter **z**, originally, and in the frontier-provinces to the present-day, sounding like the English z, in *C.* differing from ས, s, only by the following vowel being deep-toned. — 2. numer. figure: 22.

ཟ་, ཟས་ *za*, *zas*, *Ld.* any thing **small, neat, elegant, of a miniature size**, **pé-ča za žig** a little book, pocket-edition, **nod-čád za zig** a little pot or can, **čaṅ za žig** a drop of beer.

ཟྭ་ *zwa*, **nettle**, stinging nettle, gen. *zwa-tsód*, being, when young, eaten as greens (v. *tsód-ma*); *zwa(i)-p̀yi(mo)*, *'a-ya-zwa-tsód*, *Wdṅ.*, blind or dead nettle; *zwa-lčág* scourge made of stinging nettles, *zwa-lčág brgyáb-pa* to flog with it *Cs.*; *zwa-ber*, the smart produced by the stinging of nettles *Cs.*; *zwa-˳brúm Wdn* (?).

ཟ་ཁུ་ *za-k̀u Med.*, e.g. *bad-kan za-k̀ur ˳gyur Mṅg.* prob. the same word which *Sch.* spells *za-gu*, explaining it by gonorrhoea, morbid discharge of seminal fluid, semen pruriens.

ཟ་བ་ *zá-ba*, *bza-ba* I. vb., perf. *zos*, *bzas*, fut. *bza*, imp. *zo*, *zos* (*C.* **zę**) 1. **to eat**, both of men and animals, *zá-bya*, *zá-rgyu* what may or must be eaten, *za-čig-pa Dzl.* (perh. better *bza-γčig-pa*) one that takes only one meal a day, or perh.: one that takes a solitary meal; *zós-pas* having eaten *Dzl.*; *zós-pai ˏóg-tu* after he had eaten *Dzl.*; *zos-˳grogs* 'immediately after dinner' (??) *Sch.*; *ma-lús-par zá-ba Dzl.*, **dág-mo za-če** *W.*, to eat up, consume, to clear the plate, the manger; *bzá-ru rún-ba* or *mi-rún-ba* what may or may not be eaten; *Dzl.* ༢༩, 16 has also a supine *zós-su*: *bu zos-su ˏoṅ* she will even be constrained to eat her own young (s. l. c.); *žím-du zo Zam.* may you enjoy your dinner! ni f.; *zá-k̀ar* at dinner-time *Sch.*; *za-zá-ba* 'to eat often, to be a glutton' *Cs.* — 2. **to live upon, to live by,** *gla zá-ba* to gain one's subsistence as a day-labourer *Dzl.* — 3. **to itch,** *za ˳p̀rúg-pa* v. *˳p̀rug-pa*. — 4. fig. for **to steal,** **kún-ma, gòṅ-mo zos soṅ** *Ld.*, a thief, a witch, has made away with it. — 5. fig. of affections of the mind: **to entertain, to give way to,** *k̀óṅ-k̀ro*, *tsig-pa*, *té-tsom zá-ba* to give way to resentment, anger, doubts. — II. sbst. **food, meat, victuals,** *za ču žim* good eating and drinking *Mil.*; **zá-če zá-če, čó-če** *W.* to eat food, to prepare food. — *za-rkóṅ* v. *rkoṅ*. — *za-k̀aṅ* dining-room; eating-house, cook's shop *C.* — *za-k̀u* v. the preceding article. — *zá-mk̀an* one that is eating, an eater. — **za-čóg** *W.* what may be eaten, **za-mi-čóg** what may not be eaten. — **za-túr** *C.* chop-sticks. — *zá-ma* **food, victuals,** *zá-ma mi ster ruṅ* though you do not give me any food *Mil.* — *za-yón* meat-offering to saints etc. *Mil.* — For more refer to *bza*.

ཟ་མ་ *zá-ma* 1. v. above. — 2. also *zá-ma-tog Ssk.* करण्ड, **basket,** in Tibetan only fig., mostly as a title of books, but also used in connection with mysticism.

ཟ་ཟི་ *za-zí* **trouble, noise** *Cs.*, **troublesome chatting** *Sch.*; **troubled, bewildered, perplexed** *Schr.*; in the passage *rmí-lam za-zí maṅ Med.* it seems to signify troubled dreams.

ཟ་ཟོམ་ *za-zóm* a fine cotton fabric *Sch.*

ཟ་ར་ *zá-ra?* **zá-ra p̀i-mo** *W.* the later part of the afternoon, v. *rdzá-ra*.

ཟ་རུ་ *zá-ru* v. *γzár-bu*.

ཟ་འོག་ *za-ˏóg* **heavy silk cloth,** *za-ˏóg-gi gos* a garment made of it *Glr.*; *za-ˏóg dgu brtsegs k̀ri* a seat formed of nine silk quilts. — *za-báb* id.

ཟ་ཧོར་ *za-hor* n. of a town or district, acc. to *Cs.* in Bengal, acc. to *Pth.* in the north-west of India, by the statements of Lamas the present **Mandi,** a small principality under British protection, in the Punjâb, between the rivers Byās and Ravi, where there is a sacred lake, celebrated as a place of pilgrimage, from which the Brahmins residing there derive a considerable income.

ཟག་པ་ *zág-pa* 1. sometimes for *γzág-pa*, from *˳dzágs-pa*. — 2. sbst., *Ssk.* आस्रव **misery, affliction, sorrow,** esp. as a consequence of sin, hence frq. = sin, *zág-pa zad* the woe of this world is over, frq.; *zág-pa-med-pai las* works spotless or without sin *Thgy.*; *zag-méd-kyi bde-ba* untroubled happiness *Glr.*; *zag-bčás* burdened with misery and sin, *zag-bčás-kyi las γsum* the three sinful works *Thgy.*; *zag-bčas-kyi mṅon (-par)-šes(-pa) Glr.* and *Thgr.?*

ཟང་ *zaṅ? Sch.*: *zaṅ-tál-du* **penetrating.**

ཟང་ཟང་ *zaṅ-záṅ* 1. v. *dmár-po* extr. — 2. also *zaṅ-ziṅ*, *ziṅ-ziṅ*, *γziṅ-ba*, v. *˳dziṅs-pa*; *W.* also: **muddled, rather tipsy.**

ཟང་ཟིང་ *zaṅ-zíṅ* 1. sbst. **matter, object, goods,** = *rdzas*, *zaṅ-zín čúṅ-zad tsám-gyi* ṕyir even for the most trifling matter *Stg.*; *ṕyi-rol-gyi zaṅ-ziṅ* external goods, earthly possessions, (opp. to internal, spiritual gifts) *Dzl.*; also *zaṅ-ziṅ* by itself: what is earthly, pertaining to this world *Mil.* — 2. adj., **confused in mind, stupefied** *Sch.*, v. the preceding article.

ཟངས་ *zaṅs* 1. **copper,** *γsér-zaṅs* gilt copper, *záṅs-kyi btsa* prob. verdigris. — 2. **kettle** *B.*, *C.*, v. *ṕan-dil*; *záṅs-su skól-ba* to boil in a kettle *Dzl.*; *zaṅs ḱól-pa* a boiling kettle *Dzl.*; *ₒḱár-zaṅs* bronze or brass kettle, *lčags-zaṅs* iron kettle. — *zaṅs-rkyán* copper can or jug. — *zaṅs-skyógs* copper ladle. — *zaṅs-čén* a large, *zaṅs-čúṅ* a small kettle. — *zaṅs-tig* a small species of gentian. — *zaṅs-tíb* copper tea-pot. — **záṅ-ton-sa** *W.* copper-mine. — *zaṅs-ťál* copper slacks *Glr.* — *zaṅs-mdóg* copper colour. — *zaṅs-sdér* copper plate or dish *Sch.* — *zaṅs-snód* copper vessel. — **záṅ-bu** *C.*, *W.*, = *zaṅs* 2; **záṅ-bu če čuṅ nyi** two copper kettles, a large one and a little one. — *záṅs-ma* = *záṅs-bu?* *Mṅg.* — *záṅs-γya* *Cs.*: 'copper-green', prob. verdigris. — *záṅs-sa* copper-ore *Cs.*

ཟངས་དཀར་ *záṅs-dkar* south-western province of Ladak, *záṅs-dkar-pa*, *-ma* man or woman of that province.

ཟད་པ་ *zád-pa* v. *ₒdzád-pa.*

ཟན་ *zan*, *C.* **zęn**, I. resp. *bsáṅ-ma*, also *ḱam-zán* *Mil.* 1. **pap, porridge,** of flour and water, thick, boiled or not boiled, warm or cold, also called *bág-zan*, esp. as dough for baking; in *C.* porridge is gen. made of *rtsám-pa*, and if possible of tea; *ₒbrás-zan* rice-p., *ₒó-zan*, milk-p.; porridge being the daily food, as bread is with us, the word is used also 2. for **food** in gen: *zan zá-ba* to take food, to eat, *bdag daṅ zan mi zá-na* if you will not eat with me *Dzl.*; *zan-dráṅ* cold, *zan-drón* warm food, *zan-čaṅ* meat and drink, *S.g.*; *zan btsos-pa* boiled food; **zan-kón** dearth *W.*; *zan zos* 1. he was eating porridge. 2. as one word: *Bal.* wife, cf. *bza*; fig. *lkog-zán zá-ba* to take unlawful interest *Sch.* — 3. **fodder, provender,** v. *bzan.* —

II. inst. of *za* **eater,** as second part of a compound: *śa-zán* meat-eater; carnivorous animal *Glr.*; *nya-zán* fish-eater, ichthyophagist; *ṕag-zán* pork-eater.

ཟན་པོ་ *zán-po* v. *γzán-po.*

ཟབ་ *zab* **silk,** fine or heavy silk, v. *dar-záb*; *zab-čén* costly silk cloth *Sch.*; *zab-skúd* *Lt.*, *Mil.* silk-cord; *zab-ₒból* silk covering for a seat, bolster *Pth.*

ཟབ་པ་ *záb-pa*, vb., adj. and sbst., **to be deep, deep, depth,** *záb-po*, gen. *záb-mo*, adj., deep, frq.; often fig., *blo-záb* *Cs.*: a profound mind or understanding; *zab-záb byas kyaṅ záb-mo raṅ mi ₒdug* although people call it deep, it is not deep *Sch.*; *zab-lám*, *záb-moi sgom-ḱrid* a term of Buddhist mysticism, doctrine of witchcraft, = *dbú-mai lam*, or *ṕyág-rgya čén-po.* — *zab-ḱyád* depth, = *zabs*, *Dzl.*, *Mil.*

ཟབས་ *zabs* **depth,** *zábs-su ₒdom bčui doṅ* a pit ten fathoms in depth.

ཟམ་པ་ *zám-pa* **bridge,** *grú-zam* bridge of boats *Cs.*; *lcágs-zam* iron bridge, wire-bridge; *lčúg-zam* suspension-bridge, by means of cables of twisted birch-tree branches; *ₒdrén-zam* draw-bridge *Cs.*; *rdó-zam* 1. stone-bridge. 2. natural rock-bridge; *rtswá-zam* common expression for *lčúg-zam* and *ťsár-zam*; the latter: suspension-bridge by cables formed of thin split cane; *śiṅ-zam* wooden bridge; *zám-pa ₒdzúgs-pa* to throw a bridge *Cs.*; *zám-pai ká-ba* or *rkáṅ-pa* the piers or foundations, *spaṅ-léb*, *spaṅ-sgó* the boards or planks, *mda-yáb* or *lag-rtén* parapet, *γžu-ťóg* arch, *zam-γdúṅ* beam of a bridge, *Cs.*; *zam-čén* a large bridge, *zam-čúṅ* a little one *Cs.*, *zám-bu* id.

ཟར་ *zar* 1. supine of *zá-ba*; *zar ₒjúg-pa* **to give to eat.** — 2. **pitch-fork,** for shaking up the corn, hay-fork, dung-fork; forks at dinner are not yet used in Tibet, spoons and knives, and in Lhasa chop-sticks, answering their end sufficiently.

ཟར་བབས་ *zar-bábs* *Sch.*: **tassel**; acc. to our authorities: **gold-brocade.**

ཟར་བུ་ *zár-bu* *Glr.*, *Mil.* seems to be **tassel.**

ཟར་མ་ *zar-ma Dzl., Med.* **sesame-seed;** *zar-mai me-tog* flower of sesame, *Sch.*; *zar-ma-ču* is mentioned in *Pth,* as Aphrodisiacum; yet *zar-mai ras* is stated to be a fabric, manufactured from *zwa-ṫsód*, muslin?

ཟལ་ *zal Ld.* a small and uninhabited river-island.

ཟལ་མོ་ *zál-mo* 1. **young cow, heifer,** *ₒbri-zál* yak-heifer. — 2. a fabulous bird *Sch.*

ཟས་ *zas* **food, nourishment,** for men and animals, also in a wider fig. sense; *zas-bċád smyúṅ-γnas* fasting, abstaining from or withholding food *Lex.*; *zas-bzáṅ(-po)* 1. dainty food *Dzl.* 2. nourishing fare, *Wdṅ.*, *zas-ṅán(-pa)* the contrary; *zas-ni* as to diet . . . *Med.*; *zás-su ċi za* what does it feed on? *Dzl.*; *zás-suḱrag ₒṫúṅ-ba* to drink blood for nourishment *Do.*; *zas ₒṫsól-ba* to seek to obtain a livelihood *Ma.*; *ₒṫsó-ba zas, Mil.* a pleon. expression = *zas*; *ḱa-zás* (resp. *žal-zas B., sól-wa* col.) **food, meat,** for human beings; *dkár-zas* v. *dkár-ba; dmár-zas Sch.*: 'festival dishes', perh. more corr. flesh-meat, animal food? *gró-zas Sch.*: 'dry traveller's fare'; *p̓án-zas*, wholesome nutritive food *Med.* —

**Comp.** **zẹ-ḱọn** *C.* dearth, scarcity. — *zas-skom* meat and drink, solid and liquid food *Med.*; *zas-čáṅ*, id., as travelling-provisions *Glr.* — *zas-spyod* food and exercise, diet, in a wider sense *Med.* — *zas-ṫsód* the due measure of food, *zas-ṫsód ma zin* the portion or share was not full, it was not the full allowance, *S.g.* — *zas-γtsáṅ-ma* (clean food), n.p. शुद्धोदन, the father of Buddha; *bdúd-rtsi-zas, bré-bo-zas, zas-dkár* the names of his three brothers, *zas-γtsaṅ-srás* appellation of Buddha himself.

ཟི་ *zi,* I. num. figure: 52. — II. *W.* 1. something of a very **small size** or **quantity,** **zi yaṅ mi dug** not an atom is left, **zi-med-ḱan ċo** eat it up to the last crumb! **mé-zi** a spark in the ashes ever so small. — 2. **the black mark** in a target. (cf. *ža*).

ཟི་ངིལ་ *zi-ṅil* v. *zi-líṅ.*

ཟི་བ་ *zi-ba* v. *γzi-ba.*

ཟི་མ་ *zi-ma, Sch.*: **green slime** on standing water, *zi-ma-ċan* what is covered with such a slime.

ཟི་ར་ *zi-ra, Ssk.* and *Hindi* जीर, **the Asiatic caraway,** *Cuminum Cyminum,* exported from Tibet to India, of a powerful aroma, which to the taste of Europeans is often disagreeable; two kinds are distinguished, *zi-ra dkár-po*, and *nág-po.*

ཟི་རི་རི་ *zi-ri-ri* **the humming of bees,** the singing of a kettle *W.*

ཟི་རུ་ *zi-ru* col. for *γzér-bu.*

ཟི་ལིང་ *zi-líṅ* I. also **zi-ṅil, zi-lóṅ** *W.* **noise, bustle, tumult.** —

II. from the Chinese 1. also *zi-lím, zi-láṅ* **a composition metal,** similar to German silver, *zi-liṅ-pan-tse* or *baṅ-tse C.* a basin of that metal. — 2. n. p., province, adjoining the Kokonor, *zi-liṅ-ja* tea from thence.

ཟིང་ཟིང་ *ziṅ-ziṅ* v. *zaṅ-ziṅ.*

ཟིང་རེལ་ *ziṅ-rél W.*, prob. for *ₒdziṅ-sbrél*, with **ċó-ċe**, to prepare for battle, or to begin fighting.

ཟིན་པ་ *zin-pa* 1. v. *ₒdzin-pa.* — 2. = *ₒdzád-pa*, esp. in the pf. tense, **to draw near to an end, to be at an end, to be finished, exhausted, consumed;** *zin-pai p̓úṅ-po* the perishable, mortal body *Thgy.*; **to be finished, terminated,** *nam yaṅ mi zin-to Dzl.* it will never be finished; **to finish, to get done with,** building a wall *Glr.*, **zin ċúg-ċe** *W.* id.; *ₒṫuṅ ma zin dógs-pas* fearing not to be able to drink it all *Glr.*; *rtsé-ba zin-pas* as the playing has ceased, or, as he has done playing *Dzl.*; *zin(-pa) méd(-pai) las* endless working, unceasing labour *Mil.*; hence = *ṫsár-ba*, to denote an action that is **perfectly past,** esp. in *B., p̓rú-gu skyés-su zin kyaṅ* although the child is already born *Do.*; *γsón-poi tsé-na ₔú-ċag-gis de spyad zin* we had enjoyed it during our life-time; *zin-bris Cs.*: 1. **abridgment, general view, synopsis.** 2. **lecture,** so *Schf. Tar.* 210, 22. 3. **receipt, quittance; bond** (of obligation), **bill of debt.**

ཟིམ་བུ་ *zim-bu* **fine, thin, slender,** *čar zim-bu mi drág-po žig bab* a fine, drizzling rain was falling *Dzl.*, *Mil.*; *čar zim-zim dál-gyis báb-pa Mil.*, id.; *zim-zím* or *ziṅ-ziṅ* **fine, hair-shaped, capillary**, e.g. the leaves of some plants.

ཟིར་བ་ *zir-ba*, (*γzir-ba?*), gen. **zir táṅ-če** *W.*, **to aim**, *zir-po*, *zir-čan* a good aimer, marksman *W.*; *zir-sa* **aim, dispart**, **nẹ-zir** sight (of a gun) *W.*

ཟིར་མོ་ *zir-mo*, **zir-mo gyún-če** *W.* to slide down a snow-hill on the coat spread under, a winter-diversion of children.

ཟིལ་ *zil* 1. (*Cs. zil-ma*), **brightness, splendour, brilliancy, glory**, *rje-btsún-gyi ťúgs-rjei zil ma bzód-par* not being able to bear the brightness of his Reverence's grace, (the adversary fell down the mountain) *Mil.*; *zíl-čan* **brilliant, resplendent**; *zil-gyis nón-pa* to overcome, vanquish, *ǩoi zil-gyis nón-te* overpowered by him *Pth.*; *zil-bar ̥gró-ba* to increase, multiply, spread *Sch.* — 2. in botany: *stoṅ-zil*, *Corydalis meïfolia*; *γser-zíl*, *dṅul-zil? S.g.*

ཟིལ་དངར་ *zil-dṅár* v. *dṅar.*

ཟིལ་པ་ *zil pa* **dew**, *zil-pa ǩrom-mé* a sparkling dew-drop *Pth.*; *zil dkár* **hoarfrost** *Sch.*; *zil-mṅar Cs.* = *mdúd-rtsi* **nectar.**

ཟིལ་བུན་པ་ *zil-bún-pa* a slight **shuddering** from fear.

ཟུ་ *zu*, num. figure: 82.

ཟུག་ *zug* 1. also *γzug*, **pain, torment**, physical and mental; **distemper, illness, complaint**, esp. *W.* **zúg rag** I feel a pain, I am ill, **gó-la zug rág-ga** have you the head-ache? **zug čo dug** he is ill, he is suffering from pain; **só-zug** toothache; *zúg-rṅu*, *zug-γzér*, resp. *snyún* or *snyúṅ-zug*, *B.* and col. = *zug*, *mya-ṅán-gyi zúg-rṅus sdúg-bsṅal-žiṅ* weighed down by the grief of misery, *nyon-móṅs-kyi zúg-rṅu Mil.*, of the like import. — 2. also *γzug*, the principal or main pieces in cutting up an animal, **quarters**, *zug-tu ̥ṕrál-ba* to cut into such pieces *Mil.*; 1 *zug* = 3 *lhu* = 6 *dum* = 12 *rgya-ri.* — 3. v. *tsug.*

ཟུག་རྔུ་ *zúg-rṅu* v. *zug* 1.

ཟུག་པ་ *zúg-pa* I. vb. 1. v. *̥dzúgs-pa.* — 2. **to bark** *Dzl.*

II. sbst. **building, erection**, **zúg-pa gyáb-pa** *Ts.* to build (cf. *̥dzúgs-pa* 3).

ཟུང་ *zuṅ* 1. earlier literat. and *W.* **a pair, couple**, *zúṅ-du ma mčis* not occurring in pairs *Wdṅ.*; **čá-bu zuṅ čig**, *Ld.* a pair of pendants (for the ears); *nyi-zlá zuṅ γčig btsón-du bzuṅ* sun and moon are both shut up (covered by clouds) *Mil.*; *zuṅ-mčóg* the model-pair, the two principal disciples of Buddha, Sariibu and Maudgalgyibu, *Köpp.* I, 101; *zuṅ-ldán* **agreeing** in sound, **rhyming** *Cs.*; *zuṅ-̥brel* **connection, junction, union**, *zuṅ-̥brel ̥dód-na* if one wishes both things to be united *Glr.*; *zuṅ-brél-du* one after the other, or one with the other *Pth.*; *zuṅ sdébs-pa* **to join, connect, unite** *Mil.*; *zuṅ-yá* one half of a pair, a single one, e.g. shoe etc. *Cs.* — 2. **a single, separate piece** *C.* and sometimes in later literat.; *ǩa-dród zuṅ čig* a bit or mouthful of food *Thgy.*; *ťsar re zuṅ re bltás-pas* when he had seen a single piece but once, (he knew it immediately) *Tar.* — 3. symb. num.: 2; *zuṅ-ṕyógs* id. — *zuṅ-̥júg* a technical term of practical mysticism, the forcing the mind (*sems*) into the principal artery, in order to prevent distraction (of mind) (!) *Mil.* (v. *γtúm-mo*).

ཟུང་མཁར་ *zuṅ-mǩár* n. of a royal castle *Glr.*

ཟུང་བ་ *zúṅ-ba* v. *̥dzin-pa.*

ཟུངས་ *zuṅs* v. *γzuṅs.*

ཟུབ་པ་ *zúb-pa* inst. of *bsúbs-pa*, pf. of *sub-pa Glr.*

ཟུམ་པ་ *zúm-pa* 1. v. *̥dzúm-pa.* — 2. *W.* for *bzúṅ-ba*, v. *̥dzin-pa*; hence *zum-ǩáb* **pin, brooch.**

ཟུར་ *zur* 1. **edge**, *gad-zúr* edge of a steep river-bank or precipice consisting of conglomerate *Cs.*; *ču-zúr* edge of the water, border, brink, bank, *ču-zúr-pa* one that lives on the bank of a river; *zúr-na* at the border (of the place where one happens to be) *Mil.* **žiṅ-zúr-nẹ lam yod** *W.* the road leads along the field; **board**, of a ship. — 2. **edge, corner**, *ǩá-ba zur-brgyád-pa* octangular pillar *Stg.*, (v. *zúr-ċan* and *zúl-ma* below); *zur bži* the four corners *Sch.* — 3. **side,** **zúr-du* (or *lóg-su*) *žag-pa** *C.* to lay aside; *zúr(-du) bkól-ba Lex.*, *Sch.*: to lay up, put by, spare, save; *zúr-du ₒkríd-pa* to take aside, apart, for a private conversation; so also *zur ṗyin-pa Stg.*; *zúr-du, zúr-gyis B.*, **zúr-na* W.*, **indirectly, by the way, by the by, incidentally,** *zúr-du smrá-ba* to speak indirectly, by hints *Cs.*; *zúr-gyis mtsón-pa Tar.* to note, point out only by hints or insinuations *Schf.*; hence perh. *ṫsig zúr* **invective speech,** **ṫsig-zúr ma zer* W.* no invectives! don't be personal! *zur zá-ba* is prob. the same, where *Sch.* has: to address harshly; **zúr-nẹ láb-ċe* W.* to learn or study privately (out of school-time, or, not with the appointed master); *zur bžugs-pa Cs.* (prob. for *zúr-du*) **to lead a private life** (cf. *zúr-pa*); *zur mig ltá-ba* **to look sideways, askance, to leer, squint** *Sch.* — 4. **outline,** *ḱyod daṅ zur ₒdra tsam yaṅ sa steṅ med* none on earth is like you, or can be compared to you, even in a general outline *Pth.*; *ₒdi-dag zur tsam bsdú-ba yín-gyis* this is merely a brief outline, extract, sketch *Glr.* and elsewh., frq., also *zur tsam yin-gyis Glr.* —

**Comp.** *zur-bkód, zúr-ₒdébs, Sch.*: 'founded for a special purpose'. — *zúr-ċan* cornered, angular, *yi-ge Glr.* p. 31, a sort of type or printing-letter, = *klui yí-ge*, v. also no. 2 above. — *zur-ċág Sch.*: prop., having a broken edge, damaged by being knocked about; gen. fig., of words and grammatical forms: faulty, corrupted, misapplied; *Liš.* and elsewh., *Ssk.* अपभ्रंश. the most vitiated Prakrit-dialect *Was.* (267). — *zur-ₒdébs* = *zur-bkód-zur-nór* private goods *Cs.* — *zur-pa* one out of office, a private individual *Cs.* — *zúr-ma* = *zur* prov. — *zur-γsós* educated by strangers *Sch.*

ཟུར་མོ་ *zúr-mo* **pain,** = *zug*, vulg.

ཟུར་ཕུད་ *zur-ṗúd Glr.* **hair-knot, dressed hair** *Sch.*

ཟུལ་མ་ *zúl-ma W.* **cornered, angular,** = *zúr-ċan*; **ṗẹ'-zúl** lotus-edged, of bowls, dishes, plates, that are of a polygonal or radiated shape.

ཟེ་ *ze* I. num. figure: 112.

II., also *zé-ba B.*, *W.*, *zeu Cs.* 1. **hump** of a camel, zebu etc. *Cs.* — 2. **crest,** of birds, dragons etc. *Glr.*, *S.g.*; also *ze-próg Lex.* — *zé-ḱa Cs.*: 1. 'hump. 2. decorated pad or cushion'. — *ze-ṙnóg Cs.* = *zé-ba.* — *ze-ₒbrú, zeu-ₒbrú Glr.*, *Mṅg.* the anthers of a flower.

ཟེ་འབུག་ *ze-búg W.* **the maw** or **fourth stomach** of ruminating animals.

ཟེ་མ་ *zé-ma W.* **elastic spring.**

ཟེ་ཚྭ་ *zé-ṫswa* **saltpetre** *S.g.*; *zé-ṫswa-ċan* containing saltpetre, nitrous; *zé-ṫsai skyúr-rtsi* nitric acid *Cs.*

ཟེགས་མ་ *zégs-ma* **impurity, smut, dirt** *Sch.*

ཟེང་ *zeṅ*, *ṫú-ba γyás-zeṅ γyón-zeṅ byás-pa* the skirts of the coat on the right and left side folded back, tucked up *Mil.*

ཟེད་ *zed* I. sbst. 1. **brush,** *ṗag-zéd* brush of hog's bristles; *byab-zéd* clothes-brush, dust-brush *Cs.*; *so-zéd* tooth-brush *Cs.* — 2. **edge** *C.* — II. adj *Sch.*: **'broken off, damaged, injured;** *zéd-laṅs* **chink, crack, rent;** *zéd-ₒdug-pa* to crumble at the top' (?).

ཟེམ་ *zem* 1. **cask, barrel, tun,** often sonsisting merely of an excavated piece of a willow-tree, the Tibetans knowing but little of coopery *C.*, *W.* — 2. **box, chest** *W.* — *zem-šiṅ* the body or wood of a vessel, *zem-mṫil* the bottom of a vessel *Cs.*

ཟེར་ *zer* 1. v. *γzer*. — 2. **talk,** cf. *brȷod.* — 3. n of a small animal *Med.*

ཟེར་བ་ *zér-ba* 1 (seldom *ₒdzér-ba*) **to say,** esp. later literat. and vulg; *ḱyod zér-ba bdén-no* you say rightly *Dzl.* (where at other times always *smra-ba* is used inst. of it); *he he zer bgád-pas* they laughed he, he! *Glr.*; *ċos dar zer rgyai yig-ṫsaṅ-na ₒdug* then the doctrine was diffused, say the Chinese records *Glr.*; after words quoted: ... *zér-bar ₒdúg-pas* thus having been spoken, read, heard *Glr.*; *'yin' zer bsnyon byás-so* saying 'it is he', she told a lie *Glr.*, and so frq. *zer*, where in earlier literat. *žes* is used; *zér-na* 1. **if one says,** esp. for the older *že-*

*na*, frq. 2. **if I may say so, so to speak, as it were;** **di-la ci zer** what is this called? frq., also without *la;* to make a noise, e.g. **sag sag zér-wa* C.* to foam with a hissing noise, to sparkle, of wine, beer; *zér-mkan* 1. he that is saying. 2. *W.*, said, called, mentioned, esp. for the older *žes byá-ba.* — **zér-kę** *C.* rumour, report. — **zér-pog-can* W.* speaking in an uncivil or offensive manner. — *zer-ri C.* rumour. — 2 **to drive in,** nails, v. *yzér-ba.*

ཟེལ་མ་ *zél-ma* **small chip,** *šiṅ-zél* **wood-shavings** *W.*

ཟོ་ *zo* I. num. figure: 142.

II. imp. of *zá-ba.*

III. sbst. resp. *sku-zó,* = *lus-kyi kams* **physical constitution,** *sku-zo mdog légs-la* as the appearance of your majesty's bodily constitution is so excellent *Glr.; zo bzáṅ-ba* a good complexion *Cs.* — 2. **figure, delineation, representation,** perh. better to be spelt *bzo* (?) — 3. **mould,** *zo-čágs* showing mouldy spots *Sch.* (?); *zo-már* old, mouldy butter, so prob. *S.g.*; *zo-ša Lt.* mouldy meat

ཟོ་བ་ *zo-ba* 1. sbst., **pail, bucket,** *šiṅ-zo* wooden pail, *ču-zo* water-pail. — 2. vb. v. *bzó-ba.*

ཟོག་ *zog* 1. **deceit, fraud, falsehood** (*Lex.* = *rdzub*), *zóg-can* 1. **lying, deceitful; liar** *W.* 2. **adulterate, counterfeit** *W.*; *zog-ldán, zóg-po Cs.* id., *zog-méd* the opp.; *sgyu-zóg* (religious) **hypocrisy** *Pth.*; *čos-zóg* **priestcraft** *Mil.*; **zol-zóg** = *zog W.* — 2. vulg. pronunciation in *C.* and *W.*, inst. of the following.

ཟོང་ *zoṅ* (vulgo *zog*) 1. **ware, merchandise, goods,** *zoṅ-min-smár* not goods but ready money *Lex.*; *rgyágs-zoṅ* goods taken by travellers along with them to be bartered for provisions; *smán-zoṅ* drugs; *tsóṅ-zoṅ* **merchandise** *Cs.*; *zóṅ-rnams rnám-pa sna-tsógs* goods of all kinds; **zóg-gi dág-po* Ts.* owner of the goods, master of the estate, heir, = *nór-bdag.* — 2. *Sch.* **worth, price**(?). — 3. *Sch.* **doubt**(?). — 4. *Sch.* **lie**(?).

ཟོན་ *zon* **attention, heed, care,** gen. *zon byéd-pa,* **to pay attention, to take heed, to beware,** *dyrá-la* of an enemy *Pth.*; also c. accus. *Mil.*; *zon sdig-pa spoṅ mi šes* seems to mean: not knowing the attention needful for renouncing sin *Thgy.*; *zon-méd* **heedless;** *zon-grábs* **provision, precaution, preventive measure** *Sch.*

ཟོན་པ་ *zón-pa Ts.*, **stuff- or woolen shoes;** **bob-zọn** id., covered with leather.

ཟོབ་ *zob Ts.*, **zob-zób jhé-pa** **to shake thoroughly,** = *ₒdzól-ba.*

ཟོམ་ *zom* 1. **point, top,** *rdo-rjei* of the *dor-je Dom*; **summit,** of the Rirab and some other mountains *S.O.* and elsewh.; *zom-kóg* **dull, simple, stupid,** *Sch.* — 2. **cave** *Sch.*, *brag-zóm* rock-cavern.

ཟོར་ *zor,* 1. sup. of *zó-ba, bzó-ba Sch.* — 2. sbst. the weapons employed in combating the evil spirits in the *ytór-ma,* such as knife, sword, sling, bow and arrows etc.; *zor-ka* the fore- or front-part, the edge, of the weapons directed against the demons, *zór-ka ₒpén-pa Cs.:* to fling those weapons against the spirits.

ཟོར་བ་ *zór-ba* **sickle,** *zór-bas rṅá-ba Mil., ycód-pa Cs.* to cut with a sickle, *zór-lče* sickle-blade; *zor-čúṅ* small, *zor-čén* large sickle, scythe, though in Tibet as yet hardly known; *zor-rtúl* blunt, dull, *zor-rnón* sharp sickle; *zór-bu* = *zor-čúṅ.*

ཟོར་ཡང་ *zor-yáṅ Sch.:* **small, short** (?).

ཟོལ་ཚོ་ *zól-tso* v. *ₒdzól-ba.*

ཟོལ་ཟོག་ *zol-zóg* **deceit, fraud, imposture, falsehood,** *zol-zóg byéd-pa, W. *co-ce*,* **to deceive, impose on,** e.g in traffic *Thgy.*, *zól-zog-can* **deceitful, fraudulent,** *zol(-zog)-méd* without deceit, free from guile, artless *Mil.*

ཟོས་ *zos* v. *zá-ba.*

ཟླ་ *zla* 1. for *zlá-ba.* — 2. for *zlá-bo.*

ཟླ་བ་ *zlá-ba* I. sbst. 1. prov. *zla,* **moon,** frq.; *mkai zlá-ba* **celestial moon** *Lex.*, to distinguish it from 2. *dús-kyi zlá-ba* **temporal moon or month,** *zlá-ba ycig, B., W., *da cig* C.*, one month; **zlá-ba ma ₒkor šog** come before the end of the month *Sch.*; *zlá-ba tsáṅ-du nyé-bas* towards the expiration of the months (of pregnancy) *Dzl.*; *zla-dús ťém-pa daṅ* at the expiration of those months *Glr*; cf. also *ṅo* 5. — 3. symb. num: 1. — **Combinations and comp.** *zlá-bai dkyil-ˬk'or, zla-dkyil,* **da k'yir-mo** *W.* disk of the moon; **da gaṅ soṅ** *W.* the moon is full; **da gaṅ-po* or *son-te** *W. zlá-ba rgyás-pa Pth., nya-rgyás zlá-ba Pth.* full moon; *nya* day of full moon; *zla(-ba) k'ám(-pa), zla-gám, W. *da-p'éd** half moon, i.e. the first and last quarter; **semicircle,** *zlá-ba k'ám-pa ltá-bur bžág-go* they are placed round in a semicircle *Do.*; *dbyibs zla-gám ltá-bur yod* it is semicircular in shape *Glr.*; *zlá-bai ṅo* v. *ṅo*; *zla-ťéb* = *zla-šól*; *zla-nág* new moon *Sch.* (?); *zla-p'ógs* monthly wages; *zla-ťsés* 1. = *zlá-ba ťsés-pa, ťses-γsum-zlá-ba Mil.* the moon on the first two or three evenings of her being visible; **crescent,** *zla-ťsés ltá-bu* in the shape of a crescent, *S.g.*; it is also used as an image of speedy decay. — 2. **date** *Schr.* (?) — *zla-mťsán* the monthly courses; also the discharges of them, *zla-mťsán ˬdzag* the catamenial discharges flow *Cs*; *zla-mťsán-čan Stg., zla-mťsán daṅ ldán-pa S.g.* having the monthly courses; *zla(-ba)-šól, -žól, -ťéb, zla-lhág, W. *da-ṭ́úl** **intercalary month**; the separate months of the year are usually counted from *zlá-ba dáṅ-po* to *bču-γnyis-pa*, yet there are also particular names for them, viz. acc. to *Cs.*:

1. *ˬbrúg-zla, čui zlá-ba, rtá-pa zlá-ba,* माघ
2. *sbrúl-zla, k'rá-zla, dbó-zla,* उत्तरफल्गुनी
3. *rta(i) zla(-ba), nág-zla,* चैत्र
4. *lúg-zla, sá-ga-zla-ba,* वैशाख
5. *spré-zla, snrón-zla,* ज्येष्ठा
6. *byá-zla, ču-snód-zla-ba,* पूर्वाषाढा
7. *k'yi-zla, gró-bžin-zla-ba,* उत्तराषाढा
8. *p'ág-zla, k'rúm-zla,* भद्रपदा
9. *byi-zla, ťa-skár-zlá-ba,* अश्विनी
10. *glaṅ-zla, smin-drúg-zla-ba,* कार्त्तिका
11. *stág-zla, mgó-zla,* मृगशिर
12. *yós-zla, rgyál-zla,* पौष्या

II. vb., **also** *zló-ba*, *zlós-pa*, pf. *bzlas, bzlos*, fut. *bzlo*, imp. *zlos*, 1. **to say, tell, express,** *zloam mi zlo* shall you tell it or not? *Pth.*; *γžán-la zló-ba Lex.* to tell others; *yid-ma-raṅs-pa-nyid p'yir zlós-par byéd-pa* to express one's dissatisfaction *Stg.* (?). — 2. **to murmur** or **mutter over,** to recite softly or quite silently, prayers, spells etc., also *žúb-bus zlá-ba Zam.*; *yi-ge-drúg-pa lan-čig bzlás-pai bsód-nams Glr.* the merit of saying once the six-syllable prayer, and as such saying generally is done repeatedly, it is synon. with **to repeat.** — 3. **to answer, reply** *Cs.*; *Mil.* nif. — 4. undoubtedly a less correct spelling for *ˬda-ba* (for which reason the secondary forms with o are wanting), **to pass, to get beyond,** *la zlá-ba* to cross a mountain-pass, *nád-kyi la zlá-ba* to be past hope of recovery *Cs.*; also trs., *mya-ṅán-las zlá-ba* to deliver from pain, to help to eternal happiness.

ཟླ་བོ་ *zlá-bo* 1. = *grogs, W. *yá-do**, **companion, associate,** *zlá-bo byéd-pa* **to accompany, attend, assist,** *rkún-zla* a thief's accomplice *Dzl.*; *ˬgrán-zla* **rival, competitor** (v. *ˬgrán-pa* extr.); *γnyén-zla*, v. *γnyen*; *bzá-zla* **spouse, consort** (male or female) *Lex.* — *srid-zla Mil.* partner for life; *zla-γzán* a woman whose husband is dead ('who has eaten him'). — 2. **friend, acquaintance** *B.* and col. — 3. **lover, bridegroom; spouse** in *C.* To *zla* standing for *zlá-bo*, may be referred *zlas-dbyé Zam.*, expl. by द्वन्द्व, **pair, couple, combination,** viz. of a thing and its reverse, hence *zlas-p'yé-ba* **reverse, contrary,** e.g. *yód-pai zlas-p'yé-ba méd-pa Sch.*

ཟླུག(ས)པ་ *zlúg(s)-pa*, pf. *bzlugs*, fut. *bzlug*, **to give notice, send word, inform** *Sch.*, *p'rin-yig-gis bzlúgs-pa* he informed him by a letter *Stg.*, not frq.; in *Lexx.* explained by *γžán-la snyád-pa*, and *gó-bar byed ˬǰúg-pa.* —

ཟླུམ་པ་ *zlúm-pa* 1. adj., more frq. *zlúm-po*, (= **kor-kór** *C.*, **kyir-kyir** *W.*) **round, circular,** *dbyibs* in shape *Glr.*; **roundish, rounded, obtuse,** *zlúm-por rtsig-pa* to erect a round, cylindrical wall, e.g. for a monument; **clubby, clumsy,** e.g. of a short and thick tobacco-pipe; *rkáṅ-pa zlúm-pa* club-footed *Stg.*; **globular, spherical,** e.g. cavities in the human body *S.g.*; *dku-zlúm Zam.*

(acc. to the *Ssk.*) the interior rounding of the abdomen. — 2. vb. 1. **to mix together** *Sch.*; **to put together, collect,** *ṫsogs* merit *Lexx.* 2. for *btúm-pa Pth.*: *dgé-ₒdún dbu-zlúm žabs-rjén* clerics with their heads wrapt up and barefooted. 3. for *ₒdúm-pa.* — *zlum-ril* **globular** *Cs.* — **zlúm-bu** *W.* **host, swarm, troop, crowd.**

ཟླུམ་ཕུ་སེ་ *zlúm-ṕu-se* (or *rtse?*) a mole-like animal *Ld.* (whether the same as *rdza-bra?*).

ཟློ་བ་ *zló-ba* v. *zlá-ba,* II.

ཟློག་པ་ *zlóg-pa,* pf *zlogs,* fut. *bzlog,* trs. to *ldóg-pa,* **to cause to return:** 1. **to drive back, repulse,** an army *Dzl.*; **to dispel, expel,** evil spirits *Dom.*; **to send back.** — 2. in a gen. sense: **to send, dispatch,** people to fetch something *Dzl.* frq. — 3. **to turn off, divert,** *bsám-pa-las* from an intention *Dzl.*; with *blo* to divert the mind from, to dismiss a thought, to give up, to banish from one's thoughts *Thgy.*, *γnyén-gyi γduṅ-séms zlog dka* it is hard to give up the love of kindred altogether *Mil.*; *dei ṫugs slar zlóg-tu γsol* we beg you to dismiss the thought of it *Dzl.*; **to dissuade from** *Tar.* 40, 5; **to avert,** injury, evil consequences, frq.; **to prevent,** *nad-sél* the healing of a disease *S.g.* — *zlog-ṫábs* antidote *Ma.* — 4 **to subvert, overthrow** (?). 5. *mii ṅo* **to resist, to be unyielding, uncompliant** *Dzl.*

ཟློས་གར་, ཟློད་གར་ *zlós-gar*, *zlód-gar Stg.* **a dance,** *zlós-gar byéd-pa* **to dance,** *slób-pa* to teach or learn dancing; *zlós-gar-mḱan* a dancer.

ཟློས་པ་ *zlós-pa* v. *zlá-ba.*

གཟའ་ *γza* I. ग्रह 1. **planet,** *γza bdun* the well-known seven heavenly bodies called in ancient times planets, viz. Sun, Moon, Mercury, Venus, Mars, Jupiter and Saturn; sometimes the ascending knot (राहु) is added to the number, sometimes also the descending knot (केतु), and then there are *γza brgyad* or *γza dgu*, eight or nine planets. The former seven denote also the days of the week: *γza-nyí-ma* Sunday, *γza-zlá-ba* Monday, *γza-mig-dmár* Tuesday, *γza-lhág-ma* Wednesday, *γza-ṕúr-bu* Thursday, *γza-pa* (or *-wa*)*-sáṅs* Friday, *γza-spén-pa* Saturday, and the signs for them in the calendar are ༡, ༢, ༣, ༄, ༅, ༆, ༠; *γzai γnód-pa* hurtful influence of the planets. — 2. *γza-čén-po*, and often *γza* alone, = *rā́-hu*, hence *nyi-zla-γzas-ₒdzin* or *γzas-bzuṅ* **eclipse** of the sun or moon, v. *sgra-γčan*; acc. to *Pth.* every uncommon or alarming sidereal phenomenon seems to be personified as *γza.* — 3. symb. num.: 9. — 4. vulgo: **rainbow.** — *γza-skár*, 1. **planets and fixed stars,** *nyi-zla-γza-skár* the sun, moon, planets, and stars. — 2. **constellation,** *γza-skar-ṅán* an adverse configuration *S.g.* — *γza-ḱyim Cs.* 'the place', more corr. 'the house' of a planet, the constellation in which the planet stands. — *γza-nád Cs.* and *Schr.*: **apoplexy;** in *W.* it seems to be used only for **epilepsy;** *γza ṕóg-pa* id.; *γzá-ṕog-mkan*, *γzá-brgyab-pa* epileptic. — *blá-γza, sróg-γza, γšéd-γza, má-γza gróg-γza, bú-γza, dgrá-γza, klúṅ-si-dar-γza Wdk.* and several more, are astrological terms, not to be clearly defined. — II. sometimes for *bza*, q.v. — III. *W.* **rubble-stones, bowlders, detritus,** *γza-róṅ* ravine filled with detritus; a better spelling seems to be *rdza.*

གཟག་པ་ *γzág pa* v. *ₒtság-pa, ₒdzág-pa.*

གཟགས་པ་ *γzágs-pa* 1. v. *γzábs-pa.* — 2. **to magnify, multiply** *Sch.*

གཟན་ *γzan* 1. v. *bzan* and *γzan-pa*; *γčan-γzan*, q.v. — 2. esp. *W.*, commonly *γzan-gós* **plaid,** = *bla-gós* v. *bla.* *γzan-stán Zam.* id.? *rṅul-γzán* **napkin,** ni f. *Lex.*

གཟན་པ་ *γzán-pa* 1. **to eat, devour** *Cs.* — 2. **to gnaw,** mostly fig.: *ṫsér-ma žábs-la γzan* the thorn hurts, annoys, the foot *Mil.*; of clothes: **to wear out** *C.*; adj. *γzán-pa* and *γzán-po* **worn-out, threadbare;** *séms-la γzan* it gnaws at the heart *Mil.*, *sróg-la* it preys upon life *Mil.*, **ná-wa-la** *C.* it deafens the ears, = *sún-ₒbyin-pa*; *γzán-du skyúr-ba* (lit. to give to devour, e.g. a body to demons), **to scorn, slight, despise** *Mil.*; **to throw away, squander, waste, lavish,** gen. in the forms (*čud*)-*γzón-pa*, ; *són-pa*, v. *čud.*

གཟབ་པ་ γzáb-pa I. *Cs.* **'clean'**, *Sch.* also **'clear, careful'**; *bzáb-pa Cs.* **'fine, elegant'**. In books I met with neither form; in col. language, however, are used: **záb-mo** 1. **dressed up, smart,** = *mčór-po.* 2. **fond of dress, vain.** — **zab-če** *W.* to dress one's self up. — **záb-gos** *W.* festival raiment, holiday-clothes (opp. to *rgyún-gos*). — **zab-ṭód** *W.*, **zab-ṭö** *C.* (lit.: *sprod*) **taṅ soṅ** he is dressed up, very smart. — *Sch.*: *γzáb-yig*, 'elegant writing', the Tibetan printed letters, *dbú-čan.* —

II. v. *γzábs-pa.*

གཟབ་མ་ *γzáb-ma* **bundle, bunch,** of grapes *C.*

གཟབས་པ་ *γzábs-pa*, also *γzáb-pa*, *γzágs-pa Lex.*, imp. *γzobs*, **to use care, diligence,** *lo γčig zas-spyód γzábs-pas* by a careful diet continued for a year *Mṅg.*; **to take care, to beware,** *dé-las γzobs* beware of it, be on your guard against it *Sch.*

གཟར་ *γzar Lex.*, **peg, hook, wooden nail,** for hanging up things; *γzar-sláṅ* a pan that may be hung up.

གཟར་བུ་ *γzár-bu* (col. *zá-ru*) **ladle,** gen. of wood, *γzár-bu* *ˏpyar* she wields the ladle, she swings it for a blow *Mil.*; *dgáṅ-γzar* and *blúgs-γzar* two spoons or ladles, with long handles, used at burnt-offerings *Schl.* 249.

གཟར་བ་ *γzár-ba* 1. adj. *γzár-po*, **steep, rugged, precipitous,** *brag mṭó-la γzár-ba-la* near a high, precipitous rock *Mil.*; *ri γzár-po, brag γzár-po* slope, declivity, of a hill or rock; *brag-γyaṅ-γzár Mṅg.* id.; *ri γzár-gyi ṅos* steep declivity, cliff *Thgy.*; *ri-γzar-čú* waterfall, cataract *Glr.*; *γzar-ḱyóm-pa* to get dizzy on a steep height *Sch.* — 2. vb. v. *ˏdzár-ba.*

གཟས་པ་ *γzás-pa* **to be about, to be on the point, to prepare,** *mčóṅs-par, bsád-par γzás-pa-las* when he was on the point of leaping, of killing *Dzl.*; *rkó-bar γzás-so* he prepared, began, to dig out.

གཟི་ *γzi* 1. **shine, brightness, clearness, splendour;** **ṭáṅ-zi** *W.* **looming, mirage.** — 2. n. of a half-precious stone, variously coloured, brown, gray, streaked *Glr*, *Pth.* — 3. v. sub *γzir-ba.* — 4. v. *bzi.* —

**Comp.** *γzi-čan* shining, bright, e.g. a star *W.* — *γzi-brǰid* 1. **brightness, beauty,** a fair, healthy complexion, = *mdaṅs*, or joined with it, frq; **majesty,** e.g. of deities etc. *Dzl.* 2. **honour, esteem, celebrity;** *γzi-brǰid-čan* 1. bright, beautiful, majestic. 2. celebrated, famous, distinguished. — *γzi-mdáṅs* 1. **healthy appearance** *S.g.* 2. vulgo also **evening-red, evening-sky,** ni f. — *γzi-byin* = *γzi-brǰid* 1; *γzi-byin nyáms-pa* looking poor, emaciated, worn out, from hunger, sufferings *Stg.*; *γzi-byin-čan* bright, shining; *γzi-ˏód* bright gloss or lustre *Lex.*

གཟི་རུ་ *γzi-ru* col. for *γzér-bu* **a little nail** *W.*

གཟིག་ *γzig* **leopard;** *γzig-ris* its colour.

གཟིག་མོ་ *γzig-mo* **porcupine** *Ssk.*, *γzig-móṅ* id.?

གཟིགས་པ་ *γzigs-pa*, resp. for *mtóṅ-ba* and *ltá-ba* 1. **to see,** *ˏóṅs-par* seeing that he had come *Dzl.*; in indirect questions, to see whether? — what sort of? — etc.; **to see through, to get an insight** *Tar.* 94, 6, *Schf.*; **to look,** *śár-la* towards the east *Glr.*; **to look (for),** *γzígs-pas mi ˏdug* when he looked (for it), there was nothing to be seen; **to look at, to regard, mind, esteem,** *sku-tsé-la mi γzigs-pa* not regarding your Honour's life *Dzl.* — 2. equivalent to: **to give, grant,** *sá-bon žig tugs-rǰe γzigs dgos* have the goodness to give me some seed, prob. only breviloquence for *sá-bon žig γnáṅ-bar tugs-brtsé-bar γzigs śig.* — *γzigs-rtén* resp. **present, gift,** *γzigs-rtén-du skúr-ba* to charge a person with the delivery of a present *Pth.* — **zig-dod-čan** *W.* vain. — **zig-po** *W.* neat, well dressed, resp. for *mčór-po.* — — *γzígs-mo* resp. for *ltád-mo, mé-tog dé-la γzigs-mor byón-pa-las* as he came in order to look at the flower *Pth.*

གཟིང་བ་ *γziṅ-ba* for *ˏdziṅs-pa Glr.*

གཟིངས་ *γziṅs* **vessel, ship, float, ferry,** also fig.; *gru-γziṅs* id., frq.; *γziṅs čén-po žig byás-te* equipping a large vessel *Glr.*;

γziṅs-čúṅ a small vessel *Cs.*; γziṅs-pa ship-master, captain.

**གཟིམ་པ་** *γzím-pa*, also with *mnal*, resp. for *γnyid-log-pa*, 1. **to fall asleep** *Dzl.* — 2. **to sleep**, *rgyál-po γzim-pa-lus* whilst the king was sleeping *Glr.* — 3. **to expire, to die** *Tar.* 4, 20. —

**Comp.** **zim-kyoṅ** W., resp. for *rkyóṅ-rtse*, candle, lamp. — *γzim-k'aṅ* 1. sleeping-room. 2. dwelling, habitation. — *γzim-k'ebs* quilt. — *γzim-k'om* cloak-bag, portmanteau. — *γzim-k'ri* bedstead. — *γzim-gur* sleeping-tent. — **zim-gág** C. porter, door-keeper. — *γzim-ča* bedding, bed-clothes *Gyatch.* — **zim-tiṅ, zim-ter** W. lamp. — **zim-tiṅ** (lit. *-btiṅ*) *Sik.* bedstead? — *γzim-t'úl* sheep-skins for night-quarters. — *γzim-dpon* body-servant, valet-de-chambre, = *sku-mdún-pa*; *γzim-p'rúg* his subordinate servants or pages. — *γzim-mál* bed-linen. — *γzim-yól* bed-curtain.

**གཟིམ་གཟིམ་** *γzim-γzim W., C.,* **mig zim-zim ča dug** *W.* the eyes are dazzled, by a glaring light.

**གཟིར་བ་** *γzír-ba* (acc. to *Cs.* fut. of *ₒtsir-ba*, certainly related to it, but chiefly used in an intellectual sense), **to be pressed, harassed, troubled, to suffer,** to be pressed by necessity, to suffer from hunger, disease etc. *B., C.* — *Sch.* also *γzi γzir-ba* a stinging pain in the chest.

**གཟིལ་** *γzil, γzil-bun-pa C.* = *spu-ziṅ byed-pa.*

**གཟུ་བ་** *γzú-ba* **a lever, bar;** = *γšó-mo Cs.*; *γzu-ṙnás* a prop *Cs.*

**གཟུ་བོ་** *γzú-bo Cs.*: 1. **straight, right.** — 2. **upright, honest.** *Lexx.*: *t'ugs γzú-bo*, from which it appears to be a word of civility, but little known. *Sch.* has besides: *γzu-dpáṅ*, which he renders by 'witness, mediator'.

**གཟུ་ལུམ(ས)་** *γzu-lúm(s) Lexx.* = *bab-čol* and सहसा, hence signifying **rashness, impetuosity,** so *Cs.*, and therefore *γzu-lúm-čan* **inconsiderate;** *γzu-lúm byed-pa* **to act rashly;** *Sch.* also: **disobedience, pride, haughtiness.**

**གཟུག་** *γzug* 1. v. *zug.* — 2. **top,** *lai* of a mountain-pass *Mil.*

**གཟུག་གེ་བ་** *γzúg-ge-ba* **hurting, giving pain,** *žes γzúg-ge-ba žús-nas* as she spoke words that gave so much pain *Mil. nt.*

**གཟུག་པ་** *γzúg-pa* **to be able to bear, to sustain,** v. sub *tsog.*

**གཟུགས་** *γzugs, Ssk.* रूप, 1. **figure, form, shape,** *p'yi-rol-gyi γzúgs-rnams* the forms of the sensible world, the impressions that are made on the eye *Wdṅ.*; *mig-gis γzúgs-rnams mt'oṅ* the forms (of things) are seen with the eyes; *ráb-tu-byuṅ-bai γzugs* the (painted) figure of a priest *Glr.*; sim. *klui γzugs γsér-las byás-pa Tar.*; *lus-γzúgs* shape of body, stature, frq.; *srin-moi γzúgs-su byéd-pa* to transform one's self into a Rákshasi *Glr.*; *rnál-ₒbyor-pai γzugs byéd-pa* to assume the outward appearance of a hermit *Mil.*; in metaphysics: form, body, as one of the five Skandhas, v. *p'úṅ-po.* — 2. resp. *sku-γzúgs*, W **zúg-po** = *lus*, **body,** **zúg-po ṭú-ce** W. to wash the body, to bathe; **zúg-po záṅ-wa mi dug, mi-dé-wa dug** C., **dé-mo mi dug** W. euphem. for: she has just her courses. — *γzugs-ṅán* ill-formed, too short in stature *S.g.*; *γzugs ₒk'úm-pa* to bend, twist one's body, and *γzúgs-kyis ₒtsó-ba, quaestum corpore facere,* are given by *Sch.*; *γzugs riṅ-mo* long-stalked *Glr.* — 3. in physics: **body, matter, substance,** *γzúgs-čan, γzúgs-su snáṅ-ba* composed of matter, material, substantial; *γzúgs-čan ma yin-pa, γzúgs-su mi snáṅ-ba, γzugs-méd* immaterial, unsubstantial; *γzúgs-med-pai* (or *-kyi*) *skad* a ghostlike voice *Mil.*; *γzugs-k'áms* the range of the material world. — *γzugs-brnyán* v. *brnyan.*

**གཟུགས་པ་** *γzúgs-pa* v. *ₒdzúg-pa.*

**གཟུང་བ་** *γzúṅ-ba* v. *ₒdzin-pa*; *γzuṅ-ₒdzin* *Mil.* frq., **interest, inclination, bias,** *γzuṅ-ₒdzin-brál* being free from interest, unbiased, apathetic, which always is praised as an indispensable quality and the true happiness of an ascetic, and the literal equivalent to which in *Ssk.* may be regarded to be ग्राहग्राह्य; yet *Was.* p. 304 renders it by 'idea and reason'. — γzuṅ-γzér peg on a wall, = rtsig-p'úr; a hold, support, rail, balustrade (?) *Stg.*

གཟུངས་ *γzuṅs*, frq. spelt *zuṅs*, yet properly only in compounds, lit. **a hold**, i. e. 1. **power, strength** *Schr.*; *γzuṅs-žán Sch.*: **loose, weak, without a hold, untenable**; *γzuṅs-zád* **weakened, debilitated**, esp. of women by loss of blood *Cs.*; *γzuṅs-rtén* **prop, support.** — 2. *lus-zúṅs* the seven constituents necessary for **healthy life, धातु**, chyle, blood, fat, muscle, bone, marrow, semen *Med.* — 3. **धारणी**, also *γzuṅs-sṅágs*, **spells, magic sentences,** first used in the doctrine of Mahāyāna, from which the mysticism of later times originated, v. *Was.* (142, 177); they are for the most part but short, and always end in a string of Sanskrit syllables, that are devoid of any meaning. Whole volumes are filled with them.

གཟུད་པ་ *γzúd-pa*, fut. of *ₒdzúd-pa.*

གཟུམ་པ་, གཟུར་བ་, གཟུལ་བ་ *γzúm pa, γzúr-ba, γzúl-ba* v. *ₒdzúm-pa* etc.

གཟེ་བ་ *γzé-ba Sch.* 1. **pannier, dosser** *Dzl.* ༧༤༥, 14. — 2. **home, habitation, nest.** — 3. **swift,** in running *Thgy.*, **quick,** in comprehending *Sch.*

གཟེ་མ་ *γzé-ma Med.*; *Cs.*: 'a horned aquatic plant'; *γzé-mai čaṅ Med.* beer made of it.

གཟེ་རུ་ *γzé-ru*, for *γzér-bu* **a little nail.**

གཟེ་རེ་ *γze-ré* **looking poorly** *Sch.*; *γze-ré byéd-pa* **to be poorly, ailing, ill** *Sch.*

གཟེག(སྶ) *γzeg(s)*, **कण**. **a little grain, atom;** *γzeg ča čuṅ* a small particle *Lex.*; *γzég-ma* prob. id. (*Cs.* also: filth?) *γzeg-zán* **कणाद**, 'atom-eater', n. of the founder of the Vaiseshika-philosophy, also called Kāsyapa; *γzeg-zán-pa* its professors *Wdṅ.*

གཟེག་མོ་བྱི་ *γzég-mo-byi* **hedgehog** *Sch.*

གཟེངས་ *γzeṅs* **height, loftiness, sublimity, gloriousness,** esp. in *γzeṅs stód-pa*, also *yar γzeṅs stód-pa Pth.*; to praise, extol, glorify *Mil.* (cf. *seṅ*).

གཟེད་པ་ *γzéd-pa* I. vb. 1. v. *ₒdzéd-pa.* — 2. **to hit** *Sch.* — II. sbst. *Sch.*: 'a long spike'.

གཟེད་མ་ *γzéd-ma Cs*, gen. *γzéb-ma*, also *γzebs Sch.* 1. **pannier,** with lid *Kun.*; a box-shaped **basket** with lid *C.* — 2. **cage, aviary** *Lex.*; **prison** *Sch.* — 3. **net, snare** *Sch.*

གཟེམ་པ་ *γzém-pa*, 1. *Cs.* = *ₒdzém-pa.* — 2. **to do a thing gently,** *zém-te dul-wa* *C.* to walk softly, *žág-pa* *C.* to put down softly.

གཟེར་ *γzer*, also *zer*, 1. **nail, tack,** *šiṅ-γzer* wooden nail, *lčágs-γzer* iron nail; *γnám-γzer* 'plug or bolt for fastening a door (at the top)' *Cs.*; *gyáb-če* *W.*, *gyág-pa* *C.*, *γzér-ba Glr.*, *ₒdzúg-pa Lex.*, *ₒdébs-pa* and more frq. *γzér-gyis ₒdébs-pa B.* to knock in, drive in, nails; *lag-zér gyág-pa* driving red-hot tacks into the finger-ends, a kind of torture in *C.*; *γzér-bu*, vulgo *zé-ru, zi-ru* a little nail. — 2. **a help to memory,** for retaining a lesson or doctrine, **mnemonic verse** *Mil.* — 3. **ray, beam,** *nyi-γzér* sun-beam, *ₒod-γzér* ray of light; *ts̓a-γzér* 'a hot beam', *bsil-γzér* 'a cool beam' (?) *Cs.* — 4. **pain, ache, illness,** (*γ*)*zug-γzér* id., *mgo-γzér* headache, *rgyu-γzér* gripes, colic, *p̓o-γzér* stomach-ache, *rtsib-γzér* pleurisy, *so-γzér* toothache *Cs.*; *zer-kyáṅ ṅá-la gyáb-ba rag*, or *táṅ-ṅa rág* *W.* I feel the pains of labour; *zer-láṅ* *W.* spasms in the stomach or something similar; *γzer-ₒp̓rig-pa* to writhe with pain; *γzer ₒp̓o* the pain passes from one part of the body to another *S.g.*

གཟེར་བ་ *γzer-ba* 1. **to bore into, drive** or **knock into,** *zer C.* nails, *ná-da* *C.* an arrow through the ear, Chinese punishment. — 2. **to feel pain, to be suffering** (= *γzir-ba?*); *čaṅ-ₒt̓úṅ γzer* beer-tippling produces pain *Med.*

གཟེར་བུ་ *γzér-bu*, v. *γzer* 1, extr.

གཟོ་བ་ *γzó-ba* 1. v. *bzó-ba.* — 2. **to remember, keep in mind, own, acknowledge,** esp. *drin* a favour, also *byás-pa*, as much **as to be grateful;** *dé-dag-gi byas-pa γzó-bai p̓yir* from gratefulness for their kindness *Dzl.*; *byas mi γzo* they are ungrateful; *drin γzó-*

ཟ

ba, drin γzó-bai sems gratitude, drin mi γzó-ba ingratitude; drin-γzo-ċan **grateful.**

གཟོང་, གཟོང་བུ་ γzoṅ, γzóṅ-bu **chisel, graving-tool, puncheon.**

གཟོད་ γsod 1. **now, this moment,** (opp. to dá ċi, before, a little time ago) *Mil.*; at least just now, *Mil.*; da-γzod(-ċig), id.; da-γzód bu yin-par ča yod now I know that it is my son; **not until now, then for the first time** (in narratives with preterite tenses) *Pth.*; **then at length** *Pth.* — γzód-ťsor-ba, ťos-pa, -rdog-pa *Dzl.* **to hear, to receive information, to be informed, to be told,** γšégs-pa that he was gone *Dzl.* — 3. γzód-ma **beginning, commencement** v. γdód-ma.

གཟོན་པ་ γzon-pa, γsón-pa with čud, v. čud and γzán-pa extr.; bsgó-ba rnar γzón-pa the precept was wastled in the ear, it entered at one ear and left at the other; one *Lex.* gives the explanation: bsláb-bya-la mi nyán-pai don.

གཟོབ་པ་ γzób-pa 1. *Sch.* **quick, sharp, clever; caution, circumspection.** — 2. v. γzáb-pa.

བཟང་ bzaṅ 1. n. of a medicinal plant in Tibet *Wdṅ.* — 2. whatever is **good,** v. bzáṅ-ba. — 3. **agreement, treaty,** v. sgrig-pa.

བཟང་བ་ bzáṅ-ba adj. and sbst., bzáṅ-po adj 1. **good,** (**भद्र**). in every respect, answering its purpose, excellent, suited, morally good; bsam-pa bzaṅ-po a good resolution *Mil.*; bdag bzaṅ-na if I behave well, keep myself free from blame, *Do.* (cf. légs-pa). — 2. **fair, beautiful,** as to the body, frq.; nags-ťsal bzáṅ-po a beautiful wood *Mil.*; γzugs-bzáṅ of a fine, tall stature. — sbst.: bzaṅ the good, that which is good in the abstract; bzáṅ-nas byuṅ 'it came from good' i.e. from a good heart; dei γzáṅ-lan-du as an acknowledgment of his goodness *Glr.* —

**Comp.** bzáṅ-ƙyi a species of large dogs *Cs.* — bzaṅ-sgrig treaty of peace, *ǰhé'-pa* *C.*, *ċó-ċe* *W.* to make peace, to come to an agreement, to conclude a treaty, frq.; bzaṅ-sgrig-pa id. — bzaṅ-ṅán good and bad, good and ill, bzaṅ-ṅan-ₒbriṅ γsum good, bad, and indifferent; bzaṅ-ṅán ₒbyéd-pa to discern between good and evil, to choose one or the other *Schr.*; bzaṅ-ṅán rtógs-pai sems is an attempt to find an adequate expression for the word 'conscience' *Chr. P.* — bzaṅ-ťál a good exit out of the ₒƙór-ba (the cycle of transmigrations), a happy departure *Thgr.* — bzaṅ-drúg 'the six good things' (nutmeg, cloves, saffron, cardamom, camphor, sandal-wood) *C.*; used by *Mil.* also in a fig. sense; in *W.* simply: cloves. — bzaṅ-ₒdód self-complacency. — bzaṅ-spyód 1. *Cs.* good action. 2. n. of a prayer of particular efficacy *Glr.*, also called smón-lam-gyi rgyál-po. — bzaṅ-btsón v. btson. — *zaṅ-lúg* *W.* good behaviour, good treatment, *mi ži̇g-ne̥ ťób-ċe* to experience such from a person, *mí-la ċó-ċe* to show it to a person.

བཟངས་ bzaṅs, only in ƙaṅ-bzáṅs, which *Wdṅ.* explains by káṅ-pa brtségs-pa a large house of several stories, applied only to the abodes of gods; in *W.* also the cubical part of the Chodten is called so.

བཟད་པ་ bzád-pa rarely for bzod-pa; mi-bzád-pa 1. **intolerable** *Dzl.*, *Do.* — 2. **irresistible** *Do.*

བཟན་ bzan, sometimes for zan, esp. **food of animals,** bzan ₒtsól-ba to seek food *Mil*; **pasture, pasturage,** bzán-la skyél-ba to place in pasture, to let feed *Glr.*; bzán-pa *Ts.* id.

བཟབ་པ་ bzáb-pa v. γzáb-pa.

བཟའ་ bza, I. vb., fut. of zá-ba, **to eat,** bza this is to be eaten, in dietetic prescriptions; v. also zá-ba. — II. sbst. 1. (rarely γza) seems to denote the members of a family, they being conceived as **eaters** or **fellow-boarders;** bzá-tso máṅ-poi p̣a-má parents that have a large family *Mil.*; bza maṅs náṅ-na among a numerous household *Mil.*; bza-drúg a family, a company at table, of six persons, ni f. *C.*; in certain combinations: **wife, spouse,** rgyá-mo bza the Chinese spouse, bál-mo bza the Nepalese spouse (of the king), *Glr.* frq. — 2. **meat, food,** bzá-ba daṅ btúṅ-ba meat and drink, specially the quality and quantity of food, zá-

*ma bcud če-la bza če-ba* nutritive and substantial food *Mil. nt.*

**Comp.** *bza-γtád*, *bzá-bai γtád-so* store of provisions, *bzá-γtad-méd-pa* not having such a store *Mil.* — *bza-mí* 1. = *ḱyo-šug* **husband and wife,** *byéd-pa* to become husband and wife, to marry each other, *ḱyod dan̈ n̈a γnyis bza-mí byao* we will marry each other *Glr.*; *bza-mír byín-gyis rlób-pa* to give the nuptial benediction, to unite in wedlock, to marry *Glr.*; *dbúl-po bza-mi γn̈yis* a poor married couple *Glr.* 2. in a wider sense: **household,** *bza-mí nyi-šu-rtsa-γnyis* a household of twenty two persons *Mil.* — *bza-med* **ill-fed, lean** *Mil.* — *bzá-ṫso* plur. of *bza.* — **za-dá** (lit. *za-zlá*) *W.*, *C.* partner, wife. — *bza-šin̈* **fruit-tree,** *bza-šin̈-rá-ba* orchard, *bza-šin̈-ra-ba-srún̈-pa* watchman or keeper of it *Dzl.* — *bza-šúg* (vulg. *-*šúb**) = *bza-mí C.*

བཟར་ *bzar* sometimes for *zar*; *bzár-ba* v. *₀dzár-ba.*

བཟས་པ་ *bzás-pa* v. *zá-ba* and *γzás-pa.*

བཟི་ *bzi* (sometimes *γzi*, *zi*), **drunken fit, intoxication, stupefaction;** *bzi sán̈s-te* having become sober again after intoxication *Glr.*; **zi-čan** *W.* intoxicated, muddled, *bzí-ba* 1. vb. **to become intoxicated, to get drunk,** *bzí-bar ₀gyúr-ba* id.; *bzí-bar byéd-pa* to intoxicate, to make drunk *Cs.* 2. sbst. **state of intoxication.** 3. adj. **drunk, intoxicated** *C.*

བཟུང་བ་ *bzún̈-ba* v. *₀dzín-pa*; it is used as an adv. in the form of *bzún̈s-te*, e.g. *dei núb-mo-nas bzún̈s-te* from that evening (prop. beginning with that evening), ever since that evening *Mil.*; *ṫses brgyad-nas bzun̈s-te nyai bar-du* during the time from the 8th. to the 15th. (day of the month).

བཟུར་ *bzur* v. *dzúr-ba.*

བཟེ་རེ་ *bze-ré*, also *bze Sch.*: **pain,** *bze-re-čan* suffering pain, *bze-ré byéd-pa* to inflict pain, to torment. (*Cs.*: 'indignation; angry; to be angry with.')

བཟེད་ *bzed* 1. in comp.: *ṕyag-bzéd* **(hand-) basin** *Cs.*; *lhun̈-bzéd* **beggar's bowl, alms-pot,** frq.; *bzed-snód* **salver** *Sch.*; *bzed-žál Lex.*, also *žal-bzéd Cs.*: 'spitting-box; acc. to oral expl. a cup into which the higher class of people skim off the superabundant grease swimming on the tea (v. *ǰa*); *bzéd-pa* v. *₀dzéd-pa.* — 2. *bzed-snyóms-pa* **wire-drawing** *Sch.*

བཟོ་ *bzo* 1. **work, labour,** *bzoi rnam-₀gyur* the beauty of a work or workmanship *Glr.*; *bzo rgya-nág-gi lugs* as to the workmanship it is in Chinese style *Glr.* (by some the word is taken in these passages in the signification 3). — *bzó-la sréd-pa* liking labour, laborious, = *las Stg.*; **zo ṫe-rél, mi-la ma (s)tan** *W.* the work is not yet finished, do not let people see it yet! *snai bzo byed-gin ₀dug-pas* being just occupied with working out the noses *Glr.* — 2. **manufacture, art, trade, handicraft,** *rín-po-čei* art of a jeweler, *gos-* trade of a tailor, *dn̈ul-* art of a silver-smith, *lčags-* trade of a blacksmith, *ṫag-* of a rope-maker, *rdo-* of a stone-cutter, *rtsig-* of a mason, *bzan̈-* of a copper-smith, *šin̈-* of a joiner or carpenter, *γser-* art of a gold-smith, *lha-* of an image-maker, *lham-bzo* trade of a shoemaker. — 3. also *zo*, **figure, image, picture, resemblance,** = *dbyibs*, **ǎ-me zo dug** *W.* he is the exact likeness of his mother; **appearance, physical constitution,** v. *zo.* — 4. sometimes for *bzó-pa*, *bzö-bo*, so that all the words enumerated sub 2 may also denote the artist or workman. —

**Comp. and deriv.** *bzó-ḱan̈* **workshop.** — *bzo-ḱyád*, *bzoi kyad Glr.* **work of art,** masterpiece, elegant piece of workmanship. — *bzo-ḱyúd*, *bzo-ḱyun Cs.*: 1. potter's wheel. 2. a hydraulic machine(?). — *bzo-grá* academy of arts, mechanics' institution *Cs.* — *bzo-rgyú* working-materials *Glr.* — **zó-bsta*(?), *zób-sta*, *zó-sta** *W.* **form, fashion,** e.g. **style** of a house, its architecture; form, of a bottle, a lamp or candle stick, of any production of art; **zor-dö** anvil-stone *W.* (*bzo-rdo*). — *bzó-pa* **artist,** mechanic, *dn̈úl-bzo-pa*, silver-smith, and so forth. — *bzo-dpón* master, over journey-men or the students of an art. — *bzó-ba*, pf. *bzos*, **to make, to manufacture** *C.* (for the *byéd-pa* of *B.*, and **čo-če** of *W.*), **par zó-wa** to print; **sém-kyi zó-wa** *C.* to frame in one's mind, contrive, invent; **zo-*

pę tsa* manufactured salt, *zǫ-pę ser* artificial gold Wdṅ. — bzó-bo = bzó-pa, bzó-bo mḱás-pa a skilful artist Mil.; bzo-byéd 1. id. 2. **imaginative faculty, imagination,** ni f. — bzo-lás work Sch.

བཟོད་པ་ bzód-pa (rarely bžád-pa) I. vb., ཀྵམ, 1. **to suffer, bear, endure,** c. acc., mig ná-ba ma bzód-nas not being able to bear the pain in his eyes Dzl.; lus ˳dis na mi bzod with this body pain, disease, cannot be endured Thgy.; saṅs-rgyás-kyi túgs-rje čé-bas ma bzód-nas seems to imply: Buddha in his mercy not suffering this, but checking the mischief; — also c. dat.: ˳jám-po-la mi bzod he cannot bear what is soft or smooth Dzl.; ma-bdé-ba bág-tsam-la bzód-pa mi byéd-de getting so fretful through a slight indisposition Mil.; ltá-bas mi bzód-de finding it unbearable for his eyes Pth.; drán-pas mi bzód-de as much as: so that he almost lost his senses over it Pth.; bzód-tabs (or bzod-glags)-méd-par ˳byúṅ-ba or ˳gyúr-ba not to be able to bear . . . any longer, frq.; mi-bzód-pa or -bzád-pa adj., **unbearable, intolerable,** also **irresistible;** ma bzód-nas not being able to resist any longer Dzl. — 2. **to forgive, pardon,** sṅan-čad ťo-˳tsám-pa bzód-par ɣsol to pardon our former tricks is what we beg Mil.; rtá-la ma skyón-pa bzód-par bžes ˳tsal that I did not request you to mount, this I beg you to forgive me Mil.; bzód-par ɣsól-lo byas kyaṅ although she begged pardon Pth.; skyón-rnams yé-šes-spyan-ldan-rnams-la bzód-par ɣsol with respect to the deficiencies I pray for the indulgence of the very wise (readers); bzod-ɣsól byéd-pa to ask pardon, forbearance Pth. —

II. sbst. 1. **patience** (Ssk. क्षान्ति), bzód-pa sgóm-pa to exercise one's self in patience Dzl. ༢༥, 12; but also, to have patience, to show forbearance; bzód-pa bžés-pa, id. resp. (v. also above I, 2); bzód-pa-čan **patient;** bzod-srán unwearied patience; bzod-pa-čuṅ impatient Mil., bzod-med Cs. id. — 2. in asceticism: **perseverance, stedfast adherence to the four truths,** constancy in pursuing the path that has been entered upon, mi skye-bai čos-la bzod-pa acc. to Was. id., being at the same time no longer subject to re-births, p. (140). —

Observ. So far as 'to forgive' implies patience, forbearance, it may be rendered by bzód-pa; but as the Scriptural view of 'forgiveness of sin' involves more than that, other expressions, such as bú-lon sél-ba, must be resorted to with reference to the latter.

བཟོབ་པ་ bzób-pa Sch. = ɣsób-pa.

བཟོམ་ bzom **tub,** carried on the back, to convey water, v. ču-bzóm sub ču.

བཟླ་བ་ bzlá-ba v. zlá-ba.

བཟླས་བརྗོད་ bzlas-brjod (cf. zlá-ba II, 2); zlá-ba in a strict sense, is stated to be **the silent,** brjód-pa **the soft, yet audible pronouncing of spells** etc., bzlas-brjod signifying both together; bzlas-brjód byéd-pa to mutter over Glr.; mú-stegs-pai bzlas-brjód Brahmanical spell-murmuring Thgy.

བཟླུམ་པ་ bzlúm-pa v. zlúm-pa.

བཟློ་བ་ bzló-ba v. zló-ba.

བཟློག་ bzlog **the contrary, the reverse,** ṕrá-ba-las bzlog sbóm-po the contrary of thin is thick Lex.

བཟློས་ bzlos, v. zló-ba.

# འ

འ a, 1. **a letter peculiar to the Tibetan language, which, contrary to** ཨ (q.v.) **denotes the pure vowel, without any admixture of a consonant sound. The difficulty which attaches to the articulation of this vowel, requiring an opening of the glottis** before it is sounded, has occasioned a great variety of pronunciation in the different provincial dialects. Vide Phonetic Table with its explications. — 2. numerical figure: 23.

འ་ཅག་ ˛á-čag, *Cs.* **we,** v. ˛*ú-čag.*

འ་ཅི་ ˛*a-či* n. of a country *Glr.*

འདི་ཝ་ ˛*a-ti-wa,* with *lóg-pa, Sch.:* **to perform somersets, to tumble over, to roll.**

འ་ན་ཡང་ ˛*a-na-yan* **although,** *Sch.;* ˛*a-na-ma-na Sch.;* **perfectly alike, having a striking resemblance** (?).

འ་མ་ ˛*á-ma* **but,** e.g. ˛*á-ma ma rjed čig* but do not forget! *Cs.*

འ་ཨུར་ ˛*a-úr Sch.:* **'shaking or rattling sounds'** cf. ˛*ur-*˛*úr.*

འང་ ˛*an* 1. like *yan,* attached to conjunctions, and corresponding to the English **ever, soever,** after vowels, col. also after consonants, e.g. *nam-*˛*an.* — 2. ˛*án-sgra, bón-bui Cs.* the braying of an ass.

འང་ཀེ་ ˛*án-ke* (not ident. with *ăn-gi* number), a mystical character, frq. occurring in certain finical ornaments or flourishes called *sbrúl-mgo,* occasionally also in written words.

འབ་པ་ ˛*áb-pa Ts.* **to bark.**

འར་པོ་, འར་ཅན་ ˛*ár-po,* ˛*ár-čan Ts.* **angry** = *ɣtúm-po.*

འར་བ་ ˛*ár-ba C.* **lot,** *rgyáb-pa* to cast, = *rgyan rgyáb-pa.*

འར་ཨུར་ ˛*ar-*˛*úr* v. ˛*ur-*˛*úr.*

འར་ཡང་ ˛*ár-yan* **also, too, likewise** *Sch.*

ཨི་ ˛*i* 1. num. figure: 53. — 2. *W.* demonstr. pron. inst. of ˳*di,* **this,** also *'í-po.*

ཨུ་ ˛*u* 1. num. figure: 83. — 2. sbst. **kiss,** v. ˛*o.* — 3. also ˛*o, Cs.:* demonstr. pron., **this,** ˛*ú-ni-ru,* ˛*ú-nir,* ˛*ó-nir,* **hither;** *Ts.*wú-ahi** **this.**

ཨུ་སྒྲ་ ˛*ú-sgra Glr.* **noise of many foot-steps,** prob. = ˛*úr-sgra.*

ཨུ་ཅག་ ˛*ú-čag* 1. also ˛*ó-čag Glr.,* ˛*ó-čog Thgy.,* ˛*ú-bu-čag Dzl.* pers. pron. **we.** — 2. **chimney** *W.* (?).

ཨུ་ཐུག་ ˛*u-túg Sch.:* 'Lüderlichkeit, auch 'u-tsúgs'; but in *W.*'un-tug čó-če** means **to break out into a violent passion,** and **'ún-tug-k̔an* or *-čan** **angry;** in *C. *mú-tug-pa** and **dúg-tug-pa** **to be at a loss;** so also in *Mil.*

ཨུ་བུ་ ˛*ú-bu* v. ˛*ú-čag.*

ཨུ་རུ་རུ་ ˛*u-ru-rú Sch.* = *ur.*

ཨུ་ལག་ ˛*u-lág* **compulsory post-service,** the gratuitous forwarding of letters, luggage and persons, the supply of the requisite porters and beasts of burden (also more immediately these themselves), — originally a socage-service rendered to lords and proprietors, government officers and priests; in more recent times remunerated and legally regulated in those parts that are visited by European travellers; *mi-la* ˛*u-lág skúl-ba* to impose such services, by exacting porters etc. *Pth.,* ˳*gél-ba* id.; *skyél-ba* prob. to forward by Ulag; (*Cs.* limits the signification too much).

ཨུ་སུ་ ˛*ú-su Lt.* **coriander seed.**

ཨུག་པ་ ˛*úg-pa,* **owl,** *Lt.;* ˛*ug-rgán Sch.* the great horn-owl, ˛*ug(-gu)-čún* the little owl; ˛*ug-mig* owl's eyes (*Cs.* 'large languishing eyes', *Sch.:* 'large protruding eyes'); ˛*úg-mig-čan* having such eyes, ˛*úg mig-pa* or *-ma* a goggle-eyed man or woman *Cs.* — 2. *Ld.* also for *yug-po* **oats.**

ཨུག་སིངས་ ˛*ug-sins* v. *sins-po.*

ཨུད་ ˛*ud* 1. *Cs.* **swaggering, bragging, bombast, fustian;** ˛*ud čer smra-ba* to swagger, brag, gen. **wur šę-pa*, C.* — 2. = *yud Thgy.,* ˛*ud-kyis,* **in a moment, instantly, suddenly.** — 3. **command, order** (?), *Sch.:* ˛*ud-sgrog-pa* to make known an order.

ཨུབ་པ་ ˛*ub-pa* **to sweep** or **rake together** with one's hands, *pan-pas* ˛*ub-kyis bsdus-te Pth.* with the arms gathering all into one heap.

ཨུམ་བུ་གླང་མཁར་ ˛*um-bu-glan-mk̔ar* n. of the palace of the ancient Tibetan king **Thothori,** *Glr.*

ཨུར་ ˛*ur* 1. **noise, din, clashing, cracking, roar** of a tempest etc., but also and not less,

**a low, humming noise,** *rná-bai bú-ga bkág-pai tse ˬur-ˬúr žés-pai sgra* the humming in the ears produced by stopping them *Wdṅ.*, *ˬur-ˬúr-po-yi sgra* id. *Wdṅ.; rná-ba ˬúr-la ₒkrog* there is a buzzing in my ear *S.g.; ˬur ldaṅ* or *ₒbyuṅ* a noise is heard; *Cs.* more particularly: **talk, babbling, chit-chat,** *ˬur-γtoṅ-ba* to talk, to chat; **toṅ-ˬur* C.* (lit. *stoṅ*) bragging, humbug; *ˬur-sgra* = *ˬur* noise caused by many voices, many footsteps, cf. *ˬu-sgra*; of the howling of a tempest, *ˬúr-sgra če* although it (the thunder) makes a great noise *Mil.*; *ˬur-tiṅ* a brass basin, used to make a noise by striking it *Sch.*; *ˬúr-ba* sbst. **a humming insect, beetle** *Sch.*; vb., **to be noisy, chattering,** *Cs.; dga-grágs ˬúr-te* shouting, rejoicing *Mil.*; **ˬur čó-če** to set a dog on a person *W.*; **ˬur bšád-pa, ˬur-brdáb btáṅ-ba* C., W.* to exaggerate, brag, boast. — 2. *bag-dró ˬur-ˬúr Pth.* seems to describe the feeling of a genial warmth pervading the body. — 3. **wur gyág-pa* C., *'ur gyáb-če, táṅ-če* W.* to smooth, v. *dbur-ba.* — 4. *ˬúr-rdo* a sling *Sch.*, *ˬúr-rdo ₒṗén-pa* to throw with a sling.

འེ་ *ˬe* num. figure: 113.

འོ་ *ˬo* I. num. figure: 143. —

II. sbst. 1. provinc. *ˬu* **kiss** (चुम्ब), *ˬo byéd-pa* **to kiss** *Lt.*, *ḱá-la* on the mouth *Pth.; ṗyag, žabs* resp. on the hand, the foot *Cs.; ˬo γtóṅ-ba Cs., *'u lán-če* W.*, = *ˬo byed-pa.* — 2. v. *ˬo-ma.* —

III. pron. 1. pers. pron. **we**, v. *ˬu-čag.* — 2. dem. pron. **this** *Cs.* v. *ˬu* III. — IV. interj. (*o ˬŏ*) 1. like **oh, yes!** as a reply: *ˬo lágs-so* oh very well! *Mil*; **'o yóṅ-ṅog, 'o ḍig-gog, 'o gyál-log W., *ˬo yóṅ-ṅe* C.* well! it's all right to me! well, do so! — *ˬoˬo, ˬŏˬŏ*, so! well! very well! in *W.* it is a common reply, indicating nothing more, than that attention has been paid to the words spoken, like the English well! indeed! — 2. as a positive affirmative, **yes!** *W.*, cf. *ˬo-ná.*

འོ་སྐོལ་ *ˬó-skol*, also with *rnams* and *čag*, (*Cs.* also *ˬú-skol*), *Ld.' á-χo*, **we**, *Mil., Tar., Thgy.*, e.g. (if all men must die), *ˬo-skol lta či smos* of course also we *Thgy.*; it is very often used as a reciprocal pronoun: *ˬó-skol ma ši ṗrád-pa* the fact, that we have seen each other once more before we die *Mil.*

འོ་བརྒྱལ་ *ˬo-brgyál*, resp. **fatigue, weariness, want**, any kind of hardship, **ṗéb-lam-la ob-gyál ma kyód-da* W.* has not your walk hither fatigued you? *ˬo-brgyál yóṅ-lugs* the getting into difficulties *Mil.*; more frq. as vb.: *ˬo-brgyál-ba, kyéd-čag-rnams ˬo ma brgyál-lam* are you perhaps fatigued? *Glr.; žabs-tóg ˬo mi brgyal-ba ₒbul* a short expression for: everything shall be at your service, so that you shall not want anything *Mil.*; *ˬo-re-brgyál* = *ˬo-brgyál* 1. **trouble, drudgery, annoyance** *Mil.* 2. **decay, decline, ruin,** of religion, usages etc.

འོ་སྙིག་ *ˬo-snyig* **sour cream** *Sch.*

འོ་སྙིགས་ *ˬo-snyigs* **birch-tree** *Sch.*

འོ་དོད་ *ˬo-dod* **lamentation, wailing, cry for help,** gen. as vb. *ˬo-dód ₒbód-pa* to lament, to call for help *Glr., Pth., Wdṅ.*; *ˬo-dód-pa* one that seeks help, support, redress, a client, a plaintiff, more in pop. language.

འོ་ན་ *ˬo-ná* (cf. *ˬo, ˬon, ˬón-kyaṅ*), comes nearest to the Greek ἀλλά, used esp. to introduce a new thought or proposition in speech: **now,** what shall you do in that case? *Dzl.*; **well,** what did he say? *Dzl.*; **well,** I hope you have at least . . . *Dzl.*; **why, ay,** *Mil.*; **but now** *Thgy.*; **but,** the Latin *autem*, when a new clause is added *Mil., Thgy.*; **yea,** in a climax, e.g.: I met with a naked man, yea, an insane ascetic *Mil.* — 2. as an answer in the affirmative, **yes** *W.* —

འོ་མ་ *ˬó-ma* **milk,** *ˬó-ma ₒjó-ba* **to milk** *Glr.*; *snyól-ba* to let it curdle *Cs.*, *srúb-pa* to churn it *Cs.*; *ˬó-ma čags* the milk thickens, coagulates *Cs.* —

**Comp.** *ˬo-ṫáṅ* 'milk-meadow', the plain in which Lhasa now stands; of the former lake, *ˬo-ṫáṅ-gi mtso Glr.*, a sedgy moor is said to be still remaining. — *ˬo-ṫúg* milk-soup *Tar.* —, *ˬo-ṫúd* cheese, v. *ṫud.* — *ˬo-ₒṫúṅ* suckling-child, baby, = *žo-ₒṫuṅ.* — *ˬo-*

snód milk-vessel. — ˛o-spri, ˛o-sri, cream. — ˛o-már 1. milk and butter *Sch.* 2. termin. of ˛ó-ma into the milk. — ˛o-zó milk-pail.

འོ་མ་ཟི་ཟི་ ˛o-ma-zi-zi *W.* **pater-noster pea,** the seed of Abrus precatorius, used as beads for rosaries.

འོ་ཡོ་, འོ་ཡོག་ ˛o-yó, ˛o-yóg **terrier** *Sch.*

འོ་རེ་བརྒྱལ་ ˛o-re-brgyál v. ˛o-brgyál.

འོ་ཤོ་ ˛ó-šo *W.*, only in *'ó-šo táṅ-če or gyáb-če* **to laugh at,** deride, to feel a pleasure at the misfortune of others.

འོ་སེ་ ˛ó-se **mulberry,** ˛ó-se-šiṅ mulberry-tree; *ba-˛ós Med.*, perh. strawberry spinach, Blitum, which in *W.* is called *ba-o-se,* cow-mulberry.

འོག་ ˛og, *W.* *yog*, *Ts.* *wag*, 1. root signifying **below,** or with reference to time, **after,** opp. to *goṅ; ˛óg-tu, W. *yóg-la** 1. adv. **down, below, underneath; afterwards, later;** in paging books it denotes the second page of a leaf, v. *goṅ;* it is used as an expedient to correct errors in numbering, or to make additions, as with us e.g. 'page 24, b'. 2. postp. **under,** with accus., less frq. with dat., **down from; after** (as to time, rank, succession). — *˛óg-na, W. *yóg-na**, 1. adv. **underneath, below.** 2. postp. c. gen. **under, after.** — *˛óg-nas, W. *yóg-nas** 1. adv. **from under, from below.** 2. postp. c. genit. **forth from below** *˛óg-tu ˛júg-pa* to put underneath, to subject, subdue *Glr.*; *k̔a-˛óg Ts.* = *˛óg-tu,* e.g. *šiṅ-gi k̔a-wág* under the tree; sometimes (less corr.) with accus. inst. of genit., also ˛og alone, inst. of *˛óg-tu, óg-na: *Ru-tog Gu-lab-siṅ 'og mi dug** *W.* Rutog does not stand under, is not subordinate to, Gulab Singh; *ldiṅ-˛og* the division of soldiers under the Dingpon, or a century (division of hundred); *bču-˛og* a body of ten men under a *bčú-dpon* or corporal. — 2. testicles, of animals, *˛og-čan* not castrated; **wog čẹ'-pa** (*spyad-pa*) to cover, copulate *C.*

**Comp. and deriv.** *˛óg-sgo* the lower orifices of the body for the discharge of the excretions, *˛óg-sgo γnyis S.g.*; more partic. the anus *Pth.* — *˛og-rdo* anvil *Sch.* — *˛og-pag* v. *pag.* — *˛óg-ma* adj. the lower, later, following one, *dei ˛óg-ma* the one following after that, the second in turn; **lá-mẹ saṅ ge-nyén yóg-ma žig dug** *W.* a Genyen is inferior to a Lama. *˛og-min,* **अकनिष्ठ**, 'the not inferiors' i.e. the highest, the inmates of a certain heaven inhabited by gods, or also that heaven itself. — *˛óg-rol-tu* = *˛óg-tu Tar.* — *˛og-rlúṅ Lt.* vapour, flatulence. — *˛og-šál* crop, craw of birds.

འོང་བ་ ˛óṅ-ba, pf. *oṅs,* imp. *šog, B.* and *Bal.* (*'óṅ-čas*), for which in common life almost always, and in more recent literature not seldom, *yóṅ-ba, W.* *yóṅ-če*, is used, 1. **to come,** *ma ˛óṅ-ba mťóṅ-nas Dzl.* when he saw his mother coming; *náṅ-du ˛oṅs, Dzl.* he came in; *ʼpyir ˛oṅ-ba Glr.* to come back; *mi γnyis ṅai drúṅ-du ˛óṅ-rgyu yin-pa Glr.* two men that were about to come to me; *˛óṅ-bai lám-du Pth.* when being on their way; *ti-se-la sgóm-du yóṅs-pa yin Mil.* we come to the Tise in order to meditate; *˛óṅs-pa légs-so* you are welcome *Cs.*; *ṅas ˛o-dód byas kyaṅ ˛óṅ-mk̔an med Pth.* although I was crying for help, nobody came; *k̔yer ˛óṅs-so Glr.* they came to bring, they brought with them; *k̔rid-šog* bring hither! *krid ˛óṅs-so Glr.* they brought thither; with reference to time: *ma-˛óṅs-pa* not yet come, i.e. future, *dus* etc. very frq.; also poet.: *ma-˛óṅs dón-du* for the benefit of those that are to come, i.e. of posterity; *čaṅ yóṅ-bai rigs, Wdṅ.*, the kinds (of cerealia) from which beer comes (is made). — 2. **to happen,** *yód-pa yóṅ-gin ˛dúg-pas Mil.* as it sometimes happens that there are . . .; more frq. **to occur, to be met with,** *˛gréṅ-bu ˛oṅ ˛gyúr-na* whenever an e occurs, wherever an e stands *Gram.*; *mii yul-na mi ˛oṅ* such a thing does not occur on earth *Glr.*; **di-ru mi yóṅ(-če)** *W.* that is not to be met with here. — 3. **to fall to the lot of, to be given, to come upon,** c. dat., *sras ˛óṅ-bai γsól-ba btáb-bo Pth.* she prayed that a son might be given to her; **k̔o-la nad yoṅs** *W.* a disease came upon him; **sód-nyom yoṅ** I receive alms, **sod-nam yoṅ** I acquire merit *W.;* to come in, *yoṅ-sgo* income, revenue *Schr.*, cf. *yoṅ-*

འ

t̓aṅ sub t̓aṅ 2. — 4. **to be suitable, practicable, to do,** *bstán-pa γčig-la stón-pa γñ̓yis mi ˬóṅs-pas Glr.* as two preceptors for one doctrine will not do; *yúl-du lóg-pa mi ˬóṅbas Glr.* as a journey home is not practicable; *ˬo-yóṅ-ṅog* v. *ˬo*; *lús-la óṅ-bai bár-du* as long as he was fit for work; **to go on well, to do well** *C.*, **da yóṅ-ṅa* W.* will it do now? — 5. when connected with verbs, it serves to indicate futurity, like the English auxiliaries **shall** and **will**, as becomes evident from such expressions as the following: *ˬči-ba nam yoṅ č̓a med Mil.* when dying comes, i.e. when we shall die, is uncertain; *mdog ˬgyúr-ba ˬoṅ Glr.* a change of colour is coming, i.e. the colour will, or is going to, change; *ˬgró-ba mi yoṅ-bar ˬdug Mil.* I am not likely (*dúg-pa*, 4) to go there any more; **ṭel-če mi yoṅ* W.* he will not be put to shame, not be disappointed; also with the supine: *srog daṅ brál-bar ˬgyúr-du ˬoṅ Dzl.* it will even come to his dying, it will be his death; *zós-su ˬoṅ Dzl.* he will even get so far as to eat...; *ši-bar ˬoṅ* he will die; still more free and popular are those turns, in which the gerund or the mere root is used: *γnaṅ-ste ˬoṅ Pth.* he will assent to it, allow it; *γčig min kyaṅ γčig yin-te ˬoṅ Glr.* if it is not the one, it will be the other; *sleb yoṅ* he will come *Mil.* and in *C.* very common; *yid-čés mi ˬoṅ* they will not believe it; it is also used to express the passive voice, and the English **to become, to grow, to get:** *šés-na ṅa γsod ˬóṅ-bas Glr.* as I should be killed, if she heard of it; **zer yoṅ* C.* so it is said, expressed, i.e. this is the usual way of expressing it; **p̓él-te yoṅ* W.* it is getting larger, increases; or with a noun: *smin ˬoṅ Glr.* it is growing ripe; *rgyál-po ˬbaṅs-su ˬoṅ Ma.* the king becomes a subject.

འོང་མོལ་ *ˬoṅ-mól Ld.* for *ˬól-mo.*

འོད་ *ˬod*, **light, shine, brightness,** *šar* flames up, shines, *ˬp̓ro* spreads, proceeds from; *ˬod spró-ba* to emit light, *bkyé-ba* to spread *Sch.*; *ˬod lham-mér mdzád-pa* resp., to shine with a bright light *Sch.*; *ˬod k̓éṅs-pa* filled with light *Sch.*; *lús-la ˬod yód-pa* self-luminous, a property of primeval man *Glr.*; *nyi-ˬód* sun-light, *zla-ˬód* moon-light, *skar-ˬód* star-light *Cs.*; *γnam-ˬod* brightness of the night-heavens, zodiacal-light *Cs.*; *me-ˬod* fire-shine *Cs.*; lustre, brightness, of polished metal, *ˬod byin-pa* to elicit a gloss or lustre, to give a bright polish *Sch.*; metaphor. fair complexion, external beauty, **k̓áṅ-pe 'od p̓élte yoṅ** the splendour of the house increases, **bud č̓a dug** declines, decays *W.*; *ˬod daṅ ldán-pa B.*, *ˬód-čan* 1. **luminous, emitting light;** 2. **bright, polished.** 3. **light,** **da 'od-čan č̓a yin* W.* now it will grow light. 4. **of a fine colour, of a blooming appearance** *Glr.* 5. **beautiful, splendid, stately;** *ˬod-med*, vulgo *ˬod-med-k̓an*, the contrary.

**Comp.** *ˬod-kór* or *skor* a luminous circle *Lex.* — *ˬod-dkar* 1. white light. 2. symb. num.: 1. — *ˬód-čan*, v. above. — *ˬod-dpag-méd*, **अमिताभ**, also *snaṅ-ba-mt̓a-yás* the fourth Dhyani-Buddha, v. *saṅs-rgyás.* — *ˬód-spro* (or *ˬp̓ro?*) light? — **ŏd-ḷo* W.*, **ód-ṭo tog** hold up the light! **ód-ṭo bu** glow-worm, fire-fly; *ˬod-ˬp̓ro* sometimes occurring in the names of gods. — *ˬod-γzér* ray of light *Dzl.* and elsewh. frq.; *ˬod-γzér-čan* n. of a god, *ˬod-γzér-čan-ma* of a goddess *Do.* — *ˬod-srúṅ* n. p. 1. the human Buddha of the preceding period of the world. 2. a king of Tibet, son of Langdarma. — *ˬod-γsál* 1. a bright light or gloss, *ˬod-γsál mdaṅs daṅ ldán-pa* very glossy, of leaves. 2. com. of the supernatural enlightening of the saints, *ˬod-γsál-gyi ṅáṅ-nas γzígs-te Mil.* knowing, beholding, by means of prophetic light.

འོད་མ་ *ˬód-ma* **cane, bamboo,** *ˬód-ma tsal*, **वेणुवन**, cane-grove; such a grove near Rājagriha was a favourite retreat of Buddha.

འོན་ *ˬon W.* **but** (*sed, autem*); (not so often used as in English).

འོན་ཀྱང་ *ˬon-kyaṅ* **but, yet, notwithstanding** *Dzl.* and elsewh., frq. in *B.*; rarely *ˬon-yaṅ* for it *Mil.*; it stands at the beginning of sentences, but is also preceded by a gerund with *-kyi*, in which case it is almost pleonastic; *Lexx.* give **उताहो** as the

*Ssk.* word for it, which however seems not to agree with its use.

འོན་ཏང་ *˛ón-taṅ* = *˛ón-kyaṅ Lex.*

འོན་ཏེ་ *˛ón-te B.* and *C.* **or if not, or else, or also,** in double-questions after the termination *am* of the first question.

འོན་པ་ *˛ón-pa* 1. **deaf,** also **to be deaf;** *˛ón-pa-pa, ˛ón-pa-po, ˛ón-po* a deaf man, *˛ón-pa-mo, ˛on-mo* a deaf woman *Cs.*; *˛on-loṅ* deaf and blind. — 2. **to give, to bring,** chiefly as imp. *˛ón-čig Dzl.*

འོན་སེང་ *˛on-seṅ,* with *byéd-pa,* **to pay attention, to watch, to spy** *Sch.*

འོབ་ *˛ob* 1. also *˛obs* **ditch, trench, pit** *Dzl.*; *me-˛ób* fiery pit; also fig.: the fire-pool of passions. — 2. v. *yob.*

འོམ་བུ་ *˛óm-bu* 1. **tamarisk,** Myricaria *Med.* not unfrequent near the rivers of Tibet. — 2. *Sch.*: 'a town, settlement' (?).

འོར་ *˛or* 1. **dropsy,** viz. the species **anasarca,** nif., = *págs-ču*; *dbu-˛or* prob. id. *Med.* — 2. **eddy, whirlpool** *Sch.*

འོར་བ་ *˛ór-ba* 1. **to put** or **lay down** *Cs.* — 2. **to feed,** e. g. a little child *W.*

འོལ་ *˛ol* **clover, trefoil,** viz. snail-clover, medic, (Medicago); *˛ol-ťáṅ* a plain covered with such clover; **'ol-kyog* W.* snail.

འོལ་མདུད་ *˛ol-mdúd* v. *'ol-mdúd.*

འོལ་པ་ *˛ól-pa* **vulture** *Sch.* (?)

འོལ་སྤྱི་ *˛ól-spyi* **in a general way, generally speaking, about,** *˛ól-spyir* id. *Sch.*; *˛ól-spyi tsám-du dus mnyám-mo* they are about contemporaries *Tar.*

འོལ་བ་ *˛ól-ba* **black horse** *Mil., Ld.-Glr.* (*Ts.* **wál-ba**).

འོལ་མོ་ *˛ól-mo Ld.* **oṅ-mol** **besom, broom, brush,** *stag-˛ól* birch-broom, *zed-˛ól* hair-broom *Cs.*

འོལ་མོ་སེ་ *˛ol-mo-sé Wdṅ.* an officinal plant; *Cs.*: '*˛ol-ma-sa* 1. a certain small berry. — 2. a small weight'.

འོས་ *˛os* 1. v. the following. — 2. v. *˛o-se.*

འོས་པ་ *˛ós-pa* 1. vb. and adj. **to be worthy, suitable; becoming, appropriate,** with termin. inf., in later times and vulgo, with the root, *sbyin-par ˛os* it is becoming, it is meet to give; *˳di γzigs-par mi ˛os* it is not decent to see this; **ka-lón čá-če 'os* W.* he is worthy to be a vizier; **ǐ-sam la taṅ mi 'os* W.* he is not worth such high wages; **la nán-te taṅ 'os* W.* he deserves extra-pay; *yid-smón ˛os* to be wished, desirable; *p̓yag bya-bar ˛os-par ˳gyur* he becomes adorable; *stód-˛os* to be praised, laudable; *bkúr-˛os* deserving honour *Cs.*; *ťams-čád-la p̓óg-˛os-pai čád-pa* the punishment condign to all; rarely with genit.: *kún-gyis bkúr-žiṅ mčód-pai ˛os Mil.* he is deserving of universal honour and respect, and even: *rjei ˛os min* he was not worth to be a king, for which more frq. the termin. is used: *γtsó-mor ˛ós-pa žig Glr.* the one that is the most deserving of being mistress, i.e. she that has the genteelest appearance, that is most of a gentlewoman; *grógs-su ˛ós-pa* he is worthy to be his colleague, nif. *Mil.* — 2. more particularly in colloquial language: **right,** *W.* **ós-čan, ǒ-šan**; with a negative **mi-ós-pa, os-méd, os-min** *W.*, **mi-ǫ̈-pa** etc. *C.* wrong (for the *rigs-pa* and *mi-rigs-pa* of earlier lit.); *mi ˛ós-pai spyod-pa byed-pa Glr.* to entertain illicit intercourse; *rdzas ˛ós-pa* a lawful, *mi ˛ós-pa* an unlawful matter *Schr.*; **ǫ̈-min-ghi ṭim-gál** *C.* a wrong, immoral act, sinful transgression; **'os mi-ós p̓é-če** *W.* to discern between right and wrong; with regard to a man's words, **credible, trustworthy,** or the contrary. — *Sch.* has besides: *˛os či yod,* 'what other means or way is there?' and: *˛os spyí-ba* 'to finish (a thing) for the most part; to be good or tolerably good' (??).

# ཡ

ཡ *ya* 1. the consonant **y**, pronounced like the English initial **y**, in yard, yoke etc., in *C.* deep-toned; *yá-btags, yá-ta Glr.* the subscribed y or ྱ. — 2. num. fig.: 24.

ཡ་ *ya* I. often with *γčig*, one of two things that belong together as being of one kind, or forming a pair, also one of two opponents; *mig ya-γčig lóṅ-ba Pth.* blind of one eye; *lham ya-γčig Glr.* one of a pair of boots, an odd boot; *lag-pa ya-γčig-tu γser t̔ogs, lág-pa ya-γčig-tu bú-mo k̔rid-de Dzl.* in one hand holding the gold, with the other leading his daughter; *stóṅ-pa daṅ γsál-ba γnyis ya ma brál-bar Thgr.* the empty and the clear (emptiness and clearness) being inseparable from each other; *ya-gyál* one of several, e.g. of three things *Gram.*; of six *Lex.*; **yá-do** in *W.* the common word for *grogs* or *zlá-bo* **associate, companion, assistant,** **yá-do čó-če** to assist; **nyi-ka ya yo̱'** *C.* they are equal to each other, a match, one as good as the other, **k̔ó-la ya mé*, or *k̔o̱ ya ǰhé-k̔e̱n mi dug** *C.* he finds none that is a match to him, **di lé-ke̱ ya ṅe̱ mi t̔ub** *C.* I am not equal to the task; *k̔ai ya* v. *k̔á-ya*; *ya-méd* = *do-méd*; *̥t̔áb-ya* adversary, antagonist; *ya-žár* one-eyed; *ya-ma-zúṅ* and *ya-má-brla, ya-ya* v. below. —

II. root signifying **above, up** etc. (opp. to *ma*), cf. *goṅ*; adj. *yá-gi* (also *yá-ki Mil.*), *p̔u yá-gi* the upper or highest part of a valley *Glr.*, *ri-bo yá-gi* the hill up yonder *Mil.*; *yá-gi* upper = heavenly *Mil.*, opp. to *má-gi*; *yar* and *yas* v. the respective articles; the word, otherwise, occurs only in compounds: *yá-rkan* palate; *ya-gád* (for *skad*) ladder *Sch.*; *ya-góṅ* above, over *Sch.*; *ya-mgál, ya-mčú, ya-t̔ém, ya-t̔óg, ya-rábs, ya-ré, ya-só* v. *mgal* etc.; *ya-mt̔á* the upper end, i. e. the beginning e. g. of a word, opp. to *ma-mt̔a* the end *Cs.*; *yá-ša* **esteem, honour, love,** shown to a person *W.* (= *že-sa B., C.*), **yá-še̱ spé-ra** expressions of respect; **yá-še̱ p̔i-la zér-na** if one speaks respectfully; *ya-ša-méd-k̔an* uncivil, regardless, reckless, unfeeling; **yá-ša čó-če** to show love, regard, to treat with tenderness, to fondle, a child, animal etc., opp. to *má-ša*, which however is less in use.

ཡ་ཁ་ *yá-k̔a* **mutual revilings** *Ma.*: *ma smád-la yaṅ yá-k̔a sgrags* mother and children abuse one another. *Cs.*: *yá-ga* bad reputation (?).

ཡ་རྒྱལ་ *ya-gyál* v. *ya* I.

ཡ་ང(བ)་ *yá-ṅa(-ba) C.* also **yá-ṅa-bo** (prob. for *γya ṅán-pa*) **shuddering, fright, anguish,** with genit. or accus. of that which is the cause of it *Do.*; *yá-ṅa-bai dmag-ts̔ógs Mil.* a formidable host; *yá-ṅai gegs* terrible danger *Pth.*

ཡ་ཏ་ *yá-ta* v. letter *ya*.

ཡ་ཏ་ prop. ཡ་ཏྲ་ *ya-tra* (procession and feast, in honour of some idol) *W.*: **festivity, reveling,** in beer with dumplings and pastry, held in autumn or winter, in memory and for the benefit of the souls of those that died during the last year.

ཡ་དོ་ *yá-do* v. *ya* I.

ཡ་པོ་ *yá-po* **butcher; executioner** *Schr.*

ཡ་བ་ *yá-ba* prob. = *γya-ba*. — *Mil.?*

ཡ་བ་ཀྵཱ་ར་ *ya-ba-kšā-ra Ssk.* **saltpetre** *Med.*

ཡ་མ་ *yá-ma* 1. **the temples.** — 2. **a severe cold, catarrh.** *Med.*; **yá-ma rag** *W.* I have a bad cold. — 3. n. of a goddess, = *brtán-ma*.

ཡ་མ་ཟུང་ *ya-ma-zúṅ* **unsymmetrical, incongruous, not fitting together,** e. g. two unequal shoes; of religions, languages, customs, that have sprung from heterogeneous elements; of behaviour: **inconsistent; unheard of, prodigious,** *čo-ₒṕrúl* magic feats *Tar.*

ཡ་མ་བརླ་ *ya-ma-brla*, **ya-má-la**, *Ü: ya-ma-la-po*, *Ts.: *ya-ma-lẹn-te**, *Lis̀.: = snyiṅ-po-med-pa, mi-bdén-pa* **vain, unstable, fickle, not to be trusted** or **depended upon.**

ཡ་མཚན་ *yá-mtsan* 1. **wonder, miracle, supernatural occurrence,** adopted also as the term for the miracles of Scripture *Chr. Prot.*; *ltás-sam yá-mtsan ci byuṅ Dzl.* what signs and wonders have happened? *yá-mtsan-du ₒgyúr-ba Dzl.* to happen, to come to pass in a marvelous manner; *yá-mtsan-ste Pth.* being a wonderful man; *ḱyód-la ₒdí-tsam rig-pa-méd-pa ni yá-mtsan-čeo* that you are so ignorant is very strange (wonderful); **yá-tsẹm-po* C.* marvelous, miraculous; *yá-tsam-càn* id. *Schr.* — 2. **wonder, astonishment, amazement,** *rgyál-po yá-mtsan čén-po skyés-te Tar.* the king greatly wondering; **yám-tsan tsór-ce, có-ce* W.* to wonder; *yá-mtsan-gyi γnás-so Tar.* it is a thing to be wondered at; *dé-tsam yá-mtsan-rgyu med Mil.* that is not so very astonishing.

ཡ་ཡ་ *yá-ya* 1. *Cs.*: **differing, diverse,** *yá-ya-ba* **diversity;** *yá-ya-bor gyúr-ba Sch.*: a subject of dispute, contrariety of opinion. — 2. *γyá-ya.*

ཡ་ཡོ་ *ya-yó* **crooked, wry,** col. *Cs.*

ཡ་ལད་ *ya-lád* **corselet and helmet, mail, armour,** *γsér-gyi* of gold; also fig. *B.*

ཡ་ཤ་ *yá-s̀a* v. *ya* II.

ཡ་ཧུ་དཱ་ *ya-hu-dá* **Judah,** *ya-hu-dá-pa* **jew** *Chr. Prot.*

ཡ་ཧོ་ཝཱ་ *ya-ho-wá* **Jehovah** *Chr. Prot.*

ཡག་པ་ *yág-pa* **a small mattock, hoe,** *càg-yag* iron hoe, *s̀iṅ-yag* wooden hoe *Ts.*

ཡག་པོ་ *yág-po*, prov. also *ₒǰág-po*, seldom in B., but otherwise common in *C.* and *W.* **good,** in all its significations, both as to men and things, *= bzáṅ-po*; **dei ṕi-la di yág-po* W.* for that purpose this is good, fit, serviceable; **yág-po ǰhé-pa* C.*, **có-ce* W.*, c. c. *la*, **to caress, to flirt,** also in an obscene sense; *yág-po yág-po* well, well!

ཡང་ *yaṅ* 1. (accented), **again, once more; likewise, also, further,** frq., *yaṅ yaṅ Mil.*, *yaṅ daṅ yáṅ-du Tar.*, *yáṅ-nas yáṅ-du Dzl.* **again and again;** joined to adj. and adv. denoting a higher degree, **still:** *yaṅ čuṅ Mil.* still smaller, *ₒdi ci-gaṅ-las yaṅ dgá-ba z̀ig byuṅ Mil.* that was still more pleasing than any thing before; *yáṅ sgos Mil.* still more in detail; **yáṅ-ṅon-z̀ag* W.* the third day before yesterday. — 2. (unaccented, throwing the accent back on the preceding word), after the final letters g, d, b, s, gen. *kyaṅ*, after vowels often *ₐaṅ*, **also, too,** the Latin *quoque*, *ṅa yaṅ, bdag kyaṅ* I too; *bu čé-ba yaṅ Dzl.* my eldest boy too; *bsód-nams daṅ yaṅ ldáṅ-pa Dzl.* having also merit; *yaṅ — yaṅ —*, both — and —; *ₒdi yaṅ — de yaṅ* both this and that, *ṕyi-rol yaṅ naṅ yaṅ* both outside and inside; followed by a negative, **neither — nor;** *yaṅ* singly, with a negative: **not even,** *kar-s̀á-pa-ni γcig kyaṅ mi sbyin-no Dzl.* I shall not even give a cowry for it; *yaṅ* with a comparative (as above) **still,** *sṅár-bas kyaṅ lhág-par* still more than formerly; as effect of a preceding cause, **so then,** *kyeu de yaṅ tse ₒdas-so Dzl.* so then the boy died, *bsád-pa yaṅ graṅs-méd-do Dzl.* so then there were people killed without number; emphat., **even,** *ríṅ-por ma lón-par smra yaṅ s̀és-so Dzl.* within a short time he was even able to speak; *sṅa-càd kyaṅ Dzl.* even before this; *kar-s̀á-pa-ni ₒbum yaṅ* even so much as a hundred thousand cowries (I would give); also joined to a verbal root: *tams-càd ₒdus kyaṅ* even if all without exception be gathered; **although,** *btsal kyaṅ ma rnyed* although they were seeking, they did not find, or, they were seeking indeed, **but** did not find; this latter turn is frequently used, where we use **but, yet, nevertheless** etc.

ཡང་སྐྱར་ *yaṅ-skyár* 1. sbst. **postscript.** *Cs.* — 2. adv. **again, afresh, anew** *C.*

ཡང་གེ་ *yáṅ-ge* v. *yáṅ-po.*

ཡང་སྒོས་ *yáṅ-sgos* v. *yaṅ* 1.

ཡང་ཅར་ *yáṅ-čar Bhot.* and *Schr.*

ཡང་ལྕི་ *yaṅ-lči* v. *yáṅ-po.*

ཡང་འཇུག་ *yáṅ-ɔjug* the second of two final letters, viz. *s* after *g*, *ṅ*, *b*, *m*.

ཡང་ཏྲི་, ཡང་གི་ཁ་ *yáṅ-tri*, *yáṅ-gi-k̔a* (spelling uncertain), is said to be the n. of a green stone, which is worked into handles of knives etc. *W.*

ཡང་དག་པ་ *yáṅ-dag-pa* v. *dág-pa.*

ཡང་ན་ *yáṅ-na* **or,** in *B.*, com. pleon. after the affixed *am* (*gam*, *nam* etc.), which in itself already expresses the **or**; it is also preceded by *daṅ*; **further,** *Thgy.*; **either — or —**, *yaṅ-na* (*ni*) — *yaṅ-na* (*ni*) —.

ཡང་སྤྲུལ་ *yáṅ-sprul* v. *sprúl-pa.*

ཡང་པོ་ *yáṅ-po Cs.*, **yáṅ-mo** *C.* and *W.* **yáṅ-ghe** *Ts.* adj., *yáṅ-ba* adj. and sbst., **light, lightness,** opp. to *lči-ba*, q. cf.; — fig. *ɔjam-žiṅ yáṅ-ba* what is soft and light, commodious and easy *Dzl.*; of food cf. *lči-ba* II.; **weak,** **de saṅ yáṅ-mo yin** *W.* this is a weaker, less emphatic, word than that; **ṅo yáṅ-mo** *C.*, *W.* cheerful, happy.

ཡང་མ་ *yáṅ-ma* **early barley,** v. *nas* I.

ཡང་མེས་པོ་ *yáṅ-mes-po* **great-grandfather,** *yáṅ-mes-mo* **great-grandmother** *Sch.*

ཡང་རྩལ་ *yáṅ-rtsal* **very high skill, consummate art** *Mil.*

ཡང་རྩེ་ *yáṅ-rtse* **the highest point, summit,** fig. **the height of perfection.**

ཡང་ཚ་ *yáṅ-ts̔a* **great-grandson** *Sch.*

ཡང་ར་ *yáṅ-ra W.* **buck, ram, he-goat,** = *p̔á-ra.*

ཡང་ལ་ *yáṅ-la* prob. = *yáṅ-na S.g*

ཡང་སོས་ *yáṅ-sos* n. of a hell *Thgy.*

ཡངས་པ་ *yáṅs-pa* 1. also *-po*, **wide, broad, large,** *t̔aṅ*, *sa-γži* a large or wide field, plain *Glr.*; *yaṅs-šiṅ rgya-če-ba* large and spacious, of a house *S.O.*; **gú-sa* (or *nẹ́-sa*) *yaṅ-pa dug** *W.* here is much room; fig. **mig-yáṅ** *C.*, *W.* liberal, generous, bounteous; **yaṅ-méd-la*, *yaṅ-yáṅ-pa-la** *W.* sudden, unexpected, unawares; **yaṅ-lúg čó-če** *W.* to hang or throw a coat over, without getting into the sleeves; *yaṅ-šam byéd-pa* id., *Sch.*; **yaṅ-hlúb** *C.*, *W.* wide, of clothes. — 2. v. *γyéṅ-ba.*

ཡངས་པ་ཅན་ *yáṅs-pa-čan*, *Ssk.* वैशाली, *Dzl.* and elsewh., city in ancient India, now **Allahabad.**

ཡན་ *yan* (= *ya* II, opp. to *man* III q. v.) **what is uppermost,** *man-yan* **below** and **above** *Cs.*; *yán-na Cs.*: **above, in the beginning, in the first part**; gen. *yan* stands as adv. or postp. with accus., = *yán-la*, *yan-čád(-la)*, *yan-čod(-la)*, **above, in the upper part,** *lté-ba yan stéṅ-la yód-de Glr.* lit. above the navel standing out of (the water), i.e. standing in (the water) up to the navel; *sta-zúr yan-čád Dzl.* above the hips; *lo-brgyád yan-čád Pth.* above eight years old; otherwise when referring to time, always **till, to**; often preceded by *nas*, **from … forth,** *Glr.*

ཡན་གླིང་ *yan-ljiṅ* **dulcimer,** musical instrument in *Ts.*

ཡན་པ་ *yán-pa* adj., **free, vacant, unoccupied, having no owner,** of places and things that are common property, like the air, rocks and stones etc.; *k̔yi yán-pa* a dog without a master, vagrant dog; *gral yán-la yod* there are yet places unoccupied; of fields: **untilled, fallow-ground**; *yan k̔yár-la ma ča*, v. *ɔk̔yár-ba*; *yán-gar-ba* **separate, apart, by itself** *Liš.*, *rgyal-rigs yán-gar-ba žig* **a** separate dynasty, a dynasty of its own; *yán-gar-du* id., adv. *Was.* (281); *rgya-yán* the external world, *rgya-yán(-gyi) γnyén-pa Glr.* a helper from the external world; *sems rgya-yán-du ma šór-bar byos* take care that the mind be not distracted by outward things; **yan ča-če** *W.* to disperse, **lug, nor tsaṅ-ma, sam-pa yan soṅ** *W.*, the sheep have dispersed (or a sheep has strayed), the fortune is gone, the thoughts are lost, wandering; *yán-du ɔjúg-pa* to suffer (the sheep) to disperse on the pasture; *nad yán-*

*pa* wandering (contagious) disease, = *yams* *Sch.* (*yán-pa* to run about, to wander *Sch.*, is rather doubtful).

ཡན་ལག *yán-lag* 1. **member, limb,** *yán-lag lṅa* arms, legs, and head *Mṅg.*; *yán-lag skyón-čan* an injured or defective limb *Lex.*; *yán-lag nyams-pa* weak in the limbs, decrepit, crazy, = *žá-ba Lex.* — 2. fig. **branch of a river, branch of a tree;** *dge-bsnyén-gyi yán-lag γzúṅ-bar bgyio Do.* was explained: I wish to be counted a branch, i.e. a member, of the community of novices; **appendage,** something subordinate to a greater thing, like **branch-establishment** *Tar.* 175, 3; also with reference to books: **appendix, supplement** *Tar.* — 3. **branch, section, separate part** of a doctrine or science, frq., a **particular head, point, thought,** in a treatise.

ཡབ་ *yab*, resp. for *ṕa*, **father,** *rgyál-po yab yum γsum Glr.* the king and his two consorts; *rgyál-po yab yum* denotes also king and queen as father and mother to the country *Glr.*; *yab rgyál-po-la γsól-to Dzl.* he said to his royal father; *yab-srás* **father and son,** in a spiritual sense: **master and disciple;** *yab-mes* 1. **father and grandfather.** 2. **progenitor, ancestors** *Glr.*

ཡབ་པ་, གཡབ་པ་ *yáb-pa, γyáb-pa* 1. **to lock, lock up, secure, cover over** *Sch.*, *yab-ča* things well secured, under safe keeping; *yáb-yob-pa* to hide, conceal *Sch.*; *γyab* or *γyab-sa* **covered place, covert, shelter** *Sch.*; *yab riṅ-po* **portico, veranda,** e g. of the monastery at Tashilhunpo; *yab-ras* **awning, tent** *Sch.* — 2. *C.* **to skim, to scoop off,** from the surface of a fluid. — 3. *W.* **to move to and fro, hither and thither,** v. *γyób-pa.* —

ཡབ་མོ་, གཡབ་མོ་ *yáb-mo, γyáb-mo* 1. **the act of fanning, waving,** *lág-pa yáb-mo byéd-čiṅ ˳či-ba* dying whilst waving the hand to and fro, considered as a sign of peace *Do.*; *gós-kyi yáb-mo byéd-pa Glr.* to beckon by waving with one's clothes; hence fig. — 2. **the bringing on, provoking,** *dgrá-boi* of an enemy *Mil.*, *˳ṕuṅ-γžii* a calamity *Mil.*; *yáb-mo ǰhé-pa* or *γyág-pa* to beckon to come, to bring (something adverse) upon one's self. — 3. **fan,** *rṅa-yáb* a. a yak-tail fan *Cs.* b. kettle-drum stick *Sch.*; *sbraṅ-yáb* fly-brush *Cs.*; *rluṅ-yáb* ventilating- or cooling-fan *Cs.*; *bsil-yáb* **pankah** (*Hind.*), a large fan suspended from the ceiling and set in motion by means of a string. — 4. **sail** *Cs.*?

ཡམ་བུ *yám-bu* = *rdo-ťsád* v. *rdo* comp.

ཡམ་མེ་བ་ *yám-me-ba* 1. *Sch.*: **coarsely, roughly, of a coarse make, rough-hewn.** — 2. *Mil.*: *čui ḱá-na ṕár-la yám-me γšegs* he walked softly gliding across the water to the other bank.

ཡམ་ཡོམ་ *yam-yóm Cs.* also *yam-yám Thgr.* **tottering, not steady** *Cs.* *yam-yóm byéd-pa* **to totter.**

ཡམས་ *yams, yams-nád Cs.*, *nad-yáms Glr.* **epidemic** or **contagious disease, plague,** *má-yams* a plague caused by evil spirits, v. *má-mo.*

ཡར་ *yar*, from *ya*, **up, upward,** also *yár-la*, e.g. *γzigs-pa* to look up *Glr.*, *yár-˳gro már-˳gro byéd-pa Glr.* to travel up and down; *yar mar ˳čág-pa B.*, **kyód-če** *W.* resp., to walk up and down; *yár-la ḱyer šog* bring or fetch up *Pth.*; *yar ma sgyugs mar ma ˳ťón-par Pth.* as it would go off neither upward by vomiting, nor downward; *yár-nas már-la* from top to bottom; *yar ˳ťón-pa Thgy.* to come up again, from a depth; **yar mar ťsaṅ-ma-ru** *W.* in every direction, all over; in such expressions as *yar laṅ-ba* **to rise, get up,** *yar ˳ṕél-ba* **to increase,** it stands pleon.; *yár-la* also denotes a relation to that which is higher, the intercourse with, the deportment towards, superiors (*már-la* the contrary) *Glr.*; esp. with reference to the transmigration of souls and their final deliverance: *yar γčód-pa* to cut off the way to the three upper classes of beings, the so-called 'good natures', *yar skyé-ba* to be re-born in the upper classes, the reverse of which is *mar ˳gríb-pa* to sink down to the lower; *yar ˳drén-pa* to draw or lift up to heaven.

ཡར་ལྟོས་ *yár-ltos* **imitation** *Sch.*

ཡ

ཡར་བ་ *yár-ba* **to disperse, ramble, stray** *C.* (= **yan čá-če** *W.*); **to spring** or **leap off** *Cs.*; **to be scattered** *Sch.*

ཡར་ལུང་ *yar-luṅ Glr.* a large tributary of the Yangtsekyang coming from the north, in western China, east of the town of Batbang; nevertheless Tibetan historians, from a partiality to old legends, describe it as flowing near the mountain of Yarlhasampo. V. *Köpp.* II, 50.

ཡར་ལྷ་ཤམ་པོ་ *Yarlhašampo*, a snowy mountain, between Lhasa and the frontier of Bhotan, near which according to tradition the first king of Tibet, *γnya-k̔ri-γtsáṅ-po, Nyaṭ̔itsángpo*, coming from India, first entered the country.

ཡལ་ག་ *yál-ga* **branch, bough**, frq., *yál-gai tsúl-du* ramified *S.g.*, *yál-ga-čan* branchy, full of boughs; *yal-p̔rán Cs.*, *yál-ga p̔reu Sch.* small branch, twig; *yal-ₒdáb* a branch full of leaves *Cs.*

ཡལ་བ་ *yál-ba* **to dwindle, fail; disappear, vanish,** *drod yal* animal heat (in a living being) diminishes, (an inanimate object) cools down, grows cold; *ṅad yal* it evaporates *Lt.*; of beer: to get stale, dead (*W.*: **yal čá-če**); **(s)kug(s) gyál-k̔an-la yal ča dug** *W.* the stake is lost in going to the winner; *ₒja yál-ba bžin-du Glr.* like the vanishing of the rainbow; *yal-šúl Wdṅ.* in a fruit the remnants of the withered blossom; **to be obliged to yield, to be dislodged** *Glr.* fol. 25, but perh. the signification: **to disappear** is also here admissible; *lus daṅ srog yal Dzl.* body and soul are trifled away, are lost; **go-yál** (v. *sgó-po*) one who has lost himself by gambling and has thus become the slave of another; *yál-bar ₒdór-ba, ₒbór-ba*, 1. *Sch.* **to annihilate, annul.** 2. *Cs.* **to despise,** *γžan* other people. Cf. *yól-ba*.

ཡལ་ཡལ་ *yal-yál Cs.* 100 000 octillions, *yal-yál čén-po* a nonillion; yet cf. *dkrigs-pa*.

ཡལ་ཡོལ་, -ཡུལ་ *yal-yól, -yúl* **inconstancy, inattention, carelessness** *Cs.*, *Sch.*

ཡས་ *yas*, from *ya*, 1. **from above,** *ₒbáb-pa* to come down from above *Cs.*; **above,** *yás-kyi* the one above, the upper one *Do.*; *yás-nas* from above *C.*, *yas mas*, a. from above and from below *Cs.* b. upward and downward *Cs.*; *yas-byón* coming from above *Mil.* — 2. **off, away,** *yas γtóṅ-ba, ₒp̔aṅ-yás γtóṅ-ba, γtor-yas byéd-pa Glr.* and elsewh., to throw away. — 3. in comp. **without,** *mt̔a-yás* without an end, endless, frq; *bgraṅ-yás* numberless *Gram.*

ཡི་ *yi*, 1. num. fig.: 54. — 2. in some combinations inst. of *yid*, *so yi γčód-pa yi(d) čád-pa* 1. **to forget,** e.g. a benefactor *Glr.* 2. more frq. **to give up, to despair** *Dzl.*; **despondency, despair** *Mil.*; *yi-p̔ri-ba* a disliking, hatred *Cs.*; *yi(d)-múg-pa, yi-múg-par ₒgyúr-ba* to despair, frq.; *yi-ráṅ-ba* to be glad, to rejoice, v. *ráṅ-ba*; *yi-γsád-pa Cs.* = *yi-múg-pa*.

ཡི་ག་ *yi-ga* **appetite,** *yi-ga ₒgag, ldog* the appetite is lost, aversion, disgust is felt, *yi-ga sdaṅ* id. *Sch.*; *ₒčus* id. *Med.*; *yi-gar ₒoṅ* it is grateful to the taste, it tastes well *Med.*

ཡི་གེ་ *yi-ge* in comp. *yig*, 1. **letter,** *yi-ge dbú-čan*(*W.* **róm-yig**) the Tibetan printed letters, *dbu-méd*(*W.* **ṭ a-yig**) current handwriting, of which there are again different kinds: *dpé-yig* the more distinct and careful, used in copying books, *ₒk̔yúg-yig* the cursory and often rather illegible writing in letters, and *ₒbam-yig*, the very large and regular style invented for the use of elementary writing-schools (v. specimens of all of them in the lithogr. supplement to *Cs.*'s grammar). — *yi-ge-drúg-pa* the six-syllable (prayer), **the Ommanipadmehum** *Glr.* and elsewh.; *yi-ge-bdún-pa* and *brgyá-pa Mil.?* *yi-ge bsláb-pa* to learn reading and writing, *yig-rtsis* reading, writing, and cyphering; *k̔á-yig* the letter k. — 2. anything that is written, **note, card, bill, document; inscription, title** (more accurately *k̔á-yig*), esp. **letter, epistle**; *yi-ge bžág-pa* a deposited document, bond *C.*; *dge-sdig-gi yi-ge* register of virtues and iniquities; *yi-gei lan* a written answer *Glr.*; *yi-gei šubs* a. **envelope,** b. **letter-case, pocket-book**; *yi-ge ₒbri-ba* to write a letter, *spriṅ-ba W.* **kál-če** to send off, *tob-*

ཡ

*pa* to receive a letter; *yi-ge sleb* a letter arrives; *yi-ger* ₒ*bri-ba Dzl.*, ₒ*gód-pa* to compose, to pen down; *yi-ger* ₒ*brir* ₒ*ǰúg-pa* to get copied; *yi-ger bris* ₒ*ǰóg-pa literis mandatum deponere*; *skú-yig* letter, circular epistle; *ḱá-yig* v. above; *čád-yig* contract, bargain; ₒ*čáms-yig* dancing-book, rules relating to religious dances; ₒ*čól-yig* letter of recommendation *Cs.*; *rtágs-yig* 1. **stamp, signature** *Cs.* 2. **certificate, credentials** *W.*; *γnás-yig* description of a place; *spriṅs-* or ₒ*ṕrin-yig* = *skúr-yig*; *bú-yig* 1. copy. 2. commentary, opp. to *má-yig* 1. original, first copy; 2. text *Cs.*; ₒ*dzin-yig* = *rtágs-yig* 2 *W.*; *žú-yig* memorial, petition; *lán-yig* letter in answer, reply; *lám-yig* 1. **hand-book, road-book, guide,** *šám-bha-lai lam-yig* description of the road to Sambhala (a fantastical book). 2. **itinerary, travelling-journal** (?). 3. **pass-port** *Cs.*

ཡི་དྭགས་ *yi-dwags* (from etymol. subtility written also *yid-tags* or *yid-btags*), प्रेत, the fifth class of beings of Buddhist cosmography, condemned in a fore-hell to suffer perpetual hunger and thirst, a grade of punishment preceding the final and full torments of hell; they are represented as giants with huge bellies, and very narrow throats, inhabiting the air *Köpp.* I, 245.

ཡི་དམ་ *yi-dam*, less frq. *yid-dam* (= *dam-bča*) resp. *ťúgs-dam* 1. **oath, vow, asseveration, promise,** *yi-dam-la brtén-pas* because he firmly adhered to his word *Dzl.* — 2. a 'wishing prayer' (v. *smon-lam*), *yi-dam bčá-ba* to make a vow *Dzl.*, to pronounce a wishing prayer *Dzl.* — 3. **meditation** (this signification rests only on the analogy with *tugs-dam*, and has yet to be confirmed by quotations from literature). — 4. also *yi-dam-lhá* **tutelar god,** a deity whom a person chooses to be his patron, whether for his whole life, or only for some particular undertaking, and with whom he enters into an intimate union by meditation; frequently also it is a defunct saint or teacher (so e.g. the *yi-dam* of Milaraspa was *rdo-rǰe-*ₒ*čaṅ*); sometimes such a connection subsists from infancy through life, or the deity makes advances to the respective person by special revelations, so in the case of king *Sroṅ-btsan-sgam-po Glr.* — 5. acc. to *Cs.*'s proposition: **sacrament**; yet our Christian converts preferred the more popular *dam-bča.*

ཡིག་ *yig* = *yi-ge* as an affix, v. *yi-ge.*

ཡིག་བསྐུར་ *yig-bskúr*, also *yig-mgó*, **epistolary guide**, containing the different addresses and customary phrases used in writing letters *W.* — *yig-ḱáṅ* **library** *C.*, **chancery** *Schr.* — *yig-mḱan* **secretary, book-keeper, clerk** *Glr.* and elsewh. — *yig-ča Glr.*, *Tar.* **written accounts, records, books of history.** — *yig-dpon* a 'master-writer' *Cs.* — *yig-ṕréṅ* line, written or printed. — *yig-*ₒ*brú* a single letter. — *yig-tsáṅ* 1. **archives, records, documents** *Glr.* 2. **book-case** *Glr.* — *yig-*ₒ*dzin* **written contract**, *bžág-pa* to indent (articles of agreement).

ཡིད་ *yid*, resp. *ťugs*, I. 1. **soul, mind,** esp. the powers of perception, volition and imagination, cf. *blo*; *yid bžin-du* as one would wish, to heart's content, frq.; *yid-bžin-gyi nór-bu* a jewel or talisman that grants every wish; *yid-du* ₒ*óṅ-ba* adj., rarely *yid-*ₒ*óṅ-po Mil.* **engaging, winning, pleasing,** *skyé-bo máṅ-poi yid-du* ₒ*óṅ-ba Do.* beloved with many; **nice, pretty,** of girls, houses etc., frq.; also *yid-kyi* inst. of it, e.g. *yid-kyi mťo* a pretty lake *Sbh.*; *ṅai-yid* ₒ*óṅ* my dearest! my darling! *Pth.*; *yid-du-mi-*ₒ*óṅ-bai ťsig smrá-ba Wdṅ.* to say some unpleasant word; whereas *W.*: **da yid-la yoṅ* or *ǰuṅ** now it comes into my mind; *ṅa yid-du mi rag* I do not recollect; *C.*: **yi'-la ma soṅ** it would not go down with him, he had no mind for it; *ṅai yid-la mi* ₒ*bab Tar.* it does not please me, I do not like it; *yid-la šar kyaṅ ro mi myoṅ Mil.* though you may fancy it in your mind, yet you do not perceive the taste; *yid-la byéd-pa*, ₒ*dzin-pa W*: **čó-če, bór-če**, **to comprehend, perceive, remember, mind, take to heart,** frq.; *yid-kyis byéd-pa* to do a thing in one's mind, fancy, e.g. sacrificing, like *dmigs-la Thgr.*; *yid-kyis byás-pa* fancied, imaginary, ideal *Cs.*; **yi'-*

*kyi lóg-pa* C.* to read mentally, softly, inaudibly; before many verbs *yid* stands almost pleon.: **yid kul-če* W.* **to exhort;** *yid ˳kul-ba Sch.* 'mental suffering', perh. better: **to be uneasy, troubled, harassed;** *yid ˳krúl-ba* **to be mistaken;** *yid-čad-pa* v. *yi-γčod-pa;* *yid-čes-pa* **to believe,** with the accus. or dat. of the thing which one believes, with the dat. of the person whom one believes, ... *par*, that ... (cf. *dád-pa); kyód-la čuṅ žig yid ma čés-pas Mil.* having become a little distrustful towards you; **yid* (or *dén*)*-čö-čeï spé-ra* W.* credible words; *yid-brtan-dká-ba Tar.* not to be depended upon, hardly to be believed; *yid-γnyis* **doubt;** *té-tsom daṅ yid-γnyis ma byed čig Mil.*; *yid ˳pám-pa Mil.* **to be cast down, dejected, depressed;** *yid ˳próg-pa Mil.* **to prepossess, to infatuate;** *yid bloṅ-ba* **to be afraid, full of anxiety** (?) *Sch.; yid ˳byuṅ-ba*, resp. *tugs-˳byuṅ-ba Mil.* **to be sad, unhappy, discontented,** *la*, on account of; *ṅa kor-bai čos-la yid-byuṅ-nas Mil.* I was wearied of the way of (constantly moving in) the orb of transmigration; *yid-˳byín-pa* to make discontented or weary; *yid-múg-pa* v. *yi-mug-pa; yid ˳tsim-par ˳gyúr-ba Dzl.* to become satisfied, contented; **yid tsim čo-če* W.* to satisfy; *yid-log-pa* **to be tired** or **weary of** *Sch.; yid-tún Dzl.* **forward, rash, overhasty;** *yid-dúṅs* v. *duṅs;* *yid-myós* fuddled, tipsy; *yid-smón* v. *smón-pa; yid-γžúṅs* v. *γzúṅs; yid-srúbs Lexx., Sch.:* 'a refractory, stubborn mind', which however does not suit the connection. — 2. symb. num.: 14. — II. = *yud, yid-tsam* for *yud-tsam, Wdn* frq.

ཡིད་དགས *yid-tags* v. *yi-dags.*

ཡིན་པ *yin-pa*, resp. and eleg. *lágs-pa* I. **to be,** with neg. *ma yin* or *min, W.* **man*; kyod su yin* who are you? *bsa de-ka ṅa yin Mil.* I was the leopard (you saw); with genit., *ṅai yin* that is mine, belongs to me; **di-riṅ za-nyi-ma yin* W.* to-day is Sunday; *gáṅ-nas yin Mil.* whence are you? *˳di med-pas yin Pth.* it is because this is not here ...; *ṅa bú-moi dús-na yin-te Glr.* **when I was still a girl;** **yin kyaṅ* C.*, **yin-na yaṅ* W., C.* for *˳on kyaṅ* **yet, nevertheless, notwithstanding;** *yin-graṅ(-na)* v. *gráṅ-ba* extr.; *yin* for optat or imp.: *de yin* 1. **so it is, yes.** 2. **that may be,** *mi ˳dod ruṅ de yin Mil.* if you feel no inclination, never mind, let it be so! *dgrá-bo yin-na-˳aṅ yin Mil.* if he is an enemy, let him be so! *yin-na* stands also pleon. with adverbs etc.: *sṅar yin-na* = *sṅar Mil.; yin*, so it is! yes! *min, W.* **man**, no! *yin-min* truth in a relative sense, *yin-min-gyi té-tsom bsal Glr.* it removes all doubts as to the truth, e.g. the historical truth; *ma yin-pa, min-pa* 1. vb. not to be a thing. 2. adj. not being a certain thing, *ma yin-par*, adv.; *čos ma yin-par* 'not being law', i.e. contrary to the law of religion, **wrong, unjust,** = *mi rigs-par; yul, dus, tsod, rigs-pa ma yin-par spyód-pa Thgy.* to do a thing at a wrong time or place, without observing due measure, in an improper or unnatural manner; hence also *ma-yin-pa* alone: **wrong, unjust;** **ma-yim-pe čö-pa ǰhé-ken-la ten-šig zer* C.* whoever commits an improper action is called **ten-šig*;* hence also *yin-min* right and wrong. — 3. v. *min.* Cf. moreover *yód-pa* and *˳dúg-pa*, which may be used for *yin-pa*, but not inversely. Sometimes it implies **to mean, to signify:** *ṅa de či yin Glr.* what does this drumming mean? *rgyál-po koṅ-ráṅ yin dgoṅs* the king thought (the prophecy) meant him, referred to himself; *tóg-ma ṅéd-kyi pyir ma yin-pas Dzl.* as from the very beginning it was not aimed at me, had no reference to me; also in other instances, where we have to use words of a more precise character: *kyód-kyi lo gaṅ yin-pa-la kó-wo dgú-gis Tar.* whilst the sensibility that was with you, i.e. the discretion shown by you, gives me much pleasure. — II. *yin* is joined to a partic. pres., quite analogous to our English construction: *˳gró-ba yin* **I am going** *Mil., C.; kyód-la lám-mkan yód-pa é yin? Mil.* (are you having) have you a guide? *dei náṅ-na su yód-pa yin? Glr.* who is within? it is also joined to a partic. pf., when referring to the past: *ṅa-ráṅ-la skyés-pa yin Glr.* I have born him; *čád-pa yin-pas Glr.*

because he is descended from ...; *ci byúṅ-ba yiṅ, Glr.* what has become of him? *de-dus ci byas-pa yin Mil.* what were you doing just then? so esp. *W.*: **zér-pa yin, zér-pen** he has said it, **kál-pen** it has been sent off; joined to the partic. fut., (or to the partic. pres. or pf., in as far as these are sometimes used also for the fut.) it expresses futurity: *śí-ba yin Pth.* I shall die; *ṅo su śés-pa-la bskúr-ba yin Glr.* she shall be given to him, that will know her, find her out from amongst the rest; *ˌgró-ba yin mod Glr.* indeed you will have to go now. When joined to a root, it is only in *W.* that it denotes the future: **léb yin, léb-bin** he will come, **táṅ yin** he will give.

**Comp.** **yin-tog-can* W.* thinking one's self to be something (great), proud, conceited. — *yin-tsul Mil.* **property, attribute,** ni f. — *yin-lugs* 1. circumstances, **condition** (= *γnás-lugs?*); *k'ón-rnams-kyi yin-lugs brjod Mil.* she related to him her circumstances. 2. nature or essence of things *Mil.*

ཡིབ་ *yib*, v. *čar-yib* **eaves, shed** *Mil. nt.*, yet cf. the following.

ཡིབ་པ་ *yib-pa* **to hide one's self** *C., W.*; *čar yib byéd-pa Pth.* to take shelter from the rain; **yib-te bór-ce* W.* to hide, conceal; *yib-ma* **something hidden** *Sch.*; *yib-sa* **place of concealment, hiding-corner.**

ཡིས་ *yis*, termination of the instrum. case after vowels, po.

ཡུ་ *yu* 1. sbst.? *yu byéd-pa* **to calumniate** *Sch.* (?); *yu-na* if it is true *Sch.* (??) — 2. num. figure: 84.

ཡུ་གུ་, -ཁུ་ *yu-gu, -k'u* **oats**, or a similar kind of grain, which, in case of need, may serve for food *C.*

ཡུ་གུ་ཤིང་ *yú-gu-śiṅ* officinal tree, yielding a remedy for wounds and sores *S.g.*; also fig. *Wdṅ.*

ཡུ་གུར་, ཡུ་གེ་ར་ *yu-gúr, yu-gé-ra*, n. of a country and people, *Cs.*, which *Sch.* gratuitously identifies with *Taṅ-gúd*; however *Glr.* p. 32 is stated, that Tibet derived mathematical science and works of art from the east, viz. China and Minyag (i. e. *Taṅ-yúd*), laws and specimens of workmanship from the north, viz. Hor and Yugera (which are frequently mentioned together *Ma.*) — a passage which *Sch.* (History of the Eastern Monguls, 328) translated, but owing to an obscurity in the Mongul text, he failed to recognize Yugera, instead of which he has the word 'Gugi', questionable even to himself. (*Sch.* on the 'Phantom of the Turkish Uigures', v. Preface to *Dzl.* IX.).

ཡུ་བ་ *yú-ba* **handle, hilt, shaft,** *gri-yu* haft of a knife; *stár-yu* helve of an axe; *débs-yu* handle of an awl; *lhám-yu* leg of a boot *Cs.*; *yú(-ba)-can* provided with a handle, *yu-méd* without a handle *Cs.*; *yu-bcád* 'shoes, slippers' *Sch.* (?).

ཡུ་བུ་ཅག་ *yú-bu-cag Cs.* = *ˏú-bu-cag.*

ཡུ་བོ་, ཡུ་མོ་ *yú-bo, yú-mo* ox, cow, having no horns *Cs.*; for *yú-mo Sch.* has 'hind, female of a stag'; it seems to be little known. *yú-mo srol-góṅ* and *yú-mo mdeu-ˌbyin* names of plants *Wdṅ.*

ཡུག་ *yug* (= *bubs*) 1. **piece of cloth** or **stuff;** *gós-su ras-yúg γcig-las mi bdóg-ste Dzl.* as they had but one cotton cloth for their clothing. Cotton cloth is generally of very small width, but the silk fabric, designated by *dar-yúg*, seems not to exceed much the breadth of ribbons *Glr.* — 2. for *yud Mil.*

ཡུག་པོ་ *yúg-po, Ld. ˏúg-pa* **oats,** prob. the same as *yú-ku.*

ཡུག(ས)་ས་, ཡུག(ས)་ཟ་ *yúg(s)-sa, yúg(s)-za* **mourning** for a deceased husband or wife, and the state of uncleanness consequent to it, the duration of which varies according to circumstances, whether the first or second spouse has died, and also with respect to the different countries; *yúg(s)-sa-pa*, also *yúg(s)-sa* **widower,** *yúg(s)-sa-mo* **widow;** *yúg(s)-sa p'óg-pa* being unclean in consequence of mourning; *sáṅs-pa* cleansed, viz. by the expiration of the time of mourning *Cs.*

ཡུང་བ་ *yúṅ-ba Med.*, **yúṅ-pe* W.*, **turmeric.**

ཡུང་མ་ *yúṅ-ma*, for *nyúṅ-ma*, **turnip** *Glr.*

ཡ

ཡུངས་(ད)ཀར་ yuṅs-(d)kár **white mustard,** yuṅs-nág **black mustard;** yuṅs-˳brú **grain of mustard-seed,** yuṅs-˳bru tsam as small as a grain of mustard-seed *S.g.*; yuṅs-már oil of mustard.

ཡུད་ yud 1. rarely yug, a very small portion of time, **moment**, acc. to *S.g.* = कला, stated to be a space of time varying from 8 seconds to 2½ minutes; yúd tsam (žig), yud ré but one moment, yúd-tsam-pa *Do.* of a moment's duration; tse ˳di yud tsam yin p̒yi-ma-la mt̒a-méd this life is but like a moment, the future without end; yúd-kyis, yúd-du in a moment, e.g. ɣnás-su p̒yin-pa to get to a place *S.g.*; for a moment, nám-mk̒a-la ltá-ba looking up to heaven *Wdṅ.* — 2. acc. to *Stg.* k̒u, fol. 53, yud is a space of time of longer duration, 48 minutes; acc. to *Schr.* in *Bhot.* = ču-tsód 24 minutes. — 3. **a black** or coloured stripe on woven fabrics, yud-čan striped, black or white *W.*

ཡུད་བུ་ yúd-bu = yú-bu, ˴ú-bu *Cs.* (?).

ཡུད་ཡུད་ yud-yúd *Sch.*: yud-yúd bríd-pa **a dim and indistinct glimmering** before one's eyes.

ཡུན་ yun **time,** when denoting a certain space or length of time, klog ˳kyúg-pai yun tsam ma lón-par der p̒yin-nas *Mil.* in no longer time than a flash of lightning takes he arrived there; yun riṅ-po, *W.* *-mo*, a long time, yun riṅ-por, yun riṅ-du during a long time, yun riṅ-po-nas a long time since or past; *yun máṅ-po bud ča dug* *W.* a long time passes; *yun riṅ-ṅi k̒á-na* *W.* by degrees, gradually; yún-du *Glr.* for a long time to come; yun či srid-du how long? yun t̒úṅ-ba a short time.

ཡུམ་ yum, resp. for ma, 1. **mother,** btsún-mo yum, yum btsún-mo the queen mother. — 2. *Ssk.* मातृका, title of the third and latest part of the sacred writings, which contains the **Abhidharma**, or metaphysical portion (*Köpp.* I, 595. *Burn.* I, 48); *Sch.* mentions also an extract of it, yum-čúṅ.

ཡུམ་པ་ yúm-pa, only *W.* **to strew,** salt on food, ashes on the snow.

ཡུར་བ་ yúr-ba I. vb. 1. **to slumber,** *W.* also *t̒om yur-če*. — 2. v. yúr-ma.

II. sbst. **aqueduct, conduit, water-course, ditch** *Glr.*; yúr-po če a large trench, channel, canal, yur-p̒rán a small one; sbubs-yur a covered, subterraneous canal *Cs.*; yur(-bai) ču water conveyed by a canal.

ཡུར་མ་ yúr-ma **the act of weeding** *C.*, *W.*; *yur-ma yur-wa*, *C.*, *W.* also *čo-če* to pull out weeds; metaph. to purify the mind, cleanse the heart, e.g. by disburdening one's conscience.

ཡུལ་ yul 1. **place,** a. **an inhabited place,** as opp. to desolation, t̒aṅ stoṅ-pa mi daṅ yul med-čiṅ *Pth.* a desert in which there are neither men nor dwelling-places; b. **place,** with reference to a sacred community (college, monastery etc.) near it, e.g. some of the students live in the college, others in the place: so yul-dgón village and monastery, yul-dgón-rnams *Mil.* for yúl-mi daṅ dgón-pa-pa-rnams laymen and clerics. c. **place, province, country,** in a gen. sense, yúl-(gyi) skad provincial dialect, provincialism; yul-(gyi) mt̒il, mčog chief place, capital; yul čen-po brgyad chief places; as such are enumerated in *Pth.*, without any regard to geography, Singhala, Thogar, Li, Balpo, Kashmir, Zahor, Urgyan, Magata; rgya-gar(-gyi) yul India; rgyá-yul, bód-yul, sóg-yul India (or China), Tibet, Mongolia; whenever yul precedes a word, as in *yul wa-ra-ṇa-sér*, it is to be understood in this way: as to the place (situation), in Banāras; skyid-yul a lucky place, sdug-yul an unlucky one; p̒á-yul fatherland, native country, home; raṅ-yul one's own country, ɣžán-yul a foreign country; ˳bróg-yul country consisting of steppes, róṅ-yul country full of ravines; lha(i)-yul **land of gods,** abode of the lha, also fig., a particularly pleasant country or scenery; mi(i)-yul **abode of men,** (ἡ οἰκουμένη) **the inhabited world, earth,** yet in the Tibetan sense always as opp. to the abodes of good or evil deities; mii yúl-na mi ˴oṅ *Glr.* in the world such a thing is not to be found; rnám-šes dbáṅ-poi yúl-las ˳dás-pa *Wdṅ.* the soul that has left the external world, (yet cf. no. 2); *spyód-yul*, q.v. — 2. **the object or objects of perception by means of the senses**; *ṗyii yul drug* the provinces of the six senses, viz. forms (the external appearances of bodies), sounds etc. *Mil.*; so prob. also: *yúl-rnams-la lóṅs-spyod-par rmóṅs-te Wdṅ.* dead to sensual pleasures; *yul mi ₒdzín-pa*, or *γžán-du ₒdzín-pa Thgy.* to perceive things either not at all, or not correctly; *brǰód-pai yúl-las ₒdás-pa* is stated to imply: exceeding the limits of speech, unspeakable, unutterable; *bsám-byai yúl-las ₒdás-pa = bsám-gyis mi ḱyáb-pa* frq. unimaginable, inconceivable, which term, however, does not seem to be fully adequate; also *Was.* (311) translates *yul* with **object**; cf. *γnas*, 5. — 3. **weather**, or rather in a more gen. sense, **climatic state** of a country, and condition of the beings in it, v. below *yul-ṅán*, *yul-bzáṅ*.

**Comp. and deriv.** *yul-ḱáms* kingdom, e.g. of Nepal, China, *Glr.* — *yul-ₒḱór* country, province *Glr.* — *yul-gru* id. *Glr.* — *yul-dgón* v. above. — *yul-ṅán C.* tempest, *yul-ṅán-gyi ťsúb-ma* the turmoil of the tempest *Glr.*; also public calamities, such as famine, murrain etc, *Glr.* — *yúl-čan* 1. **suited, proper, being in its place, fulfilling its purpose,** *Cs.* (?) 2. **that which is treated 'objectively'** *Was* 311, cf. no. 2 above. — *yúl-čos* characteristic properties, manners etc. of a country. — *yul-ljóṅs* district, tract of country. — **yul tum-túm** *Ld.* the separate villages of a whole cluster bearing one common name. — *yul-sdé* 1. **district** *C.*, *W.* 2. **village magistrate.** — *yúl-pa* **inhabitant, native,** *gaṅ yúl-pa yin* whence are you? what is your country? — **citizen, burgher** *Mil.*; *yúl-pa-rnams* the people, the public *Mil.* — *yúl-po* gen. with *če*, a large country, *Mil.* — *yúl-dpon* village magistrate, district judge. — *yul-ṗyógs* region, neighbourhood *Mil.* — *yúl-ma* a native woman. — *yúl-mi* 1. = *yúl-pa.* 2. **countryman, compatriot** *Do.* — *yul-méd* 1. **improper, not in its place** *Cs.* 2. *ráṅ-snaṅ yul-méd bstán-du γsol Glr.* was explained: what has no place in my mind, what I do not know or understand, I beg you to teach me. — *yúl-ťso* **village, borough,** = *gróṅ-ťso.* — **yul-ťsód-zum-ḱan** *W.* land-surveyor, engineer. — *yul-γžis* v. *γžis.* — *yul-bzáṅ* fair weather *Cs.*, yet cf. *yul-ṅán.* — *yúl-yod-pa = yúl-čan Cs.* — *yúl-len* the mode of forwarding letters from village to village, instead of expediting them in longer and regular stages. — *yul-bšád* geography or topography. — *yul-sá* dwelling-place, habitation *W.* — *yul-srid* government of a country *Schr.* — *yul-sréd = yul-la ₒdód-pa* attachment to one's native place, the love of country and of home, *Mil.*

ཡུལ་བ་ *yúl-ba*, less corr. spelling for *nyúl-ba Tar.*

ཡུས་ *yus* 1. **boasting, bragging, puff,** *yus če don čuṅ Mil.* much bragging, and nothing in it, *yus če šes čuṅ Mil.* one that boasts much, and knows very little; *yus brǰod-pa, byed-pa* to boast *Cs.* — 2. **pride,** *ḱoṅ yus ma če žig* do not take too much pride in your heart *Mil.*; *lás-la byas yus čé-na ṅó-so čuṅ* the more a man is pleased with himself after his deed, the less (real) happiness. — 3. **blame, charge, accusation** *Schr.* (?), false accusation *Sch.* (?), *yus byéd-pa* to charge, accuse *Schr.* — 4. **ardour, fervour, transport,** *dád-pai yús-kyis* in the fervour of devotion, e.g. to shed tears, to fall down on the ground *Pth.* — 5. *yus ₒťúd-pa* to fasten one cord to another, **to knit or join things together** *Sch.*

ཡེ་ *ye*, 1. *Cs.*: '*yé-ma* **beginning and eternity,** *ye-ldán* **eternal'.** This word is known to me only as an adv., **completely, perfectly, highly, quite**; *yé-nas* id.; *ye-dág* quite clean, *ye-rdzógs* quite perfect, *yé-nas bzáṅ-po* altogether good; with a negative following, **not at all,** *ye ma ₒdod* I felt no inclination at all, *ye ma žig-par ₒdug Mil.* he was not hurt at all, *yé-nas mi byed dgos* that is not to be done by any means; *ye-šés* (vulgo *Ld.* **'i-šes**) ज्ञान, the perfect, absolute, heavenly, divine **wisdom**; less frq. resp. *ye-mkyén*; *ye-šés lṅa* the five kinds of divine wisdom, of which, acc. to some, every Buddha is possessed, acc. to others, only Adibuddha; *ye-šés*, in a great measure at least, is inherent to all great saints and divine beings; it will suddenly break forth from the bodies of the terrifying gods in the shape of fire, which puts the demons to flight *Glr.*; *raṅ-byúṅ ye-šés* the self-originated wisdom occasionally is personified in a similar manner, as Wisdom is in the Proverbs of Solomon; in later times this conception coincides in the popular mind also with *stoṅ-pa-nyid.* — 2. provinc. for *yin Glr.* 75. — 3. provinc. for ... *am, ǩyed blá-ma-čan ₒgró-ye Mil.* are you going to the Lama? — 4. in comp. for *ye-šés*, v. *ye-ťig.* — 5. num. figure: 114.

ཡེ་ཤིག་ *ye-ťig Sch.*: **'the trace, line, or manifestation of divine wisdom'.**

ཡེ་དངས་ *ye-dáṅs Bal.* for *nyid-ráṅ*, **you,** the pronoun of polite address.

ཡེ་འབྲོག་ *ye-ₒbróg* a contagious disease *Cs.*; acc. to oral explanation: **injury inflicted on the soul, harm done to the mind,** which may take place in 360 different ways *Mil.* —

ཡེ་རང་ *ye-ráṅ* n. of a city, next to Khobom (Katmandu), the first in Nepal *Mil.*

ཡེ་རེ་ *ye-ré* v. *yér-re-ba.*

ཡེ་ཤུ་ *yé-šu* **Jesus** *Chr. Prot.*

ཡེགས་པ་ *yégs-pa* **rough, shaggy, hairy** *Cs.*

ཡེང་བ་ *yéṅ-ba* v. *γyéṅ-ba.*

ཡེད་པོ་ *yéd-po* provinc. for *yág-po.*

ཡེན་ *yen*, prob. only in *yén-la* joined to *γtóṅ-ba* and synonyms, **to bestow liberally, amply, plentifully;** *zas daṅ spyód-lam yen-la γtad-par bya* food and exercise should be amply provided for *Lt.*

ཡེར་ *yer Lt.* = *γnyid-yer* q.v.

ཡེར་པ་ *yér-pa? ṕyág-tu yér-pa žig mdzád-nas* to raise one's hand with the palm turned upward, as a gesture of (willingly or respectfully) **offering,** *Mil.nt.* (This term might perh. be applied to the 'waving' of the wave-offerings, ordained by the Mosaic law.)

ཡེར་བ་ *yér-ba* **sprinkled, sputtered, spouted**(?) *Sch.*

ཡེར་རེ་བ་ *yér-re-ba* **pure, clear, genuine, unadulterated** *Mil.*; *sṅo ye-ré* a pure blue, *dkar ye-ré* a pure white *C.*

ཡེལ་ཡེལ་ *yel-yél, Pth.* frq., e.g. *mdaṅs yel-yél, sems-dgá yel-yél* **clear, light, bright** or something like it(?).

ཡེས་མེས་ *yes-més* **ancestor** *Sch.*

ཡོ་ *yo* numerical figure: 144.

ཡོ་ག་ *yó-ga Ssk.* = *rnal-ₒbyór*, *yó-gi* = *yo-ga-pa*, *yó-gi-ni* = *yó-ga-ma*; more about this word v. *Williams Ssk. Dict.*

ཡོ་བ་ *yó-ba* 1. adj. and sbst., **oblique, sloping, slanting, awry, crooked; obliquity, slope, slant;** *čuṅ-yó-ba* a little slanting, crooked *Glr.*; *ǩa yo* the mouth awry *S.g.*; *yón-po*, col. **yón-te**, adj., id.; *yo sróṅ-ba, yón-po bsraṅ-ba, Lexx.*, to make the crooked straight; **zám-pa yon-yón čo dug* W.* the bridge is unsteady, swings to and fro; fig. **twisted, distorted, perverted, erroneous;** *yon-dpyad* wrong interpretation, false judgment; going crooked ways, **deceitful, crafty,** and sbst. **crookedness**, deceitful dealings *Cs.*; more frq. *γyo.* — 2. **everything, altogether, whole** (?) *Sch.*

ཡོ་བྱད་ *yo-byád*, **tools, implements, chattels, household furniture, necessaries,** *ₒtsó-bai* necessaries of life; *mčod-pai* requisites for sacrificing; *yo-byád sbyór-ba* to procure the needful, to make preparations *Dzl.*; *yo-byád ťams-čád-kyis* (or *bzáṅ-pos*) *stób-pa Tar.* to provide a person with everything necessary, to fit out well; *yo-byád srél-ba* id. (?) *Sch.*; *yo-byád-kyis ₒbrál-ba* to be in want of the needful; *nor ṕyugs yo-byád* money, cattle, and furniture, as a specification of property.

ཡོ་འབོག་ *yo-ₒbóg Wdṅ.* n. of a tree, which by the Lamas of Sikim is stated to grow in Tibet; *Sch.*: **elm,** and in another place: *rii yo-ₒbóg* **linden-tree,** less prob.

ཡོག་ *yog* 1. col. but also sometimes in *B.*, for *ₒog* **below, down stairs,** *yog-ǩáṅ* **ground-floor; cellar.** — 2. v. *γyóg-pa.*

ཡོག་པོ་ *yóg-po* 1. *Sch. yóg-mo, W. yóg-šiṅ,* **pole** or **stick for stirring the fire, poker** *Mil. nt.* — 2. v. *γyóg-po.*

ཡོག་གཅིན་ *yóg-γčin* one that is wetting his bed *Sch.*

ཡོང་བ་ *yóṅ-ba*, pf. *yoṅs*, used throughout Tibet (except in Balti, where they say *'*ón-čas*'*); not unfrq. also in later literature, for *˛óṅ-ba* **to come;** *Sch.* has also *yoṅ-čad (-ṫsad?)* time and place of coming, and *yoṅ-yé* ever before, at all times (?).

ཡོངས་ *yoṅs*, **all, whole,** *mgo-nág yóṅs-kyi rje Glr.* lord of all the black-haired (i.e. of all men); *yoṅs-˳du-˳ṫsal-gyi p̔o-bráṅ Mil.* the palace in which all wish to meet, ni f.; *yóṅs-su* adv. **wholly, completely, altogether,** *yóṅs-su dág-pa* quite clean, *yóṅs-su spáṅ-ba* to give up entirely; *yóṅs-su bslád-de* quite lost in perverseness; **generally, universally,** *žes yóṅs-su grágs-so Glr.* so he was universally called; *yóṅs-grágs-kyi bu čen bži Mil. nt.*, four disciples, followers, of universal fame; *sdug-bsṅál-las yóṅs-su ma gról-la Stg.*, seems to mean: he is not yet quite delivered; cf. however *yé-nas* with a negative. — *yoṅs-grúb* **the absolute**, what is independent and complete in itself *Was.* (202). —

ཡོད་པ་ *yód-pa*, resp. and eleg. *mčis-pa* 1. **to be,** = *yin-pa, sgyu yod Dzl.* it is deceit, humbug; often with the termin., like *˳dúg-pa, dúd-pa ltá-bur yod Glr.* it is smoke-coloured; *šin-tu mṫún-par yod ˳dúg-pas Glr.* as they are very intimate with each other; with a participle joined to it (or a gerund, vulgo, esp. in *W.*), *gró-ba yod* **it is becoming, growing, getting** *Pth.; šár-p̔yogs-su bstán-pa yod* it is pointing towards the east, *stsál-nas yod* he gives, has given; *brtsig-nas yod* he is building, he was building; **léb(s)-te yod* W.* he is (has) come; with a root often pleon.: *ṅas bšags yod k̔yod-kyis k̔ol čig Mil.* I have been splitting (the tree), do you carry it away now; *ṅan čén-po byas yod Glr.* he has been committing a great evil; *soṅ yód-pas Pth.* as he was gone. — 2. **to be in a certain place,** *der rdziṅ-bu žig yód-pai náṅ-na Dzl.* in a pond which is in that place; *ṅai yúl-mi-las bú-mo yód-pa-rnam Dzl.* the girls that are among my subjects; **de náṅ-na yód-k̔an ṫsáṅ-ma* W.* all that is in it; *yód-sa*, pop. for *gáṅ-na-ba*, place of abode. — 3. **to exist, to be on hand,** *bdé-ba yod ma yin Pth.* no happiness exists; *čúṅ-zad yod kyaṅ srid-kyis Dzl.* as possibly a little might still be on hand; *'é yod* is, or are there (even now)? *Glr.; snáṅ-ba yód-pai dús-su Thgy.* whilst there is day-light. — 4. with genit. or dat. for **to have** (like the Latin *est mihi* I have): *sú-la-˛aṅ yod ma yin Pth.* nobody has . . .; *rgyál-po-la ˳dód-pa čén-po yód-par ˳dug* the king seems to have yet a great wish; *rgyál-moi γyóg-mo žig yód-pa de Pth.* a maid-servant whom the queen had; so in a like manner without a case: *gri žig yód-pa de Mil.* the knife which he had about (him); *yód-pa Thgy.* the things which one has, τὰ ὑπάρχοντα; *k̔rón-pa ˳dom bču-dgu yód-pa Glr.* a well having a depth of 19 fathoms. — 5. *yód-par ˳gyur* a. fut. of *yód-pa* **shall or will be.** b. **to originate, appear,** *bsáṅs-pai šúl-du da-rúṅ yaṅ yód-par gyúr-nas Dzl.* as in the place of (the gold-pieces) that were taken away, always new ones appeared. c. **to get, receive,** *k̔ri γdugs kyaṅ yód-par gyur čig Dzl.* the throne should also receive a canopy! *yód-par byéd-pa* **to beget, produce, effect,** frq., *bu yód-par gyis šig Dzl.* get her a child!

**Comp.** *Cs.: yod-pa-nyid* existence, *yod-min-nyid* non-existence; *Sch.: yod-ṫáṅ* 'thoroughly clear'; *yod-ṫsód yin* 'it has the semblance of being' (?); *yod-med* a. being and not being, *yod-méd go-bzlóg snaṅ* optical illusions, when one imagines to see what is not existing, or the reverse. b. in *W. yod* is also used merely to give force to *med*, as **yod med** there is not at all . . .

ཡོན་ *yon* 1. **gift, offering,** of free will, to priests and mendicant friars, frq., *zás-yon* a gift consisting in food, *yon ˳búl-ba* to bestow a gift, to bring an offering; *yón-du ˳búl-ba* to present as a gift; **fee,** *smán-yon* physician's fee *Cs.; yon sṅó-ba* to bless the gift received, to return a blessing for it. — 2. = *yon-tan.*

**Comp.** *yon-mčód* 1. = *yón-bdag Glr.* 2. for *yón-bdag daṅ mčód-γnas Mil.* dispenser (of gifts) and priest. — *yón-bdag* vulgo and in more recent literature for the *sbyín-bgag* of earlier writings, **dispenser of gifts, entertainer, host**, in point of fact identic with **house-owner, citizen, farmer,** and also at the present time used in that sense without any religious bearing; it is also the title generally used by mendicant friars in their addresses, something like 'your honour'. — *yón-γnas* the receiver of a gift *Cs.*

ཡོན་ཏན་ *yón-tan* गुण (opp. to *skyon*) 1. **good quality, excellence, valuable properties,** e.g. the medicinal virtues of plants; also **acquirements, accomplishments, attainments,** *yón-tan slób-pa* to learn something useful *Pth.* and vulgo; *ˏdi bui yóṅ-tan yin Dzl.* for that you are indebted to the boy, this is the boy's merit; **property, quality,** in gen., e.g. the different tastes and effects of medicines *Med.*; also mystic or fantastic properties *Glr.* — *bdag blus kyaṅ yón-tan med Glr.*, even if one would ransom me, it would be to no purpose, not worth while; *ˏdód(-pai) yón(-tan)* v. *ˏdód-pa*; *p̔an-yon* v. *p̔án-pa*. — 2. num.: 3.

ཡོན་པོ་ *yón-p* v. *yó-ba.*

ཡོབ་, འོབ་ *yob, ˏob,* **stirrup** *Cs.*; *yob-góṅ* instep of the foot *Cs.*; *yob-lčágs* 'the iron of the stirrup' *Cs.*; *yob-čén = yob Cs.*; *yob-t̔ág* stirrup-leather *Cs.*, *yob-mt̔il* the footing, *yob-lúṅ* (*Sch. yob-lóṅ*) the hoop of the stirrup.

ཡོབ་པ་ *yób-pa* v. *γyób-pa.*

ཡོམ་པ་ *yóm-pa Cs.* vb., adj. sbst., **to swing, totter, tremble, to be unsteady; swinging etc., the swinging etc.;** *yóm-po,* adj., *yom-yóm Pth.*, *yóm-me-ba Mil.* id.

ཡོར་པོ་ *yór-po* 1. **dull, heavy, blunt** *Cs.*; *Tar.*: *yór-yor-ba*; but the expressions *t̔om-yór* shaking, tottering, trembling, like an old man *Mil.*, and *mig-yór* mirage, seem to indicate that the proper signification is **trembling.** — 2. **oblique, slanting,** *C.*

ཡོལ་གོ་, ཡོལ་མ་ *yól-go, yól-ma* **earthenware, crockery** *Schr.*, *Cs.*, *dkar-yól* **china-ware, porcelain,** frq.; *yol-gór* **cup, bowl,** *Sch.*

ཡོལ་བ་ *yól-ba* I. sbst. **curtain,** *yól-bas ˏbré-ba Glr.* to stretch a curtain over; *yól-ba t̔en-pa Glr.* to draw a curtain; *yól-ba γčod-pa* to close the curtain (of a door), *yól-ba ˏbyéd-pa* to open it *Cs.*; *dar-yól* silk-curtain, *ras-yól* calico-curtain; *sgo-yól* curtain before a door. — II. vb. 1. **to be past,** *nyi-ma-p̔yed yol* mid-day is past, it is afternoon (about 2 o'cl.) *Wdk.* (v. *nyin-žág*); *srod yol soṅ* the evening-twilight is gone, it is complete night (about 11 o'cl.) *C.*; *nyi-ma yól-la k̔ad* day is almost over, evening is drawing on, *Dzl.* ༡༢, 6; *dús-las yól-ba* **to be past,** both impers., it is past, it is over, and pers., he is past his prime, old, decrepit *Dzl.*; *rluṅ daṅ čar dús-las mi yól-bas* wind and rain setting in and ceasing at the proper time *Dzl.* — 2. also *γyól-ba C.*, *dbyól-ba*, *ˏbyól-ba* **to evade, shun, to go not to a place,** *mig yól-ba* to look away; **lẹ-yol čém-po yin** he is very shy of work, averse to labour *C.*

ཡོས་ *yos,* 1. **slightly roasted corn,** mostly barley or wheat, which on account of its transportability is generally taken by travellers along with them, as their fare on the road; fresh prepared it is much relished by the people; *ˏbrás-yos* rice, thus prepared *S.g.* — 2. **hare,** but only as an astronomical term, *yós-lo* the hare-year.

གཡག་ *γyag,* चमर, **the yak,** Bos grunniens (reckoned by the Hindu among the antilopes), fem. v. *ˏbrí-mo*; *p̔o-γyág* male yak; *p̔a-γyág* uncastrated yak-bull; *γyag-rú* horn of a yak, also n. of a plant, Morina *Ld.*; *γyag-rog-žol-čén* a very long-haired, shaggy yak *Sch.*

གཡང་ *γyaṅ* 1. *Ssk.* श्री, synon. *dpal,* **happiness, blessing, prosperity,** *γyaṅ čágs* blessing comes (from), grows (out of), nif. *Mil.*; *šor* it departs, it is gone; *γyaṅ-skyób*, *γyaṅ-ˏgúgs Schl.* 263, **yaṅ-k̔úg* W.* a calling forth of blessing, sacrifices and other ceremonies performed, in order to secure happiness and prosperity. — *γyaṅ-skár* **propitious stars** or **aspects**; the lunar mansions no. ༦

to ꣿ v. *rgyu-skár*. — *γyaṅ-ḱúg* **beggar's bag** of the Lamas. — *γyáṅ-čan* **happy, blessed, prosperous,** *γyaṅ-méd* the contrary. — *γyaṅ-yig* a written benediction *Glr.* — *γyaṅ-lhá* a deity of the Shamans, dispensing happiness *Sch.* — 2. **gulf, abyss,** gen. *γyáṅ-sa* also *γyaṅ-γzán; ǰi-tsam mťo bžin γyáṅ-sa če* so high as you stand, so deep is the gulf; *lus γyáṅ-du γtóṅ-ba* to plunge, to precipitate one's self *Dzl.*; *γyáṅ-du* or *γyáṅ-la ltúṅ-ba* to fall down *Dzl.*; *mčóṅ-ba* to leap *Glr.*; *ṅán-soṅ-gi γyáṅ-la ˳ḱor Pth.* he totters on the brink of the abyss of hell; *γyáṅ-sa-las ˳dzin-pa* to snatch from the abyss, to save *Thgy.*; *brag-γyaṅ-γzár* rocky precipice *Mṅg.*

གཡང་ཏི་ *γyaṅ-ṭi Sch.*: 'the precious stone chas'.

གཡང་ཚེ་ *γyaṅ-tsé Mil.* nt., *C.* a bowl or cup of clay or wood.

གཡང་ལུགས་ *γyaṅ-lúgs C.* also *yaṅ-lús,* = *γzán-gos* **skin** of an animal, used for clothing; *Mil.* also fig.: *bzód-pai γyaṅ-lúgs gyon* he wrapped himself in the mantle of patience; *γyaṅ-γži Lex.* अजिन, skin of an antilope, the customary couch of the members of religious orders; also **skin, couch, covering,** in general *Pth.*

གཡན་པ་ *γyán-pa Lexx.* w.e. *Sch.*: a cutaneous eruption, akin to the itch, which is said to invade any part of the body, and to be combined with a copious discharge of matter; hereditary, and not contagious.

གཡབ་ *γyab, γyáb-pa, γyáb-mo* v. *yab* etc.

གཡམ་ *γyam Sch.*: 'the following a good or bad example, with the respective consequences(?)'.

གཡམ་པ་ *γyám-pa Sch.*: 'a certain stone'; **yam-ṕáṅ** *W.* **a slab of slate, roof-slate,** for *γya-spáṅ.*

གཡའ་ *γya* 1. **rust,** incorr. verdigris; *lčags-gyá* id.; *lčags gya čags Lt.* iron rusts; **ya ḱor,* or *ǰuṅ,* or *yoṅ** *W.* id.; **ya čád-če** *W.* to scrape the rust off (from metals), to clean, polish; *γya-dág-pa* freed from rust, clear, polished, e.g. a mirror; *γyá-pa* **rusty** *Sch.*; fig. for **infection, contamination** *Mil.*; *γya ˳drúl-ba* to be mouldy *Sch.* or more corr. **to get rusty,** to get covered with foul extraneous matter; *lčé-la γya-˳drúl byed Lt.* the tongue gets furred. — 2. also *γyá-ma,* vulgo **yá-máṅ**, **slate, slab of slate;** *γya-spáṅ* 1. id. 2. *Cs.* also **oil of vitriol, sulphuric-acid**(?) 3. in *C.* **verdigris;** *γya-tíg* 1. **a line drawn with a slate-** or **lead-pencil.** 2. **slate-pencil, lead-pencil,** also *γya-smyúg.* 3. **bolt, bar,** *γya rgáb-pa* to bolt, to bar, *γya ṕyé-ba* to unbolt, to unbar; *γyá-šir* = *γya*; **˳dzín-ya** *C.* pin. — 4. v. *γyá-ba.*

གཡའ་ཀྱི་མ་ *γyá-kyi-ma Lt.* n. of a plant, in *Lh.* a small high-alpine Saussurea.

གཡའ་བ་ *γyá-ba* 1. **to shrink, to start up,** in consequence of a sudden irritation, tickling etc., **to shudder,** *skyi-γya-ba* id. *Mil.*; *W.*: **ya čúg-če** to cause to shrink or start, **to tickle,** *Cs.* also: *γyá-ba* **to feel a horror.** — 2. **to itch,** *dei lus γyá-bas Dzl.* because he felt an itching.

གཡའ་ཡ་ *γyá-ya C.* **yá-ya** **yes!** in speaking to inferiors.

གཡའ་ལི་ *γyá-li* **maple** *Sik.*; the dried leaves of it are said to be boiled by the poor instead of tea.

གཡར་དམ་ *γyar-dám Lex.*, **oath**(?) *Sch.*

གཡར་བ་ *γyár-ba* **to borrow, to lend; to hire;** with reference to money, only provinc. (*Lh., Ts.*); *ṕo-braṅ-nas már-me γyár-te Glr.* having borrowed a lamp in the castle; *γnas-tsáṅ γyár-ba Tar., C.,* **ḍáṅ-sa yár-če** *W.* with *la,* **to ask for reception,** night-quarters; *ḱáṅ-pa γyár-mḱan* **lessee, tenant, lodger;** *γyar byed-pa* = *γyár-ba Sch.*; **ṕan-yár čo-če** *W.* to succour a person by an advance of money; *ṕa-γyár* **step-father,** *ma-γyár* **step-mother,** *bu-γyár* **adopted child;** *γyár-po* **credit** for what has been lent, advanced; **yár-po táṅ-če** *W.* to lend, a thing, *Schr.* to let, lodgings.

གཡར་ཚུས་ *γyar-tsus* **food, nourishment, victuals** *Sch.*

གཡས་པ་ *γyás-pa* **right,** *γyás-ma* the right hand, *γyás-na* on the right (hand), *γyás-su* to the right, *γyás-nas* from the right;

*mig-γyás* the right eye, *lag-γyás* the right hand, *rkaṅ-γyás* the right foot; *γyas-ṅos, -p̔yógs, -lógs* the right (hand) side: *γyas-γyón* right and left; *γyas-γyón-la ltá-ba* to look all round; *γyas-rú* 1. the right wing. 2. p.n., district in *Ts.*; **Yē-ru tsáṅ-po** n. of the principal river in Tibet v. *tsáṅ-po.*

གཡི་, དབྱི་ *γyi, dbyi* **lynx** (*Cs.* erron. ermine).

གཡིག(ས)་པ་ *γyig(s)-pa* **to be hindered** *Cs.*; *Lex.*: *γyér-mas γyigs-pa?*

གཡུ་ *γyu* **turkois,** *mdún-γyu* the front-turkois in the head-dress of females; *p̔rá-γyu* little turkois-stones; *γyui* frq. for turkois-blue; **yu-dán** *W.* the ribbon on which the turkois-stones of the head-dress are fastened; *γyu-mts̔ó* a blue-glittering lake, po. *Mil.*; **yu-žún-men-tog** forget-me-not *Sp*; *γyu-rál* a mane of turkois-colour *Glr.* — *γyu-rúṅ* for *γyuṅ-druṅ Glr.*

གཡུག་པ་ *γyúg-pa,* incorr. spelling for *dbyúg-pa.* —

གཡུང་དྲུང་ *γyuṅ-drúṅ,* स्वस्तिका (also *γža-γsaṅ*), **the cross cramponee** 卍, the principal symbol of the Bonpos, but also much in favour in Buddhist mysticism and popular superstition; *γyuṅ-drúṅ-pa* = *bón-po*; *γyuṅ-drúṅ dgón-pa* the Buddhist monastery Lama Yurru in Ladak, v. Cunningham.

གཡུང་བ་ *γyúṅ-ba* **tame,** opp. to *rgod.*

གཡུང་མོ་ *γyúṅ-mo* (*Lex.* डिम्बिका, **a libidinous woman**), *Cs.*: 'a woman having always the menses'.

གཡུར་ *γyur* 1. **sleep** *Sch.* — 2. v. *γyul-k̔a.*

གཡུར་བ་ *γyúr-ba Lex., C.* also **yór-ba** **to droop, to hang or sink down,** of fading flowers etc.; *γyur zá-ba Lex.* w.e.; *Sch.*: what has become ripe and eatable.

གཡུལ་ *γyul Schr.*: **army;** *Cs.*: **battle;** neither of the two meanings appears to be quite exact (cf. *dmag*); prob. both *γyul* and *γyul-ṅó* denote an army facing the enemy and ready for battle; *γyúl-las rgyál-ba* and *p̔ám-pa* to conquer and to be conquered frq.; *γyul ˳gyéd-pa Do., spród-pa Do., Pth., ˳t̔áb-pa* to fight, strive, struggle, *daṅ* with; *γyúl-du* or *γyul-ṅor žúgs-pa* to go to battle *Do.*; *γyul s̀óm-pa* to prepare for battle *Lex.*; *dug lṅai γyúl-ṅo zlóg-pa* to repulse the warlike host of the five poisons *Mil.*

གཡུལ་ཁ་, གཡུལ་འཐག *γyul-k̔a, γyul-˳t̔ag* **thrashing-floor;** both these words appear to be not everywhere current, but provinc., cf. *k̔o-γyu*; *γyul-k̔a γc̀óg-pa Sch.*, **yur ǰhé-pa** *C.* **to thrash.**

གཡེང་བ་ *γyéṅ-ba,* less frq. *yéṅ-ba,* pf. (*γ*)*yeṅs,* **to move a thing softly to and fro,** e.g. an infant on one's arms, to lull it to sleep *Thgy.*; esp. with reference to the water: *č̔us γyeṅs-te* moved by the waves to and fro *Dzl.*; fig. to run to and fro, like a hunted hare *Ma.*; **to stream into, to overflow,** *yul-k̔áms-su* a country, to inundate it, of floods, hostile armies etc *Ma.*; **to rummage, turn over,** *dpé-rnams* books *Mil.* — 2. **to turn off the attention, to disturb the mind,** *rgyál-po spyan γyéṅs-pa daṅ Glr.* the king looking away, directing his attention to something else; *sems bdud-kyis γyeṅs Mil.* the soul is disturbed by the devil; *č̔os ˳dód-pa-rnams γyéṅs-par byéd-pa Thgy.* to put out or confound those that are seeking religion; *ma-γyéṅs-par nyón c̀ig* now be all attention! *γyéṅ-ba, γyéṅs-pa* sbst., **inattention, wandering, absence of mind,** *γyéṅs-su ˳ǰúg-pa Thgr.* to give one's self to inattention; adj. *rnám-par γyéṅs-pa* very absent, wandering; *rnám-par mi-γyéṅ-ba* or *-γyéṅs-pa* quite attentive, not to be disturbed by anything, inexcitable, a character in which Buddha excels, and which every one of his followers must strive to attain. — 3. sbst. *γyéṅs-pa* **diversion, pleasure, recreation,** **yáṅ(s)-pa-la č̔á-c̀e**, resp. **t̔ug-yáṅ(s)-la (s)kyód-c̀e** *W.* to take a walk, **yáṅ(s)-pa sé-c̀e** *W.* to be playful, like children, kittens etc.; **jest, joke,** **yáṅ-pa man, don-dám yin** *W.* I am not joking, I am serious; **yáṅ(s)-pa-c̀an** *W.* jester, buffoon; *yéṅs-˳dod-kyi k̔a-k̔rám ma yin Mil.*, these are no falsehoods spoken in jest. — *γyéṅs-ma,* a wanton female, prostitute *Sch.*

གཡེན་ *γyen? γyen-sbyór-ba S.g.* **to calumniate** ni f.

གཡེམ་པ་ γyém-pa, *Lex.* **मिथ्याचर्या, being untrue** in one's dealings, acting **wrongfully,** which also my referees confirmed to be the general import of the word; in books, however, it is usually joined to *ₒdód-pas*, or *ₒdód-pa-la*, adding *lóg-par*, as: *ₒdód-pa-la lóg-par γyém-pa*, or it stands alone as in *γyém byéd-pa*, signifying **'to commit adultery, fornication'** *Dzl.* and elsewh.; *log-γyém* sbst. —

གཡེར་ཁ་ *γyér-ḱa* (vulg. **er-ḱa*), **bell, set of bells,** or **peal** *Glr.*

གཡེར་པོ་ *γyér-po* **wise, prudent, circumspect, thorough-going** *Sch.*

གཡེར་བག་ *γyer-bág Lex., Sch.*: **a light, luminous place.**

གཡེར་མ་ *γyér-ma Med.* frq., **Guinea pepper,** *Capsicum W.* **nyér-ma**; *γyer-śiṅ-pa* medicinal herb *S.g.*

གཡེལ་བ་ *γyél-ba* 1. **to be idle, lazy, slothful; idleness, laziness;** *γyel-ba-méd-par* incessantly, continually, e.g. to pray, to guard *Mil., S.O.* — 2. *ṭugs γyél-ba* resp. to forget *W.*

གཡོ་ *γyo* (rarely *yo*) **craft, cunning, deceit,** more frq. *γyo-sgyú, γyo-zól; γyó-čan* crafty, deceitful, *γyo-méd* honest, *γyo byéd-pa* to deceive.

གཡོ་བ་ *γyó-ba* I. vb., pf. and imp. *γyos*, 1. **to move,** to cause to change place; **to be moved,** agitated, shaken, *γnam sa γyós-so* heaven and earth were shaken *Dzl.; des ni sa ₒdi γyo-bar ₒgyur* thereby the earth may be shaken *Do.;* **to bend, incline, tilt,** e.g. a vessel; **zúg-po yos toṅ** *W.* make a bow! *sku γyós-par ₒgyúr-to* the image began to move *Glr.; sa-γyós* earthquake; **to begin to move** or to march *Ma.; tugs-rje γtiṅ-nas γyós-pai rtags* it is a sign that his heart is moved by grace *Mil. nt.*; *dgé-bai p̔yógs-la ₒdu-śés čuṅ-zad kyaṅ ma γyos* he did not [illegible]ow the least virtuous impulses to rise (in [illegible]s heart), he kept down every sense of [illegible]rtue; *γyó-ba* partic., continually moving, [illegible]stless, uneasy, of the mind *Mil., mi-γyó-[illegible]* **unmoved,** immovable, n. of Siva and of [illegible]her terrifying deities *Glr.* (cf. **अचल** *Will.*) - 2. **to prepare,** victuals for the table *γyós-su byéd-pa* id.; *γyós-ḱaṅ* kitchen, bake-house, *γyós-mḱan* baker, cook.

II. sbst. **moveableness, mobility,** *yáṅ-žiṅ γyo-ba-nyid* an easy mobility *Wdṅ.*

གཡོག་ *γyog* (v. *yog, ₒog*) *Tar.* and elsewh., usually occurring in the more definite form *γyóg-po*, **servant, man-servant,** *γyóg-mo* **maid-servant, female servant,** waiting-maid; when distinguished from *ḱól-po, ḱól-mo* and *bran*, it denotes a higher degree, e.g. *γyóg-mo γnyis* two waiting-maids and besides 500 *ḱól-mo* maid-servants *Pth.; γyóg-po daṅ yáṅ-γyog daṅ nyiṅ-γyog* servant, servant's servant, and the servant again of these *Pth.; mii γyog byéd-pa* to be in a person's service, to obey a person; *dpon-γyóg* master (mistress) and domestics, master and attendants, frq.; *nad-γyóg*, a nurse, one that tends sick persons *Dzl.; γyog-ₒḱór* attendants, e.g. *γyog-ₒḱór bču-drúg* attendants and retinue of 16 persons, *ₒḱor daṅ γyog* id.

གཡོག་ནང་ཟན་ *γyog-naṅ-zán* a house-servant *C.* —

གཡོག་པ་ *γyóg-pa*, pf. and imp. *γyogs*, rarely *yóg-pa* 1. **to cover,** *bu gós-kyis γyóg-pa* to cover a child with a garment *Dzl., mgó-la rdzá-ma γyóg-pa* to cover one's head with a pot *Glr.;* also: *rdzá-mai mgó-la drá-bas γyóg-pa* to cover the opening of a pot with a wire grate *Glr.; p̔yii págs-pa γyogs* the external cutaneous covering appears (in the embryo) *S.g.; ri-mgo ḱa-bas γyogs* the hill-tops were covered with snow *Mil.;* **to pour over** or **upon,** to cover in pouring, *ḱrág-gis* with blood *Dzl.;* **to overlay,** with gold *Dzl.;* **to sprinkle over, besprinkle,** **śig-pa-la ṭág** *W.* the wall with blood; **to strew over,** **ḱá-la gog-ṭál** *W.* ashes over the snow. — 2. **to pour away,** to throw away; so *W.;* the people in *W.* understand the words *Dzl.* ༢༩, 6: **ma yógs-pai lhág-ma** the rest which has not been thrown away, whereas others, e.g. the people of Sikkim explain it: the rest that has not been taken possession or care of.

གཡོགས་ *γyogs* 1. **cover, covering,** *mgo-γyógs Lex.* covering for the head, cap; also fig. and po. for self-delusion, self-de-

ཡ

ception (prop.: a veiling of the head) *Mil.*; *steṅ-γyógs, stod-γyógs* upper-garment, mantle, toga, *smad-γyógs* trowsers, breeches *Tar.* — 2. **cover, envelope,** *γyógs-ċan* having a cover.

གཡོད་ *γyod C.* the large intestine, colon.

གཡོན་ཅན་ *γyón-ċan Pth*; *Cs.* = *γyó-ċan* crafty; perh. also **fornicator,** as *γyón-ma*, acc. to *Lex.* and *Sch.*: harlot.

གཡོན་པ་ *γyón-pa* **left,** *γyón-ma* the left hand, *γyón-na* on the left, to the left, *γyón-du* towards the left, *γyón-nas* from the left; *γyón-lógs* the left side or hand, *γyon-lág-byed-pa Pth.* left-handed, *γyon-rú Sch.* the left wing, of an army.

གཡོབ་པ་ *γyób-pa*, pf. *γyobs* **to move about, to swing, brandish,** *γśóg-pa* the wings; *rkaṅ-lág γyób-pa* to kick, to strike, with the arms and legs.

གཡོར་མོ་ *γyór-mo* 1. **sail,** *γyor-yól* id *Cs.*, *γyor-śiṅ* sail-yard *Cs.*, also mast, in a rather obscure description of a ship in *Zam.*, where the sail is called *dar*, cloth. — 2. **wave, billow,** *rgyá-mtsoi Glr.*

Note. Tibetan writers knowing of ships and navigation about as much as a blind man of colours, the obscurity of passages relating to such matters may easily be accounted for.

གཡོར་བ་ *γyór-ba* 1. v. *γyúr-ba*. — 2. v. *γyár-ba*. — 3. v. *yor.*

གཡོལ་བ་ *γyól-ba* v. *yól-ba.*

གཡོས་ *γyos* 1. prov. for *γyas*, in *γyos-skór* circumambulation from left to right (so that the right side is towards the person or object that is reverentially to be saluted) *Wdṅ.* — 2. v. *γyo-ba.*

# ར

ར *ra* 1. the consonant **r**, always pronounced with the tongue. — 2. num. fig.: 25.

ར་ *ra* stands for: 1 *rá-ba*, 2. *rá-ma*, 3. *rá-mda*, 4. *rá-ro.*

རྭ་ *rwa* (cf. *ru*) 1. **horn** *W.* **rá-ċó** id. — 2. **sting** e.g. of the scorpion. — 3. *Sch.*: 'the inward side, the horn-side, of a bow'. — *rwa-ċan* horned. — *rwa-snyiṅ* the pith of a horn *Cs.* — *rwa-myúg* 'the first germ of seed that appears after sowing' *Cs.*; *rwá-rtsa* 'the root or bottom of a horn' *Cs.*, *rwá-rtse* 'the top or point of a horn' *Cs.*, *rwá-tsa S.g.* (?).

ར་གན་ *rá-gan*, in comp. *rag*, **brass,** *rá-gan-gyi búm-pa*, *rag-búm* brass cup, can, vessel, *rag-dúṅ* a brass trumpet; *rag-skyá Sch.*: white-copper, packfong, German silver.

ར་སྒོ་ *rá-sgo* hoof, claw *C.*, *W.*

ར་ཉེ་ *rá-nye*, provinc. for *żá-nye* **lead.**

ར་མཉེ་ *rá-mnye* an officinal root *Med.*, *Sch.*: **carrot.**

ར་ཏི་ *rá-ti Cs.*: 'a small weight, a drachm (60 grains)'; but रत्ती (not to be found in *Will.*) is prob. the Hindi word for रत्तिका, the seed or grain of *Abrus precatorius*, as a weight about = 2 grains.

ར་མདའ་ *rá-mda* **help, assistance** (*Cs.* also: companion, **assistant**), *rá-mda ˳bód-pa* to cry out for help *Glr.*, *rá-mdar sbrón-pa Cs.* to call (upon a person) for assistance, *ra ˳dégs-pa W.* **ram tág-ċe** (cf. *żabs ˳dégs-pa*) **to help,** to assist *Sch.*, *ra ˳drén-pa* id. *Mil. nt.*; *rá-mda-pa* **helper, assistant** *Glr.*; *rá-mdai dpuṅ-tsóg* **auxiliary forces** or army *Cs.*

ར་སྡོང་ *ra-sdóṅ Sch.* **weeping willow.**

ར་སྣ་ *ra-sná* n. of a medicinal herb *Wdn.* 166, = *sgrón-śiṅ* fir-tree.

ར་བ་ *rá-ba* 1. **enclosure, fence, wall,** frq., esp. in *W.*, also the space inclosed by a fence, wall etc., **yard, court-yard, pen, fold** etc.; *rá-bas skór-ba* to inclose with a fence *Stg.*, *rá-čan*(?), *ra-ldán* having an enclosure, fence, wall etc. *Cs.*; *smyúg-mai rá-ba* bamboo-hedge, bamboo-fence, *ťsér-mai rá-ba* thorn-hedge, thorn-fence, *śiṅ-gi rá-ba* wooden fence, fence of boards, pickets or rails *C.*; *rá-mo* id., *ra-mo-čé* a large pen or fold *Mil.* and *C.*; *kun-dga-rá-ba*, *kun-ra*, v. *kun*; *ḱrims-ra* place of execution; *lčáṅ-ra* garden with willow-trees; *nyág-ra*(?) wall of stones put loosely together *Ld.*; *rtá-ra* stable or pen for horses; *rdó-ra* 1. stone-wall. 2. circle of dancers; *ṗág-ra* v. *rags.* — *bá-ra* cow-house, pen for cows; *rtsig-ra Sch.*: wall round a court-yard; *brtsón-ra* v. *brtson*; *lúg-ra* sheepcot, sheepfold; *śiṅ-ra* v. above. — *ra-śúl* the remnants or traces of an old pen. — 2. the first of the three (or two) months of a season, *zla ra-ba.*

ར་མ་ *rá-ma* (rarely *ra Glr.*) **goat, she-goat,** frq. — *ra-kyál* bag made of a goat's skin. — *ra-skyés Tar.*; *Sch.*: a gelded he-goat. — *rá-gu*, col. *ri-gu*, young goat, **kid.** — *ra-rgód* wild goat, = *ra-po-čé Cunningh. Ld.* p. 199. — *ra-ťúg S.g.* and *ṗá-ra* he-goat. — *ra-ťóṅ* 1. a he-goat of two years *C.* 2. a gelded he-goat *W.* — *ra-dó*(?) thread made of goat's hair *W.* — *ra-lpágs* goat's skin. — *ra-ṗó* a gelded he-goat. — *ra-lúg* goats and sheep; *ra-ma-lúg* id., when a particular stress is laid on the impropriety of both species of animals being mixed together; also fig. of improper intermixtures. — *ra-śá* goat's flesh. — *ra-slóg* a coat made of goat's skins.

ར་མེད་ *ra-méd* **infallible,** certain, sure *Sch.*

ར་མོ་ཆེ་ *ra-mo-čé* n. of a plain near Lhasa where the Chinese wife of *Sroṅbtsansgampo* ordered a large Buddhist temple to be built *Glr.*; as a com noun v. sub *rá-ba.*

ར་རི་ *ra-ri Sch.*: *ra-ri-méd-pa* neither high nor low.

ར་རིལ་ *ra-ril* **treddles, dung** of goats.

ར་རེས་ *ra-rés* = *rés-mos*, **skyid dug ra-rés yoṅ dug** *Ld.* good fortune and misfortune come by turns.

ར་རོ་ *rá-ro* 1. **intoxication, drunkenness.** — 2. **intoxicated** *B.* and col.; *Sch.*: *rá-ro dáṅ-po bag-méd-pa*, v. sub *bag* I. *rá-ro ɣnyis-pa glaṅ-po-če smyon-pa daṅ ˳dra* drunkenness while continued resembles a furious elephant, *rá-ro ɣsúm-pa śi-ro ˳dra* the end (of it) resembles a corpse; *ra ži* or *saṅs*, also *ɣdaṅs* (?) *W.* the drunken fit is over; *rá-ro-ba B.*, *C.*, *rá-ro(-čan) W.* intoxicated, drunk, *rá-ro-bar byéd-pa* to make drunk *Dzl.*, *rá-ro-ba-las sáṅs-te* having come to one's self again after a drunken fit, being sober again *Dzl.*

ར་ས་འཕྲུལ་སྣང་ *ra-sa-˳ṗrul-snáṅ* n. of a Buddhist temple erected in Lhasa by the Nepalese wife of *Sroṅbtsansgampo Glr.*

ར་སི་ *rá-si Hind.* **rope,** in *Lh.* **hempen rope,** and as such distinguished from *ťág-pa*, rope made of goat's hair, which is the one most in use in Tibet.

ར་སིད་ *ra-sid* (Pers. رسید), **receipt,** **ra-sid ṭi-ked** money-stamp.

རཱ་ཧུ་ and རཱ་ཧུ་ལ་ *rā-hu* and *rā-hu-la* v. *sgra-ɣčán.*

རཀྟ་ *rakta Ssk.* **blood, saffron, minium, cinnabar** *Mil.*

རག་ *rag* 1. sbst. v. *ra-gán.* — 2. adj. (*Ssk.: adhīna*) subject, subservient, dependent, *rag lás-pa* or *lús-pa B.*, *C.*, *W.*, **rag-ldom-pa** *W.*, with *la*, **to depend on,** *de ḱyód-kyi nús-pa-la rag-lús* that depends on your strength *Mil.*; *dbugs rṅúb-pa sems-la rag-lás-pa yin* breathing depends on the soul *Stg.*; *˳tsó-ba ɣžán-la rag-lás-śiṅ* as they depend on others for their lives *Tar.*; *Bhar.* 22 *ḱyod rgyal-srid byed-la rag-go Schf.*: 'regno operam nava!' — 3. *W.* for *reg, grags, dregs, sbrag*, v. *rag-pa*; *rag-čan W.* for *drégs-pa-čan* **proud,** haughty; for *grágs-čan* **famous; glorious, splendid; angry** (?).

རག་པ་ *rág-pa* 1. vb. *W.* for *rég-pa* **to touch, feel,** and in a more generalized sense

= ₒtsór-ba **to perceive,** to scent, taste, hear, see, e.g. *dáń-mo rag* I feel cold, *dáń-mo rag-ga* do you feel cold? (but *dáń-mo dug* it is cold); *gó-la zug rag* (C. *rig*) my head aches; *tóg-ri rag* I feel hungry, *tóg-ri rág-ga* are you hungry? *ńai miń žód-da rag* I hear my name called; *go kád-da rag* I perceive the door sticks; *'i lúń-po kyér-ra rag* I see, the wind will carry that away; *go pé-te mi rag* the door seems to be locked. — 2. adj. **dark-russet, brownish,** of rocks, horses *W.*

རག་མ་ rág-ma 1. W. adj. to the gerund *rág-te* (sbrág-ste): *be-rág yu-dán* (lit. γdan) *rág-te* a fillet together with a strip set with turkoises. — 2. prop. n. of a village *Mil.*

རག་ཙེ་ rág-tse **stone** in fruits *W.*

རག་ཤ་ rág-ša **a bead of a rosary,** acc. to *Lis.* from रुद्राक्ष Elaeocarpus Janitrus, the berries of which are used for such beads.

རག་ཤི་ rag-ší n. of a country.

རགས་ rags 1. **dam, mole, dike, embankment,** also *ču-rágs, ču-lón* — 2. any construction of a similar shape: *pág-rags* (also *pág-ra*) **intrenchment, breast-work;** *púb-rags* stack, rick; *šiń-rags* stack of wood.

རགས་པ་ rágs-pa **coarse, thick, gross,** *lús-kyi rnám-pa pra-rágs-rnams Wdń.* the more delicate and the coarser component parts of the body; *rags-pai dbáń-du byás-na Wdń.*, reckoning one with another, on an average; **rough,** as in: *rágs-rtsis-su* by a rough estimate *Tar.*; *rágs-pai mi-rtág-pa dań prá-bai mi-rtág-pa* the perishableness of the whole mass and of the single parts *Thgy.*; *yán-lag rágs-pa* prob.: strong, firm limbs *Pth.*; of Buddhas is said that they appear *rágs-pai tsúl-gyis* i.e. **bodily,** or **substantially;** *rags-ris byed-pa Sch.:* to work, mould, form, sketch etc. roughly.

རང་ rań 1. **self** *B.* and col. (*nyid,* with few exceptions, is, in *W.* at least, colloquially not in use) *ńa-ráń kyod-ráń* **I myself, thou thyself** etc., in col. language also = **I, thou** etc.; sometimes the person is only indicated by the context, the pronoun I etc. being omitted; *rań-čag, ráń-rnams* plur.; *ráń-gi* my, thy etc.; *čúń-ma de ráń-gi lús-la čágs-pas* this wife fond of herself, in love with herself *Dzl.* (yet cf. *de-ráń,* below); *des ráń-gi ma yin-par rig-nas* he perceiving that it was his own mother *Pth.; ráń-la ráń-gis skra bčád-de* shaving one's own head *Dzl.*; also in a gen. sense: *ráń-bas ńán-pa* an inferior person than one's self *Thgy.*, in like manner: *ráń-las čé-ba Thgr.*; *ráń-la bu méd-na* if a man has no son of his own *Mil.*; *ráń-gi srúń-ba* to keep, to guard one's own property *Thgy.*; *rań mi-ₒdód-pe kyen tsáń-ma* C. all the disagreeable things that fall to one's lot; in compounds: *rań-séms* one's own soul (opp. to *γžan-lús*) *Mil.*; v. also *ₒdré-ba* extr.; *rań-rig rań-γsal rań-bde γsum* self-created knowledge, clearness, and happiness (the three fruits of the spirit) *Mil.*; *rań-sróg ráń-gis γčod* you will take your own life *Glr.* — 2. **spontaneously, of one's own accord,** *žal-zás rań-ₒóń-ńo Dzl.*; *ráń-byon-pa, ráń-byuń-ba* originated of itself, v. below; *rań ₒgról-ba* 1. to get loose, come loose of itself. 2. to become clear or intelligible spontaneously, by intuition. 3. to save one's self; *ráń-šar-ba* = *ráń-ₒgrol-ba* 2. — 3. **just, exactly, precisely, the very,** *de ráń* the very same; *de rań yin* so it is! exactly so! just so! *dhá-ta rań* C., *dá-či rań, dág-sa rań* W. just-now, *di-riń rań* just to-day *W.*; **already,** *sńá-mo rań* already early in the morning *Mil.*; **barely, merely, the mere, the very,** *ńa dań prád-pa ráń-gis* by the mere meeting with me *Mil.*; *mi rań* a person travelling all alone, i.e. without baggage, horse or companion *Kun.*; *mo-ráń* v. *mo.* — **really, indeed, actually, truly** (the verb being repeated): *mi-la-rás-pa de yin rań yín-nam?* art thou really that same Milaraspa? *yoń rań yoń-gyu yin* C. he will truly or certainly come; **even,** *sdáń-po rań byas* now they even hated him *Mil.*

**Comp.** *rań-skal* a person's own share. — *rań skyu* (?) *túb-pa Sch.:* to act after one's own mind. — *rań-skyur* vinegar *Cs.*(?)

— raṅ-ka Sch. = ráṅ-bu? — raṅ-kóṅs = raṅ-kúl territory, district C. (?) — raṅ-ₒkós one's own worth, affairs, necessities Sch. — raṅ-grub not made or produced by men, **self-produced.** — ráṅ-dga-ba **free, independent,** ráṅ-dga-pa an unmarried man Sch. — raṅ-rgyál 1. Stg.: = raṅ-saṅs-rgyás. 2. raṅ-rgyál-gyis ₒgró-ba Sch.: to live after one's own option or pleasure (?) — raṅ-rgyú Sch.: 'die eigene Ursache, Selbstfolge' (?!) — raṅ-ṅó one's own nature, šes-pa to know Mil. — raṅ-nyid himself, herself etc., one's self Mil., raṅ-nyid ₒgról-ba to deliver one's self Thgy., bdud raṅ-nyid the devil himself in his own person Tar. — raṅ-ₒtág **mill, water-mill.** — raṅ-mtóṅ **pride,** self-complacency, self-sufficiency Mil., Glr. — raṅ-dón one's own affairs, one's own profit, raṅ-dón byéd-pa to look to one's own advantage Do., raṅ-ₒdód **selfishness,** v. raṅ-rtsis. — raṅ-snáṅ v. sub snáṅ-ba; Sch. also: self-born. — raṅ-po Cs. = po-raṅ an unmarried man. — raṅ-bábs v. babs. — ráṅ-bu 1. Cs. single, alone, ráṅ-bur adv. singly, alone, without a consort. 2. Cs.: a single life (?). 3. Schr.: one's own child. — raṅ-byúṅ, raṅ-byón self-born, having originated of itself, = raṅ-grúb frq. raṅ-dbaṅ **independence, liberty,** raṅ-dbáṅ tób-pa to become free Glr.; γnás-la raṅ-dbaṅ-méd they are not master of the place i.e. they are not free to choose the place Thgy., in the same sense, gar skye raṅ-dbaṅ-med Mil.; *raṅ-wáṅ ₒǰúg-pa* to set free C.; raṅ-dbáṅ-čan **free** W. — raṅ-ₒbar Cs.: **'musket',** in W. it is only used for **pistol;** *raṅ-bár ḍug-rág* W. **a revolver.** — ráṅ-mo Cs. = mo-ráṅ an unmarried woman. — raṅ-rtsis the opinion which one has of one's self, raṅ-rtsis daṅ raṅ-ₒdód ma če žig think little of your own self! Mil. — raṅ-bžín, स्वभाव, natural **disposition,** state or **constitution, nature, temper,** raṅ-bžin-las γžán-du ₒgyúr-ba to change one's natural constitution Wdṅ., ₒbab dé-ltar čé-bai raṅ-bžin-gyis as a natural consequence of so heavy a snow-fall Mil.; raṅ-bžin-gyis **of itself, by itself,** from its very nature, **naturally, spontaneously** Dzl., in col. language, raṅ-bžin-nas id., also for **self** in the sense: I, he etc. without the **aid and** independently of others; ₒbyúṅ-ba lṅai raṅ-bžin-čan-gyi lus ₒdi this body participating of the nature of the five elements Wdṅ.; draṅ-poi raṅ-bžin-čan-gyi pýir for raṅ-bžín-čan yín-pai pýir Sbh. — *raṅ-žín ǰǒ-pa* C. needless words, where it is a matter of course; also: talk without any serious intent; *de da raṅ-žín-la zér-če žig yod* W. that is nothing but talk. — raṅ-bzó. 1. Lex.: the right, proper form (of a word)? 2. self-determination, opp. to a punctilious adhering to tradition Mil. — raṅ-raṅ **each ... himself, each ... his,** her, its etc. (not reciprocally, as Sch. has it), raṅ-ráṅ-gi krii ₒóg-tu sbas he buried each (idol) under its own seat Glr., raṅ-ráṅ-gi leur γsal each (subject) will be explained in its own chapter Lt. — raṅ-raṅ-lao each (final consonant) has itself (joined), i.e. is doubled Gram. — raṅ-ré 1. = raṅ-ráṅ: raṅ-réi sna-tág raṅ-rés zuṅ each may lead himself, may be his own guide. 2. **we,** raṅ-réi sgo drúṅ-na at our own door Mil., raṅ-ré-rnams we (the Lamas, opp. to the laymen) Mil. 3. polite way of addressing, for our **you** or the German 'Sie' Thgr.? — raṅ-šúgs-la **of itself,** spontaneously W. — ráṅ-sa, ráṅ-so one's own place, ráṅ-sa ₒdzín-pa to maintain one's place, one's station Mil., prob. like ráṅ-mgo ₒtón-pa; ráṅ-sar, ráṅ-sor 1. bžág-pa to put (a thing) in its place, fig. for: to leave undecided, to let the matter alone, ni f. Mil. 2. of itself, e.g. ráṅ-sor ži (a storm) abates of itself. — raṅ-saṅs-rgyas Pratyekabuddha, i.e. a Buddha who has obtained his Buddhaship alone by his own exercises of penance, but who does not promote the welfare of other beings.

རང་ག་བ་ ráṅ-ga-ba Cs. **coarseness, meanness.**

རང་བ་ ráṅ-ba, pf. raṅs, **to rejoice,** sems mi-ráṅs-par **discontented,** yid-ráṅ-ba or yi-ráṅ-ba id., frq.; *dhé-la ga-ráṅ-ḍhág-te* highly pleased with it C.; yid ma ráṅs-šiṅ mi mgú-bar gyúr-te being very much dissatisfied Stg.; ma-ráṅ-bžin-du unwillingly, reluctantly.

རང་རོང་ཅན་ *raṅ-roṅ-čan Cs.* **rough, craggy,** uneven.

རངས་པ་ *raṅs-pa* 1. v. *raṅ-ba.* — 2. *nyin-ráṅs-par* for *to-ráṅs-kyi dús-su* early in the morning *Tar.* 111, 17. — 3. in *W.* for *réṅs-pa.*

རངས་པོ་ *ráṅs-po Sch.* **rough, rude, unpolished.**

རད་པ་ *rád-pa W.* for *bgrád-pa.*

རད་རོད་ *rad-ród* v. *ród-po.*

རན་ད་ *rán-da* (*Pers.* رنده, رندا) **a plane** *Ld.*

རན་པ་ *rán-pa* 1. vb. and adj. to keep, or keeping, the proper mean, **to be proportionate, just right,** adv. *rán-par* **moderately,** *rán-par sro* warm yourself moderately (tolerably) *Lt.*, *zas-tsód rán-par zá-ba* to eat moderately *S.g.*; *ₒdi-tsam ni rán-no* this is about the proper measure *Dzl.*; with the root of the vb.: *žiṅ rṅá-ran-nas* as it was (the proper) time for harvest *Dzl.*, *ₒgro-ran* it is time to go *Pth.*, *ši ma rán-par ši-ba* to die an untimely death; *bág-mar γtaṅ-rán-pa daṅ* when it was time to give her in marriage *Dzl.*; not so often with a sbst.: *rtsás-ma rán-tsa-na* when harvest-time had come *Mil.* — 2. *rtsa rán-pa C.* **shave-grass,** *Equisetum arvense.* — 3. col. for *ₒdrén-pa* **to lead** (water); for *bran-pa* v. *tags.*

རབ་ *rab* I. **superior, excellent**; the eldest, of three sons, opp. to *briṅ-po* and *ta-čuṅ,* frq.; *gaṅ-zág dbaṅ-po-ráb-rnams* very able or clever persons (opp. to *ₒbriṅ-po* or *tá-ma* having moderate or very little capacity) *Mil., Thgr.*, inst. of which *rab ₒbriṅ γsum* is often used *Thgy.*; *tébs-na rab* if rightly understood, that will be the best *Thgr.*, frq. for: so it is right, that will do; **much, plentiful,** *rab-skrái ˏóg-nas* also with a full head of hair (you may be a holy man) *Mil.*; *ráb-tu* adv. **very,** with adjectives and verbs, *ráb-tu sdoms* lock (the door) well *Dzl.*; *ráb-tu krós-par gyúr-te Tar.*; it occurs also in the following phrases: *ráb-tu ₒbyin-pa* to receive or admit into a religious order, *ráb-tu ₒbyúṅ-ba* to enter into a religious community, to take orders, *slób-dpon čos-ₒbaṅs-las* being with, or being ordained by the teacher Chosbangs; *rgyál-poi rigs-las* (to take orders) as a descendant of the royal family, of the caste of noblemen *Tar.*; *ráb-(tu) byúṅ(-ba)* he that has taken orders, **a** novice, or in gen.: **a clerical person;** *rab-byúṅ* is also the name of the first year of the cycle of sixty years; *rab-(tu) γnás(-par) byéd-pa, mdzád-pa* c. acc. or *la*, prop. 'to make firm or permanent', **to consecrate, to hallow,** a new house, esp. a temple, an idol; by this act a house is secured against accidents, and an idol is supposed to acquire life and to become the abode of the respective deity, which occasionally manifests itself by sundry miracles *Glr.*; *ráb-tu ₒbyéd-pa* (also erron. *byéd-pa*) *Cs.* to analyze, but *Tar.* 96 it is equivalent to प्रकरण treatise, dissertation. *rab-ₒbyáms-pa* v. *ₒbyáms-pa*; *rab-ˏóg* the second in rank, next in value, excellence etc., thus *Dzl.* ༧༢༨, 5 (as a better reading for *ₒbriṅ-mo*); *rab-yáṅs* very wide, very extensive *Sch.*; *rab-γsál* 1. very clear, quite evident. 2. sbst. a small **balcony** or **gallery,** frequently seen in Tibetan houses. 3. *Sch.* history (?).

II. also *rabs,* **ford,** *rab-méd* without a ford, *rab-só = rabs Sch.*

རབ་རིབ་ *rab-rib*, col. also *hrab-hrib,* **mist, dimness,** e. g. before the eyes, in consequence of impaired vision; **ko šrab-šrib mán-na mi toṅ** he sees only a mist before his eyes, *W.*; *skár-ma rab-rib* the faint glimmering of a star.

རབས་ *rabs* 1. **lineage, succession of families, race, family,** *rgyal-rábs* royal family or lineage, nobility; succession of kings; *mi-rábs* human race; *rabs-čád* a person whose lineage is broken off, i.e. **childless,** issueless, *rabs-čád bza-mí γnyis* a married couple without children *Mil.*; *yá-rabs* the higher class of people, noblemen; *má-rabs* the lower class, also: one belonging to the higher or lower class; collectively: *rgán-rabs* old men, aged people, *γžón-rabs* youth, young persons; *sṅón-rabs* **the ancients** (*veteres*), *pyi-rabs* men of modern times, descendants, posterity *Glr.*, *sṅon-rabs-sgrúṅ* an old legend, ancient history *Zam.*, *snón-γyi rabs bčo-brgyad* the 18 Puranas *Tar.* 4, 11. — 2. **generation** *Dzl.*, resp. *γdun-rábs Glr.*, *ná-nas γdun-rábs lná-pa-na* in the fifth generation after me; with respect to individuals, period of life, viz. one of the many periods, which every person is supposed to pass through, or sometimes pleon. denoting a person as being the representative of his generation: *sans-rgyás rabs bdun* the seven Buddhas. — 3. in gen.; **succession, series, development**, e. g. the propagation of the Buddhist doctrine *Tar.* 205, 21; *bskal-rábs* successions of Kalpas, *bskal-rábs-nas bskal-rábs-su.*

རམ་པ་ *rám-pa* 1. *W.* **quick**-(quitch-)grass. — 2. = *rán-pa? Lt.*, *Glr.*

རམ་བུ་ *rám-bu* 1. prob. only in: *rám-bu ˳degs-pa* to join in singing, to take part in a song, to fall in with, *Dzl.* ༢༤, 13 (not: to set up a dismal cry *Sch.*), v. also *˳čol-ba.* 2. = *na-rám Polygonum viviparum.*

རམས་ *rams* 1. **indigo** *B.*, col. — 2. *Cs.*: 'degree of doctorship, *snags-* or *go-* or *drun-ráms-pa* one having such a degree'.

རལ་ *ral* 1. **goat's hair.** — 2. **rent, cleft,** *p̒u ral γnyis* a sloping valley dividing into two parts at its upper end; *ral-γsum* n. of Lahoul on account of its consisting of three valleys; cf. *rál-ba.* — 3. v. *rál-pa.*

རལ་ཀ་ *rál-ka* v. *rál-gu.*

རལ་ཁ་ *rál-k̒a* v. *rál-gri.*

རལ་ག་ *rál-ga Sch.* = *yál-ga.*

རལ་གུ་ *rál-gu* 1. *Sch.*: **cleft, chink, fissure.** — 2. *dar-dkár-gyi rál-gu* and *rál-ka Pth.?*

རལ་གྲི་ *ral-gri*, col. **ral-gyi, ra-gyi** **sword,** also for rapier and other thrust-blades *Dzl.*; *ral-grii ˳dáb-ma* or *lče* **blade,** *so* edge, *šubs* scabbard of a sword *Cs.*; *rál-gri-pa Cs.* a sword-man; a fighting man; *rál-k̒a* = *rál so*; *rál-k̒a spród-pa* 'to bring the blades together', to fight hand to hand, (*ral-k̒a sbrad-pa Sch.* is prob. a misprint).

རལ་པ་ *rál-pa* **long hair, lock, curl; mane** (of the lion, not of the horse etc.); *rál-pa-čan* having or wearing long hair, n. of a Tibetan king that distinguished himself by his bigotry and by his servility to the priests; *ral-lčan* a willow planted at the birth of a child, under which a lock of the child's hair is buried, when it is seven years old *Ld.*

རལ་བ་ *rál-ba* = *drál-ba* and *hrál-ba*, pf. of *˳drál-ba*, **torn**, of clothes etc., *mtsón-gyis* lacerated, slashed, cut to pieces by the sword *Dzl.*; *žig-rál-ba* id.; *žig-rál* breach, **destruction**, *k̒án-pa-la žig-rál byún-na* when the house gives way *Glr.*; *k̒a-rál, rna-rál, sna-rál* a lip, ear or nose, that has been lacerated by wearing rings etc.

རས་ *ras* 1. sbst. **cotton cloth**, cottons, also a piece of cotton cloth, handkerchief etc., *ras sbóm-pa* thick, strong cotton cloth; *lág-ras, p̒yis-ras Cs.* handkerchief, napkin; *tód-ras* **turban** *Cs.*; *p̒rá-ras* a fine sort of cotton stuff, = *ká-ši-kai ras.*

**Comp.** *ras-rkyán* cotton cloth. — *ras-skúd Cs.* cotton thread. — *ras-k̒úg* a small bag made of cotton. — *ras-k̒ra* **calico, chintz** *Cs.* *ras-gós* **cotton dress, gown.** — *re-˳gá* a strong cotton fabric brought from *Sik.*, *C.* *ras bčós-bu Cs.* calico, chintz. — *ras-tág* **fillet, bandage.** — *rás-pa* a person wearing cotton clothes *Mil.*, frq. — *ras-bál* raw cotton. — *ras-búbs* a whole piece of cotton cloth. — *rás-ma* a small piece, a rag *Lex.* **re-zén* C.* a long, loose cotton garment, shawl. — *ras-yúg* = *ras-búbs.* — *ras-rú* v. *re-rú.* — *ras-slág* a furred garment covered with cotton cloth *W.* — 2. adj. *k̒a-rás* (**rē**, for *rens?*) hard snow that will bear a man.

རས་པ་ *rás-pa* 1. vb., *Ld.* **ras-če** **to get or grow hoarse,** **skad ras son** the voice has grown hoarse, **skad ras-sa rag** I feel a hoarseness in my throat. — 2. sbst. v. sub *ras.*

རི་ *ri*, also *ri-bo B.*, **ri-ga* W.* 1. **mountain, hill,** *ri pó-ta-la* the mountain (called) Potala *Lis.*; *ri-bo dpal-˳bár Mil.*, *rgyal-gyi-sri ri Mil.* the mountain *Pal-bár, Gyalgyisri*; *rir* on the mountain *Mil.*, *ri-la* id.

ར

frq.; *ri-ṫaṅ-mṫsams-su* at the foot of the mountains or hills *Med.*; *rir-gán-pa* one living in close vicinity to a mountain, *W.*; *gáṅs-ri* an ice-mountain, snowy mountain, glacier, *nágs-ri* or *śiṅ-ri* a hill covered with wood, *brág-ri* a rocky mountain, *γyá-ri* a mountain or hill consisting of slate-stone or schist; *spaṅ-ri* a hill covered with grass. — 2. **brim** of a hat or cap; **side-leather**, side-piece of a shoe. — 3. symb. num.: 7. — 4. num. figure: 55. — 5. v. *ri-mo.*

**Comp. and deriv.** *ri-skéd* v. *rkéd-pa.* — *ri-skyégs Stg.*, v. *skyegs.* — *ri-ḱród* chain of mountains, assemblage of hills or mountains, esp. as abode of hermits who, on that account, are called *ri-ḱród-pa*; also directly = *dgón-pa* hermitage. — *ri-mgó* mountain top. — *ri-rgyál, rii rgyál-po* a very high mountain, e.g. Tise *Mil.*, Gandharā *Sbh.*, esp. = *ri-ráb,* q.v. — *ri-rgyúd* chain of mountains, ridge of hills. — *ri-čan* mountainous, hilly. — *ri-čén, ri-bo-čé* a great mountain. — *ri-nyin* the sunny side, the southern slope of a mountain. — *ri-rnyil* fall of a mountain, land-slip *Sch.* — *ri-stóṅ* v. *stóṅ-pa.* — *ri-deu* (or *rdeu*) *čúṅ Sch.*, **ri-bóg, ri-de-bóg** *W.*, a mountain spur abounding in stones. — **ri-dód** *W.* (perh. to be spelled *ri-ḱród*) a hermit (living) in the mountains. — *ri-sná* mountain spur. — *ri-pa* an inhabitant of the mountains, mountaineer, from a Tibetan point of view equivalent to the Latin *paganus* and *agrestis* as opp. to *urbanus*, therefore = peasant, poor uncivilized person. — *ri-ṗrán* a little hill or mountain. — *ri-bo* = *ri,* v. above. — *ri-bór-pa Tar., Cs.: ri-ʼór-pa; = ri-ḱród-pa, ri-bór-gyi groṅ* mountain village *Tar.* — *ri-brág, brág-ri* rocky mountain. — *ri-ₒbóg* spur. — *ri-sbúg* mountain cavern. — *ri-rtsá* foot, *ri-rtsé* top of a mountain, *nyi-ma ri-rtsé-la ṗóg-na* when the rising sun illumines the mountain tops. — *ri-rtsé-kan Cs.* n. of a mischievous spirit. — *ri-rdzóṅ* mountain fortress, fort. — *ri-ráb* the centre of the world and king of the mountains, the fabulous Sumeru or Meru, also *ri-rab-lhún-po, ri-rgyál, ri-bo-mčog-ráb Mil.* — *ri-lúṅ* mountain and valley. — *ri-γséb Sch.* = *ri-ḱród.* — *ri-sribs* the side not exposed to the sun, shady side, north-side of the mountains.

ར

རི་གུ་ *ri-gu* young goat, **kid** *W.*

རི་རྒྱ་ *ri-rgyá Sch.:* foxes or fox-skins(?).

རི་དྭགས་ *ri-dwags* animals of chase, **game.**

རི་བ་ *rí-ba W.* **rí-če** to be worth, gen. as adj. **worth,** **lug di ṅul čig ri-če yin** this sheep is worth one rupee *W.*; *dṅul brgya ri-bai rta* a horse worth one hundred rupees *Cs.*. cf. *rin* and *rib; rí-bai rin-ṫáṅ* the full price *Sch.*

རི་བོང་ *ri-bóṅ* **hare,** *ri-bóṅ-mo Cs.* female hare; it lives in *Ld.*, but not in the smaller valleys, e.g. not in Lahoul; *ri-bóṅ-gi rwa* the horn of a hare, a nonentity, a thing not existing, cf. *mo-śám-gyi bu.*

རི་མོ་ *rí-mo* 1. **figure, picture, painting, drawing,** *lha-ḱáṅ-gi Glr.*; *rí-mo-mḱan* **painter**; *ri-mo-čan, ri-mo-ldan* marked with figures; *ri-mor byéd-pa* to represent by means of figures and colours, to paint *Do.*; **markings** (streaks, speckles etc.) *śai* markings of a (tiger's) skin *Tar.*; *ri-ḱrá* having stripes of various colours, spotted, speckled; *ri-mo* also draught, plan, design, and fig. **pattern,** rule of conduct, law written into the heart. — 2. = *rim-gro* reverence, **veneration,** *ri-mor byéd-pa* to honour, to venerate *Stg.*

རི་ལུ་ *ri-lu* col., but also *Tar.* 63, for *ril-bu.*

རི་ཤི་ *ri-śi,* ऋषि, = *draṅ-sróṅ* q. v.

རི་ཤོ་ *ri-śó* n. of a medicinal herb *Med.*

རིག་ *rig* in *Ld.* col. and provinc. for *žig:* **maṅ-ṅa rig** or **nyuṅ-ṅu rig toṅ** give much! give little!

རིག་པ་ *rig-pa* I. vb., 1. **to know, to understand,** = *śés-pa* with the termin. of a sbst: to know (a person etc.) as, with the termin. of the inf.: to know that, **to perceive,** observe, *ḱrós-par rig-nas* perceiving that he became angry *Dzl.*; *ṗá-la rig-par gyis* let your father know it, inform your father of it *Tar.*; *zlóg-tu rig-par byed* (it or he) teaches how to avert, prevent etc. — 2. v. *sgrig-pa.*

II. sbst. 1. **knowing, knowledge; prudence, talents, natural gifts** *Glr.*; *rig-pa daṅ ldán-pa* **talented, rich in knowledge, learned** *Dzl.*; *rig-pa γsar-ba* new informations, disclosures, knowledge; **news,** *lóg-gi rig-pa bsgrés-na* if one compares the absurd news *Tar.* 174, *Schf.*; *ma-rig-pa* 1. sbst. **अविद्या ignorance,** mostly used in the specific Buddhist sense, viz. for the innate principal and **fundamental error** of considering perishable things as permanent and of looking upon the external world as one really existing, with Buddhists in a certain manner the original sin, from which every evil is proceeding, v. *Köpp.* I, 163 (but cf. *γti-mug*). 2. adj. void of reason, **unreasonable,** irrational, *dúd-ₒgro ma-rig-pa Mil.* — 2. **science, learning, literature,** *náṅ-gi rig-pa* the orthodox or sacred literature, *p̓yii rig-pa* the heterodox or profane literature *Cs.*, *t̓un-moṅ-gi rig-pa* literature or science common to both religions (Buddhists and Brahmans) *Cs.*; *rig-pai γnas* and *rig-pa* any single science (philosophy, medicine etc.) v. *rig-γnás*; *rig-pai ról-t̓so* or *rig-pai γnas t̓ams-čád Cs.* circle of science, **encyclopedia.** — 3. **soul** (prob. only in later literature), *rig-pa lus daṅ brál-ba* the soul separated from the body, *rten daṅ brál-ba* the soul separated from her hold or from her abode *Thgr.*; often opp. to *bem Mil.*

**Comp.** *rig-mk̓an*, *rig(-pa)-po Cs.*, *Sch.* a knowing person, a learned man. — *rig-rgyud* **character** *Mil.* — *rig-snágs* **a spell, charm, magic formula,** *rig-snags-mk̓an* a person skilled in charms. — *rig-γnás* a science, one of the sciences; *rig-γnás čé-ba lṅa* the five great sciences or classes of science, frq.; these are: *sgrá-rig-pa* science of language, *γtan-t̓sigs-rig-pa* dialectics, *γsó-ba-rig-pa* medicine, *bzó-rig-pa* science of mechanical arts, *naṅ-dón-rig-pa* religious philosophy; of less consequence are: *rig-γnás čúṅ-ba lṅa* the five minor sciences; and the *rig-γnás* or *rig-pa bčo-brgyad* (also *tsug-lag* ?), which need not be particularly enumerated, though they are often mentioned in the *Dzl.*; they are named by *Cs.* and *Sch.* — *rig(-pa)-po* v. *rig-mk̓an.* — *rig-byéd* 1. conveying knowledge, **instructive,** prob. also learned, *ṅa rig-byéd glú-mk̓an ma yin-te* I am no schooled, accomplished, singer *Mil.* 2. **instruction,** a book conveying knowledge, a scientific work, *bzoi rig-byéd* a technological work *Glr.* 3. **वेद** Veda, the (four) sacred writings of ancient Brahmanism, hence 4. as symb. num.: 4. — *rig-ma*, **वेदमातृ**, Veda-mother, *Gāyatrī*, a certain metre, verse and hymn of the Rigveda, personified as a deity *Mil.* — *rig-ₒdzin*, from *rig-pa ₒdzin-pa* to comprehend a science with ease, to be of quick parts *Dzl.*, as partic.: **a man of parts, a clever fellow;** but usually *rig-ₒdzin* (like *rig-ₒčaṅ*, of rarer occurrence), *Ssk.* **विद्याधर**, denotes a kind of spirits to whom a high degree of wisdom is attributed, like the Dākinis. — *rig-šés* the faculty of **reason** *Tar.* 90, 2, *Schf.*

རིག་རིག་ *rig-rig, mig rig-rig byéd-pa* or *dúg-pa* to look about, esp. in an anxious manner, shyly *Tar.*, *Mil.*

རིགས་ *rigs* 1. **family, lineage, extraction, birth, descent,** *rigs-rús* lineage and family *Glr.*, *mai rigs-su nyé-ba* or *γtógs-pa* a relation by the mother's side *Dzl.*; emph.: **noble birth** or extraction: *rígs-kyi bu* or *bú-mo* noble or honoured sir! honoured madam! a respectful address, which is also more generally applied; thus in *Thgr.* it is the regular way of addressing the soul of a deceased person; *mi-rigs* 1. the human race, mankind *Cs.* 2. **nation, tribe** *Glr.*; *sdé-rigs* **tribe** *Cs.* 3. rarely = sex, *mó-rigs* female sex *Wdṅ.* — 2. in a special sense: **caste, class** in society, **rank.** In Tibet five ranks are usually distinguished. viz.: *rgyál-rigs* royal state, royalty, *brám-ze-rigs* caste of priests (Brahman caste), *rǰé-rigs* nobility, aristocracy, *dmáṅs-rigs* the citizens, *γdól-pai rigs* the common people. When speaking of India, the appellations of these classes are applied to the castes of Brahmanism, although they do not correspond to each other in every respect. — 3. **kind, sort, species,** *groi rigs γsum yod* there are three sorts of wheat, *sk̓ád-*

ར

*rigs gós-rigs mi-˳drá-ba* different languages and costumes; *ċi-rigs* of every sort, *ċi-rigs-su* in every possible manner, e g. *čos stón-pa* to teach religion; *nyin-moi rigs-kyis* or *rigs-la* by the day, **by days, daily** *Glr.*; *rigs* is also used for **some, certain,** *nád-rigs-la mi ˳dzém-na* if one is not on his guard against certain diseases; sometimes pleon.: *yán-lag rigs bżi* the four limbs, viz. hands and feet *Glr.*; *rgyal-čén rigs bżi* the four great spirit-kings *Thgy.*, *rigs ɣsum mgón-po* the three tutelar saints (*spyan-ras-ɣzigs, ṗyag-rdór, ˳ǰam-dbyáṅs*) *Glr.*; *saṅs-rgyás rigs lṅai żiṅ-ḱams Thgr.* — *rigs-pa* vb. **to have the way, manner, custom, quality of,** *mgo ṗyir ˳byúṅ-bai rigs-so* the upper end (of a stick, part of which is in the water) has the way of sticking out, i.e. sticks out; often to be translated: **must** necessarily (according to the laws of nature or to circumstances); as partic. or adj.: **necessary,** also **proper, suitable, right, suited to its purpose,** in the earlier literature gen. with the genit. of the infin., sometimes with the termin. of the infin., in later times with the root of the verb; thus: *ťós-nas ldáṅ-bai rigs-so* you must get up as soon as you hear . . . *Dzl.*; *da ri żig snáṅ-bai rigs* now a mountain must appear *Dzl.*; *bżág-pai rigs-sam* would it not be expedient to appoint...? *Dzl.*; *rigs-kyi dús-la báb-bo* it is just the right time *Dzl.*; *mi smrá-bai mi rigs-so* it is not right to be silent *Dzl.*; *smád-par mi rigs-so* it is not right to abuse *Glr.*; *˳óṅ-rigs ˳dúg-pas* because (he) might possibly come *Mil. nt.*; *drán-pa mi zin rigs-la* if he should perhaps not retain the recollection of, if there should be any danger of his not remembering *Thgr.*; *ṅan-sóṅ-du ˳gró-bai rigs-la* as there is a possibility of going to hell *Thgr.*; *ɣdúl-bai rigs-pa* those fit for conversion *Dzl.*; *lhar skyé-ba ni rigs-pa ma lags* his being re-born as a deity is not befitting, or also: not possible, not probable *Dzl.*; *mi-rigs-pa* wrong, not right, unbecoming, improper etc., mostly as adv.: *mi-rigs-par byéd-pa* to act wrong, to do badly, frq. — *rigs-kyi rǰes-˳bráṅ Was.* (274) v. sub *luṅ*.

**Comp.** *rigs-brgyúd* race, **lineage,** extraction, **family** *Cs.*, *rigs-brgyud-˳dzín* **male issue,** *rigs-brgyúd ˳ṗél-bar ˳gyúr-ba* the rising of a numerous progeny *Dom.* — *rigs-ṅán* 1. low birth or extraction, **ḱyod mi rig-ṅán-pa daṅ nyám-po ḍé-ċe man** you must not mingle with people of low extraction, with common people *W.*; *rigs-ṅán dpón-du skó-ba* to raise a child of low extraction to the royal dignity *Glr.* 2. **hangman** *Dzl.* (cf. *ɣdól-pa*). — *rigs-ċan, rigs-ldán* of noble birth. — *rigs-mnyám-pa, mtún-pa, ˳drá-ba* of the same rank etc., of the same species. — *rigs-nyáms* **degenerated,** *rigs-nyáms dge-slóṅ* a monk disgracing his profession *Pth.* — *rigs-méd* = *rigs-ṅán* no. 1.

རིགས་པ་ *rigs-pa* 1. v. *rigs.* — 2. often erron. for *rig-pa.* — 3. adj. of *rigs*: *rgyál-rigs-pa* belonging to the reigning family or caste; *ċi-rigs-pai sgó-nas* in every possible manner *Mil.*; *ċi-rigs-par snyán-pai ťsig-gis* with ever so many kind words *Dzl.*; also: in any way, any how, to a certain degree or extent, in part, partly *Tar.* 4, 3 etc. — 4. sbst., translation of **न्याय logic, dialectics** *Trigl.* 15; an infallible, not deceptive idea *Was.* (297).

རིང་ངེ་བ་ *riṅ-ṅe-ba* **continual**(?), **daily**(?) *ḱa-tsá riṅ-ṅe-ba Mil. nt.* every day warm meals.

རིང་བ་ *riṅ-ba* I. adj., also *riṅ-po C., B.*, **riṅ-mo** *W.* 1. **long, high, tall,** relating to space; *riṅ-mo* **ḱur** *W.* carry it lengthwise; it also implies distance, in which case *ťag-riṅ* (q. v.) is the more precise form; *da-dúṅ yúl-las riṅ-ste* as he is still at a great distance from the place *Dzl.*; more frq. with *daṅ*: *ɣnas ˳di groṅ-ḱyér daṅ riṅ-bas* because this place is far from the town *Dzl.*; *mi riṅ-ba-na* at no great distance. — 2. **long,** with respect to **time,** *ťse riṅ-ba* sbst. a long life, adj. long-lived, *rgyál-ba daṅ ťse riṅ-bar šog ċig* may he be victorious and live long! *Dzl.*; *yun riṅ-po* (or *mo*) a long time; *yun riṅ-po-nas* from a long time, a long time since, *riṅ-por ma lón-par*, less accurately: *riṅ-po ma lón-par* soon afterwards, relating to things past, *riṅ-por mi ťogs-par* id. with respect to the future, = after a little while, in a short time, frq.; *mi-rín-bar* id. *Tar.*; *dé-nas mi rin-bar* not long after that *Tar.*; *rin ẑig* a long time, *rin ẑig lón-pa dan* after a long time *Dzl.*; *rin ẑig-tu* adv. **long, a long while, for a long time,** *rin ẑig-tu ma ˏons-pas* as he did not come for a long time *Dzl.*; *rin ẑig-na* after or during a long time *Glr.*; *rin-la*, resp. *sku-rín-la* c. genit. **during, at,** *nyin-gyi rín-la* in the day-time, during the day *Pth.*, *ˏdir bẑugs rin* (provinc. for *rin*?) *ˏtso-čas* or *rgyags* provisions for the time of his stay *Mil.*; esp. of kings etc.: **under** a king; during the reign or life of a king, frq.; *dé-rin B., C.*, **di-rin** (more correct form, but only in *W.*) **to-day.** — 3. **old,** *rin ẑig-na Sch.* long ago, long since, v. also *rin-lugs.* —

II. **length, distance** etc., more definite form, but of rare occurrence: *rin-ba-nyid, dé-nas mi-rin-ba-nyid-na* a very short time afterwards *Tar.*

**Comp.** *rin-ǩyád* **length.** — **rin-tab* W.* length, copiousness (of account). — *rin-túṅ* 1. long and short. 2. length, relatively. — *rin-gág*, also *stod-gág* jacket or waistcoat of a Lama, without sleeves.

རིང་ལུགས་ *rin-lúgs Cs.*: 'the sect or followers of a person', *Sch.*: 'old customs'; *Glr.* 92, 2 (?).

རིང་བསྲེལ་ *rin-bsrél* ('things which are to be preserved for a long time'), धातु, relics of a Buddha or a saint, viz. small, hard particles, acc. to Burnouf the remnants of burnt bones.

རིངས་ *rins* sometimes for *rin.*

རིངས་པ་ *rins-pa* **swift, speedy,** *rins-par rgyúg-pa* to run fast, to hasten, hurry; *rins-par yod* I am in a hurry *Mil.*; **rin-pa ton* W.* be quick! make haste! *rins run* though you be in a hurry *Mil.*; *rins-pai bsód-snyoms* alms, gifts of charity (requiring haste), urgently requested, and out of the common course, *Burn.* I, 269. 628 **za-rins, ˏtun-rins**, waiting impatiently for one's meal, **ˏgrul-rins** for setting out *W.*; *rins-stábs-su* most speedily *Mil.*

རིད་པ་ *rid-pa* 1. **meager, emaciated** *Dzl.* and elsewh. — 2. *Sch.* also: **rare.**

རིད་པང་ *rid-páṅ* the Neosa pine-tree *Kun.*

རིན་ *rin* 1. **price, value,** *rin γčód-pa* to fix, to determine the price *Cs.* (cf. *ťan*), *rin rtóg-pa* to ascertain the price, to estimate the value *Cs.*; *rin ˏbébs-pa* to abate, to lessen the price *Cs.*; *rin ˏbáb-pa, rin ˏbri-ba* to go down, to sink or fall in value *Cs.*; **rin tsam* W.*, **rin gha-tsö* C.* how dear (is it)? what does it cost? *rín-la mi čog Sch.* to sell under cost-price; *rín-čan* dear, costly; *rin-méd* worthless, also: for nothing, gratis; *rin-gón, rin-ťán, rin-tsád Tar.* ༢༠༢, 17 = *rin*; *rin-čén-po, rin-po-čé* v. the next article. — 2. for *rin*, v. *rin-ba* I, 2.

རིན་ཆེན་(པོ) *rin-čen(-po)*, also *rin-po-če*, 1. **very dear, precious, valuable;** usually: 2. sbst., रत्न, **a precious thing, treasure, jewel, precious stone, precious metal; metal** in general; *Glr.* 7, five jewels of the gods are enumerated, sapphire, indragopa and other three, prob. fabulous, stones, and five jewels as the property of man: gold, silver, pearls, corals, lapis lazuli; in other books other jewels are specified as such. In the Buddha-legends frq. mention is made of the *rin-po-če sna bdun*, i.e. the extraordinary treasures of a Tshakravartin king, viz. the precious wheel (v. *ˏǩor-lo*), the precious elephant, the precious horse, the precious jewel, the precious wife, the precious minister and the precious general (or inst. of him, the precious citizen) v. Gyatch. chap. III. Sometimes *rín-po-čei* may be understood literally: consisting of jewels, of precious stones, at other times it is merely equivalent to: valuable, precious; *rin-po-čei glin Glr.* seems frq. to signify a holy, happy land inhabited by gods. — 3. **a title,** used not only in *rgya-mťso rin-po-če* and *pan-čen rin-po-če* (the honorary titles of the high-priests of Lhasa and of Tashilunpo), but also a title of every Lama of a higher class.

རིན་དི་ *rin-di W.* (*rin-dri Bun.*) 1. **lead.** — 2. **musket-ball.**

རིབ་ *rib* = *ri-ba Sch.* (*Dzl.* ༡༡༠, 8. 15, and in *Sch.'s* dictionary): **worth,** costing, standing at; to the Tibetans asked by us the word seemed to be unknown, and the MS. of Kyelang has *ri-ba* in the above cited passage.

**རིབ་མ་** **rib-ma* W.*, **ḍib-ma* C.*, **fence, hedge, enclosure** to protect the fields from cold winds, intruders etc.

**རིམ་གྲི་** *rim-gri* resp. for **ltógs-ri** **hunger** *W.*

**རིམ་(འ)གྲོ་** *rim-gro* or *rim-ₒgro*, resp. *sku-rim* **honour, homage,** shown more esp. to gods, saints, and priests, **offerings** and other ceremonies (v. sub *sku*), *rim-gros t́ar-bar ₒgyur* he will yet be cured by religious ceremonies (if medical advise should prove insufficient) *S.g.*; *dei rim-gro-la* as a ceremony for him (the sick person) *Mil.*; *zaṅ-ziṅ-gi rim-gros* by offerings in goods, cattle etc.) *Mil.*; *rim-ₒgro čén-po byas* he arranged a great sacrificial festival *Pth.*; *rim-gro-pa* servant, waiting-man, valet de chambre.

**རིམ་པ་** *rim-pa*, *Ssk.* क्रम, 1. **series, succession,** *rim-(pa) bžin(-du) Dzl.*, *rim-par Glr.*, in a row or line, in rows, by turns, successively, one after another, also = by degrees, gradually; *rim-gyis*, *rim-pas Dzl.* id.; *rim-pas dáṅ-po mčog yin p̀yi-ma dman* v. sub *dmán-pa*; *byá-ba t́ob-rim bžin byéd-pa* to do a business by turns, each taking a certain share of the work *Glr.* — 2. **the place** in a row or file, constituent part or member of a series, *dei mi-brgyúd rim-pa lṅas rgyál-sa bzuṅ* five members of his lineage occupied the throne *Glr.*, and in a still more general sense: *sgo rim-pa bdun* a sevenfold door *Dzl.*; *rim-ldábs Sch.* and *nyis-rim S.g.* double; *rim-γčig* = *lan-γčig* one time, once. — 3. **order, method,** *ₒcád-par ₒgyúr-bai rim-pa ₒdis* by this method which will be explained immediately, *Sbh.*; *rim-bral* disorderly, irregular *Cs.* — *rim γnyis* v. *skyed-rim.*

**རིམས་(ནད་)** *rims(-nad)* contagious disease, **epidemy, plague,** *ṅan-rims* id. *Glr.*; *rims γtoṅ-ba* to send, to cause a plague, as demons do *Dzl.*; *dus γdon γnyis-kyis ma skyed rims mi ₒbyuṅ* plagues, epidemies, are caused by nothing but the season or by demons; **t́u-rim* W.* **dysentery, diarrhoea,** bloody flux; *rims-só* the 'tooth' of an epidemy, i.e. its contagium, virulency.

**རིལ་ཏིང་** *ríl-tiṅ Ld.* = *ŝa-rág.*

**རིལ་བ་** *ríl-ba* I. more frq. *ríl-po*, *ríl-mo B., C.*; **ril-ril* W.* 1. **round, globular,** in *C.* also **cylindrical;** *srán-ma ríl-mo* peas are round *Wdṅ.*; **ril-ril* W.* also sbst.: a round, globular object, such as a cabbage-head, a round lump of butter etc.; *ril-bai spyi-blugs Glr., Sch.*: 'a bottle, narrow in the middle, a gourd-bottle'. — 2. **whole, entire; wholly, quite** **k̀oṅ-ril** quite crippled, lamed *C.*; **nag-ril-ril* W.* very black, quite black; *rtág-pa daṅ ril-por ₒdzin-pa* to consider a thing lasting and entire (not compounded) *Thgy.*; *ril-por ṅa dbáṅ-na* if it belongs to me entirely *Mil.*; *ríl-po* the whole, the entire thing (opp. to a part), also in arithmetic *Wdk.*; *ril-poi lhág-ma* the remainder of the whole *Wdk.*; *bubs-ril lus* the whole body *S.g.*; *ril-gyis γyógs-pa* entirely, completely, enveloped, or wrapped up *Sch.*; *ril-mid-pa Sch.*: 'to swallow a thing entire'; *dé-dag daṅ ríl-gyis mčí-am p̀yed daṅ mčí-ba bka-stsól čig* tell me whether I am to come with all, or only with one half (of them) *Dzl.* ༡༨༢, 5 (acc. to the manuscript of Kyelang); *ril-bu*, col. **ril-lu**, **small ball, globule, pill,** *ril-bur bsgril-ba srán-ma tsam* formed into a pill of the size of a pea *Lt.*; *ril-ma* globular dung of some animals, *byi-bai ril* mouse-dung *Mṅg.* (where Piper longum is compared with it), *glá-bai ril* dung of the musk-deer; *lúg-ril* tirdles, sheep-pellets, *ŝa-ril* 1. dung of the argali *Ld.* 2. small meat-balls *C.* — II. 1. *W.*: **ril-če** (for *gril-ba*) **to fall.** — 2. *Bal.* **ril-čas** (for *sgril-ba*) **to wrap up.**

**རིས་** *ris* 1. cognate to *ri-mo* and perh. to *ₒbri-ba*: **figure, form, design,** *pádma-ris* the figure of a lotus-flower *Glr.*, *mig-maṅ-ris-su bris-pa Glr.* painted like a chess-board; *skya-ris* the blank parts of a picture, *tson-ris* the painted parts of a picture *Cs.* — 2. *Cs.*: **part, region, quarter,** hence *mt́o-ris* **heaven,** v. *mt́o*; *dbaṅ-ris* share of power or of territory; *mṅa-ris* id and **n.** of a part of

Tibet; *p̓yogs-ris* **party;** *Cs.* has also: *ráṅ-ris* one's own party, *γžán-ris* another's party, *ris-čan* **partial, prejudiced,** *ris-méd* **impartial, indifferent,** hence also **hermit,** because he ought to feel indifferent to every thing. — 3. *Sch.:* 'ris-su difference, *ris-su čád-pa* equality'(??). — 4. *ris-γza* symb. num.: 7, derived from the number of the great planets together with sun and moon.

རུ་ *ru* 1. **horn,** = *rwa*; *rá-ru* goat's horn, *lúg-ru* ram's horn. — 2. parts of vessels etc. resembling a horn, e.g. the handle of a stew-pan *Mil. nt.*; **gó-ru** *C.* door-post. — 3. **part, division,** *dmág-gi* of an army *Stg.*, wing *Cs.*; of a country, *dbu-γtsáṅ-ru-bži Mil.*; *γyás-ru* the right side or wing, *γyón-ru* the left side or wing, *γžuṅ-ru* the middle part or centre *Cs.* — 4. as num. figure: 85.

**Comp.** *ru-dár Wdk*, *Mil.*, *ru-mtsón Sch.* military ensign, **banner, colours,** *˳p̓yár-ba* to display, to hoist (a flag). — *ru-sná* division of an army *Sch.* — *rú-pa* 'troops, advanced posts of the enemy' *Sch.* — *ru-dpón* commander of a regiment, colonel.

རུ་ང་ *ru-ṅá* **hatred, grudge, malice,** (of rare occurrence); *ru-ṅa-čan* spiteful, malicious.

རུ་རྟ་ *ru-rtá Cs.:* 'a kind of spicy root'; in *Lh. Inula Helenium.*

རུ་ཐོག or རྡོག *ru-tóg* or **ru-rdóg** *Cs.* **n. of a** district in Tibet contiguous to Ladak; an extensive plain, east of lake *Paṅkoṅ.*

རུ་པ་ *rú-pa* v. *ru.*

རུ་པོ་ *rú-po* **ram** *W.*

རུ་བ་ or རེ་གུར་ *rú-ba* or *re-gur* a tent-covering made of yak's hair; *rú-ba-pa* a person living in such a tent; *rú-bai tsogs* a number of such tents, a tent-village.

རུ་མ་ *rú-ma* **curdled milk,** used as a ferment *C.*, *˯ó-mar rú-ma blug-˳dra* as when sweet and curdled milk are put together *S.g.;* as to its effect, it may also stand for **leaven.**

རུ་ཚར་ *ru-tsár* **fringes** *Ld.* = *ka-tsár.*

རུ་རཀྵ་ *ru-rakša Med.*; *Cs.*: a sort of berry.

རུ་རུ་ *ru-ru Stg.*; *Sch.*: a kind of deer; a species of fruit-trees.

རུ་ལེབ་ *ru-léb* 'flat-horn', acc. to *Sch.* the reindeer (*šá-ba ru-léb* the domesticated, and *˳bróg-gi ru-léb* the wild r.), more prob. **the elk,** v. *ka-ša.*

རུག་གེ་ *rug-gé* appearing (?), *žiṅ snum rug-gé* the field had a luxuriant appearance *Mil. nt.*

རུག་པ་ *rúg-pa* 1. *Cs.* a kind of potato. — 2. *W.* **to collect, gather, pluck,** v. *sgrúg-pa.*

རུང་ཁང་ *rúṅ-kaṅ Cs.*: **bake-house, kitchen.**

རུང་བ་ *rúṅ-ba* 1. vb. **to be fit, calculated, suitable, right,** and adj.: **fit** etc., gen. with termin., rarely with the root of the verb, *tsig ˳di ˳jigs-su ruṅ* this word is calculated to terrify, is terrible *Dzl.*; *btsoṅ-du ruṅ* it is salable, vendible *Dzl.*; *slob-dpón-du mi ruṅ* he is not fit to be a teacher *Dzl.*; *γžán-du mi ruṅ* he is good for nothing else, but also in the sense: he is too good for anything else, nothing inferior can be offered to him *Glr.*; *grub rúṅ-du yód-pa* one that is able to perform it *Tar.*; *mi rnyed mi ruṅ* it must be procured by all means *Dzl.*, *mi byar mi ruṅ* it must be done *Dzl.*; *nyál-du mi ruṅ* it would not do to sleep *Dzl.*; *med kyaṅ ruṅ* I (you etc.) can also do without (him) *Glr.*; *dei tse γtáṅ-du rúṅ-ṅam mi ruṅ* would it not be as well to let him go once more? *Dzl.*; *či-ltar yid-čes-su ruṅ* how can one believe you? *Dzl.*; **kon-čóg zun zer mi ruṅ** *W.* God cannot tell a lie; *˳di yaṅ ruṅ* this, too, is correct, will do *Gram.*; *tsab ruṅ tsam* it may perhaps be used instead *Wdṅ.*; *ṅá-la mós-pa ma byas kyaṅ rúṅ-ste* that they do not show me any honour is not so great a loss; but... *Mil.*; *˳dis ruṅ-ṅam* is that the right thing? will that do? *de-ltar ruṅ* (*W.* **čog**) well, let it be so! for aught I care! — 2. several other phrases with *ruṅ:* **a.** *lus ˳di či ruṅ* why should we care so much for this our body? *Dzl.*; esp. *či ma ruṅ*, preceded by *na* or (rarely) by *yaṅ*: **why should**

**not...?** i.e. **o that! would that!** *ₒdi bdág-gi yin-na ċi ma ruṅ* would that this were mine! *Thgy.*; *ṅai bú-mo min-na ċi ma ruṅ* I only wish, she were not my daughter! would it were not my daughter! *Pth.* b. *ruṅ* = *yaṅ* after a verbal root: *de tsam żig bsdad ruṅ* though I have been sitting so long *Mil.*; *mi dgos ruṅ* though it is not necessary *Mil.*; *śes ruṅ mi śes-pa ltar byéd-pa* to plead ignorance although one knows the thing *Mil.*; *ċi-la ṫug ruṅ* whatever may happen to me, = at all events, at any rate; *ċi yin ruṅ* whatever it may be *Mil.*; *log yin ruṅ min ruṅ* whether it be an erroneous (opinion) or not *Mil.*; *śi ruṅ γson ruṅ* whether I live or die, living or dead *Pth.*; *gaṅ yaṅ ruṅ, ċi yaṅ ruṅ* whosoever he may be, whatsoever it may be, frq.; *sa ču gaṅ yaṅ rúṅ-ba-la* on earth, water or whatever it be *Do.* c. *mi-rúṅ-ba* **illicit, improper, unfit,** v. above; *mi-rúṅ-bai γżi bċu* ten illicit actions, differently specified *Tar.* 33, 9, *Köpp.* I, 147, partly moral offences, partly only infractions of discipline; but *ma-rúṅ-ba, ma-rúṅs-pa* 1. **pernicious, dangerous, atrocious,** as enemies, beasts of prey, malignant gods and spirits, reckless destroyers etc. 2. **spoiled, destroyed, ruined,** *ma-rúṅ-bar byéd-pa* to destroy etc., *ma-rúṅ-bar ₒgyúr-ba* to be destroyed etc. *Dzl.*

རུད་ *rud* **a falling** or **fallen mass,** as: *ḱa-rúd* snow-slip, avalanche, *ču-rúd* deluge, inundation, flood (by the rupture of an embankment and the like), *sa-rúd* land-slide, descent of a great mass of earth; *rúd-zam* a snow-bridge, formed by avalanches.

རུབ་ཆུ་ *rub-ču* prop. n., a district in the south of *Ld.*

རུབ་པ་ *rúb-pa* **to rush in upon, to attack, assault,** *ṗyag żabs kún-nas rub-rúb ₒǰús-te* rushing in upon him from every side in order to touch his hands and feet *Mil.*; *bzán-la rúb-pa* **to pounce on** the prey, to fall upon the food *Glr.*; **do-rub táṅ-te sád-ċe* W.* to kill with stones, to stone; **čog-ċig-la rúb-pa* W.* to press or crowd together towards one side; *ḱa-rúb byéd-pa* to outcry, to bear down by a louder crying *Mil.*; *ₒgo-rub-rúb ₒdug* C.*, **go-rúb taṅ dug* W.* they put their heads together; **środ rub soṅ,* or *mún-ču rub soṅ* W.* darkness draws on, night is setting in, for which in *C.* **sa rub soṅ** is said to be used, so that it might also be translated by **to darken, to obscure.**

རུབ་ཤོ་ *rub-śó* **currant** *W.*

རུམ་ *rum* 1. **womb, uterus,** = *mṅal*, but less frq.: *rum mi bde-ba* sensations of pain during pregnancy *Dzl.*, *rúm-du ₒǰúg-pa* to enter into the womb. — 2. **darkness, obscurity,** *mún-pai rum Glr.*, gen. *smag-rúm.* — 3. prop. n., **Turkey, the Ottoman empire,** the site of which is but vaguely known to the Tibetans, though some commodities from thence find their way to Lhasa; *rúm-pa* a man from Turkey, a Turk; *rum-śam* (شام) Syria *Cs.*

རུལ་བ་ *rúl-ba* **to rot, to get rotten, to become putrid, to turn rancid** etc., *rúl-bar ₒgyúr-ba B.*, **rul čá-ċe* W.* id.; *ₒo-ma rul soṅ* the milk is spoiled, *ḱa rul* the snow does no longer bear, **be rul* W.* **drift-sand, quicksand;** *rul-skyúr* 'sour by putrefaction' *Sch*; *rúl-dri* a putrid smell; *rúl-po* for *hrúl-po Cs.* — Cf. *ₒdrul-ba.*

རུས་ *rus* 1., *W. rus-pa*, **lineage, family,** *miṅ daṅ rus ni ₒdi-ltar-ro* their name and lineage are such and such *Glr.*; **ṅa-raṅ-ghi* (or *ṅa-raṅ dhaṅ*) *ru-ċig-pa* or *-ḍá-wa* C. B.*, **rús-pa ċig-ċig* W.* we are of the same family; *rus-γċig-pa γsód-pa* a murderer of persons related to him by blood *Lex.*; *ṫu-mi rus Lex.*: *Thu-mi*, a family-name; *rus mṫó-ba* high extraction, *rus dmá-ba* low extraction *Cs.* — 2. v. the next article.

རུས་པ་ *rús-pa* (resp. *γduṅ*) 1. **bone,** *rus-ċág* fracture of a bone *Med.*; *rús-pai dúm-bu* prob. small bones of which the Tibetan anatomy enumerates 360. — *mi-rus* human bone; *rkáṅ-rus* bone of the foot; *mgó-rus* bone of the skull; *rús-pai rgyan Mil.* a decoration of terrifying deities and magicians, consisting of human bones suspended from the girdle; *rús-pai rgyan drug Pth.*, the like ornament, but fastened to six different parts of the body, the top of the head, the ears, the neck, the upper arm, the wrists, and the feet; *rus ₒbol-ba* mentioned as a morbid symptom *Lt.?* — 2. **the stone** of apricots and other stone-fruits *C., W.*; grape-stone *Wdṅ.* — 3. **energy,** *snyiṅ-gi Mil.*, gen. *snyiṅ-rus* q.v. — 4. v. *rus*

**Comp,** *rus-kráṅ* skeleton, **rus-ṫáṅ ṫsóg-se* W.* he is nothing but skin and bones. — *rús-k̔u Lt.* bone-broth(?). — *rus-gróg Sch.*: a dry bone (?). — *rus-bčúd Lt.?* — *rus-nád W.* caries. — *rús-bu* 1. small bone. 2. bones in general *Dzl.* — *rus-ṫsád, rus-ṫsód Med.?* — *rus-šiṅ* 1. *Sch.* firmness, perseverance, repentance. 2. n. of a part of the body (?) *Lt.*

རེ་ *re* 1. indefinite num. or pron., **single, a single one, some** (persons), **something; one to each, one at a time,** *re-ré* or *re* **every, every one, every body, each,** *ráṅ-la bu re méd-na yid-ₒp̔am-pa re yóṅ-gi ₒdug, dés-na k̔yéd-la-aṅ bu re dgos* despair comes from having no son, therefore you, too, should have a son *Mil.*; *yud re* for a moment, = *yud tsam Thgr.*; *lan re lan γnyis* once or twice *Mil.*; *mi brgya re tsam żon čóg-pa* (a horse) sufficiently (large) for being mounted by about a hundred men *Glr.*; *lo re tsam ma-γṫógs* with the exception of one year about *Glr.*; *ras-gos-rkyáṅ re* a single cotton garment *Mil.*; *čos-ₒbrél re* a small amount of spiritual instruction *Mil.*; *W.*: **bal re** some wool, **šú-gu re** some paper (= *żig*), **kú-šu re** some apples; *bčú-la p̔úr-pa re γtád-nas* handing to each of the ten a *p̔ur-pa Pth.*; *lág-na dóṅ-tse re-ré yod* in each of his hands there was a gold-coin *Dzl.*; *nyin ré-la séms-čan k̔ri re bsad Glr.* he slaughtered every day 10 000 living beings, *ra lṅa lṅa bsad* five goats (every day); *mi res lug re bsad* each man killed one sheep *Glr.*; in a somewhat different sense: **lo ré-ne lo re čúṅ-se yod* W.* they grow smaller from year to year; *nyuṅ re* little at a time *Glr.*; *re-re γnyis-γnyis* one and all, one with another, indiscriminately *Mil.*, *re-re-bżin-gyi mgo* every single person's head *Tar.*; *re żig* **somebody, something; some** (persons), **a little;** (with or without *dus*) **a little while,** *re żig sdod* wait a little! *Dzl.*; *re żig čig-na* after a little while, *Bhar.* 37; **once, one day, one time, at a future time,** also *dus re żig-gi ṫse Pth* — 2. **mutual, reciprocal** (in this sense it is perh. to be spelled *res*, though it is certainly cognate to *re*), *dpon slob re ₒk̔aṅ ₒbyuṅ Mil.* there arises mutual discord between teachers and disciples *Mil.*; **different, differing?** *ré-lta-bu* 'of a different kind or nature' *Sch.* — 3. sbst. a. the wooden parts of a door, *re bżi* the four parts of a door-frame, *yá-re* the head-piece, the lintel, *má-re* the sill or threshold (= *yá-ṫem* and *má-ṫem*), **yá-re má-re ḍal toṅ* W.* pull it down entirely! *logs-ré* the side posts (*C. sgo-ru*). b. v. *re-mos* and *reu.* — 4. In such forms as *mór-ra-re, mčis-sa-re, gyúr-ta-re* (*Dzl.* ༢༥, 1. ༡༠, 9. ༡༣༡, 2) it may be rendered by an adverb, as: certainly, undoubtedly. — 5. vb., v. *réd-pa* and *ré-ba.* — 6. particle, mostly put between two closely connected words: *nyams-re-dgá, blo-re-bdé Glr., ₒo-re brgyál, skyug-re-lóg, że-re-ₒjigs, yi-re-múg, don-re-čúṅ, snyiṅ-re-rjé* (this last very frq.), without essentially modifying the signification, yet only used in emphatic speech. — 7. num. for *drug-ču* in the abbreviated forms of the numbers 61 to 69. — 8. num. figure: 115.

རེ་སྐན་ *re-skán* (etymology?), acc. to the passages which came to my knowledge a strong negative (like οὐ μή), **by no means, never,** *yoṅ re-skan Mil.* frq., that can never happen, that is absolutely impossible (parallel to *yoṅ mi srid*); *ṫsim-par ₒgyur re-skán* they never can be satisfied with it *Tar.*

རེ་སྐོན་ *re-skón* n. of a bitter medicinal herb.

རེ་ཁ་ *re-k̔á Sch.* **a picture, painting.**

རེ་འཁན་ *re-ₒkán* v. *re-ba.*

རེ་འཁང་ *re-ₒk̔áṅ Sch.*: *re-ₒk̔áṅ ₒbyúṅ-ba* to be not too much (?).

རེ་གུར་ *re-gur* v. *ré-ba* sbst.

རེ་གྲོན་ *re-grón* **addition, increase.**

རེ་ལྕགས་པ་ or རེའུ་ལྕགས་པ་ re-lčágs-pa or reu-lčágs-pa, *Med.*, a mezereon with white blossoms in the South-Himalaya, of which paper is made.

རེ་ཏོ་ *ré-to* pumpkin *Kun.*

རེ་དོགས་ *re-dógs* v. *ré-ba.* vb.

རེ་ལྡེ་ *re-ldé* v. *ré-ba* sbst

རེ་སྣམ་ *ré-snám* v. *ré-ba* sbst.

རེ་འཕགས་ *re-ₒṗágs* prop. n., **Triloknath,** a much frequented place of pilgrimage in Chamba, with a famous image and sanctuary of *Avalokitesvara.*

རེ་བ་ *ré-ba Cs.* sbst., also *ré-bo,* acc. to some *sbré-bo, W.* *re-snam*, *Cs.* sack-cloth, a kind of cloth of yak's-hair, a tent-cloth (also *re-ldé* and *re-yól Cs.*); *re-gúr* a tent of such cloth.

རེ་བ་ *ré-ba* I. vb., 1. **to hope,** *ṫams-čád mṫóṅ-du reo* all hoped to see *Dzl.*; *dé-la ṗán-du ré-nas* hoping it might be good for it *Mil.*; *sú-la re* in whom should they place their hope, in whom should they trust? *loṅ yód-du ré-la* whilst you are hoping still to have time (enough) *Mil.*; *ré-žiṅ ltós-pa* to look up full of hope *Glr.* — 2. **to wish,** v. II. — 3. to beg, to ask alms, **to go a begging,** for victuals, **ḱo ré-a-la yoṅ** *W.* he comes to beg.

II. आशा sbst. **hope; wish,** frq., *ré-ba skóṅ-ba, ré-ba sgrúb-pa* to fulfil a hope; *rnyéd-pa, ṫób-pa* to get it fulfilled, to obtain what one has hoped for, *ré-ba ltar ₒgyur* it goes to one's wish, as well as one could wish; *ré-ba daṅ ldán-pa* hoping, full of hope, *ré-ba méd-pa* hopeless, despairing.

**Comp.** *re-ṫág* v. *ṫág-pa.* — *re-dógs* hope and fear, *re-dógs med* being without hope and without fear (the principal aim and prerogative of ascetics) *Mil.* — *ré-(bai) ɣnas Cs.:* room for hope; prob. also = *ré-sa* the person or thing whereon one's hopes are placed *C., W.*

རེ་མོས་, རེས་མོས་ *ré-mos, rés-mos* **turn, series,** or more accurately: the order or change of the series, *ṅéd-la sdúg-pai ré-mos bab* then misfortune came to be our turn *Mil.*; *re-mos-su Pth.*, **ré-mos čós-la** *Ld.* by turns, alternately, e.g. to strike one's breast with the hands; **ré-mos ré-mos** *W.* by degrees, gradually; *re-móṅs* id. *Ma.*

རེ་ཞིག་ *ré-žig* v. *re* 1.

རེ་རལ་ *re-rál* n. of a medicine *Med.*

རེ་རུ་ (རས་རུ་?) *re-rú (ras-ru?) W.* the spread- or warp-beam of a loom.

རེ་ས་ *ré-sa* v. *ré-ba.*

རེག་ *reg* 1. *Sch.*: *reg-ɣzig-pa* 'notes taken down, and extracts made, during a course of study'.—2. v. the following article.

རེག་པ་ *rég-pa* I. vb., 1. (*W.* *rág-če = nyúg-če*, the latter being more in use) **to touch,** to come in contact with, *lág-pa sá-la gar rég-par* where his hands touched the ground *Dzl.*; *rluṅ yál-ga-la rég-na* when the wind touches the branches *Dzl.*; *ḱá-reg-pa* c.dat.: to eat, to taste, to take, *dúg-la-ḱá-reg ré-ba yod* in taking poison there is hope, (viz. so bad are the times) *Ma.*; **ṫsá-big žal rag dzod** or **žál-la rag** *W.* please, taste a little of it! *sá-la ḱru gaṅ tsam-gyis ma rég-par ₒbyón-pa* to walk not touching the ground by an ell, i.e. to move in the air, about a cubit distant from the ground *Pth.*; *rég-pa-med-pa* intangible, unapproachable, out of reach, *Glr.* — 2. to feel, to perceive *Cs.?* — II. sbst. *reg* (prob. only abbreviation of *reg-bya*) feeling, touch, sense of feeling *S.g.* 10, 5?

**Comp.** *reg-dúg* ('poison that has entered the body by contact') *S.g.* 29, is said to signify now in *C.* venereal disease, syphilis. — *rég-bya* 1. what is felt or may be felt, anything palpable or tangible, *reg-bya mi ṫsor* what may be felt is felt no longer *Wdṅ.* 2. **feeling, sense of feeling,** *págs-pa-reg-bya* the feeling of the skin, *lús-po ṗyii rég-bya gráṅ-la* whilst the outside of the body appears cold to the touch, *rég-bya-rtsúb* rough to the touch *Med.* — *rég-ma Cs.* n. of a goddess.

རེང་བ་ *reṅ-ba*, pf. *reṅs* **to be stiff, hard, rigid,** *rmai reṅ sbyaṅs* to remove the hard parts, of a wound (to clear, to cleanse) *Wdṅ.*; **raṅs soṅ** *W.* (the blood) has coagulated, congealed, also of a dead body: it has grown stiff; **ráṅs-te dad dug** *W.* he makes himself stiff, he struggles against; *réṅs-pa* **solid** (opp. to liquid), **coagulated, stiff, hard;** *reṅs-par byed-pa* to make hard or stiff; fig.: **stiffnecked, obstinate, unwilling,** *Do.*

རེང་བུ་ *réṅ-bu* 1. **pastil** for **fumigating** *Lt.*, v. *spos.* — 2. *Sch.*: separate, not belonging to anything else.

རེངས་ *reṅs* sometimes for *raṅs*, v. *nyin-reṅs, ťo-reṅs.*

རེངས་པོ་ *reṅs-po Sch.* **alone, single.**

རེད་པ་ *réd-pa* 1. **to be,** = *yin-pa*, in *Sp.* and *C.*, rarely in *B.;* also *ré-pa* (*ré-ba*) is met with; *ǩyod p̓yugs-rdzi ma red rdo-rje-sems-dpar snaṅ* you are not a herdsman, no, you are *Vajrasattva* (viz. a deity)! *Pth.*; **čaṅ yǒ-pa re' mĕ-pa re'**? is there any beer here or not? *C.* — 2. *Cs.*: **to be ready,** *red mda* a ready arrow *Cs.; red daṅ ma red rma* a healed wound and one not yet healed (?) *Sch.* — 3. **to be withered** *Ts.*

རེབ་རེབ་པ་ *reb-réb-pa Sch.*: **to be in a great haste** or **hurry, to be very zealous,** *W.*: **reb log čo-če** to do something wicked again and again.

རེམ་པ་ *rém-pa* vb. and adj. (to be) strong, vigorous, durable, sound, hearty, of men and animals, **rem-pa soṅ** *W.* now I feel strong again; **gyóg-pa ḍúl-če-la rém-pa čo!** *W.* exert yourself to walk fast! *čos spyod rem* show your ability, in performing ceremonies or incantations *Mil.*; *rém-čig rém-čig* ₒ*dré-ťsogs-rnams* be strong, ye hobgoblins, show your power; do your best! (ironically) *Mil.*

རེའུ་ *reu Mil.* prob. **panel** or **square,** of a wainscoted wall, of a chessboard etc.; *re(u)-mig* id.

རེར་ *rer* termin. of *re*, to each individually; ... a piece.

རེས་ *res* 1. inst. of *re.* — 2. **change, turn, time, times,** *da ṅed byéd-pai rés-la bábste* it being now our turn of acting *Dzl.*; **di-riṅ ču-ré ǩoi yod** *W.* to-day it is his turn to irrigate (the field); *res byéd-pa* with verbal root, to do a thing by turns with another person, *čáṅ-la* ₒ*ťuṅ-rés byéd-pa*, resp.: *skéms-la ɣsol-rés mdzád-pa* to vie with one another in drinking beer *Glr.; skyes* ₒ*bul-rés byéd-pa* to send mutual presents to one another *Glr.*; *res* ₒ*jóg-pa* to change *Sch.; rés-kyis* relieving one another (in service), doing (a thing) alternately or by turns, e g. *nyál-la mél-ťse byéd-pa* to sleep and to keep watch *Dzl.*; *res* is also used as an adv.: 1. *res če res čuṅ* now great, now small, or partly great, partly small; *res yod res med* at one time it is there, at another not *Cs.* 2. **at** a time, every time, distributively: *res p̓ye ťúr-mgo re tsam* ₒ*gams* I always take the tip of a spoon full of meal at a time *Mil.*; *res ɣčig* once, once upon a time *Tar.*, *res* ₒ*ga* sometimes, *res* ... *res* now — now, **at** one time — at another, frq.; **lu-rĕ** *W.* **a** change of singing, an alternative song; *rés-mos* v. *re-mos; res-ɣzá* a changing (wandering) star, **a planet** *Cs.*; *res-*ₒ*grogs-zla-skár* the stars with which the moon is successively in conjunction *Sch.*

རེས་པོ་ *rés-po* **old,** v. *bgre-ba.*

རོ་ *ro* I. sbst. **taste, flavour, savour,** *ǩa-ro* id.; *ro-myóṅ-ba* to taste; six different kinds of taste are distinguished: *mṅár-ba* sweet, *skyúr-ba* sour, *lán-ťswa-ba* salt, *ǩá-ba* bitter, *ťsá-ba* acrid, *bská-ba* astringent, and the medicines accordingly are also divided into six classes; *ro brgya daṅ ldan-pa* of a hundred-fold taste, i.e. of the most exquisite and manifold flavour, frq. — II. sbst. 1. also *ró-ma*? resp.: *spur*, **dead body, corpse, carcass,** *mi-ro* a dead man, *rtá-ro* dead horse, *srín-bui ro* dead insects *Dzl*; *ro srég-pa* to burn a corpse. — 2. **body,** v. comp. — 3. **residue, remains, sediment,** *ťság-ro* (or ₒ*ťság-ro*) that which remains in a sieve or filter, impurities, husks etc., *já-ro*, tea-leaves in a tea-pot, *ťsil-ro* the remains of bacon after having been fried, greaves; *gál-ro, rdó-ro, sá-ro* rubbish; *skúd-ro* the ends of threads in a seam; v. also *ro-tó.*

**Comp.** *ro-ḱáṅ*, col. **rom-ḱaṅ** place for burning or burying the dead, a favourite spot for conjurations and sorceries. — *ro-gríb* defilement by contact with dead bodies. — *ro-rgyáb* **back, back part** *Lt.* — *ro-sgám* **coffin.** — *ro-tó Ld.* (= *ro* II, 3) **residue**; **raṅ-sii ro-to** **wax**; **sig-pe ro-tó** ruins of walls. — *ro-stód* the upper part of the human body, chest and back *Stg.*; esp. back *Mil.* — *ro-dóm* fees given to the Lamas for performing the burial or cremation ceremonies *Mil.* — *ro-búg Sch.* grave, tomb. — *ro-myágs* v. *myags* — *ro-smád* the lower part of the body *Med.*, *ro-smád sbrúl-du ˳ḱyil-ba* the lower part of the body like a winding serpent *Wdk.* — *ro-rás* cloth of cotton for wrapping up a dead body before cremation; upon it incantations are frequently written against demons and malignant spirits *Pth.* — *ro-laṅs* = **वेताल** (evil) spirit, or goblin that occupies a dead body (*Will.*) *Tar.* 158. — *ro-šiṅ* wood for burning a dead body.

རོ་ཉེ་ *ro-nyé Stg.* = *ra-nyé, ża-nyé* **lead.**

རོ་མ་ *ró-ma* 1. sometimes for *ro Cs., Schr.* — 2. v. *rtsa* I.

རོ་ཙ་, རོ་གཙང་ *ró-tsa, ró-γtsa* **sexual instinct, carnal desire,** lust *Med.*, *ró-tsa skyéd-pa* to excite, to increase the carnal appetite by medicine *Cs.*; also: to feel it; *ró-tsa-ba* 1. voluptuous, sensual, lustful *Mil.* 2. exciting or animating the sexual instinct *Wdṅ.*

རོག་པོ་ *róg-po* 1. *C.* **black**, cf. *bya-* and *ṕo-róg.* — 2. *W.* = *rág-pa* **reddish, yellowish-brown,** of rocks. — *róg-ge-ba* shining dimly; *żal ˳dzum-nág róg-ge-ba* with a face glowing gloomily as it were *Mil.nt.* — *rog-róg* 1. *C.* jet-black. 2. 'dark-grey' *Sch.*, prob. = *róg-po* 2. — 3. **rogue, villain** *Cs.* (a man of dark deeds?).

རོགས་ *rogs*, vulgar pronunciation of *grogs*, **friend, companion, associate, assistant** v. *grogs*; *rogs-méd γčig-pa* quite alone *Pth.*; **rog-rám čó-če** *W.* = *ra-mda byéd-pa*; **rógs-po** *Ld.* adulterer, **róg-po čó-če** (of a husband) and **róg-mo čó-če** (of a wife) to commit adultery.

རོང་ *roṅ* **narrow passage, defile, cleft** in a hill, also **valley**; *brag-róṅ* dell or chasm between rocks, **ravine,** *roṅ-rtsúb* a rough country full of ravines, so Tibet is called *Glr.*; *róṅ-yul* id.; *róṅ-mi, róṅ-rta, róṅ-lčaṅ* a man coming from, a horse bred in, a willow growing in such a country.

རོད་ *rod* **pride, haughtiness** *Ts.*

རོད་པ་, རོད་པོ་ *ród-pa, ród-po* **stiff,** unable to help one's self, *ród-lči-ba Sch.* id.; *Ld.*: **rod-da-rod-dē** of decrepit or sick people.

རོམ་ཁང་ *róm-ḱaṅ W.* for *ro-ḱaṅ.*

རོམ་པོ་ *róm-po W.* (for *sbóm-po C., B.*) **thick, big, stout,** of men, trees, sticks; **massive, massy, plump; deep,** of sounds, opp. to *ṕrá-mo.* — *róm-yig* type, types, letters used in printing, opp. to *ṕra-yig*, v. *yi-ge.*

རོལ་ *rol* 1. **side,** only in the comp.: *náṅ-rol* inside, *ṕyi-rol* outside, *ṕá-rol, ťsú-rol* etc.; *mál-gyi ṕyi-rol* the outside of the bed (e.g. has been soiled) *Glr.*; mostly as postposition: *yáṅs-pa-čan-gyi náṅ-rol-na* within the town of *Yaṅ-pa-čan*; *náṅ-rol-nas ˳búl-ba* to reach, to hand from within *Dzl.*; *čui ṕá-rol-na, ťsú-rol-na* (or *ťsú-rol-tu*) on the other side or on this side of the water; *γyás-rol, γyón-rol* the right side, the left side; also in a looser sense: *ṕyi-rol-tu bzuṅ-ba* to look upon a thing as externally or really existing *Mil.*; often pleon.: *sṅón-rol-nas* **before, previously** *Thgy.*; *˱óg-rol-tu* for *˱óg-tu* **after** *Pth., Tar.*; *˳di-nas nyi-ma-núb-kyi ṕyógs-rol-na* to the west from here. — 2. *Sch.*: *rol(-tu) bsád-pa* to destroy completely, to kill on the spot (?). — 3. (*Cs.* also *rol-mo*) **furrow;** *rol rmód-pa* to make furrows, to plough.

རོལ་རྟ་ *ról-rta Sch.*: **the near horse** in a team, the right-hand horse.

རོལ་པ་ *ról-pa* = *sprúl-pa*, v. *ról-ba* 3.

རོལ་བ་ *ról-ba* 1. **to amuse** or **divert one's self** (synon. with *rtsé-ba*), thus one of the twelve actions of a Buddha is *btsun-moi ˳ḱor-*

*du ról-ba* diverting himself with his wives; *bdag-yód daṅ ról-ba* to divert one's self with a married woman (sensu obsc.) *Schr.*; in *rgya-čer-ról-pa* (v. sub *rgya*), and in *ról-pa bkód-pa* (the n. of a certain kind of contemplation *Gyatch.*), it is used for **ललित**, playing. — 2. **to take, taste, eat, drink,** *srin-mo krág-la ról-ba* witches or ogresses reveling in blood *Mil.*; *ról-pai stábs-su bžugs* there he sits with greedy mien. — 3. = *sprúl-ba* **to practice sorcery, to cause to appear** by magic power, *rnám-par ról-pa* = *rnám-par sprúl-pa*; *yé-šes ról-pai kyeu lṅa Pth.* for: *yé-šes-kyi sprúl-pa* incarnations of the divine Wisdom; *rol-pai mtso* prob. **enchanted lake,** occurs in the description of the Sumeru, but no Lama seemed to know its exact meaning. — 4. vulg.: **to thrash,** to cudgel.

རོལ་མ་ *ról-ma* 1. v. *rol* 3. — 2. col. for *sgról-ma*.

རོལ་མོ་ *ról-mo* (cf. *ról-ba* 1). 1. **music,** *ról-mo byéd-pa*, *W.* **có-ce**, to make music, *ról-mo spyád-pa Sch.* id. — 2. **musical instrument,** = *ról-moi ča-byád Dzl.*, *ról-ča Cs.*, in *W.* esp. cymbal.

རླ་ and རླག་ *rla* and *rlag* sometimes for *bla* and *glags*.

རླག་པ་ *rlág-pa* v. *rlóg-pa*.

རླངས་པ་ *rláṅs-pa* **vapour, steam,** *ka-rláṅs* **breath, exhalation,** **ka-láṅ táṅ-ce** to breathe, to exhale *W.*; **gaṅ-láṅ** cloud-like snow-drifts on high hills, *ču-rláṅs* steam, watery vapour; *rláṅs-ču ˳dón-pa Schr.* **to distil.**

རླན་ *rlan* 1. **moisture, humidity,** *rlan spáṅ-ba* to avoid the wet *Med.*, *rlan steṅ nyál-ba* to sleep in the wet *Lt.* — 2. **a liquid,** *rlan-rlón* id., *rlan-rlón čaṅ* the liquid (called) beer *Lex.*; *rlán-can* moist, wet, humid, e.g. a country, *rlan-méd* dry. Cf. *rlón-pa, brlan.*

རླབ(ས)་པ་ *rláb(s)-pa Sch.*: 'to remove, to clear away'.

རླབས་ *rlabs* **wave, billow, flood,** *rgyá-mtsoi rlabs Med.*; *ču-rlábs* and *dba-rlábs* or *rba-rlábs* = *rlabs*; *dus-rlabs* ebb and flood, tides *Stg.*; *rlabs γyó-ba* or *˳krúg-pa* the tumult of the waves *Cs.*; *rlabs-po-čé* or *rlabs-čén*, *Lex.*: **महोर्मि**, a large wave or billow, a rolling swell of the sea, surf, surge; also fig.: a high degree, e.g. of diligence *Thgy.*

རླམ་པ་ *rlám-pa* v. *rlóm-pa*; *rlam-kyér Sch.* pride (?).

རླིག་པ་ *rlig-pa*, resp. *γsaṅ-rlíg*, **testicle, stone,** *˳byin-pa*, *˳pyid-pa*, *W.* **tón-ce** **to castrate,** emasculate (a man), to cut or geld (an animal), *rlig-pyúṅ*, *rlig-méd* castrated, emasculated, *rlig-can* having testicles, *rlig-γcig-pa* having only one testicle; *rlig-bu*, *rlig-šúbs* scrotum; *rlig-skráṅs* swollen testicles; *rlig-rlúgs Lt.*, *rlig-blúgs S.g.*, id. (acc. to *Cs.*).

རླིངས་ *rliṅs Sch.* **good, quick,** cf. *brliṅ-ba*.

རླིད་ *rlid Sch.* a closed leather-bag.

རླིད་བུ་ *rlid-bu Sch.*: 'a whole, a lump or mass'; but this seems not applicable in the phrase *dúd-˳groi rlid-bu Lex.*, and otherwise it is not known to me.

རླུག(ས)་པ་ *rlúg(s)-pa* 1. *Cs.*: **'to purge,** *mṅal rlúgs-par byéd-pa* to cause an abortion, *rlugs-byéd* purging, procuring abortion; *rlúgs-ma Sch.*: 'the casting out, effusion'; acc. to one *Lex.* excretion of indigested food. — 2. *Ts.*: to overthrow, to pull down, v. *lug-pa*.

རླུང་ *rluṅ* **वायु** 1. *W.* *rluṅ-po* **breeze, wind,** *rluṅ ló-ma-la reg* the wind touches the leaves *Dzl.*, *rluṅ-gis skyod* (a thing) is moved by the wind *Dzl.*, blown away by the wind *Glr.*; **luṅ laṅ** *C.*, **lúṅ-po pu dug** *W.*, the wind blows, also for: there is a draught (here); **lúṅ-rag máṅ-po yoṅ dug** *W.* one feels the wind (here) very much; *rluṅ čén-po Mil.*, *drág-po* a high wind, a gale; *šár-rluṅ* east-wind etc., *čar-rlúṅ* rain and wind; *skám-rluṅ* a dry wind *Cs.*; **lúṅ-po yób-ce** *W.* to fan; *˳og-luṅ* wind (from the stomach), **flatulence** *Lt.*; fig.: *lás-kyi rlúṅ-gis déd-de* impelled or pushed on by the wind of actions, i.e. involved in the consequences of one's actions; and in a similar manner in other instances, frq. — 2. **air,** atmospheric air, *rlúṅ-gyi dkyil-˳kor* **atmosphere;** *rlúṅ-gi ˳prúl-kor* air-pump *Cs.*, *rlúṅ-gi gru* air-balloon *Cs.* — 3. in physiology: one of the three humours of the body (v. *nyés-pa*) supposed to exist in nearly all the parts and organs of the body, circulating in veins of its own, producing the arbitrary and the involuntary motions, and causing various other physiological phenomena. When deranged, it is the cause of many diseases, esp. of such complaints the origin and seat of which is not known, as rheumatism, nervous affections etc. This *rluṅ* or humour is divided into five species, viz.: *srog-ₒdzin* cause of breathing, *gyén-rgyu* faculty of speaking, *k̔yab-byéd* cause of muscular motion, *me-mnyám* of digestion and assimilation, *t̔ur-sél* of excretion; *rlúṅ-las gyúr-pa yin* (the disease) arises from *rluṅ Glr.*; *rlúṅ-gis bzúṅ-ste = rluṅ-nád-kyis btáb-ste.* — These notions concerning *rluṅ* are one of the weakest points of Tibetan physiology and pathology. — 4. **in mysticism** *rluṅ ₒdzín-pa* seems to be = *dbugs bsgyáṅ-ba*, and to denote the drawing in and holding one's breath during the procedure called *γtum-mo* (q.v.), which is as much as to prepare one's self for contemplation, or enter into a state of ecstasy *Mil.*; *rluṅ séms-la dbaṅ t̔ób-pa Mil.*, frq., is said to imply that high degree of mystical ecstasy, when *rluṅ* and *sems* have been joined into one; he who has attained to the *mgyogs-rlúṅ* is able to perform extraordinary things, e.g. with a heavy burden on his back he is able to run with the greatest speed, and the like. —

**Comp.** *rlúṅ-rta* **the airy horse,** n. of little flags, frequently to be seen waving in the wind on Tibetan houses, on heaps of stones, bridges etc. The figure of a horse which together with various prayers is printed on these flags signifies (acc. to *Schl.* 253) the deity *rta-mčog.* Huc also mentions superstitious practices that may be called *rluṅ-rta.* — *rluṅ-mdá Sch.* air-gun. — *rluṅ-nád* disease caused by *rluṅ*, v. above. — *rluṅ-dmár, rluṅ nág-po* prop. dust-storm, a storm whirling up clouds of dust; further: **storm, tempest** in general, also a gale at sea *Glr.* and elsewh. — *rluṅ-t̔súb* whirlwind, **snow-storm** *Mil.* — *rluṅ-séms* v. above, *rluṅ* 4. — *rluṅ-sér, rluṅ-bsér-bu, rluṅ bsír-ba*, a violent wind *Cs.*

རླུབས་ *rlubs* 1. in *C.*: **corner, hole, place for hiding** a thing; *Lex.*: *k̔uṅ-bui rlubs.* — 2. *Sch.*: **ditch, pit, pool, abyss,** *mei rlubs* fire-pool.

རློག་པ་ *rlóg-pa*, pf. *brlags*, fut. *brlag*, imp. *rlog(s)*, *brlag*, vb. a. to *ldóg-pa*, 1. **to overthrow, to destroy**; *t̔ál-bar* or *rdál-du rlóg-pa* to reduce to powder, to destroy entirely *Thgy.* and elsewh.; *rtsa-ba-nas*, or *rnám-par*, to annihilate, e.g. all the infidels *Pth.*, **to break, to smash** e.g. a vessel *C.*; **to lose** *C.*, *'á-ma lag-soṅ* I have lost my mother *C.*, *lug čig lag soṅ* one sheep has perished *C.* — 2. fig. **to pervert, to infatuate,** *nyés-pai drí-mas yóṅs-su brlágs-te* quite corrupted by the filth of sin *Dzl.*; *č̔úṅ-mar ₒdzín-pai bsám-rlags-t̔so* those infatuated by thoughts of marriage *Glr.*; *brlág-po* **foolish, stupid,** of a little child *Thgy.*

རློང་ *rloṅ* sometimes erron. for *kloṅ* or *loṅ.*

རློན་པ་ *rlón-pa* I. 1. adj. (*Cs.* 'moist') *W.* **wet,** *tsaṅ-rlón* quite wet, wet through; hence of meat, vegetables and the like, **fresh, green, raw** *B.* and col. — 2. vb., pf. and fut. *brlan*, **to make wet, to moisten,** *č̔us*, *č̔ar-pas Dzl.*

II. *Sch.*: **to answer,** with *lan*, also *glón-pa, ldón-pa, blán-pa, zlón-pa.*

རློབ་པ་ *rlób-pa*, pf. *brlabs*, fut. *brlab*, imp. *rlobs*, v. *byin.*

རློམ་པ་ *rlóm-pa* I. vb., pf. *brlams*, fut. *brlam* 1. **to be proud of, to glory in, to boast of,** with termin., *bder rlóm-pa* to boast of one's good fortune, *γčig-par* or *γčig-tu rlóm-pa* to be proud of the identity with ... *Tar.* — 2. **to love, to adhere to, to be attached to** *W.*, **to strive after,** *γžán-gyi nór-la.* — 3. **to be possessed,** of demons, *γdón-gyis brláms-pa Lt.* — II. sbst. **pride,** *bsags kyaṅ rlóm-pas ₒk̔yer* if perhaps (any merit) has been gathered, it is taken away again by pride *Mil.* — Deriv. *rlóm-po* **a boaster,** an arrogant person *Cs.*; *rlóm-sems* **pride, arrogance.**

བརླ་(བོ་? *Cs.*) *brla* (*-bo?*) **the thigh,** *brla ná-ba* a pain in the thigh *Do.*, *brla γyas* the right thigh *Glr.*, *brla-rkáṅ* femoral bone (*Sch.*: hip-bone?). **brla-ḱuṅ** groin *W.*; *brla-bar Sch.*: junction of the legs, genitals; *brla-rús* femoral bone; *brla-ŝá* muscular part of the thigh; *brla-súl Cs.*: 'side of the thigh'.

བརླག་པ་ *brlág-pa* v. *rlóg-pa.*

བརླང་པོ་ *brláṅ-po Lex.* and *Sch.* **abusive word, invective, abusive language** (*Sch.* also: 'rude fellow, brute'?), *rtsub-brláṅ-ba ma yin-pa* refraining from abusive language *Thgy.*; *brláṅ-po-rnams byéd-pa* to make use of such language *Stg.*; *brlaṅ-spyód byéd-pa* to be coarse, churlish *Sch.*

བརླན་པ་ *brlán-pa* v. *rlón-pa.*

བརླབ་པ་ *brláb-pa* v. *rlób-pa.*

བརླམ་པ་ *brlám-pa* v. *rlóm-pa.*

བརླིང་བ་ *brlíṅ-ba C.* **firm, secure, safe** (*Sch.*: quick?), *brlíṅ-po* id., both of men and things, **liṅ-ghyi ǰhe-la ḱur** *C.* carry it safely, carefully! *brliṅ-lóg Sch.*: confused, disorderly, not to be trusted.

བརླུག་པ་ *brlúg-pa Sch.*: = *mdzá-bo* friend, assistant, helper; one *Lex.* explains *bló-brlug* by *grogs.*

བརླུབས་ *brlubs* v. *rlubs.*

# ལ

ལ *la* 1. the letter l. — 2. numeral: 26.

ལ་ *la* I. sbst. **mountain pass,** road or passage over a mountain, *lai gyen* the up-hill road or ascent of a mountain, *lai ṫur* the down-hill road or descent *Cs.*; *la rgál-ba B., C.* (*W.*: **gyáb-ċe**) to cross a mountain pass; *lá-la ˳gró-ba Cs.* id.

**Comp.** *la-rkéd* or *skéd* the declivity or slope of a mountain pass. — *la-ḱá* the highest point of the pass, *la-mgó* the head, or top, of a mountain pass. — *la-sgó*, *Sch.*: 'turnpike of a pass'. — *la-γċán-pa* a collector of duties on a ghat or pass *Cs.* — *la-čún* a small pass *Glr.* — *la-mǰúg* = *la-rtsa.* *la-stóṅ* v. *stóṅ-pa.* — *la-ṫóg* = *la-rtsé.* — *la-rtsá* (*W.* **lar-sa**) foot of a mountain pass *la-rtsé* (*W.* **lar-sé**) top of it. — *la-ŝán Sch.*: = *la-rkéd.*

II. sbst., also *lá-ba*, **wax-light, wax-candle, taper,** from the Chinese *láh* **wax,** *C.*

III. In compounds for *la-ṗug* and *la-ča.*

IV. postpos. c. acc. 1. denoting local relations in quite a general sense, in answer to the questions **where** and **whither:** *sá-la ˳gré-ba* to roll (one's body) on the ground, *sá-la ˳gríl-ba* to fall down on the ground, *nám-mka-la ˳ṗág-pa* to rise to heaven, *nám-mka-la ˳ṗúr-ba* to fly in the air, *mé-la* at, on, in, to, the fire, *ri-la* on, to, the mountain, *čú-la* in, into, to, on, the water, *ŝár-la* to, towards the east, eastward (e.g. to look), *bód-la* in, to, Tibet; also where we should say: from, as: *γnám-la ḱá-ba ˳bab* snow falls from heaven, *rtá-la ˳bab* he alights from his horse, *brág-la mčoṅs* he leaps down from the rock *Dzl.*, *lús-la ḱrag ˳byin-pa* to draw blood from the body by scratching. This latter use of *la* occurs so frequently, that it cannot always be looked upon as a misspelling for *las*, though this would be the more exact word. — 2. with reference to time: *žag γsúm-pa-la* on the third day, *lo nyi-ŝú-pa-la* in the twentieth or during the twentieth year, *zlá-ba γsúm-la* (finish it) within three months *Glr.*, *ṗyag dáṅ-po-la* at, during, the first obeisance *Glr.* — 3. in other bearings: *dé-la rtén-nas* (prop. relying on, keeping to) relative to, with respect to, in consequence of; also *dé-la*, without *rtén-nas* id.; with verbs expressing feelings of the mind: **at, off, concerning** etc., *dé-la dgá-ste* glad of, rejoicing at it; *sdíg-pa-la ˳dzém-pa* to be afraid of sin; *ma byúṅ-ba ˳di-laγdáms-ṅág γsól-to* he asked advice with respect to this not having been done *Mil.*; in introducing a new subject: *rgyál-sa me-nyág-la ṡór-bai lo-rgyús-la* now, as to the fact of the supremacy having been transferred to *Taṅ-gud*, it . . . *Glr.*; in headings of chapters etc., e.g. *gliṅ bżii míṅ-la* names of the four parts of the globe *Trig.*; *ce-čuṅ-gi t́sad-la* with respect to size *Glr.*; *bre-sráṅ-la γyo mi byéd-pa* not to cheat by measure and weight *Glr.*; for the Latin *erga* and *contra*, as: *dgra-la rgol-ba* to struggle against or with an enemy; *bu-la snyiṅ-brtse-nas* from love to her son; *nad-stóbs-kyi če-čúṅ-la dpág-pa* to proportion (the medicines) to the degree of the illness *Lt.*; *sṅár-gyi rgyún-la* in comparison with the former time *Tar.*; *rgyál-poi t́ugs-rje-la* by, or according to the king's favour; *ṅai lúgs-la* by my way of proceeding, according to my system *Mil.*; *żabs-p̀yi-la* (to go with a person) as a companion. — 4. most frq. *la* is used as sign of the dat. case, col. also of the accus. following a vb. a. — 5. in all the relations mentioned above, *la* is added to the inf., partic. and root of a vb., wherever the verb will at all admit of it, and besides it is used as gerundial particle in a similar sense as *te:* a. after the inf. (only in *B.*): *lha-rtén żig yód-pa-la* as there was in that place an idol-shrine *Dzl.*; often also to be translated by **although.** b. added to the root (*B.* and col.): *mt́óṅ-la ma btags* (though) having seen it, yet he did not fasten it *Dzl.*; col. esp. when the root is doubled, for **while, whilst:** **ṅe ṡa tub-túb-la kyod ṡiṅ k̀ur** fetch thou wood, whilst I am cutting the meat into pieces *W.*; in *C.* and *B.* = *čiṅ*, also added to adjectives, *lus mi-sdúg-čiṅ t́úṅ-la dbyaṅs snyán-pa* ugly as to his body (and) of small stature, (but) having a fine voice *Dzl.*; in sentences containing an imp. it is added to the root of it: *ṡóg-la ltos ṡig* come and look!

ལ་ཁྱི་མོ་ *la-k̀yi-mo W.* **the mountain-weasel;** = *sre-moṅ?*

ལ་རྒྱ་ *la-rgyá Sch.*: government, administration (?).

ལ་ཆ་ *la-čá* **sealing-wax,** *Wdṅ.*; **la-kyir* W.* balls of sealing-wax, with a hole for stringing them, used like our sticks of sealing-wax; *la-t́ig* drops of sealing-wax; *la-t́ig rgyág-pa* to drop melted sealing-wax upon (a person), as a torture.

ལ་ཉུང་ *la-nyúṅ Glr.*, either a sort of turnip, or (more prob.) for *lá-p̀ug daṅ nyúṅ-ma* radish and turnip.

ལ་ཉེ་ *la-nyé Sch.*: 'a mark' (?).

ལ་ཏ་ *la-tá Hind.* لتته? an imported material like flax or a sort of linen-cloth, not in general use; hence in many parts of the country unknown.

ལ་ཏུ, ལ་ཐུ, ལ་དུ་ *la-tu, la-t́u, la-du*, prop. ལཌྜུ. a sort of pastry of India, composed of suet, coarse meal, sugar and spices; the word may also be used for our gingerbread.

ལ་ཐིག་ *la-t́ig* v. *la-ča*.

ལ་ཐོད་ *la-t́ód* **turban** *Glr.*

ལ་དྭགས་ *la-dwágs*, also *mṅár-yul*, **Ladág, Ladák,** province in the valley of the Indus between *mṅa-ris* and Bálti, inhabited by Tibetans and formerly belonging to Tibet, afterwards an independent kingdom, but recently conquered by Gulab Singh of Kashmere and hindooized as much as possible by his son and successor; capital **Le.**

ལ་པ་ཤ་, ལ་པ་ཤག་ *lá-pa-ṡa* or *lá-pa-ṡag Cs.* a kind of upper garment without a girdle.

ལ་པོ་ *lá-po* **buttermilk,** boiled, but not yet dried into vermicelli (*čúr-ba*).

ལ་ཕུག་ *lá-p̀ug* **radish,** *bod lá-p̀ug* the common black radish, ni f.; *rgya lá-p̀ug* a red species, of an acidulous taste. The carrot (*Daucus carota*) is in *C.* also col. called *la-p̀ug sér-po.* — *la-bdár*, gen. **lab-*

dár*, a contrivance for grating radishes, either made of wood, or consisting of a quartz-stone with a crystallized, rough surface.

ལ་བ་ *lá-ba* v. *la* II.

ལྭ་བ, ལྭ་ཝ་ *lwá-ba, lwá-wa, Ssk.* कम्बल, *Will.*: 'a woolen blanket or cloth; a sort of deer'; *skrai lwá-ba Stg.* frq. a kind of woolen cloth. The seat of Buddha is often a slab resembling a *lwá-ba Do.*

ལ་མ་ *la-ma Sch.*: a certain herb.

ལ་མ་སྲོ་ *la-ma-sró* **raspberry** *Kun.*

ལ་འུར་ *la-ủr Cs.*, also *la-gór Sch.*, **quick, swift, speedy,** *k̔yod ma ₒdug ma ₒdug la-ủr ₒdeṅ Mil.* make haste, go without stopping (on the road).

ལ་ཡོགས་ *la-yógs* **retribution,** punishments overtaking a sinner during this life (cf. *lan-čags*) *C., W.*; **la-yóg tob yin** that will come home to you! *Sch.* has *la-yogs-pa* to return, to come back (?).

ལ་རེ་ *la-ré W.* a sort of long-legged and swift-moving centiped, frequent in houses.

ལ་ལ་ *la-la C., B.* (is said to be pronounced *la-lá* in *Sp.*, but *Thgy.* sometimes accentuates *lá-la*, according to the metre) **some, a few**; when put twice: **partly — partly, what — what;** *la-la žig* also as a singular: some body, some one *Dzl. ƲƲ*, 1.

ལ་ལ་ཕུད་ *lá-la-p̔ud* a medicinal herb; in *Lh.* a Bupleurum.

ལ་སོ་ *la-so Sch.* **list** (of cloth), **selvage.**

ལ་སོགས་ *la-sógs* v. *sogs.*

ལག་ *lag*, also *dbón-lag, dgón-lag, Sch.*: little, not much.

ལག(པ) *lág(-pa)* 1. resp. *p̔yag*, **hand, arm,** **lág-pa táṅ-če* W.* to shake hands, also to offer one's hand, as a pledge of faith (for *C.* v. *mdzúg-gu*); *lág-pa-nas ₒǰú-ba* to take, to seize by the hand *Dzl.*; *lag-pai rgyab* or *bol* the back of the hand; *lág-pai mdun* the palm of the hand *Cs.*; *lág-tu lén-pa* **to take in hand, to exercise, to practise,** *sgóm-pa* meditation *Mil.*, *tsig-dón* to study and practise the import of a word, to live accordingly *Mil.*, metaph.: *mtso-lág* **arm of the sea,** gulf, **bay,** *mtso-lag-ₒbrél* narrow sea, **straits;** *gliṅ-lág, yul-lág* tongue of land, *gliṅ-lag-ₒbrél* isthmus, neck of land *C.*; fig. for **power,** authority, *mii lág-tu ₒgró-ba* to get into a person's power, to be at his mercy *Thgy.*, *lág-nas ₒp̔róg-pa* to snatch out of a person's hand, to deliver from another's power *Glr.* — 2. **fore-paw; also paw or foot** in gen., e.g. foot of a cock *Glr.* — 3. symb. num.: 2.

**Comp.** *lag-kod* **bundle, bunch, armful,** sheaf of corn *Ld.* (?). — *lag-skór Ld.*: **hand-mill.** — *lag-k̔úg* **pouch, hand-bag** *Schr.* — *lag-mgó* 1. *lag-mgo tsam* like a fist *Glr.*, or acc. to others: both hands put together in the shape of a globe or ball. 2. a glove with only a thumb, a mitten *C.* — *lag-grám* leaning one's head on the hand *W.* — *lag-rgyúgs* **railing.** — *lag-rgyún* accustomed manner, **use, habit** *Cs* — *lag-ṅár* **the fore-arm** *Wdṅ.* — *lág-ča* **utensils, tools, implements;** object carried in the hands, e.g. royal insignia at a festival procession *Glr.*; also in a more gen. sense, like *ča-lag*, *ₒk̔or-γyóg lág-ča daṅ bčás-pa toṅ žig* supply servants and things (wanted for the journey)! *Glr.* — *lag-čág* a broken hand, a lame hand *Cs., Schr.* — **lag-čad* W.* solemn promise by shaking or joining hands. — *lag-rǰés* 1. impression, mark, of the hand, of the fingers. 2. a work which immortalizes a person's name, *lag-rǰes ₒǰóg-pa* to leave such a work behind *Glr.* — *lag-nyá*, one *Lex.* has: *lag-nyás* = *stér-mk̔an-med-par lén-pa* to take what is not given, hence *lag-nya* prob. a sbst.: a grasp, a snatch. — **lag-nyár* W.* for *lag-ṅar.* — *lag-tig* (or *dig?*) travelling-bag, pouch *Ld.* — *lag-rtags* 1. resp. *p̔yag-rtágs* q.v., sign or mark made with the hand, as a seal of verification, impressed on a legal document, but often only with the finger dipped in ink. 2. any small object, e.g. a needle, which the deliverer of a letter has to hand over together with the letter; present in general? — *lag-stábs Sch.* = *lag-*

ལ

len. — lag-mṫil **the palm** of the hand. — lag-dám Mil., lag-dám-po C. **close-fisted,** stingy, niggardly. — lag-dar Lex., prob. the same as láb-dár (W. col.) **grater.** — lag-γdúb **bracelet.** — lag-bdé Mil., C., the person that pours out the tea at a tea-carousal. — lag-ₒdón Cs. a vassal or subject paying his landlord in money or kind, opp. to rkaṅ-ₒgró who performs his services as an errand-goer or a porter. — lag-rdúm Mil. having a mutilated or crippled hand. — lag-ldán having a hand or a trunk, hence = **elephant,** Cs. — lag-brdá **sign** or signal made by the hand, **beckoning.** — lag-na-rdó-rje, lag-rdór v. rdó-rje. — lag-na-γžoṅ-ṫogs Cs. 'holding a basin in his hand', n. of a deity. — lag-snód = lag-ṫíg. — lag-dpón workmaster, overseer, esp. builder Dzl., Glr. — lag-p̔yis a piece of cloth for wiping the hands, **towel, napkin.** — lag-búbs v. ₒbúb-pa. lag-bér **walking-staff.** — lag-mí **bail,** surety. — lag-dmár C. **hangman.** — lag-btsúg **shoot, scion.** — lag-ṫsigs joint of the hand, **wrist; elbow-joint.** — lag-γzúṅs, W. *lag-zúm*, **balustrade,** banister, railing. — lág-γyog-pa **companion, assistant, associate.** — lag-rís the lines in the palm of the hand Sch. — lag-lén, resp. p̔yag-lén, Sch. also ḷag-stabs, **practice, practical knowledge, dexterity,** Cs.: čós-kyi lag-lén the practice of religion, k̔ríms-kyi of the law, rtsís-kyi of mathematics. — lag-šúbs **glove.**

ལགས་པ་ lágs-pa, resp. and eleg. for yin-pa and ₒgyúr-ba, **to be;** lágs-so like yin, as answer to a question: so it is! yes to be sure! very well! at your service! When **a Lama** asks a shepherd: k̔yéd-kyi miṅ či yin what is your name? the latter answers: N. N. byá-ba lags my name, if you please, is N.N., and asks on his part: blá-ma k̔yed či skad byá-ba lags what may be the name of your Reverence? Mil. — de k̔yed lágs-sam is it you, Sir? Pth.; dge-sloṅ de su lags who is this reverend gentleman? Dzl.; či ltar lags-pa (for gyur-pa) γsol-pa he reported (to Buddha) what had happened, Dzl.; blá-ma-la bžugs-grogs med-pa lags-sam Mil. has your Reverence no attendant? ltá-ba ma lágs-kyi that does not mean: to behold, but ... Dzl.; ₒoṅ-ba či lags 'what is it that this comes here?' i.e. how does this happen to come here? Glr.; rje či lags what is that, Sir? (when one is surprised at any thing strange or unaccountable, at an unreasonable demand etc., also when we should say: God forbid!) Glr.; yin lags, γda lags, yod lags there is, it is Glr.; žal-zás γsol lágs-nas when we shall have done dining Dzl.; a Lama asks: btsal-le (= btsal-lam) have you looked for it? and the disciple answers: btsal lags yes, I have! Mil.; in addressing a person: blá-ma lags (prop: you that are a Lama) for the mere vocative case, ὦ ἱερεῦ, Mil., frq. — In W. lags is not in use now (cf. however le 3), but in C. it is of frq. occurrence, e.g. in Lhasa: *lā, lā-so, lā yo̱', lā yin* for: yes, Sir! very well, Sir! *lā? lā-am? lā-sam?* please? what did you say?

ལགས་མོ་ lágs-mo W. **clean,** for légs-pa.

ལང་ཀ་ laṅ-ka **Ceylon,** laṅ-ka-pu-ri city of the Rakshasa in Ceylon, which island is the abode of these beings, according to the belief of many people in Tibet and northern India even at the present day; laṅ-kar γšegs-pai mdo the Sutra Laṅkāvatāra in the Kangyur.

ལང་(ང་)ལོང་(ངེ་) laṅ(-ṅa)-loṅ(-ṅe) **weak,** e.g. from hunger, disease Ld.

ལང་ཐང་ laṅ-ṫaṅ Scopolia praealta Don., a common weed with pale yellowish flowers Med.; in Lh. a species of Hyoscyamus, of frq. occurrence, seems to be understood by the same name.

ལང་བ་ láṅ-ba (provinc. lóṅ-ba), pf. laṅs, imp. loṅ(s), = ldaṅ-ba, I. **to rise, to get up,** da loṅs get up now! also with yar (pleon.); laṅs-te sdod-pa **to stand,** Lt. and col; **to arise,** e.g. of a contest W., C.; to go away, to depart, esp. fig., of the night: nam láṅs-te at daybreak; **to come forward, to step forth,** from among the crowd Do.; p̔yir láṅ-ba **to recover,** to be restored, to grow well, **to come to one's self,** after a fainting fit *Dzl.*; *bstán-pai mé-ro láṅs-pa yin* the dying embers of religion were blown into a flame again *Glr.*; **to appear, to break out,** of a disease, *nad-laṅs-dus* when a disease is in its first beginnings *Lt.* — II. *laṅ-ba* and *loṅ-ba*, pf. *loṅs* to come up to, to arrive at, **to be equal, to reach,** *ₒdi loṅ soṅ* with this it is made up, that will do *C.*; *ₒdrén-gyis ma laṅ* lit.: the serving up (of many dishes) would not do, i.e. there would be no end of serving up *Mil.*; *gráṅs-kyis láṅ-ba* to be numerable *Mil.*, cf. also *ča* (init.) and *rǰód-pa* (extr.).

ལང་ཚོ་ *láṅ-tso* **youth,** youthful age, *dei láṅ-tso-la ma čágs-pas* not falling in love with, not being enticed or led away by their youthful appearance *Glr.*, *láṅ-tso rgyás-pas* grown up to adolescence; *laṅ-tsoi dpal* the charms of youth *Pth.*; *láṅ-tso srin-moi ydoṅ* the face of the youthful Srinmo *Glr.*; *laṅ-tso-čan Cs.* adolescent, young; *laṅ-tso-ma* **girl,** maiden *Sb.*

ལང་ལིང་བ་ *láṅ-liṅ-ba Sch.* to be in a confused whirling motion (v. *loṅ-loṅ*); *laṅ-ma-liṅ Mil.* seems to be a word descriptive of the rising of a cloud, of the soaring of a bird of prey, *sprin-dkár laṅ-ma-liṅ.*

ལང་ལོང་ *laṅ-lóṅ* v. *laṅ-na-loṅ-ṅe.*

ལང་ཤོར་ *laṅ-šór Cs.* **stubbornness, obstinacy,** adj. *laṅ-šór-čan*; sometimes *laṅ-šór* (without *čan*) seems to be also used adjectively, e.g.: *ₒdre kyéd-pas láṅ-šor bág-čags yin Mil.* evil passion is more obstinate (i.e. more difficult to be got rid of) than ye hobgoblins.

ལད་པ་ *lád-pa Cs.* **weak, faint, exhausted,** of men and animals; **blunt, dull,** of knives; *Sch.* also **rotten, decayed.**

ལད་མོ་ *lád-mo* **imitation,** *lád-mo byéd-pa B., C.,* **čo-če**, *gyab-če** *W.*, **to imitate, to mimic, to say after,** *smón-lam ₒdi-skad bdág-gi lád-mo gyis* say after me the following prayer *Thgr.*; *ṅéd-kyi lád-mo kyéd-kyis mi ₒoṅ Mil.* you cannot imitate me.

ལན་ *lan* (orig. perh.: 'turn', hence): 1. **time, times,** *lan-yčig* 1. once, one time. 2. also ***dus-lan-yčig Glr.*** once, one day, both as to the past and the future. 3. once for all, decidedly *Glr.* 4. for this time, first, first of all, before all, **lan čig lé-ka ₒdi čo** this work must be done first of all; *da-lán* id.; *lan ynyis* **twice,** *lan-bču* ten times etc.; *lan bdun (nam) ysum* seven times or three times, frq. in rules about ceremonies; *bsgór-ba lan máṅ-du byás-te* circumambulating round it many times *Mil.*; *lan graṅs dpag-tu-méd-pa* innumerable times *Thgy.*; *W.*: **ži lan nyi la tsam pel** how many are 2 times 4? *bži lan ynyis-la brgyad soṅ* 2 times 4 are 8. — 2. **return, retribution, retaliation,** *lan byéd-pa* (*W.* **čó-če**), *lan ₒǰál-ba* **to return, retaliate, repay;** *pán-lan ynód-pas* or *légs-pai lan nyés-pas ₒǰál-ba B.*, **pém-pe lén-la nó-pa ǰhé-pa** *C.*, **pán-pe lán-la nód-pa čo-če** *W.* to return evil for good; **lan-zó čó-če W.* to show gratefulness, to be grateful; **punishment,** . . . *bčúg-pas lan dug* that is the punishment for having allowed . . . *Glr.*; *lan lén-pa*, *W.*: **lan kór-če, táṅ-če, dug-lan ldón-če**, to take vengeance, to revenge one's self; *mig-la mig-lan só-la só-lan šróg-la šróg-lan* eye for eye, tooth for tooth, life for life; *dei lán-la* in return for that; *lan-gráṅs* a number of retributions *Thgy.*; *drin-lan* recompense for benefits received, requital of a good action, *bzaṅ-lán* id., *dei bzáṅ-lan-du* as an acknowledgment for it *Glr.*; hence *ṅan-lan* signifies: taking revenge for an injury received, returning evil for evil, not as *Cs.* gives: *bzaṅ-lan* gratefulness, *ṅan-lan* ungratefulness (?) — 3. **answer, reply,** *kyód-kyi ysúṅ-ba dei lán-du* as answer to your majesty's question *Glr.*; *lan ₒdébs-pa* frq., also *ₒtébs-pa, klón-pa, ldón-pa Dzl.*, *W.* **zér-če** **to answer;** *lan ysól-ba, žú-ba* id. in answering to the questions of a person superior by rank, age or office, — *lan mdzád-pa* if he, the superior, answers; *ytám-lan glú-yis ₒǰal* I answer to the speech by a song *Mil.*; *drís-lan* an answer to a question, *prin-lan* a reply to a dispatch received, *rtsód-lan Cs.* a defendant's reply (in law), *yig-lan* answer to a letter.

ལན་ཀན་, ལན་གན་ *lán-kan, lán-gan* **railing, fence, enclosure** *Stg.*; *Lex.*: = *pu-šu.*

ལ

ལན་སྐྱར་ *lan-skyár W.* prob. = *lan*, **retribution, return,** **de lan-kyár yin** that is all he has gained by it!

ལན་གྱོག་ *lan-gyóg Thgy.*, prob. = *lan-čags;* or perh. the original form of *la-yógs?*

ལན་ཆགས་ *lan-čágs* **misfortune, adversity, calamity,** as a supposed punishment for what has been done in a former life; every unlucky accident, that happens to a person without his own fault, being looked upon as a retribution for former crimes. Thus *lan-čags* denotes about what Non-Buddhists would call **destiny, fate, disaster.**

ལན་བུ་ *lán-bu* **braid, plait, tress of hair** (*Cs.* curl, lock of hair? *Sch.* pigtail?) *lán-bu slé-ba* or *lhé-ba* to make plaits, to plait the hair; *lan-ťsár* ornaments, worn in the hair *Mil.*

ལན་ཚ་ *lán-ťsa*, more accurately *lańťsa* (acc. to Hodgson corrupted from रञ्जा) n. of a style of writing in use among Nepalese Buddhists. It is a kind of ornamental writing, used by caligraphists for inscriptions and titles of books.

ལན་ཚྭ་ *lán-ťswa* **salt,** prob. = *ťswa, lán-ťswa čú-la tim-pa* salt which dissolves in water *Thgy.*; *lán-ťswa ǩa-zás kún-gyi bró-ba skyed* salt gives a relish to every dish *S.g.*; *lán-tswai ču* salt-water *Lex.; lán-ťswa-ba* saline, briny *Med.*

ལབ་བདར་ *lab-bdár* v. *la-bdár* in *la-ṕúg.*

ལབ་པ་ *láb-pa* **to speak, talk, tell,** *mi-la ma lab* do not tell anybody *Mil.*; *rdzún-ɣtam láb-pa Bhot.* **to lie,** to utter a falsehood; *lab ťsól-ba Sch.*: 'to speak unseemly, to brawl(?)'. — *lab tsám-pa Sch.*: to speak while dreaming, to be delirious. *lab ɣtón-ba Cs*, **lab gyáb-če* W.* **to talk, to chat;** **ǩá-lab-čẹn** **eloquent,** fluent of words *C., W.*; *rgya-láb* a great deal of talk, *rgya-láb-čan* **talkative** *C., W.*

**Comp.** *láb-ga Cs.*, **láb-ča* C., W.* **talk.** — *lab-grógs Mil.* companion, intimate friend *Mil.* — *lab-rdól* talking unbecomingly *Sch.* — **láb-ra** (prop. *láb-sgra*) 'noise of tattling', **tattle, talk,** **láb-ra tán-če* W.* **to chat, babble.** — **lab-lób* or *lab-lo**, with **gyáb-če** to speak indistinctly, to mumble; to speak in one's sleep; **lab-lób-te ḍul** he walks speaking in his sleep, he is a somnambulist *W.*

ལབ་ཙེ་ *láb-tse* a heap of stones in which a pole with little flags is fastened, esp. on mountain passes *Schl.* 198.

ལམ་ *lam* 1. **way, road,** *lam-čén, rgyá-lam, stóṅ-lam Cs.*, **má-lam* W.* **highway, main road, high-road;** *gyén-lam* an up-hill road, an ascent, *ťúr-lam* a down-hill road, *ṕréd-lam, rtsíbs-lam* a horizontal or a sloping road, that leads alongside a hill, *lam-ṗrán* a narrow footpath, *lam dóg-mo* a strait path, *lam yáṅspa* a broad one; **lam dé-mo** a good, easy road, **lam sóg-po** a difficult, dangerous, road *W.*; *lam ťár* the road is open, may be passed, is not obstructed by snow etc. *Glr.*; *lam byéd-pa Sch.*, **lam čò-če, sál-če* W.* to clear a path, to construct a road; *rgya-gár-gyi lam* or *rgya-gar-du ˳gró-bai lam* the way to India *Pth.*; *gri-lam* the way of the knife, i.e. **a cut, slit, slash;** **'i-nẹ dúd-pẹ lam** here is the way for the smoke, here the smoke escapes *W.* — 2. way, space or distance travelled over, **journey,** *lám-du* on the road, on the journey; *bal-bód-kyi lam* the journey from Nepal to Tibet *Glr.*, *lám-du ˳júg-pa* to set out, to travel, also: to continue one's journey, *lam-ṕyéd tsám-du ṕyin-pa daṅ* as we had done about half the way *Dzl.*, *lám-nas ldóg-pa* to return home from a journey, *ǩrús-la ˳gró-bai lám-du* when he went to bathe *Dzl.* — 3. **गति,** fig. **way** or **manner** of acting, in order to obtain a certain end; *ťár(-pai) lam* the way of deliverance, viz. for Buddhists: from the cycle of transmigrations, for Christians: from sin and its consequences; hence the way to happiness, to eternal bliss. The six (sometimes only five) classes of beings (v. *˳gró-ba*) are sometimes called the six ways of re-birth within the orb of transmigration. In mystical writings *lam lṅa* are spoken of as the ways leading to the *sa bču* (q. v.) *Thgy.; lam(-gyi) rim(-pa) Cs.*: 'a degree of advance; the several steps towards perfection'; also the title of sundry mystical writings; *záb-lam* the profound method or way, *ťábs-lam* method of the (proper) means (nif.) *Mil.*; *bla-med-rdó-rjei lam*, col. *snágs-kyi lam* denotes the Uma-doctrine or mysticism, v. *dbú-ma; skyés-bu čúṅ-bai, ₒbriṅ-poi*, and *čén-poi lam* three ways: that of a natural (sinful) man, that of the more advanced believer (but not: 'the happy mean' *Cs.*) and that of the saint, or the walk and conversation of the righteous, so also in *draṅ-sroṅ-gyi lam* the saint's or hermit's course of life; *dgé-ba bčui lás-kyi lam spyód-pa* to walk the way of practising the ten virtues *Dzl.*

**Comp. and deriv.** *lám-ka* prob. = *lam*, *lám-ka-na* (another reading *lám-k̔ar*), by the road-side *Dzl.* — *lam-mk̔an* one well acquainted with the road, **a guide** *Pth.*, also fig. — *lam-gól* by-way, secret path *Sch.* — — *lam-grógs* **fellow-traveller,** travelling companion. — *lam-rgyúd* = *lam* 3? *lam-rgyúd lňa Dzl.* ༧༥༢, 18, the five classes of beings, cf. *ₒgró-ba* II. — *lam-rgyús-pa* = *lám-mk̔an*. — *lam-čén Schr.* = *rgya-lám.* — *lam-rtágs* the signs of the way being nearly accomplished i.e. the acquirements and perfections of a saint *Mil.* — *lam-ltar-snaṅ* something looking like a road, but a spurious, wrong way *Sch.* — *lam-stégs* seat, resting-place by the way-side; also fig. *Glr.* — *lam-mdó* v. *mdo.* — *lam-ₒdrén-pa, lam-sná-pa* **guide.** — *lám-pa* 1. **police-officer** stationed on high-roads for seizing thieves or fugitives; **toll-gatherer.** 2. **traveller,** wayfarer *Cs.* 3. **bell-wether** *W.* — *lám-po* = *lam, lam-po-čé.* 1. **highway** *Sb.;* also as a place for practising magic, nif. 2. **way to heaven,** = **ťar-lam** *W.*(?) — *lám-yig* v. *yi-ge.* extr. — *lam-lóg* erroneous *Mil.* — *lam-sraṅ* **lane, street.**

ལར་ *lar* 1. **but, yet, still, however** *Mil.*, *Thgy.*, *Glr.*; *lár-ni* and *lár-na* id.; occurs scarcely any more in col. language. — 2. **lar** (or **la-re**) *me' C.* none at all(?).

ལས་ *las* I. sbst., col. *lás-ka*, resp. *p̔yag-lás W.* **ṭ in-lẹ**. 1. **action, act, deed, work,** *byi-dór-gyi las* the act of sweeping *Lex.*; *las-bzáṅ, las-dkár* a good work, virtuous action, *las-ṅán, las-nág* a bad, a wicked action, frq.; *lus daṅ ṅag daṅ yid-kyi las* actions, words, thoughts *Dzl.; lás-kyi rnam-smin* retribution, reward or punishment for human actions, frq. (cf. *las-rgyu-ₒbras* below); *lás-kyi mé-loṅ* mirror of fate, mirror foreshadowing future events *Glr.; lás-kyi búm-pa* a certain vessel used in religious ceremonies *Schl.* 248; *las ma zád-pas* because the measure of his deeds was not yet full, his destiny was not yet fulfilled *Dzl.*; also **destination** in a general sense *Was.* (282); *lás-kyi lhág-ma lús-pa des* in consequence of the yet remaining rest of (unrequited) works *Stg.; snón-las* former action; *las dbaṅ-bčós-su-méd-pa Pth.* an accident which cannot be prevented; **performance, transaction, business,** *las ťams-čad nus-pa* one who can do or perform every thing *Do.*; also the **functions** of some organ of the body *Lt.; **work; labour, manual labour,*** **lé-ka ťób-pa** to get work; *las byéd-pa B., C.*, **lẹ-ka čó-če, táṅ-če* W.* to do or perform a work, **to work,** also of things: **to operate, to produce effects** *Wdṅ ; mk̔ar-las-byed-mi* workmen employed in building *Mil.; dúr-las byéd-pa* to attend to the graves, i.e. to perform the sepulchral rites and ceremonies; *zaṅ-ziṅ-las byéd-pa* to carry on business, to trade, to traffic *Mil.; lás-su* as a task, according to one's occupation, trade, or business, by virtue of one's office, **ex officio** (nif.) *Mil.; lás-su rúṅ-bar* duly, rightly, perfectly, *comme il faut Mil.; lás-su byá-ba* v. below (extr.). — 2. sometimes: **secular business,** **lé-kẹ náṅ-na** in business-affairs, in practical life. — 3. **effect** of actions, and in a special sense: **merit,** *las zád-pa* the merits being over, having an end *Thgy.* (cf. 1, above). — 4. the doctrine of works and their consequences, of retribution, *las mi bden* that doctrine is not true *Thgy.*

**Comp. and deriv.** *lás-ka* 1. col. work, labour, v. above. 2. *Sch.* and *Wts.:* **dignity, rank, title.** — *las-skál* retributive fate, = *las-p̔ró.* — *lás-mk̔an* **workman** *Cs.* — *las-rgyu-ₒbrás* either for: *las daṅ rgyu-ₒbras* works and their fruits (which in *Thgy.* are divided into *bsód-nams-ma-yin-pai las-rgyu-ₒbrás* sinful deeds, *bsód-nams-kyi las-rgyu-ₒbras* virtuous actions, *mi-γyo-bai las-rgyu-ₒbrás* ascetic or mystical works *W.*), or for *lás-kyi rgyu-ₒbrás*: **fruits** of works, retribution and the doctrine of it. — *lás-sgo* **trading-place, emporium** *Glr.* — *lás-čan* 1. laborious, industrious *Cs.* 2. (v. above *las* 3) having acquired merit, **worthy** *Mil.* — *las-čé* in *C.* used for expressing probability, as in *W.* *ₒgro* with the gerund is used, v. *ₒgro-ba* I, 5; *mtoṅ las-čé* he will probably have seen it *Mil.nt.*; *ṅas ₒdi ₒbor las-čé* as possibly I may put this yet aside; *k̕yod mi-la-ni min las-čé* you are not Mila, are you? *Mil.* — *las-t̕og-pa Sch.*: **a person employed, an official, a functionary.** — *las-rtágs Sch.* **dignity, rank, title** incident to the office held. — *las-dáṅ-po-pa* v. *daṅ-po.* — *las-dár Sch.*: 'parade, ceremonial'(?) — *lás-pa* 1. **workman, labourer** *Cs.* 2. *Sp.*: vice-magistrate of a village. — *lás-dpon* overseer of workmen. — *las-spyód* works, actions, way of life, *byaṅ-čúb-kyi las-spyód skyéd-pa* to lead a holy life *Pth.* — *las-ₒp̕ró* 'continuation, prosecution of works', blessings following meritorious deeds, *k̕yed daṅ ṅa yaṅ sṅón-gyi las-ₒp̕ró-yód-pa yin* a bond of connection is formed between you and me by the merits we acquired in former periods of life *Pth.*; — **happiness,** prosperity in consequence of good works, good luck, fortunate event, opp. to *lan-čags.* — *las-ₒbrél Glr.* prob. id. — *lás-mi* **workman.** — *las-méd* **idle, lazy, inactive.** — *las-ts̕án* 1. **office, post, service,** *las-ts̕án-du ₒjúg-pa* to put into office, to appoint, *las-ts̕án-nas ₒdón-pa* to put out of office, to dismiss *Cs.* 2. **official, functionary** **yúl-gyi lẹ-ts̕ẹ́n** elders of a village-community *C.*, *las-ts̕án-pa* id.—**lẹ-lam-k̕an** **diligent, industrious,** **lẹ-mi lám-k̕an** **idle, lazy** *W.* — *las-su byá-ba* the second case of Tibetan grammar, the **dative** case.

II. only in *B.* and *C.*: postp. c. accus. mostly corresponding in its application to the English prepos. **from,** used also for expressing the ablative case (having nearly the same sense as *nas*): 1. **from,** e.g. delivering from, coming from, often = **through,** e.g. shining into a room through the window *Dzl.*; to hear, get, borrow a thing from a person etc.; to call, to denominate a thing **from** or **after,** according to; *ts̕ád-las dpág-pa* to define **by** or **according to** measure *S.g.*; in quotations: *ₒdúl-ba-las* **out of** the, **from** the Dulva, sometimes also for: **in** the Dulva; for denoting the material **of** which a thing is made: of earth, of clay etc.; partitively: *ₒbras dé-las s̀as γčig* a part of this rice, *slób-ma-las γčig* one of the disciples *Dzl.*; *ṅai yúl-mi-las bú-mo yód-pa-rnams* the girls that are found **among** my subjects *Dzl.*, *kún-las ₒp̕ágs-pa* distinguished **amongst** all, more excellent than all the others *Dzl.*; hence 2. **than** after the comparative degree: *ná-niṅ-las bzaṅ* more beautiful than last year *Mil.*; with a negative: *lo bču-drúg-las ma lón-te* not older than sixteen years *Dzl.*; *zlá-ba lṅá-las mi sdod* I shall not stay **longer than** five months *Glr.*; *ras-yúg γčig-las mi bdóg-ste* possessing **nothing but** one sheet of cotton cloth *Dzl.*; *ṅá-las med* there is none besides myself *Glr.*; *brnyas ₒk̕yér-ba-las mi yoṅ* in the end you will probably do nothing else but despise me *Mil.*; in a brief mode of speaking: *γsa-γčig-las rje-btsun ma mt̕oṅ* we saw nothing but the leopard, your Reverence we did not see *Mil.*; *mi p̕án-žiṅ γnód-pa-las med* it is good for nothing, it only does harm *Mil.* — 3. added to the inf. of verbs it signifies not so much **from** as **after,** from doing, i.e. after doing, *nyál-ba-las láṅ-ba* to rise from lying, to rise after having been lying down; **during,** frq., the verbal root being repeated, *soṅ-sóṅ-ba-las* during my going or travelling on *Dzl.*; *náṅ-du ₒgró-bar bsám-pa-las* when (I) intended to walk in, when (I) was on the point of walking in *Dzl.*

ལས་པ་ *lás-pa Cs.* for *lús-pa*; in *rág-las-pa* and a few other expressions occurring also in *B.*

ལ

ལི་ *li* I. **bell-metal,** *li-sku, li-t̕ál, li-t̕úr, li-snód* an idol, a plate, spoon, vessel made of that metal; *li-ma* in gen.: utensil, instrument that is cast of *li Glr.*

II. **apple,** = *sli C.*

III. *li-yul Glr.*, acc. to *Was.* (74) Buddhist countries in northern Tibet, esp. Khoten; acc. to others in northern India or Nepal.

ལི་ཀ་ར་ *li-ka-ra* or *li-k̔a-ra Cs.* a sort of **sugar.**

ལི་ཁྲི་ *li-k̔ri Glr.* and elsewh., an orange-coloured powder, acc. to *Liś.* सिन्दूर red lead, **minium.**

ལི་ཐང་ *li-t̔an̄ Cs.*: 'n. of a province of Tibet near the Chinese frontier', *li-t̔an̄-pa* inhabitant of that province.

ལི་བ་ *li-ba* **squinting, squint-eyed** *Sch.*, *li-ba mig* squinting eyes *Sch.*

ལི་ཙ་བྱི་ *li-tsa-byi* n. of a noble family of ancient India, often mentioned in the history of Buddha *Dzl., Gyatch.*

ལི་ཡུལ་ *li-yul* v. *li* III.

ལི་ལམ་ *li-lam, Hind.* नीलाम, acc. to Shakspeare from the Portuguese *leilam*, **auction, public sale.**

ལི་ཤི་ *li-śi* 1. *Ssk.* लवङ्ग **cloves** *Med., C.* — 2. *Hind.* इलाएची cardamom *W.*

ལིག་བུ་མིག་ *lig-bu-mig S g., Sch.*: 'malachite'.

ལིང་ག་ *lin̄-ga Ssk.* 1. **sign, mark.** — 2. the image of an enemy which is burnt in the *sbyin-srég* in order thus to kill him by witchcraft *Lt.* — 3. membrum virile *Pth.*

ལིང་གོལ་མ་ *lin̄-gol-ma* **a large hornet** *Sik.*

ལིང་ངེ་ *lin̄-n̄é* **dangling, waving, floating,** in the wind *Mil.*; *sprin žig lin̄ byun̄-bas* a floating cloud? *Mil.*; **lin̄-lin̄ c̀ó-c̀e** *W.* **to dangle,** to hang dangling, e.g. on the gallows, **lin̄-lin̄ sé-c̀e** *W.* **to swing, to see-saw;** *rkan̄-lág p̔ra lin̄-n̄é ̥dug-pa* an infant struggling with hands and feet *Pth.*

ལིང་ཏོག་ *lin̄-tóg* or *lin̄-t̔óg* **a film** or **pellicle** on the eye *Med.*

ལིང་བ་ *lin̄-ba C.*, also *lin̄-po* or *lin̄* alone, **a whole piece,** *lin̄ γc̀ig* of one piece, *lin̄ bži* four pieces or parts, = *rnám-pa*; *γsér-gyi lin̄-ba Cs.*: a piece of unwrought gold; *dar-lin̄ Cs.* a piece of silk; *lin̄-gis ̥dril-ba* to pack up into a parcel, to roll up into one packet *Sch.*

ལིང་ཚེ་ *lin̄-t̔se* gratings, **lattice** *Cs.*

ལིང་ལིང་ *lin̄-lin̄* v. *lin̄-n̄é.*

ལིངས་ *lin̄s* **a hunting** or **chase** in which a number of people are engaged; *dmág-lin̄s* id. (cf. *k̔yi-ra*); *byá-lin̄s Cs.* falconry, hawking; *lin̄s-la ̥gró-ba* to go a shooting, a hunting; *lin̄s ̥débs-pa Sch.* to hunt, to arrange a hunting party; *lin̄s γtón-ba* to get by hunting, to hunt down, *lin̄s btán̄-ba* what has been got by hunting, game shot or caught; *lin̄s-pa* hunter, huntsman, *lin̄s-pa-mo* huntress *Cs.*; *lin̄s-k̔yi* hound, *lin̄s-k̔ra* hunting falcon or hawk.

ལིངས་སྐོར་ *lin̄s-skór* hand-mill *W.* (?)

ལིངས་པ་ *lin̄s-pa Sch.*: quite round or globular; *dkár-por lin̄s-te Pth.*: prob.: being quite white, cf. **ldin̄s-se** *Ld.* quite.

ལིབ་ *lib,* **all,** *Ld.*: **lib du-c̀e** to sweep all together with the hands; *C.*: **k̔á-we lib kab son̄** all being covered with snow.

ལུ་ *lu* 1. **knag, knot, snag,** = ̥*dzér-pa*; **lu-big** knot-hole *Ts.* — 2 num. for 86.

ལུ་ཀང་ *lu-kan̄* (perh. a misspelling for *lugs-kon̄?*) **crucible** for gold and silver *Sch.*

ལུ་གུ་, ལུག་གུ་ *lú-gu, lúg-gu,* diminutive of *lug,* **lamb,** frq.; *lu-gu-rgyúd* 1. rope to which the lambs are fastened, or strung; hence 2. small chain, e.g. watch-chain, chain or row of stitches on knitting-needles; lace-trimming and the like.

ལུ་བ་ *lú-ba* 1. vb. **to cough,** to throw up phlegm, to clear the throat. — 2. sbst. **the cough** *Cs.*

ལུ་མ་ *lú-ma Sb.* pool containing a spring, ground full of springs, *lú-ma-c̀an* rich in springs.

ལུ་ལུ་ *lú-lu* the fruit of some thorny shrubs, *śib-śi-lu-lu* hip, fruit of the wild rose-tree, *t̔ser-stár-lu-lu* berry of *Hippophaë.*

ལུག་ *lug* **sheep,** **d̥ó-lug, śi-lug, bsád-lug** *W.* sheep for slaughter. — *lúg-k̔yu* flock of sheep. — *lúg-gu* v. *lú-gu.* — *lug-sgál* sheep's load — *lug-n̄ál-ba* and *lug-c̀ún̄-ba* names of medicinal herbs *Cs., Wdn̄.* — *lug-snyid Sch.* **wether.** — *lug-t̔úg* **ram** *B., C.*; *lug-t̔úg-gi rwa dbyibs* like a ram's horn *Wdn̄.*; *rgya-ru-lug-t̔úg* a Saiga ram *S.g.* —

*lug-ťóṅ Sch.* wether. — *lúg-pa* 1. sbst. shepherd, keeper of sheep *Ma.* 2. to stick the heads together like timid sheep, to be sheepish in behaviour *Ma.* — *lug-mig* n. of a flower *Med.* — *lug-múr* and *lug-rtsi* medicinal herbs. — *lug-tsága* a sheep-skin with little wool on it *Ld.* — *lug-rá* sheep-fold, pen, sheep-cot. — *lug-rú* ram's horn; n. of several species of *Pedicularis.* — **lug-lóg** sheep-skin *Ld.*

ལུག་པ་ *lúg-pa* I. sbst. and vb., v. sub *lug.* — II. vb., **to give way, to fall down,** cf. *rlúg-pa Ts.*

ལུགས་ *lugs* 1. **the casting, founding,** of metal, *lúgs-su blúg-pa Glr.*, **lúg-la lúg-pa** col. *C.*, to found, to cast; *lúgs-ma* **a cast,** *rgya-gár lúgs-ma* an image (statue, idol) cast in India *Glr.* — 2. **way, manner, fashion, mode, method,** *bód-kyi lúgs su gyis šig Glr.* make it according to the fashion of Tibet; *ṅai lúgs-kyis bon byed dgos* you must live according to our, i.e. the Bon-fashion *Mil.*; *bsam-γtán-la yód-pai lúgs-su byas* he feigned meditation *Glr.*; *di yin-pai lúgs-su byed* they speak, act, make it appear, as if it really were so *Tar.* 184, 21; *ṅa-rán-gi lúgs-kyi mkár-las* my way of building, what I call my style of building *Mil.*; **opinion, view, judgment, way of proceeding,** *ǩyed-rán-gi lúgs-la* according to you, if we followed your advice *Mil.*; *čós-lugs* **religion,** i.e. a certain system of faith and worship, *p̓yi naṅ γnyis čós-lugs gaṅ bzaṅ* which of the two religions, the Brahman or the Buddhist be the better one *Glr.*; **established manner, custom, usage, rite,** *čá-lugs* mode of dress, fashion, *čós-lugs* religious rites, *rgyá-lugs* Chinese (or Indian) manners, *bód-lugs* Tibetan manners etc.; *rán-lugs* one's own way, *γžán-lugs* other people's way or manners; *rán-lugs-la γnás-pa* (= *raṅ-sa ˳dzin-pa*) *Glr.*; seems to be only another expression for that Buddhist virtue of absolute indifference to all objects of the outer world; *lugs* is also used concretely, meaning the adherents of a custom or religion, hence = **sect, school, religious party, denomination,** *mdo-lugs* follower of the Sutras, the Sutra sect, *sṅags-lugs* a follower of the Tantras, the Tantra sect; in a special sense: *lugs γnyis* the two principal classes with regard to religious life, *˳ǰig-rtén-gyi lugs* the laical or profane class, laymen, *čós-kyi lugs* the clerical or sacred class, priests *Cs.*; *lúgs-kyi* that which relates to manners or morals, **ethical** *Cs.* (v. As. Res. XX, 583). — 3. in conjunction with a verbal root or with the genit. of the inf. it often corresponds to the English termination **ing** as: *ldáṅ-lugs* the rising, getting up, *˳gró-lugs* the going, *sdód-lugs* the sitting *Mil.*, *˳o-rgyál yóṅ-lugs sogs šól-˳debs-kyi žú-ba* the (possibility of) getting into difficulties and other reasons for inducing him to postpone (his setting out) *Mil.*; *bsam-yás bžéṅs-lugs bris* he described the building of *Sam-yé Glr.*; *méd-lugs* the (circumstance of) not having *Mil.*; *yin-lugs* **the condition, state** *Mil.*; *dá-lta ná-lugs či-ltar na* as to your present illness, in what does it consist? *Mil.*; *ťsógs-nas skyóṅ-bai lúgs-su yód-pa* they joined in educating them, they educated them together *Mil.*; it is also added to adjectives: *čé-lugs* **greatness** *Mil.*

ལུགས་མ་ *lúgs-ma* v. *lugs* 1.

ལུང་ *luṅ* I. 1. **a strap,** slung over the shoulder or round the waist, for carrying things; **handle, ear** (curved), of vessels, baskets etc., different from *yú-ba* a straight handle, hilt. — 2. 'foot-stalk of fruits' *Cs.*; *lúṅ-ťag Cs.*: a rosary, string of beads, suspended by the girdle.

II. *Ssk.* आगम, = *bka*, used of words spoken by secular persons commanding respect: *p̓as γnáṅ-bai luṅ ťób-nas* obtaining (his) father's word of permission *Dzl*, *luṅ ˳byuṅ* an **order** is issued (by the king) *Glr.*, *tú-ru-ška-la luṅ len dgós-pa* being obliged to accept orders from the Turuskas *Tar.*; more frq.: **spiritual exhortation,** admonition, **instruction,** *luṅ γnáṅ-ba* to give it (sometimes only: to pronounce forms of prayer etc. before devotees); *luṅ γtóṅ-ba* id., **luṅ taṅ-ǩẹn** instructor, teacher, admonisher *C.*; *luṅ stón-pa*, also *lúṅ-du stón-pa* to instruct, to give spiritual precepts, also with regard to supernatural voices etc. *Mil.*; esp. **to prophesy,** predict, **to reveal secrets,** with termin.: *dā-na-śī-la yin-par luṅ bstan* it is prophesied that it is Dānaśīla, the prediction relates to D., *saṅs-rgyás-su lúṅ-bstan-to* he has received a prediction concerning (his obtaining) the Buddhaship *Dzl.*; *mdaṅ mkā-ˌgros lúṅ-bstan-pai skyés-bu de* the man foreshown yesterday by the Dākini *Mil.*, hence *lúṅ-ma-bstan-pa* unheard of, unprecedented *Mil. nt.* (*Cs.* also: to demonstrate, *lúṅ-du brtán-du yód-pa* demonstrable?); *luṅ ˌgód-pa Cs.* to make, to establish, precepts; *luṅ ˌdrén-pa Cs.* to cite, to quote, an authority *Tar.* 210, 2; *lúṅ-gi rjes-ˌbráṅ Was.* (274) those who stick to the letter (opp. to *rigs-kyi rjes-bráṅ* to the real quality, viz. the spirit); *luṅ-bstán* exhortation, precept, commandment, *lhai luṅ-bstán bśád-pa* to communicate the precept of the god *Tar.*, . . . *žes byá-bai luṅ-bstán byuṅ* there came a divine order or prophecy of this purport, to this effect; hence *luṅ-ston-pa* **prophet** *Chr. Prot.*

ལུང་ཐག *luṅ-ṫag* v. above *luṅ* I.

ལུང་པ *lúṅ-pa* 1. **valley,** *ri-lúṅ* mountain and valley; *luṅ-čén* a large valley, *luṅ-čúṅ* or *luṅ-ṗrán* a little valley; *luṅ-kóg Sch.*: 'the cavity of the valley'; *luṅ-stóṅ* a desolate, a solitary valley, as a fit abode for hermits, frq. — 2. **furrow, hollow, groove,** e.g. on the surface of a stick *Mil.*, of the liver *Med.*

ལུད *lud* **manure, dung,** *lug-lúd* sheep's dung; *lud ˌgrém-pa* to spread manure (on fields) *Cs.*, *lud ˌdrén-pa* to carry manure (to the fields) *Cs.*, **gyáb-če, táb-če, táṅ-če** *W.* to manure the ground; *lud-ku* dung-water; *lud-dóṅ* dung-hole; *lud-ṗúṅ* dung-hill; *lúd-ˌbu* grubs etc. in a dung-hill.

ལུད་པ *lud-pa* 1. sbst. **phlegm, mucus,** *rnag-kŕág-gi lúd-pas bkaṅ-ste* full of phlegm, matter and blood *Glr.*; esp. in the organs of respiration: *lúd-pa čig bskyúr-bas* throwing up some phlegm *Glr.*; *lúd-pa lú-ba* to throw up by coughing *Dzl.*, *sbrid-pa* by sneezing *S.g.*; *lúd-ṗor* spittoon, spitting-box *C.* — 2. vb., **to boil over** *ču lúd-pas* the water boiling over *Dzl.*; *mṫso lúd-pa* the running over of lakes, **inundation** *Ma.*; *ču lúd-nas lúd-nas bkáṅ-ba yin* it filled, by the water rising higher and higher.

ལུམས *lums* **a bath** used as a medical cure; **fomentation.**

ལུམ་བི, ལུམ་བི་ནི *lúm-bi, lúm-bi-ni,* n. of a queen, and of a grove called after her, situated in the north of India, where Buddha is said to have been born.

ལུས *lus,* also *lús-po,* **body,** *lus sá-la brdáb-pa* to prostrate one's self, frq., *lus stón-pa* to show one's self, to appear, to make one's self visible, as gods *Dzl.*, and in a similar manner *lus* is often used for expressing our reflective verbs, when relating to physical processes, cf. *sems; lús-kyi dbáṅ-po* the sense of feeling, in as far as it resides in the skin and the whole body of man *Med.*; *rgyál-poi ɣduṅ-brgyúd* (or *rgyal-bu*) *lús-la yod* I bear a prince under my bosom *Glr.*; *lus smád-pa* **to violate, to ravish** *Pth.*; *lus ˌgrúb-pai ṫóg-ma* the beginning of the development of a body as embryo *Wdn.*; *grúb-pa lus* v. *grúb-pa*; *lús-la čágs-śiṅ* from love of life *Dzl.*; *lus daṅ sróg-la sdó-ba* to risk or stake one's life *Dzl.*; *mi-lus ṫób-pa* or *bláṅ-ba* to be born as a human being, *lus-ñán* (to be born) as an animal, or also as a woman *Mil.*; — often for the whole person of a man: *bráṅ-gyi lus kyaṅ dpón-du ˌgyur* even a servant may become a master *S.g.*; *lús-kyis mi bzód-par nya-ñán-gyis ɣdúṅs-te* is used (*Dzl.* ༡༥༡, ༢) of an exclusively mental suffering or infirmity. — In mysticism and speculative science several expressions are employed which, however, do not differ much in their import: *sgyú-lus, ˌjá-lus, bde-ˌgro mṫo-ris-kyi lus*; *rig-pa ˌdzin-pai lus* (*Tar.* 56, 20), *yid-kyi lus* (frq.), लिङ्गशरीर, the immaterial body which is enclosed in the grosser material frame, accompanying the soul in all its transmigrations and not destroyed by death (*Köpp.* I., 66), *yid-kyi lus* might be rendered by 'spiritual body'; another explanation given by Lamas is: the body which exists only in our imagination (*yid*); in that case it would be identical with *sgyu-lús*.

**Comp.** *lus-rgyágs* a fat body *Cs.*, *lus-ríd* a mean, thin, lean body, *lus-sbóm* a thick stout figure, *lus-riṅ* a long tall body, *lus-ťúṅ* a short body *Cs.* — *lús-čan* having a body, hence as sbst. = *séms-čan* creature, being, *lús-čan kún-gyi yid-du ˳oṅ* a favourite of every creature *Stg.* — *lus-stód* upper part of the body, *lus-smád* lower part of the body. — *lus-bóṅs* the bulk of a body. — *lus-byád* form of the body. — *lus-med* having no body, incorporeal, ghostlike, ghostly, *lus-méd-pai skad* a ghostly voice *Mil.* — *lus-smád* v. *lus-stód.* — *lus-zúṅs* v. sub *γzuṅs.*

ལུས་པ་ *lús-pa*, *C.* also *lás-pa*, to remain behind or at home, *bód-du zlá-ba γnyis* to remain in Tibet for two months *Glr.*; **to be remaining or left** *Dzl.*; **to be forgotten,** omitted, left behind; *γyén-du lús-pa* to remain uppermost, floating to remain standing, sitting, lying, e.g. **ka lús-sa mi dug** *W.* the snow does not remain, will soon melt away; *lús-par byéd-pa Pth.*, *lús-su ˳ǰúg-pa*, **lus čúg-če** *Ld.* to leave behind, to leave a remainder; *ma-lús-par* entirely, wholly, without remainder, without exception, *˳gró-ba ma-lús* or *mi-lús Mṅg.*, all creatures without exception; *má-lus-par* prob. also: surely, undoubtedly, at any rate, in any case, ni f. — *lús-ma*, *rǰés-lus*, *pyír-lus*, *lhág-lus Cs.* **remainder, balance, residue.**

ལེ་ *le* 1. a small not cultivated **river-island** *C.*, = *gliṅ-ka* and *zal.* — 2. v. *leu.* — 3. *W.* a word expressive of civility and respect, and added to other words or sentences, like Sir! and Madam! in English, **zu-lé** good day, Sir! it is also added to the word *sa-heb* gentleman, and then *sa-heb-le* is about equivalent to: honoured Sir, dear Sir. — 4. num.: 16.

ལེ་བརྒན་, ལེབ་རྒན་ *le-brgan*, *leb-rgán* 1. *Med.* frq., *Lex.* = वरं saffron, whereas *Cs.* has: 'poppy, *le-brgan-rtsí* the juice of poppies, opium, *le-brgán-ghi mé-tog* the poppy flower, *le-brgán-ghi ˳brás-bu* poppy-seed', and *Sch.* adds: *le-brgan-mdóg* poppy-coloured, light-red, and he translates also *le-brgán Dzl.* ༥༤, 1, by 'poppy-coloured', although it is mentioned there amongst various species of Lotus. But in *W.* poppy and opium are usually called by the Hindi name افيم, *pīm*; neither in *W.* nor in *Sik.* did I meet with any body, who knew the significations given by *Cs.* and *Sch.*, but only: 2. **diapered design** of woven fabrics; thus also *Mil.*: *le-brgán dmár-poi γdan* a flowered carpet, *le-brgán ˳ǰol-bér Pth.* a flowered dress with a train.

ལེ་ན་ *lé-na* the soft downy wool of goats (esp. those of Jangtháng) below the long hair, **the shawl wool**; fine woolen-cloth.

ལེ་མ་ *lé-ma* v. *leu.*

ལེ་ལག་ *le-lág* **appendix, supplement, addition** *Cs.*

ལེ་ལན་ *le-lán Cs.*: consequence; *Sch.*: rebuke, reprimand, reproof, and *le-lán-pa*, *le-lán bdá-ba* to blame, rebuke, reprove; *le-lán-čan Cs.* consequential, important (?).

ལེ་ལམ་མཁན་ *le-lám-mkan* v. *las-lám-mkan.*

ལེ་ལོ་ *lé-lo*, *lé-lo-nyid* **indolence, laziness, tardiness,** *lé-lo ma byed čig* don't be lazy! *Glr.*; *γčig lé-lo byás-nas* as one (of them) had been lazy *Dzl.*; *lé-los ˳kyer* he is overcome by laziness *Mil.*; *lé-loi rǰés-su ˳gró-ba* to be given to laziness *Ld.-Glr.*; *lé-lo-čaṅ* **lazy, indolent, slothful.** — **le-šól** *W.* = *le-lo.*

ལེགས་པ་ *légs-pa B.*, *légs-po* and *-mo C.* (cf. also no. 3) 1. **good,** serving the purpose, with regard to things; adv. *légs-par* well, duly, properly, *légs-par ˳tsól-ba* to search, to investigate accurately *Glr.*; *bsú-ba légs-po gyis* do care for a proper reception! *Glr.*; *légs-par gyur čig* (*Schr.* adds *kyéd-la*) may you prosper! *Sch.*, *légs-par ˳óṅs-so* you are welcome *Sch.*; **happy, comfortable,** *bdag légs-na* when I am well off (opp. to *nyés-na*) *Do.*; *legs nyes stón-pai mé-loṅ* mirror of fate, of the future *Glr.*; *lo(-ťog) légs(-pa) B.*, **lo lag-mo** *W.*, a rich, healthy, happy year; *či ltar byás-na legs* which is the best way of doing it? *Glr.*,

*Tar.*; *sems-čan mis byás-na légs-pa gaṅ yin* which of the actions of human beings are good (in this connection it is nearly the same as *bzáṅ-po,* morally good); *legs* is also used in politely hinting or requesting, like the English 'you had better': *k̔yod p̔yín-pa légs(-so) Glr.*, and still more polite: *γšégs-par legs* your Highness had perhaps better go etc. *Pth*; *nús-na šín-tu légs-so* if you can do it, very well! *Dzl.*; also *légs-so* alone, very well! well done! *légs-so légs-so* excellent! capital! — 2. **neat, elegant, graceful, beautiful** *C.* — 3. **lág-mo* W.* **good, due,** and adv. **well, duly, properly,** like *légs-par* (v. above), e.g. **me lág-mo ₒbar ₒdug** the fire burns well, **lé-ka lág-mo čos** you have worked well; but most frq.: **clean, pure, clear,** **ču lag-mo** pure or clear water (opp. to *rtsóg-pa*); **fine,** of powder, = *žib-mo*; **lág-mo čó-če** to clean, clear, wash, wipe, sweep etc.; to reduce to fine powder, to pulverize.

**Comp.** *légs-čan Sch., legs-ldán Cs.* virtuous (?). — *legs-byás*, resp. *legs-mdzád* good deed, good work *Cs.* — *legs-sbyár*, संस्कृत, well constructed, skilfully arranged, highwrought, hence: the Sanskrit language. — *legs-smón* **patron, protector, well-wisher,** congratulator *Cs.* — *legs-bšad* a remarkable saying, a sententious remark *Mil.*, two works, called after their authors *goṅ-dkár* and *sa-skya-legs-bšád*, are recommended to students of the language. — *legs-γsol* resp. **thanks,** acknowledgment, gratitude *C.*

ལེན་པ་ *lén-pa* (rarely *lóṅ-ba, lón-pa*), pf. *bloṅs* (rarely *loṅs*), fut. *blaṅ*, imp. *lon Cs., loṅ(s) Dzl., Mil., blaṅs Cs., W.*: **lén-če, nén-če, bláṅ-če** to take, i.e. 1. **to receive, get, obtain,** *γnas-ṅán* an inferior place viz. for being re-born *Thgy.* — 2. **to accept,** what is offered or given, opp. to *ₒdór-ba*; also **to bear, to suffer patiently, to put up with.** — 3. **to seize, catch,** lay hold of, **grasp,** e.g. one that is about to leap into the water *Dzl.*; **to catch up; to catch, to take prisoner,** a culprit *Dzl.*; **to carry off,** e.g. the arms of killed enemies; *ma byin-par* to take what is not given, **to steal, to rob**; *lén-pa-ₒdra* it is as if it had been stolen from me *Glr.*; *čúṅ-ma lén-pa* to get or take a wife, frq., also to procure one for another person; *srog lén-pa* = *ₒp̔róg-pa* to deprive of life, **to kill** *Mṅg.*; **to fetch,** *lén-du* (*W. *lén-na-la**) *soṅ* go and fetch it! to take possession of, **to occupy** (by force of arms) *Glr.*

ལེབ་མོ་ *léb-mo* (*Cs.* also *léb-po*) **flat,** *mon-srán léb-mo* Indian pease are flat, lenticular; *léb-čan, leb-léb* id. col., **leb-léb-la bor** lay it down flat! *léb-ma, leb-t̔ágs* **lace, bandage, ribbon** *Cs.*, *dar-skúd-kyi leb-t̔ágs* lace of silk thread; *bhag-leb* a flat loaf of bread *C.*; *šiṅ-léb, leb-šiṅ* board, plank, *rdo-léb* a slab, cf. *gléb-pa.*

ལེའུ་ *leu* **division, section** of a speech, of a treatise, of a book, **chapter,** of very different length; *léu-čan Cs., leur byás-pa Zam.* having sections or chapters, being divided into chapters; abbreviated *le*, *bšags-le daṅ šer-le čad-pa yin* the chapters (treating) of the confession of sins and of wisdom are wanting *Tar.*; *lé-ma Cs., le-t̔sán Sch.* id.

ལོ་ *lo* 1. **year** (resp. *dgúṅ-lo*, v. *dguṅ*), *lo lṅa-bču-pa Ma.* usually *lo lṅa-bču lon-pa* (*W. *lon-k̔an**) fifty years old, of fifty years; *bú-mo lo-γnyís-ma* a girl two years old *Ma.*; *lo daṅs lo, lo-ré (-re)-bžin, ló-ltar* (*Sch.* also *bstár!*) **annually, yearly;** *ló-nas ló-ru* from year to year; *sṅá-lo, ₒdás-lo* last year; *ₒdi-lo,* usually **dá-lo**, this year; *p̔yi-lo, C. sáṅ-lo* next year; *lo ₒk̔ór-te* after one year had passed, *srás-kyis lo k̔or-te* when the prince was one year old *Glr.*; the names of the twelve years of the small cycle (v. below) are those of the following twelve animals: *byi* mouse, *glaṅ* ox, *stag* tiger, *yos* hare, *ₒbrug* dragon, *sbrul* serpent, *rta* horse, *lug* sheep, *spre* ape, *bya* hen, *kyi* dog, *p̔ag* hog; thus the first year is called *byi-lo* the mouse-year, and *byi-lo-pa* is a person born in that year etc. — 2. for *lo-tóg*, v. the compounds; for *ló-ma* leaf, for *ló-tsa-ba.* — 3. prob.: **talk, report, rumour, saying,** added (like *skad*) to the word or sentence to which it belongs, *če-gé-mo ši lo zér-ba t̔os tsá-na* when a rumour is heard, that N.N. has died

*Thgy.*; *W.*: **da lam ťar lo** they say the road is open now; also with a definitive subject: **'a-čé'kú-lig toṅ' lo** the mistress asks for the key; **ko kóm-se rag lo** he says he is thirsty (yet also in these cases a speaking on hearsay may be meant: somebody tells me that Mrs. N.N. asks for etc.); **tsór-lo** **report, rumour** *W.*, also **ťóṅ-lo** and **lób* (?)-*lo** are said to have a similar signification; **šé-lo** and **rig-lo** *W.* are expressions of which I cannot give a satisfactory explanation; *bšád-lo byas kyaṅ krám-pa yin Mil.*, prob.: though he may get a name (in the world) by his learned discussions, he is after all a liar. — *lo* 3 prob. occurs only in col. language and more recent pop. literature; *Dzl.* ༢༥༥, 17 *lo* is a corrupt reading for *ɣsol*. — 4. num.: 146.

**Comp.** *lo-skor* (*Cs.* also *lo-kor*) **cycle of years**, a period of twelve years; it is the usual manner of determining the exact time of an event, which also tolerably well suffices for the short space of a man's life. If for instance a person in a dog-year (e. g. 1874) says that he is a *byí-lo-pa*, it may be guessed by his appearance, whether he is 10 or 22, 34, 46 etc. years old, and thus also in other cases accidental circumstances must help to determine the precise date of an event. Occasionally, however, the cycles are counted, e. g. *lo-skór brgyad* 96 years *Glr.* Besides this cycle of 12 years there exists another of 60 years which is formed (in imitation of Chinese chronology) by combining those 12 names of animals with the names of the (so called) five elements, *šiṅ* wood, *me* fire, *sa* earth, *lčags* iron, *ču* water. Each of these elements is named twice, followed, the first time by *po*, and the second by *mo*; which signs of gender may also be omitted without altering any thing in the matter. Thus *šiṅ(-po)-kyi-lo*, *šiṅ(-mo)-ṗag-lo*, *me(-po)-byi-lo*, *me(-mo)-glaṅ-lo* are our years 1834, 35, 36, 37, and 1894, 95, 96, 97 etc. — *lo-krims* (v. *lo-ťóg-gi krims*) ceremonies, at the beginning of harvest. — *lo-gráṅs* prop. date (of the year), *Sch.* also: *lo-gráṅs tsán-ma* **being of** (full) **age.** — *lo-mgó Cs.* the beginning of a year, new-year's day. — *lo-rgyús* v. *rgyus.* — *lo-ṅán* a bad year, a poor harvest. — *lo-čág Cs.* 'every second year'. — *lo-čúṅ* or *nyúṅ C.* young, *lo-nyuṅ-nyúṅ* very young. — *lo-nyés* = *lo-ṅán.* — *lo-snyiṅ Sch.* 'year, period or stage of life' (?). — *lo-tóg* or *-ťóg* the produce of the year, **harvest, crop,** *lo-tóg rṅá-ba* to reap it, to gather it in. — *lo-ťó* **almanac.** — *lo-ₒdod Mil.* earthly-minded, sinner? — *lo-dpyá* annual tribute. — **lo-ṗ'ụ** = *srus-ṗúd*, *C.* — *lo-ṗyág* (*Ld.* **lob-čag**) embassy sent every year to the king to renew the oath of allegiance. — *lo-ṗyéd* half a year. — *lo-tsán* annual produce, harvest, *lo-tsan čé-ba* a rich, abundant harvest *Glr.* — *lo-légs* v. *légs-pa.* — *lo-bšád* = *lo-ťó Cs.* — *lo-ɣséb Sch.* a stack, a heap of corn (?).

ལོ་ཀ་ *ló-ka Ssk.* **world,** *lo-ke-šwa-ra* = अवलोकितेश्वर.

ལོ་ཐོག་ *lo-tóg*, or *lo-ťóg*, v. *lo*, compounds.

ལོ་འདབ་ *lo-ₒdáb* v. *ló-ma.*

ལོ་མ་ *ló-ma*, *W.* **lób-ma**, **leaf,** *ló-ma lhuṅ, brul B., C.*, **lób-ma ḍil* or *ḍul soṅ** *W.* the leaves have fallen; **lób-ma ṭ'á-mo** an acerose or pine-leaf; *lo-ₒdáb* = *ló-ma.*

ལོ་ཙ་, ལོ་ཙཱ་ *lo-tsa*, *lo-tsā* (v. *Ssk.* लोच to speak?) the (art of) **translating,** *sgra daṅ ló-tsa slób-pa* to learn the language and the (art of) translating *Glr.*; also *ló-tsa sgyúr-ba* to translate *Pth.*; *ló-tsa-ba* translator (of Buddhist works) *lo-čén* great translator, seems to be a certain title; *lo-paṇ* for *ló-tsa-ba daṅ páṇḍi-ta.*

ལོ་ལི་མ་ *ló-li-ma Ld.* (*Urd.* لولی) **prostitute, harlot.**

ལོག་གེ་བ་ *lóg-ge-ba* seems to be nearly the same as *lóg-pa* adj., *ťe-ťsom lóg-ge-bai ṅáṅ-la* prob.: entertaining irrational doubts or scruples; *baṅ-rim lóg-ge-ba* an inverted *baṅ-rim* q. v.; *lóg-ge-ba-la kyer* he took it back again *Mil.*

ལོག་པ་ *lóg-pa* I. vb., pf. and secondary form of *ldóg-pa*, q. v., 1. **to return, to go back,** *yúl-du Glr.*; **nam lóg-te ča dug** *W.*, **nam lóg-nẹ ḍó-gyu yin** *C.* when will you return? *lóg-pa* ₒ*tad Glr.*, *lóg-la* ₒ*dód-do Glr.* let us turn back, *p̀yir lóg-pai lam* **the way back.** — 2. **to come back, to come again.** — 3. **to turn round, to be turned upside down, to tumble down** *W.*, e.g. of a pile of wood etc.; *ṅo lóg-pa* or *ldóg-pa* to turn away one's face, always used fig. for to turn one's back on, to apostatize ₒ*k̀ór-bai yul ṅó-ldóg-na* if you mean to turn your back to the land of the cycle of existences, more frq.: *lóg-pa byéd-pa* **to revolt, to rebel,** *lóg-pa rtsóm-pa* to plot, to stir up, an insurrection *Glr.*, *lóg-pa-mk̀an* a rebel *Glr.*; **lóg-pa-čan** rebellious, seditious *W.*

II. adj. **reversed, inverted; irrational, wrong,** *lóg-pai lam, lam lóg-pa Mil.* a wrong way; *lóg-pa-la žúgs-pa* ('to rush into error, to turn to what is wrong?'), also euphemism **for to fornicate** *Stg.*; *lta-(ba)- log(-pa)* v. *ltá-ba; č̀os-lóg* a wrong faith, false doctrine, **heresy;** *grwa-lóg, ǰo-lóg* col. an apostate monk or nun; *lóg-par* and (col.) *log* adv. wrong, amiss, erroneously, *lóg-par sém-pa* to think evil, to have suspicions (about a thing), often = *lta-lóg skyéd-pa* **to sin**; frq.: **log* ₒ*drén-pa** to mislead, seduce *B.*; **log yóṅ-če* W.* to come back, to return, **ši-lóg yóṅ-če** to recover life, to revive (after having been nearly lifeless), to rise from the dead, prob. also: to appear as a ghost *W.*; **nad log-gyáb taṅ* W.* the disease has become worse again, there has been a relapse; **la-lóg (bla-lóg) pó-če* W.* to turn, e.g. the roast; **čud log taṅ-če** v. *yčud.*

**Comp.** *log-č̀os Ma.* = *č̀os-lóg.* — *log-rtógs* wrong judgment, false knowledge. — *lóg-lta* = *lta-lóg*, v. *ltá-ba.* — *log-spyod, Lt.*: *lóg-spyod ṅán-pa* perverse conduct, a sinful life. — *lóg-*ₒ*tso* with *sgrúb-pa* to live in a sinful manner, as much as: to live by crime, by vice *Mil.*

ལོགས་ *logs* 1. **side,** *rtsig-logs* the side of a wall, *mdún-logs* fore-side, front-side, *rgyáb-logs* back, back part of a thing; *lógs-re* 1. **side-post of a door** (opp. to *yá-* and *má-re*). 2. each side (v. *re* 3); *logs-bzáṅ* the right or upper side, *logs-ṅán* the left or lower side (of a cloth) *Cs.*; **surface,** *sai* of the earth; **side, direction, region,** *rk̀áṅ-pai-lógs-nas* from the part of the feet, up from the feet (e.g. a pain in the body proceeding up from the feet) *Sch.*; *γyas-logs* the right side, *γyón-logs* the left side, frq.; *ts̀ú(r)-logs* this side, on this side, *p̀á(r)-logs* the other side, on the other side; *lógs-su, lógs-la* **aside,** apart, **žág-pa* C.* to lay by, to put aside, to put out of the way, to clear away, *lógs-su dgár-ba, bkár-ba* means about the same; *lógs-su bkál-ba* to hang aside, to hang up in another place; *lógs-na yód-pa* to be distinct, separate, to live by one's self, solitarily *Schf.*, *Tar.* 45, 18; *lógs-pa* other, additional, by-, co-, spare-, *rgyags logs-pa* spare-provision, so also *logs γčig*: *t̀ág-pai sné-mo logs γčig* the other end of a rope. — 2. **wall,** **log-žál* W.* id.; *logs-bris* mural or fresco painting *Tar.*

ལོང་ *loṅ* 1. **leisure,** spare-time, vacant time, **time,** *loṅ yód-du ré-la nám-zla* ₒ*das* whilst you are always hoping to have (still) time (enough), you allow the favourable moment to pass away *Mil.*; similarly: *loṅ yod snyam-la mi-ts̀e zad Mil.*; *sdód-pai loṅ méd-par* without delay, immediately, directly *Glr.*; **ṅa yóṅ-loṅ med* C., W.* I have not time to come; **p̀éb-loṅ yód-na** if your honour have time to come *C*, *W.*; *rdég-loṅ yóṅ-bas* as there will be yet plenty of time to beat (me, you had better hear me now) *Mil.*; *loṅ-γtam Sch.*: 'cheerful talk, animated conversation'. — 2. imp. of *laṅ-ba* and *len-pa.*

ལོང་ཀ་, ལོང་ཁ་, ལོང་ག་ *loṅ-ka, loṅ-k̀a, loṅ-ga Med.* **intestines, entrails, guts**; strictly taken it is said to denote only the blind gut(?); *yár-loṅ, már-loṅ Cs.*: the upper gut, the lower gut or thin guts, thick guts; *loṅ-nád* a disease of the guts.

ལོང་བ་ *lóṅ-ba* 1. pf. and secondary form of *ldoṅ-ba*, as vb.: **to be blind,** and fig.: **to be infatuated**; as adj.: blind, blinded etc., as sbst.: blind man *Dzl.* — *loṅ-k̀rid* (or ₒ*k̀rid-pa*) the guide of a blind man *Lex.*; *lóṅ-po, lóṅ-ba-po* a blind man *Cs.*; **nye-lóṅ* W.* **an** empty ear of corn, a tare. — 2. also *loṅs-pa*, = *lén-pa Glr.* or *laṅ-ba* 1, 2 *Glr.*

ལོང་བུ་ *lóṅ-bu Stg*, *lóṅ-mo Mil.* **ankle-bone, astragal.**

ལོང་ལོང་ *loṅ-loṅ* being in pieces, in fragments *C.*, cf. *bun-loṅ.*

ལོངས་ *loṅs*, 1. pf. and imp. of *lóṅ-ba.* — 2. in conjunction with *spyód-pa:* **to use,** to make use of, to have the use or benefit of, **to enjoy,** e.g. *bdé-ba daṅ skyid-pa-la* happiness and prosperity; *lóṅ-spyod-par byá-bai rgyu* the object of enjoyment, the thing enjoyed *Stg.*; *loṅs-spyód* (*Ssk.* भोग) 1. **enjoyment, fruition,** use, esp. with regard to eating and drinking, *loṅs-spyód šá-la byed* they fed on meat, *loṅs-spyód šiṅ dé-las byed* they lived on (the fruits of) this tree *Pth.* 2. **plenty, abundance,** *bza-btúṅ-gi lóṅs-spyod dpag-tu-méd-pa bsag Glr.* they produced or procured an enormous quantity of food and drink; esp.: **riches,** *loṅs-spyod čé-ba* great riches; **wealth, property,** *lóṅs-spyod-kyi bdág-por gyur* he became owner of the property *Dzl.*; *mčód-pa byá-bai lóṅs-spyod med* he was not rich enough to bring an offering (to Buddha) *Dzl.*

ལོད་པ་, ལོད་པོ་ *lód-pa, lód-po,* v. *lhód-pa.*

ལོད་པོ་ *lód-po Sch.*: 'half through, through the middle, one half (?)'.

ལོན་ *lon* **notice, tidings, message,** *lon-bzáṅ* good news, *spriṅ-ba* to give notice, send word, send a message; *lon kyur* or *lon zer* has also the special sense: send in my name! *C.*; *lon žig ḱyér-la šog* let me know, send me word *Pth.*

ལོན་པ་ *lón-pa* = *lén-pa* 1. **to take, to receive** etc. *Glr.*, *Pth.*, *ču lón-nam* have you fetched the water? i. e. are you bringing the water? *Pth.*; *nór-bu mi lon* I shall not receive the jewel! *Pth.* — 2. more frq. the word is used with reference to time: **to elapse, to pass,** a. in a general sense, *lo máṅ-po žig lón-pa daṅ* after many years had elapsed *Dzl.*, *riṅ-žig lón-te* after a long time, *riṅ-por ma lón-par* after a short time. b. with regard to the age of a person: *lo či tsam lon* how old are you? *bču-drúg-lon* I am sixteen *Mil.*

ལོབ་ *lob W.* sometimes for *lo* year, and *lób-ma* for *ló-ma* leaf.

ལོབ་པ་ *lób-pa*, pf., imp. *lobs*, **to learn,** rarely for *slób-pa*; *lóbs-pa* the act of learning *Dzl.*

ལོས་ *los*, **in truth, indeed,** *mgón-skyabs raṅ los yin* he is indeed the helper (from a hymn in praise of Buddha).

# ཤ

ཤ 1. the letter *ša*, the English **sh**, but palatal; in *C.* it is distinguished from ཞ (*ža*) only by the following vowel being sounded in the high tone. — 2. num.: 27.

ཤ་ *ša* I. 1. **flesh, meat,** *γyág-ša* yak's flesh, *lúg-ša* mutton; *ša ˳tsód-pa* (*W.* **tsó-če**) to boil meat; *ša rṅod-pa* (*W.* **ṅó-če, šrág-če** or **lám-če**) to roast meat; *'p̔yi-ša* outward flesh, *náṅ-ša* or *náṅ-ča* inward flesh, or the entrails' *Cs.*(?); *šá-nas čád-pai bu Glr.* the child of my own flesh and blood; *ša ˳ḱrig-pa* sexual instinct; **'á-pe ša, 'á-me ša** in *W.* a vulgar form of attestation; **surface of the body,** *šai ri-mo* spots, stripes etc. on the skin (of an animal) *Tar.* — 2. **muscle,** *nú-ša* thoracic muscle *Mṅg.* — 2. for *ša-ḱóg* v. compounds.

II. v. *šá-ba* and *ša-mo.*

**Comp.** *ša-bkra* n. of a cutaneous disease *Med.* — *ša-skám* meat dried in the sun. — *ša-ḱáṅ* **larder**; butcher's stall. — *ša-ḱú* broth. — *ša-ḱóg* the body of a slaughtered animal, without the skin, head, and entrails, *če-śa* of a large — *čuṅ-śa* of a small animal — *śa-ḱrág* flesh and blood, meton. 1. for body, *śa-ḱrág ɣsál-ba* a sound body *Mil.* 2. for: children born of the same parents *Cs.* — *śa-rgyágs* fat meat. — **śa-ċúg** (*śa bċug*) meat cut into strips and hung up to dry in the sun *W.*, *C.* (*Hook.* II, 183). — *śa-rȷ̀én* raw meat. — *śa-nyóg Sch.*: 'soup with greens in it'. — *śa-rnyiṅ* old meat. — *śa-mdóg* colour of the skin, complexion *Dzl.* and elsewh. — *śa-mdog-lóg-pa Cs.*: *erysipelas*, St. Anthony's fire? — *śa-nág* the lean of meat *Cs.* — *śa-nád* a certain disease *Lt.* — **śá-na** (lit.-*sna*) *W.* ardour, zeal? — *śá-spu* feathers, downs. — **śa-spin** meat boiled down to jelly *W.* — *śa-₀ṗróg Mil.?* — **śá-bhag-leb** a sort of pie baked in oil *C.* — *śa-bo* sheep, cattle or other animals destined for slaughter *Mil. nt.* — *śá-₀bu* **a maggot.** — **śa-búr** *W.* **boil, abscess, ulcer;** *Sch.*: mark left by a lash, weal. — **śa-dę́** rice boiled with small pieces of meat *C.* — *śa-sbráṅ* **flesh-fly**, blue-bottle-fly. — *śa-rmén* fleshy excrescence, a little lump in the muscular flesh. — *śa-btsós* boiled meat. — *śa-ṫsá* 1. hot meat. 2. friend *Pth.*, *S.g.*, *śa-ṫsa-ċan* amicable, attached *W.* — *śa-ṫsán dmár-po Sch.*: 'a tumour resembling a weal or a wart'. — *śa-tsil* the fat of flesh. — *śá-ṫsoṅ-pa* butcher, dealer in meat. — *śa-₀dzín* 1. a hook for taking meat out of a kettle *C.*, *W.* 2. the **fork** of Europeans. — *śa-₀dzér* wart. — *śa-zá*, *śa-zán* 1. prop.: flesh-eater, carnivorous animal. 2. gen.: a class of demons, described as fierce and malignant, *Ssk.* पिशाच. — *śa-zúg*, *śa-ɣzúg* = *zug* 2. — *śa-rág* dried apricots, with little pulp, and almost as hard as stone. — *śa-rid* lean flesh. — *śa-ril* 1. little meat-pies. 2. v. *śa-ba*. — *śa-rúg* sauce, gravy *C.* — *śa-rúl* putrid meat. — *śa-ró* a disease *Wdṅ.*, is said to be an induration of the skin, callus, or perh. scirrhus. — *śa-rlón* fresh meat, raw meat, *śa-ɣsár* flesh of an animal that has just been killed.

ཤ་ *śwa* 1. *Dzl.* ༢༥༠, 1. *Sch.*: high water, flood, inundation. — 2. *Lt.*: a certain hereditary disease or infirmity?

ཤ་ཀ་ *śa-ka* some kind of game (?) *Wdṅ.*

ཤ་ཀ་མ་ *śa-ka-ma*, *ḱa-če śa-ka-ma* **saffron** *C.*

ཤ་ཀར་ *śa-kar Cs.* a kind of sugar.

ཤ་ཀོན་ *śa-kón*, or *śa-₀ḱón*, *Wdṅ.*; *Sch.*: grudge, resentment, **hatred.**

ཤཱ་ཀྱ་ *śá-kya Ssk.*, *ṗód-pa Tib.*, **the mighty, the powerful, the bold,** n. of the family of Buddha, the founder of the Buddhist religion, and hence often n. of Buddha himself, also *śā-kya-ṫúb-pa* (*Mil.* rather boldly abbreviates it into *śāk-ṫub*), *śā-kya-mú-ni*, *śā-kya-seṅ-ge*.

ཤ་དཀར་ *śa-dkár* v. *ɣśa-dkar*.

ཤ་སྐད་ *śa-skád* the cawing or croaking of ravens *W.*

ཤ་སྐྱོ་ *śa-skyó Mṅg.?* perh. dough mixed with meat.

ཤ་ཁམ་, ཤ་ཁར་ *śá-ḱa-ma*, *śá-ḱa-ra* = *śa-ka-ma* and *śa-ka-ra*.

ཤ་ཁུག་ *śa-ḱúg Sch.* a small bag or purse.

ཤ་ཁྱི་ *śa-ḱyi Sch.* a shaggy dog, a poodle.

ཤ་འཁོན་ *śa-₀ḱón* v. *śa-kón*.

ཤ་གོས་ *śa-gós*, col. for *śam-gós*.

ཤ་ཆེན་ *śa-čén Lt.?*

ཤ་ཉམ(ས)་ *śa-nyám(s) Lex.*, as explanation of *dbal?*

ཤ་སྟ་ *śa-sta*, = *klu Wdṅ.*

ཤ་སྟག་ *śá-stag* 1. also *śa-dag* **mere, merely, only,** *ḱyeu śá-dag btsás-te* only sons being born *Dzl.*; *mi dbúl-₀ṗoṅs-pa śá-stag-ste* as they are all of them poor people *Dzl.*; *bdén-pa-mṫoṅ-ba śá-stag-tu gyúr-to* they all come to the knowledge of the truth *Tar.* — 2. *Ld.* for (*rtai*) *śám*(-*la*)-*btags*(-*pa*) a pack, a bundle, fastened to the saddle behind the rider, **śá-stag-la ḱol* or *rel toṅ** tie it up, fasten it behind!

ཤ་དི་ *śá-di Ld.*, *Pur.* **ape, monkey.**

ཤ་ན་ *śa-na* 1. *Ssk.* शण **hemp,** *Cs.*: **flax,** *śá-nai ras Stg.*, *Sch.*: **'fine linen'**, *śá-nai* *gos* a garment made of fine linen. — 2. v. *ṡá-sna*, sub *ṡa*.

ཤ་པོས་ *ṡá-pos* a thick blanket *Ld.*

ཤ་བ, ཤྭ་བ་ *ṡá-ba*, *ṡwa-ba Cs. W., C., B.* **a hart, a stag,** col. usually **ṡa-wa-ra-ću* or *ru-ću**; *ṡá-po* the male animal, *ṡá-mo* the hind, roe, *ṡa-prúg* a young deer, fawn; cf. *ka-ṡwa.*

ཤ་མ་ *ṡa-ma* 1. **after-birth,** placenta. — 2. an ordinary coat made of cloth which has not been napped *W.*

ཤ་མི་ལིག་ *ṡa-mi-lig* **parsley** *Ld.*

ཤ་མོ་ *ṡá-mo C., B.* (*W. *móg-ṡa**) **mushroom**; the various species of fungus receive their appellations from their colour (*dkar-ṡá, nag-ṡa, smug-ṡa, ser-ṡa*) or from the place where they grow (*kluṅs-ṡa, ću-ṡa, lud-ṡa, ṡiṅ-ṡa*); the damp climate of Sikkim produces moreover **sọ-kẹ, ká-wa* and *ḍé-mo (sgre-mo) -ṡa-mo**, etc. *Cs.* has also *ṡa-maṅ*, a thick kind of mushroom.

ཤ་ར་ཤོ་རེ་ *ṡa-ra ṡo-ré* (cf. *γṡér-pa*) *W.* **moist.**

ཤཱ་རི་ཀ་ *ṡā-ri-ka Ssk.* n. of a bird, *Gracula religiosa;* a species of jay.

ཤཱ་རིའི་བུ་ *ṡā-rii-bu*, शारिपुत्र, n. of one of the two principal disciples of Buddha.

ཤ་རུ་ *ṡá-ru* 1. **hartshorn** *Med.* — 2. n. of a vein *Med.*

ཤ་ལོག་ *ṡa-lóg* **warped, oblique, aslant** *W.*

ཤཀ་ཏི་ *ṡák-ti Ssk.*: spear, lance, pike, sword, *Cs.* also trident; *Dzl.*

ཤག་ *ṡag*, in *ṡag-ter-gás* it broke, it burst asunder *Sch.*

ཤག་མ་ *ṡág-ma* 1. *C.* small stones or pebbles, **gravel**, *ṡág-ma-ćan* gravelly, *ṡag-táṅ* a plain abounding with gravel. — 2. *W.* **pebble,** *ṡag-rád* rocky ground, covered with a thin layer of mould which only by dint of much irrigation will yield a scanty produce; *ṡag-rúg* gravel, *ṡág-sa* earth mixed up with pebbles, stony, sterile ground.

ཤགས་ *ṡags* 1. **joke, jest, fun,** *ṡags čé-ba byéd-pa* to rally maliciously, to turn into ridicule with sarcasms *Glr.*; *ṅan-ṡágs Mil.* **a bad joke**; *ka-ṡágs* v. *ka.* — 2. cause of a contention, object of a dispute or a quarrel, **matter in dispute** *Mil.*; quarrel, dispute, contention, in gen., **ṡag gyág-pa* C.* to fight, to quarrel, to dispute.

ཤང་ *ṡaṅ* v. *γṡaṅ.*

ཤང་པོ, ཤང་སྐུལ་ཅེས, ཤང་རིག་ *ṡáṅ-po*, **ṡaṅ kúl-će**, *ṡaṅ-rig* v. *γćaṅ-po*; **ṡaṅ-lág** a kind of fur, perh. for *sbyaṅ-slág* fur-coat of wolf's skin *Lh.*

ཤང་ལང་ *ṡaṅ-láṅ* **sabre, sword** *Pth.*

ཤང་ཤང་ *ṡaṅ-ṡáṅ* a fabulous creature with wings and bird's feet, but otherwise like a human being; *ṡaṅ-ṡaṅ-téu Cs*: pheasant or partridge (**जीवजीव**).

ཤངས་ *ṡaṅs*, resp. for *sna*, **the nose**, *ṡaṅs-rgyúd Pth.*, *ṡaṅs-sna* id.; *ṡaṅs-kúṅ* nostril, *ṡaṅs-rtsé* tip of the nose.

ཤད་ *ṡad* 1. the mark of punctuation: །, also *rkyaṅ-ṡád* or *čig-ṡád;* it is a diacritical sign of about the value of our comma or semicolon; *nyis-ṡád* the double shad, །།, dividing sentences, or, in metrical compositions, verses; *bži-ṡád* the fourfold shad, །།།།, at the end of sections and chapters; *tseg-ṡád* the dotted shad (༔), an ornamental form of the ordinary shad, always made use of, when a shad is to be put after the first syllable of a line; *ṡad byéd-pa Lex.*, *˳tén-pa Sch.*, to make a shad. — 2. v. the following article.

ཤད་པ, གཤད་པ, གཤོད་པ་ *ṡád-pa*, *γṡád-pa*, *γṡód-pa Cs.* 1. **to comb, to curry,** (a horse), also *ṡad rgyág-pa.* — 2. **to brush, to stroke,** to rub gently with the hand *W.*; *ṡád-ma Sch.* **curry-comb,** horse-comb; **ṡiṅ-ṡẹ** a wooden rake, **čág-ṡẹ** an iron rake *C.*

ཤན་ *ṡan* 1. **iron hoop** of a barrel *Cs.* — 2. **small boat,** **ṡẹ́m-pa** ferry-man *C.* — 3. snow-leopard *W.* (cf. *γsa*). — 4. **difference, distinction,** *ṡan ˳byéd-pa* to distinguish, decide, determine *Mil.* and elsewh., *γžan-gyis ṡan mi byéd-pas* as nobody else is able to decide it *Glr.*; *skad-γnyis-ṡan-sbyór* is said to be the title of a certain dictionary.

ཤན་ཁ་ *ṡán-ka* 1. **oblique** *W.*, **ṡán-ka-la ḍẹ́-će** to cut off obliquely; *ṡan-tér* id.,

**lam šan-t́ér-la ča dug** the road has an oblique direction. — 2. *C.*: place of passing over a river.

ཤན་པ་ *šán-pa* 1. also *bšan-pa*, slaughterer, **butcher** *Glr.*, sometimes also **hangman;** *šán-k̔an* slaughter-house, butcher's shop, *šán-gri* butcher's knife, *šan-grib* pollution by the sin of slaughtering an animal. — 2. master or rower of a boat, **boatman.**

ཤབ་ཤུབ་ *šab-šúb* 1. *W.* **whispering,** **šab-šúb táṅ-če, zér-če** to whisper. — 2. also *šab-šób* **lie, falsehood,** *šab-šób byéd-pa* to lie, to cheat; *šab-šúb-čan* deceitful, fraudulent, crafty.

ཤམ་, གཤམ་ *šam, γšam* the lower part of a thing, e.g. of a country, *šám-pa* a lowlander (opp. to *γžúṅ-pa* and *stód-pa*); *γšám-du* adv. and postp. **below,** at foot, *ráṅ-leui šám-du ₒčad* they will be treated of in their respective chapters *Lt.*; *dei šám-du* under it, underneath (e.g. to write); *šam-gós, šam-t́abs*, resp. *sku-šám* a garment like **a petticoat,** worn by Tibetan priests and monks.

ཤམ་བུ་ *šám-bu* **flounces, fringes, trimmings.**

ཤམ་བྷ་ལ་ *šám-bha-la Ssk.* in pure Tibetan *bde-ₒbyúṅ*, n. of a fabulous country in the north west of Tibet, fancied to be a kind of paradise; *šám-bha-lai lám-yig* (not passport, but:) 'guide for the journey to Shambhala'.

ཤར་ *šar* (from *šár-ba*) 1. **east,** *šar-p̔yógs* id.; *šár-pa* inhabitant of an eastern country; *šar-lhó* south-east. — 2. termin. of *ša*, into the flesh.

ཤར་པ་ *šár-pa* 1. young men, grown-up youth (collective noun) *W.*; perh. also: a young man. — 2. v. the preceding article.

ཤར་པོ་ *šár-po* 1. *W.* **adulterer,** **šár-po čó-če* or *k̔úr-če** to commit adultery, (on the part of the husband.) — 2. = *šar-pa* 1.

ཤར་ཕོ་ *šár-p̔o* a young man, *šár-p̔o γžón-nu γsum* three young men *Mil.*

ཤར་བ་ *šár-ba* pf. and secondary form of *ₒčár-ba.*

ཤར་མ་ *šár-ma* 1. *Sch.*: **a strip** *Schr. šar rgyáb-pa* to sew in long stitches, to baste (*Sch.*: *zuṅs γdáb-pa*). — 2. *W., C.* **grown-up girls** (collective noun); **a female**(?)

ཤར་མོ་ *šár-mo* **adulteress,** cf. *šár-po.*

ཤར་ཤར་ *šar-šár* **straightway, directly,** *šar-šár ₒgró-ba Cs.*

ཤར་ཤུར་ *šar-šur Ld.* furrowed, having small elevations and hollows.

ཤལ་ *šal*, in *rna-šál* **ear-lap,** tip of the ear.

ཤལ་བ་ *šál-ba* 1. *Sch.* **stone-pavement.** — 2. **a harrow,** *šál-šal-ba Sch.*, **šál-la ḍúd-če** *Ld.* to harrow.

ཤལ་མ་ *šál-ma Cs.*: **a flint, sharp-edged stone;** *W.*: stony ground; mountain side consisting of detritus; *šál-ma-čan* full of sharp stones *Cs.*

ཤལ་མ་ལི་ *šál-ma-li Ssk.* the seven-leaved silk-cotton tree, *Bombax heptaphyllum Stg.*

ཤས་ *šas* 1. **part,** *ča-šas* id.; *ₒbras de-las šas γčig* part of this rice *Dzl.*; *šas-šás-su bgó-ba* to distribute, ... *la* among *Dzl.*; *šas-čé-ba* a good deal, much, the greater part of, *zla-mtsán šas-čé-bai k̔u-k̔rág* generative fluid in which uterine blood predominates (cf. *k̔u-k̔rág* in *k̔ú-ba*) *Wdṅ.*; *γti-mug šas-čé-bar ₒgyúr-ba* excess of dullness or stupidity *Thgr.*; *šas-čér, šas-čés, šas-čén* in an eminent degree, in an exceeding measure. — 2. **some, a few,** *žag-šás* some days *Mil.*; *ₒga-šas* some, a few *Mil.* — 3. instr. of *ša.*

ཤི་ *ši* num.: 57.

ཤི་བ་ *ši-ba* pf. and secondary form of *ₒči-ba.* 1. vb. **to die, to expire, to go out** (as light, fire); *ši-bar gyur-pa-las* when she was in a dying state *Pth.*, *ši-zin-pai ₒóg-tu* after her death; **ši-te lóg(-yoṅ)-če** *W.* to rise again from the dead, **láṅ-če** (lit. *slaṅ-čes*) to raise from the dead. — 2. sbst. the state of dying, expiring, *ši-ba-las sos* awakened from a dying state frq.; cf. also comp. — 3. partic. and adj. *ši-ba sós-par byéd-par gyur* one already dying still recovers *Do.*; *ši-bai lus* the body of the deceased *Do.*

**Comp.** *ši-ki-ma*, *˳či-k̔a-ma* 1. sbst. **dying, death,** *ši-ki-ma-ru* in dying. — 2. adj. **dying,** *ši-ki-ma yod* (or *˳či-k̔a-ma yod*) he is at the point of death, he is at death's door. — **ši-k̔an** col. the deceased, the dead. — *ši-sño* *Sch.*: 'blessing for one deceased'. — *ši-čos* religious ceremonies for the dead *Sch.* — *ši-ša* flesh of animals that have died of themselves, the only flesh which a strict Buddhist is allowed to eat, and which accordingly in Buddhist countries is frequently consumed.

ཤི་རིག་ *ši-rig* *W.* clinking, jingling.

ཤི་རོག་ *ši-róg* *W.* a sort of early barley.

ཤཱི་ལ་ *šī-la* *Ssk.* for *k̔rims*, *tsúl-k̔rims* custom, manner, moral law.

ཤིག་ *šig* 1. for *cig* (q. v.) after a final s. — 2. **louse,** *mi-šig* common louse, *lúg-šig* sheep-louse, tick, *k̔yi-šig* flea, (*lha*)-*˳dre-šig* bug; **ḍag* (lit. *brag*)-*šig-pa** *W.* mite, wood-louse, tick; *šig ˳t̔ú-ba* *B.*, **ltá-ce*, *rúg-ce** *W.* to look for lice, to louse, *šig bsál-ba* to clean from lice; *šig-čan* *Sch.* also *šig-po* or *šig-šig-po* infested with lice, lousy; *šig-nád* pedicular disease; *šig-sró* lice and nits *S.g.*

ཤིག་གེ་བ་, ཤིག་ཤིག་ *šig-ge-ba*, *šig-šig* 1. standing or lying close together, **close-banded** *Mil. nt.*, *C.* cf. *γšig-pa*, *γšib-pa*. — 2. **trembling, tottering, wavering;** with *mig:* looking this way and that, looking about, perh. also: rolling (the eyes).

ཤིགས་(སེ་)ཤིགས་ *šigs(-se)-šigs* **rocking,** as trees moved by the wind *Mil.*; *šigs-šigs yom-yóm* waving, moving to and fro, shaken etc., also fig. *Pth.*

ཤིང་ *šiṅ* I. gerundial particle for *ciṅ* after a final s.

II. sbst. 1. **tree,** *bzá-šiṅ* fruit-tree, *rtsí-šiṅ* v. *rtsi*; *ljón-šiṅ* a beautiful green leafy tree, *skám-šiṅ* a dry withered tree. — 2. **wood,** *šiṅ žig* some wood; *k̔áṅ-šiṅ* timber, timber-wood, *búd-šiṅ* firewood, fuel, *skám-šiṅ* dry wood; *yám-šiṅ* *Cs.*: 'a small quantity of wood thrown into the fire for sacrifice'. — 3. **a piece of wood, log, billet,** **šiṅ nyi sum tob** *W.* put two or three pieces (to the fire); **stump, stub** of a tree *Glr.*; **tú-pag-gi šiṅ** *W.* gun-stock; *sróg-šiṅ* axle, axle-tree.

**Comp.** *šiṅ-kir-ti* **a carrying-frame** *Lh.* — *šiṅ-kyu* a wooden hook. — *šiṅ-rkaṅ* *Schr.* **a wooden leg, a crutch.** — *šiṅ-rkéd* the upper part of the trunk of a tree. — *šiṅ-k̔an* 1. a wooden house, log-house. 2. shed or out-house for wood. — *šiṅ-k̔u* sap, juice of trees. — *šiṅ-k̔ur* a load of wood. — *šiṅ-k̔ri* wooden chair. — *šiṅ-mk̔an* worker in wood, **carpenter, joiner.** — *šiṅ-rgón* *Sch.* **wood pecker,** *šiṅ-rgon k̔rá-bo* the spotted woodpecker, *šiṅ-rgon mgo-nág* black woodpecker. — *šiṅ-rgyál* a tree of extraordinary height or circumference, **a giant-tree.** — *šiṅ-mṅár* **licorice** *Sch., Wts.*; a sort of cinnamon *W.* — *šiṅ-čás* 1. wooden utensils, implements. 2. tools for working wood *Sch.* — *šiṅ-tog*, *šiṅ-t̔og* fruits of trees, **fruit.** — *šiṅ-rta* v. that article. — *šiṅ-stan* **chopping-block** *Ld.* — *šiṅ-t̔ags* wooden enclosure. — *šiṅ-t̔ún* wood-picker, gatherer of wind-fallen wood. — *šiṅ-dúm* log, billet, block. — *šiṅ-dra* wooden lattice-work; wooden paling *C.*, *W.* — *šiṅ-druṅ-pa* one sitting under a tree, i. e. an ascetic, *Burn.* I, 309. — *šiṅ-γdúgs* the leafy crown of a tree *Sch.* — *šiṅ-sdóṅ* trunk, **stem of a tree; a tree; block.** — *šiṅ-p̔rán* **a small tree, a shrub, bush** *Sch.* — *šiṅ-bál* cotton from the cotton-tree *Cs.*, cf. *šal-ma-li-šiṅ.* — *šiṅ-bu* a small piece of wood, *šiṅ-bu sor-bži-pa* a piece of wood four inches broad or long *Tar.* — *šiṅ-˳brás* fruit. — *šiṅ-smán* medicine prepared from wood *Sch.* — *šiṅ-rtsá* root of a tree. — *šiṅ-rtsi* **resin** *Cs.* — *šiṅ-rtsé* **top of a tree.** — *šiṅ-t̔sa* **cinnamon** (having a 'saltish' taste, as is expressly stated *S.g.*); **šiṅ-t̔sẹ lób-ma** *W.* **bay-leaf, laurel-leaf.** — *šiṅ-t̔sál* **chip, shaving, splinter.** **šiṅ-tsógs** *W.* **forest.** — *šiṅ-γžoṅ* a wooden basin, trough, tub. — **šiṅ-žóg** (lit. *bžogs*) **chip, splint** *W.*; shavings brought off by the plane *C.* — *šiṅ-zán* **wood-rasp** *Sch.* — **šiṅ-žél** **a small chip,** a very small and thin piece of wood, a splinter, **šiṅ-žél zug soṅ** *W.* I have run a splinter into (my hand or foot).

— śiṅ-zóg W. **a rasp.** — śiṅ-γzér **a peg.** — śiṅ-léb board, plank. — śiṅ-śún the bark of trees. — śiṅ-séd a rasp.

ཤིང་ཀུན་ śiṅ-kun **asa foetida,** used as medicine, and (like garlic) as a spice; also n. of a mountain pass between Lahoul and Zankar.

ཤིང་རྟ་ śiṅ-rta ('wooden horse') **waggon, cart,** carriage, also fig. = *tég-pa*, e.g. *śiṅ-rta čén-po* frq. in the writings of *Tsoṅk'apa*; *śiṅ-rta-ₒk'ór-lo* id.; *śiṅ-rtai k'aṅ-bzáṅ* the body of a carriage, *śiṅ-rtai mda* the pole, beam, shaft of a cart, *ₒp'áṅ-lo* the wheel, *rjes, lam, śul, srol* the track, rut (of a cart) *Cs.*; *śiṅ-rta rkaṅ-γčig Sch.* wheelbarrow; *śiṅ-rta-mk'an Cs.* maker of carts, cartwright; *śiṅ-rta-pa* 1. carter, driver, coachman. 2. charioteer.

ཤིད་ śid 1. *Sch.* **hazel-nut.** — 2. also *γśid-γśid-ma, γśid-stón, γśid-zán* **funeral repast,** of which every body may partake; *śid-čós* religious funeral ceremony; *śid-sa Sch.* 1. burying ground, cemetery. 2. a fruitful field = *γśin-sa*. Cf. *γśin*.

ཤིན་ཏུ་ śin-tu **very, greatly,** esp. before adj. and adv., in *B.* frq.

ཤིབ་ śib v. *śib*.

ཤིབ་པ་ śib-pa v. *śúb-pa* **to whisper.**

ཤིབ་ཤི་ལུ་ལུ་ śib-śi-lú-lu or *rú-ru Ld.* **hip,** the fruit of the dog-rose.

ཤིམ་ཤ་པ་ śím-śa-pa *Cs.* a kind of tree or wood.

ཤིར་, ཤིར་ཤིར་ śir, śir-śir, with *ₒtón-pa Cs.* to gush out, to stream forth with a noise.

ཤིལ་བ་ śil-ba *W.* to drip through.

ཤིལ་ལི་ śil-li a gauze-like texture *W.*; *śil-śil* 1. id. 2. *Cs.*: 'a cant word denoting the noise of any thing'.

ཤིས་ śis **good luck, fortune, bliss;** *de ₒbyúṅ-na śis* if that happens, it will be an auspicious sign, *śis-pai miṅ* a name foreboding good *Lt.*, *mi śis-pai ltas* an omen foreboding ill *Wdṅ.*; *bstán-pai śis* acc. to *Schl.* 232 denotes the religious plays performed in the convents. *Cs.*: *śis(-pa)-po* one blessed, *śis-pa yin-pa* to be blessed, *śis-par ₒgyúr-ba* to become blessed, *śis-par byéd-pa* to make blessed, to bless; *bkra-śis* v. *bkrá-ba*.

ཤུ་ śu 1. acc. to Cunningham and other English authorities the Tibetan word for **stag;** yet as none of the many Tibetans, from different parts of the country, that were consulted by us, seemed to know this word, it is not unlikely, that in consequence of indistinct hearing it is but a corruption of *śa-ba* (q. v.). — 2. **śu-śú jhé-pa** *C.* **to whistle.** — 3. num.: 87.

ཤུ་དག་ śu-dág n. of a plant *Med.*; *Sch.*: **the rush.**

ཤུ་བ་ śú-ba I. sbst. 1. **an abscess, ulcer, sore** *Cs.*: *śú-ba ₒt'on* an abscess rises, *na* gives pain, *p'an* heals; **śu-ₒbúr** *W.*, and prob. also *śu-t'ór Med.*, id.; **śu-nág* and *bá-śu** *W.* a sore that has become inflamed and rankling. — 2. **scab, scurf, scald** *W.*

II. vb., pf. *(b)śus*, fut. *bśu*, imp. *(b)śu(s)*, 1. **to take off,** pull off, draw off, *γžán-gyi gos* to take off a person's clothes, *gó-ča* armour, *mt'són-ča* arms, weapons *Pth.*; **to strip, strip off,** e.g. leaves, twigs, *págs-pa* the skin, the peel, hence (also without *págs-pa*) **to skin, to pare, to peel** *W.*, e.g. **'á-lu śú-ce** to peel potatoes; *gyab-śús* coat of wool shorn from a sheep, fleece *Ld.* — 2. **to copy,** *dpe* a book, resp. *žal-śús byéd-pa Cs.*; *dpe-bśús* a copied book *C.*

ཤུ་བྷཾ་ su-bham *Ssk.*, sometimes at the end of books, hail! all hail!

ཤུ་ར་སེ་(ན་) śu-ra-se(-na) n. of a tract of land in the neighbourhood of Mathura, not far from Agra *Wdk.*

ཤུ་ལི་ཀ་ śú-li-ka *Tar.* 63, 8, prob. also *śu-lig Sch.*, n. of a fabulous country in the north-west.

ཤུག་ śug 1. **a thrust, push, knock,** **śug čém-po jhé-pa** **to push off,** to give a knock, to elbow, differing from *ₒp'úl-ba* to shove (by a more gentle motion) *C.* — 2. in comp.: *k'yo-śúg*, v. *k'yo*; *śúg-bza* **wife,** consort, spouse *Schr.* — 3. *W.*: **old,** but still fit for use. — 4. *śug-śúg-la* col. for *śúb-bur* **softly, gently,** e.g. *ₒgró-ba* to walk, to tread etc.

ཤུག་གུ śúg-gu W. for śóg-bu.

ཤུག་པ śúg-pa 1. the high, cypress-like **juniper-tree** of the Himalaya mountains, **the pencil cedar** (*Juniperus excelsa*). It covers large mountain tracts, is considered sacred, and much used in religious ceremonies; its berries (*śug-ₒbrás*) are burnt as incense. — *śug-dúd* the smoke or perfume of juniper. — *śug-ťsér Med.* the young pointed sprouts of this tree. — *sug-ťsód* a sort of mistletoe, *Viscum Oxycedri*, growing on it and gradually killing it. The leaves have a slightly sour taste and are used for culinary purposes *W.* — *rgya-śug* acc. to *Cs.* = *spá-ma Juniperus squamosa*, a low shrub and similar to our *Juniperus communis.* But a passage of the *Stg.* shows that its fruits are eaten like pease or rice, which cannot be imagined of juniper-berries or cypress cones; cf. *spá-ma.* — 2. in *śúg-pa ₒpúd-pa Sch.*, v. sub *ₒpúd-pa.*

ཤུགས *śugs* 1. **inherent strength, power, energy,** c. genit.: *dád-pai, byáms-pai, dgá-bai śúgs-kyis* by the power or ardour of faith, love, joy, e.g. to shed tears, = to weep with joy etc. *Glr.* and elsewh.; *γčin-gyi śugs dgag mi bya* the impulse to make water must not be suppressed *Med.*; *ₒdi-dag sṅón-gyi sbyin-śugs yin* this is the power of former alms or presents *Glr.*; *ťúgs-rǰei śúgs-kyis* by the power of grace *Do.*; *der sléb-pai śugs* the power or ability of attaining to that place *Thgr.*; without a genit.: *śúgs-kyis* = *ráṅ-śugs-kyis* spontaneously, of one's own accord, *śúgs-kyis yoṅ* they will, no doubt, come of their own accord *Mil.*; *śugs byéd-pa* to exert one's self(?); *śugs-stóbs* = *śugs*; *sṅá-śugs ₒdrén-pa Cs.*: 'the accenting the first syllable'. — 2. col. also *śubs* and *śud*, mostly in compounds: *śúgs-skad Mil.*, *śúgs-sgra*, col. **śúg-ra** **a whistling,** a whistle or whiff; *śúgs-glu* 1. a whistling. 2. a whistled tune, **śúg-ḍa ǰhé-pa** to whistle a tune *C.*; *śúgs-pa* a small whistle which, in sounding it, is put quite into the mouth.

ཤུགས་ནར *śugs-nár* (*W. *ǩóg-śúg**), *śugs-ríṅ* **sigh, groan,** *śugs nar byéd-pa* or *ₒbyin-pa* to sigh, to groan, *śugs-riṅ nar nár ₒdug* **he heaves a deep sigh** *Mil. nt.*

ཤུང་བ *śúṅ-ba*, pf. *śuṅs*, 1. **to snore.** — 2. **to hum, to buzz,** e.g. of a large beetle.

ཤུད *śud* v. *śugs* 2.

ཤུད་པ *śúd-pa* pf. fut. *bśud*, 1. **to rub,** e.g. one thing against another *C.* — 2. **to get scratched, excoriated, galled** (cf. *śún-pa*). — 3. *śud byéd-pa* (*W. *čó-če**) **to steal silently away, to sneak off** unperceived.

ཤུན་པ *śún-pa* **bark, rind, peel, skin,** *śun-kóg, śun-págs* id., the last expression is also used of the skin of animals *Lex.* — *p̀yi-śun* the outer rind or skin, *náṅ-śun* the inner rind; *bár-śun* the middle rind, the bast, esp. of willows *Sch.*: *śun-kóg láṅs-pa* the spontaneous chapping or peeling off of the skin; *śun-máṅ* **box-wood.**

ཤུབ་པ *śúb-pa*, also *śib-pa*, pf. imp. *śubs*, to speak in a low voice, **to whisper,** *śub byéd-pa* id.; **ǩog-śúb-la sil-če* W.* to read in a low voice, to read whispering; *śúb-bu* a whispering, *śúb-bus zlá-ba* to recite in a low voice *Lex.*, *śúb-bur smrá-ba B.*, **śúb-la zér-če* W.* to speak softly; *śúb-bus smód-pa* to reprehend in a whisper *B.*

ཤུབས *śubs* **case, covering, sheath, paper bag** etc. frq.; *rkaṅ-śúbs*, resp. *žabs-śúbs* stocking, sock, *gri-śúbs* knife-case or sheath, *mǰe-śúbs* v. *mǰe*; *lag-śubs*, resp. *p̀yag-śúbs* **glove.**

ཤུམ་པ *śúm-pa*, pf. (*b*)*śums*, ft. *bśum*, imp. (*b*)*śum*(*s*), 1. **to weep,** *ma śum mdzod* do not weep! *ṅu-śúm Mil.* **weeping, lamentation.** — 2. to tremble(?) *graṅ-śúm Lt.*, *Schr. graṅ-śúm byéd-pa* to tremble or shiver with cold, to shudder.

ཤུར་བ *śúr-ba*, pf. fut. *bśur*, imp. (*b*)*śur*, 1. to burn slightly, **to singe.** — 2. **to cut off.**

ཤུར་བུ *śúr-bu* 1. **girdle, belt** *Lex.*; *śur-bu-p̀réu Zam.* id. (acc. to *Sch.*). — 2. *Cs.*: **sore, ulcer.** — 3. *Ts.*: **dumpling of flour,** = *ǩo-lag.*

ཤུལ *śul* 1. **an empty place,** a place that has been left, that is no longer occupied, *ráṅ-śul stóṅs-nas* your own place becoming

ཤ

empty, by your quitting it *Mil.* *ṡúl-du lús-pai nor* all the things left behind in the camp *Glr.*; *dóṅ-tse láṅs-pai ṡúl-du* instead of the coin which had been taken away (there appeared . . .) *Dzl.*; *ḱyód-kyi ṡúl-du* in the place which you occupied during your life *Thgr.*; hence in a looser sense: *btsún-mo méd-pai ṡúl-du* on the occasion of the queen's absence *Glr.*; in the same manner *Tar.* 103, 16, 19, and also thus: *dei ṡúl-du Glr.* 51 during her absence. — 2. **track, rut,** of a carriage, **furrow,** of a plough *Dzl.*, **way, road;** also in a gen. sense: *ṡul ťag-riṅ* a long way *Glr.*; *ṡul-lám* = *ṡul*; acc. to *Cs.* also **manner, method.** — 3. any thing left behind by a person departed, or by a thing removed, as *ču-ṡul, mar-ṡul, ṕye-ṡul* that little water, butter or flour which adheres to the vessel emptied, but not washed; *me-ṡul* the extinguished cinders left by a fire; **property left** by a deceased person *ṡul ťsáṅ-ma yóg-po-la ťob* his servant gets all the property left (by his master) *W.*, *C.*, *ṕa-ṡul* paternal inheritance, patrimony; *ṕa-ṡul-ₒdzin-pa* the heir *C.*; *ṡul yaṅ mi ₒdug* nothing at all is left; **ṡúl-med-ḱan čo** *W.* finish it at once! eat it all up! *ṡū-tsaṅ-po* one that eats all up, clears his trencher (a good trencherman) *Ts.*

ཤུལ་པ་ *ṡúl-pa, bṡúl-pa Cs.*: **backbone, back, posteriors;** *ṡul - ṡá* the flesh, the muscles of the back, *ṡul-rgyús* the fibres, the nerves of the back; *Sch.*: *bṡul-dri* smell of excrements, *ṡul-byí* **polecat, fitchet.**

ཤུས་ *ṡus* 1. v. *ṡú-ba.* — 2. *ṡus ₒdébs-pa* to whistle *S.g.*

ཤུས་མ་ *ṡús-ma* any thing copied, **a copy** *Cs.*

ཤེ་ *ṡe* 1. *Cs.* *ṡe-stag, ṡe-dag* = *ṡa-stág* **mere, only,** nothing but. — 2. num.: 117.

ཤེ་ན་ *ṡé-na* v. *čé-na.*

ཤེ་པ་ *ṡé-pa* v. *ṡés-pa.*

ཤེ་བམ་ *ṡe-bám Cs.*: = *ťo-yig* a kind of contract or bargain.

ཤེ་མ་ *ṡé-ma* (for *rǰé-ma* or *γčés-ma?*) *W.* **noblewoman,** lady of rank or quality, **lady,** **ṡé-ma čuṅ-ṅu, ṡem-čúṅ** nobleman's daughter, **young lady, Miss.**

ཤེ་མོང་ *ṡe - móṅ Sch.*: 'divine predestination, divine protection; nature, fate, destiny; power; origin of power or authority; strength', force, the latter signification also in *Wts.* (?).

ཤེ་རུལ་ *ṡe-rul Sch.*: **fetid, putrid.**

ཤེག་ *ṡeg* 1. imp. of *γṡégs-pa*, resp. for *ṡog.* — 2. the Arabian شيخ, chieftain, elder, senior. — 3. *C.* col. for *ṡed* I.

ཤེད་ *ṡed* I. **strength, force,** = *stóbs, mťu, C.* also *ṡeg*; *dpá-žiṅ ṡed-čé* a mighty hero *Thgy.*; *ṡéd-čan* **strong, vigorous, powerful;** *ṡéd-mo* 1. sbst. = *ṡed?* 2. adj. = *ṡed-čan Ts.*, **ṡé-mo gyág-pa yin** he is strong and stout, *ṡed-méd* **powerless, weak,** *ṡed-méd-kyi rtá-bas rkaṅ-ťáṅ mgyogs* one travels quicker on foot than on a weak horse; *ṡed-čúṅ* **weak, feeble, frail,** e.g. *lus Lt.*; *ṡed ₒbri* strength decreases, begins to fail, *γsos* is restored, *nyams* is impaired; *ṡed skyéd-pa* to grow fat *Sch.*: 'to protect; to make haste'; **mí žig-la ṡed čúg-če** *W.* **to strengthen** a person; **ṡed daṅ nyé-če** *W.* to rub well, forcibly; **ṡed žár-te (sbyar-te) čoṅ** run and jump! **ṡed žár-te gyob** swing your arm and throw! *W.*; **ṡed-kyer-nág-po** by force, with violence, e.g. **taṅ** he forced it on (me) *W.* (cf. *nan*); *ṡed-po-čé* a strong, powerful man *Thgy.*; *ṡéd-bu Lex.* id.; *ṡed-bdág Sch.* one having power or authority, a lord, ruler. — **ṡed - wáṅ** *W.* **force, violence,** **ṡed-wáṅ daṅ** by force, e.g. to take, **ṡed-wáṅ táṅ-če** *W.* to violate, to force (a girl).

II. the approximate **direction, region, quarter,** *nyi-mai ₒog ṡéd-na* below the sun, i.e. between the sun and the horizon *Mil.*; *W.*: **gaṅ ṡéd-la** in what direction? whereto? **de ṡéd-la** about in that direction; **gaṅ ṡed nẹ* (lit. *γnas*) *ṡig-tu** to some place or other.

ཤེན་ *ṡen*(?) **floor** of a house or room *W.*

ཤེར་ཕྱིན་ *ṡer-ṕyin* abbreviation for *ṡes-ráb-kyi ṕa-rol-tu ṕyin-pa*, the title of a division of the *Kan-gyur.*

ཤེར་བ་ *s̀ér-ba*, pf. *bs̀er*, **to compare, to confront** *Cs.*

ཤེལ་ *s̀el* **crystal, glass** *Dzl.* and elsewh.; acc. to *Stg.* the moon also consists of such crystal *Cs.: rán-s̀el* native crystal, *bžú-s̀el* artificial crystal, glass; *mán-s̀el Pth.* prob. = *s̀el; spos-s̀él* amber; *me-s̀él* burning-glass, *c̆u-s̀él* चन्द्रकान्त a fabulous magic stone supposed to have the power of producing water or even rain.

**Comp.** *s̀el-kór* or *-p̔or* a tumbler. — *s̀el-dkár* = *s̀el Glr.* — *s̀el-k̔áṅ* glass-works, glass-manufactory *Schr.* — *s̀el-sgóṅ* globe of glass *Mil.* — *s̀el-sgó* glass-door. — *s̀el-rdó* crystal. — *s̀el-snód, s̀el-spyád* a crystal or glass vessel. — *s̀el-p̔réṅ* a string of glass-beads. — *s̀el-búm* glass-bottle. — *s̀el-mig* spectacles, spy-glass, telescope.

ཤེས་ *s̀es* v. *c̀es.*

ཤེས་པ་ *s̀és-pa* (synon. *rig-pa*, resp. *mk̔yén-pa*) I. vb., 1. **to know, perceive, apprehend,** *bzáṅ-bar s̀és-pa* to find, to know a thing to be good *Glr.*; *brtágs-na mi s̀es* when (the soul) is searched for, it is not to be perceived or apprehended *Mil.*; *s̀és-pai blo ingenium sapiens Dzl.*; *mi-s̀es-pa-dag* those who do not care for knowing (a thing) *Dzl.*; *su s̀és B., C.*, **c̀i s̀ē* W.* (like the Hindi क्या जाने) who can tell? may be; *c̀iaṅ mi s̀ē-k̔an* a know-nothing, ignoramus, dunce; **k̔o-ráṅ mā s̀é-k̔an c̆én-mo žig t̔sor dug* W.* he is said to be an extremely clever (learned etc.) man; *mi-s̀és dgu s̀és-pa* knowing (even) the unknown things, knowing every thing *Thgy.*; *c̀aṅ-s̀és* id.; **ṅa-ráṅ t̔oṅ s̀ē* W.* I know it from having seen it; *s̀és-par gyur* 1. he will know. 2. he comes to know, he learns; *s̀es-par gyis s̀ig* 1. know! 2. let it be known! *s̀es-bžin-du* **knowing, knowingly,** with (my) knowledge; *ṅó-s̀es-pa* = *s̀és-pa*, yet cf. sub *ṅo.* — 2. **to understand,** = *gó-ba, don* the sense *Glr.*; *ṅas rtsis s̀es* I understand mathematics; **to be able,** in a general sense, also physically: **ghaṅ s̀ē-pa* C.* to one's best ability, to the utmost of one's power (= *ji nus-kyis B.*, **c̀i t̔úb-k̔an* W.*); *k̔rág-gi goṅ ̥gul s̀és-pa* a clot of blood that could only quiver (though, in fact, a human being) *Glr.*; esp. with a negative: *smra mi s̀és-pa* not being able to speak, *dgye dgu mi s̀es* they cannot be bent or curved *Med.* — 3. **to be convinced, to be of opinion, to think,** *sú-la yaṅ mdzá-bor ma s̀es* do not think anybody to be your friend!

II. sbst. (= *rig-pa*) 1. **the knowing** (about a thing), **knowledge.** — 2. **science, learning,** *s̀és-pa-la zóg-tu ltá-ba* to look upon science as a (sort of) cheating. — 3. **intellectual power, intelligence,** *s̀és-pa t̔ibs* the intellect (of infants) is still very weak *Lt.*, *ɣsal* is clear *Pth.* — 4. **the soul** or spirit, separate from the body *Thgy., Mil.*

**Comp.** **s̀ē-gyá** talent(?) *C., W.* — **s̀ē-gyü** **character** *C., W.*, **s̀ē-gyü ṅēm-pa** a bad character. — *s̀es-̥dód* **desire of knowledge, curiosity** of mind *Mil. s̀es-ldan, s̀es-blo-ldán-pa* 1. knowing, rich in wisdom. 2. very learned Sir! — *s̀és-po, s̀és-pa-po* one that knows or understands, a knower *Cs.* — *s̀és-bya* 1. what may be known or ought to be known. *s̀és-bya kun* every thing worth knowing, all the sciences. 2. knowing, conscious, wilful? *s̀és-byai sgrib-pa* contamination by wilful sins *Do.?* — *s̀es-byed* that which knows, the understanding. — *s̀és-bžin* **consciousness** (v. above *s̀es-bžin-du*), *dran-pa daṅ s̀es-bžin-c̀an yin-te Gyatch.* ༡༡༤, 14 (cf. *Burn.* II, 806, 5); *s̀és-bžin* may, accordingly, be used for **'conscience'** in a christian sense. — *s̀és-yoṅ Ts.* = *s̀es-rgya.* — *s̀es-ráb* (प्रज्ञा) 1. 'great knowledge', **wisdom, intelligence, understanding, talent,** *s̀es-rab c̆e-ba* very talented, gifted (e.g. a boy) *Mil.*; *s̀es-ráb daṅ ldán-pa* id.; *s̀es-rab-spyan* the (mystic) eye of wisdom *Schl.* p. 210. — *s̀es-rab-rtswa Taraxacum*, dandelion, also used as food. — *s̀es-ráb-kyi p̔á-rol-tu p̔yin-pa*, प्रज्ञापारमिता, the having arrived at the other side of wisdom, n. of that section of the *Kangyur* which treats of philosophical matters.

ཤོ་ *s̀o* (*Cs.: s̀ó-mo*) I. **die, dice,** *s̀o rgyáb-pa* **to dice,** *s̀o rtsé-ba* to play at dice, *s̀o-̥gyéd-pa* (*Sch. k̔yé-žig* as imp.) id.? — *s̀o rgyál-ba* or *p̔ám-pa* to win or lose at playing;

šo-rgyán Cs. the money or stake deposited at dice-playing; *rtsis-šoi rdeu Mil.*, *šo-rdél Wdk.*, an attribute of certain deities; *šo-mig* the points of dice, *šo-mig γsúm-par* (or *-pa-la*) *ₒbáb-na* when three points are thrown. Tibetans play with three dice marked with 6 and 1, 5 and 4, 3 and 2 on opposite sides, hence from 3 to 18 points may be thrown.

II. 1. the white willow of *Spiti*, *Ld.* and other Himalayan districts. — 2. other plants *rgya-šo*, *lug-šo? Wdṅ.*

III. = *btsa-ma* blast, blight, smut, mildew *Cs.*

IV. for *šo-gam*, q. v.

V. num.: 147.

ཤོ་གམ་ *šo-gám* **custom, duty, tax,** *šo-gám lči-ba W.* **lčin-te** high duty, *šo-gam len-pa* to take toll, to levy a duty; *šo-gám bzlá-ba Sch.*: 'to smuggle, to circumvent or defraud the customs' (?); *šo-gám-gyi γnas* custom-house; *šo-gám-pa* receiver of the customs, toll-gatherer; **šo-ṭ ál, šo-dụ* Ts.* tax, duty.

ཤོ་ཆ་ *šó-ča* a kind of steel-yard *C.*

ཤོ་མ་ *šó-ma*, v. *šá-mo*, **mushroom** *Mil.*

ཤོ་མང་ *šo-máṅ* a medicinal herb *Med.*

ཤོ་ར་ *šó-ra* **saltpetre,** nitre, *šó-ra-čan* nitrous.

ཤོ་རེ་ *šo-ré*, adj., **damaged, spoiled,** by being partially broken, torn etc., sbst.: **a defect, flaw, notch, gap,** also **hare-lip;** **šo-ré soṅ** it is damaged, **šo-ré ťon soṅ** a notch, chink, crack has been caused; **ǩa-šór, na-šór**, with a slit lip, a slit nose.

ཤོ་ལོ་ཀ་ *šó-lo-ka* v. *šlo-ka.*

ཤོག་ *šog* I. *šóg-čig*, prop. from *γšégs-pa*, imp. of *ₒóṅ-ba*, 1. come! let him come! *ₒbrás-bu ťsúr-šog-gi yid-smón ṅá-la med* I do not wish that fruit should come to me from without *Mil.*; *ǩur šog, ǩyer šog bskyal šog* bring hither, (with *soṅ* inst. of *šog*: take away!) *šog zér-ba* **to invite,** *ṅed-la šog kyaṅ mi zer Glr.* we are not so much as invited, you know. — 2. with the imp. = *gyur-čig*, *bsad-par-šog* may (he, I etc.) be killed! *Dzl.* — II. v. *šos.*

ཤོག་པ་ *šóg-pa* I. sbst., also frq. *γšóg-pa*, 1. **wing,** *γšog-rkyaṅ-ba* to spread the wings, also to spread like wings; **šóg-pa dé-če, čád-če, ḍúm-če* W.* to clip the wings; *γšóg-pa-čan, γšog-ldán* provided with wings, winged, a bird. — 2. **wing-feather, pinion,** *ₒdab-γšóg, γšóg-sgro* id.; *mǰug-γšog* tail-feather. — 3. **fin,** of fishes. — 4. other things resembling a wing or a feather, *mig-γšog*, resp. *spyán-γšog* eye-lash; *raṅ-tág-gi γšóg-pa* prob.: wing or float-board of a water-mill; of course it might also be used for: wing, sail, of a windmill, though these are not yet known in Tibet.

II. vb., v. sub *γšog-pa.*

ཤོག་བུ་ *šóg-bu*, *W.* **šúg-gu**, 1. **sheet of paper,** and **paper** collectively, *rgya-šóg* China paper, *bod-šóg* Tibet paper, *dar-šóg* silk-paper, *ras-šóg* cotton-paper (also paper of linen-rags), *šiṅ-šóg* bast-paper, *pags-šóg* leather-paper, skin-paper, parchment; *mťiṅ-šóg, nag-šóg* dark-blue or black paper, for writing on in gold or silver; *mgo-šóg*, resp. *dbu-šóg*, upper leaf, i. e. cover, covering, wrapper. — 2. *Bal.*: **book.**

**Comp.** *šog-ǩáṅ* **paper-maker's form.** — *šog-gáṅ* a sheet of paper. — *šog-gráṅs* number of leaves in a book. — *šog-sgríl, šog-dríl, W.* **šog-ril** **paper-roll, codex.** — *šog-ldéb Sch.*: 'leaf, sheet'? — *šog-ťsár* scrap of paper. — *šog-šiṅ Sch.* palm-tree? — *šog-hríl γčig* = *šog-gáṅ, Sch.*

ཤོང་(ས)་, གཤོང་(ས)་ *šoṅ(s), γšoṅ(s)* (*Lex.*: सानु 'elevated plain, ridge of a mountain') 1. **mountain-ridge** *Wts.* Usual meaning: 2. **pit, hole, cavity, excavation, valley,** *ču-šoṅs* cavity filled with water *Dzl.*; *spaṅ-šoṅs* valley with meadows, low ground overgrown with grass; *snai bya-γšóg-gi γšoṅs* the cavities near the wings of the nose *Mil. nt.*; *šóṅ-du* valley-ward, down hill *Dzl.*; *šóṅs-čan, (γ)šoṅ-(γ)šóṅ* full of cavities, **uneven,** *Sch.* also: **rough, rugged, steep;** *šóṅs-bu* **furrow,** *šóṅs-bu ₒtén-pa* to make furrows, to furrow.

ཤོང་བ་ *šóṅ-ba* I. to go in, **to have room** in or on, with term., *mi šoṅ*, *W.* also: **šóṅ-če mi dug** that is not to be got in, there is no room for it; *bre lṅa ṡóṅ-bai búm-pa* a can holding five quarts *Dzl.*

II. pf. *bṡaṅs*, fut. *bṡaṅ*, imp. *ṡoṅ(s)*, **to empty, remove, carry or take away,** *W.* stones, earth etc., but gen. (with or without *rkyág-pa*) to go to stool, to ease nature, *B.* and col.

ཤོད་ *ṡod* 1. the lower, the inferior part of a thing, *rtse-ṡod* upper and lower part, top and bottom *C.*; *rgya-ṡod Wdṅ.* a low tract of land, with a milder climate, where e.g. apricots are thriving, opp. to *ṕu-lhágs* elevated cold region, scarcely fit for the cultivation of corn and barley; *ṡód-du* to or towards the bottom, **down, downwards,** *C.*, **ṡǿ-du báb-pa** to descend, come down, **ṡǿ-nẹ ˳dzég-pa** to ascend *C.* — 2. imp. of *˳čád-pa, bṡád-pa*; yet cf. also:

ཤོད་པ་ *ṡod-pa*, pf. *bṡád-pa*, 1. **to say, to declare** *C.* — 2. **to comb** *Cs.*

ཤོབ, གཤོབ་ *ṡob, γṡob* **a fib, falsehood, lie,** *smrá-ba*, *W. *gyáb-ċe**, to tell a lie.

ཤོབ་ཤོབ་ *ṡob-ṡób* **loose, soft,** as leaves etc. *W.*

ཤོམ་པ་ *ṡom-pa*, pf. *(b)ṡoms, bṡams*, fut. *bṡam*, imp. *(b)ṡom(s)*, **to prepare, make ready, arrange, put in order, fit out,** *γnas* lodgings, *γdan* a seat, *stón-mo* a festive entertainment, *bžón-pa* a carriage, i.e. to have the horses put to *Dzl.*; *dpúṅ-gi ťsogs* an army *Dzl.* — *ṡóm-ra* 1. **preparation, arrangement, fitting out,** *ṡóm-ra byéd-pa* = *ṡóm-pa C.*, so also *Cs.*; but *Sch.*: 2. *ṡóm-ra* **state, pomp, splendour,** with *byéd-pa* to show off, to dress smartly, *ṡóm-ċan* stately, grand (?).

ཤོར་ *ṡor* v. *ṡo-ré.*

ཤོར་བ་ *ṡór-ba* 1. v. *˳čór-ba.* — 2. to measure *Mil.*, v. *γṡór-ba.*

ཤོལ་བ་ *ṡól-ba* 1. **intercalation, insertion** *Cs.*, *zla-ṡól* intercalary month. — 2. *Cs*: pres. tense of *bṡól-ba* q.v.

ཤོལ་པོ་ *ṡól-po Sch.*: 'a species of willow', v. *γṡól-po.*

ཤོས་ *ṡos* 1. almost always in conjunction with *γčig*, **the other,** of two, e.g. *bud-méd γčig-ṡós* the other woman *Dzl.* — 2. *Zam.* **ཏར**, col. *ṡog*, a termination indicating the comparative or superlative degree: *čuṅ-ṡós, γžon-ṡós* the younger, the youngest, of two or of several, *btsún-mo lṅa-brgyái čuṅ-ṡós Pth.*; **riṅ-ṡóg* W.* the tallest; *yun-riṅ-ṡós Thgy.* the most long-lived; *drin-če-ṡós* the principal benefactress, cf. *drin*; *nad če-ṡós rgás-nad ˳ťébs-pas* because one is suffering under the chief disease, viz. old age, *Thgy.*

ཤྲཱི་ *ṡrī Ssk.*, = *dpal* **glory, magnificence; magnificent, splendid, grand;** *ṡrī-ri Mil.*, pr. n., a naked mountain in a sandy plain, about a ten day's journey to the west of Tashi-lhunpo, covered with monasteries, and perh. on that account considered as *nyams-mťsár-ba. ṡrī-ḱaṇḍa* v. *dpál-gyi dum-bu.*

ཤློ་ཀ་ *ṡló-ka Ssk.*, also *ṡo-lo-ka*, **strophe, stanza,** esp. one consisting of four catalectic trochaical dimeters.

གཤའ་ *γṡa* I. 1. also *γṡá-ma, bṡá-ma*, **worthy, becoming, fitting, suitable,** *˳ťsé-ba mi γṡai* as it is unworthy, unbecoming, improper, to persecute (others) *Dzl.*; **de ḱyód-la ṡa yod** or **ṡá-ċe yod* Ld.* that serves you right. — 2. **righteous, upright, honest, good,** = *skyón-med-pa, C.*; *blo γṡá-ma* an upright, true heart, *Thgy.*; **lẹ ṡá-ma ǰhē-pa* C.* to perform a work faithfully, in good earnest.

II. **only, merely; mere, nothing but,** (= *ṡá-stag*) *C.*

གཤའ་དཀར་, བཤའ་དཀར་ *γṡa-dkár, bṡa-dkár S.g., Wdṅ., C.* **tin,** *W. kar-ya*; yet cf. *ža-nye.*

གཤའ་རིང་ *γṡa-riṅ* a long skirt or coat-tail *Sch.*

གཤག་པ་ *γṡág-pa* v. *γṡóg-pa.*

གཤགས་ *γṡags* **right, justice,** *Lex.* and esp. *W.*; *γṡags ˳byed-pa Lex.* to investigate the rightfulness (of an action), = **ge dig ṕé-ċe* W.*; **ṭim-ṡág táṅ-ċe** to administer justice, to sit in judgment **ṭim-ṡág-taṅ-ḱan** judge, **ṡag (go-) lóg táṅ-ċe** to warp justice, to judge contrary to justice and right; **ṭim-ṡág žú-ċe** to go to law, to bring an action, **ṡág-pon** superior judge, chief-justice, *W* — *bka-γṡágs* v. *bka* extr.

གཤང་ γśaṅ a musical instrument, esp. used by the Bonpo, *Glr.*, *γśaṅ ˳król-ba* to play on that instrument *Mil.*

གཤང་པ་ *γśáṅ-pa Sch.* = *bśáṅ-ba.*

གཤང་གཤོང་ *γśaṅ-γśóṅ* rough, rugged places or tracts *Cs:*

གཤད་པ་ *γśád-pa* 1. = *śód-pa* **to comb.** — 2. = *˳čád-pa* II., **to explain, to relate.**

གཤམ་ *γśam* 1. **the lower part** of a thing, *γśám-du* a. adv. **down.** b. postp. **under, below, beneath**; also adv. **farther down,** more towards the end, in the course of; examples v. sub *leu*; postp. *dei γśám-du* under it. — 2. **barren,** *B.* and col., *mo-γśám, rgod-γśám, ba-γśám* a barren woman, mare, cow.

གཤར་ *γśar Sch.*: a certain style of writing.

གཤས་མ་ *γśás-ma Sch.* = *γśá-ma.*

གཤིགས་ *γśig-pa* v. *γśib-pa.*

གཤིན་པ་ *γśín-pa* 1. also *γśín-po* **good, fine,** *žiṅ śin-pa B., C.* a fertile field, *sa-ṗyógs γśin-pa* a rich country *Stg.*; *γśin-par rmó-ba* to plough well; *γśín-sa* 1. fertile field or land. 2. v. *γśín-po.* — 2. = *γśim pa.*

གཤིན་པོ་ *γśín-po* **one deceased, a dead man,** *γśín-mo* a dead woman, e.g. **śin-mó ǰor-zóm** the deceased, the late Jorzóm; it may have reference to the body, as well as to the soul, or to both together. — *γśin-rje* the god of the dead, of the lower regions, of hades, also regarded as the judge of the dead, *Ssk.* **यम**; *γśin-rjei γśed* a. id., Yama the destroyer. b. the destroyer of Yama, Siwa; *Ssk.* **यमान्तक.** cf. also *Schl.* 93. **čin-dúd** **knot,** opp. to **ṭol-dúd** a bow, a slip-knot *W.* — *γśin-˳dré* the soul as a ghost or spectre *Sch.* — *γśin-˳prás* the convulsive motions, the writhings of a dying creature. — *γśín-zas* food presented to the Lamas when a person has died (*Cs.*: food prepared, or exposed for the dead?). *śín-sa* 1. **burying ground, cemetery,** 2. fertile field.

གཤིབ(ས)་པ་, བཤིབ(ས)་པ་ *γśib(s)-pa, bśib(s)-pa,* also *γśig-pa,* 1. *Sch.*: to range, **to compare;** *Ld.* to be ranged, to draw up in files; **gral γśig rgyáb-pa** *C.* to induce assembled people by means of a stick to stand or sit closer; cf. *žal-bdág.* — 2. *ral-gri γśib-pa Wdṅ.*?

གཤིམ་པ་, གཤིན་པ་ *γśim-pa, γśin-pa Sch.*: 'ground, crushed'.

གཤིམས་བཟང་བ་ *γśims-bzáṅ-ba Sch.* to be irresolute, unsettled in opinion; to be distrustful, suspicious.

གཤིས་ *γśis,* often also *bśis,* 1. **nature, temper, natural disposition,** *γśis-ka* col. id., *raṅ-γśis yin* it is their nature, their natural disposition *Mil.* — *γśis-kyis* by the very nature of the case, without secondary causes, naturally, quite of itself *Mil.*; *γśis-ṅán Mil., Do.* was also explained by *rgyú-med-par,* prob. implying merely: not having been one's self the efficient cause. — 2. **person, body,** *γśis ṫams-čád-du ˳byúg-go* they anointed the whole body *Do.*

གཤུང་བ་ *γśuṅ-ba Cs.* to rebuke, reproach; the *Lexx.* explain it by: *śúb-bur smád-pa* to blame in a whisper, i.e. behind a person's back.

གཤུམ་པ་ *γśúm-pa* v. *śúm-pa.*

གཤེ་བ་ *γśé-ba,* pf. *γśes,* **to abuse, revile,** with *la, Dzl.* and elsewh.; *γśe yaṅ slar mi γśé-ba* even when reviled, (one should) not revile again (rule for monks) *Cs.*

གཤེག་པ་ *γśég pa* v. *γśóg-pa.*

གཤེགས་པ་ *γśégs-pa* (imp. *γśegs, Dulva* in *Feer Introd.* etc. p. 68; but *śog* is prob. the original and older form), *Bal.* **śags-čas**, resp. **to go, to go away,** opp. to *˳byón-pa* to come *Glr.*; in other passages **to come** *Dzl.*; *γśegs-grábs mdzad* he made preparations for setting out *Mil.*; *nám-mk̇a-la ˳ṗúr-žiṅ γśegs* he ascended to heaven *Tar.*; *slar γśégs-pa* **to return, to come back.** *γśégs-pa* is col. seldom used, but often in books, and mostly of Buddha and great saints; *bdé-bar γśégs-pa* **to die,** of saints and kings; *sku γśegs-pa Glr.*; *dgúṅ-du* or *dgúṅ-la γśégs-pa Mil*, *mk̇ar γśégs-pa Glr.*, id.; *bdé(-bar)-γśegs(-pa)* as partic. = **सुगत Buddha;** ***de-bžin-γśegs-pa*** **तथागत** acc. to the explanation now generally accepted: he that walks in the same ways (as his predecessors), a very frq. epithet of the Buddhas. — *γšégs-bskyés* parting-(beer-) cup, parting-feast or treat *Mil.* — *γšegs-zón Cs.* a banquet or dinner, after the death of a great person.

**གཤེད་མ་** *γšed-ma*, rarely *γšed*, 1. **executioner, hangman** *Stg.*; *γšéd-ma skó-ba* to engage a hangman, i.e. to pay a murderer *Glr*; fig.: *ṗan ṫsun γčig-gi γšed γčig-gis byá-ste Wdṅ.* prob. means: one destroying the other. — 2. in a special sense: gods of vengeance, tormenting the condemned in hell, or fighting against evil spirits, *drag-γšéd Schl.*

**གཤེན་རབ(ས)** *γšen-ráb(s) Glr.*, the founder of the Bon-religion, his full name being *bon γšen-rabs-γyuṅ-drúṅ C.* prob. identic with the Chinese philosopher *Lao-tse* — *ye-γšen Mil.* id. — *sgrub-γšén* the Bon-doctrine (opp. to *dam-čós Mil.*)

**གཤེར(བ)** *γšér(-ba) B., C.*: **wet, wetness;** *γšér-ba, γšér-pa, γšér-po* adj, *γšér-bar ₒgyúr-ba* to get thoroughly wet, to be drenched *Dzl.*, to get moist, to be moistened; *γšér-bar byéd-pa C., B.*, **šér-pa čó-če** *W.* to wet, to moisten. In *C.* and in *B.* *γšer-ba* seems to be mainly used for **wet**, in *W.* for **moist.**

**གཤེར་བ་** *γšér-ba* I. sbst. and adj. v. the preceding article.

II. vb.. 1. **to ask for, beg for,** *šér-te ṫob soṅ* I got it by asking for it (I did not buy it) *W.* — 2. **to ask** **šér-len-pa** (lit. *γšér-len-pa*) **to interrogate, to question, to try** (judicially); as partic. and sbst.; the examining or criminal judge *C.* — 3. = *γšór-ba* **to measure** *C.*

**གཤོ་བ་** *γšó-ba*, pf. *γšos*, 1. **to pour out, to pour away** *C.*, prob. the same as *bšo-ba.* — 2 (?) **ḱa šós-te ḱyer** he has **alienated** him, enticed him to join his own party *Ld.*

**གཤོ་མོ་** *γšó-mo* **lever** **šó-mo gyáb-pa** *C., W,* **taṅ-če** *W..* **šó-mo kán-pa** *W.*, **kémpa** *C.* to put a lever to (a thing).

**གཤོག་པ་** *γšóg-pa* I. sbst. v. *šóg-pa.*

II. vb., also *bšóg-pa, γšág-pa, γšég-pa, ₒčégs-pa*, pf. *γšags, bšags*, fut. *γšag, bšag*, imp. *γšog, Pth.*, 1. **to cleave, to split,** *šiṅ* wood, *rnám-par* entirely, *ṫsál-pa bžir* into four pieces *Glr*, *dúm-bur* into pieces; *sgo γšág-pa* **to break open** a door (with a hatchet) *Pth.*; **to break or pierce through,** *dkyil* through the middle *Mil.*, *gaṅs bšóg-pa Mil.* to break through the snow, by means of yaks sent in advance to beat a path (v. *Huc.*), *lam bšog-pa* in a gen. sense: to beat a path; *lam mi šog* or *ma šog-par ₒdug Glr.* the road is not practicable; *sóg-les γšég-pa Thg.* to saw lengthwise; — *γšeg-pa* is also used for: **to rend, to tear,** to make a rent or slit into a dress etc. *C., W.* — 2. **to confess,** *sdig-pa, nyés-pa, ltúṅ-ba* to confess a sin, and thus **to expiate it,** which two, according to the views of a Buddhist, are always united, at least as it regards lighter transgressions. Hence *sdig-pa bšags* frq. means: the sin is atoned for, is blotted out, and *γšeg-pa* is the usual word for **'to forgive'.** *sdig-bšágs* **atonement, expiation,** *sbrul bsád-pai-sdig-bšágs-su* as an atonement for having killed a serpent *Glr*; *mṫol-bšágs = sdig-bšágs, mṫol-bšágs-la ša-ḱóg ₒbúl-ba* to offer a killed animal (a sheep) as an atonement *Mil.*; *sdig-bšags-smón-lam Glr.* **penitential prayer.**

**གཤོང(ས)** *γšoṅ(s)* v. *šoṅ.*

**གཤོད་པ་** *γšód-pa* to comb *Cs.*

**གཤོན་པ་** *γšón-pa Cs.*: = *skyón-pa* to put on (?).

**གཤོབ་** *γšob = šob.*

**གཤོམ་པ་** *γšóm-pa Thgy. = šóm-pa.*

**གཤོར་** *γšor Sch.* a basin or **reservoir** of water, seems to be not much known; but in *Zam. yúr-bai γšor* is to be found.

**གཤོར་བ་** *γšór-ba* I. vb, *C.* also *γšér-ba*, pf. fut. *bšar, bšor*, 1. **to count,** e.g. sheep, by letting them pass one by one through one's hands, the beads of a rosary (through one's fingers), hence *čos-brjod-bšar-sbyaṅ maṅ-po byed* to read prayers etc. (cf. *sbyaṅ-ba*, 3). — 2. **to measure,** *bres* by the peck *Lex.*; **to weigh;** *γsér-la rá-gan γšár-ba* to weigh out (to exchange) brass for gold. — 3. **to hunt, to chase,** = *˳čór-ba, ri-dwags* game *Lex.*; *nya-γšór-ba* **to fish** *Dzl.* — 4. *Sch.* to cut through (?).

II. adj., also *γšér-ba,* **rough, bristly, shaggy,** *skra, spu Stg.*, opp. to *˳ǰam-po* (*Sch.* rough, gruff, rude?)

གཤོལ་ *γšol* **plough** *Glr.*, *ťoṅ, ťóṅ-γšol* id. The plough in India and Tibet consists only of a crooked beam, *γšol-mda,* (without wheels) with the share (*γšol-lčágs, toṅ-lčágs*) at the lower end; *γšol-mdá ˳dzin-pa* **to plough,** lit. to take hold of the plough-beam.

གཤོལ་པོ་ *γšól-po* **poplar-tree** *C.*

གཤོས་པ་ *γšos-pa* 1. *γšo-ba* and *bšo-ba.*

བཤའ་ *bša* 1. in *bgo-bša* **portion, share, allowance, ration** *Lex.*, evidently a secondary form of *šas.* — 2. *Dzl.* ༢༧༠, 1 **inundation,** flood; *šwa,* the reading of the manuscript of Kyelang, seems to be preferable.

བཤའ་བ་ *bšá-ba,* pf. *bšas,* **to slaughter, to kill** (animals for food); in a story of *Glr.* it follows the slaughtering and must be understood to denote the cutting to pieces of the killed animal; but our Lama preferred to read *bšús-pa* to skin.

བཤའ་མ་ *bšá-ma* v. *γšá-ma.*

བཤག་པ་ *bšág-pa* v. *γšóg-pa*

བཤང་བ་ *bšáṅ-ba, Sch.* also *γšaṅ-ba,* alvine discharges, *bšáṅ-ba ˳byin-pa* to make open bowels, of food, medicines *Med.*; *bšaṅ-dgág* **constipation** *Med.*; *bšaṅ-γči* excrements and urine, *bšaṅ-γčis skú-ba* to dirty therewith *Dzl.*; *bšaṅ-γči bsri-ba* to retain stool and urine *Sch.*; *bšaṅ-lám* the anus *Med.*

བཤངས་པ་ *bšáṅs-pa* **leaky, leaking, full of crevices,** **ču-zóm nyi-ma-la bór-na šaṅ dug** *W.* the water-pail will become leaky, if it is left standing in the sun.

བཤད་པ་ *bšád-pa* (prob. pf. of *˳čád-pa* q.v.) 1. **to explain,** expound; **to declare,** pronounce, *čos-bšád-pa* to explain religion, to lecture on religious subjects, **to preach;** *˳či-ba daṅ ˳drar bšad* he must be set down for dead *Wdṅ.*; *bú-mo skyé-bar bšad* this **indicates** that a girl will be born *Lt.*; *bšád-kyis mi láṅ-ṅo* it is **ineffable, unspeakable; to say,** *˳bab-par bšad* they say it flows down *Wdṅ.*, *ťá-mar bšad* he is said to be on the lowest stage *Thgy.*, *ṅán-par bšad* it is said or declared to be bad, *smán-du bšad* it is **mentioned** as a medicine *Wdṅ.*; **to tell, to relate,** col. the usual word. — 2. **to comb,** v. *šód-pa.* — *bšad-grwa* **school-room, lecture-room.** — **šad-dón** *W.* the subject of a talk. *bšad-yám* a public lecture *Sch.* (?). *bšad-ló byéd-pa* to make many words *Mil.*

བཤན་པ་ *bšán-pa* v *šán-pa.*

བཤར་ *bšar,* supine of *bšá-ba.*

བཤར་བ་ *bšár-ba* v *γšór-ba.*

བཤལ་བ་ *bšál-ba* 1. **to wash, to wash out or off, to clean by washing, to rinse,** plates, dishes, etc. — 2. *ltó-ba bšál-ba* **to purge** the body, hence in gen. *bšál-ba* to suffer from diarrhoea, and *W.* col. **šal** **diarrhoea, looseness, flux,** **šal rag** I have d., **šal dug** he suffers from d., **šal yoṅ** d. begins; *bšal-˳ǰám* a mild d., *bšal-˳p̀yés*(?) a violent flux *Sch.*; *bšal-nád* indisposition from d.; *bšal-byéd B.*, *bšal-smán B.* and col. **laxative,** aperient medicine.

བཤས་པ་ *bšás-pa* v. *bšá-ba.*

བཤིག་པ་ *bšig-pa* v. *˳dzig-pa* I.

བཤིབ་པ་ *bšib-pa* v. *γšib-pa.*

བཤུ་བ་ *bšú-ba* v. *šú-ba.*

བཤུག་པ་ *bšúg-pa* to sell *Cs.*

བཤུད་པ་ *bšúd-pa* 1. v. *šud-pa.* — 2. *Sch.*: to purify by fire, *bšúd-me* purifying fire (?).

བཤུབ་པ་ *bšúb-pa* to put into the scabbard, **to sheathe** *Sch.*

བཤུམ་པ་ *bšúm-pa* — བཤེར་བ་ *bšér-ba* v. ཤུམ་པ་ *šúm-pa* etc.

བཤེའུ་ *bšeu* (cf. *bša, šwa*) **inundation, flood** *Mil.*

བཤེས་པ་ *bšés-pa*, prop. pf. of *šés-pa*, **to know** (a person or thing), **to be acquainted,** *daṅ* with *Dzl.*; *γnyen-bšés* **a relation, relative,** *γnyen-bšes-la ṗán-γtogs-par sems-so* they are intent on being of use to their relatives *Dzl.*; *γnyen* and *bšes* may also be separated: *ḱyód - la γnyen med bšes kyaṅ med*, *Mil.*; *bšes-γnyén* on the other hand means: **friend,** *dgé-bai bšes- nyén* (*Ssk.* कल्याणमित्र) friend to virtue, **spiritual adviser,** opp. to *mi-dgéi bšes- nyén* **seducer,** *Glr.* (cf. *sdig-pai grógs-po*); *dge-bšés* 1. = *dgé-bai bšes-γnyén*. 2. = *dge-bsnyén* **lay-brother.** — *ṅo·bšés* v. *ṅo-šés*. — *mdza-bšés* **friend.**

བཤོ་བ་ *bšó-ba*, pf. *bšos*, 1. also *γšó-ba*, **to pour out** *Lex.* — 2. **to lie with,** to have sexual intercourse with, = *˳ḱrig-pa byéd-pa*, e.g.: *de daṅ bšós-pas bu skyes* after having slept with him, she bore him a son *Pth.*; **to engender, to generate, to beget** (v.a.), *ṗág-rdzis bšós-pai bu* the son begotten by the swine-herd *Pth.*, (*bšo-ba* seems not to be considered obscene).

བཤོག་པ་ *bšóg-pa* v. *γšóg-pa*.

བཤོད་པ་ *bšód-pa* = *bšád-pa*, **šo̱'-ri* C.* **rumour, report,** **šo̱-ri-la dhé-ḍa zer dúg-te yi' mi če** though it is rumoured I cannot believe it *C.*

བཤོར་བ་ *bšór-ba* v. *γšór-ba*.

བཤོར་པོ་ *bšór-po C., W.* **liberal, munificent,** *Schr.*: squanderer, spendthrift(?).

བཤོལ་བ་ *bšól-ba* 1. **to put off, postpone, defer, delay,** *bód-la ˳gró-ba* the going to Tibet *Glr.*; absolutely: *bšól-ba bzaṅ* it is good to wait; — **to prolong,** e.g. *mi žig-gi ˳tsó-ba* the life of a person (by a reprieve) *Dzl.*, also **to grant, to allow** viz. a respite, a reprieve, *bdág-la žag bdun žig bšól-te* granting me a respite of seven days *Dzl.*; **to stop, detain,** e.g. the sun in his course *Thgy.*, a traveller wishing to set out *Pth.*; **to omit,** to neglect doing *Mil.* (ni f.); *ṗyi bšól-ba* **to put off, postpone,** *ṗyi-bšól byéd-pai gáṅ-zag* a person that is always postponing his religious duties *Mil.*; *čós-la ṗyi-bšól byar mi ruṅ Mil.* there should be no putting off, whenever religion is concerned; *bšol ˳debs-pa* and *˳tebs-pa* = *bšol-ba* frq.; *bšol ma ťebs* he could not be detained, kept back, diverted from his purpose *Pth.*; relatives are called *bdúd-kyi bšol-˳débs* a hinderance on the way of the believer, caused by the devil.

བཤོས *bšos* resp. for *zan* or *spags*, **food, victuals, provisions of the table;** *bšos-la γšegs-pa* to go to dine, to go to dinner *Dzl.*; *dge-˳dún-la bšos γsol-ba* to treat the priests to a meal *Dzl.*; now almost exclusively applied to food **offered to the gods,** = *lha-bšos*; *bšos-bu Mil.* offering-morsels, e.g. small pieces of butter offered to the gods or the ghosts.

བཤོས་པ་ *bšos-pa* **begotten, generated,** v. *bšo-ba*.

# ས

ས *sa* 1. the letter **s,** the sharp English *s*, in *C.* distinguished from **z,** (which is sounded there also as sharp s) only by the following vowel being high-toned. — 2. num.: 28.

ས་ *sa* 1. **earth,** as elementary substance, *sa ču me rluṅ* earth, water, fire, air, the four elements, *sa nyúṅ-zad čig* a small quantity of earth, opp. to: *sa čén-poi sa* the mass of the whole earth *Dzl.*; *rdzá-sa* clay, argillaceous earth, **bé-sa* W.* sand and earth, *šág-sa* flint and earth; also for **ore, metal** (like *rdo*), *γsér-sa* gold-ore, *dṅúl-sa* silver-ore *Cs.*; *ḱyim-sa* sweepings, offscourings;

**the ground,** *sá-la* (*W.* also **se̥ k'á-na**) *˳dúg-pa* to sit on the ground, *sá-la ltúṅ-ba, gyél-ba* to fall to the ground; *sa-˷óg, sa-stéṅ, sa-blá,* under, on, above the ground; *sa-˷og-spyód* the Nagas (*klu*); **the earth,** the globe which we inhabit, usually more accurately *sa čén-po* v. above. — 2. **place, spot, space,** = *γnas,* and col. more in use than this, *rwai sa ˳búr-ba Stg.* 'swollen in the places of the horns', i.e. men that had been oxen in a former life, and in consequence of it are distinguished by little knobs corresponding to their former horns; **p'óg-sa ghá-la dug** *C.* where have you been hit or hurt? *˳dá-sa* and *˳bém-sa* sharp-shooters' stand and place of the target *C.*; *yod-sa* the place where a person lives, (in the old classical style usually expressed by *gaṅ-na-ba*); **čin-taṅ-sa** vulg. 1. orifice of the urethra. 2. privy, water-closet; *ṅá-la grós-˳dri-sa čig yod* I have a place where to ask advice, I have an oracle *Glr.*; in a wider sense: **occasion, opportunity, possibility,** *lús-la rég-sa med* one cannot get near him *Glr.*, *rje k'yód-kyi γšégs-sa dé-na med* you cannot go to that place, Sir! *Mil.*; *nor-gyis blú-sa med* you cannot ransom yourself by money *Mil.*; also with respect to men: *ṅa γžán-la zér-sa* (*žú-sa, ré-sa*) *med* I cannot address myself to any body else with my words (requests, hopes); **place, step, degree, grade,** *čuṅ-ma čé-sar bzuṅ* he took and treated his second wife in the place of the first, i.e. he showed the second the honour due to the first; *sa-bču* v. compounds. — 3. it is also said to be the name of a quadruped of the size and appearance of a badger, but not identic with *γsa Sik.*

**Comp.** *sa-dkár* = *dkar-rtsi Cs.* – *sa-skám Sch.* arid soil, dry ground, **steppe.** — *sa-skyóṅ, sa-skyór Lex.* protector of the earth i.e. king. — *sa-k'u* made dirty by earth, dust etc., **soiled, turbid.** — **sa-k'yád** *W.* (for *γnas B., sá-ča C.*) **place,** **sa-k'yád kám-po** a dry place, also: the dry land; **a piece of ground,** **sa-k'yád čig taṅ** he gave him landed property, **sa-k'yád-di dág-po** landlord; **dwelling-place, place of residence,** **k'yód-di sa-k'yád gá-ru yod** where is your home? — *sa-k'yáb Cs.* = *sa-bdag.* — *sa-k'yon Cs.:* 'the earth's extension or compass'. — **sa-ṭa** (*sa-kra*) **map** *C.* — *sá-mk'an* one who is well acquainted with a particular place or country, a guide *Dzl.* — *sa-mk'ar Glr.* a castle the walls of which consist for the most part of earth. — *sa-gyóṅ Sch.* hard ground. — *sa-dgá* and *sa-dgyés Lex.* = *ku-mu-da.* — *sa-dgra Glr.* the enemy of a country, i.e. in many cases nothing but a demon. — **saṅ-gúl** *W.* earthquake. — *sa-ṅós* surface of the earth. — *sa-sṅón Cs.* blue earth. — *sa-bčú,* दशभूमि, acc. to one explanation the ten steps or degrees of perfection which must be attained by those striving after the prize of Buddhaship; *sa t'ób-pa* to reach one step (viz. the first) *Do.*; *sa čén-po* a high degree, e.g. the eighth *Thgy.*; *Foucaux* enumerates them all *Gyatch. Transl.* p. 3. According to another supposition *sa-bču* signifies the ten worlds or dominions of the Bodhisattvas *Was.* (124). — *sa-čá Glr., Mil., C.* **place, country** (*W.* **sa-k'yád**). — *sa-čen* 1. v. above *sa* 1.; 2. v. *sa-bču*; 3. v. *sa-skya.* — *sa-stéṅ* v. above *sa* 1. — *sa-dúg* evaporation, damp, injurious to those sleeping on the bare ground. — *sa-dó* (v. *do-po*) half a load of earth, a sackful of earth, being half the load of a donkey *Mil.* — **sa-dóṅ** *W.* **pit,** hole. — *sa-bdág* 1. **landlord,** master or lord of the ground, sovereign *Stg.*, *sá-yi bdág-po sá-yi rje* are words used in addressing a king *Mil.* 2. more frq.: **god of the ground** of the country, supposed to be a jealous and angry being, of terrific appearance, to whom on many occasions sacrifices are brought, and who prob. was worshipped already before the spread of Buddhism cf. *Schl.* 271. — *sa-mda* 1. mouse-trap, also a large trap for catching leopards and other animals. 2. a fabulous plant (?). — *sa-rdó* a stone of earthy fracture; earth and stones; **sa-dó ḍa tsi-wa** to slight, to disregard, to neglect *C.* — *sa-γnás* (= *γnás-sa*) **place, region, country, landscape,** *nyams-dgá-bai sa-γnás* a lovely landscape *Glr.* — *sa-sna-lṅá* soil of five different places. — *sá-*

*pa* inhabitant of the earth, of our globe *Sch.* — *sa-spyód* possessing the earth, man *Cs.* — *sa-ṗág Glr.*, prob. = *so-ṗág* brick, dried in the sun. — *sa-ṗúg* cavern, cave. — *sa-ṗyógs* **place, region, tract,** *ˌjígs-pai sa-ṗyogs* an unsafe place or region *Thgy.* — **sá-bi-lig** *W.* 1. **mouse, rat** 2. *Ld.* also **bar, bolt,** door-bar? — *sa-blá* v. above *sa* 1. — *sa-dbáṅ Cs.* = *sa-bdág*, v. above *sa* no. 1. — *sa-ˌbol Cs.* soft earth. — *sa-ma-rdó* or *sa-min-rdó-min Sch.*: 'neither earth nor stone', i.e. a kind of conglomerate. — *sa-min Sch.*: 'white sand' (??). — *sa-mós Sch.* = *kú-mu-da* or *úd-pa-la.* — *sa-dmár* red earth; *sa-dmar-ˌbóṅ* n. of a monastery in the neighbourhood of Darjeeling, situated on a mountain-slope, which consists of a red-coloured soil (*Hook.*I, 171 calls it Simonbong). — **sa-tse** *W.* sand or gravel found in roasted barley etc. — *sa-ṙtsig, sa-rtsis, sa-ṫsig* **stage, post-station.** — *sa-mtsams, W.* **san-ṫsam**, **border, frontier, boundary** *Glr.*; *sa-mṫsáms ˌgégs-pa* to fix the borders or limits, to mark out the boundaries. — *sa-žag* dust floating on water *Pth.* — *sa-γži* **ground, soil, footing, floor; estate** *Tar.* 99. — *sa-ˌóg* v. above *sa* 1, *sa-ˌog-spyód* the Nagas (*klu*). — *sa-yáṅs* a wide place or space, an extensive tract of land. — *sa-yúl* = *sa-čá Glr.* — *sa-γyos, sa γyó-ba* earthquake. — *sa-rigs* species of earth. — *sa-ris Pth.?* — *sa-rúl Cs.* rotten or decayed earth (?) — **sa-ró** *W.* **rubbish,** (*Sch.* fallow-ground, fallow-field?) — *sa-lám Mil.*, perh. for *sa-bčui lam.* — *sa-šún Sch.* crust of the earth (?) — *sa-bšin* fertile land, rich soil. — *sa-srán* hard ground. — *sa-srúṅ Cs.* = *sa-bdag* v. above *sa* no. 1. — *sa-srós* evening twilight, dusk *Cs.*

ས

སསྐྱ *sa-skyá* a large monastery, S.W. of Lhasa, also the Lamas belonging to it, clothed in red, *Wts.* 132. *Schl.* 73. *sa (-skya)-čén(-po)* honorary title of the Lama *Kun-dga-snyiṅ-po*, born in the year 1090 after Christ; *sa-skyá páṇḍi-ṫa* a famous Lama of this monastery, born 1180.

སག *sá-ga* n. of one of the lunar mansions, v. *rgyu-skár* no. ༡༦, and hence also n. of a month, part of March and April, ni f.

སཱ་ག་ར *sā-ga-ra Skr.* **the sea.**

ས་གུ་ཙེ *sa-gu-tsé* **worm** *C.*

སཏྲ *sa-tra Tar.* 184 and 187, *Schf.*: **diploma, patent,** not to be found in *Ssk.* dictionaries.

ས་ཐེལ་ནག་པོ *sa-ṫel-nág-po* deity of the *Hór-pa.*

ས་བོན *sá-bon* 1. **seed,** *sá-bon ˌdébs-pa* to sow, *sá-bon btáb-mk̇an* sower, *sá-bon-du ḃyéd-pa* to use as seed-corn *Dzl.*; **seed-corn, corn, grain,** also green corn, *sá-bon tsám-la ṙná-ba* to mow off as if it were green corn *Ma.* — 2. = *k̇u-k̇rág*, v. *k̇ú-ba Med.*; also = *k̇ú-ba*, e.g. *sá-bon ˌdzin-pa* **conception** *S.g.*, *sa-bon zág-pa emissio seminis Glr.*; fig.: **propagation, progeny, issue,** *sá-bon byed mi nus* then no propagation can take place; *sa-bon čig žog* 'propagate thyself!' — 3. fig.: *dgé-bai sá-bon* the seeds or germs of virtue, *sdig-pai sá-bon* the germs of vice, *da sá-bon ma bskyéd-na* if I do not now produce seeds viz. of virtue (else more frq.: 'a root of virtue') *Dzl.*; *byaṅ-čúb-kyi sá-bon Tar.* — 4. *W.* **soap,** acc. to the Hind. سابن, more accurately صابن.

ས་འཚོ་མ *sa-ˌṫsó-ma* Gopa, the wife of Buddha.

ས་ཡ *sá-ya* **a million;** this number, however, is not much in use with Indians and Tibetans, whereas the lāk, *ˌbum*, 100,000, frq. serves to represent a very large sum.

ས་ཡབ *sa-yáb* (sovereign, 'father to a country') a not unfrequent perversion of the title *sa-heb W.*

ས་ར་སོ་རེ *sa-ra-so-ré* also *sar-sór*, coarse-grained and fine-grained (corn, seeds etc.) mixed together *W.*

ས་རི *sa-ri* n. of a lunar mansion, v. *rgyu-skár* ༧༤.

སཱ་ལ *sā-la Ssk.* n. of an Indian tree, *Shorea robusta,* with which also some superstitious fables are connected.

ས་ལང་གི *sa-láṅ-gi, Hind.* सारङ्गी, a kind of violin,

ས་ལུ *sa-lu Ssk.* शाली, *Oryza sativa,* **rice,** as a plant; acc. to *Sch.* also Indian corn (?).

ས་ལེ་སྦྲམ་ *sa-le-sbrám* (cf. *sbram-bu*) *Wdṅ.* **fine gold.**

ས་ཧེབ་ *sá-heb*, col. *sāb*, *sab*, *Arab.* صَاحِب, formerly in India title of Moslems of high rank, now title of every European, = **gentleman, sir.**

སག་ *sag*, also *nya-sag Cs*, 1. brawn, callosity; *Sch.* also: hair-side (of a skin); *sag-čan* brawny, *sag-ₒtúg* a thick brawn. — 2. *W.* **scale,** (of a fish) *nya-sag-čan* scaly.

སག་གདར་ *sag-γdár C.*, **sab-dár** *W.*, *γsag-brdár Sch.* **a rasp,** *sag-γdár rgyag-pa* **to rasp.**

སག་པ་ *ság-pa C.* a little bubble, **sag sag zér-wa** to sparkle, to effervesce.

སག་རམ་རྩི་ *sag-ram-rtsi* **sulphuric acid** *Cs.*

སག(ས)་རི་ *sag(s)-ri* **shagreen.**

སག་ལད་ *sag-lád*, *Pers.* سَقلات, 1. fine **cloth,** made of *lé-na*, *C.* **go-nam** (v. *snam-bu*). European broadcloth *W.* — 2. round or twisted lace, round tape, strips of cloth set with spangles? *W.*

སང་ *saṅ* 1. *B.*, *C.* **to-morrow,** *saṅ-nyin* id. *Glr.*; *sáṅ-gi γdúgs-la* for to-morrow noon *Dzl.*; *saṅ náṅ-par Cs.*, *saṅ sṅá-bar Glr.* to-morrow morning; also absolutely: on the following day *Pth.*, *dei-saṅ* id.; *saṅ-p̓ód*, more frq. *saṅ-lo* next year; *saṅ-p̓ód da ṫsám-du* a year hence, this time a year. — 2. *W.* particle denoting the comparative degree, inst. of *las* or *pas* of *B.*, **dɛ saṅ i' gyál-la** this is better than that. — 3. *Ld.*, *Balt.* sometimes for *yaṅ*.

སཾ་སྐྲྀཏའི་སྐད་ *saṅ-kritai skad* **the Sanskrit language** *Glr.*

སང་གི་ཀ་ *sáṅ-gi-ka*(?) a greenish stone of which knife-handles and similar articles are said to be made *W.*

སང་ང་ *saṅ-ṅá*, *saṅ-ṅé*, *saṅ-súṅ Ld.* **secretly, privately, whisperingly, by report,** = *sám-súm.*

སང་སེང་ *saṅ-séṅ* **hiding-place, chink, crevice,** *k̓yim-gyi* of the house *Stg.*, for hiding money and treasures, = *sbugs*; *gós-kyi* folds of the dress, that are a haunt of vermin.

སང་བ་ *sáṅ-ba*, pf. (*b*)*saṅs*, fut. (*b*)*saṅ*, 1. **to do away with,** to remove (dirt etc.), **to cleanse,** cf. *ₒṫsáṅ-ba*, where also examples are given. — 2. in a more gen. sense: **to take away** or **off,** *k̓ebs sáṅ-ba* to uncover; **k̓o-la nyi' saṅ soṅ** *C.* his sleep is gone, he cannot sleep. — 3. **to spoil,** to render unfit or useless, **wó-ma saṅ soṅ** *C.* the milk is spoiled, **zem saṅ soṅ** the cask or tub leaks *C.* Cf. *seṅ*.

སངས་རྒྱས་ *saṅs-rgyás* the Tibetan equivalent for बुद्ध; as to the etymology of the word v. sub *ₒṫsáṅ-ba*. The first historical Buddha is *Saṅs-rgyas šā-kya ṫúb-pa*, whose family name is *Gaú-ta-ma* and his personal name *Don-grúb*, सिद्धार्त, which, however, is not much used. In course of time several imaginary predecessors were given to him: *ₒOd-srúṅ*, *Gser-ṫúb* and *ₒKor-ba-ₒǰig*, as having existed and reigned in former periods of the world. A successor also, *Byáms-pa*, was assigned to him, of whom it is supposed that he will reign at the period following this present one. According to others, however, *Sākyaṫubpa* was already the seventh Buddha that appeared on earth, the four above-named having been preceded by *Tams-čad-skyób*, *Gtsug-tor-čan* and *Rnam-par-γzigs*, this last one being the first of them all. These seven Buddhas then are comprised under the name of *Saṅs-rgyas-rabs-bdún.* — But the fertile imagination of devote Buddhists has further increased the number of future Buddhas to not less than one thousand (?), appropriate names for each of them have been invented, and Prof. Schmidt has thought it worth his while, to have these thousand names reprinted in a special pamphlet. Mysticism, however, generally knows only of the five first-named Buddhas (*Gautama*, his three predecessors and his first successor) and to each of these five 'human' Buddhas a celestial Buddha corresponds, called 'Dhyani Buddha' or the Buddha of contemplation, whilst to every Dhyani Buddha again his Dhyani Bodhisattwa is associated. In later times there is even mentioned a supreme or highest god, Adi-Buddha, *tóg-mai Saṅs-rgyás*, which doctrine, however, seems not to have been generally accepted. — Cf. *Köpp.* II, 15—29.

སད་ *sad* **frost, cold air, cold, coldness,** *sád-kyis ˳kyér-ba* to be destroyed by frost *Glr.*; often in conjunction with *sér-ba*, hail.

སད་པ་ *sád-pa* I. **to examine, see, try, test,** *kyod bzód-dam mi bzod sád-par byao* I shall see, whether you are patient *Dzl.*; *γser ltar sád-nas mṅón-par ˳gyur* like gold, it is approved by testing *Dzl.*; *nyáms-sad-pa* v. *nyams*; *sád-mi mi bdun* 'the seven men of trial', i.e. the seven most distinguished and talented among the young Tibetans sent by king *Kri-sróṅ-lde-btsan* to *'Kanpo* Bodhisattwa, for being thoroughly instructed in religion and sciences *Glr.* 86, also *Tar.* 162, 22; *las sád-pai gáṅ-zag Mil.* a tried, a tested man?

II. frq. in conjunction with *γnyid*, resp. *mnal* 1. to cease to sleep, **to awake,** *rmis ma-tág-tu* directly from that dream *Dzl.*, *γzim-pa-las* from sleep *Dzl.* — 2. **to rouse,** from sleep, **to waken,** more precisely *sád-par byéd-pa*; also fig.: *dgé-bai rtsá-ba* good, virtuous, emotions *Tar.*

སན་གིན་ *san-gin*, *Pers.* سنگین, **bayonet** *W.*

སབ་ *sab*, col. for *sa-heb*.

སམ་ཏ་ *sam-ta Schr.*, *brtsam-grwa Cs.*, others: *bsám-kra*, *sáb-dra*, pocket-book, note-book, memorandum-book, tablets *C.*, *W.* (*Cs.* a small writing-desk?).

སམ་དལ་ *sam-dál Ld.*, *yar-sam Lh.* **mustaches.**

སམ་(མ་)སུམ་(མེ་) *sam(-ma)-sum(-me)* with a low voice, **lowly, softly,** e.g. **zér-če**, from politeness etc.; **sam-súm zer** speak in a low voice! *W.*

སར་ *sar* 1. termin. of *sa*, *čé-sar ˳dón-pa Cs.* to promote to high rank or dignity, *sar-γnas-dpá-bo* (in a hymn) was explained by: *sa bčú-la γnás-pai dpá-bo* i.e. Buddha. — 2. *sár-γčod-pa* v. *γsar*. — 3. sbst. **wick** *W.*

སརྫི་ཀ་ *sa-rdzi-ka Ssk.* **soda,** in *Wdṅ.* it is mentioned as a plant, yielding soda.

སར་སོར་ *sar-sor* v. *sa-ra-so-re*.

སལ་བབ་ *sal-báb W.*, and prob. also *sal-sil Mil.*, gold ornament, **gold lace,** and the like, ni. f.

སལ་ལེ་བ་ *sál-le-ba* **clear, bright, brilliant** *Mil.*, *sal-lér snáṅ-ba* lighted up brilliantly, well lighted *Pth.*, *mdaṅs sal-sál* id. *Pth.*

སས་ *sas* instr. of *sa*.

སི་ *si* 1. in some parts of *Ld.* the termination of the instrum. after vowels, like *su* in *Kun.* — 2. also *si-si*, the sound of whistling through the teeth, *si-skad*, *si-sgra* whistling, whistle; *si-brda* whistling, whistle, as a call or sign; *si-glu* a whistled tune. — 3. num.: 58.

སཱི་ཏཱ་ *sī-tā* n. of one of the four fabulous streams of the world.

སི་རི་ *si-ri* 1. **pack-thread, twine** *C.*, *W.* — 2. **bar, bolt, door-bar,** **si-ri čúg-če* or *gyáb-če** to bolt, to bolt up, **si-ri tón-če** to unbolt, unbar *W.*

སི་རི་འབུ་ *si-ri-˳bu* **centiped** *W.*

སི་རིལ་ *si-ril* a kind of inkhorn, case for carrying an inkstand in one's pocket *Ld.*

སི་ལ་ *si-la Ssk.* सिल्लकी a sort of incense.

སི་ལི་མ་ *si-li-ma* the breaking up of the ice *Sch.*

སིག་པ་ *sig-pa* **to hitch up,** to give a hitch, as porters do with a load on their back *Cs.*

སིག་བུ་ *sig-bu Sch.*, *síg-ra Schr.*, a sort of basket.

སིང་ *siṅ* v. *siṅ-siṅ*.

སིང་སྐྱུར་ *siṅ-skyúr Sch.* curdled milk, sour milk.

སིང་ག་གླིང་ *siṅ-ga-gliṅ Cs.*, *siṅ-ga-lai gliṅ Glr.*, **सिंहल, Ceylon.**

སིང་གེ་ *siṅ-ge* 1. frq. for *seṅ-ge*. — 2. v. *rtsiṅ-ge*.

སིང་བ་ *siṅ-ba* 1. vb., **bal siṅ-če** **to pick out, sort out,** wool for the third time, by which the finest is obtained. — 2. adj. in compounds: *nág-siṅ-ba* jet-black, very black *Thgy.*; *spró-siṅ-ba* v. *spro.*

སིང་བུ *siṅ-bu* liquor made of mare's milk, Tartar arrack *Sch.*

སིང་ཚུལ *siṅ-tsúl Ts.* **tea-pot, tea-kettle.**

སིང་ཡོལ *siṅ-yól* v. *seṅ-rás* in *seṅ-po.*

སིང་རི *siṅ-ri* 1. n. of a mountain *Glr.* — 2. = *siṅs-po.*

སིང་སིང *siṅ-siṅ* **thin, limpid,** of fluids *W.* (yet cf. *séṅ-po*), **siṅ čug-če** to clarify, to purify.

སིངས་པོ *síṅs-po* 1. adj. **thin, clear** *W.* — 2. sbst. *Cs.*, also *čaṅ(-ba)-siṅs Pth.*, *Lt.*, **ug-siṅ** *Ld.* **small-beer,** the fourth infusion of 'chang', a weak beverage, without any intoxicating qualities, yet not disrelished on that account.

སིད་པ *sid-pa* **to whistle** *Sch.*, *sid-sgra* = *si-sgra.*

སིནྡྷུ་ར *sindhu-ra*, for **सिन्दूर minium,** red lead, = *li-k̔ri Glr.*

སིབ་པ *sib-pa* **to evaporate, to soak in, to be imbibed,** of fluids, *sib-sib* or *sib-kyis*, also *šib-kyis tim-pa* to evaporate quickly.

སིབ་བུ *sib-bu Lt.*; *Cs.*: a sort of **small-pox;** *Schr.*: **the measles.**

སིམ་པ *sím-pa Lex.* = *bdé-ba*, **सुख**, sbst. **good health, prosperity,** vb. **to be well, to be well off.**

སིམ་བིད་(ལ) *sim-bid(-la)* adv. **sliding, glidding, slipping,** with **čá-če** to move along in this way *Ld.*

སིལ་བུ, གསིལ་བུ *sil-bu, γsil-bu* a little piece, **a fragment,** *ro sil-bur* ˳*tor* the corpse falls to pieces *Mil*; *sil-sil* col. id.; **sil čó-če** to reduce to small pieces, by breaking, crumbling, plucking etc. *W.*

སིལ་སྙན *sil-snyán* (also *sil* and *sil-sil Lex.*) **cymbal,** *lčágs-kyi sil* ˳*k̔ról-ba Lex.*, *sil snyán ról-mo* ˳*k̔ról-ba Glr.*, *Dzl.* to strike the cymbals; *sil-snyán-ma* a female cymbal-player *Tar.*

སིལ་མ *sil-ma* 1. the tinkling sound of a cymbal, *rdza-čáb sil-mas snyán-pa brjod* tunefully flows the brook over its clay-slate bed *Mil.*; *sil-čáb* gurgling water, rippling brook *Mil.*— 2. also *sil-dṅúl* the rupee of Ladak, = 4 *jau*, = $\frac{1}{5}$ of an Indian rupee, **sil-ṅul gyad-di nas** a patch of barley worth 8 Silma *Ld.*

སུ *su* I. pron., also *su žig*, 1. interrog. pron. **who?** ˳*dí-na su yod* who is here? *k̔yod su yin* who are you? *su či-skad byá-ba yod* who is it and what is his name? *Mil.*; **which?** = *gaṅ*, *rgyál-poi bu su žig* which son of the king? *Tar.*, *sú-rnams*, *sú-dag*, col. **sú-su** plural form; in certain popular phrases: **su-gyóg** race, running-match *W.*, **su tob gyáb-pa** to pounce upon, to snatch away, to plunder *C.*, *W.*— 2. correlative and indefinite pron.: *su mi di γsód-pa dé-la ... sbyin-no* to him that kills this man, I shall give ... *Stg.*; *k̔yod sṅar sú-la yaṅ γsól-ba ma btáb-bam* have not you already asked somebody before? *Dzl.* ༢༩, 14 (acc. to a better reading); *su de čáṅ-bai gán-du mčio* I shall go to him who has it *Dȯ*; *su tod-tód* whom it concerns *Sch.*(?); *su yaṅ(ruṅ)* **whosoever,** whoever, any body who, also absolutely: **every, every one, all,** *sú-bas kyaṅ p̔yis* later than all (the others) *Dzl.*, when followed by a negative: **nobody,** frq.; *su byuṅ Mil.* = *su yaṅ*; *su med kyaṅ* though nobody be present *Pth.*; *su, su žig, su gaṅ* is also used for **somebody, some one, a certain** (but not frq. and more in col. or vulg. language): *su gaṅ mdzá-bo žig* a certain friend; *su sér-sna-čan žig* a (certain) miser; also in the following manner: **su čad dug su tsem dug** one cuts out, the other sews *W.*; **bóṅ-bu su lo-čú-nyi-pa, su lo-čú-pa yin** some of the donkeys are twelve, others ten years old. — II. termination: 1. of the term. after a final s, cf. *tu, du, ru.* — 2. of the instr. in *Kun.*: *'*á-pa-su** from or by the father, inst. of the *p̔as* of *B.* (cf. **सु** in the Brāj-dialect of the Hindi). — 3. expletive after *nas Mil.* and elsewh. — III. num.: 88.

སུ་གི *sú-gi* vulgar corruption of *dzo-ki* q. v.

སུ་མི *su-mi* a medicinal root serving as an antidote *Cs.*

ས

སུ་རུ་པན་ཙ་, སུར་པན་ *su-ru-ṕan-tsá*, *sur-ṕán* Guinea pepper, *Capsicum annuum C., W.*

སུ་ལུ་ *sú-lu? sú-lui ťsúl-du bžúgs-pa* denotes perh. the usual sitting posture of Milaraspa who, while reciting his songs, used to stretch out his left leg, drawing up the other, and supporting his right arm on it, on which his head was leaning.

སུ་སུ་ *su-su* 1. v. *su.* — 2. *su-sú zer-wa* denotes **the drawing in the breath** in blowing up a fire, the lips being nearly closed, to prevent ashes or smoke from entering the mouth.

སུག་ *sug* **reward, recompense,** *sug-rṅán* id., *sug-rǰéd* mark of honour as a reward *Cs.*; *ṕag-súg* a bribe, frq.

སུག་པ་ *súg-pa* I. sbst. 1. **the hand** *Med.*; *sug-bris* handwriting *Sch.* — 2. the lower part of the leg of animals, *rtai súg-bži*; **súg-gu** *W.* id. — 3. a medicinal herb *Wdṅ.*

II. vb. **to push, jog, nudge** a person, in order to waken him, or to make him attentive; **to push open,** a door with a stick *Mil.*; *súg-pa žig byéd-pa Mil.*, **sug gyáb-pa** *C.* **to push, to shove, to displace,** **sug ča yin** it will get out of its place *W.*

སུག་སྨེལ་ *sug-rmél Cs.*: 'a kind of spice, betel, betel-nut' (?); *sug-smél Lt.* and *C.* **cardamom.**

སུད་པ་ *súd-pa* **to cough, to breathe with difficulty** *Cs.*, *súd-de ṡi-ba* to be choked or suffocated *Sch.*

སུན་པ་ *sun-pa* vb. and adj. 1. **to be tired of, weary of, sick of; tired, weary, out of humour** *rná-ba mi sún-te* not tired of hearing *Mil*; *yid sún-par ˳gyúr-ba* to become tired, to get weary of; the more precise form of the adj. is *sún-po*: **žág-daṅ ḍe zá-na sún-po rag* or *sún-na rag** *W.* if one eats rice every day, one gets tired of it; **sems sún-po** id.; *'*úm-čog sụn soṅ** *C.* one gets tired of hearing *C.*; **sá-heb nyẹn sụn ruṅ** though it may be disagreeable to you, Sir, to hear it *C.*; *ťugs-sún dgóṅs-pa yin-pa ˳dug* I suppose your Reverence will be tired of it *Mil.*; **sun** (*C.* **sụn**) **ċug-ċe** **to make** (a person) **tired of** (a thing), **to vex, annoy, to stun** or **drown with noise,** to deafen. — 2. *sún-par byéd-pa Dzl.*, and more frq. *sún-par byin-pa* 1. to drown with, to overpower by noise, to silence (thus prob. *Mil.* ch. 34 init.); hence 2. **to refute, confute, disprove** *Tar.* 3. c. acc. **to insult, defame, disgrace, dishonour** *Schr.*, *Dzl.* ༢༢༢, 1, 3, ༢༠༤, 2; *Bhar.* 67, *Schf.*; so perh. also *sun-pa* in the following passage of *Mil.*: *ťúgs-rǰe drág-po sun ma byin* we will not put to shame the great favour (of the Lama). 4. **to renounce,** to resign, *sun ˳byin-pai stobs* strength to renounce (the world).

སུབ་པ་ *súb-pa*, pf. (*b*)*subs*, fut. *bsub*, 1. **to stop up, plug up, close, cork; to keep shut,** closed, locked up, **to stop,** *ka sna lág-pas* to stop one's mouth and nose with one's hand *Lt.*; *dbugs súb-pa* to strangle, suffocate, choke (a person); **to fill up,** choke up (with earth, rubbish etc.) a lake *Glr.*; *sna-sub* a disease of the nose? *Lt.* — 2. **to cover, close, shut up** *Sch.*, more frq., fig. *rkaṅ-rǰés súb-pa* to cover the trace or track, to efface every vestige; **tí-pi ťúr-la súb-ċe** to turn down the brim of the hat; **to blot out, erase,** *ri-mo* a drawing, *bú-lon-pai miṅ* the name of a debtor; **to hush up, conceal, cover,** e.g. other people's offences; **to suppress, to avoid,** e.g. obscene words; to allow to settle, the mash, in brewing; in all these instances in *W.* also **súb-te bór-ċe** is used.

སུམ་ *sum*, for *ɣsum*, **three,** in compounds before consonants: *súm-ċu* 30, *sum-brgya* 300, *sum-stóṅ* 3000; *súm-ča*, *Sch.* also *sum-yar*, **a third,** the third part, *˳dzam-bu-gliṅ súm-ča ɣnyis* (or only *sum-ɣnyis*) two thirds of Dzambuling (i.e. of the world) *Dz.*, *bod sum ɣnyis* two thirds of (all) the Tibetans *Ma.*; *sum-skyá Sch.* a cord of three twisted threads; *sum-ċu-rtsa-ɣsum* the 33 ancient gods (of the Vedas); *súm-ċu-pa* the thirty, i.e. 30 letters, the Tibetan alphabet, *súm-ċu-pa daṅ rtags-˳ǰúg Zam.* the alphabet and the punctuation, abbreviated: *sum-rtágs Lexx.*

སུམ་(ཅུ་)ཏིག *sum(-ċu)-tig* a medicinal herb *Med.*

ས

སུམ་པ་, སུམས་པ་ súm-pa, súms-pa I. adj. **putrid, rancid, rotten.**

II. vb., pf. *bsums*? fut. *bsum*, *Sch.* **to bind** or **tie together**, to draw together; **to condense.**

སུར་ན་ *súr-na*, *Pers.* سُرنا, **hautboy,** larger than the *gliṅ-bu* and sounding sharper; for profane use.

སུར་པན་ *súr-pán* v. *su-ru-pan-tsá.*

སུར་ཡ་ or སུརྱ་ *sur-ya* or *surya Med.*, सूर्य, **colocynth.**

སུར་སུར་ *sur-sur* **coarse-grained,** e.g. grits *W.*

སུལ་ *sul* an artificial **plait** or **gather** made in a dress *W.*; **furrow, channel, groove, trench, ditch** (*Cs.*); *ri-súl* lateral valley, ravine, hollow, *ri-súl-gyi groṅ-kyér* ravine as a haunt of evil spirits; *brag-sul* narrow ravine between rocks; *ka-súl* the fluting in a column; *súl-čan* furrowed, having plaits or folds; *súl-ma* an angular, not round, vessel; *sul-mál* the third stomach of ruminating animals, the psalterium or book-tripe *Sch.*, *sul-máṅs Lt.*

སུས་ *sus* 1. instr. of *su.* — 2. *kyeu-sús Gyatch.* ༢༥, 13, also *Stg.*?

སེ་ *se* 1. *Ld.* inst. of *te* after *s*, e.g. **zós-se** — 2. num.: 118.

སེ་གོལ་ *se-gól* 1. **snapping** one's fingers. — 2. the time it takes to do this, i.e. **a very short time, a moment, a twinkling** *Cs.*, *se-gól-gyi sgra* the sound produced by snapping the fingers, *se-gól-gyi brda* a signal given by it *Cs.*; *se-gól γtóg-pa Mil.*, *byéd-pa Mil.*, *brdáb-pa Glr.* to snap one's fingers as a sign of contempt or indignation.

སེ་ཏྲང་ *se-tráṅ* yellow beads of a rosary, coming from the central part of Tibet, accounted more valuable than **rág-ša* W.*

སེ་དུག་ *se-dúg* v. *se-šiṅ.*

སེ་དྲི་, གསེ་དྲི་ *se-drí*, *bse-drí* the disagreeable smell of the sweat of the arm-pits *Lt.*, *se-drí bsnám-pa* having that smell *Pth.*

སེ་ནམ་ *se-nam* vulgar for *bsód-snyoms*, **alms.**

སེ་སྤུར་ *se-spur Sch.* **dung-beetle.**

སེ་བ་, གསེ་བ་, བསེ་བ་ *sé-ba*, *γsé-ba*, *bsé-ba* 1. **rose-bush, rose-tree; rose;** *γser-mdog-sé-ba-me* (for *mé-tog*) *Lt.*, prob. the yellow rose; wild roses with beautiful and rich blossoms frequently adorn the slopes of the lower hills in the Himalaya mountains; whether the *se-rgód Med.* and the 'wild rose' of *Cs.* are identical, seems to be questionable; **se-dúm* C.* **hip, haw.** — *šiṅ-sé-ba* is mentioned as the food of the silk-worm *Glr.*, hence = *ó-se-šin.* — 3. thorn?

སེ་བོ་ *se-bo* **gray,** *skra se-bo* gray hair; *mgo se-bo* (resp. *dbu se-bo*) a gray-headed person. — In col. language many things which we call gray, are styled white.

སེ་འབྲུ་, སེའུ་ *se-bru*, *seu* (*C.* **sen-dú**, *W.* **sem-rú**) **pomegranate.**

སེ་མོ་དོ་ *sé-mo-do* or *sé-mo-to Mil.* a kind of **ornament,** e.g. made of pearls.

སེ་མོག་ *se-móg C.* **the venereal disease;** *se-rmá* syphilitic ulcers *Sch.*

སེ་ཡབ་, བསེ་ཡབ་ *se-yáb*, *bse-yáb* **fig** *Med.*

སེ་ར་ *sé-ra*, n. of a large monastery near Lhasa.

སེ་རག་དུར་སྨན་ *se-rag-dur-smán* **carrot** *W.*

སེ་རེལ་ *se-rél* half open, **se-rél čúg-če** to open half (doors, lids, covers etc.) *W.*

སེ་ཤིང་, བསེ་ཤིང་ *sé-šiṅ*, *bsé-šiṅ Cs.*: 'a tree or shrub, good for hedges', *se-dúg* 1. poison contained in that shrub. 2. = *se-móg Cs.*

སེག་, སེག་སེག་ *seg*, *seg-ség* **obliquely, awry, sideways,** *ség-γčod-pa Cs.*, **ség-ḍhe-la ḍhá-wa* C.*, **ség-de-la dé-če* W.* to cut off obliquely (opp. to **tẹ̄-kaṅ-la** straight *C.*).

སེག་མ་ *seg-ma* **small stones, gravel** *W.*

སེང་ *seṅ* v. *γseṅ.*

སེང་གེ་ *séṅ-ge*, *W.* **siṅ-ge**, **lion,** *séṅ-ge-mo* lioness, *séṅ-gei rál-pa* the mane of a lion; *seṅ-gei kri* **सिंहासन a throne** ('said to be so called from its being supported by golden lions' *Will.*); *seṅ-mgó* lion's head *Glr.*; *seṅ-ydoṅ-ma Sch.*, = *sī-ha-mu-ka* lion's face, **a goddess,** *Glr.*; *seṅ-prúg* a lion's whelp, *seṅ-tsáṅ* a lion's den.

སེང་ལྡང་ *seṅ-ldáṅ S.g*, *seṅ-tsér Wdṅ.*, a tree growing on the southern, lower ranges of the Himalayas, having red wood, and a bark which by poor people is used for tea (*sdoṅ-ja*); its sap serves as an officinal drug, *Lt.*; acc. to *Schf.* **खदिर** *Acacia Catechu.*

སེང་པོ་, བསེང་པོ་ *séṅ-po*, *bséṅ-po* 1. **clean, white,** cf. *skya-séṅ.* — 2. *Sch.:* **thin, airy, transparent, not dense or tight,** *seṅ-séṅ* id. (*Sch.:* **open, free, roomy, spacious**); *skyé-bo seṅ-séṅ-por gyur* they became very thin, lean, pale people, **siṅ-síṅ-po, sings-po* W.* id.; *seṅ-rás Sch.*, **siṅ-yol* W.* a thin curtain, thin cotton cloth.

སེང་བ་ *séṅ-ba*, pf. *bsaṅs*, fut. *bsaṅ*, *bseṅ*, **to lift up, to raise** what was hanging down or drooping *W.* **saṅ ċo-ċe* or *taṅ-ċe** to lift up (the eyes, the hands, the dress etc.); *sku-káms bséṅ-ba-la ̥byon* (his Reverence) goes to take some recreation *Mil.*; *kams dúb-pa séṅ-ba* to refresh the wearied body *Mil.*; *kams rmúgs-pa bséṅ-bai rluṅ-ṅád* bracing air; *skyo-bsáṅ-ba* to unbend the mind, to divert one's self; *skyo-séṅ-la ̥gró-ba* (resp. *̥byón-pa*) to take a walk, *séṅ-la mdzád-pa* to drive out, to take the air in a carriage *Pth.*; *mya-ṅán bsáṅs-te* consolatory, giving comfort *Pth.*

སེང་ཤིང་, སེང་ཤང་ *seṅ-śiṅ*, *seṅ-śáṅ* v. *ysegśáṅ.*

སེད་ *sed* **a file,** **ċag-sé** id., **śiṅ-sé** **a rasp.**

ས

སེན་ཐབས་ *sen-tabs Mil.?*

སེན་མོ་ *sén-mo*, resp. *pyag-sen* or *žabs-sén*, **nail** of a finger or toe; *sen-tóg* **a gripe, pinch, nip, twitch;** a pinch (of snuff) *sén-mo ̥débs-pa*, *W.* **táb-ċe* or *gyáb-ċe** **to pinch, squeeze,** **sen-ċus gyáb-ċe** to bore with the knuckles *W.*; *sen-tsám Sch.* as much as may be put on a finger-nail, a small quantity; *sen-žó* a white spot, such as will sometimes appear on the nails of the fingers.

སེབ་ *seb* v. *yseb.*

སེམ་, སེམས་ *sem*, usually *sems*, *Ssk.* **सत्त्व**, resp. ཐུགས་, **soul;** esp. as power of perception and volition, **mind,** cf. *yid* and *blo*; *sems na* the mind is disturbed, disordered *Mṅg.*; *sem ̥krúgs-pa* a mind agitated and troubled by sorrow, affliction, vexation etc., *sem kóṅ-du* (or *kóns-su*) *ċúd-pa* one very much grieved, deeply concerned; *sem ċúṅ-ba* a timid mind, **sem tsér-ċan* W.* a compassionate disposition, **sem nyé-mo* W.* a friendly disposition; *sem ysó-ba B.*, **sem so táṅ-ċe* or *ċúg-ċe* W.* **to console,** comfort, appease; the mind as imaginative faculty, intellectual power, *sem stór-ba* to lose one's senses *Do.*; **spirit,** *kun-yžii sem* the (eternal) spirit (opp. to *̥byúṅ-ba bžii lus* the material, perishable body) *Mil.*; *sém-kyi spyód-pa* intellectual power, mental faculties *Wdṅ.*; *dṅós-po tams-ċád ráṅ-gi sems yin-te* 'as things with me are only mind', i.e. as they exist only in my mind, in my imagination *Thgr.*, cf. *Was.* (136); *sém-la ma soṅ* 'it did not enter his mind', he had no mind, did not like *W.*; *sems ̥gyur* (his) mind is changed, *sems sgyur-ba* to change one's mind, μετανοεῖν; *bzód-pai sems* patient indurance, fortitude, **constancy;** *ynod-sems* **malice;** *śes-ráb daṅ ldán-pai sems* **wisdom,** knowledge; *sems skyéd-pa*, c. genit., to suffer thoughts or inclinations to rise in one's mind, as e.g. *̥dod-ċágs-kyi* libidinous (thoughts), frq.; also: to nourish, indulge (desires, passions), to give way to them; often used for our reflective verbs: *sems smád-pa* to humble one's self (*mi žig-la* before a person); also: *bdág-gi séms-la smad* he blamed, scolded, himself *Dzl.* ༧༥, 3, cf. *lus.*

**Comp.** *séms-mkan* **intelligent, sensible,** *séms-mkan mi ycig kyaṅ ma byuṅ* not one sensible person was present *Glr.*— *sems-̥král* a mind afflicted, painfully agitated *Sch.* — *sems-ċan* animated being, **man, animal,** very frq.; *séms-ċan daṅ ldán-pa* being with child, pregnant; *sems-ċan-dmyál-ba* = *dmyál-ba*·

— *sems-nyid Glr., Thgy.*, 'the very soul', but this is often nearly the same as 'spirit', and in the language of the N. T. it may fitly be used for *πνεῦμα*, and *ťugs-nyid* for *πνεῦμα ἅγιον*, Holy Spirit. — *sems-rtén* **keepsake, token** *Pth.* and col. — *sems-dón* an intellectual or spiritual good, gift, or possession *Mil.* — *sems-bdé* **cheerful, merry** *Mil.* — *sems-nád* **heart-grief, affliction**, *séms-kyi nád-du če* he has much heart-grief *Glr.* — *sems-dpá* a brave mind; *byaṅ-čub-sems-dpá* v. *byaṅ-čúb*; *sems-dpa-čén-po*, **महासत्त्व**, a frq. apposition to it. — *séms-tsam* a mere thought, idea *Was.* (134), *séms-tsam-pa* (*Cs.*: **योगाचार्य**) a mystic *Köpp.* II, 25. — *sems-tsér* **fatigue, weariness, disgust** *Sch.*

སེམ(ས)་པ་ *sém(s)-pa*, pf. *sems, bsams*, fut. *bsam*, imp. *som*, *W.* **sám-če**, **to think**, *ₒdi snyám-du séms-so* or *bsáms-so* he thought as follows, he had the following thoughts; *lóg-par sém-pa* to think ill (of a person) *Dzl.*; **to meditate, muse, ponder**, *sém-bžin-du* absorbed in meditation, lost in thought *Dzl.*, *mi-dgá-bar sém-šiṅ* immersed in melancholy thoughts *Dzl.*; in *C.* **sém-žin-du** signifies at the present time: knowingly, wilfully, purposely, = *šes bžin-du*; *šin-tu soms šig* think over it seriously! *Dzl.*; **to think of**, c. accus., *gráṅ-bai γnas* (to think) of a cool place, i. e. to long for coolness *Dzl.*, and c. dat.: *ráṅ-gi yúl-la ma bsám-par* forgetful of home, forgetting one's native soil *Glr.*, *yi-ge ₒdi-la ma bsám-par* disregarding this contract *Glr.*; also with termin.: *γžán-du ma sems šig* do not think of anybody else; **to intend, purpose, have in view**, e.g. *γnód-par byá-bar* to do harm *Dzl.*; construed in the same manner, it also signifies: **to fancy, imagine** *Do.*; with *daṅ ₒdrá-bar* and similar expressions: **to hold, think, consider, to take for, to look upon as**; *da ₒkór-bai nyes-dmigs bsám-šes-na* (for *bsám-žiṅ*) now that you know with full consciousness the punishment of (going through) the cycle (of animal existences) *Mil.* (yet cf. *bsám-šes* in *bsám-pa*). Sometimes it denotes only an act of memory, a remembering: *lhá-čos ťos-bsam-byéd-pa-rnams* those who have heard and kept in their memory the religion of Buddha, (who remember the words even without understanding them) *Mil.* Cf. *bsám-pa*.

སེའུ་ *seu* 1. **a little tooth** *Lt.* — 2. **pomegranate.**

སེར་, སེར་རུ་ *ser, sér-ru* corruption, putrefaction? **már-la sér-ru gyab** *C.* the butter turns yellow and rancid, *sér-čan* **rancid** *S.g.*

སེར་ཀ་ *sér-ka, sér-ḱa, sér-ga* 1. **a cleft, slit, fissure, crevice, gap**, *brag-sér* chasm or cleft in a rock; *rgya-sér* a large gap, cleft, chasm; *sér-ka súb-pa* to close, stop up a hole *Pth.* — 2. v. *sér-po*.

སེར་སྐྱ་ *ser-skyá* **Lamas and laymen**, **ser-kyá kun ₒdúm-ma ǰhé-pa** a promiscuous convention, parish council *C.* — 2. v. *skyá-bo*.

སེར་ཁྱིམ་པ་ *sér-ḱyim-pa* a sect of Lamas = *dbón-po*.

སེར་ག་མ་ *sér-ga-ma Sch.* turmeric, *Curcuma*.

སེར་ཆེ་ *ser-čé Lt.* a yellow aquatic flower; **ser-čen** *W. Saxifraga flagellaris.*

སེར་སྣ་ *sér-sna* **avarice**, frq.; *sér-sna byéd-pa* to be avaricious *Dzl.*

སེར་པོ་ *sér-po* **yellow**; *ser-ₒpréṅ* clerical procession, parade *Mil.nt.*

སེར་བ་ *sér-ba* **hail**; *ser-ḱrál* a kind of insurance against damage done by hail, i.e. money paid to the Lama for his preventive ceremonies.

སེར་བུ་ *sér-bu* v. *bsér-bu*.

སེར་མོ་ *sér-mo* 1. *C.* col. **finger.** — 2. *W.* six-rowed barley, **late barley.** — *sér-mo-ba* the Lamas *Sch.*

སེལ་ *sel* 1. **discord, dissension**, *naṅ-sél* domestic dispute. — 2. a kind of **incantation**, like *brtad*, *sel ₒǰúg-pa* to exorcise, to make use of conjurations or incantations *Mil.*

སེལ་བ་ *sel-ba*, pf., fut. *bsal*, imp. *sol*, **to remove**, esp. impurities, hence **to cleanse; to pick, pick off; to blot out, cross out**, *bú-lon* a debt; **to clear**, **lam sál-če** *W.* to make a path or road; very frq. fig.: **to remove**, to remedy (an evil), to cure (a disease), to repair (a damage), to redress grievances), to dispel (darkness) etc.

སོ་ *so*, I. sbst. 1. resp. *ťsems*, **tooth**, *stéṅ-so*, *yá-so* upper tooth; *˛óg-so*, *má-so* lower tooth; *mdún-so Sch.* *ẏčád-so*, *Stg.* *so-drúṅ* fore-tooth, front-tooth; *sbúbs-so*, *grám-so*, *ráṅ-ťag-so Sch.* *ldán-so* cheek-tooth, molar-tooth, grinder, *mčé-so Cs*, **čód-ten-so* W.* eye-tooth, corner-tooth, canine-tooth. — 2. **tooth** of a saw, wheel, comb. — 3. **edge** of a knife.

II. sbst. for *sa*, in conjunction with certain words, e.g. *ṅan-sor skye-ba* to be born in an inferior place *Mil.*; v. also *ráṅ-so*, *sór-bżag-pa*, *˳k'rúl-so*.

III. sbst. **joy** (?), *so bsod-pa* id. *Cs.* and *Lex.*; cf. *ṅó-so*.

IV. sbst., also *bso*, **look-out, guard, spying**, *so byéd-pa* to spy, to look out; *só-k'uṅ* peep-hole; *só-pa* keeper, guard, watchman, spy, emissary, *zas nor bdúd-kyi só-pa yin* money and dainties are the devil's emissaries *Mil.*; *mé-bso* a guard or watch kept by several persons round a fire; *só-sgra* 1. watchword, = *sgar-miṅ*. 2. v. comp.

V. grammatical termination: **tén-so** provinc. for *rtén-no C.*, also *Glr.*

VI. num. for *súm-ču* in the abbreviated numbers 31–39.

VII. num.: 148.

**Comp.** *so-grí* a saw. — *só-sgra* the whistling through the teeth, in the magic performances of the Bonpo, *só-sgra ˳débs-pa Glr.* — *so-čág* a broken tooth. — *so-drég* tartar? *Med.* — *so-búd* a tooth that has come out. — *so-máṅ* comb. — *so-żó* a small white spot on a tooth, cf. *sén-żo*. — *so-zéd* **tooth-brush.** — *so-šiṅ* **toothpick.** — *so-srúb* gap in the teeth *Sch.*

སོ་ག་ *só-ga* = *sós-ka.*

ས

སོ་ཆ་ *só-ča* n. of an emetic *Med.*

སོ་ནམ(ས་) *so-nám(s)* **agriculture, husbandry,** *so-náms byéd-pa* to till the ground, to practise agriculture, farming, *sgrúb-pa*, *˳bád-pa* id., *so-nám-pa Cs.* husbandman, farmer.

སོ་པ་ *só-pa* v. *so* IV.

སོ་པ་རི་ *só-pa-ri Cs.* a kind of berry, beneficial to the teeth.

སོ་ཕག་ *so-p'ág* **brick, tile**; also collective noun, brickwork, tiling.

སོ་བ་ *só-ba* coarse, thick-shelled **barley,** used for fodder.

སོ་བྱ་ *só-bya* an aquatic bird *S.g.*

སོ་མ་ *só-ma* 1. sbst. *Ssk.* (prop. a climbing plant the juice of which was offered in libations to the gods and was also worshipped itself, on account of its intoxicating qualities, hence): **hemp,** also *ẏtsó-ma*, *btsó-ma*; *so-ma-rá-dza* id., *so-ma-rá-dzai ras* **hemp-linen** *Schr.*, *so-ma-rá-dzai ťág-pa* **hempen rope** *Pth.* — 2. adj. **new, fresh,** esp. *W.* **só-me nán-na zer gos** this ought to have been mentioned directly (when it was still fresh in every body's memory).

སོ་རྩིས་, སོ་རྩིགས་ *so-tsis*, *so-tsigs* **house-keeping,** management of domestic concerns, **husbandry,** cf. *so-nam* agriculture.

སོ་ལུག་ *so-lug* **lees** of liquors, yeast of beer *Sch.*

སོ་ལོག་ *so-log* **high-road, causeway** *W.*

སོ་སོ་ *so-só* distinct, separate, singly, individually, *zas so-sói lág-tu ˛óṅs-so* the victuals came into the hands of the individual persons *Dzl.*; *so-só-nas* adv. frq.: *so-só-nas snod bzéd-de* 'singulatim', each for himself, holding forth his vessel *Dzl.*; **various** e.g. **na so-só* W.* for *sna-tsogs* of *B.*; **diverse, different** *sám-pa so-só* different opinions, a dissension; **separate, distinct,** *so-só byéd-pa*, *W.* **so-só čó-če** to separate, disjoin, divide, *so-sór bżág-pa*, *W.* **so-só bór-če** to set, put, lay apart. — *so-soi skye-bo*, **पृथग्जन**, prop. one separated (from the saints), one outside the pale, a man of the lower classes, of low caste; with Buddhists: **a layman,** and as to his spiritual condition: a man in his natural state, one not yet enlightened (like ψυχικός I Cor. 2, 14, though on account of its derivation, the above term cannot well be used for the Greek word); also the lower classes of clerical persons, monks. — *so-só(s)-ťar-pa*, *so-ťár*, **प्रतिमोक्ष**,

liberation, **deliverance,** *so-só-tar-pai mdo* the book of deliverance, code of the moral law, containing about 250 precepts for the priesthood, the monastic rules of the Buddhists.

སོ་སོ་ཆ་ *so-so-čá* a medicinal herb, an emetic *Wdn.*

སོག་ *sog* 1. v. *sob.* — 2. for **srog* Ü.*

སོག་པ་ *sóg-pa* 1. sbst., also *sógs-pa,* **shoulder-blade,** scapula, *sóg-pai mé-loṅ* the flat part of it, *sog-yu* the narrow extremity of it; *sog-mó ˳débs-pa* (v. *mo* III.) to divine from the shoulder-blade; *sog-lhú* shoulder as a piece of meat for boiling (I Sam. 9, 24). — 2. vb. (also: *ɣsóg-pa, bsóg-pa, sógs-pa*) pf. (*b*)*ags,* fut. *bsag,* imp. *sogs, bsag, W. *ság-če*,* **to gather, heap up, hoard up,** *ṗral sog-˳ǰog-méd-pa* without having collected and deposited the daily requisites, the things wanted every day *Mil., bsód-nams sóg-pa Mil., ťsogs sóg-pa* frq. to collect, to hoard up merits of virtue, *las-ṅán sóg-pa* to heap up sins; *ɣsog-ldáṅ* morbid matter consisting in too great an accumulation of humours, ni f., *Med.; dmág-gi dpuṅ sóg-pa* to collect an army *Dzl.;* **to assemble,** children *Glr.;* hence **sag(s)* W.* **all** (of them), **lug sag tsam** how many sheep are there in all?

སོག་པོ་ *sóg-po* **a Mongol** *Glr., sóg-mo* a Mongol woman, *sog-ṗrúg* Mongol child, Mongol boy, *sog-čás* Mongol dress or fashion of dress, *sog-rta* Mongol horse.

སོག་མ་ *sóg-ma* **blade, stalk; straw;** *sog-˳bru Sch.* green corn that begins to sprout; *sog-ťsigs* a knot on a stalk *Cs.; sog-sbúr* a small blade of straw, chaff *Pth.; sóg-mai ˳bú-la* a shoe of straw; *sog-rú, sog-rúm, sog-ldúm* stubbles.

སོག་ལེ་ *sóg-le B., C., *čad-sóg, gya-sóg* W.* **a saw,** *sóg-les ɣčód-pa B.* to saw to pieces, **gya-sóg šrúl-ce* W.* to saw; *sog-le-ka* the toothed edge of a saw, also botanical term.: serrate, serrated (of leaves) *Wdn.*

སོགས་ *sogs* **and so forth, and the like,** mostly preceded by *la: mi-la sógs-pai srog-čágs homo et cetera animantia,* prop. the beings in addition to man; *ba-dán-la sógs-pas brgyán-te* decorated with little flags and the like; less frq.: *la sógs-te,* inst. of which always *la-sógs-pa* or *pai* may be used; often *sogs* alone, also in prose; after (*la*) *sógs*(*-pa*) usually a comma is to be supplied, and the words following are to be considered as an apposition: *yi-ge rtsis-la sógs-pa rig-pai ɣnas lṅa* writing, arithmetic and so on, the five sciences; hence often applicable, when a comprehensive noun appellative does not exist: *ɣser sogs* gold and the other, viz. metals, *Glr.; ťsa sogs ɣsum* the three *tsa*-sounds, *tsa, ťsa* and *dza Gram.*

Note. In course of time the original grammatical sense seems to have been forgotten, in as much as *la* is now read together with *sógs-pa,* and often also the dot separating the syllables is omitted.

སོང་ *soṅ* perf. and imp. of *˳gró-ba* to go, 1. **I went, I have** (thou hast etc.) **gone,** v. *˳gro-ba* 1 and 2, e.g. *der soṅ yód-pas* when he had gone thither *Pth., soṅ-sóṅ-ba-las* going on continually, *Dzl.,* continuing to do a thing *Dzl.; sóṅ-ba yin* it is gone, it is no longer extant *Mil.; dbáṅ-du soṅ* (he or it) came into the power of... *S.g.; da sdíg-pa-la sóṅ-na Thgy.* if we now go on to (the topic of sins) *W.: *da-rúṅ ṅa ma soṅ** it is not yet past five o'clock; **'i-nẹ sóṅ-pa 'a tsúg-pa** from here (adverbially, like *bzúṅs-te*) to that place *Ld.;* imp.: **di-ru ma dug! soṅ!** do not stand here! walk on! — 2. **became, turned** etc. *kyi-mo žig-tu soṅ* she became a bitch, was changed into a bitch *Mil., dkár-por soṅ* it turned white *Glr., *doṅ nág-po soṅ* W.* his face grew dark; **bi-gáṅ soṅ* W.* a hole has been made, it got a hole; **gyál-sẹ ka-čúd sóṅ-nẹ** as she got a taste for the town *W.; *nod ču gaṅ soṅ** the vessel was already full of water (when I came) *W.* — **soṅ-ťó* W.* account of expenses.

སོད་པ་ *sód-pa* 1. *C.* **to wake, rouse.** — 2. sometimes for *ɣsód-pa.*

སོན་ *son* rarely for *soṅ*; frq. only in *nár-son-pa,* v. *na.*

སོན་པ་ *són-pa* 1. v. *son.* — 2. v. *ɣsón-pa, ɣsón-po.*

ས

སོབ་ *sob* 1. also *sog, ɣsob, ɣsog,* **null, void, vain, empty, bad in its quality, not durable.** — 2. also *ɣsob* something **stuffed** (as a chair), *náṅ-sob, ḱóṅ-sob, ḱóg-sob Wdṅ.* prob. id.; *sob-stán* **cushion, bolster, mattress,** *pags-sób* the stuffed skin of an animal, *seṅ(-gei) sób* the stuffed skin of a lion *Pth.*

སོམ་ *som* 1. also *ɣsom, sóm-śiṅ* **fir-tree, pine-tree.** — 2. also *soms*, imp. of *sém-pa.*

སོར་ *sor* 1. also *ɣsor,* **gimlet,** *rús-pa ˳búgs-pai sor S.g.* prob. a sort of **trephine.** — 2. v. *sór-mo.* — 3. v. *sar, sor bžag-pa* to put in its place (*Sch.* also: 'quite the same'?); *ráṅ-sor* v. *raṅ* compounds. — 4. (cognate to *só-ma?*) *sor čúd-pa* (*Sch.* ˳*jud-pa*) **to restore, renew,** e.g. exhausted strength *Dzl.*, the doctrine of Buddha *Pth.* — 5. term. of *so.*

སོར་མོ་ *sór-mo*, resp. *ṗyag-sór Mil., žabs-sór,* 1. **finger, toe;** *sor-ɣdúb* finger-ring, *sor-ṫsigs* the joint of a finger. — 2. **inch,** *sor-bži-pa* four-inched.

སོལ་བ་ *sól-ba* **coal,** esp. charcoal, = *sol-nág; sól-bai me* coal-fire *Lt.*; **sol-mé** *W.* live coal, burning coal.

སོལ་པོ་ *sól-po* resp. **friendly, kind, affable** *C., W.*

སོས་ *sos* 1. inst. of *so, sos btáb-pa* **to bite,** *Sch.* also **to backbite,** to calumniate. — 2. v. *ɣsó-ba* and ˳*ṫsó-ba.*

སོས་ཀ་, སོ་ག་ *sós-ka, só-ga,* 1. in Tibet: **spring,** = *dpyid, Mil.* — 2. in India: **the hot season,** from about the middle of April till the middle of June.

སོས་དལ་ *sos-dál or sos-bsdal Sch.*: **slow.**

སོས་ཟིན་ *sos-zin* disease of the membrum virile, in five forms (prob. different stages of gonorrhea) *Mṅg.*

སྲ

སྲ་བ་ *srá-ba* 1. adj., also *srá-bo* and *srá-mo Cs.*, col. **srán-te** (cf. *srán-pa*), **hard, solid, compact, firm,** and abstract noun: **solidity, hardness, compactness,** of wood, meat etc., and often fig.: *ɣžu-srán* a bow difficult to be bent *S.g.*, *rgas-srá* hearty vigorous old age *S.g.*; *mṫson ḱar sra* proof against cut and thrust, also: proof against malicious words *Mil.* — *sra-brkyaṅ,* **कठिनाक्षर,** the coarse blanket of a monk. — *sa-rtsi* **varnish.** — 2. vb. *W.*, **to empty.**

སྲང་ *sraṅ* I. (cf. *sróṅ-ba*) 1. **pair of scales, balance** *B., sráṅ-la ˳dégs-pa Cs., ɣžál-ba, ṫsád-pa Sch., sráṅ-ba Sp.* to weigh, to balance. — 2. **steel-yard,** **sran tág-ce** to hold the steel-yard, in weighing. — 3. **weight,** in a general sense, *bre-sráṅ* weight and measure, *rgya-sráṅ* Chinese weights *Cs.* — 4. **an ounce,** *sraṅ gáṅ* one ounce, *sraṅ do* two ounces, *sman sráṅ-༣༢,* two pounds of medicine, the daily quantity taken by Buddha when he had caught cold *Dzl.* ༤༢, 3. — *sráṅ-ča Sch.* balance and what belongs to it. — *sraṅ-mdá* scale-beam or lever of a pair of scales *Sch.* — *sraṅ-ṗór* scale. — *sraṅ-ṫsád Cs.* weight. — *sráṅ-ba* vb. v. above.

II. **street,** *lam-sráṅ* id.; *sraṅ-yár Sch.*: tortuous path, labyrinth (?). — *rgya-sráṅ* street, lane *Glr.*; *rgyu-sráṅ* the road which a person habitually walks.

སྲན་བུ་ *srán-bu* **thread, yarn,** ˳*ḱál-ba, sgríl-ba.*

སྲད་མ་ *srád-ma* v. *srán-ma.*

སྲན་པ་ *srán-pa* (cf. *srá-ba*) *Cs.*: pf. fut. *bsran,* imp. *sron, W.* **śrán-ce** **to suffer, bear** (with patience), **endure, to be hardened** *W.* frq., **śrán-ṫub-ḱan* or *śrán-ṫeg-ḱan** one that can endure much; **ḱyod śran gos** *Ld.* you must hold out, you must stand it; in *B. sran ˳dzugs-pa* is used in the same sense; **ḱyág-śran-čan** hardened, accustomed to frost, **dúg-śran-čan** inured to hardships *W.* — **śrán-te** col. frq. adj.: 1. = *srá-ba* (opp. to *lhód-po* and ˳*ból-mo*) **hard, firm, durable, rigid, strict.** 2. fig. **hard, severe, bitter.** — *sdug-srán* hardiness *Mil.*; *sran-čé-ba* = *srán-ṫub-mḱan. Cs.*: *srán-pa* sbst. hardship, severe distress or toil, *srán-par* toilsomely, rigorously, *srán-pa-po* one that hardens himself (?).

སྲན་མ་, སྲད་མ་ *srán-ma, srád-ma* 1. **pease, beans, lentils,** *Cs.* mentions also *srad-dkár, srad-nág* and *srad-sṅón,* also *mḱal-srán,* in *W.*, however, we only met with the common field pea and some dry imported Indian sorts of it (*mon-srán*); *rgya-srán* (*Cs. mon-srán*) was the name the natives were inclined to give to our European bean. — *sran-p̓uṅ* a heap of pease, *sran-p̓ub* pease-straw, *sran-p̓yé* flour of pease, *sran-mé* blossom of pease. — 2. **grain,** like *rdóg-po*, e.g. of Indian corn; even *lčágs-kyi sran-čuṅ Wdṅ.* grains of shot(?).

སྲབ་ *srab* **bridle,** *rtai*; *srab sga stan ṫsáṅ-po* a complete riding-gear; **ṡrab čúg-če* W.* **to bridle, to bit** (a horse), **ṡrab gyúr-če** **to govern, to rein** (a horse) *srab-skyógs Cs.* **the reins,** — *srab-lčags Cs.* **the bit.** — *srab-mṫúr Sch.* **the halter.** — *srab-mdá Stg., Ld.:* **ṡram-dá** **reins.**

སྲབ་པ་ *sráb-pa B.*, **sráb-mo* W.* **thin, tender, fine,** e.g. skin *Dzl.*, cloth, leather, paper, clouds; **shallow, loose,** not close; *srab-mṫil Sch.* inner sole, welt; *srab-mṫúg* thickness, dimension.

སྲབ་སྲིབ་ *srab-srib Cs.* **dark, obscure.**

སྲམ་ *sram,* उद्र 1. **otter,** the flesh of which is considered very nourishing, the liver is used as a remedy for strangury *S.g.*, but encountering this animal is regarded as an evil omen *S.g.*; *ču-sram* id.? (*Cs.* beaver?) *nyá-sram Mil.*, either the same, or: fishes and otters; *brag-srám* rock-otter? sable? **ka-lon-ṡram* W.* prob. **sable;** it is nearly black and stated to live near Yarkand, in the mountains as well as in the flat country. The ear-coverings worn by the ladies of Ladak are made of the fur of this animal. — 2. **otter-skin, sable-skin.**

སྲར་ *srar* adv. *Sch.:* **severely, rigorously.**

སྲས་(པོ་) *sras(-po)* resp. for *bu*, **son, child,** *dpon-srás, rgyal-srás* son of the sovereign, a prince; *rgyal-srás* also: son of Buddha, a Buddha; *lha(i) sras(-po)* 1. son of a god *Dzl.* 2. a prince; *ṫugs-srás* spiritual son or daughter *Mil.;* in this sense *sras* may be applied to females: *saṅs-rgyás-kyi sras dág-pao* she has become a spotless child of Buddha *Dzl.* — *srás-bu* = *sras.* — *srás-mo* **daughter, young lady, princess.** — *sras-ṫsáb Cs.* adopted child.

སྲི་ *sri* 1. a species of **devil** or **demon,** devouring esp. children, **a vampire,** also *sri-ṅán Schl., čúṅ-sri Glr., p̓úṅ-sri Mil.* a devil bringing misfortune; they are supposed to live in underground places, and are therefore also called *ṅás-kyi sri*; *ṡri laṅ* a devil rises from below; *sri nón-pa B.*, **nán-če* W.* to lay, suppress a devil.

སྲི་བ་ *srí-ba* I. pf. *bsris*, fut. *bsri*, 1. **to retain,** e.g. *bšáṅ-ba, γčin* constipation, strangury. — 2. **to be parsimonious, niggardly,** esp. with *nor; sba-sri-méd-par γnáṅ-ba Mil.* to give unsparingly, to bestow very liberally; **ṡrí-ṡes-k̓an* W.* parsimonious.

II. *W.* **to wind, to wrap round,** for *dkrí-ba.*

སྲི་ཞུ་ *srí-žu*, less frq. *srid-žu*, **respect, reverence, deference,** *srí-žu-pa, srí-žu-mk̓an* one paying his regards, his respects, showing deference.

སྲིང་བ་ *sríṅ-ba* pf. *bsriṅs*, fus. *bsriṅ* 1. (cognate to *riṅ-ba*) **to extend, stretch, stretch out,** the arm, **to hand, reach,** **de ḍul soṅ, ṅá-la ṡriṅ toṅ** it has fallen down, hand it to me *W.;* **to fling far away** *C.* — 2. **to postpone, put off,** *ˎči-bai ṫse Glr.* the term of death; **to prolong,** *ṫse* life *S.g.;* **to wait, to tarry,** **'á-ṫsig ṡriṅ* Lh.* wait a little, **dag-sa yoṅ-ṅa ṫsa-big ṡriṅ-te yoṅ?** shall (I, you, he etc.) come directly or after a while? *Ld.;* **nam dir ṡriṅ-če ča dug?** how long shall you stay here? *W.* — 3. **to send** (*skúr-ba Lex.*) *p̓rin, yo-byád Sch.* — 4. *skyéd-sriṅ-ba* **to bring up, train up, to rear** *Glr.*

སྲིང་མོ་ *sríṅ-mo* **sister** (of a male person, cf. *míṅ-po*) *bu-sriṅ, miṅ-sriṅ*, resp. *lčam-sriṅ* brother and sister, cousins.

སྲིད་ *srid* 1. **length, extension,** *p̓ug srid-du k̓ru-bčo-brgyád-pa* a cavern 18 cubits long *Tar.*; more frq. with regard to time: *ˎdi* or *de-srid(-kyi bar)-du* (for) so long (a time), *či-srid-du*, also *či-srid-de*, how long (a time)? also: as long as; when followed by *yan*: be it ever so long (in this case *ǰi* would be more correct); also *srid-par*, or *srid* alone, for *srid-du.* — 2. **dominion, government,** *srid-la ma ˎčám-pas* falling out with one another about the government *Glr.*, esp. *rgyal-srid, dbaṅ-srid* id.; *srid byéd-pa* to reign, to govern, *srid ˎṫsó-ba* id. *Dzl.*; *ˎdi γnyis-kyi srid gaṅ yód-rnams p̓rog* he seized upon their territorial shares *Glr.*; *bla-srid Cs.* a Lama's dominion. — *sde-srid* **province**; *čos-srid* clerical government, ecclesiastical dominion. — 3. **ruler, commander, regent, reigning prince**; so also in the compounds just mentioned.

སྲིད་པ་ *srid-pa* I. vb., 1. to be, to exist (?). — 2. **to be possible,** often preceded by *yaṅ*; *skyé-ba daṅ ˳jig-pa kún-la srid-na* since springing up and passing away is the lot of all men *Dzl.*; *p̒án-pa žig srid* healing is possible *Pth.*; *˳di-las sla yaṅ srid* it might be easier (for me) then than now *Dzl.*; *de-bžin-du bden srid snyám-nas* thinking this might possibly be true; the verb is usually put in the infinitive mood terminating in *pa*: *de yin-pa-aṅ srid* after all it might be this man, it might be he *Mil.*; *˳dir ˳óṅ-ba mi srid-do, bód-du brós-pa srid* he will scarcely come back, he will have escaped to Tibet *Glr.*; sometimes with the root of the verb: *yoṅ mi srid Mil.*; *bdag t̒ar kyaṅ srid-kyis* as it is a possible case, that we might be released *Dzl.*; *ma srid čig* about the same as: God forbid! by no means! In *W.* nearly = **to be obliged:** **k̒yer-wa-la srid** now it will be my lot, now I shall be obliged, to carry (twice as much), **sád-če-la srid** (*B.*: *bab* or *t̒ug*) he deserves death, he must die.

II. sbst. भुवन 1. **existence,** state of being, **life,** *srid-pa γžan nyáms-su myóṅ-ba* to experience, to pass through, other periods of existence *Wdṅ.*, *srid p̒yi-ma Sch.*: the future period of life, of existence. — 2. things existing, **the world,** *srid(-pa) γsum* the three worlds, *srid-pai ˳k̒ór-lo Cs.*: the revolving system (the world's cycle); *srid-pai mt̒so* the ocean of existence, *srid-pai ču-klúṅ čén-po* the stream of existence *Mil.*; also a single **being,** commonly however *srid-pa-pa*; *bár-doi srid-pa, bár-srid-pa Thgy.*, *bár-ma-doi srid-pa-pa Stg.* the beings in the Bardo, v. *bár-do*. — The meaning of *srid* in *srid-pai bar-do*, and in some other expressions, have yet to be determined. — 3. symb. num.: 14.

སྲིན་ཀླད་ *srin-klád Sch.*: a sort of **flint-stone.**

སྲིན་གླང་ *srin-gláṅ Lt.?* *W.* **srin-gláṅ-čan** having the staggers (of horses); being mad.

སྲིན་པོ་ *srin-po*, *Ssk.* राचस, fem. *srin-mo*, **demons,** figuring in Indian and Tibetan mythology. They are supposed to be, for the most part, of an enormous size, generally hostile to mankind, going about at night, to ensnare and even to devour human beings. Their chief abode was Ceylon, and also Tibet was originally inhabited by them. The Tibetans are even said to be the descendants of an ape (sent by, or emanated from, Avalokitēshvara) and of a Tibetan Srinmo. *brág-srin* rock-Srinpo or Srinmo; *˳dre-srin* goblins and Srinpos; *čú-srin* v. the following article.

སྲིན་བུ་ *srín-bu*, = *˳bu*, **insect, worm, vermin;** *srin-bu pád-ma* (*srín-pa Sik.*) **leech,** *srín-bu me-˳kyér* **glow-worm;** *rgyu-srin, k̒oṅ-srin* **intestinal worm;** *p̒yi-srin* vermin living on the skin *Lt.*; *dár-srin* **silk-worm;** *srin-bál* acc. to *Wdṅ.* = *rás-bál* **cotton,** *Sch.*, *Schr.*: **flock-silk;** raw silk; *srin-byá* nocturnal bird, **owl** etc. *Lt.*; *srin-t̒ór* **small ulcer** or tumour; *srin-šiṅ Med., Sch.*: **mulberry-tree;** *ču-srin* a monster living in the water.

སྲིན་ལག་ *srin-lág* **the ring-finger.**

སྲིབ(ས)་ *srib(s)* 1. **darkness, gloom, night.** — 2. **shady side, north side** of a mountain. — *sríb-pa* vb., to grow dark or dusky, *C.*: **sa šrib soṅ** night has begun.

སྲིའུ་ནག་ *sriu-nág* **mulberry-tree.**

སྲིལ་ *sril Sch.* **silk-worm.**

སྲུ་ *sru Glr.*, *srú-mo Lex.* and *C.* mother's sister, **aunt.**

སྲུག་པ་ *srúg-pa*, *W.* for *sprúg-pa*, *srúb-pa* and *dkrúg-pa*: 1. **to shake, to shake out.** — 2. **to stir, stir up, twirl.** — 3. **to shake,** to make to totter.

སྲུང་བ་ *srúṅ-ba* I. vb., pf. (*b*)*sruṅs*, fut. *bsruṅ*, imp. (*b*)*sruṅ*(*s*), *Ssk.* रच, 1. **to watch, to keep guard** intrs.; but gen. trans., i.e. **to watch, to keep, to guard, to keep in custody,** *k̒yim* the house *Dzl.*; **to save from, to pro-**

**tect, to shelter,** e.g. *lus*, the body, but also: **to keep** unpolluted, pure, chaste; *bdag srúṅ-ba* to guard one's self, in a special sense: to live as a *bdag-srúṅ*, as a hermit *Dzl.*; **to preserve,** *bdag γnód-pa ťams-čád-las sruṅs šig* may I be preserved from every harm! *Do.*; with *la: bdág-la srúṅ-du γsol* I pray to preserve, to protect me *Do.* — 2. **to beware of, to guard against,** *lus daṅ ṅág-gi nyés-pa Dzl.*, = *lus daṅ ṅag srúṅ-ba* (v. above no. 1) *Dzl.* — 3. **to keep, to observe faithfully,** a promise, laws; *bká-sruṅ-mk̒an* **obedient, faithful, trustworthy.** — 4. **to hinder,** forbid, prohibit, *ríg̀s-kyis, bdág-pos, čós-kyis sruṅ* it is forbidden, it is prohibited, by the degree of kindred, by the husband, by religion in general *Thgy.*; **to prevent, to be a preservative** or **preventive** *S.g.* — 5. **to wait,** = *sríṅ-ba*, e.g. **žag nyi** for two days *W.*

II. sbst. 1. **the keeping, guarding, the heed, guard.** — 2. the person or the thing keeping, guarding, esp. **amulet, preventive, preservative,** *btágs-pa* to suspend (an amulet, to the neck or other part of the body).

**Comp. and deriv.** *sruṅ-skúd*, *-ₒk̒ór* or *-mdúd* an amulet consisting of threads. — *srúṅ-mk̒an* **keeper, guardian, watchman,** **ťsán-la šrúṅ-k̒an* W.* (night-) watchman; *srúṅ-pa B.* = *srúṅ-mk̒an*, *bzá-šiṅ-ra-ba srúṅ-pa* keeper of a fruit-garden *Dzl.*; *srúṅ-po Cs.* = *srúṅ-mk̒an*; *srúṅ-ma B.* id., *dmyal-bai sruṅ-ma* guardian of the infernal regions frq. *Dzl.*; *čós-skyoṅ-bai srúṅ-ma ťams-čád* all the tutelar gods of religion *Mil.*; collectively: body of watchmen, *lhá-rnams-kyi srúṅ-ma dáṅ-po* the first corps of watchmen of the gods, the Nāga; *rgyál-poi srúṅ-mai mi* the men of the king's body-guard *Stg.* —*srúṅ-sems* the taking heed, being cautious.

སྲུན་པ་, བསྲུན་པ་ *srún-pa, bsrún-pa*, **calm, soft, mild,** and: **mildness, gentleness, meekness;** *srún-po* adj. = *srún-pa*, esp. of horses: **quiet, tame;** *šín-tu mi-bsrún-žiṅ* very **malicious, malignant,** of demons *Mil.*

སྲུབ་ *srub* v. *srus.*

སྲུབ་པ་ *srúb-pa*, pf. imp. *(b)srubs*, fut. *bsrub*, 1. **to stir, stir up, stir about,** *žo srúb-pa* to churn, to make butter. — 2. **to rummage, to rake up, to stir, to turn over.** — 3. **to rub,** two pieces of wood against each other *Wdṅ.* — **šrub-šiṅ* C.* 1. twirling-stick. 2. mischiefmaker, disturber of the peace.

སྲུབས་ *srubs* 1. **a cleft, slit, gap, fissure,** *brag-srúbs* chasm or cleft in a rock, smaller than *sér-ka Mil.*; **intermediate space,** interval, interstice; **rent** in a dress; **disunion, separation; wound** *Lt.*; *srubs ₒbye Lt.*, *srubs ₒťor Sch.* a severing, a wound has been made; *srubs γtór-ba* to rend asunder, to tear *Sch.* **ťsem-šrúb ḍól-če* W.* to rip, to cut open a seam. — 2. seam? — 3. *W.* col. for *srus.*

སྲུམ་ *srum* resp. for **meat,** flesh of animals used as food, *srum-k̒óg* an animal slaughtered and cut up, for a person of quality.

སྲུལ་པོ་ *srúl-po* 1. **evil demon, malignant spirit** *Mil.*; *lús-srul-po Lex.* **sorcerer.** — 2. **putrid, rotten** *Cs.*

སྲུལ་བ་ *srúl-ba*, pf. and fut. *bsrul*, I. **to be corrupted, decomposed,** of the humours of the body *Wdṅ.*

II. *W.* **šrúl-če, = šrúg-če** 1. **to stir,** **ťúg-pa** the soup, **to mix** and stir, **čú-la ṗe** flour with water. — 2. **to shove, to move,** to and fro, **ṗág-te šrúl-če** to plane, **čad-sóg šrul-če** to saw. — 3. **ťa šrul-če** to put a horse to a gallop?

སྲུས་ *srus*, *W.* also **šrub**, **unripe ears** of wheat etc. **šrub nyé-če* W.* to rub them between the hands; the grains, thus being shelled, are considered a rural dainty; *ₒbrás-kyi srus* a shelled grain of rice.

སྲུས་པ་ *srús-pa Sch.* **to thicken, to become more consistent,** by evaporation, by boiling.

སྲེད་ *sré-da Wdṅ.*, *sred S.g.*, a species of corn (?).

སྲེ་ནག་ *sre-nág Lex.* **soot;** *W.* **šre-móg**.

སྲེ་བ་ *sré-ba* I. sbst. a certain shrub *Cs.*

II. vb., pf. bsres, fut. bsre, imp. (b)sres, trans. to ₒdré-ba 1. **to mix with, to mingle, to admix,** már-la sré-ba to mix with butter Lt., čaṅ ču sre-ba to mix beer with water Med.; dreu sré-ba to breed mules; bsrés-pa mixed up, **confused**, of a narration Tar.; fig. ḱa or lus sré-ba to communicate with another, i.e. to live, to eat, drink, smoke with a person Do.; skyid sdug sré-ba to share pleasure and pain, joy and sorrow Glr.; W., like *žé-če*, **to exchange for**: *zan daṅ śrog* to risk one's life for a subsistence. — 2. **to add; to add up**, cast up, sum up Wdk., *nyī daṅ nyī śre ži* 2 and 2 make 4 W.

སྲེ་མོག sre-móg v. sre-nág.

སྲེ་མོང་ sre-móṅ **weasel**, prob. = *la-ḱyi-mo* W.; sré-mo Lex.

སྲེ་ལོང་ sre-lóṅ 1. Sch.: the sinew above the heel. — 2 n. of a medicine?

སྲེག་པ་ srég-pa I. sbst. (W. *śrag-pa*) **partridge.**

II. vb., pf. (b)sregs, fut. bsreg, imp. (b)sreg(s), W. *śrág-če* **to burn**, i.e. 1. **to consume, to destroy by or with fire** (mes, mé-la) e.g. a corpse, dág-mo, or W. *nán-tan*, altogether, entirely, dgra an enemy (sc. in effigy); sbyin-sreg **burnt-offering; to make red-hot,** lčags-bsrégs red-hot iron Thgy. — 2. **to roast, fry, bake,** on a spit C., or in a pan, *már-la* in butter W.; *tá-gir śrág-če* to bake bread W.; **to tan,** to make swarthy, nyí-mas (to be tanned) by the sun Dzl.; bsrég-ḱaṅ Sch. shed for storing up fire-wood.

སྲེང་ sreṅ, mi-sréṅ C. = mi-rkyáṅ, v. rkyaṅ-pa.

སྲེད་ sred v. sré-da.

སྲེད་རྒྱལ་མ་ sréd-rgyal-ma a deity of the Bonpo Mil.

སྲེད་པ་ sréd-pa 1. vb., sbst., adj. **to desire, the desire, desirous,** zás-la of food Lt., ḱa-tsai ró-la of acid or hot substances Med., ról-mo-la (liking) music Stg.; yúl-sred-pa čúṅ-ba not much attached to his native country; ₒjig-rtén(-la) sréd-pa **avarice, covetousness** Mil., ₒdod-sred-čan covetous, greedy Pth., čágs-sred-čan lecherous, libidinous Pth.; sréd-pa-las yóṅs-su gról-ba quite free of any desire, (so is Buddha); sréd-po Cs. lover, sréd-ma Cs. sweet-heart. — 2. symb. num.: 8.

སྲེན་ sren (?) **floor** W.

སྲེལ་བ་ srél-ba, pf. and fut. bsrel Cs., W. *śrál če* **to bring up, to rear, to nurse up, to train,** infants, young animals, *śrál-ḱan* nourisher, fosterer, nurse etc.

སྲེས་ sres Ts. = ži-gil q.v.

སྲོ་ sro, resp. tugs-sro. W., **heat, ardour, passion, wrath, anger,** *śro yoṅ* anger rises (in a person), he (etc.) grows angry, *śro bab, śro bud* the anger abates; *śro-ríṅ-mo* slow to wrath, *śró-čan* furious, raging, *śro-túṅ* hot, ardent, passionate.

སྲོ་བ་ sró-ba, pf. (b)sros, fut. bsro, imp. (b)sro(s), **to warm,** to make warm or hot at the fire, or in the sun Glr., Lt.; ₒjám-pai dród-kyis bu bsro (a mother) foments her child with a gentle warmth Thgy.

སྲོ་མ་ sró-ma 1. **egg** of a louse, **a nit** C., W., śig-sro ₒdu nits are increasing fast S.g. — 2. small **bubble** W., *čáṅ-la śró-ma ḱol* the beer foams, froths in fermentation. — 3. sró-ma nág-po, sró-ma séṅ-ge n. of a medicinal herb Med.

སྲོ་ལོ་ sró-lo Med., Sedum and similar plants.

སྲོག་ srog **life,** srog γčód-pa to kill, frq.; srog lén-pa, ₒṕróg-pa id., esp. when done by demons; srog daṅ ₒprál-ba id., esp. to execute, to put to death Glr., srog daṅ ₒbrál-ba to die; srog ₒbúl-ba Dzl. ༢༥༢, 12 Sch.: to sacrifice, to yield up one's life, but the manuscript of Kyelang has: srog daṅ ₒbrál-lo, and śá-bai srog ḱyéd-la ₒbúl-lo (Mil.) means: I make you a present of the stag's life, i.e. I spare its life for your sake; srog ₒdór-ba to sacrifice, one's life, prop. to cast it away Dzl.; srog-la mi ltá-ba to make light of one's life frq.; srog daṅ bsdó-ba to risk, to hazard one's life, frq.; srog skyób-pa to save life Dzl., srog ₒbyin-pa, ₒdon-pa id., Thgy.: to save, to preserve (a child's) life (by well caring for it); srog ₒtsó-ba id. Dzl., S.g. (Sch. also: to recover, to grow well again); *sróg-gi ká-ba* n. of a vein; *sróg-gi snyiṅ-po Mil.?*

**Comp.** **sróg-skyób** *W.* **deliverer, redeemer, saviour.** — *sróg-ḱuṅ Mil.* the deep cut or stab, by which Tibetan butchers kill animals (*Huc* I, 443), *sróg-ḱuṅ ˳byéd-pa* to stab in this manner. — *sróg-ċan, srog-ldán* having life, living, alive. — *srog-čágs* animated being, *mí-la sógs-pai srog-čágs ťams-ċád* all men and other living beings *Dzl.*, *srog-ťág* = *dpyaṅ-ťág.* — *srog-bdág čén-po* = *pe-dkár Glr.* — *srog-méd* lifeless, inanimate. — *srog-rtsá* 'root of life, vein of life', aorta *S.g.*, chiefly used rhetor. and fig. — *srog-lén* **deadly, fatal** *Lt.* — *srog-śiṅ* **axle, axle-tree;** *mčod-rtén-gyi srog-śiṅ* the pole in a Chodten; fig. **prop,** *séms-kyi srog-śiṅ Mil.*

སྲོང་བ་ *sróṅ-ba*, pf. *bsraṅs*, fut. *bsraṅ*, imp. *sroṅ(s)*, *bsraṅ*, *W.* **śráṅ-ċe**, **to make straight, to straighten,** *yón-po* what is awry, crooked *Lex.*, *γzer sróṅ-ba* to beat out nails; **to equal** *Sch.*; *sku dráṅ-por bsráṅs-te* (he sat) straight and erect, cf. also *sraṅ* and *bsráṅ-po.* — *W.:* **sráṅ-te ča dúg-ga 'i-ru dad** will he pass straight through or does he stay here?

སྲོང་བཙན་སྒམ་པོ་ *sroṅ-btsan-sgám-po* Srongtsangampo, n. of the most famous king of Tibet, a contemporary of Mohammed; he introduced the Tibetan letters, and was the chief promoter of Buddhism and its literature.

སྲོད་, སྲོད་འཛིང་ *srod, srod-˳ǰiṅ* **dusk of the evening, twilight,** **środ rub** *W.* the dusk of evening draws near, it is getting dusky, *srod daṅ ťo-raṅs* in the evening and morning *Lt.*; *srod byiṅ soṅ* night has set in; *srod yol soṅ* id., viz. the time about 11 o'clock at night *C.; srod-la* in the dusk of evening *Mil.* — *srod-˳ḱor-ṕag Cs.* (?) the *ḱyim* of evening-twilight, v. *nyin-żag.* — *srod-loṅ* dayblind, nyctalops, seeing better in a mild than in a bright light.

སྲོལ་ *srol* **usage, custom, common use, habitual practice, habit,** *der yi-gei srol méd-pas* as the art of writing is not yet in use there *Glr.*; *sṅár-srol bzáṅ-po-la dgoṅs śig* keep in mind the good old customs *Glr.*; *srol čágs-pa, sról-du ˳gyúr-ba Cs., sról-du ˳ťsúd-pa* to grow into a habit, to become the custom (of a person, a country); *srol ˳dzúgs-pa* to introduce a practice *Glr.*; *srol γtód-pa Lex.* prob. the same; *bka-sról* = *srol,* but at the same time expressive of reverence for the originator of the custom *Zam.; ṕyag-sról Mil.* is said to be a respectful expression for *lag-lén-gyi srol* (?); *legs-pai dpe-srol btsug-ste Glr.* having introduced good customs for imitation; *ťob-sról* **claim, title, right,** founded on old custom.

སྲོས་ *sros* 1. v. *sro-ba.* — 2. *Cs.* sbst. = *srod* twilight, dusk of evening, *mún-sros-pa* dusky, dark; *Glr.: sa srós-nas* when it grew dark.

སླ(ང)་ང་ *sla(ṅ)-ṅá* a large iron **pan** for parching grain, *slaṅ-dregs* soot adhering to a pan.

སླ་བ་ *slá-ba* I. adj., also *slá-mo* 1. **thin,** of fluids (opp. to *ská-ba, ťúg-po, réṅs-pa*) *W.* **lan-te**. — 2. **easy,** opp. to *dká-bo* difficult, *śés-pa slá-ba ma yin* knowledge is not easily obtained *Dzl.*; usually with the supine: *ríg-par slao* it may easily be found out *Dzl.*, or with the root of the verb: *go-slá* easy to be comprehended.

II. vb., v. *slé-ba.*

སླག་པ་, སློག་པ་ *slág-pa, slóg-pa* **fur-coat,** *sgo-slóg Mil.*, more corr. *dgo-slog,* hunting-coat, made of the skin of an antelope; *spyaṅ-slág, W.* **śaṅ-lag** fur-coat of a wolf's skin; *ťsar-slág* coat of lamb's skins; *ras-slág* prob.: a fur-coat covered with calico *Glr.*

སླང་ *slaṅ* 1. v. sub *sla-ṅa.* — 2. v. *slóṅ-ba.*

སླང་ཁ་ *sláṅ-ka* **shelf, shelves, stand.**

སླང་བ་ *sláṅ-ba* v. *slóṅ-ba.*

སླད་ *slad,* eleg. = *ṕyi* I, II, IV, 1. *slad-ról* **hind part, back part** *Lex.*, *slád-bżin-du* or *slád-bżin-par* behind, e.g. *˳bráṅ-ba* to walk behind one, *slád-sa* = *ṕyi-sa* (**སྐྱག**) dung *Bhar.* — 2. **after,** *slád-na* c. genit. = *˳óg-tu Dzl.*; *slád-nas* adv. afterwards, hereafter, subsequently *Lex.* and *C.*; *slád-kyi* subsequent, later, posterior; *slád-ma Cs.:*

ས

the hind part, that which comes after, the later or latter part; *slád-mar, slád-kyis* afterwards, hereafter, *slád-mar yaṅ* also for the future. — 3. *slád-du* **on account of, for the sake of.**

སླད་པ་ *slád-pa*, pf. *bslad*, (cf. *lhád-pa*) **to mix,** esp. with something of an inferior quality, hence **to adulterate, vitiate, to spoil, to corrupt,** *skyón-gyis* or *lhád-kyis ma slád-pa* not marred by any defects *Lex.*, *ṗyin-ċi-lóg-gis yoṅs-su slád-de* quite unfitted by perversity *Dzl.*; *gáṅ-gis kyaṅ ma slád-pa* without any thing detrimental operating, not subject to any noxious influence *Wdṅ.*; *de myós-ṡiṅ slád-par byás-te* making him drunk and thus disabling him *Dzl.*

སླན་ *slan* 1. (?) **na-slán* W.* the furred ear-coverings of Tibetan ladies. — 2. = *slad*; *slan-čád* = *ṗyin-čád.*

སླན་ཏེ་ *slán-te* v. *slá-ba.*

སླན་པ་ *slán-pa* 1. **to mend, patch** *Sch.* — 2. v. *bslan.*

སླམ་པ་ *slám-pa*, 1. to roast slightly, **to parch,** to make brown by exposing to heat, e.g. meal *C., W.* — 2. **to roast, to fry,** **már-la* W.*

སླར་ *slar*, eleg. = *ṗyir*, 1. **again, over again, once more.** — 2. **afterwards, hereafter,** *slár-nas* id. *C.* — *slar yaṅ ̥jug-pa* to be affixed or added again (of letters, to the end of a word) *Gram.*; *slar ̥óṅ-ba* to come back, to return *Dzl.*; *slar-γṡegs* he went away again *Dzl.*; *slar stobs skyed* he regains strength *S.g.*; *slár-bsdu-ba* the final ̓o of a verb, indicating the end of a sentence *Gram.*

སླས་ *slas* 1. v. *lhas.* — 2. **retinue, train, attendants,** wives and servants, *ṗo-bráṅ-gi slas* a king's or prince's retinue, **the court,** people at court *Dzl.*

སླི་ *sli C.* acc. to some authorities: a yellowish red **apple,** or Indian apple (opp. to *kú-ṡu* Tibetan apple); acc. to *Cs.* **cherry;** cherries, however, are scarcely known in Tibet. — *sli-tsí* small, wild-growing, cherry-like dwarf-apples, *Pyrus baccata*; **bi-li-tsi* W.* gooseberry; **wám-ṗu-li-tsi** the white berries of a species of mountain-ash, *Pyrus ursina* (**wamṗu** in the Bunan language: 'bear').

སླུ་བ་ *slú-ba*, pf. *bslus*, fut. *bslu*, imp. (*b*)*slu*(*s*), **to entice, allure, ensnare, beguile, seduce,** e.g. to be ensnared by wordly sorrows; less frq. in a direct sense: **to impose on, to deceive,** *rdzun byás-te* by a falsehood *Dzl.*; *slu-k̔rid* enticement, seduction, means of seduction, bait; *bzáṅ-poi slu-k̔rid* enticement to a good purpose; *bslú-ba-mk̔an* deceiver, deluder, impostor *Glr.*; *mi-slú*(*-ba*) infallible, sure *Mil.*

སླེ་ *sle* 1. a coarse blanket *Ts.*, = *čá-ra, čá-ri.* — 2. n. of the capital of Ladak.

སླེ་ཏྲེས་ *sle-trés Med.* n. of a creeper or climbing plant.

སླེ་པོ་ *slé-po* Ü, *slé-ba, slé-bo Cs.* a flat **basket.**

སླེ་བ་ *slé-ba* I. vb., *bsle-ba*, *lhé-ba.* pf. *lhas B.*, **lá-ċe* W.* **to twist, plait, braid,** the hair, (to make) a basket etc.; **to knit.**

II. sbst. 1. v. no. I. — 2. **distortion, dislocation** (of a limb) *Cs.*; *slé-bo* one that has a distorted limb *Cs.*; *sle-mig* a distorted eye *Cs.*

སླེ་ཡོན་ *sle-yón* **craft, deceit, trickery,** *sle-yón byéd-pa* **to cheat, deceive, impose upon** *Cs.*

སླེད་ *sled* knitting-needle(?) *Ld.*

སླེབ་པ་ *sléb-pa*, pf. (*b*)*slebs*, fut. *bsleb*, resp. *̥byón-pa, ṗéb-pa* (cf. *̥óṅ-ba*), 1. **to arrive,** with termin.; *bslebs-zin* I have arrived, he has arrived; in *Ld.* however the future **slebs yin** is also pronounced **leb zin**. — 2. **to reach, to extend,** to a certain place or point *Pth.* and col. — 3. **to come in** (of interest, rent, duties), hence *sleb* income, revenue, public revenue, receipt of customs etc.; *sléb-t̔o* account of receipts.

སློ་དྲོན་ *slo-drón* warm fresh **dung** *Sch.*

སློག་པ་ *slog-pa* I. sbst. v. *slóg-pa.*

II. vb., pf. *bslogs*, fut. *bslog*, *Cs.* (trs. to *ldog-pa*) **to turn,** to turn round or about, to turn upside down, inside out, *rkyál-pa ṗyi-náṅ slóg-pa* to turn out the inside of a bag; *mig slóg-pa* to roll one's eyes; **boṅ-bu má-lag slog ̥dug** the donkey is rolling on his back; *sa slóg-pa* to plough up, turn up, to dig the soil; in arithmetic: *sum nyi lòg-pa ḍug* W. two times three are six.

སློང་བ་, སླང་བ་ slóṅ-ba, sláṅ-ba, pf. (b)slaṅs, fut. (b)slaṅ, imp. sloṅ(s), W. *láṅ-če*, I. causat. and transit. form to ldáṅ-ba. 1. **to cause to rise, to help to rise**, one lying on the ground; dgrá-ru slóṅ-ba to cause a person to rise as an enemy (cf. dgrar ldáṅ-ba), i.e. to make a person one's enemy S.g.; bsád-pai mi-ró slóṅ-ba to resuscitate the slain; **to excite, cause, inspire,** compassion, fear, terror etc.; p̀rag-dog-gis, skyo-ṡas-kyis kun-nas bslaṅs-te Glr., Mil. quite excited by envy and hatred, ni f.; esp. in pathology of the procatarctic or exciting causes of diseases: **to kindle** (a disease) **into action,** hence sloṅ-rkyén the exciting cause (of a disease); — **to raise, to erect**, a pile, post, wall Mil.; sláṅ-ṡiṅ a pile, stay, prop, erected or set up. — kun-slóṅ Lex., Mil.: nyon-móṅs-kyi sloṅ-kun-sloṅ excitement (??).

II. (perh. originally quite a different word), 1. **to ask, require,** ccdp. klu ẓig ṅá-la dpe sloṅ a Lu asks me for the book Dzl.; bú-mo čúṅ-mar slóṅ-ba to ask a man's daughter in marriage Dzl.; esp. **to beg,** to try to get by begging: čuṅ-zad bsláṅ-ṅo we beg for a little of it! Dzl., p̀á-la sláṅs-nas k̀yer he obtained it from his father by begging Mil.; bsód-snyoms slóṅ-ba to collect alms by begging (slóṅ-ba partic. and sbst. beggar, mendicant Dzl, slóṅ-mk̀an, slóṅ-ba-po id.); hence. — 2. **to collect, to gather**, nor Cs. riches. — 3. **to examine, to probe** (a wound), rma-ɣsar mdzúb-mos a fresh wound with the finger Thgy.; also: **to search** a man's **house.** — 4. **to give,** k̀a-lhág čig sdús-la sloṅ čig gather some of the remnants of the meal, and give them to me! Mil., so in Sp. and C. frq.

སློང་མོ་ slóṅ-mo **alms,** slóṅ-mo slóṅ-ba Lex., byéd-pa Cs. to ask alms, to beg; slóṅ-mos ₒtsó-ba to live on alms; slóṅ-mo-pa beggar Pth.

སློན་པ་ slón-pa 1. Sch. **to patch, to mend.** — 2. Sch.: dpáṅ-po p̀yir slón-par byéd-pa to dissemble, to feign (?) — 3. Cs.: to **thrust out.**

སློབ་ slob the act of learning, study, slob ma myóṅ-ba to have had no instruction or education; slob ₒk̀rid-pa to teach.

སློབ་པ་ slób-pa, I. vb., pf. bslabs, fut. bslab, imp. slob(s), W. *láb-če*, **to learn, to teach,** ṅa or ṅá-la slob I learn, ṅas slob I teach, dé-la mk̀an slob ɣnyis-kyis lo-tsṫsa bslabs both the abbot and the instructor taught him the art of translating Pth.; ṅa rtsis ṡig slob ₒdód-pas slobs as I should like to learn something of mathematics, teach me! Pth.; bsláb-pas ṡés-te when he had learned it Pth.; bsláb-čiṅ lóbs-pa yaṅ dka as learning is difficult, even if one is taught Dzl.; slób-tu ₒǰúg-pa to let one take lessons, to have or get one instructed Dzl.; *ṭ ú-gu-la gom-t̀áṅ láb-če* to teach a little child to walk W.; mi-la yi-ge bslabs schools were established Glr.; yón-tan slób-pa to teach (to learn) good, useful, things Pth. and frq.

II. sbst. 1. the act of **learning** Dzl. — 2. **teacher, instructor,** brám-ẓe slób-pa a Brahman as instructor Dzl.; ₒp̀ágs-pa slób-pa-rnams the venerable preceptors (more than dge-slóṅ, less than dgrá-bčom-pa) Tar. 5, 1. 31, 9.

**Comp.** *lob-k̀yád* W. **use, practice, exercise.** — slob-grwá **school, school-room, school-house;** *lob-ḍa-k̀áṅ* W. id. — slob-gróɡs school-fellow, co-disciple. — slob-ɣnyér student, scholar, slob-ɣnyér gáṅ-du bgyis where have you studied? at what college have you been a student? Mil. — slób-dpon **teacher, instructor, master,** frq.; also a college-title like our bachelor etc.; **'the teacher'** by way of eminence, is either Buddha or Padma-byuṅ-ɣnás. — slob-ₒbáṅs **scholar, pupil, disciple,** = bu-slób Mil. — slób-ma id., frq. *lob-ló* **report, rumour, fame** W. — Cf. bslabs.

སློབས་ slobs **exercise, practice, experience;** miɡ-slobs ṅan-pa skye Mil. a bad custom of seeing begins to prevail (viz. that of looking downward, and minding only earthly things).

གསའ་, བསའ་ ɣsa, bsa Mil., C. (W. *ṡan*) **the snow-leopard,** nearly white, with small clusters of black spots; living on the higher mountains.

**གསག་པ་** *γsúg-pa Sch.* **to sew together.**

**གསང་** what is **secret, hidden,** *γsaṅ šor* the secret comes out, is made known *Dzl.*

**གསང་བ་** *γsáṅ-ba* I. vb. **to do** a thing **secretly, to conceal,** *ṅa-la γsaṅ-du mi ruṅ* it is not right of you to be so close to me *Mil.*; *γsáṅ-ste brkús-nas* stealing secretly, *γsáṅ-ste bskyál-nas* sending underhand, furtively *Dzl.*; **to hide one's self, to be concealed** *dbén-pai γnas šig-tu γsáṅ-ste* betaking one's self secretly to a solitary place *Dzl.*, *yid-mťún-par γsáṅ-ste* keeping it secret with one consent *Dzl.*; **saṅ-ne dud-če* W.* to sit concealed.

II. sbst. 1. **secret things, a secret;** *γsaṅ-bai bdag-po* = *γsan-dbaṅ* v. below. — 2. **secret parts** *Med.*, also *γsaṅ-γnás Med.*, *γsáṅ-bai pád-ma Med.*, sometimes the anus included; *γsáṅ-bai nad* diseases of the sexual organs *Med.*

III. adj. 1. **secret, hidden, concealed,** *γsáṅ-bai čos* esoteric doctrine *Dzl.*; *p̔yi-naṅ-γsáṅ* v. *p̔yi* III. — 2. *k̔yi-mo nyan-gyi rna γsaṅ-ba* a female dog of very sharp hearing (v. *γseṅ-ba*).

**Comp.** *γsáṅ-kaṅ* a secret room *Cs.* — *γsáṅ-sgo* a secret door *Pth.* — *γsaṅ-sgro S.g.?* — *γsaṅ-sṅágs* secret charms, mysterious incantations, frq.; even in medical works they are praised as the 'best medicine'. — *γsaṅ-mǰe* v. *mǰe.* — *γsaṅ-γnás* 1. a secret place. 2. **mystery,** n i f.: *γsáṅ-bai γnas dú-ma γsuṅs* he taught many mysteries, many secret doctrines. 3. **privities, pudenda.** — *γsaṅ-spyód* **privy, necessary,** water-closet. — *γsaṅ-dbáṅ*, *γsaṅ-rdór Mil.*, *γsaṅ-bai-bdág-po Do.* = *rdo-rǰe-˳čaṅ*, v. *rdo-rǰe*, comp.

**གསན་པ་** *γsán-pa* resp. **to hear, to listen** *Dzl.*; *k̔yod γsan daṅ* listen (to me)! *Mil.*; *bdag-gi ťsig-la γson* id. *Glr.*; with *las* or *la:* to hear a person teaching, expounding etc. *Tar.* Cf. *γsón-pa.*

**གསབ་པ་** *γsáb-pa* v. *γsób-pa.*

**གསར་བ་** *γsár-ba, γsár-pa,* usually *γsár-po* **new, fresh,** *lúg-ša γsár-ba* fresh mutton *Lt.*; *rma γsár-pa* a raw wound *Thgy.*; *bág-ma γsár-pa* the young, (recently married) wife *Dzl.*; **bhú-mo sár-pa** a girl that is still a virgin *C.*; *γsár-du* adv., *γsár-du bsád-pai ša* flesh of animals that have just been slaughtered, lit.: fresh-slaughtered flesh *Dzl.*; *k̔a-γsár* a new edge; *kaṅ-γsár* new house, also a name of villages, castles etc.; *gos-γsár, mar-γsár Lt.*; *rta-γsár Schr.* a horse not yet broken in. — *γsar ˳grógs-pa Sch.*: 'to tell each other news; to make a new acquaintance'. **sar-zúg čó-če* W.* to plant (a piece of land) for the first time, to cultivate, to people, to stock with inhabitants. — *γsar-riṅ* old and new, stale and fresh; age, duration, existence. — *γsar γčód-pa* frq., also *ťsar γčód-pa Pth.*, **to search, inquire into, investigate thoroughly, to examine, to study,** *skad* a language. — *γsár-bu* **new beginner, tyro, novice** *Mil.*

**གསལ་བ་** *γsál-ba* vb., **to be clear, distinct, bright,** *slar šár-žiṅ γsál-na* when (the sun) shines bright again; *már-me ˳čí-k̔ar γsál-ba bžin* flaming up once more, like an extinguishing lamp *Glr.*; *lhaṅ-ṅé lham-mér γsál-te* appearing bright, clear and distinct *Dzl.*; *γsál-lo* it is clear, it is evident; it stands written, it may be read, *˳dúl-ba-na γsál-lo* it may be read in the Dulva *Glr.*. *Tar.*; *γsál-po* (प्रकाश) **visible** to a great distance, **conspicuous, distinct,** obvious, intelligible; *kun-γsál* id.; **mig sál-po ťoṅ mi ťub, ṅag sál-po zer mi še* W.* his eye, — his speech, is not clear, he is not able to see, to speak distinctly; *γsal-dag-snyan-γsúm B.* = the popular *sgra-dag-γsal-γsúm*, v. *sgra*; *yi-ge γsál-po* a plain, legible handwriting; **clear, bright,** *γsál-bai mé-loṅ* a bright mirror (a frq. title of books); **bright, light, pure,** of colours, *dkar-γsál* pure white *Glr.*; **pure,** free from faults and deficiencies, **sál-po gyáb-če* W.* **to correct;** *sa-p̔yógs kyaṅ γsál-bar gyúr-ro* also his whole neighbourhood will be freed from defects, will become **happy** *Do.*; *γsál-le-ba* = *γsal-ba*; *γsál-k̔a Tar.* prob. = *γsál-ča, Mil.*: *γsál-ča žig γnáṅ-ba žu* I request (you) to give me a detailed account, inst. of which also only *sal čig* may be said.

གསལ་ཤིང་ γsál-šiṅ (like σταυρὸς in its original meaning) **a pointed stake,** for empaling malefactors, *γsál-šiṅ-du* or *γsál-šiṅ-gi ťsé-la skyón-pa* to empale. — Cf. *rkyaṅ-šiṅ.*

གསས་མོ་ *γsás-mo Lexx.*; in *Lt.* prob.: **mother's milk.**

གསིག་པ་ *γsig-pa Cs.*, also *bsig-pa*, to throw up in a backward direction; in *Thgr.* is said of a lion: *rál-pa γsig* he shakes his mane; *dpuṅ-bsig Cs.*: 'the shaking of one's shoulder' (prob. for: **shrugging**); **to winnow, to fan, to sift** *Stg.*; *W.*

གསིང་མ་ *γsiṅ-ma* 1. **pasture-ground, meadow** *Dzl.* — 2. moor, fen *Sch.*?

གསིར་བ་ *γsir-ba Sch.*, *bsir-ba Cs.* 1. **to whirl about** or round, to twirl, *p̆aṅ* a spindle, *mda γsír-ba Cs.*: 'to whirl an arrow'. — 2. *W.* **to move** by a repeated pushing, *p̆ág-ste* a plane; **to smooth, to even,** with a plane, a knife etc.; **to slide, glide, slip,** down a slope.

གསིལ་བ་ *γsíl-ba* 1. **to cut to pieces, to divide, split,** *lhú-ru Mil.*, *dúm-bur Lex*, *γsor-gyis γsil-ba* to saw to pieces, to saw up. — 2. **to toll, sound, ring,** *dríl-bu γsil-ba* to ring a bell *Cs.*, hence *mk̆ar-γsil* v. *mk̆ar-ba.* — 3. **sil-če** *W.* **to read.** — *γsil-bu* and *γsíl-ma* v. *síl-bu.*

གསུང་ *γsuṅ*, resp. for *skad* and *γtam*, 1. **voice,** *γsuṅ byuṅ* a voice sounded, was heard *Glr.*, *γsuṅ dág-pa* a clear voice, like that of Buddha *Dzl.* — 2. **the act of speaking, talking,** *γsuṅ gléṅ-ba* to converse, discourse, *γsuṅ ͦdré-ba, γsuṅ-ͦdré mdzád-pa* id.; that which is spoken, the words uttered, **the speech,** *k̆yéd-kyi γsuṅ dei lán-du* in answer to your words *Glr.*; *γsuṅ k̆lóg-pa* to read the sayings, the apothegms (of Buddha) *Ma.*

གསུང་བ་ *γsúṅ-ba* I. vb., pf. *γsuṅs*, resp. for *smrá-ba B.* and *C.* (in *W.* **mól-če** is used inst. of it) **to speak, talk, say,** the latter also with the termin. of the infin., inst. of direct speech, but rarely; *dé-skad ma γsuṅ* your Reverence should not say so! *Mil.*; *γsuṅ ma γnaṅ* it did not please him to speak *Mil.*; *rdzun γsúṅ-ba* to tell a falsehood, to lie; **to explain,** *don Mil.*; **to ask;** *mi ͦdod mi γsuṅ bžés-par žu Mil.* please accept it without ceremonies (without a refusal); *žal-γdáms γsúṅ-ba* to give advice etc. *Glr.*; *čos γsúṅ-ba* to preach *Glr.*; *mgúr-ma γsúṅ-ba* to recite or to sing a song (but also: *mgúr-ma smrá-ba, zér-ba* is said).

**Comp.** *γsuṅ-bgrós* **report, statement, opinion.** — *γsuṅ-mčog* **principal word, main dogma** e.g. the Ommanipadmehum *Glr.* — *γsuṅ-snyán* a harmonious voice, an agreeable, pleasant speech; *Mil.* uses it also of the singing of birds (and the screaming of peacocks!) — *γsuṅ-sprós, γsuṅ-ͦp̆ró* **conversation** between persons of rank, or between such and inferior people. *γsuṅ-ráb* = *γsuṅ-mčóg*, also sacred writing, **Holy Scripture** *Chr. Pr.* — *γsuṅ-šóg* = *bka-šóg.*

གསུད་པ་, བསུད་པ་ *γsúd-pa, bsúd-pa* 1. *Sch.* **to be lost, to be dispersed.** — 2. *W.* to fill with food beyond satiety, **to stuff, to cram.** *Bhar.* 124 *smán-pa γsud* stands for *Ssk.* विसूचिका (*Will.*: spasmodic cholera), which elsewh. is rendered *zas ma žu-ba*; the meaning is prob. to overeat one's self.

གསུམ་ *γsum* three (cf. *sum*), *γsúm-k̆a, γsúm-ga* the three, all the three; *γsúm-pa* the third; containing three; *γsúm-po* the three; *γsum* also elliptically for *dkon-mčog-γsúm*: *γsúm-la skyábs-su ͦdóṅ-ba* to seek the protection of the Three Precious *Do.*; *bskál-pa gráṅs-med(-pa) γsum* three times innumerable Kalpas (appeared) *Dzl.*, *Glr.*; *rgán-mo ma smad γsum-po ͦdi* the old (woman) with her (two) sons, the three *Dzl.*; *rgyál-po yab yum γsum* the king and his (two) queens, the three *Glr.*; *rab ͦbriṅ γsum* the big, the middle (and the little one), the three. — *γsúm-sprul* emanation of the third degree, = *nyiṅ-sprul.*

གསུར་མ་ *γsúr-ma* a thing slightly burnt, **singed** *Cs.*, *γsur-drí* the smell of it.

གསུས་པ་ *γsús-pa* **belly, stomach,** *γsús-pa sbos* the belly is swollen or distended *Lex.*; *γsus-nád* dropsy of the belly; *γsus-rked* the middle part of the body, the waist *Sch.*; *γsus-ͦp̆yaṅ-po* a deity.

**གསེ་བ་** *γsé-ba* 1. v. *sé-ba.* — 2. v. *γséd-pa.*

**གསེག་བརྡར་** *γseg-brdár Sch.* **a file** (instrument), v. *sag-γdar.*

**གསེག་མ་** *γség-ma* **small stones;** *γseg-seb-čan* full of small stones.

**གསེག་གཤང་** *γseg-γšáṅ* = *mk̒ar-γsil Lex.*

**གསེང་, སེང་** *γseṅ, seṅ* 1. **cleft, chink, crevice, fissure, leak,** v. *k̒oṅ-séṅ* sub *k̒oṅ* extr.; *sgo-γséṅ* chink of a door *Tar.*; *γseṅ bsrúb-pa Sch.* to stop up, plug up, crevices etc.; *γséṅs-pa* leaky, cracked, full of fissures *Sch.* — 2. **harmonious,** well-sounding. — 3. *rná-ba γseṅ Sch.*: a sharp, acute, quick ear, cf. *γsáṅ-ba* II, 2.

**གསེད་** *γsed* several larger species of Lonicera.

**གསེད་པ་** *γséd-pa,* also *bséd-pa* (pf. *γses?*) **to pick, sort, assort,** hair, wool; **to pull or pluck in pieces.**

**གསེབ་** *γseb* I. **stallion,** a male horse or camel.

II. also *seb,* 1. the narrow **interstices** between persons or things thronged together, hence with *na, tu* and *la,* **between, among,** with *nas* **from between,** *k̒yi mii γséb-la mč̒oṅ* the dog leaps into the midst of the people, *ló-mai γséb-tu ˳ǰóg-pa* to put between leaves, *sprin-gyi γséb-nas lus p̒yed ˳t̒on* half of his body protrudes from between the clouds, = rises above etc.; *groṅ-γséb-tu bžúgs-pa* to sit among the villagers; *k̒yéd-čag-gi γséb-na Meu-dgál byá-bai bud-méd yód-dam?* is there a woman among you named *Meu-dgal?* *γséb-lam* a secret path, by-way, between rocks or underwood. — 2. **multitude, crowd,** *dmág-γseb* army, *nágs-γseb* forest.

**གསེར་** *γser* (*Pers.* زر) **gold**; *γsér-gyi* of gold, golden, *γsér-gyi mé-tog* n. of a medicinal herb.

**Comp.** *γser-skúd S.g.* n. of an officinal herb. — *γser-skyéms* v. *skyems.* — *γsér-k̒a* a gold mine. — *γser-mk̒ár* an imperial castle *Wts.* — *γser-gliṅ* Malacca *Cs.* — *γser-˳gyur-rtsi* prob. much the same as: 'philosopher's stone' *Pth.* — *γser-t̒úb* n. of the second Buddha, Kanakamuni. — *γser-mdóg* gold-colour, *γsér-mdog-čan* n. of a monastery. — *γsér-pa* gold-searcher, gold-washer *Gram.*; *γser-p̒ud* n. of a medicinal herb, an emetic *Med.* — *γser-˳p̒réṅ* a gold chain. — *γser-byé* gold-sand. — *γser-mé* = *γsér-gyi-mé-tog Med.* — *γser-γtsó-ma, γser-btsó-ma* refined gold *Glr., Pth.* — **ser-záṅ** *W.* gilt copper. — *γser-bzó-pa, γser-mgár Cs.* goldsmith. — *γser-yig-pa* 'bearer of a gold-letter', ambassador, envoy *Glr.* — *γser-šóg* leaf-gold, gold-foil, foliated gold *Sch.* — *γser-sraṅ* one ounce of gold; a coin = 16 rupees, gold-mohur.

**གསེས་** *γses?* *raṅ-γsés* **reciprocal, mutual** *Wdṅ.*

**གསོ་བ་** *γsó-ba* pf. *γsos,* (*b*)*sos* (= *˳tsó-ba*) 1. **to feed, nourish** *Dzl.*; **to bring up, nurse up, rear, train,** *bu* a child, *dúd-˳gro* an animal; also *γsó-skyoṅ-ba, γso-skyóṅ byéd-pa.* — 2. **to cure,** *nad, rma;* **to stop, remove,** to put an end to, *ṅal* fatigue, i.e. to recruit one's self, to rest; **to mend, to repair,** *k̒yim* a house *Cs.*; **to restore, rebuild, re-establish,** what had been destroyed, **to kindle again, stir up again,** a fire; *žig-* or *šig-γso-ba* id.; **to refresh, recreate,** *sems,* resp. *t̒ugs,* the soul, i.e. to comfort, console.

**Comp.** *γso-mk̒an* **restorer** *Glr.* *γso-t̒ábs* **way of curing,** manner of healing *Med.* — *γsó-ba-po* **physician** *Med.* — *γsó-bya* the thing to be cured, the disease *Med.*; *γso-byéd* the healing substance, **the remedy**; the healing person, **the physician.** — *γso-sbyóṅ-ba* v. the following article. — *γso-ts̒úl* = *γso-t̒ábs.* — *γso-rig* **pharmacology.**

**གསོ་སྦྱོང་བ་** *γso-sbyóṅ-ba,* for *ṅyés-pa γsó-ba daṅ sdig-pa sbyoṅ-ba* to get quit of sin, by making confession to a priest and thus restoring the former state of virtuousness, **to confess;** also *γso-sbyoṅ lén-pa, γso-sbyoṅ-la γnas-pa;* such confession does not entail any penalties, but only a renewal of obligations, cf. *Fouc. Gyatch.* II, 16.

**གསོ་རས་** *γso-rás Lex.*; *Sch.*: **rag, tatter.**

**གསོག་པ་** *γsóg-pa* 1. v. *sóg-pa* II. — 2. v. *sob.*

**གསོང་པོ་** *γsóṅ-po* **sincere,** *γsóṅ-por smrá-ba* to speak the truth.

**གསོང་བ་** *γsóṅ-ba Cs.* and *Lex.*; usually *γsáṅ-ba.*

**གསོད་པ་** *γsód-pa*, pf. *bsad*, fut. (*Lex. γsad*, usually:) *bsad*, imp. *sod*, *W.* **sád-če**, **1. to kill, slay, murder, slaughter.** *γsód-pa-la dgá-ba* to delight in killing *Dzl.*; *bsad ma-ťág-pai ša*, *γsár-du bsád-pai ša* v. *γsár-ba*; *rgyál-pos γsód-pa* to be executed by the authority *Dzl.*; (*ťse*) *bsád-pa-la ťúg-nas* when he was just on the point of being executed *Dzl.*; **p̔ag ǰáb-te sád-tan-če** *W.* to assassinate; *bsád-do! bčóm-mo!* I am lost! it is all over with me! *Wdṅ.* — 2. **to put out, extinguish** frq. — 3. *k̔yád-γsod-pa* to despise, v. *k̔yad* extr.

**Comp.** *γsod-γčód* **the act of murdering, murder,** slaughter, *γsod-γčód-kyi ǰigs-pa* fear of murder *Mil.*; *γsod-γčód máṅ-po byed* he is murdering, slaughtering, a great deal. — *γsod-byéd* killer, murderer, *γsod-byéd rṅán-pa* the murderous huntsman *Lex.*; *γsod-byéd-kyi γnas* slaughter-house *Stg.* — *γsód-sa* place of execution *Thgy.* — *γsód-lugs* way of killing, *sṅar ma byas* a new (way of killing) *Tar.*

**གསོན་པ་** *γsón-pa* I. A. vb., 1. intrs. **to live, to be alive,** *γsón-no* he (she etc.) is alive, **de méd-na mi són-če mi ťub** without that a man cannot live *W.*; **to remain alive, to save or preserve one's own life,** *rdzún-du smrás-na γson kyaṅ* though I could save my life by (telling) a falsehood *Dzl.*; *γsón-par mi ͦdod* I do not wish to live (any longer) *Dzl.*; of the fire: **to burn,** **da són-na** *W.* does it burn now? — 2. trs. **to wake, to rouse** from sleep **by shaking, to urge on, to hurry on** (lazy people), by force, whereas *skúl-ba* is only done by words. — B. sbst. **life,** *γsón-pai ťsé-na* or *γsón-pai dús-su* **during** (my, your etc.) **life, in lifetime,** frq.; hence: *γson-pa-nyid* for ζωή John 1, 4 etc. *Chr. P.* — C. adj. **living, alive,** frq. *γsón-po*, col. **γsón-te**, *kyé-ma bu γsón-po mťóṅ-ṅo* ah, there I see my son again alive! *Stg.*; *γsón-por byéd-pa* to call into life, to animate, *γsón-por dúr-du ͦǰúg-pa* to bury alive *Dzl.*, *γsón-pai rgyú-ma ͦdrén-pa* to tear out the bowels of a living man; **son-te** *W.* also: **healthy, whole, restored to health again,** **kaṅ-pa, mig, me són-te čó-če** to cure a foot, an eye, to blow a fire into flame again; **entire, whole, undivided,** **són-te k̔yóṅ-ṅa** am I to bring it entire (or cut into pieces etc.)? of the moon: **full.** — *γsón-ma* rarely for *γsón-po*, *p̔úg-ron γsón-ma* a live pigeon *Pth.*; *γson-γšin* both the living and the dead *Cs.*; *γson bsrégs* a creature burnt alive, *mi žig(-la) γson-bsrégs byéd-pa* to burn a person alive *Pth.*

II. vb., pf. *bsan*, fut. *γsan*, imp. *γson Cs.*, prob. the original form of *γsán-pa* **to hear.**

III. *čúd-γson-pa* v. *čud.*

**གསོབ་** *γsob* v. *sob.*

**གསོབ་པ་** *γsób-pa*, pf. *bsab*, fut. *γsab*, 1. **to fill out or up, to supply, complete, make up,** *hór-k̔oṅs* a gap (?) *Sch.*, **to cure,** wounds *W.*, **sob-mán** balm, ointment for wounds. — 2. **to pay, repay, return,** *skyin-pa* a loan *Sch.*, *drin γsób-pa* to return a kindness *Glr.*

**གསོར་** *γsor* 1. v. *sór* I. — 2. supine of *γsó-ba.*

**གསོར་བ་** *γsórba* **to brandish, flourish,** a staff *Cs.*

**གསོལ་བ་** *γsól-ba* I. vb., 1. = *žú-ba* 1, q.v.; *rgyál-po-la sróg-gi skyabs γsól-to* he besought the king to save his life *Dzl.*; *stón-pa-la smón-lam btáb-par γsol čig* ask the teacher to say the prayers *Dzl.*; *bstán-du γsol* I beg to explain, frq.; *lha γsól-ba* to worship a god, by offerings, libations etc. *Glr.* and elsewh. Tibetans when arriving on the top of a mountain-pass generally mutter the words: *γsól-lo γsól-lo*, prob. to express their thankfulness for having been preserved from harm so far, and to implore further protection. — 2. resp. for *gón-pa* and *skón-pa* **to put on:** (*skú-la*) *ná-bza*, *čos-gos*, *dbú-la ťod*, *žábs-la čag* (to put on) a garment, clerical robes, cap, shoes *Dzl.*, *Glr.*; *slób-dpon-la ber-čén skú-la γsól-te* putting the cloak on the teacher *Ma.*; for *zá-ba*, *ͦťúṅ-ba*, also for *ͦdrén-pa*, **to eat, to drink, to offer a meal** *Dzl.*; *rgyál-po ͦbras-čáṅ γsól-nas* as the king had drunk rice-wine *Glr.*; **to take, to give, administer** (medicine) *Dzl.*; **to place** (food etc.) **before, to**

**serve up for** (clerical persons) *Dzl.*, *γsól-lo mčód-čig* I place it before you, help yourself! moreover: *rgyál-pos čáb-la sku-k̔rús γsol* the king took a bath *Glr.*; *srás-la sku-k̔rús γsól-lo* they administered a bath to the prince *Glr.*; *mts̔an γsól-ba* to assume, to receive, a name *Glr.*, to give a name *Glr.*; even thus: *dei t̔ugs-la γdon γsol* a demon enters his (the king's) body (clothes himself with it) *Glr.*

**Comp.** **sol-kár* W.*, resp. for *kar-yol* earthen ware, crockery. — *γsol-skrúm* meat prepared for the table of a man of rank. *γsol-k̔á* 1. request, prayer *Sch.* 2. meat and drink *Sch.* — **sól-k̔aṅ** resp. for **yó-k̔aṅ* C.*, **t̔ab-ts̔áṅ* W.* **kitchen.** — *γsol-ṅán* poisoned food *Glr.* — *γsol-lčóg* **table.** — *γsol-mčód* **prayer** and **offerings.** — *γsol-ǰá* **tea.** — *γsol-nyá* fish destined or dressed for the table of a respected person, *rgyál-poi Pth.* — *γsol-tág*, *γsol-stégs* **table.** — *γsol-tib* **tea-pot.** — *γsol-t̔áb* **fire-place, kitchen.** — *γsol-ldóṅ* = *gur-gúr.* — *γsól-dpon* prop. head-cook, master-cook, gen. **cup-bearer, butler, waiter.** — *γsol-p̔ógs* **salary** *Sch.* — **γsol-˳biṅ* C.* = *γsol-tib.* — *γsol-már* **butter.** — *γsol-ts̔igs* **dinner.** — *γsol-žib* fine parched **barley-flour.** *γsol-γyóg* under-waiter, under-butler. — *γsol-rás* **distribution of victuals,** by a person of rank to common people, hence *Chr. P.* for **Lord's supper,** holy communion; **donation, gift, present** in gen.

II. sbst. 1. **request, demand, entreaty,** *γsol-ba ˳debs-pa* to make a request, to entreat frq. — 2. **food** **sól-wa žé-pa** to eat, dine, sup *C.*

**གསོས་པ་** *γsós-pa* v. *γsó ba*, *γsos byéd-pa* **to cure** *Sch.*; *bu mi γsos-pa* not keeping, retaining a child alive *Do.*; *γsós-bu* foster-son, **adoptive son;** *γsós-ma* cure? medicine? *γsós-ma ˳débs-pa Thgy.*

**བསའ་** *bsa* v. *γsa.*

**བསག་པ་** *bság-pa* v. *γsóg-pa.*

**བསང་བུ་** *bsáṅ-bu* resp. for *zan* **food, fare** *Glr.*; **bsáṅ-ma** id. *W.*; *bsaṅ-˳brás* resp. a dish of rice.

**བསད་པ་** *bsád-pa* v. *γsód-pa.*

**བསབ་པ་** *bsáb-pa* v. *γsób-pa.*

**བསམ་** *bsam*, **thought, thinking,** *bsám-gyis mi k̔yáb-pa* beyond the reach of human intellect, **incomprehensible** etc. frq.; *čos bzáṅ-las bsam bzaṅ lhág-pa yin* a good way of thinking is worth more than good (external) religion *Mil.*; *W.*: **sam-ṅan-čan** **malicious, wicked.**

**བསམ་པ་** *bsám-pa* I. fut. tense and secondary form of *sém-pa.*

II. sbst. सङ्कल्प, 1. **thought,** imagination, fancy, *bsám-pa ṅán-pa sém-pa* to foster bad thoughts *Do.*; *bsám-pa tsám-gyis* quick as thought; *rtág-tu ˳di snyám-du bsám-pa skyes* he was constantly haunted by these thoughts *Dzl.* — 2. **will,** *mi žig-gi bsám-pa ltar* (or *bžín-du*) *sgrúb-pa* to execute, to carry out a person's will frq.; *bsám-pa l̔ar ma gyúr-pas* as it did not go according to their **wish;** *bsam-pa ˳di-las ma zlog čig* do not try to divert me from my **purpose** *Dzl.*; *bsám-pa bzáṅ-po* good **intention** or **design** *Mil.*; **desire, mind, inclination, liking,** *γnód-pai* or *γdúg-pai* thirst for blood, murderous disposition *Glr.* — 3. **soul, heart** (of rare occurrence), *bsám-pai dón mi ˳grub* then (by doing so) you injure your own soul *Mil*

**Comp.** *bsam-γtán*, ध्यान, 1. **state of complete abstraction,** acc. to *Burn.* '*contemplation*' (cf. *tiṅ-ṅe-˳dzin*, समाधि, समापत्ति, *Burn.* '*méditation*'), *bsam-γtán byéd-pa* to transpose one's self into the state of contemplation or meditation (the difference between the two is not easily defined), v. *Köpp.* I, 586. With this extraordinary state of mind a strange conception is associated, viz. 2. of **certain regions,** where besides gods and other beings also such men have their abode, that are growing more and more perfect and are stripping off every personal quality, whether good or bad, v. *Köpp.* I, 255. — *bsam-mnó* or *-bló*, also *blo-bsám* **thinking,** wishing etc., *bsam-mnó byéd-pa* or *γtóṅ-ba*, resp. *t̔ugs-bsám γtóṅ-ba Pth.*, **to think, to meditate, consider, think upon** frq.; *bzáṅ-byed-kyi bsam-*

*bló* a mind, directed towards what is good, **honesty, probity** *Glr.* — *bsam-sbyór* **design, device, project** *Mil.*, *bzáṅ-po, ṅán-pa*; *bsam-byór byéd-pa* to plan, to scheme, to project a plan *C.* — *bsam-šés* **consciousness,** **sam-šé ṅém-pa** *C.* bad conscience (?).

བསམ་བསེའུ་ *bsam-bséu* 1. **seminal vesicle.** — 2. ovary?

བསལ་བ་ *bsál-ba* v. *sél-ba.*

བསིག་པ་ *bsig-pa* v. *ysig-pa.*

བསིད་པ་ *bsid-pa* **to mend, repair, put in order** *Sch.*

བསིར་བ་ *bsir-ba* 1. = *ysir-ba.* — 2. *W.* **to sip,** **sir-te tuṅ** he drinks sipping.

བསིལ་བ་ *bsil-ba* I. adj. and sbst. **cool, the cool** (of the day), **coolness,** *k̒áṅ-pa bsil-ba žig* a cool house *Dzl.*, *bsil-ba p̒an* coolness is wholesome *Lt.*, *ts̒á-ba bsil-bar ₒgyur* the heat changes to coolness *Dzl.*; *bsil* id., **sil-la dod** sit down in the shade *W.*, *lčaṅ-bsil* 'willow-shade', shady place under willow-trees; *bsil-žiṅ gráṅ-ba* **cold** *Dzl.*, *Glr.*; *bsil-mo* id., **sil-mo p̒i-la** *W.* for the sake of coolness.

II. vb., **to cool,** resp. for *ₒk̒rúd-pa* **to wash,** *žal* mouth and face, *žabs* the feet, *žábs-bsil* water for washing the feet *Cs.*; even: *ču drón-mos sku bsil-bar mdzád-pa* to wash the body with warm water *Cs.*; **to shed,** *spyan-čáb máṅ-po* many tears *Mil.*

**Comp.** *bsil-k̒aṅ* a cool room, a summer-house, summer-residence *Stg.* — *bsil-grib* cool shade *Cs.* — *bsil-ₒt̒úṅ* a cooling drink or beverage *Sch.* — *bsil-ydúgs* parasol *Do.* — *bsil-bu* coolness (?); *bsil-bui rluṅ* a cool breeze *Cs.* — *bsil-smán* a cooling medicine. — *bsil-zás* cooling food. — *bsil-yáb* a fan.

བསུ་བ་ *bsú-ba*, pf. and imp. *bsus,* **to go to meet,** *ma bu bsur ₒoṅ* the mother goes to meet her son *Dzl.* (usually with accus. as in the preceding case, col. also with dat.); *bsus šig* let him come to meet me *Thgr.*; **to join,** of two armies, generals, kings *Dzl.*; **to make advances, to interest one's self for;** most frq.: **to go to meet** (solemnly), **to welcome** a respected person, *p̒o-bráṅ-gi náṅ-du* into the castle *Dzl.*; *páṇḍi-ta ₒbyón-pa-la bsú-ba byéd-do* I will go to meet the arriving Pandit *Glr.*; *bsú-ba rgya-čén-po* very great festivities of reception *Pth.*; *bág-mar bsú-ba yin* we will lead her home as your bride *Mil.*; *ydóṅ-bsu-ba* = *bsú-ba Mil.*; **dan sú-če** *W.* for *dan-* or *spyan-ₒdren-pa* of *B.* — **su-k̒yel* or *k̒yal** *W.* reception and conduct of honour.

བསུ་སྨན་ *bsu-smán Sch.* **clyster,** *W.* **sur-nyig**.

བསུང་ *bsuṅ* **smell,** esp. **sweet scent** *Dzl.*; *dri-bsúṅ* id.; *dri-bsúṅ žím-pa broo* it is sweet, scented, fragrant *Dzl.*: *bsuṅ-ṅád Sch.* fragrance; *ro bsúṅ-ba* filled with a cadaverous smell *Dzl.*; **mar suṅ soṅ dog** *W.* the butter smells (rancid).

བསུན་བསྐྱུར་ *bsun-bskyúr Sch.*: irregularity of life, **dissoluteness;** *bsún-par byed-pa Sch.*: to be dissolute; to be dirty; *bsún-tsam* disgusting, obscene *Sch.*

བསུམ་པ་ *bsum-pa* 1. = *ₒdzúm-pa.* — 2. = *súm-pa Cs.*

བསུར་སྨྱིག་ *bsur-smyig W.* **clyster,** cf. *bsu-smán.*

བསེ་ *bse* 1. v. *se, se-ba, se-dri, se-šin.* — 2. also: *bse-kó,* **tanned leather,** *bse-k̒rab Lex.* a coat of mail made of leather; *bse-sgám, bsei sgróm-bu Pth.* leather-box, or a box covered with leather; *bse-sgó* leather-door, or a door-like target made of hides *Pth.* — 3. *bse* or *bse-ru* (*Lex.* ཁྭ་རྒྱ 'a certain animal') **unicorn,** *Hook.* II., 157 'tchiru', **an antelope,** prob. = *ytsod*; **rhinoceros** *Tar.* 185, 20.

བསེགས་པ་ *bségs-pa Sch.* to come from one side, to come across one's way.

བསེད་པ་ *bséd-pa* v. *yséd-pa.*

བསེད་དཔྱད་ *bsed-dpyád Sch.* the bow for setting a drill in motion.

བསེན་མོ་ *bsen-mo Sch*: a female devil.

བསེར་, སེར་, གསེར་བུ་ *bser, ser, ysér-bu* 1. **a fresh, cold breeze,** *bsér-gyis p̒og* he is exposed to a cold wind *Sch.* — 2. of persons, resp. **the feeling cold, catching cold,** *bsér-du yoṅ* you will feel cold *Mil.*; also *bsér-mo* adj. or sbst.: **sér-mo*

**sér-mo máṅ-po ma kyód-da** *W.* did you not feel very cold on your way? *bser-mai nad* resp. a catarrh, a cold *Dzl.*

བསེལ་(བ་) *bsél(-ba)*, gen. *lam-bsél* **convoy, safe-conduct, escort;** *Lex.*: *ˌǰag-skyób-kyi kyél-ma* (escort) against robbers; *bsél-pa* safeguard, guide, *(lam-) bsél byéd-pa* to accompany and protect on the way, to escort.

བསོག་པ་ *bsóg-pa* v. *ság-pa.*

བསོད་སྙོམས་ *bsod-snyóms*, **पिण्ड, alms, gifts** presented to clerical persons, *bsod-snyóms-gyis ˌťso-ba* to live on alms, on charity, *bsod-snyóms byéd-pa, sóg-pa, ˌǰúg-pa Cs., bsod-snyóms-la rgyú-ba*, resp. *śégs-pa* to beg, ask, collect alms; *bsod-snyóms sbyór-ba* to prepare an entertainment for the priesthood.

བསོད་པ་ *bsód-pa* 1. vb., **to be pleased with, to take a delight in, to like,** *W.*: **de-la kon-čoy sod-če man** God is not pleased with that. — 2. adj., **pleasing, agreeable.** **nyiṅ sod ťsor dug** *W.* I feel well, I am quite happy; *bsód-pa daṅ ṅán-pa* good and bad; *bsód-pai zas* is explained by one *Lex.*: *zas bzáṅ-poi miṅ* good food, good provisions, by another: = **प्रणीत** prepared, dressed, boiled. — *bsód-bde, bsód-nams*, resp. *sku-bsód* 1. **good fortune, happiness, felicity,** *bsód-bde-čan* happy, *bsód-bde-med* unhappy *Cs.* 2. **destiny, fate,** = *dbaṅ-ťáṅ*, **ťam-čád sód-de-nẹ ǰuṅ** every thing happens according to a decree of fate *W.*; prob. also *sku-bsód śin-tu če Ld.-Glr.* 11, b. *Schl.*, his destiny is a very high one; *ḱyód-kyi bsód-bde-la brdúṅ-ba yód-pa yin* it belongs to your destiny that you get a drubbing. — 3. **merit, virtue, good action,** *byéd-pa* to perform (a good action) *Dzl.*, *bsód-bde sóg-pa* to gather merit, *bsód-nams ma yin-pai las* sinful deed *Thgy.*

བསོས་ *bsos* **indemnification, damages** paid for bodily injury.

བསོས་པ་ *bsós-pa* v. *γsos-pa.*

བསྲང་བ་ *bsráṅ-ba* v. *sróṅ-ba*; *bsráṅ-po* **straight, upright,** **yór-po dug śráṅ-po-la żog** *C.* it stands aslant, put it straight!

བསྲད་པ་ *bsrád-pa* v. *bsród-pa.*

བསྲན་པ་ *bsrán-pa* v. *srán-pa.*

བསྲབ་པ་ *bsráb-pa*, v. *srab*, **to bridle, keep under, restrain, check, curb, refrain,** *bag-čágs* the passions, *mún-pa* or *sgrib-pa bsráb-pa Cs.* to dispel darkness (prob. only in a spiritual sense).

བསྲལ་བ་ *bsrál-ba* v. *srél-ba.*

བསྲི་བ་ *bsri-ba* etc. v. *sri-ba* etc.

བསྲུང་ *bsrun Cs.* **a tutelar genius.**

བསྲུན་པ་, བསྲུབ་པ་, བསྲུལ་བ་, བསྲེ་བ་, བསྲེག་པ་, བསྲེལ་བ་, བསྲོ་བ་ *bsrún-pa, bsrúb-pa, bsrúl-ba, bsré-ba, bsrég-pa, bsrél-ba, bsró-ba* v. *srún-pa, srúb-pa* etc.

བསྲོད་པ་, བསྲད་པ་ *bsród-pa, bsrád-pa*, = *sró-ba*, **to dry,** by exposing to the rays of the sun *Sch.*

བསླ་བ་, བསླང་བ་, བསླད་པ་ etc. *bslá-ba, bsláṅ-ba, bslád-pa* etc. v. *slá-ba, sláṅ-ba* etc.

བསླབ་པ་ *bsláb-pa* 1. vb., v. *slob-pa.* — 2. sbst. **doctrine,** *bsláb-pa γsum Glr.*, acc. to an explanation in the Triglot: *lhág-pai ťsul-ḱrims, lhág-pai sems, lhág-pai śes-ráb* (expressions which I am not able to interpret satisfactorily); our Lama explained *bsláb-pa γsúm-gyi sdóm-pa Mil.* by: *so-ťár, byaṅ-séms* and *γsaṅ-sṅágs-kyi sdóm-pa*; *bsláb-pai γnas* **dogma, tenet** *Tar.* — **lab-ḱan** *W.* **teacher.** — **lab-(s)tán táṅ-če** *W.* to teach, to keep school. — *bslab-bya* what is to be learned, **doctrine, precept, admonition,** *ˌǰig-rtén mi-čos-la dgos-pai bsláb-bya mdzád-do* he imparted to her some practical doctrines or rules of life and social intercourse *Glr.*, *bsláb-bya stón-pa B.*, **táṅ-če** *W.* to give admonitions, to exhort, reprimand.

བསླུ་བ་, བསླེ་བ་, བསླེབ་པ་, བསློག་པ་ *bslú-ba, bslé-ba, bsléb-pa, bslóg-pa* v. *slu-ba, sle-ba* etc.

# ཧ

ཧ *ha* 1. the letter *h*. — 2. numeral: 29.

ཧ་ *ha* 1. *W.* **a yawn,** **ha yoṅ dug** I cannot help yawning. 2. **breath,** *ha ͦdébs-pa* to breathe. — 3. **the sound of laughter,** **hab-gód čó-če* W.* to laugh out or aloud, cf. *ha-há.*

ཧྭ་ *hwa* 1. *gós-kyi hwa* **collar** of a coat. — 2. **shin, shin-bone** *Sch.* — 3. **hǎ, hŏ* W.* very well! — 4. col. nearly = *p̀a* II., **yonder,** farther off, **há-la gyug* C.* get you gone! be off! begone!; **há-čog = p̀á-rol** the other side, yonder side, **há-gi** that (man) there, **há-gi-ru** there, there above, up there, there behind, thither, that way *C., W.*

ཧ་གོ་བ་ *há-go-ba W.* **to understand,** **ha mi go-a** don't you understand it?

ཧ་ཅང་ *há-čaṅ* **very,** sometimes **too much, too,** *mya-ṅán-las ͦda-ba há-čaṅ yaṅ myur-čés-so* his removal (prop. disappearing) from misery happens really too soon! *Dzl.*; *há-čaṅ-nas* id., **há-čaṅ-nẹ k̀é-pa* C.* very learned, possessed of extensive information.

ཧ་ན་ཧོ་ནེ, ཧན་ཧོན་ *ha-na-ho-né, han-hón* **very angry,** much enraged *Ld.*

ཧ་ནི་ *há-ni* **all** of them, **all together, in a body** *Sch.*

ཧ་བ་ཧ་བ་ *há-ba-há-ba* **to breathe out steam** or vapour.

ཧ་བོ་ *há-bo* n. of a medicinal herb *Lt.*

ཧ་ཡེགས་ *ha-yégs* **woe** (to you etc.)! *W.*

ཧ་ར་ *há-ra,* with **gyáb-če*, W.* **to play at dice.**

ཧ་ར་ཧུ་རེ་ *ha-ra-hu-ré W.* **impetuous, violent, rude, impudent.**

ཧ་རམ་ *ha-rám* with **čó-če* W.* **to deny, disown, disavow.**

ཧ་རི་ *há-ri Ssk.* **parrot.**

ཧ་རི་ཏ་ཀ་ *ha-ri-ta-ka Ssk.* **vegetables, greens, pot-herbs** *Wdṅ.*

ཧ་རི་དྲ་ *ha-ri-dra Ssk.* the turmeric plant, **Curcuma** *S.g.*

ཧ་རི་ཙནྡན་ *ha-ri-tsan-dan Ssk.* **sandal-wood.**

ཧ་རི་ཙམ་ *ha-ri-tsam Pur.* **centipede.**

ཧ་རིབ་ *ha-rib Ld.* music (?).

ཧ་རེ་ཎུ་ཀ་ *ha-re-ṇu-ka Ssk.* a medicine *Med.*

ཧ་ལ, ཧ་ལ་ཧ་ལ་ *ha-la, ha-la-ha-la Wdṅ.,* a certain poison, also **poison** in general, *Ssk.*

ཧ་ལ་ཧ་ལ་ *ha-la-há-la Cs.:* a name of *spyan-ras-γzigs,* v. *spyan.*

ཧ་ལམ་ *há-lam* **about, near, nearly, pretty, tolerably, rather,** *de daṅ há-lam ͦdrá-ba* about or nearly like that *Wdṅ.*

ཧ་ལལ་ *ha-lál Ar., *ha-lál čó-če*, Urd.* حلال کرنا, to kill (an animal) in the manner prescribed by the Mahometan law *W.*

ཧ་ལས་ *ha-lás* col., **astonished, frightened,** **ha-la-ṡi** or **ha-la-ṡe** id., **ha-lẹ́ čá-če* W., ha-lás-pa B.* **to be astonished, frightened** *Mil., Pth.*

ཧ་ལོ་ *ha-ló* **flower,** esp. a large beautiful **garden-flower** *Glr., ha-ló rkyáṅ-pa* a simple flower, *ha-ló stoṅ-ͦdáb* a double flower; **ha-ló-ka** mallow *W.* (?)

ཧ་ཤང་ *ha-ṡáṅ* 1. *Cs.:* (Chinese word) **a Buddhist priest, doctor, scholar** *Glr.* — 2. id., represented by **a mask** in religious plays, *ha-p̀rúg* an old doctor with boys, his pupils.

ཧ་ཤིག་ *ha-ṡig* a mineral medicine, used as a remedy for the stone; acc. to *Wdṅ.* = *ṫód-le-kór,* alabaster.

ཧ་ཧ, ཧཱ་ཧཱ་ *ha-há, hā-há* the natural sound of laughter *Mil., ha-há rgód-pa* to laugh out, to set up a loud laugh;

to *Sch.* also an interjection expressive of pain (?).

ཧའི་ *hai* a Chinese word, **shoe** *C.*

ཧའུ་སྤ་བ་ *hau-spa-ba* n. of a medicinal herb *Med.*

ཧགས་ *hags Lex.* **sugar, treacle** *Cs.*, *hágs-kyi lá-tu.*

ཧང་ *haṅ? haṅ-*ₒ*dzom-pa* **to squander, to dissipate** *Sch.*, *haṅ-ča-byed* **a squanderer** *Sch.*

ཧང་བ་ *háṅ-ba, W.* **háṅ-ċe** **to pant, to gasp.**

ཧད་ཀྱིས་ *hád-kyis* **suddenly** *Sch.* — *had-po? Mil.*

ཧད་ཧད་ *had-hád* or *hur-húr*, with **ċó-ċe** **to exert one's self,** to strive *W.*

ཧན་ལྡང་ *han-ldáṅ W.* 1. **dumb, mute,** **han-dáṅ-ṅi (s)pé ra** **a stammering,** also: a confused, unmeaning speech. — 2. **imbecile, weak of mind.**

ཧན་ཧོན་ *han-hón* v. *ha-na-ho-né.*

ཧབ་ *hab* 1. **a mouthful,** *háb-za byéd-pa, hab-háb zá-ba* to devour greedily, e.g. of dogs, pigs etc., *hab-bċád* a needy wretch, a starveling, famishing person.— 2. **a stitch,** in sewing, also **háb-ka** *C.* **háb-so** *W.*, *hab-*ₒ*tsem-pa* to make here a stitch and there a stitch, as in quilting *Mil. nt.* — 3. *hab-gód* v. *ha* 3. — 4. v. the following article.

ཧབ་ཤ་ *háb-ša* **a dispute, a quarrel,** *háb-ša byéd-pa Mil., Thgr.*, to dispute, to quarrel; *hab-ťób byéd pa* to scramble for, to strive or contend for *Pth.*

ཧམ་པ་ *hám-pa* 1. **avarice, covetousness, greediness;** *W.* also vb.: to covet, **žán-ni nór-la** after a person's wealth; **to long for,** to yearn after, **ǩoi 'á-ne hám-te dad dug** his wife sits yearning (after him); *hám-pa byéd-pa Sch.*: to be covetous. — 2. **strength** *Cs.*; **courage, bravery** *W.*, of men and animals. — 3. white film on liquids etc., **mould** *C.*, **hám-ḍi* or *-ri** a musty, fusty smell *C., W.*; **hám-por čág-ǩan** *W.* **mouldy, musty,** **ham-ċe** *W.* to get mouldy. — 4. **lie,** falsehood, *C.* — *hám-pa-ċan* 1. **covetous, avaricious; greedy, voracious.** 2. **courageous;** one *Lex.* explains *rlam-ǩyér* by *hám-pas ǩyér-ba* (?); **hám-pa čúṅ-se** *W.* cowardly.

ཧམ་བུར་ *hám-bur W.* rime, hoar-frost?

ཧར་ *har* **suddenly,** *har láṅ-ba* to rise suddenly *Mil.*; **har sẹ' ǰhé'-pa** to rouse suddenly from sleep *C.*; *har-gyis* (*Sch. had-kyis*) more precise form of the adv. *Tar.*

ཧར་རེ་ *hár-re* **empty, open,** *Tar.* 115,16 *Schf.*

ཧལ་པ་ *hál-pa* a porridge, made of milk, butter and honey.

ཧལ་བ་ *hál-ba* **to pant, to wheeze, to snort,** *hal-kyi* a panting dog *Sch.*; **hal-méd** *W.* **weak.**

ཧས་ *has* **exaggeration, hyperbole,** *has-čer smrá-ba Cs*, **hẹ gyab-ċe** *W.* **to exaggerate, to talk big, to brag.**

ཧས་པོ་རི་ *hás-po-ri* n. of a mountain in *C.*, *Glr.*

ཧི་ *hi* numeral: 59.

ཧི་དིག་ *hi-dig,* or *hig-dig, W.* **zér-ċe** **to blow one's nose.**

ཧི་མཱ་ལ་ཡ་ *hi-mā-la-ya Ssk.*, = *gaṅs-ċan* the snowy mountains, **Him laya.**

ཧི་ར་ *hi-ra Ssk.* **diamond.**

ཧི་རི་ *hi-ri* **corn-stack,** **hi-ri gyáb-ċe** *W.* to pile up a stack of corn.

ཧི་ལིང་ *hi-líṅ* **noise,** **hi-líṅ táṅ-ǩan** *W.*, **bully, brawler.**

ཧི་ཧི་ *hi-hi* = *ha-há.*

ཧིའི་ཀ་ *hii ka Sch.* **breast-bone.**

ཧིག་, ཧིག་ཀ་ *hig, hig-ka* **the act of sobbing,** **hig táṅ-te dug* or *gyáb-te dug** he is sobbing *W.*; **hig ǰáṅ* (lit. *sbyaṅ*) *dug** is said to be an expression used of a Lama, when he is watching the gradual departing of the soul of a dying man.

ཧིང་ *hiṅ,* हिङ्गु, = *šiṅ-kun, Asa foetida.*

ཧིན་དུ་སྟཱ་ནི་ *hin-du-stá-ni, C.*: **hin-du-tá-ni kẹ'**, Hindoostanee, the language of the Hindoos.

ཧིས་ *his Pur.*: **hiz yoṅ** **he is panting.**

ཧུ་ *hu* 1. *W.* **breath,** **hu gyáb-ċe** to breathe. — 2. num.: 89.

ཧུ་ཀ་ *hú-ka, Ar.* حقّه **the hookah,** with an inflexible tube.

ཧུ་ཀུམ་ *hu-kúm W.,* حُکم *Urdu,* **order, command.**

ཧུ་ཁྱུ་ *hu-k̔yú* the sound of sighing *Pth.*

ཧུ་ན་ *hú-na Cs : Ssk. (hū-na)* n. of an ancient people, the Huns (?).

ཧུ་འང་དྷི་ *hu-ạn-dhí* (?) *Sch.:* title of the Chinese emperor.

ཧུ་རེ་ *hu-ré, mig hu-ré ̥dug* **he stares, he goggles,** with wonder, horror, confusion *Mil., Glr.; mig-húr Mng.*

ཧུ་ཤཱར་ *hu-šār* (from the *Hind. hōšyār?*) (grown) **well again,** being again lively, active; **diligent, sedulous** *W.*

ཧུ་ཧུ་ *hu-hú* 1. interj. expressive of pain from cold *Cs.* — 2. 'the sound of one's mouth in eating' *Cs.* — 3. **hu-hú táṅ-če* W.* **to whistle.**

ཧཱུྃ་ *hūm,* हूम्, हुम्, mystical interjection, e.g. in the prayer of six syllables, v. ཨོཾ་

ཧུན་ *hun W.* (= *ča, lon, p̔rin*) **news,** tidings, intelligence, information, **hun taṅ-če** to give account or notice, to inform, acquaint, let know, **ťsar-na hun toṅ** tell me (let me know) as soon as it is finished! **hun ťsór-če** to get intelligence, to receive news; **hun ma yoṅ* or *mi dug** we have no news yet; **disclosure, explanation, opinion, idea,** **či yód-pe hun k̔yód-la ǰuṅ yin** you shall get an idea of what kind of ... are to be found, **sém-čan ťún-čan žig yin-pe hun ṅá-la ǰuṅ** I have got the notion that this is a very quiet animal; **re-rēi hun čil-tar šē** whence have you such accurate information of every one of them? **ser-dub ḍil-te hun ma juṅ** he did not perceive it when the ring fell off; **hun-méd-la** **unexpectedly, unawares.**

ཧུབ་ *hub* as much as is swallowed at once, **a gulp, a draught,** *tóg-mar húb re ̥ťuṅ žig* at first take only one mouthful, one draught at a time *Glr.; hub ɣčig* one mouthful, *hub do* two mouthfuls *Cs.; húb-kyis* by draughts *Sch.; hub-húb byéd-pa* to drink in large draughts, to gulp.

ཧུར་ *hur* 1. v. *hu-ré.* — 2. *hur-húr* v. *had-had.*

ཧུར་བ་ *húr-ba* **dexterity, cleverness, skilfulness** *C., hur-ťág* id., also **zeal, diligence** *Sch.; húr-po* 1. **quick, alert, dexterous, clever.** 2. **hot, hasty, passionate** *Ld.; rta húr-po* a fleet, spirited, fine horse *Cs.*

ཧུས་ *hus Cs.* **moisture, humidity,** *hús-čan* wet.

ཧེ་ *he* 1. num.: 119. — 2. interj.: **o! holla!** *Cs.; he-he* 1. id. *Cs.* 2. = *ha-há, he-hé zer bgád-pas* she laughed: he, he! *Glr.*

ཧེ་ཏུ་ *hé-tu Ssk.* **cause, reason, argument, logic.**

ཧེ་བག་ *he-bag* **provocation, taunts, sarcasms.**

ཧེ་བཛྲ་ *Ssk. he-waǰra,* ཀྱེ་རྡོ་རྗེ་ *Tibet. kye-rdo-rje Cs.:* n. of a god; n. of a series of treatises.

ཧེ་རུ་ཀ་ *hé-ru-ka* **terrifying deities,** also *k̔rag-̥ťuṅ, Thgr.* frq., *hé-ru-kai rgyud* legends of wrathful deities.

ཧེག་པོ་ *hég-po* having become **putrid, rancid.**

ཧེལ་གེ་ *hél-ge Sch.:* **soft leather, wash-leather.**

ཧེལ་པོ་ *hél-po, hél-čan, *hel-hél* W.* **wide, extended;** of garments: **wide, easy;** *hél-ba* id. and sbst.: **width** *Sch.*

ཧོ་ *ho* num.: 149.

ཧོ་མ་ *hó-ma Ssk.* prop.: **burnt-offering** of butter; = *sbyin-srég* v. *Was.* (194); *Schl.* 251; *hó-ma byéd-pa* **to sacrifice;** *hom-k̔uṅ* a small pit or a triangular box used as an altar for such an offering.

ཧོ་ཧོ་ *ho-hó* interj. of admiration *Cs.*

ཧོང་ལེན་ *hoṅ-lén* a medicinal herb, *Picrorrhiza,* frequently to be found on the mountains, *Hook.* I., 272.

ཧོན་ཧོན་ *hon-hón* **stupid, foolish** *Cs.*

ཧོབ་པ་ *hób-pa, W.: *hób-te dug** it has got **bent in** or **battered,** of tin ware.

ཧོམ་ *hom* (Mongol word?) a pad, placed under a camel's load.

ཧོམ་པ་ *hóm-pa W.* **to fall away,** to lose flesh, e.g. of hollow cheeks, **to shrink, to shrivel,** of withered fruit.

ཧོར་ *hor* 1. formerly: **a Mongol** *‚hor ǰin-ǵin-k̔an* the Mongol Djingiskhan; *hor-sér Shara Sharaighol* n. of a Mongol tribe *Glr.*; *hór-yul Mongolia.* — 2. at present: in *C.* the people living near the *Tengri-nor* (*γnam-mtso*); in *W.* the Turks; *hór-zla* a Turkish month.

Note. *Cs.* has only the second of these significations, *Sch.* only the first (the latter using *Cs.*'s examples and changing all the Turks into Mongols!) The suppositions of Latham seem still less consistent with the real state of the case.

ཧོར་ཁོངས་ *hor-k̔oṅs Sch.:* deficiencies, gaps; separation' (?).

ཧོར་འདྲ་ *hór-ₒdra Sch.:* 'confiscation, *hór-ₒdra bábs-pa* to confiscate' (?).

ཧོར་པ་ *hór-pa* **wood-grouse** or cock of the wood *Sch.*, *hór-pa dkár-po* a species of hawk *Sch.* (?).

ཧོལ་ཧོལ་ *hol-hól W.* **soft, loose, light,** as the soil in spring, **hol táṅ-če, hól-te bór-če** to break up, to loosen (the soil).

ཧྲག་པ་ *hrág-pa* 1. vb., **to require more and more,** to covet incessantly *Ma.*, *W.* — 2. sbst., adj. **hardness, hard** *Cs.*

ཧྲང་བ་ *hráṅ-ba* 1. **alone,** cf. *raṅ*, **šraṅ-šráṅ-la yoṅ soṅ** I came alone *C.*, *p̔o-hráṅ, mo-hráṅ* single man and woman, = *p̔o-ráṅ* etc. *C.* — 2. with *dmar* preceding, **naked** *C.*

ཧྲད་པ་ *hrád-pa* 1. **to thrust, to push violently, to stem** firmly, **káṅ-pa sig-pa-la* W.* to stem the foot against the wall — 2. **to scratch,** *sgó-la p̔yag-hrád-pa ₒya mdzád-pa* (his Reverence) made several scratchings with his hand, scratched several times, at the door *Mil.* — 3. **to exert one's self,** to make every effort *W.*, **šrád-čan zúm-če** or *táṅ-če** id. *W.*

ཧྲབ་ཧྲིབ་ *hrab-hrib C.* **šrab-ba-šrib-be* Ld.*, v. *rab-rib.*

ཧྲལ་བ་ *hrál-ba* **to rend, tear up, tear to pieces** e.g. of a beast of prey: to tear up a person's body; **šral soṅ** he has torn it to pieces *C.*, *W*, *hral-hrál Lex.*

ཧྲི་ *hri Cs.:* '*Ssk.* essence, substance; a mystical word'.

ཧྲིག་ *hrig W.* **šrig-la táṅ-če, šrig-ga táṅ-če** **to hang** (a thief), **šrig-la ši-če** **to hang** one's self.

ཧྲིག་པ་ *hrig-pa Cs.*, *mig* (or resp. *spyaṅ*) *hrig-hrig byéd-pa* or *ₒdúg-pa*, (= *rig-rig*), to look this way and that, hither and thither *Mil. nt.*; *hríg-ge-ba* looking in that manner *Thgr.*

ཧྲིད་ *hrid*; *S.g.*; *rná-ba hrid ₒbyar* is explained by *Wdṅ.*: *rná-ba lhág-pa p̔yógs-su byar* the ear leans feebly on the neck, as a sign of death.

ཧྲིལ་པོ་ *hríl-po* 1. **round, globular,** *hril-hril byéd-pa* to writhe with pain, *hril-hril kar-kár byéd-pa* to be writhing, and then again stretching one's self or starting up *Pth.* — 2. **whole,** *tse hril-por* for the whole life *Glr.*, *mgo hril-gyis γtúm-nas* wrapping up his whole head *Glr.* — 3. **close, dense,** *hril ₒdús-te ₒdúg-pa* to sit or stand close together in rows *Mil.*, *C.*, *W.* Cf. *ríl-ba.*

ཧྲུད་པ་ *hrúd-pa* adj. and abstract noun, **rough, rugged; severe, austere; roughness** etc.; *hrúd-po* adj. id. *Cs.*

ཧྲུམ་པ་ *hrúm-pa* **to break, to smash** *Sch.*

ཧྲུལ་བ་ *hrúl-ba* adj. and abstr. sbst. **ragged, tattered; raggedness,** *hrul-bai dug-po* a ragged coat *Mil.*; *hrúl-po* id., *gos hrúl-po Dzl.* and elsewh. frq. — 2. sbst.: **rags, tatters,** *gós-su hrúl-po gyón-pa* to put on rags for a garment *Pth.*; *hrúl-k̔aṅ* a ruin, **ruins** *Sch.*

ཧྲེམ་པ་ *hrém-pa* **swollen** *Sch.*, *hrem-mé* id. *Mng.*

ལྷ་ *lha*, *Ssk.* देव. 1. the first class of beings subject to metempsychosis, **the gods,** both those of Brahminical mythology, and the various national and local gods, with whom Buddhism came in contact. These local gods were incorporated into the system of Buddhism, when they were found to be too numerous and too much endeared to the people, to be entirely discarded and given up; so, most of them are worshipped even nowadays and presented with various offerings. They are also supposed to enjoy a blissful existence (hence: *dé-riṅ lhá-yi nyi-ma ṡar* 'this day was a day of happiness to me' *Glr.*, and similar expressions are of frq. occurrence; v. also *lha-yul*) and to be possessed of qualities and capacities superior to those of ordinary human beings. Nevertheless, when compared with any Buddhist saint, they are considered to be of inferior rank and power; and a local '*lha*' can never attain to Buddhaship, without having previously assumed the nature of man; v. *Köpp.* I, 122. 248. II, 296. *lhai bu* or *sras*, *bú-mo* or *srás-mo* descendant from the gods, son or daughter of the gods *Dzl.* and elsewh.; *lha mi ṫób-pa* to obtain the birth as a god or as man *Thgy.*; *lhai yi-ge* the Lantsa-letters, v. *lan-tsa*; *lha ₒbáb-pa* the (mystical) entering of a deity into a human being, **inspiration,** so that the person inspired pronounces the oracles of the god, *lha żúgs-pa* id. pop.; also: the person thus inspired; *lha ni k̇yab-ₒǰúg-la mos* as for gods, they worshipped Vishnu *Pth.*, *lha má-mo-la byed* they worshipped the Mamo as a '*lha*' *Pth.*; *lhai dbáṅ-po, lha-bdág, = brgya-byin* Indra; in another sense: *lhai rgyál-po byéd-pa* to make the gods subject to one's self, (said to be the blessed consequence of a certain charm) *Do.*; the following gods are occasionally mentioned: *nám - mkai lha* the deity of heaven *Tar.*; that of the sea *Dzl.*; the gods of trees, of houses etc.; *dgrá-lha* and *ṗó-lha* are two personal gods of every human individual, the one being the god of the right side, the other of the left side of his body *Glr.*, *Mil.*; *yi-dam-lha* v. *yi-dam*. — 2. **the image of a god,** in as much as it is really thought to be inhabited by a deity, after having been duly inaugurated (*ráb-tu γnás-pa*) *Glr.*; the local '*lha*' are not always represented by figures resembling human beings, but even by sticks, stones and similar fetishes; gods also of non-Buddhist nations are called '*lha*' and are acknowledged as such. — 3. fig.: *mii lha* **a king** *Mil.*, and hence '*lha*' is often used in addressing a king, like the French *Sire! lha-rgyal-yab-yúm* the royal father and mother *Pth.*; *lhá-yi lha* the lord of lords, the supreme being, **Buddha** *Cs.*

**Comp.** *lha-k̇áṅ* **an idol-shrine**. — *lha-γčig* 1. dear Sir! dear Lord and King! *Pth.* 2. **princess** *Glr.* — *lha-lčám* **a princess** *Pth.* — *lha-čén* a great and mighty deity. — *lhá-čos* v. *čos* no. 2. — *lhá-rje* **physician** *Wdṅ.* — *lha-rtén* **image** or temple of a god or of the gods. — *lha-ṫó* (prob. for *lhai ṫo-yór*) **heaps of stones,** erected on mountain passes or on the tops of mountains. — *lha-ₒdre* gods and goblins, *lha klu ₒdre srin γdúg-pa maṅ Glr.* 2. **goblin, hobgoblin;** **lhá-ₒdre-ber-ka** mullein (Verbascum) *Lh.*; **lán-de non soṅ** *W.* I have had the night-mare. — *lhá-sde, mi-sde* the class of the gods, the class of men. — *lha - nád Sch.*: **hysterics; madness.** — *lha-ṗyág* honours shown to the '*lha*', worship paid to them, *ṗyogs bżir lha-ṗyág máṅ-po btsál-te* bowing towards the four points of the compass in token of reverence to the '*lha*' *Pth.*, often only: **compliments, kind regards,** offered to respected persons, in letters. — *lha-ṗyi* n. of a mountain in the south of Tibet *Mil.* — *lha-ṗrúg* a descendant from the gods, child of the gods; as a mask *Schl.* 235. — *lha-ṗrán* inferior deities. — *lha-bris-mk̇an* or *-pa* a painter of gods. — *lha-ₒbáṅs Tar.*; *Schf.*: **slaves** (doing service) **in temples.** — *lha-ma-yin, lha-min,* असुर, one of the six classes of beings, living on the slopes of the Sumeru below the '*lha*' against whom, like Titans, they are continually fighting; also *lha-ma-yin-mo* are mentioned. — *lha-ma-srín* gods, Asuras and Rakshasas, or perh. also: *lha-ma-srin sde brgyad* the eight classes of the gods, Asuras, Rākshasas etc., i.e. the whole world of spirits. — *lhá-mo* **goddess.** — *lha-ma-rtá Sch.*: a certain insect. — *lhá-bzo* 1. the art of making images of gods *Pth.* 2. also *lha-bzó-bo* a framer of gods *Glr.* — *lhá-yul* 1. the region of the world where the gods reside, the heaven, seat or abode of the gods. 2. fig.: a blessed country, a paradise. — *lhá-sa* (in early times *lha-ldán*) *Sch.*, *Köpp.* II, 332, n. of the capital of Tibet. — *lha-srin* gods and Rākshasas; *steṅ lha-*

ལ

*srin*, *˳og klu-γnyán*, *bar γži-bdág*, are often mentioned in connexion. — *lha-srúṅ* **tutelar god**, *bód-kyi Glr.*

ལྷ་ང་ *lha-ṅá* **knee-pan**, *pús-mo γyás-pai lha-ṅá sá-la ˳dzúg-pa* to kneel down on the right knee frq.; *lha-ḱúṅ* the bend of the knee *W.*

ལྷ་བ་ *lhá-ba Med.* and *Pth.*, acc. to *Wdṅ.* also *klad-rgyás*, *Sch.*: 'the bloody marrow in the bones; whilst he translates *rmai lhá-ba* by: 'the growing worse of a wound'.

ལྷ་རུ་ *lha-rú Med.*; *Sch.* **cartilage** (cf. *lha-gór* sub *lkóg-ma*).

ལྷག་ *lhag* 1. **more, beyond,** **dá-wa čig lag soṅ** more than a month has passed *W.*, **nyi-ma-ṗyéd lag soṅ* W.* it is already past noon, *rgyá-mtso-bas kyaṅ lhág-ste* as this alone would be more than the whole sea *Dzl.*; *nyi-šus lhag* more by twenty *S.g.* — 2. = *lhág-ma.* — *lhág-pa* 1. adj. **surpassing, excelling, superior,** *˳dí-las lhág-pai γžan čos med Dzl.*; *nyam-ťág-pa ṅá-las lhág-pa yód-dam* is there any one that is thinner than I? *Dzl.*; *dé-rnams-kyi náṅ-nas lhág-pa* the best amongst these *Glr.*; *rgya hor γnyis-las lhág-pa ṅed bod yin* we Tibetans surpass the Chinese and Mongols (in sagacity) *Glr.* 2. rarely = *lhág-ma*: *dé-las lhág-pa* the others, the remaining *S.g.* 6, 1. *de-lhag* **besides, moreover.** — *lhág-par* adv. **more** (magis) frq., mostly with adj., but also with verbs, *šin-tu lhág-par* **far more; very, exceedingly, uncommonly,** *lhág-par légs-pa* uncommonly beautiful *Dzl.*; *čes lhág-par* **extremely**, excessively *Stg.*; **further**, furthermore, moreover. — *lhág-ge-ba* = *lhag-pa*, *lhág-ge mdzád-nas* making it project.

*lhág-ma* 1. **remains, scrapings,** *sṅar bšad-pai lhág-ma* (the letters) which at the last discussion remained, were left, (unexplained) *Gram.*; *lha lhág-ma-rnams* the other, the remaining gods *Stg.*; **the remainder,** in subtracting *Wdk.* — 2. **razor-stone, razor-strap** *Sch.* — 3. being above, being at the upper part of, *groṅ* the place lying higher up (the valley), opp. to *˳óg-ma Dzl.*

**Comp.** *lhag-bčas* 1. having **more than** so and so much, *bhā-ra-ta šlo-ka ˳bum lhag-bčus* the Bharata of more than 100,000 verses *Tar.* 2. the gerund in *te* (*ste* etc.) *Gram.* — *lhag-mťóṅ* 'seeing more' (than other mortals), in certain states of contemplation v. *ži-γnas* sub *ži.*

ལྷག་གིས་ *lhág-gis* = *lhaṅ-ṅer*, *lhag-gis ˳čar Thgr.*, *˳byuṅ Mil.* he shines bright, *lhág-ge-ba* = *lhaṅ-ṅe-ba Mil.*

ལྷག་པ་ *lhág-pa* I. sbst., also *γza lhág-pa* 1. **Mercury.** 2. **Wednesday.** — II. adj. **more excellent**, v. *lhag.*

ལྷག(ས)་པ་ *lhag(s)-pa* I. sbst. **cold wind,** *lhág-pa ṗog* the cold wind has withered them (the flowers) *W.*; *lo-γsár lhágs-pa* the cold new year's wind *Mil.* — II. vb., **to come together,** to meet, to assemble, with other persons; perh. also: to join, to be adjacent or contiguous, of houses, beams etc.

ལྷང་ངེ་ *lhaṅ-ṅe*, *lhan-ne*, *lham-me*, also *lhag-ge*, *lam-me*, *lham-pa* **clear, distinct,** to the sight as well as to the ear; *lhaṅ-ṅe lham-mer γsal-te* (Buddha) appearing clearly and distinctly *Dzl.*, in a similar sense: *lham-me lhaṅ-ṅe lhan-ner bžúgs-so Pth.*; clear, sonorous; *ḱyi-skad lhaṅ-lhaṅ-pa Mil.* the clear (loud) barking of dogs; *ḱyod lhaṅ-lhaṅ glú-len-pa Mil* thou clear-voiced songster; *lhaṅ-lháṅ brjód-la* speaking with a clear, sonorous voice. — *Cs.* has: **majestic, glorious, sublime, august.**

ལྷད་ *lhad* a baser substance mixed with a finer one, an **alloy,** *lhad ˳júg-pa* or *sré-ba* with *la*, *lhád-kyis slád-pa* with accus. *Mil.*, **to alloy, adulterate,** *lhád-čan* **adulterated,** e.g. milk *C.*, *lhad-méd* **unadulterated, pure, genuine, real;** **tsig hlẹ̀ sor* C.* or **žug soṅ* W.* spurious words are admixed, falsehoods have been artfully introduced; *ṗyis lhád-du bčúg-pai tsig Tar.* a later interpolation. — 2. *Bal.*, **γlad**, **fatigued, exhausted.**

ལྷན་ *lhan* **together,** *lhán-gyis* (when referring to the subject of the action), *lhán-nas* (as ablative case), *lhán-du* (the most frq. form) **with one another, together,** *lhan-γčig* (*-tu*), and often *lhan-čig*(*-tu*) id.: *bdag dan lhan-γčig zan mi zá-na* if you will not eat together with me *Dzl.*, *rta bčus lhán-du rgyúgs-pa ltá-bui sgra* a noise as if ten horses were trotting together *Glr.*; *rtá-pa brgya dan lhán-du* accompanied by a hundred men on horseback *Glr.*; *lhan(-čig)-skyes(-pa)* **born together with**, e.g. the '*lha*' or '*dre*' born together with every human being *Mil.; lhan-skyes nad, rma* a hereditary disease or defect *Med. lhan-rgyás* 1. 'partner of the seal', i.e. a colleague using the same seal in official business (*lhan-rgyás-kyi ťé-tse*, or *spyi-dám*). 2. = *lhan-yčig*, **hlen-gyé-la ťsog* or *žug** they have come together.

ལྷན་པ་ *lhán-pa* I. vb., **to join, to unite,** **ka lán-če* W.* **to kiss,** **'u lán-če** id. resp.

II. sbst. 1. **a patch,** *lhán-pas klán-pa B.*, **hlém-pa gyág-pa* C.*, **gyáb-če* W.*, *débs-pa, rdáb-pa Mil.* **to patch, mend.** — 2. **spot, speck, blot,** place differently coloured, *od-zér šár-čin lhán-pa bžin-du* a sunbeam forming by reflection a bright spot *Dzl.; lhan-ťábs* **appendix, supplement,** title of a medical book.

ལྷབ་ལྷབ་པ་ *lhab-lháb-pa, lhabs-se lhabs Sch.*: 'to flutter to and fro, to glimmer, glisten' (?).

ལྷབ་ལྷུབ་ *lhab-lhúb* **wide, flowing,** *dar-bér lhab-lhúb* a wide silk cloak; prob. also sbst.: the moving to and fro, waving, *mé-tog-gi* of flowers *Do.*, **hlab-hlúb-tu sol* C.* loosen your dress! make yourself comfortable!

ལྷམ་ *lham* **boot,** also **shoe;** *mčil-lham* id.; *rgyá-lham* a Chinese boot, *sóg-lham* a Mongol boot.

**Comp.** *lham-skúd* twine, used by shoemakers *Schr.* — *lham-kan-čén* (prob. a Chinese word) strong Chinese boots *C.* — *lhám-mkan* shoemaker *Schr.* — *lham-sgróg* shoe-strap, latchet; string for lacing felt-leggings. — *lham-mťil* boot-sole. — *lham-yú* leg of a boot *Cs.*, *lham yu-rín* boots with long legs *Sch.* — *Sch.*: *lham-krád* or *-skrád* pieces of leather, used for the patching of soles; *lham-góg* worn-out boots; *lham-grám* the upper-leather, the vamp; *lham sgró-gu-čan* buskins; *lham yu-čád* a sort of slippers to which cotton leggings are sewed (?); *rtín-lham* quarter-piece (of a shoe).

ལྷམས་ཀྱིས་ *lháms-kyis* at once, all, every thing *Sch.* Cf. *lhem.*

ལྷས་(མ་) *lhas(-ma)* 1. **pen, fold,** inclosure for sheep *C., W.*; also **hlé-ra**. 2. also *lhés(-ma)* **braid; wicker-work; texture;** also of pastry, **twisted cake** or **bun, cracknel** (*W. *žim-zag**), also *lhas-dóg.*

ལྷས་བསྟན་ *lhas-bstán* n. of the birth-place of the mother of Buddha, *Ssk.* देवदर्शित.

ལྷས་པ་ *lhás-pa* v. under *slé-ba.*

ལྷས་བྱིན་ *lhas-byin,* देवदत्त, n. of a cousin of Buddha who, as the legends have it, was continually annoying Buddha by malicious artifices, whereby, however, the blameless character of the latter showed itself but the more conspicuously; hence proverbially used for any malicious character *Cs.*

ལྷིང་ *lhin*, cf. *líns-pa*; *lhin - skrán Sch.*: **a** tumor filled with matter, **an abscess,** *lhin-rtsa* a full vein; *lhin čád-pa Lt.*, acc. to *Sch.*: completely separated.

ལྷུ་ *lhu* **part, portion** of the body of an animal, = $\frac{1}{3}$ *zug*, *lhu-ťsigs bču-ynyís Sch.*: the 12 chief parts (of an animal) resulting from this way of dividing it, — but elsewhere 18 such parts are mentioned; *lhú-ru ysil-ba* to divide, to parcel out *Mil.*; **share** in plough-land, v. sub *spyod-pa* I, 2.

ལྷུག་ *lhug* v. *ldúg-pa* to pour *Cs.*

ལྷུག་པ་ *lhúg-pa, Cs.*: '*lhug-pa* and *lhug-ma* **prose;** *lhug-po* **wide, diffuse, luxurious,** *gos lhug-lhug-po* a very ample robe; *lhug-par* **amply, copiously, plentifully;** *lhug-par smra-ba* to speak diffusely, copiously, to speak in prose'. *Sch.* adds: '*lhugs* successive, continuous; *lhugs-ťsig* and *lhug-pa* continuous prose'. The principal meaning, however, seems to be: **uninterrupted, having no gaps;** unreserved; *lhúg-par bšád-pa* = *spas-ysán-med-par bšád-pa* to explain completely, without omitting any thing, **lug tán-če* Ld.* to give unreservedly, without limitation; hence also: liberally, plentifully; *mči-ma* *lhúg-par šor* or *byuṅ Mil.*, tears were flowing abundantly. — In some other passages the meaning of *lhúg-pa* is not quite clear.

ཧླུང་བ་ *lhúṅ-ba*, pf. of *ltúṅ-ba; lhuṅ lhuṅ snyán-pai sgra sgróg-čiṅ ₒbáb-bo* sweetly murmuring (the gentle stream) descends *Mil.*

ཧླུང་བཟེད་ *lhuṅ-bzéd, Ssk.* **पिण्डपात्र, the almsbowl** of Buddha and of the mendicant friars.

ཧླུན་ *lhun* **mass, bulk,** *lhún-čan* **massy, bulky; well-fed,** **lun-ťúg-po* W., lhun-čé-ba* very large; *lhun-(gyis) grub(-pa)* acc. to *Cs.*: 'formed in mass, or all at once', self-created, not contrived by human labour; *bgó-ba daṅ bzá-ba lhún-gyis grúb-pas* clothes and food coming forth of themselves *Dzl.*; also used of palaces, sacred buildings, images, though in such instances often only by way of compliment; *lhun-grúb* is also noun personal. — *lhún-po, ri-rab-lhún-po* the mountain of the universe, **Meru, Sumeru,** frq. *lhun-stúg Sch., lhun-ťúg Thgy.* very great, in reference to the mental darkness produced by sin; prob. also: considerable, sublime, grand.

ཧླུབ་པ་ *lhúb-pa* 1. sbst. **width,** *lhúb-pa-čan Cs., yan(s)-hlúb, hlub-hlúb W., C.* **wide,** of clothes. — 2. vb.: **to bind, tie, fasten,** e.g. ornaments to the ear *Ts.*, = *klúb-pa.*

ཧླུམས་ *lhums*, resp. for *mṅal* **the womb** frq., *lhúms-su žúgs-pai dus-mčód* sacrificial festival of the conception (of Buddha) *Sch.*

ཧླུར་ *lhur*, with *lén-pa* or *byéd-pa* c. acc. **to apply one's self to, bestow pains upon,** = *don-γnyér byéd-pa Dzl.* and elsewh.

ཧླེ་བ་ *lhé-ba* v. *slé-ba.*

ཧླེན་ *lhen Cs.* 'filth or dross in the bowels, causing obstruction'; acc. to others: **internal** excrescences, v. *skran*; *Sch.*: *lhen* or *lhen-sná* pit of the heart.

ཧླེབ་ *lheb, dbugs lheb-lheb-tu ₒdug-pa Pth.* **'ug leb leb ǰhed-de* C.* gasping for **breath.**

ཧླེམ་ *lhem* **now, at present, directly, instantly** *C.*; **all** (of them) cf. *lhams.*

ཧླེས་མ་ *lhés-ma* = *lhás-ma* 2; also: the act of twisting, plaiting, **hlé-ma gyáb-pa* C.* to twist, **to plait.**

ཧློ་ *lho* **south,** *lho-núb* south-west, *šar-lhó* south-east; *lhor, lho-ṕyógs-su* to the south, towards the south; *lhó-ḱa* prob. = *lho*; *lhó-ḱa món-nas ˛oṅs Mil.* they came from the Mon in the south; *lhó-pa, lho-ₒbrúg-pa* an inhabitant of Bhotan; *lhó-yul* acc. to *Cunn.* the original form of the name of that province which is now called Lāhul or Lāhōl by the Hindoos, and Lahoul by the English; *lho-búr Sch.* (also *lho-˛ú-ma*), = *ḱug-rna.*

ཧློག་པ་ *lhóg-pa, glóg-pa Cs.* **a large ulcer** or **sore,** *Sch.*: **carbuncle, anthrax,** *sbyóṅ-ba* to cure it; in *Med.* also *nya-lhóg* and *gag-lhóg* are mentioned. According to the description, however, which Tibetan physicians gave us of the *lhóg-pa*, it seems to denote a cancerous ulcer, against which they employ the *Aconitum ferox* of Nepal, or in default of it some other species of aconite.

ཧློང་ *lhoṅ Sch.* vexation, anger, wrath(?); but: '*lhoṅ šor* he has lost the *lhoṅ*', is said of one who was not equal to the exertions of incessant meditation, and who in consequence has lost his senses, v. sub *smyón-pa.*

ཧློད་པ་ *lhód-pa, glod-pa, lod-pa* or *-po, lhod, lhód-po* 1. **loose, relaxed, unstrung, slackened,** *yan-lág* of the limbs, e.g. when death approaches *S.g.*, **zúg-po lód-po čá-na* W.* when one gets tired (one cannot help yawning). *lhód-pa sgrim-pa* to tighten what is loose, *lhod lhod γtóṅ-ba* to slacken; fig. **'ó-ma lód-po* W.* the milk begins to fail, milk is scarce. — 2. of the mind: **easy, careless, unconcerned,** *lhód-de nyol čig* sleep well! sleep soundly! *Glr.*; *blo lhod gyis-la šod* relate the matter calmly, coolly *Mil.*; *šes-pa lhod-čiṅ* in good spirits, of a cheerful temper *Pth.*; *ťabs šig yod-kyi rgyal-po ťugs lhod mdzod* there is yet a help; therefore, o king, be of good cheer! *Pth.*

ཧློན་པ་ *lhón-pa, glón-pa* **to return, to give** or **pay back** *Cs.*

# ཨ

ཨ *a*, 1. the consonant which is formed in the lowest and hindmost part of the organs of speech, being produced by the opening of the glottis, like the Greek spiritus lenis, the Hebrew Aleph and the Arabian Elif. (In our modern languages the opening of the glottis is not regarded as a consonant, nor expressed by a particular letter or sign.) Combined with the Tibetan vowel-signs, ཨ, ཨི, ཨུ, ཨེ, ཨོ, it is pronounced *'a*, *'i*, *'u*, *'e*, *'o* (cf. འ). It is also called *skye-méd-pai yi-ge*, probably because all speaking depends on and is rendered possible only by a previous opening of the glottis; hence this letter is a symbol of the deity, of the *čós-sku* that was before every thing else. *Spyan-ras-zig*, therefore, addresses a celestial Buddha with *'a: 'a skye-méd rnam-dág čós-kyi dbyiṅs*. — 2. num.: 30.

ཨ་(འ?) *'a* (*ₒa?*) 1. in *Ld.* and *Kh.* the col. demonstr. pron., for *de* that (q.v.); **'á-ne** from thence, there, *'á-ru* there, thither, that way. — 2. *Lh.*, pronounced very short and sharp, **well? what is the matter? yes! here!**

ཨཿ *'a Cs.*: '*Ssk.*: अः, a mystical exclamation'.

ཨ་ཀ་(ཨ་ཁ?) *'á-ka* (*'á-ka?*) acc.to *Huc* II, 160 = *'á-ǰo Kh.*

ཨ་ཀ་རུ *'á-ka-ru Cs.*, v. *'á-ga-ru*.

ཨ་ཀཱ་ལ *'a-kā-la Lt.*, *Ssk.*: **untimely.**

ཨ་ཀྲོང *'a-kroṅ* an alpine plant, in *Lh. Arenaria Roylea.*

ཨ་ཁ་ཁ, ཨ་ཁག *'á-ka-ka*, *'a-kág* an exclamation expressive of contempt and detestation, opp. to *'á-la-la*; acc. to *Cs.* *'a-kag* is also adj. = *mi-sdug-pa*.

ཨ་ཁུ *'a-kú*, *W.* also *'a-kú*, col. for *kú-bo* 1. **father's brother, uncle** *Mil*, *C.*, *W.* — 2. **husband, consort** *W.*

ཨ་ག་རུ *'á-ga-ru*, अगरु, **aloe-wood,** agallochum, calambac.

ཨ་གྱིས *'a-gyis* caressing word used by mothers soothing their babies, prob. without any particular signification *Thgy.*

ཨ་ཅུག *'a-čúg* **ankle-bone** *Lt.*

ཨ་ཆུ, ཨ་ཆུ་ཆུ *'a-čú*, *'á-ču-čú* interj. expressive of pain from cold, hence *'a-čú-zer-ba* n. of one of the cold hells.

ཨ་ཆེ *'a-čé*, *'a-cé*, *Bal.* *'a-šé*, col. for *cé-že* 1. **an elder sister** of a female person. — 2. *W.* **wife, mistress, madam,** used as address and otherwise.

ཨ་ཇོ *'a-ǰó C.*, *W.*, *ǰo-ǰó C.* (v. *ǰó-bo*) 1. **an elder brother** of a male person. — 2. **Sir, Mr., gentleman, lord,** used in addressing and otherwise; also like our: **friend! ho there!** hollo! I say! *'a-ǰho lág C.* **the old Squire,** = *ga-gá Ld.*

ཨ་ཏི་ཤ *'a-ti-ša Ssk.*, *pŭl-du-byuṅ-ba Tib.*, n. of a celebrated Pandit of Bengal, who lived for many years in Tibet, and died there in the eleventh century of our era.

ཨ་ཐོ་བ *'a-tó-ba* beautiful, good *Sch* (?).

ཨ་འཐས *'a-ₒtas Pth.?*

ཨ་དོགས *'a-dogs Sch.* table(?)

ཨ་དོན *'a-dón Sch.*: 'without sexual distinction; sense of the letter *'a*'.

ཨ་དྲུང *'a-drúṅ C.* **horse-boy,** one tending horses.

ཨ་ན་(ན) *'á-na(-na)* an interjection expressive of grief *Sch.*

ཨ་ན་མ་ན *'a-na-ma-na Sch.*: having a striking likeness(?).

ཨ་ནུ *'á-nu* Hindi man's name, also used in Tibet *Glr.*

ཨ་ནེ *'á-ne* 1. = *né-ne-mo* **father's sister, aunt; grand-aunt** *Glr.* — 2. *Cs.*: **nun.**

3. *W.* **wife, partner, spouse,** *'*á-ne kúr-ce** to take a wife, to marry, **(s)kyá-wo 'á-ne kur cog** a layman is at liberty to marry; *'*á-ne-la có-ce** to treat, to use as a wife, sensu obsc. = to sleep with. — 4. **a woman, a female.** — 5. *Sch.* an old woman (?).

ཨ་པ་ '*á-pa* = '*á-p̓a.*

ཨ་པོ་ '*a-po Ü*: **building** (= **k̓ar-lén** *W.*), *'*á-po gyáb-pa** to construct a house, to build.

ཨ་པྲ་ '*á-pra Sch.* **zizel**, earless marmot, souslik (*Spermophilus citillus*).

ཨ་ཕ་ '*á-p̓a*, '*á-pa* col. for *p̓a*, in *B.* of rare occurrence; *'*á-pa čén-po** the elder, **čún-ṅu** the younger, of the husbands of a person's mother, hence occasionally = **uncle;** *'*á-pe ša** *W.* a vulgar oath; also (like *p̓a*) uncastrated male animal, cf. *p̓a.*

ཨ་ཕོ་ང་ '*a-p̓o-ṅá C.* col.: **I**, cf. *k̓o-bo-ṅá.*

ཨ་ཕྱི་ '*a-p̓yi Mil*, *'*a-p̓i*, '*a-pi**, for *p̓yi-mo* **grandmother.**

ཨ་ཕྱིམ་ '*a-p̓yim* **old woman, goody, dame** *Sch.*

ཨ་ཕྲག་ '*a-p̓rág Sch.*: the bosom of a garment, '*a-p̓rág-tu sdú-ba* to put into the bosom, = '*am-bág.*

ཨ་བ་དྷཱུ་ཏི་ '*a-wa-dhu-ti* v. *dhu-ti.*

ཨ་བང་ '*a-baṅ*, for *baṅ-po*, the husband of the father's or the mother's sister *Cs.*

ཨ་བི་ཥ་ '*a-bi-ša Ssk.*: 'antivenomous', n. of a medicinal herb *Wdṅ.*

ཨ་བོ་ '*a-bo* 1. *Sch.* = '*a-jo.* — 2. a medicine *S.g.*

ཨ་བོ་ཙེ་ '*a-bo-tse Sch.*: **'good, tolerable, middling'**, cf. *Bun.*: *eb-bo* good.

ཨ་བྱག་ '*a-byag* and '*a-˳bras* names of medicines *Med.*

ཨ་མ་ '*á-ma* col. and sometimes in *B.* = *ma* **mother;** *'*á-me ša** a vulgar oath; '*á-ma drin-čén* so a king addresses a wonder-working nun *Pth.*

ཨ་མ་གྱིས་ '*a-ma-gyis Cs.* interj., prob. similar to *a-gyis.*

ཨ་མི་དེ་བ་ '*a-mi-de-ba* the usual Tibetan corruption of अमिताभ, v. ˳*od-dpag-méd.*

ཨཱ་མྲ་ '*ā-mra Ssk.* **the mango tree and -fruit** *Dzl.*

ཨ་མྲི་ཏ་ '*a-mri-ta* (*Ssk.* अमृत **ambrosia;** also various fruits etc.), in the *Lt.* perh. the **guava** fruit, which in Hindoostani is now called *amrūt.*

ཨ་ཙ(་མ་) '*a-tsa(-ma)* interj. expressive of pain by touching hot objects *Sch.*; also used in various other instances, when disagreeably surprised, startled etc. *bdag ma gról-ba* ˳*di 'á-tsa-ma* alas! I am not yet released! *Thgr.*; '*á-tsa-ma yi-dwags snyiṅ re-rjé* alas! ye poor Yidags folk! *Mil.*

ཨ་ཙ་ར་ '*a-tsa-ra Mil.* a species of hobgoblins, or spectres; in *C.* a Bengalee, acc. to *Lew.* The observations of *Huc* (II, 271) concerning this word seem to be mixed with some errors.

ཨ་ཙཪྻ་ '*a-tsarya*, *Ssk.* आचार्य, **spiritual guide** or **father, instructor, professor, doctor.**

ཨ་ཚ(་ཚ་) '*a-ts̓a(-ts̓a)* an interj. expressing discomfort occasioned by heat.

ཨ་མཚར་ '*a-mts̓ar Sch.*: oh dear, what a wonder!

ཨ་ཛི་ན་ '*á-dza-na Wdṅ.*, '*á-dzi-na Stg.*, अजिन *Will.*: the hairy skin of a black antelope, which serves the religious student for a couch, seat, covering etc.; Tibetan writers use it for the animal itself: *ri-dwags 'á-dzi-nai págs-pa Stg.*

ཨ་ཞང་ '*a-žáṅ* 1. col. for *žáṅ-po* **mother's brother,** *'*a-žaṅ-ts̓á-wo** **nephew.** — 2. *Cs.*: 'an address' (?).

ཨ་ཝ་ '*á-wa* a medicinal herb *S.g.?*

ཨཱ་ཝརྟ་ '*ā-warta*, '*ā-barta* (*-na*) *Ssk.* ('whirl, whirlpool, eddy') a disease of the *rluṅ*, q.v.; perh. **dizziness?** *Med.*

ཨའུ་ཙི་ '*au-tsi* 1. *Sch.*: it is of no consequence, it does not matter. — 2. n. of a plant = *bya-po-tsi-tsi.*

ཨ་ཡ་ཟྭ་ཚོད་ '*a-ya-zwa-ts̓od* dead-nettle *Med.*

ཨ་ཡུ་ '*a-yu C.* (= *k̓u-yu*) **hornless,** of cattle.

ཨ་ར་ '*á-ra* **beard** *Ts.*

ཨ་ར༔ 'ā-rā *Hind.* **a saw.**

ཨ་ར་པ་ཙ་ན 'a-ra-pa-tsa-na a mystical and symbolical word, *Was.* (183)

ཨ་རག 'a-rág, resp. *bšes-rág C., ₒdon-rág W.*, **arrack, brandy,** the usual barley-brandy, which is distilled in the convents and in nearly every manor-house.

ཨ་རུ 'á-ru 1. prob. *Ssk.* a medicinal plant, *Med.* — 2. v. *'a.*

ཨ་རུ་ར 'á-ru-ra **myrobalan,** an astringent medicinal fruit *Med.* frq.

ཨ་རུམ 'a-rum a species of garlic, with a pale-red blossom, *Allium strictum.*

ཨ་རེ 'a-re an interj. the meaning of which is stated differently, *Mil.*; *'a-re pans* well then! throw it away!

ཨ་རོག 'a-róg *Sch.*: = *rogs-po, grogs,* **companion, mate, fellow, comrade, friend;** *'a-rog-kya* or *gya Sch.*: 'a complimentary phrase or form of salutation'.

ཨ་ལ་(ལ) 'á-la (-la) *Mil.*, also *'ál-la* id. interj. expressive of joyful surprise: aye, ah, that is capital! *dés-na 'á-la-la* well, that is excellent or splendid indeed! *Mil.;* also adjectively: **de san di 'á-la-la** *W.* this is much better than that!

ཨཱ་ལི 'á-li the Tibetan vowels, *'ā-li-kā-li* the series of the vowels together with the consonants; *'a-pren* id.

ཨ་ལི 'a-li *a* little *C.*

ཨ་ལི་ཁུག་ཏ 'a-li-kug-ta **a swallow** *Cs.*

ཨ་ལུང 'a-lún *Sch.* **buckle, clasp** (?).

ཨ་ལོང 'a-lón **a ring.**

ཨ་ཤད 'a-šád v. sub *ytúm-mo.*

ཨ་ཤུ 'a-šú **apricot.**

ཨ་ཤོ་ཀ 'a-šo-ka n. of a tree and of a king.

ཨ་སམ 'a-sám *Sch.*: a thick sauce or broth, soup; *'a-sbyár* a thin broth.

ཨ་སྲུ 'a-srú for *srú-mo* **aunt** *Sch.*

ཨ་གསལ་ལ 'a-ysál-la adv. **openly, manifestly, publicly,** = *mnon-súm-du.*

ཨ་ཧ་ཧ 'a-ha-há interj. expressing joy, pleasure, satisfaction.

ཨ་ཧོ་ཡེ 'a-ho-yé yea, nay even (?).

ཨག་པོ 'ág-po **bad** *C.*

ཨག་ཙེ 'ag-tsé *Melia Azedarachta,* **the 'neem'** of Anglo-Indians, an important remedy for cutaneous diseases.

ཨག་ཚོམ 'ag-tsóm *Glr.*, *'og-tsóm Sch.*, resp *žal-tsóm Pth.*, **beard of the chin, chin-tuft.**

ཨང 'an 1. sbst. = *ₒdoms? 'án-rta, 'án-ras* loin-cloth *C., W.*; *'an-tún* **under-garment,** χιτών, (hence also to be used for shirt and shift); *'an-rág* **trowsers,** breeches *Pth.* — 2. interj.: **well then! now then! well!** in French: *eh bien!* at the beginning of a speech also *'án-ge, 'án-ke, 'án-ki, Mil.*, without any regard to rank.

ཨང་གི 'án-gi or *'án-ki, Ssk.* अङ्क, **figure, number, cipher,** also *'an-grans, 'an-yig Cs.*; the last word, acc. to others, means **secret characters,** cryptography.

ཨང་གུ་ལི 'an-gu-li *Ssk.* **finger** *Do.*

ཨང་རྒར་འཇིག 'an-rgar-ₒjig acc. to *Lew.* **English,** *Hd. angrezi.*

ཨང་མ་ཙི 'an-ma-tsi *Sch.* **flies,** winged insects.

ཨན 'an *W.* **white chalk.**

ཨན་སྟོང 'an-ston *Med., Sch.*: cervical vertebra.

ཨན་གདོས 'an-γdos *C.*: **stocks,** **'an-dǒ-la ₒjúg-pa** to put (a person) into the stocks.

ཨན་འདར 'an-ₒdár *C.* 1. **board, plank, deal.** — 2. *lcags-kyi 'an-ₒdár Cs.* an iron instrument of torture; acc. to *Thgy.* a kind of press.

ཨནྡྲ་རྙི་ལ 'andra-rnyi-la *Lex.*, corrupted form for *'indra-ni-la.*

ཨམ་ཅོག, ཨམ་བག **'am-čog, 'am-bag** col. *C.* for *rna-mčog, snam-brag* **ear; bosom.**

ཨམ་བན am-ban a Chinese resident, Chinese superior civil officer, in the chief cities and provincial towns of the tributary countries of China.

**ཨར་ཀ་** *'ár-ka, 'ár-ga, 'ár-ka, 'ẹ́r-ka* 1. *Cs.* **marble.** — 2. **plaster-floor** made of pulverized marble and oil, also **'a-žál.**

**ཨར་མགོན་** *'ar-gon* an offspring of parents not having the same rank, nor the same religion, and not belonging to the same nation *Ld.*

**ཨ་རྒྃ་** *'a-rgam Sch.*: 'the offering of sacrifices'; *Will.*: अर्घ respectful offering to a god or Brâhman.

**ཨརྫ་ཀ་** *'ar-dza-ka Ssk., Sch.*: **cotton**, *'ár-dza-kai dóg-pa Glr.* cotton-capsule. (This signification is not to be found in our *Ssk.*-dictionaries.)

**ཨར་ལ་གཏད་པ་** *ár-la γtád-pa Sch.*: 'to be reduced to extremities, to extreme misery' (?).

**ཨལ་གཅིག་** *'al-γčig Sch.*: 'the one half of a pair, e.g. **one** eye', = *ya-γčig.*

**ཨལ་ད་** **'ál-ta** (for *da-lta*) *Bal.* 1. **now, at present.** — 2. **to-day.**

**ཨལ་ཏིང་** *'al-tiṅ, *al-tiṅ-la kur-če* W.* to carry something bulky tied up in the girdle.

**ཨལ་ཏོ་, ཨལ་ཙེ་** *'al-tó, 'al-tsé* earthen kitchen-pot *Ld.*

**ཨལ་ལ་** *'al-la* v. *'a-la-la.*

**ཨཤྨ་གརྦྷ་** *'asma-gar-bha, Tar.*: *nór-bu asma-gar-bha Schf.*: **emerald.**

**ཨི་** *'i* 1. **beer,** = *čaṅ, C.* — 2. vulgar pronunciation of *dbyi, *yi**, **the lynx.** — 3. num.: 60.

**ཨི་ཁུག་** *'i-ḱug, 'ig, W.* **hiccough, sob,** **'i-ḱug yóṅ-ṅa rag** I have got the hiccough, **'i-ḱug gyab dug** he hiccoughs.

**ཨིནྡྲ་གོ་པ་** *'indra-go-pa,* **इन्द्रगोप, cochineal;** yet among the substances devoted to a costly Chodten it is mentioned as one of the five divine jewels *Glr.* 7.

**ཨིནྡྲ་ནཱི་ལ་** *'indra-nī-la* **sapphire** (*Sch.*: emerald?).

**ཨུ་** *'u* num.: 90.

**ཨུ་ཅུག་** *'u-čúg,* with **čó-če* W.* **to persuade,** e.g. to buy something.

**ཨུ་དུམ་བ་ར་** *'u-dum-ba-ra* (*Ssk. Ficus glomerata*) in Tibetan literature a fabulous lotos of immense size.

**ཨུ་མ་** *'u-ma Ssk.*, prob. also spelled *dbú-ma,* n. of the wife of Siwa (Durga, Kāli etc.).

**ཨུ་ཚུགས་** *'u-tsúgs Sch.* = *'u-túg.*

**ཨུ་རྒྱན་** *'u-rgyán* 1. also *'oḍiyana Cs.*, (not mentioned in *Ssk.* dictionaries), often written in the abbreviated form ཨུྒྱན, a fabulous country in the north-west of India (though *Cs.* supposes it to be Ujain), frequently represented as a kind of paradise. — 2. now a noun personal of frq. occurrence; *'u-rgyan-padma* v. *padma-˳byuṅ-γnás.*

**ཨུག་ཆོས་** *'ug-čós* n. of a remedy *Med.*

**ཨུང་གུ་** *'úṅ-gu* **oil-lamp** *C.*

**ཨུཏྤ་ལ་, ཨུད་པ་ལ་** *'ut-pa-la, 'ud-pa-la* a blue lotos which is also used for medicinal purposes. In *Lh.* this name seems to be transferred to *Polemonium caeruleum.*

**ཨུན་ཐུག་** *'un-túg* v. *˳u-túg.*

**ཨུམ་** *'um* **a kiss,** **'um ǰór-wa* or *gyág-pa** **to kiss** *C.*

**ཨུར་རྒྱ་** *'ur-rgyá* a warm meal-porridge; fermenting **dough** *C.*

**ཨུར་རྡོ་** *'ur-rdó* v. *ur-rdó.*

**ཨུར་བ་** *'úr-ba* v. *dbúr-ba.*

**ཨུལ་འཐག་** *'ul-˳tág* col. for *γyul-˳tág.*

**ཨེ་** *'e* 1. in *C.* and later literature, an interrogative, pronounced short, accented, and usually put immediately before the vb. or the pron. which stands in the place of the vb.: **dé-mo ẹ́ yo'**? do you feel well? are you well? are you getting on well? *ḱyed daṅ 'e ˳prad mi śes* I do not know whether I shall see you again *Mil.*; *'e nus mi nus* whether we shall be able or not *Mil.*; rarely for **even if, though, although,** *'e sus kyaṅ mi túb-na* though nobody is really able to do it. — 2. num.: 120.

ཨེ་ཉ་ཡ་ *'e-nya-ya, 'e-na-ya, Ssk.* **एण**, a fabulous black antelope with short legs and black eyes.

ཨེ་མ་ *'é-ma, 'e-ma˳ó, 'e-ma-hó* interj. expressing joy, surprise, astonishment, **hey! hey day! indeed! you don't say so!** in asking, beseeching, requesting a person's attention: **please, pray, I say;** or expressive of lamentation, compassion: **alas! oh! would to God! O dear!** e.g.: *'é-ma séms-čan snyiṅ-re-rjé* alas, the poor people! *Glr.*

ཨེ་ཝྃ་ *'e-wam, Ssk.* **एवम्**, **yes, certainly, to be sure** *Wdk.* and elsewh.

ཨེ་ར་ཀ་ *'e-ra-ka Cs.*: 'n. of a country, Irak? Chaldaea?' (In *Ssk.* it denotes a sort of grass, or a woollen carpet.)

ཨེ་ལ་ *'e-la, Ssk.* **एला**, *'é-la prá-mo Wdṅ.* small **cardamoms**, seed of *Electeria Cardamomum.*

ཨེན་ཙམ་ *'én-tsam* **a little, some, a small bit,** *Ü* and *B.*

ཨེན་རེ་ *'en-ré* **quick, fast, speedy** *Sch.*

ཨེན་འདར་ *'en-˳dár* v. *'an-˳dar.*

ཨེམ་ཆི་ *'ém-či, 'ám-či* (Turkish word) **physician** *W.*

ཨེར་ཀ་ *'ér-ka C.* v. *'ár-ka.*

ཨོ་ *'o* 1. for འོ *˳o* **a kiss**, *Pth.* — 2. num.: 150.

ཨོ་དཀར་ *'o-dkár W.* = *lkog-dkór*, v. *lkóg-ma.*

ཨོ་ཌི་ཡན་ *'o-ḍi-yán* v. *'u-rgyán.*

ཨོནྡྲ་ *'óndra,* **ओड्र** *Oḍra*, the northern part of Orissa, *Wdk.*

ཨོ་མོ་སུ་ *'ó-mo-su* (Mongol word) **stocking** *C.*

ཨོ་ལྡོང་ *'o-ldóṅ, 'o-dóṅ,* col. **'ó-šo* Cs.*, **windpipe;** **'o-le* W.* **throat;** **'o-lé dám-te ši soṅ** he is suffocated.

ཨོ་ལོ་ *'ó-lo* (Mongol word?) *Sch.*: the place where two rivers flow together, **the confluence** of two rivers.

ཨོ་རྒྱན་ *'o-rgyán* = *'u-rgyán Pth.*

ཨོཾ་ *ōm, Ssk.* **ओम्**, mystical interjection, in later Hindooism the symbol of the Hindoo triad, in as much as it consists of the three sounds, a (Vishnu), u (Shiva), and m (Brahma). This interjection frequently occurs in the prayers of the northern Buddhists of Tibet, and especially in the famous 'six-syllable prayer', ཨོཾ་མ་ཎི་པདྨེ་ཧཱུྃ་, *ōm maṇi pad-me hūm*, the literal version of which is: 'O thou jewel in the lotus, *hūm*!' The person addressed in these words is not Buddha, but *Spyan-ras-γzigs* (v. *spyan*); by some he is thought to be the author of them. Concerning the import of this short apostrophy the best information is to be found *Köpp.* II, 59—61. — The Tibetans themselves are ignorant of the proper sense of these six syllables, if sense at all there be in them, and it is not unlikely that some shrewd priest invented this form of prayer, in order to furnish the common people with a formula or symbol, easily to be retained by the memory, and the frequent recital of which might satisfy their religious wants. And though there may be no obvious meaning in such exclamations or prayers, yet their efficacy is sure to be firmly believed in by a people, whose practical religion chiefly consists in the performance of certain rites and ceremonies, in a devout veneration of their Lamas, combined with frequent oblations to them, in abstaining from gross sins (regarding even the killing of live animals as such), and in the Pradakshina (v. *skor-ba* 2). — The numerous attempts that have been made to explain the Ommanipadmehūm satisfactorily, and to discover a deeper sense or even a hidden wisdom in it, have proved more or less unsuccessful. The most simple and popular, but also the flattest of these explanations is derived from the purely extrinsic circumstance, that the Sanskrit words of the prayer consist of six syllables, and accordingly it is suggested, that each of these syllables, when pronounced by a pious Buddhist, conveys a blessing upon one of the 'six classes of beings'. — The conjecture with which *Köpp.* closes his disquisition, is certainly nothing but a smart thought of that learned author.

ཨོཾ་ཨཱཿཧཱུྃ 'ō-'a-hūm, another mystical formula, used e. g. for transforming the *mi-γtsáṅ-ba bču* into *bdud-rtsi*, v. the explanation given under *naṅ-mčód.*

ཨོཾ་ཚུགས *'ō-tsugs Sch.*: propping one's chin on both fists, *'ō-tsúgs mdzad Mil.*

ཨོག་རྒྱ *'og-rgyá* **beard**; *'og-tsúm* = *'ag-tsóm.*

ཨོག་མ *'óg-ma* **throat, neck,** = *lkóg-ma*; *'og-žó* a beautiful white neck, a 'milk-neck' *Glr.*; *'og-skó* prob. = *'os-sko Med.*

ཨོང་གུ *'oṅ-gu* **a lamp,** *'oṅ-rás* **the wick** of a lamp *C.*

ཨོང་ལེ *'oṅ-lé W.* resp. for *'a*, at your service! at your commands!

ཨོང་ལོག *'oṅ-log* **ptarmigan** *Sch.*

ཨོམ་མོག *'om-móg* **throat and chest** *Sch.*

ཨོལ་མ *'ol-ma C.* **throat, windpipe,** = *'ol-ldoṅ*; **'ól-ma dám-te sé-pa** to strangle, throttle; *'ol-rko, 'ol-goṅ, 'ol-kroṅ* id., or acc. to others = *'ol-mdud* the fore-part of the larynx.

ཨོས་སྐོ *'os-sko*, also **ō-ku* C.* **the chin,** resp. *žal-ko.*

ཨོས་ཅོས *'os-čos Ts.* **ö-čö** *Pedicularis Hookeriana.*

ཨ

# ENGLISH-TIBETAN VOCABULARY.

# English-Tibetan Vocabulary.

The figures, here and there attached to Tibetan words, refer to the page where the respective article is to be found. — The accent is marked only when, exceptionally, it rests on the last syllable of a word.

## A

A, An, article *ċig* 140.
Abandon *skyur-ba*; *spoṅ-ba*; *˳bor-ba*.
Abate *ži-ba*.
Abbot *mḱan-po*.
Abdomen *čal*, esp. *sku-čál*.
Ability *nus-pa*; *rtsal*.
Ablative case *˳byuṅ-ḱuṅs*.
Able *mḱas-pa*; to be — *˳ḱyud-pa*; *lċogs-pa*; *nyan-pa*; *ťub-pa*; *nus-pa*; *ṕod-pa*; *˳ṫsugs-pa*; *ŝes-pa*.
Ablution *ḱrus*.
Abode *mċis-bráṅ*; *˳dug-γnas*; *˳dug-sa*; *γnas* (*-ṫsaṅ*); *γži-ma*.
Abolish *˳ǰig-pa*; *snub-pa*.
Abortion *skyur-ma*; *mṅal rlugs-pa*.
Abounding *rgyas-pa* 109, *mod-po*, *˳dzom-po*.
About *tsam-na*, *tsa-na*; round — v. *ṕyogs* 352; to be — *ča-ba* 152; *čas-pa*.
Above adv. *steṅ-na*; *bla*; *yan*, *yan-la* 506; prep. *ḱa-na*, *ḱa-ru*, *ḱa-la*, *ḱar* 34; *goṅ-du*; *ltag-nas*, *ltag*; *ťog-tu*.
Abridge *sdud-pa*.
Abridgment *zin-bris*.
Abroad v. *byes*; to go — *byes-su ˳gro-ba*.
Abscess *ču-búr*; *ṕol*.
Absolutely *ċis-kyaṅ*; *ga-na-méd*.
Abstinence *dge-ba*; *ṫsod-ŝes-pa* 452.
Abundant *ḱrigs*.
Abuse s. (reviling words) *skur-pa* 23; vb. a. (to revile) *skur ˳debs-pa* (*byed-pa*; *smra-ba*); *dma ˳bab-pa*; *smad-pa*.
Abyss *btsoṅ-doṅ*; *γyaṅ-sa*.
Academy *γtsug-lag-ḱáṅ*.
Accept *bžed-pa*, *bžes-pa*; *len-pa*.
Acceptable, to be — *ťad-pa*.
Access *˳gro-sa*; v. also *γtoṅ-ba* 208 and *m˳jal-ba* 173.
Accident *rkyen*; unfortunate — *˳gal-rkyén*; fatal — *bar-čád*; *byur*, *byus*.
Accompany *skyel-ba*; *zla-bo byed-pa*.
Accomplish v. *grub-pa*; *čom-pa*; *spyod-pa*; *rtsom-pa*.
Accomplished *pul-tu byuṅ-ba* 344.
Accomplishment *rtsal*; *yon-tan* 516.
Accord, Accordance *˳čam-pa*.
According to **naṅ-tar** *W. C.*; *daṅ sbyar-nas*; *bžin-du*.
Account s. *rtsis*, *lo-rgyús* 113; *γnas-tsúl*; on — of v. *rkyen*; *čed-du*; *ṕyir*; *slad-du*.
Account vb. a. *rtsis byed-pa* (*˳debs-pa*, *gyab-pa*).
Accountant *rtsis-pa*.
Accumulate *spuṅ-ba*.
Accurate *žib-pa*.
Accusation, false — *snyad*.
Accuse *˳gel-ba*; *rgol-ba*.
Accustomed *goms-pa*; *˳dris-pa*; to be — *˳dris-pa*.
Ache vb. n. *na-ba*.
Acid, Acidity *skyur-ba*.
Acknowledge *ḱas len-pa*; frq. only *smra-ba*, *zer-ba* etc.
Aconite *boṅ-ṅa*.
Acquaintance (friend) *ṅo-ŝés*.
Acquainted, to be — *bŝés-pa*.
Acquiesce *ḱo-ťag γċod-pa*; *mi rgol-ba*; *daṅ-du len-pa*.
Acquitted, to be — *rgyal-ba*.
Across *ṕred*, *˳ṕred*.
Act vb. *byed-pa*; *spyod-pa*; *bgyid-pa*; to — the part of *byed-pa*.
Action *spyod-pa*; *bya-ba*; *las*; former actions *sṅon-lás*.
Action (law-suit) *ḱrims*, *ŝags W.* 51.
Activity *spyod-pa*.

**Actual** *ṅes-pa-ċan*; *ṅo-rtóg*; *yáṅ-dag-pa.*
**Actually** *γži-nas.*
**Acute** *rno-ba.*
**Adage** *ḱa-dpe.*
**Add** *snon-pa*; *sre-ba*; *rǰes-su* ₒ*ǰug-pa*; v. ₒ*god-pa.*
**Addict, to** – one's self *sten-pa.*
**Adduce** v. *mťson-pa* and *dpe.*
**Adequate** ₒ*grig-pa*; *mťun-pa.*
**Adhere** ₒ*byor-ba*, ₒ*byar-ba*; *γnas-pa.*
**Adherent** *ṕyogs-pa*; ₒ*dzin-pa.*
**Adieu** v. *ṕyi-ṕyag* 347.
**Adibuddha** *kun-γži* 4.
**Adjust** *sbyor-ba*; *sgrig-pa*; ₒ*god-pa.*
**Admit** *γtoṅ-ba*; *ḱas len-pa.*
**Admonish** *skul-ba.*
**Admonition** *bskul-ba*, *bskul-ma*; *bslab-bya.*
**Adolescent** s. *ḱyeu.*
**Adore** *mos-pa.*
**Adorn** v. ₒ*god-pa*; *sgron-pa*; *brgyan-pa*; *spra-ba.*
**Adult** s. *če-mi*, *nar son-pa* 298.
**Adulterate** *slad-pa.*
**Adulterer** *šar-po*, adulteress *šar-mo.*
**Adultery, to commit** – v. ₒ*ǰug-pa* 177, *byi byed-pa*; *γyem byed-pa.*
**Advantage** *don*; *bogs*; ₒ*ḱyer-so*; *rgyal-ḱa*, *ḱa-rgyál.*
**Adversary** *ṕa-rol-po.*
**Advice** *bka-γdáms*; *ḱa-bsgos*; *ḱa-ta*, *ḱa-γdáms*; *gros*; *γdams-pa*; ₒ*dun-ma*; *man-ṅág*; to ask – *bgro-ba.*
**Advise** *γdam-pa*, ₒ*dom-pa.*
**Adviser** *bka-γdams-pa.*
**Affair** *don.*
**Affect** *bċos-pa* 147.
**Affection** *čags-pa*; *byams-pa*, *byams-sems*; *brtse-ba.*
**Affectionate** *brtse-ba-ċan.*
**Affix** *sbyor-ba.*
**Affliction** *sdug-pa*; *mya-ṅán*; *ťser-ka W.*
**Afore-said** *sňa-ma.*
**Afraid, to be** – *skrág-pa*, *dṅaṅ-ba*; ₒ*ǰigs-pa*; *bag ťsa-ba*; *bred-pa.*
**After** adv. *rgyab-tu*; *ṕyi* 349; ₒ*og*; *slad-na.*
**After** prep. *rǰes*, ₒ*og*; *slad*; *rtiṅ*; *mťar*; *nas.*
**After-birth** *ša-ma.*
**Afterwards** *rǰes-la*, *rǰes-su*; *rtiṅ-du*; *de-nas*; *ṕyin-čád*; *ṕyis*; *ṕyi-bžin*; *slad-nas*; *slar.*
**Again** *čed-du*; *ṕyir*; *slar*; *yaṅ*; – and – *yaṅ-nas yaṅ-du.*
**Age** *na-ťsód*, *na-so*; *dus.*
**Aged** *rgad-pa*; to be – *rga-ba.*
**Agent** *byed(-pa)-po*, *byed-mḱan*; *ťsab-po*, resp. *sku-ťsab.*
**Agressor** *sňa-rgol.*
**Agility** *byag-pa.*
**Agio** *non-ka*; *ṕar*; ₒ*dza.*
**Agitate** *dkrug-pa*; *skyod-pa*; *skyom-pa*; *sgul-ba*; to be agitated ₒ*gul-ba*; ₒ*ḱrug-pa.*
**Agitation** *ḱrag-*ₒ*ḱrúgs.*
**Ago** *sňun-la*; long – *sňa-mo-nas.*
**Agony** *γšin-*ₒ*ṕras*; *koṅ-*ₒ*ḱrúgs*; *sems ḱoṅ-du* ₒ*ťsul-pa.*
**Agree** ₒ*grig-pa*; ₒ*čam-pa*; *stun-pa*; *mťun-pa.*
**Agreeable** *dga-ba*; *yid-du* ₒ*oṅ-ba.*
**Agreement** *ḱa-čád*, resp. *zal-čád*; *gan-rgyá*; *čad*, *čad-šo*; ₒ*čam-pa*; *bzaṅ.*
**Agriculture** *so-nám(s).*
**Ague** *ťsad-pai nád*; *ťsan-zug W.*
**Aim** s. ₒ*gro-sa* 102; ₒ*ben.*
**Aim** vb. *zir-ba*; v. *γtod-pa* no. 3.
**Air** (atmospheric air) *ṅá-ra*; *ṅad*; *rluṅ*; cold – *ṅad.*
**Air** (tune) *mgur*, *glu*, *dbyaṅs.*
**Air** (mien) *ṅo*, *γdoṅ.*
**Alabaster** *ḱa-ma-ru*; *ťod-le-kór.*
**Alas** *kye-ma.*
**Alienism** ₒ*gron.*
**Alight** ₒ*bab-pa*, resp. *γšol-ba.*
**Alive** *γson-po.*
**All** *kun*; v. *gaṅ*; *ťams-ċád*; *mťá-dag*, *ťsad*; *yoṅs*; – right! *ťsaṅ-*ₒ*grig*; – seeing *kun-γzigs*; – uniting *kun-*ₒ*dus*; not at – *tsam yaṅ mi (ma)*; *ye mi (ma).*
**Allegory** ₒ*dra-dpe.*
**Allow** *γnaṅ-ba*; to be – ed *čog-pa*, *ruṅ-ba.*
**Almanac** *lo-ťó.*
**Almighty** *kun-dbaṅ.*
**Almond** *ba-dám.*
**Alms** *ldom-bu*; *sloṅ-mo*; *bsod-snyóms.*
**Alone** *γċig*, *γcig-γċig*, *γċig-pu*, *γċig-po.*
**Along with** *žor-la.*
**Alphabet** *ka-ṕreṅ*, *ka-ḱá*; *kā-li* 2.
**Alpine pastures** *neu-γsiṅ*; *ne-ťaṅ C.*
**Also** *yaṅ* 505.
**Altar** *mčod-stégs*, *mčod-ḱri.*
**Alter** *sgyur-ba*; *spo-ba.*
**Alteration** ₒ*gyur-ba.*
**Although** *yaṅ* 505.
**Altogether** *kun*, *yoṅs-su.*
**Alum** *ḱa-ru-ťsa*; *lče-myaṅ-ťsá.*
**Always** *rgyun-du*; *rtag-tu*; *nam-yaṅ.*
**Amalgam** *gyim-bág.*
**Ambassador** *ṕo-nya.*
**Amber** *spos-šél.*
**Ambitious** *grags-pa-la čags-pa*; *mťon-dod-ċan.*
**Ambush** v. (*lkog-*)ₒ*ǰab.*
**Amendment** *žu-dág*, *žus-dág.*
**Among** *naṅ*, *naṅ-na* 301; *las* 546.
**Amusement** *γyeṅ-rtséd.*
**Analogy** v. *dpe.*
**Anasarca** *pags-ču.*
**Anatomy** *lus-kyi γnas-lugs.*
**Ancestor** *ṕa-mes*, *mes-po*; *brgyud.*

Ancient *sña-ba*; — ly *sña-sor*; ***sňon-dús.***
And *dañ* 248; v. also *čiñ* 140.
Angel *p̓o-nya* 345.
Anger *k̓ro-ba*; *k̓oñ-k̓ro*; *k̓on-pa*; *sro*, resp. *tugs-sro W.*; *že-sdañ*.
Angle *grwa* 75; *gru*.
Angry *k̓ro-ba*, *k̓ro-bo*, *k̓ro-mo*; to be — *ₒk̓ro-ba*; *sdañ-ba*.
Angular *zul-ma*.
Animal s. *dud-ₒgro*; *srog-čágs*.
Animated being *srog-čágs*; *sems-čan*.
Animosity *ₒk̓añ*.
Annals *lo-rgyús*; — of the kings *rgyal-rábs*.
Annihilate *med-par byed-pa*; to be annihilated *med-par ₒgyur-ba*.
Annotation *mčan-bu*.
Announce *lon sgyur-ba*; *sbrón-pa*; *p̓rin smra-ba*; *šes-par byed-pa*.
Annoy *ₒk̓añ-ba*; *sñog-pa*; *sun ₒǰug-pa*.
Annually *lo-ltar*, *lo dañ lo*.
Anoint *skud-pa*; *bsgo-ba*; *ₒbyug-pa*.
Another *bdag-méd*; *γžan-ma*.
Answer vb. *lan ₒdebs-pa*.
Ant *gre-mog-ₒbu*; *grog-ma*.
Antagonist *ₒt̓ab-ya*; *p̓a-rol-pa* (or *po*).
Antelope *dgo-ba*; the Tibetan — *γtsod*, *btsod*, *γtso*.
Antidote *γnyen-po*.
Antipathy *žen-lóg*.
Antiquity *sña-dús*, *sña-ba*; *sňon-tsé*, *sňon-dus*, *sňon-rabs*.
Anus ***rkub***; *γžañ*, *γžañ-k̓a*; *bšañ-lám*.
Anxiety **k̓og-t̓úg**; col. *nyams-ña*.
Anxious (*sems*) *k̓oñ-du čud-pa*; v. also *bag-t̓sa*.
Any v. *gañ* 65; — one *gañ žig*; — thing *či žig*, *či-yañ*; — whatever *čañ*.
Apathy *btañ-snyoms*; *byar-méd*.
Aperture *sgo*; *bu-ga*.
Apostle *mi-sná*.
Apothecary's shop *sman-k̓añ*.
Apparition *snañ-ba*; *žal-γzigs*.
Appear *ₒčar-ba*; *ston-pa*; *snañ-ba*; *ₒbyuñ-ba*; *yod-par ₒgyur-ba*.
Appearance *ₒk̓yer-so*; *ča-byád*, *ča-lugs*; *čas*; *snañ-t̓súl*.
Appease *ži-bar byed-pa*.
Appendix *k̓a-skoñ*.
Appertain *γtogs-pa*.
Appetite *k̓am*; *dañ-ga*.
Apple *ku-šu*; *sli*; — of the eye *spyan-ₒbras*.
Application *ₒbad-pa*; *brtson-ₒgrus*.
Apply *bkan-pa*; to — one's self *brtson-pa*.
Appoint *skul-ba*; *sko-ba*; *ₒgel-ba*; *ₒčol-ba*; *ₒǰug-pa*.
Apprehend *γčags-pa*; *dogs-pa*.
Apprentice *mčan-bu*.
**Approach** vb. *k̓ad-pa*; *nye-ba*; *bsnyen-pa*.
**Approach** s. *ₒgro-sa*.
**Approve** ***bžed-pa***.
Appurtenance *rgyu-čá*; —s ***skor***.
Apricot *k̓am-bu*; *ču-li*, *čo-li*; dried — *ču-li C.*, *p̓a-tiñ W.*; *mña-ris k̓am-bu C.*
Apron *dun-k̓ebs*, *pañ-k̓ebs*.
Aqueduct *yur-ba*.
Arch *γžu*, *γžu-mo*.
Archer *ₒp̓oñ-mk̓an*; —y *ₒp̓oñ*.
Architect *rtsig-dpón*.
Archives *yig-t̓sáñ*.
Area v. *dkyil-ₒk̓or*; *k̓yon*, *rgya-k̓yón*; *ču-žéñ*.
Argali *γnyan*.
Argue *bgro-ba*, *rtsod-pa*.
Argument *mñon-rtágs*; *rtags*.
Arise *skye-ba*; *ₒk̓or-ba*; *ₒk̓ruñ-ba*; *čags-pa*; *ldañ-ba*.
Arm *lag*(*-pa*), resp. *p̓yag*.
Armful *lag-kód*; v. also *pañ*.
Armour *go-k̓ráb*; *go-ča*.
Armpit *mčan-kuñ*.
Arms *mt̓son*, *mt̓son-ča*, *ₒt̓ab-grabs*.
Army *dpuñ*; *dmag*; *dmag-dpúñ*.
Aroma *ñad*.
Aromatic *ñad-čan*.
Arrange *sgrig-pa*; *ₒǰog-pa*; *γtan-la ₒbebs-pa* 205.
Arrangement *grabs*; *rgyu*; *γnas-lugs*.
Arrive *sleb-pa*; *ₒbyon-pa*; *ₒbyor-ba*.
Arrogance *ña-rgyal*; *p̓o-so*.
Arrow *mda*.
Arsenal *go-k̓áñ*.
Arsenic *ba-bla*.
Art *sgyu-rtsál*; *bzo*.
Artery *rtsa-dkár*; *rluñ-rtsa*.
Artifice *sgyu*.
Artificial *bčos-pa*.
Artist *bzo-pa*.
As (like) *ltar*; *bžin-du*; (when) v. *čiñ* 140; *na* 299; *pas* 323; as — as *tsam* 430; — far — *tsam-du*, *bar-du*, *t̓ug*, *t̓sug-pa*; — much — *ga-tsám*; — soon — *ma-k̓ád*, *ma-t̓ag-tu*.
Ascend *ₒdzeg-pa*.
Ascending node *sgra-γčán*.
Ascetic s. *sgom-po*, *sgom-mk̓an*; *sdom-sruñ*.
Ashamed, to feel — *skyeñ-ba*; *k̓rel-ba*; *ₒdzem-pa*.
Ash-coloured *gro-mo*.
Ashes *gog-t̓ál*; *t̓al-ba*.
Aside *zur-du*; *logs-su*, *logs-la*.
Ask *ₒdri-ba*, *γsol-ba*, *žu-ba*; *γšer-ba*; *sloñ-ba*; 'if one asks so' v. *če-na* 142.
Asleep, to fall — *γnyid-du ₒgro-ba*.
Aspire *snyeg-pa*.
Ass *boñ-bu*, *boñ-bo*; wild — *rkyañ*.
Assailant *sña-rgol*.
Assassinate v. *ǰab-pa* 174.
Assemblage *k̓rod-pa*; *tsogs*.
Assemble vb. n. *ₒdu-ba*; *ₒtsogs-pa*; *lhags-pa*; vb. a. *sdud-pa*; *sog-pa*.
Assert *dam ₒča-ba*; *bžed-pa*.
Assiduous *brtson-pa-čan*.

Assist *zla-bo* or *grogs byed-pa.*
Assistance *skyabs*; *skyobs*; *ra-mdu.*
Assistant *grogs*; *ya-do W.*; *ra-mda-pa.*
Associate s. *grogs*; *zla-bo*; *ya-do W.*; *rogs.*
Associate vb. *ₒtsogs-pa*; to be —d *ₒgrogs-pa.*
Assume *ₒčaṅ-ba.*
Assurance *γdeṅ*; *blo-γtád, blo-γdéṅ.*
Asterism *skar-ma.*
Asthma *dbugs rdzaṅ-ba.*
Astonished, to be — *ha-las-pa.*
Astonishment *ṅo-mtsár*; *ya-mtsan.*
Astray, to go — *ₒkyar-ba*; v. also sub *yan-pa* 506.
Astride, to put — *skyon-pa.*
Astringent *bska-ba.*
Astrology *skar-dpyád, skar-rtsis.*
Astronomy *skar-rtsis* 439.
Asunder *so-sor* 578; to tear — *ₒdral-ba.*
At *kar*; *mdun-du*; *na* 298; *rtsar* 437.
Athlete *gyad.*
Atmosphere *rluṅ-gyi dkyil-ₒkor* 11.
Atom *rdul.*
Atonement *sdig-bšágs.*
Attach *ₒdogs-pa*; *sdom-pa, rtod-pa.*
Attached *zug-pa C.* 466; to be — *čags-pa*; *žen-pa.*
Attachment *ₒkri-ba*; *čags-pa*; *žen-ₒdzin.*
Attack *rub-pa.*
Attain *sgrub-pa*; *tob-pa*; *rnyed-pa*; v. also *pyin-pa.*
Attend vb. n. *skyoṅ-ba*; vb. a. *zla-bo byed-pa*; *nya-ra byed-pa.*
Attendant *ₒkor, ₒkor-mkan*; *ₒkor-γyog, γyog-ₒkor.*
Attention *γnyer-ka*; *zon.*
Attentive *γčaṅ-po.*
Attitude *stans*; *spyod-lam*; *rnam-ₒgyur, tsul, sdod-tsul.*
Attribute s. *brjod-pa* gramm.; *rtags*; *mtsan, mtsan-nyid.*
Auction *ni-lam.*
Auditory (in a monastery) *kun-dga-ra-ba* 4.
Augment vb. n. *rgyas-pa*; *ₒpel-ba*; vb. a. *spel-ba.*
Aunt *ne-ne-mo*; *'a-ne*; *sru.*
Auspice *ča*; *rten-ₒbrél.*
Authentic *ṅes-pa*
Author *byed-mkan*; *žal-γdams bris-mkan* 473.
Authority *čab*; *mtu.*
Authorize *dbaṅ skur-ba.*
Autumn *ston, ston-ka.*
Avalanche *ka-rúd.*
Avarice *ser-sna*; *ham-pa.*
Aversion *skyo-šas*; *krel*; to feel an — *skyo-ba.*
Avert *zlog-pa*; *γčod-pa.*
Avoid *γčod-pa*; *spoṅ-ba*; *ₒdzem-pa.*
Await *sgug-pa.*
Away *par* 341; *yas* 508.
Awkward *rtsal-méd*; *mi šes-pa.*
Awn *gra-ma.*
Awry *kyom-kyóm*; *ča-čús*; *yo-ba.*
Axe *sta-ré*; *ste-po.*
Axiom *γži-ma.*
Axle-tree *srog-šiṅ.*
Ay *ₒo-ná.*

# B

Babbling s. *čol-čúṅ.*
Baby *pru-gu čuṅ-ṅu.*
Back s. *rgyab*; *ltag-pa*; the small of the — *sgal-pa.*
Back adv. *rgyab-tu*; *pyir.*
Background *mtil.*
Bacon *sbo-tsil.*
Bad *ṅan-pa*; *tu-ba*; *gyi-na*; *btsog-po W.*
Badger *grum-pa.*
Bag *sgyiu, sgyig-gu*; *sgye-mo*; *pad*; leather — *rkyal-pa*; small — *rkyal-bu.*
Bail (person) *dge-rgán*; *lag-mí.*
Bakehouse *bkad-sa.*
Baker *γyos-mkan.*
Balance (pair of scales) *tu-lā*; *bat-ti*; *sraṅ.*
Balcony *rab-γsál.*
Bald *ter.*
Ball *go-la*; *bo-lo*; musket — *rdeu C., rin-di W.*; cannon — *tu-lúm.*
Ballista *sgyogs.*
Balustrade *lag-γžúṅs.*
Banana *skyes-sdóṅ.*
Band (gang) *kyu, kyu-bo.*
Bandage *ras-tág*; *leb-ma, leb-túgs.*
Bandeleer *ga-ša.*
Bandy-legged *rkaṅ-kyóg.*
Banish *spyug-pa.*
Bank (shore) *ₒkris*; *ₒgram*; *ṅogs*; *dṅo*; — of a river *ču-ka, ču-ₒgram, ču-mta.*
Banker *bun-bdág.*
Banquet s. *mgron.*
Baptism *krus* 51.
Baptize *krus γsol-ba.*
Barbarian *kla-klo.*
Barbarous *ₒkob.*
Barber *ₒbreg-mkan.*
Barberry *skyer-pa W.*
Bare *rjen-pa*; — footed *rkaṅ-rjén.*
Bark s. *pags-pa*; *šun-pa*; — of a species of willow *sgro-ba*; — of the birch-tree *gro-ga.*

Bark vb. n. *zug-pa.*
Barley *nas*; *so-ba*; boiled — *glum*; — corn *nas.*
Barm *ṕabs*; *sbaṅ-ču.*
Barter vb. *ṙje-ba*; *sdeb-pa.*
Base s. *γži*; *rmaṅ.*
Bashful *ṅo-bab-pa*; *dzem-bag-čan.*
Bashfulness *ḱrel.*
Basin *ka-to-ra*; *zi-liṅ-pan-tse.*
Basis *ₒgram-γži*; *ma-γži.*
Basket *pe-ra*; *tse-po*; *γzed-ma*; a small — of reed *bag-tse.*
Bat (animal) *ṕa-wáṅ.*
Bath *ḱrus.*
Bathe *ₒḱru-ba*, *ₒḱrud-pa.*
Battle *γyul*, *ₒṫab-mo.*
Bawling adj. *ċa-ċo-ċan.*
Bay (gulf) *ḱug*; *ċu-ḱúg*; *mṫso-lág.*
Bay-coloured *smug-po.*
Bayonet *san-gin W.*
Bazar *ḱrom.*
Be *yin-pa*, resp. *lags-pa*; *yod-pa*; *ₒdug-pa*; *mčis-pa*; *mṅa-ba*; *γnas-pa*; there is, there are *ₒdug*; *mčis.*
Beadle (in a monastery) *dge-bskós*; *dge-γyóg.*
Beam (timber) *γduṅ-ma*; — of light *γzer*; *ₒod-γzér.*
Bear vb. a. (to bring forth) *btsa-ba*; *skyed-pa*; (to carry) *ₒḱur-ba*, *ₒḱyer-ba*; *ṫeg-pa*, *ₒṫogs-pa*; (to suffer) *γzod-pa*, *ṫub-pa.*
Bear s, brown — *dom*; yellow — *dred* 264; the Great Bear *smin-bdún.*
Beard *rgya-bo*; *sma-ra*; *'ag-tsóm*; — of corn *gra-ma.*
Beast *dud-ₒgro*; — of burden *ḱal-ma*; — of prey *γċan-zán.*
Beat *rgyab-pa*; *rduṅ-ba*; *rdegs-pa*; *ₒṕam-par byed-pa*; to — the drum *skrog-pa*; to — the gong, the cymbal v. *ₒḱrol-ba*; to be beaten *ₒṕam-pa.*
Beautiful *mdzes-pa*; *bzaṅ-ba*; *legs-pa*; *sdug-pa*; *dga-ba*; *bde-ba*; — appearance or colour *bkrag*; *mdaṅs*; — form *rnam-ₒgyúr.*
Because v. *kyi* 6; *pas* 323.
Beckon *lag-brdá byed-pa.*
Become *skye-ba*; *ₒgyur-ba*; *ča-ba W.*
Becoming (comely), to be — *ₒos-pa.*
Bed *mčis-mál*; *nyal-ḱri.*
Bed (garden) *ṫsas-ḱaṅ.*
Bedding *mal-gós*, *mal-čá*; *γzim-čá.*
Bedfellow *mal-grogs*, resp. *γzim-grogs.*
Bedstead *mal-ḱri*; *mčis-mál.*
Bee *buṅ-ba*; *sbraṅ-ma.*
Beer *čaṅ*; — carousal *čaṅ-sa*; — house *čaṅ-ḱaṅ.*
Beetle *sbur-pa.*
Befool *mgo skor-ba.*
Before adv. *sṅa-ma*, *sṅa-góṅ* 135; *sṅan*, *sṅar*, *sṅun* 136; *sṅon*, *sṅon-du* 137; prep. *druṅ-du* 263; *mdun-du* 273.
Beforehand v. *sṅa*; *sṅan*, *sṅar*; to be — *sṅa-ba.*
Beg *žu-ba*; *γsol-ba.*
Beget *bšo-ba*; *skyed-pa.*
Beggar *spraṅ-po*; *ldom-bu-ba*; — boy *spraṅ-ṕrúg.*
Begin vb. n. *čas-pa*; *ǰug-pa*; *mgo ₒdzug-pa*; to — to exist *skye-ba*; vb. a. *rtsom-pa*; *ₒdzugs-pa.*
Beginner *las-daṅ-po-pa.*
Beginning s. *mgo*, *mgo-ma*; *ₒgo-ma*; *sgo-mo*; *sṅon-ma*; *ṫog-ma*; — and end (head and tail) *mgo-mǰug.*
Begotten *čad-pa*; to be — *čags-pa.*
Behalf v. *don* no. 3, 259.
Behave *ₒgrul-ba.*
Behaviour *rnam-ₒgyur*; *spyod-pa.*
Behead *ske γċod-pa.*
Behind adv. *rtiṅ*; *ṕa-rol-na* 338; *ṕyi*, *ṕyis*; prep. *ₒgab*; v. *rgyab* 107.
Behold interj. *kye-hó* 7.
Being s. *ₒgro-ba*; *lus-ċan*, *sems-ċan.*
Belch s. *sgreg-pa*; vb. n. *sgreg-pa ₒdon-pa.*
Believe vb. n. *dad-pa* 249; vb. a. *yid* (*ṫugs* or *blden*) *čes-pa.*
Bell *dril*; — metal *mḱar-ba*, *ₒḱar-ba*; — wether *ḱyu-mčóg.*
Bellows *sbud-pa.*
Belly *grod-pa*; *lto-ba*, *γsus-pa.*
Belong *γtogs-pa*; *mṅa-ba*; belonging together *ṫe-mḱan W.*
Beloved *γċes-pa*; *mon-ža-ċan.*
Below adv. *ma* 408; *man-čád*, *man-čód*; prep. *ₒog* 501.
Bench *gral.*
Bend vb. a. *ḱug-ḱúg byed-pa*; *skyil-ba*; *dgu-ba*; *gugs-pa*; *gum-pa*; *ₒdud-pa*; vb. n. *mgo dgur-ba*; *dgye-ba.*
Benefit v. *skyed* 29; *don* no. 3, 259; *ṕan-pa*, *ṕan-yón*; for the — of *ṕyogs-su*; *don-du*
Benevolence *pan-pai sems.*
Bent (crooked) *ḱoṅs*; *ₒḱyog-po*; *gug-ge-ba*; *dgu-ba.*
Benumbed v. *sbrid-pa.*
Bereave *ₒṕral-ba*; to be bereft *ₒbral-ba.*
Besides *ḱa-ru*, *ḱar*; *steṅ-du*; *min*, *min-pa.*
Besiege *skor-ba.*
Besprinkle *čag-čág byed-pa* or *ₒdebs-pa.*
Best s. *mčog* 166; *don* no. 3, 259.
Bestow *sbyin-pa*; *ster-ba.*
Better, to get the — of *ṫub-pa*; *rgyal-ba.*
Between *bar-la*, *de-bár*; *γseb-na*, *γseb-la*; from — *bar-nas.*
Beverage *skyems*; *btuṅ-ba* 244.
Beyond *ṕa-rol-na*; *ṕan-čád.*
Bhotan *ₒbrug-pa.*
Bice, blue — *sṅo-skyá.*

Bid *sgo-ba*; *ˌjug-pa*; *ˌdom-pa*.
Bier *k̔yogs*; *dgu-k̔ri*.
Big *čen-po*; — with child *sems-čan daṅ ldan-pa*; — with young *sbrum-pa*.
Bigness *k̔o-lág*.
Bile *mk̔ris-pa*.
Billet of wood *mgal-pa*; *śiṅ-dum*.
Billow *ču-ri*, *ču-rlabs*; *dba-klóṅ*.
Bind *ˌčiṅ-ba*; *ˌdogs-pa*; *sdom-pa*; *ˌk̔yig-pa*.
Biped *rkaṅ-γnyis-pa*.
Birch-tree *stag-pa*.
Bird *bya*; *dab-čágs*; little — *mčil-pa*.
Birdcage *bya-k̔áṅ*.
Birdsnest *bya-ts̔áṅ*.
Birth v. *skye-ba* 28; high — *skye-ba mto-ba*; low — *skye-ba dma-ba*.
Birthplace *skye-γnás*.
Bishop *do-dam-pa* 257.
Bison (Indian) *glaṅ-to*.
Bit (small piece) *k̔am*, *k̔am-ts̔ád*; *čag-dúm*; *brul*.
Bit (of a bridle) *srab-lčágs*.
Bitch *k̔yi-mo*.
Bite vb. *rmug-pa*; *ˌča-ba*.
Bitter *k̔a*, *k̔a-po*, *k̔a-ba* 36.
Bittern *ču-skyar*.
Bitumen *brag-žún*.
Black adj. *nag-po*.
Black s. (centre of a target) *rtags*.
Blacksmith *lčags-mgár*.
Bladder (urinary) *lgaṅ-pa*.
Blade (of grass) *ˌjag-ma*; *sog-ma*.
Blade (of a sword) *lče*.
Blame vb. a. *spyó-ba*; *smad-pa*, *smod-pa*.
Blame s. *klan-ka*.
Blank adj. *stoṅ-pa*.
Blanket *grum-tse*; *tsa-dar*; *ča-ra* 152; *śa-pos Ld.*
Blasphemy *skur-pa*.
Blast vb. *γčog-pa*.
Blaze s. *mdoṅs*.
Bleat *ˌba-ba*.
Bleed *γtar-ba*, *rtsa γčod-pa*.
Bless *sṅo-ba*.
Blessed *skal-ldán*; *bde-ˌgro*; *γyaṅ-čan*.
Blessing s. *byin*, *byin-rlábs*; *bkra-śis*; *bsṅo-ba*; *p̔an-yón*; *γyaṅ*; *rgyan* 107.
Blind *mdoṅs-pa*; *žar-ba*, *mig-žár*; *loṅ-ba*.
Blister s. (pustule) *ču-sgaṅ*; *ču-bur*; (plaster) *ˌjibs-sman*.
Blister vb. *ˌjibs-pa*; *ˌjibs-sman ˌjug-pa*.
Blood *k̔rag*; —y *k̔rag-čan*.
Blooming *bkra-ba*.
Blossom vb. *ˌbar-ba*.
Blot out *ˌp̔yid-pa*; *sel-ba*.
Blow vb. *ˌbud-pa*.
Blow s. *lčag*.
Blue *sṅon-po*, *sṅo-bo*; deep — *sṅo-nag*; pale — *sṅo-skyá*; *sṅo-saṅs*; sky — *mt̔iṅ*.
Bluff s. *gad-pa*.
Blunt *rtul-po*; vb. also *k̔a* IV. no. 5.
Blushing (the act of) *ṅo-ts̔a*.
Board s. *spaṅ-léb*; *śiṅ-léb*; *glegs*; *sgo-rnám*; — of a door *sgo-glégs*; — of a ship *zur*.
Boast vb. *rlom-pa*.
Boasting s. *k̔a-ts̔o*, *k̔a-p̔o*; *yus*.
Boat *gru*.
Boatman *gru-pa*; *ko-mk̔an*; *mnyan-pa*.
Bodily *dṅos-su*; *mṅon-sum-du*; *žal-dṅós*.
Body *lus*; *γzugs*; *sku*; — linen *gos-lág*.
Boil s. (ulcer) *ču-búr*; *śa-búr W.*
Boil vb. a. *skol-ba*; to — down *sgor-ba*; vb. n. *ˌk̔ol-ba*; to — over *lud-pa*.
Boiling adj. *k̔ol-pa*, *k̔ol-ma*.
Boldness *ṅo-mig*; *rtul-p̔od-pa*.
Bolster *sṅas*; *γdan*.
Bolt s. *bur*; v. also *γya* and *si-ri*.
Bolt vb. a. *γya rgyab-pa*; *si-ri čug-če W.*
Bond *ˌdzin*; *zin-bris*.
Bonds *bčiṅ-ba*, *bčiṅs-pa*; *ˌčiṅ-ba*.
Bone *γduṅ*; *rus-pa*; —s of fish *gra-ma*.
Book *dpe*; *glegs-bám*; *po-ti*.
Books (literature) *čos*; book-language *čos-skad*.
Bookstand *dpe-k̔ri*.
Boot *lham*; leather half-boot *krad-pa* 8.
Border s. *gru*; *mt̔a-ma*; *sna*; *mu*; *mts̔ams*.
Bore vb. *rtol-ba*; *ˌbigs-pa*.
Born *čad-pa*; to be — *skye-ba*; *btsa-ba*; *ˌk̔ruṅ-ba*, *kruṅs-pa*; *ltams-pa*.
Borough *groṅ-ts̔o*.
Borrow *skyi-ba*; *brnyan-pa*; *γyar-ba*.
Bosom *snam-brág*; *paṅ-k̔ébs*.
Botch vb. *glan-pa*.
Both *γnyis*.
Bottle *bum-pa*.
Bottom *γtiṅ*; *mt̔il*; *žabs*.
Bough *yal-ga*.
Bound vb. n. *ˌp̔ar-ba*.
Boundary *mts̔ams*, *sa-mts̔ams*.
Bow vb. *ˌdud-pa*; **skyed kug taṅ-če** 16 *W.*
Bow s. (compliment) *p̔yag*.
Bow s. (for shooting) *γžu*.
Bowels *rgyu-ma*; *naṅ-k̔ról*.
Bowl s. *ko-re W.*; *koṅ-po*; *pa-tra*; *p̔or-pa*; *γžoṅ-pa*; beggar's — *lhuṅ-bzéd*; — of a tobacco-pipe *gaṅ-mgó*.
Box s. (chest) *sgam*; *sgrom*; *gau*; *pa-ri*; — on the ear *ˌgram-lčag*.
Boy *byis-pa*; infant — *k̔yeu*.
Bracelet *γdu-bu*; *lag-γdúb*
Brag *sgeg-pa*.
Brahma *ts̔aṅs-pa*.
Brahmin *bram-ze*.
Braid vb. *γčud-pa*.
Brain *klad-pa*; *glad*; *mgo-klád*.
Bramble *ts̔er-ma*.
Bran *ts̔ag-ro*.
Branch (bough) *yal-ga*; *gel-pa*; v. also *lčug-pa* 149.

Brandish *dbyug-pa.*
Brandy *'a-rág.*
Brass *ra-gan*; — can *čab-rkyan.*
Brave adj. *des-pa*; *dpa(-ba)*; *spa-ba.*
Brawls v. *klan-ka* 8.
Bread *bag-leb C.*; *ta-gir W.*
Breadth *k̔a-žeṅ*; *žeṅ*, *γžeṅ.*
Break vb. a. *γčog-pa*; to — one's promise *˳gal-ba*; v. *˳čal-ba*; v. *˳jig-pa*; vb.n. *˳gas-pa*; *˳čag-pa*; to — forth *rdol-ba*; to - out *˳čor-ba*; *laṅ-ba.*
Breakfast s. *gro*; *dro C.*; *t̔sal-ma W.*
Breakfast vb. *t̔sal-ma za-ba.*
Breast *nu-ma*; *braṅ*, resp. *sku-bráṅ.*
Breath *rṅam-pa*; *dbugs*; *rlaṅs-pa*; to be out of — *dṅaṅ-ba.*
Breathe *rṅam-pa.*
Breeze *rluṅ.*
Bribe s. *p̔ag-súg.*
Brick *pag*, *pag-bu*; *so-pag.*
Bricklayer *rtsig-bzo-pa*
Bride *bag-ma*; —'s maid ***bag-grogs-mo.***
Bridegroom *bag-po*, ***mag-pa* col.**
Bridge ***zam-pa.***
Bridle s. *srab.*
Brier *t̔ser-ma.*
Bright *bkrag-čan*; *k̔rol-k̔ról*; *γzi-brjid-čan*; *˱od-čan*; *γsal-ba.*
Brightness *bkrag*; *dṅom-pa*; *mdaṅs*; *˳t̔ser-ba*; *zil*; *γzi*; *γzi-brjid*; *˱od.*
Brilliant *zil-čan.*
Brim *gru.*
Bring *skyel-ba*; *˳k̔yer-ba*; *˳k̔yog-pa*; *˳k̔yoṅ-ba*; *˳k̔yol-ba*; to — along with *˳k̔rid-pa*; to — on *skyed-pa*; to — round *skul-ba*; to — together *sprod-pa*; to — up *γsos skyed-pa.*
Brisk *k̔ram-pa.*
Bristle s. *k̔ab-spú.*
Bristly *rtsub-po.*
Brittle *k̔rol-mo.*
Broad *p̔al-čan*; *žeṅ-čan.*
Broken *dkrum-pa*; *čag-pa*, *čag-po*; country *lčaṅ-lčóṅ.*
Bronze v. *k̔ro* 52; *mk̔ar-ba*, *˳k̔ar-ba.*
Brook s. *grog-ču*; *ču*; *bab-ču*; *ču-p̔ran.*
Broom *p̔yag-ma*; *˱ol-mo.*
Broth *ša-k̔ú.*
Brother *spun*, resp. *mčed*; father's — *k̔u-bo*; mother's — *žaṅ-po*, *'a-žaṅ W.*; a sister's — *miṅ-po*; elder — *jo-bo*, col. *'a-jó*; resp. *γčen*; younger — *nu-bo*; *γčuṅ-po*; *no W.*; religious — *čos-spun*; brother — in law ***skud-po.***

Bruise vb. *grug-pa.*
Brush s. *pir*; *zed.*
Brute *byol-sóṅ.*
Bubble s. *ču-búr*; *lbu-ba*, *dbu-ba.*
Bubbling *k̔ol-pa.*
Bucket *ču-bzóm.*
Buckle s. *čab-ma.*
Buckler *p̔a-li*; *p̔ub.*
Buckwheat *bra-bo.*
Bud s. *sbal-míg*; leaf — *k̔yi-gu.*
Bud vb. *skye-ba.*
Buddha *saṅs-rgyas*; *rgyal-ba*; *rgyal-ba goṅ-ma.*
Buddhist *naṅ-pa.*
Buffalo *ma-he.*
Bug *ča-ré*; *(lha) ˳dre-šig.*
Build *rtsig-pa*; *˳čos-pa*; *˳god-pa.*
Building s. *bkod-pa.*
Bulk *boṅ*; *lhun.*
Bull *glaṅ-t̔úg*; *ba-glaṅ.*
Bullet *go-la*; *t̔si-gu*; — mould *ka-lib.*
Bullock *glaṅ*; *spo-to C.*
Bun *lhas(-ma)*; *lhas-dóg*; *žim-zag W.*
Bunch *čam-pód*; *čag-pa*; *čag-bu*, *čag-mo*; *čun-po*; *t̔som-pa*; *γzab-ma.*
Bundle *čun-po*; *p̔on-po*; *lag-kód.*
Bung *k̔a-˳dig.*
Burden s. *k̔al*; *k̔ur*, *k̔ur-po*; *k̔res-po*; *˳gaṅ (-po).*
Burn vb. a. *˳t̔sig-pa*; *sreg-pa*; vb. n. *˳bar-ba.*
Burning-glass *me-šél.*
Burst vb. a. *γčog-pa*; vb. n. *˳gas-pa*; *˳tor-ba*; *rdol-ba.*
Bury *skuṅ-ba.*
Bushel *k̔al-bó.*
Business *las*; *don*; *k̔ag*; *gaṅ-po*; *spros-pa*; **ḍel-wa** 382 *W.*
Busy, to be — *brel-ba.*
But adv. (only) *tsam*; v. *man* 411; conj. v. *kyi*; *˱on-kyaṅ*; *˱o-ná.*
Butcher *šan-pa*; *ša-t̔soṅ-pa.*
Butler *γsol-dpon.*
Butter *mar*; fresh — *skya-már.*
Butterfly *p̔ye-ma-léb.*
Buttermilk *da-ra*; *dar-ba.*
Buttock *rkub*; *˳p̔oṅ-t̔sos.*
Button s. ***sgrog-gu***, ***sgrog-ril***; ***tob-či***, ***t̔ob-ču.***
Buy *nyo-ba.*
Buzz vb. *˳k̔rog-pa.*
Buzzing s. *˱ur.*
By *kyi*; v. sub ***rkyen***; ***sgo-nas***; *pas*; *p̔yir*; close — ***druṅ-du.***

# C

**Cabbage** *kram*; Chinese white – *pe-tsé, pi-tsí.*
**Cairn** *t́o-yór*; *dur-ṕuṅ.*
**Calamity** *bkra-mi-ṡis*; *rkyen*; *˳gal-rkyen.*
**Calamus** *č́u-t́ág.*
**Calculate** *rtsi-ba*; *rtsis byed-pa*; *bgraṅ-ba.*
**Calculation** *rtsis.*
**Calendar** *lo-t́o.*
**Calf** *be-to, be-do*; *beu*; – of the leg *sgyid-pa*; *byin-pa.*
**Call** vb. a. *skad-pa*; *skul-ba*; *ḱug-pa*; *˳gugs-pa*; *sgrog-pa*; *˳bod-pa*; v. also *byed-pa* I, 2 and *miṅ ˳dogs-pa* 280; so-called *žes byas-pa*; vb. n. to — to a person *kẹ' taṅ-wa C.*; *skad gyab-če W.*; *sgrog-pa*; *brgyaṅ-ba.*
**Calm** adj. *gya-ma-gyú*; v. *dal-ba.*
**Calm** vb. a. *ži-bar byed-pa.*
**Calumny** *ṕra-ma.*
**Camel** *rṅa-bóṅ*; male — *rṅa-γséb,* female — *rṅa-mo.*
**Camp** *sgar.*
**Camphor** *ga-pur.*
**Can** s. *rkyan, čab-rkyán* 155.
**Cancer** (disease) *lhog-pa*; (constellation) *kar-ka-ta.*
**Candle** *rkyoṅ-tse.*
**Candy** *ḱaṇ-ḍa.*
**Cane** *spa, sba*; *smyi-gu, smyug-ma*; *˳od-ma.*
**Canine tooth** *mče-ba, mče-só.*
**Cannon** *gyogs, sgyogs*; *˳dzam-búr*; — ball *t́u-lúm.*
**Canopy** *γdugs.*
**Caoutchouc** *gyig.*
**Cap** *t́od-ḱebs.*
**Caper** vb. n. *dkyu-ba.*
**Capital** adj. *kyad-par-čan.*
**Capital** s. (stock in trade) v. *ma* I, 2; *t́og* III.; (chief city) *mt́il*; *rgyal-sa W.*
**Captain** *˳go-pa*; *brgya-dpon.*
**Captivate** *˳dzin-pa.*
**Captive** s. *btson.*
**Caravansary** *tsugs-ḱaṅ.*
**Caraway** 1. Carum *go-snyod.* 2. Cumin *zi-ra.*
**Carcass** *ro, t́eṅ-ro*; *γzugs.*
**Card** *yi-ge.*
**Cardamom** *sug-rmél*; *li-ṡi W.*
**Cardinal points** *ṕyogs* 352.
**Care** s. *nya-ra*; *γnyer-ḱa*; to take — **ka-dar čo-če**; to take — of *skyoṅ-ba*; **čag-pa ǰhé-pa* C.*; *γnyer-ba*; to use — *γzabs-pa.*
**Careless** *bag-méd.*
**Caress** vb. a. *mt́un-par byed-pa*; *yag-po*; *˳ǰag-po byed-pa.*
**Carpenter** *ṡiṅ-mḱan.*
**Carpet** *stan.*
**Carriage** (conveyance) *bčibs-pa*; *bžon-pa*; *t́eg-pa.*
**Carrion** *˳ḱrums.*
**Carrot** *guṅ-dmar-la-ṕug*; *lča-ba*; *se-rag-dur-sman W.*
**Carry** *˳ḱur-ba*; *˳ḱyer-ba, ˳ḱyog-pa*; *˳ḱyol-ba*; *skya-ba*; *skyed-pa*; to — away *skyel-ba*; *bda-ba*; to be able to — *t́eg-pa* 235.
**Cart** *ṡiṅ-rta.*
**Carter** *ṡiṅ-rta-pa.*
**Cartilage** *čag-krúm.*
**Carve** *˳ǰog-pa*; *˳bru-ba, bru-ba.*
**Case** (incident) *rkyen*; *skabs*; in — *gal-te* 68; *na* 299; (sheath) *ṡubs*; (grammar) *rnam-dbyé* 314.
**Cash** *rnags* 313.
**Cashmere** *ḱa-čúl, ḱa-čé.*
**Cask** *zem.*
**Cast** vb. a. *skyur-ba*; *rgyag-pa*; *˳debs-pa*; *˳ṕen-pa*; to — away *˳dor-ba*; to — down *˳bebs-pa*; *˳bor-ba*; to (metals) *ldugs-pa.*
**Casting-mould** *lug-koṅ.*
**Castle** *mḱar*; *ṕo-braṅ*; *rdzoṅs.*
**Castrate** *rlig-pa ˳byin-pa.*
**Cat** *byi-la*; *bi-la, bi-li, pi-ṡi W. žim-bu, žum-bu C.*
**Catapult** *sgyogs* 119.
**Cataract** *ri-γzar-čú.*
**Catarrh** *čam-pa*; *bro-˳tsál.*
**Catch** *˳dzin-pa.*
**Catgut** *rgyus-skúd.*
**Cattle** *ṕyugs*; breeding — *rkaṅ-˳grós*; hornless — *mgo-ril W.*
**Caul** (anatomy) *rgyu-sgróg.*
**Cause** s. *rkyen*; *rgyu*; *rgyu-mtsan*; original = *γži-ma.*
**Cause** vb. a. v. *gugs-pa*; *˳ǰug-pa*; *γtoṅ-ba*; *byed-pa.*
**Causeway** *so-log.*
**Caution** s. *γnyer-ḱa.*
**Cautious** v. *ka-dár*; *gya-ma-gyú*; to be — **ka-dar čo-če**; *˳gab-pa.*
**Cave, Cavern** *ṕug-pa.*
**Cavity** *ḱuṅ*; *sbugs.*
**Cease** *˳gag-pa*; *˳čad-pa*; *ži-ba.*
**Ceiling** *t́og, ya-t́og.*
**Celebrated** *gzi-brǰid-čan.*
**Cell** *grwa*; **ḍa-ṡág** 75.
**Cellar** *ṡa-ḱáṅ.*
**Cemetery** *dur-ḱrod.*
**Censer** *pog-ṕór, spos-ṕór.*
**Censor** (of a monastery) *dge-bskos* 85.
**Censure** s. *klan-ka.*
**Centiped** *la-ré W.*; *si-ri-˳bu W.*
**Centre** *lte-ba*; *mt́il*; *dbus.*
**Cerebellum** *klad-čuṅ.*
**Ceremony** *čo-ga*; *sku-rim.*

Certain *ńes-pa*; *gor-ma-čág*; *ño-rtóg*; a — one *γčig-čig*.
Certainly *γdon-mi-za-bar*.
Certainty *ńes-pa*; *ťag-čód*.
Ceylon *laṅ-ka*.
Chaff *spun-pa*, *sbun-pa*; *sbur-ma*.
Chain s. *lčags-ťág*; *nyag-ťág*.
Chair *ǩri*; *rgya-ǩrí C*.
Chairman *ǩri-pa*.
Chalk *ťo-lé dkar-po*.
Chamber *naṅ*; *ǩaṅ-mig*.
Champion *gyad*.
Chance s. *rgyu* 110.
Change s. *ₒgyur-ba*; *res*.
Change vb. a *sgyur-ba*; *rǰe-ba*; *spo-ba*; *rdzu-ba*; to — place *ₒṕo-ba*; vb. n. *ₒgyur-ba*; *ₒṕo-ba*.
Chant vb. *dgyer-ba*.
Chap vb. *ₒgas-pa*.
Chapter *leu*.
Character (disposition) *rgyud*; *naṅ*; *ño-bo-nyid*; *ťsul*; *rig-rgyud*; **šē-gyü* C*. 562.
Characteristic s. *rgyu-mťsán* 111.
Charge vb. *sko-ba*; *rgol-ba*; *mṅag-pa*; to — with (to commission) *ₒgel-ba*.
Charge s. (commission) *ǩag*.
Charity *snyiṅ-rǰe*.
Charming *dga-ba*; *yid-du ˛oṅ-ba*.
Chase vb. *ₒčor-ba*.
Chase s. *ǩyi-ra*.
Chasm s. *rgya-sér*.
Chastisement *čad-pa*; *ťul*.
Chastity *ǩrel-yod*; *ťsaṅs-par spyod-pa*.
Chat vb. *˛ur γtoṅ-ba*; *lab γtoṅ-ba*.
Chattering s. *čo-lo*.
Cheap *ǩye-mo W.*; *rin čuṅ-ba*.
Cheat vb. *blo brid-pa*; *slu-ba*; *γyo-zól byed-pa*; *mgo skor-ba*.
Cheek *ₒgram-pa*; — bone *ₒgram-rús*; — tooth *ₒgram-so*.
Cheer vb. *glod-pa*; *spro-ba skyed-pa*; *dga-bar byed-pa*.
Cheerful *ǩrul-po*; *dga-mo*; *sems-bdé*, *blo-bdé*.
Cheese *ťud*; *˛o-ťúd*.
Chess-board *mig-máṅ*; to play at chess *mig-maṅ rtse-ba*.
Chest (box) *gau*; *sgam*; *sgrom*; (thorax) *braṅ*, resp. *sku-bráṅ*.
Chew *ldad-pa*.
Chicken *bya-ṕrug*.
Chief adj. *dpon*; *γtso*; — justice *ǩrims-dpon*.
Chief s. *ₒgo-pa*; *dpon-po*; *γtso-bo*; *ǩyu-mčóg*.
Chiefly *γtso-bor*, *γtso-čér*.
Child *ṕru-gu*; *byis-pa*; *bu*; v. *ǩyeu*.
Children *bu-ṕrug*; — of the same parents (brothers, sisters) *spun*.
Chill s. *kyi-bún*.
Chin *ko-kó*; *ma-lé*.
China *rgya-nág*; *rgya-yúl*; modern name: *ma-hā-či-na*, *ma-hā-čin*; — clay *ǩam-pa*; — ware *kar-yól*; *dkar-yól*; resp. *žal-kar C.*; *sol-kar W*.
Chinese s. *rgya-nag-pa*, *rgya-bo*; fem. *rgya-nag-ma*, *rgya-mo*; *rgya-mí*; plur. *rgya-rnams*.
Chinese adj. *rgyai*, *rgya-nag-gi*, — language *rgya-skád*; — paper *rgya-šóg*.
Chink *sgo-bár*.
Chip *ťsal-pa*; *šiṅ-ťsal*.
Chirping s. *ča-čó*.
Chisel vb. *ₒbru-ba*.
Chit-chat s. *˛ur*.
Choice adj. *mčog-tu bkrab*; *ǩyad-par ṕags-pa*; *ǩyad-par-čan*.
Choke *dbugs sub-pa*; **skye tsir taṅ-če* W.*; *ske bsdam-ste γsod-pa*; to be choked *rnaṅ-ba*; *ske bsdam-ste ₒči-ba*; *ₒtsub-pa*.
Cholera *ǩoṅ-lóg W.*; *nya-lóg Sik*.
Choose vb. a. *bkrab-pa*; *ₒbyed-pa*; *ₒdzin-pa*; vb. n. (to like) *dgyes-pa*.
Chop vb. *btsab-pa*; to — off *γčod-pa*.
Chopping-block *šiṅ-stan*.
Chopsticks *ťur-ma*.
Chord *rgyud* 111
Christ *skyabs-mgón* 26; *ma-ši-ka* 410.
Chronic adj. *yun riṅ-bai*; — disease *γčoṅ-nád*.
Chronicle *lo-rgyús*.
Churn vb. *dkrog-pa*; *žo dkrog-pa*.
Churn s. v. *gur-gúr* 70.
Chutney (Indian condiment) *ťsu-u* 449.
Chyle *dwaṅs-ma* 249.
Cimeter *gri-gúg*.
Cinamon *šiṅ-ťsa*.
Cipher s. *mǩa*; *ťig-le*.
Circle s. *skor*, *ₒǩor*, *ₒǩor-lo*; *dkyil-ₒǩor*; *sgor-mo*, *sgor-ťig*.
Circular adj. *kyir-kyir*; *gor-mo*.
Circumference *dkyil-ₒǩor*; *ₒǩor*; *ǩo-ra*; *ǩyon*; *mu-ǩyúd*.
Circumstance *rkyen*; *skabs*.
Citadel *mǩar*; *rdzoṅ*.
Citizen *ǩyim-bdág*; *yul-pa*; *yon-bdag*.
Citron *gam-bu-ra W.*; *spyod-pad C*.
City *groṅ-ǩyér*.
Civilize *ₒdul-ba*.
Claim s. *ťob-ťsír*, *tob-sról*.
Clairvoyance *mṅon-šés* 133.
Clammy *rtsi-čan*.
Clamour s. *ku*, *ku-sgra*, *ku-čo*; *skad-lóg*; *ča-čó*.
Clandestinely *sbas-te W.*; v. also *lkog-tu*, *γsaṅ-ba*.
Clap vb., to — the hands *čag-čág byed-pa*.
Clap s. (crash) *sguṅ W.*; *ldim W.*; *ldir-sgra*.
Clasp vb. a. *ₒǩyud-pa*; *ₒǩril-ba*.
Clasp s. *čab-ma*; — knife *ltab-gri*.

**Class** s. *gral*; *ča-t́sán*; *bye-brág*; *dbye-ba*; *t́san*, *sde-t́sán*.
**Classify** *rnam-par bžag-pa*; *˳byed-pa*.
**Claw** *ḱron*; *sder(-mo)*; *spar-ba*.
**Clay** *˳ǰim-pa*; *rdza*; *žal-ba*; — floor *skyaṅ-nul*.
**Clean** adj. *dag-pa*, *γtsaṅ-ba*; *lag-mo W.*; — food *dkar-zás*.
**Clean, Cleanse** vb. a. *ṕyi-bdar byed-pa*; *saṅ-ba*; *sel-ba*; to be cleansed *˳byoṅ-ba*.
**Clear** adj. *mṅon-pa*; *tur-re*; *wa-lé*; *wa-le-ba*; *lag-mo W.*; *siṅs-po W.*; *lhaṅ-ṅe*.
**Clear** vb. a. *˳dag-pa*; *sel-ba*.
**Cleave** *˳ges-pa*; *˳čeg-pa*; to be cleft *˳gas-pa*.
**Cleft** s. *rgya-sér*; *ral*; *srubs*.
**Clerk** *yig-mḱan*.
**Clever** *γċaṅ-po*; *sgrin-po*; *t́abs-ċan*; *spyaṅ-po*; a — writer *rtsom-par mḱas-pa*.
**Clew** s. *gru-gu*.
**Climb** *˳dzeg-pa*; *rgal-ba*.
**Cling** *čags-pa*; *ča-bžag-pa*.
**Clip** *˳grum-pa*.
**Cloak** s. *ber*.
**Clock** *ču-t́sod*; *ču-t́sod-˳ḱor-lo*.
**Close** vb. a. *˳gegs-pa*; v. also *˳dzum-pa*.
**Close** adj. *gya-ma-gyu* 73; — fisted *ḱroṅ-po*; *lag-dam-po*; adv. *˳ǰam-pa* 174; — over *glad-la*.
**Clot** s. *goṅ-po*; — of blood *ḱrag-góṅ*.
**Cloth** *sag-lád*; *ṕrug*; *t́er-ma*; *dar*; a piece of — *yug*, *bubs*.
**Clothes** *gos*, *gos-lág*; *bgo-ba*; to change — *gos brǰe-ba*; to put on — *gos gon-pa*; to take off — *gos ˳bud-pa*; suit of — *go-lus-ča-t́saṅ W.*
**Clothes-brush** *byab-zéd*.
**Clothes-stand** *γdaṅ*, *rdaṅ*.
**Clothing** s. *bgo-ba*; *ča-byád*, *ča-lúgs*.
**Cloud** s. *sprin*; — of dust *bud*.
**Clouded**, to be — *˳ḱrig-pa*.
**Cloudy**, it has become — *ḱor-soṅ*.
**Clove** *li-ši C.*; *bzaṅ-drúg W.*; *zer-bu W.*
**Club** (mace) *ga-da*.
**Clumsy** *sbom-pa*; *zlum-pa*.
**Cluster** s. *čag-mo*.
**Clyster** s. *˳ḱos*; *bsur-smyig*; — pipe *čeu*.
**Coachman** *šiṅ-rta-pa*.
**Coagulate** *˳ḱyags-pa*.
**Coal** *sol-ba*.
**Coarse** *rtsiṅ-ba*; *rags-pa*; — grained *rtsub-po*.
**Coast** *˳ḱris*.
**Coat** s. *gos*; *dug-po Ü*; *ču-pa Ts.*; — lap *ḱud*; — of mail *ḱrab*.
**Coat** vb. a. *˳tum-pa*.
**Cock** s. *bya-ṕo*, *bya-po*; *ḱyim-bya*; of a gun *t́o-čúṅ*; *me-skám*.
**Cock** vb. a. *rdze-ba*.
**Coetaneous** *na-mnyám*, *na-˳drá*.
**Coffee** *ḱa-ba* 37, III.
**Coffer** *sgrom*.
**Coffin** *dur-sgám*, *ro-sgám*.
**Cohabit** *˳brel-ba*; *˳ḱrig-pa spyod-pa*.
**Cohabitation** *sbyor-ba*.
**Cohere** *˳brel-ba*.
**Coil** vb. (of snakes) *˳ḱri-ba*.
**Coin** s. *doṅ-tse*.
**Coition, Coitus** *˳ḱrig-pa*; *čags-spyód*; *nyal-po*.
**Colander** *t́sag-ma*.
**Cold** adj. *graṅ-ba*; — air *ṅa-ra*; *ṅad*; — wind *ṅar-ba*; *lhags-pa*; to feel — *˳ḱyags-pa*; v. *kyi-bún*; to get, to grow — *graṅ-ba*, *graṅs-pa*.
**Cold** s. *ḱyags-pa*; *graṅ-ba*; *ṅad*; *ṅar-ba*; to have a — *bro-˳t́sal-ba*; a — in the head *čam-pa*; *bro-˳t́sál*; *ya-ma*.
**Colic** *glaṅ*, *glaṅ-tábs*; *rgyu-γzér*; *t́sa-˳ḱru*.
**Collar** s. *goṅ-ba*, *gos-kyi goṅ-ba*; to seize by the — *goṅ-ba-nas ˳dzin-pa*.
**Collect** vb. a. *sgrug-pa*, *sloṅ-pa*; *sdud-pa*; *sog-pa*.
**Colonel** *ru-dpón*.
**Colour** s. *ḱa*; *ḱa-dog*; *mdog*; *t́son*; beautiful — *bkrag*; prime — *ma-γži*; to lose — *dkyug-pa*.
**Colt** *t́ur-bu*; — of an ass *ku-rúg*, *gu-rúg*.
**Comb** s. *so-máṅ*.
**Comb** vb. a. *šad-pa*, *γšad-pa*, *γšod-pa*.
**Combat** s. *˳t́ab-mo*; *˳ḱrug-pa*.
**Combat** vb. *˳t́ab-mo ˳gyed-pa*, *˳t́ab-pa*; *˳ḱrab-pa*; *rgol-ba*.
**Come** *˳oṅ-ba*, resp *˳byor-ba*, *˳byon-pa*; *ṕeb-pa*; eleg. *mči-ba*; come! *šog*; to — again *ldog-pa*, *log-pa*; to — back *ṕyir-˳gro-ba*; to — forth *čags-pa*; to — out *˳byuṅ-ba*, *˳t́on-pa*; to — to *˳ḱyol-ba*; *γnas-su ˳gyur-ba*; to — together *˳dzom-pa*; to — up (of seeds) *˳ḱruṅ-ba*, *rdol-ba*.
**Comfort** vb. a. *glod-pa*; *mya-ṅan saṅ-ba*; *spro-ba skyed-pa*.
**Comforter** *skyo-grógs*.
**Command** vb. a. *bka γnaṅ-ba*, *γnaṅ-ba*; (an army) *˳ḱrid-pa*.
**Command** s. *žal-γdáms*.
**Commander** *dmag-˳go*; *dmag-dpón*.
**Commandment** *bka*, *bka-ḱrims*, *bka-bsgos*; *ḱrims*.
**Commence** *rtsom-pa*; *˳dzugs-pa*.
**Commend** *sṅag-pa*; *˳čol-ba*.
**Comment** vb. a. *˳grel-ba*, *˳grol-ba*.
**Commerce** *t́soṅ*.
**Commissary** *sku-t́sáb*.
**Commission** vb. a. *sko-ba*; *˳gel-ba*; *mṅag-pa*.
**Commit** *skur-ba*; *˳čol-ba*; (sin etc.) *byed-pa*.
**Common** *dkyus-ma*; *tun*; *ṕal-pa*; *ṕral*; the — people *ṕal* 341.
**Communication** *bka-rgya*; *˳brel*, *˳brel-ba*.

Communion ₒ*brel-ba*; ₒ*grogs-lugs*; holy — *γsol-rás* 592.
Compact adj *mk̔ran*; ₒ*čag-čan*.
Companion *grogs*; *rogs*; *skyo-grógs*; *zla-bo*; *ya-do* W.
Company *kyu*; in — *t̔un-mon-du*; ₒ*grogs-te*.
Comparative degree v. *ǰe* 172; *las* II, *pas*, *san*.
Compare *sdur-ba*; *sgrun-pa*; *sgre-ba*.
Comparison *dpe* 327.
Compass (circumference) *mu-k̔yud*; points of the — *mt̔sams* 455.
Compasses, pair of, *skor-tig*.
Compassion *snyin-rǰe*; *snyin-brtse-ba*.
Compel v. *nan-gyis* 302; *šed-kyer-nag-pos* W.; to be compelled *dgos-pa*.
Competitor ₒ*gran-zla*.
Compile *sgrig-pa*.
Complaint *zug*, *γzug* 488, *nad*.
Complete adj. *grub-pa*; *rgyas-pa*; *t̔am-pa*; *p̔un-t̔sógs*; *rdzogs-pa*; *t̔san-ba*; to be — *t̔san-ba*.
Complete vb. a. *sgrub-pa*; *t̔og* ₒ*gel-ba*; to be completed ₒ*k̔or-ba*; ₒ*t̔sar-ba*.
Completely *γtan-du*; *ye-nas*.
Complex of fields *kluns*.
Complicate adj. *k̔rag-k̔rúg*.
Compliment s. *p̔yag*; compliments v. *stod-pa* 223.
Compose ₒ*god-pa*; *rtsom-pa*; to — verses *sdeb-pa*; *sbyor-ba*.
Comprehend *go-ba*; ₒ*dzin-pa*; *yid-la byed-pa*.
Comprehension *go-ba*.
Comprehensive *k̔yab-če-ba*.
Comprise *k̔yab-pa*; *sdud-pa*.
Compulsion *gal* 68; *nan* 302.
Computation *rtsis*.
Compute *rtsi-ba*.
Comrade *grogs*.
Concave *kon*.
Conceal *sbed-pa*; *γsan-ba*; *sgon-ba*; ₒ*čab-pa*.
Concealment *p̔ag*.
Conceited *mčor-po*.
Conception *dmigs-pa*.
Concerning (as regards) *rten-nas*; *dban-du byas-na* 387.
Concession *γnan-ba*.
Concord *mt̔un-pa*.
Condemn *žal-če γčod-pa*; *krims γčod-pa* or *γton-ba*.
Condescending *če-t̔abs-med-pa*; to be — *mt̔un-pa byed-pa*.
Condiment *skyu-rúm*; *sdor*.
Condition (state) *γnas-skabs*; *γnas-t̔súl* 311; *yin-lugs* 548.
Conduct vb. a. *skyel-ba*; ₒ*k̔rid-pa*; ₒ*dren-pa*.
Conduct s. *spyod-pa*.
Cone *t̔sa-t̔sa*.
Confess ₒ*čeg-pa*; *mt̔ol-ba*; *γšog-pa*; *γso-sbyon-ba* 590.
Confession (creed) *čos-rgyud* 164.
Confide (*yid*) *rton-pa* 215; v. *blo-γdén* 385.
Confidence *blo-γtád*, *blo-γdén*.
Confidential speaking *snyin-γtam*.
Confine vb. *dgar-ba*.
Conform vb. *sbyor-ba*.
Confound *dkrug-pa*; ₒ*dzol-ba*.
Confused, to be — *rtab-pa*.
Confusion ₒ*k̔ral*-ₒ*k̔rúl*.
Congeal ₒ*k̔yags-pa*.
Conglomerate s. *gad-pa*.
Congratulate *bkra-šis mna γsol-ba*.
Conjuncture *bsgan*; *dus*.
Conjure (implore) *nan-gyis žu-ba*.
Conjure up ₒ*gugs-pa*.
Conjurer ₒ*ba-po*.
Connect *sbyor-ba*; *sbrel-ba*; *zun sdebs-pa*.
Connected with *bčas-pa*; to be — ₒ*brel-ba*.
Connection ₒ*brel-pa*, *zun*-ₒ*brél*; v. also *rgyu-rkyén* 110.
Conquer *bčom-pa*; ₒ*ǰoms-pa*; *rgyal-ba*; ₒ*p̔am-par byed-pa* 356; to be conquered ₒ*p̔am-pa*.
Conqueror *rgyal-ba*.
Conscience *gal-mt̔un šes-pa*; *šes-bžin*; v. also *byas-čos* and *γnon-ba*.
Conscientious *krel-čan*.
Consciousness *šes-pa*; *dran-pa*; — of guilt *γnon-ba*.
Consecrate *skur-ba*; *rab(-tu) γnas(-par) byed-pa* 524.
Consequence *mǰug*; ₒ*bras-bu*; in — of *dban-gis*.
Consider vb. a. *gran-ba*; ₒ*dzin-pa*; *bsam-mnó byed-pa*; vb. n. *sgom-pa*; *mno-ba*.
Consideration *dran-pa* 262.
Consign *skur-ba*.
Consist ₒ*dus-pa*, *bsdus-pa*.
Consistence *ska-slád*.
Consistency *srab*-ₒ*t̔úg*.
Console *sems γso-ba*; *mya-nan-bsan-ba*.
Consort s. *čun-ma*; royal — *lčam-mo*; *btsun-mo*.
Conspicuous *mnon-pa*; *γsal-po*.
Constable *dge-γyóg* 86.
Constellation *skar-ma*; *γza-skár*.
Constipation *bšan-dgág*.
Constitute *gel-ba*; *sko-ba*; ₒ*ǰug-pa* II, 2.
Constraint *gal*.
Construct *bčo-ba*; v. ₒ*ča-ba*; ₒ*čos-pa*; *γton-ba*; ₒ*god-pa*; *rtsig-pa*.
Construction (grammatical) *t̔sig sgrig-pa*.
Consult *bka-bgro-ba*.
Consultation *gros-glén*; ₒ*dun-ma*.
Consume *čud γzon-pa*; *zin* ₒ*ǰug-pa*; to be

consumed *ča-ba*; *čad-pa*; *˳tsar-ba*; *˳dzad-pa*; *zin-pa*.
Consumption *γčoṅ*.
Contain v. *šoṅ-ba*; to be contained *˳gro-ba*; v. *˳dug-pa* no. 2.
Contamination *grib*.
Contemplate *sgom-pa*.
Contemplation *sgom*; *tiṅ-ṅe-˳dzin*.
Contempt *ṅan-čen*; *brnyas-pa*; *smad-pa*.
Contend (fight) *˳krug-pa*; *rtsod-pa*; (to strive) *˳gran-pa*.
Content adj. *čog šes-pa*; *tsim-pa*; to be — *mgu-ba*; to heart's — *yid bžin-du*.
Contention *˳gran-sems*; *˳dziṅ-mo*.
Contentment *snyiṅ-tsim*.
Contest s. *tob-šá*.
Continent *gliṅ*.
Continually *rgyun-du*; *čar*, *ča-ré*; *γtan-du*.
Continuation *˳pro*.
Continue *˳pro-ba*.
Contract vb. a. *skum-pa*; vb. n. *˳kor-ba*.
Contract s. *gan-rgyá*; *čad-yig*; *˳dzin*, *yig-˳dzin*.
Contradiction, to be in — *˳gal-ba*.
Contrary s. *bzlog*, *go-bzlóg*; *go-ldóg*, *go-lóg*.
Contrivance *grabs*.
Convent s. *čos-sde*; *sde*; *dgon-pa*.
Convention *ka-čád*.
Conversation *gleṅ-brjód*.
Converse vb. *gleṅ-ba*; *gleṅ-mo byed-pa*; *gros-byéd bgro-ba*.
Convert vb. *čos-su ˳jug-pa*.
Convey *skya-ba*; *skyed-pa*; *skyel-ba*; *˳kur-ba*.
Convoy s. *skyel-ma*.
Cook vb. *˳tsod-pa*.
Cook s. *gyos-mkan*; head — *γsol-dpon*, *ma-čen*.
Cool *graṅ-ba*; *bsil-ba*.
Cooly (carrier) *kur-pa*; (workman) *gla-pa*.
Coot *skyegs*.
Copious *rgyas-pa*.
Copper *zaṅs*.
Copulation *˳krig-pa*; *čags-spyod*.
Copy vb. *šu-ba*.
Copy s. (transcript) *bkod-pa*; *bu-dpe*; (pattern) *ma*, *ma-dpe*.
Coral *byi-ru*.
Cord s. *rgyud*; *sgrogs*; *ta-gu*; *˳preṅ-ba*.
Cordial s. *bčud*.
Core *kog-šiṅ*.
Coriander seed *˂u-su*.
Cork *ka-γčod*, *ka-˳dig*.
Corn (grain) *˳bru*; boiled — *čan*; slightly roasted *yos*; stack of — *rags*, *pub-rags*; *hi-ri*; corn on a toe *rkaṅ-mdzub-dzer-pa*.
Corner *kug*; *gru*; *grwa*; *zur*.
Corporal *bču-dpon*.
Corpse *ro*, resp. *spur*.
Correct adj. *skyon-méd*; *nor-méd*; to be — *˳grig-pa*.
Correct vb. *sgyur-ba*; *žu-dag byed-pa*.
Correction *žu-dág*, *žus-dág*.
Correspond (to be adequate) *˳grig-pa*.
Correspondent (in business) *tsoṅ-grogs*.
Corrupt vb. a. *slad-pa*.
Corruptness *kun-dkris*.
Costly *gus-po*, *rin-čan*.
Cottage *kan-bu*; *ku-tu*.
Cotton *ras-bal*, *srin-bal*, *šiṅ-bal*; — cloth (*ka-ši-kai*) *ras*.
Couch s. *kri*; *nyal-kri*; *mal*.
Cough s. *glo*; *kogs*; *bro-˳tsál*; vb. *kogs-pa*.
Council *gros*, *gros-gleṅ*; *˳dun-ma*.
Counsel s. *gros*; *bka-γdáms*; *˳dun-ma*.
Counselor *bka-γšags*.
Count vb. *bgraṅ-ba*; *˳dren-pa*; *rtsi-ba*; *γšor-ba*; *si kor-če W.*
Countenance *γdoṅ*; *bžin*; *ṅo*; *skye-sgo*; *sgo-lo*.
Counteract *˳gal-ba*.
Counterfeit adj. *rdzus-ma*.
Counterparty *pa-rol*.
Counting s. *rtsis*.
Country *yul*, *yul-˳kór*, *yul-grú*; *sa-čá*; *rgyal-kág*; love of — *yul-sréd*; *yul-la ˳dod-pa*.
Couple s. *zuṅ*; married — *bza-mi*.
Courage *snyiṅ-stobs*, *snyiṅ-rús*; *spobs-pa*.
Courageous *ham-pa-čan*; *dpa-ba*, *dpa-čan*.
Courier *rta-zam-pa*.
Course s. *tsir*.
Court s. (residence of a prince) *kab*; — of justice *bka-γšags*; *krims-kaṅ*.
Courtyard *kyams*; *tsoms*, *tsoms-skór*.
Cove *kug*.
Covenant s. *ka-čád*.
Cover vb. *˳keb-pa*; *˳gebs-pa*; *klub-pa*; *˳tum-pa*.
Cover, Covering s. *ka-kebs*, *ka-gab*, *ka-γčod*, *ka-leb*; *kebs*, *kyebs*, *kebs-ma*; *go-šog*; *tums*; *γyogs*; *šubs*; covering for the head *mgo-γyógs*.
Cowry *˳gron-bu*.
Crab *sdig-srin*.
Crack vb. a. *γčog-pa*; vb. n. *˳gas-pa*.
Crack s. *sguṅ*.
Craft (cunning) *dku-lto*.
Crafty *yó-ba*.
Cram *sgrim-pa*.
Crane (bird) *kruṅ-kruṅ*.
Crash s. *sguṅ*.
Crave *rṅab-pa*.
Craw *lkog-šog*.
Crawfish *sdig-srin*.
Crawl *gog-pa*; *˳pye-ba*.
Cream *spri-ma*, *spris-ma*, *sriš-ma*; *˂o-sri*; *žo-sri*.

Create ˳god-pa.
Creator ˳god-pa-po; mdzad-po.
Creature bkod-pa; ˳gro-ba, lus-ċan.
Credible ‚os-pa.
Creditor bun-bdág.
Creed čos-rgyud, čos-lugs.
Creek ḱug, ḱugs.
Creep ˳ṕye-ba, gog-pa.
Crescent s. zla-t́ses lta-bui ri-mo or dbyibs.
Crest (of fowl) ċod-pán.
Crevice γseṅ, seṅ.
Cricket (insect) ċog-ċog-pa W.
Crime nyes-pa; noṅs-pa.
Cripple ža-bo.
Crippled ḱoṅs-ḱan W.; ḱoṅ-ril C.; grum-pa.
Criticise ˳bigs-pa.
Crocodile kum-bi-ra.
Crooked kug; **kum-pa**, koṅ; kyog-po; ḱoṅs; ˳ḱyog-po; dgur; to be — dgye-ba.
Crop vb. γtog-pa.
Crop s. lo-tóg.
Cross s. brkyaṅ-šiṅ; sku-ru-ka.
Cross vb. γċod-pa; rgal-ba.
Crouch čum-pa.
Croup, he has the — ḱoi lkog-ma skraṅs soṅ (his throat is swollen).
Crow s. ḱa-ta; ṕo-róg.
Crow-bar gal-ta; lċags-bér.
Crowd s. ḱrod-pa; ḱrom; γseb.
Crowd vb. a. bċar-ba C., bċer-ba W.
Crown s. ċod-pán; — of the head spyi-bo; γtsug.
Crown vb. a. ċod-pan-gyis brgyan-pa; v. also t́og ˳gel-ba.
Crucible koṅ-po W.; žu-skyógs C.
Cruel γnyan-pa; drag-šul-ċan.
Crumb čag-dúm; brul; bir-bir W.
Crumble vb. a. grug-pa; vb. n. gog-pa.
Crupper sgal-pa; rmed.
Crush glem-pa; rdzi-ba.
Cry vb. n. ˳grags-pa, ˳grogs-pa.
Cry s. ṅa-ro; skad, skad-ṅan; ċa-ċó; — for help ‚o-dód.
Crystal man-šel, šel.
Cubit ḱru 51.
Cuckoo ḱu-byúg; kug-se W.
Cucumber ka-ka-ráṅ Kun.
Cultivate ˳bad-pa; cultivated land kluṅs.
Cunning s. dku-lto.
Cup ko-ré, kor; koṅ-po; tiṅ; ṕor-pa; — bearer γsol-dpon.
Cupboard ˳ča.
Cupping-glass me-búm, me-púṅ.
Curd žo, resp. γsol-žó.
Cure vb. γċod-pa; bċos-pa; ˳t́so-ba; γso-ba.
Curious (inquisitive) snob-zog-ċan.
Curl s. (of hair) ral-pa.
Curled tsa-ru W.
Currant nyaṅ-ka Sp.; ṙub-šo W.; (raisins) ba-šo Ld., ba-šo-ka C.
Current s. rgyun; ču-rgyún.
Current adj., to be — (of coins) ˳grul-ba, rgyug-pa.
Curse s. ṅan; dmod-pa.
Curse vb. a. ṅan ˳debs-pa; dmod-pa ˳bor-ba.
Curtain yol-ba.
Curve s. gye-gu.
Curve vb. a. kug-kug byed-pa; ˳gum-pa; curved ḱyog-po; kyag-kyóg W.; to be curving dgye-ba.
Cushion sṅas; stan; ˳bol, snye-˳ból; sob-stán.
Custom (use) ḱrims; čos; srol; (toll) šo-gám.
Cut vb. a. γċod-pa; ˳ǰog-pa; dra-ba; (to mow) rṅa-ba; to — into pieces sgral-ba; ˳t́ub-pa; v. ˳čad-pa; to — off grum-pa; ˳breg-pa, ˳dreg-pa; v. čod-pa; v. čad-pa; to — open ˳ges-pa; to — out v. γċar-ba 143; to — up γtubs-pa; dmyal-ba.
Cut s. ḱram-ka; (blow) lċag; a short — *gyog-lám*.
Cylinder ˳ḱor-lo 58; praying — čos-kyi ˳ḱor-lo.
Cylindrical ril-ba; to be — ˳gril-ba.
Cymbal sbug-žál; sbum-žól W.; sil-snyán.
Cypress spa-ma Sik.

# D

Daily adv. nyin-re-bžin(-du); žag-daṅ žag.
Dalai Lama ta-lai bla-ma.
Dam s. ču-rags; ču-lon.
Dam up vb. skyil-ba.
Damage s. skyon; gud, gun; god; nyes-pa; γnod-pa; vb. a. γnod-pa.
Damp adj. rlan-ċan.
Dance vb. ˳čam-pa; bro-brduṅ-ba or ḱrab-pa; s. gar; bro.
Dancer gar-mḱan.
Dandelion ḱur-ma, ḱur-t́sod.
Dandy ˳ṕyor-dga.
Danger nyen.
Dangerous ma-ruṅ-ba, ma-ruṅs-pa; γdug-pa-ċan; btsog-pa W.
Daring adj. rtul-ṕod-pa; spobs-pa-ċan; dpa-ċan, dpa-bo.
Dark adj. sgrib-pa; mun-pa; smag; to grow — ˳tibs-pa; ˳grib-pa.
Darken vb. a. sgrib-pa; vb. n. ˳grib-pa.

Darkness *mun-pa*; *smag-rum*.
Darling, my —! *ṅai yid˳oṅ*; cf. also *sdug-pa*.
Darn *tur-ba*; *snol-ba*.
Dart s. *mda*; vb. n. *˳ḱyug-pa* 60.
Date s. (time) *zag-gráṅs*; (fruit) *ḱa-zúr*.
Daub vb. *skud-pa*.
Daughter *bu-mo*, *bo-mo*; *sras-mo*; — in-law *mna-ma*.
Dawn s. *skya-ód*, *skya-réṅs*; *ťo-ráṅs*; vb. it dawns *skya-reṅs šar*.
Day *nyi-ma*; *nyin-mo*; *žag*; — and night *nyin-mťsán*; — by — *žag daṅ žag*; all the — long *nyin-ťse-ré*; every — *žag-daṅ W.*; from — to — *žag-nas žag-tu*; one —, some — *deu-re*; the other — *de-žag* 471 *W.*; this — five days *dgus*.
Day-break *nam-laṅs*; at — *nam-laṅs-te* or *nas*.
Dazzle vb. n. *ťom-par ˳gyur-ba*.
Dazzling *ḱrol-po*; *lčam-me-ba*.
Dead adj. v. *ši-ba*; a — man *γšin-po*; *ro*.
Deaf *˳on-pa*.
Deal with vb. *spyod-pa*.
Deal s., a good — *ga-čén*.
Dear *γčig*; *γčes-pa*; *dkon-pa*; *gus-po*; *rin-ťaṅ-čan*, *rin-čan*; to hold — *γče-ba*.
Dearth *zas-dkon C.*
Death *˳či-ba*; forebodings of — *˳či-ltas*; hour of — *˳da-ga*; to seek — *lčeb-pa*.
Debate s. *rtsod-pa*; vb. *bgro-gleṅ byed-pa*.
Debt *bu-lon*; the — is cleared *bu-lon ḱor*.
Debtor *bu-lon-pa*.
Decapitate *ske γčod-pa*.
Decay s. *˳jig-pa*.
Decay vb. *nyil-ba*; *˳ťor-ba*; *nub-pa*.
Decayed *˳ḱogs-pa*.
Deceased *γšin-po*.
Deceit *mgo-skór*; *ṅo-lkog*; *rdzub*; *zog*, *zol-zóg*.
Deceitful *lče-γnyis-pa*.
Deceive *mgo skor-ba*; *rṅod-pa*; *blo ˳brid-pa*, *˳brid-pa*; *slu-ba*.
Deceived *˳ḱrul-pa*.
Decency *ḱrel-yod*.
Decent *˳gab-pa*.
Deception *sgyu-zóg*.
Decide *γčod-pa*; *ťag-γčod-pa*.
Decided *zad*; v. *˳dzad-pa*; to be *čad-pa*.
Declare *bšad-pa*.
Declination (of the sun) v. *bgrod-pa*; north — *byaṅ-bgrod*, south — *lho-bgrod*.
Decline (decay) vb. n. *rgud-pa*.
Declivity *gud*; *ri γzar-po*, *brag γzar-po*.
Decoction *ťaṅ-gi sman*.
Decorate *sgron-pa*; *brgyan-pa*; *spra-ba*.
Decoration *rgyan*.
Decrease vb. *˳gyur-ba*; *˳grib-pa*; *˳bri-ba*.
Decree s. *bka-šog*, *bka-ḱrims*; *ḱra-ma*.
Decrepit *˳ḱogs-pa*.
Dedicate *sṅo-ba*.
Deed *las*; *bya-ba*.
Deep adj. *γtiṅ-riṅ-ba*; *zab-pa*; — (of sounds) *rom-po W.*
Deer *ka-ša Sik.*
Deface *dma ˳bebs-pa*.
Defeat vb. *˳ṗam-par byed-pa*.
Defect s. *skyon*.
Defective *skyon-čan*.
Defence *skyabs*.
Defend *skyoṅ-ba*; *skyob-pa*.
Defender (of religion) *čos-skyóṅ*.
Defer v. *˳gyaṅ-ba*.
Deficient *sgob-sgób*.
Defile s. *roṅ*.
Defile vb. *bsgo-ba*; *˳bag-pa*.
Defilement *grib*.
Deform vb. *mi sdug-par byed-pa*.
Degenerate adj. *brgyud-méd*; *rigs-nyáms*.
Degree (rank) *ťem-pa*, *ťem-rim*; *sa* no. 2; *go*, *go-ṗaṅ*; a high — v. *rlabs*; by degrees *ḱad-kyis*; *mťar-gyis*; *rim-gyis*, *rim-pa bžin du*
Dejected *žum-pa*; *mi dga-ba*, v. *dga-ba* III; *dman-pa*.
Delay s. *bšol-ba*.
Delay vb., to be delayed *˳gyaṅ-ba*.
Delegate vb. a. *mṅag-pa*.
Delegate s. *ťsab-po*, resp. *sku-ťsáb*.
Deliberate vb. *bka-bgro-ba*, *bgro-ba*.
Deliberation *grabs*, *˳dun-ma*, *˳dun-gros*.
Delight s. *dga-ba*; *dga-spró*, *dga-ťsór*, *dga-ráṅs*, *dga-mgú*; to take — in *dga-ba*, resp. *dgyes-pa* or *mnyes-pa*; *spro-ba*.
Delighted *dga-mo*, *dga-ba*, *dga-raṅs*; to be *dga-ba*.
Delightful *dga-mo*, *dga-ťsor če-ba*.
Delineation *bkod-pa*; *ris*, *ri-mo*.
Deliver (rescue) *sgrol-ba*; (transfer) *sprod-pa*; *γtod-pa*; *skur-ba*.
Deliverance (liberation) *grol-ba*.
Deliverer *skyabs-mgón*; *srog-skyób W.*
Dell *grog-po*.
Delude *mgo skor-ba*.
Deluge s. *ču-rúd*.
Delusion *snaṅ-˳ḱrúl*.
Delusive *kun-rdzób*; *˳ḱrul-snaṅ-čan*.
Demand vb. *˳dod-pa*.
Demeanour *spyod-lam*.
Demon *bgegs*; *˳goṅ-po*.
Den *ťsaṅ*.
Denomination *čos-lugs*.
Dense *stugs-po*; *˳ťug-po*.
Density *ska-slád*.
Depart *čas-pa*; *bžud-pa*; (deviate) *˳gyur-ba*.
Depend upon *rten-pa*; *blo skyel-ba W.*, *ḱel-ba C.*
Deportment *spyod-pa*.
Depository *mdzod*.

Depression (incision) *ltoṅ-ga.*
Deprive *ₒṗrog-pa*; *ₒṗral-ba*; to be deprived *ₒbral-ba.*
Depth *zab-ḱyád*; *γtiṅ*; *zab-pa*; *zabs.*
Deranged *ₒḱrul-ba* no. 3.
Derangement *skyon.*
Descend *ₒbab-pa.*
Descendants *brgyud.*
Describe *ston-pa*; *ₒbri-ba.*
Description *bšad-pa*; *bstan-pa*; *γnas-ṫsul*, *γnas-lugs*; *rnam-ṫar*; *byed-ṫsul*, *yod-ṫsul.*
Desert s. *dgon-pa*; *ₒbrog(-stoṅ).*
Deserted *stoṅ-pa.*
Deserve v. *ₒos-pa.*
Design vb. a. (delineate) *ₒbri-ba*; *ₒgod-pa*; (intend for) *sṅo-ba*
Design s. *ri-mo.*
Desirable *mḱo-ba.*
Desire s. *ṫob-bló*; *ₒdod-pa.*
Desire vb. *ₒdod-pa*; *smon-pa*; *žen-pa*; *sred-pa*; *rṅam-pa*; *rṅab-pa*; *rkam-pa.*
Desolate adj. *ṅo bab-pa*; *žum-pa.*
Despair s. *yi(d) γčod-pa*; *yi(d) mug-pa.*
Despair vb. *ḱo-tag γčod-pa*; *yi(d)-mug-pa.*
Despise *brnyas-pa*; *rṅan-čen byed-pa*; *ḱyad-du γsod-pa*; *ₒgyiṅ-ba*; *smad-pa.*
Despond *spa-sgoṅ-ba.*
Despondency *žum-pa*; *yi(d) mug.*
Destine *sko-ba*; *sṅo-ba.*
Destiny *skal-ba*; *sko-ba*; *bsod-bdé*; *dbaṅ-ṫáṅ.*
Destitute *kun-gyis btaṅ-ba*; *mgon-méd*; *rten-méd.*
Destroy *ₒgem-pa*; *rṅam-pa*; *ₒǰig-pa*; *ₒǰoms-pa*; *ṫsar-γčod-pa* 458; *ma-ruṅ-bar byed-pa*; *med-par byed-pa.*
Destruction *žig-ral*, v. *ral-ba.*
Detail s., in — *rgyas-par* 109.
Detain *skyil-ba*; *bšol-ba.*
Detect *rnyed-pa*; *ṫob-pa.*
Determine vb. a. (induce) *skul-ba*; vb. n. (resolve) *ṫag γčod-pa.*
Detest *spoṅ-ba.*
Develop vb. n. *rgyas-pa* 109.
Deviate *ₒḱyar-ba*; *ₒgol-ba.*
Devil *bdud*; *bgegs.*
Devise *dmigs-pa-nas* (or *sems-kyis*) *γzo-ba*; *dgoṅs-pa.*
Devote vb. *sṅo-ba.*
Devotion *gus-pa*, *daṅ-ba.*
Devour *čur mid-pa*; *hab-háb za-ba.*
Devout *skal-dán*; *gus-pa*; *čos-čan*; *daṅ-ba.*
Dew s. *zil-pa.*
Dexterity *sgyu-rtsál.*
Dexterous *skyen-pa*; *rtsal-čan.*
Diadem *čod-pán.*
Diagram *dkyil-ₒḱor.*
Dialect *skad-lúgs.*
Diamond *rdo-rǰe*, *dor-ǰe-ṗa-lám.*
Diaphragm *mčin-ri.*
Diarrhoea *ₒḱru-ba*; *šal W.* 567.
Dictionary *miṅ-gi mdzod.*
Die, dice s. *čo-lo*, *čol*; *šo*; to play at — *šo rtse-ba*; *šo gyed-pa.*
Die vb. n. *ₒči-ba*, *ši-ba*; resp. *dgoṅs-pa*, and *ₒgroṅ-ba*; eleg. *ₒgum-pa*; v. *ₒda-ba*; to — out *ₒčad-pa.*
Diet *spyod-lam*; lenten — *dkar-zás.*
Difference *ḱyad*, *ḱyad-par*; *bye-brag*; to find a — *γnyis-su ₒdzin-pa.*
Different *mi-γčig*; *ṫa-dad-pa*; *so-só*; *mi-ₒdra-ba*; not — *γčig-pa.*
Difficult *dka-ba*, *dka-bo*; *ḱag-po*, *ḱab-le.*
Diffuse vb. *ₒgyed-pa.*
Dig *rko-ba*; *bru-ba.*
Digest *ₒǰu-ba*; *žu-ba.*
Digestion *ₒǰu-ba.*
Dignitary *ṫsan-po.*
Dignity *go-grál*, *go-ṗáṅ*; *go-sá*; *gras*; *dbu-ₒṗáṅ.*
Dike *ču-rags*, *ču-lon*; *rags.*
Dilapidated *gog-po.*
Diligence *brtson-ₒgrus*; *snyiṅ-rús*; to use — *rtsol-ba skyed-pa.*
Diligent *brtson-pa-čan.*
Diligently *rtsol-bar.*
Dim adj. *dkrigs-pa*; *bkrag-čór*; *man-mún Ld.*; to grow — *ₒgrib-pa.*
Diminish vb. a. *ₒṗri-ba*; vb. n. *ₒgrib-pa.*
Dimness *rab-rib*, *hrab-hrib.*
Din *ₒdu-ₒdzi.*
Dip vb. *spag-pa.*
Diploma *bka-rgya*, *bka-šog*; — of nobility *dpal-gyi γnaṅ-šóg.*
Direct vb. a. *γtod-pa*; to be —ed *ston-pa*, *lta-ba.*
Direction *ṅo*, *ṅos*; *ṗyogs*; *man-ṅág*; *žal-ta*; *šed.*
Directly *de-ma-ṫag-tu.*
Director **ₒgo-pǫn* C.*
Dirt *dri-ma*; *dreg-pa*; *rkyag-pa*; *lčags-dregs.*
Dirty adj. *dri-ma-čan*; *btsog-pa*; *gos-pa*; *mi-γtsaṅ-ba*; *ṫsi-du W.*
Dirty vb. a. *ₒgo-ba.*
Disadvantage *skyon.*
Disagreeable *mi-sdug-pa*; *yid-du-mi-ₒoṅ-ba.*
Disappear *mi-snaṅ-bar ₒgyur-ba*; *yal-ba*; *med-par ₒgyur-ba*; *ₒǰig-pa*; *ₒbud-pa.*
Disapprove *ₒdor-ba*; *mi γnaṅ-ba.*
Disciple *grwa-pa*; *nye-γnas*; *slob-ₒbáṅs.*
Discontented *skyo-mo*; *mi dga-ba.*
Discontinue *γčod-pa.*
Discord *dbyen-pa*; *sel.*
Discouraged *ṅo ₒbab-pa.*
Discourse s. *gleṅ-brǰód*, *gleṅ-mo*; *lda-gu.*
Discuss *bgro-ba.*
Disdain s. *rṅan-čén.*
Disease s. *nad*; *na-ba*; *snyuṅ*; chronic — *γčoṅ*; fatal — *ₒči-nád.*
Disfigured *gya-ba.*

Disgrace s. *rkaṅ-˳drén, żabs-˳drén.*
Disgrace vb. a. *dma-˳bebs-pa.*
Disguise s. *˳bag; rdzu-ba.*
Disguise vb. a. *˳gebs-pa;* v. *čas* 156.
Disgust s. *skyo-šás; ḱrel; rnam-rtóg.*
Dish *ka-to-ra; sder-ma; spags; skyu-rúm W.*
Disheartened *skyo-mo.*
Dishonour vb. *smad-pa; dma ˳bebs-pa.*
Disk *kyir-kyír; dkyil-˳ḱór; ˳ḱor-lo; sgor-mo.*
Dislocated, to be — *˳ḱrul-ba.*
Dismay s. *żum-pa.*
Dismiss *bka ˳grol-ba; ˳gyed-pa; γtoṅ-ba; ˳don-pa.*
Disorder s. *˳ḱrug-pa; skyon; ˳ḱral-˳ḱrúl.*
Dispatch vb. *rdzoṅ-ba; zlog-pa; γtoṅ-ba, mṅag-pa.*
Dispel *zlog-pa.*
Dispense vb. (deal out) *˳brim-pa.*
Disperse vb. a. *˳gye-ba, ˳gyed-pa; γčor-ba;* vb. n. *˳byer-ba; yan ča-če W.*
Display vb. *˳grems-pa; γčal-ba.*
Disposition s. (character) *rgyud; ṅaṅ; ṅaṅ-rgyúd; raṅ-bżin; γšis.*
Disputation *rtsod-pa.*
Dispute vb. n. *rgol-ba; rtsod-pa.*
Dispute s. *ḱa-mču, rtsod-pa, ˳dziṅ-mo.*
Dissatisfaction *mi-dga-bai sems.*
Dissatisfied *mi-dga-ba;* also *˳ḱon-pa.*
Dissect *˳byed-pa.*
Dissension *˳ḱon-po; naṅ-sel, sel; dbyen-pa.*
Dissertation *rgyud, mdo.*
Dissimilarity *ḱyad-par; mi-˳dra-ba.*
Dissolute *˳čol-pa;* to be — *mi ťsaṅs-par spyod-pa.*
Dissolve vb. a. *˳ǰig-pa;* to be dissolved *ťim-pa.*
Dissuade *sgyur-ba; zlog-pa.*
Distance *rgyaṅ-ma; nye-riṅ; ťag; ṕa-ťsad, ṕa-zád.*
Distant *ťag-riṅ(-mo).*
Distend *rkyoṅ-ba.*
Distinct *ḱrol-po; čod-po; wa-lé, wal-le-ba.*
Distinction *ḱyad; dbye-ba.*
Distinguish *rnam(-par) bżag(-pa).*
Distinguished *˳ṕags-pa; ḱyad-par-čan.*
Distorted *ča-čús;* to be — *˳ḱrul-ba.*
Distress s. *sdug-bsṅal, mya-ṅan, dka-las.*
Distribute *bgod-pa; ˳brim-pa;* v. *˳gyed-pa.*
District *yul-ḱág; yul-lǰóṅs; yul-sde; ḱul; sde.*
Disturb *dkrug-pa; γyeṅs-par byed-pa; bar-du γčod-pa;* to be disturbed *˳ḱrug-pa.*
Disturber *bstan-šig.*
Ditch *ču-˂óbs; ˂obs.*
Diverse *sna-ťsogs; sna-so-só.*
Diversity *bye-ba; mi ˳dra-ba.*
Divert *sgyur-ba; rtse-ba; zlog-pa.*
Divide *bgod-pa; ˳gyed-pa; ˳byed-pa; ˳ges-pa;* to be divided *˳gye-ba.*
Dividend *bgo-byá.*
Divine s. *čos-pa.*
Division *dbye-ba; bye-brág; ḱyad, ḱyad-par; ču-tsán; rnam-pa; ḱag.*
Divisor *bgod-byéd.*
Dizzy, I am — *mgo ˳ḱor.*
Do *byed-pa; spyod-pa;* eleg. *bgyid-pa;* resp. *mdzad-pa;* that will — **dig-pa yin* C.; des čog.*
Doctrine *čos; bstan-pa.*
Dog *ḱyi,* male — *ḱyi-ṕo,* fem. *ḱyi-mo;* mad — *ḱyi smyon-pa;* — kennel *ḱyi-ḱáṅ, ḱyi-pul.*
Doll *miu.*
Domain *ḱams; ḱul; dbaṅ-ris.*
Domicile *mčis-bráṅ.*
Dominion *ḱams* 39; v. *rgyal-ḱams* 108; *ṅaṅ; mṅa; čab-˂óg; dbaṅ-ris; srid.*
Door *sgo; čab-sgo;* large — *sgo-mo;* little — *sgeu;* principal — *rgyal-sgo;* — bar *γtan-pa;* — frame *sgo-˳drig;* — hinge *sgo-ḱor, go-ṗiṅ W.;* — keeper *sgo-pa,* resp. *čabs-sgo-pa, sgo-sruṅ.*
Dose s. *ťun.*
Dosser *tse-po, tsel-po.*
Dot s. *ťseg.*
Double adj. *γnyis-ldáb;* — tongued *lče-γnyis-pa;* — barreled gun *nyi-rag W.;* (v. *sbrag-pa*); *ťsaṅ-yá.*
Double vb. a. *skum-pa.*
Doubt s. *ťe-tsóm; ťsom-pa; ťsom-ťsóm; yid-γnyis.*
Doubtful *γtol-méd.*
Dough *skyo-ma; bag-zan.*
Down adv. *ťur; ťeṅ-la C.; γšam-du;* to go — *nub-pa, ˳bab-pa.*
Downward *mar, mas; ˂og-tu, šod-du.*
Dowry *rdzoṅs.*
Doze vb. *nyid ťom-pa.*
Drag vb. *˳drud-pa.*
Dragon *˳brug.*
Dram s. (weight) *żo* 478.
Draught s. (drawing) *bkod-pa; ri-mo;* (drink) *hub.*
Draw (pull) *˳ťen-pa; ˳dren-pa;* to — in *rṅub-pa; skum-pa;* to — out *˳ťen-pa; ˳byin-pa;* to — up (to compose) *˳god-pa.*
Dreadful *˳ǰigs-pa.*
Dream s. *rmi-lam,* resp. *mnal-lam;* vb. *rmi-ba.*
Dress s. *gos, čas;* resp. *na-bza.*
Dress vb. a. (to clothe) *skon-pa;* (to cook) *˳tsod-pa, ˳tsed-pa;* to — wounds *sdom-pa.*
Dressed up *zab-mo.*
Dried *skam-po;* — up *kum-pa.*
Drink vb. *˳ťuṅ-ba.*
Drink s. *skyems; żal-skóm;* meat and *bza-btúṅ.*

**Drinkable water** *skems-ču.*
**Drinking-cup** *skyogs*; *čaṅ-čan, ṕor-pa, ko-re W.*
**Drip** vb. *₀dzag-pa.*
**Drive** vb. *₀ded-pa*; to — back *₀gogs-pa*; *zlog-pa*; to — out *skrod-pa*; *bda-ba.*
**Driver** *₀ded-mi.*
**Drop** s. *ťigs-pa.*
**Drop** vb. a. *ḱrul γtoṅ-ba*; vb. n. *₀dzag-pa*; *₀čor-ba.*
**Dropsy** *pags-ču*; *snyiṅ-ču*; *dmu-ču.*
**Dross** *lčags-drégs.*
**Drowned,** to be — *₀ťsub-pa*; *čus ₀ḱyer-ba.*
**Drum** s. *rṅa*; — skin *rṅa-lpágs*; — stick *rṅa-lčág.*
**Drummer** *rṅa-pa.*
**Drunk** *ra-ro-ba*; *bzi-čan W.*; to get — *bzi-ba.*
**Drunkard** *čaṅ-dad-čan W.*
**Drunkenness** *ra-ro.*
**Dry** adj. *skam-pa, skam-po*; *skem-pa*; — weather, drought *ťan-pa.*
**Dry** vb. a. *skem-pa.*
**Dryness** *skam-pa.*
**Duck** s. (water-fowl) *ṅur-ba.*
**Due** adj. *dgos-pa.*
**Duel** s. *₀ḱrug-pa.*
**Dulcimer** *yan-ljin Ts.*
**Dull** adj. *lkugs-pa*; *glen-pa*; *rtul-po*; *blun-pa.*
**Dullness** *rmu-ba.*
**Dumb** *lkugs-pa*; *smra-mi-nus-pa.*
**Dumpling** *ču-ta-gir W.*
**Dung** s. *lča Ld.*; *lči-ba W.*; *brun.*
**Dungeon** *ḱri-mún*; *btson-doṅ.*
**Dupe** vb. a. *mgo skor byed-pa* 25.
**During** prep. *ḱons-su*; *na* 298; *riṅ-la.*
**Dusky** *man-mún.*
**Dust** s. *ḱyim-sa*; *ťal-ba*; *rdul*; *ṕye-ma*; cloud of — *bud.*
**Duty** *ḱag*; *ḱrims*; *sdom-pa*; moral — *ťsul-ḱrims*; (tax) *dpya*; *šo-gám.*
**Dwarf** *miu.*
**Dwell** *γnas-pa*, *₀dug-pa*; *sdod-pa*; resp. *bžugs-pa*; *₀ḱod-pa.*
**Dwelling** s. *γnas-ḱaṅ*, *γnas-ťsaṅ*; eleg. *mčis-braṅ*; temporary — *₀braṅ-sa.*
**Dwindle** *yal-ba.*
**Dye** s. *ťsos*; vb. a. *ťsos rgyag-pa.*
**Dynasty** *rgyal-brgyúd*; *rgyal-rábs.*

# E

**Each** *kun*; *re, re-ré*
**Eager** *₀dod-čan, ₀dod-ldan*; to be — *₀dod-pa*; *sred-pa.*
**Eagle** *go-bo*; *glag.*
**Ear** *rna-ba*; resp. *snyan*; — ache *rna-ba na-ba*; — hole *rna-ḱúṅ*; — shot *rgyaṅ-grágs*; — wax *klog-pa*; *rna-ḱyág*; — of corn *snye-ma.*
**Early** adj. and adv. v. *sṅa* 135; earlier *sṅa-ma, sṅa-mo*; earlier or later *sṅa-rtiṅ-du.*
**Earn** *ḱug-pa.*
**Earnest** s., in good — *don-dám.*
**Earnestly** *snyiṅ-nas*; v. also *yaṅ-dag-pa*, sub. *dag-pa* 248.
**Earth** *sa*; *sa čen-po*; — quake *sa-γyós*; *saṅ-gúl W.*
**East** *šar.*
**Easy** *sla-ba*; *lhod-pa.*
**Eat** *za-ba, bza-ba*; resp. *γsol-ba*; *mčod-pa*; v. also *₀ťuṅ-ba*; to — up *ma-lus-par za-ba.*
**Echo** s. *brag-ča*; *sgra-brnyán.*
**Eclipse** of the moon *zla-₀dzin,* of the sun *nyi-₀dzin.*
**Edge** *ḱa*; *ča-ga*; *mťa*; *zur*; — of a knife *dṅo.*
**Edict** *bka-šog*, *γsuṅ-šog*; *bkar-btags-pa.*
**Edifice** *bkod-pa* 96.
**Educate** *₀ťso-ba*; *γso-ba, γso-skyon byed-pa.*
**Effect** vb. a. *byed-pa.*
**Effect** s. *₀bras-bu*; effects (goods) *ča-lag W., lag-ča, yo-byad.*
**Effervesce** *₀ḱol-ba.*
**Efficacy** *nus-pa.*
**Egg** *sgo-ṅá, ťul W.*
**Egotism** *bdag-₀dzin* 268.
**Egypt** *mi-sér yul.*
**Eight** num. *brgyad*; eighth *brgyad-pa*; eighteen *ču-brgyad*; eighteenth *ču-brgyad-pa*; eighty *brgyad-ču*; eightieth *brgyad-ču-pa.*
**Either** — or *yaṅ-na — yaṅ-na.*
**Eject** *skrod-pa*; *₀dor-ba.*
**Elapse** *₀da-ba.*
**Elbow** *gru-mo, gre-mo*; *dre-bo.*
**Elder** adj. *če-ba, čen-po*; — brother *jo-bo*; *ťu-bo.*
**Elder** s. *rgad-po.*
**Election** *γdam-ka.*
**Electuary** *lde-gu.*
**Element** *₀byuṅ-ba*; *ḱams.*
**Elephant** *glaṅ, glaṅ-po-čé, glaṅ-čén.*
**Elevate** *sgro-₀dogs-pa*; *₀degs-pa*; *spar-ba*; *seṅ-ba.*
**Eleven** *bču-γčig*; eleventh *bču-γčig-pa.*
**Elk** *ḱa-šá ša-ba.*
**Eloquence** *ḱa-sbyaṅ.*
**Eloquent** *ṅag-dbáṅ*; *ḱa-sbyaṅ-po*; *ḱa-šugs-čan W.*
**Elsewhere** *γžan-du.*

Emanate *˳p̒ro-ba.*
Emanation *sprul-ba* 336.
Emboss *p̒ur-ba.*
Embrace vb. *˳ḱyud-pa*; *˳ḱril-ba*; *˳dzin-pa*; *ḱyab-pa.*
Emerald *ma-rgád.*
Emerge *˳byuṅ-ba.*
Emetic *skyug-smán.*
Eminent *ḱyad-par-čan*; *p̒un-sum-ṫsogs-pa*; *rgyal-ba*; *p̒ul-tu byúṅ-ba.*
Emit *˳byin-pa.*
Emmet *gre-mog-bu W.*; *grog-ma.*
Empale *γsal-šiṅ-la skyon-pa.*
Emperor *rgyal-pc čen-po.*
Empire *ḱams*; *yul-ḱáms*; *rgyal-ḱág.*
Employ *skyel-ba*; *spyod-pa*; to be — ed or busy *brel-ba.*
Empty *stoṅ-pa*; to make — *stoṅs-pa.*
Emulate *˳gran-pa.*
Emulation *˳gran-sems.*
Enabled, to be — *ḱom-pa* 44.
Encampment *sgar*; *dmag-sgár.*
Enchanter *˳goṅ-po*; enchantress *˳goṅ-ba-mo.*
Encircle *skor-ba.*
Enclose *skor-ba.*
Enclosure *skor-ba*; *ra-ba.*
Encompass *˳ḱyigs-pa*; *˳ḱyud-pa*; *skor-ba.*
End s. *mǰug*; *mṫa, mṫa-ma*; *p̒ug*; *γžug*; towards or at the — *mṫa-ru, mṫar*; to be at an — *rdzogs-pa, zin-pa.*
Endeavour vb. *rtsol-ba*; *lhur len-pa*; *don-du γnyer-ba*; s. *˳grus-pa.*
Endless *mṫa-yás*; *mṫa-méd.*
Enemy *dgra, dgra-bo*; *p̒a-rol-po*; *˳ṫse-ba.*
Energy *šugs.*
Engagement (promise) *čad*; *sdom-pa*; v. also *las, brel-ba.*
Engrave *rko-ba.*
Enjoin *skul-ba.*
Enjoy *loṅs spyod-pa*; — one's self *rtse-ba.*
Enjoyment *loṅs-spyód*; *nyams-myoṅ.*
Enlarge *rgyas-pa*; *˳p̒el-ba*; *dar-ba*; — upon *spro-ba.*
Enough *ṫsad*; *čog-pa*; to be — *˳ḱyed-pa*; *˳grig-pa.*
Ensnare *dkri-ba.*
Enter vb. a. *˳ǰug-pa*; *˳ṫsugs-pa*; *˳ṫsud-pa*; vb. n. *čud-pa.*
Entertainment *mgron*; v. also *mčod-stón.*
Entire *tsaṅ-ma*; *ril-ba*; *son-te W.*
Entity *ṅo-bo-nyid* 129; *čos-nyid* 164.
Entrails *rgyu-ma, naṅ-ḱrol.*
Entrance (vestibule) *sgo-ḱáṅ.*
Entrust *˳čol-ba*; *γtod-pa, γnyer-ḱa γtad-pa.*
Enumerate *sgraṅ-ba, bsgraṅ-ba*; *˳dren-pa.*
Enumeration *rnam-gráṅs.*
Envelope *yi-gei šubs.*
Envious *p̒rag-dog-čan*; v. also *če-ré.*
Envoy *p̒o-nya.*
Envy s. *p̒rag-dóg*; *mig-sér.*
Envy vb. *p̒rag-pa.*
Epidemy *rims(-nad)*; *ṅan-rims.*
Epilepsy *ḱyab-˳ǰug*; *γza-nád*; *γza-p̒og-pa.*
Epistle *yi-ge.*
Epitaph *dur-byaṅ.*
Equal *mnyam-pa*; *snyoms-po* 201; *˳dra-ba*; *mṫsuṅs-pa.*
Equality *mnyam-pa-nyid*; *˳dra-mi-˳dra.*
Equanimity *snyoms-pa*; *btaṅ-snyóms.*
Equivalent s. *dod*; *ṫsab.*
Eradicate *rtsad-nas γčod-pa.*
Erect adj. *kye-ré*; *ḱroṅ-ṅe.*
Erect vb. a. *sgreṅ-ba*; *˳dzugs-pa*; *bžeṅ-ba.*
Err *˳ḱyar-ba*; *˳ḱrul-ba*; *˳gol-ba*; *nor-ba.*
Error *˳gal-sa*; *˳ḱrul-so, ˳ḱrul-γži.*
Eructation *skyug-ldád*; *sgreg-pa.*
Escape vb. *˳čor-ba*; *˳bud-pa.*
Escort s. *skyel-ma*; *bsel(-ba), lam-bsél.*
Escort vb. *rdzoṅ ˳debs-pa.*
Especially *ḱyad-par-du.*
Essence *ṅo-bo-nyid* 129; *bčud* (quintessence) 147.
Establish *˳god-pa.*
Estafet *rta-zam-pa.*
Esteem s. *p̒u-dúd*; *rtsis*; *ya-ša.*
Esteem vb. a. *bkur-ba*; *γčes-par byed-pa* or *˳dzin-pa.*
Estimation *rtsis*; *ṫsod* 453.
Eternal *rtag-pa*; *skye-˳či-med-pa.*
Eternity *rtag-tu-ba* (?).
Ether *mḱa.*
Etymology *ṫa-snyád.*
Eunuch *nyug-rúm.*
Euphony *sgra-dbyaṅs.*
Europe *rgya-pi-liṅ*; *p̒yi-gliṅ*, vulgo *p̒i-liṅ.*
European s. *p̒a-ráṅ, p̒e-ráṅ*; *p̒i-liṅ-pa.*
Evade *˳ǰur-ba, ˳dzur-ba*; *˳ǰol-ba*; *˳čor-ba.*
Evangelist *p̒rin-bzaṅ sgrog-pa(-po).*
Evaporate *ṫim-pa.*
Even adj. *mnyam-pa.*
Even vb. a (to level) *snyom-pa.*
Even adv. *ṫa-na*; *yaṅ*; not — v. *yaṅ* 505.
Evening *nub*; *nub-mo*; *dgoṅs.*
Evenness *nyam-pa-nyid.*
Event *rkyen*; *dṅos-po*; at all events *čis kyaṅ, gaṅ yin kyaṅ* 65; *ga-na-méd W., gar-méd W.*
Ever *rtag-tu*; *γtan-du*; *dus-rgyun-du.*
Every *kun*; *re, re-ré*; v. *gaṅ* 65; — day *dkyus-ma*; *žag daṅ žag* 248; — thing *čaṅ*; *či*; *kun.*
Everywhere *kun-tu*; v. *čir* 141.
Evidence *rgyu-mṫsan* 111.
Evident *mṅon-pa.*
Evidently v. *ṅes-pa* 128.
Evil s. *ṅan*; *nyes-pa.*
Evil adj. *ṅan-pa*; *ṫu-ba*; — spirit *˳goṅ-po.*
Exact adj. *žib-pa.*

**Exactly** *ḱo-na*; *raṅ*; — that *de-dé* 256.
**Exaggerate** *sgro-ₒdogs-pa.*
**Exalt** *sgro-ₒdogs-pa.*
**Exalted** *ₒṕags-pa.*
**Examination** *brtags-dpyad.*
**Examine** *rtog-pa*; *dpyod-pa*; *γžig-pa*; *sad-pa.*
**Example** *dpe*; *dpe-brjód.*
**Excavate** *γčoṅ-ba*; *sbug-pa.*
**Excavation** *sbugs*; *šoṅ.*
**Excellence** *dṅos-grub*; *če-ba.*
**Excellent** *rgyal ba*; *ḱyad-par-čan*; *γčes-pa*; *ṕun-ťsógs*; *ₒṕags-pa.*
**Except** prep. *ma γtogs-par*; *min, min·par.*
**Exchange** s. (agio) *ṕar.*
**Excite** *sloṅ-ba, dkrog-pa.*
**Exclaim** *ₒbod-pa.*
**Exclusively** *ḱo-na.*
**Excrement** *rkyag-pa*; *rtug-pa*; *dri-ma.*
**Excrescence** *lba-ba*; *mdzer-pa*; *ₒdzer-pa.*
**Execrate** *ṅan ₒdebs-pa*; *mṅan-pa*; *dmod-pa ₒbor-ba.*
**Exercise** s. (bodily) *spyod-lam* 335; — of religion *čos-spyod.*
**Exercise** vb. a. *sbyoṅ-ba*; *lag-tu len-pa.*
**Exert** one's self *ₒbad-pa.*
**Exertion** *ₒbad-pa*; *brtson-pa*; *don-γnyér*; *dka-ba.*
**Exhausted** *nyams-ťag-pa*; to be — (consumed) *ₒdzad-pa*; *zin-pa*; (tired) *ₒčad-pa*; *ṅal-ₒčad-pa, ťaṅ-ₒčad-pa.*
**Exhort** *skul-ba*; *skul-čag byed-pa*; *bslab-bya byed-pa*, or *ston-pa*, or *btaṅ-ba.*
**Exhortation** *bskul-ba, bskul-ma*; *snyiṅ-γtam*; *luṅ, luṅ-bstán*; *bslab-bya*; farewell — *ḱa-čéms.*
**Exile** vb. a. *γnas-nas dgar-ba.*
**Exist** cf. *ₒdug-pa*; *yod-pa*; *skye-ba.*
**Existence** *skye-ba*; *srid-pa.*
**Exorcise** *dam-la ₒdogs-pa.*
**Expanse** *kloṅ*; *ḱa-žéṅ.*
**Expect** *sgug-pa.*
**Expedient** adj. *ṕan-ₒdogs-pa, ṕan-ťogs-čan*; *rigs-pa* 528; *don-byed-nus-pa*
**Expel** *skrod-pa*; *ₒǰil-ba*; *ₒdon-pa*; *spyug-pa*; *ₒbud-pa*; *zlog-pa.*
**Expend** *skyag-pa.*
**Expenditure, Expense** *ₒgro-sgo*; *skyag-pa, skyag-sgo.*
**Expensive** *gus-po.*
**Experience** vb. a. *myoṅ-ba, nyams-su myoṅ-ba*; v. also *sbyoṅ-ba.*
**Experience** s. *slobs.*
**Experienced** (skilled) *mḱas-pa.*
**Expiation** *sdig-bšágs.*
**Expire** *ₒda-ba.*
**Explain** *ₒgrel-ba*, *ₒgrol-ba*; *ṅo sprod-pa*; *ₒčad-pa*; *bšad-pa.*
**Explanation** *brda-spród.*
**Exploit** *ḱyo ga.*
**Expressly** *čed-du.*
**Exquisite** *mčog-tu bkrab*; *kyad-par ₒṕags-pa.*
**Extend** *rkyoṅ-ba*; *bsnar-ba.*
**Extension** *ḱyon*; *gu.*
**Extensive** *rgyas-pa*; *yaṅs-pa.*
**Extent** *ḱyon*; *rgya, rgya-ḱyon, rgya-ba*; *ču-žeṅ* 158.
**Exterior** s. *rnam-pa*; *ča-byad* 152.
**External** *ṕyii*, v. *ṕyi* III 349; — appearance *ča-byad, ṕyi-rol.*
**Extinct**, to become — *ₒčad-pa*; *ši-ba.*
**Extinguish** *γsod-pa.*
**Extra** *ₒteb.*
**Extract** vb. a. *bku-ba*; *ₒbyin-pa*; *ₒdon-pa.*
**Extraction** (descent) *rigs.*
**Extremity** (end) *mťa-ma, zur.*
**Eye** s. *mig*, resp. *spyan*; — brow *smin-ma*; — lash *rdzi-ma*; *mig-γšog*, resp. *spyan-γšog*; — lid *mig-ṕág C. W.*

# F

**Fable** s. *sgruṅs.*
**Fabricate** vb. a. *ₒčos-pa*; *bčo-ba*; *byed-pa*; *bzo-ba*; to be fabricated *grub-pa.*
**Face** s. *γdoṅ*; *ṅo*; *ḱa*; *skye-sgó*; *sgo-lo*; *bžin*; in the — of *ḱa-ru, ḱar.*
**Face** vb. (to be directed towards) *ston-pa.*
**Fail** vb. (to miss) *mi ḱes-pa C.*; *mi-ₒťebs-pa W.*; (to err) *ₒgol-ba*; (to dwindle) *yal-ba.*
**Faint** adj. *nyams-čun*; to get — *γčoṅ-ba.*
**Faint** vb. n. *brgyal-ba*; *ₒḱam-pa.*
**Fair** adj. *mdzes-pa*; *mťsar-ba*; *bzaṅ-ba.*
**Faith** *dad-pa.*
**Faithful** *dad-pa*; *γdeṅs-pa*; *slu-méd*; *gyo-sgyu-méd.*
**Falchion** *gri-gug.*
**Falcon** *ḱra.*
**Fall** vb. *ₒgril-ba*; *ₒgyel-ba*; *ltuṅ-ba*; *ₒbab-pa*; to — in drops *ₒtig-pa*; to — off *ₒbyi-ba*; to — to pieces *ₒǰig-pa*; *ₒgril-ba W.*; to — upon *ₒbuṅs-pa.*
**Fall** s. *ltuṅ-ba.*
**Fallow** *yan-pa.*
**False** *mi bden-pa*; *rdzus-ma*; *γyo-čan*; — charge *ḱa-yog*; *snyad*; — conception *bčos-pa*; — sentiment *lta-lóg, log-lta.*
**Falsehood** *dkyus*; *ḱa-šób*; *rdzun.*
**Fame** *grags-pa.*
**Family** *brgyud*; *γduṅ*; *bu-smád*; *γžis-mad*; *rabs*; *rigs-brgyúd*; *rus.*

Famine *mu-ge.*
Famous *grags-čan.*
Fan s. *ṅa-yáb.*
Fan vb. a. *ₒk̓rab-pa*; v. *yab-mo.*
Fancy vb. a. *sgom-pa*; *dmigs-pa*; *sems-pa*; vb. n. *mno-ba.*
Fancy s. *dmigs-pa*; *sems-kyi snaṅ-ba.*
Fang *k̓ron*; *mče-ba, mče-so.*
Far *rgyaṅ-riṅ-po, rgyaṅs* 107; (*t̓ug-*)*riṅ-ba*; *mi nye-ba*; as — as *bar-du, k̓ad-du*; — famed *sgra-čé*; — from *lta či smos* 215.
Farewell v. *ga-le* 64; to say — v. *p̓yi-p̓yag*, sub *p̓yag.*
Farm s *groṅ-bžis*; — steward *ynyer-pa* 194.
Farmer *k̓yim-pa-pa*; *žiṅ-pa* 475.
Farsightedness *mig-rgyáṅ* 414.
Farther *p̓ar.*
Fashion s. *čos*; *lugs.*
Fast adj. *mgyogs-pa*; *myur-ba.*
Fast vb. n. *smyuṅ-ba*; *dge-ba sruṅ-ba.*
Fasten *sdom-pa*; *ₒgrogs-pa*; *ₒdogs-pa*; *sgril-ba*; *sbyor-ba*; *sbrel-ba.*
Fasting s. *bsnyen-ynas, smyuṅ-ynas.*
Fat adj. *rgyas-pa*; *t̓so-ba*; *t̓son-po.*
Fat s. *t̓sil*; melted — *t̓sil-k̓u*; *žag.*
Fatal *byur-gyi*; *nyen-čan*; *ma-ruṅ-ba*; *śrog-len, śrog-ₒp̓rog.*
Fate *skal-ba, las-bskos* v. *sko-ba* 24; *bsod-pa*; *dbaṅ-t̓áṅ*; cf. also *lun-čags* and *las-ₒp̓ro.*
Father *p̓a*, resp *yab*; — in law *gyos-po*; *skud-po.*
Fathom s. *ₒdoms-pa.*
Fatigue s. *ṅal*, resp. *ₒo-brgyál.*
Fatigue vb. a. *ṅal ₒǰug-pa*; to be fatigued *ṅal-ba*, resp. *sku-ṅal-ba, t̓ugs ṅal-ba.*
Fault *skyon*; *noṅs-pa*; *ₒt̓saṅ.*
Faulty *skyon-čan.*
Favour s. *bka-drin*; v. *ynaṅ-ba* II 309.
Favourable *mt̓un-pa*; — circumstance *mt̓un-rkyén.*
Favourite s. *snyiṅ-sdúg*; *sdug-pa.*
Fear s. *ₒǰigs-pa, ₒǰigs-skrag, ₒǰigs-ri*; *bag-t̓sa* (*-ba*).
Fear vb. *ₒǰigs-pa*; *dṅaṅ-ba*; *dogs pa.*
Fearless *ₒǰigs-méd*; *bag-méd.*
Feast s. *dga-ston*; *mgron*; *ston-mo.*
Feather *spu*; quill — *sgro.*
Fee s. *gla*; *ṅan-pa*; *bag-śis.*
Feeble *kyar-kyór*; *kyór*; *nya-ra-nyo-ré.*
Feed *stob-pa*; *snyod-pa*; *ₒor-ba W.*; *ₒt̓so-ba, yso-ba.*
Feel *reg-pa, t̓sor-ba*; to — cold *ₒk̓yags-pa.*
Feeling s. *reg-bya.*
Feign vb. n. *bčos-pa* 148; v. *lugs byed-pa* (*lugs* no. 2, 548); *t̓sul-du byed-pa* (*t̓sul* no. 1, 450).
Fellow *grogs*; *ya-do W.*; — labourer *las-grogs*; — lodger *ₒdug-grogs, braṅ-grogs*, resp. *bžugs-grogs*: — traveller *lam-grógs.*
Felt s. *p̓yiṅ-pa.*
Female *mo.*
Fen *ₒdam*; *gram-pa.*
Fence s. *k̓o-ra*; *skyor-ba*; *ta-bér W.*; *pu-śu*; *ra-ba.*
Ferment vb. *ₒk̓ol-ba*; s. *žo-ri W.* 478; *ru-ma.*
Fern *skyes-ma.*
Ferocious *ṅar-po.*
Ferry s. *gru*; *rdziṅs, yziṅs.*
Ferry-man *gru-pa*; *ču-p̓yag-pa*; *mnyan-pa.*
Festival *dus-čén.*
Fetter vb. a. *sbrel-ba*; *ₒk̓yig-pa*; *ₒčiṅ-ba.*
Fetters s. *sgrogs*; *lčags, lčags-sgrog*; *bčiṅs-pa.*
Fever *t̓sad-pai nád C.*; *t̓san-zug W.*
Few *nyuṅ-ṅu*; a few *ₒga, ₒga tsam*; *nyuṅ-ṅu žig*; *čig* 140; *la-lá C.*
Fib s. *śob, yśob.*
Fibre *rgyus-pa.*
Fickle *gyi-na*; *ya-ma-brla*; *ₒgyur-ldog*; *skad yčig kyaṅ mi t̓sugs-pa.*
Fickleness *ₒgyur-ldog, ldog-ₒgyur.*
Fictitious *bčos-pa*; *dmigs-pa-nas bzos-pa.*
Fidget vb. *ₒp̓ar-ba.*
Field *žiṅ*; *kluṅs*; — terrace *daṅ-tse W.*
Fife *gliṅ-bu.*
Fifth *lṅa-pa*; fifteen *bčo-lṅa*; fifteenth *bčo-lṅa-pa*; fifty *lṅa-bču*; fiftieth *lṅa-bču-pa.*
Fight s. *ₒt̓ab-mo.*
Fight vb. a. *gyed-pa*; *rgol-ba*; *ₒt̓ab-pa*; *ₒt̓ab-mo byed-pa*; vb. n. *ₒk̓rug-pa*; *ₒgran-pa*; *rgol-ba*; *rtsod-pa*; *ₒdziṅ-ba.*
Figure s. *dkyil-k̓or*; *skye-yzúgs*; *bk̓od-pa*; *rnam-ₒgyúr*; *dbyibs*; *yzugs*; *bzo, zo*; *ri-mo*; *ris.*
Figured (variegated) *či-tra W.*
File s. (tool) *lčags-bdar*; *sed.*
File vb. (to string) *rgyud-pa*; *star-ba.*
Fill vb. *k̓yab-pa*; *ₒgeṅs-pa.*
Filter s. *t̓sag-ma*; vb. a *ₒt̓sag-pa.*
Filth *dri-ma*; *mi-ytsaṅ-ba* 433; *grib.*
Find *t̓ob-pa*; *rnyed-pa*; *k̓ug-pa.*
Fine adj. (beautiful) *mdzes-pa*; *sdug-pa*; *mtsar-ba*; (not coarse) *žib-pa*; *lag-mo W.*; (thin) *srab-pa.*
Fine s. (penalty) *rgyal, stoṅ.*
Finger *ser-mo, sor-mo*, resp. *p̓yag-sór*; *mdzub-mo, mdzug-gu*; — ring *ser-ydúb, sor-ydúb.*
Finish vb. *sgrub-pa*; to be finished *ₒgrub-pa*; *t̓sar-ba*; *rdzogs-pa*; *ₒdzad-pa*; *zin-pa.*
Fir *t̓aṅ-śiṅ*; *som, ysom, som-śiṅ.*
Fire s. *me*; — brand *gal-mé*; — fly *ₒod-p̓ro-ₒbu W.*; — place *t̓ab, me-t̓ab*; — tongs *me-lén.*
Firm (solid) *mk̓raṅ*; *mk̓regs-pa*; *sra-ba*; (trodden) *čag-čan* 167; (tight) *t̓aṅ-po, dam-po*; (sure) *btsan*; *ṅes-pa*; **(steady)** v. *t̓sugs-pa.*

Firmness (of mind) *snyiṅ-rús.*
First *daṅ-po*; *sṅa-ma*; *mgo-ma*: born *mgo-bu*; *sṅon-skyes*; — part *stod* 223: adv. (at first) *mgo-ma W.*; *sṅa-sór*, *sṅa-góṅ*; *sṅar*; *γčig-tu*; *ťog-mar.*
Firstfruits *ṕud.*
Firstly *daṅ-por.*
Fish s. *nya*; — bone *nya-grá.*
Fish vb. *nya rṅon-pa*; *nya γšor ba.*
Fishing-hook *mčil-pa.*
Fishing-net *nya-rgya*, *nya-dól.*
Fissure *rgya-sér*; *ser-ka.*
Fist *ḱu-ťsúr.*
Fit vb. a. v. *sgrig-pa* 120; to — out *śom-pa*; to be — *ₒťad-pa*; *ruṅ-ba.*
Five *lṅa.*
Fix vb. a. *ₒgod-pa*; *sbyor-ba*; — a time *dus byed-pa.*
Flabby *kyom.*
Flag s. *dar*; — staff *dar-po-čé.*
Flageolet *gliṅ-bu*
Flame s. *lče*, *me-lče.*
Flannel *ťer-ma.*
Flap s. *gos sgáb.*
Flash vb. *ₒḱyug-pa.*
Flat adj. *leb-mo*; *mnyam-pa.*
Flatten vb. a. *gleb-pa.*
Flatter *stod-pa*; *mol-lče btaṅ-ba W.*
Flatterer *ṅo stod-ḱan.*
Flattery *γčam-bu.*
Flatulence *ṕyen*; *ₒog-rluṅ.*
Flavour s. *bro-ba*; *ro.*
Flaw s. *śo-ré W.*
Flea *ḱyi-śig*; *ₒǰi-ba.*
Flee *ₒbros-pa.*
Fleece s. *bal-rgyáb.*
Flesh *śa*; — fly *śa-sbráṅ.*
Flexible *kyom*; *mnyen-pa.*
Fling vb. *rgyab-pa*; *rgyag-pa C.*; *dbyug-pa C.*; *ₒṕen-pa*; *skyur-ba*; *ₒbor-ba.*
Flint *lčag-rdo*; *lčags-mag.*
Float vb. n. *ldiṅ-ba.*
Flock s. *ḱyu*, *ḱyu-bo.*
Flog *lčag-gis γžu-ba*, v. also *skar-ba.*
Flood s. *ču-log.*
Floor s. *γži-ma*; (bottom) *mťil* 240; *śen W.*; *'an-ₒdar C.*; ground — *ₒog-ḱaṅ.*
Flour s. *ṕye*; *žib.*
Flourish vb. *bde-ba*; *ₒťseṅ-ba.*
Flourish s. (in writing) *ri-mo kyag-kyog.*
Flow vb. *ₒbab-pa*; s. *rgyun* 112.
Flower s. *me-tog*; — bed *rka*; — garden *sdum-ra.*
Fluid s. *ḱu-ba.*
Flute *ṕred-gliṅ.*
Flutter s. *ḱrag-ḱrug* 49.
Fly vb. *ₒṕur-ba*; to — up *ₒṕar-ba* 356.
Fly s. *sbraṅ-ma.*
Foal *rteu*; — of an ass *gu-rug.*
Foam s. *lbu-ba*, *dbu-ba.*
Fodder s. *čag.*
Foe *dgra*, *dgra-bo*; *ṕa-rol-pa* and *po.*
Fog *kug-rna*; *na-bún*; *rmugs-pa.*
Fold s. (plait) *ltab-ma*; (pen) *lhas-ma.*
Fold vb. a. (to plait) *ltab-pa*; (to pen) *dgar-ba.*
Follow *ₒbraṅ-ba*, *rǰes-su ₒgro-ba*; *γčod-pa.*
Follower *bstan-ₒdzin.*
Following *ṕyi(s)*, *ṕyir* 1, 2; *ₒdi.*
Fond, to be — of ... *la čags-pa*, *žen-pa.*
Fondness *ḱri ba*; *žen-ḱris*, *žen-čags-pa.*
Fontanel *klad-sgo*; *mťsogs-ma*; *ₒťsaṅs-pai bu-ga.*
Food *zas*, resp. *žal-zás*, *bžes-pa*; *bšos*; *ka-zás*; *za-ba*, *za-ma*; *lto*; — of animals *bzan.*
Fool s. *glen-pa*; *blun-pa*, *blun-po.*
Foolish *glen-pa*; *blun-pa*; *blo-méd.*
Foot *rkaṅ pa*, resp. *žabs*; — bridge *dem-tsi Lh*; — path *rkaṅ-lam*; *ₒṕraṅ*, *lam-ₒṕraṅ*; — race *baṅ*; — ring *rkaṅ-γdub*; — soldier *rkaṅ-ťaṅ-pa*; — stool *rkaṅ-stegs*; — of a hill *rtsa-ba*; on foot *rkaṅ-ťaṅ-du* or *la.*
Footprint, Footstep *rkaṅ-rǰés.*
For *don-du*; v. *ṕyogs* 352; — forty days *žag bži-bčui bar-du*, *žag bži-bču ťug W.*
Forbear vb. a. *ₒgyod-mi rmo-ba* 98.
Forbid *ₒgegs-pa*; *mi γnaṅ-ba.*
Force s. *mťu*; *dbaṅ*; *ṅar-ba*; *śed-dbáṅ W.*
Force vb. *dbaṅ-med-du ₒčol-ba*; v. also *nan-gyis*; *śed-ḱyer-nag-pos W.*
Ford vb *rgal-ba.*
Fore, — arm *lag-ṅár*; — finger *mdzub-mo*; — part, — side *ṅar*, *ḱa*, *mdun ṅos.*
Foregoing *sṅon-gro*; *sṅa-ma.*
Forehead *ťod-pa*; *dpral-ba.*
Foreign *yan-pa*; *γžan-ma*; *ṕyii*; — country *byes.*
Forenoon *sṅa-ťóg*; *sṅa-dro.*
Foreskin *sgo-pur*; *mdun-lpags*, *ₒdom-lpags.*
Forest *nags(-ma)*, *nags-γseb*; *nags-ťsal*, *nags-ḱrod*; *ťsal.*
Forget *rǰed-pa*; *yi-γčod-pa*, resp. *ťugs γyel-ba W.*
Forgive vb. a. (not resenting) *bzod-pa* 498; (to leave unpunished) *ₒgyod-mi rmo-ba*; (to efface) *sel-ba*; (to wash away) *dag-pa.*
Fork *ḱa-bráǵ*; *śa-ₒdzin.*
Form s. (mould) *par*; (figure) *dbyibs*; *γzugs*; *čas*; grammatical — *ťsig.*
Form vb a. *skyed-pa.*
Former adj. *goṅ*, *goṅ-ma*; *sṅon-ₒgro*; *daṅ-po*; — part *stod*; — time *sṅon-rol.*
Formerly *sṅa-čád*, *sṅa-goṅ*, *sṅa-bar*; *sṅan*, *sṅar*; *sṅon.*
Fornicate *ₒčal-ba*; v. *γyem-pa.*
Fornicator *ₒčál-pa.*
Forsake *skyur-ba*; *ₒbor-ba*; *γtoṅ-ba.*
Fort *mḱar.*

Forte (in music) *rtsub-po.*
Forth *sogs*; *ṕar*; *yas.*
Fortress *rdzoṅ(s).*
Fortune (lot) *ṕya*; (wealth) *k̔a-rǰé C.*; good - *bkra-šis*; —teller *ṕya-mk̔an*; *ṅan-sṅags-mk̔an.*
Forward vb. *ₒk̔al-ba.*
Found vb. *ₒgod-pa*; *rgyag-pa*; *ₒdebs-pa*; *ₒdzugs-pa.*
Foundation *rmaṅ*; — of a house *mt̔il*; *k̔aṅ-rtsá.*
Fountain *ču-mig.*
Four *bži*; fourth *bži-pa*; fourteen *ču-bži*; fourteenth *ču-bži-pa*; forty *bži-bču*; fortieth *bži-bču-pa.*
Fourfooted *rkaṅ-bži-pa.*
Fowl *bya*; domestic - *k̔yim-bya.*
Fowler *bya-pa.*
Fox *wa*; — coloured *k̔am-pa.*
Fragile *k̔rol-mo W.*
Fragment *čag-k̔rúm, čag-dúm*: (*γ*)*sil-bu.*
Fragrance *ṅad.*
Frail, to get — *rgud-pa.*
Frame s. *k̔ri*; vb. a. *ₒgod-pa* 95.
Frankincense *bdug-pa, gu-gul.*
Fraud *ṅo-lkog*; *zog, zol-zóg.*
Free adj. *yan-pa*; *t̔ar-pa*; to become — *ₒgrol-ba*; *t̔ar-ba*; to set — *t̔ar-du ₒǰug-pá*; *ₒbud-pa.*
Freeze *ₒk̔yags-pa*; *ṕyid-pa.*
Freight s. *k̔al.*
Frenzy *ₒk̔rul-pa.*
Fresh *γsar-ba, γsar-po*; *so-ma W.*; — butter *skya-már W.*
Friday *γza-pa(-wa)-saṅs.*
Friend *grogs, rog*; *ṅo-šés, mdza-bšés, bšes-γnyén*; *mdza-bo*; *zla-bo.*
Friendly *sñyiṅ-nyé*; resp. *sol-po.*
Fright s. *ₒǰigs-pa.*
Frighten *skrag-pa.*
Frightened *skrag-pa*; to be — *rtab-pa.*
Fringes *k̔a-t̔sar.*
Frog *sbal-pa.*
From *nas* 304; *man-čad* 411; *las* 546; — within *k̔oṅ-nas* 43.
Frontier *sa-mt̔sáms.*
Front-side *k̔a*; *ṅar.*
Frost *k̔yags-pa*; *sad.*
Froth *lbu-ba, dbu-ba.*
Frozen *k̔yags-pa.*
Fruit *šiṅ-tóg*; *ₒbras-bu*; — tree *bza-šiṅ*; *rtsi-šiṅ.*
Fry vb. *sreg-pa, slam-pa, rṅód-pa.*
Fuel *bud-šiṅ.*
Fulfil *skoṅ-ba*; *sgrub-pa*; *ₒgeṅs-pa.*
Full *gaṅ-ba*; *ltem-pa*; *mt̔oṅ-po*; to be — *ltams-pa*; *ₒk̔eṅs-pa*; to make — *k̔yab-pa.*
Fully *rgyas-par.*
Fumigate *bdug-pa.*
Fun *pra-čál*; *šags.*
Functionary *blon-po*
Fundament *rtsa-ba*; *rkub.*
Fur-coat *slag-pa, slog-pa*; *t̔ul-pa.*
Furious *γtum-pa.*
Furnish (supply) *sgrub-pa.*
Furniture *yo-byád.*
Furrow s. *rka.*
Further *γžan-yaṅ, yaṅ.*
Furtherance *mt̔un-rkyen.*
Futurity *ma ₒons-pai dus*; *ṕugs.*

# G

Gain vb. a. *rgyal-ba, rnyed-pa, sgrub-pa.*
Gain s. *skyed*; *k̔e, k̔ye*; *k̔a-rgyál, rgyál-k̔a*; *rnyed-pa*; *spogs, bogs.*
Gait *bgrod.*
Galaxy *dgu-t̔sigs.*
Gale *rluṅ-dmár, rluṅ nag-po.*
Gall s. *mk̔ris-pa.*
Gallop vb. n. *rta rgyug-pa.*
Gallows *čar-šiṅ.*
Game s. (animals of chase) *ri-dwags.*
Gander *ṅaṅ-pa.*
Ganges *gaṅ-gā.*
Gap *rgya-sér*; *ser-ka, ser-ga.*
Gape vb. *sgyiṅ-ba*; *γdaṅ-ba.*
Garden *t̔sal*; *t̔sas W.*; *ldum-ra*; *sdum-ra*; — flower *ha-ló.*
Garlic *sgog-pa.*
Garment *gos*; *čas*, resp. *na-bza*; under — *ʼaṅ-t̔úṅ*; upper — *bla-gáb, bla-gós, γzan-gos.*
Garret *steṅ-k̔aṅ.*
Gate *rgyal-sgo*; *sgo-mo.*
Gather vb. a. *sgrug-pa*; *ₒt̔u-ba*; *sog-pa*; vb. n. *ₒk̔or-ba*; *ₒgugs-pa*; *ₒt̔ibs-pa.*
Gatherer *t̔un, ₒt̔un*
Gear s. *go-ča.*
Gelding s. *ṕo-rtá.*
General adj. *spyi* 333; *t̔un-moṅ.*
General s. *dmag-dpón.*
Generate *skyed-pa.*
Generation *rgyal-brgyúd*; *γduṅ-rabs, rabs.*
Genesis *čags-rábs.*
Genitals *mt̔san(-ma).*
Genitive case *ₒbrel-pa.*
Gentian *tig-ta*; *kyi-lčé.*

Gentle ˳ǰam-po, ˳bol-po; mt̔un-čan; sgye-mo.
Gentleman γtso-bo; sa-heb; old –, old squire, ga-gá Ld., 'a-ǰo-lag C.
Gently ṅaṅ-gis; ga-le C., gu-le W.
Gentry drag-rigs.
Genuine dṅos; ṅo-rtóg; lhad-méd.
Geography γnas-bšád, yul-bšád.
Germinate vb. n. skye-ba; to cause to – skyed-pa.
Gesture s. brda; rnam-gyúr; v. also t̔sul.
Get vb. a. k̔ug-pa; rnyed-pa; t̔ob-pa; ˳dzin-pa; yod-par ˳gyur-ba; vb. n. ˳gro-ba; č̔a-ba W.; to – into čud-pa; ˳bab-pa; to – through t̔ar-ba, bgrod-pa; to – up ldaṅ-ba, laṅ-ba, resp. bžeṅs-pa.
Ghost mi-ma-yin(-pa); sems-nyid.
Ghostlike γzugs-méd 494; lus-méd.
Gift s. ˳k̔yos-pa; γnaṅ-ba; bya-dgá; ˳bul-ba; sbyin-pa; yon.
Gild č̔us γtoṅ-ba, γser-č̔us ˳byug-pa.
Gills nya-skyogs.
Gimlet sor.
Ginger sga, sgeu; lča-sga.
Girdle s. ska-rágs.
Girl bu-mo; γžon-nu-ma; na-č̔uṅ.
Give k̔ur-ba; ster-ba; γnaṅ-ba; ˳bul-ba 394; ˳bogs-pa; sbyin-pa; stsol-ba; to – an entertainment ˳gyed-pa; to – up sgyur-ba; γčod-pa; spoṅ-ba; blos γtoṅ-ba; to be given to skyoṅ-ba; rten-pa.
Glacier gaṅs, gaṅs-čan.
Glad adj. dga-ba; – tidings γtam-snyán; to be – dga-ba; mgu-ba; to make – *sem t̔ad čug-če* W.
Glass šel, man-šel; – beads ga-šél; – bottle šel-búm.
Gleaner snye-t̔un.
Glide ˳dred-pa; ˳byid-pa.
Glistening k̔rom-mé, k̔rol-po; čam.
Glitter vb. ˳t̔ser-ba.
Globe ril W.
Globular zlum-pa, ril-ba; a – stone rdo-ril.
Glorious grags-čan; ˳p̔ags-pa.
Glory s. grags-pa; dpal, dpal-byór.
Glory vb. rlom-pa, p̔o-t̔sod ˳č̔ad-pa; v. p̔o-so.
Gloss bkrag; ˳od-γsál.
Glossy bkra-ba.
Glove lag-šúbs.
Glue s. spyin.
Gnash so k̔rig-k̔rig byed-pa, so bdar-ba; so sdom-pa.
Gnaw γzan-pa; ˳č̔a-ba, mur-ba.
Go ˳gro-ba; ˳doṅ-ba; č̔a-ba W.; rgyu-ba; bgrod-pa; p̔yin-pa, eleg. mči-ba, resp. p̔eb-pa: to – about ˳grim-pa; to – abroad ˳gron-du ˳gro-ba, byes-su ˳gro-ba; to – astray ˳k̔yar-ba; to away ˳gye-ba, resp. bžud-pa, γšegs-pa; to – in or into čud-pa, ˳ǰug-pa; to – out ˳t̔on-pa; spro-ba; to – round ˳k̔or-ba, skor-ba.
Goal t̔sad.
Goat ra-ma; wild – ra-rgód, ra-po-č̔é; skyin.
Goat's hair ral.
Goblet skyogs.
Goblin ˳dre, lha-˳dre.
God dkon-mčog; a god lha, a goddess lha-mo; a tutelar god yi-dam-lhá, lha-srúṅ; mgon-po.
Going s. (the act of) gros.
Goitre lba-ba.
Gold γser.
Gong ˳k̔ar-rṅá.
Good adj. bzaṅ-ba; legs-pa; dga-bdé C.; rgyal-ba W.; col. yag-po; to be – (of coins) ˳grul-ba.
Good s. (advantage) don.
Good-bye da ča yin W. 152; *ṭa-ši-šig* W.; v. ga-le C. 64.
Goods dṅos-po; ka-ča; k̔a-rǰé C.; spus; zoṅ.
Goose ṅaṅ-pa, ṅaṅ-ma.
Gorge s. (ravine) roṅ.
Gossip s. (idle talk) k̔a-bšád; rgya-láb.
Gourd ka-béd, ku-ba, gon W., čuṅ C.
Gout draṅ-nád W.; grum-bu, grum-nád, drag-grum; dreg-nad, t̔sigs-nad, t̔sigs-zúg.
Govern sgyur-ba; rgyal-srid skyoṅ-ba; dbaṅ sgyur-ba.
Government rgyal-po, rgyal-srid.
Governor sde-pa; bka-blón.
Grace s. bka-drin, t̔ugs-rǰe.
Gracious t̔ugs-rǰe-čan.
Gradually ṅaṅ-gis; gu-le gu-le W.
Graft s. pe-bán.
Grain s. č̔ag-tse, rdog-po, ˳bru.
Grammar byā-ka-ra-ṇa 372.
Grandchild t̔sa-bo; – daughter t̔sa-mo; – father mes-po; – mother ma-mo, p̔yi-mo; – son t̔sa-bo, resp. dbon-po.
Grant vb. (bka) γnaṅ-ba; ˳grub-pa; stsol-ba; γzigs-pa.
Granulous č̔ag-tse-čan W.
Grape rgun, rgun-˳brúm; č̔ag-mo.
Grasp vb. ˳ǰu-ba, ˳dzin-pa; cf. γčags-pa.
Grass rtswa.
Grasshopper čog-čog-pa, č̔a-ga-˳bu.
Grate s. dra-pa, lčags-dra.
Grateful drin-γzo-čan; to be – drin γzo-ba.
Grater lag-dár, lab-dár.
Gratitude drin dran-pa.
Grave s. dur-k̔uṅ.
Gravel s. gyo-mo; šag-ma.
Gravy spags; ša-rúg, resp. skyu-rúm.
Gray se-bo; light – skya-bo.
Grease s. snum-pa; vb. snum-gyis skud-pa.
Greasy snum-čan; t̔so-ba.
Great č̔e-ba, č̔en-po, rgyas-pa.

**Greatness** *če-ba, če-ḱyád.*
**Greedy** *ₒdod-sred-čan; blo-ₒdód; ħam-pa-čan.*
**Green** *sṅo-ba, sṅon-po; ljaṅ-ḱu.*
**Greens** s. *sṅo-ṫsód, ldum, ṫsod-ma.*
**Greensward** *na-ḱa; ne-ṫáṅ.*
**Grieve** vb. n. *skyo-ba, ₒgyod-pa.*
**Grind** *ₒṫag-pa; bdar-ba*; to — the teeth so *bdar-ba.*
**Gripes** *glaṅ, glaṅ-ṫabs.*
**Gristle** *čag-krúm.*
**Grit** (gravel) *gyo-mo.*
**Groan** s. *ₒḱog-šúgs W., šugs-nár, šugs-riṅ.*
**Groan** vb. *ₒḱun-pa.*
**Groom** *rta-rdzí.*
**Grope** *snom-pa.*
**Grotto** *gyam, ṕug-pa.*
**Ground** s. *žiṅ; γži(-ma)* 480; *sa-γži* 570.
**Grouse** *ri-skyégs; goṅ-mo.*
**Grove** *skyed-mos-ṫsal.*
**Grow** vb. n. *čer skye-ba; ₒḱruṅ-ba; ₒgyur-ba; rgyas-pa; ča-ba*; to — dark *ₒṫibs-pa*; to — old *bgre-ba*; to cause to grow *skyed-pa.*
**Growth** *skyed, skye.*
**Grudge** s. *ḱon-pa*; to bear a — *ₒḱon-pa.*
**Grumbling** s. **ṫo-ṫá** *W.*
**Grunt** vb. *ṅug-pa, ṅur-ba, ḱun-pa.*
**Guard** vb. *skyoṅ-ba, skyob-pa, sruṅ-ba.*
**Guardian** *ṕa-ṫsáb*; — of the world *jig-rten-skyoṅ.*
**Guess** s. v. *ṫsod* 453.
**Guide** s. *lam-mḱan, lam-ₒdren-pa, lam-yig.*
**Guitar** *sgra-snyan; ko-ṕoṅs W.*
**Gulf** *ḱug, ču-ḱug*; (abyss) *btson-doṅ.*
**Gullet** *lkog-ma.*
**Gulp** s. *hub; skyu-gáṅ, čor-gáṅ.*
**Gum** s. *ṫaṅ-ču.*
**Gun** *sgyogs; tu-pag W.; me-mda C.*
**Gunpowder** *tu-pag-man W.; me-rdzás C.*
**Gunstock** *ₒgu-mdá; sgum-da.*
**Gut**, great — or colon *γnye-ma.*
**Gutter** *wa.*
**Guttural** s. *lče-rtsa-čan* 150.

# H

**Habitation** *groṅ; γnas-ṫsaṅ, γnas-ḱaṅ, γži-ma.*
**Haft** *yu-ba.*
**Hail** s. (frozen rain) *ser-ba*; (salutation) v. *rgyal-ba* I 108.
**Hair** *skra; spu*, a little — *ba-spu.*
**Hairy** *ba-spu-čan; skra-čan.*
**Half** (one half) s. *ča* 151.
**Half** adj. *ṕyed*; — boot *krad-pa.*
**Hall** *bkad-sa*; — of judgment *ṫsugs-ḱaṅ.*
**Halo** *ḱyim.*
**Halter** *ṫur-mgo; srab-mṫúr.*
**Halting-place** *sti-bai γnas*; (night quarters) *ₒbraṅ-sa*, resp. *γzim-bráṅ.*
**Hammer** s. *ṫo-čúṅ*; large — *ṫo-ba.*
**Hand** s. *lag(-pa)*, resp. *ṕyag.*
**Hand** vb. a. *sriṅ-ba*; to — over *skur-ba.*
**Handicraft** *bzo.*
**Handful** *ḱyá-le; ḱyor; ₒčaṅs-pa; spar-ba; ṕul.*
**Handkerchief** *sna-ṕyis*; — of salutation *ḱa-btágs* 37.
**Handle** s. *kab-za, lčibs, yu-ba.*
**Handsome** *mčor-po, mdzes-pa.*
**Handspike** *gàl-ta.*
**Hang** vb. a. (a man) **čar-la taṅ-če** *W.*; to — up *skar-ba, dgar-ba, ₒgel-ba; ₒṕyar-ba*; vb. n. to — down *ₒjol-ba, ₒṕyaṅ-ba.*
**Hangman** *γšed-ma.*
**Hank** *gru-gu.*
**Happen** *ₒgyur-ba, ₒbyuṅ-ba, ₒoṅ-ba.*
**Happiness** *dge-ba, skyid-pa, γyaṅ; bkra-šis.*
**Happy** *bkra-šis-pa; skal-ldán, skyid-po; legs-pa*; to be — *bde-ba, skyid-pa*; may you be — *bkra-šis-šig W.*
**Hard** *kyoṅ, mḱraṅ, mḱregs-pa; sra-ba*; — to bear *ḱag-po*; — water *ču kyoṅ-po.*
**Hardened** *šran-čan.*
**Hardness** *ṅar-ba.*
**Hardship** *dka-ba, nyon-moṅs-pa* 191.
**Hardware** *lčags-čas.*
**Hare** *ri-bóṅ.*
**Harm** s. *skyon*; to do — *ṫsugs-pa, γnod-pa byed-pa* or *skyel-ba*; vb. to — *snad-pa.*
**Harmony** (musical concord) *sgra-dbyaṅs*; (agreement) *mṫun-pa*; concord amongst kinsmen *γnyen-ₒdún.*
**Harness** s. *čibs-čas.*
**Harrow** s. *šal-ba*; vb. to — *šal-ba ₒdrud-pa.*
**Harsh** *gyoṅ-po; rtsub-po.*
**Hartshorn** *ša-ru.*
**Harvest** s. *btsas-ma; lo-tóg* 552.
**Haste** s. *ṫsa-drag*; to make — *rgyug-pa*; make haste! **ṫsa-rag toṅ** *W.*; **riṅ-pa toṅ** *W.*
**Hasten** vb. n. *snyegs-pa; riṅs-pa.*
**Hasty** *spro ṫuṅ-ba; yid ṫuṅ-ba.*
**Hate** vb. *ₒḱon-pa, ₒgras-pa, sdaṅ-ba.*
**Hatred** *sdaṅ-sems, že-sdáṅ.*
**Haughtiness** *če-ṫábs, ṕo-so.*
**Haughty** *ḱa-drág, ḱeṅs-pa; če-ṫabs-čan, ṕo-so-čan*
**Hautboy** *dge-gliṅ; sur-na.*
**Have** (possess) *bdog-pa*; having v. *čan* 138,

v. *bčas-pa* 146; I have *ṅa-la yod* 515; I have to v. *rgyu* no. 3, 110.
Hawk s. *k̔ra.*
Hay *rtsa-skám*; — fork *sbrag-ma.*
Haze *k̔ug-rná.*
He *k̔o, k̔oṅ, de* 255; — who *gaṅ* no. 2 65.
Head s. *mgo*, resp. *dbu*; (chief) *k̔yu-mčog* 47; *ɣtso-bo* 434; (of an argument) *yan-lag*; — master *˳go-dpón.*
Head vb. a. *˳k̔rid-pa, sna ˳dren-pa.*
Headache *mgo-nád*; *klad-ɣzér.*
Headman *˳go-pa, rgad-po.*
Heal vb. a. *˳ts̔o-ba* 460, *ɣso-ba*; *bčos-pa.*
Health *k̔ams*; *nad-med-pa.*
Healthy *nad-méd.*
Heap s. *p̔uṅ-po.*
Heap vb. a *sgril-ba, bčer-ba, spuṅ-ba*; to — up *sog-pa.*
Heaped *byur-po, byur-byúr* 377; *gaṅ-ba W.* 66.
Hear vb. a. *t̔os-pa, t̔sor-ba W., nyan-pa*; hear! *ka-yé.*
Hearer *nyan-pa* or *-po.*
Heart *snyiṅ*, resp. *t̔ugs*; *naṅ*; *rgyud* 112; *že* 477; to know by — *k̔a-ton-du šes-pa* 35.
Heart-grief *sems-nád.*
Hearth *me-t̔áb*; *sgyid-bu* 118; — stone *sgyed-po.*
Heartily *snyiṅ t̔ag-pa-nas.*
Hearty *že-t̔ag-pa*; a — request *že-t̔ag-pai žu-ba.*
Heat *ts̔a-ba, tsad-pa*; *t̔an-pa.*
Heated *dros-pa* 264.
Heaven *mk̔a, nam-mk̔a*; *ɣnam, mt̔o-ris* 242.
Heavens *mk̔a, dbyiṅs* 390.
Heavy *lči-ba.*
Hedgehog *rgaṅ, ˳gaṅ-ɣzer-ma.*
Heed s., to give — *bya-ra byed-pa.*
Heedless *zon-méd.*
Heel s. *rtiṅ-pa.*
Heifer *zal-mo.*
Height *mt̔o-k̔yad*; *k̔yon*; *rṅams*; *dpaṅs*; *˳p̔aṅ* 355.
Heir s. *nor-bdag*; joint — *go-k̔an W.*
Hellebore *spru-ma.*
Helm s. *k̔a-lo.*
Helmet *rmog.*
Help s. *skyabs, skyobs, ra-mda.*
Help vb. a. *skyabs byed-pa, grogs byed-pa.*
Helper *skyabs-mgon, skyabs-ɣnas*; *ɣnyen-po, dpuṅ-ɣnyén, dpuṅ-grogs.*
Hem s. *sne-mo, ča-ga.*
Hemorrhoids *ɣžaṅ-nád, ɣžaṅ-brúm.*
Hemp *so-ma, ɣtso-ma, btso-ma*; *bhaṅ-ge W.*
Hen *bya-mo*; *kyim-bya.*
Henceforth *da-ste, da p̔yis* 247, *da p̔yin-čád* 350.
Herb *sṅo, sṅo-ts̔ód, rtswa.*
Herd *k̔yu, k̔yu-bo.*
Herdsman *rdzi-bo, p̔yugs-rdzi.*
Here *˳di-ru* 275.
Hereafter *p̔ugs-na, da-ste, da-p̔yis, da p̔yin-čad.*
Heresy *č̔os-lóg.*
Heritage *nor-skal.*
Hermit *dgon-pa-pa*; *bdag-bsrúṅ.*
Hermitage *dgon-pa, ɣnas.*
Hero *k̔yo-ga.*
Heron *kaṅ-ka*; *skyar-mo.*
Hesitation *t̔sam-t̔súm.*
Hew *˳ǰog-pa, ˳t̔sog-pa*; v. also cleave.
Hiccough s. *skyig-bu*; *'i-k̔ug, 'ig W.*; vb. to — *skyig-pa.*
Hide s. *ko-ba, ko-lpags, pags-pa* or *-po.*
Hide vb. a. *skuṅ-ba, sbed-pa*; to — one's self *˳gab-pa, yib-pa, ɣsaṅ-ba.*
Hiding-place *bskuṅs-sa.*
High *mt̔o-ba, mt̔on-po*; — and low *drag-žán* 261; — road, — way *rgya-lám*; *ma-lam W.*
Hill *ri*; v. *sgaṅ.*
Hilt *kab-za, lčibs, yu-ba.*
Hinder vb. a. *˳gegs-pa, ˳k̔egs-pa*; to be — ed *togs-pa.*
Hind-foot *rkaṅ-pa.*
Hind-part *mǰug.*
Hindrance *gegs, bgegs, bar-č̔ód.*
Hinge s. *sgo-˳k̔ór.*
Hip s. (joint) *sta-zúr, dpyi*; (fruit) *šib-ši-lu-lu Ld.*
Hire s. *rṅan-pa*, vb. to — *ɣyar-ba.*
History *lo-rgyús, byuṅ-t̔sul.*
Hit vb. a. *k̔es-pa, rgyab-pa, t̔ug-pa, ˳p̔og-pa, ˳t̔ebs-pa W.*
Hit s. *lčag* 148.
Hither *t̔sur*; — to *sṅa-čad.*
Hive s. *tsaṅ.*
Hoangho *rma-ču.*
Hoarfrost *ba-mo.*
Hoarse *ṅar-ṅar-po, ˳dzer-po*; to be — *˳dzer-ba*; *ras-pa Ld.*
Hoarseness *skad-gágs.*
Hoe vb. a. *rko-ba.*
Hog s. *p̔ag.*
Hoist vb. a. *˳p̔yar-ba.*
Hold vb. a. *čaṅ-ba, snom-pa, ˳dzin-pa*; to — forth *˳dzed-pa*; to — out (suffice) *˳k̔yed-pa*; vb. n. *rten-pa* 213.
Hold s. *rten*; to take — of *˳ǰu-ba.* [413.
Hole s. *k̔uṅ, bi-gán, bi-yán W., bu-ga*; *mig*
Hollo interj. *ka-yé*; *kye, kye-hó*; *W. wa!*
Hollow adj. *k̔oṅ-stóṅ.*
Hollow s. *k̔uṅ, sbug(s)*; the — of the hand *škyor.*
Holly *sgom-˳bróg.*
Holy *skal-ldán, dam-pa*; a — man, saint, *skyes-bu dam-pa.*
Homage s. *bkur-ba, bkur-sti*; *rim-gro*, resp. *sku-rim.*
Home s. *k̔yim*; to be at — *k̔yim-du sdod-pa.*

**Homeless** *ṅes-méd.*
**Hone** s. *ₒdzeṅ.*
**Honest** *draṅ-po, čos draṅ-po.*
**Honey** *sbraṅ-rtsi, raṅ-si W.*
**Honour** s. *bkur-ba, bkur-sti; sti-staṅ; ya-ša; rim-gro,* resp. *sku-rim; grags-pa, p̔u-dúd.*
**Honour** vb. a. *bkur-ba, mčod-pa, ryc-ba.*
**Honourable** *btsun-pa.*
**Hood** s. *t̔od-k̔ebs.*
**Hoof** *rmig-pa.*
**Hook** s. *kug.*
**Hookah** (Turkish pipe) *ċi-lim;* resp. *že-hór C.*
**Hoop** s. *šan.*
**Hoopoe** *p̔u-šúd.*
**Hope** s. *re-ba; blo-ydéṅ, blo-ytád;* vb. to — *re-ba.*
**Horizon** *mt̔oṅ-ₒk̔or.*
**Horn** *rwa, ru.*
**Hornet** *liṅ-gol-ma.*
**Hornless** *k̔u-yú.*
**Horse** s. *rta,* resp. *čibs;* black — *ₑol-ba;* — dung *rta-sbaṅs;* — tail *rta-ṙṅa;* — whip *rta-lċag.*
**Horseman** *rta-pa.*
**Horseshoe** *rmig-lċágs.*
**Hospital** *nad-k̔aṅ, t̔sugs-k̔aṅ.*
**Host** (number of men) *dpuṅ, p̔al-po-ċe;* (army) *dmag.*
**Hot** *t̔sa-ba, t̔san;* to be — *t̔sa-ba;* the — time of the day *dro* 264.
**Hour** *ču-t̔sod* 158; double — *k̔yim* 47.
**House** s. *k̔aṅ-pa; k̔yim; groṅ; mk̔ar; sdum-pa C.; naṅ;* — owner *k̔yim-bdag, k̔yim-pa-pa;* — rent *k̔aṅ-glá.*
**Household** *yžis-mad; bza-mí* 497.
**Housekeeping** *so-t̔sis, so-t̔sigs.*
**Housewife** *k̔yim-t̔ab-mo, k̔yim-bdag-mo.*
**How** *ċi* 139, *ċi-ltar, ċi-tsug, ga-zug, ċi-ne Bal.;* — much *ga-t̔sód; (ċi-)tsam.*
**However** *ₑon-kyaṅ.*
**Howl** vb. *ṅu-ba;* (of animals) *ṅur-ba.*
**Howling** s. (of a tempest) *ₑur-sgra* 500.
**Hug** vb. a. *ₒk̔yud-pa.*
**Hum** s. *di-ri-ri* 252; *ₑur-sgra* 500.
**Hum** vb. *ₒk̔rog-pa.*
**Human** *mii;* — being *skye-bo.*
**Humble** adj. *gus-pa.*
**Humbleness** *yċam-bu.*
**Humidity** *bad.*
**Humours** (of the body) v. *nyes-pa* 191.
**Humming** (noise) *ₑur-ₑur;* — of bees *di-ri-rí, zi-ri-ri.*
**Hump, Hunch** s. *ṙṅog; gye-gu.*
**Hundred** *brgya.*
**Hunger** s. *ltogs-pa; bkres-pa.*
**Hungry** *ltogs-pa, bkren-pa, bkres-pa.*
**Hunt, Hunting** s. *kyi-ra.*
**Hunt** vb. a. *ṙṅon-pa, ₒčor-ba, yšor-ba.*
**Hunter** *ṙṅon-pa, kyi-ra-ba, liṅs-pa.*
**Hurricane** *rluṅ-t̔súb.*
**Hurry** vb. *grim-pa; rgyug-pa.*
**Hurry** s. *tsab-tsúb.*
**Hurt** vb. a. *ynod-pa skyel-ba, ynod-pa, ₒk̔aṅ-ba, t̔sugs-pa, ₒt̔se-ba.*
**Husband** s. *k̔yo, k̔yim-t̔abs, k̔yim-bdag; skyes-pa; dga-grogs; bdag-po;* — and wife (couple) *k̔yo-šúg.*
**Husbandry** *so-t̔sís, so-t̔sigs.*
**Husk** s. *lgaṅ-bu, spun-pa, sbur-ma.*
**Hut** s. *k̔u-tu, pu-lu, spyil-po.*
**Hydrophobia** *k̔yi-smyón.*
**Hypocrisy** *k̔a-čos; sgyu-zóg; t̔sul-ₒčos.*
**Hypocrite** *k̔a-že mi mt̔suṅs-pa.*

# I

**I** pron. *ṅa, ṅed, ṅed-raṅ* 128, *ṅos* 130, *bdag-nyid* 268; I myself *ṅa-raṅ, ṅed-raṅ.*
**Ice** *dar, čab-brom, gaṅs, k̔yags-pa.*
**Icicle** *k̔yags-sdóṅ.*
**Idea** *ₒdu-šes; dmigs-pa.*
**Identic** *mi-ynyis-pa* 192.
**Idiocrasy** *ṅaṅ* 125.
**Idle** adj. *le-lo-ċan; kyaṅ-kyóṅ W.*
**If** *na* 299, *gal-te* 68; but if *ċi-ste* 140.
**Ignoble** *skye-ba dma-ba.*
**Ignorance** *yti-mug, ma-rig-pa.*
**Ill** adj. and adv. (sick) *nad-pa;* — fed *dṅos-ṅán; bza-méd;* — humoured *skyo-ba;* — looking *spus-méd;* — luck *rkyen;* to be — *na-ba.*
**Illness** *nad, na-ba, zug W.*
**Illusion** *ₒk̔rul-snáṅ, sgyu-ma.*
**Illustrate** *ₒgrel-ba;* to — by parables *dpes mt̔son-pa.*
**Image** *sku;* molten — *blugs-sku.*
**Imagine** vb. a. *go-ba, sgom-pa, dmigs-pa, sems-pa;* vb. n. *snyam-pa.*
**Imbecile** *glen-pa, han-ldáṅ W.*
**Imbibe** *ₒjibs-pa;* to be imbibed *t̔im-pa.*
**Imitate** *lad-mo byed-pa.*
**Imitation** *lad-mo; ₒbag.*
**Immaterial** (not existing) *dṅos-med, yzugs-méd.*
**Immeasurable** *t̔sad-méd, yžal-du-med-pa.*
**Immediate** *ₒp̔ral, p̔ral.*
**Immediately** *mod-la, de ma-t̔ag-tu* 227.
**Immoderate** *t̔sod-méd.*
**Immoral** *ₒčol-pa, mi tsaṅs-pa* 445.
**Impaired** *nyams-pa.*

Impart ₒbogs-pa.
Impartial p̒yogs-méd.
Impartiality mnyam-pa-nyid.
Impeded, to be — k̒ad-pa.
Impediment gegs, ₒgal-rkyén, bar-č̒ód.
Imperative mood γdams-ṅag ₒdoms-pai ts̒ig 265.
Imperishable mi-ₒjig-pa, rtag-pa.
Impetuous ṅar-ma.
Impious skal-méd; sdig-byéd.
Implements ča-byad, ča-lag, go-ča, yo-byád.
Impolite gyoṅ-po; very — k̒a-gyoṅ-čé.
Imponderable γžal-du-med-pa.
Importance k̒ag, ₒk̒os, gal, do-gál, γtsigs.
Important lc̒i-ba, k̒ag-c̒an, ₒk̒os-c̒an.
Impose vb. a. (lay on) ₒgel-ba, skul-ba; (to deceive) ₒbrid-pa, mgo skor-ba.
Imposture mgo-skór; sgyu, ṅo-lkog; rdzub.
Imprecation ṅan; byad, byad-stems.
Impress vb. (on the mind) k̒oṅ-du čud-pa; γc̒ags-pa.
Improper mi-ruṅ-ba.
Improve vb. n. ₒp̒el-ba, ts̒eṅ-ba.
Improvement skyed.
Impure skyug-bro, ma-dag-pa.
In prep. na, naṅ-na.
Inattention γyeṅ-ba, γyeṅs-pa.
Inattentive mi ₒts̒ugs-pa.
Incantation sṅags, γsaṅ-sṅags, γzuṅs.
Incense s. kun-du-ru, gu-gul, bdug-pa.
Incessantly k̒or-yug-tu. rgyun-čad-med-par, rgyun-du.
Inch sor-mo.
Inclination γzuṅ-ba, bag-čags.
Incline vb. n. (to lean) ₒk̒ra-ba.
Inclined, to be — (disposed) ₒdod-pa.
Income sleb.
Incongruous ya-ma-zúṅ.
Inconsiderate γzu-lum-c̒an, blo-gros-med.
Inconstant čol, mi ₒts̒ugs-pa, ₒgyur-ldóg.
Incorporeal lus-méd.
Incorrect skyon-c̒an.
Increase vb. a. sgro-ₒdogs-pa, snon-pa, spel-ba; vb. n. rgyas-pa, ₒp̒el-ba.
Increase s. skyed, non-ka.
Incredible mi srid-pa, ₒos-méd W.; yid-čes-su mi ruṅ-ba.
Indecorous ṅo-ts̒a.
Indeed de-ka yod 255, mod-pa.
Indefatigably skyo-mi-šes-par.
Indented c̒oṅ-c̒óṅ.
Independence raṅ-dbáṅ.
Index dkar-čag, gleṅ-γži; t̒o.
India rgya-gár, British — rgya-p̒i-liṅ.
Indian s. rgya-gar-pa.
India rubber gyig.
Indicate ston-pa.
Indication mts̒an-nyid.
Indifferent stoṅ-pa; to be — to . . . la mi lta-ba.
Indigence gyoṅ, dbul-ba, ₒp̒oṅs-pa.
Indigent dbul-po, dbul-ₒp̒oṅs.
Indigestion zas ma žu-ba.
Indigo rams; — colour mt̒iṅ.
Indirectly zur-du, zur-na W.
Indivisible mi-p̒yed-pa.
Indolent kyaṅ-kyóṅ W., rgod-bag-c̒an.
Indubitable gor-ma-čag-pa, γdon-mi-za-ba.
Induce skul-ba.
Indulge in vb. n. čags-pa; v. also bag-med-pa 363.
Industrious le-lam-k̒an W.; brtson-pa-c̒an.
Inexplicable γya-nyés; it is — to me rgyu-mts̒an mi šes or bšad mi nus.
Infallible mi-nor-ba.
Infant ču-ma-lóṅ Ld.; p̒ru-gu čuṅ-ba; — boy k̒yeu.
Infect ₒgo-ba, bsgo-ba.
Inflammation ₒts̒ig-pa; — of the eyes mig-ts̒ig (c̒e) W.
Inflate ₒbud-pa; p̒u ₒdebs-pa.
Inflection dgu-ba.
Inflict skyel-ba.
Influence s. dbaṅ; vb. a. skul-ba.
Inform vb. a. spriṅ-ba, lon zer-ba C., hun taṅ-c̒e W.
Information man-ṅág; hun W.
Infringe ₒgal-ba.
Infuse ₒjug-pa.
Infusion t̒aṅ-gi sman.
Ingenious dmigs-c̒an.
Inheritance skal-nór, nor-skal.
Inject ₒjug-pa.
Injure ₒts̒e-ba, γnod-pa.
Injured nyams-pa.
Injury γnod-pa.
Ink snag-ts̒a; — powder snag-p̒yé.
Inkstand snag-koṅ; *nag-bhum* C.
Inlet ts̒o-lág C.
Inmate naṅ-gi mi.
Inn ₒgron-k̒áṅ.
Inner naṅ-gi 301.
Innumerable graṅs-méd-pa; tsad-méd.
Inquire ₒdri-ba; to — closely žib-tu ₒdri-ba; to — rigorously *skar-tag taṅ-c̒e* W.
Inquiry brtags-pa.
Inquisitive rtogs-ₒdod-c̒an.
Insane smyon-pa; to be — ₒk̒rul-ba, smyó-ba.
Insanity smyo-ₒbóg.
Inscription byaṅ-bu, byaṅ-ma; žal-byáṅ.
Insect rkaṅ-drug-ldan-pa; ₒbu.
Insensible k̒al-k̒ól; to get — ₒk̒ol-ba.
Inseparable mi-p̒yed-pa, ₒbral-méd.
Insert ₒdzud-pa.
Inside s. k̒oṅ-pa, naṅ-rol.
Inspect lta-ba, mgo byed-pa 91, žal-ta byed-pa 473.
Inspection žal-ta.
Instance dpe; for — ₒdi-lta-ste, dper-na.
Instant s. dar, skad, yud.

Instantly *mod-la.*
Instantaneous *dar γčig-gi; ₒṗral-gyi; yud-tsam-pa.*
Instantaneously *glo-bur.*
Instead *dod-du; ṫsab-tu, šul-du.*
Instigate *ṅar ₒdon-pa.*
Instinct v. *raṅ-bžin*, v. *šugs*; sexual — *ro-tsa.*
Institute vb. a. *ₒdzugs-pa.*
Instruction *bka-γdams, bka-naṅ; ḱrid; žal-ta*; instructions *spyad-mṫsáms* 456.
Instructive *ḱrid-ₒdebs-su ruṅ-ba.*
Instructor *mḱan-po*; instructress *mḱan-mo.*
Instrument *ča-byád, ča-lag.*
Insult vb. *ₒḱu-ba; ₒḱaṅ-ba; ṫsig rtsub* (or *ṅan*) *zer-ba.*
Insurrection *sde-ḱrugs, ₒḱrug-pa.*
Intellect *blo-grós.*
Intelligence (knowledge) *rgyus*; (news) *ča.*
Intelligent *sems-mḱan, blo-rno-ba.*
Intelligible *ḱrol-po; go-sla-ba.*
Intemperate *ṫsod-méd.*
Intend *dgoṅs-pa, dga-ba, ča-ba W., ₒdod-pa; sems-pa; sṅo-ba* 137.
Intent s. *don, bsam-pa.*
Inter vb. a. *skuṅ-ba.*
Intercalary month *zla(-ba)-šol, *da-ṫul* W.* 491.
Intercessor *ṅo-čen* 129.
Intercourse *ₒbrel-ba* 402; to have — *ₒdre-ba, ḱa-bsre-ba, sdeb-pa.*
Interest s. (money) *skyed, ṗar, bed*; (concern) *γzuṅ-ba.*
Interfere *ḱa ₒJug-pa.*
Interior s. *ḱog, ḱoṅ-pa, naṅ* I 301.
Intermediate *bar* 366.
Interpret *ₒgrol-ba.*
Interpreter *skad-pa.*
Interstice *bar, dbrag.*
Interval *bar-skabs, bar-ₒṫsáms.*
Intestines *rgyu-ma, loṅ-ḱa, loṅ-ga.*
Into *naṅ-du.*
Intolerable *mi-bzad-pa.*
Intoxicated *čaṅ-čem-čan* 154, *ra-ro-ba* 521, *zi-čan W.*
Intoxication *bzi, ra-ro.*
Intrenchment *rags, ṗag-rags.*
Intrigue s. *gya-gyú.*
Introduce *ₒdzugs-pa.*
Introduction (preface) *sṅon-ₒgro.*
Inundate *γyeṅ-ba, lud-pa.*
Inundation *ču ₒḱyam-pa, ču-nag, ču-rúd.*
Inured v. *sran-pa* 580.
Invective *smad-pai ṫsig.*
Inveigh *γše-ba, ḱa kye-če W.*
Invent *dmigs-pa-nas bzo-ba; bsam-blo* or *-mno byas-te sgrub-pa; blo-ṫabs ₒṫsol-ba.*
Investigate *lta-ba, lta-rtog byed-pa.*
Invincible *γžan-gyis mi ṫub-pa* 234.
Invisible *mi-snaṅ-ba.*
Invite *ₒdren-pa, γdan-ₒdren-pa, spyan-ₒdren-pa; šog zer-ba.*
Involuntarily *ga-čád,* (*raṅ*) *dbaṅ-med-du.*
Inward *naṅ-gi* II 301.
Iron s. *lčags*; — ore *lčags-sa*; — slag *lčags-drégs.*
Iron adj. *lčags-kyi.*
Irreligious *skal-méd, čos-méd.*
Irresistible *rgol mi nus-pa.*
Irritable *rtse-reg-če* 440.
Irritate **gob-non-čo-če* W., ṫsaṅ ₒbru-ba.*
Isabel (horse) *ṅaṅ-pa.*
Ischury *ču-gags* 157.
Isinglass *nya-spyin.*
Island *gliṅ-ṗrán.*
Issue vb. n. *ₒgye-ba, ₒṗro-ba.*
Issue s. *bu-rgyúd.*
Isthmus *ču-bar, gliṅ-lag-ₒbrél* 541.
It pron. *ḱo* 42, *de* 255.
Itch s. (disease) *rkoṅ-pa.*
Itching s. *ₒbun-pa.*
Itself pron. v. *ṅo* 129; *dṅos-γži* 131.
Ivory *ba-so.*

# J

Jackal *če-spyaṅ, dur-spyaṅ, wa-spyáṅ.*
Jackdaw *skyuṅ-ka, lčuṅ-ka.*
Jacket *keu-rtse, ke-rtse.*
Jagged *čoṅ-čóṅ.*
Jar s. *rdza-búm.*
Jaundice *mig-sér*; black — *ḱsa-ya nag-po.*
Jawbone *mgal, ₒgram-rús.*
Jealous *če-ré, mig-ser-čan.*
Jealousy *gran-sems, čags-sdaṅ, mig-sér.*
Jehovah *ya-ho-wá.*
Jejune *lto-stoṅ.*
Jelly (gelatine) *ₒgrig-ₒgrig C.*
Jessamine *kun-da.*
Jesus *ye-šu.*
Jest s. *ku-ré, kyal-ka, ḱa-šágs, ga-ža.*
Jest vb. *ku-re byed-pa; rtse-ba.*
Jet of water *ču-mda.*
Jewel *rdo-rǰe; nor-bu; ṗra, ₒṗra; rin-po-če.*
Join vb. a. *sgrig-pa, ₒdogs-pa, sdud-pa, sbyor-ba, sbrel-ba, zuṅ sdebs-pa*; vb. n. *sdeb-pa*; to — (in singing) *ram-bu ₒdegs-pa.*
Joined *sbyor-la, žor-la.*
Joint s. *ₒbrel-mṫsams* 402; *ṫsigs* 448.
Jointly *skyus* 28.

Joke s. *ku-ré, kyal-ka, k̔a-śágs, ga-ża.*
Joke vb. *rtse-ba.*
Journey s. *lam* 544; a day's – *dyoṅs, dgoṅs-żág.*
Journeyman *las-grogs.*
Joy s. *dga-ba* II 83, *dga-bdé, dga-t̔sór; ṅo-só, spro-ba* II 337, *brod-pa.*
Joyful, to be – *mgu-ba.*
Joyous *dga-mo.*
Judah *ya-hu-dá.*
Judge s. *k̔rims-dpon*; district – *yul-dpon.*
Judgment-hall *bka-γśágs.*
Jug *ču-snod, ben.*
Juggler *sgyu-ma-mk̔an.*
Jugglery *˳p̔rul, čo-˳p̔rul.*
Juice *bčud, rtsi.*
Jump vb. *˳k̔rab-pa.*
Juniper *spa-ma.*
Jupiter (*γza*) *p̔ur-bu.*
Just adj. *draṅ-po, t̔sul-čan* 450.
Just adv. v. *raṅ* no. 3 522; – before *k̔a-draṅ* 35; – by *˳gram-du* 98; – he, the very, *k̔o-na* 43; – now *ma-tág* 227; – so *de-k̔a-ltar* 255.
Justice v. *k̔rims* 50; *γśags* 564; chief – *śag-dpon W.*
Justification *rnam-dag rtsi-ba* 314.

# K

Kalpa s. v. *bskal-pa* 33.
Keep vb. a. *˳čaṅ-ba, sruṅ-ba, skyoṅ-ba* 31; to – back *˳gegs-pa, skyil-ba*; to – in mind *˳čaṅ-ba*; vb. n. *rten-pa* 213.
Keeper *rdzi-bo* 468; *sruṅ-mk̔an* 583.
Kernel *rkaṅ*; *rtsi-gu, t̔si-gu.*
Kettle *zaṅs, zaṅs-bu*; – drum *ṙṅa.*
Key *lde-mig*; (*p̔e-*) *ku-lig W.*
Khams v. *k̔ams* 39.
Khatmandu v. *k̔o-bóm* 43.
Kick s. *rdog-pa, ˳p̔ra-śags.*
Kick vb. a. *˳p̔ra-ba*, v. also *rdog-pa.*
Kid *ra-gu, ri-gu W.*
Kidney *mk̔al-ma.*
Kill *γsod-pa, srog γčod-pa*, resp. *˳gum-pa, ˳gem-pa.*
Kind s. *k̔yad-par, rigs, sna* 316; *rnam-pa* 313; *bye-brag*; of every – *sna-t̔sad.*
Kind adj. *drin-čan, byams-pa*; to be – *mt̔un-po byed-pa.*
Kindle *dugs-pa, sbor-ba.*
Kindness *drin, bka-drin, bdag-rkyén, brtse-ba.*
King *rgyal-po, ṙje-bo.*
Kingdom *rgyal-k̔áms, rgyal-k̔ág.*
Kiss s. *˱o, ˱u.*
Kiss vb. *˱o byed-pa, k̔a γtugs-pa, *k̔a lan-če* W.*
Kitchen *bkad-sa, γyos-k̔aṅ; t̔ab-t̔saṅ W., sol-k̔aṅ C.*; – garden *ldum-ra W.*
Knag *mdzer-pa.*
Knapsack *k̔ab-ta-ka, k̔om*; *či-ka W.*
Knead *rdzi-ba.*
Knee *pus-mo*; – joint *sgyid-pa*; – pan *lha-ṅá.*
Knife *gri.*
Knit *slé-ba.*
Knock s. (the sound of knocking) *tag-tág*; there is a – *tag-tág zer W.*
Knocker *γtun.*
Knot s. *mdud-pa* 273; *mdzer-pa* 463.
Know *śes-pa, ṅo-śes-pa, rig-pa*, resp. *mk̔yen-pa, ṅes-pa C.*; to – by heart *k̔a-ton-du śes-pa.*
Knowledge *rgyus, rig-pa, śes-pa.*
Known adj. *rgyus-yod-pa, ča-yod-pa*; not *γtol-méd, rgyus-med-pa, ča-med-pa.*
Knuckle s. *sor-t̔sigs*; knuckles used as dice *bloṅ-mo.*
Kunawar v. *k̔u-nu* 40.

# L

Label s. *byaṅ-bu, byaṅ-ma.*
Labour s. *las*, resp. *p̔rin-las, bzo.*
Labour vb. a. *las byed-pa.*
Labourer *las-pa.*
Laconic *k̔a-nyúṅ, t̔sig-nyúṅ.*
Lad *byis-pa.*
Ladder *skad, skas-ka.*
Lade (water) *˳ču-ba.*
Ladle s. *t̔um-bu, γzar-bu, ču-γzar, skyogs.*
Lady *ǰo-mo, btsun-mo*; – of rank *ṙje-ma*, col. *śe-ma*; young – *śem-čúṅ W.*
Lahul *gar-ża* 67.
Lair *t̔saṅ.*
Lake *mt̔so.*
Lama *bla-ma*; Grand – *bla(-ma) čen-po.*
Lamb *lu-gu, lug-gu.*
Lame adj. *ża-ba, ża-bo, rkaṅ-rdúm.*
Lamed *grum-pa.*
Lament vb. n. *smre-ba, mya-ṅan byed-pa, čo-ṅe debs-pa.*
Lamentation *čo-ṅe, ˱o-dód.*
Lamp *mar-mé, sgron-ma, 'oṅ-gu, *żụm-mar-pa* C., rkyoṅ-tse W.*
Lampblack *sgron-dregs.*

Lampoon s. *sgo-yig.*
Land s. (cultivated) *kluṅs*; (dry land) *skam-sa*; — owner *žiṅ-bdág.*
Landlord (of a house) *bran-dpon*; — (of the ground) *sa-bdág.*
Landscape *sa-γnás.*
Landslip *sa-rúd.*
Lane *lam-sraṅ.*
Language *skad, sgra*; — master *skad-pa.*
Languid *nyams-čuṅ, nyams-tag-pa, γčoṅ-ba C., šed-méd W.*; to get — *rgod-pa.*
Lantern *sgron-ma*, paper — *goṅ-žu.*
Lap s. (coat-tail) *grwa*; (bosom) *paṅ*, resp. *sku-páṅ.*
Lard s. *grod-ťsil.*
Large *rgyas-pa, čen-po, rgya-čen-po, yaṅs-pa.*
Lark *čò-ga, lčo-ga; ča-čir Ld.*
Larynx *ľkol-mdúd, 'ol-mdúd.*
Last adj. *rjes* 181, *ťa-ma* 226, *ṕyi-ma, rtiṅ-ma W.*; — night *mdaṅ*; — will *ḱa-čéms, bka-čéms*; — year *ḱa-niṅ, sṅa-lo, na-niṅ.*
Last vb. n. *ₒťso-ba.*
Lasting adj. *rtag-po.*
Lastly *mťar* 240.
Latch s. *ₒḱor-gyág, ₒḱor-γya.*
Late *ṕyi-mo*; later (subsequent) *ṕyi-ma*; to be late *ₒṕyi-ba.*
Lately *da-či, *dę-zag-la** 275.
Lath *lčam, ṕyam.*
Lathe *skor-spyád.*
Latter *ṕyi-ma.*
Lattice *dra-ba.*
Laudable *stod-ₒos.*
Laugh vb. n. *dgod-pa, rgod-pa, bžad-pa.*
Laughter *gad-mo, rgod.*
Laurel, — leaf **šiṅ-ťsę lo-ma* W.*
Law *ḱrims, bka-ḱrims*; to go to — **ṭim žu-čę* W.*
Lawsuit *ḱrims, ḱrim-šágs.*
Lawyer *ḱrims-pa.*
Lax adj. *kyom.*
Laxative s. *bšal-smán.*
Lay vb. a. *snyol-ba, sgyel-ba, bsnyal-te bžag-pa; ₒgrems-pa*; to — aside *skyuṅ-ba, ₒṕud-pa*; to — on *ₒgel-ba, stad-pa*; to — out (to expend) *skyag-pa, ₒdzugs-pa*; (to plan) *ₒgod-pa*; (to display) *γčal-ba*; to — over (to spread over) *sgron-pa*; to — up *bkri-ba, bdog-pa.*
Layman *ḱyim-pa, gaṅ-zág; mi-nag skye-bo* 29.
Laziness *le-lo, le-lo-nyid.*
Lazy *le-lo-čan, kyaṅ-ḱyóṅ W.*
Lead s. *ža-nye, ža-ne, ra-nye; rin-di W.*; — pencil *γya-ṭig, ₒbri-smyúg.*
Lead vb. a. *ₒḱrid-pa, tog ₒdren-pa, sna ₒdren-pa.*
Leaf *lo-ma.*
Leak vb. n. *rdol-ba.*
Lean adj. *skam-ši, skem-po, žag-méd.*
Lean vb. (against) *snye-ba.*
Leap vb. *mčoṅ-ba, ₒṕar-ba.*
Learn *slob-pa.*
Learned adj. *mḱas-pa.*
Learning s. *rig-pa, šes-pa.*
Lease s., to take a — *nyo-ba.*
Leather s. *ko-ba, ko-lpags, bse*; — shoe *ko-ḱrád*; — sieve *ko-ťsag.*
Leave s. *γnaṅ-ba*; — of absence *bka-bkrol, dgoṅs-pa*; to take — v. *ṕyag* 347.
Leave vb. *ₒjog-pa, γtoṅ-ba, ₒbor-ba.*
Leaven s *žo-ri W.*; v. *ru-ma* 531.
Lecture s. *gleṅ-brjod, gleṅ-mo.*
Lecturer *sgrog-pa-po*; —'s chair *čos-ḱri.*
Leech s. *ḱrag-ₒťuṅ-ₒbu W.*; *srin-bu pad-ma.*
Leek *sgog-pa.*
Left adj. *γyon-pa*; — hand *γyon-ma*; — handed *γyon-lag-byed-pa; gyog-po.*
Leg *rkaṅ-pa.*
Legalize *bkar-ₒdogs-pa.*
Legend *sgruṅs.*
Legendary tales *rnam-ťár.*
Leisure *loṅ, čog-ka*; to have — *čog-pa.*
Lemon *gam-bu-ra, spyod-pád.*
Lend *γyar-ba.*
Length *dkyus, riṅ-ḱyád, srid.*
Leopard *γzig*; snow — *γsa.*
Leprosy *rňo, mdze.*
Lessen vb. n. *ₒgrib-pa; je-nyuṅ je-nyuṅ-bar ₒgyur-ba.*
Lesson s. *ḱa-ta*, resp. *žal-ta; rgyugs W.*
Lest conj. v. *dogs-pa* 258.
Let vb. (to — in, to — loose etc.) *γtoṅ-ba; ₒjug-pa* II, no. 2 178.
Letter (of the alphabet) *yi-ge*; (epistle) *yi-ge*, resp. *bka-šóg*; — case *yi-gei šubs.*
Lettuce *ldum.*
Level vb. a. *snyoms-pa.*
Lever *γšo-mo.*
Liar *ḱram-pa, zog-čan.*
Libation *mčod-pa, mčod-ston* 166.
Libel s. *sgo-yig.*
Liberal *mig-yáṅs.*
Liberate *ₒgrol-ba.*
Liberty *ťar-pa, raṅ-dbáṅ*; to be at — *čog-pa.*
Libidinous *čags-sred-čan, ₒčol-pa.*
Librarian *deb-ťer-pa.*
Library *kun-dga-ra-ba; yig-ḱaṅ.*
Lick vb. *ldag-pa.*
Lid *ḱa-ḱébs, ḱa-gáb, ḱa-γčód, ḱa-leb; čab-ma.*
Lie s. *rdzun, šob, šab-šób W.*
Lie vb. (to tell a lie) *rdzun smra-ba* or *byed-pa.*
Lie vb. (down) *nyal-ba*; to — with **ṭig-pa čo-čę* W., bšo-ba.*
Life *srog, ₒťso-ba, γson-pa, ťse* 450; — long *nam ₒťsoi bar-du.*

Lift vb. *ker-ba, ˳ḱyog-pa, ˳degs-pa, spor-ba, ˳ṕyar-ba, señ-ba.*
Light s. *˵od, snañ-ba.*
Light adj. (not heavy) *yañ-po*; (not dark) *skya-bo*; — blue *sño-skya*; — gray *dkar-skya*; — green *ljañ-skya*; — red *dkar-dmar*; — yellow *ser-skya.*
Light vb. a. *sgron-pa, sbor-ba.*
Lightning s. *glog, glog-ka, ťog.*
Like adj. (similar) *mnyam-pa, mtsuñs-pa, ťsogs-se W.*; adv. (in the same manner) *lta, ltar. nañ-tar W. C.*
Like vb. a. . . . *la dga-ba.*
Likelihood *ño.*
Likeness *bzo, zo.*
Likewise *yañ.*
Limb *yan-lag.*
Lime *rdo-žó.*
Limit s. *mťa, mu.*
Line s. *ťig; yig-ṕrén.*
Lineage *brgyud, rigs, rigs-brgyúd, rus, rus-pa.*
Linger *˳gor-ba.*
Lining s. *nañ-ša.*
Lion *señ-ge*; lioness *señ-ge-mo.*
Lip *ḱa-lpágs, mču, ḱa-mču.*
Liquid s. *ḱu-ba, rlan-rlón.*
List s. *ťo*; — of goods *rjed-byáñ.*
Listen *nyan-pa.*
Literature *čos, rig-pa.*
Litter s. (palanquin) *ḱad, ḱyogs, ˳ḱyogs*; (bier) *dgu-ḱri C.*
Little adj. *čuñ-ba, nyuñ-ba, ṕra-ba, ṕran, ṕran-bu, dman-pa.*
Little s. (a little) *čig, čuñ, čuñ-žig, ťig-ťsám, ťsa-big, 'a-ťsig W., a-li C.*; adj. *čuñ-ba.*
Live vb. n. (to be alive) *γson-pa* 591; (to dwell) *γnas-pa* 310, *˳dug-pa* 277, *˳ḱod-pa* 56; (to behave) *˳grul-ba* 100; to — by or on *za-ba* 485, *˳ťso-ba* 460.
Lively *γčañ-po, ḱram-pa.*
Liver *mčin-pa* 165.
Lizard *skyin-gór, da-byid, rgag-čig Ld.* 103, *ma-la-la-tsé Ld.* 409.
Load s. *ḱal, ḱur, rgyab, rgyab-ḱal* 107, *sgal* 114, *dos* 260.
Load vb. a. *˳gel-ba, ˳ḱel-ba*
Loadstone *ḱab-lén.*
Loaf *kor-kór, dog W.* 257.
Loan s. *skyin-pa*, resp. *kar-skyin.*
Locality *γnas, skye-γnás* 28.
Lock s. (of hair) *ral-pa.*
Lock s. (of a door) *lčags, *go-čag* C., ku-lig W.*
Lock vb. a. *γčod-pa*; to — up *˳gegs-pa*; *gar-te* or *gyañ-du bor-če W.*, v. *sgyoñ-ba* 119.
Locust *ťsa-ga-˳bu, ča-ga-˳bu.*
Lodgings *γnas-ťsañ, ˳brañ-sa.*
Log *dog W.*
Logic *ťsad-ma, rigs-pa.*
Loins *rked-pa.*
Loiter *˳gor-ba.*
Lonely *dben-pa.*
Long adj. *riñ-ba, dkyus-riñ*; as — as v. *bar* 366.
Long vb. n. *rkam-pa, skam-pa, γduñ-ba, žen-pa.*
Look vb. (to view) *lta-ba*, resp. *γzigs-pa*; (to appear) *snañ-ba*; to — at or on *ltos-pa*; to — down upon *˳gyiñ-ba*; to — upon as *sgom-pa.*
Look s. *lta-stañs, ño*; — out *so, bso.*
Loose adj. *kyom, lhod-pa.*
Loose, Loosen vb. a. *glod-pa, ˳grol-ba.*
Looseness *˳ḱru-ba.*
Lop vb. a. *˳grum-pa.*
Lord s. *mgon-po, jo-bo, rje-bo, dpon-po, dbañ-po, γtso-bo*; — of the manor *γži-bdág.*
Lose *rlog-pa, ˳bud-pa W.*; to — colour *dkyug-pa*; to be lost *stor-ba.*
Loss *gud, gun, god, god-pa, god-ma.*
Lot s. (fortune) *skal-ba*, resp. *sku-skál*; *las-bskos* (v. *sko-ba*); *ṕya*; to cast lots *mo ˳debs-pa, rgyan rgyab-pa* 107, *rtags-ril btañ-ba W.* 212.
Lotus *ku-mu-da, pad-ma* 322.
Loud *mťon-po, skad čen-po.*
Louse s. *šig.*
Love vb. a. *čags-pa, *čags-žen čo-če* W., γduñ-ba, ˳ṕreñ-ba, brtse-ba, mdza-ba* 461, **žen-˳dzin čo-če* W., γčes-par byed-pa* or *˳dzin-pa.*
Love s. *čags-pa, snyiñ-brtse-ba*, resp. *ťugs-brtse-ba, duñs-pa, dran-séms, byams-pa, byams-sems.*
Lover *˳dod-grogs, mdza-grogs, bzañ-grogs*; *˳dod-mḱan.*
Low *dma-mo, dman-pa*; *snyan-pa.*
Lower adj., — part of a thing *smad, šam, γšam, šod*; — — of the body *ro-smád.*
Lowland *smad, man-čád.*
Luck s., good — *šis*, bad — *rkyen.*
Lucky *bkra-šis-pa.*
Luggage *ča-lág.*
Lukewarm *mal-la-mul-le.*
Luminous *˵od-čan.*
Lump *goñ-po, goñ-bu, gog, dog.*
Lunar *zla-bai*; — mansions *rgyu-skar* 111.
Lunch, Luncheon s. *dro* 264.
Lungs *glo-ba.*
Lurk *sgug-pa, ˳jab-ste sdod-pa, lkog-˳jab byas-te lta-ba.*
Lurking-place *bskuñs-sa.*
Lust s *˳dod-pa, ˳dod-čags, čags-pa, ro-tsa.*
Lustful *čags-sred-čan, ˳čol-pa.*
Lustre *bkrag, ˳ťser-ba.*
Lynx *dbyi, γyi.*

# M

**Mace** (club) *ga-da.*
**Machine** *$_o$ṕrul-$_o$ḱor.*
**Mad** *smyon-pa*; to be — *smyo-ba.*
**Madam,** dear — *bżin-bzaṅ-ma.*
**Madder** *btsod.*
**Madness** *$_o$ḱrul-pa, smyo-$_o$bóg.*
**Magazine** *ťsoṅ-ḱaṅ, mdzod.*
**Maggot** *ṡa-$_o$bu.*
**Magic** s. *$_o$ṕrul*; adj. *$_o$ṕrul-gyi*; — sentence *γzuṅs*; — tricks *čo-$_o$ṕrul*; — wheel *$_o$ṕrul-$_o$ḱor.*
**Magician** *$_o$ba-po.*
**Magistrate** *$_o$go-pa, $_o$go-yod Ld.*; village — *yul-dpon.*
**Magnificence** *rṅam-pa, dpal, dpal-byór, byin.*
**Magnolia** *tsam-pa-ka.*
**Magpie** *skya-ga, ka-ta ḱra-bo.*
**Maid, Maiden** *bu-mo*; lady's — *żal-ta-ma*; — servant *ḱol-mo, γyog-mo.*
**Mail** (armour) *ḱrab, ya-lád.*
**Maim** vb.a. *ṕran γčod-pa, sug-pa $_o$ḋreg-pa.*
**Main** adj. *mčog*, v. also *γżuṅ*; — dogma *γsuṅ-mčog*; — point *don* 259, *γnad*; — substance *ṅo-bo-nyid.*
**Maintain** *smra-ba, $_o$dod-pa,* resp. *bżed-pa*; *smras-pa-la brtan-par γnas-pa.* [*tsáb* 375.
**Maitreya** *byams-pa mgon-po* 109; *rgyal-*
**Majestic** *rṅom-bag-čan, γzi-brȷid-čan.*
**Majesty** *rṅam-pa, rṅom-brȷid.*
**Make** vb. a. *byed-pa,* eleg. *bgyid-pa,* resp. *mdzad-pa, sgrub-pa, $_o$ča-ba, bzo-ba, $_o$ȷug-pa, bčo-ba*; to be made *$_o$grub-pa.*
**Maker** *mdzad-po.*
**Malabar** *ma-la-ya.*
**Male** adj. *ṕo*; — child *ḱyeu*; *bu*; — person *skyes-pa.*
**Malediction** *byad, byad-stem(s).*
**Malice** *γnod-sems.*
**Malicious** *blo-nyés.*
**Mallow** *čam-pa ta-lo.*
**Man** s. (human being) *mi, rkaṅ-γnyis-pa*; *laṅs-γro, skye-bo, skyes-bu, gaṅ-zag*; (male) *ṕo, skyes-pa*; — servant *ḱol-po, bran-ḱól*; waiting — *żal-ta-pa.*
**Mane** *rṅog, ltag-spu.*
**Manger** *ḱyi-γżóṅ*; *bres.*
**Manifest** adj. *mṅon-pa.*
**Manifestly** *ṅos-su.*
**Manifold** *sna-ťsogs, sna-maṅ-ba*; *ṕal-čér.*
**Mankind** *skye-bo, skye-dgú, skye-rgú*; *mi-rabs, mi-rigs.*
**Manly** *ḱyo-gai*; — age *dar-ma.*
**Manner** *ťsul, lugs, rnam-pa* no. 4, 313; *stabs, staṅs, sgros, čos* no. 5, 163.
**Mansion,** lunar — *rgyu-skar* 111.
**Manufacture** s. *bzo.*
**Manufacture** vb.a. *$_o$god-pa, sgrub-pa, bčo-ba, bzo-ba.*
**Manure** s. *lud*; vb. a. *lud γtoṅ-ba.*
**Many** *maṅ-po, du-ma, dgu,* a good — *ga-čén*; how —? *du*; so — *de-snyéd.*
**Map** s. *bkod-pa, żiṅ-bkod W.*; **sa-ṭa* C.*
**Maple** *γya-li Sik.*
**March** vb.n. *$_o$grod-pa, $_o$grul-ba*; to — about *$_o$grim-pa.*
**March** s. *rkaṅ-grós.*
**Mare** *rgod-ma, mo-rta.*
**Margin** *ṅos, zur, mťa.*
**Marigold** *gur-kúm.* [*bkur-sti.*
**Mark** s. *rtags, mťsan(-ma)*; — of honour
**Market** *ťsoṅ-$_o$dus*; — place *ḱrom.*
**Marmot** *ṕyi-ba, $_o$ṕyi-ba.*
**Married** adj., a — man or woman *ḱyim-ťab*; a — woman *bdag-tu byas-pai bud-med*; to get — (both of man and woman) *ḱyo-ṡug-tu $_o$du-ba* 276; (of a woman) *mi żig-gi čuṅ-mar byed-pa* 159.
**Marrow** *rkaṅ*; *ṅo-bo-nyid*; spinal — *klad-γżuṅ.*
**Marry** vb. a. (to take a wife) *čuṅ-ma len-pa*; (to unite in matrimony) *ḱyo-ṡug-tu sdud-pa.*
**Mars** *mig-dmár.*
**Marsh** *gram-pa*; *$_o$dam.*
**Marvelous** (*ṅo*) *mťsar-ba* 456; v. also *ya-mťsan-po* 505.
**Mask** s. *$_o$bag.*
**Mason** *rtsig-bzo-pa.*
**Masquerade** *$_o$bag-$_o$čam.*
**Mass** (lump) *goṅ-po,* (heap) *ṕuṅ-po,* (bulk) *lhun,* (multitude) *ḱrod-pa.*
**Mast** (flag-staff) *dar-po-čé.*
**Master** *mgon-po, mṅa-bdág, bdag-po, dpon-* [*po.*
**Mat** s. *stan.*
**Match** s. (equal) *ḱa-ya, do*; v. *čar* 156; v. *ya* 504; (lunt) *ṕa-til, pa-til.*
**Matchless** *$_o$gran-zla-med-ṕa, $_o$gran-ya-méd, do-méd, mťsuṅs-méd.*
**Mate** s. (companion) *do-zla*; *ya-do W.*
**Material** s. *rgyu.*
**Material** adj. *dṅos-čan, γzugs-čan.*
**Mathematician** *rtsis-pa.*
**Matter** s. (substance) *rgyu, dṅos-po, rdzas, zaṅ-ziṅ*; (in physics) *bem-po, γzugs*; (pus) *ču-ser, ču-rnag, rnag.*
**Matter** vb. n.; it does not — *čaṅ mi sto*; what does it —? *či sto.*
**Mattock** *$_o$ȷor, tog-tse.*
**Mattress** *sob-stán.*
**Maw** *lkog-sóg, ze-búg.*
**Maxim** *bka-rtags.*
**Meadow** *spaṅ, spaṅ-po, ne-ťán, ne-ma.*
**Meagre** *skem-pa, rid-pa.*

Meal (flour) *p̕ye.*
Mean adj. *gyi-na, ṅan-pa, btsog-pa.*
Mean vb. *go-ba, snyam-pa, ₒdu-ṡes-pa; yin-pa* 510.
Meaning s. *bsam-pa,* resp. *dgoṅs-pa; don.*
Means s. *grabs, t̕abs;* by all — *ṅes-par, gaṅ-gis kyaṅ, ċis kyaṅ;* by no — *re-skán;* by what —? *ċis;* by — of *sgo-nas* 115
Measure s. *skar-t̕sád, bre, t̕sad, t̕sod;* to take — *skad-ċe, t̕sod ₒdzin-pa;* measures (arrangements) *grabs;* to take — *grabs byed-pa.*
Measure vb.a. *ₒjal-ba, dpog-pa, t̕sod ₒdzin-pa, nyams-len-pa, ɣṡor-ba.*
Meat s. *ṡa,* resp. *skrum; za-ba,* resp. *bžes-pa;* dried — *skam-saṅ;* — and drink *bza-btúṅ;* — jelly *ṡa-spyin;* — pie *mog-móg W.*
Mecca *ma-k̕á.*
Mechanic s. *bzo-pa;* mechanics' institution *bzo-grá.*
Meddle *k̕a ₒjug-pa, t̕e-ba.*
Mediator *bar-mi.*
Medicine *sman.*
Meditate *sems-pa,* resp. *dgoṅs-pa, lta-ba, sgom-pa, bsam-mno byed-pa,* resp. *t̕ugs-bsam ɣtoṅ-ba.*
Meditation *sgom, sgom-pa, rnal-ₒbyór.*
Medley *čag-ga-čog-gé.*
Meet vb. a. *t̕ug-pa, ₒprad-pa, mjal-ba;* vb. n. *ₒdzom-pa;* to go to — *ɣdan-ₒdren-pa.*
Meeting s. *ₒdu-ba, ₒdus-pa;* — house *ₒdun-k̕aṅ, t̕sogs-k̕aṅ;* — place *ₒdus-sa.*
Melody *mgur, dbyaṅs.*
Melon *ga-gón.*
Melt vb. a. *ₒju-ba, žu-ba;* melted, molten *žun-pa, žun-mo;* melting-spoon *žu-kyóg.*
Member *yan-lag, t̕sigs* 448.
Memorandum-book *rjed-t̕o.*
Memorial stone *rjed-rdó.*
Memory *dran-pa.*
Menace vb. *ₒgam-pa.*
Mend vb. a. *glan-pa.*
Mendacious *k̕ram-sems-ċan.*
Mendicant adj. *spraṅ-po;* — friar *spraṅ-bán.*
Menses, Menstruation *k̕rag ₒdzag-pa, zla-mt̕sán.*
Mention vb. a. *ₒgod-pa;* to be mentioned (in a book etc.) *ₒbyuṅ-ba.*
Merciful *snyiṅ-rje-ċan,* resp. *t̕ugs-rje-ċan.*
Mercury (planet) *lhag-pa;* (metal) *dṅul-ču.*
Mercy *snyiṅ-rje, t̕ugs-rje.*
Mere *ₒba-žig.*
Merely *ṡa-stag, ṡa-dag.*
Merit s. *bsod-pa.*
Merry *k̕rul-po, sems-spro-ba, spro-sems-ċan; dga-ba, dga-mo.*
Mesh *ₒgug(s) W.*
Mess (dish) *skyu-rúm, spags.*
Message *p̕rin, ₒp̕rin, lon,* resp. *bka-p̕rin.*
Messenger *p̕o-nya, mi-sná.*
Metal *žu-bai k̕ams;* cast — *blugs-ma.*
Metaphor *ṅag-snyán, ₒdra-dpe.*
Meteor *ke-tu.*
Method *čo-ga, t̕abs, t̕sul, lugs.*
Metropolis *rgyal-sa, mt̕il.*
Mewing s. (of a cat) *mea̧o.*
Mid-day *nyin-guṅ, dguṅ, ɣdugs.*
Middle s. *dkyil, rked-pa, koṅs, guṅ, dguṅ, dbus, ɣžuṅ.*
Middle adj. *bar-pa, bar-ma, briṅ;* — finger *kan-ma, guṅ-mo, bar-mdzub.*
Midnight *nam-p̕yéd, mt̕san-dkyil, mt̕san-guṅ, mt̕san-p̕yed, dguṅ,* v. *guṅ* 69.
Midriff *mčin-dri*
Midst s. *koṅs, dbus.*
Might *mṅa, mṅa-t̕áṅ, dbaṅ, dbaṅ-t̕áṅ.*
Mighty *k̕a-drág, rgyas-pa, dbaṅ-ċan, btsan-po.*
Migrate *ₒp̕o-ba.*
Milch cow *bžon-ma.*
Mild *dul-ba, srun-pa, bsrun-pa.*
Mile *dpag-t̕sád.*
Milk s. *žo, ̧o-ma;* sour — *žo-ri W, ru-ma C.;* — pail *̧o-zó.*
Milk vb. a. *ₒjo-ba, ̧o-ma ₒjo-ba, ̧o-ma ₒt̕sír-ba.*
Milky-way *dgu-t̕sigs.*
Mill s. *raṅ-ₒt̕ag.*
Millet *k̕re, či-tse.*
Million *sa-ya;* ten — *bye-ba.*
Millstone *k̕od.*
Milt *mčer-pa.*
Mind s. *sems, blo, yid, nyams, snyiṅ, snyam-pa, že,* resp. *t̕ugs;* to have a — *dga-ba, ₒdod-pa;* to keep in — *dran-pa, ɣzo-ba.*
Mind vb. a. *lta-ba, ɣnyer-k̕a byed-pa* 194; never —! v. *ċis kyaṅ* 141.
Mine s. *k̕uṅs, ɣter-k̕a.*
Mine pron. *ṅai* 124.
Minister s. *blon-po;* prime — *bka-blón.*
Mint (plant) *dag-ċi Lh.*
Minute s. *ču-sraṅ.*
Minute adj. *p̕ra-ba, žib-pa.*
Miracle *ltas, ya-mt̕san.*
Mirage *dri-zai groṅ, mig-sgyu.*
Mischief *skag, ṅan;* — maker *bstan-ṡig.*
Miserable *gyi-na, ṅan-pa, t̕u-ba, sdug-bsṅal-ċan.*
Miserly *bkren-pa.*
Misery *nyon-moṅs-pa, zag-pa.*
Misfortune *bkra-mi-ṡis, rkyen, skyon, ṅan, byur, byus.*
Mishap *gal-rkyén.*
Miss s. (young lady) *ṡem-čúṅ W.*
Miss vb. *t̕al-ba, mi k̕es-pa.*
Missive s. *bka-rgya, če-dón* 160

**Mist** *na-bún, rmugs-pa.*
**Mistake** s. *ₒkrul-pa, ₒkrul-yži, ₒgol-sa, nor-ba, ₒdzol-pa.*
**Mistake** vb. *nor-ba, ₒkrul-ba.*
**Mistaken** adj. *ₒkrul-ba, ₒkrul-pa.*
**Mistress** (instructress) *mkan-mo*; (head of a household) *jo-mo, dpon-mo*; (lady) *btsun-mo* 435.
**Mix** *sdeb-pa, spel-ba* 331, *sre-ba*; to be mixed with *ₒdre-ba.*
**Mixture** *spel-ma, sbyor-ba* II no. 2, 406.
**Mock** vb. *to-ₒtsam-pa.*
**Mode** (manner) *skabs, stabs, lugs.*
**Model** s. *dpe* 327.
**Moderate** adj. *ₒbriṅ, tsod-čan.*
**Moderately** *ₒbriṅ-gis*; *ran-par.*
**Modest** *kan-man, kram-pa, ₒdzem-bag čan.*
**Modesty** *krel, krel-yod, krel-ₒdzém.*
**Mohammedan, Mohammedanism** *kla-klo.*
**Moisture** *bčud, bad.*
**Moment** *skad, bsgaṅ, yud.*
**Monastery** *dgon-pa, čos-sdé, grwa-sa.*
**Monday** *γza-zla-ba.*
**Money** *dṅul, nor*; ready — *rnags*; *smar-ba, smar-rkyáṅ*; — changer *nor-bdag.*
**Mongol** *sog-po.*
**Monk** *grwa-pa, mgo-rég, čos-pa.*
**Monkey** *spra* 335, *spre, spreu* 337.
**Month** *zla-ba*; intercalary — *da-ṭúl W.* 51.
**Moon** *zla-ba, zla*; full — *nya-rgyas zla-ba*; half — i. e. first und last quarter *da-ṗéd W.*; new — *zla-nág* 491; waxing and waning — *ṅo, ṅos* v. *ṅo* no. 5, 129.
**Moral** adj. *tsul-čan, tsul daṅ mtun-pa*; *mtsul-krims-kyi*; *dge-bai*; *čos-kyi*; also *sems-kyi, yid-kyi*; — doctrine *čos* no. 2, 163.
**More** *lhag* 600.
**Moreover** *deï steṅ-du* 222.
**Morning** *sṅa-dro, sṅa-mo W., naṅ-mo*; the next — *to-ráṅs, naṅ-par*; this — *da-náṅ*; yesterday — *ka-náṅ*; — twilight *skya-réṅs, skya-'ód W.*
**Morrow**, to — *saṅ, to-re W.*
**Mortal** s. *mi(i)-bu*; adj. (perishable) *zin-pai*; *mi rtag-pa*; (deadly) *srog-len.*
**Mortar** (for pounding) *mčig*; (short cannon) *sgyogs*; (cement) *ₒjim-pa, ka-lag W.*
**Most** *kun-las lhag* or *maṅ-po*; v. also *ṗal-čér* 342.
**Moth** *mug-pa.*
**Mother** *ma*, resp. *yum*; *'a-ma*; — in law *sgyug-mo*; *gyos-mo.*
**Motherless** *mas dben-pa.*
**Mother-of-pearl** *nya-ṗyis.*
**Motion** *ₒgul-ba, γyo-ba.*
**Motionless** adv. *ma γyo-bar, ma ₒgul-bar, ma γyens-par.*
**Motive** *rgyu.*
**Mould** s. (form) *par* 323; (fungus) *ham-pa.*
**Mould** vb. a. *ₒgod-pa, ₒčos-pa, ₒdag-pa* 274.
**Mouldy** *ham-por čags-mkan W.*
**Mound** *dur-ṗuṅ* 254.
**Mount** vb. *žon-pa*, resp. *ₒčib-pa.*
**Mountain** *ri*; — pass *la*; — pasture *ₒbrog.*
**Mourn** *mya-ṅan byed-pa.*
**Mournful** *mya-ṅan-gyi*; — song *skyo-glu.*
**Mouse** s. *byi-ba, tsi-tsi*; *sa-bi-lig W.*
**Mouth** *ka*, resp. *žal.*
**Mouthful** s. *čor-gáṅ, čor-čig.*
**Move** vb. a. *skyod-pa, sgul-ba, γyo-ba*; to — to and fro *γyeṅ-ba* 518; **šrul-če* W.* (v. *srul-ba* 583); vb. n. *rgyu-ba, ₒgul-ba*, resp. *ₒčags-pa* 167; to — a little *nur-ba* 305; to — on *ₒgro-ba*; to — quickly to and fro *ₒgyu-ba* 96; to — round *skor-ba.*
**Mow** *rṅa-ba, rṅab-pa.*
**Much** *drags, maṅ-po, rab*; as — as *ga-tsám W., tsam* 430; so — *ₒdi-snyéd, de-snyéd*; very — *maṅ-drags, šin-tu maṅ-po.*
**Mucus** *snabs, lud-pa.*
**Mud** *ka-lag, ₒjim-pa, ₒdam, mer-ba, rdzab, ₒdam-rdzáb*; — floor *skyaṅ-núl.*
**Muddy** *man-mún.*
**Mulberry** *ₒo-se.*
**Mule** *dre, dre-po, dre-mo.*
**Multiply** vb. a. *sgyur-ba, sgril-ba, sgre-ba, spel-ba, ₒṗel-ba.*
**Multitude** *krod-pa, krom, dmag, γseb.*
**Murder** vb. a. *γsod-pa*; s. *γsod-γčód.*
**Murderer** *γsod-byéd.*
**Muscle** (anatomy) *ša, nya.*
**Muse** vb. n. *rtog-pa.*
**Mushroom** *ša-mo, mog-ša W.*
**Music** *rol-mo.*
**Musk** *gla-rtsí*; — bag *gla-bai lte-ba*; — deer *gla-ba.*
**Musket** *me-dá C.*; — ball *rdeu, rdé.*
**Mustard** *ske-tsé, skye-tsé, yuṅs* 512.
**Mute** adj. *lkugs-pa, han-ldáṅ W.*
**Mutter** vb. a. *sam(-ma) sum(-me) zer-ba W.*; to — prayers *ma-ṇi taṅ-če W., zla-ba, zlo-ba* 491.
**Muzzle** s. *ka-mtsúl, mtsúl-pa.*
**My** pron. *nai*, eleg. *bdag-gi, ṅed-kyi.*
**Myriad** (*čig-*)*kri.*
**Mystic** s. *rgyud-pa.*

# N

Nail s. *γzer, zer, ṕur-pa*; a little — *γzi-ru, γzer-bu*; — of a finger or toe *sen-mo*, resp. *ṕyag-sén, žabs-sén.*
Naked *sgren-mo, γčer-bu, rǰen-pa.*
Name s. *miṅ*, resp. *mťsan.*
Name vb. *miṅ γtogs-pa, skad-pa, ₒgrag-pa, zer-ba.*
Namely *de-yaṅ, de ˬaṅ; ₒdi-lta-ste.*
Nape *ltag-pa.*
Napkin *ka-ṕyis, lag-ṕyis, paṅ-keb.*
Narcotic adj. *smyo-byéd.*
Narrative s. *lo-rgyús.*
Narrow adj. *ṕal-méd, žeṅ-méd, dog-pa.*
Nasty *btsog-pa, (b)rtsog(s)-pa.*
Nation *mi-brgyúd* 124, *sde* 295, *rigs* 527.
Native s. *yul-pa*
Native-place *γžis-ka.*
Natural *dṅos-ma, ma bčos-pa.*
Naturally *raṅ-bžin-gyis, γšis-kyis* 565.
Nature *ṅaṅ, čos-nyid, ṅo-bo-nyid* 129.
Naught (cipher) *mka.*
Naughty *ṅa-rgyal-čan.*
Nausea *skyug-bro-ba, kam-lóg, kams-rmyá.*
Navel *lte-ba.*
Near adj. *nye-ba*; adv *nye-bar, rtsar* 437, *gram-du*; *rgyaṅ ťuṅ-ba*; *ldan-la, ldan-du* 289; to be — *nye-ba, rten-pa* 214.
Neat adj. *sdug-pa, sdug-gu.*
Necessaries s. *yo-byád.*
Necessary adj. *dgos-pa, rigs-pa* 528; to be — *dgos-pa.*
Necessity *dgos-pa.*
Neck *ske, mgur, mgul, mgrin-pa, ₒǰiṅ-pa*; *γnya-ba*; — cloth *ka-dkri, ka-ras.*
Neckerchief *dkri-ma, mgul-čiṅs.*
Necklace *ske-čá.*
Need s. *gyoṅ.*
Needful *dgos-pa*
Needle *kab, ₒťsem-káb.*
Negative s. *dgag-pa* 94, *ₒgag-pai sgra.*
Neglect vb. *ₒgyiṅ-ba, . . . la mi lta-ba.*
Neigh *ₒťser-ba.*
Neighbour *kyim-mťsés, ṕa-rol-po.*
Neighbourhood *sa-ṕyógs, yul-ṕyógs.*
Nepal *bal-po, bal-yúl.*
Nephew *ťsa-bo*, resp. *dbon-po, dbon-srás.*
Nerve *ču-rtsá.*
Nest *ťsaṅ.*
Net *rgya, rgya-mo, dol*; — work *dra-ba.*
Nettle *zwa.*
Neutralize *ₒčiṅ-ba.*
Never v. *nam-yaṅ* 303.
Nevertheless *yin-kyaṅ, yin-na yaṅ W.*
New *so-ma, γsar-ba, γsar-po.*
News *ča, skad, ṕrin, ₒṕrin, lon, hun W.*; good — *lon-bzáṅ.*
Nice *sdug-pa.*
Night *nam, mťsan-mo*; — quarters *ₒbraṅ-sa*, eleg. *mčis-bráṅ*, resp. *γzim-bráṅ*; — watch *ťun.*
Nimble *skyen-pa*; — footed *rkaṅ-mgyogs-pa.*
Nine num. *dgu*; ninth *dgu-pa*; nineteen *bču-dgu*; nineteenth *bču-dgu-pa*; ninety *dgu-bču*; ninetieth *dgu-bču-pa.*
Nip vb. a. *grum-pa.*
Nipple *nu-ma* 305, *pi-pi.*
Nitre *šo-ra.*
No, none v. *gaṅ* 65.
Nobility *dpal* no. 4, 326.
Noble adj. *drag-pa, btsun-pa, skye-mťó.*
Nobleman *rǰe-bo, mi-drag-pa, no-nó* 306.
Noblewoman *btsun-mo, še-ma W.*
Nod vb. a. (beckon) *lag-brda byed-pa*; **go kug taṅ-če* W.*
Node, ascending — *sgra-γčan*; descending — *ke-tu.*
Noise *klag-čór, grag-pa, sgra, ˬur, ku, ku-sgra*; — made by thunder etc. *čems-čéms* 161; to make a — *ₒkrol-ba.*
Noisome *ṅam-pa.*
Nominate *sko-ba, ₒčol-ba.*
Nonsense *čab-čob, čal-čól*; to talk — *čal-čól smra-ba.*
Nook *kug, kugs.*
Noon *dguṅ.*
North *byaṅ.*
Nose *sna, *nam-ťsul* W.*
Nostril *sna-kúṅ.*
Not *ma* 408, *mi* 413, *med* v. *med-pa* 417.
Notch s. *kram-ka, nya-ga, ltoṅ-ga.*
Note s. *mčan-bu, yi-ge* no. 2, 508.
Nothing *čaṅ mi* 138, *či mi* 140; — but *ša-stag*, col. *ka rkyaṅ* (v. *rkyaṅ-pa*); *ₒba-žig* 391.
Notice s. *rgyus, ča, lon*; to give — *lon spriṅ-ba.*
Notion *du-šes.*
Notwithstanding *ˬon-kyaṅ* 502.
Noun substantive *dṅos-miṅ* 131
Nourish *ₒťso-ba, γso-ba.*
Nourishing adj. *nyams-brtas byed-pa.*
Nourishment *zas.*
Novice *dge-bsnyén* 85.
Now *da, da-lta, γzod, ˬo-ná* 500; — and then *bar-bar-du* or *la*; just — *ma-ťág* 227; not until — *da-γzód* 247.
Nowhere v. *čir* 141.
Noxious *mi-dgos-pa, nyes-pa, γdug-pa.*
Null adj. *sob, sog, γsob, γsog.*
Number s. *graṅs.*
Number vb. a. *bgraṅ-ba, rtsi-ba.*

Numberless *bgraṅ-yás.*
Numerous *rgyas-pa.*
Nun *čos-ma, btsun-mo, mo-btsún* 435; *ǰo-mo* 173.
Nurse s. (children's) *má-ma.*
Nurse up vb. a. *γsos skyed-pa, skyed srin-ba* 30.
Nutriment *bċud.*
Nutritious *bċud-čan, lċi-ba.*

# O

Oak *ča-ra, be-šiṅ;* — forest *be-ḱród.*
Oar *skya, gru-ḱyém.*
Oath *yi-dám,* resp. *ṫugs-dám, mna, bro.*
Oats *ka-rtsam, yug-po.*
Obedient *bka nyan-pa.*
Obey *ḱa-la* (or resp. *żal-la) nyan-pa.*
Object s. *γnas, rdzas, zaṅ-ziṅ, dṅos-po* 131; — of perception *yul* 513; mental — *dmigs-γtád.*
Oblation *mčod-pa, sbyin-pa* 405.
Oblige (compel) v. *nan-gyis* 303.
Obliged, to feel — *drin-dran-pa.*
Oblique *ḱyom-ḱyóm, yo-ba, šan-ḱa.*
Oblong *nar-mo, kyoṅ.*
Obscuration *sgrib-pa* 120.
Obscure adj. *mun-pa, go-dka-ba* 71.
Obscure vb. a. *sgrib-pa;* obscured *dkrigs-pa, rmoṅ-ba, rmoṅs-pa.*
Obscurity *mun-pa.*
Observe *sruṅ-ba, . . . la lta-ba* I no. 3, 216.
Obstinate *kyoṅ-po, go-ṫag-čan W.* (lit. *mgo-mḱregs-čan).*
Obstruct *ₒgegs-pa, bċur-ba.*
Obstruction *bgegs, ₒgag.*
Obtain *sgrub-pa, rnyed-pa, ṫob-pa, len-pa.*
Obviate *γċod-pa, zlog-pa.*
Occasion s. *rkyen, glags, skabs;* on — of *skabs-su.*
Occupy *ₒdzin-pa* no. 3, 465.
Occur *ₒgyur-ba, ₒṫon-pa, ₒoṅ-ba.*
Occurrence *rkyen, dṅos-po.*
Ocean *rgya-mṫso.*
Odour *dri, dri-ma.*
Oesophagus *lkog-ma.*
Of prep. *kyi* 6, *nas* 304, *las* 546.
Off adv. *ṗar* 341, *yas* 508.
Offence *sdig-pa;* to commit an — *nyes-pa, sdig-pa byed-pa.*
Offend *ₒḱaṅ-ba, ₒḱu-ba.*
Offensive *šin-tu ṫu-ba, mi żim-pa; yid-du mi ₒoṅ-ba.*
Offer *sbyin-pa.*
Offering s. *mčod-pa, ₒbul-ba, yon;* — lamp *mčod-sdoṅ;* — table *mčod-ḱri, mčod-stégs;* house or place of — *mčod-ḱaṅ.*
Office *ₒgaṅ-po.*
Officer *ₒgo-pa, blon-po.*
Official s. *bka-blon, bka-γšags.*
Official adj. *blon-poi, bka-blon-gyi;* — paper *bka-šog.*
Offspring *brgyud, ba-rgyúd.*
Oh interj. *ka, ka-ye, kye, kye-ma* 7; oh very well! *ₒo lags-so.*
Oil *mar, mar-nág W.;* — cake *mar-gyi tsigs-ma;* — lamp *'uṅ-gu.*
Ointment *skud; byug-pa.*
Old *rgad-pa, čen-mo W., rnyiṅ-pa, bċad-po;* — age *rgas-ka;* — man *rgad-po,* — woman *rgad-mo;* — squire *ga-ga* 63; to be — *rga-ba;* to grow — *bgre-ba.*
Oleander *ka-ra-bi-ra.*
Olive *skyu-ru, ḱa-skyur-po Sik.;* — tree *skyu-ru šiṅ, ḱa-skyur-poi šiṅ Sik.*
Omen *sṅa-ltás, ltas, rtags.*
Omit *bšol-ba.*
Omniscient *kun-mkyén*
On prep. *ḱa-ru, ḱar* 34, *ḱa-ṫog-la, ka-tod-la* 35, *dgaṅ-la, dgeṅ-la, sgeṅ-la* 114, *ṫog-tu* 237, *na* 298.
Once (one time) *lan-γċig;* — more *čed-du, da-ruṅ, ṗyir, yaṅ, slar;* at — v. *ċar* 139; (at the same time) *ṗyogs γċig-la* 352.
One num. *γċig,* — at a time *γċig-ċig* 144; — eyed *mig-żár;* — footed *rkaṅ-γċig-pa;* the one — the other *γċig . . . γċig, γċig-po.*
One pron. (French 'on') *skyes-bu* 31; — another *γċig-gis γċig* 143; by one's self *γċig* [*γċig* 144.
Onion *btsoṅ.*
Only adj. *γċig-ka, γċig-pu* 144; *zad* (v. *ₒdzad-pa* 464).
Only adv. *ka-rkyaṅ* (v. *rkyaṅ-pa* 17), *ša-stag* 555; *ḱo-na* 43, *γċig-tu* 144; *ₒba-żig* 391, *man-na mi* 411, *tsam* 430; not — *ma zad-de* 445.
Open adj. *ṗyes-pa, ṗyes-te,* vulgo *ṗe-te; bkag-pa ma yin-pa.*
Open vb. a. *ḱa ₒbyed-pa, bgrad-pa;* vb. n. *ₒbye-ba, ḱa ₒbye-ba.*
Opening s. *ḱa, bu-ga.*
Openly *ṅos-su* 130, *mṅon-sum-du* 133; *'a-γsal-la W.* 605.
Opinion *grub-mtá, lta-ba, snaṅ-ba;* in my — *ṅas bltas-pas* 216.
Opportunity *skabs, glags, rgyu, stabs, ṫabs, sa.*
Opposite *ḱa-draṅ, go-ldog;* — side *ṗar-ḱa, ṗa-rol, ṗar-ṅos.*
Opposition, to be or act in — *ₒgal-ba* c. *las* or *daṅ.*
Oppress *nón-pa.*

Optical deception *mig-ₒkrúl.*
Or *yaṅ-na* 506.
Oracle *gros-ₒdri-sa.*
Orally *ka-nas,* col. *ka-na.*
Orange *tsa-lum-pa.*
Orb *ₒkor-lo*; — of transmigration *ₒkor-ba* 58.
Orchard *bza-śiṅ-ra-ba, ldum-ra.*
Ordain *bsnyen-par rdzogs-pa, bsnyen-rdzogs mdzad-pa* 469.
Order s. (succession) *go-rim* 71; to put in — *śom-pa, ytan-la ₒbebs-pa*; (command) *bka, bka btags-pa, bka-taṅ, bka-ynaṅ-ba*; *žal-ydáms*; *hu-kúm* W.; (purpose) in — to *don-du* 259, *pyir-du* 351
Order vb. a. (command) *bka ynaṅ-ba* 13, *sgo-ba* 116.
Orderly adj. *tsul-mtún.*
Ordinarily *rgyun, pal-čér.*
Organ (of sense) *dbaṅ-po.*
Orifice *ka, bu-ga.*
Origin *kuṅs, byuṅ-kuṅs, ₒgo-ma, tog-ma, čags-tsúl, rtsa-ba.*
Originate vb. n. *kruṅ-ba, čags-pa*
Ornament s. *rgyan, čun-po.*
Orphan *da-prúg.*
Orthography *dag-yig, yi-gei sdeb-sbyór, brda-spród.*
Other *yžan, yžan-pa, yžan-ma, śos, ycig-śós.*
Otter *sram.*
Ought v. *rgyu* 110.
Ounce *sraṅ.*
Our, ours *ṅai* 124, *ṅed-kyi* 127.
Out adv. *pyir* 351, *pyi-rol-tu* 349; to be — (mistaken) *ₒkrul-ba*; out of prep. *nas, koṅ-nas.*
Outcast s. *ydol-pa.*
Outcry *grags-pa.*
Outlet *sgo.*
Outside s. *ka, pyi-rol.*
Outside adv. *pyi* III 349.
Outward adj. *pyii*; — appearance *ča-byád.*
Over prep. *goṅ-du, bar-snaṅ* or *la*; *bla*; — against *ka-draṅ, tad(-ka)*; adv. to be — (past) *tal-ba* II no. 5, 231.
Overcome vb. a. *tub-pa, non-pa*; vb. n. *sran-pa.*
Overflow vb. a. *yyeṅ-ba*; vb. n. *lud-pa.*
Overhasty *ha-čaṅ riṅs-pa, ha-čaṅ myur-čes-pa.*
Overseer *skul-kan, do-dam-pa, mgo byed-pai mi.*
Overshadow *ₒkeb-pa.*
Overtake *snyegs-pa, ytug-pa.*
Overthrow vb. *sgyel-ba, rlog-pa.*
Overturn vb. *sgyel-ba, rtib-pa.*
Owl *ₒug-pa.*
Own adj. *raṅ-gi, nyid-kyi.*
Own vb. (possess) *bdog-pa, dbaṅ-ba*; owning *mṅa-ba.*
Owner *mṅa-bdág.*
Ox *glaṅ, ba-glaṅ.*

# P

Pace s. *gom-pa*; *ₒčag-pa, gom-ₒčag-pa.*
Pace vb. *gom-pa ₒbor-ba*
Pack vb. a., to — on *ₒkel-ba*; to — up *teg-pa.*
Paddle-wheel *sku-ru.*
Padlock *doṅ-pa.*
Page s. (waiting-boy) *go-re-lón*; *sku-druṅ-pa, sku-mdun-pa*; — of a book *śog-logs.*
Pail *zo-ba.*
Pain s. (bodily) *zug, yzug*; *yzer*; (mental) *mya-ṅán* 420, *sdug-bsṅal* 294; to take pains *ₒgru-ba, ₒbad-pa*; *brtson-ₒgrus byed-pa.*
Pain vb. a. *ₒtse-ba*; to be pained *yduṅ-ba.*
Paint s. *tson*; vb. a. *skud-pa.*
Painter *ri-mo-mkan*
Painting s. *ri-mo, taṅ-ka.*
Pair s. *zuṅ, dor.*
Pairing s. (copulation) *ₒkrig-pa.*
Palace *po-braṅ.*
Palanquin *ₒkyogs*; **kyog-čáṅ* W.*, **peb-čáṅ* C.* (v. *dpyaṅ-ba* 328).
Palate *dkan, rkan*
Pale adj. **kya-ko-ré, kya-te-ré** 25.
Palm s. (of the hand) *lag-mtil, tal-mo.*
Pan (large) *sla(ṅ)-ṅa*; (small) *dra-zu*; (flat) *ta-ba.*
Pancake **tul-ta-gir** W. 234.
Pankah (fan) *bsil-yáb.*
Pannier *yzed-ma.*
Pant vb. n. *rṅam-pa, dṅaṅ-ba.*
Pap (porridge) *skyo-ma, ko-lág.*
Paper s. *śog-bu* 563; a sheet of — *gre-ga*; official — *bka-śog.*
Parable *dpe* 327, *ₒdra-dpe.*
Paradigm *dpe-brjód.*
Paradise *mto-ris*
Paragraph *rnam-bčad-pa.*
Paralyze *ₒčiṅ-ba*; *nyams-par byed-pa.*
Parasol *ydugs.*
Parcel s. (package) *tums* 234.
Parch *rṅod-pa, slam-pa.*
Pardon vb. a. (to use forbearance) *bzod-pa* 498; (to leave unpunished) *ₒgyod mi rmo-ba, čad-pas mi yčod-pa.*
Pare *kog-pa śu-ba.*
Parenthesis *yi-geï mčan-bu.*
Parents *pa-má.*
Park *skyed-mos-tsál.*

**Parrot** *ne-tso.*
**Parsimonious** *śri-śes-k̔an W.*
**Parsley** *γže-ra C., śa-mi-lig W.*
**Part** s. *ča, ča-śás, śas, rnam-pa, k̔a, k̔ag, ga-śas, lhu*; in — (partly) *ča ˳dra tsam*; at equal parts *ča-snyoms.*
**Part** vb. a. *˳p̔ral-ba*; vb. n. *˳gye-ba, ˳bral-ba.*
**Partake** *ča t̔ob-pa, t̔ob-ča ˳dzin-pa, bgo-skal t̔ob-pa.*
**Partaker** **go-k̔an* W.*
**Partial** (biased) *nye-riṅ.*
**Particle** (grammatical) *t̔sig-p̔rad.*
**Particularly** *k̔yad-par-du, mčog-tu.*
**Partition** *dbye-ba*; — wall *čod, bar-skya.*
**Partizan** *p̔yogs-pa.*
**Partly** *ča tsam, ga-śas*; v. also *la-lá* 541; *k̔a-ċig* 34.
**Partner** *k̔a-ya, ya, ya-do W., grogs, zla-bo.*
**Partridge** *sreg-pa.*
**Party** (part) *p̔yogs* 352.
**Pas** (in dancing) *gom-pa.*
**Pass** vb. n. *skyod-pa, ˳grul-ba, rgyug-pa, rgyud-pa, ˳čor-ba, t̔al-ba*; to — away *˳k̔or-ba, ˳da-ba, ˳bud-pa W.*; vb. a. (to cross) *rgal-ba, zla-ba*; to — over a certain space *˳da-ba.*
**Passage** (entrance or exit) *sgo, lam.*
**Passion** *čags-pa, ˳dod-čágs, bag-čágs.*
**Passport** *bka-śog, lam-yig.*
**Past** adj. *˳das-pa*; — ages *sṅa-rol*; to be — *yol-ba.*
**Paste** s. *skyo-ma*; vb. a. *sbyor-ba.*
**Pastry** *˳k̔ur-ba.*
**Pasturage** *bzan.*
**Pasture** s. *neu-γsiṅ*; — land *˳ol-t̔áṅ, ˳brog-γnas.*
**Pat** vb. a. *˳byug-pa.*
**Patch** s. *lhan-pa*; vb. a. *lhan-pas ˳debs-pa, glan-pa.*
**Patience** *bzod-pa.*
**Patient** adj. *bzod-pa-ċan.*
**Patron** *mgo-skyóṅ, mgo-˳drén, mgon-po.*
**Pattern** *dpe, ma, ri-mo.*
**Pauper** *dbul-p̔oṅs*; *med-po, med-mo.*
**Pavement** *skyaṅ-núl.*
**Paw** s. *spar-ba.*
**Pay** vb. a. *sprod-pa, ˳ǰal-ba.*
**Pay** s. *gla, p̔ogs.*
**Pea**, pease *sran-ma, srad-ma.*
**Peace** *žod, dus-bde, ži-bde.*
**Peach** *ka-t̔a ra, k̔am-bu, bun-ċu li.*
**Peacock** *rma-bya.*
**Peak** *rtse(-mo).*
**Pear** *nyu-ti, nyo-ti.*
**Pearl** *mu-tig.*
**Peasant** *groṅ-pa, groṅ-mi; kyim-pa-pa, žiṅ-pa.*
**Pebble** *rdeu, rde; ču-rdó; śag-ma.*
**Pedestrian** *rkaṅ-t̔aṅ-pa.*
**Peel** s. *k̔og-pa, śun-pa.*
**Peel** vb. a. *k̔og-pa śu-ba, śu-ba.*
**Peep-hole** *so-k̔uṅ* 578.
**Peg** *rtod-pa, γdaṅ-bu, p̔ur-pa.*
**Pen** s. *smyug-gu*; — knife *smyug-gri.*
**Pen** vb. a. (sheep etc.) *skyil-ba, ˳gegs-pa.*
**Penalty** *rgyal, stoṅ.*
**Penance** *dka-t̔úb, dka-spyód; brtul-žúgs.*
**Pencil** *γya-t̔ig, ˳bri-smyúg*; *pir.*
**Pencil-cedar** *śug-pa.*
**Penetrate** *k̔yab-pa, ˳dzugs-pa.*
**Penis** *mǰe, sgro-ba C.*
**Penitent** adj. *dka-t̔úb, brtul-žúgs.*
**Pent-roof** *čar-skyibs.*
**People** s. *skyes-bu*; common — *dmaṅs, smad-rigs.*
**Pepper** s. *p̔o-ba-ri*; Guinea — *γyer-ma C., *nyer-ma* or *t̔san-te* or su-ru-p̔an-t̔sá W.*
**Peppermint** *p̔o-lo-liṅ W.*
**Perambulate** *˳grim-pa.*
**Perceive** *rtogs-pa, t̔sor-ba, yid-la byed-pa, rag-pa W., rig-pa.*
**Perception** *go-ba, rtogs-pa*; object of — *yul* 513.
**Perfect** adj. *grub-pa, p̔un-t̔sógs, p̔ul-byúṅ, tsaṅ-ma, rdzogs-pa.*
**Perfection** *dṅos-grúb*; state of — *grub-pa.*
**Perfectly** *t̔saṅ, rdzogs-par.*
**Perform** *byed-pa, sgrub-pa, bċo-ba W., spyod-pa.*
**Perfume** s. *spos.*
**Perhaps** *gal-te-na, graṅ*; *su śes, ċi śes W.*
**Peril** s. *nyen, bar-čód, ˳k̔rul-so.*
**Perimeter** *mt̔a-skór.*
**Period** *dus-t̔sigs, dus-mtsams*; *γnas-skabs*; former — *sṅon-rol.*
**Perish** *˳ǰig-pa, med-par ˳gyur-ba.*
**Permission** *dgoṅs-pa, bka γnaṅ-ba*; with your — *žu W.* 476.
**Permit** *bka γnaṅ-ba*; to be permitted *čog-pa, ruṅ-ba.*
**Pernicious** *ṅan-pa*; *ma-ruṅ-ba.*
**Perpendicular** *gyen-la draṅ-po W.*
**Perpetual** *rtag-pa.*
**Perpetually** *rgyun-du.*
**Persecute** *snyeg-pa, ˳ded-pa, ˳t̔se-ba.*
**Perseverance** *yid yoṅs-su mi skyo-ba* or *mi ˳gyur-ba.*
**Persia** *ta-zig.*
**Person** *gaṅ-zág.*
**Personal** *dṅos.*
**Personally** *mṅon-sum-du, dṅos-su.*
**Perspiration** *rṅul.*
**Pertinacious** *mgo-mk̔regs-ċan.*
**Peruke** *skra-t̔sab.*
**Perverse** *go-ldog.*
**Perversity** *p̔yin-ċi-lóg.*
**Pervert** *rlog-pa.*
**Pestle** *γtun, dgog-tiṅ C.*
**Petting** adj. *mnyo-mnyo-ċan W.*

Petroleum *rdo-snúm.*
Petticoat *mo-gós, ŝam-gós.*
Pewter *dkar-γyá.*
Philology *sgra-rig-pa.*
Philosophy *naṅ-don-rig-pa* 527.
Phlegm *bad-kan, lud-pa.*
Phlegmatic *ṅaṅ-brgyud riṅ-ba*; — disposition **ŝē-gyü'-dhal-wa* C.* (lit. *ŝes-rgyud dal-ba*).
Physician *sman-pa*; *'em-či, 'am-či*; *γso-ba-po* 590.
Piccolo-flute *p̔red-gliṅ.*
Pick vb. a. *ₒbyed-pa*; to — up *sgrug-pa.*
Pickle s. *skyu-rúm.*
Picture s. *bzo, zo, ri-mo*; *t̔aṅ-ka*, resp. *ẑal-t̔aṅ*; — of a saint *bris-sku, sku-bris.*
Piebald *k̔ra-bo.*
Piece s. *čag-krum, čag-dum, dum, rnam-pa*; a single — *zuṅ* 488; a small — *k̔ol-bu*; to fall to pieces *rdib-pa.*
Pierce *ₒbig(s)-pa.*
Piety *k̔rel*; *čos-la dga-bai sems.*
Pig *p̔ag.*
Pigeon *p̔u-rón, p̔ug-rón.*
Pigtail *ču-ti W., lčaṅ-lo C.*
Pilaw *p̔u-la, p̔o-la.*
Pile vb. a. *sgril-ba, bčer-ba, rtseg-pa.*
Pilfer *byi byed-pa.*
Pilgrimage, to go on a — *mjal-ba.*
Pill s. *ril-bu.*
Pillar *ka-ba.*
Pillow *sṅas, snye-stán, snye-ₒból.*
Pin s. *p̔ur-pa, ₒdzin-γya C., zum-k̔áb W.*
Pincers *skam-čuṅ.*
Pinch vb., the shoe pinches **k̔ab-ŝa dam dug* W.* 297.
Pious *skal-ldan*; *k̔rel-čan, čos-čan, čos-sem-čan W.*; *čos-la dga-ba.*
Pisé *gyaṅ, gyeṅ* 74.
Pistol **me-dá* C., *raṅ-ₒbár* W.*
Pit s. *k̔uṅ, k̔uṅs, doṅ.*
Pitcher *ču-snód, ču-rdzá, ben, rdza-búm.*
Pitchfork *zar.*
Pith *γnad.*
Pitiable *dman-pa.*
Pity s. *snyiṅ-brtse-ba.*
Place s. *k̔ag, sa, sa-k̔yad, go, yul-gru, yul, γnas, sa-ča, groṅ*; to take — *ₒgyur-ba, ₒbyuṅ-ba.*
Place vb. a. *ₒjog-pa, ₒbor-ba, ₒdzugs-pa*; to be placed *k̔od-pa.*
Plague s. *γnyan, ₒgo-bai nad, ₒgo-bai rims*; *ṅan-rims, rims-nád.*
Plaid *γzan-gós.*
Plain s. *t̔aṅ*; *ṅos.*
Plain adj. (without ornament) *ₒjam-saṅ, rgyan-méd.*
Plaintiff **t̔im ẑu-k̔an* W.*
Plait s. *lan-bu*; vb. a. *lan-bu sle-ba*; *γčud-pa.*

Plan s. *bkob-lta, bkod-pa*; vb. a. *ₒgod-pa.*
Plane s. *p̔ag-ste W.*; vb. a. **p̔ag-sté ŝrul-če* W.*
Planet *γza* 492.
Plank *spaṅ, spaṅ-léb.*
Plant s. *sṅo, rtswa*; vb. a. *ₒdzugs-pa.*
Plantain *skyes-sdóṅ*; *ta-la*
Plaster s. (in surgery) *ₒbyor-sman.*
Plaster vb. a. (to pave) *skyaṅ-nul byed-pa.*
Plastering s. *ẑal-ba* 474.
Plate s. *glegs, gra-ti Ld., ta-bag W.*; tin — *t̔a-li W.*; iron — *lčags-t̔ál.*
Plate vb. a. *čus γtoṅ-ba* 160.
Play vb. (to sport) *rtse-ba, rtsed-pa*; to — on an instrument *ₒk̔rol-ba, skrog-pa*; to — a trick *γnod-pa skyel-ba.*
Play-fellow *rtse-grógs, grogs-k̔yeu.*
Play-ground *rtse-sa*
Pleasant *sdug-pa, yid-du ₒoṅ-ba*; to be — *ₒt̔ad-pa.*
Pleasantness *ₒk̔yer-so.*
Please vb. a. *dga-bar byed-pa*; vb. n. v. *mk̔yen-pa* 55; if you please *ẑu* 476; to be pleased *dgyes-pa, bsod-pa.*
Pleasing adj. *dga-mo, bsod-pa.*
Pleasure *dga-ba, rtsed-mo, γyeṅ-rtsed, rtsed-ₒjo*; *snyiṅ dga-ba* or *bde-ba*; at — *raṅ-dgár, yid bẑin-du.*
Plebeian *ma-rabs, p̔al-pa.*
Pledge s. *rgyan, γta-ma, γte-pa.*
Pleiades *smin-drúg.*
Plentiful *k̔rigs, rgyas-pa, mod-po*; to be — *ₒdzom-pa.*
Plenty s. *loṅs-spyód.*
Pliable, Pliant *mnyen-pa, mnyen-lčug, lčug-pa.*
Plough s. *γŝol*; vb. a. *γŝol-mda ₒdzin-pa*; *rmo-ba.*
Pluck s. (of an animal) *snyiṅ-luṅ.*
Pluck vb. *sgrug-pa.*
Plummet *ẑa-nyei γtiṅ-rdo.*
Plump *lkob*; *rom-po W.*
Plunder vb. *ₒgog-pa, *kog-te k̔yer-če W.* 95.
Pock s. *ₒbrum-pa*; — marked *mdzar-ra-mdzer-ré Ld.*
Pocket s. *čan-da, dku-mda, k̔ud-pa*; — book *yi-gei ŝubs*; *sam-ta, sab-dra*; — fire *me-lčags*; — handkerchief *na-či C., na-p̔i W.*
Pocket vb. a. *ₒk̔ur-ba.*
Pod *gaṅ-bu, lgaṅ-bu.*
Poem *ṅag-snyán*; *snyan-dṅags.*
Poetry *sdeb-sbyór.*
Point s. *t̔seg, nag-t̔seg*; main — *don, ma-γẑi*; to be on the — *ča-ba*; v. also *las* II extr. 546.
Poison *dug.*
Poker *yog-po.*
Polecat *ŝul-byi.*
Polish vb. *bdar-ba.*

**Polished** adj. *ˏod-ċan.*
**Politeness** *že-sa.*
**Pollute** *˳bag-pa.*
**Pollution** *grib.*
**Pomatum** *ṡra-skúd.*
**Pomegranate** *se-˳bru, seu.*
**Pond** *rdziṅ.*
**Ponder** *sems-pa*, resp. *dgoṅs-pa*; *bsam-blo γtoṅ-ba.*
**Pool** *ču-k̔yil, lteṅ-ka.*
**Poor** *dbul-ba, p̔oṅs-pa, ṅan-pa, gyi-na, k̔as-dmán, k̔as-žán*; the poor people! *snyiṅ-re-rǰe.*
**Poplar** *dbyar-pa*; *ma-gál W.*; *γṡol-po.*
**Popular** *mon-ža-ċan W.*
**Popularity** *mon-ža W.*
**Porcelain** *kar-yól, dkar-yól*; — clay *k̔am-pa.*
**Porch** *sgo-k̔áṅ.*
**Porcupine** *rgaṅ, byi-ṫur, γzig-mo.*
**Pore** *spui k̔uṅ-bu, ba-spui bu-ga.*
**Porridge** *zan* 486.
**Portal** *sgo-k̔áṅ.*
**Portion** s. *skal-ba, ča* 150, *ċa-ṡás*; *ṫsod, lhu* 601; — of meat *rgya-ri, sder-gáṅ.*
**Position** *go* 70.
**Positive** adj. *dṅos.*
**Possess**, to be possessed of *bdog-pa.*
**Possessing** adj. *bċas-pa* 146.
**Possession**, to hold in — *˳dzin-pa* 465.
**Possibility** *glags, go-skábs, rgyu, sa.*
**Possible**, to be — *srid-pa.*
**Post** s. (pillar) *ka-ba.*
**Posteriors** *rkub, mǰug, p̔um-p̔úm, ṡul-pa.*
**Postillion** *rta-zam-pa.*
**Postpone** *bṡol-ba, sriṅ-ba.*
**Postscript** *yaṅ-skyár.*
**Post-service** *ˏu-lág* 499.
**Post-station** *rta-zám.*
**Pot** s. *k̔og-ma, rdza-ma, p̔an-dil W.*; — cloth *tsa-lċibs*; — house *čaṅ-k̔aṅ.*
**Potato** *skyi-ba, *kyi-u* C., *ḍho-ma, gya-ḍho* C.* 78; *'a-lu W.*
**Potency** *dbaṅ.*
**Potsherd** *gyo-mo, čag-po.*
**Pouch** s. *rkyal-bu, k̔ug-ma, kab-ta-ka Ld.*
**Poultry** *k̔yim-bya.*
**Pound** vb.a. *rduṅ-ba, k̔rum-k̔rum byed-pa.*
**Pour** *ldugs-pa, ˳byo-ba, ˳bo-ba.*
**Poverty** *p̔oṅs-pa, dbul-ba.*
**Powder** s. *p̔ye-ma.*
**Power** *mṅa, mṅa-táṅ, mṫu, nus-pa.*
**Powerful** *rgyags-pa, ṅar-ma, btsan-po.*
**Powerless** *dbaṅ-méd*; to render — *dbaṅ-med-du ˳čol-ba.*
**Practice** s. *lag-lén*, resp. *p̔yag-lén*; *lob-k̔yád W.*
**Practise** vb. a. *sbyoṅ-ba.*
**Praise** s. *sṅag-γsól*; vb.a. *sṅag-pa, stod-pa.*
**Prattle** s. *ċol-ċúṅ.*
**Pray** vb. n. *γsol-ba, žu-ba.*
**Prayer** *γsol-ba*; — mill *čos-k̔or, ma-ni-čos-k̔or.*
**Preach** *čos sgrog-pa*, resp. *čos-kyi sgrog-gleṅ mdzad-pa.*
**Precede** *sṅon-du ˳gro-ba.*
**Preceding** *sṅa-ma, sṅon-˳gro.*
**Precept** *bka-bsgos, bka-rtags, k̔rims, čos, γdams-pa, bslab-bya.*
**Precious** *dkon-pa, γċes-pa, rin-čen, rin-po-če*; the most — thing *dkon-mčog* 10.
**Precipitous** *γzar-ba.*
**Precisely** *raṅ, k̔o-na.*
**Preface** s. *sṅon-˳gro.*
**Prefect** *yul-dpon, mi-dpón.*
**Preferable** *bla.*
**Prefix** s. *sṅon-ǰúg, ˳p̔ul(-yig).*
**Pregnant** *sbrum-pa*; *sems-ċan daṅ ldan-pa* 290.
**Preparation** *grabs, rgyu, sta-gón.*
**Prepare** *ṡom-pa, sbyor-ba* I, no. 2,406; *bċo-ba W., dger-ba C., ˳ča-ba* 168; to — victuals for the table *γyo-ba, γyos-su byed-pa.*
**Prepuce** *mdun-pags, ˳dom-pags.*
**Prerogative** *don.*
**Presage** s. *sṅa-ltás.*
**Presence**, in — of *mdun-du*, resp. *spyan-sṅar.*
**Present** s. (gift) *skyes, rten, žu-rtén*, resp. *γzigs-rtén, ˳k̔yos-pa, bya-dgá, sbyin-pa.*
**Preserve** vb. *skyoṅ-ba, skyob-pa, sruṅ-ba.*
**Press** vb. *bkan-pa, bċar-ba, glem-pa C., non-pa, ˳ṫsir-ba*, to — hard (in an inquest) *tsir tag ǰhe'-pa C.*
**Pressingly** *nan-gyis* 303.
**Presume** (arrogate) *k̔as-len-pa* 34.
**Pretty** adj. *mčor-po, sdug-pa, dga-mo.*
**Prevail on** *˳ǰug-pa.*
**Prevent** *˳gogs-pa, γċod-pa, zlog-pa.*
**Preventive** s. *sruṅ-ba.*
**Previous** adj. *sṅon-˳gro.*
**Previously** *sṅa-na, sṅa-goṅ, sṅan, sṅar, sṅon.*
**Price** *goṅ, ṫaṅ, rin.*
**Prick** vb. a. *snun-pa, ˳dzugs-pa* 465.
**Pricking** (pungent) *rtsub-po.*
**Pricks** fastened to the feet for climbing mountains *rkaṅ-mdzer.*
**Pride** s. *ṅa-rgyal, dregs-pa, p̔o-so, rlom-pa, rlom-sems.*
**Priest** *bla-ma.*
**Priestcraft** *čos-zog.*
**Priesthood** *dge-˳dun.*
**Primary** adj. v. *rtsa-ba.*
**Prime minister** *bka-blón.*
**Prince** *rgyal-bu, rgyal-srás.*
**Principal** adj. *mčog, γtso-bo*; — part *mgo.*
**Principal** s. *mgon-po, ˳go-dpon.*
**Principally** *γtso-bor.*
**Print** vb. *par-du ˳debs-pa, par rgyab-pa W.*

**Printer** *par-pa.*
**Printing-office** *par-k̔aṅ.*
**Prison** *btson-k̔aṅ, k̔ri-mun.*
**Prisoner** *btson.*
**Private, Privately** *sgos.*
**Privilege** s. *ynaṅ-ba.*
**Privities** *°doms, sba-ba.*
**Privy** s. *čab-k̔uṅ, ysaṅ-spyód.*
**Prize** s. (reward) *dgu-mtsán.*
**Probationer** *dge-bsnyén.*
**Proboscis** *glaṅ-sná.*
**Proceed** *°gye-ba, spro-ba*; to let — *°gyed-pa* 97.
**Proclaim** *bka bkod-pa, bka °dogs-pa, sgrog-pa, sgyur-ba W.*
**Proclamation** *bka bkod-pa, bka btags-pa, bka-°dogs-pa.*
**Procreate** *skyed-pa, bso-ba.*
**Procure** *sgrub-pa, ynyer-ba, sbyor-ba, °tsol-ba.*
**Produce** s. *t̔og.*
**Produce** vb. *skyed-pa*; to be produced *čags-pa.*
**Product** s. (sum total) *brtsis-zin.*
**Professor** *mk̔an-po.*
**Profit** s. *skyed, k̔e, k̔ye, don, spogs; p̔an-pa, p̔an-t̔ogs, bed.*
**Profitable** *drug, p̔an-°dogs-pa.*
**Profound** *zab-pa.*
**Prognostic** s. *sṅa-ltas.*
**Progress** s. *skyed.*
**Prohibit** *°k̔egs-pa, °gegs-pa.*
**Project** vb. a. *°god-pa*; vb. n. *t̔al-ba.*
**Prolong** *bsol-ba, sriṅ-ba.*
**Prolongation** *stud-ma.*
**Prominent,** to be — *t̔al-ba.*
**Promise** s. *čad*; vb. *čad-pa, °če-ba, k̔as-len-pa, dam °ča-ba.*
**Promulgate** *sgrog-pa, rjod-pa.*
**Pronounce** *°don-pa, rjod-pa.*
**Pronunciation** *lčogs, zer-lčogs, zer-t̔sul W., klog-t̔sul, rjod-dbyaṅs C.*
**Proof** s. *mṅon-rtágs, rtags, rgyu-mtsan.*
**Prop** s. *rgyab-rtén*; vb. a. *skyor-ba.*
**Propagation** *sa-bon; dar-ba.*
**Propensity** *bag-čágs.*
**Proper** *dṅos* 131; — place *go*; — time *bsgaṅ.*
**Property** *yon-tan, loṅs-spyód*; — left *sul* 561.
**Prophesy** vb. *luṅ ston-pa.*
**Prophet** *luṅ-ston-pa.*
**Prophetic sight** *mṅon-ses, °od-ysal*, resp. *t̔ugs-mk̔yén.*
**Propitious** *bkra-sis-pa, dge-ba.*
**Proportion** *t̔ig-t̔sád, byad.*
**Propound** *rjod-pa, ston-pa, °čad-pa.*
**Proprietor** *bdag-po.*
**Prospect** (likelihood) *ṅo* 129, *ča* 151.
**Prosperity** *bkra-sis.*
**Prosperous** *yyaṅ-čan.*
**Prostitute** s. *°p̔yon-ma, smad-t̔soṅ-ma.*
**Protect** *skyob-pa, °gebs-pa, sruṅ-ba, skyabs byed-pa.*
**Protection** *skyabs.*
**Protector** *skyabs-mgón; mgo-skyoṅ, mgo-°dren, mgon-po*; — of religion *čos-skyoṅ* 31.
**Proud** *k̔eṅs-pa, grags-čan, rgyags-pa, dregs-pa*; to be — *snyems-pa.*
**Proverb** *k̔a-dpe.*
**Provide** *sbyor-ba, yod-par byed-pa.*
**Provided with** (having, possessing) *čan* 138, *ldan-pa* 290.
**Province** *k̔ag, k̔ul, sde, sde-srid; yul-gyi kyad-par.*
**Provincialism** *groṅ-t̔sig.*
**Provisions** *rgyags; srog-rdzás*, resp. *bšos*; store of — *ytad-so.*
**Provoke** *nyams °bru-ba, °t̔saṅ °bru-ba.*
**Provost** *dge-bskos.*
**Prudent** *mk̔as-pa, gruṅ-ba, rgod-pa, sgriṅ-po.*
**Prune** vb. *°grum-pa.*
**Ptarmigan** *goṅ-mo.*
**Public** s. *yul-pa-rnams* 513.
**Publication** *bkar-btags-pa, bka bkod-pa, gram-yig.*
**Publicly** *mṅon-sum-du.*
**Publish** *bkar-°dogs-pa, sgyur-ba, sgrog-pa.*
**Puddle** s. *ču-°k̔yil.*
**Puff** s. (ostentation) *yus* 513.
**Puff-ball** *lgo, p̔a-ba-dgo-dgó.*
**Pull** vb. a. *°dren-pa, °t̔en-pa*; to — along *°drud-pa*; to — down *snyil-ba, rtib-pa, °dral-ba*; to — off *su-ba*; to — out *°byin-pa, °gog-pa.*
**Pulpit** *čos-k̔ri.*
**Pumpkin** *gon, čuṅ.*
**Pungency** *ber.*
**Pungent** *ber-čan, rtsub-po; t̔sa-ba, t̔san-te.*
**Punish** *°jun-pa, čad-pas yčod-pa* 155.
**Punishment** *čad-pa, k̔ral, gu-sir Ld., god, dgra, lan* 543.
**Pupil** (scholar) *mk̔an-bu; slob-ma, slob-p̔rug, slob-baṅs, bu-slob.*
**Puppy** *k̔yi-gu.*
**Purchase** vb. *nyo-ba.*
**Pure** *daṅ-ba, yt̔saṅ-ba, t̔saṅs-pa; lag-mo W.; ysal-ba, dga-mo, lhad-méd.*
**Purgative** s. *bsal-sman.*
**Purge** vb. *bsal-ba.*
**Purity** *yt̔saṅ-ba.*
**Purpose** s. *dgos-pa, don*; on — *brtson-par.*
**Purpose** vb. *dgoṅs-pa, sems-pa.*
**Purposely** *čed-du.*
**Purr** vb. n. *ṅug-pa, v. ma-ṇi.*
**Purse** s. *sgyiu, sgyig-gu, sgye-mo.*
**Pursue** *rṅon-pa, snyegs-pa, °ded-pa.*
**Pus** (matter) *ču-rnag, rnag, ču-ser.*
**Push** vb. a. *rdegs-pa, °p̔ul-ba, sug-pa.*
**Pustule** *°brum-pa.*

**Put** vb. a. *bkan-pa*, *ₒgod-pa*, *ₒǰug-pa*, *ₒǰog-pa*, *ₒbor-ba W.*; to — astride (e.g. in empaling) *skyon-pa*; to — down *grems-pa*, *ₒgrol-ba*, *sgyel-ba*, *ₒǰog-pa*; to — in or into *sgyoṅ-ba*, *čud-pa*, *ₒǰug-pa*, *teg-pa*, *ₒdzud-pa*; to — in order *sgrig-pa*; to — off *bud-pa*, *bšol-ba*; to — on *ₒgebs-pa*, *gon-pa*, resp. *ɣsol-ba*; to — together *snol-ba*.
**Putrid** *rul-ba*.
**Putty** s. *bag-sbyín* 364.

# Q

**Quadrangle** *dkyil-ₒkor gru-bži-pa*.
**Quadrate** s. *ka-gáṅ*; adj. *ka-gaṅ-ba*.
**Quadruped** *rkaṅ-bži-pa*.
**Quail** s. *big-bi-lig W.*
**Quality** *čos-nyid*; good — *yon-tan* 516.
**Quarrel** s. *ka-mču*, *ₒdziṅ-mo*, *hab-ša*, *rtsod-pa*.
**Quarrel** vb. *ₒkrug-pa*, *rgol-ba*, *ₒgran-pa*; quarreling words *ₒgran-tśig*.
**Quarrelsome**, — temper *ₒgran-sems*.
**Quarter of the heavens** *pyogs* 352.
**Quarters** *ɣnas*, *ɣnas-tsaṅ C.*, *braṅ-sa W.*
**Quartz** *čag-dkár*.
**Queen** *rgyal-mo*; — consort *btsun-mo* (*rgyal-poi*).
**Question** s. *dri-ba*, *žu-ba*.
**Queue** (pigtail) *lčaṅ-lo C.*, *ču-ti Ld.*
**Quick** adj. *mgyogs-pa*, *myur-ba*, *skyen-pa*, *kram-pa*; be —! **riṅ-pa toṅ** *W.*
**Quickly** *mgyogs-par*; *myur-du*.
**Quicksand** **be-rul** *W.*
**Quicksilver** *dṅul-ču*.
**Quiet** adj. *dal-ba*, *gya-ma-gyú*, *srun-po*; to become — *ži-ba*.
**Quill** *rkaṅ*.
**Quilt** s. *tsa-ɣčig-ma C.*
**Quintessence** *ṅo-bo-nyid*, *bčud*, *snyiṅ-po*.
**Quit** vb. a. *ₒbor-ba* 396, *ₒǰog-pa* 179, *skyur-ba* 28; *ₒgye-ba*, *ɣtoṅ-ba*.
**Quite** *ye*, *ye-nas*, *yons-su*; *lhiṅ-se Ld.*
**Quittance** *ₒprod-ₒdzín*.
**Quiver** s. *mda-dóṅ*.
**Quiver** vb. n. *ₒdar-ba*.
**Quotient** *tob-nór*.

# R

**Race** s. (generation) *mi-snà*, *rabs*.
**Race** s. (contest in running) *baṅ* 364; to run a — *dkyu-ba*.
**Radish** *la-pug*, *guṅ-la-pug*.
**Rafter** *lčam*, *gral-ma*.
**Rag** *hrul-ba*.
**Rage** vb. n. *rṅam-pa*.
**Ragged** adj. *čad-po*, *hrul-po*.
**Rail** s. *lag-rgyúgs* 541.
**Rain** s. *čar*, *čar-pa*; — cloak *čar-kebs*; — water *čar-ču*.
**Rain** vb.n. *čar ₒbab-pa*, it rains *čar ₒbab W.*
**Rainbow** *ₒǰa*, *ₒǰa-tson*.
**Rainy** *čar-čan*; — season *čar-dus*.
**Raise** *sgreṅ-ba*, *ₒdon-pa*, *ker-ba*, *ₒpyar-ba*, *ₒdzugs-pa*, *bžeṅ-ba*, *seṅ-ba*, *sloṅ-ba*.
**Raisin** *rgun-rgód*, *rgun-ₒbrúm*.
**Rake** s. (gardening) *ka-ɣzé W.*, *rgya-ɣzéb C.*
**Ram** s. *lug-túg*.
**Ramble** vb. *ₒkyam-pa*, *ₒkor-ba W.*
**Rampart** *ₒkor-yúg*.
**Range** s. (row) *gral*, *rim-pa*; — of vision *mtoṅ-ₒkor*, *mtoṅ-mta*.
**Range** vb. n. *rgyu-ba*, *ₒgrim-pa*.
**Rank** s. *go*, *go-paṅ*, *go-sá*, *go-grál*, *go-grás*, *rigs*.
**Ransom** s. *glud*, *blud*, *glud-tsab*; *blud-pa*; vb. a. *blu-ba*.
**Rare** *dkon-pa*.
**Rash** adj. *yid-tuṅ* 570.
**Rashness** *bab-čol*, *ɣzu-lúm*.
**Rasp** s. *sa-bdar*, *sag-ɣdár C.*; *šiṅ-zóg W.*, *šiṅ-séd W.*
**Rasp** vb. a. *bdar-ba*, *sag-ɣdar rgyag-pa C.*
**Raspberry** *tser-lum Sik*, *la-ma-sró Kun.*
**Rat** s. *byi-ba*, *sa-bi-lig W.*
**Rather** *ča-lam*; v. *bla* 382.
**Ration** *zas-skál*.
**Raven** *ka-ta*, *bya-róg*, *po-róg*, *bya-nág*.
**Ravine** *grog-po*, *roṅ*, *sul*.
**Raw** *rǰen-pa*.
**Ray** s. *ɣzer*, *ₒod-ɣzér*.
**Razor** *spu-gri*.
**Reach** vb. a. *ɣtug-pa*, *tug-pa*, *sriṅ-ba*, to — down *smad-pa*.
**Reach of hearing** *rgyaṅ-grágs*.
**Read** vb. *klog-pa*, *sgrog-pa*, **sil-če** *W.*
**Reading-desk** *čos-kri*.
**Ready** *pral-grig* 359; to be made — *grub-pa*, *ₒgrub-pa*; — money *rnags*, *smar-ba*, *smar-rkyáṅ*.
**Real** *ṅes-pa-čan*, *dṅos*, *dṅos-čan*; *ṅo-rtóg W.*
**Reality** *dṅos*; *yaṅ-dag-pa-nyid* 248; *ɣnas-tsul* 449.
**Really** *ṅes-pa-čan-du*; (bodily) *dṅos-su* 131.
**Realm** *kams*; *rgyal-kams* 108.

Reap *rṅa-ba.*
Reaper *žiṅ-mḱan.*
Reaping-hook *zor-ba, rgya-zór.*
Rear vb. (bring up) *srel-ba, ɣso-ba.*
Reason s. (intellect) *blo, blo-ɣrós*; (cause) *rgyu.*
Reasonable *ťsul-mťun* 450.
Rebel vb. *ṅo-log byed-pa* 553, **gyab-log ǰhe'-pa** C.
Rebel s. *ṅo-log-mḱan.*
Re-born, to be — *skye-ba* 28.
Rebound vb. n. *ₒṗar-ba.*
Rebuke s. *bka-bkyón, brgyad-kág*; vb. a. *brgyad-kag byed-pa.*
Receipt *ₒṗrod-ₒdzin, zin-bris.*
Receive *len-pa*, resp. *bžes-pa*; *ťob-pa*; *rǰes-su ₒdzin-pa.*
Receptacle *rten* no. 2, 213.
Recite *skyor-ba, sgrog-pa.*
Reckon (count) *rtsi-ba.*
Recline *bkyed-pa, snye-ba.*
Recommend *sṅag-pa*; *stod-pa.*
Recommendation, letter of — *mťun-ₒgyur-gyi yi-ge.*
Recompense s. *rṅan-pa, ɣnaṅ-sbyin, bya-dga.*
Recompense vb. a. *brṅan-pa.*
Reconcile vb. a. *sdum-pa*; to — one's self *ḱo-tág ɣċod-pa.*
Record vb. *ₒgod-pa* no. 5, 95.
Records s. *deb-ťér, yig-ča.*
Recover vb n. *ťso-ba, ṗyir laṅ-ba.*
Recreation *skyo-sáṅs*; *ɣyeṅs-pa* W.; to take — *rtse-ba*; *skyo-saṅs-la ₒgro-ba*, resp. *byon-pa.*
Rector *ₒgo-dpón* C.
Red *dmar-po, dmar-ba*; light — *dkar-dmar.*
Redeem *ₒgrol-ba, blu-ba.*
Redeemer *skyabs-mgón.*
Redemption *blud-pa.*
Reduce (the wages) *ɣċod-pa.*
Reed *ₒdam-bu*; — pen *snyug-gu, smyi-gu*, **ḍi-nyúg** W.
Reel vb. n. *ₒḱyom-pa, ₒḱyor-ba.*
Reflection (consideration) *sgom, rtog-pa.*
Refuge *skyabs-ɣnas.*
Refuse s. *gal-ró.*
Refuse vb. *ₒdor-ba, mi ɣnaṅ-ba.*
Regard vb. a. *ɣzigs-pa*; to — as *dgoṅs-pa*; as regards *dbaṅ-du byas-na, -la* 540.
Regard s., to have — to *lta-ba* I, no. 3, 216.
Regardful *ɣċaṅ-po.*
Regent *rgyal ťsáb* 109; *sde-srid, srid.*
Region *ḱams, gliṅ, lǰoṅs, sa-ṗyógs, yul-ṗyógs.*
Register s. *dkar-čág*; *ťo.*
Regular *ťsul-ċan.*
Reign s. *rgyal-srid.*
Reinforcements *dmag-ťsógs snon-ma.*
Reins (of a bridle) *srab-skyógs, srab-mdá.*
Reins (kidneys) *mḱal-ma.*
Reject *spoṅ-ba.*
Rejoice vb. n *dga-ba*, resp. *dgyes-pa*; *mgu-ba, rǰes-su yi-raṅ-ba* 182.
Relate vb. a. *skad-pa, ₒčad-pa, snyad-pa.*
Relation (kindred) *brgyud*; *nye-du, nye-brél*; (reference) *rgyud.*
Relative s. (kinsman) *nyen, ɣnyen, ɣnyen-bšés.*
Relax vb. a. *glod-pa.*
Release vb. a. *ₒgrol-ba*; to be released *ₒgrol-ba.*
Release s. *blud-pa, ťar-du ₒǰug-pa.*
Relic *riṅ-bsrél* 529.
Religion *čos, čos-lugs.*
Religious *čos-kyi*; *čos-la dga-ba*; *ḱrel-ċan* W.
Religiously, to live — *čos byed-pa.*
Reluctantly *ṅam-šúgs* Sch.
Rely *rten-pa.*
Remain *ₒdug-pa, bžugs-pa, lus-pa.*
Remainder *lus-ma, lhag-ma.*
Remains (dead body) *ro.*
Remedy s. *ɣnyen, rdzas, ɣso-byéd.*
Remember *dgoṅs-pa, dran-pa, rǰes-su dran-pa*; *yid-la byed-pa*; *ṅes-pa* 128.
Remind *yid skul-ba.*
Remove vb. *ₒgrol-ba, sgrol-ba*; *ₒbyin-pa, sbyoṅ-ba.*
Rend *ɣċod-pa, ₒdral-ba, ɣšeg-pa, hral-ba.*
Renounce *spoṅ-ba.*
Renown *grags-pa, snyan-pa.*
Renowned *grags-pa-ċan, grags-ċan, sgra-čé.*
Rent adj. *čad-po*; to be — *ₒgas-pa.*
Rent s. (fissure) *ral*; (house-rent) *ḱaṅ-gla.*
Repair vb. a. *ɣso-ba.*
Repay *ₒǰal-ba, ɣsob-pa.*
Repeat *skyor-ba, sgre-ba, stud-pa, ldab-pa.*
Repent *ₒgyod-pa.*
Repentance *ₒgyod pa.*
Repertory *ťob-yig.*
Reply s. *ḱa-lán, lan*; vb. *lan ₒdebs-pa, glon-pa.*
Report s. (of a gun) *sguṅ*; (rumour) **(s)lob-lo** W.
Representative s *ťsab-po.*
Reprimand s. *bka-bkyón.*
Reproach vb. a. *ċo ₒdri-ba, smad-pa, smad-ra ɣtoṅ-ba.*
Reproach s. *brgyad-ḱág*; *smad-pa.*
Reproduce *skyed-pa.*
Reproof *smad-pa.*
Repulse vb. *zlog-pa.*
Reputation *grags-pa.*
Request s. *žu-ba, ɣsol-ba*; vb. *žu-ba.*
Require *bžed-pa* 484.
Requisite s. *čas* 156; requisites *rdzas* 468.

**Requital** *ka-lán*; *₀bras-bu.*
**Rescue** vb. a. *sgrol-ba, skyob-pa, skyabs byed-pa, tar-bar byed-pa.*
**Resentment** *kon-pa.*
**Reserved** adj. *gya-ma-gyu* 73.
**Reside** *bžugs-pa.*
**Residence** *kab, rgyal-sa*; *γži-ma.*
**Residue** *ro.*
**Residuum** *tsigs-ma.*
**Resign** *ko-tág γčod-pa.*
**Resin** *tañ-čú.*
**Resist** *rgol-ba.*
**Resolute** *lo-na tuñ-se W.*
**Resolve** vb. n. (decide) *byro-ba, tag-γčod-pa.*
**Resound** *₀krol-ba.*
**Respect** s. *bkur-ba, bkur-sti*; *sku-rim, gus-pa*; *pu-dúd, sri-žu*; to pay one's respects *rje-sa* or *že-sa byed-pa*; best respects! *žu W.* 476; in every — *rnam-pa kun-tu*; with — to *la* 540.
**Respect** vb. a. *rtsis byed-pa.*
**Respectable** *btsun-pa.*
**Respectful** *gus-pa.*
**Respiration** *dbugs.*
**Respire** *dbugs rñub-pa dañ ₀byin-pa.*
**Responsibility** *kag.*
**Rest** s. (remainder) *mta, lus-ma, lhag-ma.*
**Rest** s. (repose) *sti-ba*; vb. *sti-ba*; *ñal γso-ba* 127.
**Resting-place** *lam-stégs.*
**Restless** *₀dug mi tsugs-pa* 459.
**Restore** *γso-ba.*
**Restrain** *₀dul-ba*; *₀jun-pa*; to be restrained *dog-par ₀gyur-ba.*
**Restrict** vb. **skar-tág tañ-če* W.*
**Retain** *skyil-ba, ₀gegs-pa* 94, *sgyoñ-ba* 119.
**Retaliation** *rnam(-par) smin(-pa)*; *lan* 543.
**Retinue** *₀kor, ₀kor-γyog, ₀kor-₀dab*; *žabs-pyi, slas.*
**Retribution** *₀bras-bu* 400, *la-yógs* 541; *lan*; doctrine of — *bgo-skál* 89.
**Return** vb. a. *lan byed-pa, lan ₀jal-ba*; to — an answer *glon-pa*; vb. n. *₀kor-ba, log-pa, pyir ₀gro-ba.*
**Revenge** s. *dugs, lan*; to take — **dug** or **lan kor-če* W.*
**Revere** *mos-pa.*
**Reverence** *sku-rim, gus-pa, bsnyen-bkúr, bag-yod(-pa), že-sa.*
**Reverend** (title) *rje-btsún, btsun-pa, dbu-rjé.*
**Reverse** s (side opposite) *rgyab-lógs*; (contrary) *zlas-pye-ba*; *bzlog, go-ldóg, go-lóg.*
**Revile** vb. a. *smad-pa, γše-ba.*
**Revise** vb. a. *sgyur-ba, lta-ba.*
**Revision** *žal-ta* 473.
**Revolt** vb. *gyab-lóg byed-pa, ño-lóg byed-pa.*
**Revolver** **rañ-bar ḍug-rág* W.* 523.
**Reward** s. *rñan-pa, sug*; vb. *rñan-pa.*
**Rheumatism** *grum-bu, grum-nád*; *grum-pa W., *zer-nẹ́* C.*
**Rhododendron** *ba-lu, da-li.*
**Rhubarb** *ču-čú, la-čú.*
**Rhyming** adj. *zuñ-ldán.*
**Rib** *rtsib(s)-ma.*
**Ribbon** *₀čiñ-ba, leb-ma.*
**Rice** *₀bras*; boiled — *₀bras-čán*; parched — *₀bras-yos.*
**Rich** adj. *pyug-po*; — in *rgyas-pa, ₀dzom-po.*
**Riches** s. *dkor, nor, dbyig(s), ₀byor-pa.*
**Rick** *pub-rags.*
**Riddle** s. (enigma) *ldem-po.*
**Ride** vb. (on horseback) *rta-la žon-te ₀gro-ba*; (in a carriage) *šiñ-ta-la žon-te ₀gro-ba.*
**Riding-beast** *bžon-pa.*
**Right** adj. (right-hand) *γyas-pa*; (not wrong) *drañ-po, ₀os-pa*; all right! *tsañ-grig*; — measure *čag-tsad*; to be — *₀grig-pa, ran-pa.*
**Right** s. *krims* 50.
**Righteous** *čos-drañ-po.*
**Rim** *kyud-mo.*
**Rind** *kog-pa.*
**Ring** s. *'a-lóñ*; — dove *ku-hu*; — worm *ke.*
**Ring** vb. a. (a bell etc.) *₀krol-ba.*
**Rinse** *bšal-ba.*
**Ripe** adj. *smin-pa.*
**Rise** vb. n. (to get up) *ldañ-ba, lañ-ba, kar* or *ker-lañ-ba*, resp. *bžeñs-pa*; (as the sun) *₀čar-ba*; (in the air) *₀pag-pa*; (to come forth) *₀bur-ba, ₀byuñ-ba.*
**Risk** s. *nyen, bar-čod.*
**Risk** vb. a. *skyel-ba, sdo-ba, blos-γtoñ-ba* 385.
**Rival** s. *₀gran-zla.*
**River** *ču, ₀bab-ču, ču-kluñ, ču-bo, γtsañ-po* 433.
**Rivet** s. *₀brel-mtsams.*
**Rivulet** *ču-pran.*
**Road** *lam, šul, šul-lám, ₀gro-sa*; — book *lam-yig.*
**Roam** *₀kor-ba, ₀pyo-ba, ₀grim-pa, yar-ba.*
**Roar** vb. n. *₀krog-pa, ñu-ba, ldir-ba, ña-ro sgrog-pa.*
**Roar, Roaring** s. *ña-ro, ñar-skad, ₀ur* 499.
**Roast** vb. a. *rñod-pa, sreg-pa.*
**Roast-flour** *rtsam-pa.*
**Rob** *rku-ba, ₀prog-pa, *kog-te kyer-če* W.*
**Robber** *mi-šér.*
**Robbery** *čoms, bčom-pa.*
**Rock** s. *brag*; — salt *rdo-tswa.*
**Rock** vb. n. *₀kyom-pa, dpyañ-ba*; vb. a. *dpyañ-la γtoñ-ba* 328.
**Rod** *lčag, lčug-ma, dbyug-gu.*
**Roll** s. *gril, ₀kor-lo*; paper — *šog-sgril, šog-ril W.*

Roll vb. a. *sgril-ba, sgre-ba*; to — one's self *ₒk̔ri-ba, ₒgre-ba*; vb. n. *ldir-ba*; the rolling of thunder *ldi-ri-ri*.
Roof s. *t̔og*.
Room s. (apartment) *k̔aṅ-pa, k̔aṅ-bu, k̔aṅ-mig, naṅ-mig C. W.*; (space) *gu, go*; to find — v. *ₒgro-ba, šoṅ-ba*.
Root s. *ba-t̔ag W.*; *rtsa-ba, rtsad*.
Root up vb. a. *rtsad-nas γčod-pa*.
Rope *sgrogs, t̔ag pa*.
Rosary *ₒp̔reṅ-ba*.
Rose *se-ba, γse-ba, bse-ba*.
Rose-coloured *dkar-rgyá*.
Rot vb. n. *ₒdrul-ba, rul-ba*.
Rouge *skeg-t̔sós*.
Rough *gyoṅ-po, rtsub-po, rags-pa, rtsiṅ-ba*.
Roughness *ṅad* 126.
Round adj. *kor-kór*; *kyir-kyir W.*; *gor-mo, sgor-mo*; *zlum-pa*; *ril-ba*; to make — *sgoṅ-ba*; to be made — *ₒgril-ba*.
Round about adv. *kun-nas, p̔yogs bžir*.
Round s., the — of transmigration *ₒk̔or-ba* 58.
Rouse *dkrog-pa*; **šaṅ skul-če* W.* 23.
Rove *ₒgrim-pa, rgyu-ba*.
Row vb. *skya rgyab-pa*.
Row s. (series) *gral, rim-pa*.
Row s. (fray) *ₒt̔ab-mo, ₒdziṅ-mo*.
Royal *rgyal-poi*; — family *rgyal-rigs*; — residence *rgyal-sa*.
Rub vb. *bdar-ba, ₒdrud-pa*.
Rubbish *gal-ró, rdo-ro, sa-ró W.*
Ruby *pad-ma-ra-ga*.
Rudder *skya-mjug*.
Rude *ₒk̔ob*; *rtsiṅ-ba*; *gyoṅ-po*, very — *k̔a-gyoṅ-če*.
Rugged *γtsaṅ-γtsoṅ, rtsub-po*.
Ruin vb. a. *ₒgud-pa*; to be ruined *ₒjig-pa*.
Ruinous *gog-po*.
Ruins s., a house in — *k̔aṅ-rul, k̔aṅ-gog*.
Rule s. (regulation) *k̔rims* 51; (special direction) *spyad-mt̔sáms* 456.
Rule vb. a. *ₒgod-pa, dbaṅ sgyur-ba* or *byed-pa*.
Ruler (governor) *mṅa-bdag*; *dbaṅ-po*; *srid*; (instrument) *t̔ig-šiṅ*.
Rumination (chewing the cud) *skyug-ldád*.
Rumour s. *grag-pa, γtam, bšod-pa*; **zer-kę'* C.*; *t̔sor-lo W.*
Rump *byaṅ-k̔óg*.
Run vb. *rgyug-pa, ₒčor-ba*; to — about *ₒkyam-pa*; to — (flow) off *rdol-ba*; to — a race *dkyu-ba*.
Rupee *dṅul*; *kyir-mo Ld.*, *gir-mo* 68, *gor-mo W.*; Tibetan — **čo̤-tán* C.* 145.
Rupture *čag-čád*.
Rush s. (reed) *snyug-ma*.
Rush vb. *ₒk̔rog-pa, rgyug-pa*.
Russia *rgya-sér*.
Russian s. *rgya-ser-pa*.
Rust s. *btsa, γya, lčags-γya*.
Rut (track) *mal, šul*.

# S

Sable s. *bka-blon sram W.*, *brag-sram W.*
Sack s. *p̔ad*.
Sacrament *dam-bča* 250.
Sacred *dag-pa*.
Sacrifice vb. a. *mčod-pa* 166.
Sacrificial, — ceremony *sku-rim* 22; — feast *mčod-ston*.
Saddle s. *sga, rta-sga*; — cloth *ka-lé, sga-k̔ébs*; — girth *glo W.*
Saddle vb. a. *sga bstad-pa*, resp. *čibs-sga bstad-pa*.
Safe adj. *brtan-pa, btsan-po*.
Saffron *gur-kúm*; *k̔a-če-skyes* 36.
Saiga-antelope *rgya-ra*.
Sail s. *dar, γyor-mo*.
Sail vb. *gru-la žon-te lam-du ₒgro-ba*; v. also *rgal-ba* 103.
Saint *grub-tób* 78; *skyes-bu dam-pa* 31; *rnal-ₒbyor-pa* 315.
Sake, for the — of *p̔yir* 351.
Sal ammoniac *rgya-t̔sá*; *t̔sa-tsé C.*
Salary *p̔ogs*.
Salt s. *t̔swa, lan-tswa*; vb. a. *t̔swa ₒdebs-pa*.
Saltpetre *ze-t̔swa, šo-ra*.
Salutation *p̔yag*.
Salute vb. a. *p̔yag ₒt̔sal-ba, ₒbul-ba* or *byed-pa*.
Same adj. *nyid*; at the — time *γčig-čar*; of the — kind *γčig-pa, γčig-γčig W.*; one and the — *γčig*; the very — *de-k̔o-na, de-ka*; *de raṅ, de-ka raṅ*.
Sample *bkod-pa*.
Sanctuary *mčod-γnas*.
Sand *bye-ma*.
Sandal-tree *tsan-dan*.
Sanskrit *nā-ga-ri*.
Sap s. *bčud, k̔u-ba*.
Satiate *ₒgraṅ-ba*.
Satisfaction *skaṅ-γso*.
Satisfied *t̔sim-pa*.
Satisfy vb. a. v. *graṅ-ba* 98; v. *ṅom-pa* 130.
Saturday, Saturn *γza-spen-pa*.
Sauce *skyu-rum, spags*.
Sausage *sgyu-ma*.
Save vb. a. (deliver) *skyabs byed-pa, skyoṅ-ba, sgrol-ba, skyob-pa, ₒp̔aṅs-pa, sruṅ-ba*; (lay up) *sri-ba* 581, *p̔aṅ-ba* 340; to be —d *t̔ar-ba* 230.

**Saviour** *skyabs-mgon* 26; *srog-skyób W.*
**Savour** s. *bro-ba.*
**Saw** s. *sog-le C.*, *ċad-* or *rgya-sóg W.*; vb. a. **ċad-sog šrul-če* W.*
**Say** *sgo-ba*, resp. *mol-ba W.*; *smra-ba, zer-ba, bšad-pa*, resp. *γsuṅ-ba*; *bka-rtsol-ba*; he says, he said *na-re* 300; to — nothing of (let alone) *lta ċi smos.*
**Scale** s. (of a fish) *ḱrab*; (of a balance) *ḱu-le*; (for measuring) *skar-ťsád*; pair of scales *sraṅ.*
**Scale off** vb. n. *gog-pa.*
**Scar** s. *rmai ǰes*, or *šul*, or *mal.*
**Scarce** adj. *dkon-pa.*
**Scarf** *ska-rugs*; — of salutation *ḱa-btágs* 37.
**Scatter** vb. a. *˳grems-pa, γtor-ba*; to be scattered *˳tor-ba.*
**Scene** *groṅ-ḱyér, ltad-mo*; v. *gleṅ-γži.*
**Scenery** *snaṅ-ťsúl.*
**Scent** s. (odour) *ṅad, dri-bsuṅ.*
**Scholar** (pupil) *grwa-pa, slob-ma, slob-baṅs, slob-ṕrug, ḱrid-ṕrúg, mḱan-bu, rgyud-pa*; (man of letters) *mḱas-po.*
**School** s. *grwa, slob-grwá, čos-gra*; — boy *grwa-ṕrug*; — house *grwa-kaṅ*; — master *grwa-dpón*; — room *bšad-grwá*; — table *čos-ḱri.*
**Science** *rig-pa*; sciences *γtsug-lág.*
**Scientific**, — work *bstan-bčos.*
**Scissors** *čan-pa* 155, *ċem-tse C.*, *grim-tse Sik.*
**Sclerotic** of the eye *gaṅs.*
**Scold** vb. *bka-bkyon-pa, spyo-ba.*
**Scoop** s. *skyogs*; vb. a. *˳ču-ba.*
**Scope** *˳gro-sa, spyod-yul.*
**Scorn** vb. *ťo-˳ťsam-pa.*
**Scrap** *čag-dúm.*
**Scrape** vb. *˳brad-pa, ˳drad-pa.*
**Scratch** vb. *spar-mos ˳brad-pa.*
**Scream** vb. *sgrog-pa.*
**Screaming** s. *skad-ṅán, skad-lóg.*
**Screw** s. *γču-ba.*
**Scripture**, Holy scripture, *γsuṅ-ráb, γsuṅ-mčóg.*
**Scrotum** *rlig-bu, rlig-šúbs.*
**Scruple** s. *rtog-pa, rnam-rtóg.*
**Scullion** *ma-γyóg, ťab-γyóg.*
**Sculpture** *brkos-ma.*
**Sea** *rgya-mťso*; — captain *ded-dpon*; — monster *ču-srin.*
**Seal** s. (stamp) *rgya*, resp. *ṕyag-rgyá*; *ťe-mo*, col. *ťe-tse*; *dam-ḱa*, resp. *ṕyag-dám*; vb. a. *dam-ḱa brgyab-pa.*
**Sealing-wax** *la-ča.*
**Seam** s. *mťa-ma, sne-mo, ťsem (-po).*
**Search** vb. *˳ťsol-ba, γžig-pa*; to — into *sar-* or *ťsar-γčod-pá.*
**Season** *dus* 255, **nam-da, nam-la** 304.
**Seat** s. *ḱri, rten, γži-ma* 480.
**Seclusion** *dben-pa, dben-γnas* 389.
**Secrecy** *lkog.*
**Secret** s. and adj. *γsaṅ-ba.*
**Secretary** *yig-mḱan*; *bka-druṅ C.*
**Sect** *čos-lugs, lugs.*
**Section** *ḱag, skubs, skor, rnam-pa, bam-po, dbye-ba*; *yan-lag.*
**Sedan-chair** *˳ḱyogs, ḱyogs-dpyaṅ, ṕeb-dpyaṅ C.*
**Sediment** *snyigs-pa, ťsigs-ma, ro.*
**Seduce** *rṅod-pa, slu-ba.*
**Seducer** *mi-dgei bšes-nyén.*
**See** vb. *mťoṅ-ba*, resp. *γzigs-pa*; to be seen *snaṅ-ba.*
**Seed** s. *sa-bon.*
**Seek** *˳ťsol-ba.*
**Seize** *˳ǰug-pa, ˳ťam-pa, ˳ťogs-pa, ˳dzin-pa, len-pa*, resp. *bžes-pa.*
**Seizure** *˳dzin.*
**Select** vb. *˳dam-pa, ˳byed-pa.*
**Self** *ṅo* 129, *ṅos, nyid, bdag, raṅ*, I myself *ṅed-raṅ* 128, *ṅa-raṅ* 522; — dependant *raṅ-dbaṅ.*
**Selfish** *dṅos-˳dzin ċan*; to be — *ṅos ˳dzin-pa.*
**Selfishness** *dṅos-˳dzin, raṅ-˳dód.*
**Sell** *˳ťsoṅ-ba*; to be sold *˳gyag-pa, ˳grim-pa W.*
**Send** *skur-ba, ˳ḱal-ba, mṅag-pa, γtoṅ-ba, rdzoṅ-ba, zlog-pa*; to — for *˳gugs-pa*; to — forth *˳byin-pa*; to — word *spriṅ-ba.*
**Senior** (elder) *rgad-po.*
**Sense** s. (intellectual power) *blo-grós* 385, *dbaṅ-po* 387; (meaning) *dgoṅs-pa* 87, *don* 258.
**Sensible** *ťsul-mťún.*
**Sentence** *žal-čé*; to pass — *žal-če γčod-pa*; *ťag-čod-pa byed-pa.*
**Sentiment** *blo* 384; false — *lta-lóg* 217.
**Sentinel** *mel-ťse, bya-ra.*
**Separate** vb. a. *dgar-ba*; vb. n. *˳gol-ba, ˳gye-ba, ˳ṕral-ba*; *so-só byed-pa*; to be separated *˳bral-ba.*
**Separate** adj. *sgos*; *so-so.*
**Separation** *gud* 69.
**Sepulchre** *baṅ-so.*
**Series** *gral, gras, rim-pa.*
**Serpent** *sbrul*; — demon *klu* 8.
**Serrated** *ċoṅ-ċóṅ.*
**Serum** *ču-sér.*
**Servant** *γyog-po, γyog-mo*; *ḱol-po, ḱol-mo*; *bran-po, bran-mo*; *bran-ḱól*; *mi-lág*; *žabs-ṕyi, mṅag-γžug*; your servant! *da čen žu W.* 152.
**Serve** vb. *žal-ta byed-pa*; to — up *˳dren-pa.*
**Service** *žabs-ťóg* 472; at your — *'oṅ-le, 'a W.*
**Sesame** *til*; — oil *til-már.*
**Set** vb. a. to — about *rtsom-pa, čas-pa*; to — at *ṕyo-ṕyó*; to — forth *rǰod-pa*; to — in order *˳god-pa, γtan-la ˳bebs-pa*; vb. n.

to — (of the sun) *nub-pa, skyod-pa W.*; to — out (depart) *čas-pa.*
Settle vb. a., to — a business *go čod-pa*; vb. n. *₀tsugs-pa* 459.
Settled adj. (decided) *zad-pa*; (at an end) *zin-pa, rdzogs-pa.*
Settlement (colony) *babs-sa.*
Seven num. *bdun*; seventh *bdun-pa*; seventeen *bču-bdun*; seventeenth *bču-bdun-pa*; seventy *bdun-ču*; seventieth *bdun-ču-pa.*
Several *ka-čig, ₀ga, mi-₀dra-ba.*
Severe *ynyan-pa, drag-pa.*
Severity *ṅad W.*
Sew *₀tsem-pa.*
Sex *rten* no. 4, 213.
Sexual *rten-gyi.*
Shackle s. *lčags, lčags-sgrog.*
Shade s. *grib.*
Shadow s. *grib-ma.*
Shake vb. a. *skyod-pa, skyom-pa, sgul-ba, sprug-pa*; vb. n. *₀gul-ba, lčogs-pa.*
Sham, to perform a — work *bčos-su byed-pa.*
Shame s. *krel, ṅo-tsa, bag-yod(-pa)* 364, *žabs-₀drén* 472; it is a —! *krel-ba yod W.* (**tel-wa yod**).
Shamefaced *ṅo-tsa-čan.*
Shameless *krel-méd; ṅo-tsa-med-pa.*
Shape s. *dbyibs, yzugs, čas, bkod-pa.*
Share vb. *bgod-pa*; s. *bgo-skal, skal-ba; ča, ča-šás.*
Sharer *go-kan W.*
Sharp adj. (not blunt) *rno-ba*; (to the taste) *tsa-ba; ber-čan.*
Sharpness (of an edge) *ka* IV, no. 5, 35.
Sharpsightedness *mig-sál W.*
Shave *₀breg-pa, bžar-ba.*
Shawl *do-šā-lā.*
She pron. *ko, koṅ* 41, *de* 255.
Sheaf *lag-kód.*
Shears v. *čan-pa* 155.
Sheath s. *šubs.*
Shed s. (slight building) *bkad-sa* 12.
Shed vb.a. *ldug-pa, blug-pa*; (tears) *bsil-ba.*
Sheep *lug*; flock of — *lug-kyu*; — fold *lug-rá.*
Sheet of paper *gre-ga C., šog-bu; šog-gáṅ W.*
Shelf *slaṅ-ka.*
Shell s. (husk) *kog-pa, gaṅ-bu, lgaṅ-bu*; (mollusk) *duṅ* 253, *₀gron-bu* 102; vb. a. *bgrud-pa.*
Shell-lac *rgya-skyégs.*
Shelter s. *skyibs; skyabs-ynás; yyam; čar-skyibs.*
Shepherd *lug-pa.*
Shield s. *pa-lí, pub.*
Shift vb. n. *₀po-ba.*
Shine vb. n. *čar-ba, ₀tser-ba, snaṅ-ba*; s. *₀od.*
Shining (bright) *čem-me-ba, lčam-me-ba; krol-krol W.*
Ship s. *gru, gru-bo, yziṅs*; — master *gru-dpon.*
Shirt s. *mgo-kár Ld.*
Shiver vb. *₀gul-ba.*
Shoe s. *lham*; soft — *ba-bu*; — of plaited straw *bu-la*; — strap *lham-sgróg.*
Shoot s. *lčug-ma*; vb. n. *₀kruṅ-ba*; vb. a. *₀pen-pa.*
Shooting-star *ke-tu, skar-mdá.*
Shore *₀gram, skam-sa.*
Short *tuṅ-ba*; in — *sgril-bas* 120, *mdor-na* 273; cf. also *zur-tsam* 489.
Shortsighted *mig-rgyaṅ-tuṅ.*
Shoulder s. *dpuṅ-pa, prag-pa*; — blade *sog-pa.*
Shout vb. *₀grags-pa, sgrog-pa.*
Shovel s. *kyem*; coal — *me-skyogs.*
Show vb. a. *ston-pa, ṅom-pa, sdigs-pa.*
Showman *ltad-mo-mkan.*
Shrewd *mkas-pa.*
Shrine *rten.*
Shrink vb. n. (to be contracted) *₀kum-pa,* (to recoil) *₀dzem-pa, čum-pa.*
Shriveled, Shrunk, *kums-pa.*
Shudder vb *yya-ba.*
Shun *spoṅ-ba, ₀dzem-pa.*
Shut vb. a. (a door) *₀gegs-pa*; (the eyes) *₀dzum-pa*; to — off or out *₀kegs-pa*; to — up *skyil-ba, sgyoṅ-ba.*
Shuttle *doṅ-po.*
Shy vb. n. (of horses) *₀drog-pa.*
Shy adj. *₀drog-čan.*
Sick *nad-pa*; v. also *yi-ga čus* 508.
Sickle *zor-ba, rgya-zór.*
Sickly *nad-bu-čan.*
Side s. *logs, ṅo, ṅos, ṅogs, ₀dabs, rol* 536, *kud-ma*; (of the body) *dku, yžogs, glo, ₀gram,* (direction) *pyogs* 352.
Sieve *lčags-tsags.*
Sigh s. *kog-šugs W., šugs-nár, sugs-riṅ.*
Sight *ltad-mo, snaṅ-ba, mtoṅ-snáṅ.*
Sign s. *rgya*, resp. *pyag-rgya; mtsan-ma, mtsan-nyid, rgyu-mtsan; rtags; brda* 297.
Signature *rgya-rtags.*
Signification *don.*
Signify v. *yin-pa* 510.
Sikim *₀bras-ljoṅs.*
Silence *čem-me-ba.*
Silent, to be — *ka-rog-pa; čaṅ mi smra-ba.*
Silk *dar, gos*; — cloth *za-₀óg*; — thread *gos-skúd*; silks *gos-čén*, col. *go-šén.*
Silk-worm *dar-srin.*
Silver s. *dṅul*; — in bars *gag.*
Similar *₀dra-ba; *tsogs-se* W.*
Similitude *dpe.*
Simple *rkyaṅ-pa.*
Simultaneously *yčig-čar.*

Sin s. *sdig-pa, nyes-pa, nyon-moṅs-pa skyon, sgrib-pa*; heinous — *rme-ba* 425; deadly — *mt̔sams-med-pa* 455.
Since adv. (ever since) *bzuṅs-te*; conj. *pas.*
Sincere *draṅ-po.*
Sinew *č̔u-ba.*
Sinful *sdig-ċan, skyon-ċan.*
Sing *glu len-pa.*
Singed, Singeing *me-γžób.*
Single adj. (separate) *γċig-ka, γċig-pu* 144; *nyag-ma, rkyaṅ-pa*; (unmarried) *k̔yo-méd*; *č̔uṅ-ma-méd*; — combat *k̔rug-pa, ˳dziṅ-mo.*
Sink vb. n. *rgud-pa, nub-pa ˳byiṅ-ba.*
Sinner *sdig-po, sgrib-pa.*
Sir *γtso-bo* 434; *sa-heb*, col. *sāb* 571; *'a-ǰó* 603; dear Sir *bžin-bzáṅ* 483.
Sister *sriṅ-mo, mċed*, resp. *lċam-mo*; elder — *'a-če* 603; younger — *nu-mo* 305.
Sit *sdod-pa*, resp. *bžugs-pa*; *˳dug-pa, ˳k̔od-pa*; sitting cross-legged *skyil-k̔rúṅ* 27.
Site *mal.*
Situated, to be — towards *lta-ba.*
Situation *γnas-skabs.*
Six num. *drug*, sixth *drug-pa*; sixteen *bċu-drug*, sixteenth *bċu-drug-pa*; sixty *drug-ċu*, sixtieth *drug-ċu-pa.*
Size *če-kyad, če-č̔uṅ, t̔sad, boṅ, k̔yon, rgya.*
Skeleton *keṅ-rus.*
Sketch s. *bkod-pa*; *zur tsam bsdu-ba* 489.
Skilful *mk̔as-pa, sgrin-po, t̔abs-šes-pa*; *t̔abs-ċan W.*; *skyen-pa, spyaṅ-po.*
Skill *sgyu-rtsál.*
Skin s. *pags-pa, ko-ba.*
Skirt s. *gos-sgab, gos-mt̔a, t̔u-ba.*
Skull *t̔od-pa.*
Sky *nam-mk̔a, γnam.*
Slab *spaṅ, γya-ma.*
Slacken vb. a. *glod-pa.*
Slackened adj. *lhod-pa, lhod-po.*
Slander s. *ṗra-ma, smad-sgra.*
Slander vb. *ṗra-ma byed-pa*, or *smra-ba*, or *˳ǰug-pa*, resp. *γsol-ba, žu-ba.*
Slanderer *ṗra-ma-mk̔an.*
Slanting *yo-ba, yon-po.*
Slate *γya-ma.*
Slaughter s. *γsod-γċod*; vb. a. *γsod-pa, ske γċod-pa*, resp. *˳gom-pa.*
Slave s. *bran, mṅag-γžúg.*
Sleep s. *γnyid*, resp. *mnal.*
Sleep vb. *nyal-ba, γnyid-log-pa*, resp. *γzim-pa.*
Sleeping-room *γzim-k̔aṅ.*
Sleet s. *k̔a-ma-č̔ár.*
Sleeve *ṗu-dúṅ.*
Slender *kyaṅ-po*; *kyaṅ-kyaṅ riṅ-mo W.*
Slide vb. n. *˳dred-pa.*
Slight adj. *ṗra-ba.*
Slight vb. a. *˳gyiṅ-ba, ˳gyiṅ-bag byed-pa*; *ċo-˳dri-ba.*
Sling s. *sgu-rdo*; — stone *rdo-γyúg.*

Slip in vb. n. *˳k̔ril-ba, ˳k̔yud-pa, ˳dzul-ba.*
Slope s. *gud, ṅogs.*
Sloping *gyiṅ-mo W.*
Slow *bul-po, dal-ba*; (irresolute) **lo-sna maṅ-ba*; *lo-sna riṅ-mo* W.*
Slowly *ṅaṅ-gis, gu! gúl*; *gu-le W., ga-le C.*
Slowness *dal-ba, dal-bu.*
Smack vb. *k̔a brdab-pa*; *dkan-sgra ˳debs-pa W.*
Small *č̔uṅ-ba, č̔uṅ-tse W.*; *ṗra-ba.*
Small-pox *˳brum-nad.*
Smart adj. (gaily dressed) *rnam-˳gyur-ċan*; *γzab-mo, γzab-sprod*; *mčor-po.*
Smash *γċog-pa, rduṅ-ba.*
Smear *skud-pa, ˳byug-pa.*
Smell s. *bsuṅ*; vb. a. *snom-pa*; vb. n. *mnam-pa.*
Smile s. *˳dzum*, vb. n. *˳dzum-pa.*
Smith *mgar-ba.*
Smoke s. *dud-pa*; vb. a. (tobacco) *˳t̔uṅ-ba.*
Smooth adj. *˳ǰam-pa.*
Smooth vb. a. *dbur-ba, ˳ur-ba, 'ur-ba.*
Smoothing-iron *lċags-bsró.*
Smuggle *ṗag-t̔soṅ byed-pa.*
Smut s. *sre-nag*; *sre-mog W.*
Snail *skyogs-lto-bu*; — clover *˳ol.*
Snake *sbrul, ˳bu-riṅ, lto-˳gro.*
Snap s. (with the fingers) *skad-ċig* 19.
Snare s. *rnyi, snyi.*
Snatch vb. *˳gog-pa.*
Sneak vb. *˳ǰab-pa.*
Sneeze vb. *sbrid-pa.*
Snipe *skyar-po, č̔u-skyar*; *tiṅ-ti-liṅ Ld.*
Snivel s. *snabs.*
Snore vb. *ṅug-pa, sṅur-ba.*
Snow s. *k̔a-ba, gaṅs*; — ball *k̔a-goṅ*; — bridge *rud-zam*; — fall *˳bab*; — leopard *γsa. bsa*; — shoe *dkyar*; — slip *k̔a-rúd*; — storm *k̔a-t̔súb, rluṅ-t̔súb, bu-yug.*
Snuff s. *sna-˳dág W.*
So *ċes* 142, *de-ltar* 256, *˳di-ltar* 275, *de-bžin-du* 256, *de-˳dras* 282; just — *de-ka-ltar* 255; so as *tsam* 430; so that *tsam-du*; so then *yaṅ* 505.
Soak *sboṅ-ba.*
Soap s. *glaṅ-glád C., sa-bon W.*
Soar *ldiṅ-ba, ˳ṗyo-ba.*
Sob s. *ṅud-mo.*
Socage *˳u-lag* 499.
Society, human — *t̔sogs* 451.
Socket of the eye *mig-k̔úṅ.*
Sod *skaṅ-ša.*
Soda *bul.*
Soft *˳ǰam-pa, mnyen-pa, snyi-ba, ˳bol-po.*
Softly *ga-le C., gu-le W.*
Soil s. *sa-γži.*
Soil vb. *bsgo-ba.*
Solder *k̔ro-č̔us sdom-pa*; **kar-ya daṅ žar-če* W.*
Soldier *dmag-mi.*

Sole of the foot *rkaṅ-mtil.*
Sole adj. *γčig, γčig-pu* 144.
Solely *k̔o-na, ₒba-žig.*
Solid adj. (not hollow) *k̔oṅ-gaṅ, gar-bu, pu-ri med-k̔an W.*; (not liquid) *reṅs-pa*; (firm) *mk̔raṅ, ₒčag-čan W., sra-ba.*
Solitary adj. *dben-pa*; — place *dgon-pa.*
Solitude *dben-pa, ₒbrog, gud.*
Some *k̔a-čig, ga-čen, ga-šas, gaṅ-žig, ₒga, res-ₒga*; *či γtoṅ W., čig, čuṅ-žig*; *ča-lam*; *re-žig*; *la-lá.*
Somebody, some one, ***γčig, γčig-čig.***
Somerset *ma-lág.*
Something *či žig*; ***či-γtoṅ W.***
Somnambulism *γnyid-rdól.*
Son *bu, bu-p̔o, **bu-ťsa W.***, resp. *sras*; — in-law *mag-pa*; — of man *mii bu, mii-sras.*
Song *glu, mgur, dbyaṅs.*
Sonorous *sgra-čan, sgra-ldaṅ.*
Soon *sṅa, mgyogs-pa*; *myur-du*; as — as *ma-k̔ad, ma ťag-tu* 227, *tsam-gyis* 431; sooner or later *sṅa-p̔yi.*
Soot *dreg-pa, sre-nág.*
Soothe *ži-bar byed-pa.*
Soothsayer *ča-mk̔an, rtsis-pa, mťsan-mk̔an.*
Sorcerer *ₒgoṅ-po, ₒba-po*; sorceress *ₒba-mo.*
Sorcery *rnam-p̔rul, p̔ra-mén*; to practise — *sprul-ba, rol-ba.*
Sorrel adj. *k̔am-pa.*
Sorrow s. *k̔oṅ-ₒk̔rugs*, col. **k̔og-ťúg*.*
Sorrowful *mi dga-ba.*
Sorry *koṅ-du čud-pa, mi dga-ba, blo mi bde-ba, sems skyo-mo.*
Sort s. *k̔yad-par, sna, rigs*; of what — *či lta-bu.*
Soul *nyams*, resp. *ťugs-nyáms, dgoṅs-pa*; *rgyud*; *rnam-šes, sems.*
Sound s *skad, k̔rol*; *sgra, sgra-skád.*
Sound vb.n. *k̔rol-ba, ₒgrags-pa*; vb.a. *sgra* [*sgrog-pa.*
Sound adj. *rem-pa, bde-ba.*
**Soup *ťug-pa.***
**Sour adj. *skyur-ba, skyur-po C.*,** *skyur-mo* ***W.***
**Source *ču-mig*,** *ču-mgo*; *k̔uṅs, ₒgo-ma.*
**South *lho.***
Sovereign s. *dbaṅ-po.*
Sow s. *p̔ag-mo*; — thistle *k̔al-pa.*
Sow vb. a. *sa-bon ₒdebs-pa.*
Space *gu, go.*
Spade *lčags-k̔yém.*
Span s. *mťo.*
Spare vb. *p̔aṅ-ba.*
Spark *me-ltág, me-ťság.*
Sparkle *ₒk̔ol-ba W., sag-ság zer-ba C.*
Sparrow *bya-po skya-bo W.*; — hawk *k̔ra, mčil-k̔ra.*
Spasm *rtsa-čus* or *-ₒdus*; *ₒčin-ba C.*
Spawn s. *sgo-ṅa, sgoṅ.*
Speak *smra-ba*, resp. *bka-stsol-ba*; *mol-ba W.*; *lab-pa*, resp. *γsuṅ-ba, zer-ba.*
Spear s. *mduṅ.*
Specimen v. *p̔ud* 344.
Speck *rme-ba, sme-ba.*
Spectacles *šel-mig*; snow — **mig-ḍa*.*
Spectator *ltad-mo-pa.*
Speech *skad, ṅag, γtam, ťsig, brǰod*, resp. *bka*, resp. *γsuṅ*; *dpe-sgra W.*
Speed, good —! **ṭam-pa čo* W.*
Speedily *myur-du, nye-bar.*
Speedy *mgyogs-pa, mgyogs-riṅs W.*; *myúr-ba, riṅs-pa.*
Spell s. *γzuṅs, γzuṅs-sṅags.*
Spend *skyag-pa, čud γzon-pa*; to be spent *ča-ba, ₒgro-ba, ₒgyag-pa, ₒťsar-ba, ₒdzad-pa.*
Sphere *dkyil-ₒk̔or* 11; *groṅ* 79, *ṅaṅ* 126; — of activity *spyod-yul.*
Spice *sdor, spod*; *ťsan-te W.*
Spider *ťags-gra-ₒbu, ₒbag-rág.*
Spin *ₒk̔al-ba, ₒk̔el-ba.*
Spindle *p̔aṅ.*
Spirit *sems, sems-nyid*; ***kun-γži*** 4; evil — *γdon* 267. *ₒgoṅ-po* 95.
Spirited *hur-po.*
Spit vb. *ťu gyab-če W., ťo-le ₒdebs-pa W.*
Spittle *mčil-ma*, resp. *žal-čab.*
Spleen (milt) *mčer-pa.*
Splendid *ₒod-čan, grags-čan.*
Splendour *rṅam-pa, dṅom-pa, rṅom-brǰid, brǰid, dpal, byin, zil, γzi, γzi-brǰid.*
Splint (for a broken limb) *čag-šiṅ.*
Splinter s. *ťsal-pa, šiṅ-ťsal*; *šiṅ-zél W.*
Split vb. a. *ₒges-pa, γčog-pa, γšog-pa, čeg-pa*; vb. n. *ₒgas-pa.*
Spoil vb. a. (plunder) *ₒǰoms-pa*; ***γčil-ba.***
Spoiled (corrupted) *k̔ag-po*; to be — *saṅ-ba.*
Spoke *rtsib-ma.*
Sponge s. *ču-ₒk̔úr.*
Spontaneously *raṅ, raṅ-bžin-gyis, šugs-kyis, rgyu med-du* 110.
Spoon *ťur-ma*; tip of a — *ťur-mgo.*
Spoon-bill *skyar-léb.*
Sport vb. n. (frolic) *rtse-ba.*
Sportsman *k̔yi-ra-ba.*
Spot s. (locality) *go*; (stain) *grib*; (mark) *tig-le.*
Spouse (wife) *čuṅ-ma, btsun-mo, k̔ab.*
Spout s. *wa-mčú.*
Sprain vb. a. *tsigs ₒbud-pa* or *ₒbog-pa*; to be sprained *ₒk̔rul-ba.*
Spread vb. a. *rkyoṅ-ba, ₒgebs-pa, ₒk̔eb-pa, γčal-ba, rdal-ba, spel-ba, ₒdiṅ-ba, ₒbre-ba, ₒgrems-pa*; vb.n. *mčed-pa, ₒgye-ba, rgyas-pa, dar-ba, ldaṅ-ba.*
Sprightly *γčaṅ-po.*
Spring up vb. n. *čags-pa* 153.

**Spring** s. (fountain) *ču-mig, ḱron-pa*; (season) *dpyid.*
**Sprinkle** *₀grems-pa, čag-čag byed-pa.*
**Sprout** s. *sbál-mig, myu-gu, myug.*
**Sprout** vb. n. *skye-ba, ₀ḱruṅ-ba, rdol-ba.*
**Spunk** *spra-ba; tsa Ld.*
**Spur** s. (of horsemen) *rtiṅ-lčags*; mountain — *sgaṅ.*
**Spy** s. *lta-nyul-pa, mel-tse*; — glass *dur-bín, šel-mig.*
**Spy** vb. *so-byed-pa*; to — out (another's faults) *₀ťsaṅ bru-ba.*
**Squander** *γzan-pa.*
**Square** s. *ḱa-gáṅ*; adj. *ḱa-gaṅ-ba, ḱa-gaṅ-ma.*
**Squash** vb. *glem-pa.*
**Squat** vb. *tsog-pur sdod-pa* 432.
**Squeeze** vb. *glem-pa, bčer-ba.*
**Squire** v. *ga-gá.*
**Stack** s. *ṕub-rags.*
**Staff** *mḱar-ba, ₀ḱar-ba, ber-ka.*
**Stag** *ša-ba* 556.
**Stage** (of a journey) *₀braṅ-sa.*
**Stain** vb. (sully) *bsgo-ba*; stained *nyams-pa.*
**Staircase** *ťem-pa, rgya-skás; gya-šrás W.*
**Stairs** *ťem-pa*; up — *ya-ťog*, down — *ma-ťog.*
**Stake** s. (in the ground) *rtod-pa*; (in a wager) *rgyal-rgyan.*
**Stalk** s. *rkaṅ, sdoṅ-po, ba-ťag, rtsa-ba, sog-ma.*
**Stallion** *γseb.*
**Stammerer** *ḱa-ldig-mḱan W.*
**Stamp** s. *rgya*, resp. *ṕyag-rgyá.*
**Stamp** vb. *₀ḱrab-pa* 61.
**Stanch** vb. (the flowing blood) *sdom-pa.*
**Stand** vb.a. (bear) *bzod pa* 498; to be able to — *ťub-pa, ťeg-pa*; vb. n *greṅ-ba, laṅs-te sdod-pa.*
**Stand** s. *stegs* 221.
**Star** *skar-ma*; shooting — *skar-mdá.*
**Start** vb. (set out) *rgyug-pa*; (from alarm) *₀drog-pa.*
**State** s. (condition) *γnas-skabs, γnas-ťsúl.*
**Stately** *₍od-čan.*
**Statue** *sku, rdo-sku.*
**Stature** *sgo-po, sgo-bo.*
**Stay** vb. n. *₀dug-pa, sdod-pa, γnas-pa, bžugs-pa.*
**Steadfast** *brtan-po.*
**Steady** *₀ťsugs-pa.*
**Steal** vb. a *rku-ba, ma-sbyin-par len-pa*; vb. n. (slip) *₀ǰab-pa, nyul-ba, ₀dzul-ba.*
**Stealth,** by — *sbas-te W.*
**Steam** *rlaṅs-pa.*
**Steel** **čag-zán*, ṕo-lád.*
**Steelyard** *rgya-ma, nya-ga; pur, spor, spo-ré, sraṅ.*
**Steep** adj. *γtsaṅ-γtsoṅ, γzar-ba.*
**Steer** vb. a. *ḱa-lo sgyur-ba.*
**Stench** *dri ṅan-pa, dri ṅa-ba, dri-mnam.*
**Step** s. *gom-pa, rdog-pa*; — of a ladder *šral-daṅ* 21; vb. n. *bgom-pa, gom-pa ₀bor-ba, ₀grul-ba, ₀čag-pa.*
**Stepfather** *ṕa-γyár*; stepmother *ma-gyár.*
**Stick** s. *ber-ka, dbyug-pa.*
**Stick** vb. n. *ḱad-pa, ₀byor-ba*; vb. a. *sbyor-ba, ₀dzugs-pa.*
**Sticky** *rtsi-čan.*
**Stiff** *reṅs-pa*; to be — *reṅ-ba.*
**Still** adj. (quiet) *dal-ba, mi γyo-bar*; (silent) v. *ḱa rog-pa.*
**Still** adv. *da-rúṅ, yaṅ.*
**Sting** s. *mduṅ*; vb. a. *₀big(s)-pa, ₀dzug-pa* 466.
**Stingy** *lag-dam-po, ťsags-₀dod-čan.*
**Stink** vb. *mnam-pa.*
**Stir** vb. a. *dkrug-pa, srub-pa*; to — up *rnyog-pa, sprug-pa.*
**Stirrup** *yob, ₍ob.*
**Stitch** vb. *sbrel-ba.*
**Stocking** *rkaṅ-šúbs*, resp. *žabs-šúbs.*
**Stomach** *grod-pa, ṕo-ba.*
**Stone** s. *rdo*; — of fruits *rus-pa*; vb. a. *rdo-rub-la btaṅ-če W.*
**Stool** *stegs* 221.
**Stoop** vb. *mgo dgu-ba, mgo dgur-ba* or *₀gug-pa.*
**Stop** vb. a. *sub-pa, ₀gegs-pa*; vb. n. *₀gag-pa, sdod-pa.*
**Stopple,** stopper *ḱa-₀dig.*
**Store** s. *mdzod*; — room *mdzod-ḱaṅ, baṅ-ba, baṅ-ḱaṅ, ťsoṅ-ḱaṅ.*
**Storm** s. *ťsub-ma, rluṅ čen-po, drag-po.*
**Story** s. (floor) *ťog*; (tale) *γnas-ťsúl, lo-rgyus.*
**Stout** adj. *sbom-pa, rom-po*; (of cloth) *ťsags-dam*; to grow — *brta-ba.*
**Stove** *ťab, me-ťáb.*
**Straight** adj. *draṅ-po, groṅs-po, bsraṅs-pa.*
**Straighten** *sroṅ-ba.*
**Strain** vb. a. (filter) *₀ťsag-pa.*
**Strainer** *ču-ťsags.*
**Straits** *sa-bár, mťso-lag-₀brél.*
**Stranger** *ṕyi-mi, byes-pa.*
**Strangle** *ske bsdam-ste γsod-pa.*
**Strangury** *γčin-₀gág.*
**Strap** s. *ko-ťág, sgrog-gu, rog-bu W., luṅ.*
**Stratagem** *dku-lto.*
**Straw** *sog-ma, ṕub-ma.*
**Strawberry** *dpal-byór W.*
**Stray** v. *yan-pa* 506.
**Street** *rgya-sráṅ, lam-sráṅ.*
**Strength** *nyams-stóbs, stobs-po; šed*; — of spirits etc. *ber.*
**Strengthen** *šed čug-če W.*
**Stretch** vb. *rkyoṅ-ba, sriṅ-ba.*
**Strew** *γtor-ba, ₀diṅ-ba.*
**Strewing-oblation** *γtor-ma* 210.

**Strict** *dam-po.*
**Stride** vb. *bgom-pa.*
**Strike** vb. *$_o$ṕog-pa, rgyab-pa, rduṅ-ba, rdeg-pa.*
**String** s. *rgyud, sgrog, $_o$čiṅ-ba, $_o$ṕreṅ-ba, ťa-gu.*
**Strip** vb. *ṡu-ba, gos $_o$bud-pa.*
**Strive for** vb. *snyegs-pa, $_o$graṅ-pa, brtson-pa.*
**Stroke** s. *lċag, $_o$ṕras-pa.*
**Stroke** vb. *byil-ba, $_o$byug-pa.*
**Strong** *gar-ba, drags-po, btsan-po, rem-pa* 535, *ṡed-ċan.*
**Structure** *bkod-pa.*
**Stubborn** *mgo-ḱregs-pa.*
**Student** *slob-γnyér.*
**Studious** *brtson-$_o$grus-ċan.*
**Study** s. *$_o$bad-pa.*
**Stuff** s. (cloth) *ras.*
**Stuff** vb. a. *$_o$ťsaṅ-ba.*
**Stunned** *ḱal-ḱól.*
**Stupid** *glen-pa, blun-pa, blo-gros-méd.*
**Style** s. *bzo, zo-sta W.* 497.
**Subdue** *$_o$ǰoms-pa.*
**Subject** s. *skor, gleṅ-γżi, mṅa-żábs, bran, $_o$baṅs.*
**Subject** vb.a. *$_o$ǰoms-pa, ˛og-tu $_o$ǰug-pa* 501.
**Subsequent** *pyi-ma.*
**Subside** *żi-ba.*
**Subsidy** *$_o$ťud-ma.*
**Subsistence** *$_o$ťso-ťabs.*
**Substance** *dṅos-po, rdzas* 468.
**Substantive** *dṅos-miṅ.*
**Substitute** s. *ťsab.*
**Subtract** *$_o$dor-ba, sbyoṅ-ba, $_o$bud-pa.*
**Succession** *ťsir, rabs* 525, *rim-pa* 530.
**Such** *$_o$di-$_o$dra-ba* 282, *de-lta-bu* 256.
**Suck** *$_o$ǰibs-pa, $_o$ťuṅ-ba.*
**Suckling baby** *żo-$_o$ťúṅs.*
**Suddenly** *glo-bur, glo-bur-du, har(-gyis); yaṅ-med-la W.*
**Suet** *grod-ťsil, ḱoṅ-ťsil.*
**Suffer** vb. a. *myoṅ-ba, bzod-pa;* vb. n. *mṅar-ba, γzir-ba.*
**Suffice** *$_o$ḱyed-pa, ldaṅ-ba; čog-pa.*
**Sugar** *ka-ra, ḱa-ra;* raw — *bu-rám;* — cane *$_o$dam-búr W.*
**Suit** s., a complete — of clothes *mgo-lus ča tsáṅ.*
**Suitable,** to be — *˛oṅ-ba* 502, *˛os-pa, ruṅ-ba.*
**Suitor** *$_o$dod-mḱan.*
**Sully** *bsgo-ba.*
**Sulphur** *mu-zi.*
**Sum** s. *brtsis-zin;* vb. to — up *sgril-ba, sdom-pa, sre-ba.*
**Summary** s. *sdom.*
**Summer** *dbyar.*
**Summit** *mgo, spo, rtse(-mo).*
**Summon** vb. a. *$_o$gugs-pa.*

**Sun** *nyi-ma;* — beam *nyi-γżér;* — dial *nyi-tsód.*
**Sunday** *γza-nyi-ma.*
**Superficies** *ṅos, ḱa, γdoṅ.*
**Superintend** *żal-ta byed-pa.*
**Superintendence** *do-dám.*
**Superior** adj. *ḱyad, goṅ-ma, rgyal-ba, bla, rab;* s. *goṅ-ma, bla-ma.*
**Supernumerary** adj. *$_o$ťeb.*
**Supine** adj. *gan-kyál.*
**Supper** *dgoṅs-zas;* Lord's — *γsol-ras* 592.
**Supple** *mnyen-pa.*
**Supplement** *ḱa-skóṅ, yan-lag, lhan-ťábs.*
**Supply** vb. *sgrub-pa.*
**Support** vb. *skyoṅ-ba, $_o$degs-pa, $_o$dzin-pa;* s. *rten-pa, rgyab-rtén.*
**Supposition** resp. *bsam-pa, snaṅ-ba, bżed-pa, bżed-ťsul.*
**Suppress** *non-pa, $_o$ǰoms-pa, snub-pa, sub-pa, $_o$gegs-pa*
**Sure** *gor-ma-čág,* eleg. *gor-ma-bkúm* 73; *btsan-po* 434; to be sure! **tig, ḍig, de-ka yod** 255.
**Surely** *ṅes-par, nan-čágs* 303.
**Surety** *brtan-pa, γdeṅ-ťsad.*
**Surface** *ḱa, ṅos, logs, $_o$ḱod, γdoṅ-pa.*
**Surpass** *$_o$da-ba.*
**Surround** *skor-ba.*
**Suspend** *dpyaṅ-ba, spyaṅ-ba* 328.
**Swaddling-cloth** *ču-stán W.*
**Swallow** s. *ḱug-ta.*
**Swallow** vb. *mid-pa, ḱyur-mid-pa.*
**Swamp** s. *gram-pa.*
**Swan** *bżad, bżad-pa; ṅaṅ-pai rgyal-po.*
**Swear** *bro $_o$ťsal-ba, dmod-mo $_o$bor-ba* 423.
**Sweat** s. *rṅul.*
**Sweep** vb. *ṕyag bdar-ba;* to — together *sdud-pa.*
**Sweepings** *pyag-dár.*
**Sweet** *dṅar-ba;* — scented *żim-po.*
**Sweet-heart** *$_o$dod-grogs, mig-grogs, mdza-grogs, bzaṅ-grogs.*
**Sweet-meats** *żim-zé, żim-żim C., żim-zág W.*
**Swell** vb. n. *skraṅ-ba, $_o$bo-ba.*
**Swift** adj. *skyen-pa, myur-ba, riṅs-pa.*
**Swim** *rkyal-ba, $_o$ṕyo-ba.*
**Swine** *ṕag.*
**Swing** vb. a. *dbyug-pa, γyob-pa.*
**Switch** s. *lċag.*
**Swoon** vb. n. *brgyal-ba.*
**Sword** *ral-gri.*
**Syllable** *sgra* 119, *ťseg-bar* 450.
**Symbol** *rten* 213.
**Symmetry** *dpe-byad, byad.*
**Symptom** *mťsan(-ma), rtags.*
**Synonym** *skad-dód* 258.
**Sypbilis** *ṕa-ráṅ, reg-dug.*
**Syria** *rum-ṡam.*
**Syringe** *γċiu.*

# T

**Tabernacle** *gur-mčóġ* 69.
**Table** *lčog-tse* 150, resp. *γsol-lčóg* 592; *γsol-stegs*; European — *rgya-lčóg*.
**Tablet**, bearing an inscription *byaṅ-bu, byaṅ-ma*.
**Taciturn** *smra-nyúṅ*.
**Tail** *rṅa-ma, mǰug-ma*.
**Tailor** *ṫsem-pa*.
**Take** vb. a. *len-pa, ˳togs-pa, ˳dzin-pa*, resp. *bžes-pa*; **nam-če** *W.*; to — for *˳dzin-pa* 465, *sems-pa*; to — off *˳bud-pa, šu-ba*; to — out *˳gog-pa, ˳doṅ-pa, ˳byin-pa*; take away! *k̔ur soṅ C., k̔ur k̔yer W.*
**Tale** *lo-rgyús, sgruṅ(s)*.
**Talent** *blo, rig-pa, yon-tan, šes-rab*.
**Talk** s. *γtam, ˬur*; vb. *smra-ba, lab-pa, gleṅ-ba, ˳bar-ba, ˬur γtoṅ-ba*.
**Talkative** *smra-˳dód, rgya-lab-čan*.
**Tall** col. *sgo-po riṅ-mo, kyaṅ-kyaṅ riṅ-mo, ˳ǰoṅ-˳ǰóṅ*.
**Tallow-candle** *tsil-sdóṅ*.
**Tamarisk** *ˬom-bu*.
**Tame** adj. *dul-ba, ˳dris-pa, γyuṅ-ba*; vb. a. *˳dul-ba, ṫul-ba*.
**Tan** vb. a. *mnyed-pa*.
**Tanner** *ko-ba mnyed-mk̔an C.*
**Tardy** *bul-po*.
**Target** *˳ben*.
**Tarry** vb. *˳gor-ba*.
**Tartar** (incrusting the teeth) *so-dreg*.
**Task** s. *k̔ag*; *rgyugs W.*
**Taste** s. (savour) *bro-ba, ro*; vb. a. *myoṅ-ba*; vb. n. *bro-ba*.
**Tattered** *čad-po*.
**Tavern** *čaṅ-k̔aṅ*
**Tax** s. *k̔ral, dpya*; *˳bab Sp*; vb. a. (appraise) *˳ǰal-ba*.
**Tea** *ǰa*, resp. *γsol-ǰá*; — pot *tib-riḱ*, resp. *γsol-tib*; — party *ǰa-mgrón*.
**Teach** vb. *ston-pa, slob-pa*.
**Teacher** *ston-pa, slob-pa, slob-dpon; rgyud-pa*.
**Team** of bullocks *glaṅ-dór*.
**Tear** s. *mči-ma*; to shed tears *mči-ma blag-pa*.
**Tear** vb. a. *γšeg-pa*; to — out *˳p̔yid-pa, ˳byin-pa*; to — to pieces *˳dral-ba, hral-ba*.
**Tease** *gob-nón čo-če W.*
**Tedder** vb. *btod-pa*; s. *btod-ṫág*.
**Tell** *˳čad-pa, snyod-pa, smra-ba, zer-ba, zlo-ba, zlos-pa*.
**Temperate** *ṫsod šes-pa*.
**Temperature** *graṅ-dro*.
**Tempest** *rluṅ čen-po* or *drag-po, rluṅ-dmár, yul-ṅán*.
**Temple** *mčod-k̔aṅ*.
**Temporal** *ṫse ˳dii*; — life *γnas-skabs*.
**Tempt** *nyams sad-pa, ṫsod ˳dzin-pa*.
**Ten** num. *bču, čig bču*; — thousand *k̔ri*; tenth *bču-pa*.
**Tenant** *k̔aṅ-pa γyar-mk̔an*.
**Tend** vb. a. *skyoṅ-ba*.
**Tender** adj. *snyi-ba, ˳ǰam-pa; byams-pa*.
**Tendon** *nya-ču*.
**Tenet** *čos*.
**Tent** *gur*, resp. *bžugs-gur*.
**Term** s. (limited time) *čad-so*.
**Terminate** vb. n. *zin-pa*; vb. a. *˳ṫsar-bar* [*byed-pa*.
**Termination** *mṫa* 239.
**Terrace** *steṅ-ka, steṅ-tse*.
**Terrify** *˳ǰigs-pa, ˳ǰigs-skrag ˳doṅ-pa C.*; **ǰig-ri skul-če** *W.*; to be terrified *skrag-pa*.
**Test** vb. a. *nyams sad-pa; ṫsod lta-ba* 216.
**Testament** *bka-čéms, k̔a-čéms*.
**Testicle** *rlig-pa*, resp. *γsaṅ-rlig*, euphem. *˳bras-bu*.
**Testimony** *če-bži*; v. *dpaṅ(-po)* 326.
**Texture** *ṫags*.
**Than** *las* 546, *pas, saṅ W.* 571.
**Thank** vb. *γtaṅ-rág byed-pa* or *˳bul-ba*.
**Thanks** s. *γtaṅ-rág, legs-γsól*; many —! *bka-drin-čé, ṅo-mṫsar-čé* 456; *žu W.*
**That** pron. *de* 255; *so-či-ltar* 218.
**The** def. art. v. *de* 255.
**Theatre** *ltad-mo lta-bai sa, ltad-mo-k̔aṅ*.
**Theft** *rkun-ma*.
**Theme** *skor*.
**Then** *de-tsa-na, der* 256.
**Theory** *lta-ba* II, no. 3, 217.
**There** *de-na, de-ru* 256, *p̔a-gir* 338.
**Therefore** *de-bas-na, des-na, des* 256.
**Therein** *naṅ-na*.
**They** *k̔o-pa*; *k̔o-wa W.*; *k̔o-ṫso, k̔o-čag C.*; *de-dag, de-rnams*.
**Thick** *˳ṫug-pa, stugs-po, sbom-pa, rom-po*; (of fluids) *ska-ba, rnyog-pa*.
**Thicket** *ṫsaṅ-ṫsiṅ* 444.
**Thickness** *srab-˳ṫug* 244.
**Thief** *rkun-ma*.
**Thimble** *lčuṅ-mo, mdzub-rtén*.
**Thin** adj. *p̔ra-ba, zim-bu, siṅs-po W.*; *srab-pa, sla-ba, sla-mo*.
**Thing** *dṅos-po, ča, ča-byád, čas, rdzas*; things (goods) *ča, ča-lag*.
**Think** (suppose) *snyam-pa*; (meditate) *sem(s)-pa; bsam-mno byed-pa* or *γtoṅ-ba*, resp. *dgoṅs-pa*; to — of *dran-pa* 261, *dgoṅs-pa*.
**Third** num. *sum-pa*; thirteen *bču-sum*; thirteenth *bču-sum-pa*; thirty *sum-ču*; thirtieth *sum-ču-pa*; a third, third part *sum-ča, sum-yar*.
**Thirst** s. *skom, skom-pa, skom-dád*; vb. *skom-pa*.

This *˳di* 275.
Thither *de-ru*, *der* 256; *ṕyogs der* 352.
Thong *ko-t́ág*.
Thorn *t́ser-ma*.
Thoroughly *ḱyon-nas*.
Thou *ḱyed*, *ḱyod*, resp. *nyid*.
Though v. *kyi* 6.
Thought *bsam-pa*, resp. *dgoṅs-pa*, *snyam-pa*, *snaṅ-ba*, *dmigs-pa*, *˳čar-sgo*, *nyams*.
Thousand num. *stoṅ*; ten — *ḱri*, *ḱri-ḱrag*, *ḱri-t́so*; hundred — *˳bum*, *˳bum-t́so*.
Thrash vb. *γyul-ḱa γċog-pa*, *γyur byed-pa* C., **ḱo-yu skor-ċe** W.
Thread s. *skud-pa*, *˳t́sem-skúd*; *snal-ma* 319, *nyag-t́ág* 185.
Threaten *gam-pa* W.
Three num. *γsum*, *sum*.
Threshold *t́em-pa*, *sgo-t́ém*.
Thrifty *paṅ-sems-ċan*.
Throat *mgul*, resp. *mgur*, *lkog-ma*, *ske*, *gre-ba*, *mgrin-pa*, *'o-lé* W.; sore — *mgul-nad*.
Throb vb. *˳ṕar-ba*.
Throne s. *rgyal-sa*, *ḱri*, *sen-ge-ḱri*.
Through *ltaṅ*, *lteṅ* 217; *ṕyir* 351.
Throughout *t́og-t́ág* 237.
Throw vb. a. *rgyab-pa*, *rgyag-pa*, *skyur-ba*, *γtor-ba*, *˳ṕen-pa*, *dbyug-pa*; *˳bor-ba* C.; to — down *˳bud-pa*, *˳bebs-pa*; to — off *spoṅ-ba*.
Thumb s. *t́e-bo*, *mt́e-bo*.
Thunder s. *˳brug*, *˳brug-skád*, *˳brug-sgrá*.
Thunderbolt *t́og*, *lċe*, *rdo-rǰe*, *γnam-lċags*.
Thursday *γza-ṕur-bu*.
Thus *de-ltar*, *˳di-ltar*, *de-bžin-du*, *de-˳dras* C., *de-tsug* W.
Thwart (frustrate) *sgyel-ba*.
Tiara *ċod-pán*.
Tibet *bod*.
Tibetan m. *bod-pa*, f. *bod-mo*; — language *bod-skad*; — printing-characters *dbu-ċan* 388; — current handwriting *dbu-méd*.
Tick s. *lug-šig*.
Tickle vb. **ki-tsi kug-ċe** W.; *gug-pa* W.
Tide s. *dus-rlábs*.
Tidings *ṕrin*; glad — *γtam-snyán*; (gospel) *ṕrin bzaṅ-po*.
Tie s. *˳čiṅ-ba*, vb. a. *˳ċiṅ-ba*, *˳kyig-pa*.
Tiger *stag*.
Tight *dam-po*, *t́aṅ-po*.
Till, until *bar-du* 366, *t́ug* C.; *t́sug-pa* W.
Till vb. a. *˳dul-ba*.
Time s. *dus*, *t́se*, *skabs*; (while) *yun*; time, times *lan*; one —, once *lan-γċig*; ten — *lan-bċu*; point of —, proper — for *bsgaṅ* 124.
Timid *˳ǰigs-pa*, *˳ǰigs-mḱan*, *˳ǰigs-pa-ċan*; *sems-čuṅ-ba*.
Tin s. *ža-nye dkar-po*, *ža-dkár*, *dkar-ya*; — plate *ta-li* W.
Tinder-box *lċags-mag*.
Tire vb. a. *ṅal ˳jug-pa*.
Tired *dub-pa*; to be — *dub-pa*, *skyo-ba*.
Tithe s. *ċu-ḱág* W.
Title s. *mt́san*; (claim) *t́ob-srol*.
To prep. *mdun* 273, *druṅ-du*, resp. *žabs-druṅ-du* 263, *rtsar* 437, *gan-du* 66.
Tobacco *t́a-ma-ḱa*; — pipe *gaṅ-zág*, *žal-zág*.
To-day *de-riṅ* C., *˳di-riṅ* W.
Toe *rkaṅ-sór*, *sor-mo*; the big — *rkaṅ-pai mt́e-bo*.
Together *γċig-tu*, *lhan-ċig-tu*; — with *bċas-pa*, *mnyam-du*.
Token *mt́san-ma*.
Tola (Indian half ounce) *dṅul*, col. *mul*.
Toll s. *šo-gam*.
Tomb *dur*, *baṅ-so*.
Tongs *rkam-pa*.
Tongue *lċe*, resp. *lǰags*.
Too adv. (too much) *ha-ċaṅ*; conj. (also) *yaṅ*.
Tool *čas*; tools *yo-byád*, *lag-ča*.
Tooth *so*, resp. *t́sems*; — ache *so-zug*; — brush *so-zéd*; — pick *t́sems-šiṅ*, *so-šiṅ*.
Top s. *rtse(-mo)*.
Topography *γnas-bšád*, *yul-bšád*.
Torch *gal-mé*, *sgron-ma*.
Torment vb. a. *˳t́se-ba*; *sdug-bsṅal* or *γnag ston-pa* W.
Torn adj. *ral-ba*, *čad-po*.
Tortoise *rus-sbal*.
Torture vb. a. *mi-la γnag ston-pa* W.
Totter *yam-yóm byed-pa*.
Touch vb. *nyug-pa*, *γtug-pa*, *t́ug-pa*, *reg-pa*.
Toupet *t́or-ċóg*, *t́or-t́súgs*.
Towards *t́og-tu* 237, *t́ad-du*, *ṕyogs-su*.
Towel *lag-˳ṕyis*.
Tower *mḱar dgu-t́og*.
Town *groṅ*, *groṅ-kyer*; *yul-gru*; *rgyal-sa* W.
Toy s. *rtsed-mo*.
Trace s. *rkaṅ-rǰés*, *mal*.
Track s. *rǰes*, *šul*.
Trackless *rǰes-méd*.
Tractable *srab-ḱa dul-mo*.
Trade s. *t́soṅ*, *bzo*.
Tradesman *ḱe-pa*.
Trading-place *las-sgo*.
Traffic s. *t́soṅ*.
Train vb. a. *sbyoṅ-ba*; to — up *skyed-sriṅ-ba*.
Trample vb. a. *rdzi-ba*, *rdog-pas rduṅ-ba*.
Tranquil *ži-ba*.
Tranquillity *žod*.
Transaction *las*.
Transfer vb. *spo-ba*, *˳god-pa*.
Transform *sgyur-ba*; to — one's self *sprul-ba* 336; to be transformed into *˳gyur-ba* 96, *˳gro-ba* 101.

**Transformation** *rdzu-˳ṗrul.*
**Transgress** *˳gal-ba*; *˳da-ba.*
**Transgression** *˳gal-krúl.*
**Translate** *sgyur-ba.*
**Transmigration**, the round of — *˳k̇or-ba* 58.
**Transplant** *spo-ba.*
**Transport** vb. *skyel-ba*, *˳k̇yer-ba.*
**Trap** s. *rnyi*, *snyi*; *ldem-pa W.*; — door *γnam-sgo*; mouse — *bi-ldém W.*, fox *wa-ldém W.*
**Travel** vb. *˳gro-ba*, *˳grod-pa*, *bgrod-pa*; *ča-ba W.*
**Tread** vb. a. *rdzi-ba*; **čag-čag ċo-če* W.*; vb. n. *˳čag-pa*, *˳čags-pa.*
**Treadle** *rkan-śiṅ.*
**Treasure** s. *γter.*
**Treasurer** *dkor-pa*, *ṗyag-mdzód.*
**Treasury** *dkor-mdzód.*
**Treat** s (feast) *mgron.*
**Treat** vb. n. (to use) *spyod-pa* 334; (to regale) *mgron-du γnyer-ba*; to — medically *bċos-pa*; *sman-dpyad byed-pa* 329; vb. n. to — of *rǰod-pa* 182.
**Treatise** *rgyud*, *rgyud-sdé.*
**Treatment**, good — *bzaṅ-lúgs W.*
**Treaty** *bzaṅ-sgrig.*
**Tree** *śiṅ*, *sdoṅ-po*, *śiṅ-sdóṅ.*
**Tremble** *˳gul-ba*, *˳dar-ba.*
**Trespass** vb. n. *bar-du γċod-pa* 367.
**Trevet** *lċags-sgyid.*
**Trial** (before a tribunal) *γtam-sdúr W.*
**Tribe** *sde.*
**Tribunal** *k̇rims-k̇aṅ.*
**Tribute** *dpya*
**Trick** s. *bar-čad*; to play tricks *ťo-˳ťsam-pa.*
**Trickle** vb. n. *˳dzag-pa.*
**Trifling** adj. *ṗra-ba.*
**Tripod** *sgyid-bu*, *lċags-sgyid.*
**Troop** s. *k̇yu*, *pal-po-če*, *ťso*; troops *dpuṅ.*
**Trophy** *rgyal-mtśan.*
**Trot** vb. *˳dur-ba*; s. *˳dur-˳gro.*
**Trouble** s. *nyon-moṅs-pa*, *dka-sdúg*, ***mya-ṅán***; vb. a. *dkrug-pa.*
**Troublesome** *ťsegs.*
**Trowsers** *rkaṅ-snam*, *gos-ťúṅ*, *dor-ma*, ***byaṅ-rkyaṅ***, *smad-γyógs.*
**True** ***bden-pa***, *ṅo-rtóg.*
**Trumpet** *duṅ.*
**Trunk** (of a tree) *sdoṅ-po*; (of an elephant) *glaṅ-sna*; (box) *sgam*, *sgrom.*
**Truss** s. *ṗon-po*; vb. to — up *rdze-ba.*
**Trustee** *ṗa-ťsáb.*
**Trustworthy** *˳os-pa.*
**Truth** *ṅes-pa*, *bden-pa*, *yin-min* 510.
**Try** *nyams sad-pa* 186, *dpyod-pa*, col. *ťsod-lta-ba.*
**Tub** *γżoṅ-pa*, *bzom.*
**Tube** *doṅ-po*, *pu-ri.*
**Tuck up** *rdze-ba.*
**Tuesday** *γza-mig-dmár.*
**Tuft** *ṗon*; — of wool *bal-˳dab W.*
**Tumble** vb. *˳gyel-ba.*
**Tumbler** (drinking-glass) ***śel-kór***, ***śel-ṗór.***
**Tumult** *˳k̇rug-pa.*
**Tun** *zem.*
**Tune** s. *glu.*
**Turban** *ťod*, *la-ťód.*
**Turbid** *ska-ba*, *nyog-pa.*
**Turf** *spaṅ*, *spaṅ-po*
**Turkey** *rum.*
**Turkois** *γyu.*
**Turmeric** *yuṅ-ba.*
**Turn** vb. a *sgyur-ba*; to — off *zlog-pa*; to — out *˳byin-pa*; to — round *˳k̇or-ba*; to — up *rdze-ba*; to — upside down *spub-pa*, *slog-pa*; vb. n. *ṗyogs-pa*, *˳gro-ba*, *ča-ba W.*; to — away *ldog-pa.*
**Turn** s. *ťsir* 448, *res* 535; by turns *ťsir-la*, *ťsir-du*, *ťsir daṅ*, *res-la.*
**Turnip** *nyuṅ-ma.*
**Turret** *speu*, *spüu.*
**Tusk** *mče-ba*, *mče-so.*
**Tutelar god** *yi-dam-lha*, *ťugs-dám.*
**Twelve** *bċu-γnyis*; twelfth *bċu-γnyis-pa.*
**Twenty** *nyi-śu*; twentieth *nyi-śu-pa.*
**Twice** *lan-γnyis.*
**Twilight** *srod*, *srod-˳ǰiṅ.*
**Twine** s. *skud-pa*, *si-ri W.*
**Twins** **ťsag-ťúg**, *mťse-ma.*
**Twirling-stick** *ǰa-bkrúg.*
**Twist** vb. a. *sgrim-pa*, *γċud-pa*, ***sle-ba.***
**Two** *γnyis*; v. also *do* 256.
**Two-legged** *rkaṅ-γnyis-pa.*
**Tyrant** *dpon-po drag-po* or *drag-śul-ċan.*

# U

**Ugly** ***mi-sdug-pa.***
**Ulcer** ***śu-ba***; *ba-śu W.*; *ṗol*, *lhog-pa.*
**Ultimately** *ṗugs-na.*
**Umbrella** *nyi-rib*, *γdugs.*
**Unable** *mi śes-pa*, *ċaṅ mi śes-pa.*
**Unaccustomed** *mi gom-pa.*
**Unadulterated** *ma-˳dres-pa*, *lhad-méd.*
**Unaware** *yaṅ-med-la W.*
**Unbearable** *mi-bzod-pa.*
**Unbecoming** *mi-rigs-pa.*
**Unbelieving** *ma-dad-pa*, *dad-méd.*
**Unbutton** vb. a. *˳grol-ba.*
**Unchangeable** *˳gyur-méd*
**Unchastity** *˳dod-lóg.*

Uncle *ku-bo*; *żaṅ(-po)*, *'a-żaṅ*, *'a-kú W.*
Unclean *mi-γtsaṅ-ba*, *dri-ma-čan*; *tsi-du W.*, *skyug-bro C.*
Uncommon *tun-min*, *tun-moṅs ma yin-pa* 234; *srol-méd*, *ta-mal-pa ma yin-pa* 227.
Undefined *ṅes-med.*
Under *og*, *og-na* 501; v. also *šam* 557.
Under-garment *'aṅ-túṅ.*
Undergo *mtoṅ-ba*, *bzod-pa*, *snyoṅ-ba.*
Understand *mkyen-pa*, *go-ba*, *ṅos-prod-pa*, *rig-pa*, *šes-pa*; *ha-go-ba W.*
Understanding s. *blo*, *blo-grós*; good — (agreement) *mtun* 241.
Undertaking s. *rtsom-pa* 441.
Undoubtedly *γdon-mi-za-bar.*
Uneasy *koṅ-du čud-pa*, *mi tsim-pa*, *mi dga-ba*, *mi dga-ste.*
Unequal *mi-dra-ba.*
Unequalled *gran-ya-med.*
Uneven *rtsub-po.*
Unexpectedly *hun-med-la W.*, *yaṅ-med-la W.*; *glo-bur-du*, *har(-gyis) C.*
Unfasten *grol-ba.*
Unfinished *te-rél W.*
Unfit adj. *mi-ruṅ-ba.*
Unfold *bu-ba*, *ka bu-ba.*
Ungracious *brtse-méd.*
Unguent *byug-sman.*
Unhappy *bkra-mi-šis-pa*, *sdug-bsṅal-čan*, *γyaṅ-med-pa.*
Unimpaired *ma-nyams-pa.*
Universally *pal-čér.*
Universe *jig-rtén.*
Unjust *tsul-méd*; *čos ma yin-pa.*
Unkind *brtse-méd.*
Unmarried (male or female) *kyim-tabs-méd*; (female) *kyo-méd.*
Unobserved adv. *ma-tsor-bar.*
Unoccupied *yan-pa.*
Unquestionable *tag-bčad-pa* 227.
Unquestionably *γdon mi za-bar.*
Unreasonable *mi-rig-pa* 528.
Unripe *rjen-pa.*
Unsought *rtsol-méd.*
Unsteady *dug mi tsugs-pa* 459.
Unsubstantial *γzugs-méd* 494.
Unsymmetrical *ya-ma-zúṅ.*
Untie *grol-ba.*
Until *bar-du*, *tug C.*, *tsug-pa W.*; *pan-la* 340, *yan-la* 506.
Untoward *mi-dod-pa.*
Untruth *šab-šob.*
Up to prep. *gan*, *druṅ-du*, *mdun-du*, *ldan-du W.* 289; *rtsar* 437; adv. *yar*, *gyen.*
Upbraid *bka-bkyon byed-pa.*
Up-hill *gyen-du.*
Upon *ka-ru*, *kar* 35, *tog-tu* 237, *steṅ-du* 222.
Upper adj. *ya-gi*; — end *tog-ma*; — part *stod.*
Upright (erect) *kye-ré*; *kroṅ-kroṅ W.*; (honest) *čos-draṅ-po.*
Up-stairs *ya-tog.*
Urge vb. a. v. *nan* 302.
Urgently *nye-bar.*
Urinary organs *ču-só.*
Urine *γčin*, *ču*, *dri-ču.*
Usage (custom) *srol.*
Use vb. a. *spyod-pa.*
Use s. *krims*; *pan-pa*; *lob-kyád W.*
Useful *dgos-pa*, *pan-togs-pa*; to be — *pan-pa.*
Useless *mi-dgos-pa*, *pan-méd*, *don-méd*; *čon W.* 162.
Usual *tun*, *tun-móṅ*, *pal-pa.*
Usurp *prog-pa.*
Utensils *lag-ča.*
Uterus *bu-snód*, *pru-ma.*
Utmost v. *bla-ma* 382, *ji* 172.
Utter *rjod-pa*, *don-pa.*
Uvula *lče-čúṅ.*

# V

Vacuity *stoṅ-pa-nyid* 223.
Vagina *mṅal-sgo* 132.
Vagrant adj. *yan-pa.*
Vain (fond of dress) *mčor-po*, *rdzob-po*, col. *zab-mo.*
Valid *stobs-čan.*
Valley *luṅ-pa*; lower part of a — *mdo*, upper part *pu.*
Valuable *dkon-pa*, *rin-po-če.*
Value s. (price) *goṅ*, *taṅ*, *rin*; (importance) *kos.*
Vanish *yal-ba*, *mi-snaṅ-bar gyur-ba* 317.
Vapour s. *ṅad*, *rlaṅs-pa.*
Variegated *bkra-ba.*
Various *sna-tsogs*, *sna-so-só*, *so-só*, *rigs mi-γčig-pa.*
Varnish s. *rtsí.*
Vegetables *sṅo-tsód*, *tsod-ma*, *ldum.*
Vehicle *teg-pa*, *bżon-pa.*
Veil s. *γdoṅ-kebs.*
Vein (of the body) *rtsa*; (of minerals) *γter-ka* 208, *rdo-ká* 287.
Venerable *btsun-pa.*
Vengeance *dugs W.*; to take — **dug kor-če*, *lan kor-če* W.*
Venture vb. *spobs-pa*
Venus *pa(-wa)-saṅs.*
Verdant, the ground becomes — *sa bo C.* 395; or *sṅo skyé* 136.

**Vermicelli** *γčur-p̔e, čur-ba.*
**Vermilion** s. *mtsal, ťsal.*
**Vermin** *srin-bu, ₒbu.*
**Verse** s. *rkaṅ-pa* 15, *ťsigs* 448.
**Vertex** *mgo-dkyil, γtsug.*
**Vertical** *gyen-la draṅ-po W.*
**Very** *rab-tu, šin-tu*; *ha-čaṅ* 595; *mā W.* 408; the very *k̔o-na* 43.
**Vessel** (receptacle) *snod*; (anatom.) *bu-ga*; (ship) *γziṅs, gru.*
**Vestibule** *sgo-k̔aṅ.*
**Vestige** *mal.*
**Vice** s. *sdig-pa, mi-dge-ba.*
**Vice-roy** *rgyal-ťsab.*
**Vicissitude** *ₒgyur-ba* II 97.
**Victorious**, to be — *rgyal-ba.*
**Victory** *rgyal.*
**Victuals** *k̔a-zás, za-ba, za-ma.*
**Vie with** *ₒgran-pa.*
**View** s. *snaṅ-ba* 317; point of — (mode of viewing things) *mťoṅ-snáṅ* 318, *γzigs-snáṅ*; vb. a. *lta-ba.*
**Vigorous** *rem-pa.*
**Vile** *btsog-pa.*
**Vilify** *smad-pa, dma-ₒbebs-pa, ma-bab kal-ba W.* 421.
**Village** *yul-gru, groṅ, groṅ-ťso, groṅ-yul, yul-ťso.*
**Villager** *groṅ-pa.*
**Vine** *rgun, rgun-šiṅ.*
**Vinegar** *skyur-k̔u, skyur-ru Sik., skyur-mo Lh.*
**Vineyard** *rgun-ťsás.*
**Violate** (infringe) *γčog-pa, ₒčal-ba*; (deflower) *lus smad-pa.*
**Violent** *drags-po, btsan.*
**Virgin** *bu-mo, bu-mo γsar-ma.*
**Virtue** *dge-ba, bsod-pa*; by — of *stobs-kyis* 224.
**Virtuous** *dge-ba, dge-ldán.*
**Viscid** *rtsi-čan.*
**Vishnu** *k̔yab-ǰúg* 46.
**Visible** *mṅon-pa, γsal-po, mťoṅ-du ruṅ-ba.*
**Vision** (act of seeing) *snaṅ-ba, mťoṅ-snaṅ*; range of — *mťoṅ-ₒk̔or*; (phantom) *žal-γzigs.*
**Visit** vb. a. *žal-lta byed-pa*; . . . *daṅ ťug-pa-la ₒgro-ba*, … *daṅ mǰal-ba* or *p̔rad-pa.*
**Visitation** (inspection) *žal-ta, žal-lta.*
**Voice** *skad, sgra, sgra-skad*, resp. *γsuṅ*; loud — *skad-čé.*
**Volcano** *me-rí.*
**Voluptuousness** *ₒdod-pa, ₒdod-čags.*
**Vomit** vb. *skyug-pa*; s. *skyugs-pa.*
**Vortex** *γtsug.*
**Vow** s. *ťugs-dám, dam, dam-ťsig, yi-dam*; to make a — *ťugs-dam bča-ba.*
**Vowel** *dbyaṅs.*
**Vulgar** s. *dmaṅs* 422; adj. *ťa-mal-pa* 227.
**Vulture** *go-bo, glag, bya-glág.*

# W

**Wag** vb. a. *sgril-ba.*
**Wages** *gla, p̔ogs.*
**Waggon** *šiṅ-rta*; — wheel *šiṅ-rtai p̔aṅ-ló.*
**Wailings** s. *smre-sṅágs.*
**Waist** *rked-pa.*
**Wait** vb. n. *sgug-pa, sdod-pa, sriṅ-ba*; to — on *mǰal-ba*; to lie in — *sgug-pa*; to keep one waiting *sgug-tu ₒǰug-pa.*
**Waiting-man** *sku-mdun-pa, žabs-p̔yi; druṅ-k̔ór.*
**Wake** vb. a. *sod-pa, γnyid sad-pa.*
**Walk** vb. n. *bgrod-pa, ₒgrul-ba, ₒgro-ba, ₒčag-pa*; resp. *skyod-pa, γšegs-pa, ₒbyon-pa*; to take a — *skyo-saṅs-la ₒgro-ba* 458; v. also *γyeṅs-pa* 518; the act of walking *ₒgros*; manner of — *spyod-ₒgrós.*
**Wall** s. *rtsig-pa, lčags-ri, skya.*
**Walnut** *star-ka, dar-sga.*
**Wand** s. *dbyug-gu, dbyu-gu.*
**Wander** *ₒk̔yam-pa, rgyu-ba.*
**Want** vb. a. *dgos-pa, ₒťsal-ba, ₒk̔o-ba*; I — *ṅa-la dgos* 87; I do not want it *ₒk̔o-če med W.* 56.
**War** s. *ₒk̔rug-pa*; *mag-ťáb C., mag-ťúg W.*
**Wardrobe** *gos-sgám.*
**Warm** adj. *dro-ba, droṅ-mo, ťsa-ba.*
**Warm** vb. a. *sro-ba*; *dugs-pa W.*; to — one's self *lde-ba.*
**Warmth** *ťsa-graṅ, drod.*
**Warp** s. *rgyu.*
**Warrior** *dmag-mí.*
**Wart** *mdzer-pa.*
**Wash** vb. a. *ₒk̔rud-pa*, resp. *bsil-ba.*
**Washing** s. *k̔rus*; water for — *k̔rus-k̔u.*
**Waste** adj. *gog-po, stoṅ-pa.*
**Watch** vb. a. *sruṅ-ba.*
**Watchman** *sruṅ-mk̔an.*
**Water** *ču*, eleg. *čab*; — carrier *ču-pa*; — channel *wa*; — closet *p̔yag-ra*; *γsaṅ-spyód*; — jar *ču-rdzá*; — snake *ču-sbrul*; — spout *ₒdre-p̔u-tsub W.*; — tub *ču-zém.*
**Wave** s. *rlabs, dba-klóṅ.*
**Wavering** s. *ťsam-ťsúm.*
**Wax** s. *spra-ťsil C., mum W.*
**Way** (road) *ₒgro-sa, lam,* (manner) *rnam-pa, ťabs, lugs, ťsul*; by or in the — of *sgo-nas* 115; to have the — of *rigs-pa* 528; to give — *ₒbyer-ba*; to make — *ₒbyol-ba, ₒdzur-ba.* [*ₒo, ₒu-čag.*
**We** pron. *ṅa* 124, *ṅa-čag, ṅed, ṅed-raṅ, ṅos,*

**Weak** adj. *żan-pa, śed-med, śed-čúṅ, hal-med W.*; *nyams-čuṅ, ₒǰam-po W.*
**Weal** (mark) col. *nya.*
**Wealth** *nor, dkor, ṗyug-ḱyád, dbyig(s), byor-pa, loṅs-spyód* 554.
**Weapon** *mṫson.*
**Wear** vb. a. *gyon-pa, bgo-ba.*
**Weariness** *ṅal-ba, ₒo-brgyál.*
**Weary** adj., to be — *skyo-ba, sun-pa.*
**Weary** vb. a. *ṅal ₒǰug-pa*; to be wearied *ṅal-ba.*
**Weather**, clear — *ɣnam daṅ-ba, ɣnam dwaṅs, ɣnam ṫaṅ*; dry — *ṫan-pa* 229.
**Weave** vb. a. *ₒṫag-pa.*
**Weaver** *ṫa-ga-pa.*
**Wedge** s. *ka-ru.*
**Wednesday** *ɣza-lhag-ma.*
**Weed** s. *rtsa-ṅan.*
**Weeding** (the act of) *yur-ma.*
**Week** *bdun-ṗrág.*
**Weep** *ṅu-ba, śum-pa.*
**Weft** *spun.*
**Weigh** vb. a. *ₒǰal-ba, ₒdegs-pa, ɣżal-ba, ɣśor-ba.*
**Weight** *rdo* 286, *sraṅ* 580.
**Welcome**, you are — *ₒoṅs-pa legs-so* 501.
**Welfare** *bde-ba, bde-ₒǰágs.*
**Well** s. *ḱron-pa, ču-doṅ, ₒbyuṅ-ḱuṅs, ču-míg.*
**Well** adj., are you —? *de-mo 'e yo C.*; adv. *ₒo-ná* 500; very — *de-ltar ₒṫsal-lo*; well, well! *yag-po yag-po*; — sounding *snyan-pa*; — tasted *żim-po.*
**Wen** *lba-ba.*
**Went**, I went *soṅ* 579.
**West** *nub.*
**Wet** adj. *rlon-pa, ɣśer-ba*; s. *rlan.*
**Wether** *ṫoṅ-pa.*
**What** interr. *či* 139, *gaṅ* 65, *či-ltar* 140, *ǰi* 172.
**Whatever** *či-yaṅ*; — it may be *či yaṅ ruṅ* 532.
**Wheat** *gro*; — flour *bag-ṗyé.*
**Wheel** s. *ₒḱor-lo*; paddle — *sku-ru.*
**When** *ḱa-ru, ḱar*; *čiṅ*; interr. *nam, dus-nam-žig* 303.
**Where** *ga-na, ga-ru, gar*; — is? *ga-ré.*
**Whetstone** *ₒdzeṅ.*
**Which** interr. *gaṅ* 65.
**While** s. *yun*; a little — *ṫen, dar-ɣčig, re žig (dus)*; a long — *riṅ žig-tu.*
**Whilst** *la* 540, *las* 546.
**Whip** s. *lčag, rta-lčag.*
**Whirl** vb. n. *ₒtsub-pa.*
**Whirlpool** *ɣtsug, ɣtsug-ₒḱyil.*
**Whirlwind** *ₒdre-pu-tsúb W.*
**Whisper** s. *śab-śúb*; vb. *śub-pa, śib-pa.*
**Whistle** vb. *śugs-sgra ɣtoṅ-ba*; v. also *hu-hú* 597.
**White** adj. *dkar-ba*; — wash *dkar-rtsí.*
**Whither** *ga-ru, ga-la* 64, *gar* 67.
**Who** interr. *gaṅ* 65, *su* 573.
**Whole** adj. *ṫams-čád* 230; *tsaṅ-ma, ril-ba, hril-po*; s. *ril-po.*
**Wholly** *yoṅs-su.*
**Why** interr. *či, či-la* 140, *čii ṗyir* 351; *ga-la rten-nas* 214; interj. *ₒo-ná* 500.
**Wick** s. *snyiṅ-po, sdoṅ-ras C., sar W.*
**Wicked** adj. *čos-méd, sdig-pa-la dga-ba.*
**Wide** *żeṅ-čan, yaṅs-pa, hel-po, hel-čan.*
**Widow** *yugs(s)-sa-mo.*
**Widower** *yug(s)-sa-pa, yug-sa*; *skyes-nág* [*C.*
**Width** *ḱyon, ɣżeṅ.*
**Wife** *čuṅ-ma, čuṅ-grogs*; *'a-ne W.*; *ḱab* 38, *ḱyo-mo* 48; (housewife) *ḱyim-ṫab-mo, ḱyim-pa-ma* 47.
**Wild** adj. *rgod-pa, ɣnyan-pa.*
**Wilderness** *dgon pa, ₒbrog.*
**Will** s. *bsam-pa, ṫugs*, resp. *ṫugs-dgoṅs.*
**Willing**, to be — *ₒdod-pa.*
**Willow** *lčaṅ-ma.*
**Wind** s. *rdzi, rluṅ*; cold — *lhag(s)-pa.*
**Wind** vb.a. *dkri-ba, ₒḱri-ba, ₒḱyil-ba, sgril-ba*; vb. n. *ₒḱril-ba.*
**Window** *rgyal-dkar C.*; — hole *dkar-ḱuṅ.*
**Windpipe** *kru-krú W., lkog-ma.*
**Wine** *rgun-čaṅ*, resp. *rgun-skyéms*; *čaṅ.*
**Wing** s. *śog-pa, ₒdab-ma.*
**Wink** vb. n. *mig ḱrab-ḱráb* or *ṫsab-ṫsáb* or *ₒdzum-ₒdzúm byed-pa.*
**Winter** s. *dgun, dgun-ka.*
**Wipe** vb. a. *ₒṗyi-ba*; to be wiped off *ₒbyi-ba.*
**Wire** *lčags-skúd.*
**Wisdom** *ye-śes, śes-ráb.*
**Wise** adj. *mḱas-pa, gruṅ-ba, mdzaṅs-pa.*
**Wish** s. *ₒdod-pa, yid-smon*; resp. *dgoṅs-pa, bżed-don*; vb. a. *ₒdod-pa, smon-pa, ₒṫsal-ba, bżed-pa.*
**Witchcraft** *mṫu, ṗra-mén.*
**With** *daṅ* 248, *mnyam-du* 195, *bčas-su.*
**Withdraw** vb. a. *ɣčod-pa, mi ster-ba*; vb. n. *ₒgye-ba.*
**Wither** vb. n. *rnyid-pa.*
**Within** *ṫsun-čád.*
**Without** prep. *med-pa(r)* 418.
**Witness** s. *dpaṅ(-po).*
**Wolf** *spyaṅ-ki.*
**Woman** *bud-méd, mo, 'a-ne W.*
**Womb** *mṅal* 132, *bu-snod* 319, *rum.*
**Wonder** s. *ya-mtsan.*
**Wonderful** *nyams-mṫsar-ba, ṅo-mṫsar-ba*; *ya-mṫsan-po C., ya-mṫsan-čan W.*
**Wont, Wonted** adj. *goms-pa.*
**Wood** (forest) *nags(-ma), ṫsal*; (timber) *śiṅ*; — shavings *śiṅ-zél.*
**Woodpecker** *śiṅ-rgón.*
**Woof** *spun.*
**Wool** *bal.*
**Word** *ṫsig, miṅ, sgra, ṅág* 125; resp. *bka.*

**Work** s. *bya-ba*, *bzo*, *las*, resp. *ṗrin-las*; vb. a. *las byed-pa.*
**Workman** *las-pa*, *las-mi.*
**Workmanship** *bzo* 497.
**Workmaster** *lag-dpón.*
**Workshop** *bzo-k̇an.*
**World** *ˏjig-rtén*, *srid-pa* 582.
**Worldliness** *ˏjig-rtén ˏdi-la čags-pai sems*; v. *bya-ba.*
**Worm** *ˏbu*, *srin-bu*, *nyal-ˏgro.*
**Worn out** *čad-po.*
**Worst**, to get the — of *ˏṗam-pa.*
**Worth** s. *ˏk̇os*, *goṅ*, *rin*, *ṫaṅ.*
**Worth** adj. *ri-ba.*
**Worthless** *rin-méd.*
**Worthy** *yśa*, *yśa-ma*; to be — *ˎos-pa.*
**Wound** s. *rma*, *rma-k̇a W.*
**Wrap** vb. a. *dkri-ba*; to — round *sgril-ba*; to — up *ˏdril-ba.*
**Wrath** *k̇ro-ba*, *že-sdaṅ.*
**Wrest** vb. a. *snol-ba.*
**Wrestle** vb. n. *snol-ba.*
**Wretched** *sdug-po*; *nyal-ba-čan W.*
**Wring** *ˏṫsir-ba.*
**Wrinkle** s. *ynyer-ma.*
**Wrist** *lag-ṫsigs.*
**Write** *ˏbri-ba.*
**Wrong** adj. *mi-rigs-pa*, *log-pa*, *mi-ˎos-pa*; *ˎos-med W.*
**Wry** adj. *ˏču-ba*, *ˏčus-pa* 170.

# Y

**Yak** *yyag*; male — *ṗo-yyág*; female — *ˏbri-mo*; wild — *ˏbroṅ.*
**Yard** (court-yard) *k̇yams.*
**Yarn** *snal-ma*, *sran-bu.*
**Yawn** vb. *glal-ba*, *sgyiṅ-ba* 118.
**Yea** *ˎo-ná* 500.
**Year** *lo*; this — *da-lo.*
**Yeast** *ṗabs*, *rtsabs.*
**Yellow** *ser-po.*
**Yes** *ˎo*, *de yin*; *'a W.*; yes, yes! *de-ka yod* 255; —, so it is *de-de-bžin-no.*
**Yesterday** *k̇a-rtsáṅ*, *mdaṅ.*
**Yet** *ˎon kyaṅ*, *yin kyaṅ*, *yin na yaṅ W.*; *gal-te.*
**Yield** vb. a. *ytoṅ-ba*; vb. n. *daṅ-du len-pa.*
**Yoke** of oxen *glaṅ-dór.*
**Yonder** *ṗa-gi.*
**You** pron. *k̇yed*, *k̇yod* 48, *nyid* 188.
**Young** adj. *yžon-pa*, *čuṅ-ba*; the youngest (son) *ṫa-čúṅ*; s. *ṗrug.*
**Youth** s. (youthful age) *laṅ-ṫso*; (boy or young man) *k̇yeu*, *yžon-nu.*

# Z

**Zeal** *rtsol-ba*, *brtson-ˏgrus*, *ˏbad-pa*, *bag-čags.*
**Zealous** *brtson-ˏgrus daṅ ldan-pa*; to be — *brtson-ˏgrus skyed-pa*, *brtson-par byed-pa.*
**Zealously** *rtsol-bar.*
**Zero** *ṫig-le.*
**Zinc** *ti-ṫsa.*
**Zodiac** *k̇yim-gyi ˏk̇or-lo.*

---

**Final remark.** The Tibetan words, given in the Vocabulary, are not in every instance to be regarded as exact equivalents for whatever word happens to be sought, but rather as hints, how to attain to the wished for expression. It will, therefore, be frequently indispensable to refer to the Tib. Engl. Dictionary for further explanation, and to examine the different bearings and relations of the word in question, so far as they may have been traced there. — Although this Vocabulary is by no means complete in itself, yet it is to be hoped that it will not prove quite unuseful, but answer the purpose for which it was intended.

# CORRECTIONS.

A revision of the Dictionary has brought such a number of misprints to light that, on second thoughts, it seems absolutely necessary not to leave them unnoticed, but to register all that are of any consequence. The unfortunate fact, that such corrections should be required, has to be ascribed to two circumstances, in regard to which the reader's indulgence has already been appealed to in the Preface, namely, the author's weak state of health, and the difficulties with which the printing of a book of this character is necessarily attended. —

---

p. page; a b the respective column, left or right; l. line; when the lines are counted from foot of page, the numerals are provided with an asterisk.

| p. | col. | l. | | |
|---|---|---|---|---|
| 2 | a | 8 | read | *ka-ma-la-ši-la* |
| 2 | b | 17 | „ | *ka-sa ǰu* |
| 3 | b | 3* | „ | to beckon |
| 8 | a | 18 | „ | *ṭad-kyi* |
| 9 | b | 21 | „ | *dka-ṫub-la* |
| 15 | a | 9 | „ | *ṭa-ši-hlum-po* |
| 16 | a | 19* | „ | *rkaṅ-˳bám* |
| 16 | b | 7* | „ | dig out |
| 17 | a | 9* | „ | affix denoting |
| 17 | a | 19* | „ | *rkyaṅ-pa* |
| 20 | b | 10* | „ | frequently |
| 21 | a | 6 | „ | *skal-nór* |
| 21 | b | 2 | „ | *ṭé* |
| 26 | a | 5 | „ | *skyaṅ* |
| 27 | a | 11* | „ | *skyil-ldír* |
| 27 | b | 13* | „ | *skyur-mo* |
| 28 | a | 6 | „ | *γyaṅ-skyúr* |
| 28 | a | 15* | „ | re-born |
| 28 | b | 19 | „ | *kyer-mẹ́n* |
| 31 | b | 16* | „ | *lag-lén* |
| 32 | b | 16 | dele | 2. to paste. — |
| 32 | b | 5* | read | *skra-šén* |
| 33 | a | 5* | „ | *k̔* |
| 33 | b | 7 | „ | *ḍá-ru skróg-pa* |
| 33 | b | 12 | „ | caste |
| 34 | a | 5 | „ | soft mouth |
| 34 | a | 15* | „ | to lie on the face |
| 35 | b | 2* | „ | *k̔a-γdáms* |
| 38 | a | 1 | „ | *lás-ka* |
| 38 | a | 10 | „ | *Ld.* |
| 39 | a | 6 | „ | *zas k̔am γčig* id. — 2. |
| 41 | a | 20 | „ | *k̔úg-tu* |
| 41 | a | 4* | „ | *rna-k̔úṅ* |
| 44 | a | 18 | „ | *kóg-pa ṅan-pa* |
| 51 | a | 14* | read | *k̔rims-k̔áṅ* |
| 52 | b | 24 | „ | **ṭó-pa** |
| 54 | b | 13 | „ | requisites |
| 56 | b | 5 | „ | འཁྱིལ་བ་ |
| 56 | b | 15 | „ | *˳k̔o-byéd* |
| 59 | a | 20* | „ | འཁྱུག(ས)་པ་ |
| 59 | a | 10* | „ | *˳k̔yam-pa* |
| 59 | b | 20* | „ | *˂ód-˳k̔yims* |
| 63 | a | 6* | „ | = *gaṅ*. — 3. bald, *W. ga-pi* (v. *spyi* 333). |
| 65 | a | 24* | „ | *˂óṅ-ba de-nè* |
| 66 | a | 16* | „ | *gaṅ-zág-* |
| 66 | a | 14* | „ | *lóg-lta-čan-gyi* |
| 66 | b | 15 | „ | *mdzod-lṅá* |
| 67 | a | 20 | „ | གན་དྷེ་ལ་ |
| 69 | b | 17* | „ | *gun-dúm* |
| 74 | a | 18 | „ | *gyád-kyi* |
| 74 | a | 13* | „ | *gyi* for *kyi* |
| 75 | a | 11 | „ | *gyón-rgyu* |
| 76 | b | 6 | „ | *ṫáb-grabs* |
| 77 | b | 18 | „ | གུ་གུ་ |
| 78 | b | 22* | „ | *gróg-ču* |
| 79 | a | 18 | „ | *mčód-rten* |
| 81 | a | 11 | „ | *-rtséd-mo* |
| 84 | b | 5 | „ | stoop |
| 85 | b | 18 | „ | उपासिका |
| 86 | b | 11 | „ | *mdo*; *dge-slóṅ-ma* a nun; *dge-slob-ma* etc. |
| 87 | a | 19 | „ | *bstán-pa-la* |

| p. | col. | l. | | |
|---|---|---|---|---|
| 89 | b | 2* | read | *ċes bgrós-nas* |
| 92 | a | 4 | „ | *'u-ṡóg* |
| 95 | a | 11* | „ | *ṅan-* |
| 95 | b | 3 | „ | འགོགས་པ་ |
| 95 | b | 21 | „ | establish |
| 96 | a | 10* | „ | *˳gor* |
| 96 | b | 1 | „ | *˳gyág-pa* |
| 96 | b | 3 | „ | *˳gyaṅ-ba* |
| 96 | b | 15 | „ | *ṡél-gyi* |
| 98 | a | 14 | „ | *˳gyód-par* |
| 111 | b | 22 | „ | རྒྱུག་པ་ |
| 112 | a | 20* | „ | *tiṅ-ṅe-˳dzin* |
| 113 | b | 7 | „ | *na-tsa* |
| 121 | a | 20 | „ | *bsgrub-* |
| 122 | a | 4 | vide | emendation p. XXII. |
| 122 | a | 8* | read | སྒྲོག(ས)་ |
| 122 | b | 24* | „ | *sgrón-pa* |
| 128 | a | 4 | „ | *ṅéd-ċag* |
| 128 | b | 4 | „ | *dé-˳dra-ba* |
| 128 | b | 6 | „ | *˳či-ba* |
| 128 | b | 2* | „ | *ṅo dkár-po* |
| 131 | a | 16*seqq. | „ | *˳dzin* |
| 132 | b | 5* | „ | *ċis* |
| 132 | b | 3* | „ | *mṅón-no* |
| 135 | a | 4 | „ | *Lex.* |
| 139 | b | 6 | „ | *ċii* of what? |
| 140 | b | 1 | „ | ཅི་ཅོ་ |
| 141 | b | 17 | „ | *ċuṅ* |
| 143 | a | 20* | „ | gallinaceous |
| 146 | b | 10*, 8* | „ | **vċu** |
| 147 | b | 23 | „ | **vċom-ldan-˳dé** |
| 158 | a | 17 | „ | *ču-búr* |
| 158 | b | 14* | „ | the water; also = |
| 161 | b | 10* | „ | *dris-pas* (instead of |
| 163 | b | 10* | „ | *čós-skad* |
| 164 | a | 3* | „ | irreligious |
| 165 | b | 18* | „ | *mčé-ba* |
| 166 | b | 15 | „ | पूज |
| 168 | b | 20* | „ | *zá-ba* |
| 170 | a | 13 | „ | *˳ču-ba* to draw etc. |
| 170 | a | 22 | „ | vb. n. to *ǰún-pa* |
| 170 | b | 2* | „ | *ḱro-bo-˳čól-pa* |
| 171 | a | 12 | „ | *Lex.* |
| 176 | b | 24 | „ | *ǰig-ṭág* |
| 177 | a | 5 | „ | *ǰiṅ-ḱúṅ* |
| 184 | b | 10* | „ | *nyá-ra byéd-pa* |
| 185 | a | 13* | „ | *dpon-gyi* |
| 186 | b | 4* | „ | *nyal-ḱri* |
| 195 | a | 21 | „ | **mnyé-ċe** |
| 195 | b | 6 | „ | སྙང་བ་ |
| 195 | b | 7* | „ | *γnyid* |

| p. | col. | l. | | |
|---|---|---|---|---|
| 200 | a | 13* | read | སྙེན་པ་ |
| 205 | a | 4 | „ | *Cs.* |
| 219 | b | 7 | „ | *ma byed* |
| 226 | a | 11* | „ | 178. 3. — *Was.* (296): 2. |
| 231 | b | 7 | „ | *ťig-skúd* |
| 232 | a | 3* | „ | *żib-ċu* |
| 233 | b | 18 | „ | *Ld.-Glr.*, |
| 233 | b | 23* | „ | translates it |
| 233 | b | 19* | „ | **ťun ċad** *W.* |
| 235 | b | 24 | „ | *mi-ťeg ḱúr-ba* |
| 237 | a | 9* | „ | *ṅá-ťog* |
| 237 | b | 15 | „ | *spyi-ťóg* |
| 238 | a | 14* | „ | *ťod* |
| 256 | a | 9 | „ | from thence |
| 256 | b | 12 | „ | དེབ་(མ)་ |
| 259 | b | 14 | „ | *don* 1. — *don-dám* |
| 264 | b | 7* | „ | དྲོན་མོ་ |
| 265 | a | 10 | „ | like an arctic sea |
| 267 | a | 14 | dele | (Pinus abies) |
| 270 | b | 14 | read | *bdé-mo* |
| 273 | b | 2* | „ | डोबी |
| 274 | a | 4* | dele | the words: marked or |
| 275 | a | 9 seqq. | read | *˳das-pa* |
| 275 | b | 6* | „ | *p̔yi* |
| 287 | b | 16 | „ | precious stone |
| 287 | b | 22 | „ | *Pth.* having obtained im mortality |
| 291 | a | 5 | „ | *˳brug* |
| 292 | b | 23 | „ | *sdáṅ-ba* |
| 293 | a | 3* | „ | *sdig-to-ċan* |
| 293 | b | 1 | „ | སྡི(ག)ས་པ་ *sdi(g)s-pa* |
| 301 | b | 22 | „ | *lo tóṅ-ṅi* |
| 303 | b | 23 | „ | *zin-to* |
| 304 | b | 22 | „ | prep. |
| 305 | b | 21* | „ | ནུར་ནུར་པོ་ |
| 312 | a | 3* | „ | མནོལ་གྲིབ་ |
| 316 | b | 8 | „ | *smin-pa* |
| 317 | b | 12* | „ | apparition |
| 318 | b | 14 | „ | brightly |
| 322 | b | 8* | „ | *dkár(-po)* |
| 325 | a | 10 | „ | *gru-˳dzin* |
| 326 | b | 4 | „ | Durga, Uma |
| 327 | a | 17 | „ | *żág-pe pe* |
| 328 | a | 18* | „ | *koṅ-ǰo* |
| 338 | a | 14* | „ | the defunct ancestors |
| 338 | b | 2* | „ | postp. c. gen. |
| 340 | a | 21 | „ | abstrusely |
| 340 | b | 17 | „ | *Gram.*; |
| 353 | b | 15 | „ | *ǰúg-pa* |
| 354 | a | 9* | „ | *˳p̔rál-ba* |

| p. | col. | l. | |
|---|---|---|---|
| 357 | b | 12* | read ˳*p̔óṅ-mk̔an* |
| 374 | a | 12* | „ བྲུག་(པ་) |
| 383 | b | 10* | „ གླ་འཚོ་ *gla-˳ts̔ó* |
| 389 | a | 12* | „ *dbón-mo* |
| 407 | a | 17* | „ སྦྲིད་པ་ |
| 410 | b | 13* | „ circle |
| 412 | b | 21*, 19* | „ *mi-k̔yim* |
| 415 | a | 24* | „ to name v. ˳*dogs-pa* 2; |
| 427 | a | 12 | „ *sman-mč̔óg* |
| 431 | a | 1* | „ *tsám-gyis* |
| 433 | a | 2* | „ *yaṅ* |
| 439 | a | 19 | „ *mii* |
| 439 | b | 14* | „ ˳*gro-* (or *č̔a-*) *rtsis yod* |
| 442 | a | 7* | „ *nyáṅ-c̀e* |
| 442 | b | 17 | „ assiduous |
| 446 | a | 3* | „ *ts̔an-zug* |
| 449 | a | 12* | „ travellers |
| 460 | b | 10 | „ ˳*ts̔ó-ba* |

| p. | col. | l. | |
|---|---|---|---|
| 466 | b | 11* | read whetstone |
| 474 | a | 20* | „ soothe |
| 480 | a | 13 | „ *γžal-med-k̔aṅ-bzaṅ* |
| 493 | b | 18 | „ *Sik.* |
| 496 | a | 5 | „ *γzod* |
| 496 | a | 18 | „ wasted |
| 508 | b | 12 | „ so *yi γc̀ód-pa, yi č̔ád-pa* |
| 522 | a | 2. 3 | „ *ḍáṅ-mo* |
| 530 | b | 5 | „ རིལ་བ་ |
| 540 | a | 4 | „ of |
| 567 | a | 5* | „ prop. |
| 576 | a | 14* | *skyo-séṅ mdzád-pa* |
| 578 | b | 3 | „ སོ་པག་ *so-pág* |
| 587 | a | 20, 21 | „ *nyon-móṅs-kyi kun-slóṅ* |
| 589 | a | 1 | „ གསལ་ཞིང་ |
| 591 | b | 23* | „ vb. 1. to beg, to pray = *žú-ba* |
| 592 | a | 9 | „ (the king's) soul |

In several of the longer articles some confusion in the use of the figures in large and small type has occurred. In order to restrict this catalogue within the smallest possible limits, these and other slight inaccuracies have not been entered.